ENCYCLOPÆDIA
Britannica

2006
BOOK OF THE YEAR®

ENCYCLOPÆDIA
Britannica®

Encyclopædia Britannica, Inc.   Chicago • London • New Delhi • Paris • Seoul • Sydney • Taipei • Tokyo

ENCYCLOPÆDIA
Britannica

BOOK OF THE YEAR®
2006

Foreword

New beginnings were on the horizon for many in 2005. After more than 25 years, Roman Catholics had a new spiritual leader; voters in a number of Latin American countries seemed fed up with politics as usual and elected leftist leaders; environmentalists rejoiced as the Kyoto Protocol came into effect; the Roma (Gypsies) of Europe began enjoying new protections enforced by the European Union; the ancient art of Japanese kabuki found a new, appreciative audience in the U.S.; and the emergency-preparedness agencies in the U.S. were evaluating their readiness in the wake of devastating hurricanes as thousands of Gulf Coast residents found themselves rebuilding their lives, many of them far from home. Pirates made a resurgence, nowadays using high-tech gadgetry to coordinate attacks on passing ships, and Einstein's theories were brought back into the limelight during celebrations held around the world devoted to the 100th anniversary of the publication of his five earth-shaking papers. All of these topics are explored in Special Reports.

A number of new trends emerged during the year, including a boom in text messaging, the popularity of poker as a spectator game on TV, an airing of social debates by Islamic writers in Europe and the U.S., and the move to reexamine ancient grains for modern use. In the realm of sports, ice skating introduced a new judging system, boxing tried to sort out its "alphabet soup" of champions, and competitors at the World Games continued their quest to gain Olympic status for their sport. Health issues that made headlines during the year included the troubling rise of childhood obesity and the possibility that bird flu might turn into a human pandemic. On the political scene, the U.K. held elections, China improved relations with most of its neighbours, and the EU experienced a setback in its adoption of a constitution. In addition, Kashmir suffered a cataclysmic earthquake, and many worried about the hundreds of thousands of survivors who were left homeless and faced the onslaught of winter. These subjects are featured in Sidebars.

While there were some significant losses, notably that of Pope John Paul II, civil rights activist Rosa Parks, Nazi hunter Simon Wiesenthal, playwrights Arthur Miller and August Wilson, architect Philip Johnson, Supreme Court Chief Justice William H. Rehnquist, Prince Rainier III of Monaco, and comedian Johnny Carson, there were a number of triumphs as well. Fiona Wood was named Australian of the Year for her invention of spray-on skin to aid burn victims; Turkish literary lion Orhan Pamuk received the German Book Trade Peace Prize; Angela Merkel became the first woman chancellor of Germany; and Camilla became duchess of Cornwall. As we look back on 2005 by paging through this volume, let us reflect on those events and people who made the year such a memorable one.

Karen Sparks, Editor

Contents
2006

Dates of 2005

In February 1,496 pairs of boots representing U.S. soldiers killed in Iraq are set out in Dallas.

© Louis DeLuca/Dallas Morning News/Corbis

January

1 With the beginning of the new year, Prime Minister Jean-Claude Juncker of Luxembourg assumes the presidency of the European Union.

A new currency goes into effect in Turkey, replacing the 1,000,000-lira notes with 1-new-lira notes and including a return of the kurus coin.

2 A car bomb goes off near Balad, Iraq, killing 18 members of the Iraqi National Guard and a civilian.

Presidential elections in Croatia result in the need for a runoff; the frontrunner, incumbent Stipe Mesic, wins only 49% of the vote. (*See* January 16.)

3 Attacks in various places in Iraq leave at least 20 people dead, including 3 British citizens and an American civilian; insurgent attacks on military and civilian targets in Iraq have become daily and continuing occurrences.

Contract negotiations involving the St. Louis Symphony Orchestra reach an impasse, leading to a work stoppage, the first in a difficult contract season for major orchestras in the United States and Canada.

4 The governor of Baghdad province in Iraq is assassinated; in four other attacks 15 people, including 5 U.S. soldiers, are killed.

James M. Zimmerman, the retired chairman and CEO of Federated Department Stores, is indicted on charges of having lied under oath during an investigation of anticompetitive practices; that investigation led to a settlement in August 2004.

The University of Southern California defeats the University of Oklahoma 55–19 in college football's annual Orange Bowl to win the Bowl Championship Series trophy and the national Division I-A championship.

Infielder and hitter Wade Boggs and second baseman Ryne Sandberg are elected to the National Baseball Hall of Fame.

5 Officials of the International Atomic Energy Agency announce that Iran has agreed to allow the agency to inspect the Parchin military complex, which the U.S. believes has been used for nuclear weapons development.

The African Union agrees to send troops to Somalia to facilitate the move of Somalia's government from Kenya to the Somalian capital of Mogadishu.

6 The pro forma counting of electoral college votes in the U.S. Congress takes place, and U.S. Pres. George W. Bush is officially certified as the winner of the presidential election.

Edgar Ray Killen, a longtime Ku Klux Klan leader, is arrested in Philadelphia,

Miss., and charged with murder in the 1964 killings of three voter-registration workers.

Nelson Mandela, former president of South Africa, announces that his son, Makgatho Mandela, has died of AIDS; it is considered very courageous of him to admit publicly that AIDS was the cause of death.

7 A fire breaks out in a garment factory in Siddhirganj, Bangladesh, killing 22 people who were trapped inside because of locked exits.

Conservative commentator Armstrong Williams acknowledges that he received payment from the U.S. Department of Education to comment favourably on his syndicated television program on the administration's No Child Left Behind education initiative.

8 Riots break out in Gilgit, in the Pakistan-administered

Northern Areas, after a prominent Shi'ite cleric is ambushed and shot; 15 people die in the violence.

9 In the first Palestinian election since 1996, former prime minister Mahmoud Abbas is elected president of the Palestinian Authority; the elections are regarded as free and fair.

In a ceremony in Nairobi, Kenya, a final peace agreement calling for a six-year transitional period is signed between the government of The Sudan and a rebel group from the south of the country led by John Garang.

10 A law banning cigarette smoking in all indoor public places, including restaurants and bars, except in walled-off and ventilated areas, goes into effect in Italy.

In Mauritius an international meeting organized by the United Nations to review the implementation of a program of action for the sustainable development of some 51 small-island less-developed states opens.

An independent panel investigating a CBS News story that was broadcast on *60 Minutes* in September 2004 about U.S. Pres. George W. Bush's service in the Texas Air National Guard during the Vietnam War concludes that the segment had been rushed onto the air without adequate vetting; CBS responds by firing four top journalists.

11 U.S. Pres. George W. Bush nominates Michael Chertoff, who headed the criminal division of the Department of Justice at the time of the 9/11 terrorist

attacks, to replace Tom Ridge as secretary of homeland security.

Officials announce that an agreement has been reached for the release of the last four Britons and one Australian citizen being detained at the U.S. military base in Guantánamo Bay, Cuba; the men have been held there for about three years.

A cow infected with mad cow disease is reported found in Alberta; this is somewhat alarming because the cow was born after a ban on certain animal protein in cattle feed went into effect.

Apple Computer introduces the Mac Mini, a low-priced Macintosh personal comput-

er intended for the home rather than work market.

12 A new constitution for the European Union is signed by a large majority of the European Parliament in Strasbourg, France; it must now be ratified by each of the EU's 25 members, a process expected to take about two years.

NASA's Deep Impact spacecraft is launched from Cape Canaveral, Florida; it is expected to reach Comet Tempel 1 in July and release an impactor that will penetrate to the comet's nucleus. *(Photo above.)*

The U.S. Supreme Court rules that sentencing guide-

lines that Congress imposed on judges in federal courts in 1994 must be regarded as advisory only and not as mandatory.

It is announced that the U.S. has abandoned the search for weapons of mass destruction in Iraq, having concluded long ago that the former Iraqi government did not possess such weapons at the time of the U.S.-led invasion.

13 Sir Mark Thatcher, son of former British prime minister Margaret Thatcher, pleads guilty in Cape Town to having helped finance mercenaries involved in a coup plot against the president of Equatorial Guinea; he receives a fine and a suspended sentence and immediately leaves the country.

A coordinated Palestinian attack on an Israeli checkpoint in the Gaza Strip leaves six Israeli civilians and three Palestinian militants dead.

Representatives of Major League Baseball and the MLB Players Association announce that in an attempt to root out the use of performance-enhancing substances in baseball, they have agreed on a new and stronger steroid-testing program than that introduced in 2002.

14 The European Space Agency spacecraft Huygens, released from the NASA orbiter Cassini, successfully lands on the surface of Saturn's moon Titan and begins transmitting photographs and data.

Israeli Prime Minister Ariel Sharon orders Israel's government officials to cut all contacts with the Palestinian Authority and orders the Gaza Strip sealed off.

Specialist Charles Graner, believed to be the leader of the U.S. soldiers responsible for the abuse of prisoners at the prison in Abu Ghraib, Iraq, is found guilty of all six charges in a court-martial in Fort Hood, Texas.

15 As has been happening increasingly for several days, large demonstrations take place in several cities in Russia in protest against a law that, upon going into effect on January 1, replaced several state benefits and subsidies for pensioners with small cash stipends.

China and Taiwan reach an agreement to allow charter flights between the mainland and Taiwan to fly non-stop over the Chinese New Year holidays, from January 29 to February 20; they will be the first nonstop flights between the two entities since 1949.

Michelle Kwan wins her ninth women's title at the U.S. figure-skating championships in Portland, Ore.

16 In a runoff election, the incumbent president of Croatia, Stipe Mesic, wins reelection to the top post with two-thirds of the votes cast. (*See* January 2.)

The 27th annual Dakar Rally finishes; the winners are French driver Stéphane Peterhansel (for the second consecutive year) in a Mitsubishi Pajero Evolution, French driver Cyril Despres on a KTM motorcycle, and Russian driver Firdaus Kabirov in a Kamaz truck; two motorcycle riders, including two-time winner Fabrizio Meoni, died in the race.

At the Golden Globe Awards in Beverly Hills, Calif., best picture honours go to *The Aviator* and *Sideways* and best director goes to Clint Eastwood for *Million Dollar Baby*.

17 Expatriate Iraqis living in places throughout the U.S. begin arriving in Chicago, Detroit, Los Angeles, Washington, D.C., and Nashville, Tenn., to register to vote in the upcoming Iraqi national elections.

Archbishop Basile Georges Casmoussa of the Eastern Rite Syrian Catholic Church is kidnapped outside his church in Mosul, Iraq; he is released the next day, but eight Chinese construction workers are then kidnapped.

In the field of children's literature, the Newbery Medal is awarded to Cynthia Kadohata for *Kira-Kira*, and Kevin Henkes wins the Caldecott Medal for illustration for his book *Kitten's First Full Moon*.

18 Ann Veneman, the outgoing U.S. secretary of agriculture, is named to replace Carol Bellamy as head of UNICEF.

A gala unveiling at the Jean-Luc Lagardère hangar in France introduces the first production model of the "superjumbo" Airbus A380 airplane, a double-decker capable of carrying as many as 850 passengers.

19 In a ceremony at the German Historical Museum in Berlin, German Chancellor Gerhard Schröder initiates a yearlong celebration of the centennial of Albert Einstein's publication of the theory of relativity.

A Moscow city official announces a plan to build a monument to leaders in the war against Nazi Germany; the monument will include a representation of Joseph Stalin, the first statue of the former dictator to be publicly displayed in Moscow in some 40 years.

Three British soldiers go on trial at a court-martial in Osnabrück, Ger., on charges of having abused Iraqi prisoners in May 2003; the abuse came to light when a soldier tried to have photographs processed in England.

20 George W. Bush is sworn in for his second term as president of the United States.

The heaviest flooding in more than a century leads the government of Guyana to declare Georgetown and the surrounding area a disaster zone and plead for international help in dealing with the situation; thousands of people have had to evacuate their homes.

The bodies of six prison employees are found outside the maximum-security prison in Matamoros, Mex.; shortly afterward army troops seize control of the prison.

21 For the second consecutive day, protesters in Beslan, North Ossetia, Russia, block a nearby highway, demanding the resignation of Aleksandr S. Dzasokhov as president of the southern republic because they believe the investigation into the school siege that killed more than 300 people in September 2004 is being mishandled.

22 Parliamentary elections, postponed from Dec. 31, 2004, because of the Indian Ocean tsunami, take place in Maldives.

23 Viktor Yushchenko is inaugurated as president of Ukraine in a ceremony in Kiev.

Sébastien Loeb of France, the 2004 world champion of automobile rally racing, wins the Monte-Carlo Rally for the third consecutive year.

24 The U.S. Supreme Court rules that the use of a trained drug-sniffing dog during a traffic stop in the absence of any suspicion of the presence of drugs does not constitute an unreasonable search and is thus permissible under the Constitution.

In Thoroughbred horse racing's 2004 Eclipse Awards, Ghostzapper is named Horse of the Year.

In Paris the Prada Group announces that Helmut Lang has resigned as head of his design house, which has been owned by Prada since 1999.

Conservative pundit William Safire publishes his final column on the opinion page of the *New York Times*, where his columns have appeared since 1973.

25 As hundreds of thousands of pilgrims approach the hilltop Mandher Devi temple near the town of Wai, Maharashtra state, India, a stampede erupts, and relatives of victims begin setting fires in anger; 258 pilgrims are killed.

France observes the 60th anniversary of the liberation of the Auschwitz death camp with the official opening in Paris of the renovated Holocaust Memorial and the unveiling of the Wall of Names, listing the 76,000 Jewish victims of the Holocaust deported from occupied France during World War II.

•

Andrea Levy wins the 2004 Whitbread Book of the Year Award for her novel *Small Island;* she previously had won the Orange Prize for the same work.

26 Condoleezza Rice is sworn in as U.S. secretary of state.

•

A U.S. Marine helicopter crashes in a sandstorm near Rutba, Iraq, killing all 31 aboard, while four U.S. soldiers are killed in battle in Anbar, another is killed in an attack in Duluiyah, and another is killed by a roadside bomb in Baghdad; this is the highest one-day death toll for the U.S. military in the war to date.

•

The inaugural Story Prize, given to honour a previously unpublished work of short fiction in the U.S., is awarded to Haitian-born Edwidge Danticat for *The Dew Breaker*.

27 A bomb goes off at a rally of the opposition Awami League in Laskarpur, Bangladesh, killing four people, among them a former finance minister.

•

A new 120-km (75-mi)-long road between Herat, Afg., and a post in the Dogharoun region of Iran is ceremonially opened by Pres. Hamid Karzai of Afghanistan and Pres. Mohammad Khatami of Iran.

28 Israel orders its army to cease offensive opera-

tions in the Gaza Strip and open the checkpoints into the region and also to cut back operations in the West Bank.

•

Leaders of Santa Cruz state, Bolivia, appoint an assembly to prepare for autonomy after Bolivian Pres. Carlos Mesa agrees to allow the state to elect its prefect rather than have him appointed and to allow a referendum on autonomy to take place in June.

•

Consumer products companies Procter & Gamble and the Gillette Co. announce a friendly merger.

•

The annual Ernst von Siemens Music Prize, which honours outstanding achievement in contemporary music, is awarded to French composer Henri Dutilleux.

29 American Serena Williams defeats her countrywoman Lindsay Davenport to win the Australian Open tennis tournament; the

following day Marat Safin of Russia defeats Lleyton Hewitt of Australia to win the men's title.

•

On the first day of the Alpine skiing world championships in Bormio, Italy, American Bode Miller wins the supergiant slalom race with a time of 1:27.55.

•

Winning films at the Sundance Film Festival awards ceremony in Park City, Utah, include *Why We Fight, Forty Shades of Blue, Murderball,* and *Hustle & Flow*.

30 Elections take place in Iraq for provincial legislatures and a national assembly empowered to write a new constitution; in spite of attacks that kill 35 people, turnout is estimated at 60%. *(Photo below.)*

•

A transport plane for the British Royal Air Force crashes in central Iraq; 10 British soldiers are killed, the highest single-day death toll for British forces since the beginning of the war.

31 A commission appointed by UN Secretary-General Kofi Annan to investigate the situation in the Darfur region of The Sudan reports that it found war crimes and crimes against humanity but not genocide; it recommends that the crimes be tried in the International Criminal Court.

•

The fifth annual World Social Forum, which grew out of the antiglobalization movement and is intended to counterbalance the World Economic Forum, wraps up after six days and thousands of workshops in Pôrto Alegre, Braz.; a record 100,000 people attended.

•

The American insurance company Metlife announces a deal in which it will purchase Citigroup's life insurance business.

•

SBC Communications, one of the companies formed by the court-ordered breakup of AT&T Co. in 1984, announces plans to buy AT&T.

© Erik De Castro/Reuters/Corbis

February

1 In a virtual coup, King Gyanendra of Nepal dismisses the government, suspends much of the constitution, and cuts off communication to and within the country.

At a meeting in Tegucigalpa, Honduras, the heads of Central American countries agree to create a plan to address narcoterrorism and other cross-border criminality on a regional basis.

China makes a deal to lend Russia $6 billion to help finance, in return for crude oil, the nationalization of the main subsidiary of the Yukos oil company, which was seized and auctioned off by Russia in December 2004.

While in Argentina, Pres. Hugo Chávez of Venezuela says that he plans to sell his country's interests in American oil refineries as part of a plan to distance his government from that of the U.S.

2 Armando Guebuza is sworn in as president of Mozambique.

U.S. Pres. George W. Bush delivers his fourth state of the union address; he emphasizes a plan to reinvent Social Security, citing the creation of a system of privately held accounts.

Vietnam appeals to the World Health Organization and the Food and Agriculture Organization for help in dealing with the A(H5N1) avian flu, which is ravaging poultry in the country and has killed 13 of the 14 people infected in the past five weeks.

The Irish Republican Army formally withdraws from peace negotiations in Northern Ireland with the governments of the United Kingdom and Ireland.

At a meeting in Sofia, Bulg., the prime ministers of Bulgaria, Bosnia and Herzegovina, the Czech Republic, Croatia, Hungary, Romania, Serbia and Montenegro, and Slovakia sign a 10-year plan for the social integration of the Roma (Gypsy) minorities in their countries.

3 The UN-appointed committee investigating the pre-occupation oil-for-food program in Iraq releases an interim report in which it cites Benon V. Sevan, head of the program in 1997–2003, for favouritism and conflict of interest.

4 Ukraine's Supreme Council approves the appointment of Yuliya Tymoshenko as prime minister.

Officials announce that Guatemala's Constitutional Court has ruled that the soldiers on trial for having killed more than 200 unarmed civilians in Dos Erres in 1982 are immune from prosecution, which thus ends the war crimes trial.

5 Gnassingbé Eyadéma, president of Togo, dies in office, and the country's military immediately installs his son Faure E. Gnassingbé in his place, in contravention of the country's constitution; the following day the National Assembly revises the constitution to allow Gnassingbé to remain in office until 2008.

Leaders of the Group of Seven industrialized countries meeting in London agree to pursue a plan to allow the entire debt owed by the poorest countries to multilateral institutions such as the World Bank to be written off.

Quarterbacks Benny Friedman, Dan Marino, and Steve Young and halfback Fritz Pollard are elected to the Pro Football Hall of Fame.

6 In parliamentary elections in Thailand, the political party of Prime Minister Thaksin Shinawatra wins lopsidedly.

In Jacksonville, Fla., the New England Patriots defeat the Philadelphia Eagles 24–21 to win Super Bowl XXXIX.

The Mazatlán Venados (Deer) of Mexico defeat the

Águilas (Eagles) from the Dominican Republic to win baseball's Caribbean Series, with a tournament record of 5–1.

7 British yachtswoman Ellen MacArthur breaks the solo around-the-world sailing record, completing the journey in 71 days 14 hours.

In the world all-around speed-skating championships in Moscow, the top overall female competitor is Anni Friesinger of Germany, and the top male competitor is Shani Davis of the U.S.

8 At a summit meeting in Egypt, Israeli Prime Minister Ariel Sharon and Palestinian leader Mahmoud Abbas agree to a formal cease-fire.

Greece's Parliament elects Karolos Papoulias, a founder of the socialist party PASOK, to the largely ceremonial post of president.

9 A court in Kazakhstan bans the country's second biggest opposition party, saying that its protests against a parliamentary election in 2004 (which was called unfair by international observers) were an incitement to public disorder.

Katsuaki Watanabe is appointed to replace Fujio Cho as president of Toyota Motor, the most profitable automobile manufacturer in the world.

The board of directors of the computer company Hewlett-Packard forces Carly Fiorina to resign as CEO.

10 In the process of announcing its withdrawal from the six-party talks on the

country's nuclear-development plans, North Korea for the first time states publicly that it has developed nuclear weaponry.

Voters in Saudi Arabia take part in the country's first-ever general election; only men are allowed to vote or run for office.

Canadian Prime Minister Paul Martin testifies before the committee investigating the money-laundering scandal that took place when Martin was minister of finance; it is the first time in more than 100 years that a sitting prime minister has testified in a case involving government corruption.

11 As protests take place in Togo, the leaders of ECOWAS (Economic Community of West African States) order the newly installed president, Faure E. Gnassingbé, to meet with them the following day in Niger; he had previously refused to meet with ECOWAS in Lomé, Togo's capital.

A judge in Pinellas county, Fla., rules that Terri Schiavo, a severely brain-damaged woman who is being sustained by a feeding tube against what her husband says are her wishes, has not been denied fair legal representation; the case has stirred public controversy for several years.

The 61st Gold Medal of the American Institute of Architects is presented to Spanish architect Santiago Calatrava.

12 A car bomber kills 17 people in front of a hospital south of Baghdad, bringing the death toll for the week to 104.

Dorothy Stang, an American nun, environmentalist, and

© John Kehe/The Christian Science Monitor via Getty Images

land rights activist, is murdered in Pará state, Braz., igniting a storm of outrage; on February 17 Brazilian Pres. Luiz Inácio Lula da Silva signs decrees that create a reserve of 3.3 million ha (8.15 million ac) and a national park of 445,000 ha (1.1 million ac) in the Amazonian rainforest in Stang's memory.

A public art project by Christo and Jeanne-Claude called *The Gates, Central Park, New York City, 1979–2005* goes on display in New York City's Central Park; it consists of 7,503 gates hung with saffron-coloured fabric along 37 km (23 mi) of walkway and remains on display until February 27. *(Photo above.)*

For the first time, the European Space Agency's Ariane-

space successfully launches its most powerful rocket, the Ariane 5-ECA, from the spaceport at Kourou, French Guiana, and places two satellites in orbit.

13 Results of the January 30 election in Iraq are reported; the United Iraqi Alliance, a Shi'ite grouping approved by Grand Ayatollah Ali al-Sistani, won 48% of the popular vote and 140 of the 275 seats in the assembly, a slim majority.

At the Grammy Awards in Los Angeles, the top winner is the late Ray Charles, who wins eight awards, including record of the year for "Here We Go Again," a duet with Norah Jones, and album of the year for *Genius Loves Company;* the song of the year is John Mayer's

"Daughters," and the best new artist is Maroon5.

14 Rafik Hariri, who resigned as Lebanon's prime minister in October 2004, is killed, along with 16 others, by a car bomb that destroys his motorcade in Beirut.

A flight test of the U.S. missile defense system fails when the interceptor missile does not launch; the previous two tests also failed.

The regional telephone company Verizon announces that it will purchase the long-distance company MCI, which had rejected overtures from Qwest Communications.

15 The U.S. recalls its ambassador to Syria because of its belief that Syria was involved in the assassination of former Lebanese prime minister Rafik Hariri.

In Uruguay, José Mujica is sworn in as chair of the Senate and Nora Castro as head of the Chamber of Deputies; both are former Tupamaro guerrillas who were imprisoned when the country was under military rule (1973–85).

Donna Orender is named president of the Women's National Basketball Association.

Kan-Point's VJK Autumn Roses, a German short-haired pointer, wins Best in Show at the Westminster Kennel Club Dog Show.

16 A ceremony is held in Kyoto, Japan, to mark the coming into force of the Kyoto Protocol, initialed in 1997; the agreement requires that the industrialized world cut emissions of greenhouse gases by 5.2% below 1990 levels by 2012.

Israel's Knesset (legislature) approves a plan to give $870 million in compensation to settlers required to leave the Gaza Strip to relocate without losing their accustomed living standards.

The Association for Computing Machinery announces that the recipients of the 2004 A.M. Turing Award are Vincent G. Cerf and Robert E. Kahn, who created the structure for TCP/IP, or transmission control protocol and Internet protocol, which allows computer networks to communicate with one another.

The Bollingen Prize in American poetry is awarded to Jay Wright.

National Hockey League commissioner Gary Bettman announces that negotiations between the owners and the players' union have been fruitless and that the entire 2004–05 season has been canceled.

17 U.S. Pres. George W. Bush nominates John D. Negroponte, the ambassador to Iraq, as the country's first national intelligence director.

18 Under international pressure, the newly installed president of Togo, Faure E. Gnassingbé, agrees to hold presidential elections within 60 days, as the constitution at the time of his installation required, but not to give up power to the speaker of the legislature, as also required by the constitution.

Scientists at a NASA news conference report that on Dec. 27, 2004, they detected a burst of light energy from interstellar space only a fraction of a second long but so powerful that it exceeded the total energy emitted from the Sun in 150,000 years; the source was identified as a distant magnetar, a rapidly spinning neutron star with an extremely intense magnetic field.

19 Suicide bombers target celebrations of the Shi'ite holy day Ashura throughout Iraq, killing some 30 people; on the previous day suicide bombers at various religious gatherings and one police checkpoint killed at least 35 people in Baghdad alone.

20 In legislative elections in Portugal, the Socialist Party defeats the ruling coalition, winning its first-ever absolute majority; José Sócrates becomes prime minister on March 12.

Spain, the first country to vote on the EU constitution in a national referendum, approves the constitution handily; the document had previously been ratified by the parliaments in Lithuania, Hungary, and Slovenia.

Beset by allegations of sexual harassment, which he denies, UN High Commissioner for Refugees Ruud Lubbers submits his resignation.

In London *The Producers* wins three Laurence Olivier Awards—best new musical, best actor in a musical (Nathan Lane), and best supporting actor in a musical (Conleth Hill)—and *The History Boys* also wins three awards—best new play, best director (Nicholas Hytner), and best actor (Richard Griffiths); Alan Bennett, the playwright of *The History Boys*, wins a special award for contributions to British theatre.

In Daytona Beach, Fla., Jeff Gordon wins the Daytona 500, NASCAR's premier race, for the third time.

In Park City, Utah, Italy's Armin Zöggeler wins a record fifth luge world championship singles title; the previous day Sylke Otto of Germany won her fourth world championship in the women's singles event, tying the record set by East Germany's Margit Schumann in the 1970s.

21 Tens of thousands of people—Muslim, Christian, and Druze—march in Beirut, Lebanon, in anti-Syrian protests *(photo right)*, while Syrian Pres. Bashar al-Assad tells the secretary-general of the Arab League that Syria intends, as it has since 1989, to withdraw its troops.

Prosecutors in Bolivia bring charges of genocide against former president Gonzalo Sánchez de Lozada, who is living in exile in the U.S., for involvement in the deaths of more than 60 people in the protests that preceded his resignation.

The British Royal Navy announces that it is planning to recruit gay enlistees to join the service.

22 An early-morning earthquake of magnitude 6.4 centred on the city of Zarand kills at least 490 people in central Iran; many villages are destroyed.

Emerging victorious in the elections, the United Iraqi Alliance chooses Ibrahim al-Jaafari as its candidate to become the prime minister of Iraq.

© Ramzi Haidar/AFP/Getty Images

23 Shigeru Omi of the World Health Organization warns that a deadly form of avian flu spreading throughout Asia, which has killed 14 people in Vietnam so far in 2005, threatens the world with a pandemic should it mutate into a form that can be transmitted easily from human to human.

In a British military court in Germany, two British soldiers, Mark Cooley and Daniel Kenyon, are convicted on charges of having abused Iraqi prisoners near Basra, Iraq, in May 2003.

24 The Palestinian legislature approves a new cabinet that is largely purged of allies of the late Yasir Arafat, though Ahmed Qurei retains his post as prime minister.

Somalian Pres. Abdullahi Yusuf Ahmed and Prime Minister Ali Muhammad Ghedi visit Somalia for the first time since attaining their posts; they are assessing conditions for moving the Somalian government-in-exile from Kenya.

Pope John Paul II is hospitalized for the second time this month and undergoes a tracheostomy because of difficulty breathing.

25 Bowing to internal and international pressure, Faure E. Gnassingbé resigns as president of Togo; Abass Bonfoh becomes interim president until a presidential election, in which Gnassingbé will be a candidate, is held.

The judge who has presided over the dispute over Terri Schiavo for the past seven years in Pinellas county, Fla., rules that he will grant no further stays and that Schiavo's husband may have the feeding tube removed on March 18.

For the first time since it was booed off the stage in 1931, the ballet *The Bolt*, with a score by Dmitry Shostakovich and originally choreographed by Fyodor Lopukhov, is performed by the Bolshoi Ballet in Moscow.

26 Egyptian Pres. Hosni Mubarak asks the parliament to amend the constitution to permit for the first time in the country's history direct, multiparty presidential elections to be held.

Japan's space agency successfully returns its H-2A heavy-lift rocket to service with a launch from its Tanegashima space centre and deploys a geostationary air traffic/weather satellite.

Wichita, Kan., police announce that they have arrested a man, Dennis L. Rader, in suburban Park City whom they believe to be the serial killer known as B.T.K., who is responsible for at least eight murders over a 30-year period.

27 Parliamentary elections are held in Kyrgyzstan and Tajikistan; international observers in both countries say the polling fell short of international standards of fairness, and runoff elections for each district in Kyrgyzstan are scheduled for March 13, while the ruling party retains power in Tajikistan.

Officials from both Iraq and Syria report that Syria has captured and turned over to Iraq Sabawi Ibrahim al-Hassan al-Tikriti, a half brother of Saddam Hussein who headed two security agencies under Saddam and who is believed to be financing the insurgency.

The Framework Convention on Tobacco Control, signed by 168 countries but ratified by only 57, comes into effect; it asks those countries to take steps to reduce tobacco smoking, which kills an estimated five million people annually.

At the 77th Academy Awards presentations, hosted by comedian Chris Rock, Oscars are won by, among others, *Million Dollar Baby* and its director, Clint Eastwood, and actors Jamie Foxx, Hilary Swank, Morgan Freeman, and Cate Blanchett.

28 In by far the deadliest bombing since the start of the war in Iraq, a car bomber detonates his weapon in a crowd of police and army recruits outside a medical clinic across the street from a market in Hilla; at least 122 people are killed.

As tens of thousands of people demonstrate in Beirut against Syrian involvement in Lebanon, the pro-Syrian Omar Karami resigns as Lebanese prime minister.

In a referendum, more than 90% of voters in Burundi approve a new constitution that lays the groundwork for a government in which the Hutu majority and the Tutsi minority would share power.

March

© Carl De Souza/AFP/Getty Images

1 A socialist, Tabaré Vázquez Rosas, is inaugurated as president of Uruguay.

In a gun battle in Ituri province in the Democratic Republic of the Congo, UN peacekeepers kill 50 members of an ethnic Lendu militia that has been terrorizing the area; also, the government says that three militia leaders have been arrested in the ambush killing and mutilation of nine UN peacekeepers in Ituri province.

The U.S. Supreme Court rules that the execution of people for crimes that they committed when they were younger than 18 years old is unconstitutional; the ruling immediately affects 72 condemned prisoners.

2 Elmar Huseynov, the founder and editor of the Azerbaijani opposition magazine *Monitor,* is shot and killed in Baku.

Hundreds of former banana plantation workers demonstrate in Managua, Nic., demanding monetary compensation for their exposure to a banned pesticide used by American companies.

3 American adventurer Steve Fossett becomes the first person to fly solo nonstop around the world when he lands in Salina, Kan., 67 hr 2 min after taking off; his plane, called the *GlobalFlyer,* was designed and built by Burt Rutan's Scaled Composites company, which also built SpaceShipOne. *(Photo above.)*

A trial involving 39 men and 27 women accused of pedophile crimes that shocked the country begins in Angers, France.

4 A car carrying Giuliana Sgrena, an Italian journalist who was kidnapped on February 4 in Baghdad, and Nicola Calipari, an Italian intelligence agent who negotiated her release, is fired on by U.S. soldiers as it approaches a checkpoint on the way to the Baghdad airport; Calipari is killed and Sgrena is wounded.

Yury F. Kravchenko, who was interior minister of Ukraine under former president Leonid Kuchma in 1995–2001, dies in an apparent suicide hours before he is to talk to government prosecutors about the 2000 murder of journalist Georgy Gongadze, in which there was widely believed to have been government involvement.

5 Syrian Pres. Bashar al-Assad makes a speech in which he declares that Syrian troops in Lebanon will gradually withdraw to border areas near Syria, but he gives no timetable.

6 In parliamentary elections in Moldova, the ruling Communist Party retains its majority.

After defeating Phil Mickelson at the Doral Open golf tournament in Miami, Tiger Woods regains the number one ranking in golf that he had lost to Vijay Singh in September 2004.

7 The Sony Corp. of Japan names Sir Howard Stringer, head of the Sony Corp. of America, its new chairman and CEO, succeeding Nobuyuki Idei.

Harry Stonecipher, who was made CEO of the aerospace company Boeing in order to restore its good name after an era of ethical missteps, is forced to resign when it is revealed that he engaged in an adulterous liaison with an executive at the company.

8 Bolivia's National Congress refuses to accept the offer of resignation given the day before by Pres. Carlos Mesa; the president reaches an agreement with most opposition parties for a plan that includes increased autonomy for the states and the drafting of a new constitution.

The prime minister of the province of Kosovo in Serbia and Montenegro, Ramush Haradinaj, surprises observers by resigning in order to surrender to the UN war crimes tribunal in The Hague.

In Beirut, Lebanon, a huge demonstration by Shi'ite supporters of the militant group Hezbollah in favour of a continued Syrian presence in Lebanon greatly outnumbers the anti-Syria demonstrations that preceded it. (*See* March 14.)

9 Omar Karami, the pro-Syrian who resigned as prime minister of Lebanon on February 28, is reelected prime minister by the legislature.

The U.S. Department of State announces that the country has withdrawn from the protocol that gives the International Court of Justice jurisdiction to hear cases involving foreigners arrested and denied the right to contact the embassies of their home countries.

The LexisNexis Group, which compiles personal, legal, and consumer information, reveals that unauthorized access to the information of some 30,000 people has occurred; in recent weeks the data broker ChoicePoint inadvertently sold the information of some 145,000 people to scam artists, and Bank of America lost backup files containing the information of more than a million people.

Charles H. Townes, a winner of the 1964 Nobel Prize for Physics, is named the winner of the Templeton Prize for Progress Toward Research or Discoveries About Spiritual Realities.

CBS news anchor Dan Rather signs off after his final broadcast, concluding a career of 42 years.

10 Tung Chee-hwa resigns as chief executive of Hong Kong two years before the end of his term; deputy Donald Tsang will serve in his place until the next election.

Members of the Chechen separatist movement announce that they have chosen Abdul-Khalim Saydullayev, a little-known religious judge, to replace Aslan Maskhadov, who was killed two days earlier, as president.

The Paris Club of creditor countries agrees to a moratorium for the remainder of the year on debt payments for the countries that were hit by the Indian Ocean tsunami in December 2004.

After winning a tournament in Linares, Spain, Russian grandmaster Garry Kasparov announces his retirement from professional chess.

11 The U.S. government announces an agreement with the U.K., France, and Germany in which the U.S. will support Iran's entry into the World Trade Organization and sell the country airplane parts if Iran agrees to a permanent end to the enrichment of uranium; the European countries pledge to bring the issue before the UN Security Council if Iran does not agree.

The British Parliament passes a controversial antiterror-ism bill that, among other things, allows the government to put suspected terrorists under strict house arrest without trial.

12 UN envoy Terje Roed-Larsen secures an agreement from Syrian Pres. Bashar al-Assad to withdraw Syrian troops from Lebanon completely and to set a timetable for the withdrawal.

At the Alpine World Cup skiing competition in Lenzerheide, Switz., Bode Miller becomes the first American in 22 years to win an overall men's World Cup championship; the following day Anja Pärson of Sweden wins the women's title for the second consecutive year.

13 Runoff legislative elections in Kyrgyzstan are widely viewed as fraudulent as domestic election observers are prevented from doing their jobs.

Canada sets a new world record time of 6 min 39.990 sec in the 5,000-m relay at the world short-track speed-skating championships in Beijing.

14 The National People's Congress of China passes a law that authorizes the use of force against Taiwan should Taiwan declare itself independent of China.

Some 800,000 Lebanese—mostly Sunni Muslims, Druze, and Christians—rally in Beirut against Syrian influence in Lebanon; it is the biggest demonstration ever seen in Lebanon. (*See* March 8.)

Israel agrees to allow the Palestinian Authority to take over security control in the West Bank cities of Jericho and Tulkarm.

Some 300 people are arrested throughout Nepal in rallies opposing the emergency rule imposed by King Gyanendra.

In its 20th induction ceremony, the Rock and Roll Hall of Fame in Cleveland inducts the solo performers Buddy Guy and Percy Sledge, the bands the O'Jays, the Pretenders, and U2, booking agency founder Frank Barsalona, and Sire Records founder Seymour Stein.

A state judge in California rules that a state law that limits marriage to opposite-sex couples violates the state's constitution.

15 People protesting elections they believe were rigged march in the streets and occupy government offices in several cities in Kyrgyzstan.

Italian Prime Minister Silvio Berlusconi says that he intends to begin withdrawing Italian troops from Iraq, where Italy has some 3,000 troops, by September.

Bernard J. Ebbers, the former CEO of the disgraced telecommunications company WorldCom (now MCI), is found guilty of securities fraud, conspiracy, and seven counts of filing false reports.

16 Iraq's newly elected National Assembly conducts its first meeting, in the heavily guarded central Green Zone in Baghdad.

On the eighth day of protests in Guatemala against a free-trade treaty with the U.S., riot police and protesters clash in Santa Cruz del Quiché.

Nicaragua declares a national health emergency in the face of a viral diarrhea that has killed at least 41 people and made tens of thousands ill.

17 During a brief visit to Afghanistan, U.S. Secretary of State Condoleezza Rice reveals that upcoming parliamentary elections in the country are being postponed for a third time, from May until September; meanwhile, in Kandahar, in the worst attack in seven months, a bomb kills at least 5 people and injures 32.

18 Wal-Mart Stores agrees to a record $11 million settlement with the federal government, which had accused the retail giant of hiring illegal immigrants as cleaning staff.

John G. Rowland, the former governor of Connecticut, is sentenced to more than a year in prison for having secretly accepted gifts from people doing business with the state while he was governor; he had pleaded guilty in December 2004.

In accordance with what her husband says would have been her wishes, in Pinellas Park, Fla., the feeding tube keeping the severely brain-damaged Terri Schiavo alive is removed. (*See* March 20.)

The U.S. government suspends military aid to Nicaragua, complaining that the country has failed to destroy its cache of Soviet-made SA-7 shoulder-launched antiaircraft missiles, which the U.S. fears could fall into the hands of terrorists.

19 A bomb goes off at a Shi'ite Muslim religious gathering in Gandhawa, Pak., killing at least 44 people.

Irina Slutskaya of Russia wins the women's world figure-skating championship in Moscow; two days earlier Stéphane Lambiel had become the first Swiss since 1947 to claim the men's title.

In the Six Nations Rugby Union championship, Wales defeats Ireland 32–20 to win the title and its first grand slam in 27 years.

20 Insurgents attack a U.S. military patrol in Salman Pak, Iraq; at least 24 insurgents are killed, while assorted attacks elsewhere in Iraq leave at least 7 people dead.

The U.S. Senate passes a bill that would give federal courts jurisdiction over whether it was legal to remove the feeding tube from a severely brain-damaged woman, Terri Schiavo, while the House of Representatives calls a special session to consider the measure; Pres. George W. Bush quickly returns to Washington, D.C., from vacation in Texas in order to sign the bill into law. (*See* March 18.)

A magnitude-7 earthquake strikes in southern Japan, devastating the island of Genkai-jima but killing only one person. (*Photo right.*)

Thousands of protesters upset by unfair elections rampage in Dzhalal-Abad, Kyrgyzstan, occupying government offices and burning down a police station.

21 Hifikepunye Pohamba is sworn in as president of Namibia; he is the country's first president elected since independence and succeeds Sam Nujoma.

Antigovernment demonstrators take over Osh, the second largest city in Kyrgyzstan.

American architect Thom Mayne is named winner of the 2005 Pritzker Architecture Prize.

Former world chess champion Bobby Fischer is granted Icelandic citizenship; under indictment by the U.S. government, Fischer has been living in detention in Japan for eight months.

22 Germany's national airline, Deutsche Lufthansa, announces a deal to take over Switzerland's troubled Swiss International Airlines.

Astronomers report that, using NASA's Spitzer Space Telescope, an orbiting infrared observatory, they have for the first time observed and directly measured light from planets outside the solar system; heretofore such extrasolar planets had been detected only by indirect methods.

23 The Arab League concludes a two-day summit in Algiers; leaders of only 13 of the 22 member countries attended the conference, at which it

was decided to create an Arab parliament.

•

Health officials warn travelers to stay out of Uíge province in Angola, where an outbreak of the Marburg virus, which is related to the Ebola virus and is fatal with no known cure, has killed at least 95 people since October 2004.

•

Composer Leonid Desyatnikov's controversial new opera *Children of Rosental*, with a book by Vladimir Sorokin, opens at the Bolshoi Theatre in Moscow after weeks of protest; it is the theatre's first new opera in 30 years.

24 Thousands of demonstrators storm the presidential palace in Bishkek, Kyrgyzstan, forcing Pres. Askar Akayev to flee the country.

•

The UN Security Council passes a resolution to send 10,000 peacekeeping troops to The Sudan, some to maintain the peace agreement in the south and some to reinforce African Union troops in the Darfur region.

•

U.S. Secretary of Defense Donald Rumsfeld announces that the country will resume giving military aid to Guatemala; aid had been suspended in 1990 in the face of atrocities committed by the Guatemalan military, including the killing of an American citizen.

25 Outside Manama, Bahrain, tens of thousands of people march in a demonstration demanding democratic reforms, including more powers for the elected legislative assembly.

•

In various places throughout Iraq, three suicide car bombings and a number of attacks with guns leave at least 23 people dead, including 5 Iraqi cleaning women.

26 A half million people march in Taipei, Taiwan, angered and frightened by the antisecession law passed in China on March 14.

After two days of looting by antigovernment protesters in Kyrgyzstan, a new government, led by Kurmanbek Bakiyev as acting president, gains control.

•

Roses in May wins the Dubai World Cup, the world's richest horse race, by three lengths.

Yokozuna Asashoryu defeats *ozeki* Kaio at the spring grand sumo tournament in Osaka, Japan, to win his 11th Emperor's Cup.

27 Pope John Paul II appears at his window in St. Peter's Square in the Vatican to deliver his traditional Easter blessing; because of his illnesses, however, he is unable to speak.

Police in Cairo arrest 100 people in preventing a demonstration by thousands of people organized by the Muslim Brotherhood to demand an end to emergency laws that have been in place in Egypt since 1981.

•

At the Nabisco championship in Rancho Mirage, Calif., Annika Sörenstam of Sweden wins her fifth consecutive Ladies Professional Golf Association Tour tournament, tying a record set by American Nancy Lopez in 1978.

•

Oxford defeats Cambridge by two lengths in the 151st University Boat Race; Cambridge leads the series 78–72.

28 An earthquake measured at magnitude 8.7 occurs with an epicentre about 200 km (125 mi) from the Indonesian island of Sumatra, killing 905 people, most on the island of Nias.

•

It is reported that King Jigme Singye Wangchuk of Bhutan has unveiled a draft of a new constitution that would establish parliamentary rule and multiparty democracy to replace what is presently a monarchy.

•

Rebels in Sa'dah province, Yemen, attack security forces, killing seven policemen; eight of the rebels are killed in turn.

•

A law is passed in Ireland that outlaws the use of English on street signs and official maps in the Gaeltacht region of the country's west coast; in more than 2,000 places, signs will appear exclusively in Gaelic.

•

Maud Fontenoy of France becomes the first woman to row across the Pacific Ocean when she arrives in Hiva Oa, Marquesas Islands, French Polynesia, 73 days after leaving the port of Callao in Peru.

29 The commission investigating misconduct in the oil-for-food program in Iraq reports having found no evidence that UN Secretary-General Kofi Annan had any involvement in the awarding of a contract to a company that employed his son.

Lord Ashdown, the international administrator of Bosnia and Herzegovina, removes the Croat member of the tripartite presidency, Dragan Covic, from office; Covic had refused to resign after being indicted for corruption.

•

Spain's Environment Ministry reports that three Iberian lynx cubs have been born at Coto Doñana National Park; the Iberian lynx is the most endangered feline species, with about 100 still alive, and these are the first cubs ever born in captivity.

30 After Palestinian Pres. Mahmoud Abbas expels members of al-Aqsa Martyrs Brigades from the presidential compound for refusing to disarm and join the Palestinian Authority security forces, the gunmen run riot in Ram Allah.

•

In the run-up to Egyptian elections on September 7, hundreds of demonstrators from the Kifaya movement, which opposes a new term of office for Pres. Hosni Mubarak, rally in Cairo, Alexandria, and Mansoura.

31 In legislative elections in Zimbabwe that independent observers say are fraudulent, the ruling Zimbabwe African National Union–Patriotic Front is said to have won handily.

The UN Security Council passes a resolution to refer war crimes suspects from the Darfur region of The Sudan to the International Criminal Court in The Hague.

•

Paul Wolfowitz is confirmed as president of the World Bank; he will begin his five-year term in June.

•

Pope John Paul II suffers a heart attack.

•

Ted Koppel, host of the ABC late-night television news program *Nightline* since 1980, announces that he will leave the network at the end of the year.

April

"

*After the great Pope John Paul II,
the cardinals have elected me, a simple, humble
worker in the Lord's vineyard.*

"

Pope Benedict XVI,
in his first public address after his election, April 19

1 Overnight, members of the state military police shoot up the streets and sidewalks of two crime-ridden suburbs of Rio de Janeiro, killing 30 people.

2 Pope John Paul II dies in his apartment in Vatican City.

The day after firing the police commander in Ram Allah, Palestinian Pres. Mahmoud Abbas asks for and receives the resignation of the security chief for the West Bank, in response to violence in Ram Allah by members of al-Aqsa Martyrs Brigades.

After months of discord that led to many canceled performances, Riccardo Muti resigns as music director of La Scala opera house in Milan.

3 In its first step toward forming a government and following months of debate, the Iraqi National Assembly appoints a Sunni as speaker and a Shi'ite and a Kurd as deputy speakers.

UN envoy Terje Roed-Larsen announces that Syrian Pres. Bashar al-Assad has agreed to remove all Syrian military and intelligence forces from Lebanon by the end of April. (*See* April 26.)

The Museum of the Shenandoah Valley opens in Winchester, Va.; the historical and cultural museum was designed by the architect Michael Graves.

4 Askar Akayev resigns as president of Kyrgyzstan after receiving assurances that he will not be prosecuted for anything that occurred during his administration.

Moldova's Parliament reelects Vladimir Voronin as president.

Hundreds of supporters of opposition leader Morgan Tsvangirai march in Harare, Zimb., to protest the results of the March 31 election.

The U.S. Supreme Court rules that creditors may not access funds in the IRAs (individual retirement accounts) of people who have filed for bankruptcy.

In New York City the winners of the 2005 Pulitzer Prizes are announced; journalistic awards go to, among others, the *Los Angeles Times* and *The Wall Street Journal*, which each win two awards; winners in letters and drama include Marilynne Robinson in fiction, Ted Kooser in poetry, and John Patrick Shanley in drama, while Steven Stucky wins in music.

The National Collegiate Athletic Association championship in men's basketball is won by the University of North Carolina, which defeats the University of Illinois 75–70; the following day Baylor University defeats Michigan State 84–62 for its first women's NCAA title.

5 Armando Falcon announces his resignation as head of the Office of Federal Housing Enterprise Oversight, the agency that oversees the mortgage companies Fannie Mae and Freddie Mac, a position in which he has served since 1999.

6 Europe's longest-reigning monarch, Prince Rainier III of Monaco, dies after 55 years as ruler; he is succeeded by his son, Prince Albert II.

The Iraqi National Assembly names Kurdish militia leader Jalal Talabani president of Iraq.

In Pretoria, S.Af., the leaders of Côte d'Ivoire's government, the opposition, and rebel forces sign an agreement to cease hostilities, begin disarmament, and make plans to hold elections.

7 Newly named Iraqi Pres. Jalal Talabani appoints Shi'ite leader Ibrahim al-Jaafari as Iraq's new prime minister.

Thousands of people assemble in Bissau, Guinea-Bissau, to welcome back from exile former president João Bernardo Vieira; a presidential election is scheduled for June.

Hundreds of thousands of people gather in Mexico City to protest the *desafuero,* the stripping of immunity from prosecution, of Mexico City Mayor Andrés Manuel López Obrador by Mexico's legislature. (*See* April 23.)

8 Pope John Paul II is buried after what is by far the largest papal funeral ever held; in the previous week more than two million people had viewed the pope's body as it lay in state.

In a presidential election that is boycotted by the opposition, Pres. Ismail Omar Guelleh, running unopposed, is reelected president of Djibouti.

In Dili, East Timor, Pres. Susilo Bambang Yudhoyono of Indonesia and Prime Minister Mari Alkatiri of East Timor witness the signing of an agreement on the demarcation of the border between the two countries.

9 Officially sanctioned anti-Japanese demonstrations in Beijing degenerate into riots in which Japanese-owned businesses are attacked before riot police gain control of the situation.

In Windsor, Eng., Charles, prince of Wales, marries Camilla Parker Bowles, who hereafter will be called Camilla, duchess of Cornwall. (*Photo right.*)

10 At the place in Jerusalem that is revered as the Temple Mount by Jews and as Al-Haram al-Sharif by Muslims, a huge deployment of Israeli police prevents a planned rally by a right-wing Israeli organization from taking place.

After police break up a roadblock set up weeks earlier by a group of elderly women in Huaxi village, Zhejiang province, China, to protest pollution from nearby factories, thousands of villagers riot in defense of the protesters, destroying police cars and driving police away.

Tiger Woods defeats Chris DiMarco on the first playoff hole to win the Masters golf tournament in Augusta, Ga., for the fourth time.

Steve Jaros wins the 2005 PBA Dexter Tournament of Champions, his first major bowling title.

11 After several days of delay, Kyrgyzstan's legislature accepts the resignation of Askar Akayev as president and sets a new presidential election for July 10.

In New Delhi, Chinese Prime Minister Wen Jiabao and Indian Prime Minister Manmohan Singh sign documents on a number of subjects; of special note is an agreement to resolve the 3,540-km (2,200-mi) border between the countries, which has been a source of friction since 1962.

Three days after filing for bankruptcy protection, MG Rover, the last major car manufacturer in the U.K., sends 6,000 factory workers home and ceases production; on April 15 the company announces that it has gone out of business.

12 The World Health Organization and the U.S. Centers for Disease Control and Prevention observe the 50th anniversary of the introduction of the polio vaccine.

The World Health Organization recommends that some 5,000 laboratories around the world destroy samples of a virus that they may have received as part of virus-testing kits; the samples contained a strain of flu that killed at least a million people in 1957 and to which no one born after 1968 has any immunity.

The European Commission recommends that the EU begin talks with Serbia and Montenegro on the first steps toward membership for that country.

13 The EU agrees to allow Bulgaria and Romania to become members of the association; it is expected that they will enter the union in 2007.

The UN General Assembly passes a nuclear-terrorism treaty that requires its signatories to prosecute or extradite individuals in possession of nuclear devices or materials.

Omar Karami for the second time resigns as prime minister of Lebanon, saying he has been unable to form a government.

At the National Magazine Awards in New York City, the big winner is *The New Yorker,* which wins five awards, including one for general excellence; other winners include *Glamour, Wired, Martha Stewart Weddings, Dwell,* and *Print.*

14 Two suicide bombers in Baghdad kill 14 people, 13 of them civilians, outside the Interior Ministry, while attacks elsewhere in Iraq kill 5 others; also, Iraqi officials describe the discovery of mass graves in Al-Nasiriyah, Al-Samawah, and Basra, the latter thought to contain as many as 5,000 bodies.

In the heaviest fighting since a five-year-old cease-fire was rescinded, 21 Kurdish rebels and 3 Turkish soldiers are killed in Turkey's southeastern Anatolia region.

Oregon's Supreme Court rules that the same-sex marriage licenses issued by Multnomah county in 2004 are invalid; the ruling affects some 3,000 couples.

© Tim Graham/Getty Images

In the first Major League Baseball game played in Washington, D.C., in 33 years, the new home team, the Washington Nationals, defeats the Arizona Diamondbacks 5–3 at R.F.K. Stadium.

15 Pres. Émile Lahoud of Lebanon appoints as prime minister Najib Mikati, a pro-Syrian businessman who has won the trust of the opposition.

Pres. Lucio Gutiérrez of Ecuador fires the Supreme Court; it is the second time in four months that the country's top court has been sacked.

In Paris a fire destroys the Paris-Opéra hotel, leaving 24 people dead, most of them African immigrants housed in the hotel by social service agencies.

16 A bomb goes off in a restaurant in Ba'qubah, Iraq, killing at least 13 people; in attacks elsewhere in Iraq, an additional 5 people are killed.

Thousands of demonstrators in Quito, Ecuador, demand the resignation of Pres. Lucio Gutiérrez.

In Port of Spain, Trinidad and Tobago, judges of the new Caribbean Court of Justice are sworn in.

17 Mehmet Ali Talat is elected Turkish Cypriot president, replacing Rauf Denktash.

Ecuador's National Congress dismisses the Supreme Court, making legal the dismissal ordered earlier by the president.

A group of ethnic Shan exiles from Myanmar

(Burma) proclaims the independence of the "Federated Shan States," with Saw Surkhanpha as president.

In the U.K., BAFTA TV Awards are won by *Little Britain*, *Sex Traffic*, *I'm a Celebrity. . . Get Me Out of Here!*, *Coronation Street*, *Omagh*, *Black Books*, and *Green Wing*.

Martin Lel of Kenya posts the fastest time in the 25th London Marathon, at 2 hr 7 min 26 sec; British runner Paula Radcliffe is the fastest woman in the race for the third time, with a finish of 2 hr 17 min 42 sec.

18 In Vatican City the conclave of 115 cardinals gathers to choose a new pope.

Prime Minister Lee Hsien Loong of Singapore announces that the government has approved the building of two casinos in the city-state in order to increase tourism.

In San Francisco the Goldman Environmental Prize is presented to Mexican forest activist Isidro Baldenegro López, Congolese botanist Corneille Ewango, Kazakh nuclear environmentalist Kaisha Atakhanova, Honduran community and forest activist José Andrés Tamayo Cortez, French-Swiss activist Stephanie Danielle Roth, and Haitian agronomist Chavannes Jean-Baptiste.

Having earlier refused the help of the UN High Commissioner for Refugees, Indonesia announces the formation of a new agency that will take over the reconstruction of the rebellious province of Aceh, which was particularly hard hit by the Indian Ocean tsunami of December 2004.

The 109th Boston Marathon is won by Hailu Negussie of

Ethiopia with a time of 2 hr 11 min 45 sec; Catherine Ndereba of Kenya is the women's winner for the fourth time, finishing in 2 hr 25 min 13 sec.

19 On its third ballot the Roman Catholic Church conclave chooses Joseph Cardinal Ratzinger, a German theologian who served for many years in the Roman Curia as defender of the faith, to be the next pope; he announces his papal name as Benedict XVI.

Greece's parliament ratifies the European Union constitution, making Greece the sixth country to approve the document.

Seventeen men return to Afghanistan after being freed from the U.S. military prison in Guantánamo Bay, Cuba; a tribunal had determined that they were not enemy combatants.

Several American dignitaries, including Pres. George W. Bush, attend the dedication of the new interactive Abraham Lincoln Presidential Library and Museum in Springfield, Ill.

20 Ecuador's National Congress dismisses Pres. Lucio Gutiérrez from office, and he flees to the Brazilian embassy; Vice Pres. Alfredo Palacio replaces him.

Connecticut becomes the second U.S. state to permit same-sex couples to enter into civil unions, a status that entails the same statutory rights and responsibilities as marriage.

The first-ever Islamic Solidarity Games, featuring 18 sports, conclude in Mecca, Saudi Arabia; 54 countries sent some 6,500 male athletes to compete.

The New York Stock Exchange and the Archipelago Exchange announce an agreement to merge in the largest-ever securities exchange merger.

Pulitzer Prize winner C.K. Williams is named recipient of the 2005 Ruth Lilly Poetry Prize; he will receive $100,000.

21 John Negroponte is sworn in as the first U.S. director of national intelligence.

The new president of Ecuador, Alfredo Palacio, names a cabinet.

The lower house of the Cortes Generales (legislature) in Spain approves a bill that gives same-sex couples the same marriage rights that opposite-sex couples now have and approves another bill making divorce easier to obtain.

22 At a regional summit meeting in Jakarta, Indon., Japanese Prime Minister Junichiro Koizumi apologizes for the suffering and damage caused by Japan during World War II.

Zacarias Moussaoui, the only person charged in the U.S. with complicity in the Sept. 11, 2001, terrorist attacks, pleads guilty—but not exactly to what he is charged with.

23 Italian Prime Minister Silvio Berlusconi forms a new coalition government three days after resigning because of the collapse of the previous government.

A judge in Mexico City rejects the request by federal prosecutors to charge Mayor

AP/Wide World Photos

28 Scientists report that an ivory-billed woodpecker, a bird thought to have been extinct since 1944, has been sighted in the Cache River National Wildlife Refuge in Arkansas.

Red Cross officials report that Togolese soldiers rampaged through the town of Aného over the previous two days, killing at least nine people, after residents protesting the election results burned a police station.

Judy Woodruff, anchor of CNN's *Inside Politics*, announces that she will leave the network at the end of her contract in June.

29 In Beijing a meeting between the leader of the Communist Party of China, Hu Jintao, and the leader of the Chinese Nationalist Party, Lien Chan, marks the first time leaders of the two parties have met in 60 years; they pledge to work together against the independence movement in Taiwan.

King Gyanendra of Nepal announces the lifting of emergency rule.

A coordinated series of 12 car bombs in the Baghdad area and other attacks in Iraq leave at least 40 people, most of them Iraqi police or military, dead.

30 A suicide bomber kills himself and injures seven people outside the popular Egyptian Museum in Cairo, and his sister and girlfriend fire guns at a tourist bus.

The death toll from bomb attacks in Baghdad and northern Iraq is more than 15, mostly civilians.

Andrés Manuel López Obrador with having violated a court order. (*See* April 7.)

24 Pope Benedict XVI is formally invested with the symbols of office and installed as the 265th pope.

Faure E. Gnassingbé wins the presidential election in Togo; the result of the ballot is accepted by international observers but not by the opposition.

Pres. Hugo Chávez of Venezuela announces that he is cutting all military ties with the U.S. and ordering U.S. military instructors to leave the country.

25 Stanislav Gross resigns as prime minister of the Czech Republic following weeks of questions about the financing of his luxury apartment; Jiri Paroubek is appointed in his place.

A Soyuz space capsule lands safely in Kazakhstan, bringing home cosmonaut Salizhan Sharipov and astronauts Leroy Chiao and Roberto Vittori; the new crew members replacing

them aboard the International Space Station are Russian Sergey Krikalev and American John Phillips.

Crown Prince Abdullah of Saudi Arabia visits U.S. Pres. George W. Bush at the latter's ranch in Crawford, Texas; the leaders discuss oil prices.

The final piece of the 1,700-year-old Aksum obelisk, which was removed from Ethiopia by Italian troops in 1937, is returned to its home in Aksum; it will be reerected in September.

26 Syria formally withdraws the last of its troops from Lebanon; Syria had maintained a military presence in the country for 29 years. (*See* April 3.)

A group of explorers led by Briton Tom Avery arrives at the North Pole by re-creating the 1909 journey of American explorer Robert Peary with replicated equipment, covering the 777 km (483 mi) in less than 37 days, a shorter time than Peary required. (*Photo above.*)

UN Secretary-General Kofi Annan appoints Kemal

Dervis, a Turkish economist, to replace Mark Malloch Brown as head of the United Nations Development Programme.

27 China rules that the chief executive to be chosen by the election committee in July to replace Tung Chee-hwa can serve only for the remainder of the term that Tung was elected to, not a full five-year term. (*See* March 12.)

Member states elected to the United Nations Human Rights Commission are Argentina, Australia, Austria, Azerbaijan, Bangladesh, Botswana, Brazil, Cameroon, China, Germany, Japan, Morocco, the United States, Venezuela, and Zimbabwe; Secretary-General Kofi Annan has proposed a smaller council that would be chosen by the General Assembly rather than, as now, by regional groups.

From Blagnac, France, the Airbus A380, the biggest-ever passenger airplane, makes a successful test flight of about four hours' duration as some 30,000 people look on.

May

> *We Germans look back with shock and shame at World War II, which was unleashed by Germany, and at the Holocaust, which was a breakdown of civilization for which Germans are responsible.*

German Pres. Horst Köhler in a speech to Parliament commemorating the 60th anniversary of the end of World War II, May 8

1 At least 35 Iraqis are killed in attacks that include a car bomb at a Kurdish funeral near Mosul and another at a scene in Baghdad where U.S. soldiers are handing out candy to children.

2 A cache of explosives stored at the home of a commander of a recently disarmed and demobilized regiment in the Afghan village of Kohna Deh explodes, leveling a portion of the village and killing at least 34 people, mostly women and children.

Six car bombs in Baghdad and one in Mosul kill at least 13 Iraqis, and American soldiers engage in a firefight near the Syrian border, killing 12.

•

A socialist, José Miguel Insulza of Chile, a candidate initially opposed by the U.S., is elected secretary-general of the Organization of American States.

•

In the telecommunications industry, Qwest abandons its attempt to purchase MCI, leaving Verizon Communications the victor in the takeover battle.

3 Iraq's newly appointed cabinet is sworn in, though seven posts remain vacant, including that of minister of defense.

•

A bomb explodes and kills at least 15 people in a stadium in Mogadishu, Somalia, where the interim prime minister, Ali Muhammad Ghedi, is speaking; top Somali officials have been living outside the country, and this is Ghedi's first visit to the capital since he was elected to office.

4 A suicide bomber kills at least 60 Kurdish Iraqis at a police recruiting station in Irbil, Iraq, in the worst single attack since early March.

•

The FBI announces that it plans to exhume from its grave in Alsip, Ill., the body of Emmett Till, whose lynching in Mississippi as a teenager 50 years ago was a catalyst for the American civil rights movement, in hopes that new forensic evidence will clarify the circumstances of his death.

•

Paleontologists in Salt Lake City, Utah, announce their discovery of a new birdlike feathered dinosaur species, *Falcarius utahensis*, that lived about 125 million years ago and appears to represent an evolutionary link between carnivorous dinosaurs and later herbivorous groups.

5 Elections in the U.K. return Prime Minister Tony Blair to office for a third term of office—unprecedented for a Labour Party leader—but with his smallest majority so far.

•

A suicide bomber at an Iraqi army base in Baghdad kills at least 13 people, and a further 9 are killed in other attacks elsewhere in Iraq.

•

On Holocaust Remembrance Day 60 years after the liberation of the Nazi death camps, some 18,000 people, including the Israeli, Polish, and Hungarian prime ministers, participate in the annual March of the Living from Auschwitz to Birkenau, former concentration camps in southern Poland; on May 10 the Memorial to the Murdered Jews of Europe, designed by Peter Eisenman, opens with a solemn ceremony in Berlin.

6 Having failed to oust Labour in the British elections, Michael Howard surprises observers by announcing that he will step down as leader of the Conservative Party before the next election.

•

A car bomber in Tikrit, Iraq, drives his car into a bus, killing at least 10 people, and a car bomber in Suwayrah kills a further 16 people.

•

Patriarch Irineos I, head of the Greek Orthodox Church in the Holy Land, flees the patriarchate after a number of bishops and archimandrites declare him persona non grata, accusing him of having allowed the leasing of two church-owned hotels in Jerusalem to Jewish renters.

·

In the world table tennis championships in Shanghai, Wang Liqin of China wins the men's singles title to give the host country a clean sweep of the championships.

7 A bombing in Baghdad kills at least 22 people; in a period of 10 minutes in Yangon (Rangoon), Myanmar (Burma), bombs go off at a trade fair in a convention centre and in two supermarkets, killing at least 11 people; and another bomb kills at least three people at an Internet cafe in Kabul, Afg.

·

The virtually unknown horse Giacomo, a 50-to-1 shot, wins the Kentucky Derby, the first race of Thoroughbred horse racing's Triple Crown; favourite Afleet Alex finishes third.

·

A new museum of contemporary art, the MARTa Museum, designed by Frank Gehry, opens in Herford, near Hannover, Ger. (Photo below.)

8 Israeli Prime Minister Ariel Sharon freezes plans for an expected release of 400 Palestinian prisoners; earlier in the week, Israeli officials had halted plans to transfer security control of three more towns in the West Bank to the Palestinian Authority.

·

A grand council of more than 1,000 representatives from throughout Afghanistan called by Pres. Hamid Karzai agrees that the country requires the continued presence of international troops but calls on the U.S. to operate in cooperation with Afghanistan's government and army.

9 A large offensive by 1,000 troops led by U.S. Marines has reportedly swept through an area of western Iraq near Syria where it is believed the insurgency is receiving logistic support; the offensive is said to have left 4 Americans and 100 insurgents dead.

·

Israeli Prime Minister Ariel Sharon announces that the official date for the beginning of the evacuation of Jewish settlements in the Gaza Strip will be pushed back about four weeks from July 25 to avoid a mourning

period ending with the Jewish fast day of Tisha be-Av.

·

Several of Tokyo's rail companies introduce women-only cars on commuter trains as a means of alleviating the problem of men groping women on overcrowded cars.

10 Russian Pres. Vladimir Putin signs an agreement with the European Union to cooperate in economic and political matters, including trade and fighting terrorism and crime.

·

A U.S. federal bankruptcy court grants United Airlines the right to default on its four employee pension plans, the largest-ever such default.

·

The World Health Organization announces that more than 40 new cases of polio have been confirmed in Yemen.

·

Iraq's National Assembly names a committee of 55 members to write a new permanent constitution for the country.

11 In Tikrit, Iraq, a car bomber kills at least 38 people,

most of them casual labourers, while in Hawijah a suicide bomber kills at least 32 people; smaller attacks in Baghdad bring the day's death toll to 79.

·

A demonstration in Jalalabad, Afg., by students upset at a report in *Newsweek* magazine that U.S. interrogators in Guantánamo Bay, Cuba, had flushed a copy of the Qur'an down a toilet turns into violent rioting; 4 people are killed and 63 wounded.

·

In Andijan, Uzbekistan, hundreds of people take part in a protest, seeking the release of 23 Muslim prisoners charged with religious extremism.

·

A judge in Mali sentences 11 Muslim men to prison for refusing to allow their daughters to be vaccinated against polio for fear it would make them sterile.

·

Slovakia's legislature ratifies the European constitution.

·

In Brasília, Braz., heads of state and officials representing 34 countries conclude the first Summit of South American–Arab Countries; the two-day meeting is intended to form an alternative grouping that is not dominated by developed countries.

12 Several bombings in Baghdad kill at least 21 people; the worst of the assaults appear not to have had a military target, unlike the vast majority of attacks.

·

A U.S. federal judge rules that an amendment to Nebraska's constitution banning same-sex marriage is unconstitutional and was written so broadly as to threaten the rights of foster and adoptive parents and people in other living arrangements.

·

In honour of the 60th birthday of Pippi Longstocking,

© Ralph Orlowski/Getty Images

Swedish writer Astrid Lindgren's child heroine, the ballet *Pippi Longstocking* has its debut at the Royal Swedish Opera of Stockholm.

13 Anti-American protests gain in intensity in Afghanistan and Pakistan and spread to Indonesia and Palestine; at least eight protesters in Afghanistan are killed.

Government troops fire on an uprising that had turned violent in Andijan, Uzbekistan, killing possibly as many as 500 people.

Australia and East Timor reach an agreement to divide equally the revenue from the Greater Sunrise gas field, in the Timor Sea between the two countries, and to defer a decision on the maritime boundary between the two for 50 years.

Reporting in the periodical *Science*, geneticists present DNA evidence from the Orang Asli people of Malaysia in support of the proposal that humans migrated out of Africa some 65,000 years ago, taking a southern coastal route into India, Southeast Asia, and Australia, while an offshoot moved north and west eventually to populate the Middle East and Europe.

Archbishop William J. Levada of San Francisco is named by Pope Benedict XVI to head the Congregation for the Doctrine of the Faith, the post the new pope occupied for many years before succeeding Pope John Paul II.

14 Protests erupt in Karasu, Uzbekistan, as hundreds of Uzbeks attempt to flee to Kyrgyzstan.

The PEN/Faulkner Award for Fiction is presented to Ha Jin for his novel *War Trash;* he also won the award in 2000 for *Waiting.*

15 *Newsweek* magazine apologizes for printing an item describing the desecration of the Qur'an that seems to have triggered massive rioting throughout the Muslim world (*see* May 11), and on the following day the magazine retracts the item.

In Vienna the Czech Republic defeats Canada 3–0 to win the gold medal in the ice hockey men's world championship tournament.

China defeats Indonesia 3–0 to win the Sudirman Cup in badminton, which thus gives China all three of the major team championship trophies in the sport.

16 Kuwait's National Assembly passes a law that for the first time gives women the right to vote and to run for office.

A celebration is held in Kinshasa to mark the ratification by the legislature of the Democratic Republic of the Congo of a new constitution; the document must still be approved in a public referendum.

17 The Paris Club of creditor countries announces that it has agreed to seek from its member governments agreement to relieve Rwanda of debts of about $90 million.

Antonio Villaraigosa is elected mayor of Los Angeles and becomes the city's first Latino mayor since 1872.

18 When a Hamas group begins firing on a Jewish settlement in the Gaza Strip,

Israel carries out an air strike on the group, its first since the beginning of the truce three months earlier.

Russia and Estonia sign a treaty ending a border dispute between the two countries; on July 27, however, days after the Estonian parliament had ratified the accord, Russia revokes its signature.

The Russian association football (soccer) club CSKA Moscow defeats Sporting Lisbon to win the UEFA Cup in Lisbon; it is Russia's first European trophy.

19 After a four-day meeting, representatives of North and South Korea announce that they have agreed to hold a cabinet-level meeting on June 15 in Pyongyang, N.Kor.

Germany begins repatriating the first of some 35,000 Roma (Gypsies) to the Kosovo region of Serbia and Montenegro, where they face an uncertain future.

US Airways and America West Airlines announce plans to merge under the US Airways name to become the fifth largest carrier in the U.S.

20 Charges are filed in Uruguay against former president Juan María Bordaberry (1972–76) and his foreign minister in the 1976 murder of two prominent opposition politicians in Argentina, where they were living in exile.

Zagir Arukhov, minister of information, ethnic policy, and external relations for the Russian republic of Dagestan, is killed by a bomb outside his home in Makhachkala; his predecessor was killed in 2003.

A U.S. federal judge orders Exxon Mobil Corp. to pay some 10,000 gas-station owners damages for having overcharged them for gasoline for a period of more than 10 years.

South Korean researchers report in the periodical *Science* that they have developed an efficient method of cloning human embryos by using the DNA of individual patients in order to procure tailor-made stem cells for therapeutic purposes and that they have already developed 11 stem cell lines by using this method.

21 Members of Hamas reach an agreement with the Palestinian Authority to cease rocket and mortar attacks on Jewish settlements and towns in and near the Gaza Strip, salvaging the three-month-old truce.

Afleet Alex recovers from a stumble to win the Preakness Stakes, the second event in Thoroughbred racing's Triple Crown, by 4¾ lengths; Kentucky Derby winner Giacomo is third.

At the Cannes Film Festival, Belgian directors Jean-Pierre Dardenne and Luc Dardenne celebrate as their film *L'Enfant* wins the Palme d'Or; the Grand Prix goes to American director Jim Jarmusch's *Broken Flowers.*

In Kiev, Ukraine, singer Helena Paparizou of Greece emerges number one in the Eurovision Song Contest with "My Number One." (*Photo right.*)

22 German Chancellor Gerhard Schröder surprises observers by calling for national elections to be held in the fall of 2005, a year earlier than scheduled.

Nambaryn Enkhbayar is elected president of Mongolia.

Yokozuna Asashoryu defeats *ozeki* Tochiazuma on the final day to win sumo's Natsu Basho with an undefeated record; it is his 12th Emperor's Cup.

Finnish driver Kimi Räikkönen wins the Monaco Grand Prix.

23 Two suicide car bombers kill 15 people in Tall 'Afar, Iraq; two attacks in Baghdad kill at least 18 people; and 5 more are killed in Tuz Khurmatu.

The government of Zimbabwe reports that authorities have detained 9,600 people in Harare for black-market peddling and lawlessness.

24 UN Secretary-General Kofi Annan appoints António Guterres, a former prime minister of Portugal, to replace Ruud Lubbers as high commissioner for refugees.

At a synod of the Orthodox Church in Istanbul, it is decided that the organization will withdraw recognition from Patriarch Irineos as head of the Greek Orthodox Church in the Holy Land in view of his loss of the support of his subordinates.

Warren Buffett's Berkshire Hathaway buys the electric utility PacifiCorp.

Star Wars: Episode III– Revenge of the Sith, which opened worldwide on May 21, breaks box-office records in the U.K. and the U.S. for the first four days of its run.

Televisora del Sur (Telesur) begins broadcasting; the 24-hour satellite news channel is owned by Venezuela, Argentina, Cuba, and Uruguay.

25 In talks with the U.K., France, and Germany, Iran agrees to extend its freeze on uranium enrichment.

A referendum in Egypt approves an amendment to the constitution to allow multiparty presidential elections.

The 1,762-km (1,094-mi)-long Baku-Tbilisi-Ceyhan pipeline, transporting oil from Azerbaijan in the Caspian basin to the Mediterranean Sea in Turkey, is ceremonially opened.

Donald Tsang, acting chief executive of Hong Kong, resigns—as is required by law—in order to become a candidate in the July 10 election.

In association football (soccer), Liverpool defeats AC Milan on penalty kicks to win the UEFA Champions League championship in Istanbul.

26 Germany's legislature votes to ratify the proposed European Union constitution.

Pascal Lamy of France, the former European Union trade minister, is selected as new director-general of the World Trade Organization.

27 Near Islamabad, Pak., a suicide bomber at a Muslim shrine kills 20 people and injures 67; on May 30, in an attack on a Shi'ite mosque in Karachi, two people are killed and at least 24 are injured.

28 Prime Minister Hama Amadou of Niger makes an emergency food-aid request; farming in the poverty-stricken country has been decimated by drought and the 2004 locust plague.

In Christchurch, N.Z., the Canterbury (N.Z.) Crusaders defeat the New South Wales (Australia) Waratahs 35–25 to win the annual tri-nation Super 12 Rugby Union championship for the fifth time in 10 years.

29 In a national referendum on the ratification of the European constitution, France votes no; the document cannot take effect until all 25 members of the European Union have ratified it.

The 89th Indianapolis 500 auto race is won by Dan Wheldon, the first British driver to do so since 1966; popular favourite Danica Patrick places fourth, the highest place a woman driver has ever achieved in the race.

Spaniard Fernando Alonso, driving for Renault, wins the European Grand Prix in Germany after Kimi Räikkönen of Finland, driving for McLaren-Mercedes, crashes in the last lap.

30 In negotiations with Georgia, Russia agrees to withdraw by 2008 its troops and equipment from two military bases in Georgia, one near Turkey and one on the Black Sea.

31 In response to France's rejection of the European constitution, Pres. Jacques Chirac replaces Jean-Pierre Raffarin with Dominique de Villepin as prime minister.

Mikhail Khodorkovsky, the founder of the oil company Yukos and once one of the richest men in Russia, is found guilty on tax charges and sentenced to nine years in prison.

Vanity Fair magazine reports that W. Mark Felt, who was second in command at the FBI in the early 1970s, has said publicly that he was the anonymous source known as "Deep Throat" who assisted *Washington Post* reporters Carl Bernstein and Bob Woodward in unraveling the Watergate story that led to the resignation of then president Richard Nixon.

The U.S. Supreme Court overturns the 2002 conviction of the once huge but now all but defunct accounting firm Arthur Andersen for obstruction of justice, ruling that the jury instructions were flawed.

June

1 In a national referendum in The Netherlands, voters reject ratification of the proposed European constitution.

Paul Wolfowitz takes office as the president of the World Bank, declaring that reducing poverty in Africa will be his top priority.

2 Israel releases 398 Palestinian prisoners as part of an agreement that Israeli Prime Minister Ariel Sharon made with Palestinian leader Mahmoud Abbas.

Three car bombs, a suicide motorcycle bomb, and a suicide attack leave at least 44 people, including 10 Sufi Muslims, dead in Iraq.

In the Scripps National Spelling Bee, Anurag Kashyap of San Diego, Calif., spells *appoggiatura* correctly to win the contest.

3 It is reported that torrential rains in three provinces in southern China have caused flooding that may have left hundreds of people dead.

Murder charges are brought against a man accused of killing Robert McCartney outside a bar in Belfast, N.Ire.; the attack, which horrified citizens, is believed to have been an act of the Provisional Irish Republican Army against Sinn Féin, the political wing of the IRA.

4 Palestinian leader Mahmoud Abbas announces that the legislative elections scheduled for July 17 will be postponed; the new date will be announced later.

Justine Henin-Hardenne of Belgium defeats Mary Pierce of France to win the women's French Open tennis title; the following day rising star Rafael Nadal of Spain defeats Mariano Puerta of Argentina in the finals to win the men's title.

The Derby, in its 226th year at Epsom Downs in Surrey, Eng., is won by Motivator, ridden by jockey Johnny Murtagh.

5 A spokesman for the Afghan armed forces reports that the army has captured two Taliban commanders who are believed to be responsible for much of the violence that has taken place in western Afghanistan.

The second round of legislative elections in Lebanon produces victories for Hezbollah and Amal, parties associated with Syria.

It is reported that Taiwan has for the first time successfully test-fired a cruise missile capable of reaching targets in China.

The 59th annual Tony Awards are presented in New York City; winners include the productions *Doubt, Monty Python's Spamalot, Glengarry Glen Ross,* and *La Cage aux folles* and the actors Bill Irwin, Cherry Jones, Norbert Leo Butz, and Victoria Clark.

6 In the face of growing and unremitting protests, Carlos Mesa Gisbert resigns as president of Bolivia.

The U.S. Supreme Court rules that the constitutional right of Congress to regulate commerce among states gives the federal government the right to enforce laws prohibiting the possession and use of marijuana even in those states that permit the use of the drug for medical purposes.

A land mine destroys a bus in Nepal; at least 37 of the passengers are killed.

7 Google becomes the largest media company in the world by stock market value when its shares reach a level on stock exchanges in New York City that make the Internet search engine company worth $80 billion.

In Hawijah, Iraq, three simultaneous suicide bombs at checkpoints kill at least 20 Iraqis; elsewhere in the country at least 7 people are killed or found dead.

8 Security forces in Addis Ababa, Eth., open fire on the continuing election protests, killing at least 22 people.

9 The National Congress of Bolivia accepts the resignation of Carlos Mesa Gisbert as president, naming Eduardo Rodríguez Veltzé, head of the Supreme Court, to replace him.

An appeals court in Mexico overturns the 1999 conviction of Raúl Salinas, brother of former Mexican president Carlos Salinas, for having ordered the 1994 murder of a politician.

10 In Iraq a roadside bomb kills 5 U.S. Marines, a car bomb kills at least 10 Iraqis, 4 Iraqi security officers are gunned down in ambushes, and some 20 bound and blindfolded bodies are found.

The banking company Citigroup settles a lawsuit by investors in Enron Corp. who accused the bank of having helped Enron defraud them; Citigroup agrees to a $2 billion payment.

11 François Bozizé is sworn in as elected president of the Central African Republic.

Finance ministers from the Group of Eight industrialized countries agree to cancel at least $40 billion of the debt owed by the poorest 18 countries in the world to international lending agencies such as the IMF and the African Development Bank.

In a boxing match with Kevin McBride in Washing-

ton, D.C., former heavyweight champion Mike Tyson fails to return to the ring after the sixth round and declares that he has retired from fighting.

Louise Stahle of Sweden becomes the first person in 30 years to win the ladies' British amateur championship in golf for two successive years when she defeats Claire Coughlan of Ireland to win the 2005 championship at Littlestone, Eng.

Preakness winner Afleet Alex comes from behind to win the Belmont Stakes, the last event in Thoroughbred horse racing's Triple Crown, by seven lengths.

At the International Indian Film Academy Awards, popularly known as the Bollywood Awards, in Amsterdam, the film *Veer-Zaara* wins six awards, including best picture, best director, best actor, and best supporting actress.

12 The third round of legislative elections in Lebanon brings victory to candidates aligned with Maronite Christian leader and former prime minister Gen. Michel Aoun.

Massouma al-Mubarak is named Kuwait's minister of planning and minister of state for administrative development affairs; she is the first woman ever to hold a position in that country's cabinet.

Hundreds of women demonstrate in favour of women's rights in Tehran in the first such demonstration since Iran's Islamic revolution of 1979.

Annika Sörenstam of Sweden wins the Ladies Professional Golf Association championship for the third consecutive year, defeating

teenage amateur Michelle Wie of the U.S. by three strokes.

13 A car bomb explodes near a security base and a high school in the town of Pulwama in Indian-administered Kashmir, killing at least 14 people and injuring 50.

The U.S. Senate formally apologizes for failing ever to enact a law making lynching a federal crime, though three bills passed by the House of Representatives were sent to it, and seven presidents asked for the legislation; some 5,000 lynchings have been recorded in U.S. history.

After a 14-week trial in Santa Maria, Calif., that became something of a media circus, pop star Michael Jackson is acquitted of child molestation charges.

© Ethan Miller/Getty Images

Philip J. Purcell announces his retirement as head of the troubled financial concern Morgan Stanley.

The European Union makes the Irish language Gaelic its 21st official language.

Jan Eliasson of Sweden is elected president of the UN

General Assembly; he will replace Jean Ping of Gabon.

14 A suicide bomber detonates his weapon among a crowd of retired people lined up to get their pensions from a bank in Kirkuk, Iraq; at least 22 people are killed.

South African Pres. Thabo Mbeki dismisses Deputy Pres. Jacob Zuma, who has been implicated in a bribery scandal.

15 The first autonomous government of the Papua New Guinean province of Bougainville, headed by newly elected Pres. Joseph Kabui, is sworn in.

The annual International IMPAC Dublin Literary Award goes to *The Known World,* by American author Edward P. Jones.

16 Donald Tsang is officially declared the new leader of Hong Kong; China appoints him chief executive on June 21.

The first case of avian flu in a human in Indonesia is confirmed by health officials.

The blockbuster exhibit from Egypt "Tutankhamun and the Golden Age of the Pharaohs" opens at the Los Angeles County Museum of Art. *(Photo left.)*

Leigh Ann Hester of the Kentucky National Guard becomes the first woman since World War II to be awarded the Silver Star; she and seven other members of her unit are decorated for their roles in stopping an insurgent attack on a convoy in March near Salman Pak, Iraq.

17 MasterCard International reveals that a computer security breach at a payment-processing company may have exposed the information of more than 40 million credit card accounts to theft.

L. Dennis Kozlowski, the former CEO of Tyco International, and Mark H. Swartz, the company's former chief financial officer, are found guilty of fraud, conspiracy, and grand larceny.

Australian Prime Minister John Howard announces a loosening of restrictions on illegal immigrants, including no more than six weeks in detention for women and children and no more than six months before claims for asylum are adjudicated.

18 A firefight takes place between U.S. armed forces and insurgents in Karabila, Iraq; U.S. Marine commanders report that at least 30 insurgents have been killed.

19 A suicide bomber attacks a restaurant in Baghdad that is popular with police officers; at least 23 persons are killed, 16 of them policemen.

A U.S. military spokesman reports that after an American patrol was attacked in Helmand province of Afghanistan, an air strike was called in and as many as 20 possibly Taliban insurgents were killed.

Vietnamese Prime Minister Phan Van Khai arrives in the U.S. for a weeklong visit; it is the first visit to the U.S. by a leader of unified Vietnam.

Denmark's Tom Kristensen, driving with J.J. Lehto and Marco Werner for Audi, wins the Le Mans 24-hour endurance race for a record seventh time.

After tire manufacturer Michelin says it cannot guarantee the safety of its tires under race conditions, which leads all 14 drivers using Michelin tires at the U.S. Grand Prix in Indianapolis, Ind., to withdraw, Michael Schumacher wins the event over the remaining 5 drivers.

In a surprising turn of events, Michael Campbell of New Zealand wins the U.S. Open golf tournament, besting American Tiger Woods by two strokes.

20 A car bomb explodes in a field behind a police station in Irbil, Iraq, killing some 15 police recruits, most of them Kurdish; other attacks in the country kill approximately 15 more people.

The Zentrum Paul Klee, designed by Italian Renzo Piano to house the works of the Swiss artist, opens in Bern, Switz.; it includes a music hall and will host workshops and a summer academy.

21 In Beirut a car bomb kills George Hawi, the former head of the Lebanese Communist Party who had campaigned for the anti-Syria slate that won the majority of the seats in the parliament.

In Philadelphia, Miss., 80-year-old Edgar Ray Killen, a former member of the Ku Klux Klan, is found guilty of manslaughter in the 1964 deaths of civil rights workers Michael Schwerner, James Earl Chaney, and Andrew Goodman; two days later he is sentenced to 60 years in prison, the maximum allowed.

22 After a two-day offensive by U.S. and Afghan military forces in response to an attack on district police in Kandahar province, at least 40 of the insurgents have been killed.

Colombia's legislature passes a law that grants leaders of right-wing paramilitaries freedom from severe punishment for atrocities or drug trafficking in return for disarmament of up to 20,000 fighters.

23 Four car bombs explode in the space of a few minutes in a commercial district of Baghdad, leaving at least 17 people dead and bringing to 700 Baghdad's death toll in the violence of the past month.

The World Customs Organization endorses a new set of standards intended to increase the inspection and tracking of freight cargo throughout the world to decrease the possibility of terrorists' making use of the cargo-shipping system.

The U.S. Supreme Court rules that governments may exercise the power of eminent domain over private property and cede the property to private developers to promote economic growth, so long as a carefully formulated plan to provide significant benefits to the community provides a rational basis for the seizure of the property.

U.S. prices for light sweet crude oil reach a record level of $60 a barrel.

The San Antonio Spurs defeat the Detroit Pistons 81–74 to win the National Basketball Association championship; Tim Duncan of the Spurs is named Most Valuable Player of the finals.

24 The presidential runoff election in Iran is won by the hard-line mayor of Tehran, Mahmoud Ahmadinejad.

The insurance company Aetna announces plans to acquire the regional health care provider HMS Healthcare.

25 In parliamentary elections in Bulgaria, the coalition led by the Bulgarian Socialist Party wins the majority of seats.

The National Association for the Advancement of Colored People appoints Bruce S. Gordon, a former business executive, to replace Kweisi Mfume as president of the organization; Gordon indicates his emphasis will be on economic equality.

At the 43rd world outdoor target archery championships in Madrid, Chung Jae Hun of South Korea wins the men's gold in recurve, while Lee Sung Jin of South Korea wins the women's recurve competition.

26 Four suicide bomb attacks in 16 hours leave 38 people dead in Iraq.

Birdie Kim of South Korea wins the 60th U.S. Women's Open golf tournament.

Three-year-old Hurricane Run, at 4–5 the favourite, comes from behind to win the Irish Derby horse race.

27 The Lebanese government decides that Palestinians born in Lebanon may henceforth be permitted to hold certain jobs in the country; this is the first time in over 50 years that immigrants from

limit on the number of terms a president may serve.

29 Venezuelan Pres. Hugo Chávez announces the formation of an energy alliance of 15 Caribbean countries to be called Petrocaribe, in which Venezuela will offer the other members oil at low prices.

•

Philippines Pres. Gloria Macapagal Arroyo announces that her husband, José Miguel Arroyo, who is accused of having taken bribes, will go into exile.

•

California's Supreme Court permits a new law granting domestic partners most of the benefits conferred by marriage to stand.

•

Brazil defeats Argentina 4–1 to win the FIFA Confederations Cup in association football (soccer).

30 Spain becomes the third European country, after The Netherlands and Belgium, to grant full marriage rights to same-sex couples; Spain's new law is the most liberal, recognizing no distinctions between same-sex and opposite-sex unions.

Police in Zimbabwe finish destroying a squatter settlement that had been home to some 10,000 people, in the process killing several people; since mid-May the government has been carrying out wholesale demolitions of such settlements and flea markets, and within six weeks some half million poor people have become homeless.

•

The World Food Programme reports that pirates have seized a ship carrying 850 metric tons of rice in food aid that was intended for tsunami victims in Somalia.

Palestine or their families have been allowed to work.

•

In two split decisions, the U.S. Supreme Court rules that long-standing outdoor displays of the Ten Commandments on government property are permissible under the Constitution, but newer indoor displays of the Ten Commandments in courthouses violate the prohibition against government establishment of religion.

•

Ismail Kadare, an Albanian novelist, is awarded the first Man Booker International Prize in Edinburgh.

28 Canada's House of Commons approves a bill permitting same-sex marriage throughout Canada, and easy approval by the Senate is expected; eight provinces and one territory already recognize same-sex marriage.

•

Emperor Akihito of Japan visits Saipan in the Northern Mariana Islands, the scene of one of the most horrific battles of World War II, to honour the war dead of Japan, Korea, the islands, and the U.S.; it is the first time a Japanese ruler has visited an overseas battle site.

The European Union, the U.S., Russia, Japan, South Korea, and China reach an agreement to build the International Thermonuclear Experimental Reactor, the world's largest fusion reactor, in Cadarache, France.

U.S. Pres. George W. Bush makes a televised speech to the country intended to shore up support for the war in Iraq; it draws fewer viewers than any of his previous televised speeches.

•

With maritime parades, a naval battle reenactment, and fireworks, the 200th anniversary of the Battle of Trafalgar, in which the British navy vanquished that of Napoleon, is celebrated in the Solent in the English Channel. *(Photo above.)*

•

Uganda's legislature approves a change to the constitution removing a

July

1 The presidency of the European Union rotates from Luxembourg's prime minister, Jean-Claude Juncker, to the prime minister of the U.K., Tony Blair.

Pres. Vladimir Putin of Russia and Pres. Hu Jintao of China sign a Declaration on the World Order in the 21st Century, seeking multilateral approaches to international disputes.

A bomb kills at least 10 Russian soldiers at a public bathhouse in the Republic of Dagestan in the worst attack against Russia's military in 2005 to date; an Islamic group connected to separatists in Chechnya claims responsibility.

U.S. Supreme Court Associate Justice Sandra Day O'Connor, the first woman appointed to the court (1981), unexpectedly announces her retirement.

2 Suicide bombers at a security forces recruiting centre in Baghdad and at a restaurant next to a police headquarters in Al-Hillah kill at least 20 people in Iraq.

Ihab al-Sharif, the head of Egypt's diplomatic mission to Iraq and its ambassador designate, is kidnapped in Baghdad; on July 7 al-Qaeda reveals that it has killed him.

A series of concerts by 100 top rock and hip-hop artists in 10 cities throughout the world are attended by some one million people; billed as Live 8, the event is intended to pressure the world leaders at the Group of Eight meeting in Scotland to pursue a policy intended to end world poverty and is believed to be the largest global broadcast in history. *(Photo below.)*

American Venus Williams defeats her countrywoman Lindsey Davenport to take the All-England (Wimbledon) women's tennis championship for the third time; the following day Roger Federer of Switzerland wins the men's title for the third consecutive year when he defeats American Andy Roddick.

AP/Wide World Photos

3 Parliamentary elections take place in Albania, coming closer to meeting international electoral standards than any previously.

Fernando Alonso of Spain wins the French Grand Prix in Formula 1 automobile racing.

4 An instrumented "impactor" released from the NASA probe Deep Impact collides with the icy nucleus of Comet Tempel I; the resulting crater and excavated debris will provide detailed information on the interior and composition of the comet.

The Nigerian writer S.A. Afolabi is awarded the 2005 Caine Prize for African Writing for his story "Monday Morning."

5 Fifteen Sunni Iraqis are accepted to the committee that is writing the new Iraqi constitution; also, Pakistan withdraws its ambassador to the country after he escapes injury in an ambush; the same day, Bahrain's top diplomat in Iraq is wounded in an ambush.

Hours after a bomb in front of a theatre is defused, another bomb explodes at a police station, killing at least two officers, in Makhachkala, the capital of the Russian republic of Dagestan on the Caspian Sea.

A group of gunmen attack the Hindu temple compound in Ayodhya, India, setting off a two-hour gun battle with guards in which six attackers are killed.

6 At its meeting in Singapore, the International Olympic Committee chooses London as the site of the Olympic Games to be held in summer 2012.

The second largest health insurer in the U.S., UnitedHealth Group, agrees to purchase PacifiCare Systems, greatly enlarging its presence in the increasingly lucrative Medicare market.

Francis Joyon smashes the world record for solo yachting of the North Atlantic when he arrives in Cornwall, Eng., 6 days 4 hr 1 min 37 sec after he left New York City; the previous record, 7 days 2 hr 34 min 42 sec, was set by Laurent Bourgnon in 1994.

7 Late in the morning rush hour in London, bombs go off almost simultaneously on three subway trains and close to an hour later on a double-decker bus in a coordinated terror attack, leaving 56 dead, including the men carrying the bombs; an al-Qaeda-affiliated group claims responsibility.

8 The Group of Eight meeting in Auchterarder, Scot., concludes after having reached a number of agreements on measures to reduce poverty in Africa as well as having addressed global warming and the Israeli-Palestinian conflict.

Ten members of the cabinet in the Philippines resign their posts, calling on Pres. Gloria Macapagal Arroyo to step down in the face of accusations that the 2004 election was rigged.

Alles auf Zucker!, a comedy, wins six prizes at the German Film Awards, including best picture, best director, and best actor.

9 In Khartoum, The Sudan's new interim constitution is signed and its transitional national government, with Omar Hassan al-Bashir as president, John Garang of the Sudan People's Liberation Army as first vice president, and Ali Osman Taha as second vice president, is sworn in.

10 A suicide bomber kills 23 people at an army recruiting centre in Baghdad, while at least 20 other people are killed in attacks elsewhere in the city and in the rest of Iraq.

Presidential elections held in Kyrgyzstan result in the election of Kurmanbek Bakiyev, who served as interim president after the uprising in March.

At the World Cup rowing championships in Lucerne, Switz., Great Britain wins seven medals, including the overall World Cup.

Juan Pablo Montoya of Colombia wins the British Grand Prix in Formula 1 automobile racing.

11 Somalian peace activist Abdulkadir Yahya Ali is killed by gunmen in Mogadishu, the capital.

After the second day of a gun battle in Tall 'Afar, Iraq, U.S. forces have killed 14 insurgents, while in Khalis an attack on an Iraqi checkpoint leaves 10 Iraqi soldiers dead.

12 With much fanfare, Prince Albert II is formally installed as the ruler of Monaco.

Uganda's Parliament amends the country's constitution to abolish term limits for the president, making it possible for Pres. Yoweri Museveni to run for a third consecutive term.

Some 150 Huaorani Indians demonstrate in Quito, Ecuador, to demand the withdrawal of the Brazilian oil company Petrobrás from Yasuní National Park, home to about 1,000 Huaorani.

13 A suicide car bomber detonates his weapon in Baghdad in the midst of a crowd of children around members of a U.S. troop patrol who possibly were giving them candy; some 27 people, almost all of them children, are killed.

Bernard Ebbers, the founder and former head of the telecommunications giant WorldCom (now MCI), is sentenced to 25 years in prison for having perpetrated an $11 billion fraud.

Tens of thousands of people demonstrate in Manila to demand the resignation of Philippine Pres. Gloria Macapagal Arroyo; an even larger demonstration by her supporters takes place on July 16.

The legislature in Chile agrees on changes to the constitution that will reduce the term of office for the president from six years to four years and limit the power of the military.

14 *Nature* magazine reports the finding of a planet about the size of Jupiter that orbits around a star that two smaller stars also orbit; it is the first time a planet has been detected in such a gravitationally complex system, a situation previously thought to be impossible.

A U.S. court of appeals lifts an injunction that barred the U.S. from resuming the import of cattle from Canada; the importation had been banned because of fears of mad cow disease.

In a crackdown on foreign oil companies, Venezuela's tax authority orders the Royal Dutch/Shell Group to pay some $131 million in back taxes and seizes financial information from the Chevron Corp.

15 A U.S. appeals court rules that the war crimes trials planned for detainees at the U.S. military base at Guantánamo Bay, Cuba, do not violate the Constitution and may resume; the trials had been stopped by a ruling by a lower court in 2004.

At least eight suicide car bombs kill 22 or more people in a 12-hour period in Baghdad.

Meeting in South Africa, UNESCO names eight new natural sites to its World Heritage list, including the Vredefort Dome in South Africa and the Wadi al-Hitan, or Whale Valley, in Egypt.

16 At one minute past midnight, *Harry Potter and the Half-Blood Prince*, the sixth book in the phenomenally successful young-adult book series by J.K. Rowling, goes on sale in bookstores throughout the U.S. and Great Britain; it breaks the record for first-day sales set in 2003 by the previous volume in the series.

In Al-Musayyib, Iraq, a suicide bomber under a fuel truck kills at least 71 people outside a Shi'ite mosque.

At the popular Turkish resort town of Kusadasi, a bomb explodes on a minibus, killing at least five people.

The longest cable-stayed suspension bridge in North America, the Arthur Ravenel Jr. Bridge in South Carolina over the Cooper River between Charleston and Mt. Pleasant, opens after a week of festivities.

Jermain Taylor wins in a split decision over Bernard Hopkins in Las Vegas to become the undisputed world middleweight boxing champion.

After 232 hands played over a period of nearly 14 straight hours in Las Vegas, Joseph Hachem of Australia emerges as the winner in the World Series of Poker.

17 In Helsinki representatives of the government of Indonesia and of the rebel Free Aceh Movement reach an agreement to end the 30-year conflict in Aceh province; the agreement calls for an amnesty for the rebels, the presence of international observers, and the formation of local political parties.

After several days of demonstrations seeking the permanent closure of a pharmaceuticals factory in Xinchang, China, by residents angry about the environmental harm it causes, some 15,000 demonstrators engage in a battle with police.

A wildfire accidentally started by picnickers in the pine forest at Spain's Cueva de los Casares, a site known for its paleolithic paintings, kills 11 volunteer firefighters during the worst drought the Iberian peninsula has experienced since the 1940s.

Tiger Woods wins the British Open golf tournament at St. Andrews in Fife, Scot., with a five-stroke victory over Colin Montgomerie of Scotland.

18 The newly elected parliament in Lebanon grants amnesty to Christian militia leader Samir Geagea, who had been serving four life sentences for having killed political rivals.

After leaving five people dead in Jamaica, Hurricane Emily comes ashore on the Yucatán Peninsula in Mexico, causing a great deal of damage but few deaths; meanwhile, Typhoon Haitang makes landfall on Taiwan, and China evacuates more than 600,000 people on the south coast.

19 The relatively unknown John G. Roberts is nominated by Pres. George W. Bush to replace Sandra Day O'Connor on the Supreme Court.

Lebanese Prime Minister Fouad Siniora introduces a new government, the first in the country since the departure of Syrian forces.

In the town of Znamenskoye in the Russian republic of Chechnya, a bomb kills some 13 people, most of them police officers.

20 Riots take place in Sanaa, Yemen, in response to government plans to cut fuel subsidies, provoking a sharp increase in fuel prices; police kill 13 people in an attempt to control the situation, a figure that rises to 36 in the next two days.

For the second consecutive day, demonstrators in Nairobi seeking changes to the Kenyan constitution to dilute the power of the presidency fight with riot police.

Some 5,000 people, many of them from the Muslim Brotherhood, demonstrate in downtown Cairo to demand greater democracy in Egypt.

Canada becomes the fourth country in the world to allow same-sex couples the same marriage rights enjoyed by opposite-sex couples.

21 During the lunch hour in London, bombs in three subway trains and one double-decker bus fail to go off as only their detonators explode, creating panic but no casualties.

After months of pressure, China revalues its currency, the yuan, allowing it to float against a basket of currencies rather than be pegged to the dollar, the strategy it had used since 1996.

German Pres. Horst Köhler dissolves the parliament and sets elections for September 18, a year earlier than they would have been held otherwise.

22 Jumpy police officers in London trail, capture, and shoot to death an innocent Brazilian electrician in full public view on a subway train.

The United Nations issues a report condemning Zimbabwe's program, begun without warning on May 19, of bulldozing urban shantytowns, a policy that has left some 700,000 people without homes or livelihood; the report demands an immediate halt to the program and compensation for its victims, as well as prosecution of those responsible.

In London, Yelena Isinbayeva of Russia sets her 17th world pole vaulting record when she becomes the first woman ever to clear 5 m (16 ft 4¾ in).

The National Hockey League officially reopens after the ratification of the agreement between the owners and the Players' Association; a number of new rules for the play of the game will be in place for the start of the new season.

23 Three bomb explosions in Egypt's premier resort town, Sharm al-Shaykh, on the Red Sea in the Sinai Peninsula, destroy one hotel and kill 88 people.

24 A truck bomber drives into barricades at a police station in Baghdad, leaving at least 25 people dead and 33 injured.

Lance Armstrong wins his seventh consecutive Tour de France bicycle race.

25 As the AFL-CIO convention celebrating the 50th anniversary of the combined organization gets under way in Chicago, the Service Employees International Union and the International Brotherhood of Teamsters announce their withdrawal from the federation.

Pres. Bingu wa Mutharika of Malawi bans the export of corn (maize), the country's staple crop, and fertilizer in an effort to stave off famine and asks citizens to contribute 10% of their income to a fund to feed the hungry.

26 The Indian city of Mumbai (Bombay) is inundated by a record 94.2 cm (37.1 in) of rain in a single day; the rain continues into the following day, leaving at least 749 people, 376 of them in Mumbai, dead.

The space shuttle *Discovery* lifts off from Cape Canaveral, Florida, on a mission to take supplies to the Inter-national Space Station; it is the first space shuttle launch since the loss of *Columbia* on Feb. 1, 2003.

Prince Walid ibn Talal of Saudi Arabia pledges to donate $20 million to the Louvre in Paris to finance a new wing to showcase Islamic art; it is the biggest donation in the museum's history.

27 In Angers, France, 62 people, including many women, are convicted in a mass pedophilia case; sentences are of as much as 28 years.

After finding that a piece of insulation foam broke off the external fuel tank of the space shuttle *Discovery* shortly after takeoff—the same problem that doomed *Columbia*—NASA once again grounds the shuttle fleet until further notice.

In a U.S. federal court in Seattle, Ahmed Ressam is sentenced to 22 years in prison for having plotted to set off a bomb in the Los Angeles International Airport during the celebrations for the start of the new millennium.

28 The Irish Republican Army formally renounces the use of violence in Northern Ireland, telling its members to disarm and inviting inspection to verify its disarmament; this is viewed as a turning point.

The Smithsonian Institution names John Berry, the executive director of the National Fish and Wildlife Foundation, the new director of the National Zoo in Washington, D.C.

29 The first plane loaded with relief supplies from the UN World Food Programme lands in Niamey, Niger; the country is threatened with mass starvation.

Pakistani Pres. Pervez Musharraf orders that all foreign students and all Pakistani students holding dual nationalities studying at madrasahs, or religious schools, in the country leave the schools; previously it had been ordered that foreign students no longer attending a madrasah had to leave the country.

Uzbekistan demands that the U.S. close its air base in the country within 180 days.

A suicide bomber kills as many as 26 people at an army recruitment centre in the northern Iraqi village of Rabi'ah.

30 In Baghdad a car bomb near the National Theatre kills at least six people; in addition, two security contractors at the British consulate in the Iraqi city of Basra are killed by a roadside bomb.

31 The founder and leader of the Sudan People's Liberation Movement and recently named first vice president of The Sudan, John Garang, is killed when the helicopter carrying him crashes into a mountain in bad weather.

Iran announces plans to restart its uranium conversion facility in Isfahan.

The National Baseball Hall of Fame in Cooperstown, N.Y., inducts second baseman Ryne Sandberg and third baseman Wade Boggs *(photo left)*; announcer Jerry Coleman and sportswriter Peter Gammons are honoured for their contributions to baseball.

The FINA world championships in swimming conclude in Montreal, with the U.S. the top medal winner, followed by Australia; nine new world records were set during the course of the competition.

© Ezra Shaw/Getty Images

August

AP/Wide World Photos

1 King Fahd of Saudi Arabia dies after 23 years on the throne; he is succeeded by his half brother Crown Prince Abdullah.

While Congress is in recess, U.S. Pres. George W. Bush appoints John Bolton ambassador to the United Nations; there had been opposition in Congress to Bolton's nomination.

The U.K.'s Northern Ireland secretary announces that the British army has begun withdrawing its forces from Northern Ireland and intends to recall about half its forces over the next two years.

Christof Wandratsch of Germany sets a new record for swimming across the English Channel when he covers 32 km (21 mi) in 7 hr 3 min, 14 minutes faster than the previous record, set in 1994.

Hungarian chess grandmaster Susan Polgar sets a record for most simultaneous games played—326, with 309 wins (another record).

2 U.S. Pres. George W. Bush signs the Central America–Dominican Republic Free Trade Agreement (CAFTA-DR); of the seven countries involved in the agreement, the U.S. is the fourth to ratify it.

The Chinese oil company CNOOC withdraws its controversial takeover bid for the American oil company Unocal, leaving the way clear for Chevron to complete its acquisition of Unocal.

At Pearson International Airport in Toronto, an Air France jet arriving from Paris overshoots a runway in severe weather, skidding off and bursting into flames; all 309 persons aboard manage to escape safely.

3 Abdullah is formally invested as king of Saudi Arabia in Riyadh.

A military junta overthrows Pres. Maaouya Ould Sid'Ahmed Taya of Mauritania while he is out of the country for the funeral of King Fahd of Saudi Arabia.

A team of scientists announce in South Korea that they have cloned a dog, an Afghan hound dubbed Snuppy; later in the year, however, the cloning research is called into question. *(Photo left.)*

The German apparel company adidas-Salomon AG reaches an agreement to buy rival Reebok International Ltd.

4 Israel's first desalination plant opens in Ashqelon; it is the largest seawater reverse osmosis plant in the world.

Prime Minister Paul Martin appoints the Haitian-born television journalist

Michaëlle Jean governor-general of Canada; the governor-general is the formal representative of Britain's Queen Elizabeth II.

Oil giant ExxonMobil announces that Lee Raymond will retire at the end of the year after 12 years as CEO, to be replaced by the company's president, Rex Tillerson.

As part of the terms of the settlement of a lawsuit, the U.S. Department of Defense agrees to make available its photographs of the coffins of U.S. soldiers killed in Iraq; a policy had been in place that forbade media coverage of photographs or videos of soldiers' coffins.

5 The World Food Programme increases its emergency funding appeal fivefold, saying the risk of mass hunger is high in Mali, Mauritania, Burkina Faso, and Niger.

The criminal trial of the American gold-mining company Newmont Mining Corp., which is accused of putting toxic waste into the sea at Buyat Bay on the northeastern Indonesian island of Celebes (Sulawesi), begins in Manado, Indon.

6 Mahmoud Ahmadinejad is inaugurated as president of Iran.

Cindy Sheehan, the mother of a U.S. soldier killed in Iraq and an antiwar activist, is turned away from U.S. Pres. George W. Bush's ranch in Crawford, Texas, where she had gone to speak with him, and vows to remain outside the ranch until Bush meets with her; over the next weeks she becomes the nucleus of a growing peace movement.

Vivid Photo, driven by Roger Hammer, wins the Hamble-

tonian, the first contest in harness racing's trotting Triple Crown.

7 Four days after a Russian submarine on a training expedition became trapped in an abandoned fishing net off Russia's Kamchatka Peninsula, a British submersible frees the submarine; with very few hours of breathable air left in the submarine, all seven aboard are saved.

Former Israeli prime minister Benjamin Netanyahu unexpectedly resigns his post as minister of finance because of his opposition to the evacuation of Israeli settlements in the Gaza Strip, scheduled to start on August 15.

Thirteen days of nuclear program talks between China, Japan, South Korea, Russia, the U.S., and North Korea end with no agreement; talks are scheduled to resume on August 29.

The Pro Football Hall of Fame in Canton, Ohio, inducts quarterbacks Benny Friedman, Dan Marino, and Steve Young and pioneering African American halfback Fritz Pollard.

8 After losing a vote on removing banking and insurance from the country's postal system and privatizing those services, Japanese Prime Minister Junichiro Koizumi dissolves the lower house of the Diet (legislature) and sets elections for September 11.

India and Pakistan announce a number of agreements relating to Kashmir, including plans to hold monthly meetings to defuse tensions and a commitment to refrain from building new military posts along the Line of Control.

The city council chief in Baghdad leads a municipal coup, removing Mayor Alaa al-Tamimi and installing in his place Hussein al-Tahaan, the head of Baghdad governorate and a member of a Shi'ite militia.

9 The results of the parliamentary election held in May in Ethiopia are released; the ruling Ethiopian People's Revolutionary Democratic Front is said to have won 296 of the 547 seats.

The space shuttle *Discovery* safely returns to Earth, landing in the Mojave Desert in California.

The Sierra Club presents the Chico Mendes Award for global environmental heroism to embattled Mexican environmentalists Felipe Arreaga, Celsa Valdovinos, and Albertano Peñaloza for their work defending forests in the Sierra de Petatlán.

10 Iran removes seals placed by the International Atomic Energy Agency on its nuclear plant in Esfahan, returning it to full operation.

Nature magazine reports that the complete genome code of rice has been sequenced.

The electoral commission of Guinea-Bissau confirms that João Bernardo Vieira won the presidential election in July; his closest challenger had demanded a recount.

America Online Inc. is awarded $13 million in its successful lawsuit against purveyors of unwanted commercial e-mail, or spam.

11 Egypt's electoral commission clears 9 candidates to run against Pres. Hosni

Mubarak in the country's first multicandidate presidential election, scheduled for September 7; 19 others are disqualified.

Pakistan successfully test-fires its first cruise missile.

As smoke from forest fires on the Indonesian island of Sumatra engulfs Malaysia's Kelang valley, the Malaysian government declares a state of emergency in the area.

12 Sri Lankan Foreign Minister Lakshman Kadirgamar is assassinated in his home; Kadirgamar was an ethnic Tamil who opposed the violence of the Liberation Tigers of Tamil Eelam.

Brazilian Pres. Luiz Inácio Lula da Silva speaks on nationwide television to plead his innocence and horror at the spreading scandal over illegal campaign financing in the election in which he gained office.

Gov. Bill Richardson of New Mexico declares a state of emergency in the four counties that border Mexico, citing violence related to illegal immigration and the trade in illegal drugs; three days later Gov. Janet Napolitano of Arizona follows suit.

13 German Chancellor Gerhard Schröder, facing an election in September, declares his opposition to the use of military force to prevent Iran from developing nuclear weapons; U.S. Pres. George W. Bush had explicitly refused to rule out that option.

Ten men are charged in a court in Kabul with the kidnapping of three United Nations election workers just before the election in Afghanistan in October 2004.

The French yacht *Iromiguy*, owned by Jean-Yves Chateau and crewed by amateurs, wins the 975-km (605-mi) Rolex Fastnet Race, sailing from the Isle of Wight in southern England around Fastnet Rock off the southwest coast of Ireland.

14 Kurmanbek Bakiyev is inaugurated as president of Kyrgyzstan.

The 46th Edward MacDowell Medal for outstanding contribution to the arts is awarded to composer Steve Reich at the MacDowell Colony in Peterborough, N.H.

The U.S. team prevents the British and Irish team from winning a fourth consecutive Walker Cup in men's golf when it wins the contest at the Chicago Golf Club in Wheaton, Ill.

15 In Helsinki a peace treaty between the government of Indonesia and the Free Aceh Movement is ceremonially signed, formalizing an agreement reached in July.

On the day that Iraq's new constitution is to be completed, according to the terms of an interim constitution, the committee writing the constitution extends the deadline by seven days.

Liberia's electoral commission approves 22 candidates to compete in the presidential election scheduled for October 11.

After seven weeks of negotiations, Bulgaria's three largest political parties agree to form a government under Sergey Stanishev of the Socialist Party.

Avian influenza H5N1 is reported in the Russian province of Chelyabinsk; it is the sixth province in Russia to report the presence of the disease.

Phil Mickelson defeats Thomas Bjorn and Steve Elkington by one stroke to win the PGA championship at the Baltusrol Golf Club in New Jersey.

16 On the day following the date for the evacuation of all Israeli settlements in the Gaza Strip, Israeli soldiers begin going door to door to persuade remaining settlers to leave voluntarily before forced evacuation begins on August 17; officials say that about half the residents left before the deadline.

17 More than 400 bombs explode within a period of half an hour in towns throughout Bangladesh, killing only two people but bringing most activities to an abrupt halt.

Three suicide bomb attacks in Baghdad kill at least 54 people; two attacks occur near a major bus station and one at a hospital.

At a site near the village of Dabene, Bulg., archaeologists report having found a trove of some 15,000 finely wrought gold artifacts believed to be about 4,150 years old.

18 China and Russia initiate an eight-day joint military exercise, taking place largely in the area of China's Shandong Peninsula; it is the largest joint exercise the two countries have conducted since the fall of the Soviet Union.

Pope Benedict XVI opens the 20th World Youth Day in Cologne, Ger., which is attended by hundreds of thousands of young people from around the world.

The Polisario Front in Western Sahara releases the last of its Moroccan prisoners of war; some of the 404 soldiers had been held as long as 20 years.

19 Burundi's new legislature elects former Hutu rebel leader Pierre Nkurunziza president of the country.

In a lawsuit in Texas, the pharmaceutical company Merck is held liable for the death of a man who was using the company's pain-killing drug Vioxx; the jury awards the man's widow some $250 million.

The government of The Netherlands orders that all commercial and domestic poultry be kept indoors to prevent them from being exposed to migratory wild birds that might have contracted H5N1 avian flu in Russia.

20 Palestinian leader Mahmoud Abbas announces that legislative elections will be held on Jan. 25, 2006; in his speech he also describes plans for the use of the area of the evacuated Israeli settlements, including new housing and a seaport.

A general strike in Bangladesh, called by the opposition Awami League to protest what it sees as the government's coddling of Islamist militants such as those who carried out the August 17 bomb attacks, leads to violent confrontations in several cities.

21 In Egypt the banned but very influential Muslim Brotherhood urges Egyptians to vote in the upcoming presidential election but does not endorse a candidate.

Kimi Raikkonen of Finland wins the inaugural Turkish Grand Prix automobile race.

In Anaheim, Calif., Xie Xingfang of China defeats her countrywoman Zhang Ning to win the International Badminton Federation women's singles world championship, and Taufik Hidayat of Indonesia defeats Lin Dan of China to win the men's singles title.

22 The last of the occupants of the Israeli settlements in the Gaza Strip are removed at the conclusion of a six-day operation.

The committee charged with writing a constitution for Iraq submits the document to the National Assembly but declares it to be incomplete and in need of three more days of work.

Violent fighting between Roman Catholic and Protestant young people continues for a third straight night in Belfast, N.Ire.

The home-appliance manufacturer Maytag agrees to be acquired by its rival, Whirlpool, in a deal that, if approved, would make Whirlpool the world's biggest appliance maker.

23 Representatives of the Red Cross from North Korea and South Korea meet in Kumgangsan, N.Kor., to discuss the destiny of hundreds of South Koreans still being detained in the north; these include prisoners of the Korean War, which ended in 1953, as well as civilians abducted later by North Korea.

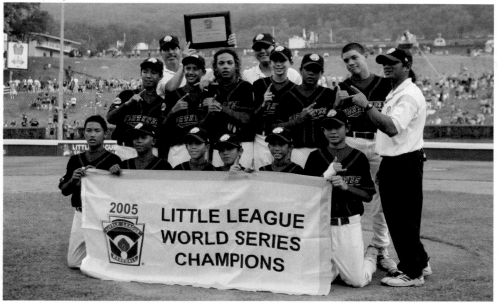

2005 LITTLE LEAGUE WORLD SERIES CHAMPIONS

France, Germany, and the U.K. cancel the resumption of negotiations with Iran over its nuclear program; the talks were to have started in late August.

24 A judge in Hong Kong strikes down a law that makes sex between two men punishable by life in prison if one or both are under 21 years of age; sex between a man and a woman or between two women over the age of 16 is legal.

Google introduces an instant-messaging and voice-communication service for PCs under the name of Google Talk.

25 The U.S. Defense Base Closure and Realignment Commission chooses to close Walter Reed Army Medical Center in Washington, D.C., founded in 1909, and merge it with the National Naval Medical Center in Bethesda, Md.

As a Category 1 storm, Hurricane Katrina makes first landfall in southern Florida, causing relatively light damage but killing seven people.

26 Sri Lanka's Supreme Court rules that a presidential election must be held in 2005, six years after the previous one, although the 1999 election was held one year earlier than necessary.

The World Health Organization declares that tuberculosis has reached emergency proportions in Africa.

The accounting firm KPMG reaches an agreement with federal prosecutors to pay a fine of $456 million and accept an outside monitor in order to avoid prosecution on charges of selling illegal tax shelters.

27 The leader of the armed wing of Hamas, Muhammad Deif, issues a video warning to the Palestinian Authority not to attempt to disarm Hamas, which holds a parade to take credit for the Israeli evacuation of its settlements in the Gaza Strip.

28 The new Iraqi constitution is presented in what seems to be its final form to the country's General Assembly; it is to be voted on in an election on October 15.

Turkmenistan revokes its full membership in the Commonwealth of Independent States, reducing its status to that of associate member; it is the first country in the alliance to downgrade its commitment.

The Goethe Prize is awarded to Israeli writer Amos Oz in a ceremony in Frankfurt, Ger.; the jury cites his literary output and moral responsibility.

Edoardo Molinari of Italy wins the U.S. amateur golf title.

The West Oahu team from Ewa Beach, Hawaii, defeats the Pabao team from Willemstad, Curaçao, 7–6 to win baseball's Little League World Series. *(Photo above.)*

29 Having strengthened from Category 1 to Category 4, Hurricane Katrina slams into the U.S. Gulf Coast, causing tremendous destruction; particularly hard hit are Gulfport and Biloxi in Mississippi and Slidell and New Orleans in Louisiana.

30 The storm surge caused by Hurricane Katrina breaks through the levees that protect New Orleans from the waters of the Mississippi River and Lake Pontchartrain, leaving some 80% of the city under several metres of water; the remaining residents are told to evacuate, and some 10,000 people are taking shelter at the Superdome, which lacks electricity, food, and water.

In accordance with the terms of the recently signed peace agreement, Pres. Susilo Bambang Yudhoyono of Indonesia signs a decree granting amnesty to 2,000 imprisoned members of the Free Aceh Movement and to group leaders living in exile.

Zimbabwe's House of Assembly approves a series of amendments to the country's constitution that restrict the rights of individuals and increase the power of the government.

31 In Baghdad Shi'ite pilgrims crossing a bridge to approach a shrine panic at shouted rumours of a suicide bomber on the bridge and stampede; at least 950 are killed, most trampled and suffocated but some drowned in the Tigris River.

Mikhail Khodorkovsky, the founder of the Yukos energy conglomerate who is in prison for tax evasion, announces that he is a candidate in the Russian legislative election scheduled for December.

September

*" Don't tell me 40,000 people are coming here.
They're not here. It's too doggone late. Now get off
your asses and do something, and let's fix the biggest
goddamn crisis in the history of this country. "*

New Orleans Mayor C. Ray Nagin,
four days after the destruction of his city by Hurricane Katrina,
on the slowness of the federal response to the emergency, September 1

1 The Socialist Albanian Prime Minister Fatos Nano concedes defeat in the July 3 election; Sali Berisha is asked to form a government two days later and takes office on September 11.

•

Buses slowly begin evacuating people from the Superdome in New Orleans to the Astrodome in Houston; some 25,000 people have been taking refuge in the Superdome, which has insufficient electricity, food, and sanitation; 20,000 more are stranded at the Ernest N. Morial Convention Center.

2 The military junta ruling Mauritania declares a general amnesty for political prisoners incarcerated by the previous government, to widespread jubilation.

•

Police in Paris make an unexpected raid on two rundown structures to evict 140 African immigrants squatting in the buildings.

3 Chief Justice of the United States William Rehnquist dies.

•

The Maoist rebels in Nepal declare a three-month unilateral cease-fire; meanwhile, some 5,000 people demonstrate in Kathmandu to demand the return of democracy.

•

In the Iraqi town of Buhruz, an attack on a checkpoint leaves nine Iraqi soldiers and two policemen dead, while an attack on a checkpoint in Ba'qubah kills six Iraqi police officers and an ambush on an Iraqi army convoy north of town kills four soldiers.

4 Simultaneous celebrations in 15 communities, all culminating in fireworks displays, mark the centennial of Saskatchewan's entry into the Canadian confederation.

•

Juan Pablo Montoya of Colombia wins the Italian Grand Prix Formula 1 automobile race.

5 U.S. Pres. George W. Bush nominates John G. Roberts, originally his choice to replace Sandra Day O'Connor on the Supreme Court, to replace instead Chief Justice William Rehnquist.

•

An Australian federal judge in Sydney rules that the peer-to-peer file-sharing network Kazaa violates music copyrights and orders the service's owner, Sharman Networks, to change its software so that it does not encourage the violation of copyrights.

6 Mayor C. Ray Nagin of New Orleans orders mandatory evacuation of the city, fearing that the hazards posed by flooding and the lack of services are too great; it is believed that between 5,000 and 10,000 people remain in their homes.

•

Typhoon Nabi makes landfall in southern Japan, forcing the evacuation of some 300,000 people; the following day, downgraded to a tropical storm, it moves north through the Sea of Japan, leaving at least 16 people dead.

7 Hosni Mubarak is reelected president in Egypt's first multi-candidate presidential election; the voting, while not free and fair, is less violent and more fair than previous elections, though the turnout is a low 23%.

•

In San Francisco, Steven Jobs of Apple Computer, Inc., introduces the next generation of the company's popular iPod music player, the solid-state iPod nano.

8 Pres. Viktor Yushchenko of Ukraine fires Prime Minister Yuliya Tymoshenko and dismisses the cabinet.

•

Russian Pres. Vladimir Putin and German Chancellor Gerhard Schröder approve an agreement to

build a pipeline to carry natural gas under the Baltic Sea between Vyborg, Russia, and Greifswald, Ger.

The Ertegun Jazz Hall of Fame inducts new members Count Basie, Roy Eldridge, Ella Fitzgerald, Benny Goodman, Earl Hines, Johnny Hodges, Jo Jones, Charles Mingus, King Oliver, Max Roach, Sonny Rollins, and Fats Waller.

9 Michael D. Brown, the head of the U.S. Federal Emergency Management Agency, is relieved of responsibility for the relief effort necessitated by Hurricane Katrina; he is replaced in that role by U.S. Coast Guard Vice Adm. Thad Allen.

The Naismith Memorial Basketball Hall of Fame in Springfield, Mass., inducts as members Brazilian player Hortencia Marcari, coaches Jim Boeheim, Jim Calhoun, and the late Sue Gunter, and broadcaster Hubie Brown.

10 U.S. and Iraqi troops begin a major offensive in the northern city of Tall 'Afar.

Waiting for the Barbarians, an opera by Philip Glass based on a novel by J.M. Coetzee, with libretto by Christopher Hampton, has its world premiere in Erfurt, Ger.; it is received with a 15-minute standing ovation.

Kim Clijsters of Belgium defeats Mary Pierce of France to win the U.S. Open tennis championship; the following day Roger Federer of Switzerland defeats American Andre Agassi to win the men's tennis tournament.

11 In an election to the lower house of the parliament in Japan, Prime Minister Junichiro Koizumi's Liberal Democratic Party wins a commanding majority of the seats.

Israeli troops begin their final evacuation of the Gaza Strip; they expect to complete the withdrawal by the following day.

Kimi Räikkönen of Finland wins the Belgian Grand Prix in Formula 1 automobile racing.

12 Parliamentary elections in Norway result in a win by the opposition Labour Party leading a centre-left bloc.

For the third night in a row, Protestant extremists riot in Belfast, N.Ire., attacking police and blockading roads; the violence began in response to a ruling that the Orange Order could not parade along streets bordering the Roman Catholic area of the city.

Michael D. Brown resigns as head of the U.S. Federal Emergency Management Agency.

In cricket, England defeats Australia in the fifth Test at the Oval in London to win the Ashes for the first time in 18 years. *(Photo above.)*

13 The UN General Assembly unanimously approves a document that will serve as a blueprint for future reforms; the plan, however, is a much-watered-down statement of goals originally proposed by Secretary-General Kofi Annan.

Six-party talks over North Korea's nuclear program resume in Beijing.

Joint air patrols by Malaysia, Singapore, Indonesia, and Thailand to combat piracy in the Strait of Malacca get under way.

The government of The Netherlands announces a plan to maintain a complete electronic database that includes information from birth to death on every person born in the country, beginning on Jan. 1, 2007.

14 Fourteen coordinated suicide bombings in Baghdad leave at least 167 people dead; in the worst of them, Shi'ite day labourers were lured to a van with the promise of work before the van exploded, killing at least 112, the highest death toll from one terrorist incident since the U.S.-led invasion of Iraq in 2003.

Delta Air Lines and Northwest Airlines, Inc., both file for bankruptcy protection.

Unite Here, a union composed of the former Amalgamated Clothing and Textile Workers, International Ladies' Garment Workers Union, and Hotel Employees and Restaurant Employees International Union, becomes the fourth major union to withdraw from the AFL-CIO during the summer.

15 Two suicide bombings within a minute of each other kill at least 31 people in Baghdad.

An audiotape by Abu Musab al-Zarqawi is released on a Web site; he declares that the al-Qaeda organization in Iraq is now at war with all Shi'ite Muslims in Iraq.

Odd Andersen—AFP/Getty Images

A UN World Food Programme ship carrying 940 metric tons of rice to aid tsunami victims is released by pirates off Somalia almost three months after it was captured.

Alison Lapper Pregnant, a sculpture by artist Marc Quinn that depicts a nude pregnant woman with vestigial arms and stunted legs, goes on display on a plinth in London's Trafalgar Square, igniting controversy. *(Photo right.)*

16 Israeli Prime Minister Ariel Sharon declares that Israel will not cooperate with planned Palestinian legislative elections if any of the candidates belong to the militant organization Hamas.

A car bomb in a Christian-majority neighbourhood in Beirut kills one person and injures many more.

Paolo Di Lauro, the head of a powerful family in the Camorra organized-crime society, is arrested in Secondigliano, Italy.

17 A car bomb kills at least 30 people in a Shi'ite neighbourhood on the outskirts of Baghdad, while outside the city a Kurdish member of the Transitional National Assembly is assassinated.

Pres. Ricardo Lagos of Chile ceremonially signs the country's new constitution, a more democratic instrument than the previous constitution promulgated by the former dictator Augusto Pinochet.

Legislative elections in New Zealand result in a slim plurality for the Labour Party of Prime Minister Helen Clark.

18 Legislative elections in Germany result in a near tie between the ruling coalition, led by Chancellor Gerhard Schröder, and the opposition coalition, headed by Angela Merkel.

Voters choose among 5,800 candidates as Afghanistan holds its first legislative elections in more than 35 years.

The winners of the 2005 Albert Lasker Medical Research Awards are announced; they are Ernest A. McCulloch and James E. Till, for work in uncovering the existence of stem cells; Edwin M. Southern and Alec John Jeffreys, for work that made it possible to search for a particular gene within a genome and for the development of genetic fingerprinting; and Nancy G. Brinker, for her creation of the Susan G. Komen Breast Cancer Foundation.

The Emmy Awards are presented in Los Angeles; winners include the television shows *Everybody Loves Raymond* and *Lost* and the actors Tony Shalhoub, James Spader, Felicity Huffman, Patricia Arquette, Brad Garrett, William Shatner, Doris Roberts, and Blythe Danner.

19 L. Dennis Kozlowski, the former CEO of industrial services manufacturing company Tyco International, and Mark Swartz, the company's former chief financial officer, are both sentenced to 8⅓ to 25 years in prison for fraud and stealing from the company.

Some 800 foreign labourers who have not been paid for more than six months march on a main highway in the city of Dubai, provoking an unprecedented response: the minister of labour orders all back pay to be delivered within 24 hours and levies

fines and restrictions on the employers of the workers.

An agreement is signed between North Korea and the U.S. and its allies that commits North Korea to abandoning all nuclear weapons and nuclear weapon programs and the other nations to providing North Korea with a civilian nuclear plant but says nothing about the timing of either provision.

20 Separatist rebels in Manipur state in India ambush and kill at least 11 Indian soldiers.

Amid allegations of corruption among members of the government, Yury I. Yekhanurov, Ukrainian Pres. Viktor Yushchenko's choice to replace Yuliya Tymoshenko as prime minister, is rejected by the legislature; on September 22, however, he is approved.

Pres. Hamid Karzai of Afghanistan suggests that U.S. military air strikes are no longer useful and that preventing militants from entering the country would be more effective; he also says that aid donations should be directed toward investment in infrastructure and industry.

The Sacramento Monarchs defeat the Connecticut Sun 62–59 to win their first Women's National Basketball Association championship.

21 The speaker of Brazil's Chamber of Deputies, Severino Cavalcanti, resigns in disgrace, accused of having extorted payments from a restaurant owner; he has been an important associate of Pres. Luiz Inácio Lula da Silva.

Lisa Dennison is named director of New York City's

Solomon R. Guggenheim Museum.

22 Some 2.5 million people attempt to evacuate Houston ahead of Hurricane Rita, a much larger evacuation than was foreseen, leading to horrific traffic jams.

23 Recently repaired levees in New Orleans begin to crumble under the assault from Hurricane Rita, and low-lying neighbourhoods are again flooded.

Lester M. Crawford resigns after having served only two months as commissioner of the U.S. Food and Drug Administration.

•

Alan Rosenberg is elected president of the Screen Actors Guild, succeeding Melissa Gilbert.

24 Hurricane Rita makes landfall near the Texas-Louisiana border as a Category 3 storm.

•

The board of the International Atomic Energy Agency votes to refer Iran to the UN Security Council as being in violation of the Nuclear Non-proliferation Treaty, to which it is a signatory.

•

A controversial conference to examine the fate of ethnic Armenians who lived in the Ottoman Empire early in the 20th century convenes at Bilgi University, Istanbul, in spite of a recent court ruling forbidding the forum.

•

The Sydney Swans defeat the West Coast Eagles to win the Australian Football League championship; it is the first title for Sydney; the Swans had won it 72 years earlier, but the team then represented South Melbourne.

25 The World Bank approves the plan put forward by the Group of Eight industrialized countries to forgive the debt owed by the poorest countries; the International Monetary Fund had approved the plan the previous day.

•

Hours after Israeli Prime Minister Ariel Sharon asserted the right to retaliate against Palestinian rocket attacks on Israel from the Gaza Strip, the militant organization Hamas announces that it has ceased making attacks on Israel from the Gaza Strip.

•

With a third-place finish at the Brazilian Grand Prix and two races to go in the season, Fernando Alonso becomes the youngest man and the first Spaniard to win the Formula 1 world automobile racing drivers' title.

•

Dan Wheldon, the winner of the Indianapolis 500 automobile race, wins the overall IndyCar championship.

•

With his defeat of *ozeki* Tochiazuma and *sekiwake* Kotooshu at the Aki Basho (the autumn grand sumo tournament), *yokozuna* Asashoryu wins a sixth consecutive Emperor's Cup, equaling a record set 38 years earlier by Taiho.

26 A new stock exchange, the Dubai International Financial Exchange (DIFX)—covering the Gulf Cooperation Council countries, the Indian subcontinent, and South Africa—begins operation in Dubai.

•

In a court-martial in Ft. Hood, Texas, U.S. Army Pvt. Lynndie England is found guilty of having mistreated prisoners in Abu Ghraib prison, Iraq; the following day she is sentenced to three years in prison and a dishonourable discharge.

•

An independent monitoring group headed by John De Chastelain confirms that the Irish Republican Army has completely destroyed its arsenal of weapons in Northern Ireland to the monitors' satisfaction.

•

Thousands of demonstrators conclude a three-day protest outside the White House in Washington, D.C., with the planned arrest of several, including Cindy Sheehan, the mother of a fallen soldier and an iconic leader of the campaign against the war in Iraq.

27 Seven American trade unions, including the four that left the AFL-CIO earlier in the year, create a new labour organization, the Change to Win Federation, which represents some 5.4 million workers.

•

US Airways and America West Airlines complete their merger; the combined company, which will operate under the name US Airways, is the sixth biggest American airline in passenger miles.

28 Tom DeLay resigns his post as majority leader of the U.S. House of Representatives after a grand jury in Texas indicts him on a charge of having conspired to violate the state's election laws.

•

The first major trial related to the collapse of the Italian food conglomerate Parmalat gets under way in Milan.

•

U.S. Secretary of the Treasury John Snow unveils the newly designed $10 bill; it includes several features meant to discourage counterfeiting, including two small images of the torch of the Statue of Liberty and colour-changing ink.

29 John G. Roberts, Jr., is sworn in as the 17th chief justice of the United States.

•

New York Times reporter Judith Miller is released from prison, where she has been for three months, after she agrees to testify about the government official who discussed a covert CIA operative with her; she says the source has released her from her promise of confidentiality.

•

In Balad, Iraq, three truck bombs go off 10 minutes apart, killing at least 62 people, nearly all Shi'ite civilians.

•

Janjawid militia members attack a refugee camp in the Darfur region of The Sudan, killing 29 people.

30 Auditors from the congressional GAO rule that the administration of U.S. Pres. George W. Bush engaged in illegal dissemination of covert propaganda when it sought favourable news coverage of its education policy—for example, by paying a commentator to promote the policy in his newspaper columns and during TV appearances.

•

The legislature of the autonomous community of Catalonia in Spain approves a measure to make the region an even more autonomous "nation" within Spain, assuming many powers that now belong to the central government.

•

The Osaka (Japan) High Court rules that visits by Prime Minister Junichiro Koizumi to the Yasukuni Shrine, a Shinto site honouring Japan's war dead, violate the constitutional separation of religion and state.

October

> *God has blessed me to be alive to see this day. When they put me on trial, it lasted five minutes, in a dark room, and I was sentenced to 20 years.*
>
> Soriya al-Sultani, a member of Iraq's interim assembly and former political prisoner, on the start of Saddam Hussein's trial, October 19

1 Three suicide bombers kill 23 people in the tourist towns of Kuta and Jimbaran on the Indonesian island of Bali.

João Bernardo Vieira is sworn in as elected president of Guinea-Bissau; he had ruled the country from 1980, when he took over in a coup, until 2000, when he was ousted by another coup.

A rocket carrying American astronaut William McArthur, Russian cosmonaut Valery Tokarev, and American space tourist Gregory Olsen takes off from the Baikonur space centre in Kazakhstan, headed for the International Space Station.

Doctor Atomic, a new opera by John Adams with libretto by Peter Sellars, has its world premiere at the San Francisco Opera.

2 When Palestinian Authority police attempt to confiscate illegal weapons from several Hamas members in Gaza City, shooting breaks out and running gun battles ensue; at least two people are killed and some 40 wounded.

With a second-place finish at the Rally of Japan, Sébastien Loeb of France wins the world rally championship title for the second consecutive year.

3 U.S. Pres. George W. Bush names Harriet E. Miers, the White House counsel and once his personal lawyer, to replace retiring Sandra Day O'Connor on the Supreme Court.

The Nobel Prize for Physiology or Medicine is awarded to Australians Barry J. Marshall and J. Robin Warren for their discovery that the bacterium *Helicobacter pylori* causes most duodenal and peptic ulcers.

The Open Content Alliance, led by Yahoo! and including the Internet Archive, the British National Archives, and the Universities of California and Toronto, among others, announces a plan to digitize and make available over the Internet hundreds of thousands of books and papers.

4 Muslims in many parts of the world begin observations of the holy month of Ramadan.

The European Union and Turkey formally open negotiations toward Turkey's eventual membership in the EU.

In Stockholm the Nobel Prize for Physics is awarded to American physicist Roy J. Glauber, for having calculated the mathematical foundation for quantum optics, and to John L. Hall of the U.S. and Theodor W. Hänsch of Germany, for having developed a method of using laser pulses to measure light frequencies precisely.

5 A suicide bomber attacks a Shi'ite mosque in Al-Hillah, Iraq, killing 25 people.

The Nobel Prize for Chemistry is awarded to a Frenchman, Yves Chauvin, and two Americans, Robert H. Grubbs and Richard R. Schrock, for their work on controlled metathesis, a low-cost method of synthesizing drugs, plastics, and other important organic substances.

American scientists announce that they have reconstructed the virus that caused the so-called Spanish influenza outbreak that killed 25 million people in 1918, and found evidence that it was a type of avian flu virus that jumped directly to humans.

The Church of England confirms John Sentamu as archbishop of York, the church's second highest position; Sentamu is the first black cleric to become an Anglican archbishop. *(Photo below.)*

AP/Wide World Photos

In 15 cities throughout North America, the National Hockey League season gets under way with its first games since the 2004–05 season was canceled.

6 NATO Secretary-General Jaap de Hoop Scheffer says that NATO will increase its force in Afghanistan to 15,000 troops and will expand its mission into southern Afghanistan.

In an attempt to stem a tide of hundreds of Africans attempting to migrate to Spain through its exclaves of Melilla and Ceuta on the North African coast, Spain reverses policy and sends 70 Malian migrants back to Morocco; also, some 400 people rush guard posts at Melilla, and six Africans are killed.

Some 50 years after it was designed by Oscar Niemeyer, the futuristic Ibirapuera Park Auditorium opens in São Paulo.

7 The Nobel Peace Prize is awarded to the International Atomic Energy Agency and its director general, Mohamed ElBaradei.

Belgium experiences its first general strike in 12 years as hundreds of thousands of workers walk out to protest a government plan to raise the retirement age from 58 to 60.

8 A shallow earthquake with a magnitude of 7.6 and an epicentre on the border of Pakistan's North-West Frontier province devastates the disputed Kashmir region, killing more than 85,000 people.

Delphi, the biggest automobile parts supplier in the U.S., files for bankruptcy protection.

The Reina Sofia Palace of the Arts, an opera house designed by Santiago Calatrava, opens in Valencia, Spain.

9 Tropical Storm Vince briefly strengthens into a hurricane and thereby makes 2005 the second busiest hurricane season since records began; two days later it becomes the first tropical cyclone to make landfall in Spain.

Kimi Raikkonen wins the Japanese Grand Prix Formula 1 auto race.

10 Three weeks after a near-tie parliamentary election in Germany, an agreement is reached to form a grand coalition government with Angela Merkel at the head.

The Nobel Memorial Prize in Economic Sciences goes to Israeli Robert J. Aumann and American Thomas C. Schelling for their respective work in game theory.

The UN General Assembly elects Ghana, the Republic of the Congo, Qatar, Slovakia, and Peru to fill the two-year regional positions on the Security Council.

The Man Booker Prize for Fiction goes to Irish writer John Banville for his novel *The Sea*.

11 Presidential and legislative elections are held in Liberia but result in the need for a presidential runoff.

Ethiopia's legislative assembly votes to strip immunity from prosecution protection from those legislators belonging to the opposition Coalition for Unity and Democracy.

U.S. Secretary of State Condoleezza Rice reaches an agreement with Kyrgyzstan that will allow the U.S. to maintain its military base in the country as long as the situation in Afghanistan makes it necessary.

12 Ghazi Kanaan, who was Syria's power broker in Lebanon for some 20 years and Syria's minister of the interior from 2004, is found dead in his office in Damascus, an apparent suicide.

Iran requests a resumption of negotiations with the U.K., Germany, and France regarding its nuclear program.

Phillip R. Bennett, the former chairman and CEO of the enormous commodities brokerage firm Refco, is charged with securities fraud.

Steven Jobs of Apple Computer introduces an iPod with a 6.4-cm (2.5-in) screen that is capable of displaying video, including music videos, short films, and television shows.

13 In Nalchik, the capital of the Russian republic of Kabardino-Balkariya, insurgents attack several police and security buildings; by the following day at least 138 people have been killed.

The Nobel Prize for Literature is awarded to British playwright and poet Harold Pinter.

It is confirmed that thousands of birds that died in the past few days around a turkey farm in Turkey were victims of the H5N1 virus, the first appearance of the disease in that country.

Nature magazine reports that scientists in China have

unearthed a bowl of what they believe to be noodles dating to 4,000 years ago near the Huang Ho in northwestern China.

14 Pres. Viktor Yushchenko of Ukraine fires the country's chief prosecutor days after he opened investigations against a close presidential aide.

The International Criminal Court reveals that it has for the first time issued arrest warrants; they are for Joseph Kony, the leader of the Lord's Resistance Army, and four of the Ugandan rebel group's commanders.

Japan's legislature approves the privatization of the country's postal service.

Veselin Topalov of Bulgaria wins the FIDE world chess championship in San Luis, Arg.

15 A national referendum on the country's new constitution is held in Iraq.

It is confirmed that ducks in Romania have died of the H5N1 avian flu; this is the first appearance of the disease in mainland Europe.

A son is born to Crown Prince Frederik and Crown Princess Mary of Denmark; he will be christened (and named) in January 2006.

A new de Young Museum designed by Jacques Herzog and Pierre de Meuron opens to critical acclaim in San Francisco.

16 U.S. air strikes against the insurgency in Ramadi, Iraq, kill some 70 people.

Annika Sörenstam wins the Ladies Professional Golf

Association Samsung world championship in Palm Desert, Calif.

Fernando Alonso's win at the China Grand Prix automobile race secures the Formula 1 constructors' championship for his team, Renault, for the first time.

17 Japanese Prime Minister Junichiro Koizumi makes his annual visit to the Yasukuni shrine to Japan's war dead, igniting criticism and anger elsewhere in Asia.

Opposition leader Rasul Guliyev is prevented from returning to Azerbaijan to run for office; he has been living in exile since 1996.

Gen. Henri Poncet, the former commander of French peacekeeping troops in Côte d'Ivoire, and two other soldiers are suspended for having covered up the death in May of an Ivoirian man in French custody.

General Motors reaches a tentative agreement with the United Automobile Workers union to cut medical benefits for workers and retirees.

18 Italian Prime Minister Silvio Berlusconi agrees to hold national elections on April 9, 2006.

The advocacy group Refugees International reports that new guidelines developed by the UN to stop sexual abuse of local women and girls by UN peacekeeping troops have not been put into practice and that abuse continues to be a problem.

19 In Baghdad former Iraqi president Saddam Hussein goes on trial with seven other men for the massacre of 148 men and boys in Dujail in 1982; Saddam refuses to recognize the court but pleads not guilty.

Five major American publishing companies file suit against Google, Inc., contending that the Internet company's plan to make searchable digitized versions of library holdings violates publishing copyrights; Google says that it plans to place only small parts of copyrighted text online.

Hurricane Wilma strengthens to Category 5 and achieves a record low pressure at its eye of 0.90 kg/cm² (12.8 psi), which makes it by that criterion the strongest hurricane ever measured.

A block of four stamps of a Curtiss JN-4 "Jenny" airplane printed upside down in 1918 is sold at auction for $2.7 million, the highest price ever paid for U.S. stamps.

20 A UN investigating committee releases a preliminary report implicating high-ranking government and military leaders in Syria in the assassination of former Lebanese prime minister Rafiq al-Hariri.

One of the defense lawyers for a co-defendant in the trial of former Iraqi president Saddam Hussein is murdered in Baghdad.

The American oil-trading company Midway Trading pleads guilty in New York to having made illegal kickback payments to Iraqi officials when buying Iraqi oil under the UN oil-for-food program.

The U.S. Congress passes a law that will shield manufacturers and dealers of firearms from civil liability lawsuits.

21 Malawi's National Assembly summons Pres.

Bingu wa Mutharika to face impeachment charges, a move supporters of the president say is illegal.

Rioting Muslims attempt to storm a Coptic Christian church in Alexandria, Egypt, angered by rumours about a play that had been performed on one occasion in the church two years ago and was recently distributed on DVD; some consider the play anti-Islamic.

Wreaths are laid on the HMS *Victory*, bells rung on all Royal Navy warships, and 1,000 beacons lit throughout the U.K in remembrance of the 200th anniversary of the death of Horatio Nelson in the Battle of Trafalgar.

22 A soldier who dies after having been injured in combat in Samarra' on October 17 is the 2,000th U.S. military death in Iraq.

A UN official reports that two weeks after the Kashmir earthquake, no aid has reached 10–20% of those affected; in addition, Indian officials have yet to agree on a plan to open the Line of Control to allow aid to flow through it.

Rafal Blechacz of Poland wins the Chopin International Piano Competition in Warsaw; he is the first Pole since 1975 to win the contest, which is held every five years.

23 In a runoff election, Lech Kaczynski, the conservative mayor of Warsaw, is elected president of Poland.

Pope Benedict XVI canonizes his first saints, two from Italy, two from Ukraine, and one from Chile; all five had been approved for sainthood by Pope John Paul II.

In Montgomery, Ala., the Civil Rights Memorial Center is ceremonially opened.

After one year and 10 months, Jesper Olsen of Denmark succeeds in running a lap around the world, completing a trek of more than 26,000 km (16,200 mi) by running an average of 41 km (25 mi) per day.

The eighth annual Mark Twain Prize for American Humor is presented to Steve Martin in a ceremony at the John F. Kennedy Center for the Performing Arts in Washington, D.C.

Timo Boll of Germany defeats Wang Hao of China to win the Men's Table Tennis World Cup in Liège, Belg.

24 U.S. Pres. George W. Bush nominates Ben Bernanke, currently head of the Council of Economic Advisers, to replace Alan Greenspan as chairman of the U.S. Federal Reserve.

Ukraine sells Kryvorizhstal, its biggest steel mill, to Mittal Steel, for $4.8 million in an auction.

Henry R. Silverman, the chairman of the huge business conglomerate Cendant, announces that the company will break into four different publicly traded companies, one each for real estate, travel, hospitality, and vehicle-rental businesses.

American Civil Rights movement icon Rosa Parks dies in Detroit.

25 Election officials in Iraq announce that the country's new constitution was narrowly approved in the referendum on October 15.

© Sean Gallup/Getty Images

responsibility for its defense and relocate some 7,000 U.S. servicepeople from Okinawa to Guam.

30 India and Pakistan agree to open the Line of Control on November 7 to make it easier to take disaster relief to victims of the Kashmir earthquake.

Officials in France report that they have arrested 22 people after three nights of rioting in Clichy-sous-Bois by people angered by the accidental death of two immigrant teenagers who were rumoured to have been fleeing from police.

The Frauenkirche in Dresden, Ger., is dedicated after having been reconstructed; the landmark was destroyed by Allied firebombing in World War II. *(Photo left.)*

31 Conservative Kazimierz Marcinkiewicz is sworn in as prime minister of Poland.

U.S. Pres. George W. Bush nominates Samuel A. Alito, a judge on the U.S. Court of Appeals, to replace Sandra Day O'Connor on the Supreme Court.

The Judicial Council of the United Methodist Church removes openly gay minister Irene Elizabeth Stroud from the ministry and orders the reinstatement of a minister who had been suspended for refusing to allow a gay man to join his congregation.

The Spanish telecommunications company Telefónica agrees to buy the British mobile phone company O_2.

Princess Letizia, the wife of Prince Felipe of Spain, gives birth to a daughter, Leonor, in Madrid.

The BBC World Service announces that it is closing 10 foreign-language broadcasts—in Bulgarian, Croatian, Czech, Greek, Hungarian, Kazakh, Polish, Slovak, Slovene, and Thai—and inaugurating the BBC Arabic Television Service, to begin broadcasting in 2007.

The European Union's top court rules that only cheese produced in Greece may be called feta cheese.

26 The UN calls for $550 million in assistance to help reach tens of thousands of survivors of the Kashmir earthquake who remain stranded in remote mountain villages.

In a speech, Iranian Pres. Mahmoud Ahmadinejad states, among other things, that Israel should "be wiped off the map."

The Chicago White Sox defeat the Houston Astros 1–0 in Houston in the fourth game of the World Series to sweep the Major League Baseball championship; it is the first World Series championship win for the White Sox since 1917.

27 The committee investigating the former UN-run oil-for-food program in Iraq releases its final report, showing that more than half of the companies participating in the program paid illegal kickbacks to Iraq and that many of those made illegal profits themselves.

Harriet E. Miers withdraws her nomination to the U.S. Supreme Court.

Switzerland releases a report indicating that the country was among those that assisted South Africa in building nuclear weapons during the apartheid era.

28 In the ongoing investigation into the leaking of a CIA operative's name to the press, U.S. Vice Pres. Dick Cheney's chief of staff, I. Lewis ("Scooter") Libby, is indicted on charges of having lied to investigators and to a grand jury.

The U.S. Fish and Wildlife Service extends the ban on the importation of beluga caviar imposed in September to include caviar from the Black Sea basin, effectively banning all beluga caviar.

29 Three coordinated bomb explosions, two in busy marketplaces and one on a public bus, kill at least 48 people in New Delhi.

A suicide car bomb in the largely Shi'ite town of Huwaider, Iraq, kills at least 20 people; in Baghdad three U.S. soldiers are killed by improvised roadside bombs.

In response to a small rally in support of a proposed new constitution in Kenya, hundreds of young people riot in Kisumu; at least three people are killed and dozens injured.

The U.S. and Japan announce an agreement on alterations to their military alliance; the changes call on Japan to take increased

November

"

The republic is completely determined . . . to be stronger than those who want to sow violence or fear.

"

French Pres. Jacques Chirac, responding to the escalating violence in working-class suburbs of Paris, November 6

1 Bolivian Pres. Eduardo Rodríguez breaks an impasse by decreeing that presidential and congressional elections will be held on December 18.

Representatives of both North and South Korea announce that the two countries will field a joint athletic team at the Asian Games in Qatar in 2006 and at the Olympic Games in Beijing in 2008, competing as a single country for the first time.

Makybe Diva wins an unprecedented third consecutive Melbourne Cup Thoroughbred horse race in Australia.

Charles, prince of Wales, and his wife, Camilla, duchess of Cornwall, make their first official overseas visit as a couple, to the United States.

2 David Blunkett resigns as U.K. secretary for work and pensions after admitting errors in his private business dealings; he had been brought back into the government by Prime Minister Tony Blair after he was forced to resign as home secretary in a scandal over improper favours granted by his office to his former lover.

Ethiopian security forces kill more than 20 protesters in Addis Ababa and injure more than 150 as unrest resulting from the May elections escalates.

Mukhtar Mai, a Pakistani woman famed for speaking out after being gang-raped on the order of a tribal council, is honoured in Washington, D.C., as *Glamour* magazine's Woman of the Year.

3 Peru's legislature passes a law mandating a redrawing of the sea boundary with Chile in order to gain better access to fishing waters in the Pacific.

At the Latin Grammy Awards in Los Angeles, which are broadcast exclusively in Spanish for the first time, Colombian rock star Juanes wins three awards, and Spanish singer Alejandro Sanz wins two, for record of the year and song of the year, both for "Tu no tienes alma."

4 As Shi'ites in Iraq begin celebrating 'Id al-Fitr, marking the end of Ramadan, insurgent attacks in the central part of the country kill at least 16 people.

Hundreds of people in Mar del Plata, Arg., riot in protest against U.S. Pres. George W. Bush's presence at the 34-country Summit of the Americas, while Venezuelan Pres. Hugo Chávez leads a huge anti-U.S. rally; the summit ends on March 5 without an agreement on the Free Trade Area of the Americas.

Colgate-Palmolive and Introgen Therapeutics announce an alliance to attempt to create an oral product, such as a mouthwash or gel, that contains genes to suppress tumours in an attempt to treat and prevent oral cancers.

5 U.S. and Iraqi forces begin a major offensive in Husayba, Iraq, a town along the Syrian border, to try to eliminate a corridor through which foreign fighters enter the country.

The luxury cruise ship *Seabourn Spirit* escapes an attempt by pirates to board and hijack it off the coast of Somalia.

6 Iran reveals that it allowed International Atomic Energy Agency inspectors access to its Parchin military complex and reports that it has sent a note to the three European countries with which it had been negotiating, requesting a resumption of talks.

As the nightly rioting in France continues, 10 police officers are shot and wounded in the suburb of Grigny.

Government officials begin a previously unannounced move of the seat of the government of Myanmar (Burma) from Yangon (Rangoon) to the remote mountain village of Pyinmana; it is expected that the move will be completed by the end of the year.

The Swaminarayan Akshardham Temple, a sandstone building dedicated to religious tolerance, is ceremonially opened in New Delhi by Indian Pres. A.P.J. Abdul Kalam, a Muslim; Indian Prime Minister Manmohan Singh, a Sikh; and L.K. Advani, Hindu leader of the main opposition party. *(Photo right.)*

7 Hours after his secret arrival in Santiago after five years of exile in Japan, former Peruvian president Alberto Fujimori is arrested; he is wanted in Peru on a number of charges, including responsibility for massacres and subversion of democracy.

Natwar Singh is removed from his post as India's foreign minister in response to allegations that he illegally profited from the UN oil-for-food program in Iraq.

Régis Jauffret wins the Prix Fémina for French novels for *Asiles de fous,* and American Joyce Carol Oates wins the foreign-novel prize for *The Falls;* the Prix Médicis for foreign literature goes to Turkish writer Orhan Pamuk for *Snow.*

8 Liberians vote in a runoff presidential election between former UN and World Bank official Ellen Johnson-Sirleaf and former association football (soccer) star George Weah.

After 12 successive nights of violence during which one person died and some 6,000 vehicles were burned, a state of emergency is declared in France, which gives the government the right to impose curfews in selected areas.

The UN General Assembly, for the 14th year in a row, passes a resolution calling for an end to the U.S. commercial embargo of Cuba; the vote is 182–4.

9 Suicide bombers in Amman, Jordan, attack the Grand Hyatt, Radisson SAS, and Days Inn hotels all within a few minutes, killing at least 59 people.

Six-country negotiations about North Korea's nuclear program resume.

U.S. Pres. George W. Bush awards the Presidential Medal of Freedom to Alan Greenspan, Muhammad Ali, Carol Burnett, Aretha Franklin, Andy Griffith, Robert Conquest, Vinton Cerf, Robert Kahn, Paul Harvey, Sonny Montgomery, Gen. Richard B. Myers, Jack Nicklaus, Frank Robinson, and Paul Rusesabagina.

10 A suicide bomber detonates his weapons in a popular Baghdad restaurant, killing at least 29 people.

The World Health Organization declares that polio has once again been eliminated from 10 sub-Saharan African countries but remains endemic in Afghanistan, Egypt, India, Niger, Nigeria, and Pakistan.

Nissan Motor Co. announces plans to move its North American headquarters from Gardena, Calif., outside Los Angeles, to Franklin, Tenn., citing lower costs; the new headquarters is expected to open in 2008.

South African Pres. Thabo Mbeki officially inaugurates the Southern Africa Large Telescope (SALT) in the Karoo region of the country.

The U.S. National Medal of Arts is awarded to Louis Auchincloss, James DePreist, Paquito D'Rivera, Robert Duvall, Leonard Garment, Ollie Johnston, Wynton Marsalis, Dolly Parton, Tina Rivera, and the Pennsylvania Academy of the Fine Arts.

11 Colombia's Constitutional Court rules that the law passed last year to allow Pres. Álvaro Uribe to run for a second four-year presidential term is permissible under the country's constitution.

Officials in Kuwait report that a migrating flamingo found on a Kuwaiti beach was ill with the H5N1 avian flu; it is the first instance of the disease in the Persian Gulf.

The journal *Science* publishes a report on the discovery of a new species of marine crocodile that lived some 135 million years ago, in the time of dinosaurs; the creature, *Dakosaurus andiniensis,* is unique among crocodiles in that its head resembled that of a *Tyrannosaurus rex.*

12 Elections are held for the House of Elders, the upper house of Afghanistan's legislature, while results from the September 18 election for the National Assembly are released, showing a majority for religious conservatives.

A meeting between the U.S. and several Muslim countries in Manama, Bahrain, concludes without the declaration in favour of democracy that the U.S. had sought.

Three new buildings designed by Italian architect Renzo Piano to expand the High Museum of Art in Atlanta open to critical acclaim.

13 In Mogadishu, Somalia, two days of fighting between the Islamic courts' militia, which is attempting to close down movie houses and video stores, and local fighters leave at least 12 people dead.

AP/Wide World Photos

American stem-cell researcher Gerald P. Schatten surprises observers by announcing that he is suspending his connections with the Seoul National University group of researchers headed by Hwang Woo Suk, citing ethical violations regarding the source of the oocytes used in producing stem cells from cloned human embryos.

In an upset the Los Angeles Galaxy wins its second Major League Soccer title in four years with a 1–0 overtime victory over the New England Revolution at the MLS Cup game in Frisco, Texas.

14 In the midst of an escalating war of words between Mexican Pres. Vicente Fox and Venezuelan Pres. Hugo Chávez, Venezuela recalls its ambassador from Mexico; Fox declares that Mexico will recall its ambassador from Venezuela as well.

Opposition leader Kizza Besigye is arrested on charges of treason in Uganda, triggering large-scale rioting in Kampala.

15 The Ministry of Agriculture in China announces its intention to vaccinate all of its 5.2 billion ducks, geese, and chickens against avian flu, a logistically overwhelming project.

Iraqi Prime Minister Ibrahim al-Jaafari announces an urgent official investigation into the circumstances behind the imprisonment and torture of 173 Iraqis in the basement of an Interior Ministry building.

Israel and the Palestinian Authority reach an agreement, brokered by U.S.

Secretary of State Condoleezza Rice, to ease travel restrictions on residents of the Gaza Strip and to open the border between Gaza and Egypt.

Illinois Gov. Rod Blagojevich signs into law a measure—the broadest such plan in the country—to give all children in the state medical-insurance coverage.

16 International officials announce that Iran has resumed the enrichment of uranium in defiance of the International Atomic Energy Agency.

China announces that it has confirmed three human cases of H5N1 avian flu; it is the fifth country to find the flu in people.

Guatemala's chief drug-enforcement investigator and two of his aides are arrested in the U.S. and charged with conspiracy to smuggle vast amounts of cocaine into the U.S.

An American businessman, Philip H. Bloom, is charged with having paid bribes to members of the Coalition Provisional Authority in Iraq in order to secure lucrative contracts for his three companies in the reconstruction of Iraq.

The National Book Awards are presented to William T. Vollmann for his novel *Europe Central,* Joan Didion for her nonfiction book *The Year of Magical Thinking,* W.S. Merwin for his poetry collection *Migration: New and Selected Poems,* and Jeanne Birdsall for her young-adult book *The Penderwicks;* Lawrence Ferlinghetti wins the inaugural Literarian Award, and Norman Mailer is given the Medal for Distinguished Contribution to American Letters.

17 Democratic U.S. Rep. John P. Murtha of Pennsylvania surprises congressional and administration members by publicly calling for the withdrawal of all U.S. troops from Iraq within six months.

Indictments are announced in Chicago against Conrad M. Black and three others on charges that they stole $51.8 million from the newspaper conglomerate Hollinger International, of which Black was a founder.

A presidential election is held in Sri Lanka; the candidate with the harder-line position against Tamil secessionists, Prime Minister Mahinda Rajapakse, narrowly wins.

18 Tropical Storm Gamma, the 24th named storm of the Atlantic hurricane season, forms near Central America and causes flooding in Honduras that leaves at least two people dead.

19 Delegates from 75 countries and organizations, including the World Bank and the Asian Development Bank, meeting in Islamabad, pledge donations of $5.8 billion to help Pakistan in the

reconstruction of its earthquake-ravaged north.

U.S. Pres. George W. Bush arrives in Beijing for talks with Chinese Pres. Hu Jintao.

20 The second round of legislative elections in Egypt is marked by violence at the polling places, particularly in places regarded as strongholds for the Muslim Brotherhood, which made a strong showing in the first round of elections.

The Muhammad Ali Center, a cultural gathering place to honour the great boxer, is ceremonially opened in Ali's hometown of Louisville, Ky.

21 At a conference of leading Iraqi Sunnis, Shi'ites, and Kurds hosted by the Arab League in Cairo, the conferees release a statement calling for the establishment of a timetable for the withdrawal of foreign military forces in the country.

Israeli Prime Minister Ariel Sharon announces that he is leaving his political party, Likud, which he helped create, in order to found a new centrist party. *(Photo below.)*

AP/Wide World Photos

Voters in Kenya reject a draft constitution backed by Pres. Mwai Kibaki.

The U.S. formally returns the Karshi-Khanabad air base to Uzbekistan.

General Motors announces a plan to improve its financial health; among other things, it plans to eliminate 5,000 jobs in addition to the 25,000 job cuts announced in June.

The centennial of the publication of Albert Einstein's equation $E = mc^2$ is observed by physicists throughout the world.

22 Angela Merkel takes office as the German chancellor.

The Chinese city of Harbin, which has a population of nearly three million, shuts off the water supply for five days after a petrochemical plant explosion in Jilin on November 13 caused an enormous benzene spill in the Songhua River, contaminating Harbin's source of water.

Maoist rebels and seven political parties in Nepal announce an agreement calling for a return to democracy and a new constitution; the rebels agree to end violence if elections are held under a new government.

The U.S. Commerce Department agrees to reduce its countervailing duties on imported Canadian softwood from 16% to under 1%.

Meeting in Washington, D.C., the Serb, Croat, and Muslim presidents of Bosnia and Herzegovina sign an agreement to pursue a major constitutional overhaul and move to a more united government structure for the country.

Microsoft's much-anticipated new video game console, the Xbox 360, goes on sale throughout the U.S. at midnight.

23 Electoral authorities in Liberia declare Ellen Johnson-Sirleaf the winner of the runoff presidential election.

Former dictator Augusto Pinochet is placed under house arrest in Chile after being charged with tax evasion and financial corruption.

A law goes into effect in England and Wales that permits bars, restaurants, and supermarkets to sell alcoholic beverages later than 11:00 PM, with even 24-hour licenses available.

24 A suicide car bomb at the entrance to a hospital in Mahmudiyah, Iraq, kills at least 30 people; it appears to have targeted a U.S. convoy, but all the victims are Iraqi.

25 The Rafah crossing between the Gaza Strip and Egypt reopens, with Palestinians responsible for security for the first time.

The journal *Science* reports the findings of the European Program for Ice Coring in Antarctica, which show that in spite of climate fluctuations over time, the current level of important greenhouse gases in the atmosphere is the highest it has been in 650,000 years.

26 An agreement is reached between Dutch Prime Minister Jan Peter Balkenende and the leaders of the Netherlands Antilles whereby the Netherlands Antilles will be dissolved as a political entity as of July 1, 2007; Curaçao and Sint Maarten will become autonomous entities within The Netherlands; the status of Bonaire, Sint Eustatius, and Saba remains to be defined.

Textile tycoon Vijaypat Singhania sets a new world record for highest flight in a hot-air balloon in Mumbai (Bombay) when he reaches an altitude of 21,290 m (69,849 ft).

27 An explosion in a coal mine in the Chinese city of Qitaihe kills at least 161 miners; more than 70 are rescued.

Presidential and legislative elections are held in Honduras; the Liberal Party candidate, Manuel Zelaya, is elected president.

Omar Bongo is reelected to the presidency of Gabon; he has been in office since 1967.

Election results in Egypt show that the outlawed Muslim Brotherhood's electoral gains continued in the second round of legislative elections, adding 29 seats to the 47 won in the first round.

The Edmonton Eskimos capture the 93rd Canadian Football League Grey Cup, defeating the Montreal Alouettes 38–35 in the Cup's first overtime game in 44 years.

The Olympic flame begins its circuitous 13,360-km (8,300-mi) journey from Olympia, Greece, for the opening of the Winter Games in Turin, Italy, on Feb. 10, 2006.

28 Canada's government loses a no-confidence vote in the House of Commons; elections will be held in January 2006.

Venezuela signs an agreement with Spain to buy patrol boats and military transport and patrol aircraft.

29 The European Union sends a note to the U.S. asking for clarifications about its practice, disclosed by the *Washington Post* on November 2, of secretly transporting terrorism suspects to unknown detention camps in Europe; the report ignited a furor in Europe.

A Vatican document that has been hotly discussed for many months is officially released; it bans candidates for the priesthood "who practice homosexuality, present deep-seated homosexual tendencies or support the so-called 'gay culture.'"

30 Surgeons in France reveal that three days earlier they performed the world's first partial face transplant, on a badly disfigured woman in Amiens.

Former Israeli prime minister Shimon Peres announces that he is leaving the Labor Party in order to support Kadima, the new party established by Prime Minister Ariel Sharon.

Ugandan-born John Sentamu is enthroned as the first black archbishop in the Church of England in a ceremony consecrating him as the 97th archbishop of York.

The *Los Angeles Times* reveals that the U.S. military has been, through a private contractor called the Lincoln Group, paying news outlets in Iraq to publish positive pieces submitted by the military in the guise of objective news or local opinion.

December

1 South Africa's Constitutional Court rules that same-sex marriage has the same legal status as opposite-sex marriage but stays its ruling for one year in order for Parliament to make laws that conform to the ruling.

A French court of appeals overturns the convictions of six people found guilty of participating in a pedophilia ring and orders a full investigation into all aspects of the miscarriage of justice.

The European Central Bank for the first time in five years raises its benchmark interest rate, by a quarter point to 2.25%.

In the Volga federal district of Russia, two subdivisions—the Perm *oblast* (province) and the Komi-Permyak autonomous *okrug* (district)—are replaced by the Perm *kray* (region).

2 Russia announces that it has made a major arms deal with Iran in which it will, among other things, sell antiaircraft missiles to the country.

© Nikola Solic/Reuters/Corbis

Legislation is passed in Belarus making it a crime punishable by prison to organize a protest or speak against the national interest; Pres. Alyaksandr Lukashenka signs the law on December 13.

In North Carolina the 1,000th prisoner to be executed in the U.S. since the reinstatement of the death penalty in 1976 is put to death.

3 At a meeting of the Group of 7 industrialized countries in London, Brazil and India offer to open their markets further, provided the U.S. and the EU decrease their farm subsidies.

Insurgents open fire on a convoy outside Adhaim, Iraq, killing 19 Iraqi soldiers.

4 Pres. Nursultan Nazarbayev overwhelmingly retains his seat in an election in Kazakhstan that fails to meet international standards.

Amr Shabana of Egypt wins the World Open men's title in squash for the second time, and Nicol David of Malaysia becomes the first Asian woman to win the women's championship.

Croatia defeats Slovakia to win its first-ever Davis Cup in men's team tennis in Bratislava, Slovakia. *(Pictured are, from left, Ivo Karlovic, Goran Ivanisevic, Nikola Pilic, Mario Ancic, and Ivan Ljubicic.)*

The annual Kennedy Center Honors are presented in Washington, D.C., to Tony Bennett, Suzanne Farrell, Julie Harris, Robert Redford, and Tina Turner.

5 Britain's Turner Prize is presented to installation artist Simon Starling; among the works Starling is known for is *Shedboatshed*, in which he turned a shed into a working boat, paddled it 11 km (7 mi) downstream, then rebuilt it into a shed.

Under the British dependency of Jersey's new system of cabinet government, replacing the former consensus system, Sen. Frank Walker is elected the island's first chief minister (head of government); Guernsey elected its first chief minister, Laurie Morgan, in 2004.

Elizabeth Vargas and Bob Woodruff are named as anchors of ABC's television news show *World News Tonight* to succeed Peter Jennings, who died in August.

6 Two suicide bombers infiltrate the main police academy in Baghdad and detonate their weapons, killing at least 36 police officers and injuring more than 70.

The Conservative Party in the U.K. chooses David Cameron as the party's leader.

U.S. Secretary of State Condoleezza Rice signs an agreement with Romanian Foreign Minister Mihai-Razvan Ungureanu that gives the U.S. permission to use military bases in Romania; it is the first such arrangement with a formerly communist country.

Eritrea decrees that all Westerners serving as UN peacekeepers in the country must depart within 10 days; the UN demands that Eritrea rescind the order.

7 British playwright Harold Pinter excoriates the U.S. during his videotaped acceptance address for the Nobel Prize for Literature in Stockholm.

At Miami International Airport, federal air marshals shoot and kill Rigoberto Alpizar, an agitated man who was running off a plane and behaving in a way that the marshals thought to be threatening.

The U.S. Supreme Court rules that the government may attach a person's Social Security benefits in order to collect unpaid student loans.

During the last day of parliamentary voting in Egypt, for runoffs resulting from the third round, Egyptian police trying to keep people from the polls leave at least six people dead; in the end, 88 seats go to members of the Muslim Brotherhood.

The signatories to the 1949 Geneva Conventions accept the addition of a new symbol, a diamond-shaped red crystal, representing the Israeli relief agency Magen David Adom, which thus joins the Red Cross and Red Crescent global relief network.

8 U.S. and Iraqi military forces find more than 600 prisoners being held in appallingly overcrowded conditions in an Iraqi government detention centre; 13 inmates are hospitalized.

A suicide bomber forces himself onto a crowded bus at Baghdad's main bus terminal and then detonates his weapon; at least 30 people are killed.

On a busy street outside a cultural centre in Netrokona, Bangladesh, a suicide bomber kills 7 people and injures some 50.

A Southwest Airlines Boeing 737 overshoots a runway on a snowy night at Chicago's Midway Airport, sliding off the runway and onto a busy street; a small boy in a car on that street is killed.

9 At the end of two weeks of UN talks on global warming in Montreal, the U.S. and China decline to accept mandatory limits on greenhouse gas emissions.

The Right Livelihood Awards are presented in Stockholm to Mexican artist Francisco Toledo, to Maude Barlow

and Tony Clarke of Canada for their work on trade justice and the right to water, to Irene Fernandez of Malaysia for her work to end abuse of women and poor and migrant workers, and to the organization First People of the Kalahari and its founder, Roy Sesana of Botswana.

10 Ethiopia agrees to pull its troops back from its border with Eritrea in compliance with a UN Security Council resolution and thereby defuses a crisis.

Shanghai opens the first five berths of its new Yangshan deepwater port; it is nearly twice as deep as its former ports.

The 2005 Heisman Trophy for college football is awarded to University of Southern California running back Reggie Bush.

11 Presidential election returns in Chile result in the need for a runoff between Michelle Bachelet, a Socialist, and conservative billionaire Sebastián Piñera.

A mob of largely drunken young white men goes on a rampage on a beach outside Sydney, attacking people they believe to be of Arab descent; the following day mobs of young men of Arab descent riot in several Sydney suburbs.

The movie studio DreamWorks SKG agrees to be acquired by Paramount Pictures, spurning what had seemed to be a done deal with NBC-Universal.

12 Standard & Poor's Ratings Services lowers its rating of the debt of General Motors two points into "junk" status; it is the lowest

rating in 52 years for the car manufacturer.

Gebran Tueni, editor of a prominent anti-Syria magazine in Lebanon and a member of the country's legislature, is killed by a car bomb, together with his driver and a bystander.

13 Stanley ("Tookie") Williams, a founder of the Crips street gang in Los Angeles, is executed in San Francisco.

Dissident members of the ruling Fatah party invade and disrupt election offices in the Gaza Strip and the West Bank, upset with the slate of candidates that they believe the party will put forward.

The U.S. National Institutes of Health announces the Cancer Genome Atlas, a new project to discover genetic abnormalities associated with all types of cancer.

Lithuania's Supreme Court exonerates former president Rolandas Paksas of charges that he disclosed state secrets to an adviser believed to have ties to organized crime in Russia.

The Committee to Protect Journalists releases its 2005 report, saying that the U.S. is tied with Myanmar (Burma) for sixth place in the list of countries holding the most journalists in prison; China, for the seventh year in a row, tops the list.

14 The first East Asia summit is held in Kuala Lumpur, Malaysia, as part of the 11th ASEAN summit; leaders from 16 countries attend.

At World Trade Organization talks in Hong Kong, an agreement to limit government subsidies to the fishing industry is reached; three-quarters of the fishing stock in the world has been severely depleted by overfishing.

Ukraine announces that the cause of the unusually large number of bird deaths this month has been confirmed as the H5N1 avian flu.

15 The long-awaited parliamentary elections, the first to be held under the country's new constitution, take place in Iraq.

After long resisting the idea, U.S. Pres. George W. Bush endorses legislation that would ban inhumane and degrading treatment of prisoners held by the U.S.

16 The *New York Times* reports that the U.S. National Security Agency has, on the sole authority of Pres. George W. Bush and without the judicial oversight ordinarily required for domestic spying, over the past three years eavesdropped on international telephone calls and e-mails placed from or to locations within the U.S.

The trial of novelist Orhan Pamuk, scheduled to begin in Turkey, for having discussed the 1915 Armenian genocide in a magazine interview, is postponed to February 2006; he is charged with having broken a law forbidding criticism of "Turkishness" and state institutions.

Peace talks between the government of Colombia and the National Liberation Army (ELN) rebel group begin in Cuba.

The inaugural Ordway Prizes, which the Penny McCall Foundation is to give every two years to a contemporary artist and a contemporary arts writer or curator,

are awarded to the Colombian artist Doris Salcedo and the curator Ralph Rugoff.

17 U.S. Pres. George W. Bush in a radio address acknowledges that he instructed the National Security Agency to conduct electronic eavesdropping within the U.S. without warrants and says that he intends to continue the program.

The UN begins repatriating refugees who fled warfare in southern Sudan to Kenya; the first 147 of 71,000 Sudanese in one camp are taken back to The Sudan, equipped with household goods and food from the UN.

18 Evo Morales, an Aymara Indian and former coca farmer, is elected president of Bolivia.

A referendum on a draft constitution is held in the Democratic Republic of the Congo.

Israeli Prime Minister Ariel Sharon suffers a transient ischemic attack, a mild stroke.

19 Afghanistan's first democratically elected legislature in 30 years convenes in Kabul.

The International Court of Justice holds Uganda responsible for attacks on civilians in the Democratic Republic of the Congo in the late 1990s and orders reparations; it also rules that the DRC must compensate Uganda for the destruction of its embassy in Kinshasa.

In Belfast, N.Ire., same-sex couples exchange vows in the first civil partnership ceremonies to be legal in the U.K.; the law goes into effect on the following day in

Scotland and on December 21 in England and Wales.

After months of pressure Antonio Fazio steps down as head of the Bank of Italy; he is accused of having improperly aided Italian companies in a battle for acquisition of the Banca Antoveneta.

Nature magazine publishes online a report by scientists in Germany who say they have reconstructed a sequence of the genome of the woolly mammoth, which has been extinct for more than 11,000 years; the genome shows that the closest living relative of the mammoth is the Asian elephant.

The International Tennis Federation names Kim Clijsters of Belgium and Roger Federer of Switzerland its 2005 world champions.

20 The Transport Workers Union in New York City goes on strike, stopping subways and buses and leaving thousands of people to find alternative ways to get to work and school; 60 hours later, on December 22, service resumes as a tentative agreement on a new contract is reached.

The UN creates a new permanent 31-member Peace-building Commission; it will be charged with overseeing and coordinating efforts to help stabilize and rebuild communities that are emerging from warfare.

Joseph P. Nacchio, the former CEO of Qwest Communications International, is indicted by the U.S. government on 42 counts of insider trading.

21 Representatives of the U.K., France, Germany, and Iran meet in Berlin and agree to resume

talks about Iran's nuclear program in January 2006; the talks had been suspended for four months.

Yunus Qanooni is chosen as the chairman of the lower house of Afghanistan's new legislature; he is Pres. Hamid Karzai's main political rival.

Canada's Supreme Court rules that group sex in private clubs is legally permissible.

22 In response to U.S. Pres. George W. Bush's request for the USA PATRIOT Act, which greatly expands the powers of the government to conduct surveillance and collect information, to be made permanent, Congress extends it for five weeks.

As a Chinese benzene spill in the Songhua River reaches the Russian city of Khabarovsk, a new chemical spill, of cadmium from a smelter in Shaoguan on the Bei River, threatens the water supplies of Guangzhou.

Barrick Gold reaches an agreement to acquire Placer Dome; the merger of the two Canadian companies will create the largest gold-producing entity in the world.

23 An investigative panel at Seoul National University finds that the research reported in the May 2005 paper in which Hwang Woo Suk said he had created patient-specific stem cell lines from 11 people was largely fabricated; Hwang resigns from the university in disgrace.

The Japanese government releases figures showing that in 2005 for the first time the number of deaths exceeded the number of births (by 10,000), for an unexpected

net decline in the population for the year.

24 Opposition leader Ayman Nour is sentenced to five years at hard labour in what is widely viewed as political persecution in Egypt.

•

UN peacekeeping forces and Congolese military forces engage in a battle with Ugandan militia members in the Ituri area of the Democratic Republic of the Congo.

25 In St. Peter's Square in Vatican City, Pope Benedict XVI delivers his first Christmas greetings as Roman Catholic pontiff; speaking in 32 languages he exhorts people not to neglect their faith.

•

Libya's Supreme Court overturns the convictions of five Bulgarian nurses and a Palestinian doctor who had been found guilty of having infected hundreds of children with HIV and had been sentenced to death; the court orders that a new trial be held.

26 Paper lanterns are released into the sky above the Andaman Sea in Khao Lok, Thai., to memorialize the 5,395 people that the South Asian tsunami killed in Thailand one year ago. *(Photo above.)*

•

In Kabul, Iranian Foreign Minister Manouchehr Mottaki and Afghan Foreign Minister Abdullah Abdullah sign an agreement on consular relations and on aid for Afghan refugees and migrant workers in Iran.

27 In Banda Aceh, Indon., leaders of the Free Aceh Movement declare that the movement's armed wing has disbanded.

•

A senior adviser to Russian Pres. Vladimir Putin, Andrey N. Illarionov, who has become increasingly critical of the government, resigns, saying the country has become politically unfree and has adopted an economic model he cannot support.

•

Wolfgang Melchior of Austria and four others complete

an unsupported ski trip across an uncharted region of Antarctica to the South Pole in a record 33 days.

28 Prime Minister Charles Konan Banny of Côte d'Ivoire announces the formation of a unity government that includes members from the governing party, the opposition party, and the rebels.

•

After weeks of exchanges of rocket fire, Israel declares a buffer zone in the northern part of the Gaza Strip, where Palestinians are not permitted to go, to prevent attacks on Israel from the area; it enforces the ban with artillery fire.

•

Kabuki actor Kotaro Hayashi ceremonially assumes the stage name Tojuro Sakata; he is the first actor since 1774 to be deemed worthy of carrying on the name of the 17th-century master.

29 The last of the 24,000 Indonesian troops in Aceh province pull out.

•

The World Bank and other Western donors reportedly have decided to withhold aid from the government of Ethiopia because of its crackdown on the opposition.

•

Donald Kennedy, editor of *Science*, says that the magazine will retract the May 2005 paper in which South Korean researcher Hwang Woo Suk reported his now thoroughly discredited claim to have cloned patient-specific human stem cell lines.

•

Wild Oats XI, the winner of the 2005 Rolex Sydney–Hobart Yacht Race in Australia, sets a new record of 1 day 18 hr 40 min 10 sec.

30 The CEO of Russia's energy company Gazprom says that if Ukraine does not accept a fourfold raise in the price of gas to make it consistent with the price paid by Western European countries, the supply to Ukraine will be cut off on Jan. 1, 2006.

•

A bomb goes off at a market in the Indonesian town of Palu in Sulawesi Tengah province, killing 6 people and injuring 45.

31 Russian Pres. Vladimir Putin states that if Ukraine will agree to start paying higher prices for Russian natural gas in April 2006, Ukraine can buy it at a lower price through March, otherwise, the flow will be cut off on Jan. 1, 2006; no accommodation in the crisis is reached before year's end.

•

The U.S. government and the Iraq Coalition Casualty Count release figures saying that 846 U.S. military service members died in Iraq in 2005, close to the 2004 total of 848; the total since the beginning of the war is 2,180.

Disasters

Listed here are major disasters that occurred in 2005. The list includes **NATURAL** and nonmilitary **MECHANICAL** disasters that claimed more than 15 lives and/or resulted in significant damage to **PROPERTY**.

Aviation

January 13, Colombia. A helicopter provided by the U.S. as part of its sponsorship of a drug-eradication system crashes during a nighttime mission; 20 Colombian soldiers are killed.

January 27, Central Vietnam. A Russian-made military helicopter crashes shortly after takeoff from Me Island; all 16 aboard perish.

February 3, Afghanistan. A Kam Air Boeing 737 flying from Herat in a snowstorm crashes shortly after being denied permission to land at Kabul; all 104 aboard are lost.

March 16, Russia. A Russian Antonov-24 airplane carrying oil workers and Lukoil subcontractors crashes near the Arctic port of Varandey; at least 28 people are killed.

April 6, Afghanistan. A U.S. military helicopter crashes in a dust storm near Ghazni, killing 18 people.

May 7, Queensland, Australia. A twin-engine propeller airplane traveling from Bamaga to Lockhart River crashes into a hillside; all 15 aboard are killed in the worst civil aviation disaster in the country since 1968.

July 16, Near Malabo, Equatorial Guinea. An overloaded Antonov-24 passenger plane bound for the mainland town of Bata crashes in a forest shortly after takeoff, killing all of the estimated 55–60 people aboard.

August 6, Off Sicily. A Tunisian ATR-72 airliner carrying tourists from Bari, Italy, to a Tunisian resort makes an emergency landing in the sea, and 16 people die; it is later learned that the plane's fuel gauge failed to indicate that the craft was out of fuel.

August 14, Near Grammatikos, Greece. A Helios Airways Boeing 737 passenger plane flying from Larnaca, Cyprus, to Prague via Athens crashes, killing all 121 aboard.

August 16, Near Machiques, Venez. A chartered Colombian MD-82 jetliner carrying French tourists from Panama to Martinique crashes in the mountains after its engines fail; all 160 aboard perish.

August 16, Near Herat, Afg. A Spanish military helicopter that is part of the NATO-led International Security Assistance Force in Afghanistan crashes, killing all 17 aboard.

August 23, Near Pucallpa, Peru. A TANS Perú Boeing 737 crashes while attempting an emergency landing during a storm; at least 40 of the 98 on board are killed.

September 5, Medan, Sumatra, Indon. A Boeing 737 belonging to the low-fare Indonesian carrier Mandala Airlines crashes into an urban neighbourhood shortly after takeoff; 101 people on board, including the governor of Sumatera Utara province, are killed, as are 44 people on the ground.

October 22, Lissa, Nigeria. Bellview Airlines Flight 210, flying from Lagos to Abuja in Nigeria, crashes after passing through an electrical storm; all 117 aboard the Boeing 737 perish.

December 6, Tehran. A military transport C-130 carrying mostly journalists crashes into an apartment building while attempting an emergency landing shortly after takeoff; all 94 passengers and crew are killed, and as many as 34 people on the ground also perish.

December 10, Port Harcourt, Nigeria. A Nigerian DC-9 with 109 aboard, many of them schoolchildren heading home from Abuja for the holidays, crashes on landing; 108 of those on board die.

Getty Images

Little remains of the Mandala Airlines 737-200 that went down in flames and crashed into a residential neighbourhood on Sumatra, Indonesia, on September 5. A total of 145 people aboard the plane and on the ground were killed.

December 19, Off Miami Beach, Fla. A 1940s-era seaplane carrying holiday shoppers home to Bimini in The Bahamas crashes shortly after takeoff; 17 adults and 3 children die.

Fires and Explosions

January 7, Siddhirganj, Bangladesh. A fire breaks out in a garment factory, killing at least 22 people who were trapped inside because the exits were locked.

January 12, Northern Shanxi province, China. An explosion in a fireworks factory kills at least 25 workers, most of them young women.

February 14, Tehran. A fire caused by a heater in a mosque kills 59 people, some of them dying as people stampede to escape.

February 23, Juba, The Sudan. High temperatures cause an explosion at an ammunition dump, and at least 24 people die.

March 2, Kecheng, Shanxi province, China. A cache of explosives being stored at the home of a coal-mine manager detonates, killing at least 20 children in an adjacent elementary school as well as the mine manager.

March 10, Karachi. A fireball engulfs the PNS *Moawin*, a naval logistics ship, during routine maintenance in port; at least 35 of those aboard are killed, and 24 are critically injured.

March 17, Jiangxi province, China. A bus traveling near the city of Shangrao is destroyed when a nearby truck carrying explosives and fireworks blows up violently; at least 30 people are killed.

March 23, Texas City, Texas. Part of a BP refinery plant explodes, killing 15 workers.

March 25, Tema, Ghana. A fire engulfs the Greek-registered MV *Polaris*, in port for repairs; 18 people lose their lives in the blaze.

April 15, Paris. A fire started by a candle flame destroys the Paris-Opéra hotel, leaving 24 people dead, most of them African immigrants.

April 20, Zambia. An explosion at a Chinese-owned explosives factory on the grounds of a copper mine kills at least 50 people.

May 2, Afghanistan. A cache of explosives stored at the home of a commander of a recently disarmed and demobilized regiment in the village of Kohna Deh detonates, killing at least 34 people.

May 3, Lahore, Pak. A gas explosion causes an apartment and factory building and several houses to collapse, killing at least 28 people.

June 10, Shantou, Guangdong province, China. A fire breaks out at the Huanan Hotel, engulfing the top three floors of the four-story building and killing at least 31 people.

July 11, Ukhta, Komi republic, Russia. A fire in a shop kills at least 24 people; the fire reportedly was deliberately set, possibly because of a business dispute.

July 12, San José, Costa Rica. A large fire on the upper floors of the Calderón Guardia hospital kills at least 18 people.

August 26, Paris. An overnight fire in an old apartment building housing African immigrants kills at least 17 people.

September 5, Bani Suwayf, Egypt. A candle being used as a prop in a production at a theatre festival falls over, starting a fire that kills at least 32 people, among them at least 13 actors.

September 5, Paris. Three girls admit to having started a fire the day before in the mailbox of a friend with whom they had fallen out; the resulting blaze killed 16 people in a low-income apartment building.

September 15, Khusropur, Bihar state, India. An explosion in a fireworks factory kills 32 people, 10 of them children.

September 23, Gaza Strip. At a celebratory Hamas military parade in the Jabaliya refugee camp during which weapons are on display, a pickup truck loaded with rockets explodes; at least 15 people are killed.

December 15, Liaoyuan, Jilin province, China. A fire in the town's largest hospital leaves at least 39 people dead.

Marine

January 17, Democratic Republic of the Congo. An overcrowded ferry traveling on the Kasai River between Ilebo and Tshikapa capsizes; at least 150 people are believed lost.

January 25, Thailand. A speedboat capsizes while carrying tourists to the resort island of Koh Samui after a full-Moon beach party; at least 15 people are killed, and possibly the same number are missing.

February 19, Near Dhaka, Bangladesh. An overcrowded ferry, the MV *Maharaj*, sinks on the Buriganga River in a storm; at least 120 people drown.

May 15, Near Golapchipa, Bangladesh. An overloaded ferry sinks; close to 60 people are found dead, and a further 20 are missing.

May 17, Manikganj district, Bangladesh. A double-decker ferry sinks in a storm on the Padma River; at least 58 people die, with an unknown number missing.

July 7, Off Papua province, Indon. As many as 200 are feared to have drowned, trapped in the ferry KMP *Digul* when it capsized in rough seas while traveling from Merauke to Tanahmerah.

July 14, Western Nepal. An overcrowded boat capsizes; at least 13 people drown, and dozens are missing.

July 26, Ondo state, Nigeria. A wooden boat traveling from Igbokoda to Awoye strikes a sharp object and breaks up; some 200 people lose their lives.

August 12, Off Colombia. An overloaded boat carrying Ecuadorans attempting to migrate to the U.S. sinks and 104 drown.

August 16, Northern Nigeria. A wooden ferry in the Lamurde River capsizes, and all 90 aboard are drowned.

August 16, Guntur district, Andhra Pradesh state, India. A boat carrying some 25 people, mainly farmworkers, on the Buckingham canal overturns; at least 19 are drowned.

August 21, Florida Straits. Rescued Cuban survivors say a speedboat on which they were traveling capsized several days earlier; 31 others who were on the boat are missing.

September 3, Gulf of Aden. Smugglers carrying would-be illegal African migrants from Ethiopia and Somalia to Yemen force their passengers to jump into the Gulf of Aden; at least 75 of them drown, and a further 100 are missing.

October 2, Adirondack Mountains, New York. The *Ethan Allen*, a tour boat carrying elderly sightseers on Lake George, capsizes and sinks; 20 passengers drown.

November 4, Off Kharo Chao, Pak. An overloaded ferry carrying people to a memorial for three people who died in a boat accident sinks in the Arabian Sea; at least 60 people lose their lives.

November 7, Bangladesh. A cargo boat carrying passengers from 'Id al-Fitr celebrations on Swandip Island home to Chittagong capsizes; at least 25 are missing.

Mining and Construction

February 9, Siberia, Russia. In the Kemerovo region, a methane gas explosion in a coal mine kills at least 21 miners.

February 14, Fuxin, Liaoning province, China. In an unusually deadly mining accident, an explosion in the Sunjiawan coal mine kills 214 miners.

March 19, Shuozhou, Shanxi province, China. An explosion at the Xishui coal mine leaves at least 65 miners dead.

April 21, Turkey. A gas explosion in a coal mine causes a cave-in and a fire, killing 17 workers.

May 12, Panzhihua, Sichuan province, China. A gas explosion kills 21 workers in a coal mine; 10 miners survive.

July 2, Ningwu county, Shanxi province, China. A gas explosion at a coal mine said to be illegal leaves 36 dead.

July 11, Fukang, Xinjiang Uygur Autonomous Region, China. An explosion in the Shenlong coal mine kills at least 83 miners.

July 19, Tongchuan, Shanxi province, China. After a gas explosion in the Jinsuo coal mine, the bodies of 26 miners are found.

August 7, Xingning, Guangdong province, China. The Daxing coal mine floods, trapping 123 miners.

October 26, Monkayo, Phil. An explosion causes a cave-in in a gold mine, killing at least 18 miners; some 50 others are still missing.

October 27, Qinglong county, Guizhou province, China. The Zhongxing Colliery suffers an explosion in which eight miners are killed outright and seven more succumb later.

November 27, Qitaihe, Heilongjiang province, China. An explosion in the Dongfeng mine kills at least 161 miners; 70 are rescued.

Natural

January 8–9, Northern Europe. Storms bring very high winds and flooding, leaving close to two million people without electricity and killing at least 11 people, 7 in Sweden and 4 in Denmark.

January 10, La Conchita, Calif. After two weeks of unusually relentless and heavy rain and snow that leave some 20 people dead in southern California, a hillside gives way, burying four blocks and killing at least 10 people.

January 22, Medina, Saudi Arabia. An unusually bad storm brings heavy rain and flash floods on the last day of the Hajj; some 29 people lose their lives.

Late January, Guyana. The heaviest flooding in 100 years leaves Georgetown and the surrounding area in disastrous shape; thousands of people are forced to evacuate, and 34 lives are lost, many from disease.

Early February, Venezuela and Colombia. Flooding caused by days of torrential rains leaves at least 86 people dead, 53 in Venezuela and 33 in Colombia.

February 10, Balochistan province, Pak. Heavy rainfall in the drought-stricken province causes the Shadi Khor Dam to give way; at least 60 people are reported dead, with more than 500 missing.

February 14, North-West Frontier Province, Pak. Authorities report 65 deaths over the previous week attributed to heavy rain and snow.

February 18, Ituri district, Democratic Republic of the Congo. The World Health Organization reports that pneumonic plague has killed at least 61 diamond miners since December 2004.

February 20, Indian-administered Kashmir. Avalanches destroy several Himalayan villages, leaving at least 278 people dead; hundreds more have perished in the region owing to frigid temperatures.

February 21, Western Java, Indon. Heavy rainfall causes a hilltop municipal dump to collapse, triggering a landslide that buries much of the village of Cimahi and leaves some 120 people either dead or missing.

February 22, Kerman province, Iran. Some 500 people are killed when a magnitude-6.4 earthquake centred on the town of Zarand takes place early in the morning.

February 25, Afghanistan. Officials report that the death toll from an unusually bitter winter is a minimum of 580.

March 20, Northern Bangladesh. A tornado in Gaibandha district leaves at least 56 people dead and thousands homeless; new storms raise the death toll in the region to above 80.

March 28, Nias island, Indonesia. An earthquake centred deep under the seabed with a magnitude of 8.7 kills at least 905 people.

April 23, Somali region, Eth. The Shebeli River overflows its banks, inundating the area and leaving at least 134 people dead.

April 28, Jiddah, Saudi Arabia. Storms and flash flooding kill some 30 people.

May 18, Chile. A blizzard catches army troops on a training march in the Andes Mountains, leaving at least 26 of them dead and a further 19 missing.

June, South Asia. A heat wave throughout the region is responsible for hundreds of deaths.

June 3, Southern China. After several days of torrential rain, the death toll reaches 204, with 79 people still missing.

June 10, Shalan, Heilongjiang province, China. Flash flooding caused when some 200 mm (8 in) of rain fall in 40 minutes leads to the drowning of at least 92 people.

June 13, Northern Andes, Chile. An earthquake of magnitude 7.9 occurs in a sparsely populated area, killing at least 11 people.

June 16, Senahú, Guat. At least 23 people are killed when a mud slide buries homes in several neighbourhoods.

June 21, Afghanistan. A government official reports that flooding in the north caused by snowmelt has killed 51 people.

June 24, China. Chinese officials report that the death toll from flooding in the past two weeks has reached 536.

June 30, Northern Italy. Italian news sources report that the death toll from a heat wave has reached 21.

July, Phoenix. A record heat wave leaves at least 30 people dead, most of them homeless.

July 1, Gujarat, India. Officials report that monsoon floods have caused the death of at least 94 people.

July 7, Haiti and Cuba. Hurricane Dennis makes landfall in Haiti, causing great destruction and leaving at least 60 people dead; the following day the hurricane swipes the south coast of Cuba, killing 16 people.

July 10, Southern China. Officials report that unusually strong and early rains have caused flooding that has left at least 29 people dead; some 26,000 homes are destroyed by floods.

July 26, Mumbai (Bombay). Rain totaling 94.2 cm (37.1 in) within 24 hours paralyzes the city and smashes the record for a one-day rainfall in India; continuing into the following day, the rains leave more than 1,000 dead in Maharashtra state, at least 736 of them in the city.

August 23, Romania. Flooding caused by heavy rains leaves 18 people dead; floods also occur in Switzerland, Austria, and Bulgaria, and by the time flooding has begun to subside, the death toll in the region has reached 26.

August 29, Gulf Coast, U.S. Hurricane Katrina at Category 4 strength roars ashore, devastating New Orleans and Slidell in Louisiana, as well as Gulfport and Biloxi in Mississippi, and leading the following day to the breach of New Orleans's levees and catastrophic flooding of 80% of the city; the death toll in Louisiana is at least 1,100 and in Mississippi some 230.

September 1, Near Padang, Sumatera Barat province, Indon. Rains trigger a landslide that kills at least 10 people and leaves an estimated 34 more buried in the rubble.

September 1, Anhui province, China. Typhoon Talim causes landslides and flooding and leaves 53 people dead.

September 6, Southern Japan. Typhoon Nabi makes landfall, forcing the evacuation of some 250,000 people and killing at least 18.

September 11, Zhejiang province, China. Typhoon Khanun kills at least 14 people and destroys well over 7,000 houses; 8 people are reported missing.

Mid-September, Bay of Bengal. Days of ferocious storms kill dozens of people, and more than 1,000 are reported missing; at least 56 people are dead in India's Andra Pradesh state, with hundreds also reported missing.

September 20, Cambodia. A government official reports that flooding on the Mekong River and storms elsewhere have left 21 people dead and ruined thousands of hectares of rice.

September 24, Gulf Coast, U.S. Hurricane Rita goes ashore near the Texas-Louisiana border, devastating the coastal areas of southwestern Louisiana and southeastern Texas but causing few deaths; the previous day the hurricane had caused recently repaired levees in New Orleans to crumble, reflooding much of the city.

September 28, East Asia. Typhoon Damrey is downgraded to a tropical depression after a week in which it killed 36 people in Vietnam, 16 in the Philippines, 16 in southern China, and at least 3 in Thailand.

October 2, Fuzhou, Fujian province, China. Floodwaters from Typhoon Longwang sweep away a military school, killing at least 80 paramilitary officers.

October 4, North and Central America. Hurricane Stan makes landfall on Mexico's Gulf Coast; resultant floods and landslides kill at least 71 people in El Salvador and 654 in Guatemala—where close to 600 more are counted as missing—while more than 60 are killed in Nicaragua, Honduras, Mexico, and Costa Rica.

October 8, Kashmir. On the border between Pakistan's North-West Frontier Province and the Pakistani-administered part of Kashmir, a magnitude-7.6 earthquake with a shallow focus devastates an enormous region, leveling cities and mountain hamlets; the death toll in Pakistan, mostly in Kashmir, is more than 87,000 people; in the India-administered part of Kashmir, more than 1,000 people also die.

October 21, Mexico. After killing 13 people in Haiti and Jamaica, Hurricane Wilma makes landfall on the Yucatán coast, stalling there for a full day and devastating the resort areas of Cancún, Cozumel, and Playa del Carmen; 6 people are killed in Mexico.

October 23, Hispaniola. Tropical Storm Alpha, which formed in the Caribbean the previous day, causes heavy rains in Haiti and the Dominican Republic, killing at least 26; Alpha is the 22nd named storm in the Atlantic, which breaks a record for the most named storms in a season, set in 1933, and makes this the most active Atlantic hurricane season ever recorded.

October 24, Florida. Hurricane Wilma enters near Marco Island on the Gulf Coast and exits six hours later near West Palm Beach on the Atlantic Ocean, leaving some 22 people dead.

October 27, Southern India. After five days of heavy rain, more than 100 people are reported dead, mostly in Tamil Nadu and Karnataka states.

November 6, Southern Indiana. A tornado that also passes through northern Kentucky leaves 24 people dead, most of them in a trailer park outside Evansville, Ind.

November 26, Jiangxi province, China. A magnitude-5.7 earthquake near the tourist destination town of Jiujiang kills at least 14 people and destroys thousands of houses.

December 28, Northern Yemen. A nighttime rock slide buries the village of Dhafir in enormous boulders, leaving at least 43 people dead and some 100 trapped in the rubble.

December 28, Northwestern Pakistan. An avalanche overwhelms gemstone miners, killing 24 of them.

Railroad

January 6, Graniteville, N.C. A freight train carrying liquid chlorine crashes into a train parked outside a textile factory; at least 8 people are killed and hundreds made sick by the poison chlorine gas, and some 5,400 residents are evacuated.

January 7, Near Bologna, Italy. A passenger train from Verona collides head-on with a freight train in heavy fog; at least 13 people are killed, including the engineers.

January 17, Bangkok. An empty subway train collides with a crowded one during the morning rush, injuring 212 passengers.

January 26, Glendale, Calif. A sport utility vehicle is left on train tracks, and a commuter train hits it and then derails and hits another commuter train, which also derails; 11 people are killed and some 200 injured.

April 21, Samlaya, Gujarat state, India. A passenger train traveling from Varanasi to Ahmedabad crashes into a stationary freight train and derails; at least 24 people are killed.

April 25, Amagasaki, Japan. An elevated commuter train that is running 90 seconds behind schedule derails while going around a curve and crashes into an adjacent apartment building; at least 107 passengers are killed.

July 13, Near Ghotki, Pak. In the predawn hours at the Sarhad train station, a Karachi Express train slams into a Quetta Express train sitting idle in the station while engine repairs are being made, and then a Tezgam Express train hits the derailed cars; at least 123 people are killed, including the engineer of the Karachi Express.

October 3, Near Gwalior, Madhya Pradesh, India. The Bendelkhand Express fails to stop and crashes into a signal cabin at the Datia station at a high speed; at least 16 people perish.

October 29, Veligonda, Andhra Pradesh, India. A train hits a section of track that had been washed away by flooding and derails, falling into a river; at least 114 passengers lose their lives.

November 28, Maniema province, Democratic Republic of the Congo. Some 60 people traveling on the tops of train cars are killed when the train, traveling from Lubumbashi to Kindu, goes over a bridge and the bridge's support beams knock them off the cars and into the river below.

Traffic

January 3, Qinghai province, China. A truck carrying Tibetan passengers from a pilgrimage to Lhasa in the autonomous region of Tibet overturns, killing at least 54 of the pilgrims.

January 3, Paulomajra, Punjab state, India. A private minibus carrying girls to work at a factory in Ludhiana collides head-on with another private minibus traveling in the opposite direction; 14 girls and a bus driver are killed.

January 4, Near Bujumbura, Burundi. An overloaded bus crashes on a hillside road, killing at least 25 people.

January 10, Bijapur district, Karnataka state, India. A bus driver loses control of his vehicle, and it falls into a canal; 57 passengers are killed.

January 11, Southwestern Nigeria. A speeding passenger bus veers into oncoming traffic and collides head-on with another bus, and a third bus plows into the wreckage; at least 21 people are killed.

January 15, Near Sabana de Torres, Colom. A passenger bus attempting to pass another vehicle on a curve late at night crashes into a truck stopped at the side of the road because of a mechanical failure; at least 27 people die.

January 19, Lagos, Nigeria. Two buses collide and are then hit by a fuel tanker truck; at least 30 commuters are burned to death.

February 3, Maharashtra state, India. A trailer carrying wedding guests that is being pulled across an unmarked railroad crossing by a tractor is hit by a train; 55 of the passengers on the trailer are killed.

February 8, Lubango, Angola. The brakes on a truck fail, and it plows into a crowd of people celebrating Carnival; at least 20 people are killed.

March 18, Punjab state, India. Floodwaters wash a tractor trailer from the road, killing 41 pilgrims in the trailer who were returning from a visit to a shrine.

March 29, Eastern China. A tire on a tanker truck carrying liquid chlorine blows out, causing the tanker to collide with a truck and overturn; chlorine fumes kill at least 27 people.

April 10, Kawambwa, Zambia. A truck carrying students home from a high school at the end of term overturns on a curve, leaving at least 44 students dead.

April 21, Kon Tum province, Vietnam. A bus carrying veterans of the Vietnam War, traveling from Hanoi to Ho Chi Minh City along the highway built on the old Ho Chi Minh Trail to celebrate the 30th anniversary of the end of the war, goes off a mountain road and falls to the valley below; 30 veterans and the bus driver are killed.

Rescuers work to free passengers trapped in railroad coaches that plunged into a rain-swollen river east of Hyderabad, India, on October 29.

AP/Wide World Photos

April 23, Khurd, Madhya Pradesh state, India. A truck carrying Hindu pilgrims to a religious meeting goes off the road and falls into a ditch, killing 23 of the passengers and injuring 38; police believe the driver fell asleep.

April 27, Near Polgahawela, Sri Lanka. The driver of a bus ignores closed gates at a railroad crossing, and the bus is hit by a passenger train; at least 35 of the bus's passengers are killed.

May 7, Near Pampa, Peru. A bus goes off the road and falls some 300 m (1,000 ft) into a ravine; at least 40 passengers are killed.

May 11, Northern Philippines. The brakes on a passenger bus traveling from the resort town of Baguio to Dagupan City fail on a mountain road, and the bus crashes into a retaining wall, killing at least 27 people.

May 17, Near Rudraprayag, Uttaranchal state, India. A bus carrying the bridegroom's party to a wedding in Chamoli falls into a gorge; at least 36 of the passengers are killed.

May 21, Near Jauja, Peru. A bus goes through a guardrail and falls from a bridge; at least 35 people lose their lives.

June 26, El Salvador. Floodwaters wash away a bus, killing 21 people aboard.

July 9, Uttaranchal state, India. A bus traveling from Srinagar leaves the road and falls into a river gorge near Rishikesh; at least 24 passengers die.

July 11, Eritrea. An overcrowded bus traveling between Adi Quala and Maimene goes off the road and falls down a mountainside, killing at least 56 people in the worst traffic accident in Eritrea's history.

July 21, Near Kallar Kehar, Pak. A bus falls into a gorge, killing at least 20 passengers; investigators suspect brake failure.

July 24, Near Kano, Nigeria. A bus falls off a bridge into a river, and 56 passengers perish; it is thought that the driver fell asleep.

August 20, Zabul province, Afg. Two passenger buses collide on a highway between Kandahar and Kabul; at least 20 passengers are killed.

September 1, Limpopo province, S.Af. When a driver leaves an overloaded minibus taxi to relieve himself, the vehicle rolls off the highway and over a cliff; 19 of the 26 passengers are killed.

September 23, Near Dallas. A bus evacuating residents of a Houston-area assisted-living centre and nursing home from the threat of Hurricane Rita explodes when sparks ignite oxygen canisters carried by the passengers; 24 die in the conflagration.

September 29, Near Tattapani, Jammu and Kashmir, India. A bus traveling from Srinagar to Sasgaldan goes out of control and falls down a mountain road; at least 40 passengers perish.

October 1, Western Tajikistan. A bus that is running on liquefied gas collides with another bus and explodes, killing all 21 passengers.

October 15, Northern Bangladesh. A bus carrying more than 50 passengers crashes into the Gangnai River; no one is rescued.

November 16, Near Los Mochis, Sinaloa state, Mex. The brakes on a truck carrying ammonia gas fail, and the truck hits a passenger bus, which falls upside-down into a ravine; 38 people are killed, some because of the poison gas.

November 25, Tamil Nadu state, India. A bus traveling from Tiruchchirappalli to Rameswaram attempts to cross a bridge against police orders and is swept from the bridge by flash floods, killing at least 27 passengers; hours later, near Pattukkottai, another bus loses control on a bridge and falls into a rain-swollen river, killing at least 50.

November 30, Western Nepal. A passenger bus carrying Hindu pilgrims to Swargadwari Temple plunges into a ravine; as many as 35 are reported killed.

Miscellaneous

January 25, Near Wai, Maharashtra state, India. As hundreds of thousands of pilgrims, mostly women, approach the hilltop Mandhar Devi temple, some begin slipping on coconut oil from devotional offerings, and this leads to a panic; angry relatives of victims begin setting fires, worsening the stampede, and a total of 257 pilgrims are killed.

February 6, Todolella, Spain. Butane gas leaking from a heating cylinder kills 18 people who were attending a weekend party at a 15th-century guesthouse.

March 9, Mabini, Phil. At least 27 schoolchildren die after eating cassava roots served at an elementary school; it is initially believed that the roots were undercooked and therefore poisonous, but later testing suggests that the children were poisoned by pesticides on the roots.

March 20, The Sudan. The government reports that 21 people have died after drinking illegally produced alcohol.

April 7, Madhya Pradesh state, India. A dam on the Narmada River releases a barrage of water that inundates some 300,000 Hindu pilgrims who were observing an annual ritual of bathing in the river, and at least 62 of them drown.

April 10, Savar, Bangladesh. A nine-story garment factory collapses, leaving at least 73 people dead.

June 7, Alexandria, Egypt. A six-story building collapses, killing at least 16 people; it is believed that the top three floors had been built illegally.

June 25, Machakos district, Kenya. After drinking homebrew made with methanol at a drinks stall, at least 51 people die and several are made blind.

July 21, Yunnan province, China. A dam collapse sends a torrent of water into the town of Xiaocaoba, drowning 15 people.

August 31, Baghdad. As Shi'ite pilgrims cross a bridge to a shrine, someone panics the crowd by shouting that there is a suicide bomber on the bridge, and at least 950 pilgrims perish in the ensuing stampede.

October 20, Gorakhpur, Uttar Pradesh, India. Village politicians attempting to curry favour with voters distribute free food and alcohol; after 19 villagers die, the alcohol is found to be laced with insecticides.

October 20, Mt. Kanguru, Nepal. A team of 7 French climbers with 11 Nepalese guides attempting to climb the 7,000-m (22,900-ft) mountain are killed by an avalanche.

December 18, Madras, Tamil Nadu, India. A crowd of flood victims waiting for food vouchers at a relief centre stampede; at least 42 people perish.

People of 2005

More than 1,000 women and children line up for food aid in Yama, Niger, hard hit by famine.

© Finbarr O'Reilly/Reuters/Corbis

Nobel Prizes

Nobels in 2005 were AWARDED to 12 men (and one institution) from eight countries for work in nuclear WEAPONS control, GAME theory, PLAYWRITING, organic chemical METATHESIS, OPTICS, and discovering the bacterial basis of stomach ULCERS.

PRIZE FOR PEACE

The 2005 Nobel Prize for Peace was shared by the International Atomic Energy Agency (IAEA) and its director general, Mohamed ElBaradei. The announcement, made on October 7, noted, "At a time when the threat of nuclear arms is again increasing, the Norwegian Nobel Committee wishes to underline that this threat must be met through the broadest possible international cooperation. This principle finds its clearest expression today in the work of the IAEA and its director general." The award was made 60 years after the dropping of atomic bombs on Hiroshima and Nagasaki, Japan, by the U.S. during World War II, the fourth time a major anniversary of the bombings had been marked with the peace prize. It was the 12th prize for the United Nations or an affiliated agency.

The IAEA, an intergovernmental organization headquartered in Vienna and linked to the UN, was established in 1957. It grew out of recommendations made by U.S. Pres. Dwight D. Eisenhower in a 1953 speech, "Atoms for Peace," before the UN. The agency promoted peaceful applications of atomic energy and also worked to prevent its use for military purposes. It gradually came to take an active role in attempts to prevent nuclear proliferation, with efforts first centred on Iraq and The Sudan, in which cases the agency claimed success, and later on North Korea and Iran. The committee remarked, "At a time when disarmament efforts appear deadlocked, when there is a danger that nuclear arms will spread both to states

and to terrorist groups, and when nuclear power again appears to be playing an increasingly significant role, IAEA's work is of incalculable importance."

Mohamed ElBaradei was born in Cairo on June 17, 1942. His father, a lawyer, was president of the Egyptian Bar Association. The son received a bachelor's degree in law from the University of Cairo in 1962 and a doctorate in international law from New York University in 1974. During the 1960s he was a member of the Egyptian diplomatic corps, twice serving on missions to the UN in New York City and in Geneva. From 1974 to 1978 ElBaradei was assistant to Egypt's foreign minister. In 1981 he became a senior fellow in

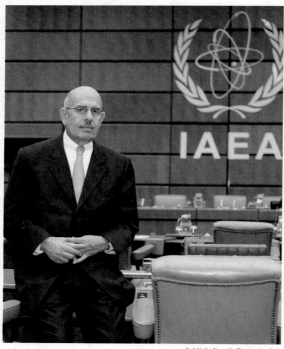

Mohamed ElBaradei in the boardroom of the International Atomic Energy Agency

charge of the International Law Program at the UN Institute for Training and Research, and he was an adjunct professor in international law (1981–87) at New York University. ElBaradei became a member of the IAEA secretariat in 1984, working as counsel and, beginning in 1993, as assistant director general for external relations. Appointed director general of the agency in 1997, he was reappointed to a second term in 2001 and, despite opposition from the United States, to a third term in 2005.

Although ElBaradei sometimes took a tough stance toward uncooperative governments, he was also known as an advocate of patient diplomacy. In 2002 he challenged U.S. claims, correctly as it turned out, that Iraqi Pres. Saddam Hussein had restarted a nuclear program, and he resisted U.S. efforts to impose sanctions on Iran. In response to the announcement that he had been given the award, he said, "The prize recognizes the role of multilateralism in resolving all of the challenges we are facing today. It will strengthen my resolve and that of my colleagues to continue to speak truth to power."

(ROBERT RAUCH)

PRIZE FOR ECONOMICS

The Nobel Memorial Prize in Economic Sciences was awarded in 2005 to Robert J. Aumann of Israel and American Thomas C. Schelling for their respective contributions to the greater "understanding of conflict and cooperation through game-theory analysis." The results of their separate work on game theory— or interactive decision theory— facilitated the development of noncooperative game theory to explain why some groups and countries are able to cooperate while others are in conflict. This widened the theory's application throughout the social sciences.

Aumann employed a mathematical approach to show that long-term social interaction could be analyzed by employing formal noncooperative game theory. Through his methodologies and analyses of so-called infinitely repeated games, he identified the outcomes that could be sustained in long-term relations and demonstrated the prerequisites for cooperation in situations where there are many participants, infrequent interaction, or the potential for a break off in relations and when participants' actions lack transparency. Aumann also extended game theory with his investigation into its cognitive foundations. He showed that peaceful cooperation is attainable in a repeated game even when the short-term interests of the parties are in conflict. Aumann's repeated game theory was applied in analyses ranging from business cartels and farming cooperatives to international territorial disputes.

Schelling extended the use of game theory to assist in the resolution of conflict and avoidance of wars. In the mid-1950s the Cold War between the U.S. and the Soviet Union prompted him to apply game-theory methods to global security and the arms race. He published his results in *The Strategy of Conflict* (1960), which became a classic. In seeking to ascertain how nuclear powers might successfully deter each other, Schelling focused on ways in which the negotiating power of the parties could be affected by such factors as the initial alternatives available to them and their ability to influence the employable alternatives in the negotiating process. He concluded that uncertain retaliation is more credible and efficient than certain retaliation and argued that a country's best defense against nuclear war is the protection of its weapons rather than its people because a government needs to demonstrate the ability to respond to a nuclear attack. In contrast to Aumann, Schelling's strength lay in his ability to generate new ideas and concepts without emphasizing the underlying mathematical techniques.

Aumann was born on June 8, 1930, in Frankfurt am Main, Ger., and immigrated to the U.S. with his family in 1938. He was educated at the City College of New York (B.S., 1950) and the Massachusetts Institute of Technology (Ph.D., 1955), followed by postdoctoral work at Princeton University. In 1956 he moved to Israel, where he served on the mathematics faculty at Hebrew University, Jerusalem, as an instructor (1956–58), lecturer (1958–64), associate professor (1964–68), professor (1968–2001), and professor emeritus (from 2001). He also held visiting professorships at various American universities. Aumann was on the editorial and advisory boards of several academic journals,

notably *International Journal of Game Theory* (from 1971), *Journal of Mathematical Economics* (from 1974), and *Games and Economic Behaviour* (from 1989). He received the Israel Prize in Economics in 1994. Aumann was the author of six books and nearly 100 scientific papers, including *What Is Game Theory Trying to Accomplish?* (1985).

Schelling was born on April 14, 1921, in Oakland, Calif., and studied economics at the University of California, Berkeley (B.A., 1944), and Harvard University (Ph.D., 1951). He began his career working for the U.S. Bureau of the Budget (1945–46), the Marshall Plan in Europe (1948–50), and the Executive Office of the President (1951–53). He then taught economics at Yale University (1953–58), Harvard (1958–90), where he was named Lucius N. Littauer Professor of Political Economy at the John F. Kennedy School of Government in 1969, and the University of Maryland (1990–2003). He was a fellow of the American Academy of Arts and Sciences and the American Economic Association (president, 1991). In addition to his work on military strategy and arms control, Schelling wrote on such varied topics as energy and environmental policy, terrorism, racial integration, and health policy. His books included *Micromotives and Macrobehavior* (1978) and *Choice and Consequence* (1984). (JANET H. CLARK)

PRIZE FOR LITERATURE

British playwright Harold Pinter was awarded the 2005 Nobel Prize for Literature for work of insight and originality that "uncovers the precipice under everyday prattle and forces entry into oppression's closed rooms." The author of more than 30 plays, Pinter was also an accomplished actor, director, poet, and writer for radio, television, and film. In addition, he was an outspoken and often controversial activist in defense of human rights. He had emerged as part of the "new wave" of postwar dramatists responsible for the renaissance of British theatre in the late 1950s and '60s, but he developed independently from his contemporaries and represented a distinct and provocative voice in contemporary theatre. As a playwright Pinter used the stage as a means to explore the anguish of the human condition through a personal mode of language and situation that came to be commonly regarded as "Pinteresque."

Pinter was born on Oct. 10, 1930, in Hackney, a working-class section in the

Harold Pinter

East End of London. He was the son of a Jewish tailor and early in childhood experienced the social and cultural ramifications of anti-Semitism. At the outbreak of World War II, he left London and lived from 1939 to 1942 in Cornwall. Pinter returned to London when he was 12 years old, and he left school at age 16. He decided to pursue an acting career and received a grant in 1948 to study in London at the Royal Academy of Dramatic Art; he later continued his studies at the Central School of Speech and Drama. In 1951 Pinter began acting with regional and provincial touring companies, performing in the 1950s under the stage name David Baron. Pinter published his first poems in the early 1950s and debuted as a dramatist with his one-act play *The Room*, performed in 1957 at the University of Bristol's Drama Studio. The play introduced the thematic elements and emotional intensity that defined Pinter's methodology and artistic sensibility, juxtaposing the known with the unknown and the mundane with the inexplicable. Within the parameters of their confined space, his characters vie with each other for position and control, searching for relevance and identity in an atmosphere pervaded by uncertainty, ambiguity, and ambivalence.

Audiences were generally unprepared for Pinter's form of drama, and critical reaction to his early so-called comedies of menace ranged from consternation and confusion to disregard and rejection. His first full-length play, *The Birthday Party*, opened in Cambridge in 1958 and then transferred to the West

End in London. Though the play was almost uniformly panned by reviewers (it closed after one week), it was later recognized as one of Pinter's most celebrated and enduring accomplishments as a dramatist. His second full-length play and first commercial success was *The Caretaker* (1960; filmed 1963 [released in the U.S. as *The Guest*]), for which he received the *Evening Standard* Award for best play.

Following *The Homecoming* (1965; filmed 1973), often cited as his most compelling work for the stage, Pinter entered a period of experimentation with plays such as *Landscape* and *Silence* (produced jointly in 1969), *Old Times* (1971), *Monologue* (1973), and *Betrayal* (1978; filmed 1983). After the overthrow (1973) of Chile's Pres. Salvador Allende, Pinter became increasingly politicized as a writer. Later plays with social and political implications included *One for the Road* (1984), *Mountain Language* (1988), *The New World Order* (1991), *Moonlight* (1993), *Ashes to Ashes* (1996), and *Celebration* (2000). He became a vocal critic of British Prime Minister Margaret Thatcher's policies and campaigned against a broad range of issues: Israeli treatment of the Palestinians, the persecution and imprisonment of dissident writers, Turkish treatment of the Kurds, and the U.S.-led invasion of Iraq.

Pinter's screenplay for *The Servant* (1963), adapted from Robin Maughman's novel, earned him Writers' Guild of Great Britain and New York Film Critics Circle awards. His critical reputation was further enhanced by *The Pumpkin Eater* (1964), which received the BAFTA Award for best screenplay; *Accident* (1967), which shared the Cannes Film Festival Special Jury Grand Prize; and *The Go-Between* (1970), which won the Grand Prize at Cannes. Later film adaptations included *The Last Tycoon* (1976), *The French Lieutenant's Woman* (1981), *Turtle Diary* (1985), *The Handmaid's Tale* (1990), and *The Trial* (1993).

Pinter received the Laurence Olivier Award for lifetime achievement in the theatre in 1996. He was made CBE in 1966 and in 2002 was appointed Companion of Honour for services to literature. In 1980 Pinter married his second wife, the novelist and historian Antonia Fraser.   (STEVEN R. SERAFIN)

PRIZE FOR CHEMISTRY

The 2005 Nobel Prize for Chemistry was awarded to three scientists—one French and two American—who developed metathesis, one of the most important types of chemical reactions used in organic chemistry. The Royal Swedish Academy of Sciences gave the $1.3 million award to Yves Chauvin, honorary research director of the French Institute of Petroleum in Rueil-Malmaison, France; Robert H. Grubbs, a professor of chemistry at the California Institute of Technology (Caltech); and Richard R. Schrock, a professor of chemistry at the Massachusetts Institute of Technology (MIT).

The term *metathesis* comes from the Greek words *meta* ("change") and *thesis* ("position"). In metathesis, substances called catalysts create and break double carbon bonds of organic molecules in a way that causes different groups of atoms in the molecules to change places with one another. (A catalyst promotes chemical reactions that otherwise would not take place or would occur very slowly.) The shift of groups of atoms from their original position to a new location yields new molecules with new properties. With the development of metathesis, the academy said, "fantastic opportunities have been created for producing many new molecules." The academy also cited many useful products that had been made through metathesis, including advanced plastics, fuel additives, agents to control harmful plants and insects, and new drugs for medical conditions such as osteoporosis and arthritis.

Researchers in the chemical industry discovered metathesis in the 1950s.

Yves Chauvin

AP/Wide World Photos

Richard Schrock

They found that various catalysts could be used to carry out metathesis reactions, although the initial catalysts did not work well. Since the scientists did not understand how the catalysts worked at a molecular level, the hunt for better catalysts was purely a hit-and-miss endeavour or, as the academy put it, "fumbling in the dark."

Chauvin, a French chemist, was born on Oct. 10, 1930. He spent most of his career conducting chemical research at the French Institute of Petroleum and was a member of the Academy of Sciences in France. In 1970 he achieved a breakthrough when he described the mechanism by which a metal atom bound to a carbon atom in one group of atoms causes the group to shift places with a group of atoms in another molecule. Although the catalyst starts the chemical reaction in which two new carbon-carbon bonds are formed, it comes away from the chemical reaction unaffected and ready to start the reaction again. Chauvin's work showed how metathesis could take place, but its practical application required the development of new catalysts.

Schrock, born on Jan. 4, 1945, in Berne, Ind., received a Ph.D. in chemistry from Harvard University in 1971 and joined the faculty of MIT in 1975. He systematically tested catalysts that contained tantalum, tungsten, or other metals in an effort to understand which metals could be used and how they worked. In a major advance in 1990, Schrock and his associates reported the development of a group of efficient metathesis catalysts that used the metal molybdenum. The new catalysts, however, were sensitive to the effects of air and water, which reduced their activity.

Grubbs was born on Feb. 27, 1942, near Possum Trot, Ky. He received a Ph.D. in chemistry from Columbia University, New York City, in 1968 and joined the faculty of Caltech in 1978. In 1992, while furthering research on metathesis, Grubbs and his associates reported the discovery of a catalyst that contained the metal ruthenium. It was stable in air and worked on the double carbon bonds in a molecule selectively, without disrupting the bonds between other atoms in the molecule. The new catalyst also had the ability to jumpstart metathesis reactions in the presence of water, alcohols, and carboxyl acids.

AP/Wide World Photos

Robert Grubbs

The academy pointed out that many other researchers had also made important contributions to the field. As scientists sought to develop new metathesis catalysts for specific applications, research in the field continued to be very active. One area of research was the synthesis of compounds found in nature that had potential commercial use in medicine or other fields. Such "natural products" usually had very complex structures and were very difficult to make in the laboratory. "Considering the relatively short time Schrock's and Grubbs's catalysts have been available, it is remarkable to note the breadth of applications they have found," the academy said.

The academy also noted that the catalysts for metathesis had played a role

in the development of "green chemistry"—the design of chemical processes and products in which the need for and the generation of various hazardous substances was reduced or eliminated. Metathesis catalysts had been used in the development of reactions for synthesizing chemical compounds that were more efficient and required fewer steps, fewer ingredients, and smaller quantities of ingredients. The reactions were simpler because they worked at ordinary temperatures and pressures, and they were more environmentally friendly because they used noninjurious solvents and produced less-hazardous waste products.

(MICHAEL WOODS)

PRIZE FOR PHYSICS

Two Americans and a German won the 2005 Nobel Prize for Physics for their contributions to the field of optics, the branch of physics that deals with the physical properties of light and its interactions with matter. The Royal Swedish Academy of Sciences gave one-half of the $1.3 million prize to Roy J. Glauber, a professor of physics at Harvard University. The other half was shared by John L. Hall, a fellow of JILA (a research institute operated by the National Institute of Standards and Technology [NIST] and the University of Colorado at Boulder), and Theodor W. Hänsch, director of the Max Planck Institute for Quantum Optics and a professor at the Ludwig Maximilians University, Munich.

Glauber was born in New York City on Sept. 1, 1925. He received a Ph.D. in physics from Harvard University in 1949 and briefly conducted research at the Institute for Advanced Studies in Princeton, N.J., and at the California Institute of Technology before he returned to Harvard in 1952. Glauber was cited by the academy for his development of a theory that advanced the understanding of light by describing the behaviour of light particles (light quanta, or photons). The theory, presented by Glauber in the early 1960s, merged the field of optics with quantum physics (which deals with the behaviour of matter on the atomic and subatomic scales), and it formed the basis for the development of a new field, quantum optics. Glauber's work helped clarify how light had both wavelike and particlelike characteristics and explained the fundamental differences between the light emitted by hot objects, such as electric light

bulbs, and the light emitted by lasers. (Hot sources of light emit incoherent light, which consists of many different frequencies and phases, whereas lasers emit coherent light, light with a uniform frequency and phase.) Practical applications of Glauber's work included the development of highly secure codes in the field known as quantum cryptography. His work also had a central role in efforts to develop the new generation of computers, so-called quantum computers, which would be extraordinarily fast and powerful and use quantum-mechanical phenomena to process data as qubits, or quantum bits, of information.

Hall was born in Denver in 1934. He received a Ph.D. in physics in 1961 from the Carnegie Institute of Technology, Pittsburgh, and joined JILA in the National Bureau of Standards (which later became the NIST) later that year. Hänsch was born Oct. 30, 1941, in Heidelberg, Ger., and he received a Ph.D. in physics from the University of Heidelberg in 1969. In awarding Hall and Hänsch the Nobel Prize, the academy specifically cited their contributions to the development of laser spectroscopy, the use of lasers to determine the frequency (colour) of light emitted by atoms and molecules. A focus of their careers had been to make precise frequency measurements. In the 1980s it led to very precise measurements of the speed of light in a vacuum (299,792,458 m per second), and as a consequence the metre, the fundamental unit of length in the International System of Units, was redefined in terms of the speed of light. Despite such advances, it was very difficult to measure optical frequencies (frequencies of visible light). It required a procedure, called an optical frequency chain, to relate them to the output frequencies of an atomic clock and was so complex that it could be performed in only a few laboratories. The optical frequency comb technique, in which ultrashort pulses of laser light create a set of precisely spaced frequency peaks that resemble the evenly spaced teeth of a hair comb, proved a practical way of obtaining optical frequency measurements to an accuracy of 15 digits, or one part in one quadrillion. Hänsch originated the idea for the technique in the late 1970s, but it took until 2000 for Hänsch, with key contributions by Hall, to work out the details. Their success soon led to the development of commercial devices with which very precise optical frequency measurements could readily be made.

Practical applications of the work of Hall and Hänsch included the development of very accurate clocks, improved satellite-based navigation systems such as the Global Positioning System, and the synchronization of computer data networks. Their work was also used by physicists to verify Einstein's theory of special relativity to very high levels of precision and to test whether the values of fundamental physical constants related to optical frequencies were indeed constant or changed slightly over time.   (MICHAEL WOODS)

PRIZE FOR PHYSIOLOGY OR MEDICINE

Two Australian scientists who discovered that stomach ulcers are an infectious disease caused by bacteria shared the Nobel Prize for Physiology or Medicine. The Karolinska Institute in Sweden, which awarded the prize, termed the discovery by Barry J. Marshall and J. Robin Warren "remarkable and unexpected." Marshall was a senior principal research fellow at the University of Western Australia in Nedlands. Warren was retired from the Royal Perth (Australia) Hospital.

Before Marshall and Warren discovered the role of the bacterium, *Helicobacter pylori*, physicians believed that peptic ulcers (sores in the stomach lining) were caused by an excess of gastric acid that was released in the stomach as the result of emotional stress, the ingestion of spicy foods, or other factors. Peptic ulcers cause pain, nausea, and—if they begin to bleed—even more serious problems. The standard treatment had included antacid medicines, hospital bed rest, and a diet in which large amounts of milk and cream were used to soothe the stomach. Some patients underwent surgery to remove parts of the stomach. Although the treatments often gave patients temporary relief, stomach pain and other symptoms often returned and caused life-long problems. "Thanks to the pioneering discovery by Marshall and Warren, peptic ulcer disease is no longer a chronic, frequently disabling condition but a disease that can be cured by a short regimen of antibiotics and acid-secretion inhibitors," said the citation from the Karolinska Institute.

Warren was born June 11, 1937, in Adelaide, S.Aus. He received a bachelor's degree from the University of Adelaide in 1961 and worked at several hospitals before he began working in 1968 as a pathologist at Royal Perth Hospital, where he remained until his retirement in 1999. In 1979 he first observed the presence of spiral-shaped bacteria in a biopsy of the stomach lining from a patient. It defied the conventional wisdom that bacteria could not survive in the highly acidic environment of the stomach. Many scientists in Australia and other countries dismissed his reports on the topic as impossible, but his research during the

© William Edwards/Reuters/Corbis

Robin Warren (left) and Barry Marshall

next two years showed that the bacteria were often in stomach tissue and almost always in association with gastritis (an inflammation of the stomach lining).

Marshall was born Sept. 30, 1951, in Kalgoorlie, W.Aus. He obtained a bachelor's degree from the University of Western Australia in 1974. He worked (1977–84) at Royal Perth Hospital and later taught medicine at the University of Western Australia. While a young staff member in Perth Hospital's gastroenterology department in 1981, Marshall became interested in Warren's research, and the two began working together to pin down the clinical significance of the bacteria. After they developed a way to grow the bacteria in laboratory culture dishes, Warren and Marshall identified the microbe as a new species. They conducted a study of stomach biopsies from 100 patients that systematically showed that the

bacteria were present in almost all patients with gastritis, duodenal ulcer, or gastric ulcer. On the basis of the findings, Warren and Marshall proposed that *H. pylori* was involved in causing those diseases.

Physicians were skeptical that peptic ulcer disease could be an infectious condition and clung to the traditional treatments for the disease. Marshall and Warren persisted in their research and continued to gather evidence. At one point Marshall chose to become his own guinea pig in what was one of the most notable instances of self-experimentation in the history of medicine. Deciding that the best way to prove their findings was to show exactly what happened when a person was infected with *H. pylori*, Marshall drank a culture of the bacterium. Within a week he began suffering stomach pain and other symptoms of acute gastritis. Stomach biopsies confirmed that he did have gastritis and showed that the affected areas of his stomach were infected with *H. pylori*. Marshall then took antibiotics and was cured.

The research solved the long-standing puzzle of why peptic ulcers often returned after traditional treatment. Bland diets and antacids reduced stomach acidity and allowed inflamed areas of the stomach lining to heal, but the bacteria responsible for the inflammation remained and were able to cause new bouts of inflammation. Studies showed that *H. pylori* infected the stomachs of at least 50% of the world's population. Although most people never experienced symptoms, 10–15% eventually developed stomach ulcers or gastritis. Infection also put people at higher risk of stomach cancer. Genetic differences were believed to influence who developed peptic ulcer disease. "The discovery that one of the most common diseases of mankind, peptic ulcer disease, has a microbial cause has stimulated the search for microbes as possible causes of other chronic inflammatory diseases," the Karolinska Institute noted in its citation. Researchers had evidence that bacterial infections might be involved in conditions ranging from arthritis to atherosclerosis, the artery-clogging disease that underlay most heart attacks and many strokes.

(MICHAEL WOODS)

Biographies

The SUBJECTS of these biographies are the people who in the editors' opinions captured the IMAGINATION of the world in 2005—the most INTERESTING and/or IMPORTANT PERSONALITIES of the year.

Abdullah, King

Upon the death of King Fahd on Aug. 1, 2005, Crown Prince Abdullah, a half brother, became king of Saudi Arabia. He formally assumed the throne, as the kingdom's sixth ruler, on August 3. Throughout the previous decade, after Fahd suffered a stroke, Abdullah had exercised control over the government. He had a reputation as a conservative leader who was, nonetheless, committed to reforming and modernizing government operations. Saudi Arabia had come under attacks by militants opposed to secularizing forces within the country, but by virtue of his character, the new king was seen as an effective power against destabilization.

'Abdullah ibn 'Abd al-'Aziz al-Sa'ud was born c. 1923 in Riyadh, in what was then Arabia. A son of Ibn Sa'ud, who had founded the Kingdom of Saudi Arabia in 1932, and his eighth wife, Abdullah was educated at court. For a time he lived among the Bedouin, and throughout his life he retained a high regard for traditional desert ways. His first government position was as mayor of the Islamic holy city of Mecca, and in 1962 then crown prince Faysal appointed him commissioner of the National Guard. Abdullah modernized the force, which was made up of descendants of the followers of Ibn Sa'ud and which was responsible for domestic security. In 1975 he was named second deputy prime minister, and in 1982 he was designated crown prince and first deputy prime minister. An Arab nationalist, he opposed the Persian Gulf War of 1991 and the stationing of U.S. troops in Saudi Arabia. When King Fahd was disabled by a stroke in 1995, Abdullah became the de facto head of the Saudi government.

Known as a religious man who had avoided the scandals frequently associated with the large royal family, Abdullah introduced a number of measured reforms, including limited political and civil liberties. As crown prince during the late 1980s and early '90s, he attempted to curb corruption among members of the royal family. He balanced the Saudi budget and introduced reforms in the government bureaucracy as well as in the country's economic institutions. Following terrorist attacks in Riyadh in 2003, he cracked down on extremist religious leaders but also introduced changes to the educational and legal systems and allowed a more open press. He was equally active in putting

Saudi King Abdullah

his stamp on Saudi foreign relations. In 2002 he proposed a comprehensive Middle East peace settlement that would include Arab recognition of Israel in exchange for the return of land to the Palestinians. He refused U.S. requests for the use of Saudi bases in the 2003 war against Iraq. In addition to holding frequent meetings with other Arab leaders, he traveled throughout the world for talks with government heads.

(ROBERT RAUCH)

Ahmadinejad, Mahmoud

The surprise winner of Iran's presidential elections in June 2005 was Mahmoud Ahmadinejad, who commanded the support of hard-line conservatives in the country. Despite having served as mayor of Tehran since 2003, Ahmadinejad was largely viewed as a political outsider when he announced his candidacy for president, and opinion polls put his support at about 7% prior to the first round of elections. Through a massive nationwide mobilization of supporters, however, Ahmadinejad managed to secure some 19.5% of the votes in that round, which propelled him into the second round of balloting, in which he handily defeated his moderate rival, former president Hashemi Rafsanjani. Ahmadinejad took office on August 3, when Supreme Leader Ayatollah Sayyed Ali Khamenei officially confirmed him as president.

Ahmadinejad, the son of a blacksmith, was born on Oct. 28, 1956, in Garmsar, Iran. He grew up in Tehran, where in 1976 he entered the Iran University of Science and Technology (IUST) to study civil engineering. During the Iranian Revolution (1978–79), he was one of the student leaders who organized demonstrations. After the revolution, like many of his peers, he joined the Revolutionary Guards, a religious militia group formed by Ayatollah Khomeini. Parallel to his service with the Revolutionary Guards in the 1980–90 Iran-Iraq War, he continued his studies at IUST, eventually earning a Ph.D. in transportation engineering and planning. Following the war he served in various positions until 1993, when he was appointed governor of the newly established Ardabil province. After his term as governor ended in 1997, he returned to IUST as a lecturer.

For the average Iranian, Ahmadinejad was an unknown figure until he became mayor of Tehran in 2003. Earlier he had helped establish a political party known as the Abadgaran (Developers of Islamic Iran), which promoted a populist agenda and sought to unite conservative factions in the country. The party gained momentum and captured the Tehran city council elections in February 2003. The city council chose Ahmadinejad to be mayor the following May. The Abadgaran also won a majority of seats in the 2004 parliamentary elections.

As mayor of the capital city, Ahmadinejad was credited with solving traffic problems and keeping prices down. He presented himself as a man of the people—an image he continued to cultivate as president as he focused on such issues as poverty and social justice. His first months in office were characterized by internal challenges brought about by a sweeping changing of the guard in all key positions. On the foreign policy front, Ahmadinejad struck an immediate defiant chord, defending Iran's controversial nuclear program and discouraging talk of reestablishing formal ties with the U.S., which had been broken in 1979. He also prompted international condemnation with comments on Israel. In an October speech, he quoted Khomeini's declaration that Israel "must be eliminated from the pages of history" and added, "This sentence is very wise." Two months later he called the Holocaust a "myth" and further suggested that Israel be moved to Europe.

(EDITOR)

Al-Aswānī, ʻAlāʼ

The appearance in 2002 of *ʻImārat Yaʻqūbiyyān* (*The Yacoubian Building*), the first novel by ʻAlāʼ al-Aswānī (Alaa Al Aswany), was in itself a novel event. The book attracted an unprecedented number of readers in Egypt and throughout the Arab world. The first edition sold out in 40 days, and nine more printings were subsequently ordered. The English version appeared in 2004 and was similarly successful. A paperback edition was scheduled for 2006.

Aswānī was born on May 27, 1957, in Cairo, the son of a lawyer enamoured of literature who was credited with reviving the *maqāmah* (assemblies in rhymed prose) genre and who won the 1972 State Award for Literature for his novel *Al-Aswār al-ʻāliya* ("High Walls"). The younger Aswānī finished the French Lycée in Cairo and graduated with an undergraduate degree (1980) in dentistry from Cairo University. He received an M.S. in dentistry from the University of Illinois at Chicago, finishing in the record time of 11 months.

Aswānī pursued dentistry and writing with equal fervour. He developed an interest in literature and culture early in life when his father allowed him to attend his literary gatherings. As a student Aswānī wrote short stories, plays, and newspaper articles dealing with politics and literary criticism. His father, however, strongly discouraged him from pursuing a career as a full-time writer. The list of Aswānī's publications included a novel, *Awrāq ʻIṣām ʻAbd al-ʻĀtī* (1989; "The Papers of ʻIṣām ʻAbd al-ʻĀti"), and two collections of short stories (1990 and 1997). *Nīrān ṣadīqah* ("Friendly Fires"), also containing some of his stories, was published in 2004. He also wrote a monthly article for the newspaper *Al-ʻArabī*. Aswānī was a staunch believer in reading national literatures in their original languages, and he studied Spanish to read the Spanish masterpieces. He also knew French and English.

The Yacoubian Building was a story of social change in Egypt, presenting a pastiche of life—good and bad—in modern Cairo. It exposed corruption, abuse of power, and exploitation of the poor. Yacoubian was the name of an actual building situated in downtown Cairo where the elder Aswānī's law offices were located, though many of the details in the novel did not correspond exactly to the real Yacoubian Building. Aswānī wanted to name his novel *Wast al-balad* ("Downtown"), but the use of the catchy name Yacoubian was inspired and probably piqued the curiosity of many readers. The novel's success also did not escape the attention of Egyptian movie producers, and a film version was expected at the beginning of 2006. (AIDA A. BAMIA)

Albert II

On April 6, 2005, His Most Serene Highness Albert, hereditary prince of Monaco and marquis of Baux, ascended to the throne of the tiny Mediterranean principality upon the death of his father, Prince Rainier III. Albert had ruled as regent during the last week of his father's life, and on July 12 he was formally enthroned as Prince Albert II. Under Rainier, Monaco had become a prosperous centre for banking, manufacturing, and tourism. Many observers wondered, however, whether Albert would be able to ensure the continued stability and prosperity of his realm. Rainier himself had expressed concern that Albert did not possess "the necessary toughness" to rule. Although the new ruler was considered intelligent and well prepared for his new role, in May news of an illegitimate son revived memories of the romantic scandals that had marred the public careers of Albert's sisters, the Princesses Caroline and Stephanie. Days before he was enthroned, Albert acknowledged that he was the father of the two-year-old son of a French-Togolese woman after the magazine *Paris-Match* published an interview in which she identified the prince as the father. In officially recognizing his relationship to the boy, Albert made his son an heir to a fortune worth more than a billion dollars—but not to the throne. In 2002 Rainier had modified Monaco's constitution to restrict the succession to "direct and legitimate" heirs, leaving the unmarried Albert without a direct heir.

Prince Albert II

Albert-Alexandre-Louis-Pierre de Grimaldi was born on March 14, 1958, in Monaco, the second child and only son of Prince Rainier III and Princess Grace. After his graduation with distinction from secondary school in 1976, Albert received training in the government of the principality. He graduated from Amherst (Mass.) College in 1981 with a B.A. in political science. Following a tour of duty with the French navy, he trained in business and in international law with firms in New York City and Paris. A lifelong sports enthusiast, Albert ran cross country while in college and attained a black belt in judo. He competed in the 1988, 1992, 1994, 1998, and 2002 Winter Olympics as a member of Monaco's bobsleigh team. Beginning in 1985 he served in various capacities with the International Olympic Committee, and in 1994 he became chairman of the Monegasque Olympic Committee. Albert also maintained an active involvement in humanitarian activities. In 1982 he was named chairman of the Monaco Red Cross, and he later founded the Monaco Aid and Presence Association to alleviate poverty in Africa and other less-developed areas. He served as president of Monaco's delegation to the United Nations from 1993, when the principality was first admitted to the UN, until his accession. (JANET MOREDOCK)

Bakiyev, Kurmanbek

On Aug. 14, 2005, Kurmanbek Bakiyev—who had been serving as interim head of state in Kyrgyzstan since March 25, when his predecessor, Askar Akayev, fled the country amid widespread demonstrations protesting government corruption—was sworn in as the country's second president after having received nearly 89% of the vote in the July 10 elections.

Kurmanbek (Saliyevich) Bakiyev, was born on Aug. 1, 1949, in the village of Masadan in the southern Kirghiz S.S.R. (or Kirghizia, now Kyrgyzstan). After graduating (1972) from the Kuybyshev (now Samara) Polytechnic Institute in Russia, he worked as an electrical engineer until 1990, when he began serving in a series of government posts in southern Kirghizia. In the late 1990s he was governor of Jalal-Abad oblast and then moved to northern Kyrgyzstan, where he assumed the post of governor of Chui oblast. In December 2000 President Akayev appointed Bakiyev to the post of prime minister. He was dismissed, however, on May 22, 2002; Bakiyev reportedly asked Akayev to allow him to return to his former position as governor of Chui but was turned down. The reason for the falling out between the two remained a matter of speculation. After threatening to join the opposition, Bakiyev then ran for a parliamentary seat in his native south.

After his election to the lower house of the national parliament in October 2002, Bakiyev joined a centrist group that sought to defend the interests of the regions. In September 2004 he became head of the newly founded opposition People's Movement of Kyrgyzstan. This position, coupled with his previous experience as prime minister, made him a likely replacement for Akayev or Prime Minister Nikolay Tanayev after both fled the country in 2005. Though the opposition leadership initially tapped Bakiyev to take over Tanayev's post, Bakiyev was quickly designated head of state as well until a presidential election could be held.

One of the first tasks of the interim president was to restore public order in the country, particularly to put an end to the looting and destruction of property that had accompanied the collapse of the previous regime. To carry out this task, Bakiyev ensured the release from prison of the popular opposition leader Feliks Kulov, a former top security official. Bakiyev then turned his attention to restoring the economy, which had been in decline for more than a decade, and to trying to reassure the international community, particularly international donors, that Kyrgyzstan was returning to normal.

International observers assessed the electoral process in the July elections as generally fair, unlike the flawed parliamentary election in February that had precipitated the revolutionary events in March. Bakiyev's problems were far from over, however. The parliament rejected several of his nominees for ministerial posts, and political tensions arose over his dismissal of the prosecutor general, prominent opposition leader Azimbek Beknazarov.

(BESS BROWN)

Banks, Tyra

Supermodel Tyra Banks, the host and executive producer of *America's Next Top Model*—a weekly prime-time reality talent show that chronicled the search for a promising fashion model from a lineup of neophytes—demonstrated in 2005 that she was a star not only on the catwalk but on television as well. In September she debuted *The Tyra Banks Show*, a daily talk show that focused on fashion, lifestyle, makeovers, and topical issues but also featured Banks at the centre of a reality twist—in taped confessional segments she divulged her own struggles with personal issues, including self-esteem as well as her failure to forge lasting romantic partnerships.

From *Top Model*'s inception in 2003, it swiftly became one of the highest-rated shows in the history of the UPN network. It also served as a springboard for *The Tyra Banks Show*, which Banks hoped would serve as a positive motivational tool for young women between the ages of 25 and 35 (its target audience). Banks also mentored contestants on *Top Model* and teenage girls who attend TZONE, an annual weeklong summer camp near Los Angeles.

Banks was born on Dec. 4, 1973, in Los Angeles. In the 1990s she launched her international modeling career, working on runways in New York City, Milan, and Paris, before her intuition led her to forge a TV career. Banks settled in New York and worked to attain the level of mass appeal that her idol, Cindy Crawford, enjoyed as both a model and a personality.

TV talk-show host Tyra Banks

In 1993 Banks was featured in a recurring role on episodes of the TV comedy *The Fresh Prince of Bel-Air.* Two years later she landed her first role in a motion picture—*Higher Learning*—a drama written and directed by John Singleton, her former boyfriend. In 2000 she starred in *Coyote Ugly*, a rowdy coming-of-age feature film. Though Banks showcased her musical talent in "Shake Ya Body," a single produced for her by Rodney Jerkins, her rendition of the song failed to become a hit when it was released in 2004. Meanwhile, her modeling career thrived. In 1997 Banks became the first black model to appear on the cover of the *Sports Illustrated* swimsuit issue, and she was the first model and first black woman to be featured on the cover of *GQ* magazine. She also had a stint as a model in the Victoria's Secret lingerie catalog and represented Cover Girl cosmetics in TV and print advertisements. In December 2005 Banks retired from modeling.

(BRONWYN COSGRAVE)

Benedict XVI, Pope

Joseph Ratzinger, a German cardinal of the Roman Catholic Church and longtime prefect (director) of the Vatican's Congregation for the Doctrine of the Faith, was elected by his fellow cardinals on April 19, 2005, as the 264th successor to St. Peter, the apostle of Jesus Christ, first bishop of Rome, and first pope. The new pope took the name Benedict XVI and embarked on a pontificate dedicated to opposing what he called "a dictatorship of relativism" infecting modern society and to reconciling the Roman Catholic, Orthodox, and Protestant Christian churches with one another.

Joseph Alois Ratzinger was born on April 16, 1927, in the Bavarian village of Marktl am Inn. German law compelled Ratzinger to join the Hitler Youth when he turned 14; he refused to attend the meetings, however, and set his sights on entering the seminary. After being drafted into the Nazi antiaircraft artillery corps, he was drafted into the German army, but his unit was never sent to the front. Briefly interned in a prisoner-of-war camp near Ulm, Ratzinger was repatriated on June 19, 1945.

Shortly after the war, Joseph and his brother Georg entered Saint Michael Seminary in Traunstein, and they then studied at the Ducal Georgianum of the Ludwig-Maximilian University of Munich. On June 29, 1951, they were ordained into the priesthood. In 1958 Ratzinger became a professor at Freising College, but the following year he joined the faculty at the University of Bonn.

By 1963, when he accepted a faculty post at the University of Münster, Ratzinger had already established a reputation as a leading theologian in the German church, so it came as no surprise when Joseph Cardinal Frings of Cologne invited him to participate at the Second Vatican Council (1962–65) as a *peritus*, or theological consultant. Ratzinger became known as a reformer at the council; he took particular interest in the debates that led to the promulgation of two key documents: *Nostra aetate*, the conciliar statement on Roman Catholicism's relationship to Judaism and to other religions, and *Dignitatis humanae*, the

Pope Benedict XVI at St. Peter's Basilica in Vatican City

startling affirmation by Vatican II of every person's inalienable right to religious freedom.

Following Vatican II, Ratzinger became (1966) a professor of dogmatic theology at the University of Tübingen, where a turning point occurred in his evolution as a Catholic theologian. Ratzinger had been an advocate of a type of Catholic federalism by which apostolic authority would be shared equally among bishops worldwide. He shared with his Tübingen colleague Hans Küng a concern about the centralization of church authority in the papacy. After a group of radical young Marxists studying at Tübingen sparked a series of riots in April and May 1968, Ratzinger, unsettled by the radicals' apparent disregard for order and law, became convinced that anarchy, including the moral "confusion" that led to the rise of the German gay rights movement, was related to a watering down of Catholic doctrine. In 1969, shaken, he left Tübingen and returned to Bavaria to teach at the University of Regensburg. Subsequently, he came to oppose certain "liberal" or "progressive" interpretations of Vatican II. One vehicle for disseminating his ideas was the international theological journal *Communio*, which Ratzinger helped to establish in 1972.

From this point Ratzinger's ecclesial fortunes ascended rapidly. In 1977 he was consecrated as the archbishop of Munich and Freising; later that year Pope Paul VI named him a cardinal. On Nov. 25, 1981, Pope John Paul II essentially made Ratzinger his second in command by appointing him prefect of the Congregation for the Doctrine of the Faith and granting him wide authority for enforcing the church's doctrine against radical and liberal Catholic theologians. These "dissident" theologians included his friend Küng, who had taken to questioning the doctrine of papal infallibility, among other traditional teachings. In assuming his new post, Cardinal Ratzinger resigned the Munich archdiocese in early 1982 and became cardinal bishop of Velletri-Segni in 1993. In 1998 he became vice-dean of the College of Cardinals and in 2002 dean, the position he commanded when that body convened in April 2005 to elect a new pope.

During the 26 years of John Paul II's pontificate, Ratzinger earned a reputation as a strict and uncompromising enforcer of the hard theological line adopted by the pope. By silencing controversial theologians or taking away their right to teach as Catholic theologians, Ratzinger attempted to eliminate dissent against received Catholic teaching on birth control, homosexuality, and the exclusion of women from the priesthood. Ratzinger applied his talents to squelching a number of innovative movements within the church, most notably the theology of liberation that emerged in Latin America in the 1980s.

In 2000 the Congregation for the Doctrine of the Faith published a document titled *Dominus Iesus*, which asserted the exclusive orthodoxy and superiority of Roman Catholic doctrine and denounced "relativistic theories which seek to justify religious pluralism." *Dominus Iesus* claimed that other religions "objectively speaking. . .are in a gravely deficient situation in comparison with those who, in the Church, have the fullness of the means of salvation." The document deeply offended other Christians, Jews, Muslims, Hindus, and Buddhists and proved a setback to the ecumenical and interreligious relationships achieved by Vatican II—advances that had been promoted by Ratzinger himself.

Nonetheless, Ratzinger's elevation to the papacy marked a new beginning for him. In his more capacious role as pope, he took great pains to position himself as a pope of reconciliation, following the example of his namesake Benedict XV. During the first six months of his pontificate, Benedict reached out to opposite theological extremes within the church by meeting with both Küng and the leader of the traditionalist followers of the late renegade archbishop Marcel Lefebvre. During his first major papal trip, to World Youth Day in Cologne, Benedict visited a historic synagogue and prayed with Jewish leaders in remembrance of the victims of the Holocaust. Despite his wariness of Islam as a global power, he addressed a small group of Muslim leaders in Cologne, offering them friendship and encouragement in the battle against radical Islamism. (R. SCOTT APPLEBY)

Bennett, Alan

The year 2005 saw a crowning achievement in the life of British dramatist Alan Bennett when his play *The History Boys* garnered both the Critics' Circle Theatre Award and the Laurence Olivier Award for best new play, and Bennett, after a career spanning five decades, received the Olivier Special Award. The play, set in Yorkshire in the 1980s, featured a clash of values between two teachers coaching a class of state-school boys through their university entrance examinations; it succeeded both as a serious-minded critique of Britain's education system—then and now—and as a superbly comic entertainment. In mid-2005 production began on a film version of *The History Boys* and a new Broadway staging due to open in 2006.

Bennett, the son of a butcher, was born on May 9, 1934, in Leeds, Yorkshire. He attended Leeds Modern School and gained a scholarship to Exeter College, Oxford, where he studied history. His fledgling career as a history don at Magdalen College, Oxford, was cut short after he enjoyed enormous success with the comedy revue *Beyond the Fringe* in 1960. He coauthored and starred in the show with Peter Cook, Jonathan Miller, and Dudley Moore, and the foursome played to packed houses in Edinburgh, London, and New York City. Bennett's first play, *Forty Years On*, was produced in 1968 and starred John Gielgud. It was followed by numerous plays, films, and television serials; a best-selling collection of Bennett's diaries and reminiscences, titled *Writing Home;* and several pieces for radio. In 1987 *Talking Heads*, a series of monologues for television, made him a household name and earned him the first of his five Oliviers. *The Madness of George III* premiered at the National Theatre in 1991, and the 1994 film adaptation, *The Madness of King George*, secured several Academy Award nominations, including one for Bennett's screenplay.

Bennett's special talent was his translation of the mundane into tragicomic dramas, and he was even able to bring his light touch to his work when referring to intellectual heavyweights such as Wittgenstein or Kafka. Bennett fearlessly scrutinized the British class system, propriety, and England's north-south cultural divide with results that were simultaneously chilling and hilarious. Meanwhile, his gift for creating an authentic dialogue for the "ordinary people" of his own background sat curiously beside his ability to portray the manners of middle and upper classes in such pieces as *An Englishman Abroad*, his 1983 TV play about the real-life meeting of actress Coral Browne and the notorious spy Guy Burgess. It was Bennett's diversity of talent that delighted audiences and led critics to hail him as perhaps the premier playwright of his day.

In September 2005 his fans were introduced to a new side of Bennett when he published the memoir *Untold Stories*, in which he looked back affectionately at his parents, poignantly reflected on his mother's descent into senility and her death in a nursing home, and revealed for the first time that in 1997 he had received treatment for what had been believed to be terminal cancer. (SIOBHAN DOWD)

Bernanke, Ben

On Oct. 24, 2005, the day that Ben Bernanke was named to replace Alan Greenspan as chairman of the U.S. Federal Reserve Board (Fed) after Greenspan's term ended in January 2006, the Dow Jones Industrial Average closed up roughly 170 points. Investors enthusiastically signaled their approval of the man Pres. George W. Bush had tapped to lead the Fed, in part because they expected Bernanke to uphold the style of fiscal management established by Greenspan, who had chaired the Fed since 1987. That vote of confidence was important because as Fed chairman, Bernanke would ultimately control the U.S. money supply, determine the direction of the federal funds interest rate, and influence the rate of inflation in the U.S. economy. A false step by the U.S.'s central bank could have negative reverberations worldwide.

Benjamin Shalom Bernanke was born on Dec. 13, 1953, in Augusta, Ga., and grew up in Dillon, S.C., where his father worked as a pharmacist and his mother was a teacher. Bernanke graduated summa cum laude in economics (1975) from Harvard University and earned a Ph.D. (1979) from the Massachusetts Institute of Technology. His first professorial appointment was at Stanford University, where he taught economics from 1979 to 1985. He became a full professor in 1985 when he moved to Princeton University. Bernanke was appointed in 2002 to the Board of Governors of the Federal Reserve System, and he became noted for thorough research and diplomacy when opinions among the governors differed. His political strengths were also evident in early 2005 when he was named chairman of the President's Council of Economic Advisors.

Bernanke coauthored an introductory economics textbook and published numerous scholarly works, many of which centred on monetary policy, the Great Depression, and business cycles. His analyses of the Great Depression suggested that as Fed chairman, he would work to prevent similar downturns—some of which, he argued, were prolonged by mistakes in fiscal policy. For some observers, however, his academic strengths represented a weakness. Past Fed chairmen usually had come from Wall Street rather than from academia, and it remained to be seen whether economic theory could prove itself in practice.

One thing analysts agreed on was that Bernanke's leadership of the Fed would not be a carbon copy of Greenspan's approach. While Greenspan was famous for indirect and vague public statements, Bernanke insisted that he would speak without ambiguity. Although Greenspan rejected inflation targeting, Bernanke preferred the stability and economic growth that he believed would result from a publicly stated inflation objective. Perhaps most important, where Greenspan expressed opinions on political topics, taxes, and economic issues outside a central banker's purview, Bernanke insisted that he would limit his comments to fiscal policy, particularly his central concerns: inflation and unemployment. Ultimately, his endorsements from investors, economists, and politicians gave Bernanke the support he would need for a smooth transition at the Federal Reserve in 2006. (SARAH FORBES ORWIG)

Blair, Tony

On May 5, 2005, Prime Minister Tony Blair led Britain's Labour Party to its third consecutive election victory—an achievement unparalleled in Labour's 100-year history. The election was also Blair's last. Seven months earlier he had announced that he would step down shortly before the next election, due in 2009 or 2010.

Anthony Charles Lynton Blair was born in Edinburgh on May 6, 1953. In July 1994, after 11 years as a member of Parliament, he was elected Labour leader on a platform of modernizing the party and abandoning its historical commitment to state socialism. On May 1, 1997, he led Labour to its biggest election victory over the Conservatives. Four years later Labour achieved a second landslide victory, which was attributed to the government's success in maintaining steady economic growth and to the continuing unpopularity of the opposition Conservative Party.

Blair's second term was overshadowed by his decision to support U.S. Pres. George W. Bush's decision to invade Iraq in March 2003. A substantial minority of Labour MPs voted against the war. Iraq cost Blair yet more support when it transpired that he had been wrong to claim that Iraqi Pres. Saddam Hussein possessed weapons of mass destruction. On the domestic front, some of Blair's reforms also proved divisive within his party—especially his proposal to charge university students up to £3,000 (about $5,000) a year in tuition fees. His personal ratings were sharply lower by the time of the May 2005 general election, but the continuing strength of the economy and the public mistrust of the Conservatives enabled Labour to retain power, albeit with a much-reduced majority.

Blair's third victory thrust him to the centre of the world stage, as the U.K. simultaneously held the presidencies of the European Union and Group of Eight (G-8) during the second half of 2005. At the G-8 summit at Gleneagles, Scot., in July, he sought to gain commitments from the world's wealthiest countries to reduce poverty in Africa and to do more to combat the effects of climate change. A $50 billion aid package for Africa was agreed on, but progress on climate change was more limited, as Blair's close relationship with Bush was not enough to overcome U.S. objections to specific measures to reduce carbon emissions. Separately, Blair made little progress on his goals of propelling the EU toward free-market measures and away from subsidies, especially for agriculture. Blair's plans were blocked, above all, by French Pres. Jacques Chirac. The two men had had a frosty relationship since the start of the Iraq war, a conflict that France opposed.

As Blair entered his third term, he was widely regarded as a lame-duck leader because of his decision to announce in advance that he would not contest another general election. His sure-footed response to the terrorist bombings in London on July 7, when he won praise from politicians of all parties for his calmness and determination, revived his authority, however, and quelled—for the time being—talk that the prime minister might be forced out of office earlier than he intended.   (PETER KELLNER)

Bolton, John R.

On Aug. 1, 2005, Pres. George W. Bush named John R. Bolton as U.S. ambassador to the UN in a recess appointment, made while Congress was not in session. Bush had nominated Bolton for the UN post on March 7, but hearings in the Senate Foreign Relations Committee were extraordinarily rancorous. When it became clear that the Republican-controlled Senate committee could not muster a majority in support of Bolton, the nomination was sent to the full Senate without a recommendation. Two attempts to end a filibuster and bring the nomination to a vote then failed.

John Robert Bolton was born on Nov. 20, 1948, in Baltimore, Md. He was educated at Yale University (B.A., 1970; J.D., 1974), and much of his subsequent career was spent in government jobs. A right-wing Republican, he began his federal service in the administration of Pres. Ronald Reagan, holding positions in the U.S. Agency for International Development and as assistant attorney general (1985–89). From 1989 to 1993, under Pres. George H.W. Bush, he was assistant secretary of state for international organization affairs. During the 1990s Bolton was active in prominent conservative organizations, including the American Enterprise Institute, at which he was a vice president during 1997–2001, and the Project for the New American Century. He also was an official of the Republican National Committee.

In the administration of George W. Bush, Bolton was undersecretary of state for arms control and international security affairs. He supported a number of reversals of U.S. foreign policy positions, including retraction of support for the International Criminal Court and withdrawal from the Anti-Ballistic Missile Treaty. Bolton ran the administration's Proliferation Security Initiative, which attempted to broker bilateral agreements on arms control between the U.S. and partner countries, and in 2001 he succeeded in torpedoing an international conference on bioweapons over verification issues. For a time he was a member of the U.S. delegation in talks with North Korea, but he was removed in 2003 after he made derogatory comments about that country's leader.

Although Bolton had supporters, particularly those who advocated a strong unilateral U.S. foreign policy and reform of the UN, there were equally fervent critics. Among the most serious charges against him were that he had consistently pursued his own notions of what U.S. diplomacy should be, even when his views were not consistent with U.S. government policy; that he had advocated an independent Taiwan despite a long-standing U.S. one-China policy; that he had pressured intelligence analysts to report findings that supported his own views and had attempted to

have workers transferred or fired when they did not do so; and that he had even given false testimony before Congress in 2003. Bolton commonly scorned the UN as well as international treaties and campaigned against a third term for International Atomic Energy Agency Director General Mohamed ElBaradei. (*See* NOBEL PRIZES.) Indeed, one of Bolton's first actions at the UN was to demand major changes to the draft of a document for reform of the body.   (ROBERT RAUCH)

Bruckheimer, Jerry

Already one of Hollywood's most successful movie producers—his explosion-laden, action-packed films had grossed some $3 billion at the U.S. box office—Jerry Bruckheimer proved he could also make a bang on the small screen. In 2005 he made television history as the first producer to have 10 shows air in a single season (2005–06). This feat came after six of his series—*CSI: Crime Scene Investigation, CSI: Miami, Without a Trace, Cold Case, CSI: NY,* and *The Amazing Race*—finished the 2004–05 season in the top 25, with *CSI: Crime Scene Investigation* the number one scripted show. Much of his success could be credited to his unique brand of "feature television," in which he brought elements of moviemaking, including high production standards and intricate story lines, to the small screen. In addition to his TV work, Bruckheimer continued to produce films, and two highly anticipated projects were the sequels to *Pirates of the Caribbean: The Curse of the Black Pearl* (2003), a family-friendly swashbuckler that starred Johnny Depp (*q.v.*) and grossed more than $650 million worldwide.

TV producer Jerry Bruckheimer

Jerome Bruckheimer was born on Sept. 21, 1945, in Detroit. After graduating from the University of Arizona in 1965, he embarked on an advertising career in New York City and eventually began producing TV commercials. His interest soon turned to film, and in the early 1970s he moved to California. He attracted attention with *American Gigolo* (1979) and had his first major success with *Flashdance* (1983). Bruckheimer worked with Don Simpson to produce the surprise hit, and the production company the two men had formed went on to churn out a string of blockbusters, including the Eddie Murphy comedy *Beverly Hills Cop* (1984); *Top Gun* (1986), which established Tom Cruise as a star; and *Bad Boys* (1995). That same year Bruckheimer ended his partnership with Simpson and launched a highly successful solo career, scoring such hits as *Armageddon* (1998), *Black Hawk Down* (2001), and *National Treasure* (2004).

In the late 1990s Bruckheimer began producing TV series, and in 2000 he had his first success with *CSI: Crime Scene Investigation*, a drama about forensic investigators in Las Vegas, Nev. The series was praised for its realism and distinct look, qualities that became trademarks of his programs, and its immense popularity eventually led to spin-offs set in Miami, Fla. (2002), and New York City (2004). Other Bruckheimer series came to include the crime dramas *Without a Trace* (2002) and *Cold Case* (2003) as well as the travel competition *The Amazing Race* (2001). The shows all aired on CBS, and by the end of the 2003–04 season, they had helped make the channel the most watched in the U.S. In the 2005–06 season Bruckheimer introduced four new shows—*E-Ring, Close to Home, Modern Men,* and *Just Legal,* although the latter was canceled after several episodes.

(AMY TIKKANEN)

Bush, Laura

First lady Laura Bush set aside her reluctance to enter the political arena and in 2004 became a very prominent and popular campaigner for her husband, George W. Bush, who sought reelection; her 80% popularity rating in the polls (the president's was 47%) was viewed by pollsters as a political asset for the president, who started his second term in office in 2005.

It soon became clear that the first lady would assume a higher profile in the president's second term. Days after the inaugural galas, in which she stepped out in a fitted Oscar de la Renta gown that accentuated a figure reshaped by yoga and weightlifting, she hired a new social secretary and fired the longtime White House chef. On May 1 she delighted attendees at a Washington press dinner with a lighthearted roast of the president when she interrupted her husband's remarks with a string of zingers. Later that month she gamely embarked alone on a five-day goodwill tour of the Middle East at a time when regard for the U.S. throughout much of the region was particularly low. Addressing the World Economic Forum in Amman, Jordan, Laura Bush called for increased attention to women's rights and greater access to education as a means of combating terrorism. In Jerusalem she conceded that the U.S. had real work to do to improve its image in the region, but she also

strongly endorsed the Bush administration's policies there. While in Cairo she taped an episode of the television show *Alam Simsim,* the Egyptian equivalent of *Sesame Street.* In July she was warmly received in South Africa, Tanzania, and Rwanda, where she served as a goodwill ambassador.

Laura Lane Welch was born on Nov. 4, 1946, in Midland, Texas. She graduated from Southern Methodist University with a B.S. in education in 1968 and taught in elementary schools in Dallas and Houston from 1969 until 1972. After earning (1973) a master's degree in library science from the University of Texas, she worked as a librarian in Houston and Austin. She met George W. Bush in June 1974, and after a whirlwind courtship they married on November 5. Soon afterward, when her husband began an unsuccessful campaign for the U.S. Congress, Laura Bush made him promise that she would never be asked to give a speech. In 1981 she gave birth to twin daughters, Barbara and Jenna. Following her husband's election to the Texas governor's office in 1994, she promoted literacy programs and raised funds for public libraries. After the presidential campaign of 2000, which saw her

© Brooks Kraft/Corbis

First lady Laura Bush

address the Republican national convention, Laura Bush pursued a similar role as the nation's first lady, continuing to promote reading and establishing a foundation to raise funds for libraries. She quietly began, however, to assume a higher profile as an advocate for her husband's administration on such issues as democracy, women's education, and health, but she maintained that her own views on such issues as abortion, the death penalty, and gay rights would remain private.

(JANET MOREDOCK)

Cameron, David

On Dec. 6, 2005, David Cameron was elected leader of Britain's Conservative Party at the age of 39 and after only four years in Parliament. He faced the daunting task of reviving the fortunes of the Tories, who had

dominated British politics for most of the 20th century but had sustained three of the heaviest election defeats (1997, 2001, and 2005) in its history.

David William Donald Cameron was born in London on Oct. 9, 1966. Unlike the previous six Conservative leaders, he was born into a family with both wealth and an aristocratic pedigree. He was a descendent of King William IV. (Cameron's wife, Samantha, could also claim royal blood: she was descended from King Charles II and his mistress Nell Gwyn.) Cameron, the son of a prosperous businessman, went to Eton College and Brasenose College, Oxford, from which he graduated (1988) with a first-class degree in philosophy, politics, and economics. At Oxford he was a member of the Bullingdon Club, a males-only dining club with a reputation for heavy drinking and occasionally riotous behaviour. In 2005 Cameron refused to answer questions about whether he had taken cocaine in his student days.

After Oxford, Cameron joined the Conservative Party Research Department. In 1992 he became a special adviser to Norman Lamont, then chancellor of the Exchequer, and the following year he undertook the same role for Michael Howard, then home secretary. Cameron joined the media company Carlton Communications in 1994 as director of corporate affairs. He stayed at Carlton until entering Parliament in 2001 as MP for Witney, northwest of London.

Cameron quickly attracted attention as the leading member of a new generation of Conservatives: young, moderate, and charismatic. He was widely compared to Labour Prime Minister Tony Blair (*q.v.*), who had acquired a similar reputation when he entered Parliament 18 years earlier. After just two years as an MP, Cameron was appointed to his party's "front bench"— making him a leading Conservative spokesman in the House of Commons. In 2004 Howard, by then party leader, appointed his young protégé to the post of head of policy coordination, which put Cameron in charge of preparing the Conservatives' 2005 election manifesto. The party's heavy defeat provoked Howard's resignation and a leadership contest.

Cameron's astonishingly self-assured speech, made without notes, at the party's annual conference in October transformed his reputation, especially when compared with the flat, uninspiring speech given by the early front-runner, the more right-wing David Davis. In the first ballot of party MPs, former chancellor Kenneth Clarke, who had been expected to be the moderates' standard-bearer, was eliminated. In the second ballot Cameron won 90 votes, versus 57 for Davis and 51 for another right-winger, Liam Fox. Under party rules the names of the top two candidates were then put to a ballot of local party members, and Cameron defeated Davis by 68–32%. In his first shadow cabinet Cameron reached across the party's political spectrum and

David Cameron, British Tory leader

offered posts to Davis, Fox, and other former opponents. (PETER KELLNER)

Camilla, duchess of Cornwall

On April 9, 2005, Camilla Parker Bowles married Charles, prince of Wales and heir to the British throne, in a civil ceremony followed by a church service of prayer and dedication. Technically, upon her marriage she became the princess of Wales, and when Charles eventually became king, she would become his queen. At the time of her wedding, however, she announced that she did not wish to be called princess and would not wish to be called queen. Instead, Camilla opted for the title duchess of Cornwall (from one of Charles's junior titles) and declared that when her husband ascended to the throne, she would adopt the title Her Royal Highness the Princess Consort. In view of her relationship with Charles over many years and her unpopularity with some sections of British public opinion—particularly in relation to the public's memory of his first wife, Diana, princess of Wales—the new duchess had little real alternative.

Camilla Rosemary Shand was born in London on July 17, 1947. She was the great-granddaughter of Alice Keppel, the mistress of Charles's great-great-grandfather King Edward VII, and was brought up to be familiar with the world of royalty and Britain's upper classes. She met Charles at a polo match in 1970, before either of them was married. Many in their circle expected Charles to propose to her, but he delayed doing so. In 1973 she married Andrew Parker Bowles, an army officer and friend of Charles; they had two children and remained in the prince's circle of friends. Camilla was a keen horsewoman and took part in rural gentry activities, including fox hunting (an activity made illegal in 2005). Her lifestyle survived largely unscathed when she was one of the "names" (investors) in Lloyds of London who lost money in a scandal that engulfed many Lloyds insurance underwriters in the 1980s.

Some years after her marriage, Camilla resumed her relationship with Charles. In 1995 she was divorced from Parker Bowles (who soon afterward married his own mistress). Diana, whom Charles had married in 1981, blamed Camilla for the 1992 breakup of her

marriage. Even though Charles and Diana divorced in 1996, it seemed unlikely that the prince would choose to offend public opinion by marrying Camilla. There was also much debate over whether Charles, as the future head of the Church of England, should be allowed to remarry. Diana's death in 1997 changed the situation to a certain extent, but Camilla had some difficulty winning the hearts of both the British people and, perhaps more important, Charles's mother, Queen Elizabeth II. Charles and Camilla began to appear together in public and gradually came to be accepted as a couple. When their engagement was announced on Feb. 10, 2005, the queen publicly bestowed her blessing.

Though the wedding was set for April 8, it had to be postponed to allow Charles to attend the funeral of Pope John Paul II. The low-key wedding proved to be a success with the British public, and by year's end even Camilla's critics were acknowledging that the duchess had settled into her new role in the royal family. (PETER KELLNER)

Chávez, Hugo

Venezuelan Pres. Hugo Chávez made headlines throughout 2005 with his escalating anti-American rhetoric and increased efforts to implement "21st-century socialism." Relations with the U.S., already contentious, rapidly worsened amid his repeated threats to end oil sales to the U.S., Venezuela's main customer, and his purchases of arms and other military equipment, acquisitions he claimed were necessary to defend Venezuela from the "imperialistic power." Chávez's allegation that the U.S. administration of Pres. George W. Bush was plotting his assassination garnered much attention in August when Pat Robertson, an influential American television evangelist, said that the U.S. should "take him out." Although the White House dismissed the statement, it viewed the firebrand leader as a destabilizing presence in South America and pursued a policy of containment. Tensions continued in November at the Summit of Americas in Argentina, where Chávez led protests against Bush ("Mr. Danger") and derided a U.S.-backed free-trade agreement. While worrisome to the U.S., his anti-American policies were extremely popular with Venezuelans, as were his efforts to end poverty in the country. After years of delays, Chávez's socialist revolution gained momentum as more cooperatives and subsidized supermarkets were established and greater access was provided to education, low-cost housing, and health care.

Hugo Rafael Chávez Frías was born on July 28, 1954, in Sabaneta, Venez. He graduated from a Venezuelan military academy in 1975 and entered the army. Chávez became increasingly critical of the government, which he viewed as corrupt, and in 1992 led an unsuccessful coup against Pres. Carlos Andrés

Pérez. Imprisoned until 1994, Chávez, an admirer of Simón Bolívar ("the Liberator"), subsequently cofounded the left-wing Fifth Republic Movement and in 1998 ran for president, promising to bring "true democracy" and populism to Venezuela. His platform proved popular with the poor, who accounted for some 80% of the population, and Chávez won a landslide victory.

After taking office in 1999, Chávez oversaw the passage of a new constitution that radically reshaped the government and granted him greater powers. He also increased control of the oil industry, using its revenues to begin his "Bolivarian Revolution." Although reelected president in 2000, Chávez faced a growing number of detractors, who viewed him as a populist demagogue and feared his growing power, and a massive protest march led to his ouster on April 12, 2002. The U.S. government—which was concerned about his close ties with Cuba and spreading influence in Latin America—appeared to support the overthrow, but it denied direct involvement. Two days later, however, Chávez was returned to power. Although unrest with his rule continued—a 2002–03 general strike greatly disrupted the country, and in 2004 enough signatures were gathered for a recall referendum, which was ultimately defeated—Chávez's power base continued to grow. In December 2005 his supporters took complete control of the legislature after most of the opposition candidates boycotted the election.

(AMY TIKKANEN)

Chertoff, Michael

In 2005 the biggest challenge for Michael Chertoff, the secretary of the U.S. Department of Homeland Security (DHS), which was created in response to the Sept. 11, 2001, attacks in the United States, was not an external terrorist threat but a domestic natural disaster. In August, Hurricane Katrina slammed into the Gulf Coast in Louisiana, Mississippi, and Alabama, killing more than a thousand Americans and leaving hundreds of thousands homeless. FEMA (the Federal Emergency Management Agency), since 2003 subordinate to DHS, bore primary responsibility for providing immediate assistance to victims of natural disasters of this sort and for managing the recovery effort. Accordingly, Chertoff was one of the federal authorities who was faulted for the slowness and inadequacy of the official response in the aftermath of Hurricane Katrina. The disjointed actions of his cabinet-level department—despite its confident statements—compounded the human tragedy among those who were stranded or made refugees by the storm.

Chertoff was born on Nov. 28, 1953, in Elizabeth, N.J., and was educated at Harvard University (A.B., 1975; J.D., 1978), graduating with top honours. He was admitted to the bar in the District of Columbia (1980), New York (1987), and New Jersey (1990). He began his career as a federal prosecutor, and, after receiving his law degree, he served as a clerk for Supreme Court Associate Justice William J. Brennan, Jr., and later worked in the U.S. Attorney's Office, becoming U.S. attorney for the District of New Jersey in 1990. In 1994–96 he was special counsel for the U.S. Senate Whitewater Committee. He worked in the private sector at Latham & Watkins in 1980–83 and again in 1994–2001. He held dual U.S. and Israeli citizenship.

Chertoff first worked for George W. Bush as an adviser in his campaign for the presidency in 2000, and following the election he served in the Department of Justice Criminal Division. There he advocated the detention of hundreds of people of Arab ancestry following the 9/11 attacks, a position for which he was later criticized. Chertoff served as a judge on the U.S. Court of Appeals for the 3rd Circuit from June 2003.

In February 2005 Chertoff was appointed secretary of homeland security, the second person to hold the post, upon the retirement of Tom Ridge and after an earlier nominee, Bernie Kerik, withdrew his candidacy. Chertoff received immediate and unanimous confirmation by the Senate, and supporters lauded him as a disciplined prosecutor who would take a hard-line stance against terrorism. He set about reorganizing the sprawling DHS, focusing on improving the screening of passengers boarding airplanes, the security of the U.S. borders with Mexico and Canada, and the safety of urban mass transit. Chertoff attempted to balance the needs for homeland security with civil liberties, on which Americans place a high value.   (TOM MICHAEL)

Coldplay

Repeatedly honoured with music industry awards but famously demeaned by tastemaker Alan McGee for producing music for "bed wetters," the guitar-based British rock group Coldplay seldom elicited neutral responses. If some hated the band, many more loved it, and Coldplay topped the charts in 2005 with its much-hyped third studio album, *X & Y*. When the album's first single, "Speed of Sound," debuted at number eight, the quartet became the first British group since the Beatles to enter the U.S. charts in the Top Ten.

Coldplay began in 1998 at University College, London, with the pairing of pianist-vocalist Chris Martin (b. March 2, 1977, Exeter, Eng.) and guitarist Jon Buckland (b. Sept. 11, 1977, London). Fellow students Guy Berryman (b. April 12, 1978, Kirkcaldy, Scot.), a bass guitarist, and Will Champion (b. July 31, 1978, Southampton, Eng.), a guitarist who later switched to the drums, rounded out the group. Following the self-financed extended-play release *Safety*, Coldplay penetrated the U.K. Top 100 in 1999 with the single "Brothers & Sisters" on the independent Fierce Panda label before signing with major label Parlophone. With the 2000 release of the hauntingly melodic single "Yellow," featuring Martin's impassioned, bittersweet vocals, Coldplay scored a huge hit. The acoustic-tinged album *Parachutes* (2000), which showcased "Yellow" as well as such other hit songs as "Shiver" and "Trouble," sold millions, drew comparisons with critics' darlings Radiohead and Tim Buckley, and earned Coldplay a Grammy Award for best alternative album.

The more ambitious *A Rush of Blood to the Head* (2002), containing another instant pop classic, "Clocks," went multiplatinum and earned Coldplay a slew of British and American awards (including two more Grammys). Together the group's first two albums sold more than 20 million copies. A concert album, *Live 2003*, followed. Determined to explore new ground, Coldplay then spent 18 months recording *X & Y*, jettisoning a number of the project's most experimental recordings on the way to an album of arena-friendly rock anthems.

A study in contradictions, Coldplay willfully sought and attained the "big band" status of its role model, U2, even as it refused to stoke the music industry's standard star-making machinery. Despite the group's democratic structure (all four members shared songwriting credits and equal royalties), Martin became the face of Coldplay, an international celebrity whose fame resulted as much from his marriage to American movie star Gwyneth Paltrow as it did from his distinctive plaintive singing, good looks, and high-profile advocacy of fair trade for small farmers in less-developed countries. Coldplay reportedly donated 10% of its earnings to a variety of social causes. Not merely content that his band had joined U2 at the top of the world, Martin, like Bono, seemed determined to save it.

(JEFF WALLENFELDT)

Coulter, Ann

Pundit Ann Coulter was not the first American commentator, on either the left or the right, to reach celebrity status by unleashing a consistent barrage of outrageous polemic invective in the national media, but the conservative Coulter could be even more extreme, more steadfast, and—perhaps most important—even more entertaining than her predecessors. In 2005 she appeared on the cover of the April 25 issue of *Time* magazine, reaffirming her worth as a media drawing card and a lightning rod for controversy. On TV, in best-selling books, and in a syndicated column, Coulter hammered the American left with accusations of hypocrisy and treason. Her brash rhetoric was intended primarily as an attempt to taunt her opposition into arguing with her. To her delight, it often worked. Coulter insisted that many of her more controversial statements were meant to be humorous—wild exaggerations used to prove a larger point and to amuse herself and her friends. One of her most publicized remarks came shortly after the Sept. 11, 2001, attacks in New York City and Washington, D.C., in which a friend of hers had died. Reacting to video footage showing Muslims celebrating in the streets, Coulter wrote, "We should invade their countries, kill their leaders, and convert them to Christianity." Coulter said that her detractors had taken that statement, and others, too literally.

Ann Hart Coulter was born on Dec. 8, 1961, in New York City and raised in New Canaan, Conn. With a father who was a corporate lawyer and two older brothers, Coulter learned to be verbally aggressive at a young age. In fact, she claimed to have argued the merits of the Vietnam War with her kindergarten teacher. She received a bachelor's degree (1984) from Cornell University, Ithaca, N.Y., and graduated with a law degree (1988) from the University of Michigan, where she served as an editor of the *Michigan Law Review*. In 1994 she left a private law firm in New York to work for U.S. Sen. Spencer Abraham in Washington, D.C. In 1996 Coulter was hired to work as a commentator on the cable news channel MSNBC and immediately made a name for herself with her sarcastic, over-the-top approach to political debate. The following year she was fired after quipping, "No

Coldplay (from left): Guy Berryman, Will Champion, Chris Martin, and Jon Buckland

Conservative pundit Ann Coulter

wonder you guys lost," during the broadcast of an argument with a disabled Vietnam veteran. Nevertheless, she continued to be invited onto other TV programs to appear as a political pundit. She was also a regular contributor to *Human Events*, a conservative weekly, and in 1999 she began writing a column for United Press Syndicate.

Coulter's first book, *High Crimes and Misdemeanors: The Case Against Bill Clinton* (1998), was a product of her work on Paula Jones's sexual-harassment suit against President Clinton. Subsequent books included *Slander: Liberal Lies About the American Right* (2002), *Treason: Liberal Treachery from the Cold War to the War on Terrorism* (2003), and *How to Talk to a Liberal (if You Must)* (2004).

(ANTHONY G. CRAINE)

Dallaire, Lieut. Gen. Roméo

By the time that Canadian Lieut. Gen. Roméo A. Dallaire left Rwanda in 1994, the ill-fated UN peacekeeping mission he led had been forced to watch helplessly as extremist ethnic Hutu butchered thousands of Tutsi and moderate Hutu. Wracked with guilt over the debacle, he sank into a despair that nearly ended in suicide in 2000. By 2005, however, Dallaire had turned his life around to become a voice of conscience for global humanitarianism. In March he was awarded the Pearson Peace Medal by Canada's governor-general for his international service, and that same month Prime Minister Paul Martin appointed him to the Senate, Canada's upper house of Parliament.

Dallaire, the son of a Canadian soldier, was born on June 25, 1946, in Denekamp, Neth. He joined the Canadian army in 1964 and earned a B.S. degree at the Royal Military College in Kingston, Ont., in 1969. During his career as an artilleryman, he held various jobs

in Canada and Germany, including command of the 5e Régiment d'Artillerie Légère du Canada. He was promoted in 1989 to the rank of brigadier general.

In 1993 Dallaire took command of the UN Assistance Mission for Rwanda. As a lightly armed force of approximately 2,500 troops, UNAMIR was given a mandate to oversee the peace agreement ending a civil war. The death of the Rwandan president, however, whose plane was shot down over Kigali airport in April 1994, triggered events that quickly became a gambit by extremist Hutu to exterminate the Tutsi population. During the bloody chaos, Dallaire ordered 10 Belgian soldiers under his command to protect the new Rwandan prime minister. The Belgians and the prime minister were taken hostage by Hutu and later found murdered. As the situation deteriorated, Dallaire pleaded with his UN superiors in New York to send reinforcements, but his requests fell on deaf ears. Confronted with an impossible situation, Dallaire consolidated his troops in a few urban areas and was able to protect some civilians. By the time the rampage subsided in July 1994, more than 800,000 people had been murdered and 2,000,000 made refugees.

Dallaire returned to Canada, and from September 1994 to October 1995, he served simultaneously as deputy commander of Land Force Command and commander of the 1st Canadian Division. Other senior appointments followed, but he sank into a despair that eventually led to a suicide attempt. Suffering from post-traumatic stress disorder, Dallaire was medically released from the army in 2000.

Palme d'Or laureates Jean-Pierre and Luc Dardenne

By 2003 Dallaire had come to terms with his Rwandan nightmare and published the autobiography *Shake Hands with the Devil—the Failure of Humanity in Rwanda*, which won the Governor General's Award for English-language nonfiction and later was made into a documentary film. He received a fellowship at

Harvard University's Carr Center for Human Rights Policy in 2004 to pursue research in conflict resolution. (PETER SARACINO)

Dardenne, Jean-Pierre and Luc

In 2005, with their film *L'Enfant*, the Belgian brothers Jean-Pierre and Luc Dardenne for the second time in six years won the Cannes Festival's Palme d'Or for best film. Only filmmakers Emir Kusturica and Imamura Shohei had previously won twice. Two other pairs of brothers—Vittorio and Paolo Taviani, in 1977, and Ethan and Joel Coen, in 1991—had earned a Palme d'Or.

Like *Rosetta* (1999), the Dardennes' first Palme d'Or winner, *L'Enfant* explored life in an impoverished, gritty, industrial region in French-speaking southern Belgium, particularly around the city of Seraing, where the brothers grew up; the region was known for its steel mills, coal mines, and endemic unemployment. Both award-winning films also examined the circumstances of people on the margins of Belgian society. Whereas *Rosetta* limned the life of a young woman determined to find work in order to escape the grinding poverty of her life, *L'Enfant* was essentially a young man's story. Its protagonist, Bruno, is a 20-year-old petty criminal whose life is changed when his 18-year-old girlfriend, Sonia, bears their child. The story was inspired, according to the brothers, by an image that haunted them during the shooting of another of their films—that of a young woman alone seen daily aimlessly pushing a baby carriage.

Jean-Pierre Dardenne was born on April 21, 1951, in Engis and Luc on March 10, 1954, in

Awirs. The elder brother studied acting in Brussels, while the younger took a degree in philosophy. The video work of one of Jean-Pierre's teachers, French director Armand Gatti, provided their inspiration to use videotape to document the lives and struggles of working-class Belgians. It also determined their signature camera style: use of the hand-held camera and a preference for improvised dialogue. Beginning in the 1970s they made a number of documentaries, establishing their own production company, Dérives, in 1975. To date the company had produced more than 60 documentaries, including *Le Chant du rossignol* (1978), about the Belgian Resistance movement in World War II, and *Leçons d'une université volante* (1982), concerning Polish immigration. The brothers expanded the production company in 1981, creating Film Dérives Fiction. With the latter company they made their first fiction feature, *Falsch* (1986), adapted from the play by Belgian playwright René Kalisky, and *Je pense à vous* (1992). In 1994 they further expanded their company to create Les Films du Fleuve. Among their other noteworthy nondocumentaries were the art-house favourites *La Promesse* (1996) and *Le Fils* (2002).　　　(KATHLEEN KUIPER)

Dell, Michael

During the first calendar quarter of 2005, Michael Dell's eponymous company, Dell, Inc., the world's leading seller of personal computers, shipped some 8.7 million PCs and attained a worldwide market share of just under 19%. In its fiscal first quarter, ended in April, the firm's net earnings per share rose 32% from a year earlier, setting a company record, while revenue rose 16%. The PC maker's phenomenal success could well be seen as a personal triumph for its 40-year-old board chairman and founder.

Dell, the son of a Houston orthodontist, was born on Feb. 23, 1965. He started his PC business (originally called PCs Limited) in 1984 while he was still a college student. Initially he operated the firm from a dormitory room at the University of Texas at Austin with $1,000 in start-up capital; by the second half of his freshman year, Dell had sold $80,000 worth of computers and had taken a leave of absence from college. He never graduated.

Dell's business philosophy was to gain PC market share through a combination of cutting costs, reducing delivery time, and providing customer service. To do so, he hired outside industry executives, both to fill jobs in the company and to act as personal mentors, and emphasized direct sales outside the usual retail outlets. In 1992 Dell became the youngest CEO in history to have his firm enter *Fortune* magazine's list of the top 500 corporations.

In his book *Direct from Dell: Strategies That Revolutionized an Industry* (1999), Dell revealed that he had been driven to achieve even when he was in grade school. When he was eight years old, he applied to take the high-school equivalency test in hopes of avoiding nine more years of school. Much later, in a 2005 video conference with college students at Abilene (Texas) Christian University, Dell said his advice to young entrepreneurs was, in part, "Don't be afraid to make mistakes. That's how you learn, so I believe a lot in trial and error and course corrections." He also urged students to think about business in global terms and to be prepared for continuous learning throughout their careers.

In 2004 Dell stepped down as CEO of the company, but he remained chairman. He served on the Foundation Board of the World Economic Forum and the executive committee of the International Business Council. He also was on the U.S. President's Council of Advisors on Science and Technology and sat on the governing board of the Indian School of Business in Hyderabad.

Through the Michael & Susan Dell Foundation, established by Dell and his wife in 1999, he used some of his personal wealth to help children around the world by focusing on health, education, safety, youth development, and early childhood care. The foundation, which in 2005 had an endowment of more than $1 billion, gave millions of dollars to help victims of the 2004 tsunami in southern Asia.

　　　(STEVE ALEXANDER)

Depp, Johnny

It was appropriate that American actor Johnny Depp, billed by many as Hollywood's ultimate outsider, would find his greatest box-office success as a pirate. His performance as Captain Jack Sparrow in *Pirates of the Caribbean: The Curse of the Black Pearl* (2003)

© Vince Bucci/Getty Images

Johnny Depp leaving his mark in Hollywood

earned Depp his first Academy Award nomination in 2004, and he spent much of 2005 at work on the next two films in the *Pirates* franchise. Depp maintained his distance from the Hollywood mainstream, though, and the film roles that he chose continued to reflect a preference for brilliant misfits. In January he received his second Oscar nomination, this time for his role as Peter Pan creator James M. Barrie in *Finding Neverland* (2004). During 2005 he starred in two films by a longtime friend, director Tim Burton. Depp's twisted turn as

the reclusive candy baron Willy Wonka in *Charlie and the Chocolate Factory* packed theatres throughout the summer, and he provided the voice of the unfortunate groom in Burton's macabre animated tale *Corpse Bride*. While some critics saw parallels between the mannerisms of Depp's Wonka and those of pop singer Michael Jackson, Depp maintained that any similarities were purely coincidental. In August Depp paid tribute to gonzo journalist Hunter S. Thompson by financing a $2 million memorial service at Thompson's Woody Creek, Colo., home.

John Christopher Depp II was born on June 9, 1963, in Owensboro, Ky. He was the youngest of four children and dealt with his family's frequent moves by acting out in school and at home. To calm him, his mother gave him a guitar. He took to it immediately, and by age 16 he had dropped out of school to focus on his music. His band, the Kids, relocated to Los Angeles, and soon after that he married Lori Anne Allison. Depp struggled as a musician, and his wife suggested that he contact her friend Nicolas Cage for some acting work. Cage arranged for him to audition with Wes Craven, and Depp made his film debut as a teen eaten by his own bed in *A Nightmare on Elm Street* (1984). More work was slow to come, and the strain led to his divorce from Allison the following year. His professional break came in 1987 with the premiere of *21 Jump Street*, a TV police series that capitalized on Depp's smoldering good looks. He left the show in 1990 and worked on distancing himself from the heartthrob image he had acquired. That year saw the release of John Waters's *Cry-Baby* and Tim Burton's *Edward Scissorhands*, two films by maverick directors that showcased Depp's range. His later work included Burton projects *Ed Wood* (1994) and *Sleepy Hollow* (1999), Jim Jarmusch's *Dead Man* (1995), Terry Gilliam's *Fear and Loathing in Las Vegas* (1998), and Roman Polanski's *The Ninth Gate* (1999). While filming *The Ninth Gate* in France, Depp met actress Vanessa Paradis. He moved to France shortly thereafter, and the couple had two children.

　　　(MICHAEL RAY)

Döpfner, Mathias

In 2005 Mathias Döpfner, the CEO of German newspaper and magazine publisher Axel Springer Verlag AG, set his sights on Springer's ambitious growth campaign, particularly the $4.4 billion purchase of ProSiebenSat.1 Media AG, Germany's largest television concern. The acquisition, endorsed by shareholders but still awaiting regulatory approval at year's end, would expand Springer's markets by adding broadcasting to its traditional print-media mix. More significant, it would move the firm into direct competition with the privately owned German media giant Bertelsmann AG.

Döpfner was born on Jan. 5, 1963, in Bonn, Ger. He studied musicology and theatrical arts before he joined (1982) the staff of the daily *Frankfurter Allgemeine Zeitung*. Later he worked in public relations (1988–90) and held various jobs in publishing, including editorial jobs with the Berlin weekly *Wochenpost*

(1994–96) and the newspaper *Hamburger Morgenpost* (1996–98). Döpfner joined Axel Springer Verlag in 1998 as editor in chief of *Die Welt*, Springer's daily news counterpart to its flashier tabloid, *Bild*. Within four years of his arrival, the 39-year-old Döpfner was named chief executive of Axel Springer. He cut costs, expanded business lines, and in 2004 increased Springer's earnings by 23%.

Döpfner's occasional forays into the editorial pages echoed the actions and opinions of the late Axel Springer, the company's notoriously outspoken founder, and earned him the crucial approval of the founder's widow, Friede Springer, who controlled 60% of the firm's stock. Indeed, Döpfner was known for expressing his politically conservative opinions in newspapers around the world, including *The Wall Street Journal*. He made a splash in 2004 when he published his provocative essay "Europe, Thy Name Is Cowardice," in which he decried European tolerance and accommodation of deadly enemies. Döpfner's managerial moves addressed a world driven by global competition and instantaneous communication. Springer's acquisition of ProSiebenSat.1, its first step outside publishing, would give the company access to five German television channels that claimed a combined 45% market share. The move would also permit advertisers to maximize their presence across Springer's newspapers, magazines, TV programming, and Web sites. Some critics, however, asserted that the deal merely expanded the outlets through which Döpfner could voice his opinions, which included support of the Christian Democratic Union, Israel, and U.S. foreign policy.

The acquisition of ProSiebenSat.1 in Springer's home country complemented the firm's expansion into emerging markets. Döpfner placed special emphasis on gaining—and holding—prominence in new markets, especially in Eastern Europe and Asia. The firm drew upon the success of its photo-rich *Bild*—Germany's best-selling newspaper—before it launched (2003) the Polish newspaper *Fakt*, which by 2005 was Poland's most popular daily. Döpfner was continuing to exploit realistic growth opportunities to expand his company's reach—and its profits.

(SARAH FORBES ORWIG)

Duncan, Tim

In game seven of the 2005 National Basketball Association (NBA) finals, Tim Duncan of the San Antonio Spurs proved why he was called the "ultimate winner." Overcoming criticism of his earlier play in the series, he registered game-high points (25) and rebounds (11) to lead the Spurs to an 81–74 victory over the defending champion Detroit Pistons. It was Duncan's third NBA title, and with his late heroics—in the second half he scored 17 points and captured 8 rebounds—the 2.13-m (7-ft)-tall power forward became just the fourth player to have won three finals Most Valuable Player (MVP) awards. Although Duncan had become one of the game's greatest players, he was a reluctant superstar whose modesty and stoicism were as legendary as his play.

Timothy Theodore Duncan was born on April 25, 1976, in St. Croix, U.S. Virgin Islands. He excelled in freestyle swimming and had hopes of competing in the Olympics. In 1989, however, Hurricane Hugo destroyed most of the island's swimming pools, and Duncan was left unable to train. He began playing basketball and proved a natural at the sport, but he attracted little interest from college scouts. In 1993 Duncan entered Wake Forest University, Winston-Salem, N.C., where he gained national attention with his all-around play and poise. He was predicted to be the number one pick in the NBA draft after his junior year, but he elected to stay in school, honouring a promise he had made to his mother, who had died of cancer in 1990. In his final season he received the John R. Wooden Award as the outstanding collegiate player in the U.S.

After graduating in 1997, Duncan was the Spurs' first overall pick. He and teammate David Robinson formed the dominating tandem known as the "Twin Towers," and in 1998 Duncan was named Rookie of the Year. The following season he averaged 24 points and 17 rebounds in the finals against the New York Knicks to give the Spurs the franchise's first NBA title and earn himself the finals MVP award. In 2000 he was named co-MVP of the All-Star game, but he later suffered a knee injury that ended the season for him and prevented the Spurs from defending their title. The injury also forced him to withdraw from the U.S. men's Olympic basketball team. Duncan's performance in the 2001–02 season—in which he became the 14th NBA player to have registered more than 2,000 points and 1,000

© Jeff Haynes/AFP/Getty Images

NBA MVP Tim Duncan at the SBC Center

rebounds in a single season—secured him the league's MVP award. In 2003 he led the Spurs to victory over the New Jersey Nets, scoring a triple double (21 points, 20 rebounds, and 10 assists) in the decisive sixth game to claim the

NBA title and his second finals MVP award. That year he again was named MVP for his regular-season play. In 2004 Duncan finally realized his dream of competing in the Olympics, helping the U.S. men's team win a bronze medal at the Athens Games.

(AMY TIKKANEN)

Dutilleux, Henri

The French composer Henri Dutilleux received the 2005 Ernst von Siemens Music Prize, considered the world's most prestigious award in music. Although his works bore influences of Claude Debussy, Albert Roussel, and Maurice Ravel, as well as of jazz, he wrote in a highly individual modernist style that conveyed a sense of spirituality. He had an affinity for variation form and liked to quote from other works, including his own. Known as a slow, painstaking worker, he produced a relatively small body of carefully crafted compositions that were frequently performed outside France, particularly in Britain and the U.S.

Henri Dutilleux was born in Angers, France, on Jan. 22, 1916, into a family that had produced painters and musicians. He was educated at the Paris Conservatoire beginning in 1933 and received the Grand Prix de Rome in 1938. Because of the outbreak of World War II, his study in Rome lasted only four months. In 1942 he worked at the Paris Opéra, and when the war ended, he began an association with Radio France that lasted until 1963. He taught composition at the École Normale de Musique from 1961 to 1970 and at the Paris Conservatoire in 1970–71. After that time he devoted himself entirely to composing.

Dutilleux wrote in a number of genres, including works for orchestra, various instrumental combinations, and solo instruments; chamber music; vocal works; and ballets, incidental music for the theatre, and film scores. He destroyed most music composed before World War II, and thus his first major work was a piano sonata premiered in 1948 by his wife, Geneviève Joy. A number of his works were written as commissions or for specific performers. These included *Symphony No. 2*, subtitled *Le double* for the use of a chamber orchestra within the orchestra, commissioned by the Boston Symphony Orchestra and the Koussevitzky Music Foundation (1959); *Métaboles*, commissioned by the Cleveland Orchestra and premiered in 1965; and *Tout un monde lointain*, for cello and orchestra, written for Mstislav Rostropovich (1970). *Ainsi la nuit*, a string quartet, also was commissioned by the Koussevitzky foundation (1977), and *Timbres, espace, mouvement* by Rostropovich for the National Symphony Orchestra in Washington, D.C. (1978). *L'Arbre des songes*, a concerto for violin, was written for Isaac Stern (1985). *Correspondances*, for soprano and orchestra, received its premiere in 2003.

Dutilleux was the recipient of many honours, including the Grand Prix National de la Musique (1967). The Koussevitzky International Recording Award for 1976 went to a recording of *Tout un monde lointain,* and a number of other recordings received Grands Prix du Disque. He was a Commander of the Legion of Honour, and in 1981 he was made an honorary member of the American Academy and Institute of Arts and Letters.

(ROBERT RAUCH)

Federer, Roger

Switzerland's Roger Federer dominated the game of tennis with unwavering assurance and athleticism in 2005, just as he had in 2004. In those two sterling seasons, the gifted shotmaker captured five of the eight major championships: one Australian Open and back-to-back All-England (Wimbledon) and U.S. Open titles. No one in the men's game had taken that many Grand Slam events over a two-year span since Australia's Rod Laver in 1968–69. Moreover, Federer became the first man since American Don Budge (1937–38) to sweep Wimbledon and the U.S. Open for two straight years and the first since Sweden's Mats Wilander in 1988 to win three Grand Slam events in one calendar year.

Federer was born in Basel on Aug. 8, 1981. He started playing tennis at the age of eight, but he was also immersed in association football (soccer). At age 12 he made tennis his top priority, and two years later he established himself as Switzerland's junior champion. In 1998 he captured the Wimbledon junior singles championship and secured the Orange Bowl junior tournament crown in Miami. The precocious Federer made his debut on the Swiss Davis Cup team in 1999 and became the youngest tennis player ever (at 18 years 4 months) to end the year among the world's top 100, finishing that season at number 64.

He reached the competition for the bronze medal at the 2000 Olympic Games in Sydney and concluded that year at number 29 in the world rankings. At Wimbledon in 2001 he toppled seven-time champion Pete Sampras of the U.S. to reach the quarterfinals, in which he lost to Britain's Tim Henman. Federer kept surging forward, however, and finished 2002 ranked number six in the world after having recorded three tournament triumphs in singles (he also won two doubles titles with partner Max Mirnyi of Belarus).

In 2003 Federer took his first Grand Slam tournament title at Wimbledon and advanced to number two in the world. He was beaten only 6 times in 80 matches that season and was victorious in 11 of 17 tournaments he played in 2004. After losing twice in August 2004, he won 17 consecutive matches to conclude his season. In 2005 his numbers were similarly remarkable; he won 11 of 15 tournaments and 81 of 85 matches, including a 35-match winning streak during June–November. Federer won a modern-record 24 straight finals he played from July 2003 until November 2005, when he was narrowly beaten by Argentina's David Nalbandian in a fifth-set tiebreaker at the Tennis Masters Cup in Shanghai. Federer finished 2005 at the top of

© Shaun Best/Reuters/Corbis

Swiss tennis champion Roger Federer took five of the eight grand-slam titles in 2004 and 2005.

the world rankings for the second straight year. Although he had already demonstrated that his game was among the most complete ever assembled by a champion, many fans, other players, and tennis experts claimed that Federer had not yet fully explored the boundaries of his potential. (STEVE FLINK)

Fitzgerald, Patrick J.

U.S. Attorney and Special Prosecutor Patrick Fitzgerald had made headlines for years by announcing convictions and indictments, but he remained largely unnoticed until October 2005, when he captivated the country during a televised press conference at which he summarized his two-year investigation into the leak of a covert CIA agent's identity. The political stakes were steep; Fitzgerald indicted I. Lewis ("Scooter") Libby, chief of staff to U.S. Vice Pres. Dick Cheney, for having made false statements and having committed perjury during a grand jury investigation of the CIA leak case. He used the press conference to outline Libby's alleged crimes and explain the consequences of revealing the identity of Valerie Plame, the formerly covert CIA operative. One month later *People* magazine endorsed Fitzgerald's celebrity status in its "sexiest men of the year" feature.

Fitzgerald was born to Irish immigrant parents in New York City on Dec. 22, 1960. He paid for his university studies by working as a janitor and—like his father—as a doorman in Manhattan. Fitzgerald studied math and economics at Amherst (Mass.) College, graduating in 1982. He earned a law degree from Harvard University in 1985 and worked in private practice until 1988, when he joined the U.S. Department of Justice (Southern District of New York) as an assistant U.S. attorney in New York City. In that job he pursued cases against drug dealers, Mafia leaders, and terrorists—including the indictment of Osama bin Laden in 1998 for the bombings of American embassies in Kenya and Tanzania. He also developed a reputation for using obscure or long-forgotten laws to clinch a case; he built his case against Sheikh Omar Abdel Rahman (convicted for the 1993 World Trade Center bombing) upon a statute that dated back to the Civil War.

Despite a portfolio brimming with high-stakes, politically charged cases, Fitzgerald shunned affiliation with any political party—a stance that lent credence to his work. This helped when in 2001 Fitzgerald became the U.S. attorney (Northern District of Illinois) in Chicago, where he brought corruption charges against Democrats and Republicans alike, among them former Illinois governor George Ryan and associates of Chicago Mayor Richard M. Daley. He again drew on the finer points of law, using mail-fraud charges to bring indictments against Ryan.

Fitzgerald continued his work as the U.S. attorney in Chicago after becoming the Justice Department's special prosecutor for the CIA leak investigation in 2003. The case became clouded in mid-November 2005 when *Washington Post* reporter Bob Woodward revealed that he had been told of Valerie Plame's identity one month before Libby exposed Plame's covert status. Taking their cue from Woodward's revelation, political pundits slammed Fitzgerald as overzealous. The following day Fitzgerald made new headlines by indicting Canadian-British media tycoon Conrad Black for fraud, and within one week he had opened a new grand jury investigation into the CIA leak case, raising the possibility of additional charges' being brought against other members of the White House inner circle. (SARAH FORBES ORWIG)

Forsythe, William

In 2005 a new ballet ensemble, the Forsythe Company, made its debut in Frankfurt am

Main, Ger. Led by William Forsythe, an internationally renowned choreographer of audaciously groundbreaking contemporary dance works, the company—with bases in both Frankfurt and Dresden and supported by both state and private funding—immediately garnered rave reviews. The company's debut featured the premiere of a new Forsythe work, *Three Atmospheric Studies*, that typified Forsythe's creations, incorporating both abstraction and theatricality.

Forsythe was born on Dec. 30, 1949, in New York City. Although he performed in musicals when he was in high school, he did not begin formal dance training until he was a drama student at Jacksonville (Fla.) University. He began studying at the Joffrey Ballet School in New York in 1969 and from 1971 to 1973 danced with Joffrey Ballet II, often appearing in the parent company's productions. Forsythe moved to Germany in 1973 to dance with the Stuttgart Ballet, and in 1976 he choreographed his first piece, *Urlicht*. He became the Stuttgart's resident choreographer in 1978 and that same year created his first piece for the the company, *Traum des Galilei*. With his first full-length ballet, *Orpheus* (1979), he began to move beyond traditional classical ballet and present his own dynamic and unconventional vision. Forsythe left the company in 1980 to freelance and created works for companies that included the Munich State Opera Ballet, Netherlands Dance Theatre, the Frankfurt Ballet, and the Paris Opéra Ballet.

© Norbert Millauer/AFP/Getty Images

Choreographer William Forsythe

In 1984 Forsythe became director of the government-sponsored Frankfurt Ballet. He continued to develop his own concepts for his dances, using spoken word, video projections, and electronic sounds and devising an extreme physical vocabulary. In works that included *In the Middle, Somewhat Elevated* (1987) and *Herman Schmerman* (1992), he dazzled—and often confused—his audiences. Numerous companies worldwide inserted his works into their repertoires. In 2002, however, the city's government began to consider removing its support in order to cut costs and to favour a more conventional dance company.

The public protested, but Forsythe decided to go his own way, and in 2004 the Frankfurt Ballet gave its last performance. Forsythe's new company was about half the Frankfurt Ballet's size, but nearly all of his dancers were from that company, and he was set to continue carrying his vision to his audiences.

(BARBARA WHITNEY)

Fossett, Steve

On March 3, 2005, Steve Fossett made history as the first person to fly an airplane around the world alone without stopping or refueling. Piloting the *GlobalFlyer*, a specialized plane that featured 13 fuel tanks and a 2-m (1 m = 3.28 ft) cockpit, the American businessman and adventurer returned to Salina, Kan., 67 hours and 1 minute after taking off on February 28. He subsisted on a liquid diet and catnaps and overcame a fuel shortage—several hours into the mission, approximately 1,178 kg (2,600 lb) of fuel inexplicably disappeared—to complete the 36,898-km (1 km = 0.62 mi) journey. It was not Fossett's first record—he had already set almost 100 records in sailing and aviation—and it did not appear to be his last. Several months after the historic flight, he announced that he would attempt to break other records. He hoped to set a distance record of 46,669 km in the *GlobalFlyer* in 2006, and he planned to fly a glider to an altitude of 30,480 m, doubling the current mark, the following year.

Fossett was born on April 22, 1944, in Jackson, Tenn., and grew up in California, where he studied economics and philosophy at Stanford University (B.A., 1966). After earning an M.B.A. (1968) at Washington University, St. Louis, he became a successful commodities broker in Chicago, and in 1980 he founded the securities company Lakota Trading. Fossett soon amassed a personal fortune that enabled him to pursue his adventures. He undertook a number of challenges, including swimming the English Channel (1985), before gaining international attention with his ballooning feats. In 1995 he registered his first record in the sport with a solo transpacific flight. The following year he began his highly publicized effort to become the first person to balloon around the world alone. The initial attempt, however, ended after three days and 3,540 km, and a series of subsequent efforts also failed. On his fourth try, in August 1998, he nearly died when the balloon was struck by lightning and crash-landed in the Coral Sea. In December of that year, he joined forces with Richard Branson, a British entrepreneur who later sponsored Fossett's 2005 flight, and Per Lindstrand of Sweden in a bid to become the first balloonists to circumnavigate the globe. Bad weather ended the trip after 19,960 km, however, and a subsequent mission was canceled after Bertrand Piccard of Switzerland and Britain's Brian Jones accomplished the feat in 1999. On June 19, 2002, in Australia, Fossett undertook his sixth attempt at a solo balloon flight around the world. He set off from Northam, W.Aus., in the *Spirit of Freedom* and made history on July 2 as he crossed his starting point, eventually landing in the outback of Queensland.

Fossett was also renowned as a speed sailor. In 2001 he recorded the quickest transatlantic crossing—4 days 17 hr 28 min 6 sec—and in 2004 he circumnavigated the globe in an unprecedented time of 58 days 9 hr 32 min 45 sec. Soon after, he retired from sailing, having set more than 20 records in the sport. His other achievements included the fastest flight (1,194.17 km/hr) in a nonsupersonic airplane (2001) as well as a number of gliding records.

(AMY TIKKANEN)

Foxx, Jamie

Stand-up comedian Jamie Foxx proved that he was not just a funnyman when in 2005 he collected a best actor Academy Award for his riveting portrayal of soul singer Ray Charles in the film *Ray*. In addition, Foxx earned a best supporting actor nomination for another serious role, that of a taxi driver abducted by a professional killer in the thriller *Collateral*. For *Ray*, Foxx not only mastered Charles's physical mannerisms but also captured the blind singer's warmth, determination, and recklessness. He spent time with Charles prior to his death in 2004 and wore prosthetic eyelids that impaired his vision. Foxx's performance also garnered best acting awards from the Golden Globes, the Screen Actors Guild, and the British Academy of Film and Television Arts.

Foxx was born Eric Bishop on Dec. 13, 1967, in Terrell, Texas. His parents split up soon after his birth, and he was adopted by his maternal grandparents. He began playing piano about the age of five and became keenly interested in music, later earning a scholarship to United States International University (now Alliant International University) in San Diego to study classical piano and music theory. (Foxx performed all the piano-playing scenes in *Ray*.)

It was while Foxx was a student in San Diego that he began performing at local comedy clubs. At open-microphone nights he delighted audiences with his bitingly funny impersonations of former U.S. president Ronald Reagan, boxer Mike Tyson, and comedian Bill Cosby. Foxx discovered, however, that it was easier for women to get stage time at "open mics," so he adopted the gender-neutral name of Jamie Foxx. In 1991 Foxx won the Bay Area Black Comedy Competition, which led to an audition for the Fox television network's hit sketch comedy show *In Living Color*. His impersonations and his drag character Wanda, an ugly yet sexually aggressive woman, impressed the show's creator and star, Keenen Ivory Wayans, and earned Foxx a job as a regular. At that time Foxx also had a recurring role on the sitcom *Roc*.

Foxx's success on television led to new opportunities in music, television, and film. In 1994 he released his debut album, *Peep This*, which he also produced and composed. He sang on the 2004 R&B hit "Slow Jamz" with rappers Twista and Kanye West, and Foxx and West again teamed up on the 2005 hit "Gold Digger." Foxx released a second album, *Unpredictable*, in late 2005. In 1996 he landed his own TV sitcom, *The Jamie Foxx Show*, on the fledgling WB network; the show lasted five seasons. Foxx's film career began in 1992, but

AP/Wide World Photos

Box-office draw Jamie Foxx

he did not land his first feature role until 1997, in the sex comedy *Booty Call*. His breakthrough performance in terms of acting came in the football drama *Any Given Sunday* (1999), in which Foxx played a young quarterback who is outwardly cocky but terrified of failure. That performance, along with his role as corner man Drew ("Bundini") Brown in the biopic *Ali*, showed that Foxx could dig much deeper than simple impersonation and led to more complex roles and greater success.

(JAMES HENNELLY)

George, Elizabeth

By her own account, American mystery writer Elizabeth George scored a great success in allowing an unprecedented calamity to befall Detective Inspector Thomas Lynley, one of the main characters in the March 2005 release *With No One as Witness*, the 13th in George's series of best-selling novels about the sleuthing British aristocrat and his working-class assistant, Detective Sergeant Barbara Havers. "It is the job of the novelist to touch the reader, and this book has clearly done that," George said in an interview following the book's release. She was referring to the magnitude of her audience's response to Lynley's tragedy, a development that some readers, writing in various Internet forums, declared could only mean the end of the detective's career—and the series. Other fans, outraged by what they considered her betrayal of their loyalty, swore off reading any future books by George. Nevertheless, one month after its release, *With No One as Witness* was in its seventh printing, and it spent six weeks on *The New York Times* best-sellers list. One bookstore owner suggested that the author's willingness to allow one of her protagonists to be harmed, a rarity in detective fiction, might have attracted new readers seeking greater realism in the genre. Indeed, it was her meticulously researched portrayal of the dreary, often harrowing work of Scotland Yard detectives—in prose as captivating as it was famously accurate—that had initially won George her huge following on both sides of the Atlantic.

Susan Elizabeth George was born on Feb. 26, 1949, in Warren, Ohio, and was a prolific writer from childhood. She studied at Foothill Community College (now Foothill College) in Los Altos Hills, Calif., and the University of California, Riverside, receiving a B.A. from the latter institution in 1970. She earned an M.S. in counseling/psychology from California State University, Fullerton, in 1979. George taught high-school English for more than 13 years in California before publishing *A Great Deliverance* (1988). The novel won the 1989 Agatha and Anthony awards for best first novel and the 1990 French Grand Prix de Littérature Policière. Its success enabled George to quit teaching and write full-time. Her third novel, *Well-Schooled in Murder* (1990), won Germany's MIMI award for international mystery fiction. Beginning in 2002, the British Broadcasting Corporation and WGBH in Boston coproduced a television series based on the Lynley novels. In addition to the Lynley books, George published two short-story collections and *Write Away* (2004), a guide for aspiring writers. She eventually returned to teaching and led writing seminars at universities in the U.S., Canada, and England.

(JANET MOREDOCK)

Gnassingbé, Faure

When the longtime president of Togo, Gen. Gnassingbé Eyadéma, died in February 2005, the military named his son Faure Gnassingbé his successor. International leaders denounced the move as a coup, in violation of Togo's 1992 constitution, so Gnassingbé stepped down, agreeing to proper democratic elections, which were held in April. He won them handily and on May 4 was officially installed as president. Gnassingbé's accession to the post, however, was accompanied by violent opposition protests. Despite finding isolated irregularities, the official delegation from the Economic Community of West African States

AP/Wide World Photos

Faure Gnassingbé, president of Togo

declared the elections free and fair, and the Constitutional Court rejected the claims of opposition leaders that Gnassingbé's victory at the polls had been rigged.

Faure Essozimna Gnassingbé was born on June 6, 1966, in the town of Afagnan in southeastern Togo. The following year his father took power in Togo during a military coup. As the son of the country's leader, Gnassingbé enjoyed a certain level of privilege. He was educated in Paris at the Sorbonne, where he studied economics and international relations. He also earned a master's degree in business administration from George Washington University, Washington, D.C. Returning to Togo, he became involved in the management of his family's business affairs, serving as a financial adviser to his father.

For some years prior to Eyadéma's death, it had seemed to some observers that Gnassingbé was being groomed to succeed him as president. In June 2002 Gnassingbé ran for the parliament as a member of the ruling Rally of the Togolese People and won a seat from the city of Blitta. Later his father appointed him minister of telecommunications, mines, and equipment. The only one of Eyadéma's many sons to enter politics, Gnassingbé was viewed as a quiet, calm figure who was trusted by the military. At the end of 2002, the constitution was amended to lower the eligibility age for the presidency from 40 to 35 (Gnassingbé was 36), and in 2003 the management of presidential elections was transferred from an independent commission to the Ministry of the Interior.

Upon taking the oath of office in 2005, Gnassingbé pledged to work toward "development, the common good, peace, and national unity" in Togo. His initial effort at forming a coalition government with the country's main opposition party failed in June, although Gnassingbé later sought to reopen talks. He also sought warmer relations with the European Union in hopes of restoring the Western aid that had been curtailed in 1993 over concerns of human rights violations in Togo.

(TOM MICHAEL)

Gregory, Rogan

In 2005 New York-based designer Rogan Gregory successfully merged the concept of cutting-edge fashion with social responsibility via the high-profile spring launch of a line called Edun. His casual clothing collection was produced from organic materials in conjunction with the Dublin-based political activist husband-and-wife duo Paul Hewson (U2 lead singer Bono) and Ali Hewson. The line was sold primarily in the U.S. at Saks Fifth Avenue department stores. Gregory's goal for Edun was twofold—to make a commercial profit and to create sustainable employment in less-developed countries. Rather than working with a Third World operation that could make items at the lowest-possible price point, Edun outsourced production to factories where work was most needed. Edun's founders hoped that their clothing would set a new precedent in the fashion industry by creating a solid foundation for new garment-manufacturing businesses to thrive in such underdeveloped economic zones as Tunisia and Peru, where the Edun collection was produced from untreated cotton as well as dyes made from coffee, blue corn, and gardenia blossoms.

Gregory was born on Sept. 17, 1972, in Denver, Colo. He arrived in New York in 1994 and worked initially in design development for fashion labels Calvin Klein and Daryl K. He became well known for independently producing an eponymous sharply tailored denim label, which launched in 2001 amid a post-new-millennium craze for relaxed apparel that ensured its success, along with sweatshirt dressing produced by Los Angeles fashion labels Juicy Couture and American Apparel. Gregory parlayed some of the profits of his denim label into the launch of Loomstate—an urban-cool clothing brand made from certified organic cotton. Gregory forged a partnership with Ali Hewson after she viewed prototypes of his Loomstate line before its 2004 retail debut; she was impressed by the line's contemporary look and Gregory's guiding business ethic. Their brand name, Edun, was the inverse of Nude, the label of a Dublin chain of organic restaurants in which the Hewsons had invested.

In 2005 American *Vogue* featured Edun in a nine-page story in its issue for March, a month normally reserved for showcasing work produced by the magazine's biggest advertisers. Meanwhile, Gregory's business continued to thrive with the September launch of A Litl Betr, a handmade collection of dressy men's clothing, and his completion of prototypes for the January 2006 unveiling of an all-natural furniture collection. Gregory attributed his success to a design process based on "trial, error, and discovery."

(BRONWYN COSGRAVE)

Guillen, Ozzie

In 2005, at the start of the baseball season, Chicago's National League (NL) Cubs and American League (AL) White Sox had gone a combined 185 years without winning a World Series title in MLB (Major League Baseball). Ozzie Guillen, the outspoken, unpredictable manager of the White Sox, turned the city upside down, however, by guiding a squad of largely unheralded players to the pinnacle of professional baseball and ending the Windy City's long dry spell.

When Guillen joined the White Sox as manager in late 2003, he was well aware of the franchise's losing tradition—he had been the team's starting shortstop for 13 years (1985–97). In his first season as manager, the White Sox hit a lot of home runs but finished well out of first place. During the off-season, he convinced general manager Kenny Williams that the team needed to sacrifice some of its power hitting to add speed, defense, and pitching. Over the course of the 2005 season, Guillen was able to draw unexpected greatness from players whom many had written off as career journeymen. He drew criticism along the way—sometimes for expressing himself too openly in the press, but mostly for his style

of game management, in which he emphasized manufacturing runs over waiting for home runs and allowed pitchers in a jam to work through it. The new approach paid immediate dividends, however, as the Sox jumped out to an early lead in the AL Central Division, finished the season with the AL's best record (99–63), and ripped through the play-offs, winning 11 of 12 games and sweeping the NL Houston Astros four games to none in the best-of-seven World Series. The national media recognized Guillen's unique skills and rewarded him with AL Manager of the Year honours.

Oswaldo José Guillen Barrios was born on Jan. 20, 1964, in Ocumare del Tuy, Venez. He grew up admiring great Venezuelan shortstops, such as Chico Carrasquel and Luis Aparicio, and signed with the San Diego Padres in 1980. After four years in the minors, Guillen was traded to the White Sox, where he was named AL Rookie of the Year in 1985. In his 16 major-league seasons (including stints with the Atlanta Braves, Baltimore Orioles, and Tampa Bay Devil Rays), Guillen was respected for his solid defense and passion for playing and was named to the AL All-Star team three times (1988, 1990, and 1991). After ending his playing career in 2000, he became the third-base coach of the Montreal Expos (2001) and then of the Florida Marlins (2002–03). Guillen—the first Venezuelan to manage a major league team and the first manager born outside the U.S. to win a World Series—remained fiercely loyal to his homeland. In November 2005 he carried the World Series trophy to Venezuela to share the White Sox success with his countrymen.

(JAMES HENNELLY)

Hawk, Tony

In 2005 Tony Hawk's Boom Boom HuckJam—a traveling show of wild skateboard, BMX bike, and motorcycle stunts all set to the head-banging beats of top punk bands—enjoyed its third consecutive year performing in sold-out arenas across North America; its success cemented the skateboarding champion's place as one of the great impresarios of alternative sports.

Anthony Frank Hawk was born on May 12, 1968, in San Diego. As a child, Hawk had an abundance of energy and little patience for failure. The fiery youngster began skateboarding at age nine, and the sport seemed to calm him immediately. He began entering competitions at age 11 and made an instant impression with his creativity and daring. His parents were supportive of his new hobby, chauffeuring him to skate parks and later organizing the California Amateur Skateboard League and the National Skateboard Association to help provide legitimacy to the sport. Hawk was 14 when he signed with the Powell Peralta professional team and starred in the famous Bones Brigade videos. Though Hawk was an accomplished street skater, his reputation rested on his skills as a "vert" (vertical) skater. In his career he invented dozens of moves, including the ollie-to-Indy, the gymnast plant, the frontside 540-rodeo flip, and the Saran wrap. In one of skateboarding's defining moments, Hawk executed a 900 twist

Skateboard pro Tony Hawk

(2 ½ turns) at the 1999 X Games, a feat only he had ever performed.

During the 1980s and '90s, Hawk dominated skateboarding competitions. He won 73 titles and was named the top vert skater every year from 1984 to 1996. Despite his consistency during those years, the sport of skateboarding experienced ups and downs. During the downs of the early 1990s, Hawk saw his income diminish and was faced with the prospect of looking for work as a computer consultant (he was a passionate "techno-geek"). Nevertheless, he persevered and pursued entrepreneurial options. In 1992 he started Birdhouse, a skateboard and accessories manufacturer, and Blitz, a skateboard products distributor. Both concerns started slowly, but when the sport regained popularity in the mid-1990s, the companies took off. In 1998 he struck a deal with the software company Activision to develop a skateboard-themed video game. The following year *Tony Hawk's Pro Skater* debuted, and it (and subsequent versions) generated more than $1 billion in sales, making it one of the most successful video games of all time. Tony Hawk, Inc., was formed to oversee all of Hawk's enterprises.

Though Hawk retired from competition in 1999, he remained active in promoting the sport and his products. In a sport that prided itself on its independence, Hawk drew some criticism for attracting too much corporate influence, but he remained keenly aware of what made skateboarding great.

(JAMES HENNELLY)

Isinbayeva, Yelena

Russian pole vaulter Yelena Isinbayeva lifted herself to a position of unchallenged mastery in her event in 2005, raising the women's outdoor world record five times during the year and becoming the first woman to soar over the 5-m (16-ft 4¾-in) mark. The 23-year-old Isinbayeva, whose career world-record tally stood at 20 (11 of them set outdoors) at the end of 2005, was named track and field's woman Athlete of the Year for a second consecutive season by the International Association of Athletics Federations (IAAF).

Isinbayeva was born in Volgograd, U.S.S.R., on June 3, 1982. She was enrolled by her parents in gymnastics school at age 4, but a growth spurt when she was 15 suddenly made her too tall to compete effectively in the sport—she eventually reached a height of 1.73 m (5 ft 8 in). Pole vault coach Yevgeny Trofimov invited her to try that sport, and the next season, in July 1998, she vaulted 4.00 m (13 ft 1½ in). She won the 1999 world youth title and the

© Michael Steele/Getty Images

Pole vaulter Yelena Isinbayeva, after clearing five metres

2000 world junior title, and in 2001 she broke both indoor and outdoor junior world records.

She defeated Russian rival Svetlana Feofanova, the reigning world champion, for the first time in March 2003. That summer Isinbayeva surpassed American Stacy Dragila's world record with a 4.82-m (15-ft 9¾-in) vault and then triumphed in two more major athletics meets over fields that included Feofanova and Dragila. Isinbayeva finished third at the 2003 IAAF world outdoor championships, but by the 2004 IAAF world indoor championships, she had taken charge, winning the title with an indoor world record. Although Feofanova claimed one more record in July 2004, Isinbayeva produced a string of five world records that summer, including the 4.91-m (16-ft 1½-in) clearance that won her the Olympic gold medal in Sydney.

Although vaulters usually followed the practice of raising the world record one centimetre (0.4 in) at a time—and only once per competition—in order to maximize performance bonuses from sponsors, Isinbayeva approached the bar differently at the London Grand Prix in July 2005. She raised the record first to 4.96 m (16 ft 3¼ in) and then to 5.00 m.

Isinbayeva, who developed a reputation for calm confidence and for jumping her highest at important competitions, was dubbed "Bubka in a skirt" by Russian sportswriters who deemed her prolific record-setting reminiscent of former men's world-record holder Sergey Bubka. After winning her first outdoor world championship title—and raising the record yet again, to 5.01 m (16 ft 5¼ in) in August 2005—

she avoided serious talk about ultimate height goals but said that she hoped to claim 36 world records in her career—one more than Bubka's total. In the fall of 2005, Isinbayeva dropped Trofimov as her coach and announced plans to train at Bubka's vault centre in Donetsk, Ukraine. (SIEG LINDSTROM)

Jaafari, Ibrahim al-

Ibrahim al-Jaafari, a physician who had spent more than 20 years outside Iraq during the reign of Saddam Hussein, became the country's new prime minister in 2005. Jaafari, the leader of the Islamic Da'wah Party, had returned to Iraq from the U.K. following the overthrow of Saddam's regime by U.S.-led coalition forces in April 2003. The general elections of January 2005 brought to power the United Iraqi Alliance, a coalition of mainly Shi'ite organizations, in which the Da'wah was a major player. After weeks of discussion and bargaining among the leading parties of the alliance, Jaafari was selected to be prime minister on April 7. He officially assumed the most powerful post in the Iraqi transitional government on May 3.

Jaafari was born Ibrahim al-Ashaiqir in 1947 in the holy city of Karbalah in central Iraq. He was an avid reader and poet from his youth, and he became an advocate of conservative religious views. In the mid-1960s he joined the Da'wah, then an underground movement. After completing high school, he left Karbalah to study medicine in the northern city of Mosul, where he obtained a medical degree in 1974. While in Mosul, he was given responsibility for the recruitment of Da'wah members in Iraqi universities.

Returning to Karbalah, Jaafari practiced medicine and remained active in the Da'wah movement. By 1979 the Da'wah had become the major Shi'ite underground party in Iraq and posed a serious threat to Hussein's regime. Saddam ruthlessly cracked down, making membership in the party punishable by death. In 1980 Jaafari was forced to escape to Iran, where he continued his anti-Saddam activities. Fearing retaliation against his family in Iraq, he changed his name from Ashaiqir to Jaafari. He moved to London in 1989, where he met leaders of the Iraqi opposition living in exile.

Before becoming prime minister, Jaafari had been appointed in July 2003 as a member of Iraq's first Governing Council. In June 2004, when sovereignty was handed over to the Iraqis, he became a vice president in the government led by Ayad Allawi. As prime minister, Jaafari expressed support for U.S. forces' remaining in Iraq as long as necessary, and he promised to continue fighting the insurgency. He also made several trips abroad to strengthen Iraqi relations with its neighbours, including Iran, a country with which he maintained close relations. During negotiations over the drafting of Iraq's basic law, Jaafari

leaned toward including conservative Islamic influences in the constitution. He was on record as saying that the constitution "should reflect, like a clear mirror, the Iraqi fabric" and that he wanted a government in which "the majority doesn't exclude the other but respects the other." (LOUAY BAHRY)

Jakab, Zsuzsanna

Hungarian epidemiologist Zsuzsanna Jakab assumed leadership of the newly formed European Centre for Disease Prevention and Control (ECDC) in 2005, taking on the task of defending the European Union against infectious diseases. Working out of ECDC headquarters in Stockholm, Jakab began to develop a surveillance network that could collect health data from, and coordinate disease prevention among, the 25 nations of the EU. At a time when borders within the EU were becoming more open, the spread of infectious diseases, such as HIV/AIDS, SARS (severe acute respiratory syndrome), and avian influenza, posed an ever-growing threat to public health. Jakab's appointment was also seen as politically significant; she was the first citizen of one of the 10 states that joined the EU in 2004 to head an EU agency.

Jakab was born on May 17, 1951, in Budapest. Her father was a surgeon, her mother an agronomist. She studied political and social sciences at Eotvos Lorand University in Budapest for five years, earning the equivalent of a master's degree in 1974. In 1999 she received a postgraduate degree in public health and epidemiology from the Nordic School of Public Health in Göteborg, Swed. For 16 years from 1975, she held a variety of external-relations posts in Hungary's Ministry of Health and Social Welfare, working as a liai-

AP/Wide World Photos

ECDC leader Zsuzsanna Jakab

son to international organizations, most notably the World Health Organization (WHO). In 1991 she accepted a post in WHO's regional office for Europe in Copenhagen, rising to director of administration in 2000. In 2002 she was invited to return home to Budapest to serve as secretary of state in Hungary's Ministry of Health, where she assisted with the nation's integration into the EU.

Jakab's lack of medical and scientific expertise was unusual for a person overseeing a disease centre, but the ECDC had no regulatory authority and no laboratories and would conduct no medical research of its own. Instead, one of its main functions would be to influence the formation of EU health policy. Jakab's extensive background in public health administration was expected to serve her well as she negotiated the EU bureaucracy. The agency was inaugurated with a minimal budget (about €5 million, or about $6 million, compared with the almost $8 billion budget of the U.S. Centers for Disease Control and Prevention), but that figure would rise incrementally to about €30 million (about $36 million) by 2007, when the ECDC was to be evaluated and perhaps have its mission broadened. Jakab's success or failure would be defined by her ability to coordinate the public health efforts of the EU's member nations, not all of whom were considered to be receptive to surrendering local control over such issues.

(ANTHONY G. CRAINE)

Jean, Michaëlle

Former journalist and television broadcaster Michaëlle Jean was officially installed as Canada's 27th governor-general on Sept. 27, 2005. She was the first black and the first Haitian immigrant ever to hold the prestigious post, in which she would serve as Queen Elizabeth II's viceregal representative in Canada. The appointment of the 48-year-old Jean reflected Canada's emergence as a multicultural society in which the highest positions were open to individuals of talent. Although her political role as governor-general was mainly ceremonial, she would be expected to travel extensively across the country, bringing the message of a united inclusive Canada to all its scattered communities. In Quebec her appointment might well dispel the tendency of the province's ethnic minorities to look favourably on the cause of a sovereign Quebec. Her task was a formidable one, but one made easier by her demonstrated skills as a communicator.

Jean was born on Sept. 6, 1957, in Port-au-Prince, Haiti. Her family was descended from slaves. Jean's father suffered imprisonment and torture under the regime of François Duvalier, a circumstance that led to the family's flight to Canada when Jean was 11 years old. The family settled in Montreal. Jean proved to be a brilliant student, studying languages and literature at the University of Montreal. From 1984 to 1986, while completing her master's degree in comparative literature, she served on the university's faculty of Italian studies. She also attended universities in Italy and France.

A social activist, Jean mixed freely in the diverse world of Montreal's ethnic communities, honing a perfect command of French and English in the process. Embarking on a career in broadcast journalism, she became a popular commentator on the French-language network of the Canadian Broadcasting Corporation and also worked frequently on the English network. From 2001 Jean worked as an anchor for Radio-Canada's *Le Téléjournal*, and in 2004 she began to host her own television interview show, *Michaëlle*. She won numerous awards for her journalism work, including the Amnesty International Journalism Award.

With her husband, French-born Canadian filmmaker Jean-Daniel Lafond, she also made several acclaimed documentary films, most notably the 1995 *Haïti dans tous nos rêve*.

Jean's appointment brought out, in a striking fashion, the changing nature of modern Canada. Since World War II, Canada had become a genuinely multicultural society, with attitudes influenced by the heavy flow of immigrants. The country's Charter of Rights and Freedoms guaranteed equality and opportunity for all citizens, and Jean's life story illustrated this promise. Her primary task would be to express the values and aspirations of the new multiracial Canada. (DAVID M.L. FARR)

Juanes

When *Time* named Colombian singer-songwriter Juanes one of the 100 most influential people in the world in 2005, the magazine was only ratifying what had become obvious to anyone who followed Latin pop music. In only four years Juanes reached the very top of the music world, and he did it without embracing the music industry practice of "crossing over." Though his music remained firmly rooted in *cumbia*, tango, and the folk music of his native Colombia, he filled arenas and topped charts throughout North and South America and the Caribbean. The handsome singer-songwriter was often compared to Bruce Springsteen and U2's Bono for his absorbing stage presence and passionate lyrics that examined both romantic love and social struggle.

Juanes was born Juan Esteban Aristizábal Vásquez on Aug. 9, 1972, in Medellín, Colom. When he was seven years old, his father and brothers taught him to play guitar, and he quickly became immersed in the musical traditions of his homeland. Later he became infatuated with rock and roll, and for 11 years he was a singer and guitarist for Ekhymosis, a heavy-metal band that enjoyed a strong

following in Colombia. Juanes grew restless with the artistic limitations of the band, however, and in 1999 he moved to Los Angeles to pursue a solo career.

In 2000 Juanes debuted with *Fíjate bien*, a brooding album that produced a handful of hits and earned the singer three Latin Grammy Awards, including best new artist. Juanes's major breakthrough came with the release of his second album, the bright and energetic *Un día normal* (2002), which included the songs "A Dios le pido," an anthem for peace that hit number one in 12 countries, and "Fotografia," a duet with Nelly Furtado that also hit the top of the charts. *Un día normal* won five awards at the 2003 Latin Grammys, including album of the year, record of the year, and song of the year. In 2004 he released his third album, *Mi sangre*, which spun off the number one hits "Nada valgo sin tu amor" and the sexy "La camisa negra." The album earned him three Latin Grammys in 2005. His passion for music was matched by the sadness he felt over the violence that plagued Colombia. Through his songs Juanes confronted his despair and anger over violence in the world but also embraced hope for the future. (JAMES HENNELLY)

Keys, Alicia

On Feb. 13, 2005, 24-year-old rhythm-and-blues singer-songwriter Alicia Keys cemented her status as one of pop music's leading lights by winning four Grammy Awards, notching wins in four R&B categories: best album, song, female vocal performance, and performance by a duo or group with vocals (with Usher [*q.v.*]). Held at Los Angeles's Staples Center, the awards show also found Keys performing her hit single "If I Ain't Got You" and then joining actor Jamie Foxx (*q.v.*) and producer Quincy Jones for an onstage tribute to the legendary Ray Charles.

Latin music phenomenon Juanes

Grammy night was only one highlight of Keys's year, which found her touring in support of her sophomore album, *The Diary of Alicia Keys* (2003). She also recorded and released *Unplugged*, an album from the MTV televised special on which the deft pianist performed stripped-down versions of past hits, two new songs, and covers of songs popularized by Aretha Franklin and the Rolling Stones. In 2005 Keys also won prizes at the NAACP Image Awards, the Soul Train Awards, and the BET Awards.

Keys was born Alicia Augello Cook on Jan. 25, 1981, in New York City and began performing at age 4 in a production of *The Wizard of Oz*. She started playing piano at age 7, concentrating on classical music and jazz, and at 14 began writing her own songs. At 16 she graduated as valedictorian from the Professional Performing Arts School in Manhattan. Keys's compositions showed modern influences but were rooted in the sounds of earlier soul artists, including Marvin Gaye and Stevie Wonder, and her piano skills, intellect, and rangy voice attracted the attention of record mogul Clive Davis. She signed to Davis's Arista Records in 1998 and went with him when he formed J Records in 1999. Keys released *Songs in A Minor* (2001), a wildly successful debut album that spawned a number one hit with "Fallin'" and went on to sell more than 10 million copies worldwide. The album was praised as an accomplished blend of classic-sounding rhythm and blues and contemporary urban music. Keys won five Grammy Awards in 2002, including those for song of the year and best new artist.

The success of her debut album established Keys as a star, and she continued her momentum in the following years. *The Diary of Alicia Keys* was another blockbuster, and Keys won seven Billboard Music Awards in 2004, the same year she released a book, *Tears for Water*, and a duet with Usher called "My Boo" that spent six weeks as the number one song on *Billboard*'s Hot 100 chart. (PETER COOPER)

Laliberté, Guy

Glitzy Las Vegas productions featuring elaborate costumes and high-stepping showgirls gave way in recent years to a new sensation—the circus. More specifically, Cirque du Soleil, the brainchild of French Canadian Guy Laliberté. By the end of 2005, Cirque du Soleil had four shows drawing large audiences in Las Vegas, including its newest production *KÀ*, which debuted in February at the MGM Grand hotel and casino. The success of Cirque du Soleil was firmly rooted in the passion and energy of Laliberté, its founder and CEO, who during a 20-year span had built a ragtag collection of street performers into one of the world's most recognizable and profitable entertainment enterprises, revitalized the circus in North America, and vaulted onto *Forbes*

magazine's billionaires list. In 2005 Cirque du Soleil boasted five permanent shows (four in Las Vegas and one at Walt Disney World in Orlando, Fla.) and six touring shows.

Each of Cirque du Soleil's productions was unique, but all of them shared the core elements of Laliberté's distinctive vision of a circus. There were no animal acts or star performers, and there was no talking. Instead, the shows were built around an imaginative fusion of varied acrobatic and artistic disciplines culled from around the world. The shows were known for their musical scores, which were rooted in global popular music; simple but engaging plot lines; fantastic costumes and special effects; and, above all, spellbinding feats of physical daring. *O*, the celebrated production at Las Vegas's Bellagio casino, was performed in, on, and above a large pool of water. *KÀ* was the fiery adventure of a set of twins that drew heavily upon the martial arts. The touring production *Corteo* was a festive parade that also examined the contradictions embodied by the character of the clown. In 2004 almost seven million people worldwide attended a Cirque du Soleil performance.

Laliberté was born on Sept. 2, 1959, in Quebec City. At age 18 he left home to hitchhike across Europe, where he earned money playing his accordion and met street performers who taught him the arts of fire-eating and stilt walking. Back in Quebec he joined a group of performers in Baie-Saint-Paul, and in 1982 he helped to organize an international festival for street performers in the town. The success of this and subsequent festivals prompted Laliberté to seek a grant to create the Cirque du Soleil as part of Quebec's 450th anniversary celebration in 1984. The circus struggled initially (the tent collapsed on the first day) but soon hit its stride. At the end of its run, it had netted a tidy $40,000 profit. Inspired by this success, Laliberté and his band of kindred spirits determined to keep the Cirque du Soleil operating. He cultivated both public and private investors who were taken by the group's originality and determination, and in 1985 Cirque du Soleil began touring North America. The success of the company grew rapidly, and by the early 1990s was mounting productions in Europe and Asia. In 1993 the troupe debuted its first permanent show, *Mystère*, at the Treasure Island casino in Las Vegas. In 1997 Laliberté was awarded the National Order of Quebec, in recognition of his contribution to Quebec's culture. (JAMES HENNELLY)

Lampert, Edward S.

On March 25, 2005, investor Edward S. Lampert saw the completion of a deal that stunned the retail industry when it was first announced in November 2004: the acquisition of Sears, Roebuck & Co. by Kmart Holding Corp.—two of the largest retailers in the United States. Lampert had spurred the merger in 2003 by gaining a controlling interest in Kmart for $1 billion (although officially bankrupt at the time, Kmart was estimated to be worth $23 billion). When the former competitors merged into a single company, Sears Holdings Corp., the new firm ranked as the country's third largest retailer.

Lampert controlled nearly 40% of the new corporation, and soon after its stock began trading on March 28, 2005, it became a favourite among the country's profit-focused hedge-fund managers.

Lampert was born on July 19, 1962, in Roslyn, N.Y. He was 14 when his father, an attorney, died. While his mother took a job at Saks Fifth Avenue to support her family, Lampert eagerly learned about the stock market from his grandmother, and by the time he was in high school, he had grown familiar with corporate reports and financial theory. He studied economics at Yale University (B.S.; 1984), where he was tapped for the elite Skull & Bones society and became a research assistant for Nobel Prize-winning economist James Tobin. Lampert then joined the arbitrage department at Goldman Sachs, where he worked under Robert E. Rubin, later the U.S. treasury secretary. Risk analysis became one of Lampert's hallmarks; even as a relatively fresh hire, he reduced his department's exposure to the stock market when he foresaw overvaluations that led to the market crash in 1987.

In 1988 he opened his own private equity fund, ESL Investments, Inc., which delivered annual returns of about 25% for its investors. Lampert gained a reputation for spotting opportunity where others did not; when he began acquiring Kmart stock in 2003, the company was little more than a distressed discount retailer with no means of reclaiming market share taken by competitors. The same held true for Sears, shares of which Lampert began amassing in 2004.

Skeptics, doubting the success of his plan to merge Kmart and Sears into a superretailer against the more stylish Target stores and the low-cost Wal-Mart outlets, questioned whether his strengths as a financial manager would supply the marketing savvy needed to pull paying customers into aging and inefficient stores. Lampert, however, had successfully increased the profits of other store chains, such as AutoZone and AutoNation, by controlling costs and tightening management. Within six months of becoming chairman of Sears Holdings, Lampert named former Kmart chief Aylwin Lewis as the corporation's CEO, causing the former Sears CEO, Alan Lacy, to move down the ranks. Even if Lampert failed, many stores still held tremendous potential value—in the form of real estate where Kmart and Sears stores were located. (SARAH FORBES ORWIG)

Lange, Jessica

Jessica Lange overcame an inauspicious start early in her career to become one of Hollywood's most respected actresses and, in 2005, one of the busiest and most versatile. In February she returned to Broadway after a 13-year absence and earned rave reviews as the domineering mother Amanda Wingfield in Tennessee Williams's *The Glass Menagerie*. This was followed by the release of the bittersweet movie *Broken Flowers*, in which Lange appeared as a lawyer turned animal communicator. Directed by Jim Jarmusch, the film won the Grand Prix at the Cannes Festival. Also premiering at Cannes was the Wim Wenders–directed drama *Don't Come Knocking*, which starred Lange opposite her longtime companion, playwright and actor Sam Shepard, as the former girlfriend of an aging actor. She had a supporting role in *Neverwas*, a psychological thriller that debuted at the Toronto Film Festival in September.

Lange was born in Cloquet, Minn., on April 20, 1949. She attended the University of Minnesota on an art scholarship but dropped out to travel. She lived in Paris, where she studied mime, before settling in New York City. A sometime model, she caught the eye of producer Dino De Laurentiis, who cast her in his big-budget remake of *King Kong* (1976). Lange's film debut was ridiculed by critics, and she did not work again for more than two years. After several small roles, she attracted attention with another remake, *The Postman Always Rings Twice* (1981). Although the sexually charged drama received mixed reviews, Lange earned praise as the adulterous wife who plots to kill her husband. Lange's double breakthrough came in 1982. In *Frances* she starred as the gifted but doomed actress Frances Farmer. The emotionally draining role almost led to a breakdown, but Lange found comic relief in the gender-bending farce *Tootsie*, playing a vulnerable soap opera actress. She earned Academy Award nominations for both films and was named best supporting actress for *Tootsie*.

Much-honoured actress Jessica Lange

Shunning conventional roles for more complex characters, Lange continued to earn acclaim for her film performances and received Oscar nominations for *Country* (1984), the Patsy Cline biopic *Sweet Dreams* (1985), and *Music Box* (1989). In 1995 she won an Academy Award for best actress for *Blue Sky* (1994). Later notable films included *Cousin Bette* (1998), based on the Honoré de Balzac novel, *Titus* (1999), an adaptation of Shakespeare's *Titus Andronicus*, and the fantasy drama *Big Fish* (2003). In addition to her screen work, Lange forged a successful stage career. After she portrayed Maggie in a 1985

television version of Williams's *Cat on a Hot Tin Roof*, Lange made her Broadway debut in 1992, playing Blanche DuBois in Williams's *A Steetcar Named Desire*. In 2000–01 she starred as the drug-addicted Mary Tyrone in the London West End production of Eugene O'Neill's *Long Day's Journey into Night*, which she hoped to take to Broadway.

(AMY TIKKANEN)

López Obrador, Andrés Manuel

During 2005 Andrés Manuel López Obrador, the popular head of Mexico's Federal District government, survived a politically motivated impeachment process and consolidated his position as the leading contender in the country's 2006 presidential contest.

López Obrador was born into a provincial middle-class family in Villa de Tepetitán, Tabasco, on Nov. 13, 1953. From 1972 to 1976 he studied political science and public administration at the National Autonomous University of Mexico.

López Obrador began his political career in Mexico's long-ruling Institutional Revolutionary Party (PRI), eventually becoming Tabasco state party president in 1983. He left the party, however, and backed the dissident presidential candidacy of Cuauhtémoc Cárdenas in 1988. López Obrador's own 1988 opposition candidacy for Tabasco's governorship ended in defeat, but he later became state president of the party founded on the basis of Cárdenas's electoral coalition, the centre-left Party of the Democratic Revolution (PRD).

During the 1990s López Obrador earned a national reputation for organizing grassroots protests against environmental damage in Tabasco caused by the state-owned Mexican Petroleum Company (PEMEX) and electoral fraud committed by the "official" PRI (most notably involving the 1994 Tabasco gubernatorial race, which he lost to 2005–06 PRI presidential candidate Roberto Madrazo Pintado). From 1996 to 1999 López Obrador served as national president of the PRD, a position he used both to promote grassroots party organization and to recruit prominent PRI members as PRD mayoral and gubernatorial candidates. In 2000 he was elected head of the Federal District government, a post he held through July 2005, when he resigned to seek the PRD's presidential nomination.

López Obrador compiled a generally successful record as head of Mexico City's government. Under the slogan "For the good of all, the poor first," he promoted a series of innovative social and cultural programs (including old-age pensions, financial support for single mothers and the unemployed, substantial investments in urban redevelopment and transportation infrastructure, and educational outreach programs) that won him widespread popularity. Nevertheless, his record was marred by sensational corruption scandals

involving several close subordinates, and public security remained a major challenge.

In May 2004 the federal attorney general initiated impeachment proceedings against López Obrador, charging him with having defied a court order by authorizing the construction of a hospital access road across private property. Mexican Pres. Vicente Fox argued that his administration sought only to uphold the rule of law, but many national and international observers believed that the underlying motive was to disqualify López Obrador as a presidential candidate. After nearly one million protesters marched through downtown Mexico City in April 2005, Fox finally ended the prolonged confrontation by dropping the impeachment charge.

(KEVIN J. MIDDLEBROOK)

MacArthur, Ellen

On Feb. 7, 2005, English yachtswoman Ellen MacArthur became a new legend in British maritime history when she crossed the finish line off Ushant, France, to complete the fastest solo nonstop voyage around the world on her first attempt. The diminutive 1.6-m (5-ft 3-in) MacArthur had sailed from Falmouth, Cornwall, in her 23-m (75-ft) carbon-fibre trimaran *B & Q* on Nov. 28, 2004, for the official start off Ushant to challenge the seemingly unassailable record set only nine months earlier by French sailor Francis Joyon. On the southward leg of the voyage, she set speed records to the Equator, the Cape of Good Hope, and Cape Leeuwin, Australia. After reaching the Southern Ocean and turning northward, she suffered a badly burned arm while changing generators. Three days later she completed her best 24-hour run—807.2 km (501.6 mi)—before passing Cape Horn. Four days south of the Equator, she fell behind Joyon's time for the first time, but when she recrossed that line on day 60, she had made up enough time to be 10 hr 50 min ahead of his record. MacArthur reached France to complete the 44,012-km (27,348-mi) journey through the

Yachtswoman Ellen MacArthur

world's most dangerous seas in 71 days 14 hr 18 min 33 sec, breaking Joyon's record by 1 day 8 hr 35 min 49 sec. On her return to Falmouth Harbour—where she was greeted by a flotilla of boats and cheering crowds—she stepped ashore as Dame Ellen MacArthur, the youngest woman in modern history to be granted a life peerage.

Ellen Patricia MacArthur was born on July 8, 1976, in the small (population 350) village of Whatstandwell, Derbyshire. She began sailing with her aunt at age four and spent her spare time reading sailing books. Four years later she started saving her school dinner money to buy her first boat. In 1994 MacArthur launched her career in yachting by working on a 18.3-m (60-ft) vessel and teaching sailing to adults at the David King Nautical School in Hull. She achieved her yachtmaster and instructor qualifications at age 18, and in 1995 she won the Young Sailor of the Year Award after sailing solo around Great Britain. The following year she finished third in her first transatlantic race, from Quebec to Saint-Malo, France. In 2003 she founded the Ellen MacArthur Trust to introduce young cancer and leukemia patients to the joys of sailing.

Seven months after completing her global record, MacArthur spent seven weeks on standby in New York waiting to challenge Joyon's solo transatlantic record of 6 days 4 hr 1 min 37 sec. The attempt would be futile without perfect conditions, but the particularly active hurricane season in the Caribbean affected the North Atlantic weather and prevented the normal pattern from forming. MacArthur would have to wait for another opportunity to set her next record.

(KEITH L. OSBORNE)

Manning, Peyton

In 2005 quarterback Peyton Manning of the National Football League (NFL) Indianapolis Colts showed that if he demanded a little less from himself, he could expect more, even perfection, from his team. In his first seven NFL seasons, Manning had routinely tried to carry the Colts to victory on his talented shoulders. The Colts' offense flourished, and the team won three division titles (1999, 2003, and 2004) and made the play-offs five times, but they never attained the ultimate goal—the Super Bowl. During the 2005 season Manning kept the Colts' no-huddle offense running at high speed, but he seemed more willing to let talented teammates, such as workhorse running back Edgerrin James, carry some of the load. Manning also showed increased confidence in an improved defense's ability to regain possession of the ball for him. As a result, the Colts thrived like never before, winning their first 13 games, gaining home-field advantage through the play-offs, and, perhaps, finally earning that elusive spot in the Super Bowl.

Peyton Williams Manning was born on March 24, 1976, in New Orleans, where his father, Archie Manning, was the star quarterback of the NFL Saints. Peyton and his brothers, Cooper and Eli (who in 2004 was named the starting quarterback for the NFL New York Giants), were immersed in football from a very young age. Peyton in particular stood out for his skill and passion for the game. He was highly regarded as a high-school player and received a national Player of the Year award in his senior season. Manning attended the University of Tennessee, where he was starting quarterback for four years. He earned the Sul-

Indianapolis Colts quarterback Peyton Manning

livan Award as the nation's top amateur athlete in 1996, was selected a first-team All-American in 1997, and finished his collegiate career in 1998 as Tennessee's career passing leader.

Although Manning was the first player picked in the 1998 NFL draft, he struggled somewhat in his first year as a professional. By his second season, however, he had proved that he was worthy of his high draft pick. Manning threw for more than 4,000 yd in six out of eight seasons and was named to the Pro Bowl six times. In 2003 he shared the league's Most Valuable Player award with Steve McNair of the Tennessee Titans. Manning won the MVP honour outright in 2004 with a sensational performance that included 49 touchdown passes and a quarterback rating of 121.1, both NFL records for a single season.   (JAMES HENNELLY)

Mayne, Thom

Iconoclastic American architect Thom Mayne received the Pritzker Architecture Prize in May 2005. He was the first American in 14 years to win the award, which honoured a living architect for lifetime achievement. Mayne, who led the Santa Monica, Calif.-based design firm Morphosis, had often been described as a "maverick" and a "bad boy" of American architecture. His bold and unconventional works were noted for their offset angular forms, layered exterior walls, incorporation of giant letter and number graphics, and emphasis on natural light. In its citation the Pritzker jury acknowledged the "audacious character" and originality of Mayne's designs and praised him as "a product of the turbulent

'60s who has carried that rebellious attitude and fervent desire for change into his practice."

Mayne was born on Jan. 19, 1944, in Waterbury, Conn., and grew up in Gary, Ind., and near Whittier, Calif. After earning a bachelor's degree in architecture from the University of Southern California in 1968, he had a brief career in urban planning, working under noted civic planner Victor Gruen. In 1972 Mayne and fellow architect Michael Rotondi launched Morphosis, taking the firm's name from the Greek word meaning "to be in formation" or "taking shape." That same year Mayne helped found the Southern California Institute of Architecture, which became a leading school in experimental design. In 1978 he completed a one-year master's degree program in architectural studies at Harvard University. He then returned to California, where he and Rotondi took projects that ranged from private residences to restaurants to a cancer centre in Los Angeles.

After Rotondi left Morphosis in 1991, Mayne achieved what was considered his breakthrough design—the Diamond Ranch High School, near Pomona, Calif. Built on a hillside, the school featured two rows of oddly angled buildings sheltering a canyonlike interior walkway. The design was widely praised and brought Mayne his first major international recognition.

Mayne celebrated the completion of a large project in Los Angeles in 2004: the Caltrans District 7 Building, which served as a regional headquarters for the California Department of Transportation. Though massive, the building had a streetscape sensitivity and was characterized by an enormous perforated aluminum shell programmed to shift throughout the day, filtering out sunlight or letting it in. In 2005 Mayne was working on another large project, a student centre at the University of Cincinnati, Ohio, and on government-commissioned projects in San Francisco, Eugene, Ore., and near Washington, D.C., as well as on an academic building at Cooper Union in New York City. He also had projects in Austria, South Korea, Spain, and Taiwan.   (TOM MICHAEL)

Mazumdar-Shaw, Kiran

By 2005 Indian businesswoman Kiran Mazumdar-Shaw had completed a remarkable rise from struggling entrepreneur to leader of India's premier biotechnology firm and winner of numerous international awards for her business achievements. As chairman and managing director of Biocon India Group, Mazumdar-Shaw headed up a pioneering enterprise that utilized India's homegrown scientific talent to make breakthroughs in clinical research.

In 2001 Biocon became the first Indian company to gain the approval of the U.S. Food and Drug Administration (FDA) for the manufacture of a cholesterol-lowering molecule, and in

2005 the company was awaiting FDA approval to begin clinical trials on the world's first orally consumed insulin. Mazumdar-Shaw was honoured as the businesswoman of the year by the *Economic Times* in late 2004. This followed a phenomenal performance by her company over the prior 12 months, during which Biocon's profits had jumped 42% to $45 million. After a wildly successful initial public stock offering held in March 2004, Biocon's stock-market value shot to $1.2 billion. With her nearly 40% stake in the company, Mazumdar-Shaw had a personal net worth of well over $400 million—enough to make her the richest woman in India.

Mazumdar-Shaw was born on March 23, 1953, in Pune, Maharashtra state, India. Her father was a brewmaster for India-based United Breweries, and Mazumdar-Shaw set out to follow in his footsteps, earning an undergraduate degree in zoology from Bangalore University in 1973 and a graduate degree in brewing from the University of Ballarat, Melbourne, in 1975. Upon returning to India, however, she found no companies willing to offer a brewing job to a woman. Instead, she did consulting work for a few years before meeting Leslie Auchincloss, then owner of an Irish firm, Biocon Biochemicals. Impressed by her drive and ambition, Auchincloss took Mazumdar-Shaw on as a partner in a new venture, Biocon India, launched in 1978 to produce enzymes for alcoholic beverages, paper, and other products.

Within a year Biocon had become the first Indian company to export enzymes to the U.S. and Europe, but progress was slowed as Mazumdar-Shaw continued to face skepticism and discrimination. She found it difficult to find employees in India who were willing to work for a woman. Investors were equally hard to come by, and some vendors refused to do business with her unless she hired a male manager. Nevertheless, the company had begun to turn a profit by the time Auchincloss sold his interest in Biocon India to Unilever in 1989. Imperial Chemical Industries bought Unilever's stake in 1997 but eventually agreed to sell its shares to Mazumdar-Shaw's husband, textile executive John Shaw, who subsequently joined Biocon's management team.

As Biocon grew steadily, awards began to pour in for Mazumdar-Shaw. The World Economic Forum recognized her as a "Technology Pioneer" in 2000, and Ernst & Young named her best entrepreneur in the health care and life sciences field in 2002. In January 2005 Mazumdar-Shaw also received the Padma Bhushan award, one of India's highest civilian honours, for her pioneering work in industrial biotechnology.   (SHERMAN HOLLAR)

McGraw, Tim
The success of singer Tim McGraw's single "Live like You Were Dying"—it spent multiple weeks atop country music charts, won best single and song at country music's two biggest awards shows, and captured best country song at the Grammy Awards—further certified McGraw's place as one of the major music stars of 2005. McGraw also won a Grammy for best country male vocal performance for that single. Though McGraw's sandy twang was decidedly Southern, his July 2 appearance in Rome on the stage of the multivenue Live 8 concert event and his vocal turn on rapper Nelly's crossover hit single "Over and Over" offered evidence that McGraw's appeal extended beyond traditional country boundaries. Since his recording career began in 1993, he had sold nearly 30 million albums and notched 20 number one country singles.

McGraw was born Samuel Timothy Smith on May 1, 1967, in Delhi, La. Raised by a single mother, he was 11 years old before he discovered that his father was famed baseball pitcher Tug McGraw. The son dropped out of college and moved in 1989 to the country music hub of Nashville. He found work as a club performer before signing a recording contract with Curb Records in 1990. McGraw's 1993 debut recording was unsuccessful, but his follow-up, *Not a Moment Too Soon*, became the biggest-selling country album of 1994 (and the sixth best-selling album of the year in any genre). *Not a Moment Too Soon* featured such

© Frank Micelotta/Getty Images

Nashville luminary Tim McGraw

hit singles as the story song "Don't Take the Girl," the rural celebration "Down on the Farm," and "Indian Outlaw," a song that critics complained portrayed Native Americans in a stereotypical manner. The controversy did not hurt sales, however, and McGraw ascended to country stardom. His celebrity spread with the 1995 release of *All I Want* and with his high-profile marriage in 1996 to country star Faith Hill. By 2000 he was well established enough to release a 15-song greatest hits package, and 2001 found McGraw and Hill accepting a Grammy for their duet "Let's Make Love."

In 2002 McGraw broke with Nashville convention by recording with his touring band, the Dancehall Doctors (most artists employed session musicians in the studio and road musicians in concert), and by releasing another single that raised controversy; a few country radio stations refused to play "Red Ragtop" because the song's story line involved an abortion. In August 2004 McGraw released the album *Live like You Were Dying;* its title song, penned by Nashville songwriters Craig Wiseman and Tim Nichols, was a tribute to his father, who died in January 2004 after battling brain cancer. In late 2004 McGraw's collaboration with Nelly, "Over and Over," spent 12 weeks at number one on *Billboard's* Top 40 singles chart, making McGraw the only contemporary country singer to enjoy a vocal turn on a hit urban record.   (PETER COOPER)

Merkel, Angela
On Oct. 10, 2005, three weeks after the German election, it was finally decided that Angela Merkel would be the next chancellor. Merkel was a rarity in German politics. Not only was she a female politician—the first woman in the federal republic's top position—and a leader of the conservative Christian Democratic Union (CDU, which contests elections with its Bavarian sister party, the Christian Social Union, CSU), but she was also one of the very few leading parliamentarians who hailed from the former communist eastern part of the country. It was also unusual that because of the CDU/CSU's razor-thin win in the elections, Merkel would be leading a "grand coalition," sharing the government with the Socialist Democratic Party (SPD).

Angela Dorothea Kasner was born on July 17, 1954, in Hamburg. She was barely a few months old when her father, a Lutheran pastor, was given a parish in Brandenburg in the German Democratic Republic. Life in East Germany was far from easy for those associated with the church, but Angela Kasner entered the University of Leipzig, graduating with a Ph.D. (1986) in physics. She then worked as a scientist at the Institute for Physical Chemistry of the GDR Academy of Sciences.

Merkel became active in politics in 1989, joining Demokratischer Aufbruch (DA), a leading pro-democracy group. Following the free elections of March 1990, she became spokeswoman for East Germany's only democratic government. She joined the ranks of the CDU when DA broke up and the faction that supported German reunification and market economics merged with the Christian Democrats. She soon became minister for women and youth in Chancellor Helmut Kohl's government, and by 1994 she had become environment minister.

Despite her apparently close relationship with Kohl, she was the first of his allies to break with him publicly during the 1999 "slush funds" scandal. Her rise was almost complete by 2000, when she was selected to lead the CDU, but in 2002 she was passed over for the nomination as the centre right's chancellor candidate in favour of CSU leader Edmund Stoiber.

Although Merkel was the only former East German in the CDU leadership, she had little electoral appeal in the east, where she was commonly viewed with suspicion. Her popularity ratings throughout 2005 were consistently lower than those of SPD Chancellor Gerhard Schröder's. Her uneasy relationship with voters was aggravated by an apparent unease in the spotlight, and she struggled with difficult relationships with some of the CDU's leading (western) regional politicians, all of which damaged her standing in the party.

Merkel assumed her new duties on November 22. She was known to be market-oriented, in favour of improving relations with the United States, and opposed to Turkish membership in the European Union. Some observers had labeled her—inaccurately—Germany's Margaret Thatcher, but in order to hold the grand coalition together, keep her party behind her, and push through the reform packages needed to revive the German economy, she might have to demonstrate a degree of determination similar to that of the former British prime minister. (ROSANNE PALMER)

Miller, Bode

In 2005 Alpine skiing had a new star and the U.S. ski team had its best male skier in two decades, perhaps ever, as Bode Miller claimed the World Cup overall championship. In doing so, he became only the second man in history to win in all four disciplines—slalom, giant slalom (GS), supergiant slalom (super-G), and downhill—during a single season. He was also the first American skier to capture a World Cup overall title since 1983.

Samuel Bode Miller was born on Oct. 12, 1977, in Easton, N.H., in the heart of the White Mountains. His parents were self-styled hippies who lived deep in the woods in a house with no electricity or running water, and Miller was home schooled until the fourth grade. After his parents divorced, his mother would take him to nearby Cannon Mountain while she worked, often leaving him in the care of the ski school staff. He learned to ski by prowling the mountain every day with various instructors and at the age of 11 began skiing competitively.

A natural athlete, Miller earned all-state honours in high school in both soccer and tennis and was an avid golfer. He was a promising snowboarder as well, but ultimately he decided to focus on skiing because snowboarding had no clear ladder for advancement. He first made the U.S. ski team in 1998 and competed that year in the Nagano (Japan) Winter Olympics. He tore ligaments in his left knee in a racing crash during the 2001 world championships in St. Anton, Austria, but rebounded in 2002 to collect silver medals in GS and the combined event at the Salt Lake City (Utah) Winter Games.

Miller went on to post increasingly better results. In 2003 he became the first American to win two golds at a single world championships, capturing the GS and combined titles. He also won three U.S. national titles that year. In 2004 he recorded six World Cup wins en route to taking the GS World Cup title—the first in any discipline by an American man since Phil Mahre won the overall and GS titles in 1983. Miller's phenomenal performances continued into 2005, when he became the only skier in the 39-year history of the World Cup tour to win the first three races of

a season. He also picked up two gold medals—in downhill and super-G—at the world championships. In the process, Miller guaranteed that the spotlight would be focused firmly on him as the American skier to watch at the 2006 Winter Olympics in Turin, Italy.
(PAUL ROBBINS)

Mittal, Lakshmi

London-based steel tycoon Lakshmi Mittal ranked third on *Forbes* magazine's 2005 list of the richest people in the world. His vault from number 62 on the 2004 list was powered by the merger of his companies, Ispat International and LNM Holdings, and the acquisition of Ohio-based International Steel Group. The newly created company, Mittal Steel Co. NV, emerged from the deal as the world's largest steelmaker, with its headquarters in Rotterdam, Neth., and some 175,000 employees at facilities in 14 countries. Mittal was regarded as a determined businessman with an unusually keen sense of the world steel market. He attributed his successful global approach to his being raised in India, where more than 300 ethnic groups found ways to work together as a nation.

Lakshmi Narayan Mittal was born on June 15, 1950, in Sadulpur, Rajasthan, India. In the 1960s his family moved to Calcutta (now Kolkata), where his father operated a steel mill. Mittal worked at the mill while studying science at St. Xavier's College. After graduating (1970), he served as a trainee at his father's mill, and in 1976 he opened his own steel mill in Indonesia, where he spent more than a decade learning how to run a mill as efficiently as possible. In 1989 Mittal purchased the beleaguered state-owned steel works in Trinidad and Tobago, which had been losing more than $100,000 a day. A year later that facility had doubled its output and had become profitable. He used a similar formula for success in a series of acquisitions all around the world, purchasing failing (mostly state-run) outfits and sending in special management teams to reorganize the businesses.

Mittal's business philosophy emphasized consolidation in an industry that had become weak and fragmented. Although demand for steel remained high, smaller steel companies had been unable to strike competitive deals with their major clients, notably automakers and appliance manufacturers. Mittal Steel, however, controlled about 40% of the American market for the flat-rolled steel used to make cars, which would allow the giant steelmaker to negotiate more favourable prices.

Mittal, who was sometimes described as being media shy, nonetheless made news frequently in the U.K., often because of the way he spent portions of his reported net worth of $25 billion. Among his more notable expenditures were a record £70 million ($128 million) for a 12-bedroom home in London; an estimated $60 million for his daughter's 2004 wedding in Paris, a six-day extravaganza that included an engagement party at the Palace of Versailles; and a donation of £125,000 (about $180,000) to the Labour Party in 2001 that created trouble for Prime Minister Tony Blair when it was learned that later that year Blair had helped Mittal purchase a steel company

in Romania even though Mittal's firms backed a U.S. tariff opposed by British steel producers. In 2005 Mittal reportedly donated £2 million (about $3.6 million) to the Labour Party.
(ANTHONY G. CRAINE)

Murakami, Takashi

By 2005 Takashi Murakami, who had been dubbed the Japanese Andy Warhol, had reached a new level of success in his career as an artist, curator, product designer, theorist, and entrepreneur. At the Japan Society Gallery in New York City, Murakami curated the exhibition "Little Boy: The Arts of Japan's Exploding Subculture," which was on view from April to July. The show, featuring young Japanese artists, examined the *otaku* movement that revolves around anime (Japanese animated films) and manga (comic books)—two industries at the heart of Japanese popular culture. From July through October, he displayed his monumental sculpture *Tongari-Kun—Mr. Pointy & the Four Guards* in Tokyo's fashionable Roppongi Hills development. This colourful, meticulously crafted work, modeled on a Buddha statue, was the fourth edition of a piece that had charmed many people in 2003 outside Rockefeller Center, New York City.

© Toru Hanai/Reuters/Corbis

Artist Takashi Murakami with his sculpture Tongari-Kun—Mr. Pointy & the Four Guards

Murakami was born on Feb. 2, 1962, in Tokyo. He studied Japanese painting at the Tokyo National University of Fine Arts and Music, where he received a Bachelor of Fine Arts degree in 1986 and a Ph.D. in 1993. Murakami's numerous solo and group exhibitions were international in scope. He made his European debut in 1995 at "TransCulture," held at the 46th Venice Biennale. The following year Murakami's paintings and sculptures were featured in many exhibitions worldwide, notably at the second "Asia-Pacific Triennial of Contemporary Art" at the Queensland Art Gallery, Brisbane, Australia.

Although many observers in Japan were surprised that a young artist with a background in traditional Japanese painting could achieve such success in contemporary art, Murakami saw similarities between the flat composition of Japanese painting and the simplified aesthetics of anime and manga. His style, which emphasized two-dimensional forms and bold, striking imagery, gave birth to what became known as the Superflat movement and allowed Murakami to move readily between the commercial and art worlds. After curating an exhibition in 2002 at the Cartier Foundation in Paris, he collaborated in 2003 with Louis Vuitton's artistic director, Marc Jacobs, to produce a fashion accessory. Murakami's brightly coloured Louis Vuitton monogram handbags became a phenomenal success, with reported sales of $300 million. He earned celebrity status in May 2003 when his *Miss Ko2* (pronounced "ko ko"), a fibreglass sculpture of a large-breasted 1.85-m (6-ft)-tall blonde in a petite waitress uniform, was auctioned in New York City for $567,500 at Christie's; the price set a record for a work by a contemporary Japanese artist.

As the founder of Kaikai Kiki Co., Ltd., an art production company with offices in both Japan and Brooklyn, N.Y., Murakami nurtured young artists and helped them gain international exposure. His company produced and sold merchandise ranging from art items to clothing and organized an art festival and convention twice a year in Tokyo. At a Murakami retrospective scheduled for 2007 at the Museum of Contemporary Art, Los Angeles, he planned to include an animated film featuring his work. (KIMIYO NAKA-MICHAELI)

Negroponte, John

Career diplomat John Negroponte was named the first director of national intelligence (DNI) of the United States in 2005. The cabinet-level position was created at the recommendation of a congressional committee in the wake of the Sept. 11, 2001, attacks in the United States. The DNI was to oversee 15 agencies responsible for intelligence and military strategy and coordinate those efforts as a way to prevent similar terrorist attacks. Negroponte was certainly familiar with the world's political and military hot spots, having served in Southeast Asia in the 1960s, Central America in the 1980s, and Iraq during the Second Gulf War in 2004. Representing his country in such volatile environments may have prepared him for the intelligence job, but it also left his reputation tainted in the eyes of many who contended that widespread abuses had occurred on his watch.

John Dmitri Negroponte was born on July 21, 1939, in London, the son of a Greek shipping magnate. He was raised in New York City and on Long Island and attended the exclusive Phillips Exeter Academy in New Hampshire, graduating in 1956. He then studied at Yale University, receiving his bachelor's degree in 1960. He attended Harvard Law School briefly but left in 1960 to join the U.S. Foreign Service. He was assigned to posts in Ecuador, Greece, Hong Kong, and Vietnam. He became a deputy assistant secretary of state, first for oceans and fisheries (1977) and then for East Asian and Pacific affairs (1980).

Negroponte was named U.S. ambassador to Honduras in 1981, at a time when the administration of Pres. Ronald Reagan was engaged in covert military operations against left-wing governments in Central America. Negroponte's

critics—including Jack Binns, his predecessor as ambassador—accused him of having ignored human rights abuses and the activities of death squads during his four years in Honduras. They claimed that Negroponte had aided the Contras, who were fighting against the government in neighbouring Nicaragua; Negroponte claimed that he had complained privately about the abuses while publicly supporting the newly elected government.

From 1985 to 1996, Negroponte held a variety of key positions, including deputy national security adviser under Reagan and ambassador to Mexico (1989–93) and the Philippines (1993–96). He worked in the private sector until 2001, when Pres. George W. Bush nominated him to serve as U.S. representative to the United Nations, where he helped build a case for war against Iraq, citing evidence of weapons of mass destruction that later proved to be flawed. In 2004 he accepted the job of ambassador to Iraq, where he was credited with reducing corruption within the U.S.-controlled administrative district of central Baghdad.

(ANTHONY G. CRAINE)

Oliver, Jamie

In a display of his passion for good food, British celebrity chef Jamie Oliver turned up the heat on government officials in 2005 with his overwhelmingly successful "Feed Me Better" campaign to improve the quality of meals served in Britain's schools. In an effort to replace unhealthy, processed food in school cafeterias with nutritious yet tasty cuisine using freshly prepared ingredients, Oliver launched a five-week petition campaign to persuade the government to increase funding for school meals. Among the critical factors in the success of his initiative was his television series *Jamie's School Dinners*, which documented the challenges Oliver faced while training a group of school "dinner ladies" to prepare the new menu items, as well as his ability to encourage the students to try the new menu. The tremendous response to his campaign resulted in the collection of 271,677 signatures that Oliver personally delivered to Prime Minister Tony Blair and Education Secretary Ruth Kelly. Consequently, the British

Activist chef Jamie Oliver

© Peter Dench/Corbis

government agreed to increase the amount spent on each school meal from 37 pence (1 pence = about 1.8¢) per student to 60 pence in some cases, with total funding raised to £280 million over a three-year period.

Oliver was born on May 27, 1975, to the owners of the Cricketers, a pub-restaurant in Clavering, Essex. After persistently begging the chefs to let him assist in the kitchen, Oliver was peeling potatoes and shelling peas at age eight, and within three years he was able to julienne vegetables with the skill of a seasoned professional. At age 16 Oliver entered the Westminster Catering College before traveling to France for additional training and experience. He landed his first job in London at the Neal Street Restaurant as head pastry chef and soon began working as sous-chef at the River Café, where his talent in front of the camera was discovered during the filming of a documentary on the restaurant. He was quickly contracted by Optomen Television to host his first series, *The Naked Chef*, in which he demonstrated how to simplify food preparation by using basic ingredients and cooking techniques. The enthusiastic young chef was often shown exiting the kitchen by sliding down a banister or zipping around town on his motor scooter from market to market collecting fresh ingredients for his menus.

In addition to starring in numerous television series, including *Oliver's Twist* and *Pukka Tukka*, Oliver authored five best-selling cookbooks, appeared in endorsements for the Sainsbury's grocery store chain, and launched his own line of cookware. In 2002 he established the Fifteen Foundation, a London-based program that gave underprivileged youths the opportunity to experience careers in the culinary industry at Oliver's Fifteen restaurant. The success of the project, chronicled in the TV series *Jamie's Kitchen*, spurred Oliver's plans to expand the program throughout the U.K. and overseas. Oliver was made an MBE in 2003. (BARBARA A. SCHREIBER)

Osteen, Joel

Riding a huge wave of popularity in 2005 was American evangelist Joel Osteen. As pastor of the nondenominational Lakewood Church in Houston, Texas, Osteen led the largest and fastest-growing congregation in the U.S. His weekly television broadcast reached households in more than 100 countries and had become the top-rated inspirational program on the air, according to Nielsen Media Research. His 2004 book, *Your Best Life Now: 7 Steps to Living at Your Full Potential*, remained a fixture on best-seller lists. In addition, he conducted a 15-city U.S. tour in 2005, preaching in front of packed crowds at virtually every stop. An affable, youthful-looking man who had earned the nickname "the smiling preacher," Osteen typically avoided heavy theology in his sermons. Instead, he delivered simple and upbeat messages that underscored his oft-repeated belief that "God wants us to have a better life." While this approach struck an obvious chord with the public, it also drew sharp criticism from those who viewed Osteen as more of a motivational speaker than a Christian minister.

Osteen was born on March 5, 1963, in Houston. His parents, John and Dodie, founded Lakewood Church in an abandoned feed store in 1959. His father served as pastor of the church and over the years built a regional following as a Pentecostal-style preacher. Osteen attended Oral Roberts University, Tulsa, Okla., but he left school in 1981 after less than a year to help his father develop Lakewood's television ministry. He worked behind the cameras as a producer of the church's television programs, and when his father died in 1999, Osteen took over as pastor.

One of Osteen's first steps as head of the church was to expand Lakewood's media strategy. This included advertising on billboards and in other venues, doubling budget allotments to purchase television airtime, negotiating with different networks for optimal time slots, and targeting the largest media markets. Church growth came rapidly. Weekly attendance at Lakewood rose from 6,000 in 1999 to more than 25,000 by 2005. To accommodate the sudden growth, Lakewood acquired the Compaq Center in Houston, where the city's professional basketball and hockey teams had formerly played. Some $95 million was spent in converting the arena into a 16,000-seat "megachurch" that officially opened its doors in July 2005.

To critics who maintained that he was offering a watered-down interpretation of Christianity or promoting what amounted to a "prosperity gospel," Osteen responded that he wanted to remain focused on the "goodness of God" and that he did not define prosperity in purely materialistic terms. He also defended Lakewood's unabashedly commercial approach to attracting new members, arguing that churches opposed to "changing with the times," as he put it, risked losing members or folding altogether. That seemed unlikely to befall Lakewood anytime soon—given weekly attendance figures that some believed could eventually top 100,000. (SHERMAN HOLLAR)

Oz, Amos

Israeli author Amos Oz added yet another branch to his impressive crown of laurels when on Aug. 28, 2005, he was awarded the Goethe Prize, one of Germany's top cultural honours.

Goethe Prize winner Amos Oz

AP/Wide World Photos

In 2004–05 alone, Oz was awarded more than half a dozen major literary prizes from organizations in France, Germany, Spain, Italy, Austria, and the United States; most of the awards were for his autobiographical *Sipour al ahava vehoshekh* (2002; *A Tale of Love and Darkness*, 2004). The novel, which culminated in the suicide of Oz's mother, was another example of his ability to interweave the complicated story of his family and his own youth with the story of Israel, the history of the Jewish people, and the Zionist movement.

Oz was born Amos Klausner on May 4, 1939, in Jerusalem. At the age of 15, following his mother's suicide, he went to live in Kibbutz Hulda. There he changed his name to Oz ("strength"), finished high school, and remained as a kibbutz member for two decades. Following his army service (1958–61), he studied (1961–63) Hebrew literature and philosophy at the Hebrew University of Jerusalem. In 1986 he moved with his wife and children to the southern town of Arad, in the Negev desert.

Oz's first collection of short stories, *Artzot hatan* (1965; *Where the Jackals Howl and Other Stories*, 1981), received high praise from critics, and his popularity soared with the publication of his second novel, *Michael shelli* (1968; *My Michael*, 1972). He became one of the leading figures among the New Wave writers (who include Amalia Kahana-Carmon, A.B. Yehoshua, and Aharon Appelfeld) and the most popular author of his generation. From his earliest fiction, his writing was marked by a unique style, in which several different levels of meaning—psychological, sociological, political, and religious—are implicitly analogous to one another. *My Michael* was followed by seven more novels, among them *Menuha nehona* (1982; *A Perfect Peace*, 1985) and *Kufsa sh'hora* (1987; *Black Box*, 1988). His writings included two collections of novellas, *Ad mavet* (1971; *Unto Death*, 1975) and *Har ha-etza h-ara'ah* (1976; *The Hill of Evil Counsel*, 1978); a novel in verse, *Oto ha-yam* (1998; *The Same Sea*, 2001); and two collections of literary essays.

Following the Six-Day War in 1967, Oz became active in the Israeli peace movement and with groups and organizations that advocated a two-state solution to the Israeli-Palestinian conflict. He became a spokesman for the Peace Now movement upon its founding in 1977. Oz's numerous essays about Israeli politics and culture were collected in *Be'or hatekhlet ha-aza* (1979; *Under This Blazing Light*, 1995), *Po va-sham be-eretz Israel* (1982; *In the Land of Israel*, 1983), *Mimordot ha-Levanon* (1988; *The Slopes of Lebanon*, 1989), *Kol hatikvot* (1998; "All Our Hopes"), and *Be'etzem yesh kan shte milhamot* (2002; "But These Are Two Different Wars").

Oz's latest work, *Pit'om be'omek ya-ya'ar* ("Suddenly in the Depth of the Forest"), defined as "a modern fairy tale," was published in 2005; the English version was scheduled for publication in 2006. (AVRAHAM BALABAN)

Pamuk, Orhan

The best of times, the worst of times—2005 had its ups and downs for Turkey's star novelist Orhan Pamuk. During the year lustre was added to his already formidable international reputation when he received the German Book Trade Peace Prize at the Frankfurt Book Fair and the French Prix Médicis for his novel *Snow*. This was also the year in which he found himself under indictment in a Turkish court and at the vortex of a human rights debate because of his political views.

Pamuk was born on June 7, 1952, in Istanbul. His family was wealthy and Western-oriented; childhood dinner-table conversations, he recalled, often centred on history and literature, especially novels, which Pamuk called "one of the cornerstones of European civilization." He was sent for secondary education to the American-run Robert College of Istanbul, and he began to train for a career as an architect at Istanbul Technical University. After three years, however, he dropped out and devoted himself full-time to writing. He graduated (1977) from the University of Istanbul with a degree in journalism. From 1985 to 1988 he lived in the United States and was a visiting scholar at Columbia University, New York City, and the University of Iowa.

Literary recognition came gradually. Pamuk began writing seriously in 1974, and his work evolved from naturalism to postmodernism over the course of eight novels that were published from 1982 to 2004. His works were often autobiographical and intricately plotted; they revealed a deep understanding of traditional Turkish Islamic culture but were tempered by a realization that Turkey's future lay in the West. Beginning in the 1990s Pamuk's work attracted international attention. His fourth novel to be translated into English, *Yeni hayat* (1994; *The New Life*, 1997), a literary mystery, was a best seller in Turkey. *Benim adım kırmızı* (1998; *My Name Is Red*, 2001), a historical murder mystery, won the International IMPAC Dublin Literary Award in 2003. *Kar* (2002; *Snow*, 2004), which was set in the city of Kars, in raw, underdeveloped eastern provincial Turkey, was also well received (if controversial) at home and much praised abroad. Pamuk followed these works with *İstanbul: hatıralar ve şehir* (2004; *Istanbul: Memories of a City*, 2005), a partly fictionalized memoir about the city of his childhood.

Pamuk was a strong advocate of Turkish integration into Europe and specifically its accession to the European Union. He was critical of those who rejected the idea of receiving Muslim Turkey into Europe, pointing out that Turks had never defined Europe in terms of its dominant Christian faith.

As if to catalyze the issue of Turkey's readiness to accept European-style human rights, Pamuk in February gave an interview to a Swiss newspaper in which he repeated charges of deliberate killing by Turks of a million Armenians in 1915 and of 30,000 Kurds more recently. For this he was charged under a provision of the Turkish penal code that made it a criminal offense to criticize "Turkishness." The case went to trial on December 16 but was promptly postponed until February 2006. (EDITOR)

Pelikan, Jaroslav

The 2004 John W. Kluge Prize for Lifetime Achievement in the Humanities and Social

Sciences was awarded to Yale University historian Jaroslav Pelikan, who shared the $1 million prize with French philosopher Paul Ricoeur, who died in May 2005. The award, the second to be given, recognized work in the humanities and social sciences for which Nobel Prizes were not given.

Pelikan was widely recognized as one of the foremost historians of the Christian church. Among his major achievements were *Luther's Works* (1955–71), a 22-volume translation of the works of Martin Luther, the five-volume *The Christian Tradition: A History of the Development of Doctrine* (1971–89), and *Credo: Historical and Theological Introduction to Creeds and Confessions of Faith in the Christian Tradition* (1994). One of the principal themes of his work was the role of Eastern Orthodoxy in church history, and in 1998 he converted from Lutheranism to Orthodoxy.

His other writings included *From Luther to Kierkegaard* (1950), *Fools for Christ* (1955), *Jesus Through the Centuries* (1985), *Bach Among the Theologians* (1986); *The Idea of the University* (1992), *The Bible and the Constitution* (1994), *Faust the Theologian* (1995), *Mary Through the Centuries* (1996), and the article "Jesus" for the *Encyclopædia Britannica*.

In 1983 the National Endowment for the Humanities invited Pelikan to deliver the Jefferson Lecture in the Humanities ("The Vindication of Tradition"), and in 1992–93 he went to Scotland to give the Gifford Lectures in natural theology, which were published under the title *Christianity and Classical Culture* (1993). He was founding chairman (1980–83; 1988–94) of the Council of Scholars at the Library of Congress and president (1994–97) of the American Academy of Arts and Sciences. In 1994 Pres. Bill Clinton appointed him to the President's Committee on the Arts and Humanities. In 2001–02 he was a visiting scholar at the John W. Kluge Center of the Library of Congress; thereafter he became scholarly director of the Institutions of Democracy Project of the Annenberg Foundation.

Jaroslav Jan Pelikan, Jr., was born on Dec. 17, 1923, in Akron, Ohio. His Slovak-born father was a Lutheran minister, as was his paternal grandfather. In 1942 Pelikan graduated from Concordia College, Fort Wayne, Ind., after which he earned a Bachelor of Divinity degree from Concordia Theological Seminary, St. Louis, Mo., and a Ph.D. (1946) from the University of Chicago. He taught at Valparaiso (Ind.) University and Concordia Theological Seminary from 1949 to 1953 and at the University of Chicago Divinity School from 1953 to 1962. In 1962 Pelikan joined the Yale University faculty as Street Professor of Ecclesiastical History. In 1972 he was appointed Sterling Professor of History, a chair he held until his retirement in 1996. He also served (1973–78) as dean of the graduate school.

(MARTIN L. WHITE)

Piano, Renzo

With construction under way in 2005 on office buildings, commercial spaces, museums, and residential complexes throughout the world, Italian architect Renzo Piano established himself as one of the most sought-after and prolific architects of the new century. Having designed just two museums in the United States prior to the turn of the century, by 2005 Piano was working on more than half a dozen projects in that country alone. Among them were a new office tower for the New York Times Co., a new campus for Columbia University in Manhattan, and the expansions of six museums, including the Whitney Museum of American Art, the Art Institute of Chicago, and the Los Angeles County Museum of Art. Although the number of museums on the list led some critics to worry that the structures might end up looking too much alike, the museum directors had no such qualms. Piano received high praise from clients for his varied portfolio, as well as for his sensitivity to a building's function and its interaction with the surrounding community. Following in the wake of such architects as Frank Gehry, Rem Koolhaas, and Michael Libeskind, all known for the audaciousness of their designs, Piano came across as a consummately practical man, one who would rather be known for the technical quality of his buildings than for a trademark style, and his designs were considered refreshingly human in scale.

© Jean-Pierre Clatot/AFP/Getty Images

Architect Renzo Piano at his 2005 Centre Paul Klee in Bern, Switz.

Piano was born on Sept. 14, 1937, into a family of building contractors in Genoa. At age 17 he decided to attend architecture school. His father's response to the decision, in which architecture compared unfavourably with construction, remained with Piano, and the architect became known for his intimate involvement with, and stringent testing of, his structures from conception through finished construction. After graduating (1964) from Milan Polytechnic Architecture School, he worked for his father's company. In the early 1970s he began a collaboration with British architect Richard Rogers that lasted until the end of the decade. In 1971 they won the international competition for the Pompidou Centre in Paris with their unmistakable inside-out design. The architecture critic Paul Goldberger described Piano's style after the Pompidou Centre as "straighter, quieter, and vastly more inventive" in its "expression of technology." Notable in this regard were the Menil Collection museum (1986) in Houston, the San Nicola Stadium (1990) in Bari, Italy, the Kansai International Airport Terminal (1994) near Osaka, the Beyeler Foundation Museum (1997) near Basel, Switz., and the Jean-Marie Tjibaou Cultural Center (1998) in Nouméa, New Caledonia. Piano's many honours included the 1995 Erasmus Prize for contributions to European culture and the 1998 Pritzker Architectural Prize. In 1994 he was named UNESCO's goodwill ambassador for architecture, and in 2000 he was made an officer in the French Legion of Honour.

(JANET MOREDOCK)

Pohamba, Hifikepunye

On March 21, 2005, Hifikepunye Pohamba was sworn in as the president of Namibia, succeeding Sam Nujoma, who had decided not to seek a fourth term in office. Pohamba had cruised to a landslide victory in the presidential election of November 2004, garnering 76% of the vote. Few were surprised at the election's outcome. At the 2004 congress held by the ruling South West African People's Organization (SWAPO), Nujoma had made clear that he favoured Pohamba to succeed him as president, and the party subsequently gave Pohamba its nomination. Pohamba, who faced little serious opposition in the general election, became Namibia's second president since the country gained independence from South Africa in 1990.

Hifikepunye Lucas Pohamba was born on Aug. 18, 1935, in the district of Okanghudi in northern Namibia. After attending Holy Cross Anglican mission school, he worked in the Tsumeb mine from 1956 to 1960, when he became a full-time organizer for SWAPO, of which he was a founding member. In June 1961 he was arrested on charges of political agitation. He was subsequently convicted by a tribal court in Ohangwena, publicly flogged, and ordered to leave the area. He made his way to Tanganyika (now mainland Tanzania), where he joined the SWAPO leadership in exile.

During the ensuing years, Pohamba returned several times to Namibia to work on behalf of SWAPO and again was charged with agitating against South African rule. In 1966 he and Nujoma were expelled from the country. It was during this time that he became Nujoma's most trusted confidant. In 1969 Pohamba was elected a member of SWAPO's Central Committee and made deputy administrative secretary of the party. By 1977 he had become the party's secretary of finance. From 1979 to 1981 he was in charge of SWAPO affairs in Zambia, and then he was transferred to party headquarters in Luanda, Angola, where he remained until the SWAPO leadership returned to Namibia in 1989.

At Namibia's independence Pohamba became a member of the National Assembly and served as the country's first minister of home affairs. In 1995 he took over as minister of fisheries and marine resources, and as minister without portfolio from 1998 to 2000, he campaigned for the constitution to be amended to allow Nujoma to serve a third term. SWAPO elected Pohamba its secretary-general in 1997 and vice president of the party in 2002. Upon taking office as president of

Namibia, Pohamba vowed to "uphold the legacy" of Nujoma, who—despite having given up the presidency—would remain chairman of SWAPO. Pohamba talked of the need to hasten land reform in a country where, according to the government, 95% of the agricultural land was controlled by 5% of the population, most of whom were white farmers. He also spoke out strongly against corruption. In August 2005 Pohamba traveled to Zimbabwe and thanked its people for having helped liberate his country.　　(CHRISTOPHER SAUNDERS)

Roberts, John G., Jr.

On Sept. 29, 2005, John G. Roberts, Jr., was confirmed by the Senate 78–22 and took the oath of office as the 17th chief justice of the United States. Pres. George W. Bush had originally nominated him on July 19 to replace Justice Sandra Day O'Connor, who was retiring from her seat on the Supreme Court. On September 5, however, two days after Chief Justice William H. Rehnquist died and just before confirmation hearings were to begin, the president named him to replace Rehnquist. Although conservative, Roberts did not emerge as an ideologue, but his refusal during the hearings to reveal his personal views or positions on questions likely to come before the court made some on both the right and the left uneasy. Nonetheless, his broad understanding of constitutional law and his thoughtful approach won him relatively easy confirmation.

John Glover Roberts was born on Jan. 27, 1955, in Buffalo, N.Y., and raised in Long Beach, Ind. In 1976 he received a B.A. degree from Harvard University—having graduated in three years—and in 1979 he was awarded a J.D. degree from Harvard Law School. Although he spent two periods, 1986–89 and 1993–2003, with a law firm in Washington, D.C., primarily handling corporate cases, much of his experience was in government. In 1979–80 he was a clerk for Henry J. Friendly on the 2nd Circuit Court of Appeals, and he often cited the influence of Friendly's approach of giving careful weight to fact, law, and precedent. In 1980–81 he was a clerk for Rehnquist, then an associate justice of the Supreme Court. From 1982 to 1986 he worked in the administration of Pres. Ronald Reagan, first as an assistant to the attorney general and then as associate counsel to the president, and from 1989 to 1993 he was deputy solicitor general in the administration of Pres. George H.W. Bush. During his years in private and government practice, he argued 39 cases before the Supreme Court, winning 25. In 2003 he was appointed to the District of Columbia Circuit Court of Appeals.

Because Roberts had been a judge for only a brief period, he had a short written record. Further, the Bush administration refused to release papers from his years in the Justice Department. Thus, members of the Judiciary Committee questioned him closely on key issues, including a constitutional right to privacy, which underlay *Roe* v. *Wade* among other matters, and the scope of the Constitution's commerce clause, on which Congress based many regulatory laws. Frequently using the words *modesty* and *humility*, he expressed the view that courts should play only a limited role and not determine social policy. At the same time, he affirmed a broader interpretation of the Constitution than one based solely on the writers' original intent.

(ROBERT RAUCH)

Rutan, Burt

In 2005 the possibility of an ordinary person's journeying to outer space was no longer restricted to the realm of science fiction. Leading the push toward commercial space travel was Burt Rutan, a visionary aircraft designer whose SpaceShipOne became the first private manned aircraft to travel into what scientists considered outer space. For his efforts Rutan received the National Academy of Sciences Award in Aeronautical Engineering in 2005.

Elbert L. Rutan was born on June 17, 1943, in Portland, Ore., and raised in Dinuba, Calif., where he and his older brother, Dick, developed a strong interest in flight at an early age. The brothers would design model airplanes and then test them by holding the models out the car window as their mother drove. Rutan took flying lessons as a teenager and flew solo at age 16. He attended California State Polytechnic College (now University) and in 1965 received a degree in aeronautical engineering. He also studied at the Space Technology Institute at the California Institute of Technology and the Aerospace Research Pilot's School at Edwards Air Force Base, California, where he worked (1965–72) for the U.S. Air Force as a civilian test project engineer.

After two years as director of the test centre at Bede Aircraft Co. in Newton, Kan., Rutan returned to California in 1974 and founded Rutan Aircraft Factory, which built light aircraft. Rutan soon gained acclaim among aviation buffs for designing airplanes that could be built at home, such as the VariEze. His designs were characterized by their unusual appearance and the use of high-tech materials such as fibreglass and plastics. Rutan's fame spread worldwide in 1986 when his aircraft *Voyager*, piloted by his brother and Jeana Yeager, set a record by making the first unrefueled flight around the world.

In 1982 Rutan launched a second company, Scaled Composites, which created research aircraft. SpaceShipOne was developed at Scaled Composites, with significant financial backing from billionaire Paul Allen, cofounder of Microsoft Corp. The craft set a new civilian altitude record of 64 km (40 mi) in May 2004. Then, in October 2004, Rutan won the $10 million Ansari X Prize by sending SpaceShipOne into suborbital flight—100 km (62 mi) above the Earth—twice in a two-week period. Shortly afterward, Virgin Galactic, a subsidiary of Virgin Atlantic Airways, announced plans to license the SpaceShipOne technology and begin producing commercial aircraft to carry paying customers into space. Rutan claimed that some 100 people had already signed contracts to pay $200,000 each to fly to outer space, but the vessels were not expected to be built until at least 2007. He predicted that at least 50,000 people would sign up for commercial trips to outer space in the venture's first dozen years.　　(ANTHONY G. CRAINE)

Sachs, Jeffrey D.

In April 2005 *Time* magazine named American Jeffrey Sachs one of the 100 most influential people in the world for the second straight year. Sachs's reputation as an international economist was long established, but as 2005 unfolded he became a household name associated with plans to rid the world of poverty. This surge in public awareness was prompted in part by the launch on March 1 of his book *The End of Poverty: Economic Possibilities for Our Time*, in which he created a blueprint for the eradication of extreme global poverty by 2025. Sachs believed that Western countries, particularly the U.S., should honour their pledges to give 0.7% of GNP to global development programs. His ambitious solution challenged traditional top-down development policies that required aid to less-developed countries to be donated and planned by Western governments and nongovernmental organizations. Instead, Sachs advocated a bottom-up approach, with recipient countries providing donors with their investment targets. Aid administered in this way would be focused where it was most needed and would avoid the problems associated with a one-size-fits-all program.

The book was a natural follow-up to the January 17 release of the official recommendations of the three-year UN Millennium Project directed by Sachs in his role as adviser to UN Secretary-General Kofi Annan. This report marked the start of a year of global initiatives to make the project's Millennium Development Goals (MDGs)—to reduce poverty, hunger, disease, illiteracy, environmental degradation, and discrimination against women—a reality. At the Group of Eight's July 6–8 summit in Gleneagles, Scot., G-8 leaders agreed to double aid to Africa by 2010 and to cancel debt to the poorest countries. The event, coupled with a series of international music concerts collectively called Live 8, attracted world attention. The meeting of more than 100 world leaders at the UN World Summit in September agreed on an action plan to meet the MDGs.

Sachs was born on Nov. 5, 1954, in Detroit. He studied economics at Harvard University (B.A., 1976; M.A., 1978; Ph.D., 1980) and remained there as an assistant professor (1980–82), associate professor (1982–83), and professor (1983–2002). In 2002 he left Harvard for Columbia University, New York City, where he became a professor of health policy and management and director of the Earth Institute. Sachs established a reputation as an expert on international finance and inflation and was an adviser to the IMF, the World Bank, and the Organisation for Economic Co-operation and Development, among others. He also advised governments in Latin America (notably Bolivia), Eastern Europe, and Asia on how to bring down excessive inflation rates, usually with great success. Sachs drew some rare criticism, however, when the shock treatment he prescribed in 1991 for Russia failed to revive the economy and an oligarchy that often acted outside the law took control of much of Russia's newly privatized resources.

(JANET H. CLARK)

Sedaris, David

Only a few years earlier, American essayist David Sedaris had refused to call himself a writer, but by 2005 he was reading his books to standing-room-only audiences, had been nominated for two Grammy Awards, and was the editor of an anthology of his own favourite short stories. Sedaris's recording of pieces from his nonfiction book *Dress Your Family in Corduroy and Denim* (2004) was nominated for the Grammy for best spoken word album, and *David Sedaris: Live at Carnegie Hall* (2003) was nominated for the award for best comedy album. Of the authors whose stories he anthologized in *Children Playing Before a Statue of Hercules* (2005), Sedaris wrote, "The authors in this book are huge to me, and I am a comparative midget, scratching around in their collective shadow." His fans, and many critics, would not have agreed, however: Sedaris was already being compared to Mark Twain, James Thurber, and Dorothy Parker, and *Time Out New York* proclaimed him "the funniest man alive."

David Raymond Sedaris was born on Dec. 26, 1956, in Johnson City, N.Y. He grew up in Raleigh, N.C., the second oldest of six siblings. His father was an IBM executive, and his mother presided over their raucous household. In 1977 Sedaris dropped out of Kent (Ohio) State University to hitchhike around the United States. On the road he took several unusual jobs and started writing a diary on placemats in diners. While attending (1985–87) the School of the Art Institute of Chicago, he began reading his diaries at a local club, and he eventually was invited to read them on the city's public radio station. In 1991 he moved to New York, where he first appeared on National Public Radio in December 1992 reading his story "The SantaLand Diaries," which recounted his experiences as a Christmas elf at Macy's department store in Manhattan. Within months of the broadcast, Sedaris's essays began to appear in such magazines as *Harper's*, *The New Yorker*, and *Esquire*. His first book, *Barrel Fever*, which included "The SantaLand Diaries," was published in 1994. *Naked* (1997) included a portrait of his wisecracking, perspicacious mother, who died prematurely from cancer. In *Me Talk Pretty One Day* (2000) Sedaris anatomized failed attempts at communication. The subjects treated in *Dress Your Family in Corduroy and Denim* could have been taken from anyone's diary, but Sedaris, by elucidating with a surgeon's skill the countless gaps and crossed wires in each interaction he described, demonstrated once again the hilarious absurdity lurking beneath the veneer of ordinariness. In 2001 he was awarded the Thurber Prize for American Humor, and *Time* magazine named him Humorist of the Year. With his sister Amy he wrote a number of plays, including *One Woman Shoe* (1995), which received an Off-Broadway Theater Award.

(JANET MOREDOCK)

Sihamoni, King Norodom

In 2005 Norodom Sihamoni completed his first full year as king of Cambodia. In October 2004 he had succeeded his father, King Norodom Sihanouk, who abdicated because of poor health—and, some speculated, because doing so would ensure that he could influence Cambodia's official nine-member Throne Council to select his choice of a successor. The 52-year-old Sihamoni, the elder of Sihanouk's two sons with his last queen, Monineath, had spent much of his life outside Cambodia. Although Sihamoni was reportedly reluctant to become king, he accepted the role of monarch after a unanimous vote of approval by the Throne Council.

Sihamoni was born in Phnom Penh, French Cambodia, on May 14, 1953. From an early age he showed an aptitude for the arts. When he was 9, he went to study in Czechoslovakia, and at the age of 14, he starred in *The Little Prince*, a film made by his father. After Sihanouk was deposed in a 1970 coup, Sihamoni remained in Prague, where he attended the National Conservatory and the Academy of Music Arts, concentrating on dance, music, and theatre. In 1975 he joined his father in North Korea and began film school there. He followed his parents and returned to Cambodia during the totalitarian regime (1975–79) of Pol Pot, and after 1976 resided with them under house arrest in the palace. Several of Sihamoni's half-brothers and half-sisters, living elsewhere, died during this period.

After the fall of Pol Pot, the family was evacuated to China, where Sihamoni served as his father's secretary for two years. In 1981 he moved to Paris, where he became a professor of classical dance and formed his own dance troupe, called Ballet Deva. He choreographed some of the troupe's performances and also made two films with a dance focus. In 1992 he was named permanent representative of Cambodia to the United Nations. In 1993, the year his father was recrowned king, Sihamoni became Cambodia's permanent representative to UNESCO, a position he held until 2004.

Sihamoni's selection as king over one of his higher-profile siblings or uncles probably represented Sihanouk's desire for someone neutral and politically untainted to succeed him. Most observers expected that it would be hard for Sihamoni to live up to the reputation of his charismatic and politically savvy father. Sihamoni's initial months as monarch, however, showed him to be a dignified king, humble toward his office and eager to reach out to the Cambodian population. In addition to formal trips abroad, Sihamoni made a series of visits in 2005 to rural Cambodian villages and towns, where he met and talked with residents. He also made known his desire to improve the state of education and health care in Cambodia and to help revive the cultural life of the country.

(JOHN A. MARSTON)

Slutskaya, Irina

On March 19, 2005, as Russian figure skater Irina Slutskaya stood before a jubilant hometown crowd that rained flowers and stuffed animals onto the ice at Moscow's Luzhniki Sports Palace, she sobbed with joy over the greatest triumph of her career. It was the day that Slutskaya capped an unbeaten season by skating an aggressive, error-free program that included seven triple jumps to win the International Skating Union (ISU) women's singles world championship for the second time in four years. Unlike her 2002 victory at Nagano, Japan—which came one month after she earned the silver medal at the Salt Lake City (Utah) Winter Olympics—Slutskaya's brilliant performance in Moscow came after she had missed almost two full seasons of skating. In 2003 she took time away from the rink to care for her ailing mother, a kidney transplant candidate who had to undergo dialysis three times a week. One year later Slutskaya was hospitalized with pericarditis, an inflamma-

© Mladen Antonov/AFP/Getty Images

World figure-skating champion Irina Slutskaya

tion of the heart lining; she also suffered with chronic asthmatic bronchitis, pneumonia, and the fear that she would never skate competitively again. The illnesses forced Slutskaya to sit out almost every competition during the 2004 season. She did skate in the 2004 world championship (after a mandatory tryout ordered by the Russian ice-skating federation), but she was less than fit and finished ninth. After all that she had gone through—and the fact that she won her latest championship at home—Slutskaya called her 2005 gold medal the dearest of her collection.

Slutskaya was born in Moscow on Feb. 9, 1979. She began skating at the age of four upon the urging of her grandmother, who thought the sport might reduce the youngster's frequent colds. Slutskaya took up serious training at a Moscow skating school two years later, and in 1996, at age 16, she became the first Russian woman to win a European figure-skating championship. She went on to conquer the field at five other European championships (1997, 2000, 2001, 2003, and 2005). Those six titles equaled the records of the legendary Sonja Henie and two-time Olympic champion Katarina Witt. Slutskaya also won both the Russian national championship and the ISU Grand Prix Final four times (2000, 2001, 2002, and 2005). At the 2000 Grand Prix Final in Lyon, France, she became the first woman to land the highly difficult triple lutz–triple loop combination. She improved on that at the 2001 world championships, when she landed a triple lutz–triple loop–double toe loop combination. She also invented the double Biellmann spin with foot change. Slutskaya's impressive record was the product of determination, superb athleticism, and technical skills that included remarkable speed, complex spins, intricate footwork, and superb jumping ability—all of which she would need as she prepared to compete at the 2006 Winter Olympics in Turin, Italy.   (RON REID)

Staples, Mavis
After more than 50 years of performing and still in top form, in 2005 American soul, blues, and gospel singer Mavis Staples accepted a Lifetime Achievement Award from the Recording Academy on behalf of her family's vocal group, the Staple Singers, in February and received three W.C. Handy Awards in May. Her chart-topping blues album *Have a Little Faith* (2004) won the Handy Awards for best blues album and best soul blues album, and she received the award for best female soul blues artist. They were her first awards as a solo performer. The smoky-voiced Staples was also nominated for a Grammy Award for best gospel performance for her duet with Dr. John "Lay My Burden Down" (2004). The honours marked the culmination of Staples's return to performing and recording following the death in December 2000 of her father, Roebuck ("Pops") Staples, who founded the Staple Singers. Mavis Staples recorded *Have a Little Faith* as a tribute to her father, whose influence—musical, parental, and spiritual—was everywhere evident on the album. Included on it was Staples's rendition of "Will the Circle Be Unbroken," a favourite of her father's, as well as "Pops Recipe," which incorporated in its lyrics biographical details from the elder Staples's life and cherished examples of his fatherly advice.

Staples was born on July 10, 1939, in Chicago. At age 11 she joined the family gospel-singing group led by her father. As a high-school graduate in 1957, she had aspirations of becoming a nurse, but her father persuaded her to stay with the group, which recorded several gospel hits by the early 1960s. The Staple Singers' transition to soul and rhythm and blues began in the late 1960s, when they signed with Stax Records, the same label on which Staples recorded her solo debut, *Mavis Staples*, in 1969. Her second solo effort, *Only for the Lonely* (1970), included the hit "I Have Learned to Do Without You," but it was the Staple Singers' string of Top 40 hits in the 1970s that made Staples and her family true pop stars. Her solo albums of the late 1970s and '80s did not fare well as she experimented unsuccessfully with disco and electropop. *Time Waits for No One* (1989) and *The*

Voice (1993), despite critics' praise, also failed to prosper, and Staples's struggle to find a suitable outlet for her music continued. In 1996 she recorded *Spirituals and Gospel: Dedicated to Mahalia Jackson* in honour of Jackson, a close friend and role model. Staples curtailed her musical activity as her father's health declined in the late 1990s. Her first recordings after his death were collaborations with other artists, including Bob Dylan and Los Lobos. Her duet with Dylan, "Gonna Change My Way of Thinking" (2003), was nominated for a Grammy Award.   (JANET MOREDOCK)

Stringer, Howard
In March 2005 the giant Japanese technology and entertainment company Sony broke with tradition by appointing Welsh-born Howard Stringer as its first non-Japanese chairman and CEO. At age 63 Stringer could have chosen a quieter life and a lesser challenge, but that would have been out of character for a man who had never taken the easy road.

Stringer was born in Cardiff, Wales, on Feb. 19, 1942. After studying modern history at Merton College, Oxford, he left in 1965 with a master's degree and no idea what he wanted to do for a living but with a passion to find his vocation in the United States. He found a job in the television industry answering telephones at CBS for the *Ed Sullivan Show* in New York City. Six weeks after he started work, Stringer's thoughts of building a career in the media were interrupted when he was drafted into the U.S. Army to fight in Vietnam. He declined to exploit his foreign nationality to avoid the draft and won five medals during his tour of duty—an achievement he later played down by saying, self-deprecatingly, that he was "in charge of medals" in his company.

After completing his military service, Stringer returned to CBS, where he stayed until 1995. For most of that time, he worked for CBS News, including three years as the executive producer of the *CBS Evening News with Dan Rather*, and two years as president of CBS News. Between 1974 and 1976 he won nine Emmy Awards as a writer, director, and executive producer. As president (1988–95) of CBS, he turned the company's fortunes around. Among his successes was hiring late-night talk-show host David Letterman from NBC in 1993.

In 1997 Stringer joined Sony as president of the company's American subsidiary. He turned its unprofitable entertainment operations around and made several successful acquisitions, including the highly profitable Spider-Man franchise and MGM's library of classic films. As an outsider, Stringer was also able to bring a new strategy to Sony's music division, which he steered into a merger with Bertelsmann. Stringer's successes prompted Sony to appoint him to head the company, hoping that he would restore the fortunes of the corporation, which had once been synonymous with Japanese technological prowess but which had slipped so badly that by early 2005 its market value was only half that of the South Korean company Samsung. Sony's failure was not just financial; although it was a longtime provider of the latest "must-have" technology products, its status among consumers had

fallen behind such innovative companies as Apple Computer Corp. On becoming chairman of Sony, Stringer said that his ambition was to make the company "cool again."

Though Stringer became a U.S. citizen in 1985, he received an honorary British knighthood in 1999.   (PETER KELLNER)

Thackeray, Bal
Published in May 2005, *Bal Keshav Thackeray: A Photobiography* commemorated the career of one of modern-day India's most controversial political leaders. Although Thackeray had never held an official post or run for elective office, the 78-year-old founder of the radical Hindu Shiv Sena ("Army of Shiva") Party was generally regarded as the most powerful man in the western Indian state of Maharashtra. He was often referred to as the "godfather of Maharashtra" or, as his legion of devout followers called him, Hindu Hridaysamrat ("emperor of the Hindu heart"). His party advocated the end of India's constitutional status as a secular state and the adoption of Hinduism as the nation's official religion. Such was Thackeray's power that when the Shiv Sena gained political control of Maharashtra in the 1990s, he had Bombay renamed Mumbai after the goddess Mumbadevi—the name by which the city is known in the regional language of Marathi—and when Thackeray was satirized by novelist Salman Rushdie in *The Moor's Last Sigh* (1995),

Hindu nationalist Bal Thackeray

the book was immediately banned in Maharashtra. Over the years, Thackeray had been accused of inciting violent conflicts between Hindus and Muslims. The most notorious incident came in 1992–93, when nearly 1,000 people were killed during several weeks of anti-Muslim rioting in Mumbai. Despite having been known to speak admiringly of Adolf Hitler and even refer to himself as the "Hitler of India," Thackeray insisted that he was "not against each and every" Muslim. "But those Muslims who reside in this country but do not go by the laws of the land," he once declared in an interview, "I consider such people traitors."

Thackeray was born on Jan. 23, 1927, in Pune, Maharashtra state, British India. He began his career in the early 1950s as a cartoonist for the *Free Press Journal* in Mumbai. His cartoons also appeared in the Tokyo daily newspaper *Asahi shimbun* and in the Sunday edition of the *New York Times*. In the 1960s he became increasingly involved in politics. He developed a strong regional following through his work for a weekly Marathi-language journal called *Marmik*, which he published with his brother and which polemicized against the influence of "outsiders" in Maharashtra. In 1966 he founded the Shiv Sena.

Amid allegations that it employed illegal and sometimes violent tactics, Thackeray's party grew into a major political force in the state. In alliance with the Bharatiya Janata Party (BJP), the Shiv Sena won 138 out of 288 seats in the Maharashtra provincial assembly in 1995—enough to form a coalition government. In power, Thackeray continued to be a lightning rod for controversy. His supporters destroyed the 16th-century Babri mosque in Ayodhya, Uttar Pradesh, in 1992, and in 2000 he was arrested on charges of having incited the deadly 1992–93 Mumbai riots. Though Thackeray never denied the charges, they were dismissed after a magistrate ruled that the statute of limitations on the case had run out.

The BJP–Shiv Sena alliance suffered a stunning setback in October 2004 when it lost six seats in the Maharashtra elections that many observers had expected the alliance to dominate, and speculation began to turn on who might eventually succeed the aging Shiv Sena leader. His nephew Raj Thackeray—who was responsible for compiling *Bal Keshav Thackeray: A Photobiography*—had been mentioned as a possibility, as had Thackeray's son Uddhav, who had already assumed the post of executive president of the Shiv Sena.

(SHERMAN HOLLAR)

Usher

Three Grammy awards and a place atop the *Los Angeles Times*'s "Pop Power List" in 2005 confirmed the extraordinary popularity of the talented rhythm-and-blues superstar Usher. His *Confessions* album sold more than a million copies during its first week of release in March 2004, and that sprawling, hour-long collection became that year's runaway best seller (with 7,978,594 copies sold). At December's Billboard Music Awards, Usher collected 11 trophies and was named overall artist of the year. He won two prizes at the People's Choice Awards on Jan. 9, 2005, and three more at the Grammy Awards on February 13—for best contemporary R&B album, best R&B performance by a duo or group (with Alicia Keys [*q.v.*] for "My Boo"), and best rap/sung collaboration (with Ludacris and Lil Jon for "Yeah!"). On March 1, one day after winning four Soul Train awards, Usher became a part owner of the Cleveland Cavaliers National Basketball Association franchise. On July 24 he was named pop's top artist in the *Los Angeles Times* poll of 21 leading industry executives.

Usher Raymond IV was born on Oct. 14, 1978, in Chattanooga, Tenn. As a youngster he sang in church choirs but sought entry into the mainstream music industry by entering talent shows. At age 12 he moved with his mother and brother to Atlanta, and two years later he secured a recording contract with LaFace Records. *Usher* was released in 1994, with the 15-year-old singer moving beyond his choirboy background by proclaiming that "it's only a sexual thing" on the slow-groove single "Can U Get Wit It." The album was not a commercial success, and Usher spent the next few years working on a follow-up.

My Way (1997) marked Usher as a major R&B star. His singles "You Make Me Wanna" and "Nice & Slow" topped R&B charts (the latter was also a number one pop song), and the performer reached greater audiences through appearances on television shows (he had a recurring role on UPN's *Moesha* series).

© Frank Micelotta/Getty Images

R&B superstar Usher

Onstage his prowess as a dancer was as notable as his fluid singing voice.

His third studio album, *8701* (2001), further defined Usher's reputation as a smooth, seductive, and bankable artist. Music from *8701* gave Usher two number one pop hits and his first two Grammy Awards. With *Confessions*, Usher extended his range beyond ballads, collaborating most famously with Atlanta rappers Lil Jon and Ludacris.

(PETER COOPER)

Vázquez Rosas, Tabaré Ramón

On March 1, 2005, Tabaré Vázquez was sworn in as the new president of Uruguay. The historic significance of this event could not be overestimated. Vázquez was the first leftist president in Uruguay's history, and the coalition he led, the Broad Front–Progressive Encounter—which was composed of former guerrillas, socialists, communists, and independent leftists—enjoyed a majority in both houses of the parliament. Vázquez's rise was emblematic of an electoral trend to the left throughout Latin America. Among the ambitious goals he established for his presidency were improving an economy that had been beset by years of negative growth, bringing greater social justice to the country, and dealing with the legacy of human rights violations that had taken place during Uruguay's 1973–85 military dictatorship.

Vázquez was born in Montevideo, Uruguay, on Jan. 17, 1940. He graduated from the medical school of the University of the Republic, Montevideo, in 1972 with a specialty in oncology and radiology. He entered private practice as an oncologist and built a reputation as one of the premier doctors in the country. Vázquez served as director of the University of the Republic medical school's department of radiology. He also founded the first medical clinic in his childhood neighbourhood of Las Teja. Vázquez further raised his public profile as president (1978–89) of the Club Progreso, an association football (soccer) team.

A lifelong militant in the Socialist Party, Vázquez became a member of the party's Central Committee in 1987. In 1989 he ran successfully as the Broad Front candidate for mayor of Montevideo, generally considered the second most important political post in the country. Since more than 40% of Uruguay's population lived in the capital, Vázquez's victory in the mayoral race represented the left's first triumph in a national election. The win also firmly established the charismatic and photogenic Tabaré, as many Uruguayans simply called him, as a political force.

Vázquez was the left's presidential candidate in 1994 and again in 1999, but he lost both of these elections. In 1999, however, he won the initial round of voting but failed to achieve the majority required by new electoral laws for avoiding a runoff. He went on to lose the runoff to Jorge Batlle by a 52–44% margin. In 2004 Vázquez was perfectly positioned for a third try for the presidency. By then polls were showing that the Broad Front–Progressive Encounter had become the largest party in the country, and Vázquez was able to claim 50.45% of the vote and avoid a second round. One of his first acts as president was to announce a $200 million National Emergency Plan to assist the estimated 20% of Uruguayans in abject poverty.

(MARTIN WEINSTEIN)

von Otter, Anne Sofie

As the Swedish mezzo-soprano Anne Sofie von Otter celebrated her 50th birthday in 2005, she continued to enjoy enormous success on the opera stage, in the concert hall, and on recordings. Stage appearances during the year included the role of Mélisande in Claude Debussy's *Pelléas et Mélisande* at the Metropolitan Opera in New York City, and her recording of Gustav Mahler's song cycle *Kindertotenlieder*, with the Vienna Philharmonic conducted by Pierre Boulez, received warm receptions from critics and listeners alike.

Von Otter was born in Stockholm on May 9, 1955. Her father was a diplomat, and she grew up not only in Stockholm but also in Bonn, then the capital of West Germany, and in London. She studied at London's Guildhall School of Music and Drama and then trained in lied performance. Her first affiliation was with the Basel (Switz.) Opera from 1983 to 1985, where she quickly gained distinction in works by Wolfgang Amadeus Mozart and Richard Strauss. She made her debut at London's Covent Garden in 1985 and at New York's Metropolitan Opera in 1988, and she was soon singing in major opera houses and concert halls worldwide. Her repertoire was extraordinarily broad, ranging from the Baroque works of Claudio Monteverdi, George Frideric Handel, and Johann Sebastian Bach to the music of 19th-century Romantics and 20th-century composers. With a small, pure lyric voice that was often described as "cool," she was especially convincing in trouser roles, including Cherubino in Mozart's *Marriage of Figaro*, Hänsel in Engelbert Humperdinck's *Hänsel and Gretel*, and Octavian in Strauss's

Swedish mezzo-soprano Anne Sofie von Otter

Der Rosenkavalier. At the same time, she was known for adventurous programs of lieder, usually accompanied by pianist Bengt Forsberg, that included not only the mainstream repertoire by composers such as Franz Schubert, Robert Schumann, and Johannes Brahms but also songs by Alexander Zemlinsky, Alban Berg, Erich Korngold, Kurt Weill, and others. In addition, she recorded two acclaimed discs of songs by Nordic composers, *Wings in the Night* (1996) and *Watercolours* (2004). In 2001 she appeared in a concert in Stockholm commemorating the 100th anniversary of the Nobel Prize, with living laureates in attendance. That same year she issued *For the Stars*, a recording with pop star Elvis Costello that she called a project of "cross-pollination" and that included songs by the Beatles and the Beach Boys.

She has received many honours, including being named the recording artist of the year (1990) by the International Record Critics Award, singer of the year by the Cannes Classical Awards (1995) and the Echo Awards (2001), and artist of the year by *Gramophone* (1996) and *Diapason d'Or* (1997) magazines. A number of her recordings also have received prizes. (ROBERT RAUCH)

Wolfowitz, Paul

Already widely known as one of the main architects of the war in Iraq, Paul Wolfowitz took on a decidedly different role on the global stage in 2005: president of the World Bank. In his post as U.S. deputy secretary of defense, Wolfowitz had spent most of the previous four years being characterized as a warmonger by opponents of the administration of Pres. George W. Bush. Now he was at the helm of an organization trying to eradicate poverty in the less-developed world. Wolfowitz and his supporters saw the move as a logical progression in a career guided by a belief in the value of economic development as a means to achieve political stability. Critics feared that Wolfowitz, a neoconservative,

would transform the World Bank into a tool to promote American interests.

Paul Dundes Wolfowitz was born on Dec. 22, 1943, in Brooklyn, N.Y. His father, a Polish immigrant whose family died in the Holocaust, taught mathematics at Columbia University, New York City, and later at Cornell University, Ithaca, N.Y., where the younger Wolfowitz, true to his father's wishes, earned his B.A. degree in mathematics in 1965. As a young man he began reading about history and politics, and in 1963 he traveled to Washington, D.C., to participate in a civil rights march. Instead of further study in mathematics, he switched to political science and received a Ph.D. from the University of Chicago in that field in 1972.

Wolfowitz went to work in Washington, first in the U.S. Arms Control and Disarmament Agency, where he was on the staff of the Strategic Arms Limitation Talks (1973–77), and then at the Pentagon as a deputy assistant secretary of defense (1977–80). During the presidency of Ronald Reagan, he served as assistant secretary of state for East Asian and Pacific affairs and then as U.S. ambassador to Indonesia. There his exposure to a moderate Muslim society friendly toward the United States convinced him that American military might could be used as a force to promote democracy around the world. Under Pres. George H.W. Bush, Wolfowitz served as undersecretary of defense for policy, working on plans for the First Gulf War under Defense Secretary Dick Cheney. During the presidency of Bill Clinton, Wolfowitz left government for academia and served as dean of the School of Advanced International Studies of Johns Hopkins University in Washington.

A soft-spoken man, Wolfowitz described himself as a "bleeding heart" when it came to social issues. His positions sometimes were no more popular with his allies than they were with his foes. He supported the overthrow of Iraqi Pres. Saddam Hussein at a time when the U.S. government still supported the dictator. He also drew the ire of other neoconservatives because he supported the formation of a separate Palestinian state in the Middle East. He said that his motivation for entering the world of politics was his desire to do what he could to prevent nuclear war. (ANTHONY G. CRAINE)

Wood, Fiona

On Jan. 25, 2005, British-born Australian plastic surgeon Fiona Wood was honoured as Australian of the Year at a ceremony in Canberra. Prime Minister John Howard presented the award to Wood, a 47-year-old mother of six who had earned an international reputation for her work in developing "spray-on-skin" technology for use in treating burn victims. Her technique was considered a significant advancement in skin repair, helping to reduce scarring in patients with extensive burns and speed their rate of recovery. In 2002

Wood, who served as head of the burns unit at Royal Perth Hospital (RPH), found herself the focus of media attention following the deadly Bali (Indon.) bombings in October of that year. A number of the bombing survivors were evacuated to RPH, where Wood led a team that was credited with saving the lives of 28 of those patients, some of whom had suffered burns over more than 90% of their bodies.

Wood was born in 1958 in a mining village in Yorkshire county, Eng. Athletic as a youth, she had originally dreamed of becoming an Olympic sprinter before eventually setting her sights on a medical career. She graduated from St. Thomas's Hospital Medical School in London in 1981 and worked for a time at a British hospital. She moved to Perth in 1987 after marrying surgeon Tony Keirath, a native of Western Australia. She became Western Australia's first—and, to date, only—female plastic surgeon. In addition to her position as head of the burns unit at RPH, she also served as a clinical professor at the School of Paediatrics and Child Health at the University of Western Australia and directed the McComb Research Foundation.

From the early 1990s Woods focused her research on improving established techniques of skin repair. Her spray-on-skin technique involved taking a small patch of healthy skin from a burn victim and using that to grow new skin cells in a laboratory. The new cells were then sprayed onto the patient's damaged skin. With traditional skin grafts, 21 days had been needed to grow enough cells to cover extensive burns. Using spray-on skin, Wood was able to lower that amount of time to just five days.

Wood patented her spray-on-skin technique and in 1993 cofounded a company, Clinical Cell Culture, to release the technology worldwide. The company went public in 2002, with much of the money it generated being used to fund further research. Wood's goals were to "continuously improve burn care" and one day achieve "scarless, woundless healing." (SHERMAN HOLLAR)

Yudhoyono, Susilo Bambang

Indonesian Pres. Susilo Bambang Yudhoyono, commonly known as SBY, had a strong mandate for pushing through reforms in 2005. He had won a landslide election victory over incumbent Pres. Megawati Sukarnoputri in September 2004, garnering 61% of the vote, to become Indonesia's sixth president and the first to be popularly elected. His election gave rise to high expectations, both within Indonesia and in the international community. A Western-educated former general, Yudhoyono was widely seen as possessing the personal traits and professional skills necessary to restore prosperity and stability to the country. He was fluent in English and well versed in economics, and his military background was seen as an asset in dealing with Indonesia's many security problems. He entered office with an ambitious reform agenda, which included promises to accelerate economic growth, crack down on corruption and terrorism, and strengthen democracy and human rights.

Yudhoyono was born into a well-to-do family of aristocratic background in Pacitan, East

Java, on Sept. 9, 1949. Following in the footsteps of his father, a middle-ranking army officer, he entered the army after graduating from the Indonesian Military Academy in 1973. He rose quickly through the ranks, a process assisted by his marriage to Kristiani Herawati, the daughter of a powerful general. As an officer he had the opportunity to acquire valuable experience abroad, undertaking the U.S. Army's Infantry Officer Advanced Course in the early 1980s and training at the U.S. Army Command and General Staff College in 1991. He also earned a master's degree in business administration from Webster University near St. Louis, Mo., in 1991. Yudhoyono eventually earned a Ph.D. in economics from the Bogor Agricultural Institute in Indonesia in 2004.

In 1995 Yudhoyono served as Indonesia's chief military observer on the UN peacekeeping force in Bosnia and Herzegovina. He later was chief of the army's social and political affairs staff. Yudhoyono left active military service in 2000 with the rank of lieutenant general. From 2000 to 2004 he held high-profile cabinet posts in the governments of both Abdurrahman Wahid and Megawati.

After his first year as president, opinion about Yudhoyono's leadership qualities and achievements was sharply divided. His admirers saw him as statesmanlike and judicious and undertaking reforms at a politically sensible pace. Some of his agenda had been implemented to promising effect. Yudhoyono had approved extensive anticorruption investigations, finalized a new peace agreement with rebel leaders in the restive province of Aceh, and succeeded in attracting greater foreign investment to Indonesia. Despite these advances, there were grounds for disappointment. In particular, Yudhoyono had proved highly cautious and rarely led public debate on contentious subjects, which led detractors to accuse him of political timidity. As a result, his public standing fell during 2005, though at year's end he remained Indonesia's most popular politician. (GREG FEALY)

Yushchenko, Viktor

Following a tumultuous political battle that had lasted for months, Viktor Yushchenko was inaugurated as the new president of Ukraine on Jan. 23, 2005. Speaking to hundreds of thousands of his orange-clad supporters who packed Independence Square in Kiev, he thanked those who had participated in the so-called Orange Revolution, the popular protest movement that helped sweep him into office. While vowing to uphold national sovereignty, the pro-Western politician also wasted little time in declaring that Ukraine's future "is in the European Union and my goal is 'Ukraine in a United Europe.'" The year 2004 had largely been taken up by the bitter election campaign between Yushchenko and Prime Minister Viktor Yanukovich. The contest included an apparent assassination attempt on Yushchenko in which a type of dioxin poison left his face disfigured and pockmarked. Mass protests followed a runoff round in which Yanukovich had been declared the winner, and the Supreme Court, after invalidating that result, ordered a second runoff to be held on

December 26. In early January 2005 Ukraine's Central Election Commission officially confirmed Yushchenko as the winner of the election by a 52–44% margin over Yanukovich.

Viktor Andriyovych Yushchenko was born on Feb. 23, 1954, in the village of Khoruzhivka in the Sumy region of northeastern Ukraine. Both of his parents were schoolteachers. He was educated at the Ternopil Finance and Economics Institute, where he graduated with a degree in economic sciences in 1975. Returning to Sumy, he became an accounting assistant on a collective farm. He briefly served in the Soviet army before accepting a position as an economist at the Sumy branch of the Soviet State Bank in 1976. In the late 1980s he served as deputy chairman of the board of directors at the Agro-Industrial Bank of Ukraine, and from 1990 to 1993 he was the first deputy chairman of the board at Bank Ukraina.

In 1993 Yushchenko was appointed governor of newly independent Ukraine's national bank. In this position he oversaw the introduction in 1996 of the national currency, the hryvnya. In 1999 Pres. Leonid Kuchma appointed Yushchenko prime minister. Over the next year and a half, many analysts credited Yushchenko with helping Ukraine emerge from a protracted financial and economic crisis. Among other measures, he introduced fiscal restraints and ended the costly practice of issuing subsidies to unprofitable companies. He also made progress with the difficult problem of tax reform. In 2001 Kuchma abruptly dismissed Yushchenko, partly because he feared his growing popularity. Yushchenko responded by forming a broad-based democratic coalition called Our Ukraine, which was victorious in the parliamentary elections later that year and gave him a platform from which to mount a credible challenge to Kuchma and his increasingly corrupt administration.

As president, Yushchenko encountered turbulence almost immediately. He faced a fuel crisis beginning in May, and in September he replaced his entire cabinet, accusing it of incompetence. He appeared, however, to make some significant first steps toward his goal of forging new ties with the West, addressing the European Parliament and attending a NATO commission meeting in February and making a four-day state visit to the U.S. in April. (DAVID R. MARPLES)

Zhang Ziyi

Young Chinese film actress Zhang Ziyi continued her rise to international stardom in 2005 with her leading role in the epic romance *Memoirs of a Geisha*, the motion-picture adaptation of Arthur Golden's best-selling 1997 novel. Produced by Steven Spielberg and directed by Rob Marshall, the film, which told the story of a famous geisha living in Kyoto, Japan, just before World War II, was only the latest in a series of high-profile projects for Zhang. She had first captured worldwide attention in 2000 in the martial-arts blockbuster *Crouching Tiger, Hidden Dragon*, in which she played a headstrong young aristocrat with a secret life as a high-flying adventuress. A lithe beauty, Zhang was noted for her physical grace in the film's action scenes and for her

solid performance alongside veteran actors Chow Yun Fat and Michelle Yeoh. Directed by Ang Lee, *Crouching Tiger, Hidden Dragon* captured four Academy Awards and became the highest-grossing foreign-language film ever. It also marked Zhang as an emerging star and one of international cinema's most intriguing new figures.

Zhang was born on Feb. 9, 1979, in Beijing. Worried about her slight build, her parents enrolled her in dance classes to help strengthen her body. From the age of 11, she attended the Beijing Dance Academy, where she specialized in folk dance. At 17 she successfully auditioned for enrollment at the prestigious China Central Drama College, where she received her first formal acting lessons. While at the college filming a commercial, director Zhang Yimou discovered her and cast her in her first film, *The Road Home* (1999). The following year he recommended her to Lee for the role in *Crouching Tiger, Hidden Dragon*.

The runaway success of *Crouching Tiger* led to a steady string of film roles for Zhang. She made her Hollywood debut in 2001 opposite Jackie Chan and Chris Tucker in the action-comedy *Rush Hour 2* and had her next big in-

Actress Zhang Ziyi

ternational hit with another Zhang Yimou-directed film, *Hero* (2002), which told the story of the first emperor of China. She also appeared in *Musa* (2001), *The Legend of Zu* (2001), *Purple Butterfly* (2003), *Jasmine Women* (2004), and *House of Flying Daggers* (2004). For her work in *2046* (2004), a science-fiction love story directed by Hong Kong filmmaker Wong Kar Wai, Zhang won best actress at the 2005 Hong Kong Film Awards.

Aside from *Memoirs of a Geisha*, Zhang also starred in *Princess Raccoon* in 2005. Directed by legendary Japanese filmmaker Seijun Suzuki, *Princess Raccoon* was an elaborate musical adaptation of a Japanese folktale. The film debuted to enthusiastic critical praise at Cannes. At year's end Zhang was in the midst of filming *The Banquet*; directed by Feng Xiaogang, the film was loosely based on *Hamlet* and was set for release in late 2006. (TOM MICHAEL)

Obituaries

In 2005 the world LOST many leaders, PATHFINDERS, newsmakers, HEROES, cultural icons, and ROGUES. The pages below RECAPTURE the lives and accomplishments of those we REMEMBER best.

Adams, Don (DONALD JAMES YARMY), American actor and comedian (b. April 13, 1923, New York, N.Y.—d. Sept. 25, 2005, Los Angeles, Calif.), portrayed the bumbling Maxwell Smart, Agent 86, in 138 episodes of the television spy-spoof series *Get Smart* (1965–70) and in a subsequent feature film, made-for-TV

© Bettmann/Corbis

Don Adams as Agent 86

movie, and another, short-lived series. He employed a number of ludicrous gadgets, including a dial phone hidden in his shoe, and with his nasal voice and clipped delivery, he gave the public such catchphrases as "Sorry about that, Chief," "Missed it by that much," and "Would you believe. . .?" He won three Emmy Awards (1967–69). Adams was also the voice of the title character in the Inspector Gadget cartoons.

Aki, Keiiti, Japanese seismologist (b. March 30, 1930, Yokohama, Japan—d. May 17, 2005, Réunion), developed the concept of the "seismic moment"—a quantitative means of measuring the amount of energy released by an earthquake. The seismic moment, first introduced by Aki in 1966, takes into consideration such factors as the length and depth of the rupture along the fault where an earthquake occurs, the strength of the displaced rocks, and the distance the rocks slip. Scientists considered Aki's seismic moment method to give a more reliable measurement of earthquake force than the Richter scale. Aki was educated at the University of Tokyo, where he earned

B.S. (1952) and Ph.D. (1958) degrees. He was a research fellow at the California Institute of Technology before returning to Japan to teach at the Earthquake Research Institute in Tokyo. From 1966 to 1984 he was a professor of geophysics at the Massachusetts Institute of Technology.

Albert, Eddie (EDWARD ALBERT HEIMBERGER), American actor (b. April 22, 1906, Rock Island, Ill.—d. May 26, 2005, Pacific Palisades, Calif.), was best remembered for his starring role as Oliver Wendell Douglas, a lawyer intent on leaving the trappings of city life to become a gentleman farmer, in the popular TV series *Green Acres* (1965–71). Albert debuted on Broadway in 1936 in the comedy *O Evening Star* and later that year landed a starring role in *Brother Rat*. He was featured in numerous Broadway productions, including *The Boys from Syracuse* (1938), *The Music Man* (1960), and *You Can't Take It with You* (1983). He appeared in nearly 100 films and received Academy Award nominations for his roles in *Roman Holiday* (1953) and *The Heartbreak Kid* (1972). Albert returned to TV in the series *Switch* (1975–78) and *Falcon Crest* (1987).

Alexander, Shana (SHANA AGER), American journalist and author (b. Oct. 6, 1925, New York, N.Y.—d. June 23, 2005, Hermosa Beach, Calif.), battled conservative columnist James Kilpatrick in "Point-Counterpoint," a political debate segment featured during the 1970s on the television program *60 Minutes*. Alexander's parents were prominent members of Manhattan's arts community but were emotionally distant, which she later discussed in her memoir *Happy Days: My Mother, My Father, My Sister & Me* (1995). After graduating (1945) from Vassar College, Poughkeepsie, N.Y., she began working as a reporter and in 1951 became the first woman staff writer at *Life* magazine. She also authored nonfiction books, several of them about notable trials.

Allen, Dave (DAVID TYNAN O'MAHONEY), Irish comedian (b. July 6, 1936, Tallaght, County Dublin, Ire.—d. March 10, 2005, London, Eng.), mocked the absurdities of society, politics, and religion—particularly the Roman Catholic Church and its clergy—usually while he perched casually on a tall chair or stool with a cigarette in one hand (until he quit smoking) and a glass of whiskey in the other. Allen offered his wry comedy monologues and introduced filmed satiric sketches on *Dave Allen at Large* (1971–76 and 1978–79) and

other British television programs from the late 1960s until the mid-1990s.

Anderson, Jack (JACKSON NORTHMAN ANDERSON), American journalist (b. Oct. 19, 1922, Long Beach, Calif.—d. Dec. 17, 2005, Bethesda, Md.), exposed political corruption in Washington, D.C., through his widely syndicated newspaper column, "Washington Merry-Go-Round" (1964–2004). He won a Pulitzer Prize in 1972 for his reports on the shifting positions of the administration of Pres. Richard Nixon on the conflict between Pakistan and India. Anderson had numerous scoops. He broke the Iran-Contra Affair, a scandal that plagued Pres. Ronald Reagan's second term; disclosed the CIA's enlistment of the Mafia to assassinate Fidel Castro; and uncovered the mystery surrounding the death of Howard Hughes. In one miscue, however, Anderson reported in 1972 that Sen. Thomas Eagleton had had drunken-driving arrests. Anderson later confessed (and apologized to Eagleton) that he could not verify the information. Anderson was the author of more than a dozen books.

Andrade, Eugénio de (JOSÉ FONTINHAS), Portuguese poet (b. Jan. 19, 1923, Póvoa de Atalia, Port.—d. June 13, 2005, Porto, Port.), was strongly influenced by Surrealism and used concrete images such as earth, water, and the human body to explore such themes as love, nature, and death. Andrade, who began publishing poetry as a teenager, worked as a civil servant in Porto from 1950 to 1983. A quiet and reclusive man, he produced some 30 volumes of poetry, prose, and translations, and his own work was widely translated. His first major verse collection was *As mãos e os frutos* (1948). Other volumes included *Coração do dia* (1958), *Obscuro domínio* (1971; *Dark Domain*, 2000), *Memória doutro rio* (1978; *Memory of Another River*, 1988), *Branco no branco* (1984; *White on White*, 1987), and *O sal da língua* (1995). He also published bilingual Portuguese- and English-language volumes, notably *Inhabited Heart* (1985) and *Forbidden Words: Selected Poetry* (2003). *Os sulcos da sede* (2001), his last original verse collection, was described as "transparent" and "luminous." Andrade was the recipient of the European Prize for Poetry (1996) and the Camões Prize (2001).

Ángeles, Victoria de los (VICTORIA GÓMEZ CIMA), Spanish soprano (b. Nov. 1, 1923, Barcelona, Spain—d. Jan. 14/15, 2005,

© Erich Auerbach/Getty Images

Victoria de los Angeles in La Bohème

Barcelona), was one of the most celebrated singers of her generation. Her voice was warm and rich, with a wide range, and her repertoire was extraordinarily broad. She sometimes ended recitals with Spanish and Catalan songs, accompanying herself on the guitar. De los Ángeles entered the Barcelona Conservatory in 1940 and completed her studies in three years, half the usual time. By the 1950s she was a star in the world's leading opera houses. Beginning in the 1960s, however, she devoted more and more time to recitals. Although she officially retired in 1979, she continued to make occasional appearances, and she sang in the closing ceremony of the 1992 Olympic Games in Barcelona. De los Ángeles was one of the most recorded singers of her time, with more than 20 operas and an even greater number of recital discs. Among her most prized recordings were those of her performances of the title role in Bizet's *Carmen* and of Mimi in Puccini's *La Bohème* and Cio-Cio-San in his *Madama Butterfly*. She was known for her recording of Joseph Canteloube's *Chants d'Auvergne*, and the recording of her performance with soprano Elisabeth Schwarzkopf of "Duetto buffo di due gatti," Rossini's "cat duet," became a best seller. De los Ángeles's many honours included six Grands Prix du Disque.

Arman (ARMAND PIERRE FERNANDEZ; ARMAND PIERRE ARMAN), French-born artist (b. Nov. 17, 1928, Nice, France—d. Oct. 22, 2005, New York, N.Y), was a founding member of the Nouveau Réalisme movement in 1960s Paris and a master of found-object sculptures, into which he incorporated everyday machine-made objects—ranging from buttons and spoons to automobiles and boxes filled with trash. Arman, who signed his work with his first name (the spelling originated from a printer's error in 1958), was educated in philosophy and mathematics, as well as art and architecture. He began painting as a child and went through periods of Surrealism and abstraction before beginning his work in found

objects in the late 1950s. He mounted his first solo exhibitions in 1956. Arman represented France at international events, including Expo '67 in Montreal, and was the subject of retrospective exhibitions in Minneapolis, Minn. (1964), and Nice, France (2001). He acquired U.S. citizenship in 1973 but also retained his French citizenship.

Atkinson, Theodore Frederick, American jockey (b. June 17, 1916, Toronto, Ont.—d. May 5, 2005, Beaver Dam, Va.), became the first jockey to win more than a million dollars in earnings in a single season (1946). Atkinson began riding professionally at age 21, and his career lasted from 1938 to 1959. He rode War Relic to an upset victory over Triple Crown winner Whirlaway in 1941, but his best mount was Tom Fool, which he rode to Horse of the Year honours in 1953. Atkinson was elected to the National Thoroughbred Racing Hall of Fame in 1957.

Ba Jin (LI YAOTANG), Chinese writer (b. Nov. 25, 1904, Chengdu, Sichuan province, China—d. Oct. 17, 2005, Shanghai, China), was one of the most critically acclaimed and widely read Chinese authors of the 20th century. He was best known for his novels and short stories of the 1930s and '40s, which first brought him international recognition; in these insightful works Ba Jin addressed social concerns and attacked the brutality of feudal life in prerevolutionary China. Born to a large and wealthy

© Lu zhengwei—Imaginechina/Zuma Press

Ba Jin at age 100

family, he received a traditional Confucian education as well as training in foreign languages. He developed an admiration for socialist and anarchist ideas before moving in 1927 to Paris to continue his studies. Ba Jin returned to China two years later, settling in Shanghai and publishing his first novel, *Miewang* ("Extinction"), to great success. He allegedly derived the pseudonym Ba Jin from the names of two Russian anarchists, Mikhail Bakunin and Peter Kropotkin. Ba Jin published perhaps his most famous novel, *Jia* ("Family"), in 1933. The work was the first volume of an autobiographical trilogy, *Jiliu* ("Torrent"), which also included *Chun* (1938; "Spring") and *Qiu* (1940; "Autumn"). Important novels of the 1940s included *Qiyuan* (1944; "Pleasure Garden") and *Hanye* (1946; "Cold Nights"). After the establishment of the

People's Republic of China in 1949, Ba Jin threw his support behind the communist government and was elected to important literary and cultural organizations. He never fully adapted to the new society, however, and his literary output dwindled for a time. Ba Jin later complained that the cultural bureaucracy severely limited what he could write. During the Cultural Revolution (1966–76), he was labeled a counterrevolutionary. He was forced to work menial jobs, and his cancer-stricken wife was denied necessary medical treatment before she died in 1972. Rehabilitated after the death of Mao Zedong in 1976, Ba Jin became a prolific essayist and was elected (1983) a vice-chairman of the Chinese People's Political Consultative Conference and chairman (1981) of the Chinese Writers' Association. Some 150 of his essays were collected in the five-volume *Suixiang lu* (1979–86; "Random Thoughts").

Bahcall, John N., American astrophysicist (b. Dec. 30, 1934, Shreveport, La.—d. Aug. 17, 2005, New York, N.Y.), made fundamental contributions to the understanding of the elusive subatomic particles called neutrinos, which are emitted by the Sun. His work helped prove that the Sun and other stars produce their energy by means of thermonuclear reactions. During his career Bahcall published more than 500 scientific papers and articles that covered not only neutrino astronomy but also such subjects as quasars and dark matter. He was a tireless advocate for the Hubble Space Telescope and was a driving force in its development. From 1971 Bahcall served on the faculty of the Institute for Advanced Study, Princeton, N.J.

Bailey, Derek, British guitarist (b. Jan. 29, 1930, Sheffield, Eng.—d. Dec. 25, 2005, London, Eng.), was the guru of free improvisation, a technique of creating arhythmic music without preset forms or melodies. Although he was first a pop and jazz musician who liked to accompany singers, he was influenced by Anton Webern and John Cage and developed an original, highly influential atonal style that combined spaced fragments of sound into coherent lines. Bailey went on to free-improvise solos and musical conversations with jazz, classical, rock, flamenco, Indian, Japanese, Latin American, and other musicians and dancers. His Incus label recorded dozens of improvisations by himself and other performers, and for his annual Company Weeks (1976–94) in London, he brought together a changing cast of 8–12 musicians from many international traditions to improvise. In his book *Improvisation: Its Nature and Practice in Music* (1980) and the television series *On the Edge* (1989–91), Bailey described how improvisers around the world create their music.

Baldry, Long John (JOHN WILLIAM BALDRY), British-born Canadian blues musician (b. Jan. 12, 1941, Haddon, Derbyshire, Eng.—d. July 21, 2005, Vancouver, B.C.), was one of the founding fathers of the 1960s British blues scene and a mentor to many later stars, including members of the Rolling Stones, Eric Clapton, and Rod Stewart. In the late 1950s

Baldry was one of the first British singers to perform folk and blues music, and in the early '60s he was the vocalist in two seminal blues bands, Alexis Korner's Blues Incorporated and the Cyril Davies R&B All Stars, which became Long John Baldry and the Hoochie Coochie Men. He later formed the groups Steampacket and Bluesology; the latter included a keyboard player who took the stage name Elton John in Baldry's honour. Although Baldry recorded more than 40 albums, he found little commercial success; his best-known songs were "Let the Heartaches Begin" and "Mexico" in Britain and "Don't Try to Lay No Boogie-Woogie on the King of Rock 'n' Roll" in the U.S.

Bancroft, Anne (ANNA MARIA LOUISA ITAL-

IANO), American actress (b. Sept. 17, 1931, Bronx, N.Y.—d. June 6, 2005, New York, N.Y.), was a versatile performer whose half-century-long career was studded with renowned successes on stage, screen, and television. She won both a Tony Award and an Academy Award for one of her most physically and emotionally demanding roles, that of Helen Keller's teacher, Annie Sullivan, in *The Miracle Worker* (Broadway, 1959; film, 1962), but it was with another Oscar-nominated film role, the seductive Mrs. Robinson in *The Graduate* (1967), that—to her bewilderment—she was most identified. Bancroft began her career in the 1950s in live television productions and in a number of grade-B or C movies. Her Broadway debut in the two-character drama *Two for the Seesaw* (1958), however, brought her wide recognition for the depth of her talent and garnered her a best supporting actress Tony. The role of Annie Sullivan followed the next year. Bancroft also received Oscar nominations for her performances in *The Pumpkin Eater* (1964), *The Turning Point* (1977), and *Agnes of God* (1985). For one of Bancroft's occasional returns to the stage— *Golda* (1977)— she received a third Tony nomination, and television roles in PBS's *Mrs. Cage* (1992) and CBS's *Oldest Living Confederate Widow Tells All* (1994) earned her Emmy Award nominations.

Barker, Ronnie (RONALD WILLIAM GEORGE BARKER), British television comedian, writer, and actor (b. Sept. 25, 1929, Bedford, Bedfordshire, Eng.—d. Oct. 3, 2005, Adderbury, Oxfordshire, Eng.), gained international recognition as the costar, with Ronnie Corbett, of the TV comedy-sketch program *The Two Ronnies*, 98 episodes of which were broadcast over a 17-year period (1971–87). The duo had worked together onstage since 1965, and Barker—a burly man—was often simply identified as "the tall one" because he towered over his much-shorter partner. Barker was one of the chief writers for *The Two Ronnies* and other TV programs, and he later appeared in several movies and the sitcoms *Porridge*, *Going Straight*, and *Open All*

The Two Ronnies: Ronnie Barker (left) and Ronnie Corbett

Hours. He abruptly retired from show business in 1988. Barker published several books, including an autobiography and collections of edited antique "saucy" postcards. He was made OBE in 1978.

Baugh, Cecil Archibald, Jamaican potter (b. Nov. 22, 1908, Bangor Ridge, Jam.—d. June 28, 2005, Kingston, Jam.), was one of the most influential Caribbean potters of the 20th century and was renowned for works that showcased his artistry and technical creativity. In 1991 the National Gallery opened a ceramics gallery bearing his name, and in 2003 he received the Order of Jamaica.

Bel Geddes, Barbara, American actress (b. Oct. 31, 1922, New York, N.Y.—d. Aug. 8, 2005, Northeast Harbor, Maine), first gained acclaim for her performances in such films as *I Remember Mama* (1948) and *Vertigo* (1958), for her roles on Broadway as the original Maggie in *Cat on a Hot Tin Roof* (1955) and as the title character in *Mary, Mary* (1961), and for television appearances in *Alfred Hitchcock Presents* in the late 1950s and early '60s. It was as Miss Ellie, the matriarch of the Ewing clan on the nighttime TV soap opera *Dallas*, however, that she found her greatest fame; she starred in that show in 1978–84 and 1985–90 and won an Emmy Award in 1980.

Bell, Mary Hayley, British playwright, novelist, and actress (b. Jan. 22, 1911, Shanghai, China—d. Dec. 1, 2005, Denham, Buckinghamshire, Eng.), turned her back on a promising stage career in the early 1940s following her marriage to actor Sir John Mills (*q.v.*) and instead began writing plays, notably *Men in Shadow* (1942) and *Duet for Two Hands* (1945), both of which starred her husband. She achieved her greatest renown, however, for her novel *Whistle Down the Wind* (1958). Its film adaptation (1961) starred her daughter Hayley Mills, and in the 1990s Andrew Lloyd Webber made it into a stage musical.

Bellow, Saul (SOLOMON BELLOWS), American

novelist (b. June 10, 1915, Lachine, near Montreal, Que.—d. April 5, 2005, Brookline, Mass.), wrote picaresque, often comic tales of thoughtful, modern urbanites and was a leading exponent of Jewish-American literature after World War II. Despite the cerebral worldliness of his characters, Bellow imbued his novels with a levelheaded realism and a fine sense of place. The setting, for example, for *The Adventures of Augie March*, his first major work, was a street-level view of Chicago. Bellow had relocated to Chicago with his family as a child and frequently featured the city as the locale for his works. He attended the University of Chicago, Northwestern University (B.S., 1937), Evanston, Ill., and the University of Wisconsin, before enlisting in the Merchant Marine in World War II. His first novels, *Dangling Man* (1944) and *The Victim* (1947), led to a Guggenheim fellowship and a tour of Europe, particularly to Paris, which enlarged his reputation and readership. (Later, in 1968, France honoured him as a Chevalier of the Legion of Honour.) *Augie March*, published in 1953, was a best seller and won a National Book Award. Bellow again received the award for *Herzog* (1964) and *Mr. Sammler's Planet* (1970), and he won the Pulitzer Prize for *Humboldt's Gift* (1975). In 1976 he was the recipient of the Nobel Prize for Literature. In addition to novels, Bellow wrote plays, criticism, and nonfiction. He was a longtime professor at various universities, notably the University of Chicago, where he was a member of the Committee on Social Thought. One of his final works, *Ravelstein* (2000), presented a fictionalized account of Allan Bloom, a Chicago colleague. Bellow had written the foreword to Bloom's landmark treatise, *The Closing of the American Mind* (1987).

Benenson, Peter James Henry Solomon,

British attorney and human rights activist (b. July 31, 1921, London, Eng.—d. Feb. 25, 2005, Oxford, Eng.), founded Amnesty International (AI) in 1961 after reading in a news story that two students in Portugal had been imprisoned by that country's dictatorial government for proposing a toast to freedom. The event spurred Benenson to submit a full-page article in *The Observer* newspaper entitled "The Forgotten Prisoners," in which he promoted an "Appeal for Amnesty," a yearlong letter-writing campaign to repressive governments on behalf of what he termed "prisoners of conscience." Support for Benenson's campaign quickly spread, and by 2005

Amnesty International was the world's largest human rights organization, with membership soaring to 1.8 million in more than 160 countries. Benenson formally resigned from AI in 1966, but he continued to work for international human rights. AI was awarded the Nobel Prize for Peace in 1977.

Benson, Obie (RENALDO BENSON), American singer and songwriter (b. June 14, 1936, Detroit, Mich.—d. July 1, 2005, Detroit,), lent his powerful bass vocals to the legendary Motown group the Four Tops. Benson founded the group with Lawrence Payton, Abdul ("Duke") Fakir, and Levi Stubbs in 1953. They initially played nightclubs, often performing with such jazz greats as Count Basie and Billy Eckstine. The group signed with Motown Records in 1963 and soon scored hits with pop-inflected tunes such as "Baby I Need Your Loving" (1964), "I Can't Help Myself" (1965), and "Reach Out, I'll Be There" (1966). In 1969 Benson wrote the protest song "What's Going On," which became a hit for Marvin Gaye.

Berberian, Ara, American opera singer (b. May 14, 1930, Detroit, Mich.—d. Feb. 21, 2005, Boynton Beach, Fla.), performed at the Metropolitan Opera in New York City for more than 20 years after having made his debut there in 1979 as Zacharie in Giacomo Meyerbeer's *Le Prophète.* His warm bass distinguished more than 100 roles, ranging from his operatic debut at age 28 with the Turnau Opera in Woodstock, N.Y., as Don Magnifico in Rossini's *La cenerentola* to such Met roles as Don Basilio in Rossini's *The Barber of Seville,* Pimen in Mussorgsky's *Boris Godunov,* and Osmin in Mozart's *The Abduction from the Seraglio.*

Berenstain, Stan (STANLEY MELVIN BERENSTAIN), American children's writer (b. Sept. 29, 1923, Philadelphia, Pa.—d. Nov. 26, 2005, Doylestown, Pa.), was the coauthor with his wife, Janice, of more than 250 books featuring the Berenstain Bears, beginning in 1962 with *The Big Honey Hunt.* The loving family of bears coped with and found solutions to the same types of problems encountered by human children and their families. The Berenstain Bears were also featured on their own animated TV show and became a commercial success, with the merchandising of such items as stuffed animals, cereal, and chocolates. In later years the Berenstains' sons, Leo and Michael, became part of the creative team.

Berman, Lazar Naumovich, Russian-born Italian concert pianist (b. Feb. 26, 1930, Leningrad, U.S.S.R. [now St. Petersburg, Russia]—d. Feb. 6, 2005, Florence, Italy), was a child prodigy who enjoyed an illustrious reputation in the U.S.S.R. and Eastern Europe for his great technical mastery. Between the late 1950s and the mid-1970s, he was not allowed to travel abroad. Berman made his American debut in 1976 and showcased not only his technical mastery but also his splendid romantic style and flair for musical interpretation. He made numerous recordings with conductor Herbert von Karajan. In 1990

Berman moved to Italy and joined the Music Conservatory in Imola as a teacher.

Best, George, British association football (soccer) player (b. May 22, 1946, Belfast, N.Ire.—d. Nov. 25, 2005, London, Eng.), electrified English soccer fans with his thrilling goal-scoring runs while playing for Manchester United (1963–74) and with his glamorous

Footballer George Best

playboy lifestyle off the field. Best was spotted at age 15 by a scout who reported to Manchester United coach Matthew Busby that he had found a "genius." Best promptly signed with United and two years later made his debut in England's first division. In his career with United, he scored 178 goals in 466 appearances. Perhaps his best year was 1968, when he was named Footballer of the Year in both England and Europe and scored the key goal in a 4–1 victory over Benfica of Portugal in the European Cup final. His star began to fade after that year as his drinking and womanizing took a toll on the quality of his play. The handsome, shaggy-haired Best was often called the "fifth Beatle" as he became a leading figure in the swinging culture of 1960s England. After a bitter departure from United, he played for numerous lesser teams in the U.K., Spain, Australia, and the U.S. His drinking continued to affect his play, however, and he became as well known for his squandered talent as for his undeniable brilliance. Best underwent a liver transplant in 2002 but was unable to overcome his alcoholism.

Bethe, Hans Albrecht, German American theoretical physicist (b. July 2, 1906, Strassburg, Ger. [now Strasbourg, France]—d. March 6, 2005, Ithaca, N.Y.), was the head of the Theoretical Physics Division of the Manhattan Project in Los Alamos, N.M., which designed and built the first atomic bomb, and the recipient of the 1967 Nobel Prize for Physics for his research on the production of energy in stars. Bethe received his doctorate

in 1928 from the University of Munich. Following appointments at several European universities, including a post working with Enrico Fermi in Rome, Bethe in 1935 accepted a position with Cornell University, Ithaca, N.Y., where he remained, except for wartime leave, until his retirement in 1975. Bethe became a U.S. citizen in 1941, shortly before the U.S. entered World War II. Following his reading in the *Encyclopædia Britannica* that the armour-piercing qualities of grenades were not well understood, he formulated a theory that became the foundation for research on the problem. His work on the subject was quickly classified, and he earned a security clearance to work on radar development at the Massachusetts Institute of Technology before moving on to Los Alamos. Bethe's main research interest to this point had been atomic nuclei. In particular, in 1938 he had discovered the main sequence of stellar nuclear chain reactions, and his contributions to the construction of the first atomic bomb were considerable. Bethe was a longtime director of and contributor to *The Bulletin of the Atomic Scientists,* a publication devoted to informing the world about the dangers of nuclear war. During the 1980s he was a vociferous opponent of the Strategic Defense Initiative, or "Star Wars." Bethe was awarded the Max Planck Medal in 1955 and the Atomic Energy Commission's Enrico Fermi Award in 1961.

Bjelke-Peterson, Sir Joh(annes), Australian politician (b. Jan. 13, 1911, Dannevirke, N.Z.—d. April 23, 2005, Kingaroy, Queen., Australia), was the idiosyncratic right-wing premier of Queensland for a record 19 years (1968–87); he ruled with autocratic, near-absolute power until he was brought down in a corruption scandal. Bjelke-Peterson, the son of Danish-born farmers, had polio as a child and was ineligible for World War II military service. He entered the Queensland parliament in 1947 as a member of the Country Party (later the National Party), joined the state cabinet in 1963, and became premier on Aug. 8, 1968. Although Bjelke-Peterson built Queensland into an economic power and Brisbane into a thriving capital city, he also demonstrated arrant chauvinism, hostility to social and environmental concerns, and disregard for alleged police corruption and brutality. In 1975 he deliberately appointed a federal senator hostile to Prime Minister Gough Whitlam and helped to precipitate Whitlam's dismissal from office. Bjelke-Peterson was forced to resign in November 1987 amid accusations of bribery and corruption, but his 1991 trial for perjury ended in a hung jury. His wife, Florence ("Lady Flo"), was a Queensland senator (1981–93) and a prominent figure in her own right. Bjelke-Peterson was knighted in 1984.

Bondi, Sir Hermann, Austrian-born British mathematician and cosmologist (b. Nov. 1, 1919, Vienna, Austria—d. Sept. 10, 2005, Cambridge, Eng.), was best known for his collaboration with astronomer Thomas Gold and astrophysicist Fred Hoyle in formulating (1948) the steady-state theory of the universe, which postulates that the universe is infinite and, though expanding, remains essentially unchanged over time through the continuous creation of new matter. The steady-state theory contributed to the development of cosmology, but it was supplanted by the big-bang theory, which (in agreement with subsequent astronomical observations) held that the universe had a specific beginning. Bondi's later study of the general theory of relativity and black holes led to a useful description of how gases would behave as they were drawn into a black hole, an effect known as Bondi accretion. After graduating (M.A., 1940) in mathematics from Trinity College, Cambridge, Bondi was briefly interned (1940–41) as an "enemy alien." He met Gold at an internment camp in Canada, but the two men were returned to England, where they did wartime research under Hoyle. Bondi taught mathematics at Cambridge (1945–54) and at King's College, London (1954–85), and was a master of Churchill College, Cambridge (1983–90). He also led a successful career in public service, first as director general of the European Space Research Organization (1967–71) and later as a scientific adviser to the British government (1971–80). Bondi was knighted in 1973.

Booth, Wayne Clayson, American literary critic (b. Feb. 22, 1921, American Fork, Utah—d. Oct. 10, 2005, Chicago, Ill.), broke from the New Criticism school, which prevailed in the mid-20th century, to explore the rhetorical techniques used by fiction writers. His groundbreaking first book, *The Rhetoric of Fiction* (1961), revealed how choices regarding structure and narrative voice and other rhetorical devices were used by writers to deepen the author-reader connection and to enrich the reader's experience. In the book Booth coined the familiar concepts of "unreliable narrator," a narrator who fails to report correctly or comprehend a story's events, and "implied author," the person of the author as conveyed through a work of fiction. Booth earned a bachelor's degree (1944) from Brigham Young University, Salt Lake City, Utah. After serving in the army during World War II, he continued his studies of literature at the University of Chicago, where he earned master's and doctorate degrees (1947 and 1950, respectively). He taught at Haverford (Pa.) College and Earlham College, Richmond, Ind., before returning to teach at Chicago in 1962. He continued to explore the use of rhetoric, extending his interest to its use in advertising and politics. He cofounded the influential journal *Critical Inquiry* in 1974, and that same year he published two major works, *The Rhetoric of Irony* and *Modern Dogma and the Rhetoric of Assent.* His book *The Company We Keep: The Ethics of Fiction* was published in 1988.

Borba, Emilinha, Brazilian singer (b. Aug. 31, 1923, Rio de Janeiro, Braz.—d. Oct. 3, 2005, Rio de Janeiro), endured as one of Brazil's most beloved radio personalities for 30 years. She made her first recording in 1939, and a year later she joined Rádio Nacional,

Radio star Emilinha Borba

where she continued to work until health problems forced her retirement in 1968. She sang rumbas and sambas and had a famous (and friendly) rivalry with the singer Marlene. Borba starred in numerous films and was a staple attraction at Rio's Carnival. She marked her 50 years of recording with the release of the album *O carnaval de João Roberto Kelly na voz de Emilinha Borba* in 1990.

Bott, Raoul, Hungarian American mathematician (b. Sept. 24, 1923, Budapest, Hung.—d. Dec. 20, 2005, Carlsbad, Calif.), was the winner of the 2000 Wolf Prize in Mathematics for his contributions in topology and differential geometry, especially applications to mathematical physics. In 1949 Bott earned a doctorate of science from the Carnegie Institute of Technology (now Carnegie-Mellon University) in Pittsburgh. After graduation he held academic appointments at the Institute for Advanced Study, Princeton, N.J. (1949–51; 1955–57), the University of Michigan (1951–55; 1957–59), and Harvard University (1959–2005). Perhaps his most famous result was his proof (with Sir Michael Atiyah) of the Atiyah-Bott fixed-point theorem, which showed the existence of "fixed points" (stable solutions) to certain types of mathematical mappings and gave a method for determining the number of such fixed points. Among Bott's awards were the 1964 Oswald Veblen Prize in Geometry from the American Mathematical Society (AMS), a 1987 National Medal of Science, and in 1990 the AMS Leroy P. Steele Prize for Lifetime Achievement.

Brainin, Norbert, Austrian-born British violinist and teacher (b. March 12, 1923, Vienna, Austria—d. April 10, 2005, London, Eng.), founded, guided, and served as first violinist of the distinguished chamber group the Amadeus Quartet through its 40-year existence. Brainin entered the Vienna Conservatory at the age of 10 and in 1938 immigrated with his family to England, where, during a period of World War II internment, three of the members of the future quartet met. The group had its debut, as the Brainin Quartet, in

1947; they changed the name to the Amadeus Quartet in 1948 and remained together until 1987. Under Brainin's leadership, the quartet performed worldwide and recorded extensively. He was made OBE in 1962.

Bromley, D(avid) Allan, Canadian-born American physicist and government official (b. May 4, 1926, Westmeath, Ont.—d. Feb. 10, 2005, New Haven, Conn.), was the founder and director (1963–89) of Yale University's A.W. Wright Nuclear Structure Laboratory, where he conducted pioneering research in heavy ion physics, and was nationally known as the most influential science adviser in U.S. history as the architect (1989–93) of Pres. George H.W. Bush's science and technology policy. Bromley was an early advocate of the so-called data superhighway (the Internet) and was instrumental in securing funds for scientific research to keep American manufacturing from falling behind that of Japan and Germany. In his worldwide travels, he gave more than 400 speeches expounding on U.S. science policy. He wrote more than 500 scientific papers and wrote or contributed to more than 20 books. In 1988 Bromley was the recipient of the National Medal of Science.

Bronfman, Edward Maurice, Canadian businessman (b. Nov. 1, 1927, Montreal, Que.—d. April 4, 2005, Toronto, Ont.), founded, with his brother Peter, Edper Investments Ltd. after their cousins forced the two out of their stake in distilling giant Seagram. The Bronfman brothers turned Edper, later known as the Brascan Corp., into a vast financial empire that became Canada's largest and included the Labatt brewing company and the Montreal Canadiens franchise of the National Hockey League. Bronfman ended his active involvement in Brascan in the 1990s and focused on charitable activities. He was awarded the Order of Canada in 2000.

Bronhill, June (JUNE GOUGH), Australian soprano (b. June 26, 1929, Broken Hill, N.S.W., Australia—d. Jan. 25, 2005, Sydney, Australia), during the 1950s and '60s, was admired for

Soprano June Bronhill.

her bright coloratura voice and clear diction in serious opera and stage musicals as well as in light opera. Her most successful role was as Hanna Glawari in Franz Lehár's operetta *The Merry Widow*. After winning contests in Australia, Bronhill traveled to England in 1952 to continue her studies. In 1954 she began performing with the Sadler's Wells Opera, and throughout her career she moved back and forth between the U.K. and Australia. Bronhill was made OBE in 1976 and retired in 1993.

Brott, Alexander, Canadian conductor, composer, and violinist (b. March 14, 1915, Montreal, Que.—d. April 1, 2005, Montreal), championed symphonic music in Canada (especially that of Canadian composers) through his work as a violinist, conductor, composer, and educator. Success as a concert violinist led to a teaching position at Montreal's McGill University in 1939. Brott founded the McGill Chamber Orchestra in 1945 and that same year began his 14-year tenure as concertmaster for the Montreal Symphony Orchestra. He served as assistant conductor for the orchestra, and from 1965 to 1981 he was artistic director of the Kingston Symphony. During his career he composed more than 100 works, many of which bore witty titles, including the violin concerto *Cupid's Quandary* (1975), *Trivial Trifles* (1984) for strings, and *Three Acts for Four Sinners* (1961) for saxophone quartet.

Brown, Gatemouth (CLARENCE BROWN), American musician (b. April 18, 1924, Vinton, La.—d. Sept. 10, 2005, Orange, Texas), synthesized blues, country, zydeco, jazz, and

Bluesman Gatemouth Brown

rhythm and blues in a unique style that influenced and won the respect of an assortment of musicians. Brown began his career at the Bronze Peacock nightclub in Houston in 1947, and club manager Don Robey signed Brown to his newly inaugurated Peacock label in 1949. Over the next 20 years, Brown made a number of locally successful recordings, leading big-band blues on guitar and singing. Though his recording career flagged in the 1960s, in 1966 Brown led the house band on a Nashville-based rhythm-and-blues music

television show, *The !!!! Beat*. In the 1970s his career revived, and he performed and recorded in a variety of styles and on a variety of instruments; one of these albums, *Makin' Music* (1979), was made with country artist Roy Clark. In 1982 his album *Alright Again!* won a Grammy Award for best traditional blues recording. Brown won eight W.C. Handy Awards, and in 1999 he was inducted into the Blues Foundation Hall of Fame.

Brown, Oscar Cicero, Jr., American jazz artist, actor, and activist (b. Oct. 10, 1926, Chicago, Ill.—d. May 29, 2005, Chicago), became noted during the civil rights movement for the songs he created and sang celebrating black American life and history. "Brown Baby," "The Snake," and "Signifyin' Monkey" were among his best-known compositions, and the lyrics he wrote to jazz standards such as "All Blues," "Dat Dere," and "Work Song" were covered by many other singers. After unsuccessfully running for political office, he turned to songwriting and performing as a tool for social change, collaborating in Max Roach's *We Insist! Freedom Now Suite* (1960). The stage musicals he crafted were timely but had short initial runs, including *Kicks & Co.* (1961), *Opportunity Please Knock* (1967), which was performed by Chicago street gang members, and *Buck White* (1969), the musical version of Joseph Dolan Tuotti's *Big Time Buck White;* the last made it to Broadway and starred Muhammad Ali as a militant black leader. Besides hosting two television series, *Jazz Scene U.S.A.* (1962) and *From Jumpstreet: A Story of Black Music* (1980), Brown appeared in the 1990s television series *Brewster Place* and *Roc*.

Bujones, Fernando, American ballet dancer (b. March 9, 1955, Miami, Fla.—d. Nov. 10, 2005, Miami), had power, elegance, and a pure technique that combined to gain him international renown as one of his generation's best dancers. He became the youngest principal dancer in the history of American Ballet Theatre two years after joining the company, with which he danced in 1972–85 and 1989–95, and in 1974 he became the first American to win a gold medal at the International Ballet Competition at Varna, Bulg. As a guest artist during his performing career, Bujones appeared with some 60 companies in more than 30 countries. He later became a choreographer and since 2000 had served as artistic director of the Orlando (Fla.) Ballet.

Burns, Richard, British race car driver (b. Jan. 17, 1971, Reading, Eng.—d. Nov. 25, 2005, London, Eng.), was at the time of his death the only English driver to have won (2001) the Fédération Internationale de l'Automobile (FIA) world rally championship. Burns became obsessed with rally driving when he was a teenager. By 1990 he had won the Peugeot Rally Series and raced in his first world championship event, and two years later he won the British national drivers' title. In 1998 (with co-driver Robert Reid) he won the Safari Rally and the first of three consecutive Rallies of Great Britain. Burns finished second in the FIA drivers' championship in 1999 and

2000 before finishing on top (with eight victories) in 2001. Contract disputes in 2002 led him to switch teams, but he failed to repeat his earlier success. Burns published his autobiography, *Driving Ambition*, in 2002. He was also the subject of a road-rally video game. Burns was forced to retire in November 2003 when he was diagnosed with a brain tumour.

Burnside, R(obert) L(ee), American blues musician (b. Nov. 21/23, 1926, Harmontown, Miss.—d. Sept. 1, 2005, Memphis, Tenn.), became widely known in the 1990s for his spare, raw style of Mississippi Delta blues. Burnside spent most of his life working as a farmer and fisherman and playing the blues in local bars in Mississippi. After folklorists George Mitchell and David Evans recorded him in the

Blues legend R.L. Burnside

late 1960s and '70s, he played in occasional blues festivals in Canada and Europe as well as locally. In 1991 he appeared in Robert Mugge's documentary film *Deep Blues*, and in 1992 he released his first album on Fat Possum Records, *Bad Luck City*. Over the next 12 years, Burnside released a number of well-received albums, including a collaboration with the Jon Spencer Blues Explosion, *A Ass Pocket of Whiskey*, and an album featuring techno redubbing, *Come On In*, which included the widely popular single "It's Bad You Know."

Cabrera Infante, Guillermo, Cuban novelist  and essayist (b. April 22, 1929, Gibara, Cuba—d. Feb. 21, 2005, London, Eng.), penned the acclaimed novel *Tres tristes tigres* (1965; *Three Trapped Tigers* [1971]), a comic and loving portrait of Havana nightlife in the years before the 1959 Cuban Revolution. Cabrera Infante developed an interest in literature and film as a young man, and he was working as a writer by the early 1950s. He was briefly jailed in 1952 after he used profanities in one of his stories. He was an outspoken critic of Fulgencio Batista's regime, as well as an ardent supporter of the 1959 revolution that brought Fidel Castro to power. Cabrera Infante founded *Lunes*, a literary weekly of the newspaper *Revolución*, and served as a cultural minister in the new regime. He soon discovered, however, that Castro was a repressive dictator, and in 1965 Cabrera Infante went into exile, living first in Spain before settling permanently in England. For the remainder of his life, he was a vocal critic of the Castro government. He collected his thoughts on his homeland in the book *Mea Cuba* (1992). His novel *La Habana para un infante difunto* (1979; *Infante's Inferno*, 1984) once again showed his love of puns and textual games; the nonfiction book *Holy Smoke* (1985; *Puro humo*, 2000) explored his passion for cigars; and his highly regarded writings on film were collected in *Un oficio del siglo veinte* (1963; *A Twentieth Century Job*, 1991). He received Spain's Cervantes Prize in 1998.

Callaghan of Cardiff, (Leonard) James Callaghan, Baron, British politician (b. March 27, 1912, Portsmouth, Hampshire, Eng.—d. March 26, 2005, Ringmer, East Sussex, Eng.), was the only person to hold the four highest offices in the United Kingdom—chancellor of the Exchequer (1964–67), home secretary (1967–70), foreign secretary (1974–76), and prime minister (1976–79)—but he was perhaps best remembered for the "Winter of Discontent" (1978–79), a period of high unemployment and massive trade-union strikes that brought the country to a standstill and ultimately toppled his government. Callaghan, who left school at age 17, became a full-time trade-union official in the mid-1930s. In 1945 he entered Parliament as a member of the Labour Party, and when Labour came to power in 1964 he joined the government. As chancellor of the Exchequer, he repeatedly resisted devaluing the pound but was compelled to do so in 1967 and subsequently resigned. Callaghan enjoyed greater success as home secretary, earning particular praise for his handling of unrest in Northern Ireland. As foreign secretary he negotiated the U.K.'s continued membership in the European Economic Community (now the European Union). After succeeding Harold Wilson as prime minister in 1976, Callaghan faced high inflation, a tight budget, and union unrest. Objections concerning pay constraints helped trigger a series of strikes in 1978–79. Callaghan was denounced for his failure to rein in the industrial actions and for his apparently cavalier attitude to the growing chaos, including understaffed hospitals and streets filled with uncollected garbage. In March 1979 his government narrowly lost a no-confidence vote, and at the subsequent general elections in May, Labour was defeated by the Conservative Party led by Margaret Thatcher. Callaghan resigned the Labour leadership in 1980 but remained active in politics. He was made a life peer in 1987.

Capaldi, Jim (NICOLA JAMES CAPALDI), British rock musician (b. Aug. 2, 1944, Evesham, Worcestershire, Eng.—d. Jan. 28, 2005, London, Eng.), was a founding member of the

© Neal Preston/Corbis

Jim Capaldi of Traffic

psychedelic rock band Traffic. Capaldi formed his first band at the age of 14 and played drums with other bands on the British music scene. Together with keyboardist Steve Winwood, Capaldi founded Traffic in 1967, and by the end of the year, the band had released the album *Mr. Fantasy*. Capaldi played drums, sang, and provided lyrics for all of the band's albums, including *Traffic* (1968), *John Barleycorn Must Die* (1970), and *The Low Spark of High Heeled Boys* (1971). Capaldi released his first solo album, *Oh! How We Danced*, in 1972 and pursued a successful solo career after the 1974 breakup of Traffic. Capaldi won several songwriting awards, and Traffic was inducted into the Rock and Roll Hall of Fame in 2004.

Cappuccilli, Piero, Italian operatic baritone (b. Nov. 9, 1926, Trieste, Italy—d. July 12, 2005, Trieste), enjoyed a 35-year career during which he was widely regarded as the leading Italian baritone of his generation; he was particularly known for his tendency to insert unwritten high notes into his performances. Cappuccilli's official debut was at the Teatro Nuovo in Milan in 1957 as Tonio in Ruggero Leoncavallo's *Pagliacci*, and he first sang at Milan's La Scala in 1964. Cappuccilli performed in opera houses throughout Europe and in the United States, where he had a long association with the Lyric Opera of Chicago. He was best known for his interpretations of Giuseppe Verdi's operas, in which he sang 17 roles. After a serious automobile accident in 1992, Cappuccilli quit performing and concentrated on teaching.

Carrasquel, Chico (ALFONSO CARRASQUEL COLÓN), Venezuelan-born baseball player (b. Jan. 23, 1928, Caracas, Venez.—d. May 26, 2005, Caracas), was the first in a long line of outstanding Venezuelan shortstops to play in Major League Baseball and the first Latin American player to appear (1951) in an All-Star Game. His 10-year career (1950–59) included stints with the Chicago White Sox (1950–55) and the Cleveland Indians (1956–58), and he was considered a national hero in Venezuela.

Carson, Johnny (JOHN WILLIAM CARSON), American comedian (b. Oct. 23, 1925, Corning, Iowa—d. Jan. 23, 2005, Los Angeles, Calif.), served as host of *The Tonight Show* for nearly 30 years, during which he established the standard format for television chat shows—including the guest couch and the studio band—and came to be considered the king of late-night TV. Although Carson was a very

American talk show host and comedian Johnny Carson

NBC Television/Getty Images

private man when he was not performing, he had an on-camera wit, self-deprecating humour, easy charm, impeccable timing, and puckish appeal that made him such a welcome presence in the lives of his audience that he became TV's most powerful performer, earning millions of dollars for himself as well as for NBC and launching the careers of numerous future stars. His decision (1972) to move his show from New York to California was instrumental in shifting the power of the TV industry to Los Angeles. Carson became intrigued with prestidigitation when he was 12 years old, and he set about to master the art of magic tricks. Following high-school graduation and World War II service in the navy, Carson enrolled at the University of Nebraska. While there, he participated in student theatrical activities and also worked for a radio station in Lincoln. Upon graduation (1949), Carson took another radio job in Omaha, and in 1951 he began working as an announcer at a TV station in Los Angeles. He was also given a Sunday afternoon comedy show, which led to his being hired as a writer for Red Skelton's show. After Carson substituted successfully for Skelton at the last minute on one occasion, he was given his own show, though it was short-lived. He then moved to New York City and in 1957 became host of the game show *Who Do You Trust?* In 1962 Carson took over as host of *The Tonight Show* after Jack Paar left that post. By the time he retired in May 1992, he had created such memorable characters as Aunt Blabby and Carnac the Magnificent, as well as a large number of classic skits, and had become one of the most beloved performers in the country. Carson won four Emmy Awards, was inducted into the Television Hall of Fame (1987), and was given the Presidential Medal of Freedom (1992) and a Kennedy Center Honor (1993).

Carvalho, Apolônio Pinto de, Brazilian politician and activist (b. Feb. 9?, 1912, Corumbá, Braz.—d. Sept. 23, 2005, Rio de Janeiro, Braz.), battled fascists at home, in Spain, and in France. He was an officer in the Brazilian army when he first embraced left-wing nationalism.

Carvalho joined the short-lived Aliança Nacional Libertadora and was jailed after his alleged involvement in a failed coup against dictator Getúlio Vargas in 1935. Carvalho was released in 1937 and sailed for Spain, where he fought on the side of the Republicans in that country's civil war. During World War II he fought in the French Resistance and was awarded the Legion of Honour, France's highest award to foreigners. In 1946 Carvalho returned to Brazil, where he was active in communist movements until he was arrested in 1969 and eventually exiled. He returned to Brazil in 1979 and helped found the Workers' Party. His autobiography, *Vale a pena sonhar*, was published in 1997.

Caulfield, Patrick Joseph, British artist (b. Jan. 29, 1936, London, Eng.—d. Sept. 29, 2005, London), was a member of the "New Generation" of 1960s British Pop and abstract artists. Caulfield's bold paintings incorporated everyday objects in still lifes and ordinary domestic interiors and were defined by strong graphic design, black outlines, and bright, saturated colours. He later introduced elements of trompe l'oeil and photorealism into his painting. He also extended his talents to graphic prints, tapestry, theatrical set design, and screen-print book illustrations. Caulfield was nominated for the Turner Prize in 1987 and shared the Jerwood Painting Prize in 1995. He was made CBE in 1996.

Cayrol, Jean-Raphaël-Marie-Noël French poet, novelist, and essayist (b. June 6, 1911, Bordeaux, France—d. Feb. 10, 2005, Bordeaux), was a pioneer in the French avant-garde *nouveau roman* ("new novel") of the 1950s. Cayrol's experiences in the French Resistance (1941–43) and in Nazi concentration camps (1943–45), notably Mauthausen in Austria, formed the heart of many of his artistic creations. The suffering he underwent in Mauthausen inspired his best-known volume of poems, *Poèmes de la nuit et du brouillard* (1946), many of which he wrote in the camp; his seminal essay *Lazare parmi nous* (1950); and his prizewinning trilogy of novels, *Je vivrai l'amour des autres* (1947–50). He was also chief literary consultant to the publishing house Éditions du Seuil and collaborated with French film director Alain Resnais on the award-winning Holocaust documentary *Nuit et brouillard* (1955; *Night and Fog*). Cayrol was elected to the Académie Goncourt in 1974.

Charles, Dame (Mary) Eugenia, Dominican lawyer and politician (b. May 15, 1919, Pointe Michel, Dominica—d. Sept. 6, 2005, Fort-de-France, Martinique), earned the nickname "Iron Lady of the Caribbean" for her uncompromising views and no-nonsense approach as prime minister of Dominica (1980–95). Charles, the granddaughter of slaves, studied in Canada and the U.K. and in 1949 became Dominica's first female lawyer. She cofounded (1968) the Dominica Freedom Party (DFP) to oppose government attempts to suppress dissent, and in 1975 she was elected to the parliament and named leader of the opposition. Two years after Dominica gained its independence (1978) from the U.K., the DFP won the general election, and Charles became the first woman prime minister in the Caribbean. In that post she fought government corruption, banned casinos, and was an effective supporter of the country's banana industry. She also oversaw rebuilding efforts following a series of hurricanes. In 1983 she made headlines for encouraging the U.S. invasion of Grenada, which was reportedly in danger of falling to communists. Charles, who was made Dame Commander of the British Empire in 1991, retired from politics in 1995.

Chen Yifei, Chinese painter, film director, and entrepreneur (b. 1946, Ningbo, Zhejiang province, China—d. April 10, 2005, Shanghai,

China), transitioned from a leading painter of the Cultural Revolution to a Western-style purveyor of lifestyle and fashion. Noted in China for his portraits of Mao Zedong and large canvases of major revolutionary events, Chen enjoyed great success there before studying in the United States. From 1980 to 1990 he blended Realist techniques with European Romanticism in paintings that featured traditional Chinese themes—colourful Tibetan landscapes and Chinese women in traditional dress—and won a following in the U.S. American industrialist Armand Hammer collected Chen's works and in 1983 presented one of them, *Shuang qiao* ("Twin Bridge"), to Chinese paramount leader Deng Xiaoping. After returning to China, Chen made documentary and feature films and developed successful fashion and design businesses.

Chisholm, Shirley Anita St. Hill, American politician (b. Nov. 30, 1924, Brooklyn, N.Y.—d. Jan. 1, 2005, Ormond Beach, Fla.), was the first black woman to serve (1969–83) as a representative in the U.S. Congress and in 1972

U.S. Rep. Shirley Chisholm

became the first woman to enter the Democratic presidential primaries. Self-described as "unbought and unbossed," she challenged the seniority system for committee assignments in Congress in order to better champion the rights of minorities and women and help improve the lives of the underprivileged. Chisholm graduated from Brooklyn College (B.A., 1946), worked in a nursery school, and then earned (1952) an M.A. at Columbia University, New York City. While working as an educational consultant in New York City, she became active in community affairs and local politics, and in 1964 she was elected to the New York state legislature. Four years later, in an upset victory, Chisholm defeated civil rights leader James Farmer for a seat in the U.S. House of Representatives. Appointed to the Agriculture Committee, she protested that assignment and got herself reassigned first to the Veterans Affairs Committee and then to the Education and Labor Committee, a post she found more relevant to her Brooklyn working-class constituency. A liberal opposed to the Vietnam War, Chisholm entered the race for the Democratic presidential nomination to run against Pres. Richard Nixon in the

1972 election. She acknowledged having no expectation of winning but wanted to emphasize the kind of changes she thought were needed in government. Following her seven terms in Congress, Chisholm taught (1983–87) at Mount Holyoke College, South Hadley, Mass., was a visiting scholar (1985) at Spelman College, Atlanta, Ga., and was a popular speaker on the lecture circuit.

Chung Se Yung ("PONY CHUNG"), Korean industrialist (b. Aug. 6, 1928, T'ongch'on, Kangwon province, Korea [now N.Kor.]—d. May 21, 2005, Seoul, S.Kor.), served (1967–96) as chairman of the Hyundai Motor Co., which under Chung's leadership grew into one of the world's largest automobile manufacturers. Chung at first steered Hyundai into working with foreign automobile companies, but in 1974 the company introduced its first production model, the Pony. Its success in South Korea prompted Chung in 1986 to market the car in the United States as the Excel. Chung was forced out of the company in 1999 by his oldest brother, Chung Ju Yung, founder of the overall Hyundai Group. Chung Se Yung was also chairman (1987–96) and honorary chairman (1996–99) of the Hyundai Group.

Clark, Kenneth Bancroft, American psychologist (b. July 14, 1914, Panama Canal Zone—d. May 1, 2005, Hastings-on-Hudson, N.Y.), conducted pioneering research into the impact of racial segregation on children. With his wife, Mamie Phipps Clark, he administered the "doll test" to African American schoolchildren in the 1940s and '50s. The test involved presenting a child with a black doll and a white doll and asking the child to select a favourite doll. In the segregated South the black children preferred the white doll by a wide margin, with many children identifying the black doll as "bad." Clark's research played a key role in arguments during the 1954 case *Brown* v. *Board of Education*, in which the U.S. Supreme Court ruled segregation to be unconstitutional. Clark helped develop integrationist educational policies for both federal and state governments. In his career he established several institutions, including in 1946 the Northside Child Development Center in Harlem, meant to foster positive identity and improved opportunities for African Americans. He was active during the civil rights movement and wrote extensively about the plight of African Americans in urban slums.

Clements, Vassar, American fiddler (b. April 25, 1928, Kinards, S.C.—d. Aug. 16, 2005, Nashville, Tenn.), taught himself to play at age seven and became one of the most versatile and sought-after stage and studio artists on the bluegrass and country music circuits. While working most of his life in nonmusical jobs to support himself, Clements mastered six stringed instruments besides the violin. He played with equal zest and success with stars of bluegrass (including Bill Monroe, Earl Scruggs, and Ricky Skaggs), rock (Linda Ronstadt, the Grateful Dead, and Paul McCartney), and jazz/blues (Stéphane Grappelli, Dave Holland, and Charlie Musselwhite). Clements, whose versatility was showcased on more than 2,000 albums, was nominated for five Grammy Awards, and he won one in 2005.

Cochran, Johnnie L., Jr., American trial lawyer (b. Oct. 2, 1937, Shreveport, La.—d. March 29, 2005, Los Angeles, Calif.), gained international prominence with his skillful (and controversial) defense of O.J. Simpson, a football star charged with a double murder in 1994. After a time as a prosecutor for Los Angeles, Cochran pursued a private career, defending both celebrity clients and minority victims of police brutality. In the high-profile Simpson trial, Cochran showed his skill for connecting with jurors and for putting the prosecution and police on the defensive. Simpson was found not guilty of having murdered his former wife and her friend.

Cohen, Isidore, American violinist and teacher (b. Dec. 16, 1922, Brooklyn, N.Y.—d. June 23, 2005, Bronx, N.Y.), was a member of two of the most distinguished chamber groups of the 20th century. From 1958 to 1968 he was second violinist in the Juilliard String Quartet, and he then joined the Beaux Arts Trio, the most celebrated piano trio of its time, where he remained until his retirement in 1992. Cohen studied at the Juilliard School in New York City and later taught at several institutions. From 1966 he was affiliated with the Marlboro (Vt.) Music School and Festival.

Cook, Robin (ROBERT FINLAYSON COOK), British politician (b. Feb. 28, 1946, Bellshill, Lanarkshire, Scot.—d. Aug. 6, 2005, Sutherland, Scot.), served as foreign secretary in the U.K. for four years following the Labour Party's return to power in 1997; he was recognized as having one of the sharpest minds in British politics and influence far beyond his official post. Cook was educated at the University of Edinburgh and taught school before entering politics. He became a Labour MP in 1974 and quickly established himself as a rousing and witty left-wing debater. In the 1980s, like many in the Labour's left wing who were shocked by the scale of the party's defeat in the 1983 general election, he became an active reformer. He worked closely with Neil Kinnock (Labour leader during 1983–92) and Tony Blair, who was elected party leader in 1994 and prime minister in 1997. As foreign secretary, Cook asserted that the U.K.'s foreign

policy would henceforth have "an ethical dimension," and in 1999 he and Blair persuaded an initially reluctant Pres. Bill Clinton to commit U.S. forces in Kosovo, in the former Yugoslavia. Following the 2001 general election, Blair demoted Cook to the lesser cabinet post of leader of the House of Commons. On March 17, 2003, Cook resigned from the government in protest against Blair's decision to support the U.S.-led invasion of Iraq. In his resignation speech, delivered from the backbenches, Cook revived his reputation as a clever and effective debater, and by 2005 it was widely predicted that he would return to the cabinet following Blair's eventual resignation. Cook died from a heart attack while hill climbing in the Scottish Highlands.

Creeley, Robert White, American poet (b. May 21, 1926, Arlington, Mass.—d. March 30, 2005, Odessa, Texas), wrote colloquial, plain-spoken, minimal verse, which was often compared to that of William Carlos Williams. In the mid-1950s Creeley taught at North Carolina's experimental Black Mountain College, where for three years he edited the highly regarded *Black Mountain Review*. The college awarded him a bachelor's degree in 1955. With poet colleagues Charles Olson and Robert Duncan, he promoted a poetics free of formalism and elitism. His collection *For Love* (1962), penned between 1950 and 1960, brought him national attention, as did the appearance of his works in Donald Allen's groundbreaking "beat" anthology *The New American Poetry 1945–1960* (1962), which showcased his intensely personal verse. Though his early poetry focused on his marriages and divorces, beginning with *Later* (1979) Creeley recalled his youth and concentrated on issues related to aging and mortality. Other works included *The Collected Poems of Robert Creeley 1945–75* (1982), *Memory Gardens* (1986), *The Old Days* (1991), and *So There: Poems 1976–83* (1998). Besides serving as visiting professor at universities in British Columbia and New Mexico, among others, Creeley was a professor at the State University of New York at Buffalo for 37 years (1966–2003). He also wrote plays, essays, and short stories. In 1988 he became a member of the American Academy and Institute of Arts and Letters, and he was awarded the Bollingen Prize for poetry in 1999.

Cresswell, Helen, British author (b. July 11, 1934, Nottingham, Nottinghamshire, Eng.—d. Sept. 26, 2005, Eakring, Nottinghamshire, Eng.), penned more than 100 children's works—ranging from picture books to intermediate-age novels—and numerous television screenplays, most of which she infused with humour and fantasy. She was perhaps best known for the Lizzie Dripping series (1973–91), about a young girl who befriends a witch, and the Bagthorpe Saga (1977–2001), a multivolume chronicle of an eccentric family's adventures. Cresswell adapted many of her books into successful television shows, and in 2000 she won a BAFTA award for children's writing.

Cruse, Harold Wright, American social and cultural critic (b. March 8, 1916, Petersburg, Va.—d. March 25, 2005, Ann Arbor, Mich.), authored *The Crisis of the Negro Intellectual* (1967), a best-selling critique of the integrationist approach of many liberal African American intellectuals. Cruse argued for black Americans to embrace their own distinctive economic, political, and cultural institutions. Together with LeRoi Jones (now Amiri Baraka), Cruse founded the Black Arts Repertory Theatre/School in Harlem, New York City. Cruse was awarded a professorship in 1968 at the University of Michigan, where he taught history and African American studies until 1984.

Cummings, Constance (CONSTANCE HALVERSTADT), American-born actress (b. May 15, 1910, Seattle, Wash.—d. Nov. 23, 2005, Oxfordshire, Eng.), enchanted audiences in Britain and the United States during a stage and screen career that spanned almost 70 years (1928–96). Cummings began as a chorus girl and appeared in such comedic films as *Movie Crazy* (1932) and *Blithe Spirit* (1945), although she later focused on increasingly dark roles. After marrying (1933) British playwright Benn W. Levy, she moved to Britain, where her acclaimed theatrical work ranged from *Goodbye, Mr. Chips* (1938) to an Oxford Playhouse production (1962) of Jean-Paul Sartre's *Huis-Clos (No Exit)* to a 1971 revival of Eugene O'Neill's *Long Day's Journey into Night*, opposite Laurence Olivier. Her most notable performance was on Broadway as a stroke victim in Arthur Kopit's *Wings* (1979), for which, at age 68, she won a Tony Award for best actress. Cummings was made CBE in 1974.

Cunhal, Álvaro Barreirinhas, Portuguese political activist (b. Nov. 10, 1913, Coimbra, Port.—d. June 13, 2005, Lisbon, Port.), returned from exile to lead the Portuguese Communist Party (PCP) after the Armed Forces Movement ousted Prime Minister Marcelo Caetano from power in a military coup (1974), which ended more than 40 years of right-wing dictatorship. Known for his hard-line Stalinist beliefs, Cunhal endured long periods of exile and imprisonment during his more than 60-year involvement with the PCP. At age 17 Cunhal joined the PCP and the League of Friends of the Soviet Union. By the time he reached his early 20s, he had become a member of the party's central committee and served as a delegate to an international communist youth congress in Moscow. He served briefly in the 1974–75 provisional administration of Vasco Gonçalves (*q.v.*). Elected as general secretary of the PCP in 1961, Cunhal continued his leadership of the party until 1992, when he retired and was made honorary president.

Curien, Hubert, French scientist and public servant (b. Oct. 30, 1924, Cornimont, France—d. Feb. 6, 2005, Loury, France), pioneered France's space program independent of U.S. or Soviet influence and supervised the debut launch of the European Space Agency's (ESA's) Ariane series of rockets in 1979. In addition to serving as professor in materials science at the University of Pierre and Marie Curie in Paris from 1956 until 1995, Curien was director-general of France's national research centre (1968–73), chairman of the national centre for space studies (1976–84), and minister of research and technology (1984–92) under three prime ministers. He was chosen to be the first president of the ESA in 1979. Curien became a member of the French Academy of Sciences in 1993 and was eventually elected president of that organization. He was also awarded the Legion of Honour.

Czerwinski, Edward Joseph, American scholar and university professor (b. June 6, 1929, Erie, Pa.—d. Feb. 16, 2005, Erie), was a specialist in Slavic languages and literatures and was also instrumental in introducing Slavic culture to Americans through promotion of theatrical, musical, and artistic events. He taught (1979–93) at the State University of New York at Stony Brook and was the founder (1970) and director of the Slavic Cultural Center at Port Jefferson, N.Y. In addition to producing numerous scholarly articles and books, Czerwinski contributed articles on Eastern European literature (1989–2000) to the *Britannica Book of the Year*.

da Silva, (José) Bezerra, Brazilian samba artist (b. March 9, 1927, Recife, Braz.—d. Jan. 17, 2005, Rio de Janeiro, Braz.), created the musical genre known as "sambandido," or bandit samba, with lyrics describing the brutality of life in the shantytowns of Brazil. Da Silva played music in nightclubs and for radio stations in Rio de Janeiro from 1950 but recorded his first single ("Viola testemunha") only in 1969 and his first album, *O rei do coco*, in 1975. Shortly afterward, he developed the persona of a *malandro*, or street hustler, and became known for singing the improvised samba style called *partido alto*. He released 28 albums, 15 of which reached at least gold status (one double-platinum); in 1995 he joined with Moreira da Silva and Dicró on *Os três malandros in Concert*.

Dalle, François Léon Marie-Joseph, French business executive (b. March 18, 1918, Hesdin, Pas-de-Calais, France—d. Aug. 9, 2005, Geneva, Switz.), in his role as CEO (1957–84), built L'Oréal SA from a small French producer of salon-based hair products into a global mass marketer of cosmetics and fragrances, which included not only consumer products under the L'Oréal name but also such presti-

L'Oréal's François Dalle

gious luxury brands as Lancôme, Garnier, Cacharel, Guy Laroche, Giorgio Armani, Helena Rubinstein, and Ralph Lauren. Dalle studied law at the University of Paris. Drafted into the army at the beginning of World War II, he was captured by the Nazis but escaped and joined the Resistance. At L'Oréal, Dalle rose through the ranks under founder Eugène Schueller, and when Schueller died in 1957, Dalle succeeded him as corporate CEO.

Dancer, Stanley Franklin, American horseman (b. July 25, 1927, West Windsor, N.J.—d. Sept. 8, 2005, Pompano Beach, Fla.), captured 3,781 races during his career as one of harness racing's most aggressive drivers. He began driving trotters in 1945 and soon after added trainer, owner, and breeder to his résumé. In 1964 Dancer became the first driver in a single year to win more than $1 million in purses. He trained and drove seven harness Horse of the Year winners, three Triple Crown winners, and four winners of the sport's premier race, the Hambletonian, for three-year-old trotters. Dancer was inducted into the Harness Racing Hall of Fame in 1969.

Dantzig, George, American mathematician (b. Nov. 8, 1914, Portland, Ore.—d. May 13, 2005, Stanford, Calif.), devised the simplex algorithm, a method for solving problems that involve numerous conditions and variables, and in the process founded the field of linear programming. Dantzig earned a bachelor's degree in mathematics and physics from the University of Maryland (1936) and a master's degree in mathematics from the University of Michigan (1937) before joining the U.S. Bureau of Labor Statistics as a statistician. In 1939 he entered the graduate mathematics program at the University of California, Berkeley. From 1941 to 1946 Dantzig was the civilian head of the Combat Analysis Branch, U.S. Air Force Headquarters Statistical Control. In 1946 he returned for one semester to Berkeley to receive his Ph.D. and then went on to Washington to work for the U.S. Department of Defense. While working on allocation of resources (materials and personnel) for various projects and deployments of the U.S. Air Force, Dantzig invented (1947) the simplex algorithm for optimization. At that time such scheduling was called programming, and it soon became apparent that the simplex algorithm was ideal for translating formerly intractable problems involving hundreds, or even thousands, of factors for solution by the recently invented computer. From 1952 to 1960 he was a research mathematician at the RAND Corporation, where he helped develop the field of operations research (essentially, the application of computers to optimization problems). From 1960 to 1966 he served as chairman of the Operations Research Center at Berkeley, and from 1966 until his retirement in 1997, he was a professor of operations research and computer science at Stanford University.

Davis, Glenn Woodward, American football player (b. Dec. 26, 1924, Claremont, Calif.—d. March 9, 2005, La Quinta, Calif.), teamed with Doc Blanchard to form arguably the greatest rushing tandem in the history of American collegiate football. The speedy and elusive Davis was "Mr. Outside" to Blanchard's "Mr. Inside" on the great Army teams of the mid-1940s. Led by their impressive backfield, the Cadets amassed a 27–0–1 record between 1944 and 1946 while collecting three national championships. Davis was a three-time All-American, and he won the Heisman Trophy in 1946. His career average of 8.26 yd per carry remains a collegiate record.

Davis, Ossie (RAIFORD CHATMAN DAVIS),

American actor, writer, director, producer, and social activist (b. Dec. 18, 1917, Cogdell, Ga.—d. Feb. 4, 2005, Miami Beach, Fla.), had a stately presence and a melifluous voice that both enriched his stage, film, and television performances and gave extra power to his work on behalf of civil rights and peace. He delivered the eulogy at Malcolm X's funeral in 1965—and repeated it for the film *Malcolm X* (1992), one of his seven Spike Lee films—and spoke at the Rev. Martin Luther King, Jr.'s funeral in 1968. He was also noted for his partnership with his wife, Ruby Dee, which was considered one of the theatre and film world's most distinguished. Their partnership extended into their activism as well; they acted as master and mistress of ceremonies for the 1963 March on Washington, which they also had helped organize. Davis studied at Howard University, Washington, D.C., but left school to move to New York City, aiming to become a playwright. In 1946 he made his Broadway debut in *Jeb*, in which Dee was also a cast member. They then performed together in *Anna Lucasta* (1946–47), and in 1948 they were married. Among Davis and Dee's most notable joint stage appearances that followed were *A Raisin in the Sun* (1959; filmed 1961) and the satiric *Purlie Victorious* (1961), which Davis wrote and in whose film version (*Gone Are the Days,* 1963) Davis and Dee also appeared; it later was made into a stage musical (*Purlie,* 1970). Television productions in which both Davis and Dee performed included *Roots: The*

Next Generation (1978), *Martin Luther King: The Dream and the Drum* (1986), and *The Stand* (1994). In addition, Davis wrote and directed such films as *Cotton Comes to Harlem* (1970) and *Countdown to Kusini* (1976). Davis and Dee were awarded the National Medal of Arts in 1995 and Kennedy Center Honors in 2004.

Dee, Sandra (ALEXANDRA CYMBOLIAK ZUCK), American actress (b. April 23, 1942, Bayonne, N.J.—d. Feb. 20, 2005, Thousand Oaks, Calif.), worked as a model and appeared in television commercials before becoming the sweetheart

Hulton Archive/Getty Images

Actress Sandra Dee.

of the teen moviegoing set. Although she had serious roles in melodramas, including *Imitation of Life* and *A Summer Place* (both 1959), she was best known as the perky star of such films as *Gidget* (1959), *Tammy Tell Me True* (1961), and *Tammy and the Doctor* (1963) and as the wife (1960–67) of pop idol Bobby Darin.

Delgado, Junior (OSCAR HIBBERT), Jamaican reggae singer (b. Aug. 25, 1958, Kingston, Jam.—d. April 11, 2005, London, Eng.), was celebrated for his distinctively gruff voice, which imbued his recordings with a feeling of anguish. He recorded his first hit, "Reaction," in 1973 as a member of the group Time Unlimited. Delgado's solo career began in 1975. He scored hits with roots reggae songs "Tition," "Sons of Slaves," and "Away with Your Fussing and Fighting." He received popular and critical acclaim for his song "Broadwater Farm" (1985), which predicted the unrest in the North London housing estate, and the album *Raggamuffin Year* (1986), which embraced the raggamuffin reggae style then sweeping Jamaica.

DeLorean, John Zachary, American automobile manufacturer and entrepreneur (b. Jan. 6, 1925, Detroit, Mich.—d. March 19, 2005, Summit, N.J.), established the DeLorean Motor Co. near Belfast, N.Ire., which produced (1981) the stainless-steel gull-winged DeLorean DMC-12 sports coupe that sparked the imagination of millions of filmgoers after being featured as a time machine in the blockbuster movie *Back to the Future* (1985). A rising star in the automotive industry, DeLorean helped to revitalize Packard before leaving in 1956 to join General Motors. While at GM, DeLorean launched (1964) the highly successful

Pontiac GTO and advanced to become at age 40 the youngest general manager in GM's history. DeLorean's tenure as an independent carmaker was brief, however, and his plant closed the year after it opened, having produced fewer than 10,000 vehicles. Though DeLorean was charged with conspiring to distribute $24 million in cocaine in 1982 in an attempt to salvage his flailing company, he was later acquitted of criminal charges. He was also accused of embezzlement, defaulting on loans, tax evasion, and defrauding investors in his company (including comedian Johnny Carson [*q.v.*]) out of millions of dollars. Although DeLorean was cleared of the fraud charges, he declared bankruptcy in 1999. The innovative DeLorean claimed more than 200 automotive patents.

Deloria, Vine, Jr., American Indian scholar and activist (b. March 26, 1933, Martin, S.D.—d. Nov. 13, 2005, Denver, Colo.), penned the influential *Custer Died for Your Sins: An Indian Manifesto* (1969) and its sequel, *We Talk, You Listen* (1970). A Standing Rock Sioux, he served as president of the National Congress of American Indians in the 1960s and was able to unify a broad range of Indian groups in dealings with the federal government. His writings helped to dispel many stereotypes and celebrated the rich spiritual and intellectual traditions of Native Americans. Deloria taught at the University of Arizona from 1978 to 1990 and the University of Colorado from 1990 to 2000.

Dennis, Clarence, American surgeon (b. June 16, 1909, St. Paul, Minn.—d. July 11, 2005, St. Paul), performed on April 5, 1951, the world's first open-heart surgery carried out with the use of a heart-lung machine that he had developed at the University of Minnesota. Though the patient died, his pioneering work revolutionized the field of cardiovascular surgery. Dennis joined the staff of the State University of New York Downstate Medical Center in Brooklyn in 1951 and remained there for 20 years. He served (1972–74) as director of technological applications at the National Heart and Lung Institute in Bethesda, Md. Dennis also developed a number of surgical instruments.

Denver, Bob (ROBERT DENVER), American actor (b. Jan. 9, 1935, New Rochelle, N.Y.—d. Sept. 2, 2005, Winston-Salem, N.C.), became a cult favourite for two roles in hit television

Bob Denver as Gilligan.

above and left: CBS Photo Archive via Getty Images

series: the beatnik Maynard G. Krebs in *The Many Loves of Dobie Gillis* (1959–63) and the title character in *Gilligan's Island* (1964–67). The latter series remained in continuous syndication and also gave rise to two animated series, an episode of the *Baywatch* TV series, and three made-for-TV movies—all of which featured Denver.

Diamond, David Leo, American composer (b. July 9, 1915, Rochester, N.Y.—d. June 13, 2005, Rochester), left a large body of works that included 11 symphonies, 10 string quartets, and many songs. His music was characterized by its classic structures and its strong melodic sense. Diamond studied with Nadia Boulanger in Paris in 1937, and his early works, from the 1940s, were met with wide acclaim. With the rise of atonality and serialism, however, his reputation suffered, although beginning in the 1980s there was a revival of interest in his music.

Dimitrova, Ghena, Bulgarian soprano (b. May 6, 1941, Beglezh, Bulg.—d. June 11, 2005, Milan, Italy), enjoyed a career in major opera houses in Europe and the U.S.; she also sang for several seasons at the Teatro Colón in Buenos Aires. Dimitrova trained at the State Conservatory in Sofia from 1959 to 1964 and made her professional stage debut in 1967 as Abigaille in Giuseppe Verdi's *Nabucco*. With her powerful voice, she specialized in dramatic roles in Italian opera, especially the works of Verdi and Giacomo Puccini, becoming known particularly for her performances in the latter's *Turandot*.

Doll, Sir (William) Richard Shaboe British epidemiologist (b. Oct. 28, 1912, Hampton, Middlesex, Eng.—d. July 24, 2005, Oxford, Eng.), with his colleague Austin (later Sir Austin) Bradford Hill, definitively established the link between cigarette smoking and lung cancer. In 1947 Doll, who was already known for a study on the causes of peptic ulcers, was asked to look into the alarming increase in lung cancer in Great Britain. Environmental causes related to the rapid increase in car ownership were suspected, but Doll, a smoker, found to his surprise that smoking was by far the dominant factor. The results were so clear that he gave up smoking himself during the study. The report, co-written with Bradford Hill, was published in 1950. Doll framed additional studies that clarified the relationship between smoking and disease. Some of his research proved that there was no link between peptic ulcers and diet and that even low-level radiation could cause cancer. Doll, the Regius Professor of Medicine at the University of Oxford from 1969, won many awards, notably the UN Award for Cancer Research in 1962. He was knighted in 1971 and made a Companion of Honour in 1996.

Doohan, James Montgomery, Canadian-born actor (b. March 3, 1920, Vancouver, B.C.—d. July 20, 2005, Redmond, Wash.), performed in character roles in hundreds of radio and television programs and in a number of movies before endearing himself to the TV-viewing public with his portrayal of the chief engineer,

Hulton Archive/Getty Images

James Doohan of Star Trek

Montgomery ("Scotty") Scott, on the TV series *Star Trek* during its three seasons (1966–69) and in seven *Star Trek* films. Because he could not shed his identification with that character, he made it his career, appearing at fan gatherings and lecturing at colleges. Doohan's autobiography, *Beam Me Up, Scotty*, was published in 1996.

Drucker, Peter Ferdinand, Austrian-born American social scientist and management consultant (b. Nov. 19, 1909, Vienna, Austria—d. Nov. 11, 2005, Claremont, Calif.), advanced the study of organizational management and popularized his findings in books about corporations, nonprofit groups, and social theory. Although Drucker was convinced that businesses had to be profitable, he also argued that companies had a larger social obligation. He opposed mass layoffs, especially when used to lift stock values and reward executives; urged managers to view employees as assets instead of commodities; strove for effectiveness in contrast to mere efficiency; and saw good management as an essential component of a healthy society. His insider's analysis of General Motors, *Concept of the Corporation* (1946), was largely ignored by GM, but it became a classic management study. The son of a prominent Austrian lawyer, Drucker completed a doctorate in international and public law (1931) at the University of Frankfurt, Ger. After the ascendant Nazi Party burned a book that he had written on a Jewish politician, Drucker moved (1933) to England, took a job in finance, and wrote for newspapers. After settling (1937) in the United States, Drucker earned wide recognition with the publication of *The End of Economic Man: The Origins of Totalitarianism* (1939), a pessimistic portrayal of the threats that he had witnessed in Germany. He thereafter devoted his life to teaching, management consulting, and writing more than 30 additional books. His university appointments included those at New York University (1950–71) and Claremont (Calif.) Graduate University (1971–2002). Drucker received the Presidential Medal of Freedom in 2002.

Dryden, Spencer, American drummer (b. April 7, 1938, New York, N.Y.—d. Jan. 11, 2005, Petaluma, Calif.), helped create the sound of the psychedelic rock band Jefferson Airplane during its heyday in the late 1960s.

Dryden was enjoying a career as a jazz drummer in Los Angeles when he was hired to replace Jefferson Airplane's original drummer, Skip Spence, in 1966. Dryden soon became one of the best-known drummers in the San Francisco firmament of rock music. He played with Jefferson Airplane on the albums *Surrealistic Pillow* (1967), *After Bathing at Baxter's* (1967), *Crown of Creation* (1968), *Bless Its Pointed Little Head* (1969), and *Volunteers* (1969) and at the storied Monterey Pop Festival in 1967 and the Woodstock and Altamont rock festivals in 1969. Dryden left the band in 1970. He played with the New Riders of the Purple Sage in 1971–78 and retired from music in 1995. Jefferson Airplane, with Dryden as its drummer, was inducted into the Rock and Roll Hall of Fame in 1996.

Duisenberg, Wim (WILLEM FREDERIK DUISENBERG), Dutch economist and banker (b. July 9, 1935, Heerenveen, Neth.—

d. July 31, 2005, Faucon, France), as the first president (1998–2003) of the European Central Bank (ECB), presided over the introduction (1999–2002) of the euro, the single currency that replaced the national currencies in 12 countries of the European Union. His calm demeanour and strong economic credentials were credited with helping to bring about a smooth transfer to the euro. After studying economics at the University of Groningen (Ph.D., 1965), Duisenberg worked (1965–69) at the International Monetary Fund and taught economics at the University of Amsterdam. He served as The Netherlands' finance minister (1973–77), governor (1982–97) of the Dutch central bank, and president (1997–98) of the European Monetary Institute, the forerunner of the ECB. Duisenberg's tenure at the ECB was not without controversy, and in 2003, five years into his statutory eight-year term, he fulfilled a campaign pledge to step down in favour of his French rival for the post, Jean-Claude Trichet.

Dutt, Sunil (BALRAJ DUTT), Indian film actor and politician (b. June 6, 1929, Khurd, Jhelum district, British India [now in Pakistan]—d. May 25, 2005, Mumbai [Bombay], India), starred in more than 100 Bollywood motion pictures between 1955 and 1993, notably the Oscar-nominated *Mother India*

(1957). Dutt settled in India after partition. A longtime advocate of social issues, he was first elected to Parliament for the Congress Party in 1984. He was reelected in 1989 and 1991, but he temporarily stood down in the late

1990s to assist his actor son, Sanjay, who was accused of involvement in Muslim-Hindu violence. Dutt returned to Parliament after his son's release in 1999, and in 2004 he was appointed sports minister. Dutt made his last screen appearance with Sanjay in *Munnabhai M.B.B.S* (2003).

Dworkin, Andrea Rita, American feminist writer, activist, and public figure (b. Sept. 26, 1946, Camden, N.J.—d. April 9, 2005, Washington, D.C.), worked to end violence against women and the subjugation of women. Born into a progressive family, Dworkin became best known for her battle against pornography. In 1983, with feminist lawyer and academic Catharine MacKinnon, she authored an ordinance that defined pornography as a violation of women's civil rights. The ordinance, adopted by several cities, was later overturned, however. Always controversial and often misunderstood, Dworkin was the author of several books, including *Woman Hating* (1974), *Pornography: Men Possessing Women* (1981). and *Heartbreak: The Political Memoir of a Feminist Militant* (2002). Her book *Scapegoat: The Jews, Israel, and Women's Liberation* won the 2001 American Book Award.

Eberhart, Richard Ghormley, American poet, playwright, and teacher (b. April 5, 1904, Austin, Minn.—d. June 9, 2005, Hanover, N.H.), received numerous awards for his lyric verse that combined a modern style with elements of Romanticism. Eberhart earned degrees at Dartmouth College, Hanover, N.H. (B.A., 1926), and St. John's College, Cambridge (B.A., 1929; M.A., 1933). Following the publication of his first poetry collection, *A Bravery of Earth* (1930), he held a series of jobs, including tutor to the son of King Prajadhipok of Siam (now Thailand) and executive at a furniture-polish company. Eberhart began teaching at universities in the 1950s and became known for mentoring aspiring poets, most notably at Dartmouth, where he taught from 1956 to 1971. Eberhart frequently explored issues of death and loss in his poems, which were often set in the natural world. His award-winning collections included *Selected Poems, 1930–1965* (1965; Pulitzer Prize) and *Collected Poems, 1930–1976* (1976; National Book Award). From 1959 to 1961 he was consultant in poetry at the Library of Congress (poet laureate), and in 1962 he was a co-winner of the Bollingen Prize for Poetry. Eberhart also wrote verse dramas, many of which were staged by the Poets' Theatre, which he helped found in 1950.

Edwards, Ralph Livingstone, American broadcasting pioneer (b. June 13, 1913, Merino, Colo.—d. Nov. 16, 2005, Hollywood, Calif.), created and emceed two of the staple programs of American television in the 1950s: *Truth or Consequences,* on which contestants performed silly tasks in public, and *This Is Your Life,* on which individuals, often celebrities (including Marilyn Monroe and Bob Hope), were taken to a studio where Edwards and their friends and relatives surprised them

by recapping their lives, frequently amid tears. A successful radio announcer, Edwards introduced both shows on that medium in the 1940s before taking them to television. He continued to produce television programs into the 1980s, including *Name That Tune* and *The People's Court.*

Ehrling, (Evert) Sixten, Swedish conductor (b. April 3, 1918, Malmö, Swed.—d. Feb. 13, 2005, New York, N.Y.), directed orchestras

© Fredrik Persson—AFP/Getty Images

Conductor Sixten Ehrling

with passion and precision; known for his high standards and fiery temper, Ehrling was unapologetic when criticized for the way he conducted or for beginning a concert before audience members who returned late from intermission were seated. He studied at Sweden's Royal Academy and spent a year at the Dresden (Ger.) State Opera before cementing his fame back in Stockholm with his 1950 performance of Igor Stravinsky's *Rite of Spring.* King Gustav VI Adolf eventually gave Ehrling the title premier royal court conductor of Sweden. His tenure as principal conductor of Stockholm's Royal Swedish Opera (1953–60) was considered its golden age, but he resigned in 1960 after an artistic dispute and moved to the U.S. He gained international renown as musical director (1963–73) of the Detroit Symphony Orchestra, for which he conducted more than 700 concerts that included 24 world premieres. From 1973 to 1987 Ehrling was director of the conducting program at the Juilliard School in New York City, and in 1993 he was named music adviser and chief conductor at the Manhattan School of Music.

Eisner, Will (WILLIAM ERWIN EISNER), American comic-book artist (b. March 6, 1917, Brooklyn, N.Y.—d. Jan. 3, 2005, Fort Lauderdale, Fla.), created the influential comic strip *The Spirit* and was generally regarded as the inventor of the graphic novel. He began his career in 1936 at the short-lived pulp *Wow What a Magazine!,* where he met fellow artist Jerry Iger. After the collapse of *Wow,* the two men formed Eisner and Iger, an independent publisher that employed comic legends Bob Kane (creator of Batman) and Jack Kirby (cocreator of Captain America, the X-Men, and the Fantastic Four). Eisner developed a number of characters during this period,

including Sheena, Queen of the Jungle, but he was best remembered for the Spirit—a working-class hero who debuted in June 1940. The Spirit's lack of gadgets, superpowers, and outrageous costumes contrasted with most of the other comic titles of the day. After he was drafted into the army in 1942, Eisner turned his attention to creating Joe Dope. The bumbling GI was featured in a series of instructional cartoons that covered everything from equipment maintenance to family issues. After the war Eisner returned to *The Spirit,* but he devoted an increasing amount of energy to educational comics. After *The Spirit* concluded in 1952, Eisner formed the American Visual Corp. For the next 25 years, the company produced visually arresting and highly effective educational comic books for schools, government, and the armed forces. In 1978 Eisner returned to the mainstream comic world with *A Contract with God,* a collection of stories that redefined the medium. The book's religious themes, mature tone, and somber look highlighted the strengths of what Eisner referred to as "sequential art." The success of *A Contract with God* brought Eisner back to comics full time, and his final work, *The Plot: The Secret Story of The Protocols of the Elders of Zion,* was published after his death.

Eorsi, Istvan, Hungarian writer and political activist (b. June 16, 1931, Budapest, Hung.—d. Oct. 13, 2005, Budapest), attempted to ignite social reform by working as an organizer during the 1956 revolt against Soviet rule in Hungary. He was a follower of Marxist philosopher George Lukacs, and two anti-Soviet poems that he published in 1956 in the journal *Elunk* ("We Are Alive") led to his arrest. Eorsi was sentenced to an eight-year prison term, and his literary works were banned from publication for 12 years. After obtaining an early release in 1960, he worked as a literary translator and wrote poetry and plays, which were distributed underground. His many works included the verse collection *Utni az ordogot!* (1956; "To Pummel the Devil!") and *Urugyeim* (1979; "My Pretexts"), a volume of essays. His play *A kihallgatas* ("The Interrogation") was written in the 1960s but was not staged until 1984 in West Germany, where he lived for a time. Eorsi was honoured with many awards, notably, in 1991, the Memorial Medal of the 1956 Revolution.

Epstein, Israel, Polish-born Chinese author and journalist (b. April 20, 1915, Warsaw, Pol., Russian Empire—d. May 26, 2005, Beijing, China), through prolific writings and his position as editor of the newsmagazine *China Today,* served as an ardent propagandist for Mao Zedong and Chinese communism. Epstein moved with his family to China at the age of two. He worked as a journalist from his teens, covering the Japanese invasion of China for Western news organizations and eventually interviewing Mao extensively in 1944. Epstein published a series of glowing portrayals of Mao, beginning with *The Unfinished Revolution in China* (1949). He became editor of *China Today* (then called *China Reconstructs*) in 1951 and held that position until 1985. His support of Chinese communism remained steadfast over the years even though Epstein himself was imprisoned for a time during the Cultural Revolution.

Evans, (Richard) Gwynfor, Welsh politician (b. Sept. 1, 1912, Barry, Glamorgan, Wales—d. April 21, 2005, Pencarreg, Carmarthenshire, Wales), devoted his life to the peaceful cause of Welsh nationalism as vice president (1943–45), president (1945–81), and honorary president (from 1982) of Plaid Cymru, the Welsh nationalist political party. A lawyer by training, Evans was educated at the University College of Wales, Aberystwyth, and St. John's College, Oxford. He represented Plaid Cymru in the British Parliament (1966–70 and 1974–79) and gained national attention for himself and his cause in 1980 when his threat of a hunger strike forced Prime Minister Margaret Thatcher's government to follow through on a promise to establish a television station for Wales.

Eyadéma, Gnassingbé (ÉTIENNE EYADÉMA), Togolese soldier and president (b. Dec. 26, 1935, Pya, Togoland [now Togo]—d. Feb. 5, 2005, en route to France from Togo), was, at the time of his death, Africa's longest-serving political leader, having ruled Togo with near-dictatorial power for more than 37 years. During his long tenure Eyadéma established a single-party state under his Rally of the Togolese People and drew frequent condemnation from Amnesty International and other groups. Despite charges of corruption and human rights abuses, he wielded considerable influence with France (Togo's former colonial master), helped to found the Economic Community of West African States, and was instrumental in several international agreements, notably the 1975 Lomé Convention. After serving as a sergeant in the French army, Eyadéma returned to Togo, where he participated in the January 1963 military assassination of Pres. Sylvanus Olympio and the installation of Nicolas Grunitzky as Togo's president. Five years later the army overthrew Grunitzky and named Eyadéma president and defense minister. Although he initially brought political stability and economic growth to Togo, the country later suffered from corruption and mismanagement, as well as internal uprisings and international economic sanctions that were imposed in 1993. Eyadéma, who took the name Gnassingbé as part of an Africanization program, ran unopposed for reelection in 1979 and 1986. He briefly relinquished power to a transitional government in 1991 but was reelected amid accusations of electoral fraud in nominally democratic ballots in 1993 and 1998. In 2001 he pledged to retire in two years, but after amending the constitution to end the presidential term limit,

he was elected again in 2003. Eyadéma, who had survived several assassination attempts, died while being flown to France for emergency medical treatment.

Fahd (FAHD IBN 'ABD AL-'AZIZ AL-SA'UD), Saudi monarch (b. 1923, Riyadh, Arabia—d. Aug. 1, 2005, Riyadh, Saudi Arabia), as crown prince (1975–82) and king (from 1982) of Saudi Arabia, oversaw the country's rapid modernization, but he later faced a number of challenges, most notably the rise of Islamic extremists. Fahd, the 11th son of Ibn Sa'ud (the founder of the Saudi kingdom), held several government positions under his half brother King Faysal before being named crown prince when his half brother Khalid ascended the throne in 1975. Owing to Khalid's poor health, Fahd became the de facto leader of Saudi Arabia, and using the country's immense oil revenues, he built roads, hospitals, and housing complexes. He also established Saudi Arabia as a moderating force in the Middle East, actively pursuing peace in the region. After succeeding Khalid upon his death in 1982, Fahd encountered a series of difficulties. In the mid-1980s oil prices fell, triggering a steady decline in the country's economy. Islamic fundamentalism also became a major concern, especially after Fahd allowed Western troops, including those from the U.S., to be stationed in Saudi Arabia following the 1990 Iraqi invasion of Kuwait. His decision was extremely unpopular and allegedly contributed to the rise of militants. Although Fahd undertook a number of measures—including the strict enforcement of Wahhabism and the funding of mosques around the world—to appease hard-liners, domestic terrorist attacks increased in the 1990s. There was also rising opposition to his autocratic rule, and Fahd responded with modest democratic reforms, including the 1993 establishment of an advisory body, the Majlis al-Shura (Consultative Council). In 1995 Fahd suffered a debilitating stroke. His younger half brother Crown Prince Abdullah became virtual ruler and succeeded Fahd as king.

Farnsworth, E(dward) Allan, American legal scholar (b. June 30, 1928, Providence, R.I.—d. Jan. 31, 2005, Englewood, N.J.), was regarded as the leading expert in U.S. contract law and wrote standard references on the subject. He taught contract law at Columbia University, New York City, from 1954 and frequently represented the U.S. at international trade conferences and at the United Nations Commission on International Trade Law. The American Law Institute in 1971 asked him to help create a reference source on contract law, and the *Restatement (Second) on Contracts* was published in 1981. His *Farnsworth on Contracts* (1990) became the standard textbook on the subject.

Fazal Mahmood, Pakistani cricketer (b. Feb. 18, 1927, Lahore, India—d. May 30, 2005, Lahore, Pak.), was a right-arm fast-medium bowler who played in 34 Test matches for Pakistan between 1952 and 1962, including 10 as captain. Fazal quickly established himself as a key bowler in the first Pakistan Test teams after the partition of India. He took 20 wickets in the first official Pakistan Test series, played against India in 1952–53. He achieved that feat again in the 1954 series against England, taking 12 wickets for 99 runs in Pakistan's victory (its first against England) at the Oval. He captained the side against the West Indies (1958–59), Australia (1959–60), and India (1960–61). In his first-class career (1943–64), Fazal played in 112 matches, scored 2,662 runs at an average of 23.35, with one century, and took 466 wickets at an average of 18.96, with a best bowling analysis of nine for 43. In 34 Test matches he scored 620 runs at an average of 14.09, with no centuries, and took 139 wickets at an average of 24.70, with a best bowling analysis of seven for 42.

Fei Xiaotong, Chinese social anthropologist (b. Nov. 2, 1910, Wujiang district, Jiangsu province, China—d. April 24, 2005, Beijing, China), wrote extensively about village life and advocated a policy of rural industrialization. Fei's contributions to anthropology ranked among the most important of the 20th century. After completing graduate studies at Qinghua University in Beijing and at the London School of Economics (where he studied with noted anthropologist Bronislaw Malinowski), he took a position at Yunnan University in Kunming, where many academics had retreated from the Japanese occupation of northeastern China. There he researched and wrote his most highly regarded works on village life, notably *Peasant Life in China: A Field Study of Country Life in the Yangtze Valley* (1939). His work brought him to prominence in China, and when he spoke out against the brutality of the Nationalist government in 1945, he was forced into a brief exile in London. Later he joined the faculty at Qinghua University and initially held some advisory positions in the communist government of Mao Zedong. In 1957 Fei was denounced as a "rightist" and stripped of his right to teach, publish, or hold any position of influence. In the early 1960s some of his privileges were restored, but during the Cultural Revolution (1966–76), he was sent to the countryside for rehabilitation. He returned to Beijing in 1972 and resurfaced in 1980 as a university professor and adviser to the reformist government of the post-Mao era.

Ferrer, Ibrahim, Cuban singer (b. Feb. 20, 1927, Santiago de Cuba, Cuba—d. Aug. 6, 2005, Havana, Cuba), became a professional musician at age 13 and went on to sing with

© Tom Craig/Corbis

Cuban singer Ibrahim Ferrer

a number of bands. He was retired and shining shoes to earn extra money when he was invited to perform on the Grammy Award-winning album *Buena Vista Social Club* (1997) and in the film that documented the group and the making of the album (1999). His subsequent albums *Buena Vista Social Club Presents Ibrahim Ferrer* (1999) and *Buenos Hermanos* (2003) also won Grammys.

Fitzgerald, Geraldine Mary, Irish-born actress (b. Nov. 24, 1913, Greystones, County Wicklow, Ire.—d. July 17, 2005, New York, N.Y.), was a versatile performer whose long career was especially notable for her supporting roles in films that included *Wuthering*

© John Springer Collection/Corbis

Actress Geraldine Fitzgerald

Heights (1939), *Dark Victory* (1939), *Watch on the Rhine* (1943), *Ten North Frederick* (1958), *The Pawnbroker* (1964), *Harry and Tonto* (1974), and *Arthur* (1981). Her most acclaimed stage portrayal was that of Mary Tyrone in a 1971 Off-Broadway production of Eugene O'Neill's *Long Day's Journey into Night.* Fitzgerald also toured with a nightclub act and directed stage productions—including *Mass Appeal* (1981), for which she received a Tony Award nomination.

Fletcher, Cyril, British entertainer (b. June 25, 1913, Watford, Hertfordshire, Eng.—d. Jan. 2, 2005, St. Peter Port, Guernsey), appeared regularly on BBC radio and television for more than six decades. He introduced his

witty "Odd Odes" on BBC TV's new service in 1937; he later revived his brand of comic rhymes—which he described as "unique in their feeble banality"—on *That's Life* (1970–81). Fletcher was a regular on the panel game show *What's My Line?* in the 1950s and starred in several other programs, notably *The*

© E. Wilson/Getty Images

Comic Cyril Fletcher

Cyril Fletcher Show (1959). He also wrote gardening books, designed ornamental gardens, and served as the host of a radio advice program and a series of TV gardening shows.

Flon, Suzanne, French actress (b. Jan. 28, 1918, near Paris, France—d. June 15, 2005, Paris), appeared in more than 60 films during a career that spanned 60 years. Flon won two César Awards, the best actress prize at the Venice Film Festival for *Thou Shalt Not Kill* (1961), and two Molière Awards for her work in the theatre. She made her screen debut in 1947 and performed in such notable films as *Moulin Rouge* (1952), Orson Welles's *Mr. Arkadin* (1955), *Le Procès* (1962), *The Train* (1964), *L'Été meurtrier* (1983), and *Les Enfants du marais* (1999). Her theatre work included plays by Shakespeare, Molière, Marguerite Duras, and, particularly, Jean Anouilh. Flon continued to perform well into her 80s and last appeared onstage in Duras's *Savannah Bay* (2004).

Foote, Shelby, American novelist and historian (b. Nov. 17, 1916, Greenville, Miss.—d. June 27, 2005, Memphis, Tenn.), wrote a masterly history of the American Civil War and appeared as a narrator and commentator on a landmark documentary about the conflict. He also wrote a number of highly regarded novels, each set in the American South. Foote embarked on a writing career after studying at the University of North Carolina for two years and serving in the military during World War II. He worked briefly as a reporter and then published his first novel, *Tournament,* in 1949. This was followed by the novels *Follow Me Down* (1950), *Love in a Dry Season* (1951), *Shiloh* (1952), and *Jordan County* (1954). Foote devoted the next two decades to completing the work for which he was best known, *The Civil War: A Narrative* (1958–74). The 3,000-page history consisted of three volumes—*Fort Sumter to Perryville* (1958), *Fredericksburg to Meridian* (1963), and *Red River to Appomattox* (1974)—and was notable for its superb storytelling. The work earned Foote a prominent role on filmmaker Ken Burns's widely acclaimed documentary

The Civil War, which first aired on the Public Broadcasting Service in 1990 and brought the reclusive Foote unwanted celebrity. He published his last novel, *September, September,* in 1978; the novel was filmed for television as *Memphis* in 1991. He also edited a 1993 short-story collection, *Chickamauga, and Other Civil War Stories.* In its 1999 list of the 20th-century's 100 best English-language nonfiction books, the Modern Library ranked *The Civil War: A Narrative* as number 15.

Forman, James (JAMES RUFUS), American civil rights activist (b. Oct. 4, 1928, Chicago, Ill.—d. Jan. 10, 2005, Washington, D.C.), served as executive secretary of the Student Nonviolent Coordinating Committee (1961–66). In that position he was a pivotal figure in the struggle for racial equality, especially in the organization of the Freedom Rides in the South and of the 1963 March on Washington.

Fowles, John Robert, British writer (b. March 31, 1926, Leigh-on-Sea, Essex, Eng.—d. Nov. 5, 2005, Lyme Regis, Dorset, Eng.), combined masterly storytelling with an unconventional, often experimental, style to explore existential themes, especially free will, in a series of acclaimed novels, most notably *The French Lieutenant's Woman* (1969; filmed 1981). After graduating (1950) from New College, Oxford, Fowles taught in Greece, France, and England. He earned critical and commercial success with his first novel, *The Collector* (1963; filmed 1965), a haunting account of a lonely butterfly collector who imprisons a woman in his basement. In *The Magus* (1965, rev. ed. 1977; filmed 1968), Fowles chronicled a young teacher's struggle to differentiate between fantasy and reality. The novel challenged readers with its ambiguity, which came to define much of Fowles's works. With *The French Lieutenant's Woman,* a 19th-century love story revolving around an engaged geologist and his obsession with an enigmatic governess, Fowles reinterpreted the classic Victorian novel by including alternate endings, social critiques, and a contemporary narrator. Among his later novels were *Daniel Martin* (1977), *Matissa* (1982), and *A Maggot* (1985). Fowles also penned several collections of essays, including *The Aristos: A Self-Portrait in Ideas* (1964) and *Wormholes* (1998), as well as poetry and nature writings.

Freas, Frank Kelly, American illustrator (b. Aug. 27, 1922, Hornell, N.Y.—d. Jan. 2, 2005, Los Angeles, Calif.), earned the designation of "the most popular illustrator in the history of science fiction" with his stylized depictions of fantastic landscapes, alien women, and painstakingly detailed robots. While his work in that genre earned him 11 Hugo Awards, Freas was best remembered as the cover artist of *Mad* magazine (1958–62) and as the spiritual father of *Mad*'s gap-toothed mascot, Alfred E. Neuman.

Freis, Edward David, American physician and medical researcher (b. May 13, 1912, Chicago, Ill.—d. Feb. 1, 2005, Washington, D.C.), successfully demonstrated the benefits of treating hypertension with drugs during a five-year study that he conducted with his colleagues during the 1960s. Freis also revealed the health risks associated with hypertension, such as heart attack and stroke, and disproved the established theory that high blood pressure was beneficial in circulating blood to the heart, brain, and other vital parts of the body. He received the Albert Lasker Award for Clinical Medical Research in 1971.

Fry, Christopher (CHRISTOPHER FRY HARRIS), British playwright and screenwriter (b. Dec. 18, 1907, Bristol, Gloucestershire, Eng.—d. June 30, 2005, Chichester, West Sussex, Eng.), wrote whimsical comedies, most notably *The Lady's Not for Burning* (1948), that were largely responsible for a verse-play revival on the post-World War II British stage. Fry, who used his maternal grandmother's maiden name, began his theatre career in the early 1930s and worked as an actor, director, and writer of plays and music before *The Lady's Not for Burning* brought him fame. A departure from the realistic theatrical style that was then prevalent, the ironic medieval comedy was written in blank verse and centred on a former soldier returned from the Hundred Years' War and a woman sentenced to be burned for witchcraft. Fry was greatly influenced by T.S. Eliot, and *The Lady's Not for Burning* was noted for its rich language and optimism, which became hallmarks of Fry's works. In 1949 John Gielgud directed and starred with a young Richard Burton in the West End production. Fry's other notable plays included *Venus Observed* (1950), which Laurence Olivier staged, *A Sleep of Prisoners* (1951), and *The Dark Is Light Enough: A Winter Comedy* (1954). From the late 1950s, with the notable exception of *A Yard of Sun: A Summer Comedy* (1970), Fry focused on writing for television, radio, and film as well as adapting and translating plays, including Henrik Ibsen's *Peer Gynt* and works by Jean Anouilh and Jean Giraudoux. Fry contributed much of the screenplay for *Ben-Hur* (1959) but was not credited.

Ganesan, Gemini (RAMASWAMY GANESH), Indian film actor (b. Nov. 17, 1920, Madras [Chennai], Tamil Nadu, India—d. March 22, 2005, Chennai), was the "kadhal mannan" ("king of romance") in southern India's Tamil-language cinema. Ganesan appeared in more than 200 films, beginning with a small role in *Miss Malini* (1947). His last significant screen appearance was in *Avvai Shanmugi* (1996), a Tamil remake of *Mrs. Doubtfire*, in which he played the romantic rival.

Garang (de Mabior), John, Sudanese rebel leader and politician (b. June 23, 1945, Wangkulei, Anglo-Egyptian Sudan [now in The Sudan]—d. July 30/31, 2005, southern Sudan), was appointed to the post of first vice president of The Sudan after having

founded and led the Sudan People's Liberation Army in 22 years of war against the Sudanese government and then negotiating an end to that war. Garang graduated from Grinnell (Iowa) College in 1969 and returned to The Sudan, where he was involved with the Anya Nya rebel group in the Christian and animist southern part of the country. After the 1972 Addis Ababa Agreement, Garang was among those rebels absorbed into the Sudanese armed forces. He became a colonel, trained at Fort Benning, Georgia, and earned advanced degrees in the U.S. The Sudanese government grew increasingly Islamist in the early 1980s, however, and when Garang was sent to put down an uprising in the south in May 1983, he instead joined the rebel forces, out of which he built the Sudan People's Liberation Army, which by 1991 was 60,000 strong. Garang engaged in peace talks with Pres. Omar Hassan Ahmad al-Bashir beginning in July 2002, and the talks culminated in the signing of a peace agreement in January 2005, under the terms of which Garang joined the government on July 9 as first vice president. He died in a helicopter crash.

Gass, J(ohn) Donald MacIntyre, American ophthalmologist (b. Aug. 2, 1928, Prince Edward Island—d. Feb. 26, 2005, Nashville, Tenn.), conducted groundbreaking research on diseases of the retina, which led to treatments that saved the eyesight of thousands of patients. Gass was among the leading developers of a diagnostic test called fluorescein angiography, which he used to identify certain forms of macular degeneration. The test revealed leakage patterns and blockage in the blood vessels of the retina through the use of an intensely fluorescent traceable dye injected into the vessels. Gass was a key figure in the discovery of the cause of macular holes, a condition in which the stretching of retinal tissue causes holes in the macula (the central area of the retina responsible for detailed vision). He was also among the first researchers to identify the macular swelling that sometimes occurs after cataract surgery, a condition called Irvine-Gass syndrome. During the 1970s Gass authored the highly influential text *Stereoscopic Atlas of Macular Diseases: Diagnosis and Treatment*. In 1999, 33,000 of his peers selected him as one of the 20th century's 10 most influential ophthalmologists. His many honours included the Helen Keller Prize for Vision Research (2001) and the Laureate Recognition Award of the American Academy of Ophthalmology (2004).

Gatski, Gunner (FRANK GATSKI), American football player (b. March 18, 1919, Farmington, W.Va.—d. Nov. 22, 2005, Morgantown, W.Va.), blocked for quarterback Otto Graham and running back Marion Motley while playing (1946–56) for the Cleveland Browns professional football team. Nicknamed Gunner for his explosive blocking, Gatski was the centre on the offensive lines that pushed the Browns to four All-America Football Conference titles (1946–49) and, after the Browns joined the National Football League, helped the team reach the championship game six

consecutive times (1950–55), with three wins. He was named to the Pro Football Hall of Fame in 1985.

Gaul, Charly, Luxembourgian cyclist (b. Dec. 8, 1932, Luxembourg—d. Dec. 6, 2005, Luxembourg), was one of international cycling's greatest climbing specialists; in 1990, long after his retirement, he was named Luxembourg's Sportsman of the 20th Century. During his 12-year career (1953–65), the "angel of the mountains" raced in the Tour de France 10 times, won 10 stages, and was the overall victor in 1958 (after finishing as the top climber in 1955 and 1956). He also won the Tour of Italy (Giro d'Italia) twice (1956, 1959) and the Luxembourg national championship four times (1959–62). The quiet, publicity-shy Gaul finished third in the 1961 Tour de France, and after quitting the sport in 1965, he retired to a reclusive rural life.

Gibbs, Sir Harry Talbot, Australian judge (b. Feb. 7, 1917, Sydney, Australia—d. June 25, 2005, Sydney), served 17 years (1970–87) on the High Court of Australia, becoming chief justice in 1981. He was much admired for his striking ability to deliver articulate, convincing arguments, along with his superior memory and knowledge of the law. Gibbs began his legal career as a barrister with the Supreme Court of Queensland in 1939. He suspended his law practice during World War II, rising to the rank of major in the Australian Imperial Force by war's end. In 1957 he was appointed a queen's counsel, and in 1961 he was named to the Supreme Court of Queensland. Gibbs presided (1967–70) over cases in the Federal Court of Bankruptcy until his appointment to the High Court. He was knighted in 1970, served on Australia's Privy Council in 1972, and was made a Companion of the Order of Australia in 1987.

Giulini, Carlo Maria, Italian conductor (b. May 9, 1914, Barletta, Italy—d. June 14, 2005, Brescia, Italy), was admired for his meticulous,

Conductor Carlo Maria Giulini

reflective performances, despite a relatively small, carefully selected repertoire of operas and orchestral works. Giulini studied violin and viola at the Academy of Santa Cecilia in Rome. Drafted into the Italian army during World War II, he conducted his debut concert with the Santa Cecilia Orchestra upon the liberation of Rome in 1944. He then worked for Italian Radio and in 1950 conducted his first staged opera. From 1953 to 1955 he was principal conductor at La Scala in Milan. He established a career in major European opera houses until, in the late 1960s, he increasingly concentrated on the orchestral literature. Giulini had a long association with London's Philharmonia and New Philharmonia orchestras and in 1955 made his American debut with the Chicago Symphony Orchestra (CSO), an affiliation that lasted until 1978. He was the CSO's principal guest conductor from 1969 to 1973. He was conductor of the Vienna Symphony Orchestra (1973–76) and of the Los Angeles Philharmonic Orchestra (1978–84). Among his opera recordings were Mozart's *Marriage of Figaro* and *Don Giovanni* and Verdi's *Don Carlos* and *Falstaff*. He also recorded Verdi's *Requiem Mass* and made several highly praised recordings with the London, Chicago, and Los Angeles orchestras.

Gonçalves, Vasco dos Santos, Portuguese military officer (b. May 3, 1921, Lisbon, Port.—d. June 11, 2005, Almancil, Port.), was a key figure in the Armed Forces Movement (MFA), which overthrew Portuguese Prime Minister Marcelo Caetano in the Revolution of the Carnations (1974), ending almost 50 years of right-wing dictatorship. Gonçalves served as prime minister of four provisional administrations from 1974 to 1975, but his national influence during that period far exceeded his official status. Under his guidance, banks and insurance companies were nationalized, paid holidays and a minimum wage were established, and most Portuguese colonies were granted independence. In April 1975 Portugal held its first free elections, with a record 91.7% of registered voters going to the polls. The radical Portuguese Communist Party, led by Álvaro Cunhal (*q.v.*), was soundly defeated by the more moderate Socialist Party, however, and Gonçalves resigned from office.

Goodpaster, Andrew Jackson, general (ret.), U.S. Army (b. Feb. 12, 1915, Granite City, Ill.—d. May 16, 2005, Washington, D.C.), wielded great influence during a lengthy military career in which he served as a presidential adviser (1954–61), most notably to Dwight D. Eisenhower; commander (1969–74) of NATO forces in Europe; and superintendent (1977–81) of the United States Military Academy at West Point following a cheating scandal. Goodpaster, a four-star general, also wrote several books and was involved with institutions that studied foreign and domestic policy. In 1984 he received the Presidential Medal of Freedom.

Gorman, R(udolph) C(arl), American artist (b. July 26, 1931, Chinle, Ariz.—d. Nov. 3, 2005, Albuquerque, N.M.), was a celebrated Navajo artist whose graceful paintings, sculptures, and lithographs—many of them featuring Native American women—earned him an international reputation. Influenced by Mexican art, he produced works that were vivid in colour and fluid in style. In 1973 New York

City's Metropolitan Museum of Art included a number of his works in an exhibition on Native American art, and in 1986 Harvard University honoured Gorman for his "notable contributions to American art and Native American culture." His admirers included Andy Warhol, who painted Gorman on several occasions and who was among the many celebrities who collected his art. Gorman was also the author of a series of popular cookbooks.

Gorshin, Frank, American actor and comedian (b. April 5, 1933, Pittsburgh, Pa.—d. May 17, 2005, Burbank, Calif.), was best known for his manic portrayal of the archvillain the Riddler on the 1960s television series *Batman*. Gorshin made a name for himself as a master impressionist, performing in nightclubs in Las Vegas and on television variety shows. In his career he appeared in more than 80 films, including *Where the Boys Are* (1960) and the cult favourite *12 Monkeys* (1995). He scored a stage hit with his portrayal of comedian George Burns in the play *Say Goodnight, Gracie* in 2002.

Gould, (Richard) Gordon, American physicist (b. July 17, 1920, New York, N.Y.—d. Sept. 16, 2005, New York City), played an important role in early laser research and coined the word *laser* (light amplification by stimulated emission of radiation). He came up with the idea of the laser and its name in 1957 while he was a physics graduate student at Columbia University, New York City. Believing that he first needed to have a working prototype, he waited until 1959 to apply for a patent, but by that time others had filed such an application and his was rejected. After many years of litigation, however, he prevailed, and in 1977 he was issued the first of the four U.S. basic laser patents that he was eventually granted. Gould was inducted into the (U.S.) National Inventors Hall of Fame in 1991.

Grant, Joseph, American animator (b. May 15, 1908, New York, N.Y.—d. May 6, 2005, Glendale, Calif.), served as both a designer and a writer on some of the classic animated works of the Disney studios. Grant joined Disney in 1933 and created the wicked queen/witch of *Snow White and the Seven Dwarfs* (1937). He played a central creative role in *Pinocchio* and *Fantasia* (both 1940) and co-wrote *Dumbo* (1941) and *Lady and the Tramp* (1955). He left Disney in the 1950s but returned to consult on popular animated films such as *Beauty and the Beast* (1991) and *The Lion King* (1994).

Gray, L(ouis) Patrick, III, American lawyer and government official (b. July 18, 1916, St. Louis, Mo.—d. July 6, 2005, Atlantic Beach, Fla.), served as interim director of the FBI after the death of J. Edgar Hoover in 1972. The Watergate scandal broke just weeks after Gray assumed the position, and he soon found himself cast as the fall guy in the White House cover-up. He was forced to resign in 1973. With the 2005 disclosure that FBI official Mark Felt had been the primary leak to the reporters who broke the Watergate story, it

became clear that Gray had been betrayed both by his friend Pres. Richard Nixon and by his top aide at the FBI.

Grimsdale, Richard Lawrence, British electrical engineer (b. Sept. 18, 1929, Australia—d. Dec. 6, 2005, Brighton, Eng.), built the first experimental fully transistorized computer, which was introduced in 1953 while he was a research student at the University of Manchester. He later collaborated on the first commercial transistor computer, contributed to the development of read-only memory (ROM), and developed digital graphics applications that eventually were used to create special effects in films and video games. Grimsdale graduated (1950) from Manchester and remained there until 1960, when he temporarily quit academia for industry. He joined the electrical engineering faculty at Sussex University in 1967.

Grunwald, Henry, Austrian-born American magazine editor (b. Dec. 2, 1922, Vienna, Austria—d. Feb. 26, 2005, New York, N.Y.), introduced the most extensive innovations to the format of *Time* magazine as its managing editor following the death of founder Henry Luce. After joining *Time* as a copy boy in 1944, Grunwald was elevated to foreign correspondent one year later and quickly advanced to become the magazine's youngest senior editor at age 28. Promoted to managing editor in 1968, Grunwald departed from *Time*'s traditional format by featuring new sections on the economy, the environment, behaviour, and gender; adding colour photographs, more original reporting that included bylines for writers, and guest essays written by famous experts; and introducing special issues devoted solely to one topic. The magazine also loosened its conservative political views; Grunwald's first editorial asked for the resignation of U.S. Pres. Richard Nixon as a result of the Watergate scandal. After serving (1979–87) as editor in chief of Time, Inc., Grunwald retired, and in 1988 Pres. Ronald Reagan appointed him ambassador to Austria.

Guerrero, Lalo (EDUARDO GUERRERO, JR.), American singer-songwriter (b. Dec. 24, 1916, Tucson, Ariz.—d. March 17, 2005, Palm Springs, Calif.), captured the spirit of daily Mexican American life and embraced the social diversity of Mexican and American communities in bilingual songs and parodies. Guerrero, who was dubbed "the father of Chicano music," incorporated a wide variety of musical styles, including Spanish boleros, *corridos*, *norteñas*, and *rancheras* as well as American blues, swing, and rock and roll. His parodies of popular American songs included "Tacos for Two," Battle Hymn of the Chicanos," "Pancho López," which lampooned Walt Disney's "The Ballad of Davy Crockett," and the satiric "Mama, Don't Let Your Babies Grow Up to Be Busboys." Other notable works included "Canción mexicana" and "Pecadora." During a six-decade career, Guerrero wrote more than 700 songs, including boogie-woogie-inspired pachuco songs, which were featured in Luis Valdez's theatrical production

Zoot Suit (1977). Guerrero was awarded a 1996 National Medal of Arts.

Gunter, Sue, American basketball coach (b. May 22, 1939, Walnut Grove, Miss.—d. Aug. 4, 2005, Baton Rouge, La.), accumulated 708 career wins, the third most in women's collegiate basketball, while serving as head coach

Coach Sue Gunter in 2003 after her 400th win for LSU

at Middle Tennessee State University (1962–64), Stephen F. Austin State University, Nacogdoches, Texas (1964–80), and Louisiana State University (1982–2004). She guided her teams to the National Collegiate Athletic Association women's basketball tournament 14 times. Gunter was inducted into the Women's Basketball Hall of Fame (2000) and the Naismith Memorial Basketball Hall of Fame (2005).

Haas, Karl, American musicologist and music broadcaster (b. Dec. 6, 1913, Speyer-am-Rhein, Ger.—d. Feb. 6, 2005, Royal Oak, Mich.), hosted a daily radio program, *Adventures in Good Music*, which he originated on a Detroit radio station in 1959. The show was syndicated nationally in 1970 and continued on the air until 2003. At times it was the most-listened-to classical music program in the world, and it won many honours, including two Peabody Awards for excellence in broadcasting. Haas, a concert pianist who fled Nazi Germany in 1936, founded the Chamber Music Society of Detroit in 1944 and headed (1967–71) the celebrated training camp for young musicians now called Interlochen (Mich.) Center for the Arts.

Haas, Peter, American business executive (b. 1918, San Francisco, Calif.—d. Dec. 3, 2005, San Francisco), was a great-grandnephew of denim blue jean manufacturer Levi Strauss and helped build Levi Strauss & Co. into a globally recognized brand. Haas joined the family business in 1945 and throughout his career at Levi Strauss worked closely with his older brother, Walter. Haas served as president and chief executive of the company (1970–81), chairman of the board (1981–89), and chairman of the executive committee (1989–2004). In the 1950s he was instrumental in bringing about racial desegregation in the company's

factories in the American South, and he later served on the city of San Francisco's Fair Employment Practices Commission—the first such commission in California.

Hackworth, David Haskell, colonel (ret.), U.S. Army (b. Nov. 11, 1930, Venice, Calif.—d. May 4, 2005, Tijuana, Mex.), was a highly decorated soldier and a scourge of the U.S. military establishment; he earned a reputation as a brilliant but rebellious battlefield commander. Hackworth lied to enlist in the army at age 15 and won a battlefield commission at 20 to become the youngest U.S. captain in the Korean War. He was the youngest American full colonel during the Vietnam War but incurred the wrath of senior officers for his harsh public criticism of U.S. strategy and policies. He was allowed to resign, however, with an honorable discharge rather than face court-martial. Hackworth earned 91 medals, including 2 Distinguished Service Crosses, 10 Silver Stars, 8 Bronze Stars, and 8 Purple Hearts. Once out of uniform, he moved to Australia, where he became a successful restaurateur and poultry farmer. His 1989 autobiography, *About Face*, became a best seller, and he was hired in 1990 by *Newsweek* magazine to report on the Gulf War; he again became a severe critic of U.S. military policy. Later his syndicated column "Defending America" appeared regularly in newspapers across the U.S.

Hallaren, Mary Agnes, colonel (ret.), U.S. Army (b. May 4, 1907, Lowell, Mass.—d. Feb. 13, 2005, McLean, Va.), helped to integrate women into the U.S. military as a director of the Women's Army Corps (WAC) in the 1940s and '50s. Hallaren was the first woman outside the Medical Corps to be commissioned into the U.S. Army when the WAC was added to the regular army in 1948. During World War II she commanded the first battalion of the Women's Army Auxiliary Corps (WAAC; later WAC) to go overseas. She then became director of WAC personnel attached to the 8th and 9th Air Forces, and by 1945 she had been named director of all WAC personnel in the European theatre. For her service she earned the Legion of Merit, the Bronze Star, and the Croix de Guerre (France). Following the passage of the 1948 Women's Armed Services Integration Act, which allowed women into the regular armed services for the first time, she continued to serve as WAC director until 1953, near the end of the Korean War. After retiring from the military in 1960, Hallaren became involved in women's labour issues, notably as director (1965–78) of Women in Community Service; in this capacity she helped enlarge the service into a national organization, known as WICS. In 1996 she was enshrined into the National Women's Hall of Fame.

Hariri, Rafiq Bahaa Edine al- Lebanese business tycoon, politician, and philanthropist (b. Nov. 1, 1944, Sidon, Lebanon—d. Feb. 14, 2005, Beirut, Lebanon), used his personal wealth, international business contacts, and charismatic personality to help broker the end of the Lebanese civil war and rebuild the country's economy and infrastructure, first as an unofficial representative of the Saudi government and then as prime minister of Lebanon (1992–98 and 2000–04). Hariri, the son of a poor Sunni Muslim farmer, studied economics and business at Beirut Arab University. He immigrated to Saudi Arabia, where he worked as a teacher and founded a construction company, Saudi Oger, which built several high-profile commissions for the Saudi royal family. Hariri's business empire eventually included holdings in construction, real estate, banking, insurance, media, and telecommunications; in 1999 *Forbes* magazine estimated his net worth at $4 billion. He also established the Hariri Foundation to provide funds for education and health care in Lebanon. In 1992 he was elected to the Lebanese parliament and was appointed prime minister under a constitution that required a Sunni head of government. A strong opponent of Syrian intervention in Lebanon, Hariri resigned from office in 1998. After being reelected in 2000, he clashed with the Syrian-backed president, Émile Lahoud, and resigned again in 2004. Hariri was assassinated in a car bombing.

Haynes, Johnny, English association football (soccer) player (b. Oct. 17, 1934, London, Eng.—d. Oct. 18, 2005, Edinburgh, Scot.), played the midfield for Fulham Football Club

England footballer Johnny Haynes

(1950–70) and England (1954–62). He was the first player to earn £100 (about $280) a week at a time (1958) when the average wage was £15 (about $42). Haynes was widely admired for his offensive skill, especially his long passes that dissected defenses. He played 56 games for England (22 as captain), scoring 18 goals, and was a member of the 1958 and 1962 World Cup squads. Haynes was particularly known for having spearheaded a six-game win streak in 1960–61 in which England scored 40 goals.

Heath, Sir Edward Richard George, British politician (b. July 9, 1916, Broadstairs, Kent, Eng.—d. July 17, 2005, Salisbury, Wiltshire, Eng.), as prime minister (1970–74) of the United Kingdom, oversaw the country's entrance into the European Economic Community (EEC; now the European Union) in 1973. After graduating (1939) from Balliol College, Oxford, Heath served in the Royal Artillery during World War II, and in 1950 he was elected to Parliament for the Conservative Party. He was a strong proponent of European unity and in his role as lord privy seal from 1960 to 1963 headed negotiations for Britain's admission into the EEC. Although the talks ultimately failed after French Pres. Charles de Gaulle blocked Britain's membership in 1963, Heath earned praise for his efforts. In 1965 he became leader of the Conservative Party and led it to victory in the 1970 election. As prime minister he continued to pursue an EEC agreement, a process that was aided by the new French president, Georges Pompidou. In 1972 Heath signed an accession treaty, and the following year the United Kingdom officially joined the EEC. Escalating violence in Northern Ireland and economic problems, including labour strikes, plagued his administration, however. In the general elections of February 1974, the Conservatives lost seats in Parliament, and Heath was unable to form a coalition government. In March he was succeeded as prime minister by Harold Wilson of the Labour Party, and in 1975 Heath was replaced as Conservative leader by Margaret Thatcher, of whom he was highly critical. Heath, who remained an MP until 2001, wrote several books, including the autobiography *The Course of My Life* (1998). He was knighted in 1992.

Heath, Percy Leroy, American musician (b. April 30, 1923, Wilmington, N.C.— d. April 28, 2005, Southampton, N.Y.), became renowned

Jazz bassist Percy Heath

© Terry Cryer/Corbis

for his melodic bass playing in the Modern Jazz Quartet (MJQ), one of the longest-lived of all jazz groups, and in the popular Heath Brothers combos. During World War II he was a fighter pilot with the Army Air Forces' Tuskegee Airmen; after the war he gradually became noted as one of the outstanding bassists in the then-new bop idiom. The MJQ's elegant ensemble sound and far-reaching repertoire offered uncommonly wide latitude for his buoyant, swinging accompaniments and lyric soloing; he played steadily with the group from 1952 to its disbanding in 1997. During the MJQ's 1974–81 hiatus, he also began playing cello, as well as bass, with his brothers—Jimmy on saxophone and Albert ("Tootie") on drums. He played in the Heath Brothers for the rest of his life. He also was bassist on classic recordings by Thelonious Monk, Miles Davis, and Ornette Coleman.

Henderson, Skitch (LYLE RUSSELL CEDRIC HENDERSON), British-born American pianist, conductor, and bandleader (b. Jan. 27, 1918, Birmingham, Eng.—d. Nov. 1, 2005, New Milford, Conn.), worked on radio with Bob Hope, Frank Sinatra, and Bing Crosby, who was responsible for his nickname, derived from Henderson's ability to sketch scores in different keys. He studied with composer Arnold Schoenberg, won a Grammy Award for the album *Great Scenes from Gershwin's Porgy and Bess* (1963), founded and conducted the New York Pops, and was a guest composer with countless symphonies, but he was best remembered as the longtime bandleader for television's *The Tonight Show*, with hosts Steve Allen and Johnny Carson (*q.v.*).

Hildegarde (HILDEGARDE LORETTA SELL), American cabaret performer (b. Feb. 1, 1906, Adell, Wis.—d. July 29, 2005, New York, N.Y.), had a career that spanned nearly seven decades, during which she was internationally known—especially at her peak in the 1930s and '40s—for her stylish, sophisticated nightclub act and such signature songs as "Darling, Je Vous Aime Beaucoup," "I'll Be Seeing You," and "The Last Time I Saw Paris." She also was credited with originating the style of being known by only one name.

Hilleman, Maurice Ralph, American microbiologist (b. Aug. 30, 1919, Miles City, Mont.— d. April 11, 2005, Philadelphia, Pa.), developed some 40 vaccines, including those for chicken pox, hepatitis A, hepatitis B, measles, meningitis, mumps, and rubella. His work was credited with having saved tens of millions of lives by making possible the virtual elimination from many countries of once-common deadly childhood diseases and by serving as the basis for public health measures against many other infectious diseases. His accomplishments included the development of vaccinations that combine vaccines against more than one disease, the discovery of patterns of genetic change in the influenza virus relating to its ability to infect persons, and the discovery or co-discovery of several viruses, including the hepatitis A virus and the rhinoviruses that cause colds. The animal vaccine he developed against Marek disease, which causes a cancer

in chickens, became of great economic importance to the poultry industry. Hilleman received a Ph.D. in microbiology from the University of Chicago in 1944. As a researcher at E.R. Squibb & Sons, he developed his first vaccine, which was used to protect U.S. troops in World War II from the Japanese B encephalitis virus. He was chief of respiratory diseases (1949–57) at Walter Reed Army Medical Center, Washington, D.C., where he began research on the influenza virus. In 1957 he joined what became Merck & Co., Inc. Following his retirement (1984) Hilleman was an adviser to public health organizations, notably the World Health Organization.

Hinds, Justin, Jamaican reggae singer (b. May 7, 1942, Steer Town, Jam.—d. March 17, 2005, Steer Town), enjoyed a four-decade-long career that began in the 1960s when his group the Dominoes recorded the reggae classic "Carry Go Bring Come." Hinds's unique vocal style reflected his rural roots and sustained him as a solo act through the ska, rocksteady, and roots reggae periods. He scored a major comeback when he recorded the acclaimed *Travel with Love* album (1985) with the original Dominoes lineup. Later he gained international acclaim by participating in an album (1997) with Keith Richards of the Rolling Stones and by touring Europe, beginning in 2002, with three other musicians in a group called the Jamaica All Stars.

Hobbs, Bruce Robertson, British jockey and trainer (b. Dec. 27, 1920, Long Island, N.Y.— d. Nov. 21, 2005, Newmarket, Suffolk, Eng.), rode 40–1 long shot Battleship to victory in the 1938 Grand National steeplechase and thereby became, at age 17, the youngest jockey ever to win the race. In 1939 his career as a rider came to a premature end when he was thrown from a horse and broke his back. Later he enjoyed a successful career as a trainer. He trained Tyrnavos, the surprise winner of the 1980 Irish Derby, and the top two-year-olds Jacinth (1973) and Tromos (1978). Hobbs retired in 1985 and that same year was elected to the Jockey Club.

Honderich, Beland, Canadian publisher and editor (b. Nov. 25, 1918, Kitchener, Ont. —d. Nov. 8, 2005, Vancouver, B.C.), transformed the *Toronto Star* from a sensationalistic newspaper of the working class to the largest and most influential paper in the country. He recruited a higher quality of writer for the *Star*, enlarged the arts and international coverage, and steered the paper toward the support of social causes. He joined the *Star* as a reporter in 1943, became editor in chief in 1955, and assumed the role of president and publisher in 1966. He later served as chairman of the paper's parent company, TorStar.

Horn, Shirley Valerie, American jazz artist (b. May 1, 1934, Washington, D.C.—d. Oct. 20, 2005, Cheverly, Md.), sang ballads in a breathy contralto voice and unforced style with a sub-

© Pascal Guyot—AFP/Getty Images

Jazz singer Shirley Horn

tle sensitivity to space and dynamics; the result was singularly intimate vocal music, enhanced by her own piano accompaniments. She recorded five albums in the 1960s but did not unveil her mature style until her 1978 trio album *A Lazy Afternoon;* she became popular through a series of Verve albums, including *You Won't Forget Me* (1990), in which she was joined by trumpeters Miles Davis and Wynton Marsalis, and especially *Here's to Life* (1992). In 1998 she won a Grammy for *I Remember Miles.* Although she appeared after 1980 in international festivals and jazz spots, she performed primarily in Washington-area clubs throughout her career.

Horner, Red (REGINALD HORNER), Canadian ice hockey player (b. May 28, 1909, Lynden, Ont.—d. April 27, 2005, Toronto, Ont.), had a reputation as the toughest and most intimidating player of his era. As a defenseman for the Toronto Maple Leafs (1928–40), he accrued 1,264 penalty minutes, leading the National Hockey League in that category eight times. During his career he scored 42 goals and was credited with 110 assists, and he helped the Maple Leafs capture the Stanley Cup in 1932. Horner was inducted into the Ice Hockey Hall of Fame in 1965.

Houston, James Archibald, Canadian artist, author, and filmmaker (b. June 12, 1921, Toronto, Ont.—d. April 17, 2005, New London, Conn.), lived for 14 years (1948–62) among the Inuit people of northern Canada, teaching printmaking and promoting native artwork throughout Canada and the United States. After leaving northern Canada, Houston worked as a designer (1962–72) for the Steuben Glass Co. in New York City. He also wrote books for children and for adults and produced documentary and animated films. Houston's memoir, *Confessions of an Igloo Dweller,* appeared in 1996.

Howells, William White, American anthropologist (b. Nov. 27, 1908, New York, N.Y.—d.

Dec. 20, 2005, Kittery Point, Maine), was a physical anthropologist who specialized in the establishment of population relationships through physical measurement. He was also known for his work in developing anthropological curricula and for his popular books in the field, including *Mankind So Far* (1944), *Back of History: The Story of Our Own Origins* (1954), and *Mankind in the Making* (1959). Howells worked as a researcher at the American Museum of Natural History from 1934 to 1939 before joining the faculty of the University of Wisconsin. He later served (1954–74) as a professor of anthropology at Harvard University. His authoritative *Cranial Variation in Man: A Study by Multivariate Analysis of Patterns of Difference Among Recent Human Populations*—which compared skull measurements from 17 distinct world populations—appeared in 1973. He received the Distinguished Service Award (1978) from the American Anthropological Association and the Charles R. Darwin Lifetime Achievement Award (1992) from the American Association of Physical Anthropologists. He was the grandson of both the novelist and literary critic William Dean Howells and the journalist Horace White.

Hunter, Bob (ROBERT HUNTER), Canadian environmental activist (b. Oct. 13, 1941, St. Boniface, Man.—d. May 2, 2005, Toronto, Ont.), served as president (1973–77) of Greenpeace, the international organization devoted to preserving the environment. He worked as a journalist with the *Vancouver Sun* newspaper before becoming actively involved in protests against U.S. nuclear testing in the Pacific Ocean. He cofounded Greenpeace in 1971 and as president steered the organization toward high-profile media-driven campaigns against whale and seal hunting, as well as toxic-waste dumping in the oceans. Hunter later returned to journalism, reporting on television and in print on environmental issues.

Hunter, Evan (SALVATORE ALBERT LOMBINO; ED MCBAIN; CURT CANNON; EZRA HANNON; JOHN ABBOTT; HUNT COLLINS; and RICHARD MARSTEN), American writer (b. Oct. 15, 1926, New York, N.Y.—d. July 6, 2005, Weston, Conn.), specialized in crime fiction and was best remembered for his series of 87th Precinct novels, which numbered more than 50 and introduced the gritty realism of police procedure to the genre. These books, written under the name Ed McBain, featured professional terminology, fast-paced action, and lively dialogue. The first in the series, *Cop Hater* (1956; filmed 1958), was followed by *Killer's Wedge* (1961), *Jigsaw* (1970), *Fuzz* (1968; filmed 1972), and *Mischief* (1993). Hunter was born Salvatore Lombino. Believing that a prejudice existed against writers with Italian names, he formally changed his name to Hunter but also wrote under other names. He penned science fiction and fantasy for juveniles for a number of magazines and produced a stream of best sellers. His stint as a teacher at a vocational school was the inspiration for the blockbuster *The Blackboard Jungle* (1954; filmed 1955). He also wrote the

screenplay for the film based on his book *Strangers When We Meet* (1958; filmed 1960) and for Alfred Hitchcock's film *The Birds* (1962). Hunter produced a series dealing with family tensions, including *Mothers and Daughters* (1961), *Last Summer* (1968; filmed 1969), and *Sons* (1969). He later started another series titled after children's stories and nursery rhymes—*Goldilocks* (1977), *Three Blind Mice* (1990), and *Mary, Mary* (1992). Other works included *Criminal Conversation* (1994), *Me and Hitch* (1997), and *Let's Talk* (2005), which recounted his bout with throat cancer. In 1986 he received the Grand Master award for lifetime achievement from the Mystery Writers of America, and in 1998 he became the first American to be honoured with a Cartier Diamond Dagger from the British Crime Writers' Association.

Hussey, Ruth, (RUTH CAROL O'ROURKE), American actress (b. Oct. 30, 1911, Providence, R.I.—d. April 19, 2005, Newbury Park, Calif.), appeared onstage, on television, and in more than 40 films, usually in roles that called for a witty, sophisticated, and worldly-wise beauty. She received a best supporting actress Academy Award nomination for her best-known role, the quick-with-a-quip photographer from *Spy* magazine in *The Philadelphia Story* (1940), and among her other notable films were *H.M. Pulham, Esq.* (1941) and *The Uninvited* (1944).

Iakovos (AGHIOI THEODOROI; DEMETRIOS COUCOUZIS), Greek Orthodox primate (b. July 29, 1911, Imroz [Imbros], Island, Ottoman Empire, [now Gokceada, Turkey]—d. April 10, 2005, Stamford, Conn.), promoted ecumenical religious unity and gained broader acceptance for the Greek Orthodox Church in the United States during his long tenure (1959–96) as primate of the Greek Orthodox archdiocese of North and South America. He was ordained a priest in 1940 in Lowell, Mass., and became a U.S. citizen in 1950. During the 1960s he served as president of the World Council of Churches and was also active in public life, marching with the Rev. Martin Luther King, Jr., in Selma, Ala., in support of civil rights; a photo of the two in action graced the March 26, 1965, cover of *Life* magazine. In the 1990s Iakovos clashed with the patriarch of Eastern Orthodoxy in Istanbul when he suggested that the 10 branches of Eastern Orthodoxy in North America unite administratively; the disagreement led to Iakovos's retirement. He was the recipient of the Presidential Medal of Freedom in 1980.

Jennings, Peter Charles, Canadian-born American television journalist (b. July 29, 1938, Toronto, Ont.—d. Aug. 7, 2005, New York, N.Y.), had an easygoing, detached manner that provided the calm delivery and knowledgeable air that earned his audience's respect and trust and, from the mid-1980s to the mid-1990s, took ABC's *World News Tonight* to the top of the ratings. One of the big three TV news anchors—along with Tom Brokaw at NBC and Dan Rather at CBS—he reported on the major news events of his era, from the world's news hot spots as well as from behind the anchor

John Paul II (Karol Jozef Wojtyla)

Pope of the Roman Catholic Church (b. May 18, 1920, Wadowice, Pol.—d. April 2, 2005, Vatican City, Vatican City State), served as the spiritual leader of the world's 1.1 billion Roman Catholics for more than 26 years—one of the longest papal reigns in church history. Elected as the 264th bishop of Rome on Oct. 16, 1978, and installed on October 22, John Paul II was the first non-Italian pope in 455 years and the first ever from a Slavic country. The youngest pope ordained in the 20th century, he became known for his energy and charisma as well as for his widely publicized crusades against political oppression. His vocal support for the dissident Solidarity movement in his native Poland, in particular, was a crucial factor in the survival of that movement and helped set the stage for the eventual peaceful dissolution of the Soviet Union. Within the church he maintained a steadfastly conservative stance on theological issues and appointed bishops and cardinals who shared his views. While he failed to reverse a decline in vocations and church attendance, he made extraordinary efforts to reach out to people around the world—to Catholics and non-Catholics alike. Dubbed the "pilgrim pope," he visited more than 120 countries during his pontificate and appeared in person before more people than had any other pope.

The early life of John Paul was marked by tragedy. His mother died when he was nine, his older brother a few years later, and his father during the first years of World War II. A brilliant student who also excelled at sports and drama, he attended the Jagiellonian University in Krakow until German troops closed the school in 1939. He continued his studies at a clandestine seminary while he worked in a quarry and then in a chemical factory—the first pope in modern times to have been a labourer. He was forced into hiding in 1944, resumed his studies after the war, and was ordained a priest in 1946. After earning a doctorate in philosophy from Pontifical Angelicum University in Rome in 1948, he returned to Poland to serve as a parish priest. He earned a second doctorate in sacred theology from the Jagiellonian University, where he also taught before being appointed (1954) to the philosophy faculty of the Catholic University of Lublin. He was named auxiliary bishop of Krakow in 1958 and, after prominent

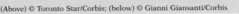

(Above) © Toronto Star/Corbis; (below) © Gianni Giansanti/Corbis

Karol Jozef Wojtyla as a young theatre actor in Poland (above) and as Pope John Paul II saying mass in Maastricht on an official visit to The Netherlands in 1985

participation in the Second Vatican Council (1962–65), was designated archbishop of Krakow in 1964 and created a cardinal in 1967 by Pope Paul VI. Although his work as archbishop in defending religious freedom under the communist regime in Poland earned him admiration in Rome, he was nevertheless a relative Vatican outsider when he was named to succeed John Paul I, who had died after only 34 days in office.

An activist pope virtually from the moment of his inauguration as John Paul II, he wasted little time in embarking on an ambitious touring schedule, making unprecedented papal visits to Mexico, Poland, and Ireland during his first year. Abandoning the customary Vatican policy of neutrality, he openly encouraged dissent in Eastern Europe. Visits by John Paul also weakened authoritarian rule in such countries as Brazil, Chile, Paraguay, the Philippines, and Haiti. His rising profile on the international stage made him an assassination target. In May 1981 he was shot by a Turkish gunman in St. Peter's Square, but he soon recovered and ultimately forgave his would-be assassin. After the collapse of the Soviet Union, John Paul increasingly came to focus criticism on what he saw as the ills of Western society. In a 1995 encyclical he used the phrase "culture of death" to encompass the practices of abortion and euthanasia and the indifference to suffering that he believed stemmed from unbridled capitalism and materialism. He spoke out on an array of other highly contentious issues, condemning divorce, artificial birth control, same-sex unions, and rights for unmarried couples—views that risked alienating many Catholics. Particularly controversial in the U.S. was the Vatican's handling of the priest sex-abuse scandal that erupted in the U.S. in 2002, with critics questioning whether the pope had been aggressive enough in addressing the problem. The last decade of his life was also consumed with ecumenical efforts, which included meetings with Jewish, Muslim, and Orthodox religious leaders. Although afflicted with Parkinson disease since the early 1990s, John Paul remained active and made a historic trip to Jerusalem in March 2000, during which he toured the Yad Vashem Holocaust memorial with Israeli Prime Minister Ehud Barak and met with Muslim leaders at the al-Aqsa Mosque before praying alone at the Western Wall. He made his final foreign trip, to Lourdes, France, in August 2004 and his last public appearance at his apartment window in the Vatican on March 30, 2005. His death three days later brought more than four million mourners to Rome.

TV anchor Peter Jennings

desk, and became one of the most familiar faces on American TV. Jennings dropped out of high school to train as a radio news reporter. In 1964 he moved to New York City to be a correspondent for ABC. The following year Jennings became the youngest national anchorman in the history of American networks. He became a foreign correspondent in 1968, and over the next 10 years, he not only reported on such events as the hostage crisis at the 1972 Summer Olympics in Munich but also established American TV's first news bureau in the Middle East, in Beirut. In 1978 Jennings again was made an anchorman, as a member of the three-man team of *World News Tonight*. He became the show's sole anchor and senior editor in 1983 and returned to New York. Jennings received many awards, including 16 Emmys. In 2003, while retaining his Canadian citizenship, he became a U.S. citizen. In April 2005, in what was to be his final broadcast, Jennings revealed that he had lung cancer.

Johannesen, Grant, American pianist (b. July 30, 1921, Salt Lake City, Utah—d. March 27, 2005, near Munich, Ger.), championed American and French piano works by such composers as Aaron Copland, Peter Mennin, Gabriel Fauré, and Francis Poulenc. Throughout his career he toured extensively, particularly with the New York Philharmonic and the Cleveland Orchestra. He enjoyed a stellar career as a teacher, most notably at the Cleveland Institute of Music from 1974 to 1985.

Johnson, John Harold, American business executive and publisher (b. Jan. 19, 1918, Arkansas City, Ark.—d. Aug. 8, 2005, Chicago, Ill.), parlayed a $500 loan, secured against his mother's furniture, into one of the largest media empires in the United States. He was the grandson of

slaves, and the harsh conditions of the Jim Crow-era South forced his family to move to Chicago when he was 15. After graduating from high school, Johnson took a job at Supreme Life Insurance Co., where he launched his first publishing venture. In 1942 he solicited 20,000 Supreme Life policyholders for advance subscriptions to *Negro Digest*, a monthly magazine that was patterned on the popular *Reader's Digest* but focused on stories and events within the African American community. Within a year *Negro Digest* had 50,000 paid subscribers, and Johnson had found his audience. His next publication, *Ebony*, debuted in November 1945. Modeled on *Life* magazine, *Ebony* was an immediate success with readers, but advertisers were initially reluctant to target what they saw as an unproven market. Skyrocketing circulation numbers and personal meetings with Johnson, however, soon convinced them of the buying power of the growing black middle class. Another Johnson publication, *Jet*, hit newsstands in 1951 and sparked a controversy when, in 1955, it ran an open-casket picture of Emmett Till—a 14-year-old boy who was abducted and brutally murdered for allegedly having whistled at a white woman. Johnson's business expanded to include a line of makeup products for women of colour, as well as a book-publishing division. In 1982 he became the first African American to appear on *Forbes* magazine's list of the 400 richest Americans, and in 1996 he was awarded the Presidential Medal of Freedom.

Johnson, Johnnie Clyde, American rock-and-roll pianist (b. July 8, 1924, Fairmont, W.Va.—d. April 13, 2005, St. Louis, Mo.), recorded, with Chuck Berry, some of the seminal songs of the early years of rock and roll, including "Maybellene," "Roll Over Beethoven," and "Brown-Eyed Handsome Man." Johnson hired Berry in 1952 to play with his group, the Sir John Trio. Berry soon became frontman for the group, but Johnson played a key role in the growth of rock and roll and inspired one of Berry's best-known hits, "Johnny B. Goode." Later Johnson played with Little Richard, Albert King, Eric Clapton, and Keith Richards. He was inducted into the Rock and Roll Hall of Fame in 2001.

Johnson, Philip Cortelyou, American architect (b. July 8, 1906, Cleveland, Ohio—d. Jan. 25, 2005, New Canaan, Conn.), wielded great influence in American architectural design, playing a defining role in several 20th-century movements, from International Style to Postmodernism to Deconstructivism. Though he graduated (1930) from Harvard University with a degree in philosophy, his abiding interest soon turned to architecture. Johnson was a student of Marcel Breuer and Walter Gropius and an apprentice of Mies van der Rohe, assisting the latter with his Seagram Building (1958) in New York City. Before and after World War II, he led the newly founded architecture department of the Museum of Modern Art in New York City. Johnson's early masterwork was built for himself: the austere, boxy Glass House (1949) with glass panel walls, in New Canaan. He drifted away from

minimalism, and in the 1970s and '80s he erected high-rise commercial buildings with historical undertones. His later masterwork was the pink granite AT&T headquarters

Philip Johnson with his AT&T building

(1984; now Sony Plaza) in New York City, which featured a split-pediment roof resembling a Chippendale cabinet, a major signpost in the arrival of Postmodernism. Other notable works included Pennzoil Place (1976) in Houston and Crystal Cathedral (1980) in Garden Grove, Calif. A public figure who positioned himself at the vanguard of new styles, Johnson was also a critic, curator, and socialite. In 1979 he became the first recipient of the Pritzker Architecture Prize for lifetime achievement.

Jones, Georgeanna Seeger, American physician (b. July 6, 1912, Baltimore, Md.—d. March 26, 2005, Norfolk, Va.), pioneered (with her husband, Howard W. Jones, Jr.) the development in the U.S. of in vitro fertilization. The couple conducted this work at a clinic that they helped establish at Eastern Virginia Medical School, which they joined in 1978 following their retirement from John Hopkins University. At Johns Hopkins they had spent more than 40 years teaching and conducting research in gynecology and obstetrics. The establishment of the clinic, later named the Jones Institute for Reproductive Medicine, was prompted by the birth in England of the world's first "test-tube baby" (a baby conceived outside the mother's body) about the time the Joneses arrived at Norfolk. The couple led an in vitro fertilization program that resulted in the first American test-tube baby, Elizabeth Jordan Carr, who was born on Dec. 28, 1981. Crucial to the success of the program was Georgeanna Jones's understanding of ovulation and fertility-inducing hormones. Jones obtained a medical degree from Johns Hopkins in 1936. Three years later she was appointed director of the reproductive physiology laboratory at the university, where she became one of the first gynecologic endocrinologists on a medical school faculty in the United States. Among the results of her research in the 1930s was the discovery that the pregnancy hormone now called human chorionic gonadotropin is produced in the placenta rather than in the pituitary gland.

Keeling, Charles David, American scientist (b. April 20, 1928, Scranton, Pa.—d. June 20, 2005, Hamilton, Mont.), presented the first evidence that carbon dioxide produced by automobiles and factories was negatively affecting the Earth's climate. In 1958 he began measuring carbon dioxide in the atmosphere with an instrument that he set up at a weather station on Mauna Loa, a dormant volcano in Hawaii. Over the next 47 years, he charted a steady increase of carbon dioxide levels and raised warnings about global warming and the dangers of continued reliance on fossil fuels. In 2002 Keeling was awarded the National Medal of Science.

Kennan, George Frost, American diplomat (b. Feb. 16, 1904, Milwaukee, Wis.—d. March 17, 2005, Princeton, N.J.), defined U.S. foreign policy during the Cold War as principal architect of the "containment policy" against the expansionism of the Soviet Union. He advocated applying counterpressure to Soviet encroachment. This was first detailed in a 5,540-word cable ("The Long Telegram") issued in 1946 while Kennan was stationed at the U.S. embassy in Moscow and in an article signed only "X" and published in 1947 in *Foreign Policy* magazine ("The Sources of Soviet Conduct"). He also helped shape the Marshall Plan for the reconstruction of Europe following World War II. Kennan was educated at Princeton University and the University of Berlin and worked as a Foreign Service officer from 1926 to 1953. He was a notable memoirist and historian, publishing from his longtime post at the Institute for Advanced Study in Princeton, N.J. Kennan undertook brief ambassadorships in Moscow (1952) and Yugoslavia (1961–63) and was awarded the Presidential Medal of Freedom (1989).

Kennedy, Graham Cyril, Australian radio and television personality and actor (b. Feb. 15, 1934, St. Kilda, Melbourne, Australia—d. May 25, 2005, Bowral, N.S.W., Australia), as one of Australia's most popular radio and television talk-show and game-show hosts, earned the nickname "King of Television." Over a 40-year career, he won 14 Logies (Australia's annual TV awards), including Star of the Year in 1959, and in 1998 he was inducted into the Logie Hall of Fame. After dropping out of school at age 15, Kennedy joined (1951) the staff at Melbourne's Radio 3. He moved to television in 1957 when it first began broadcasting in Melbourne, and despite being only 23 and having no experience in the new medium, he was named the host of *In Melbourne Tonight*, where he remained until 1969. Kennedy applied his irreverent and sometimes bawdy humour on a series of other programs, including *The Graham Kennedy Show* (1972–75), from which he was sacked in April

1975 for allegedly having squawked a banned word during a live broadcast; the game show *Blankety Blank* (1977–78); and *The Graham Kennedy News Hour* (renamed *Coast to Coast;* 1988–89). Kennedy also acted in such films as *Don's Party* (1976), *The Killing Fields* (1984), and *Travelling North* (1987). He retired in 1991 and thereafter lived as a virtual recluse. The biography *King: The Life and Comedy of Graham Kennedy* was published in 2003.

Kennedy, Rosemary, American personality (b. Sept. 13, 1918, Brookline, Mass.—d. Jan. 7, 2005, Jefferson, Wis.), was the mentally challenged sister of Pres. John F. Kennedy who at age 23 was given a prefrontal lobotomy, a procedure that left her in an infantlike state and needing institutional care for most of the rest of her life. Her younger sister, Eunice Kennedy Shriver, founded the Special Olympics in her honour.

Khachiyan, Leonid Henry, Russian-born American mathematician (b. May 3, 1952, Leningrad, U.S.S.R. [now St. Petersburg, Russia]—d. April 29, 2005, South Brunswick, N.J.), invented an algorithm for solving linear programming problems, such as the scheduling and allocation of resources. Khachiyan attended the Computing Centre of the U.S.S.R. Academy of Sciences in Moscow, where he earned a Ph.D. (1978) in computational mathematics and a D.Sc. (1984) in computer science. Before arriving in the U.S. in 1989, he held various teaching and research positions at the Computing Centre and at the Moscow Institute of Physics and Technology. After a short stay at Cornell University's School of Operations Research and Industrial Engineering, Ithaca, N.Y., Khachiyan moved to Rutgers University, New Brunswick, N.J., in 1990 and gained tenure there in 1992. He became a U.S. citizen in 2000. In 1979 Khachiyan published his algorithm in the Soviet Academy's *Doklady,* a journal little read in the West. Later that year his algorithm electrified the field when it was presented at the International Mathematical Programming Symposium in Montreal. While the simplex algorithm, developed by George Dantzig *(q.v.)* in 1947 and at the time the standard method in linear programming, was adequate for solving many problems, its method of moving from "vertex to vertex" of the intersecting linear constraints in search of an optimal solution becomes increasingly time-consuming and impractical as the number of constraints grows. Khachiyan's work opened the way for the development of new methods of solving theretofore intractable problems, with applications in fields as diverse as biology, economics, engineering, and telecommunications. He was awarded the Fulkerson Prize by the Mathematical Programming Society and the American Mathematical Society in 1982.

Kilby, Jack St. Clair, American electronics engineer (b. Nov. 8, 1923, Jefferson City, Mo.—d. June 20, 2005, Dallas, Texas), invented the integrated circuit (IC), which allowed the development of the personal computer and the cell phone and was also used in radios, televisions, and microwave ovens; for this work

he was awarded the 2000 Nobel Prize for Physics. Kilby studied electrical engineering at the University of Illinois (B.S., 1947) and the University of Wisconsin (M.S., 1950). After designing and developing circuits for Globe Union Inc.'s Centralab division in Milwaukee, Wis., for 11 years, Kilby joined (1958) semiconductor manufacturer Texas Instruments Inc. (TI) in Dallas. Shortly after his arrival at TI, Kilby designed and demonstrated the first integrated circuit, combining transistors, resistors, and capacitors on a single piece of germanium about the size of a fingernail. Soon afterward Robert Noyce (one of the cofounders of Intel Corp.) devised a similar solution while working for Fairchild Semiconductor Corp. Kilby was also the inventor in 1967, together with Jerry Merryman and James Van Tassel, of the first hand-held calculator. Kilby was inducted into the National Inventors' Hall of Fame in 1982.

Kilgore, (Wyatt) Merle, American country-music figure (b. Aug. 9, 1934, Chickasha, Okla.—d. Feb. 6, 2005, Mexico), had a versatile career that included stints as a singer and guitarist, songwriter, film actor, manager, and record company executive. He enjoyed several top 10 hits as a performer, but his greatest fame came as a songwriter; his work included "More and More," which sold a million copies for Webb Pierce in 1954, "Wolverton Mountain" (1962), which sold 10 million copies for Claude King, and "Ring of Fire," co-written (1963) with June Carter Cash and recorded by Johnny Cash, with sales of nearly 16 million. As the longtime personal manager of singer Hank Williams, Jr., Kilgore oversaw Williams's publishing and business enterprises. Kilgore also was active in country-music and songwriters' organizations in Nashville.

King of Wartnaby, John Leonard King, Baron, British industrialist (b. August 1917?, Brentwood, Essex, Eng.—d. July 12, 2005, Wartnaby, Leicestershire, Eng.), privatized the struggling state-owned British Airways (BA) and elevated it from a debt of some $1 billion to a highly prosperous enterprise that earned a profit of $284 million in six years. Appointed chairman of BA in 1981 by Prime Minister Margaret Thatcher, King introduced a number of aggressive cost-cutting techniques that included downsizing the workforce, streamlining air routes, selling surplus aircraft, cutting executive perks, and introducing more modest corporate vehicles. Much-improved customer service along with a new marketing slogan, "The World's Favorite Airline," contributed to BA's success and attracted a hoard of investors when the company sold stock to the public in 1987. King resigned as chairman of BA in 1993 but remained as president emeritus. He was knighted in 1979 and granted a life peerage in 1983.

Kishon, Ephraim (FERENC HOFFMANN), Hungarian-born Israeli satirist (b. Aug. 23, 1924, Budapest, Hung.—d. Jan. 29, 2005, Appenzell, Switz.), after surviving the Holocaust and immigrating to Israel, wrote prolifically and gained a large and appreciative audience, notably in Israel and Germany. Kishon was imprisoned in a Nazi forced-labour camp in 1944 but escaped while being transported to a death camp. He moved from Hungary to Israel in 1949, changing his name on arrival. Kishon learned Hebrew and by 1952 had a weekly column of social satire in the newspaper *Ma'ariv*. He wrote more than 50 well-received and widely translated books, as well as plays and motion pictures. Two of Kishon's movies, which he also directed, won Golden Globe Awards for best foreign-language film: *Sallah Shabati* (1964) and *Ha-Shoter Azulai* (1970; *The Policeman*). Both of these films were also nominated for Academy Awards. Kishon was awarded the Israel Prize for lifetime achievement in 2002.

Lange, David Russell, New Zealand lawyer and politician (b. Aug. 4, 1942, Otahuhu, N.Z.—d. Aug. 13, 2005, Auckland, N.Z.), during his years as prime minister (1984–89), radically transformed New Zealand's economy with free-market reforms and implemented an antinuclear policy that drew the ire of the country's traditional allies, most notably the U.S. After receiving a law degree from the University of Auckland (1966), Lange, a lay Methodist preacher, provided legal assistance to the poor. In 1977 he was elected to represent the Labour Party in Parliament, where he became noted for his oratory skills. He was named Labour leader in 1983 and led the party to victory in the general elections the following year, becoming the country's youngest prime minister of the 20th century. In 1985 Lange gained international attention after he banned nuclear-powered or nuclear-armed vessels from New Zealand's ports, a move that mainly targeted U.S. warships. Later that year he rebuked France after French agents sank a Greenpeace ship that was preparing to leave Auckland Harbour on its way to protest French nuclear-weapons testing in the South Pacific. Although his antinuclear policies proved popular with New Zealanders, Lange encountered growing resistance, particularly from within the Labour Party, over his attempts to open up the country's heavily protected economy. His privatization of state-run enterprises, including the postal service, was especially controversial. Citing poor health, Lange resigned as

prime minister in 1989, although he remained in Parliament until 1996. In 2003 he was awarded the Order of New Zealand.

Langford, Frances (FRANCES NEWBERN), American singer and actress (b. April 4, 1914, Lakeland, Fla.—d. July 11, 2005, Jensen Beach, Fla.), acted in some 30 motion pictures and, with Don Ameche, starred as the combative wife, Blanche, in the 1940s radio series *The Bickersons*. She gained her greatest fame in real combat zones, however—as an entertainer with Bob Hope's USO tours during

CBS Photo Archive/Getty Images

Big band singer Frances Langford

World War II and the Korean and Vietnam wars, singing ballads that included her trademark "I'm in the Mood for Love."

Laredo, Ruth (RUTH MECKLER), American pianist (b. Nov. 20, 1937, Detroit, Mich.—d. May 25, 2005, New York, N.Y.), was a recitalist and accompanist and also performed with orchestras and chamber groups. She graduated (1960) from the Curtis Institute of Music, Philadelphia, and married the violinist Jaime Laredo, with whom she frequently collaborated until their divorce in 1974. During the 1970s she made the first recordings of the complete solo works of Sergey Rachmaninoff and of the complete sonatas of Aleksandr Scriabin. For the last 17 years of her life, she presented a regular recital series at New York's Metropolitan Museum of Art.

Lehman, Ernest, American screenwriter and film producer (b. Dec. 8, 1915, New York, N.Y.—d. July 2, 2005, Los Angeles, Calif.), wrote screenplays for some of the most enduring Hollywood films of the 1950s and '60s. Lehman enjoyed early success as a short-story and novella writer before turning to writing for the screen. He proved adept at an original screenplay, his Academy Award-nominated *North by Northwest* (1959), and adapted screenplays, notably his Oscar-nominated work for *Sabrina* (1954), *West Side Story* (1961), and *Who's Afraid of Virginia Woolf?* (1966). Other screenplays included *Executive Suite* (1954), *Sweet Smell of Success* (1957),

and *The Sound of Music* (1965). In 2001 Lehman became the first screenwriter to receive a lifetime achievement award from the Academy of Motion Picture Arts and Sciences.

Leith, Emmett Norman, American scientist (b. March 12, 1927, Detroit, Mich.—d. Dec. 23, 2005, Ann Arbor, Mich.), revolutionized the field of holography by using continuous-wave laser beam technology to make three-dimensional holographic images. With his University of Michigan research partner Juris Upatnieks, Leith first demonstrated what they called the "off-axis" method of producing holograms at the Optical Society of America's spring conference in 1964. Using a highly coherent beam of light produced by a laser, Leith and Upatnieks created a realistic three-dimensional holographic image of a toy train and bird. This important development became the benchmark for modern holography and led to numerous applications in fields that included engineering, medicine, forensics, computer science, and credit-card technology. Among his many honours was the National Medal of Science in 1979.

Leithold, Louis, American mathematician and teacher (b. Nov. 16, 1924, San Francisco, Calif.—found dead April 29, 2005, Los Angeles, Calif.), authored *The Calculus*, a classic textbook credited with having changed the methods for teaching calculus in American high schools and universities. The textbook was first published in 1968 and saw seven printings. Leithold received a doctorate in mathematics education from the University of California, Berkeley, and later taught at California State University; Phoenix (Ariz.) College; the Open University, Milton Keynes, Eng.; and Pepperdine University, Malibu, Calif. At the age of 72 the calculus guru began teaching high school in Malibu.

Lichfield, Thomas Patrick John Anson, fifth earl of, British photographer (b. April 25, 1939, Staffordshire, Eng.—d. Nov. 11, 2005, Oxford, Eng.), was admired for his iconic images of London in the "swinging 1960s" and for his royal portraits, notably the official photographs of the 1981 wedding of Prince Charles and Lady Diana Spencer. As a cousin of Queen Elizabeth II, Patrick Lichfield (as he preferred to be called) had access to all

Photographer Lord Lichfield

AP/Wide World Photos

levels of society, and his pictorial subjects ranged from rock musicians and other artists to socialites and politicians. He showed an interest in photography as a student at Harrow and the Royal Military Academy, Sandhurst, and after a seven-year stint in the Grenadier Guards, he switched careers. He often used his natural charm, humour, and unconventional methods (such as blowing a referee's whistle) to entice his subjects to cooperate. Lichfield contributed photos to such glossy magazines as *Life* and *Vogue* and authored several photographic books. His images were the subject of an exhibition in 2003 at the National Portrait Gallery. Lichfield was named a fellow of the British Institute of Professional Photographers and was a member of the Royal Photographic Society. He succeeded his grandfather as earl in 1960.

Linowitz, Sol Myron, American diplomat, attorney, and businessman (b. Dec. 7, 1913, Trenton, N.J.—d. March 18, 2005, Washington, D.C.), served as a highly influential adviser to U.S. Presidents Lyndon B. Johnson, Jimmy Carter, and Bill Clinton and was a key negotiator during the late 1970s of the Panama Canal treaties. After serving (1944–46) in the U.S. Navy, Linowitz joined Joseph C. Wilson in the establishment of the Xerox Corp., where Linowitz served as chairman (1960–66). In October 1966 President Johnson appointed Linowitz U.S. ambassador to the Organization of American States and U.S. representative to the Inter-American Committee on the Alliance for Progress. During the Carter administration (1977–81), Linowitz smoothed relations between the U.S. and Latin America by negotiating the treaties that shifted full control of the Panama Canal from the U.S. to Panama, and from 1979 to 1981 he negotiated peace treaties with the Palestinians as special ambassador to the Middle East. In 1998 President Clinton awarded Linowitz the Presidential Medal of Freedom.

Liu Binyan, Chinese investigative journalist (b. Jan. 15, 1925, Chanchun, Jilin province, China—d. Dec. 5, 2005, East Windsor, N.J.), was a persistent critic of corruption and abuse of power within the Communist Party of China (CPC). Liu joined the CPC in 1943. He began his career in journalism as a reporter and editor for a youth newspaper and attracted widespread attention in the 1950s with forceful critiques of China's political bureaucracy. Branded a "rightist" in 1957, he was expelled from the CPC and spent much of the next two decades in labour camps. Rehabilitated in the late 1970s after Mao died, Liu returned to journalism, working as a reporter for the *People's Daily* and continuing to investigate corruption. His best-known work was perhaps a 1979 exposé entitled "People or Monsters?," which detailed the abuses of an oppressive party official in northeastern China. He was expelled from the CPC a second time in 1987. Liu was a visiting fellow at Harvard University at the time of the 1989 Tiananmen Square massacre and was never allowed to return to China. He spent the remainder of his life in the U.S., although he

continued to critique the Chinese government through such outlets as Radio Free Asia.

Lopez, Al (ALFONSO RAMON LOPEZ; "EL SEÑOR"), American baseball player and manager (b. Aug. 20, 1908, Tampa, Fla.—d. Oct. 30, 2005, Tampa), managed the Cleveland Indians (1951–56) and the Chicago White Sox (1957–65 and 1968–69) to the only American League pennants (1954 and 1959, respectively) not won by the New York Yankees from 1949 to 1964; during that period his teams also finished second to the Yankees 10 times. A two-time All-Star catcher with the Brooklyn Dodgers, Boston Braves, Pittsburgh Pirates, and Indians, he long held the record for most games played at his position. The child of Spanish immigrants, he was called "El Señor" for his gentlemanliness. Lopez entered the Hall of Fame in 1977.

Luksic Abaroa, Andrónico, Chilean business magnate (b. Nov. 5, 1926, Antofagasto, Chile—d. Aug. 18, 2005, Santiago, Chile), amassed a fortune after building one of the largest business empires in Latin America. Luksic's first investment was a copper mine in Antofagasto, which he sold to a Japanese concern in 1954. He invested the proceeds in other businesses that came to include banking and telecommunications companies, breweries, vineyards, and resorts. His business acumen allowed him to thrive in spite of political vicissitudes in Chile. His empire was divided into Antofagasto PLC, which controlled mining and railroad interests, and Quiñenco, which handled financial and industrial interests.

Luzi, Mario Egidio Vincenzo, Italian poet, essayist, and translator (b. Oct. 20, 1914, Castello, near Florence, Italy—d. Feb. 28, 2005, Florence), was an exponent of Hermeticism, an Italian modernist poetic movement whose works were characterized by unorthodox structure, illogical sequences, and highly subjective language. Luzi studied at the University of Florence (Ph.D., 1936), specializing in French literature, which he later taught in Parma, San Miniato, Rome, and at the Florence Institute of Political Science (1955–85). His earliest collections of poetry—notably *La barca* (1935), *Avvento notturno* (1940), and *Un brindisi* (1946)—showed particularly strong elements of Hermeticism. In the early 1950s he was cofounder of the literary journal *La chimera.* Much of Luzi's later verse, however, was more narrative and less Hermetic. He also wrote short stories and essays on Hermeticism and literary theory and published Italian translations of English, French, and Spanish works. In 2004 Italian Pres. Carlo Ciampi named Luzi a senator for life.

Mac Lane, Saunders, American mathematician (b. Aug. 4, 1909, Taftville, Conn.—d. April

14, 2005, San Francisco, Calif.), made significant contributions to modern algebra and topology and, with Samuel Eilenberg, was a cofounder of category theory, which established a general framework for understanding how mathematical structures, and systems of structures, relate to one another. After graduating (1930) from Yale University, Mac Lane earned (1931) a master's degree in mathematics from the University of Chicago. He moved to the University of Göttingen, Ger., where he studied under Paul Bernays, Emmy Noether, and Hermann Weyl. In 1933 Mac Lane was awarded a Ph.D. for a thesis on mathematical logic. Returning to the U.S., Mac Lane taught at Yale, Harvard University, the University of Chicago, and Cornell University, Ithaca, N.Y., before returning to Harvard, where he taught until 1946. In 1947 he moved to Chicago, where he spent the remainder of his career, serving (1952–58) as chairman of the mathematics department. In 1982 he became professor emeritus. While Mac Lane was at Harvard, his interest shifted from logic to the modern, abstract algebra developed by Noether and others. In 1941 Mac Lane and Garrett Birkhoff published *A Survey of Modern Algebra,* which for many years served as the leading English-language textbook in the field. While conducting research in homological algebra (an algebraic study of topological spaces), Mac Lane and Eilenberg, later of Columbia University, New York City, felt the need for a general theory for moving between domains of mathematics. This led to their creation of category theory, which was later applied in many areas of mathematics, as well as computer science and theoretical physics. Among Mac Lane's publications were *Homology* (1963), *Algebra* (1967; with Birkhoff), *Categories for the Working Mathematician* (1971), and *Mathematics, Form and Function* (1986). In 1989 Mac Lane was awarded the National Medal of Science.

Mangelsdorff, Albert, German musician (b. Sept. 5, 1928, Frankfurt am Main, Ger.—d. July 25, 2005, Frankfurt am Main), began as a bop

Trombonist Albert Mangelsdorff

trombonist and went on to explore modal jazz, fusions with rock and Asian musics, and free jazz, all with a stylistic integrity that made him one of Europe's leading jazz artists. Mangelsdorff was a pioneer of unaccompanied jazz trombone solos, including a memorable appearance at the 1972 Olympic Games in Munich and recordings such as "Mood Indigo," which showcased his rare mastery of multiphonics (playing several notes simultaneously). He first appeared in the U.S. in 1958, and he went on to tour throughout Europe, Asia, and the Americas with groups that included his own popular 1960s quintet and the free-jazz all-star Globe Unity Orchestra. Mangelsdorff recorded with top artists, such as saxophonist Lee Konitz and drummer Elvin Jones, and became director of the Berlin Jazz Festival in 1995. The Albert Mangelsdorff Prize was awarded regularly by the German Jazz Union from 1994.

Marín Millié, Gladys, Chilean political figure (b. July 16, 1941, Curepto, Chile—d. March 6, 2005, Santiago, Chile), opposed the brutal regime of Augusto Pinochet as a leader of the Chilean Communist Party. Marín joined the Communist Party at age 17 and served in the Chamber of Deputies during the presidency (1970–73) of Salvador Allende, but she was forced into hiding following the Sept. 11, 1973, coup that brought Pinochet to power. She eventually fled to the Soviet Union, where she remained until 1978. That year she returned to Chile by posing as a Spanish citizen, and she later held key leadership positions in the Communist Party, including those of undersecretary (1984–94), general secretary (1994–2002), and president (2002–05).

Martin, Jimmy (JAMES HENRY MARTIN), American bluegrass singer and guitarist (b. Aug. 10, 1927, Sneedville, Tenn.—d. May 14, 2005, Nashville, Tenn.), pioneered the "high lonesome sound" of bluegrass music with his high-ranging, heart-piercing vocals. Martin performed intermittently as lead vocalist with Bill Monroe and the Blue Grass Boys for several years before forming (1956) his own band, the Sunny Mountain Boys. The band recorded with Decca records for 18 years, producing such bluegrass standards as "Rock Hearts" and "Widow Maker." Martin was inducted into the International Bluegrass Music Association's Hall of Honor in 1995 and was the subject of the documentary film *King of Bluegrass* (2003).

Martino, Donald, American composer and professor (b. May 16, 1931, Plainfield, N.J.—d. Dec. 8, 2005, at sea in the Caribbean en route to Antigua), created works that were distinctly Modernist, atonal, intellectual, and complex but had elements of compositional freedom, energy, and lyricism that attracted professional musicians and concertgoers alike. His chamber work *Notturno* was awarded the 1974 Pulitzer Prize in music. Martino taught at a variety of institutions, including the Third Street Music School Settlement in New York City and Princeton, Yale, Brandeis (Waltham, Mass.), and Harvard universities.

Matsui, Robert Takeo, American politician (b. Sept. 17, 1941, Sacramento, Calif.—d. Jan. 1, 2005, Bethesda, Md.), was U.S. congressman from the 5th district of California from 1979 until his death. From 1942 to 1945 the U.S. government confined Matsui and his family in an internment camp on suspicion of disloyalty because of their Japanese ethnicity. In 1971 Matsui was elected to the city council of Sacramento, where he remained, becoming vice mayor in 1977, until his election to the U.S. House of Representatives in 1978. Matsui worked for the passage of the North American Free Trade Agreement in the 1990s and helped write legislation that was instrumental in creating the State Children's Health Insurance Program; he also led in the effort that resulted in a fund for reparations for the 120,000 Japanese-Americans who spent time in internment camps during World War II.

Mayo, Virginia (VIRGINIA CLARA JONES),  American actress (b. Nov. 30, 1920, St. Louis, Mo.—d. Jan. 17, 2005, Thousand Oaks, Calif.), appeared in more than 40 movies, many of them comedies and adventure films, but was most memorable for her dramatic portrayals of an unfaithful wife of a World War II veteran in *The Best Years of Our Lives* (1946) and of James Cagney's gun-moll wife in *White Heat* (1949). She later appeared with touring productions of stage plays and in television series.

Mayr, Ernst Walter, German-born American biologist (b. July 5, 1904, Kempten, Ger.—d. Feb. 3, 2005, Bedford, Mass.), did work in avian taxonomy that provided insights into evolution and led to his becoming one of the leading evolutionary biologists of the 20th century. In the 1940s he presented the now widely accepted definition of species as "groups of interbreeding natural populations that are reproductively isolated from other such groups," and he showed how geographic isolation played an important role in the origin of new species. In the late 1920s Mayr traveled to New Guinea and the Solomon Islands to study and collect specimens of birds. He subsequently worked with major collections of bird skins at the University of Berlin as associate curator (1926–32) and at the American Museum of Natural History as associate curator (1932–44) and curator (1944–53). Later he served (1953–75) as professor of zoology at Harvard University and led (1961–70) Harvard's Museum of Comparative Zoology. Mayr authored or coauthored more than 20 books, including *Systematics and the Origin of Species* (1942), *The Growth of Biological Thought* (1982), and *What Evolution Is* (2001). He received the U.S. National Medal of Science (1970) and the Royal Swedish Academy's Crafoord Prize in biology (1999).

McBain, Ed, *see* Hunter, Evan.

McCarthy, Eugene Joseph, American politician  (b. March 29, 1916, Watkins, Minn.—d. Dec. 10, 2005, Washington, D.C.), left an indelible mark on U.S. history by prompting fellow Democrat Lyndon B. Johnson not to seek reelection to the U.S. presidency in 1968. A largely unheralded senator from Minnesota who had initially supported Johnson's conduct of the Vietnam War, McCarthy became outraged by the escalation of the U.S. war effort and by what he saw as Johnson's imperial presidency. Though other antiwar Democrats were more prominent, McCarthy became the first to challenge Johnson's likely candidacy openly. McCarthy energized young opponents of the war, particularly college students, whom he urged to cut their long hair ("Get Clean for Gene") to campaign for him. When McCarthy won 42% of the Democratic vote in the New Hampshire primary, Johnson, who took 49% of the vote, was certain that he had lost popular support and ultimately declared that he would not run for reelection. McCarthy went on to win four more primaries, but his momentum was stolen by U.S. Sen. Robert F. Kennedy of New York, another antiwar candidate with a broader constituency. Kennedy's assassination led to a wide-open Democratic convention in Chicago, where Vice Pres. Hubert Humphrey, who had not run in any primary, beat out McCarthy for the nomination while antiwar protests raged outside the convention hall. McCarthy graduated (1935) from St. John's University, Collegeville, Minn., earned a master's degree in economics and sociology from the University of Minnesota, and taught in Minnesota high schools and colleges. He represented (1948–58) East St. Paul in the U.S. House of Representatives before serving as a U.S. senator for 12 years. McCarthy mounted increasingly quixotic and contrarian campaigns for the presidency in 1972, 1976, 1988, and 1992 and unsuccessfully sought to recapture his Senate seat in 1982.

McCarty, Maclyn, American microbiologist and physician (b. June 9, 1911, South Bend, Ind.—d. Jan. 2, 2005, New York, N.Y.), together with colleagues Oswald Avery and Colin MacLeod, provided the first evidence that genes are composed of DNA, a discovery that made possible the later development of molecular biology and genetic engineering. McCarty and his colleagues obtained their evidence from experiments, published in 1944, in which a "transforming principle" (genetic material) extracted from one type of pneumococcal bacteria and mixed with a second type would impart characteristics of the first to the second type. As a skilled biochemist, McCarty succeeded in purifying and identifying the extract. McCarty graduated from Stanford

University with a degree (1933) in biochemistry, and he received an M.D. degree (1937) from Johns Hopkins University School of Medicine, Baltimore, Md. He went to work in Avery's laboratory at the Rockefeller Institute for Medical Research (now Rockefeller University), New York City, in the early 1940s. In 1946 McCarty was appointed head of the Laboratory of Bacteriology and Immunology at Rockefeller, and he became a leader in research on streptococcus bacteria and their role in producing rheumatic fever. McCarty served as physician in chief (1960–74) at the Rockefeller University Hospital and as vice president (1965–78) of Rockefeller University. In 1994 he received an award for special achievement in medical science from the Lasker Foundation.

McLellan, Joseph, American music critic and journalist (b. 1929, Quincy, Mass.—d. Dec. 26, 2005, Hyattsville, Md.), served on the staff of the *Washington Post* for more than three decades and was the newspaper's chief music critic (1982–95). McLellan joined the *Post* in 1972. He also contributed music reviews and commentary to *American Record Guide*, *Chamber Music* magazine, the *New Grove Dictionary of Music and Musicians*, and *Britannica Book of the Year*, among other publications. In addition, he taught literature at American University and journalism at George Washington University, both in Washington, D.C. McLellan's final music review for the *Washington Post* appeared on Oct. 13, 2005.

Meehan, Tony (DANIEL JOSEPH ANTHONY MEEHAN), British drummer and music producer (b. March 2, 1943, London, Eng.—d. Nov. 28, 2005, London), was a founding member of the seminal late 1950s and early '60s instrumental rock group the Shadows, who were best known for their transatlantic hit single "Apache" (1960) and as the backing band for pop idol Cliff Richard, with whom they appeared in the film *The Young Ones* (1961). After leaving the Shadows, Meehan and former bandmate Jet Harris teamed on the British hits "Diamonds" and "Scarlett O'Hara." Meehan later worked as a record producer. He died of head injuries he suffered in a fall.

Merchant, Ismail (NOORMOHAMED ABDUL REHMAN), Indian-born film producer and director (b. Dec. 25, 1936, Bombay, British India [now Mumbai, India]—d. May 25, 2005, London, Eng.), enjoyed a 44-year collaboration with American James Ivory during which they released some 40 films, including *A Room with a View* (1985) and *Howards End* (1992), each of which won three Academy Awards. With their tasteful intelligence, careful attention to detail, and high production values, Merchant Ivory productions—featuring Merchant as producer, Ivory as director, and their friend Ruth Prawer Jhabvala as

screenwriter—came to be acknowledged as having defined the genre of literate period pieces. Merchant moved to New York City in 1958 to pursue a master's degree in business administration. He also began working on movie projects, and in 1960 he produced his first film, the short feature *The Creation of Woman*. It received an Academy Award nomination and was entered in the 1961 Cannes Festival. That same year he formed his partnership with Ivory, and in 1963 they released *The Householder*, adapted by Jhabvala from her novel of that name. *Shakespeare Wallah* (1965), gained the trio critical attention and success in art houses, but their first major hit did not come until 1983 with *Heat and Dust*. Notable among the films that followed were *The Bostonians* (1984), *Maurice* (1987), and *The Remains of the Day* (1993). At the time of his death, Merchant was finishing his work on *The White Countess*, (2005), and the team was working on the musical *The Goddess*.

Messick, Dale (DALIA MESSICK), American comic-strip artist (b. April 11, 1906, South Bend, Ind.—d. April 5, 2005, Penngrove, Calif.), created one of the top-rated comic strips of all time, *Brenda Starr, Reporter*, which featured a fiery-haired heroine modeled after actress Rita Hayworth; the strip debuted on June 30, 1940, on the Sunday page of the *Chicago Tribune*, and by 1945 it had begun appearing as a daily. In the male-dominated comic-strip industry, Messick adopted the androgenous name of Dale so that her work would be judged on its merit rather than discarded because of her sex. While encountering thrilling adventures, the glamorous Brenda paraded high fashion, presented impeccably coiffed hair, and captivated readers of both sexes. Messick, who drew some 15,000 *Brenda Starr* strips before retiring in 1985, later sketched a single-panel strip, *Granny Glamour*, until age 92.

Michels, Rinus (MARINUS HENDRIKUS JACOBUS MICHELS), Dutch association football (soccer) player and coach (b. Feb. 9, 1928, Amsterdam, Neth.—d. March 3, 2005, Aalst, Belg.), was credited with having created "total football," an aggressive style of play in which players adapt, shift positions, and improvise on the field as needed. Michels played for Ajax from 1946 to 1958, scoring 121 goals in 269 matches and contributing to the team's league championship in 1947 and 1957. He also made five international appearances for The Netherlands. As Ajax's coach (1965–71), "the General" led his old team to four league titles (1966, 1967, 1968, 1970), three cup titles (1967, 1970, 1971), and the 1971 European Cup. He guided the national team to the 1974 World Cup final, in which The Netherlands was defeated by Germany, and to the 1988 European championship title. Michels also coached professional clubs in Barcelona (1971–78), Los Angeles (1978–80), and Germany (Cologne, 1980–83; Bayer Leverkusen, 1988–89).

Mikan, George Lawrence, American basketball player and lawyer (b. June 18, 1924,

Joliet, Ill.—d. June 1, 2005, Scottsdale, Ariz.), transformed basketball as the game's first outstanding big man. His dominating play resulted in several rule changes and led the Minneapolis (now Los Angeles) Lakers to six championships (1948–50; 1952–54). Initially a clumsy player, the 2.8-m (6-ft 10-in)-tall, near-sighted Mikan developed into an offensive threat under the tutelage of coach Ray Meyer at DePaul University, Chicago. Known for his hook shot, Mikan helped DePaul win the National Invitational Tournament in 1945. After graduating the following year, he joined the Chicago American Gears of the National Basketball League (NBL), and in 1947 he led the Gears to the NBL championship. Later that year he signed with the Lakers, a team that became part of the National Basketball Association (NBA) in 1949. Mikan played for the Lakers from 1947 to 1954 and again from 1955 to 1956. Although the NBA attempted to limit his effectiveness by widening the free-throw lane (1951) and introducing the 24-second shot clock (1954), Mikan emerged as the game's first superstar. In nine seasons of professional play, he scored 11,764 points in 520 regular games, averaging 22.6 points a game. After retiring in 1956, he briefly coached (1957–58) the Lakers and served as the first commissioner (1967–69) of the American Basketball Association before concentrating on a law career. Mikan was among the first class inducted into the Basketball Hall of Fame in 1959, and in 1996 he was named one of the NBA's 50 greatest players.

Miller, Arthur Asher, American playwright (b. Oct. 17, 1915, New York, N.Y.—d. Feb. 10, 2005, Roxbury, Conn.), combined social awareness with a searching concern for his characters' inner lives. He was widely recognized as one of the most important playwrights of the mid-20th century, and Willy Loman, the tragic figure at the centre of Miller's Pulitzer Prize-winning masterpiece, *Death of a Salesman* (1949; filmed 1951), gained iconic status far beyond the English-language theatre as a symbol of a common man destroyed by the failure of the American dream and the false values at the heart of the society in which he lives. The dilemma of

Playwright Arthur Miller

above and left: AP/Wide World Photos

ordinary men struggling with moral values was central to several of Miller's other works, including his first major play, *All My Sons* (1947; filmed 1948), and *A View from the Bridge* (1955; revised 1956), *The Price* (1968), *The Ride down Mount Morgan* (1992), and the darkly comic *Resurrection Blues* (2002). *The Crucible* (1953; filmed 1996), based on the 1692 Salem witch trials, was widely interpreted as a parable criticizing the investigations by the House Un-American Activities Committee (HUAC). In 1956 Miller was called before HUAC, but he refused to testify. He was blacklisted and convicted of contempt of Congress, a conviction that was overturned on appeal. Miller's highly publicized five-year marriage (1956–61) to motion picture star Marilyn Monroe figured in two of his plays, *After the Fall* (1964) and *Finishing the Picture* (2004), the latter a thinly disguised look at the filming of Monroe's last completed movie, *The Misfits* (1961), for which Miller wrote the original screenplay. *I Don't Need You Any More*, a collection of Miller's short stories, appeared in 1967, followed by collections of essays in 1977 and 2000. His autobiography, *Timebends*, was published in 1987.

Mills, Sir John (LEWIS ERNEST WATTS MILLS), British actor (b. Feb. 22, 1908, Watts Naval Training College, North Elmham, Norfolk, Eng.—d. April 23, 2005, Denham, Buckinghamshire, Eng.), appeared in more than

© Rank/Zuma Press

John Mills in Great Expectations

100 motion pictures and dozens of stage plays and television programs during a career that spanned some seven decades. His ability to portray "everyman" characters sincerely and believably—especially humble, decent military officers—endeared him to audiences and made him one of Britain's best-loved performers. Seeking a career in the theatre, Mills moved to London when he was 19, took a sales job to pay his expenses, and studied tap dancing. His debut came in 1929 in the chorus of a musical, and he then joined the Quaints repertory company on a yearlong tour in Asia. Noël Coward saw a production, was impressed with Mills's talent, and soon was casting him in his revues and plays. Mills enlisted in the Royal Engineers at the beginning of World War II, but by 1942 an ulcer had caused him to be declared unfit for service, and he began his long string of stiff-upper-lip war-hero roles, among them one that Coward

wrote especially for him—Shorty Blake in the classic *In Which We Serve* (1942), in which his daughter Juliet also appeared, as Blake's baby. Other notable military-themed films included *Waterloo Road* (1945), *The Way to the Stars* (1945), and *Tunes of Glory* (1960). Among the best of his nonmilitary films were *Great Expectations* (1946), *Hobson's Choice* (1954), *Tiger Bay* (1959), in which his daughter Hayley made her debut, *The Wrong Box* (1966), *Ryan's Daughter* (1970), for which he won a best supporting actor Academy Award, and *Gandhi* (1982). Mills married novelist and playwright Mary Hayley Bell (*q.v.*) in 1941. He was made CBE in 1960 and was knighted in 1976.

Moog, Robert Arthur, American electronic engineer (b. May 23, 1934, New York, N.Y.—d. Aug. 21, 2005, Asheville, N.C.), invented the Moog electronic music synthesizer, which revolutionized rock, electronica, pop, and experimental music in the late 1960s and early '70s. As a teenager, Moog built a theremin from plans in *Electronics World* magazine, and in 1954 he began selling theremin-building kits by mail order. He introduced (1964) the first Moog synthesizer, a voltage-controlled machine that allowed changes in pitch, timbre, attack, and decay of sound for the use of musicians, and he continued to refine the invention for the next several years. With the release in 1968 of the popular album *Switched-On Bach*, performed by Walter Carlos entirely on the Moog synthesizer, the instrument's popularity took off. Several progressive rock bands based their sounds on the synthesizer. Moog was honoured with a Grammy Award for technical achievements in 2002.

Moores, Frank Duff, Canadian politician (b. Feb. 18, 1933, Carbonear, Nfd.—d. July 10, 2005, Perth, Ont.), ended in 1972 the 23-year tenure of Joseph Smallwood as provincial premier of Newfoundland and Labrador. Moores was elected to Parliament in 1968, and in 1970 he became leader of the Progressive Conservative Party (PCP) in Newfoundland. He was only the second premier in the province's history, and he served until 1979. In 1984 he played a key role in Brian Mulroney's successful PCP leadership campaign in the Canadian general elections.

Morita, Pat (NORIYUKI MORITA), American actor (b. June 28, 1932, Isleton, Calif.—d. Nov. 24, 2005, Las Vegas, Nev.), earned an Academy Award nomination for his role as a wise master of martial arts in the popular 1984 film *The Karate Kid*, which spawned three sequels. As a child Morita suffered from spinal tuberculosis and was confined to a sanatorium, where he entertained nurses and other children with sock puppets. During World War II, at age 11, he was transferred to a Japanese American internment camp. Before making his film debut in 1967, he spent several years doing stand-up comedy routines in nightclubs. His best-known TV role was that of Arnold, the nervous malt-shop owner in the TV series *Happy Days* (1975–76, 1982–83). Morita's later projects included roles in the films *Collision Course* (1989), *Honeymoon in*

Vegas (1992), and the animated *Mulan* (1998), for which he provided the voice of the emperor of China.

Morrison, Philip, American physicist (b. Nov. 7, 1915, Somerville, N.J.—d. April 22, 2005, Cambridge, Mass.), carried the plutonium core of the first atomic bomb on his lap as it was driven to the Trinity test sight in Alamogordo, N.M., in 1945. A protégé of J. Robert Oppenheimer, Morrison joined the Manhattan Project in 1942 and helped build the atomic bomb that was dropped on Nagasaki. After witnessing the devastation of the bomb, he became an advocate for arms control. He collaborated with Ray and Charles Eames on the film *Powers of Ten* (1977) and was host of the PBS television series *The Ring of Truth* (1987).

Motley, Constance Baker, American lawyer, jurist, and civil rights activist (b. Sept. 14, 1921, New Haven, Conn.—d. Sept. 28, 2005, New York, N.Y.), argued 10 civil rights cases before the U.S. Supreme Court and was the first African American woman to be made a federal judge. While a teenager, Motley became interested in civil rights after she was turned away from a public beach because she was black. Motley was the 9th of 12 children born to parents with blue-collar jobs. With financial help, however, from philanthropist Clarence Blakeslee, who recognized her intelligence and potential, she entered New York University and graduated in 1943. She attended Columbia University Law School, New York City, and was working with Thurgood Marshall and the Legal Defense Fund of the National Association for the Advancement of Colored People before she passed the bar. Motley was a member of Marshall's team that won the landmark 1954 case *Brown v. Board of Education of Topeka*, which declared racial segregation unconstitutional. She represented James Meredith in his effort in 1962 to gain admission to the University of Mississippi. Motley also worked to integrate universities in Alabama, Florida, Georgia, and South Carolina. She successfully defeated segregation practices in Memphis, Tenn., and Birmingham, Ala. She served (1964–65) as a New York state senator and as borough president of Manhattan (1965–66). Motley was appointed in 1966 to a federal judgeship at the U.S. District Court for the Southern District of New York, and she was made chief judge of the court in 1982 and senior judge in 1986.

Mowlam, Mo (MARJORIE MOWLAM), British  politician (b. Sept. 18, 1949, Watford, Hertfordshire, Eng. —d. Aug. 19, 2005, Canterbury, Kent, Eng.), as the United Kingdom's Northern Ireland secretary from 1977 to 1999, used her direct, earthy language to break down barriers between rival groups of politicians and paramilitary groups; she was instrumental in the successful peace negotiations between the Irish Republican Army (IRA) and Protestant Unionists that led to the 1998 Good Friday (or Belfast) Agreement. An outspoken and often irreverent supporter of the Labour Party's shift from the left wing toward the centre ground, she was also noted for her unusual ability to communicate with voters. Mowlam received a degree in anthropology from Durham University (1970) and a Ph.D from the University of Iowa (1977). She taught political science at Florida State University (1977–79) and Newcastle University (1979–83) before entering Parliament in 1987. During the run-up to the 1997 general election, she was criticized in the media for putting on weight. When she disclosed that this (and her thinning hair) was a side effect from treatment for a benign brain tumour, she gained a great deal of public sympathy. In January 1998 Mowlam entered Belfast's Maze prison and persuaded two of the key Protestant paramilitary leaders, who were serving jail sentences, to support the peace process that culminated in the Good Friday Agreement three months later. As time passed, the Unionists lost confidence in Mowlam, accusing her of being too soft on Sinn Fein, the political party associated with the IRA. In October 1999 Blair moved her to the Cabinet Office. Mowlam left the government and Parliament at the 2001 general election.

Mushtaq Ali, Syed, Indian cricketer (b. Dec. 17, 1914, Indore, India—d. June 18, 2005, Indore), was a cavalier right-hand opening batsman and slow left-arm bowler who was the first Indian to score a Test century away from home, at Old Trafford in Manchester, Eng., in 1936. Although Mushtaq and Vijay Merchant averaged 83.43 as an opening pair in four Tests (in 1936 and 1946), Mushtaq fell afoul of the selectors when he withdrew from the 1947–48 tour of Australia because of the death of his brother; he played in a total of only 11 Test matches. In his first-class career (1934–64), Mushtaq played in 226 matches, scored 13,213 runs at an average of 35.90, with 30 centuries and a high score of 233, and took 162 wickets at an average of 29.34, with a best bowling analysis of seven for 108. In 11 Test matches (1934–52), he scored 612 runs at an average of 32.21, with two centuries and a high score of 112, and took three wickets at an average of 67.33, with a best bowling analysis of one for 45.

Narayanan, K(ocheril) R(aman), Indian politician and diplomat (b. Feb. 4, 1921, Uzhavoor, India—d. Nov. 9, 2005, New Delhi, India), overcame poverty and prejudice to become the first Dalit—a member of India's lowest social caste, traditionally considered to be untouchable—to serve as India's president (1997–2002). Narayanan graduated from the University of Travancore (now the University of Kerala) in 1943 and worked as a journalist before attending the London School of Economics on a scholarship. Earning a degree in 1948, he returned to India and embarked on a diplomatic career, holding posts in numerous countries. As the first Indian ambassador

to China (1976–78) since 1962, Narayanan used his expertise and his fluent Chinese to improve Sino-Indian relations. He served as vice-chancellor of Jawaharlal Nehru University from 1979 until 1980, when Prime Minister Indira Gandhi appointed him ambassador to the U.S. Narayanan again displayed his diplomatic skills, easing tensions between the two countries. In 1984 he was elected to Parliament as a member of the Congress Party, and he held a series of ministerial positions before becoming vice president in 1992. His election to the presidency five years later was heralded as the beginning of social and political change. As president, Narayanan exhibited an assertiveness rarely seen in the largely ceremonial post and frequently spoke out against the caste system.

Nash, Joe (JOSEPH V. NASH), American dancer, historian, and archivist (b. Oct. 5, 1919, New York, N.Y.—d. April 13, 2005, New York City), performed in stage musicals, danced with the early notable figures in modern dance, and for 25 years was involved with the Christian liturgical dance known as praise dancing. Throughout his career he amassed a huge collection of African American modern dance memorabilia, and it was feared that the priceless material he had not already donated to institutions would be broken up and auctioned. It was hoped that his remaining archive collection would eventually find a home where cultural historians could have access to it.

Nelson, Gaylord Anton, American politician and conservationist (b. June 4, 1916, Clear Lake, Wis.—d. July 3, 2005, Kensington, Md.), was the founder of Earth Day—first celebrated on April 22, 1970, to focus attention on the preservation of the planet's natural resources. The inaugural Earth Day attracted more than 20 million participants across the country and sparked the passage of environmental legislation in 42 states to mark the occasion. Nelson, a Democrat, served as governor of Wisconsin (1959–62) and as a U.S. senator (1962–80). In the Senate he sponsored numerous conservation bills, including the Wilderness Act, the Wild and Scenic Rivers Act, and the Endangered Species Act. He received the Presidential Medal of Freedom in 1995.

Nilsson, Birgit (MÄRTA BIRGIT SVENNSSON), Swedish operatic soprano (b. May 17, 1918, Västra Karup, Swed.—d. Dec. 25, 2005, Västra Karup), was celebrated for her powerful, rich voice and for her interpretations of the operas of Richard Wagner. She studied with Joseph Hislop in Stockholm, where she joined the Royal Opera and made her debut (1946) in Carl Maria von Weber's *Der Freischütz.* Other successes followed, particularly in Vienna and Bayreuth, where between 1954 and 1970 her Wagnerian roles included

Isolde, Sieglinde, and Brünnhilde. In 1957 Nilsson made her debut at Covent Garden, London, as Brünnhilde in the complete *Ring* cycle, and the next year she appeared at La Scala, Milan, in the title role of Giacomo Puccini's *Turandot.* She made her debut at the Metropolitan Opera, New York City, as Isolde in 1959. Her other significant roles included Beethoven's Leonore, Weber's Rieza, and Richard Strauss's Salome, Elektra, and the Dyer's Wife. In 1969 the Austrian government gave her the honorary title of Kammersängerin ("court singer"), and in 1981 the Swedish government issued a postage stamp in her honour. Following her retirement from the stage in 1982, Nilsson returned to her birthplace, occasionally teaching master classes. At a 1992 gala at Covent Garden, she sang one last time Brünnhilde's signature battle-cry, "Ho-jo-to-ho! Heia!"

Niwa, Fumio, Japanese novelist (b. Nov. 22, 1904, Yokkaichi, Japan—d. April 20, 2005, Tokyo, Japan), was one of Japan's most prolific authors and a leading Showa literary figure known for his popular and religious novels. Many of Niwa's early works included the erotic fantasies *Ayu* (1932; "Sweet-fish") and *Zeiniku* (1933; "Superfluous Flesh"), while his later pieces featured Buddhist themes. He sensationalized post-World War II Japan with *Iyagarase no nenrei* (1947; "The Hateful Age"), a novel critical of the Japanese tradition of venerating the elderly. His self-financed magazine *Bungakusha* featured the works of young writers.

Nomura, Yoshitaro, Japanese film director (b. April 23, 1919, Tokyo, Japan—d. April 8, 2005, Tokyo), pioneered the film noir genre in Japanese cinema. The son of film director Hotei Nomura, Yoshitaro Nomura signed with the Shochiku film studio when he was 22 years old and made his directorial debut with *Hato* ("Pigeon") in 1953. Though he made samurai dramas and musicals, he was best known for his film noirs, including his masterpiece *Suna no utsuwa* (1974; "Castle of Sand"), a thriller that follows the investigation of a murdered police officer; it was considered among the finest films ever made in Japan.

Norton, Andre (ALICE MARY NORTON), American author (b. Feb. 17, 1912, Cleveland, Ohio—d. March 17, 2005, Murfeesboro, Tenn.), led many young readers into the realm

Fantasy author Andre Norton

AP/Wide World Photos; centre: © Ira Nowinski/Corbis

of science fiction with her fantasy adventure novels of the 1950s and '60s. Working as a children's librarian at the Cleveland Public Library, she kept a low public profile while penning romantic otherworldly tales about young alienated heroes. Her early works included adventure stories such as *The Prince Commands* (1934) and spy tales such as *The Sword Is Drawn* (1944). Beginning with *Star Man's Son, 2250 A.D.* (1952), she wrote in the science-fiction genre, gaining a wide readership and many accolades. Norton later concentrated on fantasy, notably with her popular *Witch World* series, launched in 1963. Fantastic animals were featured prominently in other works: *The Beast Master* (1959), *Catseye* (1961), *Iron Cage* (1974), and *Star Ka'at* (1976). In 1999 she founded a writers' research centre in Tennessee. Norton was the first woman to win (1983) the Science Fiction and Fantasy Writers of America's Grand Master Award for lifetime achievement.

Nye, Louis (LOUIS NEISTAT), American comedian (b. May 1, 1913, Hartford, Conn.—d. Oct. 9, 2005, Los Angeles, Calif.), became known in the 1950s for his television portrayal of the pretentious Gordon Hathaway, a mainstay of the man-on-the-street interviews featured on *The Steve Allen Show*; his greeting—"Hi-ho, Steverino!"—became a national catchphrase. He went on to appearances in a few films and on a number of TV shows, including *The Ann Sothern Show*, *The Beverly Hillbillies*, *St. Elsewhere*, *Laverne & Shirley*, and *Curb Your Enthusiasm*. In addition, he provided several voices for the *Inspector Gadget* cartoon series.

Obote, (Apollo) Milton, Ugandan politician (b. Dec. 28, 1924, Akoroko, Uganda British Protectorate—d. Oct. 10, 2005, Johannesburg, S.Af.), served as prime minister (1962–66) and president (1966–71, 1980–85) of Uganda, but both of his terms in the latter post were marked by repressive rule and factionalism and were ended by military coups.  After being expelled (1949) from Makerere University for his pro-independence political activities, Obote worked in Kenya before returning to Uganda in 1957. He was elected to the colonial legislative council in 1958, and two years later he formed the Uganda People's Congress. In 1962 he skillfully negotiated an alliance with King Mutesa II of Buganda (the most powerful of Uganda's five tribal kingdoms), in which Obote became the newly independent country's first prime minister. Tensions increased between the two men, however, and in 1966 Mutesa fled the country. Obote then appointed himself executive president with near-absolute powers and abolished all of the kingdoms. He attempted to implement a socialist program while ruthlessly suppressing the opposition. After being ousted in 1971 by Idi Amin, Obote settled in Tanzania,

where he agitated for Amin's overthrow. Tanzanian-led forces deposed Amin in 1979, and Obote regained the presidency in disputed elections. His second term was marred by a deadly guerrilla war and charges of human rights violations. Deposed again in 1985, Obote went into permanent exile.

O'Herlihy, Dan (DANIEL PETER O'HERLIHY), Irish actor (b. May 1, 1919, Wexford, Ire.—d. Feb. 17, 2005, Malibu, Calif.), earned an Academy Award nomination for his starring performance in Luis Buñuel's film *The Adventures of Robinson Crusoe* (1954). O'Herlihy began his 50-year acting career at the Abbey and Gate theatres in Dublin before making his film debut in *Odd Man Out* (1947). He made his Hollywood debut in *Larceny* (1948), which led to the role of Macduff in Orson Welles's Mercury Theatre Company's screen production of *Macbeth* (1948), for which O'Herlihy also designed the sets. Other notable films included *The Cabinet of Caligari* (1962), *Fail-Safe* (1964), *MacArthur* (1977), and *The Dead* (1987). His theatre work included the role of Charles Dickens in Mervyn Nelson's *The Ivy Green* (1949). O'Herlihy's final appearance was in the 1998 television movie *The Rat Pack*.

Ostrom, John Harold, American paleontologist (b. Feb. 18, 1928, New York, N.Y.—d. July 16, 2005, Litchfield, Conn.), popularized the theory that many species of dinosaurs are ancestrally linked to birds. His enthusiasm and pioneering work did much to revitalize the scholarly interest in dinosaurs. Ostrom received a Ph.D. (1960) in geology and paleontology from Columbia University, New York City, and served (1961–92) on the faculty of Yale University. He was also curator of vertebrate paleontology at Yale's Peabody Museum of Natural History. Ostrom made two key discoveries in his career. While he was conducting fieldwork in Montana in 1964 he found a fossilized claw that he determined belonged to a speedy, predatory dinosaur that lived more than 125 million years ago. He named the dinosaur Deinonychus (Greek for "terrible claw"). The discovery gave new life to the theory that dinosaurs were not cold-blooded and sluggish but rather active and warm-blooded. In 1970 while he was reviewing fossil specimens at a museum in The Netherlands, Ostrom determined that a specimen thought to be a gliding reptile was in fact a member of the genus *Archaeopteryx*, which had characteristics of both birds and dinosaurs. His discovery reenergized the theory linking dinosaurs to birds and sparked Ostrom's own research into the evolution of birds and their flight.

Packer, Kerry Francis Bullmore, Australian media magnate (b. Dec. 17, 1937, Sydney, Australia—d. Dec. 26, 2005, Sydney), was at his death the richest man in Australia, with an estimated wealth of A$7 billion (about US$5 billion). Packer was also known for having created (1977) World Series Cricket, which challenged the traditional governance of international cricket. He was the younger son of Sir Frank Packer, founder (1933) of Australian Consolidated Press. In 1956 Packer entered

the family business, and on his father's death (1974) he became chairman. After gaining control of the company in 1982, he bought out the shareholders in 1983 and took it private. In 1976 Packer bid for exclusive rights to televise Test cricket in Australia, but the national cricket board awarded the rights to the Australian Broadcasting Commission, despite Packer's having made a higher bid. In response, Packer organized World Series Cricket, which was to feature several dozen top players from the principal cricketing countries in a series of 15 five-day "Super Tests" and 49 one-day matches, many of which were to be played at night with a white ball rather than the traditional red one. The International Cricket Conference (now Council; ICC), having failed to negotiate a compromise, announced that players taking part in "disapproved" matches would be banned from Test cricket. Packer sought an injunction against the ICC ruling in the British High Court, which granted it. Although World Series Cricket lasted for only two seasons and was not a financial success, several of Packer's innovations became established in international cricket, including the predominance of one-day matches and the wearing of coloured uniforms in one-day cricket. The salaries of top players also rose substantially over what they had been before the Packer revolution. Packer's other sporting interests included horse racing and polo.

Paolozzi, Sir Eduardo Luigi, British artist (b. March 7, 1924, Leith, Scot.—d. April 22, 2005, London, Eng.), helped launch the British Pop art movement with a series of collages based on mass-media images and later became one of England's leading sculptors. Paolozzi studied art in Edinburgh and London, and in 1947 he moved to Paris, where he became immersed in Surrealism and Dada. During this time he began to craft his landmark collages, in which he juxtaposed magazine photographs, advertisements, and scientific illustrations. Returning to London in 1949, he became a member of the Independent Group, an association of artists who eschewed Modernism. At one of the group's meetings in 1952, he featured the collages in a slide show for his lecture entitled "Bunk." The event laid the foundations for the British Pop art movement. In the early 1960s Paolozzi began to craft colourful robotlike sculptures that expressed his interest in machinery and science. Paolozzi also produced abstract screen prints and taught at a number of schools. He was knighted in 1989.

Parent, Mimi (MARIE PARENT), French-Canadian painter and engraver (b. Sept. 8, 1924, Montreal, Que.—d. June 14, 2005, Switzerland), participated in most of the major Surrealist exhibitions of the mid-20th century, including the 1959 "Eros" exhibit in Paris; her masculine-feminine poster featured a tie fashioned from her own hair, set against a man's suit lapels and white shirt. She studied at the École des Beaux Artes de Montréal, where she met Jean Benoît, an artist whom she later married. She was expelled from the school in

1947 for "insubordination." Parent enjoyed a successful show at the Dominion Gallery in Montreal in 1947 and the next year relocated to Paris with Benoît. There she met the critic André Breton and became one of the key members of the Surrealist movement.

Parker, James Thomas, American football player (b. April 3, 1934, Macon, Ga.—d. July 18, 2005, Columbia, Md.), became in 1973 the first full-time offensive lineman inducted into the Pro Football Hall of Fame. Parker played under legendary coach Woody Hayes at Ohio State University, where he earned All-America honours and won the 1956 Outland Trophy as the nation's top lineman. He played 11 seasons (1957–67) with the Baltimore Colts, earning Pro Bowl honours eight times. Regarded as one of the finest linemen ever to play, Parker was part of two National Football League championship teams (1958 and '59).

Parks, Rosa (ROSA LOUISE McCAULEY), American civil rights advocate (b. Feb. 4, 1913, Tuskegee, Ala.—d. Oct. 24, 2005, Detroit,

Bettman/Corbis

Integration pioneer Rosa Parks

Mich.), became a symbol of the power of nonviolent protest after she refused to give up her bus seat to a white man in the segregated South. Her action led to the 1955–56 Montgomery, Ala., bus boycott, recognized as the spark that ignited the American civil rights movement. Parks grew up in Alabama, briefly attending Alabama State Teachers College (now Alabama State University). She married Raymond Parks, a barber, in 1932. She worked as a seamstress and became active in the National Association for the Advancement of Colored People (NAACP), serving as secretary of the Montgomery chapter from 1943 to 1956. On her way home from work one day in 1955, Parks was told by a bus driver to surrender her seat to a white man. When she refused, she was arrested and fined, an action that motivated local black leaders to take action. The Rev. Martin Luther King, Jr., led a boycott of the bus company that lasted more than a year. In 1956 the U.S. Supreme Court upheld a lower court's decision declaring Montgomery's segregated bus seating unconstitutional. The following year Parks moved to Detroit. She worked in the office of Rep. John

Conyers, Jr., from 1965 until her retirement in 1988. She remained active in the NAACP and other civil rights groups. The Southern Christian Leadership Council established the Rosa Parks Freedom Award in her honour, and in 1979 the NAACP awarded her its Spingarn Medal. In 1987 she cofounded an institute to help educate young people and teach them leadership skills. Her autobiography, *Rosa Parks: My Story,* appeared in 1993. Parks received the Presidential Medal of Freedom (1996) and the Congressional Gold Medal of Honor (1999).

Patterson, Tom (HARRY THOMAS PATTERSON), Canadian theatrical producer (b. June 11, 1920, Stratford, Ont.—d. Feb. 23, 2005, Toronto, Ont.), founded the Stratford Festival of Canada, which began in a single tent but became the largest and perhaps the most prominent repertory theatre in North America. Inspired by his visits to European opera houses and theatres while serving in World War II, Patterson aimed to boost the economy of his hometown by creating a Shakespearean theatre (complete with a River Avon) reminiscent of William Shakespeare's birthplace in Stratford-upon-Avon, Warwickshire, Eng. After much persistence, Patterson persuaded the Stratford town council and mayor to invest in his idea, and with the assistance of Tyrone Guthrie, the Stratford Shakespearean Festival opened on July 13, 1953. Eventually the festival offered non-Shakespearean performances as well, and the playwright's name was dropped from the title. Patterson served as general manager of the festival until 1967.

Peck, M(organ) Scott, American psychiatrist (b. May 22, 1936, New York, N.Y.—d. Sept. 25, 2005, Warren, Conn.), wrote the best-selling book *The Road Less Traveled* (1978), which was credited with revolutionizing the self-help genre. Self-help books had typically offered tips for succeeding in business, but Peck's book began with the premise that life is hard and then gave advice on how to lead a disciplined and spiritual life. The work eventually landed on the best-seller list, where it remained for more than eight years. *The Road* sold more than 10 million copies and was translated into 20 languages. Peck also authored several other books, including *People of the Lie* (1983), an examination of evil.

Perdue, Frank (FRANKLIN PARSONS PERDUE), American business executive (b. May 9, 1920, near Salisbury, Md.—d. March 31, 2005, Salisbury) was widely recognized for his chicken brand with his homespun advertisements in which he delivered his trademark line, "It takes a tough man to make a tender chicken." Perdue was one of the first CEOs to become an advertising spokesperson for his own company, and he was featured in some 200 television advertisements. After having served as president of Perdue Farms, Inc., from 1952, as CEO until 1988, and as chairman from 1979 to 1991, Perdue saw his company continue to prosper under the leadership of his son James, who succeeded him as CEO and chairman and as the Perdue spokesperson in 1994.

Peters, Brock (GEORGE FISHER), American actor (b. July 2, 1927, New York, N.Y.—d. Aug. 23, 2005, Los Angeles, Calif.), employed his powerful bass voice and strong presence in portrayals of a wide range of characters, the best known of which was the wrongly accused African American on trial for the rape of a white girl in *To Kill a Mockingbird* (1962). He began his motion-picture career playing villains in the musicals *Carmen Jones* (1954) and *Porgy and Bess* (1959) but changed his image to be the gay trumpet player in *The L-Shaped Room* (1962). Included among his later notable performances were roles in such films as *The Pawnbroker* (1965), *Soylent Green* (1973), *Star Trek IV: The Voyage Home* (1986), and *Star Trek VI: The Undiscovered Country* (1991); the lead role in a Broadway revival of *Lost in the Stars* (1972; filmed 1974), for which he received a Tony Award nomination; and several episodes of the television series *Star Trek: Deep Space Nine* (1996–98).

Philips, Frits (FREDERIK JACQUES PHILIPS), Dutch industrialist (b. April 16, 1905, Eindhoven, Neth.—d. Dec. 5, 2005, Eindhoven), during a 48-year career (1930–77) with Philips Electronics, oversaw its expansion from a family-run manufacturer into a vast multinational enterprise and Europe's largest electronics firm. After obtaining (1929) a mechanical engineering degree from Delft Technical University, Philips joined the company as a factory manager. He rose through the ranks to assistant managing director (1935–39), managing director (1939–61), and president and CEO (1961–71) and remained a member of the board until 1977. During World War II, Philips did not flee to the U.S. with the rest of the company's management but instead remained in Eindhoven, operating several factories, including a small concern inside the Vught concentration camp, near Eindhoven. He was credited with having saved the lives of several hundred Jewish workers, and in 1996 Israel awarded him a Yad Vashem medal. Philips was an avid supporter of the PSV Eindhoven association football (soccer) club (established by his family in 1913) and was the founder (1986) of an influential international business round table. Eindhoven's concert hall was renamed in his honour on his 90th birthday, and on his 100th birthday the city declared itself Frits Philips City for the day.

Pritam, Amrita Kaur, Punjabi writer and poet (b. Aug. 31, 1919, Gujranwala, British India [now in Pakistan]—d. Oct. 31, 2005, New Delhi, India), wrote increasingly more feminist poems and other works in which she exposed the suffering of oppressed women and the violence and misery endured by Punjabis during the Partition (1947) of India. Pritam was born into a Sikh family and published her first collection of stories at age 16. During a literary career of more than 60 years, she authored (in Hindi as well as Punjabi) some 24 novels, 23 volumes of poetry, and 15 short-story collections. She was the first woman to receive the Sahitya Akademi Award and the first Punjabi woman to be given the Padma Shri Award. In 1981 Pritam was presented with the Jnanpith Award, India's highest literary award. Her best-known works included the novel *Pinjar* (1950; "The Skeleton"), which in 2003 was made into a Bollywood film of the same name, and the poem *Aaj aakhaan Waris Shah noo* ("Ode to Waris Shah").

Proxmire, (Edward) William, American politician (b. Nov. 11, 1915, Lake Forest, Ill.—d. Dec. 15, 2005, Sykesville, Md.), was a Democratic senator from Wisconsin who crusaded against governmental waste. He joined the Senate in 1957 after winning a special election to fill the seat of Joseph McCarthy. From 1975 to 1988 Proxmire annually announced his Golden Fleece Awards, given to the year's most egregious cases of frivolous government spending. His intense dedication to a cause was not limited to fiscal waste. Between 1967 and 1986 on every day that Congress was in session, he made a speech that called for ratification of the antigenocide pact. His personal discipline was legendary; he jogged nearly 16 km (10 mi) every day, refused to accept campaign donations, and did not miss a single Senate roll-call vote in more than 20 years.

Pryor, Richard, American comedian (b. Dec. 1, 1940, Peoria, Ill.—d. Dec. 10, 2005, Los Angeles, Calif.), revolutionized American comedy with his frank and controversial style. He grew up in a brothel, and as a teenager he was expelled from school and forced to take numerous odd jobs before eventually entering the army. The hard-knock experiences of his youth inspired many of the characters in his routine and much of the emotional rawness that made his comedy so compelling. He enjoyed early success in stand-up comedy, though his act was clearly derived from the humour of Bill Cosby. By the 1970s Pryor had abandoned his safe routine for a new kind of stand-up that emphasized storytelling over punch lines and examined contemporary racial and sexual mores, using the coarse language of the streets. He became the most popular comedian in the country, bringing a uniquely black style of comedy to the American mainstream. His albums *That Nigger's Crazy* (1974) and *...Is It Something I Said* (1975) won Grammy Awards. He also wrote for television, including Emmy Award-winning work with Lily Tomlin in 1974. That same year he co-wrote (with Mel Brooks) the hit comedy film *Blazing Saddles*. In the mid-1970s Pryor also became a top box-office

draw, starring in such hits as *Silver Streak* (1976), *Stir Crazy* (1980), and *Some Kind of Hero* (1982). Despite his professional success, his personal life was plagued by drug addiction, failed marriages, and illness.

Puri, Amrish, Indian movie actor (b. June 22, 1932, Hoshiapur district, Punjab, India—d. Jan. 12, 2005, Mumbai [Bombay], India), epit-

© Sherwin Crasto—Reuters/Corbis

Film star Amrish Puri

omized the Bollywood villain. After a career of small stage roles and voice-overs, Puri was cast in *Reshma aur Shera* (1971; *Rishma and Shera*) when he was nearly 40. He gained notice playing a psychopath in *Nishaant* (1975; *Night's End*) and went on to make more than 200 movies over the next 30 years. Among his best-loved roles were those of the patriarch Babuji in *Dilwale Dulhania Le Jayenge* (1995) and Mogambo in *Mr. India* (1987). Western audiences knew him from his portrayal of the high priest Mola Ram in *Indiana Jones and the Temple of Doom* (1984).

Radcliffe, Ted (THEODORE ROOSEVELT RADCLIFFE; "DOUBLE DUTY"), American baseball player (b. July 7, 1902, Mobile, Ala.—d. Aug. 11, 2005, Chicago, Ill.), was a star Negro League pitcher and catcher who was known for his strong throwing arm and, later, for his expansive storytelling. Radcliffe played with the Negro Leagues from 1928 to 1950, starting with the Detroit Stars and going on to play for 12 other teams as well. He played in the leagues' East-West All-Star Game six times, three as a pitcher and three as a catcher. In 1932, playing for the Pittsburgh Crawfords, Radcliffe batted .325 and went 19–8 in pitching; that same year writer Damon Runyon dubbed him "Double Duty."

Rainier III (PRINCE RAINIER-LOUIS-HENRI-MAXENCE-BERTRAND DE GRIMALDI), Mone-

© Bettmann/Corbis

Prince Rainier with his fiancée Grace Kelly in 1956

gasque constitutional monarch (b. May 31, 1923, Monaco—d. April 6, 2005, Monaco), maintained Monaco's aura of glamour and intrigue while building the tiny principality into an economically thriving European nation. His 1956 marriage to American actress Grace Kelly struck many as a fairy-tale courtship and wedding, and their children (Princess Caroline, Prince Albert, and Princess Stephanie) grew up in the public eye. (This storybook image was maintained when Rainier did not remarry after Princess Grace died tragically in an automobile accident in 1982.) Rainier was the son of Prince Pierre, count de Polignac, and Princess Charlotte de Monaco, the daughter of Louis II, the reigning prince of Monaco. He was educated in England, Switzerland, and France. During World War II he served in the French army, receiving battlefield decorations. In 1944 Princess Charlotte renounced her right to succession, and when Louis II died in 1949, Rainier became the 31st hereditary ruler of Monaco. He diversified Monaco's monoculture of casino tourism to include banking and finance, and he oversaw huge construction projects. Rainier led Monaco into UN membership in 1993 and to adoption of the euro as its official currency in 2002. In 2002 he modified Monaco's constitution to ensure that his daughters and their legitimate children would continue the Grimaldi dynasty if his son, who succeeded Rainier as Albert II, did not have a legitimate heir.

Raitt, John Emmet, American actor-singer (b. Jan. 29, 1917, Santa Ana, Calif.—d. Feb. 20, 2005, Pacific Palisades, Calif.), employed his lyrical baritone voice and strong good looks to create a powerful presence in leading roles on the musical stage. His success in the role of Curly in the road company of *Oklahoma!* led to his being cast as Billy Bigelow in the Broadway production of *Carousel* (1945); that show's seven-minute-long "Soliloquy" was written especially for him. Another notable lead role was Sid Sorokin in the stage (1954) and film (1957) versions of *The Pajama Game*, and in later years he frequently collaborated with his daughter, singer Bonnie Raitt.

Rankin, Nell, American mezzo-soprano (b. Jan. 3, 1924, Montgomery, Ala.—d. Jan. 13, 2005, New York, N.Y.), was known for her warm tones in recitals and marquee opera roles during a 30-year career. Rankin made her public debut in a 1947 recital in New York City; her operatic debut was in the role of Ortrud in *Lohengrin* for the Zürich Opera Company in 1949. In 1951 Rankin made debuts at La Scala in Milan, at the Vienna State Opera, and at the Metropolitan Opera in New York City, all in the role of Amneris in *Aida*. She retired in the mid-1970s, after which she taught music until 1991.

Raskin, Jef, American computer scientist (b. March 9, 1943, New York, N.Y.—d. Feb. 26, 2005, Pacifica, Calif.), revolutionized the personal computer industry by pioneering Apple Computer Inc.'s Macintosh, which featured a user-friendly graphics interface rather than the standard text-based commands that were common in the late 1970s. The "father of the Macintosh" led a team of developers in 1979, but he left Apple in 1982, two years before the Macintosh was marketed. The interface concepts developed by Raskin had a profound impact on the industry and were incorporated into other software programs, such as Microsoft Corp.'s Windows. Raskin was also credited with having introduced the word *font* to describe digital typefaces, and he was among the originators of the "click and drag" technique, which allowed the moving of icons around a computer screen by use of a mouse.

Rehnquist, William Hubbs, American jurist (b. Oct. 1, 1924, Milwaukee, Wis.—d. Sept. 3, 2005, Arlington, Va.), served as the chief architect of the U.S. Supreme Court's conservative turn as an associate justice (1971–86) and as chief justice (1986–2005). Rehnquist, whom Pres. Richard M. Nixon appointed to the court of Chief Justice Warren E. Burger, established himself as a vocal supporter of states' rights and was a firm believer in limiting the role of the federal courts in the political landscape. During his own term as chief justice, he narrowed the focus of the Supreme Court, greatly improved its efficiency, and reduced its caseload while increasing its power relative to the legislative branch. Rehnquist attended Stanford University, where he received both a B.A. and an M.A. in 1948. He added a master's degree in government (1949) from Harvard University before returning to Stanford Law School, where he finished at the top of his class (1952). He then served as a clerk in the office of Supreme Court Justice Robert Jackson. There he authored a memorandum that would return to haunt him after he was nominated to the high court. In that memorandum he defended the "separate but equal" doctrine established in *Plessy* v. *Ferguson* (1896), saying that it "was right and should be reaffirmed." He later said that these were not his personal views and that he supported the legal reasoning behind the *Brown* v. *Board of Education* (1954) decision, which declared school segregation unconstitutional. In 1953 Rehnquist married and relocated to Phoenix. While there, he established himself in local Republican Party circles and eventually made contacts within the 1968 Nixon presidential campaign. The following year he was tapped by Nixon to serve as assistant attorney general

Chief Justice William Rehnquist

for the Office of Legal Counsel. He thrived in the position and spent much of his time articulating to Congress the constitutional justifications of the administration's policies. Rehnquist's 33 years of service on the Supreme Court were punctuated with some of the most significant decisions in American jurisprudence. He offered one of the dissenting opinions in the 1973 *Roe* v. *Wade* decision, which legalized abortion in the United States. He authored the majority opinion in *Paul* v. *Davis* (1976), a case that limited the expansion of the due process clause of the 14th Amendment. He felt that free expression extended to works of parody—as he wrote in the majority opinion of the *Hustler* v. *Falwell* (1988) decision—but not to the burning of the American flag, as articulated in his dissent in *Texas* v. *Johnson* (1989). He dissented again in *Planned Parenthood of Southeastern Pennsylvania* v. *Casey* (1992), the court's 5–4 affirmation of the Roe decision. His majority decision in *United States* v. *Lopez* (1995) checked Congress's ability to undercut state power through the use of the Constitution's commerce clause. Perhaps his most famous case was the 2000 decision *Bush* v. *Gore*, which halted the recounting of presidential ballots in Florida.

Ren Zhongyi, Chinese government official (b. September 1914, Weixian, Hebei province, China—d. Nov. 15, 2005, Guangzhou, Guangdong province, China), was one of the Communist Party of China's (CPC's) most outspoken proponents of political and economic reform. As first party secretary of Guangdong from 1980 to 1985, he was credited with ushering in reforms that led to a remarkable economic turnaround in the province. Ren was a member of the CPC from 1936. In 1961 he was appointed first party secretary of Heilongjiang province, but his service in this post was interrupted when he became a victim of the Cultural Revolution. Eventually rehabilitated, he returned briefly to his post in Heilongjiang before serving (1977–80) as first party secretary of Liaoning province. It was in Guangdong, however, that Ren became widely known as a reformer, one who pushed not only for economic liberalization but also for greater freedom of the press and the placing of limits on

the CPC's political power. He remained outspoken—and controversial—in retirement. An article he published in 2004 in the magazine *Tongzhou gongjin,* in which he offered criticisms of Deng Xiaoping, led to the dismissal of the publication's editor. Ren was also involved in the founding of a museum on the Cultural Revolution.

Ricoeur, (Jean) Paul (Gustave), French philosopher (b. Feb. 27, 1913, Valence, France—d. May 20, 2005, Châtenay-Malabry, France), was one of the foremost exponents of hermeneutics, the theory and method of interpreting texts that became a principal concern of continental philosophy under the influence of German philosopher Martin Heidegger. Ricoeur attended the University of Rennes and then went to Paris to study at the Sorbonne (Ph.D., 1950), where he was influenced by Gabriel Marcel. Ricoeur worked as a secondary-school teacher from 1935 until he was drafted (1939) into the army. Taken prisoner in 1940, he spent his time in captivity studying German philosophers such as Heidegger, Edmund Husserl, and Karl Jaspers. After the war Ricoeur taught school for three years until he was appointed a lecturer in philosophy at the University of Strasbourg. In 1957 he took a chair in general philosophy at the Sorbonne, and in 1965 he moved to the University of Nanterre. He became dean of the faculty of letters there in 1969 but resigned the next year under pressure from radical students. Ricoeur also visited several American universities and was a professor (1971–91) at the University of Chicago Divinity School. His major writings included *Freedom and Nature: The Voluntary and the Involuntary* (1966), *The Symbolism of Evil* (1967), *The Rule of Metaphor* (1977), and *Time and Narrative* (1984–88). In 2004, with Jaroslav Pelikan, he shared the $1 million John W. Kluge Prize for Lifetime Achievement in the Human Sciences.

Roa Bastos, Augusto Antonio, Paraguayan novelist and poet (b. June 13, 1917, Iturbe, Paraguay—d. April 26, 2005, Asunción, Paraguay), penned his masterpiece, *Yo el supremo* (1974; *I the Supreme;* in bilingual edition), which recounted the life of the dictator Gaspar Rodríguez de Francia and covered more than 100 years of Paraguayan history. Roa Bastos grew up in a country village where his father managed a sugar mill. The village life and its indigenous Guaran language and customs would influence his writing profoundly. A devout patriot, he volunteered as a hospital assistant in the Chaco War (1932–35) against Bolivia. In the 1930s and '40s, he lived in Asunción, working as a journalist for *El País* newspaper and writing poetry and fiction. The 1947 Civil War in Paraguay brought the dictator Gen. Alfredo Stroessner to power, and Roa Bastos, who had sided with the defeated rebels, went into exile in Buenos Aires. There he produced some of his finest works of fiction, including the short-story collection *El trueno entre las hojas* (1953) and the novel *Hijo de hombre* (1960). A military coup in Argentina in 1976 forced Roa Bastos to continue his exile in France, where he remained until the fall of the Stroessner regime in 1989. That same year he returned to Paraguay and was awarded the Cervantes Prize.

Robichaud, Louis Joseph, Canadian politician (b. Oct. 21, 1925, Saint-Antoine, N.B.—d. Jan. 6, 2005, Saint-Antoine), introduced far-reaching reforms as premier (1960–70) of New Brunswick; he was the first Acadian elected to the premiership of any of Canada's Maritime Provinces. Robichaud was elected to New Brunswick's provincial assembly in 1952, and he became provincial leader of the Liberal Party in 1958. As premier he implemented a number of controversial progressive reforms, most important among them the Equal Opportunity Program, which centralized and equalized taxation and services throughout New Brunswick. His administration also saw the establishment of the University of Moncton and the passage of the Official Languages Act. Robichaud was appointed Companion of the Order of Canada in 1971. From 1973 until 2000 he served in the Senate of Canada.

Rochberg, George, American composer (b. July 5, 1918, Paterson, N.J.—d. May 29, 2005, Bryn Mawr, Pa.), at first wrote in a Modernist vein but from the 1960s embraced an eclectic style that he felt offered greater expressive possibilities. His works included symphonies, string quartets, and songs. He taught (1948–54) at the Curtis Institute of Music, Philadelphia, where he had studied, and at the University of Pennsylvania, where he was chairman (1960–68) of the music department. An expanded edition of his 1984 book *The Aesthetics of Survival: A Composer's View of 20th-Century Music* was reissued in 2004.

Roger, Brother (ROGER LOUIS SCHUTZ-MARSAUCHE), Swiss-born religious leader (b. May 12, 1915, Provence, Switz.—d. Aug. 16, 2005, Taizé, France), was the leader of a worldwide ecumenical movement centred at the monastic community that he founded (1940) in Taizé. Brother Roger, as he preferred to be called, devoted his life to the ideals of international peace and reconciliation between Christian churches. By 2005 the Taizé commune where he was prior had drawn thousands of visitors annually and included almost 100 Protestant and Roman Catholic adherents, who took monastic vows. Schutz was the son of a Calvinist preacher and studied theology at the University of Lausanne. He spoke often (he declined to call it preaching) and wrote extensively. His many awards included the second Templeton Prize awarded (1974), the UNESCO Prize for Peace Education (1988), and the Notre Dame award for humanitarian assistance (1997).

Rogers, Adrian Pierce, American minister (b. Sept. 12, 1931, West Palm Beach, Fla.—d. Nov. 15, 2005, Memphis, Tenn.), led the conservative takeover of the Southern Baptist Convention (SBC), the largest Protestant denomination in the U.S. He assumed leadership of the Bellevue Baptist Church in Cordova, Tenn., in 1972 and transformed it into a megachurch with a congregation of 29,000. Rogers served three times as the president of the SBC and promoted the doctrine of biblical inerrancy (belief in the literal truth of the Bible). He campaigned to eliminate liberals and moderates from Baptist seminaries and to keep women out of the clergy. Rogers also led a boycott of the Disney Co. to protest the company's policies that recognized gay rights.

Rong Yiren, Chinese businessman and government official (b. May 1, 1916, Wuxi, China—d. Oct. 27, 2005, Beijing, China), served (1979–93) as president of the China International Trust and Investment Corp. (CITIC), the nation's main investment arm and one of its largest state-owned enterprises; in this position he earned the nickname "the Red capitalist" for helping launch free-market reforms and open China's economy to the West. Rong, who was listed in 1999 by *Forbes* magazine as the richest person in China (with an estimated net worth of $1 billion), also served (1993–98) as China's vice president. Educated at British-run St. John's University in Shanghai, Rong had taken over the operation of a number of businesses owned by his family at the time the communists came to power in China in 1949. Several of his siblings subsequently left China. Rong stayed, however, even though the government became a 50% partner in his businesses in 1955. From 1957 he was deputy mayor of Shanghai, and from 1959 he served as deputy minister of the textile industry, but he was stripped of both posts in 1966 when Mao Zedong launched the Cultural Revolution. Rong's businesses were seized, and he was beaten and made to work in menial jobs. He was eventually rehabilitated under Deng Xiaoping, who ascended to power following Mao's death in 1976. In 1979 Deng asked Rong to help with China's new "open door" economic reforms. After forming CITIC, Rong operated the corporation like a capitalist enterprise as he successfully sought to attract foreign capital to China. In May 1989 Rong allowed his employees to participate in prodemocracy demonstrations, but he later supported the government's military repression of the Tiananmen Square demonstrators.

Rossner, Judith Perelman, American novelist (b. March 31, 1935, New York, N.Y.—d. Aug. 9, 2005, New York City), examined the lives and experiences of modern women as they coped with loneliness, love, and their sexuality. Her best-known book, *Looking for Mr. Goodbar* (1975; filmed 1977)—inspired by a New York City schoolteacher's murder at the hands of a man she had picked up in a singles bar—became a best seller. Another best seller was *August* (1983).

Rotblat, Sir Joseph, Polish-born British physicist (b. Nov. 4, 1908, Warsaw, Pol., Russian Empire [now in Poland]—d. Aug. 31, 2005, London, Eng.), served as founding secretary-general (1957–73) and later as president (1988–97) of the Pugwash (N.S.) Conferences on Science and World Affairs, at which influential scientists and other key figures from around the world could meet informally to discuss and promote nuclear disarmament and arms control. The conferences, which first met in 1957, at the height of the Cold War, were credited with laying the groundwork for international arms-control agreements, and in 1995 Rotblat and the Pugwash Conferences were jointly awarded the Nobel Prize for Peace. Rotblat obtained a Doctor of Physics degree from the University of Warsaw in 1938. The next year he went to England, where he conducted research on neutrons at the University of Liverpool. During World War II he participated in the Manhattan Project to develop an atomic bomb, but he quit in 1944 after he learned that Nazi Germany was no longer building its own atomic bomb. As a physics professor at the University of London and a medical physicist at the university's St. Bartholomew's Hospital Medical College (1950–76), he studied the biological effects of nuclear radiation and helped to make public the dangers of fallout from the atmospheric testing of nuclear weapons. Rotblat became a British citizen in 1946 and was knighted in 1998.

Rowlands, Patsy (PATRICIA ROWLANDS), British actress (b. Jan. 19, 1934, London, Eng.—d. Jan. 22, 2005, Hove, East Sussex, Eng.), was a successful stage and film character actress for 50 years, but she was best remembered for her roles in 9 of the 31 raucous, double entendre-laden Carry On film comedies, starting with *Carry On Again, Doctor* (1969) and ending with *Carry On Behind* (1975). Rowlands also appeared with her Carry On costar Sid James in the television series *Bless This House* (1971–76).

Russell, Nipsey (JULIUS RUSSELL), American  actor and comedian (b. Oct. 13, 1924, Atlanta, Ga.—d. Oct. 2, 2005, New York, N.Y.), was considered the poet laureate of television comedy because of the clever impromptu verses he created. Russell's rhymes, his witty one-liners, and his sophisticated topical jokes gained him a number of guest stints on talk and game shows, and he became the first black to join a network game show as a regular panelist (*Missing Links*, 1964). Other TV shows on which he made frequent appearances included the game shows *Hollywood Squares, To Tell the Truth,* and *The $50,000 Pyramid.* As an actor, Russell included among his credits the roles of Officer Anderson on the TV series *Car 54, Where Are You?* (1961–62) and the Tin Man in the film *The Wiz* (1978).

Sadie, Stanley, British musicologist (b. Oct. 30, 1930, London, Eng.—d. March 21, 2005, Cossington, Somerset, Eng.), was the editor of the 20-volume *The New Grove Dictionary of Music and Musicians* (1980) and of a second, expanded edition published in 2001. He also edited several spinoffs, including *The New Grove Dictionary of Opera* (1992). After being educated at the University of Cambridge (Ph.D., 1958), Sadie taught, worked as a critic and reviewer, and, from 1967 to 1987, was editor of the *Musical Times*. Sadie was made CBE in 1982.

Sagar, Ramanand, Indian filmmaker (b. Dec. 29, 1917, near Lahore, Punjab, British India [now in Pakistan]—d. Dec. 12, 2005, Mumbai [Bombay], India), as the head of the Bollywood production company Sagar Arts Corp., wrote, directed, and produced motion pictures and television programs, notably *Ramayan* (1987), a phenomenally popular 78-part TV epic based on the life of the Hindu god Rama. After studying at the University of the Punjab, Sagar worked as a writer, newspaper journalist, and actor and technician in silent films. He settled in India after partition and in 1949 moved to Bombay, where he founded (1950) Sagar Arts. He expanded into television production in 1985. Sagar also wrote short stories, a novel, and a stage play.

Sandor, Gyorgy, Hungarian-born American pianist (b. Sept. 21, 1912, Budapest, Hung.— d. Dec. 9, 2005, New York, N.Y.), specialized in the works of Eastern European composers, notably his countrymen Zoltan Kodaly (with whom he studied composition) and Bela Bartok (with whom he studied piano). Sandor's nuanced interpretations of Bartok's piano works were especially praised, and he premiered a number of the composer's works, including the piano reduction of *Concerto for Orchestra*, which had been created in the 1940s but not performed until 1985.

Santos, Lucia de Jesus dos (LUCIA ABOBORA), Portuguese nun (b. March 22, 1907, Aljustrel, Port.—d. Feb. 13, 2005, Coimbra, Port.), was the oldest of the three shepherd children who claimed to have seen a series of visions of the Virgin Mary near Fátima, Port.—one each month between May 13 and Oct. 13, 1917. Lucia and her cousins Francisco and Jacinta Marta reported the visions, and by October tens of thousands of observers had gone to the site. The children were harshly questioned by authorities from the Roman Catholic Church, but by the time a formal church inquiry commenced in 1922, Francisco and Jacinta had died in the influenza pandemic. In 1930 the veneration of Our Lady of Fátima was authorized by the bishop of Leiria, Port., and a shrine was established at Fátima. Lucia became a nun in the 1920s. Although she wrote about her experiences, from 1948 Lucia lived in semiseclusion in a Carmelite convent. In 2000, on the occasion of the beatification of Francisco and Jacinto, the Vatican revealed that the long-debated "third secret of Fátima" referred to the 1981 attempt on the life of Pope John Paul II.

Saunders, Dame Cicely Mary Strode, British physician and humanitarian (b. June 22, 1918, Barnet, Hertfordshire, Eng.—d. July 14, 2005, London, Eng.), founded St. Christopher's Hospice in London in 1967 and was responsible for establishing the modern hospice movement worldwide. Saunders became a Red Cross war nurse in 1944 and served as a medical social worker before graduating from medical school in 1957. Research work in pharmacology inspired her idea to administer low, steady doses of pain relievers to terminally ill patients to keep them alert and comfortable. Believing that her patients were entitled to a meaningful life and to death with dignity, Saunders developed a holistic approach to their care that she hoped would also meet their emotional and spiritual needs. Among the many honours Saunders received was the Conrad N. Hilton Humanitarian Prize, awarded to St. Christopher's Hospice in 2001.

Schatz, Albert, American microbiologist (b. Feb. 2, 1920, Norwich, Conn.— d. Jan. 17, 2005, Philadelphia, Pa.), along with Selman Waksman, discovered streptomycin, the first antibiotic that effectively treated a multitude of deadly diseases such as tuberculosis, typhoid, cholera, and bubonic plague. As a graduate student at Rutgers University, New Brunswick, N.J., Schatz successfully demonstrated in 1943 that streptomycin acted as an active agent in slowing the growth of disease-causing bacteria. Initially, Schatz was denied recognition for his achievement, as well as any royalties from the sale of streptomycin, primarily because he was a graduate student. As a result, he sued Waksman and Rutgers University and eventually won recognition as co-discoverer of streptomycin, and he was awarded a portion of the royalties from its sale. When the 1952 Nobel Prize for Physiology or Medicine was awarded solely to Waksman, however, Schatz's appeals were futile.

Schell, Maria Margarethe Anna, Austrian

actress (b. Jan. 15, 1926, Vienna, Austria—d. April 26, 2005, Preitenegg, Austria), was an acclaimed actress in German-language films and stage productions in the 1940s and '50s, winning the best actress award at the Cannes Festival for *Die letzte Brücke* (1954; *The Last Bridge*) and at the Venice Film Festival for *Gervaise* (1956). Schell was admired for her delicate blonde beauty and her eloquent emotions on-screen, but her Hollywood career, which included a soulful performance as Grushenka in *The Brothers Karamazov* (1958) and several made-for-television movies, was less successful. In 2002 she was the subject of *Meine Schwester Maria* (*My Sister Maria*), a poignant documentary film by her younger brother, actor-director Maximilian Schell.

Schenkel, Chris, (CHRISTOPHER EUGENE SCHENKEL), American sports broadcaster (b. Aug. 21, 1923, Bippus, Ind.—d. Sept. 11, 2005, Fort Wayne, Ind.), provided play-by-play commentary for some of the most memorable sporting events of television's first 50 years. Though his smooth baritone voice was most commonly associated with ABC's broadcast of professional bowling events, Schenkel covered a wide range of sports, including golf, gymnastics, boxing, basketball, and football.

Schmeling, Max (MAXIMILIAN ADOLPH OTTO SIEGFRIED SCHMELING), German heavyweight boxer (b. Sept. 28, 1905, Klein Luckow, Ger.—d. Feb. 2, 2005, Hollenstedt, Ger.), became the first European boxer to become heavyweight champion of the world when he captured the title with a win by disqualification over Jack Sharkey on June 12, 1930. Schmeling held the championship until June 21, 1932, when he lost a rematch with Sharkey on a highly controversial split decision. Schmeling's two most notable fights, however, came against emerging heavyweight great Joe Louis. A 10–1 underdog in his first fight with Louis on June 19, 1936, Schmeling achieved a stunning upset with a 12th-round knockout of a fighter whom many had regarded as unbeatable. The victory made Schmeling a hero in his native Germany. Although he was never a member of the Nazi Party, he was lionized by the Nazis as a symbol of Aryan supremacy. The German and American press corps invested his rematch with the African American Louis with nationalist and racial implications. The bout, which took place on June 22, 1938, ended in the first round with Louis completely overwhelming Schmeling, knocking him out in 124 seconds. Schmeling returned to Germany and the following year won the European heavyweight title. The devastating loss to Louis and, more significantly, Schmeling's refusal to abandon his Jewish friends and associates, had resulted in his falling out of favour with the Nazi regime, which saw to it that he was drafted into the German army during World War II despite his having passed the age of conscription. After the war Schmeling staged a short-lived comeback, winning three of five fights in 1947–48 before retiring with a career record of 56 wins (40 by knockout), 10 losses, and 4 draws. In 1957 he acquired the Coca-Cola bottling and distribution franchise for the Federal Republic of Germany, and this business eventually made him a wealthy man. Over the years he also forged a strong friendship with Louis, helping his former nemesis financially and paying for Louis's funeral in 1981. Schmeling was inducted into the International Boxing Hall of Fame in 1992.

Schriever, Bernard Adolph, general (ret.), U.S. Air Force (b. Sept. 14, 1910, Bremen, Ger.—d. June 20, 2005, Washington, D.C.), led intercontinental ballistic missile (ICBM) and military space programs during the Cold War. He established a new management technique known as concurrency. Unlike the traditional method of developing a new weapon step-by-step, concurrency entailed designing all the weapon's subsystems simultaneously. This technique expedited development of the Atlas, Titan, and Minuteman ICBMs and thereby pushed the U.S. well ahead of the Soviet Union in fielding a powerful nuclear deterrent by the early 1960s.

Scott, George Lewis, American gospel singer (b. March 18, 1929, Notasulga, Ala.—d. March 9, 2005, Durham, N.C.), contributed his driving baritone to the gospel group Blind Boys of Alabama. At the Alabama Institute for the Negro Blind in Talladega, Scott met Clarence Fountain and Jimmy Carter, and in 1939 they founded their group, first known as the Happy Land Singers. As the Blind Boys of Alabama, they pioneered the jubilee style of gospel music, incorporating jazz and blues elements into their rich harmonizing. They won the first of their four consecutive Grammy Awards for the album *Spirit of the Century* (2001).

Settle, Mary Lee, American author (b. July 29, 1918, Charleston, W.Va.—d. Sept. 27, 2005, Ivy, Va.), penned the critically acclaimed Beulah Quintet—a historical fiction that traced events from Cromwellian England to 20th-century West Virginia. The saga debuted in 1956 with *O Beulah Land* and continued with *Know Nothing* (1960), *Prisons* (1973), *The Scapegoat* (1980), and *The Killing Ground* (1982). Settle won the National Book Award in 1978 for her novel *Blood Tie*. Two years later she established a new literary prize, the PEN/Faulkner Award.

Sheckley, Robert, American writer (b. July 16, 1928, Brooklyn, N.Y.—d. Dec. 9, 2005, Poughkeepsie, N.Y.), was the author of a number of novels and short stories considered classics in the science-fiction genre; his works were noted for their dark humour and nihilistic outlook. Exceedingly prolific, he wrote or co-wrote some two dozen novels and at least 400 short stories. Among his most notable novels were *The Status Civilization* (1960), *Journey Beyond Tomorrow* (1962), *Mindswap* (1966), and *Dimension of Miracles* (1968). Perhaps his most famous short story, "The Seventh Victim" (1953), became the basis for the 1965 film *La decima vittima* (also known as *The 10th Victim* and *The Tenth Victim*). It was one of four stories by Sheckley that were made into films. Sheckley served as fiction editor of *Omni* magazine in the early 1980s. Many of his later stories were collected in *Uncanny Tales* (2003).

Sheppard of Liverpool, David Stuart Sheppard, the Right Reverend Lord, British cricketer and Anglican bishop (b. March 6, 1929, Reigate, Surrey, Eng.—d. March 5, 2005, West Kirby, Wirral, Merseyside, Eng.), was the only man who played cricket for England as an ordained priest. Sheppard attended Sherborne School and Trinity Hall, Cambridge. A graceful opening batsman, David Sheppard (as he was then known) played for Cambridge (1950–52), Sussex (1947–62), and England (1950–63), serving for a time as captain of each. In 230 first-class matches, he scored 15,838 runs at an average of 43.51, with 45 centuries and 194 catches. In 22 Test matches,

he scored 1,172 runs at an average of 37.80, with 3 centuries and 12 catches. After Sheppard was ordained (1955), he gave up playing cricket full-time, but he did not retire his bat until 1963. He served as a curate of St. Mary's, Islington, in London (1955–57) and as warden at the Mayflower Family Centre in Canning Town, London (1957–69). As suffragan bishop of Woolwich (1969–75) and bishop of Liverpool (1975–97), Sheppard was known for his advocacy for the poor and for his ecumenism. He was made a life peer in 1998.

Shoman, Abdul Majeed, Palestinian banker (b. 1912, Beit Hanina, near Jerusalem, Ottoman Empire [now in Israel]—d. July 5, 2005, Amman, Jordan), was a tireless supporter of Palestinian national aspirations and for 30 years the chairman of the Arab Bank, the largest privately owned bank in the Middle East. In 1936 Shoman joined the Arab Bank, which his father had founded in Jerusalem in 1930, but after the establishment of Israel in 1948, he moved the bank's headquarters to Amman. Shoman took over the chairmanship of the bank in 1974, and under his guidance it opened 378 branches in 27 countries. He was also the first chairman of the Palestine National Fund, and the Arab Bank managed the finances of both the fund and the family of Palestinian leader Yasir Arafat. Shoman headed a number of cultural and humanitarian organizations in support of Palestinian causes. He served in Jordan's Senate in 1987–90 and 1993–97.

Short, Bobby (ROBERT WALTRIP SHORT), American cabaret singer (b. Sept. 15, 1924, Danville, Ill.—d. March 21, 2005, New York, N.Y.), began a legendary 36-year run at the Café Carlyle in Manhattan in 1968 and established himself as a New York institution, winning fans and friends among the city's social and artistic elite. His stride style of piano matched well with his velvet baritone, and he established a reputation as a master of jazz standards, especially the works of Duke Ellington, Eubie Blake, Fats Waller, and Cole Porter. Short's best-known albums included *Mabel Mercer and Bobby Short at Town Hall* (1968) and *Late Night at the Café Carlyle* (1993).

Simon, Claude (CLAUDE EUGÈNE HENRI SIMON), French author (b. Oct. 10, 1913, Tananarive [now Antananarivo], Madagascar—d. July 6, 2005, Paris, France), avoided traditional literary convention—plot, chronology, and character development—to craft challenging works that made him a leading figure in the French *nouveau roman* ("new novel," or antinovel) movement and earned him the Nobel Prize for Literature in 1985. Simon grew up in France and studied in Paris and at the Universities of Oxford and Cambridge. He fought with the Republicans in the Spanish Civil War and escaped from a German prisoner-of-war camp during World War II. His wartime experiences informed many of his works, including his first novel, *Le Tricheur* (1945). Simon, who was influenced by William Faulkner and Marcel Proust, used stream of consciousness, detailed descriptions, and

dense prose (typically lacking punctuation and often employing sentences more than 1,000 words in length) as he sought to depict the human condition. His works became prominent examples of the *nouveau roman* and were praised for their creativity and lyricism. Perhaps his most important creation was a cycle of novels that featured recurring characters—*L'Herbe* (1958), *La Route des Flandres* (1960), *Le Palace* (1962), and *Histoire* (1967), the latter of which was awarded the Prix Médicis.

Simon, Simone, French actress (b. April 23, 1910, Béthune, France—d. Feb. 22, 2005, Paris, France), was much admired for her innocent appearance and on-screen sensuality, notably in Jean Renoir's *La Bête humaine* (1938), but she was best known to American audiences for the stylish low-budget thriller *Cat People* (1942). Simon began as a model and fashion designer in Paris before making her theatrical debut in *Balthazar* and her film debut in *Le Chanteur inconnu* (both in 1931). She was offered a Hollywood studio contract in 1936, but, aside from *Cat People* and *The Devil and Daniel Webster* (1941), she enjoyed little success in Hollywood. In 1950 she returned to France, where she had well-regarded roles in Max Ophüls's *La Ronde* (1950) and *Le Plaisir* (1952). Simon's final screen performance was in *La Femme en bleu* (1973).

Sin, Jaime Cardinal, Philippine Roman Catholic cleric (b. Aug. 31, 1928, New Washington, Phil.—d. June 21, 2005, Manila, Phil.), was the spiritual leader of Roman Catholics in

Jaime Cardinal Sin

the Philippines for more than a quarter of a century; his service as archbishop of Manila from 1974 to 2003 was marked by his influential involvement in Philippine politics. Most notably, Sin played a key role in the "people power" revolts that toppled the presidencies of Ferdinand Marcos in 1986 and Joseph Estrada in 2001. Ordained a priest in 1954, Sin later served as titular bishop of Obba from 1967 to 1972 and as archbishop of Jaro from 1972 to 1974. In 1976, after his appointment as archbishop of Manila, Sin was created a cardinal by Pope Paul VI. He became a persistent and vocal critic of the authoritarian Marcos regime and urged Philippine Catholics to join the popular demonstrations against Marcos, who was widely believed to have retained the presidency in February 1986 through massive voter fraud. Marcos eventually fled the country. Sin also lent his support in 2001 to street protests that helped force Estrada from office amid corruption allegations. In declining health, Sin retired as archbishop in 2003.

Sivori, (Enrique) Omar, Argentine-born association football (soccer) player (b. Oct. 2, 1935, San Nicolas, Arg.—d. Feb. 17, 2005, San Nicolas), was revered for his audacious and brilliant play in both his homeland, Argentina, and his adopted country, Italy, although his cocky attitude earned him the sobriquet El Cabezón ("Bighead"). Sivori joined River Plate in 1954 and helped that club to three straight national titles (1955, 1956, 1957). He played 18 times for Argentina, which captured the 1957 South American championship. Instead of joining the national team for the 1958 World Cup, however, Sivori transferred to the Italian club Juventus. The diminutive 1.7-m (5-ft 7-in) Sivori's aggressive style was a perfect complement to the Welsh "Gentle Giant," John Charles, and the pair led Juventus to three Serie A titles and two Italian Cups. Sivori was named European Footballer of the Year in 1961, and the next year, by virtue of his Italian ancestry, he was selected to play for Italy in the World Cup finals. After finishing his professional career with Napoli (1965–68), Sivori returned to Argentina as a manager for Rosario Central and River Plate. He coached the national team in the 1974 World Cup qualifying rounds but quit after an argument with the Argentine football association.

Smalley, Richard Erret, American chemist and physicist (b. June 6, 1943, Akron, Ohio—d. Oct. 28, 2005, Houston, Texas), was a leading proponent of the development and application of nanotechnology, the manipulation of materials at the extremely small scale of individual atoms or groups of atoms. Seeing tremendous potential in its ability to solve many technological problems, he persuasively argued for large U.S. government funding of nanotechnology research. Smalley received a Ph.D. (1973) in chemistry from Princeton University. After postdoctoral work at the University of Chicago, he joined the faculty of Rice University, Houston, in 1976. Smalley was an adept researcher and, among other accomplishments, developed supersonic beam laser spectroscopy, which became an important tool in physical chemistry. In 1985, using an apparatus that he had helped develop, Smalley and his colleagues unexpectedly found spherical carbon molecules composed of 60 atoms that were arranged in a pattern that resembled a soccer ball or geodesic dome. The researchers called them buckminsterfullerenes (buckyballs for short), after geodesic-dome designer R. Buckminster Fuller. The molecules represented a previously unknown elemental form of carbon, and for the discovery Smalley and his colleagues Robert Curl, Jr., and Sir Harold Kroto were awarded the 1996 Nobel

Prize for Chemistry. Other large cagelike molecules of carbon, called fullerenes, were soon discovered. Smalley's later research focused on long cylindrical fullerenes called carbon nanotubes, which are extremely strong and have useful electrical properties. In 2000 he helped start Carbon Nanotechnologies, Inc., to develop the production and application of carbon nanotubes.

Smith, Jimmy (JAMES OSCAR SMITH), American musician (b. Dec. 8, 1928, Norristown, Pa.—found dead Feb. 8, 2005, Scottsdale, Ariz.), made the previously scorned electric organ into one of the most popular instruments in jazz by inventing the soul-jazz idiom, which became popular in the 1950s and '60s. Earlier, players had used two-handed chords to make organs imitate the power of big bands; Smith's innovation was to play nimble single-note melodic lines in the manner of horn players and bop pianists, accompanied by gospel music harmonies. Originally a pianist, Smith served in the U.S. Navy before studying (1948–50) at Philadelphia music schools and playing (1951–54) in Don Gardner's rhythm-and-blues group. Smith heard swing stylist Wild Bill Davis, one of the few organists in jazz, and was inspired to learn to play the Hammond organ. In 1955 Smith formed a trio that became hugely popular. His series of hit albums helped establish Blue Note as a major jazz label. His biggest hit was "Walk on the Wild Side," from his Verve album *Bashin'* (1962), accompanied by Oliver Nelson's big studio band. Smith also recorded albums with guitarist Wes Montgomery and owned his own Los Angeles supper club during the 1970s. Smith's last album, *Legacy*, was released posthumously and featured some of his greatest hits.

Soto, Jesús-Rafael, Venezuelan-born French artist (b. July 5, 1923, Ciudad Bolívar, Venez.—d. Jan. 17, 2005, Paris, France), attached himself to avant-garde modernism immediately after World War II and by the late 1960s had become known as a leader in optical and kinetic art, with works that were remarkable for their illusions of sensory vibrations. He lived in Caracas before immigrating in 1950 to Paris. There his works were shown in a number of groundbreaking exhibits, notably in 1955 as part of the group "Le Mouvement" show, which included works by Marcel Duchamp and Viktor Vasarely. Soto's experiments with the perception of movement led him to build much larger sculptural works that invited viewers to walk through, beginning with his *Pénétrables* series. He constructed enormous outdoor exhibits, some of which were public commissions. Soto exhibited widely in Europe, particularly from the mid-1960s to the mid-1970s. He remained active into the 21st century.

Spencer, John (JOHN SPESHOCK), American actor (b. Dec. 20, 1946, New York, N.Y.?—d. Dec. 16, 2005, Los Angeles, Calif.), was best remembered for his role as Leo McGarry on the hit television show *West Wing*, for which he won an Emmy Award in 2002. Spencer's television career began in the 1960s when he

had a recurring role on *The Patty Duke Show;* he later (1990–94) was a regular on *L.A. Law.* He also had supporting roles in films.

Spender, (John) Humphrey, British photojournalist and artist (b. April 19, 1910, London, Eng.—d. March 11, 2005, Ulting, Essex, Eng.), chronicled the everyday lives of working-class Britons during the 1930s and '40s in a series of candid, often surreptitiously taken, photographs for the Mass-Observation Project, the journals *Left Review* and *Picture Post*, and the *Daily Mirror*. Many of these photographs were later rediscovered and compiled in such books as *Worktown People: Photographs from Northern England, 1937–38* (1982) and *Lensman: Photographs, 1932–1952* (1987). During the 1930s he also traveled across Europe with his brother poet Stephen Spender, capturing photographs of Germany and other countries as well as of his brother's friends, including novelist Christopher Isherwood. In the 1950s Spender became a respected painter and textile designer.

Stang, Sister Dorothy, American missionary and activist (b. June 7, 1931, Dayton, Ohio—d. Feb. 12, 2005, Anapu, Pará state, Braz.), was a staunch champion of peasant farmers in the Amazon rainforest during her 22 years spent helping them to attain a sustainable living, but her advocacy was opposed by ranchers and loggers. Stang, who days before her death had met with Brazil's human rights secretary to plead for protection for the farmers, was the victim of a contract killing. Following her death, Pres. Luiz Inácio Lula da Silva created two vast Amazonian forest preserves and sent 2,000 troops to the troubled region.

Sternbach, Leo Henryk, American chemist (b. May 7, 1908, Abbazia, Austro-Hungarian Empire [now Opatija, Croatia]—d. Sept. 28, 2005, Chapel Hill, N.C.), developed a group of tranquilizing drugs known as benzodiazepines, which included Valium (diazepam), a popular sedative that became the most prescribed drug in the United States after its approval in 1963. Known as "mother's little helper," or simply as V, nearly 2.3 billion Valium pills were sold in 1978. During Sternbach's 60-year tenure with pharmaceutical company Hoffmann-La Roche, he was credited with some 241 patents, and in 1979 the American Institute of Chemists presented him with the Chemical Pioneer Award.

Stockdale, James Bond, vice admiral (ret.), U.S. Navy (b. Dec. 23, 1923, Abingdon, Ill.—d. July 5, 2005, Coronado, Calif.), received the Medal of Honor in 1976 for his bravery in the face of torture and imprisonment during the Vietnam War. He flew over 200 missions over Vietnam before he was shot down in 1965. He was imprisoned over seven years, during the first four of which he endured torture and isolation by drawing on lessons learned from his studies of ancient Greek philosophy. The navy cited his bravery as the primary cause of the North Vietnamese decision to abandon such tactics. After his release he remained in the navy and rose to the rank of vice admiral. In

1992 he was the running mate of Reform Party presidential candidate Ross Perot.

Stram, Hank (HENRY LOUIS STRAM), American football coach (b. Jan. 3, 1923, Chicago, Ill.—d. July 4, 2005, Covington, La.), steered the Kansas City Chiefs to three American

AP/Wide World Photos

Super Bowl star coach Hank Stram

Football League titles (1962 [when the franchise was in Texas], 1966, and 1969) and two Super Bowl appearances (1967 and 1970), the latter of which the Chiefs won. The colourful Stram introduced several innovations to the game, including the moving pocket and the two tight-end offense. Stram was elected into the Pro Football Hall of Fame in 2003.

Stretton, Ross, Australian dancer and artistic director (b. June 6, 1952, Canberra, Australia—d. June 16, 2005, Melbourne, Australia), began as a tap dancer but moved to ballet when he was 17, and in the 1970s and '80s—noted for his elegance and pure technique—he enjoyed performing careers with the Australian Ballet, the Joffrey Ballet, and American Ballet Theatre. In 1990 Stretton took on administrative duties, and he eventually served as artistic director of the Australian Ballet (1997–2001) and Britain's Royal Ballet (2001–02).

Struchkova, Raisa Stepanovna, Russian dancer and teacher (b. Oct. 5, 1925, Moscow, Russia, U.S.S.R.—d. May 2, 2005, Moscow, Russia), was noted for her brilliant, expressive technique in classical and dramatic ballets during her more than 30-year career with the Bolshoi Ballet. Especially in the West, she was also known for her virtuosity and athleticism in bravura pas de deux with her husband, Aleksandr Lapauri. In their most popular piece, *Moszkowski Waltz,* she followed exciting lifts and tosses with a run across the stage and a leap into his arms. Struchkova retired from performing in 1978 and became a ballet mistress and coach. In 1981–95 she served as editor in chief of *Soviet Ballet* (from 1992 *Ballet*) magazine.

Suárez Mason, Carlos Guillermo, Argentine general (b. Jan. 2, 1924, Buenos Aires, Arg.—d. June 21, 2005, Buenos Aires), ordered the execution of thousands of political opponents during the "Dirty War" of the 1970s. As part of the military junta that seized control of Argentina in 1976, Suárez Mason commanded the 1st Army Corps, which he used to brutally suppress dissent. An estimated 10,000–15,000 citizens were imprisoned, tortured, and eventually murdered. When civilians regained the government in 1983, Suárez Mason fled to the United States. He was extradited in 1988 and put on trial, but he and the rest of the regime were pardoned. In the 1990s he was found guilty of having stolen the babies born to the political prisoners of the Dirty War, and he was placed under house arrest. In 2004 his pardon was declared unconstitutional, and he was imprisoned.

Swindin, George Hedley, English association football (soccer) player (b. Dec. 4, 1914, Campsall, Yorkshire, Eng.—d. Oct. 26, 2005, Kettering, Northamptonshire, Eng.), manned the goal for Arsenal Football Club from 1936 to 1954, except for six years (1939–45) that he lost to military service during World War II. At Arsenal, Swindin was part of three first-division championships in three different decades (in 1938, 1948, and 1953). The 1947–48 championship season was perhaps his finest, as he allowed only 32 goals, a Football League record at the time. He was also in goal when Arsenal defeated Liverpool 2–0 in the 1950 Football Association Cup final. After his playing career ended, Swindin became a manager; included among his posts was a stint (1958–62) at the helm of Arsenal.

Tanaka, Atsuko, Japanese artist (b. Feb. 10, 1932, Osaka, Japan—d. Dec. 3, 2005, near Nara, Japan), was a leading avante-garde artist, best known for her experimental works of the 1950s and '60s. Tanaka was an early member of Gutai, a radical group of Osaka-based artists founded in 1954. Many of Tanaka's works involved electric light, the most famous of which, *Electric Dress* (1956), was made entirely of coloured light bulbs, cords, and fluorescent tubes that she wore as a dress during performances. She held her first solo exhibition in Osaka in 1963. The Museum of Modern Art in New York City featured some of Tanaka's works in a 1966 exhibition entitled "The New Japanese Painting and Sculpture." In later years she focused primarily on abstract paintings and drawings. Several retrospectives devoted to the work of Tanaka were held in Japan and the U.S. in the early 21st century.

Tange, Kenzo, Japanese architect and teacher (b. Sept. 4, 1913, Osaka, Japan—d. March 22, 2005, Tokyo, Japan), embodied the Japanese reverence for the past while embracing the future in such breathtaking structures as his sports stadiums—notably Yoyogi National Stadium—for the 1964 Tokyo Olympic Games. He was the first Japanese architect to gain an international reputation. As a student, he was inspired by the work of French architect Le Corbusier. In 1946 Tange became a professor of architecture at his alma mater, the Tokyo Imperial University (now the University of Tokyo). His first major commission was Peace Memorial Park at Hiroshima (completed 1955). This he followed with a number of administrative buildings in several Japanese cities. It was his Olympic stadiums, however, that won him the highest international acclaim. In awarding him the Pritzker Prize in 1987, the jury noted that his stadiums "are often described as among the most beautiful buildings of the 20th century." With each new commission, Tange sought to combine the timeless qualities of traditional Japanese architecture with the best of contemporary design. After the mid-1960s, he worked throughout the world—in China, Singapore, Australia, the Middle East, Italy, and the United States.

Taruc, Luis, Philippine freedom fighter and social reformer (b. June 21, 1913, San Luis, Phil.—d. May 4, 2005, Quezon City, Phil.), was the leader (1948–54) of the communist Huk movement, which began in 1942 as the Hukbalahap ("People's Anti-Japanese Army") and evolved in the late 1940s into the antigovernment Hukbong Magapayang Bayan ("People's Liberation Army"). Taruc and his Huk insurgents led an unsuccessful armed rebellion in the early 1950s. He surrendered to authorities in 1954 and was sentenced to 12 years' imprisonment for revolt and terrorism. After his release Taruc became active in the land-reform movement and served in the parliament.

Taube, Henry, Canadian-born American chemist (b. Nov. 30, 1915, Neudorf, Sask.—d. Nov. 16, 2005, Stanford, Calif.), revealed how electrons move between molecules during chemical reactions. For his insights in this area, he was awarded the Nobel Prize for Chemistry in 1983. Taube's studies focused on redox (reduction and oxidation) reactions of inorganic substances, such as metal compounds, dissolved in water. In experiments with isotopes, he determined that ions of metals in water form associations with a number of surrounding water molecules and that the transfer of electrons from one type of ion to another in a redox reaction requires an intermediate molecule to form a bridgelike pathway. His insight into chemical reactions led to such applications as improved selection of metallic compounds for use as catalysts and pigments. Taube received a Ph.D. (1940) in chemistry at the University of California, Berkeley. He taught chemistry at Cornell University (1941–46), Ithaca, N.Y., the University of Chicago (1946–61), and Stanford University (1961–86). Taube was a member of the National Academy of Sciences, and in addition to numerous awards in chemistry, he received (1977) a National Medal of Science.

Thaler, William John, American physicist (b. Dec. 4, 1925, Baltimore, Md.—d. June 5, 2005, Centreville, Va.), pioneered development of over-the-horizon radar for the U.S. Navy in the late 1950s. This innovation enabled early detection of Soviet ballistic missile launches and nuclear explosions up to 8,000 km (5,000 mi) away, far beyond the range of conventional radar systems. After leaving government service in 1960, Thaler became a physics professor at Georgetown University, Washington, D.C. From 1975 to 1978 he was chief scientist at the White House Office of Telecommunications Policy.

Thomas, Gerry (GERALD EHRMANN THOMAS), American marketer (b. Feb. 17, 1922, Seward, Neb.—d. July 18, 2005, Phoenix, Ariz.), while working for the C.A. Swanson & Sons frozen-food company, developed the TV dinner, utilizing multicompartment aluminum trays as a means of packaging the meals. The dinners were introduced in 1954, and 10 million were sold in their first year on the national market.

Thompson, Hunter Stockton, American  journalist and author (b. July 18, 1937, Louisville, Ky.—d. Feb. 20, 2005, Woody Creek, Colo.), blurred the line between reporting and storytelling with a signature brand of highly subjective writing that he dubbed gonzo journalism. Despite the fact that an armed robbery conviction prevented him from graduating from high school, Thompson never hesitated to use the title "doctor," in reference to a divinity degree that he purchased from a mail-order church. He began his journalism career as sports editor for a base newspaper while in the air force. Although his superior officers recognized his talent as a writer, they also saw that his rebellious streak was rubbing off on his readers, and he was honourably discharged. A series of freelance assignments followed, with Thompson spending a number of years in the Caribbean and South America. On his return to the U.S., he took an assignment that would result in the publication of his first book, *Hell's Angels* (1967). A 1970 article for *Scanlan's* magazine was intended to be a fairly straightforward treatment of a horse race. Instead, Thompson submitted "The Kentucky Derby Is Decadent and Depraved," a 7,000-word opus that signaled the birth of gonzo journalism. Two years later he followed with his best-known work, *Fear and Loathing in Las Vegas: A Savage Journey to the Heart of the American Dream* (1972)—a psychedelic travel diary set against the backdrop of a motorcycle race in the Nevada desert. Thompson's later works included *Fear and Loathing: On the Campaign Trail '72* (1973), *The Great Shark Hunt* (1979), *The Rum Diaries* (his sole novel, written in 1959 and published in 1998), and *Kingdom of Fear* (2003).

Thompson, Lucky (ELI THOMPSON), American jazz musician (b. June 16, 1924, Columbia, S.C.—d. July 30, 2005, Seattle, Wash.), played tenor saxophone solos in a romantic manner that expanded upon Ben Webster's swing era concepts of form and phrasing and

used the advanced harmonies and rhythms of bebop; he was among the major stylists of the bop era. Thompson grew up in Detroit and first became noted as a big-band soloist, most notably with Count Basie in 1945; based in Los Angeles from late 1945 to 1948 and thereafter in New York City, Thompson led his own groups and appeared on classic recordings by Charlie Parker and Thelonious Monk. Thompson reached his creative peak in mid-1950s recordings with Milt Jackson, the Miles Davis All-Stars, and his own groups, most notably with his quintet and innovative chamber jazz trio on the album *Tricrotism*. Thompson also performed in Dizzy Gillespie's 1954 big band, and he toured Europe and played baritone saxophone with Stan Kenton's band in 1956. By the 1960s Thompson had begun playing soprano saxophone, and his tenor sound became smoother and less emotionally expressive. In the mid-1960s he lived again in the U.S. but did not play music. His final creative period (1968–72) was spent mostly in Europe.

Thwaites, Michael Rayner, Australian poet and intelligence agent (b. May 30, 1915, Brisbane, Queen., Australia—d. Nov. 1, 2005, Canberra, Australia), served 21 years (1950–71) with the Australian Security and Intelligence Organisation (ASIO) and was instrumental in supervising the defection (1954) of Soviet spies Vladimir and Yevdokiya Petrov. During the 18-month period that Thwaites lived with the couple in a safe house, he served as a ghostwriter for their book *The Empire of Fear* (1956). He recounted his own version of the experience in *Truth Will Out: ASIO and the Petrovs* (1980). He penned several other important works, including the epic war poems "The Prophetic Hour" (1940) and "The Jervis Bay" (1942), the memoir *Atlantic Odyssey* (1999), and *Unfinished Journey* (2004), a volume of poems written between 1932 and 2004. Thwaites was made an Officer of the Order of Australia in 2002.

Tisch, Preston Robert, American financier and philanthropist (b. April 29, 1926, Brooklyn, N.Y.—d. Nov. 15, 2005, New York, N.Y.), owned, with his brother, the Loews Hotel chain and, with the Mara family, the New York Giants football team. In the 1970s Tisch opened the restaurant at his Regency Hotel to the civic and business leaders of New York City as they held breakfast meetings to work through the city's budget crisis; he christened these conferences "power breakfasts." He helped found Citymeals-on-Wheels in 1981 and was president of that charitable organization for 20 years. He also served (1986–88) as postmaster general of the U.S.

Todd, Ron(ald), British trade union leader (b. March 11, 1927, London, Eng.—d. April 30, 2005, Romford, Essex, Eng.), as the national organizer (1978–85) and general secretary (1985–92) of the Transport and General Workers' Union (TGWU) and chairman (1985–92) of the Trades Union Congress (TUC) International Committee, was a leading figure in the British labour union movement and the Labour Party during a period when union

membership and influence seriously declined. After his World War II military service, Todd worked as a gas fitter and autoworker until he became a full-time TGWU officer in 1962. A committed leftist, he clashed often with the antiunion government of Conservative Prime Minister Margaret Thatcher (1979–90) and with Labour leader Neil Kinnock, who he felt was abandoning the party's working-class socialist origins. Todd was also prominent in the international fights for nuclear disarmament and against apartheid in South Africa. After retiring in 1992, he published small volumes of poetry.

Toti, Andrew, American inventor (b. July 24, 1915, Visalia, Calif.—d. March 20, 2005, Modesto, Calif.), at age 16 developed the Mae West life vest, an innovation that prevented thousands of World War II pilots and sailors from drowning (including U.S. Pres. George H.W. Bush, who, as a Navy pilot, was shot down over the Pacific in 1944). The Mae West, named for the voluptuous American film idol, could be inflated either by blowing air into a tube or by pulling cords that filled the vest's two air chambers with carbon dioxide. During his career Toti patented more than 500 inventions, including the mechanical poultry feather plucker, a grape-harvesting machine for wine producers Ernest and Julio Gallo, pull tabs for beverage cans, lightweight construction beams, and various types of Venetian blinds. He also co-developed the EndoFlex endotracheal tube, a breathing apparatus used during surgery.

Tovar, Rigo (RIGOBERTO TOVAR GARCÍA),  Mexican singer (b. March 29, 1946, Matamoros, Mex.—d. March 27, 2005, Mexico City, Mex.), rose from poverty to achieve stardom not only in Mexico but in Latin America and the U.S. during a career in which he sold more than 25 million albums. He formed his band Costa Azul in 1972 and played a central role in popularizing Colombian *cumbia* music in Mexico by introducing synthesizers, electric guitars, and elements of rock and roll. Tovar and his band produced numerous hits, including "La sirenita" and "Matamoros querido." In later years he went solo, and in 1983 Tovar's free concert in Monterrey, Mex., attracted a record audience of more than 350,000 people. Tovar also starred in a handful of movies.

Trotman of Osmotherly, Alexander James Trotman, Baron, British business executive (b. July 22, 1933, Isleworth, Middlesex, Eng.—d. April 25, 2005, Yorkshire, Eng.), rose through the corporate ranks at Ford Motor Co. from his start as a management trainee in London in 1955 to become (1993) the giant automaker's first non-American chairman and CEO. During his tenure at the top, Trotman supervised the rebirth of the Mustang, oversaw the growing popularity of sport-utility vehicles, and directed a consolidation and restructuring plan that contributed to one of Ford's most prosperous periods. After stepping down in 1998, he returned to Britain, where he was chairman (2002–03) of Imperial Chemical Industries. Trotman was knighted in 1996 and was made a life peer in 1999.

Tucker, C. DeLores (CYNTHIA DELORES NOTTAGE), American political activist (b. Oct. 4, 1927, Philadelphia, Pa.—d. Oct. 12, 2005, Philadelphia), in the 1990s spearheaded a campaign against the foul language and misogyny found in the lyrics of gangsta-rap music. Tucker became politically active as a teenager. She marched in 1965 with the Rev. Martin Luther King, Jr., in Selma, Ala., and in 1984 she helped found the National Political Congress of Black Women. In her career Tucker held high-level positions with the Democratic Party, the National Women's Caucus, and the National Association for the Advancement of Colored People, and in the 1970s she served as secretary of the Commonwealth of Pennsylvania.

Turbay Ayala, Julio César, Colombian politician (b. June 18, 1916, Bogotá, Colom.—d. Sept. 13, 2005, Bogotá), served (1978–82) as

© H. John Maier Jr.—Time Life Pictures/Getty Images

Former Colombian president Julio Turbay

president of Colombia during a turbulent time. Turbay was the son of a Lebanese immigrant, and by the age of 21, he had become mayor of the town of Girardot. In 1943 he was first elected to the House of Representatives, as a member of the reformist wing of the Liberal Party. During the period known as La Violencia, Turbay's role in the Liberal Party became increasingly dominant, and in 1953 he was elected to the party's national executive. In 1957 he served as minister of energy and mines in the brief military junta, and thereafter he was a supporter of the National Front. Turbay was foreign minister in 1958–61, and he served in cabinets over the next several years. He was elected in 1962 to the first of five successive terms in the Senate. In 1978 Turbay was elected president in an extremely

close election. Within weeks, he introduced a security statute in an attempt to end Colombia's endemic violence; the measure severely limited personal freedoms and allowed civilians to be tried in courts martial. Turbay negotiated a peaceful end to a touchy international hostage situation in 1980.

Tyndall, John Hutchyns, British political activist (b. July 14, 1934, Exeter, Eng.—d. July 19, 2005, Hove, East Sussex, Eng.), was a leading figure throughout his life in Britain's far-right political fringe, notably as cofounder (1962) of the fascist British National Socialist Movement, as leader in the 1970s of the white supremacist National Front and editor of *Spearhead* magazine, and then as the founding head (1982–99) of the British National Party. On more than one occasion, Tyndall was arrested and fined or briefly jailed for inciting racial hatred. Although he was admired as a forceful speaker on behalf of the movement's right-wing goals, he was expelled twice (2002 and 2005) from the BNP for disruptive behaviour and for damaging the party's reputation.

Uppman, Theodor, American baritone (b. Jan. 12, 1920, San Jose, Calif.—d. March 17, 2005, New York, N.Y.), originated the title role of Benjamin Britten's opera *Billy Budd* at its premiere at Covent Garden, London, in 1951. Uppman enjoyed early success in opera, earning praise in 1948 for his performance as Pelléas in Claude Debussy's *Pelléas et Mélisande* in San Francisco. When his career stalled, he gave up singing and became a labourer for an oil company in California. The hard outdoor work gave him the muscular, tanned appearance he needed to win the part of the handsome sailor. His performance was widely praised, and he reprised the role for an NBC television broadcast.

Vandross, Luther Ronzoni, American singer, songwriter, and record producer (b. April 20,

R&B superstar Luther Vandross

Reuters/Corbis

1951, New York, N.Y.—d. July 1, 2005, Edison, N.J.), dominated the rhythm and blues charts in the 1980s with his smooth, romantic vocals and sold more than 25 million albums. Though he composed the song "Everybody Rejoice" for the hit musical *The Wiz* in 1972, his big break came in 1975 when he sang backup and did vocal arrangements for David Bowie's *Young Americans* album. Vandross was soon much in demand as an arranger and backup singer for Dionne Warwick, Bette Midler, Roberta Flack, Barbra Streisand, and Bowie. After several starts and stops, his solo career took off in 1981 with the release of *Never Too Much*. Other blockbuster hits included "Here and Now" (1989), "Power of Love/Love Power" (1991), and "Endless Love" (1994; duet with Mariah Carey). He won eight Grammy Awards in his career; the last came in 2004 for the song "Dance with My Father."

Vasconcellos, Josefina Alys Hermes de, British artist (b. Oct. 26, 1904, Molesey on Thames, Surrey, Eng.—d. July 20, 2005, Blackpool, Eng.), crafted bold life-size and larger naturalistic sculptures, often with religious themes. Vasconcellos, the daughter of a Brazilian diplomat and an English Quaker, studied art in London, Paris, and Florence and gained her first major commission at age 20. She married an artist and Anglican lay preacher in 1930, converted to his faith, and assimilated her newfound beliefs into her art. Vasconcellos produced her best-known piece, *Reunion* (1977)—a massive sculpture of a man and woman embracing across a piece of barbed wire—for Bradford University's department of peace studies. The work was later rededicated as *Reconciliation*, and in the 1990s casts of it were placed at peace-related sites in Hiroshima, Japan; Coventry, Eng.; Belfast, N.Ire; and Berlin. She was made MBE in 1985. *Josefina de Vasconcellos: Her Life and Art* was published in 2002.

Velthuijs, Max, Dutch children's author and illustrator (b. May 22, 1923, The Hague, Neth.—d. Jan. 25, 2005, The Hague), was best known for his series of Kikker ("Frog") books. In his "moral fables" Velthuijs used simple illustrations and childlike characters—notably the playful striped-shorts-wearing Frog and his friends Pig, Duck, and Hare—to introduce young children to such themes as friendship, loyalty, prejudice, fear, love, and death. Velthuijs trained in graphic art at the Academy of Visual Arts in Arnhem, Neth., and worked as a graphic designer in advertising and as an illustrator. His picture book *De jongen en de vis* (The Little Boy and the Big Fish) first appeared in 1969, but it was *Kikker is verliefd* (1989; *Frog in Love*) that drew international attention. Other popular Frog books included *Kikker in de kou* (1992; *Frog in Winter*) and *Kikker is bedroefd* (2003; *Frog Is Sad*). Velthuijs's books were translated into dozens of languages, and several stories were combined into a children's musical play, *Kikker* (English title, *Frog and His Friends*). In 2004 he was awarded the Hans Christian Andersen Award for Illustration.

Wang Daohan Chinese politician (b. March 27, 1915, Jiashan, Anhui province, China—d. Dec. 24, 2005, Shanghai, China), served as vice-mayor (1980–81) and mayor (1981–85) of Shanghai.. He continued to be an adviser to the Shanghai government after he was succeeded as mayor by Jiang Zemin, who later served as president of China. Named president of the mainland-based Association for Relations Across the Taiwan Straits (ARATS) in 1991, Wang held several talks with Koo Chenfu, chairman of the Taiwan-based Straits Exchange Foundation, in what were the first formal discussions between Beijing and Taipei since 1949. As president of ARATS, he also met in 2005 with visiting Taiwanese opposition leaders, Nationalist Party Chairman Lien Chan and People's First Party Chairman James Soong. Wang received an honorary Ph.D. (1985) in public administration from Tufts University, Medford, Mass.

Warrick, Ruth, American actress (b. June 29, 1916, St. Joseph, Mo.—d. Jan. 15, 2005, New York, N.Y.), had her best screen role in the first of her more than 30 films when she played the frosty first wife of newspaper magnate Charles Foster Kane in Orson Welles's *Citizen Kane* (1941). She later became better known as Phoebe Tyler Wallingford on the television daytime soap opera *All My Children*, a role she played from the show's debut in 1970 until nearly the end of her life.

Wasserman, Al(bert), American filmmaker (b. Feb. 9, 1921, Bronx, N.Y.—d. March 31, 2005, New York, N.Y.), produced award-winning television and film documentaries that examined topics ranging from civil rights to travel by rail. As a writer for *First Steps*, a documentary featuring disabled children undergoing physical therapy, Wasserman earned an Academy Award in 1947. From 1955 to 1960 he served as writer, director, and producer for *The Search*, a CBS-TV public-affairs series that demonstrated how research was conducted at universities. After co-producing (1960–67) the NBC *White Paper* series that examined numerous foreign-policy issues, Wasserman launched his own production company, which produced programs that included *A Look at the Light Side* (1969) and the film *The Making of the President 1972* (1973). Wasserman later returned to CBS as producer (1976–86) of the series *60 Minutes.*

Weber, Dick (RICHARD ANTHONY WEBER), American bowler (b. Dec. 23, 1929, Indianapolis, Ind.—d. Feb. 14, 2005, Florissant, Mo.), reigned, along with Don Carter and Earl Anthony, as one of the top three bowlers of the 20th century and captivated television audiences during the sport's heyday in the 1960s. A charter member (1959–92) of the Professional Bowlers Association (PBA),

Weber captured 26 titles, was named Bowler of the Year three times (1961, 1963, and 1965), and was crowned PBA Player of the Year in 1965. Beginning in 1955 he also played on the legendary Budweiser team (captained by Carter and including bowling greats Ray Bluth, Pat Patterson, and Billy Welu) that captured Bowling Proprietors' Association of America national titles in 1955–56, 1958–59, and 1961–62; Weber and Bluth also won four national doubles titles (1955, 1960–61, and 1964). The ambassador of bowling delighted late-night TV audiences, who watched Weber take aim at ketchup bottles, beer bottles, and lava lamps. In 1975 he became a charter member of the PBA Hall of Fame.

Weizman, Ezer, Israeli military officer and politician (b. June 15, 1924, Tel Aviv, British-mandated Palestine [now Tel Aviv, Israel]—d. April 24, 2005, Caesarea, Israel), evolved from a hawkish military leader—noted for his guidance of the Israeli Air Force (IAF) to victory in the Six-Day War (1967)—into a peace advocate who played a key role in Israel's historic 1979 treaty with Egypt. He also served as president of Israel (1993–2000). The nephew of Chaim Weizmann, Israel's first president, Weizman (who dropped the second "n" from his name) was a pilot with the British Royal Air Force during World War II. He later helped found the IAF and, as its commander (1958–66), transformed the IAF into a formidable force. He was named chief of military affairs in 1966 and the following year planned a preemptive strike against Arab forces that were preparing to attack Israel. The IAF's devastating air assault ensured Israel's victory and made Weizman a national hero. After leaving the military in 1969, he became a member of the Herut party, a forerunner of Likud, and engineered the Likud victory in 1977 that gave Menachem Begin the prime ministership. As minister of defense (1977–80), Weizman began to campaign for peace. His rapport with Egyptian Pres. Anwar el-Sadat eased the Israeli-Egyptian negotiations that culminated in the Camp David Accords (1978) and the first peace treaty between Israel and an Arab country. In the 1980s Weizman switched to the Labour Party and held several cabinet posts until 1990, when he was dismissed for unauthorized meetings with the Palestine Liberation Organization. Weizman, who was noted for his combative behaviour, was twice elected (1993, 1998) to the largely ceremonial post of president.

Westmoreland, William Childs, general (ret.), U.S. Army (b. March 26, 1914, Spartanburg county, S.C.—d. July 18, 2005, Charleston, S.C.), commanded U.S. forces in the Vietnam War from 1964 to 1968, a period during which American involvement increased from several thousand troops to more than 500,000. Westmoreland graduated (1936) from the U.S. Military Academy, West Point, N.Y., and his career was one of rapid advancement. During World War II he saw action as a battalion commander in North Africa and Sicily. Shortly after participating in the Normandy

D-Day landings in June 1944, he was promoted to colonel. He served in the Korean War and in 1955 was promoted to major general, becoming at age 42 the youngest man to have achieved that rank in the U.S. Army. Westmoreland became a full general in 1964. In Vietnam he implemented a strategy of attrition, using overwhelming firepower to try to kill enemy troops at a rate faster than they could be replaced. Senior officials in the Lyndon B. Johnson administration and a growing number of ordinary citizens began to see the war as unwinnable, and Westmoreland was recalled to Washington and given the post of army chief of staff. He retired in 1972.

Wexler, Sy (SIMON WEXLER), American filmmaker (b. Oct. 6, 1916, New York, N.Y.—d. March 10, 2005, Los Angeles, Calif.), produced more than 300 training, educational, and documentary films for students and physicians during the 1950s and '60s. While serving as a cameraman in the Army Signal Corps during World War II, Wexler worked with director Frank Capra on the documentary series *Why We Fight* and *Know Your Enemy*. Following the war he and Bob Churchill established Churchill/Wexler Film Productions, which produced classroom films that illustrated complex biological processes such as animal cognition in *Squeak the Squirrel* (1957) and protein metabolism in *How a Hamburger Turns into You;* sensitive topics, such as sex education, were also presented. After launching his own company in 1961, Wexler produced award-winning medical-training films for physicians and professionals in the pharmaceutical and medical-equipment industries.

White, Thelma (THELMA WOLPA), American actress (b. Dec. 4, 1910, Lincoln, Neb.—d. Jan. 11, 2005, Los Angeles, Calif.), appeared in more than 40 movies and was primarily a musical and comedy performer. She was best remembered for her role in the docudrama *Reefer Madness* (1936), which became a cult classic in the 1970s because of the unintentional hilarity of the way-over-the-top exaggeration of its propaganda against marijuana.

Whiteley, (John) Richard, British television personality (b. Dec. 28, 1943, Bradford, West Yorkshire, Eng.—d. June 26, 2005, Leeds, Eng.), delighted children and adults alike with his genial nature, groan-inducing puns, and hundreds of often garish neckties as the host of *Countdown*, a daily afternoon quiz show that gained cult status almost from its inception in 1982 as the first program broadcast on the then-new Channel 4. Whiteley was made OBE in 2004.

Whitley, Chris (CHRISTOPHER BECKER WHITLEY), American singer-songwriter (b. Aug. 31, 1960, Houston, Texas—d. Nov. 20, 2005, Houston), experimented with a wide variety of musical genres (from blues and folk to grunge and electronica) but arrived at his own distinctive, often hybridized version of each, winning praise from critics and musicians who included Bob Dylan but often frustrating

Singer-songwriter Chris Whitley

expectations. Following the much-praised *Living with the Law* (1991) and two other major label releases, Whitley recorded for small labels that allowed him to pursue his increasingly dark eclectic muse.

Wiesenthal, Simon, Austrian Nazi-hunter and activist (b. Dec. 31, 1908, Buczacz, Austria-Hungary [now Buchach, Ukraine]—d. Sept. 20, 2005, Vienna, Austria), after having survived imprisonment during the Holocaust, relentlessly pursued Nazi war criminals; he helped to locate and bring to justice more than 1,100 fugitives, most notably Adolf Eichmann, who was considered the main architect of the Holocaust. Wiesenthal graduated from the Technical University of Prague in 1932 and later moved to Lwow, Pol. (now Lviv, Ukraine), where he worked as an architect. After Germany occupied Lwow in 1941, he was sent to a series of labour and concentration camps, barely escaping death before being liberated in 1945 from Mauthausen, outside Linz, Austria. He then began collecting evidence on war criminals and in 1947 cofounded a documentation centre in Linz. Although the centre closed in 1954, Wiesenthal continued his work, and in 1960 he helped track down Eichmann (who was arrested in Argentina and smuggled to Israel for trial and eventual execution). The following year Wiesenthal founded the Jewish Documentation Centre in Vienna, and he served as its director until 2003. Among the other fugitives he was credited with locating were Fritz Stangl, the commandant of the Treblinka and Sobibor concentration camps, and Hermine Braunsteiner, a guard at several camps. Often called the "conscience of the Holocaust," Wiesenthal also spoke out against anti-Semitism and genocide and wrote books on his experiences. He received numerous accolades, including the French Legion of Honour (1986), the U.S. Presidential Medal of Freedom (2000), and an honourary British knighthood (2004). The Simon Wiesenthal Center, an international organization dedicated to the Holocaust, was established in 1977 in Los Angeles.

Wilson, August (FREDERICK AUGUST KITTEL), American playwright (b. April 27, 1945, Pittsburgh, Pa.—d. Oct. 2, 2005, Seattle, Wash.), chronicled the African American experience with a cycle of 10 plays, one set in each decade of the 20th century. Compared by critics to both Eugene O'Neill and Arthur Miller, Wilson used a variety of styles in his work, incorporating music, evocative language, and rich characterization to capture the atmosphere of his childhood neighbourhood in Pittsburgh's Hill District. His first major play, *Ma Rainey's Black Bottom* (1984), was praised for its portrayal of racism in the 1920s blues scene. The only one of Wilson's plays to be set outside the Hill District (it takes place in Chicago), it marked the beginning of his collaboration with Lloyd Richards, whose 1959 production of *Raisin in the Sun* was the first Broadway play to have been directed by an African American. Richards went on to direct Wilson's next five plays, and the two reestablished the once-common system of debuting plays at regional theatres and refining them prior to their Broadway openings. Wilson's father-and-son drama *Fences* (1986) swept the Tony Awards, winning in every major category. It ran for more than 500 performances, with James Earl Jones in the lead role, and established Wilson as a major Broadway force. He went on to receive a record seven New York Drama Critics' Circle

Playwright August Wilson

Awards and seven additional Tony Award nominations for best play. He earned Pulitzer Prizes for *Fences* and *The Piano Lesson* (1990), the story of a Depression-era family's attempts to exorcise the ghosts (both literal and figurative) of slavery. Wilson's other plays included *Jitney* (1982), *Joe Turner's Come and Gone* (1988), *Two Trains Running* (1992), *Seven Guitars* (1996), *King Hedley II* (1999), and *Gem of the Ocean* (2003). In 1999 he received a National Humanities Medal for his work and for his commitment to the promotion of black theatre. His final play, *Radio Golf*, opened in May 2005 and concluded the cycle with the tale, set in 1997, of the gentrification of the Hill District.

Winchell, Paul (PAUL WILCHIN), American ventriloquist and voice-over artist (b. Dec. 21, 1922, New York, N.Y.—d. June 24, 2005, Moorpark, Calif.), was a familiar presence on television in the 1950s and '60s, appearing first with his wisecracking dummy Jerry

Mahoney and later adding the dim-witted puppet Knucklehead Smiff to his act. Beginning in 1968, however, he gained additional renown as the voice of characters in film and television animations, especially Tigger in Winnie-the-Pooh cartoons, which he voiced until 1999. Winchell also achieved notable success as an inventor, with some 30 patents to his credit.

Wise, Robert Earl, American producer and director (b. Sept. 10, 1914, Winchester, Ind.—d. Sept. 14, 2005, Los Angeles, Calif.), directed films for some 56 years during which he was noted for his mastery of a number of genres in order to be true to a movie's material. For each of two of his biggest successes—*West Side Story* (1961) and *The Sound of Music* (1965)—he was rewarded with two Academy Awards, as director and as producer of the best picture. Because of the Depression, Wise had to leave college in 1933, so he moved to Hollywood and gained employment in the RKO movie studio, first as a messenger and eventually as a film editor. His work attracted the attention of Orson Welles, who hired him to edit *Citizen Kane* (1941). Wise's brilliant cutting of that film led Welles to use him the following year for *The Magnificent Ambersons*. Controversy arose, however, when the studio forced Wise to shoot new scenes and make cuts that Welles felt ruined the film. Wise next was asked to take over the direction of *The Curse of the Cat People* (1944). It became a cult classic, and Wise received a promotion to director. Among the best known of his films over the following decades were *The Body Snatcher* (1945), *The Day the Earth Stood Still* (1951), *I Want to Live!* (1958), *The Haunting* (1963), *The Sand Pebbles* (1966), and *The Andromeda Strain* (1971).

Wolf, Henry, Austrian-born American graphic designer and photographer (b. May 23, 1925, Vienna, Austria—d. Feb. 14, 2005, New York, N.Y.), influenced and energized magazine design during the 1950s and '60s with his bold layouts, elegant typography, and whimsical cover photographs while serving as art director at *Esquire, Harper's Bazaar,* and *Show* magazines. Wolf opened his own photography studio, Henry Wolf Productions, in 1971. In 1976 Wolf was awarded the American Institute of Graphic Arts Medal for Lifetime Achievement, and in 1980 he was inducted into the Art Directors Club Hall of Fame.

Woods, Rose Mary, American personality (b. Dec. 26, 1917, Sebring, Ohio—d. Jan. 22, 2005, Alliance, Ohio), served as personal secretary for Richard M. Nixon from 1951, when he entered the U.S. Senate, until some time after he resigned the presidency in 1974 because of the Watergate scandal. She achieved notoriety when it was discovered that an 18½-minute segment of one of the White House tapes she was transcribing had been mysteriously erased; she claimed that the erasure had to have been accidental, although a photograph of her re-creation of the event showed how unlikely that explanation was.

Wray, Link (FREDERICK LINCOLN WRAY), American guitarist (b. May 2, 1929, Dunn,

AP/Wide World Photos

Punk pioneer Link Wray

N.C.—d. Nov. 5, 2005, Copenhagen, Den.), pioneered the use of feedback and fuzz-tone techniques and invented the power chord—a harsh sound created by playing fifths (two notes, five tones apart)—which became the lynchpin of heavy metal and punk music. Among his admirers were Neil Young, Bob Dylan, Pete Townshend, Jeff Beck, the Kinks, and Jimi Hendrix. Wray's most famous recording, the raucous instrumental "Rumble," became a huge hit in 1958 even though many radio stations refused to play it because they believed that it incited gang violence. After serving in the army in the Korean War, Wray in 1953 bought a guitar and joined a band that included his brothers Vernon and Doug. He focused on instrumental music after his left lung was removed (1956) because of tuberculosis, which severely limited his singing. "Rumble" came about when his group, Lucky Wray and the Palomino Ranch Hands, improvised a "stroll" tune by featuring the guitar, which squealed feedback when a microphone was placed in front of Wray's amplifier. The resulting hit record was aided in the studio by the fuzz tone created when Wray punctured his amplifier with a pencil. As Link Wray and the Wraymen, the group scored big instrumental hits again with "Rawhide" (1959) and "Jack the Ripper" (1963). His music was featured in such film sound tracks as *Pulp Fiction* (1994).

Wright, Sir Edward Maitland, British mathematician (b. Feb. 13, 1906, Farnley, near Leeds, Eng.—d. Feb. 2, 2005, Reading, Berkshire, Eng.), was coauthor, with Godfrey H. Hardy, of the widely used textbook *An Introduction to the Theory of Numbers* (1938) and principal and vice-chancellor (1962–76) of the University of Aberdeen, Scot. After studying mathematics on his own while teaching school, Wright obtained a scholarship in 1926 to Jesus College, Oxford, where he studied under Hardy. Wright taught at Christ Church, Oxford, spent a year at the University of Göttingen, Ger., and taught at King's College, London, before taking up a professorship in 1935 at Aberdeen. He became vice-principal in

1961, was later appointed principal and vice-chancellor, and retired from the university in 1983. Wright's research focused on analytic number theory and graph theory.

Wright, Robert Craig, American lyricist and composer (b. Sept. 25, 1914, Daytona Beach, Fla.—d. July 27, 2005, Miami, Fla.), collaborated with George ("Chet") Forrest for more than 70 years—frequently adapting classical composers' music—to create some 2,000 songs featured in 16 stage musicals, 18 revues, and 58 movies, as well as a number of cabaret acts. Among their best-known musicals were *Song of Norway* (1944), the Tony Award-winning *Kismet* (1953), and *Grand Hotel* (1989).

Wright, (Muriel) Teresa, American actress (b. Oct. 27, 1918, New York, N.Y.—d. March 6, 2005, New Haven, Conn.), had the distinction of being the only actress to receive an Academy Award nomination for each of her first three films—*The Little Foxes* (1941), *The Pride of the Yankees* (1942), and *Mrs. Miniver* (1942), for which she was awarded the best supporting actress Oscar. Other notable films included *Shadow of a Doubt* (1943), *The Best Years of Our Lives* (1946), and *The Men* (1950).

Wriston, Walter Bigelow, American banker (b. Aug. 3, 1919, Middletown, Conn.—d. Jan. 19, 2005, New York, N.Y.), as head of the banking company now known as Citigroup, transformed the American banking industry through a series of innovations in financing and technology. Wriston began his career at what was then the National City Bank of New York in 1946 as an inspector in the controller's office. By 1960 he had become executive vice president of (since a 1955 merger) the First National City Bank of New York. The following year he introduced negotiable certificates of deposit to offer a higher interest rate to corporations. Wriston became president of the bank in 1967, the same year the bank became the largest one in New York. The following year he reorganized the company into five organizations under a holding company, an innovation that allowed it to engage in an array of financial services forbidden to banks. In 1970 Wriston became chairman of the bank (renamed Citibank in 1976) and the holding company (named Citicorp in 1974). He engaged in aggressive international expansion and diversification; one revolutionary innovation was the introduction of the automated teller machine (ATM). Wriston retired in 1984 and was awarded the Presidential Medal of Freedom in 2004.

Xue Muqiao, Chinese economist (b. Oct. 25, 1904, Wuxi, Jiangsu province, China—d. July 22, 2005, China), introduced economic reforms that pushed China toward a market-driven economy. He was imprisoned in 1927 for his activism on behalf of the Communist Party, and during his three years behind bars, he started studying economics and philosophy. Following the communist victory in 1949, Xue held several positions in the government, including head of the state statistical bureau. He was again incarcerated during the Cultural

Revolution (1966–76). Xue returned to government service in 1976 and as an ally of Deng Xiaoping, provided the underlying economic policy that led to China's market reforms of the 1980s. His book *Research into Problems in China's Socialist Economy*, first published in 1979, was regarded as a classic.

Yakovlev, Aleksandr Nikolayevich, Soviet Russian historian and government adviser (b. Dec. 2, 1923, Korolyovo, Yaroslavl oblast, Russia, U.S.S.R. [now in Russia]—d. Oct. 18, 2005, Moscow, Russia), was an important ally of Soviet Pres. Mikhail Gorbachev and a principal architect of glasnost ("openness") and perestroika ("rebuilding"), the sweeping reforms associated with Gorbachev's name. Yakovlev fought in World War II and was partially disabled. He joined the Communist Party of the Soviet Union (CPSU) in 1944, spent a year (1958–59) on a scholarly exchange program at Columbia University, New York City, and received a doctorate in history from the CPSU Academy of Social Sciences (1960). He climbed steadily in the CPSU hierarchy, working for several years (1965–73) in the party propaganda department. He served as ambassador to Canada (1973–83) before being invited back to Moscow by Gorbachev, who admired his ideas. For a Soviet apparatchik, Yakovlev was unusually outspoken, and his views did not always square with those of the top Soviet leadership.

Yao Wenyuan, Chinese propaganda official (b. 1931, Zhuji, Zhejiang province, China—d. Dec. 23, 2005, Shanghai, China?), was the last surviving member of the Gang of Four, a radical communist group that gained great political power during the Cultural Revolution (1966–76) and helped implement many of the revolution's harsh policies. Other members of the group were Wang Hongwen, Zhang Chunqiao, and Mao Zedong's third wife, Jiang Qing. Yao, a journalist, became a member of the group after he wrote a famous attack of a play by Wu Han, *Hai Jui Dismissed from Office*, in 1965. The article, which launched a fierce debate among the Chinese elite over who supported Mao and who opposed him, was said to mark the beginning of the Cultural Revolution. Yao served as the group's propagandist. After Mao's death in 1976, he was arrested, and he was eventually sentenced to 20 years in prison. Released in 1996, he returned to Shanghai, where he was reportedly working on his memoirs at the time of his death. China's official news agency did not specify where he died.

Yard, Molly (MARY ALEXANDER), American political activist (b. July 6, 1912, Shanghai, China—d. Sept. 21, 2005, Pittsburgh, Pa.), served as president of the National Organization of Women from 1987 to 1991. Though she was 75 years old when she took office, the combative and tireless Yard nearly doubled membership in the organization, substantially increased its funding, and spearheaded a successful campaign to oppose the nomination of Robert Bork to associate justice of the Supreme Court of the United States. A lifelong

Feminist Molly Yard
© Wally McNamee/Corbis

activist for liberal causes, she campaigned for passage of the Equal Rights Amendment, protection of abortion rights, and gay rights.

Yi Ku, Korean royal (b. Dec. 29, 1931, Tokyo, Japan—d. July 16, 2005, Tokyo) was heir to the throne of Korea though he was born in exile and spent most of his life in Japan. The Yi family ruled Korea for more than 500 years, but Japan ended its dynasty in 1910. Yi's father, Crown Prince Yongchin, was taken to Japan and forced to marry a member of the Japanese royal family. Yi was raised and educated in Japan and the United States, and he spoke very little Korean. He was not allowed to live in Korea until 1963. After a business failure he returned to Tokyo in 1977.

Yoshizawa, Akira, Japanese artist (b. March 14, 1911, Kaminokawa, Tochigi prefecture, Japan—March 14, 2005, Ogikubo, Japan), revived the ancient Japanese craft of origami, or paper folding, and inspired an international interest in the art. Yoshizawa used his geometric skills, precise technique, and fine design concepts to create sensational dragons, birds, and elephants from a single sheet of paper. He eschewed the traditional technique of cutting, which rendered flat creations, and invented "wet folding," the dampening of paper to mold into sculptural forms. Yoshizawa also developed a system of notation (directions for folding), still widely cited in origami primers. He gained wide renown in the 1950s and later served as a cultural ambassador for Japan. Yoshizawa was the recipient in 1983 of Japan's Order of the Rising Sun.

Zaki, Ahmed ("THE BLACK TIGER"), Egyptian motion picture actor (b. Nov. 18, 1949, Zaqaziq, Egypt—d. March 27, 2005, Cairo, Egypt), broke the unspoken colour barrier in Egyptian cinema as the first dark-skinned actor to play leading roles. Zaki was best known for his portrayals of

historical figures, notably former presidents Gamal Adbel Nasser and Anwar el-Sadat, Modernist writer Taha Hussein, and—in his last, unfinished, film—singer 'Abd al-Halim Hafiz.

Zhang Bairen, Chinese Roman Catholic cleric (b. Feb. 14, 1915, Zhangjiatai, Hubei province, China—d. Oct. 12, 2005, Beijing, China), was an influential leader of the Catholic community in China. Not formally recognized by Chinese authorities, he served as "unofficial" bishop of Hanyang diocese from 1986 until his death. Zhang was ordained in 1942. He refused to renounce his loyalty to the pope following the communist takeover of 1949 and spent nearly a quarter of a century, from 1955 to 1979, in labour camps. In later years Zhang was credited with helping to improve relations between the government-controlled Catholic Patriotic Association (CPA) and the unofficial church.

Zhang Chunqiao, Chinese government official (b. 1917, Juye, China—d. April 21, 2005, Shanghai, China), played a leading role in the Cultural Revolution (1966–76), which cost thousands of lives and forced millions into hardship and poverty. Zhang joined the Communist Party in the 1930s and worked as a journalist and propagandist in Shanghai. When Communist Party Chairman Mao Zedong called for a new class struggle in order to stave off opposition to his failed policies, Zhang quickly moved to the front of the Cultural Revolution, forming an alliance with Mao's wife, Jiang Qing, to produce propaganda and to initiate polemics against party leaders and intellectuals across China. Qing and Zhang enjoyed unprecedented power during this period, and as the revolution began to wind down, they launched new attacks on senior party members, notably Deng Xiaoping, in hopes of positioning themselves to succeed Mao. Their plan failed, and a month after Mao's death in September 1976, Zhang, Qing, and two others (Wang Hongwen and Yao Wenyuan) were arrested for treason. As defendants, they were known as the Gang of Four, and their trial was the most famous in the nation's history. In 1981 Zhang was found guilty and sentenced to death. His sentence was later commuted to life imprisonment, but he was released (1998) for health reasons.

Zhao Ziyang, Chinese politician (b. Oct. 17, 1919, Henan province, China—d. Jan. 17, 2005, Beijing, China), rose to prominence as an economic reformer and served as premier of China (1980–87) and general secretary of the Communist Party of China (1987–89). A political centrist, he split from extremist party leaders who sought to suppress pro-democracy demonstrations forcibly in the spring of 1989. Zhao's dramatic conciliatory visit to student protesters in Tiananmen Square shortly before the crackdown was his last appearance in public. He was dismissed from the government and placed under house arrest until his death. Zhao became active in the Communist Party in the 1940s even though his father, a prosperous landlord, was killed during the period of Communist reforms. A leader of Guangdong

province from 1965, Zhao was purged during the Cultural Revolution. He reemerged to take a leadership role in 1975 in populous Sichuan province, where he boosted agricultural production with his market reforms. Chinese leader Deng Xiaoping drew Zhao into the ranks of Communist Party leadership, where he was able to extend his reform plans to the

AP/Wide World Photos

Economic reformer Zhao Ziyang

entire country, halt price controls, allow foreign investment, and provide labour incentives. His extensive reforms were met with resistance from Communist hard-liners, who by mid-1989 had taken firm control.

Zhvania, Zurab, Georgian politician (b. Dec. 9, 1963, Tbilisi, Georgian S.S.R., U.S.S.R.—d. Feb. 3, 2005, Tbilisi, Georgia), was a reform-minded prime minister of Georgia. Zhvania studied biology at Tbilisi State University, graduating in 1985, but left a promising scientific career to found (1988) and lead a political party, the Georgian Greens. He was elected to the parliament in 1992, where he advanced quickly and became a protégé of then president Eduard Shevardnadze. Zhvania was elected speaker of the parliament in 1995. Distressed by the stagnation and corruption of the Shevardnadze administration, however, Zhvania left the government in 2001 and founded another party, the United Democrats. Seen as a liberal moderating influence in politics, Zhvania became prime minister in the shuffle that followed Shevardnadze's departure from office in 2004. He reportedly died from accidental carbon monoxide poisoning from a faulty space heater.

Zuleta, Emiliano, Colombian folk musician (b. Jan. 11, 1912, La Jagua del Pilar, Colom.—d. Oct. 30, 2005, Valledupar, Colom.), was the acknowledged king of the *vallenato*, a song form that originated in Zuleta's native Caribbean coast region of Colombia and became wildly popular throughout the country in the mid-20th century. He began playing the accordion as a boy and soon was leading bands and composing satiric songs and improvising performances in the *vallenato* style. Zuleta's fame began spreading to other Hispanic communities in the 1990s when international performers such as Julio Iglesias and Gloria Estefan began covering his material.

Events of 2005

Jewish settlers resist evacuation from Kfar Darom, Gaza Strip, by barricading themselves on the roof of a synagogue.

Agriculture and Food Supplies

The continued spread of BIRD FLU raised global concerns. Some BANS on beef imposed because of BSE were relaxed. Food EMERGENCIES severely affected several countries in Africa, and G-8 countries agreed to LARGE INCREASES in development aid.

AGRICULTURAL PRODUCTION AND AID

Food Production. World agricultural markets in 2005 reflected crop supplies in 2004 and 2005. The world production of grain in the 2004–05 crop year was 2,036,940,000 metric tons, which was a gain of 9.6% over the previous year and represented increases in the production of wheat, rice, and coarse grain (corn, barley, oats, sorghum, rye, millet, and mixed grains). The rise in wheat production was the result of larger harvests in China, the European Union, India, Russia, and Ukraine, which offset smaller harvests in Australia and the United States. Rice production increased in China, Pakistan, South Korea, and the United States, and coarse-grain production rose in the U.S., Argentina, China, the EU, and Ukraine. For the 2005–06 crop year, world grain production was forecast to fall 3%, with decreases in both global wheat and coarse-grain production but a slight increase in rice production. As a result of these trends, prices for wheat were stable and prices for other grains fell.

World oilseed, oilmeal, and vegetable oil production also increased. For the 2004–05 crop year, world oilseed production rose 13.4% to 379,050,000 metric tons, and most regions experienced increases. Production for 2005–06 was expected to rise 2.1%, with reduced U.S. soybean harvests more than offset by gains in South America.

Food Aid. Despite abundant global food supplies, food shortages remained in many areas, even within countries that generally had adequate supplies. In India about 20% of the population was undernourished, and the figure in China was estimated to be about 10%. Several African states faced food emergencies. Niger experienced its worst food crisis since 1985, with about 3.6 million persons threatened with famine because of inadequate rainfall, locust infestation, and restrictions on the importation of rice and wheat. Malawi, which was hurt by drought, produced only 37% of the food it needed, and five million persons were estimated to be at risk. Zambia had a poor harvest because its rains came only during a brief period, and farming in Zimbabwe continued to be hurt by poor weather, land reform, and political and economic strife. Food shortages also existed in North Korea, Ethiopia, and Eritrea.

In addition to the ongoing food aid and related assistance provided through the UN World Food Programme and individual national programs, the issue of development aid was addressed by food-donor countries at the 2005 Group of Eight (G-8) Summit in Gleneagles, Scot. The G-8 countries agreed to expand development aid by $50 billion worldwide by 2010, with $25 billion earmarked for Africa.

Rice, which was the staple food in many less-developed countries, was the focus of genetic research to increase its nutritional value. Some researchers were working with "golden rice," a strain developed to contain beta-carotene, which the human body converts into vitamin A. In 2005 a new strain of "golden rice" that contained much higher levels of beta-carotene than earlier strains was announced, and its use was seen as a potential way of overcoming vitamin-A deficiency in the diets of many children in less-developed countries. In a breakthrough that was expected to speed the development of new strains of rice, geneticists in 2005 published the complete mapping of the genetic sequence of the rice genome. (*See* LIFE SCIENCES: *Botany.*)

Animal Diseases. In 2005 outbreaks of avian influenza (bird flu) continued to appear in several East and Southeast Asian countries, including Cambodia, China, Indonesia, Thailand, and Vietnam, and spread into a number of other countries, including Russia, Turkey, and Romania. Hundreds of millions of birds, including chickens and ducks, had died from the disease or were destroyed to control it. The outbreaks, which had begun in 2003, were caused by a highly pathogenic virus strain called H5N1. The virus was also transmissible to humans who came in contact with infected birds. By the end of 2005, about 140 persons had been infected with the virus and about one-half of them, including many children, had died. Fears concerning the disease led to a decrease in the consumption of poultry meat, though cooking had been found to destroy the virus. A major concern was that the virus might mutate into a form that could be readily transmitted from human to human, which could trigger a deadly flu pandemic, and many countries and nongovernmental organizations were making contingency plans for response to such a crisis. (*See* WORLD AFFAIRS: *Vietnam:* Sidebar.)

Trade bans that had been imposed by many countries on Canadian and American beef because of concerns over bovine spongiform encephalopathy (BSE, or mad cow disease) continued to affect meat and livestock markets. Trade had been halted in 2003 after BSE was found in a cow in Canada and in a cow in the United States. A few countries, such as Chile and the Philippines, reopened their markets to some North American beef products in 2005. After lengthy negotiations the U.S. and Japan, a major importer before its 2003 ban, resolved disagreements concerning the safety of American beef. In December the U.S. government announced that the Japanese would again be buying and made a call for other beef importers also to reopen their markets. A complicating factor in the resumption of North American beef exports was the appearance of new cases of BSE. Canada reported two cases in January, and in June the U.S. reported one case in Texas. Early in the year the U.S. had agreed to relax its ban on Canadian livestock by allowing imports of cattle under 30 months of age effective March 7, but a federal injunction delayed the action until July.

In October there was an outbreak of foot-and-mouth disease in the Brazilian

Ancient Grains

In June 2005 scientists in Israel announced that they had grown the oldest-ever plant, using the 2,000-year-old seed of a long-extinct Judean palm tree, in the hope of studying its reputed medicinal properties. The project reflected growing interest in plant species outside mainstream agriculture that were gaining recognition for their powerful nutritional benefits, importance to a balanced diet, and role in maintaining biodiversity. In the forefront were so-called ancient grains, many with venerable histories stretching back to long-lost civilizations, that had fallen into obscurity but were now making a comeback among Western consumers who were health conscious and eager for exotic new tastes.

Amaranth, extolled as an elixir by the Aztecs, showed up in European and North American cereals, breads, and crackers, and quinoa, a staple of the Inca Empire, emerged as an increasingly popular rice or potato replacement in salads and casseroles or as a side dish. Both ancient grains packed more protein than wheat, and amaranth and teff, an ancient grain from Ethiopia, were touted as gluten-free wheat substitutes for those with wheat allergies.

New U.S. health guidelines issued in January 2005 recommending three daily servings of whole grains did not hurt demand for heirloom grains. Food manufacturers used spelt and kamut, ancient relatives of wheat originating in the Middle East and North Africa, respectively, and millet, first cultivated thousands of years ago in Africa, in whole grain cereals and baked goods.

The rediscovery of these grains by Western consumers was only part of the story, however. They were also championed in interna-

© Bettmann/Corbis

An illustration from the Florentine Codex, *a 16th-century account of Aztec life, shows a man threshing amaranth. Like other nutritious ancient grains, amaranth was finding new popularity in both developed and less-developed countries.*

tional development efforts. A series of reports from the U.S. National Academy of Sciences begun in the mid-1970s and including *Lost Crops of Africa, Volume I: Grains* (1996) identified and recommended underused crops, especially amaranth and sorghum, appropriate for developing economies. According to the UN Food and Agriculture Organization (FAO), some 840 million people still remained undernourished worldwide, and underutilized crops, including ancient grains, were identified as a key weapon in banishing hunger.

Quinoa and millet grow in harsh conditions, and these and other grains are rich in micronutrients (vitamins and minerals) that are typically missing in diets over-reliant on staples such as rice, wheat, and corn (maize), which constitute 60% of worldwide calorie consumption. The FAO estimated that three-quarters of the genetic diversity of agricultural crops was lost during the past century. Moreover, a report published in February 2005 by the University of California found crop gene banks that were conserving seeds to be in a parlous state, suffering underfunding and neglect. Gene banks had proved vital in reconstructing agriculture in Iraq and Afghanistan as well as areas in Asia affected by the 2004 tsunami. In October 2004 the Global Crop Diversity Trust, a UN-backed fund dedicated to providing stable funding for maintaining crop diversity collections worldwide, was launched. The importance of preserving agricultural biodiversity, the University of California report noted, was underscored by recent threats to staples in the U.S., where an epidemic of fusarium head blight had damaged wheat and barley yields and a soybean rust outbreak had affected soybean harvests.

(STEPHEN PHILIPS)

state of Mato Grosso do Sul. As a result, cattle that showed signs of infection were destroyed, and trade restrictions on Brazilian beef were imposed. Brazil had been one of the world's leading exporters of beef. Some countries refused imports from Brazil completely, but others banned only beef from the regions where the disease had been found.

AGRICULTURAL POLICY

Trade Disputes. There were numerous trade disputes during the year. In 1998 the United States and Canada had won the right from the World Trade Organization (WTO) to impose sanctions on the European Union for its ban on hormone-treated beef. In 2005 the EU claimed that it was in compliance with the WTO ruling, and it challenged the

U.S. and Canadian sanctions before a WTO panel. Among other disputes, Canada and the United States argued over trade in wheat, corn (maize), and hogs. The U.S. had imposed countervailing duties on wheat and hogs, but the wheat duties were partially overturned by administrators of the North American Free Trade Agreement, and the duties imposed on hogs were abolished. Canada moved to impose duties on American corn because of U.S. agricultural policies. In 2005 the U.S. changed the way it set fees for its export credit guarantee program after the WTO's ruling in a case in which Brazil had challenged export programs for U.S. cotton. EU policy rules for trade in sugar had been an irritant in global markets. The WTO ruled that subsidized sugar exports by the EU exceeded

the allowed limits. The EU proposed to reduce the amount of subsidized sugar exported by simplifying production quotas and reducing price guarantees 39% by 2009. Preferential access to the European market for former European colonies would also be reduced. Other decisions made by the WTO included a ruling against Mexican duties on high-fructose corn syrup and a ruling against the latest efforts by the EU to rectify its banana-import policies, against which the WTO had originally ruled in 1997 after Latin American countries and the United States filed a complaint.

Doha Development Round. The Doha Development Round of trade talks under the auspices of the WTO struggled to make headway. During the first half of 2005, there was little progress made over the major issues under negotiation—

market access, export subsidies, and domestic price support. The Cairns Group of nonsubsidizing exporters and the G-20 group of less-developed nations pressured the U.S., the EU, and Japan for concessions on policies concerning agricultural commodities. In September the U.S. proposed large reductions in U.S. agricultural supports if the Europeans and Japanese would also make bold reforms. The U.S. proposal went beyond what the Japanese could agree to, and the EU countered with a less-ambitious proposal, which triggered a negative response from France. At the December meeting of the WTO in Hong Kong, the Doha Development Round was kept moving with the goal of negotiating additional trade liberalization by April 30, 2006. Developed countries made an agreement to end export subsidies by 2013, which laid the basis for resolving complaints by West African nations that had limited progress in the negotiations. The agreement also called for imports of virtually all goods exported by the least-developed countries to be duty free by 2008. (PHILIP L. PAARLBERG)

FISHERIES

Figures published by the UN Food and Agriculture Organization indicated that in 2003, the latest year for which figures were available, the total production for the world's capture fisheries decreased by 3.09% to 90,219,746 metric tons from the 2002 figure of 93,003,701 metric tons. Marine capture fisheries recorded a 3.69% decrease of 2,997,988 metric tons to a total of 81,277,992 metric tons, while freshwater capture fisheries recorded a 2.39% increase of 214,033 metric tons to 8,941,754 metric tons. Total world production from aquaculture increased by 2,514,570 metric tons during 2003 to reach 42,304,141 metric tons. As a result, the world supply of fish showed an overall decrease of only 465,338 metric tons from the 2002 figure to the 2003 total of 132,523,887 metric tons.

The overall drop of 2.99 million metric tons in the total marine capture fisheries production during 2003 was accounted for by a 3.5-million-metric-ton fall in the anchoveta (Peruvian anchovy) catch, which also resulted in a 43.97% decrease in the total catch recorded for Peru. Following a 25.66% increase in the anchoveta catch in 2002, this subsequent decrease in 2003 confirmed the immense variability in biomass from year to year that always affected Peru's fisheries. (For Catch Trends for the Top

Five Caught Fish Species, 1994–2003, *see* GRAPH.) The effect of this variability was mirrored in the corresponding production trends for Peru and Chile, which were reliant on the anchoveta as their main catch. (For Production Trends for the Top 10 Catching Nations, 1994–2003, *see* GRAPH.)

China continued as the world's leading fishing nation and recorded a small 1.21% increase in total catch to reach 16,775,653 metric tons in 2003. This figure was more than 10 million metric tons greater than its nearest rival but paled against China's massive capability from aquaculture, which in 2003 produced 28,892,005 metric tons. Although Peru remained in second position among catching nations, the 8.9% catch increase the country recorded in 2002

was followed by a decrease of 43.97% to 6,089,660 metric tons in 2003; this reversal was due entirely to the drop in the anchoveta catch. The only change in position within the top 10 producing nations was India's rise into sixth position, which resulted from the reduction in Chile's anchoveta catch.

Among the major species of fish caught during 2003, anchoveta remained the leading species, with 6,202,447 metric tons landed, a 56.43% decline from 2002. Two other species among the top 10 caught showed decreases, while 7 recorded increases in the tonnage landed. Capelin (a pelagic species, like anchoveta) dropped out of the top 10, from 4th position in 2002 to 11th in 2003, with a 72.52% decrease to 1,148,106 metric tons. (MARTIN J. GILL)

Production Trends for the Top 10 Catching Nations, 1994–2003
(in metric tons)

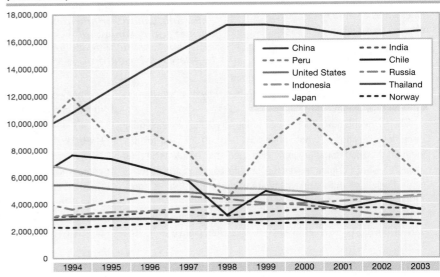

Catch Trends for the Top Five Caught Fish Species, 1994–2003
(in metric tons)

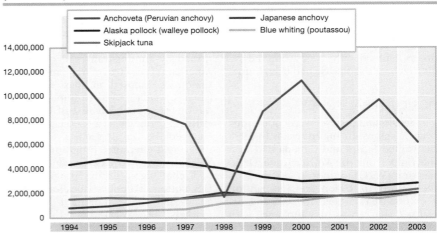

Anthropology and Archaeology

Scientists identified the first CHIMPANZEE FOSSILS and completed detailed studies of the human X CHROMOSOME. The status of a LOWER ELWHA KLALLAM ancestral village and burial grounds remained in dispute. Archaeologists discovered the OLDEST-KNOWN fishing BOAT, MUSICAL INSTRUMENT, POTTERY, and inscribed HEBREW ALPHABET.

ANTHROPOLOGY

Key developments in 2005 in the area of physical anthropology included the dating of the oldest-known fossil members of *Homo sapiens*, the first reported chimpanzee fossils, surprising findings about gene expression associated with the X chromosome, and intriguing genetic insights pertaining to the evolution of the human brain.

The Omo I and Omo II specimens, *H. sapiens* fossils from the Kibish Formation in southern Ethiopia, were originally thought to be approximately 130,000 years old, but they were re-dated with argon-isotope measurements on feldspar crystals from volcanic deposits located slightly below the fossil levels. The new preferred estimate of the age of the specimens was between 190,000 and 200,000 years, which made them the earliest well-dated members of *H. sapiens*. Prior to this redating, the oldest reported human fossils were three crania (*H. sapiens idaltu* from the Bouri Formation in the Afar depression of Ethiopia) that were argon-isotope dated to between 154,000 and 160,000 years ago. The new date for the Omo specimens was in striking agreement with many recently determined mitochondrial DNA-based dates that indicated that the origin of *H. sapiens* was approximately 200,000 years ago.

Although thousands of hominin (hominid) fossils had been reported over the last 150 years, not a single chimpanzee (*Pan*) fossil had been documented. A 2005 report described three fossil chimpanzee teeth (two upper central incisors and an upper first molar) that were found in the Kapthurin Formation, Kenya, and demonstrated that chimpanzees were present in the East African Rift Valley contemporaneously with an extinct species of *Homo*. A fourth fossil tooth (possibly an aberrant upper third molar) was also found but was not described. Argon-isotope dating bracketed the age of the specimens to between approximately 284,000 and 545,000 years old; however, stratigraphic positioning implied a date closer to the maximum age of 545,000 years. The upper incisors were nearly identical to those of modern *Pan* except that they had shorter roots. Both the extremely low crown of the upper first molar and the pronounced thinness of its enamel distinguished the tooth from those of known hominins. The three teeth probably came from one individual that died at the age of seven or eight years. The remains of the

The two fossil femur pieces (with years of discovery) are from Omo I, a Homo sapiens *specimen.*

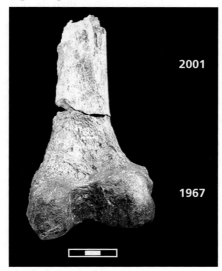

2001

1967

John Fleagle, Stony Brook University via
The New York Times

fossil chimpanzee were about 600 km (about 375 mi) east of the limit of the current range of *Pan*, which made it possible that chimpanzees and hominins were sympatric (lived in the same area) since the time of their evolutionary divergence.

An international consortium of genome centres succeeded in determining almost all of the DNA sequence of the human X chromosome and documented the extent to which the human Y chromosome had decayed in its nonrecombining regions. The X chromosome contained 1,098 genes, but exons (expressed gene regions) accounted for only 1.7% of the X-chromosome sequence. Only 54 of these genes had functional homologues (similar counterparts) on the human Y chromosome. Perhaps the most unexpected finding regarding the human X chromosome was the extensive variability in X-linked gene expression in human females. In most female mammals one of the two X chromosomes becomes randomly inactivated early in development. Since males have only one X chromosome, this inactivation results in a comparable level of gene expression for X-linked genes in females and males. Some of the genes, however, escape inactivation and are expressed from both the inactive and the active X chromosomes of a female. A comprehensive gene-expression profile for a sample of inactivated X chromosomes found that about 15% of X-linked genes regularly escape inactivation to some degree. Surprisingly, an additional 10% of X-linked genes yielded variable patterns of inactivation and are thus expressed differently in different females. These differences in gene expression might help explain both sex-specific phenotypes and variations in phenotypes between females.

Two genes that regulate brain size were shown to have undergone positive selection in human populations during the last 40,000 years. Six genetic loci were known that could lead to primary microcephaly (an abnormally small brain) as the result of recessive mutations. One of these gene loci, *microcephalin* (*MCPHI*), was thought to control the proliferation or differentiation (or both) of immature nerve cells in the formation of nervous tissue. A haplotype (haploid genotype) with a derived allele was found to have a much higher frequency than other haplotypes at this locus. Numerous statistical tests demonstrated that this haplotype was under strong positive selection. Frequencies of the favoured haplotype were found to be highest in Eurasia and the Americas and lowest in Africa. Additional calculations estimated the age of the haplotype to be approximately 37,000 years, a date that coincided with the arrival of modern humans in Europe and with the increased presence of art and symbolism that was characteristic of the Upper Paleolithic culture. The second gene locus, *abnormal spindle-like microcephaly associated* (*ASPM*), might regulate the proliferation or differentiation (or both) of neural stem cells during brain development by mediating spindle assembly during cell division. One haplotype at this locus had an unusually high frequency and differed from other haplotypes at a number of polymorphic sites, two of which were in a region that had previously exhibited particularly strong positive selection in humans. The favoured haplotype had noticeably higher frequencies in Europeans and Middle Easterners than in other populations. Additional statistical tests confirmed the indications of positive natural selection for the derived haplotype and estimated its age at approximately 5,800 years. The age and geographic distribution of this haplotype across Eurasia roughly coincided with important cultural innovations such as the domestication of plants and animals (approximately 10,000 years ago) and the development of cities and written language (5,000–6,000 years ago). As intriguing as these biocultural correlates were, their significance had not yet been established.

(STEPHEN L. ZEGURA)

ARCHAEOLOGY

Eastern Hemisphere. In 2005 the conflict in Iraq continued to take its toll on cultural treasures in the cradle of civilization, particularly at the 5,000-year-old Sumerian sites of Umma and Isin. In April the upper part of the 52-m (171-ft) 9th-century spiral minaret of Malwiya at Samarra was damaged by a mortar attack. The ongoing pillage of archaeological sites, primarily in the southern provinces, continued at an alarming rate, but few of the antiquities had yet surfaced on the international art market.

A devastating earthquake in Iran on Dec. 26, 2003, which precipitated the collapse of the massive mud-brick citadel Arg-e-Bam, proved fruitful for archaeology by revealing layers of civilization long buried by later construction. Among the finds reported in 2005 were a series of settlements and relics that dated from the time of the citadel's founding, in the Achaemenid period (6th–4th century BC), through the Islamic period and that elucidated the chronology of the inhabitation of the fortified city of Bam, the largest mud-brick construction in the world. Also in Iran, construction of the Sivand Dam threatened numerous archaeological sites, including Paleolithic rock shelters, rock-cut tombs from the Elamite period (c. 2700–c. 650 BC), and the well-known tomb at Pasargadae of Cyrus the Great (590/580–c. 529 BC).

Continued excavations at the 23,000-year-old campsite of Ohalo II on the shore of the Sea of Galilee in Israel yielded evidence for the processing of wild wheat and wild barley 10,000 years before the domestication of either grain. Dolores Piperno of the Smithsonian Institution and colleagues reported that starches and seed remains from the grains were found embedded in a grinding stone at the site. What was believed to be the earliest-known rendering of the Hebrew alphabet—22 letters carved in the correct sequence some 3,000 years ago on a 17-kg (38-lb) stone—was found by Ron Tappy of the Pittsburgh Theological Seminary and colleagues at Tel Zayit, a site in the Beth Guvrin Valley not far from Jerusalem.

Elsewhere in the Near East, excavations continued at Tell Sabi Abyad in Syria, where what was believed to be the oldest pottery in the world was found. Dated to between 6800 and 6300 BC, some two centuries earlier than the previous record holders, the dozens of rough, reddish-brown earthen water pots, jars, and jugs were simple in shape and had been made without the use of a potter's wheel, according to Peter Akkermans of the National Museum of Antiquities in Leiden, Neth., and colleagues.

In Niger, deep in the Sahara, archaeologist Elena Garcea of the University of Cassino, Italy, and her team unearthed seven Stone Age settlements, including a large cemetery, on an ancient lakeshore. Thought to have been occupied between 10,000 and 5,000 years ago—before the once-verdant landscape dried up following the last Ice Age—the sites contained abundant stone tools, personal adornments, pottery fragments, and the remains of mollusks and catfish.

The remains of a 3,250-year-old glass factory, including a glass ingot and hundreds of ceramic crucibles, were found at the ancient Egyptian capital Qantir-Piramesses in the eastern Nile delta. The find attested to ancient Egypt's role as a major producer of glass ingots. Prior to this discovery, made by Thilo Rehren of University College London and Edgar Pusch of the Pelizaeus-Museum in Hildesheim, Ger., scholars believed that the primary source for glass well into the middle of the 1st millennium BC was Mesopotamia, where glassmaking was thought to have begun around 1600 BC. Zahi Hawass of Egypt's Supreme Council of Antiquities and an international team of radiologists, pathologists, and anatomists completed a comprehensive CT scan of the mummy of King Tutankhamen (who ruled 1333–23 BC). Hawass stated that contrary to what had been previously thought, there was no evidence that King Tut had been murdered. Although

A flute made from a wooly mammoth tusk was discovered in a cave in Germany and dated to 35,000 years ago. Two views of the flute are shown.

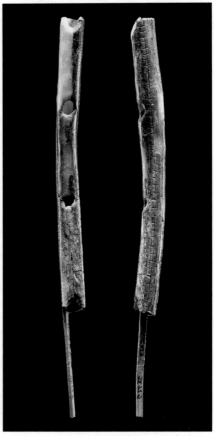

At an archaeological site in northwestern China, ancient noodles lie on a mound of sediment, at left, that scientists discovered when they lifted the bowl at right, which had been overturned. The noodles were dated to 4,000 years ago.

Tut was only 19 when he died, the team found no evidence of either a blow to the back of the head, which many believed to have been the cause of his demise, or any disease. The researchers noted that he may have broken his left femur shortly before his death but that the injury would not have been enough to kill him.

In the mountains of Swabia in southwestern Germany, archaeologist Nicholas J. Conard and co-workers from Tübingen (Ger.) University unearthed what was believed to be the world's oldest musical instruments, a 35,000-year-old flute fashioned out of a wooly mammoth tusk and two smaller flutes made of swan bones. The Ice Age instruments were found in a cave in the Ach Valley. In Hohle Fels Cave, also in the Ach Valley, the same team discovered what was considered to be one of the earliest-known representations of male genitalia, dated to 28,000 years ago. The researchers stated that the polished life-sized stone phallus had markings that indicated that it had been used to knap (split) flints. Also in Germany, archaeologists found a female counterpart to the Adonis of Zschernitz, an 8,200-year-old clay statuette, discovered in 2003, that was the earliest-known Neolithic male figurine.

Excavations in Ireland and England conducted ahead of construction projects led to more than a dozen discoveries. John Kavanagh and co-workers from the National Museum of Ireland who carried out excavations at a site

where construction was planned north of Dublin unearthed a 9th-century Viking burial of a 25–35-year-old woman who had been interred wearing a tweed garment with a bone comb and a gilded-copper brooch of Scandinavian origin. In eastern England archaeologists working ahead of the construction of a housing development at Colchester, Essex, the first Roman capital of ancient Britain, found the remains of a chariot racing track from the 2nd century AD and a well-preserved tiled bathhouse chamber. Also in England, a scrap of gold foil found in a Norfolk garden was identified as a Roman *lamella*, or magical charm, of which only a few dozen had ever been found. The charm bore an inscription that beseeches the protection of the Near Eastern god Abraxas for a soldier from the Rhineland.

What were identified as the oldest-known noodles were found in an earthen bowl at the 4,000-year-old site of Lajia on the Huang Ho (Yellow River) in China. The noodles, discovered by Maolin Ye of the Chinese Academy of Social Sciences and analyzed by Houyuan Lu of the Chinese Academy of Sciences and colleagues, were 50 cm (20 in) long and had been made with two strains of millet.

Excavators from the Kimhae (S.Kor.) National Museum found in South Kyongsang province what they purported to be the oldest fishing boat in the world. The remains of the boat were 3 m (10 ft) long and 0.6 m (2 ft)

wide and dated to around 6000 BC. The boat, which was made of pine, was believed to have been originally at least 4 m long. (ANGELA M.H. SCHUSTER)

Western Hemisphere. In New Orleans archaeologists were asked to investigate a site in the French Quarter that was slated for new construction. Accounts of the investigation in early 2005 indicated that the site was originally a French colonial garden and later possibly the location of a Spanish colonial residence. A guest house or hotel stood on the property from about 1808 until 1822, when it burned down. Excavations on the site yielded fragments of earthenware thought to be French cosmetic jars known as faience rouge pots. An 1821 newspaper advertisement for the building at the site suggested that it served primarily men, so perhaps the rouge was used by employees or prostitutes at the hotel. Experts were divided as to whether the establishment might have been a brothel. The advertisement gave the name of the building as the Rising Sun Hotel, which raised speculation that it might have been the subject of a folk song that begins "There is a house in New Orleans / they call the Rising Sun" and was later popularized by a number of musicians.

Between 5,000 and 3,500 years ago, people of what is known as the McKean complex inhabited a wide area of the Great Plains of North America. Excavations on a 4,000-year-old residential site near Parker, Colo., revealed six pithouses, which were identified from basinlike stains in the soil. The excavators believed that the partially subterranean houses, which contained hearths and storage areas, might once have been covered with hide or brush. Numerous bison-bone tools for cutting or scraping were found in the settlement. It was the first McKean-style hunting settlement found in Colorado; most were known from Wyoming.

The Chumash Indians of the Santa Barbara Channel region of southern California were expert mariners who regularly crossed open water in their *tomols*—canoes built of planks of driftwood sewn together. Archaeologist Terry Jones and linguist Kathryn Klar argued that the similarity between the Chumash word *tomol* and the term used by Polynesians for the wood with which they built sewn-plank canoes was evidence that the Chumash had acquired planked-canoe technology from visiting Polynesians by about AD 800. Polynesians were known to have colonized Hawaii and other islands in the Pacific Ocean by that time. The theory was highly controversial, since there were no traces of Polynesian artifacts along the California coast, and many archaeologists remained convinced that the Chumash developed their own distinctive canoe technology hundreds, if not thousands, of years ago to cross to the Channel Islands close offshore.

Waka', an important Maya centre located about 60 km (37 mi) west of Tikal in northern Guatemala, was founded as early as 500 BC and reached its peak development between AD 400 and 800. Some of the more than 650 monumental structures at the site formed a palace compound, which also served as a royal burial place. In 2005 Canadian archaeologist David Lee, a member of an international team of archaeologists that was studying and conserving the site, uncovered a royal burial chamber that contained the remains of a queen or other female ruler surrounded by 2,400 artifacts. The vaulted chamber had been built between AD 650 and 750 inside the shell of an existing building. The body had been richly adorned with greenstone artifacts, shell ornaments, and obsidian. A series of greenstone plaques formed a war helmet of a type associated with supreme Maya warlords, and a carved royal jade might have been part of the headdress. On the pelvis were laid stingray spines

traditionally used in royal bloodletting rites, which were believed to relate to the rituals that Maya lords used to communicate with the spiritual world.

A major controversy surrounded a construction site at Port Angeles, Wash. The Washington Department of Transportation had acquired the site to fabricate concrete pontoons to be used in rebuilding parts of a floating bridge across the Hood Canal. Soon after the work on the construction site began in August 2003,

The carved jade, believed to have been part of a headdress, was found in a newly uncovered tomb of a female Maya ruler.

David Lee/Waka Archaeology Project

bulldozers brought to light wooden hut posts, charcoal pits, and thick piles of mollusk shells. When scores of human bones were unearthed a short time later, work came to a halt. The excavations had revealed a site known as Tse-whit-zen, an ancestral village of the 850-member Lower Elwha Klallam tribe. After long negotiations with the tribe, the state resumed construction

on a limited basis in 2004 while tribal members and archaeologists investigated the site. By the end of the year, the remains of more than 300 individuals had been unearthed together with many thousands of artifacts, and the state discontinued the construction project. Archaeological evidence indicated that the area had been inhabited as long as 2,700 years ago and that it had been continuously occupied from 1,700 until about 200 years ago. In 2005 the tribe and the state attempted to work out a solution concerning where the excavated human remains would be reburied and what would be done with the site and with the large amount of material that had been transported from the site to landfill.

Caral is a complex of pyramids, plazas, and staircases in the arid Supe River valley about 115 mi (185 km) north of Lima. The site had been largely overlooked until Peruvian archaeologist Ruth Shady began investigating it in the mid-1990s. Caral, which covered 67 ha (165 ac), was radiocarbon-dated to 2627 BC, which made the city contemporary with the Pyramids of Giza in Egypt and the first cities in Mesopotamia. Among the finds presented in 2005 was an artifact that consisted of a series of knotted cords of different colours and resembled the quipu that were used several millennia later by the Inca as an apparatus for record keeping. The pyramids at Caral, some standing as high as 21 m (70 ft), were built up as terraces reinforced by grass bags packed with boulders. The circular plazas nearby were performance spaces, with acoustics that amplified the sound of the condor-bone and pelican-bone flutes found in the excavations. The city had had as many as 3,000 inhabitants, who lived on anchovies, shellfish, and sardines. Caral lay in the middle of a hierarchy of smaller population centres and presided over important trade networks that handled such commodities as fish meal and cotton. More than 18 sites were known from the Supe Valley region. Aspero, another pyramid complex, lay 32 km (20 mi) to the west on the shores of the Pacific Ocean and was dated to as early as 3022 BC. Site surveys in neighbouring valleys revealed at least seven previously unknown Caral-era sites. Caral flourished for about 1,000 years before it was abandoned, perhaps in the face of competition with inhabitants of the nearby Casma Valley, but the reasons for its abandonment were still a mystery. (BRIAN FAGAN)

Architecture and Civil Engineering

ART MUSEUMS designed by JACQUES HERZOG, PIERRE DE MEURON, RENZO PIANO, and others opened in several major cities. A fifth building by the late LOUIS KAHN won the AIA 25-Year Award. The ARCHITECTURAL HERITAGE of Louisiana and Mississippi was severely damaged by HURRICANE KATRINA.

ARCHITECTURE

The year 2005 in architecture was the year of the art museum. Celebrated architects worldwide were building new museums or adding new wings to existing art museums. Donors, both public and private, seemed eager to lavish money on such projects, and architects sometimes felt that art museums—like cathedrals in the Middle Ages—offered the best opportunity for truly daring and original design. Many of the art museums were heralded as new cultural symbols of their respective cities. According to one architectural-magazine headline, "Museum design is . . . architecture's only venue for artistic growth."

The new de Young Museum building in San Francisco, which opened in October, was designed by Swiss architects Jacques Herzog and Pierre de Meuron. A distinctive feature was the structure's outer surface, which consisted of copper shingles with different textures—some smooth, some rough. Over time the copper would oxidize into a variety of greens and earth tones, which would have the effect of making the building fade into its surrounding landscape of Golden Gate Park. Most of the museum was only two stories high, but it had a tower with an observatory where visitors could enjoy a view of the park, the city, and the ocean beyond. (*See* photograph on page 213.)

Herzog and de Meuron were also the architects of a major addition to the Walker Art Center in Minneapolis, Minn. The architects made few changes to the original museum building, which was designed in 1971 by American designer Edward Larrabee Barnes, but the wing they added was larger than the old building.

The Swiss firm Herzog and de Meuron renovated and expanded Edward Larrabee Barnes's 1971 Walker Art Center in Minneapolis, Minn., shown here behind the sculpture garden.

AP/Wide World Photos

For the exterior of the building, Herzog and de Meuron—known for inventing new kinds of "skin" for their buildings—used mesh panels of aluminum that had a slightly wrinkled surface and resembled crumpled aluminum foil. The silvery panels reflected sunlight in many directions, and from the outside the new Walker wing resembled a large gift-wrapped box of no particular shape.

The leading designer of art museums was Italian architect Renzo Piano. (*See* BIOGRAPHIES.) Piano created the Paul Klee Centre in Bern, Switz., for displaying the artwork of Klee, a Modernist painter. The building, which opened in June, had the appearance of three airplane hangers that sat side by side with their curved roofs forming a continuous wave shape. (*See* photograph on page 152.) Famed especially for his skill in handling light, Piano displayed Klee's small and delicate works beneath flat canopies of translucent cloth, which softened the illumination into a warm glow. Piano's additions to the High Museum in Atlanta also opened in 2005. They more than doubled the size of the original museum, which was designed by American architect Richard Meier. As in his celebrated Nasher Sculpture Center in Dallas, Piano created a roof of cone-shaped light scoops that allowed only indirect northern light, not direct sunlight, into the galleries. The design Piano made for an addition to the Whitney Museum in New York City had been criticized for requiring the demolition of a historic brownstone, but a revised design he made, which saved the house, was approved by the city's Landmarks Preservation Commission in May.

Another remarkable museum that opened during the year was the Yad Vashem Holocaust History Museum, which was designed by Israeli American architect Moshe Safdie on a site near Jerusalem. The basic structure of the reinforced-concrete building was essentially a hollow

Renzo Piano's Paul Klee Centre in Bern, Switz., housed some 4,000 of the Swiss artist's works and served also as a locus for activities in music, theatre, dance, and literature.

prism about 180 m (590 ft) long. The building tunneled beneath the top of a mountain from one side to the other, and at one end visitors emerged onto a lookout platform with a spectacular view of the city.

Awards. The winner of the 2005 Pritzker Prize, architecture's most coveted award, was American Thom Mayne. (*See* BIOGRAPHIES.) Mayne had been known as an outsider who ignored fashions in architecture and designed buildings that were often rough, aggressive assemblages of concrete, steel, and glass. Among the best known were the Diamond Ranch High School and the Caltrans District 7 Headquarters, both in California, and the Wayne Lyman Morse United States Courthouse in Oregon, which was under construction. The meaning of the name of Mayne's firm, Morphosis, was "the way in which an organism develops or changes."

Antoine Predock received the 2006 Gold Medal of the American Institute of Architects. Predock, who worked out of Albuquerque, N.M., spoke of deriving his architecture by "listening to the land." He was best known as an architect of the American Southwest, where his buildings seemed to grow naturally out of the open desert—its wide spaces, its long history, and its natural materials.

The AIA's 25-Year Award, for a building that had stood the test of time, was given to the Yale Center for British Art. It was the fifth building by the late Louis Kahn, an Estonian-born American architect, to win the award. The AIA also named 13 buildings for its annual honour awards. Among the better known were the Seattle Central Library, a joint venture by Dutch architect Rem

Koolhaas's firm, OMA, and Seattle-based LMN Architects, and the Jubilee Church in Rome by Meier.

The 2006 Royal Gold Medal of the Royal Institute of British Architects went to Tokyo architect Toyo Ito, best known for such works as the Sendai (Japan) Mediatheque. The Mediatheque was a kind of enormous cybercafe that exhibited all forms of media to inform the public and to support the arts.

Notable Buildings. Perhaps the most widely publicized work of architecture of the year was not a building but the Memorial to the Murdered Jews of Europe. The basic design, by American architect Peter Eisenman and American sculptor Richard Serra (who later dropped out of the project), was selected from an international competition. Situated on a prominent site across from the Tiergarten, Berlin's central park, the memorial consisted of a field of 2,711 solid blocks of dark concrete that reached up to 4.7 m (15 ft) in height. Visitors wandered among the blocks, which were separated by narrow lanes. The intent was to create a feeling of being lost or trapped and also to promote contemplation. An underground information centre, located beneath the memorial, told the story of the Holocaust. (*See* photograph on page 401.)

Also notable was the new Scottish Parliament building in Edinburgh. The architect was Spanish architect Enric Miralles, who won the international design competition for the building but died before the building was completed. Easily the year's most controversial work of architecture, it won its designers the Stirling Prize as the best building built in Britain in 2005 but

also attracted many negative comments, partly because its cost ballooned from an early estimate of £40 million (about $67 million) to a final figure about 11 times greater. Rather than a single structure, the building was a villagelike cluster of parts. It was intended to blend into the city rather than to have a single assertive or dominating presence. Many of its architectural details were playfully inventive, and the interior spaces were oddly shaped and felt highly theatrical.

A third major architectural work of 2005 was the Central Building designed by Zaha Hadid for the automobile manufacturer BMW in Leipzig, Ger. Iraqi-born Hadid, whose practice was based in London, was known for designing structures with jagged, explosive shapes or sweeping curves. The BMW building contained its Leipzig plant's main office and laboratory space. Conveyors snaked around overhead and carried partially built cars from one manufacturing area of the plant to another. By keeping the company's product always visible to the management, the design merged the white-collar and blue-collar functions of the plant and gave office workers the drama of the production line.

Other notable buildings included the Clinton Presidential Center (Little Rock, Ark.), a riverfront structure that was shaped and constructed like a bridge and designed by the New York City architectural firm Polshek Partnership; the Casa da Música (Porto, Port.), which was designed by Koolhaas as a performance venue for all types of music; and the Barajas Airport (Madrid), which was designed by British architect Richard Rogers and featured a vast concourse beneath a sensuously undulating roof.

Parks and Public Spaces. The site of the former New York City World Trade Center, destroyed in the terrorist attacks of Sept. 11, 2001, continued to be a source of confusion and disagreement. During the year two proposed museums for the site, the International Freedom Center and the Drawing Center, were both canceled. The design for the Freedom Tower, a 541-m (1,776-ft) office building designed by American architect David Childs of the firm SOM, underwent modifications to make it less vulnerable to car-bomb attacks. It was moved farther back from the street, and the lower 60 m (200 ft) of the facade would be made of solid concrete with a few small windows. The concrete was to be wrapped, said Childs, in a "shimmering metal curtain that will give the impression of movement and light." The design was widely criticized by architects and others. At the World Trade Center site, only two elements seemed fairly certain to go forward. They were the transit hub by Calatrava and a memorial to 9/11 by Israeli architect Michael Arad and American landscape architect Peter Walker, winners of a 2004 design competition.

The Casa da Música in Porto, Port., by Rem Koolhaas housed a performance hall, rehearsal space, and recording studios for the Porto National Orchestra.

Also in New York City, the so-called High Line, an abandoned overhead rail line in Manhattan, was the subject of a design competition to convert it into an aerial park. The winning design, by Field Operations and Diller Scofidio + Renfro, featured wood plank pathways that cut through a diverse array of plant life. It was hoped that new or existing buildings would eventually open onto the park at the height of their second floor.

Hurricane Katrina. The extensive destruction of buildings in Louisiana and Mississippi by Hurricane Katrina raised concerns about the adequacy of hurricane-protection measures and also sparked a debate about architecture. (*See* ECONOMIC AFFAIRS: *Special Report.*) The U.S. National Trust for Historic Preservation estimated that as many as 38,000 historic structures in New Orleans alone had been affected in some way by the storm. Many of them were beyond saving. There was disagreement over what should be built in the damaged areas of New Orleans and other places. Members of the Congress for the New Urbanism, an influential organization that advocated traditional architecture and town planning, quickly met with the governor and other officials of Mississippi and promoted guidelines that would re-create the architectural styles of the past. Some architects, however, felt that the disaster should be taken as an opportunity to explore contemporary designs. There was also the question of whether rebuilding would be handled by government contracts to a few big developers or carried out in a slower, piecemeal manner. At year's end there was no answer in sight.

Deaths. Two of the most influential architects of the 20th century, both Pritzker winners, died in 2005. Philip Johnson passed away in January at the age of 98. (*See* OBITUARIES.) Johnson was a mercurial figure who during his career tried many styles of design that always seemed to stay a step ahead of changing fashions. He was noted for having been one of the first to introduce the modern movement of architecture to the United States—in a 1932 exhibition and book, *The International Style.* Kenzo Tange died in March at the age of 91. (*See* OBITUARIES.) He reigned as the leading Modernist architect in Japan from the mid-1950s. His most celebrated works were two Olympic stadiums in Tokyo (1964), each with a membrane roof draping from a supporting pillar.

Ralph Erskine also died in March at the age of 91. Born in London, Erskine married in Sweden and became one of Scandinavia's top architects. He was especially known for his success in allowing the future inhabitants of a building to share in the process of its design. He "nobly championed humanity against its many 20th-century enemies," wrote one British critic.

(ROBERT CAMPBELL)

The Yad Vashem Holocaust History Museum near Jerusalem, designed by Moshe Safdie, was centred on the Hall of Names, dedicated to the memory of the six million Jews killed by the Nazis in World War II.

Notable Civil Engineering Projects (in work or completed, 2005)

Name	Location		Year of completion	Notes
Airports		**Terminal area (sq m)**		
Suvarnabhumi ("Golden Land")	east of Bangkok, Thai.	563,000	2006	To replace Don Muang Airport, Southeast Asia's busiest airport
Barajas International Airport (new Terminal 4)	northeast of Madrid, Spain	470,000	2006	New terminal in leading airport for Europe–Latin America flights
Changi (new Terminal 3)	eastern tip of Singapore	430,000	2008	New terminal in Asia's 6th busiest airport in passenger traffic
Central Japan International	artificial island off Nagoya, Japan	220,000	2005	Opened Feb. 17; Japan's 3rd largest airport
Dallas/Fort Worth Int'l (new Terminal D)	Irving, Texas	195,000	2005	Opened July 23; new international terminal
JFK International (new megaterminal)	New York, N.Y.	184,000	2005–06	To replace demolished terminals 8 and 9; phase I completed July 27
New Doha International (phase I)	Doha, Qatar	140,000	2009	1st airport built for world's largest passenger aircraft (Airbus A380-800)
Heathrow (new Terminal 5)	southwest of London, Eng.	70,000	2008	Biggest construction project in the U.K. from 2002
Bridges		**Length (main span; m)**		
Hangzhou Bay	near Jiaxing, China–near Cixi, China	2,600	2009	To be world's longest (35.6 km) transoceanic bridge/causeway; begun 2003
I-95 (Woodrow Wilson #2)	Alexandria, Va.–Md. suburbs of D.C.	1,829[1]	2008	2 bascule spans forming higher inverted V shape for ships; begun 2000
Nancha (1 bridge of 2-section Runyang)	Zhenjiang, China (across the Yangtze)	1,490	2005	Opened April 30; world's 3rd longest (China's longest) suspension bridge
Sutong	Nantong, China (100 km from Yangtze mouth)	1,088	2008	To be world's longest and highest cable-stayed bridge
Stonecutters	Tsing Yi–Sha Tin, Hong Kong, China	1,018	2008	To be world's 2nd longest cable-stayed bridge
Tacoma Narrows (#3)	the Narrows of Puget Sound, Tacoma, Wash.	853	2007	Built over collapsed TN #1; longest U.S. suspension bridge since 1964
Second Inchon	near Inchon, S.Kor.	800	2009	To be world's 5th longest cable-stayed bridge
Nanjing Yangtze Sanqiao	Nanjing, China (across the Yangtze)	648	2005	Opened October 7; world's 3rd longest cable-stayed bridge
Arthur Ravenel, Jr. (new Cooper River)	Charleston, S.C.–Mt. Pleasant, S.C.	471	2005	Opened July 9; longest cable-stayed bridge in North America
Shibanpe	Chongqing, China (across the Yangtze)	330	2006	To be world's longest prestressed-concrete box girder bridge
Colorado River	Boulder City, Nev. (just south of Hoover Dam)	323	2008	Final component of Hoover Dam Bypass Project—post-9/11 security measure
Buildings		**Height (m)**		
Burj ("Tower") Dubai	Dubai, U.A.E.	c. 705	2008	To be world's tallest building
Freedom Tower	New York, N.Y.	"1,776 ft" (541 m)	2010	Cornerstone laid July 4, 2004; to be tallest building in North America
Shanghai World Financial Center	Shanghai, China	492	2007	Begun 1997, resumed 2003; to be world's 2nd tallest building (in 2007)
International Commerce Centre	Hong Kong, China	484	2007	To be world's 3rd tallest (in 2007) and have world's highest hotel
Federation Tower A	Moscow, Russia	340	2007	To be tallest building in Europe
Palacio de la Bahía	Panama City, Pan.	336	2009	To be tallest building in Latin America
Eureka Tower	Melbourne, Australia	297	2006	To be Australia's 2nd tallest building and world's 2nd tallest residential
Frauenkirche (reconstruction)	Dresden, Ger.	–	2005	Baroque Lutheran cathedral firebombed in 1945; reconsecrated Oct. 30
Dams and Waterways		**Crest/channel length (m)**		
Sethusamudram Ship Canal Project	between India and Sri Lanka	89,000	2008	To create a sea route around India bypassing Sri Lanka (saving c. 780 km)
Three Gorges (3rd of 3 phases)	west of Yichang, China	1,983	2009	To create world's largest reservoir (620 km long) beginning 2003 + to be world's largest hydroelectric complex by power capacity
Sardar Sarovar (Narmada) Project	Narmada River, Madhya Pradesh, India	1,210	2007	Largest dam of controversial 30-dam project; drinking water for Gujarat
Merowe (earth core rockfill) Dam	on Nile, 350 km north of Khartoum, Sudan	841	2008	To contain 20% of Nile annual flow; to double The Sudan's power capacity
Caruachi (4th of 5-dam Lower Caroní Development scheme)	Caroní River, northern Bolívar, Venez.	360	2006	Unit of world's 3rd largest hydroelectric complex
Tucuruí (upgrade to double capacity)	Tocantins River, eastern Pará, Braz.	?	2006	Generating capacity to be 4th in world; 1st Braz. Amazon dam (1984)
Tala Hydroelectric Project	Wong River, Bhutan	?	2006	Electricity for northern India; the key to Bhutan's economic growth
Project Moses (flood-protection plan)	Venice, Italy	–	2011	78 submerged gates in 3 lagoon openings will rise in flood conditions
Highways		**Length (km)**		
Golden Quadrilateral superhighway	Mumbai–Chennai–Kolkata–Delhi, India	5,846	2006	Upgrade to 4 lanes; to link India's 4 largest metropolitan areas
Carretera Interoceánica (Peruvian part)	Iñapari–Ilo/Matarani/Marcona, Peru	c. 1,100	2007	To be paved road for Brazilian imports/exports from/to Asia
Highway 1	Kabul–Kandahar–Herat, Afg.	1,048	2006	Final, 566-km Kandahar–Herat section to open Dec. 2006
Egnatia Motorway	Igoumenitsa–Kipoi, Greece	680	2008	First Greek highway at int'l standards; 74 tunnels, 1,650 bridges
Croatian Motorway (A1)	Zagreb–Split, Croatia	380	2005	Opened June 26; mountainous terrain with unstable slopes and caves
Land Reclamation		**Area (sq km)**		
The Palms ("Jumeirah, Jebel Ali, and Deira islands")	in Persian Gulf, off Dubai, U.A.E.	"c. 20, c. 40, and c. 80 sq km"	2007–09	Three palm-tree-shaped arrays of islands; ultraexclusive
The World	in Persian Gulf, off Dubai, U.A.E.	c. 60 sq km	2008	300 private artificial islands arrayed as a map of the world
Railways (Heavy)		**Length (km)**		
Trans-Kazakhstan	Dostyq (Druzhba), Kazakh.–Gorgan, Iran	3,943	2008	China to Europe link, bypassing Russia & Uzbek.; 3,083 km in Kazakh.
Qinghai–Tibet	China: Golmud, Qinghai–Lhasa, Tibet	1,142	2006	World's highest railway (5,072 m at summit); 86% above 4,000 m
Ferronorte (extension to Rondonópolis)	Alto Araguaia–Rondonópolis, Braz.	270	2007	For soybean/cereal exports from Mato Grosso (Brazilian interior)
Bothnia Line (Botniabanan)	Nyland–Umeå, Swed.	190	2010	Along north Swedish coast; difficult terrain with 25 km of tunnels
Railways (High Speed)		**Length (km)**		
Spanish high speed	Madrid, Spain, to France (via Barcelona)	719	2009	To reach Barcelona in 2007; Madrid–Lleida corridor opened Oct. 11, 2003
Eastern France high speed	eastern Paris–near Strasbourg, France	406	2007	Will give Paris a high-speed link to the major centres of eastern France
Taiwan high speed	Hsi-chih–Tso-ying, Taiwan	345	2006	Links Taiwan's 2 largest cities (Taipei and Kaohsiung) along west coast
Italian high speed	Rome–Naples, Italy	205	2006	Naples to Turin (844 km) completed by 2009
HSL–Zuid	The Hague/Amsterdam–Belgian border	125	2008	Enables high-speed links with Brussels, London, and Paris
Beijing–Tianjin high speed	Beijing–Tianjin, China	115	2008	Construction began mid-2005
Channel Tunnel Rail Link	near Folkestone–central London, Eng.	109	2007	74-km section (Folkestone–north Kent) opened Sept. 16, 2003
Spanish high speed	Madrid–Toledo, Spain	80	2005	Opened Nov. 15
Subways/Metros/Light Rails		**Length (km)**		
Guangzhou Metro	Guangzhou (Canton), China	255.0	2010	9-line system planned; 150 km in 5 lines under construction in 2005
Shanghai Metro	Shanghai, China	87.5	2006	Length of lines under construction in late 2005
Shenzhen Metro (phase 2; lines 1, 3, and 4)	Shenzhen, China (adjacent to Hong Kong)	71.3	2009	To be part of a regional network with high-speed and heavy rail by 2010
Dubai Metro	Dubai, U.A.E.	69.7	2009–10	To be world's longest fully automated driverless transport system
Delhi Metro (Phase I)	Delhi, India	65.1	2006	Two lines (33 km) opened by July 2005; last line (32.1 km) in March 2006
Barcelona Metro (Line 9)	airport–northeast Barcelona, Spain	47.0	2008	Connections to other metro lines and future high-speed rail
Santiago Metro (Line 4)	Santiago, Chile	32.4	2005–06	18.6 km opened Nov. 30
Arizona Light Rail	Phoenix–Tempe–Mesa, Ariz.	32.2	2008	To be Arizona's first light-rail system
Copenhagen Metro (last extension)	Copenhagen, Den.	21.0	2007	4.5-km line to connect city centre to airport
Tunnels		**Length (m)**		
Apennine Range tunnels (9)	Bologna–Florence, Italy (high-speed railway)	73,400	2008	Longest tunnel (Vaglia, 18.6 km); tunnels to cover 93% of railway
Lötschberg #2	Frutigen–Raron, Switz.	34,577	2007	Breakthrough April 28, 2005; to be world's 3rd longest rail tunnel
Guadarrama	50 km north-northwest of Madrid, Spain	28,377	2007	Breakthrough June 1, 2005; to have Valladolid high-speed link
Hsüeh-shan ("Snow Mountain")	near Taipei, Taiwan	12,900	2006	Breakthrough Sept. 16, 2004; to be world's 4th longest road tunnel
East and West tunnels of A86 ring road	western outskirts of Paris, France	10,000/7,500	2007	Two tunnels under Versailles and nearby protected woodlands

1 m = 3.28 ft; 1 km = 0.62 mi; 1 ha = 2.47 ac   [1]Length of each span.

Art and Art Exhibitions

The year 2005 in art took a look at the past, with an exhibit about the terrorist RED ARMY FACTION and one on the SLIDE-SHOW PROJECTOR; projects in the works for years—*The Gates* and *The Floating Island to Travel Around Manhattan Island*—were finally REALIZED; and photo exhibits SHOWCASED images of earlier times.

ART

In 2005 the appeal of contemporary visual art and its promise of youthful provocation continued to sharpen the desire of an international art community, while visual arts strode forward at a frenzied pace.

French business mogul and art patron François Pinault made news when he halted plans to build a new Tadao Ando-designed contemporary art museum on an island in the Seine, causing an uproar among arts professionals in Paris. Following five years of bureaucratic impediments in France, Pinault purchased a controlling interest in Palazzo Grassi on the Grand Canal in Venice for the François Pinault Foundation for Contemporary Art. Pinault captured headlines again by selling for approximately $30 million Robert Rauschenberg's seminal 1955 artwork *Rebus*, a 3-m (10-ft)-wide triptych, to the Museum of Modern Art (MoMA) in New York City. Following two years of political debate over public-sanctioned funding, the year's most controversial exhibition, "Regarding Terror: The RAF-Exhibition," opened amid a public furor in Germany. Presented at Kunst-Werke in Berlin, the show included work by 50 artists who examined the "media echo" of the Red Army Faction (RAF) terrorist organization. In late 2004 curators Ellen Blumenstein and Felix Ensslin had raised more than $300,000 through an eBay auction to finance the exhibit without the aid of governmental funding.

Renewal, in both action and concept, allowed for short-term viewings of two major public art endeavours in New York City. *The Gates, Central Park, New York 1979–2005*, by Christo and Jeanne-Claude, finally materialized 26 years after its conception, with a reported price tag of $21 million. Opening only days after a blizzard had deposited 46 cm (18 in) of snow in the city, 7,503 steel gates festooned with saffron-coloured cloth panels, standing 5 m (16 ft) high, stretched across 37 km (23 mi) of walkway in Central Park. The much-anticipated project, which was financed by the artists, remained on view for only 16 days but attracted more than four million visitors. Another long-unrealized project was resurrected in tandem with the Robert Smithson survey at the Whitney Museum of American Art. *The Floating Island to Travel Around Manhattan Island*, imagined by Smithson in 1970, three years before his death, motored around the borough for nine days in September with the assistance of a tugboat; the work, which was assembled together with Smithson's artist wife, Nancy Holt, consisted of a 9 × 27-m (30 × 90-ft) barge landscaped with local earth and vegetation. Deterioration of society and material embodied the first American solo museum exhibition of Modern Gothic artist Banks Violette. For *Untitled*, Violette enlisted the sonic aid of black metal music to conjure the romantic sublime in a monumental installation at the Whitney Museum, complete with a burnt-out church cast in rock salt.

Works on paper continued to enjoy critical and mass appeal throughout the year. After a two-year buying spree conducted by trustee Harvey S. Shipley Miller, the Judith Rothschild Foundation amassed nearly 2,600 drawings from the 1930s to 2004 by more than

New York City's long-planned Floating Island *is towed past Battery Park in southern Manhattan in September. The island consisted of a barge covered with 10 trees and other vegetation, rocks, and soil.*

640 artists. Bequeathed to and accepted in 2005 by MoMA, the treasure trove included works by artists Kai Althoff, Henry Darger, Franz West, and Agnes Martin, among others. The unveiling of newly discovered works by Realist painter Edward Hopper and Abstract Expressionist master Jackson Pollock sent thrills through academic and collector communities. An East Hampton, N.Y., storage locker belonging to graphic designer Herbert Matter (1907–84) revealed 32 unrecorded paintings and drawings by Pollock executed between 1946 and 1949; the works were found in 2002, but the discovery was announced in 2005 following restoration work. Drawings by Hopper, many of which were final studies for his most iconic works, went on view at Peter Findlay Gallery in New York City. After Hopper's death in 1967, his friend and neighbour Mary Schiffenhaus had inherited the artist's Cape Cod home along with 22 drawings tucked away in drawers and cupboards; Schiffenhaus in turn gave them in 1969 to current owner Frank M. Capezzera.

The Turner Prize, which honoured a British contemporary artist, continued to reap heavy media attention. Installation artist Simon Starling took the 2005 prize, while sculptor Jim Lambie, painter Gillian Carnegie, and multimedia artist Darren Almond were shortlisted. Dubbed the "German Turner" for its aim to bridge contemporary art with wider audiences accustomed to event-driven culture, the Nationalgalerie Prize for Young Art was awarded to German-based artist Monica Bonvicini. Bonvicini's sadomasochistic installation of leather swings delivered a provocative blow, edging out other short-list contenders Anri Sala, Angela Bulloch, and John Bock. In other news painter Julie Mehretu, sculptor Teresita Fernandez, and photographer Fazal Sheikh each collected a no-strings-attached $500,000 MacArthur "genius" award, and sculptor Mark di Suvero received the 11th annual Heinz Award in the Arts and Humanities, which carried a $250,000 prize from the Heinz family foundation.

A hearty trail of shattered auction records characterized the art market's voracious appetite for modern and contemporary art, and by the beginning of the fall season, Christie's had edged ahead of Sotheby's and Phillip's auction houses with half-year sales totaling $1,653,000,000. Record sales—set by Chaim Soutine (*Le Pâtissier de Cagnes* [1924] for $9,449,856), Hopper (*Chair Car* [1965] for $14,016,000), and Joseph Cornell (*Untitled [Medici Princess]* [c. 1952] for $2,592,000)— kept Christie's ahead of the competition. Constantin Brancusi's exquisite icon of modern art, the gray marble *Oiseau dans l'espace*, or *Bird in Space* (1922–23), soared to an impressive $27,456,000. The top lot of the auction season, however, belonged to an Old Master painting—Canaletto's *Venice, the Grand Canal Looking North-East from the Palazzo Balbi to the Rialto Bridge*—which sold for $32,746,478. Several living artists emerged with new auction records, including Robert Gober, whose eerie sculpture *Untitled Leg* (1990) sold for $912,000, and Marlene Dumas, whose *The Teacher* (1987) went for $3,339,517. British artist Chris Ofili's *Afrodizzia* (1996), a glittering canvas propped atop two heaps of elephant dung, garnered $1,001,600. Additional highlights included Chuck Close's seminal painting *John* (1971–72), which reached $4,832,000; *The Cocktail Party* (1965–66), a spectacular assembly of 15 freestanding sculptural figures by Marisol (Escobar) for $912,000; and the canvas *A Nurse Involved* (2002) by Richard Prince, which sold for $1,024,000. The sale of Elizabeth Peyton's 1996 oil on masonite painting *John Lennon 1964*, an ethereal, unabashedly romantic portrait of the musician, fetched a record-breaking $800,000—quadruple its pre-sale estimate.

Female artists and curators made an impressive showing. Career-spanning presentations of work by Frida Kahlo, Rosemarie Trockel, and Diane Arbus captured the public's attention at the Tate Modern in London, Museum Ludwig in Cologne, Ger., and the Metropolitan Museum of Art in New York City, respectively. Elsewhere in New York City, emerging artists Sue de Beer and Dana Schutz maintained footing in the "Greater New York" group exhibition at P.S.1 Contemporary Art Center in Long Island City and later reasserted their position in the spotlight via American museum debuts; Schutz's mural-size painting *Presentation* (2005) was shipped by P.S.1 directly to MoMA for "Take Two. Worlds and Views: Contemporary Art from the Collection," and Sue de Beer's *Black Sun* (2004–05), a compelling video installation of psychosexual awakening, was presented at the Whitney. Rosa Martínez and María de Corral became the first female curatorial team to preside over the Venice Biennale in the

A two-channel video installation by Sue de Beer titled **Black Sun** *was shown at the Whitney Museum of American Art at Altria from March 3 to June 17, 2005. The display dealt with feminine identity, desire, and unfulfilled longing.*

Image courtesy Sammlung Goetz

110-year history of the exhibition. American artist Barbara Kruger took home the Golden Lion Award for Lifetime Achievement, and Annette Messenger garnered the prize for best national pavilion for France. Video works combining body art and political protest earned Guatemalan artist Regina José Galindo the Golden Lion for a young artist, while the indefatigable feminist artist collective Guerrilla Girls confronted the biennale's history of gender imbalance with witty posters, one of which proclaimed "French Pavilion Has Solo Show by a Woman! Who Cares if It's the First Time in 100 Years!"

(MICHAEL CLIFTON)

ART EXHIBITIONS

Art biennials and festivals vying for attendance numbers and critical attention continued to proliferate in 2005, sometimes in the same city. Dueling biennials in the Czech capital of Prague canceled each other out as critical discourse gave way to headline scandal when the publishers of *Flash Art* magazine, organizers of Prague Biennale 2, forbade local officials at Prague's National Gallery to use the name Prague Biennale when organizing their "International Biennale of Contemporary Art 2005." The 51st Venice Biennale included 70 participating countries. The United States was represented by a new cycle of Ed Ruscha paintings depicting industrial changes in Los Angeles. Curators Rosa Martínez and María de Corral presented the exhibition as two complementary shows: "Always a Little Further" and "The Experience of Art." Newcomers to the oversaturated art circuit included the Moscow Biennale of Contemporary Art in Russia and the promising Performa 05 (New York City), the first biennial devoted to visual art performance.

Nicolas Bourriaud and Jérôme Sans, the organizers of the Lyon (France) Biennale of Contemporary Art, excavated the well of hippie-era axioms to explore notions of temporality for "Expérience de la durée" or "Experiencing Duration." Setting the pace were an intergenerational mix of newly commissioned works and historical pieces, such as Andy Warhol's six-hour film *Sleep* (1963). Artworks—ranging from

La Monte Young's *Dream House* (1962), a meditation room in which time fluidity is enhanced by the vibration of minimalist electronic sounds, to Martin Creed's claustrophobic room filled with pink balloons—permitted viewers to trace the development of countercultural works of "long duration." Transcendence through artistic exploration of drugs, alcohol, and hedonism gained further critical evaluation via sprawling museum exhibitions in Los Angeles,

Carsten Höller's Upside Down Mushroom Room *was on view Oct. 9, 2005–Feb. 20, 2006, at the Los Angeles Museum of Contemporary Art, which organized the show, "Ecstasy: In and About Altered States." Paul Schimmel was the curator.*

London, and Paris. "Dionysiac: Art in Flux," presented in Paris at the Pompidou Centre, corralled 14 international artists, including Paul McCarthy, Thomas Hirschhorn, and Maurizio Cattelan, to pay tribute to the Greek deity of wine and irreverence through a variety of installations, videos, and performances. At the Los Angeles Museum of Contemporary Art, "Ecstasy: In and About Altered States" examined perceptional experimentation through artworks designed to simulate altered realities as well as artworks composed of drugs or works representing transcendental states undergone by artists. Exhibition highlights included Carsten Höller's *Upside Down Mushroom Room* (2000) and Charles Ray's 1990 photograph *Yes*, a self-portrait made while under the influence of LSD and presented in a convex frame, mounted on a convex wall. Tate Liverpool, Eng., got groovy with "Summer of Love: Art of the Psychedelic Era," comprising works culled from the 1960s and early '70s by more than 40 artists, including Yayoi Kusama, Warhol, and Robert Indiana.

In this exhibit cultural paraphernalia such as record covers held equal ground with painting and sculpture as well as a multimedia installation by Vernon Panton.

Television, film, and moving images provided artistic fodder for American group exhibitions in Baltimore, Md., Minneapolis, Minn., and Milwaukee, Wis. In "Shadowland: An Exhibition as a Film," staged at the Walker Art Center in Minneapolis, organizers Douglas Fogle and Philippe Vergne conceived the exhibition as a "movie without a camera." The curatorial configuration invited visitors to shuffle through a range of art film genres present in the work of more than 30 artists, from Bruce Nauman and Doug Aitken to Chantal Akerman. The contemporary gesture of cut and paste scored critical observation in "CUT/Film as Found Object" at the Milwaukee Art Museum. Utilizing excerpts from preexisting film and television footage, visual artists Candice Breitz, Christian Marclay, Omer Fast, and others made the familiar unfamiliar by constructing new narratives, musical scores, and emotional content. Surfacing from the shadow of the 2003 announcement by Eastman Kodak Co. that it would discontinue production of slide projectors, the Baltimore Museum of Art illuminated the role of slide as artistic medium through the exhibition "SlideShow." Signifying visual culture's shift from analog to digital technology, "SlideShow" gazed back at 40 years of art production using the unpretentious slide; the medium revealed itself in works by artists Nan Goldin, Dan Graham, and Robert Smithson.

Extending beyond New York City's five boroughs into upstate New York and New Jersey, "Greater New York 2005" at P.S.1 Contemporary Art Center in Long Island City, N.Y., offered a cacophonous array of more than 150 artists who had emerged since 2000. Remaining on view for six months, memorable works by Dana Schutz, Brock Enright, and de Beer were enlivened by the thematic loose threads of escapism and regression along with visceral depictions of beauty and horror. Elsewhere in the show, a hybrid strain of formalism as practiced by Richard Aldrich, Wade

Guyton, and Gedi Sibony humbled the high-energy proceedings. Employing similar curatorial structure, regional roundup exhibitions highlighting new directions in sculpture appeared on both coasts; the Hammer Museum, University of California, Los Angeles, mounted its "THING: New Sculpture from Los Angeles," and the Sculpture-Center in New York staged "Make It Now: New Sculpture in New York."

Significant monographic surveys of work by artists Richard Tuttle and Smithson toured multiple venues during the year and provided in-depth examinations of two of the key figures to emerge in American art during the mid-1960s. The Smithson retrospective at the Whitney Museum of American Art,

A technician adjusts El Anatsui's Cloth of Gold, *a piece constructed of thousands of bottle caps. The exhibition "Africa Remix: Contemporary Art of a Continent," which opened at London's Hayward Gallery in February, was the largest show of African art ever seen in Europe.*

New York City, presented sculptures, photographs, and documentary films of his earthworks, such as "Spiral Jetty" (1970) in Utah's Great Salt Lake, while rarely seen drawings and paintings offered a revealing glimpse into projects unrealized during the artist's lifetime. Despite his sudden death at age 35 in 1973, Smithson continued to have a profound impact on sculpture and art theory through his books, letters, and critical writings. "The Art of Richard Tuttle," presented July 2–October 16 at the San Francisco Museum of Modern Art, traced the artist's career through four decades of inventive abstraction, from drawing, collage, and painting to sculpture, design, and bookmaking. Tuttle's delicate work defied categorization; he maintained, "My work is not reduced from something. It is not abstract, it is real. It is what it is." Though his 1975 major exhibition at the Whitney Museum had been panned by the critics and that show's curator fired, Tuttle's new show would travel to the Whitney as part of its two-year tour.

Attracting cross-generational audiences by tracing the parallel creative journeys of two highly influential artists, "Pioneering Modern Painting: Cézanne and Pissarro 1865–1885," which was presented June 26–September 12 by MoMA, examined the development of Modernism through acts of artistic exchange. The exhibition reunited approximately 45 works by each artist from a period in which the two artists worked side by side in the French cities of Pontoise and Auvers. The show would later travel to the Los Angeles County Museum of Art and the Musée d'Orsay, Paris. The Neue Galerie, New York City, mounted a survey of 150 drawings and paintings by Viennese Expressionist Egon Schiele, and the Metropolitan Museum of Art, New York City, showcased "Vincent van Gogh: The Drawings," the first major American retrospective of the artist's works on paper. The transatlantic blockbuster "Turner, Whistler, Monet," presented by Tate Britain, London, focused on the artists' views of the River Thames, the Seine, and Venice to reveal connections between British and French art and the development of the symbolism and Impressionism that shaped the course of landscape painting. (MICHAEL CLIFTON)

PHOTOGRAPHY

Much of the photography exhibited in 2005 involved an exploration of "how

we looked then," in work that revisited actual and reconstructed historical sites of past interest. Returning to the early days of photography, the Eugène Atget retrospective, which was held September 10–November 27 at the Philadelphia Museum of Art, showcased 120 photographs of Paris from 1890 to 1926.

The work of Hungarian photographer André Kertész (1894–1985) traveled to the International Center of Photography (ICP), New York City, in a comprehensive exhibition organized by the National Gallery of Art, Washington, D.C., where it originated in 2004. The show then traveled to the Los Angeles County Museum of Art and was on view at the ICP from September 16 to November 27. The subtle and elegant work displayed in this exhibition brought to view Kertész's quiet observations of Paris and New York City in the years following 1925 and his unique juxtapositions of light and form.

The January–March exhibition "Peter Hujar: Night" at Matthew Marks Gallery, New York City, included 43 square-format black-and-white after-dark images from 1974 to 1985 that depicted the margins of New York City. The show, informed by Hujar's gritty sensibility and experience as a street photographer in New York City's East Village, was also mounted from March 10 to April 30 at the Fraenkel Gallery, San Francisco. P.S.1 Contemporary Art Center, Long Island City, N.Y., presented 70 images of his work, most previously unexhibited; Hujar died of AIDS in 1987. The exhibit was on view from Oct. 23, 2005, to Jan. 16, 2006. Hujar's work was also included in the New Museum of Contemporary Art's group exhibition "East Village USA."

A retrospective exhibition of the work of Lexington, Ky., optometrist and photographer Ralph Eugene Meatyard (1925–72) consisted of more than 150 prints from the archives of the University of Kentucky, organized by the ICP, where it was on view Dec. 10, 2004–Feb. 27, 2005. The show, which later traveled to the Fraenkel Gallery and the Center for Creative Photography, Tucson, Ariz., represented Meatyard's exploration of the themes of childhood and loss. Employing darkness, shadows, and masks, Meatyard developed a melancholic sensibility in the midst of a deep Southern mythology.

On display through February 27 at the ICP, which also organized the show, was "Bill Owens: Leisure"; it

This 1919 image, **The Dancing Faun,** *was one of a large collection of photographs by André Kertész organized by the National Gallery of Art, Washington, D.C., that was shown in New York and Los Angeles in 2005.*

was also exhibited March 3–April 30 at the Robert Koch Gallery in San Francisco and featured previously unseen images from Owens's "Suburbia" series, made between 1968 and 1980; these constituted the final installment of four projects, each of which focused on a different aspect of the emergence of suburban life since the late 1960s. A July–September exhibit in New York City also included images from "Suburbia" (1972), "Our Kind of People" (1976), and "Working: I Do It for the Money" (1978), as well as newly published work in the "Leisure" series.

In Beverly Hills, Calif., Gregory Crewdson's "Beneath the Roses" was on view May 21–July 16 at Gagosian Gallery and opened concurrently with shows at White Cube, London, and Luhring Augustine Gallery, New York City. Crewdson's cinematic photography, depicting extraordinary events in quite ordinary places, required the collaborative efforts of an entire movie crew to stage. Crewdson's view of middle-class America explored the psychological impact of the banal and the alienation of life in the suburbs through "disturbing dramas at play within quotidian environments."

"Turning Back: A Photographic Journal of Re-exploration," by Robert Adams, was exhibited Sept. 29, 2005–Jan. 3, 2006, at the San Francisco Museum of Modern Art (SFMoMA). Accompanied by a catalog of the same name, the show displayed Adams's newest work, which was inspired by the bicentennial of the Lewis and Clark expedition. The images on view retraced the territory covered by the famous explorers. "Robert Adams: Circa 1970," shown September 8–October 29 at the Fraenkel Gallery, presented the first exhibition of rare vintage prints from the series "The New West" and "Denver." This work, which explored the transformation of the American landscape in 1967–73, was collected in two books that were considered photographic landmarks of the past half century.

The first photography exhibition of 2005 in the newly renovated MoMA was on view March 4–May 30 and showcased Thomas Demand's work, which challenged the notion of a document through carefully constructed images that began as paper models of historically meaningful sites and were then photographed by the artist, who was trained as a sculptor. The show was the largest American survey of Demand's work to date and included 25 images from the past 12 years.

A major retrospective at MoMA of Lee Friedlander was on view June 5–August 29. The exhibition traveled to Haus der Kunst, Munich, from Nov. 16, 2005 to Feb. 12, 2006, and presented nearly 500 prints that spanned a 50-year career, revisiting the diverse interests of a multifaceted artist whose many projects included portraiture, landscape, still life, and architectural studies. Concurrent with his major retrospective at MoMA, another New York show, "Five Decades," was offered from June 11 to July 29 at the Janet Borden Gallery.

John Szarkowski was the subject of a photographic exhibition that originated at SFMoMA in February. The companion book *John Szarkowski: Photographs* featured 84 tritone images and an essay by SFMoMA curator Sandra Phillips. The show traveled in June to the Center for Creative Photography and in September to the Milwaukee (Wis.) Art Museum. MoMA was to host the exhibition in 2006.

An exhibition of topographic photographer Stephen Shore, which originated at the Akademie der Bildenden Künste in Vienna in 2004, was presented from June to mid-October 2005 at the Hammer Museum, University of California, Los Angeles, and traveled in mid-November to Presentation House Gallery, Vancouver. The show exhibited 120 prints from two major series, "Uncommon Places" and "American Surfaces," which defined the vernacular of the 1970s sociological American landscape. In the meantime, the Shore exhibition at P.S.1 Contemporary Arts Center presented a selection of more than 300 images from Shore's series "American Surfaces" and coincided with an updated publication of the landmark book of the same name.

"End of Time" at the Mori Art Museum, Tokyo, surveyed the entire body of Hiroshi Sugimoto's work. The exhibition opened in September 2005 and was scheduled to travel in February 2006 to the Hirshhorn Museum and Sculpture Garden, Washington, D.C. Sugimoto explored abstraction, focusing on the formal qualities of light and time. The retrospective exhibition included work from "Dioramas," "Seascapes," "Theatres," "Portraits," "Architecture," "Sea of Buddha," and "Conceptual Forms." The show also included "Colors of Shadow," new never-before-presented colour photographs of the changing light in the artist's studio. (MARLA CAPLAN)

159

Computers and Information Systems

These are a few of the things computer people were talking about in 2005: PHISHING, CLICK FRAUD, ZOMBIES, DARKNETS, MASHUPS, DUAL CORE, SOCIAL NETWORKING, HOTSPOTS, and TEXTING.

In 2005 people were the most wirelessly connected ever. Cellular phones were the most common electronic gadget in the world, with about 700 million expected to be sold globally in 2005. According to research firm Gartner Inc., annual sales were expected to climb to one billion cellular phones by 2009, which meant that 40% of the world's population would be using cellular phones. Adding to the appeal of the phones were features that also made them function as digital cameras or digital music players. They were also widely used as text-messaging devices. (*See* Sidebar, page 165.)

In another sign of things to come, it appeared that technology jobs were losing their lustre as demand for programmers declined. Some experts forecast a 30% decline worldwide in technology jobs by 2010. In the United States workers grew wary of seeking careers in engineering as corporate outsourcing sent tens of thousands of such jobs to other countries where wages were lower. Gartner predicted that as many as 15% of high-technology workers would leave that job category by the end of the decade, not including reductions due to natural attrition.

Computer Security and Crime. Identity theft was a growing Internet problem during 2005. Computer hackers had grown adept at stealing credit-card numbers and associated personal information from e-commerce businesses and financial institutions and then selling that data online. The U.S. Federal Trade Commission (FTC) estimated that such theft cost American consumers $5 billion and American business $48 billion each year.

There was an increase in reported breaches of security in commerce and banking Web sites, although the rise appeared to be related to new U.S. government rules that required federal banks, state-chartered banks, and savings-and-loan institutions to tell customers if their personal information had been compromised and subject to misuse. The Bank of America introduced a new security system for online banking in an attempt to recover from some embarrassing security failures. In February the bank revealed that it had lost computer tapes that contained the personal information of some 1.2 million employees of the U.S. government, and in May the Bank of America and Wachovia had to alert more than 100,000 customers after nine persons, including seven bank employees, were charged with trying to steal financial information belonging to customers. Another security breach was reported by MasterCard International, which disclosed that 40 million credit-card and debit-card numbers had possibly been obtained by someone outside the company who had gained access to the information via a firm that processed credit-card transactions. Clothing retailer Polo Ralph Lauren suffered data theft that might have affected 180,000 persons who held General Motors-branded MasterCards. The information-database firm LexisNexis reported that the personal data of 310,000 people may have been revealed inadvertently since early 2003, and competitor ChoicePoint said that fraud perpetrators who posed as businessmen had accessed data from approximately 145,000 persons.

Computer security experts blamed the leaks on several things, including the growth of data collection as a business, the poor design of software and security systems, and the lack of corporate oversight. U.S. investigators confirmed that corporations were still reluctant to report security breaches. An annual survey by the FBI and the private Computer Security Institute reported that in 2004 only about 20% of businesses were willing to report computer intrusions, a number that had changed little from previous years. Corporations feared that the disclosure of computer attacks would harm their public image and help their competitors, the FBI said.

The semiannual Internet Security Threat Report issued by the California-based security firm Symantec said that the motives of hackers appeared to have shifted from engaging in malicious behaviour (such as creating Internet viruses and worms) to seeking monetary gain, primarily through information theft. Such theft often was accomplished by means of "phishing" or "spyware." In phishing a bogus e-mail message was typically used to direct a consumer to a Web site that mimicked the appearance of a familiar bank or e-commerce Web site. Consumers were then asked to "update" or "confirm" their accounts and unwittingly disclosed confidential information such as Social Security numbers or credit-card numbers. Some types of spyware were designed to steal Social Security numbers, passwords, and other private information directly from the computer's hard drive, while others altered the results of Internet searches in order to surreptitiously redirect computer users to a Web site that would infect their PCs with even more spyware. Internet scam artists were willing to pay spyware creators for these tasks, and security-software firm Webroot Software estimated that spyware generated about $2.4 billion in annual revenue for its perpetrators. Companies and law-enforcement agencies tried to fight back with lawsuits. The state of New York sued an Internet marketer for allegedly installing spyware and adware (software that displayed unwanted pop-up advertisements) on consumer PCs. Microsoft filed 117 civil lawsuits that sought to learn the identities of people who were believed to have perpetrated phishing attempts against the customers of its Hotmail e-mail service and MSN Internet service.

Internet auction fraud was on the rise in 2005. The FTC annual report stated that complaints of such crimes over the period 2002–04 had nearly doubled. Old-fashioned fraud also prospered on the Web. Hurricane Katrina generated a wave of Internet scams that involved raising money for fake relief efforts. Spam, or junk e-mail, continued to be an enormous problem for e-mail users. Spam made up 69% of all e-mail traffic in mid-2005, up from 50% in 2003. Microsoft said that it had settled a suit it had filed against alleged spam distributor Scott Richter and his Colorado firm, OptInReal-Big.com. Richter and the firm agreed to pay Microsoft $7 million.

A much different kind of fraud troubled some Internet advertisers. Called "click fraud," it involved trying to harm Internet advertisers financially by repeatedly clicking on an Internet ad, either manually or by means of a malicious computer program. Such tactics drove up the cost of Internet advertising, since each click required the advertiser to make a payment to the owner of the Web page where the ad appeared. Likely perpetrators were said to be unhappy employees, companies that were trying to boost the ad costs of their rivals, and disreputable Web-site operators seeking to boost their revenues from advertising.

Internet service providers (ISPs) came under increasing pressure from the computer industry to rid their networks of zombies (computers that had been taken over by hackers for the purpose of launching Web-site attacks or phishing scams). The FTC promised to provide ISPs with reports of zombie PCs on their networks and asked that ISPs quarantine those machines and help customers cleanse them of infections. Some ISPs already offered their customers virus- and spam-filtering services, spyware-detection software, and firewall protection. A few also tried to regulate the outflow of e-mail from their networks in order to limit spam.

In June the British government said that there had been "industrial-scale" attacks aimed at stealing valuable data from computer networks across Britain and that the origin of the attacks had not been determined. Over several months the attackers mounted assaults on government and private-sector computer systems in such fields as communications, energy, finance, health, and transportation.

A German teenager received a suspended sentence in 2005 for having created the Sasser computer worm, which in 2004 caused thousands of computers running Microsoft's Windows 2000 or Windows XP operating systems to crash and also slowed Internet traffic. Sven Jaschan, 19, was found guilty of computer sabotage and illegal alter-

The iPod Nano digital music player, one-fifth the size of the original iPod, was introduced by Apple Computer in September.

ation of data. The celebrated case of who hacked hotel heiress Paris Hilton's cellular phone appeared solved when a Massachusetts teenager pleaded guilty in the incident. The crime was widely reported because revealing photographs and celebrity contact information from the hacked device were posted online. The 17-year-old perpetrator, who was not identified, was sentenced to 11 months of detention and two years of supervised release without access to the Internet. A British man, Gary McKinnon, was arrested in 2005 for allegedly having hacked into U.S. military computer networks in 2001 and 2002, but he sought to avoid extradition to the United States. Prosecutors said that he had caused $700,000 in damages by illegally gaining access to 97 U.S. government computers, the largest such effort on record.

E-Commerce. The issue of levying sales taxes on goods purchased online, which had been largely avoided in the United States for fear of stunting e-commerce, was raised again by a California appeals court decision that found an online bookseller liable for taxes for portions of the years 1998 and 1999 because the firm had combined its stores and online subsidiary in the state. In 1992 the U.S. Supreme Court had ruled that online retailers did not have to collect taxes unless the customer was in a state where the retailer had physical operations. The bookseller, Borders, insisted that it was protected under the 1992 ruling because its online operations and California bookstores were run by separate corporate entities. The California court disagreed and said that the two business units had worked together and therefore were not protected under the Supreme Court ruling. The California court decision led states to once again press for changes in the tax law, which they claimed unfairly deprived them of an estimated $15 billion a year in tax revenue on Internet sales.

Digital music was flourishing in 2005. Digital music players, which were also referred to as digital audio players, seemed to be everywhere, with about 95 million expected to be sold worldwide during the year. Early in 2005 a study showed that 22 million U.S. adults—about 11% of the population—owned a digital music player.

The iPod digital music player continued to drive Apple Computer's financial performance; the company's profit more than quadrupled, to $430 million, in the fourth quarter of its fiscal year. Analysts were surprised by the continued unit-sales growth for the product. At midyear the iPod accounted for about three-fourths of the digital music players sold in the United States, analysts said. Apple continued to roll out a steady stream of advances, including the iPod Nano players (which were much smaller than previous full-featured iPod models because they used flash memory instead of disk drives), a video iPod that could display music videos or TV shows, and a telephone equipped with Apple's iTunes software, manufactured by Motorola. Apple also settled a class-action suit brought on behalf of an estimated 1.4 million consumers who had battery problems with iPods that had been purchased through May 2004. The settlement gave consumers $50 vouchers for use in purchasing Apple products and extended service warranties.

The war against music piracy continued. File-sharing Web sites that aided the free trading of copyrighted music files lost key court decisions that left them open to further legal action by the music industry. The U.S. Supreme Court ruled that the creators of the Grokster and Morpheus file-sharing services could be considered liable for contributing to copyright infringement through the trading of copyrighted songs, even if their services had some legal uses. Grokster abruptly shut down in early November as part of a settlement with the recording industry. An Australian court ruled that Kazaa, another free file-sharing network, violated Australian copyright law. The music industry continued its practice of trying to curb online file sharing by suing consumers. By mid-2005 the number of suits filed over several years had reached a cumulative total of nearly 12,000, although many of the lawsuits had not yet been resolved. The research firm Yankee Group estimated that about 5 billion songs were downloaded via free file-sharing services in 2004, whereas authorized online music stores sold about 330 million songs in the same period. Moreover, the music industry's lawsuits were not always successful. Two universities in North Carolina invoked the right to privacy and successfully resisted attempts by the music industry to learn the identities of two students who allegedly shared copyrighted music on the Internet through university networks. North Carolina State University and the University of North Carolina at Chapel Hill said that they did not condone music piracy but that the privacy rights of students were more important.

Another threat to the music companies was the development of what were termed "darknets," a type of peer-to-peer file-sharing network that allowed participants to share information with far more anonymity than other file-sharing networks. The networks linked trusted members of a group and protected their communication with encryption techniques.

Other efforts were being made to prevent Internet piracy from carrying over into the world of movies. A new U.S. law sought to discourage the illegal trading of motion pictures over the Internet by providing penalties of up to three years in prison for persons who secretly videotaped films in movie theatres. Copies of movies illegally taped in theatres, together with prerelease copies surreptitiously given out by industry insiders, were said to be the chief sources of new films that were available online via file-sharing services. Meanwhile, Hollywood studios prepared to allow consumers to buy and download a wide selection of movies over the Internet, partly because they feared that the proliferation of high-speed Internet connections would increase piracy if there was not a legal alternative.

An effort by Sony BMG records to protect music CDs from unauthorized copying backfired when the copy-protection software included on the CDs came to be perceived as malicious. When played on the user's PC, the CDs automatically installed software that spied on the user's music-listening habits and opened the PC to computer-virus attacks. Attempts to remove the software left the operating system damaged. Sony offered a software patch, but experts said the patch also created PC security problems. Sony then announced that it would stop using the copy-protection software, remove three million CDs that incorporated the software from store shelves, and recall the two million such CDs that already had been sold.

Governmental Issues. Cable TV companies that offered high-speed cable modem Internet access gained a big advantage over their telephone industry rivals. The U.S. Supreme Court ruled that the cable firms did not have to open up their networks to rival ISPs that wanted to reach customers via the cable network. The ruling was based on the idea that cable TV companies provided a high-speed "information service," which was mostly unregulated by law, whereas telephone companies offered a high-speed "telecommunications service," which was regulated. The ruling disappointed consumer groups pressing for more commercial competition in high-speed Internet access and further limited the ability of slower dial-up ISPs to reach a wider audience by purchasing broadband access through the high-speed network of another company.

Cable TV's Internet rivals, the big telephone companies, also won a big victory when the Federal Communications Commission (FCC) ruled that they no longer had to provide competing ISPs with access to their lines at discounted rates. The FCC said that it believed the move would speed the growth of DSL (digital subscriber line) broadband service by giving telephone companies more incentives to upgrade their networks. Some consumer groups, however, said that the move would limit competition for broadband service and result in higher prices. The FCC said that the rule change would take effect in one year.

Legal and political action played a large role in determining the direction being taken by computer technology. A preliminary court decision limited the liability of nearly 300 technology companies that went public during the 1990s dot-com boom. The decision had the effect of diverting the wrath of investors who claimed they had been defrauded by the companies toward a group of 55 investment banks that allegedly provided favoured clients with stock from popular initial public stock offerings. Under the arrangement the companies would not have to pay if the investors recovered more than $1 billion from the investment banks. If they recovered less, the companies would have to pay the difference.

Microsoft continued its long-running fight with the European Union over its antitrust suit. Microsoft was ordered in 2004 to change the way it sold software in European countries and to pay a fine of €497 million (about $613 million), but Microsoft appealed. In 2005, as required, Microsoft introduced a version of Windows that did not include Windows Media Player, a move designed to prevent Microsoft from having an unfair advantage over other companies that sold music and video players for PCs, but Microsoft also filed a lawsuit against the European Commission over the antitrust issues. For its part the European Commission said that it had received new complaints about Microsoft that could result in a new anticompetition case against the software industry giant.

The Google Print Library Project—Google's plan to digitize the world's library books and put them online—ran into trouble, first from opposition by France and then from lawsuits by authors and publishers who were concerned about copyright infringement that could result from the unauthorized duplication and distribution of book content. French government officials, fearing that their language and culture might take a backseat under the Google plan, said that France should devise its own plan to put library collections online. The Authors Guild, which represented 8,000 writers, filed a class-action suit that alleged copyright infringement; the suit sought an injunction against the Google project and monetary damages. The Association of American Publishers, which represented five book publishers, sued Google and sought an injunction against the project to halt alleged copyright infringement. Google said that although millions of copyrighted books from five large libraries would be digitized, copyright holders could opt out of having their books scanned and, in any event, only a few sentences at a time from any book still under copyright would be viewable by readers on the Internet. No printing or downloading of the books would be allowed.

The FBI said that it had lost about $104 million on a major computer-system upgrade project that failed and that a replacement computer system would not be ready until the end of 2006. Virtual Case File, an automated case-management system, was to have cost a total of $170 million, but it was abandoned in 2005 after the FBI concluded that it was already outdated and that its performance did not meet expectations. A Department of Justice (DOJ) report said that the computer-technology problems at the FBI could affect national security.

A federal audit of the controversial E-rate program that funded Internet connections for American schools and libraries found that the $2.25-billion-a-year effort was plagued by fraud and abuse. Investigators blamed some of the schools and libraries that were recipients of the money and some of the companies that provided them with Internet connections. Investigators also said that the FCC failed to provide good oversight for the program's operation.

Companies. Google's strong financial results reflected the rapid growth of Internet advertising in general and Google's popularity in particular. The company's third-quarter profits increased 700%, and analysts attributed part of that success to a shift in advertising spending toward the Internet and away from traditional media, including newspapers, magazines, and television. Google also became the most highly valued media company in the world,

with a stock-market capitalization of more than $90 billion. A new Google technology effort captured public attention; the Google Earth service allowed people to call up on their PC screens detailed satellite images of major cities and overlay them with information as diverse as street names, crime statistics, or coffee-shop locations. Microsoft later introduced a similar online service called Virtual Earth. Some users of the online satellite images devised "mashups," in which they overlaid the images with information of their choosing, such as real-estate prices, movie filming locations, and sites where unidentified flying objects (UFOs) allegedly had been seen. Mashups proved useful to some Hurricane Katrina evacuees, who used their computers to see whether their homes had been damaged by the storm.

Carleton S. Fiorina resigned as CEO of computer manufacturer Hewlett-Packard after the board of directors asked her to do so. The resignation revolved around problems within Hewlett-Packard in the three years since she successfully completed the company's controversial merger with computer manufacturer Compaq. Among the issues facing the company was an internal debate over whether it should be broken into smaller firms—a move she had opposed—and complaints that her strategies for the company were not being executed well. Fiorina, who had been a high-profile CEO since taking the job in 1999, also was one of the best-known women executives in the U.S., where she was the first woman to head one of the 20 largest publicly owned companies. Under successor CEO Mark Hurd, Hewlett-Packard said that it would lay off 14,500 employees, or about 10% of its workforce, in 2005 and 2006. The company also froze its pension plan for employees not yet vested in it. The two-pronged plan was intended to save the company about $1.9 billion annually beginning in 2007. Meanwhile, Dell, the eponymous PC company founded by Michael Dell (*see* BIOGRAPHIES), showed record earnings in early 2005.

Microsoft settled the last of the big antitrust suits that it faced in the U.S. by agreeing to pay RealNetworks $761 million. Chief among RealNetworks' claims was that Microsoft had used its dominant position in operating systems to promote its free Windows Media Player, which hurt sales of the RealNetworks Real Player software. Earlier in the year, Microsoft had settled

claims brought by IBM for $850 million and settled antitrust and other claims brought by Gateway for $150 million over four years. Microsoft had cleared accounts with Sun Microsystems in 2004 and AOL in 2003. Microsoft settled another antitrust suit by agreeing to pay Burst.com $60 million. Burst had sued Microsoft in 2002 over alleged antitrust violations and patent infringement related to Burst's video-playing software; Microsoft had denied the claims. Burst alleged that its technology and trade secrets were improperly used in Microsoft's Windows Media Player.

Computer-chip manufacturer Advanced Micro Devices (AMD) sued microprocessor industry leader Intel for alleged antitrust violations, including claims that Intel threatened to retaliate against companies that purchased from AMD. Intel denied doing anything wrong and claimed that AMD's problems were of its own making. Both companies remained at the forefront of chip technology, introducing new microprocessors using "dual core" technology, which was designed to combat the problem of heat generated by computer chips inside computers. As the speed of traditional chips increased, their heat output had risen to the point that the need to dissipate it had become a serious problem. The dual-core chips used two processors on a chip, each running at a speed slow enough to keep temperatures manageable.

Time Warner was poised to pay $2.4 billion to settle a class-action suit based on allegations of fraudulent business practices at AOL, both before and after it merged with Time Warner in 2001. Time Warner earlier had agreed to pay $300 million to the Securities and Exchange Commission to settle civil fraud charges related to the improper inflation of AOL revenues and to pay $150 million to settle an investigation by the DOJ. AOL laid off hundreds of employees and repositioned itself as a group of free Web sites rather than a proprietary online service. Time Warner reportedly was negotiating to sell an interest in AOL to one of three suitors, Google, Microsoft, or Yahoo! All were interested in the 112 million unique monthly visitors that AOL could bring to their advertising-supported Web sites.

IBM showed improved earnings while it completed the sale of its PC business to Lenovo of China, settled an antitrust case it had filed against Microsoft, and laid off 13,000 employees, most of them in Europe. Analysts believed that the company's stronger financial results showed that spending on information technology, which had been in a lull, was increasing slowly. IBM also bought software company Ascential Software for $1.1 billion; Ascential's software helped organize large quantities of raw data for business customers.

Apple dropped IBM and Freescale Semiconductor as its longtime suppliers of the computer chips used in Macintosh computers in favour of Intel, whose microprocessors were also used in Windows-based computers. Amazon.com, with an eye on the popularity of downloaded music, said that it would download short literary works to online customers for 49 cents each. The book industry was divided over whether the downloads, called Amazon Shorts, posed a threat or boon to traditional publishers.

Howard Stringer (see BIOGRAPHIES), Sony's new CEO and its first top executive from outside Japan, promised to improve the firm's electronics division, which had been badly hurt by competing consumer electronics products, including Apple's iPod music player, and by declining prices for items such as digital cameras. The electronics business contributed about two-thirds of Sony's revenue. When Apple introduced new iPod models late in the year, Sony said that it intended to challenge Apple's dominance in digital music players. Sony also announced it would eliminate 10,000 jobs as part of a reorganization, however, and that it expected to lose about $90 million in the fiscal year ending in March 2006. Sony had predicted a profit of $90 million.

Mergers and Acquisitions. Oracle bought Siebel Systems, which made software for managing customer relationships, for $5.85 billion. It was part of Oracle's continuing effort to be a consolidator in the business software market; Oracle said that the Siebel acquisition would make it the world's leader in that field. Oracle's biggest rival was the German business software company SAP. The relatively quiet acquisition of Siebel was less than a year after Oracle's year-and-a-half pursuit and hostile takeover of business software firm PeopleSoft for $10.3 billion. Early in 2005 Oracle outbid SAP for Retek, a retail-oriented business software maker, for which Oracle paid $643.3 million.

Sun Microsystems acquired Storage Technology for $4.1 billion in cash. Analysts said that Sun was trying to revitalize its business by strengthening its storage capabilities, which was likely to

please corporate customers concerned about the long-term storage and security of data. Sun's revenue had reached a peak in 2001 and had lost money the next three years on diminished revenues.

Adobe Systems, creator of the Acrobat document-and-graphics software, acquired Macromedia, a multimedia firm, for $3.4 billion in stock. The deal promised a combined firm that would have both document-sharing and Web-design capabilities.

There was a consolidation in the online brokerage business as online trading continued a two-year decline. Ameritrade bought TD Waterhouse for an estimated $3 billion. E*Trade Financial Corp. paid $700 million in cash for competitor Harrisdirect. The deals were made in the belief that size would be a key factor in determining which companies prospered.

In an unusual purchase of a technology firm by private investors, Agilent Technologies sold its semiconductor business for $2.66 billion to two equity companies, Kohlberg Kravis Roberts and Silver Lake Partners. At the same time, Agilent, itself a spin-off from Hewlett-Packard five years earlier, said that it would spin off its chip-testing operations as two companies in 2006.

EBay bought Internet phone company Skype Technologies of Luxembourg for about $2.6 billion in cash and stock, although that amount could rise based on performance, the companies said. Skype software users could talk over the Internet for free, using their PCs instead of phones. The company also offered a premium service that allowed PC users to make calls to and receive calls from traditional telephones. EBay made the acquisition after Google, Microsoft, and Yahoo! began to offer online phone-calling services.

IAC/InterActiveCorp, the owner of travel Web site Expedia as well as television's Home Shopping Network, bought search engine company Ask Jeeves for $1.85 billion. While most search engine Web sites searched for key words or phrases, Ask Jeeves was designed to search for answers to specific questions.

Internet marketer DoubleClick was acquired for $1.1 billion by Hellman & Friedman LLC, a firm that specialized in buying out media companies. Despite a sharp increase in spending for online advertising, competition between firms that provided Internet ads to Web sites had driven down prices and left DoubleClick in a commodity market, some analysts said.

The Internet. In 2005 the United States insisted that it would indefinitely retain control of a group of Internet "root servers," which acted as traffic directors for PCs navigating the Web. The move was a departure from previous U.S. policy and came at a time when many nations favoured putting an international body in charge of overseeing the root servers. The U.S. government said that its decision was both a response to security threats and a way of ensuring Internet dependability for communications and business, but some countries believed that the United States was improperly tightening its grip on the Internet. In the end an international forum was created to discuss Internet issues, but the U.S. remained in control of the Internet's address system.

A resolution was reached in a long-running dispute between the Internet Corporation for Assigned Names and Numbers (ICANN), an Internet oversight group, and VeriSign, the company whose computers controlled much of the flow of traffic destined for Internet addresses that ended in ".com" and ".net." VeriSign in 2003 created a service that provided Web surfers who misspelled an Internet address with suggestions about what they might have intended to type. Because VeriSign sometimes profited from directing traffic to some of the Web sites it suggested, ICANN pressured the company to halt the service. VeriSign then sued ICANN on the grounds of business interference. ICANN and VeriSign reached a settlement that extended VeriSign's control of the ".com" addresses an extra five years beyond the existing 2007 contract expiration date but gave ICANN the right to review new services that might affect the Internet's address system.

Bloggers, persons who published personal opinions at their own Internet addresses, continued to gain more recognition and, in some cases, instant fame. A number of bloggers became self-appointed public watchdogs, and a few were credited with precipitating the resignations of prominent persons in the mainstream news media, such as Dan Rather, who quit the *CBS Evening News* several months after bloggers exposed flaws in a major news story that he had reported. Some observers, however, feared that blogs (a shortened form of the words *Web logs*) gave individuals the power of the press without the accompanying accountability for accuracy and fairness. Some blog-

Text Messaging: WAN2TLK?

In 2005 some 45 billion text messages were expected to be sent by cellular phone users in the United States. The sending of messages to and from mobile phones via Short Messaging Service (SMS) had been developed in the United Kingdom in the late 1980s, and the first text message was sent on Dec. 3, 1992. An SMS commercial service was launched in the U.K. in 1995. Text messaging, also called "texting" or TXT, did not take off until 1998, however, when it became possible to send messages between the four main British cell phone networks. The number of messages sent in the U.K. grew from one billion in 1999 to an expected 30 billion in 2005, according to the Mobile Data Association. In the U.S., text messaging emerged later but expanded rapidly. From 30 million messages sent in the U.S. in June 2001, the number grew to 14 billion in all of 2003 and skyrocketed to 25 billion in 2004.

Because tapping text into a telephone keypad was cumbersome and the number of characters in a text message was limited, a form of shorthand evolved, especially among young people. This included such shortcuts as UR for "your" or "you're," IMHO for "in my humble opinion," BTW for "by the way," and CUL8R for "see you later," as well as the employment of "emoticons," or "smileys," to express emotions. Even the plots of major literary works were being condensed into short text messages for use as a study aid. Meanwhile, educators were banning cell phones from the classroom to discourage cheating, and there was concern that standards of English would drop as text abbreviations entered the mainstream.

© Corbis

Text messaging on personal computers and, especially, handheld devices such as this cellular phone had blossomed hugely by 2005. Abbreviations and other keyboard shortcuts contributed to a unique "texting" language.

In addition to basic communication and entertainment, texters developed a wide variety of more serious uses, including the announcement by activists of demonstrations on the streets of China, Ukraine, and Kuwait and clandestine flirting in societies in which informal contact with the opposite sex was frowned upon. In South Africa counselors were sending information on patients' use of antiretroviral drugs to combat HIV/AIDS via text message to researchers at Cape Town University. Indian politicians were being summoned by staff members via text message to vote on new laws or make up a quorum in Parliament. A new computer system was being rolled out in the U.K. that would enable text reminders of criminal court sessions to be sent to witnesses. In May 2005 AMBER Alert warnings of U.S. child abductions began to be sent by text to those who opted to receive them, while Indonesia planned to use text messaging to spread early warnings of impending disasters. Individual politicians around the world—even the pope—were making use of text messaging. Shortly after his inauguration in April 2005, Pope Benedict XVI sent a "thought of the day" text message, a service that had been started by his predecessor, Pope John Paul II, in 2003.

With so many messages being sent, it came as no surprise that overactive texters around the world were developing a form of repetitive strain injury. The American Society of Hand Therapists warned in January 2005 that overuse of handheld devices could lead to carpal tunnel syndrome and tendinitis and advised users to switch hands frequently and take hourly breaks.

(ALAN STEWART)

oriented businesses that specialized in "social networking" became hugely successful. MySpace.com, begun in 2003 as a social network in which members could share their likes and dislikes about popular music, attracted an audience of more than 30 million members, many of them aged 14 to 20. In 2005 the Internet traffic of MySpace rose 840% over the previous year, and News Corp. acquired MySpace's parent company, Intermix Media, for about $580 million.

High-speed Internet access, also called broadband, continued to spread and grow in popularity. The extent to which broadband had become established in a country was viewed by some people as a measurement of the country's preparedness for the future. South Korea ranked first in broadband use as a percentage of its population, whereas the United States ranked 12th, according to the Organisation for Economic Co-operation and Development. In terms of the number of broadband users, however, the United States ranked first and South Korea was third. In the U.S., broadband service was not evenly distributed, and because of costs the rollout of broadband service sometimes skipped over areas that were too lightly populated, too distant from network equipment, or—some charged—too poor to afford the service. A few large U.S. cities planned their own broadband networks to make certain their entire population would be served. Philadelphia sought to construct a network using Wi-Fi, or wireless fidelity technology, to cover the entire city (350 sq km [135 sq mi]) with wireless broadband service. In San Francisco the establishment of a city wireless Internet network was opposed by commercial broadband providers—telephone and cable TV companies. Broadband services that transmitted data signals over electrical power lines became available in a small number of U.S. cities, but questions remained whether that form of broadband service would be economically viable.

Wi-Fi hotspots, which functioned as short-range wireless connections to a broadband Internet connection, proliferated in coffee shops, bookstores, hotels, and airports. Some hotspots offered free connections; others required a payment. The business of providing Wi-Fi for a fee proved to be less profitable than originally thought, and many commercial providers who sought to charge consumers for Wi-Fi underwent a consolidation. Security software firm McAfee acquired Wireless Security; networking firm Cisco Systems bought Wi-Fi firm Airespace; and electronics giant Siemens AG acquired Chantry Networks.

Computer Games. The game industry prepared for the next generation of video-game consoles. Microsoft's new Xbox 360 debuted in late 2005, but the competing Sony PlayStation 3 and Nintendo Revolution consoles were not expected to reach consumers until mid-2006. Microsoft hoped to pull ahead of Sony by introducing its game console earlier; in the previous generation of consoles, the Sony PlayStation 2 outsold the Microsoft Xbox nearly four to one, with Nintendo's GameCube coming in third. In the handheld video-game market, the Nintendo DS and various Game Boy models from Nintendo got some competition from Sony's new handheld unit, the PlayStation Portable, which was dubbed the PSP.

Grand Theft Auto: San Andreas, the latest in a series of controversial video games known for their casual attitude toward violence, had its rating changed from "mature" to "adults only" after a controversy erupted over sexually oriented material that was found hidden in the game's code. (Games rated "mature" could be purchased by those 17 or older; games rated "adults only" could be purchased only by persons 18 or older.) Hackers discovered they could unlock hidden animated sex scenes that had been part of the game during its development but had been eliminated before the game was introduced by its creator, Rockstar Games. The hackers then used the Internet to distribute the code that unlocked the sex scenes. The code was widely downloaded, which created an outcry in Congress and prompted the Entertainment Software Rating Board to change the rating of the game. As a result, many retailers removed the game from their shelves, which dealt a financial blow to Rockstar, whose *Grand Theft Auto* series of video games had collectively sold more than 21 million copies over four years. Rockstar later offered

Microsoft's next-generation Xbox 360 video-game machine, shown here mounted in large demonstration units, draws visitors at the Tokyo Game Show.

a software patch for the game that disabled the code for the sex scenes, and it also released a new mature-rated version of the game.

New Technology. A battle over standards threatened to disrupt the introduction in 2006 of next-generation DVD players that would be able to play high-definition TV programs and movies. It was feared that consumers might be reluctant to purchase next-generation players for fear that one of the two incompatible standards, Blu-ray from Sony and HD DVD from Toshiba, would lose out to the other and thereby render the purchase worthless. Movie studios faced a potentially expensive situation if they produced movies for the losing format. Computer and software firms such as Intel and Microsoft were concerned because new computers would need to have a DVD disk drive that used one or the other standard, since the technology would be a key to making PCs the centre of home multimedia networks. The first Toshiba HD DVD player was expected to appear in the U.S. in the spring of 2006, whereas the first Blu-ray DVD player to hit the American market would likely be the disk drive in Sony's PlayStation 3 video-game console, which would probably ship in late 2006. Microsoft rechristened its upcoming version of Windows for consumers. The

company changed the development codename, Longhorn, to its product name, Windows Vista. Microsoft promised security enhancements, better graphics, and new ways of searching for data. Vista was to be introduced in 2006, but test versions became available in mid-2005 as part of the company's efforts to refine the product before releasing it.

Disk-drive manufacturers rushed to make smaller drives, which they hoped would be used in consumer devices such as cellular phones. Hitachi and Seagate Technologies developed drives with capacities of several gigabytes that used disks only 2.5 cm (1 in) in diameter. Anticipating that such consumer devices would sometimes accidentally be dropped, drive makers were developing motion-sensing technology for hard drives that would detect when the hard drive was falling. The technology would make it possible to move sensitive components of the drive into a safe position before impact. In another area of disk-drive technology, Toshiba was the first manufacturer to introduce a commercial disk drive that used "perpendicular recording," a method of orienting the magnetically recorded data on a disk in a way that dramatically increased storage capacity.

(STEVE ALEXANDER)

Earth Sciences

New findings on MANTLE PLUMES were reported, while the very existence of mantle plumes came into question. GEONEUTRINOS were detected for the first time. The North Atlantic region experienced a record-breaking HURRICANE season, and scientists debated possible tropical-cyclone effects from GLOBAL WARMING.

GEOLOGY AND GEOCHEMISTRY

The dramatic red Navajo sandstone cliffs of the Colorado Plateau in southern Utah contain many iron-rich concretions, some of which appear to be very similar to the small spherical gray rocks, known as "blueberries," that were discovered on Mars by the Exploration Rover Opportunity. In 2005 Marjorie Chan of the University of Utah and coauthors presented a detailed geologic and geochemical study of the processes that led to the formation of the concretions in the Navajo sandstone. The processes involved the breakdown of iron minerals in a source rock by the action of groundwater and the formation of thin films of iron oxide (hematite), which coloured the rocks red. At a later time a different aqueous solution percolated through the rock and dissolved some of the iron oxide. When the solution reached locations that were more oxidizing than the solution, the iron minerals were precipitated and formed solid concretions of various shapes, including marble-shaped bodies that resembled the Mars blueberries. Listing six characteristics that indicated that the spherical concretions found in Utah were a good analog for the Mars blueberries, Chan's team concluded that the formation of the blueberries required the percolation of two separate aqueous solutions. The question that remained was whether the water that percolated through the rock on Mars also supported life.

A 2005 paper published by Aivo Lepland of the Geological Survey of Norway and coauthors delivered a strong shock in the continuing debate about whether traces of early life are recorded by the geochemistry of 3.85-billion-year-old rocks found in southwestern Greenland. In 1996 it had been reported that apatite, a mineral that was widely distributed in these old rocks, had inclusions of graphite (a carbon mineral) whose isotope ratios indicated that the carbon was of biogenic origin, and it was proposed that the apatite-graphite combination was derived from bacteria. Geologic and geochemical evidence supported the view that some of the rocks were sedimentary in origin and therefore indicative of the presence of water necessary for the existence of early bacteria.

Although it was well established that the geochemistry of tiny mineral bodies might facilitate the interpretation of the geologic environments of rock formation, these rocks had been strongly metamorphosed during their long history, which obscured the geologic environment of their original formation. The new results, which used optical microscopy and electron microscopy, denied the existence of any graphite in the apatite minerals described in the 1996 report, despite a diligent search that was extended to many associated rocks. The authors of the 2005 paper concluded that claims for the existence of early life in the rocks "cannot be founded on an occurrence of graphite inclusions in apatite."

Joseph V. Smith of the University of Chicago in 2005 presented evidence to support the hypothesis that mineralogy and geochemistry, particularly as related to volcanic eruptions, played significant roles in the emergence and evolution of a self-replicating biochemical system—that is, life. After the first living cells were generated by geochemistry on internal mineral surfaces about four billion years ago, life evolved through the utilization of energy from the Sun and the incorporation of selected chemical elements. Smith described

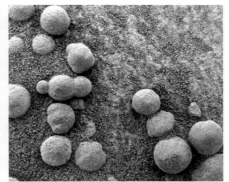

The loose round stones resting on the red sandstone ledges in Utah, shown at left, are iron-rich concretions and resemble the small round rocks found on Mars, shown below. A geologic study of the Utah nodules determined that they had formed in the presence of water and it therefore implied that water had also been present on Mars.

(Above) Photo by Marjorie A. Chan—University of Utah; (right) NASA—Jet Propulsion Laboratory—Cornell University

how volcanic activity would have been a major source of such biologically important elements as carbon, phosphorus, sulfur, iron, zinc, and manganese. Drawing on emerging evidence from studies of metabolism, gene regulation, and medicine, he noted a connection between geochemistry and the evolution of large-brained hominids. The East African Rift Valley, which opened about 30 million years ago, is associated with alkali-rich carbonatite volcanoes. Local soils derived from material erupted from these volcanoes would have been abundant in phosphorus and other trace elements that are known to be biochemical nutrients essential for the growth and enhancement of primate brains. Only in the Rift Valley was there the unique coincidence of this rather rare type of volcano and an evolving large-brained primate population. A test of the possible influence of alkali-rich volcanism in the evolution of hominids in Africa might come from advanced synchrotron X-ray measurements of the trace elements in the mineral apatite of fossil teeth.

In 2005 Ralf Tappert of the University of Alberta and coauthors demonstrated how major geologic processes might be elucidated by the geochemistry of diamonds and their inclusions. Diamonds from Jagersfontein, S.Af., contain tiny inclusions of garnet with two geochemical properties of interest. First, their content of the trace-element europium showed that they grew from material of the Earth's crust. Second, their unusual composition (majoritic garnet) proved that they nucleated and grew at depths of 250–500 km (about 155–310 mi) or more. This evidence indicated that crustal rocks were carried into the Earth's interior. The most likely geologic process that satisfied these observations was subduction of the oceanic crust. In addition, the ratio of carbon isotopes in the diamonds indicated that the source of the carbon may have been organic. Organic carbon would have been introduced from surface rocks (such as from dead organisms buried in the seafloor), which was consistent with the inferred subduction process. The study confirmed the idea of the long-term survival of crustal material within a heterogeneous mantle, at least to a depth of 500 km.

The geochemistry of lavas from Hawaii provided information about the mantle plume that many geologists assumed transports source rocks from deep in the mantle to a near-surface hotspot, where melting occurs. The

Hawaiian volcanoes comprise the parallel Loa and Kea chains, whose lavas are distinguished by slightly different but overlapping geochemical properties. Two papers in 2005 countered previous interpretations that described the mantle plume as having a concentrically zoned structure in terms of composition. Wafa Abouchami of the Max Planck Institute for Chemistry, Mainz, Ger., and coauthors presented high-precision lead-isotope data from the lavas and demonstrated that the plume had a bilateral composition structure between the two chains and that there were small-scale variations in composition along the chains. The results indicated that there were compositional bands less than 50 km (about 30 mi) in diameter within the plume and that they stretched out vertically like spaghetti over tens to hundreds of kilometres. Zhong-Yuan Ren of the Tokyo Institute of Technology and coauthors analyzed trace elements in inclusions of magma solidified within olivine crystals, which recorded the complexities of the magma sources in the mantle during the process of melting, magma uprise, and crystallization. They inferred that the plume was not concentrically zoned and that the geochemistry was controlled by the thermal structure of the plume, which contained streaks or ribbons of deformed ocean crust that had been subducted much earlier.

The phenomenon of volcanism within tectonic plates, such as that which occurs in Hawaii, was understood by most geologists to be caused by plumes of material that rises from the mantle to the Earth's surface. Two 2005 publications, however, presented powerful challenges to the existence of mantle plumes and suggested that geologists had reached an important revolutionary stage in theories of mantle dynamics and plate tectonics. Yaoling Niu of the University of Durham, Eng., organized an issue of the *Chinese Science Bulletin* that featured the "Great Plume Debate," and the Geological Society of America published *Plates, Plumes, and Paradigms*, a compendium that included several articles by one of the most influential skeptics of mantle plumes, Don L. Anderson of the California Institute of Technology.

(PETER J. WYLLIE)

GEOPHYSICS

Geophysicists of many different stripes spent much of the year in 2005 sifting through data from the great

earthquake of Dec. 26, 2004, which produced the tsunami that devastated coastal regions of the Indian Ocean. Seismologists determined that the earthquake lasted about 500 seconds, rupturing a 1,200-km (about 750-mi) segment of plate boundary from Sumatra, Indonesia, to the Andaman Islands, India, with maximum offsets of 15–20 m (49–66 ft). Debate continued about the precise moment magnitude of the event. It was originally inferred to be 9.0, but later analyses suggested values ranging from 9.15 to 9.3. Although these differences appear to be numerically small, they actually represent a large difference in the amount of energy released in the earthquake because earthquake magnitude scales are logarithmic. Geodesists contributed to the debate by using GPS (global positioning system) stations to measure the offset of the ground, which suggested a moment magnitude of 9.2. Remarkably, they found measurable offsets at distances as far as 4,500 km (2,800 mi) from the epicentre. Oceanographers used coastal tide-gauge records and satellite altimetry records to delineate the region where the tsunami originated and found several "hot-spot" regions of variable slip (motion) that acted as distinct tsunami sources. Geodynamicists calculated that the redistribution of mass that occurred during the earthquake should have decreased the length of day by 2.68 microseconds and shifted the rotation axis of the Earth so that the North Pole would have moved by about 2 cm (0.8 in). The change in rotational speed was probably too small to observe; however, the change in rotational axis might be detectable with observations made over an extended period of time. Some geomagneticists also speculated that the earthquake altered conditions in the fluid core of the Earth, and they were expecting a "jerk" in the strength of Earth's magnetic field to become observable within the following few years.

On March 28, 2005, an earthquake of moment magnitude 8.7 occurred off the west coast of Sumatra. It was located on the boundary of the Australia and Sunda tectonic plates, about 160 km (100 mi) to the southeast of the epicentre of the earthquake of December 26. Some seismologists considered this earthquake an aftershock because it was likely triggered by a change in stress induced by the December event. As an aftershock it would have the distinction of being the largest ever recorded. Incredibly, a group of seismologists in the United

Kingdom had forecast such an event in a paper published on March 17, just 11 days before the earthquake occurred. The technique used by the scientists did not allow for specific earthquake predictions (for example, a forecast of a magnitude–7.4 earthquake next Tuesday at 11:40 AM in southern California), but it might be able to provide information that would be useful in preparing for future earthquakes and so reduce the damage they could cause. The slip of the March 28 earthquake was concentrated beneath the Indonesian islands of Nias and Simeulue. It caused widespread damage and the deaths of about 1,300 persons, but the fact that it occurred mainly beneath these islands may have kept the death toll from being even larger. Scientists who modeled the earthquake found that the presence of the islands severely reduced the amount of water displaced during the earthquake so that only a mild, and largely unnoticed, tsunami was produced.

Although most earthquakes happen at the boundaries of tectonic plates, large damaging earthquakes occasionally occur within a tectonic plate. A notable example is the New Madrid seismic zone, which lies approximately in the middle of the North America tectonic plate. Four large earthquakes occurred near New Madrid, Mo., in 1811–12, and debate about the present-day seismic hazard in the region was vigorous. In June researchers published results from a four-year study of ground motion in the New Madrid region. The scientists drove H-beams 20 m (66 ft) into the ground and continuously tracked their relative positions, using GPS equipment. They found relative motion of about 3 mm (0.12 in) per year for two H-beams on opposite sides of an active fault and argued that this implied a strain (deformation) in the New Madrid region as great as that found in plate-boundary regions such as the San Andreas Fault zone in California. This interpretation, though it was at odds with previous GPS studies in the region, was consistent with previous geologic results that suggested that large, damaging earthquakes happened in the New Madrid seismic zone about every 500 years. If the new interpretation came to be supported by future work, the seismic hazard to residents of the New Madrid region, including the city of Memphis, Tenn., would be recognized to be just as high as for those living in earthquake-prone California.

A new subfield of geophysics was established in 2005 when an international team of scientists announced the first-ever detection of geoneutrinos. Neutrinos are nearly massless subatomic particles that travel close to the speed of light and interact very weakly with matter. They are emitted during the radioactive decay of certain elements, such as uranium and thorium, and solar neutrinos from nuclear reactions on the Sun had been detected and studied on Earth for many years. Using a detector buried in a mine in Japan and cleverly screening out neutrinos emitted by nearby nuclear-power plants, the scientists were able to identify conclusively neutrinos that were emitted by the decay of radioactive elements within the Earth. Ultimately, the scientists hoped to be able to use geoneutrino observations to deduce the amount of radioactive heat generated within the Earth, which is generally thought to represent 40–60% of the total heat the Earth dissipated each year. Furthermore, by combining geoneutrino observations from many detectors, scientists might be able to make tomographic maps of radiogenic heat production within the Earth. Such maps would lead to a better understanding of the convection currents within the mantle that drive the motion of tectonic plates at the surface of the Earth. (KEITH D. KOPER)

METEOROLOGY AND CLIMATE

The devastation that resulted from Hurricanes Katrina and Rita along the Gulf of Mexico during the 2005 hurricane season increased investigators' interest in short-term and seasonal forecasts of tropical storms and hurricanes as well as the role that climate might be playing in the recent surge in storm activity. (A tropical storm is a tropical cyclone with sustained winds of 63–118 km/hr [39–73 mph]; a hurricane is a tropical cyclone with sustained winds of 119 km/hr [74 mph] or greater.) Although the seasonal forecasting of where tropical storms and hurricanes might make landfall remained a difficult task, forecasts of broader measures of storm activity had become quite successful. A press release by the National Oceanic and Atmospheric Administration (NOAA) on May 16, 2005, forecast an active tropical-cyclone season, with 12–15 named storms and 7–9 hurricanes. (A tropical cyclone is named when it reaches tropical-storm status.) This forecast was in contrast to the long-term mean of 11 named storms and 6 hurricanes. On August 2, only two months into the six-month-long tropical-cyclone season, the forecast was updated to 18–21 named storms and 9–11 hurricanes. When the phenomenal season officially ended November 30, a record 26 named storms had formed, including a record 13 hurricanes. (On December 2 the 26th storm, Epsilon, became the 14th hurricane of the year, and one additional tropical storm, Zeta, formed on December 30. After the original, preselected list of 21 names from Arlene to Wilma was exhausted, letters of the Greek alphabet were used.) The NOAA forecasts, which have been issued since 1998, were a combined effort of the National Hurricane Center, the

NOAA

From a research aircraft within the eye of Hurricane Katrina, the surrounding eyewall had the appearance of an immense "stadium" of clouds, an effect characteristic of intense hurricanes.

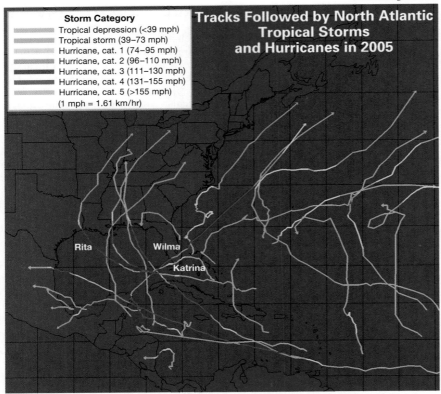

www.wunderground.com

Tracks Followed by North Atlantic Tropical Storms and Hurricanes in 2005

Storm Category
Tropical depression (<39 mph)
Tropical storm (39–73 mph)
Hurricane, cat. 1 (74–95 mph)
Hurricane, cat. 2 (96–110 mph)
Hurricane, cat. 3 (111–130 mph)
Hurricane, cat. 4 (131–155 mph)
Hurricane, cat. 5 (>155 mph)
(1 mph = 1.61 km/hr)

The map shows the tracks of 24 tropical cyclones in the North Atlantic region that reached tropical-storm strength or greater in 2005. (Three storms that formed in the eastern North Atlantic are not shown.) Hurricanes Katrina, Rita, and Wilma at their peak were among the most intense hurricanes on record and had maximum sustained surface winds that reached 173 mph (278 km/hr).

Climate Prediction Center, and the Hurricane Research Division. Forecasts of above-normal activity were also made within the private sector and by academics. For example, a team led by William Gray, a professor at Colorado State University (CSU), forecast as early as December 2004 that there was an above-average probability that a major hurricane would make landfall in the U.S. during 2005. By the end of May, the CSU team had bumped up their forecast from 11 named storms to 15, and on August 5 the team raised it to 20.

The ability to make such seasonal forecasts hinges on the fact that several large-scale oceanic and atmospheric patterns have been identified as having an influence on tropical-cyclone activity. The NOAA forecasts rely upon observations in the Atlantic basin of wind and air-pressure patterns and of multidecadal (decade-to-decade) variations in such environmental factors as sea-surface temperatures. In addition, most seasonal-storm forecasters closely monitored the status of the El Niño/Southern Oscillation (ENSO), a large-scale weather pattern associated with the warming and cooling of the equatorial Pacific Ocean, because it can affect the strength of wind shear—which inhibits storm development—over the Atlantic Ocean. In 1995 the Atlantic multidecadal signal turned favourable for storm development, and all the tropical-storm seasons from that year through 2005 exhibited above-normal activity except for the years 1997 and 2002, when there were ENSO-related increases in Atlantic-basin wind shear.

Although the idea that multidecadal climate variations influence tropical-storm activity in the Atlantic had become generally accepted, the role of long-term climate change and global warming was under debate. Since warmer ocean waters tend to fuel hurricane development, it was tempting to consider possible links between a warmer climate and more frequent or intense hurricanes. Kerry Emanuel of the Massachusetts Institute of Technology determined that there was a high correlation between an increase in tropical ocean temperatures and an increase in an index that he developed to gauge the potential destructiveness of hurricanes. His results suggested that future warming could lead to a further increase in the destructive potential of hurricanes. Kevin Trenberth of the National Center for Atmospheric Research noted that human-influenced changes in climate were evident and that they should affect hurricane intensity and rainfall. He cautioned, however, that there was no sound theoretical basis for determining how these changes would affect the number of hurricanes that would form or the number that would make landfall.

Theoretical and numerical simulations of global warming on hurricanes by Thomas Knutson of NOAA's Geophysical Fluid Dynamics Laboratory in Princeton, N.J., and colleagues suggested that hurricane wind intensity would gradually increase by about 5% over the next 80 years. Given the normal large multidecadal variations that occur in hurricane frequency and intensity, it appeared therefore that any effects of global warming on the impact of hurricanes would be difficult to determine for some time. Another study, however, presented observational evidence that an increase in storm intensity might already be occurring. Using hurricane data from weather satellites, Peter Webster of the Georgia Institute of Technology and colleagues found nearly a doubling in the number of the most severe (category 4 and 5) storms worldwide in the previous 35 years. Yet they also cautioned that a longer period of observations was needed in order to attribute the increase to global warming.

Less controversial was the steady improvement in the forecasts of tropical-storm tracks. Accurate and timely landfall forecasts are crucial to the effectiveness of evacuations in the face of dangerous storms. In the early 1970s the mean 48-hour error in the storm tracks forecast by the National Hurricane Center was about 510 km (320 mi). With steady improvement through the years, the mean error shrank to less than 290 km (180 mi) in the late 1990s, and the mean error of 175 km (108 mi) in 2004 was the best to date. Both statistical and numerical forecast models had contributed to the improving forecasts, with numerical forecast models taking the lead since the 1990s. Hurricane forecasting is clearly a case where better models resulting from advances in physics and computational power have the potential to save lives.

(DOUGLAS LE COMTE)

Economic Affairs

In 2005 rising U.S. DEFICITS, tight monetary policies, and higher OIL PRICES triggered by HURRICANE DAMAGE in the Gulf of Mexico were MODERATING INFLUENCES on the world economy and on U.S. stock markets, but some other countries had a ROBUST year, the U.S. dollar strengthened, and oil companies reported RECORD profits.

In 2005 the world economy expanded by 4.3%, in contrast to the 30-year high of 5.1% in 2004. Several factors contributed to the more moderate growth that affected nearly all regions (notable exceptions were India and Japan). Higher oil and other commodity prices, which had begun causing capacity constraints at the end of 2004, were reducing incomes of importers. In the U.S., monetary policy was tighter. Other developed countries' macroeconomic policies were also less accommodative, and the booming housing markets of 2004 were becoming more subdued. Against this, at least for the time being, inflation and interest rates remained low, however, and a global slowdown in manufacturing output was offset by the strengthening services sector.

The global economy continued to be led by the U.S. and China. Higher oil prices, short-term interest rates that were still low but rising, and the exceptionally disruptive hurricane season slowed expansion in the U.S. to 2.5% (3.3% in 2004). Insurance brokers estimated that Hurricanes Katrina, Rita, and Wilma could cost global insurance and reinsurance sectors up to $80 billion. Although past experience of natural disasters suggested that the hurricanes would not have an impact on overall U.S. growth in the longer term, in the short term a major cost resulted from the shutdown of oil-refinery capacity that accounted for 13% of national capacity. In China economic momentum moderated only slightly, and the country's importance as a global player became increasingly evident. In July, in

recognition of this development, the outgoing secretary-general of the Organisation for Economic Co-operation and Development stated that China should be admitted as a member.

The slowdown in global growth, intense competition in many industries, and higher oil and commodity prices provided a stimulus for foreign direct investment (FDI) as major firms sought to improve their competitive positions. More than 100 countries introduced

© Louis DeLuca—Dallas Morning News/Corbis

A Dallas service station's price sign uses humour to underline the strong feelings among Americans in response to sharply rising gasoline prices in August.

new regulations to improve their investment appeal. Total inflow of FDI was up 2% in 2004 to $648 billion, bringing the total stock to an estimated $9 trillion. Less-developed countries (LDCs) were the main beneficiaries, and after three years of declining flows, FDI in 2004 rebounded to rise 40%, giving the LDCs a record 36% share of the total. All less-developed regions had increased inflows, led by China, which accounted for a quarter of the total. LDCs offered new growth markets in

which companies could boost their sales and gave access to rich supplies of natural resources when demand for oil and other commodities was forcing up prices.

NATIONAL ECONOMIC POLICIES

The International Monetary Fund projected a 2.5% rise in the GDP of the developed economies, compared with a 3.1% rise in 2004.

United States. In the first half of the year, the U.S. economy grew 3.6% year-on-year. Events in the third quarter temporarily dislocated output and dented U.S. and international confidence, but GDP was likely to exceed the IMF's projected expansion of 3.5% (4.3% in 2004). The economy quickly moved back on course, and third-quarter output rose much faster than expected, at an annual rate of 4.3%. The immediate effect of Hurricanes Katrina and Rita was the loss of oil, natural gas, and petroleum-products processing in New Orleans and the Gulf of Mexico, which resulted in a short-term extreme escalation of energy prices. The area represented only 2% of total U.S. GDP, but it accounted for a much larger share of oil and oil-derivatives activities. The hurricanes, together with a strike at aircraft manufacturer Boeing, caused industrial output and employment to fall in September, but there was a recovery in October when industrial output rose a modest 1.9% above year-earlier levels.

The buoyancy in the economy was due to strong consumer demand. This was partly fueled by the strength of the housing market, where the median established-home price rose by 14.4% in the year-to-August. At the same time, the rate of unemployment fell steadily and at 5% in October was below the year-earlier level (5.5%). Fears that consumer confidence would be dented by high energy prices proved unfounded. Retail sales (excluding autos) rose 10.3% year-on-year in October.

Headline inflation, which included food and energy, rose fast relative to rates over the previous decade, reflecting the higher oil prices. In October consumer prices rose 4.3%, compared

Table I. Real Gross Domestic Products of Selected OECD Countries
% annual change

Country	2001	2002	2003	2004	2005[1]
United States	0.8	1.6	2.7	4.2	3.5
Japan	0.2	–0.3	1.4	2.7	2.0
Germany	1.2	0.1	–0.2	1.6	0.8
France	2.1	1.3	0.9	2.0	1.5
Italy	1.8	0.4	0.3	1.2	0.0
United Kingdom	2.2	2.0	2.5	3.2	1.9
Canada	1.8	3.1	2.0	2.9	2.9
All developed countries	1.2	1.5	1.9	3.3	2.5
Seven major countries above	1.0	1.1	1.8	3.2	2.5
European Union	2.0	1.3	1.3	2.5	1.6

[1]Estimated.
Note: Seasonally adjusted at annual rates.
Source: OECD, *IMF World Economic Outlook*, September 2005.

Table II. Standardized Unemployment Rates in Selected Developed Countries
% of total labour force

Country	2001	2002	2003	2004	2005[1]
United States	4.8	5.8	6.0	5.5	5.1
Japan	5.0	5.4	5.3	4.7	4.4
Germany	6.9	7.6	8.7	9.2	9.3
France	8.7	9.0	9.7	10.0	10.0
Italy	9.6	9.1	8.8	8.1	7.7
United Kingdom	5.1	5.2	5.0	4.7	4.8
Canada	7.2	7.7	7.6	7.2	6.8
All developed countries	6.2	6.7	6.9	6.7	6.5
Seven major countries above	5.9	6.5	6.7	6.4	6.1
Euro zone	7.8	8.2	8.7	8.8	8.7

[1]Projected.
Source: OECD, *Economic Outlook*, November 2005.

with 3.2% a year earlier. The underlying rate (excluding food and energy) was well contained and slowed to 1.7% in the first half of the year but began rising toward the end of the year, which was attributed to the tighter labour market and higher unit-labour costs.

Given a continuing decline in the national savings rate and a growing U.S. current-account deficit, public finances continued to be a cause of domestic as well as international concern. At 2.6% of GDP, the federal deficit for fiscal 2005 was lower than expected. Corporate income taxes and other revenue increases offset increased military expenditure.

United Kingdom. The rate of economic growth slowed much more than expected in 2005, and the U.K.'s GDP was likely to fall slightly short of the IMF-projected 1.9% increase. This was in stark contrast to the 3.2% consumer-led growth in 2004. The 1.5% growth in output early in the year was the lowest in a decade. A modest improvement in the second quarter brought the annual rise to 1.7%. The slowdown was due to sluggish private consumption, which declined to 1.8% from 3.6% in 2004.

Higher interest rates, which were subsequently lowered in August, contributed to the slowdown, as did the rapid cooling of the housing market. The rise in house prices peaked at 15.2% in August 2004, and in September 2005 the annual increase of 3.2% represented a nine-year low. At the same time, the rise in fuel prices contributed to the two-percentage-point decline in real income in the year to the second quarter.

Despite the slowdown, the rate of inflation increased. Year-on-year the September consumer price index rose 2.5% before falling back in October to 2.3%. Higher oil prices added 0.7 percentage point to the September index, compared with 0.25 percentage point a year earlier. Import prices for consumer goods rose, which was surprising given that U.K. companies were increasingly outsourcing to countries such as China that had lower labour costs.

Labour-market trends were more positive in the U.K. The 4.7% unemployment rate in September was unchanged over the same year-earlier period. Tight labour conditions were eased by the substantial net inflow of immigrants

attracted to the U.K. by the abundance of jobs. There were an estimated 75,000 potential workers from countries that had joined the EU in 2004 who were eligible to join the U.K. workforce. The increase in the labour supply also eased pressure on the average wage, which rose 4.1%. Public-sector wages were rising much faster (5.6% annually) than those in the private sector (3.8%), with take-home pay some 13% higher for public-sector workers than that of their private-sector counterparts.

Japan. Expansion over the year looked set to exceed the 2% (2.7% in 2004) projected by the IMF, and business confidence in Japan was at its highest level in a decade. For the fourth straight quarter, output rose in the three months to September, exceeding expectations with an annualized increased of 1.7%. This was despite adverse factors that included cuts in public expenditure and the increased cost of imported oil. Japan moved away from its traditional export-led growth to private domestic demand. This was helped by increasing household incomes and a drop in the unemployment rate to 4.2% in September (compared with 4.6% a year earlier), which brought it to the lowest level since August 1998. For the first time in a decade, firms were increasing the number of full-time jobs and reducing the amount of part-time work.

Badly needed reforms were made in the banking sector, and bank lending increased for the first time since 1988. The sector had long underperformed because of the large number of bad loans being supported—they were estimated at $362 billion in 2002—but it was at last becoming more profitable. By March the major banks had exceeded government targets in reducing the share of nonperforming loans down to 2.9% from 8.4% in 2002.

Although deflation persisted, it was on a downward trend. The core inflation rate (excluding fresh food but not energy products) fell 0.1% in the third quarter. Land prices nationwide were falling more slowly, and in Tokyo they rose for the first time in 15 years.

Euro Zone. In 2005 Europe's long-awaited economic recovery did not materialize, and the euro zone remained weak and vulnerable. The IMF revised downward its forecast rise for GDP to 1.2% (2% in 2004), and the zone once again lagged the performance of Japan, the U.K., and the U.S. Second-quarter output slowed to 0.3% (down from 0.5% in the first quarter). The economic malaise that this generated was exacerbated by political turmoil surrounding the rejection of the proposed EU constitution by voters in France and The Netherlands (*see* WORLD AFFAIRS: *European Union:* Sidebar) and the failure of national governments at the June EU summit to agree on a budget. The EU institutions came under criticism, and for the 11th straight year the Court of Auditors refused to approve the EU's own accounts because of waste and fraud in the €100 billion (about $118 billion) budget. In March the once-sacred Stability and Growth Pact, which set a 3% limit on the budget deficits of national governments, was amended to give governments more time to reduce excessive deficits. This made it more difficult to enforce discipline, and the pact lost credibility. Several major countries, including Germany, France, and Italy, exceeded the limits, and Hungary's deficit was expected to reach nearly 7%.

Economic performance across the zone varied widely, and monetary management was difficult. Unemployment remained high at 8.6%, and labour reforms were long overdue in several countries, notably Germany, Spain, and France, where unemployment was nearly 10%. The future of the monetary union was questioned, and the European Central Bank (ECB) once again came under pressure to cut interest rates. Headline inflation, which included the cost of energy, remained above the ECB's 2% ceiling and in September jumped to 2.6% owing to higher oil prices, though it dipped in October (2.5%) and November (2.4%). Core inflation was much lower, but the ECB moved to subdue prices and on December 1 raised interest rates for the first time since 2000, from 2% to 2.25%.

The Countries in Transition. Overall, the region, excluding the Commonwealth of Independent States (CIS), grew by 4.3%, which reflected a marked slowdown from 2004 (6.6%). The eight "emerging Europe" countries of Central and Eastern Europe (Czech Republic, Estonia, Hungary, Latvia, Lithuania, Poland, Slovakia, and Slovenia) that became members of the EU in May 2004 continued to benefit from EU accession, but the pace of expansion eased following the initial high level of activity and investment boom in the run-up to EU membership. Among the top performers were Estonia (7%) and Slovakia (5%), which were establishing reputations for being business-friendly and were attracting strong investment interest.

Table III. Changes in Output in Less-Developed Countries
% annual change in real gross domestic product

Area	2001	2002	2003	2004	2005[1]
All less-developed countries	4.1	4.8	6.5	7.3	6.4
Regional groups					
Africa	4.1	3.6	4.6	5.3	4.5
Asia	5.6	6.6	8.1	8.2	7.8
Middle East and Europe	3.7	4.2	6.5	5.5	5.4
Western Hemisphere	0.5	0.0	2.2	5.6	4.1
Central and Eastern Europe	0.2	4.4	4.6	6.5	4.3
Commonwealth of Independent States	6.3	5.3	7.9	8.4	6.0

[1]Projected.
Source: *IMF World Economic Outlook*, September 2005.

Table IV. Changes in Consumer Prices in Less-Developed Countries
% change from preceding year

Area	2001	2002	2003	2004	2005[1]
All less-developed countries	6.7	5.9	6.0	5.8	5.9
Regional groups					
Africa	12.2	9.6	10.4	7.8	8.2
Asia	2.7	2.1	2.6	4.2	4.2
Middle East	5.4	6.5	7.1	8.4	10.0
Western Hemisphere	6.1	8.9	10.6	6.5	6.3

[1]Projected.
Source: *IMF World Economic Outlook*, September 2005.

The 12 transition counties of the CIS grew faster. Output in the seven low-income CIS countries (Armenia, Azerbaijan, Georgia, Kyrgyzstan, Moldova, Tajikistan, and Uzbekistan) accelerated to 8.9% (8.3% in 2004), led by an 18.7% increase in GDP in Azerbaijan, where oil production rose sharply. Output in the larger CIS countries (Russia, Ukraine, Kazakhstan, Belarus, and Turkmenistan) increased more slowly at 6% (8.4% in 2004). GDP growth in Russia slowed to 5.5% (7.2% in 2004), as the oil sector was hampered by a lack of investment and manufacturing was hurt by capacity constraints. While inflation rates in most of the EU transition countries declined, in the CIS countries inflationary pressures were increasing, largely because of high oil prices and, in some countries, excessive private consumption. In Russia social spending contributed to a 12.6% rise in consumer prices. Bribery and corruption were less of an obstacle to doing business in 2005, compared with 2002, according to a survey by the European Bank for Reconstruction and Development. Nevertheless, bribes were accepted as a business cost and still accounted for some 1% of annual revenues.

Less-Developed Countries. The IMF projected a deceleration in LDC output from 7.3% in 2004 to a still-robust 6.4%, and all regions grew more slowly. China and India again boosted overall LDC expansion. Regional disparities were not as wide as in many previous years. On a per capita basis, the lowest growth was in Africa (2.4%).

Output in Africa slowed to 4.5% from a higher-than-expected 5.3% in 2004. The resource-rich countries boosted growth in sub-Saharan Africa (4.8%). The GDP of South Africa, the region's largest economy, increased 4.3%, with higher metal prices helping to offset increased oil prices and rising unit-labour costs. Unemployment remained a problem. Zimbabwe continued to deteriorate, with output down 7.1% and consumer prices up 200%. Output in Seychelles also fell, for the third straight year, by 2.8%. The Angolan economy expanded strongly for the second straight year, at 14.7%. GDP in Nigeria, the region's second largest economy, slowed to around 4% (6% in 2004) as oil output was constrained by capacity constraints, but the non-oil sector was buoyant and at risk of overheating. The CFA franc zone lagged, with output falling to 3.3%.

In Asia GDP was forecast to increase 7.3%, led by China (9%) and India (7.1%), but growth was mixed across the region. Pakistan grew by 7.4%, its fastest pace in two decades, as past macroeconomic reforms began to bear fruit. In Indonesia GDP expanded 5.8%, while the inflation rate reached a six-year high of 17.9% in October as fuel prices rose in response to government cuts in subsidies. Poor harvests and higher oil prices were detrimental in the Philippines, where growth slowed from 6% in 2004 to 4.7%, and in Thailand, where it declined from 6.1% to 3.5%. The newly industrializing Asian economies (Hong Kong, Singapore, South Korea, and Taiwan) grew by 4%, led by Hong Kong, where GDP rose 6.3%. Higher oil prices and slower growth in information technology exports adversely affected South Korea (3.8%) and Taiwan (3.4%). Singapore expanded 3.9% and earned the distinction of overtaking the U.S. as the world's most successful economy in exploiting new information and communications technology.

The better-than-expected recovery in Latin America in 2004 continued at a more sustainable pace in 2005, with output forecast at 4.1% (5.6% in 2004). Argentina expanded by 7.5% (9% in 2004); Uruguay grew 6% (12.3% in 2004); and though Venezuela rose 7.8%, that was much lower than the 17.9% growth recorded in 2004. Weaker manufacturing output was offset by the strong demand for the region's commodities, particularly coffee, copper, and oil, which accounted for 65% of the region's exports. The low interest rates and improved risk profile of the region also helped to stimulate an 11% increase in investment. The region's annual inflation rate fell to around 5% in September. Only Venezuela experienced high consumer price rises (16.6%), but the rate was declining with price controls and tighter monetary policy.

Despite the continuing terrorism and insurgency in some countries in the

With high oil prices hurting economies across Asia in 2005, environmentalists campaign in South Korea. The writing on the barrel says, in part: "Oil is as pricey as gold; a barrel is worth $100."

AP/Wide World Photos

Middle East, overall economic growth was estimated at 5.4%. Bahrain, Kuwait, Oman, Qatar, Saudi Arabia, and the United Arab Emirates, which constituted the Gulf Cooperation Council, generated nearly 40% of both oil imports and the world's oil reserves. Continuing high oil revenues enabled double-digit public spending, much of it on infrastructure improvements. The strong demand for labour in these countries assisted the non-oil-producing countries in the region through higher remittances and intraregional travel flows. Nevertheless, growth in the oil-importing countries fell from 4.6% in 2004 to 4%, partly because of the removal of quotas under the Agreement on Textiles and Clothing.

INTERNATIONAL TRADE AND PAYMENTS

The volume of world trade in goods and services was expected to rise 7%, which would make 2005 the fourth year of strong recovery. The deceleration from the exceptional 10.3% expansion in 2004 largely reflected the slowdown in the industrialized countries.

Current-account balances in 2005 became a source of international debate and concern. The U.S. economy was being largely driven by the willingness of Americans to spend heavily on imported goods, while much of the world was building up dollar savings, providing support for the U.S. currency. This situation made the U.S. extremely vulnerable to externalities. The U.S. deficit continued to burgeon and was expected to exceed $760 billion. It was being counterbalanced, not only by the huge surpluses in Asia but also by the commodity-producing countries in the Middle East and Russia and, to some extent, by Latin America and Canada.

Overall, the current-account deficit of the developed countries rose from $314 billion to $451 billion, with the value of exports rising more slowly than imports. The trade deficit closely matched that on current account, increasing from $314 billion to $476 billion. Continuing the well-established trend, the U.S. current-account deficit—which at $760 billion was well above the 2004 figure ($668 billion) and was expected to rise further in 2006—exceeded the total surplus of the other developed countries. In Japan the surplus fell for the first time in four years, to $153 billion. The traditional deficits in the Anglo-Saxon countries continued, with a slight fall in the U.K. to $41 billion and

Australia unchanged at $39 billion. In the euro zone, however, the surplus halved to $24 billion, despite a 20% surge in Germany's surplus to $121 billion. Spain, Italy, and France saw their deficits rise. A 12% drop in the surplus of the newly industrialized Asian countries to $78 billion was accounted for by a decline in South Korea.

Most notable were the changes in the LDCs. For the sixth straight year, the overall surplus rose dramatically, from $228 billion in 2004 to a record $410 billion. Significantly, the Middle East surplus more than doubled to $218 billion as higher oil prices sent the region's exports soaring to $543 billion ($388 billion in 2004). China accounted for a quarter of the surplus ($116 billion). Exports from LDCs in Asia rose by 21%, contributing to the $110 billion surplus. The surplus in Latin America rose slightly to $22 billion, and in Africa it was a record $12 billion, up from $600 million. Increased oil revenues produced a doubling of the surplus in Russia to $102 billion. Indebtedness of the LDCs rose in absolute terms by around 5% to almost $3.2 trillion. Measured as a share of exports of goods and services, it fell for the seventh straight year to 3.8%, compared with 4.2% in 2004 and 9.6% in 1998. The rate fell in all regions except in less-developed Asia, where it was unchanged at 2.4%.

Interest and Exchange Rates. For the early part of 2005, interest rates were benign and reflected the low-inflation environment. Low interest rates were particularly beneficial for the LDCs, which were able to reschedule debt and meet their financing commitments early. At the same time, the low rates contributed to much stronger economic growth, which in itself became inflationary through the act of raising commodity prices. These, in turn, had consequences for the industrialized countries, where inflationary pressures were building and creating uncertainty in central banks, which feared that the increased costs of fuel and other raw materials would feed into consumer prices and wages.

It was against this background that monetary policies were being tightened, and interest rates, rather than the nature of public and current accounts, had the most bearing on exchange rates. The U.S. Federal Reserve (Fed) raised interest rates in quarter-point hikes from 2.25% at the beginning of the year to 4.25% at year's end. The Bank of England (BOE) cut interest rates for the first time in two years, by

AP/Wide World Photos

Textile workers at a factory in Fanchang, China, produce garments for export. China's growing trade surplus in 2005 raised concerns in the developed world, particularly in the U.S. and the European Union.

a quarter point to 4.5%. The ECB, prompted by signs of economic recovery in France and Germany, raised the interest rate to 2.25%, ending two years of inactivity. In Japan the zero-interest policy continued, but in much of Asia rates were rising modestly in the second half of the year. In Hong Kong monetary policy was kept in line with that of the U.S. Despite a modest rise, interest rates were declining in real terms in Asian LDCs.

In contrast to 2004, in 2005 the dollar demonstrated considerable strength and resilience. In the first half of the year, the U.S. dollar appreciated against its trading partners, and in July the dollar was up 3.5%. This was due partly to the rise in U.S. interest rates, which had created a wider differential with Europe and encouraged investors to hold dollar- rather than euro-denominated assets. From the end of July, the dollar was more volatile. In mid-October it was reported that the September consumer price increase of 1.2% was the biggest in 25 years, while core inflation was only 0.1%. This news dampened speculation concerning more interest-rate increases, and the dollar slid. Good economic news and higher interest rates caused it to recover, and on November 10 the dollar reached two-year highs against the euro, British sterling, and the Japanese yen. The dollar fell back following comments by Fed Chairman Alan Greenspan, who warned against complacency about the current-

account deficits and the buildup of dollar assets outside the U.S. By year's end the dollar had recovered to end its steep three-year decline.

In late November the yen reached seven-year lows against the euro, sterling, the Australian dollar, and the South Korean won. The fall was prompted by positive economic news that sent the Nikkei 225 stock index soaring to a five-year high. The weakening yen was good news for exporters, and the Japanese government appeared complacent.

On July 21 the People's Bank of China (PBC) announced long-awaited currency reforms following pressure on China from the U.S. and other industrialized countries to change the fixed exchange rate under which the renminbi was pegged to the dollar. The perceived undervaluation of the renminbi was seen as giving China an unfair trading advantage. Under the new regime the renminbi was revalued by 2.1% and moved to a managed float against a basket of currencies that included the dollar, the yen, the euro, and the won. This allowed the renminbi to fluctuate by 0.3% against the dollar. The Malaysian government announced that the ringgit, which was pegged to the dollar, would be subject to a managed float; it soon rose 0.7% against the dollar. The moves toward more flexible exchange rates were widely welcomed. In a further—and unexpected—move on September 25, the PBC announced a widening of

the band in which currencies other than the dollar might trade against the renminbi. No reasons were given for the move, but it was likely that the wider band would ease pressure on China to intervene in the market to keep the yen and euro within the band.   (IEIS)

STOCK MARKETS

High energy prices, such as those experienced in 2005, usually push up inflation and interest rates, put companies under pressure, and undermine stock markets. Other economic shocks—such as the impact of natural disasters on the scale of the December 2004 tsunami in the Indian Ocean on Asia, Hurricanes Katrina and Rita on the United States in 2005, and the massive earthquake in October 2005 on the Indian subcontinent—traditionally unnerve stock market investors. In 2005, however, despite causing local economic disruptions and loss of life, these events had little effect on global stock markets.

Inflation generally remained low and less volatile, as did output growth, thanks to three recent major structural changes: global economic liberalization; the maturing of financial markets, particularly in emerging economies; and the success of central banks in controlling inflation.

Following a shaky first quarter, equity markets around the world performed strongly, buoyed by unexpectedly good corporate earnings. Investors had expected markets to slow from 2004's pace, but in Europe and the U.S., corporate earnings rose by more than 10% year-on-year in the second quarter of 2005. Terrorist attacks in London in July failed to disrupt the momentum. The equity markets were also resilient to the long-expected revaluation of the Chinese renminbi. Shares of Japanese exporters were hard hit at first by expectations that a major yen appreciation might follow, but although the yen did appreciate sharply at first, the currency returned to prerevaluation levels within a week. During the third quarter an improvement in the economic outlook reinforced the rally in equity markets, particularly in the U.S. and in Japan, where July's favourable Tankan survey of business confidence and an encouraging machinery-orders report in August prompted economists to upgrade growth forecasts.

At first, further rises in oil prices did little to sour investors' enthusiasm. In the first half of 2005, firms appeared to have offset rising raw materials and

Table V. Selected Major World Stock Market Indexes[1]

Country and Index	2005 range[2] High	2005 range[2] Low	Year-end close	Percent change from 12/31/2004
Argentina, Merval	1731	1276	1543	12
Australia, Sydney All Ordinaries	4715	3905	4709	16
Belgium, Brussels BEL20	3575	2959	3549	21
Brazil, Bovespa	33,629	23,610	33,456	28
Canada, Toronto Composite	11,296	9006	11,272	22
China, Shanghai A	1384	1062	1221	−8
Denmark, Copenhagen 20	400	285	394	37
Finland, HEX General	8230	6084	8167	31
France, Paris CAC 40	4773	3816	4715	23
Germany, Frankfurt Xetra DAX	5459	4178	5408	27
Hong Kong, Hang Seng	15,466	13,355	14,876	5
Hungary, Bux	23,672	14,587	20,785	41
India, Sensex (BSE-30)	9398	6103	9398	42
Indonesia, Jakarta Composite	1192	995	1163	16
Ireland, ISEQ Overall	7364	5798	7364	19
Italy, S&P/MIB	35,962	30,645	35,704	16
Japan, Nikkei Average	16,344	10,825	16,111	40
Mexico, IPC	18,054	11,740	17,803	38
Netherlands, The, AEX	441	347	437	26
Pakistan, KSE-100	10,295	6220	9557	54
Philippines, Manila Composite	2166	1813	2096	15
Poland, Wig	36,069	25,207	35,601	34
Russia, RTS	1129	592	1126	83
Singapore, Straits Times	2377	2066	2347	14
South Africa, Johannesburg All Share	18,312	12,467	18,097	43
South Korea, Composite Index	1389	871	1379	54
Spain, Madrid Stock Exchange	1177	951	1156	21
Switzerland, SMI	7620	5670	7584	33
Taiwan, Weighted Price	6576	5633	6548	7
Thailand, Bangkok SET	742	638	714	7
United Kingdom, FTSE 100	5638	4784	5619	17
United States, Dow Jones Industrials	10,941	10,012	10,718	−1
United States, Nasdaq Composite	2273	1904	2205	1
United States, NYSE Composite	7852	6935	7754	7
United States, Russell 2000	691	575	673	3
United States, S&P 500	1273	1138	1248	3
World, MS Capital International	1272	1114	1258	7

[1]Index numbers are rounded.   [2]Based on daily closing price.
Sources: *Financial Times, Wall Street Journal.*

energy costs against higher sales prices and cost cutting and thus maintain or even widen their profit margins. In late August investors started to doubt that this would continue into the latter part of 2005, and markets gave up some of their earlier gains. The price of Brent crude oil rose steadily from $47 a barrel in mid-May to $67 in mid-August, though it eased to just over $58 at year's end. High energy prices were one of the factors most often cited in profit warnings by companies.

Other concerns also surfaced as the year continued. In September the International Monetary Fund warned of the excessive dependence of global demand on high spending by consumers and high asset prices, particularly housing, as well as the high and volatile

price of oil. Low inflation also carried its own problems as low interest rates forced investors in search of yield to take on greater risk. Yet the Morgan Stanley Capital International (MSCI) world index, which ended the first quarter of 2005 in negative territory, rose to 3.5% by the end of the third quarter and ended the year up about 7.5%. (For Selected Major World Stock Market Indexes, see TABLE V.)   (IEIS)

United States. A combination of rising domestic interest rates and volatile fuel markets left U.S. stocks trading flat to lower for much of 2005 before a rally late in the year pushed the broad market into positive territory. The Standard & Poor's (S&P) 500 index ended up 3.00%. The Nasdaq (National Association of Securities Dealers automated

quotations) composite index gained 1.37%, but the Dow Jones industrial average (DJIA), composed of 30 of the market's most respected stocks, ended the year down 0.61%. (See GRAPH.)

The Federal Reserve (Fed) set the more cautious tone by raising short-term interest rates eight times during the year in order to relieve emerging inflationary pressures. The rate-setting Federal Open Market Committee raised the benchmark federal funds rate two percentage points to a four-year high of 4.25%, curbing the economy's expansive momentum in the process. As a result, the practice of borrowing money to fund corporate growth became more expensive.

High oil prices remained a persistent drag on shares in many sectors as the rally in the energy markets that began in 2004 continued into 2005. Between greater global consumption of fossil fuels, occasionally precarious conditions in various oil-supplying regions, and more widespread speculation in energy markets, the price of a barrel of light sweet crude oil broke multiple records as the spring and summer wore on, with the benchmark contract eventually settling at $61.04. Because higher fuel prices generally act as a drain on both corporate profits (by raising the effective cost of doing business) and consumer budgets, equity markets grew increasingly fixated on official stockpile inventories, production forecasts, and even the weather. Both Hurricane Katrina in August and Hurricane Rita in September took their toll on stock prices before coming to shore as investors gauged the damage that the storms would wreak on oil and natural-gas production in the Gulf of Mexico.

Investors also grappled with various political concerns, including the $319 billion federal budget deficit, increasingly vocal public displeasure with the Iraq war, and the spectre of high-level government scandals in Congress and White House inner circles. On the bright side, the markets applauded the nomination and almost certain confirmation of Ben S. Bernanke (see BIOGRAPHIES), chairman of the President's Council of Economic Advisors, to replace Alan Greenspan as Fed chairman when Greenspan's tenure expired in January 2006. The perception that Bernanke's expertise, clear communication style, and approach to fighting inflation would work to investors' favour was considered a major factor in the overall stock market's year-end upturn.

The U.S. economy proved resilient despite the combined effect of rising interest rates and fuel prices and the disruptions caused by the year's destructive storms. On a sector-by-sector basis, 8 of the 10 major Dow Jones industry benchmarks advanced during the year. The automotive industry, however, suffered especially sharp declines amid General Motors' dramatic operating losses and mounting retiree expenses on the one hand and the high-profile October bankruptcy of former GM subsidiary Delphi Corp., the nation's largest automotive parts supplier, on the other. Massive obligations to retiring employees raised doubts about American automakers' ability to compete in global markets profitably; credit evaluation agency Standard & Poor's cut both GM's and Ford's credit ratings to "junk" status on May 5, and Moody's followed suit on August 25. As the year closed, the Securities and Exchange Commission was pursuing a wide-ranging investigation of GM and DaimlerChrysler for possible accounting irregularities surrounding the automakers' pension and retiree health care practices. Meanwhile, GM had announced plans to lay off 30,000 employees, and Ford was preparing to close at least eight manufacturing plants.

Pension-related woes, coupled with the soaring cost of jet fuel, also spelled trouble for American airlines. Shares of Delta Air Lines, Inc., and Northwest Airlines Corp.—the country's third and fourth largest domestic carriers, respectively—plunged after both companies filed for bankruptcy protection on September 14 and their stocks were delisted from major exchanges. Bankruptcy allowed the companies to restructure their own pension funds and other aspects of their relationships with organized labour groups.

On the bullish side, the energy sector led the market for the second consecutive year by delivering a 34% total return, followed by utilities. After achieving market capitalization of $385 billion in February, oil producer Exxon Mobil Corp. became the world's largest publicly traded enterprise for several months (briefly surpassing General Electric Co.) and went on in October to report the highest quarterly profit ($9.92 billion) and revenue ($100.72 billion) ever recorded by any company.

Companies playing other roles in the energy industry also delivered outstanding investment returns in 2005. Coal providers led the market, up 77% as the high price of oil brought coal-fired power plants back into favour as an alternative, while shares in oil-field service providers and pipeline operators jumped 64% and 27%, respectively. Other standouts included water utilities, diversified mining companies, heavy construction, and health care providers.

While 66 of the 104 subsector groups in Dow Jones' reorganized market-classification system saw gains in 2005, two were unchanged and 36 ended in the red. Losers included the previously mentioned automotive group and auto parts makers, down 39% and 29%, respectively, as well as a broad swath of the chemical industry, which relied extensively on increasingly expensive petroleum products. U.S. forestry stocks also suffered, with the paper products group down 20%.

Mutual funds investing in U.S. stocks delivered an average return of 6.89%. As in the stock market itself, the year's greatest funds' gains were concentrated in the natural-resources sector, where oil-heavy funds ended up an average 38.11%. More broadly based funds investing in large-capitalization stocks

AP/Wide World Photos

Striking mechanics picket Northwest Airlines on August 22. Northwest and Delta Air Lines, faced with high labour and jet fuel costs, filed for bankruptcy protection in September.

ended the year up 6.04% on average, while their small-cap counterparts rose 6.13%. The largest U.S. mutual fund, the Vanguard Group's passively managed $107 billion 500 Index Fund, ended the year up 4.8%, while the actively managed $51 billion Fidelity Magellan Fund gained 6.4%.

On the New York Stock Exchange (NYSE), the nation's oldest, the pace of trading activity picked up substantially, with 1.61 billion shares being bought and sold every day, up 10% from the 1.46 billion shares traded daily in 2004. The dollar value of all trades surged 11% to an average of $56 billion a day, while computerized trading programs expanded their domination of the market to account for 57% of all shares exchanged.

Closing Prices of Selected U.S. Stock Market Indexes, 2005

Sources: [1]Dow Jones, [2]National Association of Securities Dealers, [3]Standard & Poor's.

Table VI. Change in Share Price of Selected U.S. Blue-Chip Stocks[1]
(in U.S. dollars)

Company	Starting price January 2005	Closing price year-end 2005	Percent change
General Electric Co.	36.50	35.05	–3.97
Exxon Mobil Corp.	51.26	56.17	9.58
Microsoft Corp.	26.72	26.15	–2.13
Citigroup, Inc.	48.18	48.53	0.73
Wal-Mart Stores, Inc.	52.82	46.80	–11.40
Johnson & Johnson	63.42	60.10	–5.23
American International Group, Inc.	65.67	68.23	3.90
Pfizer, Inc.	26.89	23.32	–13.28
Altria Group, Inc.	61.10	74.72	22.29
Intel Corp.	23.39	24.96	6.71
J.P. Morgan Chase & Co.	39.01	39.69	1.74
Procter & Gamble Co.	55.08	57.88	5.08
International Business Machines Corp.	98.58	82.20	–16.62
Coca-Cola Co.	41.64	40.31	–3.19
Home Depot, Inc.	42.74	40.48	–5.29
Verizon Communications, Inc.	40.51	30.12	–25.65
Hewlett-Packard Co.	20.97	28.63	36.53
AT&T Corp.	25.77	24.49	–4.97
Merck & Co., Inc.	32.14	31.81	–1.03
American Express Co.	56.37	51.46	–8.71

[1]In order of market capitalization as of Dec. 31, 2005.

Between a relatively thin calendar of initial public offerings (IPOs) and a steady stream of mergers and acquisitions taking companies off the market, the number of securities traded on the NYSE edged up only slightly to 3,669 stocks issued by 2,775 companies. Nonetheless, rising share prices helped lift the aggregate value of all securities listed on the exchange 9.6% to $21.7 trillion. Losers outnumbered winners, with 2,008 issues falling over the course of the year, 1,642 advancing, and 19 closing unchanged. Lucent Technologies remained the exchange's most heavily traded stock; high trading volume also surrounded shares of Pfizer and Time Warner.

The NYSE announced on April 20 that it planned to acquire electronic trading platform Archipelago to form the world's largest securities market and become a publicly traded entity in its own right. The deal would have awarded the exchange's 1,366 seatholders $300,000 in cash for their seats plus 70% of the new company's stock, while Archipelago shareholders would receive the other 30% of the shares. At least one NYSE seatholder balked at the terms of the arrangement, however, spurring debate for months before the membership eventually voted December 5 to approve the merger. Meanwhile, anticipation helped to fuel interest among investors hoping to buy seats on the exchange. A total of 94 seats traded hands in 2005, three times

the number seen in the previous year, while the price per seat quadrupled, with three selling for a record-high price of $4 million.

Trading sentiment on the NYSE revealed the market's ambivalent outlook. On the one hand, investors who believed that stock prices were likely to fall increased their short-selling activity, borrowing shares to sell in order to repurchase them later at what they hoped would be a lower price. In late December short interest on the NYSE was up 10% at 8.5 billion shares, representing 2.3% of all shares listed on the exchange. On the other hand, those investors who had equally fierce bullish convictions continued to buy stocks on credit or "margin," pushing the total level of margin debt on the exchange to a five-year high of $219 billion by November.

On the Nasdaq, the nation's largest electronic share exchange, the average number of shares traded surged to 1.7 billion shares a day, with an average of $3.9 billion a day changing hands. The market's long-standing technological focus remained in force, with Microsoft ending the year as the most heavily traded Nasdaq stock, followed by equally computer-driven companies Intel, Cisco Systems, and Sun Microsystems. In all, 216 companies debuted on the market, but the number of securities delisted from the Nasdaq owing to mergers, acquisitions, or other reasons outstripped the number of IPOs, leaving 2,775 issues on the market at the

end of the year. Nasdaq also engaged in a merger of its own, buying rival electronic-trading network Instinet in April for $1.9 billion in cash.

While stock trading on the NYSE and Nasdaq expanded dramatically in 2005, the activity on the American Stock Exchange (Amex) was increasingly dominated by exchange-traded funds (ETFs), with the number of equities listed on the exchange edging up only slightly to 1,156. Moreover, the Amex's leading role in the popular but competitive ETF arena was challenged several times during the year. In July Barclays Global Investors announced plans to move its 81 ETF products to the NYSE and Archipelago.

Given the lack of high-profile market scandals compared with previous years, investors were less inclined to file complaints against financial advisory firms. The number of arbitration cases filed with NASD, the primary U.S. market regulatory organization, sank 35% to 5,480 by November.

Despite a background of rising short-term interest rates and inflation, both of which have historically had a negative effect on the bond market, U.S. Treasury securities displayed unexpected strength through much of the year and gained ground from May through July and again in early September. As the Fed's campaign to guide rates higher continued, long-term bond prices finally retreated in late September, pushing Treasury yields higher. (As demand for bonds falls, prices also decline, pushing yields higher.)

The benchmark 10-year Treasury note ended the year paying an effective interest rate of 4.39%, above its closing 2004 level of 4.22%. Shorter-term securities followed the Fed more closely, with five-year Treasury rates climbing to 4.36% from 3.61% and the 13-week Treasury bill yield going to 3.98% from 2.18%. In fact, at the end of the year, short-term securities briefly paid a higher effective interest rate than their longer-term counterparts, which created a condition known as an "inverted yield curve," generally considered to presage slower economic growth ahead. Short-term government funds ended the year up 1.23%; middle-term funds gained 1.79%; and long-term funds rose 3.29% on average.

Once again, investors willing to accept higher risk for a larger return on their money pursued emerging market debt and more speculative or "junk"-rated bonds issued by companies with a proportionally high risk of defaulting on their debt. Emerging-markets bond funds gained 11.63% in 2005, far and away outperforming the rest of the fixed-income field. Demand for junk-rated corporate bonds pushed the associated yields lower, reducing the difference, or spread, between them and ultrasafe Treasury rates to 3.65%, versus a spread of more than 10% in 2002.

Canada. Global thirst for oil and other natural resources ensured that stocks in Canada (the world's fifth largest energy producer) outperformed not only their U.S. counterparts but also every other developed economy's equity market in U.S.-dollar terms. Not even the collapse of Prime Minister Paul Martin's minority Liberal government on November 28 managed to curtail the market's year-end performance. As a broad measure of all issues traded on the Toronto Stock Exchange (TSX), the S&P/TSX Composite index climbed 21.92%. The S&P/TSX 60, a basket of the nation's biggest companies, advanced 37.35%.

Most sectors shared in the gains, but oil was the primary contributor to the market's bullish year. Shares in energy companies, which accounted for 24% of the weight of the S&P/TSX Composite, ended the year up 59%, while the nation's major utility stocks (including several power-generation companies and pipeline operators) gained 34%. Demand for industrial metals sent mining company shares up 45%. Shares in the volatile information technology sector ended the year in the red, as did health care and consumer staples companies.

Nortel Networks, a leading global communications equipment maker, remained the most heavily traded stock on the TSX, but shares shed 14% of their value as investors continued to reevaluate that company's prospects. Semiconductor maker ATI Technologies and wireless network provider Research in Motion were also heavily traded, as were shares of industrial manufacturer Bombardier and several of the nation's gold-mining companies.

Trade remained the primary driver of Canada's economic expansion in 2005, led by continued export of oil, natural gas, minerals, and forestry products. The Bank of Canada encouraged economic activity by keeping domestic interest rates relatively low. The central bank raised interest rates only three times during the year (on September 7, October 18, and December 6), leaving the key overnight rate target at 3.25% at year's end. As a result of this relatively loose monetary policy, global capital

flows continued to favour the Canadian dollar, pushing the loonie to a 13-year high against its U.S. counterpart.

On average, 255.6 million shares a day were traded on the TSX, representing a 5% increase from 2004 as activity hit a new record pace. The value of those trades jumped 30% to $4.28 billion to reflect the overall increase in individual stock prices. A steady stream of 137 IPOs and 46 graduations from the small-cap Venture Exchange helped to swell the number of issuers listed on the exchange to 1,537 by the end of the year.

(BETH KOBLINER)

Western Europe. As the year began, the region's equity markets were the strongest performers in local currency terms, despite poor economic news (the IMF projection was for GDP growth of 1.8% in 2006) and the persistent inability of Germany and France to institute structural reforms. Investors were encouraged by the pace of corporate restructuring, which was seen as a driver of continued gains in productivity and profits; the level of merger and acquisition activity; and the opportunities opened up for companies in the developed markets by the new markets of the Central and Eastern European countries that joined the EU in 2004. Other positive factors included the demand from Asia for European industrial products and the opportunity in Germany to back companies likely to benefit from any restructuring programs once the political uncertainty surrounding the national elections in September was over. The inconclusive election result did cause stock market performance to waver a little. The German DAX 30 initially fell 1.1%, and the DJ Euro STOXX 50 index of leading euro zone shares slid by less than half a percentage point. Optimism returned with the confirmation in November of pro-reform politician Angela Merkel (*see* BIOGRAPHIES) as German chancellor, and the DAX ended the year up 27.1%. There were substantial returns to investors who braved the EU's political and economic uncertainties. The S&P 350 Index, a broad measure of European stocks, was up 22.7% at year's end.

European markets were judged to be attractively valued in comparison with other major markets, particularly the U.S. Europe's lower labour costs and low real-rates of interest were considered conducive to more growth, and despite the possibility of a global stock-market correction, investors expected companies with exposure to domestic European demand to be better able

than most to weather it. In London the *Financial Times* Stock Exchange index of 100 stocks (FTSE 100) rose steadily throughout most of 2005, though the 16.7% increase for the year lagged most other European bourses.

Interest in European stocks was reflected in takeover bids for the London Stock Exchange (LSE), Europe's biggest stock market. The total value of companies trading on the LSE was estimated at £1.3 billion (about $2.3 billion). A bid by Deutsche Börse, operator of the Frankfurt stock exchange, was rebuffed by the LSE in February. Euronext, which already operated the French, Dutch, Belgian, and Portuguese securities markets—as well as Europe's second biggest derivatives exchange, Liffe, in London—also expressed interest, and in August Australian company Macquarie Bank Ltd. stepped into the ring. By year's end Macquarie looked like the strongest contender, even though the LSE rejected the bank's offer.

Other Countries. Globally, emerging markets looked to be maturing—displaying a widening investor base, improved credit standing, and better hedging instruments that decreased the dependence of securities on global liquidity and thereby allowed markets to deepen. On September 26 trading began on the Dubai International Financial Exchange (DIFX). The DIFX was expected to provide a market for international investors in a region that had previously been underrepresented.

Judicious investment in emerging-markets equities had delivered some

Traders arrive for business on September 26, the opening day of the new Dubai International Financial Exchange. The DIFX was the first international stock exchange based in the Middle East.

spectacular returns, but there was wide disparity of stock-market performance between regions and between countries. By year's end, the MSCI Emerging Markets Standard Index had risen 30.3% from just over 1% up at the end of the first quarter. The regional breakdown showed Emerging Markets Far East to have risen 22% over the period, compared with 46% by Eastern Europe. The Emerging Markets Asia index rose by little more than 23%, compared with Latin America's rise of nearly 45%. Country indexes showed the same wide disparities, with tsunami-wrecked Sri Lanka producing an index return of more than 30.7% over the year to end December and Thailand just 4.8%. Analysts were bullish about Asia, despite worries about sustained high oil prices. Growing domestic demand in a number of countries was expected to counter the effect of weakening export markets. Corporations had repaired their balance sheets, and returns on equity were running at record-high levels, particularly in the financial, consumer, and industrial sectors.

Disparity of country returns was generally less dramatic in the developed-world equity markets. While the MSCI World Index was up just under 5% by the end of the third quarter, in China economic momentum moderated only slightly to 9% (from 9.5% in 2004), helped by the 29% growth in exports in the first half of the year. This was spurred by the ending of textile quotas, which were subsequently reinstated. (See BUSINESS OVERVIEW.) At the same time, import growth slowed. MSCI country index returns ranged from Norway's 20%, on the strength of its drilling services and shipping companies, to Spain's 1.5%. Nordic bourses, however, quoted gains of up to 40% for the year, and Spain's Ibex-35 ended the year up 18.2%. Throughout 2005, Japan's markets performed consistently strongly against a steady improvement in private consumption and investment and the reduction of the country's reliance on exports to drive growth. Japan's benchmark Nikkei index of 225 stocks ended the year up 40.2%.

Commodities. Investment success depended heavily on positioning in energy, and in June the energy sector was the strongest, recording a gain of 7.4% for the month. By August the impact of higher energy prices was beginning to weigh more heavily on businesses and consumers, particularly in the wake of Hurricane Katrina and the damage

As the price of gold hit record highs in 2005, small investors collected bullion coins such as this one-ounce solid-gold Panda from China.

AP/Wide World Photos

caused to oil refineries in the Gulf of Mexico. Although energy prices trended lower in October and, in aggregate, economic news was positive, markets still tended to drift down. Nevertheless, the *Economist* Commodity Price All Items Dollar index ended the year up 18.5%.

A sign that 2005's high oil and natural-gas prices were possibly beginning to dampen demand came from Brazil, where sales of a biofuel based on sugar cane rose sharply. Shortage of refining capacity around the world, particularly following Hurricane Katrina in August, forced gasoline prices higher than other fuel prices to make it 70% more expensive than bio-ethanol. By the end of 2005, most new Brazilian-built cars were powered by "flex fuel" engines.

Whatever the likely success of new technologies and new fuels, commodity prices, including oil and gas, were expected to moderate as supply caught up with demand. The extent and timing of this event, however, was more problematic. Oil and gas prices were generally expected to remain relatively high and volatile into 2006, but in November the World Bank reported that growth in demand for oil had slowed from more than 3.5% in 2004 to an annualized rate of 1.4% in the first three quarters of 2005.

The price of gold reached a 24-year high in November of $528.40 an ounce, as the metal again became popular as a store of value. At the same time,

supply fell owing to decreased production and a five-year agreement by central banks to limit the sale of official reserves. The World Gold Council reported at the end of November that global demand was up 18% in dollar terms and investment demand was up 56% from a year earlier. Gold ended the year at $502 per ounce, for an increase over the year of 24%.

Platinum and silver prices were strong because of increased use in industrial processes, and demand for steel held up, driven by China's continued boom. China was increasingly an important producer as well as a consumer of these commodities and was likely to produce 30% of the world's steel by 2006.

The World Bank reported that, overall, commodity prices showed signs of stabilizing after a long bull run, supported in part by the higher energy costs that kept production tight. Agricultural prices fell by around 5% over the second and third quarters, but the price of agricultural raw materials such as rubber was rising, which reflected the use of those products as crude-oil substitutes.   (IEIS)

BUSINESS OVERVIEW

The U.S. economy in 2005 endured a host of catastrophes, both natural and man-made, yet it managed not to fall into recession. To analysts this indicated that either the economy had levels of unfathomable resilience or old indicators of economic decline no longer had significance. One image that defined the economic year was that of gasoline pumps with a posted price of more than $3 per gallon. High energy costs were a hard fact of life throughout the year, and they affected every sector of the U.S. economy. The destruction caused by hurricanes in the Gulf of Mexico—particularly the damage to oil refineries by Hurricane Katrina—helped knock both oil and natural gas prices skyward. Prices for crude oil, which had been hovering around $50 per barrel in late 2004, reached $60 per barrel in June 2005 and hit a high of $70.85 per barrel on August 30. Natural gas prices by October had risen above $13 per million BTU, compared with $7 per million BTU one year earlier. Earlier in the year David O'Reilly, the chairman and CEO of Chevron Corp., stated his belief that the era of "easy" oil and natural gas was over, a sentiment that was shared by producers and energy traders alike. Natural disasters and the continued threat of terrorist attacks led oil-futures traders to add a risk premium of as much as $15 per barrel.

For the top oil producers, it was an astonishingly profitable year. The five largest oil companies in the world—ExxonMobil, BP, Royal Dutch/Shell Group, Total, and Chevron—reported record-breaking combined third-quarter earnings of about $33 billion. Top American oil producer ExxonMobil, which had a massive $9.9 billion profit in the third quarter alone, overtook General Electric as the most valuable company in the world. Shell posted the highest annual profit in British corporate history. The cash-fueled resilience of these oil companies was demonstrated by their having been able to cope with Hurricane Katrina and still post major profits. For example, BP managed to post a 34% increase in net profit for the third quarter despite having lost $700 million in pretax profit because of hurricane-related production shutdowns.

As global spare petroleum capacity fell below one million barrels per day—the lowest in more than 20 years—expenditures for exploration and development soared. By May an average of 2,585 drilling rigs were active worldwide, the highest level of activity in 20 years. (In addition, the cost of drilling an onshore well in the U.S. had risen dramatically, topping $1,000,000 in 2005, compared with $800,000 in 2003.)

The biggest challenge for the major oil companies was that much of the world's untapped oil reserves lay in countries that were hostile to Western interests or were wracked by political chaos. Furthermore, many reserves were owned by nationalized oil companies. Nine of the top 20 oil companies, as ranked by existing reserves, were state-owned; privately held ExxonMobil ranked 12th. Power was expected to shift further to such companies as Saudi Arabia's Aramco, Iran's NIOC, Venezuela's PDV, and Nigeria's NNPC in the years to come.

In a sign of the growing dominance of nationalized oil companies, China National Offshore Oil Corp. (CNOOC) attempted to purchase Unocal, which had been bid on by Chevron. CNOOC ultimately withdrew its offer after U.S. government officials expressed concern about the purchase and Chevron upped its offer, but analysts expected CNOOC and other Chinese producers to continue on the acquisition hunt. In Russia state-controlled Gazprom purchased a majority share, worth roughly $13 billion, in Russia's fifth largest producer, Sibneft, in what was the country's largest corporate takeover. As the Russian government continued to dismantle privately owned Yukos, which had been the country's largest oil producer, Gazprom emerged as Russia's champion energy power.

The impact of rising oil and gas prices on utilities was varied. Among those

utility companies that prospered was Texas-based TXU, which posted a net income of $791 million for the first half of 2005, compared with a loss of $425 million in the same period in 2004. Other utilities, such as Calpine, posted losses. The main difference between a winning and a losing utility often lay in whether it had locked in a long-term energy-pricing agreement. PECO Energy, for example, had an agreement in place to pay set, relatively low prices for the rest of the decade.

In Europe a flurry of mergers occurred because European utilities were eager to expand beyond their national markets. The EU was to deregulate gas and electricity markets in July 2007, and some producers already had begun jockeying for position; France's Suez in August acquired the remaining shares of Belgium's Electrabel, and Spanish natural gas producer Gas Natural launched a $27 billion hostile takeover for utility Endesa. (The takeover of Endesa would leave Spain with two large energy companies, Gas Natural and Iberdrola.)

Higher energy prices also at last ended the infatuation in the United States with low-mileage sport utility vehicles (SUVs), which proved terrible news for American automakers Ford Motor and General Motors. These companies had over the preceding half decade increasingly relied on the SUV to drive sales, and when SUV sales deteriorated, the results were brutal. GM, which controlled 60% of the large SUV market, watched its sales fall 24% year over year in September, while Ford's sales plummeted 19.5%. (By contrast, DaimlerChrysler, which relied far less on large SUVs, reported a 3.7% sales increase in the same period.)

GM had been considered to be the healthiest of the Big Three automakers, but it was hit the hardest. GM's stock fell to its lowest level in more than a decade, and analysts said that GM's three consecutive quarterly losses (a $1.6 billion loss in the third quarter alone) represented the failure of CEO Rick Wagoner's efforts to streamline the company's North American operations without drastically cutting employees and downsizing brands. As the year went on, Wagoner, who personally took charge of GM's North American unit in April, said that he would cut approximately 25,000 jobs by 2008, eliminating about 22% of GM's hourly workforce. When its purges ended, GM would likely be left with 125,000

(continued on page 184)

A worker adjusts a valve at a natural gas compressor station in Opari, Ukraine. A price dispute between Ukraine and the Russian state-owned energy company Gazprom in late 2005 led to strained relations between the two countries.

© Baran Alexander—ITAR-TASS/Corbis

Preparing for Emergencies

by Susan L. Cutter

When Hurricane Katrina devastated the U.S. Gulf Coast in 2005, it became not only a natural disaster but a social catastrophe as well. While there are many lessons to be learned from this tragic event, among the most significant involve the failures in the emergency management system of the United States. An emergency management system consists of four primary elements: preparedness, response, recovery, and mitigation. The system is often depicted as a cycle showing how one phase morphs into the next one and then the process starts again with the next event. Emergency management is an essential concern of government at all levels. Local agencies (police, fire, and emergency services) bear first-response accountability for public health and safety. Larger-scale disasters may require state intervention. Only when the magnitude of an event has overwhelmed local resources and a state's capacity to respond must the federal government assist.

Emergency Management History. The U.S. federal government did not become actively involved in disaster response until the 1930s and then did so only on an ad hoc basis, providing funding to repair highways and bridges damaged by natural disasters or building flood-control projects. During the 1950s the preeminent perceived risks were nuclear war and nuclear fallout, and most emergency management efforts were funneled into civil defense programs at all levels of government. During the 1960s and '70s, a number of large natural disasters beset the country, notably the Ash Wednesday storm (1962), the Alaskan earthquake (1964), Hurricane Camille (1969), and the San Fernando Valley earthquake (1971). Each of these events required federal

response and recovery assistance, yet public policies governing emergency management continued on an ad hoc basis, with a multiplicity of government agencies and departments each having partial responsibility for or governing authority over disaster response.

In 1979 the Federal Emergency Management Agency (FEMA) was created in order to centralize emergency management functions at the federal level. The priority at the time still was preparing for a nuclear attack. Two

© Jim Watson/AFP/Getty Images

Pres. George W. Bush, standing with (from left) New Orleans Mayor Ray Nagin, FEMA Director Michael Brown, and Louisiana Gov. Kathleen Blanco, speaks at New Orleans International Airport on September 2, four days after Hurricane Katrina struck the Gulf Coast. The picture at top was drawn by a nine-year-old evacuee living in the Houston Astrodome.

large natural disasters in 1989, however, were turning points for the agency. Under fire for its slow response and lack of attention to Hurricane Hugo and the Loma Prieta earthquake, FEMA was an agency in trouble. In 1992 when Hurricane Andrew hit south Florida, FEMA's relevance again was questioned. Many politicians and officials called for its abolishment.

FEMA's stock began to rise in 1993, when James Lee Witt became agency director. Witt, a former head of Arkansas's emergency management agency, was

the first and so far only director of FEMA with experience in emergency management. During his tenure the agency was professionalized, became more technologically sophisticated, focused more on natural-hazards mitigation, and proved more willing to engage local and state partners. The value and centrality of emergency management to the country was recognized when Pres. Bill Clinton elevated FEMA to a cabinet-level position. After the 2000 presidential election, however, FEMA reverted to its pre-1993 status; though still an independent agency, it was again led by a director with no emergency management experience, focused on civil defense threats, and exhibited little or no interest in natural-disaster mitigation. The attacks of Sept. 11, 2001, catalyzed national attention on preparedness for terrorist threats and homeland security issues. In 2003 FEMA was combined with 22 other federal agencies and programs into the new Department of Homeland Security (DHS). The emphasis of FEMA (which became a department within DHS) was now counter-terrorism training and providing equipment for first responders.

All Disasters Are Local. Preparedness is the foundation of emergency management and helps to reduce vulnerability to threats. Local, state, and federal preparedness is vital to securing the safety of the country, yet as was clear from the Hurricane Katrina disaster, not all places enjoy the same levels of preparedness. When a disaster strikes, lack of preparedness often translates into loss of life and property and longer recovery periods at the local level, but often there are regional, national, or even international repercussions for such losses.

Preparedness includes the establishment of warning systems (such as tornado sirens, weather bulletins, and reverse-911 telephone notification) to alert residents of impending danger. Evacuation plans designed especially for high-risk communities, such as those along the nation's hurricane coast or around nuclear or chemical facilities, are another aspect of preimpact preparedness. Evacuation planning takes time and resources, however, and often lies beyond the technical and financial reach of local communities and is not readily financed by state and federal bodies. In particular, evacuation planning must identify special-needs populations—people who are homeless, elderly, infirm, or poor—that is, individuals who may require extra assistance to get out of harm's way. All too often evacuation planning in the U.S. has comprised little more than an elegant traffic analysis that shows poor understanding of human behaviour and overlooks the needs of vulnerable populations (such as residents who do not have a personal automobile).

Preparedness also entails the establishment of longer-term mitigation strategies aimed at reducing the vulnerability of the built environment. There are many obvious mitigation opportunities—elevating homes in flood-prone areas, requiring wind-resistant construction in hurricane-prone areas, retrofitting buildings to withstand seismic events—but these all require partnerships between residents and various

A volunteer team from the Bay Saint Louis (Miss.) Emergency Management Agency rescues a family from the roof of their SUV, which was trapped on U.S. 90 in heavy flooding from Hurricane Katrina.

levels of government. Citizens must be aware of the risks and demand better safety measures; local jurisdictions must show the will to pass and enforce building codes and zoning ordinances; and resources from state and federal agencies must be available.

Disaster Relief: Entitlement or Responsibility? At present there is no policy in the U.S. that discourages people from moving into high-risk hazard-prone areas. Quite the contrary. Through FEMA the federal government underwrites the National Flood Insurance Program, which allows residents to obtain insurance for properties in flood-prone areas. Private underwriters gave up providing flood insurance directly to consumers because the premiums did not cover the losses. Instead of encouraging disaster-resilient communities, the federal government rewards communities by providing resources to rebuild "bigger and better" after disasters. Rather than preparing for emergencies, individuals and communities wait for a disaster to occur and then seek federal payments to cover the losses. The mechanism of "presidential disaster declarations" rewards rather than penalizes bad siting and land-use decisions. Accordingly, residences are rebuilt time and time again in flood-prone areas.

How much more prepared might all people be if this federal safety net was not there and communities and individuals had to pay for disaster losses themselves? If citizens and local authorities were required by the government to build disaster-resistant structures and to be more responsible in their choices of construction sites, then

rather than being an entitlement for everyone, federal disaster relief could be delivered in larger measure to the truly needy victims. Individual and community responsibility for development (how, where, and for whom) would create a more resilient future for these high-hazard areas.

Learning from Katrina. Hurricane Katrina brought home the lesson that the emergency management system in the U.S. is broken and needs to be fixed—but this has been known since at least 2001. The country needs a highly visible coordinating agency (FEMA) to attend to all phases of the emergency management cycle—preparedness, response, recovery, and mitigation. Preparedness and mitigation must have equal status in such an agency and must be funded to the same levels as response and recovery. FEMA needs to be independent and report directly to the president. All appointees within the agency, political or not, should have professional experience in emergency management. Finally, federal disaster policies cannot be nonfunded mandates to state and local governments; such federally mandated programs must be resourced appropriately and flexibly. Only in this way can communities optimize their federal dollars and mitigate the threats that pose the greatest real risk—not just the politically determined hazard du jour.

Susan L. Cutter is Carolina Distinguished Professor of Geography at the University of South Carolina and Director of its Hazards Research Lab; she is an internationally respected scholar in the fields of risk and hazards and is the author/editor of 12 books.

In the Houston Astrodome, a Red Cross volunteer comforts a victim of Hurricane Katrina on September 2.

This metal-fabricating plant in Lansing, Mich., was among those expected to be shuttered after General Motors announced in 2005 that it would lay off some 30,000 employees and close 12 North American automotive factories.

(continued from page 181)
employees, compared with more than 600,000 in 1979. Furthermore, GM was seriously considering ending two of its most storied brands, Buick and Pontiac.

The corporate ratings of both GM and Ford were cut in May to non-investment-grade status by the credit-rating agency Standard & Poor's, which said that it no longer had confidence in either company's business strategies. Along with declining sales, a major concern was the massive benefits-related cost obligations carried by GM and Ford. GM alone covered roughly 1.1 million current and former employees' health care—about 0.4% of the entire U.S. population—and the obligation was estimated to be in the $77 billion range. Negotiations between GM and the United Auto Workers produced a proposed $15 billion reduction in health care costs, but GM still was in dire straits as the year ended and was considering selling off its lucrative financial arm, General Motors Acceptance Corp., to achieve a massive cash infusion.

Ford, although not as battered as GM, did not have a promising year either. In the third quarter, it posted a $284 million loss, and for the first nine months of 2005, net income was $1.9 billion, down from $3.38 billion in the same period in 2004. Ford blamed higher prices of oil and steel, the weak dollar,

and rising health care costs, but analysts said that the largest factor was the decline in sales of the large pickup trucks and SUVs that had been the backbone of Ford's revenues for the past decade. By September the automaker had shaken up its top executive ranks. Mark Fields, Ford's top European executive, took over the company's ailing North American operations and became the fourth person to head that division in as many years. Ford also said that it planned to eliminate up to 30% of its white-collar workforce.

DaimlerChrysler, which posted a profit during the first half of 2005, was by far the healthiest of the Big Three. One reason was the success of the company's hemi V8 engine, which was used in about one-half of Chrysler's Magnum, Dodge Ram, and Durango vehicles and retailed for $10,000 more than a standard engine even though it cost no more to build. DaimlerChrysler's CEO Jürgen Schrempp said that he planned to retire at year's end, three years before his contract expired. It would mark the end of a decade-long tumultuous tenure during which he had spearheaded the controversial merger of Daimler and Chrysler in 1998. He was to be succeeded by Dieter Zetsche, who would be aided by new Chrysler head Tom LaSorda.

In contrast to Detroit's woes, Japanese automakers thrived in 2005. Honda

Motor, for example, posted an 11.7% increase in sales in September, buoyed by sales of its compact Civic models. Toyota Motor sales were up 11.3% year-to-date as of September, and the Japanese automaker was one step closer to its goal of unseating General Motors as the world's largest carmaker. Toyota planned to ramp up its global production to 9.06 million units by 2006, compared with GM's estimated 2005 figure of 9 million units, and said that it intended to control 15% of the global auto market sometime in the following decade. Toyota's spending on research and development had grown from $4.5 billion annually at the beginning of the decade to roughly $7 billion a year, a figure that reflected the aging of the company's product lines. Moreover, the Japanese automaker was making a substantial bet that high energy prices would continue to spur sales of gasoline/electric hybrid cars, such as its Prius model. (The energy bill signed into law by U.S. Pres. George W. Bush in August provided a tax credit of as much as $3,400 per car to purchasers of the first 60,000 hybrids sold by an automaker.) By 2008 Toyota planned to have rolled out 10 hybrid models, and its hybrid sales already accounted for 64% of new hybrids registered in the United States. Honda was in second place, with 31%. If hybrids flopped, Toyota could be left with massive numbers of unsold cars, but the company was still in solid shape, with low pension-related costs and $30 billion in cash.

Chinese automaker Chery said that it planned to introduce its first ultracheap imports to the U.S. in the next two years. China could provide a way for automakers to reduce costs, however. DaimlerChrysler said that it planned to build a subcompact car in China, where the hourly cost of wages and benefits for autoworkers was $1.96, compared with $49.60 in Germany.

For European automakers one event of note in 2005 was the appearance for the first time of a single executive running two major automakers. Carlos Ghosn, already at the helm of Nissan Motor, became the CEO of French carmaker Renault in April. Ghosn had come full circle—Renault had bought a near-majority stake in Nissan in 1999 and installed Ghosn as Nissan's CEO. In subsequent years he helped convert Nissan's losses into a $7 billion profit while he reduced $23 billion in debt and pushed Nissan's operating profit margin up 11%. He had made Nissan the world's most profitable volume carmaker, and Renault was hoping that Ghosn could work the same magic at home.

For auto suppliers it was an equally grim season. The world's second largest auto-parts supplier, Delphi, filed for bankruptcy protection in October after the company said that it could not come to terms with either its unions or GM, its largest customer. Delphi claimed that because it had to pay its employees the same wages as auto-workers (Delphi was spun out of GM in 1999), it was at a competitive disadvantage. Delphi planned to cut wages from $27 per hour to $10–$12 per hour. The auto-supply sector attracted the interest of financier Wilbur Ross, who had spent much of the decade consolidating companies in the steel industry. Ross's group bought stakes in Oxford Automotive, a French supplier that had recently emerged from bankruptcy, and Collins & Aikman, a Michigan-based supplier that was still in bankruptcy. Ross also expressed interest in Delphi.

In 2005, for the first time since the terrorist attacks on Sept. 11, 2001, airline passenger traffic had been expected to return to pre-2001 levels. The chaos wreaked by Hurricane Katrina, however, proved to be a crippling blow to some already reeling airlines and played a large part in the decision by Delta Air Lines and Northwest Airlines—the nation's third and fifth largest airlines—to file for federal bankruptcy protection. With the two bankruptcies, both filed on the same day in September, four of the seven largest American carriers were operating under Chapter 11 protection.

Delta, which had lost $12 billion since 2001, said that it would use its time under bankruptcy protection to reduce its fleet. It was cutting as many as 80 planes and retiring 4 of its 11 aircraft types. Delta also intended to cut its workforce by 17% (after having already reduced it by 20% since 2001) and lower employee wages and benefits by more than $600 million. Its goal was to save $3 billion annually. Northwest, which had lost $3.6 billion since 2001, said that it was seeking $1.4 billion in concessions from its unions. United Airlines, which was already under bankruptcy protection, received permission from a federal court to end its four employee pension plans, which thereby released the airline from about $3.2 billion in pension obligations over the next five years. It was the largest pension default in the three decades that the U.S. government had guaranteed pensions.

Boeing 737 jets are assembled at a plant in Renton, Wash., in June. The success of the 737 and other Boeing airplanes in 2005 helped the American aircraft manufacturer surpass its European rival, Airbus, in selling and delivering jets.

High energy costs in the form of skyrocketing jet-fuel prices played a part in the downfall of Northwest and Delta and squeezed the other large "legacy" airlines. Jet-fuel prices over the course of 2005 rose even more sharply than crude oil prices, and by early September jet fuel was selling for $92 a barrel. Northwest had a $3.3 billion fuel bill in 2005, an increase of $1.1 billion over 2004, but some low-cost carriers were able to hedge fuel costs dramatically through the use of futures contracts. Southwest Airlines had much of its fuel needs hedged at a set price of $26 a barrel. There was some positive news for legacy U.S. airlines; US Airways gained federal approval to merge with low-cost carrier America West Airlines and emerged in late September from its second round of bankruptcy protection in as many years.

Aircraft manufacturers unexpectedly had a very strong year. Both Europe's Airbus and U.S.-based Boeing experienced upticks in aircraft orders and deliveries. The two rivals together were expected to deliver about 670 jetliners in 2005, compared with a six-year low of 586 planes in 2003. After five years of trailing Airbus, Boeing retook the lead with the help of its new 787, the first Boeing plane to be designed since Sept. 11, 2001. Deliveries were expected to begin in mid-2008. Boeing's CEO Harry Stonecipher was forced out in March because of an indiscretion with a female executive and was replaced by

James McNerney, who had run General Electric's jet-engine unit.

The chemicals industry was shaken up by the combination of high energy costs and hurricane-related damage. DuPont posted an $82 million loss in the third quarter because of both a tax-related charge and Hurricane Katrina. DuPont said that storm damage to its Gulf Coast facilities would force it to spend $115 million to replace equipment and would result in about $250 million in lost sales revenue in the fourth quarter of 2005. Meanwhile, Dow Chemical, the nation's largest chemical company, escaped serious damage to its Gulf Coast sites and posted $801 million in net income in the third quarter, despite an $850 million increase in raw material and energy costs.

In April London-based steel tycoon Lakshmi Mittal (*see* BIOGRAPHIES) acquired Ohio-based International Steel Group to create the world's largest steelmaker. Mittal Steel in October bought Kryvorizhstal, Ukraine's biggest steel mill. Meanwhile, American domestic steel producers had to contend with price softening throughout the year after having experienced a return to profitability in 2004 because of heavy demand from China. Nevertheless, the steel industry was in better shape to contend with a downturn than it had been in many preceding years, during which it had endured massive bankruptcies, mergers, wage reductions, and increased energy costs. In 2005 steel

Lakshmi Mittal (right), head of Mittal Group, the world's largest steelmaker, and Subir Raha (far left) of India's Oil and Natural Gas Corp. celebrate the completion in July of an Indian government-approved agreement to form a new joint venture.

minimills, which used low-cost electric furnaces, produced about 48% of American steel, compared with 8% in 1995.

Aluminum producers were also victims of the year's hurricanes and higher energy costs. Top producer Alcoa said that its energy costs increased by $374 million in the first nine months of 2005 and that Hurricane Rita knocked out some of its alumina refineries. Alcoa still managed to post a 13% increase in revenue for the first nine months of 2005. Alcoa CEO Alain Belda, who had run the company since 2000, began new measures to increase business, including courting airlines and increasing such foreign ventures as the purchase of Russian aluminum mills. Although global aluminum production was up 9% in 2005, much of that demand came from China, which was already taking action to curb aluminum exports.

Not all metals faced price deterioration. Gold futures hit a 17-year high of $483 an ounce in mid-October before soaring to well over $500 per ounce by year's end. The price increases in gold came in tandem with increases in the value of the U.S. dollar, which was unusual. Analysts cited increased demand for jewelry as the cause. Gold jewelry fabrication in India was up 50% for the first half of 2005.

For much of the year, the main issue for textile manufacturers was the confrontation between China, the European Union, and the U.S. over the growth of Chinese textile exports. On Dec. 31, 2004, decades-old quotas that had controlled worldwide trade in textile and apparel products expired, which opened the door for a massive increase in Chinese exports. In the first four months of 2005, U.S. imports of Chinese-manufactured shirts, blouses, and trousers were up more than 1,000%, compared with the same period in 2004. Even though import growth cooled as the year went on, the U.S. imported $9.43 billion in Chinese textiles in the first seven months. Some analysts predicted that in the next two years, China could capture up to 70% of the U.S. market, compared with its 16% market share before quotas were lifted.

Pushed by domestic textile manufacturers, which feared that their business would collapse, the U.S. launched a number of trade investigations and threatened to impose annual limits on Chinese apparel imports. In May the Bush administration said that it would impose new quotas on items such as cotton shirts and trousers. As the year ended, China and the U.S. were still in disagreement on the growth rate that should be set for Chinese imports in 2007 and 2008, and the U.S. continued to impose "safeguard" quotas—annual growth caps of 7.5%—on specific categories of textiles. In September China and the EU came to an agreement after many European countries called for new quotas on Chinese textile exports to Europe, which had ballooned by 82% in the first four months of 2005 alone. The agreement imposed limits of 8–12.5% on imports of Chinese textiles until 2007.

In the pharmaceutical industry Merck faced ongoing repercussions from its painkiller Vioxx, which it withdrew from the market in 2004. In August a Texas jury ordered the company to pay $253 million in damages to the widow of a man who had died after taking Vioxx, but in a similar case in New Jersey, Merck was found not liable. Merck, which had seen its stock value fall 60% since 2000, looked to shore itself up by replacing longtime CEO Raymond Gilmartin 10 months before his scheduled retirement in favour of longtime veteran Richard Clark. Rumours that Merck would seek a big merger persisted throughout the year, since the company faced other challenges, including the fact that its top-selling drug, Zocor, would become available as a generic in 2006. Other drugmakers faced similar problems. Pfizer had to take its painkiller Bextra off the market in April at the request of the U.S. Food and Drug Administration (FDA) and European regulators, who said that the drug posed substantial risks that included skin reactions and heart-related complications. The FDA also ordered labeling that would carry warning language on a number of painkillers, including Pfizer's Celebrex.

The generic-drug sector continued to prosper, and generic-drug sales were expected to grow by more than 20% a year for the rest of the decade. Ties between generic and name-brand pharmaceutical companies continued as Swiss drug giant Novartis in February purchased two generic-drug makers—Germany's Hexal and its sister American company, Eon Labs—for $8.3 billion. The deal turned Novartis into the world's largest seller of generic drugs, with 600 generic products that together accounted for more than $5 billion in annual sales.

The U.S. Supreme Court unanimously ruled in June that name-brand-drug companies had broad exemption from patent infringement during early-stage research. At the same time, the U.S. National Institutes of Health offered to pay for and run early clinical trials of experimental drugs through a $13 million program that was intended to encourage drug companies to pursue drug trials that might be unprofitable.

The tobacco industry also benefited from a favourable decision by the Supreme Court. In October the court declined without comment to overturn a lower court's decision that the Department of Justice could not sue Philip Morris, R.J. Reynolds, and other tobacco companies under the federal antiracketeering RICO Act for allegedly misleading the public about smoking-related ailments.

(CHRISTOPHER O'LEARY)

Education

IMPROVED national **TEST SCORES** in the U.S., a trend toward establishing small high schools, controversies over history **TEXTBOOK CONTENT**, discussion about the role of **RELIGION** in the classroom, rising university enrollments, and dominance by Finnish students in **PISA TESTING** were some of the highlights in education in 2005.

PRIMARY AND SECONDARY EDUCATION

The highest reading and mathematics exam scores in 30 years were reported in 2005 for nine-year-old Americans in the National Assessment of Educational Progress testing program, known as the nation's report card. Math scores among 13-year-olds also reached their highest point in three decades. Also, the gap narrowed between black and Hispanic pupils and their white age-mates. Analysts credited the improvement to school reforms introduced by the states over the past two decades. The greatest gains appeared in southern states that traditionally had lagged behind the rest of the nation. Reading and math scores of 17-year-olds remained essentially unchanged over the 30-year period. Pres. George W. Bush's No Child Left Behind education program was also cited as having had an influence on rising test scores.

Efforts to improve American high schools focused chiefly on dividing large comprehensive schools into multiple small academies that specialized in such areas as fine arts, science, business, finance, leadership, engineering, theatre, communications, health sciences, and advanced college preparation. Nationwide, an estimated 1,400 small schools had recently been created. An important financial boost to the movement came from the Bill and Melinda Gates Foundation, which had furnished $2.3 billion for various school-reform projects over the past several years. In another attempt to upgrade high schools, the governors of 13 states that enrolled 35% of the nation's students pledged to make core classes and tests more rigorous and to match high-school graduation standards to the expectations of employers and colleges. Public support for such efforts was reflected in an opinion poll that found that only 9% of the American populace believed that high schools set high-enough academic expectations for students.

By 2005 about half of U.S. states had adopted high-school exit exams used to determine if students deserved to graduate. The dual intent of the exams was to motivate students to study hard and to assure employers that graduates had adequate skills in the tested subjects. Critics, however, denounced such an evaluation system, which, regardless of the quality of the students' years of classroom performance, would deny them a diploma for failing multiple-choice tests in a limited set of subject fields (usually language and math).

Conflicts over the content of history textbooks continued in Bosnia and Herzegovina, France, Germany, India, Israel, Japan, Northern Ireland, Russia, South Africa, and Zimbabwe. Most confrontations concerned the question of how much of a nation's sordid past, in comparison with its glorious accomplishments, should be included for study. In an effort to enhance youths' sense of national pride, should Russian texts avoid mentioning the vicious treatment of minorities in Stalin's era? Should Japanese texts gloss over atrocities committed by soldiers in China and Korea? Should German texts downplay the Holocaust of Hitler's day? Should France's curricula ignore the French army's repressive tactics in North Africa during colonial times?

Critics complained of religious bias in Jordanian and Pakistani public-school textbooks. Though Jordanian texts generally advocated tolerance toward other religions, debate continued over the support for jihad, the Islamic principle of waging holy war against non-Muslims. Pakistan's government-sanctioned textbooks for state schools were censured by foreign observers for including such passages as "Islam preaches equality, brotherhood, and fraternity [whereas] the foundation of Hindu [society] is injustice and cruelty."

South Korean schoolboys hold up anti-Japanese placards in a demonstration at the Japanese embassy in Seoul in April. Among other issues, the Koreans were protesting what they saw as distortions in Japanese school textbooks over the history of Japan's 1910–45 occupation of Korea.

© Kim Kyung-Hoon/Reuters/Corbis

Attempts to renovate education in Iraq's 16,000 schools resulted in both success and failure. The U.S. Agency for International Development reported that it had built or refurbished 2,405 schools. Although textbooks were rewritten to expunge references to Saddam Hussein's fallen regime, the revised versions still included passages urging Iraqis to fight "against invasion and foreign powers." The production of new civics books that promoted democracy was stalled by inaction in the highly centralized Ministry of Education, and the safety of students was threatened by street violence that caused many to avoid attending class.

Following terrorist bombings in London, the British government rejected demands that the nation's five state-funded Muslim schools be closed. Instead, officials intended to increase the number of such schools to 150 in an effort to move thousands of Muslim children from independent Islamic schools into government-controlled mainstream education. Muslim schools would be offered the same voluntary-aided status held by almost 7,000 Anglican, Roman Catholic, and Jewish schools. Complaints that Muslim schools in the United Kingdom failed to teach tolerance of other faiths led the British Office of Standards in Education to inspect 50 Muslim schools and 40 evangelical Christian schools. Investigators discovered that a higher proportion of evangelical schools (43%) than Muslim schools (36%) were guilty of intolerance.

In the wake of Hurricane Katrina, which devastated the Gulf Coast area in late August, thousands of American refugee students from the disaster area were enrolled in schools across the nation. Storm damage had left more than 135,000 children in Louisiana and 35,000 in Mississippi without a nearby school to attend.

A South African research centre reported that while sub-Sahara African countries were moving slowly toward universal schooling, more than half of the 80 million children of primary-school age in the region were still not in school. Enrollment in secondary schools in 22 countries was below 20%, while less than 10% of the workforce had a secondary-school education. In an effort to reduce the AIDS epidemic in Uganda, MP Sulaiman Madada offered to pay the university fees for girls who were virgins when they graduated from high school.

French students organized massive street demonstrations to protest changes that Minister of Education François Fillon proposed for the traditional baccalaureate test ("le bac"), which for two centuries had been high-school graduates' passport to a university education. Faced with such furor, Fillon withdrew his proposal so that 634,168 high-school seniors in France and its overseas territories could sit for the exam, which annually confronted students with the analysis of complex philosophical issues; "le bac" dated back to Napoleon's time.

Education officials in Finland credited the quality of the nation's teachers when Finnish 15-year-olds scored at the top in the PISA (Programme for International Student Assessment) testing plan that compared pupils' educational achievement across 41 industrialized countries. The generally poor showing on PISA exams by students in Germany (ranked 25 out of the 41 countries) prompted the German government to extend the length of the school day and offer improved and expanded German-language instruction for immigrant children.

The proper role of religion in schools concerned officials in Canada and the U.S. The government in Quebec gave church-sponsored schools three years to replace their religious curriculum with classes focusing on ethics and comparative religious cultures. In the U.S. more school districts considered supplementing the study of Darwin's theory of evolution with either biblical creationism (the belief that human life began as depicted in the Bible in the first chapter of Genesis) or creationism's recent modification—intelligent design (attributing life's beginning to an unidentified supreme being). Efforts to introduce such religion-based beliefs in science classes attracted increased attention after President Bush recommended adding intelligent design to science curricula. In December, however, a judge in Pennsylvania ruled that high-school biology teachers should not have been permitted to read a statement to students to the effect that intelligent design is an acceptable alternative theory to evolution.

The use of computers as learning tools continued to expand. A survey in the U.S. showed that 67% of nursery-school children and 80% of kindergartners used computers at school, with 23% of children in nursery schools and 32% of those in kindergartens accessing the Internet. In higher grades the proportions of students using computers were 91% in grades 1–5, 95% in grades 6–8, and 97% in grades 9–12. Data from the PISA testing program showed, however, that the more time children spent on computers at home, the lower test scores they were likely to earn. Analysts estimated that much of the home time was spent on computer games and Internet chatting that contributed nothing toward test performance. In contrast to the PISA evidence, a study in the U.S. found that children with computers at home—but no television sets in their bedrooms—earned higher test scores.

Problems caused by students' carrying cell phones motivated school officials to restrict or ban cell phone use. Teachers complained that mobile phones in classrooms diverted students from learning tasks and interrupted class sessions by ringing at inopportune times. In Britain 1,013 penalties were imposed on students who used cell phones inappropriately, a 16% increase over the previous year. More than 2,500 British students had their test scores reduced because they had cheated, with the 9% rise in cheating partly due to students' using mobile phones' text messaging features to seek answers from classmates. (See COMPUTERS AND INFORMATION SYSTEMS: Sidebar.)

To cope with a shortage of teachers in the U.S., more than 1,000 schools imported more than 1,900 teachers from abroad, thereby continuing a recruiting practice that accounted for more than 10,000 foreign teachers in the country's public elementary and secondary schools and another 5,000 in charter and private schools.

HIGHER EDUCATION

By 2005 more people worldwide were completing postsecondary schooling than ever before, according to the Organisation for Economic Co-operation and Development. In the 30 OECD member nations, half of young adults attended some form of tertiary education, with an average of 32% completing a first-level university degree. The rate of enrollment varied across countries, ranging from below 20% in Austria, the Czech Republic, Germany, and Switzerland to 45% in Australia and Finland. Between 1995 and 2002, attendance in postsecondary education rose by more than 20% in Australia, Finland, Ireland, Mexico, Portugal, Spain, Sweden, and the U.K. and by more than 50% in the Czech Republic, Greece, Hungary, Iceland, South Korea, and Poland.

AP/Wide World Photos

Students and fans of the University of Utah express their support for their team name, Utes—an Indian people—at a football game in September. In 2005 the NCAA tightened its policy on permitting college team names and mascots that might be offensive to Native Americans.

The number of students in colleges and universities outside their own country continued to grow during the year. The figure of two million studying abroad in 2005 was expected to double by 2015 and double again by 2025. More Japanese universities opened offices in China to recruit students who could make up for the dwindling pool of university students in Japan, which was attributed to a declining Japanese birthrate.

Rising college costs increased the financial burden of British students. A study of 1,200 graduates in Britain found that 60% were still financially supported by their parents three years after graduation, with the situation expected to become worse after higher tuition costs (top-up fees) were imposed in 2006. In Britain's private schools a decline in students from China, Hong Kong, Russia, and the United States was blamed on the dou-

bling of visa fees and an average tuition increase of 5.8%. To raise more operating funds, the University of Oxford planned to reduce the number of British students enrolled in order to admit more foreign students, who were charged tuition fees that were 10 times higher than those paid by British students. The plan drew a sharp response from members of Parliament, who argued that the large sums of taxpayers' money Oxford received obligated the university to give top priority to educating British youths rather than foreigners.

A growing movement in American college libraries found reading rooms being emptied of books to make way for computers. At the University of Texas at Austin, 90,000 volumes in the undergraduate library were transferred to other libraries on the campus, leaving only 1,000 reference books in the resulting "information commons," where students could download information from the Internet and work on multimedia projects under the guidance of Internet-wise librarians.

China continued to achieve unprecedented growth in higher education. Between the years 1998 and 2005, college enrollment tripled to 20 million. Education officials predicted that by 2010 at least 20% of high-school graduates would be pursuing some form of tertiary education; that number was expected to reach 50% by 2050. Much of the enrollment growth was attributed to the recent creation of 1,300 private institutions. Though the Internet was credited with providing China's scholars a worldwide outlet for writings critical of conditions in their country, Chinese officials feared that such a channel for free speech would foment unrest. As a result, officials restricted Internet access to students and defined the research topics of professors who were dissidents.

Zimbabwe celebrated the 25th anniversary of independence from British colonial rule by noting several advances that occurred over the past quarter century: the number of the nation's universities had increased from one to 12, with enrollment rising from 1,000 students to 54,000; teacher-training colleges increased from one to 15, and enrollment expanded from 1,000 to 20,000 students; the number of technical colleges grew from 2 to 10, and student admissions rose from 2,000 to 15,000.

The disastrous consequences of educated Africans' moving abroad was a

key concern at an immigration conference in South Africa, where participants learned that an estimated 20,000 professionals had left the continent each year since 1990. Conference speakers noted that for the welfare of African societies, the time and money invested in the emigrants' schooling had been wasted.

A report from Human Rights Watch criticized the Egyptian government for censoring reading lists in colleges, harassing student activists, and creating a harsh climate of repression that drastically restricted universities' teaching and research activities. The report not only condemned the state's repressive measures against Islamic student activists but also criticized Islamic activists' efforts to intimidate non-Muslim professors and students.

In Mexico, as government funding of public universities stagnated, the nation's 1,500 private colleges and universities that had been founded in recent decades increased their enrollment from 1.3 million in 1993 to 2.5 million in 2005. Private institutions' share of the country's total number of students rose from 15% in 1985 to 33% in 2005 and was projected to reach 40% by 2010.

The U.S. Department of Defense announced that it was compiling personal information about high-school and college students that would aid the department in recruiting youths for the armed forces. As the Iraq war dragged on, however, American college and high-school officials became increasingly reluctant to provide military recruiters access to student information on the grounds that sharing such information violated students' privacy rights.

The use by U.S. colleges of American Indian peoples or personalities for athletic team names and mascots came under criticism as the National Collegiate Athletic Association asked 33 colleges to explain why their nicknames were not offensive to Native Americans.

College officials in the U.S. worried about the accelerating pace of drinking on campuses. Researchers announced that fatal injuries related to alcohol rose from 1,500 in 1998 to more than 1,700 in 2001 among students aged 18–24. Over the same period, the number of students who drove cars under the influence of alcohol increased by half a million (2.3 million to 2.8 million), a trend that was apparently continuing through 2005.

(R. MURRAY THOMAS)

The Environment

The UN completed a comprehensive ASSESSMENT of the world's ECOSYSTEMS. The KYOTO PROTOCOL came into force, and in the European Union CARBON EMISSIONS TRADING with "carbon credits" began. Studies showed a link between TOP PREDATORS and biodiversity, and a study of bird species yielded important findings concerning BIODIVERSITY HOTSPOTS.

INTERNATIONAL ACTIVITIES

The results of a four-year, $24 million survey ordered in 2000 by UN Secretary-General Kofi Annan were published on March 30, 2005. Known as the Millennium Ecosystem Assessment and produced by 1,360 scientists in 95 countries, the survey aimed to assess the state of ecosystems from the point of view of the people who depend on the benefits that they provide. These benefits included food, timber, and other materials, protection from floods and soil erosion, and recreation. The survey found that 15 of the 24 ecosystem benefits it studied were being degraded or used in an unsustainable manner. Where some ecosystem benefits had improved, mostly through an increase in food production, the improvement had been achieved at the cost of degrading others. Instead of making recommendations, the assessment outlined four different scenarios that might result from particular sets of policies. (1) "Order from strength" was a scenario in which nations were obsessed with security and became fragmented into regional markets and alliances. In this scenario every type of ecosystem would deteriorate, and less-developed countries would bear the worst changes. (2) "Global orchestration" was a scenario in which free trade was encouraged together with an emphasis on poverty reduction. Food production would rise sharply in less-developed countries, but climate change would accelerate and there would be a loss of environmental cultural benefits such as ecotourism. (3) "TechnoGarden," which emphasized green technologies, was a scenario in which the production of food would rise but would not be maximized. Many environmental problems would decrease, but so would biodiversity. (4) "Adapting mosaic" would use low-technology local-based solutions that would maximize benefits and minimize problems. If it was adopted widely, it would allow all ecosystem-related benefits to improve.

The Kyoto Protocol came into force on February 16, following Russia's ratification of the treaty in November 2004. Two additional countries, Indonesia and Nigeria, ratified the protocol in December 2004. (*See* Special Report.)

In June the European Court of Human Rights, sitting in Strasbourg, France, ruled that European governments had a duty to prevent serious damage to their citizens' health caused by pollution from industrial installations, even when those installations were privately owned and operated. The ruling concerned the case of Nadezhda Fadeyeva, who lived near a privately held steel plant in a town northeast of Moscow. The court found that the state had failed to protect Fadeyeva, either by resettling her or by reducing pollution from the plant, and it ordered the government to pay her compensation of €6,000 (about $7,200) and to resolve her situation.

At a June meeting held in Stockholm, 28 countries with research interests in Antarctica agreed to rules that would make individual nations responsible for taking immediate action to deal with any incident that resulted in environmental pollution and to meet the cleanup costs. The rules went into effect June 15 as the Stockholm Annex to the 1959 Antarctic Treaty.

Scientists met in London in February to mark the completion of the five-year, £7 million (about $13 million) Global

The Kyoto Protocol, which came into force in 2005, allowed the planting of trees—which take up carbon dioxide—as credits to help meet emissions-reduction targets. At the Aichi (Japan) World Exposition to attend a program on the protocol, Kenyan Nobel Peace Prize winner Wangari Maathai helps plant a tree while flanked by two expo mascot characters.

Nitrogen Enrichment (GANE) Programme to map the worldwide effects of excess nitrogen on rivers, forests, and grasslands. John Lawton, chief executive of the U.K.'s Natural Environment Research Council, said that the massive increase in the amount of chemically reactive forms of nitrogen that was in circulation was one of the three major environmental challenges facing the world, together with the loss of biodiversity and climate change. The GANE study noted that parts of the Gulf of Mexico were losing marine animals because of high levels of eutrophication (the process by which the nutrient-stimulated growth of aquatic plants depletes oxygen from the water). Researchers suspected that shallow freshwater lakes in the U.K. and Poland might be losing plant species for the same reason.

The pan-European Göteborg protocol on air pollution became binding following its ratification by Portugal on May 17. The protocol set national ceilings for emissions of sulfur oxides, nitrogen oxides, ammonia, and volatile organic compounds from industry, agriculture, and transport. International restrictions on the emissions of sulfur oxides and nitrogen oxides from ships went into force on May 19 as part of Annex VI to the International Convention for the Prevention of Pollution from Ships (MARPOL).

Bob Hunter, cofounder of Greenpeace, died on May 2, and Gaylord Nelson, the former U.S. senator who founded the Earth Day movement, died on July 3. (See OBITUARIES.) At a ceremony held at United Nations headquarters in New York City on April 19, the UN Environment Programme's executive director, Klaus Töpfer, presented the first annual Champions of the Earth awards, which were intended to recognize outstanding contributions to the environment made by people in all parts of the world. The seven recipients were King Jigme Singye Wangchuk and the people of Bhutan, the late Sheikh Zayid ibn Sultan Al Nahyan of the United Arab Emirates, Pres. Thabo Mbeki and the people of South Africa, Patriarch Bartholomew of the Eastern Orthodox Church, Julia Carabias Lillo of Mexico, Sheila Watt-Cloutier of Canada, and Zhou Qiang and the All-China Youth Federation.

NATIONAL DEVELOPMENTS

Europe. The European Union plan for the trading of carbon emissions came into force on Jan. 1, 2005. Approximately 12,000 industrial installations, which accounted for about one-half of all EU carbon-dioxide output, had their emissions capped. Any factory that emitted more than a specified amount of carbon dioxide would be penalized unless it covered the excess by purchasing "carbon credits" from other factories that emitted less than their allowance. The European Commission had endorsed the national allocation plans for all but four countries (Italy, Poland, the Czech Republic, and Greece), and the plan for Spain was conditional pending minor changes. The first stage, to run from 2005 to 2007, covered the cement, glass, paper-and-pulp, electric-power, and iron-and-steel industries. The second stage, to run from 2008 to 2012, was expected to impose tighter restrictions and would perhaps be extended to cover additional producers, such as the chemical and aluminum industries and, possibly, the aviation industry. The opening price was about €8 (about $11) per metric ton of carbon dioxide, and the trade in unused emission allowances was expected eventually to be worth billions of euros.

The Eurobarometer survey published in May by the European Commission found that 85% of respondents wished that policy makers would consider environmental policies to be as important as economic and social policies, 88% thought that environmental concerns should be taken into consideration when decisions in other areas were made, and 72% believed that the condition of the environment significantly influenced their quality of life. The survey was the first to include the 10 new member states of the EU. Climate change was rated as the most serious worry among respondents from old-member countries, but it ranked only seventh among those from the new-member countries.

Peter Calow, a British scientist, was appointed director of Denmark's Environmental Assessment Institute in November 2004. The post was formerly held by Bjørn Lomborg, who had generated controversy in his criticism of views held by many environmentalists. Calow, former professor of zoology at the University of Sheffield, Eng., and a specialist in ecology and ecological risk assessment, was a member of the EU scientific committee on health and environmental risks.

The Obrigheim nuclear reactor closed down on May 11. The 36-year-old 340-MW plant was the oldest in Germany and was the second of the original 19 reactors in the country to close under Germany's plan to phase out nuclear power by 2021.

A four-year study of the Russian Arctic, conducted by the Arctic Monitoring and Assessment Program and reported in November 2004, found that samples of human breast milk and umbilical-cord blood contained very high levels of a number of persistent toxic substances, including hexachlorobenzene, dioxins, DDT, PCBs, mercury, and lead. The mean concentrations of these substances were similar to those found in Canada and Greenland, with the highest concentrations in the Chukotka peninsula, in the Russian Far East, where people ate large amounts of marine mammals and fish. About 5% of the population, mainly male, had very high PCB levels (0.01 mg/g of blood lipid, or one part in 100,000).

In February it appeared that the national commitment to phase out nuclear power in Sweden was unlikely to be fulfilled. The four-party opposition alliance was said to be prepared to retain all but one of the existing nuclear plants, and the Social Democratic government was said to have approved a 15 billion Swedish kronor (about $2.1 billion) modernization program to increase capacity at 7 of the existing 10 reactors. Nevertheless, the Barsebäck 2 nuclear reactor was shut down on May 31. Vattenfall, the Swedish energy company that ran Barsebäck, announced plans to replace it with the largest wind farm in northern Europe. The 8 billion Swedish kronor (about $1.1 billion) turbine park would be built offshore near Copenhagen.

A March opinion poll showed that approximately 80% of Swedes favoured continuing the use of nuclear power, which was supplying one-half of Sweden's electricity, and only 10% supported phasing it out. People feared that abandoning nuclear power would make it necessary to import power generated elsewhere in Europe from fossil fuels.

Asia. In March it was reported at a symposium on water management that one-third of China's rural population, which amounted to 360 million persons, lacked access to safe drinking water and that more than 70% of the country's rivers and lakes were polluted. The vice-minister for water resources, Zhai Haohui, said that the provision of clean drinking water should be made a priority. *China Daily*

A woman collects bottles near a polluted river in Dongxiang, China. One-third of China's rural population was reported to lack access to safe drinking water.

cited a 2002 study that revealed that more than two million persons had been made ill by drinking water and burning coal containing arsenic.

On August 11 the authorities declared a state of emergency in the Kelang Valley and Kuala Lumpur when air quality deteriorated because of fires that had been started to clear land in Sumatra, Indonesia. Schools were closed, and people were advised to remain indoors or to wear masks if they went outdoors. Air-quality readings were rated "hazardous" in Port Kelang and Kuala Selangor. After Malaysia helped Indonesian authorities extinguish the fires, air quality reached an acceptable level, and on August 13 the state of emergency was lifted.

United States. Addressing an audience in San Francisco on World Environment Day, June 2, California Gov. Arnold Schwarzenegger announced an executive order that set targets for reducing greenhouse-gas emissions in the state. The order called for a reduction in emissions to year 2000 levels by 2010, to 1990 levels by 2020, and to 80% below 1990 levels by 2050. The Californian economy was the sixth largest in the world, and the state was the world's 10th largest emitter of greenhouse gases.

In August officials in Connecticut, Delaware, Maine, Massachusetts, New Hampshire, New Jersey, New York, Rhode Island, and Vermont agreed to restrict power-plant emissions of carbon dioxide in 2009 to their 2000–04 average level and then reduce them by 10% between 2015 and 2020. The

agreement, which affected more than 600 power plants, would go into effect when all nine states had passed the necessary legislation.

ENVIRONMENTAL ISSUES

Climate Change. The 10th conference of parties to the UN Climate Change Convention, held in Buenos Aires Dec. 6–17, 2004, was attended by representatives from about 200 countries. Harlan Watson, the U.S. chief negotiator, stated that the United States had no intention of signing the Kyoto Protocol, which he said was a political document based on bad science. The aim of the Buenos Aires conference had been to open discussions on emission targets to be introduced after 2012, but no agreement was reached. The delegates decided to meet again in May 2005 to discuss post-2012 targets, but it also proved impossible to agree to any post-2012 measures at the May meeting.

During his visit to Brussels in February, days after the Kyoto Protocol came into force, Pres. George W. Bush said that U.S. determination to stay outside the Kyoto framework remained strong and that all countries should still work together in order to make progress with emerging technologies that would encourage environmentally responsible economic growth. This approach led to the Asia-Pacific Partnership, an agreement reached in July between Australia, China, India, Japan, South Korea, and the United States. The partnership aimed to combat climate change by promoting clean-energy technologies,

including natural gas, methane capture from waste, hydroelectricity, and nuclear power. Each signatory country would set its own goals for reducing emissions, with no outside mechanism for enforcement.

In September the German Economics Institute reported that during 2004 global carbon-dioxide emissions from energy generation and use increased by 4.5% over 2003, the highest rate of growth since 2000. The rise was greatest in China, whose 2004 carbon-dioxide emissions were 579 million metric tons more than in the previous year, a rise of 15%. Global emissions, at 27.5 billion metric tons, were 26% above their 1990 level. Total 2004 emissions of all six greenhouse gases from the countries bound by the Kyoto Protocol were 4.1% below their 1990 level.

Ozone Layer. In late June an extraordinary meeting of parties to the Montreal Protocol on Substances that Deplete the Ozone Layer agreed to cap 2006 production of methyl bromide at 13,000 metric tons, a reduction of 20% from the amount permitted in 2005. Developed countries were required to phase out the use of methyl bromide by 2005 but were allowed to negotiate annual exemptions. Less-developed countries, which had consumed 12,000 metric tons in 2003, were to phase out use by 2015.

Ozone depletion in 2005 was severe in both the Antarctic and the Arctic. Readings from the Scanning Imaging Absorption Spectrometer for Atmospheric Chartography on the European satellite *Envisat* suggested that ozone depletion over Antarctica in August covered a larger area than in any other year since 2000. Measurements of the Arctic ozone layer made between January and March by scientists at the Alfred Wegener Institute for Polar and Marine Research in Potsdam, Ger., showed ozone losses to have been the largest ever recorded. An analysis of satellite records and surface-monitoring instruments led scientists who worked with the Center for Integrating Statistical and Environmental Science at the University of Chicago to report that the ozone layer was no longer thinning. The study found that in some parts of the world the ozone layer had thickened slightly, although ozone levels remained below levels that existed before ozone depletion began.

Chernobyl. In September the Chernobyl Forum published a three-volume, 600-page report assessing the impact on public health of the 1986 nuclear accident at Chernobyl. Approximately 50 emergency workers died of acute radiation syndrome shortly after the accident, and 9 children died from thyroid cancer because of radiation exposure. As a result of the accident, an additional 3,940 people—from among the 200,000 emergency workers who were present at the site in the first year following the accident, the 116,000 people who were evacuated, and the 270,000 residents of the most heavily contaminated areas—were likely to die from cancer. These deaths represented a 3% increase over the number of deaths that would be expected from naturally occurring cancer—an increase that would be difficult to detect. Although 4,000 cases of thyroid cancer had been reported in individuals who were children or adolescents at the time of the accident, their survival rate from the cancer was expected to be almost 99%. The report also found that the trauma of being evacuated, combined with persistent myths and misperceptions about the threat of radiation, had produced harmful effects. The report was compiled by more than 100 scientists, economists, and health experts. The Chernobyl Forum comprised seven UN organizations and programs, the World Bank, and the governments of Belarus, Russia, and Ukraine.

The former Danish ferry Kong Frederik IX (Ricky) *lies at anchor near the Alang ship-breaking yard in Gujarat, India.*

Marine Pollution. A report from the Swedish environmental advisory council (SEAC), delivered to the government on February 22, expressed the fears of scientists that the marine ecology of the Baltic Sea had become locked into permanent eutrophication. SEAC found that measures to control the release of nutrients from agricultural runoff, drainage, and road traffic had resulted in some improvement in the waters around Stockholm and the Swedish west coast but had not had a discernible effect in the open sea.

In May Danish authorities failed in their attempt to secure the return of the 51-year-old ferry *Kong Frederik IX* (later renamed *Frederik* and finally *Ricky*), which had been sent to India for scrapping. The ship, which contained asbestos insulation, had docked at the Alang ship-breaking yard in Gujarat on April 19. The Basel Action Network, an environmental group, protested what it considered to be a clear violation of the UN Basel Convention on Trade in Hazardous Waste. Danish authorities said the ship had been exported illegally, but Environment Minister Connie Hedegaard said on May 3 that her Indian counterpart, A. Raja, had refused to return the ship. Raja maintained that the Indian authorities did not regard it as waste and were confident of their ability to dispose of it legally and in an environmentally defensible fashion. The Danish government planned to seek measures through the International Maritime Organization to prevent future incidents of this kind, although the Danish press reported that two more old ferries, the *Dronning Margrethe II* and the *Rügen*, were on their way to India to be scrapped. The *Ricky* remained beached at Alang, and 150 kg (330 lb) of asbestos had been recovered from it by November. (MICHAEL ALLABY)

WILDLIFE CONSERVATION

The June 2005 meeting of the International Whaling Commission in Ulsan, S.Kor., opened to fears among the antiwhaling bloc, led by New Zealand, Australia, and the United Kingdom, that pro-whaling nations might finally gain a majority among the 66 member states and overturn the 19-year-old ban on commercial whaling, but the status quo did not change. Japan stood by its plans to increase its so-called scientific catches, stating that it intended to increase its annual minke-whale quota to 935, more than double the previous

A worldwide study in 2005 noted an increase in eutrophication, which was blamed for the death of these fish in a lake near Bangalore, India.

quota, and take 50 humpbacks and 50 fin whales.

Sakhalin Energy Investment Co. Ltd., of which Royal Dutch Shell was the main stakeholder, agreed in March to reroute a controversial undersea oil pipeline so that it would avoid the feeding grounds of the critically endangered western gray whale near Sakhalin Island in Russia's Far East. Environmentalists said that the offshore oil platforms the company was developing posed the greater problem, and whale experts recommended that the platforms be placed as far from the shore as possible.

In June a report commissioned by Britain's Royal Society showed that the oceans were becoming more acidic as they absorbed some of the excess carbon dioxide that was being released into the atmosphere through the burning of fossil fuels. The change could be catastrophic for marine ecosystems and for economies that rely on reef tourism or fishing. Seawater is naturally alkaline, with an average pH of 8.2. (On the pH scale, values above 7 are alkaline, values below 7 are acidic, and lower values correspond to greater acidity.) The study suggested that by the year 2100 anticipated increases in atmospheric carbon dioxide would lead to a fall of 0.5 in the *(continued on page 196)*

The Kyoto Protocol:
What Next?

by Roger A. Pielke, Jr.

The Kyoto Protocol to the UN Framework Convention on Climate Change (UNFCCC), an international treaty that was named after the Japanese city in which it was proposed in December 1997, came into effect in February 2005 following its ratification by Russia. Despite the ratification of the treaty, its future is cloudy. Although some have hailed the protocol as the most significant environmental treaty ever negotiated, others have labeled it a dead end, and international responses to climate change remained mired in political uncertainty. How nations and other interests respond to this uncertainty will shape international climate policy for years to come.

The Kyoto Protocol addresses the issue of climate change, which the UNFCCC considers to be the direct or indirect result of human activity that alters the composition of the atmosphere. In particular, the protocol is concerned with the release of greenhouse gases, such as carbon dioxide and methane, which affect the energy balance of the global atmosphere in ways expected to lead to an overall increase in temperature, popularly referred to as "global warming." Although climate change is most often discussed in terms of the global average temperature, the reasons for concern are far less abstract. Among the tangible effects of such climate change would be a general rise in sea level around the world; the melting of glaciers, sea ice, and Arctic permafrost; and possible changes in the number and distribution of extreme climate-related events such as floods and drought.

The Kyoto Protocol is focused on reducing the emission of six greenhouse gases in 38 developed countries to a level 5.2% below a 1990 baseline by a commitment period of 2008–12. Different emissions-reduction targets were negotiated with each country on the basis of its unique circumstances. Under the protocol, countries have several means at their disposal to reach their targets. One approach is to make use of natural processes, called "sinks," that remove greenhouse gases from the atmosphere. The planting of trees, which

take up carbon dioxide from the air, would be an example. Another approach is the international program called the Clean Development Mechanism (CDM), which encourages developed countries to invest in technology and infrastructure in less-developed countries, where there are often significant opportunities to reduce emissions. Under the CDM the investing country can claim the effective reduction in emissions as a credit toward meeting its obligations under the protocol. An example would be an investment in a clean-burning natural-gas power plant to replace a proposed coal-fired plant. A third approach is emissions trading, which allows participating countries to buy and sell emissions rights and thereby places an economic value on greenhouse-gas emissions. European countries have initiated a fledgling emissions-trading market as a mechanism to work toward meeting their commitments under the Kyoto Protocol.

Without a doubt, the Kyoto Protocol is a landmark diplomatic accomplishment, and it represents a tremendous effort by many countries around the world, most notably the major members of the European Union. Yet the future of the protocol is uncertain for at least three reasons.

First, there are signs that most participants under the protocol will fail to meet their commitments to reduce emissions. For example, the European Environment Agency reported in 2004 that 11 of the 15 EU "member states are heading towards overshooting their emission targets [mandated under the protocol], some by a substantial margin." Furthermore, the remaining 4 member states are meeting their targets only because of unique, nonrepeatable circumstances of politics, economics, or geography that are independent of the protocol, such as the long-term move away from coal-based energy generation in the U.K.

Second, the U.S. (the leading greenhouse-gas emitter) is not party to the protocol, and China (the next leading emitter) and other less-developed countries that are party to the protocol are not required to restrict their greenhouse-gas emissions. The architecture of the Kyoto Protocol focuses on a country-by-country accounting of emissions and tends to place countries that have a moderate to high population growth at a disadvantage. For example,

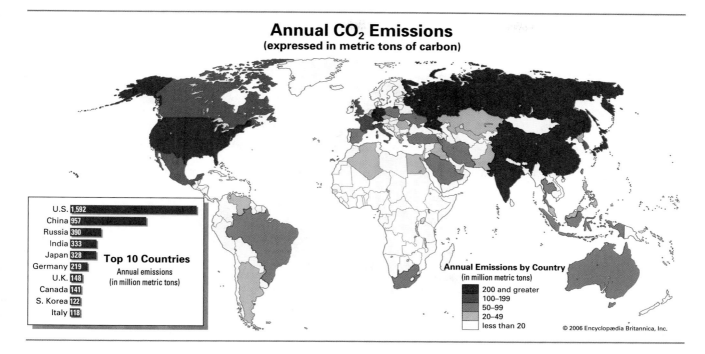

Annual CO₂ Emissions
(expressed in metric tons of carbon)

Top 10 Countries
Annual emissions
(in million metric tons)

U.S. 1,592
China 957
Russia 390
India 333
Japan 328
Germany 219
U.K. 148
Canada 141
S. Korea 122
Italy 118

Annual Emissions by Country
(in million metric tons)
- 200 and greater
- 100–199
- 50–99
- 20–49
- less than 20

© 2006 Encyclopædia Britannica, Inc.

the U.S. is expected to see a 40% increase in its population between 1990 and 2025, whereas the population of Europe as a whole is expected to be about the same in 2025 as it was in 1990. Assuming that greenhouse-gas emissions remain constant on a per capita basis, then most countries in Europe need only follow business as usual to equal its 1990 emissions, whereas the U.S. would need to achieve a 30% decrease in its per capita emissions.

Third, and perhaps most crucial, even complete success in meeting the emissions targets under the protocol would do little to address projected climate change. In 1998 Tom Wigley, a scientist at the National Center for Atmospheric Research in Boulder, Colo., and a longtime participant in climate-change-assessment activities, sought to study the effectiveness of the protocol by using a climate model similar to those underlying assessment reports by the Intergovernmental Panel on Climate Change. He ran the climate model under one scenario in which greenhouse-gas emissions were reduced as called for by the Kyoto Protocol and under another scenario in which no reductions were made. He found that the influence of the protocol would be not detectable for many decades.

Since the world is certain to undergo some amount of climate change and the economic and human toll of weather-related disasters is inexorably rising, many less-developed countries have advocated that improved adaptation to climate variability and change receive an equal standing to greenhouse-gas reduction in order to address their priorities of poverty reduction and development. This approach, however, has proved to be challenging for several reasons, not least of which is the explicit focus of the UNFCCC on greenhouse gases. There is also a sense among the protocol's advocates that discussion of adaptation will necessarily divert attention from efforts to control emissions.

The challenges that implementation of the protocol has faced to date raise questions whether the protocol can form the basis for international climate-change policies or whether a new approach may be needed. For example, U.K. Prime Minister Tony Blair, who has been a leader on the issue of climate change, has called into question the viability of the Kyoto framework. In the United States not only did Republican Pres. George W. Bush in 2001 withdraw U.S. participation in the Kyoto Protocol, but the major Democratic presidential candidates in 2004 did not support the treaty (although some favoured participation in international climate-change negotiations). In addition, China, the country with the world's largest population, has routinely emphasized poverty reduction through continued development as a higher national priority than

reductions in greenhouse-gas emissions, and India, the country with the world's second largest population, has signed the Kyoto Protocol but has not agreed to adopting emissions-reduction targets. These positions suggest the possibility that post-Kyoto climate policy may see dramatic changes.

There is reason for optimism that progress will be made on dealing with climate change. Europe remains steadfastly committed to the issue, and Japan and Russia have both agreed to emphasize it during their upcoming turns as hosts of G-8 summits. In the U.S., municipalities and several states have taken proactive steps to reduce their greenhouse-gas emissions by using strategies that some observers say foreshadow broader actions by the federal government. Also, less-developed countries have continued to emphasize the importance of adaptation in the face of their significant vulnerability. As nations and other interests grapple with climate policy in the first year following the ratification of the Kyoto Protocol, it is clear that much has been learned about the challenges of confronting climate change but the task of turning those lessons into improved climate policies has only just begun.

Roger A. Pielke, Jr., is a Professor in the Environmental Studies Program at the University of Colorado and the Director of the Center for Science and Technology Policy Research.

(continued from page 193)

average pH of ocean surface waters. The increasing acidity might affect animals that have high oxygen demands, such as squid, since dissolved oxygen would become more difficult to extract from water. The change might also have serious consequences for organisms with calcium-carbonate shells, including lobsters, crabs, shellfish, certain plankton species, and coral polyps, because increasing acidity would affect how readily calcium carbonate dissolves in seawater.

A study published in January 2005 by the British Antarctic Survey identified the year-round habitats of gray-headed albatrosses. The birds were tracked as they flew from their breeding sites near South Georgia Island in the South Atlantic Ocean to areas of the southwestern Indian Ocean. More than one-half then completed a round-the-world journey, some in just 46 days. By identifying the areas where the birds feed, the report was expected to help governments and fisheries take measures to reduce the number of albatrosses that were dying each year from preying on hooked bait used in longline fishing.

The charisma of top vertebrate predators was often used to help solicit funds for conservation projects. Although this promotional strategy had been criticized, it received some justification on scientific grounds from a study published in July of habitat data for five raptor species. The study found that the sites occupied by the five apex predators, which differed greatly in diet and habitat, were associated with high biodiversity and thereby ecologically important. In a related matter, a study published in June showed that the large

Two fjords in southwestern Norway were selected as a World Heritage site in 2005. Geirangerfjord, shown here, and Nærøyfjord were among the longest and deepest fjords in the world.

specimens of game fish prized by anglers were also important for maintaining fish populations and thereby called into question fishing regulations that allowed large fish to be kept and required that small fish be released. The study found that the fecundity of female fish often increased with size and that the larvae of large individuals were bigger and better able to survive than the larvae of small individuals. Moreover, the young of some fish species needed to follow older fish to learn how to reach their spawning areas.

A study published in August of a newly compiled database of the breeding distribution of all the birds in the world found an alarming lack of congruence, or overlap, in the areas defined by three different criteria for biodiversity hotspots (areas with an exceptional concentration of species). The analysis of the three types of hotspots—based, respectively, on the total number of species, the number of endemic species (species with the smallest breeding ranges), and the number of rare or threatened species in the area—showed that only 2.5% of hotspot areas were common to all three types of hotspots and more than 80% were unique to only one type. From the analysis it appeared that separate mechanisms were associated with the different types of diversity and that the

different types of hotspots should be used together in setting priorities for conservation efforts.

Another study published in August showed that the illegal removal of coral from reefs along the coastline of Sri Lanka led to greater destruction than otherwise would have been caused by the tsunami of December 2004. The tsunami reached significantly farther inland through the gaps that were left by the illegal removal of coral. The coral was typically taken to provide souvenirs for tourists or to be ground up for use in house paint.

The World Heritage Committee inscribed seven new sites on the World Heritage list in July. The sites included two fjords (Geirangerfjord and Nærøyfjord) in Norway, marine ecosystems within the Gulf of California in Mexico, Coiba National Park and its special zone of marine protection within the Gulf of Chiriquí in Panama, part of the Shiretoko Peninsula of Hokkaido and associated marine ecosystems in Japan, and a mosaic of tropical forests in Thailand. The committee also considered the future delisting of Garamba National Park in the Democratic Republic of the Congo if it failed to protect its last remaining northern white rhinoceroses. Only 10 individuals of this subspecies were believed to be left in the wild.

(MARTIN FISHER)

As part of an effort to protect gray-headed albatrosses, scientists tracked the birds and identified the areas at sea where they feed.

Fashions

The colour WHITE cheered the fashion scene amid the troubling times of 2005, and CELEBRITIES once again stole the spotlight with new clothing lines and EXPOSÉS written about them; PEASANT SKIRTS and RUFFLED BLOUSES crammed the runways, while LUXURY brands continued to enjoy ROBUST sales.

As the war in Iraq raged, the threat of terrorist bombings escalated, and hurricane devastation gripped the U.S. in 2005, the fashion industry delivered its antidote to the troubled times—clothes and accessories that were defined by bold, cheerful colours, whimsical shapes, and romantic patterns. After New York designer Narciso Rodriguez displayed bright white empire-line day and evening dresses on his spring-summer runway, the positive pallid shade defined the year's colour palette. The Gap's summer line of white denim became hugely popular, and Tod's and Valextra, Italian makers of expensive handbags, produced stylish models from ashen crocodile. Designers Diane von Furstenberg and Kenneth Cole offered fitted white tank tops as an alternative to blouses. Christian Dior's John Galliano displayed Op art–inspired black-and-white mini sweaterdresses on his autumn-winter runway. Helmut Lang revived classic pearls, displaying them as oversize rope necklaces, at his spring-summer show. In January Lang left his New York fashion house after a 15-year tenure as an arbiter; he had gradually sold off his brand to the Prada Group, which experienced financial woes while trying to revive the brand. In October London-based designer Roland Mouret resigned from his thriving eponymous fashion label. Sharai Meyers, the creative director and financial backer of Roland Mouret, told the *New York Times*, "We have very different views of how the collection should evolve and grow."

Lang's departure heralded a change of the guard within the fashion industry. In February newcomer Riccardo Tisci was appointed creative director of Givenchy; Bruno Frisoni, the new design director of Roger Vivier, the mid-century influential French shoe-design label, successfully relaunched the line in spring; and avant-garde Belgian designer Raf Simons was elevated by Prada in July to helm its moribund Jil Sander ready-to-

The bright white of designer Narciso Rodriguez's empire-line dresses for day and evening, as shown here in New York City, defined the trend for the spring-summer 2005 shows.

© Petre Buzoianu/Corbis

wear label. Three months later Matthew Williamson succeeded Paris couturier Christian Lacroix as the creative force behind Pucci. Alber Elbaz, the 43-year-old Israeli designer of venerable French dress label Lanvin, was regarded as fashion's most influential aesthetic force owing to his continued ability to produce coveted feminine cocktail dresses and decorative accessories that were instantly copied by others, notably his silk-ribbon jeweled choker. Lanvin's opulent loft apartment-like Paris flagship store became a retail destination where high-profile personalities—notably actresses Sarah Jessica Parker, Kirsten Dunst, and Nicole Kidman; film director Sofia Coppola; and fashion designer Vera Wang—could be spotted shopping. In June Wang was named Womenswear Designer of the Year by the Council of Fashion Designers of America (CFDA). In November Tom Ford introduced a pricey cosmetics line and a perfume, Youth Dew Amber Nude, marketed by Estée Lauder. Meanwhile, Liya Kebede, American *Vogue* cover girl and Ethiopian fashion model, was appointed the World Health Organization's goodwill ambassador for maternal, newborn, and child health. Supermodel Tyra Banks (*see* BIOGRAPHIES), host of the popular UPN reality program *America's Next Top Model*, debuted in September *The Tyra Banks Show*, a talk show.

The first spring-summer collection produced by Stefano Pilati—Ford's successor as designer in chief of YSL Rive Gauche, Yves Saint Laurent's ready-to-wear line—led fashion's new direction. Pilati's saucy ruffled YSL minidress was previewed on the February cover of Paris *Vogue*, while American *Vogue* showcased YSL's violet suede stacked-heel loafers and thigh-grazing bell-shaped "tulip bubble" skirts rendered in canary yellow and perky white polka dots. Giles Deacon, the designer of the eponymous London women's luxury fashion label, shared Pilati's voluminous sartorial preference, producing a knee-skimming variation of the tulip skirt. Rigorously tailored knee-hovering poufs were introduced for autumn as well. Marc Jacobs produced an ankle-length "balloon," Balenciaga introduced the "bubble," and Oscar de la Renta's "carnation" featured festooned pleats.

Actress and director Jada Pinkett Smith arrives at the 2005 Nickelodeon Kids Choice Awards in April decked out in white denim, a top fashion choice during the year.

Floral prints proved another yearlong women's fashion trend. In January Gucci introduced Flora—a range of handbags, shoes, and watches that featured zingy Mediterranean wildflowers. Jacobs displayed his spring-summer collection at Pier 54, transforming the otherwise cold lower-Manhattan location into a bucolic paradise where models parading down the runway in his feminine clothes passed beneath an archway adorned with 500,000 pink and white roses. For Louis Vuitton's ready-to-wear collection, Jacobs introduced flirty summer dresses, featuring 1940s-inspired floral prints. Leather rosettes topped flats produced in autumn for his eponymous shoe line, while handmade silk buds decorated a peplumed jacket that Giorgio Armani displayed at his second showing of Privé, his new couture line. English garden blossoms covered classic trench coats and handbags at the spring-summer Burberry Prorsum line. Feathers were a spring-summer alternative to flowers, with Milan design duo Dolce & Gabbana producing a skirt from fluffy peacock plumes, and a quill-print dress proved a coveted item of Miu Miu, Miuccia Prada's diffusion line. For men the answer to the feminine blossom was paisley, which was featured on spring neckties, while hot pink proved the masculine alternative to bright yellow, a popular shade for women's wear. Purple came on strong for both men's and women's wear.

In urban capitals women embraced fashion's upbeat direction by taking to the streets in summer in romantic peasant skirts. Numerous design labels, from Etro to Alberta Ferretti and Dries Van Noten, displayed such "gypsy" skirts, topping the ankle-length floaty silhouette with billowy ruffled blouses. Popular variations of high fashion's gypsy skirts were produced by Club Monaco and Old Navy. The fashionable sought brightly coloured 1970s-inspired beads as well as ethnic-inspired caftans, such as those produced by French retailer BCBG Max Azria and Tory by TRB, a mid-priced resort-inspired sportswear line designed by New York socialite Tory Burch. At OG2, a women's fashion boutique on London's Portobello Road, Nigerian owner Duro Olowu reported selling 1,000 of his $900 knee-length kimono-caftan creations, which he designed from bright vintage silk.

Baggy trousers—which *Harper's Bazaar* magazine deemed "de rigueur"— proved functional amid the summer's heat wave. More popular, however, were women's walking shorts. Actress Gwyneth Paltrow, photographed on a London street wearing knee-length shorts with frilly ankle-tied high-heeled espadrilles, displayed a gradual move toward a more polished, feminine spin on comfort dressing. A high-low mix of casual and expensive dressy items became trendsetting fashion. American *Vogue*'s August issue promoted a relaxed chic look that combined a Marni fur capelet with a pair of $500 Chloé jeans.

Celebrities remained powerful fashion marketing tools. Uma Thurman successfully promoted Louis Vuitton, while Madonna and Demi Moore appeared in advertisements for Versace. Celebrity fashion labels proliferated; British actress Elizabeth Hurley produced an eponymous resort collection, and pop star Justin Timberlake sold his William Rast 60-piece collection of men's and women's casuals at Bloomingdale's. Other celebrity labels were launched by Jennifer Lopez, Beyoncé, Gwen Stefani, Jessica Simpson, and Paula Abdul, who premiered her Skirtz clothing line. Sarah Jessica Parker launched Lovely, a signature fragrance in a pink egg-shaped bottle, and Ali and Paul Hewson collaborated with Manhattan denim designer Rogan Gregory (*see* BIOGRAPHIES) in the launch of Edun, a casual sportswear line. *W* magazine reported sales of nearly double the 75,000 copies sold at newsstands of its July issue, which featured a 58-page Steven Klein fashion shoot in which the Hollywood love match Brad Pitt and Angelina Jolie romped as suburban parents of five children. Photographer Steven Meisel used Italian *Vogue* as the forum for the public's fascination with celebrity fashion. The magazine's January issue featured Meisel's "Hollywood Style" story, inspired by the glossy tabloid *Star*, in which his *Vogue* models were sloppily dressed to resemble stars such as Simpson and Mary-Kate and Ashley Olsen caught unawares by the paparazzi. In July Italian *Vogue* published "Makeover Madness," a controversial 80-page Meisel portfolio that portrayed supermodel Linda Evangelista and other models portraying plastic-surgery patients. Meisel described his images as a "reaction to where entertainment is right now—everything is makeovers and plastic surgery, altering oneself at any cost."

firstVIEW

Colourful high-fashion ankle-length "gypsy" skirts, as in this creation by Alberta Ferretti, typified a trend in 2005 toward happy, ethnic-inspired designs.

During New York City's Fashion Week in February, a model shows a pair of diamond-studded jeans from Jennifer Lopez's fall 2005 line that were valued at $2 million. Film star Lopez was one of several celebrities who launched fashion lines in 2005.

© Mark Mainz/Getty Images

Retail sales figures appeared both buoyant and bumpy during the year. Two days after the July 7 terrorist bombings in London's public transport network, *Women's Wear Daily* magazine noted brisk business on Bond Street, the city's luxury-goods retail thoroughfare. After the second wave of London attacks two weeks later, retail consultancy SPSL reported a 26.9% decline in the number of shoppers on that day compared with 2004. The retail consequences of Hurricane Katrina, which battered the U.S. Gulf Coast, were catastrophic. Gap Inc. reported shuttering 70 stores in affected areas in Mississippi, Alabama, and Tennessee. Saks Inc. closed its Saks Fifth Avenue New Orleans branch, and it was reported in September that some of the city's major retail chains, such as Macy's and Coach, would remain shut down for weeks or perhaps months. Though the arrival in mid-September of Hurricane Rita to the same blighted area sent the U.S. Conference Board's Consumer

Confidence Index plunging 18.9 points—its lowest level since October 2003—the bullish stock market helped buoy sales in luxury markets. LVMH Moët Hennessy Louis Vuitton, owner of fashion labels Louis Vuitton, Givenchy, and Dior, revealed a promising 19% rise in net profit in the first half of the year. PPR, proprietor of avant-garde fashion names, including Balenciaga, Stella McCartney, and Alexander McQueen, reported a healthy 12.5% gain in net profits during the first six months of the year but also divulged that retail sales were weak, owing to a tepid European economic climate.

Premium accessories—designer shoes, must-have handbags, and expensive watches—were the deluxe items purchased by high-spending consumers. A group of specialty boutique retailers surveyed by *Women's Wear Daily* reported a year-on-year 30% increase in September sales. Such hip independent outposts as Kitson on South Robertson Boulevard in Los Angeles were the new

In Comme des Garçons' spring 2006 collection for men, designer Rei Kawakuba scored a hit with her use of rock music iconography, particularly references to the Rolling Stones.

firstVIEW

Kristine A. Strom

Lance Armstrong's yellow "Live Strong" rubber bracelet was just one of the wristbands worn by men and women to show support for various causes. Each cause had a different colour: breast cancer (pink), environment (green), and poverty (white).

zones where young men and women shopped for fashion ephemera, such as designer jeans, collectors item T-shirts, bright cashmeres, and fun fur, as well as essential autumn seasonal accessories such as modish newsboy caps and knee-high boots in leather or suede. Geox, a line of functional Italian footwear with a "breathable" flexible perforated sole that staved off perspiration, opened its first freestanding American store in March on New York City's 57th Street and announced sales of more than nine million pairs of shoes in 68 countries. For men *GQ* magazine deemed the loafer "versatile" footwear. Both men and women continued to sport the "Live Strong" yellow wristbands that were launched in 2004 as a cancer fund-raising initiative by cyclist Lance Armstrong, the seven-time Tour de France champion.

Starkly contrasting fashion's positive direction was a September front-page photo story published by Britain's *Daily Mirror* tabloid newspaper, which reproduced images from video footage that captured 31-year-old supermodel Kate Moss snorting cocaine in a London music studio. In June the CFDA had awarded Moss its Award for Fashion Influence, an accolade based on her continued success as a designer fashion muse. Days after the news of Moss's Class A illicit-drug use was circulated, the plan was halted for her to appear in an advertising campaign to promote a McCartney collection of affordable fashion set to launch worldwide on November 10 at 400 outlets of the popular Swedish retail chain H&M. After Rio de Janeiro-based jeweler H. Stern, Burberry, and Chanel also terminated relationships with Moss, she checked into a rehabilitation clinic near Phoenix. (BRONWYN COSGRAVE)

Health and Disease

Outbreaks of **BIRD FLU** in poultry spread and government officials prepared for a potential **PANDEMIC** among humans. **POLIO** reemerged in Indonesia and elsewhere. Physicians reported the first successful treatment for a patient with advanced **RABIES**, and researchers identified the animal reservoir for **SARS**.

"We don't know when it will start, we don't know where it will start, we don't know how severe it will be, we don't even know for certain from where the causative virus will come." So said David Nabarro, senior coordinator of the UN response to avian influenza, or "bird flu," in a BBC News interview in November 2005. Those were the unknowns. Nabarro went on to list the things he knew—that sooner or later there would be a flu pandemic, that such a pandemic would cause widespread deaths, and, above all, that the world was not prepared. Since mid-2003 a deadly influenza A strain known as H5N1 had been circulating among poultry flocks in Southeast Asia, and in 2005 outbreaks spread to other areas of Asia and to Eastern Europe. Although H5N1 influenza remained essentially an illness in birds, by late 2005 more than 140 people in six Asian countries—Cambodia, China, Indonesia, Thailand, Turkey, and Vietnam—had come down with the particularly virulent flu after having had contact with infected poultry; more than half of them died. Vietnam was the most severely affected, with more than 90 cases. (*See* WORLD AFFAIRS: *Vietnam:* Sidebar.) The first human cases outside China and Southeast Asia occurred in eastern Turkey at the end of December.

The expanding geographic range of H5N1-infected birds sharply increased opportunities for human exposure, and influenza experts warned that each additional human case increased the opportunity for the virus to transform itself into a strain capable of being spread easily among humans and setting off a pandemic. The best defense against pandemic flu would be a vac-cine, and vaccine manufacturers were developing and testing vaccines against the H5N1 virus present in birds. It would take many months to prepare hundreds of millions of doses, however, and existing global vaccine production capacity was not sufficient to meet the demand. Antiviral medications were also expected to play an important role in treatment plans. Two existing antiviral drugs—oseltamivir (Tamiflu), a pill, and zanamivir (Relenza), a nasal spray—were likely to be able to shorten the duration and severity of flu caused by an H5N1 influenza strain if they were used soon after a person became infected with the virus. A pandemic-preparedness plan for the United States was announced by the administration of Pres. George W. Bush on November 1. The plan included the purchase of 20 million doses of a vaccine against the existing H5N1 virus and the stockpiling of enough antiviral medication for another 20 million people. In addition, $2.8 billion was allotted toward research into more reliable and faster ways to produce vaccines.

As the world was scrambling to prepare for a flu pandemic, American scientists working in a high-security laboratory at the Centers for Disease Control and Prevention in Atlanta discovered that the deadliest influenza in history, the 1918–19 "Spanish flu," which killed 50 million people, was in fact a bird flu that became an extremely lethal human flu through the slow accumulation of genetic mutations. The timely research not only offered insights into the evolution of avian influenza viruses but also revealed that the H5N1 virus that was circulating in Asia in 2005 shared some of the mutations found in the 1918 virus.

On November 5, veterinarians in the northern Vietnamese province of Bac Giang pass a barrier with a sign warning that the area is infected with avian influenza. Some 4,000 birds had died of the flu in three villages in the area.

200

HIV and AIDS. The highly ambitious 3 by 5 Initiative of the World Health Organization (WHO) and the Joint UN Program on HIV/AIDS aimed to provide life-prolonging antiretroviral drugs to three million people living with HIV/AIDS in less-developed countries (mainly in Africa) by the end of 2005. In June the sponsoring UN agencies issued a progress report that described clear accomplishments since the launching of the initiative in December 2003 but acknowledged that the 2005 goal would not be met.

Problems with drug procurement were greater than expected, and donors had delivered only about $9 billion of the $27 billion pledged. WHO Director-General Lee Jong Wook was not discouraged. When the initiative began, there were only about 400,000 persons who were receiving treatment in the target countries; a year and a half later, there were one million. "This is the first time that complex therapy for a chronic condition has been introduced at anything approaching this scale in the developing world," said Lee. "The challenges in providing sustainable care in resource-poor settings are enormous, as we expected them to be. But every day demonstrates that this type of care can and must be provided." The UN special envoy for HIV/AIDS in Africa, Stephen Lewis, expressed his belief that the 3 by 5 Initiative would "be seen one day as one of the UN's finest hours." As he traveled through Africa, Lewis observed governments "moving heaven and earth to keep their people alive, and nothing will stop that driving impulse."

Researchers had been struggling for two decades to produce a vaccine against HIV that would be safe and effective in diverse populations. More than 100 candidates had been tested in animals and humans, but none had achieved that goal. A trial that was under way in six countries and involved 1,500 healthy volunteers had scientists excited, however. The vaccine used a disabled common cold virus to deliver three HIV genes into cells to stimulate an immune response against HIV. (No live HIV was used in the production of the vaccine, so it could not cause HIV infection.) The early results were so promising—the vaccine had generated a potent, lasting response—that the researchers were doubling the number of enrollees in the trial.

Polio Eradication. The suspension of polio vaccination in Muslim states in Nigeria in 2003–04 led to polio out-

A nurse hands out information about HIV/AIDS to migrant workers in Chengdu, southwestern China, on December 1. China made a commitment to keeping the number of persons living with HIV/AIDS to below 1.5 million by 2010.

breaks in children and set back the Global Polio Eradication Initiative, which aimed to wipe polio off the face of the Earth by the end of 2005. Polio vaccination resumed in Nigeria in late 2004 but not before 788 youngsters had been afflicted, and the polio strain that crippled Nigerian children spread across Africa. Thanks to a massive international public-health effort and $135 million in emergency vaccination funds, an estimated 100 million children in 23 African countries received multiple doses of polio vaccine over an 18-month period, and epidemics of polio in 10 countries—Benin, Burkina Faso, Cameroon, the Central African Republic, Chad, Côte d'Ivoire, Ghana, Guinea, Mali, and Togo—were stopped.

Approximately 1,500 polio cases in 16 countries were recorded during the year—a 99% reduction since the global eradication initiative began in 1988. For the first time the number of cases was greater in countries that had been reinfected after having been polio-free than in countries in which the chain of polio transmission had never been interrupted.

In May polio reemerged in Indonesia, which was the world's fourth most populous country and which had been without polio for a decade. By the end of November, there were nearly 300 cases. In response to the outbreaks, an estimated 24 million Indonesian children were vaccinated. In Yemen, which had not seen a case of polio since 1999, a 2005 polio outbreak was thought to

have been started by pilgrims returning from Mecca. In May and July five million Yemeni children were immunized. Alarmed by the reemergence of polio in the Middle East, Iraq undertook a vaccination drive to deliver drops of polio vaccine to an estimated five million children. The UN even partnered with mobile-phone service providers to send text messages to Iraqi parents with cellular phones, urging them to take their children to clinics to be vaccinated. To curb the spread of polio during the 2005–06 hajj, or pilgrimage to Mecca, Saudi Arabia took the unprecedented step of requiring all children from countries experiencing polio to bring proof of polio vaccination.

Since 1963 most polio vaccines given around the world had included weakened forms of the three existing polioviruses (types 1, 2, and 3) in one oral dose. In May researchers in Egypt and India began testing a new polio vaccine composed solely of type 1 virus. Experts believed that mass immunization with the new vaccine in areas where types 2 and 3 had already been eliminated could rapidly finish the job of eradication. (Wild poliovirus type 2 had not been found anywhere in the world since 1999; type 3 continued to circulate in Africa, Pakistan, and Afghanistan.) On the basis of the success of the trials of type 1 vaccine, WHO contracted with a French vaccine maker to produce tens of millions of doses.

Other Infectious Diseases. HIV/AIDS and polio, of course, were not the only

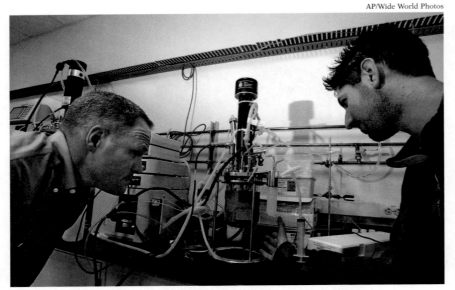

Supported by a multimillion-dollar grant from the Bill & Melinda Gates Foundation, these scientists at the Lawrence Berkeley National Laboratory in California are researching genetically engineered yeast, a precursor to the antimalaria drug artemisinin.

infectious diseases that were causing misery and death around the world. Between March and the end of August, Uíge province in Angola experienced an outbreak of highly infectious Marburg hemorrhagic fever—the largest such outbreak the world had ever seen. More than 300 persons died from the viral illness, including most of the patients in the pediatric ward of one hospital and more than a dozen health care workers who treated victims of the disease.

Marburg is a close relative of the Ebola virus, which had previously caused lethal epidemics in Angola. A WHO epidemiologist who had witnessed outbreaks of both viruses in the country, noted, "Marburg is a very bad virus, even worse than Ebola." Symptoms included high fever, diarrhea, vomiting, and bleeding from bodily orifices; most of those infected died within one week. The virus was spread via contact with the bodily fluids (such as blood, saliva, sweat, or semen) of an infected person. Corpses too were highly infectious; thus, victims had to be buried rapidly. Some families were reported to have hidden sick loved ones rather than allow them to be put in the isolation unit of a hospital, where they were likely to die and then be buried without a traditional family funeral.

The mosquitoborne viral illness Japanese encephalitis, which causes high fever, blinding headaches, coma, and sometimes death, took an especially harsh toll on young people in the state of Uttar Pradesh, India. In the month of August alone, the viral disease was responsible for more than 1,100 deaths. Those who survived were at risk of mental retardation and other neurological problems. (The virus grows mainly in pigs; mosquitoes transmit it from pigs to humans, and children are the most susceptible.) An effective Japanese encephalitis vaccine existed, but only 200,000 of Uttar Pradesh's 7,000,000 children had received it. At least 300 Japanese encephalitis deaths were also reported in neighbouring Nepal.

There had been woefully little progress in the fight against another mosquitoborne illness, malaria, which killed more than one million persons a year, the vast majority of them children in Africa. In October a major infusion of funds, three grants totaling $258.3 million from the Bill & Melinda Gates Foundation, offered hope that the suffering and deaths associated with malaria could finally be reduced. "It's a disgrace that the world has allowed malaria deaths to double in the last 20 years, when so much more could be done to stop the disease," said Bill Gates, cofounder of the foundation. One grant would support advanced human trials of a malaria vaccine that had shown promise in early trials in children in Mozambique. Another grant would support research into new antimalarial drugs, which were desperately needed in Africa because malaria

parasites had developed high levels of resistance to available drugs. At least 20 promising compounds were in the pipeline, and several were in clinical trials. The third grant would support efforts to find more effective methods of controlling mosquitoes—among them, improved insecticide-treated bed nets. "As we step up malaria research, it's also critically important to save lives today with existing tools. Bed nets cost just a few dollars each, but only a fraction of African children sleep under one," said Gates. The Gates Foundation gave another $35 million to help establish a program in Zambia to use proven malaria-control strategies—such as bed nets—to cut malaria deaths by 75% over three years.

The life of a 15-year-old Wisconsin girl was saved by a first-of-its-kind treatment after she contracted rabies from a bat bite. (Rabies is a viral illness; the virus travels from the site of a bite via nerves to the spinal cord and brain, where it multiplies and causes serious neurological damage.) The disease had always been fatal if an infected person did not immediately receive multiple doses of rabies vaccine. In this case the girl ignored her bite for a month, so by the time she developed symptoms—including nausea, blurred vision, fever, numbness, slurred speech, and tremours—it was too late for the vaccine to be effective. Rather than watch her die, her parents allowed a team of Milwaukee physicians to try an aggressive experimental treatment. To protect her brain from injury, the doctors gave her drugs that put her into a deep coma. They also gave her antiviral medications, which they hoped would stimulate her immune system to mount a response against the rabies virus. After a week the physicians tapered the drugs. Once she woke from her coma, her senses returned gradually. A month after she entered the hospital, tests showed that she no longer had transmissible rabies, so she was able to move out of isolation. Over the next couple of months, she progressed rapidly; by the time she left the hospital— 76 days after she entered it—she was able to walk with the aid of a walker, feed herself, and speak intelligibly. Five months after her treatment, she still had some neurological impairment, including a condition characterized by involuntary bodily movements, but she was able to attend high school part time and enjoy many normal teenage activities. She was the first

Confronting Childhood Obesity

The beloved blue Muppet Cookie Monster debuted his hit song, "C Is for Cookie," on the Public Broadcasting Service television program *Sesame Street* in 1972. For more than 30 years, he sang the praises of the sweet caloric treat that he devoured in quantity. In recent years, however, the creators of *Sesame Street* recognized that Cookie Monster, in his own lovable way, might have been contributing to the growing crisis of childhood obesity in the United States. In April 2005 the show introduced "Healthy Habits for Life," a segment in each episode that featured tips on exercise and healthy eating. In addition, Cookie Monster learned a new tune from a more enlightened Muppet, Hoots the Owl: "Won't you listen to what Hootsy tells you. / . . . A cookie can be scrumptious / Crunchy, sweet and yumptious / But . . . / A cookie is a sometime food. / . . . Try an orange or some cherries / Try a melon or some berries. / . . . Yes, a fruit is an anytime food!"

Cookie Monster's introduction to fruit was long overdue, given that nine million American children over age six, including teenagers, were overweight, or obese (the terms were typically used interchangeably in describing excess fatness in children). Moreover, in the previous two decades, the prevalence of obesity had more than doubled among 2- to 5-year-olds (from 5.1% to 10.4%) and 6- to 11-year-olds (from 6.1% to 15.3%). The American Academy of Pediatrics called obesity "the pediatric epidemic of the new millennium."

Overweight youngsters faced stigma and suffered emotional, psychological, and social problems. Increasingly, fat children were being diagnosed with high blood pressure, elevated cholesterol, and type 2 diabetes, all conditions that were once seen almost exclusively in adults, and one study indicated that overweight children had broken bones and problems with joints more often than other children. The long-term consequences of obesity in young people were of great concern to pediatricians and public-health experts because obese children were at high risk of becoming obese adults. In the past year, experts on longevity concluded that the current generation of American youth might "live less healthy and possibly even shorter lives than their parents" if the rising prevalence of obesity was left unchecked.

The root causes of childhood obesity were complex and not fully understood, but it was clear that most fat children got that way because they ate too much and exercised too little. Many child health experts believed that one reason kids ate too much was that "junk foods" were so prevalent and so aggressively and cleverly marketed to them (in 2004 food and beverage companies spent over $10 billion on marketing fattening products directly to American youngsters). The lack of calorie-burning exercise was highlighted by a 2005 Kaiser Family Foundation survey, which found that respondents aged 8–18 spent an average of about six hours a day watching television, videos, and DVDs, playing video games, and using computers.

Curbing the rise in childhood obesity was the aim of the Alliance for a Healthier Generation, a partnership formed in 2005 by the American Heart Association, former U.S. president Bill Clinton, and the children's television network Nickelodeon. Clinton, who had been a fat child, knew firsthand the life-threatening consequences of unhealthy lifestyle habits. "After my bypass surgery last year, I wanted to develop a program for young people so they know about the dangers of eating poorly and living an unhealthy lifestyle," said the reformed junk-food lover. The alliance intended to reach kids through a vigorous public-awareness campaign. Speaking of his media company's role in the partnership, Nickelodeon Networks president Herb Scannell said, "We want kids to become personally invested in living strong, healthy lives. And if we do our jobs right, kids will believe that being healthy is cool."

(ELLEN BERNSTEIN)

---

unvaccinated person known to have survived rabies. During the year doctors in Germany used a similar strategy in an unsuccessful attempt to cure three transplant recipients who had contracted rabies from infected donor organs.

On the research front, two independent international teams of scientists reported that they had identified the animal reservoir of the virus responsible for severe acute respiratory syndrome (SARS), which infected more than 8,000 persons and killed about 800 in 26 countries in 2002–03. (Animal reservoirs are hosts for an infectious organism that causes illness in other species; the host generally does not become ill.) At the time of the frightening SARS outbreak, attention was focused on Himalayan palm civets and raccoon dogs that were sold in live food markets in Guangdong province in China as the source of SARS. According to the new findings, however, they were only intermediaries. Chinese horseshoe bats, which were also sold at the markets, were the actual reservoir. The most likely scenario, according to the scientists, was that the bats in markets infected civets and raccoon dogs, and humans who had contact with the latter animals then became infected.

Cancer. The findings of four large clinical trials published in the October 20 issue of *The New England Journal of Medicine* were called "revolutionary," "simply stunning," and "truly life-saving results in a major disease." The studies found that the drug trastuzumab (Herceptin) dramatically reduced the chances of cancer recurrence in patients with early-stage disease when the drug was given for one year following standard chemotherapy. Trastuzumab had been used since 1998 to prolong survival in women with advanced-stage breast cancer. The drug is a mono-clonal antibody that specifically blocks the activity of human epidermal growth factor receptor 2 (HER2), which is found on the cells of up to 30% of breast cancers. HER2-positive tumours tend to be aggressive and unresponsive to most chemotherapy agents. The latest results were so impressive that a leading breast cancer specialist who was not involved in the studies declared, "Our care of patients with HER2-positive breast cancer must change today."

Cardiovascular Disease. Cardiologists in the United States reported in the February 10 issue of *The New England Journal of Medicine* on a unique cardiac syndrome that they had seen in 18 previously healthy women and one man. Each of the patients had been hospitalized with heart-attack-like symptoms after having been "stunned" in some profound way (ranging from a car crash to a surprise birthday party). The

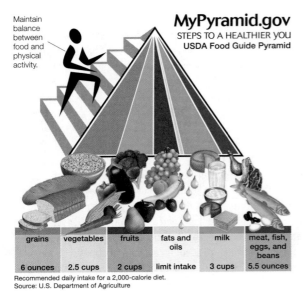

Maintain balance between food and physical activity.

MyPyramid.gov
STEPS TO A HEALTHIER YOU
USDA Food Guide Pyramid

grains	vegetables	fruits	fats and oils	milk	meat, fish, eggs, and beans
6 ounces	2.5 cups	2 cups	limit intake	3 cups	5.5 ounces

Recommended daily intake for a 2,000-calorie diet.
Source: U.S. Department of Agriculture

cases were unique in that none of the patients had blood clots, clogged arteries, or other signs of heart attack; all had distinctly abnormal electrocardiograms not indicative of heart attack; and all recovered completely with no lasting damage to the heart. After extensive tests, the authors concluded that in each case a stunning event had triggered a significant burst of the stress hormone adrenaline, which temporarily impaired the heart's contractions. They dubbed the syndrome "stress cardiomyopathy."

Numerous trials had shown that a low-dose regimen of aspirin reduced the risk of a first heart attack in men (although it did not lower their risk of stroke to any substantial degree), and many women therefore also followed such a regimen in hope of staving off heart attacks. During the year the surprising results of the Women's Health Study, which involved almost 40,000 initially healthy women, were published. Most of the women who took 100 mg of aspirin every other day had outcomes that were essentially the opposite of those in men: their risk of heart attack and of dying from heart disease was not reduced, but they did have a significantly lower likelihood of stroke. (For a subset of women in the trial—those aged 65 years and older—the risk of heart attack was reduced.)

Pharmaceuticals. In the United States the advertising of prescription drugs directly to consumers—particularly on television—came under fire in the fall of 2004 when the widely advertised arthritis medication and pain reliever Vioxx (rofecoxib) was forced off the

market because postmarketing studies had found that it doubled the risk of heart attacks and strokes. Critics of direct-to-consumer (DTC) drug advertising contended that commercials such as those for Vioxx prompted patients to ask their doctors for expensive prescription medications that they did not need, and that, with considerable regularity, doctors complied. Indeed, 93 million prescriptions were written for Vioxx from the time it was approved in 1999 to the time it was taken off the market in September 2004.

The pharmaceutical industry, which spent more than $4 billion on advertising in 2004, called DTC advertising "an invaluable communications tool" that both increased public awareness of diseases and symptoms and potentially averted underuse of effective treatments. Nonetheless, in response to widespread criticism, the Pharmaceutical Research and Manufacturers of America, which represented pharmaceutical research and biotechnology companies, drew up new guidelines on DTC advertising. The guidelines called for pharmaceutical manufacturers to put off advertising new drugs directly to consumers for "an appropriate amount of time" in order for drug companies "to educate health professionals about new medicines." The guidelines also discouraged TV commercials that promoted drugs without saying what they were for (such ads instead encouraged consumers to "ask your doctor if . . . is right for you"). Those ads were popular with drug companies because by not saying what a drug was for, they were not required to list the side effects and risks that were associated with it.

Starting Jan. 1, 2006, Medicare—the U.S. government's health care program for people aged 65 and older and for some people with disabilities—would begin offering insurance coverage for prescription drugs, known as Medicare Part D. Between Nov. 15, 2005, and May 15, 2006, beneficiaries could enroll in one of the private insurance plans that Medicare had approved. In most states more than 40 prescription-drug plans were available, which had widely varying benefits and costs. The government estimated that with the

average plan beneficiaries would pay a monthly premium of about $37, with a yearly deductible of up to $250. Plan beneficiaries would also pay a share of their yearly prescription-drug costs. For the first $2,000 in prescription-drug costs beyond the deductible, they would pay a 25% share; for the next $2,850, they would pay a 100% share; and for prescription-drug costs beyond $5,100, they would pay a 5% share. People with limited income and resources would be eligible for extra help to pay for prescription drugs.

President Bush called the plan "the greatest advance in health care for seniors" in 40 years, but many seniors found Part D in general and the enrollment process in particular to be complicated and confusing. In a letter to the editor of the *New York Times*, a senior citizen from New Jersey wrote, "I have two engineering degrees and an M.B.A. and find it almost impossible to compare the different plans offered for the new Medicare drug benefit. It is not an apples-to-apples comparison, but rather apples to every other kind of fruit." The U.S. secretary of health and human services, Michael O. Leavitt, responded to such criticism by saying, "Health care is complicated. We acknowledge that. Lots of things in life are complicated: filling out a tax return, registering your car, getting cable television. It is going to take time for seniors to become comfortable with the drug benefit."

Other developments. In 2005 the U.S. Department of Agriculture released a redesigned food-guide pyramid, which presented the government's newly revised dietary guidelines as a graphic for use by the general public. The new pyramid, known as MyPyramid, was available as an online tool that could be personalized.

Surgeons in France performed the first partial face transplant. The surgeons grafted the nose, lips, and chin from a deceased donor onto the face of a woman who had been severely disfigured in an attack by a dog.

An advance in human-cloning research reported in May 2005 by a team led by Hwang Woo Suk, a South Korean scientist, raised expectations that stem cells derived from embryos cloned from the skin cells of individuals with a disease or injury could be readily obtained for therapeutic use. By the end of the year, however, the report had been discredited, and the results of his other stem-cell work had fallen under scrutiny.　　(ELLEN BERNSTEIN)

Law, Crime, and
Law Enforcement

Trials of former **HEADS OF STATE**, U.S. Supreme Court rulings on **EMINENT DOMAIN** and the **DEATH PENALTY**, and **HIGH-PROFILE** cases against former **EXECUTIVES** of large corporations were leading legal and criminal issues in 2005.

INTERNATIONAL LAW

On Oct. 19, 2005, the trial of former Iraqi dictator Saddam Hussein began. The Iraqi Special Tribunal had been established by the United States in 2003, when Iraq was first under U.S. military occupation. The initial case against Saddam and several of his top officials centred on the 1982 execution of more than 140 men and teenage boys in Dujail, a mostly Shi'ite town 56 km (35 mi) north of Baghdad. An estimated 300,000 Iraqis, mostly Shi'ites and Kurds, were killed by Saddam's regime. Human rights groups expressed concern about the tribunal and what many perceived to be the impossibility that Saddam would receive a fair trial, and Saddam's chief strategy was to challenge the legitimacy of the tribunal. The trial resumed on November 28 for a few hours, was recessed, and resumed December 5 to 7 and December 21 to 22, when it was again recessed until Jan. 24 2006.

The International Court of Justice. The International Court of Justice (ICJ) dismissed Liechtenstein's case against Germany regarding confiscation of the principality's property following World War II. The court held that it had no jurisdiction because the states had not given the ICJ jurisdiction over their disputes in 1945. It also dismissed a case brought by Serbia and Montenegro against NATO stemming from the NATO air campaign that brought an end to the Serbian conflict with Kosovo. The court found that Serbia and Montenegro did not have standing to sue because former Yugoslavia was not an official member of the United Nations or the ICJ when it initiated the case in 1999.

Ruling on a dispute between Niger and Benin, the court determined that the island of Lété Goungou in the Niger River belonged to the former. In September Costa Rica brought suit against Nicaragua for navigational rights of the San Juan River. In a nod to the advisory opinion handed down by the ICJ in 2004, the Israeli Supreme Court said that the security wall that Israel was building in the West Bank must not run through five Arab villages that were threatened to be divided by the structure; earlier the ICJ had stated that the wall stood in violation of international law.

International Tribunals and Special Courts. At the International Criminal Tribunal for the Former Yugoslavia (ICTY) at the end of 2004, the lawyers representing former Serbian leader Slobodan Milosevic, upon his initiative, had asked to be removed from the case; the judges denied the request, and Milosevic continued to serve as his own primary counsel. In March the ICTY indicted Ramush Haradinaj, the prime minister of Kosovo, who resigned in order to face trial. The Bosnian war crimes court still had 1,000 cases pending. While prosecutions of major war criminals continued at the International Criminal Tribunal for Rwanda (ICTR), a network of 12,000 traditional community courts called *gacaca* was established in Rwanda to alleviate the burden on the ICTR. These local courts were charged with reviewing charges against about 63,000 people implicated in the 1994 genocide.

In May the United Nations closed its special prosecution unit investigating crimes committed during East Timor's 1999 struggle for independence from Indonesia. More than 600 cases were left pending, including an indictment of General Wiranto, the former head of the Indonesian armed forces.

Several countries besides Iraq had established special domestic courts to try persons charged with human rights abuses. Problems beset these courts, however. In Sierra Leone there was a shortage of funding for its tribunal, and in Cambodia similar money problems, coupled with concerns over fairness, hampered progress in trying leaders from the Khmer Rouge era. The UN Security Council called upon Burundi to establish a special court to prosecute war crimes associated with the decades of civil war in that country.

The International Criminal Court. During 2005 the International Criminal Court (ICC) investigated war crimes in The Sudan, the Democratic Republic of the Congo (DRC), and Uganda. The ICC began pretrial hearings into abuses in the DRC. In February the UN issued a report that described war crimes—but not genocide—in the Darfur region of The Sudan. In March the UN Security Council adopted Resolution 1593, which referred the ongoing conflict in Darfur to the ICC. The Sudan was not a signatory to the ICC, but under the Rome Statute charter for the ICC, the court's jurisdiction extended to investigation and prosecution of those responsible for severe human rights crimes when domestic governments were unwilling or unable to do so. The U.S. abstained on the 11–0 Security Council vote on the resolution. The Security Council submitted a list of 51 Sudanese suspects to the ICC for investigation. Following this international pressure, in June The Sudan established its own special court to try those accused of war crimes in Darfur. Human rights groups expressed concern about the impartiality of such courts and the desire and ability of The Sudan to bring the perpetrators of the human rights abuses to justice.

In October the ICC unsealed its indictments of war criminals in Uganda. Rebel leader Joseph Kony and his Lord's Resistance Army (LRA) were accused of gross human rights violations during the 19-year war against the Ugandan government. Kony and his four top deputies, who were believed to be hiding in southern Sudan, were indicted. The Sudan gave the Ugandan army permission to enter the region to search for the LRA leaders.

Universal Jurisdiction. Universal jurisdiction is the policy of allowing courts in one country to judge human rights crimes committed in another, regardless of the nationality of the accused. In April Adolfo Scilingo, a former Argentine naval officer, was convicted in Spain of crimes against humanity for his role in the so-called Dirty War in Argentina in the 1970s. It was the first conviction under a Spanish law that allowed courts to prosecute crimes committed in other countries if they constituted violations of international law. A ruling in September by the Spanish Constitutional Court stated that universal jurisdiction over genocide and crimes against humanity was allowed in Spain and thereby overturned a Spanish Supreme Court decision that Spain's judiciary could deal only with crimes committed against Spanish citizens. The case was sparked by 1992 Nobel Peace Prize winner Rigoberta Menchú's request that Spain prosecute members of the Guatemalan government who were allegedly responsible for genocide and crimes against humanity during their 1978–86 rule.

In July a British jury sentenced a former Afghan commander living in Great Britain to 20 years in a British prison for torture and hostage taking in Afghanistan during the Taliban rule. Two other Afghans, Heshamuddin Hesam and Habibulla Jalalzoy, faced Dutch war-crimes charges for their actions in Afghanistan during the 1980s. These cases were made possible by Dutch law making domestic law parallel international law, in this case the Geneva Conventions and the Convention Against Torture. The defendants had applied for political asylum in The Netherlands, were denied, but stayed anyway. The two men were high-ranking officials in the KhAD secret police. Both were convicted; Hesam was ordered to serve 12 years in prison and Jalalzoy to serve 9.

In September a Belgian court issued an indictment and arrest warrant for former (1982–90) Chadian dictator Hissène Habré for crimes against humanity for his treatment of thousands of citizens. In 2003 under international pressure, especially from the United States, Belgium repealed its universal jurisdiction law. The Habré case, however, was allowed to continue because the investigation had already begun and three of the plaintiffs were Belgian citizens. Habré was arrested in Senegal on November 15 but later released. Senegal's Court of Appeals stated that it was not competent to rule on the

matter and decided to turn the case over to the African Union summit in January 2006.

Treaties. Two international treaties took effect in 2005. The Kyoto Protocol on global warming, having been ratified by 140 countries following its negotiation in Japan in 1997, entered into force in February. The United Nations Convention Against Corruption became law in December, 90 days after ratification by the 30th signatory state. It had been signed by more than 100 countries and provided for international cooperation in the return of assets illicitly acquired by corrupt leaders as well as the institution of preventive measures to detect the plundering of national wealth as it occurred.

In February in compliance with an ICJ ruling in a case known as *Avena,* in which the court determined that the U.S. was in violation of its obligations under the Vienna Convention to notify consular officials of the arrest of a foreign national, the administration of Pres. George W. Bush agreed to grant 51 Mexicans on death row in Texas new state court hearings. In March, however, President Bush withdrew the U.S. from the Vienna Convention's Optional Protocol Concerning the Compulsory Settlement of Disputes and thus rejected ICJ jurisdiction over future domestic death-penalty cases.

(VICTORIA C. WILLIAMS)

COURT DECISIONS

The 2004–05 term of the U.S. Supreme Court was the last term with Chief Justice William H. Rehnquist, who died Sept. 3, 2005. (*See* OBITUARIES.) Rehnquist's death marked the end of a dozen years of institutional stability in which there had been no changes in the membership of the court. On September 29 the U.S. Senate confirmed John G. Roberts, a conservative judge on the District of Columbia Circuit Court of Appeals, to succeed Rehnquist as chief justice of the United States. (*See* BIOGRAPHIES.)

In the 2004–05 term the voting behaviour of the court as an institution remained centre-right, but the voting blocs had become considerably less stable than at any point in recent history. Justices Antonin Scalia and Clarence Thomas, who often voted together, took opposing sides in 12 cases, and Justices Ruth Bader Ginsburg and Stephen Breyer—who were the only two Democratic-appointed justices—took opposite sides 11 times.

By far the court's most controversial decision of the year was the ruling that concerned eminent domain in the case of *Kelo* v. *City of New London.* Although there was little debate over the authority of government to exercise eminent domain, questions had arisen regarding the constitutional provision of "public use." Historically, governments claimed private property for public use in the furtherance of such things as bridge construction, highway development, and services in the public interest. Commerce, which was a corollary to economic vitality, had always been a concern in eminent domain cases, but in *Kelo,* New London, Conn., argued that the public-use provision could be satisfied via *private* economic development. Specifically, New London condemned private property as part of a municipal development plan and transferred it to the New London Development Corp., a private development company. Writing for the court in a 5–4 ruling, Justice John Paul Stevens upheld the city's action by arguing that "public purpose" was the functional equivalent of "public use" and that private economic development fostered by the government fell within the court's "traditionally broad understanding of public purpose."

In 2005 the U.S. Supreme Court refused to intervene in court rulings that concerned Terri Schiavo, a Florida resident who suffered severe brain damage in 1990 and was being sustained by means of a feeding tube. Asserting that it would have been her wish not to continue artificial life-prolonging procedures, her husband filed a petition in 1998 to authorize the removal of the feeding tube, but her parents insisted that her wish would be to live. After extensive court proceedings and appeals, the tube was removed March 18 by a county court order, and she died March 31. The case brought widespread attention to the issue of health care surrogates in cases such as Shiavo's in which a person became incapacitated and had not established an advance directive (living will) or a health care guardian. (*See* MAP.)

In the field of criminal law, the death penalty—once a dormant area of constitutional law—occupied centre stage and was addressed in three separate cases: *Miller-El* v. *Dretke, Rompilla* v. *Beard,* and *Roper* v. *Simmons.* In the first case the central question focused on the civil rights of a criminal defendant who had been convicted of murder almost 20 years earlier. The prosecutors in the original case had used peremptory (discretionary) challenges to exclude 10 of 11 African Americans summoned for jury duty. In overturning the conviction, the court reasoned that the jury-selection process had been rooted in racial discrimination and therefore compromised Miller-El's right to a fair trial. In *Rompilla* v. *Beard* the court again upheld the rights of the criminally accused and overturned the death sentence of Ronald Rompilla on the grounds of inadequate counsel. In the third and most compelling case, *Roper* v. *Simmons*, the court ruled 5–4 that the Constitution prohibited the death sentence for defendants under the age of 18. In raising the protective age for capital punishment from 16 to 18, the court overruled a precedent set only 16 years earlier.

The court also addressed two cases of consequence for the civil liberties and civil rights of prisoners. In a 5–3 decision the court ruled in *Johnson* v. *California* that the state's policy of temporarily segregating new and transferred inmates by race was inherently suspect and that the deference that was commonly owed to prison administrators should not be afforded in light

of apparently discriminatory policies and practices. In the case of *Cutter* v. *Wilkinson*, the court upheld the Religious Land Use and Institutionalized Persons Act, which required prison officials to satisfy the religious needs of inmates. Despite the arguments made on behalf of Reginald Wilkinson, the director of the Ohio Department of Rehabilitation and Correction, the court ruled unanimously that the law did not violate the establishment clause of the U.S. Constitution's First Amendment.

Two other cases dealt squarely with the establishment clause. In *McCreary County* v. *American Civil Liberties Union* and in *Van Orden* v. *Perry*, the court was asked to address, separately, questions that involved the display of the Ten Commandments on public property. At first glance a reasonable assumption would have been that the court would rule identically in the two cases, given their similarity. In the *McCreary County* case, the court ruled that framed displays of the Ten Commandments in two Kentucky courthouses constituted an endorsement of religion and therefore violated the establishment clause. In *Van Orden* v. *Perry*, however, the court ruled that a 1.8-m (6-ft) granite monolith that displayed the Ten Command-

ments on the grounds of the Texas State Capitol did not violate the clause. A pivotal matter in the rulings may have been the centrality of the Ten Commandments to the government buildings—framed in the courthouses in the first case and displayed among 17 monuments and 21 historical markers over a 9-ha (about 20-ac) site in the other.

In three cases that dealt with discrimination, the court extended constitutional protection to individuals in matters that concerned sex, age, and disabilities. Title IX was a well-known law that prohibited sex discrimination in schools. In 2005 the law was broadened in *Jackson* v. *Birmingham Board of Education* to include whistle-blower protection. Under the law, third parties who filed complaints of discrimination as well as those who were directly subjected to sex discrimination were now protected from retaliatory action by school officials. In *Smith* v. *City of Jackson*, the court broadened the scope of the Age Discrimination in Employment Act by ruling 5–3 that proof of intentional discrimination was not necessary to sustain a suit based upon age discrimination. By appropriating the theory of "disparate impact" to age and

Health Care: Who Decides When the Patient Cannot

First priority surrogate
(in absence of an advance directive or an appointed agent or guardian with health powers)

- Spouse
- Individual designated by patient
- Physician and next of kin
- Consensus of "interested persons"
- Equal status for spouse and parent
- No priority specified

Source: American Bar Association Commission on Law and Aging

NOTE: Limits on what a surrogate can decide vary from state to state.

© 2006 Encyclopædia Britannica, Inc.

employment, employees did not have to prove discriminatory motivation or intent, only effect. With regard to individuals with disabilities, the court ruled 6–3 that the Americans with Disabilities Act applied to cruise ships that sailed under foreign flags and stopped at American ports. Absent a controlling doctrine of international law, the court in *Spector* v. *Norwegian Cruise Line Ltd.* decided that although the American government cannot compel foreign charters to make structural changes to vessels, passengers of cruise ships that stop at American ports were otherwise protected by the act.

In a marginally related case that involved medical treatment for the ill, the court in *Gonzales* v. *Raich* upheld the authority of Congress to ban the use of medicinal marijuana and to prosecute those who violated the law. The law had a controlling effect even in the 11 states that had legalized the substance for medicinal purposes. Part of the irony of the case was that Stevens, the most liberal member of the bench, wrote the decision. Stevens's action was less concerned with marijuana than it was with the conflict between state laws and federal laws. As the court had moved to the ideological right and championed states' rights along the way, Stevens had sought to curtail what he perceived to be a subversion of federal authority by the states. As the final term of the Rehnquist era drew to a close, the legacy of states' rights had become less secure. The ultraconservative court that some had predicted and desired under Rehnquist never grew to fruition; instead, the centre-right position, dominated by Justice Sandra Day O'Connor and joined by Republican appointees Justice David Souter and Justice Kennedy, held sway.

(BRIAN SMENTKOWSKI)

CRIME

Terrorism. Despite a bounty of $25 million on his head, Osama bin Laden continued to elude captors in 2005 as his radical Muslim al-Qaeda supporters and affiliated terror groups perpetrated new and lethal attacks. On July 7, during the morning rush hour in London, bomb explosions ripped through three subway trains and a double-decker bus in a coordinated assault that left 52 persons dead and 700 injured. Responsibility for the action was claimed by a group called the Group of al-Qaeda of Jihad Organization in Europe, which said that the as-

sault was mounted to avenge British involvement in the wars in Afghanistan and Iraq.

London police revealed that the blasts were the work of four suicide bombers who had detonated explosives carried in backpacks. On July 21 four more would-be suicide bombers attempted a similar but unsuccessful attack on London's transport network. Within days, five members of a suspected gang of bombers believed responsible for the failed attack were arrested. The bombers, like their July 7 predecessors, were mainly young Muslim men who were British residents or from families of recent immigrants to the U.K. Because two of the July 7 bombers had visited Pakistan during 2004, investigations intensified into possible links between the bombers and extremist groups in that country.

On July 23 three suicide bombers drove vehicles into the popular Egyptian tourist resort town of Sharm al-Shaykh, killing at least 64 people and wounding more than 200. Two groups claimed immediate responsibility for the atrocity—the Abdullah Azzam Brigades of al-Qaeda in Syria and Egypt and the previously unknown Holy Warriors of Egypt. On October 1 three suicide bombers killed 23 people and injured more than 100 in explosions at two Indonesian beachside restaurants in the village of Jimbaran and at a café in the town of Kuta, both on Bali. The attack was thought to have been committed by the al-Qaeda-linked Indonesian Muslim extremist group Jemaah Islamiyah.

Imad Eddin Barakat Yarkas, the leader of an al-Qaeda cell in Spain, was sentenced on September 26 in Madrid to 27 years in prison for conspiracy to commit terrorist murders in the Sept. 11, 2001, attacks on New York City and Washington, D.C. The Syrian-born Yarkas, known as Abu Dahdah, was said to have conspired with suicide pilot Mohamed Atta and other members of the al-Qaeda cell based in Hamburg that carried out the 9/11 attacks. Zacarias Moussaoui, a Frenchman, was the only other person in jail for 9/11-related crimes.

In April the newly established National Counterterrorism Center (NCTC), assuming a statistical reporting responsibility previously undertaken by the U.S. Department of State, announced that 651 "significant" terrorist attacks took 1,907 lives during 2004. In July the NCTC issued revised figures, which increased its 2004 estimates to 3,192

terrorist attacks, with 28,433 people killed, wounded, or kidnapped.

Drugs and Human Trafficking. According to the 2005 World Drug Report, published in June by the UN Office on Drugs and Crime (UNODC), 200 million people, or 5% of the world's population aged 15–64, had consumed illegal drugs at least once during the previous 12 months. Of these drug consumers, close to 160 million had used cannabis, 26 million amphetamines, 14 million cocaine, 16 million opiates (11 million of whom had used heroin), and 8 million ecstasy. For the first time, on the basis of data for 2003, UNODC presented an estimate of the volume of the illicit drug market, which was calculated at $13 billion at the production level, $94 billion at the wholesale level (taking into account seizures), and $322 billion at the retail level (also taking seizures and other losses into account).

In its annual report released in March, the International Narcotics Control Board (INCB) expressed concern about the continuing opium production in Afghanistan, with the illicit drug crop and related activities reaching an unprecedented level in 2004. The Pentagon subsequently announced plans to quadruple spending on its antinarcotics campaign in Afghanistan, which in 2004 was reportedly responsible for almost 90% of the world's supply of heroin and opium.

Murder and Other Violence. Preliminary figures released in June from the FBI's Uniform Crime Reporting Program indicated that compared with 2003, the overall number of violent crimes reported in 2004 to law-enforcement agencies in the U.S. decreased 1.7%; murder declined by 3.6%, and property crimes fell by 1.8%.

Over the past decade in England and Wales, overall crime decreased 44%, with a fall of 7% reported in 2004. There was an increase in reports of incidents of violence against individuals, a small rise in the number of murders, and a continuing increase in crimes involving guns.

In South Africa, one of the world's most crime-ridden countries, police reported that 18,793 murders had been recorded in the financial year ended March 2005, a 5.2% decrease from the previous year. Police officials attributed the reduction to a government amnesty that persuaded citizens to surrender more than 90,000 unlicensed firearms.

A bloody feud in which more than 130 people were murdered in the city of Naples in 2004 continued unabated between rival families of the notorious Neapolitan mafia. The feud, fueled by the desire to gain control of the multi-million-dollar local drug trade, also led to the death of innocent bystanders, including that of a 14-year-old girl who was killed while being used as a human shield by a fleeing gangster.

In Pakistan a woman who had accused 14 men of orchestrating her gang rape in 2002 received legal support from the nation's Supreme Court, which in June overturned the acquittals of some of the men and ordered that all of them be rearrested.

On March 21 teenager Jeff Weise shot dead nine people, seven of them in a rampage through a high school, before taking his own life on a Native American reservation in Minnesota. The attack was the deadliest school shooting in the U.S. since the Columbine killings in 1999.

Following a sensational trial and a week of deliberation, a California jury on June 14 acquitted American pop star Michael Jackson on all charges surrounding the alleged molestation of a teenage boy at his Neverland Ranch.

White-Collar Crime, Corruption, and Fraud. Bernard Ebbers, the former WorldCom CEO who was alleged to have orchestrated the $11 billion accounting debacle that forced the company into bankruptcy in 2002, was found guilty in March on all nine counts, involving conspiracy, securities fraud, and filing false reports with regulators. Ebbers was sentenced in July to 25 years in prison. In June John Rigas, the founder and former head of Adelphia Communications, received a 15-year prison sentence, and his son, the former CFO, was sentenced to 20 years. Earlier in the year Andrew Fastow, the former CFO of Enron, was sentenced to 10 years in prison under a plea deal in which he agreed to cooperate with prosecutors in their pursuit of those responsible for that corporate ruination.

Nearly two years after the collapse of the Italian dairy giant Parmalat, its founder, Calisto Tanzi, and 15 other company executives went on trial in September in Milan on charges of false auditing, market rigging, and obstructing regulators.

In May a Moscow court sentenced Mikhail Khodorkovsky, former chief of the Russian oil giant Yukos, to nine years in jail for tax evasion and fraud. Though authorities described Khodorkovsky as a robber baron who bought Yukos at a bargain during the privatization of state assets in the 1990s,

many Western observers characterized his conviction as a case of political persecution. Khodorkovsky had provided funding for politicians opposing Russian Pres. Vladimir Putin.

Law Enforcement. In a report censored in part for security reasons and published in September, the U.S. Department of Justice's (DOJ's) Office of the Inspector General (OIG) revealed that the FBI's efforts since the 9/11 terrorist attacks to transform itself into a more proactive, intelligence-driven counterterrorism law-enforcement agency had been largely achieved but at a considerable cost. The OIG analyses of FBI agent utilization data showed that the agency had reduced its efforts to combat transnational crime, such as narcotics trafficking, organized crime, and white-collar crime, even more than planned. The OIG review said that other law-enforcement bodies claimed that the reduction in the FBI's investigative capacity had hurt its ability to address crime and left an investigative gap, particularly in dealing with financial institutional fraud and bank robberies.

In Britain a top-level review was initiated by the Independent Police Complaints Commission (IPCC) of a controversial shoot-to-kill policy after its first use resulted in the death of an innocent man. On July 22 a Brazilian man residing and working in London was mistaken for a suicide bomber and shot by police seven times in the head at close range after he boarded a train.

Doubts were expressed about the safety of the nonlethal Taser stun gun, which fires two darts that deliver a debilitating 50,000-v electrical charge to the intended target. The Taser was used in 43 countries, including the U.S., where almost 8,000 police forces and 150,000 officers were armed with the device. Amnesty International alleged that 130 people had died after being hit by a Taser, but U.S. proponents of the Taser claimed that it had resulted in a marked reduction in fatal police shootings.

On February 28 in the Iraqi town of Hilla, insurgents mounted one of the bloodiest single attacks since the fall of Saddam Hussein when a suicide bomber drove a car into a line of men waiting to take medical tests in order to join the Iraqi army and police. At least 122 people were killed and 130 wounded in the assault. Despite repeated attacks on Iraqi police and security-force recruits, the promise of a regular $200 monthly salary and the lack of alternative jobs kept Iraqi police-recruiting centres filled. Some U.S.

officials were concerned about the quality of the vetting process for new police recruits, many of whom were said to be marginally literate, while others had criminal records, were physically handicapped, or were members of insurgent groups.

(DUNCAN CHAPPELL)

DEATH PENALTY

Countries that had abolished the death penalty for all crimes numbered 84 at the start of 2005, following the addition of Greece and Senegal to the list at the end of 2004. The gradual movement toward universal abolition continued. The death penalty was abolished for all crimes in Mexico. Uzbekistan's Pres. Islam Karimov signed a decree abolishing the death penalty from Jan. 1, 2008. Indian leaders proposed amending the penal code by replacing the death penalty with life imprisonment without parole. Kenyan Justice Minister Kiraitu Murungi stated that his country was committed to abolishing the death penalty and that death row inmates in Kenya would have their sentences commuted to life imprisonment. In Uganda 417 prisoners on death row sought a declaration that the punishment violates a constitutional prohibition of cruel, inhuman, and degrading treatment. Steps were taken to begin the gradual abolition of the death penalty in Taiwan; the country's criminal code was amended to prohibit the execution of those aged under 18 or over 80. The U.S. also stopped the use of the death penalty against individuals aged under 18 at the time they committed their offenses; the Supreme Court concluded by a slim majority that such executions were unconstitutionally cruel. By contrast, in Nigeria the Committee on Judicial and Legal Reform recommended the use of the death penalty against juveniles who had committed "heinous offenses." Four men who had confessed to murders were executed by Palestinian security forces, reversing a stay imposed by the late leader Yasir Arafat in 2001. Despite a 29-year moratorium on executions in Sri Lanka, the country's Justice Ministry and attorney general recommended that the death sentences imposed on the men who in 1998 had gang-raped and murdered Rita John, a newlywed Indian woman, be carried out. In the U.S. confessed serial killer Michael B. Ross was put to death in Connecticut's first execution in 45 years.

(STUART MACDONALD)

Piracy
on the High Seas

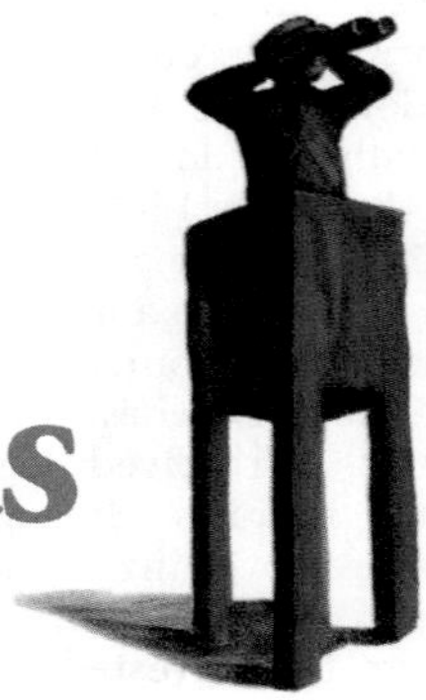

by John S. Burnett

To the astonishment of many, high-seas piracy, a crime thought long relegated to legend, made headlines in late 2005 when a luxury cruise ship was attacked off the Somali coast. The *Seabourn Spirit*, carrying 151 Western tourists, managed to evade capture but not without one of its security officers wounded and the ship itself damaged by rocket-propelled grenades. It was a miracle that the ship escaped; since March, 28 vessels had been attacked in the same waters, many of which were hijacked.

In 2005 modern-day piracy was as violent, as costly, and as tragic as it ever had been in the days of yore. Pirates no longer fit the Hollywood image of plundering buccaneers—with eye patches, parrots on their shoulders, cutlasses in their teeth, and wooden legs—but were often ruthless gangs of agile seagoing robbers who attacked ships with assault rifles and antitank missiles. According to the International Maritime Bureau, the organization that investigates maritime fraud and piracy, there were 325 reported attacks on shipping by pirates worldwide in 2004. These latest statistics, the IMB said, reflected only reported incidents directed at commercial shipping and represented a fraction of the actual number. Most acts of piracy went unreported because shipowners did not want to tie up a vessel, costing tens of thousands of dollars a day to operate, for lengthy investigations. The human cost was also high—399 crew members and passengers were killed, were injured, were held hostage, or remained missing at the end of 2004. These sobering statistics did not include, however, those innocent passengers, tourists, commercial fishermen, or yachtsmen whose mysterious disappearances were unofficially attributed to acts of piracy or maritime terrorism.

Piracy, a crime that is as old as mankind, has occurred since the earliest hunter-gatherer floated down some wilderness river on a log raft and was robbed of his prized piece of meat. Homer first recorded in *The Odyssey* an act of piracy around 1000 BC. In many parts of the world, the culture of piracy

Eric Pasquier—TCS/ZUMA Press

A band of pirates in the Philippines prepares for a raid in the South China Sea in January. Heavy armaments, speedy boats, and small regard for human life made 21st-century pirates a serious menace to maritime traffic.

dates back generations; ransacking passing ships was considered part of local tradition and an acceptable though illegal way of earning a living.

Nowadays, pirates have found it relatively easy to attack a ship and make a clean getaway. Sea robbers on small, fast boats sneak up on the rear of a ship within the blind spot of its radar, toss grappling hooks onto the rail, scamper up the transom, overpower the crew, and loot the ship's safe. In less than 20 minutes, raiders are back in their boats, often $20,000 to $40,000 richer. Only a few pirates are ever caught, and they have discovered that plundering a ship is far less risky than robbing a bank. Recent events and innovations have also conspired to make modern piracy much easier to commit. Following the end of the Cold War, superpower navies ceased to patrol vital waterways, and local nations were left to deal with problems that heretofore had been international in nature. Pirates no longer had to rely on cotton sails, oars, sextants, and dead reckoning to mount an attack. Modern-day pirates use mobile phones, portable satellite navigation systems, handheld VHF ship-to-ship/shore radios, and mass-produced fibreglass and inflatable dinghies that can accommodate larger and faster inexpensive Japanese outboard motors. Indeed, the pirates who attacked the *Seabourn Spirit* had taken a page from Blackbeard and had launched their attack from a mothership stationed far offshore.

Several types of piracy exist. The most common one is the random attack on a passing ship—a mugging at sea. Merchant vessels are slow-moving lumbering beasts of trade that parade in a line down narrow shipping lanes. They present easy targets. The booty for these pirates is crew members' possessions—watches and MP3 players—as well as the cash aboard the ship. A second type of attack is one that is planned in advance against vessels that are known to be carrying tens of thousands of dollars in crew payoff and agent fees. With the complicity and connivance of local officials, transnational crime syndicates employ pirates to pillage these vulnerable ships. Though little known outside

The luxury cruise ship Seabourn Spirit *lies peaceably at anchor off the Seychelles in November after having been attacked by pirates in the Indian Ocean two days earlier. Two boats full of pirates fired assault rifles and rocket-propelled grenades, but the ship sped away before the marauders could board.*

the maritime industry, crime syndicates also organize the hijackings of entire ships and cargo. With military precision, a ship carrying cargo that is easily sold on the black market is taken over, and it simply disappears off the face of the Earth; the bodies of the crew are often found washed up on a deserted shore some days later. The stolen vessel becomes a phantom ship, with a new name, new paint job, new home port, and bogus registration under a different national flag. The vessel is used to transport drugs, arms, or illegal immigrants or is utilized in cargo scams.

During the past 24 months, piracy has taken a new turn. Pirates discovered that kidnapping the master and another officer is more lucrative than merely stealing the captain's Rolex watch. In 2004 a record 86 seafarers were kidnapped, and in nearly every case the ransom was paid.

There is a long-standing link between piracy and terrorism, and the possibility of post-9/11 terrorism at sea is a growing concern. Maritime terrorism is not new, however. In 1985 the Palestine Liberation Organization attacked the Italian cruise ship *Achille Lauro,* and one of the passengers was shot and thrown overboard; in 2001 Basque separatists attempted to bomb the *Val de Loire* on a passage between Spain and the U.K.; and in February 2004 Abu Sayyaf, a terrorist group associated with al-Qaeda, admitted having planted the explosives that sank SuperFerry 14 in Manila Bay. Of the 900 persons aboard that ferry, 116 lost their lives.

Merchant ships have no real defenses against an attack. Fire hoses blast outboard, the decks are well lighted, and an extra crew member with a handheld radio patrols the decks, but these precautions are not adequate. They merely indicate to pirates lying in wait that a ship is aware that it has entered pirate territory and that another ship in the vicinity without these obvious defenses might present a softer target. The *Seabourn Spirit* had been a little better equipped than most. She repelled the pirates by use of firehoses as well as a nonlethal acoustic weapon that aimed an earsplitting noise at the attackers; one of the passengers said the pirates fled because they thought the ship was returning fire. Even the most modern and sophisticated vessel is vulnerable to attack. Suicide bombers in October 2000 nearly sank the U.S. destroyer *Cole,* a state-of-the-art warship, and in 2002 suicide terrorists attacked the modern supertanker *M/V Limburg,* laden with Persian Gulf crude oil in the Gulf of Aden.

Maritime officials are concerned that terrorists will target the world's strategic maritime passages, blocking the movement of global trade. Most recently, attention has focused on the Malacca Strait, the gateway to Asia, conduit of a third of world commerce, and a prime hunting ground for pirates.

About 80% of the oil bound for Japan and South Korea is shipped from the Persian Gulf through the strait. In addition, some 50,000 ships transit this narrow channel annually. U.S. officials have expressed fears that one day terrorists trained to be pirates—as terrorists trained to be pilots for attacks on 9/11—will take over a high-profile ship and turn it into a floating bomb and close the strait. Disrupting the flow of half the world's supply of oil that is transported through the passage would have a catastrophic effect on the world economy.

Though the U.S. government offered Malaysia and Indonesia (nations through which the strait passes) military patrol boats and personnel to guard the waterway, the offer was quickly rejected by both littoral states on the grounds that the patrolling of their waters by American forces was a violation of territorial sovereignty. Those nations were also mindful that an American military presence in the strait would stir an already restive Muslim population within their countries. By 2005 Malaysia and Indonesia together with the city-state of Singapore, located at the mouth of the strait, had established joint patrols, increased intelligence sharing, and formed a joint radar surveillance project. Issues regarding the employment of hot pursuit—one of the most indispensable tools for combating piracy, involving the right to chase pirates back to their lairs in another country's territory—have not been resolved, however, and this has rendered much of the effort to halt piracy in the region less effective.

Following the devastating tsunami that struck the west coast of Indonesia on Dec. 26, 2004, piracy in this region suddenly disappeared. It is unclear whether the attacks stopped because of the large international military presence that aided relief efforts off the coast of Sumatra or because the villages from which the pirates launched their raids had been wiped out. During the first few weeks of 2005, however, pirates began attacking ships anew, and because pirates were using the tactics and weapons of Islamist militants, insurers acknowledged finally that there was a threat to global trade and for the first time gave the sea lane a war-risk rating.

John S. Burnett was attacked by pirates in the South China Sea. He is a maritime security consultant and author of Dangerous Waters, Modern Piracy and Terror on the High Seas *(2002).*

Libraries and Museums

During 2005 libraries coped with REQUIREMENTS of the USA PATRIOT Act, and museums instituted SECURITY measures to prevent theft and thwart TERRORISM; HURRICANE KATRINA walloped libraries and museums on the U.S. Gulf Coast; and GOOGLE's plan to digitize the books of five major libraries had worldwide implications.

LIBRARIES

The year 2005 again offered proof that libraries were not immune to matters that shaped society. Google, the ubiquitous Internet search service, in late 2004 had announced plans to digitize books from the collections of five great research libraries in the U.S. and Britain. *The Christian Science Monitor* compared the project to Gutenberg's invention of the printing press in its importance to the dissemination of knowledge. A test service, Google Print, was launched as digitalization efforts progressed, but in August 2005 Google suspended the operation owing to copyright disputes with publishers and publishing associations. In September a number of authors filed suit on the basis of copyright issues.

Google's bold venture, however, sparked international ramifications. Hungarian Prime Minister Ferenc Gyurcsany wrote to his counterparts in France, Germany, Italy, Spain, and Poland to propose that all these countries begin digitizing the contents of their libraries. Without this effort, he wrote, "this heritage will perhaps not occupy its deserved place in the scholarship of the future." The director of the French Bibliothèque Nationale publicly worried about "the risk of America reinforcing its crushing domination of future generations' understanding of the world." Worldwide, digitalization of library materials was drawing attention. The U.S. National Archives and Records Administration (NARA) awarded a six-year, $308 million contract to Lockheed Martin to build NARA's Electronic Records Archives. An op-ed article in the *Toronto Star* urged the Canadian government to commence work on digitizing much of

the content of the national library, and libraries everywhere, notably the British Library (BL), were digitizing their unique materials and mounting them on the Web.

At the Anna Amalia Library in Weimar, Ger., a previously unknown aria composed by Johann Sebastian Bach was discovered. A 27-year campaign by the Italian city of Benevento resulted in an order for the BL to surrender a 12th-century illuminated missal believed to have been looted during World War II. The BL was also facing the loss of the world's oldest Bible, the *Codex Sinaiticus*, to a

monastery in Egypt. The *Codex*, which had been housed in the monastery since the 6th century, was removed in the 19th century and purchased by the BL in 1933 from the Imperial Library in Leningrad (now St. Petersburg).

A provision of the USA PATRIOT Act that allowed federal police agencies to demand circulation records and placed a gag order on library workers was hotly debated in both the U.S. House of Representatives and the Senate as Congress considered renewal of the law. Despite stiff resistance from a coalition of liberals, libertarians, and librarians, the renewals passed, and a conference committee was to attempt to resolve differences in the respective versions. Before that could happen, however, a federal judge lifted a gag order on a Connecticut library that sued the government over the constitutionality of the gag order permitted by the PATRIOT Act. Government lawyers promptly and successfully appealed the ruling, and the gag order was reinstated.

The International Federation of Library Associations and Institutions convened in Oslo as an expanded and renovated National Library of Norway

An exhibit in the Abraham Lincoln Presidential Library in Springfield, Ill., depicts a slave auction such as the young Lincoln might have seen in New Orleans in the 1820s. The library was dedicated on April 19.

was inaugurated in August. In Bahrain the Shaikh Isa National Library opened, and in Iran the inauguration of a new National Library occasioned a diplomatic incident following the detainment at the airport and subsequent deportation of the editor of *American Libraries* magazine, the membership magazine of the American Library Association. In the U.S. the Abraham Lincoln Presidential Library and Museum opened in Springfield, Ill.

Four public libraries opened in small communities in Nepal through a partnership of individual villages with the U.S.-based READ literacy-advocacy organization. Over the past 15 years, some 35 public libraries had opened in that country. In Imphal, India, protesters torched the Central Library of the state of Manipur. The group that took credit for the act also threatened newspapers and publishing companies that used Bengali script, the language of the library's 145,000-volume collection.

Hurricane Katrina devastated libraries along the U.S. Gulf Coast. Public libraries in Gulfport and Biloxi, Miss., and in the parishes surrounding New Orleans were destroyed. A branch library in Pass Christian, Miss., was described simply as "gone." In New Orleans the first floor of Dillard University's library was under water, and the entire Southern University campus might have to be rebuilt. A card catalog in the school's library had drawers exploded by water-swollen cards. Tulane University and the New Orleans Public Library's main branch, however, seemed to have escaped major damage. In most areas of the affected region, roofs were ripped off and library collections destroyed. In many cases library workers who evacuated could not learn the fate of their workplaces, and across the country evacuees inundated libraries to communicate with loved ones and file applications for aid from FEMA (the Federal Emergency Management Agency). The Houston Public Library set up temporary libraries in some emergency shelters, and libraries across the country collected books to send to the devastated area. Recovery of libraries and library services, however, would likely take years; the impact of Hurricane Rita was still undetermined.

The Bill and Melinda Gates Foundation awarded $1 million to Shidhulai Swanirvar Sangstha, a nongovernmental organization that used boats to take Internet access and computer training to impoverished villages in Bangladesh.

AP/Wide World Photos

San Francisco's 110-year-old M.H. de Young Memorial Museum reopened in October with double the previous exhibition space in an earthquake-resistant building. The design, by the Swiss firm Herzog & de Meuron, drew a range of comments pro and con.

In The Netherlands a public library instituted a program to "lend out," for 45 minutes of conversation in the library's coffee shop, people from minority groups. Among these people available to be "checked out" were Roma (Gypsies), Muslims, gays, lesbians, noncriminal drug addicts, and asylum seekers.

(THOMAS GAUGHAN)

MUSEUMS

Following a five-year closure, San Francisco's M.H. de Young Memorial Museum celebrated its 110th anniversary in 2005 by reopening in a landmark building designed by Swiss architects Herzog & de Meuron. In addition to offering double the exhibition space of the museum's previous home, the new building was seismically designed to be a stable base for the city's art collections; the original de Young Museum had sustained extensive damage in the 1989 Loma Prieta earthquake. A dramatic reminder of the threat that natural disasters posed to museums came in August when punishing Hurricane Katrina devastated the U.S. Gulf Coast. Although the New Orleans Museum of Art survived intact, other Gulf Coast museums suffered significant damage, including the Louisiana State Museum and the Old Capitol Museum of Mississippi History.

In March a $56 million Holocaust Museum opened in Jerusalem, with dignitaries and heads of state from more than 40 countries attending the inauguration. The museum, which replaced Yad Vashem's old museum, focused on the individual tragedies of the Holocaust victims. Oslo's Munch Museum reopened in June after a 10-month closure following the theft of Edvard Munch's masterpieces *The Scream* and *Madonna*. In the new museum, Munch's paintings were secured behind glass and bolted to the walls.

Herzog & de Meuron was the firm in demand for the museum sector in 2005. Besides completing de Young in April, the Pritzker Prize-winning practice completed the Walker Art Centre in Minneapolis, Minn., and continued its work on cultural projects, ranging from the Parrish Museum in Long Island, N.Y., to Madrid's CaixaForum exhibition space.

The global boom in museum building and expansion continued apace during the year. The variety of new museum developments underlined the public's burgeoning appetite for a wide range of culture. In Naples a museum of contemporary art opened in the 18th-century Palazzo Roccella. In the Swiss capital of Bern, architect Renzo Piano (*see* BIOGRAPHIES) designed a radical museum dedicated to the work of artist

Paul Klee. King Abdullah of Jordan inaugurated in Amman the new wing of the National Gallery dedicated to temporary exhibitions. The Museum of World Culture opened in Göteborg, Swed., to show ethnographic treasures from across the world. In San Juan, P.R., Espacio 1441 opened its doors to showcase cutting-edge works of art from Latin America.

There was anxiety among many, however, that the costs for some high-profile buildings were spiraling out of control. Washington's Corcoran Gallery of Art abandoned its long-planned expansion by superstar architect Frank Gehry when only half of the $170 million funds needed were secured. In January the chairman of the Guggenheim Foundation, Peter B. Lewis, resigned after accusing the trustees and director Thomas Krens of profligacy. In Madrid the Reina Sofía's new wing opened a year late and €17 million (about $21 million) over budget. There were signs that less-expensive architects were once more gaining favour. Leipzig's minimalist Museum der bildenden Künste was the first major new museum to be built in eastern Germany since 1945. It was met with wide praise and was built by Hufnagel Putz Rafaelian, a little-known Berlin practice.

In London the terrorist attacks of July 7 and 21 caused a severe drop in the number of museum visits; the National Gallery reported 46% fewer visits in the aftermath of the bombings than it had during the same week a year earlier. New security measures were put in place, and searches of bags became commonplace. Previously, the number of visitors had been at an all-time high, and the success of the abolition of entrance fees in December 2001 continued to buoy attendance. In 2004 there were 75% more visits to museums in the U.K. than in 2001. In 2005 Sweden also dropped admission fees for all state museums. In Paris artists demonstrated outside the Louvre in January after the museum withdrew a traditional exemption that allowed them free admission.

Inside the Louvre the world's most famous painting, the *Mona Lisa* by Leonardo da Vinci, was moved to a renovated and expanded viewing gallery in

April. In July Saudi Prince Walid ibn Talal agreed to donate $20 million to the Louvre for the construction of a wing to house Islamic art. The Guggenheim in Bilbao, Spain, unveiled one of the most ambitious and expensive sculptures in modern history when it installed in its vast ground-floor lobby *A Matter of Time* by American artist

A visitor at the Guggenheim museum in Bilbao, Spain, is dwarfed by A Matter of Time, *Richard Serra's monumental steel sculpture. The display was opened to the public on June 8.*

Richard Serra. Commemorative dates continued to frame many art exhibitions. The most important anniversary in 2005 was the centenary of the foundation of the Brücke artist group of German Expressionists, including Ernst Ludwig Kirchner, Emil Nolde, and Erich Heckel. Unprecedented displays of their art were mounted in museums in Berlin, Hamburg, Madrid, and other European cities.

A number of museums highlighted the art of Africa in 2005. "Africa Remix," a show on display in London and then Paris, was an attempt to introduce the diversity of contemporary

African art. (*See* photograph on page 158.) The exhibition coincided with political attempts at the Group of Eight summit to alleviate poverty on the continent. The art and archaeology of Egypt also continued to attract crowds, with a range of exhibitions that showcased treasures from Cairo. In Europe, Egyptian art shows were on display in Paris; Bonn, Ger.; and Cremona, Italy. In the U.S. a dazzling exhibition of artifacts from the tomb of the pharaoh Tutankhamen opened in June at the Los Angeles County Museum of Art, beginning a 27-month tour of the country. The show's organizers hoped that the latest "Tut" would emulate the success of the seminal Tutankhamen show, which attracted some eight million visitors and set traveling show attendance records when it toured the U.S. in 1976–79. Another touring exhibition, "The Quest for Immortality: Treasures of Ancient Egypt," thrilled audiences in Denver, Las Vegas, and Dayton, Ohio. New York's Museum for African Art, operating from a temporary location in Queens, started construction work on its new site in Harlem. The federal government agreed to a grant of $3.9 million for the creation of a National Museum of African American History and Culture in Washington, D.C. American talk-show host Oprah Winfrey was named as a member of the museum's board.

Major exhibitions of Russian art introduced the country's collections to a Western audience. The blockbuster "Russia!" at the Guggenheim Museum in New York City presented art ranging from 13th-century religious icons to Moscow's present day avant-garde. Across the city in the East Village, the Ukrainian Museum moved to a new $9 million home with two floors of galleries for temporary exhibitions. The Musée d'Orsay in Paris and the Art Gallery of Ontario in Toronto also staged Russian shows, borrowing many works from St. Petersburg's State Hermitage Museum. The Hermitage's director, Mikhail Pyotrovsky, announced plans for a museum in St. Petersburg celebrating Fabergé, the world-famous brand established by Peter Carl Fabergé, goldsmith and jeweler to the tsars of Russia.

(SAM PHILLIPS)

Life Sciences

Geneticists completed the mapping of the RICE GENOME. Zoologists identified the LAOTIAN ROCK RAT and classified it within a new RODENT family. The FDA approved BIDIL as a drug for a specific racial group. Scientists studied the snap of the VENUS FLYTRAP, and paleontologists found SOFT TISSUE preserved in DINOSAUR FOSSILS.

ZOOLOGY

In 2005 zoological research explained how honeybees navigate from their hive to a food source. Honeybees had been the focus of behavioral studies for decades, and many researchers were especially fascinated by the implications of the "waggle dance" performed by honeybees on the vertical surface of the honeycomb within the hive when they return from a newly discovered food source. The function originally ascribed to the dance, now accepted by most zoologists, is to allow the returning bee to convey to other bees (the recruits) the direction and distance of the new food source from the hive. Some investigators, however, challenged this interpretation. They suggested that the recruits that attend the dance do not decode the motions of the dancing bee but merely pick up odours of the food source from particles still clinging to the bee. The recruits then search for the food by tracking down the source of these food odours borne on the wind. Joe R. Riley of Rothamsted Research in Harpenden, Hertfordshire, Eng., and colleagues tested the effectiveness of the waggle dance as a navigational guide. They placed tiny antennae that functioned as radar transponders on recruits that left the hive in search of the designated food source, an unscented artificial feeder 200 m (660 ft) east of the hive. They released some of the recruits at the hive and others at sites 200–250 m (660–820 ft) southwest of the hive. Using signals from the transponders, the scientists mapped the flight paths of the bees. Of the recruits released at the hive, most flew unerringly to the immediate vicinity of the feeder. A small number of these recruits succeeded in locating the feeder itself, but most were unable to do so, presumably because no scents or visual cues were available to them. These results not only provided very strong support for the hypothesis that the waggle dance communicates distance and direction but also showed that the target is ultimately located by cues that are related to natural food sources. The flight paths taken by the recruits released from the locations away from the hive provided even stronger support for the hypothesis; these bees did not fly toward the feeder but instead flew in the same direction and for the same distance as the bees

The antenna attached to this nectar-gathering honeybee was used to track the bee's flight patterns.

Photo by Ingrid Williams, Rothamsted Research

released at the hive. The radar tracks also demonstrated that most of the recruits compensated accurately for lateral drift caused by the wind, even though they were flying to destinations that they had never visited.

Birds have always been noted for sexual dichromatism (differences in colouring between males and females), with males characteristically being the more brightly coloured. Sexual dichromatism is particularly dramatic in tropical parrots. In most species of tropical parrots, the males have bright plumage and the females are much less colourful. Robert Heinsohn of the Australian National University, Canberra, and colleagues reported on an eight-year study of an Australian parrot (*Eclectus roratus*) in which the opposite is true—the red-and-blue females are more brightly coloured than the green males. The females and males of *E. roratus* are so distinctly different in appearance that in the original descriptions of the birds, they were classified as separate species. In all other bird species in which females are more colourful than males (a characteristic referred to as reversed sexual dichromatism), there is also a sex-role reversal; that is, females compete with each other for male mates, and males care for the eggs and young. Despite the disparate colour patterns of the sexes of *E. roratus*, however, males compete for mates and females tend the nests while males feed them. The investigators attributed independently operating selection pressures related to ecology and behaviours of the female and male parrots to explain how they could evolve to have reverse sexual dichromatism without sex-role reversal. The females live most of the year in tree hollows where they also nest. They forage near the hollows, to which they can quickly retreat from aerial predators. The females are therefore freed from the need for camouflage, but there are relatively few tree hollows in which the females can nest, and the conspicuous display of a female helps ward off other females from its nesting place. In contrast, males have been selected for green plumage, which makes them less conspicuous to predators against the leaves in the tree canopy yet more visible against tree trunks, where they compete for female mates.

A newly identified species of rodent from Southeast Asia was described by Paulina D. Jenkins of the Natural History Museum, London, and colleagues. It was so distinctive that the scientists placed it in a new family—the first new family of mammals to be described by scientists in more than three decades. The Laotian rock rat (*Laonastes aenigmamus*), known as the Kha-nyou in food markets in the Khammouan province of Laos, where the scientists first found a specimen, reaches approximately 0.3 m (1 ft) in length and most closely resembles a squirrel or rat in general appearance. The skull and other bone structures, however, are atypical of those of other rodents. DNA analysis confirmed the genetic individuality of the species and showed that its closest relatives are rodents from Africa and South America rather than Asia.

The rediscovery in an Arkansas forest of the ivory-billed woodpecker (*Campephilus principalis*), believed to be extinct in the United States since the mid-1950s, was reported by John W. Fitzpatrick of Cornell University, Ithaca, N.Y., and colleagues who included ornithologists and conservationists. They confirmed the presence of at least one male ivory-billed woodpecker in the Big Woods area in eastern Arkansas. The sightings were first made in 2004 but were not disclosed until 2005. A video of a brief visual encounter and recordings of tree-drumming sounds characteristic of ivory-billed woodpeckers gave further evidence that the species still existed.

Discoveries were also made in the global-distribution patterns of well-studied groups of animals, as reported by M.S. Min of Seoul National University and colleagues. They described the

The Laotian rock rat, or Laonastes aenigmamus, *was discovered by scientists in a food market in Laos. The species was assigned a new genus and family.*

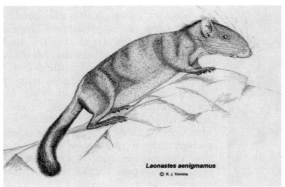

Laonastes aenigmamus
© R J. Timmins

AP/Wide World Photos

first plethodontid (lungless) salamander known from Asia. The salamander, *Karsenia koreana*, was given the common name Korean crevice salamander. With the exception of six species from the Mediterranean region, all members of the family were known only from the Western Hemisphere. The family Plethodontidae comprises more than 377 of the 550 species of salamanders. Characteristic of plethodontids, the new species has nasolabial grooves but no lungs or pterygoid bone. The species differs from those of other genera in the bone structures of its feet and skull. The investigators determined that there was a high level of genetic divergence between *Karsenia* and other plethodontids. This finding, coupled with its geographic isolation in Asia, suggested that *Karsenia* was possibly separated from North American members of the family before the Tertiary, at least 65 million years ago.

Julia A. Clarke of North Carolina State University and colleagues challenged a long-held conviction among many paleontologists that modern birds arose as a distinct phylogenetic lineage after the extinction of nonavian dinosaurs at the end of the Cretaceous Period (about 65 million years ago). The lack of convincing evidence of true bird fossils prior to the Tertiary has suggested that birds did not coexist with dinosaurs. The investigators described a new species of bird, *Vegavis iaai*, from Antarctica, that was associated with sediments dated to be from about 66 million to 68 million years ago. The researchers placed the specimen in the avian group Anseriformes (waterfowl) and suggested that the specimen was closely related to the Anatidae (ducks and geese). Their conclusions, based on where they located the new species in the bird evolutionary tree, indicated that avian relatives not only of ducks but also of other modern birds lived in the Cretaceous contemporaneously with nonavian dinosaurs.

An explanation for how changes in climatic conditions could lead to concurrent changes in the sizes of spatially distributed populations of a species was given by Isabella M. Cattadori and Peter J. Hudson of Pennsylvania State University and

Daniel T. Haydon of the University of Glasgow, Scot., based on more than a century of records of red grouse (*Lagopus lagopus scoticus*) in northern England. The investigators tested competing hypotheses to explain the concurrent decreases and increases of grouse populations in each of the five distinct regions they investigated. One hypothesis, the climate hypothesis, was that fluctuations in grouse populations were caused directly by the effects of the climate on the breeding success of the grouse and on the survival of grouse chicks. Alternatively, the climate-parasite hypothesis held that the climate affected the interaction between the grouse and the parasitic nematode *Trichostrongylus tenuis*, which reduces fecundity in the grouse and is known to affect the abundance of the bird populations. Using elaborate modeling and detailed weather data for each region, the researchers verified that environmental conditions favourable for the spread of the parasitic infection among grouse led to widespread declines in grouse populations, whereas unfavourable years for the parasitic infection resulted in increases in grouse survival. The findings were seen not only to be applicable to the management of grouse populations but also to be indicative of how regional changes in climate could result in local changes in parasite burdens that lead to concurrent changes in the size of host populations.   (J. WHITFIELD GIBBONS)

BOTANY

A major milestone in plant science reported in 2005 was the completion of the mapping of the complete sequence of the rice genome. This achievement was expected to pave the way for making critical improvements in rice, the staple food for more than one-half of the world's population. The genome project took six years and involved 32 research groups from more than 10 countries. Although the function of many of the rice genes remained unknown, about 70% of them mirror those in *Arabidopsis thaliana* (thale cress), the only other completely sequenced plant genome. By teasing out the roles of the newly sequenced genes, researchers hoped to identify beneficial genes much more quickly and accurately and to develop strains of rice with the most advantageous combinations. They believed that the genetic modification and traditional plant breeding of rice would gain from a more complete understanding of the genome. Breeding of other major cereal crops also stood to benefit, because all of the major cereal crops—including rice—descended from a common, grasslike ancestor. "The rice genome is the Rosetta Stone of all the bigger grass genomes," said Joachim Messing of Rutgers University, Piscataway, N.J., one of the research leaders. After analyzing the completed genome, the scientists found that rice has more genes than humans do—37,544 genes compared with the estimated 25,000 genes of the human genome.

Botanists were astonished by the remarkable discovery of plants whose reproduction seemed to shatter the laws of inheritance of all living things, as first described by Gregor Mendel in the mid-1800s. The plants were mutant specimens of *Arabidopsis thaliana* with closed, deformed flowers in which some flower parts were fused together. Each plant had two copies of a mutant, defective gene. When two such plants are cross-pollinated, the expectation under the Mendelian laws of inheritance is that all the progeny of the two plants will produce deformed flowers. Instead, the botanists observed that 10% of the progeny had normal flowers. Genetic analysis determined that the normal offspring had somehow replaced the defective gene in their DNA. Robert Pruitt, whose team at Purdue University, West Lafayette, Ind., made the extraordinary discovery, believed that the normal offspring somehow acquired genetic information from an earlier generation than their parents'. The team had not determined the source of the genetic instructions for repairing the defective gene, but one possibility was RNA, molecules that are used by cells for the manufacture of proteins and that can also be passed directly from parent to offspring. The circumstances that would trigger the plant to revert to healthier ancestral genes also remained a mystery, but they might be related to stress or to the severity of a mutation. "This means that inheritance can happen more flexibly than we thought in the past," said Pruitt. "If the inheritance mechanism we found in the research plant *Arabidopsis* exists in animals, too, it's possible that it will be an avenue for gene

therapy to treat or cure diseases in both plants and animals."

Advances continued to be made in 2005 in the genetic modification of plants. Chinese scientists who were led by Jingxue Wang of the Agri-Biotechnology Research Centre of Shanxi Province inserted two animal genes—one from a scorpion and one from a moth—into rape plants (the source of rapeseed oil, or canola) to make them poisonous to insects that feed on them. The researchers said that the use of two foreign genes instead of one would reduce the likelihood that insect pests would develop resistance to the geneti-

The complete genetic sequence of rice, published in 2005, was expected to help in the development of new varieties. Shown is a high-yielding variety of rice called Lemont.

cally introduced toxins. Researchers at the University of Victoria, B.C., succeeded in inserting a modified frog gene into potato plants to give the plants resistance against a range of microbial diseases. The gene was taken from *Phyllomedusa bicolor*, a poisonous frog of South American rainforests, and it produces dermaseptin B1, a skin toxin that helps protect the frog against fungi and bacteria that thrive in the hot and humid conditions. The scientists found that the toxin also inhibits the growth of some of the fungi and bacteria that cause plant diseases.

Scientists at Max Planck Institute of Molecular Plant Physiology, Golm, Ger., reported a role for hemoglobins in plants. Hemoglobins are proteins best known for their function of carrying oxygen in human blood, but they are also found in high concentrations

in the root nodules of legume plants. The nodules are home to symbiotic bacteria, called rhizobia, that take nitrogen from the air and turn it into ammonia, a nitrogen compound that plants can use readily. The nitrogen supplied by the bacteria is vital for plant growth in nitrogen-poor soils. (In return, the bacteria obtain food and shelter from the plant.) Thomas Ott and his team of scientists at the institute found that the plant hemoglobin carries away oxygen from the nodules and thereby helps protect nitrogenase, an oxygen-sensitive enzyme found in the nodules, from damage. Nitrogenase is needed by the bacteria for nitrogen fixation.

Scientists have long been astonished by the speed at which the Venus flytrap snaps shut—its two leaf lobes close together to entrap prey in a mere tenth of a second. The movement was believed to involve the pumping of water into or out of motor cells within the plant, but the release of water in these tissues is about 10 times too slow to explain the speed of the trap. A study by Yoël Forterre and colleagues at the University of Cambridge used high-speed video to record the snapping-shut motion of the Venus flytrap. Fluorescent reference dots painted onto the leaf lobes helped reveal how the lobes suddenly snapped and buckled. As the plant lies in wait for an insect, the leaf is curved outward. When an insect wanders into the trap and trips over a trigger hair on the leaf, the plant pumps water into the motor cells along the outside of the leaf. This action alters the curvature of the leaf until it flips rapidly from a convex to concave shape, similar to the way a bowed plastic lid will spring inward and outward. It is likely that other uncommon fast motions in plants—such as the explosive propulsion of seeds by the squirting cucumber—depend on similar mechanisms. (PAUL SIMONS)

MOLECULAR BIOLOGY AND GENETICS

The Genetics of Race. The human genome, like every other naturally occurring genome, is a rainbow of variation. Indeed, there is not one human genome; there are as many distinct human genomes as there are distinctly conceived individuals on Earth. To be sure, the differences between these genomes are minute—single-base substitutions, small additions, deletions, or rearrangements that involve only a tiny fraction of the more than three billion base pairs of DNA sequence that make up a haploid human genome. Nonetheless, it is these differences, working in concert with environmental factors, that make people who and what they are—that make them unique.

DNA sequence variations are passed from parents to children in the normal Mendelian fashion; parents carry two independent copies, or alleles, of every gene, and from each pair one is passed to each child, with random distribution. Humans also share relationships that extend beyond immediate family boundaries. As successive waves of human emigration out of Africa populated the continents of the globe, groups became isolated from one another by distance, by physical barriers such as mountains, deserts, or oceans, and by social factors such as language, religion, and culture. This separation, coupled with differing founder groups and differing selective pressures, resulted in detectable and heritable genetic differences between distinct human populations. Some of these genetic differences are visible in terms of physical appearance and give rise to the commonly held notion of race. Other genetic differences are not visible but instead are evident in differing carrier frequencies for specific disease genes; for example, thalassemia mutations are most common in peoples of Mediterranean and Southeast or East Asian descent, cystic fibrosis mutations are most common in peoples of northern European descent, and Tay-Sachs disease mutations are most common in peoples of Eastern European Jewish or French Canadian descent. Beyond differences in disease frequency, distinct human populations can also show varying degrees of disease severity. For example, although many different populations in Africa suffer from a high prevalence of sickle cell anemia, some tend to be more mildly affected than others because they continue to produce fetal hemoglobin, which blocks or limits aggregation of the mutant "sickle cell" hemoglobin protein. From these observations it is reasonable to conclude that different human groups might also have strikingly disparate response rates to specific disease treatments.

In June 2005 the U.S. Food and Drug Administration (FDA) approved the use of BiDil, the first medication targeted to a specific racial group. BiDil, a product of NitroMed, Inc., in Lexington, Mass., is prescribed to prevent heart failure and is a combination of isosorbide dinitrate (a medication used to treat angina) and hydralazine (a medication used to lower blood pressure). Originally tested on a racially mixed population, BiDil appeared unimpressive. When a reanalysis of the study data took self-declared race into account, however, a striking outcome emerged—African American patients responded much better to the drug than did their Caucasian counterparts. In the original analysis, this response was masked owing to the preponderance of Caucasian patients in the study. In a subsequent study of more than 1,000 self-declared African American patients with congestive heart failure, BiDil reduced deaths by 43%, a result so dramatic the trial was stopped early, in 2004. Largely on the basis of these results, the FDA approved the sale of BiDil with its racially designated target population.

The implications of the BiDil study were both simple and complex. If a medication worked well in some patients but not in others, the best medical practice clearly was to target the medication to those patients most likely to benefit. Ignoring factors, such as race, that might influence patient response would be negligent. Nevertheless, as pointed out by Francis Collins, director of the National Human Genome Research Institute in Bethesda, Md., self-declared race was a "biologically inaccurate and socially dangerous" surrogate for the more specific genetic and environmental factors that underlay the different responses that different patients had to any given treatment. The challenge was to identify and characterize those factors so that every patient could be assessed as an individual rather than as a member of a preestablished group and could thereby be treated with whatever medications were most likely to provide personal benefit. Classifying patients strictly by race assumes that all members of a race are identical, which clearly they are not. Further, racial classification discounts the existence of mixed-race individuals, who make up a significant and growing segment of most societies.

Another concern raised by the BiDil example stemmed from the design of the follow-up study on which the new FDA approval was granted. Although the initial, smaller study suggested a racial disparity in drug response, the follow-up study lacked a racial control group—only one group was studied. By itself, therefore, the study could not claim differential drug efficacy in different racial groups, and marketing BiDil as a racially targeted therapy potentially limited access of non-African Americans to a treatment from which they also might benefit. Clearly, resolving this issue would require further studies involving a large number of patients from many different racial groups.

How Auxin Works. Indole 3-acetic acid, or auxin, is a plant hormone that helps plants to grow their shoots upward and roots downward and to flower and bear fruit. The process by which auxin works was not determined until 2005, some 70 years after the hormone was first identified in plants. (Since that time other auxins have been discovered, but it became common practice to use the term to refer specifically to indole 3-acetic acid, the most important one.) In May two groups working independently, one headed by Mark Estelle from Indiana University and the other headed by Ottoline Leyser from the University of York, Eng., reported that auxin binds to a protein complex called SCF^{TIR1} and that, once bound, the complex acts to target a specific set of proteins, called Aux/IAAs, for degradation. Since Aux/IAA proteins normally repress the transcription of growth-related genes, auxin effectively induces transcription and thereby promotes cell growth.

The discovery that auxin binds directly to SCF^{TIR1} and results in the degradation of a transcriptional repressor was striking for at least two reasons. First, this mechanism of action is distinct from those of other hormone receptors that had been studied either in plants or in animals. Most hormone receptors influence gene expression by entering the nucleus in response to hormone binding or through a complex cascade of signaling enzymes. Second, SCF^{TIR1} is an F-box ubiquitin protein ligase. Like other such molecules, it tags specific proteins for degradation by attaching a small protein marker called ubiquitin to them. Given that plants express about 700 different F-box proteins, the new findings suggested that at least some of these other F-box proteins might serve similar functions, perhaps mediating responses to other plant hormones. Indeed, the group headed by Estelle further reported that SCF^{TIR1} is highly related to the F-box proteins AFB1, AFB2, and

AFB3, each of which also functions as an auxin receptor, ostensibly triggering the degradation of different Aux/IAA targets. By controlling which F-box auxin receptors and which Aux/IAA proteins are expressed in specific cells and tissues, the plant could facilitate the many diverse physiological responses attributed to auxin.

Much remained unknown about the newly discovered process. For example, it was unclear how auxin interacts with SCF^{TIR1} and how binding this small ligand alters the activity of SCF^{TIR1} with respect to Aux/IAAs. In addition, the F-box proteins might represent only one of many auxin-receptor-and-response pathways. Finally, and perhaps most important, if indole 3-acetic acid could modulate the function of SCF^{TIR1}, were other ubiquitin protein ligases in plants and perhaps also in animals similarly subject to regulation by small-molecule ligands?   (JUDITH L. FRIDOVICH-KEIL)

PALEONTOLOGY

Perhaps the most astonishing event in paleontology in 2005 was the discovery of blood vessels and other soft tissues inside the femur (thighbone) of a *Tyrannosaurus rex* from a remote field site in the Hell Creek Formation in Montana. This amazing find fueled discussion as to whether protein or DNA might have survived within the tissues, which were about 70 million years old. Experts on fossil preservation were skeptical, saying DNA could not be preserved for so long a time. In one study of the tissues inside the bone, researchers identified a way of determining the gender of a dinosaur for the first time. Some of the tissue they found was similar to specialized bone tissue that forms in female birds during ovulation. In female birds the tissue, pitted with channels through which blood vessels run, serves as a source of calcium to produce egg shells. Based on the presence of such tissue in the *T. rex* bone the researchers concluded that the specimen was a female.

In the summer of 2001, a team from the Burpee Museum of Natural History in Rockford, Ill., that was conducting fieldwork in the Hell Creek Formation discovered what it later determined to be the world's most complete juvenile tyrannosaurid. In 2005 the museum unveiled the mounted skeleton, named "Jane." (*See* photograph on p. 220.) The museum also cosponsored (with Northern Illinois University) a major symposium at which most of the world's experts on tyrannosaurs presented pa-

Reprinted with permission from Fig. 1 A, D, G from
MH Schweitzer et al., SCIENCE 308:1456–60 (2005) AAAS

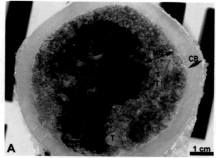

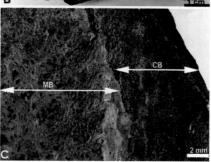

The fossilized Tyrannosaurus rex *femur shown in images* **B** *and* **C** *reveals bone tissue similar to the medullary bone (**MB**) that occurs in a domestic hen femur (image* **A***) within denser cortical bone (**CB**). The find indicated that the* T. rex *bone was from a female.*

pers. The primary point of debate at the symposium was the status of *Nanotyrannus*, a genus of small tyrannosaurs. Although some paleontologists contended that it was a valid taxon, others argued that the specimens that represented it were juveniles of *T. rex*. The Burpee Museum specimen lay at the heart of the controversy, since the museum and some of the presenters claimed that it was a juvenile (11-year-old) *T. rex*, whereas other presenters contended that it was a new specimen of *Nanotyrannus*.

Until recently most specimens of deinonychosaurs, the theropods most closely related to birds, had been found only in North America and Asia. In 2005 the specimen of a new species was described that provided the first non-controversial evidence of the existence of deinonychosaurs in the Southern Hemisphere. The specimen, *Neuquenraptor argentinus*, was found in Patagonia (Argentina). Another new species of dinosaur, *Falcarius utahensis*, was described from the Early Cretaceous Cedar Mountain Formation in Utah. It represented the earliest-known therizinosauroid dinosaur from North America. Previously, this enigmatic group of theropods had been known mainly from China. *F. utahensis* lay at the base of the therizinosauroid clade and therefore documented the earliest stage in the transition from carnivorous to herbivorous traits that took place within the evolution of this group.

The discovery of an oviraptorosaurian pelvis and a pair of eggs with shells within the pelvic cavity helped answer questions about the reproductive biology of oviraptorosaurians and other theropods collectively known as maniraptoran dinosaurs. The specimen was from the Upper Cretaceous Nanxiong Formation near Ganzhou, China. The relatively large size of the eggs, their placement within the pelvic cavity, and the anatomy of the pelvis led the authors to conclude that maniraptoran dinosaurs, like crocodilians, had two functional oviducts but that, like birds (which have only one oviduct), each oviduct produced only one egg at a time.

Other dinosaur research during the year included a study of a new specimen of the theropod *Majungatholus atopus*. Openings within the vertebral column of the specimen were compared with similar structures for pulmonary air sacs that are found in living birds. The study concluded that the dinosaur had both cervical (neck) and abdominal air-sac systems, which implied, in turn, that it and other nonavian theropods had an avianlike pulmonary system. The finding supported other evidence that dinosaurs had relatively high metabolic rates.

The discovery of embryos of the primitive dinosaur *Massospondylus carinatus*, which was believed to be related to the sauropods, provided insights into its developmental growth. Although adult members of this species had forelimbs significantly shorter than their hind limbs, the embryos had large forelimbs relative to body size. As the animal grew, therefore, the hind limbs must have grown rapidly in relation to the forelimbs. The authors suggested that the four-legged posture that

Photo by M. Graham

The exhibit "Jane: Diary of a Dinosaur," which opened June 30 at the Burpee Museum in Rockford, Ill., featured a notable well-preserved specimen that the museum identified as a juvenile **Tyrannosaurus rex.** *It stood about 2.3 m (7.5 ft) high at the hips and was about 8.5 m (28 ft) long.*

evolved in sauropods might have been the result of a reduction in this disparate growth.

Although fossil bird embryos had been previously reported in the scientific literature, no specimen had been found with its feathers preserved. A newly discovered embryo from the Early Cretaceous of Liaoning, China, had a hardened, nearly complete skeleton with sheets of feathers. The embryo was in the final stages of development prior to hatching and represented some type of early precocial bird (a bird capable of independent survival immediately after birth). A rare partial skeleton of a new bird, *Vegavis iaai*, from the Cretaceous of Antarctica, was the first Cretaceous bird that could be definitely placed within the lineages of living birds, which suggested, therefore, that living-bird lineages emerged prior to the Cretaceous/Tertiary mass-extinction event. (See *Zoology*, above.)

Other excavations of the Early Cretaceous deposits of Liaoning yielded a new species of mammal, *Repenomamus giganticus*, that was the largest known from the Mesozoic—larger than some small dinosaurs. The body of the specimen was more than 1 m (3.3 ft) long, including the tail, and was estimated to have weighed up to 14 kg (30 lb). A specimen of a related smaller species, *R. robustus*, from the same deposit was found with the skeleton of a juvenile *Psittacosaurus* near where its stomach would have been. This finding provided the first evidence that some primitive mammals fed on dinosaurs.

Taxonomists had long suggested that the nearest living relatives of the hippopotamus were the pigs and the peccaries. A recent study argued instead that hippos are the only surviving members of anthracotheres, a group that shared ancestry with the cetaceans (whales, dolphins, and porpoises). This view supported genetic studies that had shown that the whales were the nearest living relatives of the hippopotamus. New North American fossil material from Paleocene to Eocene apheliscine "condylarths" (early primitive ungulates) showed that a close relationship exists between this group and the extant African Macroscelidea (elephant shrews). This finding countered the idea that placental diversification was driven by the breakup of Gondwana.

Research on the oldest known monotreme, *Teinolophos trusleri* from the Early Cretaceous, indicated that the complex structures of the mammalian inner ear evolved independently in the evolutionary lines of monotremes and therians (placentals and marsupials). Another study showed that *Fruitafossor windscheffeli*, a recently described Late Jurassic mammal from the Morrison Formation of Colorado, had highly specialized teeth similar to those of some placental mammals and very different from the generalized dentitions of most Jurassic mammals. This specimen also exhibited forelimb features that were specialized for digging.

A new study of Late Permian terrestrial vertebrate faunas from the Karoo Basin of South Africa claimed that the fossil record showed a gradual extinction in the Late Permian followed by an increased rate of extinction at the Permian-Triassic boundary (particularly of small herbivorous reptiles called dicynodonts). This paper argued that the fossil record did not support theories in which the impact of an asteroid or meteorite caused the Permian-Triassic mass extinction and that the extinction event was protracted, lasting tens or hundreds of thousands of years. Another study of Late Permian fossils—of temnospondyl amphibians from the Moradi Formation of Niger—revealed characteristics of faunas that lived in the dry climate that prevailed at low latitudes at that time. These specimens were found to be surprisingly different from the much better-known Late Permian fauna of higher latitudes and thereby indicated that Late Permian faunas were less homogeneous than had previously been theorized.

(WILLIAM R. HAMMER)

Literature

The ORANGE PRIZE proved its staying power; ESTABLISHED authors led the list of top U.S. novels; French authors fretted about the VITALITY of their literature; the 400th anniversary of *DON QUIXOTE* overshadowed much Spanish work; ORHAN PAMUK and KENZABURŌ ŌE were names in the news; and Arabs flocked to read a novel by a Cairo DENTIST.

ENGLISH

United Kingdom. The Orange Prize for Fiction, an award dedicated to women writers, celebrated its 10th anniversary in 2005. Although some had predicted at its inception that the prize would not achieve meritoriousness, the prize showed itself to be firmly established as one of Britain's most prestigious literary awards (alongside the Whitbread Book Awards and the Man Booker Prize), attracting massive press attention and generating book sales in the tens of thousands. It nonetheless continued to provoke controversy. Defending the need for a women-only award, judge Joanne Harris said, "Year after year the short list for the Booker is mostly old men." Kate Mosse, the co-founder and honorary director of the Orange Prize, noted that it helped promote writers who had previously been ignored: "This is about getting great books read more widely." Its detractors, however, agreed with critic John Walsh, who said, "There is nothing more condescending than the idea that there is women's fiction. It's extreme bigotry."

A sure sign of the award's efficacy was the fate of the 2004 winner, Andrea Levy's *Small Island* (2004), which—besides being voted Best of the Best, the overall winner from the 10 novels that had won the Orange Prize to date—captured the Whitbread Book of the Year Award and Novel Award, beating the 2004 Man Booker winner, Alan Hollinghurst's *The Line of Beauty* (2004). Levy's social comedy about Caribbean immigration to Britain also took the 2005 Commonwealth Writers' Prize.

Those who argued that women writers were still more likely than men to concern themselves with domestic and so-called women's issues might have felt their views confirmed by the Orange Prize's 2005 short list. Of the six short-listed books, five had female protagonists and most of the plots revolved around family relations. Marina Lewycka's *A Short History of Tractors in Ukrainian* explored the dynamics that emerge when two sisters join forces to prevent their father from marrying a glamorous Ukrainian divorcée. Meanwhile, Sheri Holman's *The Mammoth Cheese* (2004 [published in the U.S. in 2003]) touched on fertility medication, postpartum depression, and what happens when one woman's obsession with politics blinds her to the plight of her teenage daughter. A favourite with bookmakers was *Old Filth* (2004) by Jane Gardam, a Yorkshire-born writer and two-time winner of the Whitbread. Gardam's subject was the devastating emotional cost of separating young children from their parents. Her protagonist, an 80-year-old retired international lawyer, was once a "raj orphan"; he now seeks to come to terms with memories of a loveless childhood in a Welsh foster home. The winner was American novelist Lionel Shriver for *We Need to Talk About Kevin* (2003), a novel about a career woman who gives birth to a son she is unable to love. Years later the boy commits a Columbine-style massacre, killing nine people in his high school. Jenni Murray, chair of the judging panel, said *Kevin* "is a book that acknowledges what many women worry about but never express—the fear of becoming a mother and the terror of what kind of child one might bring into the world."

On the whole, however, British literature of 2005 gave evidence of a country preoccupied as much with global concerns as with domestic ones, and books on terrorism and the war in Iraq were abundant. Ian McEwan's latest novel, *Saturday*, traced a day in the life of a London neurosurgeon. The day is Feb. 15, 2003, when more than a million people took to the streets to protest the incipient war in Iraq. Unlike much fiction provoked by post-Sept. 11, 2001, politics, however, *Saturday* did not take a clear position; the arguments for and against the war were distributed with ambiguity. *The Guardian* journalist James Meek's much-lauded novel *The People's Act of Love* delved into the twin ideologies of self-sacrifice and terror. Meek's tale, featuring castrates, cannibals, and torturers, was set in remote Siberia after the Russian Revolution of 1917, but it cast light on how destructive belief systems might operate in any context. One revolutionary, describing himself in the third person, says, "He's not a destroyer, he is destruction, leaving these good people who remain to build a better world on the ruins. . . . What looks like an act of evil to a single person is the people's act of love to its future self."

American author Lionel Shriver took home Britain's Orange Prize for a novel by a woman for her 2003 work, **We Need to Talk About Kevin.**

© Jerry Bauer

In the nonfiction realm, books attempting to understand terrorism continued to proliferate. An original approach was taken by leading critic Terry Eagleton. Billed as "a metaphysics of terror with a serious historical perspective," *Holy Terror* traced the concept throughout the ages, citing writers from Euripides to D.H. Lawrence. John Gray, author of another study of terrorism, *Al Qaeda and What It Means to Be Modern* (2003), commended Eagleton's effort, saying, "Very few of the thousands of books on the subject have explored it in a larger context of ideas."

Current world affairs were also brought into focus by the Nobel Committee's decision to award the doyen of British theatre, Harold Pinter, the Nobel Prize for Literature. (*See* NOBEL PRIZES.) In recent years Pinter had attracted attention for his vocal opposition to the bombing of Afghanistan and the war in Iraq. Early in 2005, having written more than 30 plays, he announced that he was giving up playwriting to concentrate on political writing, including poetry: "I'm using a lot of energy more specifically about political states of affairs, which I think are very worrying as things stand." Despite grumbles in some camps over the award's alleged political dimension, most commentators agreed that Pinter had had a seminal influence on British theatre during his nearly 50-year career. His distinctive style, it was widely remarked, had given rise to the well-used term *Pinteresque* to describe "a work of drama full of atmospheric silences peppered with half-stated insights." In describing Pinter's contribution, Nobel permanent secretary Horace Engdahl commented, "Pinter restored theatre to its basic elements: an enclosed space and unpredictable dialogue, where people are at the mercy of each other and pretense crumbles."

In *The Times* (London) newspaper, Michael Gove drew meaningful comparisons between recent fiction and the literature of prewar Edwardian Britain. As he observed, three of the six Man Booker Prize finalists were inspired by authors or events of the first decades of the past century. Julian Barnes's *Arthur & George*, a semifictional life of Sherlock Holmes's creator, Sir Arthur Conan Doyle, was set in fin de siècle Britain. It also was written in the formal style of the period, a fact that publisher Jonathan Cape underscored by binding it in embossed dark mustard cloth. *On Beauty*, Zadie Smith's latest foray into the dynamics of race relations, also looked backward, with Smith unabashedly borrowing elements of plot and style from E.M. Forster's 1910 masterpiece *Howards End*. Finally, Sebastian Barry's *A Long Long Way* treated the end of Edwardian innocence: World War I. Gove attributed the parallels to similarities in the eras: "Iraq, like the Boer War, divides opinion and is proving a profound test of leadership. The rise of China, like the growth of Imperial Germany, has led to deep questioning of what difficult changes we need to make to prepare for a shift in the geopolitical balance. Just as new social forces within Edwardian England forced a recasting of politics, so questions of national cohesion and multiculturalism are creating new alliances and new strains in British public life."

The winner of the Man Booker Prize, however, was inspired neither by politics nor by Edwardian classics. Veteran Irish writer John Banville's novel *The Sea* told the story of a man who escapes the recent loss of his wife by revisiting an Irish coastal resort where he spent a holiday in his youth. There he unravels his memories of a life-shaping encounter with the Grace family. *The Sunday Times* called it a novel "concerned with rites of passage: coming-of-age and coming of old age; awakening and dying." *The Sea* narrowly beat the front-runner—Kazuo Ishiguro's more topical dystopia about cloning, *Never Let Me Go*. Man Booker Prize chairman John Sutherland had cast the deciding vote for *The Sea*. This was a reversal of fortunes for Banville, whose novel *The Book of Evidence* had lost the Booker Prize in 1989 to Ishiguro's *The Remains of the Day*. It also represented the second consecutive win for the publishers Picador. Nevertheless, *The Sea* provoked ambivalent reviews. Many critics complained that Banville's "jewelled sentences" and "fancy epithets" interfered with the book's narrative flow. "Banville's text is one that constantly demands admiration and analysis," wrote one reviewer, "There's lots of lovely language, but not much novel."

Banville's themes of loss, identity, and remembrance recurred in Sheila Hancock's memoir, *The Two of Us: My Life with John Thaw* (2004), chronicling her turbulent 28-year marriage to the British actor and her grief following his death from cancer. Hancock was named Reader's Digest Author of the Year at the British Book Awards. In *Rules for Old Men Waiting*, Peter Pouncey, a retired classics professor, made his debut as a novelist with works in which characters deal with bereavement and memory. An old man waiting to die retreats to his decrepit summer house on Cape Cod to finish writing a story about World War I. As the novel progresses, he realizes that he is making "some kind of tally of his memories, as though completing the inventory might tell him what his life amounted to."

Other notable newcomers on the literary scene included Diana Evans, whose novel *26a*, about a pair of identical twins growing up in an eccentric mixed-race family in northwestern London, won the Orange Award for New Writers. Susan Fletcher's *Eve Green* (2004) won the 2004 Whitbread First Novel Award. It had sold fewer than 1,000 copies before its nomination.

The 2004 Whitbread Biography Award went to John Guy for *My Heart Is My Own: The Life of Mary Queen of Scots* (2004). Guy's study joined a crowded arena of books about the "unluckiest ruler in British history" but distinguished itself by portraying a less-romanticized queen, based on previously overlooked evidence. A shocked reviewer noted the disparity between Guy's modern Mary and earlier accounts: "Although she was only 42 years old, her legs were so swollen and her feet so inflamed by arthritis that she had to be helped into the execution chamber by two soldiers." History received a far more devastating update, however, in *Mao: The Unknown Story*. Jung Chang, the author of *Wild Swans*, and her historian husband, Jon Halliday, revealed Mao as "one of the greatest monsters of the 20th century alongside Hitler and Stalin," responsible for 70 million deaths. Based on a decade of interviews, the book promised to undermine the distortions of history perpetuated by the Communist Party of China. Nicholas Shakespeare in the *Daily Telegraph* predicted that "when China comes to terms with its past this book will have played a role."

On a lighter note, Geraldine McCaughrean's alternative version of the Noah story, *Not the End of the World* (2004), won the 2004 Whitbread Children's Book Award, which made her the first writer to have won the award three times. McCaughrean's version named the wives of Noah's sons, added a daughter to the biblical cast, and filled out the story with graphic details. A reviewer in *The Guardian* commented, "McCaughrean embraces the sheer physical reality of what surviving the flood means: the pleading of the drowning people as

(continued on page 224)

WORLD LITERARY PRIZES 2005

All prizes are annual and were awarded in 2005 unless otherwise stated. Currency equivalents as of July 1, 2005, were as follows: €1 = $1.210; £1 = $1.792; Can$1 = $0.816; ¥1 = $0.009; SKr 1 = $0.128; and DKr 1 = $0.162.

Nobel Prize for Literature

Awarded since 1901; included in the behest of Alfred Nobel, who specified a prize for those who "shall have produced in the field of literature the most outstanding work in an ideal direction." The prizewinners are selected in October by the Swedish Academy and receive the award on December 10 in Stockholm. Prize: a gold medal and an award that varies from year to year; in 2005 the award was SKr 10,000,000.
Harold Pinter (U.K.)

International IMPAC Dublin Literary Award

First awarded in 1996, this is the largest international literary prize; it is open to books written in any language. The award is a joint initiative of Dublin City Council, the Municipal Government of Dublin City, and the productivity-improvement company IMPAC. It is administered by Dublin City Public Libraries. Prize: €100,000, of which 25% goes to the translator if the book was not written in English, and a Waterford crystal trophy. The awards are given at Dublin Castle in May or June.
The Known World by Edward P. Jones (U.S.)

Neustadt International Prize for Literature

Established in 1969 and awarded biennially by the University of Oklahoma and World Literature Today. Novelists, poets, and dramatists are equally eligible. Prize: $50,000, a replica of an eagle feather cast in silver, and a certificate.
Adam Zagajewski (Poland), awarded in 2004

Commonwealth Writers Prize

Established in 1987 by the Commonwealth Foundation. In 2005 there was one award of £10,000 for the best book submitted, as well as an award of £3,000 for the best first book. In each of the four regions of the Commonwealth, two prizes of £1,000 are awarded: one for the best book and one for the best first book.

Best Book	*Small Island* by Andrea Levy
Best First Book	*Purple Hibiscus*
	by Chimamanda Ngozi Adichie (Nigeria)
Regional winners-Best Book	
Africa	*Boy* by Lindsey Collen (South Africa)
Caribbean & Canada	*Runaway* by Alice Munro (Canada)
Eurasia	*Small Island* by Andrea Levy (U.K.)
Southeast Asia & South Pacific	*White Earth* by Andrew McGahan (Australia)

Booker Prize

Established in 1969, sponsored by Booker McConnell Ltd. and, beginning in 2002, the Man Group; administered by the National Book League in the U.K. Awarded to the best full-length novel written by a citizen of the Commonwealth or the Republic of Ireland and published in the U.K. during the 12 months ended September 30. Prize: £50,000.
The Sea by John Banville

Whitbread Book of the Year

Established in 1971. The winners of the Whitbread Book Awards for Poetry, Biography, Novel, and First Novel as well as the Whitbread Children's Book of the Year each receive £5,000, and the winner of the Whitbread Book of the Year prize receives an additional £25,000. Winners are announced in January of the year following the award.
Small Island by Andrea Levy (2004 award)

Orange Prize for Fiction

Established in 1996. Awarded to a work of published fiction written by a woman in English and published in the U.K. during the 12 months ended March 31. Prize: £30,000.
We Need to Talk About Kevin by Lionel Shriver (U.S.)

PEN/Faulkner Award

The PEN/Faulkner Foundation each year recognizes the best published works of fiction by contemporary American writers. Named for William Faulkner, the PEN/Faulkner Award was founded by writers in 1980 to honour their peers and is now the largest juried award for fiction in the U.S. Prize: $15,000.
War Trash by Ha Jin

Pulitzer Prizes in Letters and Drama

Begun in 1917, awarded by Columbia University, New York City, on the recommendation of the Pulitzer Prize Board for books published in the previous year. Five categories in Letters are honoured: Fiction, Biography, and General Non-Fiction (authors of works in these categories must be American citizens); History (the subject must be American history); and Poetry (for original verse by an American author). The Drama prize is for "a distinguished play by an American author, preferably original in its source and dealing with American life." Prize: $10,000 in each category.

Fiction	*Gilead* by Marilynne Robinson
Biography	*de Kooning: An American Master*
	by Mark Stevens and Annalyn Swan
Poetry	*Delights & Shadows* by Ted Kooser
History	*Washington's Crossing*
	by David Hackett Fischer
General Non-Fiction	*Ghost Wars* by Steve Coll
Drama	*Doubt, a Parable* by John Patrick Shanley

National Book Awards

Awarded since 1950 by the National Book Foundation, a consortium of American publishing groups. Categories have varied, beginning with 3—Fiction, Nonfiction, and Poetry—swelling to 22 awards in 1983, and returning to 4 (the initial 3 plus Young People's Literature) in 2001. Prize: $10,000 and a bronze statue.

Fiction	*Europe Central* by William T. Vollmann
Nonfiction	*The Year of Magical Thinking* by Joan Didion
Poetry	*Migration: New and Selected Poems*
	by W.S. Merwin

Frost Medal

Awarded annually since 1930 by the Poetry Society of America for distinguished lifetime service to American poetry.
Marie Ponsot

Governor General's Literary Awards

Canada's premier literary awards. Prizes are given in 14 categories altogether: Fiction, Poetry, Drama, Translation, Nonfiction, and Children's Literature (Text and Illustration), each in English and French. Established in 1937. Prize: Can$15,000.

Fiction (English)	*A Perfect Night to Go to China* by David Gilmour
Fiction (French)	*Hotaru* by Aki Shimazaki
Poetry (English)	*Processional* by Anne Compton
Poetry (French)	*Vingtièmes siècles* by Jean-Marc Desgent

Griffin Poetry Prize

Established in 2001 and administered by the Griffin Trust for Excellence in Poetry, the award honours first-edition books of poetry published during the preceding year. Prize: Can$40,000 each for the two awards.

Canadian Award	*Short Journey Upriver Toward Ōishida* by Roo Borson
International Award	*Selected Poems: 1963–2003* by Charles Simic (U.S.)

Büchner Prize

Georg-Büchner-Preis. Awarded for a body of literary work in the German language. First awarded in 1923; now administered by the German Academy for Language and Literature. Prize: €40,000.
Brigitte Kronauer (Germany)

Hooft Prize

P.C. Hooftprijs. The Dutch national prize for literature, established in 1947. Prize: €60,000.
Frédéric Bastet

Nordic Council Literature Prize

Established in 1961. Selections are made by a 10-member jury from among original works first written in Danish, Norwegian, or Swedish during the past two years or in other Nordic languages (Finnish, Faroese, Sami, etc.) during the past four years. Prize: DKr 350,000.
Skugga-Baldur by Sjón (Sigurjón Birgir Sigurðsson) (Iceland)

Prix Goncourt

Prix de l'Académie Goncourt. First awarded in 1903 from the estate of French literary figure Edmond Huot de Goncourt, to memorialize him and his brother, Jules. Prize: €10.
Trois jours chez ma mère by François Weyergans

Prix Femina

Established in 1904. The awards for works "of imagination" are announced by an all-women jury in the categories of French fiction, fiction in translation, and nonfiction. Announced in November together with the Prix Médicis. Prize: Not stated (earlier the award was F 5,000 [about €690]).

French Fiction	*Asiles de fous* by Régis Jauffret

Cervantes Prize for Hispanic Literature

Premio Cervantes. Established in 1976 and awarded for a body of work in the Spanish language. Announced in December and awarded the following April. Prize: €90,000.
Sergio Pitol (Mexico)

Planeta Prize

Premio Planeta de Novela. Established in 1951 by the Planeta Publishing House for the best unpublished original novel in Spanish. Awarded in Barcelona in October. Prize: €600,000 and publication by Planeta.
Pasiones romanas by Maria de la Pau Janer

Camões Prize

Premio Luis da Camões da Literatura. Established in 1988 by the governments of Portugal and Brazil to honour a "representatative" author writing in the Portuguese language. Prize: €100,000.
Lygia Fagundes Telles (Brazil)

Russian Booker Prize

Awarded since 1992, the Russian Booker Prize has sometimes carried the names of various sponsors—e.g., Smirnoff in 1997–2001. In 2004 it was underwritten by the Open Russia Charitable Organization and called the Booker/Open Russia Literary Prize. Awards: $15,000 for the winner; $1,000 for each finalist.
Bez puti-sleda ("Neither Hide nor Hair") by Denis Gutsko

Naguib Mahfouz Medal for Literature

Established in 1996 and awarded for the best contemporary novel published in Arabic. The winning work is translated into English and published in Cairo, London, and New York. Prize: $1,000 and a silver medal.
Laylat 'urs ("Wedding Night") by Yusuf Abu Rayyah (Egypt)

Jun'ichirō Tanizaki Prize

Tanizaki Jun'ichirō Shō. Established in 1965 to honour the memory of novelist Jun'ichirō Tanizaki. Awarded annually to a Japanese author for an exemplary literary work. Prize: ¥1,000,000 and a trophy.
Kō Machida for Kokuhaku ("Confession") and Eimi Yamada for Fūmi zekka ("Superb Flavours")

Ryūnosuke Akutagawa Prize

Akutagawa Ryūnosuke Shō. Established in 1935 and now sponsored by the Association for the Promotion of Japanese Literature, the prize is awarded in January and June for the best serious work of fiction by a promising new Japanese writer published in a magazine or journal. Prize: ¥1,000,000 and a commemorative gift.
"Gurando finaare" ("Grand Finale") by Abe Kazushige (132nd prize)
"Tsuchi no naka no kodomo" ("A Child Buried in the Earth") by Fuminori Nakamura (133rd prize)

Mao Dun Literary Award

Established in 1981 to honour contemporary Chinese novels and named after novelist Shen Yanbing (1896-1981), whose nom de plume was Mao Dun; awarded every five years. The latest awards were announced in April 2005.
Zhang Juzheng ("Chang Chü-cheng") by Xiong Zhaozheng
Wuzi ("Without Words") by Zhang Jie
Lishi de tiankong ("The Sky of History") by Xu Guixiang
Dong cang ji ("Hidden Away in the East") by Zong Pu
Yingxiong shidai ("The Era of Heroes") by Liu Jianwei

(continued from page 222)

Noah refuses to take them aboard, in the name of fulfilling God's design, the muck, the parasites, the lack of food."

A battle over intellectual property was launched when 15 eminent literary figures banded together to stem the flow of writers' archives to universities in the U.S. The group, which included Poet Laureate Andrew Motion and biographer Michael Holroyd, called for tax breaks and government funding to assist British universities in competing more effectively with their wealthier American counterparts. Salman Rushdie, Smith, and Ishiguro were among the British writers said to have been recently approached by American institutions for their papers. Motion stated, "This is about our cultural heritage as well as the obvious research opportunities."

Lest anyone doubt the value of culture in the modern world, popular intellectual John Carey produced *What Good Are the Arts?* The second half of the book puts "The Case for Literature" as an art form superior to any other because it is capable of criticism, reasoning, and moralizing. "Literature does not make you a better person, though it may help you to criticize what you are. But it enlarges your mind and it gives you thoughts, words and rhythms that will last you for life."

Deaths during the year include those of biographer Humphrey William Bouverie Carpenter, novelist and editor Alice Thomas Ellis, playwright Christopher Fry, children's author Helen Cresswell, and Postmodern author John Fowles. (See OBITUARIES.)

(CAROL PEAKER)

United States. The death on April 5, 2005, of Saul Bellow (see OBITUARIES), one of the giants of modern American literature, precipitated accolades by Herbert Gold and Philip Roth, among many others. For half a century Bellow had stood at the forefront of American letters and set the highest standard for 20th-century American prose and serious thought about life and culture in the U.S.

Roth himself was singled out during the year as a major living American writer; he became one of three writers (Eudora Welty and Bellow were the others) whose work was published during his or her lifetime in the admirable Library of America series—the U.S. version of France's "Pléiade" editions. Two volumes of Roth's work—which included short stories, his first novel, *Letting Go*, his still-audacious 1969 novel

Portnoy's Complaint, and other early work—appeared between the covers of the distinctive Library of America binding.

Far and away the best new novel of the year came in the fall when E.L. Doctorow published *The March*, his fictionalized version of Civil War Gen. William Tecumseh Sherman's 1864 march across the South.

And, as they watched, the brown cloud took on a reddish cast. It moved forward, thin as a hatchet blade in front and then widening like the furrow from the plow. It was moving across the sky to the south of them. When the sound of this cloud reached them, it was like nothing they had ever heard in their lives. It was not fearsomely heaven-made, like thunder or lightning or howling wind, but something felt through their feet, a resonance, as if the earth was humming. . . .The symphonious clamor was everywhere, filling the sky like the cloud of red dust that arrowed past them to the south and left the sky dim, it was the great processional of the Union armies, but of no more substance than an army of ghosts.

John Irving used his own childhood and adolescent experience of sexual transgressions as the basis for his weighty new novel *Until I Find You*, the story of a Hollywood actor in search of the father who abandoned him. California octogenarian Oakley Hall issued the entertaining *Ambrose Bierce and the Ace of Shoots*. Jim Harrison delivered to his faithful following of readers another trio of novellas, under the title *The Summer He Didn't Die*. Mary Gordon's novel *Pearl* featured a mother-daughter struggle, and Francine Prose drew a portrait of an American neo-Nazi in *A Changed Man*.

Paul Theroux carried readers into the Amazon jungle in *Blinding Light*, and Michael Cunningham, winner of the 1999 Pulitzer Prize for *The Hours*, straddled New York City's past and future in *Specimen Days*; neither book met with complete acclaim, however. Rick Moody's *The Diviners*, his first novel in seven years, worked as an uproarious send-up of the world of television and film, though it did not win the credit it deserved. Although another decidedly experimental work, *Europe Central* by William T. Vollmann, an 811-page novel about the rise of Nazism and the Russian front, did not garner

© Jerry Bauer

Veteran novelist E.L. Doctorow scored again in 2005 with The March.

much initial praise, it won the National Book Award for Fiction.

In his much-praised novel *The Hummingbird's Daughter*, Luis Alberto Urrea beautifully combined family and Mexican history.

Mexico was too big. It had too many colors. It was noisier than anyone could have imagined, and the voice of the Atlantic was different from the voice of the Pacific. . . . The east was a swoon of green, a thick-aired smell of ripe fruit and flowers and dead pigs and salt and sweat and mud, while the west was a riot of purple. Pyramids rose between llanos of dust and among turgid jungles. Snakes as long as country roads swam tame beside canoes. Volcanoes wore hats of snow. Cactus forests grew taller than trees. Shamans ate mushrooms and flew.

David Anthony Durham went all the way back to the Punic Wars for his successful novel *Pride of Carthage*, the story of Hannibal and his civilization. *The German Officer's Boy* by Harlan Greene used the Third Reich as the background for a story of thwarted sexuality and corruption. New York City and the construction of the Empire State Building put its special stamp on Thomas Kelly's *Empire Rising*.

A number of authors borrowed everyday themes for their works. In his second novel, *Drives like a Dream*, Porter Shreve, the author of *The Obituary Writer*, sprinkled auto-industry gossip in a story about a woman's quest to lure her grown children home. Jonathan Safran Foer's *Extremely Loud & Incredibly Close* took its cue from the Sept. 11, 2001, terrorist attack in New York City. In the background of *Wounded*, Percival Everett's new novel, there is a hate crime taken almost directly out of the newspaper headlines. Marc Estrin's quirky coming-of-age novel, *The Education of Arnold Hitler*, chronicled the life of the protagonist as he moves from a Texas high school fraught with racial tensions to antiwar demonstrations at Harvard University to encounters with Al Gore and Leonard Bernstein, among others, in a quest for meaning.

Mother of Sorrows by Richard McCann drew on personal history. Nancy Rawles's *My Jim* played off traditional fiction and told the story of the escaped slave Jim, a character from Mark Twain's *The Adventures of Huckleberry Finn*. Among numerous first novels there were a number of standouts: *Music of the Mill* by Luis J. Rodriguez, *The Coast of Akron* by Adrienne Miller, and *The Lake, the River & the Other Lake* by Steve Amick.

It was a good year for short-story offerings. James Salter, one of the few reigning American masters of short fiction, published *Last Night*, a new collection of short stories, in which he melded sharp observation with lyric intensity in the service of deep characterization. Several other elder statesman published short-story collections, including San Francisco octogenarian Leo Litwak with *Nobody's Baby and Other Stories* and Chicago craftsman Richard Stern with his collection of short fiction under the title *Almonds to Zhoof*. Ann Beattie and Roxana Robinson, both in the middle of their careers, issued new collections, *Follies* and *A Perfect Stranger and Other Stories*, respectively. John Edgar Wideman signed in with *God's Gym*, Amy Hempel with *The Dog of the Marriage*, and Edith Pearlman with *How to Fall*. New collections also came from Florida writer John Dufresne (*Johnny Too Bad*) and New York writer Jay Neugeboren (*News from the New American Diaspora and Other Tales of Exile*), and there was some experimental new work from National Book Award nominee Christine Schutt (*A Day, a Night, Another Day, Summer*).

A number of younger writers came out with first or second books, including Daniel Alarcón (*War by Candlelight*), Elizabeth McKenzie (*Stop That Girl*), William Henry Lewis (*I Got Somebody in Staunton*), Judy Budnitz (*Nice Big American Baby*), and Thomas McConnell (*A Picture Book of Hell and Other Landscapes*). Perhaps the most extraordinary debut of the year was that of Chinese émigré and California resident Yiyun Li, whose collection of

stories titled *A Thousand Years of Good Prayers* was set in both modern China and the contemporary U.S. The book drew numerous laudatory reviews.

The year in nonfiction prose had a number of highlights, beginning with Joan Didion's starkly told and remarkably moving *The Year of Magical Thinking*, her 2005 National Book Award-winning memoir of life in the wake of the death in 2003 of her husband, novelist John Gregory Dunne. Novelist Kurt Vonnegut published a group of brief contrarian essays under the title *A Man Without a Country*. Jonathan Harr's *The Lost Painting* garnered great attention with a beautifully turned narrative about a quest for a lost Caravaggio: "The Englishman moves in a slow but deliberate shuffle, knees slightly bent and feet splayed, as he crosses the piazza, heading in the direction of a restaurant named Da Fortunato." Harr's book reads like a novel and wears rather lightly its scholarship about the world of art history and the restoration of masterpieces. Award winner Dava Sobel attracted attention for her delightful prose in the treatment of the bodies in the solar system in *The Planets*.

Pulitzer Prize-winning novelist Jane Smiley turned to casual literary criticism in *13 Ways of Looking at the Novel*. Vietnam War veteran and novelist Larry Heinemann wrote in *Black Virgin Mountain* of his return to the sites in Vietnam that had haunted him. Novelist Howard Norman wrote a slender, delicate tribute to a long-lost friendship in *In Fond Remembrance of Me*, and in

God's Gym, *a collection of stories, won attention for the artistry of author John Edgar Wideman.*

© Jerry Bauer

The Language of Baklava fiction writer Diana Abu-Jaber turned to childhood as her subject (*see* Sidebar, page 237). Craig Lesley's *Burning Fence: A Western Memoir of Fatherhood* was his take on that subject. *The Coldest Winter: A Stringer in Liberated Europe* by Paula Fox focused on her adventures in Europe just after the end of World War II.

Harry Mathews spoofed the genre of memoir and politics in *My Life in CIA*. In *Uncensored: Views & (Re)views*, prodigious and celebrated novelist Joyce Carol Oates showed off a fascinating miscellany of recent work. Meanwhile, Pulitzer Prize-winning literary critic Michael Dirda showcased his work in *Bound to Please*.

Efforts at formal literary biography were masterly in the case of Andrew Delbanco's *Melville* and Lewis M. Dabney's *Edmund Wilson: A Life in Literature*. Midwestern critic and scholar Barbara Burkhardt won accolades for *William Maxwell: A Literary Life*. Former poet laureate Robert Pinsky wrestled with biblical scholarship and received much praise for *The Life of David*, his study of King David. Independent scholar Megan Marshall proved 20 years of work worthwhile in *The Peabody Sisters: Three Women Who Ignited American Romanticism*.

Other literary biographies that merited attention were Sherill Tippins's *February House*—a work that focused on the little community formed in Brooklyn in 1940 by W.H. Auden, Paul Bowles, Carson McCullers, and Gypsy Rose Lee—as well as novelist Jerome Charyn's *Savage Shorthand: The Life and Death of Isaac Babel*.

Other biographies of note included *Jean-Jacques Rousseau: Restless Genius* by Leo Damrosch, *American Prometheus: The Triumph and Tragedy of J. Robert Oppenheimer* by Kai Bird and Martin J. Sherwin, *Stepin Fetchit: The Life and Times of Lincoln Perry* by Mel Watkins, *Andrew Jackson: His Life and Times* by H.W. Brands, and *The River of Doubt: Theodore Roosevelt's Darkest Journey* by Candice Millard.

Also noteworthy in nonfiction were Peter L. Bernstein's *Wedding of the Waters: The Erie Canal and the Making of a Great Nation*, James Reston, Jr.'s *Dogs of God: Columbus, the Inquisition, and the Defeat of the Moors*, Edward G. Lengel's *General George Washington: A Military Life*, Sean Wilentz's *Andrew Jackson*, historian John Hope Franklin's autobiographical *Mirror to America*, and A. Roger Ekirch's *At Day's Close: Night in Times Past*.

The late author Jane Kenyon had her *Collected Poems* published during the year ("I got out of bed / on two strong legs. / It might have been / otherwise"); Robert Bly offered *My Sentence Was a Thousand Years of Joy* ("It is not yet dawn, and the sitar is playing. / Where are the footsteps that were so clear yesterday?"); and W.S. Merwin signed in with *Migration: New & Selected Poems*. Other books of verse included Lorna Dee Cervantes' *Drive: The First Quartet*, Charles Simic's *My Noiseless Entourage*, and two collections by Lawrence Joseph (*Into It* and *Codes, Precepts, Biases, and Taboos: Poems 1973–1993*). Also appearing were MacArthur Fellowship winner Campbell McGrath's *Pax Atomica* (2004), Kevin Young's *Black Maria* ("He loves me slow / as gin, then's out / light-switch quick"), and *A Wild Perfection: The Selected Letters of James Wright*, edited by Anne Wright and Saundra Maley. "Maud went to college. / Sadie stayed at home. / Sadie scraped life / With a fine-tooth comb": the voice of the late Gwendolyn Brooks took on new strength as the Library of America's American Poets Project issued *The Essential Gwendolyn Brooks*, edited by Elizabeth Alexander.

Poet Laureate Ted Kooser wrote *The Poetry Home Repair Manual*, a textbook on the writing of poems. His book seemed part of a burgeoning new subgenre, the writing-instruction memoir. Other works in that vein included *Before We Get Started: A Practical Memoir of the Writer's Life* by Bret Lott and *From Where You Dream: The Process of Writing Fiction* by Robert Olen Butler.

The 2005 Pulitzer Prizes were awarded for works that appeared in 2004. The Pulitzer for fiction was awarded to Marilynne Robinson's *Gilead*, and the history prize went to David Hackett Fischer for *Washington's Crossing*. The Pulitzer biography winners were Mark Stevens and Annalyn Swan for *De Kooning: An American Master*. Kooser took the Pulitzer for poetry for *Delights & Shadows*. Merwin won the National Book Award for poetry. Ha Jin, winner in 2000 of the PEN/Faulkner Award for fiction for his novel *Waiting*, collected the prize for a second time—for his novel *War Trash*.

Besides the deaths of Bellow, historian Shelby Foote, poet Richard Eberhart, and authors Mary Lee Settle, Frank Conroy, Judith Rossner, Larry Collins, and Andrea Rita Dworkin (*see* OBITUARIES), other losses in American arts and letters included those of poet

Philip Lamantia, author Max Steele, and screenwriter and biographer Gavin Lambert, best known for his novel *Inside Daisy Clover* (1963) and its screenplay. (ALAN CHEUSE)

Canada. The past was present, sometimes forcefully, sometimes stealthily, in many Canadian novels in 2005. Joseph Boyden's *Three Day Road* wielded the horrors of World War I like an oyster knife, opening up prevailing myths for examination. Similarly, Ethiopia's violence-torn history was evident at every turn in Camilla Gibb's *Sweetness in the Belly*. A father's mysterious return to Vietnam 30 years after the Vietnam War led his daughter and son to follow in search of him in David Bergen's *The Time in Between*. Edeet Ravel's *A Wall of Light* showed what happens when a family's most dangerous and treasured secrets are dragged into the open, and the repressed histories of three women affected by one man's death were relentlessly uncovered in Joan Barfoot's *Luck*.

Undoing the past was the theme of Margaret Atwood's *The Penelopiad*, which retold the Greek myth of Odysseus from the perspective of his wife, Penelope. Victorian London was the setting for Audrey Thomas's *Tattycoram*, in which Charles Dickens played a pivotal role, and 19th-century Ontario formed the backdrop of Jane Urquhart's *A Map of Glass*.

The geography of Newfoundland loomed large in three novels: Lisa Moore's *Alligator*, a study of class and family lines fractured on the edges of hardened emotions; Donna Morrissey's *Sylvanus Now*, set in an outport village

Ontario writer Jane Urquhart's partly historical novel A Map of Glass *was one of 2005's top sellers.*

© Jerry Bauer

in the 1950s; and Michael Crummey's *The Wreckage*, in which long-divided lovers, meeting again by chance, strive to bridge their divergent lives.

Caribbean islands were the setting for Shanti Mootoo's story of fate-denied lovers in *He Drown She in the Sea*, Neil Bissoondath's exploration of impossible choices in *The Unyielding Clamour of the Night*, and Rabindranath Maharaj's dissection of independence, personal and political, in *A Perfect Pledge*. Leon Rooke's *The Beautiful Wife* romped from the Philippines to Winnipeg.

Novels situated in contemporary Canada included two set in Toronto—Dionne Brand's *What We All Long For*, about a Vietnamese refugee family, and David Gilmour's Governor General's Literary Award-winning book for fiction *A Perfect Night to Go to China*, in which a father searches for the child he lost through his own selfishness. Andrew Pyper's *The Wildfire Season* featured a pyromaniac and a wounded grizzly wreaking their particular forms of havoc in the Yukon. Sandra Birdsell's *Children of the Day* covered a single day in a small Manitoba town, where children are left to fend for themselves while their mother spends most of the day in bed; and Golda Fried's *Nellcott Is My Darling* depicted a young McGill University student's sweetly cruel dilemma—she is afraid to lose her virginity and afraid not to.

An ironic humour ran through several collections of short stories, from the laid-back realism of Thomas King's *A Short History of Indians in Canada* to Aaron Bushkowsky's *The Vanishing Man*, in which encounters in the contemporary world come to ambivalent, inconclusive ends, to Matthew Kneale's sardonic versions of karma in *Small Crimes in an Age of Abundance*.

A more somber note was struck in the sad lives exposed in Charlotte Gill's *Ladykiller* and in the horrific experiences of Hungarian exiles in Canada presented in Tamas Dobozy's *Last Notes, and Other Stories*. Vivette J. Kady's stories in *Most Wanted* were reminiscent of post-office bulletin boards that advertised the painful peccadilloes of domestic desperadoes. In *The Far Away Home*, Marci Denesiuk's characters displayed a gritty resilience despite the many disappointments in their lives.

Poets ranged in mood and style from the dour visions expressed in Paul Vermeersch's *Between the Walls* and Evelyn Lau's grim, lyrical conflicts of sex and selfhood in *Treble* to the adept playfulness of bill bissett's *northern wild roses:*

deth interrupts th dansing and Leon Rooke's *Hot Poppies*, which pushed the boundaries between illusion and stark reality, and to the silences explored in Jan Zwicky's *Thirty-Seven Small Songs & Thirteen Silences* and in Anne Compton's *Processional*, which won the Governor General's Literary Award for Poetry. Lorna Crozier sharpened her observations of nature, wild and human, in *Whetstone;* Barry Dempster provided sometimes irreverent musings on loss, illusion, and illness in *The Burning Alphabet;* and Olive Senior offered subtle graces in *Over the Roofs of the World.*

Water and music formed the matrix for the musings in Ross Leckie's *Gravity's Plumb Line* and, in a different form, in Robert Hilles's *Calling the Wild,* which harkened back to the days of true wilderness. In *Little Theatres* Erin Mouré deftly directed language like actors on the page's small, revealing stage.　　　(ELIZABETH RHETT WOODS)

Other Literature in English. English-language writing from sub-Saharan Africa, Australia, and New Zealand was represented in 2005 by a wide range of authors—literary novices, experienced writers, and Nobelists.

Africa provided its usual fare of outstanding works, including much-anticipated novels by two Nobel laureates in literature from South Africa. Nadine Gordimer, the 1991 Nobelist, weighed in with *Get a Life,* the story of a South African ecologist who, after receiving thyroid treatment, becomes radioactive to others; and J.M. Coetzee, the 2003 Nobel winner, explored ideas, the power of literature, and the theme of displacement in *Slow Man.* Nigerian Wole Soyinka, Africa's first recipient of the Nobel Prize for Literature (1986) and the continent's most prominent dramatist, made the news when his first and perhaps most famous play, *The Lion and the Jewel* (1963), was performed at the Barbican Theatre in London. His countryman S.A. Afolabi won the sixth Caine Prize for African Writing for his short story "Monday Morning," which first appeared in 2004 in the journal *Wasafiri.* Short-listed for the award were Doreen Baingana (Uganda), Jamal Mahjoub (The Sudan), Muthal Naidoo (South Africa), and Ike Okonta (Nigeria). A 20-year-old student at the University of Cambridge, Nigerian-born Helen Oyeyemi, who already had two plays to her credit, made her debut as a novelist to critical acclaim with *The Icarus Girl.* The story was of a mixed-race youth who confronts her double, ghosts, and

© Jerry Bauer

Nadine Gordimer, winner of the 1991 Nobel Prize for Literature, offered a new book in 2005, Get a Life.

confusion growing up between cultures and races. Nigerian Chimamanda Ngozi Adichie received the grand 2005 Commonwealth Writers' Prize for Best First Book for her novel *Purple Hibiscus* (2003). Ghanaian-born award-winning author William Boyd continued his string of important works with the publication of his first book of nonfiction, *Bamboo.* Poet Kwame Dawes, who was born in Ghana but grew up in Jamaica, teamed with noted illustrator Tom Feelings—who died in 2003—to produce *I Saw Your Face* (2004), a delight for readers young and old.

Noted South African novelist and playwright Zakes Mda presented his fifth novel, *The Whale Caller,* which was set in the Western Cape coastal resort town of Hermanus, whose cliffs attract throngs of whale-watchers. The book, which appeared in paperback in April 2004, found greater acclaim when it was released in hardback by Penguin Books in 2005. Compatriot Lindsey Collen explored a young man's social and sexual coming-of-age in her novel *Boy* (2004), regional winner for Africa of the 2005 Commonwealth Writers' Prize for Best Book.

Prolific and best-selling Australian author Colleen McCullough offered her novel *Angel.* Other fiction from Australians included Janette Turner Hospital's short-story collection *North of Nowhere, South of Loss* (2003; U.S. and U.K. publication 2004) and Tim Winton's *The Turning* (2004), which included 17 overlapping stories. Meanwhile, veteran poet and critic Chris Wallace-Crabbe offered *Read It Again,* an incisive collection of essays on poetry, art, and Australia. Also noteworthy were Fabienne Bayet-Charlton's novel *Watershed* and N.A. Bourke's new fiction, *The True Green of Hope.*

The year was marked by sadness with the death of novelist and short-story writer Yvonne Vera of Zimbabwe as well as that of Australian poet Denis Kevans, whose close identification with Aborigines, Irish political prisoners, environmental causes, and the antiwar movement earned him a reputation as "the people's poet."
　　　(DAVID DRAPER CLARK)

GERMANIC

German. In 2005 the Federation of German Booksellers awarded its German Book Prize, with a first prize of €25,000 (about $30,200), to the Austrian Arno Geiger for his novel *Es geht uns gut,* which, like several other well-received works of 2005, returned to the time-honoured tradition of the German family novel pioneered by Thomas Mann in *Buddenbrooks* (1901). Geiger's novel had as its main character Philipp Erlach, a man in his mid-30s who must come to terms with the difficult legacy of earlier eras, particularly the generation of his two grandfathers, one an opponent of the Nazis and the other a supporter. Meanwhile, Gila Lustiger, a German-language writer living in Paris, published *So sind wir,* an autobiographical novel that dealt with the experiences of Lustiger's father, the writer Arno Lustiger, a Holocaust survivor. In her novel Lustiger explored the effects of this past on the family in the present.

The year also saw the publication of Kerstin Hensel's novel *Falscher Hase,* which focused on the life of an East German policeman, Heini Paffrath, who had moved from West Berlin to East Berlin shortly after the erection of the Berlin Wall in 1961. Paffrath finds solace in East Berlin's lack of freedom, since it protects him from the frightening openness of the life he had experienced in the West. His life collapses not with the fall of the wall in 1989 but with his retirement from the police force more than a decade later. This event forces him to confront a reality he had previously repressed—the reunification of his country and his city. In the novel Hensel demonstrated the way in which geography, history, and psychology are mapped onto each other in Germany's new capital, and she provided a much-needed psychological explanation for some Berliners' willingness to put up with the long-term division of their city.

Andreas Maier published *Kirillow,* a novel whose title was an allusion to a

Austrian Arno Geiger shows off the 2005 German Book Prize of the Federation of German Booksellers, which he received during the Frankfurt Book Fair in October. Geiger was the first recipient of the award.

nihilist character from Fyodor Dostoyevsky's novel *Demons* (1873). *Kirillow,* set in contemporary Frankfurt, focused on the lives of a group of privileged but directionless young people seeking to understand the meaning of life and the structure of the contemporary world. In their search the young people encounter a group of Russian emigrants and a mysterious manuscript by a contemporary Russian thinker.

The 60th anniversary of Germany's defeat in World War II was marked in 2005, and Jochen Missfeldt's novel *Steilküste* was an attempt at reconciliation with part of that unpleasant past. It recounted the story of two young sailors who, even though the war has ended, are executed for desertion from the *Wehrmacht.* Uwe Tellkamp, who had won the Ingeborg Bachmann Prize in 2004 for an unpublished manuscript, published his first novel, *Der Eisvogel,* in 2005. Like Maier's *Kirillow,* it dealt with large political and existential dilemmas, particularly neo-Nazism, right-wing conspiracies, and the apparent emptiness of contemporary consumer life.

Bernd Cailloux's novel *Das Geschäftsjahr 1968/69,* like Missfeldt's *Steilküste,* was an attempt to come to terms with German history—but in this case with the history of Cailloux's so-called 1968 generation, not with the legacy of World War II. This was the late 1960s, a time of cultural and political protest that produced the generation that

dominated German politics during Socialist Gerhard Schröder's chancellorship. Cailloux focused not so much on the politics of this generation as on its cultural rebelliousness, particularly its experimentation with mind-bending drugs, free love, and rock music.

The highly respected Austrian writer Friederike Mayröcker published her novel *Und ich schüttelte einen Liebling,* a poetic and philosophical reflection on her relationship with, and mourning for, the great Austrian poet Ernst Jandl (1925–2000). Like Jandl's writing, Mayröcker's is full of linguistic play. Ulrike Draesner's well-received novel *Spiele,* meanwhile, dealt with yet another aspect of 20th-century German history—the hostage taking at the 1972 Olympic Games in Munich. Draesner's protagonist, Katja, is a photojournalist who must come to terms with terrorism.

Wilhelm Genazino, who had won the Georg Büchner Prize in 2004, published his novel *Die Liebesblödigkeit* in 2005, an exploration of the consciousness of a middle-aged man who, while trying to satisfy two female lovers, must also face the reality of aging and his diminishing sexual energy. Karl-Heinz Ott's novel *Endlich Stille* addressed the problems of men living in a world supposedly dominated by sexually liberated and independent women, while Annette Mingels's *Die Liebe der Matrosen*—a novel in four parts, each narrated by a different character—examined the current state

of relations between the sexes from a variety of perspectives. Finally, Martin Mosebach's novel *Das Beben,* which dealt with tensions between the Western world and an imagined Orient, featured a German protagonist who seeks to escape what he sees as the cultural dead end of contemporary German life by moving to a supposedly idyllic India. (STEPHEN BROCKMANN)

Netherlandic. In 2005 Dutch readers marked the passing of several writers who held unusual positions in the literary landscape: Theun de Vries, an extremely prolific and talented writer; Nel Benschop, the most widely read poet in The Netherlands; and Marten Toonder, a writer known for his innovative graphic novels. Though they represented different literary areas, each was influential. Works by de Vries (b. 1907) and Nel Benschop (b. 1918) reflected their epistemic commitments more explicitly than was usual in 20th-century literature. Though some judged that the religious and political aspects of the texts diminished the artistry of the prose, these works reached broad audiences and were influential. De Vries—an exceptionally prolific novelist-historian and a Marxist who had been imprisoned for his resistance to the Nazi occupation during World War II—focused on the social context of his characters in his prose and poetry rather than on their psychological makeup. He was acclaimed as a master storyteller, but his late repudiation of his membership in the Dutch Communist Party tarnished his standing somewhat. Benschop was known for her religious poetry. While her work was not highly valued by the literary establishment, three million copies of her 15 volumes were sold, which made her the best-read Dutch-language poet of her time. Her poem *In memoriam voor een vriend* was often quoted at funerals. Toonder (b. 1912) had a respected place in the literary canon as well as in the world of comic books. He founded the first cartoon studio in The Netherlands, but he was especially influential because his works were serialized in newspapers for more than 50 years.

Novels that treated religious themes still won major literary prizes. The 2005 Libris Literatuur Prijs went to Willem Jan Otten for *Specht en zoon,* an investigation of creation, incarnation, and knowledge narrated by the canvas rather than its painter. Jan Siebelink received the AKO Literatuur Prijs for *Knielen op een bed violen,* a study of a gentle man's conversion in midlife to a severe Calvinism and its effects on his family and loved ones, and Frédéric Bastet won the P.C. Hooftprijs, the Dutch national prize for literature.

(JOLANDA VANDERWAL TAYLOR)

Danish. Danish writers explored new horizons, melded fantasy and reality, and offered new insights in 2005. The master of the historical novel, Maria Helleberg, continued her abiding interest in history with *Den hellige Knud (Slægten, Bind 1)*, the first in a series on the family founded by Valdemar Dane, Knud (Canute) the Holy's liege. In *Drengen fra dengang* (2004), Janina Katz depicted the tragedy of Ania and Joachim, Holocaust victims with no past and scant hope of ever belonging in Denmark. Janne Teller's *Kattens tramp* (2004) focused on two strangers searching for connection in a Europe torn by war and xenophobia.

Contemporary Denmark also proved excellent subject matter for writers. In *En kvinde med hat*, Inge Eriksen portrayed the experiences of a woman determined to make her mark. Helle Helle's novel *Rødby-Puttgarden* chronicled the lives of two sisters who sold perfume on a ferry and shared mundane commutes that were enlivened only by exotic fragrances. In *En have uden ende*, Christina Hesselholdt reflected on modest lives, the promise of the past, and the problematic present. Merete Pryds Helle's *Det glade vanvid* followed life in an ordinary family and tested the boundaries of self and other. Jens-Martin Eriksen's novel *Forfatteren forsvinder ind i sin roman* described what happens when the roles of the writer-protagonist reverse and reality and fantasy intermingle. Eriksen's second work of 2005, *Dunkle katastrofer*, consisted of three crime stories. In *Grill* Ib Michael focused on a love story set amid the war in Iraq, and Christian Jungersen's novel *Undtagelsen* (2004) was a combination of psycho-thriller, story of workers' solidarity, and essay on evil.

Following her success with *København* (2004), Katrine Marie Guldager told tales about Africa in *Kilimanjaro*. Hanne Marie Svendsen's new novellas in *Skysamleren* revealed the author's delight in her craft and natural surroundings. Bo Green Jensen's poetry collection *Den store epoke* (2004) joined the story of Everyman with social history. Maise Njor and Camilla Stockmann, both young career-and-family women, published their correspondence on ordinary and extraordinary days in *Michael Laudrups tænder*. Jens

Christian Grøndahl's essay *Sihaya ti amo* was a discourse on Danish Finnish painter Seppo Mattinen.

The Booksellers' Golden Laurels Award was given to Jungersen for *Undtagelsen;* Guldager received the Danish Critics' Prize for *København;* and Suzanne Brøgger garnered the Rungstedlund Prize. The recipient of the BG Bank's Annual Literary Prize was Bjarne Reuter for his 2004 novel *Løgnhalsen fra Umbrien;* the other nominees were Helle Helle (*Rødby-Puttgarden*) and Katz (*Drengen fra dengang*).

(LANAE HJORTSVANG ISAACSON)

Norwegian. Several well-established authors published noteworthy novels in 2005. Jan Kjærstad's momentous *Kongen av Europa* probed significant philosophical and existential questions. Lars Saabye Christensen's *Modellen* confronted the sacrifices that a person makes in life in pursuit of his or her art. Roy Jacobsen's *Hoggerne* portrayed a Finnish village fool turned heroic leader during the Russo-Finnish Winter War. Edvard Hoem was nominated for the 2005 Nordic Council Literature Prize for *Mors og fars historie*, which recounted his mother's love for a German World War II soldier and her eventual marriage to Hoem's father.

Øivind Hånes was also nominated for the Nordic Council Literature Prize for his melancholic novel *Pirolene i Benidorm*. Anne B. Ragde's best seller *Eremittkrepsene*, about three grown village brothers, was awarded the Booksellers' Prize. Frode Grytten's well-received *Flytande bjørn* criticized the tabloid press. In *Volvo Lastvagnar* cherished author Erlend Loe mocked the obsession with perfection.

Marita Fossum was awarded the Brage Prize for Fiction for *Forestill deg*, which focused on a middle-aged woman in the aftermath of her mother's death. Other nominees in that category were Linn Ullmann for *Et velsignet barn*, a story about the fears and secrets that can haunt children, and Tore Renberg for *Kompani Orheim*, which also depicted childhood struggles. Merethe Lindstrøm's commended *Barnejegeren* portrayed adults' helplessness in dealing with children's vulnerability.

Among notable debuts were Adelheid Seyfarth's *Fars hus*, about growing up as a mixed-race girl in the small country of Norway before going to Africa to find her father, and Edy Poppy's *Anatomi.Monotoni*, which won the publisher Gyldendal's competition for best new love story as well as attention for its erotic depictions. Olaug Nilssen's

third novel, *Få meg på, for faen*, was applauded for its humour in portraying women's lust and sexual fantasies.

Established author Arne Svingen was awarded the Brage Prize for Youth Literature for *Svart elfenben*, about two wandering friends who travel to war-torn Côte d'Ivoire.

The mystery novel affirmed its popularity with best-selling publications by Jo Nesbø (*Frelseren*) and Unni Lindell (*Orkestergraven*). Graphic novels also became increasingly popular. John Arne Sæterøy ("Jason") won the prize in the Open Category of the Brage Prize: Animation for *La meg vise deg noe . . . .* Internationally renowned dramatist Jon Fosse was awarded the Honorary Brage Prize and the Royal St. Olav's Order. *Flokken og skuggen* by much-admired poet Eldrid Lunden was widely acclaimed. (ANNE G. SABO)

Swedish. The depicting of everyday events with detailed care but underpinning them with a feeling of threat was a recurring characteristic of many Swedish novels in 2005. Reasons to reflect on Swedish society from an estranged point of view were often presented in novels concerned with illness and crime. In John Ajvide Lindqvist's *Hanteringen av odöda*, estrangement is turned into horror—a well-balanced mix of realism and shock—when a strange weather phenomenon over Stockholm calls all the newly dead back to life. In Ulf Eriksson's *Varelser av glas*, the theme was less explicitly demonstrated through a mysterious tendency among certain people to break their legs. In Klas Östergren's *Gangsters*, the long-expected sequel to *Gentlemen*, the novel that made his name in 1980, threat is turned into pure narrative delight, and the author is free to elaborate upon an intrigue involving a never-explained dark centre of illusion and disillusion.

Ethnic estrangement in sitcom-inspired depictions of social relations was a technique successfully used in first novels by the ethnic Pole Zbigniew Kuklartz in *Hjälp jag heter Zbigniew* and Iranian-born Marjaneh Bakhtiari in *Kalla det vad fan du vill*. In Bakhtiari's novel the Swedish way of showing thankfulness causes problems. (See *Arabic Literature:* Sidebar, below.) One can see why when reading *Leendet*, Magnus Florin's skillfully revealing short-fiction exploration of the Swedes' unwillingness to owe a debt of gratitude to anyone.

Gender estrangement from the female point of view was another common motif. Male authors including Stewe Claeson in *De tiotusen tingen* and Mats Kolmisoppi in *Ryttlarna* explored this theme, as did several women. Ann-Marie Ljungberg's *Simone de Beauvoirs hjärta* told the story of a group of well-educated but marginalized single mothers, while Eva Adolfsson's hero in *Förvandling* was a pregnant woman wandering the streets of her small town as a lone seeker of existential meaning. The August Prize went to Monika Fagerholm for *Den amerikanska flickan*, which dealt with friendship between girls. In her grand, well-researched *Mästarens dröm* Carola Hansson told a story of twin sisters and their total isolation from everything while working as missionaries in China in the 1920s and '30s—a fascinating investigation into the Western mind completely at a loss in the East and a novel for anyone interested in history or ethics. (IMMI LUNDIN)

FRENCH

France. France's fear of literary decline, already exacerbated in 2005 by *Harry Potter*'s and *The Da Vinci Code*'s domination of best-seller lists, took a blow from within with the publication of *Harcèlement littéraire*, in which the writer Richard Millet, interviewed by two doting critics, savaged contemporary French literature as a wasteland devoid of style, theme, and interest. Millet named names, specifying why his contemporaries were failures as writers; the "literature business," as he put it, in its rush to sell the ever more numerous (633 in 2005) titles published at the *rentrée littéraire*, the mass marketing of books in September, had lowered standards, favouring rubbish that would sell over art. For Millet the dumbing down of culture had brought about the destruction of grammar, syntax, and style as "authors"—not to be confused with the more lofty "writers," among whom Millet counted himself—produced more and more drivel.

Even the one bona fide literary sensation of 2005 brought grist to Millet's mill. Michel Houellebecq, the most celebrated contemporary French author but one whom Millet had specifically named as short on style though long on showmanship, published *La Possibilité d'une île* in a media-frenzied shock release, without the usual prepublication fanfare. Despite its meteoric rise through the best-seller lists and its immediate purchase by American publishing houses—sure signs to Millet of literary worthlessness—even detractors could not deny the appeal of this long-awaited novel, in which Daniel1, a self-loathing comic who pops pills to avoid the dehumanization of modern life and his own miserable emptiness, falls in with a sect that promises to clone him. Two thousand years from the present, his clones Daniel24 and Daniel25—from whom all destructive emotions, including love, have been removed—read their "ancestor's" memoirs, discovering with mystification his sentimental torments.

Millet's attack centred on style, but many felt that France's international literary decline was due rather to its relentless bleakness, known as *déprimisme*, and to the trend toward navel-gazing novelizations of authors' lives, known as *autobiofictions*, whose hold on French literature seemed only to tighten with time, despite the growing sense of tedium with which they were met. During the year three established novelists published autobiofictions instead of novels. One of the previous decade's most celebrated writers, Marie NDiaye, published *Autoportrait en vert*, her musings on women who have been important in her life and who are all mysteriously connected by the leitmotif of greenness. Patrick Chamoiseau, one of the leading writers of the Antilles' *Créolité* movement, wrote *À bout d'enfance*, the story of his own adolescent sexual awakening. The book received much criticism for its author's seeming fascination with his genitalia. Finally, Patrick Modiano, one of the most important writers of the 1970s and '80s, published an autobiofiction, by no means his first, titled *Un pedigree*, which detailed the author's miserable childhood as his parents abandoned him in a series of boarding schools.

Yet amid the depression and self-fascination, there were also breaks in the gloom, novels showing that beneath the crust there was still life in French literature. The ever-original Eric Chevillard published an ironic take on the traditional dream of exoticism with *Oreille rouge*, in which an author travels to Mali, hoping to capture Africa in literature, only to find that in the end he has understood nothing at all. Eric Nonn, too, explored the world outside France in *Museum*, in which a man comes to grips with his sad childhood and cruel mother as he travels through Cambodia with an Italian woman, herself still reeling from a childhood spent with an abusive father. Together they learn to forgive in a land of genocide.

Patrick Rambaud, best known for his novelizations of the Napoleonic wars, left epic behind for humour and irony with his new novel, *L'Idiot du village*, in which a man from 1995 suddenly and inexplicably finds himself transported to 1953 Paris, the time of his childhood, only to find that the good old days were not as good as nostalgia would have them.

The strangest novel of note was Maurice G. Dantec's fascist-leaning *Cosmos Incorporated*, in which a mechanically enhanced contract killer in a postapocalyptic future begins to wonder if he himself is not the last hope for freedom and creation in a world where humans have willingly enslaved themselves to machines as machines have become more human.

In 2005 two of the most prestigious literary prizes crowned autobiofictions. François Weyergans won the Prix Goncourt for his *Trois jours chez ma mère*, in which the author's alter ego, François Weyergraf, suffering from writer's block, tries in vain to write the very novel we are reading, an homage to his mother that would serve as a pendant to his 1997 homage to his father, *Franz et François*. The Prix Renaudot went to Algerian French Nina Bouraoui's *Mes mauvaises pensées*, in which the author, thinly veiled as the narrator, confesses her lesbianism to her psychoanalyst. The two other top prizes were awarded to nonautobiofictional novels. The Prix Femina went to Régis Jauffret for *Asiles de fous*, a sarcastically humorous novel in which a romantic breakup is told through the four contradictory and neurotic points of view of the couple and the man's parents. Jean-Philippe Toussaint won the

Marseille native Régis Jauffret won the 2005 Prix Femina for his mordantly humorous novel Asiles de fous.

Prix Médicis for *Fuir*, the story of a man, caught between lovers and countries, who abandons himself to jet lag and endless travel as he is called back from China to Elba by a series of coincidences that he never quite understands. (VINCENT AURORA)

Canada. Two major public events brought attention to French Canadian literature during 2005. The first was the opening in April of the Grande Bibliothèque, a new public library in Montreal. Unfortunately, in June the exterior decorative-glass panels fell onto the sidewalk, keeping some citizens away. Montreal was also named World Book Capital—a UNESCO designation awarded annually—and this set in motion a large number of public events based on books and reading.

Former hockey coach Jacques Demers shocked the public with his as-told-to story *Jacques Demers: en toutes lettres*, in which he admitted (to author Mario Leclerc) his illiteracy and described the shame associated with this handicap.

The province of Quebec continued to be intensely interested in the life of René Lévesque, its late premier. Pierre Godin issued the fourth and final volume of his biography, *René Lévesque: l'homme brisé*, in which the politician was portrayed as a broken man at the end of his life as a result of his frustrated ambitions.

Notable among literary works was Nicolas Dickner's novel *Nikolski*, which was published by Éditions Alto, a new imprint of Éditions Nota Bene. Popular writer Pan Bouyoucas offered the new work *L'Homme qui voulait boire la mer* and was also recognized for the evocative *Anna pourquoi* (2003), which won the 2005 Prix Littéraire des Collégiens. The Governor General's Literary Awards for French-language writers went to Aki Shimazaki, who won the fiction prize for *Hotaru* (2004), and Jean-Marc Desgent, who captured the poetry prize for *Vingtièmes siècles*. Yvon Rivard, a past recipient of the Grand Prix du Livre de Montréal, in 2005 won a second time, for his novel *Le Siècle de Jeanne*.

A number of writers solidified their reputations. Suzanne Jacob's lyrical novel *Fugueuses* was greeted with great acclaim; poet, essayist, and philosopher Pierre Nepveu published his collection of poems *Le Sens du soleil;* and Victor-Lévy Beaulieu, a writer who specialized in controversy, continued his ways with an attack on his younger peers, whom he accused of being self-centred. He also delivered the fictional *Je m'ennuie*

de Michèle Viroly. Michel Vézina, who had previously worked as a musician and a clown, revisited the road-novel genre with *Asphalte et vodka*.

(DAVID HOMEL)

ITALIAN

Some established trends in the Italian literary scene were maintained in 2005. Detective stories continued to enjoy wide success, as attested in particular by the publication of *Crimini*, an anthology of short stories penned by the most popular authors of the genre, including Carlo Lucarelli, Marcello Fois, and Giorgio Faletti. Andrea Camilleri also confirmed his extraordinary creativity by producing *Privo di titolo*, a historical novel inspired by the accidental killing in 1921 of a young fascist by fellow party members. Historical documents and narrative sections alternate to reconstruct the attempts of the fascists to exploit the murder to their advantage by attributing it to a communist and thereby provide Sicily with a fascist martyr while at the same time getting rid of a political enemy. A secondary story line, skillfully woven into the main plot, deals with Mussolinia, a model city planned by the fascist regime but never brought to completion. Later in the year Camilleri went back to writing detective stories and published *La luna di carta*, a new Inspector Montalbano adventure in which the aging hero is haunted by thoughts of his own mortality; this does not prevent him, of course, from shedding light on yet another mystery.

The year also offered some surprises, such as Claudio Magris's *Alla cieca*. The story begins as 80-year-old Salvatore Cippico (a survivor of both a Nazi concentration camp and the Soviet Gulag) reflects on his life. Soon, however, his voice merges with those of others who, like him, have been disillusioned in their hope for the betterment of humanity. The identity of the narrator of this ambitious and thought-provoking novel shifts as he sails various seas, traveling from Friuli to New Zealand, and crosses several centuries. The voyage of Jason and the Argonauts provides the central metaphor and unifying theme in this epic tale characterized by disenchantment and despair.

Maurizio Maggiani's *Il viaggiatore notturno* (winner of the 2005 Strega Prize) focused on the destruction brought by war. The protagonist is a zoological researcher who is determined to prove that swallows migrate to the middle of

the Sahara. As he waits for the birds' passage, he listens to the stories around him and is haunted by memories of his previous travels. Animals (apart from the swallows, Maggiani tells of a wounded lion and of a very special she-bear) and humans share the same enigmatic qualities in this novel. In particular, mystery seems to surround Amapola, the bear, whose movements the zoologist had tracked years earlier, and Perfetta, a woman who, after having been victim of gratuitous violence during the Bosnian war, leaves the hospital without a word, taking with her a plastic bag containing her belongings.

Sandro Veronesi's *Caos calmo* presented personal tragedy as a means of self-discovery and internal serenity. The protagonist is a successful manager who tries to help his 10-year-old daughter cope with her mother's death; he receives unexpected comfort and guidance from the girl and the world of childhood. Love and loss were also at the centre of Milo De Angelis's *Tema dell'addio*, a collection of powerful poems that earned its author a 2005 Viareggio Prize. A line from one of Osip Mandelshtam's poems provided the title for Elisabetta Rasy's novel *La scienza degli addii*, which centred on the relationship between the Russian poet and his wife, Nadezhda, who preserved his work and memory after his death in the Gulag.

In *Un giorno perfetto*, Melania G. Mazzucco abandoned the historical reconstructions that had brought her success (*Vita* [2003], which dealt with

In 2005 best-selling and prizewinning author Melania G. Mazzucco published a new novel, Un giorno perfetto, *which focused on events and the feelings of nine characters during a single day in her native Rome.*

© Jerry Bauer

early 20th-century Italian immigration to the U.S., won the Strega Prize) to recount an uneventful day in the very recent past. During the 24 hours of May 4, 2001 (and in the 24 chapters that constitute the novel), the stories of nine characters are woven together to present a picture of contemporary life. The city of Rome provides the background to the protagonists' struggle against solitude and their search for meaningful human interaction. In *Il maestro magro*, Gian Antonio Stella followed the protagonist's voyage from Sicily to northern Italy, his attempts to start a school, and his will to succeed against all prejudice in a country that is rediscovering its vitality after the trauma of World War II. The title alludes to his new status as a teacher as well as to his thinness, induced by the meagre compensation typical in his new profession.

Two important cultural figures died in 2005: poet Mario Luzi, who in 2004 had been appointed a lifetime member of the Senate for his extraordinary contributions to Italian culture (*see* Obituaries), and Cesare Cases (born in 1920), a scholar who greatly facilitated Italians' knowledge and understanding of literary critics and philosophers such as Gyorgy Lukacs, Walter Benjamin, Max Horkheimer, and Theodor Adorno.

(LAURA BENEDETTI)

SPANISH

Spain. In 2005, the year of the 400th anniversary of the publication of *Don Quixote*, the literature coming from Spain confirmed once again that pretty much everything had already been said by Miguel de Cervantes in his masterpiece.

Doctor Pasavento, the latest novel by Enrique Vila-Matas, starts as a dissertation about reality and fiction and becomes an inquiry into the writer's obsession, the paradox in the creative mind between vanity and oblivion. The Primavera Prize went to José R. Ovejero's *Las vidas ajenas*, a novel about worldwide commercial exploitation, bribery, the underground world, and the need to escape from a doomed social class.

In *Escribir es vivir* José Luis Sampedro presented a vision of life as he described through personal anecdotes his childhood in Morocco, his years as a young adult in Madrid, and the hardships of the Spanish Civil War. Another book about the Civil War, *Los girasoles ciegos* by Alberto Méndez, who died in late 2004, was awarded the National

Prize for Narrative. Rosa Montero published *Historia del rey transparente*, a novel set in troubled 12th-century France, where Leola, a young countrywoman, disguises herself as a man by dressing in the clothes of a dead soldier in order to protect herself. The Argentines Graciela Montes and Ema Wolf received the Alfaguara Prize for their work *El turno del escriba*, about Marco Polo's journeys. The National Prize for Poetry went to José Corredor Matheos for his book *El don de la ignorancia*, which demonstrated the author's deep immersion in Eastern culture and Buddhist philosophy. The Planeta Prize went to Maria de la Pau Janer for her novel *Pasiones romanas*, a love story, and the Peruvian writer and journalist Jaime Bayly was awarded second place for *Y de repente, un ángel*. The Rómulo Gallegos Prize, one of the most important Latin American awards, was given to the Spaniard Isaac Rosa for his novel *El vano ayer*, about the vicissitudes of a professor during the agitated 1960s in Spain. It described a student's disappearance, which Rosa re-created through the testimonies of the oppressors and the victims of repression. The top Spanish-language literary award, the Cervantes Prize, was awarded to Mexican author Sergio Pitol.

In *La sombra del viento*, a complex narrative with overtones of Poe and Borges, Carlos Ruiz Zafón told a story full of mystery, dark family secrets, tragic loves, revenge, and murder, all set in Barcelona between 1932 and 1966. Almudena Grandes presented

Juan Marsé wrote about nightlife in his newest novel.

© Jerry Bauer

Estaciones de paso, a book of short stories united by one underlying idea: adolescence as the setting of circumstantial experiences, a transitory stage that nonetheless can determine the entire course of a life. Juan Marsé invited readers to enter the nightclub world in *Canciones de amor en Lolita's Club*, where a woman seated at a bar waiting for clients meets a man who has lost everything and whose life is a mystery.

(VERÓNICA ESTEBAN)

Latin America. History and travel—and historical travels—were recurring themes in the best works of Spanish-language literature in Latin America in 2005. *El turno del escriba*, masterfully written by Graciela Montes and Ema Wolf, both from Argentina, received the Alfaguara Prize. The novel dealt with Marco Polo's travels as narrated to the scribe Rustichello de Pisa while the two share a cell in a Genoese prison. The erudite and imaginative Rustichello works as a calligrapher for his captors and during the day writes down what the Venetian explorer has narrated the previous night. The novel revealed the glory and misery of writing and shows the inevitable distance between spoken and written word and between the memories of the narrator and the imagination of the scribe.

The Argentine writer Juan José Saer died in Paris on June 11 before completing *La grande*. The novel was divided into seven journeys, but of the last one Saer was able to write only one sentence; the book, almost 500 pages in length, was published unfinished. It dealt with the obsessions of the narrator, the characters of the province where he was born, and its landscape. Yet another Argentine, Eduardo Belgrano Rawson, published *Rosa de Miami*, a carnivalesque version of the 1961 Bay of Pigs invasion to overthrow the Cuban government. Belgrano Rawson cultivated the grotesque, showing the characters' weakest side and how they acted according to a fixed destiny.

In Mexico the insurrectionist Subcomandante Marcos collaborated with Paco Ignacio Taibo II on *Muertos incómodos: falta lo que falta*, which was first serialized in the Mexico City newspaper *La Jornada*. A great sense of humour and a keen vision of the corruption of power in Mexico dominated this detective story and political satire written with singular linguistic accomplishment.

Margo Glantz published *Historia de una mujer que caminó por la vida con zapatos de diseñador*, a fragmented rewriting of the narrator's obsessions, which return in the person of Nora García, a fictitious double of the Mexican author. Mario Bellatin published *Lecciones para una liebre muerta* and reissued *La escuela del dolor humano de Sechuán* (2001). The former work was a narrative constructed with intertwining fragments, featuring some real and some fictitious characters and reading like a rewriting of the author's earlier works. Both Glanz and Bellatin cultivated a half-hearted humour, a light surrealism, and a measure of frivolity.

In *Mil y una muertes* (2004), Nicaraguan writer Sergio Ramírez told how he came to know the life of a unique person, his compatriot the photographer Castellón, who traveled through Europe at the end of the 19th century. The novel alternated between the narrator's present and the past of the Castellones, father and son, and the personages they met, including Frederick I, Napoleon III, Frédéric Chopin, George Sand, and Ruben Darío. The novel is not only a delirious family saga but a comprehensive chronicle of the small Central American country where Ramírez once served as vice president.

From Gioconda Belli, also a Nicaraguan, came *El pergamino de la seducción*, a novel that explored the author's fascination with the personality of the Spanish queen known as Joan the Mad. The queen's life seems to play counterpoint to that of Lucía, a contemporary character who is seduced by her history professor, a descendent of King Philip the Handsome—Joan's consort. The professor locks up Lucía after having his way with her, which thus duplicates the destiny of Queen Joan. During the year the young and successful Colombian writer Santiago Gamboa published the linear and predictable *El síndrome de Ulises*, a novel whose title referred to the sufferings and psychological problems of exiled and displaced people fighting for survival in a hostile milieu.

Carlos Franz, a Chilean born in Geneva, won the La Nación–Sudamericana Prize for his novel *El desierto*, which dealt with the return to Chile of a political exile and the trauma of the crimes committed by the Augusto Pinochet regime during her absence. Santiago Roncagliolo, a young Peruvian writer living in Spain, published *Pudor*, a novel that treated familiar themes, with all their grandeur and misery, mostly in a humorous vein.

The Menéndez Pelayo International Prize was awarded in Spain to Uruguayan Mario Benedetti in recognition of his contribution to the Spanish language as a culturally unifying force. The year 2005 was good to Argentine poet Juan Gelman, who was doubly honoured for *País que fue será*. The collection of poems received the Buenos Aires Book Fair Prize as well as Chile's Pablo Neruda Iberoamerican Prize in Poetry. In October Gelman's life work was honoured in Spain with the Queen Sofía Award in Iberoamerican Poetry. The Prince of Asturias Prize for Letters was awarded to Brazilian Nélida Piñón, and the Juan Rulfo Prize went to Spanish-born Mexican poet Tomás Segovia. Chile's University of Talca recognized Argentine Ricardo Piglia with the José Donoso Iberoamerican Prize in Letters for his oeuvre and his stylistic innovations.

(LEDA SCHIAVO)

PORTUGUESE

Portugal. The prolific Vasco Graça Moura—a poet, translator, essayist, novelist, politician (currently serving in the European Parliament), and, in his own words, "man of action"—won the 2005 Fiction Prize of the Association of Portuguese Writers for the novel *Por detrás da magnólia* (2004). The story takes place in the Douro port wine region, through the author's reconstructed and subtly disguised recollection of his aristocratic family and childhood. Also in the realm of well-established fictionists, the most internationally renowned of Portuguese novelists—1998 Nobel Prize winner José Saramago and his literary rival António Lobo Antunes—both published new books in 2005. With his novel *As intermitências da morte*, Saramago once again wrote an allegory, presenting a "what if" fictional world in which death goes on strike. Antunes's *D'este viver aqui neste papel descripto: cartas da guerra* was a collection of the author's vivid letters to his wife, written while he was fighting (1971–73) in the colonial war in Angola.

In May the Camões Prize, the most prominent literary award of the Portuguese-speaking world, went to Brazil's Lygia Fagundes Telles. Although most of her books were collections of short stories, Telles was also recognized for her novels, including *Ciranda de pedra* (1954), *Verão no aquário* (1963), *As meninas* (1973), and *As horas nuas* (1989). The adaptation in 1981 of *Ciranda de pedra* as a television series by the network Globo was highly popular in both Brazil and Portugal.

In 2005 readers marked the death of Eugénio de Andrade (*see* OBITUARIES), the pastoral and musical poet of *As mãos e os frutos* (1948). His influence in contemporary Portuguese poetry and his critical fortune were evaluated in the collection *Ensaios sobre Eugénio de Andrade* (2003), edited by José de Cruz Santos. Alexis Levitin had translated into English some of Andrade's books, including *Memory of Another River* (1988), *Solar Matter* (1995), *The Shadow's Weight* (1996), and *Another Name for Earth* (1997), as well as *Forbidden Words* (2003), a volume of selected poetry. Among the many notable poetry collections in 2005 were surrealist Alexandre O'Neill's *Anos 70—Poemas dispersos* (published posthumously); monarchist (and one of the most important lyric voices since the 1970s) João Miguel Fernandes Jorge's *Invisíveis correntes;* and Manuel António Pina's *Os livros*, which was awarded the 2005 Poetry Prize by the Association of Portuguese Writers.

(VICTOR J. MENDES)

Brazil. Brazil's most successful novel of 2005 was Jô Soares's *Assassinatos na Academia Brasileira de Letras.* In this tale of events in Rio de Janeiro in the 1920s, the author continued his almost obsessive preoccupation with historical detail as a key element of his fiction. Reginaldo Ferreira da Silva, known by his nom de plume Ferréz, published a children's novel called *Amanhecer Esmeralda*, which he described as a work of *literatura marginal*, or "literature for the nonprivileged." The protagonist is a young São Paulo slum dweller whose life is changed when she experiences some small surprises. Paulo Henriques

In 2005 Brazil's Jô Soares, a dramatist and social critic as well as a novelist, had another best seller—his third—with Assassinatos na Academia Brasileira de Letras.

© Jerry Bauer

Britto, the poet and translator into Portuguese of American fiction, published a volume of short stories, *Paraísos artificiais*, with a clear poetic and philosophical bent. While the title of the volume invoked Baudelaire's poetry, the stories showed the linguistic and stylistic inventiveness of a writer who has read widely and integrated a variety of approaches into his own act of writing. Hilda Hilst's (1930–2004) death was noted through the reissue in 2005 of her poetry, including the collection *Poemas malditos, gozosos e devotos*, originally published in 1984, in which the author offered provocative insights into human frailties and views of her personal relationship with God.

Outros escritos, edited by Teresa Montero and Lícia Manzo, brought together miscellanea and heretofore-uncollected works of Clarice Lispector (1925–77). The texts, stories, and interviews, organized according to the writer's life's events, highlighted the enigmatic relationship between her personal life and literary career as a critic of her contemporaries and as a writer and mother plagued by self-doubts. The first volume of *Caio 3D*, titled *O essencial da década de 1970*, gathered the early short fiction and other writings by Caio Fernando Abreu (1948–96), one of the most prolific and prized writers during the 1960s through the 1980s. The writer's strife with his art and his bisexuality, as well as Brazil's existence as a political and cultural entity, was revealed through numerous letters to his family and friends as well as other assorted writings.

As part of an homage to playwright Nelson Rodrigues (1913–80), a major Rio de Janeiro cultural centre celebrated the 25th anniversary of his death with new productions of his plays, including *Anjo negro*, in an updated version directed by his son, Nelson Rodrigues Filho. The distinguished novelist Lygia Fagundes Telles was awarded the Camões Prize, the highest literary honour in the Portuguese-speaking world, for her contributions to literature in Portuguese. The city of Olinda in the northeastern state of Pernambuco, founded in 1537, was awarded the title of the first Brazilian Cultural Capital for the year 2006.

(IRWIN STERN)

RUSSIAN

The year 2005 in Russian literature had both controversy and scandal but also saw the continuing emergence of a new literary generation and the deaths of several leading lights of the generation of the 1960s.

Among already established authors Mikhail Shishkin, winner of the 2000 Russian Booker Prize for *Vzyatiye Izmaila* ("The Taking of Izmail"), garnered the most critical attention with the publication of his latest novel, *Venerin volos* ("Maidenhair"). More autobiographical than *Vzyatiye Izmaila*, *Venerin volos* made use of many of the literary devices employed in the preceding novel, and, overall, the work had less compositional wholeness than the last. Nevertheless, it received excellent notices and was awarded the National Bestseller Prize. The prolific journalist, fiction writer, and poet Dmitry Bykov published three books in rapid succession: a fantasy novel *Evakuator* ("The Evacuator"), a biography of Boris Pasternak, and a collection of his political columns. The poet Vladimir Aleynikov, whose career began in the 1960s avant-garde, published a fictionalized memoir entitled *Pir* ("The Feast"), in which several legendary figures of the late Soviet period appeared, including the writers Sergey Dovlatov and Venedikt Yerofeyev and the artist Anatoly Zveryev. Although Anatoly Nayman's *Kablukov* was a work of fiction, among its secondary figures were Dovlatov and an almost caricatural version of Joseph Brodsky. Inna Lisnyanskaya produced a more conventional memoir of the poet Arseny Tarkovsky titled *Otdelny* ("Separate"). The talented and skillful Oleg Yermakov, renowned for his early work about the Afghanistan war, depicted life among the Russian provincial artistic intelligentsia in his new novel *Kholst* ("The Canvas").

The literary journals *Zvezda* and *Oktyabr* published special issues devoted to young writers. One very promising debut was made by a young author publishing under the humourous pseudonym of Figl-Migl. Her novella, entitled *Myusli* ("Muesli"), stood out for its subtle irony and mastery of literary form, reminiscent of Konstantin Vaginov's works of the 1920s and 1930s. By contrast, the short stories gathered in Lev Usyskin's first book, *Meditsinskaya sestra Anzhela* ("Nurse Angela"), were remarkable for their precise reproduction of contemporary language, attention to detail, and finely crafted plots. Also making names for themselves were younger critics such as Sergey Gedroyts and Viktoriya Pustovaya.

Russia's complex literary reality of 2005 was only marginally reflected in the distribution of literary prizes.

Besides the already-mentioned books of Yermakov and Nayman, the short list for the Russian Booker Prize included Denis Gutsko's *Bez puti-sleda* ("Neither Hide nor Hair"), Boris Yevseyev's *Romanchik* ("A Little Novel"), two books by Roman Solntsev about economic struggle in the metal works of eastern Siberia, *Zolotoe dno* ("The Golden Bottom") and *Minus Lavrikov*, and Yelena Chizhova's *Prestupnitsa* ("The Criminal"), which explored the "Jewish question" in one of Leningrad's research institutes in the 1980s. The choice of these books, in which the level of literary accomplishment in many cases barely exceeded that of journalistic prose, provoked both bewilderment and charges of bias on the jury, which was led by the previous year's Booker Prize laureate, Vasily Aksyonov. The eventual winner was Gutsko; Bykov won the Student Booker Prize. The popular Moscow novelist Aleksandr Kabakov was awarded the Apollon Grigoryev Prize. The Andrey Bely Prizes went to the veteran avant-gardists Yelizaveta Mnatsakanova (poetry), Viktor Sosnora ("special service" to Russian literature), Mikhail Yampolsky (humanities), and Sergey Spirikhin (prose).

Several important figures of the generation of the 1960s died, perhaps marking the end of an era: the prose master Rid Grachyov, whose literary career was cut short by mental illness; the talented poet and prose writer Sergey Volf, who did some of his most important writing later in life; and the poet and singer-songwriter Aleksey Khvostenko, who lived the last decades of his life in Paris.

Perhaps the most significant volume of poetry to be published during the year came from the still youthful but already accomplished Mariya Stepanova, *Fiziologiya i malaya istoriya* ("Physiology and a Little Story"). In St. Petersburg the publisher Platforma put out a flawed but representative anthology of local poetry titled *Stikhi v Peterburge* ("Poems in Petersburg"). The Moscow publisher OGI published an anthology dedicated to the Russian poetic diaspora. Nevertheless, the "imperial" heritage of Russian literature did, somewhat comically, still make itself felt. It was revealed that three Russian poets (including the renowned Yevgeny Reyn) had written a letter to Turkmenistan's Pres. Saparmurad Niyazov requesting that they be permitted to translate his poetic works into Russian. (Press reports suggested that the translators were to be handsomely compensated by a leading

Russian energy company hoping to receive a gas concession). Threatened with expulsion from the Russian PEN Centre, however, the Russian poets were forced to renounce their compromising project.   (VALERY SHUBINSKY)

JEWISH

Hebrew. With a new wave of women writers joining the ranks of Hebrew literature in the late 1980s and the 1990s, motherhood emerged as one of the most pivotal themes in contemporary Hebrew fiction in 2005. The most intriguing novel about motherhood was Avirama Golan's *Ha-'Orvim* ("The Ravens" [2004]), which described every mother as a possible Medea. Motherhood played a major role in the novels of Tseruya Shalev (*Terah,* "Late Family"), Mira Magen (*Parparim ba-geshem,* "Butterflies in the Rain"), Ronit Yedaya (*Shosh*), and Irith Dankner-Kaufmann (*Australia*). The Arab-Israeli conflict was the focus of two best-selling novels: *Yasmin* ("Jasmine") by Eli Amir and *Yonim bi-Trafalgar* ("Pigeons at Trafalgar Square") by Sami Michael. Novels by veteran writers included Nathan Shaham's *Pa'amon be-Kyong'u* ("The Bell in Ch'ongju"), Aharon Appelfeld's *Polin erets yerukah* ("Poland, a Green Country"), Israel Segal's *Ve-khi nahash memit?* ("My Brother's Keeper"), and Alex Epstein's *La-Kahol en darom* ("Blue Has No South"). The title of Dalia Ravikovitch's new collection of short stories, *Ba'ah ve-halkhah* ("Come and Gone") tragically turned out to be a fitting title for the popular poet, who died during the year.

Maya Bejerano collected her poems in *Tedarim* ("Frequencies"), and Aharon Shabtai published his raging political poems in *Semesh, semesh* ("Sun, Oh Sun"). Other notable books of poetry included Ayin Tur-Malka's *Shuvi nafshi li-tekheltekh* ("Go Back My Soul to Your Azure"), Ronny Someck's *Mahteret he-halav* ("The Milk Underground"), Israel Bar-Cohav's *Be-Karov ahavah* ("History of Thirst"), Nurit Zarchi's *Ha-Nefesh hi Afrika* ("The Soul Is Africa"), and Zali Gurevitch's *Zeman Baba* ("Time Baba").

The most important event in literary scholarship was the publication of Yig'al Schwartz's *Mah she-ro'im mi-kan* ("Vantage Point"), which dealt with a pivotal topic in the historiography of modern Hebrew fiction. Malkah Shaked studied the role of the Bible in modern Hebrew poetry (*La-Netsah anagnekh,* "I'll Play You Forever"), and Avner Holtzman collected his articles on contemporary Hebrew fiction in

Works of Israeli author Tseruya Shalev (shown here at a reading in Erfurt, Ger.) were translated into 21 languages.

Mapat derakhim: siporet 'Ivrit ka-yom ("Road Map, Hebrew Narrative Fiction Today").   (AVRAHAM BALABAN)

Yiddish. The notable Yiddish literary events of 2005 included an autobiography, a novel, a bilingual dictionary, and a unique recognition. Barukh Mordekhai Lifshits's *Zikhroynes fun gulag* (2004; "Memoirs of the Gulag") was a chronicle of Lubavitcher Jewish life during the Stalin era. Bukovina-born Aleksander Shpigelblat wrote *Krimeye: an altfrenkishe mayse* ("Krimeve: An Old Frankish Story"), a gripping tale about Transylvanian Jews told through the persona of Itche Meyer. Peter David and Lennart Kerbel collaborated on a pioneering 7,000-word *Jiddisch-Svensk-Jiddisch Ordbok* ("Yiddish-Swedish-Yiddish Dictionary") with a historical essay and a minigrammar.

Bronx poet and ballad singer Beyle Schaechter-Gottesman received a National Heritage fellowship from the National Endowment for the Arts at a September 22 ceremony on Capitol Hill. Her work was described as a "blend of traditional folk idiom and original material" with "a certain quality of naïveté . . . but also an immense sophistication." This was the first time a Yiddish writer had received the nation's highest honour in the folk and traditional arts. Her works included *Stezshkes tsvishn moyern* (1972; "Footpaths amid Stone Walls"), *Sharey* (1980; "Dawn"), *Zumerteg* (1990; "Summer Days"), *Lider* (1995; "Poems"),

Perpl shlengt zikh der veg (2002; "Winding Purple Road"), and *Af di gasn fun der shtot* (2003; "On the Streets of the City," a two-disc CD-ROM). Schaechter-Gottesman was also recognized as a major contributor to the renaissance of klezmer music in the U.S.

While Yiddish-language titles were few in 2005, the third millennium saw the publication of several important volumes of translation and titles about Yiddish literature. Among them were Ken Frieden's *Classic Yiddish Stories of S.Y. Abramovitsh, Sholem Aleichem, and I.L. Peretz* (2004), a collection of fiction by the three authors who laid the foundation for contemporary Yiddish literature with three biographical essays that related their work to the literary and cultural currents of their time, and *Proletpen: America's Rebel Yiddish Poets*, edited by Amelia Glaser and David Weintraub, with an introduction by Dovid Katz, an anthology of 30 American Yiddish poets of the 1920s through the 1950s who were members or fellow travelers in the Communist Party of the United States of America.   (THOMAS E. BIRD)

TURKISH

Growth and controversies enlivened Turkey's literary scene in 2005. Hopes were raised again for a Nobel Prize for Orhan Pamuk (*see* BIOGRAPHIES), whose candidacy, according to the *Manchester Guardian* newspaper, had split the Nobel Committee. At home he was roundly criticized for trying to curry favour in Europe with a statement that

Turkish novelist Orhan Pamuk greets a crowd on December 15, just before the beginning of his trial in Istanbul for a reference he made to mass killings of Armenians and Kurds that took place in Turkey in the early and later 20th century, respectively.

"one million Armenians and 30,000 Kurds were killed in Turkey" early in the 20th century. Later, however, Pamuk won the German Book Trade Peace Prize at the Frankfurt Book Fair as well as the French international Prix Médicis.

One phenomenal success—sales of an unprecedented million copies—was achieved by a 748-page docu-narrative related to the Turkish War of Liberation (1919–22), titled *Şu çılgın Türkler* ("Those Crazy Turks"), compiled by Turgut Özakman. The much-honoured nonagenarian poet Fazıl Hüsnü Dağlarca earned the $100,000 award of the Vehbi Koç Foundation. Former prime minister Bülent Ecevit published his complete poetry under the title *Bir şeyler olacak yarın* ("Things Will Happen Tomorrow"). *Tevfik Fikret ve Haluk gerçeği* ("Tevfik Fikret and the Truth About Haluk") by Orhan Karaveli treated the poet and social critic Tevfik Fikret (1867–1915) and presented new findings about his son, who became a Presbyterian minister in the United States.

Vüs'at O. Bener, a virtuoso of fiction, passed away shortly before he was to be feted as "the author of the year" at the Istanbul Book Fair. A new work by the popular novelist Ahmet Altan, *En uzun gece* ("The Longest Night"), sold half a million copies (a record for a novel). Other best sellers included *Metal fırtına* ("Metallic Storm") by Orkun Uçar and Burak Turna, a farcical work of science fiction that pitted staunch allies—the U.S. and Turkey—against one another, and *Bir gün* ("One Day") by the perennially popular novelist Ayşe Kulin. Significant fiction came from Hasan Ali Toptaş, Mario Levi, Ayşe Sarısayın (winner of the 2005 Sait Faik Short Story Prize), Aslı Erdoğan, İhsan Oktay Anar, Feridun Andaç, Mehmet Eroğlu, Tahsin Yücel, Özen Yula, and Adnan Binyazar.   (TALAT SAIT HALMAN)

PERSIAN

Despite the collapse of the reform movement following the election of a hard-line president, 2005 marked advances in literary production in Iran. While Muḥammad Ḥusaynī's *Ābītar az gunāh* ("More Blue than Sin") was perhaps the most impressive novel by a young writer, more established figures also made their mark, as exemplified by Amīr Ḥasan Chihil'tan's *Sipidih dam-i Irani* ("Iranian Dawn") and *Āb va khāk* ("Water and Earth") by veteran novelist Ja'far Mudarris Ṣadīqī.

The decades-long march of Iranian women to the forefront of literary production continued, culminating in several noteworthy works of fiction and poetry. Sūdabāh Ashrafī's *Māhī'hā dar shab mī'khvāband* ("The Fish Sleep Through the Night"), Bīhnāz Gaskarī's *Biguzarīm* ("Let's Get off It"), and Shahla Ma'sumnijad's *Imuz naubat-i man nist* ("Not My Turn Today") were the most notable among numerous works chronicling the social forays and private experiences of urban women. *Kilid* ("The Key") by Sīmā Yārī was the most successful example of a poetry book by a woman. Like many other recent publications, this slim volume was accompanied by a compact disc with the author reading the text.

The perils of such literary ambitions by women became apparent when in November a 25-year-old Afghan poet named Nadia Anjuman was beaten to death by her husband, only a few days after *Gul-i dudi* ("Dark-Colored Flower"), her first book of verse, rolled off the press. Two months earlier the BBC had reported that the government of Uzbekistan had placed Hayot Ni'mat, an ethnic Tajik poet, under house arrest and held him incommunicado. Ni'mat had founded a cultural centre for the Persian-speaking poets and writers of Samarkand and thus challenged the Uzbekistan government's official position that Persian poetry was no longer extant in that city.

The appearance in the U.S. in April of *Strange Times, My Dear: The PEN Anthology of Contemporary Iranian Literature* constituted the most important literary event of the Persian diaspora. Modernist Iranian poet Manūchihr Ātishī died in November at age 74.

(AHMAD KARIMI-HAKKAK)

ARABIC

In 2005 writer and filmmaker Assia Djebar gave Algerians a very good reason to be proud of a native daughter as she was elected to the Académie Française, the first Maghribi writer to receive such an honour. The novel, which continued to occupy pride of place on the Arab world's literary scene, was used as a platform by the intellectuals to contest both national and international politics. The Osama bin Laden saga was at the centre of Driss Chraïbi's *L'Homme qui venait du passé* (2004). Through the book's protagonist, police inspector Ali, a parody of American TV's Inspector Colombo, Chraïbi ridiculed the West's obsession

with al-Qaeda and its founder. In her novel *Rabi'un ḥār* (2004; "A Hot Spring Season"), Saḥar Khalīfeh narrated the events of the second *intifadah* and the destruction of Yasir Arafat's compound, focusing on the role of the international observers and the risks they take to protect Palestinian rights. Khalīfeh was critical of the Palestinian Authority, its demagoguery, and the parasites of the organization.

In Egypt literary officials scrambled to rehabilitate the novel, following the embarrassing rejection in February of the Ministry of Culture Award by Ṣun 'Allah Ibrāhīm, who called it "worthless." The 2005 award finally went to the Sudanese author of the well-known *Season of Migration to the North*, al-Ṭayyib Ṣāliḥ. After a long silence, Ṣāliḥ published a nine-volume autobiography, each volume bearing a different title and covering topics that included friends, conferences, literary festivals, personalities encountered, work experience in Europe and the Arab world, and the author's peregrinations across Arab and Western countries. Jamāl al-Ghīṭānī published *Nithār al-maḥw* ("Fragments of Effacement"), the fifth volume of *Dafātīr al-tadwīn*, an autobiographical work. Although Ghīṭānī evoked numerous events from his youth, the book was mostly a reflection on the ominous approach of his

Dentist and best-selling novelist 'Alā' al-Aswānī poses for a photo in his office in Garden City, Cairo.

Literary Voices for Islam in the West

The Muslim population in Europe and North America is growing quickly, but even more significant is the degree of attention being paid to this very articulate minority. More than ever before, Westerners and Easterners are struggling to understand one another and explain themselves through their writings. An especially fertile topic for Muslim writers has been the pressures on Muslim women living in Western society.

When Sudanese author Leila Aboulela published *The Translator* (1999), it was hailed in the *Muslim News* as "the first halal novel written in English." (*Ḥalāl* ["permissible"] is the opposite of *ḥarām* ["forbidden"].) The Islamic message in the novel and in Aboulela's collection of short stories, *Coloured Lights* (2001), was subtle, however, compared with her latest novel, *Minaret* (2005). For this work Aboulela adopts an openly didactic approach, and the book abounds in information about Islamic religious practices. Her message is clearly that salvation is to be found in Islam. Herself a veiled woman, Aboulela studied in London and lived for a decade in Scotland; she probably experienced many of the misconceptions described in her novel. Najwa, the protagonist, is slowly transformed from a modern Sudanese university student into a devout Muslim who interacts with her "sisters" at the mosque and speaks their devotional language. Readers learn in detail the various ways to wear the veil and the importance of reading the Qur'an and seeking God's help and protection. One wonders if the novel was not written in reaction to the banning in recent years of the public display of religious symbols in France and elsewhere. Aboulela appears to be aligning herself with French revisionist and Muslim convert Roger Garaudy's call for an "Islamization of modernity" rather than a "modernization of Islam."

The virtue of the veiled woman that Aboulela portrays, however, is questioned by Diana Abu-Jaber, an Arab American writer, in *Crescent* (2003). Rana, a veiled Muslim student in the U.S., relates her numerous love affairs and affirms her ability to seduce any man she wants. She explains her veiling by saying simply, "This reminds me that I belong to myself. And to God." If Islam represents an identity for Aboulela's protagonist Najwa, Francophone Algerian author Assia Djebar approaches her faith from a cultural angle. Her motivation to speak out during the tragic events in her homeland in the 1990s emanated from a desire "to defend Algerian culture, which appeared threatened."

Arab writers have been generally eager to inform the West about their true selves. The ethnographic novels of the mid-20th century were followed by more sophisticated works revealing various aspects of Arab-Islamic societies. Despite her staunch rejection of her country's customs and religion, for example, Algerian Malika Mokaddem clearly values many of the desert traditions she describes in *Mes hommes* (2005).

A "dialogue of civilizations"—to use the phrase of Jamal M. Ibrahim, Sudanese ambassador in London—is under way. A lively discussion of the religious and cultural content of Islam has now been brought to Europe and the Americas and is being conducted by writers in Western languages as well as in Arabic.

(AIDA A. BAMIA)

retirement. The book escaped banality not only because of its reflection on universal themes but also because of the style of the five-volume work. In her usual polemical style, Nawāl al-Saʿdāwī authored *Al-Riwāyah* ("The Novel"), a story-within-a-story written by a young woman of illegitimate birth who is herself pregnant out of wedlock. Her pregnancy is described as "a divine seed in the womb of a virgin," a description that angered both al-Azhar (the powerful Islamic cultural centre in Cairo) and the church. Meanwhile, a best-selling novel, *ʿImārat Yaʿqūbiyyān* (2002; *The Yacoubian Building*, 2004) by Egyptian dentist ʿAlāʾ al-Aswānī (Alaa Al Aswany; *see* BIOGRAPHIES), received a broader readership during the year owing to its English translation.

In Maghribi Francophone literature, Malika Mokeddem—known for shedding light on the Algerian desert in her semiautobiographical novels—released *Mes hommes*, a defiant rejection of all kinds of restrictions, be they social or religious, on her freedom of action and expression. In Anglophone literature the Sudanese author Leila Aboulela published her second novel, *Minaret*, with the clear aim of informing the English-reading public of the teachings of Islam. (*See* Sidebar.)

If the novel was still king, poetry nonetheless continued to register the interest of its adepts and serve as a vehicle for protest. Tamīm al-Barghoutī published his third collection of colloquial poems, *ʿAlūlī bithib Maṣr, ʿult mish ʿāref* ("They Asked Me Whether I Liked Egypt. I Said, I Do Not Know"). The poet, much like his father before him, is torn between his affiliation to his mother's country, Egypt, and the difficulties he endures as a Palestinian living there. He asks a poignant question regarding his mother, the writer Radwa ʿAshour: "Oh, people of Egypt, tell me how many times do you want to punish her for loving a Palestinian?" Another strong proponent of poetry was Aḥmad ʿAbd al-Muʿṭī Ḥijāzī, who believed in the responsibility of poets to fight despair and promote hope during periods of darkness, to "announce the arrival of spring."

Ashtar, a Palestinian association that performs onstage and trains young actors, shared Ḥijāzī's vision. Its play *The Story of Mona*, described as "legislative" theatre, involved the public in the search for an alternative to the unfair laws imposed on the people. The company's struggle was cultural and aimed at salvaging Palestinian cultural identity. In an effort to revive the theatrical tradition in Morocco, Al-Ṭayyeb al-Ṣiddīq fulfilled a long-held dream by establishing a private theatre complex in Casablanca. At the annual Cairo Festival for International Experimental Theatre, interesting performances of original Arabic dramas, such as Alfrid Farag's *Al-Amīra waʾl suʿlūk*, or adaptations from Western literature helped strengthen a lingering interest in the theatre.

The 2005 Naguib Mahfouz Medal was awarded to Egyptian writer Yusuf Abu Rayyah for his 2002 novel *Laylat ʿurs* ("Wedding Night"). Algerian intellectual and poet Jamal Eddine Bencheikh (1930–2005) died on August 8. He greatly contributed to the field of classical Arabic literature and cooperated with André Miquel in a new translation of *The Thousand and One Nights*.

(AIDA A. BAMIA)

CHINESE

By 2005 at long last, after years of hesitation and evasion, Chinese writers began to react directly and strongly to the harsh social realities in the country, especially the bitter life of the *ruo shi qun ti* ("socially vulnerable groups"). Since mid-2004 more than half the stories and novels published in the nine leading literary monthlies and quarterlies in Beijing (three), Shanghai (two), and Guangzhou, Haikou, Nanjing, and Guiyang (one each) had concentrated on the sufferings of the poor as the main theme.

Among works published in 2005 were some by top writers. In the novelette *Bao gao zheng fu* ("Reporting, Sir"), author Han Shaogong adopted an ingenious structure for his story, which took place in a jail and in which "I," the first-person narrator, a young imprisoned journalist, converses in turn with each of his cell mates: a thief, a murderer, a swindler, and so on. The position of "I" changes both as to his point of view and moral response when he speaks with a different cell mate. In this way the point emerges, which might be summarized in the words of one of the prisoners: "The reason you turned out a bad person rather than a good one is only that you have encountered poverty."

Fu nü xian liao lu ("A Woman's Chatting"), a novel by Lin Bai, a leading women writer, used meticulously designed—if on occasion somewhat disorganized—transcriptions of a recording made by the author of her chats with her housecleaner. The book painted a lifelike picture of a rural woman's harsh life.

Generally considered one of the best literary works of the year was *Ma si ling xue an* ("Bloody Murder on Ma-si Hill"), a novelette by Chen Yingsong, a serious writer of fiction from rural central China. The story was cast as the recollections of a young farmer on death row. The young man joins his uncle, a poor widower living with five daughters, to work as a labourer for a professor leading a six-person scientific expedition team to the wild Ma-si Hill to prospect for gold. Misunderstandings between the two farmers and the professor and his team grow and fester, even though neither the farmers nor the academics wish it and strive to maintain amicable relations. The situation quickly deteriorates, the farmers kill the others, and the uncle goes mad. The author's description of the changing mental states of the murderers was carefully and truly crafted. In his bloody story Chen made the shocking inference that men of different social and cultural status could reach a state of total misunderstanding, even hatred, although they all were good men who bore no malice toward the others. Clearly the novelette was a harsh reaction to the current social reality in China.

Ba Jin, one of China's best-known authors, died in October. (*See* OBITUARIES.) (WANG XIAOMING)

JAPANESE

In 2005 premier author Kenzaburō Ōe's new work of fiction, *Sayonara, watashi no hon yo!* ("Goodbye, My Book!"), again featured the protagonist Cogito, who had appeared in two previous works, *Torikaeko* ("Changeling") and *Ureigao no dōji* ("A Child with a Melancholy Face"). On this occasion Cogito, a storyteller and activist, meets an old friend, the architect and renovation specialist Shige, who is connected to a secret society called Geneva. Shige believes that it is his job to bomb high-rise buildings in Tokyo. These two strange old men represented, as Ōe said, the author now and a fictional visualization of the author as an old man. Through them Ōe again explored the individual's ability to face the veiled violence of the state.

Ōe made news of another kind in 2005. In October he announced the founding of the Kenzaburō Ōe Prize, to be given out starting in 2007 for a work published in 2006. Ōe was to be the sole judge, and there would be no prize money, but the winning story would be translated into English and published worldwide. Ōe told the *Asahi shimbun* that he was seeking to promote the revival of literature as an alternative to the culture of the Internet and the mobile phone.

"I, Murakami, am the narrator of these stories. Almost all the stories will be told in the third person, but the narrator himself happens to appear in the beginning." So begins Haruki Murakami's new collection of stories, *Tōkyō kitanshū* ("Twilight Zone Stories of Tokyo"), as if the author and the narrator were the same person, suggesting that the stories may be nonfiction. Five years after *Kami no kodomotachi wa mina odoru* (*After the Quake*, 2002), which featured Murakami's stories inspired by the 1995 Great Hanshin Earthquake, he returned to his pattern of crafting mysterious tales to unveil the reality hidden behind life in modern Tokyo.

Haruki Murakami himself was the narrator of his new book of stories.

For the first half of 2005, the Akutagawa Prize, awarded semiannually to the most promising new Japanese writers of fiction, went to Kazushige Abe's short story "Gurando fināre" ("Grand Finale"), first published in the December 2004 issue of *Gunzo*. A man whose wife and daughter abandoned him because of his liking for nymphets somehow puts his life back on course by helping out in girls' primary-school theatres in his hometown. The Akutagawa Prize for the second half of the year was given to Fuminori Nakamura's "Tsuchi no naka no kodomo" ("A Child Buried in the Earth"), the story of a young taxi driver who grapples with an old trauma caused by his stepparents' violence.

The Yomiuri Prize for Literature went to Hisaki Matsuura's *Hantō* (2004; "The Peninsula"). The Jun'ichirō Tanizaki Prize, given to the year's most accomplished novel, was awarded to Kō Machida's *Kokuhaku* ("Confession") and Eimi Yamada's *Fūmi zekka* ("Superb Flavours"). Noboru Tsujihara's "Kareha no naka no aoi honoo" ("Blue Flame in a Dead Leaf") won the Yasunari Kawabata Prize, awarded annually to the best short story. Among the best-selling books of the year were Ryū Murakami's *Hantō o deyo* ("Get Out of the Peninsula") and Banana Yoshimoto's book of talks with Toshiko Okamoto, the wife of the late internationally known artist Tarō Okamoto, "Renai ni tsuite hanashimashita" ("We Talked About Love"). The popular fiction writers Fumio Niwa (*see* OBITUARIES) and Yumiko Kurahashi died in 2005. (YOSHIHIKO KAZAMARU)

Media and Publishing

American TV broadcasters coped with the DEPARTURE of four longtime news ANCHORS, and "PODCASTING" spread quickly; in the publishing realm, newspapers continued to STRUGGLE to attract readers, *Vanity Fair* magazine disclosed the identity of DEEP THROAT, and the latest book in the HARRY POTTER series sold millions of copies.

TELEVISION

Organization. Rupert Murdoch, who bought Internet companies IGN Entertainment, MySpace.com, and Scout Media, was reelected chairman of the News Corp. in 2005 despite a shareholders' revolt. Murdoch's son Lachlan unexpectedly resigned from his executive post at News Corp. in August. Lachlan's brother, James, remained chief executive of BSkyB, which acquired EasyNet in order to be able to offer Internet access, pay TV, and telephony. British terrestrial broadcasters ITV and Channel 4 each acquired a 20% stake in Freeview, a digital free-to-air TV service launched in 2002.

The British Broadcasting Corporation was hit on May 23 with a 24-hour strike in which 11,000 of 28,000 BBC journalists and technicians protested 4,000 job cuts. On August 15 Canadian Broadcasting Corporation locked out 5,500 workers. Seven weeks later, after protests from unions in London, Jerusalem, and the U.S., the dispute was resolved when CBC backed down from its plan to hire more contractual workers.

The U.S. Securities and Exchange Commission charged Spanish-language production company TV Azteca and its chairman, Ricardo B. Salinas Pliego, with not having properly disclosed transactions from which they had benefited. Meanwhile, TV Azteca sued independent TV CNI Canal 40 for having accepted a loan from the Mexican unit of General Electric, which had violated Mexican laws that barred foreigners from running local media. Telesur, a 24-hour Spanish-language satellite station based in Caracas, was inaugurated by Venezuela's Pres. Hugo Chávez. (*See* BIOGRAPHIES.) The state-run regional TV station was receiving assistance from Cuba and Brazil state TV networks and from the governments of Argentina and Uruguay.

The European Commission cleared the joint venture by DirecTV and Sky-Terra Communications (an affiliate of equity firm Apollo Group) to buy DirecTV unit Hughes Network Systems. In other sales-and-acquisitions news, private equity firms Permira and Kohlberg Kravis Roberts & Co. bought Luxembourg-based SBS Broadcasting; under new CEO Mathias Döpfner (*see* BIOGRAPHIES), German publisher Axel Springer purchased a majority in ProSiebenSat. 1 Media; and Russia's last independent network station, REN TV, was sold to state-controlled Evrofinans Bank. Japan's conservative broadcast industry was rocked by the takeover bid made by the Internet firm Livedoor Co. for Fuji Television Network Inc. A $1.6 billion deal ended the feud. Hong Kong broadcaster Television Broadcasts Ltd. bought the remaining 30% stake that it did not own in Taiwan broadcast firm Liann Yee Production Co., and Star TV, a satellite and cable operator in Hong Kong, bought 20% of the Indonesian national network ANTV, which was owned by the family of the chief economy minister, Aburizal Bakrie.

Early in the year China tightened controls on TV ventures by foreign companies, an action that was viewed unfavourably by several media chiefs. Time Warner's Dick Parsons declared an unwillingness to compromise the integrity of its news broadcasting in response to criticism by Chinese officials even if the decision affected business prospects, and the Walt Disney Co.'s Robert Iger intended to postpone building a Disneyland on mainland China until he was assured of having permission to broadcast on Chinese TV. Rupert Murdoch stated that News Corp., which was under investigation for having used unauthorized local Chinese cable networks, had hit "a brick wall" in China.

Marking the 25th anniversary of CNN, the first 24-hour news network in the U.S., founder Ted Turner remarked that the network was started as an "adventure." Ten years after the network was launched, its coverage of the 1991 Gulf War turned CNN into a household name.

Programming. By late 2005, within an 11-month period, all four of the men who had dominated American television news since the early 1980s had vacated their posts, and their bosses were left trying not only to replace them but to determine what kind of program a 21st-century network newscast ought to be. First to leave was NBC's Tom Brokaw. He retired in December 2004, when he handed over the reins to Brian Williams in a long and carefully planned succession. CBS's Dan Rather left less of his own volition. His departure in March came as a direct result of a bungled report he did for a *60 Minutes Wednesday* telecast the previous year. The report had used what turned out to be unverified documents to try to raise questions about U.S. Pres. George

American news icon Ted Koppel prepares to tape his last Nightline *show on November 22. Koppel was a pioneer of late-night in-depth political programming on network television.*

W. Bush's service in the National Guard as a young man. ABC's Peter Jennings, who might have been in position to gain viewers from his departing rivals, instead suddenly left the air in early April with the announcement that he was fighting lung cancer. Jennings, known for his strong reporting in the field and calm erudition from the anchor desk, died August 7, at age 67. (*See* OBITUARIES.) Then, in November, ABC *Nightline* anchor Ted Koppel kept a promise he had made earlier in the year to step away from the program because of disagreement with ABC management over the show's mission and format. *Nightline* had taken its nightly place on the ABC schedule in 1980, when it was created to provide coverage of the taking of American hostages in Iran. Brokaw had been network anchor since 1983, Rather since 1981, and Jennings since 1983. Filing occasional reports, Brokaw and Rather remained affiliated with their respective networks.

The big guns were gone, and in a sign of confusion or uncertainty, ABC and CBS did not immediately chose successors for their nightly news anchors. ABC employed morning-show host Charles Gibson and correspondent Elizabeth Vargas as temporary replacements for Jennings and only in December did it name Vargas and correspondent Bob Woodruff as his successors. CBS used veteran Washington, D.C., correspondent Bob Schieffer as its temporary anchor and by the end of the year had not selected anyone to succeed Rather. CBS network chief Leslie Moonves openly longed for a more contemporary kind of news program, and he replaced news-division president Andrew Heyward with Sean McManus, who had headed CBS Sports but had not put in time at the network's fabled news operation. (NBC also fired its news chief, Neil Shapiro, primarily over ratings trouble at the network's top-rated *Today* morning show.) ABC's decision to replace Koppel with three anchors—Martin Bashir, Cynthia McFadden, and Terry Moran—signaled a turn away from *Nightline*'s reliable one-story format toward a look similar to that of other TV newsmagazines. British journalist Bashir was best known in the U.S. for having interviewed pop star Michael Jackson in the documentary that was the impetus for Jackson's latest round of legal woes.

Despite the changes and uncertainty, network newscasts continued to draw more than 20 million viewers nightly. The numbers were a far cry from those of the 1970s and '80s but still well ahead of the combined audience for cable news channels on any given night. Indeed, the Fox network talked of launching a nightly network newscast on its broadcast stations by spinning off the work of its top-rated cable operation, Fox News Channel. Longtime cable king CNN took steps to try to reclaim viewers after Fox supplanted it in the ratings, owing to its more opinionated brand of news delivery. CNN in late 2004 installed former CBS News executive Jonathan Klein as president of its U.S. operation. Among other steps, Klein replaced anchor Aaron Brown with Anderson Cooper.

In prime time the annual Emmy Awards honoured one old favourite and one newcomer to American television. The Academy of Television Arts and Sciences gave its outstanding comedy series honour to *Everybody Loves Raymond*, the venerable CBS family series that had gone off the air in May. Top drama series was ABC's first-year mystery *Lost*, about the survivors of a plane wreck on a not-deserted-enough tropical island. In another sign of its ascendancy to the top of the topical comedy heap—in critical and popular buzz, if not in overall viewership—*The Daily Show with Jon Stewart* won two Emmys. *Daily Show* later spun off a nightly half-hour program called *The Colbert Report*, which was adored by critics for the manner in which former *Daily* correspondent Stephen Colbert sent up the bluster of top-rated cable-news talker Bill O'Reilly. In a sign of its popular and critical resurgence, the recently moribund ABC network finished with 16 Emmys overall, first among broadcast networks. Its comeback was fueled not only by *Lost* but also by the runaway popularity of another first-year series, the suburban caricature *Desperate Housewives*. Part comedy and part murder mystery, the show captured the American imagination instantly in a manner few series had done in recent times. The Emmy Awards were also notable for late-night host David Letterman's tribute to the dean of his genre, Johnny Carson, who died January 23, almost 13 years after he had retired as host of *The Tonight Show*. (*See* OBITUARIES.)

While ABC made the biggest ratings gains, CBS won the overall battle for most viewers, and Fox just barely won the lead among the advertiser-coveted 18-to-49-year-old demographic. The big loser of the season—in a trend continued into the new fall season—was NBC, which suffered from losing the ratings powerhouse *Friends* and from its inability to develop new hit shows. NBC finished the season fourth both among the 18-to-49 group and in total viewers, a giant comedown for a network that had been the most successful through the late 1990s and into the 2000s.

On the business front, turmoil was the order of the day as television began a transition toward the likely day when much of what it did would also be offered on the Internet. ABC, in a deal with Apple Computer, made episodes of *Lost* and *Desperate Housewives* available for purchase and downloading via Apple's iTunes media service. Each episode would become available the day after it aired and cost $1.99. NBC began video streaming its *Nightly News* free of charge over its Web news site MSNBC.com and later joined ABC in offering

On September 18 in Los Angeles, the cast of Lost *gathers to celebrate the winning of the 2005 Emmy Award for outstanding drama series.*

Poker Fever

By 2005 the disreputable image of card hustlers, seedy card rooms, hard liquor, and concealed pistols long associated with the game of poker had been dispelled as earnest individuals could be seen—on planes, trains, and buses—poring over poker manuals to study methods of scoring a jackpot payday.

Many believed that poker's newfound popularity was sparked in 2003 when—filming from Binion's Horseshoe casino in Las Vegas— the cable television Travel Channel began using a "lipstick camera" embedded in the poker gaming table to film the cards held by each player at the World Poker Tour. For the first time, television viewers could vicariously play along, and many dreamed of amassing riches for themselves as a player with the unlikely name of Chris Moneymaker parlayed a $39 entrance fee for an Internet "satellite" contest into a $10,000 entrance fee into the 2003 World Series of Poker No-Limit Texas Hold'em Championship in Las Vegas, where the rookie won the top prize of $2,500,000.

The synergy between film, television, and the Internet grew stronger in 2004 with the showcasing of entertainers and even sports figures on television's *Celebrity Poker*. That year Hollywood stars such as Ben Affleck and Jennifer Tilly crossed over from the make-believe world of charity poker tournaments to play in open events. *Tilt*, a drama series about poker players, debuted on TV in 2005.

The latest gambling craze was not limited to men. Women made up about one-third of the nearly two million poker players on the Internet. In September 2004 Annie Duke won the World Series of

© Ethan Miller/Getty Images

Lebanese-born Australian Joseph Hachem is virtually wallowing in cash after he won $7.5 million on the final day of the World Series of Poker No-Limit Texas Hold'em event in Las Vegas on July 16.

Poker Tournament of Champions. Her victory in the $2 million winner-take-all pot in this high-profile TV event led to another surge in Internet and tournament play, especially among women. On the Internet hundreds of international poker sites attracted novices and those who preferred the Web's anonymity. That anonymity also extended to cheaters, such as those who used computer software to help figure out what actions to take, and to poker "bots" (computer programs capable of playing the game) disguised as people.

The 2005 No-Limit Texas Hold'em Championship drew a record 5,619 entrants, which translated into a prize fund of more than $52 million and a first-place prize of $7.5 million. The 2005 event was won by Australian Joseph Hachem, a Lebanese-born former chiropractor and another example of those who had forsaken their careers or educational pursuits, and sometimes their families, in hopes of making the big time.

The first invitation-only World Poker Robot Championship was held in 2005 to coincide with the World Series of Poker Championship at Binion's in Las Vegas. PokerProbot, written by Hilton Givens, a car salesman from Indiana, won the $100,000 first prize. Poker pro Phil ("the Unabomber") Laak took three hours to defeat PokerProbot in the ensuing exhibition match, however, with the crowds cheering, "Hu-mans! Humans!" As had happened in the game of chess, it might be only a matter of time before man was eclipsed again by machines.

(WILLIAM L. HOSCH)

shows through iTunes. Respected trade journal *Television Business Report* reported that many mainstream media channels were going online and that arrangements for video-on-demand content were commonplace. In response to the declining television advertising market, product placement— the insertion of sponsors' products inside TV series, rather than just in ads aired during ad breaks—was on the rise and was predicted to increase greatly. In September, for example, CBS reportedly added a Chevrolet Impala logo into five of its shows through digital methods. Meanwhile, and not coincidentally, late in the year *The Wall Street Journal* reported that ad inventory on the front pages of the leading Web portal sites AOL, Yahoo!, and MSN was sold out.

In programming relating to children, The Walt Disney Co. asked the U.S. Federal Communications Commission to review rules that limited the use of interactive ads that mentioned the names of Web sites that kids could visit. Viacom's Nickelodeon children's TV network also opposed the restrictions. *PBS Kids Sprout* began as the first national 24-hour channel aimed at American toddlers, and Nickelodeon launched seven international services. Arabic satellite TV broadcaster al-Jazeera launched *Al-Jazeera Children's Channel* to teach Arab children and adolescents open-mindedness and tolerance.

The continuing worldwide coverage of the aftermath of the Dec. 26, 2004, South Asian tsunami was eclipsed by the April 2 death of Pope John Paul II. (*See* OBITUARIES.) The global scale of the media coverage of the pope's death was unprecedented; ABC News.com reported that it was generating 35,000 stories a day. In their media coverage Arabic broadcasters al-Jazeera and al-

Arabiya both cited the pope's support of Muslim and Arab causes.

The Hindi-language quiz show *Kaun banega crorepati* ("Who Will Be a Ten-Millionaire"), which offered a prize of 20 million rupees ($450,000), was closely followed by 11.7 million Indians. Meanwhile, the Indian government banned the adult satellite channel Free X-TV for having shown programs that violated good taste and morality. In other controversial programming, Dutch TV presenter Filemon Wesselink was shown taking drugs during the show *Spuiten & Slikken*. *Big Brother* in The Netherlands featured a pregnant woman who during the series gave birth to a baby that she kept with her in the house in which the series was taking place. In its first week the Filipino version of the series was suspended and given a stern warning by the Movie and Television Review and

Classification Board of the Philippines for showing what it called intimate scenes that included bathing and bodypainting. Producers of the series in Germany had a village built specifically for the program, a move that imitated the movie *The Truman Show*, but the series had poor ratings and was to end in early 2006, a year after it began.

Technology. Countries began imposing deadlines on media organizations to switch from analog to digital broadcasting even as the Internet and mobile telephone became new venues for TV programming. Free digital TV started to spread in Britain, Sweden, Italy, Germany, and France. Conventional broadcasters saw digital terrestrial TV as a means to reach new audiences and sell more ads, and pay-TV providers competed with special offers and expanded services.

The conventional TV cathode-ray tube (CRT) metamorphosed. Samsung, RCA, and LG Electronics introduced 75-cm (30-in) screen CRT TV receivers that were one-third slimmer than earlier models. Sony unveiled BRAVIA, a series of nine models of flat-panel liquid-crystal-display (LCD) TV receivers. With 38- to 101-cm (15- to 40-in) screens, BRAVIA's picture quality was equivalent to images with one-megapixel resolution.

Internet-based TV typically came along with personal computers that had built-in TV capabilities and a broadband connection. *POV* magazine founder Drew Massey financed ManiaTV, an Internet company that on a 24-hour basis served up film clips, music videos, and chatter from "cyberjockeys" (CJs) to college students and 20-somethings. Yahoo! launched a made-for-the-Web program called *Kevin Sites in the Hot Zone* (an audio-video-photo-blog-chat room run by Sites), Google offered on-demand stream video of the premiere of Chris Rock's new TV comedy *Everybody Hates Chris*, and Viacom's Nickelodeon created TurboNick, a free Internet-based 24-hour access to its programs.

As part of a growing role of the Internet in marketing, cosmetics maker Coty Inc. launched its new fragrance, Lovely, on *Vogue* magazine's Web site, Style.com. Featuring actress and model Sarah Jessica Parker, the online commercial appeared before the TV airing of the same ad.

French telecommunications provider Alcatel and Microsoft agreed to share

AP/Wide World Photos

ManiaTV—shown here broadcasting from a bus in Denver in March—was one of several companies that took television programming directly to the Internet in 2005.

development of Internet-based TV services provided by telephone companies. Nordic telecommunications operator TeliaSonera was already broadcasting Swedish broadcaster TV4's channels to high-speed Internet customers.

The cellular (mobile) phone became the latest venue for TV programming. SmartVideo Technologies and V Cast started the year with live and prerecorded TV programs sent to American cell phones equipped with Microsoft's Windows Mobile operating system. Australian telephone subscribers were introduced to cell-phone video by Telstra, Optus, and Vodafone via the Hutchison 3 network. Germany's Vodafone D2 was one of the first European operators to offer cell-phone TV service with shows, sports, news, and movies. Norway's state broadcaster NRK used a cross-country ski marathon in Sweden for testing the transmission from a camera-equipped cell phone to Norwegian TV watchers. French mobile telecommunications operators Orange and Bouygues Telecom began testing the Digital Video Broadcast Handheld (DVB-H) service, which enabled subscribers to watch broadcast TV on a cell phone. Nokia, the world's largest cell-phone manufacturer, launched a pilot project with Finnish Broadcasting Company and commercial TV channels as well as with mobile service providers TeliaSonera and Elisa.

By the last quarter of 2005, Apple Computer had introduced the video iPod, which was capable of playing short movies, music videos, and ABC or Disney TV shows. Satellite broadcaster EchoStar released PocketDISH, a

portable personal video recorder equipped with a hard drive for recording programs and a screen for watching what had been recorded.

Yet a different type of broadcasting venue was being pursued by Sirius Satellite Radio and auto-parts-maker Delphi, which separately unveiled more programming choices for their in-vehicle backseat video displays. Sirius and Microsoft were to develop a video companion to the satellite radio service, and Delphi and Comcast were to create an in-vehicle system that would enable owners to transfer selected video programming to their cars. Although prohibitively expensive and questioned by transportation safety advocates, satellite TV in cars was popular in 2005 as an accessory in SUVs, recreational vehicles, and pickup trucks.

RADIO

A new audio genre, called podcasting, came into vogue in 2005. Named after the iPod portable media player but not restricted to it, podcasting was essentially a system for posting a file with audio content onto the World Wide Web and for providing an automatic online notification to the computer of a subscriber to download the file. Subscribers could then copy the downloaded file to a portable media player and play the program whenever and wherever they wanted. The podcaster could be anyone from an amateur husband-and-wife team in Wisconsin to NBC's top-rated morning *Today* show, which launched its own podcast during the year. Podcasting took off about midyear when Apple Computer's popular iTunes online store added tens of thousands of podcasts to its offerings. The Pew Internet and the American Life Project estimated in April that six million Americans listened to podcasts, but a *New York Times* story in August asked, "Podcasts: All the Rage or About to Fizzle?" One expert quoted in the article estimated that in 2010 some 57 million people would be using podcasts, but another, more pessimistic, expert said that the number would be 30 million. Either way, it was a large audience, and traditional radio executives in 2005 debated how much impact podcasting would have on their industry.

The New York City "shock jock" Howard Stern, meanwhile, spent much of his last year on what was being labeled "terrestrial" (as opposed to satellite-based) radio running down that medium, a situation that caused much tension with his employers at Infinity Broadcasting. He signed a five-year, $500 million contract with Sirius. Sirius and rival XM were the two players in the emerging field of subscription-based satellite radio. At the end of the year, Sirius was ramping up its campaign to convert Stern's imminent arrival into new subscribers and new buyers for the proprietary receivers necessary for the services. With about five million subscribers, XM had more than double the number of Sirius subscribers, and executives were predicting continued rapid growth. Kagan Research, a leading media analyst, predicted that the total number of subscribers would grow to 46 million by 2014.

To replace Stern, the Infinity conglomerate came up with two new morning shows, an East Coast effort fronted by David Lee Roth (former lead singer for the rock band Van Halen) and a West Coast show headed by Adam Carolla, a comic who also had his own comedy talk show on Comedy Central and cohosted Comedy Central's *The Man Show*. Infinity also signed magician Penn Jillette to head a one-hour daily syndicated show. Leslie Moonves, the CBS/Viacom executive who oversaw Infinity operations, said that not all the new shows would succeed but that losing Stern would not be as painful as it seemed because the profit margins on his high salary were thin. A number of stations that were losing Stern began to market themselves as "free radio" to

emphasize that there would be a cost for those who followed Stern to satellite. The radio advertising market, which was the basis of free radio, remained soft throughout 2005, however, and toward the end of the year, Wall Street analysts were predicting that little would change in 2006.

In Nepal in February, King Gyanendra declared a state of emergency and imposed a media law that barred FM radio stations from broadcasting news and criticism of the king and the royal family. BBC Nepal news service was stopped, and all community radio stations were locked shut.

Channel Africa, the international radio service of the South African Broadcasting Corporation, formed a partnership with the Southern African Broadcasting Association. Channel Africa took over production of a weekly magazine program named *SADC Calling*, which discussed regional activities and developments on such issues as HIV and AIDS.

BBC announced that to launch its Arabic TV service, it was ceasing radio services in Bulgarian, Croatian, Czech, Greek, Hungarian, Kazakh, Polish, Slovak, Slovene, and Thai. The language services would be continued online. BBC began operating an Arabic radio service in 1938.

Palestinian radio station Voice of Love and Peace (VOLP) planned to sue Radio Sawa, the U.S. government's Arabic network, for using 94.2 FM. Assigned to VOLP since 1996, the frequency was reassigned by the Palestinian Ministry of Information, which went to court to stop VOLP from continuing to broadcast. The Ram Allah Magistrates Court granted an injunc-

tion on the ministry's order, but Radio Sawa continued broadcasting.

(RAMONA MONETTE SARGAN FLORES;
STEVE JOHNSON)

NEWSPAPERS

In 2005 newspapers continued to face challenges on the advertising and circulation fronts—the very battlegrounds that permitted their existence. Some critics said that newspapers had been too slow to change to meet the needs of the news consumer, particularly in the developed world, where revenue advertising share and circulation declines were more pronounced than in populous Third World countries such as China and India. Robert Cauthorn, the former vice president for digital media at the *San Francisco Chronicle* and an ardent advocate for change in the industry, declared in the International Newspaper Marketing Association's *Ideas* magazine that "readership, the engine that powers everything, has been falling for 25 years. The ugly fact is that with each new day our readers open our newspapers, and they find another reason to want us less." From a worldwide perspective newspaper circulations and advertising revenues were up, but the elevated numbers reflected a short-term increase following the 2001–03 worldwide advertising downturn. Though advertising sales had recovered solidly, the newspaper industry continued to lose ad market share over time. In 1994 newspapers worldwide commanded 36.1% of the advertising market share, second only to TV advertising. ZenithOptimedia, which supplied the annual statistical data to the World Association of Newspapers' "World Press Trends" report, projected that newspapers' ad share would slide to 29.3% of the ad market share by 2007.

Advertising share declines were most prominent in developed countries in Europe and North America. Analysts said that the ad market share dropped as circulation declined because advertisers paid more to reach larger audiences. In 2000 Canada's newspaper advertising share was 43.8%, compared with 31.5% for TV and 13.1% for radio. In 2004 newspaper ad share had dropped to 38.4%, compared with 33.3% for TV and 13.9% for radio. In 2007 Canadian newspapers were projected to garner 37.3% of the ad market. Meanwhile, in South Korea newspaper ad share fell from 49.8% in 2000 to 44.1% in 2004; the projection for 2007 was 41.3%. The share for TV increased

In June radio journalists in Kathmandu protest a clampdown on radio and other media by King Gyanendra and Nepalese communications officials.

from 30.4% in 2000 to 33.6% in 2004. In the United Kingdom newspaper ad share dropped from 40.2% in 2000 to 39.1% in 2004 to a projected 38.2% in 2007, compared with 31.4% and 30.2% for TV in 2000 and 2004, respectively.

Though newspaper circulation was booming in such countries as South Africa, Poland, and India, with 25.94%, 53.67%, and 14.04% circulation increases from 2000 to 2004, respectively, circulations were shrinking in the developed world; from 2000 to 2004 declines were experienced in the United Kingdom (8.74%), the U.S. (2.06%), and Hong Kong (78.46%).

In the U.S. the circulation statistics for 2005 told a much different story. *Editor & Publisher* magazine headlined the dramatic drops in major newspaper circulations across the country in its May 2 publication as "Bloody Monday." The statistics showed marked circulation declines from first-quarter 2004 to the same period in 2005 for the *Baltimore Sun* (11.5% daily), the *Chicago Tribune* and Denver's *Rocky Mountain News* (6.6%), the *Los Angeles Times* (6.4%), and the *San Francisco Chronicle* (6%).

Several reasons were cited for the steep drops, including the federal "no call" rule, which barred telemarketers from contacting those who had declared in writing that they did not want to be called. Prior to the 2005 ruling, the majority of newspaper subscription sales had been made by telemarketers. Another factor was the 2004 scandal in which a number of popular newspapers—the *Chicago Sun-Times*, owned by Hollinger Inc.; New York's *Newsday* and *Hoy*, owned by the Tribune Co.; and the *Dallas Morning News*, owned by Belo, among others—inflated circulation figures to attract larger advertising revenue. This caused several newspapers to "right size" their 2004 statistics in 2005.

The reduced circulation and advertising figures sent some newspaper investors reeling. Though newspaper profit margins remained higher than those for other industries (the American newspaper industry recorded a profit of 22.9% in 2004) and were expected to grow in 2005, investors were agitated by declining stock values. Following a 14% stock-price free fall from July to November 2005, the largest investor of Knight Ridder, the second largest U.S. newspaper chain, demanded in November that the company be sold. During that same period, Gannett, the country's largest newspaper chain, experienced an 11% stock price decline, and the New York Times Co. faced a 13% drop.

Convergence—the integration of a company's media operations, including TV, radio, print, and online to achieve editorial and business efficiencies and economies—continued in 2005. Some media companies that owned only print and Web sites were also converging by integrating their operations into one newsroom and one advertising department. The New York Times Co. announced the convergence of its print and Web operations in preparation for a move in 2007 to a new office tower. Nordjyske Medier, based in Ålborg, Den., completely merged its newsroom and cross-trained its 249 journalists to be able to report in all types of media. The company's advertising staff was also trained to sell advertising in multimedia campaigns. The strategy, launched in 2001, was credited with shifting the company to profitability.

Another strategy to increase readership was to provide, according to the usage patterns and desires of news consumers, around-the-clock news operations that provided relevant content anytime and anywhere. Media companies were providing content for traditional and nontraditional news channels, such as mobiles/PDAs, iPods, video screens in subways and in hotel elevators, shopping mall kiosks, and electronic ticker billboards on busy city streets.

Part of the audience-focus strategy was to embrace the idea of community-generated content. OhmyNews.com (international site <english.ohmynews.com>), a South Korean-based Web site, employed 40,000 registered community journalists worldwide to write stories about which they were passionate. The community journalists were paid on the basis of where on the site the editors placed the material. Hundreds of new stories, edited by a small team of paid journalists, were published daily. The community-generated content strategy was also popular in the U.S. The Georgia-based Morris chain of newspapers launched BlufftonToday.com, a Web site whose main purpose was to encourage "a community in conversation with itself." The content from the community-generated blogs also appeared in the newspaper of the same name. The site and newspaper, launched in April, increased circulation, and Morris decided to use the model elsewhere.

The most popular community-generated content was not deep, intellectual, journalistic-style stories, however. Jacksonville.com reported that in 2004 more than 80,000 community photos

were submitted, including images of babies, dogs, cats, sunsets, and vacations. About 13% of all Web-site traffic, or 21 million page views in 2004, was for community-generated photos. Media companies followed the craze and asked readers to contribute text, photos, and video, especially for breaking news stories. The July 7 London transit bombings generated hundreds of video, audio, and text reports from eyewitnesses to online news sites. On the day of the bombings, the 100 reader-originated photos and video clips generated about one-third of the traffic on the BBC.co.uk Web site—about 15 million page views. During the Hurricane Katrina disaster, CNN.com and NOLA.com solicited content from readers and received hundreds of pictures, eyewitness accounts, and pleas to reunite loved ones scattered by the catastrophe.

The shrinkage of newspapers for the convenience of the reader from the large broadsheet size to the tabloid size, a trend that began in earnest in 2003, was in full swing in 2005. Venerable brands such as *The Wall Street Journal Europe*, *The Wall Street Journal Asia*, and *The Guardian* (London) all downsized in an effort to capture a larger audience and reduce costs. The WSJ estimated that it would save $17 million in production costs alone. In London both *The Times* and *The Independent* converted in 2003; *The Times* had a 1% increase in circulation year on year, and *The Independent* registered a 15% rise in circulation, its highest increase since 1997. The free commuter newspaper, most notably Stockholm-based *Metro*, was now considered the most circulated type of newspaper in the world. According to "World Press Trends," from 2000 to 2004 free-daily-newspaper circulation grew dramatically in several countries, most notably in Hungary (66.67%), the U.K. (81.82%), Singapore (123.11%), and Italy (900%). *Metro* reported that it supplied seven million free daily newspapers in 18 languages to 86 major cities in 19 countries.

Though Lord Black had stepped down in 2003 as chief executive of global media giant Hollinger Inc. following a scandal in which he was investigated for alleged fraud and other abuses, the company continued to recover from huge losses allegedly stemming from the scandal. Hollinger filed suit to recover $425 million that it claimed Black and some former executives took in the form of unauthorized bonuses and excessive salaries. In November Black was indicted for fraud.   (MARTHA L. STONE)

MAGAZINES

In 2005 *Vanity Fair* magazine shocked the world when, in its July issue, it became the first publication to reveal that W. Mark Felt, the 91-year-old former associate director of the FBI, was the Watergate Scandal informant known as "Deep Throat." John D. O'Connor, the attorney who wrote the article, had been in negotiations with the magazine for two years prior to publication. Felt's daughter, Joan, disclosed in an interview that the family had many reasons for revealing her father's role in Watergate but said she would not deny "that to make money was one of them."

The biggest controversy of the year involving a magazine occurred when *Newsweek* published an article in its May 9 issue that claimed that U.S. interrogators, in an attempt to rattle suspects at Guantánamo Bay, Cuba, had flushed a Qur'an down a toilet. Many attributed to the article's impact a wave of anti-American protests in Afghanistan and Pakistan that left at least 15 dead. *Newsweek* retracted the story a week later, after the U.S. Department of Defense challenged its veracity. In a note to readers, editor Mark Whitaker said that the report had been based on information from "a knowledgeable U.S.

The eye-catching cover of Rolling Stone *for Jan. 22, 1981, featuring a photo of John Lennon and Yoko Ono and published a month after Lennon's death, was selected as the greatest magazine cover of the past 40 years by the American Society of Magazine Editors.*

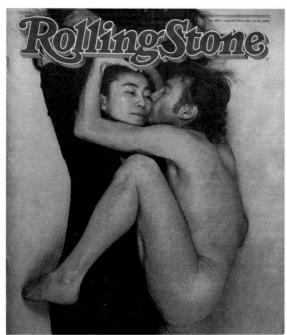

© Evan Agostini/Liaison/Getty Images

government source." He went on to say, however, that his source was no longer certain that he had read about the alleged incident in the still-unreleased Pentagon report cited in the article.

In a competition sponsored by the American Society of Magazine Editors to determine the 40 greatest magazine covers of the past 40 years, the Jan. 22, 1981, *Rolling Stone* cover of a nude John Lennon curled around a fully clothed Yoko Ono was chosen as first; the cover appeared the month after Lennon's death. The *Vanity Fair* August 1991 cover that portrayed the nude and pregnant actress Demi Moore took second place, followed by the April 1968 *Esquire* cover that featured boxer Muhammad Ali with arrows piercing his body. *Esquire, Time,* and *Life* each had four winning covers. A panel of 52 editors, design directors, and photography editors selected the winners from 444 entries representing 136 magazines.

A July report by PQ Media revealed that product placement, which influenced every segment of media, would increase 17.5% in magazines—to $161 million—in 2005. With the increased pressure for product placement in magazine articles, the American Society of Magazine Editors in October announced revised guidelines for editors and publishers to ensure that there was a clear demarcation between advertising and editorial content. ASME's newly revised "Ten Commandments" included the statements "Advertisements should look different enough from editorial pages that readers can tell the difference" and "Advertisers should not pay to place their products in editorial pages nor should they demand placement in return for advertising."

In June the Meredith Corp., best known for publishing *Better Homes and Gardens* and *Midwest Living,* became the second largest U.S. publisher with its $350 million purchase of *Family Circle, Parents, Fitness,* and *Child* magazines from Gruner + Jahr USA, a division of the German-owned Bertelsmann AG. In announcing the purchase, Meredith chairman William Kerr said,

"One of our growth strategies is to broaden our magazine portfolio to reach younger women and to serve the rapidly growing Hispanic market." The purchase was the largest in the Des Moines, Iowa-based company's 103-year history.

Gruner + Jahr's U.S. division, which was the sixth largest U.S. magazine publisher, fired Dan Brewster, its top American official, after having suffered a major setback with the demise in 2002 of its *Rosie* magazine and subsequent accusations of circulation mismanagement that arose during its court battle with the magazine's editor, talk-show host Rosie O'Donnell. Brewster later sued the company, accusing it of having made him a scapegoat.

People was named *Advertising Age's* "Magazine of the Year" in October "for handling the [Hurricane] Katrina disaster more deftly than the government. . .[and] reaching the highest circulation in its 31 years, holding its position atop Time Inc.'s formidable magazine portfolio and confidently navigating the foamy, sometimes filthy, currents of celebrity weeklies." Just hours before *People* was set to close its annual "best- and worst-dressed" issue, the editors decided to change the cover and include an additional eight pages of Hurricane Katrina coverage.

Time Inc. strengthened its place as the largest U.S. magazine publisher by expanding its international operations with the purchase of Grupo Editorial Expansión, Mexico's second largest magazine publisher. Its 15 titles brought Time Inc.'s total to 155 magazines. The Mexican publisher's stable included the business magazine *Expansión,* the celebrity-centric *Quién,* the women's lifestyle review *Balance,* and the men's title *Life and Style.*   (DAVID E. SUMNER)

BOOK PUBLISHING

United States. Though the American publishing industry's bottom-line profits in 2005 highlighted the realities expressed in one industry executive's quip that "flat is the new growth," initiatives in digital search and delivery spurred speculation that five years into the new millennium, publishing might indeed be entering the 21st century.

In 2005 sales figures again bore out that the American industry was a mature one. The Book Industry Study Group's (BISG's) *Book Industry Trends 2005* projected that total publishers' net dollar sales in 2004 had risen only 2.75% over 2003, reaching $28,584,000,000.

Though BISG was predicting a compound annual growth rate of 3.4% in publishers' net dollar sales between 2004 and 2009, the compound annual growth rate in unit sales for the same period was projected to be only 1.4%. Regarding trade-book sales, BISG's *Trends* quoted Ingram Book Co. president Jim Chandler's observation that "the pie is about as big as it's going to get."

The market-research firm Ipsos-Insight estimated that in 2004 consumer spending for books (across all channels) held at $13.3 billion for the second straight year. Unit sales, it said, were up 2.5% from 2003, reaching 1.7 billion. One distribution channel that showed growth was that of independent/small-chain bookstores. That market share accounted for 9% of the dollars spent by consumers, up 2.1% from 2002. According to Ipsos, the independents' overall performances exceeded the industry average for the past several years.

The 2005 year-to-date bookstore sales, according to the U.S. Bureau of the Census, were $10,332,000,000, a 2.2% decline from August 2004, the most recent figures available. In six of the first nine months of 2005, participating bookstores—including trade, college, religious, chain stores (including superstores), and others—reported lower sales than in 2004. These reports came during a year in which total retail sales were relatively robust; August sales were 9.9% ahead of those for that month in 2004.

The religious-book sector was a major engine in industry growth, in both revenue and units, with net sales of $1,946,300,000 in 2004. BISG projected a 37.3% increase in net revenues for the sector over the next five years. The success of the Rev. Rick Warren's *The Purpose Driven Life*, which had sold 23 million copies since 2003, prompted many trade publishers to focus on the religious market.

J.K. Rowling's *Harry Potter and the Half-Blood Prince* sold a record 6.9 million copies in the first 24 hours after its publication on July 16, and there were 13.5 million books in print before publication. Reflecting this, the Association of American Publishers reported a 71% increase in gross domestic sales in the children's and young-adult hardcover category as of September (the most recent figures available). Overall, sales of titles for teens were up 23% since 1999.

BISG reported that used books were one of the fastest-growing segments of the industry, driven by large increases in online sales and characterized by positive purchasing experiences for consumers. In 2004 sales of used trade titles (noneducational books) were $589 million; that number reached $2.2 billion when used textbook sales of $1.6 billion were included. This was an 11.1% increase over 2003. The fastest-growing component of the used-book market was online sales, which in 2004 saw a 33.3% revenue growth totaling $609 million.

It was a Silicon Valley interloper, however, that introduced the most intriguing possibilities into the often staid world of publishing. In December 2004 Internet company Google Inc. had announced that it was launching a project to digitize and index the collections of titles still protected by copyright in the libraries of the University of Michigan, Harvard University, and Stanford University (along with titles in the public domain in the collections of the New York Public Library and the University of Oxford). Google's plan to offer brief excerpts of the titles via free online searches—and to possibly link the searches to ad sales—garnered a strong reaction from many in the industry. On the legal front, authors and publishers sought an injunction to halt the initiative. In addition, Amazon.com and industry giant Random House announced new business models for the online viewing of titles on a pay-per-page basis. (DAN CULLEN)

International. It was no surprise that J.K. Rowling's *Harry Potter and the Half-Blood Prince*, whether in English or in translation, proved to be the worldwide publishing sensation of 2005. In South Africa, for example, where the weekly average sale required for a book to qualify as a best seller was 1,000, *Harry Potter* sold 40 times that number in a single day in July.

The vicious discounting in the U.K., led by the supermarket groups, was much resented by independent booksellers. That strategy had previously been unknown in South Africa; as a result, the decision by supermarket chain Pick 'n Pay to undercut the standard bookseller price by 40% introduced a significant element of instability into the book market. Booksellers in countries such as France, where resale price maintenance (RPM) remained in force, breathed a sigh of relief. The inconclusive debate about the desirability of RPM within the EU continued. In May 2005 Polish publishers roundly condemned a government proposal to reintroduce RPM. Some argued that the reintroduction of RPM was likely to provide further stimulus to the already sizable markets in illegal photocopies and unlicensed books.

Takeover activity slowed significantly during the year, following the mega-merger activity of 2004, which left little scope for further restructuring, especially in the U.K., where the top four publishing groups—Bertelsmann, Hachette (now incorporating Hodder Headline), Pearson, and News Corp.—accounted for almost one-half of total sales by value. In June 2005, however, Editis, the second largest French publisher, bought independent publisher Le Cherche Midi for a rumoured €10 million (about $12.6 million), and Éditions Privat agreed in May to purchase Éditions du Rocher for an undisclosed sum.

Having achieved some success in stemming book piracy in India and China, the U.K. Publishers Association (PA) turned its efforts toward Pakistan and Turkey. In India 500,000 pirated copies had been seized since the campaign began, although piracy remained widespread, in part because the penalties imposed by the courts were proving to be an insufficient deterrent. In China success hinged on convincing the authorities that the problem existed. Progress was proving to be slow in Pakistan, where the trade was vast; seemingly legitimate traders were involved, and the penalties were wholly inadequate. Turkish authorities were more cooperative. The PA admitted, however, that piracy was partly fostered by the setting of unreasonably high prices in less-developed markets.

The phenomenon of newspapers' promoting their own book series took hold, with the emphasis on low pricing and heavy promotion. In Germany at least eight different series had been launched by midyear; the most recent, a library of management books, sold 21 million copies. Four of the five national daily newspapers in The Netherlands also launched their own series, and the phenomenon became well-established in France, Italy, and Spain. U.K. newspapers, however, preferred to give away DVDs and music CDs.

When search engine Google began digitizing works from major libraries, the action was met with protests over its right to digitize copyrighted material. In an effort to compete with Google, the French National Library responded with a proposal, supported by other EU member states, to create a European digital library that would offer 15 million books online. (*See also* COMPUTERS AND INFORMATION SYSTEMS; LIBRARIES AND MUSEUMS: *Libraries.*) (PETER CURWEN)

Military Affairs

The main ENEMY in 2005 was MOTHER NATURE, and military forces worldwide were charged with rescuing SURVIVORS and delivering HUMANITARIAN AID. Major military combat dragged on in IRAQ AND AFGHANISTAN, and deadly violence persisted elsewhere as well.

DISASTER RELIEF

Getting assistance to the areas worst affected by the massive tsunami that struck the Indian Ocean region in December 2004 proved difficult. In early 2005 armed forces from around the world found themselves at the centre of relief efforts. The U.S. responded with Operation Unified Assistance, which included 25 ships and 16,000 personnel assisting stricken countries. India deployed 14 ships, nearly 1,000 military personnel, and dozens of helicopters and fixed-wing aircraft to Sri Lanka in what was India's largest foreign relief mission since independence in 1947. Japan sent 1,000 troops to Indonesia to help the sick and injured—also Japan's largest overseas deployment since World War II. Australia, Brazil, Bulgaria, Canada, France, Germany, Greece, Israel, Italy, Malaysia, Mexico, The Netherlands, New Zealand, Norway, Pakistan, Portugal, Russia, Singapore, Spain, Sweden, Tunisia, and the United Kingdom also contributed military personnel and equipment to the largest relief effort ever mounted.

After Hurricane Katrina struck the U.S. Gulf Coast in August, the U.S. military effort included nearly 75,000 National Guard and active-duty troops, 350 helicopters, more than 80 fixed-wing aircraft, and 50 ships. The National Guard, the branch of the military charged with civil defense and disaster relief, did not arrive in force until four days after the hurricane struck, however. Critics suggested that the delay was linked to the deployment of 40,000 National Guard soldiers and their equipment to fight the war in Iraq. (*See* ECONOMIC AFFAIRS: *Special Report.*) Canada, France, Germany, and the U.K. also sent military personnel to assist in the aftermath of Katrina. For the first time ever, Mexican troops—including nearly 100 engineers, doctors, and nurses—entered the U.S. to deliver humanitarian assistance. When Hurricane Rita hit the same area in September, more than 7,000 U.S. National Guard and active-duty troops were sent to assist in recovery operations.

International efforts in the form of military personnel and equipment were again deployed after an earthquake devastated northern Pakistan and the disputed Kashmir region in October. (*See* WORLD AFFAIRS: *Pakistan:* Sidebar.) NATO announced that it would send up to 1,000 soldiers—including a battalion of engineers, some medics, and helicopters. The organization also coordinated the military relief efforts of 41 countries that were either NATO members or partners. The U.K. and the U.S. sent military helicopters to help fly supplies and medical personnel to remote Kashmiri villages left isolated by the destruction.

WMD, ARMS CONTROL, AND DISARMAMENT

After seven years of negotiations, the UN General Assembly adopted the International Convention for the Suppression of Acts of Nuclear Terrorism. States that signed the treaty would be required to criminalize acts of nuclear terrorism, including attacks on nuclear facilities such as electricity-generating stations. The U.S. broke with nearly three decades of nonproliferation policy in July when Pres. George W. Bush struck a deal with Indian Prime Minister Manmohan Singh to share civil nuclear technology, despite India's refusal to sign the Nuclear Non-proliferation Treaty. The deal followed an announcement in March that the U.S. would resume arms sales to Pakistan, which had been suspended in 1990 in view of Islamabad's nuclear-weapons program. The resumption included the sale of approximately 75 F-16 aircraft at up to $40 million each. (Pakistan postponed the deal after the earthquake.) In October nuclear-armed rivals India and Pakistan agreed to notify each other in advance of ballistic missile test flights and to ensure that missiles were not permitted to fly close to each other's borders.

Soldiers of the Mexican navy were deployed to Biloxi, Miss., in September to help in the cleanup operations after Hurricane Katrina struck the U.S. Gulf Coast.

AP/Wide World Photos

CONFLICTS

Middle East. Violence intensified as the war in Iraq entered its third year. Civilians were the primary target of suicide and car bombings, mortar attacks, and assassinations. More than 26,000 Iraqi civilians were estimated to have been killed since the 2003 U.S.-led invasion, and the U.S. military reported its 2,000th fatality in October. The leading cause of death of troops of the U.S.-led coalition was remotely detonated roadside bombs, known in military parlance as IEDs (improvised explosive devices).

Nine U.S. soldiers—the best-known being Pvt. Lynndie England—were convicted during the year of having abused prisoners at Iraq's Abu Ghraib jail in 2003. In other incidents, soldiers from Denmark and the U.K. were charged with abuse of Iraqi prisoners. Iraq's government began investigating allegations that many of the 173 detainees discovered in November in an Interior Ministry building had been tortured by their Iraqi captors. The war in Iraq also involved a growing number of private security personnel. Approximately 70,000 civilian contractors—30,000 of them armed—were estimated to be supporting coalition military or security operations.

Fighting between Turkish armed forces and Kurdistan Workers' Party (PKK) separatists heated up in 2005. In April, 21 PKK fighters and 3 Turkish soldiers were killed near the border with Iraq in the biggest clash in the area since the PKK declared a unilateral truce in 1999. Almost 6,000 PKK guerrillas were thought to be based in Iraq.

In August and early September, Israel dismantled all its settlements and military bases in the Gaza Strip. Thousands of Israeli troops were used to remove settlers—some by force—who refused to leave. In April, Syria announced that it had withdrawn all of its military forces from Lebanon, as demanded by the UN. Syrian troops had been in the country since they intervened in the Lebanese civil war in 1976.

Caucasus. Attacks against government and civilian targets in several Caucasian republics throughout the year increased fears that separatist violence that had long beset the Russian republic of Chechnya might engulf the Caucasus region. The war in Chechnya itself continued, but the extent of the civilian casualties was largely unknown because of restrictions that Russian authorities had placed on journalists.

South and Central Asia. Hostilities in Afghanistan entered one of the bloodiest periods since the U.S.-led invasion

in 2001. Attacks by Taliban rebel forces increased, leading to the deaths of approximately 1,500 people. A 20,000-strong U.S. force shouldered the bulk of the fighting against the Taliban in the east of the country, while more than 8,000 troops from 36 countries made up the International Security Assistance Force (ISAF), which was charged with security in the area of Kabul.

King Gyanendra dismissed Nepal's government in February, declared a state of emergency, and assumed direct power, citing the need to defeat Maoist rebels, who for nine years had been fighting to end the monarchy. The state of emergency was lifted in April, and in September the rebels announced a three-month unilateral cease-fire, the first truce since peace talks broke down in 2003. The civil war in Nepal had left more than 12,000 people dead on both sides. Rebels of the separatist Liberation Tigers of Tamil Eelam organization attacked government forces in Sri Lanka on several occasions, threatening a truce agreed to in 2002.

Southeast Asia. In Indonesia the daunting task of recovering from the 2004 tsunami helped persuade the government and the separatist Free Aceh Movement (GAM) to agree in August to end the 30-year-old civil war in Aceh province. Under the agreement the European Union, together with Thailand, Malaysia, Brunei, the Philippines, Singapore, Norway, and Switzerland, provided monitors to oversee the decommissioning of GAM weapons and the relocation of Indonesian military and police forces out of the province. GAM gave up its goal of a separate state in return for local political representation.

A 2003 cease-fire between the Philippines government and Moro Islamic Liberation Front (MILF) rebels broke down in January. The army said nearly 200 MILF fighters attacked its forces, and it responded with helicopter gunships and heavy artillery. After three days of talks in Malaysia in April, however, the two sides reached an agreement. The MILF had been fighting for autonomy on the southern island of Mindanao.

Africa. In January, Burundi's president signed a law to set up a new national army that would incorporate into the government force all but one of the Hutu rebel groups. The Forces Nationales de Libération continued to reject offers of peace talks and launched a series of attacks, including one in September on the capital, Bujumbura. Fighting erupted between ethnic militias and UN troops

in the Democratic Republic of the Congo (DRC) following an attack in February on a UN convoy. The UN responded with an offensive that killed at least 50 militiamen. Numbering more than 13,000, the UN force in the DRC was the largest anywhere. Congolese troops backed by UN peacekeepers mounted their first combat operation against Hutu rebels since a deadline for the departure of all foreign armed groups expired in September. Thousands of ethnic Hutu from neighbouring Rwanda had fled to the eastern DRC after taking part in the 1994 genocide against Tutsi.

The UN Security Council threatened Eritrea and Ethiopia with sanctions in November following reports that both countries were increasing troop levels along their disputed border. In December, Eritrea expelled European and North American personnel from the UN mission that had been monitoring implementation of the 2000 peace agreement.

In March the UN Security Council established the UN Mission in the Sudan (UNMIS) to support implementation of a peace agreement signed by the government and the Sudan People's Liberation Movement/Army (SPLM/A) in January. The agreement brought to an end the conflict that had been waged in the country's south for most of the period since 1955 and had cost more than two million lives. Attacks by Arab militias on villages continued in the Darfur region in The Sudan's west, however. Tens of thousands of people had been killed and more than 1.8 million displaced since the militias took up arms in early 2003. In March the UN Security Council voted to allow the International Criminal Court (ICC) to try persons accused of war crimes in Darfur, but The Sudan insisted on prosecuting any suspects itself. NATO launched its first mission to Africa in June when it agreed to help the African Union expand its peacekeeping mission in Darfur. NATO then airlifted approximately 2,000 African Union Mission in Sudan (AMIS) troops from their home countries into Darfur and provided training. By October there were nearly 7,000 AMIS military, police, and civilian personnel in Darfur. The ICC issued its first five arrest warrants for leaders of the rebel Lord's Resistance Army (LRA) in October. The LRA was accused of widespread murder, torture, and the kidnapping of thousands of children during nearly 20 years of fighting in northern Uganda.

Latin America and the Caribbean. More than 11,000 members of the 19,000-strong United Self-Defence Forces of

Colombia (AUC) right-wing paramilitary group surrendered their weapons in return for government amnesty. The guerrilla war being waged by the Revolutionary Armed Forces of Colombia (FARC) intensified, however, which led to the deaths of more than 300 members of the security forces in the first nine months of the year. Tens of thousands of civilians had died during Colombia's 40-year civil war, which involved left-wing rebels, right-wing paramilitaries, and government forces. Throughout 2005 troops of the 7,500-strong UN Stabilization Mission in Haiti (MINUSTAH) clashed with armed gangs and supporters of Jean-Bertrand Aristide, the Haitian president ousted in 2004. Eight MINUSTAH peacekeepers and hundreds of civilians had been killed in the fighting, which took place mostly in crowded urban slums.

MILITARY TECHNOLOGY

The U.S. Air Force Research Laboratory unveiled a "nonlethal" laser rifle designed to dazzle enemy personnel without causing them permanent harm. The Personnel Halting and Stimulation Response (PHaSR) rifle could be used, for example, temporarily to blind suspects who drove through a roadblock. In March, Pakistan successfully tested its nuclear-capable Shaheen-2 ballistic missile, which had a range of 2,000 km (1,240 mi), and in August test-fired its first nuclear-capable cruise missile, the 500-km (310-mi)-range Babur. Cruise missiles normally fly at subsonic speeds and at low altitudes to avoid detection by radar. The U.S. Navy christened *Sea Jet*, an advanced electric ship built to demonstrate new technologies. Powered by an underwater waterjet the 40-m (133-ft)

vessel could operate in shallow water with great maneuverability. Unlike conventional waterjets, the system was completely submerged, reducing noise and surface wake and improving stealth.

ARMED FORCES, POLITICS, AND THE ENVIRONMENT

China opened its military procurement process to private contractors in 2005 and in November launched a Web site allowing anyone to view public tenders for matériel that ranged from weapons to livestock for feeding troops.

Indonesia, Malaysia, and Singapore agreed in August to begin coordinated air patrols over the pirate-infested waters of the Malacca Strait, one of the world's busiest sea-lanes. (*See* LAW, CRIME, AND LAW ENFORCEMENT: *Special Report.*) The area was so dangerous that private security firms started to offer armed escorts for ships traversing the strait. In October, Malaysia set up its own coast guard to strengthen maritime security in the Malacca Strait.

The largest warship ever sunk was sent to the bottom of the Atlantic Ocean in May. The decommissioned 79,700-ton, 319.3-m (1,047.5-ft)-long aircraft carrier USS *America* was sunk by the U.S. Navy following a series of test explosions over 25 days to gather data on the survivability of modern warships. In September the U.S. retired from service the last of its most powerful intercontinental ballistic missiles (ICBMs)—the MX, also known as the Peacekeeper. The 10-warhead MX was first deployed in 1986 during the Cold War. A 10-year, $7 billion environmental project to clean up the former Rocky Flats nuclear weapons plant in the U.S. was declared complete in

October. The Colorado facility made plutonium triggers for nuclear warheads until it was shut down in 1992.

Japan agreed to sweeping changes in the deployment of U.S. forces on its territory. The plan included the basing of a nuclear-powered aircraft carrier south of Tokyo and the withdrawal of about 7,000 of the 18,000 Marines from the island of Okinawa. Japan had previously refused to allow a nuclear-powered ship to be based in its waters. The U.S. lost a key air base in southeastern Uzbekistan that supported its operations in Afghanistan. Uzbek Pres. Islam Karimov evicted the Americans after Washington called for an independent inquiry into the shooting of demonstrators in the city of Andijan by Uzbek troops in May. In September, Russia and Uzbekistan held their first joint military exercise. The U.S. and Kyrgyzstan reached an agreement in October to allow U.S. forces to continue using a military base near the Kyrgyz capital, Bishkek. The base had been used to launch missions in Afghanistan since the 2001 invasion to oust the Taliban. The U.S. garnered its first military base on the Black Sea in November when it reached an agreement with Romania. The deal was part of Washington's strategy to eliminate bases in Western Europe and move operations closer to hot spots in the Middle East and Central Asia.

In an important symbol of the reconciliation that had taken place since Bosnia and Herzegovina's civil war ended in 1995, 36 soldiers from the country's three constituent groups—Serbs, Croats, and Bosnian Muslims—were sent to Iraq to support coalition forces.

MILITARY AND SOCIETY

The Canadian military hosted its first gay wedding in May after a Supreme Court ruling effectively changed the definition of marriage to include same-sex couples. In October the government of Sierra Leone banned civilians from wearing army combat fatigues; violators and anyone who sold army clothing risked being fined or jailed. The measure was being taken to stop criminals from dressing up as soldiers. Recruitment proved a problem in a number of countries involved in the war in Iraq. For the fiscal year the British army fell short of its goal of 15,000 recruits by nearly 2,000, while the U.S. Army needed approximately 7,000 more enlistees to meet its goal of 80,000.   (PETER SARACINO)

Sea Jet, *an advanced electric ship demonstrator, was christened at the Naval Surface Warfare Center facilities in Bayview, Idaho, in August.*

Performing Arts

Classical music moved into the 21st century, AFRICAN music flourished; works by choreographers WILLIAM FORSYTHE and JÉRÔME BEL fascinated the dance world; *THE LIGHT IN THE PIAZZA* brightened Lincoln Center Theater; and films about animals—*The March of the* PENGUINS, *The Chronicles of* NARNIA, and *KING KONG*—were smash hits.

MUSIC

Classical Music. Any cultural tradition that endures and flourishes for a thousand years must move at a considered pace. Thus it was that a mere five years late, in 2005 classical music entered the 21st century. The move was not heralded by a revolution in sound—as with the new music of Igor Stravinsky and Arnold Schoenberg at the turn of the previous century—as much as a new sensibility, one that opened the doors to fresh ideas and realities.

In June the BBC offered free downloads of Beethoven's nine symphonies on the Internet. The performances, by conductor Gianandrea Noseda and the BBC Philharmonic, were drawn from the network's *The Beethoven Experience* series. Initially the offer was made as an experiment to gauge interest in the music on the part of the public. By the end of the month, the experiment had turned into a phenomenon; listeners downloaded the music 1.4 million times in two one-week periods (Beethoven's Ninth Symphony proved to be the most popular, drawing 220,461 downloads). The immensity of the response—comparable to that of hit recordings by pop music artists—attested to the enduring popularity of classical music. In a more tangible sense, however, it offered the flagging classical music industry new insights and business models for making the product available to the public via the distribution of "virtual" classical recordings that could expand the form's accessibility and commercial viability.

Classical music also combined with the digital realm in February when the world's largest music publisher, London-based Boosey & Hawkes, concluded a deal with the Music Solution, London, in which the former made available the rights to themes from 300 popular classical music pieces, including "Russian Dance" from Stravinsky's *Petrushka* and Aaron Copland's "Fanfare for the Common Man," for use as ringtones on cellular phones.

The classical world flirted with another pop culture phenomenon in the form of the "Dear Friends" concert tour, which traversed the U.S. during the year. The program featured music by Japanese composer Nobuo Uematsu from the immensely popular video game series *Final Fantasy*.

In a more traditional sense, composers and orchestras continued their public outreach efforts by launching their own labels. Following the lead of the London Symphony Orchestra and the San Francisco Symphony, the London Philharmonic Orchestra founded its own record label and in April issued its initial releases, which included two archive recordings and two recent live performances of works by Dmitry Shostakovich and Sergey Rachmaninoff. Released from a contract with Deutsche Grammophon, which had undertaken to fund his project of recording all of Johann Sebastian Bach's sacred cantatas, conductor John Eliot Gardiner started his own label, Soli Deo Gloria, which issued its first recordings during the year. Meanwhile, two British composers were taking matters into their own hands. Michael Nyman (best known for film scores such as that for *The Piano* [1993]) and the venerable Scottish iconoclast Peter Maxwell Davies also formed their own respective record labels.

The classical world was rocked when Marin Alsop was named music director of the Baltimore Symphony. She thus became the first woman to attain such a post at a major American orchestra.

Space—and a galaxy far, far away—figured in two new musical works that made their debuts in 2005. In June conductor Erich Kunzel's adaptation of composer John Williams's score for the six *Star Wars* films was presented by the Toronto Symphony Orchestra. Also in June the British Institute of Physics paid tribute to physicist Albert Einstein with its Heavenly Music workshop event at the National Maritime Museum in Greenwich, in which the recorded sounds of stars, planets, and galaxies were mixed into a celestial musical work.

On CD and DVD, classical music celebrated the new and old. The January 2000 world premiere of English composer John Tavener's choral work *Fall and Resurrection* was released on an Opus Arte DVD, while up-and-coming Danish virtuoso Nikolaj Znaider was highlighted in performances of the Beethoven and Mendelssohn violin concertos. The independent Bridge label began to release a series of historic recordings of performances at the Coolidge Auditorium of the Library of Congress, which marked its 80th anniversary in 2005. On a similar note, officials of Germany's Bayreuth Festival released a 13-CD set of the 1956 staging of Richard Wagner's *Ring* cycle, featuring Hans Hotter in the role of Wotan and Astrid Varnay as Brünnhilde. The digital clarity of DVDs came to the assistance of two French baroque operas, highlighting the visuals and dancing that were as important to that form as the music itself. Jean-Baptiste Lully's *Persée* (EuroArts) was captured in a production by Hervé Niquet and the Tafelmusik Baroque Orchestra and Chamber Choir, while Jean-Philippe Rameau's *Les Indes galantes* (Opus Arte) was given a fanciful reading by William Christie and Les Arts Florissants. Herbert Henck demonstrated the delicate, surprisingly melodic side of the young John Cage on piano pieces that included "The Seasons" and "Metamorphosis" on an ECM New Series CD. Alsop and the Bournemouth Symphony Orchestra provided a look at Kurt Weill—before he was seduced by the musical theatre—on performances of his first and second symphonies on the Naxos label. Arguably one of the most intriguing recordings of the year was *The Five Browns* (RCA), which showcased five siblings performing energetic and vivacious five-piano adaptations of such warhorses as Rimsky-Korsakov's *The Flight of the Bumblebee* and Paul Dukas's *The Sorcerer's Apprentice*.

Older works were given a rebirth during the year. A fragment from a previously unheard piano concerto by Beethoven was given its premiere in The Netherlands in February by pianist Ronald Brautigam and the Rotterdam Chamber Orchestra. Two works by Antonio Vivaldi were given their modern premieres; a concert version of the Italian Baroque master's opera *Motezuma* was presented in Rotterdam in June, and a full production was staged in Düsseldorf, Ger., in September, its first performances since 1733. An aria, "De torrente in via bibet," recently reattributed to Vivaldi, was performed in Melbourne in August. A manuscript of a "ritornello aria" by J.S. Bach was found in the Anna Amalia Library in Weimar, Ger., in May; it was the first discovery of a previously unknown vocal work by Bach since 1935. At year's end music scholars at Vienna's Musikverein were attempting to authenticate a manuscript that bore the name of Wolfgang Amadeus Mozart.

A host of new operas appeared during the year, two of which illustrated the ways in which the worlds of classical and pop music were merging. In October the Royal Danish Opera presented the world premiere of a 10-song cycle from pop songwriter Elvis Costello's opera-in-progress, *The Secret Arias*, based on the unrequited love of Danish author Hans Christian Andersen for Swedish soprano Jenny Lind. In September Roger Waters, formerly of the psychedelic rock group Pink Floyd, unveiled his first opera, *Ça Ira*, on CD and DVD. Electronics composer Charles Wuorinen delved deeply into his 12-tone abstractions in his opera *Haroun and the Sea of Stories*, which received its premiere at the New York City Opera late in 2004. James Fenton's libretto was based on the book by Salman Rushdie. Also in New York, composer Tobias Picker's *An American Tragedy* was given its debut by the Metropolitan Opera. Philip Glass's *Waiting for the Barbarians* debuted in Erfurt, Ger., in September. The two-and-a-half-hour work was based on South African writer J.M. Coetzee's book about the evils of state-sponsored repression. In October, two months after the 60th anniversary of the bombings of Hiroshima

and Nagasaki, John Adams's *Doctor Atomic* was presented by the San Francisco Opera. The work was based on the efforts of a team of scientists led by J. Robert Oppenheimer that led to the detonation of the atomic bomb in 1945. The Glass and Adams works were acclaimed by critics and the public, but other new operas—and new productions of older operas—did not fare as well. Conductor Lorin Maazel's operatic version of George Orwell's novel *1984* was lambasted by critics following its debut at London's Royal Opera, and in August the British premiere of Adams's 1991 opera *The Death of Klinghoffer* created a furor over its staging, in which members of the Scottish Opera stormed the stage from the audience as terrorists with mock machine guns.

Some new stagings of Wagner operas created controversies as well. German film producer and director Bernd Eichinger came under critical fire in March for his depiction in a production at Berlin's Staatsoper of the knights in *Parsifal* as punk rockers. At Bayreuth, Swiss director Christoph Marthaler's new staging of *Tristan und Isolde* was booed during its unveiling in July, and the English National Opera raised the ire of critics and public with its version of *Götterdämmerung*, which called for Brünnhilde to strap on a bomb and blow up herself and the cast in a simulated suicide attack.

All those controversies paled in comparison to the exit of longtime music director Riccardo Muti from Milan's fabled La Scala. Muti, who had led the company for 19 years, was accused by his staff and musicians of running La Scala like a fiefdom. The dispute ended acrimoniously in April, when Muti resigned, citing irreconcilable differences. One of opera's most generous and ostentatious benefactors, the Cuban-American investor Alberto Vilar, suffered a similarly operatic downfall. Vilar, who had donated millions of dollars to various major opera companies, was arrested in May and charged with having defrauded a business client of $5 million. Oboist Blair Tindall raised eyebrows with her book *Mozart in the Jungle: Sex, Drugs, and Classical Music* when it was published in June; the tell-all tome recounted alleged cases of orchestral in-fighting and substance abuse by classical musicians. Welsh baritone Bryn Terfel lowered brows when in January, after suddenly losing his voice, he mimed a portrayal of Wotan at London's Covent Garden while another singer sang the role.

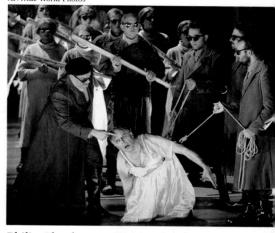
AP/Wide World Photos

Philip Glass's opera Waiting for the Barbarians *received an enthusiastic reception at its world premiere in Erfurt, Ger., on September 10.*

Recipients of top musical awards in 2005 included French composer Henri Dutilleux (*see* BIOGRAPHIES), who was honoured with the Ernst von Siemens Music Prize. The Pulitzer Prize for Music went to Steven Stucky's *Second Concerto for Orchestra*, while the Grammy Award for best classical recording was given to John Adams for *On the Transmigration of Souls* (2002), his large-scale work commemorating the victims of the 9/11 terrorist bombings in New York City.

The music world lost composers David Diamond and George Rochberg; conductors Carlo Maria Giulini, Sergiu Comissiona, Alexander Brott, and Sixten Ehrling; opera luminaries Victoria de los Angeles, Birgit Nilsson, June Bronhill, Ghena Dimitrova, Nell Rankin, Ara Berberian, and Theodore Uppman; pianists Ruth Laredo, Lazar Berman, and Grant Johannesen; violinists Norbert Brainin and Isidore Cohen; and music critic Joseph McLellan. (*See* OBITUARIES.)   (HARRY SUMRALL)

Jazz. In 2005 the jazz world reeled from the devastation wreaked by Hurricane Katrina on the New Orleans jazz community. Though most musicians scattered for safety, some outlasted the storm in the city, including noted trumpeter Marlon Jordan, who was discovered after having spent five days clinging to a rooftop. In the following weeks, radio station WWOZ, though it did not broadcast, maintained a list on its Web site of musicians who had survived the storm. Even if musicians were able to return home, the city's jazz venues remained closed. Two noted New Orleans bands, Astral Project and the

Preservation Hall Jazz Band, toured widely during the autumn. Hurricane relief efforts were established quickly, most notably by the New York-based Jazz Foundation of America, through its Jazz Musician Emergency Fund. The most famous of the many fund-raising concerts was held by New Orleans native Wynton Marsalis at Lincoln Center in New York City and included, along with his Lincoln Center Jazz Orchestra, a parade of jazz, pop music, and movie stars. The New Orleans Jazz Museum, housed in the old U.S. Mint building, was reportedly battered by the storm. The Historic New Orleans Collection, where Jelly Roll Morton's papers and other valuable research material were safeguarded, was not damaged, however, and reopened in its French Quarter location six weeks after the storm. The important collection of the Hogan Jazz Archive, housed at Tulane University, was unscathed. The lack of electricity in the hot, humid weeks that followed the storm, however, could have damaged some archived documents that might have deteriorated as a result of the absence of climate-controlled conditions.

In New York City, Lincoln Center began living up to its promise as a major jazz centre, with concerts on three stages that included during September a Women in Jazz Festival in its nightclub, Dizzy's Club Coca-Cola. On the Lower East Side, the Vision Festival's six evenings of music included a stunning performance by trumpeter Bill Dixon's quintet and a nightlong tribute to 76-year-old tenor saxophonist Fred

Anderson. Though real-estate developers in Chicago announced plans to level Anderson's nightclub, the Velvet Lounge, successful fund-raising efforts would allow Anderson to move his popular jazz spot.

Actor Rome Neal portrayed composer-pianist Thelonious Monk in the New York City one-man show *Monk*, written by Laurence Holder. Bassist Christian McBride was named co-director, along with arranger Loren Schoenberg, of the Jazz Museum in Harlem, a project that had yet to find a permanent home. Saxophonist John Zorn, whose Tzadik label issued CDs by exploratory composers and improvisers, opened a nightclub, the Stone, which featured jazz six nights a week.

The 40th anniversary of the cooperative Association for the Advancement of Creative Musicians was celebrated in the AACM's Chicago and New York City concerts and at a conference during the Ai Confini tra Sardegna e Jazz Festival in Sant'Anna Arresi, on the Italian island of Sardinia. The festival's performers included AACM members Muhal Richard Abrams (piano), Anthony Braxton (saxophones), and the Art Ensemble of Chicago, as well as Japan's Shibura Shirazu Orchestra. During a two-day Brazilian cultural symposium in Fort Lauderdale, Fla., the bossa nova was featured in the North American premiere of *Jobim sinfônico*, composed by Antonio Carlos Jobim and performed by the Symphony of the Americas, with Claudio Cruz conducting. Jobim and Vinicius de Moraes's seldom-heard 1960 work

Brasília, sinfonia da alvorada, honouring the building of Brazil's new capital, Brasília, was featured in a version of *Jobim sinfônico* recorded by the São Paulo State Symphony Orchestra and conducted by Roberto Minczuk.

Two discoveries of major performances by jazz greats highlighted the year's recordings. The Dizzy Gillespie Quintet with Charlie Parker played the electrifying *Town Hall, New York City, June 22, 1945*. A 1957 Voice of America broadcast, unearthed in the Library of Congress, was the source of *Thelonious Monk Quartet with John Coltrane at Carnegie Hall*. One of the first appearances by a Miles Davis fusion group was the historically important six-CD set *The Cellar Door Sessions 1970*. The highlight of the 2005 reissues was *The Complete Library of Congress Recordings* by pioneer pianist-composer Morton, recorded in 1938 and finally available in an eight-CD set.

Though only two major labels still focused on jazz, musician-owned labels proliferated. Trumpeter Dave Douglas's Greenleaf label issued his *Mountain Passages*, and saxophonist Branford Marsalis's Marsalis Music offered Miguel Zenón's *Jíbaro* and Harry Connick, Jr.'s *Occasion*, duets by the pianist and Marsalis. Saxophonist Evan Parker's Psi label reissued the free-improvisation landmark recording *The London Concert* with Parker and guitarist Derek Bailey (*see* OBITUARIES).

More than 70 Monk songs were offered, almost all he ever composed, in the three-CD *Monk's Casino* by pianist Alexander von Schlippenbach's quintet. *Not in Our Name* by bassist Charlie Haden's Liberation Music Orchestra featured a composition by Carla Bley, and pianist Dave Brubeck's quartet offered *London Flat, London Sharp*.

Deaths included those of bassist Percy Heath, singer-songwriter Oscar Brown, Jr., trombonist Albert Mangelsdorff, saxophonist Lucky Thompson, and pianist Shirley Horn. (*See* OBITUARIES.) Other losses during the year were those of bassist Niels-Henning Ørsted Pedersen and guitarist Billy Bauer.

(JOHN LITWEILER)

Popular. *International.* Much of the world's finest and most varied music of 2005 originated in the landlocked African state of Mali. There were three notable albums by Malian artists during the year. The most commercially successful came from Amadou and Mariam, a middle-aged blind couple who had been singing and playing together since the 1970s. Their dramatic

Among the jazz artists with New Orleans roots who helped raise money for aid to the victims of Hurricane Katrina was trumpeter Wynton Marsalis, shown here (second from left) with his band at a televised benefit concert on September 2.

NBC Universal/WireImage

change of fortune came about when the Spanish star Manu Chao offered to produce, co-write, and perform on their latest album, *Dimanche à Bamako*. Sections of the recording echoed Chao's own work, but other tracks focused on the duo's easygoing songs, embellished by slick singing and impressive blues-influenced guitar work from Amadou. The album was a major success in Europe.

The two other great Malian albums came from established veterans. Five years earlier guitarist Ali Farka Touré had announced that he had retired to his farm in the town of Niafunké, where he became mayor. In 2005, however, he made a welcome return, accompanied for the first time by Toumani Diabate, the greatest exponent of the kora, the African classical harp. Their album *In the Heart of the Moon* mixed Touré's hypnotic blueslike guitar work with virtuoso flurries of rapid-fire improvised kora playing. Diabate made a further appearance on the new album by Salif Keita, Mali's finest male singer. After years of working abroad, Keita had returned to Bamako to live and record, and his magnificent homecoming album, *M'Bemba*, was a gently rhythmic, largely acoustic set in which he was also backed by guitarist Kante Manfila and his own foster sisters.

It was a good year for African music. A series of Africa-related events across the U.K. were mounted to inspire and encourage the politicians. These included concerts, art exhibitions, and a lecture by Senegalese musician Baaba Maal at the British Museum. Rock musician and humanitarian Bob Geldof helped to organize the ambitious Live 8 concert in London and nine other cities to call attention to world poverty on the eve of the G-8 meeting. The London Live 8 event included such notables as U2, Madonna, Paul McCartney, and Pink Floyd. Senegal's Youssou N'Dour appeared there too before flying to another awareness-raising concert in Cornwall that featured African stars Tinariwen and Thomas Mapfumo, among others.

New collaborations and fusions were another highlight of music in 2005. The veteran Indian singer Asha Bhosle, who had recorded thousands of songs for the Bollywood film industry, joined forces with the adventurous Kronos Quartet from the U.S. to record an album of classic movie songs written by her late husband, R.D. Burman. Adventurous musical fusion work came from Mexico as well. The acoustic-gui-

Tony Barson/WireImage

The duo Amadou and Mariam from Mali appears at the 23rd Fête de la Musique, a celebration of many genres of music, in Versailles, France.

tar-playing duo of Rodrigo y Gabriela followed up their album *Live Manchester and Dublin* with a series of virtuoso concerts in which they mixed anything from jazz to Spanish influences to heavy metal. Other Mexican musicians, Los de Abajo, provided an even greater contrast of styles with their album *LDA v the Lunatics*, which included a Latin treatment of the 1980s hit by the Fun Boy Three, "The Lunatics (Have Taken Over the Asylum)," along with songs that ranged from salsa to punk and Mexican styles.

Brazil's minister of culture, veteran singer-songwriter Gilberto Gil, followed his live album *Eletracústico* with a series of rousing shows proving that politics had not harmed his impressively varied musical skills. Brazil's latest celebrity, Seu Jorge, came to worldwide attention through his appearances in the films *City of God* and *The Life Aquatic with Steve Zissou*, but his album *Cru* and live shows demonstrated his ability to switch from a quirky treatment of David Bowie songs in Portuguese to light dance songs and thoughtful ballads.

(ROBIN DENSELOW)

United States. The year 2005 in American pop music began with hoots and howls as pop singer and reality-television star Ashlee Simpson was booed lustily during her off-pitch performance at halftime of college football's national championship game at the

Orange Bowl in Miami. It was the second nationally televised embarrassment for Simpson, who had been caught using a prerecorded vocal track on *Saturday Night Live* two months earlier. Simpson sang her way to some measure of redemption in October, however, when she reappeared on *Saturday Night Live*, offered a truly live performance, and was cheered.

Also, January 2005 saw the start of a year of benefit concerts as Madonna, Stevie Wonder, Elton John, Kenny Chesney, and numerous other artists participated in *Tsunami Aid: A Concert of Hope*, a telethon broadcast from New York City, Los Angeles, and London. The effort raised an estimated $18 million for relief of the victims of the December 2004 Indian Ocean tsunami. Later, performers banded together for charity shows that included July's massive Live 8 event and numerous concerts in September to raise money for Hurricane Katrina relief efforts.

The late Ray Charles received the lion's share of accolades at the Grammy Awards in Los Angeles in February. Charles was remembered with eight Grammys, including the album and record of the year prizes. Together, rhythm and blues superstars Alicia Keys and Usher (*see* BIOGRAPHIES) won a total of seven Grammys, and Kanye West and rock band U2 each won three. Country music's Tim McGraw (*see* BIOGRAPHIES) won the awards for best country male vocal and best song for "Live like You Were Dying." The show's considerable star power did not save television ratings, however, which were the lowest for a Grammy presentation show since 1995.

The year saw some significant stylistic developments. A subgenre of Latin music called reggaeton, which combined elements of hip-hop and reggae, galvanized young Spanish-speaking audiences and became a springboard to stardom for Don Omar, Daddy Yankee, Luny Tunes, and others. The hushed avant-folk sounds of acts such as Devendra Banhart and Iron and Wine garnered substantial popularity and critical praise. Meanwhile, the ubiquitous nature of technology such as Apple Computer's iPod—a digital audio player that could store music downloaded via computer—made nonmainstream music more readily available to consumers.

Rock music made something of a comeback in 2005, with Coldplay (*see* BIOGRAPHIES), Nine Inch Nails, Audioslave, and other rock acts topping the *Billboard* all-genre album chart.

Wearing enormous angel wings, singer Kanye West performs "Jesus Walks" at the 47th annual Grammy Awards in the Staples Center in Los Angeles.

Country artist Chesney had an eventful year as well. His *Be as You Are: Songs from an Old Blue Chair* album debuted at number one on the *Billboard* Top 200 album chart in February; he won the Academy of Country Music Awards top entertainer prize; and his album *The Road and the Radio*, released in November, was a commercial standout.

The sales story of the year was hardcore rapper 50 Cent, whose album *The Massacre* sold more than four million copies. Other commercial successes included Mariah Carey's *The Emancipation of Mimi*, which had sold 3.4 million by mid-October, and Kanye West's *Late Registration*, which sold nearly a million copies in its first week of release. West's "Gold Digger," 50 Cent's "Candy Shop," Carey's "We Belong Together," and Gwen Stefani's "Hollaback Girl" were some of the biggest radio singles.

The Pretenders, The O'Jays, Percy Sledge, U2, and Buddy Guy were inducted into the Rock and Roll Hall of Fame in 2005. Losses included blues, gospel, and R&B greats George Lewis Scott, Clarence ("Gatemouth") Brown, Obie Benson, Luther Vandross, and Tyrone Davis; bluegrass and country stars Jimmy Martin, Vassar Clements, and Merle Kilgore; rock drummers Jim Capaldi of Traffic and Spencer Dryden of Jefferson Airplane; and synthesizer pioneer Robert Moog. (*See* OBITUARIES.)   (PETER COOPER)

DANCE

North America. One of the dance highlights of 2005 was the collaboration between Toronto's National Ballet of Canada and the Suzanne Farrell Ballet, which brought former-ballerina-turned-ballet-mistress Farrell's staging of George Balanchine's *Don Quixote* (1965), a work not seen since 1978, to the Kennedy Center for the Performing Arts in Washington, D.C. Farrell's newly designed (by Zack Brown) and arranged production showed the ballet to be its strange and yet haunting self. Farrell, once primarily associated with New York City Ballet (NYCB), was working mostly out of the Kennedy Center, where her troupe presented (November 22–27) works by Balanchine. In December Farrell was the recipient of one of the Kennedy Center's annual honours.

Performances at the Kennedy Center included two appearances by the Mariinsky Ballet of St. Petersburg, including one that offered a three-act *Cinderella,* the first major American showing of the choreography of Aleksey Ratmansky, artistic director of Moscow's Bolshoi Ballet. Later in the year Ratmansky toured with the Bolshoi and offered his mostly well-received reworking of a 1935 Dmitry Shostakovich ballet called *The Bright Stream.* In October the Kennedy Center focused on the performing arts of China, with samplings of that country's fledgling modern dance traditions as well as its ballet offerings, most notably *Raise the Red Lantern,* based on the film of the same name.

American Ballet Theatre (ABT) and NYCB, the U.S. flagship ballet troupes, had fairly standard years. ABT went into historical mode and, to the luscious score of Léo Delibes, put on a splendid staging of Sir Frederick Ashton's marvelous mythological classical ballet *Sylvia.* Standout interpreters included Gillian Murphy as Sylvia and the ever-radiant Angel Corella as Aminta, the narrative's lovesick shepherd. In addition, ABT put on a full evening of ballets by the once-ubiquitous Michel Fokine. Some of these were more reliable than others, with *Le Spectre de la rose* among the highlights and *Petrouchka* among the lesser lights. Ballerina Amanda McKerrow took her farewell bows with ABT in a summer performance of *Giselle,* while ballerina Julie Kent celebrated her 20th anniversary with the company during its fall season. One of the new roles added to her repertory was that of the ballerina in the company's first-ever staging of Jerome Robbins's *Afternoon of a Faun.* NYCB offered

a number of new works, the most distinguished of which was resident choreographer Christopher Wheeldon's *After the Rain,* a winter premiere. Otherwise, season highlights included the recognition of departing dancers; Jock Soto retired from the stage, and Peter Boal left to assume artistic directorship of the Pacific Northwest Ballet. Robbins's impressive *New York Export Opus Jazz* was staged by NYCB for the first time in a strong production presented by former Joffrey Ballet dancer Edward Verso.

Boston Ballet, which appointed Jorma Elo of Finland its new resident choreographer, already had a Finnish artistic director, Mikko Nissinen. The company's repertory included not only new works by Lucinda Childs and Peter Martins but also traditional works, such as *The Sleeping Beauty* and *La Sylphide.* Houston Ballet proceeded under the fairly new direction of Stanton Welch to offer a mix of contemporary works and narrative standards, such as Welch's own *Divergence* and John Cranko's *Onegin.* Oregon Ballet Theatre, under the direction of the recently appointed Christopher Stowell, included Robbins's *In the Night* in its mixed repertory and ended the year with an ambitious staging of Balanchine's blue-chip version of *The Nutcracker.* Edward Villella's Miami City Ballet managed to acquire Twyla Tharp's 1976 landmark crossover ballet *Push Comes to Shove.* The Joffrey Ballet of Chicago launched its 50th anniversary in October with a mixed bill featuring *The Dream,* Ashton's now-classic one-act rendering of *A Midsummer Night's Dream.* Pacific Northwest Ballet had a year of "farewell and hail" as long-time artistic directors Francia Russell and Kent Stowell left their positions, and Boal took over the reins with a gala program that featured works specially brought in by him, notably Balanchine's *Symphony in Three Movements,* set to the music of Igor Stravinsky.

The 2004 "Fall for Dance" series at the New York City Center returned in 2005, with local and visiting groups featured in ballet, modern dance, and in-between aesthetics—all for the flat rate of $10 a ticket. The series participants were wide-ranging, from the Lyon (France) Opéra Ballet to the Urban Bush Women, a New York City-based group that celebrated its 20th anniversary during the year. The Paul Taylor Dance Company spent the year wending its way on a 50th-anniversary celebratory tour to all 50 states.

The Martha Graham Dance Company had ambitious seasons in New York City and the Kennedy Center, with notable revivals of its namesake's too-little-seen *Deaths and Entrances*. At midyear the legal battle with Ron Protas, Graham's legal heir, moved closer to an end when a New York federal judge ruled that the Martha Graham Center of Contemporary Dance owned the rights to seven of Graham's unpublished works. Graham artistic directors Terese Capucilli and Christine Dakin were removed in what was termed an administrative "streamlining" in favour of Janet Eilber.

Merce Cunningham Dance Company, which toured abroad and at home, presented Cunningham and John Cage's large-scale *Ocean* in a run at the Lincoln Center Festival. The Mark Morris Dance Group moved into its 25th-anniversary season with a 26-city tour; Morris's masterly *L'allegro, il penseroso, ed il moderato* made a strong showing at Lincoln Center's Mostly Mozart series, his *Sandpaper Ballet* helped launch Houston Ballet's year, and his *Gong* was revived for ABT's fall New York City season.

The American Dance Festival's season in Durham, N.C., included 17 companies, one of which traveled from Indonesia; the festival's annual Scripps award went to Bill T. Jones, whose new politically motivated *Blind Date* had its premiere there in September at Montclair State University before touring elsewhere. The Alvin Ailey American Dance Theater moved into handsome and practical quarters in midtown New York City, where the troupe climaxed a busy year of touring with its annual monthlong winter season, for which artistic director Judith Jamison produced a specially made new work called *Reminiscin'*—set to the music of female jazz greats.

Karole Armitage offered a three-week season with her company Armitage Gone! Dance in New York City. Although she had spent a good part of her postpunk choreographic career abroad, she recently had reestablished herself in the U.S. The Japan Society produced a series called "Cool Japan: *Otaku* Strikes!," which was highlighted by the amusing antics of the Condors all-male dance troupe in the freewheeling *Mars: Conquest of the Galaxy II.* The older and similarly geared modern dance companies Pilobolus and MOMIX had multiweek runs in New York City, with each showing programs of works under single umbrella titles, such as the Moses Pendleton-directed *Lunar Sea* for MOMIX. Matthew Bourne's choreography-based *Play Without Words* helped greatly distinguish the offerings at the

Brooklyn (N.Y.) Academy of Music (BAM). Avant-garde and experimentalist aesthetics were highlighted by Jérôme Bel at New York City's Dance Theater Workshop, with his witty *The Show Must Go On;* by Dean Moss at the Kitchen in New York City, with his complex *Figures on a Field;* and by Sarah Michelson's intense *Daylight* series, which debuted at P.S. 122 (New York City) before traveling to the Walker Art Center (Minneapolis, Minn.) and On the Boards in Seattle.

The directorship at the National Ballet of Canada changed shortly after the company brought then current director James Kudelka's *The Contract (The Pied Piper)* to BAM. The new director of the Canadian company was former ballerina Karen Kain; Kudelka remained as resident choreographer. Veteran ballerina Martine Lamy gave a farewell performance for that company during the year, dancing the lead in *Études*. The Royal Winnipeg (Man.) Ballet toured its atypical versions of *The Magic Flute*, by Mark Godden, and *A Cinderella Story*, by Val Caniparoli. Les Grands Ballets Canadiens de Montréal toured to the Jacob's Pillow Dance Festival in Becket, Mass., and won high praise for its modernist mixed bill. The Montreal-based Marie Chouinard Company took part in the "Fall for Dance" festival and also performed at the Joyce Theater.

Deaths during the year included those of choreographers Warren Spears, Onna

Christophe Jeannot and Miki Orihara are featured in the revival of the Martha Graham Dance Company's production of Deaths and Entrances *at New York City Center.*

Photo by John Deane

White, and Alfredo Corvino, dancers Joe Nash and Fernando Bujones (*see* OBITUARIES), and NYCB music adviser Gordon Boelzner.　　(ROBERT GRESKOVIC)

Europe. The European dance world's major events in 2005 ranged from triumph, with the emergence in Germany of a new company led by choreographer William Forsythe (*see* BIOGRAPHIES), to disaster, with the sudden closure of the Ballet Gulbenkian in Portugal. The year's big anniversary celebration took place in Denmark, where the Royal Danish Ballet commemorated the bicentenary of the birth of its great choreographer August Bournonville.

In the United Kingdom the Royal Ballet joined in the Bournonville party with a new production of his most famous ballet, *La Sylphide*, by its Danish principal dancer Johan Kobborg. The Royal Ballet concluded its season of homage to its own founder choreographer Sir Frederick Ashton with some fine performances of his masterpiece *Symphonic Variations*. Contemporary choreographer Christopher Bruce made a new piece for the company, *Three Songs—Two Voices*, using music by Jimi Hendrix, which was a bold choice on paper but less successful in reality. The contract of Royal Ballet director Monica Mason was extended to 2010, giving her four more years in the post than was originally planned.

The Birmingham Royal Ballet became the first British company to mount the reconstructed version of Vaslav Nijinsky's *Rite of Spring;* later in the year the company looked back on its own history for a triple bill, including early works by Kenneth MacMillan (*Solitaire*), Ninette de Valois (*Checkmate*), and John Cranko (*The Lady and the Fool*). MacMillan also featured in the programming of English National Ballet, which gave the first European performances of the production of *The Sleeping Beauty* that he had originally made for ABT. English National Ballet artistic director Matz Skoog resigned in the spring and was replaced by Wayne Eagling, previously artistic director of the Dutch National Ballet.

Scottish Ballet continued on the upward curve it had been climbing since 2002, when Ashley Page launched his regeneration of the company; the highlight of the year was the company's appearance, after a long absence, at the Edinburgh International Festival, with a program of ballets by George Balanchine, including the rarely seen *Episodes*. The most unusual commission of the year saw Rambert Dance

Company's artistic director, Mark Baldwin, creating a dance at the request of the Institute of Physics, London, to mark the centenary of the year in which Albert Einstein published his three most revolutionary ideas. Although the relationship between science and choreography was difficult to detect, the resulting work, *Constant Speed,* was colourful and energetic, and the Einstein connection generated a gratifyingly large amount of publicity.

It was a busy year for choreographer Matthew Bourne, with revivals of his famous *Swan Lake* and the less-well-known *Highland Fling* (his updating of *La Sylphide*) and a new work, *Edward Scissorhands,* all being shown at Sadler's Wells. The original star of Bourne's *Swan Lake,* Adam Cooper, made a dance version of *Les Liaisons dangereuses;* though originally produced in Japan, it had a summer season in London and was much enjoyed by audiences despite strong reservations in most of the reviews. The Ballet Nacional of Cuba and the Paris Opéra Ballet made welcome appearances in London for the first time in many years.

The third Bournonville Festival in Copenhagen combined performances, exhibitions, and lecture-demonstrations; nine of Bournonville's surviving ballets were shown, as well as several shorter pieces in the end-of-festival gala. New versions of *The Kermesse in Bruges* and *The King's Volunteers on Amager* were coolly received by some of the foreign visitors, but there was some memorable dancing throughout the week, especially from the men—Thomas Lund and Mads Blangstrup—who led the company in this repertoire; new principal dancer Kristoffer Sakurai also made a fine impression. The company's Bournonville training was based on six daily classes arranged by Bournonville's successor, Hans Beck, and the company recorded the classes in their entirety and published them on DVD to coincide with the festival. The recordings were important documentation of both the technical foundation of the company and a talented generation of performers.

Earlier in the season the Royal Danish Ballet had premiered a new full-evening work by John Neumeier in honour of the great storyteller Hans Christian Andersen. Neumeier's *The Little Mermaid* used music by Lera Auerbach, and Marie-Pierre Greve danced the title role at the first performance. Another, very different children's tale inspired the Royal Swedish Ballet's new production;

choreographer Pär Isberg translated Swedish writer Astrid Lindgren's *Pippi Longstocking* into a highly successful ballet for younger audiences, with Anna Valev and Marie Lindqvist alternating as the spirited young heroine.

The Paris Opéra Ballet showed a creation by étoile Nicolas Le Riche, who put Vivaldi's *Four Seasons* to new and unexpected uses in his full-length version of *Caligula,* originally inspired by *The Twelve Caesars* of Suetonius. Wilfried Romoli was promoted to étoile at the unusually late age of 42, and Emmanuel Thibault, a very stylish virtuoso dancer long admired by the public, was made premier danseur after years of having been overlooked at the annual competitions. The most talked-about choreographer of the year was Jérôme Bel, whose work delighted some as much as it scandalized others.

The Forsythe Company gave its first performances in April in Frankfurt am Main, Ger. The company, which was based jointly in Frankfurt and Dresden and funded by both cities, allowed Forsythe to resume his creative journey with a new sense of security. His first work for his ensemble, *Three Atmospheric Studies,* was a critical triumph. Australian choreographer Graeme Murphy made his first ballet for a European company; in Munich the Bavarian State Ballet premiered *The Silver Rose,* telling the same story as *Der Rosenkavalier* but using music by Carl Vine instead of Richard Strauss.

On March 24 the Mariinsky Ballet in St. Petersburg added Forsythe's *Approximate Sonata* to its growing collection of his works and at the same performance gave the premiere of *Reverence* by David Dawson, a British-born choreographer who was establishing a serious reputation from his base in the Dutch National Ballet. Kirill Simonov made a new version of *Daphnis and Chloe,* using only some of Ravel's music and abandoning the traditional story altogether. The company continued its punishing touring schedule, and there were complaints from knowledgeable viewers about young dancers' being featured in roles for which they were not properly prepared. In Moscow the Bolshoi Ballet showed director Aleksey Ratmansky's new version of the Shostakovich ballet *The Bolt* and also gave its first performances of three ballets by Léonide Massine—*Le Tricorne, Les Présages,* and *Gaîté Parisienne.* The Bolshoi Theatre closed for a period to be measured in years, for desperately needed renovations.

The announcement of the closure of the 40-year-old Ballet Gulbenkian, based in Lisbon, came with no advance warning for its dancers, who reacted with shock and an appeal to the rest of the dance world to join in their protest against the decision.

Deaths during the year included those of former Bolshoi Ballet dancer Raisa Struchkova and Australian dancer and artistic director Ross Stretton. (*See* OBITUARIES.)   (JANE SIMPSON)

Highland Fling, "a romantic wee ballet," presented by the New Adventures company, was one of two revivals of work by choreographer Matthew Bourne in 2005. Bourne also mounted a new production, Edward Scissorhands.

Linda Rich. Dance Picture Library

THEATRE

Great Britain and Ireland. Three days after *Talking to Terrorists* opened on July 4, 2005, at the Royal Court Theatre, bombs were detonated in the London transport system. Robin Soans's verbatim play for the Out of Joint touring company crisscrossed testimonies from former terrorists and their victims with the views of workers, politicians, and British ambassadors abroad. The play was a fascinating revelation of the sociology of terrorism.

Meanwhile, an exciting revival of *Julius Caesar,* directed by Deborah Warner at the Barbican Theatre, cast a powerful light on what goes wrong when politicians act illegally in the name of democracy. Ralph Fiennes bounded on as a hyperactive Mark Antony in a white vest, while Simon Russell Beale as Cassius and Anton Lesser as Brutus locked horns in argument against the background of a huge, seething crowd in the first half and an abandoned aircraft hangar in the second.

The British theatre was again politicized by world and local events. The National Theatre followed the 2004 response to the Iraq war in David Hare's *Stuff Happens* with *The UN Inspector,* David Farr's sparky, satiric rewrite of Nikolay Gogol's comedy about a nonentity mistaken for a government official. In addition, Hampstead Theatre had a big success with Denis Kelly's *Osama the Hero,* in which a schoolboy tries to understand what makes Osama bin Laden tick. Tom Brooke, a brilliant new young actor, played the boy and scored again later in the year at the Edinburgh Festival in another impressive Kelly play, *After the End,* set in an underground bunker after a catastrophe of some kind at ground level.

As an antidote to all this edginess, the new musical *Billy Elliot* was greeted with relief and acclaim, one critic even suggesting that it was the best new British musical since *Oliver! Billy Elliot* was a huge popular success, even if one felt that the score by Elton John was way below his best and Stephen Daldry's direction was surprisingly flat-footed. The story of a boy escaping from a grim industrial background—meticulously evoked in the miners' strike of 1984—in dance classes and

artistic endeavours seemed to pack more of a punch in the theatre than it did in the 2000 film.

Ewan McGregor returned to the stage as Sky Masterson in the 1950 classic musical *Guys and Dolls,* directed by Michael Grandage against a bare black brick wall that evoked the Donmar Warehouse space (the Donmar Warehouse production company was co-producer with Howard Panter's Ambassador Theatre Group and Clear Channel Entertainment). McGregor's

© Gareth Cattermole/Getty Images

Billy Elliot, a new stage production adapted from the film of the same name, was a critical and popular success at the Victoria Palace Theatre in the West End following its opening in September.

insinuating charm almost made up for his weak vocal chords. There were standout performances by Jenna Russell as Sarah Brown, Douglas Hodge as a flustered, emotionally chaotic Nathan Detroit, and, especially, Jane Krakowski as a downright sexy Miss Adelaide, leading the Hot Box girls in a vaudeville striptease (minxes with minks).

A third big musical, *The Big Life,* transferred from the Theatre Royal, Stratford East, and fared equally well with the critics but not with the public. It closed after a few months. This was a free-and-easy update on Shakespeare's *Love's Labour's Lost,* focusing on the first wave of black immigrants

to Britain after World War II. The musical numbers—ska, tap, and blues—were performed with relish, but the show was loose at the seams and finally fell apart as a trite, good-natured revue.

Admirable star turns in the West End came from *Friends* television favourite David Schwimmer, relaxed and rakish in Neil LaBute's *Some Girl(s);* Sir Tom Courtenay as a befuddled Anglo-Irish landowner in Brian Friel's glorious Chekhovian *The Home Place* at the Comedy Theatre (Adrian Noble's production was first seen at the Gate in Dublin); and two Hollywood B-listers, Val Kilmer and Rob Lowe, in plays better known as film titles, *The Postman Always Rings Twice* and *A Few Good Men,* respectively.

More adventurous, perhaps, were a pair of postwar signature classics, John Osborne and Anthony Creighton's 1958 *Epitaph for George Dillon* and Simon Gray's 1975 *Otherwise Engaged,* which attracted, respectively, Joseph Fiennes and Richard E. Grant into meaty roles first undertaken by Robert Stephens and Alan Bates. There were also rewarding revivals of Harold Pinter's 1958 debut play, *The Birthday Party,* with Eileen Atkins and Henry Goodman offering definitive new readings of Meg and Goldberg; Terence Rattigan's 1963 *Man and Boy,* with David Suchet wrestling the ghost of Laurence Olivier to the ground as a wheeler-dealer con man; and Bill MacIlwraith's 1966 *The Anniversary,* with Sheila Hancock blazingly funny as a monstrous mother-in-law from hell.

It was hard to deny Beale his accolades as "actor of the year," especially after three more sensationally intelligent and captivating performances: his Cassius was flanked by a surprisingly imaginative and compelling Macbeth at the Almeida Theatre (Emma Fielding was his porcelain-featured troubled Lady) and a predictably brilliant and tentative academic in David Grindley's fine revival of Christopher Hampton's *The Philanthropist* at the Donmar.

A new fringe venue, the Menier Chocolate Factory in Southwark, had an impressive season of plays by Philip Ridley and David Greig and also gave a British premiere of Jonathan Larson's

(continued on page 260)

Kabuki
Goes West

by Shōzo Satō

Traditional Japanese popular theatre—kabuki and nō—is making inroads in the West. In 2005 *Kabuki Lady Macbeth*, a version of Shakespeare's *Macbeth*, had its world premiere at the Chicago Shakespeare Theater. In that same city three months earlier, audiences had marveled at a nō program from Japan's Nōgaku Kyokai, one of the first visits to the United States by this troupe, which includes artists designated as "intangible cultural assets" (an official state distinction for artists who have achieved the pinnacle of their field). Their program replicated the one that was given for Pres. Ulysses S. Grant during his visit to Japan in 1879. For the Chicago nō performances, the 900 available tickets were snapped up in less than two

Michael Brosilow

Actress Barbara Robertson appears as Lady M in Chicago Shakespeare Theater's world premiere production of Kabuki Lady Macbeth *during the spring of 2005.*

hours. The 60 performances of *Kabuki Lady Macbeth* were similarly well-received and well-attended.

The history of kabuki parallels and is roughly contemporaneous with the development of such Western genres as Shakespearean drama, ballet, and opera. In all of these theatrical forms, the plot is already well known, but audiences attend new productions to savour the production values: acting, singing, orchestral playing, direction, set and costume design, and so forth. Tradition is especially strong in kabuki; actors are organized into "families" and often assume the name of a famous line of kabuki masters, adding a number after the name to indicate his generation. For example, in a recent celebration in the kabuki world, Nakamura Kankuro took on the title of his late father, becoming Nakamura Kanzaburō XVIII, a line that dates back to 1624. Thus, the nuances, characterizations, and skills of a production will vary depending upon which kabuki family is performing. Moreover, an actor known for portraying virile males might appear the following month as an old woman. A young kabuki actor may become very popular, but until he receives a historically important name, he cannot perform certain roles on the main stage.

Ka-bu-ki translates as "song-dance-acting," but originally it was called *kabuku*, meaning "extraordinary." The genre began in 1603 as a sort of all-female street theatre, with a simply-clad priestess chanting a sutra, ringing a handbell, and dancing. In time, other priestesses joined in, and they performed on street corners and empty temporary nō stages. Early kabuki gained popular appeal, so much so that prostitutes began to imitate the performances for their own ends. This prompted the officials of the shogunate to prohibit females from performing in public, which in turn was the start of

all-male kabuki troupes. Kabuki flourished and gained a reputation for harbouring antiestablishment influences, which troubled the authorities. Other official restrictions led to ingenuity and innovation on the part of the kabuki troupes. In the 17th century, for example, adult males customarily shaved the tops of their heads. In order to perform

Michael Brosilow

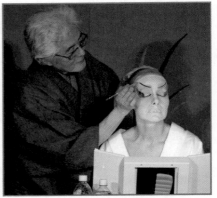

Author Shōzo Satō, who created and directed Kabuki Lady Macbeth, *applies makeup to actress Barbara Robertson (Lady M) before a performance.*

female roles, the actors needed wigs, and this led to the creation of one of the most advanced wig-making technologies in the world. When the government prohibited the use of wigs, however, *onnagata* (males portraying females) covered their foreheads with a rich purple cloth, although silk and gold brocades were reserved for the warrior classes and prohibited for actors. Other official prohibitions included steel swords (the spirit of the samurai; kabuki henceforth used bamboo) and suits of armour (kabuki uses papier maché). *Onnagata* perfected stylized femininity, another departure from realism. Over 400 years kabuki troupes developed some of the greatest theatrical innovations in the world, including the revolving stage, the elevator stage, and the *hanamichi,* a walkway through the audience for performers.

Some influences of Japanese kabuki were felt in professional theatre in New York City beginning in the 1950s, but they were generally short-lived. In the 1970s a few American universities began teaching mostly academically oriented courses on Japanese theatre. The one significant exception was the University of Illinois at Urbana-Champaign (UIUC), where what is now called "fusion kabuki" was developed.

When the UIUC's Krannert Center for the Performing Arts opened in 1969, I had the honour to be appointed artist in residence. We began staging kabuki plays each year, but our productions were based on translations of the kabuki classics and performed with traditional stage settings, costumes, and conventions. Certainly the American student actors lacked the inheritance and training of the generations of kabuki families, but they nonetheless began to attract attention and were invited to perform at institutions across the country during university vacations.

Fusion kabuki melded plots of well-known Western dramas with kabuki conventions. When traditional kabuki plays were presented in English, the plot-oriented audience most often did not understand the theatrical conventions. What was needed was a kabuki play in which the audience would focus on the acting and staging rather than the story line. Over the years we have produced *Kabuki Macbeth* (1978), *Kabuki Medea* (1983), *Kabuki Othello* (1986), *Kabuki Faust* (1986), *Achilles: A Kabuki Play* (1991), and, most recently, *Kabuki Lady Macbeth.* We have moved beyond student productions and even for a time enjoyed a professional theatre company, the Wisdom Bridge Theatre of Chicago. Fusion kabuki has been seen at the John F. Kennedy Center for the Performing Arts in Washington, D.C., the Sherover Theatre in Jerusalem, the Deutsches National Theater in Weimar, Ger., in Cairo, and elsewhere.

For *Kabuki Lady Macbeth,* based loosely upon Shakespeare's *Macbeth* and told from the lady's point of view, a script was written in contemporary poetic form. The play was performed by American actors using English dialogue. Eastern aesthetics and spiritual values were retained, and all the traditional kabuki staging conventions were

followed, including makeup, costuming, stylized body language, and kabuki intonation of the dialogue. A music synthesizer accompanied the *ki* player (a percussionist garbed in black and seated at stage right), who punctuated

Macbeth (Michael F. Goldberg) prepares to kill Duncan (Peggy Roeder) in the Chicago Shakespeare Theater production of **Kabuki Lady Macbeth.**

action with the sharp sounds of wood striking a board on the floor. Actors began each rehearsal on their hands and knees purifying the work space by polishing the floor with a cloth. A system of warm-up stretching exercises helped clear their mind, and time was allotted for *zazen* (seated meditation) in order to get into character.

Unquestionably, influences from kabuki now have permeated theatre in the West, not only with innovations in stage technology such as those mentioned earlier but also in such novelties as *koken* (onstage assistants to an actor) and *hikinuki* (a quick change of costume for an actor that reveals a change in character of the actor and his true state of mind). Of even greater significance, however, is the fusion of

Eastern and Western aesthetics that is taking place. American performers are going beyond mere imitation of a style of acting and developing an understanding of the basis for Japanese aesthetics. This was encouraged at UIUC by having all kabuki students take lessons in other Japanese art forms, such as *chadō* (the tea ceremony), ikebana (flower arrangement), *sumi-e* (black-ink painting), and Japanese classical dance. Among other things, students learned the eloquence of silence and the value of empty space. Through universalization of such aesthetic principles, we are gradually transcending our cultural differences.

Shōzo Satō is professor emeritus of the Art and Design Faculty of the University of Illinois at Urbana-Champaign and visitng professor at Northwestern University, Evanston, Ill. In additon to his theatre work he is a master in the Japanese tea ceremony, ikebana, and classical dance and has published widely in these and other areas of Japanese culture.

(continued from page 257)
posthumous *Tick, Tick. . .Boom!*, written before *Rent* and poignant as both prelude and postscript.

The Young Vic, peripatetic while its premises were being rebuilt, co-presented at the Wyndhams Theatre in the West End a David Lan production of Shakespeare's *As You Like It*, with Helen McCrory as a delightful Rosalind and Sienna Miller as a feisty Celia. Miller attracted unjust scorn for her performance, undoubtedly as a punishment for conducting a well-publicized on-off romantic relationship with Jude Law.

Other West End incursions were made by the Donmar, with a scintillating production by Phyllida Lloyd of Friedrich Schiller's *Mary Stuart*, starring Harriet Walter and Janet McTeer, and the Almeida, with Richard Eyre's incandescent revival—in his own translation—of Henrik Ibsen's *Hedda Gabler*, starring Eve Best, another brilliant actress entering her peak period.

Kevin Spacey weathered the storm of critical disapproval at the Old Vic to give a blistering performance in Dennis McIntyre's *National Anthems;* Spacey had also performed in the play's 1988 American premiere. He then eased into the Cary Grant role in *The Philadelphia Story* (minus six weeks in Hollywood to shoot the film *Superman Returns*) before diving into rehearsals for *Richard II* in an Armani-suited production by Sir Trevor Nunn. Spacey remained bullish about his artistic directorship, saying his job at the Old Vic would take him 10 years, with a few breaks for filming. He was determined to win a new audience and face down his critics.

There was no such problem for Nicholas Hytner, artistic director at the National Theatre, which had another hugely successful year of full houses and well-reviewed work. *The History Boys*, the hit play by Alan Bennett (*see* BIOGRAPHIES), won several awards early in the year and continued to do sellout business until a new cast embarked on a national tour in the fall. The play, with some of the original cast restored, returned to the South Bank in December. An international tour was planned prior to the Broadway opening in April 2006. Michael Gambon's Falstaff in Hytner's panoramic revival of Shakespeare's great historical diptych, *Henry IV, Parts One and Two*, was inevitably admired; even when he blurred his lines, Gambon just was Falstaff, and there was an incisive and acidulous old Justice Shallow from John Wood

for him to bounce off in the great recruitment scenes in the Gloucestershire orchard. The most eagerly anticipated new plays at the National were film director Mike Leigh's first stage work in more than a decade, *Two Thousand Years*, an elegiac inquiry into the meaning of Jewishness in a suburban north London family, and David Edgar's *Playing with Fire*, an ambitious, argumentative take on the recent racist riots in northern British towns.

The Royal Shakespeare Company announced a collaboration with Sir Cameron Mackintosh in his West End theatres. The Strand was to be renovated and renamed the Novello (composer Ivor Novello formerly kept an apartment in the building) and would be a new winter home for the RSC's summer Shakespeare comedies in Stratford-upon-Avon. The RSC was settling down nicely under Michael Boyd, and a Gunpowder Plot season of rare Elizabethan and Jacobean plays at the Swan in Stratford (including Shakespeare's "banned play" *Thomas More* and Ben Jonson's superb political thriller *Sejanus: His Fall*) was also destined for the capital at year's end, in the reconfigured Trafalgar Studios, formerly the Whitehall Theatre.

After months of speculation in the press, Andrew Lloyd Webber (Lord Lloyd-Webber) finally sold off four of his London theatres—the Apollo, the Garrick, the Duchess, and the Lyric—in an £11.5 million (about $20 million) deal with a newly formed alliance of Nica Burns (formerly Lloyd Webber's production director at the Really Useful Group) and Broadway producer and oil millionaire Max Weitzenhoffer.

Dan Crawford, American fringe impresario and founder-director of the King's Head in Islington, died shortly before the opening of his last presentation, *Who's the Daddy?* His smash hit was a curiously bumptious, crude, and naive farce about sex scandals at a weekly magazine, *The Spectator*, that involved former home secretary David Blunkett; the magazine's proprietor, Kimberly Quinn; the magazine's editor, MP Boris Johnson; various columnists; and a Chilean chef. The characters were all named in the play and impersonated with varying degrees of accuracy and competence, but the script was dross. The authors, Toby Young and Lloyd Evans, doubled as joint theatre critics for *The Spectator*, which made the whole event even more bizarre.

Though Ray Cooney usually excelled at farce, his latest, *Tom, Dick & Harry*—

coauthored with his son Michael, a Hollywood screenwriter—was a gruesome misfire owing to the use of body parts in plastic bags as key properties in the escalating mayhem. In addition, Cooney's direction was far too frantic to be funny, and the only point of interest was that three acting McGann brothers—Joe, Stephen, and Mark—played the three brothers named in the title.

In other news, actor Samuel West (son of Timothy West and Prunella Scales) succeeded Michael Grandage as director of the Sheffield Crucible and began by appearing as Benedick in Shakespeare's *Much Ado About Nothing*. The Chichester Festival Theatre directorate of Martin Duncan, Ruth Mackenzie, and Steven Pimlott resigned after three eventful years. The summer's highlights included a fizzing primary-coloured revival by Duncan of *How to Succeed in Business Without Really Trying* and David Warner as a tearjerking King Lear.

Farther along the south coast, the Brighton Festival's centrepiece was the visit of the Maly Theatre of St. Petersburg in Lev Dodin's incomparable production of *Uncle Vanya* (which also visited the Barbican). Sir Peter Hall's third annual season at Bath featured his 50th-anniversary production of *Waiting for Godot*.

Irish actor Richard Dormer plays Lucky the slave in the 50th-anniversary production of Samuel Beckett's **Waiting for Godot** *at the Theatre Royal, Bath.*

The Edinburgh Festival presented the complete cycle of six plays by J.M. Synge, including his masterpiece, *The Playboy of the Western World,* and his last, the mythical tragedy *Deirdre of the Sorrows.* Garry Hynes's superb Druid Theatre Company, based in Galway, Ire., revealed Synge to be a harsher, more death-fixated playwright than was commonly supposed.

At the Abbey in Dublin, artistic director Ben Barnes resigned amid revelations of financial chaos and accusations of mismanagement. Instead of basking in the afterglow of its 2004 centenary year, the Abbey was struggling for survival, solvency, and artistic credibility. The Abbey was due to move to a new home—yet to be built—in five years' time, and incoming artistic director Fiach MacConghail promised that his theatre would still be worth celebrating in another 100 years. Meanwhile, Druid had resoundingly stolen the Abbey's thunder with its Synge cycle and growing international reputation, and around the corner from the Abbey, the Gate Theatre under Michael Colgan continued to thrive on a diet of old and new classics.

(MICHAEL COVENEY)

U.S. and Canada. A whirlwind of leadership changes made an impact on major American regional theatres in 2005, altering established patterns of new-play development and raising fieldwide questions about strategies for cultural inclusion and audience diversification. Among the companies taken over by new artistic directors were New York City's high-profile Public Theater, famously founded and nurtured by Joseph Papp and overseen in recent seasons by the redoubtable George C. Wolfe; Los Angeles's powerful, hydra-headed Center Theater Group (CTG), which had been steered for nearly four decades by the liberal/activist vision of director Gordon Davidson; and the flagship arts institution of Colorado, the well-appointed Denver Center Theatre Company, which had been the fiefdom for 21 years of its company-minded artistic director, Donovan Marley.

Younger artists with sterling producing credits assumed the helm at all three companies. Moving into what was perhaps the toughest act to follow—Wolfe's 12-year stint at the Public, which generated Pulitzer- and Tony-winning plays (*Topdog/Underdog, Angels in America*) and commercial hits (*Bring in 'da Noise, Bring in 'da Funk*) as well as a few misfires (*The Wild Party*)—was Oskar Eustis, 46, a sharp administrator and champion of new writers who had previously headed Trinity Repertory Company in Providence, R.I., and San Francisco's Eureka Theatre. Surrounding himself with youthful talent, Eustis set a progressive tone at the Public, and he was expected to build upon Wolfe's legacy of artistic diversity.

A bluster of controversy accompanied the appointment in January of Michael Ritchie, former artistic head of Massachusetts's actor-centred Williamstown Theatre Festival, to the top job at CTG. In marked contrast to Eustis's approach, Ritchie, 48, declared that "attention has to go to production," not readings and workshops. He immediately jettisoned several new-play-development programs that had become a staple of CTG's Mark Taper Forum, including the African American, Asian American, and Latino play labs that had been in place since the early 1990s and another that had been supporting disabled writers since 1982. The loss of these resources for developing and minority writers prompted heated criticism from the expected quarters and was likely to lead to seismic shifts in writer-support programs nationwide.

Becoming only the third artistic director in the Denver Center's 26-year history, Kent Thompson, 51, moved west from a highly successful tenure at the Alabama Shakespeare Festival in Montgomery. Thompson, a Shakespeare specialist as well as a fan of new plays, affirmed that he would retain Denver's resident acting company—one of only a handful in the U.S.—and would rev up rather than reduce the company's assets for new and underrepresented voices.

If 2005 was any indication, fresh theatrical voices would continue to emerge across the country no matter how the argument over play development shook out. Among the provocative new works making their debuts during the year were Noah Haidle's *Mr. Marmalade,* which mounted an oblique but sharp-toothed critique of trashy American culture by entering the vivid imagination of an abused four-year-old girl (played, at New York's Roundabout Theatre Company, by the adult actress Mamie Gummer, a daughter of Meryl Streep); Adam Rapp's *Red Light Winter,* an edgy, nudity-heavy drama about college buddies who become involved with a prostitute in Amsterdam, which earned kudos at Chicago's Steppenwolf Theatre Company; and *Thom Pain (based on nothing),* Will Eno's existential monologue that became an unexpected Off-Broadway hit and prompted the *New York Times* to dub the young playwright a "Samuel Beckett for the Jon Stewart generation." Two new plays by the inimitably negative Neil LaBute appeared: *Fat Pig,* at Manhattan's MCC Theater, in which a man who sees beyond his overweight girlfriend's girth to discover the beautiful person underneath is unable to survive social pressures to dump her;

The lead actresses Victoria Clark (left) and Katie Clarke perform a scene from **The Light in the Piazza** *at the Tony Awards ceremony in New York City in June.*

© Frank Micelotta/Getty Images

and *This Is How It Goes*, a twisty, acidic love triangle that brought film stars Ben Stiller, Amanda Peet, and Jeffrey Wright together for a glitzy run at the Public. At California's Berkeley Repertory Theatre, a docudrama, *The People's Temple*, penned by director Leigh Fondakowski and several colleagues, movingly revisited the 1978 mass suicide of 913 American religious cult members in the Guyana jungle.

The most significant theatrical event of the year was likely the masterful Lincoln Center Theater production of Adam Guettel and Craig Lucas's unusual musical drama *The Light in the Piazza*, a show that had been seen to lesser advantage in 2004 in Seattle and Chicago. Based on Elizabeth Spencer's 1960 novella (which also became a sentimental Olivia de Havilland film) about a protective American mother and her mentally challenged daughter on a life-changing excursion in Italy, the musical marked the mainstream emergence of composer Guettel, grandson of Richard Rodgers, and also brought its first-rate director, Seattle-based Bartlett Sher, to national prominence. *Piazza* swept most of the musical categories in the 59th annual Tony Awards in June (except for the top trophy, best musical, which went to the jokey pastiche *Monty Python's Spamalot*, and the musical-directing prize, which went to that show's Mike Nichols), and captured similar accolades for Guettel, its lead actress Victoria Clark, and its impeccable design team from the Drama Desk, the Outer Critics Circle, and other quarters. The year's other big Tony winners were John Patrick Shanley's carefully crafted religious drama *Doubt;* former clown Bill Irwin, who defied expectation as a compellingly cerebral George in Edward Albee's *Who's Afraid of Virginia Woolf?;* and Albee, who won a lifetime achievement award. His once-controversial plays such as *Woolf* and *Seascape* had proved to be big 2004 attractions for Broadway's middlebrow throngs.

Also on Broadway, television mogul Oprah Winfrey made her theatrical producing debut by signing on as one of 16 individuals and organizations underwriting a $10-million-plus musicalization of Alice Walker's *The Color Purple*. The show's critical reception was less than enthusiastic, as was the response to a pair of miscast Tennessee Williams dramas—Edward Hall's staging of *A Streetcar Named Desire*, in

which John C. Reilly failed to ignite Stanley Kowalski's fuse, and David Leveaux's rendition of *The Glass Menagerie*, in which Jessica Lange (*see* BIOGRAPHIES) struggled in vain to be frumpish and overbearing as Amanda Wingfield.

Headlines were made in Canadian theatre circles when *The Lord of the Rings*, a multimillion-dollar musical stage version of J.R.R. Tolkien's trilogy, began rehearsals at Toronto's Princess of Wales Theater. Featuring a 65-member Canadian cast and sets described by *Variety* as "three interconnected turntables containing 16 elevators," the production was scheduled to open officially in February 2006 and clearly had its hobbit-hat cocked for eventual engagements in London's West End and on Broadway. British director Matthew Warchus, who supervised the production, immodestly described the undertaking as "a hybrid of text, physical theatre, music and spectacle never previously seen on this scale."

A less-publicized but nevertheless significant landmark was the retirement of veteran Stratford Festival of Canada actor William Hutt, who had led Shakespearean casts at the classical theatre centre for nearly four decades. Hutt, 85, capped off his career by playing Prospero in *The Tempest* for the fourth and last time, to reverential notices, and Stratford's artistic director, Richard Monette, praised him as "arguably the greatest Shakespearean actor alive."

Theatre figures who passed away in 2005 included actor and activist Ossie Davis; legendary American playwright Arthur Miller; Tom Patterson, founder of the Stratford Festival of Canada; and August Wilson, who completed *Radio Golf*, the final drama in his epic 10-play series chronicling African American life in the 20th century, before he succumbed to cancer in October. (*See* OBITUARIES.) Other losses included longtime *New York Times* theatre critic Mel Gussow and T. Edward Hambleton, a theatrical producer and a cofounder of the Phoenix Theater.   (JIM O'QUINN)

MOTION PICTURES

United States. The world box office was again dominated by Hollywood's magic-themed epics for the juvenile audience. *Harry Potter and the Goblet of Fire* (Mike Newell, director) carried Harry and his budding wizard friends into their teen years. *The Chronicles of Narnia: The Lion, the Witch and the Wardrobe*

(Andrew Adamson), an adaptation of the first in C.S. Lewis's series of children's books, was Disney's answer to *The Lord of the Rings*. *Charlie and the Chocolate Factory* (Tim Burton), the second screen version of Roald Dahl's fantasy, centred on the androgynous performance of Johnny Depp (*see* BIOGRAPHIES) as Willy Wonka, the factory owner. Burton was also co-director, with Mike Johnson, of the macabre animated musical *Corpse Bride*, set in the Victorian era and rather less suited to a very young audience. An uncompromisingly British work, Nick Park and Steve Box's *Wallace & Gromit: The Curse of the Were-Rabbit*—the first venture of the animated clay man and his dog into feature-length film—also enjoyed major box-office success. The year ended with the runaway triumph of Peter Jackson's high-budget but honourable remake of the 1933 classic *King Kong*, enriching the original characters and their backgrounds and using new digital techniques to create a monster as totally characterful as the original.

The year was marked by a rise of politically themed fiction films. *The Constant Gardener*, directed by Fernando Meirelles, was an effective adaptation, if more hectically paced than the original, of John le Carré's political thriller about the efforts of a man to investigate the death of his wife and expose the international effects of corporate and political corruption. Sydney Pollack's *The Interpreter*—the first film to have scenes shot in the United Nations building—fictitiously linked U.S. policies with oppression in a far-off African state. Stephen Gaghan's *Syriana* explored the political, corporate, and intelligence-service machinations involved in the oil business of the Middle East. Richard Curtis's script for David Yates's made-for-TV romantic comedy *The Girl in the Café* interpolated protest against the Group of Eight's insufficient concern for Third World distress. *Lord of War* (Andrew Niccol) was a bold attempt to turn the evils of the arms trade into black comedy. *Thank You for Smoking* (Jason Reitman) used its portrait of a persuasive and conscienceless spokesman for the tobacco industry as sharp satire on the morality and rhetoric of George W. Bush's America. Historical events were recalled in Sam Mendes' *Jarhead*, which depicted a group of U.S. Marines chafing for action in the First Persian Gulf War, and in Steven Spielberg's *Munich*, a rather undeveloped reflection on the massacre of Israeli athletes at the 1972

Actress Naomi Watts as Ann Darrow is the object of contention in a scene from Peter Jackson's 2005 blockbuster film **King Kong.**

Olympics and the subsequent attempts at retaliation. Spielberg also directed an update of H.G. Wells's 1898 novel *War of the Worlds*, depicting with startling realism the terror of an interplanetary invasion.

This was a fruitful year for film biographies, one of the best being Bennett Miller's *Capote*, a perceptive portrait of Truman Capote (played by Philip Seymour Hoffman) at the time of his coverage of the Kansas killings that inspired the nonfiction novel *In Cold Blood*. In George Clooney's *Good Night, and Good Luck*, David Strathairn played commentator Edward R. Murrow courageously defying McCarthyist hysteria. Ron Howard's *Cinderella Man* was a profound and feeling account of the boxer James J. Braddock and his changing fortunes in the hard world of the Great Depression. *Coach Carter* (directed by Thomas Carter) was the true story of an inspirational school basketball coach who was no less concerned with the academic development of his students than with their athletic prowess. Tony Scott's *Domino* chronicled the troubled daughter of the actor Laurence Harvey.

The erratic lives of pop musicians inspired Irish director Jim Sheridan's *Get Rich or Die Tryin'*, based on the career of rap megastar and small-time gangster Curtis ("50 Cent") Jackson; James Mangold's *Walk the Line*, with Joaquin Phoenix playing Johnny Cash and Reese Witherspoon as June Carter; and Gus Van Sant's oddly disconnected presentation of the end of a rock idol's

self-destruction, transparently based on Kurt Cobain, in *Last Days*. A host of remakes indicated nostalgia for the 1960s and '70s, among them *Yours, Mine and Ours* (Raja Gosnell, director), from the 1968 comedy with Henry Fonda and Lucille Ball; *The Longest Yard* (Peter Segal), from Robert Aldrich's 1974 story of a crucial football match in a prison; *Bad News Bears* (Richard Linklater), from the 1976 comedy; *Assault on Precinct 13* (Jean-François Richet), from John Carpenter's 1976 thriller; *Fun with Dick and Jane* (Dean Parisot), an update of the 1977 comedy with Jane Fonda; and *The Fog* (Rupert Wainwright) from Carpenter's 1980 horror film. Mel Brooks's 1968 comedy *The Producers* returned to the screen via its Broadway musical reincarnation, this time directed by Susan Stroman.

Costume films were few, the most notable being Martin Campbell's *The Legend of Zorro*, a sequel to 1998's *The Mask of Zorro*, with Antonio Banderas in the title role; *Casanova*, glamorously and wittily filmed in Venice by Swedish director Lasse Hallström with the Australian Heath Ledger in the leading role; and Ridley Scott's *Kingdom of Heaven*, a spectacular epic that viewed the Crusades with greater respect for the Muslim world than earlier attempts had done.

An outstanding critical success of the year and winner of the Venice Film Festival's Golden Lion, Ang Lee's *Brokeback Mountain* was the story of two Western sheepherders who develop a

barely understood and troubling mutual love that is not ended with years of separation and heterosexual lives. Other films that made an impact at international festivals were Rob Marshall's *Memoirs of a Geisha*, adapted from Arthur Golden's best seller and starring the luminous Chinese actress Zhang Ziyi (*see* BIOGRAPHIES), and Jim Jarmusch's lively and quirky *Broken Flowers*, with a poker-faced Bill Murray encountering a series of former flames in his search for the son he might or might not have fathered. David Cronenberg's *A History of Violence* was a thriller that gradually stripped the externals of an apparently normal citizen, husband, and father. Tommy Lee Jones's debut as a feature director, *The Three Burials of Melquiades Estrada*, was the unrelenting story of an old ranch foreman who painstakingly avenges the killing of his friend, a Mexican "illegal," by a stupid young border patrolman. *Kiss Kiss Bang Bang*, the directorial debut of writer Shane Black, was a quirky and well-sustained comedy thriller.

Noteworthy among independent films of the year were Craig Brewer's *Hustle & Flow*, about a black man from a bad area of Memphis fired with determination to fulfill his aspirations as a rapper; Mike Mills's *Thumbsucker*, a finely acted portrait of the people around a maladjusted teenager; and Jim McKay's *Angel*, an uncompromisingly truthful account of the relationship between a social welfare counselor and a deeply troubled youngster.

British Isles. Woody Allen chose to make a British variant of Theodore Dreiser's *An American Tragedy* (unacknowledged) in *Match Point*. Michael Caton-Jones's *Shooting Dogs* was a deeply felt impression of the Rwandan genocide tragedy seen through the eyes of two Europeans. Stephen Frears's *Mrs. Henderson Presents* was slight but engaging, the true story of a rich widow who created the Windmill nudie shows as a lucrative hobby. Lexi Alexander's *Hooligans* took an unsparing look at the gang culture of English football hooliganism. Actor Richard E. Grant's directorial debut, *Wah-Wah*, was a partly autobiographical story of a boy growing up in the narrow and overheated white colonial society of the last days of British Africa. *The White Countess*—the final Merchant Ivory production (Ismail Merchant died before its release—*see* OBITUARIES)—was directed by Ivory from a script by Kazuo Ishiguro about the liaison of a blind American and a White Russian noblewoman who is reduced to poverty and prostitution after the 1917 Revolution.

The British predilection for literary adaptation was vindicated by Joe Wright's bright, original, and thoughtful rendering of *Pride & Prejudice*. Michael Hardy's script for Michael Winterbottom's *Tristram Shandy: A Cock and Bull Story* ingeniously made Laurence Sterne's unmanageable digressive novel a film within a film, with the actors moving in and out of their contemporary and 18th-century roles.

The best comedy productions were Brian W. Cook's *Colour Me Kubrick*, the true story of a con man who masqueraded as director Stanley Kubrick in the 1990s, and Julian Jarrold's *Kinky Boots*, a characteristic English realist–outrageous situation comedy about a shoe factory that is saved when it launches a line of kinky boots for transvestites. *Nanny McPhee*, directed by Kirk Jones, was scripted by Emma Thompson, who also played the main role of a magical nanny who tames a large rambunctious family.

Some excellent work came from low-budget independent production, including Kolton Lee's *Cherps*, a black *Alfie* for 21st-century Britain, and Jason Ford's *New Town Original*, which took a fresh and lively view of the life of a young office worker.

Canada, Australia, and New Zealand. Canadian director Atom Egoyan followed a disappointing melodrama, *Where the Truth Lies*, with his production of Ruba Nadda's *Sabah* (also called *Coldwater*), a more rewarding story of a Syrian Canadian woman invigilated by her strict Muslim family but defiantly in love with a Canadian carpenter. Claude Gagnon's *Kamataki* was a subtle character drama about a troubled young man who finds calm and maturity working in a Japanese pottery. After long production difficulties Toronto-based Deepa Mehta completed the third film in her trilogy (after *Fire* [1996] and *Earth* [1998]); *Water* was a forceful and moving exposé of the plight of widows ostracized by strict Hindu observance.

The most notable Australian production of the year was the former animator Sarah Watt's *Look Both Ways*, a well-observed and well-structured study of a group of characters all confronted by sudden catastrophe. In New Zealand, Roger Donaldson directed *The World's Fastest Indian*, based on the true story of Burt Munro (played by Anthony Hopkins), who at age 72 set out to break the world's motorcycle record—an undertaking that Donaldson chronicled in a 1972 documentary.

Western Europe. French films with international appeal were led by Michael Haneke's *Caché*, a finely paced open-ended thriller, with the implicit theme of the fear the "haves" feel toward the "have-nots." *La Moustache* (Emmanuel Carrère, director) offered a disturbing fable about human relations, centred on the phenomenon that even those closest to him do not notice when the protagonist shaves off his moustache. Christian Carion's subtle and delicate *Joyeux Noël* presented an ideal subject for such pan-European production, the legendary Christmas truce on the front line in 1914. In *Gabrielle*, Patrice Chéreau adapted a short novella by Joseph Conrad about the breakup of a marriage, set in the Belle Epoque and employing intriguing stylized staging.

A few filmmakers looked at the urgent issues of mixed ethnic communities in poor-grade housing; examples were Pierre Jolivet's *Zim and Co.* and Malik Chibane's *Voisins, voisines*. Other exceptional productions of the year were *Le Promeneur du champ de Mars*, Robert Guédiguian's portrait of former president François Mitterrand reflected through a young journalist's collaborating on his memoirs; Richard Dembo's posthumous *La Maison de Nina*, a moving description—rooted in autobiographical reminiscence—of life in orphanages for Jewish children set up in France after the Holocaust; and Antoine Santana's *La Ravisseuse*, with its unprecedented subject—the relations of a young couple of 1877 and their peasant wet nurse. *L'Enfant*, a Belgian film directed by the brothers Jean-Pierre and Luc Dardennes (*see* BIOGRAPHIES), the story of a feckless young couple thrown into crisis by the arrival of a child, deservedly won the Cannes Festival Palme d'Or.

Among the best Italian films were Alessandro d'Alatri's *La febbre*, an involved and passionate film study of a very ordinary young man whose dreams are progressively crushed by his killing civil-service job. Gianpaolo Tescari's *Gli occhi dell'altro* offered a subtly constructed study of prejudice through the irrational suspicions that fester in the mind of a politically correct man who with his girlfriend has aided a young Kurdish emigré. Roberto Faenza's *Alla luce del sole* told the story of Don Pino Puglisi, a priest who was killed for his fight against violence in Palermo. Marco Tullio Giordana's *Quando sei nato non puoi più nasconderti* was a brave essay on the issues of illegal immigration, motivated by an accidental encounter between the son of a rich family and intriguing young "illegals."

Marc Rothemund's *Sophie Scholl—die letzten Tage* was the third film about the fate of Germany's most celebrated anti-Nazi heroine, who was

Paradise Now, a suspenseful international production directed by Dutch Palestinian Hany Abu-Assad, plumbs the thoughts of two young men as they prepare for a suicide bombing.

beheaded in 1943 for distributing literature advocating the ending of the war. This version earned a number of international prizes, notably for the leading actress, Julia Jentsch. Other outstanding German productions were Werner Herzog's ironic science-fiction fantasy ingeniously spun out of actuality and staged material, *The Wild Blue Yonder*, and Yilmaz Arslan's *Brudermord*, a tragic account of the struggle of young Kurdish émigrés in contemporary Germany.

In Denmark, Lars von Trier, founder of the Dogme movement, completed *Manderlay*, a new lesson in American history to follow *Dogville* (2003). Still in the 1930s, Grace (played in the first film by Nicole Kidman but here by Bryce Dallas Howard) arrives at an old plantation where slavery still survives. Her efforts to bring democracy to the place meet with very dubious success. Another script by von Trier, *Dear Wendy*, about footloose youngsters fascinated by firearms, was directed by Thomas Vinterberg.

Among Spain's flourishing production of genre films, idiosyncratic exceptions were Carlos Saura's musical composition *Iberia*, a follow-up to his earlier *Flamenco*, in this instance derived from Isaac Albéniz's *Iberia* suite; and Fernando León de Aranoa's *Princesas*, a socially committed and generous study of the life of prostitutes.

In Portugal the 97-year-old Manoel de Oliveira, the oldest continuously active filmmaker in history, made *O espelho mágico*, a mysterious movie about time and memory, through the story of a religion-obsessed woman befriended by a dubious young man. In *Alice*, Marco Martins, a disciple of Oliveira, offered an involving study of the obsessive daily routines of a man searching for his lost young daughter.

Eastern Europe. The production of the former communist countries was largely dedicated to readily marketable genre pictures—thrillers and situation or character comedies, but original works continued to surface. In Russia, with *Solntse* ("The Sun") Aleksandr Sokurov completed the third part of his tetralogy of portraits of dictators (the first were about V.I. Lenin and Adolf Hitler) with a keen and often sardonically humorous picture of the last days of the reign of Japanese Emperor Hirohito. Other films worth note were Valery Akhadov's *Parnikovy effekt* ("The Greenhouse Effect"), a finely detailed portrayal of the friendship of a 12-year-old homeless Muscovite and a pregnant

teenager, and Pavel Lungin's *(Bedniye rodstvenniki)* ("Poor Relations"), a fierce black comedy about a con man who specializes in providing supposed long unseen or unknown relatives for foreign tourists.

In Poland veteran Krzysztof Zanussi returned in top form with *Persona non grata*, a study of the complex world of career diplomats—in this case aging men with aching memories of Cold War years, politics, and personal lives. Among the best of a cycle of Czech films about ordinary lives was Martin Šulík's *Sluneční stát* ("The City of the Sun"), relating the misadventures of four unemployed friends, and Petr Zelenka's *Příběhy obyčejného šílenství* ("Wrong Side Up"), from his own play about the sexual and social adventures of a deadpan airport worker. An outstanding work from Romania—and an international prizewinner—Cristi Puiu's *Moartea domnului Lazarescu (The Death of Mr. Lazarescu)* was a remarkably compelling account of an old alcoholic's efforts to find medical treatment in uncaring and inhuman public hospital facilities.

Hungary's major production of the year was *Sorstalanság (Fateless)*, directed by the distinguished cinematographer Lajos Koltai, a calm yet harrowing account of a young Jewish boy's Holocaust experiences based on the autobiographical novel of Imre Kertész. Roland Vranik's *Fekete kefe* ("Black Brush") was an engaging offbeat comedy about four incompetent chimney sweeps in search of money. Péter Gárdos's *A porcelánbaba* ("The Porcelain Doll") related three stories that interwove the naturalistic, magical, and political and were acted by authentic village people.

Latin America. Tristán Bauer's *Iluminados por el fuego* was the first Argentine film to deal with the 23-year trauma of the Falklands Islands War. A noteworthy film from Brazil's prolific production, Andrucha Waddington's *Casa de areia* related the lives of three generations of women living in remote sand dunes in Brazil's northern Maranhão state between 1910 and 1969.

Middle East. Veteran filmmaker Yavuz Turgul's *Gönül yarası* ("Lovelorn") was the portrait of a retiree who returns to Istanbul from teaching in a poor village and finds disillusionment on all sides. *Paradise Now*, directed by Dutch Palestinian Hany Abu-Assad, though perhaps somewhat compromised by the number of its national partners (Israel, The Netherlands, Germany, and

France), remained an intelligent and sensitive study of two young men's preparation for a suicide bombing mission to Tel Aviv. From Palestine, Rashid Masharawi's *Attente* was a road movie in which a theatre director travels from Gaza to Jordan, Syria, and Lebanon, visiting refugee camps and ostensibly auditioning actors for a Palestinian national theatre.

Iran continued its production of polished, intelligent, and often surprisingly outspoken films dealing with contemporary life and people. Kianoush Ayari's *Wake up, Arezu!* was a drama centred on the 2003 earthquake that destroyed the ancient city of Bam. Hamid Ramanian's *Dame sobh* ("Daybreak") was a harrowing study of a murderer awaiting the death penalty, which is by Islamic law the personal responsibility of the injured family. Directed by Rakhshan Bani Etemad and Mohsen Abtolvahab, *Gilaneh* related the human tragedies of the Iran-Iraq War and the subsequent Iraq catastrophe through the experiences of a simple countrywoman. Bizhan Mir Baqeri's *Ma hameh khoubim* ("We Are All Fine") was a delicate and feeling study of a family left behind when a key member migrates to Western Europe and is absorbed by the life there.

India. Bollywood continued to extend its range in search of international markets. *The Rising: Ballad of Mangal Pandey* (Ketan Mehta, director) was an effective costume spectacle, relating the story of the Indian Mutiny of 1857. *Paheli* (Amol Palekar) was an equally lively historical picture from a classic tale by the writer Vijaydan Detha. *Black* (Sanjay Leela Bhansali) treated the theme of *The Miracle Worker*, with superstar Amitabh Bachchan in the role of a tired and bibulous teacher who transforms a blind and deaf girl's life. Less successful was the glossy *Taj Mahal: An Eternal Love Story* (Akbar Khan), reputedly India's most costly film ever and timed to coincide roughly with the 350th anniversary of the Taj Mahal.

East and Southeast Asia. With *Haru no yuki* ("Spring Snow"), Japan's Isao Yukisada made a handsome adaptation of Yukio Mishima's tale of a love affair in the Taisho era, 1912–26. In China, Zhang Yimou returned to an intimate, contemporary theme with *Qian li zou dan ji* ("Riding Alone for Thousands of Miles"), the strange odyssey of a Japanese man who sets out to fulfill his dying son's frustrated ambition to record

(continued on page 267)

INTERNATIONAL FILM AWARDS 2005

Golden Globes, awarded in Beverly Hills, California, in January 2005

Best motion picture drama	*The Aviator* (U.S./Japan/Germany; director, Martin Scorsese)
Best musical or comedy	*Sideways* (U.S.; director, Alexander Payne)
Best director	Clint Eastwood (*Million Dollar Baby*, U.S.)
Best actress, drama	Hilary Swank (*Million Dollar Baby*, U.S.)
Best actor, drama	Leonardo DiCaprio (*The Aviator*, U.S./Japan/Germany)
Best actress, musical or comedy	Annette Bening (*Being Julia*, Canada/U.S./Hungary/U.K.)
Best actor, musical or comedy	Jamie Foxx (*Ray*, U.S.)
Best foreign-language film	*Mar adentro* (*The Sea Inside*) (Spain/France/Italy; director, Alejandro Amenábar)

Sundance Film Festival, awarded in Park City, Utah, in January 2005

Grand Jury Prize, dramatic film	*Forty Shades of Blue* (U.S.; director, Ira Sachs)
Grand Jury Prize, documentary	*Why We Fight* (U.S.; director, Eugene Jarecki)
Audience Award, dramatic film	*Hustle & Flow* (U.S.; director, Craig Brewer)
Audience Award, documentary	*Murderball* (U.S.; directors, Henry Alex Rubin and Dana Adam Shapiro)
Special Jury Prize, dramatic film	*O herói* (*The Hero*) (Angola/France/Portugal; director, Zézé Gamboa); *Brødre* (*Brothers*) (Denmark; director, Susanne Bier)
Special Jury Prize, documentary	*Stand van de Maan* (*Shape of the Moon*) (Netherlands; director, Leonard Retel Helmrich); *Shake Hands with the Devil: The Journey of Roméo Dallaire* (Canada; director, Peter Raymont)
Best director, dramatic film	Noah Baumbach (*The Squid and the Whale*, U.S.)
Best director, documentary	Jeff Feuerzeig (*The Devil and Daniel Johnston*, U.S.)

Berlin International Film Festival, awarded in February 2005

Golden Bear	*U-Carmen e-Khayelitsha* (South Africa; director, Mark Dornford-May)
Silver Bear, Grand Jury Prize	*Kong que* (China; director, Gu Changwei)
Best director	Marc Rothemund (*Sophie Scholl—Die letzten Tage*, Germany)
Best actress	Julia Jentsch (*Sophie Scholl—Die letzten Tage*, Germany)
Best actor	Lou Taylor Pucci (*Thumbsucker*, U.S.)

Césars (France), awarded in February 2005

Best film	*L'Esquive* (France; director, Abdel Kechiche)
Best director	Abdel Kechiche (*L'Esquive*, France)
Best actress	Yolande Moreau (*Quand la mer monte…*, Belgium/France)
Best actor	Mathieu Amalric (*Rois et reine* [*Kings and Queen*], France)
Most promising actor	Gaspard Ulliel (*Un long dimanche de fiançailles* [*A Very Long Engagement*], France/U.S.)
Most promising actress	Sara Forestier (*L'Esquive*, France)

British Academy of Film and Television Arts, awarded in London in February 2005

Best film	*The Aviator* (U.S./Japan/Germany; director, Martin Scorsese)
Best director	Mike Leigh (*Vera Drake*, U.K./France/New Zealand)
Best actress	Imelda Staunton (*Vera Drake*, U.K./France/New Zealand)
Best actor	Jamie Foxx (*Ray*, U.S.)
Best supporting actress	Cate Blanchett (*The Aviator*, U.S./Japan/Germany)
Best supporting actor	Clive Owen (*Closer*, U.S.)
Best foreign-language film	*Diarios de motocicleta* (U.S./Germany/U.K./Argentina/Chile/Peru/France; director, Walter Salles)

Academy of Motion Picture Arts and Sciences (Oscars, U.S.), awarded in Los Angeles in March 2005

Best film	*Million Dollar Baby* (U.S.; director, Clint Eastwood)
Best director	Clint Eastwood (*Million Dollar Baby*, U.S.)
Best actress	Hilary Swank (*Million Dollar Baby*, U.S.)
Best actor	Jamie Foxx (*Ray*, U.S.)
Best supporting actress	Cate Blanchett (*The Aviator*, U.S./Japan/Germany)
Best supporting actor	Morgan Freeman (*Million Dollar Baby*, U.S.)
Best foreign-language film	*Mar adentro* (*The Sea Inside*) (Spain/France/Italy; director, Alejandro Amenábar)

Cannes Film Festival, France, awarded in May 2005

Palme d'Or	*L'Enfant* (*The Child*) (Belgium/France; directors, Jean-Pierre Dardenne and Luc Dardenne)
Grand Jury Prize	*Broken Flowers* (U.S.; director, Jim Jarmusch)
Special Jury Prize	*Qing hong* (*Shanghai Dreams*) (China; director, Wang Xiaoshuai)
Best director	Michael Haneke (*Caché* [*Hidden*], France/Austria/Germany/Italy)
Best actress	Hanna Laszlo (*Free Zone*, Israel/Belgium/France/Spain)
Best actor	Tommy Lee Jones (*The Three Burials of Melquiades Estrada*, U.S./France)
Caméra d'Or	*Sulanga enu pinisa* (France/Sri Lanka, director, Vimukthi Jayasundara); *Me and You and Everyone We Know* (U.S./U.K.; director, Miranda July)

Locarno International Film Festival, Switzerland, awarded in August 2005

Golden Leopard	*Nine Lives* (U.S.; director, Rodrigo García)
Silver Leopard	*Brudermord* (Luxembourg/Germany/France; director, Yilmaz Arslan)
Special Jury Prize	*Un couple parfait* (Japan/France; director, Nobuhiro Suwa)
Best actress	the ensemble of the actresses of *Nine Lives* (*Nine Lives*, U.S.)
Best actor	Patrick Drolet (*La Neuvaine*, Canada)

Montreal World Film Festival, awarded in September 2005

Best film (Grand Prix of the Americas)	*Off Screen* (Netherlands/Belgium; director, Pieter Kuijpers)
Best actress	Adriana Ozones (*Heroína*, Spain)
Best actor	Jan Decleir (*Off Screen*, Netherlands/Belgium)
Best director	Claude Gagnon (*Kamataki*, Canada/Japan)
Grand Prix of the Jury	*Itsuka dokusho suruhi* (Japan; director, Akira Ogata); *Schneeland* (Germany; director, Hans W. Geissendörfer)
Best screenplay	*Tapas* (Spain; writers, José Corbacho and Juan Cruz)
International cinema press award	*Kamataki* (Canada/Japan; director, Claude Gagnon)

Toronto International Film Festival, awarded in September 2005

Best Canadian feature film	*C.R.A.Z.Y.* (director, Jean-Marc Vallée)
Best Canadian first feature	*Familia* (director, Louise Archambault); *The Life and Hard Times of Guy Terrifico* (director, Michael Mabbot)
Best Canadian short film	*Big Girl* (director, Renuka Jeyapalan)
International cinema press award	*Sa-Kwa* (South Korea; director, Kang Yi Kwan)
People's Choice Award	*Tsotsi* (U.K./South Africa; director, Gavin Hood)

Venice Film Festival, awarded in September 2005

Golden Lion	*Brokeback Mountain* (U.S.; director, Ang Lee)
Jury Grand Prize	*Mary* (France/U.S.; director, Abel Ferrara)
Volpi Cup, best actress	Giovanna Mezzogiorno (*La bestia nel cuore*, Italy/U.K./France/Spain)
Volpi Cup, best actor	David Strathairn (*Good Night, and Good Luck*, U.S.)
Silver Lion, best direction	Philippe Garrel (*Les Amants réguliers*, France)
Marcello Mastroianni Prize for new actor or actress	Ménothy Cesar (*Vers le sud*, France/Canada)
Luigi De Laurentis Award for best first film	*13* (*Tzameti*) (France/Georgia; director, Géla Babluani)

San Sebastián International Film Festival, Spain, awarded in September 2005

Best film	*Stestí* (Czech Republic/Germany; director, Bohdan Slama)
Special Jury Prize	*Iluminados por el fuego* (Argentina/Spain; director, Tristán Bauer)
Best director	Yang Zhang (*Xiang ri kui* [*Sunflower*], China/Netherlands)
Best actress	Anna Geislerová (*Stestí*, Czech Republic/Germany)
Best actor	Juan José Ballesta (*7 vírgenes*, Spain)
Best photography	Jong Lin (*Xiang ri kui* [*Sunflower*], China/Netherlands)
New directors prize	Jan Cvitkovič (*Odgrobadogroba*, Croatia/Slovenia)
International film critics award	*Tideland* (Canada/U.K.; director, Terry Gilliam)

Vancouver International Film Festival, awarded in October 2005

Federal Express Award (most popular Canadian film)	*Eve and the Fire Horse* (director, Julia Kwan)
AGF People's Choice Award	*Va, vis et deviens* (*Go, See, and Become*) (France/Belgium/Israel/Italy; director, Radu Mihaileanu)
National Film Board Award (documentary feature)	*Un silenzio particolare* (Italy; director, Stefano Rulli)
Citytv Western Canadian Feature Film Award	*Lucid* (director, Sean Garrity)
Bravo!FACT Award (best young Western Canadian director of a short film)	Jamie Travis (*Patterns*)
Dragons and Tigers Award for Young East Asian Cinema	*Niu pi* (China; director, Jiayin Liu)

Chicago International Film Festival, awarded in October 2005

Best feature film	*Mój Nikifor* (Poland; director, Kyzysztof Krauze)
Special Jury Prize	*Moartea domnului Lazarescu* (Romania; director, Cristi Puiu)
International Film Critics' Prize	*La Moustache* (France; director, Emmanuel Carrère)

European Film Awards, awarded in December 2005

Best European film of the year	*Caché* (*Hidden*) (France/Austria/Germany/Italy; director, Michael Haneke)
Best actress	Julia Jentsch (*Sophie Scholl—die letzten Tage*, Germany)
Best actor	Daniel Auteuil (*Caché* [*Hidden*], France/Austria/Germany/Italy)

(DAVID ROBINSON)

March of the Penguins *focused on the compatibility of the birds and their environment; for example, the flatness of the* *terrain at St. Andrew Bay on South Georgia Island is perfect for these penguin mothers-to-be.*

(continued from page 265)
a great Chinese singer performing the song of the title. The distinguished cinematographer Gu Changwei made his directorial debut with *Kong que* ("Peacock"), a probing and observant picture of an urban working-class family in the years of transition from 1977 to 1984. In *Zui hao de shi guang* (*Three Times*), Taiwanese master Hou Hsiao-Hsien told three love stories with the same pair of actors in three different historical periods (1911, done as a silent film, 1966, and 2000).

South Korea offered a number of exceptional productions. Im Sang Soo's *Geuddae geusaramdeul* ("The President's Last Bang") offered the region's first true political satire by restaging the 1979 assassination of Pres. Park Chung Hee. *Welcome to Dongmakgol*, directed by Park Kwang Hyeon, was a curious comedy fable about groups of soldiers from the North and South, together with an American, stranded together in a remote village during the Korean War. In Yoon Jong Bin's *Yongseobadji mothanja* (*The Unforgiven*), two young soldiers meet after their period of service to find their roles of protector and protected reversed. Kim Ki Deok's *Hwal* ("The Bow") offered a strange, graceful, and occasionally violent fable about an elderly man who has brought up a child

on his boat, intending her as his eventual bride.

Malaysian filmmakers were inclined to deal with pressing contemporary issues. Deepak Kumaran Menon's *Chemman chaalai* ("The Gravel Road"), Malaysia's first production shot in Tamil (and as such ineligible for official funding), provided a gentle and often humorous picture of life on a rubber plantation. Ming Jin Woo's *Lampu merah mati* (*Monday Morning Glory*) was a story about the official manipulation of a terror incident for political expediency.

Africa. Two contrasting films from Africa attracted international attention. From South Africa, Mark Dornford-May's *U-Carmen e-Khayelitsha* exuberantly transposed Bizet's *Carmen* into the Xhosa language and contemporary Africa. From Burkino Faso, S. Pierre Yaméogo's *Delwende*, partly filmed in Ouagadougou shelters for women accused of witchcraft, offered a fierce attack on the brutalities of superstition.

(DAVID ROBINSON)

Nontheatrical Films. To some extent films about animals dominated nontheatrical releases in 2005. The most widely distributed was French director Luc Jacquet's beautifully photographed *March of the Penguins*, which documented the life cycle of penguins and their struggle for survival

in the harsh conditions of Antarctica. *Being Caribou* sought to bring attention to the plight of animals should drilling be allowed in Alaska's Arctic National Wildlife Refuge. The film followed a Canadian wildlife biologist and his filmmaker wife on a 1,500-km (930-mi) round-trip journey by foot from the Yukon Territory to the calving grounds of the caribou on the northern coast of Alaska. Directed by Leanne Allison and Diana Wilson, the film earned numerous festival awards and screenings. In *Grizzly Man* accomplished German director Werner Herzog told the harrowing story of one man's ill-fated obsession with grizzly bears. The film won the Alfred P. Sloan Feature Film Prize at the 2005 Sundance Film Festival.

Ross Kauffman and Zana Briski's *Born into Brothels* won the Academy Award and the International Documentary Association Award for feature documentaries. Their film told the story of the children of prostitutes in Kolkata (Calcutta) and portrayed the challenges they faced. Marilyn Agrelo's *Mad Hot Ballroom* followed inner-city youth as they trained for a New York City-area competition in ballroom dancing. This exuberant, inspiring film illustrated how children could increase their pride and self-esteem through engaging in an unlikely pursuit.

(BEN LEVIN)

Physical Sciences

Researchers reported on the fast SPEED of electron transfers, the high TEMPERATURE of collapsing bubbles, and the SUPERFLUIDITY of a fermionic condensate. Space probes PARACHUTED onto Titan, SLAMMED into a comet, and HOVERED over an asteroid. Astronomers discovered a remote solar system object LARGER THAN PLUTO.

CHEMISTRY

Industrial Chemistry. Acetylene is a starting material used in making many important products in the electronics and petrochemical industries. Storage of the highly reactive gas, however, is difficult, because the gas explodes when compressed under a pressure of more than two atmospheres (about 2 kg/cm²) at room temperature. In 2005 Susumu Kitagawa and colleagues at Kyoto (Japan) University reported the synthesis of a copper-organic microporous material that allowed acetylene to be compressed and stored safely at a pressure almost 200 times higher. Greater amounts of the gas thus could be stored in smaller containers. The new material was $Cu_2(pzdc)_2(pyz)$. Pzdc is pyrazine-2,3-dicarboxylate, and pyz is pyrazine. The compound contains nanoscale-dimensioned channels that adsorb large amounts of acetylene at room temperature. Unlike conventional adsorbants, such as activated carbons and zeolites, the new compound showed a selective adsorption of acetylene (C_2H_2) compared with carbon dioxide (CO_2), its molecular cousin. Kitagawa's group said that the discovery could be used as the basis for the design and synthesis of metal-organic compounds that could hold other gases. Two prime candidates were nitrogen oxides (NO_x) and sulfur oxides (SO_x), air pollutants that must be removed from industrial emissions.

Applied Chemistry. Individual carbon nanotubes, which resemble minute bits of string, can be assembled to form ribbons or sheets that are ultrathin but extraordinarily strong, light, and electrically conductive. Many trillions of these microscopic fibres must be assembled in order to make useful commercial or industrial products. In one technique, similar to that used for making paper, nanotubes dispersed in water were allowed to collect on a filter, dried, and then peeled off the filter—a process that typically took about a week. Ray H. Baughman and colleagues at the University of Texas at Dallas in 2005 reported the development of a dry process for assembling carbon nanotube sheets 5 cm (2 in) wide at rates of 7 m (23 ft) per minute. Nanotubes were first gathered into an aerogel, a highly porous solid with extremely low density, and then were compressed into a sheet. The nanotube sheets made by this process had been used as a medium for the microwave bonding of plastics and for such objects as flexible light-emitting diodes and electrically conducting film. Baughman said that their laboratory method appeared to be suitable for scaling up to an industrial process that could make nanotube sheets available commercially.

Chemists at the University of California, Los Angeles, developed the first nanoscale valve, which could be opened and closed on demand to trap and release molecules. Jeffrey I. Zink, who headed the research group, said that the valve had potential applications in new drug-delivery systems that would be small enough to work inside living cells. It joined a wide array of microscopic gears, shafts, motors, and other microelectromechanical systems that had been produced with nanotechnology. The moving parts of the valve were formed by rotaxanes, molecules in which a ring component fits around the central portion of a separate dumbbell-shaped component and can move up and down in a linear motion. The rotaxane molecules were attached by one end to openings of minute holes, a few nanometres in diameter, on the surface of a piece of porous silica. When the movable ring structure of the rotaxane molecule was in the down position, it blocked the hole and trapped molecules. When the ring structure was in the up position, it allowed the molecules to escape. The energy for the operation of the switch was obtained through redox reactions.

Environmental Chemistry. Green chemistry, or "sustainable chemistry," is the effort to use techniques that minimize pollution in chemistry. One major focus was the development of chemical reactions that reduced or eliminated the use of toxic substances and the production of toxic by-products. A notable advance in this area in 2005 concerned the Barton-McCombie deoxygenation, an important reaction used by organic

Microscopic carbon fibres called nanotubes can be used to form strong, extremely thin sheets. The droplets of orange juice, water, and grape juice shown here are each tens of thousands of times heavier than the two transparent nanotube sheets that support them.

Shaoli Fang of the NanoTech Institute of the University of Texas at Dallas

chemists to replace hydroxyl (–OH) groups with hydrogen atoms. The ingredients for the reaction had traditionally included tin hydrides that were not only toxic but also expensive and difficult to handle. John L. Wood and co-workers at Yale University reported the development of a less-toxic deoxygenation reaction, in which water and trimethylborane were used in place of the tin hydride. The new reaction also works under mild conditions because of the low energy that is needed to break the O–H bond when water forms a chemical complex with trimethylborane.

Nanoparticles, such as buckyballs (soccer-ball-shaped molecules [C_{60}] made of 60 carbon atoms), are ultrasmall particles whose unusual properties sparked substantial interest for their potential use in commercial and industrial products. Their properties also led to concern about their potential hazard to the environment and how they should therefore be regulated. Scientists had assumed that buckyballs—because they are insoluble—posed no potential hazard to living organisms and their environment. Joseph Hughes of the Georgia Institute of Technology and co-workers reported, however, that buckyballs form into clumps called nano-C60 upon contact with water and that nano-C60 is readily soluble. The researchers also found that even at low concentrations the nanoparticles inhibited the growth of soil bacteria, which potentially would have a negative environmental effect. Hughes suggested that the antibacterial property of nano-C60 might be harnessed for beneficial uses.

Physical Chemistry. For more than 30 years, scientists had been trying to verify the existence of a "liquid" magnetic state. In theory, such a state would occur when the magnetic spins of the electrons in a material fluctuated in a disorderly fluidlike arrangement in contrast to the ordered alignment of magnetic spins that produces magnetism. Liquid magnetic states might be related to the way that electrons flow in superconducting materials. Satoru Nakatsuji and co-workers at Kyoto University synthesized a material, nickel gallium sulfide ($NiGa_2S_4$), that might demonstrate its existence. The Japanese team and researchers from

Courtesy Joseph Hughes, Georgia Institute of Technology/John Fortner, Rice University

Carbon molecules known as buckyballs clump together in water to form particles called nano-C60, which appear here in an image from a transmission electron microscope.

Johns Hopkins University, Baltimore, Md., and the University of Maryland at College Park studied a polycrystalline sample of the material that had been cooled to an extremely low temperature. They found that the triangular arrangement of the atoms in the material appeared to prevent the alignment of the magnetic spins of the electrons. The scientists concluded that for an instant the material appeared to have been a magnetic liquid, but they said that verification would be needed.

The transfer of electrons from one atom to another is a key step in photochemical reactions, including those that underlie photosynthesis and commercial processes such as photography and xerography. Alexander Föhlisch of the University of Hamburg and co-workers reported a new and more accurate measurement of the time required for electron transfer. Their study of sulfur atoms deposited on the surface of ruthenium metal found that electrons jumped from the sulfur to the ruthenium in about 320 attoseconds (billionths of a billionth of a second, or 10^{-18} second). For the experiment the researchers beamed X-rays at the sulfur, exciting an inner-shell, or core, electron so that it jumped to a higher energy level and left an empty "core hole" in its place. The electron then moved onto the ruthenium metal in less time than it took for the hole to be filled by

another electron, a process known to take 500 attoseconds. Föhlisch believed that the research would enable studies of electrodynamics on the attosecond scale. Knowledge of how electrons move would be a crucial step for the development of spintronic computing, in which information is stored in the spin state of electrons.

In sonochemistry, high-frequency sound waves are used to introduce energy into a liquid-reaction medium. The energy forms bubbles in the liquid, a phenomenon called acoustic cavitation. The bubbles quickly collapse and release tremendous amounts of energy in a burst of heat and light. Some scientists believed that the collapse could be exploited to produce "desktop" nuclear fusion. Ken Suslick and David Flannigan of the University of Illinois at Urbana-Champaign reported the first direct measurement of the process that takes place inside a single collapsing bubble in a sonochemical experiment. They recorded the spectra of light emitted from the collapse, much as astronomers use spectra to measure the temperature of stars, and determined that the gases in the collapsing bubble reached a temperature of 15,000 K, more than two times hotter than the surface of the Sun. The experiment showed that a plasma was formed but did not provide evidence for nuclear fusion.

Organic Chemistry. The growing public health problem caused by the emergence of bacteria that were resistant to existing antibiotics was encouraging pharmaceutical chemists to search for new antibiotics. One common way of finding new antibiotics was to modify the complex molecular structures of old standbys, such as tetracycline and erythromycin, because slight alterations in their structure could enable an antibiotic to slip past the defenses that had evolved in resistant bacteria. After 50 years of research, all the tetracycline antibiotics in use were either natural products or semisynthetics—that is, products made by modifying the structure of the natural product. In 2005 Mark G. Charest and co-workers in the department of chemistry and chemical biology at Harvard University reported a method for synthesizing a broad range of structural variants of

(continued on page 272)

Celebrating the Centennial of

Einstein's

"Miraculous Year"

by John J. Dykla

By his 26th birthday, in 1905, Albert Einstein had not yet obtained his doctorate in physics or obtained an academic teaching position. He had published five papers in the premier German physics journal, *Annalen der Physik*, but they were relatively undistinguished. Other than perhaps those closest to him—his wife (and former fellow physics student), Mileva Maric, and his fellow patent-office clerk Michele Besso—it is unlikely that anyone would have anticipated the significance of the next five papers that Einstein submitted to the journal. Those five papers, completed within a seven-month period in 1905, were landmarks in their respective fields that laid the foundation for modern physics. Not only did Einstein forever leave his mark on theoretical physics, but he also influenced mankind's view of science and of the universe.

To commemorate the centennial of Einstein's remarkable achievement, the year 2005 was celebrated as the World Year of Physics throughout the world. Under the endorsement of the United Nations and the International Union of Pure and Applied Physics, many organizations and educational institutions throughout the world marked the occasion by seeking to promote public awareness of the importance of physics and to build interest in its ideas and study. A multitude of events and activities planned for the year officially began with the conference "Physics for Tomorrow," held January 13–15 at the Paris headquarters of UNESCO, with more than 1,000 participants, including many Nobel Prize winners and some 500 students from 70 countries. On December 1 a 12-hour live Webcast that included programs on Einstein and the legacy of his physics from leading science museums and physics research laboratories helped bring the year to a close. Among the many independently organized events—in addition to many symposia, lectures, and exhibitions—were activities that ranged from a competition in which schoolchildren used a household item to explain simple concepts in physics to a project by the Rambert Dance Company to mount a work inspired by Einstein's theories.

What were these five physics papers that provided so much inspiration? Einstein's 1905 papers covered three fundamental topics: the photoelectric effect, Brownian motion, and the special theory of relativity.

The photoelectric effect is a phenomenon in which light that strikes a metal surface ejects electrons from the metal. Physicists understood light to consist of electromagnetic waves, as had been well demonstrated, but to explain the photoelectric effect, Einstein's first paper showed that light also consists of "light quanta"—that is, particlelike bundles of energy (later called photons). It was especially for his explanation of the photoelectric effect that Einstein was awarded the Nobel Prize for Physics in 1921.

The second and fourth papers helped establish the idea that bulk matter consists of vast numbers of small particles (molecules) that are in constant motion. Einstein's second paper demonstrated that for this idea to be true, small particles suspended in a liquid should move in random erratic patterns. This type of movement, called Brownian motion, had been observed in studies of microscopic pollen grains in water, for example, but it could not be explained well by classical physics. Einstein, intent on demonstrating the physical reality of molecules, showed in his fourth paper how the size of molecules could be estimated from the effect that a suspension of small particles within a fluid would have on the viscosity of the fluid. (As it turned out, one of the calculations in this paper was incorrect, and he issued a correction in 1911. Even Einstein's published calculations were not always perfect!) Because of their practical applications in fields as diverse as the study of aerosol particles and semiconductor solid-state physics, these two papers are the most frequently cited of Einstein's 1905 work.

The third paper that Einstein submitted in 1905, bearing the title "On the Electrodynamics of Moving Bodies," presented the foundation of what is now known as the special theory of relativity. The paper dealt with the apparent contradictions between the laws of motion for physical objects in nonaccelerating reference frames (that is, reference frames at rest or moving at an unchanging velocity) and the property that light and other electromagnetic waves have of always traveling at the same speed in all such reference frames. Einstein's insight was that the contradictions could be resolved by radically modifying the concept of absolute time and what it means for two events to be simultaneous. As a consequence, he showed that the three dimensions of space and the dimension of time are unified in a single entity, space-time. The fifth 1905 paper, a follow-up to the third, presented the relationship between the physical quantities of energy, mass, and momentum. For an object at rest, Einstein obtained the famous equation of special relativity, $E = mc^2$ ("energy equals mass times the speed of light squared").

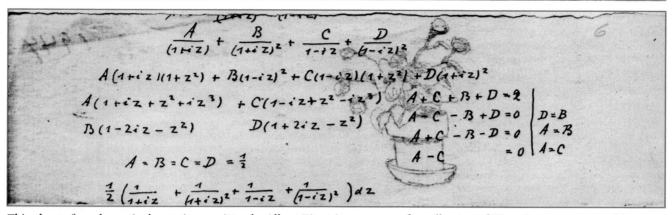

$$\frac{A}{(1+iz)} + \frac{B}{(1+iz)^2} + \frac{C}{1-iz} + \frac{D}{(1-iz)^2}$$

$$A(1+iz)(1+z^2) + B(1-iz)^2 + C(1-iz)(1+z^2) + D(1+iz)^2$$

$$A(1+iz+z^2+iz^3) + C(1-iz+z^2-iz^3) \qquad A+C+B+D=2$$

$$B(1-2iz-z^2) \qquad\qquad D(1+2iz-z^2) \qquad A-C-B+D=0 \qquad D=B$$

$$A+C-B-D=0 \qquad A=B$$

$$A-C \qquad\qquad =0 \qquad A=C$$

$$A=B=C=D=\frac{1}{2}$$

$$\frac{1}{2}\left(\frac{1}{1+iz} + \frac{1}{(1+iz)^2} + \frac{1}{1-iz} + \frac{1}{(1-iz)^2}\right)dz$$

This sheet of mathematical notations written by Albert Einstein was part of a collection of Einstein mementos and letters put up for auction in 1998. The sketch of flowers that he drew on the back of the sheet is reproduced on the facing page. The portrait below is from the series **Ten Portraits of Jews of the Twentieth Century** *by Andy Warhol (1980).*

Einstein's work was not immediately accepted, and the idea of light quanta, in particular, was considered so radical that few physicists immediately adopted it. In 1913, when recommending him for a membership in the Prussian Academy of Sciences, the eminent German physicist Max Planck was not yet convinced and still felt it necessary to excuse Einstein's work on the photon concept, writing "that he may sometimes have missed the target in his speculations, as for example in his theory of light quanta, cannot really be held against him." In time,

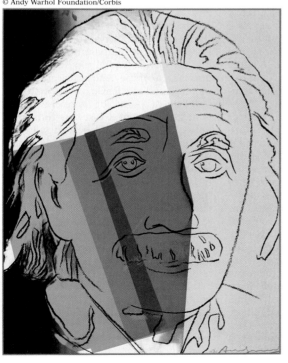

however, the idea of quanta, or discrete units, in many physical properties came to pervade physics and formed the basis of the field of quantum mechanics. By the end of the 1920s, quantum mechanics and its implications for basic atomic structure and interactions had been established, and today they inform the way scientists and nonscientists alike think about matter. Einstein's pioneering work in statistical mechanics and random fluctuations are fundamental to many areas of science, including molecular biology, physical chemistry, and theoretical economics. The equivalence of matter and energy derived from special relativity was borne out with the development of both nuclear reactors and nuclear weapons.

Einstein's importance to the modern world in the 100 years since 1905 goes well beyond his achievements in science. After observations of a solar eclipse in 1919 showed that the gravitation of the Sun deflects starlight—as predicted by Einstein's general theory of relativity from a few years before—Einstein soon gained international renown in a way that gave weight to many of his opinions and beliefs even outside physics. In the 1920s he started to engage actively in political and social issues, including pacifism, the establishment of a Jewish state, civil liberty, and the promotion of world government. He also sought to make the ideas of physics and of social issues understandable to the general population. The scientific ideas that Einstein developed beginning with his 1905 papers influenced the world view not only of physicists but also of other scientists, intellectuals, and the common person. Indeed, *Einstein* is now synonymous with *genius*, and Einstein's likeness is a cultural icon. Einstein believed that all human genius springs from one source: "The fairest thing we can experience is the mysterious. It is the fundamental emotion which stands at the cradle of true art and true science."

In addition to celebrating past achievements, a World Year of Physics looks forward. Perhaps Einstein's most lasting legacy is the search throughout the latter part of his life for a unified theory of the fundamental interactions in physical phenomena. Einstein's efforts were to unify gravitation and electromagnetism. Others have expanded the quest for a "theory of everything" to include the other two fundamental forces, the weak and strong nuclear interactions. The theoretical basis for the unification of electromagnetism and the weak interaction has been achieved, and various theories that would unify the electromagnetic, weak, and strong interactions await confirmation with the next generation of particle accelerators. Einstein's legacy inspires the theoretical physics of the future even as it points to the problems he left unsolved.

John J. Dykla is Associate Professor in the Physics Department of Loyola University, Chicago.

(continued from page 269)
tetracycline. The synthetic-chemical breakthrough involved 14- to 18-step processes that began with benzoic acid, a widely available and inexpensive compound. (MICHAEL WOODS)

PHYSICS

Particle Physics. The Standard Model of particle physics describes the basic composition of nature in terms of fundamental particles, such as quarks and electrons, and fundamental forces, which act between these particles through the exchange of massless particles. Quarks are bound tightly together in composite particles such as protons and neutrons and have never been observed directly. Nevertheless, the mass of a quark can be estimated through a complex calculation that involves the known mass of a composite particle such as the proton and an assumed value for the force that binds the quarks together. A good test of the Standard Model, therefore, is to use this value to predict the mass of a new type of composite particle. In 2005 this calculation was carried out for the first time on a so-called charmed B meson—a bound state of two types of quark—by a team from Glasgow (Scot.) University, Ohio State University, and Fermi National Accelerator Laboratory (Fermilab), near Chicago. Only days after the prediction was published, Darin Acosta and fellow experimentalists associated with the Tevatron accelerator at Fermilab found 19 examples of a meson whose mass agreed well with the theoretical prediction—a result that was seen as a strong vindication of the model.

There were still problems in particle physics to be solved, however. Researchers at the High Energy Accelerator Research Organization (KEK) at Tsukuba, Japan, and the BaBar Experiment at Stanford Linear Accelerator Center (SLAC), Menlo Park, Calif., discovered a number of new perplexing particles, including the Y(3940) and the Y(4260). A few appeared to be composite particles that consisted of four quarks, but some researchers speculated that they might be completely new types of particles.

The existence of pentaquarks (particles made up of five quarks bound together), which a number of laboratories reported to have found in 2003, came to appear more doubtful in 2005. The Large Acceptance Spectrometer collaboration at Jefferson Laboratory, Newport News, Va., conducted the most precise experiments made to date for detecting pentaquarks but found no evidence for them.

SLAC researchers who analyzed the results of experiments in which accelerated electrons were scattered off electrons in a target material found a small asymmetry that depended on whether the accelerated electron had a left- or right-handed spin. The asymmetry was the first observed example of the violation of parity (the principle that physical phenomena are symmetrical) in electron-electron interactions, and its magnitude was in agreement with theoretical predictions based on the Standard Model.

Optics and Photonics. It had become possible to observe physical processes with extremely high time resolution. The observational technique involved exciting the system of interest with a "pump" pulse of electromagnetic radiation and then probing it with a precisely timed second pulse. In the visible region of the electromagnetic spectrum, laser pulses with lengths of several femtoseconds (one femtosecond = 10^{-15} second) could be produced, but in the extreme ultraviolet and X-ray region, pulses as short as 0.2 femtosecond (or 200 attoseconds) could be realized. The temporal evolution of a system could be followed as a function of the time delay between the pulses. Such a setup was used by Ferenc Krausz at the Technical University of Vienna and co-workers to observe directly the time variation of the electric field in a light wave at a frequency of approximately 10^{15} Hz. Alexander Föhlisch of the University of Hamburg and co-workers used the technique to study ultrafast electron transfer in a solid—an important process in photochemistry and electrochemistry. (See *Chemistry,* above.) At the same time, Tsuneto Kanai and co-workers from the University of Tokyo developed a similar technique that might make it possible to investigate molecular structures to a precision of a fraction of a nanometre (one-billionth of a metre). These techniques were expected to become increasingly important in the study of atomic and molecular processes. The extension of their application depended on the production of coherent (in-phase) sources of radiation in the X-ray region of the spectrum. Jozsef Seres from the Technical University of Vienna and co-workers built a source of coherent one-kiloelectronvolt X-rays (at a wavelength of about one nanometre). It relied on the generation of high-order harmonics in a jet of helium gas ionized by a five-femtosecond laser pulse.

Mario Paniccia and associates from Intel Corp. succeeded in producing the first continuous-wave silicon laser based on the Raman effect, the phenomenon in which the wavelength of light shifts when the light is deflected by molecules. Pumped by an external diode laser, the device emitted continuous radiation at a wavelength of 1,686 nanometres with power in the milliwatt range. The creation of lasers from relatively inexpensive silicon components held promise for the development of many new applications. Other devices were being developed that did away with the external pump laser. A group of researchers headed by Federico Capasso of Harvard University produced one such device, an electrically pumped laser made from alloys of aluminum, gallium, indium, and arsenic. It worked by means of a "quantum cascade" of electrons that passed through hundreds of precisely grown layers of silicon. The device produced electromagnetic radiation with a wavelength of 9 micrometres, and the researchers planned to modify it in order to produce radiation with a wavelength between 30 and 300 micrometres, a region of the spectrum for which no cheap and practical lasers existed.

Superconductivity. The discovery of superconductors (materials in which electrical resistance can be reduced to essentially zero) had long been an empirical process, but in 2005 work conducted by F. Lévy and colleagues at the Atomic Energy Commission of France suggested a possible path to follow for devising totally new superconductors. Working with a ferromagnetic material called URhGe, they found that the critical point, or temperature, at which the material loses its ferromagnetic properties could be varied by applying pressure to a block of the material. As the pressure was increased, the critical point moved to lower and lower temperatures so that fluctuations in the magnetic properties of the material became predominantly quantum mechanical rather than thermal—a so-called quantum critical point. At the quantum critical point, the application of a strong magnetic field produced superconducting phenomena.

Quantum Physics. The next development in computing might well involve quantum computing—the storage and transport of qubits, quantum-system states that can be used to represent bits of data. A great advantage of devices based on quantum computing is that their interaction might not be limited by the speed of light; through the phenomenon called quantum entanglement, it might be possible for two qubit devices to interact instantaneously. There were many candidates for quantum-mechanical systems upon which such devices could be based, including atoms, trapped ions, or "quantum dots" (tiny isolated clumps of semiconductor atoms with nanometre dimensions). Although practical systems to store and manipulate qubits had not yet been constructed, a number of laboratories had produced devices that might form part of such a system. Sébastien Tanzilli of the University of Geneva and colleagues built an interface between states of alkaline atoms and photons at wavelengths suitable for transmission along optical fibres, and Robert McDermott of the University of California, Santa Barbara, and colleagues employed a Josephson junction (a type of superconducting switching device) to measure the qubit states of two interconnected quantum devices virtually simultaneously. Hans-Andreas Engel and Daniel Loss of the University of Basel, Switz., suggested a mechanism by which the spin states of a pair of electrons in a quantum dot could be measured without the destruction of the spin states. This mechanism might well form the basis for a qubit memory device.

Condensed-Matter Physics. Experiments that involved cooling a few thousand gas atoms to temperatures less than a millionth of a degree above absolute zero (0 K, −273.15 °C, or −459.67 °F) had by 2005 become almost commonplace. A cooled gas that consists of atoms with zero or integral intrinsic spin (atoms called bosons) yields a state of matter known as a Bose-Einstein condensate (BEC); the atoms act together as one "superparticle" described by a single set of quantum-state functions. For atoms with multiples of half-integral spins (atoms called fermions), a similar cooling process can take place to produce fermionic condensates. These atoms, however, cannot fall to the same state (as described by the Pauli exclusion principle) but instead tidily fill up all available states starting from the lowest energy. In this case it was postulated that atoms should pair up and each strongly interacting pair would act like a boson. A series of experiments had suggested that such pairing did take place, but the first conclusive evidence

of it was obtained in 2005 by Martin Zwierlein and colleagues at the Massachusetts Institute of Technology. They produced a rotating sphere of a fermionic gas with ultracold lithium atoms and observed the formation of a framework of minute vortices, a phenomenon unambiguously associated with superfluids (a fluid with a vanishingly small viscosity). The formation of a superfluid is characteristic of BECs and showed that pairing had occurred. (DAVID G.C. JONES)

ASTRONOMY

Solar System. In planetary space science, the year 2005 began with the precision landing of the Huygens (European Space Agency) space probe on Saturn's moon Titan on Jan. 14, 2005. The probe had been released from the Cassini (NASA) spacecraft, which had been in orbit around Saturn since July 2004. Huygens parachuted through the atmosphere of Titan for about 2.5 hours and then continued to take measurements for about another 70 minutes while on the surface. Titan is perpetually covered in clouds, and the mission provided the first opportunity to examine the moon's atmospheric layers and surface geology directly. The probe revealed deep surface channels, which were probably carved by flowing liquid methane. The surface temperature is far too low (−180 °C, or −290 °F) to allow water to exist in liquid form. Grapefruit-sized objects that were shown lying on the surface were probably composed of water ice.

On July 4, 2005, after a journey of more than 431 million km (268 million mi), NASA's Deep Impact space probe fired a 370-kg (816-lb) copper projectile, or impactor, into the nucleus of Comet Tempel 1, which was only about 14 km (8.7 mi) wide and 4 km (2.5 mi) long. The crash excavated a crater about 30 m (about 100 ft) deep and 100 m (about 325 ft) across. Cameras aboard the main spacecraft took pictures before, during, and after the strike, which produced a bright flash of light as matter was ejected from the comet. (*See* photograph, page 276.) The large cloud of ejected material was observed by some 80 ground-based telescopes at radio, infrared, optical, and ultraviolet wavelengths. Preliminary analyses of the observations were at odds with the standard "dirty snowball" model of comets, which had described comets as agglomerates of graphite and silicate dusts held together by ices such

as frozen carbon dioxide, water, and methane. The ejected material behaved more like fine dust particles, which suggested that the comet "may resemble an icy dirt ball more than it does a dirty snowball," according to Deep Impact research team member Carey Lisse of the University of Maryland. Other scientists said that the data implied that the object had a layered structure. Overall, astronomers concluded that Tempel 1 was an extraordinarily fragile object that was only weakly held together by gravity.

For several years the status of Pluto as the most distant planet of the solar

Earth Perihelion and Aphelion, 2006	
Jan. 4	Perihelion, approx. 15:00[1]
July 3	Aphelion, approx. 23:00[1]
Equinoxes and Solstices, 2006	
March 20	Vernal equinox, 18:26[1]
June 21	Summer solstice, 12:26[1]
Sept. 23	Autumnal equinox, 04:03[1]
Dec. 22	Winter solstice, 00:22[1]
Eclipses, 2006	
March 14–15	Moon, penumbral (begins 21:21[1]), the beginning visible in Africa, Europe, most of Asia (except the northeastern part), western Australia; the end visible in Africa, Europe, South America, and most of North America (except Alaska, and the far western parts of Canada and the United States).
March 29	Sun, total (begins 7:37[1]), visible along a path beginning at the eastern tip of South America; extending through northern Africa, ending in central Asia; with a partial phase visible in northern areas of the South Atlantic Ocean, southern areas of the North Atlantic Ocean, Europe, most of Africa, western and central Asia.
Sept. 7	Moon, partial umbral (begins 16:42[1]), the beginning visible in the western Pacific Ocean, Asia, Australia, the Indian Ocean, eastern Africa; the end visible in Asia (except the northeastern part), western Australia, the Indian Ocean, Africa, Europe, the eastern Atlantic Ocean.
Sept. 22	Sun, annular (begins 8:40[1]), visible along a path beginning in northeastern South America; extending through the southern North Atlantic Ocean, the South Atlantic Ocean; ending in the southwestern Indian Ocean; with a partial phase visible in most of the Atlantic Ocean (except the northern and western parts), South America, western and southern Africa, the southwestern Indian Ocean, and parts of Antarctica.

[1] Universal time.
Source: *The Astronomical Almanac for the Year 2006* (2004).

273

NASA

system had been questioned because of the discovery of other similar icy bodies in the Kuiper Belt, which lies beyond the orbit of the planet Neptune and extends well beyond the orbit of Pluto. Pluto—discovered in 1930—was known to have one moon, called Charon, which was detected by ground-based telescopes in 1978. In May 2005 a team of astronomers, who used the Advanced Camera for Surveys on the Hubble Space Telescope, discovered that Pluto has not one but three moons. The two newly discovered moons have diameters estimated to be between 32 and 70 km (20 and 45 mi) and are about two to three times as far as from Pluto as Charon. The existence of two additional moons lent strength to the claim by some astronomers that Pluto should still be viewed as a planet in its own right. Then, in the summer of 2005, astronomers Michael E. Brown of the California Institute of Technology, Chadwick Trujillo of the Gemini Observatory in Hilo, Hawaii, and David Rabinowitz of Yale University announced the discovery of the largest object found in the outer solar system since the discovery of Neptune and its moon Triton in 1846. The object was originally recorded in images taken in October 2003 with the 122-cm (48-in) Schmidt telescope on Mt. Palomar, near San Diego, and the astronomers designated the object 2003 UB313. Observations in January 2005 showed that the object had been slowly moving and that it was more than twice the distance from the Sun as Pluto. By analyzing these observations, the team was able to conclude that the diameter of the object is at least 1.5 times that of Pluto. The object, unofficially called Xena, moves in a highly elliptical orbit that is inclined by about 44 degrees to the plane in which most of the planets move, and it takes about 560 years to orbit the Sun. While using the giant Keck II telescope on Mauna Kea, Hawaii, in September, the team spotted a small moon that orbits Xena. Whether Pluto and Xena are, indeed, the 9th and 10th planets in the solar system or merely exotic members of the Kuiper Belt, their very existence could be expected to help scientists unravel the mysteries of how the solar system was formed.

Stars. For more than a decade, astronomers had been finding planets around stars other than the Sun, and by late 2005 at least 160 such extrasolar planets had been detected. Since a planet is small compared with its parent star, it was extraordinarily difficult to detect extrasolar planets directly in

Using two dozen exposures from the NASA Hubble Space Telescope, astronomers produced a highly detailed image of the Crab Nebula. The nebula was formed by a supernova explosion recorded in 1054.

photographic images. Instead, every extrasolar planet had been found indirectly by looking for and detecting the wobble it induced in the motion of its parent star, as shown by shifts in the star's spectra or, in a few cases, by the small amount of light the planet blocked when passing in front of the star. In March 2005 two separate groups reported the direct detection of extrasolar planets. Each team used the infrared Spitzer Space Telescope to record the thermal radiation from hot Jupiter-sized planets just as they passed in front of and behind their central star. One object, called TrES-1, was found to have a surface temperature of about 790 °C (1,454 °F), with an atmosphere rich in carbon monoxide. The other planet, called HD 209458b, had a temperature of about 960 °C (1,760 °F). Both were far too hot to support any life like that known on Earth.

The year 2005 brought with it a host of spectacularly detailed images of the remnants of supernovae that had exploded in the Milky Way galaxy during the past millennium. Supernova explosions produce the heavy chemical elements, leave behind magnetized and rapidly rotating neutrons stars, and are

likely sources of the highly energetic particles called cosmic rays. In 1572 the Dutch astronomer Tycho Brahe noticed a "new star" in the sky, which faded from sight several months after its appearance. NASA's Chandra X-ray Observatory produced the most detailed image to date of the remnant of Tycho's supernova explosion. Studies made by a group from Rutgers University at Piscataway, N.J., used the data to offer the first strong evidence that supernovae accelerate heavy subatomic particles, which make up the preponderance of cosmic rays. Perhaps even more spectacular than these findings was a photograph of the Crab Nebula, the remnant of a supernova that exploded on July 4, 1054. It was produced from a mosaic of images taken with the Hubble Space Telescope and showed in great detail the complex structure of filaments and wisps within the nebula.

Galaxies and Cosmology. Gamma-ray bursts were first detected in the late 1960s. These extremely powerful bursts of photons last from less than a second to several minutes. Their cause and origin were subject to a great deal of theoretical conjecture until the late 1990s, when distant galaxies were definitively identified as a source of long-lived gamma-ray bursts. Long-lived bursts were thought to be associated with supernova explosions that occurred with the death of massive stars. The year 2005 brought a host of new observations of gamma-ray bursts and insights into their nature. In January detectors aboard NASA's Swift spacecraft recorded the X-rays from the relatively long-lived burst designated GRB 050117. Within about three minutes of the burst, Swift was able to point its X-ray imaging telescope in the direction of the burst and, for the first time, recorded an X-ray image of such an event. During the year Swift also recorded for the first time the precise location of two relatively short-lived gamma-ray bursts, GRB 050509B and GRB 050709. On the basis of their positions, both events were shown to have arisen in relatively nearby galaxies, which meant that the luminosities of the events were approximately a thousand times less than those of long-lived gamma-ray bursts detected from distant galaxies. Some astronomers thought that the short bursts arose from the merger of compact objects, such as when two neutron stars coalesced and produced jets of high-energy particles and radiation. On September 4 the Swift satellite recorded its 68th burst event of the year, GRB 050904. A team of astronomers led by Nobuyuki Kawai of the Tokyo Institute of Technology used the infrared Subaru Telescope on Mauna Kea to determine that the source of the burst lay about 12.8 billion light years from Earth, which made it the most distant such event recorded to date. The burst occurred a mere 900 million years after the universe was formed and suggested that supernovae existed early in the history of the universe.   (KENNETH BRECHER)

SPACE EXPLORATION

In March 2005 Michael Griffin, a former NASA manager, was named to succeed Sean O'Keefe as NASA administrator. Griffin quickly made radical changes such as the cancellation of much of the space research program, including the study of the effects of zero-g (microgravity) environments on both humans and physical phenomena. Most of the cuts were intended to make it possible to fund the Vision for Space Exploration program announced by Pres. George W. Bush in 2004. The program included the return of humans to the Moon by 2020 to determine what lunar resources could be utilized for the

purpose of beginning human exploration of Mars and beyond. Key elements were to be the creation of an infrastructure to support long-term exploration and the use of "go-as-you-pay" funding rather than set political deadlines. In September 2005 NASA presented its plans for the spacecraft it would develop for the post-space-shuttle era. They included a four-person Crew Exploration Vehicle (CEV) and a heavy-lift launch vehicle. The CEV would resemble the Apollo Command/Service Module of the 1960s and '70s but would be large enough to carry four to six persons. It would have a two-stage launch vehicle, the first stage powered by a space-shuttle-derived solid-rocket booster and the second powered by a space-shuttle main engine. The heavy-lift launch vehicle (which could be used for launching cargo or a manned spacecraft) would also use shuttle-derived components—two solid-rocket boosters and five main engines powered by fuel from a redesigned external tank—and would be able to place up to 100 metric tons into orbit. These spacecraft were also to be used as building blocks for manned lunar and Mars missions. In October 2005 NASA announced the selection of two contractors, Lockheed Martin and a team formed by Northrop Grumman and Boeing, to produce preliminary designs. An accelerated development schedule was planned to lead to a 2012 launch.

Manned Spaceflight. In July the U.S. space shuttle program resumed flight with launch of the orbiter *Discovery*. It was the first space shuttle flight since the loss of the orbiter *Columbia* and its crew of seven astronauts on Feb. 1,

2003. The shedding of foam from the external tank that had occurred just seconds after liftoff of the *Columbia* led to damage of the high-temperature heat-shield tiles on the leading edge of the left wing that doomed the craft during its descent for landing. Despite a range of engineering design changes to the insulating foam on the shuttle's external tank since the accident, video cameras installed on *Discovery* to monitor its launch showed a section of foam from the external tank breaking off and whipping backward through the slipstream after the separation of the boosters. The foam lost during the *Discovery* launch did not strike the vehicle, but the incident required NASA to reevaluate the production program for external tanks and to postpone the next space shuttle launch until 2006.

The remainder of *Discovery*'s mission, STS-114, went well. It docked to the International Space Station (ISS) two days after launch, and fresh supplies and experiment gear were delivered to the ISS. The *Discovery* crew used a camera on the orbiter's robotic arm to inspect the heat shield for damage. No holes from impacts with lost foam were found, but the camera revealed two areas where felt insulating pads had been pulled from between heat-shield tiles and the orbiter's aluminum skin. Because of uncertainties about excessive heating that might occur around the protrusions during reentry, two astronauts were dispatched on a spacewalk and they gingerly removed the strips from the tiles. It was the first time that astronauts had worked around the orbiter's belly; all previous spacewalks had been in or above the payload bay.

Human Spaceflight Launches and Returns, 2005

Country	Flight	Crew[1]	Dates[2]	Mission/payload
Russia	Soyuz TMA-6 (up)	Sergey Krikalyov John Phillips Roberto Vittori	April 15	transport of replacement crew to ISS
Russia	Soyuz TMA-5 (down)	Salizhan Sharipov Leroy Chiao Roberto Vittori	April 25	return of departing ISS crew to Earth
U.S.	STS-114, *Discovery*	Eileen Collins James Kelly Charles Camarda Wendy Lawrence Soichi Noguchi Steve Robinson Andy Thomas	July 26–August 9	space shuttle's return to flight; ISS supplies
Russia	Soyuz TMA-7 (up)	William McArthur Valery Tokarev Gregory Olsen[3]	October 1	transport of replacement crew to ISS
Russia	Soyuz TMA-6 (down)	Sergey Krikalyov John Phillips Gregory Olsen[3]	October 10	return of departing ISS crew to Earth
China	Shenzhou 6	Fei Junlong Nie Haisheng	October 12–17	China's second human spaceflight

[1] For shuttle flight, commander and pilot are listed first; for Soyuz flights, ISS commander is listed first.
[2] Flight dates for shuttle and Shenzhou missions; Soyuz launch or return date for ISS missions.
[3] Flew as a paying passenger.

A camera aboard the Deep Impact spacecraft captured this image of the nucleus of Comet Tempel 1 and the flash of light that was produced by the high-speed collision with an impactor probe.

Two crew-exchange missions, Soyuz TMA-6 and 7, were flown to the International Space Station (ISS). Each carried an American and Russian replacement for American and Russian crew members who had completed a six-month stay on the ISS. In addition, the TMA-6 mission carried an Italian scientist and TMA-7 a space tourist.

China continued its manned space program with its second manned mission, Shenzhou 6, which carried two taikonauts (astronauts). The first manned mission, Shenzhou 5, lasted one day and carried a single taikonaut. Although it had started its space program cautiously, China announced long-range plans that included complex rendezvous maneuvers, assembly of a space station, and possible manned missions to the Moon.

Space Probes. One of the most notable events in space exploration in 2005 was the collision on July 4 of the Deep Impact impactor probe with the short-period comet Tempel 1. The 370-kg (816-lb) impactor, which had been released by the main Deep Impact spacecraft the day before, slammed into the comet at a relative speed of 37,000 km/hr (23,000 mph). To obtain information about the composition of the comet nucleus, high-resolution infrared and medium-resolution visible cameras on the main Deep Impact spacecraft observed the collision and the material

that it ejected from the comet. The impactor was largely made of pure copper to ensure clean spectral data of the material. The collision was also observed by the Hubble Space Telescope, the Spitzer Infrared Space Telescope, the Chandra X-Ray Observatory, and many ground-based observatories. (See *Astronomy*, above.)

The Spirit and Opportunity rovers on Mars continued their work more than a year after the completion of their primary 90-day missions. The European Space Agency's Mars Express orbiter deployed the Mars Advanced Radar for Subsurface and Ionosphere Sounding instrument, which was designed to use microwave pulses to search for radar signatures of subsurface water. NASA's Mars Global Surveyor and Mars Odyssey continued their observations of the planet and were to be joined in early 2006 by the Mars Reconnaissance Orbiter (MRO). The MRO, launched August 12, carried instruments for studying the atmosphere of Mars and for searching for signs of water on the planet. Its shallow subsurface radar was to probe the surface to a depth of 1 km (0.6 mi) to detect variations in electrical conductivity that might be caused by water.

The Huygens probe, which was released in December 2004 by the Cassini spacecraft in orbit around Saturn, parachuted to the surface of Titan, Saturn's largest moon, on Jan. 14, 2005. Data that Huygens transmitted during its final descent and for about 70 minutes from the surface included 350 pictures that showed a shoreline with erosional features and a river delta that scientists believed had been formed by liquid methane. In error one radio channel on the satellite was not turned on, and data were lost concerning the winds Huygens encountered during its descent. As the Cassini spacecraft continued to orbit Saturn, it made several flybys of the moons Titan, Mimas, and Enceladus. During the flybys Cassini used its radar mapper and instruments for infrared, visible, and ultraviolet observations to study surface features on the moons.

Japan's Hayabusa probe (formerly called MUSES-C) arrived at asteroid Itokawa (named after Hideo Itokawa, Japan's rocket pioneer) on September 12 and became only the second spacecraft to have visited an asteroid. Hayabusa then hovered above the asteroid, which is only 600 m (about 2,000 ft) long, and mapped its surface in preparation for several descents to collect surface samples that it would

return to Earth. A 600-g (21-oz) MINERVA lander released by Hayabusa was to have studied the asteroid as it hopped around the surface, but the small probe was lost after it was released on November 12. Hayabusa attempted brief landings on November 20 and November 26. It was unclear whether it succeeded in collecting any soil samples, and control and communications problems with the spacecraft raised doubts whether it would be able to return to Earth.

Europe's Venus Express spacecraft was launched November 9 by a Russian Soyuz-Fregat rocket and was scheduled to go into orbit around Venus in April 2006. Near-infrared and other instruments were to study the structure and composition of the middle and upper Venusian atmosphere.

Unmanned Satellites. Japan's Suzaku (Astro-E2) spacecraft, launched in July, was designed to complement the U.S. Chandra X-Ray Observatory and Europe's XMM-Newton spacecraft. Suzaku was equipped with X-ray instruments to study hot plasmas that occurred in star clusters, around black holes, and other regions. The mission of Gravity Probe B ended in October when the last of its liquid-helium coolant ran out. The satellite carried high-precision quartz gyroscopes whose precession (shift in rotational axis) provided extremely accurate measurements of the subtle effects predicted by Einstein's general theory of relativity. China launched the Shijian 7 spacecraft July 6 on a three-year mission to study the space environment. The U.S. Department of Defense launched the XSS-11 experimental satellite, which was designed to approach to within 500 m (1,640 ft) of target spacecraft, including several dead American satellites, and inspect them. NASA's DART (Demonstration of Autonomous Rendezvous Technology) spacecraft made a successful rendezvous with a target satellite, but during its final approach a propulsion system failure aborted the mission at a distance of 91 m (300 ft) from the target.

Launch Vehicles. Europe's most powerful rocket to date, the Ariane 5 ECA, became operational in 2005, with launches on February 12 and November 16. Using liquid-propellant engines and solid-propellant boosters, it was capable of lifting a 9,600-kg (21,000-lb) payload to geostationary transfer orbit. The premier flight of the Ariane 5 ECA, in 2002, had failed shortly after liftoff.

(DAVE DOOLING)

Religion

Top NAMES in religious news in 2005 were those of popes JOHN PAUL II and BENEDICT XVI and the Rev. BILLY GRAHAM. Deadly ATTACKS on worshippers in mosques occurred in several countries, and relations between CHURCH AND STATE and SAME-SEX UNIONS were also key areas of concern.

Religious Leadership. Pope John Paul II, who died on April 2 at the age of 84 (*see* OBITUARIES), was the first non-Italian to be elected pope in 455 years when he was chosen in 1978. Other historic milestones of his papacy included his becoming the first pope since the 1st century to visit a Jewish house of worship when he visited the Rome synagogue in 1986, becoming the first to visit an Islamic house of worship when he visited a mosque in Syria in 2001, and in the same year becoming the first pope to visit Greece since the Great Schism between the churches of the East and the West in 1054.

On April 19 Joseph Cardinal Ratzinger was chosen to succeed John Paul II, at the age of 78 becoming the 265th Roman Catholic pontiff. The first Germanic pope since the 11th century, he took the name Benedict XVI (*see* BIOGRAPHIES) to honour both the 6th-century saint who is considered the father of Western monasticism and Pope Benedict XV, who tried to promote the cause of peace during World War I. A month after taking office, the new pope named Archbishop William J. Levada of San Francisco to become prefect of the Congregation for the Doctrine of the Faith, the office that Benedict had headed for 24 years. At a meeting with leaders of the World Council of Churches at the Vatican in June, Benedict assured them that the Roman Catholic Church's commitment to the search for Christian unity was "irreversible." In a visit to Germany in August, the pope went to a synagogue in Cologne and lamented what he called "the rise of new signs of anti-Semitism and various forms of a general hostility toward foreigners." The following day he met with 10 representatives of the country's Muslim community and urged them to work to combat terrorism and steer young people away from "the darkness of a new barbarism." The main purpose of the pope's visit to Cologne was to preside over World Youth Day, a weeklong festival that drew an estimated 700,000 young Catholics from nearly 200 countries. Later in August the Vatican and Israel resolved a dispute that had arisen in July when Israeli officials complained that Benedict had failed to include Israel in a list of countries that had recently been targeted by terrorist attacks. The Vatican responded by saying that the pope could not condemn every Palestinian attack because Israel often retaliated with actions that would also have to be condemned. After a meeting between Vatican and Israeli diplomats, both sides said the dispute had been resolved, and Israeli Prime Minister Ariel Sharon called Benedict "a true friend of Israel."

Billy Graham, 86, whose preaching career had extended through six papacies, drew 230,000 people in June to a three-day evangelistic rally at New York City's Flushing Meadows–Corona Park. During the event, 8,400 attendees indicated that they wanted to make or renew a commitment to faith in Jesus Christ. Graham, a Southern Baptist who had preached to more than 210 million people in 185 countries, announced later that he would conduct no more evangelistic crusades because of his poor health.

Sectarian and Political Violence. Deadly attacks that appeared to be directed against Shiʿite Muslims by members of extremist Islamic movements killed worshippers at mosques in Iraq, Pakistan, and Afghanistan. Abdul Fayaz, leader of the Council of Clerics in Kandahar, Afg., and a supporter of Afghan Pres. Hamid Karzai, was gunned down in May after he convened a gathering of hundreds of Muslim leaders to strip fugitive Taliban leader Mohammed Omar formally of the religious title "leader of the faithful," which he had been granted when he assumed political power in the early 1990s. Deadly bombings in July in the Egyptian resort of Sharm al-Shaykh were denounced by Muhammad Sayyed Tantawi, grand imam of al-Azhar University in Cairo, one of the world's leading Sunni institutions. During a service at Sharm al-Shaykh's Peace Mosque, he declared that if people who carried out such attacks on innocents claimed they were obedient to Islamic teachings, they were "liars and charlatans."

Terrorist attacks on three underground trains and a bus in London on July 7 were condemned by two gatherings of British Muslim leaders. Sayed Mohammed Musawi, the head of the London-based World Islamic League, however, later called for "a clear distinction between the suicide bombing of those who are trying to defend themselves from occupiers, which is something different from those who kill civilians, which is a big crime." American Muslims also disagreed about the proper response to terrorist attacks. The Fiqh Council of North America, an advisory

Billy Graham appears before a large crowd at the end of his crusade at Flushing Meadows–Corona Park, Queens, N.Y., June 26.

© Keith Bedford/Reuters/Corbis

committee on Islamic law, issued an edict in August declaring that nothing in Islam justified terrorism targeting civilians. Muzammil H. Siddiqi, chairman of the council, said the edict applied even when a Muslim country had been taken over by a foreign power. Several American Muslim academics said the edict was too broad to be meaningful, however, and that it should have named specific terrorist groups. Some also noted that Islam had no ordained clergy or central authority and that Islamic leaders frequently issued conflicting edicts.

Doctrine and Interfaith Issues. In another intra-Muslim disagreement, Amina Wadud, a professor of Islamic studies at Virginia Commonwealth University, drew the ire of Mideast Muslims when she led a mixed-gender prayer service at the Cathedral of St. John the Divine in New York City, an Episcopal house of worship, even after three mosques and an art gallery refused to host the event. After the service Wadud said that men had distorted the teachings of the Qur'an that put men and women on equal footing. Her action was denounced by Grand Mufti 'Abd al-Aziz al-Sheikh in Saudi Arabia and by Soad Saleh, the head of the Islamic department of the women's college at al-Azhar University, who said that a woman's leadership of a mixed-gender prayer service "intentionally violates the basics of Islam."

Jordan's King Abdullah II hosted a conference of 180 scholars from 45 countries in Amman in July that issued a declaration condemning the practice of *takfir,* or declaring other Muslims to be apostates. In a speech at Catholic University in Washington, D.C., in September, he called on the "quiet majority" of Muslims to "take back our religion from the vocal, violent, and ignorant extremists." Another notable interfaith event, the First World Congress of Imams and Rabbis for Peace, met for four days in Brussels in January. Notable addresses at the gathering included a talk by Sheikh Talah Sedir, the Palestinian Authority's representative for interreligious affairs, who declared that "anybody who is pleased when a woman or child is killed in a refugee camp or bus does not belong to any religion."

In the first major Protestant-Catholic accord on devotion to the Virgin Mary, the Anglican–Roman Catholic International Commission released a statement in May declaring that differences on the subject need no longer be seen as "communion-dividing." The statement, titled "Mary: Grace and Hope in Christ," affirmed that the Catholic doctrines of

AP/Wide World Photos

On July 29, in the days following the deadly terrorist bombings in Sharm al-Shaykh, Egypt, Sunni Imman Muhammad Sayyed Tantawi calls for the public to assist the police in finding the perpetrators.

Mary's Immaculate Conception and Assumption were consonant with scripture. It added, however, that the question remained for Anglicans "as to whether these doctrines concerning Mary are revealed by God in a way which must be held by believers as a matter of faith." While Protestants and Catholics made progress in this area, their 16th-century split was commemorated in April at the opening of the International Museum of the Reformation in Geneva, the Swiss city that was the birthplace of Calvinism and that now hosted the headquarters of the World Council of Churches, the Lutheran World Federation, and the World Alliance of Reformed Churches. Leaders of two of the largest mainline Protestant denominations in the United States, the 8.3-million-member United Methodist Church (UMC) and the 4.9-million-member Evangelical Lutheran Church in America, approved an interim agreement under which members of the two churches might share in the sacrament of Holy Communion.

Homosexuality and Gender Issues. In July the Antiochian Orthodox Christian Archdiocese of North America announced that it was planning to leave the National Council of Churches because of its disagreement with positions some other member denominations had taken supporting same-sex unions and the ordination of homosexuals to the ministry. At a gathering in Dromantine, N.Ire., in February, 35 Anglican primates asked the U.S. Episcopal Church and the Anglican Church of Canada to forgo attending meetings of the Anglican Consultative Council be-

cause of tensions in the worldwide Anglican Communion caused by the election and consecration of a homosexual bishop in the American church and blessings of same-sex unions in the American and Canadian church. The primates also called for a moratorium on such actions.

The 1.3-million-member United Church of Christ became the largest Christian church to have endorsed same-sex marriage when it adopted a resolution to that effect at its General Synod in Atlanta in July. Delegates to the Churchwide Assembly of the Evangelical Lutheran Church in America, meeting in Orlando, Fla., in August, rejected a proposal that would have allowed gay people in committed relationships to serve as clergy in certain situations. The gathering adopted another resolution calling for the church to stay united despite differences over the issue of homosexuality. In September leaders of the Pacific Southwest Region of the American Baptist Churches USA said that they planned to leave the denomination as a group because of what they saw as its failure to discipline congregations that defied the church's position that gay relationships are incompatible with Christianity.

The United Methodist Judicial Council, the denomination's highest court, in October overturned the ruling of an appeals committee and upheld the December 2004 conviction of the Rev. Irene Elizabeth Stroud of Philadelphia for having violated the denomination's ban on "self-avowed practicing homosexuals" in the ordained ministry. The General Synod of the Reformed Church in America, meeting in Schenectady, N.Y., in June, found that the Rev. Norman J. Kansfield had violated church law by officiating at the marriage of his daughter, Ann, to her partner, Jennifer Aull, a year earlier. Delegates voted to suspend him from the ministry and to remove his standing as a professor of theology until he changed his views. In January trustees of New Brunswick (N.J.) Theological Seminary in New Jersey had decided not to renew his contract as president because of his action.

In September the Vatican ordered an examination of American Catholic seminaries to look for what it called "evidence of homosexuality," and two months later its Congregation for Catholic Education released an instruction stating that men with "deep-seated homosexual tendencies" should not be ordained to the priesthood. Both actions reflected studies undertaken when the church's sexual-abuse scandal exploded into public view in 2002. The Standing Conference of Canonical Orthodox Bishops in the Americas, which represented the nine major ethnic Eastern Orthodox churches in North America, declared in August that "sexual abuse or misconduct will find no safe haven" in their churches. The bishops added that they would require new priests to undergo criminal background checks.

Women gained new positions in the Seventh-day Adventist Church and the Christian Church (Disciples of Christ) during 2005. In July, Ella Simmons, a top administrator at the Adventists' La Sierra University in Riverside, Calif., became the first woman chosen as one of the nine vice presidents of the worldwide church. Adventist spokesman John Banks said that the election was "an incredible development," because the church "traditionally has not dealt with women's leadership issues in an adequate way." The Rev. Sharon Watkins, a pastor in Bartlesville, Okla., was elected general minister and president of the Disciples at the 750,000-member denomination's General Assembly in Portland, Ore., in July, becoming the first woman to attain the top elected position in a major mainline Protestant denomination.

Church and State. Two rulings by the U.S. Supreme Court on public displays of the Ten Commandments on government property stirred bewilderment when they were issued June 27. In one of the 5–4 rulings, *McCreary County* v. *ACLU,* the court said that displays on the wall of two rural Kentucky courthouses had had the unconstitutional purpose of favouring monotheistic religions. In the other case, *Van Orden* v. *Perry,* the court said that a Texas monument had secular historical and educational meaning because it was displayed as part of a group of similar markers. In the Kentucky case, the majority opinion written by Justice David Souter declared, "Trade-offs are inevitable, and an elegant interpretive rule to draw the line in all the multifarious situations is not [to] be had."

In a unanimous ruling issued in May, the high court upheld a federal law that barred government policies that substantially burdened the free exercise of religion by prison inmates and by a person or institution in land-use cases. The decision, written by Justice Ruth Bader Ginsburg, said the law "alleviates exceptional government-created burdens on private religious exercise." In September U.S. District Judge Lawrence Karlton ruled in Sacramento that recit-

ing the Pledge of Allegiance in public schools was unconstitutional because of its reference to one nation under God. The case had been brought by atheist Michael Newdow, who had had a similar case dismissed by the U.S. Supreme Court in 2004 on the ground that he lacked standing. Newdow brought the new case on behalf of three parents and their children, and Karlton said he was bound by a ruling issued by an appeals court in Newdow's previous case.

A federal judge ruled in December that a school board in Dover township, Pa., had acted improperly in requiring high-school biology teachers to read a statement asserting that intelligent design offers an alternative theory to evolution regarding the origin of life. In a 139-page opinion, U.S. District Judge John Jones declared that intelligent design "is a religious view, a mere relabeling of creationism, and not a scientific theory."

In March the Israeli Supreme Court ruled in a 7–4 decision that certain types of non-Orthodox conversions to Judaism had to be recognized by the state. The ruling was hailed by leaders of the Reform and Conservative movements and weakened the monopoly that the Orthodox chief rabbinate had exercised over religious affairs.

A task force report in June concluded that evangelical Christianity had been given a preferred status at the U.S. Air Force Academy in Colorado Springs, Colo. The report contained guidelines on how the air force could allow service members to express their faith while

Greek Orthodox Metropolitan Theofilos is enthroned as patriarch of Jerusalem in ceremonies on August 22.

Hazem Bader/AFP/Getty Images

on duty without promoting intolerance. A Pentagon report issued in June confirmed that the Qur'an had been abused in several incidents at the prison in Guantánamo Bay, Cuba, used to house terrorism suspects. Earlier, in response to unconfirmed reports of abuse of the Muslim holy book, the Department of State had told U.S. embassies to spread the word that the U.S. respects all religious faiths. In September Ontario Premier Dalton McGuinty announced that he would propose legislation to outlaw religious tribunals that had been used by Roman Catholics and Jews to settle family and civil disputes in the Canadian province. The voluntary practice had been used since adoption of an arbitration act in 1991 but had received little attention until some Muslims demanded the same rights.

Personalities. Ireneos I was deposed in May as patriarch of the Greek Orthodox Church in the Holy Land by 12 of its 18 bishops because of his having approved a long-term lease of church property in Jerusalem to Jewish investors. He was replaced in August by Metropolitan Theofilos, who was elected by a unanimous vote of the church's Holy Synod after promising to return all the properties that were leased to Israelis. The Rev. Roger Haight, a Jesuit priest, in February was forbidden to teach as a Catholic theologian because of what the Vatican called "serious doctrinal errors" in his work. He had submitted his resignation from the faculty of Weston Jesuit School of Theology in Cambridge, Mass., in October 2004 and was lecturing at the nondenominational Union Theological Seminary in New York City when the order was announced. The Rev. Thomas J. Reese resigned in May as editor of the Jesuit magazine *America* after his publishing of articles critical of church positions had come under fire at the Vatican. Russia's chief rabbi, Beryl Lazar, was denounced by the World Union for Progressive Judaism in April after he declared in a magazine article that Reform Judaism violated the Torah and "can't be labeled as a religion."

Charles Townes, a Nobel laureate in physics and a coinventor of the laser, was the 2005 recipient of the Templeton Prize for Progress Toward Research or Discoveries About Spiritual Realities. The 89-year-old scientist was raised in a liberal Baptist household in South Carolina. His 1966 article "The Convergence of Science and Religion" was one of the first by a major scientist to examine commonality between the two disciplines.   (DARRELL J. TURNER)

Roman Catholicism at a Crossroads

by R. Scott Appleby

© Elio Ciol/Corbis

The death on April 2, 2005, of Pope John Paul II (*see* OBITUARIES) put an end to the third longest pontificate in two millennia of Roman Catholic history. The Polish pontiff left to his German successor, Pope Benedict XVI (*see* BIOGRAPHIES), a global church whose demographic, spiritual, and theological centres had shifted dramatically during the 26 years of John Paul's papacy.

Demographically, Africa, Latin America, and parts of Asia are now the areas of dramatic growth and vitality. Catholic practice and affiliation, however, have waned considerably in Europe, especially in the historic Catholic communities of Italy, France, Spain, Portugal, and Austria. The largest Catholic populations in the world reside in Brazil, Mexico, the Philippines, and the United States; the total number of Catholics worldwide is estimated to be approximately 1.2 billion.

While the seeming loss of Europe is much bemoaned (and a particular concern of Pope Benedict XVI, who has pledged to reverse the tide of secularism and Islamism now shaping the continent), even the good news of growth elsewhere comes at a cost. The increasing number of lay Catholics needing pastoral care poses a profound institutional challenge because it has been accompanied by a startling decline in the percentage of priests and religious.

For hundreds of years prior to the 1960s, numerous and well-enrolled religious orders of priests, brothers, and nuns served with little or no material reward (most of them took vows of poverty and lived celibate lives under the direction of a religious superior) while building and staffing Catholic parishes, schools, colleges, seminaries, hospitals, and orphanages. As their numbers have dwindled (along with the numbers of

diocesan or "secular" priests, those who work under the direct authority of the local bishop), concerns have arisen about the ability of the church to provide even the sacraments to all the faithful—not to mention Catholic education, catechesis, and health care. The sacramental crisis revolves around the Eucharist, or Holy Communion, the bread and wine that, Catholics believe, is transformed at mass into the body and blood of Jesus Christ. The mass is the foundation of Catholic worship, but increasing numbers of Catholics worldwide are being denied access to the Eucharist on a weekly basis owing to the shortage of priests, who alone can consecrate the bread and wine.

In the U.S., for example, the "full pews, empty altars" phenomenon is reaching crisis proportions. One-fourth to one-third of the country's 19,000

parishes no longer have a priest in residence. In 1960 approximately 55,000 priests and 160,000 women religious (i.e., "nuns" or "sisters") served 40 million American Catholics. Today the number of Catholics has grown to 65 million, while the number of priests (average age: 60) has fallen to 35,000, and the number of women religious (average age: 70) has been cut in half, to approximately 80,000. Catholic colleges and universities, feeling the absence of the clergy who once taught in the classroom and served as chaplains, struggle with their religious identity, as do Catholic hospitals now led by Catholic laity or by health care professionals with little or no personal connection to Roman Catholicism.

Pope John Paul II will go down in history as one of the church's greatest evangelists, teachers, and world leaders.

© Illustration by Alex Abajian

He preached the gospel to more people and in more nations than all of his 262 predecessors combined; he authored almost 60 encyclicals and apostolic letters as well as several best-selling books; and he will be remembered for proclaiming religious freedom around the world and for his role in inspiring the Solidarity labour movement in his native Poland, which eventually brought down the communist regime. He will not be lauded universally, however, for his governance of the church itself.

Rather than support and expand lay ministries in their own right, as authentic and permanent forms of ministry in the church, John Paul curtailed them and insisted on an exclusive policy of attempting to foster more priestly vocations. This policy has enjoyed only modest success. A new clericalism (emphasis on clergy as the sole spiritual religious leaders, with laity in a passive or merely "temporal" role) was the dubious result. Rather than empower his fellow bishops, in line with the Second Vatican Council's affirmation of collegiality (the sharing of authority among the bishops), he treated them as his subordinates and stifled innovation and creativity that might have led to needed reforms. Rather than appoint women to positions of real authority within the church bureaucracy, John Paul emphasized and reinforced their exclusion from the priesthood.

Pope John Paul II also moved to shore up traditional Catholic teaching after a period of experimentation and theological pluralism that followed Vatican II. During his reign prominent departures from the ethical positions and theological approach favoured by the pope were seen as "dissent" and silenced.

The doctrinal enforcer assigned the task of overseeing and sometimes rejecting the work of fellow Catholic theologians was Joseph Cardinal Ratzinger, a brilliant German theologian whom John Paul appointed in 1981 as the prefect of the Congregation for the Doctrine of the Faith. Cardinal Ratzinger quickly established a formidable reputation as a doctrinally conservative, unbending "inquisitor" who brooked no dissent and seemed, with John Paul, to steer the church away from some of the more progressive implications of Vatican II. Ratzinger, for example, presided over the weakening of national episcopal conferences, the elimination of gender-inclusive language in Catholic liturgy and in the *Universal Catechism of the Catholic Church,* and the attempted termination of theological discussion on controversial issues such as the ordination of women.

When Ratzinger was elected to succeed Pope John Paul II after the latter's death, however, he took the name Benedict XVI in an effort to convey his intention, he explained, to emulate the

role of peacemaker in the world and reconciler in the church that Pope Benedict XV had embraced before and during World War I. As was his predecessor, Benedict XVI is a virulent opponent of war; he has been a strong critic of the U.S.-led invasion and occupation of Iraq and of the doctrine of preemptive war that was developed to justify the invasion and other aspects of the administration of George W. Bush's "global war on terrorism."

Within the church Benedict XVI was expected to focus much more energy than his predecessor had on its internal life and administration. Whereas John Paul was a natural performer who loved the stage and skillfully exploited the world spotlight, Benedict is retiring and professorial. He eschews the cult of personality that seemed the birthright of John Paul II. Rather than crisscross the globe as a cultural superstar-evangelist, Pope Benedict XVI is more likely to focus on fortifying the morale of the clergy and restoring the proper authority of the college of bishops. Indeed, the relatively open and deliberative procedures of the International Synod of Bishops held in Rome in October 2005 (and devoted to the question of the Eucharist) raised hopes that Benedict would restore a measure of collegiality to the church.

Benedict is unlikely to depart, however, from his predecessor's policies forbidding birth control, a married clergy, or women priests. Yet it is far from certain that these policies, which both Pope John Paul II and Pope Benedict XVI consider to have deep foundations in Christ's original example and teaching, will serve the goal of solving the "full pews, empty altars" crisis afflicting not only the American church but, increasingly, the church universal.

The scandal of the sexual abuse of minors by a small but nonetheless appalling number of priests has served only to exacerbate the crisis in the priesthood. Though the United States was the epicentre of the scandal that broke in 2002, the sexual-abuse scandals had an international dimension. Sexual abuse, a crime that stretches across decades and national boundaries, has already cost the Catholic Church hundreds of millions of dollars and invaluable prestige and trust ("social capital") built up over generations. Many American Catholics were dismayed by the Vatican's initial response to the crisis, which fell short, they believed, of fully acknowledging and addressing both the causes and the consequences of the scandal. In light of the fact that Pope John Paul placed Cardinal Ratzinger in charge of formulating that response, it will be important to see how Pope Benedict XVI addresses its subsequent phases.

R. Scott Appleby is a Professor of History at the University of Notre Dame; he is the author of The Ambivalence of the Sacred: Religion, Violence and Reconciliation.

THE 2005 ANNUAL MEGACENSUS OF RELIGIONS

Statistical data about religions and churches have been generated from various sources at least since 1750, and the amount of data available has been growing quickly. In addition to the religious groups' own statistics, much of the information comes from decennial governmental censuses; about half the countries of the world ask their populations to state their religions, if any. The United States has never asked a religious question in the federal censuses, which have been conducted since 1790. In its 2000 census the British government introduced a religion question for the first time since 1851, acknowledging that the information is valuable for enumerating and serving the social needs of ethnic minorities. Less-developed countries began to drop religion questions owing to the high cost of including them, but this trend seems to have been reversing in recent years. A second major source of church membership data is

Worldwide Adherents of All Religions, Mid-2005

	Africa	Asia	Europe	Latin America	Northern America	Oceania	World	%	Number of Countries
Christians	410,973,000	350,633,000	553,271,000	517,107,000	275,364,000	26,458,000	2,133,806,000	33.1	238
Affiliated Christians	389,304,000	344,834,000	530,967,000	511,908,000	220,913,000	22,258,000	2,020,184,000	31.3	238
Roman Catholics	147,123,000	123,781,000	276,559,000	483,033,000	79,915,000	8,580,000	1,118,991,000	17.3	235
Independents	90,262,000	181,645,000	24,696,000	46,311,000	80,484,000	1,772,000	425,170,000	6.6	221
Protestants	118,513,000	57,641,000	70,760,000	55,141,000	65,990,000	7,770,000	375,815,000	5.8	232
Orthodox	38,865,000	13,244,000	159,042,000	886,000	6,684,000	780,000	219,501,000	3.4	134
Anglicans	44,480,000	743,000	25,656,000	914,000	2,950,000	4,975,000	79,718,000	1.2	163
Marginal Christians	3,395,000	3,183,000	4,551,000	10,812,000	11,561,000	649,000	34,151,000	0.5	215
Multiple affiliation	*−53,334,000*	*−35,403,000*	*−30,297,000*	*−85,189,000*	*−26,671,000*	*−2,268,000*	*−233,162,000*	*−3.6*	*163*
Unaffiliated Christians	21,669,000	5,799,000	22,304,000	5,199,000	54,451,000	4,200,000	113,622,000	1.8	232
Muslims	357,846,000	910,375,000	33,303,000	1,745,000	5,259,000	412,000	1,308,941,000	20.3	206
Hindus	2,637,000	853,371,000	1,465,000	770,000	1,469,000	421,000	860,133,000	13.3	116
Chinese universists	35,900	403,564,000	266,000	203,000	719,000	134,000	404,921,900	6.3	94
Buddhists	150,000	372,698,000	1,643,000	709,000	3,110,000	498,000	378,808,000	5.9	130
Ethnoreligionists	107,162,000	143,174,000	1,233,000	3,159,000	1,279,000	325,000	256,332,000	4.0	144
Neoreligionists	114,000	105,197,000	382,000	774,000	1,578,000	86,200	108,131,200	1.7	107
Sikhs	58,700	24,457,000	239,000	0	598,000	25,000	25,377,700	0.4	34
Jews	226,000	5,327,000	2,015,000	1,221,000	6,179,000	105,000	15,073,000	0.2	134
Spiritists	3,100	2,000	135,000	12,721,000	162,000	7,400	13,030,500	0.2	56
Baha'is	1,964,000	3,730,000	146,000	827,000	859,000	124,000	7,650,000	0.1	218
Confucianists	300	6,402,000	16,700	800	0	51,100	6,470,900	0.1	16
Jains	76,100	4,505,000	0	0	8,000	700	4,589,800	0.1	11
Shintoists	0	2,721,000	0	7,200	61,000	0	2,789,200	0.0	8
Taoists	0	2,722,000	0	0	12,000	0	2,734,000	0.0	5
Zoroastrians	900	2,471,000	90,500	0	82,400	3,200	2,648,000	0.0	23
Other religionists	80,000	70,000	260,000	110,000	670,000	10,000	1,200,000	0.0	78
Nonreligious	6,042,000	602,308,000	108,304,000	16,139,000	32,656,000	3,930,000	769,379,000	11.9	237
Atheists	595,000	123,781,000	21,952,000	2,787,000	2,090,000	407,000	151,612,000	2.3	219
Total population	**887,964,000**	**3,917,508,000**	**724,722,000**	**558,280,000**	**332,156,000**	**32,998,000**	**6,453,628,000**	**100.0**	**238**

Continents. These follow current UN demographic terminology, which now divides the world into the six major areas shown above. *See* United Nations, *World Population Prospects: The 2002 Revision* (New York: UN, 2003), with populations of all continents, regions, and countries covering the period 1950–2050, with 100 variables for every country each year. Note that "Asia" includes the former Soviet Central Asian states and "Europe" includes all of Russia eastward to the Pacific.

Countries. The last column enumerates sovereign and nonsovereign countries in which each religion or religious grouping has a numerically significant and organized following.

Adherents. As defined in the 1948 Universal Declaration of Human Rights, a person's religion is what he or she professes, confesses, or states that it is. Totals are enumerated for each of the world's 238 countries following the methodology of the *World Christian Encyclopedia*, 2nd ed. (2001), and *World Christian Trends* (2001), using recent censuses, polls, surveys, yearbooks, reports, Web sites, literature, and other data. *See* the World Christian Database <www.worldchristiandatabase.org> for more detail. Religions are ranked in order of size in mid-2005.

Christians. Followers of Jesus Christ, enumerated here under **Affiliated Christians**, those affiliated with churches (church members, with names written on church rolls, usually total number of baptized persons, including children baptized, dedicated, or undedicated); total in 2005 being 2,020,184,000, shown above divided among the six standardized ecclesiastical blocs and with (negative and italicized) figures for those persons with **Multiple affiliation** (all who are baptized members of more than one denomination and not to be added to other denominations here) and **Unaffiliated Christians,** who are persons professing or confessing in censuses or polls to be Christians though not so affiliated.

Independents. This term here denotes members of Christian churches and networks that regard themselves as postdenominationalist and neo-apostolic and thus independent of historic, mainstream, organized, institutionalized, confessional, denominationalist Christianity.

Marginal Christians. Members of denominations who define themselves as Christians but who are on the margins of organized mainstream Christianity (e.g., Unitarians, Mormons, Jehovah's Witnesses, Christian Science, and Religious Science).

Muslims. 84% Sunnites, 14% Shi'ites, 2% other schools.

Hindus. 68% Vaishnavites, 27% Shaivites, 2% neo-Hindus and reform Hindus.

Chinese universists. Followers of a unique complex of beliefs and practices that may include: universism (yin/yang cosmology with dualities earth/heaven, evil/good, darkness/light), ancestor cult, Confucian ethics, divination, festivals, folk religion, goddess worship, household gods, local deities, mediums, metaphysics, monasteries, neo-Confucianism, popular religion, sacrifices, shamans, spirit writing, and Taoist and Buddhist elements.

Buddhists. 56% Mahayana, 38% Theravada (Hinayana), 6% Tantrayana (Lamaism).

Ethnoreligionists. Followers of local, tribal, animistic, or shamanistic religions, with members restricted to one ethnic group.

Neoreligionists. Followers of Asian 20th-century neoreligions, neoreligious movements, radical new crisis religions, and non-Christian syncretistic mass religions.

Jews. Adherents of Judaism. For detailed data on "core" Jewish population, *see* the annual "World Jewish Populations" article in the American Jewish Committee's *American Jewish Year Book*.

Confucianists. Non-Chinese followers of Confucius and Confucianism, mostly Koreans in Korea.

Other religionists. Including a handful of religions, quasi-religions, pseudoreligions, parareligions, religious or mystic systems, and religious and semireligious brotherhoods of numerous varieties.

Nonreligious. Persons professing no religion, nonbelievers, agnostics, freethinkers, uninterested, or dereligionized secularists indifferent to all religion but not militantly so.

Atheists. Persons professing atheism, skepticism, disbelief, or irreligion, including the militantly antireligious (opposed to all religion).

Total population. UN medium variant figures for mid-2005, as given in *World Population Prospects: The 2002 Revision*.

the decentralized censuses taken by many religious headquarters. Almost all 37,000 Christian denominations ask statistical questions each year on at least some of 180 major religious subjects. All Roman Catholic bishops, for instance, are required to answer 141 statistical questions about their activities over the previous 12 months. Each year about 27,000 new books on the religious situation in a single country, as well as some 9,000 printed annual yearbooks or official handbooks, appear in print. Although not centralized or coordinated, these publications are the third significant source of data for the megacensus of world religion. The two tables below are the result of a combination and synthesis of these data around the major characteristic, namely individuals' religious profession and/or affiliation. The first table summarizes worldwide adherents by the 19 major or largest religions. The second goes into more detail for the United States. (DAVID B. BARRETT, TODD M. JOHNSON, PETER F. CROSSING)

Religious Adherents in the United States of America, 1900–2005

	1900	%	mid-1970	%	mid-1990	%	mid-2000	%	mid-2005	%	Annual Change, 1990–2000 Natural	Conversion	Total	Rate (%)
Christians	73,260,000	96.4	190,732,000	90.8	218,335,000	85.4	239,575,000	84.1	250,042,000	83.3	2,501,000	−377,000	2,124,000	0.93
Affiliated Christians	54,425,000	71.6	152,874,000	72.8	175,500,000	68.6	194,498,000	68.2	200,614,000	66.9	2,010,000	−110,000	1,900,000	1.03
Independents	5,850,000	7.7	35,666,000	17.0	66,900,000	26.2	75,218,000	26.4	78,786,000	26.3	766,000	66,000	832,000	1.18
Roman Catholics	10,775,000	14.2	48,305,000	23.0	56,500,000	22.1	62,970,000	22.1	65,900,000	22.0	647,200	−200	647,000	1.09
Protestants	35,000,000	46.1	58,568,000	27.9	60,216,000	23.5	60,497,000	21.2	61,295,000	20.4	690,000	−662,000	28,100	0.05
Marginal Christians	800,000	1.1	6,126,000	2.9	8,940,000	3.5	10,188,000	3.6	11,018,000	3.7	102,000	23,000	125,000	1.32
Orthodox	400,000	0.5	4,189,000	2.0	5,150,000	2.0	5,733,000	2.0	5,992,000	2.0	59,000	−700	58,300	1.08
Anglicans	1,600,000	2.1	3,196,000	1.5	2,450,000	1.0	2,325,000	0.8	2,206,000	0.7	28,100	−40,600	−12,500	−0.52
Multiple affiliation	*0*	*0.0*	*−3,176,000*	*−1.5*	*−24,656,000*	*−9.6*	*−22,433,000*	*−7.9*	*−24,583,000*	*−8.2*	*−282,000*	*504,000*	*222,000*	*−0.94*
Evangelicals	*32,068,000*	*42.2*	*35,248,000*	*16.8*	*38,400,000*	*15.0*	*42,600,000*	*14.9*	*44,800,000*	*14.9*	*440,000*	*−20,000*	*420,000*	*1.04*
evangelicals	*11,000,000*	*14.5*	*45,500,000*	*21.7*	*88,449,000*	*34.6*	*98,326,000*	*34.5*	*103,500,000*	*34.5*	*1,013,000*	*−25,000*	*988,000*	*1.06*
Unaffiliated Christians	18,835,000	24.8	37,858,000	18.0	42,835,000	16.8	45,077,000	15.8	46,428,000	16.5	491,000	−267,000	224,000	0.51
Jews	1,500,000	2.0	6,700,000	3.2	5,535,000	2.2	5,659,000	2.0	5,764,000	1.9	63,400	−51,000	12,400	0.22
Muslims	10,000	0.0	800,000	0.4	3,471,600	1.4	4,291,000	1.5	4,745,200	1.6	39,800	42,100	81,900	2.14
Black Muslims	0	0.0	200,000	0.1	1,250,000	0.5	1,650,000	0.6	1,850,000	0.6	12,700	17,300	30,000	2.29
Buddhists	30,000	0.0	200,000	0.1	1,880,000	0.7	2,517,000	0.9	2,721,000	0.9	21,500	42,200	63,700	2.96
Neoreligionists	10,000	0.0	560,000	0.3	1,155,000	0.5	1,428,000	0.5	1,509,000	0.5	13,200	14,100	27,300	2.14
Ethnoreligionists	100,000	0.1	70,000	0.0	780,000	0.3	1,083,000	0.4	1,158,000	0.4	8,900	21,400	30,300	3.34
Hindus	1,000	0.0	100,000	0.0	750,000	0.3	1,056,000	0.4	1,144,000	0.4	8,600	22,000	30,600	3.48
Baha'is	2,800	0.0	138,000	0.1	600,000	0.2	774,000	0.3	829,000	0.3	6,900	10,500	17,400	2.58
Sikhs	0	0.0	1,000	0.0	160,000	0.1	239,000	0.1	270,000	0.1	1,800	6,100	7,900	4.09
Spiritists	0	0.0	0	0.0	120,000	0.0	142,000	0.0	149,000	0.0	1,400	800	2,200	1.70
Chinese universists	70,000	0.1	90,000	0.0	76,000	0.0	80,000	0.0	86,700	0.0	870	−370	500	0.63
Shintoists	0	0.0	0	0.0	50,000	0.0	57,600	0.0	60,600	0.0	570	190	760	1.43
Zoroastrians	0	0.0	0	0.0	42,400	0.0	54,000	0.0	56,800	0.0	490	670	1,160	2.45
Taoists	0	0.0	0	0.0	10,000	0.0	11,400	0.0	12,000	0.0	110	30	140	1.32
Jains	0	0.0	0	0.0	5,000	0.0	7,100	0.0	7,700	0.0	60	140	200	3.57
Other religionists	10,200	0.0	450,000	0.2	530,000	0.2	577,000	0.2	600,000	0.2	6,100	−1,400	4,700	0.85
Nonreligious	1,000,000	1.3	10,070,000	4.8	21,442,000	8.4	26,123,000	9.2	29,390,000	9.8	246,000	222,000	468,000	1.99
Atheists	1,000	0.0	200,000	0.1	770,000	0.3	1,328,000	0.5	1,493,000	0.5	8,800	47,000	55,800	5.60
US population	**75,995,000**	**100.0**	**210,111,000**	**100.0**	**255,712,000**	**100.0**	**285,003,000**	**100.0**	**300,038,000**	**100.0**	**2,929,000**	**0**	**2,929,000**	**1.09**

Methodology. This table extracts and analyzes a microcosm of the world religion table. It depicts the United States, the country with the largest number of adherents to Christianity, the world's largest religion. Statistics at five points in time from 1900 to 2005 are presented. Each religion's **Annual Change** for 1990–2000 is also analyzed by **Natural** increase (births minus deaths, plus immigrants minus emigrants) per year and **Conversion** increase (new converts minus new defectors) per year, which together constitute the **Total** increase per year. **Rate** increase is then computed as percentage per year.

Structure. Vertically the table lists 30 major religious categories. The major categories (including nonreligious) in the U.S. are listed with largest (Christians) first. Indented names of groups in the first column are subcategories of the groups above them and are also counted in these unindented totals, so they should not be added twice into the column total. Figures in italics draw adherents from all categories of Christians above and so cannot be added together with them. Figures for Christians are built upon detailed head counts by churches, often to the last digit. Totals are then rounded to the nearest 1,000. Because of rounding, the corresponding percentage figures may sometimes not total exactly to 100%. Religions are ranked in order of size in 2005.

Christians. All persons who profess publicly to follow Jesus Christ as God and Savior. This category is subdivided into **Affiliated Christians** (church members) and **Unaffiliated** (nominal) **Christians** (professing Christians not affiliated with any church). See also the note on Christians to the world religion table. The first six lines under "Affiliated Christians" are ranked by size in 2005 of each of the six blocs (Anglican, Independent, Marginal Christian, Orthodox, Protestant, and Roman Catholic).

Evangelicals/evangelicals. These two designations—italicized and enumerated separately here—cut across all of the six Christian traditions or ecclesiastical blocs listed above and should be considered separately from them. The **Evangelicals** (capitalized "E") are mainly Protestant churches, agencies, and individuals who call themselves by this term (for example, members of the National Association of Evangelicals); they usually emphasize 5 or more of 7, 9, or 21 fundamental doctrines (salvation by faith, personal acceptance, verbal inspiration of Scripture, depravity of man, Virgin Birth, miracles of Christ, atonement, evangelism, Second Advent, et al.). The **evangelicals** (lowercase "e") are Christians of evangelical conviction from all traditions who are committed to the evangel (gospel) and involved in personal witness and mission in the world.

Jews. Core Jewish population relating to Judaism, excluding Jewish persons professing a different religion.

Other categories. Definitions are as given under the world religion table.

Social Protection

With medical costs SKYROCKETING and government programs scaled back, citizens bore more RESPONSIBILITY for their health care costs; irregular migration, human TRAFFICKING, and migrant SMUGGLING posed challenges for governments; and the protection of human rights in the face of TERRORISM and efforts to prevent it remained at the forefront of social protection policies in 2005.

BENEFITS AND PROGRAMS

North America. Social protection programs were in the spotlight in the United States in 2005 as Pres. George W. Bush stumped for a ground-breaking change in Social Security, the nation geared up for the biggest, most expensive expansion of Medicare ever, and Congress considered controversial cutbacks in spending on several programs for the poor.

President Bush's number one domestic priority was a plan that would let younger workers divert part of their payroll taxes into private individual retirement accounts that they could decide how to invest. He spearheaded an intensive 60-day, 60-city campaign to sell the idea, and versions of the proposal were introduced in Congress. However, when public opinion remained cool to the change and Congress became engulfed by issues stemming from Hurricane Katrina and Supreme Court nominations, Social Security reform slid to the back burner, its fate uncertain.

Advocates of the private accounts argued that they would produce higher returns for workers and give them greater control over their money. Critics contended that workers' retirement nest eggs would be left to the vagaries of the stock market and that siphoning off part of payroll taxes from the Social Security trust fund would hasten the system's looming financial troubles. Officials estimated that Social Security would start paying out more in benefits than it collected in taxes in 2017 (a year sooner than they had projected in 2004) and would have to start dipping into reserves at that time. They said

that the reserves would be exhausted around 2041, at which time retirees would receive only about 74% of scheduled benefits.

Established in 1935 as part of Pres. Franklin D. Roosevelt's New Deal, Social Security became the largest segment of the American social safety net, one in which current workers financed the benefits of retirees with a 6.2% tax on their earnings (up to a maximum wage of $94,200 in 2006); their payment was matched by employers. With workers far outnumbering retirees, taxes had exceeded payments, and the excesses went into the Social Security Trust Funds. As the huge baby-boom population reached retirement age,

however, the present three-to-one ratio of workers to retirees would shrink to two-to-one. The aging, longer-lived population was cited as the chief cause of future financial problems.

Social Security benefits represented the sole source of income for about one-fifth of the 52 million recipients and at least half the income for another 45%. Beneficiaries would receive a 4.1% cost-of-living increase for 2006, the largest since 1990, bringing the average payment for a retired worker to just over $1,000 a month.

As historic change was debated for Social Security, it was being implemented in its partner program, Medicare, which provided health insurance for 41 million elderly and disabled persons. In 2003 Congress passed legislation that added prescription-drug coverage to Medicare, starting Jan. 1, 2006. Ten large private insurers were chosen to market drug coverage nationwide, and several more were selected to sell it regionally. The insurance plans, which were subsidized and regulated by Medicare, would offer a variety of options, each covering different drugs and carrying different co-payments and benefits. Though participation in the new program was voluntary, 28 million to 30 million people were expected to sign up.

Printed materials in support of Pres. George W. Bush's Social Security-reform plan await distribution in Louisville, Ky., in March. Early in the year the reform plan topped the administration's agenda, but it was later overtaken by more pressing issues.

While most of the costs would be paid by the government, seniors would pay premiums, co-payments, and deductibles. The average premium was estimated to be $32 a month, with some plans costing as little as $20 a month and additional subsidies available for low-income enrollees. Most participants would pay a $250 deductible, 25% of drug costs from $251 to $2,250, then all of the next $2,850 in charges. After the total tab reached $5,100, individuals would pay only 5% of charges beyond that. In addition to payments for drug coverage, the Medicare premium for doctors and outpatient care was slated to rise in 2006 by 13%, to $88.50 a month, reflecting a large increase in the use of doctors' services.

Prescription-drug coverage, the cost of which was estimated to top $700 billion dollars over the next 10 years, put additional pressure on a system that already faced daunting fiscal problems because of demographic factors and runaway health care costs. Medicare's hospital insurance fund had started paying out more than it collected in 2004, and officials warned that it would run out of money in 2020, two decades earlier than Social Security, unless changes were made. The price tag for Medicare was projected to soar at a rate of 9% a year, compared with 5.6% for Social Security and 3.2% for general inflation; the cost of Medicare accounted for 15% of the federal budget in 2005 and by some estimates could reach 25% by 2020.

Financing was also an issue for other social protection programs. With cost cutting required by the fiscal 2006 budget resolution and expenditures mounting in the wake of hurricane relief and the war in Iraq, Congress for the first time in nearly a decade targeted several programs for the needy. The most severe cuts were proposed in Medicaid, the health care program for the poor that was administered by states under guidelines set by Washington and whose costs were split between states and the federal government. Those costs had shot up over 60% in the past five years to more than $320 billion annually, and the program consumed more than $1 of every $5 spent by states, which made it the second largest item in many state budgets, behind education.

Even as they acknowledged that their Medicaid operations were sometimes riddled with waste and abuse, state officials lobbied for greater latitude in managing the program and experimenting with new approaches, such as importing cheaper drugs from Canada and tightening regulations to prevent the elderly from transferring assets in order to qualify for nursing-home payments. The National Governors Association proposed sweeping changes to cut costs, and the Bush administration set up a commission to find ways to slow Medicaid's rapid growth. One of the challenges reformers faced was reflected in a Census Bureau report showing that 45.8 million Americans, almost one in six, did not have health insurance. The number of uninsured increased by 4.5 million between 2001 and 2004, largely as a result of employers' reducing their coverage.

States also moved to fill the gap when Congress continued to balk at raising the federal minimum wage, which had been $5.15 an hour since 1997. Fifteen states and the District of Columbia set their own minimums at higher levels, ranging up to $7.35 an hour.

For the third straight year, Congress failed to reauthorize the 1996 welfare-reform act, which had replaced cash assistance to needy families with block grants to states and new work requirements. Lawmakers passed a series of temporary extensions as the House and Senate tried to reach compromises on Republican demands for greater work requirements and the call by Democrats for more money for child care. Although welfare rolls were down sharply since passage of the 1996 law, the Census Bureau reported that poverty in the United States rose from 12.5% in 2003 to 12.7% in 2004, the fourth year in a row that an increase had been registered.

In Canada a landmark ruling by the Supreme Court left the country's heralded national public health care system in a state of limbo and challenged some long-held ideas about health care delivery. The high court struck down a Quebec law banning private health insurance. Although the ruling applied only to Quebec province and the impact elsewhere was unclear, some observers speculated that it could presage fundamental changes in the universal health care system, which provided mostly free, tax-funded medical care and inexpensive drugs for everyone.

The one-tier system generally was a point of pride for Canadians, but in recent years it had been marred by reports of a shortage of doctors and long waiting periods for diagnostic tests and elective surgery. The case that led to the ruling was brought by a physician and one of his patients, who had waited a year for hip-replacement surgery. In its 4–3 decision, the court majority said that "access to a waiting list is not access to health care" and that "delays in the public system are widespread and have serious, sometimes grave, consequences." They ruled that banning private insurance in cases in which the public system failed to provide reasonable service violated the provincial charter's protection of life and personal security.

The decision triggered a broad new debate over strategies to cure Canada's ailing $130 billion health-delivery system. On one side were those who feared that it would open the door for a hybrid two-tier health-delivery system in which the wealthy would get one level of care and the less affluent another. They also worried that some doctors would drop out of the public system and set up private clinics. Others argued that the present system needed to be improved and suggested that Canada consider moving in the direction of European countries that allowed private health insurance to cover the same benefits as public insurance. (DAVID M. MAZIE)

Europe. In an effort to address budget deficits, many countries in Europe proposed reforms in 2005 that would lower the costs for health care provision and future pension payments. One solution was to increase the responsibility of program beneficiaries, particularly when the shift would offer people more flexibility and choice. European countries also sought to create a better balance between time spent at work and life away from the job, especially in efforts to generate additional employment opportunities.

The government of the Czech Republic proposed a health reform bill that established a closer link between the salaries of insured persons and both their health-insurance contributions and the amount of their sickness cash benefits. Employers had their contributions reduced but were made responsible for continued wage payments during the first 14 days of their employees' illnesses. Beginning in January employers in Sweden, who already had a similar obligation, were in addition required to cofinance cash benefits from day 15 of an employee's illness. Employers would bear 15% of the social insurance office's expenditures, but this cost was subject to exemptions (such as cases in which a worker took part in rehabilitation measures or was listed as only part-time sick).

The Netherlands embarked on a major health reform that abolished the two-tiered system that provided compulsory social health insurance for people below a certain income threshold and private health-insurance coverage for people better-off financially. Private insurers would run the new system and not be allowed to base their premiums on the age or health status of the insured and would be required to accept anyone residing in their area of operation. As a provision of the Dutch Work and Care Act, employees were given the option of taking additional unpaid leave to care for a sick relative, preferably on a part-time basis; employers would be required to grant leave unless they could prove that the employee absence would cause serious business problems.

In November the two largest German parties, the Christian Democratic Union/Christian Social Union and the Social Democratic Party, concluded negotiations on the formation of a new coalition government that would address the budget deficit and combat unemployment. The parties did not reach a consensus on health policy but agreed to increase the retirement age to 67 years. Current pensioners would not enjoy pension increases in the next few years. Though contributions to the old-age-pension system would rise slightly, those to the unemployment insurance would decrease; the overall objective was to arrive at a combined contribution rate of less than 40% for all social benefits. Employment protection for new hires would begin after they had been on the job for 24 months.

In France the maximum probation period for new hires in companies with fewer than 10 employees was raised from six months to two years. New French Prime Minister Dominique de Villepin outlined ideas for boosting economic growth and employment, including facilitating return to work of the long-term unemployed and providing employment assistance to young people and workers over the age of 50, including a reorganization of government services to provide more personalized assistance. Following suburban riots in the fall, he announced that the government would step up measures to combat discrimination and inequity at the workplace and in the labour market.

The Norwegian government proposed a new integrated employment and welfare administration with the long-term goal of establishing a one-stop service of combined municipal and central government employment and welfare offices in each municipality. Finland gave more flexibility to self-employed persons in paying their pension contributions. In good years additional contributions could be paid to compensate for reduced payments in financially difficult times. Spain worked on providing incentives for people with disabilities to return to work. The Spanish government introduced regulations that made the receipt of a disability pension more easily compatible with remunerated work.

Austria streamlined its pension provision by including all persons who on Jan. 1, 2005, were younger than 50 years in a new uniform system that would grant a pension of 80% of lifetime average earnings to people with 45 years of contributions at age 65. The government of the United Kingdom announced the principles for a future pension reform that included measures to tackle poverty effectively and provide an opportunity for all, including women and caregivers, to build an adequate retirement income. To build up some capital for children living in poor households, a Child Trust Fund system was established, and an initial voucher of at least £250 (about $450) was sent to all eligible families to open savings accounts for children from which moneys could be drawn only after a child's 18th birthday.

Industrialized Asia and the Pacific. Prosperous countries in the Asia-Pacific region were also concerned with the long-term stability of their social programs and sought to increase the participation of their populations in the labour market. The Australian government considered that it would become increasingly important for people to keep connected to the labour market at older ages and introduced new rules to ease the transition to retirement. Beginning in July, persons who became entitled to superannuation (mandatory occupational pensions) could draw on a portion of their benefits without having to retire permanently from the workforce. The government also announced the introduction of the Australian Fair Pay and Conditions Standard, a package of workplace reforms that included legislation that defined minimum conditions of employment regarding annual leave, caregiver's leave, parental leave, and the maximum

number of ordinary working hours. Collective agreements would have to be assessed against this new standard and conform to it.

Facing an aging population and rising health care costs, Singaporean Prime Minister Lee Hsien Loong called for increasing the effective retirement age that tended to be below the legal retirement age of 62 years for about half of the country's male working population and more than half of working women. Possibly this could be achieved through an increase in the legal retirement age. In an effort to provide short-term assistance to families, a Self-Reliance Programme was launched that would provide rental subsidies, medical coverage, or children's educational assistance. Those eligible for the program would have to attend counseling and casework sessions with community social workers.

For the period September 1 to December 31, the South Korean government eliminated two public holidays and increased the hourly minimum wage by 9.2% in comparison with the previous year. The two major trade union federations protested because they feared that those workers employed in enterprises with 300 or more employees would end up with lower weekly wages because their workweek had been reduced from 44 to 40 hours in July. As a result, the government obliged those businesses to guarantee the minimum wage amount based on the prior 44-hour week. In an effort to increase the employment of nonregular female workers and to boost birthrates, the government declared that social security would pay the entire 90-day maternity benefit from 2006. Currently the social security benefit compensated for 30 days, and the employer paid the remaining 60 days.

Japan considered allowing corporate health-insurance societies (health insurers for larger companies) to merge across industry sectors in the hope that removing barriers to consolidation would help slow the rate at which these societies were ceasing operation. In May a panel of experts appointed by the government proposed the decentralization of the government-managed employee's health insurance operated by the Social Insurance Agency (the health insurer for small- and medium-sized firms).

Emerging and Less-Developed Countries. China merged its basic-subsistence guarantee system for workers laid off in state-owned enterprises with its system

Schoolchildren in Panama City, Pan., flee police during the second consecutive day of public protests against proposed reforms in the country's social security system.

for unemployment insurance. In July Pakistan launched a voluntary pension system in which individual retirement accounts would be managed by asset-management and life-insurance companies. Any Pakistani national over the age of 18 who had a national tax number and was not a member of an occupational pension scheme was allowed to open an account.

Azerbaijan increased pension levels and more than doubled the lump sum payable upon childbirth. Under the state pension system, Kazakhstan added a new basic payment to all retired citizens regardless of their current level of benefits. This was a step toward a three-pillar pension system that would include a basic pension, individual retirement accounts, and voluntary or occupational insurance. Kazakhstan also embarked on a reform of its health care, for which initial emphasis was placed on primary medical care.

Countries in Africa made efforts to provide better benefits and services and launch structural reform. South Africa increased the maximum amounts of various social grants for people with low incomes. Lesotho introduced universal old-age pensions, mirroring regional developments. Uganda's National Social Security Fund implemented a new electronic database that made it easier to reach beneficiaries and identify employers with unpaid contributions. Burkina Faso, Ghana, Guinea, Kenya, and Mali all had ongoing reform discussions pertaining to health care and/or pensions.

In Latin America the four members (Argentina, Brazil, Paraguay, and Uruguay) of the regional common market Mercosur concluded a multilateral social security agreement that was expected to affect 2.1 million workers. The accord would allow companies and their employees on assignment within the zone to contribute only to the social programs of their home country. Chile enacted legislation to regulate private health care institutions. Among the measures included were the standardization of price variations and prohibition of the arbitrary termination of contracts. Proposed social security reforms that included using up to 25% of the Social Security Fund's reserves for national development projects were greeted in Panama by protests and strikes; the reforms would have made the access to benefits more difficult and increased contributions for both employees and employers.   (CHRISTIANE KUPTSCH)

HUMAN RIGHTS

Terrorism and efforts to prevent it remained at the forefront of many of the most significant human rights developments in 2005. With the threat posed by major new attacks in Indonesia, Great Britain, Egypt, India, and Iraq, many countries adopted stronger measures to monitor potential threats and to provide new and more expedited methods of punishment and prevention. Many of these measures, however, involved serious erosions of well-established human rights protections, such as freedom of speech, freedom from arbitrary arrest and from long-term, indefinite detention, and the absolute prohibition against torture or involvement in sending anyone to a situation of torture in another country.

The expanding recognition that human rights should encompass economic and social factors as well as the more traditional political and civil rights protections was demonstrated by the increasing attention being paid to the threat of famine in major portions of Africa, health needs (particularly those related to AIDS and HIV) in less-developed countries (LDCs), and the

In June a child under threat of famine in the Maradi region of Niger eats a packet of "plumpy nut," an emergency foodstuff. The high-calorie peanut-based product manufactured in France revolutionized famine-aid work in Africa and elsewhere.

substantial human needs created by an unusually harsh series of natural disasters associated with the 2004 tsunami in the Indian Ocean and such 2005 events as the widespread flooding that Hurricane Katrina caused in the U.S Gulf Coast, the Guatemala mud slides triggered by Hurricane Stan, and the October earthquake in the Kashmir region of the Indian subcontinent.

Terrorism. Statistics compiled by the U.S. Department of State for its annual report on terrorism to the Congress indicated that the number of serious international terrorist incidents more than tripled in 2004, with 651 reported attacks. Britain responded to the major bombings that took place in the London transport system on July 7 and 21, 2005, by passing laws that limited free-speech protections in situations that could be characterized as involving incitement to terrorism and by seeking the deportation of one prominent Islamic cleric accused of promoting attacks. The USA PATRIOT Act was renewed just days after the second wave of London bombings, providing U.S. law-enforcement agencies with broad powers to monitor private actions and to conduct emergency investigations in secrecy, including having access to library and bookstore records.

Responding to these human rights restrictions, the U.S. Supreme Court ruled that U.S. judges had jurisdiction to review the legality of the treatment of suspected terrorist detainees being held at Guantánamo Bay, Cuba, while a number of other courts grappled with challenges to the use of special military tribunals (rather than regular criminal courts) to prosecute suspected terrorists and with the practice of rendition to torture. In August the U.S. government announced that it was seeking to short circuit some of these legal challenges by repatriating many of the Guantánamo Bay detainees back to their home countries, where they would continue to be held in prisons constructed there with U.S. funding and assistance. Critics pointed out that this could well continue the practice in other countries of arbitrary, indefinite detention of suspected terrorists without judicial determination of their status and amounted to little more than another form of "extraordinary rendition."

The UN Human Rights Committee, which is responsible for monitoring national compliance with the International Covenant on Civil and Political Rights and recognizing the special importance of the human rights infringements taking place in connection with antiterrorism efforts, took the unprecedented step of notifying the U.S. government that it would examine these issues at its October session without waiting for submission of the U.S. government's periodic compliance report. The UN Committee Against Torture also scheduled hearings on torture-related issues involving the U.S. to take place in May 2006, after receiving the U.S. government's report on compliance under the Convention Against Torture as well as "shadow reports" from human rights nongovernmental groups that critiqued the U.S. submission.

As an indicator that the abuses at Abu Ghraib prison in Iraq were taken seriously by the government, the U.S. military initiated court-martial prosecutions against nine lower-echelon soldiers implicated in the torture inflicted on detainees there in 2004. Former Abu Ghraib prison guard Lynndie England was convicted and sentenced in September to three years' imprisonment for her part in the abuse of prisoners in her care. The U.S. had yet to file criminal charges, however, against any of the higher-level officials whom many considered to have authorized or encouraged this type of conduct as an interrogation method. In June a prosecutor in Milan ordered the arrest and criminal prosecution of 13 CIA agents who had participated in the "extraordinary rendition" of an Egyptian cleric to Cairo, where, he claimed, he was beaten and tortured.

On a more positive note, in March the U.S. Supreme Court abolished the use of the death penalty for juvenile offenders, successfully ending a long-standing effort to remove the U.S. from an increasingly shorter list of nations (now reduced to Iran, China, and Pakistan) that still permitted juvenile executions. Prior to the ruling, 19 states still allowed juvenile executions, though since 1976 only 6 had used the practice.

Genocide in The Sudan. The campaign of genocide against the black African (non-Arab) population in Darfur remained a major problem in The Sudan, despite efforts by individual countries (including the U.S.) and the international community to put pressure on the government to bring an end to the assaults. A British parliamentary report estimated that in the two-year conflict 300,000 persons had died, half of them by execution and half through disease and malnutrition. The UN estimated 180,000 deaths, with up to 1,800,000 more displaced as refugees, more than 200,000 of whom fled to neighbouring Chad. The killing continued despite the negotiation of a cease-fire in November 2004 and a promised end to attacks on towns in the Darfur region by the Janjawid paramilitary groups conducting the genocide, with help from government forces, and the arrival of a small (2,000-member) peacekeeping force sent by the African Union to help protect the cease-fire monitors. In October 18 members of the AU peacekeeping force were abducted and later released by the Janjawid, and the AU released a statement condemning the government's continued "acts of calculated and wanton destruction." Juan Méndez, the UN special adviser on the prevention of genocide, found the situation "much more dangerous and worrisome" than he expected, with growing lawlessness. Two unprecedented attacks on refugee camps indicated an escalation of the violence.

The violence in Darfur included the frequent use of rape as a method of intimidation and "ethnic cleansing." Many women and girls were sexually abused during the attacks or when they left their villages or refugee camps to obtain water, food, or firewood.

Promoting Accountability for Major Human Rights Abusers. The trial of former Iraqi leader Saddam Hussein, along with seven of his high-level former officials, began in October. Charges against him included crimes against humanity associated with a series of summary executions and arbitrary detentions in the town of Dujayl, a Shi'ite village north of Baghdad; a 1988 aerial attack using chemical weapons on a Kurdish town; and the violent suppression of demonstrations in 1991 in the Kurdish and Shi'ite communities. Saddam pleaded not guilty, but little progress was made in his trial due to several delays. After years of continued delay in commencing the prosecution of Gen. Augusto Pinochet, the former dictator of Chile, the Chilean Supreme Court in September voted 10–6 to confirm removal of his immunity and in December ruled that he was fit to stand trial, paving the way for a trial in a case involving the disappearance and execution of at least 119 political dissidents, whose bodies were found in 1975 in Argentina. The trial of Slobodan Milosevic proceeded before the International Tribunal for Former Yugoslavia, though at a very slow pace. Progress was also plodding for the international tribunals created to deal with the problems in former Yugoslavia, Rwanda, Sierra Leone, Cambodia, and East Timor.

The International Criminal Court began work on its initial cases, including its investigation of genocide in Darfur. The ICC began to take action in three other pending cases involving the Democratic Republic of the Congo (DRC), Côte d'Ivoire, and abuses by the Lord's Resistance Army in Uganda. In the DRC case the ICC issued a protective order for witnesses involved in testifying in the closed proceedings.

Economic and Social Rights. The international community continued to place greater emphasis on the economic and social rights aspects of human rights. At the Group of Eight Summit meeting held July 6–8 in Gleneagles, Scot., British Prime Minister Tony Blair took the leadership role, supported by a series of Live 8 rock concerts in cities around the globe, in seeking a substantial increase in economic support for the LDCs of Africa and progress in fighting AIDS/HIV and malaria. He obtained commitments from developed nations to double their financial aid to Africa to $50 billion by 2010, but he did not achieve all of the debt-relief and environmental-protection measures he had been seeking. According to the UN, at the beginning of 2005 there were 37.2 million adults and 2.2 million children living with HIV/AIDS, 95% of them in LDCs.   (MORTON SKLAR)

INTERNATIONAL MIGRATION

In 2005 there were nearly 200 million migrants worldwide, and although the overall percentage of migrants in the global population was low (2.9%), their social, economic, and political visibility was often very high. The demographic impact of migration, however, was felt disproportionately in the less-developed world; from 1990 to 2000 international migration accounted for 56% of the population growth in less-developed countries (LDCs), compared with 3% in developed countries.

According to the UN High Commissioner for Refugees, the global number of refugees fell by 4%, to 9.2 million, in 2004. That year there were about 676,400 asylum claims lodged globally, a decrease of 19% compared with 2003. In 38 industrialized countries the number of new asylum seekers fell in 2004 to its lowest level in 16 years, and the number of internally displaced persons

Spain was the target of many migrants, especially from North Africa, during the year. These two women were among a group of 70 in a makeshift boat who were intercepted by officials off the southern coast of Spain on October 31.

remained stable at about 25 million worldwide.

General Policy Orientations. In 2005 the international discourse on migration strongly acknowledged the existence of close policy linkages between human mobility and other global issues such as employment, development, trade, security, human rights, and health. There were also increased calls for cross-disciplinary efforts aimed at improving levels of policy coherence in migration management at national, regional, and international levels.

Countries and companies looked abroad increasingly for personnel to improve their competitiveness and to address shortages, especially at the higher skills level of labour markets. Though goods, capital, services, and information flowed freely across borders, the movement of labour was still closely managed. The largest established migration programs continued to be run by the traditional countries of origin. In 2004, 946,000 persons were granted permanent residence in the United States, 236,000 in Canada, and 149,000 in Australia. Elsewhere, policy experimentation continued, particularly in new immigration countries that had begun only recently to attract migrant workers.

In Ireland a new Irish Naturalisation and Immigration Service was created— a new "one stop shop"—for applica-

tions for entry into the country. In April 2005 the Department of Justice, Equality and Law Reform published a discussion paper that outlined policy proposals on a comprehensive Immigration and Residence Bill, and in June the Irish government announced that it would introduce a new employment permits bill that would give migrant workers greater protection in the workplace. Italy introduced an innovative program that enabled the training and placement of personal-care workers from Sri Lanka. The Doha Development Round of World Trade Organization talks devoted significant attention to the temporary movement of persons across borders as suppliers of services pursuant to Mode 4 of the General Agreement on Trade in Services.

The link between migration and development remained the subject of much research and policy debate. Migrants injected more than $230 billion into the global economy through remittances that they sent back to their countries of origin. LDCs received $167 billion, or more than twice the level of official development aid offered worldwide. Remittances sent through informal channels could boost that figure by at least 50%. Though the countries receiving the most in recorded remittances were India ($21.7 billion), China ($21.3 billion), Mexico ($18.1 billion),

(continued on page 292)

The Roma—Europe's Largest Minority

by Erika Schlager

Europe's Roma (Gypsies) were much in the news in 2005. Claims of discrimination and racism—including appeals to the U.K. Human Rights Act of 1998—filled the British press. In May Germany returned to their native Kosovo 60 of the estimated 34,000 Roma who had enjoyed a temporary protected status since the outbreak of the Kosovo conflict in 1999. In the Czech Republic the government ombudsman began an investigation into claims that Romani women had been sterilized without informed consent. In October a Bulgarian court upheld a claim brought against the Ministry of Education alleging racial

Photo by Sofia News Agency (www.novinite.com)

Celebrations for the launch of the Decade of Roma Inclusion take place in Sofia, Bulg., in early February. Several nongovernmental organizations and European countries banded together to improve the social and political status of Europe's fastest-growing ethnic minority.

segregation in schools. Meanwhile, Roma continued to make inroads into political participation when Livia

Jaroka, the first Romani member of the European Parliament, took her seat in that organization after Hungary joined the EU in 2004.

Who Are the Roma? By the early part of the second millennium, the ancestors of today's Roma had migrated from what is now India to Europe and taken with them their own language (Romani, related to Sanskrit) and distinct cultural traditions. The name Gypsy, used commonly in English-speaking countries, is a corruption of the word *Egyptian,* reflecting a mistaken belief that Roma had come from Egypt. Roma are also known in many European countries as Tsigani (or a variant thereof). Many Roma reject the terms *Gypsy* and *Tsigan* as pejorative and instead prefer designations such as Roma, Sinti, or Manouches (all based on Romani words for "man," "human," or "person"). For the purposes of international political discourse, the word *Roma* has become the most widely accepted term for this dispersed people.

Today Roma live throughout all European countries (as well as the Americas and Australasia); taken together, there are an estimated 8 million–10 million Roma in Europe, with large concentrations in central, eastern, and southern Europe. The number of Roma in Europe is comparable to the population of Sweden or Belgium. Constituting Europe's largest ethnic minority, Roma in many countries are the fastest-growing ethnic group.

Historical Background. Historically, experiences of European Roma were characterized by exclusion and intolerance, although there have been occasional periods of toleration and even some romanticization of Romani life. At various times Roma have been subjected to expulsion or arrest solely on the basis of their ethnicity. In Spain, for example, Roma suffered mass race-based imprisonment (1749). Roma

© Peter Turnley/Corbis

Romani women dressed in traditional scarves and long skirts pose for a photograph in Romania in May. Long the object of discrimination, Europe's Roma made great political and social strides in 2005.

have also been forcibly assimilated. In the Habsburg Empire in the late 18th century, for example, Roma were subject to banishment if they did not submit to apprenticeship, and children were forcibly removed from Romani homes for "reeducation." The Romani language and dress were forbidden. In the provinces of Wallachia and Moldova, Roma were actually enslaved to the crown, nobility, and the monasteries from the 14th century until the founding of modern Romania in the mid-19th century.

The Fate of Roma Under Nazism and Communism. Calculating either the size of Europe's Roma population before World War II or the number of Roma killed in the 1930s and '40s is not yet possible because of the dearth of reliable statistics and the inaccessibility even of official documentation. Clearly, the Nazis targeted Roma for extermination, and the losses were horrendous. A widely used estimate for the number of Roma killed during World War II is 500,000. The fate of Roma varied considerably from one country to another, however. In Croatia, for example, virtually all Roma were murdered, while in neighbouring Bosnia, Muslim leaders intervened on behalf of their coreligionists, and the survival rate of Roma was much greater. The genocide eviscerated Romani cultural and political movements that had begun to emerge in Europe by the early 20th century.

Roma political development was further stunted by the totalitarian regimes that took over in Eastern Europe, the area where Roma were most numerous, after the war. The communist regimes nominally sought to integrate Roma into the new class structure of society as part of the proletariat. In practice Roma were largely channeled into unskilled or semiskilled labour. Communist regimes undertook forcible assimilation of the Roma, suppressed the use of the Romani language, confiscated their private property, and restricted their freedom of movement. During this period de facto segregated education emerged in several Eastern European countries, and in Czechoslovakia Roma women were even coerced into submitting to sterilization.

Current Situation. Ironically, after the fall of communism in Europe, the situation for Roma deteriorated markedly in many respects. They experienced a sharp increase in racially motivated violence, pogroms in Romania, and the denial of citizenship in the Czech Republic and some countries emerging from the breakup of Yugoslavia and the Soviet Union. As British social anthropologist Michael Stewart wrote in his 1997 book *The Time of the Gypsies*, "More Gypsies had their houses burned, were expelled from their villages, and were killed in racist attacks between 1989 and 1996 than in all the time that has passed since World War II." Roma were also disproportionately affected by the dislocations associated with the transition

Estimated Roma Population of Europe: 1939, 1945, and 1998			
Country	1939	1945	1998
Romania	300,000	(. . .)[1]	2,341,000
Yugoslavia	100,000	(. . .)[2]	
Serbia and Montenegro			444,000
Macedonia			349,000
Croatia			57,000
Bosnia and Herzegovina			49,000
Slovenia			12,000
Bulgaria	80,000	(. . .)[3]	892,000
Spain & Portugal	(. . .)	(. . .)	786,000
Czechoslovakia			
Slovakia	80,000	(. . .)[4]	598,000
Czech Republic	10,000	c. 200–300	319,000
U.S.S.R. including			600,000–
Baltic States	207,000	(. . .)[5]	1,000,000[6]
Hungary	100,000	(. . .)[7]	585,000
France	40,000	c. 13,000	310,000
Greece	(. . .)	(. . .)	183,000
Germany	18,800 ⎫	c. 7,000	123,000
Austria	11,200 ⎭		23,000
Albania	20,000	(. . .)	123,000
Italy	25,000	(. . .)	97,000
British Isles	(. . .)	(. . .)	89,000
Poland	20,000	c. 6,000	77,000
Low Countries	1,200	(. . .)	50,000
Scandinavia	(. . .)	(. . .)	43,000[8]
Switzerland	4,200	(. . .)	(. . .)
Total	**1,017,400**	**c. 417,000– 797,000**	**8,150,000– 8,550,000**

(. . .) - insufficient data

[1]No outright extermination policy, but tens of thousands met their death through expulsion. [2]Unknown number of 30,000 Croatian and Bosnian Roma murdered at Jasenovac concentration camp, Croatia. [3]Roma population not deported. [4]Hundreds of Roma murdered in pogromlike rampages by fascists. [5]Many nomadic Roma murdered by Nazi secret army field police; sedentary Roma treated as citizens of country. [6]International Federation for Human Rights, *The Roma of Russia* (November 2004); estimate is for all countries of the former Soviet Union. [7]31,000 deported to camps; 3,000 returned from camps. [8]Excludes Norway.

Principal sources: United States Holocaust Memorial Museum (for 1939 data), *Encyclopedia of the Holocaust* (for most 1945 data), European Roma Rights Centre (for most 1998 data). Note: 1998 population estimates of the European Roma Rights Centre are higher than most official country census estimates.

in Eastern Europe from a command to a market economy, with correspondingly high levels of unemployment relative to non-Roma. The outbreak of war in Yugoslavia, the European country with perhaps the largest Roma minority, turned significant numbers of Roma into refugees and internally displaced persons. In 2003 the United Nations Development Programme issued a report on the situation in five Central European countries, concluding that "by measures ranging from literacy to infant mortality to basic nutrition, most of the region's Roma endure living conditions closer to those of sub-Saharan Africa than to Europe."

A variety of international organizations, including the Organization for Security and Co-operation in Europe (OSCE), the Council of Europe, and the European Union, have increased their engagement with Roma issues. In 1990 the OSCE adopted the Copenhagen Document, the first international agreement that recognized the human rights problems faced by Roma. In 2000 the OSCE High Commission on National Minorities issued a report stating that "discrimination and exclusion are fundamental features of the Roma experience."

The conditions of Roma in Eastern Europe sparked heightened attention to their plight and, eventually, reexamination of their condition in Western European countries as well. With the accession of 10 new countries to the EU in 2004, Roma are today its largest ethnic minority group. Romani activists and a small but growing cadre of Romani government officials have called attention to issues such as discrimination in education, employment, housing, public assembly, and public services; spotlighted the plight of Roma refugees as well as internally displaced persons in and from the Balkans; improved political participation of Roma; and lobbied for the inclusion in school curricula dealing with World War II of information about the genocide of Roma.

Some progress has been made toward these goals. Racially motivated murders of Roma have declined since the early 1990s, and increased publicity has drawn public attention to human rights abuses. Currently eight countries—Bulgaria, Croatia, the Czech Republic, Hungary, Macedonia, Romania, Serbia and Montenegro, and Slovakia—are participating in a Decade of Roma Inclusion, a multilateral initiative to identify measurable national goals for improvements in the social and political status of this ancient and vital people.

Erika Schlager is Counsel for International Law at the Commission on Security and Co-operation in Europe (U.S. Helsinki Commission), an independent government agency.

(continued from page 289)
France ($12.7 billion), and the Philippines ($11.6 billion), remittance flows had the greatest economic impact on small economies, such as those of Tonga, Lesotho, and Haiti, where remittances accounted for at least 25% of each country's GDP.

Irregular migration, human trafficking, and migrant smuggling continued to challenge the ability of countries to regulate the entry and stay of migrants. This was demonstrated most dramatically in October by the highly publicized attempts of several hundred irregular migrants to cross from Morocco into the tiny Spanish enclaves of Ceuta and Melilla. In the ensuing rush, several persons died, and the Moroccan government later introduced deportation programs. Global figures were difficult to compile, but it was estimated that between 2.5 million and 4 million migrants crossed international borders annually without authorization, including 600,000–800,000 trafficked men, women, and children. It was believed that the U.S. hosted some 10 million migrants with irregular status and that the number in Europe was about 5 million. At year's end more than 90 countries had ratified or acceded to the Trafficking Protocol to the UN Convention Against Transnational Organized Crime, and many others were taking concrete steps to tackle the problem. Biometric technologies, including fingerprinting, iris scanning, and facial imaging, were used more widely to control entry.

The human rights of migrants remained an issue of great concern for governments and migrants. The committee tasked with monitoring the implementation of the International Convention on the Protection of the Rights of All Migrant Workers and Members of their Families continued its work with the current 34 countries party to the convention. A draft of the International Labour Organization Multilateral Framework on Labour Migration was finalized at an experts' meeting convened by the ILO in November and would be submitted to the ILO governing body in early 2006.

While migration in itself did not constitute a health risk, a number of large-scale humanitarian disasters, both natural and man-made, showed that conditions surrounding forced migration could have serious adverse health effects. Physical injuries were obviously of immediate concern, but malnutrition, lack of shelter, and a general breakdown of community infrastructures required long-term and expensive responses. The continuing spread of HIV/AIDS and the appearance of new infectious diseases, particularly the avian influenza, were reminders of the interdependencies between population mobility and health and the need for effective preventive action. Another quite distinct and much-debated health-related policy issue surrounded the migration of skilled health personnel from LDCs to developed countries, which resulted in the depletion of health care resources in the LDCs.

Regional Developments. Following the European Union's adoption in 2004 of The Hague Programme, the EU continued its efforts to forge an agreement on a common asylum and immigration policy for its 25 member states. The particulars included a special emphasis on the development of partnerships with countries of origin and transit, the establishment of a European agency (Frontex) for coordination of national-level operations at the external borders of the enlarged EU, and the issuance by the European Commission of a Green Paper on economic migration. Though the latter did not provide specific policy prescriptions, it did discuss future labour-market needs in light of Europe's changing demographic profile. Given the continued relevance of the issue of transit migration from the Maghrib to the EU, the 5+5 Dialogue on Migration in the Western Mediterranean remained an important platform for informal dialogue, exchange of information, and analysis of migration-related topics in the region.

The 10th Meeting of the Regional Conference on Migration, held in Vancouver, highlighted the importance of integration and citizenship policies through which the economic, social, and cultural aspirations of both migrants and host societies could be fulfilled. Following the December 2004 Cuzco Declaration, in which presidents of 12 South American countries announced the formation of the South American Community of Nations modeled after the EU, plans were developed for closer regional integration of migration policies. Similarly, the Central American countries of El Salvador, Guatemala, Nicaragua, and Honduras agreed to harmonize their national policies on key migration and integration issues.

In Africa a number of regional economic communities worked toward the development of migration-management strategies and the inclusion of migration within broad economic-development strategies. The African Union's overarching Strategic Framework for a Migration Policy in Africa was reviewed at the 10th Ordinary Session of the Permanent Representatives' Committee in Sirte, Libya. If approved, the framework would be submitted for adoption at the AU's January 2006 Ordinary Session in Khartoum, Sudan.

At the third Ministerial Consultations on Overseas Employment and Contractual Labour for Countries of Origin in Asia (previously the Asian Labour Ministerial Consultations), held in September in Bali, Indon., ministers and senior officials of countries of origin responsible for overseas employment were joined for the first time by their counterparts from destination countries, including many from the Gulf States and Europe. Participants identified strong common interests in the establishment of effective training programs for migrant workers, in the operation of fair recruitment procedures, and in the protection of migrant workers abroad. The earthquakes in South and Southeast Asia led to significant internal displacement and forced the international community to seek a better understanding of the migratory impacts of large-scale natural disasters.

The Global Dimension. Three ground-breaking policy reports on the global dimensions of migration appeared in 2005. The International Organization for Migration's (IOM's) biennial *World Migration Report* addressed costs and benefits of international migration in broad social, economic, and political terms and, drawing on extensive research, outlined and assessed the range of available policy choices. The Global Commission on International Migration report, *Migration in an Interconnected World*, provided a comprehensive examination of the way states and other stakeholders were addressing the issue of international migration and put forward global principles for action and recommendations for enhanced interinstitutional cooperation. The World Bank's 2006 *Global Economic Prospects* report dwelled on the economic implications of remittances and migration, particularly how the application of appropriate policies could decrease the role of migrant-created capital in efforts to reduce poverty.

(GERVAIS APPAVE)

Sports and Games

Baseball's Chicago WHITE SOX swept to the franchise's first WORLD SERIES victory since 1917, while England's cricketers upset Australia in the ASHES series. Outstanding athletes included tennis star Roger FEDERER, pole vaulter Yelena ISINBAYEVA, and sumo champion ASASHORYU.

AUTOMOBILE RACING

Grand Prix Racing. In 2005 Renault and Spanish driver Fernando Alonso won the Fédération Internationale de l'Automobile (FIA) Formula 1 (F1) world championship for constructors and drivers, respectively. This confirmed the prediction made in 2003 by Renault team chief Flavio Briatore, who suggested that his squad would probably be ready to mount a world championship challenge in 2005. Briatore could see that his team was maturing in tandem with Alonso's emergence as one of the best new drivers of his era, and in 2005 the partnership blossomed with perfect timing. At the end of the season, the longest in the 56-year history of the FIA's F1 title contest, the 24-year-old Alonso had captured 7 of 19 races to become Grand Prix racing's youngest world champion.

Alonso and his Renault team faced a season-long battle for the crown with Kimi Räikkönen (McLaren-Mercedes),

who also won seven races. Alonso's season started steadily and built up consistently. Räikkönen's year was more unpredictable, as his McLaren team failed to capitalize on its apparent performance edge early in the season and then fumbled a second chance to press home a counterattack for the title in the middle of the year. By finishing third in the Brazilian Grand Prix, Alonso scored enough points to clinch the title with two races left in the season. Even more significantly, he emerged as the most likely challenger to seven-time champion driver Michael Schumacher (Ferrari) of Germany. Alonso performed with a consistent and inarguable genius, with the sole exception of a slip in the Canadian Grand Prix, where he broke his Renault R25's suspension against a retaining wall. The disciplined fashion in which the young Spaniard paced himself in the San Marino Grand Prix at Imola, Italy, and kept Schumacher's obviously faster Ferrari bottled up behind his Renault demonstrated every facet of Alonso's skill; he

was quick, unflappable, precise, and consistent. He also kept the pressure on Räikkönen in the European Grand Prix at Nürburgring, Ger., allowing his rival no respite as the Finnish driver struggled with a flat-spotted tire that finally became completely unbalanced and broke the McLaren-Mercedes car's front suspension.

The intense rivalry between Renault and McLaren-Mercedes ensured an epic season of changing fortunes during which Ferrari, the top manufacturer for the previous five years, was reduced to the role of also-ran. Ferrari and its tire supplier, Bridgestone, had a disastrous season. Ferrari secured a single victory from the still-motivated Schumacher in the ill-starred U.S. Grand Prix at Indianapolis. Only six Bridgestone-equipped cars started after the teams that used Michelin tires were obliged to withdraw prior to the start when Michelin could not guarantee that the tires the company had provided for the race were safe. In the event, Michelin picked up the estimated $20 million cost of reimbursing the disappointed spectators and bought a large number of tickets for the 2006 U.S. race. The biggest disappointments of the 2005 F1 season were the Williams-BMW and BAR-Honda teams.

The arrival in November 2004 of Austrian billionaire Dietrich Mateschitz and his takeover of the Jaguar squad, which he renamed for his Red Bull beverage, signaled that commercial value could still be leveraged from this global sport. Barely nine months later Mateschitz purchased the Minardi racing team as a training ground for fledgling F1 talent. Russian-born Canadian businessman Alex Shnaider of Midland Group took a similarly upbeat if lower-key attitude to his takeover of the Jordan racing squad. BMW, having determined that the chemistry was not right in its partnership with Williams, purchased the Swiss-based Sauber team as a vehicle for the company's fully branded long-term ambitions. Williams later signed a deal with British engine supplier Cosworth. With Honda taking total ownership of the BAR squad, only DaimlerChrysler was left without 100% ownership of an F1 team for the 2006 season, although the German-based automaker's 40% stake in McLaren yielded an impressive tally of 10 race wins in 2005.

© Jimin Lai/AFP/Getty Images

Spanish driver Fernando Alonso (Renault) is first across the finish line in the Malaysian Grand Prix auto race on March 20. Alonso won 7 of the 19 Formula 1 races in 2005 to capture his first drivers' world championship.

BMW's decision to abandon Williams for Sauber had another side effect. British driver Jenson Button, who had previously announced that he would switch from BAR-Honda to Williams, declared in August that he did not want to drive for Williams now that the team's cars had lost their BMW engines. The FIA's Contract Recognition Board had already ruled in 2004 that Button's BAR contract took priority. Eventually Button and Williams reached an agreement, and the driver had to pay Williams for the privilege of remaining with BAR-Honda in 2006. (ALAN HENRY)

U.S. Auto Racing. Tony Stewart collected the 2005 National Association of Stock Car Auto Racing (NASCAR) Nextel Cup (formerly the Winston Cup) and the prize money of more than $6 million that went with it. During the season Stewart, driving a Chevrolet Monte Carlo for Joe Gibbs Racing, triumphed in 5 races, but none of them in the 10-event Chase for the Championship that was supposed to determine the champion stock-car driver. Stewart, however, earned points for finishing in the top 10 in 25 events, including 7 races in the Chase, and his total of 6,533 points put him 35 points ahead of Ford Taurus drivers Greg Biffle and Carl Edwards, both part of the Jack Roush racing team. Stewart's fifth victory was the Brickyard 400 on August 7 at the Indianapolis Motor Speedway. That triumph fulfilled a childhood dream for the Indiana native, who had raced in five Indianapolis 500s and six Brickyard 400s at the Speedway but had never finished better than fifth prior to his 2005 victory (Jeff Gordon and Dale Earnhardt, Jr., two of NASCAR's most popular drivers, did not qualify for the Chase). Jimmie Johnson, who in May won $470,000 at NASCAR's longest race, the Coca-Cola 600 in North Carolina, led the point standings periodically, but he crashed in the season-finale Ford 400 at Homestead, Fla. Chevrolet won the manufacturer's championship over Ford and Dodge, but all three awaited the entry of tough competitor Toyota into the billion-dollar competition of carmakers after NASCAR mandated new specifications for the automotive package over which each carmaker would hang its stock-appearing body beginning in the 2007 season.

NASCAR began the 2005 season with its richest event, the $17,590,647 Daytona 500-miler. Gordon, driving a Hendricks Team Monte Carlo, averaged 135.173 mph in the race and edged Kurt Busch in a Roush Ford Taurus by

1.58 sec to win and claim $1,497,154 of the purse. Prerace favourite Earnhardt, Scott Riggs, and Johnson, all in Monte Carlos, finished third, fourth, and fifth, respectively.

NASCAR used its subsidiary Busch Series to seek new Hispanic fans north and south of the Mexican border. About 95,000 spectators crowded into Mexico City's Autodromo Hermanos Rodríguez to see Martin Truex, Jr. (Chevrolet), beat Nextel Cup drivers Kevin Harvick and Carl Edwards in the Telcel Motorola 200. Truex went on to defend his Busch season crown.

Toyota entries, led by former Winston Cup driver Tod Bodine, posed a serious challenge in Craftsman Truck racing. Bodine finished third to new champion Ted Musgrave (Dodge) and Dennis Setzer (Chevrolet).

In American open-wheel competition, the Indy Racing League (IRL) and the Champ Car World Series drew farther apart in the type of races offered, the star drivers, and the specifications of the cars. Champ Car favoured street courses all over the world, while the IRL schedule included mostly oval tracks in the United States. Frenchman Sébastien Bourdais easily defended his Champ Car crown over Oriol Servia of Spain. Bourdais, driving for Newman-Haas Racing, won 6 of the 13 races in the 2005 series, which included events in Canada, Australia, and Mexico.

The 89th Indianapolis 500, the jewel of the IRL season, fell to British driver Dan Wheldon, who also won the IRL season championship. Wheldon, driving an Andretti Green Dallara-Honda, won $1,537,805 in the Indy 500, which had an average speed of 157.603 mph and 27 lead changes among seven drivers. Wheldon scored four victories in the first five IRL races and then preserved his lead over teammate Tony Kanaan of Brazil for the season crown. The most-talked-about driver in the series, however, was Danica Patrick, a photogenic 23-year-old American who finished fourth in the Indy 500 in her Rahal-Letterman Panoz-Honda. Patrick, who was named the race's Rookie of the Year, led three times for 19 laps—something no woman had ever done before. She went on to earn $1,037,655 for the season. Both Toyota and Chevrolet announced that they would no longer provide engines for IRL, yet each won a race, courtesy of American Sam Hornish and South African Tomas Schekter, respectively. (ROBERT J. FENDELL)

Rallies and Other Races. Sébastien Loeb (Citroën) of France dominated the

world rally championship (WRC) in 2005. He overwhelmed all challengers, winning a record 10 of the 16 WRC races, including 6 in a row and his third straight season-opening Monte Carlo Rally. Loeb secured the driver's title (and the constructors' championship for Citroën) after finishing second to Marcus Grönholm of Finland in the Rally of Japan with three races left, two of which he won. Loeb would have wrapped up the title in Wales one race earlier had it not been for a crash in which co-driver Michael Park of England was killed. Loeb, who was in the lead on the last leg in Wales but backed off after the accident to allow Petter Solberg (Subaru) of Norway to win the race, did not gain enough points to clinch his second consecutive title. Although Park's driver, Markko Martin (Peuguot) of Finland, was not injured in the crash, he did not race again in 2005. England's only world rally champion, Richard Burns, died in November on the fourth anniversary of his WRC title. (*See* OBITUARIES.)

On June 19 Tom Kristensen of Denmark, sharing an Audi R8 with co-drivers J.J. Lehto and Marco Werner, captured the 24-hour Le Mans Grand Prix d'Endurance. It was a record seventh win for Kristensen in nine attempts.

The Rolex 24 Hours of Daytona, sanctioned under the Grand American Sports Car series, saw the amateur trio of Wayne Taylor, Max Angelelli, and Emmanuel Collard cover 4,067.8 km (2,527.6 mi) in their Pontiac-Riley and easily defeat a field of 28 other prototypes co-driven by such professional superstars as Sébastien Bourdais and Tony Stewart, respectively the Champ Car and Nextel Cup titlists. The margin of victory was 11 laps on the 5.73-km (3.56-mi) Daytona Speedway road course. A Pontiac-Crawford co-driven by NASCAR's Johnson finished second.

Two Audi R8s in their last year of eligibility contested the 12 Hours of Sebring race, the opening event in the American Le Mans Series. Lehto, Werner, and Kristensen edged Alan McNish, Emanuele Pirro, and Frank Biela by 6.365 sec for the victory. Aston-Martin topped Corvette for the GT1 manufacturers honours. (ROBERT J. FENDELL; MELINDA C. SHEPHERD)

BADMINTON

Chinese players dominated the 2005 All England badminton championships, held in Birmingham in March. In the men's singles final, Chen Hong defeated the top seed, defending champion Lin Dan. The women's events also featured all-Chinese finals as Xie Xingfang bested Zhang Ning in the singles competition and Gao Ling and Huang Sui triumphed over Zhao Tingting and Wei Yili in the doubles event. The Chinese team of Cai Yun and Fu Haifeng defeated Lars Paaske and Jonas Rasmussen of Denmark for the men's doubles title. England's Nathan Robertson and Gail Emms delighted the home crowd by winning the mixed doubles.

The Sudirman Cup, an international mixed-team event, was contested in Beijing in May. After having lost to South Korea in the 2003 final, China gained revenge in the 2005 competition with an easy semifinal victory over its rival. Indonesia surprisingly dominated Denmark in the other semifinal, but the Indonesians were no match in the final round against an incredibly strong Chinese team. With the win, China, which in 2004 captured the Thomas and Uber Cups, became the first nation to hold all three international team titles at the same time.

The world championships, which were staged in August in Anaheim, Calif., produced both expected and unexpected results. The women's events had all-Chinese finals; Xie again defeated Zhang for the singles title, and Yang Wei and Zhang Jiewen overcame

China's Gao Ling (right) and her partner, Zhang Jun, reach for the birdie in the mixed-doubles final of the Sudirman Cup badminton team championships. China beat Indonesia 3–0 in the final round to take the title.

AP/Wide World Photos

Gao and Huang in the doubles competition. Taufik Hidayat of Indonesia beat Lin to become the first men's singles player to capture the world championship after having won Olympic gold the previous year. The men's doubles team of Tony Gunawan and Howard Bach also made history when they secured the first world championship gold medal for the U.S. Gunawan (who formerly played for Indonesia) and Bach scored three stunning upsets, including a final-round win over the Indonesian team of Sigit Budiarto and Candra Wijaya. Indonesia won gold in the mixed doubles for the first time in 25 years. Competitors from Taiwan, Germany, New Zealand, and Thailand won bronze medals for their respective countries.   (DONN GOBBIE)

BASEBALL

North America. Despite adverse publicity stemming from a U.S. congressional probe on allegations of substance abuse by players (past and present), Major League Baseball continued to thrive during the 2005 season. An all-time attendance mark of 74,915,268 (up from 73,022,969 in 2004) was established; a sixth different champion in as many seasons was crowned; and the sport returned to Washington, D.C., when the Montreal Expos (formed in 1969) relocated and became the Washington Nationals. The former Washington Senators franchise left in 1972 to become the Texas Rangers.

World Series. The Chicago White Sox defeated the Houston Astros 1–0 in Houston on October 26 to complete a four-game sweep in the best-of-seven 2005 World Series. The White Sox thus achieved the franchise's first championship since 1917. The franchise had not appeared in a World Series since 1959. A two-out single in the eighth inning by Jermaine Dye accounted for the only run in the final game as Freddy Garcia pitched seven innings and was credited with the victory. Dye, who batted .438 for the series, was voted World Series Most Valuable Player (MVP). The Series culminated a surge by the White Sox, which won 11 of 12 postseason games. Chicago manager Ozzie Guillen (*see* BIOGRAPHIES) earned much of the credit and the American League (AL) Manager of the Year honours.

In game one, played in Chicago on October 22, the White Sox defeated the Astros 5–3. Joe Crede hit a fourth-inning home run to break a 3–3 tie. José

Contreras was credited with the victory, after a strong effort by the White Sox relief pitchers. The Sox won game two in Chicago 7–6 on a ninth-inning home run by Scott Podsednik, who had not hit any home runs during the regular season. Paul Konerko hit a grand-slam home run for the White Sox, the 18th in World Series history. When the Series moved to Houston on October 25, the White Sox prevailed to win game three 7–5 in 14 innings. This tied the record set in the 1916 Boston versus Brooklyn Series for the most innings in a World Series game and set a record of 5 hours and 41 minutes as the longest game in Series history. Geoff Blum, a utility player, broke a 5–5 tie with a home run in the top of the 14th inning.

Play-offs. The White Sox secured the team's first pennant in 46 years by defeating the Los Angeles Angels of Anaheim four games to one in the American League Championship Series (ALCS). After the Sox lost the opener at home 3–2, they recorded four consecutive victories, with all four starting pitchers—Mark Buehrle, Jon Garland, Garcia, and Contreras—pitching complete games. The White Sox advanced to the ALCS by eliminating the defending world champion Boston Red Sox three games to none in the best-of-five AL Division Series. The Angels won their ALDS matchup with the New York Yankees three games to two.

Houston, which at one point during the regular season was 15 games under .500, achieved the first National League (NL) pennant in the franchise's 44-year history by defeating the St. Louis Cardinals four games to two. Roy Oswalt won the clinching game 5–1 and was MVP of the NLCS. The Astros eliminated the Atlanta Braves three games to one in the NL Division Series (NLDS). In the clincher the Astros prevailed 7–6 in 18 innings, the longest game in postseason history, when Chris Burke hit the game-winning home run. The Cardinals swept the San Diego Padres three games to none in the NLDS. Reggie Sanders of the Cardinals set an NLDS record with 10 runs batted in.

The White Sox won a league-high 99 games to claim the AL Central title by six games over the Cleveland Indians. The Yankees won their eighth consecutive AL East division title with a record of 95–67. The Red Sox had the same record but lost the season series to the Yankees and thus became the league's wild-card play-off entry. The Angels won the AL West by seven games over

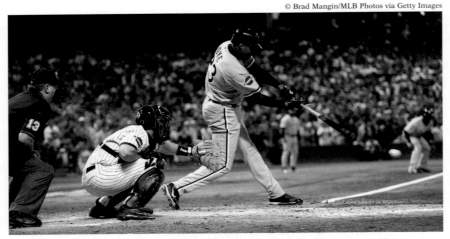

In game four of the World Series on October 26, Jermaine Dye of the Chicago White Sox hits an eighth-inning single to drive in the winning run. Chicago completed a four-game sweep over the Houston Astros in the best-of-seven series.

the Oakland Athletics. The Braves won the NL East by two games over the Philadelphia Phillies for their 14th consecutive division championship. The Cardinals registered 100 victories, the most in either league, to win the NL Central by 11 games over Houston, which qualified as the wild card. The Padres, despite a record of 82–80, won the NL West by five games.

Drug Investigation. On March 17 several baseball figures—including commissioner Bud Selig and Players Association director Donald Fehr—were called to Washington to participate in a congressional hearing on baseball's policy regarding performance-enhancing drugs, specifically steroids. The congressional panel questioned Selig, Fehr, and players about the effectiveness of baseball's existing penalties, under which a player who tested positive for the first time had been subject to a suspension of 10 days, for the second time 30 days, for the third time 60 days, and for the fourth time one year. In November, facing congressional pressure, the union agreed to significantly stricter measures. Beginning in 2006, a first-time offense would result in a 50-game suspension, a second-time offense would mean a 100-game suspension, and there would be a lifetime suspension for a third-time offender, with the right of appeal for reinstatement after two years. There was also a provision to institute the testing of players for use of amphetamines. The Baltimore Orioles' Rafael Palmeiro, one of the active players who testified during the hearing that he had never used steroids, was suspended in July for 10 days after a failed drug test. He was the highest-

profile player of the nine who were suspended during the 2005 season.

Individual Accomplishments. Bartolo Colon, who led the AL with 21 victories for the Angels, was voted winner of the Cy Young Award. Cy Young honours in the NL went to Chris Carpenter, who won 21 games for St. Louis. The Yankees' Alex Rodriguez, who led the AL with 48 home runs, was named the league's regular-season MVP; Albert Pujols of St. Louis was MVP in the NL. Michael Young of the Texas Rangers won the AL batting title with an average of .331. Derrek Lee of the Chicago Cubs took NL batting honours with a .335 average. Andruw Jones of the Braves hit 51 home runs to lead the NL. Boston's David Ortiz amassed 148 runs batted in to lead the AL; Jones had 128 to top the NL. Dontrelle Willis of the Florida Marlins set the NL pace with 22 victories. Chone Figgins of the Angels led both leagues in stolen bases with 62. Chad Cordero of the Nationals led relief pitchers in both leagues with 47 saves. Palmeiro reached 3,000 career hits during the season and thus joined Hank Aaron, Willie Mays, and Eddie Murray as the only players to have amassed 3,000 hits and 500 or more home runs. Atlanta's Bobby Cox was named NL Manager of the Year for the second consecutive season. Ken Griffey, Jr., of the Cincinnati Reds was voted NL Comeback Player of the Year, while Jason Giambi of the Yankees received that honour in the AL.

The American League defeated the National League 7–5 in the annual All-Star Game, played in Detroit on July 12. The victory, the ninth straight for the AL, ensured that the league's World

Series representative, which turned out to be the White Sox, would have home-field advantage in the Series. Baltimore's Miguel Tejada, who hit a home run and drove in two runs, was voted the game MVP.

Little League World Series. A team from Ewa Beach, Hawaii, rallied to defeat the defending champion Pabao Little League of Willemstad, Curaçao, Netherlands Antilles, 7–6 and win the Little League World Series on August 28 in Williamsport, Pa. Hawaii scored three runs in the bottom of the sixth inning to tie the title game. In the seventh inning Michael Memea hit the second game-ending home run in Little League World Series championship game history and thereby prevented Curaçao from becoming the first repeat champion since Long Beach, Calif., won in 1992 and 1993.

(ROBERT VERDI)

Latin America. The 2005 Caribbean Series was held in Mazatlán, Mex., on February 1–6. The Mazatlán Deer (Venados), representing Mexico, won the title with a 5–1 record. The Aragua Tigers (Tigres) from Venezuela and the entry from the Dominican Republic, the Cibao Eagles (Águilas Cibaeñas), tied for second place with 3–3 records. The Mayagüez Indians (Indios) of Puerto Rico were in last place with a 1–5 record.

In Cuba, Santiago de Cuba defeated Havana four games to two to win the 44th Serie Nacional (National Series) championship. Santiago had defeated Granma three games to none in the quarterfinals and Villa Clara four games to none in the semifinals to advance. Las Tunas outfielder Osmani Urrutia hit .385 to win his fifth consecutive batting title.

During the year it was announced that baseball would be cut from the Olympic Games beginning in 2012. Since the official recognition of baseball as an Olympic sport, Cuba had won three of the four gold medals (1992, 1996, and 2004), while the U.S. had captured the title in 2000.

Major League Baseball (MLB) and the Players Association announced that the inaugural World Baseball Classic would be held in March 2006. The 16-team event—in which MLB players were eligible to participate—would include teams from Canada, Cuba, the Dominican Republic, Mexico, Panama, Puerto Rico, Venezuela, and the U.S. The World Baseball Classic would be played again in 2009 and every four years thereafter.

The Angelopolis Tigers defeated the Saltillo Sarape Makers (Saraperos) four games to two to win the Mexican League championship series. It was the ninth league title for the Tigers, who had captured their first league title in 1955. (MILTON JAMAIL)

Japan. The Chiba Lotte Marines swept the Hanshin Tigers in four games in the 2005 Japan Series for their first Japanese baseball title since 1974, when they were known as the Lotte Orions. Bobby Valentine became the first foreign manager to win the series. The Marines dominated the first three games with scores of 10–1, 10–0, and 10–1. In game four they edged the Tigers 3–2 as South Korean slugger Lee Seung Yeop blasted a two-run home run and added a run-scoring double, while the Tigers' rally fell short. Marines third baseman Toshiaki Imae was named the series Most Valuable Player (MVP) after going 10-for-15 with four runs batted in (RBIs). The 22-year-old Imae also set a series record when he made eight consecutive hits in his first eight at bats.

The Marines finished the regular season 4½ games behind the Fukuoka Softbank Hawks in the Pacific League (PL). The Marines reached the Japan Series by beating the league's third-place Seibu Lions in the first stage of the play-offs and the Hawks in the second stage. The Tigers cruised to their second Central League (CL) title in three years.

In the regular season Hawks first baseman Nobuhiko Matsunaka led the PL with 46 home runs and 121 RBIs and became the first player in Japanese baseball to drive in at least 120 runs for three consecutive seasons, but in the MVP balloting he lost out

© Masanori Genko/Yomiuri/Reuters/Corbis

Chiba Lotte Marines manager Bobby Valentine (right) and third baseman Toshiaki Imae celebrate winning the team's first Japan Series since 1974. Imae was named the series Most Valuable Player.

to his teammate pitcher Toshiya Suguichi. Tigers outfielder Tomoaki Kanemoto was the CL regular-season MVP.
(HIROKI NODA)

BASKETBALL

Professional. Though the defending 2003–04 National Basketball Association champions the Detroit Pistons wanted to prove their team-oriented approach could create a new NBA dynasty, that plan got derailed in the 2005 NBA finals when the San Antonio Spurs beat the Pistons at their own game in a bruising best-of-seven series. By the time the Spurs wrapped up the title at home on June 23 with an 81–74 victory in game seven, it was hard to tell whether the players or their fans were more exhausted.

In this hard-fought final series, the Spurs were extended to the limit, mentally and physically. Detroit, which had erased a 0–2 series deficit by winning games three and four, appeared poised to take command at home in the pivotal fifth game. The Spurs trailed in the closing seconds of overtime and were heading toward a third consecutive defeat in the Pistons' stadium, the Palace of Auburn Hills. Canny Spurs veteran Robert Horry, however, seized an opening that saved his team. Seeing his defender, Rasheed Wallace, rotate away from him to prevent an open shot from the corner, the 2.08-m (6-ft 10-in) Horry calmly stepped just outside the three-point line, got the ball, and sank a shot that gave San Antonio the lead for good. The victory set the stage for the Spurs to claim their second NBA title in three seasons and their third since 1999.

Horry's thrilling shot left Detroit with the daunting challenge of attempting to win the last two games in San Antonio. The Pistons refused to quit, evening the series with a 95–86 victory in game six, but the Spurs then rode their home-court advantage into the winner's circle in the decisive battle. As usual, their clutch performer, Tim Duncan (*see* BIOGRAPHIES), led the way with 25 points and 11 rebounds. Duncan was named the Most Valuable Player of the series.

In the Women's National Basketball Association (WNBA), a new champion was crowned to cap the 2004–05 season. The Sacramento Monarchs swept to victory, dealing the Connecticut Sun a second straight setback in the WNBA finals. A crowd of 15,002 spectators in Sacramento's Arco Arena touched off a noisy celebration when the Monarchs

hung on to wrap up the title with a 62–59 decision in game four of the best-of-five series. Sacramento's Yolanda Griffith led the way with 15 points, earning MVP laurels in the finals. The WNBA also added a new franchise, the Chicago Sky, to the 2005–06 lineup.

College. The University of North Carolina's (UNC's) Sean May grew up with a championship pedigree as the son of former Indiana Hoosier great Scott May, and he lived up to that legacy in the 2005 National Collegiate Athletic Association (NCAA) basketball tournament. The spectacular forward scored a game-high 26 points to lead the Tar Heels (33–4) to a nerve-racking 75–70 victory over Illinois (37–2) in the dramatic closing match of the tournament. Without May's performance, the Illini would probably not have been vanquished in this St. Louis matchup between the nation's top-ranked teams. Besides making 10 of 11 field goal attempts and going 6 for 8 at the foul line, the 2.06-m (6-ft 9-in), 120.6-kg (266-lb) junior grabbed 10 rebounds. May's imposing presence under the basket forced Illinois to shoot from outside. The Big Ten Conference champs—who had entered the tournament having lost just one game all season—took 40 shots from three-point range. The Illini made only 12 of those shots, however, and got just 15 baskets from inside the bonus arc. It was that imbalance in the usually consistent Illini offense that frustrated them just one step short of capping a miracle season with their first NCAA crown. The Tar Heels led by 15 points soon after halftime and spent the remainder of the game fighting off frantic Illinois rallies. Instead, it was May—along with rugged defense and some clutch free throws by point guard Raymond Felton—that put the Tar Heels on top and earned UNC its fourth national championship. May, who was named Most Outstanding Player of the Final Four, scored 16 points during an 11-minute stretch of that explosive closing half, and, in a neat repeat of history, his 26 points overall exactly matched the total scored by his father when Indiana beat Michigan in the 1976 NCAA final.

For UNC coach Roy Williams, the championship was the fulfillment of a dream that he had been pursuing since he first became a collegiate head coach in 1988. Williams had left the University of Kansas after losing the NCAA title game in 2003 to return to North

Sean May of the University of North Carolina goes for a slam dunk in the final of the NCAA men's basketball championship on April 4. May was named MVP as North Carolina defeated the University of Illinois 75–70 for the title.

Carolina, where he had served as an assistant under college basketball's all-time winningest coach, Dean Smith. By winning it all in his fifth appearance in the Final Four—and third appearance in the title game—Williams was finally able to silence critics who had said he was unable to win the big one.

In the women's NCAA tournament, new faces emerged to provide an unexpected ending to the 2004–05 season. Neither Baylor (33–3) nor Michigan State University (33–4) had got to the doorstep of a national championship until they collided in Indianapolis on April 5. Both teams made it to the title game the hard way. In the semifinals Baylor shocked highly regarded Louisiana State University 68–57, and the MSU Spartans upset Tennessee 68–64, dashing Volunteers coach Pat Summitt's hopes for a seventh NCAA title.

The Lady Bears of Baylor had too much firepower for MSU when they met in the final. Emily Niemann made five of her seven three-point shots in the first half, and 1.85-m (6-ft 1-in) Sophia Young, a native of Saint Vincent and the Grenadines, racked up 18 of her game-high 26 points after the break. That one-two punch gave Baylor a convincing 84–62 victory over the Spartans and the first NCAA crown for coach Kim Mulkey-Robertson.

(ROBERT G. LOGAN)

International. Throughout the summer and early autumn of 2005, men's international basketball focused on the continental championships. The competing countries had two targets—to win medals and to secure places in the Fédération Internationale de Basketball (FIBA) men's world championships, to be held in Japan in August and September 2006.

The U.S. ended 2005 at the top of FIBA's rankings but did little better than stumble into qualification through the Americas championship. Brazil won the Americas tournament for the first time, beating defending champion Argentina 100–88 in the final. Venezuela handed the U.S. its third straight loss in the third-place play-off to gain a place in Japan. An extra qualification spot was given to fifth-place Panama because Argentina automatically qualified for Japan as the 2004 Olympic champion.

Greece crowned its qualification for Japan with a stunning 78–62 triumph over Germany in Eurobasket, the European championship, held in Belgrade, Serbia and Montenegro. Australia and New Zealand had no competition to claim Oceania's two world championship places, but the Boomers earned the better seeding with a 3–0 series sweep over the Tall Blacks. China defeated Lebanon 77–61 in the Asia championship final held in Qatar. The host country also qualified with an 89–77 third-place win over South Korea. In the African championship, held in Algiers, Angola retained the title and secured a place in Japan by beating Senegal 70–61.

Twenty teams qualified for the men's world championships through tournament play: Angola, Argentina (as the reigning Olympic champion), Australia, Brazil, China, France, Germany, Greece, Japan (as the host country), Lebanon, Lithuania, New Zealand, Nigeria, Panama, Qatar, Senegal, Slovenia, Spain, the U.S., and Venezuela. Four others—Italy, Puerto Rico, Serbia and Montenegro (which as part of Yugoslavia won the title in 2002), and Turkey—were issued wild-card invitations to complete the field.

São Paulo was scheduled to host the 15th world championship for women in September 2006. Only three countries had ever won gold—the U.S. (seven times), the former Soviet Union (six times), and Brazil (once). The qualifiers in 2005 were Argentina, Australia, Brazil, Canada, China, Cuba, the Czech Republic, France, Lithuania, Nigeria, Russia, Senegal, South Korea, Spain, Chinese Taipei (Taiwan), and the U.S.

(RICHARD TAYLOR)

BILLIARD GAMES

Carom Billiards. In January 2005 Sonny Cho of Flushing, N.Y., won his first U.S. championship in three-cushion (carom) billiards by beating defending champion Pedro Piedrabuena 50–45 in the deciding game. Piedrabuena scored the event's high runs, getting a 14 and a 13 in a single game. The 24-player event was sponsored by the U.S. Billiard Association and hosted by the Elks Lodge in Tacoma, Wash. The Japanese national championship was captured for the first time by 32-year-old Hideaki Kobayashi, the son of 13-time winner Nobuaki Kobayashi.

Spain's Daniel Sánchez won the annual Union Mondial de Billard (UMB) world championship in Lugo, Spain, in June. The surprise runner-up was Jean-Paul De Bruijn of The Netherlands. The victory moved the 30-year-old Sánchez ahead of Dick Jaspers of The Netherlands, the 2004 UMB champion, in world point rankings. Sánchez solidified his ranking in July by winning the three-cushion competition at the World Games in Bottrop, Ger. Jaspers, however, continued his string of successes at the Crystal Kelly invitational in Monte-Carlo, winning for the fifth consecutive time, with an average of 2.012. Jaspers collected $21,375 from the purse of $88,563.

The first Sang Lee memorial tournament was staged in early August at Carom Café in Flushing. Almost all of the top players in the world participated in the $100,000 event—the richest carom event in history—to honour Sang Chun Lee, the South Korean-born 12-time U.S. champion, who had died in 2004. Seventy-six players from 18 countries played a record 479 matches before Sweden's Torbjörn Blomdahl defeated Semih Sayginer of Turkey 40–19 in the final.

Three-cushion legend René Vingerhoedt of Belgium died on February 14 at age 83. Between 1939 and 1959 Vingerhoedt won three world, six European, and nine Belgian national championships.

Pocket Billiards. In 2005 came news of a series of eight-ball competitions

Shaun Murphy of England lines up a shot at the snooker world championship final on May 2. Murphy, who came into the tournament as a 150–1 long-shot qualifier, defeated three former world champions en route to the title.

with prizes surpassing anything ever before seen in the game. The International Pool Tour (IPT) was sponsored by Kevin Trudeau, an entrepreneur known for his aggressive television marketing. The tour began with a battle-of-the-sexes match between retired champions Mike Sigel and Loree Jon Jones staged on August 20 at the Mandalay Bay Resort & Casino in Las Vegas. Sigel won easily and pocketed $150,000, while Jones consoled herself with $75,000—the biggest paydays in either of their long careers. The next IPT event was a King of the Hill tournament on November 30–December 4 at the Orlando (Fla.) Convention Center. Thirty invited players from around the world and 12 members of the Billiard Congress of America's (BCA's) Hall of Fame competed for a share of the $1 million purse and the right to challenge Sigel. After four days of round-robin play, a challenger was determined: Efren Reyes of the Philippines, who easily beat Sigel 8–0 and 8–5 and pocketed $200,000. Trudeau promised to sponsor five more tournaments in 2006, with fields of 150 players and purses ranging from $1 million to $3 million.

The most surprising winner of a professional nine-ball event in 2005 was Taiwan's 16-year-old Wu Chia-ching, who took the $75,000 first prize at the World Pool–Billiard Association (WPA) world championship, held in July in

Kaohsiung, Taiwan. Wu topped a field of 128 players from 43 countries. Another surprise champion was 23-year-old Raj Hundal of England, who in September won the World Pool Masters tournament in Doncaster, Eng. Former WPA world champion Thorsten Hohmann of Germany in July defeated American Johnny Archer 7–0 for the BCA Open nine-ball title and followed up with the World Pool League championship, which took place in Poland in October. The final event of the year was the Mosconi Cup, held in Las Vegas on December 15–18. The team event, which pitted the United States against Europe, was won by the U.S. for the third time in a row.

At the beginning of the year, England's Allison Fisher, the top-ranked player in the Women's Professional Billiard Association (WPBA), commented that the level of play had risen so much in the women's ranks that it had become difficult for anyone to dominate. Ireland's Julie Kelly and Kim Ga Young of South Korea had broken through to win major WPBA tournaments at the end of 2004, thus ending the near stranglehold on first-place finishes enjoyed by Fisher and Karen Corr of Northern Ireland. Fisher, however, belied her own statement in 2005 as she captured the Carolina Classic, the Great Lakes Classic, the BCA Open, the Midwest Classic, and the U.S. Open, an unprecedented level of success. She also won the $24,000 top prize at the Amway Cup in Taipei. The year's only other significant WPBA winners were Kelly Fisher (no relation to Allison) at the West Coast Classic in April, Corr at the Southeast Classic in June, and Kim, who took home the $16,000 first prize at the Cuetec Cues national nine-ball championship in November.

Deaths in 2005 included those of BCA Hall of Famer Eddie Taylor and former straight-pool champions Johnny Ervolino and Jack Colavita.

Snooker. The year 2005 saw three memorable snooker performances. At the China Open in Beijing, Ding Junhui, who turned 18 during the competition, became the first Chinese player to win a ranking event. In the April 7 final against Scotland's Stephen Hendry, Ding showed his phenomenal shot-making ability in winning eight of the last nine frames. The mayor of Beijing was in the audience of 1,500, and an estimated 100 million people watched on television. A month later at the world championship in Sheffield, Eng., 22-year-old Shaun Murphy, a

150–1 shot at the start of the tournament, became the first qualifier to take snooker's most prestigious event. Murphy won £250,000 (about $475,000) for his efforts, which included victories over three former champions: Steve Davis, John Higgins, and Peter Ebdon. At the Preston Grand Prix, Higgins set a record in the final on October 16 against Ronnie O'Sullivan by making four consecutive century breaks: 103, 104, 138, and 128, a total of 494 unanswered points.

Other winners during 2005 included O'Sullivan at the Welsh Open and the Wembly Masters, Hendry at the Malta Cup, Northern Ireland's Joe Swail at the Irish Professional Championship, and Higgins at the British Open. At the U.K. championship in December, the unlikely finalists were Davis, age 48, and Ding Junhui, 18, respectively the oldest and youngest players in the field. The sensational Chinese teenager was the winner 10–6.   (ROBERT BYRNE)

BOBSLEIGH, SKELETON, AND LUGE

Bobsleigh. During the 2004–05 bobsleigh season, three drivers dominated the circuit—Switzerland's Martin Annen, Canadian Pierre Lueders, and Aleksandr Zubkov of Russia. In two-man racing Annen drove consistently throughout the World Cup season, winning three golds and the two-man overall title. He was unable to capture the title at the world championships, held in Calgary, Alta., however, and finished third behind Lueders and second-place André Lange of Germany. In four-man action Zubkov medaled in six of seven races; he failed to medal only on the track built for the 2006 Winter Olympics in Turin, Italy. The Russian claimed the World Cup overall four-man title, but he failed in his quest to win the four-man race at the world championships in Calgary, where he finished second to Lange. Lueders earned third place.

In women's bobsleigh Germany dominated, medaling in every race on the circuit and taking the top three spots for the overall World Cup season title. Sandra Prokoff Kiriasis led the charge for the Germans, winning five races and the overall title, as well as the gold medal at the world championships. Cathleen Martini, at the helm of Germany 3, finished the World Cup season in second place overall, with Susi-Lisa Erdmann, driving Germany 2, taking third place. At the world championships British driver Nicola Minichiello and

American Shauna Rohbock finished in second and third, respectively.

Skeleton. American Noelle Pikus-Pace, in her second season on the World Cup skeleton circuit, surprised the world by winning the overall title for the 2004–05 season. Pikus-Pace collected three gold, one silver, and one bronze medal on the tour and finished the season with a silver medal at the world championships in Calgary. Maya Pedersen of Switzerland was second in the overall World Cup standings but won gold in Calgary. Michelle Kelly of Canada took third place at the world championships.

In men's skeleton Jeff Pain of Canada started and ended the season on top of the podium. Pain earned one gold, two silver, and two bronze medals on his way to the World Cup overall title. Pain, who lived in Calgary, also slid to the gold medal in the world championships on his home track. American Chris Soule had a strong season and finished second in the overall standings. In third place for the overall title was Canadian Duff Gibson, who also earned bronze at the world championships, behind silver medalist Gregor Stähli of Switzerland.

(JULIE URBANSKY)

Luge. Christian Oberstolz and Patric Gruber of Italy captured the 2004–05 overall World Cup luge doubles title. A win in the eighth race of the season gave them enough total points for the title; the final race, scheduled to be held on the 2006 Olympic track in Turin, was canceled for safety concerns. Perennial leaders Patric Leitner and Alexander Resch of Germany, sidelined for most of the season, returned to win two of the final three World Cup races and the silver medal at the 2005 world championships in Park City, Utah, behind their teammates André Florschütz and Torsten Wustlich. Americans Mark Grimmette and Brian Martin finished third in Park City.

Italy's Armin Zöggeler raced to his fifth world championship victory, but the surprise men's singles World Cup winner was Russian Albert Demchenko, who earned gold in half the season's races to capture the overall title. Georg Hackl and David Möller of Germany finished silver and bronze, respectively, in both the world championships and the World Cup standings.

Germans dominated women's luge. Sylke Otto added another world championship title to her collection, with Barbara Niedernhuber in second and Anke Wischnewski taking third. In the

© Harry How/Getty Images

World Cup champion Noelle Pikus-Pace of the U.S. concentrates on the track during her silver-medal-winning slide at the skeleton world championships in Calgary, Alta., in February.

World Cup standings, Niedernhuber captured gold, Silke Kraushaar won the silver, and Otto took bronze.

(JANELE M. URBANSKY)

BOWLING

World Tenpins. The 40th AMF World Cup, the biggest singles tenpin bowling tournament of the 2004–05 season, was held in Singapore in December 2004. A record-breaking 167 players (93 men and 74 women) from 95 countries participated. American Shannon Pluhowsky celebrated her second victory in three years, defeating Canada's Kerrie Ryan-Ciach in the women's final, while 35-year-old Kai Virtanen of Finland outclassed Norway's Petter Hansen in the men's final.

The World Ranking Masters tournament, a showcase for the top eight men and women from each of the three regional zones of the World Tenpin Bowling Association (WTBA), took place in April in Lake Wales, Fla. In the men's division Kimmo Lehtonen of Finland was victorious over his countryman Jouni Helminen. Clara Guerrero of Colombia defeated Malaysia's Wendy Chai in the women's final.

Finland ruled at the men's European championships in Moscow in June, winning gold medals in all six events: singles (Virtanen), doubles, trios, teams, all-events (Petteri Salonen), and masters (Petri Mannonen). The Finnish team added two silver and two bronze medals in the individual competitions.

The 2005 World Games for non-Olympic events was held July 14–24 in Duisburg, Ger. Virtanen added one more gold to his collection when he defeated Belgian Gery Verbruggen in the

men's tenpin final. Kim Soo Kyung of South Korea beat Zara Glover of Great Britain by one pin to win the women's event. Bowling was one of several sports at the World Games seeking Olympic status. (See *Squash*: Sidebar, below.)

For the first time, the WTBA voted to sponsor separate men's and women's world championships in alternating years. The women's tournament was held August 4–13 in Ålborg, Den., with 216 participants representing 53 countries. The team from Taiwan won the trio and team events as well as the individual all events (Wang Yu-ling). Malaysia's Esther Cheah captured the singles title, and Yang Suiling of China took the masters. The only gold medal that the Asian competitors missed was in the doubles event, which was won by Germany. The next men's world championship was scheduled to take place in 2006.

(YRJÖ SARAHETE)

U.S. Tenpins. Just four years after he captured his first career title, Patrick Allen of the U.S. emerged as the bowler ranked number one in the world, earning honours as the 2005 Professional Bowlers Association (PBA) Player of the Year and claiming the PBA's Harry Smith Point Leader Award. Allen finished in the top five at all four major events of the PBA Tour during the season, including a win at the PBA Denny's world championship, held on April 3 in Ypsilanti, Mich. Allen placed second at two other major tournaments, the American Bowling Congress (ABC) Masters event and the U.S. Open. He also led the PBA Tour in season earnings with more than $350,000—the second highest single-season earnings total in tour history.

A highlight of the PBA season was the first appearance of a female bowler, Liz Johnson of Cheektowaga, N.Y., in a nationally televised PBA tournament, the Banquet Open, held in Grand Rapids, Mich. Johnson, who had won 11 meets in the Professional Women's Bowling Association before that organization was disbanded in 2003, finished second in the tournament. She established an even greater milestone later in the year when she became the first woman to win a PBA Tour title. Johnson triumphed in August at the PBA's East Region Kingpin Games Open in Rome, N.Y., prevailing 244–171 over Michael Fagan in the title match.

One of the growing issues facing tenpin bowling during the year was the effect of advancing technology on the sport. The improvement in bowling balls and the weakening of regulations governing the application of oil on the lanes had caused the number of high-score awards to increase dramatically. In the 1979–80 season, for example, when membership in the ABC peaked at 4,799,195, there were 5,373 perfect (300) games sanctioned. In the 2000–01 season, with ABC membership down to 1,866,023, the number of 300s approved was 39,470, and the trend toward higher scoring had only increased by 2005. The U.S. Bowling Congress did not propose any specific measures for limiting the number of high-score awards, however.

(JOHN J. ARCHIBALD)

BOXING

The retirement of World Boxing Council (WBC) heavyweight titleholder Vitali Klitschko (Ukraine) on Nov. 9, 2005, ended an uneventful year for the sport's so-called glamour division, which had been in the doldrums since the retirement of Lennox Lewis (U.K.) in 2004. Klitschko, who won the vacant title by knocking out Corrie Sanders (S.Af.) in 2004, suffered a series of injuries and did not fight at all in 2005. He announced his retirement after having surgery to repair his right knee, which was injured while training for a bout with former champion Hasim Rahman (U.S.). The WBC subsequently awarded the title to Rahman.

World Boxing Association (WBA) heavyweight titleholder John Ruiz (U.S.) made two defenses. He lost a 12-round decision to James Toney (U.S.) on April 30 in New York City, but the result was later changed to "no contest" when Toney tested positive for steroids. The title reverted to Ruiz, and Toney was suspended for 90 days and fined $10,000. Ruiz filed a $10 million lawsuit against Toney, claiming that despite having gotten the title back, he had incurred significant financial damage as a result of Toney's use of an illegal substance. Ruiz's suit was believed to be the first case of one professional athlete suing another for using a performance-enhancing drug. Nikolay Valuev (Russia) won a controversial 12-round decision over Ruiz on December 17 in Berlin to take the title. At 2.13 m (7 ft), Valuev was the tallest boxer to win a major title. Chris Byrd (U.S.) made a solitary defense of his International Boxing Federation (IBF) title, winning a 12-round decision over DaVarryl Williamson (U.S.) on October 1 in Reno, Nev. The lacklustre bout was widely criticized as one of the most boring heavyweight title fights in the history of the sport.

Antonio Tarver (U.S.) regained recognition as the world's top light heavyweight with a 12-round decision over former IBF champion Glen Johnson (Jamaica) on June 18 in Memphis, Tenn. None of the alphabet organizations' belts was on the line because Tarver and Johnson had refused to allow the organizations to dictate whom they should fight, but the match was recognized as a world title bout by *The Ring* magazine and the majority of the boxing industry. (*See Sidebar.*) Tarver's next bout was a rubber match with former champion Roy Jones, Jr. (U.S.), whom he had lost to in a close decision in 2003 and then knocked out in a 2004 rematch. The third Tarver-Jones bout, on October 1, drew a capacity crowd of 20,895 to the St. Pete Times Forum in Tampa, Fla., and the pay-per-view television broadcast sold to approximately 405,000 households. Although it was one of the most financially successful bouts of the year, it was a relatively tame fight, which Tarver won in a unanimous 12-round decision.

IBF super middleweight titleholder Jeff Lacy (U.S.) impressed critics and fans alike with a trio of successful defenses. On March 5 he scored a seventh-round knockout of Rubin Williams (U.S.) in Las Vegas. Lacy followed on August 6 with a seventh-round knockout of former WBC titleholder Robin Reid (U.K.) in Tampa, Fla., and on November 5 finished the year with a second-round knockout of Scott Pemberton (U.S.) in Stateline, Nev.

Undisputed middleweight champion Bernard Hopkins (U.S.) lost his titles to Jermain Taylor (U.S.) in a controversial 12-round bout on July 16 in Las Vegas. The 40-year-old Hopkins, who won the IBF belt in 1995 and unified the title with successful WBA and WBC title bouts in 2001, started slowly, rallied in the late rounds, and lost in a split decision. Taylor and Hopkins fought again on December 13 in Las Vegas, and again Taylor won a close but unanimous 12-round decision in a lacklustre bout that attracted approximately 410,000 pay-per-view customers.

The attempted comeback of Félix Trinidad (P.R.) came to a sudden halt when he lost a 12-round unanimous decision to Ronald ("Winky") Wright (U.S.) on May 14 in Las Vegas. Wright, a skillful, defensive-minded southpaw, gave the favourite a one-sided boxing lesson. The pay-per-view event sold to approximately 510,000 households and generated $25.5 million in revenue, which helped to make it the largest-grossing match of the year. Less than two weeks after the fight, Trinidad retired again.

On June 4 Ricky Hatton (U.K.) scored one of the year's biggest upsets when he forced unified junior welterweight champion Kostya Tszyu (Australia) to quit on his stool at the end of the 11th round of their bout held in Manchester, Eng. Hatton was a popular boxer in the U.K., and his bout with Tszyu drew a capacity crowd of 22,000. Hatton defended the title (and added the WBA belt) with a ninth-round knockout of WBA titleholder Carlos Maussa (Colom.) on November 26 in Sheffield, Eng.

By far the most spectacular fight of the year was the lightweight title bout between WBC titleholder José Luis Castillo (Mex.) and Diego Corrales (U.S.) on May 7 in Las Vegas. It was a toe-to-toe battle from the start, with both men landing numerous flush punches in every round. The bout was very close as the 10th round of the scheduled 12-round fight began, but when Castillo twice knocked down Corrales with left hooks to the head, victory for the Mexican boxer seemed imminent. On both occasions, however, Corrales spit out his mouthpiece as he went down. Although he was penalized for doing so, the delay caused by having the

During the 10th round of the May 7 lightweight title bout between Diego Corrales (right) of the U.S. and José Luis Castillo of Mexico, the referee steps in to stop the fight. Corrales was declared the winner and awarded Castillo's WBC belt.

Boxing's "Alphabet Soup" of Champions

There was a time when virtually every sports fan could name all of the world boxing champions. That was during the first half of the 20th century, however, when there were only eight weight classes, with one champion each. By 2005 professional boxing was plagued by a confusing and counterproductive situation with 17 weight classes, and dozens of so-called champions under the control of a group of self-appointed governing bodies, collectively known as the "alphabet organizations." The three most prominent governing bodies were the World Boxing Association (WBA; originally formed in 1920), the World Boxing Council (WBC; founded in 1963), and the International Boxing Federation (IBF; formed in 1983), though several less-well-known bodies also endorsed their own champions.

All of the alphabet organizations were funded by dues and by "sanctioning fees," money paid to them by promoters to approve bouts in which each organization's titles were on the line. These fees were based on a percentage of the fighters' purses and could be as high as several hundred thousand dollars per fight.

The alphabet organizations gained little traction until the 1970s, when television networks began to insist that virtually every televised fight be a title bout. Eager to please their paymasters, promoters and managers embraced the various groups, regardless of their titles' authenticity. This proved profitable in the short run, but soon fans and the mainstream media became more and more confused as to who were the legitimate champions.

It also became clear that the alphabet organizations' rankings of contenders were not based solely on merit. In 1983 promoter Bob Arum told *The Ring* magazine that he had paid the WBA $500,000

© Corbis

to get American boxer Ray Mancini a shot at the organization's lightweight title.

In 1999 the U.S. attorney for New Jersey indicted the IBF president, Robert W. Lee, on racketeering charges, alleging that Lee and others had accepted bribes to manipulate ratings. In 2000 Lee was acquitted on 27 counts of bribery and racketeering but was convicted of money laundering, two counts of tax evasion, and three counts of interstate travel in aid of racketeering. Lee was sentenced to 22 months in prison, fined $25,000, and banned permanently from the sport.

In 2002 German boxer Graciano Rocchigiani won a $30 million judgment against the WBC when a U.S. district court ruled that the organization had cheated Rocchigiani of his claim to the WBC light heavyweight title. Unable to pay the judgment, the WBC filed for Chapter 11 bankruptcy in August 2003, but the organization reached a settlement with Rocchigiani before being forced into liquidation.

In an effort to impose some order in the ranking of professional boxers, *The Ring*, a leading boxing magazine, revitalized its championship policy in its April 2002 issue. *The Ring* had begun awarding championship belts shortly after its debut in 1922. The practice became dormant during much of the 1990s but was revived as part of the new policy. ESPN and HBO, two of the leaders in televised boxing, came to accept the boxers designated by *The Ring* as the legitimate world champions. Nonetheless, by 2005 much of the boxing industry had become comfortable with the ability to manipulate the alphabet organizations and continued to do business with them, and many fans were left increasingly confused and unhappy with the sport.

(NIGEL COLLINS)

---

mouthpiece retrieved, washed, and replaced gave him extra time to recover. When action resumed and an overeager Castillo went for the finish, Corrales caught him with several hard blows to the head that rendered Castillo helpless and prompted the referee to stop the fight and declare Corrales the winner.

The nature of the Corrales-Castillo fight and the controversy surrounding the ending led to a much-anticipated rematch on October 8 in Las Vegas. This time the controversy came before the bout started, when Castillo failed to make the lightweight-division weight limit. Although Corrales's WBC title would not be at stake, the fight went on as scheduled after Castillo was fined $120,000 of his $1.2 million purse—half of the fine money went to the Nevada State Athletic Commission, and half was given to Corrales. Although it

was another give-and-take affair, Castillo dominated and knocked out Corrales in the fourth round with a left hook to the chin. Negotiations began almost immediately for a rubber match in 2006. (NIGEL COLLINS)

CHESS

The year 2005 in chess was filled with surprises. Vladimir Kramnik, the official world champion, continued to play in uncertain form and dropped as low as sixth in the international ratings in July. Garry Kasparov, the strongest player of the past two decades, announced early retirement, while chess legend Bobby Fischer succeeded in regaining his freedom after eight months of detention in Japan. Finally, the elite Dortmund (Ger.) Sparkassen Tournament was won by 19-year-old Arkady

Naiditsch, the lowest-rated player in the event.

Kasparov and Fischer were the two strongest players of the second half of the 20th century, and their actions in 2005 ensured headline coverage in the media, yet reverses suffered by leading human players against the latest enhanced supercomputers, such as the 5.5–0.5 victory by Hydra against English grandmaster Michael Adams in London on June 21–27, resulted in diminished sponsorship and sparser media coverage than a decade earlier.

The retirement of Kasparov at the age of 41 while still at the top of the ratings was a bombshell. Most grandmasters continued to play until the age of 50 or beyond, and exceptional figures such as Viktor Korchnoi were enjoying success even in their 70s. Kasparov, in top form, won the Linares, Spain, tournament in

February–March, but he was disillusioned by the continuing failure of chess officials to implement the Prague agreement of May 2002 that was intended to mend the rift in the chess world. He had been unable to secure a rematch with Kramnik, who had taken the world title from him in 2001, and his planned match with Rustam Kasimjanov, scheduled for Dubai in January–February and part of the Prague unification process, was canceled by the Fédération Internationale des Échecs (FIDE), the world ruling body, after sponsorship fell through. Because Kasparov had held this slot open in his schedule, he was denied the chance to play in the tournament at Wijk aan Zee, Neth., in January, where his archrivals Peter Leko of Hungary, Viswanathan Anand of India, and Veselin Topalov of Bulgaria took the top three spots.

Kasparov stated at the end of the Linares meet, where he was declared winner on tiebreak ahead of Topalov, that he was seeking a new challenge and intended to go into Russian politics on a platform opposing Pres. Vladimir Putin.

Fischer benefited from strong support from sympathizers in Iceland in the face of pressure by the U.S. authorities, who still wished to punish the former child prodigy for having broken sanctions against Yugoslavia by playing a match there against Boris Spassky in 1992. Legal wrangles and appeals in Japan throughout 2004 delayed the implementation of the U.S. request for Fischer's extradition; further, the charges against him, based on a presidential executive order, might not stand up in court. The matter was additionally complicated by Fischer's application for political asylum in several countries. On March 22 the Icelandic parliament passed a special bill to grant the American maverick Icelandic citizenship, whereupon he was released from Japan and given the chance to return to Reykjavík, the scene of his epic defeat of the world champion Spassky in 1972.

Fischer did not envisage returning to orthodox chess, however, which he regarded as compromised by results fixed in advance, especially in matches involving former Soviet players. He continued to promote "random chess," an unorthodox form of the game in which the players draw lots not only for colour but also for a randomly determined positioning of the pieces on the back row, which nullifies any advantages of having mastered stock chess openings.

A move to reduce the large number of lacklustre draws reached by agreement early in games was conducted in the one new top tournament of the year, that in Sofia, Bulg., sponsored by M-Tel, the Bulgarian telecommunications company, on May 12–22. The players were forbidden to speak to each other during the game or otherwise signal that they were agreeable to a draw, so halving the point for the game could come about only by natural attrition of material, stalemate, threefold repetition of a position, or authorization of the tournament arbiter. Topalov, on home ground, scored 6.5/10, a full point ahead of Anand, and advanced his claim as a world championship contender. Former child prodigy Judit Polgar of Hungary, returning after a long maternity leave, showed that she had retained her playing strength by coming equal third in the double-round contest, while Kramnik scored a disappointing four points to finish equal at fifth–sixth with Adams.

The Dortmund tournament on July 8–17 also saw a welcome reduction of draws. Naiditsch, the local man, scored the biggest surprise of recent years, emerging on top at 5.5/9; second through fifth places were claimed by Topalov, Étienne Bacrot of France, Loek van Wely of The Netherlands, and Peter Svidler of Russia. Kramnik and Adams were tied for fifth–sixth, and Leko was seventh. The performances of the last three men were surprising, especially as Kramnik and Leko had drawn a world championship match only 10 months earlier.

A step toward the long-awaited world title unification process took place in San Luis province, Arg., September 27–October 16, when Topalov took the FIDE world championship in a double-round event over Anand and Svidler (tied for second) and Aleksandr Morozevich of Russia (third). In another development a new Association of Chess Professionals was formed to protect the interests of second-echelon players on the chess circuit in the harsher economic climate that had prevailed since the turn of the century.

(BERNARD CAFFERTY)

CRICKET

In 2005 England outplayed Australia in an enthralling five-match Test series to end 16 years of defeat by its oldest cricketing foe and regain possession of the small but symbolic Ashes urn. England recovered from losing the first Test at Lord's by 239 runs to win the second Test by just two runs and then failed by one wicket to win the third Test as Australia's last pair of batsmen, Brett Lee and Glenn McGrath, survived the final 24 balls of the match to eke out a draw. Needing 129 runs to win the fourth Test, England collapsed to 116 for 7 before Ashley Giles scored the winning runs. Never in the 128-year history of Test cricket had three consecutive matches produced such thrilling finishes. Australia had to win the final Test at the Oval to tie the series and retain the Ashes, but some timely rain and a second-innings score of 158 by Kevin Pietersen, England's South African-born batsman, on the final day earned the draw that took the Ashes trophy back to its spiritual home. There was national rejoicing, and the England team, led by captain Michael Vaughan and inspired by Andrew ("Freddie") Flintoff, was feted in a parade through the streets of London. A set of special postage stamps was issued to commemorate the historic victory. To cap an unforgettable summer, England's women cricketers also won back the Ashes after a gap of 42 years.

Flintoff, England's Ashes Player of the Series, scored 402 runs, including a century, at an average of 40.20 and took 24 wickets (average 27.29), easily the most effective all-round contribution from either side. Pietersen, in his first Test series, was the leading run scorer with 473, and Marcus Trescothick, who had been a conspicuous failure in Australia two years before, erased those memories with 431 runs. England outperformed Australia in every department, batted more solidly, and with a battery of four fast bowlers (Stephen Harmison, Flintoff, Simon Jones, and Matthew Hoggard) bowled more aggressively.

Australia's resistance was led by Shane Warne, who during the third Test became the first bowler to pass 600 wickets in Test cricket and ended the series with 40 wickets (average 19.92). Only a brilliant innings of 156 runs by captain Ricky Ponting staved off defeat in the third Test, while at times it seemed that only Warne's genius as a leg spinner stood between England and certain victory. Ironically, Warne dropped the decisive catch in the fifth Test that would have put Pietersen out when he had scored just 15 runs. Justin Langer was the top scorer for Australia, with 394 runs, and McGrath took 19 wickets (including match figures of 9 for 82 at Lord's) despite having missed two Tests through injury. McGrath and Warne, both age 35, left the Oval to a standing ovation at the end of their final Tests in England.

Despite the Ashes loss, Australia ended the 2004–05 season as officially the best team in the world, with England second. Only India came close, though its first home series against Pakistan in five years ended in stalemate. After a drawn first Test, Rahul Dravid scored a century in both innings to help India win the second. Younis Khan replied with innings of 267 and 84 not out to bring Pakistan level in the third Test. Sourav Ganguly, the Indian captain, was banned by the International Cricket Council (ICC) for six matches for having deliberately slowed down the over rate in the one-day series between the two countries.

South Africa lost narrowly to England at home, but in Jacques Kallis the South Africans had one of the game's most consistent all-rounders. The decline of West Indies cricket continued, though the side, captained by Shivnarine Chanderpaul, managed to draw against Pakistan and Brian Lara became the fourth batsman—after Australia's Steve Waugh and India's Sunil Gavaskar and Sachin Tendulkar—to beat Sir Don Bradman's record of 29 Test centuries.

In Sri Lanka the December 2004 tsunami devastated the country's prettiest cricket ground at Galle and took the lives of a generation of young cricketers in the area. On the day the tsunami struck, a local representative side and a touring team from England's Harrow School were about to play a match at Galle. Both teams escaped by climbing to the top of the pavilion. To the dismay of the cricketing community, the authorities announced that they might not restore Galle but rather intended to build a new ground farther from the sea. Not surprisingly, the Sri Lankan players had little appetite for the game in 2005 and lost in New Zealand before beating both West Indies and Bangladesh. Zimbabwe's political troubles continued to blight its cricket team, which suffered a series of humiliating defeats, including a loss to South Africa in less than two days. It seemed only a matter of time before the ICC withdrew Zimbabwe's Test status.

In English domestic cricket, Nottinghamshire won the county championship, Hampshire took the one-day knockout trophy, Essex gained the one-day league title, and Somerset secured the Twenty20 Cup. In the West Indies, Trinidad and Tobago won the one-day President's Cup, and Jamaica captured the Carib Beer Cup. A reorganization of the regional structure in South Africa brought victory for the Eagles, one of six new franchises, in the one-day Standard Bank Cup and a share of the SuperSport Series for the Eagles and the Dolphins. Tasmania (in the ING one-day cup) and New South Wales (in the Pura Cup) took the domestic honours in Australia.   (ANDREW LONGMORE)

CURLING

The men's and women's world curling championships were divided into two separate competitions in 2005 after having run as a combined event for the previous 16 years.

In Victoria, B.C., Randy Ferbey's Canadian team won its third men's world championship in four years. Ferbey won eight consecutive games, including a tiebreaker, and easily defeated Scotland's David Murdoch 11–4 in a final that lasted only eight ends. Andy Kapp of Germany took the bronze after losing 8–6 to Canada. The rest of the men's field were, in order, Norway, Finland, the U.S., Switzerland, New Zealand, Sweden, Australia, Denmark, and Italy.

At the women's world championship in Paisley, Scot., Anette Norberg of Sweden won her first world title after having finished third four times and second once. Norberg went undefeated

Canadian skip Randy Ferbey (crouching centre) encourages his team at the men's curling world championship in Victoria, B.C., in April. Canada won its third men's title in four years.

through the round-robin at 11–0 and beat American Cassie Johnson 10–4 in the final. Norway's Dordi Nordby took the bronze. The rest of the field were, in order, Canada, Russia, Scotland, China, Switzerland, Japan, Denmark, Italy, and Finland.

Canada's Kyle George won the men's title at the world junior championships in Pinerolo, Italy, with a 6–5 victory in an extra end over Sweden's Nils Carlsén. Logan Gray of Scotland went undefeated in the round-robin at 9–0 but was upset 10–2 by Canada in the semifinal and finished with a bronze medal. Switzerland's Tania Grivel captured the women's world junior title with a 10–2 victory over Stina Viktorsson of Sweden. Canada's Andrea Kelly won the bronze medal.

At the world senior championships, held in Glasgow, Scot., Canada's Bas Buckle defended his men's title with a 5–4 win over the U.S. team, skipped by David Russell. Scotland's Carolyn Morris captured the women's senior championship with a 9–5 win over Hatoni Nagaoka of Japan.   (DONNA SPENCER)

CYCLING

American Lance Armstrong extended his record sequence of wins in the Tour de France, cycling's premier road event, to seven with his triumph in the 2005 race, which began on July 2 in Fromentine, on the Atlantic coast, and finished on July 24 on the Champs-Élysées in Paris. Armstrong, who announced in April that he would retire at the end of the Tour, was again the dominant rider in the high mountains of the Alps and Pyrenees before sealing victory with his only individual stage win of the race in the 55.5-km (1 km = about 0.62 mi) St. Étienne time trial on the penultimate day. After 3,608 km of racing, he finished 4 min 40 sec ahead of his nearest challenger, Ivan Basso of Italy. Thor Hushovd became the first rider from Norway to win one of the subsidiary competitions, the green jersey for the most consistent daily finisher.

In September, Spaniard Roberto Heras won the Tour of Spain (Vuelta a España) for a record fourth time. Cycling's other major national tour, the Tour of Italy (Giro d'Italia) in May, was won by Paolo Savoldelli of Italy, the 2002 victor. The inaugural ProTour, introduced by cycling's governing body, the Union Cycliste Internationale (UCI), as an expanded replacement for the World Cup, ran through the road-race season from March to October.

After winning a record seventh Tour de France on July 24, American cyclist Lance Armstrong shows off the victor's trophy to his three children.

The overall winner on points was Italy's Danilo Di Luca.

At the UCI world track championships, held in Los Angeles in March, Great Britain, with four gold medals, was the leading nation. Women's keirin winner Clara Sanchez of France was the only 2004 champion to successfully defend a title.

In July unheralded Czech rider Ondrej Sosenka broke the UCI's world one-hour record for rides on conventional bicycles without technological and aerodynamic aids. Sosenka covered 49.7 km in one hour at the Krylatskoye Olympic Velodrome in Moscow, beating by 259 m (about 850 ft) the record set in 2000 by Britain's Chris Boardman.

Cycling's fight to eliminate drugs and doping from the sport continued. The French sports daily *L'Équipe* claimed in August that Armstrong had taken the banned human hormone erythropoietin (EPO) during his first Tour de France win in 1999. The newspaper published leaked laboratory results of tests carried out on urine samples taken during that race and subsequently frozen. The urine test for EPO was introduced by the UCI in 2001, and the leftover 1999 samples were being analyzed to improve testing techniques. Armstrong denied the allegation, and no action was taken by the UCI. American Tyler Hamilton, a gold medalist at the 2004 Olympic Games, was banned for two years by the U.S. Anti-Doping Agency after testing positive for blood doping at the 2004 Tour of Spain. His appeal to the international Court of Arbitration for Sport was heard in September 2005, but there was no immediate decision. (JOHN R. WILKINSON)

EQUESTRIAN SPORTS

Thoroughbred Racing. *United States.* Problems continued in 2005 for the beleaguered New York Racing Association (NYRA), operator of Aqueduct, Belmont Park, and Saratoga racetracks since 1955. The franchise agreement was scheduled to end on Dec. 31, 2007, and after losing $15 million in 2004 and $22 million in 2003, the association was struggling to remain solvent. Clerk of scales Mario Sclafani and his assistant Braulio Baeza, a former jockey and member of racing's Hall of Fame, were arraigned on criminal charges of falsifying records in 2004 by allowing jockeys to ride over the prescribed weight without informing the public. The pair were removed from their positions on January 12 and fired on September 21. Meanwhile, a deferred-prosecution agreement struck in 2003 for the NYRA's involvement in tax evasion and money laundering by its pari-mutuel clerks was dismissed by the U.S. Attorney's Office for the Eastern District of New York.

On the track, Giacomo scored the second biggest upset in the 131-year history of the Kentucky Derby by rallying from far back under jockey Mike Smith to prevail by a length over Closing Argument and paying $102.60 to win. (Donerail paid $184.90 in 1913.) After finishing third in the Derby, Afleet Alex won both the Preakness and the Belmont Stakes to complete the 2005 Triple Crown. In the Preakness Afleet Alex stumbled to his knees and nearly fell when interfered with by another horse as they approached the stretch, yet he went on to win convincingly for jockey Jeremy Rose. In the Belmont Afleet Alex ran his final quarter mile in only 24.50 sec. He became the 49th horse and the 10th in the past 12 years to win two legs of the Triple Crown. Afleet Alex underwent surgery in July, however, for a fracture in his left foreleg that was detected shortly after the Belmont. He was retired to stud in December, having won 8 of 12 career starts and $2,765,800 in purses.

The eight Breeders' Cup World Thoroughbred Championship races were held on October 29 at Belmont Park. A record $116,465,923 was wagered at the host track and at simulcast locations around the world, breaking the previous mark of $109,838,668 established in 2004 at Lone Star Park in Grand Prairie, Texas. Saint Liam, the 2–1 favourite, won the $4,680,000 Breeders' Cup Classic. The victory established his claim to the Eclipse Award for top older male horse and put him into contention for Horse of the Year honours.

Hollywood Park in Inglewood, Calif., was purchased in July for $260 million from Churchill Downs, Inc., by Bay Meadows Land Co., a subsidiary of Stockbridge Capital Group. All turf racing for Hollywood Park's 31-day fall meeting was canceled when the track's newly renovated one-mile grass course was deemed unsatisfactory. Eight graded stakes were affected. Zia Park in Hobbs, N.M., opened on September 23. It was the first racetrack in the country specially constructed and designed to accommodate both racing and slot machines and was the first major North American racetrack to open since Lone Star Park in 1997. The revolutionary synthetic all-weather racing surface Polytrack was used for the first time at a pari-mutuel meeting in North America at Turfway Park in Florence, Ky.

As a result of the damage inflicted on Louisiana racetracks by Hurricanes Katrina and Rita, the scheduled 83-day meeting at the Fair Grounds in New Orleans was shortened to 37 days and moved to Louisiana Downs in Bossier City beginning on November 19, while the 88-day meeting at Delta Downs in Vinton was moved to Evangeline Downs in Opelousas with a December 1 start date.

Hall of Fame jockey Pat Day announced his retirement at age 51. Day,

Afleet Alex, with jockey Jeremy Rose on board, races to victory in the Preakness Stakes on May 21. The colt nearly fell after being interfered with by another horse but recovered to win by 4¾ lengths.

305

who ranked fourth all time with 8,803 victories, earned $297,912,019 in purses during a career that began in 1973. He rode in the Kentucky Derby a record 21 straight years (1984–2004) and won with Lil E. Tee in 1992. He also won the Preakness five times and the Belmont three times while earning four Eclipse Awards for outstanding jockey. Another Hall of Fame jockey, 42-year-old Gary Stevens, in November announced his retirement, citing chronic knee problems. During a 26-year career, Stevens rode more than 5,000 winners, including 8 in Triple Crown races, and earned more than $221 million in purses, which ranked him fifth on the all-time list. Angel Cordero, Jr., a two-time Eclipse Award winner, emerged from a 10-year retirement for one day to ride a horse in the $300,000 Cotillion Handicap at Philadelphia Park as part of a promotion to raise money for hurricane relief efforts. West Coast-based Russell Baze became the second jockey to win 9,000 races, behind Laffit Pincay, Jr., who retired in 2003 with 9,530 wins.

Hall of Fame jockey Ted Atkinson died on May 5 at age 88. (*See* OBITUARIES.) Owner and breeder John Ryan Gaines, who was considered the founding father of the Breeders' Cup World Thoroughbred Championships, died in February.   (JOHN G. BROKOPP)

International. The Asian Mile Challenge, which involved one race in Hong Kong and one in Japan, was introduced in 2005. Races in Australia and Dubai (U.A.E.) were scheduled to be added in 2006. The more ambitious Global Sprint Challenge was composed of two races each in Australia, the U.K., and Japan and was expected to add a final event in Hong Kong in December 2006. In the Champions Mile in Hong Kong, Bullish Luck beat his stablemate Silent Witness by a short head. Silent Witness was unbeaten in 17 shorter-distance races, but he had never before attempted a one-mile race. In the Yasuda Kinen, the Japanese half of the Mile Challenge, Silent Witness and Bullish Luck finished third and fourth, respectively, behind Asakusa Den'en. On October 2 Silent Witness showed that his real merit was at shorter distances when he beat 15 rivals in the Sprinters Stakes at Nakayama, Japan, the final race of the Global Sprint Challenge. Undefeated Deep Impact became the first winner of the Japanese Triple Crown since 1994. The colt, sired by the 1989 Kentucky Derby and Preakness winner Sunday Silence, was so dominant that his backers had their stakes returned, without

increment, when he beat 15 rivals in the Kikuka Sho (Japanese St. Leger).

All of the big races traditionally run at England's Ascot racecourse were shared out between other courses in 2005 while new grandstands were being built at Ascot and parts of the racecourse were realigned. Kempton Park was also closed and would reopen in March 2006 as an all-weather track with floodlit racing and the same kind of Polytrack surface that was introduced in 2005 at Turfway Park in Kentucky. On July 9 Lingfield Park, the first English course to use Polytrack, staged the first Group race to be run in Europe on an artificial surface.

Motivator looked like a good prospect in June when he won the Epsom Derby by five lengths over Walk in the Park. Up to that point Motivator was undefeated in four races, but he was beaten twice by Oratorio before finishing fifth to Hurricane Run in the Prix de l'Arc de Triomphe at Longchamp in Paris. Motivator was the third consecutive Derby winner that seemed to be unable to win again. Hurricane Run, the sixth Arc winner trained by André Fabre, also won the Irish Derby ahead of Scorpion. The latter redeemed himself with a victory in the St. Leger at Doncaster, Eng. Hurricane Run lost to Shamardal in the Prix du Jockey-Club (French Derby) at Chantilly, which was run for the first time over 2,100 m (about 1⅓ mi). Shamardal and 2,000 Guineas winner Footstepsinthesand both suffered midsummer injuries, and their owners, Coolmore Stud and Godolphin, respectively, retired them to stud in Australia before retrieving them for the Northern Hemisphere breeding season.

Coolmore, with the help of its new stable jockey, Kieren Fallon, enjoyed an excellent year after the disappointments of 2004. Shamardal and Dubawi both excelled for Godolphin, but the stable's Kentucky Derby hope, Blues and Royals, which won the UAE Derby in March by 12 lengths, developed colitis and had to be put down in June. Godolphin suffered other disappointments during the season and ended the year at odds with Coolmore, as its owners refused to buy any yearling sired by a Coolmore stallion.

Jamie Spencer, a failure as the stable jockey for Coolmore in 2004, returned to Britain and became the champion rider. Robert Winston led Spencer by two wins when he suffered serious injuries in a fall at Ayr on August 6. He missed the rest of the season. Lanfranco ("Frankie") Dettori, the 2004

champion, missed eight weeks of riding because of injury, and Ioritz Mendizábal, his French counterpart, suffered a similar misfortune. That left the door open for Christophe Soumillon to reclaim the jockey title in France and to set a new French record for the number of wins. Many of Soumillon's 226 winners were owned by the Aga Khan, who expanded his racing and breeding operation with the purchase of all the bloodstock owned by the late Jean-Luc Lagardere.

Three different horses were victorious in the Canadian Triple Crown. On June 26 Wild Desert captured the Queen's Plate by half a length, but three weeks later he managed only to finish third behind Ablo in the Prince of Wales. Both horses skipped the Breeders' Stakes, which was won by Jambalaya in his first major stakes race.

In Australia the seven-year-old mare Makybe Diva became the first winner of three Melbourne Cups. She carried a joint top weight in a field of 24 horses for Australia's richest race and started as the favourite for the 2-mi handicap. Ten days earlier, Makybe Diva had won the Cox Plate, the richest weight-for-age race in the Southern Hemisphere, over 1¼ mi. Railings captured the Caulfield Cup.   (ROBERT W. CARTER)

Harness Racing. Vivid Photo and Classic Photo battled for supremacy in the ranks of three-year-old trotters for most of the 2005 North American harness racing season. Pennsylvania horseman Roger Hammer (with co-owner Todd Schadel) had first raced Vivid Photo for a meager $2,115 purse at a fair in Bloomsburg, Pa., in June 2004. The young colt was so rambunctious early in his training that he was castrated so that he would keep his mind on racing. In the 2005 Hambletonian, Hammer positioned Vivid Photo behind the favoured Classic Photo until the stretch and then roared past the favourite to victory and a $750,000 first-place check. Vivid Photo's Hambletonian win was one of the most popular triumphs of the season. Strong Yankee, however, came on late in the season to defeat Vivid Photo in the Kentucky Futurity and the Breeders Crown.

In the Little Brown Jug, held at the county fair in Delaware, Ohio, three-year-old pacer P-Forty-Seven faced a powerful three-horse combination from the same stable—Rocknroll Hanover, Village Jolt, and Cam's Fool. Rocknroll Hanover, at that time the victor in seven of his nine starts, including two $1 million races, loomed as the heavy favourite. P-Forty-Seven seemed to have fate on his side, however. He showed incredible tenacity in winning both heats and set off a winner's circle celebration for his Ohioan owners and trainer.

The season's top older trotters were the gelding Mr. Muscleman and the mare Peaceful Way. Mr. Muscleman won 12 of his 14 starts, banking $1,364,220 in the process and bringing his career earnings to $3,250,000. Peaceful Way was equally successful in her abbreviated campaign, but her season was marred when she broke stride and lost her chance in the Maple Leaf Trot on September 17 in Toronto. Mr. Muscleman won the race, which had been publicized as a "battle of the sexes."

Hall of Fame trainer-driver Stanley Dancer, who won the trotting Triple Crown twice (1968 and 1972) as well as the 1970 pacing Triple Crown, died in September. (See OBITUARIES.)

In European racing, the French endurance classic, the Prix d'Amerique, was raced on January 30 at the Vincennes racecourse near Paris, and fans cheered wildly as the French star Jag De Bellouet defeated the Swedish challenger Gigant Neo. The race was contested over 2,700 m (1⅔ mi) for a purse of €1 million (about $1.2 million). Four months later Europe's best sprinters gathered at the Solvalla track in Stockholm to contest the Elitlopp. Norwegian harness racing devotees had traveled to Sweden to support their native hero Steinlager, hoping he could show up Swedish defending champion Gidde Palema. When Steinlager won the duel, delighted Norwegian spectators sang and waved national flags. At year's end six-time Elitlopp winner Stig Johansson of Sweden announced at age 60 that he was retiring from driving, though he would continue as a trainer. During a 42-year career in the sulky, Johansson attained more than 6,220 victories, including 3 on his last day.

New Zealand pacer Elsu dominated the 2005 Inter-Dominion Carnival held in Auckland, N.Z. Elsu's driver, David Butcher, allowed the field of 14 horses to settle into position early in the 2,700-m race before making his move. Elsu paced with authority and electrifying speed and won impressively. Racegoers "down under" agreed that they had not seen a pacer of Elsu's stature in a decade.   (DEAN A. HOFFMAN)

Steeplechasing. Irish horses dominated the big steeplechase meetings at Cheltenham and Aintree racecourses in 2005. Kicking King won the Cheltenham Gold Cup as well as the King George VI Chase

at Kempton. Hardy Eustace captured the Champion Hurdle, in which the first five finishers were trained in Ireland. Moscow Flyer, unbeaten in six races during the British season, was victorious in the Queen Mother Champion Chase. Nine-year-old Hedgehunter, the 7–1 favourite in 2005 after having fallen tired at the last fence in the 2004 race, won the Grand National. Best Mate, winner of three Cheltenham Gold Cups, was out of action from Dec. 28, 2004, until Nov. 1, 2005, when he suffered a heart attack and died after a comeback race at Exeter. Sleeping Jack, ridden by Christophe Pieux, beat 17 rivals in the Grand Steeple-Chase de Paris, the largest field for the race since 1978. Pieux was bidding for a record 16th French jockey championship in 2005, but he was beaten by Jacques Ricou. In Britain Martin Pipe was champion trainer for the 15th time in 17 seasons, and Tony McCoy was the top jockey for a record 10th time. Irish-bred but Australian-trained Karasi won the Nakayama Grand Jump, the world's richest chase.
(ROBERT W. CARTER)

FENCING

Following the July 2005 announcement that the 2012 Olympic Games would be held in London, the International Olympic Committee (IOC) turned its attention to the composition of the Games. Contrary to ill-founded rumours of fencing's demise as an Olympic event, the sport's unbroken record of inclusion since 1896 remained intact. The decision to retain fencing as an Olympic sport was the direct result of the modernization program forced through by Fédération Internationale d'Escrime (FIE) Pres. René Roch following advice from IOC Pres. Jacques Rogge and Rogge's predecessor, Juan Antonio Samaranch. The situation illustrated the imperative to continue the sport's modernization initiatives.

Among the most successful initiatives were Internet broadcasting, which was due for further development, and the acceptance by fencers of the transparent mask. Other areas in which fencing scored were the sport's growing international popularity (with 118 affiliated national federations), the near parity of men and women fencers, environmentally friendly policies (such as the traceability of materials for equipment manufacture), the modest costs of staging fencing events, and various health-related initiatives.

Throughout 2005 the new timings used to register hits at foil and sabre were hotly debated. After about a year of deliberation and controversy, the earlier FIE Congress decision on foil and sabre timings was reaffirmed. At the 2005 Congress the vexing question of which of the 12 disciplines to exclude from the 2008 Beijing Olympics, in which only 10 sets of fencing medals would be available, was discussed, but a decision was postponed.

At the 2005 senior world championships, held October 8–15 in Leipzig, Ger., France topped the medals table with 10 (4 gold), followed by Russia with 7 medals (2 gold) and Italy with 6 (2 gold). South Korea and the U.S. won gold in women's team foil and sabre, respectively. Valentina Vezzali of Italy captured her sixth world individual foil title in seven years.
(GRAHAM MORRISON)

AP/Wide World Photos

At the fencing world championships in October, American Mariel Zagunis (left) lunges to score a hit against Sofiya Velikaya of Russia in the final of the women's team sabre competition. The U.S. defeated Russia to take the title.

FOOTBALL

Association Football (Soccer). *Europe.* In 2005 the majority of European national association football (soccer) teams were concerned with qualifying matches for the 2006 Fédération Internationale de Football Association (FIFA) World Cup finals to be held in Germany. The first European country to qualify was Ukraine, coached by Oleg Blokhin (who held the Soviet Union record of 112 international appearances as a player). The standout on Ukraine's team was AC Milan striker Andriy Shevchenko, the 2004 European Footballer of the Year.

As a prelude to those finals, Germany staged the seventh FIFA Confederations Cup in June, featuring the champions of the five geographic areas covered by the world governing body, both European and South American champions, and the hosts. The final game, which took place in Frankfurt, was a South American duel, with Brazil comfortably defeating Argentina 4–1.

In contrast, the Union des Associations Européennes de Football (UEFA) Champions League final on May 25 at Atatürk Olympic Stadium in Istanbul proved to be one of the most dramatic matches in the competition's 50-year history. AC Milan, in its 10th final, faced England's Liverpool FC, which had last appeared at this level in the 1985 European cup final at Heysel Stadium in Brussels, where 39 fans died and more than 400 were injured. Liverpool had reached the 2005 final by eliminating the favourite, Chelsea FC, in the semifinal.

In Istanbul the Italian team took the lead after just 53 seconds. Andrea Pirlo's free kick reached the veteran Milan defender, Paolo Maldini, playing in his 149th European cup game, who scored with a shot that bounced down to deceive Liverpool's Polish goalkeeper, Jerzy Dudek. In the 39th minute Brazilian Ricardo Izecson Santos Leite (known as Kaká) combined with Shevchenko to provide the second goal for Argentine striker Hernán Crespo from close range. Five minutes later the enterprising Kaká again carved out the opening for Crespo to score and give Milan a 3–0 lead.

At halftime Liverpool coach Rafael Benítez was forced into a tactical rethink in view of the team's parlous position, and in a sensational five-minute period in the second half, the English team leveled the game at 3–3. After 54 minutes John Arne Riise crossed the ball from the left, and Liverpool team

© Clive Brunskill/Getty Images

Liverpool's Steven Gerrard outmaneuvers Gennaro Gattuso of AC Milan in the UEFA Champions League final in Istanbul on May 25. The English team won the match 3–2 in a penalty shootout after overtime play failed to break a 3–3 tie.

captain Steven Gerrard headed it in. Liverpool pressed forward, and within two minutes Vladimir Smicer hit a long shot that Milan's Brazilian goalkeeper Nélson de Jesús Silva (Dida) could only help into his own net. In noticeable disarray Milan conceded the equalizer in the 59th minute from the penalty spot. Gerrard was balked by Gennaro Gattuso, and though Xabi Alonso's kick was saved by Dida, the Liverpool player scored from the rebound.

It was only in overtime that stunned Milan coach Carlos Ancelotti was able to regroup his players. The turning point of the match came in the 117th minute, when Dudek brilliantly parried two close-range shots from Shevchenko. The initiative remained with Liverpool, however, and in the penalty shoot-out that followed, the Milan players appeared distinctly unnerved by the dancing tactics of Dudek, who saved shots from Pirlo and Shevchenko as Liverpool won the match 3–2 on penalties.

In the UEFA Cup final on May 18, Sporting Lisbon had home-ground advantage in its own José Avalade Stadium against CSKA Moscow and scored first after 28 minutes through a drive by Brazilian Rogério Fidelis

Régis. The Portuguese team held the lead until the 57th minute, when Aleksey Berezutsky equalized the score from a free kick taken by Daniel Carvalho of Brazil. In the 66th minute another Carvalho free kick set up CSKA's Yury Zhirkov to make it 2–1. Fifteen minutes before the end, Vagner Love, CSKA's other Brazilian player, scored a third goal after Carvalho had sprinted down the flank before finding his colleague in a scoring position. CSKA, which was sponsored in part by a company held by Roman Abramovich (Chelsea's Russian oil-billionaire owner), became the first Russian team to win a European final.

There was even more satisfaction for Abramovich; his personal wealth and the shrewd leadership of Portuguese coach José Mourinho provided the dual incentive for Chelsea, celebrating the club's centenary year, to achieve its first English championship title in half a century. Chelsea also won the League Cup and set several Premier League records: 29 wins, fewest goals conceded (15), and 25 shutouts. Of the 30 cosmopolitan players called upon, 22 were full international players. The leading goal scorer in England was Thierry Henry of Arsenal with 25 goals; he tied with Uruguayan Diego Forlán, who was traded to the Spanish club Villarreal by Manchester United after he failed to gain a regular starting place with the Old Trafford club.

Manchester United was itself taken over by American tycoon Malcolm Glazer and his family, who acquired ownership of Manchester United PLC for £790 million (about $1.4 billion). It was not an entirely popular move among many fans, and a minor breakaway club, to be called FC United, was formed in protest. At the other end of the financial spectrum, Germany's Borussia Dortmund had a debt of €135 million (about $160 million), but a restructuring saved it from bankruptcy.

The English Premier League claimed the top spot as a spectator attraction, with attendance of 12.88 million people during 2004–05, in front of the German Bundesliga with 11.57 million and the Spanish La Liga with 10.92 million. Surprisingly, in fourth place ahead of Italy's Serie A was the English Football League's newly designated Championship—effectively the second division in the country—which drew 9.8 million and pressed for entry into the UEFA Intertoto Cup.

Problems for Italy remained after Roma had to play Champions League matches behind closed doors when Swedish referee Anders Frisk was hit by a cigarette lighter thrown from the crowd. The quarterfinal between Internazionale and AC Milan was abandoned because of fan violence. This resulted in a similar ban and fine for Internazionale. During the 2004–05 season, 335 arrests were made in Italy resulting from some 231 incidents. In addition, Genoa was relegated from Serie A to Serie C1 after a match-fixing scandal. Italian referee Pierluigi Collina was allowed to continue after the retirement age of 45 but resigned when he felt a car sponsorship deal created a conflict of interest for him. Bribery and match-fixing as a consequence of betting scams also came to light in Germany, where referee Robert Hoyzer was among numerous people implicated. Portugal had similar concerns.

Though some progress had been made in the fight against racism, an upsurge of fascist and racist behaviour at matches in Romania alarmed the UEFA, which could sanction only its own competitions and not domestic games. Bulgaria also had problems, and Spain experienced some disturbing outbreaks, with even national coach Luis Aragones fined for remarks he made concerning Arsenal's Henry, a black French international player.

In France, where Lyon won its fourth successive championship, Guy Roux, the 66-year-old coach of Auxerre, retired after 44 years with the club following its Cup final victory. A record three-year television deal was struck in France when Canal Plus agreed to pay €600 million ($793 million) annually. Partizan Belgrade of Serbia and Montenegro, which had 25 wins and 5 draws, was the sole champion in Europe to remain unbeaten in League matches. League and Cup double winners were Brøndby (in Denmark), Levadia Tallinn (Estonia), HB Torshavn (Faeroes), Bayern Munich (Germany), Olympiakos (Greece), PSV Eindhoven (Holland), and FBK Kaunas (Lithuania). In Scotland, Rangers won its 51st championship and the League Cup.

The sport responded generously to the tsunami tragedy in late 2004, with donations from various organizations. FIFA pledged $2 million, and a world all-stars match held in Barcelona on February 15 was earmarked as another fund-raiser. FIFA was at odds with the World Anti-Doping Agency, however, and refused to observe the agency's code, preferring individual case assessment rather than blanket sentencing.

European football lost one of its greats with the death in November of former Manchester United and Northern Ireland player George Best. (*See* OBITUARIES.) (JACK ROLLIN)

The Americas. In 2005 Brazil continued to take all the major association football (soccer) honours in the Americas, defeating Argentina 4–1 in the Confederations Cup final and coming out just ahead of Argentina in the regional qualifying tournament for the 2006 World Cup. Argentina, Paraguay, and Ecuador were the other South American qualifiers, while the U.S., Mexico, Costa Rica, and Trinidad and Tobago (for the first time) qualified from the CONCACAF (Confederation of North, Central American and Caribbean Association Football). The U.S. was almost upset by Panama in the CONCACAF Gold Cup final but won 3–1 in a penalty shoot-out after a 0–0 extra-time draw.

Brazil's São Paulo Football Club won the Libertadores de América Cup over another Brazilian club, Atlético Paranaense, and captured the Club World Championship in Japan with a 1–0 final victory over England's Liverpool, thanks mainly to outstanding goalkeeper Rogerio Ceni (who had also scored well over 50 goals since his club debut in 1992). Argentina's Boca Juniors completed a rare treble; the team won the Recopa between the 2004 Libertadores and South American Cup champions with 3–1 and 1–2 scores against Once Caldas of Colombia, secured the national opening championship (the team's 21st domestic title), and defeated Mexico's UNAM on penalties after two 1–1 draws in the South American Cup. A Costa Rican club won the CONCACAF club championship for the second straight year as Deportivo Saprissa defeated UNAM 2–0 and 1–2.

The Los Angeles Galaxy captured the U.S. Major League Soccer Cup for the second time in four years, beating the New England Revolution 1–0 in the final. Rocha became the first club from outside Montevideo to win Uruguay's first division (opening) championship. Universidad Católica, which won Chile's closing championship, was undefeated through 19 games with a 33–3 goals record, and goalkeeper José Buljubasich set a Chilean record with 1,361 minutes unbeaten. Two teams celebrated becoming Brazil's champion—the Corinthians and Internacional Porto Alegre—as 11 games that were controlled by a corrupt referee were replayed and changed results. A court ordered the replays to be annulled, and the Brazilian Football

Confederation declared the Corinthians the champions. (ERIC WEIL)

Africa and Asia. In 2005 Japan and South Korea, cohosts of the 2002 association football (soccer) World Cup, were among the first countries to qualify for the 2006 finals to be held in Germany. Iran and Saudi Arabia were the other Asian qualifiers. China failed to qualify but won the East Asia championship, held July 31–August 7 in South Korea.

Enyimba of Nigeria maintained its record as the leading club in Africa, beating the Ghanaian club Hearts of Oak 2–0 in overtime in the African Super Cup on February 20. The COSAFA Castle Cup for the Southern African championship produced a surprise winner when Zimbabwe defeated Zambia 1–0 in the final on August 14 with a goal by Francis Chandida in the 84th minute. (JACK ROLLIN)

U.S. Football. *College.* The University of Texas won the 2005–06 college football championship on quarterback Vince Young's dramatic "fourth-and-five" touchdown run from the 8-yd line with 19 seconds to play, defeating the University of Southern California (USC) 41–38 in the Rose Bowl at Pasadena,

University of Texas quarterback Vince Young evades a tackle as he rushes for a gain in the Rose Bowl on Jan. 4, 2006. Texas defeated the University of Southern California 41–38 to capture the 2005 college football national championship.

Calif., on Jan. 4, 2006. The victory gave Texas (13–0) its first national crown in 35 years, as well as a 20-game winning streak, and ended USC's (12–1) streaks of 34 victories and two national championships. Young, the game's Most Valuable Player (MVP), ran 19 times for 200 yd, three touchdowns, and a two-point conversion, setting a Rose Bowl record with 467 yd total offense on runs and passes.

Texas and USC were the highest-scoring teams in the big-budget Division I-A of the National Collegiate Athletic Association (NCAA), with 50.2 and 49.1 points per game, respectively. Pacific-10 champion USC led with 579.8 total yards per game, while Big 12 champion Texas ranked third in total yards and second in rushing, behind Navy. Young ranked third in passing efficiency, winning the top national quarterbacks award and the Maxwell Award as player of the year, although USC tailback Reggie Bush won the Heisman Trophy and the Walter Camp award for player of the year. Bush led Division I-A with 8.7 yd per carry and 2,890 all-purpose yards on catches, kick returns, and 1,740 yd rushing. Bush was USC's third Heisman winner in four years and joined quarterback Matt Leinart as the first Heisman-winning teammates since Army's Doc Blanchard and Glenn Davis in 1945–46.

Big Ten cochampions Penn State (11–1) and Ohio State (10–2) ranked third and fourth, respectively, in both major polls, by writers and broadcasters for the Associated Press (AP) and coaches for ESPN. Penn State coach Joe Paterno, who had been heavily criticized for a 7–16 record the previous two years, was Coach of the Year at age 79, while Paul Posluszny won the top linebackers award and the Chuck Bednarik Award for defensive players. Ohio State's only losses were to Texas and Penn State as linebacker A.J. Hawk won the linemen's Lombardi Award in leading the top rushing defense. Penn State won the Orange Bowl 26–23 in triple overtime over Atlantic Coast Conference winner Florida State (8–5), and Ohio State won the Fiesta Bowl 34–20 over Notre Dame, the latter's record-setting eighth consecutive bowl defeat.

Big East champion West Virginia (11–1) defeated Southeastern Conference champion Georgia (10–3) by 38–35 in the Sugar Bowl, which was moved to Atlanta from New Orleans because of the damage caused by Hurricane Katrina. West Virginia received the AP's fifth ranking, which ESPN gave to hurricane-affected Louisiana

State (11–2), while each ranked the other team sixth. Virginia Tech (11–2) was seventh, and eighth-ranked Alabama's (10–2) defense allowed a division-low 10.7 points per game while trailing only Virginia Tech's 247.6 yd allowed per game. The polls split their ninth ranking between Notre Dame (9–3) and Mountain West champion Texas Christian (11–1) but agreed on Georgia at number 10. Nevada (9–3) won the Western Athletic Conference; Tulsa (9–4) took Conference USA; and Akron (7–6) came out atop the Mid-American Conference.

Louisville defensive end Elvis Dumervil won the Bronko Nagurski Award for defenders, and Minnesota centre Greg Eslinger received the Outland Trophy for interior linemen. Hawaii's Colt Brennan led Division I-A with 4,301 yd passing, 4,455 yd total offense, and 35 touchdown passes.

Winners of the lower-budget NCAA divisions' championship tournaments were 12–3 Appalachian State (N.C.) in division I-AA, 13–0 Grand Valley State (Mich.) in Division II, and 14–1 Mount Union (Ohio), which won its eighth Division III title in 13 years after a 21–14 loss to Northern Iowa on October 22 ended its 110-game regular-season winning streak. Carroll (Mont.) went 14–0 for its fourth consecutive National Association of Intercollegiate Athletics championship, while quarterback Tyler Emmert won his third straight NAIA Most Valuable Player (MVP) award.

Professional. The New England Patriots of the American Football Conference (AFC) won Super Bowl XXXIX and the 2004–05 National Football League (NFL) championship in a 24–21 victory over the Philadelphia Eagles of the National Football Conference (NFC) on Feb. 6, 2005, in Jacksonville, Fla. With their second championship in a row, the Patriots became the first team to win three Super Bowls in four years, each of them by three points. Wide receiver Deion Branch was MVP with 11 catches for 133 yd, and coach Bill Belichick replaced the team's usual three linemen–four linebackers defense with a two–five alignment in winning his 10th of 11 postseason games, the best ever in the NFL.

Philadelphia then became the fifth consecutive league runner-up to miss the play-offs in the following season, and New England barely avoided the Eagles' fate by winning the AFC East with a 10–6 record, the worst of any 2005–06 division winner. Seven teams reached the play-offs after missing

them in 2004–05, and the records of 15 teams in the 32-team league improved or declined by at least four games. Chicago and Tampa Bay went from last place to first in the NFC North and South divisions, respectively, each improving by a league-best six games to 11–5, while Philadelphia's seven-game decline was the worst. Cincinnati (11–5) won the AFC North with its first winning record—or play-off berth—since 1990. The other division winners were Seattle (13–3) in the NFC West, the New York Giants (11–5) in the NFC East, Indianapolis (14–2) in the AFC South, and Denver (13–3) in the AFC West, the division's fourth champion in four years. "Wild-card" play-off teams, as their conferences' best runners-up, were Pittsburgh (11–5), Carolina (11–5), Washington (10–6), and Jacksonville (12–4), with the last two ending six-year play-off absences.

Under quarterback Peyton Manning (*see* BIOGRAPHIES) Indianapolis won its first 13 games by at least seven points, an NFL record. Green Bay had its first losing record in 13 years. The New Orleans Saints, displaced by Hurricane Katrina, played "home" games in San Antonio, Texas; Baton Rouge, La.; and suburban New York City in a 3–13 season that began with an uplifting 23–20 victory two weeks after the storm. Quarterback Doug Flutie scored an extra point in New England's last regular-season game with the NFL's first successful dropkick since 1941. Seattle led the league with 28.25 points per game, and Chicago and Tampa Bay built their improvements on defense, with league-best per-game yields of 12.6 points and 277.8 yd, respectively. Kansas City coach Dick Vermeil retired at 69 after his Chiefs (10–6) led the league with 387 yd per game of total offense but missed the play-offs.

An unusually high number of MVP candidates included league leaders Shaun Alexander with 1,880 yd rushing, 168 points, and a record 28 touchdowns for Seattle, Tiki Barber with 2,390 yd from scrimmage for the Giants, Tom Brady with 4,110 yd passing for New England, Carson Palmer with 32 touchdown passes for Cincinnati, and Manning with a 104.1 passer rating. Carolina's Steve Smith led NFL receivers with 1,563 yd and tied Arizona's Larry Fitzgerald with 103 catches. Arizona's Neil Rackers kicked a record 40 field goals with a league-best .952 percentage on 42 attempts. Kansas City's Larry Johnson ran for 1,351 yd in the last nine games.

Running back Shaun Alexander of the Seattle Seahawks talks to reporters after being named the NFL's 2005–06 regular-season MVP.

Emmitt Smith retired on February 3 after 15 seasons, with NFL rushing records of 18,355 yd and 164 touchdowns, and Jerry Rice called it quits on September 5 after 20 seasons, with 38 league records, including 1,549 catches and receptions for 22,895 yd and 197 touchdowns. On December 26 ABC broadcast its last Monday Night Football game after 36 seasons. ESPN won the rights to Monday night games for 2006 and beyond, with Sunday night games moving to NBC in a new television package that was worth nearly a 50% increase to $3.7 billion a year.

(KEVIN M. LAMB)

Canadian Football. The Edmonton Eskimos won the 2005 Canadian Football League (CFL) championship by defeating the Montreal Alouettes 38–35 in the Grey Cup on November 27 at Vancouver in the second overtime game of the Cup's 95-year history and the first in 44 years. Quarterback Ricky Ray won the game's Outstanding Player Award with a Cup-record 35 completions on 45 passes for 359 yd and two touchdowns. Ray, who had been replaced during Edmonton's previous two play-off victories, ran one yard for the touchdown that put Edmonton ahead 28–25 with 1 minute 3 seconds left in regulation play, but Damon Duval's field goal at the gun forced overtime (in which each team takes possession at its opponent's 35-yd line). Sean Fleming's 36-yd field goal on the second possession won the game after Edmonton's defense held Montreal.

Division winners Toronto (11–7) in the East and the B.C. Lions (12–6) in the West lost in the division finals to Montreal (10–8) and Edmonton (11–7),

respectively, but 42-year-old Toronto quarterback Damon Allen won the first CFL Outstanding Player Award of his 21-year career. Outstanding Special Teams Player Corey Holmes of Saskatchewan led the CFL with 3,455 yd total offense. Other awards went to Calgary linebacker John Grace for defensive players, Saskatchewan's Gene Makowsky for linemen, Winnipeg defensive end Gavin Walls for rookies, and Lions defensive end Brent Johnson, who was the top Canadian and sack leader with 16. (KEVIN M. LAMB)

Australian Football. After 72 years the Red and the White was finally rewarded with the Australian Football League (AFL) premiership when the Sydney (formerly South Melbourne) Swans defeated Perth's West Coast Eagles by a score of 8.10 (58) to 7.12 (54) in the Grand Final on Sept. 24, 2005, at the Melbourne Cricket Ground. (South Melbourne had last won a premiership in 1933, and after years of financial insecurity the team had relocated to Sydney in 1982.) With the crowd of 91,898 spectators at fever pitch, the Eagles made a last-ditch effort to snatch the 2005 title, but a great high mark by Sydney's Leo Barry deep in the Eagles' forward line turned them away as the final siren sounded. In the home-and-away regular season, Sydney (15–7) finished third behind the Eagles, which had a record of 17–5. Adelaide (17–5), which finished atop the ladder,

did not make it beyond the preliminary finals.

Chris Judd of the Eagles was awarded the Norm Smith Medal as best on the ground in the Grand Final. His teammate Ben Cousins won the Brownlow Medal for the best and fairest player in the regular season, St Kilda full-forward Fraser Gehrig received the Coleman Medal for the most goals kicked (74), Richmond youngster Brett Deledio was chosen the AFL Rising Star, and Adelaide captain Mark Ricciuto was named captain of the All-Australian side. (GREG HOBBS)

Rugby Football. In Rugby Union 2005 was the year of the New Zealand All Blacks. After being knocked out of the 2003 World Cup in the semifinals by Australia, the All Blacks had embarked on a rebuilding process that culminated in their stunning form in 2005. New Zealand rugby underwent top-to-bottom changes, including the installation of a new coaching team and the emergence of an inspirational on-field leader in Tana Umaga.

In May New Zealand's Canterbury Crusaders outplayed Australia's New South Wales Waratahs 35–25 and lifted the last Super 12 trophy (the tri-nation tournament would expand to 14 teams in 2006). Many of the Crusaders players, including Justin Marshall, Daniel Carter, and Richie McCaw, formed the backbone of the national side that welcomed to New Zealand in June and

The New Zealand All Blacks perform the team's customary pregame haka *(a traditional Maori war chant) before the September 3 match against the Australia Wallabies in the Rugby Union Tri-Nations series. New Zealand won the game and the title.*

July the British and Irish Lions (made up of the best players from England, Ireland, Scotland, and Wales). The All Blacks were clearly in world-class form and won all three Test matches by record margins: 21–3, 48–18, and 38–19. In more than 100 years of trying to clutch victory, the Lions had only once (in 1971) won a Test series in New Zealand, but no one expected them to lose all three Tests so badly. Although the Lions, coached by Sir Clive Woodward, lost their captain, Brian O'-Driscoll, to injury inside the first minute of the first Test, the All Blacks still produced three stunning performances. Following that series victory, it came as no surprise in November when the All Blacks won all four Tests in New Zealand's "grand slam" tour of Great Britain and Ireland. The New Zealanders suffered their only defeat of 2005 in the Tri-Nations tournament when on August 6 they lost 22–16 to South Africa, the defending champion, in Cape Town. Home and away wins against Australia and a 31–27 victory over South Africa in the return match, however, gave New Zealand the Tri-Nations title.

Wales achieved its first Six Nations grand slam since 1978. The young Welsh side, employing an expansive new playing style, completed a clean sweep, with wins over all of the other five nations. It was a huge turnaround for the Welsh players; as Captain Gareth Thomas remarked, "We've been shot down and written off but we've come through."

Domestically, the London Wasps lifted the team's third consecutive English title, the Neath-Swansea Ospreys won the Celtic League, and Biarritz proved too strong for Stade Français in the French championship. In the European Cup final, held on May 22 in Edinburgh, Toulouse defeated Stade Français 18–12 to capture a record third Heineken Cup.

In Rugby League the Bradford Bulls avenged their 2004 loss to the Leeds Rhinos with a 15–6 victory over their rivals on October 15 in the English Super League Grand Final. Wests Tigers capped an incredible come-from-behind season by securing the team's first Australian National Rugby League championship in its first finals appearance. In June the Tigers fell to 12th place in the league, but they surged back to win 12 of their last 14 matches, including a 30–16 triumph on October 2 over the North Queensland Cowboys for the title. (PAUL MORGAN)

GOLF

Having seen his five-year reign as world number one ended by Fijian Vijay Singh late in the 2004 season, Eldrick ("Tiger") Woods did not need long in 2005 to reclaim the position and reestablish himself as golf's leading light. In the process the American took two more steps toward Jack Nicklaus's record 18 major championship titles. Woods improved his total to 10 with victories in the Masters at the Augusta (Ga.) National Golf Club and the British Open at the Old Course, St. Andrews, Scot., and he accomplished it as Nicklaus made his final appearances in the two events.

Nicklaus received standing ovations as he brought down the curtain on what was the greatest career in golf's history. There was added emotion in the British Open because his caddie was his son Steve, whose own son Jake had died earlier in the year in a hot-tub accident at age 17 months. The 65-year-old Nicklaus failed in his stated goal of surviving the halfway cut at St. Andrews, but he did bow out with a birdie.

The two Woods successes were contrasting affairs. At the Masters, which he had won in 1997, 2001, and 2002, Woods trailed Ryder Cup teammate Chris DiMarco by six strokes at halfway before equaling the tournament record of seven successive birdies in a third-round 65, which took him three clear. Although DiMarco faltered with a third-round 74—and Woods had never lost a major when he held the lead after 54 holes—the fourth round turned out to be an unexpectedly thrilling climax. DiMarco appeared to have a chance to draw level on the par-three 16th hole, only for Woods to produce one of the most memorable shots of his career. Long and left off the tee, he chose to play his chip shot up and down the steep slope in the green. In what was perhaps the most dramatic moment of the entire 2005 season, the ball lingered on the edge of the hole before it toppled in accompanied by a huge roar from the crowd. DiMarco missed his putt and was two behind. He was handed a lifeline when Woods bogeyed the final two holes, and, tied at 12 under par, they went into a play-off. DiMarco, who had nearly chipped in for victory on the last hole, faced a similar shot at the first extra hole but missed again, and Woods grabbed the victory for his fourth green jacket with a 4.6-m (15-ft) birdie putt.

There was no such late excitement in the British Open. Back on the course where he had won in 2000 by eight strokes with a major-championship record of 19 under par, Woods was in a league of his own. An opening-round 66 gave him the lead; he followed with a second-round 67 to surge into the

New Zealander Michael Campbell takes a fairway shot on the 16th hole in the final round of the U.S. Open golf tournament on June 19. Campbell, who went into the event ranked 80th in the world, won his first PGA major by two strokes.

lead by four strokes. Closing scores of 71 and 70 were sufficient to give Woods a five-stroke victory with a 14-under-par score of 274. In front of his home fans, 42-year-old Colin Montgomerie was second, the fourth time he had come up just shy in pursuit of a first major title.

Woods also figured prominently in the other two major championships of the season, finishing second to New Zealander Michael Campbell in the U.S. Open at Pinehurst, N.C., and fourth behind American Phil Mickelson in the Professional Golfers' Association (PGA) championship at Baltusrol Golf Club in Springfield, N.J.

Campbell's victory was a real surprise. The 36-year-old, who was 80th in the world rankings, would not have entered the tournament had it not been for a qualifying tournament that was held in Europe for the first time. At Pinehurst, with a round to play, he was in joint fourth position. The defending champion, South African Retief Goosen, who was seeking a third win in five years, led by three strokes over little-known American Jason Gore, but both those players collapsed with final rounds of 81 and 84, respectively, while Campbell's fourth-round 69 for a level-par total of 280 gave him a two-stroke triumph over Woods. Campbell became New Zealand's first major golf champion since Bob Charles captured the 1963 British Open; he later added the record £1 million ($1.8 million) first prize in the HSBC World Match Play championship.

Mickelson had achieved his first major win in the 2004 Masters and had come close in the other three majors of that season, but it was not until the 2005 PGA championship that he put himself in position to win again. Bad weather forced the event into a Monday-morning finish, and Australian Steve Elkington and Denmark's Thomas Bjorn posted three-under-par aggregates of 277. Mickelson chipped from the rough to within one metre (3 ft) of the final hole and sank the birdie putt to win by one stroke. Woods finished at two under par on Sunday evening and unexpectedly flew home to Florida without waiting to see if he might be required for a play-off.

Woods was quickly back on the winning trail; he again pushed DiMarco into second place at the NEC Invitational at Firestone Country Club, Akron, Ohio, and then beat American John Daly in a play-off for another of the World Golf Championships events,

At the Women's British Open golf tournament in July, a triumphant Jang Jeong of South Korea (right) shares the moment with American Michelle Wie, who finished third and won the trophy for lowest-scoring amateur.

the American Express championship at Harding Park, San Francisco. Remarkably, that made it 11 victories for Woods in the 21 WGC tournaments in which he had played since the series was introduced in 1999. Not surprisingly, he topped the PGA Tour money list for the sixth time; his 2005 earnings of $10,628,024 took his worldwide career total to nearly $70 million, not including endorsement, promotional, and appearance fees. Montgomerie became the European tour's leading money winner for a remarkable eighth time, with earnings of £1,888,613 (about $3.3 million).

DiMarco had some compensation for his two narrow losses to Woods when he sank the winning putt to give the United States an 18½–15½ victory over the International side in the Presidents Cup at the Robert Trent Jones Club, Gainesville, Va.

One of the hottest stories in women's golf was American Michelle Wie, whose potential was recognized in 2005 when she decided to turn professional on reaching the age of 16. Without having won any significant titles, Wie signed contracts with Nike and Sony for a reported $10 million. As an amateur she gained worldwide fame in 2004 by missing the halfway cut by only one shot in the PGA Tour's Sony Open. She made two more appearances on the men's circuit in 2005 and finished second and third (in a tie with South Korea's Young Kim), respectively, in the

Ladies Professional Golf Association (LPGA) championship at Bulle Rock, Havre de Grace, Md., and the Women's British Open at Royal Birkdale Golf Club, Southport, Eng., two of the women's four major championships. Wie's professional debut came at the world championship at Bighorn Golf Club, Palm Desert, Calif., but after posting a total that would have given her fourth place, she was disqualified when officials ruled that she had taken an incorrect drop away from a bush during the third round.

Sweden's Annika Sörenstam won that event as well as the Kraft Nabisco championship at Mission Hills Country Club, Rancho Mirage, Calif., and the LPGA championship to bring her number of major titles to nine. The U.S. Women's Open was captured by South Korea's Birdie Kim at Cherry Hills Country Club, Cherry Hills Village, Colo., where amateurs Morgan Pressel and Brittany Lang tied for second. Victory in the Women's British Open went to another South Korean, Jang Jeong. The United States regained the Solheim Cup trophy from Europe by a 15½–12½ margin at Crooked Stick Golf Club, Carmel, Ind.

In men's amateur competition, the Walker Cup returned to American hands, but only just. After three successive defeats, the U.S. narrowly beat Britain and Ireland by 12½–11½ at the Chicago Golf Club, Wheaton, Ill., despite having lost their number one player, Ryan Moore, to the professional ranks two months after his brilliant 13th-place finish in the 2005 Masters. Moore's successor as U.S. amateur champion was Edoardo Molinari, the first Italian ever to have entered the event. Molinari won at Merion Golf Club, Ardmore, Pa. The British amateur championship was won by Ireland's Brian McElhinney at the Royal Birkdale course. (MARK GARROD)

GYMNASTICS

At the artistic gymnastics world championships, held in Melbourne during Nov. 21–27, 2005, the United States was the dominant force in the women's competition, winning 9 out of the 10 medals for which it was eligible (4 gold, 4 silver, and 1 bronze). This was the U.S. women's best performance at a world championships since 1993, when they collected five medals (three gold and two silver). Americans Chellsie Memmel (37.824 points) and Anastasia Liukin (37.823 points) finished first and second, respectively, in the all-around competition. It marked the first 1–2 finish by the U.S., and the .001-point margin of victory was the closest since Soviet teammates Yelena Shushunova and Oksana Omelyanchik tied for gold at the 1985 world championships. Local favourite Monette Russo won Australia's first individual medal in the all-around, scoring 37.298 points for the bronze medal. During the

event finals, Liukin secured the gold medal on the uneven bars and the balance beam. (Liukin came from a strong gymnastics background—her father and coach was an Olympic gymnastics champion for the Soviet Union, and her mother was a former Soviet world champion in rhythmic gymnastics.) American Alicia Sacramone took top honours on floor exercise. China's Cheng Fei won her country's first gold medal on vault. The world championships did not include team events.

In the men's all-around competition, Japan's Hiroyuki Tomita, the bronze medalist from the 2003 world championships, and Hisashi Mizutori were first and second, respectively. It was Japan's first 1–2 finish since 1970, when it swept the top three all-around places. Denis Savenkov of Belarus took home the bronze. During the men's individual event finals, Slovenian gymnasts won two gold medals; Mitja Petkovsek finished first in the rankings on parallel bars, while his teammate Aljaz Pegan won the high bar with a routine in which he used three consecutive release moves and then dismounted with a triple back. Diego Hypolito captured the floor exercise for Brazil's first title in men's gymnastics. China's Xiao Qin took first on pommel horse with a score of 9.85, earning his third world medal in the event in his fourth consecutive final. Yuri van Gelder of The Netherlands claimed the gold medal on rings for the first world gymnastics

Gold medalist Hiroyuki Tomita of Japan performs on the parallel bars in the men's all-around finals at the world gymnastics championships in Melbourne on November 24.

medal for his country. Romania's Marian Dragulescu took first on vault.

The rhythmic gymnastics world championships took place October 3–9 in Baku, Azerbaijan. The Russian team overwhelmingly prevailed, with a total of 12 medals and 7 of the 9 golds awarded, including the group all-around title. Ukraine was second overall, with seven medals but no golds. Olga Kapranova, age 17, almost swept the individual apparatus titles, with solid triumphs in ball, rope, clubs, and the four-event individual all-around final. Her teammate Vera Sesina won gold in the ribbon competition. Only Italy and Bulgaria broke through the Russian domination, with one victory each in the group apparatus finals.

(LUAN PESZEK)

ICE HOCKEY

North America. For the severely troubled National Hockey League (NHL), the unplayed season of 2004–05 was the most worrisome in its 87-year history. In what long had been an economic certainty, owners throughout the league began a lockout of their players at midnight on Sept. 15, 2004, when the collective-bargaining agreement with the players' union ran out. Over the next 4½ months and through sporadic negotiations between management and the union, the two sides remained $6.5 million apart on the

(From left to right) Olga Kapranova, Irina Chachina, and Vera Sesina of Russia wave to the crowd after winning the group final at the European rhythmic gymnastics championships in June. Four months later the Russian trio dominated the world championships with 12 medals, including 8 in individual competition.

owners' quest for a salary cap, the issue that stalemated negotiations until the 11th hour. With 20 of the league's 30 franchises claiming to have lost money and player salaries at an all-time-high average of $1,830,126, the deadlock induced NHL commissioner Gary Bettman to cancel the 2004–05 season on Feb. 16, 2005.

By that time the lockout had cost the NHL more than 900 games and an exodus of players who signed with European teams or minor league clubs in the U.S. The cancellation was the second in 10 years on Bettman's watch, and it left the NHL with the dubious honour of becoming the first North American professional sports league to cancel an entire season. It also eliminated the Stanley Cup play-offs, historically the most compelling segment of the season for NHL fans.

The future loomed even worse for the NHL because the canceled season generated hardly a blip of protest, outrage, or media reaction outside Canada. Critics of the NHL and its players pointed out that the league's television ratings had fallen to infomercial status in the U.S., chiefly because rule changes and defensive-oriented coaches had robbed the game of much of its excitement. Rule changes that favoured mucking, grinding, trapping defensive play increased fan boredom through a succession of low-scoring games. Nor did it help scoring that goalie pads had grown ever bigger and bulkier over time. Since the cost of attending an NHL game could easily reach $300 for a family of four, diminished attendance was the logical outcome of boring contests.

Bettman drew heavy criticism for putting the season on ice, as did Bob Goodenow, the dogmatic executive director of the NHL Players' Association. Goodenow repeatedly refused to compromise on the salary cap issue until there was time sufficient only for a 28-game season. The union then came up with a cap number—$52 million per team—and a 24% salary rollback, but neither offer satisfied the team owners. In the wake of the cancellation, team officials, players, and season-ticket holders pondered what the future would hold for the NHL. No reasonable person expected the league to operate as it had in previous seasons. That assessment was virtually guaranteed on June 1, when the cable television network ESPN called off negotiations with the NHL, saying that even if a new labour contract could be reached and play resumed in October, ice hockey

Goalkeeper Tomas Vokoun of the Czech Republic blocks a shot in the final of the men's world ice hockey championships in May. Vokoun made 29 saves in the game and helped his team defeat Canada 3–0 for the gold medal.

was not worth half the $60 million the network paid for rights fees in 2003–04. ESPN's decision not to pick up its $60 million option for 2005–06 left the NHL without a national television partner for the first time since the late 1970s. The NHL also lost a valuable corporate owner when the Walt Disney Co. sold the Mighty Ducks of Anaheim for roughly $75 million on June 16. Disney had bought the team as an expansion franchise in 1992 for $50 million.

In July the 301-day lockout ended after players and owners agreed to a new contract. Highlights of the six-year deal included a 24% rollback of players' salaries and an initial salary cap of $39 million per team. The NHL also announced rule changes designed to create a more exciting game. Among the notable changes was the introduction of a shoot-out to decide regular-season games that were still tied after an overtime period. In August the NHL reached a television agreement with the cable network OLN. The three-year deal was worth more than $200 million.

Given the absence of NHL games, some fans turned to competition provided by the American Hockey League (AHL), whose Philadelphia Phantoms franchise captured the AHL Calder Cup title with a 5–2 victory over the Chicago Wolves on June 10. The Phantoms' triumph iced the cake in the final series four games to none and gave the team its second AHL title since 1998. The

Phantoms got two goals each from centre John Sim and left wing Patrick Sharp, while Antero Niittymaki, the team's goalkeeper, made 28 saves. Niittymaki stopped 132 of Chicago's 136 shots on goal during the finals and was named Most Valuable Player (MVP) of the play-offs.

In September Mark Messier, one of the most recognized figures in professional ice hockey, announced his retirement from the sport after having played 25 seasons in the NHL. The 44-year-old Messier won five Stanley Cups during his stint with the Edmonton Oilers from 1979 to 1991. He spent much of the remainder of his career with the New York Rangers and led the team to victory in the Stanley Cup finals in 1994. Messier's 1,887 regular-season points placed him second, behind Wayne Gretzky, on the NHL's all-time scoring list.

International. The Czech Republic ended Canada's two-year hold on the International Ice Hockey Federation (IIHF) championship on May 15, 2005, in Vienna. With flawless defense at the heart of a dominating performance, the Czechs powered to a 3–0 victory that denied Canada its 24th international gold medal. Earlier in the day, Russia had defeated Sweden 6–3 in the bronze-medal game.

It was the first championship victory for the Czechs since 2001, and it marked the first shutout loss for

Canada since an uncharacteristic 9–0 loss to Sweden in 1987. The tournament also brought a measure of revenge for the Czechs, whom the United States had eliminated in a quarterfinals shoot-out a year earlier in Prague. In 2005 it was the Czechs who beat the U.S. in the quarterfinals—in a shoot-out. Tomas Vokoun, hailed as the tournament's best goalkeeper, stopped 29 Canadian shots in the gold-medal final. The Czechs also got a standout performance from Jaromir Jagr, the five-time NHL scoring champion, who became one of only 15 players to have won the Stanley Cup and a gold medal in both the Olympic Games and the world championships.

The Czechs got their first goal at 4:13 of the first period, when Vaclav Prospal knocked a rebound shot past Canadian goalie Martin Brodeur. Martin Rucinsky made it 2–0 at 3:12 of the third period, when his slap shot beat Brodeur to the glove side from the top of the left circle. Canada replaced Brodeur with an extra attacker during a last-minute power play, but the strategy backfired when Josef Vasicek fired a length-of-the-rink empty-net goal that sealed the Czech victory with 53 seconds left. Tournament MVP honours went to Canada's Joe Thornton, who led his team with 6 goals and 10 assists.

In the IIHF women's world championships, contested at Linköping, Swed., in April, the U.S. settled an old score when it beat Canada in the gold-medal game for the first time in nine tries. The long-sought American victory came in a shoot-out—the first in the history of the tournament—after neither team could score through the first three periods and an overtime session. Natalie Darwitz, Angela Ruggiero, and Krissy Wendell each scored for Team USA in the shoot-out, while Canada got only one goal, from Sarah Vaillancourt. Chanda Gunn of the U.S. was named the tournament's top goaltender, while Wendell, the leading American scorer, received the MVP award. (RON REID)

ICE SKATING

Figure Skating. The happiest moment achieved by any figure skater in 2005 undoubtedly belonged to Russia's Irina Slutskaya (see BIOGRAPHIES) on March 19, when the 26-year-old won her second world championship gold medal and the soaring adoration of her hometown fans in Moscow's Luzhniki Sports Palace. Slutskaya's victory not only completed a remarkable comeback

Figure Skating's New Judging System

The tidal wave of criticism spawned by the judging scandal at the 2002 Winter Olympics in Salt Lake City, Utah, prompted the International Skating Union (ISU) to devise a reformed judging system that went into effect in 2005. The new system, based on cumulative points, replaced the traditional 6.0 scoring system that had been used for more than a century. The addition of technical experts to assist in the judging process was a part of the new reforms, as was the use of videotape replays. There were also changes in the way scores were tabulated and displayed. Skaters under the new system were to be awarded points for a technical score combined with points for five additional qualities—skating skills, transitions, performance/execution, choreography/composition, and interpretation. Ice dancing included an additional component—timing. When the new system was first tested in the U.S., on Oct. 21, 2004, at Reading, Pa., some skaters complained that it did not necessarily prize the performance of difficult jumps but rather rewarded doing easier jumps well. Nevertheless, the ISU felt that its reforms would result in more objective judging and an end to controversy.

Key aspects of the new system included:
• A technical specialist who identifies each of the skating elements.
• A technical controller overseeing the judging panel who can ask for video reviews of specific elements if there is uncertainty about what has been identified.
• A panel of 10 judges that gives numerical marks for every element of a skater's program. Judges would no longer be responsible for ranking each skater relative to the other skaters in the competition. They would now be responsible for simply evaluating the qualities of each performance.
• A base value for each element, from spins to footwork to jumps and—for pairs and dance—lifts. A triple toe loop has a 4.8 base, for example, while a quadruple loop is worth 9.0. A judge can add from +3 points to –3 points to the base value of a jump or element and +1.5 to –1 for a spin.

While the 6.0 system tended to award higher scores to skaters who started late in the competition, starting order would not have an impact on skaters' scores in the new system. Competitors should have a greater opportunity to win by coming from a lower position than was the case under the 6.0 system. Hoping to reduce the risk of outside influences on judges, the ISU also ruled that the names of judges working ISU championships and senior Grand Prix events would not be linked to their scores. In addition, the scores that counted in the final tally were to be randomly selected from among the panel of judges. Separate scores would be posted for technical elements and for program components, and the winner would be determined by the highest combined score. Although the ISU expressed confidence in the new judging system, a number of skaters and coaches voiced concerns. The anonymous scoring, in particular, gave corrupt judges greater protection from scrutiny, some believed, and might inhibit the ability of competitors to get crucial feedback from judges. (RON REID)

from the disappointments she had endured in 2004, when health problems forced her to withdraw from several major events, but also finished off a 2005 season that saw her win every competition she entered. Slutskaya secured the world title with her highest score of the season, despite a penalty imposed under the sport's new scoring system (see Sidebar) for executing an extra triple loop.

Slutskaya graced her home ice with seven clean triple jumps, including a triple lutz–triple loop reminiscent of her superb performances of the past.

After being penalized for minor flaws in some of her jumps and for landing a triple flip off-balance, American Sasha Cohen finished second, about eight points behind Slutskaya. Italy's Carolina Kostner took the bronze medal with a score that was 0.37 point better than that of American Michelle Kwan, who finished out of the top three for the first time since 1995. Kwan fell on a triple salchow, and her other jumps did not match the more energized efforts of her rivals.

Stéphane Lambiel of Switzerland won the men's gold medal, the first of his

At the world figure-skating championships in Moscow in March, Tatyana Totmyanina and Maksim Marinin of Russia execute a spectacular lift in the free-skating program that secured their second straight pairs title.

career in a major competition. His victory owed less to a program that was not without errors than to the late withdrawal of defending champion Yevgeny Plushchenko of Russia. Plushchenko, a three-time world champion, pulled out of the competition because of a groin injury. Lambiel's score was almost 17 points better than that of Jeffrey Buttle, who won the silver medal for Canada. American Evan Lysacek made his world championships debut at age 20 memorable by winning the bronze medal. Johnny Weir, the two-time U.S. champion, was bothered by an ailing foot and finished fourth.

The Russian pairs team of Tatyana Totmyanina and Maksim Marinin successfully defended their world title, taking their second consecutive gold medal. Mariya Petrova and Aleksey Tikhonov earned silver for Russia, while China's Zhang Dan and Zhang Hao took the bronze. Russia also struck gold in ice dancing when Tatyana Navka and Roman Kostomarov beat their competition for the second straight year. Tanith Belbin and Ben Agosto captured the silver medal, the first in ice dancing for a team from the United States in 20 years. Ukraine's Yelena Grushina and Ruslan Goncharov were third.

The 2005 season had looked more promising for Kwan two months earlier, when she won her ninth women's singles title at the U.S. championships in Portland, Ore. As the crowd's cheers almost drowned out the music, Kwan enjoyed a victory that tied the career record for U.S. championships held since 1937 by Maribel Vinson. Cohen had two bad jumps but hung on for second place ahead of 15-year-old Kimmie Meissner, who made history herself by landing the first triple axel in the U.S. women's nationals since 1991. In the men's competition, Weir won his second straight title, while Timothy Goebel, the bronze medalist at the 2002 Salt Lake City (Utah) Winter Olympics, finished second.

In the 2005 European championships, held January 23–27 in Turin, Italy, site of the 2006 Winter Olympics, Slutskaya skated to her sixth gold medal, equaling the career records of Germany's Katarina Witt and Norway's Sonja Henie. Susanna Pöykiö of Finland took the silver medal, the first for her country, while Yelena Lyashenko of Ukraine won the bronze. Plushchenko won his fourth European men's title, despite a spirited challenge from Brian Joubert of France, who won his second European silver. Germany's Stefan Lindemann took the bronze medal.

Speed Skating. In early February 2005 in Moscow, Anni Friesinger of Germany won her fourth world all-around speed-skating championship, while Shani Davis of the U.S. captured the men's all-around title. Friesinger was clearly the class act of the women's competition, winning the 500-, 1,500-, 3,000-, and 5,000-m races. Cindy Klassen of Canada, the 2003 world champion, won the silver medal, while three-time Olympic champion Claudia Pechstein of Germany took the bronze. Davis had a tougher time, but he won the 1,500-m race, finished second in the 500-m, and placed fifth in both the 5,000- and 10,000-m finals. Teammate Chad Hedrick won the silver medal ahead of Sven Kramer of The Netherlands with the bronze.

At the world short-track speed-skating championships in Beijing on March 11–12, South Korea's Ahn Hyun Soo won his third straight overall title. American Apolo Anton Ohno, an Olympic gold and silver medalist in 2002, got off to a rocky start, however. He was disqualified twice before making an impressive showing in the 1,000-m final, when he came from last place to win the gold in little more than 90 seconds. Ohno also took the 3,000-m final and skated a leg that helped the U.S. capture gold in the 5,000-m relay. Three weeks earlier, at the U.S. short-track championships in Milwaukee, Wis., Ohno had captured the men's overall title for the seventh time. Jin Sun Yu of South Korea won the women's overall title in Beijing.　　(RON REID)

Shani Davis of the U.S. rounds a turn in the 1,500-m final at the world all-around speed-skating championships in February. Davis won the race and added enough points at the other distances to secure the men's overall title.

RODEO

When the Professional Rodeo Cowboys Association's (PRCA's) 2005 season concluded in December, the sport witnessed an upset in the all-around cowboy championship—awarded to the cowboy with the most earnings in two or more rodeo events. Newcomer Ryan Jarrett of Summerville, Ga., dethroned reigning titleholder Trevor Brazile of Decatur, Texas, who had won the title the previous three years. Brazile faltered while Jarrett soared at the National Finals Rodeo (NFR), the 10-day title-determining competition that took place December 2–11 at the Thomas & Mack Center in Las Vegas. Jarrett competed in tie-down roping and steer wrestling and amassed $114,718 in earnings to boost his season total to $263,665. At age 21 he was the second youngest cowboy to win the all-around crown; record setter Ty Murray of Stephenville, Texas, won the first of his seven all-around awards in 1989 at age 19. Lee Graves of Calgary, Alta., a veteran NFR competitor and Canadian national champion in steer wrestling, emerged as the runner-up to Jarrett in the all-around title chase. The Canadian did not return home empty-handed, however; his total earnings in steer wrestling ($206,415) established a new record in the event. The last Canadian to win the steer-wrestling championship was Blaine Pederson of Amisk, Alta., who claimed the honour in 1994.

PRCA ProRodeo Hall of Fame inductee Fred Whitfield of Hockley, Texas, with earnings of $168,782 for the year, added another award to his list of professional accomplishments,

staving off fellow Texan Cody Ohl by a mere $4,000 on the closing day to capture his seventh tie-down roping championship. Whitfield ended the season just one title shy of the all-time record for tie-down roping set by Dean Oliver in the 1960s. Other repeat champions were Will Lowe of Canyon, Texas, and Kelly Kaminski of Bellville, Texas. Lowe, the top money earner in bareback riding with $185,486, handily defeated his nearest rival, Kelly Timberman of Mills, Wyo., by a margin of nearly $20,000. Kaminski, who led going into the barrel-racing competition, was challenged in the early rounds by NFR first timer Shali Lord of Lamar, Colo., who captured three successive early rounds. Kaminski, however, placed among the money winners in 9 of 10 rounds and banked season earnings of $191,702. First-time world champions in the remaining events included saddle-bronc rider Jeffery Willert of Belvidere, S.D. ($278,169), team ropers Clay Tryan of Billings, Mont., and Patrick Smith of Midland, Texas ($167,204 each), and bull rider Matt Austin of Wills Point, Texas ($320,766). Austin's total broke the all-time single-season earning record of $297,896 set by Murray in 1993.   (GAVIN FORBES EHRINGER)

ROWING

Australia, New Zealand, and Great Britain were the top nations at the 2005 Fédération Internationale des Sociétés d'Aviron (FISA) world rowing championships, held August 29–September 4 on the Nagara River in Gifu, Japan.

Although the region was narrowly missed by Typhoon Mawar, racing conditions were difficult, varying from tail winds to head winds on different days. Of the 56 teams competing, 27 won at least one medal. Italy took home the most medals (10), followed by the U.S. (7), but Australia and New Zealand won the most gold, with four each. The U.S., which won in men's eights at the 2004 Athens Olympics, continued its supremacy in 2005. Great Britain and New Zealand did likewise in men's coxless fours and women's double sculls, respectively. In women's eights Australia defeated the reigning Olympic champion, Romania. New Zealand's Mahe Drysdale became the new men's single sculling champion, and Yekaterina Karsten of Belarus won the women's single sculls by 3.34 sec. Five titles were decided by less than one second, and the medalists in many finals were overlapping at the finish. Germany won women's lightweight double sculls over the U.S. by 0.30 sec, with Finland just 0.25 sec behind in third place. Great Britain defeated Germany, the 2004 Olympic champion, by 0.34 sec in women's quadruple sculls, and Poland was only 0.50 sec faster than Slovenia in men's quadruple sculls. Canada's win over Denmark in women's lightweight quadruple sculls was achieved by 0.82 sec.

The ninth World Cup series was held in Munich; Eton, Eng.; and Lucerne, Switz. Titleholder Germany (153 points) continued undefeated, with Great Britain (111 points) in second place for the sixth year. Germany, with 12 medals (4 gold, 6 silver, and 2

The powerful University of Oxford Dark Blue rowing crew surges past its Light Blue opponents from the University of Cambridge to win the 151st Boat Race by two lengths on March 27.

bronze), also dominated at the FISA world junior championships in Brandenburg, Ger. A landslide of success by European countries in the 13 events was halted only by the U.S, which beat Germany by 1.67 sec in men's eights, and the defeat of Italy by New Zealand in women's single sculls. In the two closest finals, Germany lost by only fractions of a second to Romania in men's coxless fours and to Italy in men's quadruple sculls. The world under-23 championships, held in Amsterdam, were contested by 50 nations, of which 21 won medals.

At the 156th Henley Royal Regatta in England, entries from eight overseas countries won 10 trophies. American Wyatt Allen of Princeton, N.J., won the Diamond Challenge Sculls (men's singles), and the crew from Trinity College, Hartford, Conn., completed a second success for the U.S. in the Temple Challenge Cup (college eights). Ireland was also a double winner in the men's quadruple sculls and the intermediate coxless fours. Germany's Dortmund Rowing Centre took the Grand Challenge Cup (top men's eights). The quadruple sculls champions were Poland in the Queen Mother Challenge Cup (men), Ukraine (women), and Australia (junior). Former world champion Rumyana Neykova of Bulgaria was victorious in the women's single sculls.

In the 151st University Boat Race, Oxford fielded the heaviest crew of all time, averaging 15 stone 6.5 lb (98.2 kg, or 216.5 lb). The Cambridge crew averaged a stone and a half (about 9.5 kg, or 21 lb) lighter. Winning by two lengths, Oxford became the fastest successful Dark Blue crew in history and reduced the Cambridge lead in the series to 78–72 with one dead heat. Later in the year one of the oldest sculling races in the world—Doggett's Coat and Badge Race—took place on the River Thames from London Bridge to Cadogan Pier in Chelsea for the 291st time since 1715.   (KEITH L. OSBORNE)

SAILING

In 2005 the International Sailing Federation's new president, Göran Petersson, a veteran sailor and competition judge, completed his first full year in office, but the big story was how technology dramatically influenced sailing during the year. Records fell quickly in offshore competition as boats using Canting Ballast Twin Foil (CBTF) designs joined the races. There were also failures in the evolving technology,

© Stephen Hird/Reuters/Corbis

Ellen MacArthur's trimaran **B & Q** *is escorted into Falmouth Harbour in Cornwall, Eng., on February 8 at the conclusion of the English yachtswoman's record-setting solo sail around the world.*

however, and some boats had to be abandoned when they lost their keels. Hull and rig technology followed aircraft-manufacturing practice in the use of exotic composite structures. The challenge remained in finding the right balance between strength and weight and in marrying the canting keel to the yacht. More foil-borne dinghies were evident, and one captured a world championship against conventional boats (in the Moth class). In April a highly modified sailboard raised the bar for fastest sailboat in the world when Finian Maynard of Ireland clocked 48.7 knots.

In round-the-world competition, several new records were set. In a fully crewed giant catamaran, Bruno Peyron of France circumnavigated in just over 50 days (slicing almost 8 days off the previous record) and in the process sailed 706.2 nm (nautical miles; 1 nm = 1.85 km) in 24 hours. Britain's Dame Ellen MacArthur (*see* BIOGRAPHIES) established a new single-handed nonstop record of 71 days 14 hr 18 min 33 sec in a trimaran. Twenty entries in Open 60 monohulls started the Vendée Globe race in November 2004, and 13 finished the race in 2005 after numerous retirements along the way. Vincent Riou came first in 87 days 10 hr 47 min 55 sec. The last finisher, Karen Leibovici, arrived 39 days later.

In late May, 19 large yachts and the tall ship *Stad Amsterdam* began the Rolex Transatlantic Challenge Race from New York Harbor to the Lizard in England, attempting to break the record set in 1905 by the schooner *Atlantic*. The boats had a challenging sail across, and six broke the record. Two canting-keel speedsters led the way and shared the honours; *Mari-Cha IV* crossed first in 10 days, but *Maximus* was declared the winner on corrected time. Seventeen of the starters eventually made it to Cowes, Isle of Wight, although the chartered tall ship had to use its engine in order to keep up and make its next charter window.

The America's Cup spectacle, under way in Valencia, Spain, was attracting 12 teams from 10 countries, including newcomers South Africa and China. Although the official regatta against defending champion Switzerland was scheduled for 2007, activity among the potential challengers continued. The Admiral's Cup was canceled in 2005 by its organizer because of a lack of entries. This was largely due to the transition that was taking place in the choice of handicapping systems. With two systems (IMS and IRC) vying for acceptance, organizers were forced to choose one or the other and in so doing drove half the fleet away. IRC was employed in the U.S. at several major regattas in 2005 with mixed results, but it appeared to be gaining adherents all over the world and might become the system of choice in 2006.

Although the 2004 Sydney–Hobart race was tough, with nearly half the fleet of 116 retired and one of the three big CBTF boats capsized and abandoned, the 2005 race went smoothly. On Dec. 28, 2005, *Wild Oats XI* completed the first "treble" since *Rani* won the inaugural race in 1945. *Wild Oats*, an Australian super maxi under the direction of skipper Mark Richards, claimed line honours (as the first boat to finish), set a race record, and was confirmed as the IRC handicap winner. (JOHN B. BONDS)

SKIING

Alpine Skiing. American Bode Miller (*see* BIOGRAPHIES) won the first 3 races of the Alpine skiing 2004–05 World Cup season—the first skier to do so in the 39-year history of the tour—and 6 of the first 10 events en route to capturing the World Cup overall crown in 2005. He was the first American skier to win a World Cup overall title since Phil Mahre in 1983. Miller also took the World Cup supergiant-slalom (super-G) title and was the gold medalist in downhill and super G at the world championships in Bormio, Italy. For the third straight season, Miller competed in every tour event, running his historic streak to 111 consecutive World Cup races.

Miller dominated from the start of the season, just holding off Austrian Benjamin Raich for the overall title. Raich, who finished every race in which he competed, chipped away at Miller's points lead late in the season. Miller, however, turned up the heat at the World Cup finals, winning one race and finishing second in two others. Raich finished 194 points off Miller's overall total but skied consistently well enough to earn the slalom and giant slalom (GS) World Cup titles. At the world championships, while Miller won the two speed events but failed to finish in the other events, Raich left with four medals, including gold in slalom and combined. Austrian Hermann Maier reached another milestone in his glittering career when he claimed his 50th World Cup victory. The win moved him into a tie with Italy's Alberto Tomba for second place on the all-time victory list behind Ingemar Stenmark of Sweden, who retired in 1989 with 86 World Cup wins.

The women's World Cup points race was contested by Anja Pärson of Sweden and Croatian superstar Janica Kostelic. At season's end,

Pärson defended her 2004 overall championship by a mere three points. Her number of victories dropped from 11 in 2004 to 4 in 2005, but she had seven other top-three results. Austrian Renate Götschl earned her second consecutive downhill title, while teammate Michaela Dorfmeister won her first super-G crown. Rising Finnish star Tanja Poutiainen won both the slalom and GS titles. At the world championships in Bormio, it was Kostelic and Pärson battling again in each race—Kostelic won three gold medals (slalom, combined, and downhill), while Pärson took two titles (super G and GS).

Nordic Skiing. Norwegian Marit Bjørgen dominated the 2004–05 season in women's cross-country skiing with a stunning display of speed, technique, and power. She won 10 of 22 races, including sprints in both classic and free technique as well as distance events, en route to taking the overall title by an overwhelming 569 points. At the Nordic world championships in Oberstdorf, Ger., Bjørgen won five medals but somehow failed to qualify for the sprint final. For the men, Germany's Axel Teichmann jumped out to a lead early in the season, winning three of his first four World Cup races, and then held on to bring home the overall

Bode Miller of the U.S. becomes airborne in the final of the men's supergiant slalom at the world Alpine ski championships in January. Miller won the gold medal by 0.14 sec.

AP/Wide World Photos

title by 68 points over Frenchman Vincent Vittoz.

In ski jumping, Finland's Janne Ahonen won 11 of the first 13 World Cup meets—and a record 12 overall—to claim his second straight World Cup title. In 2004 he had won by 10 points over Norway's Roar Ljøklsøy, and in 2005 he beat the Norwegian, who had two wins and eight other top-three finishes, by 275 points. In Nordic combined another Finn, Hannu Manninen, breezed to his second title in a row, this one by nearly 400 points over former champion Ronny Ackermann of Germany, who nonetheless secured two individual golds and a team silver at the world championships.

Freestyle Skiing. American Jeremy Bloom, the 2002 World Cup freestyle moguls champion, caught fire in 2004–05 at midseason, stringing together a record six consecutive wins to earn his second World Cup moguls crown. Meanwhile, aerialist Jeret Peterson of the U.S. won the first three events of his career en route to seizing his first aerials World Cup title. On the women's scene, Canadian Jennifer Heil won the moguls title for a second straight season, while Li Nina of China took the women's aerials title.

At the freestyle world championships, held in Ruka, Fin., Americans Hannah Kearney, a four-time world juniors champion, and Nate Roberts won the moguls gold medals. Another American, Toby Dawson, surged to victory in dual moguls, while Heil won the women's duals title. In the aerials competition, it was 2004 World Cup champion Steve Omischl of Canada and Li taking the gold medals.

Snowboarding. Snowboard cross (SBX) was scheduled to be the new snowboarding event at the 2006 Winter Olympics in Turin, Italy, and there was plenty of attention paid to the sport at the 2005 snowboard World Cup and world championships. Frenchman Xavier Delerue won the men's World Cup title in SBX, while Austrian Doresia Krings was the women's champion. At the world championships in Whistler, B.C., Americans Seth Wescott and Lindsey Jacobellis were the gold medalists.

Swiss riders Philipp Schoch and Daniela Meuli won their respective World Cup parallel titles; at the world championships,

Canadian Jasey Jay Anderson fired up the home crowd by winning both the men's parallel giant slalom (PGS) and parallel slalom (PSL), while Austrian Manuela Riegler was the women's PGS champion. Meuli took the women's gold medal in PSL. On the World Cup tour, Mathieu Crepel of France was the men's halfpipe champion, and Mero Narita of Japan was the women's halfpipe winner. In Whistler, Finland's Antti Autti won gold in both the halfpipe and the men-only big air events, while French veteran Doriane Vidal took gold in the women's halfpipe.

(PAUL ROBBINS)

SQUASH

The highs and lows of the squash world were not confined to the court during 2005. After the 2004 Athens Olympics, squash had appeared on the short list of five sports vying for entry into the program for 2012 were any sports to be dropped. At the International Olympic Committee meeting in July 2005 in Singapore, the IOC delegates decided that baseball and softball would be eliminated but no new sports would be added. (See Sidebar.)

In the Professional Squash Association men's tour, Frenchman Thierry Lincou took over the top ranking at the beginning of 2005 and—despite notching up only one title, the Pakistan Open—retained the top spot for the entire year. Australian Anthony Ricketts returned to form after knee surgery and won the Tournament of Champions in New York City in February and the British Open title in October. Former world champion Jonathon Power of Canada showed a strong resurgence and captured five titles. England's Peter Nicol, another former world titleholder, won two events, and the other top English players, Lee Beachill and James Willstrop, secured the U.S. Open crown and the Qatar Classic, respectively.

At the World Open, held in Hong Kong in December, Egyptian left-hander Amr Shabana won the event for the second time. The majority of players then decamped to Islamabad, Pak., for the men's world team championship. The top two seeds, England and Egypt, contested the final, with England coming out on top to regain the trophy that it had last held in 1997.

The Women's International Squash Players Association Tour saw the balance of power shifting during the year. Australian Rachael Grinham lost the

World Games and the Quest for Olympic Status

The seventh World Games, held in Duisburg, Ger., July 14–24, 2005, was an international event that drew some 500,000 spectators and featured a diverse palette of more than 30 sports in six categories: artistry and dance sports, precision sports, trend sports, martial arts, ball sports, and strength sports. The individual events contested ranged from bodybuilding and mountaineering to bowling and waterskiing. Russia and Germany tied in the overall medal count with 57 medals each, though Russia won more gold (27).

Held every four years in the year following the Summer Olympic Games—and with the support of the International Olympic Committee (IOC)—the World Games were created in 1981 to help celebrate the Olympic movement while allowing non-Olympic sports to have their own elite international competition. Some events, such as triathlon and beach volleyball, were later accepted into the Olympics, while others, such as rugby and tug-of-war, were former Olympic sports.

In order for a sport to be included in the Olympic program, it must be voted into the program seven years prior to the Games in which it would appear. To be eligible, a sport needs to be under the control of an international sports federation (IF) that is responsible for the integrity of the sport on the international level and is recognized by the IOC. The IFs can petition the IOC to become official Olympic sports. They are evaluated on the following principles: history of the sport, worldwide reach, popularity, image, athletes' health and welfare, development of the IF, and venue costs. Each sport in the Games is later reevaluated to make sure that it appeals to Olympic fans.

Four sports contested in the 2005 World Games—karate, roller sports, rugby, and squash—vied to be added to the program for the 2012 Olympics in London. IOC members cast their ballots during the 117th IOC Session, held in July in Singapore. Since the IOC eliminated baseball and softball from the 2012 Games, supporters of the five candidate sports (the four World Games sports and golf) were optimistic. Only squash and karate advanced past the initial vote, gaining the 50% of the preliminary votes needed to be considered, but on the second vote neither sport gained the necessary two-thirds majority to be included in the 2012 Games. After the 2008 Olympics in Beijing, each sport would have the opportunity to come up again for an IOC vote into the Olympic program.

(JANELE M. URBANSKY; JULIE URBANSKY)

number one spot to Dutch player Vanessa Atkinson, who won the Qatar Classic at the end of November. Malaysian Nicol David, however, stole the limelight by taking six tour titles, including the British Open, before becoming the first Asian woman to win the World Open, beating Grinham in the final in Hong Kong in December. This win took David into the number one spot going into 2006.

(ANDREW SHELLEY)

SWIMMING

In 2005 swimming superstars Ian Thorpe of Australia and Amanda Beard of the U.S. decided to skip the entire year of competition—Thorpe to focus on his burgeoning commercial empire and Beard to concentrate on her budding acting and modeling career. Their absence was scarcely noticed, however, as 11 world long-course records were set, 9 of them in July at the 11th Fédération Internationale de Natation (FINA) world championships, held in Montreal. Records held by Thorpe and Beard were among those to fall.

The American men and Australian women dominated the competition in Montreal. The U.S. claimed the overall team title with a total of 32 medals (15 gold, 11 silver, and 6 bronze). Australia was a strong second with 22 medals (13 gold, 5 silver, and 4 bronze). Swimmers from 12 countries earned gold medals, and 24 countries had at least one medalist. Though eight athletes won

Grant Hackett of Australia turns toward victory in the 1,500-m freestyle final at the Australian national swimming championships in March. Hackett later won three events, including the 1,500 m, at the world championships and was named male World Swimmer of the Year.

two individual events apiece, Australia's Grant Hackett was the only swimmer to win three events. Hackett took the 400-m freestyle (3 min 42.91 sec), 800-m freestyle (7 min 38.65 sec), and 1,500-m freestyle (14 min 42.58 sec) and led from the first stroke to the last in every race. His performance in the 800 m broke by 0.51 sec the previous world record, set by Thorpe at the 2001 world championships. With his win in the 1,500 m, Hackett became the only swimmer ever to win the same event in four consecutive world championships. It was also his 7th individual world championship gold medal—more than any other swimmer in history. At year's end Hackett was named by *Swimming World* magazine as the male World Swimmer of the Year, just edging Aaron Peirsol of the U.S.

Peirsol took the 100-m and 200-m backstroke events in Montreal, lowering his own world record to 1 min 54.66 sec in the latter race. Brendan Hansen of the U.S. renewed his credentials as the world's fastest breaststroker by taking the 100-m and 200-m events. Meanwhile, another American, Michael Phelps, the star of the 2004 Athens Olympics, passed up two events in Montreal in which he held the world record—the 200-m butterfly and 400-m medley—to try to extend his dominance to two new events. The experiment proved less than spectacular, however, as Phelps finished seventh in the 100-m freestyle and failed to qualify for the 400-m freestyle final. He nevertheless emerged from Montreal with come-from-behind victories in the 200-m medley and 200-m freestyle. Rounding out the 10-victory performance by the

American men, Ian Crocker stopped the clock in the 100-m butterfly in the world-record time of 50.40 sec.

Roland Schoeman of South Africa broke the world record in the 50-m butterfly twice in two consecutive days in Montreal. He ultimately clocked 22.96 sec in the event. The explosive Schoeman also won the 50-m freestyle in 21.69 sec, just five-hundredths of a second off Russian Aleksandr Popov's world standard.

In the women's competition, Australia's Leisel Jones broke Beard's world record in the 200-m breaststroke, finishing in 2 min 21.72 sec, and edged American Jessica Hardy to claim another world title in the 100-m breaststroke final (though Hardy had scored her own world record of 1 min 6.20 sec in the semifinals). Jones's performance earned her *Swimming World*'s female World Swimmer of the Year honours. Hardy also finished second behind Australian Jade Edmistone's world-record time of 30.45 sec in the 50-m breaststroke. Distance phenomenon Kate Ziegler of the U.S. secured wins in the 800-m and 1500-m freestyle races. Zimbabwe's Kirsty Coventry upset American Natalie Coughlin to win the 100-m backstroke in 1 min 0.24 sec before cruising to a second gold medal in the 200-m backstroke. Katie Hoff of the U.S. staked her claim as the world's most versatile female swimmer with victories in the 200-m and 400-m individual medley.

Otylia Jedrzejczak of Poland lowered her own world record in the 200-m butterfly to 2 min 5.61 sec, finishing just four-hundredths of a second ahead of Jessicah Schipper of Australia. The

thrilling finish was marred by controversy, however, as television replays seemed to show Jedrzejczak touching the wall with one hand instead of two as required under FINA rules. Nevertheless, officials failed to call the apparent transgression, and FINA rejected the Australian protest that requested that videotapes be used to determine the legality of Jedrzejczak's finish. On October 1 Jedrzejczak was seriously injured in an auto accident that claimed the life of her brother and put her future in swimming in doubt.

In the open-water competition at Montreal, Dutch star Edith Van Dijk ended her career in spectacular fashion. After more than five hours of swimming, the 32-year-old Van Dijk won the 25-km event by a mere three-tenths of a second. She had a much easier time winning the 10-km race, and she took bronze in the 5-km event, which was won by Russian teenager Larisa Ilchenko. Van Dijk planned to retire at the end of the season. Among the men, Thomas Lurz of Germany and 17-year-old Chip Peterson of the U.S. shared top honours. Peterson, swimming in his first major international meet, nipped Lurz in the 10-km race and finished second to the German in the 5-km contest. Spain's David Meca took the 25-km event.

FINA made several rule changes during the year, including the decision to allow breaststrokers to take one dolphin kick following the start of a race and after each turn. Even more controversial was the governing body's decision to require athletes to advertise FINA corporate sponsors on their swim caps and on the bibs worn over their national team uniforms. The move prompted complaints from several swimmers. The issue was expected to be resolved in 2006.

Four short-course world records were broken during 2005. Lisbeth Lenton of Australia set new marks in the 100-m freestyle (51.70 sec) in August and the 200-m freestyle (1 min 53.29 sec) in November. Sweden's Anna-Karin Kammerling lowered her own 50-m butterfly record to 25.33 sec, while in men's competition, Schoeman and Ryk Neethling of South Africa both shattered the 100-m medley mark, with Neethling establishing a new standard of 51.52 sec.

Diving. China won gold in 5 of the 10 diving events contested at the FINA world championships, but the Chinese divers were no longer seen as invincible. Canada captured three golds in Montreal, and the U.S. and Russia each earned one. Divers from 10 countries won at least one medal, with China leading the way with 12.

Blythe Hartley gave Canada its first gold medal of the championships with a dominating performance on the women's 1-m springboard. Guo Jingjing and Wu Minxia finished first and second, respectively, in the 3-m event. Laura Wilkinson of the U.S. won the 10-m platform event in a contest marred by numerous blown dives. Wilkinson, the Olympic champion in 2000, led through all three rounds. The Chinese dominated both women's synchronized events. Li Ting

and Guo Jingjing teamed up to take the 3-m springboard crown with 349.80 points, more than 30 ahead of Germany. In the 10-m platform, Jia Tong and Yuan Peilin—aged 15 and 14, respectively—breezed to victory with 351.60 points.

Canada's Alexandre Despatie won both of the men's springboard events with brilliant performances. In the 1-m competition, he outclassed the field with 489 points. His victory in the 3-m event was even more stunning as he tallied a record 813.60 points. In an exciting 10-m platform contest, China's Hu Jia came from behind on the final dive to overtake Cuba's José Guerra and win with a score of 698.01. Teenagers Wang Feng and He Chong scored a decisive victory for China in the men's 3-m synchronized event. Russia won its only gold when Dmitry Dobroskok and Gleb Galperin pulled away on the final two dives to take the 10-m synchronized crown.

Synchronized Swimming. At the FINA world championships, Russia managed to surpass its dominant performances in synchronized swimming at the 2004 Olympics and at the 2003 world championships. Led by Anastasiya Davydova and Anastasiya Yermakova, the Russians won three of the four gold medals in Montreal and added a silver. Davydova and Yermakova, winners of the duet competition in 2003, claimed the world title once again, easily besting second-place Spain and third-place

Japan. The Russians collected their two additional titles in the team and free routine events. Only France's Virginie Dedieu was able to prevent a clean sweep by the Russians. She scored seven perfect 10s and three 9.9s en route to becoming the first synchronized swimmer to repeat as world champion in the solo competition.

(PHILLIP WHITTEN)

TENNIS

In 2005 Roger Federer (*see* BIOGRAPHIES) dominated men's tennis with grace, panache, and strategic acumen and was the game's top player for the second year in a row. The Swiss stylist captured 11 of the 15 tournaments in which he played, made it to the quarterfinals or beyond in every event he entered, and finished the year with $6,137,018 in winnings. Spain's Rafael Nadal—a left-hander with unflagging competitive spirit and superbly crafted topspin ground strokes—surged to number two in the world, matching Federer's feat of capturing 11 tournament titles.

Among the women, the four Grand Slam tournaments were controlled by players from only two nations. Sisters Serena and Venus Williams of the U.S. prevailed at the Australian Open and Wimbledon, respectively, while Belgians Justine Henin-Hardenne and Kim Clijsters secured the top honours at the French and U.S. opens, respectively. American Lindsay Davenport was the number one ranked woman for the year for the fourth time in her career, but number two ranked Clijsters made the most prize money of any female player ($3,983,654), won nine events, and was named the International Tennis Federation's women's world champion.

Australian Open. Russia's Marat Safin collected his second career Grand Slam singles championship, coming through at a major event for the first time since the 2000 U.S. Open. Safin, the number four seed, ousted number three seed Lleyton Hewitt 1–6, 6–3, 6–4, 6–4 in the first evening final at the event. Hewitt made a valiant attempt to become the first Australian man since Mark Edmondson in 1976 to take the title, but he could not exploit a 4–1 lead in the third set as Safin overwhelmed him in the latter stages of the contest. Safin's mightiest effort was in the semifinals; in a magnificent 4-hour 28-minute epic that ended at 12:35AM on his 25th birthday, Safin saved a match point in the fourth-set tiebreaker and contrived

At the world championships in Montreal in July, Canadian diver Alexandre Despatie rotates in midair in the 1-m springboard semifinals. The 20-year-old Despatie added the gold medal to the one he had already earned in the 3-m springboard competition.

© Robyn Beck—AFP/Getty Images

an astonishing 5–7, 6–4, 5–7, 7–6 (7), 9–7 triumph over defending champion Federer.

Serena Williams—seeded seventh—staged two stirring comeback matches to capture her second Australian and seventh Grand Slam championship. Facing Mariya Sharapova of Russia in the semifinals, Williams was down 3–5 in the final set. Sharapova served for the match at 5–4, but Williams cast aside three match points against her with audacious shot making to win 2–6, 7–5, 8–6. Then in the final against the top-seeded Davenport, Williams swept the last nine games for a 2–6, 6–3, 6–0 victory.

French Open. Federer had lost only one match since his Australian Open setback against Safin, and many knowledgeable observers believed that he was primed to rule at Roland Garros for the first time. Nadal was simply too confident and consistent on the slow clay courts, however, and the charismatic Spaniard took the trophy. In an eagerly awaited semifinal, Nadal's slow-court instincts and impeccable counterattacking methodology were too much for the world's top-ranked player. Nadal, who was playing in his first French Open, bested Federer 6–3, 4–6, 6–4, 6–3 to reach the final. It was his 19th birthday. In the final against Argentina's Mariano Puerta, Nadal was a 6–7 (6), 6–3, 6–1, 7–5 victor after confronting some precarious moments in the fourth set, when Puerta served at 5–4 and had three set points. It was Nadal's 24th straight match win and the culmination of a clay-court run that included four consecutive titles.

Henin-Hardenne needed to fight ferociously to win her second French Open and fourth Grand Slam. As with Nadal, however, the 10th-seeded Belgian was overflowing with confidence on the clay after winning three tournaments in a row en route to Paris. She lifted her season winning streak to 24 straight matches by easily dispatching a jittery Mary Pierce of France 6–1, 6–1. Pierce, the 2000 French Open winner, was thoroughly outclassed by an unerring adversary who was primed for the occasion. Henin-Hardenne's sternest test came in the fourth round against 2004 U.S. Open winner Svetlana Kuznetsova of Russia. Serving at 3–5 in the third set, Henin-Hardenne was twice down match point before escaping 7–6 (6), 4–6, 7–5 in a match that lasted 3 hours 14 minutes.

Wimbledon. A revitalized Federer—determined to record his first major win

A jubilant Venus Williams of the U.S. jumps for joy after winning her third Wimbledon women's singles tennis championship on July 2.

© Adrian Dennis/AFP/Getty Images

of the season—emerged the victor at Wimbledon for the third year straight. He conceded only one set in seven matches, cutting down the big-serving American Andy Roddick in a repeat of the 2004 final and prevailing 6–2, 7–6 (2), 6–4 with one of his finest performances of the season. The second-seeded Roddick built a 3–1 second-set lead and tried every tactic he could in an attempt to break up Federer's smooth rhythm, but it was futile.

In the women's final Venus Williams overcame Davenport in a classic encounter to win her first Grand Slam championship since the U.S. Open of 2001. In a captivating and bruising battle of American veterans, Williams held back a purposeful and daring Davenport 4–6, 7–6 (4), 9–7 in 2 hours 45 minutes, the longest women's final ever recorded in the tournament. Davenport served for the match at 6–5 in the second set and led 4–2, 40–15 in the third set, but Williams would not surrender. With Williams serving at 4–5, Davenport arrived at championship point. Williams responded emphatically with a clean backhand winner. The 14th-seeded Williams was unshakable under extreme duress, willing her way to a fifth Grand Slam title. In the tournament's biggest surprise, two-time champion Serena Williams was beaten in the third round by American Jill Craybas, the world's 85th-ranked player.

U.S. Open. In a sparkling final pitting the defending champion against a two-time former titlist, Federer came from behind to defeat 35-year-old Andre Agassi. Agassi (the oldest man to reach the final round since 39-year-old Australian Ken Rosewall was beaten by Jimmy Connors of the U.S. in 1974) put forth an honourable effort. After losing the opening set, the immensely popular Agassi took the second set and established a 4–2, 40–30 lead in the third. Federer surged back to 4–4 and then swept majestically through a tiebreaker and coasted to a 6–3, 2–6, 7–6 (1), 6–1 victory for his sixth major championship title. The second-seeded Nadal was knocked out in the third round by an inspired James Blake of the United States, who squandered a two-sets-to-love lead against Agassi in the round of 16.

Clijsters finally took her place among the elite as a major champion, claiming her first Grand Slam title by subduing Pierce 6–3, 6–1. Clijsters, forced out of action for much of 2004 by a wrist injury, had slipped to number 133 in the world early in the season but had already won six tournaments on the Women's Tennis Association (WTA) tour by the time she arrived in New York City for the season's last Grand Slam event. In their brief skirmish under the lights, the 4th-seeded Clijsters was never unduly threatened by 12th-seeded Pierce, who repeatedly made flagrant unforced errors. Clijsters removed the top-seeded Sharapova in the semifinals; Pierce upset Henin-Hardenne in the fourth round, Amélie Mauresmo of France in the quarterfinals, and Russian Yelena Dementyeva in the semifinals.

Other Events. Argentina's David Nalbandian—a former Wimbledon finalist but long an underachiever, celebrated the most significant win of his career when he halted Federer in a fifth-set tiebreaker to garner the Tennis Masters Cup title in Shanghai. Federer had won his previous 24 final-round matches since July 2003, setting a modern record with that run. Pierce fell in three high-quality sets to Mauresmo in the final of the WTA tour's season-ending championships in Los Angeles.

Croatia—led by Ivan Ljubicic and Mario Ancic—was victorious in the Davis Cup for the first time, toppling Slovakia 3–2 in the final in Bratislava, Slovakia. In the Fed Cup final, Russia, spurred on by Dementyeva and Anastasiya Myskina, defeated France 3–2 at Roland Garros.   (STEVE FLINK)

TRACK AND FIELD SPORTS (ATHLETICS)

The International Association of Athletics Federations (IAAF) world outdoor championships highlighted the schedule in 2005 as four world records were set and a young American team collected a record 14 gold medals. Ethiopian runners and Russian field-event athletes dominated the season in setting records.

World Outdoor Championships. For its 10th staging, on August 6–14, the world outdoor championships returned to Helsinki, where the first edition of the meet had been held 22 years earlier. Cold rainstorms challenged athletes at times and forced the rescheduling of some finals. Justin Gatlin of the U.S., the 100-m champion at the 2004 Athens Olympics, won a sprint double in the 100 m and 200 m in Helsinki. His 9.88-sec winning time in the 100 m led silver medalist Michael Frater of Jamaica by 0.17 second, the largest margin ever in a world championships men's 100 m. In the 200 m, Gatlin's 20.04-sec time led the U.S. to the first 1–2–3–4 sweep by one nation in a world championships event. Gatlin and his American teammates Jeremy Wariner (men's 400 m), Bershawn Jackson

Moroccan-born Rashid Ramzi, competing for Bahrain, races in the 800-m final on August 14 for the second of his two gold medals at the IAAF world outdoor championships in Helsinki.

© Francois-Xavier Marit—AFP/Getty Images

© Olivier Morin—AFP/Getty Images

Gold medalist Tirunesh Dibaba outruns fellow Ethiopian Berhane Adere in the women's 10,000-m final on August 6 at the world outdoor track championships in Helsinki; a week later Dibaba also won the 5,000-m title.

(men's 400-m hurdles), Lauryn Williams (women's 100 m), Allyson Felix (women's 200 m), Michelle Perry (women's 100-m hurdles), and Tianna Madison (women's long jump) all won gold in the first world championships finals of their respective careers.

The IAAF passed a rule during the year that extended the period of international championships ineligibility for athletes who change citizenship in future years, but two athletes who had already switched made history in 2005. Rashid Ramzi, a former Moroccan competing for Bahrain, became the first man to win a world championships 800-m/1,500-m double. In the steeplechase Saïf Saaeed Shaheen, a former Kenyan competing for Qatar, repeated his victory of 2003. Although relations between Shaheen (formerly Stephen Cherono) and Kenyan athletics officials had been acrimonious, it was the eighth straight gold medal for Kenyan-born steeplechasers.

In the men's 110-m hurdles, Ladji Doucouré's win in 13.07 sec brought France's first medal in the event. Jaouad Gharib of Morocco became the second man to defend a world championships marathon title, winning in 2 hr 10 min 11 sec. Adam Nelson of the U.S. put the shot 21.73 m (71 ft 3½ in) to end a string of second-place finishes at the previous two world championships and two Olympic Games. Battling rain and gusty winds, Bryan Clay of the U.S. took the decathlon lead in

the 400 m (the fifth event) and held it to the finish.

Nineteen-year-old Tirunesh Dibaba of Ethiopia won the first women's 5,000-m/10,000-m double in a global championships. Dibaba, whose cousin Derartu Tulu was twice Olympic champion in the 10,000 m, took the 10,000 m in only her second race at the distance. Dibaba covered the final 400 m in a stunning 58.4 sec for a final time of 30 min 24.02 sec. A week later her victory in the 5,000 m came with a world championships record of 14 min 38.59 sec that included a 58.2-sec time for the final 400 m and 28.1 sec for the last 200 m. In both events Dibaba led an Ethiopian sweep, with her sister Ejegayehu in third place. Olimpiada Ivanova of Russia won the 20-km walk in 1 hr 25 min 41 sec, cutting 41 seconds from the world record and 1 minute 11 seconds from the world championships record.

With $100,000 bonuses on offer for world records, in addition to the $60,000 prizes for all champions, Russian pole vaulter Yelena Isinbayeva (*see* BIOGRAPHIES) and javelin thrower Osleidys Menéndez of Cuba took their titles by raising their own world records. Isinbayeva won the pole vault with no misses through 4.70 m (15 ft 5 in) and then had the bar raised to 5.01 m (16 ft 5¼ in), one centimetre above her world mark, and cleared the bar on her second try by an astounding margin. Although she lightly brushed the crossbar on her way down, it stayed up.

Menéndez launched her javelin out to 71.70 m (235 ft 3 in) on her first throw, a 16-cm (6-in) improvement on her global standard. Germany's Christina Obergföll hurled a surprising 70.03 m (229 ft 9 in), a European record.

Olympic heptathlon champion Carolina Klüft of Sweden triumphed in a close battle with France's Eunice Barber, the 1999 champion. The win made Klüft the first successful defender of a world championships heptathlon title. She overcame an ankle injury to take the lead from Barber in the fifth event, the long jump. Barber narrowed Klüft's lead to 18 points with a longer javelin throw, but Klüft ran faster in the 800 m to finish 63 points ahead with a final score of 6,887 points.

International Competition. Jamaican sprinter Asafa Powell began the season with a clear intention of dethroning 100-m king Gatlin and ran a 9.84-sec race in early May. In early June Powell lost an extremely close race to Gatlin in Eugene, Ore., as both recorded a wind-aided 9.84. Powell attributed his lack of a lean at the finish line to caution over a thigh injury that he had sustained three weeks earlier, but 10 days later he stormed down the track in Athens to a new world record of 9.77 sec. An intense rivalry with Gatlin was projected for Powell, but the Jamaican's injury forced him to withdraw from competition until the London Grand Prix in late July. Ten metres into that race, which was won by Gatlin, Powell pulled up with a groin injury. He failed to finish the race and was forced to cancel the rest of his season. American Tim Montgomery, who had set the 9.78-sec 100-m record that Powell broke, had a lacklustre 2005 as a U.S. Anti-Doping Agency case alleging that he had used banned drugs dragged slowly through the international arbitration system. In December the Court of Arbitration for Sport ruled against Montgomery and his U.S. teammate Chryste Gaines, imposed a two-year ban on each, and stripped Montgomery of his record.

Ethiopian distance star Kenenisa Bekele's fiancée, Alem Techale, the 2003 world youth 1,500-m champion, died in January from a heart attack as the couple trained in the forest outside Addis Ababa. Although Bekele said that his heart was not in the 2005 season, he came within three seconds of his world record for 5,000 m at the Paris Golden League meeting in July. In Brussels in September he ran 10,000 m in 26 min 17.53 sec to cut 2.78 seconds from his world record for that distance.

In the elite Golden League series, which offered a share of a $1 million jackpot to any athlete who could win his or her events at six meetings (in Paris, Rome, Oslo, Zürich, Brussels, and Berlin), the field was narrowed quickly. After Rome only three women—100-m sprinter Christine Arron of France, 400-m hurdler Lashinda Demus of the U.S., and Russian triple jumper Tatyana Lebedeva—remained in the chase. Demus lost in Oslo, and Arron was eliminated in Zürich. The 29-year-old Lebedeva, whose domination of the early season included three meets in which she surpassed 15.00 m (49 ft 2½ in), aggravated an Achilles tendon injury in the world championships qualifying trials. Although a win in Helsinki would have made her world champion for the third time in a row, she bowed out of the final in order to preserve her shot at the $1 million. Lebedeva's decision paid off richly; she kept her win streak alive through Berlin and became just the second Golden League winner (after 800-m runner Maria Mutola of Mozambique in 2003) who did not have to share the jackpot. Late in the year the IAAF announced a reduction in the number of events in its World Athletics Tour from 34 meets in 2005 to 24 in 2006. Revisions to the Golden League jackpot format were promised, but no details were announced before year's end.

Cross Country and Marathon Running. A trio of distance greats in their 30s showed that they could still win. Haile Gebrselassie of Ethiopia, who had retired from track racing after his quest for a third Olympic 10,000-m gold came up short in 2004, ran the fastest marathon of the year. In the Amsterdam Marathon in October, Gebrselassie passed through the half-marathon in 1 hr 2 min 3 sec in an aggressive attack on Paul Tergat's marathon world record (2 hr 4 min 54 sec). In the final 12 km, Gebrselassie slowed as he ran solo through a hindering wind to finish in a personal-best 2 hr 6 min 20 sec for his first marathon victory. Tergat ran the New York Marathon, where he waged a nail-biting battle with defending champion Hendrik Ramaala of South Africa and Olympic silver medalist Meb Keflezighi of the U.S. over the closing kilometres to snatch the win from Ramaala in the last five metres—the closest finish in race history. Tergat was timed in 2 hr 9 min 30 sec. World record holder Paula Radcliffe of the U.K. won the London Marathon in a time that only she had ever bettered, 2 hr 17 min 42 sec.

Bekele won his fourth consecutive double at the world cross country championships. Dibaba matched Bekele's short-course/long-course double in the women's races as Ethiopia took all four senior team titles, relegating archrival Kenya to a single victory in the men's junior race. (SIEG LINDSTROM)

VOLLEYBALL

In 2005 Brazil continued to show why it was the world's top-rated volleyball nation. The men's team won its fourth Fédération Internationale de Volleyball (FIVB) World League title in

Kerri Walsh (left) and Misty May-Treanor of the U.S. compete in the final of the beach volleyball world championships in Berlin in June. The duo, who were the gold medalists at the 2004 Olympics, earned their second consecutive world title.

five years, downing host Serbia and Montenegro 14–25, 25–14, 25–19, 25–16 on July 10 to capture the world's top event. Cuba edged Poland in five sets to collect the bronze medal. Ivan Milkovic of Serbia and Montenegro was named Most Valuable Player (MVP) in his nation's fourth successive World League medal performance. In the women's Grand Prix championship, staged a week later in Sendai, Japan, MVP Paula Pequeno helped Brazil beat Italy 25–20, 22–25, 25–21, 27–29, 15–7 to capture the title for a fifth time. Cuba garnered the bronze medal in the six-team round-robin final. At the $2 million Grand Champions Cup, held in November in Japan, the Brazilian men defeated all five opponents to capture the title. The U.S. and Italy finished second and third, respectively. The women from Brazil also went unbeaten in five matches, and the U.S. placed second, followed by China. Brazil's André Nascimento and Sheilla Castro were named the tournament MVPs.

The 2005 FIVB beach volleyball world championships were held in Berlin in June. Misty May-Treanor and Kerri Walsh of the U.S., the 2004 Olympic gold medalists, won their second successive world championship crown. The American duo beat Juliana Felisberta da Silva and Larissa França of Brazil 21–17, 21–17 for the title. China's Tian Jia and Wang Fei scored the bronze with a 21–13, 21–17 win over Dalixia Fernández Grasset and Tamara Larrea Peraza of Cuba. The men's final was an unexpected matchup between Brazil's Marcio Araujo and Fábio Magalhães and Sascha Heyer and Paul Laciga of Switzerland. The Brazilians won 22–20, 21–12 for their first world championship. In the all-German bronze-medal match, Julius Brink and Kjell Schneider defeated Marvin Polte and Thorsten Schoen 16–21, 21–17, 15–10. (RICHARD S. WANNINGER)

WEIGHTLIFTING

The 2005 International Weightlifting Federation world championships were held in Doha, Qatar, on November 9–17, together with the IWF's centenary celebration. A total of 281 athletes (169 men and 112 women) from 70 countries entered the championships. In the eight men's and seven women's body-weight categories, 45 overall medals (combined snatch and clean and jerk) were awarded to athletes from 16 countries. A total of 54 world records were set in both men's

and women's competitions: 26 at the senior level and 28 at the junior.

In the women's events, China topped the medal rankings with seven (four gold, two silver, and one bronze), followed by Russia (six medals) and Thailand (five). South Korea won one gold medal. The U.S. and the Dominican Republic each won a bronze. Jang Mi Ran of South Korea won the superheavyweight division, with a 300-kg (661.4-lb) overall total.

China also topped the rankings in the men's competition, with five medals (three gold and two silver), followed by Russia with four medals and Romania, Qatar, and South Korea with two each. Nine other countries each took home one medal. Hossein Rezazadeh from Iran, the reigning superheavyweight Olympic champion from the 2004 Athens Games, won the division's overall title with a 461-kg (1,016.3-lb) total result. He was the only repeat winner from Athens. (DRAGOMIR CIOROSLAN)

WRESTLING

Freestyle and Greco-Roman. Wrestling medals were contested in three disciplines—men's Greco-Roman, men's freestyle, and women's freestyle—at the 2005 Fédération Internationale des Luttes Associées world championships, held September 26–October 2 in Budapest. In men's freestyle Russia won the team competition, with four gold medals and 54 points. Cuba (39 points) placed second, and Georgia (33 points) was third. Buvaysa Saytyev of Russia, a two-time Olympic champion, won his sixth world gold medal in the 74-kg division, defeating local favourite Arpad Ritter of Hungary 3–0, 3–1 in the finals.

In women's freestyle competition Japan was the top-ranked team, with 61 points and four individual champions. Japan was followed by China (52 points) and the U.S. (42 points). American Iris Smith defeated five-time world champion Kyoko Hamaguchi of Japan to win the gold medal at 72 kg. It was Smith's second appearance at the world level and her first medal.

Host country Hungary (41 points) won the Greco-Roman team title, ahead of Russia (27 points) and Turkey (26 points). Mijail López of Cuba won his first world title in Greco-Roman competition. López hit a five-point throw in the first period of the 120-kg final and handed Mihaly Deak-Bardos of Hungary his fifth career world silver medal.

AFP/Getty Images

Sumo yokozuna *Asashoryu acknowledges cheers after winning the Aki Basho in September. Asashoryu dominated all six* basho *in 2005.*

In American collegiate wrestling Oklahoma State University captured its 33rd (and third straight) National Collegiate Athletic Association wrestling championship, with a record-tying five individual champions. The University of Michigan finished second, and the University of Oklahoma edged Cornell for third place. (ANDRÉ REDDINGTON)

Sumo. Mongolian-born *yokozuna* (grand champion) Asashoryu had another year of sumo dominance in 2005, sweeping all six of the 15-day *basho* (grand tournaments) with a record-setting 84 of a possible 90 victories. He became the first *rikishi* ("strong man") to mark seven consecutive *yusho* (championships) and achieved a perfect 15–0 record in the Hatsu (New Year's) Basho and the Natsu (summer) Basho. At midyear Bulgarian-born Kotooshu proved the only man capable of challenging Asashoryu, and in November Kotooshu became the first European to be promoted to *ozeki* (champion), breaking the record set by Asashoryu for the quickest rise to that rank.

Kotonowaka was required to retire during the Kyushu Basho in November 2005 when his master, the former *yokozuna* Kotozakura, reached mandatory retirement age. Kotonowaka inherited ownership of Kotozakura's powerful *Sadogatake beya* (sumo stable). Other notable retirements during the year included those of Asanowaka, Kotoryu, Wakanoyama, Gojoro, and Yotsukasa. (KEN COLLER)

Sporting Record

ARCHERY

FITA Outdoor World Target Archery Championships*

Year	Men's individual			Men's team	
	Winner	Points		Winner	Points
2001	Yeon Jung Ki (S.Kor.)	115		South Korea	247
2003	M. Frangilli (Italy)	113		South Korea	238
2005	**Chung Jae Hun (S.Kor.)**	**102**		**South Korea**	**244**

Year	Women's individual			Women's team	
	Winner	Points		Winner	Points
2001	Park Sung Hyun (S.Kor.)	111		China	232
2003	Yun Mi Jin (S.Kor.)	116		South Korea	252
2005	**Lee Sung Jin (S.Kor.)**	**111**		**South Korea**	**251**

*Olympic (recurve) division.

South Korea's Chung Jae Hun after winning the men's individual recurve final at the world target archery championships.

AUTOMOBILE RACING

Formula One Grand Prix Race Results, 2005

Race	Driver	Winner's time (hr:min:sec)
Australian GP	G. Fisichella (Italy)	1:24:17.336
Malaysian GP	F. Alonso (Spain)	1:31:33.736
Bahrain GP	F. Alonso (Spain)	1:29:18.531
San Marino GP	F. Alonso (Spain)	1:26:19.670
Spanish GP	K. Räikkönen (Fin.)	1:27:16.830
Monaco GP	K. Räikkönen (Fin.)	1:45:15.556
European GP	F. Alonso (Spain)	1:31:46.648
Canadian GP	K. Räikkönen (Fin.)	1:32:09.290
United States GP	M. Schumacher (Ger.)	1:29:43.181
French GP	F. Alonso (Spain)	1:31:22.233
British GP	J.P. Montoya (Colom.)	1:24:29.588
German GP	F. Alonso (Spain)	1:26:28.599
Hungarian GP	K. Räikkönen (Fin.)	1:37:25.552
Turkish GP	K. Räikkönen (Fin.)	1:24:34.454
Italian GP	J.P. Montoya (Colom.)	1:14:28.659
Belgian GP	K. Räikkönen (Fin.)	1:30:01.295
Brazilian GP	J.P. Montoya (Colom.)	1:29:20.574
Japanese GP	K. Räikkönen (Fin.)	1:29:02.212
Chinese GP	F. Alonso (Spain)	1:39:53.618

WORLD DRIVERS' CHAMPIONSHIP: Alonso 133 points; Räikkönen 112 points; Schumacher 62 points.
CONSTRUCTORS' CHAMPIONSHIP: Renault 191 points; McLaren-Mercedes 182 points; Ferrari 100 points.

National Association for Stock Car Auto Racing (NASCAR) Nextel Cup Champions*

Year	Winner
2003	M. Kenseth
2004	K. Busch
2005	**T. Stewart**

*Winston Cup until 2004.

Daytona 500

Year	Winner	Avg. speed in mph
2003	M. Waltrip	133.870
2004	D. Earnhardt, Jr.	156.345
2005	**J. Gordon**	**135.173**

Indy Car Champions*

Year	Driver
2003	P. Tracy (Can.)
2004	S. Bourdais (Fr.)
2005	**S. Bourdais (Fr.)**

*Champ Car (formerly CART) champion.

Indianapolis 500

Year	Winner	Avg. speed in mph
2003	G. de Ferran	156.291
2004*	B. Rice (U.S.)	138.518
2005	**D. Wheldon (Eng.)**	**157.603**

*Race stopped because of rain after 450 mi.

Le Mans 24-Hour Grand Prix d'Endurance

Year	Car	Drivers
2003	Bentley	T. Kristensen, R. Capello, G. Smith
2004	Audi R8	T. Kristensen, R. Capello, S. Ara
2005	**Audi R8**	**T. Kristensen, J.J. Lehto, M. Werner**

Monte-Carlo Rally

Year	Car	Driver
2003	Citroën Xsara	S. Loeb (Fr.)
2004	Citroën Xsara	S. Loeb (Fr.)
2005	**Citroën Xsara**	**S. Loeb (Fr.)**

BADMINTON

All England Open Championships—Singles

Year	Men	Women
2003	Muhammad Hafiz Hashim (Malay.)	Zhou Mi (China)
2004	Lin Dan (China)	Gong Ruina (China)
2005	**Chen Hong (China)**	**Xie Xingfang (China)**

Uber Cup (women)

Year	Winner	Runner-up
1999–2000	China	Denmark
2001–02	China	South Korea
2003–04	China	South Korea

Thomas Cup (men)

Year	Winner	Runner-up
1999–2000	Indonesia	China
2001–02	Indonesia	Malaysia
2003–04	China	Denmark

World Badminton Championships

Year	Men's singles	Women's singles	Men's doubles	Women's doubles	Mixed doubles
2001	Hendrawan (Indon.)	Gong Ruina (China)	T. Gunawan, H. Haryanto (Indon.)	Gao Ling, Huang Sui (China)	Zhang Jun, Gao Ling (China)
2003	Xia Xuanze (China)	Zhang Ning (China)	L. Paaske, J. Rasmussen (Den.)	Gao Ling, Huang Sui (China)	Kim Dong Moon, Ra Kyung Min (S.Kor.)
2005	**T. Hidayat (Indon.)**	**Xie Xingfang (China)**	**H. Bach, T. Gunawan (U.S.)**	**Yang Wei, Zhang Jiewen (China)**	**N. Widianto, L. Natsir (Indon.)**

BASEBALL

Final Major League Standings, 2005

AMERICAN LEAGUE

East Division				Central Division				West Division			
Club	W.	L.	G.B.	Club	W.	L.	G.B.	Club	W.	L.	G.B.
*New York	95	67	—	*Chicago	99	63	—	*Los Angeles	95	67	—
*Boston	95	67	3	Cleveland	93	69	6	Oakland	88	74	7
Toronto	80	82	15	Minnesota	83	79	16	Texas	79	83	16
Baltimore	74	88	21	Detroit	71	91	28	Seattle	69	93	26
Tampa Bay	67	95	28	Kansas City	56	106	43				

NATIONAL LEAGUE

East Division				Central Division				West Division			
Club	W.	L.	G.B.	Club	W.	L.	G.B.	Club	W.	L.	G.B.
*Atlanta	90	72	—	*St. Louis	100	62	—	*San Diego	82	80	—
Philadelphia	88	74	2	*Houston	89	73	11	Arizona	77	85	5
Florida	83	79	7	Milwaukee	81	81	19	San Francisco	75	87	7
New York	83	79	7	Chicago	79	83	21	Los Angeles	71	91	11
Washington	81	81	9	Cincinnati	73	89	27	Colorado	67	95	15
				Pittsburgh	67	95	33				

*Gained play-off berth.

Caribbean Series

Year	Winning team	Country
2003	Cibao Eagles	Dominican Republic
2004	Licey Tigers	Dominican Republic
2005	**Mazatlán Deer**	**Mexico**

World Series*

Year	Winning team	Losing team	Results
2003	Florida Marlins (NL)	New York Yankees (AL)	4–2
2004	Boston Red Sox (AL)	St. Louis Cardinals (NL)	4–0
2005	**Chicago White Sox (AL)**	**Houston Astros (NL)**	**4–0**

*AL—American League; NL—National League.

Japan Series*

Year	Winning team	Losing team	Results
2003	Fukuoka Daiei Hawks (PL)	Hanshin Tigers (CL)	4–2
2004	Seibu Lions (PL)	Chunichi Dragons (CL)	4–3
2005	**Chiba Lotte Marines (PL)**	**Hanshin Tigers (CL)**	**4–0**

*CL—Central League; PL—Pacific League.

BASKETBALL

NBA Final Standings, 2004–05

EASTERN CONFERENCE

Team	Won	Lost	G.B.	Team	Won	Lost	G.B.	Team	Won	Lost	G.B.
Atlantic Division				**Central Division**				**Southeast Division**			
*Boston	45	37	—	*Detroit	54	28	—	*Miami	59	23	—
*Philadelphia	43	39	2	*Chicago	47	35	7	*Washington	45	37	14
*New Jersey	42	40	3	*Indiana	44	38	10	Orlando	36	46	23
Toronto	33	49	12	Cleveland	42	40	12	Charlotte	18	64	41
New York	33	49	12	Milwaukee	30	52	24	Atlanta	13	69	46

WESTERN CONFERENCE

Team	Won	Lost	G.B.	Team	Won	Lost	G.B.	Team	Won	Lost	G.B.
Northwest Division				**Pacific Division**				**Southwest Division**			
*Seattle	52	30	—	*Phoenix	62	20	—	*San Antonio	59	23	—
*Denver	49	33	3	*Sacramento	50	32	12	*Dallas	58	24	1
Minnesota	44	38	8	L.A. Clippers	37	45	25	*Houston	51	31	8
Portland	27	55	25	L.A. Lakers	34	48	28	*Memphis	45	37	14
Utah	26	56	26	Golden State	34	48	28	New Orleans	18	64	41

*Gained play-off berth.

National Basketball Association (NBA) Championship

Season	Winner	Runner-up	Results
2002–03	San Antonio Spurs	New Jersey Nets	4–2
2003–04	Detroit Pistons	Los Angeles Lakers	4–1
2004–05	**San Antonio Spurs**	**Detroit Pistons**	**4–3**

Women's National Basketball Association (WNBA) Championship

Season	Winner	Runner-up	Results
2003	Detroit Shock	Los Angeles Sparks	2–1
2004	Seattle Storm	Connecticut Sun	2–1
2005	**Sacramento Monarchs**	**Connecticut Sun**	**3–1**

*Best-of-three final series until 2005; thereafter best-of-five series.

Division I National Collegiate Athletic Association (NCAA) Championship—Men

Year	Winner	Runner-up	Score
2003	Syracuse	Kansas	81–78
2004	Connecticut	Georgia Tech	82–73
2005	**North Carolina**	**Illinois**	**75–70**

Division I National Collegiate Athletic Association (NCAA) Championship—Women

Year	Winner	Runner-up	Score
2003	Connecticut	Tennessee	73–68
2004	Connecticut	Tennessee	70–61
2005	**Baylor**	**Michigan State**	**84–62**

World Basketball Championship—Men

Year	Winner	Runner-up
2000*	United States	France
2002	Yugoslavia	Argentina
2004*	Argentina	Italy

*Olympic champion.

World Basketball Championship—Women

Year	Winner	Runner-up
2000*	United States	Australia
2002	United States	Russia
2004*	United States	Australia

*Olympic champion.

BILLIARD GAMES

World Three-Cushion Championship*

Year	Winner
2003	S. Sayginer (Tur.)
2004	D. Jaspers (Neth.)
2005	**D. Sánchez (Spain)**

*Union Mondiale de Billard champion.

WPA World Nine-Ball Championships

Year	Men's champion
2003	T. Hohmann (Ger.)
2004	A. Pagulayan (Can.)
2005	**Wu Chia-Ching (Taiwan)**

Year	Women's champion
2002	*not held*
2004	Kim Ga Young (S.Kor.)
2005	***not held***

World Professional Snooker Championship

Year	Winner
2003	M. Williams
2004	R. O'Sullivan
2005	**S. Murphy**

BOBSLEIGH AND LUGE

Bobsleigh and Skeleton World Championships

Year	Two-man bobsleigh	Four-man/driver	Women's bobsleigh	Men's skeleton	Women's skeleton	Team
2003	A. Lange, K. Kuske (Ger.)	Germany/A. Lange	S. Erdmann, A. Dietrich (Ger.)	J. Pain (Can.)	M. Kelly (Can.)	
2004	P. Lueders, G. Zardo (Can.)	Germany/A. Lange	S. Erdmann, K. Bader (Ger.)	D. Gibson (Can.)	D. Sartor (Ger.)	Germany
2005	**P. Lueders, L. Brown (Can.)**	**Germany/A. Lange**	**S. Kiriasis, A. Schneiderheinze (Ger.)**	**J. Pain (Can.)**	**M. Pedersen (Switz.)**	

Luge World Championships*

Year	Men	Women	Doubles	Team
2003	A. Zöggeler (Italy)	S. Otto (Ger.)	A. Linger, W. Linger (Austria)	Germany
2004	D. Möller (Ger.)	S. Kraushaar (Ger.)	P. Leitner, A. Resch (Ger.)	Germany
2005	**A. Zöggeler (Italy)**	**S. Otto (Ger.)**	**A. Florschütz, T. Wustlich (Ger.)**	**Germany**

*Artificial track.

BOWLING

ABC Bowling Championships—Regular Division

Year	Singles	Score	All-events	Score
2003	R. Bahr	837	S. Kloempken	2,215
2004	J. Janawicz	858	J. Janawicz	2,224
2005	**D. Adam**	**791**	**S. Craddock**	**2,131**

WIBC Bowling Championships—Classic Division

Year	Singles	Score	All-events	Score
2003	M. Feldman	764	M. Feldman	2,048
2004	S. Smith	754	K. Adler	2,133
2005	**L. Barrette**	**774**	**L. Barrette**	**2,231**

World Tenpin Bowling Championships—Men

Year	Singles	Pairs	Triples	Team (fives)
1995	M. Doi (Can.)	Sweden	Netherlands	Netherlands
1999	G. Verbruggen (Belg.)	Sweden	Finland	Sweden
2003	M. Luoto (Fin.)	Sweden	United States	Sweden

World Tenpin Bowling Championships—Women

Year	Singles	Pairs	Triples	Team (fives)
1995	D. Ship (Can.)	Thailand	Australia	Finland
1999	K. Kulick (U.S.)	Australia	South Korea	South Korea
2003	Z. Glover (Eng.)	England	Philippines	Malaysia

PBA Tournament of Champions

Year	Champion
2002–03	J. Couch
2003–04	P. Healey, Jr.
2004–05	**S. Jaros**

PBA World Championship*

Year	Winner
2002–03	W.R. Williams, Jr.
2003–04	T. Baker
2004–05	**P. Allen**

*PBA National Championship until 2002.

BOXING

World Heavyweight Champions
No Weight Limit

WBA

John Ruiz (P.R.; 2/24/04)
Nikolay Valuev (Rus.; 12/17/05)

WBC

Vitaly Klitschko (Ukr.; 4/24/04)
  gave up title in 2005
Hasim Rahman (U.S.; 11/10/05)

IBF

Chris Byrd (U.S.; 12/14/02)

World Cruiserweight Champions
Top Weight 195 Pounds (WBC 200 Pounds)

WBA

Jean-Marc Mormeck (Fr.; 2/23/02)
  declared super champion in 2005

WBC

Wayne Braithwaite (Guyana; 10/11/02)
Jean-Marc Mormeck (Fr.; 4/2/05)

IBF

Kelvin Davis (U.S.; 5/1/04)
  stripped of title in 2005
O'Neil Bell (U.S.; 5/20/05)

Jermain Taylor (right) defeats Bernard Hopkins to become the new undisputed middleweight champion.

AP/Wide World Photos

BOXING (continued)

World Light Heavyweight Champions
Top Weight 175 Pounds

WBA

Fabrice Tiozzo (Fr.; 3/20/04)

WBC

Antonio Tarver (U.S.; 5/15/04)
    gave up title in 2004
Tomasz Adamek (Pol.; 5/21/05)

IBF

Glencoffe Johnson (Jam.; 2/6/04)
    gave up title in 2004
Clinton Woods (U.K.; 3/4/05)

World Super Middleweight Champions
Top Weight 168 Pounds

WBA

Mikkel Kessler (Den.; 11/12/04)

WBC

Markus Beyer (Ger.; 10/9/04)

IBF

Jeff Lacy (U.S.; 10/2/04)

World Middleweight Champions
Top Weight 160 Pounds

WBA

Bernard Hopkins (U.S.; 12/13/03)
    declared undisputed champion in 2003
Maselino Masoe (N.Z.; 5/1/04)
Jermain Taylor (U.S.; 7/16/05, defeated Hopkins)
    declared undisputed champion in 2005

WBC

Bernard Hopkins (U.S.; 4/14/01)
Jermain Taylor (U.S.; 7/16/05)

IBF

Bernard Hopkins (U.S.; 4/29/95)
Jermain Taylor (U.S.; 7/16/05)
    gave up title in 2005
Arthur Abraham (Arm.; 12/10/05)

World Junior Middleweight Champions
Top Weight 154 Pounds
(also called super welterweight)

WBA

Ronald (Winky) Wright (U.S.; 3/13/04)
    declared unified champion in 2004
    gave up title in 2004
Alejandro García (Mex.; 5/21/05)

WBC

Ronald (Winky) Wright (U.S.; 3/13/04)
    gave up title in 2004
Ricardo Mayorga (Nic.; 8/13/05)

IBF

Kassim Ouma (Uganda; 10/2/04)
Roman Karmazin (Rus.; 7/14/05)

World Welterweight Champions
Top Weight 147 Pounds

WBA

Ricardo Mayorga (Nic.; 3/30/02)
    declared super champion in 2003
Jose Rivera (U.S.; 9/13/03)
Cory Spinks (U.S.; 12/13/03, defeated Mayorga)
    declared undisputed champion in 2003
Zab Judah (U.S.; 2/5/05, defeated Spinks)
    declared undisputed champion in 2005
Luis Collazo (U.S.; 4/2/05, defeated Rivera)

WBC

Cory Spinks (U.S.; 12/13/03)
Zab Judah (U.S.; 2/5/05)

IBF

Cory Spinks (U.S.; 3/22/03)
Zab Judah (U.S.; 2/5/05)

World Junior Welterweight Champions
Top Weight 140 Pounds
(also called super lightweight)

WBA

Vivian Harris (Guyana; 10/19/02)
Carlos Maussa (Colom.; 6/25/05)
Ricky Hatton (U.K.; 11/26/05)
    declared unified champion in 2005

WBC

Arturo Gatti (Can.; 1/24/04)
Floyd Mayweather, Jr. (U.S.; 6/25/05)

IBF

Kostya Tszyu (Austl.; 11/3/01)
Ricky Hatton (U.K.; 6/4/05)

World Lightweight Champions
Top Weight 135 Pounds

WBA

Juan Diaz (U.S.; 7/17/04)

WBC

José Luis Castillo (Mex.; 6/5/04)
Diego Corrales (U.S.; 5/7/05)

IBF

Julio Diaz (U.S.; 5/13/04)
    gave up title in 2005
Leavander Johnson (U.S.; 6/17/05)
Jesus Chavez (U.S.; 9/17/05)

World Junior Lightweight Champions
Top Weight 130 Pounds
(also called super featherweight)

WBA

Yodsanan Nanthachai (Thai.; 4/13/02)
Vicente Mosquera (Pan.; 4/30/05)

WBC

Marco Antonio Barrera (Mex.; 11/27/04)

IBF

Erik Morales (Mex.; 7/31/04)
    stripped of title in 2004
Robbie Peden (Austl.; 2/23/05)
Marco Antonio Barrera (Mex.; 9/17/05)

World Featherweight Champions
Top Weight 126 Pounds

WBA

Juan Manuel Márquez (Mex.; 11/1/03)
    declared unified champion in 2003
    stripped of title in 2005
Chris John (Indon.; 9/26/03)
    interim champion 2003–05

WBC

Chi In Jin (S.Kor.; 4/10/04)

IBF

Juan Manuel Márquez (Mex.; 2/1/03)
    stripped of title in 2005

World Junior Featherweight Champions
Top Weight 122 Pounds
(also called super bantamweight)

WBA

Mahyar Monshipour (Fr.; 7/4/03)

WBC

Oscar Larios (Mex.; 11/1/02)
Israel Vázquez (Mex.; 12/3/05)

IBF

Israel Vázquez (Mex.; 3/25/04)

World Bantamweight Champions
Top Weight 118 Pounds

WBA

Johnny Bredahl (Den.; 4/19/02)
    gave up title in 2004
Vladimir Sidorenko (Ukr.; 2/26/05)

WBC

Veeraphol Sahaprom (Thai.; 12/29/98)
Hozumi Hasegawa (Japan; 4/16/05)

IBF

Rafael Márquez (Mex.; 2/15/03)

World Junior Bantamweight Champions
Top Weight 115 Pounds
(also called super flyweight)

WBA

José Martin Castillo (Mex.; 12/3/04)

WBC

Katsushige Kawashima (Japan; 6/28/04)
Masamori Tokuyama (Japan; 7/18/05)

IBF

Luis Pérez (Nic.; 1/4/03)

BOXING (continued)

World Flyweight Champions
Top Weight 112 Pounds

WBA

Lorenzo Parra (Venez.; 12/6/03)

WBC

Pongsaklek Wonjongkam (Thai.; 3/2/01)

IBF

Vic Darchinyan (Austl.; 12/16/04)

World Junior Flyweight Champions
Top Weight 108 Pounds

WBA

Rosendo Álvarez (Nic.; 3/3/01)
  stripped of title in 2004
Roberto Vásquez (Pan.; 4/29/05)

WBC

Jorge Arce (Mex.; 7/6/02)
  gave up title in 2005
Eric Ortiz (Mex.; 3/11/05)
Brian Viloria (U.S.; 9/10/05)

IBF

Víctor Burgos (Mex.; 2/15/03)
Will Grigsby (U.S.; 5/14/05)

World Mini-flyweight Champions
Top Weight 105 Pounds
(also called strawweight)

WBA

Yutaka Niida (Japan; 7/3/04)

WBC

Isaac Bustos (Mex.; 12/18/04)
Katsunari Takayama (Japan; 4/4/05)
Eagle Kyowa (Japan; 8/6/05)

IBF

Muhammad Rachman (Indon.; 9/14/04)

CHESS

FIDE Olympiad—Open

Year	Winner	Runner-up
2000	Russia	Germany
2002	Russia	Hungary
2004	Ukraine	Russia

FIDE Olympiad—Women

Year	Winner	Runner-up
2000	China	Georgia
2002	China	Russia
2004	China	United States

CRICKET

Cricket World Cup

Year	Result			
1996	Sri Lanka	245 for 3	Australia	241
1999	Australia	133 for 2	Pakistan	132
2003	Australia	359 for 2	India	234

Test Match Results, October 2004–September 2005

Host/Ground	Date	Scores	Result
India/Bangalore	Oct. 6–10	Austl. 474 and 228; India 246 and 239	Austl. won by 217 runs
India/Chennai	Oct. 14–18	Austl. 235 and 369; India 376 and 19 for 0	Match drawn
India/Nagpur	Oct. 26–29	Austl. 398 and 329 for 5 dec; India 185 and 200	Austl. won by 342 runs
India/Mumbai	Nov. 3–5	India 104 and 205; Austl. 203 and 93	India won by 13 runs; Austl. won series 2–1
Bangladesh/Dhaka	Oct. 19–22	Bangl. 177 and 126; N.Z. 402	N.Z. won by an innings and 99 runs
Bangladesh/Chittagong	Oct. 26–29	N.Z. 545 for 6 dec; Bangl. 182 and 262	N.Z. won by an innings and 101 runs; N.Z. won series 2–0
Pakistan/Faisalabad	Oct. 20–24	SriL. 243 and 438; Pak. 264 and 216	SriL. won by 201 runs
Pakistan/Karachi	Oct. 28–Nov. 1	SriL. 208 and 406; Pak. 478 and 139 for 4	Pak. won by 6 wickets; series drawn 1–1
Australia/Brisbane	Nov. 18–21	N.Z. 353 and 76; Austl. 585	Austl. won by an innings and 156 runs
Australia/Adelaide	Nov. 26–30	Austl. 575 for 8 dec and 139 for 2 dec; N.Z. 251 and 250	Austl. won by 213 runs; Austl. won series 2–0
India/Kanpur	Nov. 20–24	S.Af. 510 for 9 dec and 169 for 4; India 466	Match drawn
India/Kolkata	Nov. 28–Dec. 2	S.Af. 305 and 222; India 411 and 120 for 2	India won by 8 wickets; India won series 1–0
Bangladesh/Dhaka	Dec. 10–13	Bangl. 184 and 202; India 526	India won by an innings and 140 runs
Bangladesh/Chittagong	Dec. 17–20	India 540; Bangl. 333 and 124	India won by an innings and 83 runs; India won series 2–0
Australia/Perth	Dec. 16–19	Austl. 381 and 361 for 5 dec; Pak. 179 and 72	Austl. won by 491 runs
Australia/Melbourne	Dec. 26–29	Pak. 341 and 163; Austl. 379 and 127 for 1	Austl. won by 9 wickets
Australia/Sydney	Jan. 2–5	Pak. 304 and 325; Austl. 568 and 62 for 1	Austl. won by 9 wickets; Austl. won series 3–0
South Africa/Port Elizabeth	Dec. 17–21	S.Af. 337 and 229; Eng. 425 and 145 for 3	Eng. won by 7 wickets
South Africa/Durban	Dec. 26–30	Eng. 139 and 570 for 7 dec; S.Af. 332 and 290 for 8	Match drawn
South Africa/Cape Town	Jan. 2–6	S.Af. 441 and 222 for 8 dec; Eng. 163 and 304	S.Af. won by 196 runs
South Africa/Johannesburg	Jan. 13–17	Eng. 411 for 8 dec and 332 for 9 dec; S.Af. 419 and 247	Eng. won by 77 runs
South Africa/Centurion	Jan. 21–25	S.Af. 247 and 296 for 6 dec; Eng. 359 and 73 for 4	Match drawn; Eng. won series 2–1
Bangladesh/Chittagong	Jan. 6–10	Bangl. 488 and 204 for 9 dec; Zimb. 312 and 154	Bangl. won by 226 runs
Bangladesh/Dhaka	Jan. 14–18	Zimb. 298 and 286; Bangl. 211 and 285 for 5	Match drawn; Bangl. won series 1–0

CRICKET (continued)

Test Match Results, October 2004–September 2005 (continued)

Host/Ground	Date	Scores	Result
New Zealand/Christchurch	March 10–13	N.Z. 433 and 131; Austl. 432 and 135 for 1	Austl. won by 9 wickets
New Zealand/Wellington	March 18–22	Austl. 570 for 8 dec; N.Z. 244 and 48 for 3	Match drawn
New Zealand/Auckland	March 26–29	N.Z. 292 and 254; Austl. 383 and 166 for 1	Austl. won by 9 wickets; Austl. won series 2–0
South Africa/Cape Town	March 4–5	Zimb. 54 and 265; S.Af. 340 for 3 dec	S.Af. won by an innings and 21 runs
South Africa/Centurion	March 11–13	Zimb. 269 and 149; S.Af. 480 for 7 dec	S.Af. won by an innings and 62 runs; S.Af. won series 2–0
India/Mohali	March 8–12	Pak. 312 and 496 for 9 dec; India 516 and 85 for 1	Match drawn
India/Kolkata	March 16–20	India 407 and 407 for 9 dec; Pak. 393 and 226	India won by 195 runs
India/Bangalore	March 24–28	Pak. 570 and 261 for 2 dec; India 449 and 214	Pak. won by 168 runs; series drawn 1–1
West Indies/Guyana	March 31–April 4	W.Ind. 543 for 5 dec; S.Af. 188 and 269 for 4	Match drawn
West Indies/Trinidad	April 8–12	W.Ind. 347 and 194; S.Af. 398 and 146 for 2	S.Af. won by 8 wickets
West Indies/Barbados	April 21–24	W.Ind. 296 and 166; S.Af. 548 for 9 dec	S.Af. won by an innings and 86 runs
West Indies/Antigua	April 29–May 3	S.Af. 588 for 6 dec and 127 for 1; W.Ind. 747	Match drawn; S.Af. won series 2–0
New Zealand/Napier	April 4–8	N.Z. 561 and 238; SriL. 498 and 7 for 0	Match drawn
New Zealand/Wellington	April 11–14	SriL. 211 and 273; N.Z. 522	N.Z. won by an innings and 38 runs; N.Z. won series 1–0
England/London (Lord's)	May 26–28	Bangl. 108 and 159; Eng. 528 for 3 dec	Eng. won by an innings and 261 runs
England/Durham	June 3–5	Bangl. 104 and 316; Eng. 447 for 3 dec	Eng. won by an innings and 27 runs; Eng. won series 2–0
West Indies/Barbados	May 26–29	W.Ind. 345 and 371; Pak. 144 and 296	W.Ind. won by 276 runs
West Indies/Jamaica	June 3–7	Pak. 374 and 309; W.Ind. 404 and 143	Pak. won by 136 runs; series drawn 1–1
England/London (Lord's)	July 21–24	Austl. 190 and 384; Eng. 155 and 180	Austl. won by 239 runs
England/Birmingham	Aug. 4–7	Eng. 407 and 182; Austl. 308 and 279	Eng. won by 2 runs
England/Manchester	Aug. 11–15	Eng. 444 and 280 for 6 dec; Austl. 302 and 371 for 9	Match drawn
England/Nottingham	Aug. 25–28	Eng. 477 and 129 for 7; Austl. 218 and 387	Eng. won by 3 wickets
England/London (the Oval)	Sept. 8–12	Eng. 373 and 335; Austl. 367 and 4 for 0	Match drawn; Eng. won series 2–1
Sri Lanka/Colombo	July 13–16	W.Ind. 285 and 113; SriL. 227 and 172 for 4	SriL. won by 6 wickets
Sri Lanka/Kandy	July 22–25	SriL. 150 and 375 for 7 dec; W.Ind. 148 and 137	SriL. won by 240 runs; SriL. won series 2–0
Zimbabwe/Harare	Aug. 7–8	N.Z. 452 for 9 dec; Zimb. 59 and 99	N.Z. won by an innings and 294 runs
Zimbabwe/Bulawayo	Aug. 15–17	Zimb. 231 and 207; N.Z. 484	N.Z. won by an innings and 46 runs; N.Z. won series 2–0
Zimbabwe/Bulawayo	Sept. 13–16	Zimb. 279 and 185; India 554	India won by an innings and 90 runs
Zimbabwe/Harare	Sept. 20–22	Zimb. 161 and 223; India 366 and 19 for 0	India won by 10 wickets; India won series 2–0
Sri Lanka/Colombo	Sept. 12–14	Bangl. 188 and 86; SriL. 370 for 9 dec	SriL. won by an innings and 96 runs
Sri Lanka/Colombo	Sept. 20–22	SriL. 457 for 9 dec; Bangl. 191 and 197	SriL. won by an innings and 69 runs; SriL. won series 2–0

AP/Wide World Photos

Triumphant English cricketers (from left) Michael Vaughan, Kevin Pietersen, and Andrew Flintoff. Vaughan holds aloft a replica of the Ashes urn England won for beating Australia 2–1 in the five-Test series.

CURLING

World Curling Championship—Men

Year	Winner	Runner-up
2003	Canada	Switzerland
2004	Sweden	Germany
2005	**Canada**	**Scotland**

World Curling Championship—Women

Year	Winner	Runner-up
2003	United States	Canada
2004	Canada	Norway
2005	**Sweden**	**United States**

CYCLING

Cycling Champions, 2005

Event	Winner	Country
WORLD CHAMPIONS—TRACK		
Men		
Sprint	R. Wolff	Germany
Individual pursuit	R. Bartko	Germany
Kilometre time trial	T. Bos	Netherlands
Points	V. Rybin	Ukraine
Team pursuit	S. Cummings, R. Hayles, P. Manning, C. Newton	Great Britain
Keirin	T. Mulder	Netherlands
Team sprint	C. Hoy, J. Queally, J. Staff	Great Britain
Madison	M. Cavendish, R. Hayles	Great Britain
Scratch	A. Rasmussen	Denmark
Women		
Sprint	V. Pendleton	Great Britain
Individual pursuit	K. Mactier	Australia
500-m time trial	N. Tsylinskaya	Belarus
Points	V. Carrara	Italy
Scratch	O. Slyusareva	Russia
Keirin	C. Sanchez	France
WORLD CHAMPIONS—ROAD		
Men		
Individual road race	T. Boonen	Belgium
Individual time trial	M. Rogers	Australia
Women		
Individual road race	R. Schleicher	Germany
Individual time trial	K. Thürig	Switzerland
WORLD CHAMPION—CYCLO-CROSS		
Men	S. Nijs	Belgium
Women	H. Kupfernagel	Germany

Event	Winner	Country
WORLD CHAMPIONS—MOUNTAIN BIKES		
Men		
Cross-country	J. Absolon	France
Downhill	F. Barel	France
4-cross	B. Lopes	United States
Women		
Cross-country	G.-R. Dahle	Norway
Downhill	A.-C. Chausson	France
4-cross	J. Kintner	United States
MAJOR ELITE ROAD-RACE WINNERS		
Tour de France	L. Armstrong	United States
Tour of Italy	P. Savoldelli	Italy
Tour of Spain	R. Heras	Spain
Tour of Switzerland	A. González	Spain
Milan–San Remo	A. Pettacchi	Italy
Tour of Flanders	T. Boonen	Belgium
Paris–Roubaix	T. Boonen	Belgium
Amstel Gold	D. Di Luca	Italy
Liège–Bastogne–Liège	A. Vinokurov	Kazakhstan
HEW–Cyclassics Cup	F. Pozzato	Italy
San Sebastian Classic	C. Zaballa	Spain
Zürich Championship	P. Bettini	Italy
Paris–Tours	E. Zabel	Germany
Tour of Lombardy	P. Bettini	Italy
Paris–Nice	B. Julich	United States
Ghent–Wevelgem	N. Mattan	Belgium
Flèche Wallonne	D. Di Luca	Italy
Tour of Romandie	S. Botero	Colombia
Dauphiné Libéré	I. Landaluze	Spain
Tirreno–Adriatico	O. Freire	Spain

EQUESTRIAN SPORTS

The Kentucky Derby

Year	Horse	Jockey
2003	Funny Cide	J. Santos
2004	Smarty Jones	S. Elliott
2005	**Giacomo**	**M. Smith**

The Preakness Stakes

Year	Horse	Jockey
2003	Funny Cide	J. Santos
2004	Smarty Jones	S. Elliott
2005	**Afleet Alex**	**J. Rose**

The Belmont Stakes

Year	Horse	Jockey
2003	Empire Maker	J. Bailey
2004	Birdstone	E. Prado
2005	**Afleet Alex**	**J. Rose**

2,000 Guineas

Year	Horse	Jockey
2003	Refuse To Bend	P. Smullen
2004	Haafhd	R. Hills
2005	**Footstepsinthesand**	**K. Fallon**

The Derby

Year	Horse	Jockey
2003	Kris Kin	K. Fallon
2004	North Light	K. Fallon
2005	**Motivator**	**J. Murtagh**

The St. Leger

Year	Horse	Jockey
2003	Brian Boru	J. Spencer
2004	Rule of Law	K. McEvoy
2005	**Scorpion**	**L. Dettori**

Triple Crown Champions—U.S.

Year	Horse
1973	Secretariat
1977	Seattle Slew
1978	Affirmed

Triple Crown Champions—British

Year	Winner
1918	Gainsborough
1935	Bahram
1970	Nijinsky

Melbourne Cup

Year	Horse	Jockey
2003	Makybe Diva	G. Boss
2004	Makybe Diva	G. Boss
2005	**Makybe Diva**	**G. Boss**

The Hambletonian Trot

Year	Horse	Driver
2003	Amigo Hall	M. Lachance
2004	Windsong's Legacy	T. Smedshammer
2005	**Vivid Photo**	**R. Hammer**

EQUESTRIAN SPORTS (continued)

Major Thoroughbred Race Winners, 2005

Race	Won by	Jockey
United States		
Acorn Stakes	Round Pond	S. Elliott
Alabama Stakes	Sweet Symphony	J. Bailey
American Oaks Invitational	Cesario	Y. Fukunaga
Apple Blossom Handicap	Dream of Summer	P. Valenzuela
Arlington Million	Powerscourt	K. Fallon
Ashland Stakes	Sis City	E. Prado
Beldame Stakes	Ashado	J. Velazquez
Belmont Stakes	Afleet Alex	J. Rose
Beverly D. Stakes	Angara	G. Stevens
Blue Grass Stakes	Bandini	J. Velazquez
Breeders' Cup Classic	Saint Liam	J. Bailey
Breeders' Cup Distaff	Pleasant Home	C. Velasquez
Breeders' Cup Filly and Mare Turf	Intercontinental	R. Bejarano
Breeders' Cup Juvenile	Stevie Wonderboy	G. Gomez
Breeders' Cup Juvenile Fillies	Folklore	E. Prado
Breeders' Cup Mile	Artie Schiller	G. Gomez
Breeders' Cup Sprint	Silver Train	E. Prado
Breeders' Cup Turf	Shirocco	C. Soumillon
Breeders' Futurity	Dawn of War	J. Jacinto
Carter Handicap	Forest Danger	R. Bejarano
Champagne Stakes	First Samurai	J. Bailey
Cigar Mile Handicap	Purge	G. Gomez
Coaching Club American Oaks	Smuggler	E. Prado
Diana Stakes	Sand Springs	J. Velazquez
Donn Handicap	Saint Liam	E. Prado
Eddie Read Handicap	Sweet Return	A. Solis
Florida Derby	High Fly	J. Bailey
Flower Bowl Invitational	Riskaverse	J. Santos
Frizette Stakes	Adieu	J. Velazquez
Haskell Invitational	Roman Ruler	J. Bailey
Hollywood Futurity	Brother Derek	A. Solis
Hollywood Gold Cup	Lava Man	P. Valenzuela
Hollywood Starlet	Diplomat Lady	T. Baze
Hollywood Turf Cup	Pellegrino	G. Stevens
Hopeful Stakes	First Samurai	J. Bailey
Jockey Club Gold Cup	Borrego	G. Gomez
Joe Hirsch Turf Classic	Shakespeare	J. Bailey
Kentucky Derby	Giacomo	M. Smith
Kentucky Oaks	Summerly	J. Bailey
Man o' War Stakes	Better Talk Now	R. Dominguez
Matron Stakes	Folklore	E. Prado
Metropolitan Mile Handicap	Ghostzapper	J. Castellano
Mother Goose Stakes	Smuggler	E. Prado
Pacific Classic	Borrego	G. Gomez
Personal Ensign Handicap	Shadow Cast	R. Albarado
Pimlico Special	Eddington	E. Coa
Preakness Stakes	Afleet Alex	J. Rose
Queen Elizabeth II Challenge Cup	Sweet Talker	R. Bejarano
Santa Anita Derby	Buzzards Bay	M. Guidry
Santa Anita Handicap	Rock Hard Ten	G. Stevens
Santa Anita Oaks	Sweet Catomine	C. Nakatani
Secretariat Stakes	Gun Salute	C. Velasquez
Spinster Stakes	Pampered Princess	E. Castro
Stephen Foster Handicap	Saint Liam	E. Prado
Suburban Handicap	Offlee Wild	E. Prado
Travers Stakes	Flower Alley	J. Velazquez
Turf Classic	America Alive	R. Albarado
Turf Mile	Host	R. Bejarano
United Nations Handicap	Better Talk Now	R. Dominguez
Whitney Handicap	Commentator	G. Stevens
Wood Memorial Stakes	Bellamy Road	J. Castellano
Woodward Stakes	Saint Liam	J. Bailey
Yellow Ribbon Stakes	Megahertz	A. Solis

Race	Won by	Jockey
England		
One Thousand Guineas	Virginia Waters	K. Fallon
Two Thousand Guineas	Footstepsinthesand	K. Fallon
Epsom Derby	Motivator	J. Murtagh
Epsom Oaks	Eswarah	R. Hills
St. Leger	Scorpion	L. Dettori
Coronation Cup	Yeats	K. Fallon
Ascot Gold Cup	Westerner	O. Peslier
Coral-Eclipse Stakes	Oratorio	K. Fallon
King George VI and Queen Elizabeth Diamond Stakes	Azamour	M. Kinane
Sussex Stakes	Proclamation	M. Kinane
Juddmonte International Stakes	Electrocutionist	M. Kinane
Dubai Champion Stakes	David Junior	J. Spencer
France		
Poule d'Essai des Poulains	Shamardal	L. Dettori
Poule d'Essai des Pouliches	Divine Proportions	C. Lemaire
Prix du Jockey-Club	Shamardal	L. Dettori
Prix de Diane	Divine Proportions	C. Lemaire
Prix Royal-Oak	Alcazar	M. Fenton
Prix Ganay	Bago	T. Gillet
Grand Prix de Paris	Scorpion	K. Fallon
Grand Prix de Saint-Cloud	Alkaased	L. Dettori
Prix Jacques Le Marois	Dubawi	K. McEvoy
Prix Vermeille	Shawanda	C. Soumillon
Prix de l'Arc de Triomphe	Hurricane Run	K. Fallon
Prix Jean-Luc Lagardere	Horatio Nelson	K. Fallon
Ireland		
Irish Two Thousand Guineas	Dubawi	L. Dettori
Irish One Thousand Guineas	Saoire	M. Kinane
Irish Derby	Hurricane Run	K. Fallon
Irish Oaks	Shawanda	C. Soumillon
Irish St. Leger	Collier Hill	D. McKeown
Irish Champion Stakes	Oratorio	K. Fallon
Italy		
Derby Italiano	De Sica	M. Monteriso
Gran Premio del Jockey Club	Cherry Mix	L. Dettori
Germany		
Deutsches Derby	Nicaron	D. Bonilla
Grosser Preis von Baden	Warrsan	K. McEvoy
Preis von Europa	Gonbarda	F. Minarik
Australia		
Melbourne Cup	Makybe Diva	G. Boss
Caulfield Cup	Railings	G. Childs
Cox Plate	Makybe Diva	G. Boss
United Arab Emirates		
Dubai World Cup	Roses in May	J. Velazquez
Asia		
Japan Cup	Alkaased	L. Dettori
International Cup	Mummify	D. Nikolic
Canada		
Queen's Plate Stakes	Wild Desert	P. Valenzuela
Prince of Wales Stakes	Ablo	G. Olguin
Breeders' Stakes	Jambalaya	J. Jones
Canadian International Stakes	Relaxed Gesture	C. Nakatani

FENCING

World Fencing Championships—Men

| Year | Individual | | | Team | | |
	Foil	Épée	Sabre	Foil	Épée	Sabre
2003	P. Joppich (Ger.)	F. Jeannet (Fr.)	V. Lukashenko (Ukr.)	Italy	Russia	Russia
2004*	B. Guyart (Fr.)	M. Fischer (Switz.)	A. Montano (Italy)	Italy	France	France
2005	**S. Sanzo (Italy)**	**P. Kolobkov (Russia)**	**M. Covaliu (Rom.)**	**France**	**France**	**Russia**

*Olympic champions.

World Fencing Championships—Women

| Year | Individual | | | Team | | |
	Foil	Épée	Sabre	Foil	Épée	Sabre
2003	V. Vezzali (Italy)	N. Conrad (Ukr.)	D. Mihai (Rom.)	Poland	Russia	Italy
2004*	V. Vezzali (Italy)	T. Nagy (Hung.)	M. Zagunis (U.S.)	Italy	Russia	Russia
2005	**V. Vezzali (Italy)**	**D. Dmowska (Pol.)**	**A.-L. Touya (Fr.)**	**South Korea**	**France**	**United States**

*Olympic champions, except for team foil and team sabre.

FOOTBALL

FIFA World Cup—Men

Year	Result			
1994	Brazil*	0	Italy	0
1998	France	3	Brazil	0
2002	Brazil	2	Germany	0

*Won on penalty kicks.

FIFA World Cup—Women

Year	Result			
1995	Norway	2	Germany	0
1999	United States*	0	China	0
2003	Germany	2	Sweden	1

*Won on penalty kicks.

Association Football National Champions, 2004–05

Nation	League Champions	Cup Winners	Nation	League Champions	Cup Winners
Argentina	Newell's Old Boys (Opening)	Velez Sarsfield (Closing)	Mexico	Pumas (Opening)	América (Closing)
Australia	no league competition in 2005		Morocco	FAR Rabat	Raja Casablanca
Austria	Rapid Vienna	FK Austria	Nigeria	Dolphin	Dolphin
Belgium	FC Brugge	Beerschot	Northern Ireland	Glentoran	Portadown
Bolivia	Bolivar (Special)		Norway	Rosenborg	Brann
Brazil	Corinthians	Paulista	Paraguay	Cerro Porteno (Opening)	Cerro Porteno (Closing)
Bulgaria	CSKA Sofia	Levski Sofia	Peru	Cienciano (Opening)	Sporting Cristal (Closing)
Cameroon	Cotonsport	Cotonsport	Poland	Wisla	Groclin
Chile	Unión Española (Opening)	Universidad Católica (Closing)	Portugal	Benfica	Setúbal
China	Dalian Shide	Shandong	Romania	Steaua	Dinamo Bucharest
Colombia	Atlético Nacional (Opening)	Deportivo Cali (Closing)	Russia	Lokomotiv Moscow	CSKA Moscow
Costa Rica	Pérez Zeledón (Opening)	Alajuelense (Closing)	Saudi Arabia	Al-Hilal	Al-Hilal
Croatia	Hajduk Split	Rijeka	Scotland	Rangers	Celtic
Czech Republic	Sparta Prague	Banik Ostrava	Senegal	Port Autonome	AS Douanes
Denmark	Brøndby	Brøndby	Serbia & Montenegro	Partizan Belgrade	Zeleznik
Ecuador	LDU Quito (Opening)	El Nacional (Closing)	Slovakia	Artmedia	Bystrica
England	Chelsea	Arsenal	Slovenia	Gorica	Publikum
Finland	Haka	MyPa	South Africa	Kaizer Chiefs	SuperSport United
France	Lyon	Auxerre	South Korea	Suwon Samsung	Suwon Samsung
Georgia	Dinamo Tbilisi	Lokomotivi	Spain	Barcelona	Betis
Germany	Bayern Munich	Bayern Munich	Sweden	Malmö	Djurgården
Greece	Olympiakos	Olympiakos	Switzerland	Basel	Zürich
Holland	PSV Eindhoven	PSV Eindhoven	Tunisia	CS Sfaxien	ES Zarzis
Hungary	Debrecen	Matav	Turkey	Fenerbahce	Galatasaray
Ireland	Shelbourne	Longford Town	Ukraine	Shakhtar Donetsk	Dynamo Kiev
Israel	Maccabi Haifa	Maccabi Tel Aviv	United States (MLS)	DC United	Los Angeles Galaxy
Italy	Juventus	Internazionale	Uruguay	Nacional (Special)	
Japan	Yokohama F. Marinos	Tokyo Verdy 1969	Venezuela	Unión Atlético (Opening)	Unión Atlético (Closing)

UEFA Champions League

Season	Result			
2002–03	AC Milan (Italy)*	0	Juventus (Italy)	0
2003–04	Porto (Port.)	3	Monaco (Fr.)	0
2004–05	**Liverpool FC (Eng.)***	**3**	**AC Milan (Italy)**	**3**

*Won on penalty kicks.

UEFA Cup

Season	Result			
2002–03	Porto (Port.)*	3	Celtic (Scot.)	2
2003–04	Valencia (Spain)	2	Olympique de Marseille (Fr.)	0
2004–05	**CSKA Moscow (Rus.)**	**3**	**Sporting (Port.)**	**1**

*Won on "Silver Goal" in overtime.

FIELD HOCKEY

World Cup Field Hockey Championship—Men

Year	Winner	Runner-up
1994	Pakistan	Netherlands
1998	Netherlands	Spain
2002	Germany	Australia

World Cup Field Hockey Championship—Women

Year	Winner	Runner-up
1994	Australia	Argentina
1998	Australia	Netherlands
2002	Argentina	Netherlands

FOOTBALL (continued)

Libertadores de América Cup

Year	Winner (country)	Runner-up (country)	Scores
2003	Boca Juniors (Arg.)	Santos FC (Braz.)	2–0, 3–1
2004	Once Caldas (Colom.)	Boca Juniors (Arg.)	0–0, 1–1, 2–0*
2005	**São Paulo (Braz.)**	**Atlético Paranaense (Braz.)**	**1–1, 4–0**

*Winner determined in penalty shoot-out.

Copa América

Year	Winner	Runner-up	Score
1999	Brazil	Uruguay	3–1
2001	Colombia	Mexico	1–0
2004	Brazil	Argentina	2–2, 4–2*

*Winner determined in penalty shoot-out.

MLS Cup

Year	Result			
2003	San Jose Earthquakes	4	Chicago Fire	2
2004	D.C. United	3	Kansas City Wizards	2
2005	**Los Angeles Galaxy**	**1**	**New England Revolution**	**0**

U.S. College Football National Champions

Season	Champion
2003–04	Louisiana State* Southern California†
2004–05	Southern California
2005–06	**Texas**

*BCS champion.   †AP champion.

Rose Bowl

Season	Result			
2003–04	Southern California	28	Michigan	14
2004–05	Texas	38	Michigan	37
2005–06	**Texas**	**41**	**Southern California**	**38**

Orange Bowl

Season	Result			
2003–04	Miami	16	Florida State	14
2004–05	Southern California	55	Oklahoma	19
2005–06	**Penn State**	**26**	**Florida State**	**23**

Fiesta Bowl

Season	Result			
2003–04	Ohio State	35	Kansas State	28
2004–05	Utah	35	Pittsburgh	7
2005–06	**Ohio State**	**34**	**Notre Dame**	**20**

Sugar Bowl

Season	Result			
2003–04	Louisiana State	21	Oklahoma	14
2004–05	Auburn	16	Virginia Tech	13
2005–06	**West Virginia**	**38**	**Georgia**	**35**

NFL Final Standings, 2005–06

AMERICAN CONFERENCE

East Division	W	L	T	North Division	W	L	T	South Division	W	L	T	West Division	W	L	T
*New England	10	6	0	*Cincinnati	11	5	0	*Indianapolis	14	2	0	*Denver	13	3	0
Miami	9	7	0	*Pittsburgh	11	5	0	*Jacksonville	12	4	0	Kansas City	10	6	0
Buffalo	5	11	0	Baltimore	6	10	0	Tennessee	4	12	0	San Diego	9	7	0
New York Jets	4	12	0	Cleveland	6	10	0	Houston	2	14	0	Oakland	4	12	0

NATIONAL CONFERENCE

East Division	W	L	T	North Division	W	L	T	South Division	W	L	T	West Division	W	L	T
*New York Giants	11	5	0	*Chicago	11	5	0	*Tampa Bay	11	5	0	*Seattle	13	3	0
*Washington	10	6	0	Minnesota	9	7	0	*Carolina	11	5	0	St. Louis	6	10	0
Dallas	9	7	0	Detroit	5	11	0	Atlanta	8	8	0	Arizona	5	11	0
Philadelphia	6	10	0	Green Bay	4	12	0	New Orleans	3	13	0	San Francisco	4	12	0

*Qualified for play-offs.

Super Bowl

	Season	Result			
XXXVII	2002–03	Tampa Bay Buccaneers (NFC)	48	Oakland Raiders (AFC)	21
XXXVIII	2003–04	New England Patriots (AFC)	32	Carolina Panthers (NFC)	29
XXXIX	**2004–05**	**New England Patriots (AFC)**	**24**	**Philadelphia Eagles (NFC)**	**21**

CFL Grey Cup*

Year	Result			
2003	Edmonton Eskimos (WD)	34	Montreal Alouettes (ED)	22
2004	Toronto Argonauts (ED)	27	British Columbia Lions (WD)	19
2005	**Edmonton Eskimos (WD)**	**38**	**Montreal Alouettes (ED)**	**35**

*ED—Eastern Division; WD—Western Division.

FOOTBALL (continued)

AFL Grand Final

Year	Result			
2003	Brisbane Lions	20.14 (134)	Collingwood	12.12 (84)
2004	Port Adelaide Power	17.11 (113)	Brisbane Lions	10.13 (73)
2005	**Sydney Swans**	**8.10 (58)**	**West Coast Eagles**	**7.12 (54)**

Rugby Union World Cup

Year	Result			
1995	South Africa	15	New Zealand	12
1999	Australia	35	France	12
2003	England	20	Australia	17

Rugby League World Cup

Year	Result			
1992	Australia	10	Great Britain	6
1995	Australia	16	England	8
2000	Australia	40	New Zealand	12

Six Nations Championship

Year	Result
2003	England*
2004	France*
2005	**Wales***

*Grand Slam winner.

GOLF

Masters Tournament

Year	Winner
2003	M. Weir (Can.)
2004	P. Mickelson (U.S.)
2005	**T. Woods (U.S.)**

United States Open Championship (men)

Year	Winner
2003	J. Furyk (U.S.)
2004	R. Goosen (S.Af.)
2005	**M. Campbell (N.Z.)**

British Open Tournament (men)

Year	Winner
2003	B. Curtis (U.S.)
2004	T. Hamilton (U.S.)
2005	**T. Woods (U.S.)**

U.S. Professional Golfers' Association (PGA) Championship

Year	Winner
2003	S. Micheel (U.S.)
2004	V. Singh (Fiji)
2005	**P. Mickelson (U.S.)**

United States Amateur Championship (men)

Year	Winner
2003	N. Flanagan (Austl.)
2004	R. Moore (U.S.)
2005	**E. Molinari (Italy)**

British Amateur Championship (men)

Year	Winner
2003	G. Wolstenholme (U.K.)
2004	S. Wilson (U.K.)
2005	**B. McElhinney (Ire.)**

United States Women's Open Championship

Year	Winner
2003	H. Lunke (U.S.)
2004	M. Mallon (U.S.)
2005	**B. Kim (S.Kor.)**

Women's British Open Championship

Year	Winner
2003	A. Sörenstam (Swed.)
2004	K. Stupples (U.K.)
2005	**Jang Jeong (S.Kor.)**

Ladies Professional Golf Association (LPGA) Championship

Year	Winner
2003	A. Sörenstam (Swed.)
2004	A. Sörenstam (Swed.)
2005	**A. Sörenstam (Swed.)**

United States Women's Amateur Championship

Year	Winner
2003	V. Nirapathpongporn (Thai.)
2004	J. Park (U.S.)
2005	**M. Pressel (U.S.)**

Ladies' British Amateur Championship

Year	Winner
2003	E. Serramia (Spain)
2004	L. Stahle (Swed.)
2005	**L. Stahle (Swed.)**

World Cup (men; professional)

Year	Winner
2003	South Africa (T. Immelman and R. Sabbatini)
2004	England (P. Casey and L. Donald)
2005	**Wales (S. Dodd and B. Dredge)**

Solheim Cup (women; professional)

Year	Result
2002	United States 15½, Europe 12½
2003	Europe 17½, United States 10½
2005	**United States 15½, Europe 12½**

Ryder Cup (men; professional)

Year	Result
1999	United States 14½, Europe 13½
2002	Europe 15½, United States 12½
2004	Europe 18½, United States 9½

American Tiger Woods hits a drive at the British Open golf championship, where he earned his second major title of 2005.

© Andrew Redington/Getty Images

GYMNASTICS

World Gymnastics Championships—Men

Year	All-around team	All-around individual	Horizontal bar	Parallel bars
2003	China	P. Hamm (U.S.)	T. Kashima (Japan)	Li Xiaopeng (China)
2004*	Japan	P. Hamm (U.S.)	I. Cassina (Italy)	V. Goncharov (Ukr.)
2005	*not held*	**H. Tomita (Japan)**	**A. Pegan (Slvn.)**	**M. Petkovsek (Slvn.)**

Year	Pommel horse	Rings	Vault	Floor exercise
2003	Teng Haibin (China)† T. Kashima (Japan)†	I. Iovchev (Bulg.)† D. Tampakos (Greece)†	Li Xiaopeng (China)	P. Hamm (U.S.)† I. Iovchev (Bulg.)†
2004*	Teng Haibin (China)	D. Tampakos (Greece)	G. Deferr (Spain)	K. Shewfelt (Can.)
2005	**Xiao Qin (China)**	**Y. Van Gelder (Neth.)**	**M. Dragulescu (Rom.)**	**D. Hypolito (Braz.)**

*Olympic champions. †Tied.

World Gymnastics Championships—Women

Year	All-around team	All-around individual	Balance beam
2003	United States	S. Khorkina (Russia)	Fan Ye (China)
2004*	Romania	C. Patterson (U.S.)	C. Ponor (Rom.)
2005	*not held*	**C. Memmel (U.S.)**	**A. Liukin (U.S.)**

Year	Uneven parallel bars	Vault	Floor exercise
2003	C. Memmel (U.S.)† H. Vise (U.S.)†	O. Chusovitina (Uzbek.)	D. Dos Santos (Braz.)
2004*	E. Lepennec (Fr.)	M. Rosu (Rom.)	C. Ponor (Rom.)
2005	**A. Liukin (U.S.)**	**Cheng Fei (China)**	**A. Sacramone (U.S.)**

*Olympic champions. †Tied.

© David Callow/Reuters

Gold medalist Alicia Sacramone of the U.S. performs her routine in the final of the world gymnastics floor-exercise competition.

ICE HOCKEY

NHL Final Standings, 2004*

EASTERN CONFERENCE

Northeast Division	W	L	T	OTL†
‡Boston	41	19	15	7
‡Toronto	45	24	10	3
‡Ottawa	43	23	10	6
‡Montreal	41	30	7	4
Buffalo	37	34	7	4

Atlantic Division	W	L	T	OTL†
‡Philadelphia	40	21	15	6
‡New Jersey	43	25	12	2
‡New York Islanders	38	29	11	4
New York Rangers	27	40	7	8
Pittsburgh	23	47	8	4

Southeast Division	W	L	T	OTL†
‡Tampa Bay	46	22	8	6
Atlanta	33	37	8	4
Carolina	28	34	14	6
Florida	28	35	15	4
Washington	23	46	10	3

WESTERN CONFERENCE

Central Division	W	L	T	OTL†
‡Detroit	48	21	11	2
‡St. Louis	39	30	11	2
‡Nashville	38	29	11	4
Columbus	25	45	8	4
Chicago	20	43	11	8

Northwest Division	W	L	T	OTL†
‡Vancouver	43	24	10	5
‡Colorado	40	22	13	7
‡Calgary	42	30	7	3
Edmonton	36	29	12	5
Minnesota	30	29	20	3

Pacific Division	W	L	T	OTL†
‡San Jose	43	21	12	6
‡Dallas	41	26	13	2
Los Angeles	28	29	16	9
Anaheim	29	35	10	8
Phoenix	22	36	18	6

*2004–05 season canceled. †Overtime losses, worth one point. ‡Qualified for 2004 playoffs.

The Stanley Cup

Season	Winner	Runner-up	Games
2002–03	New Jersey Devils	Anaheim Mighty Ducks	4–3
2003–04	Tampa Bay Lightning	Calgary Flames	4–3
2004–05	*canceled*		

World Ice Hockey Championship—Men

Year	Winner
2003	Canada
2004	Canada
2005	**Czech Republic**

World Ice Hockey Championship—Women

Year	Winner
2003	*canceled*
2004	Canada
2005	**United States**

ICE SKATING

World Figure Skating Champions—Men

Year	Winner
2003	Ye. Plushchenko (Russia)
2004	Ye. Plushchenko (Russia)
2005	**S. Lambiel (Switz.)**

World Figure Skating Champions—Women

Year	Winner
2003	M. Kwan (U.S.)
2004	S. Arakawa (Japan)
2005	**I. Slutskaya (Russia)**

World Figure Skating Champions—Pairs

Year	Winners
2003	Shen Xue, Zhao Hongbo (China)
2004	T. Totmyanina, M. Marinin (Russia)
2005	**T. Totmyanina, M. Marinin (Russia)**

World Ice Dancing Champions

Year	Winners
2003	S. Bourne, V. Kraatz (Can.)
2004	T. Navka, R. Kostomarov (Russia)
2005	**T. Navka, R. Kostomarov (Russia)**

ICE SKATING (continued)

World Ice Speed-Skating Records Set in 2005 on Major Tracks*

Event	Name	Country	Result
MEN			
500 m	Joji Kato	Japan	34.30 sec
1,000 m	Shani Davis	United States	1 min 07.03 sec
1,500 m	Shani Davis	United States	1 min 43.33 sec
	Chad Hedrick	United States	1 min 42.78 sec
3,000 m	Chad Hedrick	United States	3 min 39.02 sec
	Eskil Ervik	Norway	3 min 37.28 sec
5,000 m	Chad Hedrick	United States	6 min 09.68 sec
	Sven Kramer	Netherlands	6 min 08.78 sec
10,000 m	Carl Verheijen	Netherlands	12 min 57.92 sec
	Chad Hedrick	United States	12 min 55.11 sec
small combo	Erben Wennemars	Netherlands	146.365 points
big combo	Shani Davis	United States	149.359 points
team pursuit	Canada National Team (Arne Dankers, Steven Elm, Denny Morrison)	Canada	3 min 39.69 sec
WOMEN			
1,500 m	Cindy Klassen	Canada	1 min 53.87 sec
	Cindy Klassen	Canada	1 min 53.77 sec
	Anni Friesinger	Germany	1 min 53.22 sec
	Cindy Klassen	Canada	1 min 51.79 sec
3,000 m	Cindy Klassen	Canada	3 min 55.75 sec
small combo	Cindy Klassen	Canada	159.605 points
team pursuit	German National Team (Daniela Anschütz, Anni Friesinger, Claudia Pechstein)	Germany	2 min 56.04 sec

*May include records awaiting ISU ratification at year's end.

World Ice Speed-Skating Records Set in 2005 on Short Tracks*

Event	Name	Country	Time
MEN			
3,000 m	Mathieu Giroux	Canada	4 min 32.193 sec
5,000-m relay	Canada National Team (Charles Hamelin, François-Louis Tremblay, Steve Robillard, Mathieu Turcotte)	Canada	6 min 39.990 sec
WOMEN			
1,000 m	Wang Meng	China	1 min 30.216 sec

*May include records awaiting ISU ratification at year's end.

World All-Around Speed-Skating Champions

Year	Men	Women
2003	G. Romme (Neth.)	C. Klassen (Can.)
2004	C. Hedrick (U.S.)	R. Groenewold (Neth.)
2005	**S. Davis (U.S.)**	**A. Friesinger (Ger.)**

World Short-Track Speed-Skating Championships—Overall Winners

Year	Men	Women
2003	Ahn Hyun Soo (S.Kor.)	Choi Eun Kyung (S.Kor.)
2004	Ahn Hyun Soo (S.Kor.)	Choi Eun Kyung (S.Kor.)
2005	**Ahn Hyun Soo (S.Kor.)**	**Jin Sun Yu (S.Kor.)**

World Speed-Skating Sprint Champions

Year	Men	Women
2003	J. Wotherspoon (Can.)	M. Garbrecht-Enfeldt (Ger.)
2004	E. Wennemars (Neth.)	M. Timmer (Neth.)
2005	**E. Wennemars (Neth.)**	**J. Rodriguez (U.S.)**

© Mladen Antonov/AFP/Getty Images

Germany's Anni Friesinger speeds to victory in the 1,500-m race at the world all-around speed-skating championships.

JUDO

World Judo Championships—Men

Year	Open weights	60 kg	66 kg	73 kg
2001	A. Mikhaylin (Russia)	A. Lounifi (Tun.)	A. Miresmaeili (Iran)	V. Makarov (Russia)
2003	K. Suzuki (Japan)	Choi Min Ho (S.Kor.)	A. Miresmaeili (Iran)	Lee Won Hee (S.Kor.)
2005	**D. Van der Geest (Neth.)**	**C. Fallon (Gr.Brit.)**	**J. Derly (Braz.)**	**A. Braun (Hung.)**

Year	81 kg	90 kg	100 kg	+100 kg
2001	Cho In Chul (S.Kor.)	F. Demontfaucon (Fr.)	K. Inoue (Japan)	A. Mikhaylin (Russia)
2003	F. Wanner (Ger.)	Hwang Hee Tae (S.Kor.)	K. Inoue (Japan)	Y. Muneta (Japan)
2005	**G. Elmont (Neth.)**	**H. Izumi (Japan)**	**K. Suzuki (Japan)**	**A. Mikhaylin (Russia)**

World Judo Championships—Women

Year	Open weights	48 kg	52 kg	57 kg
2001	C. Lebrun (Fr.)	R. Tamura (Japan)	Kye Sun Hui (N.Kor.)	Y. Lupetey (Cuba)
2003	Tong Wen (China)	R. Tamura (Japan)	A. Savon (Cuba)	Kye Sun Hui (N.Kor.)
2005	**M. Shintani (Japan)**	**Y. Bermoy (Cuba)**	**Li Ying (China)**	**Kye Sun Hui (N.Kor.)**

Year	63 kg	70 kg	78 kg	+78 kg
2001	G. Vandecaveye (Belg.)	M. Ueno (Japan)	N. Anno (Japan)	Yuan Hua (China)
2003	D. Krukower (Arg.)	M. Ueno (Japan)	N. Anno (Japan)	Sun Fuming (China)
2005	**L. Decosse (Fr.)**	**E. Bosch (Neth.)**	**Y. Laborde (Cuba)**	**Tong Wen (China)**

ROWING

World Rowing Championships—Men

Year	Single sculls	Min:sec	Double sculls	Min:sec	Quadruple sculls	Min:sec	Coxed pairs	Min:sec
2003	O. Tufte (Nor.)	6:46.15	A. Hardy, S. Vieilledent (Fr.)	6:13.93	Germany	6:12.26	D. Berry, M. Rich (U.S.)	7:10.11
2004*	O. Tufte (Nor.)	6:49.30	A. Hardy, S. Vieilledent (Fr.)	6:29.00	Russia	5:56.85	M. Palmisano, M. Trombetta (Italy)	6:54.46
2005	**M. Drysdale (N.Z.)**	**7:16.42**	**I. Cop, L. Spik (Slvn.)**	**6:37.61**	**Poland**	**5:34.96**	**S. Conrad, H. Cubasch (Austl.)**	**7:16.61**

Year	Coxless pairs	Min:sec	Coxed fours	Min:sec	Coxless fours	Min:sec	Eights	Min:sec
2003	D. Ginn, J. Tomkins (Austl.)	6:19.31	United States	6:04.68	Canada	5:52.91	Canada	6:00.44
2004*	D. Ginn, J. Tomkins (Austl.)	6:30.76	Italy	6:11.53	Great Britain	6:06.98	United States	5:42.48
2005	**G. Bridgewater, N. Twaddle (N.Z.)**	**6:52.51**	**France**	**6:02.42**	**Great Britain**	**6:11.59**	**United States**	**5:22.75**

*Olympic champions, except coxed pairs and coxed fours.

World Rowing Championships—Women

Year	Single sculls	Min:sec	Coxless pairs	Min:sec
2003	R. Neykova (Bulg.)	7:18.12	C. Bishop, K. Grainger (Gt.Brit.)	7:04.88
2004*	K. Rutschow-Stomporowski (Ger.)	7:18.12	G. Andrunache-Damien, V. Susanu (Rom.)	7:06.55
2005	**Ye. Karsten (Bela.)**	**7:48.35**	**N. Coles, J. Haigh (N.Z.)**	**7:43.83**

Year	Double sculls	Min:sec	Coxless fours	Min:sec
2003	C. Evers-Swindell, G. Evers-Swindell (N.Z.)	6:45.79	United States	6:53.08
2004*	C. Evers-Swindell, G. Evers-Swindell (N.Z.)	7:01.79	France	6:36.28
2005	**C. Evers-Swindell, G. Evers-Swindell (N.Z.)**	**7:08.03**	**Australia**	**6:55.56**

Year	Quadruple sculls	Min:sec	Eights	Min:sec
2003	Australia	6:46.52	Germany	6:41.23
2004	Germany	6:29.29	Romania	6:17.70
2005	**Great Britain**	**6:09.59**	**Australia**	**5:58.10**

*Olympic champions, except coxless fours.

© Kazuhiro Nogi/AFP/Getty Images

Single sculls world champion Yekaterina Karsten of Belarus raises her fist in celebration.

SAILING (YACHTING)

America's Cup

Year	Winning yacht	Owner	Skipper	Losing yacht	Owner
1995	*Black Magic* (N.Z.)	P. Blake and Team New Zealand	R. Coutts	*Young America* (U.S.)	Pact 95 syndicate
2000	*Black Magic* (N.Z.)	Team New Zealand	R. Coutts	*Luna Rossa* (Italy)	Prada Challenge
2003	*Alinghi* (Switz.)	Alinghi Swiss Challenge	R. Coutts	*New Zealand* (N.Z.)	Team New Zealand

World Class Boat Champions, 2005

Class	Winner	Country
Etchells 22	T. Gonzales/B. Mouk/ J. Linton/D. Gonzales	United States
Europe	Xiaoying Shen	China
Finn	B. Ainslie	Great Britain
J/24	A. Kotoun	Virgin Islands
Laser	R. Scheidt	Brazil
Lightning	A. González	Chile
Mistral (men's)	N. Huguet	France
Mistral (women's)	B. Manchon	Spain
470 (men's)	N. Wilmot/M. Page	Australia
470 (women's)	M. de Koning/L. Berkhout	Netherlands
49er	R. Luka/G. Leonchuk	Ukraine
2.4 metre	N. Scandone	United States
Optimist	T. Lutz	Germany
Snipe	A. Diaz/P. Kelly	United States
Star	X. Rohart/P. Rambeau	France
Tornado	F. Echavarri/A. Paz	Spain
Yngling (women's)	S. Barkow/C. Howe/ D. Capozzi	United States
Farr 40	R. Perini	Australia

Admiral's Cup

Year	Winning team
2001	*canceled*
2003	Australia
2005	*canceled*

Transpacific Race

Year	Winning yacht	Owner
2001	*Bull*	S. Radow
2003	*Alta Vita*	B. Turpin
2005	***Rosebud***	**R. Sturgeon**

Bermuda Race*

Year	Winning yacht	Owner
2000	*Restless*	E. Crawford
2002	*Zaraffa*	S. Sheldon
2004	*Alliance*	D. Porco

*St. David's Lighthouse Trophy winner from 2002.

SKIING

World Alpine Skiing Championships—Slalom

Year	Men's slalom	Men's giant slalom	Men's supergiant	Women's slalom	Women's giant slalom	Women's supergiant
2002*	J.-P. Vidal (Fr.)	S. Eberharter (Austria)	K.A. Aamodt (Nor.)	J. Kostelic (Cro.)	J. Kostelic (Cro.)	D. Ceccarelli (Italy)
2003	I. Kostelic (Cro.)	B. Miller (U.S.)	S. Eberharter (Austria)	J. Kostelic (Cro.)	A. Pärson (Swed.)	M. Dorfmeister (Austria)
2005	**B. Raich (Austria)**	**H. Maier (Austria)**	**B. Miller (U.S.)**	**J. Kostelic (Cro.)**	**A. Pärson (Swed.)**	**A. Pärson (Swed.)**

*Olympic champions.

World Alpine Skiing Championships—Downhill

Year	Men	Women
2002*	F. Strobl (Austria)	C. Montillet (Fr.)
2003	M. Walchhofer (Austria)	M. Turgeon (Can.)
2005	**B. Miller (U.S.)**	**J. Kostelic (Cro.)**

*Olympic champions.

World Alpine Skiing Championships—Combined

Year	Men	Women
2002*	K.A. Aamodt (Nor.)	J. Kostelic (Cro.)
2003	B. Miller (U.S.)	J. Kostelic (Cro.)
2005	**B. Raich (Austria)**	**J. Kostelic (Cro.)**

*Olympic champions.

World Nordic Skiing Championships—Men

Year	Sprint	Team sprint	Double pursuit	10-km	15-km	30-km	50-km	Relay
2002*	T.A. Hetland (Nor.)			T. Alsgaard (Nor.)†‡ F. Estil (Nor.)†‡	A. Veerpalu (Est.)	C. Hoffmann (Austria)	‡M. Ivanov (Russia)	Norway
2003	T. Fredriksson (Swed.)		P. Elofsson (Swed.)		A. Teichmann (Ger.)	T. Alsgaard (Nor.)	M. Koukal (Cz.Rep.)	Norway
2005	**V. Rochev (Russia)**	**Norway**	**V. Vittoz (Fr.)**		**P. Piller Cottrer (Italy)**		**F. Estil (Nor.)**	**Norway**

*Olympic champions. †Tied. ‡Original winner disqualified after failed drug test.

World Nordic Skiing Championships—Women

Year	Sprint	Team sprint	Double pursuit	5-km	10-km	15-km	30-km	Relay
2002*	Yu. Chepalova (Russia)			B. Scott (Can.)†	B. Skari (Nor.)	S. Belmondo (Italy)	G. Paruzzi (Italy)	Germany
2003	M. Bjørgen (Nor.)		K. Smigun (Est.)		B. Skari (Nor.)	B. Skari (Nor.)	O. Savyalova (Russia)	Germany
2005	**E. Öhrstig (Swed.)**	**Norway**	**Yu. Chepalova (Russia)**		**K. Neumannova (Cz.Rep.)**		**M. Bjørgen (Nor.)**	**Norway**

*Olympic champions. †Original winner disqualified after failed drug test.

World Nordic Skiing Championships—Ski Jump

Year	Normal hill (90 m)*	Large hill (120 m)	Team jump (normal hill)	Team jump (large hill)	Nordic combined (7.5-km)	Nordic combined (15-km)	Nordic combined Team
2002†	S. Ammann (Switz.)	S. Ammann (Switz.)	Germany	Germany	S. Lajunen (Fin.)	S. Lajunen (Fin.)	Finland
2003	A. Malysz (Pol.)	A. Malysz (Pol.)	Finland	Finland	J. Spillane (U.S.)	R. Ackermann (Ger.)	Austria
2005	**R. Benkovic (Slvn.)**	**J. Ahonen (Fin.)**	**Austria**	**Austria**	**R. Ackermann (Ger.)**	**R. Ackermann (Ger.)**	**Norway**

*95-m in 2003. †Olympic champions.

Alpine World Cup

Year	Men	Women
2003	S. Eberharter (Austria)	J. Kostelic (Cro.)
2004	H. Maier (Austria)	A. Pärson (Swed.)
2005	**B. Miller (U.S.)**	**A. Pärson (Swed.)**

Nordic World Cup

Year	Men	Women
2003	M. Fredriksson (Swed.)	B. Skari (Nor.)
2004	R. Sommerfeldt (Ger.)	G. Paruzzi (Italy)
2005	**A. Teichmann (Ger.)**	**M. Bjørgen (Nor.)**

Freestyle Skiing World Cup

Year	Men	Women
2003	D. Arkhipov (Russia)	K. Traa (Nor.)
2004	S. Omischl (Can.)	K. Traa (Nor.)
2005	**J. Bloom (U.S.)**	**Li Nina (China)**

Snowboard World Cup

Year	Men	Women
2003	J.J. Anderson (Can.)	K. Ruby (Fr.)
2004	J.J. Anderson (Can.)	J. Pomagalski (Fr.)
2005	**P. Schoch (Switz.)**	**D. Meuli (Switz.)**

Agence Zoom/Getty Images

Freestyle skier Jeremy Bloom of the U.S. takes to the air in a World Cup moguls event in February; Bloom won the World Cup moguls crown and the overall title.

SQUASH

British Open Championship—Men

Year	Winner
2002–03	D. Palmer (Austl.)
2003–04	D. Palmer (Austl.)
2004–05	**A. Ricketts (Austl.)**

British Open Championship—Women

Year	Winner
2002–03	R. Grinham (Austl.)
2003–04	R. Grinham (Austl.)
2004–05	**N. David (Malay.)**

World Open Championship—Men

Year	Winner
2003	A. Shabana (Egypt)
2004	T. Lincou (Fr.)
2005	**A. Shabana (Egypt)**

World Open Championship—Women

Year	Winner
2003	C. Owens (N.Z.)
2004	V. Atkinson (Neth.)
2005	**N. David (Malay.)**

SWIMMING

World Swimming Records Set in 2005 in 25-m Pools*

Event	Name	Country	Time
MEN			
100-m freestyle	Roland Schoeman	South Africa	46.25 sec†
200-m backstroke	Markus Rogan	Austria	1 min 50.43 sec
50-m butterfly	Kaio Márcio de Almeida	Brazil	22.60 sec
100-m individual medley	Roland Schoeman	South Africa	52.51 sec
	Ryk Neethling	South Africa	52.11 sec
	Ryk Neethling	South Africa	52.01 sec
	Ryk Neethling	South Africa	51.52 sec
200-m individual medley	Laszlo Cseh	Hungary	1 min 53.46 sec
400-m individual medley	Laszlo Cseh	Hungary	4 min 00.37 sec
WOMEN			
100-m freestyle	Lisbeth Lenton	Australia	51.91 sec
	Lisbeth Lenton	Australia	51.70 sec
200-m freestyle	Lisbeth Lenton	Australia	1 min 53.29 sec
400-m freestyle	Laure Manaudou	France	3 min 56.79 sec
800-m freestyle	Laure Manaudou	France	8 min 11.25 sec
50-m butterfly	Anne-Karin Kammerling	Sweden	25.33 sec
4 × 50-m medley relay	Netherlands National Team (Hinkelien Schreuder, Moniek Nijhuis, Inge Dekker, Marleen Veldhuis)	Netherlands	1 min 47.44 sec

World Swimming Records Set in 2005 in 50-m Pools*

Event	Name	Country	Time
MEN			
800-m freestyle	Grant Hackett	Australia	7 min 38.65 sec
100-m backstroke	Aaron Peirsol	United States	53.17 sec
200-m backstroke	Aaron Peirsol	United States	1 min 54.66 sec
50-m butterfly	Roland Schoeman	South Africa	23.01 sec
	Roland Schoeman	South Africa	22.96 sec
100-m butterfly	Ian Crocker	United States	50.40 sec
WOMEN			
50-m backstroke	Janine Pietsch	Germany	28.19 sec
50-m breaststroke	Jade Edmistone	Australia	30.45 sec
100-m breaststroke	Jessica Hardy	United States	1 min 6.20 sec
200-m breaststroke	Leisel Jones	Australia	2 min 21.72 sec
200-m butterfly	Otylia Jedrejczak	Poland	2 min 5.61 sec

*May include records awaiting FINA ratification at year's end.

*May include records awaiting FINA ratification at year's end.   †Equals world record.

World Swimming and Diving Championships—Men

	Freestyle					
Year	50 m	100 m	200 m	400 m	800 m	1,500 m
2001	A. Ervin (U.S.)	A. Ervin (U.S.)	I. Thorpe (Austl.)	I. Thorpe (Austl.)	I. Thorpe (Austl.)	G. Hackett (Austl.)
2003	A. Popov (Russia)	A. Popov (Russia)	I. Thorpe (Austl.)	I. Thorpe (Austl.)	G. Hackett (Austl.)	G. Hackett (Austl.)
2005	**R. Schoeman (S.Af.)**	**F. Magnini (Italy)**	**M. Phelps (U.S.)**	**G. Hackett (Austl.)**	**G. Hackett (Austl.)**	**G. Hackett (Austl.)**

	Backstroke			Breaststroke		
	50 m	100 m	200 m	50 m	100 m	200 m
2001	R. Bal (U.S.)	M. Welsh (Austl.)	A. Peirsol (U.S.)	O. Lisogor (Ukr.)	R. Sludnov (Russia)	B. Hansen (U.S.)
2003	T. Rupprath (Ger.)	A. Peirsol (U.S.)	A. Peirsol (U.S.)	J. Gibson (U.K.)	K. Kitajima (Japan)	K. Kitajima (Japan)
2005	**A. Grigoriadis (Greece)**	**A. Piersol (U.S.)**	**A. Piersol (U.S.)**	**M. Warnecke (Ger.)**	**B. Hansen (U.S.)**	**B. Hansen (U.S.)**

	Butterfly			Individual medley		Team relays
	50 m	100 m	200 m	200 m	400 m	4 × 100-m freestyle
2001	G. Huegill (Austl.)	L. Frölander (Swed.)	M. Phelps (U.S.)	M. Rosolino (Italy)	A. Boggiatto (Italy)	Australia
2003	M. Welsh (Austl.)	I. Crocker (U.S.)	M. Phelps (U.S.)	M. Phelps (U.S.)	M. Phelps (U.S.)	Russia
2005	**R. Schoeman (S.Af.)**	**I. Crocker (U.S.)**	**P. Korzeniowski (Pol.)**	**M. Phelps (U.S.)**	**L. Cseh (Hung.)**	**United States**

	4 × 200-m freestyle	4 × 100-m medley	Diving				
			1-m springboard	3-m springboard	Platform	3-m synchronized	10-m synchronized
2001	Australia	Australia	Wang Feng (China)	D. Sautin (Russia)	Tian Liang (China)	China	China
2003	Australia	United States	Xu Xiang (China)	A. Dobrosok (Russia)	A. Despatie (Can.)	Russia	Australia
2005	**United States**	**United States**	**A. Despatie (Can.)**	**A. Despatie (Can.)**	**Hu Jia (China)**	**China**	**Russia**

SWIMMING (continued)

World Swimming and Diving Championships—Women

	Freestyle					
Year	50 m	100 m	200 m	400 m	800 m	1,500 m
2001	I. de Bruijn (Neth.)	I. de Bruijn (Neth.)	G. Rooney (Austl.)	Ya. Klochkova (Ukr.)	H. Stockbauer (Ger.)	H. Stockbauer (Ger.)
2003	I. de Bruijn (Neth.)	H.-M. Seppälä (Fin.)	A. Popchanka (Bela.)	H. Stockbauer (Ger.)	H. Stockbauer (Ger.)	H. Stockbauer (Ger.)
2005	**L. Lenton (Austl.)**	**J. Henry (Austl.)**	**S. Figues (Fr.)**	**L. Manaudou (Fr.)**	**K. Ziegler (U.S.)**	**K. Ziegler (U.S.)**

	Backstroke			Breaststroke		
	50 m	100 m	200 m	50 m	100 m	200 m
2001	H. Cope (U.S.)	N. Coughlin (U.S.)	D. Mocanu (Rom.)	Luo Xuejuan (China)	Luo Xuejuan (China)	A. Kovacs (Hung.)
2003	N. Zhivanevskaya (Spain)	A. Buschschulte (Ger.)	K. Sexton (U.K.)	Luo Xuejuan (China)	Luo Xuejuan (China)	A. Beard (U.S.)
2005	**G. Rooney (Austl.)**	**K. Coventry (Zimb.)**	**K. Coventry (Zimb.)**	**J. Edmistone (Austl.)**	**L. Jones (Austl.)**	**L. Jones (Austl.)**

	Butterfly			Individual medley		Team relays
	50 m	100 m	200 m	200 m	400 m	4 × 100-m freestyle
2001	I. de Bruijn (Neth.)	P. Thomas (Austl.)	P. Thomas (Austl.)	M. Bowen (U.S.)	Ya. Klochkova (Ukr.)	Germany
2003	I. de Bruijn (Neth.)	J. Thompson (U.S.)	O. Jedrzejczak (Pol.)	Ya. Klochkova (Ukr.)	Ya. Klochkova (Ukr.)	United States
2005	**D. Miatke (Austl.)**	**J. Schipper (Austl.)**	**O. Jedrzejczak (Pol.)**	**K. Hoff (U.S.)**	**K. Hoff (U.S.)**	**Australia**

			Diving				
	4 × 200-m freestyle	4 × 100-m medley	1-m springboard	3-m springboard	Platform	3-m synchronized	10-m synchronized
2001	United Kingdom	Australia	B. Hartley (Can.)	Guo Jingjing (China)	Xu Mian (China)	China	China
2003	United States	China	I. Lashko (Austl.)	Guo Jingjing (China)	E. Heymans (Can.)	China	China
2005	**United States**	**Australia**	**B. Hartley (Can.)**	**Guo Jingjing (China)**	**L. Wilkinson (U.S.)**	**China**	**China**

TABLE TENNIS

World Table Tennis Championships—Men

Year	St. Bride's Vase (singles)	Iran Cup (doubles)
2001	Wang Liqin (China)	Wang Liqin, Yan Sen (China)
2003	W. Schlager (Austria)	Wang Liqin, Yan Sen (China)
2005	**Wang Liqin (China)**	**Kong Linghui, Wang Hao (China)**

World Table Tennis Championships—Women

Year	G. Geist Prize (singles)	W.J. Pope Trophy (doubles)
2001	Wang Nan (China)	Wang Nan, Li Ju (China)
2003	Wang Nan (China)	Wang Nan, Zhang Yining (China)
2005	**Zhang Yining (China)**	**Wang Nan, Zhang Yining (China)**

World Table Tennis Championships—Mixed

Year	Heydusek Prize
2001	Qin Zhijian, Yang Ying (China)
2003	Ma Lin, Wang Nan (China)
2005	**Guo Yue, Wang Liqin (China)**

World Table Tennis Championships—Team

Year	Swaythling Cup (men)	Corbillon Cup (women)
2000	Sweden	China
2001	China	China
2004	China	China

Table Tennis World Cup

Year	Men
2003	Ma Lin (China)
2004	Ma Lin (China)
2005	**T. Boll (Ger.)**

Year	Women
2003	Wang Nan (China)
2004	Zhang Yining (China)
2005	**Zhang Yining (China)**

TENNIS

Australian Open Tennis Championships—Singles

Year	Men	Women
2003	A. Agassi (U.S.)	S. Williams (U.S.)
2004	R. Federer (Switz.)	J. Henin-Hardenne (Belg.)
2005	**M. Safin (Russia)**	**S. Williams (U.S.)**

Australian Open Tennis Championships—Doubles

Year	Men	Women
2003	M. Llodra, F. Santoro	S. Williams, V. Williams
2004	M. Llodra, F. Santoro	V. Ruano Pascual, P. Suárez
2005	**W. Black, K. Ullyett**	**S. Kuznetsova, A. Molik**

French Open Tennis Championships—Singles

Year	Men	Women
2003	J.C. Ferrero (Spain)	J. Henin-Hardenne (Belg.)
2004	G. Gaudio (Arg.)	A. Myskina (Russia)
2005	**R. Nadal (Spain)**	**J. Henin-Hardenne (Belg.)**

French Open Tennis Championships—Doubles

Year	Men	Women
2003	B. Bryan, M. Bryan	K. Clijsters, A. Sugiyama
2004	X. Malisse, O. Rochus	V. Ruano Pascual, P. Suárez
2005	**J. Bjorkman, M. Mirnyi**	**V. Ruano Pascual, P. Suárez**

All-England (Wimbledon) Tennis Championships—Singles

Year	Men	Women
2003	R. Federer (Switz.)	S. Williams (U.S.)
2004	R. Federer (Switz.)	M. Sharapova (Russia)
2005	**R. Federer (Switz.)**	**V. Williams (U.S.)**

All-England (Wimbledon) Tennis Championships—Doubles

Year	Men	Women
2003	J. Bjorkman, T. Woodbridge	K. Clijsters, A. Sugiyama
2004	J. Bjorkman, T. Woodbridge	C. Black, R. Stubbs
2005	**S. Huss, W. Moodie**	**C. Black, L. Huber**

TENNIS (continued)

United States Open Tennis Championships—Singles

Year	Men	Women
2003	A. Roddick (U.S.)	J. Henin-Hardenne (Belg.)
2004	R. Federer (Switz.)	S. Kuznetsova (Russia)
2005	**R. Federer (Switz.)**	**K. Clijsters (Belg.)**

United States Open Tennis Championships—Doubles

Year	Men	Women
2003	J. Bjorkman, T. Woodbridge	V. Ruano Pascual, P. Suárez
2004	M. Knowles, D. Nestor	V. Ruano Pascual, P. Suárez
2005	**B. Bryan, M. Bryan**	**L. Raymond, S. Stosur**

Davis Cup (men)

Year	Winner	Runner-up	Results
2003	Australia	Spain	3–1
2004	Spain	United States	3–2
2005	**Croatia**	**Slovakia**	**3–2**

Fed Cup (women)

Year	Winner	Runner-up	Results
2003	France	United States	4–1
2004	Russia	France	3–2
2005	**Russia**	**France**	**3–2**

Double gold medalist Justin Gatlin of the U.S. on the track in the 200 m at the world outdoor championships.

TRACK AND FIELD SPORTS (ATHLETICS)

World Outdoor Track and Field Championships—Men

Event	2003	2005
100 m	K. Collins (S.Kitts)	J. Gatlin (U.S.)
200 m	J. Capel (U.S.)	J. Gatlin (U.S.)
400 m	J. Young (U.S.)	J. Wariner (U.S.)
800 m	D. Saïd-Guerni (Alg.)	R. Ramzi (Bahrain)
1,500 m	H. El Guerrouj (Mor.)	R. Ramzi (Bahrain)
5,000 m	E. Kipchoge (Kenya)	B. Limo (Kenya)
10,000 m	K. Bekele (Eth.)	K. Bekele (Eth.)
steeplechase	S.S. Shaheen (Qatar)	S.S. Shaheen (Qatar)
110-m hurdles	A. Johnson (U.S.)	L. Doucouré (Fr.)
400-m hurdles	F. Sánchez (Dom.Rep.)	B. Jackson (U.S.)
marathon	J. Gharib (Mor.)	J. Gharib (Mor.)
20-km walk	J. Pérez (Ecua.)	J. Pérez (Ecua.)
50-km walk	R. Korzeniowski (Pol.)	S. Kirdyapkin (Russia)
4 × 100-m relay	United States (J. Capel, B. Williams, D. Patton, J.J. Johnson)	France (L. Doucouré, R. Pognon, E. De Lépine, L. Dovy)
4 × 400-m relay	France (L. Djhone, N. Keïta, S. Diagana, M. Raquil)*	United States (A. Rock, D. Brew, D. Williamson, J. Wariner)
high jump	J. Freitag (S.Af.)	Y. Krymarenko (Ukr.)
pole vault	G. Gibilisco (Italy)	R. Blom (Neth.)
long jump	D. Phillips (U.S.)	D. Phillips (U.S.)
triple jump	C. Olsson (Swed.)	W. Davis (U.S.)
shot put	A. Mikhnevich (Bela.)	A. Nelson (U.S.)
discus throw	V. Alekna (Lith.)	V. Alekna (Lith.)
hammer throw	I. Tikhon (Bela.)	I. Tikhon (Bela.)
javelin throw	S. Makarov (Russia)	A. Värnik (Est.)
decathlon	T. Pappas (U.S.)	B. Clay (U.S.)

*Original winner disqualified after one runner failed drug test.

World Outdoor Track and Field Championships—Women

Event	2003	2005
100 m	T. Edwards (U.S.)*	L. Williams (U.S.)
200 m	A. Kapachinskaya (Russia)*	A. Felix (U.S.)
400 m	A. Guevara (Mex.)	T. Williams-Darling (Bah.)
800 m	M. Mutola (Mozam.)	Z. Calatayud (Cuba)
1,500 m	T. Tomashova (Russia)	T. Tomashova (Russia)
5,000 m	T. Dibaba (Eth.)	T. Dibaba (Eth.)
10,000 m	B. Adere (Eth.)	T. Dibaba (Eth.)
steeplechase		D. Inzikuru (Uganda)
100-m hurdles	P. Felicien (Can.)	M. Perry (U.S.)
400-m hurdles	J. Pittman (Austl.)	Yu. Pechonkina (Russia)
marathon	C. Ndereba (Kenya)	P. Radcliffe (U.K.)
20-km walk	Ye. Nikolayeva (Russia)	O. Ivanova (Russia)
4 × 100-m relay	France (P. Girard, M. Hurtis, S. Félix, C. Arron)	United States (A. Daigle, M. Lee, M. Barber, L. Williams)
4 × 400-m relay	United States (M. Barber, Washington, J. Miles Clark, S. Richards)	Russia (Yu. Pechonkina, O. Krasnomovets, N. Antyukh, S. Pospelova)
high jump	H. Cloete (S.Af.)	K. Bergqvist (Swed.)
pole vault	S. Feofanova (Russia)	Ye. Isinbayeva (Russia)
long jump	E. Barber (Fr.)	T. Madison (U.S.)
triple jump	T. Lebedeva (Russia)	T. Smith (Jam.)
shot put	S. Krivelyova (Russia)	N. Ostapchuk (Bela.)
discus throw	I. Yatchenko (Bela.)	F. Dietzsch (Ger.)
hammer throw	Y. Moreno (Cuba)	O. Kuzenkova (Russia)
javelin throw	M. Manjani (Greece)	O. Menéndez (Cuba)
heptathlon	C. Klüft (Swed.)	C. Klüft (Swed.)

*Original winner disqualified after failed drug test.

TRACK AND FIELD SPORTS (ATHLETICS) (continued)

World Indoor Track and Field Championships—Men

Event	2003	2004
60 m	J. Gatlin (U.S.)	J. Gardener (Gr.Brit.)
200 m	M. Devonish (Gr.Brit.)	D. Demeritte (Bah.)
400 m	T. Washington (U.S.)	A. Francique (Grenada)
800 m	D. Krummenacker (U.S.)	M. Mulaudzi (S.Af.)
1,500 m	D. Maazouzi (Fr.)	P. Korir (Kenya)
3,000 m	H. Gebrselassie (Eth.)	B. Lagat (Kenya)
60-m hurdles	A. Johnson (U.S.)	A. Johnson (U.S.)
4 × 400-m relay	United States (J. Davis, J. Young, M. Campbell, T. Washington)	Jamaica (G. Haughton, L. Colquhoun, M. McDonald, D. Clarke)
high jump	S. Holm (Swed.)	S. Holm (Swed.)
pole vault	T. Lobinger (Ger.)	I. Pavlov (Russia)
long jump	D. Phillips (U.S.)	S. Stringfellow (U.S.)
triple jump	C. Olsson (Swed.)	C. Olsson (Swed.)
shot put	M. Martínez (Spain)	C. Cantwell (U.S.)
heptathlon	T. Pappas (U.S.)	R. Sebrle (Cz.Rep.)

World Indoor Track and Field Championships—Women

Event	2003	2004
60 m	Z. Block (Ukr.)	G. Devers (U.S.)
200 m	M. Collins (U.S.)	N. Safronnikova (Bela.)*
400 m	N. Nazarova (Russia)	N. Nazarova (Russia)
800 m	M. Mutola (Mozam.)	M. Mutola (Mozam.)
1,500 m	R. Jacobs (U.S.)	K. Dulecha (Eth.)
3,000 m	B. Adere (Eth.)	M. Defar (Eth.)
60-m hurdles	G. Devers (U.S.)	P. Felicien (Can.)
4 × 100-m relay	Russia (N. Antyukh, Yu. Pechonkina, O. Zykina, N. Nazarova)	Russia (O. Krasnomovets, O. Kotlyarova, T. Levina, N. Nazarova)
high jump	K. Bergqvist (Swed.)	Ye. Slesarenko (Russia)
pole vault	S. Feofanova (Russia)	Ye. Isinbayeva (Russia)
long jump	T. Kotova (Russia)	T. Lebedeva (Russia)
triple jump	A. Hansen (Gr.Brit.)	T. Lebedeva (Russia)
shot put	I. Korzhanenko (Russia)	S. Krivelyova (Russia)*
pentathlon	C. Klüft (Swed.)	N. Gomes (Port.)

*Original winner disqualified after failed drug test.

2005 World Indoor Records—Men*

Event	Competitor and country	Performance
400 m	Kerron Clement (U.S.)	44.57 sec

*May include records awaiting IAAF ratification at year's end.

2005 World Indoor Records—Women*

Event	Competitor and country	Performance
5,000 m	Tirunesh Dibaba (Eth.)	14 min 32.93 sec
4 × 200-m relay	Russia (Yekaterina Kondratyeva, Irina Khabarova, Yuliya Pechonkina, Yuliya Gushchina)	1 min 32.41 sec
pole vault	Yelena Isinbayeva (Russia)	4.87 m (15 ft 11¾ in)
	Yelena Isinbayeva (Russia)	4.88 m (16 ft)
	Yelena Isinbayeva (Russia)	4.89 m (16 ft ½ in)
	Yelena Isinbayeva (Russia)	4.90 m (16 ft ¾ in)

*May include records awaiting IAAF ratification at year's end.

2005 World Outdoor Records—Men*

Event	Competitor and country	Performance
100 m	Asafa Powell (Jam.)	9.77 sec
10,000 m	Kenenisa Bekele (Eth.)	26 min 17.53 sec
half marathon	Samuel Wanjiru (Kenya)	59 min 16 sec
10,000-m walking†	Ivano Brugnetti (Italy)	37 min 58.60 sec
30-km road race	Takayuki Matsumiya (Japan)	1 hr 28 min 00 sec

*May include records awaiting IAAF ratification at year's end.   †Not an officially ratified event; best performance on record.

2005 World Outdoor Records—Women*

Event	Competitor and country	Performance
2,000-m steeplechase†	Dorcus Inzikuru (Uganda)	6 min 04.46 sec
sprint medley relay†	United States Red Team (Allyson Felix, Kia Davis, Debbie Dunn, Hazel Clark)	3 min 37.42 sec
pole vault	Yelena Isinbayeva (Russia)	4.93 m (16 ft 2 in)
	Yelena Isinbayeva (Russia)	4.95 m (16 ft 2¾ in)
	Yelena Isinbayeva (Russia)	4.96 m (16 ft 3¼ in)
	Yelena Isinbayeva (Russia)	5.00 m (16 ft 4¾ in)
	Yelena Isinbayeva (Russia)	5.01 m (16 ft 5¼ in)
hammer throw	Tatyana Lysenko (Russia)	77.06 m (252 ft 10 in)
javelin throw	Osleidys Menéndez (Cuba)	71.70 m (235 ft 3 in)
decathlon	Austra Skujyte (Lith.)	8,366 points
20,000-m walking	Olimpiada Ivanova (Russia)	1 hr 25 min 41 sec
5-km road race†	Tirunesh Dibaba (Eth.)	14 min 51 sec‡
25-km	Mizuki Noguchi (Japan)	1 hr 22 min 13 sec
30-km	Mizuki Noguchi (Japan)	1 hr 38 min 49 sec

*May include records awaiting IAAF ratification at year's end.   †Not an officially ratified event; best performance on record.   ‡Equals world record.

World Cross Country Championships—Men

Year	Individual	Team
2003	K. Bekele (Eth.)	Kenya
2004	K. Bekele (Eth.)	Ethiopia
2005	**K. Bekele (Eth.)**	**Ethiopia**

World Cross Country Championships—Women

Year	Individual	Team
2003	W. Kidane (Eth.)	Ethiopia
2004	B. Johnson (Austl.)	Ethiopia
2005	**T. Dibaba (Eth.)**	**Ethiopia**

Boston Marathon

Year	Men	hr:min:sec
2003	R.K. Cheruiyot (Kenya)	2:10:11
2004	T. Cherigat (Kenya)	2:10:37
2005	**H. Negussie (Eth.)**	**2:11:45**

Year	Women	hr:min:sec
2003	S. Zakharova (Russia)	2:25:20
2004	C. Ndereba (Kenya)	2:24:27
2005	**C. Ndereba (Kenya)**	**2:25:13**

Chicago Marathon

Year	Men	hr:min:sec
2003	E. Rutto (Kenya)	2:05:50
2004	E. Rutto (Kenya)	2:06:16
2005	**F. Limo (Kenya)**	**2:07:04**

Year	Women	hr:min:sec
2003	S. Zakharova (Russia)	2:23:07
2004	C. Tomescu-Dita (Rom.)	2:23:45
2005	**D. Kastor (U.S.)**	**2:21:24**

London Marathon

Year	Men	hr:min:sec
2003	G. Abera (Eth.)	2:07:56
2004	E. Rutto (Kenya)	2:06:18
2005	**M. Lel (Kenya)**	**2:07:26**

Year	Women	hr:min:sec
2003	P. Radcliffe (U.K.)	2:15:25
2004	M. Okayo (Kenya)	2:22:35
2005	**P. Radcliffe (U.K.)**	**2:17:42**

New York City Marathon

Year	Men	hr:min:sec
2003	M. Lel (Kenya)	2:10:30
2004	H. Ramaala (S.Af.)	2:09:28
2005	**P. Tergat (Kenya)**	**2:09:30**

Year	Women	hr:min:sec
2003	M. Okayo (Kenya)	2:22:31
2004	P. Radcliffe (U.K.)	2:23:10
2005	**J. Prokopcuka (Latvia)**	**2:24:41**

VOLLEYBALL

Beach Volleyball World Championships		
Year	**Men**	**Women**
2001	M. Baracetti, M. Conde (Arg.)	A. Behar, Shelda (Braz.)
2003	R. Santos, E. Rego (Braz.)	M. May, K. Walsh (U.S.)
2005	**M. Araujo, F. Magalhães (Braz.)**	**M. May-Treanor, K. Walsh (U.S.)**

World Volleyball Championships		
Year	**Men**	**Women**
2000*	Yugoslavia	Cuba
2002	Brazil	Italy
2004*	Brazil	China

*Olympic champions.

WEIGHTLIFTING

World Weightlifting Champions, 2005

MEN			WOMEN		
Weight class	**Winner and country**	**Performance**	**Weight class**	**Winner and country**	**Performance**
56 kg (123 lb)	Wang Shin-yuan (Taiwan)	281 kg (619.5 lb)	48 kg (105.5 lb)	Wang Mingjuan (China)	213 kg (469.6 lb)
62 kg (136.5 lb)	Qiu Le (China)	322 kg (709.9 lb)	53 kg (116.5 lb)	Li Ping (China)	224 kg (493.8 lb)
69 kg (152 lb)	Shi Zhiyong (China)	350 kg (771.6 lb)	58 kg (127.5 lb)	Gu Wei (China)	241 kg (531.3 lb)
77 kg (169.5 lb)	Li Hongli (China)	361 kg (795.9 lb)	63 kg (138.5 lb)	P. Thongsuk (Thai.)	256 kg (564.4 lb)
85 kg (187 lb)	I. Ilin (Kazakh.)	386 kg (851 lb)	69 kg (152 lb)	Z. Kasayeva (Russia)	275 kg (606.3 lb)
94 kg (207 lb)	N. Pashaev (Azer.)	401 kg (884 lb)	75 kg (165 lb)	Liu Chunhong (China)	285 kg (626.3 lb)
105 kg (231 lb)	D. Klokov (Russia)	419 kg (923.7 lb)	+75 kg (+165 lb)	Jang Mi Ran (S.Kor.)	300 kg (661.4 lb)
+105 kg (+231 lb)	H. Rezazadeh (Iran)	461 kg (1,016.3 lb)			

WRESTLING

World Wrestling Championships—Freestyle

Year	55 kg	60 kg	66 kg	74 kg
2003	D. Mansurov (Uzbek.)	A.A. Yadulla (Azer.)	I. Farnyev (Russia)	B. Saytyev (Russia)
2004*	M. Batirov (Russia)	Y.M. Quintana (Cuba)	E. Tedeyev (Ukr.)	B. Saytyev (Russia)
2005	**D. Mansurov (Uzbek.)**	**A. Dudayev (Russia)**	**M. Murtazaliyev (Russia)**	**B. Saytyev (Russia)**

Year	84 kg	96 kg	120 kg
2003	S. Sazhidov (Russia)	E. Kurtanidze (Georgia)	A. Taymazov (Uzbek.)
2004*	C. Sanderson (U.S.)	K. Gatsalov (Russia)	A. Taymazov (Uzbek.)
2005	**R. Mindorashvili (Geo.)**	**K. Gatsalov (Russia)**	**A. Polatci (Tur.)**

*Olympic champions.

World Wrestling Championships—Greco-Roman Style

Year	55 kg	60 kg	66 kg	74 kg
2003	D. Jablonski (Pol.)	A. Nazaryan (Bulg.)	M. Kvirkelia (Georgia)	A. Glushkov (Russia)
2004*	I. Majoros (Hung.)	Jung Ji Hyun (S.Kor.)	F. Mansurov (Azer.)	A. Dokturishivili (Uzbek.)
2005	**H. Sourianreyhanpour (Iran)**	**A. Nazaryan (Bulg.)**	**N. Gergov (Bulg.)**	**V. Samurgashev (Russia)**

Year	84 kg	96 kg	120 kg
2003	G. Ziziashvilly (Israel)	M. Lidberg (Swed.)	K. Baroyev (Russia)
2004*	A. Michine (Russia)	K. Ibrahim (Egypt)	K. Baroyev (Russia)
2005	**A. Selimav (Bela.)**	**H. Yerlikaya (Tur.)**	**M. López (Cuba)**

*Olympic champions.

Sumo Tournament Champions, 2005

Tournament	Location	Winner	Winner's record
Hatsu Basho (New Year's tournament)	Tokyo	Asashoryu	15–0
Haru Basho (spring tournament)	Osaka	Asashoryu	14–1
Natsu Basho (summer tournament)	Tokyo	Asashoryu	15–0
Nagoya Basho (Nagoya tournament)	Nagoya	Asashoryu	13–2
Aki Basho (autumn tournament)	Tokyo	Asashoryu	13–2
Kyushu Basho (Kyushu tournament)	Fukuoka	Asashoryu	14–1

Russian freestyle wrestler Buvaysa Saytyev (in blue) en route to his third straight 74-kg title.

© Attila Kisbenedek/AFP/Getty Images

The World in 2005

Pakistani children rest on a hill above a tent camp following the massive Kashmir earthquake.

© Kimimasa Mayama/Reuters/Corbis

World Affairs

ROCKETING fuel prices; the end of the textile QUOTA; a plethora of natural disasters, including a CATACLYSMIC earthquake in Kashmir and a string of HURRICANES in the U.S.; and fears about BIRD FLU and the possibility of its becoming a human PANDEMIC were among the chief concerns of a number of countries during 2005.

UNITED NATIONS

In 2005 the member states of the United Nations celebrated the 60th anniversary of the world body. The occasion was marked more by critical reflection than grand hoopla. What was the role of the UN in the 21st century? How could the institutional structures and mechanisms established well over half a century earlier be made more responsive to problems and issues in a greatly transformed world order? The largest gathering ever of heads of state and government met in September at the UN headquarters in New York City to ponder these and other critical questions concerning the future of the world organization. Any celebratory atmosphere that might have been expected to accompany such a milestone event was greatly tempered by the weight of important issues to be decided—as well as by news of scandal involving the UN and by political attacks on the organization and its administration, particularly from Washington.

Terrorism. An International Summit on Democracy, Terrorism, and Security was held in Madrid in March, and in April the 59th session of the General Assembly adopted its 13th antiterrorist convention. The International Convention for the Suppression of Acts of Nuclear Terrorism was opened for signature in September.

Despite this progress, an internationally accepted definition of *terrorism* continued to be elusive as thorny issues such as state-sponsored use of force against civilians and the right of people to resort to violence to resist foreign occupation also remained unsettled. The December 2004 report issued by the High-level Panel on Threats, Challenges and Change, *A More Secure World: Our Shared Responsibility*, proposed language to resolve the matter that was endorsed by UN Secretary-General Kofi Annan in his March 2005 report, *In Larger Freedom: Towards Security, Development and Human Rights*. Conferees at the September World Summit failed to achieve closure on a definition or on a comprehensive antiterrorist convention.

Iraq. National elections were held on Jan. 30, 2005, to select the 275 members of the provisional National Assembly. Although the United Iraqi Alliance won a bare majority (140) of the seats, no single party won enough seats to control the government unilaterally. In April Ibrahim al-Jaafari (*see* BIOGRAPHIES) of the Islamic Da'wah Party was selected

UN Secretary-General Kofi Annan unveils the "One Laptop per Child" initiative in Tunis, Tun., in November.

© Eric Feferberg/AFP/Getty Images

as prime minister. Jalal Talabani of the Patriotic Union of Kurdistan took office as president. A successful referendum on the ratification of a new constitution was held on October 15, and on December 15 parliamentary elections were held. The UN reiterated its pledge to help bring peace and stability to the country, with Annan remarking in November, "We have a clear mandate from the Security Council to do whatever we can to work with the government and people of Iraq to ensure that Iraq takes charge of its own future and develops a stable, peaceful society."

Afghanistan. Parliamentary elections were held in Afghanistan in September. The security situation continued to be precarious, and the institutions of governance remained weak. Opium production and drug trafficking persisted as major concerns. As in 2004, Secretary-General Annan prodded the Security Council and the General Assembly during the year to address these and other sources of insecurity. At year's end the UN had more than 800 staff members in the field in Afghanistan, yet the security situation remained unstable. In December 2005 the UN restricted staff movements following two suicide bombings near UN offices in Kabul that killed four persons, including one NATO peacekeeper.

Iran. Confrontation continued in 2005 between the Iranian government and the UN, the International Atomic Energy Agency (IAEA), and EU and U.S. officials over the issue of uranium enrichment and other nuclear activities in Iran. Although an apparent agreement between European diplomats and the Iranian government had been concluded in 2004, under which Iranian officials promised to halt all uranium-enrichment measures and permit inspectors to verify compliance with IAEA safeguards, the Iranians later refused to follow through. Diplomatic initiatives continued throughout 2005, but as the year drew to a close, Iran, led by new hard-line Pres. Mahmoud Ahmadinejad (*see* BIOGRAPHIES), declared that it planned to move forward with its uranium-enrichment activities.

Development. At the Millennium Summit in 2000, world leaders had set forth a declaration that contained eight primary goals and a set of associated targets and social indicators, called the

Millennium Development Goals (MDGs), for eradicating extreme poverty and the conditions associated with it by 2015. One primary purpose of the World Summit in September 2005 was to assess the MDG process to date and make any mid-course correction that might be necessary. The Millennium Project produced an interim report, *Investing in Development: A Practical Plan to Achieve the Millennium Development Goals*. According to the report, although some countries and regions were making progress, the world was not on track for achieving any of the project's stated goals. The situation in sub-Saharan Africa was particularly dire. "There is still time to meet the Millennium Development Goals—though barely," proclaimed the report, which added that meeting the MDGs would require launching "a decade of bold action."

Health. Global health issues were again much in the news. The number of people infected with HIV/AIDS stood at more than 40 million, with some 8,000 persons per day dying from AIDS-related causes. The crisis was especially acute in sub-Saharan Africa, where three-quarters of the world's annual AIDS-related deaths occurred. Almost two-thirds of all persons living with HIV/AIDS resided on the continent, and two-thirds of all new infections occurred there as well. At the same time, a problematic "second wave" of the global pandemic was rapidly penetrating parts of Europe and Asia.

Although HIV/AIDS still topped the list of world health concerns, new infectious diseases splashed onto the front pages. Avian influenza (bird flu), Marburg virus, and SARS (severe acute respiratory syndrome) were of special immediate concern. UNAIDS continued to coordinate the global response to HIV/AIDS, although global funding commitments remained far short of projected financial needs. The UN Environment Programme had taken the lead in an international alliance to develop an early-warning system for the transmission of the avian flu virus. These diseases vied for attention and resources among a long list of persisting ills such as malaria, tuberculosis, and polio.

Refugees. The number of refugees in the world dropped in 2004 to its lowest total in two and a half decades as 35% more refugees were repatriated to their homes than in the year before. Nevertheless, the number of "persons of concern" who fell under the mandate of the UN High Commissioner for Refugees—

which excluded more than 4 million refugees and internally displaced persons (IDPs) in Palestine—increased from 17.1 million to 19.2 million.

Humanitarian Affairs. UNICEF dubbed 2005 the "Year of Emergencies" as humanitarian crises abounded. Acute conflict-related emergencies persisted in Iraq, Uganda, the Democratic Republic of the Congo, and The Sudan. Nutrition and food emergencies prevailed in Niger, Malawi, Ethiopia, and Eritrea. Tsunami-, earthquake- and hurricane-related crises plagued regions as diverse as South and Southeast Asia and North and Central America. The death toll was devastating and the scope of human misery awesome. In northern Uganda, however, the international community seemed to have turned a blind eye as the government persisted in its policy of forcibly removing 1.6 million Acholi people from their traditional lands, entrapping them in conditions of squalor in IDP camps.

Peace Operations. The year was an active one for peace operations, with UN forces reaching an unprecedented level. In late November 2005 there were 16 active UN peacekeeping missions, involving some 70,000 military and police personnel from 107 countries and 15,000 support staff. In addition, there were 10 peacemaking and peacebuilding operations and a total of 26 conflicts or potential conflict situations being monitored by the UN Department of Political Affairs.

Eight of the UN peacekeeping operations and the vast majority of peacekeepers were based in Africa. Initiatives in Burundi and Liberia met with much success. The Burundi mission facilitated stabilization of security in the country and moved the postconflict peacebuilding process forward. In Liberia presidential elections were concluded peacefully in November 2005 with the election of Ellen Johnson-Sirleaf to the post. After six years of operation, the UN peacekeeping mission in Sierra Leone was brought to a successful conclusion on December 31 in what the world body billed as a "prototype for the UN's new emphasis on peacebuilding." The situation in Western Sahara, however, continued to elude a peaceful solution.

There was some positive movement on one of the world's greatest humanitarian crises—civil strife in The Sudan. On January 9, following two decades of civil war, a Comprehensive Peace Agreement was signed between the Sudanese government and the Sudan People's

Liberation Movement. The UN Mission in Sudan was created to replace the UN Advance Mission in Sudan, which had been established nine months earlier. A new National Unity government took office in July. Despite this progress, the civil strife in Darfur raged on, with the Arab militia known as Janjawid continuing to terrorize civilians and perpetuate human rights abuses. In March the Security Council moved to refer allegations of war crimes violations to the International Criminal Court. There was hope that the Declaration of Principles for the Resolution of the Sudanese Conflict in Darfur signed in Abuja, Nigeria, on July 5 would facilitate a peaceful end to the violence.

Digital Divide. The global disparities in access to the Internet and other information and communication technologies that propelled globalization had led to what many termed a "digital divide" between technological haves and have-nots. This was one of the central issues during the three-year World Summit on the Information Society (WSIS) that had begun in 2003. Heads of state and their representatives met again on Nov. 16–18, 2005, in Tunis, Tun. This final phase of the WSIS yielded four documents: the Geneva Declaration of Principles, the Geneva Plan of Action, the Tunis Commitment, and the Tunis Agenda for the Information Society. World politics dominated the proceedings, and one of the most hotly contested issues at the summit was Internet governance. Conferees agreed to permit the American-based firm ICANN, the Internet Corporation for Names and Numbers, to continue its role as primary governor of the World Wide Web.

Reform. The December 2004 report of the High-Level Panel on Threats, Challenges and Change contained 101 recommendations for improving the capabilities of the UN to respond to global threats. Foremost among the recommendations was a proposal to enlarge the Security Council from 15 to 24 members. Annan endorsed most of the panel's recommendations and commended them for adoption at the September World Summit.

With respect to enhancing the capacity of the UN to fulfill its many mandates, the results of the summit were mixed at best. World leaders agreed, for example, to create a Human Rights Council to replace the Commission on Human Rights and on establishing a new Peacebuilding Commission to deal with creating the conditions necessary for maintaining peace in postconflict situations. Consensus was also reached on the collective responsibility of states to protect people from genocide, ethnic cleansing, and war crimes. In the wake of the oil-for-food scandal, leaders further agreed to establish an internal UN ethics office. No agreement could be reached on expanding the role of the secretary-general to make major management changes. Also, the entire section in the draft of the final document on nuclear nonproliferation and disarmament had to be dropped.

Administration and Finance. The financial situation of the UN remained tenuous despite the fact that arrearages to the regular budget had decreased in comparison with previous years. Its financial reserves remained depleted. As 2005 drew to a close, the proposed regular budget of $3.6 billion for 2006–07 continued to be challenged by the U.S. In exchange for its acquiescence, the U.S. wanted agreement from the other 190 member states on a number of management and structural reforms. One of the first moves by John R. Bolton (*see* BIOGRAPHIES), the newly appointed U.S. ambassador to the UN, was to demand significant changes to the draft of a document for reform of the world body.

Allegations about corruption surrounding the UN's oil-for-food program in Iraq continued to unfold throughout the year as the Independent Inquiry Committee, chaired by former U.S. Federal Reserve Board chairman Paul Volcker, issued several reports. The fifth and final report of the IIC's 18-month investigation was issued in late October. It told a story of $1.8 billion in kickbacks and illicit surcharges paid to Saddam Hussein's government by more than 2,200 corporations. Individuals and diplomats from more than five dozen countries were involved. Substantial surcharges for humanitarian contracts and kickbacks for oil contracts had been illegally paid by major corporations in the U.S., Russia, France, Germany, South Korea, and elsewhere. The report strongly criticized the UN Secretariat and Security Council for having failed to monitor the $64 billion program.

Revelations also surfaced of a sexual-abuse scandal involving some UN peacekeepers. In November 2004 the secretary-general acknowledged allegations of sexual abuse by a number of UN peacekeepers in the Democratic Republic of the Congo. Annan expressed his outrage at the conduct of those who

were involved and pledged that appropriate action would be taken.

In the 17 months preceding December 2005, 177 UN staff members lost their lives in the service of the world body and international community.

(ROGER A. COATE)

EUROPEAN UNION

The year 2005 would be remembered as one in which Europe's political elite received a reality check when voters in referenda held in two of the European Union's founding members—France and The Netherlands—rejected the EU's proposed constitution. These negative verdicts created the biggest crisis in the EU's history—one that was to dominate EU affairs throughout the year.

In October 2004 the EU members signed a treaty in which they agreed on the text for a proposed Constitution of Europe. (*See* Sidebar.) Under EU law, for any treaty to come into force, all member countries had to ratify it either in referenda or in votes of their national parliaments, so any "no" votes would put a halt to the momentum.

As 2005 began, the momentum toward further integration and expansion seemed irresistible. Two parliaments—in Lithuania and Hungary—had already voted to ratify the treaty, and on February 20 a referendum in Spain drew a 76.7% "yes" vote. Plans to move one step farther by binding member countries together under a written constitution were to prove a step too far for some Europeans, however. In four momentous days the people of France (on May 29) and The Netherlands (on June 1) rejected the constitutional treaty. Although several other member parliaments ratified the treaty during the year, pro-constitution leaders in Europe were forced to slow down, take stock, and ponder how to reconnect with the people who opposed the planned changes.

France's rejection of the constitution had been widely predicted in opinion polls, but that did nothing to lessen the sense of shock when the result came through. Almost 55% voted "no," and the unusually high turnout of more than 69% left no doubt that this was a clear verdict that could not be ignored. Pres. Jacques Chirac, who had fought hard for a "yes" vote, appeared uncertain how to react. In a brief statement after the result was announced, he said merely that the outcome would make it "difficult to defend French interests in Europe."

The reasons that the French rejected the constitution were many and complex. Centre-left politicians argued that the document was too Anglo-American in its view of Europe's economic objectives, placing too much emphasis on the free market and too little on the principles of protection for citizens against the ravages of the global marketplace. They argued that the constitution echoed too enthusiastically the EU's long-standing commitment to "free and fair competition" and the goal of "free movement of goods, people, and capital." Opponents on the right, however, criticized the treaty for transferring power from the national government to Brussels and thus promoting a multicultural Europe with open borders in which decisions on immigration and border controls would be made by the EU. Their fear was that as the EU membership stretched farther eastward, there would be a multinational free-for-all in which Eastern European workers could move to Paris, undercut local wages, and put French workers out of their jobs overnight. France's rejection of the treaty reflected a multifaceted distrust of the country's and the EU's leaders.

Another disheartening blow for Chirac and other Brussels supporters was the speed with which The Netherlands—which until a few years before had been one of the most pro-EU countries—followed France's lead. Discontent among the Dutch people about rising immigration into their crowded if prosperous country was coupled with a sense that the euro had not proved good for the local economy. Dutch voters rejected the proposed constitution by 61.6–38.4% in a turnout of 63%.

Dutch cows are recruited for the campaign against the EU constitution in May. **Boe** *in Dutch means both "boo" and "moo," the sound a cow makes.*

AP/Wide World Photos

The European Union's Proposed Constitution

The ratification process for the Constitution of Europe stalled in 2005. The constitution was established through a European Union treaty signed in Rome in 2004 and was intended to make a community originally designed for six founding members in the 1950s more workable with a membership of 25 disparate countries. Governments that were faced with selling the document to a heavily skeptical electorate, such as that in the U.K., claimed that the treaty did not amount to a large extension of the EU's powers and was little more than a "tidying-up exercise." Meanwhile, many pro-integration political leaders in France and Germany billed it as a significant move toward the full "political union" to which they had always aspired. The document, which would supersede all previous community treaties (except the so-called Euratom Treaty, which established the European Atomic Energy Community), contained several significant—and highly controversial—changes to the structure and functioning of the 25-member European Union.

- The constitution changed the way that EU members voted on European issues so that majority voting—where no one country could block a decision—would become the norm. A qualified majority would consist of "at least 55% of the members of the Council, comprising at least fifteen of them and representing Member States comprising at least 65% of the population of the Union." The national veto would disappear in 39 policy areas, including sensitive matters such as justice and home affairs.

- In an effort to achieve better management of EU business and improve continuity in policy making, the document called for the creation of the post of EU president, who would be voted in by the heads of governments for a period of up to five years. The president replaced the system of rotating presidencies, under which member

states took turns chairing EU meetings and coordinating business for six-month terms.

- An EU foreign minister would be chosen by national governments for up to five years. The foreign minister would have his or her own supporting diplomatic service, the European External Action Service, and would represent the EU's interests in foreign affairs—for example, in official dealings with the UN.

- A formal Charter of Fundamental Rights was incorporated into the constitution and given legal force. It stated: "Any discrimination based on any ground such as sex, race, colour, ethnic or social origin, genetic features, language, religion or belief, political or any other opinion, membership of a national minority, property, birth, disability, age or sexual orientation shall be prohibited."

- The constitution confirmed that EU law had "primacy" over national law and gave the EU the power to sign international treaties on behalf of its member countries.

- It created the post of European public prosecutor and devised common policies on foreign affairs and defense matters, though national vetoes would remain in these areas.

To come into force the new constitutional treaty had to be ratified by all 25 member states either through referenda or by votes in the national parliaments. Its rejection in France and The Netherlands therefore meant that it had to be abandoned for the foreseeable future, though proponents insisted that the constitution was not dead. Until agreement on a new set of rules was reached—and no alternative had been announced as of year's end—the EU would have to work under the existing treaty rules. Many of the failed constitution's advocates argued that this situation would mean ineffectual decision making and would leave the EU less effective than it should be in international affairs.   (TOBY HELM)

A few weeks later Luxembourg, the chief beneficiary of EU funds in per capita terms, approved the constitution by a surprisingly narrow margin (56.5–43.5%), which reinforced the impression that support for the treaty was fading. A period of indecision followed. Should referenda proceed in other countries, while a rescue plan was devised? If they did, would there be a chain reaction of "no" votes that would further damage the EU's reputation and morale?

Pro-EU British Prime Minister Tony Blair (*see* BIOGRAPHIES) had committed his people to a referendum that looked impossible to win. The collapse of the constitution might have come as a relief, although he was at pains not to say so publicly. In a landmark speech on June 23 to the European Parliament in Brussels, Blair took the lead in arguing for a profound rethink about the direction in which Europe should go. The "no" votes, he said, had been a "wake-up call" for the EU. Europe's

leaders could no longer kid themselves that it was "business as usual," and the community would need to redefine its economic priorities and develop a more modern economic philosophy before it thought again about how to expand its powers and enlarge its institutions. Blair insisted, "It is a time to recognize that only by change will Europe recover its strength, its relevance, its idealism, and therefore its support amongst the people."

During the second half of the year, after the U.K. took over the EU presidency, Blair led calls for reform of the so-called Europe social model of high social protection (put in place after World War II), which he said had failed to adapt to the challenges of globalization and the threat from such emerging economies as India and China. Europe's labour markets were too inflexible and contributed to unemployment, which had risen to 20 million in Europe—with almost 5 million people out of work in Germany, the former engine of the EU

economy. Blair asserted that the community's common agricultural policy desperately needed reform so that more of the EU budget would go to support training and industries of the future rather than to prop up unproductive farmers through overly generous farm support and export subsidies.

Blair's approach infuriated the French and German governments. Chirac immediately hit back, saying that he would refuse to accept any change to agricultural subsidies, which benefited millions of small French farmers. Blair offered to give up Britain's 21-year-old deal, known as the rebate, under which the U.K. received £3 billion (about $5.5 billion) back from Brussels in recognition of its lower farm-subsidy payments. German Chancellor Gerhard Schröder also fell out spectacularly with the British prime minister, who, Schröder said, wanted to abandon Europe's political project and return the EU to a mere free-trade area. Europe was locked in bitter stalemate as it tried to address its next big challenge—the shape of the EU budget from 2007 to 2013. In September Schröder, a Social Democrat, narrowly lost the German election to his centre-right opponent, Angela Merkel (*see* BIOGRAPHIES).

Arguments were also opening up on other fronts. Turkey, which with 70 million citizens would become the EU's most populous country, was hoping to open negotiations in October on its entry into the community in several years' time. There was strong opposition, particularly from Austria, which feared an influx of Turks and threatened to block the opening of talks. Not only deeper integration but the goal of further expansion was under threat. The deadlock over Turkey was broken, and in a rare success negotiations opened in October.

At a summit in October at Hampton Court near London, EU leaders agreed to commit themselves to economic reform. In Brussels in December a new budget defined support for the economies of the 10 new members and required the European Commission to undertake a full review of the budget.

(TOBY HELM)

MULTINATIONAL AND REGIONAL ORGANIZATIONS

High oil prices, natural disasters, insurgency in Iraq, terrorism, and interregional trade ties were among the issues of concern to multinational and regional organizations in 2005. There were also increased efforts to address Africa's needs.

The 2004 Indian Ocean tsunami that killed more than 200,000 people in 12 countries triggered responses by the Association of Southeast Asian Nations (ASEAN), Asia-Pacific Economic Cooperation (APEC), and the Intergovernmental Oceanographic Commission (IOC), which operates under UNESCO. Beginning on January 6 with a Special ASEAN Summit in Jakarta, the focus was on creating a tsunami-warning system for the Indian Ocean and strengthening disaster-response capabilities. A series of subsequent meetings involving 21 countries in the Indian Ocean region as well as other states and organizations led in June to the creation of the Intergovernmental Coordination Group for the Indian Ocean Tsunami and Mitigation System. The IOC was charged with coordinating the establishment of this system, which was expected to be fully operational by July 2006. In addition, APEC created the Emergency Response Preparedness Task Force and the Virtual Task Force for Emergency Preparedness to strengthen preventive measures, enhance preparedness, build disaster-management capacity, and develop disaster-reduction technologies throughout the region. ASEAN, in turn, initiated the Agreement on Disaster Management and Emergency Response and conducted the first Regional Disaster Emergency Response Simulation Exercise in September. (*See* ECONOMIC AFFAIRS: *Special Report.*)

ASEAN members continued discussions of the possibility of free-trade areas with India, the European Union, China, South Korea, Australia, and New Zealand, as well as progressing toward full implementation of the ASEAN Free Trade Area. At the ASEAN summit held in December in Kuala Lumpur, Malaysia, ASEAN hosted the first ASEAN-Russia Summit and the inaugural East Asia Summit.

At its annual summit in November in Pusan, S.Kor., APEC issued a joint statement of support for the World Trade Organization Doha round of negotiations. In addition, the Pusan Declaration included trade and investment-related commitments, several counter-terrorism initiatives, measures aimed at strengthening cooperation and technical assistance to address the threat of avian flu, and the APEC initiative on Preparing for and Mitigating an Influenza Pandemic.

The Arab League free-trade zone went into effect on January 1 and covered 94% of Arab trade volume. In May the league also explored new trade and investment cooperation opportunities at the Arab–South American summit. Disagreements over the Saudi peace initiative kept eight leaders away from the March summit; no action was taken on the political crisis in Lebanon or Iraq or on demands for withdrawal of Syrian troops from Lebanon. In November the Arab League hosted a reconciliation conference for leaders of Iraqi political groups that called for withdrawal of foreign troops on a timetable linked to a national program for rebuilding Iraq's security forces.

Arab League members met with African Union (AU) members in June for the first Afro-Arab summit that discussed the situation in the Darfur region of The Sudan and aid to African Arabs. The AU itself mediated talks to end the Darfur conflict and enlarged the African Union Mission in The Sudan (AMIS II) from 3,320 to more than 7,000 troops and police from five countries. In May the United States, Canada, the European Union, and some African states pledged almost $300 million to AMIS II. The AU's fourth Extraordinary Summit on August 4 reaffirmed the common AU position on several UN reform issues, most notably the enlargement of the Security Council.

The Group of Eight summit in July in Gleneagles, Scot., produced major commitments to helping Africa, including a comprehensive agreement to double aid to the world's poorest countries by 2010, cancel debt for the 18 poorest African nations, realize universal health care and education for children by 2015, and train up to 25,000 African peacekeeping troops. Little headway was made, however, on the climate-change plan of action.

Energy issues were a major concern in 2005, particularly the record-high oil prices throughout the year. The conflict in Iraq and the hurricanes on the U.S. Gulf Coast contributed to prices that topped $70 a barrel in September. OPEC sought to stabilize the market with production increases and a comprehensive long-term strategy that emphasized investment in refineries and technology to lower prices.

The fourth Summit of the Americas in Mar del Plata, Arg., in November was marked by riots and demonstrations against U.S. Pres. George W. Bush, free-market policies, and the war in Iraq. Opponents of free trade, led by Venezuelan Pres. Hugo Chávez (*see* BIOGRAPHIES), blocked any advance in negotiations on the proposed Free Trade Area of the Americas (FTAA). Small Latin American countries feared that the agreement would benefit the United States and larger countries at the expense of the poor; Brazil and Argentina opposed the U.S. version of FTAA. The summit's outcome, along with the election in May of the first Organization of American States secretary-general not endorsed by the U.S. (Chilean José Miguel Insulza), signaled the erosion of U.S. influence in the Americas. (MARGARET P. KARNS)

DEPENDENT STATES

Europe and the Atlantic. It was reported in May 2005 that as of January 1, Greenland had 56,969 inhabitants, including 14,874 in the capital, Nuuk. The ruling coalition of Prime Minister Hans Enoksen's centrist Siumut Party and the Inuit Ataqatigiit (IA) collapsed amid budget negotiations in September. In the subsequent general elections on November 15, Siumut retained its 10 seats in Greenland's 31-seat parliament. After more than a week of deliberations, Enoksen formed a new "Northern Lights coalition" with the IA (seven seats) and the centre-right Atassut party (five seats). Denmark and Canada reached agreement in September on the means to resolve their dispute over the ownership of tiny uninhabited Hans Island, which lies between Greenland and Ellesmere Island.

On May 9 the U.K.'s Queen Elizabeth II and the duke of Edinburgh visited Guernsey and Jersey as part of the commemoration of the 60th anniversary of the Channel Islands' liberation from Nazi occupation. Late in the year, Jersey followed Guernsey's lead in the creation of a new ministerial system of government. On December 5 Frank Walker was elected Jersey's first chief minister at the head of a nine-member Council of Ministers. Guernsey's first chief minister, Laurie Morgan, had been elected in May 2004. Sark, the smallest of the four main Channel Islands, held its last election under its ancient system of feudal law on December 7; a new constitution was scheduled to go into effect in 2006. The annual Commonwealth Parliamentary Association British Islands and Mediterranean Region conference took place in Jersey in June. At that meeting and at various other international forums during the year, Gibraltar Chief Minister Peter Caruana and opposition leader Joe Bossano spoke out in defense of the right of self-determination not only for Gibraltar but also for the Falkland Islands/Islas Malvinas.

(MELINDA C. SHEPHERD)

Caribbean and Bermuda. On Nov. 26, 2005, the Dutch government signed a formal agreement resolving that the Netherlands Antilles would cease to exist as a group on July 1, 2007. Aruba, which had long enjoyed control of its own internal affairs, would be joined by Curaçao and Sint Maarten as separate "countries" within the Kingdom of The Netherlands. Bonaire, Saba, and Sint Eustatius opted for a slightly different status as "royal" islands. The Netherlands would retain all responsibility for foreign relations and defense. In March the Dutch government dispatched additional police and customs personnel to the Netherlands Antilles, primarily Curaçao, to intensify the anti-drug-trafficking effort. Venezuela filed a formal protest over the visit of a U.S. warship to Curaçao, but local authorities in

At a press conference in Palm Beach, Aruba, in July, Jug Twitty and his wife, Beth Holloway Twitty, the mother of the disappeared teenager Natalee Holloway, appeal for help.

Willemstad explained that such visits were normal and that the government would not permit any act of aggression to be launched from Curaçao. The disappearance on May 30 of American teenager Natalee Holloway, who was last seen leaving a nightclub on Aruba, drew worldwide media attention but had little effect on Aruba's legislative elections in September. The ruling People's Electoral Movement campaigned on the issues of immigration and economic growth and easily retained its majority.

Puerto Rico's Planning Board projected in February that the economy would grow by 2.3% in 2005, compared with the 2004 growth rate of 2.8%. Gov. Aníbal Acevedo-Vilá stressed the importance of reducing the size of the public sector in Puerto Rico, where 25% of the workforce, or 250,000 people, were government employees; he promised in March to eliminate 23,000 government jobs and close several public agencies. Two months later Moody's Investors Services cut Puerto Rico's credit rating from Baa1 to Baa2. In April a U.S. government audit criticized the U.S. Virgin Islands Port Authority for "mismanaging" millions of dollars on 11 government projects, mainly by not following the rules on competitive bidding.

The Anguilla United Front (AUF), led by Osbourne Fleming, retained its hold on power with a four-seat majority in Anguilla's February general elections. The AUF campaigned on its development record, specifically the $25 million expansion of the island's airport. The Anguilla National Strategic Alliance (two seats) remained the official opposition party. In the Cayman Islands the ruling United Democratic Party (UDP) was voted out of office in the May general elections. The People's Progressive Movement, led by Kurt Tibbets, won 9 of the 15 legislative seats, while the UDP retained only 5 seats, including that of its leader, McKeeva Bush. Montserrat, which had been virtually cut off from the outside world following the 1995 volcanic eruption, had commercial air links finally restored in July, when a scheduled service with Antigua was inaugurated.

Throughout 2005 Bermuda celebrated its quincentennial, the 500th anniversary of the first sighting of the island by Spanish explorer Juan de Bermúdez. The Bermuda Independence Commission, which pro-independence Premier Alex Scott had appointed in December 2004, issued its report in September 2005. Although the British government had indicated that it was open to discussions on independence for the overseas territory, polls showed that a majority of Bermudians remained opposed to it.   (DAVID RENWICK)

Pacific Ocean. In French Polynesia in 2005, there was continuing political instability, which reflected the rivalry between pro-France and pro-independence groups. After disputed Territorial Assembly elections in May 2004, a court ruling identified electoral irregularities in the Windward constituency and declared void results in 37 of the 57 seats in Tahiti and Moorea. In the subsequent by-election in February 2005, a six-party coalition headed by pro-independence leader Oscar Temaru secured an overall majority, and Temaru assumed power.

Leadership struggles within the proFrench Rassemblement-UMP party had little impact on New Caledonia's political life, which was dominated by a proindependence coalition. Goro Nickel, a $1.8 billion venture, secured tax concessions of some $500 million from the French government. The company's local position was also strengthened by the sale of a 10% stake to provincial governments. France settled a dispute on Wallis Island between customary leaders by reaffirming its support for 86-year-old King Tomasi Kulimoetoke, the last remaining monarch in the French state.

Following contentious legislative elections in September 2004 and weeks of uncertainty, Jim Marurai emerged in December 2004 as the Cook Islands' new prime minister. Marurai emphasized the importance of political stability and public-sector reform. The Cook Islands were affected by five cyclones early in the year, with the capital, Rarotonga, and the northern islands of Pukapuka and Nassau the worst affected. Marurai met in October with New Zealand Prime Minister Helen Clark to discuss repairs and reconstruction of damaged areas. Elections in Niue in April installed three new members (and three women) in the 20-member parliament; Young Vivian was reelected as premier. A year after being devastated by Cyclone Heta, Niue escaped any serious damage from the 2005 cyclones. Construction began on a replacement hospital, to be funded by New Zealand, and plans were under way for an industrial and commercial park.

American Samoa, following allegations that Samoans were abusing the U.S. territory's 14-day permit system, tightened controls. Samoa did likewise and then insisted that all travelers carry passports. This particularly affected visitors who traveled on U.S. military IDs, especially American Samoan military reservists. In March armed FBI agents arrived in American Samoa's capital, Pago Pago, to execute search warrants as part of an ongoing investigation into public corruption. Despite the protests of officials, the agents removed a number of individual and company tax records.

Guam projected a significant deficit for 2005 after government finances were affected by U.S. federal tax cuts, volatility in the tourism industry, and overexpenditure by government. The Commonwealth of the Northern Marianas faced similar difficulty, with an accumulated deficit exceeding $100 million, much of it arrears in contributions to the retirement fund for government employees. The local tourism industry coped with an anticipated decline of 45% after Japan Airlines suspended flights between Tokyo and the Marianas, and the local garment-manufacturing industry, which was based on immigrant labour, dealt with the implications of increases in the U.S. minimum wage.   (BARRIE MACDONALD)

Indian Ocean. Problems continued in 2005 with illegal travel from Comoros to Mayotte, which had voted to remain under French jurisdiction when the other three islands (Anjouan, Grand Comore, and Mohéli) in the archipelago formed independent Comoros in 1975. The Italian-based Missionary International Service News Agency estimated that some 60,000 Comorans were in Mayotte illegally. In response, François Baroin, the French minister for overseas territories, considered radical steps to fight illegal immigration. These measures included a review of the right to nationality based on place of birth, a principle that allowed anyone born in a French territory to acquire French citizenship. Meanwhile, activists seeking to reintegrate Mayotte into Comoros established committees on Mayotte throughout the archipelago and in France.

On Christmas Island work continued on the construction of a $220 million "immigration reception and processing centre" despite concerns that the structure was not needed and warnings by Christmas Island shire Pres. Gordon Thompson that there were no psychiatric services on the island should asylum seekers require them. The facility, which was being paid for by the Australian government, was intended to replace a detention centre that was closed in July. It was reported in November, however, that the shuttered facility would be temporarily reopened to house a group of Indonesian detainees. Christmas Island's isolation was reduced in 2005 when Air Pacific, Fiji's national airline, began a new service from Nadi, Fiji.   (A.R.G. GRIFFITHS)

ANTARCTICA

Ice averaging 2,160 m (7,085 ft) in thickness covers more than about 98% of the continent of Antarctica, which has an area of 14 million sq km (5.4 million sq mi). There is no indigenous human population, and there is no land-based industry. Human activity consists mainly of scientific research. The 45-nation Antarctic Treaty is the managerial mechanism for the region south of latitude 60° S, which includes all of Antarctica. The treaty reserves the area for peaceful purposes, encourages cooperation in science, prescribes environmental protection, allows inspections to verify adherence, and defers the issue of territorial sovereignty.

More than 300 representatives from over 50 governments and international organizations met in Stockholm in June 2005 for the 28th Antarctic Treaty Consultative Meeting (ATCM). The 28 consultative parties (voting members) approved Annex VI to the Protocol on Environmental Protection to the Antarctic Treaty. For almost 14 years the consultative parties had been negotiating the terms of this last piece of the Antarctic environmental regime. Annex VI dealt with "liability arising from environmental emergencies," and once it entered into force, any Antarctic operator who failed to respond promptly and effectively to "environmental emergencies arising from its activities" would be liable for the costs incurred by another operator. The governments of all 28 consultative parties had to ratify the measure, however, before the annex would enter into force.

Tourism in Antarctica, which had tripled in the past decade, was also discussed in Stockholm. During the 2004–05 austral summer, more than 27,000 tourists visited Antarctica by ship. Another 878 flew to Antarctica and landed on the continent. Working with the International Association of Antarctic Tour Operators, representatives of Australia, the U.K., and the U.S. proposed *Site Guidelines for Visitors*, which the consultative parties adopted. These guidelines provided recommendations for the most frequently visited sites, including guidance on how tour operators and guides should conduct site visits and take into account environmental sensitivities.

On February 12 Norway's Queen Sonja officially opened the expanded Troll Station in Dronning Maud Land,

Dependent States[1]	
Australia	**United Kingdom**
Christmas Island	Anguilla
Cocos (Keeling) Islands	Bermuda
Norfolk Island	British Virgin Islands
	Cayman Islands
Denmark	Falkland Islands
Faroe Islands	Gibraltar
Greenland	Guernsey
	Isle of Man
France	Jersey
French Guiana	Montserrat
French Polynesia	Pitcairn Island
Guadeloupe	Saint Helena
Martinique	Tristan da Cunha
Mayotte	Turks and Caicos
New Caledonia	Islands
Réunion	
Saint Pierre and	**United States**
Miquelon	American Samoa
Wallis and Futuna	Guam
	Northern Mariana
Netherlands, The	Islands
Aruba	Puerto Rico
Netherlands Antilles	Virgin Islands
	(of the U.S.)
New Zealand	
Cook Islands	
Niue	
Tokelau	

[1]Excludes territories (1) to which Antarctic Treaty is applicable in whole or in part, (2) without permanent civilian population, (3) without internationally recognized civilian government (Western Sahara), or (4) representing unadjudicated unilateral or multilateral territorial claims.

East Antarctica. Troll Station, with its airfield, was managed by the Norwegian Polar Institute, which would conduct year-round research ranging from glacier studies to greenhouse-gas monitoring to meteorological observations. France and Italy in November completed winter operations at Concordia Station, located in East Antarctica on the polar plateau near Dome C—one of only three inland Antarctic stations and the first multinational station. A team of nine technical staff and four scientists planned to monitor the new structure and conduct research in astronomy, glaciology, atmospheric chemistry, earth sciences, microbiology, and remote medicine.

By February the main station modules had been completed on the U.S. Amundsen-Scott South Pole Station at the geographic South Pole. Later in the year the communications facility was moved to the new station. The new station was scheduled to be dedicated in January 2007. The old station's geodesic dome would be dismantled and removed from Antarctica in accordance with environmental regulations. The British Antarctic Survey (BAS) announced the selection of a design for the Halley Research Station on the Brunt Ice Shelf in Coats Land. The winning design by Faber Maunsell and Hugh Broughton Architects was one of 86 schemes submitted. The modular station would be built on ski-based jackable legs in order to avoid burial by snow. The structure was devised to be towable so that the modules could be relocated inland periodically as the ice shelf flowed toward the sea.

Polar researchers throughout the world began preparations for the 2007–08 International Polar Year (IPY). Under the auspices of the International Council for Science and the World Meteorological Organization, the IPY science planning group published the *IPY Science Plan and Implementation Strategy*, a document that included input from 40 government and nongovernmental organizations and 32 national IPY planning committees. A program office was established in December 2004 at the BAS, and in May 2005 David Carlson of the U.S. National Center for Atmospheric Research in Boulder, Colo., was named director.

In November 2004 the iceberg B-15A began to drift away from Ross Island along the coast of Victoria Land. B-15A—which was 115 km long (1 km = about 0.62 mi) and had an area of more than 2,500 sq km (about 965 sq mi)—

had been grounded for nearly five years in McMurdo Sound. It disrupted ocean currents, wind circulation, and supply operations to the U.S. and New Zealand research stations located on Ross Island, caused sea ice in McMurdo Sound to reach record thicknesses, and disturbed the breeding habits of the region's Adélie penguin population. Scientists forecast that the iceberg would collide with the Drygalski ice tongue, a 20-km-wide ice projection that extended into McMurdo Sound. Although some predicted the "collision of the century," B-15A did only a small amount of damage to the ice tongue before breaking up in November 2005.

By comparing the genetic code retrieved from 6,000-year-old remains of Adélie penguins with that of modern Adélies living at the same site as their ancestors, a team of researchers from Italy, New Zealand, and the U.S. showed that microevolution—the process of evolutionary change at or below the species level—had occurred in the population. The alleles (slight variations in the genetic coding) from ancient birds differed in several significant ways from those in the modern populations. The data also suggested that the remarkable lack of genetic differentiation between current Adélie populations around Antarctica might have been prompted by changes in migration patterns caused by giant icebergs similar to B-15A. Previous studies had shown genetic similarities across modern Adélie colonies, despite each individual bird's natural instinct to return to its natal location to breed, a behaviour that would be expected over time to promote genetic differences between colonies.

Scientists from the BAS and the U.S. Geological Survey found that over the last 61 years, 87% of 244 marine glacier fronts in the Antarctic Peninsula had retreated and that this glacial retreat was moving progressively south. Although there was evidence in 2005 that atmospheric warming in the peninsula region was driving the retreat, the researchers' observations suggested that other forces were working to accelerate the process. The scientists found that temperatures had increased in that area of Antarctica by as much as 2 °C (3.6 °F) since the 1950s. These increased temperatures were bringing about the collapse of ice shelves along the peninsula, and the research teams believed that the loss of the ice shelves was accelerating the retreat and contributing significantly to a rise in sea level.

The European Project for Ice Coring (EPICA), a consortium of 10 European countries, retrieved a 3,270.2-m (about 10,700-ft) ice core at Concordia Station, Dome C. Covering some 900,000 years, the core was composed of the oldest ice ever retrieved and contained an equally long, uninterrupted record of Antarctic climate. Although EPICA scientists had only begun to study this core, their analysis had already demonstrated that the four earliest interglacials (warmer periods between cold glacial periods) were cooler but lasted longer than the more recent interglacials.　　(WINIFRED REUNING)

ARCTIC REGIONS

The Arctic regions may be defined in physical terms (astronomical [north of the Arctic Circle, latitude 66° 30′ N], climatic [above the 10 °C (50 °F) July isotherm], or vegetational [above the northern limit of the tree line]) or in human terms (the territory inhabited by the circumpolar cultures—Inuit [Eskimo] and Aleut in North America and Russia, Sami [Lapp] in northern Scandinavia and Russia, and 29 other peoples of the Russian North, Siberia, and East Asia). No single national sovereignty or treaty regime governs the region, which includes portions of eight countries: Canada, the United States, Russia, Finland, Sweden, Norway, Iceland, and Greenland (part of Denmark). The Arctic Ocean, 14.09 million sq km (5.44 million sq mi) in area, constitutes about two-thirds of the region. The land area consists of permanent ice cap, tundra, or taiga. The population (2005 est.) of peoples belonging to the circumpolar cultures is more than 450,000 (Aleuts [in Russia and Alaska], 3,000; Athabascans [North America], 32,000; Inuits [or Eskimos, in Russian Chukhotka, North America, and Greenland], 155,000; Sami [Northern Europe], 70,000; and 40 indigenous peoples of the Russian North, totaling nearly 200,000). International organizations concerned with the Arctic include the Arctic Council, the Barents Euro-Arctic Council, the Inuit Circumpolar Conference, and the Indigenous Peoples' Secretariat. International scientific cooperation in the Arctic is the focus of the International Arctic Research Center of the University of Alaska at Fairbanks.

In 2005 the "pipeline race" continued between the proposed natural gas pipeline from Alaska's Prudhoe Bay south through the Yukon to the U.S. Midwest and a separate gas pipeline project from the Mackenzie River Delta to serve the rapidly developing oil-sands developments in northern Alberta. The Alaska pipeline, expected to cost some $20 billion, was proposed in the 1970s to carry an estimated 991 billion cu m (1 cu m = 35.3 cu ft) of natural gas—enough to supply about one-tenth of the country's natural gas needs. In September Alaska Gov. Frank Murkowski announced that state officials and the major North Slope producers, led by Exxon Mobil Corp., had made enough progress on negotiating fiscal terms to be able to sign a contract by the end of the year. To help spur the pipeline forward, the state also had agreed to invest $3 billion in return for part ownership in the project. In November the president of Exxon Mobil indicated that he believed the Mackenzie Valley gas pipeline would be built before the Alaska pipeline.

In February the panel conducting the environmental analysis of the Mackenzie pipeline halted the review process for the third time until Imperial Oil and the other pipeline proponents provided additional information to supplement their 6,500-page submission on how the project would affect the communities along its 1,200-km (1 km = 0.62 mi) route. Imperial Oil and its partners announced in May that they were halting all nonregulatory work on the project because of unanticipated regulatory delays and higher-than-expected demands from the First Nations for compensation and for permission to access their lands for the pipeline route. In July a study by the engineering firm Sproule Associates Ltd. estimated that a larger-capacity pipeline should be built because revised estimates of gas reserves indicated that there could be about 1.3 trillion cu m of undiscovered gas in the Mackenzie Delta and the Beaufort Sea, more than four times the estimate used by Imperial in its original project proposal.

In March the U.S. Senate voted narrowly in favour of allowing exploratory drilling in the environmentally and politically sensitive Arctic National Wildlife Refuge (ANWR). Canada continued to oppose exploration in this area, citing a 1987 Canada-U.S. agreement to refrain from activities in the refuge that could have a negative impact on the environment and wildlife. Canadian Prime Minister Paul Martin suggested that U.S. access to the enormous reserves in the oil sands of northern Alberta would be more than adequate to offset any loss of potential oil production if the U.S. continued to protect the ANWR. Congress was expected to vote on the drilling provision, which was included in the annual budget bill, by the end of the year. Oil exploration in the ANWR was approved by the U.S.

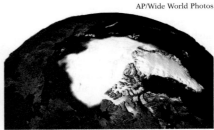

The two satellite images show the minimum extent of Arctic sea ice in 1979 (left) and in 2005 (right). Scientists reported that average air temperatures in the Arctic were rising and that in September 2005 the area covered by sea ice in the Arctic was the least ever recorded through satellite observations.

House of Representatives as a part of a Department of Defense appropriations bill, but passage of the ANWR provision was blocked by the U.S. Senate.

An Arctic Climate Impact Assessment report issued in March noted that the average temperature in the Arctic had risen by 0.4 °C (0.7 °F) per decade since the mid-1960s. The study also indicated that the current warming in the Arctic was without precedent since the last ice age. According to a Woods Hole Research Center study, rising temperatures and concentrations of carbon dioxide were causing a "greening" of the frozen tundra and permafrost. Indications were that more plant growth and longer growing seasons were occurring in northern Canada and Alaska and that there was a decline in the immense boreal forests from the interior of Alaska into northern Canada. In August the British newspaper *The Guardian* reported that Exit Glacier in Alaska's Kenai Fjords National Park had receded 300 m (1 m = 3.28 ft) in the past 10 years, while Muir Glacier in Glacier Bay had retreated eight kilometres in the past 30 years. In September the U.S.-based National Snow and Ice Data Center (NSIDC) reported a continuing decay in the polar ice cap for the fourth consecutive year. Satellite images showed 5.3 million sq km (1 sq km = 0.39 sq mi) of sea ice. According to the NSIDC, this was the lowest measurement of sea ice ever recorded and represented a decrease of 1.66 million sq km (an area more than twice the size of Texas) from the average 6.96-million-sq-km end-of-summer ice-pack data recorded since 1979. It also was reported that the sea-ice change appeared to be self-sustaining because solar energy was being absorbed by the increased amount of open water instead of being reflected back into space by bright white ice, thus raising ocean temperatures. Early in the year the Inuit Circumpolar Conference, representing 155,000 Inuit around the

world, began legal proceedings to convince the Inter-American Commission on Human Rights that global warming caused by the emission of greenhouse gases was a violation of Inuit human rights.

Ottawa continued to fend off challenges to Canadian sovereignty over its northern regions. In September Canadian and Russian officials met to discuss sharing responsibility for surveillance of the Arctic. The unprecedented cooperation included trading images from satellites and unmanned aerial vehicles. The Canadian military expanded its presence in the Arctic by sending troops and warships north for training purposes and by patrolling its northern waters.

Substantial progress was made on planning for the 2007–08 International Polar Year, the fourth time in some 125 years that scientists from around the world would collaborate on researching environmental and social phenomena in the polar regions. It was reported that 50 countries had already submitted approximately 12,000 proposed studies. For the first time, a priority was being placed on involving people who lived in the northern regions, making use of their indigenous knowledge, and scrutinizing the impact of climate change.

In July it was announced that Canada was set to establish its first marine sanctuary for bowhead whales in the waters of Baffin Island's Isabella Bay. Wildlife officials and local Inuit reported that during the summer open-water season, more than 300 of the 20-m-long whales visited the area, which was dotted with the remains of 19th-century stations whose whalers almost exterminated the bowheads and with remains of Inuit hunting campsites dating back to prehistory. The Inuit population was hoping to benefit from the increasing popularity of the Arctic for cruise ships looking for destinations that could offer authentic wildlife and cultural experiences.   (KENNETH DE LA BARRE)

AFGHANISTAN

Area: 645,807 sq km (249,347 sq mi)
Population (2005 est.): 23,867,000 (excluding 1,900,000 Afghan refugees, numbering about 950,000 in Pakistan and about 950,000 in Iran at the beginning of the year)
Capital: Kabul
Chief of state and head of government:
President Hamid Karzai

In 2005 Afghanistan appeared to move toward constitutional stability and economic growth, but widespread incidents of violence made it clear that the Taliban, driven from power in 2001 by U.S. forces, and other fundamentalist guerrillas remained a serious threat to the government of Pres. Hamid Karzai. Supported by some 30,000 U.S. and NATO soldiers, the Karzai government struggled to broaden its control beyond Kabul and its surroundings.

In February the Taliban announced plans to increase attacks on the government when the weather improved, and throughout the year it carried out drive-by shootings and bombings, mainly directed at local officials and pro-government clergy, and ambushed U.S. soldiers, mostly in the south and east of the country. May saw a dramatic increase in attacks, and on June 1 a suicide bomber killed 20 people in Kandahar's main mosque. The dead included Kabul's security chief, who was attending the funeral of an anti-Taliban

cleric killed three days earlier by two men on a motorcycle. In late June, 16 U.S. servicemen were killed when their helicopter crashed during operations against guerrillas in Kunar province; it was the deadliest year for U.S. forces in Afghanistan since the overthrow of the Taliban. In May anti-American demonstrations in several locations were stoked by a U.S. press report that claimed that U.S. authorities at a prison in Guantánamo Bay, Cuba, had desecrated the Qur'an. At least 14 deaths were reported. After Uzbekistan asked the U.S. in July to vacate the airbase it used there to support operations in Afghanistan, U.S. officials announced that bases in Kyrgyzstan and Afghanistan would be used instead. In December the U.S. announced that in 2006 it would reduce its military presence in Afghanistan from 19,000 troops to about 16,000.

The process outlined in the Bonn agreement of December 2001 by which Afghanistan's state structure would be rebuilt approached completion with the September 18 election of the Wolesi Jirga, the lower house of Afghanistan's National Assembly, and provincial and local councils across the country. That process included the adoption of a constitution and the 2004 election of Karzai as president. Zalmay Khalilzad, the U.S. ambassador to Afghanistan who had played a very active role in implementing the Bonn agreement, left in June to represent the U.S. in Iraq. The September parliamentary elections had been scheduled together with the presidential election in October 2004 but were twice delayed. The constitution required at least two female delegates

from each of Afghanistan's 34 provinces in the 249-member Wolesi Jirga, and election officials said that almost 350 of some 2,900 candidates were female. Almost 280 women sought places on provincial councils. One-third of the National Assembly's Meshrano Jirga (upper House of Elders) was to be chosen from these newly elected provincial councils. Though Taliban guerrillas had promised not to disrupt the polling, they carried out a deadly campaign of violence leading up to the elections and killed several candidates and election workers.

Afghanistan's economic situation in 2005 generated both optimism and alarm. Obvious enthusiasm from international investors focused on opportunities arising from the need for goods and services to satisfy domestic demand and the promise of traditional exports of agricultural products and minerals. President Karzai spoke of the positive effects of Afghanistan's role as a land bridge connecting the Middle East, China, and India and welcomed investment in transportation and power generation. In addition to security concerns and the weakness of the central government, economic progress was stymied by bad roads, land mines, lack of electricity, and a poor educational system. The greatest threat to economic recovery, however, remained the nationwide economic dependence on opium production. Afghanistan supplied most of the world's opium, which was smuggled through Central Asia and Pakistan to be processed into heroin for the world market. UN sources reported that while the area under cultivation had decreased in 2005, yield per hectare had increased.

Relations with neighbouring Pakistan were strained as Kabul officials continued to assert that madrasahs and camps in Pakistan were providing training and refuge for fighters carrying out antigovernment attacks and killings inside Afghanistan. Pakistan's government denied official responsibility, but stories from individuals seemed to corroborate Kabul's position. India, which had traditionally sought good relations with Afghanistan, stepped up its effort when India's Prime Minister Manmohan Singh visited in August. One of the most generous aid donors to Afghanistan, India directed its assistance at education, health care and power sectors, and training for civil servants and police.

(STEPHEN SEGO)

Claims that U.S. authorities had desecrated a Qur'an in their detention facilities at Guantánamo Bay, Cuba, stoked popular demonstrations in Afghanistan. On May 12 some 200 students march in Kabul, holding up copies of the Islamic holy book and chanting anti-American slogans.

ALBANIA

Area: 28,703 sq km (11,082 sq mi)
Population (2005 est.): 3,130,000 (not including Albanians living abroad)
Capital: Tirana
Chief of state: President Alfred Moisiu
Head of government: Prime Ministers Fatos Nano and, from September 11, Sali Berisha

Sali Berisha addresses his followers at a rally in Tirana on July 4 after he claimed victory for his Democratic Party in the general elections. Berisha was president of Albania from 1992 to 1997.

Albania experienced a major political turnaround in 2005 when on July 3 the centre-right coalition of former president Sali Berisha won the general elections. Berisha had led the opposition to the governing Socialist Party of Prime Minister Fatos Nano since he was ousted as president in 1997. His Democratic Party won the 2005 elections largely by charging the Nano government with nepotism and by pledging to root out corruption and organized crime. Furthermore, Berisha promised tax cuts and the creation of attractive conditions for foreign direct investment. His coalition received 81 of the 140 seats in the parliament. The Socialist-led centre-left coalition received the remaining 59 seats. International observers approved the conduct of the election campaign and of the elections. The appointment of the new government was delayed, however, because voting in three constituencies had to be repeated owing to irregularities. Pres. Alfred Moisiu presented Berisha's new government on September 7, and the parliament approved it three days later. Berisha appointed the writer Besnik Mustafaj of his Democratic Party the new foreign minister, and the party received nine other key ministries. Leaders of four smaller coalition parties were given portfolios in the new government. Fatmir Mediu (Republican Party) took defense, Genc Pollo (New Democratic Party) received education, Lufter Xhuveli (Agrarian Party) was given environment, and Kosta Barka (of the mainly ethnic Greek Human Rights Union Party) took on social affairs. Nano resigned as chairman of the Socialist Party and was succeeded by Edi Rama, the mayor of Tirana.

The new government said it would increase its efforts to pursue Euro-Atlantic integration. Albania had begun negotiations for an EU Association and Stabilization Agreement in 2003, but the European Commission repeatedly postponed the signing, arguing that Albania had to show better results in fighting corruption and organized crime. An agreement with the EU was signed in Luxembourg on April 14 that obligated Albania to take back illegal migrants who had entered the EU via its territory.

Albania continued to pursue regional military cooperation. Defense Minister Pandeli Majko signed a memorandum on military cooperation with his Bulgarian and Macedonian counterparts on May 17. Along with Macedonia and Croatia, Albania was a founding member of the U.S.-backed Adriatic Charter, which promoted NATO membership. Furthermore, Albania participated in two international peacekeeping missions. On March 7 Majko and the EU high representative for common foreign and security policy, Javier Solana, signed an agreement on Albania's participation in EUFOR, the EU's peacekeeping mission in Bosnia and Herzegovina. The Albanian government also increased its military contingent in Mosul, Iraq, by 50 troops, reaching a force level of 120 in April. Joint military exercises with the U.S. were overshadowed by the crash of a U.S. C-130 transport plane on March 31, in which nine people were killed.   (FABIAN SCHMIDT)

ALGERIA

Area: 2,381,741 sq km (919,595 sq mi)
Population (2005 est.): 32,854,000
Capital: Algiers
Chief of state: President Abdelaziz Bouteflika
Head of government: Prime Minister Ahmed Ouyahia

The year 2005 in Algeria was one of consolidation. Despite a brief upsurge in violence in May, the capture in January in Algiers of Noureddine Boudiafi, the head of the Armed Islamic Group, meant that only the Salafist Group for Preaching and Combat (GSPC) continued to be active. In June the GSPC was accused of having organized an attack on a Mauritanian army outpost just as the United States, Algeria, and Sahel countries were organizing military exercises in the Sahara. After a referendum held on September 29 on a plan for national reconciliation received 97% support from the 79% of the electorate who voted, some dissidents in western Kabylia submitted to the authorities, and others were expected to follow.

The reconciliation plan was criticized by international human rights organizations in April because it implicitly offered immunity to the security forces for their involvement in abuses during the eight-year-long civil war. Their criticisms came after the official human rights monitoring organization in Algeria confirmed, in a report to the president on March 31, that 6,146 persons had "disappeared" in the struggle. As part of the complex legal package adopted after the referendum, the government offered families of the disappeared financial compensation rather than investigation. The public in Algeria was outraged by the kidnapping and murder of two Algerian diplomats in Baghdad on July 27. Ali Belhadj, the former deputy leader of the banned Islamic Salvation Front, was accused of having supported the murders; he was arrested and faced a 10-year prison sentence.

In keeping with his hegemony over the domestic political scene, Pres. Abdelaziz Bouteflika was elected head of the newly unified National Liberation Front (FLN), which had supported an alternative candidate in the 2004 presidential elections. The government's plans to end the crisis in Kabylia—which had begun in 2001 when a teenager was killed in gendarmerie custody—was abruptly thrown into confusion in mid-September when President Bouteflika unexpectedly reversed his policy to give the Berber language of Tamazight official status alongside Arabic in the constitution. The by-elections that were demanded by Kabylia as part of the deal did go ahead as planned at the end of November.

On March 30 President Bouteflika met the king of Morocco at an Arab League summit in Algiers, raising hopes that they might negotiate a settlement to end the Western Sahara conflict and that the border between the two countries might reopen, but the situation was not resolved. Despite Algerian criticism of French legislation over colonialism, France and Algeria signed a Treaty of Amity at the end of the year. High oil prices ensured a buoyant economy, with foreign debt falling to $18.8 billion and foreign reserves rising to $50 billion, despite a poor cereals harvest in July of 2.5 million metric tons, compared with 4 million metric tons the previous year. Direct private foreign investment rose to $2.1 billion, and in March the parliament passed an energy-liberalization law that was expected to allow the Algerian oil concern Sonatrach to become an international company. The move

came as Algeria sought to increase its oil-production capacity significantly.

(GEORGE JOFFÉ)

ANDORRA

Area: 464 sq km (179 sq mi)
Population (2005 est.): 74,800
Capital: Andorra la Vella
Chiefs of state: Co-princes of Andorra, the president of France and the bishop of Urgell, Spain
Head of government: Chief Executives Marc Forné Molné and, from May 27, Albert Pintat Santolària

More than 80% of Andorran voters cast their ballots in parliamentary elections held on April 24, 2005. The ruling Andorran Liberal Party (PLA) won 14 of the 28 seats in the General Council. The Social Democratic Party (PS) captured 11 seats; the Democratic Center of Andorra (CDA) won 2; and Democratic Renovation (RD) claimed 1.

Chief Executive Marc Forné Molné stepped down after the elections. Albert Pintat Santolària, also a PLA member and former foreign minister, succeeded him on May 27. The new government's immediate concerns were to ease the restrictions on citizenship—only about

one-third of the population were citizens—and deal with the scarcity of housing. Andorra continued to work toward developing its relationship with the EU, having signed a series of accords in June 2004 involving economic, social, and cultural cooperation. A major task for Andorra was to institute reforms required by the Organisation for Economic Co-operation and Development so that Andorra would be removed from the OECD's list of countries that were deemed tax havens.

The economy continued to thrive as investment in new ski facilities and hotels attracted more long-term visitors.

(ANNE ROBY)

ANGOLA

Area: 1,246,700 sq km (481,354 sq mi)
Population (2005 est.): 11,827,000
Capital: Luanda
Chief of state and head of government: President José Eduardo dos Santos, assisted by Prime Minister Fernando da Piedade Dias dos Santos

An epidemic of hemorrhagic fever caused by the Marburg virus, which had first been noticed in Angola's northern province of Uige toward the

In Uige, northern Angola, on April 19, World Health Organization workers examine the home of a suspected victim of Marburg virus. The virus causes a hemorrhagic fever and is often fatal, especially for young children.

end of 2004, aroused grave concern as the death toll rose steadily into 2005. By early May it had reached nearly 300, many of the victims being children less than five years old. In June, however, the outbreak was thought to have peaked, and fears that the illness might spread even further were calmed.

The government's failure to answer the IMF's questions as to what had become of a $600 million oil-revenue windfall forecast in November 2004 led to the repeated postponement of an IMF mission to Angola and a consequent delay in the provision of financial aid to promote development. China did not share the IMF's reservations. Its offer of a $211 million loan, to be repaid in oil deliveries, was rapidly producing results. Early in the year Chinese workers were already restoring Angola's railway system and constructing new government buildings. Some economists, however, expressed doubts as to whether the government in Luanda had the capacity to maintain such substantial projects. Angolan businessmen and workers protested that the Chinese activities failed to provide them with either contracts or opportunities for employment, and the IMF was worried because the Chinese loan made it easier for the government to cover up its financial position.

Onofre dos Santos, a lawyer who had been director-general of the national electoral council at the time of the last Angolan elections in 1992, was also concerned about the government's lack of transparency regarding its preparations for the parliamentary and presidential elections scheduled for 2006. His doubts, set out in a book published early in 2005, gained wider support when Pres. José Eduardo dos Santos asked the Supreme Court in June whether sections of the new electoral law were unconstitutional. The swift resolution of the matter by the court provided temporary reassurance that this was not a delaying tactic. In August, however, the main opposition party, the National Union for the Total Independence of Angola, protested that the government was itself breaking the electoral law to promote its own case for reelection.

A report published in March claimed that the profits from the diamond industry benefited only a wealthy few. Issues of a similar nature also created trouble in the Cabinda exclave, where a major offensive was launched in June against the Front for the Liberation of the Enclave of Cabinda, which led to protests that the government was trying to destroy its critics rather than address their concerns, foremost among which was the unfair distribution of the region's oil revenues. In Eastern Angola problems persisted over the resettlement and reintegration of the hundreds of thousands who had fled over the border into Zambia or who had been displaced within Angola itself during the civil war. Organizers of the World Food Programme said that in spite of improving harvests, the agency was still feeding 700,000 people.

(KENNETH INGHAM)

ANTIGUA AND BARBUDA

Area: 442 sq km (171 sq mi)
Population (2005 est.): 77,800
Capital: Saint John's
Chief of state: Queen Elizabeth II, represented by Governor-General Sir James Carlisle
Head of government: Prime Minister Baldwin Spencer

The new United Progressive Party (UPP) government in Antigua and Barbuda overturned one of its predecessor's key policies in April 2005 when it restored personal income tax, which would be paid by individuals earning at least EC$3,000 (about U.S.$1,110) a month. Also in April former prime minister Lester Bird, who lost his seat in the election, was nevertheless voted back as leader of the Antigua Labour Party (ALP), which had governed for 28 straight years before being deposed in 2004 by the UPP. Though he faced strong competition from a former planning minister, Gaston Browne, Bird prevailed. His elder brother, however, Vere Bird, Jr., lost his bid for party chairman.

Prime Minister Baldwin Spencer said in May that he would create a special task force to curb organized crime and corruption by government officials; he blamed inaction by past ALP administrations for the upsurge in such ongoing problems.

Venezuela deepened its relations with Antigua and Barbuda in August as part of a wider initiative by Pres. Hugo Chávez to assist Caribbean territories that were hard hit by rising inflation and foreign-exchange shortages largely caused by high oil prices. Besides soft loans for oil purchases, Antigua and Barbuda also received Venezuelan assistance for its outage-plagued electricity system.   (DAVID RENWICK)

ARGENTINA

Area: 2,780,092 sq km (1,073,400 sq mi)
Population (2005 est.): 38,592,000
Capital: Buenos Aires
Head of state: President Néstor Kirchner

In 2005 Pres. Néstor Kirchner of the Justicialist (Peronist) Party (PJ) greatly consolidated his dominance over the country's political system. Kirchner, elected in 2003 with the support of then president Eduardo Duhalde—at the time the undisputed boss of the PJ in the province of Buenos Aires (PBA)—had maintained a tacit alliance with Duhalde under which the former president supported Kirchner in national-level affairs and Kirchner did not interfere with politics in the PBA. Chafing at the continued power wielded by Duhalde, Kirchner broke with him and challenged Duhalde's party machine in the PBA in the October 23 midterm elections.

Kirchner's challenge proved to be very successful. The PBA Senate race was the marquee battle of the day. The race featured Kirchner's spouse, Sen. Cristina Fernández de Kirchner, running under the Front for Victory banner against Duhalde's spouse, former congressional deputy Hilda ("Chiche") González de Duhalde, of the Justicialist Front. "Cristina" soundly defeated "Chiche" by a margin of 46% to 20%, which thereby strengthened Kirchner's control of the PJ at the national level and in the PBA and severely weakened Duhalde politically.

Throughout the country members of the governing PJ ran on numerous party lists, often competing among themselves (for instance, in many provinces a pro-Kirchner faction competed as the Front for Victory and an anti-Kirchner or neutral PJ faction as either the official PJ or using a province-specific name). The PJ (including a handful of non-Peronists placed on the Peronist lists at Kirchner's behest as well as a handful of anti-Kirchner Peronists) won 21 of the 24 Senate seats and 78 of the

127 Chamber seats. A very fragmented non-Peronist opposition won the remaining seats. The Radical Civic Union garnered the 3 other Senate seats as well as 21 Chamber seats. Only two other parties won 5 or more seats in the Chamber: Affirmation for an Equitable Republic and Republican Proposal, each of which won 9 seats.

Argentina enjoyed robust growth in 2005 as the economy benefited from elevated world prices for the country's principal agricultural and mineral exports, a booming industrial sector (aided by a purposefully undervalued peso), and a high level of consumer confidence. While the country's GDP grew by 9% during the year, Argentina's economic future was uncertain. Investors remained reluctant to invest in medium- and long-term projects for a host of reasons, including the prospect of energy shortages in 2006 and beyond, the government's frequent failure to respect legal contracts and negotiate in good faith, the government's often hostile treatment of foreign (in particular) and domestic companies, and a rising inflation rate (12% in 2005).   (MARK P. JONES)

ARMENIA

Area: 29,743 sq km (11,484 sq mi). About 16% of neighbouring Azerbaijan (including the 4,400-sq-km [1,700-sq-mi] disputed region of Nagorno-Karabakh [Armenian: Artsakh]) has been under Armenian control since 1993.
Population (2005 est.): 2,983,000 (plus 145,000 in Nagorno-Karabakh)
Capital: Yerevan
Chief of state: President Robert Kocharyan
Head of government: Prime Minister Andranik Markaryan

A public spat in Armenia in February–March 2005 between Prime Minister Andranik Markaryan and parliament speaker Artur Baghdasaryan highlighted dissent within the three-party ruling coalition. On May 11 the parliament approved in the first reading government-drafted constitutional amendments intended to curtail the powers of the president and augment those of the legislature, expand basic freedoms, and formalize dual citizenship. Those amendments were reworded following harsh

In 2005 Armenians remembered the 90th anniversary of the "Great Slaughter," the massacre of as many as 1.5 million of their people by the Turks. This granite monument to the events of 1915 was raised in Yerevan in 1965.
AP/Wide World Photos

criticism on May 27 by the Council of Europe's Venice Commission, which approved the revised draft on July 21. Opposition parties nonetheless continued to demand further changes and boycotted an emergency debate on August 29–31 and September 28 during which lawmakers approved the revised draft.

In early September the opposition National Accord Party and eight of the nine parties aligned in the Artarutyun ("Justice") bloc announced the end of the boycott of legislative proceedings they had begun in February 2004 and launched a campaign to persuade voters to reject the draft constitutional amendments. Former prime minister Aram Sarkisyan's Republic Party continued its parliament boycott; seven prominent members of that party defected in early September and later founded a new party, National Rebirth. According to official returns, 65.3% of Armenia's 2.4 million voters endorsed the constitutional changes in a nationwide referendum on November 27. Artarutyun, however, claimed that fewer than the required minimum one-third of all voters approved the changes, and it convened a rally on November 29 to protest the apparent falsification, which Baghdasaryan indirectly admitted.

The economic upswing of recent years continued, with a 12.2% increase in GDP during the first 10 months. On May 25 the IMF approved a new three-year, $34.2 million loan program.

In late April Armenia formally commemorated the 90th anniversary of the mass killings of some 1.5 million ethnic Armenians in Ottoman Turkey. An exchange of letters in April–May between Armenian Pres. Robert Kocharyan and Turkish Prime Minister Recep Tayyip Erdogan did not culminate in the hoped-for meeting between the two

men on the sidelines of the Council of Europe summit in Warsaw on May 16–17, and bilateral relations remained strained.

In November Armenia began talks with the EU on an Action Plan within the framework of the European Neighborhood Policy. In mid-December NATO formally endorsed the Individual Partnership Action Plan that Armenia had submitted in June. Close military and economic cooperation also continued with Russia.   (ELIZABETH FULLER)

AUSTRALIA

Area: 7,692,208 sq km (2,969,978 sq mi)
Population (2005 est.): 20,345,000
Capital: Canberra
Chief of state: Queen Elizabeth II, represented by Governor-General Michael Jeffery
Head of government: Prime Minister John Howard

Domestic Affairs. Prime Minister John Howard dominated the Australian political scene in 2005. His control of both chambers of the federal Parliament—the House of Representatives and the Senate—left him free to set an achievable agenda for significant changes to society. It was the first time in 25 years that an Australian prime minister had been in such a position, and Howard, confident that his plans would eventually become law, moved decisively. The centrepiece of his strategy involved reform to replace the existing Industrial Relations Commission

363

with a unitary industrial relations system. Under a proposed Fair Play Commission, unfair dismissal laws were to be abolished for workplaces with up to 100 employees. Howard kept the labour movement in the dark until the last possible moment, not releasing details of the new laws until late in the year, and thereby deflected criticism and potential strike action.

Following comments by the premier of New South Wales, Bob Carr, that Muslim suicide bombers might strike in Sydney, Howard attempted to bring Muslim citizens into the mainstream of Australian political life by organizing a summit of Muslim leaders to decide how to weed out extremists and stop inappropriate overseas speakers from entering Australia. Howard defended the right of Muslim public-school children to wear headscarves and rejected the views of more conservative members of his government. He did, however, accept the need to release refugee families with children from detention centres, and he assisted Immigration Minister Amanda Vanstone in the difficult task of changing a system that had led to inappropriate imprisonment of the mentally ill and was unduly harsh in its application of visa and residence regulations. The prime minister remained firm in his attitude toward alleged Taliban supporter David Hicks, insisting that the best way to determine whether the U.S. Military Commissions would provide Hicks with a fair trial was to subject the prisoner to one.

In January Mark Latham resigned as leader of the opposition Australian Labor Party (ALP) and gave up his seat in Parliament. Latham, who had failed to defeat Howard's Liberal-National Party coalition in the 2004 general election, had been on leave since December 2004 because of illness. Former ALP leader Kim Beazley was chosen to replace Latham. At the end of July, Carr announced his retirement after a decade at the head of the New South Wales government, though he expressed a desire to remain involved in the ALP.

The Economy. While rising fuel prices had a dampening effect on consumer spending, overall the Australian economy performed well in 2005. Helped by a surplus of $A13.6 billion ($A1 = about U.S.$0.76), Treasurer Peter Costello's 10th budget provided tax cuts for all. The budget axed an unpopular superannuation surcharge, and economists commented that Costello had virtually eliminated the top marginal tax rate of 47%. In the budget there were losers as

Australian Prime Minister John Howard (second from left) makes a surprise visit to Iraq on July 25. He is shown here in Baghdad's Green Zone with Air Marshal Angus Houston (second from right) and Ambassador Howard Brown (right).
© Andrew Taylor/Reuters/Corbis

well as winners, however. The treasurer expressed concern that disability welfare recipients had grown to 6.5% of the workforce and his doubts that 6.5% of Australian workers could be disabled.

The centrepiece of what Costello hoped would be his last budget was the creation of a Future Fund to be seeded with $A16 billion in addition to proceeds from the sale of Australia's major telecommunications company, Telstra. The Future Fund was designed to reduce an unsustainable welfare burden, which was expected to become worse as the elderly population doubled while the workforce remained static. On September 7 the federal government introduced to Parliament the first of its bills for the full sale of Telstra. The sale, which the prime minister described as an impossible quagmire of conflicting interests, proved difficult to manage smoothly. Competing interests struggled for some of the proceeds from the share float, and arguments broke out over whether the assets of the Future Fund should be held in currency or in unsold Telstra shares. Telstra's share price dropped dramatically as an embarrassing row between the government and the Telstra board over deregulation gathered steam.

Foreign Affairs. Australia's new ambassador to Washington, Dennis Richardson, worked hard to explain Canberra's goal of balancing its trading and strategic relationships with China and the U.S. During a midyear visit to the U.S., Prime Minister Howard had positive talks with Pres. George W. Bush, Secretary of State Condoleezza Rice, and Defense Secretary Donald H. Rumsfeld. Howard reaffirmed Australian commitment to the U.S. alliance and the war on terrorism through the continued engagement of troops in Iraq and Afghanistan. When Howard visited London on

his way home from the U.S., there was a second attempt to explode terrorist bombs in that city, and this gave Howard and British Prime Minister Tony Blair the opportunity to reaffirm their joint determination not to let foreign policy be dictated by terrorists. (*See* UNITED KINGDOM.) Howard asserted that a secure future for Australia could lie only in narrowing the productivity gap between high-income countries such as Australia and rising economic powers, notably China and India. To do this, he formed a close team with Foreign Minister Alexander Downer to create networks of strong support with Australia's significant Asian allies, including Singapore, Japan, and Indonesia. Downer also made great progress in improving Australia's standing with its Asian neighbours. At an Association of Southeast Asian Nations (ASEAN) meeting in Vientiane, Laos, Downer announced a new Asia-Pacific climate-control partnership between Australia, the U.S., and several Asian nations. Speaking warmly of the new environmental-development partnership, U.S. Deputy Secretary of State Robert B. Zoellick explained that the U.S. saw this breakthrough as a complement to the Kyoto Treaty and the UN convention on climate change. On July 13 Downer committed Australia to acceding to the ASEAN Treaty of Amity and Cooperation. This opened the way for Australia to be invited to the inaugural East Asian Summit, a meeting of the key leaders of ASEAN, Australia, China, India, Japan, South Korea, and New Zealand to be held in Kuala Lumpur, Malaysia, in December. Earlier in the year Australian Trade Minister Mark Vaile had agreed to free-trade negotiations with China and Malaysia and free-trade agreements with Thailand.

(A.R.G. GRIFFITHS)

AUSTRIA

Area: 83,871 sq km (32,383 sq mi)
Population (2005 est.): 8,168,000
Capital: Vienna
Chief of state: President Heinz Fischer
Head of government: Chancellor Wolfgang Schüssel

Heavy rains and landslides in the western Austrian Tirol region in August caused great damage to structures and closed the road into the Paznauntal valley.

Austria officially designated 2005 a jubilee year as it celebrated 60 years since the founding of the Second Republic after World War II, 50 years since the country regained full independence following the signing of the State Treaty, and 10 years since it joined the EU. Chancellor Wolfgang Schüssel, the leader of the senior party in the ruling coalition, the centre-right Austrian People's Party (ÖVP), might have hoped that these celebrations would help boost his standing (and that of the ÖVP) among the electorate prior to the general election in 2006.

Attention was focused instead on the ÖVP's junior coalition partner, the far-right Freedom Party (FPÖ). In April a bitter dispute between opposing factions in the party came to a head when Jörg Haider—the populist former party leader and governor of Carinthia—together with most of the FPÖ leadership and parliamentarians broke away to form a new party, the Alliance for the Future of Austria (BZÖ). This unexpected development followed a period of acrimonious fighting within the FPÖ; tensions flared between the party leadership, which mostly comprised representatives of its moderate wing, and prominent hard-line members of the FPÖ over the future course of the party in the wake of a stream of poor election results. The BZÖ was formally established on April 17 and subsequently replaced the FPÖ as the junior partner in government; the new coalition retained a small majority in the Nationalrat (lower house of parliament). To the surprise of many Austrians and to the frustration of opposition parties, which had demanded an early general election amid claims that the ÖVP-BZÖ coalition no longer had the support of the electorate, the new right-of-centre alliance held together. Despite a disappointing performance by both parties in important state elections held in three of Austria's nine states in Oc-

tober, the government seemed likely to remain in office until the end of the legislative term in 2006.

Having implemented a range of structural-reform measures in recent years, including a major tax reform (cuts in business and income tax came into effect at the start of 2005) and a significant restructuring of the state pension system, the government turned its focus to rising unemployment. In May job-creation measures were unveiled, and in August the government presented a €1.2 billion (about $1.5 billion) Regional Employment and Growth Campaign. Meanwhile, a controversial new asylum bill was approved, and the length of compulsory military service was reduced as part of a wider military reform. The more expansive fiscal policy adopted by the government contributed to a deterioration in the budget deficit, but overall the economy continued to grow at a slightly faster rate than the average for the euro area.

In May the Austrian parliament ratified the EU constitutional treaty, although the entire ratification process was then thrown into disarray when the constitution was rejected by French and Dutch voters. The start of accession negotiations between Turkey and the EU in October prompted fierce debate in Austria; there was considerable opposition to Turkey's future EU membership. Meanwhile, surveys showed that support for the EU in general in Austria was among the lowest of all member states—a situation that was not improved following a ruling by the Euro-

pean Court of Justice in July that forced Austria to revise its admission rules for foreign students. In August torrential rain caused flooding in western Austria, with areas of Tirol particularly badly hit. Nine German tourists died in September in the Tyrolean ski resort of Sölden after a helicopter accidentally dropped a concrete block onto their cable car.

In November Austria arrested British historian David Irving for speeches he made in 1989 that allegedly violated an Austrian law against Holocaust denial.

(NEIL PROTHERO)

AZERBAIJAN

Area: 86,600 sq km (33,400 sq mi), including the 5,500-sq-km (2,100-sq-mi) exclave of Nakhichevan and the 4,400-sq-km (1,700-sq-mi) disputed region (with Armenia) of Nagorno-Karabakh
Population (2005 est.): 8,381,000
Capital: Baku
Head of state and government: President Ilham Aliyev, assisted by Prime Minister Artur Rasizade

Seven opposition politicians jailed in November 2004 for violent protests following the October 2003 presidential election in Azerbaijan were pardoned and released in March 2005.

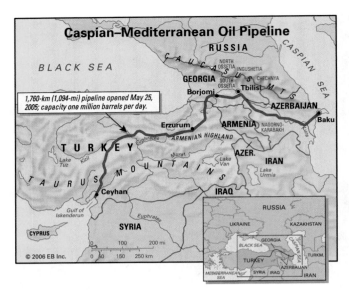

Caspian–Mediterranean Oil Pipeline

1,760-km (1,094-mi) pipeline opened May 25, 2005; capacity one million barrels per day.

© 2006 EB Inc.

Opposition parties aligned in two blocs to participate in the November 6 parliamentary elections. On March 18 the opposition Musavat and Democratic parties and the progressive wing of the Azerbaijan Popular Front Party formed the Liberty Bloc, and in mid-April Eldar Namazov, a former adviser to the late president Heydar Aliyev, formed the New Policy, together with the Azerbaijan National Independence Party chairman, Ali Aliyev, and former president Ayaz Mutalibov. In August Ruslan Bashirli, leader of the youth organization Yeni Fikir, was arrested and charged with colluding with Armenian intelligence to provoke unrest.

On May 11 and October 25, Pres. Ilham Aliyev issued decrees instructing local officials to ensure that the ballot was free and fair. Opposition candidates encountered few problems in registering as candidates, although some 500 of the initial 2,000 candidates later withdrew. Police resorted to violence to break up opposition rallies on September 25 and on October 1, 9, and 23.

Former parliament speaker and parliamentary candidate Rasul Guliyev was detained in Ukraine on October 17 en route to Baku, but he was released after several days. Several senior officials were subsequently arrested and charged with conspiring with Guliyev to stage a coup, including former finance minister Fikret Yusifov, Economic Development Minister Farkhad Aliyev, Health Minister Ali Insanov, and former Academy of Sciences president Eldar Salayev. Salayev, 73, was released on bail on November 16.

Opposition candidates won only 9 of the 125 seats in the parliament, and international monitoring organizations complained that the election did not meet international standards. Up to 20,000 people attended protest rallies on November 9, 13, 19, and 26 to demand that the results be annulled and new elections held.

GDP grew by 25.2% during the first 11 months of the year. U.S. Defense Secretary Donald Rumsfeld visited Baku in April, but rumours that the U.S. would establish a military base in Azerbaijan proved premature. An anticipated official visit by President Aliyev to Washington did not take place.

The Organization for Security and Co-operation in Europe Minsk Group mediated talks held in January, April, and June between the Armenian and Azerbaijani foreign ministers, at which progress was reportedly achieved on undisclosed aspects of a plan to resolve the Nagorno-Karabakh conflict. At a December 6 meeting, however, the two foreign ministers failed to reach agreement on a further meeting between President Aliyev and Armenian Pres. Robert Kocharyan, who had met in Warsaw on May 15 and in Kazan, Russia, on August 27 to discuss that peace plan.

(ELIZABETH FULLER)

BAHAMAS, THE

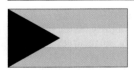

Area: 13,939 sq km (5,382 sq mi)
Population (2005 est.): 323,000
Capital: Nassau
Chief of state: Queen Elizabeth II, represented by Governor-General Dame Ivy Dumont
Head of government: Prime Ministers Perry Christie, Cynthia Pratt (acting) from May 4, and, from June 22, Christie

After suffering what officials referred to as a "slight stroke," Prime Minister Perry Christie was replaced on May 4, 2005, by Deputy Prime Minister Cynthia Pratt, who served as acting prime minister until doctors pronounced Christie recovered on June 22.

In May it was announced that Florida Power & Light had temporarily shelved its search for a long-term provider of liquefied natural gas (LNG) because none of the bidders planning to regasify LNG in The Bahamas could meet all of the requirements. The news put the government's hope for two LNG regas projects in jeopardy. Committed to privatizing the Bahamas Telecommunications Co., the government talked directly to interested parties until it found one that had the necessary expertise and financial capability to operate the country's telecommunications system.

American independent oil and gas producer Kerr-McGee was reportedly encouraged to continue evaluating The Bahamas offshore region as an exploration location for hydrocarbons. Though the country currently had no domestic production, the company felt that there was potential for oil. Kerr-McGee held licenses for 2.6 million ha (6.5 million ac) on The Bahamas continental shelf.

Hurricane Wilma struck The Bahamas on October 24, causing much damage to Grand Bahama and the Bimini Islands. The Biminis were further shaken in December after a seaplane carrying mostly Bimini passengers crashed near Miami, killing all 20 people on board. (DAVID RENWICK)

BAHRAIN

Area: 720 sq km (278 sq mi)
Population (2005 est.): 715,000
Capital: Manama
Chief of state: King Hamad ibn Isa al-Khalifah
Head of government: Prime Minister Khalifah ibn Sulman al-Khalifah

The year 2005 in Bahrain was marked by social and political agitation, mainly among the Shi'ites, who composed about 70% of the Muslim population. Shi'ites were protesting the lack of political reforms and the use of force by the government against protesters and political prisoners. The Shi'ites also organized street demonstrations to demand jobs for their unemployed. (More than 16% of Shi'ite males in Bahrain were unemployed.) Though the government promised to train 8,000 unemployed annually, that number would still fall short of providing jobs for all of those having to compete with some 250,000 foreign workers who were less expensive to employ and often better trained.

Political groups, called associations, bitterly protested a new Law of Associations that forbade such groups from receiving financial aid from abroad and raised the age of potential members from 18 to 21 years of age.

On July 20 King Hamad ibn Isa al-Khalifah ratified a free-trade treaty, signed in 2004, between Bahrain and the U.S. The Bahraini government expected the treaty to improve its trade balance and acquire an outlet for its exports in American markets. The U.S. Congress was expected to ratify the treaty in 2006.

After three years of discussion, the Bahraini parliament passed a law that made it a crime to prevent children from learning about respect for human rights and the need for religious tolerance. This ambitious law required changes in the school curriculum. If applied correctly, it could encourage respect for all religions and sects.   (LOUAY BAHRY)

BANGLADESH

Area: 147,570 sq km (56,977 sq mi)
Population (2005 est.): 137,636,000
Capital: Dhaka
Chief of state: President Iajuddin Ahmed
Head of government: Prime Minister Khaleda Zia

For Bangladesh the year 2005 was a rude awakening from a mode of denial. On the morning of August 17, the country was shaken as more than 500 bombs went off within a span of half an hour in a precisely coordinated manner in 63 of the country's 64 districts. At every bomb location, leaflets were recovered belonging to a banned Islamic militant group, Jama'atul Mujahideen Bangladesh (JMB). Though casualties were minor—2 deaths and slight injuries to 100 persons—it was nonetheless a moment of great embarrassment for the

Police officers try to disperse women participating in a general strike on August 20 in Dhaka, the capital, to protest a coordinated series of more than 500 bomb explosions throughout Bangladesh a few days earlier. The government later admitted that the acts were the work of a local Islamist militant group thought to have ties to al-Qaeda.

AP/Wide World Photos

government, which had flatly denied local and international media reports saying that terrorists linked to al-Qaeda were organizing in Bangladesh. Though the government finally admitted that JMB was behind the blasts, it also suggested that there were "foreign forces" behind such a well-organized attack plan. The government subsequently embarked upon an antimilitant drive and apprehended some 170 terrorists, but this effort created a stir among the country's Islamic political parties, two of which were coalition partners in the government. The parties warned that harassing mullahs in the name of catching militants would not be tolerated.

Earlier in the year, the killing on January 27 of S.A.M.S. Kibria, an Awami League (AL) party leader and a former UN undersecretary-general, shocked the country. Two grenades were tossed at him at a rally in the northeastern district of Habiganj. At least 3 other people were killed, and some 50 more were injured. The government's already rocky relationship with the opposition AL only worsened in the wake of the attack. The AL, angered by an unfinished probe into an earlier grenade attack that had killed 21 people at another party rally in August 2004, remained skeptical about the government's commitment to investigating Kibria's murder. Charges were ultimately brought against 10 people, 8 of whom had connections to the

ruling Bangladesh Nationalist Party (BNP). Kibria's family rejected the investigation, however, saying that the masterminds of the attack were still at large.

Bangladesh once again came under international scrutiny when reports surfaced that the Ahmadiyya community was being persecuted. In particular, Islamic fundamentalist parties Jamaat-e-Islami and Islami Oikyo Jote demanded that the government declare the Ahmadiyyas non-Muslims in the fashion of Pakistan, but the government—which had banned the Ahmadiyya religious book in 2004—remained silent to the demands. The persecution of the Ahmadiyyas evoked international reaction, including one from the U.S. assistant secretary of state for South Asian affairs, Christina Rocca, who during a visit to Dhaka in May expressed her concern over the treatment of the Ahmadiyyas.

On the economic front, Bangladesh came under severe pressure from a few sides. Despite a healthy 8.71% growth in exports from January to June, as well as a 32.1% rise in foreign assistance and a 14.13% rise in remittance from overseas workers in fiscal 2004–05, the country's foreign-exchange reserves dwindled to $2.73 billion in September from $3.02 billion in June. This followed a sudden 18.45% jump in imports during the January–June period. Inflation rose to 7.35% in June from 5.5% in January. In September the government increased state-controlled fuel prices by 18%, stoking fears of a further price hike and demand squeeze. As a reaction to inflationary pressure, the government embarked on a tighter monetary policy.   (INAM AHMED)

BARBADOS

Area: 430 sq km (166 sq mi)
Population (2005 est.): 270,000
Capital: Bridgetown
Chief of state: Queen Elizabeth II, represented by Governor-General Sir Clifford Husbands
Head of government: Prime Minister Owen Arthur

In 2005 it was estimated that about $2 billion would be invested during the next three to five years in the Barbados tourism sector, which included the construction or refurbishment of 2,000 hotel rooms.

In July Standard & Poor's revised its outlook on Barbados's long-term foreign and local currency sovereign credit rating, lowering it to negative from stable because of rising external pressures due to high current-account deficits. An increase in mostly short-term external debt was also a factor in the decision.

In an unusual act for a politician, Prime Minister Owen Arthur decided in August not to accept a 20% pay raise, which formed part of an overall increase for public officers endorsed by the parliament. The increase amounted to the equivalent of $16,565 a year. Some other government ministers and MPs later indicated that they might follow Arthur's lead. In October the parliament approved a bill that allowed for a referendum to determine if Barbados should become a republic.

In an effort to make the country's Grantley Adams International Airport the tourism hub of the Caribbean, Barbados neared completion on a major expansion and renovation project. The upgraded airport would be capable of accommodating about 2,000 passengers an hour. In the first four months of 2005, long-staying visitors to Barbados rose by 1.3%.   (DAVID RENWICK)

BELARUS

Area: 207,595 sq km (80,153 sq mi)
Population (2005 est.): 9,776,000
Capital: Minsk
Head of state and government: President Alyaksandr H. Lukashenka, assisted by Prime Minister Syarhey Sidorski

The year 2005 saw significant moves by the political opposition to prepare for the Belarusian presidential elections of 2006. Following nationwide meetings to nominate 839 delegates to the Congress of Democratic Forces of Belarus, and after delays in obtaining a building for the event, the congress was opened on October 1 at the Palace of Culture of the Minsk Automobile Factory. Initially there were four candidates to oppose incumbent Pres. Alyaksandr

Among the popular demonstrations in Belarus in 2005 was a commemoration of the disappearance in September 1999 of Viktar Hanchar, a vice-speaker of the parliament, and a businessman friend. Here a police officer manhandles one of the unauthorized protesters in Minsk.

AP/Wide World Photos

Lukashenka: Stanislau Shushkevich, Syarhey Kalyakin, Anatol Lyabedzka, and Alyaksandr Milinkevich. After Shushkevich withdrew from the contest, Milinkevich, a 58-year-old moderate leader of Polish ancestry and a former physics professor at Hrodna State University, defeated Lyabedzka in the second round by 399 votes to 391.

The vote was a triumph for the opposition, which was excluded from using the official media and suffered harassment and arrest of its members. On May 31, for example, Mikola Statkevich, an opposition leader from the Social Democratic Party, and Pavel Severinets, a leader of the youth wing of the Popular Front, received terms of three years of hard labour for group activities that violate civic order.

Relations with Poland featured large in Belarus in 2005. In March Tadeusz Kruczkowski, the leader of the Belarusian Union of Poles (BUP), was replaced by Andzelika Borys. The Ministry of Justice overturned the action in May, against the wishes of the country's 400,000-strong Polish minority. In mid-July Belarus and Poland each expelled diplomats from the other country, and on July 27 Borys was detained overnight after a raid on the BUP headquarters. Several Polish journalists reporting the event were arrested. On July 28 Poland recalled its ambassador to Belarus, while the Belarusian government accused Poland of heading an international plot to overthrow the Lukashenka regime.

The Belarusian government had been especially sensitive to all opposition following the Orange Revolution in neighbouring Ukraine in late 2004. On March 25 it brutally broke up a Day of Freedom march organized by a leader of the opposition, Andrey Klimau, and

it also responded harshly to a rally by youth leaders on the anniversary of the Chernobyl nuclear power plant disaster. In March and May the government faced strikes from entrepreneurs who were protesting against a value-added tax of 18% on all imports from Russia. On April 16 the Supreme Court ordered the closure of the Independent Institute of Socio-Economic and Political Research (NISEPI) on the grounds that it was not operating out of its official headquarters. NISEPI had disputed the official results of the October 2004 referendum on the president's running for a third term in office. *Narodnaya Volya*, the country's only major independent newspaper, was forced off the streets from October 1, after pressure was brought to bear on its distributors. In December the parliament approved legislation, submitted by Lukashenka, that criminalized protests and other acts that "discredited" the government.

Economic figures for the year 2005 indicated a 9.2% rise in GDP and a 10% rise in industrial output. Relations with Russia were complicated by further delays in the plans to issue a common currency and over the basis of the Russia-Belarus Union.   (DAVID R. MARPLES)

BELGIUM

Area: 30,528 sq km (11,787 sq mi)
Population (2005 est.): 10,432,000
Capital: Brussels
Chief of state: King Albert II
Head of government: Prime Minister Guy Verhofstadt

Belgium observed twin celebrations in 2005. The country marked the 175th anniversary of the relatively painless revolution of 1830, when citizens took to the streets and ended 15 years of Dutch rule, and commemorated Belgium's 25th birthday as a federal state in which most internal powers had been devolved to the three regions. In January, looking ahead to the year of festivities, Prime Minister Guy Verhofstadt said: "We want to use the occasion to show that our country is modern and dynamic. The aim is not to wallow in nostalgia but to look ahead to the future, focusing on youth, meetings, and conviviality."

Verhofstadt's coalition government faced one of its toughest tests, however, with a linguistic dispute that echoed the bitter language battles of the 1970s between the country's French- and Dutch-speaking communities. At stake was the Brussels-Hal-Vilvoorde parliamentary constituency. Not only was it the largest in Belgium, but it was also the only bilingual constituency in the country, with both French- and Dutch-speaking parties putting forward candidates in elections. The Dutch-speaking parties wanted to split the constituency by adding Hal and Vilvoorde to nearby Leuven to create a purely Flemish unit. French-speaking parties objected, however, fearing that such a division would undermine the rights of francophone residents in the constituency itself and

AP/Wide World Photos

The 175th anniversary of Belgian independence was the theme of the sand sculpture festival at Blankenberge on June 30. Famous Belgian landmarks, icons, and public figures were popular subjects for the sand artists.

in some other communes around Brussels. After months of negotiations, a compromise was reached that put the issue on hold for two years; it would be addressed again after the next general election, due in May 2007 at the latest.

On the economic front, the government announced in October that it had kept within its budget for the sixth straight year. The government also received a boost from the proceeds of the fiscal amnesty that it had organized during 2004 to encourage Belgians to repatriate funds that they had lodged in foreign banks in order to escape the country's high tax rates. The initiative brought the government €496 million (€1 = about $1.28) from the levies it applied to the returning funds. Officially, €5.7 billion returned to Belgium, but it was widely believed that as much as €10 billion more had gone back into the country without being declared. The government continued to reduce the country's national debt, paring it by €3.06 billion in the year leading up to May 2005; however, the debt, at €268.18 billion, represented 95.5% of GDP—one of the highest percentages in the European Union.

It was a good year for Belgium's top two tennis players, Kim Clijsters and Justine Henin-Hardenne, after both had suffered injuries and fallen in the rankings during 2004. Clijsters won the U.S. Open—her first Grand Slam title after having been beaten in four previous finals. Henin-Hardenne won her second French Open, taking her Grand Slam wins to four.

Cycling, which had been personified in Belgium by five-time Tour de France winner Eddy Merckx, saw the emergence of a new Belgian champion, Tom Boonen. The 24-year-old Boonen crowned an outstanding year by becoming world road-race champion at the end of September. He had previously won three other road races during the year, including the Paris–Roubaix and the Tour of Flanders, as well as two road-race stages in the 2005 Tour de France.

In the world of culture, the brothers Luc and Jean-Pierre Dardenne (*see* BIOGRAPHIES) joined the rare group of film directors to have twice won the Palme d'Or at the Cannes Film Festival. Their entry, *L'Enfant*, about the lives of two young parents, was voted best film six years after they won their first award at Cannes with *Rosetta*.

(RORY WATSON)

BELIZE

Area: 22,965 sq km (8,867 sq mi)
Population (2005 est.): 291,000
Capital: Belmopan
Chief of state: Queen Elizabeth II, represented by Governor-General Sir Colville Young
Head of government: Prime Minister Said Musa

Concern about grave failures in government management of Belize's finances continued with full force in 2005. During the first half of the year, the government entered into a historic agreement with social partners—made up of members of labour unions, the private sector, and churches—to provide greater transparency in its management of public finances. Accusing the government of duplicity in the implementation of this agreement, however, the labour unions mounted unprecedented strikes that paralyzed the country for more than a week in late April. Telephone company employees and teachers were among the most visible groups to strike. Also contributing to the unrest among Belizeans during the year were crippling increases in the cost of fuel, a spike in criminal activity, and dropping prices for sugar and bananas, two of the country's chief exports.

Despite the civil unrest, some notable cultural gains were witnessed in Belize in 2005. Aided by support from volunteers and the National Institute of Culture and History (NICH), several groups promoted a revival of interest in poetry, music, dance, and folklore. A long-awaited new national museum, located in Belmopan and administered by the NICH, was nearing completion.

(JOSEPH O. PALACIO)

BENIN

Area: 112,622 sq km (43,484 sq mi)
Population (2005 est.): 7,649,000
Capital: Porto-Novo (executive and ministerial offices remain in Cotonou)
Head of state and government: President Mathieu Kérékou

A group of Togolese refugees move out of a Roman Catholic mission in eastern Benin in May. Tens of thousands of persons fled the violence in Togo following the election of Faure Gnassingbé as president.
© Issouf Sanogo/AFP/Getty Images

In July 2005 Pres. Mathieu Kérékou stated that he would retire in 2006 and thus scotched rumours that he planned to reform Benin's constitution to allow him to stand for a third term in 2006.

Although the 2005 budget predicted a 5.3% economic growth rate, Benin remained one of the world's poorest and most heavily indebted countries. On June 13 the Group of Eight summit canceled $800 million owed by the nation to the World Bank, an amount representing 63% of Benin's foreign debt. The following day the World Bank announced a new loan of $30 million for continuation of Benin's program of government decentralization. On August 5 the IMF announced a $9 million grant for the country's poverty-reduction initiatives.

At a meeting held in Cotonou in May, Benin and other West African cotton producers demanded that industrialized nations discontinue export subsidies to their own growers. Falling world prices were seriously threatening domestic production in African countries.

Benin continued to participate in UN peacekeeping operations and on April 9 sent a new contingent of 102 soldiers to Côte d'Ivoire. On July 12 the International Court of Justice resolved a 45-year boundary dispute between Benin and Niger as well as the ownership of 25 islands in the Niger River. Sixteen were awarded to Niger. Both countries agreed to abide by the ruling.

The election on April 24 of Faure Gnassingbé (see BIOGRAPHIES) as the new president of Togo prompted more than 24,000 people from that country to take refuge in Benin. With reassurances from the new Togolese government, several thousand returned home.

(NANCY ELLEN LAWLER)

BHUTAN

Area: 38,394 sq km (14,824 sq mi)
Population (2005 est.): 776,000 (excluding more than 100,000 refugees in Nepal)
Capital: Thimphu
Head of state: Druk Gyalpo (King) Jigme Singye Wangchuk
Head of government: Prime Ministers Lyonpo Yeshey Zimba and, from September 5, Lyonpo Sangay Ngedup

While maintaining its record of internal tranquility, Bhutan headed toward political reform in 2005. King Jigme Singye Wangchuk forwarded a document to every household proposing a new democratic constitution that would authorize the parliament to impeach the king and form a multiparty system with the government accountable to the legislature. Economically, the country enjoyed expanded electricity sales to India and a growth rate of 7%.

In the traditional annual rotation of prime ministers, Lyonpo Ngedup took office in September. During the year Bhutan banned foreign television channels—including Indian channels, which were considered a threat to the country's deeply Buddhist cultural values—and smoking in public places.

Despite several rounds of talks, more than 100,000 Bhutanese refugees were still languishing in refugee camps in Nepal after more than 15 years waiting for repatriation. In August Indian police prevented a group of Bhutanese refugees from crossing into India to reach their native land. During the year

Bhutanese and Chinese officials discussed ways to settle an ongoing border dispute between the two countries.

In December King Wangchuk announced that he would abdicate in 2008 and be succeeded by his son Crown Prince Dasho Jigme Khesar Namgyal Wangchuk.   (KESHAB POUDEL)

BOLIVIA

Area: 1,098,581 sq km (424,164 sq mi)
Population (2005 est.): 8,858,000
Capitals: La Paz (administrative) and Sucre (judicial)
Head of state and government: Presidents Carlos Mesa Gisbert and, from June 9, Eduardo Rodríguez Veltzé

Saying Bolivia was "on the verge of civil war," Pres. Carlos Mesa submitted his resignation on June 6, 2005. It was accepted by Congress three days later and marked the third time in less than four years that a Bolivian president had left office before completing his term. Mesa was forced from his post by massive protests and road blockades mounted by leaders of Bolivia's poor Indian majority. The chief justice of the Supreme Court, Eduardo Rodríguez Veltzé, was installed as caretaker president. The fall of Mesa's government underscored the deep ethnic, regional, and socioeconomic divisions in South America's poorest country and the persistent failure of its political system to deal with them.

The issue at the root of the protests was the management of Bolivia's huge natural gas reserves. For several years leftist and indigenous movements had demanded sharp increases in taxes on gas firms and a halt to exports. Bloody street clashes drove Pres. Gonzalo Sánchez de Lozada from office in 2003, and he was succeeded by Mesa, his vice president. The protests were rekindled in 2005 as Congress considered and eventually voted for a sharp increase in taxes on gas production. At the same time, a backlash against the Indian movements gathered steam in the gas-rich eastern lowlands, where many believed the political turmoil was slowing investment and robbing them of an energy bonanza.

Over Mesa's objection the gas-tax measure became law in May, which led energy firms to scale back exploration and development. The protests intensified, with demands now including nationalization of the gas industry, and Mesa promised before resigning to convene a constitutional assembly to redistribute political power in the Indians' favour. Earlier, he had agreed to allow states to elect their governors instead of having them appointed by the central government.

The protests abated once Rodríguez was installed. Soaring world energy prices gave hope that Bolivian gas revenue might finally be used to alleviate the country's crushing poverty. Bolivia's wealthier neighbours, whose industries depended on a steady supply of gas, invited it to join a South American pipeline network. Meanwhile, the jockeying to succeed Rodríguez got under way. The front-runners were socialist Evo Morales, a key protest leader who had placed second in the 2002 presidential election, and Jorge Quiroga, a former vice president who had served out the term of Pres. Hugo Bánzer. Quiroga accused Morales of being under the influence of Venezuelan Pres. Hugo Chávez (see BIOGRAPHIES), while Morales denounced Quiroga as a puppet of the U.S. On December 18 Morales won an absolute majority. Scheduled to take office in early 2006, he would be the country's first Indian president.

The furor over natural gas overshadowed developments in the coca trade. The UN reported sharp increases in production of cocaine and in the area devoted to growing coca leaf, the drug's chief ingredient. The Bolivian government scaled back U.S.-supported eradication campaigns. (PAUL KNOX)

BOSNIA AND HERZEGOVINA

Area: 51,209 sq km (19,772 sq mi)
Population (2005 est.): 3,853,000
Capital: Sarajevo
Heads of state: Nominally a tripartite (Serb, Croat, Muslim) presidency with a chair that rotates every eight months; members in 2005 were Borislav Paravac (Serb); Dragan Covic to March 29 and, from June 28, Ivo Miro Jovic (Croat); and Sulejman Tihic (Muslim); final authority resides in the Office of the High Representative, Paddy Ashdown, Baron Ashdown (U.K.)
Head of government: Prime Minister Adnan Terzic

Two anniversaries in 2005 served as reminders that multiethnic Bosnia and Herzegovina had a long way to go in terms of reconciliation among the republic's Croats, Muslims, and Serbs. In July the 10th anniversary of the Srebrenica massacre of more than 7,000 mainly Muslim men and boys by Bosnian Serb forces was indicative of how little progress had been made to reconcile Serbs and Muslims and to bring to trial the main perpetrators, namely Bosnian Serb Gen. Ratko Mladic. More than 50,000 people, including leaders from Croatia and Serbia and Montenegro, attended the solemn ceremonies. Many Serbs remained doubtful that Serb forces committed the atrocity, however, despite growing evidence from confessions by former Serb officers and a televised videotape broadcast throughout the region showing Serb paramilitary troops executing Bosnian Muslim males near Srebrenica.

In November the U.S.-sponsored Dayton Peace Agreement, which ended the 1992–95 conflict, was commemorated. Though widely credited with preserving the peace, it remained a target of harsh criticism, mainly for its alleged political shortcomings and biases. To mark the accord's 10th anniversary, the country's leaders agreed to constitutional reforms, including the elimination of a three-president system, that they hoped to implement by March 2006.

The Croat, Muslim, and Serb nationalist parties that had led the republic into war were still in power and were actively preparing for the general election slated for October 2006. Muslim members of the federal parliament proposed a new constitutional arrangement calling for the redefinition of the republic as a decentralized state with five economic regions. Croat and Serb representatives opposed the plan, however, believing that it would weaken their nationalist agendas. In the RS the parliament leveled criticism against Mladic, an indicted war criminal, and renewed calls for former RS president Radovan Karadzic to surrender to the UN War Crimes Tribunal. In what was seen as a breakthrough, the Bosnian Serb leaders later issued their first public statement calling for the surrender or arrest of the two fugitives. Bosnian Serbs agreed to the creation of a joint army and defense ministry with the federation by July 2007 and in early October approved plans calling for the integration of its police with the federation. Both reforms were seen as crucial to Bosnia and Herzegovina's acceptance into the EU and NATO.

The economy continued to record high levels of unemployment, unsteady productivity, and widespread poverty. Hundreds of farmers staged protests throughout the year demanding government action to develop a national agricultural policy to curb the tide of cheap imports from Croatia and Serbia and improve farm technology. The government suggested a plan to combat poverty, but no steps were taken to legislate such a program, and protesting farmers ended

In July 2005, the same month that citizens of Bosnia and Herzegovina were remembering the 10th anniversary of the Srebrenica massacre, the International Commission on Missing Persons was excavating the Budak mass grave in the city, where more than 7,000 men and boys were killed by Bosnian Serbs.

© Marco Di Lauro/Getty Images

up distributing food to the urban poor. Among these poor were thousands of disabled veterans who received monthly government pensions of about €50 (about $60). (MILAN ANDREJEVICH)

BOTSWANA

Area: 582,356 sq km (224,848 sq mi)
Population (2005 est.): 1,765,000
Capital: Gaborone
Head of state and government: President Festus Mogae

Though the Botswana Democratic Party had consolidated 40 years in power with its ninth successive electoral victory in 2004, the year 2005 was one in which economic setbacks were accompanied by political disquiet.

In May 2005 the pula currency was devalued by 12% in an attempt to increase government revenue from diamond exports sold abroad against a declining U.S. dollar and to reduce the relative cost of wages and development projects in government service and the export sector. Construction, manufacturing, and retail sectors were in recession, and foreign investors crossed the border to South Africa.

Much of the criticism leveled against Pres. Festus Mogae and Vice Pres. Ian Khama centred on Australian academic Kenneth Good, whose expulsion from Botswana after 15 years in residence was ordered by presidential fiat in February. Good challenged the order but in July the appeals court ruled that the constitution did not oblige the president to offer a reason, and Good was deported. The example of Good's case added to criticism of arbitrary presidentialism, reinforced by the ongoing critique of insufficient representation of ethnic minorities and their languages in education, broadcasting, and the House of Chiefs.

The high court case of the ǁGana and ǀGwi people, challenging their relocation from the Central Kalahari Game Reserve, was suspended in September 2005 to give the applicants time to raise more funds to cover legal costs. Frustration over this delay led to clashes between game scouts and those people who had returned to live in the reserve. (NEIL PARSONS)

BRAZIL

Area: 8,514,877 sq km (3,287,612 sq mi)
Population (2005 est.): 184,016,000
Capital: Brasília
Head of state and government: President Luiz Inácio Lula da Silva

The year 2005 in Brazil was marked by challenges to the government of Pres. Luiz Inácio Lula da Silva. For much of the year, a series of corruption scandals consumed the government and prevented it from making significant progress on its agenda. In early May the weekly newsmagazine *Veja* reported that a hidden camera had captured Maurício Marinho, a top official in the Brazilian postal service's Department of Contracts and Administration, accepting a bribe of 3,000 reais (R$1 = about U.S.$0.45) from two businessmen seeking a procurement contract with the state-run entity. Played on network television, the videotape also showed Marinho implicating Roberto Jefferson, a federal deputy and the president of the Brazilian Labour Party, which was allied with the Lula government. The exposé created a maelstrom of accusations and investigations. On May 17 Congress began an inquiry into the postal service and the Brazilian Reinsurance Institute. On June 7 Lula sacked all of the directors at both institutions.

Facing expulsion from the Chamber of Deputies, Jefferson blew the whistle on a payola scheme orchestrated by the ruling Workers' Party (PT) to curry favour with politicians from smaller political parties. The *mensalão* ("monthly allowance") scandal, as the payola scheme was dubbed, implicated dozens of deputies and top PT leaders. Moreover, Jefferson accused the president's chief of staff, José Dirceu, of being the scheme's mastermind. The Senate launched an inquiry into the *mensalão* scandal on July 20. While Lula himself was not directly linked to either the postal service or the *mensalão* affairs, the top echelon of the PT soon began to fall. The party president, treasurer, and executive secretary were replaced. Dirceu resigned as Lula's chief of staff on June 16. Former minister of mines and energy Dilma Rousseff was named the new chief of staff on June 20. On September 14 Jefferson

was expelled from Congress, and on November 30 Dirceu, who after his resignation had returned to the Chamber of Deputies, was also forced out of Congress. Both officials lost their right to hold public office for eight years.

Scandal also stalked the president of the Chamber of Deputies, Severino Cavalcanti. On September 21 Cavalcanti resigned his post and federal deputy seat over looming corruption charges. He was accused of having accepted bribes in exchange for granting food-service contracts at the congressional building. A São Paulo federal deputy, Aldo Rebelo of the Brazilian Communist Party, was elected to replace him as chamber president. In November the Chamber of Deputies voted to extend the parliamentary inquiry of the postal service scandal to the following April, guaranteeing that corruption and ethics would be major themes during the presidential election year of 2006.

On February 12, near Anapu, Pará state, gunmen shot and killed Sister Dorothy Stang (*see* OBITUARIES), a 72-year-old American nun and naturalized Brazilian citizen who had been assisting rural families living in an area of the Amazon rainforest near the BR-163 federal highway. In the days leading up to the killing, Stang had reportedly complained to Human Rights Minister Nilmário Miranda of death threats made against peasant farmers by illegal loggers and ranchers in the area. The shooting called national and international attention to the problems of uncontrolled expansion and land-related violence along BR-163, which had been used as an access route to the rainforest. After Stang's murder the government announced the establishment of an approximately 37,000-sq-km (14,000-sq-mi) forest-protection area on the western side of BR-163 as well as plans to strengthen security in the area. In December two men were convicted of killing Stang and received sentences of 27 and 17 years. Three others accused of ordering the murder were awaiting trial.

On April 15 Lula signed a controversial decree delimiting the Raposa Serra do Sol Indian Reserve in northeastern Roraima state as "continuous," which meant that all non-Indian villages and settlements within the reserve would have to be abandoned. This touched off violence by some area residents against the federal police. On April 17 four federal policemen were kidnapped by Macuxi tribesmen. Although most Macuxi and other tribespeople who lived in the reserve supported the "continuous" demarcation, some feared the negative impact it might have, particularly when non-Indian employers left the area. On April 30, following discussions between the hostage takers and Roraima Gov. Ottomar Pinto, the four police officers were released unharmed. While the government did not revoke the decree, as the hostage takers had demanded, it promised to help improve living conditions on the reserve.

On March 28 Finance Minister Antônio Palocci announced that Brazil would not renew its standby loan agreement with the International Monetary Fund, an agreement that had been in place since 1998 and renewed in 2002. The announcement underscored the strength of the country's economic recovery over the past several years. Successful economic policy had engendered lower inflation, GDP growth, a trade surplus, stable balance of payments, reduced unemployment, and increased foreign direct investment. On November 18 foreign reserves were estimated at $49 billion. The accumulated trade surplus for the first 10 months of 2005 reached $36.35 billion, compared with $28 billion in 2004. The economy continued to meet or surpass export targets. By the end of October, exports had exceeded 2004 totals and reached $96.6 billion. Brazilian monetary policy continued to mandate high interest rates to meet inflation targets set at 4.5–5.1%. The central bank's open-market committee began the year with a series of interest-rate increases; the discount rate began at 17.75% in January and rose to 19.75% by May before falling to 18.5% in November. Brazil's real interest rate stood at approximately 13–14%. (JOHN CHARLES CUTTINO)

BRUNEI

Area: 5,765 sq km (2,226 sq mi)
Population (2005 est.): 364,000
Capital: Bandar Seri Begawan
Head of state and government: Sultan and Prime Minister Haji Hassanal Bolkiah Mu'izzaddin Waddaulah

In May 2005 a major cabinet reshuffle was carried out in Brunei by Sultan Haji Hassanal Bolkiah Mu'izzaddin Waddaulah. Several senior ministers who had served in the government since the country gained independence in 1984 ceased to hold their portfolios. These included Pehin Isa Haji Ibrahim, the minister of home affairs and a special adviser to the sultan, and Pehin Abdul Aziz Haji Umar, the minister of education. The latter was regarded as a leading Islamist and had been promoting the expansion of religious teaching in Brunei; he was replaced by Pehin Abdul Rahman Taib, who moved from the Ministry of Industry and Primary Resources. The new cabinet also included several Western-educated young technocrats—among them a former permanent secretary, Pehin Yahya Bakar, who was tapped to head up the newly created Ministry of Energy.

Perhaps the most significant appointment, however, was that of the sultan's elder son, Crown Prince Haji Al-Muhtadee Billah, to a senior minister's post in the prime minister's office. He spent much of the rest of the year making working visits to many government departments—a clear indication that a grooming process was under way for the 31-year-old crown prince eventually to succeed his father.

The sultan visited Russia in early June, holding talks with Pres. Vladimir Putin that the latter described as initiating "a promising new stage" in relations between the two states. The sultan also made news later in the year when in August he married Azrinaz Mazhar Hakim, a 26-year-old television personality from Malaysia, in a private ceremony in Kuala Lumpur. (B.A. HUSSAINMIYA)

BULGARIA

Area: 111,002 sq km (42,858 sq mi)
Population (2005 est.): 7,740,000
Capital: Sofia
Chief of state: President Georgi Purvanov
Head of government: Prime Ministers Simeon Saxecoburggotski and, from August 16, Sergei Stanishev

The year 2005 was an eventful one in Bulgaria. The country exceeded most expectations and achieved notable economic development. Though the state-owned Bulgarian Telecommunication Co. was successfully privatized and awarded a license to operate Bulgaria's third cellular telephone network, the general public deemed this a failure because of suspicions of corruption by government officials. Tourism continued to be one of the most prosperous sectors of the economy, with the Black Sea resorts remaining the major attraction for 2.7 million vacationers from West and Central Europe. Bulgaria's improving economy encouraged a number of foreign investors to look for opportunities in the country. During January–May 2005, direct foreign investment amounted to €421.6 million (about $526 million). The Bulgarian government resumed construction of a nuclear plant complex in Belene and initiated negotiations with possible buyers.

On April 25 Bulgaria, together with Romania, signed an accession treaty to the European Union; the country would be admitted to the EU on Jan. 1, 2007, if it implemented the promised judicial and administrative system reforms and successfully dealt with corruption. Failure to comply with these European Commission requirements could delay admission to the EU by a year.

Starting in July torrential rains, alternating with hail and high temperatures, left a number of towns and villages across the country in ruins and displaced their inhabitants. The floods destroyed river ports, crops, and cultural monuments. The damages, excluding the lost crops, were estimated to be more than €128 million (about $155 million).

In the June 25 elections, seven parties, none of which had enough representatives to form a government, were elected to the 240-seat parliament. The party possessing the biggest share of seats was the left-wing Bulgarian Socialist Party. The right wing was occupied by two opposing factions of the once-strong United Democratic Forces. After each of the two most populous parties in the parliament took turns holding a mandate to construct a government and did not find broad-enough support, Pres. Georgi Purvanov granted a mandate to the third parliamentary power, the Movement for Rights and Freedoms (MRF), which represented the country's Turkish minority. After weeks of negotiations, the parties with the largest representation in the parliament—the Socialists, the centrist National Movement for Simeon II, and the MRF—formed a coalition government on August 15, with Socialist leader Sergei Stanishev, nominated by the MRF, installed the following day as the country's new prime minister.

(IVA IOVTCHEVA; BORIS YOVCHEV)

BURKINA FASO

Area: 267,950 sq km (103,456 sq mi)
Population (2005 est.): 13,492,000
Capital: Ouagadougou
Chief of state: President Blaise Compaoré
Head of government: Prime Minister Ernest
Paramanga Yonli

Pres. Blaise Compaoré—in power in Burkina Faso since the 1987 violent coup and twice elected (1991 and 1998) president—brushed aside objections to his plan to seek a third term in the Nov. 13, 2005, presidential elections. Though opposition parties claimed that Compaoré was not eligible to run again, citing the passage of a constitutional amendment in April 2000 that reduced a president's term to five years and barred a second term, Compaoré's ruling Congress for Democracy and Progress insisted that the law could not be applied retroactively.

The food crisis in neighbouring Niger threatened to spill over into Burkina Faso as prices of basic commodities soared. With the region still suffering from the effects of the 2004 drought and locust invasion, the government distributed grain at prices 75% lower than those prevailing in the market. At least 500,000 Burkinabes in the north were short of food, and they began to move south. A good 2005 harvest was expected to ease the situation.

The World Bank approved grants of $60 million on May 3 as part of its poverty-reduction program and a further grant of $5 million on May 5 for Burkina Faso's anti-AIDS initiative. The government planned to double the number of those receiving antiretroviral treatment to 10,000 by the end of the year. On June 15 the Group of Eight canceled the country's outstanding debts of $18 million. Also, the drastic fall in world cotton prices had severely shaken the economy.   (NANCY ELLEN LAWLER)

BURUNDI

Area: 27,816 sq km (10,740 sq mi)
Population (2005 est.): 7,795,000 (including about 450,000 refugees in Tanzania)
Capital: Bujumbura
Head of state and government: Presidents Domitien Ndayizeye and, from August 26, Pierre Nkurunziza

On Aug. 26, 2005, Pierre Nkurunziza, the former leader of the rebel group Forces for the Defense of Democracy (FDD), was sworn in as Burundi's first democratically elected president following the 1993 genocide that sparked a 12-year civil war that killed more than 300,000 people. The election of Nkurunziza, who received amnesty for war crimes as part of the South African-sponsored peace accords, marked the end of the five-year peace deal and the transitional government of Pres. Domitien Ndayizeye. The presidential election, originally scheduled for November 2004, was postponed until April 2005 because of power-sharing disputes between the Hutu majority and the Tutsi minority in the drafting of the country's new constitution. A referendum on the constitution was to be held before the presidential election could take place. Ongoing violence by the Forces for National Liberation (FNL), a Hutu guerrilla group, led to another election postponement. A new schedule was drafted by Burundi's Independent National Electoral Commission, with an election date finalized for August 19. The new power-sharing constitution had been passed by a referendum vote in March, and July elections for a new parliament ushered in the FDD as the ruling party.

Despite the steps taken toward peace and stability, much of the year in Burundi was marred by bouts of violence, threats to peace efforts, and severe food shortages. Following the failure of the 2004 harvest, the UN World Food Programme began a two-month food-distribution program in January to assist more than 520,000 people at risk of starvation in two of Burundi's northeastern provinces. Relations with neighbouring Rwanda were strained in April when some 2,000 Hutu being tried for crimes of genocide in the Rwandan *gacacas* (traditional courts) fled to Burundi, fearing that they would not receive fair treatment in these courts. After months of sporadic violence, the main rebel group outside the peace process, the FNL, signed a peace pact with the government in May only to break the truce with renewed attacks against the army a few days after signing the accords. In mid-September the FNL rejected President Nkurunziza's offer to renew peace talks.   (MARY F.E. EBELING)

CAMBODIA

Area: 181,035 sq km (69,898 sq mi)
Population (2005 est.): 13,327,000
Capital: Phnom Penh
Chief of state: King Norodom Sihamoni
Head of government: Prime Minister Hun Sen

Perhaps the most significant political development in Cambodia in 2005 was the passing of legislation to remove parliamentary immunity from Sam Rainsy and two members of his eponymous opposition party (SRP). When the dominant Cambodian People's Party (CPP) formed an alliance in mid-2004 with the country's second-ranking party, the

Poor children in Ouagadougou, the capital of Burkina Faso, are treated to free film showings during the Pan-African Festival of Cinema and Television.

National United Front for an Independent, Neutral, Peaceful and Cooperative Cambodia (Funcinpec), many analysts interpreted the move as part of a strategy to actively undermine the growing SRP. When parliamentary immunity was revoked on February 3, SRP politician and National Assembly member Cheam Channy was immediately arrested. Rainsy fled the country with the help of the U.S. embassy, and Chea Poch, another SRP and National Assembly member, soon followed him. Accused of raising an army to overthrow the government, Channy was tried by a military court in August and sentenced to seven years in prison. Human rights organizations claimed that the charges were unfounded and pointed to irregularities in the trial procedures. Rainsy and Poch faced charges of criminal defamation against Prime Minister Hun Sen and Funcinpec leader Norodom Ranariddh, an older half-brother of Cambodia's new monarch, King Norodom Sihamoni. (*See* BIOGRAPHIES.)

For several months SRP legislators boycotted the National Assembly, but they returned on August 22. Poch returned to Cambodia in mid-August and testified in court regarding the defamation allegations but was not arrested. From exile Rainsy campaigned internationally for support. He stated publicly his intention to return to Cambodia and face trial, but in December he was tried in absentia and found guilty. His sentence of 18 months in prison raised concerns about the future of his party and Cambodia's multiparty democracy.

During the year significant progress was made toward setting up a three-year international tribunal to try leaders of Pol Pot's regime (1975–79) for genocide and crimes against humanity. By late 2005 there was still a shortfall in funds needed to finance the tribunal. Despite this, most observers believed that the trials would begin in 2006. A venue was designated on the outskirts of Phnom Penh, and the UN named as its chief administrator Michele Lee, a Chinese staff member who had served as a ranking administrator on the International Criminal Tribunal for Rwanda.

Early in 2005 there was much concern about Cambodia's garment industry, which accounted for 90% of the country's exports. New regulations by the World Trade Organization meant the end of a quota system with the U.S., and this left Cambodia vulnerable to competition with China. Some 20,000 mostly female workers lost their jobs when 12 factories closed and 24 more suspended

operations. By midyear, however, the crisis seemed to have passed after both the U.S. and the European Union moved to limit the yearly increase in Chinese imports. (JOHN A. MARSTON)

CAMEROON

Area: 475,442 sq km (183,569 sq mi)
Population (2005 est.): 16,988,000
Capital: Yaoundé
Chief of state: President Paul Biya
Head of government: Prime Minister Ephraim Inoni

In 2005, three years after the International Court of Justice had delineated the 1,600-km (1,000-mi) border between Cameroon and Nigeria, the implementation of the ruling remained stalled. The Cameroon-Nigeria Mixed Commission met on July 28 for its first session of the year to continue discussions under the auspices and funding of the UN. An agreement was reached on July 29 to establish a new committee to draw up a final timetable for the withdrawal of Nigerian troops from the oil-rich peninsula.

Cameroon Prime Minister Ephraim Inoni's campaign to eliminate government corruption and inefficiency targeted the attendance records of civil servants. Two high officials in the Ministry of Education were sacked in early January for failing to appear at their desks. On January 14 hundreds of workers who arrived after 8 AM found themselves locked out of their ministries. Three senior civil servants at the Ministry of Public Service, arrested on charges of embezzlement on June 3, were convicted of having appropriated 450 million CFA francs ($865,000) of ministry funds. This anticorruption program did not prevent the government from imprisoning editor Joseph Ahanda on July 6, after his weekly newspaper, *Le Front*, published articles about the alleged embezzlement of 300 million CFA francs (about $575,000) by the head of Cameroon's postal service.

During the second week of a strike, two students were killed on April 28 in a clash with security forces at the University of Buéa. Students demanded the abolition of tuition fees and called for improved teaching and the modernization of laboratory and living conditions. In May the strike spread to the Universities of Douala and Dschang, and hundreds of students were arrested and at least five more killed. By the end of the month, the government released nearly $5 million to meet some of the students' demands. Secondary schools were also disrupted by a series of teacher strikes and unofficial walkouts. (NANCY ELLEN LAWLER)

CANADA

Area: 9,984,670 sq km (3,855,103 sq mi)
Population (2005 est.): 32,227,000
Capital: Ottawa
Chief of state: Queen Elizabeth II, represented by Governors-General Adrienne Clarkson and, from September 27, Michaëlle Jean
Head of government: Prime Minister Paul Martin

Domestic Affairs. During 2005 the eyes of Canadians were fixed on Parliament, where a government, outnumbered by members of opposition parties, struggled to survive. In the 2004 election the Liberal Party, under a new prime minister, Paul Martin, had won 135 seats in the House of Commons. Among the three opposition parties, the Conservatives held 99 seats, the separatist Bloc Québécois 54 seats (all from Quebec), and the New Democratic Party (NDP) 19 seats. There was also one independent. Under the British parliamentary system—which was the basis for Canada's—the party forming the government had to command a majority in Parliament. The prime minister's task therefore was to bring forward legislation that would win support. However, a corruption scandal in the Liberal Party seriously undermined the Martin government, which lost a confidence vote in November.

The scandal that brought down the Liberal government had been disclosed during the 2004 election. The movement for a separate Quebec had been worrying to national governments for a generation, and in 1995 a referendum within the province on the subject was narrowly defeated. The Liberal administration headed by Jean Chrétien had established a fund to enhance the image of Canada in the province, principally by sponsoring cultural and sporting events. The funds were distributed by advertising agencies, many with connections to the Liberal Party. It was discovered that some of this money had been improperly spent according to government accounting practices. The news was angrily received by Canadians, and Martin set up a judicial inquiry under Quebec Superior Court Justice John Gomery to look into the matter. Gomery's inquiry was wide-ranging, involving ministers, their staffs, public servants, and advertising executives. In February the judge called on the two prime ministers, Chrétien and Martin, to reveal their knowledge of the affair. A prime minister had not been called before a judicial inquiry to explain his conduct in office since 1873. The prime ministers defended themselves by stating they had had no part in the distribution of funds. The testimony before the inquiry damaged the Liberal Party across the country, especially in Quebec. The separatist movement, which had seemed to be in decline, was revived by the scandal, and there were calls for another referendum. Martin pleaded with Canadians to allow the inquiry to complete its work before they made judgments.

The first part of Judge Gomery's report was released on November 1, and it sharply censored Chrétien, who had conceived the advertising campaign and had administered it from his office with lax oversight, which thus allowed illegal kickbacks to the Liberal Party in Quebec. Although the report exonerated Martin from any part in the scandal, the three opposition parties combined to pass a no-confidence motion 171–133 on November 28. The Martin government resigned the next day to face a general election on Jan. 23, 2006.

A long-standing grievance from Nova Scotia and Newfoundland and Labrador concerned their revenues from oil and gas reserves lying off their shores. The federal government had appropriated some of these revenues to build an equalization fund intended to help the provinces provide a uniform level of social services. The premiers of the two provinces, however, argued that the appropriations were unfair and that Nova Scotia and Newfoundland and Labrador had not sufficiently benefited under the equalization scheme. After long bargaining, Martin agreed that the two

Michaëlle Jean and her husband, Jean-Daniel Lafond, wave to crowds on Parliament Hill in Ottawa after she was sworn in as Canada's governor-general.

provinces could keep their offshore revenues. In addition, Newfoundland and Labrador received an immediate payment of Can$2 billion (Can$1 = about U.S.$0.85), and Nova Scotia was given a grant of Can$830 million.

Ontario also raised complaints. Its premier claimed that Ontario contributed Can$23 billion more each year to the federal treasury than it received in grants from Ottawa. Another grievance concerned the payment the province received for providing services, such as language and skills training, to immigrants. It was asserted that the benefits Ontario received were not on the same scale as those given to Quebec. A long negotiating session on May 7–8 resulted in Martin's agreeing to pay the province Can$5.75 billion over the next five years to compensate for this imbalance. Ontario would use the money for immigrant services, job training, and postsecondary education.

On April 13 Canada announced long-awaited plans for the 1997 Kyoto Protocol, intended to reduce greenhouse gas emissions. The government committed itself to expenditures of Can$10 billion over the next seven years to reduce emissions to 6% below 1990 levels. This ambitious goal would be achieved through major reductions in the use of fossil fuels, the promotion of energy-saving measures, and the purchase of emission credits from both home and abroad.

The Commons passed an important piece of legislation on June 28, just before the summer recess. This law changed the definition of marriage to

include couples of the same sex. Earlier the Supreme Court had approved such a change, and nine of the provincial higher courts had concurred. Although some party members broke ranks on the issue, only the Conservatives opposed the change.

Martin announced an appointment on August 4 that surprised many Canadians. The prestigious post of governor-general, representing Canada's head of state, Queen Elizabeth II of England, would be filled on September 27 by a black immigrant from Haiti. Michaëlle Jean (*see* BIOGRAPHIES) was a gifted television journalist well known in Quebec. As an experienced communicator, she would be expected to express the values and aspirations of Canadians.

The Economy. The Canadian economy performed strongly in 2005. A booming energy sector, profiting from high international demand, stimulated economic growth. It was estimated that GDP would expand by 2.9% during the year. Inflation remained under control, with the consumer price index settling at 1.7% in the middle of the year. The unemployment rate stood at 6.7% of the labour force, with jobs in the service sectors showing marked growth.

A budget was presented by Finance Minister Ralph Goodale on February 23. Spending was to be increased by 23% over the five years between 2005 and 2010. The largest increase would come in the last years of the plan. Social goals, including national child care, received the largest attention, but there was also money to strengthen the Canadian armed forces and to increase foreign aid from its present 2.5% of GDP to 3% within the coming year. A share of the federal gas tax (1.5 cents per litre in 2005, gradually increasing to 5 cents per litre in 2009–10) was to be channeled to cities to help them improve public transportation. Goodale promised that a robust economy would support these expenditures and that a balanced budget, the eighth in a row, would be achieved. He predicted a surplus of $3.1 billion for the first two months of the year, almost twice as large as the one posted in the previous year.

Spending did not stop with the Goodale budget. On April 26 Martin announced that he had reached an agreement with Jack Layton, the leader of the NDP, for a further Can$4.6 billion to be disbursed over the next two years. This would be used for projects dear to the party: social housing, the environment, and development assistance. In return, Layton and his party promised to support the government's budget as it made its way through Parliament. The crucial vote on the budget occurred on May 19. There was uncertainty regarding the votes of the independent members, but when their votes were cast, it was found that 152 members had supported the budget, 152 had opposed it. Under British parliamentary practice the elected speaker, in a tie, votes with the government, and the budget was thus approved. It was the first time this had happened in the history of Canada's Parliament.

Foreign Affairs. Canada-U.S. relations were marked by further differences in 2005. Two years earlier Canada had stood apart from the U.S. in its intervention in Iraq. In 2005 it declined to join in Pres. George W. Bush's missile defense shield. The decision was announced on February 24 and led to a vigorous debate in the Commons. A majority of members supported the decision, with only the Conservative Party unhappy. In point of fact, many Canadians were confused over the issue, since two days before the Commons debate, the recently appointed Canadian ambassador to the U.S., former New Brunswick premier Frank McKenna, had stated that Canada was already involved in the preparations for missile defense. McKenna referred to a 2004 change in the treaty setting up the North American Aerospace Command (NORAD). This change allowed NORAD to communicate aerial-surveillance information to the U.S. Northern Command, the operating agency for the missile shield. Thus, McKenna claimed that Canada had at least partial participation in the missile shield. McKenna's claim was not denied by the Martin government.

Canada showed sympathy toward U.S. objectives in the Middle East by embarking on a plan to station 2,500 troops in Afghanistan by early 2006. A Canadian force had been sent to Kabul in 2003. The new contingent would be posted to Kandahar, a city in which conservative Taliban elements were strong.

Canada-U.S. commercial disputes showed mixed results in 2005. The mad cow issue, which had seen the closing of the U.S. border to Canadian cattle after the disease infected a single Canadian animal in 2003, was resolved. Thorough inspection of animals on each side of the border led the U.S. Department of Agriculture to declare that the trade in animals could be resumed. The action was resisted by Montana ranchers, who secured an injunction against the opening of the border. A judgment of the U.S. Court of Appeals on July 14 set aside the injunction. The border was again open to the movement of cattle under 36 months of age.

Another dispute, dating back to 2002, failed to be settled. The U.S. had imposed a 28% duty on Canadian softwood or construction lumber entering the country, claiming that a subsidy had been given to Canadian lumber producers. More than $5 billion had been collected through these duties. Five rulings by North American Free Trade Association (NAFTA) panels had supported Canada's position that its lumber-cutting practices did not constitute a subsidy, but the U.S. refused to accept the decisions. On August 10 a three-member special appeal panel declared unequivocally that there was no basis for the duties. It directed the U.S. to remove them and return the moneys collected. Again the U.S. rejected the ruling, urging Canada to settle the dispute through negotiation. The Canadian government rejected this option, arguing that the dispute should be settled under NAFTA procedures. Further talks on the subject were broken off, an indication that the softwood lumber dispute would continue.

(DAVID M.L. FARR)

CAPE VERDE

Area: 4,033 sq km (1,557 sq mi)
Population (2005 est.): 476,000
Capital: Praia
Chief of state: President Pedro Pires
Head of government: Prime Minister José Maria Neves

In February 2005 former Portuguese president Mário Soares called on his country to press the European Union to admit Cape Verde as a member. Soares saw Cape Verde as a bridge between the EU and Africa and Latin America. More than 70% of the people were literate in Portuguese, and the government sought to encourage tourism from the EU. In May the IMF confirmed that the country's macroeconomic policies were sound. GDP growth went down in 2004 to 4.5% because of difficulties in the agricultural sector. Remittances from Cape Verdeans living aboard continued to be important, but the government's privatization program was moving toward completion. When Prime Minister José Maria Neves visited Washington, D.C., in July, his country was praised for good governance and was promised greatly increased aid under the Millennium Challenge Account, a fund to reward less-developed nations making progress in political and economic reform. NATO's elite Response Force agreed to hold major military maneuvers in Cape Verde in 2006. In the parliament, however, a bill promoted by the ruling African Party for the Independence of Cape Verde creating a Republican Intelligence Service, meant in part to deal with the increase in organized crime, especially drug trafficking, was rejected by the opposition on the grounds that the new force might not act impartially.

(CHRISTOPHER SAUNDERS)

CENTRAL AFRICAN REPUBLIC

Area: 622,436 sq km (240,324 sq mi)
Population (2005 est.): 4,038,000
Capital: Bangui
Chief of state: President François Bozizé
Head of government: Prime Ministers Célestin Gaombalet and, from June 13, Élie Doté

Two years after he seized power in a military coup in the Central African Republic (CAR), Pres. François Bozizé ran against 10 rival candidates in the March 13, 2005, presidential elections. Bozizé took 42.9% of the vote, nearly double that of his nearest rival, former prime minister Martin Ziguélé. In the May 8 runoff election, Bozizé easily defeated Ziguélé. Although former ruler Ange-Félix Patassé had been barred from the contest, international observers generally applauded the moves toward the restoration of constitutional rule. On June 21 newly appointed Prime Minister Élie Doté named a 27-member cabinet that included several of the defeated presidential candidates.

The CAR's continuing struggle to pay its civil servants was considered by

François Bozizé, who had assumed power in the Central African Republic after a coup two years earlier, takes the presidential oath in Bangui on June 11.

international donors to be the cause of much political instability. The European Union withheld the release of development funds for the CAR until a new cooperative agreement with the IMF was reached. In a belt-tightening measure, President Bozizé on September 1 suspended the recruitment of new government employees.

As a result of renewed fighting in early June between government and rebel forces in the north, more than 8,000 people were forced to flee across the border into Chad. An additional 2,000 others followed in mid-July after an operation was launched to clear the area of armed dissidents. By year's end the UN High Commissioner for Refugees estimated that more than 43,000 CAR refugees were living in southern Chad.

(NANCY ELLEN LAWLER)

CHAD

Area: 1,284,000 sq km (495,755 sq mi)
Population (2005 est.): 9,657,000, excluding some 200,000 refugees from The Sudan
Capital: N'Djamena
Chief of state: President Lieut. Gen. Idriss Déby
Head of government: Prime Ministers Moussa Faki Mahamat and, from February 3, Pascal Yoadimnadji

In 2005, despite its wealth as a new oil exporter, Chad remained one of the world's poorest nations, with 80% of the population living on less than a dollar a day by UN estimates. For months early in the year, civil servants and other workers were not paid. After a series of protest strikes, Prime Minister Moussa Faki resigned in February and was replaced by Pascal Yoadimnadji, a former agriculture minister. After the army quelled a mutiny that Pres. Idriss Déby said was aimed at him, his ruling Patriotic Salvation Movement (MPS) pushed a series of constitutional amendments through the parliament, where the MPS held 113 of the 155 seats. The measure that aroused most criticism repealed the two-term limit for presidents. This would allow Déby to stand in 2006 for a third five-year term as elected chief of state. Despite rumours that the president was seriously ill, the amendments were endorsed by 77% of those who voted in a referendum held on June 6. Another amendment replaced the Senate with an Economic, Social and Cultural Council, the members of which would all be nominated by the president. Most newspapers and radio stations stopped work in August to protest what one reporter called Déby's "creeping dictatorship."

Meanwhile, the some 200,000 refugees from the conflict in the Darfur region of The Sudan who had fled into Chad strained the extremely poor east of the country. The refugees were supplied with food rations by the UN, but providing them with enough water posed major problems. In mid-2005 waves of refugees began entering southern Chad from the Central African Republic.

In December tensions between Chad and The Sudan increased following a deadly rebel attack in eastern Chad. Although The Sudan denied involvement, Chad declared "a state of war."

(CHRISTOPHER SAUNDERS)

CHILE

Area: 756,096 sq km (291,930 sq mi)
Population (2005 est.): 16,295,000
Capitals: Santiago (national) and Valparaíso (legislative)
Head of state and government: President Ricardo Lagos Escobar

Chile continued to demonstrate its unique position in Latin America during 2005, achieving a high level of economic growth while strengthening its democratic institutions. On the political front, the 2004 financial scandal surrounding Gen. Augusto Pinochet's secret foreign bank accounts continued to expand, sullying not only his own reputation but his family's as well and creating ripple effects far into Chile's political waters. By the end of 2005, both Pinochet's wife and his youngest son had been arrested for illegal financial dealings, and Pinochet found himself stripped of immunity not only for illegal financial dealings but for yet another human rights violation, the disappearance of 119 people in Operation Colombo. At the end of 2004, the report of the National Commission on Political Imprisonment and Torture, dubbed the Valech Report, confirmed more than 35,000 cases of torture and underscored the moral lapses of the Pinochet regime.

The cumulative ripple effect of these scandals could not be overestimated. The scandals virtually destroyed whatever remained of Pinochet's political standing, even among many Chileans on the right, and neutralized him as a political force. After many years' efforts, a series of constitutional reforms were approved overwhelmingly by Congress on August 16. The reforms eliminated most of the residual nondemocratic features of the 1980 constitution that had been written and promulgated under military rule, and they reflected a broad political agreement achieved through negotiations between the ruling centre-left Concertación coalition and the right-wing Alliance for Chile coalition. The constitutional reforms included the restoration of the president's authority to dismiss heads of the branches of the armed forces and national police; the elimination of nonelected senators in the Senate; an end to military influence in the National Security Council, which became a presidential advisory group; and a shortening of the presidential term (from six) to four years. Though another long-anticipated reform—modification of the binomial electoral system—was not achieved, future change was facilitated by moving it from the constitutional realm to that of the organic election law.

In the campaign for the upcoming presidential elections, the Concertación candidacy was won by Socialist Michelle Bachelet, who scored an easy victory over the more moderate Christian Democrat Soledad Alvear. Bachelet represented the victory of the more progressive wing of the Concertación.

The daughter of Air Force Gen. Alberto Bachelet, a democratic loyalist who was tortured and killed in the aftermath of the coup, she was herself tortured by the military. Bachelet also epitomized generational change within the Concertación and the flowering of a new kind of politics, one that was more open and transparent; if elected, she would become the first woman president in the country's history.

The political ripples from the Pinochet affair were also felt within the right-wing Alliance. Competition for the presidential nomination erupted between its two parties, pitting Joaquín Lavín of the Independent Democratic Union (UDI), the presumed candidate until then, against the more moderate Sebastián Piñera of the National Renewal, who had supported the "no" vote in the 1988 plebiscite on Pinochet's continuing in office. Lavín's UDI represented more hard-line Pinochet supporters. In the December 11 election, Bachelet fell short of the absolute majority needed, winning 46% of the vote. She was scheduled to face Piñera, who had captured 25% to edge out Lavín for second place, in a runoff election on Jan. 15, 2006.

The economy showed great dynamism in 2005, with growth topping 6%. Inflation sped up as well, estimated at over 4%. The country's trade balance continued to be positive, and unemployment, while still high, declined. Relations with both Bolivia and Peru, which had been rocky for a few years, improved.　　(LOIS HECHT OPPENHEIM)

CHINA

Area: 9,572,900 sq km (3,696,100 sq mi), including Tibet and excluding Taiwan and the special autonomous regions of Hong Kong and Macau
Population (2005 est., excluding Taiwan, Hong Kong, and Macau): 1,304,369,000
Capital: Beijing
Chief of state: President Hu Jintao
Head of government: Premier Wen Jiabao

Domestic Politics. Chinese Pres. Hu Jintao consolidated his power in 2005 through a series of political maneuvers and policies. Under Hu's leadership, the Communist Party of China (CPC) launched a campaign early in the year to "preserve the vanguard character" of the party. A program was undertaken to engage all of the CPC's 69 million members in six months of workshops and evaluations. By midyear some 14 million CPC members had gone through this process aimed at strengthening their beliefs and commitment to the party.

Hu also continued to wage a high-profile campaign against institutional corruption, which many feared had begun to erode governmental authority. A spate of financial scandals led to a crackdown on corruption in banking and other industries. Zhang Enzhao, president of China Construction Bank—one of the leading state-owned commercial banks in China—resigned in March over allegations that he had taken bribes from an American contractor. He was the latest of four high-ranking banking officials who had been removed from their posts. The China Banking Regulatory Commission concluded its investigation of the four major state-run banks, the "Big Four," and claimed to have saved $61 million from being lost to fraud. One branch manager of the Bank of China had embezzled about $102 million from several bank accounts before fleeing abroad. Among government officials arrested or sentenced for corruption during the year were the deputy governor of Sichuan province, the deputy party secretary of Shanxi province, the transportation bureau chiefs in Henan, Heilongjiang, and Yunnan provinces, and the deputy mayor of Suzhou. Quite a few others who lost their jobs over corruption charges had been promoted by Hu's predecessor, Jiang Zemin. These included Zhang Enzhao, Lanzhou's Mayor Zhang Zhiyin, and Li Yizhen, the deputy party secretary of Shenzhen. China also took steps in 2005 to join the Financial Action Task Force on Money Laundering, an intergovernmental body established to counter the manipulation of financial systems by criminals.

In a departure from the previous administration, the government began to take active measures to ease rural poverty. The widening wealth gap in Chinese society had prompted social protests and distrust in government. The Gini coefficient (a measure of income distribution in a society by which 0 = perfect equality and 1 = perfect inequality) in China had already exceeded the 0.4 threshold—widely viewed as an indicator of potential serious social disruption and instability. While the country's economy had been on the fast track in recent years, a significant portion of its rural population had not been lifted from poverty. Toward this end the People's National Congress in March moved to eliminate most of the basic agricultural taxes

Chilean soldiers meet with their Bolivian counterparts on July 21 to inaugurate the process of removal of Chilean land mines along the border between the two countries. The border was mined during the revival of an old territorial dispute in 1962, and there had been no diplomatic relations between Chile and Bolivia since.

© David Mercado/Reuters/Corbis

imposed on rural families and to increase agricultural subsidies for grain production. Agricultural reforms, however, fell short of granting peasants greater control over their land.

The government also kept a vigilant eye on public health issues during the year. It pledged to control the spread of AIDS and took aggressive measures to curb the threat posed by avian influenza (bird flu), including a plan to vaccinate all 14 billion of its poultry. The drastic move was intended to impede the spread of avian influenza and hopefully reduce human exposure to the virus. The world's largest poultry-producing nation, China had by year's end reported at least 30 outbreaks of bird flu in poultry in 2005 and at least three cases of bird-to-human infections, two of which resulted in death. Other antiflu measures taken by the government included the establishment of warning networks across the country and the stockpiling of antiviral drugs and other emergency supplies.

One interesting phenomenon that had developed in China in the early 21st century was the rapidly increasing number of Chinese returning from abroad. Most of the estimated 200,000 Chinese who had returned in recent years had obtained academic degrees or concluded short-term academic training outside the country. Some of these had begun to assume prominent government and business positions in China. Among a long list of notable returnees were the People's Bank of China governor, Zhou Xiaochuan, and Education Minister Zhou Ji from the U.S.; the Chinese Academy of Sciences president, Lu Yongxiang, from Germany; and Science and Technology Minister Xu Guanhua from Sweden. Three foreign affairs vice ministers, Yang Jiechi, Zhang Yesui, and Zhou Wenzhong, had also returned from the U.K. These officials, all of whom were young and poised to take up challenges, were expected to have a broader worldview and greater practical knowledge of the West as well as to be generally more open to reform than the previous generation of leaders.

The Economy. China's economy continued to grow impressively, at 9.4% in the first quarter of 2005 and at more than 9% overall for the third consecutive year. There were still no ready answers, however, to the long-term energy shortage that China faced. As economic growth greatly boosted demand for electricity, the country experienced a third straight year of crippling power blackouts. The State Electricity Regulatory Commission reported a 25,000-MW shortfall during the summer, when electricity consumption typically peaked—though this was a marginal improvement over the 30,000-MW shortfall experienced the previous summer. Forecasts also indicated that China's demand for petroleum could rise 8% every year for the next quarter of a century. Although China accelerated oil and gas production in Xingjiang and other areas—and although PetroChina planned a $3.3 billion refinery expansion—close to half of the country's oil consumption continued to be met by imports.

China searched for energy resources from East Africa to Central and Southeast Asia. China Petroleum & Chemical Corp. (Sinopec) signed a $300 million deal to develop natural gas resources in Saudi Arabia, near the huge Ghawar oil and gas field in the eastern region of the country. China also concluded a $70 billion deal with Iran to buy 250 million tons of natural gas over 30 years. China National Petroleum Corp. (CNPC) purchased the Iranian subsidiary of Sheer Energy of Canada for $121 million, which gave CNPC a 49% stake in the Masjed Soleyman oil field. It also purchased PetroKazakhstan, a Canadian-owned company, for $4 billion. President Hu himself traveled to Indonesia, Brunei, and the Philippines on missions that were focused largely on securing energy supplies. China provided $6 billion to Russia in hopes of securing oil, and in May it signed a $600 million agreement on energy cooperation with Uzbekistan.

After much speculation on the outside and preparation on the inside, the central bank made two significant currency reforms. One was to enlarge the span of currency fluctuation and allow the yuan to appreciate by more than 2%. The other was to adopt a new formula to valuate the yuan against a basket of foreign currencies instead of just the U.S. dollar. These foreign currencies included the U.S. dollar, the euro, the Japanese yen, and the South Korean won. The currencies of Singapore, Britain, Malaysia, Russia, Australia, Canada, and Thailand were similarly considered in setting the yuan's foreign exchange rate. As a result, the yuan was revaluated on July 21 to 8.11 per dollar from a long-standing trading point of 8.278 per dollar. The revaluation was preceded by a 20-minute floating of the yuan on April 29 and by Hong Kong's loosening its currency peg on May 19. China hitherto had had no experience of a floating yuan. Although the central bank might broaden the span of currency fluctuation in the future, currency liberalization was not on its reform agenda.

In addition to these significant currency changes, China pressed ahead with reforms of its troubled banking system and markedly opened the door to foreign investment in its financial institutions. State-run banks were encouraged to list their shares abroad. Bank of Communications became the second Chinese bank—following the Bank of China—to list its operations on the Hong Kong exchange market. Bank of America acquired a 9% stake in the country's third largest lender, China Construction Bank. Dutch bank ING Group and British bank HSBC bought a 19.9% stake and a 20% stake, respectively, in the Bank of Beijing. An investor group led by the Royal Bank of Scotland and Merrill Lynch agreed to pay $3.1 billion to acquire a 10% stake in the Bank of China. American Express and a group of investors led by Goldman Sachs and Allianz Group signed a $3 billion deal to purchase a stake in Industrial & Commercial Bank of China. General Electric bought a 7% stake in Shenzhen Development Bank

Vegetable vendors in a market in Beijing count their money on July 22. On the previous day China's central bank had declared that it no longer would peg the yuan to the U.S. dollar alone but rather would peg it to a basket of currencies.

© Guang Niu/Getty Images

China's Relations with Its Neighbours

During the administration of Chinese Pres. Hu Jintao, who took office in 2003, China adopted a so-called Good Neighbour Policy as part of a new strategy of "peaceful development," in which China sought to promote an interdependent, rather than competitive, relationship with its neighbours and the world. In the second half of the 20th century, China had experienced three military conflicts with neighbouring countries—India in 1962, the Soviet Union in 1969, and Vietnam in 1979—each of which had been over disputed territories along their borders. By 2005, however, effects of the Good Neighbour Policy were increasingly evident. In 2004 China had reached an agreement with Russia that put an end to their decades-long border disputes. The two countries agreed on the final demarcation of two areas totaling some 375 sq km (145 sq mi) along their eastern border, with China gaining control over Tarabarov Island (Yinlong Island) and 50% of Bolshoy Ussurisky Island (Heixiazi Island). In 2005 China signed an agreement with India to resolve their dispute over a territory covering 130,000 sq km (50,000 sq mi) in the Himalayan region. This was only the latest sign of a warming in Sino-Indian relations. Recent years had seen India officially accept China's definition of Tibet and China reopen a trade route into India through the border region of Sikkim. The latter move appeared to signal China's recognition for the first time of Indian sovereignty over Sikkim.

During a visit to Vietnam in late 2005, President Hu offered a five-point proposal for developing political and economic relations. In one of those points, China proposed to complete the full demarcation of the border between the two countries, a first step toward resolving the disputes that lingered from the 1979 war. During Hu's visit, a joint statement was also released that announced the countries' plans to expand bilateral trade from $7 billion to $10 billion by 2010. This visit was preceded by Hu's trip to North Korea.

Throughout the year China persistently attempted to persuade North Korea to return to six-party talks on nuclear disarmament.

In another attempt to promote regional cooperation, China continued to push "ASEAN-plus-one" (China) and "ASEAN-plus-three" (China, South Korea, and Japan) initiatives to expand the free-trade area of the Association of Southeast Asian Nations. China also remained committed to building relations with Central Asian states, mainly via the Shanghai Cooperation Organization (SCO). This intergovernmental body had originated as the "Shanghai Five" in 1996, when China, Kazakhstan, Kyrgyzstan, Russia, and Tajikistan signed the Treaty on Deepening Military Trust in Border Regions at a summit meeting held in Shanghai. Uzbekistan joined the group in 2001, when the SCO was formally established. Its basic goals were regional security and economic cooperation.

Despite the many positive developments in foreign relations that China's Good Neighbour Policy had helped to bring about by 2005, tensions in Sino-Japanese relations heightened sharply. Several issues had led to an increasingly acrimonious atmosphere. One was Japan's adoption of new history textbooks that whitewashed its wartime atrocities against China. A second issue was over continual visits by Japan's top leaders, including Prime Minister Junichiro Koizumi, to Tokyo's Yasukuni Shrine, a war memorial that China's Foreign Ministry had called "a symbol of militarism" that "honours Class A war criminals." A third issue concerned Japan's bid for a permanent seat on the UN Security Council—a bid that China successfully helped to thwart. Toward the end of 2005, however, both governments called for resolutions of sensitive problems and promised to work on their differences. In China's case it appeared evident that it would continue to regard a good relationship with neighbouring countries as vital to its economic development as well as to political stability. (XIAOBO HU)

for $100 million, and Citigroup planned to raise its stake in Shanghai Pudong Development Bank to 20%.

China continued to reform its state-owned enterprises (SOEs) by planning to close down more than 2,000 debt-ridden SOEs in the next four years and transferring a limited number of state-held shares to the private market. In early May the government picked 4 companies for the pilot project of selling off state-held shares and then expanded that to 42 additional companies, including some of the country's largest. The number of private companies in China had increased tremendously since 1993, growing by an annual rate of 24% on average. In 2004 there were more than three million private companies in the country employing some 47 million workers.

Special Administrative Regions and Tibet. Macau's gaming industry continued to see explosive growth. Building upon his previous year's profits, gaming tycoon Stanley Ho, who controlled 15 of Macau's 17 casinos, planned to expand his operation by as much as 30%. Gaming revenue in Macau was forecast to rise 20% over the next four years as banks rushed to finance additional casino projects. Goldman Sachs and Lehman Brothers led the new round of financing. At least one project was expected to run up to $2.5 billion in loans and bond sales.

Hong Kong democracy advocate Martin Lee continued his calls for the Chinese government to set a timetable for full democracy in the special administrative region. Lee voiced his concerns during trips to Europe and to the U.S., where he had a closed-door meeting in November with U.S. Secretary of State Condoleezza Rice. He warned the secretary of state that "democracy is limping" in Hong Kong and that "we are not making any headway at all." According to her spokesman, Rice told Lee that while the U.S. supported democracy and universal suffrage for Hong Kong, it would be up to the people of Hong Kong to "determine the pace and scope of political reform in accordance with the Basic Law."

In August the Chinese government held celebrations marking the 40th anniversary of the establishment of the Tibet Autonomous Region. While members of a government delegation sent to Lhasa for a parade in the regional capital trumpeted the "tremendous changes" that had taken place in Tibet under Chinese rule, human rights activists decried policies in the region and labeled the celebrations a "major propaganda opportunity" for the government.

Foreign Relations. China strengthened regional cooperation (see Sidebar) and expanded its economic diplomacy during the year. The second Greater Mekong Subregion (GMS) Summit was

Chinese Premier Wen Jiabao (right) traveled to New Delhi in April to meet with his Indian counterpart, Manmohan Singh, and sign a number of bilateral accords.

held in Kunming on July 4–5, with government leaders from China, Laos, Myanmar (Burma), Thailand, Cambodia, and Vietnam participating. China agreed to lend Vietnam more than $1 billion for a series of projects. China promoted GMS cooperation as a first step toward building a China-ASEAN Free Trade Area. President Hu visited Indonesia and signed nine agreements on April 25 to establish a "strategic partnership" and engage in more trade, investment, and maritime cooperation. During another year of active diplomacy, Hu also paid visits to Brunei, the Philippines, Russia, Kazakhstan, the U.K., the U.S., Canada, Mexico, North Korea, Vietnam, Germany, Spain, and South Korea.

Premier Wen Jiabao visited India in April and signed an agreement aimed at resolving a long-running dispute over the countries' shared Himalayan border, a territory that covered some 130,000 sq km (50,000 sq mi). The agreement followed a model of successful resolution between China and Russia over the eastern sector of their border that had been under dispute until 2004. Cooperation between China and Russia continued in 2005 in the form of joint military exercises beginning in August. Although the two states had participated in multilateral military exercises in the past, this was the first time that they had conducted bilateral drills. India also extended an invitation to China for joint military exercises.

Beijing hosted the 2005 Korea-China Economic Conference, aimed at fostering "super economic cooperation in East Asia." China and Australia launched

free-trade negotiations in late May, while China continued to work on a free-trade agreement with New Zealand. China also signed a free-trade agreement with Chile in November.

Joining the World Trade Organization in 2001 had bound China irreversibly in a global supply chain for industrial products. In the wake of its entry into the WTO, China experienced a considerable increase in its textile exports. China and the U.S. concluded protracted negotiations over restrictions on such exports during the year. Trade between China and South Korea surpassed $100 billion in 2005, and robust economic growth in both Russia and China was expected to lead to increased trade between those countries.

Although China became Japan's number one trading partner, Sino-Japanese relations delved to perhaps their lowest point in 30 years. Early in 2005 Japan approved a set of new middle-school textbooks that in the eyes of many Asians justified and glorified its wartime wrongs. The textbooks offered little or no coverage of Japan's wartime atrocities. In addition, top Japanese leaders continued to make pilgrimages to Tokyo's Yasukuni Shrine, where some two million of Japan's war dead were honoured, including 14 convicted Class A war criminals linked to atrocities committed during World War II. Mass protests were staged in all major cities in China. In August, as it joined 110 UN member states in blocking Japan's bid for a permanent seat on the Security Council, China charged that Japan was not mature enough to take leadership responsibilities in international affairs. Earlier in the year, Japanese Foreign Minister Nobutaka Machimura had called China's criticism of visits to the war shrine "absurd" and accused China of ignoring Japan's pacifist record.

U.S. Pres. George W. Bush paid a two-day visit to Beijing in November during a multicountry tour that included attendance at the APEC (Asia-Pacific Economic Cooperation) Summit in Pusan, S.Kor. Although he called for greater human rights in China, Bush struck a generally conciliatory tone during his visit, reiterating the "one-China" policy of the U.S. government and focusing much of his discussions on economic matters. For its part China expressed its commitment to continuing to reform its currency, taking serious measures to crack down on violations of intellectual property rights, and pressuring North Korea to

return to the six-party nuclear disarmament talks that it had abandoned in February.   (XIAOBO HU)

COLOMBIA

Area: 1,141,568 sq km (440,762 sq mi)
Population (2005 est.): 42,954,000
Capital: Bogotá
Head of state and government: President Álvaro Uribe Vélez

In 2005 the administration of Pres. Álvaro Uribe struggled against guerrillas on the left and paramilitaries on the right, but it chose widely divergent strategies when dealing with the two sides. The government offered positive incentives to encourage demobilization by the paramilitary United Self-Defense Forces of Colombia (AUC) but continued to pursue the Revolutionary Armed Forces of Colombia (FARC) and the National Liberation Army (ELN) militarily—though the government showed some softening in its dealings with both leftist guerrilla groups at the end of the year. Neither strategy was without its critics, but tellingly the president's popular approval remained high, and his close relationship with the administration of U.S. Pres. George W. Bush remained strong.

At least some factions within the officer corps continued their collaboration with the AUC, and the president worked hard to stall a bill that would determine the fate of demobilized combatants. The law that eventually passed required that demobilizing paramilitaries with criminal charges against them confess their crimes, receive a sentence, and then have that sentence commuted to a significantly lesser "alternative penalty." Given the record of past atrocities committed by paramilitaries, human rights groups complained that demobilization was being purchased at too high a price. Still, the law was sufficient to persuade foreign governments to reinstitute the aid necessary to pay for the demobilization.

A military defeat of the FARC was far from achieved, but the Uribe administration held fast to its position that a weakened FARC was more likely to participate seriously in peace negotiations. Political violence declined in

2005, but noncombatants continued to be displaced at a rate of well over 100,000 annually. Plan Colombia, an aid package agreed to during the administration of U.S. Pres. Bill Clinton, expired, but the Bush administration continued aid at a similar level. The aid was used for more widespread spraying to eradicate coca crops and for beefing up the military's abilities. The amount of land under coca cultivation declined, but spraying had diminishing returns. The government expanded its effort to simply pull up the plants by hand. Whatever the strategy, the price and the supply of cocaine in Europe and in the U.S. did not appear to be affected.

The movement of paramilitaries, guerrillas, and others involved in the drug trade back and forth across Colombia's borders created tensions with neighbours. Most notably, the Colombian government used bounty hunters to seize Rodrigo Granda, a roving envoy for the FARC, while he was in Caracas. Claiming a violation of its sovereignty, the administration of Venezuelan Pres. Hugo Chávez (see BIOGRAPHIES) recalled its ambassador and froze trade. Rightist Uribe and leftist Chávez were relatively slow to

normalize relations. In June the FARC attacked a military base in Putumayo, just north of the Ecuadoran border. Colombia charged that the guerrillas had been allowed to stage their attack from Ecuador, and the Ecuadoran government quickly countered that Colombia needed to control its own border. Despite tensions on several fronts, diplomacy prevailed between governments.

Presidential and legislative elections were scheduled for 2006. A bill that Uribe pushed through Congress amended the constitution to allow him to run for a second term, and late in 2005 the law was upheld by the Constitutional Court. The newly formed left-of-centre Independent Democratic Pole nominated popular Sen. Antonio Navarro Wolff as its presidential candidate. A former mayor of Bogotá, Antanas Mockus, planned to run as an independent. At its national convention in June, the Liberal Party chose former president César Gaviria as its leader, and a nasty fight for the right to be the party's standard-bearer in the presidential race seemed likely.

In 2006 each party would be able to run only one list of candidates per district; in 2002, 64 parties had presented

321 lists for the Senate race, and 75 parties had presented 962 lists for races for the House of Representatives. Combined with new minimum vote thresholds, the single-list requirement might encourage candidates to coalesce under fewer banners. How the banners fared would be influenced heavily by whether Uribe was allowed to run and by the popularity of his opponents. Elections could clarify the political scene.

(BRIAN F. CRISP)

COMOROS

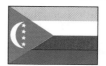

Area: 1,862 sq km (719 sq mi), excluding the 374-sq-km (144-sq-mi) island of Mayotte, a de facto dependency of France since 1976
Population (2005 est.): 614,000 (excluding 181,000 on Mayotte)
Capital: Moroni
Chief of state and head of government: President Col. Azali Assoumani

Following the Indian Ocean tsunami in December 2004, representatives of island states, including Comoros, met in January 2005 at a UN-sponsored conference in Mauritius to ask for help amid a decline in donor aid. Several student and teacher protests occurred in Moroni in January, and others in early March on Anjouan resulted in two deaths and an islandwide curfew. Hundreds were forced to flee their homes on Mt. Karthala on Grande Comore in April, when the volcano erupted in smoke.

Pres. Col. Azali Assoumani made a historic state visit in January to France, the first since Comoros gained its independence in 1975. The visit helped to repair relations between the two countries, which had been strained since the 1999 coup that brought Assoumani to power. In April a controversial bill that would have allowed Assoumani to run for a second term as federal president was withdrawn. Under the 2001 constitution, the federal presidency rotated between the three islands' presidents every four years. In an effort to strengthen the country's economy and to receive donor funds and attract investors, the government submitted austerity measures in February to the International Monetary Fund.

(MARY F.E. EBELING)

Under the watchful gaze of liberation leader Simón Bolívar, Colombia's rightist Pres. Álvaro Uribe (left) and Venezuela's leftist Pres. Hugo Chávez (right) meet on February 15 at Miraflores Palace in Caracas to resolve a number of diplomatic problems dividing the neighbour states.

© Jorge Silva/Reuters/Corbis

CONGO, DEMOCRATIC REPUBLIC OF THE

Area: 2,344,858 sq km (905,354 sq mi)
Population (2005 est.): 57,549,000
Capital: Kinshasa
Head of state and government: President Joseph Kabila

Work progressed toward a new constitution for the Democratic Republic of the Congo (DRC) in 2005. On May 14 the parliament adopted a draft constitution that proposed the division of the country into 25 provinces in addition to Kinshasa, the recognition of all ethnic groups living in the country at the time of independence in 1960, and the reduction of the minimum age for presidential candidates from 35 to 30. The latter would allow 33-year-old DRC Pres. Joseph Kabila—who had succeeded his father, Laurent Kabila, after the elder's assassination in 2001—to stand for election. There was also provision for the election by parliament of a prime minister who in certain instances might act as a check on the powers of the president. Having been officially adopted by the legislature, the draft constitution was subjected to a national referendum in December and was overwhelmingly approved by voters.

The new constitution was a bold initiative in view of the troubles that continued to disturb the eastern provinces of the country. The year began under threat of an invasion from Rwanda, whose president, Paul Kagame, claimed that the UN Observer Mission in Congo (MONUC) had failed to bring under control the Hutu rebels who menaced his country's borders. The invasion did not materialize, owing to UN pressure, and on March 31 leaders of the rebel groups said that they would put an end to their attacks on Rwanda. As a result, the number of refugees returning peacefully to Rwanda increased markedly, but there was no parallel reduction in the number and severity of attacks by the rebels upon citizens inside the DRC.

In the Ituri district of Orientale province, which bordered Uganda, a MONUC patrol was ambushed on February 25 and nine of its members killed. Although MONUC responded vigorously and seemed to meet with considerable success in disarming rebels—15,000 of whom had been disarmed in Ituri by June—fighting between militia groups from the Lendu and Hema tribes continued unabated, and any prospect of the government's gaining control of the district seemed illusory.

In the southern province of Katanga, it was reported in May that government forces had thwarted an attempt at secession, and in that same month violence broke out between rival parties in the capital of the central province of Kasai. In Kinshasa seven demonstrators were killed and hundreds more arrested in June, while further heavy fighting between government forces and Hutu militias took place in July in the province of North Kivu. South Africa agreed to provide technical and financial aid to the DRC to help in the restoration of public services.

(KENNETH INGHAM)

CONGO, REPUBLIC OF THE

Area: 342,000 sq km (132,047 sq mi)
Population (2005 est.): 3,602,000
Capital: Brazzaville
Head of state and government: President Denis Sassou-Nguesso

New attempts were made in 2005 to disarm the remnants of the militiamen who had fought the government of the Republic of the Congo during the 1998–2003 civil wars. On January 31 former rebel leader Frédéric Bitsangou announced a drive to implement the peace agreement signed on March 17, 2003, to collect all guns belonging to his "Ninjas" in the Pool district, north of Brazzaville. The government responded by launching a three-month program to demobilize, disarm, and finally reintegrate into the community 450 Ninjas who had already surrendered. An estimated 43,000 former rebels had yet to accept the pact, however. Sporadic outbreaks of violence by Ninjas continued, and on April 26, using grenades and rifles, one group attacked a UN aid convoy. Bitsangou's disarmament program was suspended on June 13, when he announced that Ninja weapons would not be destroyed until an unspecified "political compromise" had been reached with the government.

On August 17 the trial ended for 15 high-ranking military and security officials who had been charged with the 1999 disappearance and presumed murder of 353 Congolese who were returning to Brazzaville from refuge in

Thousands of opposition sympathizers in the Democratic Republic of the Congo, disgruntled by delays in elections, demonstrate in Kinshasa on July 9.

the Democratic Republic of the Congo; the returnees were suspected of being supporters of the Ninjas. The defendants were acquitted of the murder charges on the grounds that they had not been personally responsible for the disappearances.

Despite world record oil prices, Congo's economy continued to lose ground. Though government revenues depended principally on exports of timber and oil, the majority of government expenditure went toward debt servicing and civil-service salaries. Economic-development strategies provided little in the way of job creation or poverty reduction. Health services were poor, and severe power shortages hampered growth in both the private and public sectors. Though relatively little revenue was left for improvements in infrastructure, on August 3 construction began on an electrical plant to serve Brazzaville.

(NANCY ELLEN LAWLER)

COSTA RICA

Area: 51,100 sq km (19,730 sq mi)
Population (2005 est.): 4,221,000
Capital: San José
Head of state and government: President Abel Pacheco de la Espriella

Corruption scandals, trade agreements, and preelection fever dominated the attention of Costa Ricans in 2005. In late 2004 Costa Rica's immediate past three presidents were accused of accepting bribes. Former president Rafael Ángel Calderón Fournier, Jr. (1990–94), was accused of having negotiated a multimillion-dollar bribe from a Finnish medical supply firm and was placed under house arrest. Former president Miguel Ángel Rodríguez Echeverría (1998–2002) was accused of having taken a huge bribe from the French telecommunications firm Alcatel for helping negotiate a deal. Rodríguez had just taken over as secretary-general of the Organization of American States and was forced to resign in order to return to Costa Rica to respond to the corruption charges. He too remained under house arrest. Former president José María Figueres Olsen (1994–98) was also tainted with

AP/Wide World Photos

On May 16 students and trade union workers in San José, Costa Rica, demonstrate against CAFTA-DR, the Central America–Dominican Republic Free Trade Agreement, being negotiated with the United States. President Abel Pacheco was moving cautiously on endorsing the pact.

bribery accusations related to Alcatel. Figueres had not returned from his residence in Geneva to respond to the charges.

The administration of the current president, Abel Pacheco, was itself rocked by accusations of secret bank accounts in Panama, problems arising at a time when the administration seemed bogged down. Only a handful of Pacheco's original cabinet ministers remained. Hopes to reduce a persistent 20% poverty rate went unrealized, and inflation remained several points above the 10% target. Pressure grew on Pacheco to bring the issue of accession to the Central America–Dominican Republic Free Trade Agreement (CAFTA-DR) to a vote in the legislature, but he deferred, establishing instead a five-member "council of notables" to advise him. In August Costa Rica approved another free-trade agreement, however, this one with CARICOM, the Caribbean free-trade community.

Presidential and legislative elections were scheduled for February 2006. The leading contender was former president and Nobel Peace Prize laureate Óscar Arias. His National Liberation Party included many women on its slate of legislative candidates.

(MITCHELL A. SELIGSON)

CÔTE D'IVOIRE

Area: 320,803 sq km (123,863 sq mi)
Population (2005 est.): 17,298,000
De facto capital: Abidjan
Chief of state: President Laurent Gbagbo
Head of government: Prime Minister Seydou Diarra

International efforts to reconcile and reunify Côte d'Ivoire met with little success in 2005. The January 2003 peace agreement between the government and rebel groups that controlled the north had not been implemented, and plans to hold legislative and presidential elections on October 30 seemed doomed. On September 9 UN Secretary-General Kofi Annan deemed it impossible to conduct elections, citing the failure to create an electoral commission acceptable to all sides and the absence of updated voter registration lists. He warned that the Security Council would soon be forced to place new sanctions on the country, in addition to the arms embargo that had been imposed

Fighters of the Liberation Front for the Great West, a pro-government militia, patrol the Guiglo area of western Côte d'Ivoire in March. Fragmentation and violence between various ethnic groups continued throughout the year.

in November 2004 and strengthened in February 2005. The government eventually decided to postpone the October 30 elections. New elections were to be held no later than Oct. 31, 2006.

Vigilante and militia bands, most of which supported Pres. Laurent Gbagbo, continued to operate in Abidjan and other cities. The government repeatedly ignored UN calls for swift disarmament of these groups. UN peacekeepers and French troops guarded the buffer zone between north and south and, with members of the Ivorian army, patrolled Abidjan. In an effort to maintain public order, police fought with militia in the capital on February 4. At least two people were killed. In a series of violent clashes in early June, at least 100 people were killed near Duekoué, 400 km (about 250 mi) west of Abidjan. Local officials blamed the conflict on ethnic tensions between the Djula and Guéré peoples.

Rebel commanders, declaring the peace process dead, accused the government of having masterminded a militia attack on March 1 in the north. South African Pres. Thabo Mbeki brokered three days of peace talks in Pretoria between Gbagbo and rebel leader Guillaume Soro. As a result, two ministers of the northern New Forces Party rejoined the cabinet on April 15 after an absence of five months. Negotiations continued, but no agreement was reached on the key issues of nationality and eligibility to vote and whether President Gbagbo was obliged to step down before new elections were held. The dispute over the repeal of Article 35 of the constitution, a clause that had been invoked to prevent opposition leader Alassane Ouattara from running in the past two presidential elections, appeared no closer to resolution.

(NANCY ELLEN LAWLER)

CROATIA

Area: 56,594 sq km (21,851 sq mi)
Population (2005 est.): 4,440,000
Capital: Zagreb
Chief of state: President Stipe Mesic
Head of government: Prime Minister Ivo Sanader

Croatia entered 2005 with incumbent Stipe Mesic winning a second five-year term as president on January 16, defeating Jadranka Kosor, the candidate backed by Prime Minister Ivo Sanader. The same month, Foreign Minister Miomir Zuzul resigned under fire and was succeeded by Kolinda Grabar-Kitarovic, the minister of European integration, which highlighted the government's principal foreign-policy objective of EU membership.

On March 16, however, the EU ministers decided to postpone accession negotiations with Croatia following a critical report by the International Criminal Tribunal for the Former Yugoslavia (ICTY) that charged the Croatian government with failing to locate Gen. Ante Gotovina and arrest him for war crimes. The EU decision prompted Prime Minister Sanader to launch more robust efforts, and by May two alleged members of Gotovina's support network had been arrested. In late August, Hrvoje Petrac, considered a major figure in the criminal underworld, was arrested in Greece. Because Petrac too was considered to be a key figure in the Gotovina support network, his arrest, it was hoped, would satisfy ICTY Chief Prosecutor Carla del Ponte and spur a more favourable EU view later in the year. Indeed, after del Ponte met with officials in Zagreb, she expressed her satisfaction, and talks with the EU began in early October. Gotovina was arrested in the Canary Islands on December 7 and quickly flown to the ICTY in The Hague.

Attitudes were also changing within the country toward war crimes committed by members of Croatia's security forces during the country's war of independence. On Aug. 19, 2004, the Supreme Court had ordered a retrial of eight men charged with acts of torture and murder while serving as guards at the Lora military prison in Split. In July the chief prosecutor ordered the investigation of crimes committed in Osijek in 1991–92. In September a Zagreb court sentenced five members of a reserve police unit to a total of 30 years in prison for torture and murder committed in an illegally run prison camp in the Slavonian village of Pakracka Poljana.

Regional relations generally soured. On August 5 Croatia celebrated the 10th anniversary of Operation Storm, the military action that liberated much Croatian territory from Serbian occupation. The event, however, sparked a row with Serbia after its president, Boris Tadic, equated Operation Storm with the July 1995 Srebrenica massacre of thousands of Bosniacs by Bosnian Serb forces. August also saw a deterioration in Croatia's relations with Slovenia after that country's government endorsed a bill claiming sovereignty over disputed waters in the Adriatic Sea.

The Croatian government came under heavy criticism for having awarded a majority share of the profitable state-owned Liburnia Riviera Hotels chain to two private funds, ostensibly to settle a debt incurred during the privatization campaign of the late 1990s. The government was obliged to overturn its decision after an investigation found that the Croatian Privatization Fund, which was responsible for the preparation of documents pertaining to the case, had conducted itself improperly. Overall, there was little change in the economy from the previous year, but signs of an emerging recovery could be detected. The Central Bureau of Statistics reported that industrial production reached an annual growth rate of 5.4% for the first half of the year. Inflation was expected to stay low at 3.5%, and GDP growth was estimated at 3.6%. Although the rise in foreign debt had slowed, it was expected to reach $26.5 billion—83% of the country's GDP—by the end of the year.

Tourism continued its upward trend and achieved its highest level since 1990, growing at 10% over the previous year and generating more than $7 billion in revenues.　　　　　(DAVORKA MATIĆ)

CUBA

Area: 110,860 sq km (42,804 sq mi)
Population (2005 est.): 11,269,000
Capital: Havana
Head of state and government: President of the Council of State and President of the Council of Ministers Fidel Castro Ruz

In 2005 Cuban Pres. Fidel Castro marked his 79th birthday, having fully recovered from a serious fall that fractured his knee and arm in 2004. Cuba's warm relationship with the government of Venezuelan Pres. Hugo Chávez (see BIOGRAPHIES) continued to intensify, and Castro declared 2005 to be "the Year of the Bolivarian Alternative for the Americas." In February Venezuela increased its discounted oil shipments to Cuba to 90,000 bbl a day. Castro responded by pledging to send 30,000 health professionals to Venezuela. The two countries promoted hemispheric proposals, including a new television station called Telesur and a regional oil pact known as PetroCaribe.

In July Hurricane Dennis struck Cuba, killing 16 people and causing an estimated $1.4 billion in damage. After Hurricane Katrina devastated New Orleans in September, Castro offered to send doctors and medical supplies, but U.S. authorities rebuffed the offer.

In January U.S. Secretary of State Condoleezza Rice identified Cuba as an "outpost of tyranny." New restrictions decreased the number of U.S. citizens traveling to the island, and remittances from Cuban-Americans to their families in Cuba declined. In response to U.S. support for dissidents, Cuba erected a billboard showing Iraqi prisoners being abused by U.S. soldiers outside the U.S. interests section in Havana. The long-term detention of hundreds of prisoners at the U.S. Naval Base in Guantánamo Bay, Cuba, remained controversial.

In May Luis Posada Carriles, a long-time anti-Castro militant accused of having plotted from Venezuela the 1976 Cuban airline bombing that killed 73 people, resurfaced in Miami. Posada Carriles asked for asylum but was charged with illegal entry to the U.S. and was detained while Venezuela sought his extradition. In a separate case a U.S. federal court overruled the convictions of five Cuban citizens accused of spying on exile groups.

By early 2005 U.S. agricultural sales under new legislation passed in 2000 had exceeded $1 billion, transforming Cuba into the 25th largest market for American food exports. The Cuban government estimated 5% GDP growth in 2004 and predicted even better economic performance in 2005. Cuba projected that 2.5 million tourists would visit in 2005, the highest number on record. The government recentralized control over state-owned enterprises, reduced the number of licenses available for small-scale entrepreneurs, and scaled back foreign-investment partnerships with European and Canadian companies. Cuba's three largest trading partners in 2004 were Venezuela, Spain, and China, which planned major investments in Cuba's nickel industry. Oil and gas companies from Spain, Norway, and India continued to explore for offshore energy deposits along the island's northern coast.

During the summer, energy shortages and frequent blackouts plagued the island and fueled citizen complaints about government incompetence. Cuban authorities struggled to address the problem with energy-saving light bulbs but failed to address the basic problem of dilapidated electrical infrastructure. A Cuban agency issued a critical assessment of the island's housing crisis, reporting a deficit of 500,000 houses and describing 43% of existing dwellings as in mediocre or poor condition. By September the U.S. Coast Guard had intercepted more than 2,000 Cuban migrants at sea, the highest number since 1994.

Independent opposition groups remained active following the release of several more of the 75 dissidents arrested during the crackdown in the spring of 2003. In May 2005 more than 100 government opponents attended the Assembly for the Promotion of Civil Society, organized by opposition leader Marta Beatriz Roque. The gathering was boycotted by noted dissident Oswaldo Payá of the Christian Liberation Movement. Cuban authorities allowed the meeting to occur undisturbed with a number of foreign observers in attendance, but several visiting European parliamentarians were ejected from the country. Tensions with Mexico continued when that country supported a UN resolution condemning the human rights situation in Cuba, but the island retained cordial relations with most other Latin American countries. In March Uruguay restored diplomatic relations with Cuba that had been severed for several years, and Panama later followed suit.

(DANIEL P. ERIKSON)

CYPRUS

Area: 9,251 sq km (3,572 sq mi) for the entire island; the area of the Turkish Republic of Northern Cyprus (TRNC), proclaimed unilaterally (1983) in the occupied northern third of the island, 3,355 sq km (1,295 sq mi)
Population (2005 est.): island 968,000; TRNC only, 221,000 (including Turkish settlers and Turkish military)
Capital: Lefkosia/Lefkosa (also known as Nicosia)
Head(s) of state and government: President Tassos Papadopoulos; of the TRNC, Presidents Rauf Denktash and, from April 24, Mehmet Ali Talat

In 2005 Cyprus was adapting to membership in the European Union. The island's complex political situation was

Mehmet Ali Talat and his wife, Oya, greet well-wishers in Turkish Cyprus on February 21 following his party's victory in legislative elections. Talat was elected president on April 17.

complicated further by Turkey's progress in negotiations to join the EU. Accession to the EU was not universally acclaimed; only 41% of Cypriots saw membership as a benefit. Nevertheless, belonging to the EU became a fact of life, and Cyprus benefited from assistance in clearing mines and opening the border. Cyprus approved the proposed EU constitution and began the process of adopting the euro.

In April Turkish Cyprus elected a new president, Mehmet Ali Talat. Talat was born in 1952 and was educated as an electrical engineer. He became a member of the parliament in 1998, held various cabinet posts, and was appointed prime minister shortly before becoming president. His platform sought a unification of Cyprus as a federal state, with the Turkish zone retaining its identity.

As intraisland tensions eased, people and goods crossing the interzonal border became routine. Some 5,000 Turkish Cypriots worked in the Greek zone and sent $36 million home during the year. Perhaps because of these practical advances, no significant new reunification negotiations took place. With contacts on the increase, the problem of land ownership in Turkish Cyprus increased. The UN force remained but at reduced strength.

Turkish Cyprus underwent a building and tourist boom. Imports were up about 48%, much of the increase attributable to growth of trade in building

materials. Greek Cyprus remained an offshore business centre, and many banks showed double-digit profit increases. (GEORGE H. KELLING)

CZECH REPUBLIC

Area: 78,866 sq km (30,450 sq mi)
Population (2005 est.): 10,235,000
Capital: Prague
Chief of state: President Vaclav Klaus
Head of government: Prime Ministers Stanislav Gross and, from April 25, Jiri Paroubek

The year 2005 in the Czech Republic was characterized by political conflicts and an unexpectedly strong economy. Having taken over as prime minister in August 2004, Stanislav Gross was struck by a scandal in January 2005 in connection with the uncertain provenance of property held by him and his wife. Gross's defenders argued that the scandal's emergence was part of a political campaign designed to weaken his position prior to the Social Democrats' (CSSD's) party congress, held on March 25–27. Gross's only competitor for the CSSD chairmanship was Labour and Social Affairs Minister Zdenek

Skromach, who wanted to see the party shift to the left. In contrast, Gross backed a more centrist approach. Gross was elected chairman even though it was clear before the congress that one of the CSSD's two junior partners, the Christian Democrats (KDU-CSL), would likely leave a Gross-led cabinet.

In a parliamentary vote of confidence on April 1, the KDU-CSL joined the opposition Civic Democrats (ODS) in voting against the Gross cabinet, which survived only thanks to the abstention of deputies from the opposition Communists. Just as the country appeared to be on the verge of early elections, the CSSD managed to make a new deal with the KDU-CSL and its other junior partner, the Freedom Union (US-DEU), by putting forward a new candidate for the post of prime minister. Thus, Gross resigned and was replaced by Jiri Paroubek on April 25, with only a few minor changes in the government lineup. Gross decided to leave politics altogether in September after his name was raised in connection with a privatization scandal.

A relative political unknown who had served as local development minister, Paroubek demonstrated surprising agility in political maneuvering, having convinced his party's junior coalition partners to remain in the government, forged agreement on a new policy statement, and persuaded left-wing CSSD rebels to vote in favour of the new cabinet. Paroubek's government won a vote of confidence on May 13, receiving the support of 101 of 200 parliamentary deputies who represented the CSSD and its two junior partners. After Paroubek assumed the post of prime minister, his popularity grew rapidly, putting him in first place in the CSSD in public opinion polls. He also helped the party improve its standing.

In the latter part of 2005, Czech politics became increasingly focused on the next parliamentary elections, scheduled for June 2006. Under Paroubek, the CSSD shifted back toward the left, and in September the party joined forces with the opposition Communists to approve several key bills, which angered the KDU-CSL. Desperate to raise public support before the elections, the CSSD was reluctant to approve any major economic reforms.

The economy performed much better than expected in 2005. Many indicators reached their best levels since the mid-1990s, which demonstrated the benefits of the Czech Republic's membership in

Jiri Paroubek (left), the new prime minister, is toasted by Czech Pres. Vaclav Klaus at a reception in Prague's Hradcany castle on April 25.

the European Union. GDP reached its highest growth rate since 1996, while the country's trade balance recorded the first surplus since 1993. Moreover, the Czech Republic attracted record inflows of direct foreign investment, partly thanks to the privatization of several key firms. That investment helped to bring down unemployment rates after 2004's record highs. Interest rates were cut to a historic low in April, 25 basis points below those of the European Central Bank. Despite those cuts, the Czech koruna strengthened substantially against the euro, helping to keep inflation down, despite surging energy prices. The country's fiscal results were also better than expected as strong economic growth helped to boost revenues.　　(SHARON FISHER)

DENMARK

Area: 43,098 sq km (16,640 sq mi)
Population (2005 est.): 5,416,000
Capital: Copenhagen
Chief of state: Queen Margrethe II
Head of government: Prime Minister Anders Fogh Rasmussen

The incumbent centre-right Liberal-Conservative coalition of Prime Minister Anders Fogh Rasmussen won the February 2005 general elections with a comfortable margin, trouncing the opposition Social Democrats, who scored their worst result since 1973. The outcome gave Rasmussen's bloc—including the government's far-right ally, the ultranationalistic, anti-immigration Danish People's Party (DF)—a total of 95 seats in the 179-seat Folketing (parliament) and left the opposition in tatters. Social Democrat leader Mogens Lykketoft tendered his resignation as party chairman, and Helle Thorning-Schmidt became the party's first woman leader; she pledged to adopt a more centrist political line. Since the economy was booming, the main themes of the election were immigration and the maintenance of Denmark's streamlined womb-to-tomb welfare state. The new government was quick to pass legislation further tightening control on immigrants, including the establishment of a so-called integration pact that required immigrants to make an active effort to learn Danish, find employment, and eschew criminal activity on pain of having state social benefits withdrawn. Although the refugee and foreigner inflow had dipped dramatically owing to the government's restrictive policies, immigration—especially when involving Muslims—remained a major issue. The matter was underscored by an (abortive) arsonist attack on the home of Refugees, Immigration and Integration Affairs Minister Rikke Hvilshøj and the racist tone of much of the DF's political rhetoric.

U.S. Pres. George W. Bush paid a 17-hour visit to Copenhagen in early July ahead of the Group of Eight summit in Scotland to thank Denmark for its military support in Iraq. The visit sparked demonstrations to protest the U.S. intervention in Iraq and Denmark's involvement. President Bush's stopover in Denmark took place just one day before the terrorist bombings in London, and fears were triggered among Danes that Copenhagen could be next on the bombers' list; in a statement posted on the Internet, the Group of al-Qaeda of Jihad Organization in Europe, the group claiming responsibility for the London blasts, threatened similar attacks against "crusader" states with troops in Iraq and Afghanistan, mentioning Denmark by name. As a result, the government intensified security throughout the transport system.

In the realm of European affairs, Denmark postponed a planned September 27 national referendum on the EU's new constitution, following the rejection of the treaty by French and Dutch voters in the late spring and the subsequent decision by EU heads of state to hold a "pause for thought" on the issue. Faced with strong public resistance to Turkish membership in the EU, Prime Minister Rasmussen urged consolidation rather than enlargement of the current union.

At a children's hospital in her native Australia, Danish Crown Princess Mary reads Hans Christian Andersen's story "The Ugly Duckling" in March. The 200th anniversary of the birth of the beloved Danish storyteller was celebrated in 2005.

On the cultural front, two events dominated all else: the opening in January of Copenhagen's stunning new opera house, designed by leading architect Henning Larsen, and events throughout the year to celebrate the bicentenary of the birth of fairy-tale writer Hans Christian Andersen (1805–75). On October 15, amid a wave of patriotic fervour, Crown Prince Frederik, heir to the Danish throne, and Australian-born Crown Princess Mary announced the birth of their first child, a boy to be named Prince Christian, who would be second in line to the throne, after his father.

(CHRISTOPHER FOLLETT)

DJIBOUTI

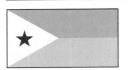

Area: 23,200 sq km (8,950 sq mi)
Population (2005 est.): 477,000
Capital: Djibouti
Chief of state and head of government: President Ismail Omar Guelleh, assisted by Prime Minister Dileita Muhammad Dileita

Djibouti was threatened early in 2005 with the possibility of severe food shortages resulting from two seasons of drought. When the rainy season failed to materialize in April, appeals were made for $7.5 million and 5,000 metric tons of food aid in an effort to avert a famine faced by an estimated 47,000 people. The appeal fell on deaf ears, however; the governments of Germany and the United States in June committed to providing aid for non-food relief, which covered only 5.3% of the total aid needed. The food crisis deepened in August as appeals for food aid were still unmet. Amid drought and food insecurity, campaigning in the run-up to the presidential election hit a snag when the only opposition candidate, Mohamed Daoud Chehem, withdrew from the race because he was unable to raise sufficient campaign funds. As a result, on April 8 Pres. Ismail Omar Guelleh won 100% of the vote in an election that registered a voter turnout of 78.9% but was boycotted by the opposition. Election day was marred when police used tear gas to disperse hundreds of protesters who had blockaded streets with burning tires. (MARY F.E. EBELING)

DOMINICA

Area: 750 sq km (290 sq mi)
Population (2005 est.): 69,000
Capital: Roseau
Chief of state: President Nicholas Liverpool
Head of government: Prime Minister Roosevelt Skerrit

The IMF, which under its Poverty Reduction and Growth Facility had allocated $11.7 million to Dominica over three years, gave the country a thumbs up in March 2005 for its economic recovery program; the IMF rated Dominica's overall performance as very strong.

Dominica began reaping the benefits of having established diplomatic relations with China in 2004, following its break with Taiwan. China agreed in March to construct a 12,000-seat $12.3 million sports stadium, build roads and schools, and renovate a hospital.

The Dominica Labour Party (DLP) was returned to office in the general election in May, winning 12 of the 21 elected seats in the parliament. The United Workers Party (UWP), which obtained eight seats, would remain in opposition. One seat went to an independent. DLP leader Roosevelt Skerrit, who was again sworn in as prime minister, also held the portfolios of finance, economic planning, national security, and Caribbean affairs. Former prime minister Eugenia Charles died in September. (See OBITUARIES.)

In September universal secondary education was achieved; all pupils leaving primary school were able to be placed in high schools. Prime Minister Skerrit said that the government's next goal for education was to have a university graduate in every home in Dominica. (DAVID RENWICK)

DOMINICAN REPUBLIC

Area: 48,671 sq km (18,792 sq mi)
Population (2005 est.): 8,895,000
Capital: Santo Domingo
Head of state and government: President Leonel Fernández

Pres. Leonel Fernández restored sound fiscal management to the Dominican Republic in 2005 as the country continued to rebound from the profligacy and mismanagement of his predecessor, Hipólito Mejía. Despite the weight of public debt, which had doubled under Mejía's government, GDP growth exceeded 4% during the year, and positive results encompassed most sectors of the economy. In January the Dominican Republic signed a $665 million standby agreement with the International Monetary Fund, and the government's fiscal discipline under the terms of this agreement outperformed expectations. Inflation, which had been running at nearly 60% during the previous two years, fell to 8% in 2005.

In July a closely divided U.S. Congress approved the Central America–Dominican Republic Free Trade Agreement. With control of the Dominican legislature, the Dominican Revolutionary Party initially opposed ratification of the CAFTA-DR agreement, but negotiations—which focused on cushioning measures for local industry and tax and institutional reform—yielded congressional approval in September.

Economic success on many fronts did not insulate President Fernández from rising public disapproval. Major planks of his 2004 campaign had been the revitalization of the chronically inadequate national electricity grid and robust action to combat equally chronic public and private corruption. Although a petroleum agreement with Venezuelan Pres. Hugo Chávez (see BIOGRAPHIES) offered some solace, there was no viable energy plan in sight, and daily outages continued throughout the country. Despite his pledge, Fernández did not press for effective anticorruption measures, and hopes that significant steps would be taken to improve the quality of public governance were not realized. (JOHN W. GRAHAM)

EAST TIMOR (TIMOR-LESTE)

Area: 14,604 sq km (5,639 sq mi)
Population (2005 est.): 975,000
Capital: Dili
Chief of state: President Xanana Gusmão
Head of government: Prime Minister Mari Alkatiri

East Timor was accepted as the 25th member of the ASEAN (Association of Southeast Asian Nations) Regional Forum in July 2005. Equally important, the increasing integration of the new state into the international community was strongly supported by the U.S., which donated almost $25 million to help the strengthening of democracy in East Timor. Because the oil industry made the biggest contribution to the East Timorese economy, Prime Minister Mari Alkatiri sought broader investment for oil and gas exploration from companies in Singapore, the U.K., Canada, and the U.S. He stressed, however, that he wanted East Timor to avoid being dependent on petroleum and wished to develop the country's fisheries, agriculture, and tourism. In September, Foreign Minister José Ramos-Horta broke new ground by asking Israeli Prime Minister Ariel Sharon to send an economics expert to offer advice on East Timor's economy. In response, Sharon offered to send former Israeli finance minister (and former prime minister) Benjamin Netanyahu. (A.R.G. GRIFFITHS)

ECUADOR

Area: 272,045 sq km (105,037 sq mi), including the 8,010-sq-km (3,093-sq-mi) Galápagos Islands

Population (2005 est.): 13,003,000 (Galápagos Islands, about 20,000)

Capital: Quito

Chief of state and head of government: Presidents Lucio Gutiérrez Borbúa and, from April 20, Alfredo Palacio González

The removal of Pres. Lucio Gutiérrez from office in April 2005 sparked growing uncertainty about Ecuador's economic and political future. Gutiérrez, who won the 2002 presidential election with the support of Indian and social-reform movements, had become estranged from his political base after adopting the austerity policies favoured by the International Monetary Fund. He engineered the removal of most Supreme Court judges and eventually dissolved the court, apparently to forestall legal action against former president Abdalá Bucaram, his political ally. Bucaram's return to Ecuador from

Panama in early April angered the well-to-do, who joined calls for the president's ouster. With thousands of protesters in the streets, a session of Congress attended chiefly by Gutiérrez's opponents declared that he had abandoned his office by acting unconstitutionally and replaced him with Vice Pres. Alfredo Palacio. Gutiérrez and his wife, legislator Ximena Bohórquez, were granted asylum in Brazil, although Bohórquez soon returned to Ecuador and her husband moved on to Colombia. Bucaram resumed his exile in Panama.

Palacio, a 66-year-old cardiologist, modified some of his predecessor's policies. He reinstated Indian representatives to government posts. His foreign minister, Antonio Parra, said that the agreement allowing U.S. antidrug forces to operate out of Ecuador should not be renewed when it expired in 2009. Palacio won a promise from Venezuela to buy $300 million of Ecuadoran bonds, which stoked fears about the potential influence of mercurial Venezuelan Pres. Hugo Chávez (*see* BIOGRAPHIES). Finally, an oil-revenue fund that was

mostly earmarked for debt service was abolished, and the percentage of oil proceeds allocated to social programs was increased. In response, the World Bank, under its new president, Paul Wolfowitz (*see* BIOGRAPHIES), suspended disbursement of a $100 million loan.

Ecuador's oil policies continued to attract criticism from all sides. Demonstrators demanding a larger share of oil income for producing regions shut down most operations for a week in August. Long-running legal actions involving foreign firms remained unsettled, and oil executives complained about the difficulty of doing business in Ecuador. The Canadian firm EnCana announced in September that it would sell its interests to a Chinese joint venture for $1.4 billion.

Calls for a crackdown on migrant smuggling were renewed after 94 Ecuadorans bound for the U.S. drowned on August 12 when their fishing boat sank off the Pacific Coast. Meanwhile, several major seizures of illegal drugs pointed to growing Ecuadoran involvement in the Andean cocaine trade. (PAUL KNOX)

Police tear gas fills the streets of Quito on April 19 as demonstrators demand the removal of Ecuador's Pres. Lucio Gutiérrez. He was deposed by Congress and went into exile in Brazil on April 25.

AP/Wide World Photos

EGYPT

Area: 997,739 sq km (385,229 sq mi)
Population (2005 est.): 70,457,000
Capital: Cairo
Chief of state: President Hosni Mubarak
Head of government: Prime Minister Ahmad Nazif

Egypt in 2005 saw, for the first time, the emergence of secular opposition to the regime of its authoritarian Pres. Hosni Mubarak. The Kifaya ("Enough") movement and the al-Ghad ("Tomorrow") Party, both of which had emerged in late 2004, became forces for mobilizing the secular opposition. Hitherto the main opposition to Mubarak had been the Muslim Brotherhood. This militant Islamist movement was tolerated because its very radicalism made Mubarak and his allies seem to be the only reasonable choice to govern the country. Fear of this new popularism prompted the authorities to arrest al-Ghad leader Ayman Nur on January 29. He was detained on fabricated charges that he had falsified petitions for the legalization of al-Ghad in October 2004. Nur was kept in prison for six weeks and was released only because of foreign pressure on the Egyptian authorities. Washington's call for democratic reforms forced Mubarak for the first time to allow multiple candidates in the presidential election and permit political opposition parties and organizations to demonstrate publicly. Some even shouted anti-Mubarak slogans; in one Kifaya rally on February 21, antiregime demonstrators chanted, "A quarter of a century in power is enough" and "Mubarak, admit you're a despot."

Many members of the Coptic Christian minority (estimated at 10 million) supported the Kifaya Movement and the al-Ghad Party, but Pope Shenuda III, the head of the Coptic Christian community, publicly professed his support for Mubarak's reelection bid, probably to deflect possible further government pressure on the Copts. Some members of the Christian community were critical of his stance, however, arguing that the head of the Coptic Church should not play a political role.

The presidential elections took place on September 7, and Mubarak won

© Aladin Abdel Naby/Reuters/Corbis

In Cairo on March 1, supporters of politician Ayman Nur enjoy a new relaxation of rules against rallies by Egyptian opposition parties. Nur was arrested in January on trumped-up charges but was released six weeks later; he challenged incumbent Hosni Mubarak for the presidency in September but lost.

88.5% of the ballots, while Nur, his main challenger, got 7.6% The elections, however, were neither free nor fair. Television, radio, and most print periodicals were controlled by the regime, and opposition parties were prevented from early campaigning and establishing branches in the provinces.

President Mubarak continued to be active in the peace process between the Israelis and the Palestinians. On February 8 in the Egyptian resort of Sharm al-Shaykh, he hosted a summit between Israeli Prime Minister Ariel Sharon and Palestinian Pres. Mahmoud Abbas at which a cease-fire between the two sides was declared after four years of violence. A new Egyptian ambassador, Muhammad Assem Ibrahim, arrived in Israel in March after the post had stood vacant for four years.

On July 23 a terrorist group linked to al-Qaeda targeted Sharm al-Shaykh—chosen undoubtedly because it was a major tourist resort and was the site of the Israeli-Palestinian peace summit. More than 60 persons were killed in three coordinated operations. A few days later in a videotaped message, the

Egyptian-born Ayman al-Zawahiri, al-Qaeda's second in command, attacked American policy in the Middle East.

Intellectual life in Egypt, too, was reinvigorated by the Kifaya Movement because it had dared to break the government's lock on freedom of thought. Hundreds of intellectuals organized themselves into an organization called Writers for Change, which actively worked against the Mubarak regime. Continuing tensions between Christian Copts and Muslims came to a head on October 21 when more than a thousand Muslims demonstrated outside the Coptic St. Gergis Church in a poor neighbourhood of Alexandria in protest against the DVD release of a play that they claimed was offensive to Muslims. The play, which was entitled *I Was Blind but Now I Can See*, had been performed at the church; it depicted a poor Christian university student who converts to Islam when a group of Muslim men promise him money. When he becomes disillusioned and decides to return to his original faith, he is threatened with physical violence.

(MARIUS K. DEEB)

EL SALVADOR

Area: 21,042 sq km (8,124 sq mi)
Population (2005 est.): 6,881,000
Capital: San Salvador
Head of state and government: President Elías Antonio Saca González

Despite widespread popular protest, El Salvador in 2005 became the first country to ratify the Central America–Dominican Republic Free Trade Agreement (CAFTA-DR), which would go into effect on Jan. 1, 2006. The Salvadoran government headed by Pres. Antonio Saca and his National Republican Alliance Party argued that CAFTA would bring significant increases in Salvadoran exports to the U.S. Aware of the rising demand for energy sources, the government hoped to expand greatly production of ethanol from sugarcane and other agricultural produce. Led by the opposition Farabundo Martí National Liberation Front, oppo-

© Yuri Cortez/AFP/Getty Images

On October 3 Red Cross rescuers work to retrieve the bodies of several family members who were killed in a mud slide in the community of 12 de Abril, El Salvador. Hurricane Stan killed some 30 persons in El Salvador and at least 8 elsewhere in Central America.

nents claimed that CAFTA would jeopardize the rights and job security of Salvadoran workers.

Saca's government also faced a rising tide of gang violence. In collaboration with the U.S. and other Central American states, it attacked gangs such as the Mara-18 and Mara Salvatrucha. The lack of jobs for young males and the U.S. deportation of Salvadoran criminals back to the country had exacerbated the problem of gang violence. Saca's government invoked hardline police methods, and there were charges that police turned a blind eye toward paramilitary death squads that targeted gang leaders for assassination. The U.S. offered funding for establishment in El Salvador of an international police academy to fight the gangs. The murder rate in El Salvador had risen from 37 per 100,000 in 2002 to 45 per 100,000 in 2005.

Moderate economic growth, fueled by rising coffee prices and increased exports, was offset by rising oil prices. Agreements with other Central American states in an emergency energy plan had only limited success. Another negative economic indicator was a decline in textile exports because of Asian competition, with significant job losses in El Salvador as a result. Hurricane Katrina's devastating blow to the U.S. Gulf Coast (*see* DISASTERS) also had an impact on El Salvador, for nearly 10,000 Salvadoran émigrés lived in the affected area, and the storm greatly reduced the remittances that they sent back to relatives and associates in El Salvador. Disruption of New Orleans and other Gulf Coast ports also reduced Salvadoran coffee and other exports to the U.S., while closure of refineries sent oil prices even higher. In early October heavy rains and landslides from Hurricane Stan caused deaths and inflicted serious damage to roads and bridges in El Salvador.

(RALPH LEE WOODWARD, JR.)

EQUATORIAL GUINEA

Area: 28,051 sq km (10,831 sq mi)
Population (2005 est.): 504,000
Capital: Malabo
Chief of state: President Brig. Gen. Teodoro Obiang Nguema Mbasogo
Head of government: Prime Minister Miguel Abia Biteo Boricó

In 2005 the consequences of the failed February 2004 coup continued to be felt in Equatorial Guinea. In November 2004 the conspirators held in Equatorial Guinea were sentenced to terms of up to 34 years in jail. Amnesty International condemned their trial as unfair and expressed alarm over the conditions under which they were imprisoned. Severo Moto, the exiled politician who was to have been installed as president in place of Teodoro Obiang Nguema, fled from Spain fearing assassination and in April 2005 was discovered to be in Croatia.

Meanwhile, the boom in oil exploration and production in the Gulf of Guinea continued, and Equatorial Guinea was set to become the third largest producer in sub-Saharan Africa, after Nigeria and Angola. Output by the end of 2005 was projected to reach 380,000 bbl a day. With the rise in oil prices through the year, Equatorial Guinea's bonanza was even greater, with economic growth expected to be 50%. What did not go into the bank accounts of the leading politicians went mainly into infrastructure development, particularly the creation of a new city at the capital, Malabo. A dispute with Gabon over uninhabited islands in Corisco Bay remained unsettled, but there was talk of creating a joint development zone for the two countries to share the hydrocarbon wealth of the area.

(CHRISTOPHER SAUNDERS)

ERITREA

Area: 121,144 sq km (46,774 sq mi)
Population (2005 est.): 4,670,000
Capital: Asmara
Head of state and government: President Isaias Afwerki

Despite extreme poverty exacerbated by drought, shortfalls in international relief funding, and a weak economy, Eritrea spent its energy in 2005 threatening to renew war with its large neighbour Ethiopia over a five-year border dispute. The shaky peace agreement signed between the two countries in December 2000, following two years of warfare that claimed 70,000 lives, tottered on the brink of collapse. The

Red Cross workers unload food at a warehouse in the Eritrean capital, Asmara, on August 22. The country had not yet recovered economically from its 1998–2000 war with neighbouring Ethiopia, and shortages of food and other necessities were still widespread.

biggest obstacle to peace remained the small town of Badme, which Ethiopia continued to hold despite pressure from the UN Security Council and an earlier ruling by a border commission that placed it in Eritrean territory. The escalating tensions forced the UN Security Council to extend the mandate of UN troops keeping peace between Eritrea and Ethiopia, even as the two countries increased their own military presence at the tense border.

Eritrean Foreign Minister Ali Said Abdella died of a heart attack in August, before the UN Security Council convened. He was a former military commander in the Eritrean People's Liberation Front, which later became the People's Front for Democracy and Justice (Eritrea's ruling party under the leadership of Pres. Isaias Afwerki).

Eritreans continued to suffer from dire shortages of food and basic necessities throughout the year, which prompted aid agencies to make further appeals for food aid and funding. Though rains increased in the March–May rainy season, giving a boost to agricultural production, Eritrea was expected to meet only 45% of its food needs for the year. The food situation was worsened, however, by what should have been a positive development—the return and resettlement

of 19,000 Eritreans displaced by war and previous droughts.

Afwerki's government marked another year of repressive rule with the arbitrary arrest and detention of political opponents and journalists. Despite pleas from Western governments, humanitarian groups, and press organizations, Afwerki's government refused to release the 15 journalists who had been imprisoned since 2001.

On the economic front, Eritrea stayed on the list of the world's poorest nations, with a per capita GDP of about $130. The country's balance of trade remained terribly skewed, with nearly $426 million in imports, compared with $16 million in exports. Military spending accounted for about 20% of the nation's GDP.

(PATRICK L. THIMANGU)

ESTONIA

Area: 45,227 sq km (17,462 sq mi)
Population (2005 est.): 1,345,000
Capital: Tallinn
Chief of state: President Arnold Rüütel
Head of government: Prime Ministers Juhan Parts and, from April 13, Andrus Ansip

Despite remaining the largest party in the parliament, Res Publica's fortunes continued to decline in Estonian political life during 2005. In late March the cabinet of Prime Minister Juhan Parts, Res Publica's leader, resigned following a vote of no confidence. It was replaced by a three-party coalition (Reform Party, Centre Party, and People's Union), headed by the Reformist Andrus Ansip. The new government pledged to increase child support and pensions while also gradually reducing personal income taxes. Local government elections in October offered a boost to the ruling coalition, as the Centre Party won an outright majority in Tallinn, and the Reform Party dominated in Tartu. A pioneering innovation was Internet voting, although fewer than 1% of eligible voters took advantage of this option. The turnout of only 47% signified an all-time low in postcommunist local elections and suggested continued voter alienation.

Relations with Russia remained troubled. Pres. Arnold Rüütel refused an invitation from Russian Pres. Vladimir Putin to attend the Moscow ceremonies commemorating the 60th anniversary of the end of World War II in Europe. Although Rüütel acknowledged the U.S.S.R.'s role in the defeat of Nazism, he also stressed the far-reaching repression suffered by Estonia under Soviet rule, a fact still not fully recognized by Russia. An apparent thaw in relations appeared on May 18 as the two countries finally signed border treaties that Estonia quickly ratified. Russia objected to a preamble added by the Estonian parliament, however, and withdrew its signature, insisting that the agreements be renegotiated.

Like most Eastern European countries in the aftermath of communism's collapse, Estonia faced the challenge of demographic decline as birthrates plummeted and death rates remained high among an aging population. A pronatalist policy by recent governments, strongly reinforced by the Parts and Ansip cabinets in 2005, was finally paying dividends in a rising birthrate, lower infant mortality, and fewer abortions. (TOIVO U. RAUN)

ETHIOPIA

Area: 1,127,127 sq km (435,186 sq mi)
Population (2005 est.): 73,053,000
Capital: Addis Ababa
Chief of state: President Girma Wolde-Giyorgis
Head of government: Prime Minister Meles Zenawi

Turnout was high for parliamentary elections held in Ethiopia on May 15, 2005. Voters returned the ruling party, the Ethiopian People's Revolutionary Democratic Front to power, albeit with a much-reduced majority. Opposition parties went from 12 seats in the parliament to 176 and won every constituency in the capital, Addis Ababa. Announcement of the election results was delayed for eight weeks owing to complaints of irregularities from more than half of the country's electoral constituencies. The elections themselves were delayed for over two months in the Somali region owing to security concerns. European election observers noted that the polling was marked by

Heavy rains in late April caused flooding in the Somali region of Ethiopia and made the lot of the many internally displaced persons—such as this woman at the Hartesheik camp—much more difficult. Ironically, this area had earlier suffered from a long drought that claimed the lives of at least 40 children.

© Boris Heger/Reuters/Corbis

irregularities. The outcome of the elections and accusations of fraud led to massive protests in Addis Ababa. As a result of clashes between protesters and security forces, 38 people were confirmed dead, hundreds injured, and 3,000 arrested. The United Kingdom temporarily froze aid to Ethiopia in protest against the violent crackdown. Further riots in early November over alleged election fraud left at least 23 more people dead.

In September 43 members of the opposition political party, the Coalition for Unity and Democracy (CUD), were arrested in the Amhara region for "violent activities aimed at subverting the constitutional order." The CUD did not take its 109 seats in the parliament at the start of the session in protest against alleged government vote-rigging in the election. Clashes between Oromo and Somali groups continued throughout 2005 in the Oromiya region and led to the deaths of more than 70 people and the internal displacement of thousands.

Economically, Ethiopia posted an estimated growth rate of 7.3% and had an excellent harvest. Food aid was still needed for the acutely undernourished, however. Historically, most of Ethiopia's GDP revenue came from agriculture, the primary export crop being coffee. Low world coffee prices over the past five years prompted a diversification into the production of flowers,

vegetables, and khat for the export market. Ethiopia was one of 18 countries that benefited from 100% multilateral debt relief of loans from the International Monetary Fund, the World Bank, and the African Development Bank in a deal agreed to by the Group of Eight finance ministers in June 2005.

The border dispute resulting from the 1998–2000 war with Eritrea continued without resolution. Ethiopia rejected the 2002 ruling of the Eritrea-Ethiopia Boundary Commission, which was created by the 2000 Algiers Peace Agreement. The UN Mission in Ethiopia and Eritrea (UNMEE) noted continued violence along the border. The UN Security Council extended the mandate of UNMEE until March 2006 and called upon Ethiopia to accept fully the ruling of the boundary commission. As further conflict threatened Somalia, Ethiopia gave political and military support to Somali Pres. Abdullahi Yusuf Ahmed. Ethiopia benefited from an economic relationship with the self-declared republic of Somaliland that included access to the port of Berbera for exports. Ethiopia welcomed the peace agreement between northern and southern Sudan, anticipating that it would help put an end to ethnic violence along the Sudanese border with Ethiopia and increase trade between the two countries.

(SANDRA F. JOIREMAN)

FIJI

Area: 18,272 sq km (7,055 sq mi)
Population (2005 est.): 846,000
Capital: Suva
Chief of state: President Ratu Josefa Iloilo
Head of government: Prime Minister Laisenia Qarase

In Fiji the 2000 coup continued to cast a shadow over political life in 2005. The number of people charged with related offenses, including treason, sedition, murder, and unlawful assembly, had reached 566, and most of those charged had been convicted, including 122 serving military personnel. A number of politicians were also implicated, with some returning to high political office after serving a prison sentence.

The government's reconciliation, tolerance, and unity bill, introduced in May, aroused further controversy. Proposals for a commission that could grant amnesty to perpetrators and approve compensation for victims were seen as an attempt to undermine the judicial process, an attack on human rights, and a device for absolving those still under investigation. The provisions were criticized by opposition parties, the military commander, and the governments of the U.S., Australia, and New Zealand. In September, Prime Minster Laisenia Qarase announced that the amnesty provisions would be revised.

Although the economy achieved 3.8% growth in 2004, largely on the back of strong tourism growth, 2005 was less buoyant. Fiji faced the end of a garment-industry quota for the American market as well as a decline in sugar revenues projected from 2007 with the phasing out of a European Union price-support scheme. As partial compensation, the EU offered to provide development assistance to the industry.

In September heavy rain caused serious flooding in southeastern Viti Levu, which led to one death, serious disruption of services, hospital evacuations, and many residents left homeless.

(BARRIE MACDONALD)

FINLAND

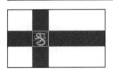

Area: 338,145 sq km (130,559 sq mi)
Population (2005 est.): 5,244,000
Capital: Helsinki
Chief of state: President Tarja Halonen
Head of government: Prime Minister Matti Vanhanen

A prolonged labour dispute in Finland's paper industry, which accounted for as much as 20% of the country's exports, dominated much of 2005. The conflict began when the Finnish Forest Industries Federation announced that it would not join in the comprehensive collective labour agreement reached in late 2004. At the end of March 2005, after months of fruitless negotiations, the Finnish Paper Workers' Union (Paperiliitto) announced an overtime ban that brought production lines to a halt at several paper mills. After alternating company lockouts and union walkouts—and intervention by National Conciliator Juhani Salonius and Prime Minister Matti Vanhanen—the crisis was finally resolved in June. The repercussions of the dispute were widely felt. The Central Organization of Finnish Trade Unions (SAK) had contemplated a general strike, while contractors to the paper industry and related industries had suffered great financial losses.

In Helsinki on August 25, Finland's Martti Ahtisaari (centre) joins hands with Indonesia's Hamid Awaludin (left) and the representative of the Free Aceh Movement, Malik Mahmud (right), to mark the successful conclusion of negotiations to end three decades of secessionist strife in Indonesia.

© Olivier Morin/AFP/Getty Images

Even some newspapers had refrained from publishing their usual Sunday supplements.

The generous option benefits of the state-owned energy group Fortum raised questions in the fall when their value skyrocketed to astronomical figures as Fortum share prices rose. Politicians who had given their approbation to the option scheme at the time it was drawn passed the buck to one another, toyed with the idea of a law that would grant exceptions, and finally resorted to asking option beneficiaries to give up their benefits voluntarily. Fortum CEO Mikael Lilius was among those called to a hearing in front of the parliamentary Commerce Committee. Lilius staunchly refused to give up his options or to discuss the details of his contract and blamed the imbroglio for the sudden downward trend of Fortum share prices. Pres. Tarja Halonen came out in support of the option beneficiaries, pointing out that in a country enjoying the rule of law, one could not very well back away from legitimate agreements.

Russian military aircraft violated Finnish airspace repeatedly during the year. After Finnish media reported the incidents, government officials admitted to having known of a dozen violations. While on a visit to Moscow in early June, Vanhanen took up the issue with Russian Prime Minister Mikhail Fradkov. Four months later Russia apologized, blaming navigational errors, and Finland accepted the apology.

Former president Martti Ahtisaari won international praise for his key role in the peace negotiations that took place in Helsinki early in the year between the Indonesian government and the Free Aceh Movement.

(SUSANNA BELL)

FRANCE

Area: 543,965 sq km (210,026 sq mi)
Population (2005 est.): 60,733,000
Capital: Paris
Chief of state: President Jacques Chirac
Head of government: Prime Ministers Jean-Pierre Raffarin and, from May 31, Dominique de Villepin

The events of 2005 with undoubtedly the deepest impact on France itself were the ethnic minority riots that began in late October in satellite towns around Paris and during three weeks spread to the rest of the country. This dispelled any justified sense of French superiority in terms of racial and religious integration. Of wider consequence was the refusal of the French people in a May 29 referendum to endorse a new constitution for the European Union. This decision, in which France more or less brought to a halt the process of European integration that it had helped launch half a century earlier, left the EU functioning under existing treaty rules. On June 1 the Dutch also voted "no" in a similar referendum. The constitution's failure to win popular approval in these two founder states effectively doomed it. Another 9 of the 25 EU member states had already ratified it through their parliaments, but the constitutional blueprint required unanimous approval by all 25 for the new constitution to enter into effect.

The unexpected May 29 result had widespread consequences. At home it looked likely to hasten the political demise of Pres. Jacques Chirac well before his second term expired in 2007 and possibly to realign the political left along the lines on which it split over the EU. Abroad it put France—for the first time—on the opposite side of a major EU issue from Germany, its longtime special partner, and sparked a wider debate about the EU's purposes and goals. One reason for the French "no" vote was dislike of the recent EU enlargement to Eastern Europe and an accompanying aversion to further enlargement that would incorporate Turkey and countries in the Balkans in coming years.

Domestic Affairs. The spark for the autumn riots was the accidental death on October 27 of two teenagers who were electrocuted when they hid from police in an electricity substation. This was the immediate pretext for the start of the riots, but the reason they spread so rapidly was the high unemployment, discrimination, and lack of opportunity in France's heavily immigrant suburbs. The protests peaked on the night of November 7, affecting 274 communes around the country. The following day President Chirac declared a state of emergency. It was not until November 17, after nearly 9,000 cars had been torched and nearly 3,000 arrests made, that the French police declared that the level of car burning had returned to "normal." The state of emergency continued through the end of the year.

Expressing discontent in a milder way, French voters rejected the draft EU constitution (by 54.68% to 45.32%) and thereby turned their back on some-

thing that was largely their country's creation. President Chirac said, in the closing stages of the referendum campaign, that the constitution was "essentially of French inspiration in terms of its ideas and authors." One of his presidential predecessors, Valéry Giscard d'Estaing, had presided over the special convention that provided the blueprint for the EU constitution. Giscard had ensured that the draft constitution provided for a more permanent presidency of the EU and for unified control of foreign policy so that the EU could assume a higher profile in the world—very much a preoccupation of Paris.

The draft constitution, however, failed to cater to the French people's more pressing worry about unemployment and, in particular, to provide some "social protection" against market deregulation coming from Brussels and globalization from outside France. Against a background of increasing disenchantment with EU liberalization and disciplines such as state aid controls, many French took exception to the European Commission's so-called Bolkestein directive on services. This controversial directive, proposed in 2004 by then European commissioner Frits Bolkestein, sought to open up all service sectors to cross-border competition. The domestic context was also conducive to a "no" in the referendum campaign. Unemployment in France remained persistently high, and the government's political stock fell further when Finance Minister Hervé Gaymard was forced to resign on February 25 after it emerged that the

state was paying €14,000 (about $18,500) a month to house Gaymard, his wife, and their eight children when the couple already owned a Paris apartment. Gaymard was succeeded by Thierry Breton, who came from France Télécom to be France's fourth finance minister in a year.

At the start of 2005, the polls showed the "yes" camp standing at 65%, and on February 28 the constitution was easily endorsed by a special session of both houses of Parliament. By mid-March, however, polls were showing a majority of voters opposed, with pro-European support slipping particularly among Socialists, who were worried that EU policies were threatening France's "social model" built around high job protection. Chirac complained to fellow leaders at a March EU summit that free-market economics had become "the new communism [or totalitarian doctrine] of our age." The French government offered pay concessions to civil servants and pressed the European Commission to impose emergency quotas on surging Chinese textile imports but never regained control of the referendum campaign. Chirac had a rough ride in a mid-April television debate that brought him face to face with the tendency of referenda to become a magnet for extraneous issues. In early May polls showed that the "yes" camp had briefly regained the lead, but it did not hold.

While refusing to take the referendum defeat personally, Chirac nonetheless sacked Prime Minister Jean-Pierre Raffarin, who had lingered on borrowed time since the centre-right's election setbacks of 2004. Chirac faced the awkward choice of a successor as prime minister: his longtime protégé Dominique de Villepin or his rival and head of the ruling Union for a Popular Movement (UMP) party, Nicolas Sarkozy. In the end the president named Villepin prime minister and allowed Sarkozy to return to government (as interior minister) and to run the UMP, the very combination of party and government jobs that Chirac had earlier refused to allow Sarkozy to hold. The other immediate consequence of the referendum was a further deepening of divisions within the Socialists, the main opposition party. Former prime minister Laurent Fabius had defied an earlier party decision to support the EU constitution and had become the most prestigious politician in the "no" camp.

There was also serious rivalry on the centre-right. Villepin focused the first few months of his premiership on a

Beneath a huge sign that makes quite clear his far-right party's views in the referendum on ratifying the EU constitution, National Front leader Jean-Marie Le Pen addresses supporters in Paris on May 1. The voters' "no" on May 29 was an embarrassment for Pres. Jacques Chirac and French foreign policy.

AP/Wide World Photos

modest attack on unemployment (changing the labour code for small firms and making it harder for the unemployed to refuse job offers) and on a modest boost to consumption (proposing some income-tax exemptions and simplification). These policies, together with public appreciation of his dashing style, raised Villepin's standing in the polls by early autumn to the level enjoyed by Sarkozy. Chirac's hospitalization for several days in early September because of a vascular problem affecting his vision underlined the unlikelihood that the 72-year-old president would seek a third term in 2007.

Foreign Affairs. Chirac's close partnership with Chancellor Gerhard Schröder came to an end with the latter's defeat in Germany's general election on September 18. The slightly more reform-minded and pro-American Angela Merkel, who succeeded Schröder as chancellor, had to share power in a "grand coalition" with Schröder's Social Democrats. The German election's clearest lesson for Chirac and Villepin was to confirm their view that in continental Europe reform could be only a gradual process.

Relations with London were cooler. The friction was due to the resurgence, at every EU summit during the year, of the Anglo-French differences over the EU budget; the budget was eventually finalized in a deal in December. Paris, which had been the hot favourite to host the 2012 Olympics, also had to bear the disappointment of being beaten out by London. The bombings in London the day after its Olympic selection, however, served to toughen U.K. antiterrorist policy, a move welcomed by French authorities, who had complained of British laxity on this score.

France's relations with the U.S. improved, starting with a conciliatory visit to Paris in February by U.S. Secretary of State Condoleezza Rice and a meeting between Chirac and Pres. George W. Bush later that month. One reason for the warming of relations was that the EU in general, and France in particular, backed off the idea of ending the EU's long-standing arms embargo on China. There was a broader coincidence of Franco-American policies on the Middle East, although not on Iraq, where the two countries' views remained as divided as ever. France and the U.S. jointly pressed Syria to end its occupation of Lebanon, while France worked with the U.K., Germany, and the U.S. to try to persuade Iran to halt its nuclear program. (DAVID BUCHAN)

GABON

Area: 267,667 sq km (103,347 sq mi)
Population (2005 est.): 1,384,000
Capital: Libreville
Chief of state: President Omar Bongo Ondimba
Head of government: Prime Minister Jean-François Ntoutoume-Emane

Gabon continued to benefit from skyrocketing oil prices in 2005, but its reserves were rapidly being depleted. The IMF strongly recommended that a portion of oil revenues be set aside to repay external debts and to diversify the economy in order to prepare for a future with diminishing petroleum exports.

The latest official results from the 2003 census were disputed by demographers and a government statistician, who stated that current birth and death rates would make a growth rate of 50% over a 10-year period impossible. Opposition parties accused the government of inflating the figures in order to qualify for increased international aid.

Typhoid spread to the capital by the end of January as water shortages caused by a broken pump at the Libreville filtration centre forced people to turn to untreated water supplies. On February 1 the government announced that it would build an Ebola Surveillance Centre in the eastern forest region to monitor and respond to any new outbreaks of the deadly disease. On November 27 Pres. Omar Bongo, who had ruled Gabon since 1967, was overwhelmingly reelected. The Interior Ministry reported that Bongo won 79% of the votes cast to opposition leader Pierre Mamboundou's 13%. Bongo thus secured another seven-year term in office. (NANCY ELLEN LAWLER)

GAMBIA, THE

Area: 10,689 sq km (4,127 sq mi)
Population (2005 est.): 1,517,000
Capital: Banjul
Head of state and government: President Col. Yahya Jammeh

In January 2005 five opposition parties in The Gambia, under the leadership of Halifa Sallah, minority leader in the parliament, launched a coalition—the National Alliance for Democracy and Development—to challenge Pres. Yahya Jammeh and his ruling Alliance for Patriotic Reorientation and Construction in the 2006 elections. The same month Jammeh, who had ruled since 1994, was defeated in a contest for chair of the UN Economic Community of West African States by the president of Niger, who was supported by Nigeria. It was thought that Jammeh's links with Charles Taylor, the former strongman of Liberia, had counted against him. In March Jammeh dismissed his ministers of economy, health, and agriculture and reduced the size of his cabinet.

In December 2004 the parliament had approved media legislation that imposed mandatory prison terms for press offenses and made operating licenses for private newspapers and radio stations prohibitively expensive. Shortly thereafter Deydra Hydara, a leading critic of the new laws and editor of the Banjul newspaper *The Point,* was shot dead. Opposition groups claimed the murder was politically motivated. The country's police chief was sacked in February 2005, but by then no one had been charged with the crime.
(CHRISTOPHER SAUNDERS)

GEORGIA

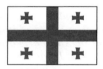

Area: 70,152 sq km (27,086 sq mi), of which 8,640 sq km (5,336 sq mi) in the breakaway Republic of Abkhazia and 3,900 sq km (1,506 sq mi) in the breakaway Republic of South Ossetia
Population (2005 est.): 4,496,000, of which in Abkhazia 176,000 and in South Ossetia 48,000
Capital: Tbilisi
Head of state and government: President Mikheil Saakashvili, assisted by Prime Ministers Zurab Zhvania and, from February 17, Zurab Nogaideli

Georgia's Prime Minister Zurab Zhvania was found dead at a friend's apartment early on Feb. 3, 2005; his family rejected the official verdict, endorsed

© Vano Shlamov/AFP/Getty Images

A herdsman tends to his sheep in Tbilisi, Georgia, on May 8, the eve of U.S. Pres. George W. Bush's visit to the country. No U.S. president had ever before visited the Caucasian country.

by the U.S. Federal Bureau of Investigation, of accidental asphyxiation from a malfunctioning gas heater. On February 17 Pres. Mikheil Saakashvili appointed Finance Minister Zurab Nogaideli as Zhvania's successor. Accusations in August that parliament deputy Koba Beqauri tried to bribe a journalist not to publicize his dubious business activities reflected badly on Saakashvili's administration, as did opposition allegations that the authorities spent millions of laris to ensure the victory of candidates from Saakashvili's National Movement in five by-elections on October 1 in each of which four opposition parties aligned to field a single candidate. On October 19 Nogaideli acceded to the parliament's demand that he dismiss Foreign Minister Salome Zurabishvili, and she was replaced by National Security Council Secretary Gela Bezhuashvili on the following day.

On January 12 Sergey Bagapsh was elected president of the breakaway unrecognized Republic of Abkhazia and pledged closer ties with Russia. The abduction in early June of four Georgian residents of the unrecognized Republic of South Ossetia revived latent tensions with the Georgian government. A September 20 mortar attack on the South Ossetian capital, Tskhinvali, injured 10

people. The Ossetians accused Georgia, which in turn sought to incriminate Russia. The Georgian parliament adopted a resolution on October 11 proposing that the Russian peacekeepers deployed in the Abkhaz and South Ossetian conflict zones be replaced in mid-2006 by an international force if they continued to act in contravention of their mandate.

Visiting Tbilisi on May 9–10 to demonstrate support for Saakashvili, U.S. Pres. George W. Bush escaped injury when a hand grenade was thrown at him during a public address. Georgian police apprehended the perpetrator after a shoot-out on July 20. On September 12 an agreement was signed allocating Georgia $295 million from the Millennium Challenge Account.

Following fruitless talks in February and mid-May, the Georgian and Russian governments reached agreement on May 30 on the closure by 2008 of the two remaining Russian military bases in Georgia. Military hardware from those bases was withdrawn on schedule during the summer.

Georgia's GDP grew by 7.5% during the first six months of the year. In September the World Bank approved a new Country Partnership Strategy with Georgia for 2006–09.

(ELIZABETH FULLER)

GERMANY

Area: 357,023 sq km (137,847 sq mi)
Population (2005 est.): 82,443,000
Capital: Berlin; some ministries remain in Bonn
Chief of state: President Horst Köhler
Head of government: Chancellors Gerhard Schröder and, from November 22, Angela Merkel

Events in Germany in 2005 were dominated by the decision to call an early federal election in September, 12 months ahead of schedule. The election followed disastrous regional election results for the Social Democratic Party (SPD) in May and the continued unpopularity of the Social Democrat–Green federal government. Weak economic performance, high unemployment rates, and unpopular welfare-state reforms were the key factors in public discontent. The

election outcome—a hung Parliament—left Germany in limbo for several weeks while the shape of a new government coalition was hammered out.

Domestic Affairs. In January the payment scheme for unemployment benefits was altered, which caused discontent among those on benefits and contributed to the unpopularity of the federal government. Germany also faced a number of commemorative events marking the 60th anniversary of the end of World War II in Europe, including a trip by the federal president in January to the site of the Auschwitz concentration camp in Poland. Measures were put in place to prevent neo-Nazi groups from disrupting such events after deputies of the far-right National Democratic Party boycotted the Saxony state parliament in protest against commemorations of the liberation of Auschwitz.

During the year Germany was involved in a number of high-profile trials relating to global terrorism. Metin Kaplan, a Muslim radical, was jailed for life in Turkey for conspiring to overthrow the Turkish secular system. Kaplan, known as the caliph of Cologne, was extradited to Turkey from Germany to face charges in 2004 after Turkey banned the death penalty. The case of the Moroccan Mounir al-Motassadeq was also finally resolved following a year-long retrial. Motassadeq, who was convicted in 2003 of having been an accessory to the September 11 attacks in the United States, had had his 15-year sentence overturned in 2004 because the German courts had been unable to directly question suspects held by the U.S. In the retrial, with fresh evidence from the U.S., Motassadeq was found guilty of belonging to a terrorist organization and given a seven-year sentence, though he was not convicted of charges relating directly to the September 11 attacks.

In February the SPD, with help from a local ethnic Danish party, narrowly managed to avoid defeat in the Schleswig-Holstein state elections and to stay in office. Real damage to the SPD was done, however, by the party's disastrous defeat in the North Rhine–Westphalia state election on May 22. The rout was attributed largely to high unemployment, the sluggish economy, and the unpopularity of welfare-state and labour-market reforms.

The cumulative effect of the SPD's poor regional election results in 2004 and 2005 left the Christian Democratic Union (CDU) and its sister party, the

Christian Social Union (CSU), holding a strong position in the Bundesrat, the upper chamber of Parliament. The ruling SPD–Green Party coalition was seriously short of room for legislative maneuvering. In effect, there came into being an informal "grand coalition" in which negotiations between the two large parties were needed in order to realize legislative progress.

The SPD defeat in North Rhine–Westphalia, Germany's largest state economy but an area that suffered from industrial decline and high unemployment rates, was what finally provoked Chancellor Gerhard Schröder to seek early elections. In order for early elections to be called, the chancellor had to engineer—and lose—a vote of confidence in the Bundestag and thereby prove that his government lacked the support of a stable parliamentary majority and could not stand. Schröder's tactic was highly unusual and controversial. It could have been blocked at either of two points: by the German president, who had the responsibility to dissolve the Bundestag, or by the Federal Constitutional Court (FCC), which could declare the move unconstitutional. In fact, the issue was referred to the FCC by two backbench deputies in protest against Schröder's move, but neither Pres. Horst Köhler nor the FCC would intervene, which probably reflected the perceived popular and parliamentary will. The confidence vote in the Bundestag took place on July 1; 296 deputies voted against the government and 151 in favour, with 148 abstentions. The stage was set for the critical federal election to take place on September 18.

The campaign revolved around the state of the economy, the need for labour-market and tax-system reform, and the personalities of the chancellor candidates, Schröder for the SPD and Angela Merkel (*see* BIOGRAPHIES) for the CDU/CSU. In the opinion polls the CDU/CSU enjoyed substantial leads for most of the year. The biggest question for most people seemed to be whether Merkel (who would be the country's first woman chancellor) would be able, as the CDU/CSU had usually done, to form a coalition with the liberal Free Democratic Party (FDP).

The SPD election campaign managed to gather momentum, however, despite the unpopularity of the Socialists' reform measures and the fact that it was being squeezed on the left by a new Linke ("Left") party, which brought together the former communists of eastern Germany's Party of Democratic

Conservative challenger Angela Merkel and incumbent Socialist Chancellor Gerhard Schröder are all smiles on September 4 at their television debate two weeks before the German elections. Neither candidate won a clear mandate, however, and a grand coalition government was formed in November.

Socialism (PDS) and disaffected traditional social democrats from the west, led by former finance minister Oskar Lafontaine and the PDS's Gregor Gysi. The SPD's impetus was driven largely by the personality of Schröder, who enjoyed consistently high personal popularity ratings.

The Union parties' cause was not helped by the image of Merkel herself, who repeatedly showed as less popular than Schröder in opinion polls and was apparently uneasy in the media spotlight. Nor was her candidacy advanced by two political colleagues whose presence seemed only to divide party and electors. The outspoken CSU leader Edmund Stoiber had been the Union's unsuccessful candidate for chancellor in 2002; he stirred up problems for the Union by making critical statements about the eastern electorate. Paul Kirchhof, Merkel's choice for finance minister, was an academic who mired the Union in controversy with his ideas for the introduction of a flat-rate income tax.

The two candidates went head to head in a television debate on September 4. Schröder, the more accomplished media performer, was generally adjudged to have been the winner, but Merkel put in a stronger performance than many expected. Two weeks before the election, a large number of voters were still undecided. Opinion polls in

the week before the election were still indicating a comfortable victory for the Union parties, although the gap was narrowing.

Exit polls revealed the thinness of the CDU/CSU's margin. There was a mere 1% difference between the CDU and the SPD, a scant majority for the Union parties. Both Merkel and a jubilant Schröder claimed a mandate to be chancellor.

The CDU/CSU received four seats more than the SPD (226 to 222). The FDP showed strongly (61 seats), but the Union and the FDP were unable to form a parliamentary coalition with a workable majority. The Linke received 54 seats and the Greens 51, so a number of coalition permutations were possible. The two main parties began the delicate task of looking for a workable alliance. Three possibilities dominated—a grand coalition of CDU/CSU and SPD, a "traffic light" coalition of SPD (red), Green, and FDP (yellow), and a "Jamaica" coalition of CDU/CSU (black), Green, and FDP (named for the colours of the Jamaican flag). During the course of the campaign, the SPD had ruled out an arrangement that included the Linke, even though together the SPD, the Greens, and the Linke could muster more than 50% of the vote.

During the three weeks that followed the election, it gradually became clear that the only way forward would be the formation of a grand coalition. Serious negotiations were delayed by the continued insistence of both Merkel and Schröder that they be chancellor in the new government. Schröder finally ceded to his rival, and on October 10 it was announced that Germany would indeed have its first female chancellor. Merkel would, however, lack the strong popular mandate that she had anticipated. The cabinet seats were effectively divided up between three parties (the CDU shares posts with the CSU). The SPD was given eight cabinet portfolios (foreign affairs, finance, justice, economic cooperation and development, labour, health, transport, and environment) and the CDU/CSU six (economy; interior; defense; family; consumer rights, nutrition, and agriculture; and education) as well as the posts of chancellor and state secretary in the Chancellery. Negotiations over the detailed government program continued through the end of the year and focused in particular on labour-market reform, improvement of economic performance, and cuts in government expenditure.

The Economy. The country continued to suffer from weak growth and high unemployment in 2005. In January unemployment reached the psychologically important figure of five million for the first time, though the number fell slightly in subsequent months. Real growth was elusive and remained export-driven, and domestic demand, badly affected by weak consumer confidence, remained feeble. The effects of the limitations imposed by the euro zone's Growth and Stability Pact continued to have a negative impact, and the government remained unable to use its own spending to encourage domestic demand.

"Co-determination," the German system of industrial relations, came under attack once again. The traditionally strong German trade unions began to be undermined as large companies threatened to move jobs outside Germany. Volkswagen AG was embroiled in a succession of scandals concerning leading figures in the company, which resulted in three major resignations, including that of Peter Hartz, director of personnel at VW and a close economic adviser to Chancellor Schröder. A further scandal embroiled VW's operations in India, with accusations of bribery relating to the setting up of a plant in the country. Sportswear manufacturer Adidas sought to reposition itself in the global market by divesting itself of Salomon, its winter sports

Visitors walking through the Memorial to the Murdered Jews of Europe, which opened in May, are dwarfed by the 2,711 close-set concrete slabs. The site, near the Brandenburg Gate in central Berlin, was designed by architect Peter Eisenman.

AP/Wide World Photos

branch, and moving to purchase Reebok in order to secure a stronger footing in the American sportswear market.

Foreign Affairs. Together with the U.K. and France, Germany led negotiations with Iran throughout the year about the cessation of Iran's nuclear fuel enrichment program. Failure of the talks and the reopening of the nuclear plant at Esfahan, which had been sealed by the International Atomic Energy Agency, would likely lead to the question's being referred to the UN Security Council. At the UN Germany continued to press for reform of the Security Council and lobby for a permanent seat on the Council.

Both houses of the German Parliament, the Bundestag and the Bundesrat, approved the draft EU Constitution, although the charter was rejected a few weeks later in referenda in France and The Netherlands. Arguments over the EU budget for the period 2007–13 continued in 2005 and focused largely on reform of the Common Agricultural Policy and the anomaly of the budget rebate received by the U.K.; Germany wanted to see the rebate abolished. Relations with the U.S. were boosted somewhat in February as U.S. Pres. George W. Bush visited Germany during his tour of Europe, which was aimed in part at mending fences with those European states, such as Germany, that had been critical of the U.S.-led coalition's intervention in Iraq in 2003. Papering over their differences, the German and U.S. leaders made much of Germany's troop contributions in Afghanistan as evidence of its commitment to the global war on terrorism.

The prospects for a consistent foreign policy after the election were uncertain. Foreign policy was an area in which the ideas of the grand coalition partners diverged markedly. The union parties wanted to concentrate on rebuilding relations with the U.S.; Schröder was sharply critical of the U.S. attitude toward Iran. The SPD would welcome Turkey into the EU; the union parties would not. Schröder's SPD government had developed close ties between Germany and Russia; Merkel wanted to loosen these ties somewhat. In terms of policy making and control of the foreign-policy apparatus, from late November the Foreign Ministry was in the hands of the SPD, yet Chancellor Merkel too had a key role to play in Germany's relations with the rest of the world.

(ROSANNE PALMER)

GHANA

Area: 238,533 sq km (92,098 sq mi)
Population (2005 est.): 21,946,000
Capital: Accra
Head of state and government: President John Agyekum Kufuor

On Jan. 4, 2005, Ghanaian Pres. John Agyekum Kufuor concluded his first presidential term with his statutory state of the union address that reviewed his government's achievements. It had established multiparty democracy, reduced ethnic and political tensions, overhauled the national communications and transportation infrastructures, and revamped the education system. Acceptance of the Heavily Indebted Poor Countries (HIPC) initiative had strengthened the economy, reduced inflation, and stabilized the currency. By mid-2004 Ghana qualified for the cancellation of more than $2 billion of its external debts, and it anticipated the cancellation of a further $2 billion over the next 20 years. In addition, it qualified for a second tranche of $1 billion from the U.S. Millennium Challenge Account. Sworn in for his second term of office on January 7, Kufuor reconfirmed his government's commitment to "positive change," and he stressed government accountability, capacity building, agricultural development, and privatization.

Throughout the year economic development dominated international policy. On August 29 the government signed the Third Poverty Reduction Support Credit Agreement with the World Bank in Washington, D.C., to facilitate implementation of Ghana's Poverty Reduction Strategy. As one of the world's poorest countries, Ghana was awarded total debt cancellation in late September by the Group of Eight.

In January women leaders complained about the small number of females elected to the national legislature and participating in other public bodies. Concerned medical professionals argued that the country's health care program was seriously undermined by nurses' and doctors' leaving for better economic opportunities in the developed world. Ghanaians in the diaspora began campaigning for political rights in future elections. (LARAY DENZER)

GREECE

Area: 131,957 sq km (50,949 sq mi)
Population (2005 est.): 11,088,000
Capital: Athens
Chief of state: Presidents Konstantinos Stephanopoulos and, from March 12, Karolos Papoulias
Head of government: Prime Minister Konstantinos Karamanlis

On Feb. 8, 2005, the parliament elected Karolos Papoulias the new president of Greece. The 75-year old Papoulias, a veteran politician of the Panhellenic Socialist Movement (PASOK) and former foreign minister, received 279 votes in the 300-member parliament and became the first Socialist to accede to the Greek presidency. Papoulias's candidacy had been put forward by Prime Minister Konstantinos (Kostas) Karamanlis of the centre-right New Democracy (ND) party and was supported by ND and PASOK. Papoulias took office on March 12.

On March 3–6 PASOK held its seventh congress, adopting a new manifesto and new party statutes. Following the congress the PASOK National Council on March 16 elected as its secretary

Mariliza Xenogiannakopoulou, the first woman to hold this post. Throughout the year dissatisfaction was voiced at what was widely perceived as meek and ineffective opposition by party leader Georgios Papandreou, but there were no serious challenges to his leadership. In February the Communist Party of Greece (KKE) held its 17th congress, reelecting Secretary-General Alexandra (Aleka) Papariga.

Major scandals rocked the Greek Orthodox Church and the judiciary in 2005. Senior members of the church hierarchy were accused of corruption, embezzlement, the smuggling of antiquities, sexual harassment, and other misdeeds. Several bishops, including the patriarch of Jerusalem and the metropolitan bishop of Attica, were deposed or resigned. While Archbishop of Athens and All Greece Christodoulos publicly apologized for the scandals, he said he did not intend to step down. Both church and government rejected calls for the complete separation of church and state. Within the judiciary several judges and prosecutors were dismissed for unprofessional and unethical conduct, partly in connection with the scandals involving the church.

On April 19 the parliament ratified the EU constitution by a vote of 268–17. A proposal by UN mediator Matthew Nimetz regarding the name of Macedonia was assessed as a basis for further talks by Greece; the Skopje

government, however, rejected the proposed compromise of using the name Republika Makedonija–Skopje without translation in international relations. Greece's relations with Turkey remained stable despite repeated violations of Greek airspace by Turkish fighter planes, and Athens continued to support the opening of EC membership talks with Turkey and the prospect of eventual Turkish accession.

The government vowed to press ahead with its economic-reform course despite numerous protests against its perceived neoliberal policies. On June 13 the government won a vote of confidence, which Karamanlis had requested in connection with his fiscal and economic policies. Throughout the summer numerous strikes were held in protest against the government's plans for labour and social security reforms. The Finance Ministry announced that GDP was expected to grow by 3.5–3.6% in 2005, while the budget deficit would drop below 4%. Unemployment dropped to 10.4% in the first quarter, from 11.3% one year earlier, while inflation stood at 3.7% in August. Tourist arrivals were estimated to have increased by more than 10% over 2004.

The parliament on January 20 passed the so-called Main Shareholder Law, which would prevent companies "interconnected" with Greek media businesses from participating in procedures for the awarding of public contracts, starting June 14, 2005. The European Commission in April requested changes to the law, arguing that it violated the EC treaty and Commission directives. Although the government defended the law, saying it was in line with the Greek constitution, it was suspended.

The government unsuccessfully tried to find a lasting solution for the country's ailing national carrier, Olympic Airlines. Attempts to sell the company failed to produce the desired results. Olympic's future was further cast in serious doubt after the European Commission in September demanded the return of €568 million (about $700 million) in what it considered illegal state subsidies and gave the government two months to take necessary measures regarding Olympic. In December Greece announced that it was preparing a privatization plan, expected to be presented to the Commission in early 2006.

On August 14 a jetliner of the Cypriot carrier Helios Airways en route from Larnaca, Cyprus, to Athens and Prague crashed north of Athens, killing all 121 people on board. Initial investigations

On March 17 student demonstrations in Athens are countered by police. Widespread strikes by transportation workers and civil servants to protest changes in labour rules disrupted airline and other transport services.

AP/Wide World Photos

suggested that cabin depressurization was the cause of the crash, the worst ever to occur on Greek territory.

One year after winning the European football championship, Greece again scored a major sports success as the men's national basketball team on September 25 won the Eurobasket 2005 championship. On May 21 Helena Paparizou became the first Greek singer to win the Eurovision Song Contest.

Former archbishop of North and South America Iakovos, who headed the Greek Orthodox Church in the Western Hemisphere for 37 years until his resignation in 1996, died on April 10, aged 93. (*See* OBITUARIES.) On May 22 veteran Communist Party politician and former KKE secretary-general Harilaos Florakis died, aged 90.

(STEFAN KRAUSE)

GRENADA

Area: 344 sq km (133 sq mi)
Population (2005 est.): 103,000
Capital: Saint George's
Chief of state: Queen Elizabeth II, represented by Governor-General Sir Daniel Williams
Head of government: Prime Minister Keith Mitchell

Following the devastation wrought by Hurricane Ivan in September 2004, the International Monetary Fund noted in February 2005 that the Grenadan economy remained in a difficult state. The country could achieve only 1% growth in 2005, and restoring its economy would require extraordinary reconstruction expenditures.

Grenada began to enjoy the fruits of diplomatic relations with China, which offered in March to rebuild its national stadium, damaged extensively by Ivan. In July China put Grenada on its list of approved destinations for Chinese tourists. An offer of $50 million in aid from Taiwan did not induce the Grenadan government to continue to maintain links with Taipei.

The commission of inquiry into allegations of wrongdoing by Prime Minister Keith Mitchell during his 2000 visit to EU countries and Kuwait commenced hearings in June. He was alleged to have accepted improper

payments of $187,265 from Eric Resteiner, Grenada's former trade representative. Mitchell insisted that the money was for reimbursement of legitimate expenses but agreed to take part in the inquiry in an effort to clear his name. In September the opposition National Democratic Congress accused the government of spying on its MPs.

In July Grenada was hit by Hurricane Emily, which caused approximately $175 million in damages to crops and buildings; an estimated 90% of the bananas planted after Ivan were destroyed by Emily.   (DAVID RENWICK)

GUATEMALA

Area: 109,117 sq km (42,130 sq mi)
Population (2005 est.): 12,599,000
Capital: Guatemala City
Head of state and government: President Óscar Berger Perdomo

More than 1,000 people perished in early October 2005 as Hurricane Stan's torrential rains triggered mud slides on lands already saturated by a heavier-than-usual rainy season. Especially

hard hit were the western highlands around Lake Atitlán, where whole communities washed away. Together with rising energy costs, the damage to roads and bridges threatened the moderate economic growth that Guatemala had enjoyed. In May the World Bank agreed to provide $780 million between 2005 and 2008 to promote Guatemalan economic development and fight poverty in collaboration with President Óscar Berger's "Vamos Guatemala" program. That program sought to stimulate economic growth through investment in housing, infrastructure, tourism, finance, and forestry and to increase productivity through technological innovation and growth of exports. Guatemala also signed agreements with Mexico and the other Central American states to conserve energy and reduce fuel costs.

Guatemala ratified the Central America–Dominican Republic Free Trade Agreement (CAFTA-DR) in March. Amid noisy protests from labour unions, the government argued that CAFTA-DR, scheduled to go into effect on Jan. 1, 2006, would increase exports and reverse the trend of Guatemala's losing markets to Asian producers, especially in the garment industry. Soon thereafter, U.S. Secretary of Defense Donald Rumsfeld visited Guatemala and declared that the U.S. would resume military aid to the country. U.S. military aid had been frozen because of human

Residents of Las Cuchillas village, Guat., search through mud and debris that resulted from torrential rains accompanying Hurricane Stan in early October. More than 1,000 persons were killed in Guatemala and elsewhere in Central America.

© Orlando Sierra/AFP/Getty Images

rights violations by the Guatemalan military. Rumsfeld said that the restoration of aid would help the Guatemalan army combat terrorism, drug trafficking, and juvenile gangs. Following the catastrophic landslides in October, Rumsfeld met again with Guatemala's security ministers to discuss both disaster relief and U.S. security concerns. President Berger also met with Brazilian Pres. Luiz Inácio Lula da Silva, which resulted in several new agreements between the two countries, including a plan to import more Brazilian goods for reexport to the U.S. under CAFTA-DR.

Gang violence and drug-related crimes continued to be a problem in Guatemala. The vigilante death squads, which had assassinated gang leaders and others, appeared to be privately organized and tolerated by the government. Criticism of the police led to the firing of more than 500 of the National Civil Police's 22,000 officers for corruption, kidnapping, assault, drug trafficking, homicide, and rape. Of particular concern was the rising incidence of violent crimes against women. The government announced in June that it would try to attack the socioeconomic roots of juvenile gang violence, but on August 15 at least 35 gang members died in Guatemalan prison riots that some believed were encouraged by officials.　(RALPH LEE WOODWARD, JR.)

GUINEA

Area: 245,836 sq km (94,918 sq mi)
Population (2005 est.): 9,402,000
Capital: Conakry
Head of state and government: President Gen. Lansana Conté, assisted by Prime Minister Cellou Dalein Diallo

Antoine Soromou, the longtime political ally of Alpha Condé, the leader of the Rally of the Guinean People (RPG), was arrested for unspecified reasons on Jan. 6, 2005, following a meeting with Prime Minister Cellou Dalein Diallo designed to reopen dialogue with the Guinean government. Soromou was released on bail on January 13. Dozens of people were arrested in Conakry after gunmen fired on a convoy carrying Pres. Lansana Conté on January 19. Among those detained in the apparent coup attempt

were Benn Pepito, editor of an opposition newspaper, and Yomba Korouma, the lawyer for Soromou. Though all of the initial detainees were released without charge within a few days, additional arrests were made later, and lawyers refused to attend court sessions in protest. Soromou had not been seen since the incident.

Tensions ran high on May 15 when rumours of an army mutiny swept through Conakry after heavy gunfire broke out. The governor of the capital told reporters that the barrage erupted as a number of civilian and military prisoners escaped from the central jail.

New protests against rocketing food prices hit the capital in June. The price of rice, the main staple, doubled in one month, partly owing to increased demand from much of drought- and locust-stricken West Africa. The cost of fuel also rose by more than 50%. Unions demanded an immediate quadrupling of their wages to cope with inflation.

On July 3 Condé returned from his self-imposed exile in Paris to a huge welcome from his RPG supporters. Though the opposition remained splintered, it agreed that the ailing President Conté should step down. On September 10 the opposition coalition called for his resignation and the installation of a government of national unity. In the December 18 municipal elections, the ruling Party for Unity and Progress scored a landslide victory amid allegations of fraud.　(NANCY ELLEN LAWLER)

GUINEA-BISSAU

Area: 36,125 sq km (13,948 sq mi)
Population (2005 est.): 1,413,000
Capital: Bissau
Chief of state: Presidents Henrique Pereira Rosa (acting) and, from October 1, João Bernardo Vieira
Head of government: Prime Ministers Carlos Gomes Júnior, and from November 2, Aristides Gomes

President-elect João Bernardo Vieira and his wife, Isabel, greet supporters after his narrow victory in the second round of Guinea-Bissau's elections in July. Vieira was president of the small West African country from 1980 to 1999.

Familiar faces dominated the Guinea-Bissau presidential elections in 2005. The first presidential election since the 2003 coup was due to take place in March 2005 but was postponed to June. For a time it seemed that neither deposed former president Kumba Ialá, now leader of the main opposition Social Renovation Party, nor João Bernardo ("Nino") Vieira, who had held power from 1980 to 1999 and was facing murder charges, would be allowed to stand, but they were both eventually admitted. The other main contender for the five-year presidential term was Malam Bacai Sanhá, who had headed the interim administration after Vieira's ouster. The leader whom the military installed after the coup, Henrique Rosa, did not stand.

In the election Sanhá won 35.3% of the vote, Vieira 28.5%, and Ialá 25.7%. International monitors found the election free, fair, and well-organized. The runoff on July 24 went smoothly, and this time Vieira emerged as the victor. Sanhá's supporters claimed electoral fraud and lodged an appeal with the Supreme Court, but that was dismissed. Prime Minister Carlos Gomes Júnior then stated that he would not recognize the new president, and Ialá's supporters also remained disaffected. In October Vieira dismissed Gomes's government and later named Aristides Gomes prime minister. A new government was installed in November. Political stability, however, remained fragile.

(CHRISTOPHER SAUNDERS)

GUYANA

Area: 215,083 sq km (83,044 sq mi)
Population (2005 est.): 751,000
Capital: Georgetown
Chief of state: President Bharrat Jagdeo
Head of government: Prime Minister Sam Hinds

Severe flooding following torrential rainfall wreaked havoc in Guyana beginning in January 2005. The downpour, which lasted about six weeks, inundated the coastal belt, caused the deaths of 34 people, and destroyed large parts of the rice and sugarcane crops. The UN Economic Commission for Latin America and the Caribbean estimated in March that the country would need $415 million for recovery and rehabilitation. About 275,000 people—37% of the population—were affected in some way by the floods.

At the end of 2004, Guyana's external debt stood at $1.1 billion, but in June 2005 the Group of Eight wrote off $336.6 million of the country's debt. A month later Guyana and OPEC reached an agreement in which OPEC would provide $5.4 million in debt relief. Guyana's hopes of finally becoming an oil producer were again dashed in September when Canada's CGX Energy discontinued its onshore exploration program in the Berbice Block after having drilled three unsuccessful wells.

In June the government launched a $3.3 million, five-year plan to combat drug trafficking; the scheme included the hiring of 600 new police officers and greater deployment of security forces along the border with Venezuela.

(DAVID RENWICK)

HAITI

Area: 27,700 sq km (10,695 sq mi)
Population (2005 est.): 8,528,000
Capital: Port-au-Prince
Chief of state and government: President Boniface Alexandre (provisional), assisted by Prime Minister Gérard Latortue (interim)

Throughout 2005 reverberations from the tumult surrounding the departure in 2004 of Pres. Jean-Bertrand Aristide continued to dominate Haiti's political, economic, and social developments, as well as its international relations. Polarization, tension, and conflict between the ousted president's supporters and detractors resulted in hundreds of deaths, politically related detentions, and international accusations of interim-government human rights violations. Haiti's dysfunctional judiciary and violence-prone police contributed to criminal impunity and unrest. Instability and eroded confidence in the government slowed disbursements of the $1.08 billion in development assistance pledged in 2004 by international donors. Remittances from overseas Haitians, however, increased to more than $1 billion, which enabled the foundering country to stay afloat.

The interim government moved toward fulfilling its principal mandate of shepherding presidential, legislative, and municipal/local elections by year's end, with the inauguration of an elected president on Feb. 7, 2006. Most Haitians and international observers viewed elections as a prerequisite for addressing Haiti's myriad problems. With security and technical support provided by the United Nations Stabilization Mission in Haiti (MINUSTAH) and the Organization of American States, respectively, election mechanisms were established; a voter-registration drive ultimately enrolled more than three million voters, some 75% of those eligible.

By year's end, however, elections had not been held. Contributing to their postponement was a nationwide atmosphere of crime and insecurity, particularly in Port-au-Prince where politically linked gangs reigned with virtual impunity in the city's massive slums and where hundreds of kidnappings fueled an environment of fear. After the midyear extension of MINUSTAH's mandate to February 2006 and its augmentation to 7,500 military personnel and 1,897 civilian police, however, the Brazilian-led mission effectively quelled the violence fueled by inner-city gangs, rogue elements within the Haitian National Police, and members of the disbanded Haitian army.

The apparent inability of the Haitian authorities to organize and deliver a

Through the auspices of Yele Haiti, an initiative of singer Wyclef Jean and the UN World Food Programme, food is distributed in the Port-au-Prince slum of Cité Soleil on November 14. Continued instability in Haiti's government throughout 2005 hampered social development.

© Eduardo Munoz/Reuters/Corbis

credible electoral exercise, however, pushed the ballot into 2006. By year's end former president René Préval (1996–2001) had emerged as the leading presidential candidate in a field of 35 that included veteran politician Marc Bazin as the standard-bearer of Aristide's Lavalas Family (FL) and several noteworthy newcomers, including former insurrectionist Guy Philippe and businessman Charles Baker, leader of an anti-Aristide civil society group. Préval, eschewing his affiliation with FL to accept the nomination of a coalition of several minor political parties and a national peasant organization appeared to be attracting significant support among Haiti's demographically dominant rural and urban poor, formerly attracted to the FL.   (ROBERT MAGUIRE)

HONDURAS

Area: 112,492 sq km (43,433 sq mi)
Population (2005 est.): 7,187,000
Capital: Tegucigalpa
Head of state and government: President Ricardo Maduro

On Nov. 27, 2005, Honduras held its sixth elections since democracy was installed in 1982. Manuel Zelaya Rosales of the Liberal Party won the presidency and would take office in January 2006. The Liberal Party won 62 seats in the

Manuel Zelaya of the Liberal Party greets supporters in Tegucigalpa on December 2, a few days after the presidential election in Honduras but before he had been declared the winner. Zelaya was to take over in January.

National Congress, the National Party 55 seats, with the remaining 11 seats divided between three parties. Electoral competition had begun in earnest on February 20, when the Liberal and National parties held primaries to select their presidential and mayoral candidates and slates for Congress.

On March 3 the Honduran Congress voted to ratify the Central America–Dominican Republic Free Trade Agreement (CAFTA-DR). Honduras was the second country to ratify the treaty. In August the CAFTA-DR was ratified by the U.S. The agreement would allow duty-free import of many Honduran products into the U.S. after the Caribbean Basin Initiative expired in 2008. Under CAFTA-DR, U.S. imports into Honduras would also be duty free.

Honduras began to receive benefits during the year from the Heavily Indebted Poor Country program. Total debt relief over time would exceed $1.2 billion. On June 13 Honduras became the second country, after Madagascar, to take part in the U.S.-sponsored Millennium Challenge Account program, with a 5-year, $215 million aid package to promote good governance and poverty reduction.

A December 2004 attack in San Pedro Sula by members of the international Mara Salvatrucha criminal gang that claimed the lives of 28 people prompted Congress to pass penal reforms in 2005 and to strengthen Pres. Ricardo Maduro's zero-tolerance crime program. The attack also made crime and security major issues in the presidential campaign.

In February international environmental groups discovered harpy eagles in the heavily forested region of La Mosquitia in easternmost Honduras. The animals had been thought to be extinct in the Americas.

(MICHELLE M. TAYLOR-ROBINSON)

HUNGARY

Area: 93,030 sq km (35,919 sq mi)
Population (2005 est.): 10,078,000
Capital: Budapest
Chief of state: Presidents Ferenc Madl and, from August 5, Laszlo Solyom
Head of government: Prime Minister Ferenc Gyurcsany

In 2005 the initial pledges of the new Hungarian government headed by Ferenc Gyurcsany focused on generating employment and improving social equality during its first year in office. From the start the government proved a better communicator and used the media more adroitly than its predecessor, and the image of the Hungarian Socialist Party was much improved. Some government promises, including a review of Hungary's military involvement in Iraq and public disclosure of the documents of the former communist secret services, failed to materialize, however. In April Gyurcsany announced a program of "100 steps," a reform package with proposed changes primarily in the fields of taxes and social benefits. Some measures, such as the transformation of the housing support system initiated by the previous government, were introduced within a few months. New tax brackets that would reduce burdens on low-income families were to enter into force in January 2006, as would a reduction from 25% to 20% of the highest value-added-tax bracket and an increase in taxes on banks and financial service companies. Large-scale projects such as reform of the health care system and the state administration were stalled, however.

In late 2004 the opposition Fidesz–Hungarian Civic Alliance collected more than 300,000 signatures to press for referenda on two issues—granting citizenship to the nearly three million Hungarians living outside the country and ending privatization in the health care sector. The two main coalition parties argued that the citizenship law would contravene EU regulations and that the issue should be solved in a different way. The coalition members also favoured pressing forward with health care privatization. Turnout for the referenda, held on Dec. 5, 2004, was too low, however—with only 37.4% of voters participating—and was declared invalid.

Allegations of involvement of politicians and high-ranking law-enforcement officials in the "Brokergate" scandal, a complicated affair involving illegal accounting practices and large-scale embezzlement at the brokerage firm of a large commercial bank, first became public in January 2005. The slow and often controversial investigations in the case generally heightened public distrust of politics.

The presidential election in June offered an opportunity for political parties to put their strength to the test. The opposition emerged successful; with the support of Fidesz and the Hungarian Democratic Forum, independent candidate Laszlo Solyom won the election by a narrow margin against Katalin Szili, the chair of the parliament, who had been nominated for the post by the Socialist Party. The election of Solyom, the former chair of Hungary's Constitutional Court, was possible because coalition partner Free Democrats did not support either presidential candidate. Politicians were also already readying themselves for parliamentary elections in April 2006. Economic issues were uppermost in discussions, and Fidesz continued to lead the polls, although its margin began shrinking later in the year. Opposition leader Viktor Orban and Socialist Prime Minister Gyurcsany were neck and neck in public opinion polls in September.

Economic growth and macroeconomic indicators remained relatively stable throughout the year, although the disappointingly high budget deficit raised concerns that Hungary would not be able to meet the criteria for joining the euro zone even at the new target date, 2010, postponed from the government's original deadline of 2008 or 2009.   (AGNES CSONKA)

ICELAND

Area: 102,928 sq km (39,741 sq mi)
Population (2005 est.): 295,000
Capital: Reykjavík
Chief of state: President Ólafur Ragnar Grímsson
Head of government: Prime Minister Halldór Ásgrímsson

Iceland's economy continued its brisk expansion in 2005, with GDP growth exceeding 6%, the second year of such a high growth rate. The source of this expansion was the ongoing construction of a 690-MW hydropower project and a huge aluminum plant in the northeastern part of the country, both scheduled for completion in 2006–07. The GDP growth rate for 2006 was expected to be 4½–5%, although the economy was expected to cool down upon completion of the construction projects.

Several Icelandic companies embarked upon a series of takeovers abroad, notably the food and apparel retailer Baugur Group, which was aggressively buying British and Scandinavian retail firms, including a number of well-known names in the fashion industry. The head of the group, Jón Ásgeir Jóhannesson, was indicted in 2005 for illegally using company funds and for accounting irregularities. In the first round of litigation, the court rejected many of the charges on the grounds of insufficient preparation. The government later revised the charges for another indictment. FL Group, the owner of Icelandair, was an active investor in the U.K.-based Easy-Jet and also acquired Sterling Airways, a Danish low-cost carrier.

On September 27 former prime minister David Oddsson resigned his post as foreign minister to become the head of the central bank. He also stepped aside as chairman of the Independence Party in favour of Geir H. Haarde, who had been finance minister since 1998 and was succeeding Oddsson at the Foreign Ministry.

In recent years the U.S. had indicated that it would like to withdraw from its air base at Keflavík (established in 1951) or maintain only a minimal presence there. The Icelandic government had urged the U.S. to stay, both because the base provided employment and because Iceland had no domestic defense force. In late 2005 negotiations for the future of the base seemed to have broken down, apparently over the issue of cost-sharing.   (BJÖRN MATTHÍASSON)

INDIA

Area: 3,166,414 sq km (1,222,559 sq mi)
Population (2005 est.): 1,103,371,000
Capital: New Delhi
Chief of state: President A.P.J. Abdul Kalam
Head of government: Prime Minister Manmohan Singh

Domestic Politics. The coalition government of the United Progressive Alliance (UPA), headed by Indian Prime Minister Manmohan Singh, succeeded in consolidating its position in Parliament in 2005. The UPA had been able to form a government in 2004 only after it had

gained the support of the Left Front, an alliance of communist and radical groups, but predictions of a short-lived unity between politically diverse allies proved incorrect. In part this was due to disarray within the main opposition Bharatiya Janata Party (BJP). Internecine quarrels following the BJP's shocking electoral defeat of 2004 and the continuing jockeying for power as the party's aging leadership retired kept the BJP divided.

The UPA, however, also had its own share of internal squabbles and ideological differences. The Left Front, led by the Communist Party of India (Marxist) (CPI-M), stepped up its campaign against certain economic and foreign policies of the Singh government. On the economic side, the Left Front's main objection was to the government's proposals to sell its equity in public-sector enterprises. The Left insisted that privatization be restricted to unprofitable public enterprises and not include moneymaking large enterprises. A second area of difference related to the government's policy on foreign investment. The Left Front was willing to accept foreign direct investment in the infrastructure sector, but it opposed such investment in banking, insurance, and other financial services as well as in retail trading.

Complicating matters for the UPA was the fact that the Left Front had been trying to create a "Third Front," a new coalition led by itself and including a clutch of regional parties. These attempts were stepped up after Prakash Karat, a former student activist, took over as the general secretary of the CPI-M in the spring of 2005. Unlike his moderate predecessor, Harkishen Singh Surjeet, Karat was a hard-line Marxist with an ambition to increase the Left's presence in Parliament and its relevance to national politics. In addition to criticisms aimed at the government, Karat chose to target foreign policy initiatives pushed by the opposition Congress Party, especially an India-U.S. agreement on cooperation in such matters as civil nuclear energy. Sharp differences between the Left and the Congress over India's decision to vote along with the U.S. and the EU on an International Atomic Energy Agency resolution regarding Iran's adherence to Nuclear Non-proliferation Treaty obligations also came to the fore.

A corruption scandal hit Parliament in December after 11 MPs were filmed allegedly accepting bribes; all were quickly expelled from Parliament.

In Poonch village, Indian-administered Kashmir, a survivor of the South Asian earthquake comforts her grandson in front of a collapsed house on October 12. Some 1,200 people died on the Indian side of the "line of control" and 87,000 on the Pakistani side.

K.R. Narayanan, the first Dalit (member of the lowest social caste) to serve as president of India (1997–2002), died on November 9. (*See* OBITUARIES.)

The Economy. The Indian economy grew at a rate above 7% in 2005, following two years of 7% growth. There were no major concerns on the economic front, apart from the inflationary pressure exerted by the continued rise of global energy prices. The domestic inflation rate approached 5%, well above the 3% level at which it had been contained in recent years. This in part forced the central bank, the Reserve Bank of India, to announce a marginal increase in interest rates. The short-term outlook for the Indian economy was positive. The stock market continued to attract inflows of portfolio investment. While foreign-exchange reserves remained at high and comfortable levels, the current and trade accounts registered a deficit, owing to a sharp increase in imports. India's trade deficit was balanced by a surplus on the capital account, owing to sustained high inflows of foreign-exchange remittances from Indians overseas.

The focus of the government throughout much of the year remained on securing new investments in infrastructure. The government launched new initiatives to step up investment in roads, railways, airports, sea ports, and power. A rural infrastructure program was launched to focus public expenditure on rural housing, power, telecommunications, and irrigation. The government continued to push for trade liberalization, entering into a range of new free-trade agreements, including ones with ASEAN (Association of Southeast Asian Nations) member states. Investment in roads, railways, and new urban infrastructure increased the demand for steel, cement, and other related industries.

Foreign Policy. India made several momentous decisions on foreign policy during the year. The underlying theme was the attempt to improve relations with major powers, especially the U.S., Japan, and the EU, and with its neighbours, including China, Pakistan, Afghanistan, and Myanmar (Burma). A U.S.-India joint statement was released in July, with Prime Minister Singh and U.S. Pres. George W. Bush initialing an agreement to cooperate in defense matters and in civil nuclear-energy development. India also signed bilateral strategic partnership agreements with the EU, Japan, and Russia and agreed to pursue strategic cooperation with China. Visits were paid to India by Chinese Prime Minister Wen Jiabao, Japanese Prime Minister Junichiro Koizumi, and British Prime Minister Tony Blair during the year, while India sent representatives to the Group of Eight summit meeting at Gleneagles, Scot., and to the first East Asian Summit in Kuala Lumpur, Malaysia.

India's relations with Pakistan continued to improve; during Pakistani Pres. Pervez Musharraf's visit to India in April, Singh and Musharraf spoke about the need to convert the "line of control" in Jammu and Kashmir into a "soft border" across which there could be freer and increased trade and movement of people. A first, but important, step toward that end was the resumption of bus service between Srinagar on the Indian side and Muzaffarabad on the Pakistani side. Crossing points were also opened along the line of control to facilitate humanitarian efforts following the massive earthquake that struck northern Pakistan in October. (See *Pakistan:* Sidebar, below.)

Singh's visit to Kabul in midyear revived a once-close relationship between India and Afghanistan. With India's help, a new parliament building was being constructed in Afghanistan, and Singh and Afghan Pres. Hamid Karzai pledged to build "a new partnership for the 21st century." In July Singh also addressed the U.S. Congress, placing new emphasis on the importance of nurturing democracy around the world and vowing cooperation in efforts to fight global terrorism. (SANJAYA BARU)

INDONESIA

Area: 1,890,754 sq km (730,024 sq mi)
Population (2005 est.): 222,781,000
Capital: Jakarta
Head of state and government: President Susilo Bambang Yudhoyono

The government of Pres. Susilo Bambang Yudhoyono (*see* BIOGRAPHIES), who was elected to office in October 2004 with 61% of the vote, had a year of mixed results in 2005. Yudhoyono assumed office promising to make a number of improvements: to accelerate economic growth, push through political and judicial reforms, and launch strong anticorruption measures. While praised by foreign observers for delivering on some of these promises, particularly those regarding the economy, he was strongly criticized for not achieving more.

An early challenge for the Yudhoyono government was responding to the Dec. 26, 2004, tsunami that had struck Aceh province on the island of Sumatra. The magnitude-9.15 tsunami, the greatest natural disaster to befall Indonesia in more than a century, destroyed most of the infrastructure and buildings on the eastern and northern coasts of Aceh. The death toll was estimated at 132,000 people; another 37,000 were missing; and some 100,000 were seriously injured. Another 700,000 persons were displaced. A multibillion-dollar international relief and rebuilding program was under way but was proceeding slowly, which caused it to draw criticism from the United Nations and other international agencies. Some 60,000 survivors were still living in tents, and 100,000 persons were reliant on food aid for survival.

One positive outcome from the tsunami and the extensive international relief effort that followed was renewed impetus to find peace in Aceh, a province beset by decades of violent separatist conflict. Negotiations between the central government and the Free Aceh Movement (GAM) began in April in Helsinki, moderated by former Finnish prime minister Martti Ahtisaari. (*See* photograph on page 396.) A deal was struck in July whereby the government would grant amnesty to GAM members, reduce troop numbers, and restore GAM members' political, social, and economic rights; GAM agreed to surrender all weapons and accept Indonesian sovereignty. Much progress was made as GAM disarmament and the withdrawal of Indonesian troops were completed by year's end. Plans were under way to integrate GAM members into local politics and the economy. Violence in Aceh was at its lowest level in many years.

The government's anticorruption measures dominated local media for much of the year. A newly instituted Anticorruption Commission (KPK) and the establishment of ad hoc anticorruption courts proved surprisingly effective. Aceh Gov. Abdullah Puteh was jailed for 10 years for his role in a multimillion-dollar bribery scandal. Several members of the national Election Commission were on trial for corruption; dozens of regional heads and legislators were found guilty of malfeasance; and a number of prominent judges and lawyers were under investigation. Detractors said that these actions were selective and that many well-connected corrupt businessmen

and politicians had been left untouched.

Another controversial case concerned the 2004 murder of respected human rights activist Munir Said Thalib on a Garuda (the national airline) flight to The Netherlands. After a sluggish start, police investigators charged a Garuda pilot, who was also a part-time National Intelligence Agency (BIN) spy, with involvement in the murder, though there was open speculation in the media that senior BIN leaders, including its former head, Hendropriyono, might have been implicated in Munir's poisoning. No charges were filed against BIN officials, and the government was accused of lacking resolve.

Terrorism continued to be a serious problem in Indonesia. For the fourth year in row, there was a major terrorist attack in the third trimester, this time on October 1. Twenty-two people died and dozens more were seriously injured in the attack, the second such incident on the tourist island of Bali. The latest bombing brought the total number of people killed in terrorist attacks since 2000 to more than 260. The attack was carried out by three suicide bombers using shrapnel-filled backpack bombs, rather than the massive car bombs of the preceding three attacks. In early November authorities eventually identified the suicide bombers as part of the network led by two Malaysian terrorists, Azhari Husin and Noordin Mohammad Top, both of whom had been senior operatives of Jemaah Islamiyah (JI) but now seemed to be acting independently of that organization. Azhari, an expert bomb maker, had been involved in at least five major terrorist attacks and was tracked down by police and killed in a shoot-out on November 9. Recent attacks added to indications that Indonesia's terrorist threat was becoming more diffuse, owing in part to a fracturing of JI. In the two previous major bombings, operatives from outside JI circles had been recruited to stage attacks, and it was possible that non-JI groups were involved in the most recent attack. Aside from the Bali attack, there were also a number of other bombings, including an attack in May in Tentena, in central Sulawesi, where 25 Indonesians were killed.

Economically, Indonesia experienced fluctuating fortunes. In early 2005 the economy was growing at an annual rate of more than 5%, and there were predictions that growth would reach Suharto-era levels of 7–8% by the end of the year. The rise was partly due to

increased confidence among investors regarding the government's economic policies. Spiraling oil prices in mid-2005, however, led to a giant boost in the generous government subsidies for petroleum and gas and placed the budget under severe pressure. Amid fears that the economic recovery would stall, the value of the rupiah slid to 11,000 rupiah to U.S.$1. The government cut subsidies in October, which led to a doubling of fuel prices. Despite the amount of the increase, protests were muted. Economic commentators applauded the government for taking politically unpopular steps but were unimpressed by its tardiness.

Indonesian politics continued to be dogged by party instability and the poor performance of its representative institutions. Five of the seven largest political parties experienced serious internal splits, and most parties remained elite driven, with ramshackle branch structures and little genuine grassroots participation. The national parliament became notorious for its graft, the absenteeism of its members, and its inability to meet legislative timetables—only 10 of the promised 55 bills were passed during the year. Relations between the parliament and the executive had improved in late 2004 when Vice Pres. Jusuf Kalla gained the chairmanship of Golkar, the biggest party, and thereby ensured a less-hostile legislature than had been the case during the early months of the new government. There was widespread speculation that Kalla might challenge Yudhoyono in the next presidential election, scheduled for 2009.

(GREG FEALY)

IRAN

Area: 1,648,200 sq km (636,374 sq mi)
Population (2005 est.): 69,515,000
Capital: Tehran
Supreme political and religious authority:
Rahbar (Spiritual Leader) Ayatollah Sayyed Ali Khamenei
Head of state and government: Presidents Mohammad Khatami and, from August 3, Mahmoud Ahmadinejad

The Islamic Republic of Iran in 2005 remained firmly on a course of consolidation of hard-line government. The first half of the year was dominated by preparations for the ninth presidential election. On May 23 the Guardian Council determined that only 7 nominations, including one reinstated candidate, of a total of 1,014 would be accepted, most from the conservative camp. The elections on June 17 were inconclusive, and a second round of voting to choose the winner from the top two contenders—Ali Akbar Hashemi Rafsanjani and Mahmoud Ahmadinejad (*see* BIOGRAPHIES)—took place on June 24. In a voter turnout of almost 60%, the surprise result was the election of Ahmadinejad, who took 62% of the vote against 36% for Rafsanjani.

During the election Ahmadinejad campaigned on a program of a return to revolutionary Islamic values. He promised to bring about social equity, maintain subsidies on staple commodities, and end corrupt practices in state-run agencies. The nominations to the cabinet were delivered to the Majlis (parliament) on August 14, and all but four were ratified on August 24. Key appointments to the cabinet were allocated to centrist conservatives such as Mostofa Purmohammadi as minister of the interior and Hussain Saffar as minister of culture and Islamic guidance. The foreign affairs portfolio was taken by Manuchehr Mottaki, a supporter of Ahmadinejad's rival in the presidential race, Ali Larijani. It was assumed in the Iranian press that the new administration would be more politically coherent than the outgoing Khatami regime because all the groups in power, from the supreme leader to the president and the Majlis, were aligned on a broadly similar set of policies. First signs indicated that the segments of government shared Islamic sympathies but had markedly differing aims.

The minister of foreign affairs took over a difficult situation in which an impasse affected Iran-EU negotiations on nuclear development as a result of Iran's threat in March to resume its uranium-enrichment program. Hossein Mousavian, the head of the Iranian team that dealt with France, Germany, and the U.K. acting on behalf of the EU, also warned in January that only complete

On June 25 a young supporter of Mahmoud Ahmadinejad holds up a campaign poster for the dark-horse candidate in the Iranian presidential election. The conservative Ahmadinejad won in a landslide.

EU cooperation with Iran on nuclear power would lead to a continuing suspension of uranium enrichment. Three months of talks in Switzerland ended in March without a firm outcome. The announcement by U.S. Secretary of State Condoleezza Rice on March 11 that the U.S. officially supported the EU initiative gave some impetus to negotiations but increased pressures for a referral of the case to the UN Security Council. An offer on August 5 by the EU of concessions in areas of nuclear technology transfer was dismissed by Iran. On August 11 the IAEA (International Atomic Energy Agency) passed a resolution demanding suspension of all enrichment-related activities, but the situation was made ambivalent by Mohamed ElBaradei (*see* NOBEL PRIZES), the top IAEA

official, who issued an indecisive report on Iran on September 3. Iranian policy under the Ahmadinejad government was defiant of foreign intervention in the nuclear field, and chances of an agreement's being found with the EU diminished.

During the elections Ahmadinejad took an anti-U.S. stance but later did not pursue this theme, concentrating instead on denying the right of Israel to exist, in speeches on October 26 and November 14, and denying the Holocaust in a speech in Mecca on December 8. Rice took a hard line against suggestions of a U.S. military intervention to remove Iran's nuclear industry, however, while the administration of Pres. George W. Bush remained critical of the lack of real legitimacy of the Islamic regime.

Iran increasingly looked to Asia for allies, cultivating China and India as strategic and commercial partners. Relations with Russia were rewarded with strong support by Moscow of the Iranian nuclear program, for which an agreement for the supply of nuclear fuels was signed on February 27. Within the Middle East the Iranian political link with Syria was sustained, and a visit was made to Tehran by Pres. Bashar al-Assad in August. Elsewhere the Iranian government made little progress. Turkey was alienated as a result of the changes enforced in its important contracts for telecommunications and airfield developments in Iran. The Islamic Republic attempted to forge closer ties with Iraq but was increasingly drawn into the sectarian strife as a result of its support for the Iraqi Shi'ite population.

The domestic economy was buoyed by high oil revenues, estimated to run at $70 billion, in the year March 2005–March 2006. The slow pace of privatization and economic reform persisted after the June election, although fears that the new government would stop modernization and return to a welfare economy did not immediately materialize. Unemployment remained high at 13% of the labour force. Inflation was officially claimed to have fallen to 10.3% annually but was independently estimated as high as 20%.

(KEITH S. MCLACHLAN)

IRAQ

Area: 434,128 sq km (167,618 sq mi)
Population (2005 est.): 27,818,000
Capital: Baghdad
Head of state: Presidents Ghazi al-Yawer and, from April 7, Jalal Talabani
Head of government: Prime Ministers Ayad Allawi and, from May 3, Ibrahim al-Jaafari

The first general elections to be held in Iraq following the U.S. occupation took place as scheduled on Jan. 30, 2005. While the Kurdish and Shi'ite populations voted massively in their areas of concentration, Sunni Arabs generally stayed home, either because of intimidation by insurgents or because they were boycotting the election. In the view of many Sunni, the elections were illegal, since they took place under foreign occupation. The vote produced a transitional National Assembly in which the Shi'ite religious parties won 51% of the seats, the Kurdish alliance claimed 27%, and the secular Shi'ite list led by Prime Minister Ayad Allawi took 14%. Only 16 of the 275 Assembly members elected were Sunni. On April 6 the new parliament elected Jalal Talabani, leader of the Patriotic Union of Kurdistan, as the new Iraqi president. Chosen as prime minister was Ibrahim al-Jaafari (see BIOGRAPHIES), head of the Islamic Da'wah Party. Jaafari was sworn in, along with the cabinet he selected, on May 3.

The main task of the transitional parliament was to write a permanent constitution for Iraq by mid-August. To this end a constitutional committee of 55 members was selected from the parliament. Since the majority of its members were either Shi'ites or Kurds, the Sunni protested that their representation was insufficient. To rectify this problem, some Sunni were added, but they were able to join the committee only after its work was well under way. The committee had difficulty meeting its schedule, but a draft was finally approved by the National Assembly, and it was submitted to a popular referendum on October 15.

The draft constitution was narrowly approved. A two-thirds rejection in three separate provinces was required for defeat. Two of Iraq's 18 provinces did reject the document by a two-thirds vote, while a simple majority rejected it in a third province. In contrast to the January elections for the parliament, there was substantial Sunni participation in the referendum, and it was mainly the Sunni-dominated provinces that voted "no." The new Iraqi constitution called for a federated state in Iraq with a weak central government. Many of the details, which were left vague or unfinished, were to be filled in after a permanent National Assembly was elected on December 15. Preparations for the December elections started immediately after the referendum. Some 228 candidates or entities were registered to run. This time a number of Sunni parties and candidates decided to compete. Iraqis voted along ethnic and sectarian lines. The religiously oriented Shi'ite bloc won a large plurality but fell short of a majority. They were followed by Sunni and Kurdish blocs. This result guaranteed that Iraq's next government would be a coalition.

During the year there was a noticeable deterioration of public services, including electricity, clean water, and garbage collection. As a result of acts of sabotage, especially against pipelines and petroleum facilities, oil exports

Iraqi children in the southern city of Najaf sort through a newly arrived load of garbage on November 15. Iraq's economic infrastructure remained marginal in 2005, and many citizens were living at a subsistence level.

were disrupted. Among males, unemployment reached 50–60%; the rate was even higher among women. Random acts of kidnapping, assassination, and murder ravaged areas of the country. University professors, medical doctors, and other members of the Iraqi elite were targeted, and many left the country. Militias belonging to political parties or individuals were active and visible in policing certain areas. Corruption reportedly expanded among government officials at all levels despite repeated promises by the Iraqi government to investigate and punish offenses.

A rising tide of tensions and hostilities became apparent between the Shi'ite and Sunni communities. There were increasing reports of killings, kidnappings, and reprisals between members of these two communities, reportedly reaching tens of thousands of victims. These attacks were encouraged by Abu Musab al-Zarqawi, head of the al-Qaeda terrorist network in Iraq. He declared war on the Shi'ites, accusing them of being "infidels" and of cooperating with the American "occupiers."

Insurgents and terrorist groups in Iraq—foreign terrorists, Iraqi nationalists, and loyalists to deposed Iraqi president Saddam Hussein—attacked both Iraqis and U.S. troops. Their attacks took many forms—armed street fights, suicide bombings, roadside bombs, and car bombings. In particular, insurgents aimed attacks at police stations, police and military recruiting centres, U.S. forces and facilities, and other public places such as markets and even mosques. In one tragic case, on August 31—after rumours spread of a terrorist attack—some 1,000 Shi'ite pilgrims in Baghdad on their way to visit a holy shrine died in a stampede as they crossed a bridge over the Tigris River. Attacks were also aimed at foreign diplomats working in Iraq; Ihab al-Sharif, the Egyptian envoy to Baghdad, was kidnapped on July 2 and executed five days later.

At least half of all attacks occurred in four Sunni-dominated provinces—Anbar, Salah al-Din, Nineveh, and Baghdad. Iraq's borders, especially with neighbouring Syria, were only lightly guarded, and hundreds of fighters crossed to join the Iraqi insurgents. The new government in Baghdad, eager to restore law and order, began increasing the number of police and armed forces. In an effort to assuage Sunni discontent, the government on November 2 called junior officers in Saddam's disbanded army back into service, openly canceling a U.S. directive issued in 2003. The trial of Saddam and of a number of his aides officially began on October 19. The prosecution started with the case of the 1982 massacre of 143 people in the village of Dujail, which Saddam allegedly ordered after an attempt on his life was made. His trial was expected to take several months.

An Arab League meeting aimed at national reconciliation among Iraqis was held in Cairo in November. The talks were attended by high-level Iraqi government leaders, including the president and the prime minister, as well as leading Sunni opposition groups, among them the Association of Muslim Scholars and the National Dialogue Council. On November 21, at the end of the three-day meeting, the group called for the "withdrawal of foreign troops according to a timetable," a position that satisfied an important demand of the Sunni opposition.

A crisis between Iraq and Kuwait over border demarcation was averted in the summer of 2005 as leaders of the two countries called for calm and restraint. Although top officials in Iraq and Iran exchanged visits, many Iraqis voiced concern over increased Iranian influence in Iraq, especially in the south. Relations with Syria deteriorated, with Iraqi officials accusing the country of tolerating the infiltration of foreign fighters into Iraq from Syria. In October and November, Iraqi and U.S. troops launched joint operations against suspected insurgents in western Iraqi towns near the Syrian border. These operations led to the killing or capture of hundreds of suspected insurgents.　　　　　(LOUAY BAHRY)

IRELAND

Area: 70,273 sq km (27,133 sq mi)
Population (2005 est.): 4,152,000
Capital: Dublin
Chief of state: President Mary McAleese
Head of government: Prime Minister Bertie Ahern

The strong growth that had characterized the Irish economy since the late 1990s continued through 2005, although some signs of a possible slowdown became apparent toward year's end. Third-quarter estimates published by Ireland's Department of Finance supported the budget projections presented in December 2004. The government's economic report in August predicted GDP growth of 5.1% for 2005, and unemployment was expected to remain at about 4%, with an additional 54,000 jobs to be created. This number, however, represented a significant increase from the 35,000 additional jobs estimated at the start of the year. Inflation was projected to run at 2.4% for the year, compared with 2.2% in 2004. Government economists claimed the upward pressure was attributable to rising oil prices.

Some independent economists, opposition parties in the Dail (lower house of parliament), and media commentators were less upbeat in their analysis of the economy. Opposition spokespersons accused the government of complacency and claimed that exports and industrial output were dropping in the latter part of the year. The *Irish Times* reported that the government was "holding out hostages to fortune" in its optimistic projections. The newspaper highlighted data from the Central Statistics Office (CSO) showing that while GDP growth had been running at 6% at the beginning of the year, it was down to less than 3% in the summer.

The trend for older industries to relocate out of Ireland to low-wage destinations continued. Manufacturing and assembly plants in Donegal, Dublin, Louth, and elsewhere closed. Although new jobs outnumbered those lost by three to one, the closures created localized unemployment difficulties, especially in rural areas.

Notwithstanding the strong performance of the economy, the year saw rising public concern over consumer prices. Figures from the Organisation for Economic Co-operation and Development showed that for nearly all goods or services, Dublin remained close to the top of the prices league among EU capitals. CSO figures also showed an upward convergence in prices between Dublin and rural areas. High prices were cited as a contributory factor in dwindling tourist figures. While Dublin remained a popular destination, there was a marked drop in visitors to other regions—as much as 30% in some areas. Real-estate prices

continued to rise, although the rate of increase showed a year-on-year drop. Real-estate agents predicted that house prices would rise on average by 5–6% during the year—less than half the rate of increase during 2004.

A number of judicial tribunals, established by order of the Oireachtas (joint houses of the parliament), continued to investigate allegations of political corruption during the year. The most dramatic tribunal revelations, however, concerned the operation of the Garda Siochana (the national police service) rather than the political establishment. A tribunal chaired by the former president of the High Court, Frederick Morris, revealed systemic corruption, the fabrication of evidence, and the failure to investigate abuses in the Garda's Donegal division. A number of senior officers resigned, and others were dismissed. The Morris tribunal continued to take evidence through the latter part of the year. In October a report by former judge Frank Murphy into the sexual abuse of children by Roman Catholic clergy in the Wexford area caused widespread anger. The government established a tribunal to investigate similar allegations in Dublin.

The government continued its efforts to further the Northern Ireland peace process, with Irish ministers and civil servants working in close cooperation with their counterparts in the U.K. Their combined efforts appeared to be rewarded in July when the Irish Republican Army (IRA) declared an end to all paramilitary activity and committed itself to purely constitutional action in the future. The gesture was not expected to lead to an immediate restoration of the power-sharing executive that had been established in 1998 under the Belfast Agreement but had been suspended for more than two years. Nonetheless, the IRA's action was seen as a step toward the resumption of full dialogue between the political parties in Northern Ireland.

Levels of paramilitary violence remained low as the IRA maintained its cease-fire, first declared in 1994; however, violence by Loyalist paramilitaries, opposed to any rapprochement with republicanism, increased. Four murders were attributed to Loyalists over the summer months. In September serious rioting by Loyalist factions took place in Belfast and other centres.

The peace process was strained by the return to Ireland of three IRA associates who had been convicted in Colombia of assisting the rebel movement there. The so-called Colombia Three had jumped bail in Colombia. Irish Justice Minister Michael McDowell accused republican leaders, including Sinn Fein leader Gerry Adams, of having engineered the men's return to Ireland and jeopardized the peace process.

In April Ireland's national theatre, the Abbey Theatre, declared a crisis in its funding. The Abbey, strongly associated with the Irish independence movement of the early 20th century, had been through a sequence of creative and organizational difficulties, and in May the managing and artistic directors both resigned. The government stepped in, abolished the controlling company, and announced a reorganization of the institution. (CONOR BRADY)

On August 18 hard-line Israeli settlers, camped out on the roof of the synagogue in Kfar Darom, Gaza Strip, watch as Israeli riot police are delivered by helicopter to oust them forcibly.

ISRAEL

Area: 21,671 sq km (8,367 sq mi), including the Golan Heights and disputed East Jerusalem, excluding the Emerging Palestinian Autonomous Areas
Population (2005 est.): 6,677,000
Capital: Jerusalem is the proclaimed capital of Israel (since Jan. 23, 1950) and the actual seat of government, but recognition has generally been withheld by the international community
Chief of state: President Moshe Katzav
Head of government: Prime Minister Ariel Sharon

The Emerging Palestinian Autonomous Areas (the West Bank and the Gaza Strip)
Total area under disputed administration: West Bank 5,900 sq km (2,278 sq mi); Gaza Strip 363 sq km (140 sq mi)
Population (2005 est.): West Bank 2,632,000, including 2,386,000 Arabs and 246,000 Jews; Gaza Strip 1,481,000, including 1,481,000 Arabs and no Jews (as of late August 2005)
Principal administrative centres: Ram Allah and Gaza
Head of government: Presidents Rauhi Fattouh (acting) and, from January 9, Mahmoud Abbas, assisted by Prime Minister Ahmad Quray

---

Israel's unilateral withdrawal or "disengagement" from Gaza and the northern West Bank was the seminal event of 2005 and could prove to be a historical turning point in relations between Israel and the Palestinians. The action seemed to herald the beginning of the end of Israel's 38-year occupation and opened up possibilities for a new Israeli-Palestinian peace dialogue. The pullout also reinforced an earlier cease-fire. After more than four years of fighting, the lull helped to change the economic climate on both sides.

The withdrawal was not easily achieved; it entailed the evacuation of more than 9,000 Jewish settlers and encountered strong domestic opposition. Prime Minister Ariel Sharon's right-wing opponents challenged him in the Knesset (parliament) and in the courts. They also held mass demonstrations and blocked major roads. The violent clashes that many feared would erupt during the evacuation, however, failed to materialize. Palestinian militiamen, who had threatened to snipe at the retreating Israelis, also held their fire.

The removal in August of 21 settlements in the Gaza Strip and 4 in the northern West Bank took less than a week, and no one was seriously hurt. More than 50,000 soldiers and police participated in the operation, and by sheer weight of numbers, they succeeded in evacuating the settlers with minimal force and in deterring Palestinian attacks. On September 12, 38 years after Israel conquered the Strip in the 1967 Six-Day War, the last Israeli soldiers left Gaza.

Addressing the UN General Assembly three days later, Sharon announced that Israel was ready to make more "painful concessions," at the same time recognizing the Palestinians' right to statehood. The Palestinians "are also entitled to freedom and to a national, sovereign existence in a state of their own," he declared. The Israeli withdrawal was widely acclaimed by the international community. It left the Palestinian Authority in control of Gaza, except for its airspace and territorial waters, and was hailed as a significant step toward the establishment of a Palestinian state. In the fierce domestic debate, Sharon argued that the pullout was of vital strategic importance; it consolidated Israel's Jewish majority, improved its defensive lines, and assured it of wide international backing. Sharon's opponents chastised him, however, for unilaterally handing over land to the Palestinians, and they argued that in doing so he was simply inviting more terrorism.

Spearheaded by the Judea, Samaria, and Gaza Settlers' Council, a well-financed antidisengagement campaign failed to win over public opinion or to deter the prime minister. The antidisengagement forces lost key battles in the Knesset, the Supreme Court, and on the streets. Their Knesset campaign imploded on March 28 when, by a vote of 72 to 39, the legislators rejected their call for a national referendum on the withdrawal plan. Their legal struggle disintegrated when on June 9 the Supreme Court denied 12 petitions against the evacuation legislation. In late July antidisengagement forces lost a crucial standoff with the authorities when police prevented an estimated

413

200,000 demonstrators from marching on the Gaza settlements.

The most serious challenge to Sharon, however, came from within his hawkish Likud Party; his disengagement policy sparked an internal rebellion. Months of ferment against the prime minister came to a head when his chief rival, Benjamin Netanyahu, resigned as finance minister on August 7, just 10 days before the scheduled withdrawal, and challenged him for the leadership. In a first trial of strength, Sharon narrowly defeated a motion by Netanyahu, a former prime minister, to bring forward to November a party leadership primary that was scheduled for spring 2006. In late November, however, frustrated by continued sniping at his leadership, Sharon dramatically broke away from Likud, taking party moderates with him to form a new centrist party he would lead in early elections scheduled for March 2006.

There were also major changes in Palestinian politics. The death of Yasir Arafat on Nov. 11, 2004, paved the way for the emergence of a more moderate Palestinian leadership. Mahmoud Abbas, who was elected on January 9 to succeed Arafat as president, renounced the use of terrorism against Israel and began negotiating a cease-fire. During a summit in early February at the Egyptian resort town of Sharm al-Shaykh, Sharon and Abbas announced a mutual suspension of hostilities, ostensibly ending more than four years of Israeli-Palestinian fighting, in the so-called second *intifadah*. Abbas, however, could not guarantee the compliance of Hamas and other radical Palestinian militia groups, and it took several more weeks of Egyptian mediation before the groups agreed to honour the temporary truce until the end of 2005. Though Hamas and other radical militias observed the cease-fire for the most part, sporadic terror continued. There were several suicide bombings, and hundreds of Qassam rockets and mortars were fired at Israeli settlements in and around Gaza before and immediately after the evacuation.

The disengagement from Gaza and the renewed dialogue with the Palestinians enhanced Israel's international and regional standing, and there were some significant foreign policy achievements, particularly with Arab and Muslim countries. Soon after the Sharm al-Shaykh summit in February, Jordan and Egypt sent back the ambassadors they had recalled after the outbreak of the second *intifadah*. Speculation arose about an imminent breakthrough in

relations between Israel and Pakistan, a Muslim country that had ostracized the Jewish state, after a highly publicized meeting on September 1 in Istanbul between the two countries' foreign ministers. The strongest opposition to these winds of change came from Shi'ite Iran, whose new president, Mahmoud Ahmadinejad (*see* BIOGRAPHIES), raised a storm of international protest in late October when—at a conference in Tehran entitled "The World Without Zionism"—he called for Israel to be "wiped off the map."

Most important for Israeli foreign policy, the disengagement led to unprecedentedly close ties with the U.S. government. Still, there were some differences. Washington was critical of Israel's plans to build in an area outside Jerusalem known as "E-1" and of its delay in removing 24 unauthorized West Bank outposts. The two countries also clashed over Israel's military relationship with China, and Israel was forced to scrap a contract to upgrade unmanned air vehicles that it had sold to Beijing. To prevent future misunderstandings, on August 16 Israel and the U.S. signed a memorandum of understanding providing for prior consultations on potentially problematic Israeli-Sino arms deals.

The cease-fire with the Palestinians and the disengagement fueled an economic turnaround in Israel and hopes for economic growth in Gaza. For the second consecutive year, Israel's GNP grew by about 4%, and in the months after disengagement, the Tel Aviv Stock Exchange reached record levels. On the Palestinian side, the Group of Eight meeting of industrialized nations promised to raise $3 billion annually over the next three years for investment in Gaza. By year's end, however, there was little sign of the economic transformation that the fund-raisers had hoped would underpin the cease-fire.

(LESLIE D. SUSSER)

ITALY

Area: 301,336 sq km (116,346 sq mi)
Population (2005 est.): 57,989,000
Capital: Rome
Chief of state: President Carlo Azeglio Ciampi
Head of government: Prime Minister Silvio Berlusconi

In 2005 the government of Italian Prime Minister Silvio Berlusconi suffered a stinging electoral defeat at the hands of the opposition during a year that was marked by differences with the United States over the death of an Italian agent in Iraq and a kidnapping in Iraq, as well as by a major scandal involving the national Bank of Italy.

In April 41 million Italians were called to vote in key elections in 14 of Italy's 20 regions. The vote was seen as a test of the popularity of the House of Liberties, Berlusconi's right-of-centre governing coalition, which had been in power since 2001. In the event, the coalition won only 2 of the regions at stake, with the other 12 going to the left-leaning Union alliance led by the moderate former prime minister Romano Prodi. Among the 12 was the crucial region of Lazio, which includes Rome. The Union also reaped victories from voting in two provincial contests and nine provincial capitals. A triumphant Prodi proclaimed, "Italians have called upon us to prepare to govern next." Berlusconi acknowledged on television the "severe defeat" of his own Forza Italia party, the strongest component in the House of Liberties, which dropped to 18% of the vote in the regions, down from a 25% share in 2000.

His defeat was preceded by spiraling prices, economic decline, the hardship of families trying to make ends meet, controversial reforms of the judiciary and school system, and what was generally seen as the lacklustre leadership of Berlusconi himself.

Thanks to a healthy majority in the national Parliament, however, he won a vote of confidence in April after a minor cabinet reshuffle, but from then on repeated fissures appeared in his coalition; its future direction and leadership were questioned.

In early March Italians learned on television of the release of Giuliana Sgrena, an Italian journalist who had been kidnapped a month earlier in Iraq and taken hostage. Their relief vanished, however, when a news flash revealed that Nicola Calipari, the Italian intelligence agent who had been instrumental in the negotiations to secure Sgrena's freedom and was escorting her to the airport, had been killed by U.S. forces at a Baghdad checkpoint. It was reported that Calipari had thrown his body over Sgrena's to save her life when the Americans opened fire. In Rome Berlusconi summoned U.S. Ambassador Mel Sembler for clarification

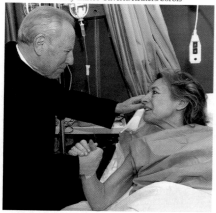

Italian Pres. Carlo Azeglio Ciampi comforts Giuliana Sgrena, a former hostage in Iraq, in her hospital room in Rome on March 7. Sgrena, a journalist, had been fired upon and wounded by U.S. troops outside Baghdad in an incident that claimed the life of an intelligence officer traveling with her.

following testimony from a carabiniere riding in the car with Calipari at the time. The carabiniere reported that they had been issued passes by the Americans allowing them to move about Baghdad armed and, how, after the handing over of the journalist in a Baghdad alley, the car had been on the way to the airport when a lamp had been shone into the windshield, followed immediately by shooting that lasted some 10 seconds. The U.S. command in Iraq called Calipari's death an "unfortunate accident." Public reaction in Italy was emotional. In Rome some 10,000 people flocked to the Unknown Soldier's monument, where the hitherto-unknown Calipari was lying in state, and covered the monument with flowers. One anonymous message read: "Goodbye Nicola, you are the pride of all Italians." At Calipari's state funeral, central Rome was brought to a standstill as huge crowds converged on the church.

Two months later a joint investigating commission failed to agree on the sequence of events, and the two sides produced conflicting versions. The Pentagon released its own report first, clearing the 10 U.S. troops at "checkpoint 541" on the grounds that they had properly followed rules of engagement and had fired on the car, which was approaching at high speed, only after using arm signals, lights, and warning shots to get it to stop. No one at the checkpoint had known of the Italians' imminent arrival. The Italians

on the commission refuted the U.S. version point by point. The Italian report noted an absence of road signs warning of the checkpoint, denied that the car was speeding, and said that an American machine gunner had shone a high-powered flashlight at the car while firing the first shots and had then dropped the light to be able to continue firing with both hands. The Italian report accused the "inexperienced" American unit of acting instinctively and under stress and declared that it was "undeniably certain" that the Americans knew of the presence of the two Italians in Baghdad, adding that the later removal of the car itself, as well as the destruction of U.S. military logs, had precluded a proper inquiry. In Rome magistrates continued their own investigation and months later examined the car, which was shipped to Italy after being purchased in Iraq.

In July Berlusconi summoned the U.S. ambassador for the fourth time following a report in the *Washington Post* that in February 2003 the CIA had, with the prior knowledge of Italian intelligence, kidnapped from Milan and taken to Egypt for torture Abu Omar, an Egyptian imam suspected of links with terrorism. A junior minister testified that the report was false and denied that the Italian government had authorized such an operation.

A simmering scandal centring on Antonio Fazio, governor of the supposedly impartial Bank of Italy, finally exploded in September when prosecutors in Rome disclosed that Fazio faced a charge of abuse of authority after having been under investigation for a takeover bid that he had authorized in July despite opposition from the bank's own inspectors. Berlusconi told Parliament that Fazio's governorship was no longer "compatible with the international credibility of our country" but that he had failed to induce the governor to resign. In refusing to quit, Fazio had remained within the legal rights of his lifetime appointment. Economy Minister Domenico Siniscalco resigned, however, and was replaced by the man he had supplanted in 2004, Giulio Tremonti, who promptly forbade Fazio to speak for Italy at a World Bank meeting in Washington, D.C. Prosecutors reportedly wanted Fazio to explain why in July he had given the green light for the Italian Banca Popolare Italiana (BPI) to bid for Italy's far-larger Antonveneta Bank despite a more solid rival bid by the Dutch bank

ABN Amro. In a taped phone conversation, BPI president Gianpiero Fiorani—on hearing from Fazio of the authorization—exclaimed, "I'd kiss you on the forehead!" The two men were close friends, and Fazio was widely known to oppose foreigners' moving in on Italian banks. Prosecutors wanted to know if Fazio had been aware of alleged irregularities on the part of Fiorani, which had led to the freezing of BPI's bid by Italy's stock-market regulator, to Fiorani's suspension as bank president, and eventually to the charges by prosecutors of market rigging, false accounting, abuse of authority, and obstructionism. The investigators also sought to question Fazio on how BPI had managed to boost its financial ability to be able to compete for Antonveneta.

In September, after a nine-year trial, a Milan court acquitted Berlusconi on a charge of having "cooked the books" of his Fininvest empire between 1988 and 1995. The case was dismissed on the grounds that under a 2002 law—passed by Berlusconi's government—false accounting was no longer a criminal offense. The verdict raised to 12 the number of cases that had been brought against Berlusconi and then "neutralized."　　　　(DEREK WILSON)

JAMAICA

Area: 10,991 sq km (4,244 sq mi)
Population (2005 est.): 2,736,000
Capital: Kingston
Chief of state: Queen Elizabeth II, represented by Governor-General Sir Howard Cooke
Head of government: Prime Minister Percival J. Patterson

Experienced Jamaican politician Bruce Golding in February 2005 assumed the leadership of the official opposition Jamaica Labour Party, replacing longtime JLP leader and former prime minister Edward Seaga. In April Golding also took over Seaga's West Kingston seat in a by-election and thus consolidated his hold on the party by taking charge of the JLP MPs in Parliament.

In April Jamaica began considering whether its old sugar industry had a future exporting against the background of analysts' predictions that as many as 40,000 jobs could be lost owing to changes in the EU preferential price-quota system. Another option was to use raw sugar to feed into value-added products, such as ethanol, rather than exporting it directly.

The two main political parties, the governing People's National Party (PNP) and the JLP, decided in May to require their elected members publicly to disavow ties to criminal gangs operating in the country. This followed a demand by business groups that MPs no longer be seen to be giving "comfort" to gang leaders.

In another attempt to kick-start so-far-unsuccessful efforts to find oil in Jamaica, the government offered 24 offshore and onshore blocks to international companies in an auction that closed in July. The outcome was considered a disappointment, however; only three companies showed interest. Jamaica's oil-import bill was expected to top $1.2 billion in 2005. In September the JLP led protests against government-imposed price increases for water, electricity, and public transport.   (DAVID RENWICK)

JAPAN

Area: 377,899 sq km (145,908 sq mi)
Population (2005 est.): 128,085,000
Capital: Tokyo
Symbol of state: Emperor Akihito
Head of government: Prime Minister Junichiro Koizumi

Domestic Affairs. An election that nobody wanted produced a hallmark in Japanese politics in 2005 that nobody expected. For the first time since the end of World War II, Japanese voters handed a government more than two-thirds of the seats in the powerful lower house of the Diet (parliament). The September 11 election came about as a result of Prime Minister Junichiro Koizumi's refusal to accept defeat on postal reform—a goal he had been seeking throughout much of his political career. In early August some 30 members of Koizumi's own Liberal Democratic Party (LDP) joined the opposition in the upper house of the Diet to vote down Koizumi's plan to privatize

© Yuriko Nakao/Reuters/Corbis

In September elections Japan's ruling Liberal Democratic Party won in a landslide that also saw a record number of women elected to seats in the Diet. Three of these (from left)—Yukari Sato, Satsuki Katayama, and Kuniko Inoguchi—enjoy their victory.

Japan's postal service, the country's largest savings and insurance institution. The plan had earlier passed the lower house by a mere five votes. Rejecting the advice of advisers who warned him against staging an election when his party was split, Koizumi carried through on his threats to dissolve the lower house should his privatization bills end in defeat. He then purged antireform members of his party and handpicked high-profile, pro-reform candidates (described by the media as "assassins") to run against them. The prime minister also made a direct appeal to voters for postal reform and declared that he would resign if his coalition government lost its majority "even by one seat."

Koizumi's gamble paid off. Predictions that Japanese voters would for the first time carry out a change of government evaporated as the LDP won the largest percentage of seats in any election since 1969 and scored the biggest-ever single-election gain. With the LDP claiming 296 of the 480 contested seats (a pickup of 84 seats) and its coalition partner, the Buddhist-backed New Komeito Party, taking another 31 seats, the ruling coalition increased its presence in the lower house to a commanding 327 seats. The main opposition Democratic Party of Japan (DPJ) saw its share dwindle from 175 to 113 seats. So overwhelming was the coalition victory that leaders of both

the LDP and the New Komeito Party called for Koizumi to continue serving as prime minister after his term as party president ended in September 2006. Koizumi, however, said that he had promised many times to step down on schedule and would not change his mind now.

DPJ leader Katsuya Okada resigned even before the vote counting ended. He was replaced by Seiji Maehara, who at the age of 43 became the youngest Japanese politician ever selected to head a major party. In a vote by party members, Maehara, an expert on security issues who favoured strong ties with the U.S., won by two votes over former DPJ leader Naoto Kan. Maehara promised to "revitalize" the DPJ, eliminate waste in government spending, and push for a revision of Japan's no-war constitution to include the right of "collective self-defense."

Several factors that had an impact on the election underscored the current strength of the LDP. One was that an unprecedented number of highly qualified women agreed to run for the LDP instead of for the opposition. A record 26 female LDP candidates won seats. A second factor was the resumption of political contributions to the LDP from the powerful Japan Keidanren, a pro-business lobby group. In 1994 the group had halted contributions when the LDP appeared to be losing power. Another factor was the success of politicians who took over seats in the Diet formerly occupied by their fathers, grandfathers, or other relatives. Of all winning candidates this time, 125 won "inherited seats." Of those, 107 were Liberal Democrats.

The only negative for the LDP was its continuing reliance upon the New Komeito Party. Drawing upon members of a Buddhist laymen's group, the Soka Gakkai, who were expected to support the party as part of their religious practices, the New Komeito had been a coalition partner of the LDP since 1999. It had backed Liberal Democratic candidates running in single-seat districts in exchange for the LDP's support for the New Komeito's proportional representation lists from which the bulk of its politicians was elected. Many Japanese observers believed that the LDP could not win a majority without the New Komeito's support.

In the aftermath of the election, Koizumi returned his postal reform bills to the Diet, where the legislation sailed through the lower house and won approval in the upper house by a 134–100 vote in October. Privatization of the postal service was to be completed in stages by the year 2017, with shares going on sale to the public beginning in 2007. Whether the postal service's estimated ¥330 trillion (about $2.9 trillion) in assets would actually be put under the control of the private sector and how many jobs the privatized postal company would maintain remained unclear.

By year's end, speculation had begun to mount over possible successors to the prime minister. Shinzo Abe, the 51-year-old chief cabinet secretary, was viewed by many as the front-runner, but he, like Koizumi and Yasuo Fukuda, 69, a former chief cabinet secretary who also was touted as a potential leader, belonged to the faction of LDP politicians headed by former prime minister Yoshiro Mori. Choosing a third consecutive prime minister from the same faction would violate the ruling party's tradition of balancing power. Other possibilities were Finance Minister Sadakazu Tanigaki, 60, and Taro Aso, 65, who was appointed foreign minister in a new cabinet Koizumi formed on October 31.

The Economy. The Japanese economy took an upturn in 2005. Stock prices rose 40.2%, the biggest spurt since 1986, while corporate profits expanded and unemployment dropped. The government announced that the economy grew at an annualized rate of 5.3%

during the first quarter of the year and at an annualized 3.3% during the second quarter. *The Economist* magazine predicted that Japan's economy would grow by 2.2% in 2005 and by 2% in 2006—better than the average 1% real annual growth since 1992. Toshihiko Fukui, governor of the Bank of Japan, indicated that by the third quarter of 2005, rising oil prices had begun to "subdue" growth but would not send it back into decline.

Fukui also pointed to the likelihood that by the summer of 2006, the central bank would move away from its decade-long policy of suppressing interest rates to virtually zero. Koizumi opposed such a move, however. "It's too early. Deflation still exists," he declared in mid-November. Fukui admitted that the zero-interest policy had deprived Japanese households of interest income totaling ¥154 trillion (about $1.34 trillion) between 1993 and 2002. Nonetheless, Fitch Ratings, in a special report issued on May 6, predicted that Japan could grow 2% a year in real terms over the next five years, with corporate investment providing the main domestic driving force. Externally, Japan's burgeoning trade with China and the U.S. provided a huge prop.

According to figures announced in September by the National Tax Agency, average wages for full-time employees in 2004 fell to ¥4.39 million (about $38,000), down 1.2% from the previous year. Much of the decline occurred as companies hired more part-time workers to trim personnel costs. The percentage of workers who were not in full-time jobs rose to 35% in 2004. Japan's unemployment rate, however, dropped to 4.2% in June—the lowest it had been since mid-1998.

In central Tokyo a construction boom helped drive up land prices for the first time after 15 years of decline. In Nagoya, Japan's fourth largest city, the new Chubu International Airport opened—astonishingly ¥130 billion (about $1.13 billion) under budget. The 2005 World Expo, held over the course of six months in central Aichi prefecture, was an overwhelming success. The event attracted an estimated 22 million visitors—7 million more than originally anticipated—and infused some ¥1.3 trillion (about $11.3 billion) into the regional economy.

Major corporations in Japan announced new plans during the year that were aimed at trimming losses. Sony Corp. unveiled a plan to slash 10,000 jobs and close 11 factories as the once

high-flying electronics and entertainment giant faced its first annual loss in more than a decade. In March Sony appointed Howard Stringer (*see* BIOGRAPHIES) its chairman and CEO. Sanyo Electric said that it would eliminate 15,000 jobs by 2008, but as it later announced an outlook for a 72% drop in operating profits, the company decided to move up 10,000 of the cuts to January 2006. Wal-Mart Stores, Inc., announced that it would spend ¥68 billion (about $600 million) to take over control of Seiyu as the Japanese supermarket chain projected its fourth consecutive loss since the American giant first purchased a stake in the company in 2002.

Mitsubishi UFJ Financial Group, Inc., came into existence on October 1 as the world's largest banking group in terms of assets. The Bank of Tokyo-Mitsubishi and UFJ Bank were scheduled to join the group on Jan. 1, 2006, and become its core units. The new group would hold an estimated ¥190 trillion (about $1.64 trillion) in assets—a sum that was roughly 40% of Japan's GDP. It would assume responsibility for repaying the ¥1.5 trillion (about $12.9 billion) that the government had injected into UFJ Bank to help it clean up its bad loans. Repayment was to be completed by March 2008.

Deaths exceeded births by about 10,000 persons, which indicated that Japan's decline in population had started two years earlier than expected.

Foreign Affairs. Although Prime Minister Koizumi's cozy relations with U.S. Pres. George W. Bush continued, Japan's overall diplomacy suffered a series of setbacks in 2005.

Frictions with China reached a new high. The trouble began when Japan's Ministry of Education approved a textbook for use in junior high schools that mentioned only that "many" Chinese were victimized during the 1937–38 Nanking Massacre without describing details of the mass atrocities of murder and rape committed by the Japanese military while destroying the Chinese city. Although fewer than 1% of the schools in Japan actually selected the textbook, demonstrations ensued in Beijing, Shanghai, and other Chinese cities that turned into near riots. Chinese police stood by as more than 10,000 protesters hurled bottles, stones and other objects at the Japanese embassy in Beijing and consulate general in Shanghai. Vandals also trashed private shops that served Japanese food or sold Japanese goods.

The Japanese government issued an official protest on April 16 against China's failure to halt the vandalism. When Foreign Minister Nobutaka Machimura demanded an apology and payment for damages, his Chinese counterpart, Li Zhaoxing, responded that "the Chinese government has never done anything for which it has to apologize to the Japanese people." Later, when Vice Premier Wu Yi became the most senior Chinese official to have visited Japan in two years, Japanese exploded with anger after Wu flew home on May 23 without a word of apology, snubbing a scheduled meeting with Koizumi. Beijing officials explained that her abrupt departure was meant to protest remarks that Koizumi had made justifying his visits to the Yasukuni Shrine in Tokyo, where Japan's war dead—including 14 World War II leaders executed for "war crimes"— were enshrined. On June 7 Machimura called China's criticism of the Yasukuni visits "absurd" and defended the controversial textbook.

The uproar attracted major international attention, inducing Koizumi to make two blanket apologies on top of some 20 previous statements of remorse for Japan's wartime aggression and colonialism. He made one of the apologies at a meeting of Asian and African nations in Jakarta and the other in Tokyo on the 60th anniversary of the end of World War II. Nonetheless, as an autumn religious festival began at Yasukuni on October 17, Koizumi paid his fifth visit to the shrine since he became prime minister in 2001. China and South Korea immediately protested, and China canceled a scheduled visit to Beijing by Foreign Minister Machimura. Koizumi declared that he visited the shrine to pay respects to Japan's war dead and to pledge that Japan would remain "a country of peace that will never launch a war again." Foreign governments, he added, "should not intervene in a matter of the heart" for Japanese people.

Also exacerbating relations between Japan and China were disputes over an island chain held by Japan in the South China Sea, Chinese drilling for natural gas in waters near Japan's exclusive economic zone, and Japan's worries about burgeoning increases in China's military budget. In addition, China launched a campaign against Japan's bid to win a permanent seat on the UN Security Council. (*See* CHINA: *Sidebar.*) Although President Bush and U.S. Secretary of State Condoleezza

Rice, during separate visits to Japan, declared that Washington supported Japan's becoming a permanent member of the UN Security Council, both refrained from offering to Japan veto power that was now held by all of the current permanent Security Council members, including China. American officials explained that the U.S. did not want to weaken the decision-making power of the council. The snub, however, dealt a major blow to Japan's prestige. In September Machimura announced that Japan would seek to reduce its 19.4% share of contributions to the UN budget—an amount that exceeded the combined 15.3% that permanent members Britain, France, China, and Russia paid together. Japan's payments ranked second only to those of the U.S., which contributed 22% of the UN budget.

Lesser issues with the U.S. added irritations to the Tokyo-Washington relationship throughout the year. By September, U.S. congressmen demanded that the White House impose sanctions against Japan for failing to lift a ban on imports of American beef imposed in 2003 when a single cow in Washington state had tested positive for mad cow disease. Only in December did Japan finally lift the ban after asserting that the U.S. had to limit its exports to cattle not older than 20 months (an age group in which no cases of mad cow disease had been found). Japan and the U.S. finally agreed—after nine years of negotiations—on a plan to relocate a U.S. Marine air station on the island of Okinawa. Ambassador Thomas Schieffer, meanwhile, announced that the U.S. Navy would base a nuclear-powered aircraft carrier for the first time at the Yokosuka naval base after the conventionally powered USS *Kitty Hawk* was decommissioned in 2008. Local residents in both Okinawa and Yokosuka immediately opposed the moves despite a revelation that 7,000 Marines would be relocated to Guam "to reduce the footprint" of American troops in Japan. In December, Koizumi authorized an extension for up to one year of Japan's deployment of 550 noncombat troops in Iraq.

New tensions arose in Japan's relations with the two Koreas. South Korean Pres. Roh Moo Hyun retracted a promise to stop making a political issue of Japan's colonial rule of Korea and condemned Japan for continuing to claim sovereignty over two tiny islands off the coast of South Korea. North Korea, which Koizumi had visited twice in an attempt to establish diplomatic rela-

tions, told Japan that negotiations were "finished" over Tokyo's demands for detailed explanations of what had happened to the more than 100 Japanese citizens believed to have been abducted by North Korean agents between the 1970s and the late '90s.

Relations with Russia, meanwhile, remained in a stalemate. Even before he visited Tokyo in November, Pres. Vladimir Putin declared in a televised "town hall" meeting with Russian citizens in September that four northern islands claimed by Japan were "under Russian sovereignty"—a status he said was "fixed in international law." He and Koizumi agreed to enlarge business cooperation but were unable to issue any statement on the territorial dispute. Soviet troops had seized the four islands off the coast of Hokkaido after World War II ended. The two countries restored diplomatic relations in 1956, but they had yet to sign a peace treaty.

(SAM JAMESON)

JORDAN

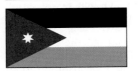

Area: 89,342 sq km (34,495 sq mi)
Population (2005 est.): 5,182,000 (including about 1,800,000 Palestinian refugees, most of whom hold Jordanian citizenship)
Capital: Amman
Head of state and government: King Abdullah II, assisted by Prime Ministers Faisal al-Fayez and, from April 7, Adnan Badran

In 2005 Jordan's King Abdullah II continued his active involvement in the Israeli-Palestinian peace process. He participated in the summit negotiations in Sharm al-Shaykh, Egypt, on February 8 that brought together Israeli Prime Minister Ariel Sharon, Palestinian Pres. Mahmoud Abbas, and the host, Egyptian Pres. Hosni Mubarak. Meeting again with Abbas in the Jordanian capital on October 16, Abdullah confirmed that Jordan would exert all its efforts on the regional and international level to ensure the continuation of the Mideast peace process.

In early December 2004 the king had expressed apprehension that if militant Shi'ites beholden to Iran were to take over power in Iraq "a Shi'ite crescent" could result in the Middle East linking

© Shawn Baldwin/Corbis

Explosions on November 9 in the Radisson, Days Inn, and Hyatt hotels in Amman brought the violence in the Middle East directly to Jordan. The destruction in this room, used for wedding receptions in the Radisson Hotel, was typical of the damage.

Iran, Iraq, Syria, and Lebanon. Jordanian-Iraqi relations worsened when a Jordanian suicide bomber killed more than 120 Iraqis in the predominantly Shi'ite city of Hilla, Iraq, on Feb. 28, 2005. The suspected bomber's family held a public condolence service, which led to demonstrations outside the Jordanian embassy in Baghdad by thousands of Iraqi Shi'ites on March 18. The protesters burned Jordanian flags and pictures of King Abdullah and demanded an official apology. In order to mend relations, Iraqi Pres. Jalal Talabani traveled for an official visit to Amman on May 7 and was given a red-carpet reception and a 21-gun salute. The Iraqi and Jordanian leaders issued a statement expressing their determination to wage all-out war against terrorism.

Asked on April 5 to form a government, Adnan Badran, an academic, assembled a cabinet that after a July 3 reshuffle consisted of 28 members, including 3 women. The major agenda of the new cabinet was to modernize laws and legislation and fight corruption. The Islamic Action Front, an Islamist parliamentary bloc, constituted Badran's main opposition. On July 21 the new cabinet received a vote of confidence. Badran's cabinet was determined to introduce reforms especially in education, culture, and media. As

deputy prime minister, veteran diplomat Marwan Muasher was tapped to spearhead the government's anticorruption and reform-minded program and took on the task of selling the reforms to the Jordanian people.

On November 9 the Hyatt, Days Inn, and Radisson hotels in Amman were attacked by three suicide bombers; 58 people were killed and scores of others wounded. It was confirmed that al-Qaeda was behind the operation and that the bombings were masterminded by Jordanian-born Abu Musab al-Zarqawi. King Abdullah called these terrorists "heretics of Islam" and said that "terrorism is a sick and cross-border phenomenon. Therefore, eradicating it is the whole world's responsibility."

(MARIUS K. DEEB)

KAZAKHSTAN

Area: 2,724,900 sq km (1,052,090 sq mi)
Population (2005 est.): 15,186,000
Capital: Astana
Head of state and government: President Nursultan Nazarbayev, assisted by Prime Minister Daniyal Akhmetov

Authoritarian tendencies increased in Kazakhstan's political life during 2005; some observers attributed the government's growing intolerance of opposition to the run-up to the presidential election in December. In the event, incumbent Pres. Nursultan Nazarbayev won a third seven-year term in office with 91% of the vote; foreign observers stated that the election fell short of international standards. The most common explanation for the government's actions was that the Kazakh leadership feared that the country could experience a political overturn such as had occurred in Georgia, Ukraine, and, in March 2005, neighbouring Kyrgyzstan. The danger of such a "revolution" to the country's social and economic stability was a frequent theme in the public statements of President Nazarbayev and other government officials.

In early January one of the country's major opposition political parties, the Democratic Choice of Kazakhstan (DVK), was shut down by court order for having allegedly called publicly for civil disobedience in protest against the outcome of parliamentary elections in 2004. An appeal against the court order failed in February, and other political parties saw the fate of the DVK as a precedent that would be used against others. In the same month, the most important opposition parties announced that they would back a single candidate in the presidential contest; they chose former parliamentary speaker Zharmakan Tuyakbay, a former leader of the pro-presidential Otan Party who had joined the opposition in protest against vote rigging in the 2004 election. In April Parliament adopted a law banning protest rallies before election results were announced; the opposition declared that the law would restrict rights of citizens that were guaranteed in the constitution.

Kazakhstan's independent media also fared poorly in 2005, with a number of major publications being closed by court order or being forced out of business by large fines. In a speech in May, Nazarbayev rejected unlimited freedom of speech, reacting to a rally in Almaty in support of free speech, in which participants called on the government to stop persecuting the media for criticizing the authorities.

In mid-July Parliament adopted a law strengthening government control over nongovernmental organizations, especially NGO funding from foreign sources. This action was explained by supporters and opponents of the legislation as a reaction to assertions in the Russian and other regional media that foreign funding had played a major role in events in Georgia and Ukraine. Kazakhstan NGOs protested the restrictions, and in August the Constitutional Court declared the law unconstitutional.

During the year Kazakhstan drew closer to the Russian Federation as Kazakh officials praised Russia as a bulwark against political instability.

(BESS BROWN)

KENYA

Area: 582,646 sq km (224,961 sq mi)
Population (2005 est.): 33,830,000
Capital: Nairobi
Head of state and government: President Mwai Kibaki

On November 21 two elderly Masai are shown the way to the polling station by a Kenyan army officer. The couple are going to vote in a referendum on the country's new constitution.

Clashes in Kenya in January 2005 between Masai pastoralists and Kikuyu farmers over access to water supplies resulted in several deaths and the displacement of hundreds of people. Mindful of the importance of agriculture and cattle ranching to Kenya's economy, Pres. Mwai Kibaki on February 23 announced plans to assist the country's farmers. He also said that the government had launched an economic-recovery program for the mainly pastoralist region in the north and northeast. Nevertheless, similar clashes took place in March, April, and July between rival groups of Borana and Gabra pastoralists in the semiarid region along the border with Ethiopia and Somalia. These skirmishes exacerbated the problems already caused by prolonged drought. In May, however, flash floods drove thousands of people from their homes in the west and the northeast.

The government's alleged failure to fulfill its electoral promise to tackle corruption at the highest levels attracted the most attention both inside and outside the country. A survey by the World Bank and the Kenya Institute for Public Policy Research claimed that the awarding of government contracts was still subject to bribery. Early in the year Sir Edward Clay, the British high commissioner in Nairobi,

renewed his verbal attacks on government corruption. His remarks resonated on February 7 when John Githongo, Kibaki's highly regarded adviser in the president's anticorruption campaign, resigned. Githongo complained that he was not getting adequate support.

Following Clay's lead, the Canadian high commissioner announced that Canada could not continue to give aid that would only be pocketed by fraudulent businessmen or corrupt civil servants. The U.S. government in turn decided to suspend its $2.5 million in funding for Kenya's anticorruption campaign. Public opinion in Kenya also began to turn against Kibaki because of his apparent reluctance to act decisively against senior members of his government who were widely believed to be involved in fraud. The president was in a difficult position; he had come to power at the head of an unlikely coalition of political parties, the leaders of which had only two aims in common—to overthrow then president Daniel arap Moi and to take office themselves. To antagonize any one of them now might seriously damage an already fragile grouping.

In July police dispersed demonstrators in Nairobi who were protesting that the government was assuming the right to amend a draft constitution

that had been prepared by a constituent committee. The draft contained a number of contentious proposals, notably the suggestion that a strong prime minister be appointed who could act as a check on the powers of the president. The protesters' fears were compounded when the parliament voted against that measure on July 22. The opposition, which included several members of Kibaki's cabinet, showed its strength in November when the president put the draft constitution, as revised by the parliament, to a national referendum. The motion was defeated, with 57% of the voters opposing it. Kibaki then dismissed the entire cabinet and banned political demonstrations. Early in December he swore in a new cabinet but was immediately accused of appointing only timeservers or members of his own clan.

In midyear Washington threatened to suspend payment of military aid if the government refused to sign a bilateral agreement granting U.S. soldiers serving in Kenya immunity from being handed over to the International Court of Justice. In September, however, UN agencies joined the Kenyan government in appealing to the U.S. for $29 million to feed the 1.2 million people who still needed food aid.

(KENNETH INGHAM)

KIRIBATI

Area: 811 sq km (313 sq mi)
Population (2005 est.): 95,300
Capital: Government offices on three islets of South Tarawa
Head of state and government: President Anote Tong

In 2005 Kiribati was in the diplomatic spotlight as it joined the International Whaling Commission, which continued to focus on the debate between whaling nations, especially Japan, and those that promoted bans on both commercial and scientific whaling (the latter of which was seen as a device for circumventing the commercial ban). With Japan accused of seeking to buy votes in the IWC with aid funds, the issue remained controversial for small Pacific Island countries.

In May 2005 Taiwanese Pres. Chen Shui-bian visited Kiribati and other countries in the region with which Taipei had diplomatic relations. In 2003 Kiribati had shifted its formal recognition from Beijing to Taiwan. During Chen's visit the police banned demonstrations (both for and against the current arrangement). Taiwan also had a role in resolving difficulties in Nauru's phosphate-mining industry. As part of a regional aid contribution, Taipei agreed to meet the $3.5 million cost of repatriating 1,000 workers from Kiribati and Tuvalu who had been unpaid for a year and stranded on Nauru.

To address urban overcrowding and public health issues on South Tarawa, the government of Pres. Anote Tong sought to decentralize some services to regional centres. (BARRIE MACDONALD)

KOREA, DEMOCRATIC PEOPLE'S REPUBLIC OF

Area: 122,762 sq km (47,399 sq mi)
Population (2005 est.): 22,488,000
Capital: Pyongyang
Head of state and government: Chairman of the National Defense Commission Kim Jong Il

Cooling tower with small steam plume →

A satellite image of North Korea's Yongbyon five-megawatt (electric) nuclear reactor site dated September 11 shows a steam plume, which indicates that the facility is in operation.

North Korea ended 2005 with a tenuous agreement, forged in September, to end its nuclear-weapons program. It had spent much of the year in negotiations in Beijing, where meetings were held involving six countries—North Korea, South Korea, China, Japan, Russia, and the United States. Though the talks were dominated by North Korea and the United States, South Korea and China played positive roles in the process.

South Korea announced in July and reaffirmed in September that it would provide electrical energy to North Korea. It was hoped that this provision might lessen demands by North Korea that South Korea, the United States, and Japan pay for construction of a new nuclear-generating light-water reactor to replace the heavy-water reactors that had been at the centre of the controversy for several years. Heavy-water reactors could easily produce radioactive material that could be used in making nuclear weapons.

The greatest breakthrough in the difficult nuclear disarmament talks came when on September 19 North Korea announced that it would abandon its nuclear-weapons program. Within days of the declaration, however, Pyongyang stated that prior to relinquishing its program, it wanted the civilian light-water reactor to be built. When the six-party talks resumed in November, at the top of the agenda was the clarification of the July agreement. Although progress was made, the finer points of agreement and implementation would continue to take time and further negotiations.

Progress between North Korea and South Korea, however, was substantial. Exchanges of visitors increased at all levels. Government delegations at the ministerial level made visits to each other's capitals; sporting events took place (marathons for unification in which runners from both Pyongyang and Seoul participated); and reunions were held in August and November that brought together family members who had been separated. In addition, the special tourist zone in the Diamond Mountains, just north of the border between the two countries, celebrated the arrival of its one millionth visitor from South Korea. In November the two countries agreed in principle to have their athletes compete as a unified team at the 2008 Olympic Games in Beijing.

Periodically, refugees who had fled North Korea and hidden in China would make their way to safety in South Korea. There were an estimated 200,000 North Korean escapees hiding in China. (MARK PETERSON)

KOREA, REPUBLIC OF

Area: 99,601 sq km (38,456 sq mi)
Population (2005 est.): 48,294,000
Capital: Seoul
Head of state and government: President Roh Moo Hyun, assisted by Prime Minister Lee Hai Chan

The split between South Korea and its longtime ally the United States over policy toward North Korea marked many of the events of 2005. Since the outbreak of the Korean War in 1950, the U.S. and South Korea had maintained a close military alliance vis-à-vis their common enemy, North Korea, and though both countries agreed on the objective—defense against possible hostilities from North Korea and eventual reunification—they began to diverge from concordance on the method of achieving that objective.

South Korea had moved farther to the left in such matters as the election in 2002 of a new president and in its attitude toward North Korea, whereas the U.S. had moved farther to the right under the policies of Pres. George W. Bush. In 2005 South Korea continued

© You Sung-Ho/Reuters/Corbis

In March South Korean demonstrators loudly protest a declaration by a Japanese prefectural assembly of a Takeshima Day. The protesters objected that the declaration added weight to Japanese claims of authority over a group of tiny islands, which Japan called Takeshima and Koreans called Tokdo, lying between Japan and South Korea.

to pursue a policy of engagement with North Korea, aimed at increased levels of trade, economic assistance, and visitor exchanges, while the U.S. continued its confrontational rhetoric regarding North Korea's cessation of nuclear-weapons production.

South Korea increased trade with both the U.S. and North Korea and moved up one notch to become the U.S.'s seventh largest trading partner. In addition, Seoul replaced Beijing as the single-largest trading partner with North Korea.

South Korean–Japanese relations deteriorated on two fronts. The first was an argument over the ownership of an island group that South Korea called Tokdo and that Japan referred to as Takeshima (some maps used a neutral term—the Liancourt Rocks). The issue came to the fore when the Shimane Prefectural Assembly—not the Japanese government—declared that February 22 was Takeshima Day. The South Korean government immediately lodged protests with the Japanese government, which said that it could not become involved in local matters. The second issue, which had boiled to the surface in the past, involved the issuance of Japanese history books that South Korea and China charged had toned down the atrocities committed by Japanese soldiers during World War II. A solution was reached, however, when South Korea, China, and Japan

formed a committee to write a history acceptable to all parties.

Pres. Roh Moo Hyun made four overseas trips that were a boost to his sagging approval ratings at home. He visited seven countries: Costa Rica, Germany, Mexico, Russia, Turkey, Uzbekistan, and the U.S. twice, including one stop in New York City to address the United Nations. In addition, Roh played host in June to Japanese Prime Minister Junichiro Koizumi. The crowning event of the year, however, was South Korea's hosting in November of the 13th Asia-Pacific Economic Cooperation (APEC) meeting, where leaders of 21 countries in the Pacific region attended meetings in Pusan.

On the domestic front, a controversial redevelopment project that included the removal of the overhead Cheonggye Highway—which was built during the 1970s and covered a hopelessly polluted stream and blighted area but provided a rapid exit from downtown Seoul to the east side of town and eastern suburbs—turned into an unmitigated success. Though Mayor Lee Myung Bak's plan to tear down the crumbling highway and restore the stream was initially met with skepticism, concerns about greater traffic congestion were swept away after the stream was restored and beautifully landscaped along its banks with bridges, stepping stones, walkways, and jogging/biking paths. These areas became a tourist attraction and an example of an urban-beautification success story.   (MARK PETERSON)

KUWAIT

Area: 17,818 sq km (6,880 sq mi)
Population (2005 est.): 2,847,000
Capital: Kuwait
Head of state and government: Emir Sheikh Jabir al-Ahmad al-Jabir al-Sabah, assisted by Prime Minister Sheikh Sabah al-Ahmad al-Jabir al-Sabah

Security forces were active in uncovering the mounting activities of Islamic extremists in Kuwait in 2005. In January the country witnessed several armed confrontations between police and members of militant Islamic groups organized in underground cells.

The confrontations left several dead and wounded. Soon after, more than 30 people linked to the Lions of the Peninsula—a militant group that allegedly took part in the clashes and was suspected of planning attacks on U.S. troops—were arrested, and in December a Kuwaiti court sentenced six to death. In an effort to quell religious extremism, the government undertook several measures, including an amnesty for those surrendering their arms and closer surveillance of mosques and religious associations.

On January 29, in an unprecedented move, several Islamist personalities announced the establishment of Hizb al-Umma ("the Nation's Party"). This not only was the first such organization in Kuwait but represented the first time a political party had been publicly established in any Gulf Cooperation Council country. Hizb al-Umma leaders demanded that they be allowed to register as a party, but the Kuwaiti government refused, emphasizing that Kuwaiti law did not allow political parties.

The year also saw major improvements in the status of women in Kuwait. After years of unsuccessful efforts by the government and Kuwaiti women to compel the conservative parliament to grant women the right to vote and run for office, the parliament finally amended the election law to give women these rights. The vote of approval was 35 to 23. Soon after, on June 12, Masouma al-Mubarak, a U.S.-educated professor, was appointed planning minister, the first woman to serve as a cabinet member in Kuwait. Women were expected to register and

Masouma al-Mubarak, who took over responsibility for Kuwait's Ministry of Planning from Sheikh Ahmad al-Abdullah al-Ahmad al-Sabah (left) in June, was her country's first woman minister.

© Stephanie McGehee/Reuters/Corbis

vote in the country's parliamentary election in 2007.

The Shi'ites in Kuwait were able to achieve some of their demands in the spring when Prime Minister Sheikh Sabah al-Ahmad al-Jabir al-Sabah agreed to allow them to have their own *husainiyyas*—religious clubs or associations in which people gathered to perform religious ceremonies and social functions. In addition, Shi'ites would be allowed to establish a *hawza,* or religious seminary, to teach Shi'ite theology. (LOUAY BAHRY)

KYRGYZSTAN

Area: 198,500 sq km (76,641 sq mi)
Population (2005 est.): 5,146,000
Capital: Bishkek
Head of state: Presidents Askar Akayev (de jure to April 11; actually deposed March 24), Ishenbay Kadyrbekov (acting) on March 24–25, and, from March 25, Kurmanbek Bakiyev
Head of government (appointed by the president): Prime Ministers Nikolay Tanayev, Kurmanbek Bakiyev from March 25, and, from August 15, Feliks Kulov

Kyrgyzstan drew international attention in March 2005 when it became the first Central Asian country in which popular disaffection had forced the post-Soviet regime out of office. The anger of large segments of the population had been growing for many years; there was a widespread conviction that the millions of dollars of international aid that had been given to the country to counter the effects of the post-1991 economic collapse and resulting poverty had been siphoned off by corrupt relatives and cronies of Kyrgyzstan's first president, Askar Akayev.

A parliamentary election was held on February 27, preceded by a campaign in which Akayev accused the political opposition of trying to destabilize the country. Prime Minister Nikolay Tanayev called on international organizations not to try to import revolution to Kyrgyzstan, and other top officials warned of the possibility of a civil war. Opposition rallies and the independent media were severely harassed. Election authorities disqualified a number of popular candidates, including former foreign

© Vladimir Pirogov/Reuters/Corbis

On March 21 elderly citizens of Jalal-Abad in southern Kyrgyzstan rally against the president, Askar Akayev, and the improper conduct of recent elections. A few days later Akayev was deposed and forced to flee the country.

minister Roza Otunbayeva, sparking demonstrations in various parts of the country. The day after the election, large-scale protests against alleged vote rigging began in Bishkek and in the south.

On March 4 some 300 protesters stormed the regional administration building in the southern city of Jalal-Abad, while 2,000 protesters in the main square called on the president to resign. Akayev reacted by asserting that "irresponsible politicians" were fomenting unrest. On March 18 protesters in Osh, the country's "southern capital," set up an alternate administration headed by a prominent opposition member. On March 24 protesters in Bishkek stormed government buildings; Akayev and his family fled the country. The unrest in Bishkek and other cities was accompanied by massive looting and a number of fatalities; Kurmanbek Bakiyev (*see* BIOGRAPHIES), a former prime minister and head of the opposition People's Movement of Kyrgyzstan, took over as interim leader with the blessing of the Constitutional Court. He formed an interim government of prominent opposition figures. Opposition leader Feliks Kulov was released from prison and given responsibility to restore order.

A presidential election was set for July 10, at which Bakiyev received almost 89% of the vote. In a preelection deal with his most credible rival, Bakiyev had promised the premiership to Kulov. Stresses appeared in the new government within a few months, however, and in September the parliament

elected in February rejected several of Bakiyev's ministerial appointees, sparking rumours that Kulov too would be forced to resign. (BESS BROWN)

LAOS

Area: 236,800 sq km (91,429 sq mi)
Population (2005 est.): 5,924,000
Capital: Vientiane
Chief of state: President Khamtay Siphandone
Head of government: Prime Minister Bounngang Vorachith

For Laos 2005 was a year for self-congratulation. On Nov. 29–30, 2004, for the first time since joining the Association of Southeast Asian Nations in 1997, Laos hosted the annual ASEAN summit. This brought together not only the leaders of the 10 member states but also leaders of countries with official dialogue status (China, Japan, South Korea, India, Australia, and New Zealand). This was followed by the 38th ASEAN Ministerial Meeting in Vientiane on July 26, 2005.

Both meetings taxed the capacity of Vientiane to the maximum in terms of accommodations and security. Four small explosions were reported in the days leading up to the summit, all well outside the city limits and causing no casualties or significant damage. Security was understandably tight for both occasions, with limits imposed on the movement of people and vehicles. Elsewhere in the country, the Hmong insurgency seemed to have all but collapsed as bedraggled remnants gave themselves up to authorities.

The importance of these international meetings for Laos lay not just in the agreements signed—notably the Vientiane Action Programme (VAP), designed to reduce the socioeconomic gap between the wealthier ASEAN states and the poorer ones, including Laos—but also in the international attention Laos received and the boost given to the country's self-esteem. Establishment of an ASEAN Development Fund under the VAP was especially likely to benefit Laos.

Confidence was also boosted by the agreement of the World Bank finally to back construction of the massive $1.2 billion Nam Theun II Dam in central Laos. The dam would produce 1,070 MW of power when completed in six years. Income from the project was to be earmarked for the country's poverty-reduction program.

Laos was also looking forward to increased revenue from mining. In early 2005 copper production began at the Australian-owned mine in southern Sepone province. Other new mines were in the planning stage elsewhere in the country. The government expected revenue from mining taxes and royalties to reach $460 million annually by 2020, a figure almost double the country's total revenue for 2003–04.

(MARTIN STUART-FOX)

LATVIA

Area: 64,589 sq km (24,938 sq mi)
Population (2005 est.): 2,299,000
Capital: Riga
Chief of state: President Vaira Vike-Freiberga
Head of government: Prime Minister Aigars Kalvitis

As a full-fledged member of the EU, NATO, and a number of other international organizations, Latvia participated actively in their work in 2005.

© ELTA/Reuters/Corbis

Latvia's first gay-pride parade goes forward in the capital, Riga, on July 23. The Riga town council had prohibited the procession on grounds that it might spark violence from antigay groups, but a court found this reasoning unjustified and reversed the ban.

The Latvian Parliament endorsed the EU constitutional treaty on June 2. On an invitation from UN Secretary-General Kofi Annan, Latvia's Pres. Vaira Vike-Freiberga served as a special envoy for UN reforms. As EU commissioner for energy, Andris Piebalgs dealt with the increasingly complex energy challenges facing Europe. Latvian doctors, policemen, and soldiers served in international missions in Iraq, Afghanistan, and the Balkans. U.S. Pres. George W. Bush visited Riga on May 7, and President Vike-Freiberga was in Georgia, Azerbaijan, and Armenia in October. Latvia opened an embassy in Turkey on April 19.

Unlike the heads of the other two Baltic States, President Vike-Freiberga accepted an invitation to attend the commemoration on May 9 in Moscow of the 60th anniversary of the end of World War II in Europe. The run-up to the event provided an opportunity for Latvia's leaders to remind the world that the Soviet Union's occupation of the Baltic states had lasted from 1940 until 1991. They welcomed the urging of international organizations that Russia, as the successor state of the U.S.S.R., condemn the occupation of the Baltic States; Russia, however, refused to do so.

In 2004 Latvia's GDP had increased by 8.5% over 2003 levels. The high growth rate continued into 2005 but was offset by a steadily rising annual inflation rate, anticipated at 6.5% (against 7.3% in 2004). The mounting cost of living, aggravated by a world-wide increase in oil and gas prices, prompted people with low incomes to stage protests and seek employment abroad. Municipal elections were held on March 12. Some politicians and traditionalists protested against Latvia's first gay-pride parade on July 23, while the mainstream of society deplored the sporadic signs of intolerance.

(DZINTRA BUNGS)

LEBANON

Area: 10,400 sq km (4,016 sq mi)
Population (2005 est.): 3,577,000 (excluding unnaturalized Palestinian refugees estimated to number about 400,000)
Capital: Beirut
Chief of state: President Gen. Émile Lahoud
Head of government: Prime Ministers Omar Karami, Najib Mikati from April 19, and, from July 19, Fouad Siniora

Lebanon had a tumultuous year in 2005. The UN Security Council reasserted its 2004 resolution, which stipulated that Syria was to evacuate its forces from Lebanon and called on the Lebanese army to take control of the southern borders and disarm all militias. These included the powerful Hezbollah, which considered itself a resistance movement and defense force

Following a massive car bombing in Beirut on February 14, a man calls for help for a wounded victim. Former prime minister Rafiq al-Hariri was killed in the blast, which shocked the citizenry and changed the course of political life in Lebanon.

© Mohamed Azakir/Reuters/Corbis

against Israel. Hezbollah enjoyed the backing of Pres. Émile Lahoud.

On February 14 former prime minister Rafiq al-Hariri was assassinated in a huge explosion in Beirut (*see* OBITUARIES); two dozen security officers and a former minister were also either killed on the spot or severely wounded. The incident heightened the tension between Lahoud and the political opposition, notably the parliamentary bloc that had been led by Hariri and Druze leader Walid Jumblatt.

Demonstrations erupted in Beirut. Hezbollah protested against the UN resolution, and the opposition replied with a demonstration on March 14 in which an estimated one million people demanded the ouster of Syrian forces and the resignation of the heads of the Lebanese security apparatus. Another UN resolution called for an international investigation of the assassination of Hariri and the removal of Syrian forces from Lebanon. An expert UN investigation team arrived later in Beirut, and its initial findings led to the arrest of the top leaders of the presidential guard, the general security apparatus, the internal security forces, and military intelligence. Citing a lack of Syrian cooperation, the UN Security Council in December extended the inquiry. Yet another resolution renewed the mandate of the UN peacekeeping forces to monitor Lebanon's southern borders for another six months.

Syrian forces withdrew from Lebanon by the end of April. Parliamentary elections were carried out in May and June, after the parliament passed motions allowing two Christian leaders to participate in them. The first of these pardoned Gen. Michel Aoun, who was living in exile in Paris; the second released Samir Geagea, who had served 11 years in prison. The opposition, led by Jumblatt and Hariri's son Saad, won the majority of seats and nominated Fouad Siniora as prime minister, but the minority party led by Aoun as well as the Amal Shi'ite coalition and Hezbollah, backed by President Lahoud, insisted on strong representation in the new government. This effectively led to a hung cabinet, in which only after great difficulty was the majority able to nominate replacements for the security chiefs accused of participation in Hariri's assassination. Lebanese-Syrian relations remained poor.

More than a dozen explosions, assassinations, and attempts on the lives of prominent journalists and politicians followed over a period of seven months, but the security forces were unable to pinpoint those responsible.

Largely owing to the security situation in Lebanon, the economic growth rate was expected to be nil in 2005, but the budget deficit to August dropped to 24.7% from 26.4% year on year. External and internal debt were at least 180% of GNP.　　(MAHMOUD HADDAD)

LESOTHO

Area: 30,355 sq km (11,720 sq mi)
Population (2005 est.): 2,031,000
Capital: Maseru
Chief of state: King Letsie III
Head of government: Prime Minister Bethuel Pakalitha Mosisili

In early May 2005 Lesotho's Independent Electoral Commission announced that the ruling Lesotho Congress for Democracy had won most of the 1,000 seats in the country's first-ever municipal election. Voter turnout was only about 30%, however, and for most people the election was clearly an irrelevance in the face of increasing poverty.

Poverty increased for a number of reasons; agricultural production continued to decline, in part because of endemic soil erosion in the very limited arable land combined with repeated droughts and in part as a consequence of the impact of the HIV/AIDS pandemic on the workforce. Up to half a million people in the rural areas of the small mountainous country suffered from food shortages. While a government Poverty Reduction Strategy Paper put the country's unemployment rate at 31%, most observers estimated that more than 70% of the workforce was jobless. Whereas in the late 1980s almost half the gross national product had come from remittances from over 120,000 migrant workers in the South African gold mines, with the retrenchment of such workers, only half that number were employed in 2005. Hopes that the textile and clothing industry would be the key engine of growth were hard hit by the end on Jan. 1, 2005, of the World Trade Organization Agreement on Textiles and Clothing. This led to the closure of a number of factories and put many of the 56,000 jobs in the sector at risk, for while Lesotho still enjoyed duty-free access to the American market under the Africa Growth and Opportunity Act, it could no longer compete with goods from countries such as China.　　(CHRISTOPHER SAUNDERS)

LIBERIA

Area: 97,754 sq km (37,743 sq mi)
Population (2005 est.): 2,900,000
Capital: Monrovia
Head of state and government: Chairman of the National Transitional Government Charles Gyude Bryant

In a runoff election on Nov. 8, 2005, Liberia made history when voters elected Africa's first woman president. With 59% of the vote, Ellen Johnson-Sirleaf overturned the impressive lead

Ellen Johnson-Sirleaf greets crowds in front of a church in Monrovia, Liberia. Several weeks after a runoff election, she was confirmed as having been elected Africa's first woman president on November 23.

that her opponent, international association football (soccer) star George Weah, had secured in the first-round voting on October 11. In that contest, according to a National Elections Commission estimate, about 1.3 million of an estimated 1.5 million eligible voters registered. Hundreds of thousands turned out to vote for a president, 30 senators, and 64 representatives. Observers, among them former U.S. president Jimmy Carter, were upbeat about the lack of violence and the apparent general desire for peace. The runoff election also took place peacefully, which clearly indicated that Liberians looked forward to an end to chaos and violence. Although Weah challenged the election results in the courts, his postelection statesmanlike behaviour set a high standard for democracy in the West African state; in December Weah dropped his fraud case.

Meanwhile, 15,000 UN peacekeepers remained in Liberia in a supervisory role. The new government faced the enormous task of restoring a stable democratic government, rebuilding the economy, ending corruption, and bringing about reconciliation among 17 ethnic groups. Public opinion identified education as the main priority.

From exile in Nigeria the long hand of former Liberian head of state Charles Taylor stirred up political intrigue.

Maintaining contact with his well-developed business network, Taylor contributed funds to some of the new parties and was suspected of involvement in corrupt activities. Throughout the year international pressure to review the terms of his exile intensified, but Nigerian Pres. Olusegun Obasanjo resisted calls to hand him over to the special court in Sierra Leone, which had indicted him on 17 counts of war crimes for his role in the civil war in that country. (LARAY DENZER)

LIBYA

Area: 1,759,540 sq km (679,362 sq mi)
Population (2005 est.): 5,853,000
Capital: Tripoli (policy-making body intermittently meets in Surt)
Chief of state: (de facto) Col. Muammar al-Qaddafi; (nominal) Secretary of the General People's Congress Zentani Muhammad al-Zentani
Head of government: Secretary of the General People's Committee (Prime Minister) Shukri Ghanem

Libya's international relations continued to improve in 2005, especially on the African continent. The Libyan leadership cooperated with the U.S. in Africa south of the Sahara, and the leaders of African countries were frequent visitors to Tripoli and to Col. Muammar al-Qaddafi's tent in Surt. U.S. strategic goals in Africa—diversifying sources for U.S. energy needs, stabilizing the continent to create a good investment climate, and containing global terrorism—were no longer in conflict with Libya's objectives. Libya's new capacity to cultivate its old alliances was significantly reinforced by the high level of its oil revenues.

In 2005 the economic mood in Libya paralleled that of the 1970s, when unlimited supplies of capital fueled high investment and rapid infrastructure development. The problems of managing the economy were also remarkably similar, with absorptive capacity the main constraint then and in 2005. Libya was also, however, finding that the earlier socialist development model was no longer the obvious way forward. The necessary transition from a radical socialist mode to an economically mixed

and substantially privatized system was proving very difficult to bring about. Qaddafi was not yet able to redirect the socialist mind set of the loyal group of officials and advisers close to him. Old beliefs from the 1970s were running smack into reform initiatives, which Qaddafi was trying to ventriloquize through the person of his prime minister, Shukri Ghanem.

Libya sought to increase oil exports from about 1.7 million bbl a day to 3 million; investments of $30 billion would be required. The international oil companies all clamoured to share in the exploration. Libya had always enjoyed a sound relationship with international oil companies and had a well-functioning petroleum law. In the first round of bidding in January 2005, most exploration lots went to American companies. American producers Occidental Petroleum, Chevron, and Amerada Hess won 11 of 15 permits alone or jointly with other companies; no producer from Europe or Japan was successful in this round of bidding. In October Italy's ENI Spa gained four permits; Japan's Mitsubishi Oil and the British BG Group also gained acreage, while ExxonMobil was the only successful American company. These arrangements were all preliminary, but by year's end a number of contracts had been signed. The winners would cooperate with Libya's state-owned National Oil Corp. (J.A. ALLAN)

LIECHTENSTEIN

Area: 160 sq km (62 sq mi)
Population (2005 est.): 34,800
Capital: Vaduz
Chief of state: Prince Hans Adam II
Head of government: Otmar Hasler

In 2005 Liechtenstein lost its demand for millions of dollars in damages from Germany for land and property assets seized in 1945. The International Court of Justice in The Hague threw out Liechtenstein's claim on February 10, stating that the dispute was too old for it to rule on. The suit claimed that Germany had turned over artworks and other property of Liechtenstein citizens to Czechoslovakia as war reparations, while Germany contended that

Czechoslovakia had seized the assets after the German defeat in 1945. The ICJ had had the case before it since 1980.

Meanwhile, the Independent Commission of Historians Liechtenstein–Second World War found the principality not guilty of war crimes during the Nazi era. Accusations by the World Jewish Congress in 2000 had led to the four-year investigation. On April 13 the commission concluded that Liechtenstein had done little wrong.

Legislative elections on March 11 and 13 for the 25-seat Landtag produced a turnout of 86.47%. The Progressive Citizens Party (FBP) captured 12 seats (with 48.74% of the vote), the Patriotic Union (VU) 10 seats (38.23%), and the green Free List 3 seats (13.03%), having picked up one from each of the larger parties. On April 21 Prime Minister Otmar Hasler (leader of the FBP), in coalition with the VU, formed a new government, the first to begin operations since the 2003 constitutional changes that gave Prince Hans Adam II the power to veto legislation and dismiss governments.

(ANNE ROBY)

LITHUANIA

Area: 65,300 sq km (25,212 sq mi)
Population (2005 est.): 3,413,000
Capital: Vilnius
Chief of state: President Valdas Adamkus
Head of government: Prime Minister Algirdas Brazauskas

Lithuania actively participated in the promotion of democracy in the Eastern European region during 2005. Together with his Polish counterpart, Pres. Valdas Adamkus had helped mediate during the "Orange Revolution" in Ukraine in late 2004. With his Estonian counterpart he rejected an invitation by the Kremlin to celebrate in Moscow on May 9 the end of World War II in Europe because the Baltic States had been subjected to Soviet occupation. On July 22 the U.S. Congress unanimously passed a resolution demanding that Russia "issue a clear and unambiguous statement of admission and condemnation of the illegal occupation and annexation by the Soviet

Union from 1940 to 1991 of the Baltic countries of Estonia, Latvia, and Lithuania," but Russia refused to make an apology.

Lithuania's relationship with Russia became even more tense when on September 15 a fighter aircraft accompanying a Russian spy plane over the Baltic Sea violated Lithuanian airspace for about 20 minutes before crashing near Kaunas. The plane, en route from St. Petersburg to the heavily militarized Russian exclave of Kaliningrad, was carrying four air-to-air missiles and at least 2 kg (4.4 lb) of radioactive metal. Embarrassingly, the incident coincided with negotiations in Washington, D.C., by Russian Pres. Vladimir Putin regarding the acquisition of Lithuania's main petroleum refinery at Mazeikiai by the Russian state oil company Lukoil. In response, Lithuania called for the demilitarization of the Kaliningrad region.

Lithuania's GDP was growing at the rate of 7%, and the foreign direct investment reached $6.1 billion by the beginning of the second quarter. Average annual wages remained low, however, at approximately $5,600.

Lithuanians were proud when Virgilijus Alekna won the gold medal in discus at the Helsinki IAAF world athletics championship in August and set a new world record.

(DARIUS FURMONAVIČIUS)

LUXEMBOURG

Area: 2,586 sq km (999 sq mi)
Population (2005 est.): 457,000
Capital: Luxembourg
Chief of state: Grand Duke Henri
Head of government: Prime Minister Jean-Claude Juncker

Luxembourg continued to prosper in 2005. In May it was reported that there were 161 banks in the country, with 22,711 employees and total banking assets exceeding $725 billion. There were also 13,569 holding companies, with total capital of €36.4 billion (about $46 billion) established in Luxembourg, and financial services contributed the greatest share (28%) of the grand duchy's income. According to a CIA report, Luxembourg again led the world with the highest GDP per capita: about $64,000 in 2004.

Luxembourg continued to be one of the European Union's firmest supporters in 2005. In January, Prime Minister Jean-Claude Juncker began a two-year term as the first permanent president of the 12-nation Eurogroup, and on

The grand ducal family of Luxembourg and the Belgian royals attend the funeral of Luxembourg's Grand Duchess Joséphine-Charlotte on January 15. In front, from left, are Grand Duke Jean (seated), Grand Duke Henri and Grand Duchess Maria Teresa, Crown Prince Guillaume, and Belgian King Albert II and Queen Paola.

June 30 he finished his term as president of the EU. Luxembourg approved the proposed EU constitution in a referendum on July 10.

Grand Duchess Joséphine-Charlotte, mother of Grand Duke Henri, died at age 77 on January 10. In her honour the grand duke named Luxembourg's new concert venue the Grande-Duchesse Joséphine-Charlotte Concert Hall. The stunning $70 million structure was designed by Christian de Portzamparc. Its main auditorium was the new home of the Luxembourg Philharmonic Orchestra, and smaller rooms played host to chamber music and experimental music.   (ANNE ROBY)

MACEDONIA

Area: 25,713 sq km (9,928 sq mi)
Population (2005 est.): 2,034,000
Capital: Skopje
Chief of state: President Branko Crvenkovski
Head of government: Prime Minister Vlado Buckovski

Local elections held in Macedonia on March 13 and 27, 2005, were marred by serious, albeit isolated, irregularities. The coalition "Together for Macedonia," led by the Social Democratic Union of Macedonia, the main governing party, emerged as the strongest single bloc; its coalition partner, the ethnic Albanian Democratic Union for Integration, and the main opposition party, the Macedonian Internal Revolutionary Organization—Democratic Party of Macedonian National Unity (VMRO-DPMNE), also scored well. Trifun Kostovski, a businessman running as an independent with the backing of VMRO-DPMNE, replaced the Liberal Democratic Party chairman, Risto Penov, as mayor of Skopje.

The dispute between the Macedonian and Serbian Orthodox churches continued as the Serbian Orthodox Church decided to recognize only the breakaway Archbishopric of Ohrid as canonical. On June 23 an appeals court in Bitola confirmed a lower-court verdict sentencing Bishop Jovan, the highest-level cleric to join the Serbian church, to 18 months in prison for embezzlement and for inciting religious and ethnic hatred. The Supreme Court on September 16 turned down the bishop's appeal against his sentence. The case put a strain on relations between Skopje and Belgrade.

On February 25 Croatian prosecutors charged former interior minister Ljube Boskovski with murder in connection with the killing of seven immigrants in 2002. After Boskovski was also charged with war crimes by the International Criminal Tribunal for the former Yugoslavia (ICTY) on March 14, the Croatian authorities handed him over to the ICTY. Three former senior police officers and a fourth man charged in connection with the killing of the immigrants were acquitted in April for insufficient evidence. On June 27 three former ethnic Albanian rebel commanders were sentenced to seven years in prison each for bomb attacks during ethnic tensions in 2003.

On July 15 the parliament passed a law allowing national minorities to fly their flags on official occasions alongside the Macedonian flag in communes where they constituted the majority of the population.

On February 14 the Macedonian government presented to the European Commission its official answers to the EU's questionnaire on Macedonia's preparedness to start membership talks. Following the European Commission's recommendation in November, EU leaders granted Macedonia the status of candidate country at a December summit, although no timetable was given for the talks.

The dispute with Greece over Macedonia's name remained unresolved. A compromise proposal by UN mediator Matthew Nimetz to use the name Republika Makedonija–Skopje without translation in international relations was rejected by the Macedonian side. A new proposal that Nimetz proposed in October was rejected by the Greek side.

The issue of the demarcation of Macedonia's borders with Kosovo also remained unsettled despite repeated talks between the Macedonian government, officials of Serbia and Montenegro, Kosovar politicians, and representatives of the United Nations mission UNMIK. In May EU officials announced that the EU had no plans to extend further its Proxima police mission in Macedonia after its mandate expired in December 2005.

On May 20 Prime Minister Vlado Buckovski announced a plan for a large-scale government program to revive the country's economy, which continued to be in a precarious state despite an expected growth in GDP of 3.8% and a slight drop in unemployment.   (STEFAN KRAUSE)

MADAGASCAR

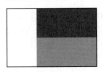

Area: 587,051 sq km (226,662 sq mi)
Population (2005 est.): 18,606,000
Capital: Antananarivo
Chief of state and head of government: President Marc Ravalomanana

After having gradually gained acceptance among other African countries in the aftermath of the political crisis of 2002–03, Madagascar welcomed the news in 2005 that it had been accepted into the Southern African Development Community. Madagascar remained one of the poorest countries in the world, but its economy was gradually being reformed under the government of Pres. Marc Ravalomanana, which took a strong line against corruption. Some 7 of 10 people still lived on less than a dollar a day, and one child in 10 was chronically malnourished, but child mortality rates had dropped by almost half since 1997, and the government's Poverty Reduction Strategy Paper (PRSP), prepared in consultation with the IMF and the World Bank, aimed to halve poverty by 2015.

In the poor south of the country, however, polio reemerged in August, and the authorities had to launch a nationwide immunization campaign for children under five. Farmers in the northeast suffered as the price of vanilla, the country's chief export, fell from $180 per kilogram in 2004 to $50 in early 2005. The price had been artificially high, however, because of cyclones in the area and the political crisis, and Madagascar remained the largest producer of vanilla in the world in terms of value. With unemployment high and inflation soaring to 27% in 2004, antigovernment demonstrations continued to take place, and the abolition of the international agreement guaranteeing clothing and textile export quotas to less-developed countries cost jobs in the clothing and textile sector, but there was hope for new jobs in mining and tourism. After the country had reached the completion point under the World Bank/IMF's highly indebted poor countries initiative in October 2004, the Bank approved $239 million in 2005 to help Madagascar implement its PRSP programs, fight HIV/AIDS, and stimulate economic growth.

(CHRISTOPHER SAUNDERS)

MALAWI

Area: 118,484 sq km (45,747 sq mi)
Population (2005 est.): 12,707,000
Capital: Lilongwe; judiciary meets in Blantyre
Head of state and government: President Bingu wa Mutharika

In February 2005 Pres. Bingu wa Mutharika resigned from Malawi's ruling United Democratic Front (UDF) to form the Democratic Progressive Party. He said that he had done so to preserve the integrity of his office in light of the corruption among members of his government. The UDF called for the impeachment of the president for quitting the party that had sponsored him. Debate on the proposal was adjourned after the unexpected death of the speaker of the parliament on June 27. Nevertheless, demonstrations for and against impeachment grew more violent, leading to the suspension of the parliament on October 24 and the arrest of three UDF members of the parliament who were among the fiercest critics of the president.

Early in the year an IMF team praised the government for its control of public spending and the president for his campaign against corruption. Opposition in the parliament to the contents of the budget delayed its approval, however, until local protest and UN pressure persuaded the government to make concessions that averted the prospect of a holdup in securing debt relief. In October the donor community expressed its concern over the impact of the impeachment proceedings on a country suffering from an acute food crisis, an intervention that opposition leaders regarded as an unwelcome interference in Malawi's internal affairs.

(KENNETH INGHAM)

MALAYSIA

Area: 329,847 sq km (127,355 sq mi)
Population (2005 est.): 26,130,000
Capital: Kuala Lumpur; some government offices have moved to Putrajaya (the new planned capital)
Chief of state: *Yang di-Pertuan Agong* (Paramount Ruler) Tuanku Syed Sirajuddin ibni al-Marhum Tuanku Syed Putra Jamalullail
Head of government: Prime Minister Datuk Seri Abdullah Ahmad Badawi

When Malaysia's minister of science and technology announced in August 2005 his government's plan to put an astronaut on the Moon by 2020, the declaration generated little surprise, consistent as it was with the country's record of technological advancement. Despite this latest sign of progress, however, Malaysia continued to struggle in 2005 with corruption, a troubled human rights record, and conflicts between Islamic law and individual rights. Although the devastating Indian Ocean tsunami that struck in late December 2004 had caused relatively light damage in Malaysia, in June the government reported receiving complaints that the recovery in some areas had been hampered by the misappropriation of relief funds by aid distributors. Prime Minister Abdullah Ahmad Badawi's effort to root out government corruption yielded only one notable case during the year; Isa Samad, a cabinet minister and high-ranking officer in the ruling United Malays National Organization, was suspended from the party on charges of vote buying and asked to resign his cabinet post. In May a royal commission investigating corruption and human rights abuses in the Malaysian police

force published its recommendations for reform, which included the establishment of an independent panel to review complaints of police misconduct. Earlier in the year, human rights groups had called for restrictions on state Islamic departments after Kuala Lumpur's Islamic department arrested some 100 Muslim patrons of a popular nightclub for immoral conduct. Activists charged that such actions violated constitutional guarantees of individual privacy. Responding to the furor over "state-sponsored snooping," the Badawi administration ordered Islamic departments to seek permission from the police before arresting anyone for immoral behaviour. In August further protests greeted the government's order that police begin checking mobile telephones for pornography, which was illegal in Malaysia.

After announcing the opening of free-trade talks with Australia in April, Malaysia sealed a free-trade pact with Japan in May. In October the government began trying to persuade oil companies to produce fuel made from a combination of petroleum and palm oil, of which Malaysia was the world's leading producer. With rising fuel prices exerting pressure on the

Civilian security forces in Kuala Lumpur, Malaysia, round up migrant workers in March to inspect their documents. Many thousands of illegal foreign workers were expelled during the year, but the government then found itself facing labour shortages.

© Jimin Lai/AFP/Getty Images

economies of major trading partners, Malaysia's export-driven economy was projected to grow 4.9% in 2005, down significantly from the previous year's 7% growth rate. Early in the year the Badawi administration clashed with business leaders after the expulsion of hundreds of thousands of undocumented immigrants created a critical labour shortage. Undocumented immigrants, most of them from Indonesia, previously had made up one-tenth of Malaysia's workforce. In May the government invited the workers back and even set up centres in Indonesia to help expedite applications for work visas.

Relations with neighbouring Thailand remained tense owing to the ongoing Muslim insurgency in southern Thailand. In late December 2004 the Thai government claimed to have obtained evidence that some insurgents had received training in the northern Malaysian state of Kelantan. When 131 Thai Muslims fled into Malaysia in early September to escape the fighting, the government refused to repatriate them immediately, despite the Thai prime minister's assertion that some of the refugees were Islamic separatists.

(JANET MOREDOCK)

MALDIVES

Area: 298 sq km (115 sq mi)
Population (2005 est.): 294,000
Capital: Male
Head of state and government: President Maumoon Abdul Gayoom

In 2005 Maldives faced a tough task of rebuilding after the December 2004 Indian Ocean tsunami. The country lost assets equivalent to about 62% of GDP, and its economic growth declined to 1% from a 20-year average of 8%. Maldives needed $239 million for emergency relief and another $1.3 billion for reconstruction over the next five years, but the aid pledged by the international community was inadequate, leaving a $113 million shortfall. In view of the mounting cost of reconstruction, the decline in tourist arrivals, and surging oil prices, the government prepared a supplementary budget in August. Pres. Maumoon Abdul Gayoom's visit to India, which donated $2.4 million to help

© Prakash Singh/AFP/Getty Images

Maldives Pres. Maumoon Abdul Gayoom (right) talks with the president of India's Congress Party, Sonia Gandhi, during his visit to India in late March. In addition to New Delhi, Gayoom visited the southern Indian cities of Chennai (Madras) and Trivandrum.

ease Maldives' budgetary restraints, was an acknowledgement of India's role in posttsunami relief work.

The election to choose 42 members of the Majlis (parliament), originally scheduled for the end of 2004, was held on January 22. In late January Gayoom announced a 31-point proposal for a constitutional amendment to establish a multiparty democracy with more fundamental rights, a separation of powers, and a criminal justice system. Registration of political parties began after the Majlis passed legislation in June. Beginning August 12, several days of antigovernment protests demanding the president's resignation led to the arrest of more than 160 people.

(PONMONI SAHADEVAN)

MALI

Area: 1,248,574 sq km (482,077 sq mi)
Population (2005 est.): 11,415,000
Capital: Bamako
Chief of state: President Amadou Toumani Touré
Head of government: Prime Minister Ousmane Issoufi Maïga

Spiraling fuel costs coupled with poor crops, owing to the 2004 locust invasions and near drought, led to huge price increases for staple grains in Mali during 2005. With 70% of the population living on less than one dollar a day, many faced a food crisis during the year. An estimated three million people were facing shortages, although the government denied any risk of actual famine. Among the worst hit economically were the Tuareg nomads, who had seen prices for their animals drop at a time when water shortages had greatly reduced the size of most herds.

On June 11 the government welcomed the news that the Group of Eight had canceled debts of €1.6 billion (about $2 billion). Despite another announcement declaring that the G-8 would double aid to the world's poorest nations by 2010, organizers of a "People's Forum"—held July 6–9 in Fana, 129 km (80 mi) west of Bamako—still condemned the industrialized nations for not doing enough.

Eleven men were convicted and imprisoned in May for refusing to allow their children to receive the polio vaccine. On September 18 an armed confrontation broke out between the police and members of a sect known as the "Barefoots," who were opposed to the immunization campaign. Four people were killed and several injured.

Timbuktu was removed from the list of world heritage sites classified as endangered. The reason cited was Mali's actions to implement preservation-and-conservation programs, particularly for the vast collection of historic manuscripts held at the Ahmed Baba Institute.

(NANCY ELLEN LAWLER)

MALTA

Area: 315 sq km (122 sq mi)
Population (2005 est.): 404,000
Capital: Valletta
Chief of state: President Eddie Fenech Adami
Head of government: Prime Minister Lawrence Gonzi

On July 6, 2005, the Maltese parliament unanimously ratified the European Union constitution. The opposition Labour Party, however, stated that its vote was conditioned to five reservations, one of which was meant to ensure Malta's neutrality. Meanwhile, the government announced its plan to entrench in the Maltese constitution the law prohibiting abortion. Shortly after the government decided to adopt the euro, the ministers of the euro zone member states included the Maltese lira in the Exchange Rate Mechanism II, and on May 2 the central rate of the lira was set at 1 euro to 42.93 cents.

The dominant theme of the year was the influx of illegal immigrants from the African continent, which for Malta reached crisis proportions. In June a conference of five European and five African countries (so-called 5+5) in Malta agreed on the need to adopt a holistic approach toward tackling the problem. A high-level meeting in Rome between Malta and Italy was held in October.

On October 3 Prime Minister Lawrence Gonzi met U.S. Pres. George W. Bush in Washington, D.C. Among the matters discussed were the reinstatement of an agreement to avoid double taxation, the removal of visa requirements for Maltese citizens traveling to the U.S., the immigration problem, and international terrorism. The government and people of Malta donated €8 million (about $10.5 million) to help Asian tsunami victims, while Malta in September wrote off $8 million owed by Iraq as a show of solidarity with the Iraqi people. (ALBERT GANADO)

MARSHALL ISLANDS

Area: 181 sq km (70 sq mi)
Population (2005 est.): 56,300
Capital: Majuro
Head of state and government: President Kessai Note

In May 2005 the U.S. Congress finally held hearings on a 2000 Marshall Islands petition seeking increased compensation for nuclear tests carried out by the U.S. between 1946 and 1958 at Bikini atoll and other sites. Although there was some sympathy for the Marshall Islands' position in committee hearings, the administration of U.S. Pres. George W. Bush had already rejected the case. The U.S. maintained that a 1983 settlement, under which some $270 million had been distributed since 1986, was a final payment covering all claims and that substantial contributions to health, resettlement, and land-remediation costs had been made. Claims in 2004 from several island communities south of the nuclear zone were also rejected by the U.S. for a lack of evidence of any direct impact from nuclear tests on the locals' health or land.

Under the renewed Compact of Free Association, the U.S. provided financial assistance covering some two-thirds of the Marshall Islands' projected 2006 budget of $146 million. In July, however, the U.S. Government Accountability Office expressed concern over the low rate of return being achieved by the trust funds, the lack of strategic planning, and other issues.

In May Pres. Chen Shui-bian of Taiwan paid an official visit to the Marshall Islands and acknowledged the Marshall Islands' support for Taiwan's continuing bid for international recognition. (BARRIE MACDONALD)

MAURITANIA

Area: 1,030,700 sq km (398,000 sq mi)
Population (2005 est.): 3,069,000
Capital: Nouakchott
Chief of state: President Col. Maaouya Ould Sid'Ahmed Taya and, from August 3, Chairman of the Military Council for Justice and Democracy Ely Ould Mohamed Vall
Head of government: Prime Ministers Sghair Ould M'Barek and, from August 7, Sidi Mohamed Ould Boubakar

Taking advantage of Pres. Maaouya Ould Sid'Ahmed Taya's absence at the funeral of Saudi Arabian King Fahd (*see* OBITUARIES), dissident Mauritanian army officers launched a successful coup on Aug. 3, 2005. A former close ally of Taya, Col. Ely Ould Mohamed Vall, emerged as the leader of the Military Council for Justice and Democracy. All but one of its 17 members were

Maltese marines negotiate with illegal would-be immigrants packed onto a small boat and stranded at sea some 30 km (19 mi) southwest of Malta on September 25. Illegal immigration reached crisis proportions in the small Mediterranean country in 2005.

colonels. News of the bloodless coup was greeted by huge celebrations in the streets. Vall sought to reassure the international community that democracy would be swiftly restored, with a referendum on a new constitution to be held within a year and legislative elections to follow immediately. The African Union, the European Union, and the U.S. initially condemned the coup, but after talks with Vall and members of the Council, they expressed guarded support for the new regime.

On September 2 Vall proclaimed a general amnesty for political prisoners. Many were freed immediately. Among them were scores of men arrested earlier in the year on suspicion of being Islamic militants, as well as two of the four army officers sentenced to life imprisonment on February 3 for having participated in the failed June 2003 coup. On September 13 thousands of opposition supporters mobbed the airport to welcome 30 former dissidents back from exile. (NANCY ELLEN LAWLER)

MAURITIUS

Area: 2,040 sq km (788 sq mi)
Population (2005 est.): 1,245,000
Capital: Port Louis
Chief of state: President Sir Anerood Jugnauth
Head of government: Prime Ministers Paul Bérenger and, from July 5, Navin Ramgoolam

In the wake of the massive Indian Ocean tsunami that occurred on Dec. 26, 2004, Mauritius hosted a meeting in early January 2005 of the Small Island Developing States (SIDS), a group of 51 small island countries and territories, to address plans for an early-warning system and other economic and social needs. The economies had been worsening in many of the SIDS member countries and territories, including Mauritius, owing to environmental threats, trade barriers, and political instability.

In April, Prime Minister Paul Bérenger dissolved the parliament and announced new elections for July. The move signaled that pressure had been mounting on Bérenger to address the woes of the once-strong Mauritian economy after massive job cuts in the

island's two main industries, textiles and sugar production. Despite efforts to diversify the economy by attempting to make Mauritius a high-tech hub, the economy was hit hard when preferential trade deals on sugar exports and textiles were scrapped in January by the European Union and the U.S. The parliamentary elections held on July 3 resulted in the opposition party Social Alliance's sweeping 38 of 62 seats. Navin Ramgoolam, the son of Mauritius's first postindependence leader, became prime minister. (MARY F.E. EBELING)

MEXICO

Area: 1,964,375 sq km (758,449 sq mi)
Population (2005 est.): 107,029,000
Capital: Mexico City
Head of state and government: President Vicente Fox Quesada

Political maneuvering in advance of the July 2006 presidential election dominated events in Mexico during 2005. In May Pres. Vicente Fox was finally forced to halt legal proceedings against Andrés Manuel López Obrador (*see* BIOGRAPHIES), the popular head of the

Federal District government and the leading presidential candidate of the Party of the Democratic Revolution (PRD). In May 2004 the federal attorney general had requested that the Chamber of Deputies lift López Obrador's immunity from prosecution as an elected official (an action that might eventually have permitted his removal from office), on the grounds that he had authorized construction of a hospital access road across private land in defiance of a judicial order. Fox failed signally, however, in his efforts to convince domestic and international publics that the case against López Obrador represented a test of the rule of law.

López Obrador maintained that Fox's real motive was his desire to disqualify the leading leftist candidate and thereby tilt the upcoming presidential race in favour of his own centre-right National Action Party (PAN). Following a march in Mexico City by nearly one million people protesting the government's political manipulation of judicial proceedings, the Fox administration was compelled to drop the charges. The outpouring of public support for López Obrador paved the way for his nomination in September as the PRD's presidential standard-bearer.

In October and November both the PAN and the long-dominant Institutional Revolutionary Party (PRI) also chose their presidential candidates.

On April 7 tens of thousands of supporters of Mexico City's Mayor Andrés Manuel López Obrador fill the Zócalo, the main square, to protest moves to impeach him. López Obrador was seen as a strong bet to run against incumbent Vicente Fox for the presidency in 2006.

Felipe Calderón won the PAN's party primaries decisively. The son of a PAN founder, a former president of the party (1996–99), a leader of the PAN's Chamber of Deputies delegation (2000–03), and a former minister of energy (2003–04), Calderón appealed to party traditionalists long at odds with "neopanistas" such as President Fox. Calderón's principal opponent was Santiago Creel, who was minister of the interior between 2000 and 2005 and President Fox's apparent favourite for the nomination.

The PRI's candidate-selection process was the most conflictive. Former PRI president Roberto Madrazo, a former governor of Tabasco (1994–2000) who had held the party together in the wake of its historic defeat in the 2000 presidential election, won the party primary in November. His principal opponent had been Arturo Montiel, a former governor of the state of México who—until he was forced to resign following press revelations concerning his family's unexplained accumulation of wealth—had represented an anti-Madrazo coalition of PRI notables. The divisions that emerged around Madrazo's nomination increased the risks of serious defections from the PRI, a development that would hurt its electoral performance in 2006.

The intense partisan rivalries surrounding the presidential contest raised unsettling questions regarding Mexico's future. Some observers worried that if the election was marred by significant irregularities and the reported results did not indicate a clear winner, the country's electoral institutions might not be capable of managing the ensuing tensions. Others were concerned that a tumultuous presidential succession might undercut the country's hard-won financial stability.

In an effort to safeguard against such outcomes, in September the prominent entrepreneur Carlos Slim convoked 300 public figures in support of a National Agreement for Unity, the Rule of Law, Development, Investment, and Employment. Slim, head of the Grupo Carso conglomerate and Mexico's (and Latin America's) wealthiest individual, and his fellow opinion leaders used the 12-page document to underscore the multiple economic, social, and political challenges facing contemporary Mexico and to argue that all sectors—not just the government—had to work together constructively to address these problems. The Fox administration itself sought to reassure the business communities

at home and abroad by maintaining strict macroeconomic discipline. The government held the annual rate of inflation to a very low 3.8% during 2005, and the government's budget deficit was estimated at 0.2% of GDP. In part because international oil prices remained high, Mexico's international financial reserves reached $65.6 billion in June. The country's GDP rose by an estimated 2.7% during the year.

Elsewhere on the domestic political front, in February the special prosecutor appointed to investigate human rights crimes committed during Mexico's "dirty war" of the late 1960s and early 1970s lost his case against former president Luis Echeverría (1970–76)—involving the killing of at least a dozen demonstrators in Mexico City on June 10, 1971—when the Supreme Court ruled that the crime of genocide was not applicable in cases originating before 1982. In June Raúl Salinas, older brother of former president Carlos Salinas (1988–94), was freed after having served more than 10 years in prison on charges associated with the 1994 assassination of PRI secretary-general José Francisco Ruiz Massieu. Although Raúl Salinas still faced charges of illegal enrichment, prosecutors had failed to produce reliable evidence in their main case against him. In August the secretary-general of the Confederation of Mexican Workers (CTM), Leonardo Rodríguez Alcaine, died at age 86. He was succeeded by Joaquín Gamboa Pascoe, leader of the Federal District Workers' Federation.

Mexico's always-complex relations with the United States also generated considerable controversy during 2005. Immigration-reform legislation remained stalled in the U.S. Congress, and the two governments made no further progress in negotiating a bilateral accord on migration issues. Yet the northward flow of undocumented Mexican migrants continued unabated, and U.S. immigration officials reported a record number of deaths as migrants seeking to evade U.S. border controls were forced into inhospitable desert and mountainous terrain. The governors of Arizona and New Mexico declared states of emergency in their border areas to draw the U.S. government's attention to escalating migration problems.

It was drug trafficking-related violence along the border, however, that was the principal flash point in Mexico-U.S. relations. Protracted fighting between rival drug cartels over border-

crossing routes in the Nuevo Laredo, Tamaulipas, area resulted in multiple deaths and greatly heightened concerns about public security in the region. The U.S. ambassador to Mexico, Antonio O. Garza, Jr., briefly closed the U.S. consulate in Nuevo Laredo to underscore the U.S. government's frustration with Mexico's handling of the situation—an action that provoked heated reactions from senior Mexican officials.　　(KEVIN J. MIDDLEBROOK)

MICRONESIA, FEDERATED STATES OF

Area: 701 sq km (271 sq mi)
Population (2005 est.): 113,000
Capital: Palikir, on Pohnpei
Head of state and government: President Joseph J. Urusemal

In the March 2005 elections for state representatives to the Federated States of Micronesia (FSM) Congress, 9 of 10 incumbents were returned. Results for one district were withheld and investigated because the number of votes cast substantially exceeded the number of registered voters.

Under the Compact of Free Association signed in 2004, the U.S. had agreed to provide annual funding of $76 million for 20 years and contributions to trust funds intended for longer-term income. In July 2005 the U.S. Government Accountability Office expressed concern over the rate of return being achieved by the trust funds, the lack of strategic planning, and the quality of reporting. The U.S. also noted that some financial assistance was not being spent in the intended areas.

The Asian Development Bank reported that although the FSM had received some $2.4 billion in development assistance between 1987 and 2003 (and currently received aid per capita at three to four times the regional average), there had been negative growth (a shrinkage of GDP) over the period. Despite the investment of some $300 million in public-sector enterprises, no successes in turning the tide had been reported.

In January the nuclear-powered submarine USS *San Francisco* struck an uncharted undersea mountain in the FSM exclusive economic zone with the loss of one life. The government sought assurances that there was no nuclear leakage or other hazard to the area.

(BARRIE MACDONALD)

MOLDOVA

Area: 33,845 sq km (13,068 sq mi)
Population (2005 est.): 4,206,000 (including more than a quarter million persons working abroad and about 600,000 persons in Transnistria)
Capital: Chisinau
Chief of state: President Vladimir Voronin
Head of government: Prime Minister Vasile Tarlev

Moldova's parliamentary elections held on March 6, 2005, saw a reform-based consensus among previously divergent parties. Pres. Vladimir Voronin's Communists held on to power with a reduced majority. In April pro-Western opposition leaders supported his election for a second term. Despite grassroots misgivings, he hoped to transform his party into a social democratic force. In June 2005, while on a visit to the European Union and NATO headquarters in Brussels, Voronin asked for EU assistance in establishing international customs control on the Transnistrian segment of the Moldovan-Ukrainian border. Ukrainian leaders supported this move, as evidence mounted that the separatist enclave of Transnistria was at the centre of a vast smuggling racket involving liquor, consumer goods, and small arms.

On July 22 Parliament unanimously passed a law stating that negotiations with Transnistria had to be based on democratization, demilitarization, and decriminalization of the territory rather than sharing power with the existing authorities there. Voronin welcomed growing Western involvement in seeking to end the secession. On October 6–7 the EU commissioner for external relations paid an official visit following the launch of an EU action plan designed to strengthen links with Moldova and stabilize the new eastern borders established in 2004 with the accession to the EU of eight states formerly in the communist bloc.

Moldova's relations worsened with Russia, which continued to station troops in Transnistria and preferred a settlement that would increase the dependence on Moscow of a united Moldova. Some 85% of Moldova's wine, its main source of revenue, was exported to Russia; in September 2005 Russian authorities blocked its shipment. On October 4 President Voronin declared that he was ready to face an interruption in energy supplies from Russia in order to defend the country's sovereignty.

(TOM GALLAGHER)

MONACO

Area: 1.97 sq km (0.76 sq mi)
Population (2005 est.): 32,700
Chief of state: Prince Rainier III and, from April 6, Prince Albert II
Head of government: Ministers of State Patrick Leclercq and, from June 1, Jean-Paul Proust

Monaco was greatly saddened by the death of Prince Rainier III (see OBITUARIES) on April 6, 2005. Europe's longest-reigning monarch, Rainier had ruled Monaco for 56 years and had transformed the "sunny place for shady people" into a vibrant modern state.

Prince Albert II (see BIOGRAPHIES) succeeded to the throne, with the official ceremony held at the cathedral on July 12 followed by celebrations at the palace for the people of Monaco. A formal investiture that included foreign heads of state was held on November 19. Just days before he was enthroned, Albert acknowledged paternity of a two-year-old son, who lived in Paris with his mother, a former Air France flight attendant from Togo. The child was not eligible to succeed to the throne.

Jean-Paul Proust was appointed to succeed Patrick Leclercq as Monaco's minister of state on June 1. Proust was chosen from a list of three French national candidates presented by the French government.

Monaco reached agreement with the EU on a tax on savings accounts held abroad by EU residents. The law, which came into force on July 1, targeted interest income from savings and bonds but exempted earnings from stocks and other assets.

(ANNE ROBY)

MONGOLIA

Area: 1,564,116 sq km (603,909 sq mi)
Population (2005 est.): 2,550,000
Capital: Ulaanbaatar
Chief of state: Presidents Natsagiyn Bagabandi and, from June 24, Nambaryn Enhbayar
Head of government: Prime Minister Tsahiagiyn Elbegdorj

Political events in Mongolia in 2005 were dominated by the May 22 presidential elections, which were won by the candidate of the Mongolian People's Revolutionary Party (MPRP), Nambaryn Enhbayar, with an overall majority of votes over his three opponents. Enhbayar had served as prime minister in 2000–04 and as chairman (speaker) of the Great Hural (national assembly) in 2004–05; he was the first politician to serve in Mongolia's three top posts. To stand for the presidency, he had given up the post of chairman of the MPRP, which passed to the mayor of Ulaanbaatar, Miyeegombyn Enhbold. Tsendiyn Nyamdorj, the minister of law and home affairs and a member of the MPRP leadership under Enhbayar, was elected the new Great Hural chairman.

In late December 2004 Radnaasumbereliyn Gonchigdorj had replaced Mendsayhany Enhsayhan as leader of the Democratic Party (DP), which led to the "Motherland"–Mongolian Democratic New Socialist Party's withdrawing from the "Motherland-Democracy" coalition. As a result, Civil Courage–Republican Party leader Sanjaasurengiyn Oyuun lost her post as deputy chairperson of the Great Hural. The DP members of the Great Hural were unable to maintain their own parliamentary group, and most opted to join the MPRP faction, of which Gonchigdorj became deputy chairman. This politically ambiguous situation continued until July, when the MPRP parliamentary group leader, Doloonjongiyn Idevhten, expelled the DP members. A DP parliamentary group was enabled, however, following the approval of amendments to the Law on the Great Hural.

The "grand coalition" government of the MPRP and DP survived to adopt budgets and development plans, as well as finalize arrangements for celebrating the 800th anniversary of the Mongolian state in August 2006. The remains of the revolutionary leaders Suhbaatar (died 1923) and Choybalsan (died 1952) were removed from the mausoleum in front of the State Palace on Ulaanbaatar's Suhbaatar Square, and the mausoleum was demolished to make way for the Great Lord Genghis Khan Memorial and Worship Complex with a 9-m (30-ft)-high statue of the founder of the Mongol Empire.   (ALAN J.K. SANDERS)

MOROCCO

Area: 710,850 sq km (274,461 sq mi), including the 252,120-sq-km (97,344-sq-mi) area of the disputed Western Sahara annexation
Population (2005 est.): 30,230,000, of which Western Sahara 341,000 (excluding 170,000 Saharawi refugees living near Tindouf, Alg., from 1975)
Capital: Rabat
Head of state and government: King Muhammad VI, assisted by Prime Minister Driss Jettou

The Western Sahara issue continued to dominate Morocco's diplomatic horizons in 2005 as the government struggled for a solution after having rejected the Baker Plan in 2004. At the start of the year, an attempted mediation by France and Spain ran up against Algerian intransigence, which was not mitigated by the meeting in March between King Muhammad VI and Algeria's Pres. Abdelaziz Bouteflika in Algiers. In the wake of riots in the region in May, 100 Western Saharans were arrested amid accusations of police brutality. In June, Moroccan Prime Minister Driss Jettou met his Spanish counterpart, José Luis Rodríguez Zapatero, for discussions on the issue and on the growing problem of illegal immigration via Morocco into Spain. Shortly afterward Kenya recognized the Arab Saharan Democratic Republic, forcing Morocco to recall its ambassador from Nairobi.

Despite the Polisario Front's late August goodwill gesture of releasing the remaining 404 prisoners it held, the Moroccan government offered it no concessions. Instead, in November the king offered Western Saharans full internal autonomy in return for recognition of Moroccan sovereignty over the region. The immigration issue came to a head

Having traversed the Sahara desert, migrants from sub-Saharan Africa are detained on October 9 in a camp in Bouarfa, eastern Morocco. Illegal migration of Africans seeking to get to Spain through Morocco was a major concern in 2005.
© Samuel Aranda/AFP/Getty Images

in the same month as illegal immigrants from sub-Saharan Africa and elsewhere tried to rush the border fences between Morocco and the two Spanish presidios of Ceuta and Melilla. For the first time, Spain began to return illegal immigrants to Morocco, which in turn tried to force them across its frontiers until deterred by United Nations complaints.

Anxieties were voiced about press freedom in Morocco after Ali Lamrabet was fined and banned from practicing journalism for 10 years as a result of his comments about the Western Sahara. At the same time, the radical weekly *TelQuel* survived its publication of the detailed expenditures of the royal court. Moroccans also saw televised testimony about the "Years of Lead"— the repression under the king's father.

Morocco continued to be in the economic doldrums, despite further attempts at liberalizing the economy, with promises of full dirham convertibility soon. Global increases in oil prices forced the government to increase fuel prices twice—by 8% in May and 5% in October. Irregular rainfall patterns meant a poor harvest, with agricultural production falling by 21% in value by August, and Morocco's GDP fell by 3% as a result.   (GEORGE JOFFÉ)

MOZAMBIQUE

Area: 812,379 sq km (313,661 sq mi)
Population (2005 est.): 19,407,000
Capital: Maputo
Head of state and government: Presidents Joaquim Chissano and, from February 2, Armando Guebuza, assisted by Prime Minister Luisa Diogo

On Jan. 20, 2005, the results of the Mozambique elections of December 2004, in which the ruling party, Frelimo, and its candidate, Armando Guebuza, were victorious, were validated by the Constitutional Council. The Council commented, however, that it would like to see greater transparency in the conduct of future elections. The demand of the main opposition party, Renamo, for a rerun of the elections was rejected, Renamo having already agreed, for the sake of the country, not to carry out its threat to boycott the parliament.

The economic outlook was good, and the country, according to a report from the Bank of Mozambique, had achieved all its targets for 2004. Work on the infrastructure was going well, but the bank recommended that investors place more emphasis on encouraging labour-intensive projects that would have a greater impact on employment prospects for ordinary people. This latter theme was taken up in May by an economist, Manuel Araujo, who, while echoing the growing criticism of the widening gap between the wealthy and the poor, also suggested that foreign investors were linked too closely with industry rather than developing the country's agricultural potential, an area in which the majority of the population was involved. Prime Minister Luisa Diogo also pointed out that tariff barriers set up by wealthier countries seriously restricted Mozambique's trading opportunities.

Nevertheless, foreign donors remained friendly. On a visit to Mozambique in January, U.K. Chancellor of the Exchequer Gordon Brown said that Britain would cancel the country's total debt of $154 million. The IMF also promised to support Mozambique's economic-reform program into 2006, and in September the World Bank approved credit to a total of $120 million to assist the government's action plan to reduce absolute poverty. These economic benefits, however, were overshadowed by the impact of prolonged drought, which later in the year threatened hundreds of thousands of people with acute food shortages.

A strike in April by mine clearers claiming unpaid wages underlined the continuing problems posed by the aftereffects of the civil war and the inefficiency of the administration. In June workers declared that an increase of 14% in the statutory minimum wage was wholly inadequate for meeting the rising cost of living.

Guebuza's vigorous campaign against corruption, which had won widespread approval from the international community, encountered criticism in September when the replacement of the temporary Anti-Corruption Unit by a Central Office for Combating Corruption was accompanied, without explanation, by the dismissal of the highly regarded head of the unit, Isabel Rupia, under whose leadership a number of high-profile investigations had met with opposition.   (KENNETH INGHAM)

MYANMAR (BURMA)

Area: 676,577 sq km (261,228 sq mi)
Population (2005 est.): 46,997,000
Capital: Yangon (Rangoon); movement to new capital complex at Pyinmana began in 2005
Head of state and government: Chairman of the State Peace and Development Council Gen. Than Shwe, assisted by Prime Minister Lieut. Gen. Soe Win

Internal bickering and tensions within Myanmar's ruling junta, the State Peace and Development Council (SPDC), escalated in 2005 following the sacking of former prime minister and once-powerful intelligence chief Gen. Khin Nyunt in late 2004. Rumours of coups accompanied the purge of Khin Nyunt's supporters; the general himself received a 44-year suspended sentence for corruption. In July former home, agriculture, and foreign ministers were also arrested on corruption charges. Security concerns about future invasions or uprisings prompted the SPDC's decision to move the military headquarters, together with several ministries, from

Yangon to Pyinmana, a location about 320 km (200 mi) to the north in the remote Mandalay division.

Tasked with drafting a new constitution, the National Convention met in February–March and was scheduled to resume before the end of the year. Myanmar's constitutional talks lacked any credibility, however, because a number of political and ethnic groups, including Myanmar's main opposition party, the National League for Democracy, were not involved. Some cease-fire agreements with armed rebel ethnic groups showed signs of unraveling. Several bomb blasts rocked Yangon and Mandalay in April–May. The U.S. and the EU maintained sanctions against Myanmar. U.S. Secretary of State Condoleezza Rice branded the country an "outpost of tyranny" because of its poor human rights record and continuing repression of democracy, including its detention of Nobel Peace Prize winner Aung San Suu Kyi. According to UN human rights investigator Paulo Sérgio Pinheiro, Myanmar was holding more than 1,100 political prisoners. In June China and Russia used the threat of a veto to block a U.S. move in the UN Security Council to impose sanctions on Myanmar. Russia also reportedly resumed talks on helping Myanmar build a nuclear research reactor. In August the UN Global Fund to Fight AIDS, Tuberculosis, and Malaria withdrew from Myanmar because of fresh travel restrictions on aid workers. AIDS had become a "generalized epidemic" in the country, with 1.2% of the population infected with HIV. About 100,000 new cases of tuberculosis were also being detected every year in Myanmar.

Faced with intense pressure from fellow member states in ASEAN (Association of Southeast Asian Nations), Myanmar agreed to forgo its turn on the rotating chairmanship in 2006. This decision avoided a major rupture in ASEAN's relations with the U.S. and the EU, which had threatened to boycott ASEAN meetings if Myanmar assumed the chair. The final communiqué of the ASEAN Regional Forum (ARF) expressed concern over the slow pace of democratic reform and national reconciliation in Myanmar. However, in a gesture of camaraderie with Myanmar and disapproval of ASEAN pressure on Yangon to give up its ASEAN chairmanship, Chinese Foreign Minister Li Zhaoxing chose to skip the ARF's security deliberations and travel to Myanmar to express solidarity with the beleaguered military regime.

Myanmar's economy would have been in an even more parlous state were it not for the support of fellow ASEAN countries, China, India, and the country's large illegal trade in narcotics. The UN ranked it among the least-developed countries in Asia, on a par with Cambodia and Bangladesh. The only sector that registered strong growth was oil and gas, owing to Chinese, Thai, South Korean, and Indian investments. Thailand's imports from Myanmar (mostly consisting of gas) rose in 2005 by 51.2% year on year. In September the kyat fell to a record low of 1,330 to the U.S. dollar, from about 880 at the start of the year, pushing the price of oil imports yet higher. Inflation again returned to double digits, driven by rising global prices for oil and rice.   (MOHAN MALIK)

NAMIBIA

Area: 825,118 sq km (318,580 sq mi)
Population (2005 est.): 2,031,000
Capital: Windhoek
Chief of state and head of government: Presidents Sam Nujoma and, from March 21, Hifikepunye Pohamba, assisted by Prime Ministers Theo-Ben Gurirab and, from March 21, Nahas Angula

On March 21, 2005, the 15th anniversary of Namibia's independence, Pres. Sam Nujoma, after three terms in office, handed over power to his hand-picked successor, Hifikepunye Pohamba. (*See* BIOGRAPHIES.) Nujoma remained president of the South West African People's Organization (SWAPO), which he helped found in 1960 and which continued to enjoy a two-thirds majority in the National Assembly. The other, mostly small parties in Namibia were unable to put up any effective opposition to the government.

Pohamba appointed former minister of education Nahas Angula his new prime minister, and initially the change of leadership seemed to herald little change in policy. It was expected, however, that the program of land reform would be stepped up. Between the program's launch in 1996 and 2005, the government had bought 146 commercial farms covering more than 900,000 ha (1 ha = about 2.5 ac), but critics pointed out that posttransfer support was necessary if the reform was to be a success. The government said that it intended to acquire 15 million ha by 2020 to resettle 240,000 people on its waiting list.

In the 2005 UN Human Development Report, Namibia moved up only slightly from 126th of 177 countries to 125th place. An estimated 40% of the population lived below the poverty line, and about 230,000 Namibians were HIV-positive; of those only 17,000 had received antiretroviral medication. The UN granted Namibia $44.7 million to fight against HIV/AIDS, to help deal with food insecurity, and to improve the delivery of social services.

(CHRISTOPHER SAUNDERS)

NAURU

Area: 21.2 sq km (8.2 sq mi)
Population (2005 est.): 10,200
Capital: Government offices in Yaren district
Head of state and government: President Ludwig Scotty

A report from the Asian Development Bank showed the economy of Nauru to be in a critical condition in 2005. According to the ADB, the fiscal 2004–05 budget approved by Nauru's Parliament in late October 2004 represented a fundamental change in the country's approach to fiscal management and indicated that Nauru had acknowledged that it was in financial crisis and that expenditures needed to be reduced. Pres. Ludwig Scotty's government scaled down diplomatic representation in Australia and the U.S., cut expenditure on Nauruans receiving medical treatment and studying in Australia, and transferred overseas Nauruan students from Australian to Fijian educational institutions. Outstanding loans were called in, including one from the Cook Islands, which had borrowed funds from Nauru to build a national auditorium. Nauru reduced the interest on the loan, and the Cook Islands arranged for early repayment of the final installments, which had been due in December 2005 and June 2006.

Criticism continued over Australia's policy of holding on Nauru asylum seekers who were said to be depressed and suicidal. In September, Australian

Immigration Minister Amanda Vanstone approved a visit to Nauru by mental health experts to assess the condition of the remaining 27 detainees, most of whom were Iraqis and Afghans. (A.R.G. GRIFFITHS)

NEPAL

Area: 147,181 sq km (56,827 sq mi)
Population (2005 est.): 27,133,000
Capital: Kathmandu
Head of state: King Gyanendra Bir Bikram Shah Dev
Head of government: Prime Minister Sher Bahadur Deuba until February 1

Nepal's 15-year democratic exercise—which was marked by deep political instability—came to an end on Feb. 1, 2005, after King Gyanendra Bir Bikram Shah Dev dismissed the government of Prime Minister Sher Bahadur Deuba, who was later imprisoned on corruption charges; the claims were leveled by a highly controversial anticorruption body formed by the king. Meanwhile, the king took over absolute executive power, imposed a three-month state of emergency, and suspended all fundamental rights, including press freedom. The U.S., the U.K., and India suspended military aid to Nepal. Some European countries and international human rights groups, however, compelled the king to withdraw the state of emergency and restore civil rights. The Office of the UN High Commissioner for Human Rights opened an office in Nepal to monitor the situation. Amid protests, the king promised in September to hold elections in 2006. Meanwhile, in Beijing the Chinese government welcomed Pyar Jung Thapa, the chief of the Royal Nepalese Army, and announced on October 25 that it would provide $1 million in weapons to arm the Royal Nepalese Army; this marked the first time that China had provided military aid to Nepal. In January 2005 Nepal closed the Dalai Lama's office, which had been operating there for 45 years. The government ratified the Kyoto Protocol in September.

On September 3 the Communist Party of Nepal (Maoist) announced a three-month unilateral cease-fire; in the nine-year "people's war," more than 12,000 people had been killed.

On October 9 the government announced a controversial media ordinance that imposed restrictions on free press, curtailed freedom of speech, and decreed punishment of $3,000 in fines and two years' imprisonment for criticism of the government or the royal family. Later that month King Gyanendra announced that elections for the House of Representatives would be held by April 2007.

As a result of the expiration on January 1 of the Multi-Fiber Agreement, which set textile quotas, the country's export of garments (the number one export) was reduced by 40%; the livelihood of tens of thousands of people, particularly women and the poor, depended upon that industry. The escalation in the violent insurgency in Nepal caused tremendous loss in protected conservation areas because security forces that had been used against poaching were needed elsewhere; the population of the rare one-horned rhinos dwindled alarmingly from 600 (five years earlier) to fewer than 400. (KESHAB POUDEL)

NETHERLANDS, THE

Area: 41,528 sq km (16,034 sq mi)
Population (2005 est.): 16,306,000
Capital: Amsterdam; seat of government, The Hague
Chief of state: Queen Beatrix
Head of government: Prime Minister Jan Peter Balkenende

The start of 2005 saw The Netherlands still reeling from the murder of filmmaker Theo van Gogh in November 2004. Radical Islamist Mohammed Bouyeri, who had been promptly arrested for the murder, refused all legal defense (including psychiatric consideration) and demanded that he be held fully accountable for van Gogh's death. Several letters that Bouyeri had written to friends and relatives stated that he had intended to die in the commission of the murder. On July 26 he was sentenced to life in prison. Bouyeri was also indicted as a member of the Hofstad group, considered a terrorist organization; several other Hofstad members were prosecuted for complicity in the death of van Gogh, as well as for threats to politicians and for obstructing the democratic process.

Member of the Dutch parliament Ayaan Hirsi Ali, who was forced to go into hiding near the end of 2004 after the murder of filmmaker Theo van Gogh, returns to work in The Hague on January 18.

In January politician Ayaan Hirsi Ali, who had collaborated with van Gogh on his film *Submission* and had been in hiding for two months following a death threat by Bouyeri at the time of the murder, returned to her seat in the parliament. The cabinet instituted increased security policies in the country.

Dutch citizens and politicians continued their contentious discussions about policies and attitudes toward minorities, immigrants, and asylum seekers. Studies on the status of immigrants showed discouraging data; those minorities forced to enroll in Dutch-language courses did not typically improve dramatically. This result cast doubt on the effectiveness of the forthcoming compulsory language and culture courses for recent immigrants. In some cities ethnic segregation increased. Many citizens (including those of immigrant descent) stated in a poll that they viewed Western lifestyles as inconsistent with Islam. Very few ethnically Dutch citizens reported personal contacts with members of Islamic communities.

On June 1, 62.8% of the electorate participated in the first Dutch national referendum in two centuries. The voters rejected the proposed European Constitution by 61.6–38.4%, in spite of a last-ditch public-relations campaign by the government. Various reasons were offered for the "no" vote, including distaste for the current national administration, a perception that a united Europe offered a less-direct form of democracy, concern that liberties cherished by some Dutch citizens would be curtailed (e.g., gay rights, animal rights, a liberal drug policy), and a lack of comprehension of the constitution. Those who had voted "yes" also cited a

variety of reasons. It became clear that part of the populace demanded from the government more—and clearer—efforts at communication.

Consequently, in a controversial and telling revision of tradition, Queen Beatrix's formal address at the opening of the parliament in September featured a new format and content. In light of public opinion research, the monarch and the Council of Ministers decided to replace the speech from the throne's customary listing of policies (from each ministry in turn) with a more coherent text that grouped policy statements and their rationales and presented the information in a style that targeted a broad audience. The text set out goals in four themes: security, employment, a reduction in rules coupled with an increase in the quality of public service, and greater mutual respect among the populace.

(JOLANDA VANDERWAL TAYLOR)

NEW ZEALAND

Area: 270,534 sq km (104,454 sq mi)
Population (2005 est.): 4,096,000
Capital: Wellington
Chief of state: Queen Elizabeth II, represented by Governor-General Dame Silvia Cartwright
Head of government: Prime Minister Helen Clark

The New Zealand election on Sept. 17, 2005, broke new constitutional ground as mixed member proportional (MMP) voting returned 121 members of Parliament, an increase of one from the previously fixed 120-member House of Representatives. Prime Minister Helen Clark's government was elected to a third three-year term, but Clark was obliged to negotiate support from four minor parties to form an administration. Clark's Labour Party (with 50 seats) concluded a formal coalition with the Progressive Party (1 seat), agreed to various arrangements with New Zealand First (7) and United Future (3), and made policy concessions to the Greens (6) in return for a pledge from the Greens to abstain on financial issues and votes of confidence. The opposition comprised the National Party (48 seats), ACT New Zealand (2), and the Maori party (4). Former attorney general Margaret Wilson, who had successfully legislated in

2003 for a new Supreme Court to replace the Privy Council as the nation's final appellate court, became the first female speaker of the House of Representatives.

In a move she called "constitutional evolution," Clark appointed New Zealand First leader Winston Peters foreign minister and United Future leader Peter Dunne revenue minister. Both men remained outside the cabinet, however, and each had unprecedented dispensation to disagree with any government policies apart from his respective portfolio. Labour's preelection-year program had offered incentives to stimulate personal savings, boost productivity, and encourage more women into the workforce. Finance Minister Michael Cullen's 2005–06 budget projected an operating surplus of $NZ 6.6 billion ($NZ 1 = about U.S.$0.70), which prompted other parties to run election campaigns in which they promised tax cuts.

It was a busy legislative year for Clark's government. A law authorizing civil unions took effect on April 26, ending discrimination against both de facto heterosexual and same-sex relationships under more than 100 statutes. The qualifying period for New Zealand citizenship was increased from three years' residency to five years', and from Jan. 1, 2006, the automatic right to citizenship of a child born in New Zealand would be replaced by a requirement that one parent had to be a citizen or permanent resident. New passports were reduced from 10 years' validity to 5 years' and could be refused or withdrawn for reasons of national security. New Zealand's troop deployment for reconstruction work in Afghanistan was extended for an additional year to September 2006. The government announced $NZ 4.6 billion in extra spending over the next decade to modernize equipment and increase military personnel by 10,000 in the three armed services; this constituted a 51% increase in defense funding since 1999. Seventeen Skyhawk strike jets and 17 Aermacchi jet trainers, which had been mothballed in 2001 when the air force strike wing was scrapped, were sold to the U.S. Tactical Air Services for training purposes.

Graham Capill, a lawyer, moral crusader, and one-time police prosecutor, was convicted in Christchurch district court on July 14 and sentenced to nine years' imprisonment for having sexually molested three girls (aged 5–11) over a span of years when he was leader of the Christian Heritage political party. In September former ACT party MP Donna Awatere Huata and her husband, Wi

Huata, were jailed for 33 months and 24 months, respectively, for having fraudulently misused $NZ 82,409 in public funds that had been allocated to a trust to help underprivileged Maori children.

Former prime minister David Lange died in August from renal failure. He had been diagnosed in 2002 with amyloidosis. (*See* OBITUARIES.) Rod Donald, coleader of the Green Party from 1995 and a member of Parliament since 1996, died suddenly from viral myocarditis on November 5 at age 48. Donald had led the campaign to introduce MMP voting. In June New Zealand golfer Michael Campbell won the $1.17 million U.S. Open. (*See* SPORTS AND GAMES: *Golf.*)   (NEALE MCMILLAN)

NICARAGUA

Area: 130,373 sq km (50,337 sq mi)
Population (2005 est.): 5,487,000
Capital: Managua
Head of state and government: President Enrique Bolaños Geyer

Nicaragua spent much of 2005 in crisis as the standoff continued between Pres. Enrique Bolaños and the main opposition parties—Daniel Ortega's left-wing Sandinista Front (FSLN) and Arnoldo Alemán's right-wing Constitutionalist Liberal Party (PLC). The crisis stemmed from constitutional reforms passed by the National Assembly in November 2004 limiting presidential powers. In January the three sides began a national dialogue after Bolaños threatened to declare a state of emergency. The dialogue ended in April when Bolaños vetoed the reforms.

José Miguel Insulza, secretary-general of the Organization of American States (OAS), intervened with a visit to the country, and a special envoy was appointed to persuade the sides to resume negotiations. In June the National Assembly threatened to revoke Bolaños's immunity from prosecution for electoral crimes allegedly committed during the 2001 presidential campaign, and it eventually did revoke the immunity of two of Bolaños's cabinet members. In August the Supreme Court of Justice (CSJ) upheld the reforms, and in September the OAS reiterated its call for a

return to dialogue. The political crisis was defused in October when an agreement was reached under which the constitutional reforms would take effect after Bolaños left office in January 2007.

Alemán, the former president of Nicaragua convicted of money laundering and other crimes in 2003, continued to be allowed to carry out his 20-year prison sentence at his private ranch, though in September restrictions on his movements were eased slightly. U.S. envoys unsuccessfully attempted to unite the country's right-wing parties, with an eye toward preventing an FSLN victory in the 2006 presidential elections.

There were transport strikes in April and September. The weeks-long April strike in several cities saw many violent clashes. For two weeks in September, Nicaragua's Spanish-owned electric utility, Unión Fenosa, rationed power, causing sweeping blackouts, after the CSJ rejected rate increases. In October the International Monetary Fund insisted on a 25% rate increase.

In October the National Assembly ratified the Central America–Dominican Republic Free Trade Agreement, set to take effect on Jan. 1, 2006. Nicaragua was among 18 countries that would benefit from a $40 billion debt-relief package approved in June by the Group of Eight.

In October Hurricane Beta caused considerable damage to homes, crops, infrastructure, and the ecosystem, mostly around cays and isolated communities on the Caribbean coast. A forestry law passed in November called for a 10-year ban on cutting and selling certain kinds of trees.   (NADINE JUBB)

NIGER

Area: 1,189,546 sq km (459,286 sq mi)
Population (2005 est.): 12,163,000
Capital: Niamey
Head of state and government: President Mamadou Tandja, assisted by Prime Minister Hama Amadou

The legacy of the 2004 plague of locusts and drought in Niger manifested itself in a massive food crisis in 2005. In May the UN estimated that more than a quarter of Niger's population faced severe

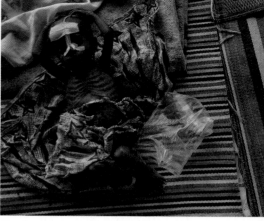

On August 6, 10-month-old Umaya Hamidou is suffering from malnutrition but has been under the care of a Médecins sans Frontières medical clinic at Maradi, Niger, for a week.

shortages and called for $16 million from the international community to tide the country over until the October harvest. Emergency stockpiles were virtually exhausted when, on May 29, Prime Minister Hama Amadou announced to the National Assembly that he was launching an "anguished appeal" for food aid. At least 2,000 demonstrators marched through Niamey on June 2 to protest the government's failure to have responded earlier to the situation and to demand free distribution of foodstuffs in the interior. Officials responded by claiming they had no resources to distribute free food in the famine-threatened areas. Prices of staples, such as rice and millet, had increased fourfold over 2004. Until the world media publicized the crisis, response to the UN's appeals had been minimal, and it was not until mid-August that the World Food Programme airlift of emergency food finally got under way as donors came to recognize the magnitude of the problem.

Pres. Mamadou Tandja was reelected to his second five-year term on Dec. 4, 2004. Throughout 2005 he faced widespread demonstrations by large segments of the population. On March 15 thousands took to Niamey's streets to denounce price increases and the imposition of a 19% value-added tax on a broad variety of essential goods and services. Protests continued for three weeks, and a general strike was threatened. On April 20 the government agreed to drop the tax on flour and milk and to reduce it on both water and electricity.   (NANCY ELLEN LAWLER)

NIGERIA

Area: 923,768 sq km (356,669 sq mi)
Population (2005 est.): 131,530,000
Capital: Abuja
Head of state and government: President Olusegun Obasanjo

The year 2005 was critical for Pres. Olusegun Obasanjo's government as it sought to push through its reform program before the national focus turned to the 2007 electoral campaign. From February to July the National Political Reforms Conference deliberated on wide-ranging constitutional issues that included federalism versus regionalism, resource control and revenue allocation, rotation of the presidency, tenure of presidential and gubernatorial officials, creation of new states, the banning of former military rulers from contesting elections, and judicial immunity for some public-office holders. At times the debate was heated, and on the issues of resource control and revenue allocation, consensus could not be reached. The delegates from the oil-producing Niger Delta walked out in protest against the conference's decision that their region should receive only 17% of oil income; they had wanted their share to rise to 50% over five years.

The Economic and Financial Crimes Commission (EFCC), set up in 2000, estimated that 45% of the nation's oil revenues were being either stolen or wasted. Intent on improving the situation, President Obasanjo intensified his anticorruption campaign. In the spring he dismissed two federal ministers, forced the Senate president to resign, publicly identified legislators known to have received huge bribes, and ordered the arrest of a former inspector of police on charges of financial misconduct. In a nationwide broadcast he announced that the Independent Corrupt Practices Commission would undertake further investigations and arraignments without regard to who was involved—not even himself or his family. In August he imposed even more stringent measures against corrupt practices and ordered the monitoring of the movement and utilization of all state or federal funds at home and abroad. On

August 3 the U.S. Federal Bureau of Investigation raided the Maryland home of Vice Pres. Atiku Abubakar, and on September 15 Bayelsa state Gov. Diepreye Alamieyeseigha was arrested in London on charges of having laundered some £1.8 million (about $3.2 million). Alamieyeseigha later skipped bail and returned to Nigeria, where he was arrested again.

The judicial system moved slowly, and no high-profile public officials were convicted for economic crimes during the year. Obasanjo's opponents questioned his sincerity and dismissed his drive against corrupt officials as hypocritical and motivated by a desire to undermine the political aspirations of his opponents, especially Vice President Abubakar, who was known to have ambitions to succeed Obasanjo in office in 2007. Abia state Gov. Orji Uzor Kalu publicly accused the president of taking bribes himself. In response Obasanjo instructed the EFCC to investigate the allegations and publish its findings. By September relations between the president and his vice president had broken down and their feud threatened to split the ruling party.

As world crude-oil prices rose over $60 a barrel, tensions in the Niger Delta increased. Local communities

Citizens in Lagos protest the fact that despite Nigeria's position as the number one petroleum producer in sub-Saharan Africa, prices of gas and diesel fuel were raised by as much as 40% in late August.

AP/Wide World Photos

resented government policy on resource control and what they saw as high-handed oil-company practices. Federalists, led by Alamieyeseigha, and militants, led by militia leader Alhaji Mujahid Dokubo-Asari, who in 2004 had threatened war against the federal government, vied for public support. Several times during the summer, militant youth organized kidnappings of oil workers and shut down oil-extraction operations. After Alamieyeseigha was detained, the federal government quickly moved to arrest Dokubo-Asari on charges of treason. His followers retaliated by forcing the shutdown of two oil-flow stations, vowing to "kill every iota of oil operations in the Niger Delta" until he was freed. Although the government later reclaimed control of the stations, the situation remained volatile.

Nigeria won its case for repatriation from Switzerland of $458 million that had been stolen by former head of state Gen. Sani Abacha. The country played important roles in the campaigns for debt relief for African nations presented to the Group of Eight powers and for African representation in the UN Security Council. (LARAY DENZER)

NORWAY

Area: 385,199 sq km (148,726 sq mi), including the overseas Arctic territories of Svalbard (61,020 sq km [23,560 sq mi]) and Jan Mayen (377 sq km [145 sq mi])
Population (2005 est.): 4,617,000
Capital: Oslo
Chief of state: King Harald V
Head of government: Prime Ministers Kjell Magne Bondevik and, from October 17, Jens Stoltenberg

The Norwegian economy remained strong in 2005, thanks to income from the export of oil, natural gas, and fish. Oil and gas prices were high, and spokesmen advised increasing production, especially since new methods had been developed to pump carbon dioxide (a serious pollutant) back into the ground or to clean it from the smoke generated. The new techniques were expensive, but in a wider perspective the government, environmental activists, and oil companies agreed that it

Norwegian Prime Minister Kjell Magne Bondevik (left), Swedish Prime Minister Göran Persson (right), and their wives mark the 100th anniversary year of Norwegian independence from Sweden at the historic site of Eidsvoll, Nor., in May.

would be more expensive to continue polluting the environment. Oil production was about to start in the Russian part of the Barents Sea, and many observers feared that the increased offshore oil production and transport could affect some of the most vulnerable Arctic fishing areas. Meanwhile, Norwegians debated whether to boost domestic oil production in the Barents region. Drilling would attract more jobs to the north, but increased production could threaten the fisheries that traditionally had provided livelihoods for families in the region.

Despite the healthy economy and the fact that the UN Development Programme again ranked Norway as having the world's highest standard of living, Prime Minister Kjell Magne Bondevik's centre-right coalition lost the general election on September 12. The so-called Red-Green alliance, led by former prime minister Jens Stoltenberg's Labour Party, had promised to take on more social responsibility and was rewarded with 48% of the vote and 87 of the 169 seats (up from 165 in the 2001 election) in the Storting (parliament). Turnout was high, with about 77% of the electorate voting. Labour received 32.7% of the vote and 61 seats,

followed by the Socialist Left Party with 8.8% (15 seats), and the Centre (Agrarian) Party with 6.5% (11 seats). The right-wing anti-immigration Progress Party, which had previously allied itself with the outgoing coalition, gained new power in the opposition as the second largest party, with 38 seats. Stoltenberg was sworn in as prime minister on October 17. The new government announced that Norway would continue to participate in UN and NATO-led military operations while reducing Norwegian forces in Iraq and Afghanistan to near nil, but the country would not pursue EU membership.

During the year Norway and Sweden commemorated the 100th anniversary of the peaceful end of the Swedish-Norwegian union. King Harald recovered from heart surgery in time to take part in the celebration on June 7 (the date in 1905 when Norwegian Prime Minister Christian Michelsen declared that King Oscar II had not fulfilled his duty as Norwegian king and the union was thus ended). On December 3 Crown Princess Mette-Marit gave birth to a son. His name was Sverre Magnus, and he was the third in line to the throne, behind his father, Crown Prince Haakon, and his sister, Ingrid Alexandra. Leah Isadora Behn, the second daughter of Princess Märtha Louise and her husband, Ari Behn, was born on April 8. (HILDE SANDVIK)

OMAN

Area: 309,500 sq km (119,500 sq mi)
Population (2005 est.): 2,409,000
Capital: Muscat
Head of state and government: Sultan and Prime Minister Qaboos bin Said (Qabus ibn Sa'id)

The conclusion of a free-trade agreement (FTA) with the United States in October 2005 was an important breakthrough for Oman; it was to go into effect by the end of 2005. The FTA was emblematic of Oman's commitment to increased commercial liberalization en route to integrating its economy further with the global marketplace. The agreement would eliminate tariff and other barriers to trade between the two countries, and it was signed at a time when the six-country Gulf Cooperation Council (GCC) was its closest ever to concluding a free-trade agreement with the European Union. The trade accord followed a major Omani military strategic decision in 2004 to reconfigure the lead segments of its air force with advanced American-built F-16 fighter aircraft.

Other highlights were the construction of massive coastal hotel and resort complexes at Barka, Yiti, Seeb, and Bandar Jissah, together with eight similar but smaller-scale investment schemes elsewhere in the sultanate. Costing a total of $17.5 billion, the dozen projects were designed to attract vacationers and purchasers of second homes in top income brackets. The benefits of Oman's ever-widening economic engagement with the international tourist industry and increased levels of foreign direct investment in development sectors were mainly targeted at expanding employment opportunities for the country's burgeoning population of youth leaving school. (JOHN DUKE ANTHONY)

PAKISTAN

Area: 796,096 sq km (307,374 sq mi), excluding the 84,159-sq-km Pakistani-administered portion of Jammu and Kashmir
Population (2005 est.): 153,960,000 (excluding nearly 4,350,000 residents of Pakistani-administered Jammu and Kashmir as well as 950,000 Afghan refugees)
Capital: Islamabad
Head of state and government: President Gen. Pervez Musharraf, assisted by Prime Minister Shaukat Aziz

A magnitude-7.6 earthquake struck on Oct. 8, 2005, in Pakistan near the city of Muzaffarabad near the border between Pakistani- and Indian-administered Kashmir. The quake was one of the largest and most damaging in modern times; by mid-November the death toll in Pakistan alone exceeded 87,000. (*See* SIDEBAR.)

Pres. Pervez Musharraf's decision on Dec. 30, 2004, to renege on his promise to yield his role as commanding officer of the Pakistani army influenced developments significantly in 2005. In April the Supreme Court dismissed all constitution petitions relating to the 17th amendment and the dual office of the president, and Musharraf remained head of the army as well as of the government.

The president sustained peace talks with India and met with his Indian counterpart in September at the 60th session of the UN General Assembly in New York. In October Islamabad and New Delhi signed an agreement on prenotification of flight testing of ballistic missiles. Pakistan had been especially irked by India's repeated accusations that Islamabad harboured an "infrastructure for terrorism," and, given continued violence in Kashmir, Islamabad rejected a proposal by UN Secretary-General Kofi Annan calling for the decades-old UN Military Observers Group in Kashmir to be disbanded. The first round of high-level negotiations was completed in October, and a second round of foreign ministers' meetings was set for January 2006. Islamabad also announced that Pakistan would not be the first country to resume nuclear testing. The Kashmir earthquake prompted the opening in November of a single crossing point in the Line of Control to help the flow of relief aid.

Tensions between Pakistan and Afghanistan were in evidence when Kabul accused Islamabad of not adequately

Cataclysm in Kashmir

On Oct. 8, 2005, a magnitude-7.6 earthquake on the border between Pakistan's North-West Frontier Province and Kashmir brought tragedy not only to Pakistan but to India and Afghanistan as well. The epicentre was near the city of Muzaffarabad. Several towns were effectively leveled. Schools collapsed and children and teachers were crushed. Some 80,000 people perished, the vast majority of them in the Pakistani-administered region of Kashmir. Compounding the horror, destruction from the earthquake and bad weather made the arrival of aid, particularly to remote mountain areas, painfully slow in arriving. With hospitals in Muzaffarabad destroyed, makeshift trauma centres had to be contrived. A week after the quake, millions were still without food, water, and shelter, and the UN estimated that two weeks after the event, only 30–40% of the affected villages had even been inspected. The acute shortage of aid increased the death toll, and hundreds of thousands were left homeless.

A number of political adjustments followed the massive destruction. In places where the Pakistani army could not reach to give aid, Islamist militant groups were often able to assist. India, which had long contested control of the Kashmir region with Pakistan but itself was badly damaged, offered aid. Pakistan agreed to receive relief supplies—tents, blankets, food, and medicine—but refused an offer of helicopters. Weeks of negotiation resulted in an agreement to temporarily open points along the India-Pakistan Line of Control to allow aid to pass through. At year's end, however, UN relief workers said that they were still working on rescue and survival, and aid still had not reached many of those survivors who faced the onslaught of winter.   (PATRICIA BAUER)

preventing terrorists from infiltrating Afghanistan. In August Islamabad announced that it intended to relocate remaining Afghan refugees away from the border. The Pakistani army sustained its campaign against terrorists secreted in the mountains along the Afghan frontier. Major operations continued in Waziristan. In May a suicide bomber detonated a device amid hundreds of Shi'ite Muslims at a shrine near Islamabad, and suicide bombings in Karachi provoked riots that spread to many neighbourhoods. In September bombs were detonated in Lahore, where victims were numerous, and in

December Hamza Rabia, a senior al-Qaeda operative, was killed in North Waziristan along the Afghan border.

Musharraf's political opposition continued its threats to disrupt routine in the National Assembly, but repeated walkouts by the Alliance for the Restoration of Democracy and the Muttahida Majlis-i-Amal (MMA) failed to energize public response. In exile former president Benazir Bhutto and former prime minister Nawaz Sharif agreed to a "Charter of Democracy," but this too failed to move the Pakistani public.

The leader of the MMA and the Jamaat-e-Islami Party, Qazi Hussain Ahmed, rejected accusations that his followers were principally responsible for sectarian conflict. Citing Musharraf's ties with the United States, the MMA leader insisted that the president had given renewed impetus to "secularism" in the country and if not challenged would lead Pakistan away from its Islamic roots. Musharraf further angered fundamentalists by signing the Criminal Law Bill that called for enhanced punishment for "honour-related crimes." The law also provided some protection for women against arbitrary treatment by vigilante religious orders. Musharraf strongly opposed efforts by the MMA in the North-West Frontier Province to prevent women from voting in local elections. In mid-August

A woman in the village of Comsar mourns the deaths of 53 children and a teacher in the school that collapsed in the earthquake that struck Pakistani-administered Kashmir on October 8.

Musharraf promulgated an ordinance, repudiated by the religious opposition, amending the Societies Registration Act requiring the country's 11,882 seminaries to register with the government. Earlier, all non-Pakistanis allegedly studying in Pakistani religious schools had been ordered to leave the country. The religious leaders condemned these actions as well as the general's "chance" meeting with the Israeli prime minister at the UN and his address to the American Jewish Congress during his New York visit.

Sectarian riots broke out in the Himalayan region of Gilgit, and unrest in Balochistan threatened to cut the natural gas supply from the Sui fields. Musharraf urged mutual consultation with local leaders and cited the recently completed Makran Coastal Highway and the nearly completed Mirani Dam, Gwadar Port, and Kachhi Canal as examples of government desire to elevate living standards in Balochistan.

In January Pakistan gave the United States custody of Ahmad Khalfan Ghailani, a Tanzanian affiliated with al-Qaeda and linked with the bombing of the American embassies in East Africa in 1998. In May the alleged third most senior leader of al-Qaeda, Abu Farraj al-Libbi, was captured near Peshawar and transferred to American custody. Musharraf nonetheless held to his decision not to permit American intelligence officials to interview 'Abd al-Qadir Khan, the father of Pakistan's nuclear program. Following the July London bus and subway bombings, which had possible connections with Pakistani extremist groups, Musharraf ordered a national crackdown on Islamist "extremists." The MMA called the action "state terrorism" and accused Musharraf of becoming a "Western puppet."

The U.S. announced allocations of $691 million to Pakistan for fiscal year 2006, including $300 million for foreign military financing. Washington also lifted long-imposed sanctions and allowed Pakistan to purchase two dozen F-16 warplanes. Islamabad's external debt increased by $1.52 billion to $34.82 billion in the first half of the fiscal year. The trade deficit amounted to $2.4 billion, up from $723 million in 2004. Inflation was pegged at 8.8%, up from 3.4% in 2004. Food prices increased by 13.33%, rent for housing soared 12.3%, and transport and communications services rose 10.65%. Defense expenditure for 2004–05 was 9.2% over budget, and for 2005–06 the government requested still higher expenditures (15%) despite a sharp decline in revenues. (LAWRENCE ZIRING)

PALAU

Area: 488 sq km (188 sq mi)
Population (2005 est.): 21,100
Provisional capital: Koror; new capital buildings at Melekeok (on Babelthuap) scheduled to be completed in 2006
Head of state and government: President Tommy Remengesau, Jr.

In 2005 Palau continued to enjoy one of the highest living standards in the Pacific region, thanks to disbursements by the U.S. under the Compact of Free Association. Palau was allocated $12.8 million in direct assistance from the U.S. during the year. Major building projects included an 85-km (53-mi) highway on the island of Babelthuap and the continuing construction of a new national capital complex at Melekeok. As part of a strategy to improve public health in Palau, Pres. Tommy Remengesau, Jr., declared September 2005 as Alcohol and Addiction Recovery Month. Remengesau stressed the need to support family members and encourage addicts in the community to seek help.

Palau remained a conspicuous supporter of Taiwan. In New York City on September 14, President Remengesau urged the UN to fulfill its goal of universal representation by admitting Taiwan as a member. Taiwanese Pres. Chen Shui-bian went to Palau to attend the inauguration ceremony for Remengesau, who won reelection in 2004. Chen's visit provoked an angry response from China. (A.R.G. GRIFFITHS)

PANAMA

Area: 75,040 sq km (28,973 sq mi)
Population (2005 est.): 3,140,000
Capital: Panama City
Head of state and government: President Martín Torrijos

Panamanian Pres. Martín Torrijos began 2005 with his approval ratings above 60% and ended the year with his ratings below 20%. The fall was among the fastest seen by any Panamanian president since democracy was restored to the country in 1989 and shattered any honeymoon the president might have enjoyed since coming to office in September 2004. The decline was due in part to increasing evidence of government corruption, particularly in the judicial branch, and a series of massive protests against reform legislation proposed by Torrijos to overhaul the social security and tax systems.

Charges of corruption swirled around the Supreme Court. Several of the justices were accused of receiving bribes in exchange for favourable rulings toward drug traffickers and money launderers. Amid the controversy, Torrijos appointed a State Commission for Justice to investigate corruption in the judiciary and to develop possible judicial reforms.

In early 2005 Torrijos proposed a sweeping tax-reform initiative that would close many tax loopholes, but he was forced to revise his proposal after intense protests from leading business groups. More troubling for Torrijos was the reaction to his proposed changes to the social security system. The reforms were aimed at dealing with a $3 billion deficit in the Social Security Fund. The proposed changes, which included a gradual raise in the retirement age and an increase in pension contributions by both employers and workers, sparked violent protests in early May. Despite the protests, the National Assembly approved the reforms on June 1. This led the National Front for the Defense of Social Security, an organization created to oppose the reforms, to escalate the demonstrations, paralyzing the streets of Panama City for several weeks. Bowing to popular pressure, the president on June 21 announced the opening of a "national dialogue" to propose changes to the new social security law.

U.S. Pres. George W. Bush visited Panama on November 6–7. The visit by Bush was the first by a sitting U.S. president since Pres. George H.W. Bush visited Panama in 1992. Bush's visit to Panama in November reciprocated Torrijos's April 28 visit to the U.S. The talks between the two leaders centred on negotiations for a bilateral free-trade agreement and enhanced security cooperation. (ORLANDO J. PÉREZ)

© Torsten Blackwood/AFP/Getty Images

To join celebrations of the 30th anniversary of Papua New Guinea's independence from Australia on September 16, this group of Manubada islanders is traveling to the capital, Port Moresby, on a lagatoi, *a large Papuan trading canoe.*

PAPUA NEW GUINEA

Area: 462,840 sq km (178,704 sq mi)
Population (2005 est.): 5,887,000
Capital: Port Moresby
Chief of state: Queen Elizabeth II, represented by Governor-General Sir Paulias Matane
Head of government: Prime Minister Sir Michael Somare

On Sept. 16, 2005, Prime Minister Sir Michael Somare, who had steered Papua New Guinea through its achievement of statehood in 1975, presided over the country's official celebration of 30 years of independence from Australia. Throughout the year Somare gave top priority to reducing economic reliance on donor aid from Australia, New Zealand, China, South Korea, and the EU. Somare's government adopted an export-focused strategy for economic recovery based on improvements to infrastructure and a public-works program of port, jetty, bridge, and road construction.

Papua New Guinea had to resolve several diplomatic disputes with Australia in advance of the September festivities. These included a disagreement over the local deployment of Australian Federal Police and the subsequent collapse in May of Australia's U.S.$750 million aid program. In March Prime Minister Somare was incensed when Brisbane Airport security staff, who were searching for explosives as part of the war on terrorism, asked him to remove his shoes. Minister of Inter-Government Relations Sir Peter Barter stressed the need to maintain good relations with Australia and pointed to the potential significance of a proposed natural gas pipeline between the two Pacific Ocean neighbours.

In May–June the secessionist province of Bougainville held its first elections under the terms of the 2001 peace agreement. Former rebel leader Joseph Kabui was elected to lead the province's new autonomous government.

(A.R.G. GRIFFITHS)

PARAGUAY

Area: 406,752 sq km (157,048 sq mi)
Population (2005 est.): 5,905,000
Capital: Asunción
Head of state and government: President Nicanor Duarte Frutos

In 2005 former Paraguayan army chief Gen. Lino Oviedo was back in the news. Imprisoned since June 2004 for having led a 1996 military rebellion, Oviedo was acquitted in January of charges that he had conspired in 1999 to destabilize then president Luis González Macchi's government. It was the second court victory for Oviedo since he began serving a 10-year prison sentence after having returned voluntarily from exile in Brazil. In October 2004 he had also been acquitted of having masterminded a military plot in 2000. Oviedo, who retained a popular following in Paraguay, still held out hopes of becoming president and had expressed a wish to participate in the upcoming 2008 elections. It was unclear, however, if he would be able to overcome his current sentence and other charges pending.

Paraguay continued to reel from waves of lawlessness during the year. On February 16 the country's highest-profile kidnapping case ended tragically when the body of Cecilia Cubas, daughter of former president Raúl Cubas, was found buried behind an abandoned house in suburban Asunción. The 32-year-old Cubas had been abducted by gunmen five months earlier. Officials in Paraguay asserted that evidence linked an extremist group known as Free Fatherland to the crime and that the group had received training and advice regarding the kidnapping from Colombia's guerrilla insurgency FARC (the Revolutionary Armed Forces of Colombia). Pres. Nicanor Duarte soon afterward ordered the deployment of military troops to reinforce police in some rural departments. Duarte also unveiled a security plan that would amend the constitution to institutionalize the military's role in "public security" tasks. The Roman Catholic Church, however, condemned what it described as "creeping authoritarianism" in the country and singled out Duarte's repression of social protests by landless peasant groups, considered by the government as vulnerable to left-wing subversion.

In July a rumour spread that 500 U.S. Marines had landed in the northern Chaco desert as part of a plan to establish a secret military base that would eventually quarter 16,000 troops near Bolivia's gas deposits. In reality, the Paraguayan Senate had authorized the arrival of some 400 American soldiers in small groups over 18 months to run courses in counterinsurgency and antidrug operations. Several joint military exercises were planned as well. In August the Senate also approved the expropriation in the Chaco of 52,000 ha (about 128,000 ac) of land owned by a firm that was affiliated with controversial Sun Myung Moon's Unification Church. The move burnished the reformist image of President Duarte, who had argued for the expropriation to bolster government efforts toward land reform. (PAUL C. SONDROL)

PERU

Area: 1,285,198 sq km (496,218 sq mi)
Population (2005 est.): 27,968,000
Capital: Lima
Head of state and government: President Alejandro Toledo

As 2005 unfolded, Peru increasingly looked ahead to presidential and congressional elections scheduled for April 2006. A great deal of posturing and negotiating occurred as candidates, parties, and various movements all sought to position themselves for these elections. Early presidential favourites included well-known politicians such as former president Alan García, former interim president Valentín Paniagua, and Popular Christian Party leader Lourdes Flores Nano, but all polls suggested that much of the electorate had yet to decide on their candidate. Former president Alberto Fujimori, who had been residing in Japan and resist-

Supporters of fugitive former Peruvian president Alberto Fujimori rally in the streets of Lima on November 6. Fujimori had declared that he would return home from exile in Japan and seek the presidency again.

ing extradition to Peru on a variety of charges, surprised nearly everyone by traveling to Chile in November—apparently as a first step toward returning to Peru to challenge for the right to participate in the elections. His future remained uncertain, however, after Chilean authorities decided to detain him. By year's end the Peruvian government was preparing a formal request for Chile to extradite Fujimori.

In overall economic terms, Peru enjoyed a good year. GNP growth was nearly 5%; inflation was nil; exports as well as imports were up; and most financial indicators were favourable. Nevertheless, Pres. Alejandro Toledo continued to have very low levels of public support, with his approval rating hovering around 10%. Problems arose for him in January when his sister was placed under house arrest for allegedly having masterminded the forgery of thousands of signatures to help get Toledo's party, Peru Posible, on the 2000 presidential ballot. Toledo denied his sister's involvement in the so-called signature scandal and that he had ever had knowledge of such a scheme. His credibility was further eroded by the allegations and by the fact that several other members of his family had been linked to corruption cases.

Toledo was also hurt by a cabinet crisis in August that threatened briefly to bring down the government. The crisis was precipitated when a key Toledo ally, Fernando Olivera, was appointed minister of foreign affairs. Olivera, who was known for taking controversial stands such as supporting the legalization of coca production in southern Peru, was seen as a divisive figure by many, and his appointment was widely criticized. Prime Minister Carlos Ferrero resigned in protest, a move that under Peruvian law required the rest of the cabinet, including Olivera, to resign as well. The situation was diffused when Toledo named Pedro Pablo Kuczynski, a former finance minister who enjoyed virtually unanimous support, as the country's new prime minister. A new cabinet was also named, with the foreign affairs portfolio going to Oscar Maurtua de Romana, a former Peruvian ambassador to Thailand.

Peru also dealt with a variety of other political and social problems. A series of strikes and demonstrations by numerous groups—including rice growers, coca farmers and producers, and nurses—as well as a number of violent clashes between mining companies and

the inhabitants of mining communities contributed to unease throughout the year. Progress did occur on some fronts, however. The Camisea gas pipeline was operational and successful; a new transcontinental highway linking Peru with Brazil and other countries was inaugurated; and the country carried out its first nationwide population and housing census since 1993. In addition, a new government program was launched that would eventually provide monthly stipends to about 25% of Peru's lowest-income families. (HENRY A. DIETZ)

PHILIPPINES

Area: 316,294 sq km (122,121 sq mi)
Population (2005 est.): 84,191,000
Capital: Quezon City (designated national government centre and the location of the lower house of the legislature and some ministries); many government offices are in Manila or other suburbs
Head of state and government: President Gloria Macapagal Arroyo

In September 2005 the lower house of the Philippine Congress rejected an effort to impeach Pres. Gloria Macapagal Arroyo over charges that she had cheated during the 2004 elections, in which Arroyo won a six-year term by more than a million votes. Arroyo's political opponents went public in June with recordings of telephone conversations she had during the 2004 vote counting. On one recording a woman's voice could be heard asking an election commissioner if her lead could fall below a million ballots. "We will do our best," the man replied, without elaborating. Accusing Arroyo of vote rigging, her opponents organized demonstrations in an effort to force her from office. Unlike the "people power" rallies that ousted Pres. Joseph Estrada in 2001 and Pres. Ferdinand Marcos in 1986, however, the protests against Arroyo failed to draw the massive numbers of participants who had mobbed Manila in those earlier demonstrations. Arroyo's supporters, in fact, turned out for counterdemonstrations that were larger than the rallies staged by the opposition.

In a television address on June 27, Arroyo acknowledged having phoned an

In Manila, Gloria Macapagal Arroyo is burned in effigy by protesters on July 25, the day of her state of the nation message that followed new allegations regarding her contentious reelection as president of the Philippines in 2004.

© Jay Directo/AFP/Getty Images

election commissioner during vote counting, but she said her conversations were only an attempt to keep her votes from disappearing, not to influence the election's outcome. Denying any impropriety, she apologized for a "lapse in judgment" in making the phone calls. Arroyo's apology failed to mollify her opponents. To vote rigging they added other charges, including the padding of government contracts and responsibility for unjustified army killings of leftist activists. They also accused her husband, businessman José Miguel Arroyo, their son Juan, and a brother-in-law of receiving kickbacks from illegal gambling. Her husband and son later went into exile in San Francisco. When members of Arroyo's cabinet discussed her quitting on the grounds that she could no longer govern effectively, she fired 10 of them on July 7. They and former president Corazon Aquino called on Arroyo to resign. Although the Justice Committee of the lower house rejected impeachment charges, Arroyo's opponents took the charges to the full house. After almost 24 hours of acrimonious debate, the house voted 158 to 51 on September 6 to uphold the committee's decision.

Before the impeachment effort, Arroyo had advocated changing the Philippines' American-style presidential system to a European-style parliamentary system, with the chief executive being a prime minister dependent on majority backing in the lower house of Congress. She contended that this would eliminate the turmoil caused by replacing a chief executive through demonstrations and that it might make it easier for the executive to get laws through Congress, which had often stymied presidential efforts. Arroyo reiterated the need for

such a change in her annual state of the nation speech to Congress on July 25, but many congressional members were skeptical, partly because the upper house's power would be reduced.

Bombs exploded in Manila and two southern cities on February 14, killing eight people and wounding more than a hundred. In October an Indonesian and two Filipinos were sentenced to death for the bombings, which police attributed to Abu Sayyaf, an affiliate of the al-Qaeda terrorist network.

One of the most influential Filipinos, Jaime Cardinal Sin (*see* OBITUARIES), died on June 21. As Roman Catholic archbishop of Manila for three decades, he played key roles in the ousters of Marcos and Estrada. Luis Taruc (*see* OBITUARIES), leader of the communist Huk movement from 1942 to 1954, died on May 4.   (HENRY S. BRADSHER)

POLAND

Area: 312,685 sq km (120,728 sq mi)
Population (2005 est.): 38,164,000
Capital: Warsaw
Chief of state: Presidents Aleksander Kwasniewski and, from December 23, Lech Kaczynski
Head of government: Prime Ministers Marek Belka and, from October 31, Kazimierz Marcinkiewicz

The year 2005 in Poland was special because of the number of anniversaries, all having their origin in the

country's recent history. Preeminent among these was the 25th anniversary of the trade union Solidarity, which triggered the transformation not only of communist Poland but the whole of the former Eastern Bloc. The celebrations in Gdansk gathered many top European politicians, including the president of the European Commission, José Barroso, and the heads of most of the European states that owed the end of communism to the Polish unionists. The events of 1980, in the words of German Pres. Horst Köhler, "helped to overcome the division of Europe, and, consequently, Germany."

Another momentous event for Poland—this one sad and almost overshadowing the Solidarity celebrations—was the death earlier in the year of Pope John Paul II. (*See* OBITUARIES.) It was the Polish-born pontiff's messages of encouragement that had had Poles chanting the slogan "There's no liberty without solidarity," which ultimately led to the decentralization of the political system and democratic elections. The 15th anniversary of these elections was yet another date to be remembered in 2005. August turned out to be a month not only for celebration but also for reflection and some soul-searching over some disappointments and a growing decline in public confidence in the country's political leaders.

Despite promises for the early dissolution of the government, the politicians of the ruling Democratic Left Alliance continued to cling to power, although its public support dropped to 11% and party membership fell drastically. The two centre-right opposition parties, Civic Platform (PO) and Law and Justice (PiS)—both with a Solidarity pedigree—were not idle and used this time to prepare for the parliamentary elections on September 25. Both parties were conservative, and they basically agreed on moral and historical issues, but they had little in common when it came to economic matters. The PO had a free-market stance, while the PiS was more populist and nationalist, promising social protection, a safeguarding of Christian values, and restoration of the integrity of the state.

The two main candidates for the presidency were Donald Tusk and Lech Kaczynski, the leaders of the PO and the PiS, respectively. On October 23, in the second round of voting, Poles chose Kaczynski, the twin brother of PiS leader Jaroslaw Kaczynski. A mere 4% of the vote secured the PiS the right to appoint the prime minister in the coali-

446

tion that, despite fierce rivalry, the two parties were destined to form. In a surprise move, PiS economist Kazimierz Marcinkiewicz took the post on October 31, and despite some differences between him and Kaczynski, for the first time in postwar Poland both the government and the presidency were completely free of all communists and communist influence.

In 2005 Poland also celebrated the first anniversary of its joining the European Union, which provided an occasion to count some of the gains of EU membership, mainly in the agricultural sector (structural funds and subsidies), the opening of markets, as well as expanded opportunities for travel, jobs, and education.

Poland's GDP, expected to end the year at 3.5%, was still acceptable by EU standards, but the country's economy had slowed down considerably in comparison with most of the other former communist states that had joined the EU in 2004. An unemployment rate of 17.6% (the highest in the EU), a budget deficit of 6.8% of GDP, and a debt-to-GDP ratio of 53% (the constitutional limit was 55%) in October posed a real challenge for the new government, which started off its term with generous social benefits promises.

Internationally Poland began to engage more in affairs of significance, both religious and political. "The Europe of Dialogue," the sixth Gniezno Congress held in Poland's historic first capital in September, attracted some 800 representatives of different religions, including for the first time members of the Jewish and Islamic faiths. One activity that could have far-reaching consequences was Poland's overt involvement in Ukraine's "Orange Revolution." Also, Poland was demonstrating increased self-confidence and influence in Brussels and in EU affairs generally. (IWONA GRENDA)

PORTUGAL

Area: 92,152 sq km (35,580 sq mi)
Population (2005 est.): 10,513,000
Capital: Lisbon
Chief of state: President Jorge Sampaio
Head of government: Prime Ministers Pedro Santana Lopes and, from March 12, José Sócrates

Portugal suffered a year of turmoil in 2005. Pres. Jorge Sampaio called early elections following infighting in the centre-right coalition led by Prime Minister Pedro Santana Lopes of the Social Democratic Party (PSD). Santana Lopes ran a lame-duck government until the election on February 20 and was unable to make any major policy decisions in the run-up to the vote. The Socialist Party (PS) swept to victory, winning an absolute majority in the parliament. José Sócrates, the young and charismatic PS leader who had served as environment minister from 1999 to 2002, became prime minister. His first challenge was the budget deficit, which a Bank of Portugal audit estimated would increase to more than 6.8% of GDP in 2005—more than twice the European Union's limit—if no steps were taken to reduce it. The Sócrates government moved to raise sales taxes and started cracking down on tax dodgers to boost revenue, while at the same time promising to rein in public spending. The deficit target remained a high 6.2% of GDP for the year, though it was expected to shrink to 4.8% in 2006 and to 3% by 2008.

The austerity measures heightened the country's gloomy outlook. Economic growth stumbled, heading back toward recession after a brief recovery in 2004. The country also was hit by a severe drought that dried up reservoirs and seriously reduced key agricultural output. The long dry season—which followed a stretch of low-rainfall years—resulted in an outbreak of fires, some of which were thought to have been caused by arson. More than 280,000 ha (about 700,000 ac) of forested terrain burned, and renewed questions were raised over the country's land-management regime and its emergency preparedness for what had seemingly become an annual tragedy.

The fires, the drought, and the struggling economy made Sócrates's first months in office difficult. The initial burst of postelection euphoria as the Socialists resumed control of the country faded quickly. Finance Minister Luis Campos e Cunha, a former central bank vice president, tendered his resignation, and in October municipal elections, the

Portugal's Socialist Party leader José Sócrates greets his followers at a Lisbon hotel on February 21 following the party's victory in an early general election. Sócrates became prime minister on March 12.

Socialists stumbled to their biggest loss at the polls. The centre-right PSD held such key cities as Lisbon, Porto, and Sintra and won about half of the country's total mayoral victories. While the vote was seen as a clear defeat for Sócrates and the PS, it was unlikely to spark an early general election, given the party's control of the parliament.

The next political battle was expected to be the January 2006 presidential election pitting former PSD prime minister Aníbal Cavaco Silva, who was seen as the front-runner, against former president and Socialist prime minister Mário Soares, as well as another PS stalwart, poet Manuel Alegre. Although the presidency was largely a ceremonial position, the next president was expected to confront the growing "democratic gap" between politicians and citizens, which had led to rising abstention rates and general political apathy. The mayoral elections contributed to the problem; three of the winners were under investigation for corruption, including one who had fled to Brazil for two years before returning to campaign.

Two significant Portuguese figures died during the year: Álvaro Cunhal, who was a force in the Portuguese Communist Party (PCP) for more than half a century, and former prime minister Vasco Gonçalves. (See OBITUARIES.) Although its support had fallen, the PCP remained an active minority force in domestic politics. In the February general election, the PCP and its coalition partner, the Ecology Party, saw a modest increase in their share of the vote—to 7.6% from 7% in the 2002 election. (ERIK T. BURNS)

QATAR

Area: 11,427 sq km (4,412 sq mi)
Population (2005 est.): 773,000
Capital: Doha
Head of state and government: Emir Sheikh Hamad ibn Khalifah al-Thani, assisted by Prime Minister Sheikh Abdullah ibn Khalifah al-Thani

Major accomplishments in Qatar in 2005 included the ground breaking for a new international airport and the announcement of plans for the establishment of a United Nations human rights centre. The latter would be the first of its kind in the Arabian Peninsula and Persian Gulf. Focusing on southwestern Asia and the Arab world, the centre's role would be to facilitate cooperation and exchange of information among civil society organizations and governments with a view to safeguarding and implementing human rights.

Qatar increased its role as a provider of liquefied natural gas (LNG) to Europe and North America. Doha signed deals with global energy giants Shell, Exxon Mobil, Total, and Chevron valued at more than $20 billion. In addition, it concluded a 25-year agreement to supply substantial amounts of LNG to Great Britain. Qatar also continued to pursue the possibility of providing gas on a long-term basis to the U.S. The latter prospect took on added importance as the effects of major hurricanes revealed the extent to which the large energy component of the U.S. economy was constrained by distribution bottlenecks and an inadequate number of refineries.

Qatar hosted its fifth annual international Forum on Democracy and Free Trade. As a result of exchanges between the more than 500 conference participants from virtually every corner of the globe, a heightened emphasis was placed on two global requirements. One was the need to enhance living standards in the world's poorest countries, particularly among rural populations and women. The other was increased attention to improving the effectiveness of political systems and representative governance worldwide. Within Arabia and the Gulf region, these and related initiatives furthered Qatar's activist profile in selected areas of international affairs.   (JOHN DUKE ANTHONY)

ROMANIA

Area: 238,391 sq km (92,043 sq mi)
Population (2005 est.): 21,602,000
Capital: Bucharest
Chief of state: President Traian Basescu
Head of government: Prime Minister Calin Popescu-Tariceanu

In 2005 the parliament in Romania was deadlocked, owing to the inconclusive 2004 elections, which resulted in a weak centre-right coalition government that included several smaller parties. Members of the Social Democratic Party (PSD), usually the dominant political force, continued to chair the Senate and the Chamber of Deputies. This enabled the PSD to stall government business in the vital year that Romania had to pass numerous laws necessary before it could join the European Union in 2007. The EU demanded a reform of the justice system, which the PSD had packed with its own appointees when it was in power. The minister of justice, human rights lawyer Monica Macovei, the most energetic member of a lacklustre government, was in constant conflict with

branches of the judicial system opposed to her reformist agenda. In July the Constitutional Court voted down her proposals to modify the separation of powers principle, which involved a more rapid promotion for younger judges and magistrates who were trained after the communist era. In August, however, she scored a victory with the appointment to the National Anticorruption Prosecutor's Office of a new chief, Daniel Morar, who reopened cases against numerous figures from the elite. Much of the progress acknowledged by the EU in its October 25 report on Romania stemmed from improvements in the justice system.

Pres. Traian Basescu shared power with the government and demonstrated during the year that he planned to be an activist head of state. His calls for early elections to break the parliamentary deadlock, the introduction of a single-chamber parliament, and electoral reform (in an effort to restore popular confidence in the political system) were rejected, however, by Prime Minister Calin Popescu-Tariceanu. In response, President Basescu in August accused the prime minister, a former businessman, of remaining too close to influential economic interests.

After initial optimism over the ability of the new government to show a higher commitment to public service than its predecessor had, more than

In October police in eastern Romania dispose of bags containing birds that were culled because of suspected infection with avian flu. Discovery of the virus in some Romanian ducks was the first evidence that the disease had reached Europe.

50% of Romanians who took part in a poll in October declared that the country was moving in the wrong direction. Corruption remained endemic; a report released by the Health Ministry on September 25 showed that in 2004 Romanians had paid bribes to health staff totaling $360 million, almost half the amount the ministry had paid to its employees. The gloom was compounded by severe flooding in many parts of the country from April to October. As a result, agricultural output was severely affected, and 2005 became one of the worst years ever for wine production. In October Romania reported avian flu in poultry, which led to a cull of the domestic bird population in areas affected by the virus.

Though the PSD continued to wield power in the state bureaucracy, it was unable to exploit the government's difficulties. Infighting among PSD leaders made it challenging for Mircea Geoana, the party's new leader, to establish his authority. His promise in September to transform the PSD into a modern leftist force seemed destined for failure, especially when those who became multimillionaires while serving as government ministers remained in the top echelons of the party.

(TOM GALLAGHER)

RUSSIA

Area: 17,075,400 sq km (6,592,800 sq mi)
Population (2005 est.): 143,420,000
Capital: Moscow
Chief of state: President Vladimir Putin
Head of government: Prime Minister Mikhail Fradkov

Domestic Politics. The year 2005 began with thousands of angry pensioners taking to the streets all over Russia to protest against changes in the way welfare benefits were paid. These apparently spontaneous demonstrations took the authorities by surprise. They occurred, moreover, at a time when the Russian leadership was struggling to come to terms with the outcome of Ukraine's "Orange Revolution" of December 2004, seen by the Kremlin as a significant setback for Russia's geopolitical position. The combination of the two events plunged the Kremlin into

apparent alarm that Russia might be the next post-Soviet state to experience a "coloured" revolution—that is, a change of regime brought about as a result of peaceful popular protest.

This was remarkable in that Pres. Vladimir Putin had barely completed the first year of his second term in office. Parliamentary elections were not due until 2007, and the next presidential election—when Putin would be obliged to leave office, since the constitution restricted a president to no more than two successive terms in office—would be held in 2008. Putin had used his first term (2000–04) to wage a sustained campaign aimed at restoring stability to Russian society, recentralizing power, and modernizing the economy. He and his team had also succeeded in neutralizing the electronic media, taming the parliament, forcing the political opposition to the margins, launching a pro-Kremlin youth movement, and concentrating almost all the levers of state power in the hands of the presidency. As a result, Putin faced no credible opposition. His approval ratings dipped following the monetization of welfare benefits in January but soon returned to their previously high levels of 70% or above. Putin was described as the most powerful Russian leader since Leonid Brezhnev or even, some said, Joseph

Pensioners demonstrate in front of the mayor's office in St. Petersburg to protest changes in government benefits. Such seemingly spontaneous protests in various cities were the largest outburst of public anger in the five-year tenure of Pres. Vladimir Putin.

AP/Wide World Photos

Stalin. Having consolidated power in his first term, he had been expected to use the second to enact tough but necessary reforms to enable the Russian economy to catch up with those of the advanced Western world.

Instead the Kremlin seemed in the first half of 2005 to fall into indecision. The main concerns of the members of Putin's entourage appeared to be fear of civil disorder (however improbable that looked to outside observers), determination to ensure that nothing undermined the president's approval ratings or hindered an orderly transfer of power in 2008 to a Putin-nominated successor, desire to safeguard their own positions in the post-Putin period, and professed fear of Western plans to weaken Russia and dismember its territory. As a result, the Kremlin appeared for much of 2005 able to focus on little other than the upcoming elections, far off though these were.

By year's end the leadership appeared to have recovered its composure. In September Putin announced the creation of new national programs. In November he carried out a major government reshuffle. Mikhail Fradkov remained prime minister, but the head of the Presidential Administration, Dmitry Medvedev, was appointed first deputy prime minister with responsibility for the new national projects, while Defense Minister Sergey Ivanov became deputy prime minister. There was speculation that the appointments put Medvedev and Ivanov, both close Putin confidants, in line as possible presidential candidates. Meanwhile, Sergey Sobyanin succeeded Medvedev as head of the Presidential Administration.

At the beginning of the year, Putin began to exercise his new power to appoint regional governors (previously they were popularly elected). At first he tended merely to reappoint incumbents, but as the year wore on, he began to appoint new faces. In March he used his power for the first time to sack a governor whose performance was deemed unsatisfactory.

In May a Moscow court sentenced billionaire Mikhail Khodorkovsky to nine years in prison after he was convicted of fraud and tax evasion. Reduced to eight years on appeal, the sentence was widely seen as punishment for meddling in politics. The Yukos oil company, which Khodorkovsky had headed, was broken up, and its largest production unit, Yuganskneftegaz, was taken into state ownership and subsumed into the state oil company, Rosneft.

Taking the hint, other Russian businessmen took care to avoid political activity and to pay their taxes in full and on time. After former prime minister Mikhail Kasyanov suggested that he might be a candidate in the 2008 presidential election, prosecutors launched an investigation into his business dealings. While the Kremlin denied any involvement, commentators said the probe showed that the authorities were determined not only to choose Putin's successor but even to decide who else would contest the election.

Legislation came into force in August that was expected to have a major impact on future election campaigns. Single-mandate constituencies in the State Duma, the lower house of the parliament, were to be abolished, and all 450 deputies would in future be elected by proportional representation on the basis of party lists; parties would also be prohibited from campaigning in blocs. To secure representation a party would have to win at least 7% of the votes cast (previously the threshold was 5%). These changes were accompanied by new regulations, due to enter into force in 2006, requiring parties running for election to meet tighter registration criteria, including providing proof of membership in each of Russia's 89 republics and regions. The new system was expected to reduce sharply the number of parties eligible to run in national elections, eliminate parties formed on a regional or minority basis, and end the election of locally popular maverick politicians. New restrictions were also announced banning independent domestic monitors and journalists from observing vote counts, while international monitors would be permitted only by invitation. There was alarm at the end of the year when the Duma moved to adopt legislation that would severely restrict the work of foreign-funded nongovernmental organizations. Putin promised to soften the bill's harshest clauses but insisted that Russia would not permit foreign governments and organizations to finance political activities in its territory.

The situation in Chechnya remained highly unstable. In March federal security forces announced that they had killed separatist leader Aslan Maskhadov, who had been Chechnya's first democratically elected president; observers opined that with Maskhadov out of the picture, what was probably the last chance of a negotiated settlement between Moscow and the separatist forces had disappeared. His place

AP/Wide World Photos

Investigators, a child, and an amateur photographer examine the scene after a gunfight in the restive southern Russian republic of Dagestan. In all, two police officers and four suspected militants died in the clash in October.

was taken by a previously little-known cleric, Abdul-Khalim Sadulayev. Sadulayev represented a younger, more radicalized, and more devoutly Muslim generation of Chechen fighters. In November Chechens took part in the first local parliamentary elections since Russia wrested control from the rebel government in 2000.

Meanwhile, instability appeared to be spreading from Chechnya into other parts of the North Caucasus. In July Putin's representative to the region, Dmitry Kozak, warned that tensions were close to the boiling point in Dagestan, which adjoined Chechnya. Experts agreed that the causes of the tensions, while complex, were largely local. They included rampant corruption, poverty, unemployment, and high birthrates as much as religious extremism or interethnic conflict. In October more than a hundred people were killed when Islamic militants launched a coordinated attack on Nalchik, the capital of Kabardino-Balkaria.

Economy. Russia recorded its seventh consecutive year of economic growth since the prolonged output collapse of 1989–98. The economy grew robustly and had high international liquidity. For 2005 as a whole, gross domestic product was projected to grow at a rate

of 6%, compared with the 7.1% officially reported in 2004. Growth was largely attributable to record world oil prices, which generated big export revenues. As a result, Russia maintained a high trade surplus and was able to meet its external-debt repayments ahead of schedule. In January it fully repaid its outstanding $3.3 billion debt to the International Monetary Fund. The state budget recorded its sixth successive surplus. For much of the year, Russia continued to accumulate foreign-currency reserves, which exceeded a year's supply of merchandise imports. The Stabilization Fund—based on tax revenues from high oil prices and designed to protect the budget against any subsequent fall in the oil price—largely offset the potentially inflationary impact of large capital inflows.

With oil at record world prices, however, Russia was awash with petrodollars that many politicians and spending departments of the government said should be used to lay the groundwork for a more diversified economy. The pressure to spend this money—whether on public-sector pay, infrastructure projects, or both—was hard to resist. The Finance Ministry, supported for much of the time by Putin, resisted this pressure for many months, citing the need for macroeconomic stability. A compromise was reached in the spring whereby the threshold price at which oil-tax revenues would be diverted into the Stabilization Fund was raised from $20 per barrel of Ural crude to $27, with effect from the beginning of 2006. Oil-tax revenue accruing from prices between $20 and $27 would be allocated to a new investment fund. The plans Putin announced in September included initiatives to spend an additional $4.7 billion in 2006 on human capital development: education, health care, housing, and rural development. This alarmed some economists, who saw it as a sign of reduced fiscal prudence. Others viewed it as the first shot in the campaign for the 2008 presidential election. Meanwhile, the authorities continued to put off many structural reforms. Liberal economists warned that, in so doing, Russia was laying itself open to the so-called resource curse and long-term stagnation.

Economic growth slowed considerably from summer 2004 through summer 2005. While there was some improvement in the third quarter of 2005, the year as a whole showed a clear slowdown from 2003 and 2004. On the demand side the slowdown came above all from fixed investment, particularly in the natural-resource sector. This had an immediate impact on oil output, which slowed sharply, bringing the overall growth of the industrial sector down to quite modest rates. The causes of the slowdown were a fall in business confidence following the Yukos affair in addition to a sudden upsurge in large back-tax demands against other companies. Foreign direct investment did increase, thanks partly to Russian-controlled money returning from abroad, but these inflows were outweighed by large and increasing flows of capital out of the country. A further probable factor in the slowdown in the oil industry was increases in oil-industry taxation in late 2004 and 2005. Household consumption continued to grow strongly as the inflow of petrodollars helped to boost personal income.

In January Soviet-era welfare benefits such as free transportation and prescription drugs ceased to be dispensed in kind and were replaced by cash payments. The reform was sensible, but its implementation was bungled. Thousands of angry pensioners, suddenly unable to pay for bus rides, medicines, and utilities, came out in protest. Some demonstrations became violent. Clearly shaken, the government backed down.

A compromise was reached in which the monetary value of the benefits was increased and recipients were given the choice of taking the benefits, as of 2006, in money or kind. Inflation began to rise and, as of August, was running at 13% year on year—well above the 8.5% targeted by the central bank for the year as a whole. Concessions to pensioners over welfare payments were one factor that helped fuel inflation, as did the inflow of petrodollars arising from high oil prices, insofar as this was not offset by payments to the Stabilization Fund.

Meanwhile, the state was taking over the "commanding heights" of the economy. The most dramatic illustration of this was the state's reacquisition of Yuganskneftegaz. The presidential administration strengthened its hold over natural-resource companies in the state sector through the appointment to board positions of close associates of the president. This was not, however, a well-coordinated process. The leading state-controlled energy companies, Gazprom and Rosneft, engaged in a long battle over which of them should acquire Yuganskneftegaz. Rosneft was the eventual winner. This indicated that there was infighting over the control of assets within the president's entourage and that the leadership was fragmented. In September Gazprom bought a 72.7% share in Sibneft, Russia's fifth largest producer of crude oil, from Russia's richest man, Roman Abramovich. This, plus another minor acquisition of Sibneft shares, gave Gazprom a stake in Sibneft of just over 75%. This meant that under Russian law no other Sibneft shareholder would have a blocking vote on major decisions.

Accession negotiations with the World Trade Organization (WTO) reached a stage at which, it was generally believed, Russia could become a member in 2006. Bilateral negotiations had been completed with a majority of the WTO members concerned. Some bilateral and some multilateral issues remained unresolved, however.

Foreign, Military, and Security Policy. The former Soviet republics on Russia's borders remained the chief focus of Moscow's attention, with Russian leaders in shock over the "loss" of Ukraine in the Orange Revolution. The Kremlin looked on with dismay as Ukraine and Georgia talked of setting up an alternative alliance to the Commonwealth of Independent States (CIS) and when mass demonstrations in the spring led to the ouster of Kyrgyzstan's Pres.

Askar Akayev. In May Russia agreed to a timetable for closing its two remaining military bases in Georgia by the end of 2008; no plans were announced, however, for the withdrawal of Russian troops from Moldova's breakaway Transnistria.

Moscow paid increasing attention to the Collective Security Treaty Organization (CSTO), set up in 2003 and including Armenia, Belarus, Kazakhstan, Kyrgyzstan, Russia, and Tajikistan, and the Shanghai Cooperation Organization (SCO), set up in 1996 and now including China, Kazakhstan, Kyrgyzstan, Russia, Tajikistan, and Uzbekistan. Russia's relations with China remained excellent, with the two countries engaging in joint military exercises in August for the first time.

In May Putin invited world leaders to Moscow for celebrations marking the 60th anniversary of the defeat of Nazi Germany. The event was preceded by mudslinging with Polish and Baltic leaders who urged Russia to use the opportunity to publicly disavow the 1939 Molotov-Ribbentrop Pact, which opened Hitler's path to war; Moscow angrily refused. In September Russia formally withdrew its signature from the border treaty that it had earlier negotiated with Estonia but that the Russian parliament had yet to ratify.

Russia clashed with Western countries over the election-observation missions run by the Organization for Security and Co-operation in Europe, which Moscow complained were characterized by "double standards" and pro-Western bias. At the end of the year, as the West continued to express concern over Iran's planned nuclear program, Moscow proposed a possible compromise whereby the final stage of the fuel-enrichment process would be carried out not in Iran but in Russia.

In February the European Court of Human Rights in Strasbourg, France, passed a landmark judgment for the first time obliging the Russian authorities to pay compensation to six Chechen civilians whose family members had been killed by Russian forces.

The defense budget for 2005 was sharply up from that of 2004. This, however, was before adjusting for inflation. In real terms the increase was more modest. The officially declared national defense budget was narrower in coverage than the definition of defense spending in NATO countries; adjusted for comparability, the 2005 budget was reckoned to be 4.4% of GDP rather than the officially declared

2.7%. There appeared to be problems in the acquisition of new military hardware, and it was not clear that increased spending would substantially improve the equipping of the Russian military.   (ELIZABETH TEAGUE)

RWANDA

Area: 26,338 sq km (10,169 sq mi)
Population (2005 est.): 8,574,000
Capital: Kigali
Head of state and government: President Maj. Gen. Paul Kagame, assisted by Prime Minister Bernard Makuza

Rwanda attained relative stability in 2005 under the regime of Pres. Paul Kagame and the Rwanda Patriotic Front (RPF), although the government had not yet shed its authoritarian rule. The country made steady progress in reconstructing its economy. The government set up a poverty-alleviation program designed to implement a system of sustainable development that met the requirements of the debt-relief program of the World Bank and the International Monetary Fund. To further Rwanda's case, President Kagame visited the United States from September 13 to 19 and addressed the UN General Assembly on the challenges of coping with worldwide poverty and postconflict reconstruction.

Throughout the year Rwanda sought to project a positive international image. In July, Finance Minister Donald Kaberuka was elected president of the African Development Bank, which signaled that the country was ready to take its place in pan-African policy making and diplomacy.

Tense relations continued with neighbouring states in the Great Lakes region, particularly the Democratic Republic of the Congo (DRC), which accused Rwanda of backing rebel leaders in its eastern region in attacks against Hutu refugees who after the 1994 genocide had sought refuge there. In July UN peacekeepers destroyed the main Rwandan base in eastern Congo and warned the rebels to disarm and return to Rwanda. Rebel leaders, however, had resisted earlier attempts to push them back, declaring that they wanted a guarantee of amnesty. Elsewhere efforts to persuade refugees to return home achieved some success. In October a small group returned from Uganda. Still, an estimated 48,000 refugees remained scattered in 14 African countries.

The 1994 genocide still preoccupied the nation. In March local courts called *gacaca* began the process of identifying the victims and perpetrators of massacres. This process reached deep into sociopolitical and religious hierarchies. Catholic leaders and priests were accused of having had close relations with extremist politicians prior to the genocide or even helped Hutu militias. In July, Archbishop Thaddée Ntihinyurwa, the head of the Roman Catholic Church of Rwanda, was summoned to testify before the Nyamasheke court about his role in the massacre of thousands of Tutsi in the district church. On September 19 the United Nations Appeals Chamber in The Hague upheld the life sentence of former Rwandan minister Jean de Dieu Kamuhanda. On September 23 it was announced that genocide suspect Joseph Serugendo had been extradited from Libreville, Gabon, to Arusha, Tanz., in order to stand trial before the UN International Criminal Tribunal for Rwanda; this brought the number of arrests by the court to 71.

(LARAY DENZER)

SAINT KITTS AND NEVIS

Area: 269 sq km (104 sq mi)
Population (2005 est.): 46,600
Capital: Basseterre
Chief of state: Queen Elizabeth II, represented by Governor-General Sir Cuthbert Montraville Sebastian
Head of government: Prime Minister Denzil Douglas

Taxpayers in Saint Kitts and Nevis breathed a sigh of relief in February 2005 when Prime Minister and Minister of Finance Denzil Douglas decided not to reintroduce personal income tax in the national budget. Fuel prices, however, were increased in light of rising world oil costs.

A milestone in the history of Saint Kitts and Nevis came in March with commencement of the last sugar harvest. The industry had sustained Saint Kitts and Nevis and most other insular Caribbean territories for generations,

A group of Rwandan refugees prepares to return home from neighbouring Burundi in May. Thousands of Rwandans had fled the country in fear of the gacaca, *local courts empowered to seek out and try persons suspected of involvement in the 1994 ethnic massacres.*

© Jean Pierre Harerimana/Reuters/Corbis

but the steady erosion of preferential markets in the European Union had undermined its viability in the Caribbean. The final sugar crop was expected to be about 12,000 metric tons. The government was considering 20 different investment projects that could provide alternative employment for sugar workers.

Saint Kitts and Nevis bucked the trend among Caricom (Caribbean Community and Common Market) countries in 2005 by reaffirming its intention to retain diplomatic relations with Taiwan rather than establish formal ties with China. Prime Minister Douglas in May described the territory's association with Taiwan as special. Taiwan agreed to provide a $12 million aid package, which would help build the modern stadium required for the 2007 Cricket World Cup. (DAVID RENWICK)

SAINT LUCIA

Area: 617 sq km (238 sq mi)
Population (2005 est.): 161,000
Capital: Castries
Chief of state: Queen Elizabeth II, represented by Governor-General Dame Pearlette Louisy
Head of government: Prime Minister Kenny Anthony

In March 2005, 79-year-old Sir John Compton returned as the leader of Saint Lucia's official opposition party, the United Workers' Party (UWP). Compton, who replaced Vaughan Lewis, had cofounded the UWP in 1964 and led it for three decades before relinquishing control.

Prime Minister Kenny Anthony insisted in May that the apparent antihanging stance of the Privy Council in London—the country's final court of appeal—would not stop Saint Lucia from executing convicted murderers; four condemned men were on death row. He declared that violence had become "a tidal wave that is threatening the entire Caribbean" and needed to be deterred. At the time of Anthony's speech, Saint Lucia had already had 17 murders for the year. Anthony was criticized by the country's Centre for Legal Aid and Human Rights, however, for his "premature" announcement.

A motion of no confidence in the St. Lucia Labour Party (SLP) government was defeated in Parliament in June. The motion, filed by a newly reinvigorated UWP opposition, was inspired by the alleged improper use of funds by a government agency operating under the aegis of the Ministry of Social Transformation. In June the government announced that a commission would review and reform the country's constitution, which was more than 25 years old. (DAVID RENWICK)

SAINT VINCENT AND THE GRENADINES

Area: 389 sq km (150 sq mi)
Population (2005 est.): 119,000
Capital: Kingstown
Chief of state: Queen Elizabeth II, represented by Governor-General Sir Frederick Ballantyne
Head of government: Prime Minister Ralph Gonsalves

The IMF in April 2005 urged the government of Saint Vincent and the Grenadines to accelerate the country's economic growth in order to lift income levels and reduce poverty. The IMF recommended such measures as improving investment attractiveness, encouraging remittances from the large overseas community of Vincentians, and providing better preparation for natural disasters, including hurricanes. Prime Minister Ralph Gonsalves reported in September that offshore exploration for oil would soon begin. Gonsalves secured a second term in office on December 7 as his Unity Labour Party won 12 of the 15 seats in the House of Assembly.

The country came under fire in June for its alleged sluggishness in tackling the transshipment of marijuana through its territory to other Caribbean islands. Barbados Prime Minister Owen Arthur insisted that Saint Vincent and the Grenadines could do far more to crack down on trafficking. Gonsalves maintained that Barbados should improve its own drug-monitoring mechanisms. Comments by police spokesmen in which they suggested that drug mules were more "opportunistic" than "criminal" in intent seemed to lend

On September 29 Taiwan's Pres. Chen Shui-bian (left) receives a traditional welcome from Prime Minister Ralph Gonsalves of Saint Vincent and the Grenadines, one of a shrinking list of countries that recognized Taiwan rather than mainland China.

credence to Arthur's observations. Saint Vincent and the Grenadines, after 24 years, remained one of only four insular Caribbean territories still aligned with Taiwan rather than mainland China. Taiwanese Pres. Chen Shui-bian visited the territory in September. (DAVID RENWICK)

SAMOA

Area: 2,831 sq km (1,093 sq mi)
Population (2005 est.): 185,000
Capital: Apia
Chief of state: *O le Ao o le Malo* (Head of State) Malietoa Tanumafili II
Head of government: Prime Minister Tuila'epa Sa'ilele Malielegaoi

Following a series of well-publicized cases, the Samoa Land and Titles Court in 2005 ruled that village councils could not impose the traditional punishment of banishment on either individuals or families without recourse to the court, which ruled on matters of custom as part of its official responsibilities. Banishment had a long history of being used to control antisocial activity or to curtail political rivalries. Recent cases were prompted by incidents that ranged from drunken and disorderly behaviour to campaigning in national elections against a high chief or candidate supported by a village council.

There was friction between Samoa and American Samoa over migration between the two island groups. American Samoa tightened controls following allegations that Samoans were abusing its 14-day permit system by overstaying. Samoa, which had traditionally allowed American Samoans into the country without permits, retaliated by introducing a reciprocal system. Talks eased but did not solve the issue, which had an impact on regional airlines and businesses.

After Cyclone Percy stuck the region in late February, Samoa provided coordination and assistance for the small atoll communities of Tokelau, a New Zealand dependency of some 1,400 people administered from an office in Samoa.　　　(BARRIE MACDONALD)

SAN MARINO

Area: 61.2 sq km (23.6 sq mi)
Population (2005 est.): 30,100
Capital: San Marino
Heads of state and government: The republic is governed by two *capitani reggenti,* or coregents, appointed every six months by a popularly elected Great and General Council.

In 2005 San Marino proposed reforms in response to economic difficulties evident in the relative decline in the purchasing power of the average Sammarinese family, but these reform efforts were often met with hostility. The rationalization of state-delivered heath care services was criticized as an attack on the welfare state. The liberalization of labour markets, which was intended to stimulate economic growth through labour flexibility, was met with stern union opposition. There was also debate on the prospects of liberalizing retail activities. One modern trend that met with determined resistance was the secularization of public life, and a campaign directed at abolishing the display of crucifixes in public places was ruled out by the majority Christian Democratic Party.

Reform on the domestic front was matched by a range of international initiatives. New commercial prospects were explored in China and the Middle East, and an important collaborative agreement was signed with Serbia and Montenegro. In August San Marino established diplomatic relations with Nepal. Meanwhile, there was deliberation on the possibility of seeking membership in the European Union, but it was not clear that such membership would bring unqualified advantages. San Marino also expressed the hope that its territory would be declared part of the UNESCO World Heritage program.　　　(GREGORY O. SMITH)

SÃO TOMÉ AND PRÍNCIPE

Area: 1,001 sq km (386 sq mi)
Population (2005 est.): 157,000
Capital: São Tomé
Chief of state: President Fradique de Menezes
Head of government: Prime Ministers Damião Vaz d'Almeida and, from June 8, Maria do Carmo Silveira

Though an oil bonanza was set to transform the fortunes of São Tomé and Príncipe, the country was mired in allegations of high-level corruption in 2005. In February the National Assembly removed the indemnity from prosecution of five of its members, two of them former prime ministers, who were alleged to have embezzled funds from a government aid-management agency. As a special tribunal was set up to investigate the allegations, some claimed that the president, whose own cement company was also under investigation, was trying to destroy political rivals ahead of the 2006 legislative and presidential election. The resignation in May of the minister of natural resources was followed by that in June of Prime Minister Damião Vaz d'Almeida, who disagreed with Pres. Fradique de Menezes over how to deal with a civil-service strike for higher wages and the president's awarding of five offshore blocks in the Joint Development Zone that São

Army soldiers in newly oil-rich São Tomé and Príncipe receive training from U.S. Coast Guard instructors in July. U.S. officials cited the dangers of political instability, terrorism, and piracy as justification for a growing U.S. presence there.

Tomé shared with Nigeria to the Texas-based but Nigerian-controlled oil company Environmental Remediation Holding Corp. This award would bring São Tomé $113 million, in addition to the $49 million the country was to receive from the consortium led by ChevronTexaco and ExxonMobil for an exploration and production-sharing agreement that was signed in February. As relations between the president and the ruling MLSTP-PSD Party deteriorated, the latter demanded that presidential and parliamentary elections be brought forward.

　　　(CHRISTOPHER SAUNDERS)

SAUDI ARABIA

Area: 2,149,690 sq km (830,000 sq mi)
Population (2005 est.): 23,230,000
Capital: Riyadh
Head of state and government: Kings Fahd and, from August 1, Abdullah

On Aug. 1, 2005, King Fahd of Saudi Arabia died. (*See* OBITUARIES.) His half brother Crown Prince Abdullah was

Members of the Saudi royal family, including Prince Abdul Aziz ibn Fahd (centre), carry the shrouded body of King Fahd before a special prayer ceremony in Riyadh on August 2. Fahd had been king since 1982.

named the new monarch, and a full brother, Prince Sultan, became the new crown prince. The succession process went very smoothly, and the investiture ceremony was extremely simple. The new king personally retained direct command of the Saudi Arabian National Guard and continued as chairman of the Supreme Economic Council (SEC), a high-level policy unit. At the same time, Crown Prince Sultan continued as general inspector of the Royal Saudi Air Force.

The new king made an important symbolic gesture in September when he ordered citizens not to kiss his hand, saying that the traditional gesture of respect was degrading and violated Islam. Abdullah asked everyone to refrain from kissing the hands of anyone but their parents.

The economic situation improved tremendously owing to the international increase in crude-oil prices. It was predicted that 2005 would be the best year in Saudi economic history, with a growth forecast of 26%. Oil-export revenue would reach $180 billion, about a 70% increase over the 2004 level. The internal national debt of around $150 billion was to be reduced by a third to about $100 billion. Western leaders called on oil producing countries to increase their production in order to reduce the rise in oil prices; King Abdullah concurred but also asked Western countries to reduce their taxes on petroleum products in order to help achieve this result.

The country's prosperity was likely behind King Abdullah's decree on August 22 awarding a 15% salary raise to all Saudi government employees, both civilian and military, as well as to retired persons. At the same time, he put solving the unemployment problem as one of his priorities. About $700 million in additional funds were made available for education and training. Concurrently, the Ministry of Education announced that it was revising the school curriculum, with a greater emphasis on science and job-oriented education. The point was made about a direct link between the large number of jobless young people and the increase in support for militant Islamic groups. In regard to these latter groups, Saudi authorities were successful in gunning down two dozen Muslim extremists who belonged to an al-Qaeda organization and were intent on carrying out acts of sabotage in different parts of the kingdom.

After four years of negotiations and a visit in April by then crown prince Abdullah with Pres. George W. Bush in Crawford, Texas, Saudi Arabia reached a decisive agreement with the U.S. in September that paved its way to joining the World Trade Organization. A U.S. statement pointed out that the agreement also promised to open up Saudi trade with Israel, as the kingdom had explicitly undertaken to allow free trade with all WTO members. Saudi Arabia formally joined the WTO on December 11. The Saudi ambassador to Washington, Prince Bander ibn Sultan,

was replaced by Prince Turki al-Faysal, who had served as ambassador in London and was earlier the head of the Saudi intelligence service, but little change in policy was expected. On the other hand, Prince Saud al-Faysal, the Saudi foreign minister, criticized U.S. policy in Iraq as divisive. Nonetheless, President Bush certified that Saudi Arabia was cooperating with efforts to combat international terrorism, which thus qualified Riyadh to receive direct U.S. aid to combat such activities.

(MAHMOUD HADDAD)

SENEGAL

Area: 196,722 sq km (75,955 sq mi)
Population (2005 est.): 11,706,000
Capital: Dakar
Chief of state: President Abdoulaye Wade, assisted by Prime Minister Macky Sall

The year 2005 in Senegal opened on a hopeful note, the signing of a peace treaty on Dec. 30, 2004, that was expected finally to end the 22-year-long Casamance rebellion, in which at least 3,500 people died, 50,000 refugees fled into The Gambia and Guinea-Bissau,

Many Senegalese were among the thousands of Africans who sought to immigrate illegally to Spain by crossing from Moroccan territory into the Spanish North African enclaves of Ceuta and Melilla.

and the region's once booming tourist economy virtually collapsed.

The growing rift between Pres. Abdoulaye Wade and former prime minister Idrissa Seck threatened the unity of the ruling Senegalese Democratic Party (PDS). In April, 12 PDS deputies considered loyal to Seck, long regarded as the likely successor to the 79-year-old head of state, walked out of the ruling coalition to establish their own party. On July 15 Seck was arrested and interrogated for alleged corruption. Eight days later he was charged with the far more serious crime of jeopardizing state security, and on August 3, the parliament voted to bring Seck before a special tribunal. Opposition parties, already angered by the May 30 arrest of Reform Party leader Abdourahim Agne on charges of inciting rebellion, called the parliamentary action unconstitutional.

A cholera outbreak in central Senegal in January threatened to get out of control after an estimated million Muslims, members of the Murid brotherhood, made the annual pilgrimage to Touba, 200 km (125 mi) east of Dakar. Nearly 5,000 new cases were recorded between March 28 and April 6, with 64 deaths reported. The heavy rains that flooded much of Dakar in September gave the epidemic new strength.

(NANCY ELLEN LAWLER)

SERBIA AND MONTENEGRO

Area: 102,173 sq km (39,449 sq mi), including 10,887 sq km (4,203 sq mi) in the UN interim-administrated region of Kosovo
Population (2005 est.): 9,960,000, including 1,900,000 in Kosovo
Administrative centres: Belgrade (Serbia) and Podgorica (Montenegro)
Chief of state: President Svetozar Marovic
Head of government: Prime Ministers Vojislav Kostunica (Serbia) and Milo Djukanovic (Montenegro)

Efforts by Serbia and Montenegro to begin the process of integration into Europe, address issues of the country's future status—including that of the restive province of Kosovo—face up to corruption and war crimes, and deal with the economy dominated headlines in 2005. In October the International

A woman holds a leaflet representing an EU passport under road signs to Brussels and other European capitals during a political rally in Belgrade on October 6. Serbia and Montenegro began EU accession talks later that month.

Monetary Fund temporarily suspended high-level talks with Belgrade following disagreements over Serbia's monetary and public-spending policies and the country's higher-than-planned inflation rate of 17%. The negotiations aimed at extending a nearly $1 billion standby credit arrangement were crucial for Serbia's transition process because they were linked to a $730 million debt write-off by the Paris Club of creditors, which had already canceled $2.3 billion of Serbia's $13 billion debt. In response Serbia's government approved a 2006 budget proposal of $6.9 billion, calling for more spending cuts in health services, aid to state-run companies, and salaries in the public-services sector. The government projected a surplus in 2006 of $560 million, compared with the budget deficit of $533 million the previous year. Serbian Deputy Prime Minister Miroljub Labus announced in November that he expected that Serbia and Montenegro would sign its first contract with the EU by November 2006. The International Criminal Tribunal for the Former Yugoslavia (ICTY), however, gave Serbia a strong warning that Belgrade had to deliver Bosnian Serb war-crimes fugitive Ratko Mladic by the end of the year or face "excommunication" from any Euro-Atlantic integration process.

Officials contended that the main obstacles for economic development in Serbia were unemployment and the lack of investments, compounded by political issues such as cooperation with the ICTY, the status of Kosovo, and relations with Montenegro. In November a

European Commission report found that economic growth in Serbia and Montenegro had improved, but problems regarding human rights, freedom of expression, corruption, and "inappropriate political interference" in the courts interfered with the country's development.

Media intimidation and intolerance of ethnic and religious minorities increased somewhat. Journalists and nongovernmental organizations investigating Serbia's role in the wars that led to the dissolution of Yugoslavia were frequently threatened, beaten, and harassed by right-wing extremists and hooligans. Incidents involving discrimination were largely ignored by officials, and talk of independence for Kosovo and Montenegro increased fears that the northern province of Vojvodina, with more than 20 different ethnic groups, might also seek to leave Serbia. Serbia's Jewish community reported an increase in anti-Semitism.

In November the government of Serbia brought criminal charges against 40 judges in an effort to fight corruption. Media and reformers repeatedly accused government prosecutors of serving the interests of politicians. The most publicized case came in August, when charges of extortion against Marko Milosevic, the son of former Serbian president Slobodan Milosevic, were dropped. A damning government report in September alleged the acquisition of military equipment by top Montenegrin officials and further damaged the already-tense relations between Serbia and Montenegro. It was widely expected that a referendum on Montenegro's future status would be held in April 2006.

Public support for Serbian right-wing nationalists remained strong. According to several polls, the Serbian Radical Party of indicted war criminal Vojislav Seselj, which held the largest bloc of seats in Parliament, was the most popular, with Serbian Pres. Boris Tadic's Democratic Party a distant second and Serbian Prime Minister Vojislav Kostunica's Democratic Party of Serbia in either third or fourth place. In October Tadic recommended new parliamentary elections, alleging that the governing coalition under Kostunica had lost the trust of the voters.

Kosovo's political landscape remained polarized, despite efforts by the international community to broker a peaceful settlement over the future status of the province. Kosovo Pres. Ibrahim Rugova and Prime Minister Bajram Kosumi stressed that the province would accept nothing less than full independence after the completion of UN-sponsored final-status talks. Several proposals, notably from within the EU, had called for "conditional independence" for Kosovo, which would not enjoy full sovereignty until it joined the EU and adopted its rules and restrictions. Serb political leaders in Kosovo were divided about how to approach the negotiations, and even Tadic was not immune from using nationalist rhetoric. On a visit to a Kosovo Serb enclave in February, he stated that "this [Kosovo] is Serbia" and emphasized that independence for the predominantly Albanian-populated province was "unacceptable." Kostunica said Belgrade would grant Kosovo broad autonomy but warned that outright independence could provoke a major crisis.

(MILAN ANDREJEVICH)

SEYCHELLES

Area: 455 sq km (176 sq mi)
Population (2005 est.): 82,800
Capital: Victoria
Head of state and government: President James Michel

In 2005 Seychelles began recovering from the Indian Ocean tsunami that devastated several Asian countries and the east coast of Africa on Dec. 26, 2004. The tsunami claimed two lives in Seychelles and displaced 900 families. The archipelago sustained widespread flood damage to roads and bridges, residential neighbourhoods, hotels and tourist facilities, and fisheries. The largest island, Mahé, bore the brunt of the damage when flooding washed out two bridges connecting the capital city, Victoria, to the airport. Total damage had been estimated at nearly $30 million. The Paris Club, a group of creditor nations, froze debt repayments of tsunami-affected countries, including

Seychelles, until the end of 2005 to allow them to focus on recovery efforts. Less than a month after the tsunami, Seychelles representatives attended a meeting of the Small Island Developing States in neighbouring Mauritius to address plans for a tsunami early-warning system and other needs. By July an estimated $1 million in foreign aid had been donated to help rebuild the fishing and farming industries and restore the environment in Seychelles. Tourism numbers had also rebounded strongly by August, another sign that the economy was recovering after the tsunami.

(MARY F.E. EBELING)

SIERRA LEONE

Area: 71,740 sq km (27,699 sq mi)
Population (2005 est.): 5,018,000
Capital: Freetown
Head of state and government: President Ahmad Tejan Kabbah

By 2005 Sierra Leone's recovery from the status of a failed state had become an important test case in African development. Ranked by the United Nations Development Programme's (UNDP's) human development index as the world's poorest country, Sierra Leone faced enormous difficulties in rebuilding socioeconomic and political infrastructures. The restoration of civil authority over all areas of the country depended on the reintegration of former combatants and displaced citizens and the restructuring of the security forces. Throughout the year public discourse focused on the impact of the civil war as a result of the activities of the Truth and Reconciliation Commission and the trial in the Special Court of members of the former military government on charges of crimes against humanity. On March 1 a National Victims Commemoration Conference provided a forum for citizens to discuss their experiences and views about justice. The government joined in the international campaign to extradite former Liberian head of state Charles Taylor to Sierra Leone for trial.

The government prioritized policies for economic revitalization, but progress was slow. In the capital, Freetown, reconstruction of public buildings and roads made good headway. In

January the government quickly reached an agreement with workers about wages, conditions of service, and fuel prices after the trade unions launched the first major strike since the end of civil conflict in 2002. In February the Poverty Reduction Strategy Paper formulated grassroots projects to improve conditions for the poor, estimated to make up 70% of the population. The government thereafter obtained approval for full debt relief from the Group of Eight as well as substantial new loans from the International Monetary Fund and World Bank.

Reflecting confidence in the country's future, company representatives announced plans to revive operations in bauxite and rutile mines closed during the civil war. Diamond mining also recovered rapidly. The designation of "conflict" or "blood" diamonds was removed because greater transparency in the system had channeled gemstone exports through legitimate channels, which thus met the requirements of the Kimberley Process Certification Scheme established in 2003. Still, diamond smuggling remained a serious problem.

On June 30 the Security Council announced that the United Nations Mission in Sierra Leone (UNAMSIL) would pull out its peacekeeping force of 17,500 troops by the end of the year and replace it with an Integrated United Nations Office to coordinate the work of international agencies, oversee long-term development, and consolidate peace.   (LARAY DENZER)

SINGAPORE

Area: 699 sq km (270 sq mi)
Population (2005 est.): 4,291,000
Head of state: President S.R. Nathan
Head of government: Prime Minister Lee Hsien Loong

Two subjects dominated public discourse in Singapore in 2005—casinos and charities. Early in the year, the government overcame a decades-old aversion to casinos to announce that it had decided to allow two to set up operations in the island republic. The reason for the move was to create jobs and help boost tourism. Among Southeast Asian countries, Singapore was not

In 2005 the government of Singapore broke a long-standing practice and decided to allow two casinos/resorts to open on its territory. Here one of the contending casino companies uses costumed models in a mock-up of the facilities that might be built.

alone in this decision. Thailand indicated that it would do the same. Singapore's closest neighbour, Malaysia, had long had casinos. Still, the decision was vehemently opposed by conservatives, especially on the religious right. The decision even split the cabinet; in an unprecedented break with a tradition of collective responsibility, Deputy Prime Minister Tony Tan publicly announced that he was against casinos. Tan retired from politics at the end of 2005 and became chairman of Singapore Press Holdings, the largest publisher of newspapers in the country. Casino licenses were likely to be awarded in 2006.

A second controversy erupted when a libel suit brought by the National Kidney Foundation (NKF)—Singapore's most successful charity in terms of fund-raising—against the *Straits Times* newspaper went to court in July. The NKF denied the newspaper's reports of extravagant expenditures at the charity's headquarters, including gold-plated bathroom fixtures in the office of its CEO, T.T. Durai. Two days into the court proceedings, however, Durai acknowledged a host of such expenditures as well as an annual salary of S$600,000 (about U.S.$355,000). The subsequent public furor was exacerbated by the fact that NKF patron Tan Choo Leng—wife of former prime minister Goh Chok Tong—called the salary "peanuts." Disclosures of the NKF's extravagance prompted housecleaning at other charities and a review of charity governance issues.

Economic growth was expected to top 5% for the year and to stay in that range for several years. This performance outpaced early official forecasts of 3.5–4.5% for 2005. Former prime minister Lee Kuan Yew enthused over the positive economic numbers, remarking, "If you ask me, we have never had it more promising." There was, however, considerable apprehension in the country over the threat posed by avian influenza (bird flu), with the government outlining a Disease Outbreak Response System and stepping up efforts to stockpile antiviral drugs.

The much-anticipated presidential election scheduled for late August proved an anticlimax as no credible contender to Pres. S.R. Nathan emerged. Singapore's Presidential Elections Committee, responsible for evaluating the eligibility of candidates, rejected all applications save that of Nathan, who was declared the winner without a vote's being taken. Singaporeans looked forward to early 2006, when the next general election was widely expected to be held.

(CHUA LEE HOONG)

SLOVAKIA

Area: 49,035 sq km (18,933 sq mi)
Population (2005 est.): 5,384,000
Capital: Bratislava
Chief of state: President Ivan Gasparovic
Head of government: Prime Minister Mikulas Dzurinda

Despite economic success, the position of the government of Slovakia was somewhat shaky in 2005. Three ministers were replaced during the course of the year, and the government came close to collapse in September. Within the four-party ruling coalition, relations were especially tense between the Christian Democratic Movement (KDH) and the New Citizen's Alliance (ANO), owing partly to personality conflicts within the Education Ministry. In May an education-reform bill failed after ANO rejected the legislation, marking the first time that the government had been disunited over an important reform matter. The situation calmed down after the ministry's state secretary, Frantisek Toth of ANO, replaced Rudolf Chmel as culture minister.

Political tensions heightened again in August when the KDH demanded ANO leader Pavol Rusko's dismissal as economy minister because of a financial scandal. After failing to heed Prime Minister Mikulas Dzurinda's call to resign voluntarily, Rusko was fired on August 24, and he subsequently withdrew ANO from the ruling coalition. Nonetheless, a majority of ANO parliamentary deputies, led by former journalist Lubomir Lintner, opted to continue supporting Dzurinda's cabinet and forged an agreement with the three remaining ruling coalition partners: the KDH, Dzurinda's Slovak Democratic and Christian Union, and the Party of the Hungarian Coalition. Lintner's group was therefore able to keep ANO's two remaining ministers in place and name a replacement to head the Economy Ministry, with Jirko Malcharek taking that post in October.

Rusko's departure made the achievement of a parliamentary majority uncertain, particularly since Dzurinda had been running a minority government since late 2003, dependent on backing from political independents. The opposition refused to attend the mid-September parliamentary session, and the necessary quorum of 76 out of 150 deputies was not reached for several days, which led to calls for early parliamentary elections. After more than a week of delay, the parliament finally started operating on September 21, with 77 deputies present. That followed the surprising shift of two deputies from the opposition Movement for a Democratic Slovakia (HZDS) to Lintner's group, accompanied by allegations that they had been

© Petr Josek/Reuters/Corbis

Slovak traditional dancers entertain the crowd awaiting the arrival of U.S. Pres. George W. Bush in Hviezdoslavovo Square in central Bratislava on February 24.

"bought." In an apparent effort to improve the government's image, Dzurinda backed the resignation in October of controversial Labour and Social Affairs Minister Ludovit Kanik in connection with questionable financial dealings. The sociologist Iveta Radicova replaced Kanik, becoming the first woman in Dzurinda's cabinet. Despite weak public support, Slovakia's ruling parties fared surprisingly well in the November regional elections, which were plagued by a very low turnout.

On the economic front Slovakia continued to record rapid GDP growth in 2005, owing partly to a recovery of real wages. Inflation and unemployment dropped sharply, and the country appeared to be in good shape to meet its goal of euro adoption by 2009, joining the European exchange-rate mechanism in late November. In regard to foreign affairs, Bratislava hosted a summit between U.S. Pres. George W. Bush and his Russian counterpart, Vladimir Putin, in February; this marked the first visit of a sitting U.S. president to Slovakia. In May Slovakia became the seventh European Union member state to ratify the constitution, approving it through a parliamentary vote. In October Slovakia was elected for the first time as a nonpermanent member of the United Nations Security Council. (SHARON FISHER)

SLOVENIA

Area: 20,273 sq km (7,827 sq mi)
Population (2005 est.): 1,999,000
Capital: Ljubljana
Chief of state: President Janez Drnovsek
Head of government: Prime Minister Janez Jansa

In October 2005 the centre-right coalition government led by Prime Minister Janez Jansa of the Slovenian Democrat Party proposed an extensive reform of the country's tax and social-welfare system. The goal was to make taxation fairer, ease the tax burden on business, and reduce the level of state control of the economy by promoting privatization. Of those Eastern European countries that had joined the EU in 2004, Slovenia had the highest percentage (45%) of state ownership of the economy.

The reform program generated intense opposition from the left-centre political parties as well as most organized-labour and retiree groups. They accused the government of trying to dismantle key aspects of the social-welfare system established during the communist era (1945–90) and largely maintained after independence by the primarily centre-left governments of Slovenia.

On September 25, voters in a national referendum confirmed (by a 50.2% majority) a law enacted by the parliament designed to provide a more representative leadership for the national radio and television network, including a separate channel to transmit sessions of the parliament. This was seen as a way of pluralizing the media, which in the eyes of the government and its supporters retained a strong leftist bias in reporting the news.

In foreign affairs Slovenia and neighbouring Croatia remained unable to reach agreement on defining their common border, and it became clear that international mediation was the only feasible solution. Despite these difficulties, Slovenia continued strongly to support Croatia's candidacy for membership in the European Union. Slovenia ratified the EU's proposed new constitution in February, when the parliament voted 79–4 in favour of the measure. That month the government

introduced a plan to take the steps necessary for Slovenia to adopt the euro on Jan. 1, 2007. In November the central bank of Slovenia revealed the design of Slovenia's euro coins.

Church-state relations improved during the year. Most Slovenes belonged to the Roman Catholic Church, and the Jansa government was favourably inclined toward it. In addition, the new Roman Catholic archbishop, Alojz Uran, adopted a less-confrontational manner than that of his predecessor, Franc Rode. In October the Slovene Bishop's Conference asked the Vatican for permission to establish three new dioceses in the cities of Celje, Murska Sobota, and Novo Mesto. The action was taken after several years of discussion, and there were indications that the Vatican would approve the request. (RUDOLPH M. SUSEL)

SOLOMON ISLANDS

Area: 28,370 sq km (10,954 sq mi)
Population (2005 est.): 471,000
Capital: Honiara
Chief of state: Queen Elizabeth II, represented by Governor-General Sir Nathaniel Waena
Head of government: Prime Minister Sir Allan Kemakeza

In 2005 Solomon Islands continued its recovery from the civil disorder that destroyed infrastructure and effectively caused a cessation of government activity. By midyear the Australian-led Regional Assistance Mission, which brought some 250 police from 11 countries as well as technical advisers, had largely restored public order and government systems and had contributed to the reconciliation of rival factions. Audit reports confirmed widespread fraud, corruption, and poor public-sector management; revenue-gathering systems had fallen into abeyance, and some government activities had not been audited for 20 years. In March militia leader Harold Keke and two associates were convicted and sentenced to life imprisonment for the murder of a cabinet minister in 2002.

The economy, which had been in contraction since 2000, showed signs of recovery. The government discontinued

exemptions on customs duties for log exports amid long-standing allegations that the system had been subject to corruption and misuse. Leaked documents from the forestry industry showed that businesses in the Solomon Islands were receiving only half of the world price for exports that remained a mainstay of the economy and revealed that forests were being logged at unsustainable levels. The flow of aid increased, with Japan, the EU, Australia, and New Zealand committing to major projects.
(BARRIE MACDONALD)

SOMALIA

Area: 637,000 sq km (246,000 sq mi), including the 176,000-sq-km (68,000-sq-mi) area of the unilaterally declared (in 1991) and unrecognized Republic of Somaliland
Population (2005 est.): 8,228,000 (including 3,500,000 in Somaliland); nearly 400,000 refugees are in neighbouring countries
Capital: Mogadishu; Hargeysa is the capital of Somaliland
Head of state and government: Somalia's government under President Abdiqassim Salad Hassan was barely functioning in 2005; a new transitional government in exile (until June 13) comprised President Abdullahi Yusuf Ahmed, assisted by Prime Minister Ali Muhammad Ghedi

Despite the announcement of a new transitional federal government in October 2004, Somalia passed its 15th successive year in 2005 without a functioning central government. Parts of the country, including the separatist state of Somaliland in the northwest and the semiautonomous region of Puntland in the northeast, enjoyed relative stability and exhibited signs of recovery; other zones, notably the central and southern regions, continued to suffer from instability and armed conflict.

The interim government was paralyzed by internal discord virtually from the moment of its inception. The most contentious issue was a request by interim Somali president Abdullahi Yusuf Ahmed for a 20,000-strong regional protection force to deliver the Transitional Federal Institutions (TFIs) back into Somalia from Kenya, where they had been created. The plan initially was backed by the Intergovernmental

A gunman armed with a long-range machine gun guards a vessel carrying food aid to Somalia, a country without a functioning government. Incidents of piracy off the east coast of Africa were on the increase.

Authority on Development and the African Union, but it was rejected on March 19 at a turbulent session of the Somali parliament. The United Nations Security Council also withheld authorization for the deployment, calling for political dialogue first.

Disagreement within the TFIs over relocation to Somalia further undermined the peace process. One wing of the TFIs, led by interim president Yusuf and his prime minister, Muhammad Ghedi, established itself in Jowhar, 90 km (56 mi) north of Mogadishu, asserting that the capital was insecure. The other wing, led by the speaker of the parliament, Sharif Hassan, relocated to Mogadishu, arguing that the Transitional National Charter did not allow for an alternative seat of government. Prospects for reconciliation between the two factions receded in June when President Yusuf instructed his parliamentary allies to take a recess, effectively crippling the transitional legislature. Although MPs from both sides attempted to revive the institution, the parliament had still not met by the end of 2005.

The political stalemate was matched by a military buildup on both sides, in violation of a United Nations arms embargo. A report by UN monitors identified Ethiopia and Yemen as major arms suppliers. Violence, much of it linked to the struggle within the TFIs, continued to plague central and southern Somalia. Armed clashes in the Mudug, Bay, and Gedo regions generated scores of

casualties and displaced tens of thousands of people. Hopes for peace were dealt a further blow in July when one of Somalia's most respected peace activists, Abdulqadir Yahya Ali, was assassinated at his Mogadishu home.

Concern about terrorism continued to inform international perspectives on Somalia. American military officials voiced fears that militants from Iraq and other parts of the world would seek refuge in the Horn of Africa. A Somali extremist group with alleged links to al-Qaeda emerged in Mogadishu and was accused of having murdered four foreign-aid workers in Somaliland between 2003 and 2004. The country's coastline retained its reputation as one of the most dangerous in the world, with over two dozen incidents of piracy reported to the International Maritime Organization in 2005. (*See* LAW, CRIME, AND LAW ENFORCEMENT: *Special Report.*)

On September 29 the self-declared Republic of Somaliland held its first parliamentary elections, both advancing the consolidation of democracy in the territory and enhancing Somaliland's prospects for international recognition. Somaliland's ruling party, led by Pres. Dahir Riyale Kahin, obtained only 33 of the 82 seats in the parliament, in a contest that international observers described as reasonably free and fair. Somalis everywhere applauded the poll as a goal that leaders should work toward.
(MATT BRYDEN)

SOUTH AFRICA

Area: 1,219,912 sq km (471,011 sq mi)
Population (2005 est.): 46,888,000
Capitals (de facto): Tshwane/Pretoria (executive); Mangaung/Bloemfontein (judicial); Cape Town (legislative)
Head of state and government: President Thabo Mbeki

Domestic Affairs. The most important developments in South Africa in 2005 were the events surrounding the dismissal in June by Pres. Thabo Mbeki of Jacob Zuma, his deputy president; the action led to the most severe crisis for the African National Congress (ANC) since it came to power in 1994. In June, after an eight-month trial, Schabir

Shaik, a businessman and close colleague of Zuma, was sentenced to 15 years in jail after being convicted of fraud and corruption. The judge found that there was a generally corrupt relationship between Shaik and Zuma, who was subsequently charged with two counts of corruption. Zuma also recused himself from all ANC activities at the request of the organization's national working committee. He was replaced as deputy president by the first woman to have the job, Phumzile Mlambo-Ngcuka.

Following pro-Zuma demonstrations at ANC events, however, the national general council of the ANC in June defied Mbeki by reinstating Zuma in ANC activities. In August the central committee of the Congress of South African Trade Unions (COSATU), the ANC's ally along with the South African Communist Party (SACP) in the "Tripartite Alliance," resolved that the charges against Zuma were politically motivated to prevent his succession as president.

In response, Mbeki proposed an internal ANC commission to investigate the charges, but this was rejected by the SACP and COSATU. In the same month, the investigative arm of the National Prosecuting Authority (the "Scorpions") conducted armed raids on Zuma's several homes and offices and those of his attorney; Zuma challenged the legality of the raids. Supported by thousands of demonstrators, Zuma appeared in court twice. Zuma was indicted on November 12. Following this, allegations of rape surfaced against him stemming from an incident that month, and he was indicted on charges of rape on December 6. Zuma again withdrew from ANC activities, and many of his supporters distanced themselves from him.

In May former South African president Nelson Mandela took legal action against his former lawyer to stop what he claimed were unauthorized sales of artworks and other merchandise involving the use of his name. In June, 21 current and former MPs and six travel agencies appeared in court on charges of fraud for the misuse of parliamentary travel vouchers, and later in the month 5 of the ANC MPs resigned. In September there was a third "floor-crossing window," in which parliamentarians were allowed to switch parties. In KwaZulu/Natal the Inkatha Freedom

Party was struck by the resignation of its chairperson, Ziba Jiyane, who formed the National Democratic Convention, which picked up four seats. After 90 years the New National Party, which in April had voted to disband after the impending local elections, lost its last members in the national parliament. Since parliamentarians were elected on party lists and not as individuals, however, floor crossing was heavily controversial and was said to deprive voters of the ability to hold their representatives accountable.

In defiance of the government, COSATU called two one-day general strikes, in June and August, to protest poverty and job losses, which COSATU blamed on trade liberalization and an

© Mike Hutchings/Reuters/Corbis

South African Pres. Thabo Mbeki greets the new deputy president, Phumzile Mlambo-Ngcuka, after she was sworn into office in Cape Town on June 23.

incoherent government industrial strategy. The strikes were supported by more than one million workers, including an unprecedented number of white workers, and were followed by a series of one-day provincial general strikes. At an ANC national general council, COSATU secured the defeat of a two-tier labour-market proposal: a dual wage system in which young workers would earn less than what was stipulated in prevailing South African wage agreements.

There was a substantial increase in strike activity over wages, which drew particular attention to lucrative increases for executives. For the first time ever, black and white workers united for a national mine strike, the first in 18 years. There was also a wave of demonstrations in small towns as well as big cities by people impatient with the lack of service delivery.

Economy. The GDP growth of 3.7% in 2004 was expected to increase to 4.3% in 2005. The rand's appreciation by 18% against the dollar in 2004 led to severe job losses in sectors such as mining, clothing, and textiles. Gold production sank to its lowest level since 1931. In the first quarter of 2005, 130,000 jobs were lost in the nonfarming formal economy. Though the official unemployment rate was put at 26.5% at the end of the first quarter of 2005, the unofficial estimate was more than 40%. In the year to late September, however, the rand fell by 11% against the dollar. As a result of the decline in inflation, the main interest rate was cut in April from 7.5% to 7%. Largely as a result of the increase in fuel prices, however, the inflation index CPIX, which had averaged 3.9% in the year from July 2004, increased to 4.8% in August 2005.

The 2005 February budget promised 115 billion rand (1 rand = about $0.16) in infrastructure spending over the next three years, tax cuts of 10.6 billion rand, and 23.3 billion rand for social grants. The deficit for 2004–05 was later revised downward to 1.5% of GDP and was estimated at 1% for 2005–06.

Foreign Relations. Despite objections by Zimbabwean opposition parties, the South African parliamentary observer mission declared in March that general elections held that month in Zimbabwe had been legitimate and fair. After a COSATU fact-finding mission to Zimbabwe was twice expelled, COSATU and the SACP marched to the Beit Bridge border crossing shortly before the elections to protest violations of democracy by the regime of Zimbabwean Pres. Robert Mugabe and implicitly to show displeasure against the ANC government's appeasement of Zimbabwe. The South African government continued to assist the peace process in Burundi and tried to play a role in securing peace in the renewed Côte d'Ivoire civil war. In September, when President Mbeki was in New York for the special UN summit on reform, he questioned whether Europe and the U.S. were really committed to ending world poverty and called on them to end farm subsidies within three years. He also criticized the UN for its failure to reform its structures.

(MARTIN LEGASSICK)

SPAIN

Area: 505,988 sq km (195,363 sq mi)
Population (2005 est.): 44,079,000
Capital: Madrid
Chief of state: King Juan Carlos I
Head of government: Prime Minister José Luis Rodríguez Zapatero

Philippe Desmazes—AFP/Getty Images

Thousands of Spanish students demonstrate in Madrid on December 14 against a plan by the Socialist government to make religious education optional in state schools.

On Feb. 20, 2005, Spaniards became the first Europeans to vote in a referendum on the proposed EU constitution. The overwhelming "yes" vote (77%) came as no surprise in a country that had long been one of the largest net recipients of EU funds, where support for European integration had always been high, and where all of the major parties supported the constitutional text. The very predictability of the result and a lacklustre campaign, however, helped keep participation down to a mere 42% of the electorate, the lowest turnout at the polls in Spain's recent democratic history.

The European referendum constituted a rare instance of political consensus during a year in which the conservative Popular Party (PP) headed a series of demonstrations against the governing Socialist Party's policies. On two of these occasions, the PP enjoyed the support of the Roman Catholic Church. Twenty bishops joined hundreds of thousands of demonstrators in the streets of Madrid in protest against same-sex marriage, but it was nevertheless legalized on June 30. In November some 500,000 people joined church and PP leaders to protest alleged antireligious and pro-public-school biases in the Socialists' educational reforms.

The government breathed a sigh of relief in the wake of regional elections in the Basque Country in April. The centre-right Basque Nationalists regained power—but without sufficient support in the regional assembly to press ahead with controversial plans to move unilaterally toward semi-independence through "freely associated state" status with Spain. Hopes also spread of an end to almost four decades of violence at the hands of the armed Basque separatist organization Euzkadi Ta Askatasuna (ETA). While the organization continued its campaign of low-intensity

urban warfare, the year ended without any fatalities (the last of more than 800 victims of ETA attacks since 1968 died in May 2003). Several developments provided grounds for cautious optimism, including unconfirmed reports of contacts between the Socialists and ETA, ambiguous but favourable statements by the organization's banned political wing, Batasuna, and a parliamentary declaration inviting negotiations with ETA if it definitively abandoned the armed struggle. The PP led demonstrations in January and June in support of the victims of terrorism and in opposition to any idea of dialogue with ETA.

The real headache for Prime Minister José Luis Rodríguez Zapatero, however, involved Catalonia, where the Socialist-dominated regional parliament approved a major overhaul of the statute of autonomy. Accepted for consideration by the Madrid parliament in November, the text defined Catalonia as "a nation" and provided for a substantial increase in self-government and fiscal independence for the region. The problem was that the text was considered unconstitutional by many Spaniards and unacceptable by many more, including a number of Zapatero's own ministers. Intense efforts continued at the end of the year to come up with a text that would satisfy both the Socialists and the Catalan proponents of the proposal. Most analysts attributed the Socialists' dramatic slump in opinion polls to widespread hostility both to the

proposal and to Zapatero's vacillating handling of the issue.

In the international arena, the Socialists made halfhearted attempts to patch up relations with the U.S., which had been severely strained after Spanish troops were pulled out of Iraq in April 2004. The government dispatched a stream of senior ministers to Washington and more troops to join NATO peacekeeping forces in Afghanistan, where 17 Spanish soldiers died in a helicopter crash in August. Any goodwill generated by these gestures, however, was offset by the active role that Spain played in persuading the EU to reestablish normal diplomatic relations with Cuba, by its signing of a high-profile arms deal with the government of Hugo Chávez in Venezuela, and by Zapatero's championing of an "Alliance of Civilizations." Conceived as an alternative to the U.S.-led war on terrorism, the Spanish initiative advocated dialogue and cooperation between the world's major religions and political powers as the only effective long-term solution to international conflict and violence.

It was a year of celebrations for the Spanish royal family. The 30th anniversary of the coronation of King Juan Carlos in November came just weeks after Crown Princess Letizia gave birth to her first child, a daughter, Leonor. While Spain's 1978 constitution allowed a woman to inherit the throne only if she had no brothers, a broad consensus immediately emerged in support of a constitutional amendment that would one day enable Leonor to succeed her grandfather and father, Crown Prince Felipe, even if she were to have younger male siblings. (JUSTIN BYRNE)

SRI LANKA

Area: 65,610 sq km (25,332 sq mi)
Population (2005 est.): 20,743,000
Capitals: Sri Jayawardenepura Kotte (legislative and judicial); Colombo (executive)
Head of state and government: Presidents Chandrika Kumaratunga, assisted by Prime Minister Mahinda Rajapakse, and, from November 19, Rajapakse, assisted by Prime Minister Ratnasiri Wickremanayake from November 21

Sri Lanka entered 2005 still reeling from the disastrous Indian Ocean tsunami of December 2004, which caused at least 31,000 deaths along the country's coasts. It damaged schools, hospitals, tourist facilities, and some 99,000 dwellings, displaced 443,000 people, and destroyed two-thirds of the fishing fleet. Donors pledged $3 billion in reconstruction aid. A dispute arose over how to handle assistance to areas controlled by the rebel Liberation Tigers of Tamil Eelam (LTTE), where two-thirds of the assistance needs were located. The government, led by Pres. Chandrika Kumaratunga, signed a cooperative agreement with the LTTE, causing the government's coalition partner, the Janata Vikmuthi Permuna, to withdraw its parliamentary support in June. This left Kumaratunga's United People's Freedom Alliance (UPFA) in a minority position.

In August the Supreme Court rejected Kumaratunga's claim that she could remain in office until late 2006, ruling that she had to leave office as scheduled on Dec. 22, 2005. In presidential elections held on November 17, UPFA nominee Mahinda Rajapakse, a hard-liner in dealings with the LTTE, scored a narrow victory over United National Party candidate Ranil Wickremasinghe. Ratnasiri Wickremanayake was appointed prime minister on November 21.

A February 2002 truce between the government and the separatists held, despite the suspension of Norwegian-brokered peace negotiations in April 2003, but ethnic tensions rose during

A Buddhist monk in Colombo, Sri Lanka, warns off an antiriot policeman who was sent to break up a demonstration against the president's plan to extend aid to the Tamil Tiger guerrillas.

2005. One reason was the assassination of Foreign Minister Lakshman Kadirgamar on August 12. Although the LTTE denied responsibility for the minister's death, many blamed it for the crime.

Economic growth in 2005 sagged to about 4.7% (from the 5.4% in 2004), primarily because of a drop in tourism following the tsunami. If violence did not resume, a recovery was expected in 2006. Inflation spiked, owing to a large government deficit and rising oil prices. According to the Asian Development Bank, political instability, poor access to finance, and weak infrastructure (particularly frequent power cuts) combined to make Sri Lanka less attractive to investors than some other Asian countries. (DONALD SNODGRASS)

SUDAN, THE

Area: 2,503,890 sq km (966,757 sq mi)
Population (2005 est.): 36,233,000, including nearly 200,000 refugees in Chad
Capitals: Khartoum (executive and ministerial) and Omdurman (legislative)
Head of state and government: President and Prime Minister Lieut. Gen. Omar Hassan Ahmad al-Bashir

The Comprehensive Peace Agreement (CPA) signed in Nairobi on Jan. 9, 2005, by the National Islamic Front (NIF) government and the Sudan People's Liberation Army/Movement (SPLA/M) was greeted with widespread relief. Under the terms of the CPA, the south gained the autonomy for which it had fought, with the prospect of a referendum in six years' time to determine whether it would become totally independent of the north. The distribution of seats in the central parliament was satisfactorily negotiated, even in the three disputed oil-rich districts between the north and the south. Offices of state were allocated between the signatories, and agreement was reached on the sharing of oil revenues. Equally significant was the ruling that Shari'ah (Islamic) law would only apply to Muslims, even in the north.

Nevertheless, questions still remained about the future. Even in the north the NIF was not universally popular, and the minimal share of political power accepted grudgingly by the National Democratic Alliance, an umbrella group of several other northern political

A crowd numbering more than a million assembles to greet former rebel leader John Garang, who arrived in Khartoum on July 8, the day before his inauguration as first vice president of The Sudan.

parties, was insufficient to satisfy the group's aspirations indefinitely. In the south the SPLA had spearheaded the fight for autonomy, but 17 other armed forces, representing a variety of ethnic groups and political objectives, had also participated in the battle and were determined not to be marginalized. Also, the granting of autonomy to the south provided a precedent that disgruntled elements in the east might be tempted to pursue.

Above all, there remained the problem of the large western province of Darfur, where—in spite of deliberations at the UN and intermittent attempts by the African Union to mediate between the Sudanese government and the rebels—sporadic fighting continued, and the death toll grew while the number of refugees multiplied steadily. Although the African-sponsored and the Western-funded-and-equipped peace-keeping force achieved some success, its numbers were insufficient and its mandate inadequate to protect the civilians at risk, and in spite of exhortations and promises, reinforcements were not forthcoming.

The arrival in Khartoum of SPLA/M leader John Garang (*see* OBITUARIES), who was sworn in on July 9 as first vice president of the entire country, was greeted with great jubilation. Garang was widely regarded as the person most capable of holding the south together as well as encouraging hope of a united Sudan and a settlement of the Darfur crisis. The rejoicing turned to anger and dismay on July 30, however, when the helicopter carrying Garang back from a meeting with Ugandan Pres. Yoweri Museveni crashed, killing all on board. Although the crash appeared to have been accidental, conspiracy theories proliferated, and hostile black Africans in Khartoum and Juba turned on the Arab population, killing more than 100 of them and damaging many homes and businesses. The SPLM moved rapidly to calm the situation by appointing Salva Kiir Mayardit, a staunch supporter of Garang, to succeed him as leader of the party, and in September Pres. Lieut. Gen. Omar Hassan Ahmad al-Bashir was able to swear in a cabinet that represented the entire country. Later in the month, however, the situation in Darfur deteriorated sharply, and divisions among the leadership of the main rebel group in October posed a further threat to the resolution of the conflict and had repercussions in other parts of the country.   (KENNETH INGHAM)

SURINAME

Area: 163,820 sq km (63,251 sq mi)
Population (2005 est.): 493,000
Capital: Paramaribo
Head of state and government: President Ronald Venetiaan, assisted by Prime Ministers Jules Rattankoemar Ajodhia and, from August 12, Ram Sardjoe

The dominant event of 2005 in Suriname was the reelection of Pres. Ronald Venetiaan to a third term in office. His solid record included an increase in GDP and a significant decline in inflation, which had been reduced from 82% to 9% during the previous five years. Growth and a favourable trade balance were attributed to bauxite receipts, a prosperous Canadian gold mine, and an increase in tourism. In addition, stable financial management and the privatization of several agricultural enterprises encouraged increased foreign investment.

Less encouraging was the paper-thin margin by which Venetiaan was returned to office. His New Front coalition lost one-third of its seats, mostly to the New Democratic Party of former police sergeant and dictator Desi Bouterse, and governed with an enlarged but less-cohesive coalition.

Ronnie Brunswijk, a former rebel chief and leader of the party representing the minority Bush Negroes (Maroons), attends the opening session of Suriname's parliament on June 30.

AP/Wide World Photos

Though Bouterse faced murder charges for having assassinated political opponents in 1982, he controlled approximately 30% of the legislature. Gains were also made by the party representing the Bush Negroes (descendants of escaped slaves), including the election of Ronnie Brunswijk, the former Bush Negro commander in the civil war and convicted drug smuggler.

The outlook for settlement of the long-standing offshore border dispute with Guyana improved, with arbitration scheduled to terminate in 2007. Less promising was resolution of an additional dispute with Guyana involving the border demarcation along the Courantyne River. Another dark note was the magnitude of the drug-trafficking trade. Suriname remained a major transshipment base for South American cocaine destined for Europe.
(JOHN W. GRAHAM)

SWAZILAND

Area: 17,364 sq km (6,704 sq mi)
Population (2005 est.): 1,032,000
Capitals: Mbabane (administrative and judicial); Lozitha and Ludzidzini (royal); Lobamba (legislative)
Chief of state: King Mswati III, with much power shared by his mother, Queen Mother Ntombi Latfwala
Head of government: Prime Minister Absalom Themba Dlamini

On July 26, 2005, King Mswati III signed a new constitution for Swaziland, nine years after he had appointed a Constitution Review Commission. Swaziland had been without a constitution since 1973, when King Mswati's father, King Sobhuza II, abolished the 1968 constitution signed at independence. Though long-awaited, the new constitution was met with protests by a number of civil society organizations and labour groups that rejected key areas of the document and the manner by which it was adopted. Critics were particularly dismayed that the new constitution upheld a ban on opposition political parties.

A five-year period of chastity imposed on young Swazi women in 2000 ended during the year. This cultural rite—known as *umcwasho* after the tasseled headgear worn by women to indicate their celibacy—had last been observed in the 1970s. King Mswati had reintroduced the rite partly in an attempt to reduce the high levels of HIV infection in the Swazi nation. There were many claims that the custom of *umcwasho* contributed to a significant reduction in the HIV infection level among teenagers between 2000 and 2005. Surveillance reports revealed, however, that the national HIV infection rate in 2005 stood at 42.6%, up from 38.6% in 2002.

At the end of August, Swaziland held its first-ever jobs summit, which was aimed at boosting employment and reducing poverty. It helped raise 1.6 billion emalangeni (about $252 million), which would be deposited in a special fund to support small- and medium-sized business enterprises. An estimated 70% of Swaziland's population lived below the poverty line, and about 300,000 people needed food aid, up from 257,000 the previous year.

(ACKSON M. KANDUZA)

SWEDEN

Area: 450,295 sq km (173,860 sq mi)
Population (2005 est.): 9,024,000
Capital: Stockholm
Chief of state: King Carl XVI Gustaf
Head of government: Prime Minister Göran Persson

Sweden began 2005 still reeling from the devastating loss of life caused by the Indian Ocean tsunami that struck in late December 2004. Some 20,000 Swedes were vacationing in Thailand when the tsunami hit, and early estimates indicated that the Swedish death toll from the disaster could top 3,000. At midyear the number of Swedes believed killed or missing in the tsunami stood at 544, with 428 deaths confirmed.

The Social Democratic government of Prime Minister Göran Persson faced withering public criticism of its handling of the crisis. In particular, concerns were raised over the apparent sluggishness of the government's response, with Persson and Foreign Minister Laila Freivalds singled out for not having interrupted their vacations sooner. In the immediate aftermath of the disaster, Persson's approval ratings

sank to 32%. A final report by the Swedish commission set up to evaluate the government's tsunami response concluded that Persson "bears the overall responsibility for the shortcomings" of the response and recommended the creation of a "crisis-management unit" in the prime minister's office. Persson resisted calls that he resign and further indicated that he had no plans to dismiss anyone in his administration. Late in the year the government announced its intention to become a key donor to a UN trust fund to support the creation of a tsunami early-warning system for the Indian Ocean.

As Sweden's immigrant population continued to swell (by 2005 more than one million of the country's nine million inhabitants were foreign-born), a new report by the Organisation for Economic Co-operation and Development claimed that immigrants were being forced to live in areas where jobs were scarce and where they would therefore likely become dependent on welfare. There were also concerns over the high number of asylum seekers who had gone into hiding in the country after having their applications for resident permits rejected. In November the Riksdag (parliament) voted in favour of granting thousands of rejected applicants an opportunity to resubmit their petitions for legal status.

Debate also focused on Sweden's nuclear-energy policy, and some environmentalists questioned the industry's plan to store massive amounts of spent nuclear fuel in a permanent repository some 500 m (1,640 ft) underground. At the same time, many in Sweden had begun to reevaluate the nuclear-phase-out plan altogether, especially in light of growing concerns over global warming and fears that the phaseout could lead to increased reliance on coal and gas imports. Though an opinion poll taken in March suggested that more than 80% of Swedes wanted to maintain or even increase nuclear power, the Barsebäck 2 reactor was closed on schedule at the end of May.

On the economic front, export growth ground to a virtual halt in the first quarter of the year. By the end of 2005, total exports of goods had risen by just 4.2%, a sharp decline from the robust 10.5% growth witnessed a year earlier. GDP growth sank to 2.4% for the year, down from 3.6% in 2004. The slowdown led to an interest-rate cut of half a percentage point at midyear. Sweden's most troubling economic news by far,

however, was a jump in the unemployment rate from 5.5% in 2004 to 7.1% by June 2005. In response, the government, which had made job creation one of its key priorities, approved an ambitious two-year employment package that was set to go into effect on Jan. 1, 2006.

In the general elections scheduled for Sept. 17, 2006, the Social Democrats and their allies were expected to face a stiff challenge from an opposition headed by Fredrik Reinfeldt, leader of the conservative Moderate Party.

(SHERMAN HOLLAR)

SWITZERLAND

Area: 41,284 sq km (15,940 sq mi)
Population (2005 est.): 7,519,000
Capitals: Bern (administrative) and Lausanne (judicial)
Head of state and government: President Samuel Schmid

Fiercely independent Switzerland edged closer to the European Union in June 2005 when voters approved by 55–45% the country's participation in the passport-free Schengen zone. Pres. Samuel Schmid hailed the outcome of the referendum as a vote of confidence in the government's policy to promote closer links with the EU while retaining full political sovereignty. Switzerland was due to join the Schengen zone under an arrangement that would allow it to retain customs controls. The pro-European mood also prevailed in a September vote that approved a proposal to allow citizens of the 10 new EU members to work in Switzerland. The scheme would extend an agreement to open labour markets that was signed in 1999 with the original 15 EU members. Opponents of the move warned that Eastern European labourers would take jobs from higher-paid Swiss workers.

In another key referendum 58% voted in favour of granting more rights to registered same-sex couples, which would thus allow them to receive the same tax and pension status as married couples. The referendum stopped short of letting same-sex couples adopt children or undergo fertility treatment.

Swiss engineers completed drilling for the 34.6-km (1 km = 1.6 mi) Lötschberg tunnel, which would link northern and

Swiss miners await the breakthrough in the Lötschberg tunnel in Bern canton on April 28. It was one of two major north-south railroad tunnels being dug beneath the Alps with the aim of keeping truck-trailers off Swiss roads.

southern Europe and cut travel times between Germany and Italy when it opened in 2007. The more ambitious 57-km Gotthard tunnel remained under construction. The aim of the two multi-billion-dollar construction projects was to shift heavy trucks in transit through Europe from the roads to the railways and ease congestion on Alpine highways.

The Swiss railway system—famous for its punctuality—in June suffered an embarrassing and unprecedented power failure that halted the entire network for several hours and stranded tens of thousands of commuters and tourists. Swiss International Airlines, which accumulated losses of 2 billion Swiss francs (about $1.7 billion) in the three years of its existence, was sold to Germany's Lufthansa during the year. The newly integrated company announced plans for scaled-down European short-haul flights to cut costs.

Many Swiss were relieved at the news that another national symbol—the Swiss army knife—was to remain in local hands after Victorinox purchased its smaller, struggling rival, Wenger. The two companies, which previously had shared the rights to supply the Swiss army, produced nearly 26 million knives annually. Sales fell after the Sept. 11,

2001, terrorist attacks in the U.S., as tighter security measures led to airline bans on pocket knives, which had been a popular item at airport stores.

In a long-running money-laundering scandal, Switzerland agreed to return to Nigeria $290 million in funds held in accounts linked to the late dictator Sani Abacha. The announcement came after Nigeria agreed to allow the World Bank to monitor the funds to ensure that the money was spent on development projects in areas such as health, education, and infrastructure. A second installment of $170 million was due to be sent back to Nigeria at a subsequent date once the assets had been converted to cash. The funds, allegedly plundered from Nigerian state coffers by Abacha and transferred to Swiss bank accounts, had been held by Switzerland since 1999.

The sluggish economies in most EU countries—the main export markets for Switzerland—dashed hopes of economic revival in 2005, even though the weakening of the Swiss franc against the U.S. dollar helped make Swiss exports more competitive. Government figures showed that GDP grew by only 0.9%, largely because of buoyant consumer demand, compared with initial predictions of 1.5%. Unemployment remained below 4%.   (CLARE KAPP)

SYRIA

Area: 185,180 sq km (71,498 sq mi)
Population (2005 est.): 17,794,000
Capital: Damascus
Head of state and government: President Bashar al-Assad, assisted by Prime Minister Muhammad Naji al-Otari

Syria's leaders reeled from setback after setback during 2005. The most important reverse surrounded the assassination on February 14 in Beirut of former Lebanese prime minister Rafiq al-Hariri. (*See* OBITUARIES.) Accusations that Syrian agents were involved in the bombing that killed him were quickly voiced by Lebanese and U.S. leaders, despite Damascus's immediate and unequivocal condemnation of the killing. Syrian labourers in Sidon and the Ba'th Party office in Beirut were attacked the following day in retaliation.

U.S. Pres. George W. Bush reiterated the call for Syria to pull its forces out of Lebanon. Syria responded by moving its troops to the eastern edge of Al-Biqa' valley. As February ended, some 25,000 Lebanese demonstrated at Hariri's grave site, and the pro-Syrian government in Lebanon collapsed. Saudi and Egyptian leaders then joined in lobbying Damascus for a full withdrawal, while the UN issued a provisional report charging that Syria "bears primary responsibility for the political tension that preceded the assassination." In late March, Foreign Minister Faruq al-Shar' promised the Security Council that all Syrian forces would be out of Lebanon before that country's parliamentary elections in May. The last Syrian soldiers left Lebanese territory on April 26.

Tensions steadily escalated between Beirut and Damascus. Syrian border guards harassed Lebanese commercial vehicles; Lebanese police carried out raids against suspected smugglers in disputed border districts; and Syrian patrol boats seized Lebanese fishing vessels in contested waters north of Tripoli, Lebanon. In these circumstances a UN commission headed by Detlev Mehlis started to collect evidence and testimony regarding the Hariri assassination. As the investigation proceeded, the two countries resumed discussions over border demarcation and the supply of Syrian natural gas to Lebanese electricity plants. The Mehlis report, released in late October, implicated senior Syrian intelligence officers in the assassination. A second UN commission then charged that Syrian agents remained active in Lebanese affairs. At the end of October, Lebanese troops took up positions around training camps of Syrian-sponsored Palestinian guerrillas in Al-Biqa' valley.

Meanwhile, relations with Washington went from bad to worse. Heightened Syrian efforts to reduce the flow of insurgents and supplies into Iraq elicited only disdain from U.S. officials. Washington gave Damascus little credit for turning over to authorities in Baghdad 30 high-ranking Iraqi Ba'thists in late February. The U.S. joined Britain and France in sponsoring a Security Council resolution at the end of October that demanded greater Syrian cooperation with subsequent inquiries into the Hariri affair. Only firm opposition from Russia and China prevented the new resolution from including sanctions should Damascus hesitate or continue to support militant Palestinian and Lebanese organizations.

On the domestic front, Pres. Bashar al-Assad dismissed Gen. Hasan Khalil as chief of military intelligence in the wake of the Hariri assassination and appointed his brother-in-law, Gen. Asaf Shawkat, to the post. The long-postponed 10th Regional Congress of the Ba'th Party that took place in early June adopted minor reforms and occasioned the resignation of longtime Vice Pres. 'Abd al-Halim Khaddam. Two weeks before the publication of the Mehlis report, Minister of the Interior Ghazi Kan'an was found dead, apparently by his own hand. As commander of Syrian intelligence in Lebanon, General Kan'an had supervised Lebanese affairs from 1982 to 2002. (FRED H. LAWSON)

TAIWAN

Area: 36,188 sq km (13,972 sq mi)
Population (2005 est.): 22,726,000
Capital: Taipei
Chief of state: President Chen Shui-bian
Head of government: Presidents of the Executive Yuan (Premiers) Yu Shyi-kun and, from February 1, Frank Hsieh

In Taiwan the major events of 2005 centred mostly on the island's relations with China. The year began with the government's announcement to permit Taiwanese banks to set up branches in China, a move that was preceded by Taiwanese insurance and securities companies' being allowed on the mainland. Negotiations were also under way for Chinese banks to be allowed to establish offices in Taiwan. An even more significant breakthrough came in the form of the first direct commercial flights between the island and mainland China in 55 years. The two sides had long talked about cross-straits flights, but political tension had hitherto delayed progress on the matter. A three-week-long experimental period was finally planned. From January 29 to February 20—a span that encompassed the Chinese Lunar New Year holidays—chartered flights exclusively for

Taiwanese businesspeople and their families were operated between Taipei and Kaohsiung and the mainland cities of Beijing, Shanghai, and Guangzhou. In the wake of this experiment, which was generally enthusiastically received on the island, China encouraged Taiwan to consider more direct flights. This proposal was met by initial opposition from Taiwanese pro-independence leaders, who expressed fears that such flights could undermine the island's political and economic security. In late November, however, Taiwan's Mainland Affairs Council and China's Taiwan Affairs Office respectively announced that direct charter flights would also be operated during the 2006 Lunar New Year holidays. The mainland city of Xiamen was added to the schedule, and flights would be available to any Taiwanese who had valid travel documents.

Another historical breakthrough in cross-straits relations occurred in April–July when the heads of three major Taiwanese opposition parties—the Nationalist Party (KMT), the People's First Party (PFP), and the New Party—made separate visits to Beijing for face-to-face talks with Chinese Pres. Hu Jintao. Each of the opposition leaders recognized Taiwan as part of China but did not necessarily regard reunification as a policy priority. While reshaping political communications across the Taiwan Strait, such direct talks between the Chinese leadership and nonseparatist elements within Taiwan put added pressure on the pro-independence government of Pres. Chen Shui-bian.

Lien Chan, the honorary chairman of the Taiwanese KMT party, and his wife visit a panda research centre during a tour of mainland China in October. China offered a pair of pandas as a gift to Taiwan.

© China Newsphoto/Reuters/Corbis

An antisecession law passed by China in March aroused widespread protests in Taiwan. The law authorized the use of military force should Taiwan seek independence. In response, President Chen threatened to propose an antiannexation law and reannounced the bid to purchase a number of advanced weapons, including 3 PAC-3 missiles, 8 diesel-electric submarines, and 12 P-3C antisubmarine aircraft. The KMT and PFP succeeded in blocking Chen's military budget at year's end, however.

The Taiwanese business community continued to invest money in mainland projects. According to the Ministry of Economic Affairs, more than $42 billion from Taiwan had been invested in some 33,000 projects in China since 1991. Investment in the mainland during 2004 totaled $7.2 billion—about 67% of the island's total investment abroad. The electronics industry alone invested $3 billion that year. In early 2005 Chi Mei Optoelectronics Corp., a major manufacturer of large-size TFT-LCD panels for televisions, notebook computers, and desktop monitors, won approval from Taiwanese authorities for its first investment ($1 million) in the mainland.

Since democratization Taiwan had hardly gone a year without elections. To prevent the KMT and PFP from joining forces in the December 2005 elections of county chiefs and city mayors, the ruling Democratic Progressive Party (DPP) approached the PFP regarding possible cooperation. No deal was reached, however, and as the elections neared, the DPP's popularity declined to a low point of 36%. This prompted young leaders in the DPP to lambaste corruption in the party and call for reforms, which the DPP chairman, Su Tseng-chang, promised. The KMT witnessed its own share of infighting as the party chairman, Ma Ying-jeou, and the Legislative Yuan speaker, Wang Jin-pyng—two leaders expected to compete for the party's 2008 presidential nomination—vied for power. Within the DPP, Vice Pres. Annette Lu, Premier Frank Hsieh, and Su were among those who had begun positioning themselves for a possible run in 2008. The DPP's big loss in the December elections probably eliminated Su, who was forced to submit his resignation as party chairman. Out of 23 counties and cities, the DPP won only six election contests—a result that was sure to intensify intraparty power struggles in the coming years. (XIAOBO HU)

TAJIKISTAN

Area: 143,100 sq km (55,300 sq mi)
Population (2005 est.): 6,849,000
Capital: Dushanbe
Chief of state: President Imomali Rakhmonov
Head of government: Prime Minister Akil Akilov

Tajikistan's parliamentary election on Feb. 27, 2005, passed off quietly, despite previous criticism by opposition political figures that the Popular Democratic Party, the party of the president, enjoyed an unfair advantage after the independent media had been muzzled in the months leading up to the election. Opposition parties asserted that local election boards had denied many of their candidates places on the ballot. There was little active campaigning. Opposition claims of election fraud were rejected in March by the Central Election Commission, and final results gave 52 of the 63 seats in the lower house to the Popular Democratic Party. Only six newly elected deputies represented opposition parties.

In mid-April Mahmadruzi Iskandarov, head of the opposition Democratic Party, was abducted in Moscow, where he had sought refuge to avoid what he said were politically motivated charges in Tajikistan. He later turned up in custody in Dushanbe, and, after a lengthy trial, in October he received a 23-year sentence on various charges, including terrorism, embezzlement, and illegal possession of firearms. Other opposition leaders warned that Iskandarov's harsh treatment could lead to popular disturbances.

The authorities continued to restrict the independent media throughout the year. Prior to the February election, the National Association of Independent Media complained that government officials were refusing to give information to independent journalists while willingly sharing it with state media. In January the popular weekly *Nerui Sukhan* was closed for alleged tax evasion. It was allowed to resume publication in

July but was almost immediately shut down again, and in August its editor in chief was sentenced to two years in prison for stealing electricity.

In July Russian border guards stationed on the Tajik-Afghan frontier completed the handover to Tajik troops of responsibility for protecting Tajikistan's southern border. Some Russian media questioned whether Tajik troops were adequately prepared to guard the border, in particular to stop the flow of illegal drugs from Afghanistan into the Commonwealth of Independent States. During the year the international community promised assistance to Tajikistan to strengthen the country's border security.

Economic officials reported rising indicators in all spheres, but international organizations questioned whether the country would be able to reach its Millennium Development Goals that were meant to cut the poverty level in half by 2015. In September the Russian Aluminum Co. launched construction of the Rogun power station, which had been started in the Soviet era but later abandoned. The firm intended to use the plant's electricity to power an expansion of Tajikistan's aluminum industry. (BESS BROWN)

TANZANIA

Area: 945,090 sq km (364,901 sq mi)
Population (2005 est.): 36,766,000
De facto capital: Dar es Salaam; only the legislature meets in Dodoma, the longtime planned capital
Chief of state and head of government: Presidents Benjamin William Mkapa and, from December 21, Jakaya Kikwete, assisted by Prime Ministers Frederick Tulway Sumaye and, from December 30, Edward Lowassa

Beginning on Jan. 1, 2005, as a result of an agreement reached in 2004 between the presidents of Tanzania, Kenya, and Uganda, passport holders of the three countries were able to travel in the region free from immigration requirements. Together with the simultaneous implementation of a customs union, this marked a significant advance toward the federal relationship envisaged for 2012. In June the government suggested that primary education would be available by

the end of the year for all who required it and that at least 100,000 people suffering from HIV/AIDS would receive free antiretroviral drugs by the end of 2006. Also in June, a company involved in producing an antimalarial drug stated that it would soon make the treatment available cheaply to Tanzanians.

These hopeful signs, however, were set against the continuous struggle against poverty. Teachers complained that their profession was being denigrated by poor pay and difficult working conditions, and junior doctors at the Muhimbili National Hospital went on strike for a week in June for similar reasons. There also remained the ongoing problem of feeding and housing 400,000 refugees located in the northwest, although that situation improved slightly with a steady increase in the second half of the year in the numbers returning to Burundi. In May there were warnings of food shortages in 13 districts in the north of the country, and the government's contract with a company supplying water to Dar es Salaam was terminated because of poor performance, which meant that thousands of people continued to suffer acute shortages.

The local elections for the president and the parliament of the islands of Zanzibar and Pemba were preceded by violent clashes between supporters of the two main parties, Chama Cha Mapinduzi (CCM) and the Civic United Front (CUF), but went ahead as scheduled on October 30. Pres. Amani Abeid Karume was reelected, and the ruling CCM won a majority of parliamentary seats. Though the defeated CUF accused authorities of intimidation, complained about irregularities in the registration of voters, and questioned the legitimacy of Karume's government, its members agreed to take up their seats in the parliament.

The national elections were postponed because of the death of one of the vice presidential candidates. When elections eventually took place on December 14, there was a high turnout; 11 million of the 16 million registered voters cast their ballots. The ruling CCM's presidential candidate and former foreign minister Jakaya Kikwete won 80.2% of the vote and succeeded retiring Pres. Benjamin Mkapa. The CCM also won 206 of the 232 seats in the parliament. Although there were some disturbances on Zanzibar when the results were announced, the African Union monitor submitted a favourable report on the general conduct of the elections. (KENNETH INGHAM)

THAILAND

Area: 513,120 sq km (198,117 sq mi)
Population (2005 est.): 64,186,000
Capital: Bangkok
Chief of state: King Bhumibol Adulyadej
Head of government: Prime Minister Thaksin Shinawatra

In Thailand the year 2005 began amid profound chaos following the devastating Indian Ocean tsunami that struck several of the country's southern provinces on Dec. 26, 2004. Some 5,400 people, including foreign tourists, were killed. Although Thailand was not as seriously damaged as Indonesia and Sri Lanka, the tsunami did wreak havoc on Phuket, Krabi, and other beach resorts that depended heavily on tourism.

Economically disastrous, the tsunami turned out to be a boon for the political fortunes of Prime Minister Thaksin Shinawatra. Having come under fire for his growing authoritarian inclinations throughout 2004, Thaksin was praised for his swift response to the tsunami. Refusing foreign relief aid, he personally toured the tsunami-ravaged areas in January and allocated more than $750 million worth of government aid. The disaster helped unite Thailand behind his decisive leadership.

The parliamentary election held on February 6 produced a staggering result; the Thai Rak Thai (TRT) Party, led by Thaksin, gained 376 of the 500 seats in the parliament. This was the first time in Thailand's history that any one party had obtained an absolute majority. The Democrat Party, TRT's main rival, won only 96 seats. The other two parties, Chart Thai and the Great People's Party, took 26 and 2 seats, respectively. Buoyed by the parliamentary majority, Thaksin formed a one-party government—another unprecedented phenomenon in Thailand, where a coalition government had been the norm.

The most serious problem facing Thaksin was persistent Muslim insurgency in the southern provinces of Yala, Pattani, and Narathiwat. In March he invited Anand Panyarachun, a respected former prime minister, to establish a National Reconciliation Commission. Criticizing the brutal repression of Muslim insurgents in the past, the 48-member commission advocated a peaceful solution. On July 16, however, a defiant Thaksin, following a spate of renewed militant attacks by Muslims, issued an emergency decree that granted him absolute power to detain suspects without charge, censor the media, tap telephones, and confiscate property. Most ominous was the fact that security forces were granted immunity from criminal prosecution. The decree only exacerbated the insurgency that it was designed to contain.

Thaksin's infringement on freedom of expression continued. In October he filed a defamation lawsuit against Sondhi Limthongkul, political talk show host and owner of the Manager Media Group, and another prominent television host over stories in which they had criticized the prime minister. Such moves, coupled with his unchallenged dominance in the parliament and his draconian handling of Muslim insurgency, reinforced his detractors' criticism that Thailand had lapsed into an "electoral dictatorship."

The economy showed mixed results. On the one hand, exports kept growing, tourism recovered from the tsunami, and consumer spending remained relatively high. On the other hand, rising oil prices increased fuel costs, and inflation rose. On balance, however, the problems remained manageable, and popular discontent remained minimal.

Overall, Thaksin's position remained unshaken. Criticized by academics and human rights activists in urban areas, he nonetheless maintained good standing with the majority of the rural population, his main base of support. Even the insurgency in the south remained essentially a "local" problem in predominantly Muslim provinces, which did not seriously affect Buddhist Thais elsewhere. (YOSHINORI NISHIZAKI)

TOGO

Area: 56,785 sq km (21,925 sq mi)
Population (2005 est.): 5,400,000
Capital: Lomé
Chief of state: Presidents Gen. Gnassingbé Eyadéma, Faure Gnassingbé from February 5 (acting from February 21), Abass Bonfoh (acting) from February 25, and, from May 4, Gnassingbé
Head of government: Prime Ministers Koffi Sama and, from June 9, Edem Kodjo

AP/Wide World Photos

Emotions ran high in the run-up to the Togolese presidential elections of April 24. Here a car full of opposition supporters armed with sticks speeds past a campaign poster for Faure Gnassingbé, the eventual winner.

Gnassingbé Eyadéma, Africa's longest-serving ruler, died of a heart attack on Feb. 5, 2005 (*see* OBITUARIES), ending 38 years of near total control of Togo. Within hours army chiefs overrode the constitution by naming Faure Gnassingbé (*see* BIOGRAPHIES), the president's son, as successor. The parliament, dominated by Eyadéma's party, moved to legalize the takeover by passing a retroactive constitutional amendment the next day. The son was officially sworn in on February 7, amid protests from the international community and opposition parties. The African Union described the actions as a "military coup." A two-day general strike called by opposition parties to protest Gnassingbé's accession was only partially successful. Subsequent riots and demonstrations in the capital, however, and pressure by the African Union, the United Nations, individual African leaders, and Western donors forced the new president to agree to hold elections. On February 21 the parliament rescinded its amendment and reinstated the old constitution, which contained the provision that elections were to be held within 60 days of the death of a sitting president. Further pressure forced Gnassingbé to resign three weeks after his inauguration, but he announced that he would be a candidate in the election then scheduled for April 24.

Togo's opposition parties formed an election coalition and, on March 15, named 75-year old Emmanuel Bob-Akitani as their sole candidate. Scattered violence in Lomé and other urban centres disrupted the campaign throughout much of April as fears of poll-rigging grew. Dozens of people were killed and hundreds injured in violent street fighting throughout the campaign. More disturbances erupted after the Constitutional Court threw out opposition protests of voting irregularities and declared Faure Gnassingbé the victor with 60% of the vote. Fearing reprisals from the new government, at least 30,000 Togolese fled into Benin and Ghana.

On June 9 Gnassingbé appointed Edem Kodjo prime minister. Kodjo, although a member of the opposition coalition, had been prime minister under Eyadéma in the mid-1990s. On June 20 the prime minister announced his 30-member cabinet, most of whom were close allies of Gnassingbé. Kpatcha Gnassingbé, the president's older brother, was appointed defense minister.   (NANCY ELLEN LAWLER)

TONGA

Area: 750 sq km (290 sq mi)
Population (2005 est.): 98,600
Capital: Nuku'alofa
Head of state and government: King Taufa'ahau Tupou IV, assisted by Prime Minister of Privy Council Prince 'Ulukalala Lavaka Ata

For several weeks in mid-2005, Tongan civil servants went on strike for higher wages. Their action was prompted by wages that had fallen behind inflation and by the dramatic increase to T$100,000 (T$1 = about U.S.$0.51) of government ministers' salaries compared with the income of most civil servants (T$2,000–T$5,000). There was also discontent over the transfer of privatized government activities to members of King Taufa'ahau Tupou IV's family. In unprecedented demonstrations 10,000 people marched on the king's palace, government vehicles were firebombed, and a royal residence was destroyed in a suspected arson. In Auckland, N.Z.,

where the ailing 87-year-old king kept a home, Tongan immigrants staged protests. The Tongan government finally agreed to most of the strikers' demands, conceding wage increases of 60–80%. More significant for the longer term, however, was an agreement to establish a royal commission on democratic reform, though this was unlikely to bring significant change during the lifetime of the current monarch.

A review of the Tongan economy by the World Bank and the government found that more than 20% of the communities surveyed were living in poverty. The king called for T$1 billion in investment to revitalize the economy.   (BARRIE MACDONALD)

TRINIDAD AND TOBAGO

Area: 5,128 sq km (1,980 sq mi)
Population (2005 est.): 1,298,000
Capital: Port of Spain
Chief of state: President Maxwell Richards
Head of government: Prime Minister Patrick Manning

In January 2005 the ruling People's National Movement (PNM) party strengthened its hold on the institutions of government in Trinidad and Tobago. The PNM retained control of the Tobago House of Assembly, winning 11 of the 12 seats for a net pickup of 3. The last seat went to the opposition Democratic Action Committee.

The United National Congress (UNC), the official opposition party in Trinidad and Tobago's House of Representatives, was, by contrast, weakened in April when two of its MPs, Fuad Khan and Gillian Lucky, declared themselves no longer bound by the party whip. They expressed dissatisfaction over the path the party was taking and were particularly troubled by UNC leader and former prime minister Basdeo Panday's declaration that "politics has its own morality and that if one wishes to hold on to one's professional integrity one ought to leave politics." Panday spent a week in jail in May–June after refusing bail on a corruption charge linked to the construction of a new international airport while he was prime minister. His wife, Oma, and former UNC works

minister Carlos John were also charged alongside Panday, who eventually agreed to step down as leader of the UNC in October. Winston Dookeran, an MP for the St. Augustine constituency, succeeded him.

Explosions rocked Port of Spain throughout the year. Some form of terrorism appeared evident as bombs went off in the capital city's main shopping area, Frederick Street, in July, in a nearby street in August, outside a restaurant in downtown Independence Square in September, and outside a popular bar in St. James, west of Port of Spain, in October. No one claimed responsibility for the bombings, and there were no fatalities.   (DAVID RENWICK)

TUNISIA

Area: 163,610 sq km (63,170 sq mi)
Population (2005 est.): 10,038,000
Capital: Tunis
Chief of state: President Gen. Zine al-Abidine Ben Ali
Head of government: Prime Minister Mohamed Ghannouchi

In March 2005 Tunisia announced that as host in Tunis to more than 170 countries participating in November in the World Summit on the Information Society, it had invited Israeli Prime Minister Ariel Sharon to attend. The news, however caused demonstrations that month in major towns. In the process of preventing a demonstration in central Tunis, police, using brutal tactics, injured celebrated human rights lawyer Radia Nasraoui. Demonstrating students arrested in Safaqis (Sfax) in late February were said to have been tortured in custody.

The previous week Nasraoui had attended a demonstration in which hundreds of lawyers gathered in Tunis before the Palais de Justice to protest the arrest of human rights activist Mohamed Abbou, who had been accused of disseminating false information in articles he published on the Sharon visit and on torture in Tunisia in 2004. Abbou, who had previously been imprisoned for two years on charges of attacking a lawyer, was sentenced in April to a three-and-a-half-year term for his comments on a

Two supporters of imprisoned lawyer Mohamed Abbou (in background photo), human rights activist Radia Nasraoui (left) and fellow lawyer Sonia Ben Amor, flash victory signs during their sit-in in May to secure Abbou's release. Human rights were still a major concern in Tunisia in 2005.

Web site comparing conditions in Tunisian prisons to those at the U.S.'s Abu Ghraib prison in Iraq.

In other government crackdowns, the Association of the Tunisian Magistrates (AMT) was banned in August after its members called for greater independence; the Trade Union of Tunisian Journalists (SJT) was prevented from holding its first congress in September; and the Federation of the Leagues of Human Rights (FIDH) was prevented from holding its sixth annual congress that same month. In mid-September Hussein Sumaida, an Iraqi-Tunisian asylum seeker returned from Canada, was arrested by state security.

A cabinet reshuffle in mid-August brought new faces into government as Tunisia's old guard was quietly shunted aside. Hedi Mhenni was named the new secretary-general of the ruling Democratic Constitutional Assembly (RCD). Despite the collapse of the Tunisian textile-export trade as a result of the end on January 1 of the Multi-Fibre Agreement, which set quotas for the international trade in textiles, and anxieties over the EU's Barcelona Process and European Neighbourhood Policy, the Tunisian economy remained buoyant in 2005.

An aircraft belonging to Tuninter, a subsidiary of Tunis Air, plunged into the sea near Sicily in August while on a flight from Bari to Jarbah (Djerba). Alhough 23 of the 39 passengers and crew survived, several were injured seriously. In July Tunisia's second privately owned radio station began to broadcast in Susah (Sousse).

(GEORGE JOFFÉ)

TURKEY

Area: 783,562 sq km (302,535 sq mi)
Population (2005 est.): 72,083,000
Capital: Ankara
Chief of state: President Ahmet Necdet Sezer
Head of government: Prime Minister Recep Tayyip Erdogan

The government headed by Recep Tayyip Erdogan, leader of the Justice and Development Party (AKP), which had been in power since the November 2002 elections, achieved its immediate foreign-policy objective when negotiations for Turkey's accession to the European Union opened formally in Luxembourg on Oct. 3, 2005. Earlier in the year, Turkey had extended to the 10 new EU members, including Cyprus, the customs union that it had signed with the original membership in 1995.

The Turkish government declared simultaneously, however, that it did not recognize the Greek Cypriot administration as the government of the republic of Cyprus. The EU issued a counterdeclaration, stating that it expected Turkey to meet its obligations to all members. The decision to open accession negotiations was difficult for the EU Council of Ministers; public-opinion surveys showed that in most EU countries the majority of voters did not want Turkey as a full member. As a result, the document setting out the framework within which the negotiations were to be carried out was replete with conditions and reservations, and Turkey was warned not to expect membership for at least 10 years. Nevertheless, full membership remained the goal of the negotiations, and the Austrian government withdrew at the last moment its demand that a "privileged partnership" be specified as an alternative. This helped Prime Minister Erdogan answer opposition claims that he had made concessions to the EU, notably on Cyprus and on the rights of Turkey's Kurdish citizens, to no good effect.

Turkey's hope that Cypriot Turks would be rewarded for backing the UN plan to reunify the island was not realized. The fact that Turkish Cypriot leader Mehmet Ali Talat—who favoured the UN plan—increased his

The injured are helped after a suicide bomber caused an explosion that killed at least four people in the Turkish Aegean beach resort of Kusadasi in July. Authorities assumed that the blast was the work of Kurdish separatists who were targeting Turkey's tourist areas.

representation in the Turkish assembly in parliamentary elections (held on February 20) and then on April 17 was elected president of the Turkish Republic of Northern Cyprus ([TRNC], recognized only by Turkey) suggested that Erdogan was in step with Turkish Cypriot opinion.

The tone of the Turkish opposition became more nationalistic following the reelection on January 29 of Deniz Baykal to the leadership of the main opposition Republican People's Party (CHP) and the revival of the Motherland Party (ANAP), which mustered 22 seats in the parliament, after its leadership was passed on April 3 to 42-year-old Erkan Mumcu, a minister in the former AKP government.

Turkey's efforts to secure EU membership continued to be supported by the United States, which Erdogan visited three times during the year; he met Pres. George W. Bush on June 8. Relations were hampered, however, by the failure of the U.S. to take action against the presence in northern Iraq of armed militants of the Kurdistan Workers Party (PKK, now renamed KONGRA-GEL), which was banned in the U.S. and in the EU as a terrorist organization. Terrorists calling themselves Freedom Falcons of Kurdistan (TAK), believed to be an offshoot of the PKK, tried to disrupt Turkey's tourist industry with bomb attacks in Istanbul and in coastal resorts. In the face of mounting popular anger, Erdogan broke with tradition by declaring on August 10 that Turkey faced a Kurdish problem that he intended to solve by democratic means. The PKK responded by offering a truce until the end of September. Terrorist attacks and sweeps by Turkish security forces continued, however, and tension rose in November when an explosion in the remote mountainous province of Hakkari was blamed on a death squad of paramilitary policemen.

The growth of the economy slowed from 9.9% in 2004 to 3.4% in the second quarter of 2005, but these figures were still high by EU standards. Exports increased by 18%, and imports rose by 21% in the first nine months of the year. The consequent increase of the trade deficit to $32 billion was the main cause for disquiet. Inflation continued to drop, and consumer prices increased by only 6% in the first 10 months. Despite the threat of terrorism, the number of foreign visitors increased by 21%, to a record 19 million in the first 10 months of the year. Though the IMF was satisfied with the progress of the Turkish economy as a whole, popular discontent focused largely on unemployment, which remained high, about 9% in August, at a time when only 45% of the population of working age was employed.

(ANDREW MANGO)

TURKMENISTAN

Area: 488,100 sq km (188,500 sq mi)
Population (2005 est.): 4,833,000
Capital: Ashgabat
Head of state and government: President Saparmurad Niyazov

In August 2005 Turkmenistan became the first post-Soviet state to leave the CIS (Commonwealth of Independent States). During a CIS summit, Turkmenistan's representative—a deputy prime minister—announced that the country was moving from full to associate membership. Turkmen Pres. Saparmurad Niyazov said later that the move was because of Turkmenistan's status as a neutral country (formally recognized by the UN 10 years earlier) and that he would maintain relations with CIS states on a bilateral basis.

Throughout the year Niyazov continued his practice of replacing government officials after relatively short periods in office, apparently with the objective of preventing anyone from starting to establish an independent power base. Some longtime Niyazov associates also fell from grace. In March Foreign Minister Rashid Meredov was removed from his deputy prime ministership, but he was left in charge of the Foreign Ministry even after Niyazov complained that the country's foreign policy lacked consistency and decisiveness. In May the president dismissed Yolly Gurbanmuradov, the deputy prime minister responsible for the oil and natural gas industries, and in July longtime presidential aide Rejep Saparov was fired after being accused of nepotism. Niyazov commented that Saparov's replacement, a former mayor of the Caspian city of Turkmenbashi, had few relatives. Saparov later received a 20-year prison sentence for corruption.

After a period of relative relaxation, harassment of Turkmenistan's minority religious communities by law-enforcement officials worsened in 2005. Such groups as Baptists and Seventh-day Adventists, which had been allowed to register with the authorities, were told that despite having registered, they had no right to gather for worship.

After Uzbekistan demanded that the U.S. air base at Karshi-Khanabad be closed down, some Russian and other international media speculated that the Americans might move their military presence to Turkmenistan, though this would undermine Turkmenistan's official neutrality. Some high-level U.S. officials visited the country, fueling the speculation, but the Turkmen authorities adamantly denied having any intention of accepting an American military presence.

Turkmenistan, one of the world's most important producers of natural gas, started the year in a dispute over prices and cut off gas supplies to Russia and Ukraine. Ukrainian officials quickly agreed to a price increase, but Russia's powerful Gazprom did not settle until April. The Ukrainian side subsequently promised to pay Turkmenistan in full for previous gas deliveries; by November Ukrainian energy officials were asserting that the debt had been paid.

(BESS BROWN)

TUVALU

Area: 25.6 sq km (9.9 sq mi)
Population (2005 est.): 9,700
Capital: Government offices in Vaiaku, Fongafale islet, of Funafuti Atoll
Chief of state: Queen Elizabeth II, represented by Governors-General Faimalaga Luka and, from April 15, Filoimea Telito
Head of government: Prime Minister Maatia Toafa

In 2005 Tuvalu Prime Minister Maatia Toafa, who won office by a single vote in the 15-member legislature in October 2004, consolidated his position and named his predecessor, Saufatu Sopoanga, deputy prime minister. Early in the year Parliament met only occasionally because Toafa initially depended on the vote of one MP, Sio Patiale, who was having medical treatment overseas. By mid-September by-elections triggered by resignations, including Patiale's, had given the prime minister a working majority. In June Tuvalu hosted a meeting of regional ministers of finance and other officials to discuss strategies for the strengthening of the private sector, especially in the smaller aid-dependent island states. That same month the government participated in regional talks aimed at increasing income from the exploitation of fisheries in island states' exclusive economic zones. Former prime minister Faimalaga Luka died in August; he had resigned as governor-general in April because of failing health.

As part of a regional aid contribution, Taiwan in July agreed to meet the $3.5 million cost of repatriating hundreds of unpaid phosphate-mining employees from Tuvalu and Kiribati who had been stranded in Nauru, which was near bankruptcy and unable to pay the workers.   (BARRIE MACDONALD)

UGANDA

Area: 241,038 sq km (93,065 sq mi)
Population (2005 est.): 27,269,000
Capital: Kampala
Head of state and government: President Yoweri Museveni, assisted by Prime Minister Apolo Nsibambi

Some sectors of the international community continued to lavish praise on the government of Uganda for its achievements, especially after it was announced in July 2005 that the government had reached its target six months early for the number of HIV-positive people having access to antiretroviral treatment. Another significant advance was the completion in May in Kampala of a 50-MW thermal electricity plant, which would lessen the demands on the water supply provided by Lake Victoria, the main source of the country's hydroelectric power. Meanwhile, the World Bank gave $4.2 million to help resettle an estimated 11,000 former rebels in the north, and the U.S. was gratified by the government's agreement to grant U.S. personnel in Uganda immunity from prosecution by the International Criminal Court.

There were signs, however, that several foreign donors were beginning to

© Hudson Apunyo/Reuters/Corbis

Children, such as these in a day-care centre at a camp for internally displaced persons in the Pader district of Uganda, were among the most significant victims of the violence and disorder in the northern part of the country.

have doubts about the goodwill they had consistently shown Pres. Yoweri Museveni. The change in attitude occurred for two main and several subsidiary reasons. There were growing concerns over the government's ability to deal with the long-running rebellion of the Lord's Resistance Army (LRA) in the north, despite Kampala's heavy defense expenditures. Though there were several limited cease-fire agreements made early in the year between the government and the LRA and government forces claimed occasional successes against the rebels, the LRA's attacks continued unabated, and 1.6 million displaced persons, many of them ill-fed and troubled by disease, looked in vain for protection even when located in refugee camps.

The second troubling issue was the uncertainty surrounding the country's constitutional future. The U.K., a long-time generous aid donor to Uganda, decided in July to freeze a portion of its financial assistance because it lacked confidence in the long-promised transition to a multiparty political system. Ireland followed suit, and Norway also contemplated taking similar action. The concerns were reinforced when the Ugandan Parliament amended the constitution so that President Museveni could stand for reelection for an additional term, despite the fact that by the

time elections took place, he would have held office for 20 years. When Museveni did launch a national referendum on July 28 and urged voters to support the introduction of a multiparty system, his action was received with suspicion rather than satisfaction, because for 19 years he had rejected the system, which he said encouraged ethnic divisions.

In November rioting broke out in Kampala when Kizza Besigye was arrested and charged with treason, among other offenses. After returning from voluntary exile in South Africa, Besigye had mounted a powerful political campaign for the 2006 presidential elections, which government critics believed led to his arrest. Tensions rose when his trial was transferred from the civilian court to a closed court martial.

In addition, there was a growing lack of confidence in the government's ability to control its finances. Economic growth no longer reached the high levels it had achieved in the 1990s, and despite having been the first beneficiary of the IMF and World Bank's debt-relief program to assist poorer countries, Uganda's foreign debt had soared 50% over the previous 10 years. On October 10 former president Milton Obote died in exile. (*See* OBITUARIES.)

(KENNETH INGHAM)

UKRAINE

Area: 603,628 sq km (233,062 sq mi)
Population (2005 est.): 47,075,000
Capital: Kiev
Chief of state: Presidents Leonid Kuchma and, from January 23, Viktor Yushchenko
Head of government: Prime Ministers Viktor Yanukovich, Mykola Azarov (acting) from January 5, Yuliya Tymoshenko from January 24 (acting to February 4), and, from September 8 (acting to September 22), Yury Yekhanurov

The year 2005 in Ukraine was dominated by the tribulations of the new government headed by Pres. Viktor Yushchenko (*see* BIOGRAPHIES), who was inaugurated on January 23. His cabinet comprised 15 members of his Our Ukraine Party, 3 Socialist Party members, and a member each from the Yuliya Tymoshenko Bloc and the Union of Industrialists and Entrepreneurs. Tymoshenko, a key figure in the Orange Revolution, was appointed prime minister on February 4, with the unanimous endorsement of the parliament.

Yushchenko came to office with promises that Ukraine would take immediate steps to join Euro-Atlantic structures, particularly the EU and NATO. As a result, he attended a NATO commission meeting in Brussels in March and in April had a four-day state visit to the United States, where he delivered an address to a joint session of the U.S. Congress. He also tried to mend the ruptured relationship with Russian Pres. Vladimir Putin, visiting Moscow in January and for the May celebrations of the 60th anniversary of the end of World War II in Europe.

The new government soon ran into serious problems over several key issues, including personality conflicts and mutual accusations of continuing corruption among cabinet ministers; a fuel crisis, which materialized in May and was accompanied by a 15% rise in oil prices, leading the president to accuse his cabinet of incompetence; and an apparent failure to deal with the irregular practices of the regime of former president Leonid Kuchma, notably the reprivatization of companies undersold to favoured oligarchs, including the giant Kryvyy Rih steelworks, and the unsolved 2000 murder of opposition journalist Georgy Gongadze.

On March 1 Yushchenko confirmed that the journalist had been murdered by Ukrainian police officers, and two suspects were arrested. Tapes released by Kuchma's former bodyguard, however, clearly implicated the involvement of government officials. On March 4, shortly before he was scheduled for interrogation, former internal affairs minister Yury Kravchenko was discovered dead in his home. Thereafter, the investigation appeared stalled.

In the eyes of some critics, the Yushchenko administration was viewed as insufficiently different from its predecessor. At a July press conference, the president angrily dealt with a reporter's questions about the lavish lifestyle of his son by accusing the speaker, Serhy Leshchenko, of acting "like a hired killer." In a similar fashion the president and several ministers defended the credentials of Justice Minister Roman Zvarych, whom the Internet newspaper *Ukrainska Pravda* accused of padding his résumé with an unearned doctorate and law degree.

The Ukrainian economy slowed down sharply compared with recent years. GDP rose by 4.7% in the first five months of the year, and the anticipated annual rate was likely to be lower than the official prognosis of 8.2%. The slowdown was accompanied by rising inflation and sluggish rates of privatization as a result of the crisis over the Kryvyy Rih steelworks—an issue that remained unresolved until that company's sale in October to the Rotterdam, Neth.-based Mittal Steel Co. for $4.8 billion.

Nevertheless, there was general surprise when Yushchenko dismissed his entire cabinet on September 8, including Prime Minister Tymoshenko and Petro Poroshenko, secretary of the National Security and Defense Council. Chief of Staff Oleksandr Zinchenko also resigned. Over the next two weeks, Yushchenko reached an agreement with Viktor Yanukovich, his former adversary for the presidential post, in order to secure the approval of a new prime minister, Yury Yekhanurov, a Siberian-born resident of Dnipropetrovsk. At the same time, the president granted an amnesty to election officials accused of having manipulated the December 2004 vote.

The new cabinet had eight new faces, as well as a new portfolio—the Ministry for Construction and Architecture. Key appointees were Anatoly Kinakh in the National Security and Defense Council, Arseny Yatsenyuk as minister of the economy, and Serhy Holovaty (appointed in October) as minister of justice. The restructured government faced a period of preparation for the 2006 parliamentary elections, when Yushchenko would likely face opposition from Tymoshenko, his former ally. Though constitutional reforms that were to take effect in January 2006 would provide the

Russian Pres. Vladimir Putin (left) and Ukrainian Pres. Viktor Yushchenko address a press conference in Kiev on March 19. Relations between the two Eastern European powers were problematic throughout 2005.

AP/Wide World Photos

new prime minister with enhanced powers vis-à-vis the president, Our Ukraine currently had the support of only about 20% of MPs; Regions of Ukraine (Yanukovich) and the Tymoshenko Bloc had similar standings.

Further political conflict in Ukraine appeared inevitable, and with an economic slowdown and little progress made on EU membership, the road ahead for the Orange government appeared rocky. (DAVID R. MARPLES)

UNITED ARAB EMIRATES

Area: 83,600 sq km (32,280 sq mi)
Population (2005 est.): 4,690,000, of whom about 800,000 are citizens
Capital: Abu Dhabi
Chief of state: President Sheikh Khalifah ibn Zayid Al Nahyan
Head of government: Prime Minister Sheikh Maktum ibn Rashid al-Maktum

In 2005 the United Arab Emirates witnessed a smooth transition of power from Sheikh Zayed ibn Sultan Al

Boys who had been working as camel jockeys in the emirates are returned home to Lahore, Pak., in June. The boys were kept in severe conditions and were underfed to keep their weight down so they could participate in the sport of camel racing.

Nahyan, who died in 2004, to his eldest son, Sheikh Khalifah ibn Zayid Al Nahyan. International observers were concerned that instability would result in this oil-rich country during the first presidential succession in its history, but the transition was relatively uneventful. Some intellectuals used the opportunity to renew a call for the Federal National Council, an appointed body that advises the ruling sheikhs, to be democratized. As a result, the president announced that half of the council would be selected by a limited election at a future date. The government reiterated its stance on promoting a moderate form of Islam and rooting out radical elements in the country. This position was underscored in August when Maulana Fazlur Rahman, the hard-line leader of Pakistan's Jamiat Ulema-i-Islam party, was refused entry into the country while on holiday.

The U.A.E.'s economy continued to blossom, with an expected growth rate of 10% in 2005, and real GDP was expected to grow 6.7%. Though the majority of national wealth was derived from oil, the tourist industry was also booming. Earlier in the year, developers in Dubai unveiled the Dubai waterfront project, which would be the largest waterfront development in the world. The U.A.E. relied mainly on foreign labour (only 20% of the population were nationals), and, amid heavy criticism, reforms were enacted to ensure workers' rights. These included a ban on working outdoors during the hottest hours of the day and the return of child camel jockeys to their home countries. (RUMEE AHMED)

UNITED KINGDOM

Area: 242,514 sq km (93,635 sq mi)
Population (2005 est.): 60,020,000
Capital: London
Chief of state: Queen Elizabeth II
Head of government: Prime Minister Tony Blair

Three of the most significant events for the United Kingdom in 2005 took place in the space of just three days. On July 6 London was named as the city that would host the 2012 Olympic Games.

Londoners celebrate in Trafalgar Square on July 6 following the announcement that the city has won its bid to host the 2012 Summer Olympic Games.

The following day 56 people were killed in central London by four separate, almost simultaneous, suicide bombs. A day later Prime Minister Tony Blair (*see* BIOGRAPHIES) announced that the Group of Eight (G-8) summit being held in Gleneagles, Scot., had agreed to a massive increase in aid to Africa to help alleviate poverty in the world's poorest continent.

Domestic Affairs. In May Blair led the Labour Party to its third successive general-election victory, despite a drop from 412 seats in Parliament to 356. (*See* Sidebar, page 477.) Immediately after the election, there was widespread speculation that he might not remain prime minister for more than about a year. Blair had indicated in September 2004 that he would step down as Labour leader shortly before the next election, due in 2009 or 2010. Following the 2005 victory—and in light of Labour's sharply reduced majority—a number of Labour MPs and media commentators predicted that Blair would be forced to resign much earlier.

The events of July 6–8 extinguished such speculation for the time being. Blair played a major role in London's victory in the contest to stage the 2012 Olympics. He had flown to Singapore, where the International Olympic Committee was meeting, and lobbied a number of IOC members personally. His efforts were credited in part for London's defeat of Paris, the favourite to host the Games, in the final days of the committee's deliberations.

The suicide bombers on July 7 struck without warning and exploded bombs in three underground (subway) trains and one bus. Within a week the police had analyzed enough forensic evidence and tapes from closed-circuit-television cameras to identify the bombers as three British-born Muslims from Leeds and one Jamaican-born man living in Aylesbury, Buckinghamshire. These were the first suicide bombings ever carried out in Great Britain, and they caught the U.K.'s intelligence services completely by surprise. London's bus and underground system was immediately closed down, but within days the network was back to normal, except for the areas of the underground directly affected by the bombs.

Blair was hosting the summit of G-8 leaders in Gleneagles when he was informed about the bombings. He interrupted the meeting to fly back to London to oversee the governmental and police response to the attacks and then returned to Scotland. By the time he announced on July 8 the progress that he had made at Gleneagles, especially on aid to Africa, talk of an early handover to Gordon Brown, the chancellor of the Exchequer, had subsided.

On July 21 London's transport system was targeted by four more bombers, but on this occasion none of the devices exploded. In the days that followed, police arrested three men in London for terrorist offenses and traced a fourth man to Rome, where he was held by the Italian police and subsequently extradited to Britain. Blair and the London police were widely hailed for their handling of the two sets of bombings. Praise for the police was short-lived, however, when on July 22 they shot dead an innocent Brazilian worker, Jean Charles de Menezes, at Stockwell Station in south London. At first the police said that Menezes was

A photograph taken by a commuter on his mobile phone camera shows passengers being evacuated from an underground train through a tunnel near London's King's Cross station after an explosion aboard a train, one of four coordinated terrorist bomb attacks on July 7.

acting suspiciously and had run from the police when challenged. It was later learned that he had not run from the police and had indeed been restrained by police officers before being shot eight times.

Following his summer holiday, the prime minister sought to increase the pace of his planned reforms, especially of the public services. In his speech to Labour's annual conference in September, Blair admitted, "Every time I've ever introduced a reform in government, I wish in retrospect I had gone further." Four weeks later he unveiled controversial plans to give each state secondary school far greater independence and to reduce the powers of the elected local education authorities. These proposals built on previous reforms, which allowed new kinds of state schools to be created, including some run and/or partly financed by private businesses. By the end of 2005, Blair was well on the way to dismantling the system of comprehensive schools that had dominated the education of 11–18-year-old pupils for more than 30 years.

Blair knew that his proposals would face opposition from some politicians in his own party, but he had become used to that. As part of his attempts to combat terrorism, he backed a number of measures that critics alleged would harm civil liberties without, in practice, making Britain any safer. These schemes included the issuance of control orders (akin to house arrest) against people suspected of terrorism in cases in which there was insufficient

usable evidence to bring them to trial, plans to allow the police, in exceptional circumstances, to hold suspects for up to 90 days without charge, and the introduction of national identity cards. On November 9 some Labour MPs joined forces with the opposition parties to reduce the maximum time for holding terrorist suspects to 28 days. It was the first time that the Blair government had been defeated in the House of Commons since it came to power in 1997.

On November 2 one of Blair's closest allies, David Blunkett, resigned from the cabinet for the second time in less than 12 months. Blunkett had been appointed secretary of state for work and pensions in May, five months after he had resigned as home secretary in the fallout from a failed love affair. During his period out of office, Blunkett joined the board of (and received shares in) a small British company. At the end of October, the news emerged that Blunkett had failed to seek the permission of a committee created to regulate the private work that ministers who had recently left office were allowed to accept. This disclosure provoked a controversy that forced Blunkett to resign again.

Meanwhile, the opposition Conservative Party, which had failed to topple Blair despite a net gain of parliamentary seats, sought a new leader. On the day after the general election, Michael Howard announced his intention to resign as soon as his successor had been chosen. This process was unusually protracted. Howard wanted to change the party rules first, so that the final choice of leader was made by the party's MPs rather than by the wider party membership. A party ballot was held on this proposal, but it did not quite obtain the two-thirds majority it needed to take effect. In early October a two-month contest was started under the old rules. After two ballots by party MPs, the names of the top two candidates were submitted to the wider party membership. One was David Davis, a 56-year-old right-winger who had been brought up by his mother in a south London council house and had served as minister for Europe in the 1990s. His rival was a 39-year-old centrist, David Cameron. (*See* BIOGRAPHIES.) Despite having no government experience and very little experience of opposition politics at the highest level, Cameron quickly captured the imagination of party members as a charismatic speaker. He defeated Davis by 68–32% in the ballot of party members and became party leader on December 7. Cameron immediately signaled a shift away from the right and toward more centrist policies, including greater emphases on improving public services, redistributing wealth to Britain's poor, and combating global poverty.

On April 9, after considerable legal debate, Prince Charles, the heir to the British crown, was married to his longterm partner, Camilla Parker Bowles, who would henceforth be called Camilla, duchess of Cornwall. (*See* BIOGRAPHIES.) The civil wedding took place in Windsor and was followed by a service of prayer and dedication in St. George's Chapel at nearby Windsor Castle. In November the newlywed couple made an official visit to the United States; it was their first overseas tour together.

The Scottish Parliament, established in 1999, continued to set its own distinct priorities, especially in social policies. In October 2005 it decided to abolish charges for eye tests by 2007. Scotland and England also moved at slightly different speeds toward a ban on smoking in enclosed public spaces. In June the Scottish Parliament voted to ban smoking in all bars, restaurants, offices, and enclosed public spaces from March 2006. England seemed likely to follow suit, but a dispute between members of Blair's cabinet erupted in October. The result was a decision to impose a slightly weaker ban in England, under which smoking would continue to be allowed in private clubs and in bars that did not serve food, while it would otherwise be banned in offices, restaurants, and bars that did serve food.

Economic Affairs. In the view of many commentators, Gordon Brown's luck ran out in 2005. In his annual budget statement on March 16, the chancellor predicted that Britain's economy would grow by 3–3.5% in 2005. Later in the year, when it became clear that both consumer spending and export markets were growing far more slowly than expected—partly because of rising world oil prices—the forecast for domestic growth was revised down to 1.75%.

On its own, slower economic growth was not fatal. Brown could boast that Britain's economy had grown in every quarter for 13 years—"the longest period of sustained economic growth since records began in the year 1701."

The British Election of 2005

On May 5, 2005, Prime Minister Tony Blair (*see* BIOGRAPHIES) led the U.K.'s Labour Party to its third consecutive election victory—the first time in Labour's 105-year history that it had won three such victories in succession. Continuing arguments about Blair's role in the U.S.-led invasion of Iraq in 2003, however, contributed to a sharp drop in Labour's vote and to a reduction of Labour's majority from 167 in the previous Parliament to just 66 (out of 646 members of Parliament) in the new House of Commons.

Labour won 356 seats (47 fewer than in 2001), the Conservative Party captured 198 (a net gain of 33), the Liberal Democrats took 62 (a net gain of 11), and other parties combined for a total of 30 seats (a net gain of 3). Although Labour won 55% of the seats, it secured only 35.2% of the popular vote, down 5.5% from the 2001 election. This was the lowest level of support ever achieved by any party winning an outright victory in a British general election. The Conservatives won 32.3% (up 0.6% from 2001), and the Liberal Democrats secured 22.1% (up 3.8%). Overall turnout was 61.3%, low by historical standards but 1.9% higher than in 2001.

Labour's main advantage was that it had presided over a steadily growing economy during the eight years since it returned to power. Previous Labour governments had been dogged by economic failure, but under the stewardship of Gordon Brown, chancellor of the Exchequer since 1997, unemployment, inflation, and mortgage rates all fell to their lowest levels in 30 years or more. Whereas Brown enjoyed consistently high public ratings, Blair suffered from sustained criticisms (which he rejected forcefully) that he had misled the British public at the time of the 2003 Iraq war. These criticisms widened into a general argument about Blair's honesty.

The Conservatives made this one of their central campaign themes, but they were more successful at denting Blair's and Labour's support than at building their own. This was partly because the public did not warm to their leader, Michael Howard, who was handicapped by his past record as a right-wing cabinet minister. More fundamentally, the Conservatives suffered from long-standing problems with a "brand" image, which could not be solved during a four-week campaign. This point was made forcibly by Lynton Crosby, the Australian political strategist hired by Howard to run the election campaign, in a speech to Conservative MPs after the defeat: "You can't fatten a pig on market day," he told them.

Lord Saatchi, the joint chairman of the Conservative Party, acknowledged after the election that the party had concentrated too much on specific populist issues such as tighter immigration controls and not enough on providing a broader vision for Britain. On May 6 Howard announced his decision to step down as party leader, saying that in 2009, the likely year of the next election, he would be 67, and he felt that this was too old for an opposition leader seeking to become prime minister.

Many discontented Labour supporters switched to the Liberal Democrats, who ended the election with the biggest thirdparty block of MPs since 1923. Yet their 62 seats fell short of the informal party target of 70–80 seats that they hoped to win in an election when both the Labour and Conservative parties were unpopular. Nevertheless, the public regarded the Liberal Democrats' Charles Kennedy as easily the most attractive personality among the three main party leaders.

(PETER KELLNER)

The slowdown caused a slight rise in unemployment to almost 5% by the end of the year, as well as a deterioration in the public finances. In March Brown promised that public borrowing would fall from £38 billion (£1 = about $1.75) in 2004–05 to £32 billion in 2005–06. By the end of 2005, however, it was clear that public borrowing in the 2005–06 fiscal year would be higher than the year before. Partly in response to the slowdown in the country's economy, the Bank of England reduced the benchmark "repo" interest rate in August from 4.75% to 4.5%.

A telling sign of the long-term decline of British manufacturing was the sale of two once-dominant companies to foreign owners. Automaker MG Rover Group was sold in July to China's Nanjing Automotive Corp., and the electronics company Marconi Corp. (formerly General Electric Co.) was acquired in October by the Swedish telecommunications giant Ericsson. A generation earlier Rover and General Electric had been two of Britain's biggest employers.

Foreign Affairs. The U.K. held the G-8 presidency for 2005 and the presidency of the European Union for the second half of the year. Blair sought to use the combination of the two roles to achieve three objectives—extra aid for Africa, agreement on further measures to tackle climate change, and agreement on a new EU budget strategy for 2007–13.

The greatest progress was made on aid for Africa. On June 11 the finance ministers representing the G-8 members agreed to write off the debts of 18 African countries. Brown, chairing the London meeting that reached the deal, said that an additional 20 countries would be eligible for debt relief if they met targets for good governance and tackling corruption. At the summit of G-8 leaders in Scotland in July, agreements were reached to increase aid to Africa substantially. The deal was praised by, among others, rock-concert organizer Sir Bob Geldof and economist Jeffrey Sachs. (*See* BIOGRAPHIES.)

Less progress was made on climate change. In the face of U.S. opposition to the Kyoto Protocol, the final G-8 communiqué contained no targets for the reduction of emissions, no help for new low-carbon technologies, and no assistance for less-developed countries. Blair defended the weak wording of the communiqué by saying that it was vital to involve the U.S. in discussions about climate change. Without U.S. cooperation, it would be impossible to ensure that large emerging economies such as China and India also contributed to global attempts to curb climate change. (*See* ENVIRONMENT: Special Report.)

Reform of the EU's budget fared the worst. For 20 years the U.K. had received an annual rebate, mainly to compensate for the fact that the U.K. had a relatively small farm sector and thus received little money from the EU's Common Agricultural Policy (CAP). Blair was willing to give up most or all of the rebate in return for radical reform of the CAP. Such reform was rejected by other countries, notably France. A compromise was agreed on

Bridgeen Hagans (left), the fiancée of Robert McCartney, and McCartney's five sisters leave the White House after three of them met with U.S. Pres. George W. Bush in March. McCartney was murdered outside a bar in Belfast on January 30.

© Jim Bourg/Reuters/Corbis

December 17 whereby the U.K. would give up part of its rebate in return for a program of support for the EU's new member countries in Central and Eastern Europe and a review of the EU's budget, including the CAP. Critics complained that there was no guarantee that the review would propose substantial changes to the CAP or that such proposals would be accepted by other EU governments. Meanwhile, Blair put off any referendum on the proposed EU constitution after it was rejected by voters in France and The Netherlands. (*See European Union:* Sidebar, above.)

Northern Ireland. The early months of 2005 saw two setbacks for the Provisional Irish Republican Army (IRA). British ministers blamed the IRA for having organized a £26.5 million bank raid in Belfast in December 2004, and the group was forced to admit that on January 30 its members murdered a locally popular nationalist, Robert McCartney, in Belfast. The IRA subsequently expelled three of its members for the murder and offered to shoot the offenders. McCartney's family rejected this offer and asked that the men be handed to the police for prosecution. The family won support from many quarters for their campaign—including from U.S. Pres. George W. Bush, who met with McCartney's sisters and fiancée in Washington, D.C. On June 1 two men were arrested and charged with McCartney's murder.

The U.K. general election on May 5 was a disaster for the once-dominant Ulster Unionist Party (UUP), which lost five of its six seats, including that of its leader, David Trimble, who had been Northern Ireland's first minister during the brief period of devolved government following the 1998 Good Friday Agreement. Trimble resigned as UUP leader immediately after his defeat. The Democratic Unionist Party (DUP), which had opposed the Good Friday Agreement, emerged as the province's biggest party, with 9 of Northern Ireland's 18 seats, a gain of 4 since 2001. On the nationalist side, Sinn Fein (five seats; up one from 2001) increased its lead over the Social Democratic and Labour Party (SDLP; unchanged with three seats). Thus, the two moderate parties, UUP and SDLP, which had worked closely to bring peace to the province, found themselves outflanked by the more militant DUP and Sinn Fein, between which communication was virtually nonexistent.

Few observers were surprised that little political progress was made in 2005 toward a new agreement that would allow a resumption of devolved government. In response to continuing pressure, however, the IRA announced on July 28 that it had ordered all its units to "dump arms." On September 26 Gen. John de Chastelain, the head of the independent decommissioning body, said that he was satisfied that all the IRA's arms were now beyond use. DUP leaders refused to accept this statement, as no firm evidence, such as photographs of the decommissioned weapons, had been provided to support de Chastelain's statement. (PETER KELLNER)

UNITED STATES

Area: 9,366,008 sq km (3,616,236 sq mi), including 204,083 sq km of inland water but excluding the 156,049 sq km of the Great Lakes that lie within U.S. boundaries
Population (2005 est.): 296,748,000
Capital: Washington, D.C.
Head of state and government: President George W. Bush

In 2005, amid world skepticism and domestic opposition, the administration of U.S. Pres. George W. Bush forged ahead with its bold and aggressive response to international terrorism. Progress in pacifying a determined Iraqi insurgency and in establishing capable Iraqi security forces proved far more difficult than expected, however. American deaths in Iraq continued at a rate of nearly three per day. A drumbeat of criticism from a unified Democratic opposition helped tax American patience and weaken Bush's base of support. Even a purring U.S. economy failed to assuage doubters. By the fall of 2005, with more than 60% of Americans disapproving of his job performance and his conduct of the Iraqi war, President Bush appeared to be in serious danger, perhaps lacking the political support necessary for him to be able to continue pursuing his plan.

War on Terrorism. The American-led effort to establish a functioning democracy in Iraq again dominated world news during 2005. A determined resistance, including both Iraqi and foreign fighters, continued incessant bombing, small arms, and suicide attacks, and U.S. military deaths—846—were only slightly fewer than the 848 recorded in 2004.

Iraq showed unmistakable signs of progress during the year, starting with a historic election on January 30, in which 57% of the voters turned out for elections to the National Assembly. Voter turnout in an October election to ratify the constitution was even higher (63%), and a third "purple-finger" election, held on December 15, produced a voter turnout of 70%. (See *Iraq,* above.)

Allegations of widespread illegality in the UN's Iraq oil-for-food program in the months leading up to the U.S.-led 2003 invasion produced an independent investigation led by former U.S. Federal Reserve chairman Paul Volcker. The inquiry found "corrosive corruption" at the UN and blamed UN Secretary-General Kofi Annan for mismanagement. The report stated that Saddam Hussein had collected at least $229 million in bribes from a majority of companies involved in the program and that $10 billion in Iraqi oil had been illegally smuggled into adjacent countries. The report showed that French and Russian companies received $23.7 billion in Iraqi contracts from 1996 to 2003, during the period when both countries were strong critics of Iraqi sanctions and ultimately opposed the U.S.-led invasion.

Even while violence continued in Iraq and Afghanistan, a potent political battle was being waged in the U.S. over the war on terrorism. Democrats continued to hammer at President Bush's decision to invade Iraq, suggesting that his stated fear of Iraq's harbouring weapons of mass destruction had been concocted. The controversy eroded Bush's polling numbers, and by October surveys were finding that the majority of the public believed that the decision to invade Iraq was a mistake.

After Rep. John Murtha, a Democrat from Pennsylvania, called for the U.S. withdrawal from Iraq in November, the public focus turned from President Bush's 2003 decision and his credibility

At the president's state of the union address on February 2, women's rights activist Safia Taleb al-Suhail, specially invited to the occasion, shows an ink-stained finger, indicating that she voted in the Iraqi election on January 30, and is applauded by first lady Laura Bush.

AP/Wide World Photos

to the future. Murtha's remarks delighted antiwar activists. Polling soon showed, however, that many Americans disagreed with that assessment and believed that the U.S. should stay the course in the war on terrorism. Defense Secretary Donald Rumsfeld announced plans to reduce U.S. troop strength from 160,000 to below 138,000 in early 2006, saying that trained Iraqi security forces would make up the difference. At year's end Bush's approval rating stood at 40%, up 5% from a month earlier.

Domestic Policy. President Bush laid out an unusually ambitious agenda following his second inauguration. He announced plans to regularize the national system of immigration and border control, which had fallen into disrepair. He promised a revamping of the nation's tax code and offered proposals to reform controversial legal liability procedures covering medical malpractice, class-action lawsuits, and asbestos cases. Finally, as the centrepiece of his 2005 agenda, Bush tackled the "third rail" of American politics, the Social Security retirement system, by suggesting an alternation of the current scheme, in which wage earners effectively fund benefits paid to retired Americans. Instead, Bush proposed that workers be given the opportunity to fund their own private retirement accounts, which they would own.

Little of Bush's agenda became law. Instead of receding after their 2004 election defeat, congressional Democrats showed unusual unity and organized to stop the administration agenda; they were occasionally joined by key Republicans. Ethics problems sapped the majority party. When the U.S. House's GOP leader, Tom DeLay, was forced to step down after a Texas grand jury indicted him on election-law charges, Republican effectiveness frayed noticeably. The result was the worst political and legislative season of Bush's presidency.

In early 2005 Bush traveled the country extensively, touting his Social Security proposals to enthusiastic, carefully selected crowds. He claimed that reform was needed to avoid the system's bankruptcy as baby boomers retired and laid claim to system payments. Democrat critics, however, rallied opposition by suggesting that Bush was attempting to "privatize" the system, throwing guaranteed benefits into doubt, and by pointing out that the transition period in Bush's plan would actually require more funding than the current plan. Political support for Bush's program was so anemic that the president never offered specific legislation, and the issue had died by year's end.

Bush's immigration proposals also met with a storm of criticism from both the left and the right, with the most-heated comments coming from his own party. Instead of amnesty for the estimated 12 million illegals living within the U.S., Bush proposed establishing a "guest worker" program that would grant them legal status and the opportunity for eventual citizenship. Outraged conservatives said that the Bush plan rewarded illegality and called instead for tighter border security and enforcement of often-ignored immigration statutes. The U.S. House, in a largely symbolic vote before adjourning, approved the establishment of a 1,100-km (700-mi) fence along key portions of the U.S.–Mexico border, and Bush was forced to add border-security language to his proposal for congressional consideration in 2006.

Congress approved a limited portion of Bush's legal reform, moving many class-action lawsuits from state to federal courts, which had historically been less receptive to innovative claims from plaintiff's lawyers. No progress was made, however, on administration proposals to reform the tax system, asbestos litigation, or medical malpractice lawsuits.

Some significant legislation was passed in the Congress, but little of it met with Bush's full approval. After nearly a decade under consideration, a

Cindy Sheehan, founder of Gold Star Families for Peace, addresses supporters of her anti-Iraq-war movement. Sheehan, whose son was killed in the conflict, held a vigil outside the Texas ranch of Pres. George W. Bush in August.

bankruptcy-reform bill was signed into law; supporters claimed that by requiring more overextended debtors to adopt a long-term repayment plan instead of having their debts discharged, the measure would reduce credit abuse. Another long-stalled measure, a national energy bill, was approved amid claims that it mostly benefited highly profitable energy companies. Moderate Republicans joined most Democrats to strip from the bill an administration-backed provision allowing energy exploration in the Arctic National Wildlife Refuge.

After promising to veto any highway-construction legislation that exceeded $256 billion over five years, the president in August signed a $286 billion measure that contained a record 6,371 congressional "earmarks"—special provisions that individual senators and representatives had inserted for pet projects. One earmark inserted by powerful Alaska legislators was funding for a $223 million bridge from Ketchikan (pop. 8,000) to Gravina Island (pop. 50), currently served by an efficient ferry. After a nationwide protest, the bridge spending was rescinded, but Alaska authorities were allowed to take control of the funds for use on any project—including a Gravina bridge. Despite taxpayer group complaints over excessive spending by Congress, Bush completed his fifth consecutive year in office without casting his first veto.

Legislative setbacks were almost directly tied to public antipathy over Bush's handling of the Iraq war. As violence continued and U.S. casualties mounted, Democrats concentrated on Bush's credibility, suggesting that he had deliberately misled the country about the threat of Iraqi weapons of mass destruction, never found following the Iraq invasion. When Bush spent his usual August recess month at his ranch in Crawford, Texas, he was dogged by Cindy Sheehan, the antiwar mother of a slain U.S. serviceman, who attracted daily news media attention as she demanded to meet with Bush. He declined.

Bush's poll ratings, adversely affected by growing public impatience over Iraq, declined even further when government authorities proved incapable of dealing promptly with the fallout from Hurricane Katrina, a major disaster that devastated parts of Louisiana, Alabama, Mississippi, and Florida. Bush eventually took responsibility for the failed federal effort and promised a broad rebuilding package that some experts thought would reach $200 billion. Louisiana's congressional

Lewis ("Scooter") Libby (on crutches), a former chief of staff of Vice Pres. Dick Cheney, leaves the U.S. District Court in Washington, D.C., on November 3 after having pleaded not guilty to charges of lying to investigators and a grand jury looking into a leak of CIA information.

delegation proposed federal aid for that state alone that exceeded $250 billion. By year's end Congress had set aside about $64 billion for storm relief. (*See* ECONOMIC AFFAIRS: *Special Report*.)

Republicans were hard hit by a series of scandals. Shortly after DeLay was indicted, Senate Majority Leader Bill Frist revealed that he was being investigated by two federal agencies for having sold stock in a hospital company controlled by his family, shortly before bad news drove its stock price down. A long-running special counsel investigation into the 2003 naming of an undercover CIA operative by Washington columnist Robert Novak culminated in the indictment of a top White House aide. Lewis ("Scooter") Libby, chief of staff to Vice Pres. Dick Cheney, was indicted for lying to Special Prosecutor Patrick J. Fitzgerald (*see* BIOGRAPHIES) before a grand jury; Libby immediately resigned. Fitzgerald's probe continued into 2006. In a development that threatened to expose corrupt fund-raising and trading of favours on Capitol Hill, federal investigators in November obtained a guilty plea on a conspiracy charge and $19.7 million in restitution from Michael Scanlon, a former DeLay aide. Scanlon promised to testify against another grand jury target, lobbyist Jack Abramoff, over alleged bilking of Indian tribe clients whom they represented on gambling issues.

A long-running dispute over confirmation of federal appellate judges was at least partially resolved during the summer, with a "Gang of 14" centrist senators, 7 from each party, agreeing to a compromise that seated eight contested Bush nominees. The agreement came just before two seats opened on the U.S. Supreme Court, one caused by the death of Chief Justice William Rehnquist (see OBITUARIES) and the other by the retirement of Justice Sandra Day O'Connor. Under terms of the agreement forbidding filibusters except in "exceptional circumstances," a Washington, D.C., judge, John Roberts (see BIOGRAPHIES), was quickly confirmed as chief justice. Bush suffered another setback when his choice to replace O'Connor—Bush confidant and White House counsel Harriett Miers—was judged unacceptable by conservative activists and withdrew. Bush then nominated New Jersey appellate judge Samuel Alito, whose confirmation was being opposed at year's end by an alliance of liberal interest groups.

The administration suffered a final setback in December when Congress attempted to renew expiring portions of the 2001 USA PATRIOT Act designed to update law-enforcement tools against terrorism. After House and Senate conferees approved a compromise extension, a bipartisan coalition of senators refused to sign off, with four key Republicans claiming that the renewal potentially infringed on civil liberties. As the vote approached, the *New York Times* published details of a National Security Agency eavesdropping program on international calls; although technically unrelated, the article reinforced fears about the PATRIOT Act's reach. After applying political pressure by threatening to veto any temporary extension, President Bush in late December signed a mere five-week extension.

The Economy. On paper the U.S. economy enjoyed a banner 2005, shaking off natural disasters and spiking energy prices and growing at a robust 3.5% rate for the third consecutive year. Nearly two million new jobs were created, and the nation's unemployment rate fell from 5.4% to 4.9%. Interest rates and inflation, while rising modestly, remained at historically low levels. Labour productivity rose for a fifth consecutive year.

The economic performance was particularly impressive in the third quarter as Hurricanes Katrina and Rita devastated the Gulf Coast region. The storms eliminated 600,000 jobs, disrupted

John G. Roberts, Jr., nominated as associate justice of the U.S. Supreme Court, smiles confidently after a breakfast meeting with Pres. George W. Bush on July 20. In September Bush nominated Roberts as chief justice, and he was promptly confirmed.

shipping traffic, and shut down refining and energy infrastructure, sending gasoline prices nationwide temporarily over $3 per gallon. Relief from the federal government and from private insurers helped to jump-start rebuilding efforts, and the national economy grew by a healthy 4.1% during the August–October period.

As the U.S again provided its traditional economic leadership among industrialized nations, however, there were disquieting signs of excess. The U.S. trade deficit, which had hit a record $618 billion in 2004, topped $700 billion in 2005.

As the U.S. economy expanded, the Federal Reserve pursued its 18-month policy of nudging short-term interest rates higher, to combat anticipated inflation. The key federal funds rate was boosted by 0.25% on eight occasions during the year, to 4.25%, up from 1% in early 2004. U.S. consumer price inflation, pushed by rising fossil-fuel prices, rose more than 4% for the year, but core inflation (excluding food and energy) remained at modest levels, just over 2%. The gradual interest-rate rise finally contributed at year's end to a cooling of an extended boom in housing construction, sales, and refinancing. Meanwhile, property values in some major urban areas had doubled over the previous five years.

In another cautious indicator, the solid economic growth failed to impress major equity markets. Stock averages dipped during the spring

months, recovered later in the year, but ended 2005 with only slight gains. Overall, smaller companies outperformed major firms. Most broad market gauges rose less than 5%, and the Dow Jones Industrial Average actually dropped by nearly 0.5% for the year.

Foreign Policy. As the year began, the U.S., Japan, India, and Australia led the world's humanitarian response to the December 2004 tsunami disaster in the Indian Ocean, which claimed an estimated 212,000 lives. U.S. Navy helicopter carriers arrived off Aceh, Indon., only five days after the devastation and were particularly effective in preventing additional disease and hardship by delivering fresh water, medical care and supplies, food, and other relief. The U.S. allocated about $1 billion in official aid, and private U.S. citizens donated another $700 million to the relief effort. The U.S. also provided significant aid when a cataclysmic earthquake struck Kashmir on Oct. 8, 2005, killing more than 87,000 people. (See *Pakistan:* Sidebar, above.)

In his second inaugural address, President Bush ambitiously pledged to end tyranny around the globe and spread liberty and freedom "to the darkest corners of the world." As he spoke, the U.S. was fully extended, financially and militarily, in Iraq and Afghanistan, arguably doing what Bush promised, but the strenuous effort seriously hampered U.S. ability to deliver further on Bush's goal.

Even so, the administration could point to numerous advances in self-government, human rights, and democracy worldwide, all encouraged by U.S. policy. The breakthroughs included Syria's withdrawal from Lebanon, political progress by women in Muslim countries such as Kuwait and Saudi Arabia, advances toward free elections in Egypt and Liberia, and the historic seating of the first democratic national parliament in Afghanistan. The scheduled Palestinian vote, in addition to Israel's unilateral withdrawal from the occupied Gaza Strip, provided a glimmer of hope for that region.

International efforts to stop persistent rogue nuclear-weapons-development programs in Iran and North Korea went nowhere during 2005. President Bush had dubbed both countries, with Iraq, "the axis of evil" in 2001, in part because of their nuclear ambitions. With allied military efforts overextended in Iraq and Afghanistan, the U.S. was forced to rely on diplomacy to bring pressure on North Korea and Iran.

When six-nation talks were belatedly resumed in Beijing in July, North Korea agreed to curb its nuclear program and return to international safeguards provided that it received trade concessions, economic assistance, and security guarantees. Within days, however, the apparent deal broke down as the North Koreans demanded renewed assistance on two substitute light-water reactors, and the U.S. publicly accused North Korea of counterfeiting currency and assisting illegal nuclear proliferation. Pyongyang repudiated its concessions and claimed openly that it had already manufactured several atomic weapons in apparent violation of international law.

Iran successfully stalled ongoing efforts by France, Great Britain, and Germany to negotiate an end to an illegal enrichment plan. The U.S. favoured a hard-line approach, threatening to seek economic sanctions against Iran at the UN Security Council, but did not press the issue because Russia and China, both with veto power over UN sanctions, opposed the move. At year's end, in an effort to break the impasse, Russia offered to host Iran's enrichment efforts and ensure that the uranium would be used only for energy production.

U.S. relations with the United Nations, never smooth, suffered through an especially tumultuous year. As details of bribery and corruption in the UN's Iraq oil-for-food program came to light, the Bush administration appointed a vocal UN critic, conservative John Bolton (*see* BIOGRAPHIES), as U.S. ambassador, over substantial U.S. Senate opposition. Bolton arrived at UN headquarters in August and immediately began pushing for significant reforms in transparency and efficiency. At one point Bolton unsuccessfully sought postponement of the UN budget until the management, finance, and appointment changes enacted at a September UN summit had been approved by the General Assembly.

With China rapidly emerging as a world economic and military power, U.S. policy makers attempted to find a delicate balance in bilateral relations that were superficially correct but laden with serious tensions just below the surface. As the country's trade deficit with China topped a record $200 billion, its options were narrow in pursuing complaints about Chinese currency manipulation, political suppression, DVD and computer software piracy, and arms exports. The U.S. forged historically strong ties with

Japan, Pakistan, and especially India in an attempt to counter steadily increasing Chinese influence all over Asia.

As a wave of populism swept across Latin America, U.S. policy suffered several setbacks. President Bush's attempt to expand a free-trade zone was rejected by major South American countries at a November Western Hemisphere summit in Buenos Aires. A vocal critic of the U.S., Pres. Hugo Chávez (*see* BIOGRAPHIES) of oil-rich Venezuela, continued to taunt the U.S.; to highlight U.S. internal problems, he sent subsidized heating oil to low-income families in Boston and New York City. A Chávez admirer, Evo Morales, was elected the president of Bolivia after promising to defy U.S. antidrug objections and facilitate coca-leaf production.

(DAVID C. BECKWITH)

DEVELOPMENTS IN THE STATES

Party Strengths. An often-difficult relationship with the federal government marked 2005 for the 50 U.S. states; differences over funding, power, and responsibility frequently roiled the federalism partnership. State officials stepped up complaints over unfunded federal mandates and U.S. preemption of authority over traditional state powers. Uneven state/federal response to major natural disasters created major news, but the differences extended to numerous additional areas, including education, health care, and economic development. Meanwhile, the national economic recovery allowed states to restore some services that had been cut in previous years and prompted setbacks for antitax activists. All 50 states held regular legislative sessions during the year, and 24 of them staged special sessions on matters ranging from hurricane relief to school finance.

Democrats fared well in limited 2005 state elections, capturing a handful of legislative seats and retaining governorships in Virginia and New Jersey. The partisan gubernatorial lineup across the country was therefore maintained at 28 Republicans and 22 Democrats. State legislatures remained at virtual parity between the parties nationwide. Republicans would enter 2006 with a two-house control of 20 states, Democrats dominated in 19 states, and the two parties split legislative authority in 10 states, all unchanged from 2005. Nebraska had a nonpartisan unicameral legislature.

Structures, Powers. Voters decided a record 18 citizen initiatives during off-year elections and rejected 16 of them.

A recent trend toward limiting state spending, which was pushed by low-tax advocates, stalled during the year as states recovered from a national economic downturn.

Voters in California and Ohio decisively rejected proposals to shift contentious legislative redistricting authority away from the state legislature. The California initiative would have turned redistricting over to a panel of retired judges, while Ohio's measure would have substituted a nonpartisan citizen commission.

New Jersey became the 43rd state to establish the office of lieutenant governor, with power to succeed when the governorship became vacant. In 2004 when that state's governor resigned, the job had devolved to the state Senate president, who simultaneously served as acting governor and as a legislator. New York voters rejected a proposal to overhaul the state's chronically tardy budget process; the measure would have shifted significant budget responsibility from the governor to the legislature. Washington voters approved an initiative requiring periodic audits of local governments.

In a late-night July vote, the Pennsylvania legislature approved a pay raise for legislators and judges without public notice or comment. Although no legislative elections were scheduled, the resulting public furor resulted in one state Supreme Court justice's losing his position in November balloting—the first judicial rejection in state history. The pay raise was rescinded later that month.

Alabama, Delaware, and Texas approved new laws restricting eminent domain powers of local officials. The laws were approved after a divided U.S. Supreme Court, in the controversial *Kelo* v. *City of New London* (Conn.) decision, affirmed that local governments could condemn and seize private property to make way for commercial development that paid higher taxes. (*See* LAW, CRIME, AND LAW ENFORCEMENT: *Court Decisions.*)

Government Relations. Arguments over allocation of power between state and federal governments were front-page news during most of 2005. With fallout from Hurricane Katrina the most glaring example, state officials struggled to maintain productive relationships—and their traditional lines of authority in the U.S. system of federalism—during often-contentious dealings with Washington. Some state officials claimed that the federal government was neglecting its responsibility in vital areas, such as

Thousands of New Orleans residents gather at an evacuation staging area along Interstate 10 in suburban Metarie following Hurricane Katrina.

curbing global warming, lowering the prices of costly drugs, and funding stem-cell research. In other instances states asserted that federal authorities were not providing resources to pay for mandates that they imposed on the states. The National Council of State Legislatures claimed that over a two-year period it had identified $51 billion in largely uncompensated annual costs that states incurred as a result of federal mandates, not including the additional mandates that were on the drawing board. The officials also complained about increased federal preemption of state power to regulate health care, land use, technology, and other programs.

In May Congress approved the REAL identification act, which set rigorous national standards for documents needed in order to obtain a driver's license. The new law effectively prohibited licenses for undocumented aliens and mandated costly new documentation requirements without providing any funding for state compliance.

After Hurricane Katrina swept over Louisiana, Mississippi, Florida, and Alabama in late August, the devastation was exacerbated by arguments over responsibility for rescue, relief, and rebuilding. Disaster planning had traditionally been the purview of states, but the federal government had taken a steadily expanding role in recent years, blurring lines of authority and responsibility. With news media accounts blaming FEMA (the Federal Emergency Management Agency) for delays in pro-

viding relief services and supplies, federal officials made ill-disguised attempts to take control. Officials in Louisiana, Florida, and other affected states pushed back—even while demanding that the U.S. government pay for virtually all rebuilding efforts. The year ended in an uneasy truce, with lines of authority and responsibility remaining largely undefined. (*See* ECONOMIC AFFAIRS: *Special Report.*)

Finances. States completed their recovery from the 2001–03 economic downturn during the year. An expanding economy generated revenue beyond projections and outpaced increased outlays for programs such as Medicaid and allowed states to replenish "rainy day" reserve funds that had been tapped in previous years. Legislatures avoided significant tax changes. Several states produced large surpluses, notably California, which boasted $3.4 billion of black ink and its first surplus since 2000. The year saw only a modest overall increase in state taxes, and a majority of the states were preparing for tax reductions in 2006.

As fiscal restrictions eased, many states increased their spending on both K–12 and higher education, which had been

targeted for unpopular reductions in previous years. Often by tightening eligibility and reducing some benefits, states managed to slow growth of Medicaid spending from the nearly 15% increase in 2004. Tennessee, for example, started trimming 190,000 recipients from its generous TennCare program. State expenditures on correction facilities increased but also at a slower rate as a 10-year prison expansion stalled. Hurricane-battered Louisiana was forced to make major reductions across the board in state expenditures.

Ohio was the only state to increase overall taxes significantly, enacting a new commercial-activities tax and boosting both sales and tobacco taxes. Idaho, Iowa, and Virginia approved modest tax reductions. Seven states increased cigarette taxes, and most states increased fees for motor vehicles, driver's licenses, court costs, and other state services.

Efforts to curb state spending suffered setbacks in several state elections. In a significant setback for antitax enthusiasts, Colorado voters approved a suspension of a landmark 1992 Taxpayer Bill of Rights law that limited revenue increases to population growth plus inflation. Though the moratorium resulted in a refund of more than $3 billion to state taxpayers, it also prompted a shrinkage in state government relative to the state's economy and crimped state education and highway funding. The Colorado plan was being eyed as a model by several other state legislatures.

California voters rejected an initiative backed by Gov. Arnold Schwarzenegger that would have capped state spending

In October members of Janitors for Justice rally in Los Angeles against California Gov. Arnold Schwarzenegger's special election initiatives that would have a negative impact on unions and state workers.

and given additional budget authority to the governor. Washington voters turned down a spending limit and refused to overturn a 9.5-cent gasoline-tax increase approved by the state legislature.

Marriage, Gay Rights. Activists seeking equal marital and other rights for homosexuals made additional progress during the year in the aftermath of a 2003 Massachusetts high-court decision that legalized gay marriage. Maneuvering to exploit or blunt the ruling's effect accelerated in courts, legislatures, and at the ballot box across the country. Voters in two additional states, Kansas and Texas, overwhelmingly approved a state constitutional amendment banning recognition of same-sex unions, bringing to 19 the number of states that rejected gay marriage in their basic state document.

Equal-rights advocates also made breakthroughs, however. Connecticut's legislature voluntarily joined Vermont in recognizing same-sex civil unions. A similar measure, approved by the Maryland legislature, was vetoed by the state's governor. The Alaska Supreme Court ordered state and local governments to grant the same benefits to employees' same-sex partners as those offered to spouses. A federal judge in Nebraska added a new wrinkle to the debate in striking down that state's prohibition of same-sex marriage. The ruling said that state law went impermissibly beyond regulating marriage and denied gay couples fundamental rights guaranteed by the U.S. Constitution. California lawmakers failed in an attempt to recognize same-sex marriage. Maine voters rejected a measure that would have overturned a legislature-approved state law banning discrimination against homosexuals in housing, employment, and education.

Law, Justice. Continuing a recent trend, states including California, Montana, and New Hampshire toughened laws governing sex crimes against children. Iowa's new law was particularly dramatic, mandating life imprisonment for a major second offense.

Arkansas, Nevada, North Dakota, and Texas joined California in prohibiting government use of data from chip-recording devices that were contained in most new cars. South Dakota authorities had used information from the chip—which recorded speed, brake and seat-belt use, and other data recoverable after a crash—to convict Gov. William Janklow of vehicular homicide in 2003. The new state laws required an owner's permission or a court order

before insurers or law-enforcement personnel could access the data.

Health, Welfare. Continuing a recent trend, 11 states approved new laws that further restricted abortion. Mississippi, a state with only one abortion clinic, required that an abortion be done in a hospital or surgical centre in cases in which the pregnancy had exceeded three months. Arkansas, Florida, and Idaho approved new laws requiring consent of a parent or guardian before a minor could receive an abortion. California voters, however, rejected a similar law. Though 35 states now required parental involvement for abortions obtained by minors, courts struck down those laws in 9 additional states. Georgia mandated a 24-hour waiting period for most abortions; Indiana required doctors to offer ultrasound images to prospective abortion seekers; and Arkansas ordered that applicants who were seeking abortions after their 20th week of pregnancy receive mandatory counseling on the possibility of fetal pain during the procedure.

States were badly split on their approach to a "morning-after" pill to prevent pregnancies. New Hampshire and Massachusetts became the seventh and eighth states to allow purchase of the pill specifically without a prescription, and Bay State legislators overcame a gubernatorial veto. New York Gov. George Pataki successfully vetoed a similar bill. Some pharmacists balked at dispensing the drug, but Illinois Gov. Rod Blagojevich and the California legislature enacted measures that required pharmacies that sold birth-control pills to also stock the morning-after pill. Mississippi joined Arkansas, Georgia, and South Dakota in giving pharmacists the right to refuse to dispense the pill.

State relationships with federal authorities on health care were uneven at best. The federal government's 2003 reform of Medicare included a new prescription-drug benefit that was initially expected to save significant state funds. Congress imposed a last-minute "clawback" provision, however, that required offsetting state payments, and nearly 30 states instead projected increased costs from the program. The U.S. Supreme Court, in a major blow to states' rights, declared that laws in California and 10 other states that allowed the medical use of marijuana had to give way to federal antidrug enforcement laws.

Education. A grassroots rebellion over federal mandates for K–12 schools simmered in numerous states throughout

the year, despite Washington's efforts to accommodate complaints. Critics charged that the No Child Left Behind (NCLB) and Individuals with Disability Education (IDEA) acts were excessively costly and underfunded and usurped traditional local and state control of public schools. Connecticut and Michigan filed unsuccessful legal challenges to require full NCLB reimbursement from the federal government; states estimated that the unfunded mandates would cost $18 billion annually. Utah's legislature allowed school districts to ignore NCLB requirements that necessitated state financing or conflicted with state test guidelines. The Texas education commissioner declared that the state would ignore NCLB guidelines on the testing of special-education students.

Federal officials attempted to mollify state critics by granting increased flexibility. The U.S. Department of Education announced that up to 10 states would be allowed to use a "growth-based" NCLB assessment scheme similar to that of Utah's testing regimen.

Texas became the first state to require public schools to spend 65% of funding on classroom expenses. The gubernatorial mandate came after the state legislature had turned down the proposal. Legislatures in Kansas and Louisiana also approved measures that encouraged the "65-cent solution." The proposal, which was aimed at reducing administrative spending, also had an impact on school buses, counselors, libraries, and ancillary educational services. Support for another reform idea, school vouchers, remained sluggish during the year. Utah joined Florida in enacting a statewide voucher program but limited its application to special-education students.

Consumer Protection. Georgia and Washington approved tough statewide smoking bans, bringing to 13 the number of states that prohibited smoking in most public areas. The Washington ballot initiative was particularly sweeping; it outlawed smoking in all public buildings and workplaces, including private clubs, and even lighting up within 7.6 m (25 ft) of doorways, windows, and air vents of public buildings. New York, in an attempt to protect students, prohibited the "unrestricted marketing" of credit cards on college campuses. Georgia declared the sending of multiple unsolicited "spam" e-mails—10,000 in a month or 1,000,000 in a year—to be a felony punishable by up to five years in prison.   (DAVID C. BECKWITH)

URUGUAY

Area: 176,215 sq km (68,037 sq mi)
Population (2005 est.): 3,256,000
Capital: Montevideo
Head of state and government: Presidents Jorge Batlle Ibáñez and, from March 1, Tabaré Ramón Vázquez Rosas

On March 1, 2005, Uruguay experienced the inauguration of its first leftist president, Tabaré Vázquez (*see* BIOGRAPHIES) of the Broad Front–Progressive Encounter coalition. The event marked the culmination of a long struggle by the left to achieve national political power. The success of the leftists in the previous October's election also gave them a majority in both houses of the parliament. Their momentum continued in the municipal elections held in May, when Broad Front–Progressive Encounter won 8 of the 19 departments. In the past the coalition had won only in the department of Montevideo. This victory gave the left control of departments representing some 80% of the country's GDP. (*See* Special Report, below.)

The new government quickly moved on two fronts: the economy and human rights. A National Emergency Plan was approved to deal with the 20% of Uruguayans who found themselves in abject poverty. The plan, with a projected $200 million budget, offered a combination of cash stipends, health care, educational access, and job training to the target population. The government hoped to showcase this effort as a demonstration of the left's ability to deliver social and economic justice. Fortunately, the economy continued its recovery in 2005, growing at a rate of 6%. Inflation remained contained at around 4%, but the cost of energy was putting upward pressure on prices.

On the human rights front, the government sought to deal with the legacy of disappearances that had taken place during Uruguay's 1973–85 military dictatorship. Pressured by the government, the military submitted two reports that indicated where some victims were buried. Months of forensic digging at an army installation turned up nothing until early December, when remains were found on one army installation and near the city of

© Miguel Rojo/AFP/Getty Images

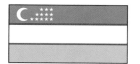

Newly installed Pres. Tabaré Vázquez (left) and Vice Pres. Rodolfo Nin Novoa greet supporters in the Plaza Independencia in Montevideo, Uruguay, on March 1.

Pando. Nevertheless, a frustrated Vázquez administration proposed legislation that would permit the courts to reopen some of the investigations that were closed by an amnesty law passed in 1986.   (MARTIN WEINSTEIN)

UZBEKISTAN

Area: 447,400 sq km (172,700 sq mi)
Population (2005 est.): 26,593,000
Capital: Tashkent
Chief of state and head of government: President Islam Karimov, assisted by Prime Minister Shavkat Mirziyayev

Uzbekistan's standing in much of the international community declined precipitously in 2005 following an incident in the town of Andijan, where several hundred ordinary citizens may have died at the hands of government troops. Beginning in January, unrest was reported from various parts of the country, and groups of up to 1,000 people demonstrated against cuts in gas and electricity supplies. In February, Pres. Islam Karimov called for economic liberalization, but, as usual, no concrete steps were taken. In March the International Monetary Fund demanded deeper reforms, including the privatization of all banks as well as the

removal of state restrictions on agriculture and trade. The following month an independent journalist was beaten in the town of Jizzak, apparently in retaliation for his articles, which accused local authorities of taking the best farmlands for themselves.

In February, 23 successful businessmen were put on trial in Andijan, in eastern Uzbekistan's Fergana Valley, traditionally a region of strong Muslim piety. The defendants were charged with having established a group of religious extremists; some observers asserted that the success in business of those on trial had angered the authorities. On May 13 a demonstration in the main square of Andijan turned violent as supporters of the imprisoned businessmen broke into the prison, freed the inmates, and then crashed into the mayor's office and other public buildings, taking hostages and setting fires. According to eyewitnesses, troops then fired on the demonstrators in the square. Accounts of the event varied widely—the government insisted that there had been 173 deaths of law-enforcement personnel and criminals, while independent observers insisted that up to 1,000 persons—mostly unarmed civilians—had been killed. Several hundred Uzbek citizens fled into Kyrgyzstan.

Karimov described events in and around Andijan as the work of terrorists, at least some of whom had come from abroad, and rejected international demands for an independent investigation. As international pressure increased, Uzbekistan demanded that the

Residents of Andijan view bodies of people who were killed in fighting that followed government troops' suppression of an uprising in the eastern Uzbekistan town on May 13.

U.S. leave its air base at Khanabad and strengthened its ties with Russia and China, both of which had supported the actions of the Uzbek authorities in Andijan. Relations with Kyrgyzstan deteriorated sharply when the Kyrgyz authorities allowed the United Nations High Commissioner for Refugees to evacuate 440 Uzbek refugees to a third country.

On September 9, 15 persons went on trial in Tashkent for their role in the Andijan events. All pleaded guilty; some observers compared the conduct of the trial to the Stalinist show trials of the 1930s. On November 14 all defendants were sentenced to prison terms ranging from 14 to 20 years.   (BESS BROWN)

VANUATU

Area: 12,190 sq km (4,707 sq mi)
Population (2005 est.): 211,000
Capital: Vila
Chief of state: President Kalkot Mataskelekele
Head of government: Prime Minister Ham Lini

In 2005 Prime Minister Ham Lini, president of the Penama Provincial Council and brother of founding prime minister the Rev. Walter Lini, made the restoration of Vanuatu's warm relations with China a high priority. In December 2004 the government of Prime Minister Serge Vohor had been defeated on a vote of no confidence when a number of ministers and other government supporters crossed the floor in opposition to Vohor's unilateral decision to shift diplomatic recognition from China to Taiwan. Lini, who was elected unopposed to lead a new coalition of 11 parties, consolidated his position in mid-2005 with a cabinet reshuffle.

The government budget for 2005 was set at 8.9 billion vatu (about $84.2 million), with the minister of finance promising a surplus at year's end. Increased activity in the region by budget airlines and a buoyant Australian economy helped GDP growth in Vanuatu. The economy grew 3.5% in 2004, an improvement on 2003 (2.4%) and the preceding two-year recession. Australia and the EU increased aid in 2005, but both called for better governance and a willingness by Vanuatu to tackle mismanagement and corruption. An import fee levied on Fiji-made biscuits drew retaliatory licensing of Vanuatu exports to Fiji.   (BARRIE MACDONALD)

VATICAN CITY STATE

Area: 44 ha (109 ac)
Population (2005 est.): 920; about 3,000 workers live outside the Vatican
Chief of state: (sovereign pontiff) Pope John Paul II, (chamberlain) Eduardo Cardinal Martínez Somalo from April 2, and, from April 19, (sovereign pontiff) Pope Benedict XVI
Head of administration: Secretary of State Angelo Cardinal Sodano, who heads a pontifical commission of five cardinals

The year 2005 was a critical turning point for the Vatican City State. Pope John Paul II died on April 2 after a pontificate that had lasted since 1978. (See OBITUARIES.) Political leaders around the world acknowledged John Paul as having been one of the most remarkable figures of the 20th century. During his tenure as pope, the number of Roman Catholic faithful in the world grew significantly, as did the number of countries having diplomatic relations with the Vatican City State. (See RELIGION: Special Report.)

An estimated one million pilgrims flowed into Rome to pay homage to Pope John Paul II in Saint Peter's Basilica. The funeral (and burial in the Vatican Grottos) was followed by nine days of mourning. During the interim between John Paul's death and the election of a new pope, the affairs of the Vatican City State were in the hands of the College of Cardinals, presided over by the dean, Joseph Cardinal Ratzinger. On April 18 the conclave of 115 cardinals convened to select a new pope. After two days of deliberation, they announced the election of Ratzinger, who took the name Benedict XVI. (See BIOGRAPHIES.)

The new pope made his first trip outside Italy in August when he traveled to his native Germany to preside over the World Youth Day festival in Cologne. Pope John Paul had been scheduled to attend. Ecumenical Patriarch Bartholomew I of the Eastern Orthodox Church invited Benedict to visit Turkey later in the year, but the Turkish government requested that the trip be delayed until 2006. A dispute with Israel that arose in July when Benedict failed to include Israel in a list of countries targeted by terrorist attacks was settled in August after a meeting between Vatican and Israeli diplomats.   (GREGORY O. SMITH)

VENEZUELA

Area: 916,445 sq km (353,841 sq mi)
Population (2005 est.): 26,749,000
Capital: Caracas
Head of state and government: President Hugo Chávez Frías

Pres. Hugo Chávez (see BIOGRAPHIES) continued reshaping Venezuela in 2005. He increased his political control, weakened his critics in the private sector, and widened the breach with the United States. Elections held on August 7 for municipal and neighbourhood councils resulted in a doubling of the proportion of seats that Chávez supporters held to 80%. A survey of public opinion by the Venezuelan polling firm Datanálisis in November indicated that political parties loyal to the government would capture an overwhelming majority of seats in the National Assembly elections scheduled for December 4. This prospect, coupled with distrust of the electoral system, led the opposition political parties to withdraw from the field of electoral competition. Thus, President Chávez's Fifth Republic Movement and its political allies claimed all of the 167 seats in the National Assembly.

Chávez's clean sweep of the parliamentary elections marked the culmination of a year during which the opposition had steadily weakened. The National Assembly had passed legislation in 2004 that required all media outlets to prove the truth of the political information that they broadcast, and the implementation of this legislation reduced criticism of the government dramatically. The military promotion list, published in July 2005, allowed the president to promote officers loyal to him. The government-authorized 50–60% pay raise to the armed forces gave noncommissioned officers a salary level that exceeded that of most university-educated professionals. In addition, funding for opposition political parties dried up as potential backers concluded that supporting the opposition carried unacceptable risks.

Venezuela's economy grew at an annual rate of roughly 8% during the first 10 months of 2005. This was less than half the rate achieved in 2004; however, most growth in the previous year restored activity lost in the political and economic turmoil of 2002. High oil prices in 2005 provided Venezuela with an estimated $36 billion in revenue—triple the amount that the government received in 1998, the last full year of Rafael Caldera's presidency. Oil revenue accounted for 80% of Venezuelan exports. The country's proven oil reserves stood at 78 billion bbl, although estimated production for 2005 was 2.1 million bbl per day, 20% below the production level recorded in 2002.

National income experienced a modest rise. The consumer price index rose 12.3% in the first 10 months of the year, which was a slight decline from the rate experienced in 2004. Nevertheless, 53% of Venezuelan households remained in poverty. Still, many residents of the urban slums began to receive free health care from the 13,000 Cuban

doctors sent to Venezuela in a barter arrangement that saw an average 98,000 bbl of petroleum per day delivered to Cuba. An estimated 46% of Venezuelans also received subsidized food from government supermarkets. Many products sold in these supermarkets came from expropriated agricultural estates.

The Chávez government continued to deliver services to the poor through the "missions" program managed directly out of the president's office and aimed at increasing basic literacy, access to primary education, and cultural opportunities. One special mission, Barrio Adentro, provided housing and public services to slum neighbourhoods. Funding for these programs bypassed established bureaucratic channels and came directly from the state petroleum company, PDVSA (Petróleos de Venezuela).

Chávez used wealth from increased petroleum revenue to exert Venezuelan influence throughout the Caribbean Basin and South America. (*See* Special Report.) On several occasions he claimed that U.S. Pres. George W. Bush was plotting to assassinate him and invade Venezuela to seize its oil, charges that the U.S. government denied. The Chávez government also orchestrated opposition to President Bush's Free Trade for the Americas project, which he claimed would enslave Latin American workers. In this effort he received support from Brazil, Argentina, and Uruguay, each of which preferred strengthening Mercosur (the Southern Cone Common Market) before creating a hemispheric trading bloc. On December 9 Venezuela gained admission to Mercosur as a full voting member.

Venezuela maintained cordial relations with its South American neighbours, although the kidnapping of a Colombian dissident in Caracas raised tensions for a time between Caracas and Bogotá. The dissident, Luis Rodrigo Granada, oversaw diplomatic efforts for Colombia's rebel FARC (Revolutionary Armed Forces of Colombia). His abduction was reportedly carried out by Colombian intelligence agents, and Chávez voiced anger over this violation of Venezuelan sovereignty. Notwithstanding this incident, Venezuela cooperated with its neighbours on a broad range of issues of mutual interest, ranging from developing the Amazon to creating a television network geared to the interests of South Americans. Finally, Venezuela

extended the preferential oil-trade deal that it had negotiated in the 1970s with selected Caribbean Basin countries to include a total of 13. A newly created petroleum company, PetroCaribe, was intended to challenge U.S. domination of energy in the subregion.

(DAVID J. MYERS)

VIETNAM

Area: 329,241 sq km (127,121 sq mi)
Population (2005 est.): 82,628,000
Capital: Hanoi
Chief of state: President Tran Duc Luong
Head of government: Prime Minister Phan Van Khai

The year 2005 commenced with the convening in January of the 11th plenum of the Vietnam Communist Party's Central Committee. The plenum focused on development strategies, the strengthening of party leadership, and preparations for the 10th national congress, scheduled for mid-2006. In preparation for the congress, party committees from the grassroots level and above were to review and offer comments on major draft policy documents. Provincial party congresses were to select delegates to the national congress, and these delegates would also have the responsibility of electing the new party leadership.

Reports from Vietnam emerged during the year that there was intense and often heated intraparty debate over policy matters and political leadership. Following the 11th plenum, the Politburo held three off-the-record meetings to hear the opinions of various focus groups. At one such meeting, Le Dang Doanh, who had served as economic adviser to former prime minister Pham Van Dong, offered this blunt assessment: "The Party clings to power, its members are corrupt and wasteful, leading to a huge gap between rich and poor and cruel injustice everywhere."

Former prime minister Vo Van Kiet privately circulated a document that was highly critical of the party's leadership-selection process. While at another meeting held in Ho Chi Minh City, senior retired officials voiced criticism of the leadership style of the

(continued on page 490)

A Leftist Surge in Latin America

by Paul Knox

Presidents (from left) Fidel Castro (Cuba), Hugo Chávez (Venezuela), Luiz Inácio Lula da Silva (Brazil), and Néstor Kirchner (Argentina).

The visit of Venezuelan Pres. Hugo Chávez (see BIOGRAPHIES) to New York City in September 2005 provided a dramatic illustration of the growing power of populist leaders in Latin America. Having positioned himself as a champion of the poor throughout the region, Chávez sought to take the same message to the United States. He proposed to provide cheap home heating oil at a deep discount to poor Americans during the coming winter through the American subsidiary of Venezuela's state-owned petroleum company. The gesture turned the tables on the U.S., historically a major contributor of foreign aid to Latin America. With energy prices soaring and Chávez sitting atop some of the world's largest oil reserves, few doubted that he would be able to honour the pledge.

Though Chávez was the most outspoken of Latin America's left-wing leaders, eclipsing even Cuba's Fidel Castro in political theatrics, he had plenty of company. Since Chávez came to power in 1999, leaders with solid left-of-

centre credentials had been elected in Brazil (Luiz Inácio Lula da Silva in 2002), Argentina (Néstor Kirchner in 2003) and Uruguay (Tabaré Vázquez [see BIOGRAPHIES] in 2005). Leftist candidates had also mounted strong campaigns in Mexico (Andrés Manuel López Obrador [see BIOGRAPHIES]) and Bolivia (Evo Morales). All rejected the political and economic formulas of U.S.-supported leaders in the region, and most of them were backed by well-organized social movements demanding greater popular participation in state affairs and policies more favourable to the poor and Indians. In the early years of the 21st century, Latin America was experiencing more grassroots ferment than at any other time since the 1970s, when radical political experiments were snuffed out by military coups d'état.

The leftist surge was rooted in reaction to the so-called Washington consensus, a set of economic policies adopted in most Latin American countries during the 1990s at the behest of the U.S. government, the International

Monetary Fund (IMF), and foreign bankers—often as a condition for relief of crippling debts. The prescriptions included tax increases, tight curbs on public spending, trade liberalization, and the sale of state-held assets to private interests. For a time the market-oriented policies provided stability, but delivering sustained increases in prosperity proved difficult. Farmers and small manufacturers found themselves unable to compete with foreign-made goods. Privatized utilities sharply increased rates for services such as electricity, water, and telephones. Some Latin Americans prospered by producing for export markets or selling their skills to foreign firms, but stark income disparities remained and in some countries widened. In the absence of effective judicial reform, corruption often accompanied the market opening. Alarmingly, in a region with a history of shocking abuses under military rule, a poll taken for the United Nations Development Programme found a decline in support for democracy from 61% in 1996 to 57% in 2002.

It was against this backdrop that Chávez was elected. A former army officer who had led an unsuccessful coup attempt in 1992, he vowed a clean break with a discredited political class that squandered oil wealth as millions languished in poverty. He proclaimed a "Bolivarian revolution," named after 19th-century independence hero Simón Bolívar, that would include land redistribution and an overhaul of education and welfare policies. After decisively winning a referendum on his rule in 2004, Chávez moved to expand Venezuela's sphere of influence. His chief tool was oil, which he agreed to provide on friendly terms to Cuba, Uruguay, Argentina, and the island countries of the Caribbean. A grateful Castro sent hundreds of Cuban doctors to work in Venezuelan clinics. Chávez also developed Telesur, a continental television network and rival to U.S.-based CNN. He labeled capitalism a "savage" system, called on Venezuelans to support socialism, and, after his referendum victory, moved to confiscate some large landholdings.

Argentina's Kirchner, a former state governor in Patagonia, had little of Chávez's style, but his roots were in the left wing of the Peronist movement, and he frequently railed against foreign speculators and multinational companies. He suspended dealings with the IMF and pulled off an audacious debt swap, persuading most of the country's bondholders to accept new bonds for defaulted ones at a 70% discount. Kirchner's government repurchased several privatized utilities and forced multinational Royal Dutch Shell to roll back a gasoline price increase. He also successfully allied himself with elements of the *piqueteros*—movements of unemployed and impoverished Argentines that arose during the 1990s—and his popularity level in mid-2005 remained high. In Bolivia Morales forced the resignation of Pres. Carlos Mesa in June, and Morales was elected president in December. He observed that Latin leaders who aligned themselves with the World Bank and the IMF were faring poorly, while "those who yield to their people, such as Fidel or Chávez, do well."

Elsewhere, evidence of a marked shift to the left was less decisive.

Vázquez was installed in March as Uruguay's first socialist president and immediately restored diplomatic relations with Cuba, but he remained within the mainstream in a country renowned for its generous social-welfare policies. The same was true of Chilean Socialists such as Pres. Ricardo Lagos and the front-runner to succeed him, Michelle Bachelet. In Brazil Lula built on two decades of groundwork laid by his Workers' Party in city and state administrations. A former trade union leader with a grade-school education, he played a key role in stalling the

Leftists in Latin America

MEXICO
CUBA
JAMAICA
DOMINICAN REPUBLIC
BELIZE
HONDURAS
HAITI
GUATEMALA
EL SALVADOR
NICARAGUA
COSTA RICA
PANAMA
VENEZUELA
GUYANA
SURINAME
FRENCH GUIANA (FR.)
COLOMBIA
ECUADOR
PERU
BRAZIL
BOLIVIA
PARAGUAY
CHILE
URUGUAY
ARGENTINA

- ▨ Communist government (Cuba)
- ■ Leftist government allied with Cuba
- ▨ Left-leaning government
- ▨ Major left-wing opposition presence
- □ Leftist electoral coalitions on the rise
- □ Important mass-based social movements

0   500   1,000 mi
0   800   1,600 km

© 2006 Encyclopædia Britannica, Inc.

U.S.-led push for a Free Trade Area of the Americas, whose original implementation date of Jan. 1, 2005, was postponed indefinitely. Lula also made a war on hunger the first priority of his administration, but its implementation was spotty. In office he proved a moderate, unwilling to challenge conventional economic tenets in the style of Chávez or Kirchner.

Castro, the 79-year-old Cuban leader, was content to leave much of the political showmanship to Chávez, whose oil-fueled exploits attained prominence in the U.S. American Christian evangelist Pat Robertson went so far as to call for Chávez's assassination (he quickly recanted), and Otto Reich, a former U.S. Department of State official warned of a Castro-Chávez "axis."

The more common approach was to note that Chávez had been careful not to threaten American firms or oil security directly. "Venezuela's President Pushes Foreign Companies Only So Far," was *The Wall Street Journal's* conclusion in late August. Defense Secretary Donald Rumsfeld and other U.S. officials expressed irritation with Chávez, and Venezuela was deemed to have failed to cooperate with U.S. antinarcotics efforts. Allegations that Venezuela's oil wealth was financing leftist subversion were prevalent but not supported by strong evidence.

There were worrying abuses and excesses, such as Chávez's curbs on Venezuela's privately owned media and Kirchner's tolerance of *piquetero* strong-arm tactics, but nothing the new Latin leaders were doing was a match for Castro's radical collectivization of Cuba in the 1960s or his support for armed guerrilla movements. Indeed, the range of thought and action on display was so broad that some questioned whether the "left-wing" tag was appropriate. "The 'leftist' label is by now an artificial construct that should be jettisoned," wrote Michael Shifter and Vinay Jawahar of the Inter-American Dialogue, a Washington think tank. "It confuses more than it clarifies."

In 2005 Kirchner struggled to realize significant gains against poverty and unemployment. In addition, it was an open question whether Chávez's "revolution" would survive a fall in world oil prices. Despite Lula's personal reputation for honesty, his prospects for reelection in 2006 were seriously damaged by a bribery and campaign-spending scandal that tainted key associates. Structural inequality, the boom-and-bust commodity cycle, and dirty politics have historically conspired to thwart many a Latin American visionary. For all the sound and fury over the latest generation of leaders, it was hard to discern in their programs a pathway to sustainable, transformative change.

Paul Knox is Chair of the School of Journalism at Ryerson University in Toronto and a former Latin America correspondent for the Globe and Mail *of Toronto.*

Bird Flu—The Next Human Pandemic?

In 2005 an epidemic of a viral respiratory disease called bird flu (avian influenza) continued to devastate poultry farms in many countries. The epidemic, which began in 2003, had by the end of the year infected poultry in Cambodia, China, Indonesia, Japan, Kazakhstan, Laos, Malaysia, Mongolia, North Korea, Romania, Russia, South Korea, Thailand, Turkey, Ukraine, and Vietnam. Hundreds of millions of birds had been killed by the disease or slaughtered in efforts to limit its spread.

The deadly disease is caused by the H5N1 strain of type A influenza virus. The H5N1 strain, which was first isolated from terns in South Africa in 1961, is now common in waterfowl such as wild ducks, which can then infect domesticated birds, among which the disease spreads easily. The H5N1 virus was first found to have the capability of infecting humans in 1997, when an outbreak of bird flu in Hong Kong poultry caused severe illness in 18 persons, 6 of whom died.

The idea of influenza's passing from birds to humans seems

© Jason Lee/Reuters/Corbis

frightening, but there is nothing new in it. Genetic research suggests that all flu strains originated from birds. By year's end the current epidemic of bird flu had led to human cases of the disease in Cambodia, China, Indonesia, Thailand, Turkey, and Vietnam. Vietnam was the worst hit, with 93 cases. Of those, 42 died. According to the World Health Organization, the total number of cases by the end of 2005 stood at more than 140, with about a 50% mortality rate. Sustained transmission of bird flu from person to person had not been observed, but health officials were aware that the H5N1 virus could rapidly mutate or combine genetically with a human influenza virus to yield a virulent new strain that might easily spread through the human population.

Can a bird-flu pandemic be prevented? Laboratory tests suggest that two popular antiviral drugs, amantadine (Symmetrel) and rimantadine (Flumadine), do not work against H5N1. Hopes are pinned on two others, oseltamavir (Tamiflu) and zanamavir (Relenza). The National Institute of Allergy and Infectious Diseases, part of the U.S. National Institutes of Health, awarded contracts for the production and clinical testing of an investigational vaccine based on the H5N1

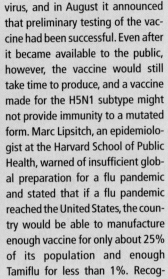

virus, and in August it announced that preliminary testing of the vaccine had been successful. Even after it became available to the public, however, the vaccine would still take time to produce, and a vaccine made for the H5N1 subtype might not provide immunity to a mutated form. Marc Lipsitch, an epidemiologist at the Harvard School of Public Health, warned of insufficient global preparation for a flu pandemic and stated that if a flu pandemic reached the United States, the country would be able to manufacture enough vaccine for only about 25% of its population and enough Tamiflu for less than 1%. Recognizing the need for greater preparation, in November U.S. Pres. George W. Bush outlined a $7.1 billion plan to provide funding for the early detection and containment of any pandemic flu outbreaks both in the United States and in other countries, improved methods for creating flu vaccines, and the stockpiling of flu vaccines and antiviral drugs. The sense of urgency in Southeast Asia in dealing with the spread of the bird flu is great. In some countries taxis even have signs warning passengers who feel ill to go straight to a hospital. The influenza pandemics of 1957 and 1968 each killed millions of people, and the great influenza pandemic of 1918 killed tens of millions. Another flu pandemic is clearly a possibility, and preparing for the threat is a serious and difficult problem.   (BRIAN J. FORD)

(continued from page 487)
party secretary-general, Nong Duc Manh.

The Central Committee took stock of the situation at its 12th plenum in July. This meeting was primarily concerned with determining how to accelerate economic growth and strengthen party leadership and with carrying out the final editing of draft documents for the national congress. The plenum resolved to achieve an annual growth rate of between 7.5% and 8% of GDP in order to end Vietnam's status as a less-developed state by 2010. Press accounts revealed that the draft party statutes included a provision to permit

individuals working in the private sector to join the party for the first time. Also under discussion was a proposal to combine the offices of state president and party secretary-general, as had been done in China. In light of backroom bickering, the plenum "severely condemned . . . factionalism, opportunism, [and] individualism." The plenum also adopted measures "to combat 'the plot of peaceful evolution' and schemes to incite unrest and overthrow, as well as distortions by hostile forces."

Vietnam continued carefully to balance its external relations. Nong Duc Manh visited France in early June on

the eve of a working visit to the U.S. later that month by Prime Minister Phan Van Khai. Khai was received at the White House by Pres. George W. Bush and at the Pentagon by Secretary of Defense Donald Rumsfeld. Khai pleased his hosts by agreeing to Vietnam's participation in the U.S. Defense Department's International Military and Education Program. In October Vietnam dispatched its defense minister to Beijing, where he signed an agreement with his counterpart on joint naval patrols in the Gulf of Tonkin. Later that month Vietnam hosted a visit by Chinese Pres. Hu Jintao.   (CARLYLE A. THAYER)

YEMEN

Area: 555,000 sq km (214,300 sq mi)
Population (2005 est.): 20,043,000
Capital: Sanaa
Chief of state: President Maj. Gen. 'Ali 'Abdallah Salih
Head of government: Prime Minister 'Abd al-Qadir al-Ba Jamal

In 2005 the government of Yemen continued to cooperate closely with the U.S. on its "war on terrorism" and arrested hundreds of al-Qaeda suspects in the process. Yemeni authorities engaged in clashes with the followers of radical cleric Hussein al-Houthi, who had been killed in September 2004 after starting an uprising. These clashes led to the death of more than 200 people in 2005. Pres. Maj. Gen. 'Ali 'Abdallah Salih, responding to criticism that Yemen was one of the world's most heavily armed countries, continued his program to disarm tribal Yemenis who were carrying weapons in public. This led to a number of skirmishes between troops and tribesmen.

Nurses in Sanaa, Yemen, demonstrate against the large number of firearms in the country, saying that the heavily armed populace creates problems for security and investment and results in a high crime rate.

AP/Wide World Photos

The Yemeni government undertook drastic economic reforms in an effort to address its budget deficit. A tax increase coupled with a cut in fuel subsides—which more than doubled the cost of fuel—resulted in riots and the death of both civilians and government officers. Yemen was one of the poorest countries in the world.

Though Yemen was officially considered polio-free, more than 100 cases of polio were reported. The World Health Organization described this outbreak as an epidemic, and WHO became heavily involved in orchestrating a national immunization drive to combat the polio outbreaks.

(AYESHA SIDDIQUA CHAUDHRY)

ZAMBIA

Area: 752,612 sq km (290,585 sq mi)
Population (2005 est.): 11,262,000
Capital: Lusaka
Head of state and government: President Levy Mwanawasa

Pres. Levy Mwanawasa began 2005 with a frank admission that he had been unable to reduce poverty in Zambia. A high proportion of the population lived below the poverty level, and after two years of good harvests, during which surpluses of corn (maize) were exported to neighbouring countries, drought forced the imposition of a ban on exports. In June the government warned that up to 1.2 million people would require food aid for at least eight months. There were also serious shortages of fuel.

Certain key sectors of the economy showed a promising upturn, however. Soaring prices for copper—stimulated by heavy demands from China and India and the discovery of extensive new deposits of the mineral in North-Western province—encouraged an increase in copper output. Plans were made in March to restore the rail link with the Angolan port of Benguela to counter the holdups that sometimes occurred along the rail routes via Zimbabwe and South Africa. Copper prices reached a record high in September in anticipation of increased demand following the damage caused by hurricanes in the Caribbean. Good prices for coffee and a shortfall in

coffee production in Brazil also encouraged a marked increase in Zambia's coffee-growing industry. In addition, the tourist industry benefited from the celebrations marking the 150th anniversary of David Livingstone's naming of Victoria Falls. There was a further boost to the economy in June when Zambia qualified for debt cancellation under the IMF and World Bank's scheme to help poorer countries.

President Mwanawasa's anticorruption campaign continued to garner widespread international approval. In June a senior official in the Ministry of Health was charged with corrupt practices, and it was announced in September that the U.K. High Court's trial of former president Frederick Chiluba on corruption charges would take place in Lusaka to avoid the possibility of Chiluba's disappearance if he was allowed to leave Zambia. Chiluba challenged the legitimacy of a foreign court acting in Zambia but said that he was prepared to face a Zambian court.

Although the High Court of Zambia on February 16 had rejected a challenge to President Mwanawasa's victory in the presidential election of 2001, former vice president Nevers Mumba, in a bid for power, renewed the allegation of corruption against Mwanawasa and threatened to oppose him in the presidential election scheduled for 2006. The ruling party rallied around the president and expelled Mumba in May. His attempt to seek redress failed when the court stated that it had no jurisdiction over the rules governing the management of political parties.

(KENNETH INGHAM)

ZIMBABWE

Area: 390,757 sq km (150,872 sq mi)
Population (2005 est.): 12,161,000, of which about 3 million–4 million people might be living outside the country
Capital: Harare
Head of state and government: President Robert Mugabe

The parliamentary elections held on March 31, 2005, were preceded by dire predictions from critics of the government both inside and outside Zimbabwe who maintained that free and

Ten-year-old Nashel Chisvo looks at what is left of his house in Porta Farm, west of Harare, after the Zimbabwean government razed it as part of a campaign to eliminate "illegal" structures and shantytowns in the country.

fair elections would be impossible. The Southern African Development Community's observer mission, the only foreign group permitted to monitor the elections, drew attention to several matters that, it said, should be investigated but nevertheless praised both the behaviour of voters and the conduct of the elections. SADC concluded that the result reflected the free will of the people of Zimbabwe.

Of the parliamentary seats determined by voters, the ruling Zimbabwe African National Union–Patriotic Front won 78 and the Movement for Democratic Change (MDC) 41. Morgan Tsvangirai, leader of the MDC, immediately claimed that there had been massive vote rigging, pointing to the serious discrepancies between the number of people registered as having voted and the total number of votes cast for the candidates, but his call for fresh elections was ignored.

Western critics were incensed in late April by the news that Zimbabwe had been reelected to the UN Human Rights Commission. They were angered too when on May 19 the government launched a cleanup campaign that involved the destruction of thousands of shanty dwellings on the outskirts of Harare and other urban centres. Critics were quick to claim that this was a punitive measure aimed at the supporters of the opposition, who were mainly located in the towns, while churches and other charitable bodies denounced the manner in which thousands of people were made homeless. In June Pres. Robert Mugabe announced a scheme to build two million replacement houses in the next five years, but UN Secretary-General Kofi Annan had already dispatched Anna Kajumulo Tibaijuka, a Tanzanian, on a fact-finding mission to investigate the cleanup program. Her critical report was submitted a month later, but Mugabe cast doubts on her impartiality, citing an earlier comment by U.K. Prime Minister Tony Blair, his arch critic, that Tibaijuka would "do a good job."

A proposal in May by the governor of the Bank of Zimbabwe to invite back some of the white farmers whose land had been seized under the government's land-reform program was rejected by Mugabe, who in July flew to China to solicit financial support. His efforts bore little fruit, and the Zimbabwe dollar consequently fell to an all-time low.

The courts retained a considerable degree of independence and in May, despite government opposition, released the 62 alleged mercenaries who were said to have been plotting to overthrow the president of Equatorial Guinea. The detainees had been jailed in Zimbabwe on various charges of immigration infringement and security regulations. In August all charges of treason leveled against Tsvangirai were dropped, but any hopes that this might lead to talks between the opposition leader and Mugabe were immediately quashed by the president. Mugabe then demonstrated his contempt for the opposition by arbitrarily creating a Senate, or second chamber of the parliament. His move was effective; it caused a serious split in the MDC between those who wished to challenge Mugabe by voting for their own candidates in the Senate elections and the supporters of Tsvangirai, who insisted on boycotting the elections.

At a farewell banquet Benjamin Mkapa, the retiring president of Tanzania, voiced the opinion of several African leaders when he said that they should be guided by elders such as President Mugabe and not be dictated to by the West.   (KENNETH INGHAM)

Ahmed, Inam. News Editor, *The Daily Star*, Bangladesh. Contributor to *Rivers of Life.* •WORLD AFFAIRS: *Bangladesh*

Ahmed, Rumee. Ph.D. Candidate, Religious Studies, University of Virginia. •WORLD AFFAIRS: *United Arab Emirates*

Alexander, Steve. Freelance Technology Writer. •BIOGRAPHIES *(in part)*; COMPUTERS AND INFORMATION SYSTEMS

Allaby, Michael. Freelance Writer. Author of *Encyclopedia of Weather and Climate* and *Basics of Environmental Science.* •THE ENVIRONMENT: *Environmental Issues; International Activities*

Allan, J.A. Professor of Geography, School of Oriental and African Studies, University of London. Author of *The Middle East Water Question.* •WORLD AFFAIRS: *Libya*

Andrejevich, Milan. Professor of History, Ivy Tech Community College; Adjunct Professor of Communication, Valparaiso (Ind.) University. •WORLD AFFAIRS: *Bosnia and Herzegovina; Serbia and Montenegro*

Anthony, John Duke. President and CEO, National Council on U.S.-Arab Relations; Secretary, U.S. Gulf Cooperation Council Corporate Cooperation Committee. Author of *The United Arab Emirates: Dynamics of State Formation.* •WORLD AFFAIRS: *Oman; Qatar*

Appave, Gervais. Director, Migration Policy, Research and Communications, International Organization for Migration. •SOCIAL PROTECTION: *International Migration*

Appleby, R. Scott. Professor of History, University of Notre Dame. Author of *The Ambivalence of the Sacred: Religion, Violence, and Reconciliation.* •BIOGRAPHIES *(in part)*; RELIGION: *Special Report: Roman Catholicism at a Crossroads*

Archibald, John J. Retired Feature Writer, *St. Louis* (Mo.) *Post-Dispatch.* Member of the American Bowling Congress Hall of Fame. •SPORTS AND GAMES: *Bowling: U.S. Tenpins*

Aurora, Vincent. Lecturer in French and Romance Philology, Columbia University, New York City. Author of *Michel Leiris' Failles: immobile in mobili.* •LITERATURE: *French*

Bahry, Louay. Adjunct Professor of Political Science, University of Tennessee. Author of *The Baghdad Bahn.* •BIOGRAPHIES *(in part)*; WORLD AFFAIRS: *Bahrain; Iraq; Kuwait*

Balaban, Avraham. Professor of Modern Hebrew Literature, University of Florida. Author of *Mourning a Father Lost: A Kibbutz Childhood Remembered.* •BIOGRAPHIES *(in part)*; LITERATURE: *Jewish: Hebrew*

Bamia, Aida A. Professor of Arabic Language and Literature, University of Florida. Author of *The Graying of the Raven: Cultural and Sociopolitical Significance of Algerian Folk Poetry.* •BIOGRAPHIES *(in part)*; LITERATURE: *Arabic*; LITERATURE: Sidebar

Barrett, David B. Research Professor of Missiometrics, Regent University, Virginia Beach, Va. Author of *World Christian Encyclopedia* and *Schism and Renewal in Africa.* Coauthor of *World Christian Trends, AD 30–AD 2200: Interpreting the Annual Christian Megacensus.* •RELIGION: *Tables (in part)*

Baru, Sanjaya. Media Adviser to Prime Minister, Government of India. Author of *The Political Economy of Indian Sugar: State Intervention and Structural Change.* •WORLD AFFAIRS: *India*

Bauer, Patricia. Assistant Editor, Encyclopædia Britannica. •CALENDAR; DISASTERS; OBITUARIES *(in part)*; WORLD AFFAIRS: *Pakistan: Sidebar*

Beckwith, David C. Vice President, National Cable Television Association. •WORLD AFFAIRS: *United States; United States: State and Local Affairs*

Bell, Susanna. Producer, the Finnish News Agency STT. •WORLD AFFAIRS: *Finland*

Benedetti, Laura. Laura and Gaetano De Sole Associate Professor of Contemporary Italian Culture, Georgetown University, Washington, D.C. Author of *La sconfitta di Diana: un percorso per la Gerusalemme liberata.* •LITERATURE: *Italian*

Bernstein, Ellen. Freelance Writer and Editor, specializing in health and medicine. •HEALTH AND DISEASE; HEALTH AND DISEASE: Sidebar

Bird, Thomas E. Professor of European Languages, the Jewish Studies Program, Queens College, City University of New York. Coeditor of *Hryhorij Savyč Skovoroda: An Anthology of Critical Articles.* •LITERATURE: *Jewish: Yiddish*

Bonds, John B. Visiting Assistant Professor of History, The Citadel, Charleston, S.C. Author of *Bipartisan Strategy: Selling the Marshall Plan.* •SPORTS AND GAMES: *Sailing (Yachting)*

Bradsher, Henry S. Foreign Affairs Analyst, Author, and Lecturer. •WORLD AFFAIRS: *Philippines*

Brady, Conor. Editor Emeritus, *The Irish Times*, Dublin. •WORLD AFFAIRS: *Ireland*

Brecher, Kenneth. Professor of Astronomy and Physics; Director, Science and Mathematics Education Center, Boston University. •PHYSICAL SCIENCES: *Astronomy*

Brockmann, Stephen. Professor of German, Carnegie Mellon University, Pittsburgh, Pa. Editor of *The Brecht Yearbook.* Author of *Literature and German Reunification* and *German Literary Culture at the Zero Hour.* •LITERATURE: *German*

Brokopp, John G. Media Relations Consultant; Freelance Journalist; Syndicated Columnist on casino gambling. Author of *Thrifty Gambling* and *Insider's Guide to Internet Gambling.* •SPORTS AND GAMES: *Equestrian Sports: Thoroughbred Racing: United States*

Brown, Bess. Economic Officer, Organization for Security and Co-operation in Europe Centre in Dushanbe, Tajikistan. Author of *Authoritarianism in the New States of Central Asia.* •BIOGRAPHIES *(in part)*; WORLD AFFAIRS: *Kazakhstan; Kyrgyzstan; Tajikistan; Turkmenistan; Uzbekistan*

Bryden, Matt. Director, Horn of Africa Project, International Crisis Group. •WORLD AFFAIRS: *Somalia*

Buchan, David. Foreign Editorial Writer, *Financial Times*, London. Author of *The Single Market and Tomorrow's Europe: A Progress Report from the European Commission.* •WORLD AFFAIRS: *France*

Bungs, Dzintra. Senior Research Fellow, Latvian Institute of International Affairs, Riga. Author of *The Baltic States: Problems and Prospects of Membership in the European Union.* •WORLD AFFAIRS: *Latvia*

Burnett, John S. Maritime Security Consultant. Author of *Dangerous Waters: Modern Piracy and Terror on the High Seas.* •LAW, CRIME, AND LAW ENFORCEMENT: *Special Report: Piracy on the High Seas*

Burns, Erik T. Bureau Chief, Dow Jones Newswires, Lisbon. •WORLD AFFAIRS: *Portugal*

Byrne, Justin. Acting Director of Graduate Studies, New York University in Madrid. •WORLD AFFAIRS: *Spain*

Byrne, Robert. Writer. Member of the Billiard Congress of America's Hall of Fame. Author of *Byrne's Complete Book of Pool Shots* and others. •SPORTS AND GAMES: *Billiard Games*

Cafferty, Bernard. Associate Editor, *British Chess Magazine.* Author of *The Soviet Championships.* •SPORTS AND GAMES: *Chess*

Campbell, Robert. Architect and Architecture Critic. Author of *Cityscapes of Boston: An American City Through Time.* •ARCHITECTURE AND CIVIL ENGINEERING: *Architecture*

Caplan, Marla. Photographer, International Center of Photography, New York City; MFA Candidate, Bard College, Annandale-on-Hudson, N.Y. •ART AND ART EXHIBITIONS: *Photography*

Carter, Robert W. Journalist. •SPORTS AND GAMES: *Equestrian Sports: Steeplechasing; Thoroughbred Racing: International*

Chappell, Duncan. President, Mental Health Review Tribunal, Sydney. Author of *Preventing and Responding to Violence at Work.* •LAW, CRIME, AND LAW ENFORCEMENT: *Crime*

Chaudhry, Ayesha Siddiqua. Ph.D. Candidate, Middle Eastern and Islamic Studies Program, New York University. •WORLD AFFAIRS: *Yemen*

Cheuse, Alan. Writing Faculty, English Department, George Mason University, Fairfax, Va.; Book Commentator, National Public Radio. Author of *The Light Possessed* and *Listening to the Page: Adventures in Reading and Writing.* •LITERATURE: *English: United States*

Chua, Lee Hoong. Review Editor, *The Straits Times*, Singapore. •WORLD AFFAIRS: *Singapore*

Cioroslan, Dragomir. USA Weightlifting, Inc., Board of Directors Member; Vice President, International Weightlifting Federation. Coauthor of *Banish Your Belly.* •SPORTS AND GAMES: *Weightlifting*

Clark, David Draper. Editor in Chief, *World Literature Today.* •LITERATURE: *English: Other Literature in English*

Clark, Janet H. Editor, Independent Analyst, and Writer on economic and financial topics. •BIOGRAPHIES *(in part)*; NOBEL PRIZES *(in part)*

Clifton, Michael. Independent Curator and Writer. Curator, "SCREAM: 10 Artists × 10 Writers × 10 Scary Movies." •ART AND ART EXHIBITIONS: *Art; Art Exhibitions*

Coate, Roger A. Professor of International Organization, University of South Carolina. Coauthor of *The United Nations and Changing World Politics.* •WORLD AFFAIRS: *United Nations*

Coller, Ken. President, West Seattle Productions. •SPORTS AND GAMES: *Wrestling: Sumo*

Collins, Nigel. Editor in Chief, *The Ring, KO, World Boxing,* and *Boxing 2005.* •SPORTS AND GAMES: *Boxing; Boxing: Sidebar*

Cooper, Peter. Music Journalist, *The Tennessean.* •BIOGRAPHIES *(in part)*; PERFORMING ARTS: *Music: Popular (United States)*

Cosgrave, Bronwyn. Author, Journalist, Broadcaster. Author of *Costume and Fashion: A Complete History.* •BIOGRAPHIES *(in part)*; FASHIONS; OBITUARIES *(in part)*

Coveney, Michael. Theatre Critic in London. Author of *The World According to Mike Leigh; The Andrew Lloyd Webber Story;* and others. •PERFORMING ARTS: *Theatre: Great Britain and Ireland*

Craine, Anthony G. Writer. •BIOGRAPHIES *(in part)*

Crisp, Brian F. Associate Professor of Political Science, Washington University, St. Louis, Mo. Author of *Democratic Institutional Design.* •WORLD AFFAIRS: *Colombia*

Crossing, Peter F. Data Analyst, World Christian Database; Associate Editor, *World Christian Encyclopedia;* Missions Information Coordinator, Sydney Centre for World Mission, Australia. •RELIGION: *Tables (in part)*

Csonka, Agnes. Journalist. •WORLD AFFAIRS: *Hungary*

Cullen, Dan. Director, American Booksellers Association, Information Department. •MEDIA AND PUBLISHING: *Book Publishing (United States)*

Curwen, Peter. Professor of Telecommunications, Strathclyde University, Glasgow, Scot. Author of *The U.K. Publishing Industry* and others. •MEDIA AND PUBLISHING: *Book Publishing (international)*

Cutter, Susan L. Carolina Distinguished Professor and Director, Hazards Research Lab, University of South Carolina. Editor, *American Hazardscapes: The Regionalization of Hazards and Disasters.* •ECONOMIC AFFAIRS: *Special Report: Preparing for Emergencies*

Cuttino, John Charles. Lyndon B. Johnson School of Public Affairs, University of Texas at Austin. •WORLD AFFAIRS: *Brazil*

Deeb, Marius K. Professor of Middle East Studies, SAIS, Johns Hopkins University, Washington, D.C. Author of *Syria's Terrorist War on Lebanon and the Peace Process* and others. •WORLD AFFAIRS: *Egypt; Jordan*

de la Barre, Kenneth. Fellow and Research Associate, Arctic Institute of North America; Research Associate, Yukon College, Northern Research Institute. •WORLD AFFAIRS: *Arctic Regions*

Denselow, Robin. Correspondent, BBC Television's *Newsnight.* Author of *When the Music's Over: The Story of Political Pop.* •PERFORMING ARTS: *Music: Popular (international)*

Denzer, LaRay. Visiting Scholar, Department of History, Northwestern University, Evanston, Ill. Author of *Folayegbe M. Akintunde-Ighodalo: A Public Life.* •WORLD AFFAIRS: *Ghana; Liberia; Nigeria; Rwanda; Sierra Leone*

Dietz, Henry A. Professor, Department of Government, University of Texas at Austin. •WORLD AFFAIRS: *Peru*

Contributors

Dooling, Dave. Education and Public Outreach Officer, National Solar Observatory, Sacramento Peak, New Mexico. Coauthor of *Engineering Tomorrow.* •PHYSICAL SCIENCES: *Space Exploration*

Dowd, Siobhan. Columnist, *Glimmer Train* (U.S.). Author of *A Swift Pure Cry.* Editor, *This Prison Where I Live* and *Roads of the Roma.* •BIOGRAPHIES *(in part)*

Dykla, John J. Theoretical Astrophysicist and Associate Professor of Physics, Loyola University Chicago. Contributor to *Encyclopedia of Physical Science and Technology.* •PHYSICAL SCIENCES: *Special Report:* Celebrating the Centennial of Einstein's "Miraculous Year."

Ebeling, Mary F.E. Department of Sociology, University of Surrey, Guildford, Eng. •WORLD AFFAIRS: *Burundi; Comoros; Djibouti; Mauritius; Seychelles*

Ehringer, Gavin Forbes. Sports Columnist, *Rocky Mountain News* and *Western Horseman.* Author of *Rodeo Legends.* •SPORTS AND GAMES: *Rodeo*

Erikson, Daniel P. Director, the Caribbean Program, Inter-American Dialogue, Washington, D.C. Coeditor, *Transforming Socialist Economies: Lessons for Cuba and Beyond.* •WORLD AFFAIRS: *Cuba*

Esteban, Verónica. Journalist and Bilingual Editor. •LITERATURE: *Spanish:* Spain

Fagan, Brian. Professor of Anthropology, University of California, Santa Barbara. Author of *The Little Ice Age: How Climate Made History, 1300–1850; Floods, Famines, and Emperors: El Niño and the Fate of Civilizations;* and *The Long Summer: How Climate Changed Civilization.* •ANTHROPOLOGY AND ARCHAEOLOGY: *Archaeology:* Western Hemisphere

Farr, David M.L. Professor Emeritus of History, Carleton University, Ottawa. •BIOGRAPHIES *(in part)*; WORLD AFFAIRS: *Canada*

Fealy, Greg. Research Fellow and Lecturer in Indonesian Politics, The Australian National University, Canberra. Coauthor of *Joining the Caravan?: The Middle East, Islamism and Indonesia.* •BIOGRAPHIES *(in part)*; WORLD AFFAIRS: *Indonesia*

Fendell, Robert J. Freelance Writer on automobiles and racing. Author of *The Encyclopedia of Auto Racing Greats.* •SPORTS AND GAMES: *Automobile Racing:* U.S. Auto Racing *(in part)*; Rallies and Other Races *(in part)*

Fisher, Martin. Editor, *Oryx;* Coeditor, *The Natural History of Oman: A Festschrift for Michael Gallagher.* •THE ENVIRONMENT: *Wildlife Conservation*

Fisher, Sharon. Central European and Balkan Specialist, Global Insight, Inc., Washington, D.C. Author of *Political Change in Post-Communist Slovakia and Croatia: From Nationalist to Europeanist.* •WORLD AFFAIRS: *Czech Republic; Slovakia*

Flink, Steve. Senior Correspondent, *Tennis Week.* Author of *The Greatest Tennis Matches of the Twentieth Century.* •BIOGRAPHIES *(in part)*; SPORTS AND GAMES: *Tennis*

Flores, Ramona Monette Sargan. Professor, Department of Speech Communication and Theatre Arts, University of the Philippines, Quezon City; Freelance Journalist. •MEDIA AND PUBLISHING: *Radio* (international); *Television* (international)

Follett, Christopher. Denmark Correspondent, *The Times;* Editor, *Copenhagen This Week.* •WORLD AFFAIRS: *Denmark*

Ford, Brian J. NESTA Fellow, London; Member of Gonville and Caius College, Cambridge. Author of *The Secret Language of Life: How Animals and Plants Feel and Communicate.* •WORLD AFFAIRS: *Vietnam:* Sidebar

Fridovich-Keil, Judith L. Professor, Department of Human Genetics, Emory University School of Medicine, Atlanta. •LIFE SCIENCES: *Molecular Biology and Genetics*

Fuller, Elizabeth. Editor, *Newsline,* Radio Free Europe/Radio Liberty, Prague. •WORLD AFFAIRS: *Armenia; Azerbaijan; Georgia*

Furmonavičius, Darius. Doctor and Research Fellow, Department of Languages and European Studies, University of Bradford, Eng. •WORLD AFFAIRS: *Lithuania*

Gallagher, Tom. Professor of Ethnic Peace and Conflict, University of Bradford, Eng. Author of

Modern Romania: The End of Communism, the Failure of Democratic Reform, and the Theft of a Nation; The Balkans After the Cold War: From Tyranny to Tragedy; and others. •WORLD AFFAIRS: *Moldova; Romania*

Ganado, Albert. Lawyer; Chairman, Malta National Archives Advisory Committee; President, Malta Historical Society. Author of *Valletta Città Nuova: A Map History (1566–1600).* •WORLD AFFAIRS: *Malta*

Garrod, Mark. Golf Correspondent, PA Sport, U.K. •SPORTS AND GAMES: *Golf*

Gaughan, Thomas. Library Director, Muhlenberg College, Allentown, Pa. •LIBRARIES AND MUSEUMS: *Libraries*

Gibbons, J. Whitfield. Professor of Ecology, Savannah River Ecology Laboratory, University of Georgia. Coauthor of *Ecoviews: Snakes, Snails, and Environmental Tales.* •LIFE SCIENCES: *Zoology*

Gill, Martin J. Executive Director, Food Certification (Scotland) Ltd. •AGRICULTURE AND FOOD SUPPLIES: *Fisheries*

Gobbie, Donn. CEO, American Badminton League. •SPORTS AND GAMES: *Badminton*

Graham, John W. Chair, Canadian Foundation for the Americas; Former Canadian Ambassador. •WORLD AFFAIRS: *Dominican Republic; Suriname*

Grenda, Iwona. Senior Lecturer in English, the Faculty of Law and Administration, Adam Mickiewicz University, Poznan, Pol. •WORLD AFFAIRS: *Poland*

Greskovic, Robert. Dance Writer, *The Wall Street Journal.* Author of *Ballet 101.* •PERFORMING ARTS: *Dance:* North America

Griffiths, A.R.G. Associate Professor in History, Flinders University of South Australia. Author of *Contemporary Australia* and *Beautiful Lies.* •WORLD AFFAIRS: *Australia; Dependent States: Indian Ocean and Southeast Asia; East Timor; Nauru; Palau; Papua New Guinea*

Haddad, Mahmoud. Associate Professor of History, the University of Balamand, Lebanon. Contributor to *Altruism and Imperialism: Western Cultural and Religious Missions in the Middle East.* •WORLD AFFAIRS: *Lebanon; Saudi Arabia*

Halman, Talat Sait. Professor and Chairman, Department of Turkish Literature, and Dean, Faculty of Humanities and Letters, Bilkent University, Ankara, Turkey. Editor and Translator, *Nightingales and Pleasure Gardens: Turkish Love Poems.* •LITERATURE: *Turkish*

Hammer, William R. Professor and Chair, Department of Geology, Augustana College, Rock Island, Ill. Author of *Gondwana Dinosaurs from the Jurassic of Antarctica.* •LIFE SCIENCES: *Paleontology*

Hayes, David C. Science Editor, Encyclopædia Britannica. •OBITUARIES *(in part)*

Helm, Toby. Chief Political Correspondent, *The Daily Telegraph.* •WORLD AFFAIRS: *European Union; European Union:* Sidebar

Hennelly, James. Associate Editor, Encyclopædia Britannica. •BIOGRAPHIES *(in part)*; OBITUARIES *(in part)*

Henry, Alan. Editor, *Autocourse;* Motor Racing Correspondent, *The Guardian.* Author of *50 Years of World Championship Grand Prix Motor Racing* and *Four Seasons at Ferrari: The Lauda Years.* •SPORTS AND GAMES: *Automobile Racing:* Grand Prix Racing

Hobbs, Greg. Senior Contributing Writer, Football Historian. Author of several books on Australian football and long-time writer with newspapers and the Australian Football League. •SPORTS AND GAMES: *Football:* Australian

Hoffman, Dean A. Senior Editor, *Hoof Beats.* Author of *Castleton Farm: A Tradition of Standardbred Excellence; Quest for Excellence: Hanover Shoe Farms: The First 75 Years;* and *The Hambletonian: America's Trotting Classic.* •SPORTS AND GAMES: *Equestrian Sports:* Harness Racing

Hollar, Sherman. Associate Editor, Encyclopædia Britannica. •BIOGRAPHIES *(in part)*; OBITUARIES *(in part)*; WORLD AFFAIRS: *Sweden*

Homel, David. Freelance Writer; Lecturer, Concordia University, Montreal. Author of *The Speaking Cure: A Novel* and others. •LITERATURE: *French:* Canada

Hosch, William L. Editor, Encyclopædia Britannica. •MEDIA AND PUBLISHING: Sidebar; OBITUARIES *(in part)*

Hu, Xiaobo. Associate Professor of Political Science, Clemson (S.C.) University. Coeditor of *China After Jiang.* •WORLD AFFAIRS: *China; China:* Sidebar; *Taiwan*

Hussainmiya, B.A. Associate Professor, Department of History, University of Brunei Darussalam. Author of *The Brunei Constitution of 1959: An Inside History.* •WORLD AFFAIRS: *Brunei*

IEIS. International Economic Information Services. •ECONOMIC AFFAIRS: *World Economy; Stock Markets* (international)

Ingham, Kenneth. Professor Emeritus of History, University of Bristol, Eng. Author of *Politics in Modern Africa: The Uneven Tribal Dimension* and others. •WORLD AFFAIRS: *Angola; Congo, Democratic Republic of the; Kenya; Malawi; Mozambique; Sudan, The; Tanzania; Uganda; Zambia; Zimbabwe*

Iovtcheva, Iva. Ph.D. Student, Operations and Management Science, Stephen M. Ross School of Business, University of Michigan. •WORLD AFFAIRS: *Bulgaria (in part)*

Isaacson, Lanae Hjortsvang. Editor, *Nordic Women Writers.* Contributor to *Dictionary of Literary Biography: Twentieth-Century Danish Writers* and *Dictionary of Literary Biography: Twentieth-Century Norwegian Writers.* •LITERATURE: *Danish*

Jamail, Milton. Lecturer, Department of Government, University of Texas at Austin. Author of *Full Count: Inside Cuban Baseball.* •SPORTS AND GAMES: *Baseball:* Latin America

Jameson, Sam. Visiting Fellow, Yomiuri Research Institute and Institute for International Policy Studies. •WORLD AFFAIRS: *Japan*

Joffé, George. Affiliated Lecturer, Centre of International Studies, University of Cambridge; Visiting Professor, Department of Geography, King's College, University of London. Editor, *Jordan in Transition.* •WORLD AFFAIRS: *Algeria; Morocco; Tunisia*

Johnson, Steve. Television Critic, *Chicago Tribune.* •MEDIA AND PUBLISHING: *Radio* (U.S.); *Television* (U.S.)

Johnson, Todd M. Director, Center for the Study of Global Christianity. Coauthor of *World Christian Encyclopedia.* •RELIGION: *Tables (in part)*

Joireman, Sandra F. Associate Professor of Politics and International Relations, Wheaton (Ill.) College. Author of *Property Rights and Political Development in Ethiopia and Eritrea.* •WORLD AFFAIRS: *Ethiopia*

Jones, David G.C. Author of *Atomic Physics.* •PHYSICAL SCIENCES: *Physics*

Jones, Mark P. Associate Professor of Political Science, Rice University, Houston, Texas. Author of *Electoral Laws and the Survival of Presidential Democracies.* •WORLD AFFAIRS: *Argentina*

Jubb, Nadine. Political Scientist; Research Associate, Centre for Research on Latin America and the Caribbean, York University, Toronto. •WORLD AFFAIRS: *Nicaragua*

Kanduza, Ackson M. Associate Professor, Department of History, University of Swaziland. Author of *Political Economy of Democratisation in Swaziland* and "Tackling HIV/AIDS and Related Stigma in Swaziland Through Education" (*Eastern Africa Social Science Research Review,* XIX, no. 2, June 2003). •WORLD AFFAIRS: *Swaziland*

Kapp, Clare. Freelance Journalist; Contributor to *The Lancet.* •WORLD AFFAIRS: *Switzerland*

Karimi-Hakkak, Ahmad. Professor and Founding Director, The Center for Persian Studies, University of Maryland. Poetry Editor, *Strange Times, My Dear: The PEN Anthology of Contemporary Iranian Literature.* •LITERATURE: *Persian*

Karns, Margaret P. Professor of Political Science, University of Dayton, Ohio. Coauthor of *International Organizations: The Politics and Processes of Global Governance.* •WORLD AFFAIRS: *Multinational and Regional Organizations*

Kazamaru, Yoshihiko. Literary Critic. •LITERATURE: *Japanese*

Kelling, George H. Lieutenant Colonel, U.S. Army (ret.). Author of *Countdown to Rebellion: British Policy in Cyprus 1939–1955.* •WORLD AFFAIRS: *Cyprus*

Kellner, Peter. Chairman, YouGov PLC. Author of *The New Mutualism* and others. •BIOGRAPHIES *(in part)*; OBITUARIES *(in part)*; WORLD AFFAIRS: *United Kingdom; United Kingdom:* Sidebar

Knox, Paul. Associate Professor and Chair, School of Journalism, Ryerson University, Toronto. •WORLD AFFAIRS: *Bolivia; Ecuador; Special Report: A Leftist Surge in Latin America*

Kobliner, Beth. Journalist. Author of *Get a Financial Life.* •ECONOMIC AFFAIRS: *Stock Markets: Canada, U.S.*

Koper, Keith D. Assistant Professor of Geophysics, Saint Louis (Mo.) University. •EARTH SCIENCES: *Geophysics*

Krause, Stefan. Freelance Analyst. •WORLD AFFAIRS: *Greece; Macedonia*

Kuiper, Kathleen. Senior Editor, Encyclopædia Britannica. Editor, *Merriam-Webster's Encyclopedia of Literature.* •BIOGRAPHIES (in part); OBITUARIES (in part)

Kuptsch, Christiane. Senior Research Officer, International Institute for Labour Studies, International Labour Office. Coeditor of *Social Security at the Dawn of the 21st Century.* •SOCIAL PROTECTION (international)

Lamb, Kevin M. Health and Medical Writer, *Dayton* (Ohio) *Daily News.* Author of *Quarterbacks, Nickelbacks & Other Loose Change.* •SPORTS AND GAMES: *Football: Canadian, U.S.*

Lawler, Nancy Ellen. Professor Emerita, Oakton Community College, Des Plaines, Ill. Author of *Soldiers, Airmen, Spies, and Whisperers: The Gold Coast in World War II* and others. •WORLD AFFAIRS: *Benin; Burkina Faso; Cameroon; Central African Republic; Congo, Republic of the; Côte d'Ivoire; Gabon; Guinea; Mali; Mauritania; Niger; Senegal; Togo*

Lawson, Fred H. Professor of Government, Mills College, Oakland, Calif. Author of *Why Syria Goes to War.* •WORLD AFFAIRS: *Syria*

Le Comte, Douglas. Meteorologist, Climate Prediction Center, National Oceanic and Atmospheric Administration. •EARTH SCIENCES: *Meteorology and Climate*

Legassick, Martin. Professor of History, University of the Western Cape, Bellville, S.Af. Author of *Skeletons in the Cupboard: South African Museums and the Trade in Human Remains 1907–1917.* •WORLD AFFAIRS: *South Africa*

Levin, Ben. Documentary Filmmaker; Professor, Department of Radio, Television and Film, University of North Texas. Coproducer and Codirector, *Verso Negro: Black Verse Poetry of the Spanish Caribbean.* •PERFORMING ARTS: *Motion Pictures: Nontheatrical Films*

Lindstrom, Sieg. Managing Editor, *Track & Field News.* •BIOGRAPHIES (in part); SPORTS AND GAMES: *Track and Field Sports (Athletics)*

Litweiler, John. Jazz Critic. Author of *The Freedom Principle: Jazz After 1958* and *Ornette Coleman: A Harmolodic Life.* •OBITUARIES (in part); PERFORMING ARTS: *Music: Jazz*

Logan, Robert G. Sports Journalist. Author of *Bob Logan's Tales from Chicago Sports* and *More Tales from the Cubs Dugout.* Coauthor of *Gerry Faust's Tales from the Notre Dame Sideline.* •SPORTS AND GAMES: *Basketball: United States*

Longmore, Andrew. Senior Sports Writer, *Sunday Times;* Former Assistant Editor, *The Cricketer.* Author of *The Complete Guide to Cycling.* •SPORTS AND GAMES: *Cricket*

Lundin, Immi. Freelance Journalist and Literary Critic. •LITERATURE: *Swedish*

Macdonald, Barrie. Professor of History, Massey University, Palmerston, N.Z. •WORLD AFFAIRS: *Dependent States: Pacific; Fiji; Kiribati; Marshall Islands; Micronesia, Federated States of; Samoa; Solomon Islands; Tonga; Tuvalu; Vanuatu*

Macdonald, Stuart. Lecturer in Law, University of Wales, Swansea. •LAW, CRIME, AND LAW ENFORCEMENT: *Death Penalty*

Maguire, Robert. Director, Trinity University Haiti Program, Washington, D.C. Author of *Haiti Held Hostage: International Responses to the Quest for Nationhood 1986–1996.* •WORLD AFFAIRS: *Haiti*

Malik, Mohan. Professor, Asia-Pacific Center for Security Studies, Honolulu. Author of *Dragon on Terrorism: Assessing China's Tactical Gains and Strategic Losses Post-September 11.* •WORLD AFFAIRS: *Myanmar (Burma)*

Mango, Andrew. Foreign Affairs Analyst. Author of *Atatürk: The Biography of the Founder of Modern Turkey* and *The Turks Today.* •WORLD AFFAIRS: *Turkey*

Marples, David R. Professor of History, University of Alberta. Author of *Belarus: A Denationalized Nation* and *Motherland: Russia in the Twentieth Century.* •BIOGRAPHIES (in part); WORLD AFFAIRS: *Belarus; Ukraine*

Marston, John A. Professor, Centro de Estudios de Asia y África, El Colegio de México. Coeditor of *History, Buddhism, and New Religious Movements in Cambodia.* •BIOGRAPHIES (in part); WORLD AFFAIRS: *Cambodia*

Matić, Davorka. Assistant Professor, Department of Sociology, Faculty of Philosophy, University of Zagreb, Croatia. •WORLD AFFAIRS: *Croatia*

Matthíasson, Björn. Economist, Ministry of Finance, Iceland. •WORLD AFFAIRS: *Iceland*

Mazie, David M. Freelance Journalist. •SOCIAL PROTECTION: *Benefits and Programs:* North America

McLachlan, Keith S. Professor Emeritus, School of Oriental and African Studies, University of London. Coeditor of *Landlocked States of Africa and Asia.* Author of *Boundaries of Modern Iran.* •WORLD AFFAIRS: *Iran*

McMillan, Neale. Managing Editor, South Pacific News Service. Author of *Top of the Greasy Pole: New Zealand Prime Ministers of Recent Times.* •WORLD AFFAIRS: *New Zealand*

Mendes, Victor J. Associate Professor and Graduate Program Director, University of Massachusetts Dartmouth. Author of *Almeida Garrett: crise na representação nas Viagens na minha terra.* •LITERATURE: *Portuguese:* Portugal

Michael, Tom. Editor, Encyclopædia Britannica. •BIOGRAPHIES (in part); OBITUARIES (in part)

Middlebrook, Kevin J. Reader in Latin American Politics, Institute for the Study of the Americas, University of London. Editor of *Dilemmas of Political Change in Mexico.* •BIOGRAPHIES (in part); WORLD AFFAIRS: *Mexico*

Moredock, Janet. Freelance Writer and Editor. •BIOGRAPHIES (in part); WORLD AFFAIRS: *Malaysia*

Morgan, Paul. Editor, *Rugby World.* •SPORTS AND GAMES: *Football: Rugby Football*

Morrison, Graham. Press Officer, British Fencing Association; Correspondent, *Daily Telegraph* and *Jewish Chronicle.* •SPORTS AND GAMES: *Fencing*

Myers, David J. Professor of Political Science, Pennsylvania State University. Coauthor of *Capital City Politics in Latin America: Democratization and Empowerment.* •WORLD AFFAIRS: *Venezuela*

Naka-Michaeli, Kimiyo. International Editorial Project Coordinator, Encyclopædia Britannica. •BIOGRAPHIES (in part); OBITUARIES (in part)

Nishizaki, Yoshinori. Postdoctoral Fellow, National University of Singapore. •WORLD AFFAIRS: *Thailand*

Noda, Hiroki. Sporting News Reporter, *Kyodo News,* Tokyo. •SPORTS AND GAMES: *Baseball:* Japan

O'Leary, Christopher. Contributing Editor and Writer, *Investment Dealers Digest.* •ECONOMIC AFFAIRS: *Business Overview*

Oppenheim, Lois Hecht. Professor of Political Science, University of Judaism, Los Angeles. Author of *Politics in Chile: Democracy, Authoritarianism, and the Search for Development.* Coeditor, *After Pinochet: The Chilean Road to Democracy and the Market.* •WORLD AFFAIRS: *Chile*

O'Quinn, Jim. Editor in Chief, *American Theatre.* •PERFORMING ARTS: *Theatre:* U.S. and Canada

Orwig, Sarah Forbes. Associate Editor, Encyclopædia Britannica. Contributor to *The Next Phase of Business Ethics: Integrating Psychology and Ethics.* •BIOGRAPHIES (in part); OBITUARIES (in part)

Osborne, Keith L. Editor, *British Rowing Almanack.* Author of *1000 Years of Rowing on the Dee; Berlin or Bust; Boat Racing in Britain, 1715–1975;* and *One Man Went to Row.* •BIOGRAPHIES (in part); SPORTS AND GAMES: *Rowing*

Paarlberg, Philip L. Professor of Agricultural Economics, Purdue University, West Lafayette, Ind. •AGRICULTURE AND FOOD SUPPLIES: *Agriculture*

Palacio, Joseph O. Ph.D. Former Resident Tutor and Head, University Centre, University of the West Indies School of Continuing Studies, Belize. Author of *Development in Belize, 1960–1980: Initiatives at the State and Community Levels.* •WORLD AFFAIRS: *Belize*

Palmer, Rosanne. Lecturer in European Studies, Cardiff (Wales) University. •BIOGRAPHIES (in part); WORLD AFFAIRS: *Germany*

Parsons, Neil. Professor of History, University of Botswana. Author of *King Khama, Emperor Joe, and the Great White Queen.* •WORLD AFFAIRS: *Botswana*

Peaker, Carol. D.Phil. Candidate, Wolfson College, Oxford. Author of *The Penguin Modern Painters: A History.* •LITERATURE: *English:* United Kingdom

Pérez, Orlando J. Associate Professor of Political Science, Central Michigan University. Editor of *Post-Invasion Panama: The Challenges of Democratization in the New World Order* and others. •WORLD AFFAIRS: *Panama*

Peszek, Luan. Publications Director and Editor, *U.S.A. Gymnastics.* Author of *Gymnastics Almanac.* •SPORTS AND GAMES: *Gymnastics*

Peterson, Mark. Associate Professor of Korean Studies, Brigham Young University, Provo, Utah. Author of *Korean Adoption and Inheritance* and others. •WORLD AFFAIRS: *Korea, Democratic People's Republic of; Korea, Republic of*

Phillips, Sam. Assistant Editor, *Royal Academy of Arts Magazine,* London. •LIBRARIES AND MUSEUMS: *Museums*

Phillips, Stephen J. United States Correspondent, *The Times Educational Supplement,* London. •AGRICULTURE AND FOOD SUPPLIES: Sidebar

Pielke, Roger A., Jr. Professor, Environmental Studies, University of Colorado. Coeditor, *Prediction: Science, Decision Making, and the Future of Nature.* •THE ENVIRONMENT: *Special Report: The Kyoto Protocol: What Next?*

Ponmoni Sahadevan. Associate Professor, Jawaharlal Nehru University, New Delhi. Author of *Conflict and Peacemaking in South Asia.* •WORLD AFFAIRS: *Maldives*

Poudel, Keshab. Freelance Journalist. •WORLD AFFAIRS: *Bhutan; Nepal*

Prothero, Neil. Editor and Economist, Economist Intelligence Unit, Europe. •WORLD AFFAIRS: *Austria*

Rauch, Robert. Freelance Editor and Writer. •BIOGRAPHIES (in part); NOBEL PRIZES (in part); OBITUARIES (in part)

Raun, Toivo U. Professor of Central Eurasian Studies, Indiana University. Author of *Estonia and the Estonians.* Contributor to *Nations and Nationalism.* •WORLD AFFAIRS: *Estonia*

Ray, Michael. Copy Editor, Encyclopædia Britannica. Contributor to *Trimtab* (the newsletter of the Buckminster Fuller Institute). •BIOGRAPHIES (in part); OBITUARIES (in part)

Reddington, André. Assistant Editor, *Amateur Wrestling News.* •SPORTS AND GAMES: *Wrestling: Freestyle and Greco-Roman*

Reid, Ron. Staff Writer, *Philadelphia Inquirer.* •BIOGRAPHIES (in part); SPORTS AND GAMES: *Ice Hockey; Ice Skating; Ice Skating:* Sidebar

Renwick, David. Freelance Journalist. •WORLD AFFAIRS: *Antigua and Barbuda; Bahamas, The; Barbados; Dependent States: Caribbean and Bermuda; Dominica; Grenada; Guyana; Jamaica; Saint Kitts and Nevis; Saint Lucia; Saint Vincent and the Grenadines; Trinidad and Tobago*

Reuning, Winifred. Editor and Web Manager, Office of Polar Programs, National Science Foundation. •WORLD AFFAIRS: *Antarctica*

Robbins, Paul. Freelance Writer; Correspondent, *Ski Trax* and *Ski Racing.* •BIOGRAPHIES (in part); SPORTS AND GAMES: *Skiing*

Robinson, David. Film Critic and Historian. Author of *A History of World Cinema* and others. •PERFORMING ARTS: *Motion Pictures*

Roby, Anne. Freelance Journalist; Program Associate, Institute for Mathematics and Science Education, University of Illinois at Chicago. •WORLD AFFAIRS: *Andorra; Liechtenstein; Luxembourg; Monaco*

Rollin, Jack. Editor, *Sky Sports Football Yearbook* and *Playfair Football Annual.* Author of *Soccer at War 1939–45* and others. •SPORTS AND GAMES: *Football: Association Football (Soccer): Africa and Asia; Europe*

Contributors

Sabo, Anne G. Associate Professor of Norwegian, St. Olaf College, Northfield, Minn.; Contributor to *LIT: Literature Interpretation Theory; Journal of Popular Culture; NORA: Nordic Journal of Women's Studies; Journal of European Studies; Scandinavian Studies;* and others. •LITERATURE: *Norwegian*

Sanders, Alan J.K. Freelance Mongolist; Former Lecturer in Mongolian Studies, School of Oriental and African Studies, University of London. Author of *Historical Dictionary of Mongolia;* Coauthor of *Colloquial Mongolian.* •WORLD AFFAIRS: *Mongolia*

Sandvik, Hilde. Dr. Philos., Associate Professor of History, University of Oslo. Author of *Norsk historie 1300–1625.* •WORLD AFFAIRS: *Norway*

Saracino, Peter. Freelance Defense Journalist. •BIOGRAPHIES *(in part);* MILITARY AFFAIRS; OBITUARIES *(in part)*

Sarahete, Yrjö. Secretary Emeritus, Fédération Internationale des Quilleurs. •SPORTS AND GAMES: *Bowling: World Tenpins*

Satō, Shozō. Visiting Professor, Northwestern University, Evanston, Ill.; Professor Emeritus, University of Illinois at Urbana-Champaign. Author of *Soul of Japan: Introducing Traditional Japanese Arts to the New Generations.* •PERFORMING ARTS: *Special Report: Kabuki Goes West*

Saunders, Christopher. Professor of Historical Studies, University of Cape Town. Coauthor of *Historical Dictionary of South Africa* and *South Africa: A Modern History.* •BIOGRAPHIES *(in part);* WORLD AFFAIRS: *Cape Verde; Chad; Equatorial Guinea; Gambia, The; Guinea-Bissau; Lesotho; Madagascar; Namibia; São Tomé and Príncipe*

Schiavo, Leda. Professor Emerita, University of Illinois at Chicago. Author of *El éxtasis de los límites: temas y figuras del decadentismo.* •LITERATURE: *Spanish: Latin America*

Schlager, Erika. Counsel for International Law, Commission on Security and Cooperation in Europe. •SOCIAL PROTECTION: *Special Report: The Roma—Europe's Largest Minority*

Schmidt, Fabian. Head of the Bosnian and Albanian Programs, Deutsche Welle. •WORLD AFFAIRS: *Albania*

Schreiber, Barbara A. Editorial Assistant, Encyclopædia Britannica. •BIOGRAPHIES *(in part);* OBITUARIES *(in part)*

Schuster, Angela M.H. Editor in Chief, historic preservation quarterly *ICON;* Contributing Editor, *Archaeology;* Contributor, *New York Times.* •ANTHROPOLOGY AND ARCHAEOLOGY: *Archaeology: Eastern Hemisphere*

Sego, Stephen. Freelance Journalist; Former Director, Radio Free Afghanistan. •WORLD AFFAIRS: *Afghanistan*

Seligson, Mitchell A. Centennial Professor of Political Science, Vanderbilt University, Nashville. Editor of *Elections and Democracy in Central America, Revisited.* •WORLD AFFAIRS: *Costa Rica*

Serafin, Steven R. Director, Writing Center, Hunter College, City University of New York. Coeditor of *The Continuum Encyclopedia of American Literature* and *The Continuum Encyclopedia of British Literature.* •NOBEL PRIZES *(in part)*

Shelley, Andrew. Executive Director, Women's International Squash Players Association; Technical Director, World Squash Federation. Author of *Squash Rules: A Players Guide.* •SPORTS AND GAMES: *Squash*

Shepherd, Melinda C. Senior Editor, Encyclopædia Britannica. •OBITUARIES *(in part);* SPORTS AND GAMES: *Automobile Racing:* Rallies and Other Races *(in part);* WORLD AFFAIRS: *Dependent States:* Europe and the Atlantic

Shubinsky, Valery. Freelance Critic and Journalist. Author of *Nikolay Gumilyov: zhizn poeta.* •LITERATURE: *Russian*

Simons, Paul. Freelance Journalist. Author of *The Action Plant.* •LIFE SCIENCES: *Botany*

Simpson, Jane. Freelance Writer. •PERFORMING ARTS: *Dance: European*

Sklar, Morton. Executive Director, World Organization for Human Rights USA; Judge, Administrative Labor Tribunal, Organization of American States. Editor, *The Status of Human Rights in the United States* and *Torture in the U.S.* Author of *The Right*

to Travel and others. •SOCIAL PROTECTION: *Human Rights*

Smentkowski, Brian. Professor of Political Science and Assistant Director, Center for Scholarship in Teaching and Learning, Southeast Missouri State University. •LAW, CRIME, AND LAW ENFORCEMENT: *Court Decisions*

Smith, Gregory O. Academic Director, European School of Economics, Rome. •WORLD AFFAIRS: *San Marino; Vatican City State*

Snodgrass, Donald. Institute Fellow Emeritus, Harvard University. Coauthor of *Economics of Development,* 5th ed. •WORLD AFFAIRS: *Sri Lanka*

Sondrol, Paul C. Associate Professor of Political Science, University of Colorado at Colorado Springs. Author of *Power Play in Paraguay: The Rise and Fall of General Stroessner.* •WORLD AFFAIRS: *Paraguay*

Sparks, Karen J. Editor, Encyclopædia Britannica. •OBITUARIES *(in part)*

Spencer, Donna. Journalist, The Canadian Press. •SPORTS AND GAMES: *Curling*

Stern, Irwin. Teaching Assistant Professor of Foreign Languages, North Carolina State University. Editor, *Dictionary of Brazilian Literature.* Coauthor of *Paso a Paso: Spanish for Health Professionals.* •LITERATURE: *Portuguese:* Brazil

Stewart, Alan. Freelance Journalist. Author of *Gathering the Clans: Tracing Scottish Ancestry on the Internet.* •COMPUTERS AND INFORMATION SYSTEMS: Sidebar; OBITUARIES *(in part)*

Stone, Martha L. Training Director, Ifra Newsplex. Author of *Convergence: Fact or Fiction?* and *Cross Media Advertising.* •MEDIA AND PUBLISHING: *Newspapers*

Stuart-Fox, Martin. Professor Emeritus, University of Queensland. Author of *A History of Laos.* •WORLD AFFAIRS: *Laos*

Sumner, David E. Professor of Journalism and Head of the Magazine Program, Ball State University, Muncie, Ind. General Editor, Peter Lang Media Industry Series. Coauthor of *Feature and Magazine Writing: Action, Angle and Anecdotes.* Contributor to *Encyclopedia of International Media and Communications.* •MEDIA AND PUBLISHING: *Magazines*

Sumrall, Harry. Editor in Chief, RedLudwig.com; Classical Music Editor, Gracenote, Inc. •PERFORMING ARTS: *Music: Classical*

Susel, Rudolph M. Editor, *American Home.* •WORLD AFFAIRS: *Slovenia*

Susser, Leslie D. Diplomatic Correspondent, *The Jerusalem Report.* Coauthor of *Shalom Friend: The Life and Legacy of Yitzhak Rabin.* •WORLD AFFAIRS: *Israel*

Taylor, Jolanda Vanderwal. Associate Professor of Dutch and German, University of Wisconsin at Madison. Author of *A Family Occupation: Children of the War and the Memory of World War II in Dutch Literature of the 1980s.* •LITERATURE: *Netherlandic: The Netherlands*

Taylor, Richard. Basketball Correspondent, *The Independent;* Production Editor, Midland Weekly Media (Trinity Mirror). •SPORTS AND GAMES: *Basketball: International*

Taylor-Robinson, Michelle M. Associate Professor of Political Science, Texas A&M University. Coauthor of *Negotiating Democracy: Transitions from Authoritarian Rule.* •WORLD AFFAIRS: *Honduras*

Teague, Elizabeth. Foreign & Commonwealth Office, London. (The opinions expressed are personal and do not necessarily represent those of the British government.) •WORLD AFFAIRS: *Russia*

Thayer, Carlyle A. Professor of Politics, Australian Defence Force Academy, Canberra. Author of *The Vietnam People's Army Under Doi Moi.* •WORLD AFFAIRS: *Vietnam*

Thimangu, Patrick L. Reporter, *St. Louis Business Journal.* •WORLD AFFAIRS: *Eritrea*

Thomas, R. Murray. Professor Emeritus of Education, University of California, Santa Barbara. Author of *Recent Theories of Human Development* and *High-Stakes Testing: Coping with Collateral Damage.* •EDUCATION; EDUCATION: Sidebar

Tikkanen, Amy. Associate Editor, Encyclopædia Britannica. •BIOGRAPHIES *(in part);* OBITUARIES *(in part)*

Turner, Darrell J. Freelance Writer; Former Religion Writer, *Fort Wayne* (Ind.) *Journal Gazette;* Former Associate Editor, Religion News Service. •RELIGION

Urbansky, Janele M. Account Executive, Crowley Webb & Associates. •SPORTS AND GAMES: *Bobsleigh, Skeleton, and Luge:* Luge; SPORTS AND GAMES: Sidebar *(in part)*

Urbansky, Julie. Retail Marketing Manager, Nextel Partners, Inc. •SPORTS AND GAMES: *Bobsleigh, Skeleton, and Luge:* Bobsleigh; Skeleton; SPORTS AND GAMES: Sidebar *(in part)*

Verdi, Robert. Senior Writer, *Golf Digest, Golf World;* Contributing Columnist, *Chicago Tribune.* •SPORTS AND GAMES: *Baseball* (U.S. and Canada)

Wallenfeldt, Jeff. Senior Editor, Encyclopædia Britannica. •BIOGRAPHIES *(in part);* OBITUARIES *(in part)*

Wang Xiaoming. Professor of Modern Chinese Literature at East China Normal University; Director, Program of Cultural Studies, Shanghai University. Author of *Life Cannot Be Faced Straight-On: A Biography of Lu Xun.* •LITERATURE: *Chinese*

Wanninger, Richard S. Freelance Journalist. •SPORTS AND GAMES: *Volleyball*

Watson, Rory. Freelance Journalist specializing in European Union affairs; Brussels Correspondent, *The Times.* Coauthor of *The American Express Guide to Brussels.* Contributor to *The European Union: How Does It Work?* •WORLD AFFAIRS: *Belgium*

Weil, Eric. Columnist and Contributor, *Buenos Aires Herald;* South America Correspondent, *World Soccer Magazine;* Contributor to *FIFA Magazine.* •SPORTS AND GAMES: *Football: Association Football (Soccer): The Americas*

Weinstein, Martin. Professor of Political Science, William Paterson University of New Jersey. Author of *Uruguay: Democracy at the Crossroads.* •BIOGRAPHIES *(in part);* WORLD AFFAIRS: *Uruguay*

White, Martin L. Freelance Writer. •BIOGRAPHIES *(in part);* OBITUARIES *(in part)*

Whitney, Barbara. Copy Supervisor, Encyclopædia Britannica. •BIOGRAPHIES *(in part);* OBITUARIES *(in part)*

Whitten, Phillip. Editor in Chief, Swiminfo.com, *Swimming World, Swim,* and *Swimming Technique* magazines. Author of *The Complete Book of Swimming* and others. •SPORTS AND GAMES: *Swimming*

Wilkinson, John R. Sportswriter, Coventry Newspapers. •SPORTS AND GAMES: *Cycling*

Williams, Victoria C. Assistant Professor of Political Science, Alvernia College, Reading, Pa.; Independent Consultant on international affairs. •LAW, CRIME, AND LAW ENFORCEMENT: *International Law*

Wilson, Derek. Former Correspondent, BBC. Author of *Rome, Umbria and Tuscany.* •WORLD AFFAIRS: *Italy*

Woods, Elizabeth Rhett. Writer. Author of *Absinth of Desire; Family Fictions: Poems; If Only Things Were Different (I): A Model for a Sustainable Society;* and others. •LITERATURE: *English: Canada*

Woods, Michael. Science Editor, *Toledo* (Ohio) *Blade.* Author of *Ancient Technology.* •PHYSICAL SCIENCES: *Chemistry;* NOBEL PRIZES *(in part)*

Woodward, Ralph Lee, Jr. Professor Emeritus of Latin American History, Tulane University, New Orleans. Author of *Central America, a Nation Divided.* •WORLD AFFAIRS: *El Salvador; Guatemala*

Wyllie, Peter J. Professor Emeritus of Geology, California Institute of Technology. Author of *The Dynamic Earth* and *The Way the Earth Works.* •EARTH SCIENCES: *Geology and Geochemistry*

Yovchev, Boris. Ph.D. Candidate, University of Michigan. •WORLD AFFAIRS: *Bulgaria (in part)*

Zegura, Stephen L. Professor of Anthropology, University of Arizona. •ANTHROPOLOGY AND ARCHAEOLOGY: *Anthropology*

Ziring, Lawrence. Arnold E. Schnieder Professor Emeritus of Political Science, Western Michigan University. Coauthor of *The United Nations: International Organization and World Politics.* Author of *Pakistan in the Twentieth Century: A Political History* and *Pakistan: At the Crosscurrent of History.* •WORLD AFFAIRS: *Pakistan*

World Data

The damage caused by Hurricane Katrina and various other hurricanes interrupted production of petroleum products in the late summer of 2005 and helped to drive the prices of gasoline, natural gas, and crude petroleum to all-time highs in the United States and around the world.

CONTENTS

INTRODUCTION

Britannica World Data provides a statistical portrait of some 217 countries and dependencies of the world, at a level appropriate to the significance of each. It contains 214 country statements (the "Nations of the World" section), ranging in length from one to six pages, and permits, in the 20 major thematic tables (the "Comparative National Statistics" [CNS] section), comparisons among these larger countries and 4 other states.

Updated annually, *Britannica World Data* is particularly intended as direct, structured support for many of Britannica's other reference works—encyclopaedias, yearbooks, atlases—at a level of detail that their editorial style or design do not permit.

Like the textual, graphic, or cartographic modes of expression of these other products, statistics possess their own inherent editorial virtues and weaknesses. Two principal goals in the creation of *Britannica World Data* were up-to-dateness and comparability, each possible to maximize separately, but not always possible to combine. If, for example, research on some subject is completed during a particular year (x), figures may be available for 100 countries for the preceding year ($x - 1$), for 140 countries for the year before that ($x - 2$), and for 180 countries for the year before that ($x - 3$).

Which year should be the basis of a thematic compilation for 217 countries so as to give the best combination of up-to-dateness and comparability? And, should $x - 1$ be adopted for the thematic table, ought up-to-dateness in the country table (for which year x is already available) be sacrificed for agreement with the thematic table? In general, the editors have opted for maximum up-to-dateness in the country statistical boxes and maximum comparability in the thematic tables.

Comparability, however, also resides in the meaning of the numbers compiled, which may differ greatly from country to country. The headnotes to the thematic tables explain many of these methodological problems; the Glossary serves the same purpose for the country statistical pages. Published data do not always provide the researcher or editor with a neat, unambiguous choice between a datum compiled on two different bases (say, railroad track length, or route length), one of which is wanted and the other not. More often a choice must be made among a variety of official, private, and external intergovernmental (UN, FAO, IMF) sources, each reporting its best data but each representing a set of problems: (1) of methodological variance from (or among) international conventions; (2) of analytical completeness (data for a single year may, successively, be projected [based on 10 months' data], preliminary [for 12 months], final, revised or adjusted, etc.); (3) of time frame, or accounting interval (data may represent a full Gregorian calendar year [preferred], a fiscal year, an Islamic or other national or religious year, a multiyear period or average [when a one-year statement would contain unrepresentative results]); (4) of continuity with previous data; and the like. Finally, published data on a particular subject may be complete and final but impossible to summarize in a simple manner. The education system of a single country may include, for example, public and private sectors; local, state, or national systems; varying grades, tracks, or forms within a single system; or opportunities for double-counting or fractional counting of a student, teacher, or institution. When no recent official data exist, or they exist, but may be suspect, the tables may show unofficial estimates, a range (of published opinion), analogous data, or no data at all.

The published basis of the information compiled is the statistical collections of Encyclopædia Britannica, Inc., some of the principal elements of which are enumerated in the Bibliography. Holdings for a given country may include any of the following: the national statistical abstract; the constitution; the most recent censuses of population; periodic or occasional reports on vital statistics, social indicators, agriculture, mining, labour, manufacturing, domestic and foreign trade, finance and banking, transportation, and communications. Further information is received in a variety of formats—telephone, letter, fax, microfilm and microfiche, and most recently, in electronic formats such as computer disks, CD-ROMs, and the Internet. So substantial has the resources of the Internet become that it was decided to add uniform resource locators (URLs) to the great majority of country pages and a number of the CNS tables (summary world sites with data on all countries still being somewhat of a rarity) so as to apprise the reader of the possibility and means to access current information on these subjects year-round.

The recommendations offered are usually to official sites (national statistical offices, general national governments, central banks, embassies, intergovernmental organizations [especially the UN Development Programme], and the like). Though often dissimilar in content, they will usually be updated year-round, expanded as opportunity permits, and lead on to related sites, such as parliamentary offices, information offices, diplomatic and consular sites, news agencies and newspapers, and, beyond, to the myriad academic, commercial, and private sites now accessible from the personal computer. While these URLs were correct and current at the time of writing, they may be subject to change.

The great majority of the social, economic, and financial data contained in this work should not be interpreted in isolation. Interpretive text of long perspective, such as that of the *Encyclopædia Britannica* itself; political, geographic, and topical maps, such as those in the *Britannica Atlas;* and recent analysis of political events and economic trends, such as that contained in the articles of the *Book of the Year,* will all help to supply analytic focus that numbers alone cannot. By the same token, study of those sources will be made more concrete by use of *Britannica World Data* to supply up-to-date geographic, demographic, and economic detail.

GLOSSARY

A number of terms that are used to classify and report data in the "Nations of the World" section require some explanation.

Those italicized terms that are used regularly in the country compilations to introduce specific categories of information (*e.g., birth rate, budget*) appear in this glossary in italic boldface type, followed by a description of the precise kind of information being offered and how it has been edited and presented.

All other terms are printed here in roman boldface type. Many terms have quite specific meanings in statistical reporting, and they are so defined here. Other terms have less specific application as they are used by different countries or organizations. Data in the country compilations based on definitions markedly different from those below will usually be footnoted.

Terms that appear in small capitals in certain definitions are themselves defined at their respective alphabetical locations.

Terms whose definitions are marked by an asterisk (*) refer to data supplied only in the larger two- to four-page country compilations.

access to services, a group of measures indicating a population's level of access to public services, including electrical power, treated public drinking water, sewage removal, and fire protection.*

activity rate, *see* participation/activity rates.

age breakdown, the distribution of a given population by age, usually reported here as percentages of total population in 15-year age brackets. When substantial numbers of persons do not know, or state, their exact age, distributions may not total 100.0%.

area, the total surface area of a country or its administrative subdivisions, including both land and inland (nontidal) water area. Land area is usually calculated from "mean low water" on a "plane table," or flat, basis.

area and population, a tabulation usually including the first-order administrative subdivisions of the country (such as the states of the United States), with capital (headquarters, or administrative seat), area, and population. When these subdivisions are especially numerous or, occasionally, nonexistent, a planning, electoral, census, or other nonadministrative scheme of regional subdivisions has been substituted.

associated state, *see* state.

atheist, in statements of religious affiliation, one who professes active opposition to religion; "nonreligious" refers to those professing only no religion, nonbelief, or doubt.

balance of payments, a financial statement for a country for a given period showing the balance among: (1) transactions in goods, services, and income between that country and the rest of the world, (2) changes in ownership or valuation of that country's monetary gold, SPECIAL DRAWING RIGHTS, and claims on and liabilities to the rest of the world, and (3) unrequited transfers and counterpart entries needed (in an accounting sense) to balance transactions and changes among any of the foregoing types of exchange that are not mutually offsetting. Detail of national law as to what constitutes a transaction, the basis of its valuation, and the size of a transaction visible to fiscal authorities all result in differences in the meaning of a particular national statement.*

balance of trade, the net value of all international goods trade of a country, usually excluding reexports (goods received only for transshipment), and the percentage that this net represents of total trade.

Balance of trade refers only to the "visible" international trade of goods as recorded by customs authorities and is thus a segment of a country's BALANCE OF PAYMENTS, which takes all visible and invisible trade with other countries into account. (Invisible trade refers to imports and exports of money, financial instruments, and services such as transport, tourism, and insurance.) A country has a favourable, or positive (+), balance of trade when the value of exports exceeds that of imports and negative (−) when imports exceed exports.

barrel (bbl), a unit of liquid measure. The barrel conventionally used for reporting crude petroleum and petroleum products is equal to 42 U.S. gallons, or 159 litres. The number of barrels of crude petroleum per metric ton, ranging typically from 6.20 to 8.13, depends upon the specific gravity of the petroleum. The world average is roughly 7.33 barrels per ton.

birth rate, the number of live births annually per 1,000 of midyear population. Birth rates for individual countries may be compared with the estimated world annual average of 22.5 births per 1,000 population in 2000.

budget, the annual receipts and expenditures— of a central government for its activities only;

Abbreviations

Measurements

cu m	cubic metre(s)
kg	kilograms(s)
km	kilometre(s)
kW	kilowatt(s)
kW-hr	kilowatt-hour(s)
metric ton-km	metric ton-kilometre(s)
mi	mile(s)
passenger-km	passenger-kilometre(s)
passenger-mi	passenger-mile(s)
short ton-mi	short ton-mile(s)
sq km	square kilometre(s)
sq m	square metre(s)
sq mi	square mile(s)
troy oz	troy ounce(s)
yr	year(s)

Political Units and International Organizations

ASEAN	Association of Southeast Asian Nations
CACM	Central American Common Market
Caricom	Caribbean Community and Common Market
CFA	Communauté Financière Africaine
CFP	Comptoirs Françaises du Pacifique
CIS	Commonwealth of Independent States
CUSA	Customs Union of Southern Africa
EC	European Communities
ESCWA	Economic and Social Commission for Western Asia
EU	European Union
FAO	United Nations Food and Agriculture Organization
IMF	International Monetary Fund
OECD	Organization for Economic Cooperation and Development
OECS	Organization of Eastern Caribbean States
Serb.–Mont.	Serbia and Montenegro

U.A.E.	United Arab Emirates
UNDP	United Nations Development Programme

Months

Jan.	January	Oct.	October
Feb.	February	Nov.	November
Aug.	August	Dec.	December
Sept.	September		

Miscellaneous

AIDS	Acquired Immune Deficiency Syndrome
avg.	average
c.i.f.	cost, insurance, and freight
commun.	communications
CPI	consumer price index
est.	estimate(d)
excl.	excluding
f.o.b.	free on board
GDP	gross domestic product
GNP	gross national product
govt.	government
incl.	including
mo.	month(s)
n.a.	not available (in text)
n.e.s.	not elsewhere specified
no.	number
pl.	plural
pos.	position
pub. admin.	public administration
SDR	Special Drawing Right
SITC	Standard International Trade Classification
svcs.	services
teacher tr.	teacher training
transp.	transportation
VAT	value-added taxes
voc.	vocational
$	dollar (of any currency area)
£	pound (of any currency area)
…	not available (in tables)
—	none, less than half the smallest unit shown, or not applicable (in tables)

does not include state, provincial, or local governments or semipublic (parastatal, quasi-nongovernmental) corporations unless otherwise specified. Figures for budgets are limited to ordinary (recurrent) receipts and expenditures, wherever possible, and exclude capital expenditures—*i.e.*, funds for development and other special projects originating as foreign-aid grants or loans.

When both a recurrent and a capital budget exist for a single country, the former is the budget funded entirely from national resources (taxes, duties, excises, etc.) that would recur (be generated by economic activity) every year. It funds the most basic governmental services, those least able to suffer interruption. The capital budget is usually funded by external aid and may change its size considerably from year to year.

capital, usually, the actual seat of government and administration of a state. When more than one capital exists, each is identified by kind; when interim arrangements exist during the creation or movement of a national capital, the de facto situation is described.

Anomalous cases are annotated, such as those in which (1) the de jure designation under the country's laws differs from actual local practice (*e.g.,* Benin's designation of one capital in constitutional law, but another in actual practice), (2) international recognition does not validate a country's claim (as with the proclamation by Israel of a capital on territory not internationally recognized as part of Israel), or (3) both a state and a capital have been proclaimed on territory recognized as part of another state (as with the Turkish Republic of Northern Cyprus).

capital budget, *see* budget.

causes of death, as defined by the World Health Organization (WHO), "the disease or injury which initiated the train of morbid events leading directly to death, or the circumstances of accident or violence which produced the fatal injury." This principle, the "underlying cause of death," is the basis of the medical judgment as to cause; the statistical classification system according to which these causes are grouped and named is the *International List of Causes of Death,* the latest revision of which is the Tenth. Reporting is usually in terms of events per 100,000 population. When data on actual causes of death are unavailable, information on morbidity, or illness rate, usually given as reported cases per 100,000 of infectious diseases (notifiable to WHO as a matter of international agreement), may be substituted.

chief of state/head of government, paramount national governmental officer(s) exercising the highest executive and/or ceremonial roles of a country's government. In general usage, the chief of state is the formal head of a national state. The primary responsibilities of the chief of state may range from the purely ceremonial—convening legislatures and greeting foreign officials—to the exercise of complete national executive authority. The head of government, when this function exists separately, is the officer nominally charged (by the constitution) with the majority of actual executive powers, though they may not in practice be exercised, especially in military or single-party regimes in which effective power may reside entirely outside the executive governmental machinery provided by the constitution. A prime minister, for example, usually the actual head of government, may in practice exercise only Cabinet-level authority.

In communist countries an official identified as the chief of state may be the chairman of the policy-making organ, and the official given as the head of government the chairman of the nominal administrative/executive organ.

c.i.f. (trade valuation): *see* imports.

colony, an area annexed to, or controlled by, an independent state but not an integral part of it; a non-self-governing territory. A colony has a charter and may have a degree of self-government. A crown colony is a colony originally chartered by the British government.

commonwealth (U.K. and U.S.), a self-governing political entity that has regard to the common weal, or good; usually associated with the United Kingdom or United States. Examples include the Commonwealth (composed of independent states [from 1931 onward]), Puerto Rico since 1952, and the Northern Marianas since 1979.

communications, collectively, the means available for the public transmission of information within a country. Data are tabulated for: daily newspapers and their total circulation; radio and television as total numbers of receivers; telephone data as "main lines," or the number of subscriber lines (not receivers) having access to the public switched network; cellular telephones as number of subscribers; and facsimile machines and personal computers as number of units. For each, a rate per 1,000 persons is given.

constant prices, an adjustment to the members of a financial time series to eliminate the effect of inflation year by year. It consists of referring all data in the series to a single year so that "real" change may be seen.

constitutional monarchy, *see* monarchy.

consumer price index (CPI), also known as the retail price index, or the cost-of-living index, a series of index numbers assigned to the price of a selected "basket," or assortment, of basic consumer goods and services in a country, region, city, or type of household in order to measure changes over time in prices paid by a typical household for those goods and services. Items included in the CPI are ordinarily determined by governmental surveys of typical household expenditures and are assigned weights relative to their proportion of those expenditures. Index values are period averages unless otherwise noted.

coprincipality, *see* monarchy.

current prices, the valuation of a financial aggregate as of the year reported.

daily per capita caloric intake (supply), the calories equivalent to the known average daily supply of foodstuffs for human consumption in a given country divided by the population of the country (and the proportion of that supply provided, respectively, by vegetable and animal sources). The daily per capita caloric intake of a country may be compared with the corresponding recommended minimum daily requirement. The latter is calculated by the Food and Agriculture Organization of the United Nations from the age and sex distributions, average body weights, and environmental temperatures in a given region to determine the calories needed to sustain a person there at normal levels of activity and health. The daily per capita caloric requirement ranges from 2,200 to 2,500.

de facto population, for a given area, the population composed of those actually present at a particular time, including temporary residents and visitors (such as immigrants not yet granted permanent status, "guest" or expatriate workers, refugees, or tourists), but excluding legal residents temporarily absent.

de jure population, for a given area, the population composed only of those legally resident at a particular time, excluding temporary residents and visitors (such as "guest" or expatriate workers, refugees, or tourists), but including legal residents temporarily absent.

deadweight tonnage, the maximum weight of cargo, fuel, fresh water, stores, and persons that may safely by carried by a ship. It is customarily measured in long tons of 2,240 pounds each, equivalent to 1.016 metric tons. Deadweight tonnage is the difference between the tonnage of a fully loaded ship and the fully unloaded tonnage of that ship.

See also gross ton.

death rate, the number of deaths annually per 1,000 of midyear population. Death rates for individual countries may be compared with the estimated world annual average of 9.0 deaths per 1,000 population in 2000.

density (of population), usually, the DE FACTO POPULATION of a country divided by its total area. Special adjustment is made for large areas of inland water, desert, or other uninhabitable areas—*e.g.,* excluding the ice cap of Greenland.

dependent state, constitutionally or statutorily organized political entity outside of and under the jurisdiction of an independent state (or a federal element of such a state) but not formally annexed to it (*see* Table).

Dependent states[1]

Australia
Christmas Island
Cocos (Keeling) Islands
Norfolk Island

Denmark
Faroe Islands
Greenland

France
French Guiana
French Polynesia
Guadeloupe
Martinique
Mayotte
New Caledonia
Réunion
Saint Pierre and Miquelon
Wallis and Futuna

Netherlands, The
Aruba
Netherlands Antilles

New Zealand
Cook Islands
Niue
Tokelau

United Kingdom
Anguilla
Bermuda
British Virgin Islands
Cayman Islands
Falkland Islands
Gibraltar
Guernsey
Isle of Man
Jersey
Montserrat
Pitcairn Island
Saint Helena and Dependencies
Turks and Caicos Islands

United States
American Samoa
Guam
Northern Mariana Islands
Puerto Rico
Virgin Islands (of the U.S.)

[1]Excludes territories (1) to which Antarctic Treaty is applicable in whole or in part, (2) without permanent civilian population, (3) without internationally recognized civilian government (Western Sahara, Gaza Strip), or (4) representing unadjudicated unilateral or multilateral territorial claims.

direct taxes, taxes levied directly on firms and individuals, such as taxes on income, profits, and capital gains. The *immediate* incidence, or burden, of direct taxes is on the firms and individuals thus taxed; direct taxes on firms may, however, be passed on to consumers and other economic units in the form of higher prices for goods and services, blurring the distinction between direct and indirect taxation.

distribution of income/wealth, the portion of personal income or wealth accruing to households or individuals constituting each respective decile (tenth) or quintile (fifth) of a country's households or individuals.*

divorce rate, the number of legal, civilly recognized divorces annually per 1,000 population.

doubling time, the number of complete years required for a country to double its population at its current rate of natural increase.

earnings index, a series of index numbers comparing average wages in a collective industrial sample for a country or region with the same industries at a previous period to measure changes over time in those wages. It is most commonly reported for wages paid on a daily, weekly, or monthly basis; annual figures may represent total income or averages of these shorter periods. The scope of the earnings index varies from country to country. The index is often limited to earnings in manufacturing industries. The index for each country applies to all wage earners in a designated group and ordinarily takes into account basic wages (overtime is normally distinguished), bonuses, cost-of-living allowances, and contributions toward social security. Some countries include payments in kind. Contributions toward social security by employers are usually excluded, as are social security benefits received by wage earners.

economically active population, *see* population economically active.

education, tabulation of the principal elements of a country's educational establishment, classified as far as possible according to the country's own system of primary, secondary, and higher levels (the usual age limits for these levels being identified in parentheses), with total number of schools (physical facilities) and of teachers and students (whether full- or part-time). The student-teacher ratio is calculated whenever available data permit.

educational attainment, the distribution of the population age 25 and over with completed educations by the highest level of formal education attained or completed; it must sometimes be reported, however, for age groups still in school or for the economically active only.

emirate, *see* monarchy.

enterprise, a legal entity formed to conduct a business, which it may do from more than one establishment (place of business or service point).

ethnic/linguistic composition, ethnic, racial, or linguistic composition of a national population, reported here according to the most reliable breakdown available, whether published in official sources (such as a census) or in external analysis (when the subject is not addressed in national sources).

exchange rate, the value of one currency compared with another, or with a standardized unit of account such as the SPECIAL DRAWING RIGHT, or as mandated by local statute when one currency is "tied" by a par value to another. Rates given usually refer to free market values when the currency has no, or very limited, restrictions on its convertibility into other currencies.

exports, material goods legally leaving a country (or customs area) and subject to customs regulations. The total value and distribution by percentage of the major items (in preference to groups of goods) exported are given, together with the distribution of trade among major

trading partners (usually single countries or trading blocs). Valuation of goods exported is free on board (f.o.b.) unless otherwise specified. The value of goods exported and imported f.o.b. is calculated from the cost of production and excludes the cost of transport.

external debt, public and publicly guaranteed debt with a maturity of more than one year owed to nonnationals of a country and repayable in foreign currency, goods, or services. The debt may be an obligation of a national or subnational governmental body (or an agency of either), of an autonomous public body, or of a private debtor that is guaranteed by a public entity. The debt is usually either outstanding (contracted) or disbursed (drawn).

external territory (Australia), *see* territory.

federal, consisting of first-order political subdivisions that are prior to and independent of the central government in certain functions.

federal republic, *see* republic.

federation, union of coequal, preexisting political entities that retain some degree of autonomy and (usually) right of secession within the union.

fertility rate, *see* total fertility rate.

financial aggregates, tabulation of seven-year time series, providing principal measures of the financial condition of a country, including: (1) the exchange rate of the national currency against the U.S. dollar, the pound sterling, and the International Monetary Fund's SPECIAL DRAWING RIGHT (SDR), (2) the amount and kind of international reserves (holdings of SDRs, gold, and foreign currencies) and reserve position of the country in the IMF, and (3) principal economic rates and prices (central bank discount rate, government bond yields, and industrial stock [share] prices). For BALANCE OF PAYMENTS, the origin in terms of component balance of trade items and balance of invisibles (net) is given.*

fish catch, the live-weight equivalent of the aquatic animals (including fish, crustaceans, mollusks, etc., but excluding whales, seals, and other aquatic mammals) caught in freshwater or marine areas by national fleets and landed in domestic or foreign harbours for commercial, industrial, or subsistence purposes.

f.o.b. (trade valuation), *see* exports.

food, *see* daily per capita caloric intake.

form of government/political status, the type of administration provided for by a country's constitution—whether or not suspended by extralegal military or civil action, although such de facto administrations are identified—together with the number of members (elected, appointed, and ex officio) for each legislative house, named according to its English rendering. Dependent states (*see* Table) are classified according to the status of their political association with the administering country.

gross domestic product (GDP), the total value of the final goods and services produced by residents and nonresidents within a given country during a given accounting period, usually a year. Unless otherwise noted, the value is given in current prices of the year indicated. The *System of National Accounts* (SNA, published under the joint auspices of the UN, IMF, OECD, EC, and World Bank) provides a framework for international comparability in classifying domestic accounting aggregates and international transactions comprising "net factor income from abroad," the measure that distinguishes GDP and GNP.

gross national product (GNP), the total value of final goods and services produced both from within a given country *and* from external (foreign) transactions in a given accounting period, usually a year. Unless otherwise noted, the value is given in current prices of the year indicated. GNP is equal to GROSS DOMESTIC PRODUCT (*q.v.*) adjusted by net factor income from abroad, which is the income residents

receive from abroad for factor services (labour, investment, and interest) less similar payments made to nonresidents who contribute to the domestic economy.

gross ton, volumetric unit of measure (equaling 100 cubic feet [2.83 cu m]) of the permanently enclosed volume of a ship, above and below decks available for cargo, stores, or passenger accommodation. Net, or register, tonnage exempts certain nonrevenue spaces—such as those devoted to machinery, bunkers, crew accommodations, and ballast—from the gross tonnage. *See also* deadweight tonnage.

head of government, see chief of state/head of government.

health, a group of measures including number of accredited physicians currently practicing or employed and their ratio to the total population; total hospital beds and their ratio; and INFANT MORTALITY RATE.

household, economically autonomous individual or group of individuals living in a single dwelling unit. A family household is one composed principally of individuals related by blood or marriage.

household income and expenditure, data for average size of a HOUSEHOLD (by number of individuals) and median household income. Sources of income and expenditures for major items of consumption are given as percentages.

In general, household income is the amount of funds, usually measured in monetary units, received by the members (generally those 14 years old and over) of a household in a given time period. The income can be derived from (1) wages or salaries, (2) nonfarm or farm SELF-EMPLOYMENT, (3) transfer payments, such as pensions, public assistance, unemployment benefits, etc., and (4) other income, including interest and dividends, rent, royalties, etc. The income of a household is expressed as a gross amount before deductions for taxes. Data on expenditure refer to consumption of personal or household goods and services; they normally exclude savings, taxes, and insurance; practice with regard to inclusion of credit purchases differs markedly.

immigration, usually, the number and origin of those immigrants admitted to a nation in a legal status that would eventually permit the granting of the right to settle permanently or to acquire citizenship.*

imports, material goods legally entering a country (or customs area) and subject to customs regulations; excludes financial movements. The total value and distribution by percentage of the major items (in preference to groups of goods) imported are given, together with the direction of trade among major trading partners (usually single countries), trading blocs (such as the European Union), or customs areas (such as Belgium-Luxembourg). The value of goods imported is given free on board (f.o.b.) unless otherwise specified; f.o.b. is defined above under EXPORTS.

The principal alternate basis for valuation of goods in international trade is that of cost, insurance, and freight (c.i.f.); its use is restricted to imports, as it comprises the principal charges needed to bring the goods to the customs house in the country of destination. Because it inflates the value of imports relative to exports, more countries have, latterly, been estimating imports on an f.o.b. basis as well.

incorporated territory (U.S.), *see* territory.

independent, of a state, autonomous and controlling both its internal and external affairs. Its date usually refers to the date from which the country was in effective control of these affairs within its present boundaries, rather than the date independence was proclaimed or the date recognized as a de jure act by the former administering power.

indirect taxes, taxes levied on sales or transfers of selected intermediate goods and services, including excises, value-added taxes, and tariffs, that are ordinarily passed on to the ultimate consumers of the goods and services. Figures given for individual countries are limited to indirect taxes levied by their respective central governments unless otherwise specified.

infant mortality rate, the number of children per 1,000 live births who die before their first birthday. Total infant mortality includes neonatal mortality, which is deaths of children within one month of birth.

invisibles (invisible trade), see balance of trade.

kingdom, see monarchy.

labour force, portion of the POPULATION ECONOMICALLY ACTIVE (PEA) comprising those most fully employed or attached to the labour market (the unemployed are considered to be "attached" in that they usually represent persons previously employed seeking to be reemployed), particularly as viewed from a short-term perspective. It normally includes those who are self-employed, employed by others (whether full-time, part-time, seasonally, or on some other less than full-time, basis) and, as noted above, the unemployed (both those previously employed and those seeking work for the first time). In the "gross domestic product and labour force" table, the majority of the labour data provided refer to population economically active, since PEA represents the longer-term view of working population and, thus, subsumes more of the marginal workers who are often missed by shorter-term surveys.

land use, distribution by classes of vegetational cover or economic use of the land area only (excluding inland water, built-up areas, and wasteland), reported as percentages. The principal categories utilized include: (1) arable land under temporary cultivation including land left fallow less than five years, (2) land under permanent cultivation (significantly tree crops but also grapes, pineapples, and bananas), (3) pastures and rangeland, which includes land in temporary or permanent use whose principal purpose is the growing of animal fodder, and (4) forest areas, whose definition overlaps with other land use classes per the FAO *State of the World's Forests;* forest areas include scrub forests, forest plantations, and recently afforested or reforested land.

life expectancy, the number of years a person born within a particular population group (age cohort) would be expected to live, based on actuarial calculations.

literacy, the ability to read and write a language with some degree of competence; the precise degree constituting the basis of a particular national statement is usually defined by the national census and is often tested by the census enumerator. Elsewhere, particularly where much adult literacy may be the result of literacy campaigns rather than passage through a formal educational system, definition and testing of literacy may be better standardized.

major cities, usually the five largest cities proper (national capitals are always given, regardless of size); fewer cities may be listed if there are fewer urban localities in the country. For multi-page tables, 10 or more may be listed.* Populations for cities will usually refer to the city proper—*i.e.,* the legally bounded corporate entity, or the most compact, contiguous, demographically urban portion of the entity defined by the local authorities. Occasionally figures for METROPOLITAN AREAS are cited when the relevant civil entity at the core of a major agglomeration had an unrepresentatively small population.

manufacturing, mining, and construction enterprises/retail sales and service enterprises, a detailed tabulation of the principal industries in these sectors, showing for each industry the number of enterprises and employees,

wages in that industry as a percentage of the general average wage, and the value of that industry's output in terms of value added or turnover.*

marriage rate, the number of legal, civilly recognized marriages annually per 1,000 population.

material well-being, a group of measures indicating the percentage of households or dwellings possessing certain goods or appliances, including automobiles, telephones, television receivers, refrigerators, air conditioners, and washing machines.*

merchant marine, the privately or publicly owned ships registered with the maritime authority of a nation (limited to those in Lloyd's of London statistical reporting of 100 or more GROSS TONS) that are employed in commerce, whether or not owned or operated by nationals of the country.

metropolitan area, a city and the region of dense, predominantly urban, settlement around the city; the population of the whole usually has strong economic and cultural affinities with the central city.

military expenditure, the apparent value of all identifiable military expenditure by the central government on hardware, personnel, pensions, research and development, etc., reported here both as a percentage of the GNP, with a comparison to the world average, and as a per capita value in U.S. dollars.

military personnel, see total active duty personnel.

mobility, the rate at which individuals or households change dwellings, usually measured between censuses and including international as well as domestic migration.*

monarchy, a government in which the CHIEF OF STATE holds office, usually hereditarily and for life, but sometimes electively for a term. The state may be a coprincipality, emirate, kingdom, principality, sheikhdom, or sultanate. The powers of the monarch may range from absolute (*i.e.,* the monarch both reigns and rules) through various degrees of limitation of authority to nominal, as in a constitutional monarchy, in which the titular monarch reigns but others, as elected officials, effectively rule.

monetary unit, currency of issue, or that in official use in a given country; name, spelling, and abbreviation in English according to International Monetary Fund recommendations or local practice; name of the lesser, usually decimal, monetary unit constituting the main currency; and valuation in U.S. dollars and U.K. pounds sterling, usually according to free-market or commercial rates.

See also exchange rate.

natural increase, also called natural growth, or the balance of births and deaths, the excess of births over deaths in a population; the rate of natural increase is the difference between the BIRTH RATE and the DEATH RATE of a given population. The estimated world average during 2000 was 13.5 per 1,000 population, or 1.35% annually. Natural increase is added to the balance of migration to calculate the total growth of that population.

net material product, see material product.

nonreligious, see atheist.

official language(s), that (or those) prescribed by the national constitution for day-to-day conduct and publication of a country's official business or, when no explicit constitutional provision exists, that of the constitution itself, the national gazette (record of legislative activity), or like official documents. Other languages may have local protection, may be permitted in parliamentary debate or legal action (such as a trial), or may be "national languages," for the protection of which special provisions have been made, but these are not deemed official. The United States, for example, does not yet formally identify English as "official," though it uses it for virtually all official purposes.

official name, the local official form(s), short or long, of a country's legal name(s) taken from the country's constitution or from other official documents. The English-language form is usually the protocol form in use by the country, the U.S. Department of State, and the United Nations.

official religion, generally, any religion prescribed or given special status or protection by the constitution or legal system of a country. Identification as such is not confined to constitutional documents utilizing the term explicitly.

organized territory (U.S.), see territory.

overseas department (France), see department.

overseas territory (France), see territory.

parliamentary state, see state.

part of a realm, a dependent Dutch political entity with some degree of self-government and having a special status above that of a colony (*e.g.,* the prerogative of rejecting for local application any law enacted by The Netherlands).

participation/activity rates, measures defining differential rates of economic activity within a population. Participation rate refers to the percentage of those employed or economically active who possess a particular characteristic (sex, age, etc.); activity rate refers to the fraction of the total population who *are* economically active.

passenger-miles, or **passenger-kilometres,** aggregate measure of passenger carriage by a specified means of transportation, equal to the number of passengers carried multiplied by the number of miles (or kilometres) each is transported. Figures given for countries are often calculated from ticket sales and ordinarily exclude passengers carried free of charge.

people's republic, see republic.

place of birth/national origin, if the former, numbers of native- and foreign-born population of a country by actual place of birth; if the latter, any of several classifications, including those based on origin of passport at original admission to country, on cultural heritage of family name, on self-designated (often multiple) origin of (some) ancestors, and on other systems for assigning national origin.*

political status, see form of government/political status.

population, the number of persons present within a country, city, or other civil entity at the date of a census of population, survey, cumulation of a civil register, or other enumeration. Unless otherwise specified, populations given are DE FACTO, referring to those actually present, rather than DE JURE, those legally resident but not necessarily present on the referent date. If a time series, noncensus year, or per capita ratio referring to a country's total population is cited, it will usually refer to midyear of the calendar year indicated.

population economically active, the total number of persons (above a set age for economic labour, usually 10–15 years) in all employment statuses—self-employed, wage- or salary-earning, part-time, seasonal, unemployed, etc. The International Labour Organisation defines the economically active as "all persons of either sex who furnish the supply of labour for the production of economic goods and services." National practices vary as regards the treatment of such groups as armed forces, inmates of institutions, persons seeking their first job, unpaid family workers, seasonal workers and persons engaged in part-time economic activities. In some countries, all or part of these groups may be included among the economically active, while in other countries the same groups may be treated as inactive. In general, however, the data on economically active population do not include students, persons occupied solely in family or household work, retired persons, persons living entirely on their own means, and persons wholly dependent upon others.

See also labour force.

population projection, the expected population in the years 2010 and 2020, embodying the country's own projections wherever possible. Estimates of the future size of a population are usually based on assumed levels of fertility, mortality, and migration. Projections in the tables, unless otherwise specified, are medium (*i.e.,* most likely) variants, whether based on external estimates by the United Nations, World Bank, or U.S. Department of Commerce or on those of the country itself.

price and earnings indexes, tabulation comparing the change in the CONSUMER PRICE INDEX over a period of seven years with the change in the general labour force's EARNINGS INDEX for the same period.

principality, see monarchy.

production, the physical quantity or monetary value of the output of an industry, usually tabulated here as the most important items or groups of items (depending on the available detail) of primary (extractive) and secondary (manufactured) production, including construction. When a single consistent measure of value, such as VALUE ADDED, can be obtained, this is given, ranked by value; otherwise, and more usually, quantity of production is given.

public debt, the current outstanding debt of all periods of maturity for which the central government and its organs are obligated. Publicly guaranteed private debt is excluded. For countries that report debt under the World Bank Debtor Reporting System (DRS), figures for outstanding, long-term EXTERNAL DEBT are given.

quality of working life, a group of measures including weekly hours of work (including overtime); rates per 100,000 for job-connected injury, illness, and mortality; coverage of labour force by insurance for injury, permanent disability, and death; workdays lost to labour strikes and stoppages; and commuting patterns (length of journey to work in minutes and usual method of transportation).*

railroads, mode of transportation by self-driven or locomotive-drawn cars over fixed rails. Length-of-track figures include all mainline and spurline running track but exclude switching sidings and yard track. Route length, when given, does not compound multiple running tracks laid on the same trackbed.

recurrent budget, *see* budget.

religious affiliation, distribution of nominal religionists, whether practicing or not, as a percentage of total population. This usually assigns to children the religion of their parents.

republic, a state with elected leaders and a centralized presidential form of government, local subdivisions being subordinate to the national government. A *federal republic* (as distinguished from a unitary republic) is a republic in which power is divided between the central government and the constituent subnational administrative divisions (*e.g.,* states, provinces, or cantons) in whom the central government itself is held to originate, the division of power being defined in a written constitution and jurisdictional disputes usually being settled in a court; sovereignty usually rests with the authority that has the power to amend the constitution. A *unitary republic* (as distinguished from a federal republic) is a republic in which power originates in a central authority and is not derived from constituent subdivisions. A *people's republic,* in the dialectics of Communism, is the first stage of development toward a communist state, the second stage being a *socialist republic.* An *Islamic republic* is structured around social, ethical, legal, and religious precepts central to the Islamic faith.

retail price index, *see* consumer price index.

retail sales and service enterprises, *see* manufacturing, mining, and construction enterprises/retail sales and service enterprises.

roundwood, wood obtained from removals from forests, felled or harvested (with or without bark), in all forms.

rural, see urban-rural.

self-employment, work in which income derives from direct employment in one's own business, trade, or profession, as opposed to work in which salary or wages are earned from an employer.

self-governing, of a state, in control of its internal affairs in degrees ranging from control of most internal affairs (though perhaps not of public order or of internal security) to complete control of all internal affairs (*i.e.,* the state is autonomous) but having no control of external affairs or defense. In this work the term self-governing refers to the final stage in the successive stages of increasing self-government that generally precede independence.

service/trade enterprises, see manufacturing, mining, and construction enterprises/retail sales and service enterprises.

sex distribution, ratios, calculated as percentages, of male and female population to total population.

sheikhdom, *see* monarchy.

social deviance, a group of measures, usually reported as rates per 100,000 for principal categories of socially deviant behaviour, including specified crimes, alcoholism, drug abuse, and suicide.*

social participation, a group of measures indicative of the degree of social engagement displayed by a particular population, including rates of participation in such activities as elections, voluntary work or memberships, trade unions, and religion.*

social security, public programs designed to protect individuals and families from loss of income owing to unemployment, old age, sickness or disability, or death and to provide other services such as medical care, health and welfare programs, or income maintenance.

socialist republic, *see* republic.

sources of income, *see* household income and expenditure.

Special Drawing Right (SDR), a unit of account utilized by the International Monetary Fund (IMF) to denominate monetary reserves available under a quota system to IMF members to maintain the value of their national currency unit in international transactions.*

state, in international law, a political entity possessing the attributes of: territory, permanent civilian population, government, and the capacity to conduct relations with other states. Though the term is sometimes limited in meaning to fully independent and internationally recognized states, the more general sense of an entity possessing a *preponderance* of these characteristics is intended here. It is, thus, also a first-order civil administrative subdivision, especially of a federated union. An associated state is an autonomous state in free association with another that conducts its external affairs and defense; the association may be terminated in full independence at the instance of the autonomous state in consultation with the administering power. A *parliamentary state* is an independent state of the Commonwealth that is governed by a parliament and that may recognize the British monarch as its titular head.

structure of gross domestic product and labour force, tabulation of the principal elements of the national economy, according to standard industrial categories, together with the corresponding distribution of the labour force (when possible POPULATION ECONOMICALLY ACTIVE) that generates the GROSS DOMESTIC PRODUCT.

sultanate, *see* monarchy.

territory, a noncategorized political dependency; a first-order administrative subdivision; a dependent political entity with some degree of self-government, but with fewer rights and less autonomy than a colony because there is no charter. An *external territory* (Australia) is a territory situated outside the area of the country. An *organized territory* (U.S.) is a territory for which a system of laws and a settled government have been provided by an act of the United States Congress. An *overseas territory* (France) is an overseas subdivision of the French Republic with elected representation in the French Parliament, having individual statutes, laws, and internal organization adapted to local conditions.

ton-miles, or ton-kilometres, aggregate measure of freight hauled by a specified means of transportation, equal to tons of freight multiplied by the miles (or kilometres) each ton is transported. Figures are compiled from waybills (nationally) and ordinarily exclude mail, specie, passengers' baggage, the fuel and stores of the conveyance, and goods carried free.

total active duty personnel, full-time active duty military personnel (excluding militias and part-time, informal, or other paramilitary elements), with their distribution by percentages among the major services.

total fertility rate, the sum of the current age-specific birth rates for each of the child-bearing years (usually 15–49). It is the probable number of births, given present fertility data, that would occur during the lifetime of each woman should she live to the end of her child-bearing years.

tourism, service industry comprising activities connected with domestic and international travel for pleasure or recreation; confined here to international travel and reported as expenditures in U.S. dollars by tourists of all nationalities visiting a particular country and, conversely, the estimated expenditures of that country's nationals in all countries of destination.

transfer payments, *see* household income and expenditure.

transport, all mechanical methods of moving persons or goods. Data reported for national establishments include: for railroads, length of track and volume of traffic for passengers and cargo (but excluding mail, etc.); for roads, length of network and numbers of passenger cars and of commercial vehicles (*i.e.,* trucks and buses); for merchant marine, the number of vessels of more than 100 gross tons and their total deadweight tonnage; for air transport, traffic data for passengers and cargo and the number of airports with scheduled flights.

unincorporated territory (U.S.), *see* territory.

unitary republic, see republic.

urban-rural, social characteristic of local or national populations, defined by predominant economic activities, "urban" referring to a group of largely nonagricultural pursuits, "rural" to agriculturally oriented employment patterns. The distinction is usually based on the country's own definition of urban, which may depend only upon the size (population) of a place or upon factors like employment, administrative status, density of housing, etc.

value added, also called value added by manufacture, the gross output value of a firm or industry minus the cost of inputs—raw materials, supplies, and payments to other firms—required to produce it. Value added is the portion of the sales value or gross output value that is actually created by the firm or industry. Value added generally includes labour costs, administrative costs, and operating profits.

The Nations of the World

Afghanistan

Official name: Islamic Republic of Afghanistan (Jomhūrī-ye Eslāmī-ye Afghānestān [Dari]); Da Afghanestan Eslami Jamhuriyat (Pashto)[1].
Form of government: Islamic republic[1] with two legislative bodies (House of Elders [102]; House of the People [249]).
Head of state and government: President.
Capital: Kabul.
Official languages: Dari; Pashto[2].
Official religion: Islam.
Monetary unit: 1 (new) afghani (Af) = 100 puls (puli); valuation (Sept. 1, 2005) 1 U.S.$ = Af 43.00; 1 £ = Af 79.17[3].

Population (2003–04 estimate)

Province	population ('000)	Province	population ('000)	Province	population ('000)
Badakhshān	725.7	Kābol (Kabul)	3,445.0	Paktīkā	357.3
Bādghīs	305.6	Kandahār	913.9	Parvān[4]	737.2
Bāghlān	726.6	Kāpīsā	364.9	Samangān	318.5
Balkh	949.6	Khowst	304.6	Sar-e Pol	474.8
Bāmīān	391.7	Konar	328.1	Takhār	761.4
Farāh	343.4	Kondūz	833.2	Uruzgān	636.0
Fāryāb	794.1	Laghmān	378.1	Vardak	448.7
Ghaznī	914.8	Lowgar	315.4	Zābol	249.1
Ghowr	492.4	Nangarhār	1,105.7	**Other**	
Helmand	756.4	Nīmrūz	151.5	nomadic pop.	1,500.0
Herāt	1,208.0	Nūrestān	111.0	TOTAL	22,191.5
Jowzjān	447.5	Paktīā	401.3		

Demography

Area: 249,347 sq mi, 645,807 sq km.
Population (2005): 23,867,000[5].
Density (2005): persons per sq mi 95.7, persons per sq km 37.0.
Urban-rural (2003): urban 22.4%; rural 77.6%.
Sex distribution (2004): male 51.19%; female 48.81%.
Age breakdown (2004): under 15, 44.7%; 15–29, 26.8%; 30–44, 15.9%; 45–59, 8.5%; 60–74, 3.5%; 75 and over, 0.6%.
Population projection: (2010) 28,926,000; (2020) 38,981,000.
Ethnolinguistic composition (2000): Pashtun *c.* 49%; Tajik *c.* 18%; Ḥazāra *c.* 9%; Uzbek *c.* 8%; Chahar Aimak *c.* 4%; Turkmen *c.* 3%; other *c.* 9%.
Religious affiliation (2000): Sunnī Muslim 89.2%; Shīʿī Muslim 8.9%; Zoroastrian 1.4%; Hindu 0.4%; other 0.1%.
Major cities (2003–04): Kabul 2,799,300[6]; Kandahār (Qandahār) 323,900; Herāt 254,800; Mazār-e Sharīf 187,700; Jalālābād 97,900.

Vital statistics

Birth rate per 1,000 population (2004): 47.3 (world avg. 21.1).
Death rate per 1,000 population (2004): 21.1 (world avg. 9.0).
Total fertility rate (avg. births per childbearing woman; 2004): 6.8.
Life expectancy at birth (2004): male 42.3 years; female 42.7 years.

National economy

Budget (2003–04). Revenue: U.S.$208,000,000[7] (tax revenue 63.0%, of which import duties 53.4%; nontax revenue 37.0%). Expenditures: U.S.$2,826,-000,000 (development expenditure 84.0%; current expenditure 16.0%).
Gross domestic product (2003): U.S.$7,000,000,000[8] (U.S.$340 per capita).

Structure of gross domestic product and labour force

	2003		1992–93	
	in value U.S.$'000,000	% of total value	labour force	% of labour force
Agriculture (legal)	2,310	33.0	} 4,276,100	67.2
Opium (illegal)	2,450	35.0		
Mining	—	—		
Manufacturing	630	9.0	} 298,900	4.7
Public utilities	} 560	8.0		
Transp. and commun.			139,900	2.2
Construction	210	3.0	81,400	1.3
Trade	420	6.0	420,600	6.6
Pub. administration	210	3.0	} 929,300	14.6
Services	210	3.0		
Other	—	—	214,300	3.4
TOTAL	7,000	100.0	6,360,500	100.0

Public debt (external, outstanding; 2000): U.S.$5,319,000,000.
Production (metric tons except as noted). Agriculture, forestry, fishing (2003): wheat 4,361,000, grapes 558,000, rice 434,000, barley 410,000, corn (maize) 310,000, sugarcane 83,000, opium poppy (2004) 4,200[9]; livestock (number of live animals) 8,700,000 sheep, 7,200,000 goats, 3,600,000 cattle; roundwood 1,415,474 cu m; fish catch (2001) 800. Mining and quarrying:

salt (2000) 13,000; gemstones (2004) n.a. Manufacturing (by production value in [old] Af '000,000; 1988–89): food products 4,019; leather and fur products 2,678; textiles 1,760; printing and publishing 1,070; industrial chemicals 1,053. Energy production (consumption): electricity (kW-hr; 2003) 805,000,000 (721,000,000); coal (metric tons; 2002) 1,000 (1,000); petroleum products (metric tons; 2002) none (115,000); natural gas (cu m; 2002) 108,915,000 (108,915,000).
Household income and expenditure (2003). Average household size 8.0; sources of income: wages and salaries 49%, self-employed 47%, other 4%.
Population economically active (1994)[10]: total 5,557,000; activity rate of total population 29.4% (participation rates: female 9.0%; unemployed [2004] *c.* 30%).

Price index (March 2001 = 100)

	2001	2002	2003	2004
Consumer price index[11]	100.0	143.4	218.4	241.3

Tourism (1997): receipts U.S.$1,000,000; expenditures U.S.$1,000,000.
Land use as % of total land area (2000): in temporary crops 12.1%, in permanent crops 0.2%, in pasture 46.0%; overall forest area 2.1%.

Foreign trade[12]

Balance of trade (current prices)

	2001–02	2002–03	2003–04
U.S.$'000,000	−1,628	−2,352	−1,957
% of total	92.3%	92.2%	87.2%

Imports (2003–04): U.S.$2,101,000,000 (machinery and equipment 22.8%, fabrics, clothing, and footwear 16.2%, food 14.7%, chemicals 10.5%). *Major import sources:* China 18.2%; Japan 14.2%; Pakistan 8.6%; India 5.8%.
Exports (2003–04): U.S.$144,000,000 (dried fruits 41.0%, skins 20.1%, carpets and handicrafts 14.6%). *Major export destinations:* Pakistan 68.9%; India 7.6%; Russia 5.6%.

Transport and communications

Transport. Railroads (2002): 25 km. Roads (2001): total length 20,720 km (paved 12%). Vehicles (2003–04): passenger cars 176,723; trucks and buses 116,278. Air transport: passenger-km (2000) 143,000,000; (2000) metric ton-km cargo 21,000,000; airports (2002) 2.

Communications

Medium	date	unit	number	units per 1,000 persons
Daily newspapers	2000	circulation	129,000	5.0
Radio	2000	receivers	2,950,000	114
Television	2000	receivers	362,000	14
Telephones	2003	main lines	36,700	1.8
Cellular telephones	2003	subscribers	135,000	6.5
Internet	2003	users	700	0.03

Education and health

Educational attainment: n.a. Literacy (2003)[10]: total population age 15 and over literate 29%; males 43%; females 14%.

Education (2003)

	schools	teachers	students	student/teacher ratio
Primary	4,876[13]	58,312[13]	3,900,000	52.9[13]
Secondary	1,994[13]	34,271[13]	400,000	18.1[13]
Higher[14]	1	462	13,000	28.1

Health (2002): physicians 3,617 (1 per 5,675 persons); hospital beds 12,668 (1 per 1,620 persons); infant mortality rate per 1,000 live births (2004) 166.0.
Food (2003): daily per capita caloric intake 2,802 ([1999] vegetable products 79%, animal products 21%); 114% of FAO recommended minimum.

Military

Total active duty personnel (August 2004): 13,000 (army 100%); size of planned army is 65,000, size of planned air force 8,000[15]. *Military expenditure as percentage of GDP* (2003): *c.* 9%; per capita expenditure *c.* U.S.$28.

[1]From promulgation of new constitution on Jan. 26, 2004. [2]Six additional locally official languages per the 2004 constitution are Uzbek, Turkmen, Balochi, Kafiri (Nuristani), Pashai, and Pamiri. [3]The afghani was re-denominated on Oct. 7, 2002; from that date 100 (old) afghanis equaled 1 (new) afghani. [4]Includes Panjsher province created May 2004. [5]Excludes Afghan refugees in Pakistan and Iran and other Afghans abroad; includes 1.5 million nomads. [6]Urban agglomeration. [7]Domestic revenue only; excludes heavy reliance on foreign assistance. [8]$1/3$ of which is illegal opiate receipts. [9]Represents 87% of world production. [10]Based on settled population only. [11]March 21 to March 20 fiscal year. [12]Per Afghan authorities; exports are f.o.b. and imports are c.i.f. [13]2002. [14]University of Kabul only. [15]Foreign troops (March 2005): 8,000-member, NATO-controlled International Security Assistance Force (ISAF) and the 17,000-member, non-ISAF U.S. troops searching for al-Qaeda and Taliban fighters.

Internet resources for further information:
• **Central Statistics Office http://www.aims.org.af/cso/index.htm**

Albania

Official name: Republika e Shqipërisë (Republic of Albania).
Form of government: unitary multiparty republic with one legislative house (Assembly [140]).
Chief of state: President.
Head of government: Prime Minister.
Capital: Tirana (Tiranë).
Official language: Albanian.
Official religion: none.
Monetary unit: 1 lek = 100 qindars; valuation (Sept. 1, 2005)
1 U.S.$ = 99.50 leks;
1 £ = 183.20 leks.

Area and population

Provinces	Capitals	area sq mi	area sq km	population 2001 census
Berat	Berat	353	915	127,837
Bulqizë	Bulqizë	277	718	42,968
Delvinë	Delvinë	142	367	10,765
Devoll	Bilisht	166	429	34,641
Dibër	Peshkopi	294	761	85,699
Durrës	Durrës	176	455	181,662
Elbasan	Elbasan	498	1,290	221,635
Fier	Fier	328	850	199,082
Gjirokastër	Gjirokastër	439	1,137	54,647
Gramsh	Gramsh	268	695	35,750
Has	Krumë	144	374	19,660
Kavajë	Kavajë	152	393	78,179
Kolonjë	Ersekë	311	805	17,161
Korçë	Korçë	676	1,752	142,909
Krujë	Krujë	144	372	63,517
Kuçovë	Kuçovë	43	112	35,338
Kukës	Kukës	369	956	63,786
Kurbin[1]	Laç	91	235	54,392
Lezhë	Lezhë	185	479	67,734
Librazhd	Librazhd	425	1,102	72,387
Lushnjë	Lushnjë	275	712	143,933
Malësi e Madhe	Koplic	346	897	36,692
Mallakastër	Ballsh	125	325	39,529
Mat	Burrel	397	1,028	61,187
Mirditë	Rrëshen	335	867	37,056
Peqin	Peqin	74	191	32,964
Përmet	Përmet	359	929	25,780
Pogradec	Pogradec	280	725	70,471
Pukë	Pukë	399	1,034	34,386
Sarandë	Sarandë	282	730	35,089
Shkodër	Shkodër	630	1,631	185,395
Skrapar	Çorovoda	299	775	29,845
Tepelenë	Tepelenë	315	817	32,404
Tiranë	Tirana (Tiranë)	461	1,193	519,720
Tropojë	Bajram	403	1,043	27,947
Vlorë	Vlorë	621	1,609	147,128
TOTAL		11,082	28,703	3,069,275

Demography

Population (2005): 3,130,000.
Density (2005): persons per sq mi 282.4, persons per sq km 109.0.
Urban-rural (2001): urban 42.1%; rural 57.9%.
Sex distribution (2001): male 49.88%; female 50.12%.
Age breakdown (2004): under 15, 26.4%; 15–29, 26.3%; 30–44, 20.3%; 45–59, 15.0%; 60–74, 9.0%; 75 and over, 3.0%.
Population projection: (2010) 3,216,000; (2020) 3,420,000.
Ethnic composition (2000): Albanian 91.7%; Vlach (Aromanian) 3.6%; Greek 2.3%; other 2.4%.
Religious affiliation (2000): Muslim 38.8%; Roman Catholic 16.7%; nonreligious 16.6%; Albanian Orthodox 10.4%; other Orthodox 5.7%; other 11.8%.
Major cities (2001): Tirana (Tiranë) 343,078; Durrës 99,546; Elbasan 87,797; Shkodër 82,455; Vlorë 77,691.

Vital statistics

Birth rate per 1,000 population (2004): 15.1 (world avg. 21.1).
Death rate per 1,000 population (2004): 5.0 (world avg. 9.0).
Natural increase rate per 1,000 population (2003): 10.1 (world avg. 12.1).
Total fertility rate (avg. births per childbearing woman; 2003): 2.1.
Life expectancy at birth (2003): male 72.1 years; female 78.6 years.

National economy

Budget (2002). Revenue: 153,197,000,000 leks (tax revenue 67.3%, of which taxes on goods and services 43.9%, income taxes 13.6%, taxes on international trade 8.7%; nontax revenue 16.3%; grants 2.7%; other revenue 13.7%). Expenditures: 187,109,000,000 leks (general public services 26.2%, of which public debt transactions 13.2%; social protection 24.7%; economic affairs 15.0%; education 10.2%; health 7.3%; defense 4.0%).
Production (metric tons except as noted). Agriculture, forestry, fishing (2004): vegetables and melons 667,000, cereals 527,100, potatoes 175,000; livestock (number of live animals) 1,800,000 sheep, 1,025,000 goats, 700,000 cattle, 4,300,000 chickens; roundwood (2003) 296,200 cu m; fish catch (2002) 3,955. Mining and quarrying (2003): chromium ore 85,000. Manufacturing (value added in U.S.$'000,000; 2001): textiles 17; glass products 14; leather (all forms) 11; iron and steel 11; office machinery 9. Energy production (consumption): electricity (kW-hr; 2002) 3,686,000,000 (5,791,000,000); lignite (metric tons; 2002) 87,000 (100,000); crude petroleum (barrels; 2002) 2,591,000 (2,591,000); petroleum products (metric tons; 2002) 204,000 (795,000); natural gas (cu m; 2002) 13,941,000 (13,941,000).

Gross national product (2004): U.S.$6,641,000,000 (U.S.$2,080 per capita).

Structure of gross domestic product and labour force

	2002 in value '000,000 leks	2002 % of total value	2001 labour force	2001 % of labour force
Agriculture	219,100	33.3	767,000	61.7
Manufacturing, mining, public utilities	84,200	12.8	55,000	4.4
Construction	71,100	10.8	13,000	1.0
Transp. and commun.	69,700	10.6	24,000	1.9
Trade			56,000	4.5
Pub. admin., defense	214,000	32.5	148,000	11.9
Services				
Other			181,000[2]	14.5[2]
TOTAL	658,100	100.0	1,244,000	100.0[3]

Public debt (2003): U.S.$1,230,000,000.
Population economically active (2002): total 1,318,114; activity rate of total population 42.4% (participation rates: ages 15–64, 65.9%; female 43.7%; unemployed [2004] 14.6%).

Price and earnings indexes (2000 = 100)

	1998	1999	2000	2001	2002	2003	2004
Consumer price index	99.6	99.9	100.0	103.0	108.5	111.0	114.1
Monthly earnings index[4]	82.6	91.7	100.0	120.1	122.4	...	...

Household income and expenditure (2000). Average household size (2002): 4.2; sources of income[5]: wages and salaries 64.2%, self-employment 15.7%, transfers 14.8%; expenditure[5]: food, beverages, and tobacco 57.8%, transportation and communications 7.9%, housing and energy 6.9%.
Tourism (2003): receipts U.S.$522,000,000; expenditures U.S.$489,000,000.
Land use as % of total land area (2000): in temporary crops 21.1%, in permanent crops 4.4%, in pasture 16.2%; overall forest area 36.2%.

Foreign trade[6]

Balance of trade (current prices)

	1998	1999	2000	2001	2002	2003
U.S.$'000,000	−604	−663	−814	−1,033	−1,157	−1,411
% of total	59.2%	54.6%	61.4%	62.9%	63.6%	61.3%

Imports (2003): U.S.$1,857,000,000 (nonelectrical and electrical machinery 15.3%; mineral products 11.8%; textiles and clothing 10.9%; base and fabricated metals 9.5%). *Major import sources:* Italy 33.6%; Greece 20.1%; Germany 5.7%; China 3.5%.
Exports (2003): U.S.$446,000,000 (textiles and clothing 34.8%; footwear, headgear, and umbrellas 29.9%; base and fabricated metals 11.1%). *Major export destinations:* Italy 74.9%; Greece 12.8%; Germany 3.4%.

Transport and communications

Transport. Railroads (2001): length 670 km; passenger-km 138,000,000; metric ton-km cargo 19,000. Roads (2002): total length 18,000 km (paved 39%). Vehicles (2002): passenger cars 148,531; trucks and buses 72,986. Air transport (2003)[7]: passenger-km 121,061,000, passenger-mi 75,224,000; short ton-mi, none, metric ton-km; none; airports (2002) 1.

Communications

Medium	date	unit	number	units per 1,000 persons
Daily newspapers	2000	circulation	109,000	35
Radio	2000	receivers	756,000	243
Television	2001	receivers	480,000	157
Telephones	2003	main lines	255,000	83
Cellular telephones	2003	subscribers	1,100,000	358
Internet	2003	users	30,000	9.8

Education and health

Educational attainment (1989). Population age 10 and over having: primary education 65.3%; secondary 29.1%; higher 5.6%. *Literacy* (2001): total population age 10 and over literate 85.3%; males 92.5%; females 77.8%.

Education (2000–01)

	schools	teachers	students[8]	student/ teacher ratio
Primary (age 6–13)	1,811[9]	28,293	523,253	18.5
Secondary (age 14–17)	409[9]	5,760	100,082	17.3
Voc., teacher tr.	...	2,174[10]	18,495	8.5[10]
Higher	10	1,683	42,160	24.3

Health: physicians (2002) 4,100 (1 per 753 persons); hospital beds (2003) 9,514 (1 per 327 persons); infant mortality rate per 1,000 live births (2003) 16.8.
Food (2002): daily per capita caloric intake 2,848 (vegetable products 71%, animal products 29%); 118% of FAO recommended minimum requirement.

Military

Total active duty personnel (2004): 21,500 (army 74.4%, navy 9.3%, air force 16.3%). *Military expenditure as percentage of GDP* (2003): 1.2%; per capita expenditure U.S.$25.

[1]Name changed from Laç to Kurbin in 1999. [2]Unemployed. [3]Detail does not add to total given because of rounding. [4]Manufacturing only. [5]Urban areas only. [6]Imports c.i.f.; exports f.o.b. [7]Albanian Air only. [8]2001–02. [9]1997–98. [10]1996.

Internet resources for further information:
• Albanian Economic Development Agency http://www.aeda.gov.al
• Instituti i Statistikës http://www.instat.gov.al

Algeria

Official name: Al-Jumhūrīyah al-Jazāʾirīyah ad-Dīmuqrāṭīyah ash-Shaʿbīyah (Arabic) (People's Democratic Republic of Algeria).
Form of government: multiparty republic with two legislative bodies (Council of the Nation [144][1]; National People's Assembly [389]).
Chief of state: President.
Head of government: Prime Minister.
Capital: Algiers.
Official language: Arabic[2].
Official religion: Islam.
Monetary unit: 1 Algerian dinar (DA) = 100 centimes; valuation (Sept. 1, 2005) 1 U.S.$ = DA 72.28; 1 £ = DA 133.09.

Population (1998 census)

Provinces	population	Provinces	population	Provinces	population
Adrar	313,417	El-Bayadh	172,957	Ouargla	444,683
Aïn Defla	658,897	El-Oued	525,083	Oum el-Bouaghi	529,540
Aïn Temouchent	337,570	Et-Tarf	350,789	Relizane	646,175
Alger	2,423,694	Ghardaïa	311,678	Saïda	313,351
Annaba	559,898	Guelma	444,231	Sétif	1,299,116
Batna	987,475	Illizi	34,189	Sidi bel-Abbès	535,634
Béchar	232,012	Jijel	582,865	Skikda	793,146
Bejaïa	836,301	Khenchela	345,009	Souk Ahras	365,106
Biskra	568,701	Laghouat	326,862	Tamanrasset	138,704
Blida	796,616	Mascara	651,239	Tébessa	565,125
Bordj Bou Arreridj	561,471	Médéa	859,273	Tiaret	770,194
Bouira	637,042	Mila	663,578	Tindouf	27,053
Boumerdes	608,806	Mostaganem	636,884	Tipaza	507,959
Constantine	807,371	M'Sila	835,701	Tissemsilt	274,380
Djelfa	805,298	Naâma	131,846	Tizi Ouzou	1,100,297
Ech-Cheliff	874,917	Oran	1,208,171	Tlemcen	873,039
				TOTAL	29,273,343

Demography

Area: 919,595 sq mi, 2,381,741 sq km.
Population (2005): 32,854,000.
Density (2005): persons per sq mi 35.7, persons per sq km 13.8.
Urban-rural (1998): urban 80.8%; rural 19.2%.
Sex distribution (2004): male 50.40%; female 49.60%.
Age breakdown (2004): under 15, 29.9%; 15–29, 32.3%; 30–44, 20.6%; 45–59, 10.6%; 60–74, 5.0%; 75 and over, 1.6%.
Population projection: (2010) 35,420,000; (2020) 40,624,000.
Doubling time: 53 years.
Ethnic composition (2000): Algerian Arab 59.1%; Berber 26.2%, of which Arabized Berber 3.0%; Bedouin Arab 14.5%; other 0.2%.
Religious affiliation (2000): Muslim 99.7%, of which Sunnī 99.1%, Ibāḍīyah 0.6%; Christian 0.3%.
Major cities (1998): Algiers 1,519,570; Oran 692,516; Constantine 462,187; Annaba 348,554; Batna 242,514; Blida 226,512; Sétif 211,859.

Vital statistics

Birth rate per 1,000 population (2004): 17.8 (world avg. 21.1).
Death rate per 1,000 population (2004): 4.6 (world avg. 9.0).
Natural increase rate per 1,000 population (2004): 13.2 (world avg. 12.1).
Total fertility rate (avg. births per childbearing woman; 2004): 2.0.
Marriage rate per 1,000 population (2002): 7.0.
Life expectancy at birth (2004): male 71.2 years; female 74.3 years.
Notified cases of infectious diseases per 100,000 population (1996): measles 67.8; typhoid fever 15.2; hepatitis 11.3; dysentery 10.1; meningitis 9.4.

National economy

Budget (2003). Revenue: DA 1,966,600,000,000 (hydrocarbon revenue 68.7%, nonhydrocarbon revenue 31.3%). Expenditures: DA 1,752,700,000,000 (current expenditure 68.4%, capital expenditure 31.6%).
Public debt (external, outstanding; 2003): U.S.$21,741,000,000.
Production (metric tons except as noted). Agriculture, forestry, fishing (2004): wheat 2,600,000, potatoes 1,800,000, barley 1,200,000, tomatoes 820,000, dates 450,000, onions 450,000, oranges 360,000, grapes 280,000, olives 170,000; livestock (number of live animals) 18,700,000 sheep, 3,200,000 goats; roundwood (2003) 7,523,973 cu m; fish catch (2002) 134,320. Mining and quarrying (2004): iron ore 1,414,000; phosphate rock 784,000; zinc (metal content; 2003) 5,201; mercury 90. Manufacturing (value added in U.S.$'000,000; 1997): food products 463; cement, bricks, and tiles 393; iron and steel 118; tobacco products 114; paints, soaps, and related products 105; electrical machinery 79. Energy production (consumption): electricity (kW-hr; 2004) 30,885,000,000 (25,909,000,000); coal (metric tons; 2002) none (894,000); crude petroleum (barrels; 2002) 361,890,000 (163,117,000); petroleum products (metric tons; 2002) 41,458,000 (10,179,000); natural gas (cu m; 2002) 81,227,000,000 (22,942,000,000).
Land use as % of total land area (2000): in temporary crops 3.2%, in permanent crops 0.2%, in pasture 13.4%; overall forest area 0.9%.
Household income and expenditure. Average household size (2002) 6.2; disposable income per household (2002) c. U.S.$5,700; sources of income (2003): self-employment 40.5%, wages and salaries 38.9%, transfers 20.6%; expenditure (1989)[3]: food and beverages 44.1%, clothing and footwear 11.6%, transportation and communications 11.5%, furniture 6.8%.
Gross national product (2004): U.S.$73,676,000,000 (U.S.$2,280 per capita).

Structure of gross domestic product and labour force

	2000		2002	
	in value DA '000,000	% of total value	labour force	% of labour force
Agriculture	325,751	8.0	1,438,000	15.5
Petroleum and natural gas	1,666,236[4]	40.9[4]		
Other mining	5,022	0.1	504,000	5.4
Manufacturing	234,624[4]	5.8[4]		
Public utilities	44,108	1.0		
Construction	292,046	7.2	860,000	9.2
Transp. and commun.	272,697	6.7		
Trade, restaurants	478,840	11.7	1,157,000	12.4
Finance, real estate	194,698	4.8		
Services				
Pub. admin., defense	359,744	8.8	1,476,000	15.9
Other	204,909[5]	5.0[5]	3,868,000[6]	41.6[6]
TOTAL	4,078,675	100.0	9,303,000	100.0

Population economically active (2002): total 9,303,000; activity rate of population 29.2% (participation rates: ages 15–64 [1998] 52.6%; female, n.a.; unemployed [2003] 23.7%).

Price index (2000 = 100)

	1998	1999	2000	2001	2002	2003	2004
Consumer price index	98.6	100.6	100.0	103.5	105.8	109.5	114.5

Tourism: receipts from visitors (2003) U.S.$161,000,000; expenditures by nationals abroad (2002) U.S.$248,000,000.

Foreign trade

Balance of trade (current prices)

	1998	1999	2000	2001	2002	2003
U.S.$'000,000	+435	+3,363	+12,879	+9,609	+6,690	+11,147
% of total	2.4%	15.5%	41.3%	33.6%	21.8%	29.6%

Imports (2003): U.S.$13,322,000,000 (industrial equipment 34.9%, semifinished products 20.1%, food 18.9%, consumer goods 14.9%). *Major import sources* (2002): France 22.7%; U.S. 9.8%; Italy 9.6%; Germany 7.2%; Spain 5.3%.
Exports (2003): U.S.$24,469,000,000 (crude petroleum 31.6%, natural and manufactured gas 30.7%, condensate 14.6%, refined petroleum 12.3%). *Major export destinations* (2002): Italy 20.1%; U.S. 14.2%; France 13.6%; Spain 12.1%; The Netherlands 9.0%; Turkey 5.1%; Canada 5.0%.

Transport and communications

Transport. Railroads (2003): route length 2,468 mi, 3,973 km; (2000) passenger-km 1,142,000,000; metric ton-km cargo 2,029,000,000. Roads (1999): total length 64,600 mi, 104,000 km (paved 69%). Vehicles (2001): passenger cars 1,692,148; trucks and buses 948,553. Air transport (2003)[7]: passenger-km 3,343,000,000; metric ton-km cargo 19,091,000; airports (1996) 28.

Communications

Medium	date	unit	number	units per 1,000 persons
Daily newspapers	2000	circulation	817,000	27
Radio	2000	receivers	7,380,000	244
Television	2000	receivers	3,300,000	110
Telephones	2003	main lines	2,199,600	69
Cellular telephones	2003	subscribers	1,447,310	45
Personal computers	2003	units	242,000	7.6
Internet	2004	users	500,000	15.5

Education and health

Educational attainment (1998). Percentage of economically active population age 6 and over having: no formal schooling 30.1%; primary education 29.9%; lower secondary 20.7%; upper secondary 13.4%; higher 4.3%; other 1.6%.
Literacy (1998): total population age 10 and over literate 15,314,109 (68.1%); males literate 8,650,719 (76.3%); females literate 6,663,392 (59.7%).

Education (1996–97)

	schools	teachers	students	student/ teacher ratio
Primary (age 6–11)	15,426	170,956	4,674,947	27.3
Secondary (age 12–17)	3,954[8]	151,948	2,618,242	17.2
Higher[8]	...	19,910	347,410	17.4

Health: physicians (2002) 28,642 (1 per 1,095 persons); hospital beds (1996) 34,544 (1 per 827 persons); infant mortality rate per 1,000 live births (2004) 32.2.
Food (2002): daily per capita caloric intake 3,022 (vegetable products 90%, animal products 10%); 126% of FAO recommended minimum requirement.

Military

Total active duty personnel (2004): 127,500 (army 86.3%, navy 5.9%, air force 7.8%). *Military expenditure as percentage of GDP* (2003): 3.3%; per capita expenditure U.S.$69.

---

[1]Includes 48 nonelected seats appointed by the president. [2]The Berber language, Tamazight, became a national language in April 2002. [3]Weights of consumer price index components; Algiers only. [4]Petroleum and natural gas includes (and Manufacturing excludes) refined petroleum and manufacture of hydrocarbons. [5]Import taxes and duties. [6]Includes 2,412,000 unemployed and 1,456,000 military draft and irregular employment. [7]Air Algérie. [8]1995–96.

Internet resources for further information:
• Statistiques Algérie http://www.ons.dz/them_sta.htm

American Samoa

Official name: American Samoa (English); Amerika Samoa (Samoan).
Political status: unincorporated and unorganized territory of the United States with two legislative houses (Senate [18]; House of Representatives [20]).
Chief of state: President of the United States.
Head of government: Governor.
Capital: Fagatogo[1] (legislative and judicial) and Utulei (executive).
Official languages: English; Samoan.
Official religion: none.
Monetary unit: 1 dollar (U.S.$) = 100 cents; valuation (Sept. 1, 2005) 1 U.S.$ = £0.54.

Area and population	area		population
			2000
Districts and islands	sq mi	sq km	census
Eastern District	25.9	67.1	23,441
Tutuila Island (part)	25.3	65.5	21,673
Aunu'u Island	0.6	1.6	1,768
Western District	28.8	74.6	32,435
Tutuila Island (part)	28.8	74.6	32,435
Manu'a District (Manu'a Islands)	21.9	56.7	1,378
Ofu Island	2.8	7.2	289
Olosega Island	2.0	5.2	216
Ta'u Island	17.1	44.3	873
Rose Island[2]	0.1	0.3	0
Swains Island[2]	0.6	1.5	37
LAND AREA	77.3	200.2	—
INLAND WATER (HARBOUR) AREAS	7.1	18.4	—
TOTAL AREA	84.4	218.6	57,291

Demography

Population (2005): 63,900.
Density (2005)[3]: persons per sq mi 826.6, persons per sq km 319.2.
Urban-rural (2003): urban 54.0%; rural 46.0%.
Sex distribution (2000): male 51.08%; female 48.92%.
Age breakdown (2000): under 15, 38.8%; 15–29, 25.5%; 30–44, 19.4%; 45–59, 10.8%; 60–74, 4.5%; 75 and over, 1.0%.
Population projection: (2010) 71,000; (2020) 86,000.
Doubling time: 33 years.
Ethnic composition (2000): Samoan 88.2%; Tongan 2.8%; Asian 2.8%; Caucasian 1.1%; other 5.1%.
Religious affiliation (1995): 4 major Protestant groups 60.1%; Roman Catholic 19.4%; Mormon 12.5%; other 8.0%.
Major villages (2000): Tafuna 8,406; Nu'uuli 5,154; Pago Pago 4,278 (urban agglomeration [2001] 15,000); Leone 3,568; Fagatogo 2,096[1].

Vital statistics

Birth rate per 1,000 population (2004): 24.5 (world avg. 21.1); legitimate (2001) 71.7%; illegitimate 28.3%.
Death rate per 1,000 population (2004): 3.4 (world avg. 9.0).
Natural increase rate per 1,000 population (2004): 21.1 (world avg. 12.1).
Total fertility rate (avg. births per childbearing woman; 2004): 3.4.
Marriage rate per 1,000 population (2000): 4.7.
Divorce rate per 1,000 population (1993): 0.5.
Life expectancy at birth (2004): male 72.1 years; female 79.4 years.
Major causes of death per 100,000 population (2002): diseases of the circulatory system 147; malignant neoplasms (cancers) 62; diabetes mellitus 48; injuries 43; diseases of the respiratory system 18.

National economy

Budget (1997). Revenue: U.S.$144,438,095 (U.S. government grants 67.4%; taxes 23.6%; insurance claims 4.9%; other 4.1%). Expenditures: U.S.$152,912,308 (education and culture 28.5%; health and welfare 27.3%; general government 14.1%; public works and parks 12.8%; public safety 6.9%; economic development 6.1%; capital projects 3.4%; debt 0.9%).
Gross national product (2000): U.S.$379,000,000 (U.S.$6,320 per capita).

Structure of labour force		
	2000	
	labour force	% of labour force
Agriculture, forestry, and fishing	517	2.9
Manufacturing	5,900	33.4
Construction	1,066	6.0
Transp. and commun.	1,036	5.9
Trade	1,790	10.1
Finance, real estate	311	1.8
Public administration	1,550	8.8
Services	4,548	25.7
Other	946[4]	5.4
TOTAL	17,664	100.0

Production (metric tons except as noted). Agriculture, forestry, fishing (2004): coconuts 4,700, taros 1,500, fruits (excluding melons) 1,195, bananas 750, vegetables and melons 490; livestock (number of live animals) 10,500 pigs, 38,000 chickens; forestry, n.a.; fish catch (2002) 6,963, of which tunas, bonitos, and billfish 6,925. Mining and quarrying: n.a. Manufacturing (value of export in U.S.$; 2003): canned tuna 467,700,000; pet food 9,800,000; other manufactures include garments, handicrafts, soap, and alcoholic beverages. Construction (value of building permits in U.S.$; 2000) 12,801,000. Energy production (consumption): electricity (kW-hr; 2002) 135,000,000 (135,000,000); coal, none (n.a.); crude petroleum, none (n.a.); petroleum products (metric tons; 2002) none (93,000); natural gas, none (n.a.).
Public debt: n.a.
Population economically active (2000): total 17,664, activity rate of total population 30.8% (participation rates: ages 16 and over 52.0%; female 41.5%; unemployed 5.1%).

Price index (2000 = 100)						
	2000	2001	2002	2003	2004	2005[5]
Consumer price index[6]	100.0	101.4	103.5	108.6	116.4	120.2

Household income and expenditure. Average household size (2000) 6.0; income per household (2000): U.S.$24,000; sources of income: n.a.; expenditure (1995): food and beverages 30.9%, housing and furnishings 25.8%, church donations 20.7%, transportation and communications 9.4%, clothing 2.9%, other 10.3%.
Tourism: receipts from visitors (1998) U.S.$10,000,000; expenditures by nationals abroad (1996) U.S.$2,000,000.
Land use as % of total land area (2000): in temporary crops c. 10%, in permanent crops c. 15%, in pasture, n.a.; overall forest area c. 60%.

Foreign trade[7]

Balance of trade (current prices)						
	1996	1997	1998	1999	2000	2001
U.S.$'000,000	−157.8	−104.3	−83.4	−107.5	−159.6	−203.0
% of total	20.1%	10.9%	9.1%	13.5%	18.7%	24.2%

Imports (2001): U.S.$520,000,000 (fish for cannery 50.9%, consumer goods 16.4%, other food 12.8%, mineral fuels 5.0%). *Major import sources* (2000): United States 56.7%; Australia 14.9%; New Zealand 11.1%; Fiji 5.7%; Samoa 3.1%.
Exports (2001)[7]: U.S.$317,000,000 (tuna in airtight containers 86.3%, fish meal 8.9%, pet food 4.8%). *Major export destination* (2000): United States 99.6%.

Transport and communications

Transport. Railroads: none. Roads (1991): total length 217 mi, 350 km (paved, 43%). Vehicles (2001): passenger cars 6,579; trucks and buses 625. Air transport (2001): passenger arrivals 74,543; passenger departures 81,669; cargo unloaded 897 metric tons, cargo loaded 659 metric tons; incoming cargo 890 metric tons; airports (2000) with scheduled flights 3.

Communications				units per 1,000
Medium	date	unit	number	persons
Daily newspapers	2000	circulation	4,900	85
Radio	1997	receivers	57,000	929
Television	2000	receivers	13,200	211
Telephones	2002	main lines	14,700	252
Cellular telephones	2001	subscribers	2,156	38

Education and health

Educational attainment (2000). Percentage of population age 25 and over having: no formal schooling to some secondary education 33.9%; completed secondary 39.3%; some college 19.4%; undergraduate degree 4.8%; graduate degree 2.6%. *Literacy* (2000): total population age 10 and over literate 33,993 (99.4%); males literate 17,704 (99.4%); females literate 16,589 (99.5%).

Education (2001)				student/
	schools	teachers	students	teacher ratio
Primary (age 6–14)	32	...	11,343	...
Secondary (age 14–18)	10	...	4,217	...
Vocational[8]	...	21	160	7.6
Higher[9]	1	77	1,178	15.3

Health (2003): physicians 49 (1 per 1,253 persons); hospital beds 128 (1 per 480 persons); infant mortality rate per 1,000 live births (2004) 9.5.
Food: daily per capita caloric intake, n.a.

Military

Military defense is the responsibility of the United States.

[1]The seat of the legislature, as defined by the Constitution of American Samoa, is at Fagatogo, one of a number of villages within an urban agglomeration collectively known as Pago Pago. [2]Not within district administrative structure. Swains Island is administered by a village government and a representative of the governor. [3]Based on land area. [4]Includes 909 unemployed and 37 in military. [5]First quarter average. [6]Excludes rent. [7]Based on exports to the United States only. [8]1997–98. [9]American Samoa Community College at Mapusaga.

Internet resources for further information:
• U.S. Department of the Interior: Pacific Web http://www.pacificweb.org
• Bank of Hawaii: Economics Research Center http://www.boh.com/econ/pacific
• American Samoa Government Department of Commerce http://www.amsamoa.com

Andorra

Official name: Principat d'Andorra (Principality of Andorra).
Form of government: parliamentary coprincipality with one legislative house (General Council [28]).
Chiefs of state: President of France; Bishop of Urgell, Spain.
Head of government: Head of Government.
Capital: Andorra la Vella.
Official language: Catalan.
Official religion: none[1].
Monetary unit[2]: 1 euro (€) = 100 cents; valuation (Sept. 1, 2005) 1 U.S.$ = €0.80; 1 £ = €1.47.

Area and population		area		population
				2003
Parishes	**Capitals**	sq mi	sq km	estimate
Andorra la Vella	Andorra la Vella	11	27	22,035
Canillo	Canillo	47	121	3,707
Encamp	Encamp	29	74	11,832
La Massana	La Massana	23	61	7,264
Les Escaldes–Engordany	—	12	32	16,402
Ordino	Ordino	34	89	2,767
Sant Julià de Lòria	Sant Julià de Lòria	23	60	8,313
TOTAL		179	464	72,320

Demography

Population (2005): 74,800.
Density (2005): persons per sq mi 417.9, persons per sq km 161.2.
Urban-rural (2003): urban 93%; rural 7%.
Sex distribution (2003): male 51.97%; female 48.03%.
Age breakdown (2003): under 15, 14.9%; 15–29, 18.9%; 30–44, 29.1%; 45–59, 20.3%; 60–74, 10.7%; 75 and over, 6.1%.
Population projection: (2010) 78,000; (2020) 82,000.
Doubling time: 100 years.
Ethnic composition (by nationality; 2003): Spanish 38.3%; Andorran 36.7%; Portuguese 11.5%; French 6.5%; British 1.4%; Moroccan 0.7%; German 0.5%; other 4.4%.
Religious affiliation (2000): Roman Catholic 89.1%; other Christian 4.3%; Muslim 0.6%; Hindu 0.5%; nonreligious 5.0%; other 0.5%.
Major urban areas (2002[3]): Andorra la Vella 20,787; Les Escaldes–Engordany 15,519; Encamp 10,627.

Vital statistics

Birth rate per 1,000 population (2003): 10.0 (world avg. 21.1).
Death rate per 1,000 population (2003): 3.1 (world avg. 9.0).
Natural increase rate per 1,000 population (2003): 6.9 (world avg. 12.1).
Total fertility rate (avg. births per childbearing woman; 2004): 1.3.
Marriage rate per 1,000 population (2003): 2.7.
Life expectancy at birth (2004): male 80.6 years; female 86.6 years.
Major causes of death per 100,000 population (1998–2002 avg.): malignant neoplasms (cancers) 107.2; diseases of the circulatory system 93.6; injuries and poisoning 30.8; diseases of the respiratory system 26.9; diseases of the digestive system 19.9.

National economy

Budget (2003). Revenue: €246,610,000 (indirect taxes 75.0%, taxes from government enterprises 15.6%, revenue from capital 9.4%). Expenditures: €253,835,000 (current expenditures 51.3%, of which education 13.9%, tourism 7.7%, public order 6.5%, health 4.3%, environment 3.5%; development expenditures 48.7%).
Production. Agriculture (2002): tobacco 319 metric tons; other traditional crops include hay, potatoes, and grapes; livestock (number of live animals; 2002–03) 2,807 sheep[4], 1,428 cattle, 830 horses, 459 goats. Quarrying: small amounts of marble are quarried. Manufacturing (value of recorded exports in €'000; 2003): motor vehicles and parts 17,513; electrical machinery and apparatus 11,433; optical, photographic, and measuring apparatus 10,658; fabricated metal products 6,107; perfumery and cosmetic preparations 5,008. Construction (approved new building construction; 2002): 309,918 sq m. Energy production (consumption): electricity (kW-hr; 2003) 95,200,000 ([2004] 526,000,000); coal, none (n.a.); crude petroleum, none (n.a.); petroleum products, none ([2000] 201,677,000 litres); natural gas, none (n.a.).
Household expenditure (1997)[5]: food, beverages, and tobacco 25.5%, housing and energy 19.4%, transportation 17.7%, clothing and footwear 9.2%.
Land use as % of total land area (2000): in temporary and permanent crops c. 4%, in pasture c. 45%; overall forest area c. 35%.
Population economically active (2003): total 39,372; activity rate of total population 54.5% (participation rates: ages 15–64, 75.1%; female, n.a.; unemployed, n.a.[6]).

Price and earnings indexes (1997 = 100)[7]							
	1996	1997	1998	1999	2000	2001	2002
Consumer price index	...	100.0	101.6	104.3	108.9	111.9	115.7
Annual earnings index	98.6	100.0	101.6	103.7	105.8	...	...

Gross domestic product (at current market prices; 2001): U.S.$1,462,000,000 (U.S.$22,120 per capita)[8].

Structure of labour force		
	2003	
	labour force	% of labour force
Agriculture	134	0.3
Mining	...	...
Manufacturing	1,573	4.0
Construction	5,862	14.9
Public utilities	156	0.4
Transp. and commun.	1,496	3.8
Trade[9]	11,087	28.2
Restaurants, hotels	5,393	13.7
Finance, real estate, insurance	4,789	12.2
Pub. admin., defense	3,620	9.2
Services	4,794	12.2
Other	470	1.2
TOTAL	39,374[10]	100.0[11]

Public debt (1995): c. U.S.$500,000,000.
Tourism (2004): 11,668,460 visitors; number of hotels (2003) 272.

Foreign trade

Balance of trade (current prices)						
	1998	1999	2000	2001	2002	2003
€'000,000	–918	–989	–1,054	–1,103	–1,204	–1,258
% of total	89.9%	92.5%	91.4%	90.4%	90.3%	88.9%

Imports (2003): €1,337,100,000 (food, beverages, and tobacco 19.1%; chemicals and chemical products 15.6%; machinery and apparatus 13.5%; transport equipment 10.3%; textiles and wearing apparel 8.9%; photographic and optical goods and watches and clocks 5.1%). *Major import sources:* Spain 54.1%; France 25.7%; Germany 5.4%; Italy 3.5%; U.K. 1.9%.
Exports (2003): €78,960,000 (motor vehicles and parts 22.3%; electrical machinery and apparatus 22.2%; optical and photo equipment 14.1%; chemicals and chemical products 8.0%; textiles and clothing 4.8%). *Major export destinations:* Spain 55.7%; France 19.2%; Germany 12.4%.

Transport and communications

Transport. Railroads: none; however, both French and Spanish railways stop near the border. Roads (1999): total length 167 mi, 269 km (paved 74%). Vehicles (2003): passenger cars 46,560; trucks and buses 4,246. Airports with scheduled flights: none.

Communications				units per 1,000
Medium	date	unit	number	persons
Daily newspapers	1996	circulation	4,000	62
Radio	1997	receivers	16,000	247
Television	2000	receivers	36,000	461
Telephones	2003	main lines	45,065	623
Cellular telephones	2003	subscribers	32,199	445
Internet	2001	users	24,500	371

Education and health

Educational attainment (mid-1980s). Percentage of population age 15 and over having: no formal schooling 5.5%; primary education 47.3%; secondary education 21.6%; postsecondary education 24.9%; unknown 0.7%. *Literacy:* resident population is virtually 100% literate.

Education (1999–2000)				student/
	schools	teachers	students	teacher ratio
Primary/lower secondary (age 7–15)	12	...	5,996	...
Upper secondary	6	...	1,136	...
Higher	1	...	1,341	...

Health (2003): physicians 244 (1 per 296 persons); hospital beds 233 (1 per 310 persons); infant mortality rate per 1,000 live births (1999–2001 avg.) 4.1.
Food: n.a.

Military

Total active duty personnel: none. France and Spain are responsible for Andorra's external security; the police force is assisted in alternate years by either French gendarmerie or Barcelona police. Andorra has no defense budget.

---

[1]Roman Catholicism enjoys special recognition in accordance with Andorran tradition. [2]The French franc and Spanish peseta were the former monetary units; on Jan. 1, 2002, F 6.56 = €1 and Pta 166.39 = €1. [3]January 1. [4]Large herds of sheep and goats from Spain and France feed in Andorra in the summer. [5]Weights of consumer price index components. [6]The restricted size of the indigenous labour force has in the near past necessitated immigration to serve the tourist trade. [7]All indexes are end of year. [8]Tourism (including winter-season sports, fairs, festivals, and income earned from low-duty imported manufactured items) and the banking system are the primary sources of GDP. [9]Includes motor vehicle maintenance and repair. [10]Sum total; reported total is 39,372. [11]Detail does not add to total given because of rounding.

Internet resources for further information:
• **Department d'Estudis i d'Estadística**
  http://www.finances.ad
• **Cambra de Comerç Indústria i Serveis d'Andorra**
  http://www.ccis.ad/index.htm

Angola

Official name: República de Angola (Republic of Angola).
Form of government: unitary multiparty republic with one legislative house (National Assembly [220])[1].
Head of state and government: President assisted by Prime Minister[2].
Capital: Luanda.
Official language: Portuguese.
Official religion: none.
Monetary unit: 1 refloated kwanza (Kz) = 100 lwei; valuation (Sept. 1, 2005) 1 U.S.$ = refloated kwanza 89.20; 1 £ = refloated kwanza 164.24.

Indian Ocean

Structure of gross domestic product and labour force				
	2003		1999	
	in value Kz '000,000	% of total value	labour force	% of labour force
Agriculture	79,579	7.7	4,132,000	72.1
Mining	549,284	53.0		
Manufacturing	37,063	3.6		
Construction	34,413	3.3		
Finance				
Trade				
Public utilities	154,772	14.9	1,597,000	27.9
Transp. and commun.				
Pub. admin., defense				
Services	155,832	15.0		
Other	26,097	2.5	...	...
TOTAL	1,037,040	100.0	5,729,000	100.0

Population economically active (1999): total 5,729,000; activity rate of total population 57.7% (participation rates over age 10 [1991] 60.1%; female 38.4%; unemployed [2002] 70%).

Price and earnings indexes (2000 = 100)					
	2000	2001	2002	2003	2004
Consumer price index	100.0	252.6	527.6	1,045.8	1,501.2
Monthly earnings index	...	...	...	...	...

Land use as % of total land area (2000): in temporary crops 2.4%, in permanent crops 0.2%, in pasture 43.3%; overall forest area 56.0%.

Area and population		area		population
				2004
Provinces	Capitals	sq mi	sq km	estimate
Bengo	Caxito	12,112	31,371	...
Benguela	Benguela	12,273	31,788	...
Bié	Kuito	27,148	70,314	...
Cabinda	Cabinda	2,807	7,270	...
Cunene	N'Giva	34,495	89,342	...
Huambo	Huambo	13,233	34,274	...
Huíla	Lubango	28,958	75,002	...
Kuando Kubango	Menongue	76,853	199,049	...
Kuanza Norte	N'Dalatando	9,340	24,190	...
Kuanza Sul	Sumbe	21,490	55,660	...
Luanda	Luanda	934	2,418	...
Lunda Norte	Lucapa	39,685	102,783	...
Lunda Sul	Saurimo	17,625	45,649	...
Malanje	Malanje	37,684	97,602	...
Moxico	Lwena	86,110	223,023	...
Namibe	Namibe	22,447	58,137	...
Uíge	Uíge	22,663	58,698	...
Zaire	M'Banza Kongo	15,494	40,130	...
TOTAL		481,354[3]	1,246,700	11,521,000

Demography

Population (2005): 11,827,000.
Density (2005): persons per sq mi 24.6, persons per sq km 9.5.
Urban-rural (2001): urban 34.9%; rural 65.1%.
Sex distribution (2004): male 50.52%; female 49.48%.
Age breakdown (2004): under 15, 43.5%; 15–29, 26.6%; 30–44, 16.8%; 45–59, 8.5%; 60–74, 4.0%; 75 and over, 0.6%.
Population projection: (2010) 13,262,000; (2020) 16,157,000.
Doubling time: 37 years.
Ethnic composition (2000): Ovimbundu 25.2%; Kimbundu 23.1%; Kongo 12.6%; Lwena (Luvale) 8.2%; Chokwe 5.0%; Kwanyama 4.1%; Nyaneka 3.9%; Luchazi 2.3%; Ambo (Ovambo) 2.0%; Mbwela 1.7%; Nyemba 1.7%; other 10.2%.
Religious affiliation (2001): Christian 94.1%, of which Roman Catholic 62.1%, Protestant 15.0%; traditional beliefs 5.0%; other 0.9%.
Major cities (2004): Luanda 2,783,000; Huambo 173,600; Lobito 137,400; Benguela 134,500; Namibe 132,900.

Vital statistics

Birth rate per 1,000 population (2004): 45.1 (world avg. 21.1).
Death rate per 1,000 population (2004): 25.9 (world avg. 9.0).
Natural increase rate per 1,000 population (2004): 19.2 (world avg. 12.1).
Total fertility rate (avg. births per childbearing woman; 2004): 6.3.
Life expectancy at birth (2004): male 36.1 years; female 37.6 years.
Major causes of death (percentage of total deaths; 1990): diarrheal diseases 25.8%; malaria 19.4%; cholera 7.3%; acute respiratory infections 6.8%.

National economy

Budget (2003). Revenue: U.S.$5,186,000,000 (oil revenue 75.0%; non-oil revenue 25.0%, of which tax on goods 7.8%, income tax 7.2%, import duties 5.9%, other 4.1%). Expenditure: U.S.$6,284,000,000 (social security 9.8%, education 6.8%, defense and internal security 6.4%, health 5.2%, interest payment 4.1%, other 67.7%).
Public debt (external, outstanding; 2003): U.S.$8,576,000,000.
Household income and expenditure. Average household size (2000) 4.7; annual income per household: n.a.; sources of income: n.a.; expenditure: n.a.
Production (metric tons except as noted). Agriculture, forestry, fishing (2004): cassava 5,600,000, corn (maize) 510,000, sweet potatoes 430,000, sugarcane 360,000, bananas 300,000, oil palm fruit 280,000, millet 96,000, dry beans 66,000, pineapples 40,000, peanuts (groundnuts) 30,000, coffee 1,250; livestock (number of live animals) 4,150,000 cattle, 2,050,000 goats, 780,000 pigs, 340,000 sheep, 6,800,000 chickens; roundwood (2003) 4,518,302 cu m; fish catch (2002) 260,797. Mining and quarrying (2003): diamonds 6,063,000 carats. Manufacturing (2000): fuel oils 1,064,000; cement 201,000; bread 105,000; wheat flour 69,000; frozen fish 41,600; beer (2002) 1,685,000 hectolitres. Energy production (consumption): electricity (kW-hr; 2002) 1,786,000,000 (1,786,000,000); coal, none (none); crude petroleum (barrels; 2002) 326,329,000 (15,300,000); petroleum products (metric tons; 2002) 1,829,000 (1,353,000); natural gas (cu m; 2002) 604,000,000 (604,000,000).
Tourism: receipts from visitors (2003) U.S.$71,000,000; expenditures by nationals abroad (2002) U.S.$19,000,000.
Gross national product (at current market prices; 2004): U.S.$14,441,000,000 (U.S.$1,030 per capita).

Foreign trade

Balance of trade (current prices)						
	1998	1999	2000	2001	2002	2003
U.S.$'000,000	+1,464	+2,077	+4,881	+3,355	+4,568	+4,028
% of total	26.0%	24.1%	44.5%	34.6%	37.8%	26.9%

Imports (2003): U.S.$5,480,000,000 (consumer goods 63.3%, capital goods 26.1%, intermediate goods 10.6%). *Major import sources:* Portugal 18.1%; South Africa 12.3%; U.S. 12.1%; The Netherlands 11.6%; France 6.5%.
Exports (2003): U.S.$9,508,000,000 (crude petroleum 89.8%, diamonds 8.3%, refined petroleum 1.4%, liquefied natural gas 0.2%). *Major export destinations:* U.S. 47.1%; China 23.1%; Taiwan 8.7%; France 7.3%; Belgium 3.1%.

Transport and communications

Transport. Railroads (2001): route length 1,722 mi, 2,771 km; (2001) passenger-km 3,722,300,000; metric ton-km cargo, n.a. Roads (2001): total length 31,956 mi, 51,429 km (paved 10%). Vehicles (2001): passenger cars 117,200; trucks and buses 118,300. Air transport (2001)[4]: passenger-mi 455,400,000, passenger-km 732,968,000; short ton-mi cargo 35,800,000, metric ton-km cargo 57,662,000; airports (1999) with scheduled flights 17.

Communications				units per 1,000 persons
Medium	date	unit	number	
Daily newspapers	2000	circulation	111,000	11
Television	2000	receivers	193,000	19
Telephones	2003	main lines	96,300	6.7
Cellular telephones	2002	subscribers	130,000	9.3
Personal computers	2002	units	27,000	1.9
Internet	2002	users	41,000	2.9

Education and health

Educational attainment: n.a. *Literacy* (1998): percentage of population age 15 and over literate 41.7%; males literate 55.6%; females literate 28.5%.

Education (1997–98)	schools	teachers	students	student/ teacher ratio
Primary (age 7–10)	...	31,062[5]	1,342,116	...
Secondary (age 11–16)	...	5,138[6]	267,399	...
Voc., teacher tr.	...	566[6]	...	...
Higher	...	776	8,337	10.7

Health (1997): physicians 736 (1 per 12,985 persons); hospital beds (1990) 11,857 (1 per 845 persons); infant mortality rate per 1,000 live births (2004) 192.5.
Food (2002): daily per capita caloric intake 2,083 (vegetable products 92%, animal products 8%); 89% of FAO recommended minimum requirement.

Military

Total active duty personnel (2004): 108,400 (army 92.3%, navy 2.2%, air force 5.5%). *Military expenditure as percentage of GDP* (2003): 4.7%; per capita expenditure U.S.$58.

---

[1]Civil war begun in 1975 was officially declared over on Aug. 2, 2002. A cease-fire agreement had been signed earlier in April 2002. [2]Post of Prime Minister abolished in January 1999 and reinstated in December 2002. [3]Detail does not add to total given because of rounding. [4]TAAG airline. [5]1991–92. [6]1989–90.

Internet resources for further information:
• **Official Home Page of the Republic of Angola** http://www.angola.org
• **Bank of Angola** http://www.bna.ao

Antigua and Barbuda

Official name: Antigua and Barbuda.
Form of government: constitutional monarchy with two legislative houses (Senate [17]; House of Representatives [17[1]]).
Chief of state: British Monarch represented by Governor-General.
Head of government: Prime Minister.
Capital: Saint John's.
Official language: English.
Official religion: none.
Monetary unit: 1 Eastern Caribbean dollar (EC$) = 100 cents; valuation (Sept. 1, 2005) 1 U.S.$ = EC$2.70; 1 £ = EC$4.97.

Area and population	area		population
			2001
Parishes (of Antigua)[2]	sq mi	sq km	census
Saint George	9.3	24.1	6,447
Saint John's (city)	2.9	7.5	24,061
Saint John's (rural)	25.6	66.3	21,371
Saint Mary	22.0	57.0	6,475
Saint Paul	18.5	47.9	7,779
Saint Peter	12.7	32.9	4,817
Saint Phillip	17.0	44.0	3,352
Other islands[2]			
Barbuda	62.0	160.6	1,439
Redonda	0.5	1.3	0
TOTAL	170.5	441.6	75,741[3]

Demography

Population (2005): 77,800.
Density (2005): persons per sq mi 456.3, persons per sq km 176.2.
Urban-rural (2001): urban 36.9%; rural 63.1%.
Sex distribution (2001): male 47.56%; female 52.44%.
Age breakdown (2001): under 15, 26.4%; 15–29, 25.4%; 30–44, 23.9%; 45–59, 13.9%; 60 and over, 10.4%.
Population projection: (2010) 80,000; (2020) 84,000.
Ethnic composition (2000): black 82.4%; U.S. white 12.0%; mulatto 3.5%; British 1.3%; other 0.8%.
Religious affiliation (1991): Protestant 73.7%, of which Anglican 32.1%, Moravian 12.0%, Methodist 9.1%, Seventh-day Adventist 8.8%; Roman Catholic 10.8%; Jehovah's Witness 1.2%; Rastafarian 0.8%[4]; other religion/no religion/not stated 13.5%.
Major city (2004): Saint John's 23,600[5].

Vital statistics

Birth rate per 1,000 population (2004): 17.7 (world avg. 21.1); (2001) legitimate 25.7%; illegitimate 74.3%.
Death rate per 1,000 population (2004): 5.6 (world avg. 9.0).
Natural increase rate per 1,000 population (2004): 12.1 (world avg. 12.1).
Total fertility rate (avg. births per childbearing woman; 2004): 2.3.
Marriage rate per 1,000 population (2001): 23.6.
Life expectancy at birth (2004): male 69.3 years; female 74.1 years.
Major causes of death per 100,000 population (1999): diseases of the circulatory system 296, of which hypertension 102; malignant neoplasms (cancers) 111; diabetes mellitus 53; accidents and injuries 52.

National economy

Budget (2002). Revenue: EC$418,000,000 (tax revenue 92.9%, of which taxes on international transactions 49.8%, consumption taxes 18.9%, corporate income taxes 14.7%; grants 4.3%; other 2.8%). Expenditures: EC$535,-500,000 (current expenditures 94.5%, of which interest payments 10.8%; development expenditures 5.5%).
Public debt (external, outstanding; 2004): more than U.S.$740,000,000.
Production (metric tons except as noted). Agriculture, forestry, fishing (2004): tropical fruit (including papayas, guavas, soursops, and oranges) 7,900, mangoes 1,430, eggplants 340, lemons and limes 285, carrots 240, "Antiguan Black" pineapples 210; livestock (number of live animals) 19,000 sheep, 14,300 cattle; roundwood, n.a.; fish catch (2001) 1,583. Mining and quarrying: crushed stone for local use. Manufacturing (1994): beer and malt 166,000 cases; T-shirts 179,000 units; other manufactures include cement, handicrafts, and furniture, as well as electronic components for export. Energy production (consumption): electricity (kW-hr; 2002) 105,000,000 (105,000,000); coal, none (none); crude petroleum, none (none); petroleum products (metric tons; 2002) negligible (121,000); natural gas, none (none).
Population economically active (1991): total 26,753; activity rate of total population 45.1% (participation rates: ages 15–64, 69.7%; female 45.6%; unemployed [2001] 11.0%).

Price and earnings indexes (1996 = 100)						
	1996	1997	1998	1999	2000	2001
Consumer price index	100.0	98.9	103.6	104.4	104.6	106.3
Annual earnings index[6]	100.0	100.0	106.0	106.0	106.0	106.0

Household income and expenditure (2001). Average household size 3.1; income per household: n.a.; sources of income: n.a.; expenditure[7]: housing 21.8%, food 21.4%, transportation and communications 15.4%, household furnishings 12.6%, clothing and footwear 11.1%.

Gross national product (2004): U.S.$800,000,000 (U.S.$10,000 per capita).

Structure of gross domestic product and labour force				
	2003		1991	
	in value EC$'000,000	% of total value	labour force	% of labour force
Agriculture, fishing	65.2	3.2	1,040	3.9
Quarrying	29.8	1.5	64	0.2
Manufacturing	40.1	2.0	1,444	5.4
Construction	243.9	11.9	3,109	11.6
Public utilities	50.6	2.5	435	1.6
Transp. and commun.	348.4	17.0	2,395	9.0
Trade, restaurants, and hotels	348.9	17.0	8,524	31.9
Finance, real estate	291.9	14.2	1,454	5.4
Pub. admin., defense	322.0	15.7	2,572	9.6
Services	126.7	6.2	5,207	19.5
Other	187.5[8]	9.1[8]	509	1.9
TOTAL	2,054.9[9]	100.0[9]	26,753	100.0

Land use as % of total land area (2000): in temporary crops *c.* 18%, in permanent crops *c.* 5%, in pasture *c.* 9%; overall forest area *c.* 20%.
Tourism: receipts from visitors (2003) U.S.$301,000,000; expenditures by nationals abroad U.S.$35,000,000.

Foreign trade[10]

Balance of trade (current prices)						
	1996	1997	1998	1999	2000	2001
U.S.$'000,000	−302	−297	−304	−335	−322	−318
% of total	90.0%	91.9%	91.1%	91.4%	90.8%	90.4%

Imports (1999): U.S.$356,000,000 (machinery and equipment 32.2%, agricultural products 24.7%, basic manufactures 15.4%, petroleum products 10.5%). *Major import sources:* United States 49.5%; Japan 10.2%; United Kingdom 6.3%; Trinidad and Tobago 6.0%; Netherlands Antilles 5.5%.
Exports (1999): U.S.$37,800,000 (reexports [significantly, petroleum products reexported to neighbouring islands] 60.3%; domestic exports 39.7%). *Major export destinations* (1998): Barbados 9.5%; Trinidad and Tobago 7.3%; St. Lucia 7.3%; United Kingdom 6.1%; unspecified 52.5%.

Transport and communications

Transport. Railroad[11]. Roads (1999): total length 155 mi, 250 km (paved, n.a.). Vehicles: passenger cars (1998) 24,000; trucks and buses (1995) 1,342. Air transport (2001): passenger-mi 189,000,000, passenger-km 304,000,000; short ton-mi cargo 137,000, metric ton-km cargo 200,000; airports (2001) with scheduled flights 2.

Communications				units per 1,000
Medium	date	unit	number	persons
Daily newspapers	1996	circulation	6,000	87
Radio	1997	receivers	36,000	523
Television	1999	receivers	33,000	501
Telephones	2004	main lines	38,000	494
Cellular telephones	2004	subscribers	54,000	701
Internet	2004	users	20,000	260

Education and health

Educational attainment (1991). Percentage of population age 25 and over having: no formal schooling 1.1%; primary education 50.5%; secondary 33.4%; higher (not university) 5.4%; university 6.2%; other/unknown 3.4%. *Literacy* (2000): percentage of total population age 15 and over literate 86.6%.

Education (2000–01)				student/
	schools	teachers	students	teacher ratio
Primary (age 5–11)	55	525	10,427	19.9
Secondary (age 12–16)	14	361	5,794	16.0
Higher[12]	1	16	46	2.9

Health: physicians (1999) 76 (1 per 867 persons); hospital beds (1996) 255 (1 per 269 persons); infant mortality rate per 1,000 live births (2004) 20.2.
Food (2002): daily per capita caloric intake 2,349 (vegetable products 68%, animal products 32%); 100% of FAO recommended minimum requirement.

Military

Total active duty personnel (2004): a 170-member defense force (army 73.5%, navy 26.5%) is part of the Eastern Caribbean regional security system. *Military expenditure as percentage of GDP* (2003): 0.6%; per capita expenditure U.S.$52.

[1]Directly elected seats only; attorney general and speaker may serve ex officio if they are not elected to House of Representatives. [2]Community councils on Antigua and the local government council on Barbuda are the organs of local government. [3]Estimated total de jure census population including institutionalized persons and long-term guests; same population definition excluding institutionalized persons and long-term guests equals 75,078. The enumerated 2001 de jure census total equals 70,737. [4]Increased to more than 3% of population by 2000. [5]Large settlements include (2001): All Saints 3,412; Liberta 2,239; Potters 2,067; Codrington 980. [6]Public sector only. [7]Weights of consumer price index components. [8]Net indirect taxes less imputed bank service charges. [9]Detail does not add to total given because of rounding. [10]Balance of trade excludes reexports; data for commodities and destinations includes reexports. [11]Mostly nonoperative privately owned tracks. [12]1994–95.

Internet resources for further information:
• **Eastern Caribbean Central Bank** http://www.eccb-centralbank.org
• **Reports and Statistics** http://www.antigua.gov.ag/gov_v2/government/statsandreports/index.html

Argentina

Pacific
Ocean

Atlantic
Ocean

Official name: República Argentina
(Argentine Republic).
Form of government: federal republic
with two legislative houses (Senate
[72]; Chamber of Deputies [257]).
Head of state and government:
President[1].
Capital: Buenos Aires.
Official language: Spanish.
Official religion: Roman Catholicism.
Monetary unit: 1 peso (Arg$; pl.
pesos) = 100 centavos; valuation
(Sept. 1, 2005) 1 U.S.$ = Arg$2.91;
1 £ = Arg$5.36.

Area and population

Provinces	area sq km	population 2001 census	Provinces	area sq km	population 2001 census
Buenos Aires	307,571	13,827,203	Neuquén	94,078	474,155
Catamarca	102,602	334,568	Río Negro	203,013	552,822
Chaco	99,633	984,446	Salta	155,488	1,079,051
Chubut	224,686	413,237	San Juan	89,651	620,023
Córdoba	165,321	3,066,801	San Luis	76,748	367,933
Corrientes	88,199	930,991	Santa Cruz	243,943	196,958
Entre Ríos	78,781	1,158,147	Santa Fe	133,007	3,000,701
Formosa	72,066	486,559	Santiago del Estero	136,351	804,457
Jujuy	53,219	611,888	Tierra del Fuego[2]	21,263	101,079
La Pampa	143,440	299,294	Tucumán	22,524	1,338,523
La Rioja	89,680	289,983	**Autonomous city**		
Mendoza	148,827	1,579,651	Buenos Aires	200	2,776,138
Misiones	29,801	965,522	TOTAL	2,780,092	36,260,130

Demography

Population (2005): 38,592,000.
Density (2005): persons per sq mi 36.0, persons per sq km 13.9.
Urban-rural (2003): urban 90.1%; rural 9.9%.
Sex distribution (2001): male 48.70%; female 51.30%.
Age breakdown (2001): under 15, 28.3%; 15–29, 25.0%; 30–44, 18.6%; 45–59, 14.7%; 60–74, 9.3%; 75 and over, 4.1%.
Population projection: (2010) 40,519,000; (2020) 44,247,000.
Doubling time: 71 years.
Ethnic composition (2000): European extraction 86.4%; mestizo 6.5%; Amerindian 3.4%; Arab 3.3%; other 0.4%.
Religious affiliation (2000): Roman Catholic 79.8%; Protestant 5.4%; Muslim 1.9%; Jewish 1.3%; other 11.6%.
Major cities (2001): Buenos Aires 2,776,138 (12,046,799[3]); Córdoba 1,267,521; San Justo 1,253,921; Rosario 908,163; La Plata 563,943; Mar del Plata 541,733.

Vital statistics

Birth rate per 1,000 population (2003): 17.5 (world avg. 21.1).
Death rate per 1,000 population (2003): 7.6 (world avg. 9.0).
Natural increase rate per 1,000 population (2003): 9.9 (world avg. 12.1).
Total fertility rate (avg. births per childbearing woman; 2003): 2.3.
Marriage rate per 1,000 population (2003): 3.2.
Life expectancy at birth (2003): male 71.7 years; female 79.4 years.
Major causes of death per 100,000 population (2002): diseases of the circulatory system 272.6; malignant neoplasms (cancers) 155.8; communicable diseases 73.3; accidents and violence 44.2; diabetes mellitus 25.7.

National economy

Budget (2001). Revenue: Arg$37,019,700,000 (tax revenue 90.5%, of which sales tax 36.0%, social security tax 22.8%, income tax 18.0%, property tax 9.3%; nontax revenue 9.5%). Expenditure: Arg$46,013,400,000 (social security 47.8%; debt service 22.1%; education 5.7%; defense 3.8%; health 1.8%).
Public debt (external, outstanding; 2003): U.S.$99,300,000,000.
Gross national product (at current market prices; 2004): U.S.$142,338,000,000 (U.S.$3,720 per capita).

Structure of gross domestic product and labour force

	2002 in value Arg$'000,000	2002 % of total value	2001 labour force	2001 % of labour force
Agriculture	31,904	10.2	910,996	6.0
Mining	18,674	6.0	37,979	0.2
Manufacturing	63,603	20.4	1,245,544	8.2
Construction	7,888	2.5	638,566	4.2
Public utilities	5,352	1.7	90,165	0.6
Transp. and commun.	23,116	7.4	717,573	4.7
Trade, restaurants	40,372	12.9	2,213,065	14.5
Finance, real estate	56,342	18.0	898,264	5.9
Pub. admin., defense	16,867	5.4	969,280	6.3
Services	34,524	11.0	2,762,447	18.1
Other	13,939[4]	4.5[4]	4,780,904[5]	31.3[5]
TOTAL	312,580[6]	100.0	15,264,783	100.0

Production (metric tons except as noted). Agriculture, forestry, fishing (2004): soybeans 32,000,000, sugarcane 19,500,000, wheat 14,800,000, corn (maize) 13,000,000, sunflower seeds 3,100,000, grapes 2,365,000, sorghum 2,160,000, potatoes 2,150,000; livestock (number of live animals) 50,768,000 cattle, 12,450,000 sheep, 3,655,000 horses; roundwood (2003) 9,307,000 cu m; fish catch (2002) 944,346. Mining and quarrying (2003): copper (metal content)

199,020; silver 133,917 kg; gold 29,744 kg. Manufacturing (value added in U.S.$'000,000; 1999): food products 5,601; beverages 2,146; refined petroleum products 1,361; fabricated metal products 1,321; plastic products 985. Energy production (consumption): electricity (kW-hr; 2002) 84,492,000,000 (90,411,000,000); coal (2002) 97,000 (708,000); crude petroleum (barrels; 2002) 278,000,000 (185,000,000); petroleum products (metric tons; 2002) 20,849,000 (15,074,000); natural gas (cu m; 2002) 51,449,000,000 (45,237,000,000).
Land use as % of total land area (2000): in temporary crops 12.2%, in permanent crops 0.5%, in pasture 51.9%; overall forest area 12.7%.
Tourism (2003): receipts U.S.$2,097,000,000; expenditures U.S.$2,575,000,000.
Population economically active (2001): total 15,264,783; activity rate of total population 42.1% (participation rates: ages 14 and over 57.2%; female 40.9%; unemployed [2004] c. 12%).

Price and earnings indexes (2002 = 100)

	1999	2000	2001	2002	2003	2004	2005[7]
Consumer price index	81.1	80.0	79.5	100.0	113.4	118.5	124.1
Monthly earnings index	...	...	...	100.0	119.9	136.7	148.7

Household size and expenditure. Average household size[8] (2003) 3.4; expenditure (1996–97): food products 26.8%, transportation and communications 15.0%, housing and energy 13.4%, health 10.2%.

Foreign trade[9]

Balance of trade (current prices)

	1998	1999	2000	2001	2002	2003
U.S.$'000,000	–3,097	–794	+2,452	+7,385	+17,178	+16,448
% of total	5.5%	1.7%	4.9%	16.2%	50.3%	38.5%

Imports (2001): U.S.$20,321,100,000 (chemicals and chemical products 20.4%, motor vehicles 9.0%, nonelectrical machinery 6.7%, electrical machinery 6.5%, telecommunications equipment 5.5%). *Major import sources:* Brazil 26.0%; U.S. 18.6%; Germany 5.2%; China 5.2%; Italy 4.1%; Japan 3.8%.
Exports (2001): U.S.$26,610,100,000 (food products and live animals 31.6%, of which soybean oilcake 9.0%, wheat 4.9%, corn (maize) 3.7%; crude petroleum 9.0%, road vehicles 7.4%, fixed vegetable oils 5.8%, refined petroleum products 4.8%, iron and steel 3.4%). *Major export destinations:* Brazil 23.3%; U.S. 10.9%; Chile 10.7%; China 4.2%; Spain 4.1%.

Transport and communications

Transport. Railroads: (2002) route length 35,753 km; (2001) passenger-km 7,934,000,000; (2001) metric ton-km cargo 8,989,000,000. Roads (2001): total length 143,053 mi, 230,222 km (paved 30%). Vehicles: passenger cars (2000) 5,386,700; commercial vehicles and buses (1998) 1,496,567. Air transport (2003)[10]: passenger-km 9,514,000,000; metric ton-km cargo 103,435,000.

Communications

Medium	date	unit	number	units per 1,000 persons
Daily newspapers	2000	circulation	1,320,000	37
Radio	2000	receivers	24,300,000	681
Television	2001	receivers	11,800,000	311
Telephones	2004	main lines	8,700,000	224
Cellular telephones	2004	subscribers	13,512,400	348
Personal computers	2004	units	3,000,000	80
Internet	2004	users	5,120,000	132

Education and health

Educational attainment (2001). Percentage of population age 15 and over having: no formal schooling 3.7%; incomplete primary education 14.2%; complete primary 28.0%; secondary 37.1%; some higher 8.3%; complete higher 8.7%. *Literacy* (2001): percentage of total population age 10 and over literate 97.4%; males literate 97.4%; females literate 97.4%.

Education (1999–2000)

	schools	teachers	students	student/ teacher ratio
Primary (age 6–12)	22,283	307,874	4,609,077	15.0
Secondary (age 13–17)[11]	21,492	127,718	3,281,512	25.7
Higher	1,744	126,224	1,336,800	10.6

Health: physicians (1999) 99,358 (1 per 373 persons); hospital beds (1996) 115,803 (1 per 304 persons); infant mortality rate (2004) 15.7.
Food (2002): daily per capita caloric intake 2,992 (vegetable products 70%, animal products 30%); 127% of FAO recommended minimum requirement.

Military

Total active duty personnel (2004): 71,400 (army 58.0%, navy 24.5%, air force 17.5%). *Military expenditure as percentage of GNP* (2003): 1.2%; per capita expenditure U.S.$40.

---

[1]Assisted by the cabinet chief (ministerial coordinator) who exercises general administration of the country. [2]Area of Tierra del Fuego excludes claims to British-held islands in the South Atlantic Ocean. [3]Urban agglomeration. [4]Import duties and VAT less imputed bank service charges. [5]Includes 427,307 (2.8%) not defined and 4,351,596 (28.5%) unemployed. [6]Detail does not add to total given because of rounding. [7]January and February only. [8]Urban areas only. [9]Import figures are f.o.b. in balance of trade and c.i.f. in commodities and trading partners. [10]Aerolineas Argentinas. [11]Secondary includes vocational and teacher training.

Internet resources for further information:
• National Institute of Statistics and Censuses http://www.indec.mecon.ar

Armenia

Official name: Hayastani Hanrape-
tut'yun (Republic of Armenia).
Form of government: unitary multiparty
republic with a single legislative body
(National Assembly [131]).
Head of state: President.
Head of government: Prime Minister.
Capital: Yerevan.
Official language: Armenian.
Official religion: none[1].
Monetary unit: 1 dram = 100 lumas;
valuation (Sept. 1, 2005)
1 U.S.$ = 463.50 drams;
1 £ = 853.42 drams.

Area and population		area		population
Districts	**Centres**	**sq mi**	**sq km**	**2004 estimate**
Aragatsotn	Ashtarak	1,063	2,753	138,800
Ararat	Artashat	809	2,096	272,700
Armavir	Armavir	479	1,242	277,300
Gegharkunik	Gavar	2,065[2]	5,348[2]	238,500
Kotayk	Hrazdan	807	2,089	273,100
Lori	Vanadzor	1,463	3,789	284,500
Shirak	Gyumri	1,035	2,681	282,200
Syunik	Kapan	1,740	4,506	153,100
Tavush	Ijevan	1,044	2,704	134,300
Vayots-Dzor	Yeghegnadzor	891	2,308	55,800
City				
Yerevan	—	88	227	1,101,900
TOTAL		11,484[3]	29,743[3]	3,212,200[4]

Demography

Population (2005)[5]: 2,983,000.
Density (2005): persons per sq mi 259.8, persons per sq km 100.3.
Urban-rural (2003): urban 65.1%; rural 34.9%.
Sex distribution (2001): male 46.87%; female 53.13%.
Age breakdown (2001): under 15, 24.8%; 15–29, 24.9%; 30–44, 21.8%; 45–59,
13.6%; 60–74, 12.1%; 75 and over, 2.8%.
Population projection[5]: (2010) 2,967,000; (2020) 3,017,370.
Ethnic composition (2001): Armenian 97.9%; Kurdish 1.3%; Russian 0.5%;
other 0.8%.
Religious affiliation (2000): Christian 84.0%, of which Orthodox (nearly all
Armenian Apostolic) 78.2%, Roman Catholic 4.6%; Muslim 2.7%; nonreli-
gious 8.4%; atheist 4.9%.
Major cities (2001[5]): Yerevan 1,091,235; Gyumri 150,917; Vanadzor
(Kirovakan) 107,394; Vagharshapat 56,388; Hrazdan 52,808.

Vital statistics

Birth rate per 1,000 population (2003): 11.2 (world avg. 21.1); legitimate 88.2%;
illegitimate 11.8%.
Death rate per 1,000 population (2003): 8.1 (world avg. 9.0).
Natural increase rate per 1,000 population (2003): 3.1 (world avg. 12.1).
Total fertility rate (avg. births per childbearing woman; 2004): 1.3.
Marriage rate per 1,000 population (2003): 4.8.
Divorce rate per 1,000 population (2003): 0.6.
Life expectancy at birth (2003): male 69.9 years; female 75.8 years.
Major causes of death per 100,000 population (2003): diseases of the circula-
tory system 443.8; malignant neoplasms (cancers) 135.7; diabetes mellitus
53.2; diseases of the respiratory system 48.6; accidents and violence 32.3.

National economy

Budget (2003). Revenue: 250,087,100,000 drams (tax revenue 84.9%, of which
value-added tax 43.1%, excise tax 15.6%, profit tax 7.0%, stamp duties 6.1%;
government duty 6.1%; grants 3.9%; nontax revenue 3.8%; other 1.3%).
Expenditures: 241,963,000,000 drams (defense 18.3%; education and science
13.6%; public services 12.4%; social security 12.1%; health 7.8%).
Public debt (external, outstanding; 2003): U.S.$875,000,000.
Tourism (2003): receipts from visitors U.S.$73,000,000; expenditures by nation-
als abroad U.S.$67,000,000.
Land use as % of total land area (2000): in temporary crops 17.6%, in per-
manent crops 2.3%, in pasture 28.4%; overall forest area 12.4%.
Gross national product (2004): U.S.$3,424,000,000 (U.S.$1,120 per capita).

Structure of net material product and labour force				
	2001		**2003**	
	in value '000,000 drams	% of total value	labour force	% of labour force
Agriculture	294,160	25.0	509,000	41.3
Manufacturing, mining }	245,775	20.9	138,800[6]	11.3[6]
Public utilities				
Construction	125,751	10.7	37,200	3.0
Transp. and commun.	87,810	7.5	41,800	3.4
Trade	115,770	9.8	105,000	8.5
Finance, real estate	59,895	5.1	37,600[6]	3.1[6]
Pub. admin., defense	39,475	3.4	25,000	2.0
Services	110,640	9.4	204,800	16.6
Other	96,209[7]	8.2[7]	133,200[8]	10.8[8]
TOTAL	1,175,487[9]	100.0	1,232,400	100.0

Production (metric tons except as noted). Agriculture, forestry, fishing (2004):
potatoes 510,000, wheat 350,000, tomatoes 180,000, watermelons 120,000,
grapes 80,000, barley 62,000, apples 40,000; livestock (number of live animals)

573,703 sheep, 565,800 cattle, 85,400 pigs, 54,800 goats, 3,600,000 chickens;
roundwood (2003) 67,000 cu m; fish catch (2002) 465. Mining and quarrying
(2001): copper concentrate (metal content) 7,056; molybdenum (metal content) 5,770; gold (metal content) 400 kg. Manufacturing (value of production
in '000,000 drams; 2003): food products and beverages 143,700; base metals
46,200; jewelry 22,000; tobacco products 14,300; bricks, cement, and tiles
14,000. Construction (2003): residential 512,275 sq m. Energy production
(consumption): electricity (kW-hr; 2003) 5,501,000,000 (5,225,000,000); coal
(metric tons; 2002) none (none); crude petroleum (barrels; 1998) none
(1,035,000); petroleum products (metric tons; 2002) none (254,000); natural
gas (cu m; 2002) none (1,022,000,000).
Population economically active: total (2003) 1,232,400; activity rate of total
population (2001) 49.5% (participation rates: ages 15–64 [2001] 72.1%;
female [2003] 49.5%; unemployed [2003] 10.1%).

Price and earnings indexes (2000 = 100)							
	1998	1999	2000	2001	2002	2003	2004
Consumer price index	100.2	100.8	100.0	103.1	104.3	109.2	117.6
Earnings index	...	...	...	...	...	...	...

Household income and expenditure. Average household size (2002) 4.1; income
per household (2002) 750,400 drams (U.S.$1,300); sources of income (1999):
agricultural income 32.1%, wages and salaries 24.6%, transfers 19.3%, help
from abroad 12.8%, self-employment 10.6%, other 0.6%; expenditure (2003):
food and beverages 66.3%, non-food goods 14.1%, services 13.1%, tobacco
6.5%.

Foreign trade[10]

Balance of trade (current prices)						
	1998	1999	2000	2001	2002	2003
U.S.$'000,000	−574	−471	−459	−412	−358	−430
% of total	56.5%	50.4%	43.3%	38.9%	26.2%	23.9%

Imports (2003): U.S.$1,279,490,000 (2002; rough diamonds 18.1%; mineral
fuels 17.9%, of which refined petroleum 9.4%; food 14.8%). *Major import
sources* (2003): Russia 15.9%; Belgium 10.1%; Israel 9.7%; U.S. 8.7%; U.K.
6.5%; Iran 5.5%.
Exports (2003): U.S.$685,600,000 (2002; cut diamonds 37.5%; wine and grape
brandy 8.7%; metal ores and scrap 8.5%; wearing apparel 4.1%). *Major
export destinations* (2003): Israel 20.8%; Belgium 18.1%; Russia 13.8%; U.S.
8.2%; Germany 6.5%; U.K. 6.2%.

Transport and communications

Transport. Railroads (2003): length 442 mi, 711 km; passenger-mi 25,600,000,
passenger-km 41,200,000; short ton-mi cargo 335,700,000, metric ton-km
cargo 529,200,000. Roads (2003): length 4,743 mi, 7,633 km (paved 91%).
Vehicles (2003): passenger cars 1,300; trucks and buses 4,460. Air transport
(2003): passenger-mi 446,900,000, passenger-km 719,200,000; short ton-mi
cargo 3,490,000, metric ton-km cargo 5,500,000; airports (2003) 1.

Communications				units per 1,000
Medium	date	unit	number	persons
Daily newspapers	2000	circulation	18,700	6.2
Radio	2000	receivers	700,000	225
Television	2001	receivers	696,000	230
Telephones	2004	main lines	582,500	191
Cellular telephones	2004	subscribers	203,300	67
Personal computers	2004	units	200,000	66
Internet	2004	users	150,000	49

Education and health

Educational attainment (2001). Percentage of population age 25 and over having: no formal schooling 0.7%; primary education 13.0%; completed secondary and some postsecondary 66.0%; higher 20.3%. *Literacy* (2001): total
population age 15 and over literate 99.4%; male 99.7%; female 99.2%.

Education (2003–04)	schools	teachers	students	student/ teacher ratio
Primary (age 6–13) }	1,439	46,000	498,500	10.8
Secondary (age 14–17) }				
Voc., teacher tr.	81	3,386	28,600	8.4
Higher	20	6,628	55,900	8.4

Health (2003): physicians 11,728 (1 per 256 persons); hospital beds 14,208 (1
per 211 persons); infant mortality rate per 1,000 live births (2003) 12.0.
Food (2002): daily per capita caloric intake 2,268 (vegetable products 84%,
animal products 16%); 89% of FAO recommended minimum requirement.

Military

Total active duty personnel (2004): 44,874 (army 93.0%, air force 7.0%);
Russian troops (August 2004) 3,500. *Military expenditure as percentage of
GDP* (2003): 2.7%; per capita expenditure U.S.$26.

[1]The Armenian Apostolic Church (Armenian Orthodox Church) has special status per
1991 religious law. [2]Includes area of Lake Sevan. [3]In addition, about 16% of neighbouring Azerbaijan (including the 4,400-sq km geographic region of Nagorno-Karabakh
[Armenian: Artsakh]) has been occupied by Armenian forces since 1993. [4]January 1
de jure estimate; January 1 de facto estimate equals 2,997,000. [5]De facto population.
[6]Finance, real estate includes Public utilities. [7]Taxes less imputed bank service charges.
[8]Includes 8,400 not adequately defined and 124,800 unemployed. [9]Detail does not add
to total given because of rounding. [10]Imports f.o.b. in balance of trade and c.i.f. in commodities and trading partners.

Internet resources for further information:
• **National Statistical Service http://www.armstat.am**

Aruba

Official name: Aruba.
Political status: nonmetropolitan territory of The Netherlands with one legislative house (States of Aruba [21]).
Chief of state: Dutch Monarch represented by Governor.
Head of government: Prime Minister.
Capital: Oranjestad.
Official language: Dutch.
Official religion: none.
Monetary unit: 1 Aruban florin[1] (Af.) = 100 cents; valuation (Sept. 1, 2005) 1 U.S.$ = Af. 1.79; 1 £ = Af. 3.30.

Area and population	area[2]		population
Census region	sq mi	sq km	2000 census
Noord/Tanki Leendert	14	37	16,944
Oranjestad East	5	13	14,224
Oranjestad West	4	10	12,131
Paradera	10	25	9,037
San Nicolas North	9	23	10,118
San Nicolas South	4	10	5,730
Santa Cruz	18	47	12,326
Savaneta	11	28	9,996
TOTAL	75	193	90,506

Demography

Population (2005): 97,400.
Density (2005): persons per sq mi 1,298.7, persons per sq km 504.7.
Urban-rural (2003): urban 45.4%; rural 54.6%.
Sex distribution (2003): male 47.80%; female 52.20%.
Age breakdown (2003): under 15, 22.0%; 15–29, 18.5%; 30–44, 27.2%; 45–59, 20.3%; 60–74, 9.3%; 75 and over, 2.7%.
Population projection: (2010) 102,000; (2020) 111,000.
Linguistic composition (2000): Papiamento 69.4%; Spanish 13.2%; English 8.1%; Dutch 6.1%; Portuguese 0.3%; other 2.0%; unknown 0.9%.[3]
Religious affiliation (2000): Christian 96.2%, of which Roman Catholic 81.9%, Protestant 7.3%, other Christian (Jehovah's Witness) 1.3%; Spiritist 1.0%; nonreligious 1.4%; other 1.4%.
Major urban areas (2000): Oranjestad 26,355[4]; San Nicolas 15,848[5].

Vital statistics

Birth rate per 1,000 population (2003): 12.3 (world avg. 21.1); legitimate (2001–03) 56.0%; illegitimate 44.0%.
Death rate per 1,000 population (2003): 5.2 (world avg. 9.0).
Natural increase rate per 1,000 population (2003): 7.1 (world avg. 12.1).
Total fertility rate (avg. births per childbearing woman; 2004): 1.8.
Marriage rate per 1,000 population (2003): 5.5.
Divorce rate per 1,000 population (2003): 5.1.
Life expectancy at birth (2004): male 75.6 years; female 82.5 years.
Major causes of death per 100,000 population (2000–02): diseases of the circulatory system 181.1, malignant neoplasms (cancers) 126.4, accidents and violence 45.3, diabetes mellitus 28.3, diseases of the respiratory system 26.4, infectious and parasitic diseases 24.6.

National economy

Budget (Oct. 1, 2003–Sept. 30, 2004). Revenue: Af. 854,200,000 (tax revenue 84.4%, of which taxes on income and profits 40.4%, sales tax 28.7%; nontax revenue 8.4%; grants 7.2%). Expenditures: Af. 953,900,000 (wages 29.3%, goods and services 19.4%, subsidies 12.1%, social security contributions 8.0%).
Production (metric tons except as noted). Agriculture, forestry, fishing: aloes are cultivated for export; small amounts of tomatoes, beans, cucumbers, gherkins, watermelons, and lettuce are grown on hydroponic farms; divi-divi pods, sour orange fruit, sorghum, and peanuts (groundnuts) are nonhydroponic crops of limited value; livestock (number of live animals) Aruba has very few livestock; roundwood, n.a.; fish catch (2002) 163. Mining and quarrying: excavation of sand for local use. Manufacturing[6]: refined petroleum, rum, cigarettes, aloe products, and soaps. Energy production (consumption): electricity (kW-hr; 2002) 810,000,000 (810,000,000); coal, none (none); crude petroleum (barrels; 2002) none (2,400,000); petroleum products (metric tons; 2002) none (316,000); natural gas, none (none).
Gross domestic product (2003): U.S.$2,011,000,000 (U.S.$21,160 per capita).

Structure of gross domestic product and labour force

	2000			
	in value Af. '000,000	% of total value	labour force	% of labour force
Agriculture	14	0.4	212	0.5
Mining			38	0.1
Manufacturing	91[7]	2.7[7]	2,440	5.4
Construction	202	6.1	3,892	8.6
Public utilities	212[8]	6.4[8]	500	1.1
Transp. and commun.	287	8.6	2,905	6.5
Trade, restaurants	796	23.9	14,763	32.8
Finance, real estate	877	26.4	5,206	11.6
Pub. admin., defense	390	11.7	3,528	7.8
Services	365	11.0	8,129	18.1
Other	92[9]	2.8[9]	3,423[10]	7.6[10]
TOTAL	3,326	100.0	45,036	100.0[11]

Population economically active (2000): total 45,036; activity rate of total population 49.8% (participation rates: ages 15–64, 70.9%; female 46.6%; unemployed [2003] 8.0%).

Price and earnings indexes (2000 = 100)					
	2000	2001	2002	2003	2004
Consumer price index	100.0	103.1	106.7	110.2	113.0
Monthly earnings index[12]	100.0	103.8	103.8	103.8	...

Public debt (external, outstanding; 2003): U.S.$407,800,000.
Household income and expenditure: average household size (2000) 3.1; average annual income per household (1999): Af. 39,000 (U.S.$21,800); sources of income: n.a.; expenditure (September 2000)[13]: housing 23.0%, transportation and communications 19.7%, food 14.7%, clothing and footwear 10.9%, household furnishings 10.0%, recreation and education 8.0%.
Tourism: receipts from visitors (2003) U.S.$852,000,000; expenditures by nationals abroad U.S.$191,000,000.
Land use as % of total land area (2000): in temporary crops *c.* 11%, in permanent crops, none, in pasture, negligible; overall forest area, negligible.

Foreign trade

Balance of trade (current prices)							
	1997	1998	1999	2000	2001	2002	2003
U.S.$'000,000	−391	−354	−594	−58	+55	−530	−334
% of total	10.2%	13.2%	17.3%	1.1%	1.1%	15.2%	7.5%

Imports (2003): U.S.$2,378,800,000 (petroleum [all forms] 64.4%, food and beverages 7.0%, electrical and nonelectrical machinery 6.3%, free-zone imports 2.3%). *Major import sources*[14]: United States 55.2%; The Netherlands 13.0%; Netherlands Antilles 3.1%; Venezuela 3.0%.
Exports (2003): U.S.$2,045,100,000 (petroleum [all forms] 95.9%, free-zone exports 3.1%, food and beverages 0.2%). *Major export destinations*[14]: The Netherlands 33.7%; Colombia 12.9%; Panama 12.3%; Netherlands Antilles 11.7%; Venezuela 11.1%; United States 8.8%.

Transport and communications

Transport. Railroads: none. Roads (1995): total length 497 mi, 800 km (paved 64%). Vehicles (2003): passenger cars 45,217; trucks and buses 1,093. Air transport (2001)[15]: passenger-mi 497,000,000, passenger-km 800,000,000; metric ton-mi cargo, n.a.; airports (2003) with scheduled flights 1.

Communications				units per 1,000 persons
Medium	date	unit	number	
Daily newspapers	1996	circulation	73,000	851
Radio	2000	receivers	51,000	562
Television	2000	receivers	20,000	224
Telephones	2002	main lines	37,100	397
Cellular telephones	2001	subscribers	53,000	500
Internet	2002	users	24,000	257

Education and health

Educational attainment (2000). Percentage of population age 25 and over having: no formal schooling or incomplete primary education 9.7%; primary education 33.9%; secondary/vocational 39.2%; advanced vocational/higher 16.2%; unknown status 1.0%. *Literacy* (2000): percentage of total population age 13 and over literate 97.3%.

Education (2002)	schools	teachers	students	student/ teacher ratio
Primary (age 6–12)	36	478	9,595	20.1
Secondary (age 12–17)	15	568	8,160	14.4
Voc., teacher tr.	1	34	178	5.2
Higher	2	21	203	9.7

Health (2003): physicians 129 (1 per 740 persons); hospital beds 305 (1 per 315 persons); infant mortality rate per 1,000 live births (2002–04) 6.1.

Military

Total active duty personnel (2004): a small Dutch naval/coast guard contingent is stationed in Aruba and the Netherlands Antilles to combat organized crime and drug smuggling.

[1]The Aruban florin (Af.) is pegged to the U.S. dollar at a fixed rate of Af. 1.79 = 1 U.S.$. [2]Areas for census regions are approximate. [3]Most Arubans are racially and ethnically mixed; ethnic composition (1998): Amerindian/other 80%; other (primarily Dutch, Spanish and/or black) 20%. [4]Combined population of Oranjestad East and Oranjestad West. [5]Combined population of San Nicolas North and San Nicolas South. [6]Service facilities include a free zone, offshore corporate banking facilities, casino/resort complexes, a petroleum transshipment terminal, a cruise ship terminal, and ship repair and bunkering facilities. [7]Excludes refined petroleum. [8]Includes refined petroleum. [9]Taxes less subsidies and imputed bank service charges. [10]Includes 3,118 unemployed. [11]Detail does not add to total given because of rounding. [12]Minimum wage for the manufacturing and service industries. [13]Weights of consumer price index components. [14]Excludes petroleum (all forms) imports and exports. [15]Air Aruba only.

Internet resources for further information:
• Centrale Bank van Aruba
  http://www.cbaruba.org

Australia

Official name: Commonwealth of Australia.
Form of government: federal parliamentary state (formally a constitutional monarchy) with two legislative houses (Senate [76]; House of Representatives [150]).
Chief of state: British Monarch represented by Governor-General.
Head of government: Prime Minister.
Capital: Canberra.
Official language: English.
Official religion: none.
Monetary unit: 1 Australian dollar ($A) = 100 cents; valuation (Sept. 1, 2005) 1 U.S.$ = $A 1.31; 1 £ = $A 2.41.

Area and population		area[1]		population
				2005
States	**Capitals**	sq mi	sq km	estimate[2]
New South Wales	Sydney	309,130	800,642	6,769,604
Queensland	Brisbane	668,207	1,730,648	3,939,507
South Australia	Adelaide	379,725	983,482	1,540,413
Tasmania	Hobart	26,410	68,401	485,199
Victoria	Melbourne	87,806	227,416	5,019,777
Western Australia	Perth	976,790	2,529,875	2,005,583
Territories[3]				
Australian Capital Territory	Canberra	910	2,358	324,415
Christmas Island	The Settlement	52	135	1,510
Cocos (Keeling) Islands	West Island	5	14	600
Jervis Bay	—	28	73	560
Norfolk Island	Kingston	13	35	2,037[4]
Northern Territory	Darwin	520,902	1,349,129	201,282
"Statistical discrepancy"		—	—	2,600
TOTAL		2,969,978	7,692,208	20,293,087[4]

Demography

Population (2005): 20,345,000.
Density (2005): persons per sq mi 6.9, persons per sq km 2.6.
Urban-rural (2003): urban 91.0%; rural 9.0%.
Sex distribution (2003): male 49.80%; female 50.20%.
Age breakdown (2003): under 15, 20.3%; 15–29, 20.7%; 30–44, 22.7%; 45–59, 19.3%; 60–74, 11.0%; 75 and over, 6.0%.
Population projection: (2010) 21,401,000; (2020) 23,537,000.
Ethnic composition (2001): white c. 92%; Asian c. 6%; aboriginal c. 2%.
Religious affiliation (2001): Christian 68.0%, of which Roman Catholic 26.6%, Anglican Church of Australia 20.7%, other Protestant 15.8% (Uniting Church 6.7%, Presbyterian 3.4%), Orthodox 2.8%, other Christian 2.1%; Buddhist 1.9%; Muslim 1.5%; Hindu 0.5%; Jewish 0.4%; no religion 15.5%; other 12.2%.
Metropolitan areas (2001): Sydney 3,997,321; Melbourne 3,366,542; Brisbane 1,627,535; Perth 1,339,993; Adelaide 1,072,585; Newcastle 470,610; Gold Coast 444,077; Canberra 353,149; Wollongong 257,510; Caloundra 192,397; Hobart 191,169.
Place of birth (2002): 76.8% native-born; 23.2% foreign-born, of which Europe 10.3% (United Kingdom and Republic of Ireland 6.0%, Italy 1.2%, Serbia and Montenegro 1.1%, Greece 0.7%, Germany 0.6%, The Netherlands 0.5%, Poland 0.3%), Asia and Middle East 4.4% (China [including Hong Kong] 1.2%, Vietnam 0.9%), New Zealand 2.1%, Africa, the Americas, and other 6.4%.
Mobility (1999). Population age 15 and over living in the same residence as in 1998: 84.4%; different residence between states, regions, and neighbourhoods 15.6%.
Households (2002). Total number of households 7,510,000. Average household size 3.0; 1 person 25.1%, 2 persons 33.4%, 3 or more persons 41.5%. Family households 5,357,000 (71.3%), nonfamily 2,153,000 (28.7%), of which 1-person (2001) 24.1%.
Immigration (2002–03): permanent immigrants admitted 93,914, from United Kingdom and Ireland 14.0%, New Zealand 13.2%, China 7.1%, India 6.2%, South Africa 4.9%, Philippines 3.4%, Indonesia 3.2%, Iraq 3.0%, Sudan 3.0%, Malaysia 2.9%. Refugee arrivals (2003–04): 13,851. Emigration (2002–03): 50,463.

Vital statistics

Birth rate per 1,000 population (2003): 12.6 (world avg. 21.1); (2000) legitimate 69.3%; illegitimate 30.7%.
Death rate per 1,000 population (2003): 7.3 (world avg. 9.0).
Natural increase rate per 1,000 population (2003): 5.3 (world avg. 12.1).
Total fertility rate (avg. births per childbearing woman; 2003): 1.8.
Marriage rate per 1,000 population (2002): 5.4.
Life expectancy at birth (2003): male 77.3 years; female 83.1 years.
Major causes of death per 100,000 population (2002): diseases of the circulatory system 222.5; cancers 190.4; respiratory diseases 47.3; accidents, poisoning, and violence 24.8; diabetes 16.9; suicides 11.8.

Social indicators

Quality of working life (2003). Average workweek: 34.7 hours. Working 50 hours a week or more 28.8%. Annual rate per 100,000 workers for: accidental injury and industrial disease, 3,200[5]; death, n.a. Proportion of employed persons insured for damages or income loss resulting from injury

100%; permanent disability 100%; death 100%. Working days lost to industrial disputes per 1,000 employees (2002): 32. Means of transportation to work (2003): private automobile 74.5%; public transportation 12.0%; motorcycle, bicycle, and foot 5.7%. Discouraged job seekers (2002): 78,000 (0.8% of labour force).

Distribution of household income (1999–2000)				
percentage of household income by quintile				
lowest	second	third	fourth	highest
3.8%	9.0%	15.0%	23.8%	48.4%

Educational attainment (2003). Percentage of population age 15 and over having: no formal schooling and incomplete secondary education 50.9%; completed secondary and postsecondary, technical, or other certificate/diploma 31.0%; bachelor's degree 13.0%; incomplete graduate and graduate degree or diploma 5.1%.
Social participation. Eligible voters participating in last national election (2004): 94%; voting is compulsory. Trade union membership in total workforce (2002): 23.1%.
Social deviance (2003). Offense rate per 100,000 population for: murder 1.5; sexual assault 92; assault 798; auto theft 497; burglary and housebreaking 1,776; armed robbery 99. Incidence per 100,000 in general population of: prisoners 139[6]; suicide 13.0[6].
Material well-being (1995). Households possessing: automobile 85%; telephone 95%; refrigerator 99.7%; washing machine 90.0%.

National economy

Gross national product (2004): U.S.$541,173,000,000 (U.S.$26,900 per capita).

Structure of gross domestic product and labour force				
	2002–03		2003	
	in value $A '000,000	% of total value	labour force	% of labour force
Agriculture	20,059	2.7	395,000	3.9
Mining	34,943	4.6	77,000	0.8
Manufacturing	80,741	10.7	1,128,000	11.2
Construction	45,568	6.0	786,000	7.8
Public utilities	16,906	2.2	76,000	0.7
Transportation and communications	56,438	7.5	622,000	6.2
Trade, restaurants	94,015	12.5	2,574,000	25.6
Finance, real estate	201,044	26.7	1,537,000	15.3
Pub. admin., defense	29,743	3.9	566,000	5.6
Services	108,353	14.4	2,144,000	21.3
Other	65,442[7]	8.77	162,000[8]	1.6[8]
TOTAL	753,252	100.0[9]	10,067,000	100.0

Budget (2003–04). Revenue: $A 187,559,000,000 (tax revenue 93.3%, of which individual 52.7%, corporate 19.4%, excise duties and sales tax 17.6%; nontax revenue 6.7%). Expenditures: $A 181,238,000,000 (social security and welfare 44.2%; health 17.5%; economic services 7.8%; education 7.4%; public services 7.3%; defense 7.1%; interest on public debt 2.2%; other 6.5%).
Public debt (2002–03): $A 69,926,000,000.
Tourism (2003): receipts from visitors U.S.$11,269,000,000; expenditures by nationals abroad U.S.$7,329,000,000.

Retail and service enterprises				
	no. of establishments	no. of employees	total wages and salaries ($A '000,000)	annual turnover ($A '000,000)
Retail[10]				
Motor vehicle dealers, gasoline and tire dealers	37,305	220,661	...	44,954
Food stores	53,166	406,299	...	63,340[11]
Department and general stores	459	87,148	...	13,714[11]
Clothing, fabric, and furniture stores	21,688	91,138	...	11,005[11]
Household appliances and hardware stores	14,268	75,355	629	20,554[11]
Recreational goods	...	...	...	7,393[11]
Services				
Real estate agents[12]	7,589	52,079	1,847.5	3,902.7
Pubs, taverns, and bars	4,792[13]	81,724[13]	...	9,007.2[11]
Dental services[13]	5,257	24,108	568.4	1,685.2
Consulting engineering services[14]	5,514	30,736	1,242	3,233.3
Legal services[12]	10,819	73,186	2,181.0	7,034.3
Accounting services[14]	8,389	66,792	...	4,939.1
Computing services[12]	14,731	74,395	4,065.0	10,474.0
Travel agency services[15]	3,266	24,451	647.9	1,979.5
Market research services[12]	272	10,744	203.4	455.8
Private security services[12]	1,714	31,752	756.2	1,394.8

Production (gross value in $A '000 except as noted). Agriculture, forestry, fishing (2002–03): livestock[16] 10,676,000 (cattle 6,411,100, sheep and lambs 2,036,900, poultry 1,280,500, pigs 911,300); wool 3,317,800, wheat 2,691,900, fruits and nuts 2,216,100, vegetables 2,125,600, grapes 1,370,800, sugarcane 1,018,900, barley 984,200, seed cotton 853,000, canola 389,000, oats 209,700, rice 153,000, corn (maize) 72,000, tobacco 41,000, other cereal crops 723,600; livestock (number of live animals) 99,252,000 sheep, 26,664,000 cattle, 2,658,000 pigs, 85,535,000 poultry (July 2003); roundwood (2002) 31,212,000 cu m; fish catch 249,012 metric tons. Mining and quarrying (metric tons except as noted; 2002): iron ore (metal content) 113,548,000 (world rank: 2), bauxite 54,024,000 (world rank: 1), ilmenite 1,917,000 (world rank: 3), zinc (metal content) 1,469,000 (world rank: 2), copper (metal content) 883,000 (world rank: 4), lead (metal content) 683,000 (world rank: 1), rutile 218,000 (world rank: 1), nickel (metal content) 186,000 (world rank: 2), cobalt (metal content) 6,600 (world rank: 2), opal (value of production) U.S.$34,000,000 (world rank: 1), diamonds 33,636,000 carats (world rank by volume: 1), gold 273,010 kilograms (world rank: 3). Manufacturing (value added in $A '000,000;

2000–01): food products 11,026; printing and publishing 6,599; chemicals and chemical products 5,756; nonferrous base metals 5,678; fabricated metal products 5,402; motor vehicles and parts 4,657; electrical machinery and apparatus 3,366; beverages 3,185.

Population economically active (2003): total 10,067,000; activity rate of total population 50.6% (participation rates: ages 15–64, 74.2%; female 44.8%; unemployed [September 2003–August 2004] 5.7%).

Price and earnings indexes (2000 = 100)

	1998	1999	2000	2001	2002	2003	2004
Consumer price index	94.3	95.7	100.0	104.4	107.5	110.5	113.1
Weekly earnings index	92.8	95.3	100.0	105.0	110.3	116.5	...

Household income and expenditure. Average household size (2002) 3.0; average annual disposable income per household (2002–03) $A 44,252 (U.S.$25,055); sources of income (1999–2000): wages and salaries 56.7%, transfer payments 28.0%, self-employment 6.0%, other 9.3%; expenditure (1998–99): food and nonalcoholic beverages 18.2%, transportation and communications 16.9%, housing 13.9%, recreation 12.7%, household durable goods 6.0%.

Financial aggregates

	1998	1999	2000	2001	2002	2003	2004
Exchange rate, $A 1.00 per[17];							
U.S. dollar	0.63	0.65	0.58	0.51	0.57	0.75	0.78
£	0.38	0.40	0.38	0.35	0.38	0.42	0.40
SDR	0.44	0.48	0.43	0.41	0.42	0.50	0.50
International reserves (U.S.$)[17]							
Total (excl. gold; '000,000)	14,641	21,212	18,118	17,955	20,689	32,189	35,803
SDRs ('000,000)	18	72	94	109	136	170	195
Reserve pos. in IMF ('000,000)	1,256	1,633	1,243	1,412	1,934	2,053	1,706
Foreign exchange ('000,000)	13,366	19,507	16,782	16,434	18,618	29,966	33,901
Gold ('000,000 fine troy oz)	2.56	2.56	2.56	2.56	2.56	2.56	2.56
% world reserves	0.3	0.3	0.3	0.3	0.3	0.3	0.3
Interest and prices							
Govt. bond yield (short-term; %)	5.02	5.55	6.18	4.97	5.30	4.90	5.30
Industrial share prices							
(2000 = 100)	83.8	92.7	100.0	103.2	100.2	96.1	111.7
Balance of payments[17]							
(U.S.$'000,000)							
Balance of visible trade	−5,332	−9,761	−4,813	+1,786	−5,431	−15,312	...
Imports, f.o.b.	61,215	65,857	68,865	61,890	70,530	85,852	...
Exports, f.o.b.	55,884	56,096	64,052	63,676	65,099	70,540	...
Balance of invisibles	−12,682	−12,534	−10,668	−10,498	−11,955	−15,066	...
Balance of payments, current account	−18,014	−22,295	−15,481	−8,712	−17,386	−30,377	...

Energy production (consumption): electricity (kW-hr; 2002) 222,182,000,000 (222,182,000,000); hard coal (metric tons; 2002) 273,200,000 (63,600,000); lignite (metric tons; 2002) 68,600,000 (68,600,000); crude petroleum (barrels; 2002) 227,000,000 (244,000,000); petroleum products (metric tons; 2002) 34,716,000 (32,296,000); natural gas (cu m; 2002) 36,849,000,000 (25,753,000,000).

Land use as % of total land area (2000): in temporary crops 6.5%, in permanent crops 0.04%, in pasture 52.7%; overall forest area 20.1%.

Foreign trade[18]

Balance of trade (current prices)

	1997	1998	1999	2000	2001	2002	2003
$A '000,000	+1,422	−7,746	−14,551	−6,376	+5,307	−6,974	−20,073
% of total	0.8%	4.2%	7.7%	2.8%	2.2%	2.8%	8.4%

Imports (2002–03): $A 133,131,000,000 (machinery and transport equipment 45.5%, of which road motor vehicles 7.7%, office machines and automatic data-processing equipment 3.7%, telecommunications equipment 3.2%; chemicals and related products 11.3%, of which medicines and pharmaceuticals 3.2%; mineral fuels and lubricants 8.0%; food and live animals 3.8%). *Major import sources:* U.S. 16.9%; Japan 12.3%; China 10.4%; Germany 6.0%; U.K. 4.3%; New Zealand 3.8%; South Korea 3.6%; Indonesia 3.5%; Singapore 3.3%; Malaysia 3.2%; Italy 3.1%.

Exports (2002–03): $A 115,442,000,000 (mineral fuels 20.6%, of which coal [all forms] 10.3%, petroleum products and natural gas 5.1%; crude materials excluding fuels 18.6%, of which metalliferous ores and metal scrap [mostly iron ore and alumina] 4.6%; food 15.9%, of which meat and meat preparations 3.4%, cereals and cereal preparations 2.6%; machinery and transport equipment 11.7%). *Major export destinations:* Japan 18.8%; U.S. 9.0%; South Korea 7.9%; China 7.6%; New Zealand 7.0%; U.K. 6.3%; Singapore 4.0%; Taiwan 3.7%; Hong Kong 2.8%; Indonesia 2.5%.

Trade by commodity group (2003–04)

SITC Group	imports U.S.$'000,000	%	exports U.S.$'000,000	%
00 Food and live animals	3,762	3.8	13,666	16.7
01 Beverages and tobacco	675	0.7	2,025	2.5
02 Crude materials, excluding fuels	1,448	1.5	15,592	19.1
03 Mineral fuels, lubricants, and related materials	7,569	7.7	15,326	18.8
04 Animal and vegetable oils, fat, and waxes	276	0.3	269	0.3
05 Chemicals and related products, n.e.s.	11,306	11.5	3,974	4.9
06 Basic manufactures	11,819	12.0	8,518	10.4
07 Machinery and transport equipment	45,266	46.1	8,957	11.0
08 Miscellaneous manufactured articles	14,030	14.3	3,209	3.9
09 Goods not classified by kind	2,113	2.1	10,146	12.4
TOTAL	98,265[9]	100.0	81,680[9]	100.0

Direction of trade (2003–04)

	imports U.S.$'000,000	%	exports U.S.$'000,000	%
Africa	962	1.0	1,559	1.9
Asia	48,176	49.0	49,846	61.0
Japan	12,076	12.3	14,849	18.2
South America	371	0.4	383	0.5
North and Central America	16,775	17.1	8,699	10.7
United States	14,959	15.2	7,090	8.7
Europe	23,528	23.9	9,763	11.9
European Union	22,439	22.8	9,419	11.5
United Kingdom	4,073	4.1	3,849	4.7
Other Europe	1,089	1.1	344	0.4
Oceania	5,012	5.1	6,988	8.6
New Zealand	3,792	3.9	6,060	7.4
Other	3,442	3.5	4,442	5.4
TOTAL	98,265[9]	100.0	81,680	100.0

Transport and communications

Transport. Railroads (2003): route length 25,763 mi, 41,461 km; passengers carried[19] 595,000,000; short ton-mi cargo 112,630,000,000, metric ton-km cargo[19] 164,437,000,000. Roads (2004): total length 503,709 mi, 810,641 km (paved 42%). Vehicles (2003): passenger cars 10,404,000; trucks and buses 2,382,000. Merchant marine (2002): vessels (150 gross tons and over) 77; total deadweight tonnage 2,028,637. Air transport (2003)[20]: passenger-mi 42,827,000,000, passenger-km 68,923,000,000; short ton-mi cargo 879,000,000, metric ton-km cargo 1,284,000,000; regulated airports (2004) with scheduled flights 256.

Communications

Medium	date	unit	number	units per 1,000 persons
Daily newspapers	2000	circulation	5,630,000	293
Radio	2000	receivers	36,700,000	1,908
Television	2001	receivers	14,168,000	730
Telephones	2004	main lines	10,872,000	546
Cellular telephones	2004	subscribers	16,449,000	826
Personal computers	2004	units	13,720,000	689
Internet	2004	users	13,000,000	653

Education and health

Literacy (2003): total population literate, virtually 100%[21].

Education (2003)

	schools	teachers	students	student/ teacher ratio
Primary (age 6–12) } Secondary (age 13–17) }	9,607	229,576	3,330,300	14.5
Vocational[22]	1,949	32,300[19]	1,717,800	
Higher	46	84,435	929,952	11.0

Health: physicians (2003) 52,404 (1 per 375 persons); hospital beds (2001–02) 78,868 (1 per 249 persons); infant mortality rate per 1,000 live births (2003) 4.8.

Food (2002): daily per capita caloric intake 3,054 (vegetable products 66%, animal products 34%); 115% of FAO recommended minimum requirement.

Military

Total active duty personnel (2004): 51,800 (army 48.8%, navy 24.8%, air force 26.4%). *Military expenditure as percentage of GDP* (2003): 1.9%; per capita expenditure U.S.$488.

[1]Mainland and island areas only; excludes coastal water. [2]As of March. [3]With permanent civilian population only. [4]Total includes 2001 census population for Norfolk Island. [5]1992–93. [6]2001. [7]Taxes on products less subsidies ($A 66,693,000,000) less statistical discrepancy ($A 1,251,000,000). [8]Represents remainder. [9]Detail does not add to total given because of rounding. [10]1991–92. [11]2001–02. [12]1998–99. [13]1997–98. [14]1995–96. [15]1996–97. [16]Slaughtered value. [17]At end of year. [18]Imports and exports f.o.b. [19]2002–03. [20]Qantas only. [21]A national survey conducted in 1996 put the number of persons who had very poor literacy and numeracy skills at about 17% of the total population (age 15 to 64). [22]Includes special education.

Internet resources for further information:
• Australian Bureau of Statistics http://www.abs.gov.au

Austria

Official name: Republik Österreich (Republic of Austria).
Form of government: federal state with two legislative houses (Federal Council [64]; National Council [183]).
Chief of state: President.
Head of government: Chancellor.
Capital: Vienna.
Official language: German.
Official religion: none.
Monetary unit: 1 euro (€) = 100 cents; valuation (Sept. 1, 2005) 1 U.S.$ = €0.80; 1 £ = €1.47[1].

Area and population		area		population
States	**Capitals**	**sq mi**	**sq km**	**2003 estimate**
Burgenland	Eisenstadt	1,531	3,965	276,419
Kärnten	Klagenfurt	3,682	9,536	559,440
Niederösterreich	Sankt Pölten	7,404	19,178	1,552,848
Oberösterreich	Linz	4,626	11,982	1,387,086
Salzburg	Salzburg	2,762	7,154	521,238
Steiermark	Graz	6,329	16,392	1,190,574
Tirol	Innsbruck	4,883	12,648	683,317
Vorarlberg	Bregenz	1,004	2,601	356,590
Wien (Vienna)	—	160	415	1,590,242
TOTAL		32,383[2]	83,871	8,117,754

Demography

Population (2005): 8,168,000.
Density (2005): persons per sq mi 252.3, persons per sq km 97.4.
Urban-rural (2003): urban 65.8%; rural 34.2%.
Sex distribution (2003): male 48.52%; female 51.48%.
Age breakdown (2003): under 15, 16.4%; 15–29, 18.4%; 30–44, 24.7%; 45–59, 18.8%; 60–74, 14.2%; 75 and over, 7.5%.
Population projection: (2010) 8,232,000; (2020) 8,304,000.
Ethnic composition (2000): Austrian 86.5%; German Swiss 4.0%; German 3.5%; Bosniac 0.9%; Turkish 0.9%; Polish 0.5%; other 3.7%.
Religious affiliation (2000): Christian 89.8%, of which Roman Catholic 75.5%, unaffiliated Christian 5.6%, Protestant (mostly Lutheran) 5.0%, Orthodox 1.9%; Muslim 2.2%; nonreligious 6.8%; other 1.2%.
Major cities (2001): Vienna 1,550,123 (urban agglomeration 2,179,000[3]); Graz 226,244; Linz 183,504; Salzburg 142,662; Innsbruck 113,392; Klagenfurt 90,141.

Vital statistics

Birth rate per 1,000 population (2003): 9.5 (world avg. 21.1); (2003) legitimate 64.7%; illegitimate 35.3%.
Death rate per 1,000 population (2003): 9.6 (world avg. 9.0).
Natural increase rate per 1,000 population (2003): −0.1 (world avg. 12.1).
Total fertility rate (avg. births per childbearing woman; 2003): 1.4.
Marriage rate per 1,000 population (2003): 4.6.
Divorce rate per 1,000 population (2003): 2.3.
Life expectancy at birth (2003): male 76.0 years; female 81.8 years.
Major causes of death per 100,000 population (2003): diseases of the circulatory system 432.2; malignant neoplasms (cancers) 238.1.

National economy

Budget (2004). Revenue: €59,237,000,000 (tax revenue 97.3%, of which turnover tax 32.0%, individual income taxes 29.2%, corporate income tax 7.3%, other taxes 28.8%; nontax revenue 2.7%). Expenditures: €62,667,000,000 (social security, health, and welfare 34.4%; education 14.3%; interest 13.3%; transportation 9.6%; public safety 3.8%; defense 2.8%).
Public debt (2001): U.S.$117,420,000,000.
Production (metric tons except as noted). Agriculture, forestry, fishing (2004): sugar beets 3,045,000, wheat 1,718,000, corn (maize) 1,603,000, barley 1,007,000, potatoes 685,000, apples 482,000, grapes 351,000, triticale 236,000, rye 213,000, cabbages 118,000; livestock (number of live animals) 3,125,000 pigs, 2,051,000 cattle, 11,000,000 chickens; roundwood (2003) 17,055,000 cu m; fish catch (2002) 2,683. Mining and quarrying (2002): iron ore 1,941,800; magnesite 728,200; talc 140,000. Manufacturing (value added in U.S.$'000,000; 2000): nonelectrical machinery and apparatus 3,907; electrical machinery and apparatus 3,786; food products and beverages 3,112; fabricated metals 2,896; chemicals and chemical products 2,246; base metals 2,050. Energy production (consumption) (kW-hr; 2004) 64,285,000,000 (67,365,000,000); hard coal (metric tons; 2002) none (3,890,000); lignite (metric tons; 2002) 1,411,800 (1,587,000); crude petroleum (barrels; 2003) 7,200,000 ([2002] 63,299,000); petroleum products (metric tons; 2003) 6,700,000 (11,900,000); natural gas (cu m; 2004) 1,898,000,000 (8,993,000,000).
Tourism (U.S.$'000,000; 2003): receipts U.S.$14,036; expenditures U.S.$11,735.
Population economically active (2003): total 3,967,000; activity rate of total population 49.2% (participation rates: ages 15–64, 71.8%; female 44.6%; unemployed [November 2003–October 2004] 7.1%).

Price index (2000 = 100)							
	1998	1999	2000	2001	2002	2003	2004
Consumer price index	94.2	94.8	100.0	102.7	104.5	105.9	108.1

Gross national product (2004): U.S.$262,147,000,000 (U.S.$32,300 per capita).

Structure of gross domestic product and labour force				
	2002			
	in value €'000,000	% of total value	labour force	% of labour force
Agriculture, forestry	4,685	2.1	215,300	5.4
Mining	744	0.3	8,300	0.2
Manufacturing	42,219	19.3	747,100	18.7
Construction	15,151	6.9	338,000	8.5
Public utilities	4,477	2.1	35,200	0.9
Transp. and commun.	14,791	6.8	251,800	6.3
Trade, restaurants	34,133	15.6	818,900	20.5
Finance, real estate	48,538	22.2	436,200	10.9
Pub. admin., defense	11,835	5.4	248,400	6.2
Services	29,005	13.3	736,500	18.4
Other	12,755[4]	5.8[4]	161,000	4.0
TOTAL	218,333	100.0[2]	3,996,700	100.0

Household income and expenditure. Average household size (2003) 2.4; average annual disposable income per household (2003) €28,709 (U.S.$32,403); sources of income (1995): wages and salaries 54.8%, transfer payments 25.9%; expenditure (2001): housing and energy 19.3%, transportation 12.6%, food and nonalcoholic beverages 12.6%, cafe and hotel expenditures 12.2%.
Land use as % of total land area (2000): in temporary crops 16.9%, in permanent crops 0.9%, in pasture 23.2%; overall forest area 47.0%.

Foreign trade[5]

Balance of trade (current prices)						
	1999	2000	2001	2002	2003	2004
€'000,000,000	−5.05	−5.25	−4.44	+0.30	−2.09	−0.29
% of total	4.0%	3.6%	2.9%	0.2%	1.3%	0.2%

Imports (2004): €89,420,000,000 (2002; machinery and transport equipment 38.9%, of which road vehicles 11.2%, electrical machinery and apparatus 7.6%; chemicals and related products 11.3%; mineral fuels 7.4%; food products 5.2%). *Major import sources:* Germany 42.6%; Italy 6.8%; France 4.0%; United States 3.3%; Czech Republic 3.2%; Hungary 3.0%.
Exports (2004): €89,131,000,000 (2002; machinery and apparatus 32.9%; chemical products 10.2%; transportation equipment 9.8%; paper and paper products 4.6%; fabricated metals 4.3%; iron and steel 4.1%). *Major export destinations:* Germany 32.1%; Italy 8.6%; United States 6.0%; Switzerland 4.5%; United Kingdom 4.2%; France 4.2%; Hungary 3.8%.

Transport and communications

Transport. Railroads[6]: (2002) length 5,616 km; (2003) passenger-km 8,248,700,000; (2004) metric ton-km cargo 17,931,100,000. Roads (2002): total length 200,000 km (paved 100%). Vehicles (2004): passenger cars 4,109,129; trucks and buses 342,384. Air transport (2003)[7]: passenger-km 17,965,000,000; metric ton-km cargo 442,549,000; airports (2002) with scheduled flights 6.

Communications				units per 1,000
Medium	**date**	**unit**	**number**	**persons**
Daily newspapers	2000	circulation	2,380,000	296
Radio	2000	receivers	6,050,000	753
Television	2002	receivers	4,364,000	542
Telephones	2004	main lines	3,763,000	463
Cellular telephones	2004	subscribers	7,990,000	984
Personal computers	2004	units	3,420,000	421
Internet	2004	users	3,900,000	480

Education and health

Educational attainment (2002). Percentage of population age 25 and over having: no formal schooling through lower-secondary education 22%; upper secondary/higher vocational 63%; university 14%. *Literacy:* virtually 100%.

Education (2002–03)				student/
	schools	teachers	students	teacher ratio
Primary/lower secondary (age 6–13)	4,458	67,152	649,198	9.7
Upper secondary/voc. (age 14–17)	734	41,840	326,891	7.8
Higher[8]	19	16,099	242,598	15.1

Health: physicians (2004[9]) 37,447 (1 per 216 persons); hospital beds (2003[9]) 65,025 (1 per 124 persons); infant mortality rate per 1,000 live births (2003) 4.5.
Food (2002): daily per capita caloric intake 3,673 (vegetable products 67%; animal products 33%); 140% of FAO recommended minimum requirement.

Military

Total active duty personnel (2004): 35,000 (army 82.9%; air force 17.1%).
Military expenditure as percentage of GDP (2003): 0.8%; per capita expenditure U.S.$245.

[1]The Austrian Schilling (S) was the former monetary unit; on Jan. 1, 2002, S 13.76 = €1. [2]Detail does not add to total given because of rounding. [3]2003. [4]Value-added tax less imputed bank service charges and subsidies. [5]Imports c.i.f., exports f.o.b. [6]Federal railways only. [7]Austrian Airlines Group. [8]Universities only. [9]January 1.

Internet resources for further information:
• **Austrian Central Office of Statistics** http://www.statistik.at
• **Austrian Press and Information Service (Washington, D.C.)** http://www.austria.org/index.html

Azerbaijan

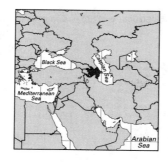

Official name: Azərbaycan Respublikası (Republic of Azerbaijan).
Form of government: unitary multiparty republic with a single legislative body (National Assembly [124¹]).
Head of state and government: President assisted by Prime Minister.
Capital: Baku (Azerbaijani: Bakı).
Official language: Azerbaijani.
Official religion: none.
Monetary unit: 1 manat (A.M.) = 100 gopik; valuation (Sept. 1, 2005) free rate, 1 U.S.$ = A.M. 4,613; 1 £ = A.M. 8,493.

Area and population

Economic regions²	area sq km	population 2000 estimate
Absheron	5,400	2,182,000
Gyadza	5,400	529,000
Kazakh	7,100	568,000
Kelbadjar	7,400	259,000
Khachmas	7,000	455,000
Lenkoran	6,100	744,000
Mil-Karabakh	6,500	696,000
Mugan-Salyan	9,000	621,000
Priarak	4,300	323,000
Sheki	9,000	531,000
Shirvan	11,200	661,000
Upper-Karabakh³	2,700	143,000
Autonomous republic		
Nakhchivan	5,500	363,000
TOTAL	86,600	8,075,000⁴

Demography

Population (2005): 8,381,000.
Density (2005): persons per sq mi 250.9, persons per sq km 96.8.
Urban-rural (2005⁵): urban 51.5%; rural 48.5%.
Sex distribution (2004): male 49.10%; female 50.90%.
Age breakdown (2005⁵): under 15, 26.4%; 15–29, 27.8%; 30–44, 24.0%; 45–59, 12.6%; 60 and over, 9.2%.
Population projection: (2010) 8,710,000; (2020) 9,350,000.
Doubling time: 70 years.
Ethnic composition (1999): Azerbaijani 90.6%; Lezgian 2.2%; Russian 1.8%; Armenian 1.5%; other 3.9%.
Religious affiliation (2000): Muslim *c.* 84%, of which Shī'ī *c.* 59%, Sunnī *c.* 25%; Orthodox *c.* 4%; nonreligious *c.* 11%; other *c.* 1%.
Major cities (2003): Baku 1,828,800; Gäncä 302,200; Sumqayıt (Sumgait) 289,700; Mingäçevir (Mingechaur) 94,900; Äli Bayramlı (2002) 68,700.

Vital statistics

Birth rate per 1,000 population (2004): 16.1 (world avg. 21.1); legitimate 89.5%; illegitimate 10.5%.
Death rate per 1,000 population (2004): 6.1 (world avg. 9.0).
Natural increase rate per 1,000 population (2004): 10.0 (world avg. 12.1).
Total fertility rate (avg. births per childbearing woman; 2002): 1.8.
Life expectancy at birth (2004): male 69.6 years; female 75.2 years.
Major causes of death per 100,000 population (2004): diseases of the circulatory system 345.5; malignant neoplasms (cancers) 77.2; diseases of the respiratory system 38.7; accidents, poisoning, and violence 25.9.

National economy

Budget (2004). Revenue: A.M. 7,405,800,000,000 (tax revenue 83.2%, of which value-added tax 30.6%, enterprise profits tax 15.1%, personal income tax 15.0%, import duties 6.9%, excise taxes 4.9%; nontax revenue 16.8%). Expenditures: A.M. 7,505,000,000,000 (education 19.6%; national economy 19.4%; social security 15.8%; defense 10.4%; health 4.9%).
Public debt (external, outstanding; 2003): U.S.$1,132,000,000.
Production (metric tons except as noted). Agriculture, forestry, fishing (2004): cereals 2,158,200, vegetables (except potatoes) 1,076,200, potatoes 930,400, fruit (except grapes) 424,600, cotton 135,700, sugar beets 56,800, grapes 54,900, tobacco leaves 6,500, tea 1,000; livestock (number of live animals) 7,488,100 sheep and goats, 2,315,700 cattle; roundwood (2003) 13,500 cu m; fish catch (2002) 11,334. Mining and quarrying (2001): alumina 95,000; gypsum 60,000. Manufacturing (gross value of production in A.M. '000,000; 2003): food, beverages, and tobacco products 4,216,600; petroleum products 3,162,800; chemicals and chemical products 697,000; fabricated metal products 684,100. Energy production (consumption): electricity (kW-hr; 2004) 21,500,000,000 ([2003] 18,407,000,000); coal (metric tons; 2002) none (none); crude petroleum (barrels; 2004) 114,000,000 ([2002] 47,000,000); petroleum products (metric tons; 2003) 5,476,000 ([2002] 3,079,000); natural gas (cu m; 2004) 4,900,000,000 ([2003] 5,100,000,000).
Household income and expenditure. Average household size (2003) 4.4; income per household (2003) A.M. 2,254,450 (U.S.$459); sources of money income (2003): self-employment 55.2%, wages and salaries 7.5%, transfers 7.5%, other 29.8%; expenditure, n.a.
Tourism (2003): receipts U.S.$57,700,000; expenditures U.S.$111,400,000.
Gross national product (at current market prices; 2004): U.S.$7,828,000,000 (U.S.$950 per capita).

Structure of gross domestic product and labour force

	2003 in value A.M. '000,000	% of total value	labour force	% of labour force
Agriculture	4,592,000	13.1	1,499,600	39.5
Petroleum and natural gas	10,025,300	28.6	42,300	1.1
Manufacturing	2,839,300	8.1	169,900	4.5
Public utilities	385,600	1.1	39,800	1.0
Construction	4,241,500	12.1	180,000	4.7
Transp. and commun.	3,330,100	9.5	178,500	4.7
Trade	2,769,200	7.9	630,100	16.6
Finance, real estate	} 4,416,700	} 12.6	110,500	2.9
Pub. admin., defense			330,000	8.7
Services			566,300	14.9
Other	2,453,700⁶	7.0⁶	54,400⁷	1.4⁷
TOTAL	35,053,400	100.0	3,801,400	100.0

Population economically active (2003): total 3,801,400; activity rate of total population 46.0% (participation rates: n.a.; female 47.8%; unemployed 1.4%).

Price index (2000 = 100)

	1997	1998	1999	2000	2001	2002	2003
Consumer price index	108.2	107.3	98.2	100.0	101.5	104.4	106.7

Land use as % of total land area (2000): in temporary crops 19.2%, in permanent crops 2.8%, in pasture 29.6%; overall forest area 13.1%.

Foreign trade

Balance of trade (current prices)

	1999	2000	2001	2002	2003	2004
U.S.$'000,000	−106	+573	+883	+502	−35	+100
% of total	5.4%	19.6%	23.6%	13.1%	0.7%	1.4%

Imports (2004): U.S.$3,516,000,000 (2002; machinery and equipment 23.8%, natural gas 12.9%, iron and steel 11.6%, food 10.3%, transport equipment 7.4%). *Major import sources* (2004): Russia 16.2%; United Kingdom 12.0%; Kazakhstan 6.7%; Turkey 6.4%; Germany 5.6%; Ukraine 4.9%.
Exports (2004): U.S.$3,615,500,000 (2002; crude petroleum 68.1%, refined petroleum 19.6%, food products 1.8%). *Major export destinations* (2004): Italy 44.7%; Israel 9.0%; Russia 5.8%; Georgia 5.2%; Turkey 5.1%.

Transport and communications

Transport. Railroads (2004): length 2,122 km; passenger-km 792,000,000; metric ton-km cargo 7,670,000,000. Roads (2002): total length 45,870 km (paved 94%). Vehicles (2004): passenger cars 403,964; trucks and buses 99,909. Air transport (2004): passenger-km 1,443,000,000; metric ton-km cargo 312,000,000; airports (2002) 3.

Communications

Medium	date	unit	number	units per 1,000 persons
Daily newspapers	2000	circulation	217,000	27
Radio	2000	receivers	177,000	22
Television	2001	receivers	2,604,000	321
Telephones	2004	main lines	983,600	116
Cellular telephones	2004	subscribers	1,782,900	211
Personal computers	2004	units	149,000	18
Internet	2004	users	408,000	48

Education and health

Educational attainment (1999). Percentage of population age 25 and over having: primary education 4.1%; some secondary 9.3%; secondary 50.1%; vocational 4.2%; some higher 0.9%; higher 13.3%. *Literacy* (1999): percentage of total population 15 and over literate 98.8%.

Education (2004–05)

	schools	teachers	students	student/ teacher ratio
Primary (age 6–13) } Secondary (age 14–17)	4,553	173,819	1,634,341	9.4
Voc., teacher tr.	59	7,028	55,794	7.9
Higher	42	13,630	127,248	9.3

Health (2004): physicians 30,000 (1 per 278 persons); hospital beds (2003) 68,600 (1 per 120 persons); infant mortality rate per 1,000 live births 9.8.
Food (2002): daily per capita caloric intake 2,575 (vegetable products 85%, animal products 15%); 101% of FAO recommended minimum requirement.

Military

Total active duty personnel (2004): 66,490 (army 85.5%, navy 2.6%, air force 11.9%). *Military expenditure as percentage of GDP* (2003): 1.9%; per capita expenditure U.S.$17.

¹Excludes one vacant seat reserved for Nagorno-Karabakh representative. ²Administratively, Azerbaijan is divided into 59 regions, 7 cities, and 1 autonomous republic. ³Controlled in part by Armenian forces from 1993. ⁴Sum of grossly rounded parts; beginning of year 2003 population estimate is 8,202,500. ⁵January 1. ⁶Taxes and subsidies on goods and services. ⁷Unemployed.

Internet resources for further information:
• The National Bank of Azerbaijan Republic
  http://www.nba.az/eng
• The State Statistical Committee of Azerbaijan Republic
  http://www.azstat.org

Bahamas, The

Official name: The Commonwealth of The Bahamas.
Form of government: constitutional monarchy with two legislative houses (Senate [16]; House of Assembly [40]).
Chief of state: British Monarch represented by Governor-General.
Head of government: Prime Minister.
Capital: Nassau.
Official language: English.
Official religion: none.
Monetary unit: 1 Bahamian dollar (B$) = 100 cents; valuation (Sept. 1, 2005) 1 U.S.$ = B$1.00; 1 £ = B$1.84.

Area and population

Islands and Island Groups[2]	area[1] sq mi	area[1] sq km	population 2000 census
Abaco, Great and Little	649	1,681	13,170
Acklins	192	497	428
Andros	2,300	5,957	7,686
Berry Islands	12	31	709
Bimini Islands	9	23	1,717
Cat Island	150	388	1,647
Crooked and Long Cay	93	241	350
Eleuthera	187	484	7,999
Exuma, Great, and Exuma Cays	112	290	3,571
Grand Bahama	530	1,373	46,994
Harbour Island	3	8	1,639
Inagua, Great and Little	599	1,551	969
Long Island	230	596	2,992
Mayaguana	110	285	259
New Providence	80	207	210,832
Ragged Island	14	36	72
Rum Cay	30	78	80
San Salvador	63	163	970
Spanish Wells	10	26	1,527
Other uninhabited cays and rocks	9	23	—
TOTAL	5,382	13,939[3]	303,611

Demography

Population (2005): 323,000.
Density (2005)[4]: persons per sq mi 83.0, persons per sq km 32.1.
Urban-rural (2003): urban 89.5%; rural 10.5%.
Sex distribution (2004): male 48.93%; female 51.07%.
Age breakdown (2004): under 15, 28.3%; 15–29, 26.1%; 30–44, 22.5%; 45–59, 14.2%; 60–74, 6.8%; 75 and over, 2.1%.
Population projection: (2010) 344,000; (2020) 385,000.
Doubling time: 74 years.
Ethnic composition (2000): local black 67.5%; mulatto 14.2%; British 12.0%; Haitian black 3.0%; U.S. white 2.4%; other 0.9%.
Religious affiliation (2000): non-Anglican Protestant 54.5%; Roman Catholic 15.6%; Anglican 8.9%; nonreligious 5.3%; Spiritist 1.5%; other (mostly independent and unaffiliated Christian) 14.2%.
Major cities (2002): Nassau 179,300; Freeport 42,600; West End 7,800; Cooper's Town 5,700; Marsh Harbour 3,600.

Vital statistics

Birth rate per 1,000 population (2004): 18.2 (world avg. 21.1); (2000) legitimate 43.2%; illegitimate 56.8%.
Death rate per 1,000 population (2004): 8.8 (world avg. 9.0).
Natural increase rate per 1,000 population (2004): 9.4 (world avg. 12.1).
Total fertility rate (avg. births per childbearing woman; 2004): 2.2.
Marriage rate per 1,000 population (2001): 5.8.
Life expectancy at birth (2004): male 62.2 years; female 69.1 years.
Major causes of death per 100,000 population (2000): diseases of the circulatory system 145.0; HIV/AIDS 80.7; malignant neoplasms (cancers) 73.8; accidents and violence 71.8; diabetes 34.6.

National economy

Budget (2004). Revenue: B$1,051,623,000 (import taxes 43.7%, stamp taxes from imports 9.5%, departure taxes 6.6%, business and professional licenses 6.6%). Expenditures: B$1,184,555,000 (education 19.0%, health 15.8%, public order 11.9%, interest on public debt 10.4%, defense 3.2%).
National debt (2004): U.S.$1,813,300,000.
Production (metric tons except as noted). Agriculture, forestry, fishing (2004): sugarcane 55,000, citrus fruits 21,700; livestock (number of live animals) 3,000,000 chickens; roundwood (2003) 17,000 cu m; fish catch (2002) 9,300 (mainly lobsters, crayfish, and conch). Mining and quarrying (2002): aragonite 1,200,000; salt 900,000. Manufacturing (value of export production; 2001): rum 38,190; chemical products 13,842. Energy production (consumption): electricity (kW-hr; 2003) 1,797,029,000 (1,656,600,000); petroleum products (metric tons; 2002) none (677,000).
Tourism (U.S.$'000,000; 2003): receipts 1,782; expenditures 305.
Household income and expenditure. Average household size (2000) 3.5; income per household (2004) B$39,626 (U.S.$39,626); sources of income: n.a.; expenditure (1995)[5]: housing 32.8%, transportation and communications 14.8%, food and beverages 13.8%, household furnishings 8.9%.
Gross national product (at current market prices; 2003): U.S.$3,280,000,000 (U.S.$10,450 per capita).

Structure of gross domestic product and labour force

	2002[6] in value B$'000,000	2002[6] % of total value	2000 labour force	2000 % of labour force
Agriculture, fishing	205	4.6	5,058	3.3
Manufacturing	125	2.8	6,108	4.0
Mining			412	0.2
Public utilities	356	8.0	1,813	1.2
Construction	73	1.6	16,980	11.0
Transp. and commun.	432	9.8	10,776	7.0
Trade, restaurants	867	19.6	46,908	30.4
Finance, real estate			15,900	10.3
Pub. admin., defense			13,069	8.5
Services	2,372	53.5	29,630	19.2
Other			7,742[7]	5.0[7]
TOTAL	4,430	100.0[3]	154,396	100.0[3]

Population economically active (2000): total 154,396; activity rate of total population 50.9% (participation rates: ages 15–64, 76.6%; female 47.5%; unemployed [2003] 10.8%).

Price index (2000 = 100)

	1998	1999	2000	2001	2002	2003	2004
Consumer price index	97.2	98.4	100.0	102.0	104.3	107.4	108.3

Land use as % of total land area (2000): in temporary crops 0.7%, in permanent crops 0.4%, in pasture 0.2%; overall forest area 84.1%.

Foreign trade[8]

Balance of trade (current prices)

	1998	1999	2000	2001	2002	2003
B$'000,000	–1,515	–1,325	–1,447	–1,551	–1,450	–1,509
% of total	71.6%	60.9%	56.6%	67.4%	65.1%	67.4%

Imports (2003): B$1,874,000,000 (2001; machinery and apparatus 16.0%; food products 14.2%; refined petroleum 14.1%; transport equipment 10.3%). *Major import sources* (2003): South Korea 19.6%; U.S. 18.1%; Italy 9.9%; Norway 9.6%; France 7.9%.
Exports (2003): B$365,000,000 (2001; crustaceans and mollusks [primarily crayfish] 19.1%; polystyrene 19.1%; refined petroleum 18.3%; rum 10.2%). *Major export destinations* (2003): U.S. 35.2%; Peru 10.0%; Germany 9.7%; Spain 9.7%; France 7.7%.

Transport and communications

Transport. Railroads: none. Roads (2000): total length 1,673 mi, 2,693 km (paved 57%). Vehicles (2001): passenger cars 80,000; trucks and buses 25,000. Air transport (2001)[9]: passenger-mi 232,000,000, passenger-km 374,000,000; short ton-mi cargo 1,208,000, metric ton-km cargo 1,764,000; airports (1997) with scheduled flights 22.

Communications

Medium	date	unit	number	units per 1,000 persons
Daily newspapers	1996	circulation	28,000	99
Radio	1997	receivers	215,000	744
Television	2001	receivers	76,600	247
Telephones	2004	main lines	139,900	441
Cellular telephones	2004	subscribers	186,000	587
Internet	2004	users	93,000	293

Education and health

Educational attainment (2000). Percentage of population age 15 and over having: no formal schooling 1.5%; primary education 8.7%; incomplete secondary 19.9%; complete secondary 53.7%; incomplete higher 8.1%; complete higher 7.1%; not stated 1.0%. *Literacy* (2002): total percentage age 15 and over literate 95.5%; males literate 94.7%; females literate 96.4%.

Education (1996–97)

	schools	teachers	students	student/teacher ratio
Primary (age 5–10)	113	1,540	34,199	22.2
Secondary (age 11–16)[10]	...	1,352	27,970	20.7
Higher[11]	1	160	3,463	21.6

Health (2001): physicians 458 (1 per 672 persons); hospital beds 1,540 (1 per 200 persons); infant mortality rate per 1,000 live births (2004) 25.7.
Food (2002): daily per capita caloric intake 2,755 (vegetable products 67%, animal products 33%); 114% of FAO recommended minimum requirement.

Military

Total active duty personnel (2004): 860 (paramilitary coast guard 100%). *Military expenditure as percentage of GDP* (2003): 0.6%; per capita expenditure U.S.$92.

[1]Includes areas of lakes and ponds, as well as lagoons and sounds almost entirely surrounded by land; area of land only is about 3,890 sq mi (10,070 sq km). [2]For local administrative purposes, The Out Islands of the Bahamas are divided into 31 districts; New Providence Island is administered directly by the national government. [3]Detail does not add to total given because of rounding. [4]Land area only. [5]Weights of retail price index components. [6]Derived figures from UN source. [7]Includes 552 not adequately defined and 7,190 unemployed. [8]Imports c.i.f.; exports f.o.b. [9]Bahamasair only. [10]Public sector only. [11]College of The Bahamas only; 1997–98.

Internet resources for further information:
• **The Central Bank of The Bahamas** http://www.bahamascentralbank.com
• **The Commonwealth of The Bahamas**
  http://www.bahamas.gov.bs/bahamasweb2/home.nsf

Bahrain

Official name: Mamlakat al-Baḥrayn (Kingdom of Bahrain).
Form of government: constitutional monarchy with a parliament comprising two bodies (Chamber of Deputies [40]; Consultative Council [40])[1].
Chief of state: Monarch.
Head of government: Prime Minister.
Capital: Manama.
Official language: Arabic.
Official religion: Islam.
Monetary unit: 1 Bahrain dinar (BD) = 1,000 fils; valuation (Sept. 1, 2005) 1 BD = U.S.$2.66 = £1.44.

Area and population

Governorates[2]	Principal cities	area		population 2001 census
		sq mi	sq km	
Capital	Manama	...	...	163,696
Central	Ar-Rifāʿ	...	...	167,691
Muharraq[3]	Muharraq[3]	...	...	103,576
Northern	Madīnat Ḥamad	...	...	166,824
Southern	ʿAwālī	...	...	44,764
TOTAL		278[4]	720[4]	650,604[5]

Demography

Population (2005): 715,000.
Density (2005): persons per sq mi 2,571.9, persons per sq km 993.1.
Urban-rural (2003): urban 90.0%; rural 10.0%.
Sex distribution (2003): male 57.47%; female 42.53%.
Age breakdown (2004): under 15, 28.3%; 15–29, 23.2%; 30–44, 25.6%; 45–59, 17.7%; 60–74, 4.2%; 75 and over, 1.0%.
Population projection: (2010) 778,000; (2020) 895,000.
Doubling time: 49 years.
Ethnic composition (2000): Bahraini Arab 63.9%; Indo-Pakistani 14.8%, of which Urdu 4.5%, Malayali 3.5%; Persian 13.0%; Filipino 4.5%; British 2.1%; other 1.7%.
Religious affiliation (2000): Muslim 82.4%, of which Shīʿī *c.* 58%, Sunnī *c.* 24%; Christian 10.5%; Hindu 6.3%; other 0.8%.
Major urban areas (2001): Manama 143,035; Muharraq 91,307; Ar-Rifāʿ 79,550; Madīnat Ḥamad 52,718; Madīnat ʿĪsā 36,833.

Vital statistics

Birth rate per 1,000 population (2004): 18.5 (world avg. 21.1).
Death rate per 1,000 population (2004): 4.0 (world avg. 9.0).
Natural increase rate per 1,000 population (2004): 14.5 (world avg. 12.1).
Total fertility rate (avg. births per childbearing woman; 2004): 2.7.
Marriage rate per 1,000 population (2003): 7.8.
Divorce rate per 1,000 population (2003): 1.3.
Life expectancy at birth (2004): male 71.5 years; female 76.5 years.
Major causes of death per 100,000 population (2003): diseases of the circulatory system 86.6; malignant neoplasms (cancers) 39.3; injury and poisoning 26.5; metabolic and immunity diseases 24.4; diseases of the respiratory system 20.7; diseases of the digestive system 13.8; infectious and parasitic diseases 11.9; ill-defined conditions 39.3.

National economy

Budget (2003). Revenue: BD 1,145,500,000 (petroleum revenue 73%, non-petroleum revenue 27%). Expenditures: BD 1,080,300,000 (infrastructure 32%, public administration 29%, social services 21%, transfers 14%, economic services 3%, other 1%).
Production (metric tons except as noted). Agriculture, forestry, fishing (2003): dates 17,000, fruit (excluding dates; 2002) 8,336, vegetables 7,922 (of which tomatoes 3,067, onions 2,159), hen's eggs 60,133,000 eggs, cow's milk 6,728 litres; livestock (number of live animals; 2003) 17,500 sheep, 16,000 goats, 13,000 cattle; roundwood, n.a.; fish catch (2003) 13,638. Manufacturing (barrels; 2003): gas oil 32,037,000; fuel oil 20,030,000; kerosene and jet fuel 19,297,000; naphtha 12,217,000; gasoline 6,913,000; aluminum 531,000 metric tons. Energy production (consumption): electricity (kW-hr; 2003) 7,768,000,000 (7,171,000,000); crude petroleum (barrels; 2003) 68,900,000[6] ([2002] 91,000,000); petroleum products (metric tons; 2002) 10,618,000 (882,000); natural gas (cu m; 2003) 9,622,000,000 (9,622,000,000).
Gross national product (2003): U.S.$8,610,000,000 (U.S.$11,880 per capita).

Structure of gross domestic product and labour force

	2003		2001	
	value in BD '000,000	% of total value	labour force[7]	% of labour force[7]
Agriculture, fishing	22.5	0.6	4,483	1.5
Crude petroleum, nat. gas	899.5	24.9	} 2,780	0.9
Quarrying	10.9	0.3		
Manufacturing	403.7	11.2	49,979	16.2
Construction	139.1	3.8	26,416	8.6
Public utilities	49.6	1.4	2,515	0.8
Transp. and commun.	262.6	7.3	13,769	4.5
Trade, restaurants	369.4	10.2	47,570	15.5
Finance, real estate	1,031.9	28.6	24,797	8.1
Pub. admin., defense	360.4	10.0	52,389	17.0
Services	343.8	9.5	61,256	19.9
Other	−281.3[8]	−7.8[8]	21,560[9]	7.0[9]
TOTAL	3,612.0[10]	100.0	307,514	100.0[11]

Population economically active (2002): total 319,000; activity rate of total population 46.3% (participation rates: ages 15 and over 64.1%; female 21.7%; unemployed [2001] 5.5%).

Price index (2000 = 100)

	1997	1998	1999	2000	2001	2002
Consumer price index	102.4	102.2	100.7	100.0	100.2	101.5

Public debt (2001): BD 773,600,000 (U.S.$2,057,800,000).
Tourism (2003): receipts from visitors U.S.$740,000,000; expenditures by nationals abroad U.S.$327,000,000.
Household income and expenditure. Average household size (2001) 6.2; expenditure (1984): food and tobacco 33.3%, housing 21.2%, household durable goods 9.8%, transportation and communications 8.5%, recreation 6.4%, clothing and footwear 5.9%.
Land use as % of total land area (2000): in temporary crops *c.* 3%, in permanent crops *c.* 6%, in pasture *c.* 6%; overall forest area, negligible.

Foreign trade[12]

Balance of trade (current prices)

	1998	1999	2000	2001	2002	2003
BD '000,000	−111.3	+166.5	+420.0	+482.0	+297.5	+454.1
% of total	4.3%	5.6%	10.8%	13.1%	7.3%	10.1%

Imports (2003): BD 2,027,700,000 (petroleum products 38.3%, machinery and transport equipment 22.5%, chemicals and chemical products 7.9%). *Major import sources*[13]: Japan 12.4%; Saudi Arabia 9.1%; Australia 8.0%; Germany 7.3%; U.K. 5.7%.
Exports (2003): BD 2,481,800,000 (petroleum products 70.9%, base metals, including aluminum [all forms] 13.8%, textiles and clothing 4.3%). *Major export destinations*[13]: Saudi Arabia 24.0%; U.S. 14.6%; Taiwan 10.2%; India 5.8%; U.A.E. 5.7%.

Transport and communications

Transport. Railroads: none. Roads (2003): total length 3,498 km (paved 79%). Vehicles (2002): passenger cars 176,261; trucks and buses 36,231. Air transport (2003)[14]: passenger-km 3,369,800,000; metric ton-km cargo 140,000,000; airports (2002) with scheduled flights 1.

Communications

Medium	date	unit	number	units per 1,000 persons
Daily newspapers	1996	circulation	67,000	117
Radio	2000	receivers	48,500	76
Television	2001	receivers	256,000	430
Telephones	2004	main lines	191,600	259
Cellular telephones	2004	subscribers	649,800	879
Personal computers	2004	units	121,000	164
Internet	2004	users	152,700	207

Education and health

Educational attainment (2001). Percentage of population age 15 and over having: no formal education 24.0%; primary education 37.1%; secondary 26.4%; higher 12.5%. *Literacy* (2002): percentage of population age 15 and over literate 89.1%; males literate 91.9%; females literate 85.0%.

Education (2001–02)

	schools	teachers	students	student/ teacher ratio
Primary (age 6–11)	241	9,970	150,054	15.1
Secondary (age 12–17)				
Higher[15]	2	696	14,187	20.4

Health (2003): physicians 1,189 (1 per 580 persons); hospital beds 1,912 (1 per 361 persons); infant mortality rate per 1,000 live births (2004) 17.9.

Military

Total active duty personnel (2004): 11,200 (army 75.9%, navy 10.7%, air force 13.4%)[16]. *Military expenditure as percentage of GDP* (2003): 5.1%; per capita expenditure U.S.$688.

[1]Constitutional monarchy declared Feb. 14, 2002. Seats of Chamber of Deputies are elected, and seats of the Consultative Council are appointed by the monarch. [2]As of the administrative reorganization announced July 2002. [3]Official name is Al-Muḥarraq. [4]Includes the area of Ḥawār island and other nearby islets awarded to Bahrain by the International Court of Justice in 2001. [5]Includes 4,053 living abroad. [6]Including offshore production totaling 55,100,000 barrels. [7]Excludes small number of unemployed non-Bahrainis. [8]Includes import duties less imputed bank service charges. [9]Includes 5,424 inadequately defined and 16,136 unemployed Bahrainis. [10]Detail does not add to total given because of rounding. [11]Of which *c.* 59% non-Bahrainis. [12]Imports c.i.f. [13]Excludes trade in petroleum. [14]One-fourth apportionment of international flights of Gulf Air (jointly administered by the governments of Bahrain, Oman, Qatar, and the United Arab Emirates). [15]Bahrain and Arabian Gulf universities only. [16]U.S. troops in Bahrain (end of 2004): 1,750.

Internet resources for further information:
• **Bahrain Government Homepage**
  http://www.bahrain.gov.bh/english/index.asp
• **Bahrain Monetary Agency http://www.bma.gov.bh**

Bangladesh

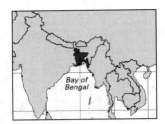

Official name: Gana Prajatantri
Bangladesh (People's Republic of
Bangladesh).
Form of government: unitary multiparty
republic with one legislative house
(Parliament [300[1]]).
Chief of state: President.
Head of government: Prime Minister.
Capital: Dhaka.
Official language: Bengali (Bangla).
Official religion: Islam.
Monetary unit: 1 Bangladesh taka
(Tk) = 100 paisa; valuation (Sept. 1,
2005) 1 U.S.$ = Tk 65.73;
1 £ = Tk 121.02.

Area and population		area		population
		sq mi	sq km	2001 census[2]
Divisions	**Administrative centres**			
Barisal	Barisal	5,134	13,297	8,514,000
Chittagong	Chittagong	7,906	20,476	23,796,682
Dhaka	Dhaka	12,015	31,119	40,592,431
Khulna	Khulna	8,600	22,274	15,185,026
Rajshahi	Rajshahi	13,326	34,513	31,477,606
Sylhet	Sylhet	4,863	12,596	8,290,857
Tribal region				
Chittagong Hill Tracts[3]	Rangamati	5,133	13,295	1,390,631
TOTAL		56,977[4]	147,570[4]	129,247,233

Demography

Population (2005): 137,636,000.
Density (2004)[5]: persons per sq mi 2,558.4, persons per sq km 987.8.
Urban-rural (2003): urban 24.2%; rural 75.8%.
Sex distribution (2004): male 51.29%; female 48.71%.
Age breakdown (2004): under 15, 33.5%; 15–29, 32.6%; 30–44, 18.2%; 45–59, 10.4%; 60–74, 4.3%; 75 and over, 1.0%.
Population projection: (2010) 150,491,000; (2020) 175,954,000.
Doubling time: 32 years.
Ethnic composition (1997): Bengali 97.7%; tribal 1.9%, of which Chakma 0.4%, Saontal 0.2%, Marma 0.1%; other 0.4%.
Religious affiliation (2000): Muslim 85.8%; Hindu 12.4%; Christian 0.7%; Buddhist 0.6%; other 0.5%.
Major cities/urban agglomerations (2001): Dhaka 5,644,235/10,403,597; Chittagong 2,199,590/3,361,244; Khulna 811,490/1,287,987; Rajshahi 402,646/678,728.

Vital statistics

Birth rate per 1,000 population (2004): 30.0 (world avg. 21.1).
Death rate per 1,000 population (2004): 8.5 (world avg. 9.0).
Natural increase rate per 1,000 population (2004): 21.5 (world avg. 12.1).
Total fertility rate (avg. births per childbearing woman; 2004): 3.2.
Marriage rate per 1,000 population (1998): 9.2.
Life expectancy at birth (2004): male 61.8 years; female 61.6 years.
Major causes of death per 100,000 population (2001): old age 65.3; diseases of the respiratory system 57.6; high blood pressure and heart disease 49.8; typhoid fever, influenza, and other fever 44.5; suicide, accidents, and poisoning 43.0.

National economy

Budget (2004–05). Revenue: Tk 431,900,000,000 (tax revenue 77.9%, of which value-added tax 25.0%, import duties 20.6%, income and profit taxes 14.5%; nontax revenue 17.7%; grants 4.4%). Expenditures: Tk 572,500,000,000 (development program 38.4%, interest payments 11.4%, education 8.1%, defense 4.8%, social security 2.8%, health 2.7%).
Production (metric tons except as noted). Agriculture, forestry, fishing (2004): paddy rice 37,910,000, sugarcane 6,484,000, potatoes 3,908,000, wheat 1,253,000, jute 800,000, bananas 700,000, sweet potatoes 320,000, oilseeds 312,300, mangoes 243,000, tea 60,000; livestock (number of live animals) 34,500,000 goats, 24,500,000 cattle, 1,260,000 sheep, 850,000 water buffalo, 140,000,000 chickens, 13,000,000 ducks; roundwood (2003) 28,009,946 cu m; fish catch (2002) 1,103,855. Mining and quarrying (2002): marine salt 350,000; industrial limestone 32,000. Manufacturing (value added in U.S.$'000,000; 1998): wearing apparel 839; tobacco products 634; textiles 567; industrial chemicals 499; food products 382; footwear 315; iron and steel 153. Energy production (consumption): electricity (kW-hr; 2003) 18,458,000,000 (16,132,000,000); coal (metric tons; 2002) none (700,000); crude petroleum (barrels; 2003) 2,200,000 ([2002] 11,000,000); petroleum products (metric tons; 2002) 865,000 (2,895,000); natural gas (cu m; 2002) 11,472,000,000 (11,472,000,000).
Household income. Average household size (2000) 5.7; average annual income per household Tk 52,389 (U.S.$1,277); sources of income: self-employment 56.9%, wages and salaries 28.1%, transfer payments 9.1%, other 5.9%; expenditure (2002–03): food and drink 64.5%, housing and energy 15.0%, clothing and footwear 5.9%, transport 3.3%, other 11.3%.
Population economically active (2000): total 52,847,000; activity rate of total population 47.3% (participation rates: over age 15, 58.8%; female 37.5%; unemployed 3.3%[6]).

Price index (2000 = 100)							
	1997	1998	1999	2000	2001	2002	2003
Consumer price index	85.1	92.2	97.8	100.0	102.0	105.4	111.4

Public debt (external, outstanding; 2003): U.S.$18,088,000,000.
Gross national product (2004): U.S.$61,230,000,000 (U.S.$440 per capita).

Structure of gross domestic product and labour force				
	2002–03		1999–2000	
	in value Tk '000,000	% of total value	labour force	% of labour force
Agriculture	630,590	21.1	36,217,000	60.1
Mining	33,020	1.1	364,000	0.6
Manufacturing	462,380	15.4	4,300,000	7.1
Construction	234,830	7.8	1,144,000	1.9
Public utilities	40,350	1.3	135,000	0.2
Transp. and commun.	312,150	10.4	2,672,000	4.4
Trade	406,810	13.5	7,045,000	11.7
Finance	301,660	10.0	415,000	0.7
Public admin., defense	77,850	2.6	} 5,775,000	9.6
Services	402,000	13.4		
Other	103,210[7]	3.4[7]	2,224,000[8]	3.7[8]
TOTAL	3,004,850	100.0	60,291,000	100.0

Land use as % of total land area (2000): in temporary crops 62.5%, in permanent crops 2.7%, in pasture 4.6%; overall forest area 10.2%.
Tourism (2003): receipts U.S.$57,000,000; expenditures U.S.$165,000,000.

Foreign trade[9]

Balance of trade (current prices)						
	1998–99	1999–2000	2000–01	2001–02	2002–03	2003–04
U.S.$'000,000	–1,904	–1,814	–1,963	–1,711	–2,151	–2,237
% of total	15.2%	13.6%	13.2%	12.5%	14.1%	13.1%

Imports (2003–04): U.S.$10,903,000,000 (capital goods 26.4%; textile yarn, fabrics, and made-up articles 14.8%; imports for export processing zone 8.1%; cotton 5.4%; rice and wheat 4.0%). *Major import sources* (2003): India 15.5%; China 13.8%; Singapore 9.5%; Japan 6.7%; Hong Kong 4.9%.
Exports (2003–04): U.S.$7,603,000,000 (woven garments 46.5%; hosiery and knitwear 28.3%; frozen fish and shrimp 5.1%; jute manufactures 3.3%). *Major export destinations* (2003): U.S. 24.6%; Germany 13.3%; U.K. 10.9%; France 5.6%; The Netherlands 3.9%.

Transport and communications

Transport. Railroads (1998–99): route length 1,699 mi, 2,734 km; passenger-mi 3,094,000,000, passenger-km 4,980,000,000; short ton-mi cargo 567,000,000, metric ton-km cargo 828,000,000. Roads (1999): total length 128,925 mi, 207,486 km (paved 10%). Vehicles (2004): passenger cars 185,000; trucks and buses 88,000. Air transport (2003)[10]: passenger-mi 2,831,000,000, passenger-km 4,556,000,000; short ton-mi cargo 94,619,000, metric ton-km cargo 149,160,000; airports with scheduled flights (2001) 8.

Communications				units per 1,000 persons
Medium	date	unit	number	
Daily newspapers	2000	circulation	6,880,000	53
Radio	2000	receivers	6,360,000	49
Television	2001	receivers	2,209,000	17
Telephones	2003	main lines	742,000	5.5
Cellular telephones	2003	subscribers	1,365,000	10.1
Personal computers	2003	units	1,050,000	7.8
Internet	2003	users	243,000	1.8

Education and health

Educational attainment (1991). Percentage of population age 25 and over having: no formal schooling 65.4%; primary education 17.1%; secondary 13.8%; postsecondary 3.7%. *Literacy* (2000): total population age 15 and over literate 41.3%; males literate 52.3%; females literate 29.9%.

Education (2000)				student/ teacher ratio
	schools	teachers	students	
Primary (age 6–10)	63,658	259,441	17,378,000	67.0
Secondary (age 11–17)	16,095	187,338	7,746,885	41.4
Voc., teacher tr.	138	2,560	44,832	17.5
Higher[11]	13	5,172	85,224	16.5

Health: physicians (2000) 29,746 (1 per 4,306 persons); hospital beds (2001) 44,030 (1 per 2,951 persons); infant mortality rate per 1,000 live births (2004) 64.3.
Food (2002): daily per capita caloric intake 2,205 (vegetable products 97%, animal products 3%); 95% of FAO recommended minimum requirement.

Military

Total active duty personnel (2004): 125,500 (army 87.6%, navy 7.2%, air force 5.2%). *Military expenditure as percentage of GDP* (2003): 1.2%; per capita expenditure U.S.$5.

---

[1]Excludes 45 seats reserved for women to be reinstated as of 2006 elections. [2]Preliminary figure. [3]Autonomous region for non-Bengali tribal people was created by accord signed in December 1997, formally established in May 1999, but mostly not implemented by the government as of mid-2005. [4]The total area excluding the river area equals 53,797 sq mi (139,334 sq km). [5]Based on the total area excluding the river area. [6]For year ending in June. [7]Import duties. [8]Includes not adequately defined and unemployed. [9]Import figures are f.o.b. in balance of trade and c.i.f. in commodities and trading partners. [10]Bangladesh Biman only. [11]Universities only.

Internet resources for further information:
• **National Data Bank** http://www.bbsgov.org
• **Bangladesh Bank** http://www.bangladesh-bank.org

Barbados

Official name: Barbados.
Form of government: constitutional monarchy with two legislative houses (Senate [21]; House of Assembly [30]).
Chief of state: British Monarch represented by Governor-General.
Head of government: Prime Minister.
Capital: Bridgetown.
Official language: English.
Official religion: none.
Monetary unit: 1 Barbados dollar (BDS$) = 100 cents; valuation (Sept. 1, 2005) 1 U.S.$ = BDS$2.00; 1 £ = BDS$3.68.

Area and population

Parishes[1]	area		population
	sq mi	sq km	1990 census
Christ Church	22	57	47,050
St. Andrew	14	36	6,346
St. George	17	44	17,905
St. James	12	31	21,001
St. John	13	34	10,206
St. Joseph	10	26	7,619
St. Lucy	14	36	9,455
St. Michael[2]	15	39	97,516
St. Peter	13	34	11,263
St. Philip	23	60	20,540
St. Thomas	13	34	11,590
TOTAL	166	430[3]	260,491

Demography

Population (2005): 270,000.
Density (2005): persons per sq mi 1,627, persons per sq km 627.9.
Urban-rural (2003): urban 51.7%; rural 48.3%.
Sex distribution (2003): male 48.26%; female 51.74%.
Age breakdown (2003): under 15, 21.2%; 15–29, 23.1%; 30–44, 25.8%; 45–59, 17.8%; 60–74, 8.1%; 75 and over, 4.0%.
Population projection: (2010) 273,000; (2020) 278,000.
Ethnic composition (2000): local black 87.1%; mulatto 6.0%; British expatriates 4.3%; U.S. white 1.2%; Indo-Pakistani 1.1%; other 0.3%.
Religious affiliation (2000): Christian 97.0%, of which Protestant 60.1% (including Anglican 28.6%), unaffiliated Christian 24.1%, independent Christian 6.5%, Roman Catholic 4.1%; Bahā'ī 1.3%; Muslim 0.8%; nonreligious/other 0.9%.
Major cities (1990): Bridgetown 6,070 (urban agglomeration [2003] 140,000); Speightstown *c.* 3,500.

Vital statistics

Birth rate per 1,000 population (2004): 13.0 (world avg. 21.1).
Death rate per 1,000 population (2004): 8.8 (world avg. 9.0).
Natural increase rate per 1,000 population (2004): 4.2 (world avg. 12.1).
Total fertility rate (avg. births per childbearing woman; 2004): 1.6.
Marriage rate per 1,000 population (2000): 13.1.
Divorce rate per 1,000 population (1995): 1.5.
Life expectancy at birth (2004): male 70.4 years; female 74.4 years.
Major causes of death per 100,000 population (1995): diseases of the circulatory system 369.7; malignant neoplasms (cancers) 163.6; endocrine and metabolic disorders 151.3; diseases of the respiratory system 56.3; accidents, poisonings, and violence 36.4; diseases of the digestive system 34.5.

National economy

Budget (2003). Revenue: BDS$1,843,800,000[4] (tax revenue *c.* 94%, of which personal income and company taxes 31.4%, value-added tax 29.8%, import duties 9.3%; nontax revenue *c.* 6%). Expenditures: BDS$2,009,200,000 (current expenditure 86.4%, of which wages and salaries 31.5%, debt payment 13.5%; capital expenditure 13.6%).
Production (metric tons except as noted). Agriculture, forestry, fishing (2004): raw sugar (2003) 36,300, sweet potatoes 2,700, cucumbers and gherkins 2,100, coconuts 1,800, okra 1,550, yams 1,375, chilies and green peppers 1,300, tomatoes 1,250, carrots 1,110, string beans 960; livestock (number of live animals) 27,000 sheep, 16,600 pigs, 14,300 cattle; roundwood (2003) 5,000 cu m; fish catch (2002) 2,500. Manufacturing (value added in U.S.$'000,000; 1997): industrial chemicals 87; food products 63; beverages (significantly rum and beer) 58; paper and paper products 32; fabricated metal products 23. Energy production (consumption): electricity (kW-hr; 2003) 806,000,000 (806,000,000); crude petroleum (barrels; 2002) 580,000 (none); petroleum products (metric tons; 2002) none (331,000); natural gas (cu m; 2002) 29,000,000 (29,000,000).
Household income and expenditure. Average household size (2000) 2.8; income per household (1988) BDS$13,455 (U.S.$6,690); sources of income: n.a.; expenditure (1994): food 39.4%, housing 16.8%, transportation 10.5%, household operations 8.1%, alcohol and tobacco 6.4%, fuel and light 5.2%, clothing and footwear 5.0%, other 8.6%.
Tourism: receipts from visitors (2003) U.S.$747,000,000; expenditures by nationals abroad U.S.$105,000,000.
Population economically active (2004): total 148,800[5]; activity rate of total population 54.6%[5] (participation rates: ages 15 and over, 70.7%[5]; female 49.1%[5]; unemployed [October 2003–September 2004] 9.9%).

Price index (2000 = 100)

	1997	1998	1999	2000	2001	2002	2003
Consumer price index	97.4	96.1	97.6	100.0	102.6	102.7	104.4

Public debt (external, outstanding; September 2004): U.S.$647,750,000.
Gross national product (2003): U.S.$2,512,000,000 (U.S.$9,270 per capita).

Structure of gross domestic product and labour force

	2003			
	in value BDS$'000,000	% of total value	labour force[6]	% of labour force[6]
Agriculture, fishing	160.2	3.0	5,000	3.9
Mining	31.0	0.6	[7]	[7]
Manufacturing	292.7	5.4	7,200	5.6
Construction	232.5	4.3	12,200[7]	9.4[7]
Public utilities	146.5	2.7	2,700	2.1
Transp. and commun.	374.6	6.9	4,500	3.5
Trade, tourism	1,251.0	23.2	32,400	25.0
Finance, real estate	847.1	15.7	9,000	7.0
Pub. admin., defense	780.5	14.5	28,700	22.2
Services	222.0	4.1	27,600	21.3
Other	1,055.1	19.6	...	...
TOTAL	5,393.2	100.0	129,300	100.0

Land use as % of total land area (2000): in temporary crops *c.* 37%, in permanent crops *c.* 2%, in pasture *c.* 5%; overall forest area *c.* 5%.

Foreign trade[8]

Balance of trade (current prices)

	1999	2000	2001	2002	2003	2004
BDS$'000,000	−1,689	−1,767	−1,619	−1,659	−1,592	−2,269
% of total	61.5%	61.9%	60.9%	63.2%	63.5%	67.1%

Imports (2003): BDS$2,050,000,000 (capital goods 20.9%; food and beverages 15.5%; mineral fuels 11.1%; chemicals and chemical products 5.1%). *Major import sources* (2002): U.S. 44.1%; Trinidad and Tobago 11.7%; U.K. 7.9%; Japan 4.5%; Canada 3.7%.
Exports (2003): BDS$458,000,000 (food and beverages 25.3%, of which sugar and molasses 9.2%, rum 7.0%; chemicals and chemical products 8.3%; electrical components 5.2%; other manufactures 17.5%). *Major export destinations* (2002): U.S. 16.5%; U.K. 11.9%; Trinidad and Tobago 11.0%; Jamaica 7.0%; bunkers and ships' stores 9.3%.

Transport and communications

Transport. Railroads: none. Roads (2002): total length 9,942 mi, 1,600 km (paved 99%). Vehicles (2002): passenger cars 81,648; trucks and buses 7,698. Air transport: (2001) passenger arrivals and departures 1,760,000; (2000) cargo unloaded and loaded 14,000 metric tons; airports (2002) with scheduled flights 1.

Communications

Medium	date	unit	number	units per 1,000 persons
Daily newspapers	1996	circulation	53,000	199
Radio	2001	receivers	202,000	749
Television	2001	receivers	83,700	310
Telephones	2003	main lines	134,000	497
Cellular telephones	2004	subscribers	171,000	631
Personal computers	2004	units	34,000	126
Internet	2004	users	150,000	554

Education and health

Educational attainment (1990). Percentage of population age 25 and over having: no formal schooling 0.4%; primary education 23.7%; secondary 60.3%[9]; higher 11.2%; other 4.4%. *Literacy* (2002): total population age 15 and over literate 99.7%; males literate 99.7%; females literate 99.7%.

Education (2002)

	schools	teachers	students	student/teacher ratio
Primary (age 3–11)	109	1,823	29,502	16.2
Secondary (age 12–16)	32	1,389	21,436	15.4
Higher	4	339	11,226	33.1

Health (2002): physicians 376 (1 per 721 persons); hospital beds 501 (1 per 541 persons); infant mortality rate per 1,000 live births (2004) 12.2.
Food (2002): daily per capita caloric intake 3,091 (vegetable products 75%, animal products 25%); 128% of FAO recommended minimum requirement.

Military

Total active duty personnel (2004): 610 (army 82.0%, navy 18.0%). *Military expenditure as percentage of GDP* (2003): 0.5%; per capita expenditure U.S.$49.

[1]Parishes and city of Bridgetown have no local administrative function. [2]Includes city of Bridgetown. [3]Detail does not add to total given because of rounding. [4]Current revenue only. [5]End of 2nd quarter (June) figure. [6]Employed only. [7]Construction includes Mining. [8]Imports c.i.f.; exports f.o.b. [9]Includes composite senior.

Internet resources for further information:
• Central Bank of Barbados http://www.centralbank.org.bb
• Profile of Barbados http://labour.gov.bb/blmis2/WEBDOC/ trends/profile_of_barbados.asp?stats-quart

Belarus

Official name: Respublika Belarus (Republic of Belarus).
Form of government: republic with two legislative bodies (Council of the Republic [64[1]]; House of Representatives [110[1]]).
Head of state and government: President assisted by Prime Minister.
Capital: Minsk.
Official languages: Belarusian; Russian.
Official religion: none.
Monetary unit: rubel[2] (Rbl; plural rubli); valuation (Sept. 1, 2005)
1 U.S.$ = (new) Rbl 2,154;
1 £ = (new) Rbl 3,965.

Area and population		area		population
		sq mi	sq km	2004[3] estimate
Provinces	**Capitals**			
Brest	Brest	12,700	32,800	1,462,900
Homyel (Gomel)	Homyel	15,600	40,400	1,505,400
Hrodna (Grodno)	Hrodna	9,700	25,100	1,146,100
Mahilyow (Mogilyov)	Mahilyow	11,200	29,100	1,169,200
Minsk (Myensk)	Minsk	15,500[4]	40,200[4]	1,503,000
Vitsyebsk (Vitebsk)	Vitsyebsk	15,500	40,000	1,321,100
City				
Minsk (Myensk)	—	4	4	1,741,400
TOTAL		80,200[5]	207,600[5]	9,849,100

Demography

Population (2005): 9,776,000.
Density (2005): persons per sq mi 122.0, persons per sq km 47.1.
Urban-rural (2004): urban 71.5%; rural 28.5%.
Sex distribution (2004): male 46.61%; female 53.39%.
Age breakdown (2004): under 15, 16.3%; 15–29, 23.7%; 30–44, 22.5%; 45–59, 19.0%; 60–74, 12.8%; 75 and over, 5.7%.
Population projection: (2010) 9,504,000; (2020) 8,958,000.
Ethnic composition (1999): Belarusian 81.2%; Russian 11.4%; Polish 3.9%; Ukrainian 2.4%; Jewish 0.3%; other 0.8%.
Religious affiliation (2000): Belarusian Orthodox 48.7%; Roman Catholic 13.2%; other (mostly nonreligious) 38.1%.
Major cities (2004): Minsk 1,682,900; Homyel 497,200; Mahilyow 365,400; Vitsyebsk 355,200; Hrodna 315,500.

Vital statistics

Birth rate per 1,000 population (2004): 10.5 (world avg. 21.1); (2000) legitimate 81.4%; illegitimate 18.6%.
Death rate per 1,000 population (2004): 14.1 (world avg. 9.0).
Natural increase rate per 1,000 population (2004): –3.6 (world avg. 12.1).
Total fertility rate (avg. births per childbearing woman; 2004): 1.4.
Marriage rate per 1,000 population (2002): 6.7.
Divorce rate per 1,000 population (2002): 3.8.
Life expectancy at birth (2004): male 62.8 years; female 74.7 years.
Major causes of death per 100,000 population (2003): diseases of the circulatory system 693.5; malignant neoplasms (cancers) 171.2; accidents, poisoning, and violence 161.6; diseases of the respiratory system 45.0.

National economy

Budget (2003). Revenue: Rbl 12,154,223,000,000 (tax revenue 76.8%, of which value-added tax 23.8%, income tax 8.4%, profit tax 7.7%, excise tax 6.9%, property tax 6.0%, other 24.0%; nontax revenue 23.2%). Expenditures: Rbl 12,646,135,000,000 (education 18.5%, target budgetary fund 15.3%, health 14.3%, subsidies 7.4%, public order 5.2%, capital expenditure 4.2%, defense 3.0%).
Public debt (external, outstanding; 2003): U.S.$678,000,000.
Household income and expenditure. Average household size (2000) 3.4; income per household, n.a.; sources of money income (2003): wages and salaries 49.2%, business activities 31.6%, transfers 18.1%; expenditure (2001): food and nonalcoholic beverages 53.6%, clothing and footwear 9.4%, housing and energy 7.2%, transport 6.3%, alcoholic beverages and tobacco products 5.9%.
Population economically active (2003): 4,480,000[6]; activity rate of total population 45.5% (participation rate [1999]: ages 15–64, 69.7%; female 53.4%; unemployed [2004] 1.9%).

Price and earnings indexes (2000 = 100)						
	1998	1999	2000	2001	2002	2003	2004
Consumer price index	9.4	37.2	100.0	161.1	229.6	294.8	351.7
Annual earnings index	7.9	33.2	100.0	208.8	321.1	425.5	439.1

Production (metric tons except as noted). Agriculture, forestry, fishing (2004): potatoes 8,500,000, maize for forage 6,500,000, sugar beets 2,500,000, barley 2,200,000, rye 1,725,000, wheat 1,254,000, cabbages 690,000, carrots 300,000; livestock (number of live animals) 3,924,000 cattle, 3,287,000 pigs, 192,000 horses, 30,600,000 poultry; roundwood (2003) 7,542,800 cu m; fish catch (2002) 5,575. Mining and quarrying (2004): potash 4,650,000; peat 2,100,000. Manufacturing (2000): fertilizers 4,056; cement 1,847; steel 1,623; wheat flour 924; alcoholic beverages 10,323,000 hectolitres; cigarettes 10,346,000,000 units; footwear 18,736,000 pairs. Energy production (consumption): electricity (kW-hr; 2003) 26,615,000,000 (33,228,000,000); coal (2002) none (334,000);

crude petroleum (barrels; 2003) 13,300,000 (116,000,000); petroleum products (2003) 15,774,000 (6,240,000); natural gas (cu m; 2003) 254,000,000 (18,448,000,000).
Gross national product (2004): U.S.$20,856,000,000 (U.S.$2,120 per capita).

Structure of gross domestic product and labour force				
	2003			
	in value Rbl '000,000	% of total value	labour force[7]	% of labour force
Agriculture	2,985	8.3	493,000	11.1
Mining	} 9,180	25.5	987,000	22.2
Manufacturing				
Public utilities	8	8	...	...
Construction	2,151	6.0	231,000	5.2
Transp. and commun.	3,735	10.4	265,000	5.9
Trade	3,560	9.9	257,000	5.8
Finance			57,000	1.3
Public admin., defense	} 14,319[8]	39.9[8]	84,000	1.9
Services			1,033,000	23.2
Other			1,039,000[9]	23.4[9]
TOTAL	35,930	100.0	4,446,000	100.0

Tourism (2003): receipts U.S.$267,000,000; expenditures U.S.$493,000,000.
Land use as % of total land area (2000)[10]: in temporary crops 29.6%, in permanent crops 0.6%, in pasture 14.4%; overall forest area 45.3%.

Foreign trade[11]

Balance of trade (current prices)						
	1999	2000	2001	2002	2003	2004
U.S.$'000,000	–765	–1,320	–835	–882	–1,541	–2,593
% of total	6.1%	8.3%	5.3%	5.2%	7.2%	8.6%

Imports (2004): U.S.$16,345,000,000 (2002; crude petroleum 16.8%, machinery and apparatus 15.5%, chemicals and chemical products 10.2%, food and beverages 8.8%, natural and manufactured gas 6.3%, iron and steel 6.2%). *Major import sources* (2004): Russia 68.2%; Germany 6.6%; Ukraine 3.3%; Poland 2.9%; Italy 1.8%.
Exports (2004): U.S.$13,752,000,000 (2002; refined petroleum 18.3%, road vehicles 8.9%, nonelectrical machinery 8.3%, food 6.7%, potassium chloride 5.7%, electrical machinery 5.7%). *Major export destinations* (2004): Russia 47.0%; United Kingdom 8.3%; The Netherlands 6.7%; Poland 5.3%; Ukraine 3.9%.

Transport and communications

Transport. Railroads (2004): length (2002) 5,533 km; passenger-km 13,893,000,000; metric ton-km cargo 40,331,000,000. Roads (2002): total length 79,990 km (paved 86.7%). Vehicles: passenger cars (2002) 1,548,472; trucks and buses (2001) 85,791. Air transport (2004): passenger-km 674,000,000; metric ton-km cargo 49,000,000; airports 1.

Communications				units per 1,000 persons
Medium	date	unit	number	
Daily newspapers	2000	circulation	1,550,000	155
Radio	2001	receivers	1,187,000	199
Television	2000	receivers	3,420,000	342
Telephones	2003	main lines	3,071,300	311
Cellular telephones	2003	subscribers	1,118,000	113
Internet	2004	users	1,600,000	162

Education and health

Education (2003–04)	schools	teachers	students	student/ teacher ratio
Primary (age 6–13)	} 4,460	138,744	1,369,000	9.9
Secondary (age 14–17)				
Voc., teacher tr.[12]	248	14,772	138,593	9.4
Higher	58	21,684	337,000	15.5

Literacy (2001): total population age 15 and over literate 99.7%; males literate 99.8%; females literate 99.6%.
Health (2003): physicians 44,800 (1 per 220 persons); hospital beds 112,007 (1 per 88 persons); infant mortality rate per 1,000 live births (2004) 13.6.
Food (2002): daily per capita caloric intake 3,000 (vegetable products 74%, animal products 26%); 117% of FAO recommended minimum requirement.

Military

Total active duty personnel (2004): 72,940 (army 40.6%, air force and air defense 24.9%, other 34.5%). *Military expenditure as percentage of GDP* (2003): 1.3%[13]; per capita expenditure U.S.$23[13].

[1]Statutory number. [2]Rubel re-denominated Jan. 1, 2000; 1,000 (old) rubli = 1 (new) rubel. [3]January 1. [4]Minsk province includes Minsk city. [5]Rounded area figures; exact area figures are 80,153 sq mi (207,595 sq km). [6]Based on official estimate. [7]Based on annual survey. [8]Public utilities included with Services. [9]Includes 136,000 registered unemployed and 799,000 undistributed self-employed and unregistered unemployed. [10]25% of Belarusian territory severely affected by radioactive fallout from Chernobyl. [11]Imports c.i.f.; exports f.o.b. [12]2000–01. [13]Excludes expenditures on military pensions and paramilitary.

Internet resources for further information:
• **Ministry of Statistics and Analysis**
  http://www.belstat.gov.by/homep/en/main.html
• **National Bank of the Republic of Belarus**
  http://www.nbrb.by

Belgium

Official name: Koninkrijk België (Dutch); Royaume de Belgique (French) (Kingdom of Belgium).
Form of government: federal constitutional monarchy with two legislative bodies (Senate [71[1]]; House of Representatives [150]).
Chief of state: Monarch.
Head of government: Prime Minister.
Capital: Brussels.
Official languages: Dutch; French; German.
Official religion: none.
Monetary unit: 1 euro (€) = 100 cents; valuation (Sept. 1, 2005) 1 U.S.$ = €0.80; 1£ = €1.47[2].

Area and population

Regions[3] Provinces	Capitals	area sq mi	area sq km	population 2004[4] estimate
Brussels[5]	—	62	161	999,899
Flanders	—	5,221[6]	13,522	6,016,024
Antwerp	Antwerp	1,107	2,867	1,668,812
East Flanders	Ghent	1,151	2,982	1,373,720
Flemish Brabant	Leuven	813	2,106	1,031,904
Limburg	Hasselt	935	2,422	805,786
West Flanders	Brugge	1,214	3,145	1,135,802
Wallonia	—	6,504[6]	16,844[6]	3,380,498
Hainaut	Mons	1,462	3,786	1,283,200
Liège	Liège	1,491	3,862	1,029,605
Luxembourg	Arlon	1,714	4,440	254,120
Namur	Namur	1,415	3,666	452,856
Walloon Brabant	Wavre	421	1,091	360,717
TOTAL		11,787	30,528[6]	10,396,421

Demography

Population (2005): 10,432,000.
Density (2005): persons per sq mi 885.0, persons per sq km 341.7.
Urban-rural (2003): urban 97.2%; rural 2.8%.
Sex distribution (2003): male 48.95%; female 51.05%.
Age breakdown (2003): under 15, 17.2%; 15–29, 18.2%; 30–44, 22.5%; 45–59, 20.1%; 60–74, 14.1%; 75 and over, 7.9%.
Population projection: (2010) 10,511,000; (2020) 10,589,000.
Ethnic composition (2000): Flemish 53.7%; Walloon (French) 31.6%; Italian 2.6%; French 2.0%; Arab 1.8%; German 1.5%; Berber 0.9%; other 5.9%.
Religious affiliation (2000): Roman Catholic 80.9%; other Christian 7.4%, of which unaffiliated Christian 4.4%, Protestant 1.2%; Muslim 3.6%; nonreligious 7.5%; other 0.6%.
Major cities (2004[4]): Brussels 999,899[5]; Antwerp 455,148; Ghent 229,344; Charleroi 200,608; Liège 185,488; Brugge 117,025.

Vital statistics

Birth rate per 1,000 population (2003): 10.7 (world avg. 21.1).
Death rate per 1,000 population (2003): 10.2 (world avg. 9.0).
Natural increase rate per 1,000 population (2003): 0.5 (world avg. 12.1).
Total fertility rate (avg. births per childbearing woman; 2003): 1.6.
Marriage rate per 1,000 population (2003): 4.0.
Divorce rate per 1,000 population (2003): 3.0.
Life expectancy at birth (2003): male 75.9 years; female 81.7 years.
Major causes of death per 100,000 population (1997): diseases of the circulatory system 388.4; malignant neoplasms (cancers) 294.1; diseases of the respiratory system 78.9; accidents and violence 54.3.

National economy

Budget (2004). Revenue: €139,949,000,000 (social security contributions 29.0%, income tax 24.8%, taxes on goods and services 23.3%, property tax 7.6%). Expenditures: €140,272,000,000 (social security payments 26.2%, wages 24.1%, health 13.1%, interest on debt 9.8%, capital expenditure 4.5%).
Public debt (2004): U.S.$361,645,000,000.
Production (metric tons except as noted). Agriculture, forestry, fishing (2004): sugar beets 5,914,000, potatoes 3,030,000, wheat 1,871,000, corn (maize) 556,000, barley 311,000, apples 280,000, tomatoes 250,000; livestock (number of live animals) 6,366,000 pigs, 2,684,000 cattle; roundwood (2003) 4,765,000 cu m; fish catch (2002) 29,028. Mining and quarrying (2003): Belgian bluestone 1,200,000 cu m. Manufacturing (value added in €'000,000; 2003): chemicals and chemical products 8,667; base and fabricated metals 6,155; food/beverages/tobacco 6,105; transport equipment 3,808; paper products, printing, and publishing 3,364; value of traded polished diamonds handled in Antwerp U.S.$13,000,000,000. Energy production (consumption): electricity (kW-hr; 2004) 81,540,000,000 ([2002] 90,202,000,000); coal (metric tons; 2002) 173,000 (9,042,000); lignite (metric tons; 2002) none (204,000); crude petroleum (barrels; 2003) none (261,000,000[7]); petroleum products (metric tons; 2002) 29,327,000 (15,892,000); natural gas (cu m; 2002) none (19,558,000,000).
Household income and expenditure (2003). Avg. household size 2.4; sources of income: wages and transfer payments 69.3%, property income 11.1%, mixed income 19.6%; expenditure: housing and energy 23.5%, transportation 14.3%, food and nonalcoholic beverages 13.7%, recreation and culture 9.1%.
Tourism (2003): receipts U.S.$8,130,000,000; expenditures U.S.$12,124,000,000.
Population economically active (2004): total 4,797,000; activity rate 46.1% (participation rates: ages 15–64, 70.3%; female [2002] 43.0%; unemployed 12.0%).

Price and earnings indexes (2000 = 100)

	1998	1999	2000	2001	2002	2003	2004
Consumer price index	96.4	97.5	100.0	102.5	104.2	105.8	108.0
Annual earnings index	95.3	97.9	100.0	102.8	105.4	107.4	…

Gross national product (2004): U.S.$357,285,000,000 (U.S.$34,370 per capita).

Structure of gross domestic product and labour force

	2003 in value €'000,000	2003 % of total value	2002 labour force[8]	2002 % of labour force[8]
Agriculture	3,329	1.2	71,800	1.6
Mining	308	0.1	7,300	0.2
Manufacturing	43,555	16.2	785,600	17.8
Construction	11,990	4.4	276,000	6.3
Public utilities	5,801	2.2	30,600	0.7
Transp. and commun.	17,328	6.4	327,400	7.4
Trade, restaurants	34,471	12.8	776,500	17.6
Finance	71,437	26.5	552,600	12.6
Pub. admin., defense	20,491	7.6	405,600	9.2
Services	41,235	15.3	1,037,800	23.6
Other	19,603[9]	7.3[9]	130,600[10]	3.0[10]
TOTAL	269,546[6]	100.0	4,401,800	100.0

Land use as % of total land area (2000): in temporary crops 25.6%, in permanent crops 0.7%, in pasture 20.5%; overall forest area 21.1%.

Foreign trade[11]

Balance of trade (current prices)

€'000,000	1998	1999	2000	2001	2002	2003
	+11,600	+13,500	+14,600	+12,500	+18,841	+17,700
% of total	3.7%	4.2%	3.8%	3.1%	4.3%	4.0%

Imports (2002): €209,720,700,000 (machinery and apparatus 16.3%, road vehicles 12.0%, medicine and pharmaceuticals 10.6%, food 6.8%). *Major import sources* (2003–04): The Netherlands 19.6%; Germany 16.5%; France 14.0%; U.K. 8.2%; U.S. 5.6%.
Exports (2002): €228,561,700,000 (machinery and apparatus 14.0%, road vehicles 13.8%, pharmaceuticals 10.1%, food 7.6%, organic chemicals 5.9%). *Major export destinations* (2003–04): Germany 17.4%; France 17.1%; The Netherlands 13.0%; U.K. 8.6%; Italy 5.5%.

Transport and communications

Transport. Railroads (2003): route length 3,521 km; passenger-km 8,276,000,000; metric ton-km cargo 7,293,000,000. Roads (2002): total length 149,028 km (paved 78%). Vehicles (2002): passenger cars 4,787,359; trucks and buses 555,406. Air transport (2001): passenger-km 15,320,000,000; metric ton-km cargo, n.a.; airports 5.

Communications

Medium	date	unit	number	units per 1,000 persons
Daily newspapers	2000	circulation	1,640,000	160
Radio	2000	receivers	8,130,000	793
Television	2000	receivers	5,550,000	541
Telephones	2004	main lines	4,756,600	491
Cellular telephones	2004	subscribers	9,131,700	883
Personal computers	2004	units	3,627,000	351
Internet	2004	users	4,200,000	406

Education and health

Educational attainment (2002). Percentage of population age 25 and over having: no formal schooling through lower-secondary education 39%; upper secondary/higher vocational 33%; university 28%.

Education (2002–03)

	schools	teachers	students	student/ teacher ratio
Primary (age 6–12)	4,596	89,445[12, 13]	755,447	…
Secondary (age 12–18)	1,911	112,487	795,590	7.1
Higher	226	26,454	298,387	11.3

Health: physicians (2002) 46,268 (1 per 223 persons); hospital beds (2001) 71,907 (1 per 143 persons); infant mortality rate (2004) 4.8.
Food (2002): daily per capita caloric intake 3,584 (vegetable products 69%, animal products 31%); 134% of FAO recommended minimum requirement.

Military

Total active duty personnel (2004): 40,800 (army 60.8%, navy 6.0%, air force 25.1%, medical service 4.4%, other 3.7%); U.S. troops (Dec. 2004) 1,450.
Military expenditure as percentage of GDP (2003): 1.3%; per capita expenditure U.S.$375.

[1]Excludes children of the monarch serving ex officio from age 18. [2]The Belgian franc (BF) was the former monetary unit; on Jan. 1, 2002, BF 40.34 = €1. [3]Corresponding to three language-based federal community councils: Dutch (Flanders), French (Wallonia), and bilingual (Brussels) having authority in cultural affairs; a fourth (German) community council (within Wallonia; 2002 population 71,287) lacks expression as an administrative region. [4]January 1. [5]Officially, Brussels Capital Region. [6]Detail does not add to total given because of rounding. [7]Includes Luxembourg. [8]As of June. [9]Taxes on products less subsidies on products and less imputed bank service charges. [10]Including 118,700 unemployed not previously employed. [11]Imports c.i.f.; exports f.o.b. [12]Includes preschool teachers. [13]2001–02.

Internet resources for further information:
• National Bank of Belgium http://www.bnb.be/sg/index.htm
• Belgian Federal Government On Line http://belgium.fgov.be

Belize

Official name: Belize.
Form of government: constitutional monarchy with two legislative houses (Senate [8[1]]; House of Representatives [29[2]]).
Chief of state: British Monarch represented by Governor-General.
Head of government: Prime Minister.
Capital: Belmopan.
Official language: English.
Official religion: none.
Monetary unit: 1 Belize dollar (BZ$) = 100 cents; valuation (Sept. 1, 2005) 1 U.S.$ = BZ$2.00; 1 £ = BZ$3.68.

Area and population

Districts	Capitals	area sq mi	area sq km	population 2004 estimate
Belize	Belize City	1,663	4,307	84,200
Cayo	San Ignacio/Santa Elena	2,006	5,196	63,900
Corozal	Corozal	718	1,860	35,000
Orange Walk	Orange Walk	1,790	4,636	43,800
Stann Creek	Dangriga	986	2,554	28,900
Toledo	Punta Gorda	1,704	4,413	26,800
TOTAL		8,867[3]	22,965[3, 4]	282,600

Demography

Population (2005): 291,000.
Density (2005): persons per sq mi 32.8, persons per sq km 12.7.
Urban-rural (2004): urban 49.9%; rural 50.1%.
Sex distribution (2004): male 50.50%; female 49.50%.
Age breakdown (2004): under 15, 40.8%; 15–29, 27.7%; 30–44, 17.4%; 45–59, 8.1%; 60–74, 4.3%; 75 and over, 1.7%.
Population projection: (2010) 326,000; (2020) 393,000.
Doubling time: 29 years.
Ethnic composition (2000): mestizo (Spanish-Indian) 48.7%; Creole (predominantly black) 24.9%; Mayan Indian 10.6%; Garifuna (black-Carib Indian) 6.1%; white 4.3%; East Indian 3.0%; other or not stated 2.4%.
Religious affiliation (2000): Roman Catholic 49.6%; Protestant 31.8%, of which Pentecostal 7.4%, Anglican 5.3%, Seventh-day Adventist 5.2%, Mennonite 4.1%; other Christian 1.9%; nonreligious 9.4%; other 7.3%.
Major cities (2004): Belize City 59,400; San Ignacio/Santa Elena 16,100; Orange Walk 15,000; Belmopan 12,300; Dangriga 10,400.

Vital statistics

Birth rate per 1,000 population (2004): 29.9 (world avg. 21.1); (1997) legitimate 40.3%; illegitimate 59.7%.
Death rate per 1,000 population (2004): 5.6 (world avg. 9.0).
Natural increase rate per 1,000 population (2004): 24.3 (world avg. 12.1).
Total fertility rate (avg. births per childbearing woman; 2004): 3.8.
Marriage rate per 1,000 population (2003): 6.3.
Divorce rate per 1,000 population (2003): 0.6.
Life expectancy at birth (2004): male 66.5 years; female 70.6 years.
Major causes of death per 100,000 population (1997–2000): diseases of the circulatory system 164.3; accidents and violence 77.0; communicable diseases 69.9; malignant neoplasms 64.9.

National economy

Budget (2003–04). Revenue: BZ$487,200,000 (tax revenue 78.0%, of which import duties 33.8%, general sales tax 24.6%, income tax 18.3%; nontax revenue 9.1%; capital revenue 8.0%; grants 4.9%). Expenditures: BZ$645,400,000 (current expenditure 62.1%; capital expenditure 37.9%).
Production (metric tons except as noted). Agriculture, forestry, fishing (2004): sugarcane 1,100,000, oranges 168,000, bananas 70,000, grapefruit and pomelos 40,000, corn (maize) 35,000, plantain 28,500, papayas 12,000; livestock (number of live animals; 2004) 59,000 cattle, 22,000 pigs, 1,600,000 chickens; roundwood (2003) 187,600 cu m; fish catch (2002) 29,152, of which marine fish 22,639, crustaceans 5,010. Mining and quarrying (2002): limestone 700,000; sand and gravel 415,000. Manufacturing (value added in U.S.$'000,000; 2003): food products and beverages (significantly citrus concentrate, flour, sugar, and beer) 63.7; textiles, clothing, and footwear 6.1; other (incl. cigarettes) 11.1. Energy production (consumption): electricity (kW-hr; 2002) 162,000,000 (189,000,000); coal, none (none); crude petroleum, none (none); petroleum products (metric tons; 2002) none (257,000); natural gas, none (none).
Household income and expenditure. Average household size (2002) 4.6; average annual income of employed head of household (1993) BZ$6,450[5] (U.S.$3,225[5]); sources of income, n.a.; expenditure (1990): food, beverages, and tobacco 34.0%, transportation 13.7%, energy and water 9.1%, housing 9.0%, clothing and footwear 8.8%, household furnishings 8.0%.
Tourism: receipts from visitors (2003) U.S.$156,000,000; expenditures by nationals abroad (2002) U.S.$43,000,000.
Land use as % of total land area (2000): in temporary crops 2.8%, in permanent crops 1.7%, in pasture 2.2%; overall forest area 59.1%.
Population economically active (2002): total 94,172; activity rate of total population 35.9% (participation rates: ages 14 and over 57.3%; female 32.8%; unemployed [April 2004] 11.6%).

Price index (2000 = 100)

	1999	2000	2001	2002	2003	2004
Consumer price index	99.4	100.0	101.2	103.4	106.1	109.4

Gross national product (2004): U.S.$1,115,000,000 (U.S.$3,100 per capita).

Structure of gross domestic product and labour force

	2003 in value BZ$'000	2003 % of total value	2002 labour force	2002 % of labour force
Agriculture, fishing, forestry	279,400	14.1	19,131	20.3
Mining	9,800	0.5	342	0.4
Manufacturing	161,300	8.2	6,385	6.8
Construction	77,700	3.9	7,098	7.5
Public utilities	60,700	3.1	739	0.8
Transp. and commun.	183,100	9.3	3,131	3.3
Trade, restaurants	396,000	20.0	22,872	24.3
Finance, real estate, insurance	266,500	13.5	3,122	3.3
Pub. admin., defense	202,800	10.3 }	20,024	21.3
Services	120,000	6.1 }		
Other	219,500[6]	11.1[6]	11,330[7]	12.0[7]
TOTAL	1,976,800	100.0[4]	94,172[4]	100.0

Public debt (external, outstanding; 2002): U.S.$789,600,000.

Foreign trade[8]

Balance of trade (current prices)

	2000	2001	2002	2003
BZ$'000,000	−405.2	−425.7	−376.5	−418.6
% of total	26.5%	28.4%	23.3%	24.9%

Imports (2003): BZ$1,131,700,000 (machinery and transport equipment 18.0%; mineral fuels and lubricants 14.3%; manufactured goods 11.4%; food 10.5%; chemicals and chemical products 7.3%). *Major import sources:* U.S. 42.2%; EU 8.5%; Mexico 7.9%; Caricom 2.8%.
Exports (2003): BZ$632,600,000 (domestic exports 60.4%, of which seafood products [significantly shrimp] 17.4%, citrus concentrate 12.4%, raw sugar 11.2%, bananas 8.3%, garments 5.0%; reexports [principally to Mexico] 39.6%). *Major export destinations*[9]: U.S. 55.6%; U.K. 24.3%; other EU 5.4%; Caricom 9.1%.

Transport and communications

Transport. Railroads: none. Roads (1999): total length 1,785 mi, 2,872 km (paved 18%). Vehicles (1998): passenger cars 9,929; trucks and buses 11,755. Air transport (2001)[10]: passenger arrivals 256,564, passenger departures 240,900; cargo loaded 186 metric tons, cargo unloaded 1,272 metric tons. Airports (1997) with scheduled flights 9.

Communications

Medium	date	unit	number	units per 1,000 persons
Radio	1997	receivers	133,000	571
Television	1998	receivers	42,000	183
Telephones	2004	main lines	33,800	129
Cellular telephones	2004	subscribers	97,800	375
Personal computers	2003	units	35,000	127
Internet	2004	users	35,000	134

Education and health

Educational attainment (2000). Percentage of population age 25 and over having: no formal schooling 36.6%; primary education 40.9%; secondary 11.7%; postsecondary/advanced vocational 6.4%; university 3.8%; other/unknown 0.6%. *Literacy* (2001): total population age 14 and over literate 93.4%; males 93.6%; females 93.3%.

Education (2003–04)

	schools	teachers	students	student/ teacher ratio
Primary (age 5–12)	275	2,618	62,074	23.7
Secondary (age 13–16)	43	1,074	15,344	14.3
Higher[11]	12	228	2,853	12.1

Health: physicians (1998) 155 (1 per 1,558 persons); hospital beds (1999) 598 (1 per 406 persons); infant mortality rate per 1,000 live births (2004) 26.3.
Food (2002): daily per capita caloric intake 2,869 (vegetable products 79%, animal products 21%); 127% of FAO recommended minimum requirement.

Military

Total active duty personnel (2004): 1,050 (army 100%).[12] *Military expenditure as percentage of GDP* (2003): 2.4%; per capita expenditure U.S.$69.

---

[1]Excludes president of the Senate, who may be elected by the Senate from outside its appointed membership. [2]Excludes speaker of the House of Representatives, who may be elected by the House from outside its elected membership. [3]Includes offshore cays totaling 266 sq mi (689 sq km). [4]Detail does not add to total given because of rounding. [5]Estimated figure for about 33,000 employed heads of household. [6]Taxes less subsidies on products. [7]Includes 245 not adequately defined and 8,910 unemployed. [8]Imports are f.o.b. in balance of trade and c.i.f. in commodities and trading partners. [9]Domestic exports only. [10]Belize international airport only. [11]1997–98. [12]Foreign forces (2002): British army 30.

Internet resources for further information:
• **Central Statistical Office—Belize** http://www.cso.gov.bz
• **Central Bank of Belize** http://www.centralbank.org.bz

Benin

Official name: République du Bénin (Republic of Benin).
Form of government: multiparty republic with one legislative house (National Assembly [83]).
Head of state and government: President, assisted by Prime Minister[1].
Capital[2]: Porto-Novo.
Official language: French.
Official religion: none.
Monetary unit: 1 CFA franc (CFAF) = 100 centimes; valuation (Sept. 1, 2005) 1 U.S.$ = CFAF 522.78; 1 £ = CFAF 962.57[3].

Atlantic Ocean

Gulf of Guinea

Area and population		area		population
				2002
Departments	**Capitals**	sq mi	sq km	census
Alibori	Kandi	9,916	25,683	521,093
Atacora	Natitingou	7,899	20,459	549,417
Atlantique	Ouidah	1,248	3,233	801,683
Borgou	Parakou	9,772	25,310	724,171
Collines	Savalou	5,236	13,561	535,923
Couffo	Dogbo	928	2,404	524,586
Donga	Djougou	4,128	10,691	350,062
Littoral	Cotonou	31	79	665,100
Mono	Lokossa	539	1,396	360,037
Ouémé	Porto-Novo	1,095	2,835	730,772
Plateau	Sakété	720	1,865	407,116
Zou	Abomey	1,971	5,106	599,954
TOTAL		43,484[4]	112,622	6,769,914

Demography

Population (2005): 7,649,000.
Density (2005): persons per sq mi 175.9, persons per sq km 67.9.
Urban-rural (2002): urban 38.9%; rural 61.1%.
Sex distribution (2002): male 48.51%; female 51.49%.
Age breakdown (2003): under 15, 47.1%; 15–29, 27.7%; 30–44, 14.5%; 45–59, 7.0%; 60–74, 3.1%; 75 and over, 0.6%.
Population projection: (2010) 8,731,000; (2020) 10,886,000.
Doubling time: 25 years.
Ethnic composition (2002): Fon 39.2%; Adjara 15.2%; Yoruba (Nago) 12.3%; Bariba 9.2%; Fulani 7.0%; Somba (Otomary) 6.1%; Yoa-Lokpa 4.0%; other 7.0%.
Religious affiliation (2002): Christian 42.8%, of which Roman Catholic 27.1%, Protestant 5.4%, indigenous Christian 5.3%; Muslim 24.4%; traditional beliefs 23.3%, of which voodoo 17.3%; other 9.5%.
Major cities (2004): Cotonou 818,100; Porto-Novo 234,300; Parakou 227,900; Djougou 206,500; Abomey 126,800.

Vital statistics

Birth rate per 1,000 population (2004): 40.2 (world avg. 21.1).
Death rate per 1,000 population (2004): 12.7 (world avg. 9.0).
Natural increase rate per 1,000 population (2004): 27.5 (world avg. 12.1).
Total fertility rate (avg. births per childbearing woman; 2004): 5.4.
Life expectancy at birth (2004): male 51.2 years; female 53.4 years.

National economy

Budget (2003). Revenue: CFAF 342,934,000,000 (tax revenue 89.6%, of which tax on international trade 46.4%, income tax 20.8%, sales tax 19.8%; nontax revenue 10.4%). Expenditures: CFAF 436,400,000,000 (current expenditures 67.3%, of which transfers 35.0%, salaries 29.5%, interest on debt 2.8%; development expenditure 32.7%).
Production (metric tons except as noted). Agriculture, forestry, fishing (2004): cassava 4,000,000, yams 2,500,000, corn (maize) 800,000, seed cotton 425,000, oil palm fruit 244,000, sorghum 190,000, tomatoes 170,000, peanuts (groundnuts) 130,000, pineapples 106,000, dry beans 105,000, okra 86,000; livestock (number of live animals) 1,745,000 cattle, 1,350,000 goats, 700,000 sheep, 309,000 pigs, 13,000,000 chickens; roundwood (2002) 6,297,969 cu m; fish catch (2002) 40,663. Mining (2003): gold 20 kg. Manufacturing (value added in U.S.$'000,000; 1999): food products 74; textiles 42; beverages 36; bricks, tiles, and cement 21. Energy production (consumption): electricity (kW-hr; 2002) 92,000,000 (625,000,000); coal, none (none); crude petroleum (barrels; 2002) 290,000 (negligible); petroleum products (metric tons; 2002) none (585,000); natural gas, none (none).
Gross national product (2004): U.S.$3,667,000,000 (U.S.$530 per capita).

Structure of gross domestic product and labour force					
	2003		2002		
	in value CFAF '000,000,000	% of total value	labour force[5, 6]	% of labour force[5, 6]	
Agriculture	720.7	35.7	1,324,000	46.8	
Mining	4.9	0.3	39,400	1.4	
Manufacturing	182.5	9.0	253,100	8.9	
Public utilities	21.0	1.0	2,800	0.1	
Construction	81.9	4.1	70,300	2.5	
Transp. and commun.	164.0	8.1	95,600	3.4	
Trade, restaurants	365.5	18.1	815,400	28.8	
Finance	194.4	9.6	2,800	0.1	
Pub. admin., defense } Services }	121.6	6.0	205,300	7.2	
Other	163.5[7]	8.1[7]	22,200	0.8	
TOTAL	2,020.0	100.0	2,830,900	100.0	

Public debt (external, outstanding; 2003): U.S.$1,964,000,000.
Population economically active (2002): total 2,830,900; activity rate of total population 41.4% (participation rates: ages 15–64 [1997] 84.3%; female [1998] 50.8%; unemployed in Cotonou [April 2003] 6.8%).

Price index (2000 = 100)						
	1998	1999	2000	2001	2002	2003
Consumer price index	95.7	96.0	100.0	104.0	106.6	108.2

Household income and expenditure. Average household size (2002) 5.6; income per household: n.a.; sources of income: n.a.; expenditure (1996)[8]: food and nonalcoholic beverages 38.2%, transportation 10.1%, expenditures in cafés and hotels 9.8%, housing and energy 9.5%, clothing and footwear 6.9%.
Land use as % of total land area (2000): in temporary crops 17.6%, in permanent crops 2.4%, in pasture 5.0%; overall forest area 24.0%.
Tourism (2002): receipts from visitors U.S.$60,000,000; expenditures by nationals abroad U.S.$7,000,000.

Foreign trade[9]

Balance of trade (current prices)						
	1998	1999	2000	2001	2002	2003
CFAF '000,000,000	−93.4	−131.6	−88.1	−131.8	−161.0	−109.4
% of total	16.0%	20.2%	13.6%	19.3%	20.5%	14.5%

Imports (2003): CFAF 432,200,000,000 (food products 28.6%; machinery and transport equipment 18.2%; petroleum products 16.6%). *Major import sources* (2001): France c. 23%; China c. 8%; free trade zones c. 6%; Côte d'Ivoire c. 5%; Ghana c. 5%; Nigeria c. 5%.
Exports (2003): CFAF 322,800,000,000 (domestic exports 66.2%, of which cotton yarn 28.9%; reexports 33.8%). *Major export destinations* (2001): India c. 31%; Brazil c. 6%; Indonesia c. 6%; Ghana c. 6%; Nigeria c. 5%.

Transport and communications

Transport. Railroads (2002): length 360 mi, 579 km; passenger-mi 38,646,000, passenger-km 62,194,000; short ton-mi cargo 60,845,000, metric ton-km cargo 88,832,000. Roads (1999): total length 4,217 mi, 6,787 km (paved 20.0%). Vehicles (1996): passenger cars 37,772; trucks and buses 8,058. Air transport[10]: passenger-km (1999) 235,000,000; airports (2002) with scheduled flights 1.

Communications				units per 1,000
Medium	date	unit	number	persons
Daily newspapers	2000	circulation	12,900	2
Radio	2000	receivers	2,820,000	439
Television	2000	receivers	289,000	45
Telephones	2004	main lines	72,800	11
Cellular telephones	2003	subscribers	236,200	34
Personal computers	2004	units	30,000	4.3
Internet	2004	users	100,000	14

Education and health

Educational attainment (1992). Percentage of population age 25 and over having: no formal schooling 78.5%; primary education 10.8%; some secondary 8.2%; secondary 1.2%; postsecondary 1.3%. *Literacy* (2002): total percentage of population age 15 and over literate 32.6%; males literate 45.0%; females literate 21.9%.

Education (2001–02)				student/
	schools	teachers	students	teacher ratio
Primary	4,682	21,766	1,152,798	53.0
Secondary	145[11]	4,447[12]	188,035[12]	42.0[12]
Voc., teacher tr.[11]	14	283	4,873	17.2
Higher	16[11]	962[13]	14,085[13]	14.6[13]

Health (2001): physicians 923 (1 per 7,183 persons); hospital beds 590 (1 per 11,238 persons); infant mortality rate per 1,000 live births (2004) 82.9.
Food (2002): daily per capita caloric intake 2,548 (vegetable products 96%, animal products 4%); 111% of FAO recommended minimum requirement.

Military

Total active duty personnel (2004): 4,550 (army 94.5%, navy 2.2%, air force 3.3%). *Military expenditure as percentage of GNP* (2003): 1.6%; per capita expenditure U.S.$8.

[1]Office of Prime Minister vacant from May 1998. [2]Porto-Novo, the official capital established under the constitution, is the seat of the legislature, but the president and most government ministers reside in Cotonou. [3]Formerly pegged to the French franc and since Jan. 1, 2002, to the euro at the rate of €1 = CFAF 655.96. [4]Detail does not add to total given because of rounding. [5]Age 10 years and over. [6]Based on census. [7]Indirect taxes. [8]Weights of consumer price index components. [9]Import figures are f.o.b. in balance of trade and commodities and c.i.f. in trading partners. [10]Air Afrique, an airline jointly owned by 11 African countries (including Benin) was declared bankrupt in February 2002. [11]1993–94. [12]1997–98. [13]1996–97.

Internet resources for further information:
• **Institut National de la Statistique et de l'Analyse Economique**
  http://www.insae.bj/index_haut.htm
• **La Banque de France: La Zone Franc**
  http://www.banque-france.fr/fr/eurosys/zonefr/zonefr.htm

Bermuda

Official name: Bermuda.
Political status: overseas territory (United Kingdom) with two legislative houses (Senate [11]; House of Assembly [36]).
Chief of state: British Monarch, represented by Governor.
Head of government: Premier.
Capital: Hamilton.
Official language: English.
Official religion: none.
Monetary unit: 1 Bermuda dollar (Bd$) = 100 cents; valuation (Sept. 1, 2005) 1 U.S.$ = Bd$1.00[1]; 1 £ = Bd$1.84.

Area and population	area		population
			2000
Municipalities	sq mi	sq km	census
Hamilton	0.3	0.8	969
St. George	0.5	1.3	1,752
Parishes			
Devonshire	2.0	5.1	7,307
Hamilton	2.0	5.1	5,270
Paget	2.1	5.3	5,088
Pembroke[2]	1.8	4.6	10,337
St. George's[3, 4]	3.5	8.0	3,699
Sandys	2.1	5.4	7,275
Smith's	1.8	4.7	5,658
Southampton	2.2	5.6	6,117
Warwick	2.0	5.1	8,587
TOTAL	20.5[5, 6]	53.1[5, 6]	62,059[7]

Demography

Population (2002): 65,400.
Density (2005): persons per sq mi 3,190, persons per sq km 1,232.
Urban-rural (2003): urban 100.0%; rural, none.
Sex distribution (2004): male 48.90%; female 51.10%.
Age breakdown (2004): under 15, 19.1%; 15–29, 17.8%; 30–44, 24.0%; 45–59, 22.5%; 60–74, 12.3%; 75 and over, 4.3%.
Population projection: (2010) 67,000; (2020) 70,000.
Ethnic composition (2000): black 50.4%; British expatriates 29.0%; mulatto 10.0%; U.S. white 6.0%; Portuguese 4.5%; other 0.1%.
Religious affiliation (2000): Protestant 64.3%, of which Anglican 22.6%, Methodist 14.9%; Roman Catholic 14.9%; nonreligious 13.8%; other 6.0%; unknown 1.0%.
Major cities (2000): St. George 1,752; Hamilton 969.

Vital statistics

Birth rate per 1,000 population (2004): 11.8 (world avg. 21.1); (2001) legitimate 62.3%; illegitimate 37.7%.
Death rate per 1,000 population (2004): 7.5 (world avg. 9.0).
Natural increase rate per 1,000 population (2004): 4.3 (world avg. 12.1).
Total fertility rate (avg. births per childbearing woman; 2004): 1.9.
Marriage rate per 1,000 population (2002): 15.1.
Divorce rate per 1,000 population (2002): 3.7.
Life expectancy at birth (2004): male 75.5 years; female 79.7 years.
Major causes of death per 100,000 population (1998): diseases of the circulatory system 313.9; malignant neoplasms (cancers) 252.7; accidents and violence 38.6; AIDS 27.4.

National economy

Budget (2002–03). Revenue: Bd$671,100,000 (payroll tax 30.3%; customs duty 27.6%; tax on international companies 7.1%; land tax 6.0%; stamp duties 5.2%; other 23.8%). Expenditures: Bd$641,400,000 (current expenditure 84.2%, of which wages 38.7%, goods and services 23.6%, grants and contributions 21.9%; development expenditure 11.0%).
Production (value in Bd$'000 except as noted). Agriculture, forestry, fishing (2003): vegetables 3,060, milk 1,834, eggs 322, fruits 312, honey 77; livestock (number of live animals; 2004) 900 horses, 600 cattle, 45,000 chickens; roundwood, n.a.; fish catch (metric tons; 2002) 393, of which crustaceans 30. Mining and quarrying: crushed stone for local use. Manufacturing: industries include pharmaceuticals, cosmetics, electronics, fish processing, handicrafts, and small boat building[8]. Energy production (consumption): electricity (kW-hr; 2003) 664,000,000 (664,000,000); coal, none (none); crude petroleum, none (none); petroleum products (metric tons; 2002) none (162,000); natural gas, none (none).
Land use as % of total land area (2000): in temporary crops, n.a., in permanent crops, n.a., in pasture, n.a.; overall forest area, n.a.
Tourism: receipts from visitors (2003) U.S.$370,000,000; expenditures by nationals abroad (1997) U.S.$148,000,000.
Population economically active (2000): total 37,879; activity rate of total population 61.0% (participation rates: ages 16–64, 84.8%; female 48.3%; unemployed 2.6%).

Price index (2000 = 100)							
	1998	1999	2000	2001	2002	2003	2004
Consumer price index	91.3	97.4	100.0	102.9	105.3	108.6	112.5

Gross national product (at current market prices; 2003): U.S.$4,470,000,000 (U.S.$54,820 per capita).

Structure of gross domestic product and labour force				
	2000–01		2002	
	in value Bd$'000,000	% of total value	labour force	% of labour force
Agriculture, fishing	24	0.7	648	1.7
Quarrying	8	0.2		
Manufacturing	86	2.5	1,107	2.9
Construction	207	6.1	2,917	7.7
Public utilities	77	2.3	412	1.1
Transp. and commun.	245	7.2	2,859	7.6
Trade, restaurants	571	16.8	9,969	26.4
Finance, real estate	1,638	48.2	7,245	19.2
International business			3,587	9.5
Pub. admin., defense	191	5.6	3,896	10.3
Services	340	10.0	5,175	13.7
Other	10[9]	0.3[9]	—	—
TOTAL	3,397	100.0[6]	37,815	100.0[6]

Public debt (external, outstanding): n.a.
Household income and expenditure. Average household size (2004) 2.3; median annual gross income per household (2004) Bd$84,350 (U.S.$84,350); sources of income (1993): wages and salaries 65.3%, imputed income from owner occupancy 10.6%, self-employment 9.0%, net rental income 4.8%, other 10.3%; expenditure (2002): housing 26.1%, food and nonalcoholic beverages 16.0%, household furnishings 15.0%, clothing and footwear 4.2%, other goods and services 38.7%.

Foreign trade

Balance of trade (current prices)						
	1998	1999	2000	2001	2002	2003
Bd$'000,000	−564	−661	−668	−671	−696	−781
% of total	80.3%	86.6%	86.5%	87.0%	86.7%	88.2%

Imports (2002): Bd$746,000,000 (food, beverages, and tobacco 20.2%; machinery 16.5%; chemicals and chemical products 13.9%; mineral fuels 7.8%; transport equipment 6.0%). *Major import sources:* United States 76%; Canada 5%; United Kingdom 5%; Caribbean countries (mostly Netherlands Antilles) 3%.
Exports (2002): Bd$57,000,000 (nearly all reexports; diamond market was established in 1990s). *Major export destinations* (2002): mostly United States, United Kingdom, Norway, and Spain.

Transport and communications

Transport. Railroads: none. Roads (2000): total length 140 mi, 225 km (paved 100%)[10]. Vehicles (2003): passenger cars 21,770; trucks and buses 3,818. Air transport (2001): passenger arrivals 826,000, passenger departures 826,000; cargo loaded and unloaded 4,200 metric tons; airports (2002) with scheduled flights 1.

Communications				units per 1,000
Medium	date	unit	number	persons
Daily newspapers	2003	circulation	17,000	268
Radio	1997	receivers	82,000	1,328
Television	1999	receivers	70,000	1,135
Telephones	2001	main lines	56,300	872
Cellular telephones	2002	subscribers	30,000	476
Personal computers	2002	units	34,000	535
Internet	2003	users	34,500	543

Education and health

Educational attainment (2000). Percentage of total population age 15 and over having: no formal schooling 0.4%; primary education 7.0%; secondary 39.3%; postsecondary technical 25.7%; higher 26.8%; not stated 0.8%. *Literacy* (1997): total population age 15 and over literate, 98%.

Education (2002)	schools	teachers	students	student/ teacher ratio
Primary (age 5–11)	...	1,291[11]	10,474	...
Secondary (age 12–16)				
Higher	1	...	544	...

Health (2003): physicians 121 (1 per 525 persons); hospital beds 226 (1 per 281 persons); infant mortality rate per 1,000 live births (2004) 8.8.
Food (2002): daily per capita caloric intake 2,225 (vegetable products 74%, animal products 26%); 88% of FAO recommended minimum requirement.

Military

Total active duty personnel (2003): 700; part-time defense force assists police and is drawn from Bermudian conscripts.

[1]The Bermuda dollar is at par with the U.S. dollar. [2]Excludes the area and population of the city of Hamilton. [3]Excludes the area and population of the town of St. George. [4]Includes the 2.0 sq mi (5.2 sq km) area of the former U.S. military base closed in 1995. [5]Includes 0.4 sq mi (1.1 sq km) of uninhabited islands. [6]Detail does not add to total given because of rounding. [7]Excludes 8,335 short-term visitors, 901 institutionalized persons, and 39 transients. [8]The economy of Bermuda is overwhelmingly based on service industries such as tourism, insurance companies, offshore financial centres, e-commerce companies, and ship repair facilities. [9]Taxes less imputed bank service charges. [10]Excludes 138 mi (222 km) of paved private roads. [11]Includes preschool teachers.

Internet resources for further information:
• **Bermuda Online: Economy http://bermuda-online.org/economy.htm**

Bhutan

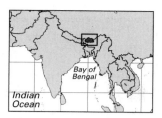

Official name: Druk-Yul (Kingdom of Bhutan).
Form of government: monarchy[1] with one legislative house (National Assembly [152[2]]).
Chief of state: Monarch[1].
Head of government: Prime Minister[1].
Capital: Thimphu.
Official language: Dzongkha (a Tibetan dialect).
Official religion: Mahayana Buddhism.
Monetary unit: 1 ngultrum[3] (Nu) = 100 chetrum; valuation (Sept. 1, 2005) 1 U.S.$ = Nu 43.87; 1 £ = Nu 80.77.

Area and population

Districts	Capitals	area sq mi	area sq km[4]	population 2003 estimate
Bumthang	Jakar	1,008	2,611	...
Chhukha	Chhukha	667	1,728	...
Chirang	Damphu	237	614	...
Dagana	Dagana	519	1,344	...
Gasa	...	1,616	4,185	...
Gaylegphug	Gaylegphug	845	2,188	...
Ha	Ha	637	1,651	...
Lhuntshi	Lhuntshi	1,067	2,764	...
Mongar	Mongar	726	1,881	...
Paro	Paro	474	1,229	...
Pema Gatsel	Pema Gatsel	193	499	...
Punakha	Punakha	356	922	...
Samchi	Samchi	578	1,497	...
Samdrup Jongkhar	Samdrup Jongkhar	860	2,227	...
Shemgang	Shemgang	786	2,035	...
Tashi Yangtse	Tashi Yangtse	534	1,382	...
Tashigang	Tashigang	845	2,188	...
Thimphu	Thimphu	712	1,843	...
Tongsa	Tongsa	667	1,728	...
Wangdi Phodrang	Wangdi Phodrang	1,497	3,878	...
TOTAL		14,824	38,394	734,000[5]

Demography

Population (2005): 776,000.
Density (2005): persons per sq mi 52.3, persons per sq km 20.2.
Urban-rural (2003): urban 8.5%; rural 91.5%.
Sex distribution (2003): male 50.50%; female 49.50%.
Age breakdown (2003): under 15, 42.1%; 15–29, 23.7%; 30–44, 16.4%; 45–59, 10.6%; 60–74, 5.9%; 75 and over, 1.3%.
Population projection: (2010) 866,000; (2020) 1,059,000.
Doubling time: 27 years.
Ethnic composition (1993): Bhutiā (Ngalops) 50.0%; Nepalese (Gurung) 35.0%; Sharchops 15.0%.
Religious affiliation (2000): Buddhist 74.0%; Hindu 20.5%; other 5.5%.
Major cities (2002): Thimphu 45,000; Phuntsholing (1997) 45,000.

Vital statistics

Birth rate per 1,000 population (2002): 34.9 (world avg. 21.1).
Death rate per 1,000 population (2002): 8.7 (world avg. 9.0).
Natural increase rate per 1,000 population (2002): 26.2 (world avg. 12.1).
Total fertility rate (avg. births per childbearing woman; 2003): 4.9.
Life expectancy at birth (2002): male 62.0 years; female 64.0 years.
Major causes of death (percentage distribution; 1989): respiratory tract infections 19.5%; diarrhea/dysentery 15.2%; skin infections 12.2%; parasitic worm infestations 10.0%; malaria 9.4%.

National economy

Budget (2004–05). Revenue: Nu 11,352,000,000 (domestic revenue 51.1%, grants 38.5%, other 10.4%). Expenditures: Nu 13,621,700,000 (capital expenditures 52.6%, current expenditures 43.8%, repayments 2.9%).
Public debt (external, outstanding; 2002): U.S.$376,900,000.
Production (metric tons except as noted). Agriculture, forestry, fishing (2004): rice 45,000, corn (maize) 40,000, potatoes 40,000, oranges 36,000, sugarcane 12,800, apples 6,000, nutmeg, mace, and cardamom 5,800, wheat 4,800, ginger 3,100, millet 3,000, green peppers and chilies 2,800, pulses 1,600; livestock (number of live animals) 372,000 cattle, 41,000 pigs, 30,000 goats, 28,000 horses, 20,000 sheep; roundwood (2003) 4,545,689 cu m; fish catch (2002) 300. Mining and quarrying (2003): limestone 285,000; dolomite 270,000; gypsum 56,000; iron ore (2001) 3,100. Manufacturing (value in Nu '000,000; 2000): cement 696.7; chemical products 474.6; alcoholic beverages 255.0; wood board products 228.6; processed fruits 108.5. Energy production (consumption): electricity (kW-hr; 2002) 1,898,000,000 (494,000,000); coal (metric tons; 2002) 52,000 (62,000); crude petroleum, none (none); petroleum products (metric tons; 2002) none (51,000); natural gas, none (none).
Household income and expenditure. Average household size (2003) 5.5; income per household: n.a.; sources of income: n.a.; expenditure: n.a.
Population economically active (1999): total 358,950; activity rate of total population 52.9% (participation rates: ages 15 and over 69.6%; female, n.a.; unemployed 1.4%).

Price index (2000 = 100)

	1997	1998	1999	2000	2001	2002	2003
Consumer price index	81.4	90.0	96.1	100.0	103.4	106.0	107.6

Gross national product (2004): U.S.$677,000,000 (U.S.$760 per capita).

Structure of gross domestic product and labour force

	2003 in value Nu '000,000	2003 % of total value	1999 labour force	1999 % of labour force
Agriculture	10,595	33.2	...	...
Mining	612	1.9	...	...
Manufacturing	2,445	7.7	...	...
Construction	6,431	20.2	...	...
Trade	1,768	5.5	...	...
Public utilities	3,097	9.7	...	...
Transportation and communications	2,772	8.7	...	...
Finance	2,089	6.6	...	...
Pub. admin., defense } Services	2,554	8.0	...	...
Other	−479[6]	−1.5[6]	...	...
TOTAL	31,884	100.0	358,950	100.0

Tourism (2003): receipts from visitors U.S.$8,000,000; expenditures by nationals abroad, n.a.
Land use as % of total land area (2000): in temporary crops 3.0%, in permanent crops 0.4%, in pasture 8.8%; overall forest area 64.2%.

Foreign trade[7]

Balance of trade (current prices)

	1997–98	1998–99	1999–2000	2000–01	2001–02
U.S.$'000,000	−24.7	−57.5	−70.7	−103.0	−90.6
% of total	10.0%	21.5%	23.6%	31.4%	31.6%

Imports (2001): U.S.$188,300,000 (1999; machinery and transport equipment 41.7%, of which computers and related goods 11.0%, road vehicles 10.5%; food 13.9%, of which cereals 7.6%; refined petroleum 7.2%). *Major import sources* (2001): India 81.1%; Japan 7.2%; Thailand 3.4%; Singapore 2.5%.
Exports (2001): U.S.$97,700,000 (electricity 48.1%, calcium carbide 13.3%, ferro-silicon 12.6%, cement 9.6%). *Major export destinations* (2001): India 94.1%; Bangladesh 4.5%; Nepal 0.8%.

Transport and communications

Transport. Railroads: none. Roads (2003): total length 2,489 mi, 4,007 km (paved 60%). Vehicles (2003): passenger cars 10,574; trucks and buses 3,852. Air transport (1999): passenger-mi 30,000,000, passenger-km 49,000,000; short ton-mi cargo 2,700,000, metric ton-km cargo 4,000,000; airports (2002) with scheduled flights 1.

Communications

Medium	date	unit	number	units per 1,000 persons
Radio	1997	receivers	37,000	60
Television	2001	receivers	17,000	26
Telephones	2004	main lines	29,600	42
Cellular telephones	2004	subscribers	17,800	25
Personal computers	2004	units	11,000	16
Internet	2004	users	20,000	29

Education and health

Educational attainment: n.a. *Literacy* (1995 est.): total population age 15 and over literate 42.2%; males literate 56.2%; females literate 28.1%.

Education (2004)

	schools	teachers	students	student/ teacher ratio
Primary (age 7–11) } Secondary (age 12–16)	433	4,376	135,988	31.1
Institutes	14	321	3,381	10.5

Health (2002): physicians 122 (1 per 6,019 persons); hospital beds 1,023 (1 per 696 persons); infant mortality rate per 1,000 live births 55.0.
Food: daily per capita caloric intake, n.a.

Military

Total active duty personnel (2002): about 6,000 (army 100%).

[1]Constitution commissioned by the monarch may become effective by 2008; reforms in July 1998 curtailed the powers of the monarchy. [2]Includes 36 nonelective seats occupied by representatives of the King and religious groups. [3]Indian currency is also accepted legal tender; the ngultrum is at par with the Indian rupee. [4]Estimated district areas are derived from district area percentages of total national area as published in the *Statistical Yearbook of Bhutan* (2003). [5]Official estimate (UN estimate for mid-2003 is 2,071,000); prior to 1994 official and UN estimates were in close agreement. [6]Imputed bank service charges. [7]Imports c.i.f.; exports f.o.b.

Internet resources for further information:
• **Planning Commission: Royal Government of Bhutan**
  http://www.dop.gov.bt
• **Royal Monetary Authority of Bhutan**
  http://www.rma.org.bt

Bolivia

Official name: República de Bolivia (Republic of Bolivia).
Form of government: unitary multiparty republic with two legislative houses (Chamber of Senators [27]; Chamber of Deputies [130]).
Head of state and government: President.
Capitals: La Paz (administrative); Sucre (judicial).
Official languages: Spanish; Aymara; Quechua.
Official religion: Roman Catholicism.
Monetary unit: 1 boliviano (Bs) = 100 centavos; valuation (Sept. 1, 2005) 1 U.S.$ = Bs 8.05; 1 £ = Bs 14.83.

Area and population

Departments	Capitals	area sq mi	area sq km	population 2001 census
Beni	Trinidad	82,458	213,564	362,521
Chuquisaca	Sucre	19,893	51,524	531,522
Cochabamba	Cochabamba	21,479	55,631	1,455,711
La Paz	La Paz	51,732	133,985	2,350,466
Oruro	Oruro	20,690	53,588	391,870
Pando	Cobija	24,644	63,827	52,525
Potosí	Potosí	45,644	118,218	709,013
Santa Cruz	Santa Cruz	143,098	370,621	2,029,471
Tarija	Tarija	14,526	37,623	391,226
TOTAL		424,164	1,098,581	8,274,325

Demography

Population (2005): 8,858,000.
Density (2005): persons per sq mi 20.9, persons per sq km 8.1.
Urban-rural (2003): urban 63.4%; rural 36.6%.
Sex distribution (2004): male 49.82%; female 50.18%.
Age breakdown (2001): under 15, 38.6%; 15–29, 27.4%; 30–44, 17.0%; 45–59, 10.0%; 60–74, 5.2%; 75 and over, 1.8%.
Population projection: (2010) 9,499,000; (2020) 10,747,000.
Doubling time: 41 years.
Ethnic composition (2000): Amerindian c. 65%, of which Quechua c. 40%, Aymara c. 24%; mestizo c. 27%; white c. 8%, of which German c. 3%.
Religious affiliation (2000): Roman Catholic 88.3%; Protestant 6.4%; other 5.3%.
Major cities (2001): Santa Cruz 1,116,059; La Paz 789,585 (urban agglomeration [2003] 1,477,000); El Alto 647,350[1]; Cochabamba 516,683; Oruro 201,230; Sucre 193,873.

Vital statistics

Birth rate per 1,000 population (2004): 24.7 (world avg. 21.1).
Death rate per 1,000 population (2004): 7.8 (world avg. 9.0).
Natural increase rate per 1,000 population (2004): 16.9 (world avg. 12.1).
Total fertility rate (avg. births per childbearing woman; 2004): 3.1.
Life expectancy at birth (2004): male 62.5 years; female 67.9 years.
Major causes of death per 100,000 population (2000)[2]: circulatory system diseases 370.3; communicable diseases 122.6; external causes 109.7; malignant neoplasms (cancers) 73.5.

National economy

Budget (2004). Revenue: Bs 18,390,300,000 (tax revenue 90.5%, of which value-added taxes 22.1%, taxes on hydrocarbons 18.9%, import duties 3.6%; nontax revenue 9.5%). Expenditures: Bs 22,337,800,000 (current expenditure 71.8%; capital expenditure 28.2%).
Public debt (external, outstanding; 2004): U.S.$4,945,900,000.
Production (metric tons except as noted). Agriculture, forestry, fishing (2004): sugarcane 4,800,000, soybeans 1,551,000, potatoes 786,765, corn (maize) 707,738, bananas 626,779, rice 424,454, cassava 392,268, plantains 185,000, sunflower seeds 178,500, sorghum 176,400, tomatoes 135,167; livestock (number of live animals) 8,550,000 sheep, 6,822,200 cattle, 2,984,000 pigs, 1,900,000 llamas and alpacas, 1,501,000 goats, 635,000 asses, 323,300 horses; roundwood (2002) 10,237,753 cu m; fish catch (2002) 5,800. Mining and quarrying (metric tons of pure metal; 2003): zinc 145,490; tin 16,386; lead 9,353; silver 466; gold 9,361 kg. Manufacturing (value added in Bs '000,000; 2003)[3]: food products 1,513; beverages and tobacco products 505; petroleum products 453; textiles, clothing, and leather products 422; nonmetal mineral products 290. Energy production (consumption): electricity (kW-hr; 2003) 4,318,000,000 (2,905,000,000); coal, none (none); crude petroleum (barrels; 2002) 12,000,000 (9,400,000); petroleum products (metric tons; 2002) 1,593,000 (1,763,000); natural gas (cu m; 2002) 6,724,000,000 (2,704,000,000).
Population economically active (2002): total 3,823,500; activity rate of total population 44.5% (participation rates: ages 10 and over 78.2%; female 45.9%; unemployed [2003] 9.2%).

Price and earnings indexes (2000 = 100)

	1998	1999	2000	2001	2002	2003	2004
Consumer price index	93.8	96.7	100.0	100.9	103.4	105.0	109.7
Annual earnings index[4]	87.0	95.0	100.0	106.5	111.7		

Tourism (2003): receipts U.S.$111,000,000; expenditures U.S.$97,000,000.
Gross national product (2004): U.S.$8,656,000,000 (U.S.$960 per capita).

Structure of gross domestic product and labour force

	2003 in value Bs '000	2003 % of total value	2002 labour force[5]	2002 % of labour force[5]
Agriculture	7,803,017	13.0	1,609,700	42.1
Mining	1,915,861	3.2	38,200	1.0
Crude petroleum, nat. gas	2,681,293	4.5		
Manufacturing	7,802,059	13.0	435,900	11.4
Construction	1,580,631	2.6	206,500	5.4
Public utilities	1,830,107	3.0	7,700	0.2
Transp. and commun.	7,111,128	11.8	175,900	4.6
Trade, hotels	6,034,473	10.0	722,600	18.9
Finance	6,943,527	11.5	95,600	2.5
Pub. admin., defense	7,797,324	12.9	68,800	1.8
Services	3,242,255	5.4	462,600	12.1
Other	5,510,008[6]	9.1[6]	—	—
TOTAL	60,251,682[7]	100.0	3,823,500	100.0

Household income and expenditure (2000). Average household size 4.0; annual income per household (1999): Bs 16,980 (U.S.$2,920); expenditure: food 28.6%, transportation and communications 23.1%, rent and energy 10.3%, expenditures in cafes and hotels 9.5%, recreation and culture 7.1%, household furnishings 6.3%.
Land use as % of total land area (2000): in temporary crops 2.7%, in permanent crops 0.2%, in pasture 31.2%; overall forest area 48.9%.

Foreign trade[8]

Balance of trade (current prices)

	1998	1999	2000	2001	2002	2003
U.S.$'000,000	−721.0	−487.9	−375.0	−212.7	−253.6	+158.8
% of total	24.6%	18.8%	13.2%	7.6%	9.0%	5.3%

Imports (2003): U.S.$1,684,600,000 (machinery 18.8%; transport equipment 12.0%; chemicals and chemical products 11.0%; food 9.4%). *Major import sources:* Brazil 20.4%; U.S. 18.2%; Argentina 16.7%; Chile 7.2%; Peru 6.2%.
Exports (2003): U.S.$1,656,800,000 (natural gas 23.0%; food 18.3%, of which soybean oilcake 13.1%; zinc ores and concentrates 7.4%; petroleum 5.8%; soybean oil 5.4%; silver 4.5%). *Major export destinations:* Brazil 29.9%; U.S. 14.2%; Colombia 10.3%; Switzerland 10.0%; Venezuela 9.4%.

Transport and communications

Transport. Railroads (2004): route length 2,187 mi, 3,519 km; (1997) passenger-mi 139,746,000, passenger-km 224,900,000; short ton-mi cargo 574,600,000, metric ton-km cargo 838,900,000. Roads (2002): total length 37,457 mi, 60,282 km (paved 7%). Vehicles (2001): passenger cars 254,175; trucks and buses 194,510. Air transport (2003): passenger-mi 1,058,800,000, passenger-km 1,704,000,000; short ton-mi cargo 16,660,000, metric ton-km cargo 24,348,000; airports (2000) with scheduled flights 14.

Communications

Medium	date	unit	number	units per 1,000 persons
Daily newspapers	2000	circulation	448,000	65
Radio	2000	receivers	5,510,000	676
Television	2000	receivers	970,000	119
Telephones	2004	main lines	625,400	70
Cellular telephones	2004	subscribers	1,800,800	201
Personal computers	2002	units	190,000	23
Internet	2003	users	350,000	39

Education and health

Educational attainment (2002). Percentage of population age 19 and over having: no formal schooling 13.0%; some to complete primary education 45.4%; some to complete secondary 24.7%; some to complete higher 16.7%; not specified 0.2%. *Literacy* (2001): total population age 15 and over literate 86.0%; males literate 92.3%; females literate 79.9%.

Education (2002)

	schools	teachers	students	student/teacher ratio
Primary (age 6–13)	...	72,433	1,718,000	23.7
Secondary (age 14–17)	...	15,823	443,470	28.0
Higher	12[9]	13,929	298,668	21.4

Health: physicians (2002) 2,987 (1 per 2,827 persons); hospital beds (2003) 12,464 (1 per 689 persons); infant mortality rate per 1,000 live births (2004) 54.6.
Food (2002): daily per capita caloric intake 2,235 (vegetable products 84%, animal products 16%); 94% of FAO recommended minimum requirement.

Military

Total active duty personnel (2004): 31,500 (army 79.4%, navy 11.1%, air force 9.5%). *Military expenditure as percentage of GDP* (2003): 1.7%; per capita expenditure U.S.$15.

[1]Within La Paz urban agglomeration. [2]Based on a study of 10,744 deaths in the nine departmental capitals. [3]In 1990 prices. [4]Private sector only. [5]Population 10 years of age and over. [6]Import duties and indirect taxes less imputed bank service charges. [7]Detail does not add to total given because of rounding. [8]Import figures are f.o.b. in balance of trade and c.i.f. for commodities and trading partners. [9]2000.

Internet resources for further information:
• **Instituto Nacional de Estadística** http://www.ine.gov.bo
• **Banco Central de Bolivia** http://www.bcb.gov.bo/sitio/introduccion_f.html

Bosnia and Herzegovina[1]

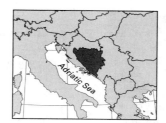

Official name: Bosna i Hercegovina (Bosnia and Herzegovina).
Form of government: emerging republic with bicameral legislature (House of Peoples [15[2]]; House of Representatives [42]).
Chiefs of state: nominally a tripartite presidency.
International authority: High Representative[1].
Head of government: Prime Minister (Chairman of the Council of Ministers).
Capital: Sarajevo.
Official language: Bosnian.
Official religion: none.
Monetary unit: 1 marka[3, 4, 5] (KM) = 100 fenning; valuation (Sept. 1, 2005) 1 U.S.$ = KM 1.56; 1 £ = KM 2.87.

Area and population

Autonomous regions Cantons	Principal cities	area		population
		sq mi	sq km	2002[6] estimate
Federation of Bosnia and Herzegovina	Sarajevo	10,081	26,110	2,312,000
Central Bosnia	Travnik	1,231	3,189	240,000
Goražde	Goražde	195	505	35,000
Neretva	Mostar	1,699	4,401	217,000
Posavina	Orašje	125	325	44,000
Sarajevo	Sarajevo	493	1,277	401,000
Tuzla-Podrinje	Tuzla	1,023	2,649	507,000
Una-Sava	Bihać	1,593	4,125	306,000
Western Bosnia	Livno	1,905	4,934	84,000
Western Herzegovina	Ljubuški	526	1,362	81,000
Zenica-Doboj	Zenica	1,291	3,343	397,000
Republika Srpska	Banja Luka	9,496	24,594	1,392,000[7]
District				
Br ko	Br ko	190	493	85,000
WATER		5	12	—
TOTAL		19,772	51,209	3,789,000

Demography

Population (2005): 3,853,000.
Density (2005): persons per sq mi 194.9, persons per sq km 75.2.
Urban-rural (2003): urban 44.3%; rural 55.7%.
Sex distribution (2004): male 49.32%; female 50.68%.
Age breakdown (2004): under 15, 16.7%; 15–29, 21.6%; 30–44, 25.0%; 45–59, 18.7%; 60–74, 12.9%; 75 and over, 5.1%.
Population projection: (2010) 3,875,000; (2020) 3,768,000.
Ethnic composition (1999): Bosniac 44.0%; Serb 31.0%; Croat 17.0%; other 8.0%.
Religious affiliation (1999): Sunnī Muslim 43.0%; Serbian Orthodox 30.0%; Roman Catholic 18.0%; other (mostly nonreligious) 9.0%.
Major cities (2004): Sarajevo 428,600 (urban agglomeration 602,500); Banja Luka 170,000; Zenica 139,800; Tuzla 123,500; Mostar 94,100.

Vital statistics

Birth rate per 1,000 population (2003): 9.2 (world avg. 21.1); (2003) legitimate 88.7%; illegitimate 11.3%.
Death rate per 1,000 population (2003): 8.3 (world avg. 9.0).
Natural increase rate per 1,000 population (2003): 0.9 (world avg. 12.1).
Total fertility rate (avg. births per childbearing woman; 2004): 1.2.
Marriage rate per 1,000 population (2003): 5.4.
Life expectancy at birth (2002): male 65.0 years; female 70.7 years.
Major causes of death per 100,000 population (2003): circulatory diseases 441.0; malignant neoplasms (cancers) 149.8; endocrine and metabolic disorders 25.2; accidents, violence, and poisoning 24.7; respiratory diseases 22.7.

National economy

Budget (2003)[8]. Revenue: KM 5,061,800,000 (tax revenue 56.5%, social contributions 35.2%, grants 0.8%, other 7.5%). Expenditures: KM 5,009,100,000 (transfers 33.6%, wages and contributions 27.8%).
Gross national product (2004): U.S.$7,841,000,000 (U.S.$2,040 per capita).

Structure of gross domestic product and labour force

	2002		1999	
	in value KM '000,000	% of total value	labour force	% of labour force
Agriculture	1,144	9.8	21,000	2.0
Manufacturing, mining	1,383	11.9	} 224,000	21.6
Construction	482	4.1		
Public utilities	592	5.1	36,000	3.5
Transp. and commun.	1,045	9.0	45,000	4.3
Trade, restaurants	1,463	12.5	91,000	8.8
Finance, real estate	612	5.3	42,000	4.1
Pub. admin., defense	1,450	12.4	73,000	7.0
Services	1,270	10.9	96,000	9.3
Other	2,210[9]	19.0[9]	409,000[10]	39.4[10]
TOTAL	11,651	100.0	1,037,000	100.0

Production (metric tons except as noted). Agriculture, forestry, fishing (2004): corn (maize) 750,000, potatoes 350,000, wheat 250,000, cabbages 78,000, plums 73,000, oats 55,000, tobacco 4,000; livestock (number of live animals) 670,000 sheep, 440,000 cattle, 300,000 pigs; roundwood (2003) 4,095,000 cu m; fish catch (2002) 2,500. Mining (2001): iron ore (gross weight) 100,000; bauxite 75,000; kaolin 3,000; barite (concentrate) 2,000. Manufacturing (value of exports in KM '000,000; 2003): base metals and fabricated metal products 498.3; wood and wood products 398.9; machinery and apparatus 286.1; textiles, wearing apparel, and footwear 228.0. Energy production (consumption): electricity (kW-hr; 2002) 10,785,000,000 (9,671,000,000); hard coal (metric tons; 2002) 3,584,000 (3,196,000); lignite (metric tons; 2002) 5,377,000 (5,339,000); crude petroleum, none (none); petroleum products (metric tons; 2002) none (918,000); natural gas (cu m; 2002) none (302,000,000).
Public debt (external, outstanding; 2003): U.S.$2,629,000,000.
Population economically active (2002): total 1,056,900; activity rate of total population 27.6% (participation rates: ages 15–64 [1991] 35.6%; female 40.9%; unemployed [2003] 41.5%).

Price index (2000 = 100)

	1998	1999	2000	2001	2002	2003	2004
Retail price index	108.1	99.0	100.0	98.4	95.8	95.7	96.1

Household income and expenditure. Average household size (1991) 3.4; income per household: n.a.; sources of income (1990): wages 53.2%, transfers 18.2%, self-employment 12.0%, other 16.6%; expenditure: n.a.
Tourism (2003): receipts from visitors U.S.$235,000,000; expenditures by nationals abroad U.S.$59,000,000.
Land use as % of total land area (2000): in temporary crops 13.0%, in permanent crops 3.0%, in pasture 23.7%; overall forest area 44.6%.

Foreign trade

Balance of trade (current prices)

	1998	1999	2000	2001	2002	2003
KM '000,000	–4,077	–4,673	–4,317	–4,692	–5,805	–5,571
% of total	66.2%	63.0%	48.8%	49.7%	58.1%	54.2%

Imports (2003): KM 7,920,191,000. *Major import sources:* Croatia 17.3%; Germany 13.2%; Italy 9.6%; Slovenia 9.6%; Serbia and Montenegro 7.6%.
Exports (2003): KM 2,349,189,000. *Major export destinations:* Croatia 17.9%; Germany 15.4%; Serbia and Montenegro 15.3%; Italy 13.4%; Slovenia 9.7%.

Transport and communications

Transport. Railroads (2001)[11]: length 1,031 km; passenger-km 38,740,000; metric ton-km cargo 239,138,000. Roads (2001): total length 21,846 km (paved 64%). Vehicles (1996): passenger cars 96,182; trucks and buses 10,919. Air transport (2001): passenger-km 44,000,000; metric ton-km, n.a.; airports (2000) with scheduled flights 1.

Communications

Medium	date	unit	number	units per 1,000 persons
Daily newspapers	2000	circulation	563,000	152
Radio	2000	receivers	900,000	243
Television	2000	receivers	411,000	111
Telephones	2003	main lines	938,000	244
Cellular telephones	2003	subscribers	1,050,000	274
Internet	2004	users	225,000	54

Education and health

Educational attainment: n.a. *Literacy:* n.a.

Education (2002–03)

	schools[12]	teachers	students	student/ teacher ratio
Primary (age 7–14)	955	20,874	363,072	17.4
Secondary (age 15–18)	184	10,792	169,497	15.7
Higher	55	2,833	34,477	13.4

Health (2003): physicians 5,576 (1 per 691 persons); hospital beds 11,981 (1 per 322 persons); infant mortality rate per 1,000 live births 7.7.
Food (2002): daily per capita caloric intake 2,894 (vegetable products 86%, animal products 14%); 114% of FAO recommended minimum requirement.

Military

Total active duty personnel (2004): federal level: none; Federation of Bosnia and Herzegovina forces 16,400 (army 100%); Republika Srpska forces 8,200 (army 100%). EU peacekeeping troops[13] (March 2005) 7,000. *Military expenditure as percentage of GDP* (2003): 2.9%; per capita expenditure U.S.$53.

[1]Government structure provided for by Dayton accords and constitutions of 1993 and 1994 is being implemented in stages since formal signing of peace accord on Dec. 14, 1995. [2]All seats are nonelective. [3]An interim currency, the marka (or "convertible mark"; KM), was introduced on June 22, 1998, to replace another interim currency, the Bosnian dinar (BD), at a rate of 1 KM to 100 BD. [4]The KM is pegged to the euro from Jan. 1, 2002. [5]The euro also circulates as semiofficial legal tender. [6]January 1. [7]Estimated figure by Republika Srpska government. [8]Combined total for the separately constructed budgets of the Federation of Bosnia and Herzegovina, Republika Srpska, and Brčko District. [9]Taxes on products and imports less subsidies. [10]Unemployed. [11]1991–95 war destroyed much infrastructure; limited service resumed in 1998. [12]1997–98. [13]Also includes Canadian and Turkish troops.

Internet resources for further information:
• **Agency for Statistics of Bosnia and Herzegovina**
  http://www.bhas.ba
• **Central Bank of Bosnia and Herzegovina** http://www.cbbh.gov.ba

Botswana

Official name: Republic of Botswana.
Form of government: multiparty
   republic with one legislative body[1]
   (National Assembly [63[2]]).
Head of state and government:
   President.
Capital: Gaborone.
Official language: English[3].
Official religion: none.
Monetary unit: 1 pula (P) = 100 thebe;
   valuation (Sept. 1, 2005)
   1 U.S.\$ = P 5.29; 1 £ = P 9.75.

Area and population

Districts	Capitals	area sq mi	area sq km	population 2001 census
Central	Serowe	57,039	147,730	501,381
Ghanzi	Ghanzi	45,525	117,910	33,170
Kgalagadi	Tsabong	41,290	106,940	42,049
Kgatleng	Mochudi	3,073	7,960	73,507
Kweneng	Molepolole	13,857	35,890	230,335
North East	Masunga	1,977	5,120	49,399
North West				
Chobe		8,031	20,800	18,258
Ngamiland	Maun	33,359	86,400	75,070
Okavango		8,776	22,730	49,642
South East	Ramotswa	687	1,780	60,623
Southern	Kanye	10,991	28,467	171,652
Towns				
Francistown	—	31	79	83,023
Gaborone	—	65	169	186,007
Jwaneng	—	39	100	15,179
Lobatse	—	16	42	29,689
Orapa	—	7	17	9,151
Selebi-Pikwe	—	23	60	49,849
Sowa	—	61	159	2,879
TOTAL		224,848[4]	582,356[4]	1,680,863

Demography

Population (2005): 1,765,000.
Density (2005): persons per sq mi 7.8, persons per sq km 3.3.
Urban-rural (2003): urban 51.6%; rural 48.4%.
Sex distribution (2001): male 48.40%; female 51.60%.
Age breakdown (2000): under 15, 40.6%; 15–29, 30.8%; 30–44, 15.0%; 45–59, 7.7%; 60–74, 4.3%; 75 and over, 1.6%.
Population projection: (2010) 1,729,000; (2020) 1,671,000.
Ethnic composition (2000): Tswana 66.8%; Kalanga 14.8%; Ndebele 1.7%; Herero 1.4%; San (Bushman) 1.3%; Afrikaner 1.3%; other 12.7%.
Religious affiliation (2000): Christian 59.9%, of which independent Christian 30.7%, unaffiliated Christian 13.6%, Protestant 11.7%; traditional beliefs 38.8%; other 1.3%.
Major cities (2001): Gaborone (2003) 198,822; Francistown 83,023; Molepolole 54,561; Selebi-Pikwe 49,849; Maun 43,776.

Vital statistics

Birth rate per 1,000 population (2004): 24.0 (world avg. 21.1).
Death rate per 1,000 population (2004): 28.9 (world avg. 9.0).
Natural increase rate per 1,000 population (2004): –4.9 (world avg. 12.1).
Total fertility rate (avg. births per childbearing woman; 2004): 3.0.
Marriage rate per 1,000 population: n.a.
Life expectancy at birth (2004): male 34.0 years; female 34.4 years.
Adult population (ages 15–49) *living with HIV* (2004[5]): 37.3% (world avg. 1.1%).

National economy

Budget (2003–04). Revenue: P 16,197,300,000 (tax revenue 87.3%, of which mineral royalties 50.4%, customs duties and excise tax 13.9%, income tax 12.8%, value-added tax 9.7%; nontax revenue 12.3%, of which property income 6.0%; grants 0.4%). Expenditures: P 16,275,800,000 (general services, including defense 30.6%, education 24.2%, health 10.0%, public utilities 4.9%).
Population economically active (2001): total 587,882; activity rate of total population 35.0% (participation rates: ages 15–64, 57.6%; female 43.8%; unemployed [June 2002–August 2003] 23.8%).

Price and earnings indexes (2000 = 100)

	1998	1999	2000	2001	2002	2003	2004
Consumer price index	85.5	92.1	100.0	106.6	115.1	125.7	134.4
Monthly earnings index[6]	82.1	96.4	100.0	111.7	127.3	...	...

Production (metric tons except as noted). Agriculture, forestry, fishing (2004): sorghum 32,000, pulses 17,500, corn (maize) 10,000; livestock (number of live animals) 2,250,000 goats, 1,700,000 cattle, 400,000 sheep; roundwood (2003) 754,570 cu m; fish catch (2002) 139. Mining and quarrying (2003): soda ash 234,520; nickel ore (metal content) 27,400; copper ore (metal content) 24,289; diamonds 30,371,000 carats. Manufacturing (value added in U.S.\$'000,000; 1997): motor vehicles 33; beverages 26; bricks, cement, and tiles 20; rubber products 15. Energy production (consumption): electricity (kW-hr; 2003) 624,000,000 ([2000] 1,450,000,000); coal (metric tons; 2003) 822,780 ([2000] 971,000); crude petroleum (2001) none (n.a.); natural gas (2000) none (none).
Tourism: receipts (2003) U.S.\$356,000,000; expenditures (2002) U.S.\$184,-000,000.

Gross national product (2004): U.S.\$7,490,000,000 (U.S.\$4,340 per capita).

Structure of gross domestic product and labour force

	2003–04 in value P '000,000	2003–04 % of total value	2000 labour force	2000 % of labour force
Agriculture	931	2.3	95,283	16.6
Mining	13,534	33.9	11,219	2.0
Manufacturing	1,617	4.1	42,626	7.4
Construction	2,103	5.3	44,940	7.8
Public utilities	1,062	2.7	2,222	0.4
Transp. and commun.	1,404	3.5	13,800	2.4
Trade, hotels	4,490	11.3	73,446	12.8
Finance	4,589	11.5	22,068	3.8
Pub. admin., defense	6,265	15.7	73,217	12.8
Services	1,522	3.8	104,613	18.2
Other	2,364[7]	5.9[7]	90,728[8]	15.8[8]
TOTAL	39,881	100.0	574,160[4]	100.0

Public debt (external, outstanding; 2003–04): U.S.\$427,258,000.
Household income and expenditure (2002–03). Average household size 4.1; average annual disposable income per household P 29,095 (U.S.\$5,320), of which cash income P 25,519 (U.S.\$4,670); sources of income, n.a.; expenditure: food and nonalcoholic beverages 23.7%, transportation 15.6%, housing and energy 12.9%, alcoholic beverages and tobacco 9.6%, household furnishings 8.0%, clothing and footwear 6.8%.
Land use as % of total land area (2000): in temporary crops 0.7%, in permanent crops 0.01%, in pasture 45.2%; overall forest area 21.9%.

Foreign trade[9]

Balance of trade (current prices)

	1997	1998	1999	2000	2001	2002
P '000,000	+2,135	–816	+2,063	+3,222	+3,750	+4,814
% of total	11.4%	4.5%	9.2%	13.2%	15.1%	19.1%

Imports (2002): P 10,169,000,000 (machinery and apparatus 19.6%; food, beverages, and tobacco 13.9%; transport equipment 12.1%; chemical and rubber products 10.3%; wood and paper products 8.8%). *Major import sources:* Customs Union of Southern Africa (CUSA) 77.6%; Europe 12.3%, of which U.K. 4.4%; Zimbabwe 3.2%; U.S. 1.8%.
Exports (2002): P 14,983,000,000 (diamonds 83.3%; copper-nickel matte 3.2%; textiles 2.0%; meat products 1.9%). *Major export destinations:* U.K. 85.9%; CUSA 6.5%; Zimbabwe 2.6%.

Transport and communications

Transport. Railroads (2000–01): length 705 mi, 1,135 km; passenger-km 106,000,000; metric ton-km cargo 747,000. Roads (2003): total length 5,540 mi, 8,916 km (paved [2002] 55%). Vehicles (2003): passenger cars 64,681; trucks and buses 70,923. Air transport (2002)[10]: passenger-km 96,000,000; metric ton-km cargo 300,000; airports (2000) 7.

Communications

Medium	date	unit	number	units per 1,000 persons
Daily newspapers	2000	circulation	44,200	27
Radio	2000	receivers	254,000	155
Television	2000	receivers	40,900	25
Telephones	2004	main lines	136,500	76
Cellular telephones	2004	subscribers	563,800	314
Personal computers	2004	units	80,000	45
Internet	2004	users	60,000	33

Education and health

Educational attainment (1993). Percentage of population age 25 and over having: no formal schooling 34.7%; primary education 44.1%; some secondary 19.8%; postsecondary 1.4%. *Literacy* (2001): total population over age 15 literate 78.1%; males literate 75.3%; females literate 80.6%.

Education (2003)

	schools	teachers	students	student/ teacher ratio
Primary (age 6–13)	770	13,153	328,825	25.0
Secondary (age 14–18)	275	9,597	205,093	21.4
Teacher training	6	...	2,899[11]	...
Higher	1	697[12]	12,286[11]	...

Health (2003): physicians 510 (1 per 3,261 persons); hospital beds 3,816 (1 per 464 persons); infant mortality rate per 1,000 live births (2004) 55.6.
Food (2002): daily per capita caloric intake 2,151 (vegetable products 82%, animal products 18%); 93% of FAO recommended minimum requirement.

Military

Total active duty personnel (2004): 9,000 (army 94.4%, navy, none [landlocked], air force 5.6%). *Military expenditure as percentage of GDP* (2003): 4.1%; per capita expenditure U.S.\$169.

---

[1]In addition, the House of Chiefs, a 15-member body consisting of chiefs, subchiefs, and associated members, serves in an advisory capacity to the government. [2]Includes 4 specially elected members. [3]Tswana is the national language. [4]Detail does not add to total given because of rounding. [5]Beginning of year. [6]Includes noncitizens. [7]Import duties and indirect taxes less subsidies and less imputed bank service charges. [8]Unemployed. [9]Imports c.i.f.; exports f.o.b. [10]Air Botswana only. [11]2002. [12]1999.

Internet resources for further information:
• **Central Statistical Office http://www.cso.gov.bw**
• **Bank of Botswana http://www.bankofbotswana.bw**

Brazil

Official name: República Federativa
do Brasil (Federative Republic
of Brazil).
Form of government: multiparty
federal republic with 2 legislative
houses (Federal Senate [81]; Chamber
of Deputies [513]).
Chief of state and government:
President.
Capital: Brasília.
Official language: Portuguese.
Official religion: none.
Monetary unit: 1 real[1] (R$; plural
reais) = 100 centavos; valuation
(Sept. 1, 2005) 1 U.S.$ = 2.34 reais;
1 £ = 4.31 reais.

Area and population

States	Capitals	area sq mi	area sq km	population 2003 estimate
Acre	Rio Branco	58,912	152,581	600,595
Alagoas	Maceió	10,721	27,768	2,917,664
Amapá	Macapá	55,141	142,815	534,835
Amazonas	Manaus	606,468	1,570,746	3,031,068
Bahia	Salvador	218,029	564,693	13,435,612
Ceará	Fortaleza	57,462	148,826	7,758,441
Espírito Santo	Vitória	17,791	46,078	3,250,219
Goiás	Goiânia	131,308	340,087	5,306,459
Maranhão	São Luís	128,179	331,983	5,873,655
Mato Grosso	Cuiabá	348,788	903,358	2,651,335
Mato Grosso do Sul	Campo Grande	137,887	357,125	2,169,688
Minas Gerais	Belo Horizonte	226,460	586,528	18,553,312
Pará	Belém	481,736	1,247,690	6,574,993
Paraíba	João Pessoa	21,792	56,440	3,518,595
Paraná	Curitiba	76,956	199,315	9,906,866
Pernambuco	Recife	37,958	98,312	8,161,862
Piauí	Teresina	97,116	251,529	2,923,725
Rio de Janeiro	Rio de Janeiro	16,871	43,696	14,879,118
Rio Grande do Norte	Natal	20,385	52,797	2,888,058
Rio Grande do Sul	Porto Alegre	108,784	281,749	10,510,992
Rondônia	Porto Velho	91,729	237,576	1,455,907
Roraima	Boa Vista	86,602	224,299	357,302
Santa Catarina	Florianópolis	36,813	95,346	5,607,233
São Paulo	São Paulo	95,834	248,209	38,709,320
Sergipe	Aracaju	8,459	21,910	1,874,613
Tocantins	Palmas	107,190	277,621	1,230,181
Federal District				
Distrito Federal	Brasília	2,240	5,802	2,189,789
TOTAL		3,287,612[2, 3]	8,514,877[2, 3]	176,871,437

Demography

Population (2005): 184,016,000.
Density (2005): persons per sq mi 56.0, persons per sq km 21.6.
Urban-rural (2003): urban 83.1%; rural 16.9%.
Sex distribution (2004): male 49.45%; female 50.55%.
Age breakdown (2004): under 15, 26.6%; 15–29, 28.1%; 30–44, 22.8%; 45–59, 13.9%; 60–74, 6.6%; 75 and over, 2.0%.
Population projection: (2010) 195,954,000; (2020) 216,384,000.
Doubling time: 64 years.
Racial composition (2000): white 53.7%; mulatto and mestizo 39.1%; black and black/Amerindian 6.2%; Asian 0.5%; Amerindian 0.4%.
Religious affiliation (2000)[4]: Catholic 73.9%, of which Roman Catholic 73.6%; Protestant 15.4%, of which Pentecostal 10.4%; nonreligious 7.4%; Spiritist 1.3%; Jehovah's Witness 0.7%; Umbanda 0.2%; Buddhist 0.1%; other 1.0%.
Major cities[5] and metropolitan areas (2003): São Paulo 10,041,500 (18,628,444); Rio de Janeiro 5,974,100 (11,226,729); Salvador 2,555,400 (3,183,327); Belo Horizonte 2,305,800 (5,100,359); Fortaleza 2,256,200 (3,164,225); Brasília 2,094,100 (3,199,451); Curitiba 1,671,200 (2,930,772); Manaus 1,517,500 (1,527,314); Recife 1,461,300 (3,466,214); Porto Alegre 1,353,300 (3,815,447); Belém 1,333,500 (1,916,982); Goiânia 1,138,600 (1,766,588); Guarulhos 1,135,500[6]; Campinas 990,100 (2,483,594).

Other principal cities[5] (2003)

	population		population		population
Aracaju	479,800	Maceió	847,700	São Gonçalo	925,400[6]
Campo Grande	697,800	Natal	744,800	São Jose dos	
Contagem	560,300[7]	Nova Iguaçu	792,200[8]	Campos	562,200
Cuiabá	501,000	Osasco	678,600[6]	São Luís	889,100
Duque de Caxias	805,400[8]	Ribeirão Preto	525,500	Sorocaba	521,500
Jaboatão	596,900[9]	Santo André	659,300[6]	Teresina	711,700
João Pessoa	628,800	São Bernardo		Uberlândia	529,300
Juiz de Fora	474,600	do Campo	732,200[6]		

Families. Average family size (2000) 3.5; (1996) 1–2 persons 25.2%, 3 persons 20.3%, 4 persons 22.2%, 5–6 persons 23.3%, 7 or more persons 9.0%.
Number of emigrants/immigrants (1986–96): 2,355,057/169,303. Emigrants' most popular destinations in order of preference are the United States, Japan, and the United Kingdom.

Vital statistics

Birth rate per 1,000 population (2004): 17.3 (world avg. 21.1).
Death rate per 1,000 population (2004): 6.1 (world avg. 9.0).
Natural increase rate per 1,000 population (2004): 11.1 (world avg. 12.1).
Total fertility rate (avg. births per childbearing woman; 2004): 2.0.
Life expectancy at birth (2004): male 67.5 years; female 75.6 years.

Marriage rate per 1,000 population (2002): 4.1.
Divorce rate per 1,000 population (2001): 0.7.
Major causes of death per 100,000 population (1998; based on incomplete registration of deaths): diseases of the circulatory system 153.2; accidents, murder, and violence 70.3; malignant neoplasms (cancers) 66.2; diseases of the respiratory system 55.0; infectious and parasitic diseases 29.1; diseases of the digestive system 24.3; endocrine, metabolic, and nutritional disorders 23.8; ill-defined conditions 82.8.

Social indicators

Educational attainment (2000). Percentage of population age 25 and over having: no formal schooling or less than one year of primary education 14.6%; lower primary only 17.8%; incomplete upper primary 30.6%; complete primary to some secondary 12.8%; complete secondary to some higher 16.3%; complete higher 6.8%; unknown 1.1%.

Distribution of income (2000)

percentage of national income by decile/quintile

1	2	3	4	5	6	7	8	9	10 (highest)
1.0	1.6	2.5	3.2	4.2	5.5	7.3	10.1	16.1	48.5

Quality of working life. Proportion of employed population receiving minimum wage (2002): 53.5%. Number and percentage of children (age 5–17) working: 5,400,000 (12.6% of age group).
Access to services (1999)[10]. Proportion of households having access to: electricity 94.8%, of which urban households having access 99.2%, rural households having access 75.4%; safe public (piped) water supply 79.8%, of which urban households having access 92.3%, rural households having access 24.9%; public (piped) sewage system 43.6%, of which urban households having access 52.5%, rural households having access 4.5%; no sewage disposal 8.5%, of which urban households having no disposal 2.9%, rural households having no disposal 32.9%.
Social participation. Voting is mandatory for national elections; abstention is punishable by a fine. Trade union membership in total workforce (2001): 19,500,000. Practicing Roman Catholic population in total affiliated Roman Catholic population (2000): large cities 10–15%; towns and rural areas 60–70%.
Social deviance. Annual murder rate per 100,000 population (2002): Brazil 28, Rio de Janeiro only 56, São Paulo only 54.
Leisure. Favourite leisure activities include: playing soccer, dancing, rehearsing all year in neighbourhood samba groups for celebrations of Carnival, and competing in water sports, volleyball, and basketball.
Material well-being (2003). Households possessing: television receiver 89.9%, of which urban 94.5%, rural 69.4%; refrigerator 86.7%, of which urban 91.7%, rural 60.0%; washing machine 34.0%, of which urban 38.1%, rural 10.0%.

National economy

Gross national product (at current market prices; 2004): U.S.$552,096,000,000 (U.S.$3,090 per capita).

Structure of gross domestic product and labour force

	2003 in value R$'000,000	2003 % of total value	2000 labour force[10,11]	2000 % of labour force
Agriculture	138,191	8.9	12,119,389	15.6
Mining	54,888	3.5	234,869	0.3
Public utilities	47,594	3.1	328,918	0.4
Manufacturing	337,457	21.7	8,757,040	11.3
Construction	100,951	6.5	4,568,396	5.9
Transportation and communications	78,337	5.0	3,318,814	4.3
Trade[12]	107,501	6.9	13,970,811	18.0
Finance, real estate	240,003	15.4	4,587,510	5.9
Pub. admin., defense	144,884	9.3	3,522,868	4.5
Services	220,459	14.2	14,221,277	18.4
Other	85,917[13]	5.5[13]	11,837,581[14]	15.3[14]
TOTAL	1,556,182	100.0	77,467,473	100.0[3]

Budget (2002). Revenue: R$321,855,000,000 (tax revenue 75.5%, of which income tax 26.7%, social security contributions 16.2%, value-added tax 6.2%, profit tax 4.2%; social welfare contributions 22.1%; other 2.4%). Expenditures: R$289,596,000,000 (social security and welfare 30.4%; personnel 25.3%; transfers to state and local governments 19.4%; other 24.9%).
Public debt (external, outstanding; 2003): U.S.$94,985,000,000.
Production ('000 metric tons except as noted). Agriculture, forestry, fishing (2004): sugarcane 411,009, soybeans 49,205, corn (maize) 41,947, cassava 24,230, oranges 18,263, rice 13,356, bananas 6,593, wheat 6,036, seed cotton 3,623, tomatoes 3,395, dry beans 3,054, coconuts 2,960, potatoes 2,883, coffee 2,454, sorghum 2,103, cashew apples 1,603, papayas 1,600, pineapples 1,436, grapes 1,280, dry onions 1,133, apples 950, lemons and limes 950, tobacco 928, maté 550, oil palm fruit 516, cashews 224, peanuts (groundnuts) 221, sisal 192, cacao beans 177, natural rubber 96, garlic 89, Brazil nuts 29; livestock (number of live animals) 192,000,000 cattle, 33,000,000 pigs, 14,182,000 sheep, 5,900,700 horses; roundwood (2003) 238,536,476 cu m, of which fuelwood 135,542,476 cu m, sawlogs and veneer logs 49,290,000 cu m, pulpwood 45,861,000 cu m; fish catch (2002) 1,068, of which freshwater fishes 385. Mining and quarrying (metric tons; 2003): iron ore (metal content) 115,693,000; bauxite 13,147,900; manganese ore and concentrate 2,500,000; kaolin (marketable product) 1,444,200; zinc 152,823; columbium-tantalum ores and concentrates 41,640; nickel (metal content) 31,100; copper (metal content) 27,300; tin (metal content) 12,100; quartz 4,300; gold 40.4. Manufacturing (value added in U.S.$'000,000; 2001): food products 15,387; petroleum products 11,046; transport equipment 10,632, of which cars 8,103; electrical machinery 7,248; iron, steel, and nonferrous metals 7,209; indus-

trial chemicals 5,457; paper and paper products 4,740; printing and publishing 4,304; plastics and rubber products 4,201.
Land use as % of total land area (2000): in temporary crops 6.8%, in permanent crops 0.9%, in pasture 23.2%; overall forest area 64.3%.

Manufacturing enterprises (2001)			
	number of employees	wages of employers as a % of avg. of all mfg. wages	value added at factor cost (in U.S.$'000,000)
Food products	894,457	67.1	15,387
Petroleum products	23,385	494.9	11,046
Transport equipment	323,485	184.9	10,632
Nonelectrical machinery and apparatus	368,050	132.8	8,855
Paints, soaps, pharmaceuticals, and related products	226,848	181.6	8,016
Electrical machinery and apparatus	216,030	160.5	7,248
Industrial chemicals	72,088	229.8	5,457
Iron and steel	97,513	184.9	5,151
Beverages	137,197	106.1	5,115
Paper and paper products	138,268	131.8	4,740
Clothing and footwear	762,034	44.4	4,727
Fabricated metal products	315,417	87.8	4,310
Printing and publishing	194,903	125.4	4,304
Bricks, tiles, cement, and related products	262,184	67.3	4,042
Plastics	210,099	90.3	2,976
Textiles	244,882	71.5	2,831
Nonferrous base metals	40,262	165.5	2,058
Furniture	193,388	56.2	1,479
Rubber products	69,630	117.2	1,225

Population economically active (2000): total 77,467,473; activity rate of total population 45.6% (participation rates: ages 15–59, 69.1%; female 39.9%; unemployed [December 2003–November 2004] 11.6%).

Price and earnings indexes (2000 = 100)							
	1998	1999	2000	2001	2002	2003	2004
Consumer price index	89.1	93.4	100.0	106.8	115.9	132.9	141.7
Monthly earnings index	94.0	98.6	100.0	110.7	118.2	...	...

Tourism (2003): receipts from visitors U.S.$2,479,000,000; expenditures by nationals abroad U.S.$2,261,000,000.

Retail trade enterprises (1996)				
	no. of businesses	total no. of employees	annual wage as a % of all trade wages	annual values of sales in R$'000,000[1]
General merchandise stores (including food products)	10,382	437,452	131.2	35,766
Vehicles, new and used	9,348	202,892	229.9	30,926
Gas stations	20,388	210,250	124.7	23,199
Electronics, kitchen equipment, musical instruments	18,245	158,755	143.7	14,855
Metal products, lumber, glass, and construction materials	81,303	386,285	90.1	14,047
Vehicles, parts	55,534	252,731	110.6	10,881
Pharmaceutical and cosmetic products	50,778	240,633	94.2	9,658
Clothing and apparel	128,908	428,150	76.4	9,023
Food, beverages, and tobacco	135,672	378,102	60.7	6,900

Households. Average household size (2002) 3.8.
Family/household income and expenditure. Average family size (2000) 3.5; average annual income per household (2000) R$14,065 (U.S.$7,686), median annual income per household (2000) R$6,744 (U.S.$3,685); sources of income, n.a.; expenditure (1995–96)[15]: housing, energy, and household furnishings 28.8%, food and beverages 23.4%, transportation and communications 13.8%, health care 9.2%, education and recreation 8.4%.

Financial aggregates[16]						
	1999	2000	2001	2002	2003	2004
Exchange rate, reais per:						
U.S. dollar	1.79	1.96	2.32	3.53	2.89	2.65
£	2.89	2.92	3.36	5.69	5.15	5.13
SDR	2.46	2.55	2.92	4.80	4.29	4.12
International reserves (U.S.$)						
Total (excl. gold; '000,000)	34,796	32,488	35,740	37,683	49,111	52,740
SDRs ('000,000)	10	—	11	275	2	4
Reserve pos. in IMF ('000,000)						
Foreign exchange ('000,000)	34,786	32,488	35,729	37,409	49,108	52,736
Gold ('000,000 fine troy oz)	3.17	1.89	0.46	0.44	0.45	0.45
% world reserves	0.44	0.20	0.05	0.05	0.05	0.05
Interest and prices						
Central bank discount (%)	21.37	18.52	21.43	30.42	23.92	24.55
Govt. bond yield (%)	...	...	...	...	...	...
Industrial share prices	...	...	...	...	...	...
Balance of payments (U.S.$'000,000)						
Balance of visible trade	−1,261	−698	+2,650	+13,121	+24,801	...
Imports, f.o.b.	49,272	55,783	55,572	47,240	48,283	...
Exports, f.o.b.	48,011	55,086	58,223	60,362	73,084	...
Balance of invisibles	−24,139	−23,527	−25,865	−20,758	−20,785	...
Balance of payments, current account	−25,400	−24,225	−23,215	−7,637	+4,016	...

Energy production (consumption): electricity (kW-hr; 2002) 345,000,000,000 (310,000,000,000); coal (metric tons; 2002) 5,140,000 (17,800,000); crude petroleum (barrels; 2002) 536,000,000 (597,000,000); petroleum products (metric tons; 2002) 70,603,000 (73,178,000); natural gas (cu m; 2002) 8,205,000,000 (13,435,000,000).

Foreign trade[17]

Balance of trade (current prices)						
	1998	1999	2000	2001	2002	2003
U.S.$'000,000	−6,623	−1,284	−753	+2,642	+13,121	+24,831
% of total	6.1%	1.4%	0.7%	2.3%	12.2%	20.5%

Imports (2001): U.S.$55,581,000,000 (machinery and apparatus 43.0%; chemicals and chemical products 18.1%; mineral fuels 14.4%; motor vehicles 9.5%; food products 5.0%). *Major import sources* (2002): United States 21.8%; Argentina 10.1%; Germany 9.3%; Japan 5.0%; Italy 3.7%; France 3.7%; China 3.3%; U.K. 2.8%; Algeria 2.3%; South Korea 2.3%.
Exports (2001): U.S.$58,223,000,000 (food products 20.0%, of which meat 5.0%, sugar 4.1%, animal food 3.7%, coffee 3.0%; transportation equipment 13.6%, of which road vehicles 7.4%; machinery and apparatus 13.1%; iron and steel 5.5%; chemicals and chemical products 5.4%; iron ore and concentrates 5.0%; soybeans 4.7%). *Major export destinations* (2002): United States 25.4%; The Netherlands 5.3%; Germany 4.2%; China 4.2%; Argentina 3.9%; Mexico 3.9%; Japan 3.5%; Belgium 3.1%; United Kingdom 2.9%; France 2.5%.

Transport and communications

Transport. Railroads (2000)[18]: route length 18,196 mi, 29,283 km; passenger-mi 3,636,000,000, passenger-km 5,852,000,000; short ton-mi cargo 106,077,000,000, metric ton-km cargo 154,870,000,000. Roads (2000): total length 1,071,816 mi, 1,724,924 km (paved 10%). Vehicles (2001): passenger cars 23,241,966; trucks and buses 3,897,140. Air transport (2003)[19]: passenger-mi 24,283,000,000, passenger-km 39,079,000,000; short ton-mi cargo 761,900,000, metric ton-km cargo 1,201,000,000; airports (1995) with scheduled flights 139.

Communications				units per 1,000 persons
Medium	date	unit	number	
Daily newspapers	2000	circulation	7,390,000	43
Radio	2000	receivers	74,400,000	433
Television	2000	receivers	58,900,000	343
Telephones	2004	main lines	42,382,000	234
Cellular telephones	2004	subscribers	65,605,000	363
Personal computers	2004	units	19,350,000	107
Internet	2005	users	17,945,000	98

Education and health

Literacy (2002): total population age 15 and over literate 86.0%; males literate 85.8%; females literate 86.2%.

Education (2002)				student/ teacher ratio
	schools	teachers	students	
Primary (age 7–14)	172,508	1,581,044	35,150,362	22.2
Secondary (age 15–17)	21,304	468,310	8,710,584	18.6
Higher	1,180	197,712	2,694,245	13.6

Health: physicians (2001) 357,888 (1 per 485 persons); hospital beds (2002) 471,171 (1 per 371 persons); infant mortality rate per 1,000 live births (2004) 30.7.
Food (2002): daily per capita caloric intake 3,049 (vegetable products 78%, animal products 22%); 128% of FAO recommended minimum requirement.

Military

Total active duty personnel (2004): 302,909 (army 62.4%, navy 16.0%, air force 21.6%). *Military expenditure as percentage of GDP* (2003): 1.6%; per capita expenditure U.S.$44.

[1]The real (R$) replaced the cruzeiro real (CR$) on July 1, 1994, at a rate of 2,750 cruzeiros reais to 1 real (a rate par to the U.S.$ on that date). [2]Total area including inland water per survey of 2002. [3]Detail does not add to total given because of rounding. [4]Christian data include nominal Christians. [5]Populations are for *municípios*, which may include adjacent urban or rural districts. [6]Within São Paulo metropolitan area. [7]Within Belo Horizonte metropolitan area. [8]Within Rio de Janeiro metropolitan area. [9]Within Recife metropolitan area. [10]Excludes rural population of Acre, Amapá, Amazonas, Pará, Rondônia, and Roraima. [11]Excludes members of armed forces in barracks. [12]Includes restaurants and hotels. [13]Import duties less imputed bank service charges. [14]Unemployed. [15]Based on survey of 11 metropolitan areas only. [16]End-of-period figures. [17]Imports f.o.b. [18]Includes suburban services. [19]TAM, VARIG, and VASP airlines only.

Internet resources for further information:
• IBGE: Instituto Brasileiro de Geografia e Estatística
  http://www.ibge.gov.br/english/default.php
• Central Bank of Brazil: Economic Data
  http://www.bcb.gov.br/defaulti.htm

Brunei

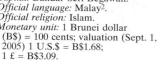

Official name: Negara Brunei Darussalam (State of Brunei, Abode of Peace).
Form of government: monarchy (sultanate) with one advisory body (Legislative Council [29][1]).
Head of state and government: Sultan.
Capital: Bandar Seri Begawan.
Official language: Malay[2].
Official religion: Islam.
Monetary unit: 1 Brunei dollar (B$) = 100 cents; valuation (Sept. 1, 2005) 1 U.S.$ = B$1.68; 1 £ = B$3.09.

Area and population		area		population
				2003
Districts	Capitals	sq mi	sq km	estimate
Belait	Kuala Belait	1,052	2,724	58,000
Brunei and Muara	Bandar Seri Begawan	220	571	242,600
Temburong	Bangar	504	1,304	8,600
Tutong	Tutong	450	1,166	39,600
TOTAL		2,226	5,765	348,800

Demography

Population (2005): 364,000.
Density (2005): persons per sq mi 163.5, persons per sq km 63.1.
Urban-rural (2003): urban 76.2%; rural 23.8%.
Sex distribution (2003): male 50.54%; female 49.46%.
Age breakdown (2002): under 15, 30.2%; 15–29, 27.0%; 30–44, 25.2%; 45–59, 13.2%; 60–74, 3.6%; 75 and over, 0.8%.
Population projection: (2010) 403,000; (2020) 478,000.
Doubling time: 45 years.
Ethnic composition (2003): Malay 66.6%; Chinese 10.9%; other indigenous 3.6%; other 18.9%.
Religious affiliation (2000): Muslim 64.4%; traditional beliefs 11.2%; Buddhist 9.1%; Christian 7.7%; other religions and nonreligious 7.6%.
Major cities: Bandar Seri Begawan (2001) 27,285 (urban agglomeration [2002] 74,700); Kuala Belait (2002) 27,200; Seria (2002) 23,200.

Vital statistics

Birth rate per 1,000 population (2004): 19.3 (world avg. 21.1).
Death rate per 1,000 population (2004): 3.4 (world avg. 9.0).
Natural increase rate per 1,000 population (2004): 15.9 (world avg. 12.1).
Total fertility rate (avg. births per childbearing woman; 2004): 2.3.
Marriage rate per 1,000 population (2002): 6.7.
Divorce rate per 1,000 population[3] (2002): 0.9.
Life expectancy at birth (2004): male 72.1 years; female 77.1 years.
Major causes of death per 100,000 population (2002): diseases of the circulatory system 98.8; malignant neoplasms (cancers) 52.3; accidents and violence 35.6; diseases of the respiratory system 31.2; diabetes mellitus 26.5; transportation accidents 12.6; congenital anomalies 8.5.

National economy

Budget (2004). Revenue: B$6,126,400,000 (tax revenue 57.9%, of which taxes on petroleum and natural gas companies 53.7%; nontax revenue 42.1%, of which government property income 37.4%, commercial receipts 4.6%). Expenditures: B$4,908,700,000 (current expenditure 83.1%; capital expenditure 16.9%).
Production (metric tons except as noted). Agriculture, forestry, fishing (2004): cassava 1,800, pineapples 1,000, bananas 640, rice 400, roots and tubers 350, oranges 320; livestock (number of live animals) 6,800 pigs, 6,000 buffalo, 13,000,000 chickens; roundwood (2003) 228,590 cu m; fish catch (2002) 2,058. Mining and quarrying: other than petroleum and natural gas, none except sand and gravel for construction. Manufacturing (2003): cement 235,000; gasoline 1,717,000 barrels; kerosene 634,000 barrels; distillate fuel oils 1,195 barrels. Energy production (consumption): electricity (kW-hr; 2002) 3,036,000,000 (3,036,000,000); coal, none (none); crude petroleum (barrels; 2004) 75,000,000 ([2002] 1,600,000); petroleum products (metric tons; 2002) 923,000 (928,000); natural gas (cu m; 2003) 12,000,000,000 ([2002] 1,273,000,000).
Gross national product (at current market prices; 2003): U.S.$7,290,000,000 (U.S.$20,360 per capita).

Structure of gross domestic product and labour force				
	2003		2001	
	in value B$'000,000	% of total value	labour force	% of labour force
Agriculture	294.5	3.6	1,994	1.3
Mining }	3,402.3	41.3	3,954	2.5
Manufacturing }			12,455	7.9
Construction	334.0	4.1	12,301	7.8
Public utilities	62.1	0.7	2,639	1.7
Transportation and communications	431.9	5.2	4,803	3.0
Trade	803.7	9.8	20,038	12.7
Finance	722.2	8.8	8,190	5.2
Pub. admin., defense } Services }	2,441.1	29.6	79,880	50.7
Other	−254.8[4]	−3.1[4]	11,340[5]	7.2[5]
TOTAL	8,236.9[6]	100.0	157,594	100.0

Population economically active (2001): total 157,594; activity rate of total population 45.2% (participation rates: ages 15–64, 65.9%; female 41.2%; unemployed [2003] 4.3%).

Price index (2000 = 100)						
	1998	1999	2000	2001	2002	2003
Consumer price index	98.8	98.7	100.0	100.6	98.3	98.6

Public debt (external, outstanding; 1999): U.S.$902,000,000.
Household income and expenditure. Average household size (2000) 6.1; income per household: n.a.; sources of income: n.a.; expenditure (July–September 2003)[7]: food and nonalcoholic beverages 28.8%, transportation 22.5%, housing and energy 8.8%, household furnishings 8.6%, recreation and entertainment 8.1%, clothing and footwear 5.6%, communications 5.5%.
Tourism (1998): receipts from visitors U.S.$37,000,000; expenditures by nationals abroad U.S.$1,000,000.
Land use as % of total land area (2000): in temporary crops 0.6%, in permanent crops 0.8%, in pasture 1.1%; overall forest area 83.9%.

Foreign trade[8]

Balance of trade (current prices)						
	1998	1999	2000	2001	2002	2003
B$'000,000	+856	+2,074	+4,826	+4,446	...	+5,513
% of total	15.5%	31.5%	55.8%	51.7%	...	55.7%

Imports (2004): B$2,412,500,000 (basic manufactures 37.1%, machinery and transport equipment 34.9%, food and live animals 14.7%, chemicals and chemical products 8.0%). *Major import sources* (2003): ASEAN countries 47.4%; United States 11.5%; Japan 10.0%; Hong Kong 6.6%; China 4.9%.
Exports (2004): B$8,562,700,000 (crude petroleum and partly refined petroleum 57.4%, natural gas 34.0%, garments 3.6%). *Major export destinations* (2003): Japan 41.0%; ASEAN countries 20.2%; South Korea 11.2%; Australia 8.4%; China 6.7%.

Transport and communications

Transport. Railroads[9]: length 12 mi, 19 km. Roads (2000): total length 2,033 mi, 3,272 km (paved 73%). Vehicles (2003): passenger cars 212,000; trucks and buses (2002) 20,000. Air transport (2003)[10]: passenger-mi 2,229,000,000, passenger-km 3,588,000,000; short ton-mi cargo 101,853,000, metric ton-km cargo 148,703,000; airports (2003) with scheduled flights 1.

Communications				units per 1,000
Medium	date	unit	number	persons
Daily newspapers	2002	circulation	72,000	213
Radio	2000	receivers	362,712	1,120
Television	2001	receivers	215,000	648
Telephones	2003	main lines	81,900	235
Cellular telephones	2003	subscribers	177,372	509
Personal computers	2004	units	31,000	85
Internet	2004	users	56,000	153

Education and health

Educational attainment (1991). Percentage of population age 25 and over having: no formal schooling 17.0%; primary education 43.3%; secondary 26.3%; postsecondary and higher 12.9%; not stated 0.5%. *Literacy* (2002): percentage of total population age 15 and over literate 93.9%; males literate 96.3%; females literate 91.4%.

Education (2003)				student/
	schools	teachers	students	teacher ratio
Primary (age 5–11)[11]	207	4,828	58,837	12.2
Secondary (age 12–20)	33	2,913	37,743	13.0
Voc., teacher tr.	8	538	3,024	5.6
Higher	2	392	3,805	9.7

Health (2002): physicians 391 (1 per 870 persons); hospital beds 934 (1 per 364 persons); infant mortality rate per 1,000 live births (2004) 13.1.
Food (2002): daily per capita caloric intake 2,855 (vegetable products 82%, animal products 18%); 127% of FAO recommended minimum requirement.

Military

Total active duty personnel (2004): 7,000 (army 70.0%, navy 14.3%, air force 15.7%). British troops (a Gurkha batallion [2004]): 1,120; Singaporean troops (2002) 500. *Military expenditure as percentage of GDP* (2003): 5.1%; per capita expenditure U.S.$740.

[1]Legislative Council (suspended from 1984) reinstated September 2004 and enlarged August 2005; all seats are nonelected. [2]All official documents that must be published by law in Malay are also required to be issued in an official English version. [3]Muslim divorces only. [4]Less imputed bank service charges. [5]Unemployed. [6]Detail does not add to total given because of rounding. [7]Weights of consumer price index components. [8]Imports c.i.f.; exports f.o.b. [9]Privately owned. [10]Royal Brunei Airlines. [11]Includes preprimary.

Internet resources for further information:
• **The Government of Brunei Darussalam**
  http://www.brunei.gov.bn/index.htm
• **Brunei Economic Development Board**
  http://www.bedb.com.bn

Bulgaria

Official name: Republika Bŭlgaria (Republic of Bulgaria).
Form of government: unitary multiparty republic with one legislative body (National Assembly [240]).
Chief of state: President.
Head of government: Prime Minister.
Capital: Sofia.
Official language: Bulgarian.
Official religion: none[1].
Monetary unit: 1 lev (Lw; leva) = 100 stotinki; valuation (Sept. 1, 2005) 1 U.S.$ = 1.56 leva; 1 £ = 2.87 leva.

Area and population

Districts	area sq km	population 2005[2] estimate	Districts	area sq km	population 2005[2] estimate
Blagoevgrad	6,449	334,907	Ruse	2,803	259,173
Burgas	7,748	418,925	Shumen	3,390	199,577
Dobrich	4,720	206,893	Silistra	2,846	135,701
Gabrovo	2,023	137,461	Sliven	3,544	211,005
Khaskovo	5,533	268,335	Smolyan	3,193	133,015
Kurdzhali	3,209	159,878	Sofiya[3]	7,062	262,032
Kyustendil	3,052	154,468	Sofiya-Grad[4]	1,349	1,221,157
Lovech	4,129	161,190	Stara Zagora	5,151	362,090
Montana	3,636	170,217	Targovishte	2,559	136,806
Pazardzhik	4,457	300,092	Varna	3,819	458,392
Pernik	2,394	142,251	Veliko Turnovo	4,662	285,677
Pleven	4,335	310,449	Vidin	3,033	120,192
Plovdiv	5,973	709,861	Vratsa	3,938	212,656
Razgrad	2,640	140,743	Yambol	3,355	147,906
			TOTAL	111,002	7,761,049

Demography

Population (2005): 7,740,000.
Density (2005): persons per sq mi 180.6, persons per sq km 69.7.
Urban-rural (2005)[2]: urban 70.0%; rural 30.0%.
Sex distribution (2005)[2]: male 48.55%; female 51.45%.
Age breakdown (2005)[2]: under 15, 13.8%; 15–29, 21.2%; 30–44, 20.9%; 45–59, 21.3%; 60–74, 15.9%; 75 and over, 6.9%.
Population projection: (2010) 7,459,000; (2020) 6,871,000.
Ethnic composition (2001): Bulgarian 83.9%; Turkish 9.4%; Rom (Gypsy) 4.7%; other 2.0%.
Religious affiliation (2001): Christian 83.7%, of which Bulgarian Orthodox *c.* 72%, independent Christian *c.* 7%; Sunnī Muslim 12.2%; other/nonreligious 4.1%.
Major cities (2005)[2]: Sofia 1,138,950; Plovdiv 341,464; Varna 312,026; Burgas 189,529; Ruse 158,201.

Vital statistics

Birth rate per 1,000 population (2004): 9.0 (world avg. 21.1).
Death rate per 1,000 population (2004): 14.2 (world avg. 9.0).
Natural increase rate per 1,000 population (2004): −5.2 (world avg. 12.1).
Total fertility rate (avg. births per childbearing woman; 2004): 1.3.
Life expectancy at birth (2004): male 68.9 years; female 76.0 years.
Major causes of death per 100,000 population (2003): diseases of the circulatory system 967.3; malignant neoplasms (cancers) 201.8; ill-defined conditions 64.9; accidents, poisoning, and violence 51.6.

National economy

Budget (2003). Revenue: 13,222,000,000 leva (tax revenue 77.7%, of which value-added tax 23.5%, social insurance 21.2%, income and profit tax 16.8%; nontax revenue 20.0%; grants 2.3%). Expenditures: 13,221,000,000 leva (social insurance 35.0%; capital expenditure 10.3%; health 9.5%; administration and defense 8.4%; interest on debt 5.5%).
Public debt (external, outstanding; 2003): U.S.$7,749,000,000.
Gross national product (2004): U.S.$21,326,000,000 (U.S.$2,740 per capita).

Structure of gross domestic product and labour force

	2003 in value '000,000 leva	% of total value	labour force	% of labour force
Agriculture, forestry, and fishing	3,435	10.0	285,900	8.7
Manufacturing, mining	5,959	17.3	718,100	21.9
Construction	1,341	3.9	151,400	4.6
Transp. and commun.	4,231	12.3	214,800	6.6
Trade	2,142	6.2	551,900	16.8
Public utilities	1,720	5.0	60,000	1.8
Finance	1,105	3.2	146,400	4.5
Pub. admin., defense	10,155[5]	29.5[5]	230,200	7.0
Services			473,600	14.4
Other	4,321	12.6	450,800[6]	13.7[6]
TOTAL	34,410[7]	100.0	3,283,100	100.0

Production (metric tons except as noted). Agriculture, forestry, fishing (2004): wheat 3,300,000, corn (maize) 1,400,000, barley 1,000,000, sunflower seeds 700,000, potatoes 600,000, grapes 400,000; livestock (number of live animals) 2,074,699 sheep, 1,031,000 pigs, 800,000 goats, 668,311 cattle; roundwood (2002) 4,833,000 cu m; fish catch (2002) 15,007. Mining and quarrying (2001): copper (metal content) 115,000; iron (metal content) 92,000; gold 2,540 kg.

Manufacturing (value added in U.S.$'000,000; 2001): refined petroleum products, n.a.; nonelectrical machinery and apparatus 188; wearing apparel 168; food products 158; paints, soaps, and pharmaceuticals 122. Energy production (consumption): electricity (kW-hr; 2002) 42,679,000,000 (36,384,000,000); hard coal (metric tons; 2002) 129,000 (3,640,000); lignite (metric tons; 2003) 27,200,000 ([2002] 24,970,000); crude petroleum (barrels; 2004) 370,000 (31,000,000); petroleum products (metric tons; 2002) 4,392,000 (3,155,000); natural gas (cu m; 2002) 21,000,000 (3,184,000,000).
Household income and expenditure (2004). Average household size (2002) 2.7; income per household 6,356 leva (U.S.$4,035); sources of income: wages and salaries 37.5%, transfers 22.7%, self-employment in agriculture 15.1%; expenditure: food and nonalcoholic beverages 37.0%, housing and energy 13.0%, transportation 5.0%, communications 4.6%, health 4.2%.
Population economically active (2003): total 3,283,100; activity rate of total population 47.0% (participation rates: ages 15–64, 60.9%; female 46.8%; unemployed [2004] 12.0%).

Price index (2000 = 100)

	1998	1999	2000	2001	2002	2003	2004
Consumer price index	88.4	90.6	100.0	107.4	113.6	116.0	123.4

Tourism (2003): receipts U.S.$1,658,000,000; expenditures U.S.$750,000,000.
Land use as % of total land area (2000): in temporary crops 40.0%, in permanent crops 1.9%, in pasture 14.6%; overall forest area 33.4%.

Foreign trade[8]

Balance of trade (current prices)

	1999	2000	2001	2002	2003	2004
U.S.$'000,000	−1,081	−1,175	−1,576	−1,619	−2,474	−3,375
% of total	11.9%	10.9%	13.4%	12.7%	14.3%	14.5%

Imports (2004): €11,617,400,000 (machinery and apparatus 15.7%; crude petroleum and natural gas 12.8%; textiles 11.7%; transport equipment 10.5%; plastics and rubber 4.8%). *Major import sources:* Germany 14.6%; Russia 12.7%; Italy 9.8%; Turkey 6.0%; Greece 5.7%; France 5.3%.
Exports (2004): €7,993,900,000 (base and fabricated metals 19.5%, of which iron and steel 10.1%; clothing and footwear 19.4%; mineral fuels 10.1%, of which petroleum products 7.8%; machinery and transport equipment 9.7%). *Major export destinations:* Italy 13.1%; Germany 10.2%; Turkey 10.0%; Greece 9.9%; Belgium 6.0%; France 4.5%; U.S. 4.5%.

Transport and communications

Transport. Railroads (2002): track length 6,384 km; passenger-km (2003) 2,517,000,000; metric ton-km (2003) cargo 5,274,000,000. Roads (2002): length 37,077 km (paved 92%). Vehicles (2002): cars 2,254,222; trucks and buses 306,896. Air transport (2001): passenger-km 1,795,400,000; metric ton-km cargo 2,335,000; airports (2000) with scheduled flights 3.

Communications

Medium	date	unit	number	units per 1,000 persons
Daily newspapers	2000	circulation	2,060,000	257
Radio	2001	receivers	4,340,000	543
Television	2002	receivers	3,620,000	453
Telephones	2004	main lines	2,770,200	354
Cellular telephones	2004	subscribers	4,729,700	604
Personal computers	2004	units	461,000	59
Internet	2004	users	2,200,000	281

Education and health

Educational attainment (1992). Percentage of population age 25 and over having: no formal schooling 4.7%; incomplete primary education 12.5%; primary 31.9%; secondary 35.7%; higher 15.0%. *Literacy* (2003): total population age 15 and over literate 98.6%; males 99.1%; females 98.2%.

Education (2002–03)

	schools	teachers	students	student/ teacher ratio
Primary (age 6–14)	2,720	61,354	825,668	13.5
Secondary (age 15–17)				
Voc., teacher tr.	513	21,103	217,313	10.3
Higher	42	18,710	215,712	11.5

Health (2003): physicians 28,243 (1 per 277 persons); hospital beds 54,854 (1 per 143 persons); infant mortality rate per 1,000 live births (2004) 11.6.
Food (2002): daily per capita caloric intake 2,848 (vegetable products 76%, animal products 24%); 114% of FAO recommended minimum requirement.

Military

Total active duty personnel (2004): 51,000 (army 49.0%, navy 8.6%, air force 25.7%, other 16.7%). *Military expenditure as percentage of GDP* (2003): 2.6%[9]; per capita expenditure U.S.$66[9].

---

[1]Bulgaria has no official religion; the constitution, however, refers to Eastern Orthodoxy as the "traditional" religion. [2]January 1. [3]District nearly encircles Sofiya-Grad district on north, east, and south. [4]Sofiya-Grad includes Sofia city and immediately adjacent urban and rural areas. [5]Includes Trade and with Finance). [6]Includes 449,100 unemployed. [7]Detail does not add to total given because of rounding. [8]Imports f.o.b. in balance of trade and c.i.f. for commodities and trading partners. [9]Excludes expenditures for military pensions.

Internet resources for further information:
• National Statistical Institute http://www.nsi.bg
• Bulgarian National Bank http://www.bnb.bg

Burkina Faso

Atlantic Ocean

Gulf of Guinea

Official name: Burkina Faso (Burkina Faso).
Form of government: multiparty republic with one legislative body[1] (National Assembly [111]).
Chief of state: President.
Head of government: Prime Minister.
Capital: Ouagadougou.
Official language: French.
Official religion: none.
Monetary unit: 1 CFA franc (CFAF) = 100 centimes; valuation (Sept. 1, 2005) 1 U.S.$ = CFAF 522.78; 1 £ = CFAF 962.57[2].

Population (1996 census)

Provinces	population	Provinces	population	Provinces	population
Balé	169,543	Komondjari	49,389	Passoré	271,216
Bam	212,295	Kompienga	73,949	Poni	196,568
Banwa	214,234	Kossi	217,866	Sanguié	249,169
Bazèga	214,450	Koulpélogo	188,760	Sanmatenga	460,684
Bougouriba	76,444	Kouritenga	250,699	Séno	202,972
Boulgou	415,414	Kourwéogo	117,370	Sissili	153,560
Boulkiemdé	421,083	Léraba	93,351	Soum	253,867
Comoé	240,942	Loroum	111,707	Sourou	189,726
Ganzourgou	257,707	Mouhoun	237,048	Tapoa	235,288
Gnagna	307,386	Nahouri	121,314	Tuy	160,249
Gourma	221,956	Namentenga	251,909	Yagha	116,985
Houet	674,916	Nayala	136,273	Yatenga	443,967
Ioba	159,422	Noumbiel	51,449	Ziro	117,774
Kadiogo	976,513	Oubritenga	198,130	Zondoma	127,580
Kénédougou	198,936	Oudalan	136,583	Zoundwéogo	196,698
				TOTAL	10,373,341

Demography

Area: 103,456 sq mi, 267,950 sq km.
Population (2005): 13,492,000.
Density (2005): persons per sq mi 130.4, persons per sq km 50.4.
Urban-rural (2003): urban 17.8%; rural 82.2%.
Sex distribution (2004): male 49.75%; female 50.25%.
Age breakdown (2004): under 15, 47.0%; 15–29, 28.1%; 30–44, 14.4%; 45–59, 6.5%; 60–74, 3.3%; 75 and over, 0.7%.
Population projection: (2010) 15,667,000; (2020) 20,915,000.
Doubling time: 23 years.
Ethnic composition (1995): Mossi 47.9%; Fulani 10.3%; Lobi 6.9%; Bobo 6.9%; Mande 6.7%; Senufo 5.3%; Grosi 5.0%; Gurma 4.8%; Tuareg 3.1%.
Religious affiliation (2000): Muslim 48.6%; traditional beliefs 34.1%; Christian 16.7%, of which Roman Catholic 9.5%.
Major cities (1996): Ouagadougou 709,736; Bobo-Dioulasso 309,771; Koudougou 72,490; Ouahigouya 52,193; Banfora 49,724.

Vital statistics

Birth rate per 1,000 population (2004): 46.3 (world avg. 21.1).
Death rate per 1,000 population (2004): 16.2 (world avg. 9.0).
Natural increase rate per 1,000 population (2004): 29.8 (world avg. 12.1).
Total fertility rate (avg. births per childbearing woman; 2004): 6.6.
Life expectancy at birth (2004): male 46.6 years; female 49.5 years.
Adult population (ages 15–49) *living with HIV* (2004[3]): 4.2% (world avg. 1.1%).

National economy

Budget (2002). Revenue: CFAF 377,000,000,000 (tax revenue 63.9%, of which sales tax 34.5%, income taxes 16.4%, import duties 11.2%; grants 31.5%; non-tax revenue 4.6%). Expenditures: CFAF 489,100,000,000 (current expenditure 52.9%, of which wages and salaries 21.1%, transfers 14.3%, goods and services 12.8%, debt service 3.4%; investment expenditure 47.1%).
Public debt (external, outstanding; 2003): U.S.$1,652,000,000.
Household income and expenditure. Average household size (2000) 6.0; average annual income per household: n.a.; sources of income: n.a.; expenditure (1998)[4]: food 33.9%, transportation 15.6%, electricity and fuel 10.5%, clothing 6.4%, health 4.2%, education 3.4%.
Production (metric tons except as noted). Agriculture, forestry, fishing (2004): sorghum 1,600,000, millet 1,250,000, corn (maize) 738,500, seed cotton 575,000, sugarcane 420,000, dry cowpeas 330,000, peanuts (groundnuts) 321,000, rice 97,000, shea nuts 70,000, sesame 29,000; livestock (number of live animals) 8,800,000 goats, 7,000,000 sheep, 5,200,000 cattle, 24,000,000 chickens; roundwood (2003) 7,335,000 cu m; fish catch (2002) 8,500. Mining and quarrying (2003): gold 400 kg[5]. Manufacturing (2002): sugar 47,743; edible oils 19,626; flour 10,005; soap 9,923; beer 546,000 hectolitres; soft drinks 250,000 hectolitres; bicycles 20,849 units; mopeds 19,702 units; cigarettes 78,000,000 packets. Energy production (consumption): electricity (kW-hr; 2002) 400,000,000 (400,000,000); crude petroleum (barrels; 2002) none (none); petroleum products (metric tons; 2002) none (347,000); natural gas (cu m; 2002) none (none).
Tourism: receipts (2002) U.S.$39,000,000; expenditures (2001) U.S.$22,000,000.
Population economically active (1996): total 5,075,615; activity rate 49.2% (participation rates: over age 10, 70.0%; female 48.2%; unemployed 1.4%).

Price index (2000 = 100)

	1998	1999	2000	2001	2002	2003	2004
Consumer price index	101.4	100.3	100.0	105.0	107.3	109.5	109.0

Gross national product (2004): U.S.$4,436,000,000 (U.S.$360 per capita).

Structure of gross domestic product and labour force

	2002		1996	
	in value CFAF '000,000	% of total value	labour force	% of labour force
Agriculture	692,600	31.8	4,513,868	88.9
Mining	} 274,600	} 12.6	3,979	0.1
Manufacturing			71,565	1.4
Construction	96,600	4.4	21,076	0.4
Public utilities	31,700	1.4	2,813	0.1
Transp. and commun.	84,000	3.9	20,580	0.4
Trade	306,800	14.1	224,581	4.4
Finance	...	...	13,131	0.3
Pub. admin., defense	} 671,900	} 30.8	103,926	2.0
Services				
Other	21,000[6]	1.0[6]	100,096[7]	2.0[7]
TOTAL	2,179,200	100.0	5,075,615	100.0

Land use as % of total land area (2000): in temporary crops 13.9%, in permanent crops 0.2%, in pasture 21.9%; overall forest area 25.9%.

Foreign trade

Balance of trade (current prices)

	1997	1998	1999	2000	2001	2002
CFAF '000,000,000	−164.0	−183.8	−201.2	−222.4	−204.5	−217.5
% of total	38.0%	32.5%	39.2%	43.2%	37.7%	39.8%

Imports (2002): CFAF 381,700,000,000 (capital equipment 32.6%, petroleum products 18.6%, food products 12.7%, raw materials 10.1%). *Major import sources:* France 19.6%; Côte d'Ivoire 18.8%; Japan 9.3%; Germany 6.0%; U.S. 3.3%.
Exports (2002): CFAF 164,200,000,000 (raw cotton 54.1%, hides and skins 11.0%, live animals 8.8%, shea nuts 2.6%, gold 2.0%). *Major export destinations:* France 45.3%; Côte d'Ivoire 9.2%; Singapore 5.1%; Mali 4.0%; Japan 3.0%.

Transport and communications

Transport. Railroads: (2002) route length 386 mi, 622 km; (2002) passenger-km 129,403,000; (2001) metric ton-km cargo 597,447,000. Roads (1999): total length 6,505 mi, 10,469 km (paved 19%). Vehicles (2001): passenger cars 26,500; trucks and buses 22,600. Air transport (2001)[8]: passenger-km 154,000,000; metric ton-km cargo, n.a.; airports 2.

Communications

Medium	date	unit	number	units per 1,000 persons
Daily newspapers	2000	circulation	12,200	1.0
Radio	2000	receivers	428,000	35
Television	2000	receivers	147,000	12
Telephones	2004	main lines	81,400	6.1
Cellular telephones	2004	subscribers	398,000	30
Personal computers	2004	units	29,000	2.1
Internet	2004	users	53,200	3.9

Education and health

Educational attainment (1985). Percentage of population age 10 and over having: no formal schooling 86.1%; some primary 7.3%; general secondary 2.2%; specialized secondary and postsecondary 3.8%; other 0.6%. *Literacy (2003):* percentage of total population age 15 and over literate 26.6%; males literate 36.8%; females literate 16.6%.

Education (1995–96)

	schools	teachers	students[9]	student/teacher ratio
Primary (age 7–12)	3,568	14,037	816,393	50.0
Secondary (age 13–19)	252	4,162	} 173,200	33.0
Vocational	41	731		13.0
Higher	9	632	9,900	15.1

Health (2001): physicians 326 (1 per 35,653 persons); hospital beds 15,801 (1 per 735 persons); infant mortality rate per 1,000 live births (2004) 94.4.
Food (2002): daily per capita caloric intake 2,462 (vegetable products 95%, animal products 5%); 104% of FAO recommended minimum requirement.

Military

Total active duty personnel (2004): 10,800 (army 98.1%, air force 1.9%).
Military expenditure as percentage of GDP (2003): 1.3%; per capita expenditure U.S.$4.

[1]In addition, the 90-member Economic and Social Council is an advisory board. [2]Formerly pegged to the French franc and since Jan. 1, 2002, to the euro at the rate of €1 = CFAF 655.96. [3]January 1. [4]Weights of consumer price index components; Ouagadougou only. [5]Officially marketed gold only; does not include substantial illegal production. [6]Includes indirect taxes less imputed bank service charges and subsidies. [7]Includes 71,280 unemployed. [8]Air Afrique, an airline jointly owned by 11 African countries (including Burkina Faso), was declared bankrupt in February 2002. [9]1998–99.

Internet resources for further information:
• Embassy of Burkina Faso
  http://www.burkinaembassy-usa.org
• La Banque de France: La Zone Franc
  http://www.banque-france.fr/fr/eurosys/zonefr/zonefr.htm

Burundi

Official name: Republika y'u Burundi
(Rundi); République du Burundi
(French) (Republic of Burundi).
Form of government: republic[1] with
two legislative bodies (Senate [54[2]];
National Assembly [100[2]]).
Head of state and government:
President assisted by Vice Presidents.
Capital: Bujumbura.
Official languages: Rundi; French.
Official religion: none.
Monetary unit: 1 Burundi franc
(FBu) = 100 centimes; valuation
(Sept. 1, 2005) 1 U.S.$ = FBu 1,036;
1 £ = FBu 1,907.

Area and population		area		population
				1999
Provinces	Capitals	sq mi	sq km	estimate
Bubanza	Bubanza	420	1,089	289,060
Bujumbura	Bujumbura	476	1,232	755,994[3]
Bururi	Bururi	952	2,465	437,931
Cankuzo	Cankuzo	759	1,965	172,477
Cibitoke	Cibitoke	631	1,636	385,438
Gitega	Gitega	764	1,979	628,872
Karuzi	Karuzi	563	1,457	384,187
Kayanza	Kayanza	476	1,233	458,815
Kirundo	Kirundo	658	1,703	502,171
Makamba	Makamba	757	1,960	357,492
Muramvya	Muramvya	269	696	481,846[4]
Muyinga	Muyinga	709	1,836	485,347
Mwaro	Mwaro	324	840	4
Ngozi	Ngozi	569	1,474	601,382
Rutana	Rutana	756	1,959	244,939
Ruyigi	Ruyigi	903	2,339	304,567
Urban Province				
Bujumbura	—	34	87	3
TOTAL LAND AREA		10,020	25,950	
INLAND WATER		721	1,867	
TOTAL		10,740[5]	27,816[5]	6,490,518

Demography

Population (2005): 7,795,000.
Density (2005)[6]: persons per sq mi 777.9, persons per sq km 304.6.
Urban-rural (2003): urban 9.9%; rural 90.1%.
Sex distribution (2003): male 49.57%; female 50.43%.
Age breakdown (2003): under 15, 46.7%; 15–29, 28.8%; 30–44, 13.4%; 45–59,
7.1%; 60–74, 3.1%; 75 and over, 0.9%.
Population projection: (2010) 9,281,000; (2020) 12,266,000.
Doubling time: 24 years.
Ethnic composition (2000): Hutu 80.9%; Tutsi 15.6%; Lingala 1.6%; Twa
Pygmy 1.0%; other 0.9%.
Religious affiliation (2000): Roman Catholic 57.2%; Protestant 19.5%; unaf-
filiated Christian 14.7%; traditional beliefs 6.7%; Muslim 1.4%[7]; other 0.5%.
Major cities (2004): Bujumbura 340,300; Gitega 46,900; Muyinga 45,300; Ngozi
40,200; Ruyigi 36,800.

Vital statistics

Birth rate per 1,000 population (2004): 42.6 (world avg. 21.1).
Death rate per 1,000 population (2004): 14.1 (world avg. 9.0).
Natural increase rate per 1,000 population (2004): 28.5 (world avg. 12.1).
Total fertility rate (avg. births per childbearing woman; 2004): 6.7.
Life expectancy at birth (2004): male 49.2 years; female 50.4 years.
Adult population (ages 15–49) *living with HIV* (2004[8]): 6.0% (world avg. 1.1%).

National economy

Budget (2004). Revenue: FBu 218,892,500,000 (tax revenue 53.6%, of which
income tax 16.4%, sales tax 15.9%, taxes on international trade 10.3%; grants
32.8%; nontax revenue 13.6%). Expenditures: FBu 292,854,900,000 (current
expenditure 64.4%, of which debt service 11.7%; capital expenditure 30.6%;
other 5.0%).
Public debt (external, outstanding; 2003): U.S.$1,234,000,000.
Production (metric tons except as noted). Agriculture, forestry, fishing (2004):
bananas 1,600,000, sweet potatoes 834,394, cassava 709,574, dry beans
220,218, sugarcane 180,000, corn (maize) 123,199, sorghum 74,171, yams and
taros 71,615, rice 64,532, peas 33,500, potatoes 26,091, coffee 20,100, wheat
7,493, tea 6,600; livestock (number of live animals) 750,000 goats, 325,000 cattle, 230,000 sheep, 4,300,000 chickens; roundwood (2002) 8,428,000 cu m; fish
catch (2002) 9,000. Mining and quarrying (2001): gemstones 16,500 kg; gold
(2003) 2,855 kg. Manufacturing (2003): beer[9] 580,226 hectolitres; carbonated
beverages[9] 82,367 hectolitres; cottonseed oil 125,000 litres; sugar 20,268 tons;
cigarettes 354,395,000 units; blankets 123,217 units; fabrics 7,158,943 sq m.
Energy production (consumption): electricity (kW-hr; 2004) 92,000,000
(165,000,000); coal, none (none); crude petroleum, none (none); petroleum
products (metric tons; 2002) none (78,000); natural gas, none (none); peat
(metric tons; 2004) 4,580 ([2000] 12,000).
Household income and expenditure (2004)[10]. Average household size 5.6; average annual income per household: *c.* FBu 30,000 (*c.* U.S.$27); sources of
income: agriculture/livestock *c.* 91%, other *c.* 9%; expenditure: food *c.* 46%,
housing n.a., debt service *c.* 14%, alcoholic beverages and tobacco *c.* 8%,
transportation *c.* 6%, health *c.* 5%, clothing *c.* 4%.
Land use as % of total land area (2000): in temporary crops 35.0%, in permanent crops 14.0%, in pasture 36.4%; overall forest area 3.7%.

Gross national product (2004): U.S.$669,000,000 (U.S.$100 per capita).

Structure of gross domestic product and labour force				
	2002		1990	
	in value FBu '000,000	% of total value	labour force	% of labour force
Agriculture	213,200	36.5	2,574,443	93.1
Mining			1,419	—
Public utilities }	6,000	1.0	1,672	0.1
Manufacturing	67,500	11.5	33,867	1.2
Construction	24,300	4.2	19,737	0.7
Transp. and communications	29,000	5.0	8,504	0.3
Trade	27,600	4.7	25,822	0.9
Finance			2,005	0.1
Pub. admin., defense }	158,400	27.1 }	85,191	3.1
Services				
Other	58,600[11]	10.0[11]	13,270	0.5
TOTAL	584,600	100.0	2,765,945[5]	100.0

Population economically active (1997): total 3,475,000; activity rate of total
population 63.1% (participation rates [1991]: ages 15–64, 91.4%; female
48.9%; unemployed, n.a.).

Price index (2000 = 100)							
	1998	1999	2000	2001	2002	2003	2004
Consumer price index	77.8	80.4	100.0	109.2	102.9	119.3	128.7

Tourism (2003): receipts from visitors U.S.$700,000; expenditures by nationals
abroad U.S.$15,000,000.

Foreign trade

Balance of trade (current prices)						
	1999	2000	2001	2002	2003	2004
U.S.$'000,000	−42.3	−58.8	−69.1	−73.8	−92.5	−128.0
% of total	27.8%	37.5%	46.8%	54.3%	55.2%	57.2%

Imports (2004): U.S.$175,900,000 (mineral fuels 15.1%, food and food prod-
ucts 13.1%, transportation equipment 9.7%, pharmaceuticals 9.4%, fabricated metal products 8.7%). *Major import sources* (2003): Belgium-Luxembourg
14.8%; Kenya 14.4%; Tanzania 11.7%; Uganda 5.9%; Zambia 5.2%; France
4.8%.
Exports (2004): U.S.$47,900,000 (coffee 61.4%, tea 21.3%, refined sugar 6.2%,
beer 3.9%). *Major export destinations* (2003): Switzerland 32.0%; United
Kingdom 16.4%; Rwanda 5.7%; Belgium-Luxembourg 5.7%; The Netherlands 4.5%.

Transport and communications

Transport. Railroads: none. Roads (2001): total length 8,997 mi, 14,480 km
(paved 7%). Vehicles (1999): passenger cars 6,900; trucks and other vehicles 9,300. Air transport (2004)[12]: passenger arrivals and departures 117,386;
cargo loaded and unloaded 3,237 metric tons; airports 1.

Communications				
				units per 1,000
Medium	date	unit	number	persons
Daily newspapers	1996	circulation	20,000	3.2
Radio	2000	receivers	1,260,000	220
Television	2002	receivers	220,000	31
Telephones	2003	main lines	23,900	3.4
Cellular telephones	2003	subscribers	64,000	9.0
Personal computers	2004	units	34,000	4.8
Internet	2004	users	25,000	5.3

Education and health

Educational attainment: n.a. *Literacy* (2003): percentage of total population age
15 and over literate 51.6%; males literate 58.5%; females literate 45.2%.

Education (1998)				
	schools	teachers	students	student/ teacher ratio
Primary (age 6–11)	1,512	12,107	557,344	46.0
Secondary (age 12–18) }	400	3,548	56,872	16.0
Vocational and teacher training				
Higher	...	379	5,037	13.3

Health (2004): physicians 323 (1 per 23,270 persons); hospital beds (1999) 3,380
(1 per 1,657 persons); infant mortality rate per 1,000 live births 65.6.
Food (2002): daily per capita caloric intake 1,649 (vegetable products 98%,
animal products 2%); 71% of FAO recommended minimum requirement.

Military

Total active duty personnel (2004): 50,500 (army 100%); UN peacekeeping
troops (June 2005) 5,600. *Military expenditure as percentage of GDP* (2003):
5.9%; per capita expenditure U.S.$5.

---

[1]New constitution approved by referendum on Feb. 28, 2005; transitional regime ended
August 2005. [2]Statutory membership. [3]Bujumbura (province) includes Bujumbura urban
province. [4]Muramvya includes Mwaro. [5]Detail does not add to total given because
of rounding. [6]Based on land area. [7]Unofficial 2005 estimate of Muslim population is
c. 9%. [8]Beginning of year. [9]First eight months only. [10]Based on a survey of 4,300 households. [11]Indirect taxes less subsidies. [12]Figures for Bujumbura airport only.

Internet resources for further information:
• **Banque Centrale du Burundi**
  http://brb.bi

Cambodia

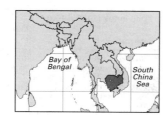

Official name: Preah Reach Ana Pak Kampuchea (Kingdom of Cambodia).
Form of government: constitutional monarchy with two legislative houses (Senate [61]; National Assembly [123]).
Chief of state: King.
Head of government: Prime Minister.
Capital: Phnom Penh.
Official language: Khmer.
Official religion: Buddhism.
Monetary unit: 1 riel = 100 sen; valuation (Sept. 1, 2005) 1 U.S.$ = 4,160 riels; 1 £ = 7,660 riels.

Area and population

Provinces	Capitals	area sq mi	area sq km	population 2004 estimate[1]
Banteay Mean Chey	Sisophon	2,579	6,679	752,392
Bat Dambang	Bat Dambang	4,518	11,702	979,823
Kampong Cham	Kampong Cham	3,783	9,799	1,830,722
Kampong Chhnang	Kampong Chhnang	2,132	5,521	501,455
Kampong Spueu	Kampong Spueu	2,709	7,017	713,967
Kampong Thum	Kampong Thum	5,334	13,814	668,895
Kampot	Kampot	1,881	4,873	595,036
Kandal	Ta Khmau	1,378	3,568	1,224,433
Kaoh Kong	Krong Kaoh Kong	4,309	11,160	183,648
Kracheh	Kracheh	4,283	11,094	325,097
Mondol Kiri	Senmonorom	5,517	14,288	41,201
Otdar Mean Cheay	Phumi Samraong	2,378	6,158	95,410
Pousat	Pousat	4,900	12,692	421,528
Preah Vihear	Phum Tbeng Mean Cheay	5,324	13,788	148,407
Prey Veaeng	Prey Veaeng	1,885	4,883	1,035,672
Rotanak Kiri	Lumphat	4,163	10,782	117,664
Siem Reab	Siem Reab	3,976	10,299	841,268
Stueng Traeng	Stueng Traeng	4,283	11,092	101,136
Svay Rieng	Svay Rieng	1,145	2,966	532,478
Takaev	Takaev	1,376	3,563	889,777
Municipalities				
Kaeb	—	130	336	36,592
Pailin	—	310	803	31,442
Phnom Penh	—	112	290	1,272,386
Preah Sihanouk	—	335	868	201,981
TOTAL LAND AREA		68,740	178,035	
INLAND WATER		1,158	3,000	
TOTAL		69,898	181,035	13,542,410[1]

Demography

Population (2005): 13,327,000.
Density (2005)[2]: persons per sq mi 193.9, persons per sq km 74.9.
Urban-rural (2003): urban 18.6%; rural 81.4%.
Sex distribution (2004): male 48.70%; female 51.30%.
Age breakdown (2004): under 15, 37.6%; 15–29, 29.5%; 30–44, 18.7%; 45–59, 9.1%; 60–74, 4.1%; 75 and over, 1.0%.
Population projection: (2010) 14,574,000; (2020) 17,442,000.
Ethnic composition (2000): Khmer 85.2%; Chinese 6.4%; Vietnamese 3.0%; Cham 2.5%; Lao 0.6%; other 2.3%.
Religious affiliation (2000): Buddhist 84.7%; Chinese folk religionist 4.7%; traditional beliefs 4.3%; Muslim 2.3%; Christian 1.1%; other 2.9%.
Major urban areas (1998): Phnom Penh (2003) 1,157,000; Bat Dambang 124,290; Sisophon 85,382; Siem Reab 83,715; Preah Sihanouk 66,723.

Vital statistics

Birth rate per 1,000 population (2004): 27.0 (world avg. 21.1).
Death rate per 1,000 population (2004): 9.2 (world avg. 9.0).
Natural increase rate per 1,000 population (2004): 17.8 (world avg. 12.1).
Total fertility rate (avg. births per childbearing woman; 2004): 3.5.
Life expectancy at birth (2004): male 56.6 years; female 60.6 years.
Major causes of death per 100,000 population: n.a.; however, major health problems include tuberculosis, malaria, and pneumonia. Violence and military ordnance (especially unexploded mines) remain hazards.

National economy

Budget (2003). Revenue: 1,694,300,000,000 riels (indirect taxes 37.4%, of which VAT 22.7%; taxes on international trade 23.3%; direct taxes 8.8%; nontax revenue 30.5%). Expenditures: 3,086,700,000 riels[3] (current expenditure 59.7%, of which civil administration 35.8%, defense and security 13.3%; development expenditure 40.3%, of which externally financed 29.5%).
Public debt (external, outstanding; 2003): U.S.$2,814,000,000.
Land use as % of total land area (2000): in temporary crops 21.0%, in permanent crops 0.6%, in pasture 8.5%, overall forest area 52.9%.
Production (metric tons except as noted). Agriculture, forestry, fishing (2004): rice 4,710,000, sugarcane 220,000, corn (maize) 200,000, bananas 148,000, cassava 140,000, coconuts 71,000, oranges 63,000, rubber 46,000, soybeans 39,000, tobacco leaves 7,361; livestock (number of live animals) 3,000,000 cattle, 2,180,000 pigs, 625,000 buffalo; roundwood (2003) 9,683,046 cu m; fish catch (2002) 406,182. Mining and quarrying: legal mining is confined to fertilizers, salt, and construction materials. Manufacturing (value added in U.S.$'000,000; 2000): wearing apparel 626; textiles 479; leather products 105; food products 81; rubber products 66. Energy production (consumption): electricity (kW-hr; 2002) 129,000,000 (129,000,000); petroleum products (metric tons; 2002) negligible (178,000); crude petroleum (barrels; 2002) none (none); natural gas (cu m; 2002) none (none).

Household income and expenditure. Average household size (2004) 5.1; household expenditure (2002): food, beverages, and tobacco 62.6%, housing and energy 19.7%, health 6.0%, transportation and communications 3.4%.
Gross national product (2004): U.S.$4,430,000,000 (U.S.$320 per capita).

Structure of gross domestic product and labour force

	2002 in value '000,000,000 riels	% of total value	labour force	% of labour force
Agriculture	5,231.8	33.4	4,479,773	70.0
Mining	46.6	0.3	10,751	0.2
Manufacturing	2,969.5	19.0	556,388	8.7
Construction	1,023.1	6.5	100,123	1.6
Public utilities	75.8	0.5	4,704	0.1
Transp. and commun.	960.0	6.0	174,711	2.7
Trade	2,140.2	13.7	661,406	10.3
Finance	964.8	6.2	16,224	0.3
Public admin., defense	390.5	2.5	143,513	2.2
Services	902.9	5.8	252,084	3.9
Other	962.0[4]	6.1[4]	—	—
TOTAL	15,667.2	100.0	6,399,677	100.0

Population economically active (1998): total 5,118,945; activity rate of total population 44.8% (participation rates: ages 15–64, 79.0%; female 51.6%; unemployed[5] [November 2001] 1.8%).

Price index (2000 = 100)

	1998	1999	2000	2001	2002	2003	2004
Consumer price index	96.9	100.8	100.0	102.4	102.6	103.8	107.8

Tourism (2003): receipts U.S.$389,000,000; expenditures U.S.$36,000,000.

Foreign trade

Balance of trade (current prices)

	1998	1999	2000	2001	2002	2003
U.S.$'000,000	−365	−462	−538	−523	−564	−537
% of total	18.6%	17.0%	16.1%	14.3%	13.9%	11.5%

Imports (2003): U.S.$2,613,000,000 (retained imports 96.6%; imports for reexport 3.4%). Major import sources: Thailand 27.0%; Hong Kong 14.7%; Singapore 12.1%; China 11.6%; Korea 5.2%.
Exports (2003): U.S.$2,076,000,000 (domestic exports 94.4%, of which garments c. 80%, rubber 4.7%[6], rice 4.3%[6], fish 1.8%[6], sawn timber and logs 1.2%[6]; reexports 5.6%). Major export destinations: U.S. 59.8%; Germany 10.4%; U.K. 7.4%.

Transport and communications

Transport. Railroads (1999): length 403 mi, 649 km; passenger-km 49,894,000; metric ton-km 76,171,000. Roads (2000): total length 7,657 mi, 12,323 km (paved 16%). Vehicles (2002): passenger cars 209,128; trucks and buses 33,164. Air transport (2002)[7]: passenger-km 60,900,000; metric ton-km cargo 4,100,000; airports (1997) with scheduled flights 8.

Communications

Medium	date	unit	number	units per 1,000 persons
Daily newspapers	2000	circulation	24,000	2.0
Radio	2000	receivers	1,480,000	119
Television	2002	receivers	100,000	8.0
Telephones	2003	main lines	36,400	2.6
Cellular telephones	2003	subscribers	498,400	35
Personal computers	2004	units	38,000	2.6
Internet	2004	users	41,000	2.8

Education and health

Educational attainment (2004). Percentage of literate population age 25 and over having: no formal schooling 4.3%; some primary education 54.1%; primary 23.7%; some secondary 11.3%; secondary, vocational, and above 6.4%.
Literacy (2000): percentage of total population age 15 and over literate 68.5%; males literate 79.8%; females literate 57.1%.

Education (2002–03)

	schools	teachers	students	student/ teacher ratio
Primary (age 6–10)	5,915	48,433	2,747,411	56.7
Secondary (age 11–16)	594	22,830	543,885	23.8
Voc., teacher tr.[8]	...	2,315	9,983	4.3
Higher[8]	...	1,001	8,901	8.9

Health (2002): physicians 2,083 (1 per 6,610 persons); hospital beds 9,800 (1 per 1,405 persons); infant mortality rate per 1,000 live births (2004) 73.0.
Food (2002): daily per capita caloric intake 2,046 (vegetable products 91%, animal products 9%); 92% of FAO recommended minimum requirement.

Military

Total active duty personnel (2004)[9]: 124,300 (army 60.3%, navy 2.3%, air force 1.2%, provincial forces 36.2%). Military expenditure as percentage of GDP (2003): 2.5%[10]; per capita expenditure U.S.$8[10].

[1]Projection based on 1998 census; 2004 population estimate based on 2004 intercensal survey is 13,091,000. [2]Based on land area. [3]Summed total; officially reported total equals 2,913,700,000 riels. [4]Indirect taxes less imputed bank service charge. [5]For population age 10 and over. [6]Includes estimates for illegal exports. [7]Combined total of Imtrec Aviation, Phnom Penh Airways, President Airlines, and Siem Reap Airways. [8]1997–98. [9]Figures exclude paramilitary forces. [10]Includes expenditures for police.

Internet resources for further information:
• National Institute of Statistics http://www.nis.gov.kh

Cameroon

Official name: République du Cameroun (French); Republic of Cameroon (English).
Form of government: unitary multiparty republic with one legislative house (National Assembly [180]).
Chief of state: President.
Head of government: Prime Minister.
Capital: Yaoundé.
Official languages: French; English.
Official religion: none.
Monetary unit: 1 CFA franc (CFAF) = 100 centimes; valuation (Sept. 1, 2005) 1 U.S.$ = CFAF 522.78; 1 £ = CFAF 962.57[1].

Area and population		area		population
				2001
Regions	Capitals	sq mi	sq km	estimate
Adamoua	Ngaoundéré	24,591	63,691	723,600
Centre	Yaoundé	26,613	68,926	2,501,200
Est	Bertoua	42,089	109,011	755,100
Extrême-Nord	Maroua	13,223	34,246	2,721,500
Littoral	Douala	7,814	20,239	2,202,300
Nord	Garoua	25,319	65,576	1,227,000
Nord-Ouest	Bamenda	6,877	17,810	1,840,500
Ouest	Bafoussam	5,356	13,872	1,982,100
Sud	Ebolowa	18,189	47,110	534,900
Sud-Ouest	Buea	9,448	24,471	1,242,700
LAND AREA		179,519	464,952	
INLAND WATER		4,051	10,492	
TOTAL		183,569[2]	475,442[2]	15,731,000[2]

Demography

Population (2005): 16,988,000.
Density (2005)[3]: persons per sq mi 94.6, persons per sq km 36.5.
Urban-rural (2003): urban 51.4%; rural 48.6%.
Sex distribution (2004): male 50.19%; female 49.81%.
Age breakdown (2004): under 15, 41.9%; 15–29, 28.7%; 30–44, 15.6%; 45–59, 8.8%; 60–74, 4.1%; 75 and over, 0.9%.
Population projection: (2010) 18,780,000; (2020) 22,463,000.
Doubling time: 33 years.
Ethnic composition (1983): Fang 19.6%; Bamileke and Bamum 18.5%; Duala, Luanda, and Basa 14.7%; Fulani 9.6%; Tikar 7.4%; Mandara 5.7%; Maka 4.9%; Chamba 2.4%; Mbum 1.3%; Hausa 1.2%; French 0.2%; other 14.5%.
Religious affiliation (2000): Roman Catholic 26.4%; traditional beliefs 23.7%; Muslim 21.2%; Protestant 20.7%.
Major cities (2002): Douala 1,239,100; Yaoundé 1,122,500; Garoua 185,800; Maroua 169,200; Bafoussam 151,800.

Vital statistics

Birth rate per 1,000 population (2004): 34.7 (world avg. 21.1).
Death rate per 1,000 population (2004): 13.8 (world avg. 9.0).
Natural increase rate per 1,000 population (2004): 21.0 (world avg. 12.1).
Total fertility rate (avg. births per childbearing woman; 2004): 4.6.
Life expectancy at birth (2004): male 50.5 years; female 50.9 years.
Adult population (ages 15–49) *living with HIV* (2004[4]): 6.9% (world avg. 1.1%).

National economy

Budget (2004). Revenue: CFAF 1,241,000,000,000 (taxes on goods and services 28.8%; oil revenue 26.2%; direct taxes 18.8%; customs duties 14.2%; nontax revenue 7.5%). Expenditures: CFAF 1,318,000,000,000 (current expenditure 88.6%, of which wages and salaries 34.0%, goods and services 31.6%, transfers 10.6%, interest on public debt 10.5%; capital expenditure 11.4%).
Gross national product (2004): U.S.$13,138,000,000 (U.S.$800 per capita).

Structure of gross domestic product and labour force				
	2003		1985	
	in value CFAF '000,000,000[5]	% of total value	labour force	% of labour force
Agriculture, fishing, forestry	1,087	19.6	2,900,871	74.0
Mining	201	3.6	1,793	0.1
Manufacturing	1,033	18.6	174,498	4.5
Construction	...	...	66,684	1.7
Public utilities	66	1.2	3,522	0.1
Transp. and commun.			51,688	1.3
Trade			154,014	3.9
Finance	2,836	51.2	8,009	0.2
Services			292,922	7.5
Public admin., defense				
Other	320[6]	5.8[6]	263,634	6.7
TOTAL	5,543	100.0	3,917,635	100.0

Household income and expenditure. Average household size (2000) 5.5; average annual income per household: n.a.; sources of income: n.a.; expenditure (1993)[7]: food 49.1%, housing 18.0%, transportation and communications 13.0%, health 8.6%, clothing 7.6%, recreation 2.4%.
Tourism (2000): receipts U.S.$39,000,000; expenditures (1995) U.S.$105,-000,000.
Population economically active (1991): total 4,740,000; activity rate of total population 40.0% (participation rates [1985]: ages 15–69, 66.3%; female 38.5%; unemployed[8] 5.8%).

Price index (2000 = 100)							
	1997	1998	1999	2000	2001	2002	2003
Consumer price index	86.5	97.2	98.9	100.0	104.5	107.4	108.1

Public debt (external, outstanding; 2003): U.S.$7,882,000,000.
Production (metric tons except as noted). Agriculture, forestry, fishing (2004): cassava 1,950,000, sugarcane 1,450,000, plantains 1,200,000, oil palm fruit 1,200,000, corn (maize) 750,000, bananas 630,000, sorghum 550,000, tomatoes 370,000, yams 265,000, seed cotton 200,000, peanuts (groundnuts) 200,000, sweet potatoes 175,000, cacao 140,000, coffee 69,000, avocados 53,000, natural rubber 45,892; livestock (number of live animals) 5,900,000 cattle, 4,400,000 goats, 3,800,000 sheep; roundwood (2003) 10,880,353 cu m; fish catch (2002) 120,135. Mining and quarrying (2003): cement 930,000; pozzolana 600,000; aluminum 77,000; gold 1,000 kg. Manufacturing (value added in U.S.$'000; 1999): beverages 182; food products 149; textiles 112; wood products excluding furniture 68; nonferrous base metals 41; rubber products 38. Energy production (consumption): electricity (kW-hr; 2002) 3,249,000,000 (3,249,000,000); coal (metric tons; 2002) negligible (negligible); crude petroleum (barrels; 2004) 33,000,000 ([2002] 8,900,000); petroleum products (metric tons; 2002) 1,146,000 (917,000); natural gas, none (none).
Land use as % of total land area (2000): in temporary crops 12.8%, in permanent crops 2.6%, in pasture 4.3%; overall forest area 51.3%.

Foreign trade

Balance of trade (current prices)						
	1999–2000[9]	2000–01[9]	2001–02[9]	2002	2003	2004
CFAF '000,000,000	+386.7	+380.6	−8.8	+54.6	+137.1	+130.8
% of total	16.0%	13.7%	0.3%	2.0%	5.3%	4.8%

Imports (2004): CFAF 1,294,600,000,000 (semifinished goods 15.3%, minerals and other raw materials 14.5%, industrial equipment 14.0%, food, beverages, and tobacco 12.7%, transport equipment 9.7%). *Major import sources* (2003): France 30.5%; Nigeria 13.5%; Belgium 5.9%; Italy 3.9%; U.S. 3.9%.
Exports (2004): CFAF 1,425,400,000,000 (crude petroleum 49.9%, aluminum 7.3%, cocoa beans 7.0%, cotton 6.6%, lumber 6.5%, coffee 2.9%). *Major export destinations* (2003): Spain 20.3%; Italy 15.0%; The Netherlands 11.9%; France 10.6%; U.S. 8.4%.

Transport and communications

Transport. Railroads (2001): route length 631 mi, 1,016 km; passenger-km 237,800,000; metric ton-km cargo 854,600,000. Roads (1999): total length 30,630 mi, 49,300 km (paved 8%). Vehicles (2000): passenger cars 115,900; trucks and buses 47,400. Air transport (2001): passenger-km 796,567,000; metric ton-km cargo 23,255,000; airports (1998) with scheduled flights 5.

Communications				units per 1,000
Medium	date	unit	number	persons
Daily newspapers	2004	circulation	35,000[10]	2.2
Radio	2000	receivers	2,410,000	163
Television	2000	receivers	503,000	34
Telephones	2003	main lines	95,200	5.9
Cellular telephones	2004	subscribers	1,536,600	94
Personal computers	2004	units	160,000	9.8
Internet	2004	users	167,000	10

Education and health

Educational attainment: n.a. *Literacy* (2003): percentage of total population age 15 and over literate 74.6%; males literate 81.5%; females literate 67.9%.

Education (1998)				student/
	schools	teachers	students	teacher ratio
Primary (age 6–14)	9,459	41,142	2,133,707	51.9
Secondary (age 15–24)	700[11]	19,515	341,439	17.5
Vocational	324[11]	7,245[11]	122,122	...
Higher[12]	7	2,223	58,251	26.2

Health: physicians (1996) 1,031 (1 per 13,510 persons); hospital beds (1988) 29,285 (1 per 371 persons); infant mortality rate per 1,000 live births (2004) 66.2.
Food (2002): daily per capita caloric intake 2,273 (vegetable products 94%, animal products 6%); 98% of FAO recommended minimum requirement.

Military

Total active duty personnel (2004): 14,100 (army 88.7%, navy 9.2%, air force 2.1%). *Military expenditure as percentage of GDP* (2003): 1.5%; per capita expenditure U.S.$12.

---

[1]Formerly pegged to the French franc and since Jan. 1, 2002, to the euro at the rate of 1 € = CFAF 655.96. [2]Detail does not add to total given because of rounding. [3]Based on land area. [4]Beginning of year. [5]At constant prices of 1999–2000. [6]Indirect taxes less subsidies. [7]Weights of consumer price index components. [8]Ages six and over. [9]Based on fiscal year July 1–June 30. [10]Le Nouvelle Expression only. [11]1995–96. [12]Universities only; 2003–04.

Internet resources for further information:
• **La Banque de France: La Zone Franc**
　http://www.banque-france.fr/fr/eurosys/zonefr/zonefr.htm
• **Republic of Cameroon; Prime Minister's Office**
　http://www.spm.gov.cm

Canada

Official name: Canada.
Form of government: federal multiparty parliamentary state with two legislative houses (Senate [105]; House of Commons [308]).
Chief of state: Queen of Canada (British Monarch).
Representative of chief of state: Governor-General.
Head of government: Prime Minister.
Capital: Ottawa.
Official languages: English; French.
Official religion: none.
Monetary unit: 1 Canadian dollar (Can$) = 100 cents; valuation (Sept. 1, 2005) 1 U.S.$ = Can$1.19; 1 £ = Can$2.19.

Area and population

Provinces	Capitals	area sq mi	area sq km	population 2004 estimate
Alberta	Edmonton	255,541	661,848	3,201,900
British Columbia	Victoria	364,764	944,735	4,196,400
Manitoba	Winnipeg	250,116	647,797	1,170,300
New Brunswick	Fredericton	28,150	72,908	751,400
Newfoundland and Labrador	St. John's	156,453	405,212	517,000
Nova Scotia	Halifax	21,345	55,284	937,000
Ontario	Toronto	415,599	1,076,395	12,392,700
Prince Edward Island	Charlottetown	2,185	5,660	137,900
Quebec	Quebec	595,391	1,542,056	7,542,800
Saskatchewan	Regina	251,367	651,036	995,400
Territories				
Northwest Territories	Yellowknife	519,735	1,346,106	42,800
Nunavut	Iqaluit	808,185	2,093,190	29,600
Yukon Territory	Whitehorse	186,272	482,443	31,200
TOTAL		3,855,103	9,984,670	31,946,400

Demography

Population (2005): 32,227,000.
Density (2005)[1]: persons per sq mi 9.1, persons per sq km 3.5.
Urban-rural (2003): urban 80.4%; rural 19.6%.
Sex distribution (2004): male 49.51%; female 50.49%.
Age breakdown (2004): under 15, 17.9%; 15–29, 20.4%; 30–44, 23.1%; 45–59, 21.1%; 60–74, 11.5%; 75 and over, 6.0%.
Population projection: (2010) 33,668,000; (2020) 36,428,000.
Ethnic origin (2000): Anglo-Canadian 45.5%; French-Canadian 23.5%; Chinese 3.4%; British expatriates 3.3%; Indo-Pakistani 2.6%, of which Punjabi 2.3%; German 2.4%; Italian 2.2%; U.S. white 1.8%; Métis (part-Indian) 1.8%; Indian 1.5%, of which detribalized 0.5%; Jewish 1.4%; Arab 1.3%; Ukrainian 1.2%; Eskimo (Inuit) 0.1%; other 8.0%.
Religious affiliation (2001): Christian 77.1%, of which Roman Catholic 43.2%, Protestant 28.3%, unspecified Christian 2.6%, Orthodox 1.7%, other Christian 1.3%; Muslim 2.0%; Jewish 1.1%; Hindu 1.0%; Buddhist 1.0%; Sikh 0.9%; nonreligious 16.5%; other 0.4%.
Major metropolitan areas (2004): Toronto 5,202,300; Montreal 3,607,200; Vancouver 2,173,100; Ottawa-Hull 1,145,500; Calgary 1,037,100; Edmonton 1,001,600; Quebec 710,800; Hamilton 710,100; Winnipeg 702,400; London 459,600.

Other metropolitan areas (2004)

	population		population		population
Abbotsford	157,600	Regina	198,600	Sherbrooke	162,300
Halifax	379,800	St. Catharines–		Sudbury	161,100
Kingston	156,500	Niagara	394,900	Victoria	330,200
Kitchener	450,000	St. John's	179,900	Windsor	330,900
Oshawa	329,000	Saskatoon	234,000		

Place of birth (2001): 81.6% native-born; 18.4% foreign-born, of which U.K. 2.0%, other European 5.7%, Asian countries 5.8%, U.S. 0.8%, other 4.1%.
Mobility (2001). Population living in the same residence as in 1996: 58.1%; different residence, same municipality 22.4%; same province, different municipality 3.3%; different province 12.7%; different country 3.5%.
Households. Total number of households (2003) 12,214,000. Average household size (2003) 2.7; 1 person (1997) 25.2%, 2 persons 33.0%, 3 persons 16.7%, 4 persons 16.3%, 5 or more persons 8.8%. Family households (2001): 8,371,020 (72.4%), nonfamily 3,191,955 (27.6%, of which 1 person 75.6%).
Immigration (2002): permanent immigrants admitted 228,830; from Asia 61.7%, of which India 12.6%, Philippines 4.8%; Europe 17.0%, of which U.K. 2.2%, France 1.7%; U.S. 2.3%; refugee arrivals (2003) 28,413; overall refugee population (end of 2003) 133,094.

Vital statistics

Birth rate per 1,000 population (2003–04): 10.4 (world avg. 21.1); (1997) legitimate 72.3%; illegitimate 27.7%.
Death rate per 1,000 population (2003–04): 7.3 (world avg. 9.0).
Natural increase rate per 1,000 population (2003–04): 3.1 (world avg. 12.1).
Total fertility rate (avg. births per childbearing woman; 2004): 1.6.
Marriage rate per 1,000 population (2004): 4.6.
Divorce rate per 1,000 population (2003): 2.2.
Life expectancy at birth (2004): male 76.6 years; female 83.5 years.

Major causes of death per 100,000 population (2002): diseases of the circulatory system 240.6; malignant neoplasms (cancers) 207.5; diseases of the respiratory system 56.6; accidents and violence 44.1 (including suicide 11.6).

Social indicators

Educational attainment (2003). Percentage of population age 15 and over having: incomplete primary and complete primary education 9.1%; incomplete secondary 16.0%; complete secondary 19.2%; some university/higher vocational 38.6%; bachelor's degree or higher 17.1%.

Distribution of income (1999)

percentage of household income by quintile

1	2	3	4	5 (highest)
7.4%	11.6%	15.3%	24.2%	41.5%

Quality of working life. Average workweek (2004): 33.3 hours. Annual rate per 100,000 workers for (1997): injury, accident, or industrial illness 1,330; death 2.7. Average days lost to labour stoppages per 1,000 employee-workdays (2001): 0.7. Average commuting distance (2001): 4.5 mi, 7.2 km; mode of transportation: automobile 80.7%, public transportation 10.5%, walking 6.6%, other 2.2%. Labour force covered by a pension plan (2001): 33.6%.
Access to services. Proportion of households having access to: electricity (2002) 100.0%; public water supply (1996) 99.8%; public sewage collection (1996) 99.3%.
Social participation. Eligible voters participating in last national election (June 2004): 60.5%. Population over 18 years of age participating in voluntary work (2000): 26.7%. Union membership as percentage of civilian labour force (2003) 25.0%. Attendance at religious services on a weekly basis (2001): 20.0%.
Social deviance (2003). Offense rate per 100,000 population for: violent crime 962.8, of which assault 746.5, sexual assault 74.1, homicide 1.7; property crime 4,121, of which auto theft 541, burglary 900.
Leisure (1998). Favourite leisure activities (hours weekly): television (2002) 21.6; social time 13.3; reading 2.8; sports and entertainment 1.4.
Material well-being (2001). Households possessing: automobile 64.0%; telephone 97.4%; cellular phone 47.6%; colour television 99.2%; central air conditioner 35.9%; cable television 68.3%; home computers 59.9%; Internet access 49.9%.

National economy

Gross national product (2004): U.S.$905,000,000,000 (U.S.$28,390 per capita).

Structure of gross domestic product and labour force

	2004 in value Can$'000,000[2]	% of total value	labour force	% of labour force
Agriculture, fishing, forestry	23,201	2.2	334,300[3]	1.9[3]
Mining	38,699	3.7	297,800[4]	1.7[4]
Manufacturing	181,120	17.3	2,282,400	13.2
Construction	58,572	5.6	983,700	5.7
Public utilities	25,875	2.4	131,400	0.8
Transportation	50,191	4.8	800,500	4.6
Trade, hotels	149,382	14.2	3,513,500	20.3
Finance, real estate[5]	256,550	24.5	2,634,500	15.3
Pub. admin., defense	57,424	5.5	820,600	4.8
Services	207,252	19.8	4,221,800	24.5
Other	—	—	1,248,700[6]	7.2[6]
TOTAL	1,048,266[7]	100.0	17,269,200	100.0

Budget (2003–04)[8]. Revenue: Can$204,075,000,000 (income tax 60.8%, sales tax 21.6%, contributions to social security 10.8%, other 6.8%). Expenditures: Can$197,296,000,000 (social services and welfare 37.9%, defense and social protection 13.0%, public debt interest 12.1%, economy 3.9%, health 3.1%, education 2.4%).
Public debt (2004): U.S.$483,344,000,000.
Tourism (2003): receipts U.S.$10,579,000,000; expenditures U.S.$13,252,000,000.

Manufacturing, mining, and construction enterprises (2000)

	no. of employees	weekly wages as a % of avg. of all wages[9]	annual value added (Can$'000,000)[10]
Manufacturing			
Transport equipment	255,500	148.4	27,656
Food and beverages	239,500	100.2	21,577[11]
Chemicals and related products	95,700	147.5	14,884
Electrical and electronic products	139,700	140.1	13,264
Metal fabricating	191,500	123.2	11,418
Primary metals	87,300	153.9	11,171
Wood products (excl. furniture)	150,700	111.9	11,163
Paper and related products	105,400	154.4	11,132
Nonelectrical machinery	95,700	145.9	9,756
Rubber and plastic products	98,700	111.3	9,271
Furniture and fixtures	67,300	99.7	4,928
Nonmetallic mineral products	54,300	121.5	4,362
Printing, publishing, and related products	157,100	109.6	4,184
Wearing apparel	93,200	72.6	2,799
Textiles	54,700	101.9	2,048
Petroleum and coal products	15,400	186.1	1,815
Tobacco products industries	4,400	201.3	[11]
Mining	140,900	180.5	36,517
Construction	557,700	115.4	51,117

Production (metric tons except as noted). Agriculture, forestry, fishing (2004): wheat 24,462,300, barley 13,040,300, corn (maize) 8,360,200, rapeseed 7,001,100, potatoes 5,000,000, oats 3,488,400, dry peas 3,307,500, soybeans 2,919,600, lentils 938,000, tomatoes 733,900, sugar beets 680,000, linseed 671,900, apples 382,000, carrots 293,400, cabbages 186,400, onions 183,700;

livestock (number of live animals) 15,090,000 cattle, 14,680,000 pigs, 642,000 sheep; roundwood (2002) 193,168,000 cu m; fish catch (2003) 1,129,287. Mining and quarrying (value of production in Can$'000,000; 2004): nickel 3,348; gold 2,206; diamonds 2,140; copper 2,031; potash 1,930; iron ore 1,371; sand and gravel 1,079; stone 1,071; zinc 997. Manufacturing (value added in Can$'000,000; 2004)[2]: transportation equipment 27.5; chemicals 17.6; food 17.3; fabricated metal products 13.5; wood industries 13.2; machinery 12.3; primary metals 12.0; paper products 11.6; rubber and plastic products 10.3; computers and electronic products 8.4.

Retail trade (2002)

	no. of employees[12]	weekly wages as a % of all wages[9, 12]	annual sales (Can$'000,000)
Motor vehicle dealers	326,400[13]	143.5	89,979.0
Food stores	496,700	84.2	66,424.8
Clothing and footwear stores	144,600	79.4	27,229.0
Home furnishings and electronics	173,200	81.7	24,501.5
Automotive stores	[13]	143.5	23,078.5
Service stations	[13]	143.5	22,679.5
Furniture and appliance stores	87,000	119.2	18,275.9
Pharmacies	54,200	...	14,356.7
Sporting goods	...	...	11,686.9
Hardware stores	...	81.7	8,113.0
Electronics, including computers	[14]	92.0	8,108.2
Personal care products	[14]	79.4	7,620.0
Other	235,300[14]	92.0	53,767.7

Energy production (consumption): electricity (kW-hr; 2004) 567,600,000,000 (556,600,000,000); hard coal (metric tons; 2002) 29,500,000 (18,800,000); lignite (metric tons; 2002) 37,000,000 (42,900,000); crude petroleum (barrels; 2004) 1,146,000,000 (840,000,000); petroleum products (metric tons; 2002) 110,753,000 (98,234,000); natural gas (cu m; 2003) 180,500,000,000 (87,400,000,000).

Population economically active (2004): total 17,269,200; activity rate of total population 54.1% (participation rates: ages 15 and over 65.9%; female 46.6%; unemployed 7.2%).

Price and earnings indexes (2000 = 100)

	1998	1999	2000	2001	2002	2003	2004
Consumer price index	95.7	97.3	100.0	102.5	104.8	107.7	109.7
Hourly earnings index[15]	96.2	97.5	100.0	101.6	104.4	107.3	110.7

Household income and expenditure (2003). Average household size 2.7; average annual income per family Can$72,700 (U.S.$51,888); sources of income (2001): wages, salaries, and self-employment 71.8%, transfer payments 14.0%, other 14.2%; expenditure: housing 26.5%, transportation 19.1%, food 15.5%, recreation 9.5%, household operations 6.6%, clothing 5.6%, household furnishings 4.0%, health 3.6%, alcoholic beverages and tobacco 3.4%, education 2.3%, other 3.9%.

Financial aggregates

	1999	2000	2001	2002	2003	2004
Exchange rate, Can$ per:						
U.S. dollar[16]	1.49	1.49	1.55	1.57	1.40	1.30
£[16]	2.33	2.24	2.29	2.37	2.29	2.38
SDR[16]	1.98	1.95	2.00	2.15	1.92	1.87
International reserves (U.S.$)						
Total (excl. gold; '000,000)[16]	28,126	31,924	33,962	36,984	36,222	34,430
SDRs ('000,000)[16]	527	574	614	719	838	924
Reserve pos. in IMF ('000,000)[16]	3,168	2,509	2,863	3,580	3,847	3,338
Foreign exchange ('000,000)[16]	24,432	28,841	30,484	32,685	31,537	30,167
Gold ('000,000 fine troy oz)[16]	1.81	1.18	1.05	0.60	0.11	0.11
% world reserves	0.19	0.12	0.11	0.06	0.01	0.01
Interest and prices						
Central bank discount (%)[17]	5.00	6.00	2.50	3.00	3.00	2.75
Govt. bond yield (%)[17]	5.69	5.89	5.78	5.66	5.28	5.08
Industrial share prices (2000 = 100)[17]	73.5	100.0	80.5	73.2	74.5	90.0
Balance of payments (U.S.$'000,000)						
Balance of visible trade,	+28,291	+45,047	+45,275	+36,436	+41,513	+51,733
of which:						
Imports, f.o.b.	220,203	243,975	226,528	227,318	244,281	279,337
Exports, f.o.b.	248,494	289,022	271,803	263,754	285,794	331,070
Balance of invisibles	−26,526	−25,425	−29,066	−21,989	−24,245	−25,863
Balance of payments, current account	+1,765	+19,622	+16,209	+14,447	+17,268	+25,870

Land use as % of total land area (2000): in temporary crops 4.9%, in permanent crops 0.02%, in pasture 3.1%; overall forest area 26.5%.

Foreign trade

Balance of trade (current prices)

	1999	2000	2001	2002	2003	2004
Can$'000,000,000	+42.0	+66.9	+70.1	+57.3	+57.6	+67.2
% of total	6.0%	8.5%	9.1%	7.4%	7.8%	8.5%

Imports (2004): Can$363,123,400,000 (machinery and apparatus 25.1%; transport equipment 24.8%, of which road vehicles and parts 21.3%; chemicals and chemical products 7.4%; food products 5.9%; base metals 5.8%; crude petroleum 4.6%). *Major import sources* (2002): U.S. 62.6%; China 4.6%; Japan 4.4%; Mexico 3.6%; U.K. 2.8%; Germany 2.4%; France 1.7%.
Exports (2004): Can$430,357,600,000 (transport equipment 25.6%, of which road vehicles and parts 21.0%; machinery and apparatus 16.7%; base metals and alloys 7.5%; food products 7.1%; natural gas 6.5%; chemicals and chemical products 6.3%; wood and wood pulp 6.3%; crude petroleum 6.1%; paper and paperboard 2.8%). *Major export destinations* (2002): U.S. 87.2%; Japan 2.1%; U.K. 1.1%; China 1.0%; Germany 0.7%.

Trade by commodities (2002)

SITC Group	imports U.S.$'000	imports %	exports U.S.$'000	exports %
00 Food and live animals	11,285,900	5.1	16,230,800	6.4
01 Beverages and tobacco	1,371,900	0.6	1,002,600	0.4
02 Crude materials, excluding fuels	6,095,900	2.8	18,507,000	7.3
03 Mineral fuels, lubricants, and related materials	10,928,100	4.9	31,904,000	12.6
04 Animal and vegetable oils, fats, and waxes	303,900	0.1	420,700	0.2
05 Chemicals and related products, n.e.s.	20,909,300	9.4	14,789,900	5.9
06 Basic manufactures	29,427,100	13.2	38,240,600	15.1
07 Machinery and transport equipment	109,498,100	49.3	96,048,800	38.1
08 Miscellaneous manufactured articles	27,382,200	12.3	17,056,100	6.8
09 Goods not classified by kind	5,043,100	2.3	18,222,700	7.2
TOTAL	222,241,000[18]	100.0	252,418,500[18]	100.0

Direction of trade (2002)

	imports U.S.$'000	imports %	exports U.S.$'000	exports %
Africa	2,000,200	0.9	1,049,400	0.4
Asia	34,300,700	15.4	13,961,100	5.5
China	10,185,300	4.6	2,608,900	1.0
Japan	9,824,800	4.4	5,352,700	2.1
South Korea	3,098,300	1.4	1,273,200	0.5
Other	11,192,300	5.0	4,726,300	1.9
Americas	151,657,300	68.2	224,005,000	88.7
Mexico	8,100,700	3.6	1,537,300	0.6
United States	139,157,900	62.6	220,111,300	87.2
Other Americas	4,398,700	2.0	2,356,400	0.9
Europe	29,360,200	13.2	12,505,900	5.0
EU	24,830,300	11.2	11,085,900	4.4
Other Europe	4,529,900	2.0	1,420,000	0.6
Oceania	1,466,400	0.7	895,500	0.4
TOTAL	222,241,000[18, 19]	100.0[18, 19]	252,418,500[18]	100.0

Transport and communications

Transport. Railroads (2000): length 65,403 km; passenger-km (2001) 1,553,000,000; metric ton-km cargo (2001) 330,067,000,000. Roads (2002): total length 1,408,800 km (paved *c.* 35%). Vehicles (2002): passenger cars 17,543,659; trucks and buses 723,665. Air transport (2003): passenger-km 59,016,000,000; metric ton-km cargo 1,284,800,000; airports (2002) with scheduled flights 263.

Communications

Medium	date	unit	number	units per 1,000 persons
Daily newspapers	2000	circulation	4,890,000	159
Radio	2000	receivers	32,200,000	1,047
Television	2000	receivers	21,700,000	691
Telephones	2003	main lines	19,950,900	658
Cellular telephones	2003	subscribers	13,221,800	417
Personal computers	2002	units	15,300,000	487
Internet	2002	users	16,110,000	513

Education and health

Literacy (2004): total population age 15 and over literate virtually 100%.

Education (1999–2000)

	schools	teachers	students	student/teacher ratio
Primary (age 6–14) }	15,595	302,977	5,397,000	17.8
Secondary (age 14–18) }				
Postsecondary[20]	199	27,832	407,000	14.6
Higher[21]	75	33,801	591,000	17.5

Health: physicians (2002) 59,294 (1 per 529 persons); hospital beds (2002–03) 115,120 (1 per 274 persons); infant mortality rate per 1,000 live births (2004) 4.8.
Food (2002): daily per capita caloric intake 3,589 (vegetable products 73%, animal products 27%); 135% of FAO recommended minimum requirement.

Military

Total active duty personnel (2004): 52,300 (army 36.9%, navy 17.2%, air force 25.8%, not identified by service 20.1%). *Military expenditure as percentage of GDP* (2003): 1.2%; per capita expenditure U.S.$317.

[1]Based on land area of 3,551,023 sq mi (9,093,507 sq km). [2]At prices of 1997. [3]Excludes fishing, forestry. [4]Includes fishing, forestry. [5]Includes professional, scientific, and technical services. [6]Unemployed. [7]GDP at current values in 2004 was Can$1,290,185,000,000. [8]Federal government revenue and expenditure. [9]Excludes agriculture, fishing and trapping, private household services, religious organizations, and the military. [10]For 2002 in constant dollars of 1997. [11]Food and beverages includes tobacco. [12]2000. [13]Motor vehicle dealers includes Service stations and Automotive stores. [14]Other includes Electronics and Personal care products. [15]Manufacturing only. [16]End of period. [17]Period average. [18]Detail does not add to total because of discrepancies in estimates. [19]Total for imports includes U.S.$3,456,300,000 (1.6% of total imports; mostly special transactions) not distributable by region. [20]Community colleges. [21]Universities only.

Internet resources for further information:
• **Statistics Canada** http://www.statcan.ca

Cape Verde

Official name: República de Cabo Verde (Republic of Cape Verde).
Form of government: multiparty republic with one legislative house (National Assembly [72]).
Chief of state: President.
Head of government: Prime Minister.
Capital: Praia.
Official language: Portuguese.
Official religion: none.
Monetary unit: 1 escudo (C.V.Esc.)[1] = 100 centavos; valuation (Sept. 1, 2005) 1 U.S.$ = C.V.Esc. 88.90; 1 £ = C.V.Esc. 163.69.

Area and population

Island Groups Islands/Counties[2] Counties	Capitals	area		population 2000 census
		sq mi	sq km	
Leeward Islands		694[3]	1,798	287,323
Brava	Nova Sintra	25	64	6,820
Fogo				
Mosteiros	Mosteiros	} 184	476	9,479
São Filipe[4]	São Filipe			27,930
Maio	Porto Inglês	103	267	6,742
Santiago		383	991	236,352
Praia[4]	Praia	153	396	106,052
Santa Catarina[4]	Assomada	94	243	49,970
Santa Cruz[4]	Pedra Badejo	58	149	32,822
São Domingos	São Domingos	}		13,296
São Miguel	São Miguel	78	203	16,153
Tarrafal	Tarrafal			18,059
Windward Islands		858	2,223	147,489
Boa Vista	Sal Rei	239	620	4,193
Sal	Santa Maria	83	216	14,792
Santa Luzia		14	35	0
Santo Antão		300	779	47,124
Paúl	Pombas	21	54	8,325
Porto Novo	Porto Novo	215	558	17,239
Ribeira Grande	Ponta do Sol	64	167	21,560
São Nicolau[4]	Ribeira Brava	134	346	13,536
São Vicente	Mindelo	88	227	67,844
Other islets		5	12	0
TOTAL		1,557	4,033	434,812

Demography

Population (2005): 476,000.
Density (2005): persons per sq mi 305.7, persons per sq km 118.0.
Urban-rural (2003): urban 55.9%; rural 44.1%.
Sex distribution (2004): male 48.46%; female 51.54%.
Age breakdown (2004): under 15, 40.0%; 15–29, 27.5%; 30–44, 16.8%; 45–59, 7.4%; 60–74, 5.6%; 75 and over, 2.7%.
Population projection: (2010) 523,000; (2020) 630,000.
Doubling time: 36 years.
Ethnic composition (2000): Cape Verdean *mestico* (black-white admixture) 69.6%; Fulani 12.2%; Balanta 10.0%; Mandyako 4.6%; Portuguese white 2.0%; other 1.6%.
Religious affiliation (2000): Roman Catholic 91.4%; Muslim 2.8%; other 5.8%.
Major cities (2000): Praia 94,757; Mindelo 62,970; São Filipe 7,894.

Vital statistics

Birth rate per 1,000 population (2004): 26.1 (world avg. 21.1).
Death rate per 1,000 population (2004): 6.7 (world avg. 9.0).
Natural increase rate per 1,000 population (2004): 19.4 (world avg. 12.1).
Total fertility rate (avg. births per childbearing woman; 2004): 3.6.
Life expectancy at birth (2004): male 66.8 years; female 73.5 years.
Major causes of death per 100,000 population (1999): diseases of the circulatory system 151.0; diseases of the respiratory system 58.3; infectious and parasitic diseases 55.9; malignant neoplasms (cancers) 48.7; accidents, poisoning, and violence 48.0.

National economy

Budget (2003). Revenue: C.V.Esc. 18,889,000,000 (tax revenue 81.5%, of which income and profit taxes 31.1%, taxes on international trade 26.1%, taxes on goods and services 19.6%; nontax revenue 18.5%). Expenditures: C.V.Esc. 32,149,000,000 (current expenditure 55.9%, of which wages and salaries 30.9%, transfers 10.2%, public debt 6.7%, goods and services 1.1%; capital expenditure 44.1%).
Public debt (external, outstanding; 2002): U.S.$385,000,000.
Production (metric tons except as noted). Agriculture, forestry, fishing (2004): sugarcane 14,000, corn (maize) 10,000, bananas 6,000, mangoes 4,500, tomatoes 4,500, sweet potatoes 4,000; livestock (number of live animals) 205,000 pigs, 112,500 goats, 22,500 cattle; roundwood (2003) 1,542 cu m; fish catch (2002) 8,000. Mining and quarrying (2003): salt 1,600. Manufacturing (1999): flour 15,901; bread 5,628[5]; soap 833; paint 628[6]; canned tuna 337[5]; cigarettes and cigars 77 kg; beer 4,105,000 litres; soft drinks 923,000[6] litres. Energy production (consumption): electricity (kW-hr; 2002) 45,000,000 (45,000,000); coal, none (none); crude petroleum, none (none); petroleum products (metric tons; 2002) none (48,000); natural gas, none (none).
Tourism (2003): receipts from visitors U.S.$85,000,000; expenditures by nationals abroad U.S.$71,000,000.
Gross national product (2004): U.S.$852,000,000 (U.S.$1,770 per capita).

Structure of gross domestic product and labour force

	2001		1990	
	in value C.V.Esc. '000,000	% of total value	labour force	% of labour force
Agriculture	6,888.7	10.3	29,876	24.7
Manufacturing			5,520	4.6
Public utilities }	6,098.3	9.1	883	0.7
Mining			410	0.3
Construction	5,196.2	7.8	22,722	18.9
Transp. and commun.	12,197.7	18.3	6,138	5.1
Trade	12,402.2	18.6	12,747	10.6
Finance	7,686.1	11.5	821	0.7
Pub. admin., defense	9,311.9	14.0	17,358	14.4
Services	1,967.8	3.0 }		
Other	4,943.6[7]	7.4[7]	24,090	20.0
TOTAL	66,692.5	100.0	120,565	100.0

Population economically active (2000): total 174,644; activity rate of total population 40.2% (participation rates: ages 15–64 [1990] 64.3%; female 39.0%; unemployed 17.4%).

Price index (2000 = 100)

	2000	2001	2002	2003	2004	2005
Consumer price index	100.0	99.6	105.4	106.5	104.5	103.4[8]

Household income and expenditure. Average household size (2000) 4.6; income per household: n.a.; sources of income: n.a.; expenditure (1988): food 51.1%, housing, fuel, and power 13.5%, beverages and tobacco 11.8%, transportation and communications 8.8%, household durable goods 6.9%, other 7.9%.
Land use as % of total land area (2000): in temporary crops 9.7%, in permanent crops 0.5%, in pasture 6.2%; overall forest area 21.1%.

Foreign trade[9]

Balance of trade (current prices)

	1997	1998	1999	2000	2001	2002
C.V.Esc. '000,000	−20,469	−21,582	−25,746	−26,313	−29,317	−31,034
% of total	88.8%	91.4%	91.7%	91.2%	92.4%	92.6%

Imports (2000): C.V.Esc. 27,585,000,000 (food 32.8%, machinery and apparatus 16.1%, transport equipment 9.5%, base and fabricated metals 6.5%). *Major import sources* (2003): Portugal 48.4%; The Netherlands 14.7%; Belgium 5.7%; U.S. 3.4%; France 3.1%.
Exports (2000): C.V.Esc. 1,272,000,000 (shoes and shoe parts 51.8%, clothing 35.1%, fish 4.8%). *Major export destinations* (2003): Portugal 70.8%; U.S. 22.5%; Germany 1.1%.

Transport and communications

Transport. Railroads: none. Roads (2001): total length 870 mi, 1,400 km (paved [1996] 78%). Vehicles (2000): passenger cars 13,473; trucks and buses 3,085. Air transport (2001)[10]: passenger-mi 171,000,000, passenger-km 276,000,000; short ton-mi cargo (1998) 16,200,000, metric ton-km cargo 26,000,000.

Communications

Medium	date	unit	number	units per 1,000 persons
Radio	1997	receivers	71,000	179
Television	2001	receivers	45,000	101
Telephones	2004	main lines	73,400	156
Cellular telephones	2004	subscribers	65,800	139
Personal computers	2004	units	48,000	102
Internet	2004	users	25,000	53

Education and health

Educational attainment (1990). Percentage of population age 25 and over having: no formal schooling 47.9%; primary 40.9%; incomplete secondary 3.9%; complete secondary 1.4%; higher 1.5%; unknown 4.4%. *Literacy* (2002): total population age 15 and over literate 75.7%; males 85.4%; females 68.0%.

Education (1997–98)

	schools	teachers	students	student/teacher ratio
Primary (age 7–12)	370[11]	3,219	91,636[12]	...
Secondary (age 13–17) }	...	1,372	40,214[12]	...
Vocational				
Higher	...	...	1,600[13]	...

Health (2000): physicians 102 (1 per 4,274 persons); hospital beds 689 (1 per 631 persons); infant mortality rate per 1,000 live births (2004) 49.1.
Food (2002): daily per capita caloric intake 3,243 (vegetable products 86%, animal products 14%); 138% of FAO recommended minimum requirement.

Military

Total active duty personnel (2004): 1,200 (army 83.3%, air force 8.3%, coast guard 8.4%). *Military expenditure as percentage of GDP* (2003): 0.7%; per capita expenditure U.S.$12.

---

[1]Formerly pegged to the Portuguese escudo and since Jan. 1, 2002, to the euro at the rate of €1 = C.V.Esc. 110.27. [2]Island/county areas are coterminous except Fogo, Santiago, and Santo Antão islands. [3]Detail does not add to total given because of rounding. [4]County divided into two parts as of 2005 administrative reorganization; new county is not listed. [5]1995. [6]1997. [7]Taxes and duties on imports less imputed bank service charges. [8]March. [9]Imports c.i.f., exports f.o.b.; excludes reexports of fuel. [10]TACV airline only. [11]1991. [12]1999–2000. [13]Students abroad in 1996–97.

Internet resources for further information:
• Instituto Nacional de Estatística de Cabo Verde http://www.ine.cv
• Banco de Cabo Verde http://www.bcv.cv

Central African Republic

Official name: République Centrafricaine (Central African Republic).
Form of government: multiparty republic with one legislative body (National Assembly [105])[1].
Chief of state: President.
Head of government: Prime Minister.
Capital: Bangui.
Official languages: French; Sango.
Official religion: none.
Monetary unit: 1 CFA franc (CFAF) = 100 centimes; valuation (Sept. 1, 2005) 1 U.S.$ = CFAF 522.78; 1 £ = CFAF 962.57[2].

Area and population		area		population
				2003
Prefectures	Capitals	sq mi	sq km	census[3]
Bamingui-Bangoran	Ndélé	22,471	58,200	38,437
Basse-Kotto	Mobaye	6,797	17,604	203,887
Haut-Mbomou	Obo	21,440	55,530	38,184
Haute-Kotto	Bria	33,456	86,650	69,514
Kemo	Sibut	6,642	17,204	98,881
Lobaye	Mbaïki	7,427	19,235	214,137
Mambéré-Kadéï	Berbérati	11,661	30,203	289,688
Mbomou	Bangassou	23,610	61,150	132,740
Nana-Gribizi	Kaga-Bandoro	7,721	19,996	87,341
Nana-Mambéré	Bouar	10,270	26,600	184,594
Ombella-M'poko	Boali	12,292	31,835	304,025
Ouaka	Bambari	19,266	49,900	224,076
Ouham	Bossangoa	19,402	50,250	280,772
Ouham-Pendé	Bozoum	12,394	32,100	325,567
Sangha-Mbaéré	Nola	7,495	19,412	89,871
Vakaga	Birao	17,954	46,500	37,595
Autonomous commune				
Bangui	Bangui	26	67	531,763
TOTAL		240,324	622,436	3,151,072

Demography

Population (2005): 4,038,000.
Density (2005): persons per sq mi 16.8, persons per sq km 6.5.
Urban-rural (2003): urban 42.7%; rural 57.3%.
Sex distribution (2003): male 49.47%; female 50.53%.
Age breakdown (2003): under 15, 43.1%; 15–29, 28.9%; 30–44, 14.6%; 45–59, 8.2%; 60–74, 4.2%; 75 and over, 1.0%.
Population projection: (2010) 4,333,000; (2020) 4,960,000.
Doubling time: 44 years.
Ethnolinguistic composition (1988): Gbaya (Baya) 23.7%; Banda 23.4%; Mandjia 14.7%; Ngbaka 7.6%; Sara 6.5%; Mbum 6.3%; Kare 2.4%; French 0.1%; other 15.3%.
Religious affiliation (2000): Christian 67.8%, of which unaffiliated Christian 23.3%, Roman Catholic 18.4%, Protestant 14.4%, independent Christian 11.6%; Muslim 15.6%; traditional beliefs 15.4%; other 1.2%.
Major cities (2003): Bangui 531,763; Bimbo 114,086; Berbérati 59,414; Carnot 37,339; Bambari 33,273.

Vital statistics

Birth rate per 1,000 population (2004): 34.8 (world avg. 21.1).
Death rate per 1,000 population (2004): 18.9 (world avg. 9.0).
Natural increase rate per 1,000 population (2004): 15.9 (world avg. 12.1).
Total fertility rate (avg. births per childbearing woman; 2004): 4.6.
Life expectancy at birth (2004): male 43.1 years; female 43.5 years.
Adult population (ages 15–49) *living with HIV* (2004[4]): 13.5% (world avg. 1.1%).

National economy

Budget (2003). Revenue: CFAF 53,700,000,000 (taxes 84.4%, of which indirect domestic tax 38.2%, taxes on income and profits 26.1%, international trade tax 19.9%; nontax receipts 15.6%). Expenditures: CFAF 85,500,000,000 (current expenditure 77.2%, of which wages 40.4%; capital expenditure 22.8%).
Public debt (external, outstanding; 2003): U.S.$917,000,000.
Production (metric tons except as noted). Agriculture, forestry, fishing (2004): cassava 563,000, yams 350,000, peanuts (groundnuts) 133,600, corn (maize) 119,000, bananas 110,000, taro 100,000, sugarcane 90,000, plantains 80,000, sesame seeds 42,800, sorghum 42,480, pulses 30,000, seed cotton 30,000, paddy rice 29,700, oranges 20,000; livestock (number of live animals) 3,423,000 cattle, 3,087,000 goats, 805,000 pigs, 4,769,000 chickens; roundwood (2003) 2,824,000 cu m; fish catch (2002) 15,000. Mining and quarrying (2003): gold 2 kg[5], diamonds (2004) 352,000 carats[6]. Manufacturing (2002): refined sugar 10,570; palm oil 2,743; soap 1,625; aluminum products 812; cigarettes (2003) 16,100,000 packets; beer (2003) 121,700 hectolitres; soft drinks (2003) 38,400 hectolitres. Energy production (consumption): electricity (kW-hr; 2003) 120,000,000 (112,000,000); coal, none (none); crude petroleum, none (none); petroleum products (metric tons; 2002) none (90,000); natural gas, none (none).
Household income and expenditure. Average household size (2002) 6.1; average annual income per household (1988) CFAF 91,985 (U.S.$435); sources of income: n.a.; expenditure (1991)[7]: food 70.5%, clothing 8.5%, other manufactured products 7.6%, energy 7.3%, services (including transportation and communications, recreation, and health) 6.1%.
Gross national product (2004): U.S.$1,226,000,000 (U.S.$310 per capita).

Structure of gross domestic product and labour force

	2003		1988	
	in value CFAF '000,000	% of total value	labour force	% of labour force
Agriculture	378,800	54.4	1,113,900	80.4
Mining	46,100	6.6	15,400	1.1
Manufacturing	16,100	2.3	22,400	1.6
Construction	30,900	4.4	7,000	0.5
Public utilities	5,400	0.8	1,500	0.1
Transp. and commun.	26,600	3.8	1,500	0.1
Trade	72,300	10.4	118,000	8.5
Services	42,100	6.0	15,600	1.1
Pub. admin., defense	47,000	6.8	91,700	6.6
Other	31,300[8]	4.5[8]	—	—
TOTAL	696,400[9]	100.0	1,387,000	100.0

Population economically active (2000): total 1,752,000; activity rate of total population 50.0% (participation rates [1988]: ages 15–64, 78.3%; female 46.8%; unemployed [2001] *c.* 8%).

Price index (2000 = 100)							
	1997	1998	1999	2000	2001	2002	2003
Consumer price index	100.2	98.3	96.9	100.0	103.4	106.9	110.2

Land use as % of total land area (2000): in temporary crops 3.1%, in permanent crops 0.1%, in pasture 5.0%; overall forest area 36.8%.
Tourism (2002): receipts U.S.$3,000,000; expenditures U.S.$29,000,000.

Foreign trade

Balance of trade (current prices)						
	1997	1998	1999	2000	2001	2002
CFAF '000,000,000	+9.6	+2.8	+10.3	+26.6	+25.6	+19.6
% of total	5.5%	1.6%	6.0%	13.6%	14.0%	10.7%

Imports (2002): CFAF 81,700,000,000 (imports for public improvements 15.9%, petroleum products 9.8%, unspecified 74.3%). *Major import sources:* France *c.* 43%; African nations *c.* 19%; U.S. *c.* 7%; Spain *c.* 5%; Belgium *c.* 4%.
Exports (2002): CFAF 101,300,000,000 (wood 49.0%, diamonds 35.8%, cotton 6.3%, coffee 1.0%). *Major export destinations:* Belgium *c.* 71%; Spain *c.* 7%; Italy *c.* 4%; African nations *c.* 3%; France *c.* 3%.

Transport and communications

Transport. Railroads: none. Roads (1999): total length 14,795 mi, 23,810 km (paved *c.* 3%). Vehicles (1996): passenger cars 8,900; trucks and buses 7,000. Air transport (2001)[10]: passengers arriving and departing 44,000; freight loaded and unloaded 1,500 tons; airports (2003) 1.

Communications				units per 1,000
Medium	date	unit	number	persons
Daily newspapers	2000	circulation	7,000	2.0
Radio	2000	receivers	280,000	80
Television	2002	receivers	22,800	6.0
Telephones	2004	main lines	10,000	2.6
Cellular telephones	2004	subscribers	60,000	15
Personal computers	2004	units	11,000	2.8
Internet	2004	users	9,000	2.3

Education and health

Educational attainment (1988). Percentage of population age 10 and over having: no formal schooling 59.3%; primary education 29.6%; lower secondary 7.5%; upper secondary 2.3%; higher 1.3%. *Literacy* (2002): total population age 15 and over literate 48.6%; males literate 64.7%; females literate 33.5%.

Education (1998)	schools	teachers	students	student/ teacher ratio
Primary (age 6–11)	...	3,125	284,398	91.0
Secondary (age 12–18)	46[11]	845[11]	42,263[12]	...
Vocational	13	13	1,477[12]	...
Higher[14]	1	154	6,474	42.0

Health (2001): physicians 189 (1 per 20,291 persons); hospital beds 4,365 (1 per 879 persons); infant mortality rate (2004) 89.0.
Food (2002): daily per capita caloric intake 1,980 (vegetable products 90%, animal products 10%); 86% of FAO recommended minimum requirement.

Military

Total active duty personnel (2004): 2,550 (army 54.9%; navy, none; air force 5.9%; paramilitary [gendarmerie] 39.2%); [2004] 200 French troops. *Military expenditure as percentage of GDP* (2003): 1.3%; per capita expenditure U.S.$4.

---

[1]Transitional government begun March 15, 2003, officially ended in June of 2005. [2]Formerly pegged to the French franc and since Jan. 1, 2002, to the euro at the rate of €1 = CFAF 655.96. [3]Preliminary unadjusted figure. [4]January 1. [5]Reported figure. Actual gold production in 2003 was estimated at 1,000 kg. [6]Official figure; at least an equal amount was smuggled out of the country in 2004. [7]Weights of consumer price index components. [8]Indirect taxes and customs duties. [9]Detail does not add to total given because of rounding. [10]Bangui airport. [11]1990–91. [12]1991–92. [13]Included with secondary. [14]2002; University of Bangui only.

Internet resources for further information:
• **Statistics, Economic Studies, and Social Division**
   http://www.stat-centrafrique.com

Chad

Official name: Jumhūrīyah Tshad
(Arabic); République du Tchad
(French) (Republic of Chad).
Form of government: unitary republic
with one legislative body (National
Assembly [155]).
Chief of state: President.
Head of government: Prime Minister.
Capital: N'Djamena.
Official languages: Arabic; French.
Official religion: none.
Monetary unit: 1 CFA franc
(CFAF) = 100 centimes; valuation
(Sept. 1, 2005) 1 U.S.$ = CFAF 522.78;
1 £ = CFAF 962.57[1].

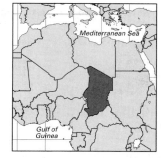

Area and population		area		population
				1993
Préfectures[2]	Capitals	sq mi	sq km	census
Batha	Ati	34,285	88,800	288,458
Biltine	Biltine	18,090	46,850	184,807
Borkou-Ennedi-Tibesti	Faya Largeau	231,795	600,350	73,185
Chari-Baguirmi	N'Djamena	32,010	82,910	1,251,906
Guéra	Mongo	22,760	58,950	306,253
Kanem	Mao	44,215	114,520	279,927
Lac	Bol	8,620	22,320	252,932
Logone Occidental	Moundou	3,357	8,695	455,489
Logone Oriental	Doba	10,825	28,035	441,064
Mayo-Kebbi	Bongor	11,625	30,105	825,158
Moyen-Chari	Sarh	17,445	45,180	738,595
Ouaddaï	Abéché	29,436	76,240	543,900
Salamat	Am Timan	24,325	63,000	184,403
Tandjilé	Laï	6,965	18,045	453,854
TOTAL		495,755[3]	1,284,000	6,279,931

Demography

Population (2005): 9,657,000[4].
Density (2005): persons per sq mi 19.5, persons per sq km 7.5.
Urban-rural (2003): urban 24.9%; rural 75.1%.
Sex distribution (2002): male 48.62%; female 51.38%.
Age breakdown (2002): under 15, 47.8%; 15–29, 26.2%; 30–44, 14.1%; 45–59, 7.5%; 60–74, 3.6%; 75 and over, 0.8%.
Population projection: (2010) 11,170,000; (2020) 14,839,000.
Doubling time: 23 years.
Ethnolinguistic composition (1993): Sara 27.7%; Sudanic Arab 12.3%; Mayo-Kebbi peoples 11.5%; Kanem-Bornu peoples 9.0%; Ouaddaï peoples 8.7%; Hadjeray (Hadjaraï) 6.7%; Tangale (Tandjilé) peoples 6.5%; Gorane peoples 6.3%; Fitri-Batha peoples 4.7%; Fulani (Peul) 2.4%; other 4.2%.
Religious affiliation (2000): Muslim 59.1%; Christian 22.8%, of which Protestant 10.3%, Roman Catholic 6.6%; traditional beliefs 17.0%; other 1.1%.
Major cities (1993): N'Djamena (2003) 609,600; Moundou 282,103; Bongor 196,713; Sarh 193,753; Abéché 187,936; Doba 185,461.

Vital statistics

Birth rate per 1,000 population (2004): 46.6 (world avg. 21.1).
Death rate per 1,000 population (2004): 17.0 (world avg. 9.0).
Natural increase rate per 1,000 population (2004): 29.6 (world avg. 12.1).
Total fertility rate (avg. births per childbearing woman; 2004): 6.4.
Life expectancy at birth (2004): male 45.3 years; female 48.6 years.
Adult population (age 15–49) living with HIV (2004[5]): 4.8% (world avg. 1.1%).

National economy

Budget (2004). Revenue: CFAF 239,000,000,000 (tax revenue 52.3%; petroleum revenue 38.9%; nontax revenue 8.8%). Expenditures: CFAF 296,000,000,000 (current expenditure 55.3%, of which wages and salaries 20.9%, materials and supply 13.2%, defense 9.8%, transfer payments 7.7%, debt service 3.7%; capital expenditure 44.7%).
Tourism (2002): receipts from visitors U.S.$25,000,000; expenditures by nationals abroad U.S.$80,000,000.
Production (metric tons except as noted). Agriculture, forestry, fishing (2004): sorghum 560,000, peanuts (groundnuts) 450,000, millet 430,000, sugarcane 355,000, cassava 325,000, yams 230,000, seed cotton 200,000, corn (maize) 120,000, rice 109,000; livestock (number of live animals) 6,400,000 cattle, 5,716,800 goats, 2,568,500 sheep, 735,000 camels; roundwood (2003) 7,000,038 cu m; fish catch (2003) 70,000. Mining and quarrying (1997): aggregate (gravel) 170,000; limited commercial production of natron (10,000) and salt; artisanal gold production. Manufacturing (2002): cotton fibre 67,200; refined sugar 23,100; gum arabic (2000) 3,420; woven cotton fabrics (2000) 1,000,000 metres; beer 124,200 hectolitres; edible oil 90,000 hectolitres; cigarettes 36,000,000 packs; bicycles (1998) 3,444 units. Energy production (consumption): electricity (kW-hr; 2002) 98,000,000 (98,000,000); coal, none (none); crude petroleum (barrels; 2004) 71,000,000 (n.a.); petroleum products (metric tons; 2002) none (43,000); natural gas, none (none).
Household income and expenditure. Average household size (2002) 5.0; average annual income per household (1993) CFAF 96,806 (U.S.$458); sources of income (1995–96; urban): informal-sector employment and entrepreneurship 36.7%, transfers 24.8%, wages 23.6%, ownership of real estate 8.6%; expenditure (1983)[6]: food 45.3%, health 11.9%, energy 5.8%, clothing 3.3%.
Population economically active (1997): total 3,433,000; activity rate of total population 47.9% (participation rates: over age 15, 72.3%; female 44.5%; unemployed [1993] 0.6%).

Price index (2000 = 100)

	1997	1998	1999	2000	2001	2002	2003
Consumer price index	92.2	103.4	96.5	100.0	112.4	118.3	116.0

Public debt (external, outstanding; 2003): U.S.$1,371,000,000.
Gross national product (2004): U.S.$2,277,000,000 (U.S.$260 per capita).

Structure of gross domestic product and labour force

	2002		1993	
	in value CFAF '000,000	% of total value	labour force	% of labour force
Agriculture	476,900	34.3	1,903,492	83.0
Mining, fishing[7]	99,600	7.2	756	—
Manufacturing	119,500	8.6	33,670	1.5
Construction	20,000	1.4	10,885	0.5
Public utilities	7,600	0.5	2,026	0.1
Transp. and commun.	342,000	24.6	13,252	0.6
Trade	} 149,900	} 10.8	211,812	9.2
Finance, real estate			1,071	—
Pub. admin., defense	...	...	61,875	2.7
Services	125,700	9.0	45,453	2.0
Other	50,700[8]	3.6[8]	9,271	0.4
TOTAL	1,391,800[3]	100.0	2,291,577[9]	100.0

Land use as % of total land area (2000): in temporary crops 2.8%, in permanent crops 0.02%, in pasture 35.7%; overall forest area 10.1%.

Foreign trade

Balance of trade (current prices)

	1998	1999	2000	2001	2002	2003
CFAF '000,000,000	−11.5	−22.1	−40.2	−239.4	−466.3	−198.8
% of total	3.6%	7.3%	13.4%	46.4%	65.3%	27.7%

Imports (2003): CFAF 458,200,000,000 (petroleum sector 65.1%; non-petroleum sector 34.9%). Major import sources: France c. 29%; U.S. c. 21%; Cameroon c. 15%; The Netherlands c. 5%; Germany c. 4%.
Exports (2003): CFAF 259,400,000,000 (petroleum products 49.3%; cattle, sheep, and goats 21.0%; cotton fibre 15.8%). Major export destinations: U.S. c. 25%; Germany c. 17%; Portugal c. 16%; France c. 7%; Morocco c. 5%.

Transport and communications

Transport. Railroads (2002): none. Roads (1999): total length 33,400 km (paved 1%). Vehicles (1996): passenger cars 10,560; trucks and buses 14,550. Air transport (1999): passenger-km 235,000,000; metric ton-km cargo 36,000,000; airports (2000) with scheduled flights 1.

Communications

Medium	date	unit	number	units per 1,000 persons
Daily newspapers	1997	circulation	2,000	0.2
Radio	2000	receivers	1,990,000	236
Television	2002	receivers	16,600	2.0
Telephones	2003	main lines	12,400	1.5
Cellular telephones	2003	subscribers	65,000	8.0
Personal computers	2004	units	15,000	1.7
Internet	2004	users	60,000	6.8

Education and health

Educational attainment (1993). Percentage of economically active population age 15 and over having: no formal schooling 81.1%; Qur'anic education 4.2%; primary education 11.2%; secondary education 2.7%; higher education 0.3%; professional education 0.5%. Literacy (2002): percentage of total population age 15 and over literate 45.8%; males 54.5%; females 37.5%.

Education (1996–97)

	schools	teachers	students	student/ teacher ratio
Primary (age 6–12)	2,660[10]	10,151	680,909	67.1
Secondary (age 13–19)	153[10]	2,598	97,011	37.3
Voc., teacher tr.	18[10]	194	2,778	14.5
Higher[11]	8	288	3,274	11.4

Health: physicians (2000) 1,667 (1 per 4,471 persons); hospital beds (1998) 4,105 (1 per 1,908 persons); infant mortality rate (2004) 94.7.
Food (2002): daily per capita caloric intake 2,114 (vegetable products 93%, animal products 7%); 89% of FAO recommended minimum requirement.

Military

Total active duty personnel (2004): 30,350 (army 82.4%; air force 1.2%; paramilitary [gendarmerie] 16.4%); French peacekeeping troops (July 2005) c. 1,000. Military expenditure as percentage of GDP (2003): 1.5%; per capita expenditure U.S.$4.

[1]Formerly pegged to the French franc and since Jan. 1, 2002, to the euro at the rate of €1 = CFAF 655.96. [2]Pre-1999 local administrative structure (Chad was administratively reorganized in both 1999 and 2002); effective implementation of 2002 reorganization had not occurred as of April 2005. [3]Detail does not add to total given because of rounding. [4]Excludes about 200,000 Sudanese refugees in eastern Chad in mid-2005. [5]January 1. [6]Capital city only. [7]Includes petroleum sector. [8]Indirect taxes less subsidies. [9]Official census total; summed total equals 2,293,563. [10]1995–96. [11]Universities and equivalent institutions only.

Internet resources for further information:
• **National Institute of Statistics and Economic and Demographic Studies**
  http://www.inseed-tchad.org
• **La Banque de France: La Zone Franc**
  http://www.banque-france.fr/fr/eurosys/zonefr/zonefr.htm

Chile

Official name: República de Chile (Republic of Chile).
Form of government: multiparty republic with two legislative houses (Senate [38[1]]; Chamber of Deputies [120]).
Head of state and government: President.
Capital: Santiago[2].
Official language: Spanish.
Official religion: none.
Monetary unit: 1 peso (Ch$) = 100 centavos; valuation (Sept. 1, 2005) 1 U.S.$ = Ch$535.40; 1 £ = Ch$985.81.

Area and population[3]

Regions	Capitals	area sq mi	area sq km	population 2002 census[4]
Aisén del General Carlos Ibáñez del Campo	Coihaique	41,890	108,495	91,492
Antofagasta	Antofagasta	48,668	126,049	493,984
Araucanía	Temuco	12,294	31,842	869,535
Atacama	Copiapó	29,026	75,176	254,336
Bío-Bío	Concepción	14,310	37,063	1,861,562
Coquimbo	La Serena	15,668	40,580	603,210
Libertador General Bernardo O'Higgins	Rancagua	6,327	16,387	780,627
Los Lagos	Puerto Montt	25,874	67,013	1,073,135
Magallanes y Antártica Chilena	Punta Arenas	51,080	132,297	150,826
Maule	Talca	11,697	30,296	908,097
Región Metropolitana	Santiago	5,947	15,403	6,061,185
Tarapacá	Iquique	22,818	59,099	428,594
Valparaíso	Valparaíso	6,331	16,396	1,539,852
TOTAL		291,930	756,096	15,116,435

Demography

Population (2005): 16,295,000.
Density (2005): persons per sq mi 55.8, persons per sq km 21.6.
Urban-rural (2003): urban 87.0%; rural 13.0%.
Sex distribution (2004): male 49.55%; female 50.45%.
Age breakdown (2004): under 15, 25.8%; 15–29, 24.5%; 30–44, 22.0%; 45–59, 16.2%; 60–74, 8.6%; 75 and over, 2.9%.
Population projection: (2010) 17,134,000; (2020) 18,639,000.
Ethnic composition (2000): mestizo 72.4%; local white 20.8%; Araucanian (Mapuche) 4.7%; European 1.0%; other 1.1%.
Religious affiliation (2002)[5]: Roman Catholic 70.0%; Protestant 15.4%; other Christian 2.1%; atheist/nonreligious 4.6%; other 7.9%.
Major cities[6] (2002): Greater Santiago 4,647,444; Puente Alto 501,042; Concepción 376,043; Viña del Mar 298,828; Antofagasta 298,153.

Vital statistics

Birth rate per 1,000 population (2004): 15.8 (world avg. 21.1).
Death rate per 1,000 population (2004): 5.7 (world avg. 9.0).
Natural increase rate per 1,000 population (2004): 10.1 (world avg. 12.1).
Total fertility rate (avg. births per childbearing woman; 2004): 2.1.
Life expectancy at birth (2004): male 73.1 years; female 79.8 years.
Major causes of death per 100,000 population (2002): diseases of the circulatory system 154.3; malignant neoplasms (cancers) 130.5; accidents, poisoning, and violence 52.0; communicable diseases 43.6[7]; diabetes mellitus 20.3.

National economy

Budget (2001). Revenue: Ch$9,537,200,000,000 (income from taxes 76.2%, nontax revenue 23.5%, capital 0.3%). Expenditures: Ch$9,932,200,000,000 (pensions 29.5%, wages 19.0%, capital expenditure 15.0%, interest 2.1%).
Public debt (external, outstanding; 2003): U.S.$8,053,000,000.
Population economically active (2003): total 6,128,200; activity rate of total population 38.7% (participation rates: ages 15–64, 58.8%; female 34.3%; unemployed [July 2003–June 2004] 8.6%).

Price and earnings indexes (2000 = 100)

	1998	1999	2000	2001	2002	2003	2004
Consumer price index	93.2	96.3	100.0	103.6	106.1	109.1	110.3
Hourly earnings index	89.7	95.0	100.0	105.2	110.0	114.2	117.5

Production (metric tons except as noted). Agriculture, forestry, fishing (2004): sugar beets 2,500,000, wheat 1,850,000, grapes 1,750,000, tomatoes 1,300,000, corn (maize) 1,200,000, apples 1,100,000, potatoes 1,093,728, oats 425,000, onions (dry) 290,000; livestock (number of live animals) 4,170,000 sheep, 3,989,000 cattle, 3,450,000 pigs; roundwood (2003) 40,203,371 cu m; fish catch (2002) 4,271,475. Mining (metal content; 2003): copper 4,904,000; iron ore 4,500,000; molybdenum 33,375; zinc 33,051; silver 1,313,000 kg; gold 38,954 kg. Manufacturing (value added in U.S.$'000,000; 2000): food products 3,251; nonferrous base metals 1,947; paints, soaps, pharmaceuticals 1,206; beverages 1,169; industrial chemicals 1,047; paper and paper products 1,020; refined petroleum 705. Energy production (consumption): electricity (kW-hr; 2002) 45,483,000,000 (45,483,000,000); hard coal (metric tons; 2002) 433,000 (3,629,000); crude petroleum (barrels; 2002) 1,600,000 (71,000,000); petroleum products (metric tons; 2002) 8,762,000 (9,872,000); natural gas (cu m; 2002) 2,248,000,000 (7,099,000,000).
Tourism (2003): receipts U.S.$860,000,000; expenditures U.S.$768,000,000.
Gross national product (2004): U.S.$78,407,000,000 (U.S.$4,910 per capita).

Structure of gross domestic product and labour force

	2001 in value Ch$'000,000[9]	2001 % of total value	2003[8] labour force	2003[8] % of labour force
Agriculture	2,052,900	5.6	796,000	13.0
Mining	3,050,700	8.4	74,600	1.2
Manufacturing	5,722,100	15.7	858,500	14.0
Public utilities	1,214,800	3.3	32,800	0.5
Construction	2,952,500	8.1	493,100	8.0
Transp. and commun.	2,727,900	7.5	518,800	8.5
Trade	3,904,100	10.7	1,145,400	18.7
Finance	4,557,200	12.5	494,500	8.1
Pub. admin., defense			1,643,300	26.8
Services	10,350,800[10]	28.3[10]		
Other			71,200[11]	1.2[11]
TOTAL	36,533,000	100.0[12]	6,128,200	100.0

Household income and expenditure. Average household size (2002) 3.4; average annual income per household (1994) Ch$5,981,706 at November prices (U.S.$12,552); sources of income (1990): wages and salaries 75.1%, transfer payments 12.0%, other 12.9%; expenditure (1989): food 27.9%, clothing 22.5%, housing 15.2%, transportation 6.4%.
Land use as % of total land area (2000): in temporary crops 2.6%, in permanent crops 0.4%, in pasture 17.3%; overall forest area 20.7%.

Foreign trade[13]

Balance of trade (current prices)

	1999	2000	2001	2002	2003	2004
U.S.$'000,000	+2,427	+2,119	+1,844	+2,386	+3,015	+9,019
% of total	7.6%	5.8%	5.3%	7.0%	7.7%	16.4%

Imports (2003): U.S.$19,413,000,000 (intermediate goods 57.4%, of which crude petroleum 11.1%; capital goods 19.2%; free zone imports 6.8%). *Major import sources:* Argentina 19.4%; U.S. 13.0%; Brazil 10.4%; China 6.6%; Germany 3.7%.
Exports (2003): U.S.$20,652,000,000 (copper 36.3%; foodstuffs 16.0%, of which salmon and trout 5.5%; chemicals and chemical products 8.4%; fruits 8.1%). *Major export destinations:* U.S. 16.2%; Japan 10.5%; China 8.6%; South Korea 4.7%; Mexico 4.3%.

Transport and communications

Transport. Railroads (2001): route length 5,282 mi, 8,501 km; passenger-km 870,836,000; metric ton-km cargo 3,318,000,000. Roads (2001): total length 49,465 mi, 79,605 km (paved 20.2%). Vehicles (2002): passenger cars 1,373,121; trucks and buses 731,000. Air transport: passenger-km (2001) 8,308,000,000; metric ton-km cargo (1999) 2,107,000,000; airports (1998) 23.

Communications

Medium	date	unit	number	units per 1,000 persons
Daily newspapers	2004	circulation	816,000	52
Radio	2000	receivers	5,230,000	354
Television	2000	receivers	3,580,000	242
Telephones	2004	main lines	3,318,300	215
Cellular telephones	2004	subscribers	9,566,600	621
Personal computers	2004	units	2,138,000	139
Internet	2004	users	4,300,000	279

Education and health

Educational attainment (1995). Percentage of population age 25 and over having: no formal schooling 5.1%; primary education 45.8%; secondary 35.4%; higher 13.7%. *Literacy* (2001): total population age 15 and over literate 95.9%; males literate 96.1%; females literate 95.7%.

Education (1995)

	schools	teachers	students	student/ teacher ratio
Primary (age 6–13)	8,702	80,155	2,149,501	26.8
Secondary (age 14–17)[14]	...	51,042	679,165	13.3
Higher	...	18,084[15]	367,094	...

Health: physicians (2000) 17,720 (1 per 834 persons); hospital beds (1999) 42,163 (1 per 346 persons); infant mortality rate (2004) 9.1.
Food (2002): daily per capita caloric intake 2,863 (vegetable products 79%, animal products 21%); 117% of FAO recommended minimum requirement.

Military

Total active duty personnel (2004): 77,700 (army 61.4%, navy 24.4%, air force 14.2%). *Military expenditure as percentage of GDP* (2003): 3.5%; per capita expenditure U.S.$158.

[1]Elected seats only; seats occupied by appointees or former heads of state are to be eliminated as of March 2006. [2]Legislative bodies meet in Valparaíso. [3]Excludes the 480,000-sq mi (1,250,000-sq km) section of Antarctica claimed by Chile (and administered as part of Magallanes y Antártica Chilena region) and "inland" (actually tidal) water areas. The 2002 census population of Chilean-claimed Antarctica is 130. [4]Final. [5]For population age 15 years and older. [6]Preliminary census populations of single communes except for Greater Santiago and for Concepción, which is a total for 3 communes. [7]Includes infectious and parasitic diseases and acute respiratory infections. [8]Excludes all or some classes or elements of the military. [9]In constant prices of 1996. [10]Less imputed bank service charges, import duties, and value-added tax on imports. [11]Unemployed, not previously employed. [12]Detail does not add to total given because of rounding. [13]Imports f.o.b. in balance of trade and c.i.f. in commodities and trading partners. [14]Includes vocational. [15]Universities only.

Internet resources for further information:
• **Instituto Nacional de Estadísticas http://www.ine.cl**
• **Banco Central de Chile http://www.bcentral.cl/eng**

China

Official name: Chung-hua Jen-min Kung-ho-kuo (People's Republic of China).
Form of government: single-party people's republic with one legislative house (National People's Congress [2,980[1]]).
Chief of state: President.
Head of government: Premier.
Capital: Peking (Beijing).
Official language: Mandarin Chinese.
Official religion: none.
Monetary unit: 1 Renminbi (yuan) (Y) = 10 jiao = 100 fen; valuation (Sept. 1, 2005) 1 U.S.$ = Y 8.09; 1 £ = Y 14.90.

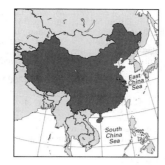

Area and population[2, 3]

Provinces	Capitals	area[4] sq mi	area[4] sq km	population 2002[5] estimate
Anhwei (Anhui)	Ho-fei (Hefei)	54,000	139,900	63,380,000
Chekiang (Zhejiang)	Hang-chou (Hangzhou)	39,300	101,800	46,470,000
Fukien (Fujian)	Fu-chou (Fuzhou)	47,500	123,100	34,660,000
Hainan (Hainan)	Hai-k'ou (Haikou)	13,200	34,300	8,030,000
Heilungkiang (Heilongjiang)	Harbin	179,000	463,600	38,130,000
Honan (Henan)	Cheng-chou (Zhengzhou)	64,500	167,000	96,130,000
Hopeh (Hebei)	Shih-chia-chuang (Shijiazhuang)	78,200	202,700	67,350,000
Hunan (Hunan)	Ch'ang-sha (Changsha)	81,300	210,500	66,290,000
Hupeh (Hubei)	Wu-han (Wuhan)	72,400	187,500	59,880,000
Kansu (Gansu)	Lan-chou (Lanzhou)	141,500	366,500	25,930,000
Kiangsi (Jiangxi)	Nan-ch'ang (Nanchang)	63,600	164,800	42,220,000
Kiangsu (Jiangsu)	Nanking (Nanjing)	39,600	102,600	73,810,000
Kirin (Jilin)	Ch'ang-ch'un (Changchun)	72,200	187,000	26,990,000
Kwangtung (Guangdong)	Canton (Guangzhou)	76,100	197,100	78,590,000
Kweichow (Guizhou)	Kuei-yang (Guiyang)	67,200	174,000	38,370,000
Liaoning (Liaoning)	Shen-yang (Shenyang)	58,300	151,000	42,030,000
Shansi (Shanxi)	T'ai-yüan (Taiyuan)	60,700	157,100	32,940,000
Shantung (Shandong)	Chi-nan (Jinan)	59,200	153,300	90,820,000
Shensi (Shaanxi)	Sian (Xi'an)	75,600	195,800	36,740,000
Szechwan (Sichuan)	Ch'eng-tu (Chengdu)	188,000	487,000	86,730,000
Tsinghai (Qinghai)	Hsi-ning (Xining)	278,400	721,000	5,290,000
Yunnan (Yunnan)	K'un-ming (Kunming)	168,400	436,200	43,330,000
Autonomous regions				
Inner Mongolia (Nei Monggol)	Hu-ho-hao-t'e (Hohhot)	454,600	1,177,500	23,790,000
Kwangsi Chuang (Guangxi Zhuang)	Nan-ning (Nanning)	85,100	220,400	48,220,000
Ningsia Hui (Ningxia Hui)	Yin-ch'uan (Yinchuan)	25,600	66,400	5,720,000
Sinkiang Uighur (Xinjiang Uygur)	Wu-lu-mu-ch'i (Urumqi)	635,900	1,646,900	19,050,000
Tibet (Xizang)	Lhasa	471,700	1,221,600	2,670,000
Municipalities				
Chungking (Chongqing)	—	31,700	82,000	31,070,000
Peking (Beijing)	—	6,500	16,800	14,230,000
Shanghai (Shanghai)	—	2,400	6,200	16,250,000
Tientsin (Tianjin)	—	4,400	11,300	10,070,000
TOTAL		3,696,100[4]	9,572,900[4]	1,275,180,000

Demography

Population (2005): 1,304,369,000.
Density (2005): persons per sq mi 352.9, persons per sq km 136.3.
Urban-rural (2003)[6]: urban 38.6%; rural 61.4%.
Sex distribution (2003): male 51.05%; female 48.95%.
Age breakdown (2003): under 15, 20.3%; 15–29, 22.8%; 30–44, 26.7%; 45–59, 18.2%; 60–74, 9.4%; 75 and over, 2.6%.
Population projection: (2010) 1,342,723,000; (2020) 1,411,530,984.
Ethnic composition (2000): Han (Chinese) 91.53%; Chuang 1.30%; Manchu 0.86%; Hui 0.79%; Miao 0.72%; Uighur 0.68%; Tuchia 0.65%; Yi 0.62%; Mongolian 0.47%; Tibetan 0.44%; Puyi 0.24%; Tung 0.24%; Yao 0.21%; Korean 0.15%; Pai 0.15%; Hani 0.12%; Kazakh 0.10%; Li 0.10%; Tai 0.09%; other 0.54%.
Religious affiliation (2000): nonreligious 42.1%; Chinese folk-religionist 28.5%; Buddhist 8.4%; atheist 8.1%; Christian 7.1%; traditional beliefs 4.3%; Muslim 1.5%.
Major cities (2003[7]): Shanghai 10,030,800; Beijing 7,699,300; Tianjin 4,933,100; Guangzhou 4,653,100; Wuhan 4,593,400; Chongqing 4,239,700; Shenyang 3,995,500; Nanjing 2,966,000; Harbin 2,735,100; Chengdu 2,664,000; Xi'an 2,657,900; Jinan 2,346,000; Changchun 2,283,800; Dalian 2,181,600; Hangzhou 2,059,800; Shijiazhuang 1,971,000; Taiyuan 1,970,300; Qingdao 1,930,200; Zhengzhou 1,770,800; Kunming 1,597,800; Lanzhou 1,576,400; Changsha 1,562,200; Zibo 1,519,300.
Households. Average household size (2000) 3.4; total households 351,233,698, of which family households 340,491,197 (96.9%), collective 10,742,501 (3.1%).

Vital statistics

Birth rate per 1,000 population (2004): 13.0 (world avg. 21.1).
Death rate per 1,000 population (2004): 6.9 (world avg. 9.0).
Natural increase rate per 1,000 population (2004): 6.1 (world avg. 12.1).
Total fertility rate (avg. births per childbearing woman; 2004): 1.7.
Marriage rate per 1,000 population (2002): 6.1.
Divorce rate per 1,000 population (2001): 1.0.

Life expectancy at birth (2004): male 70.4 years; female 73.7 years.
Major causes of death per 100,000 population (2002)[8]: malignant neoplasms (cancers) 119.7; cerebrovascular disease 88.4; diseases of the respiratory system 78.1; heart diseases 74.1; accidents, violence, and poisoning 43.5.

Social indicators

Educational attainment (2000). Percentage of population age 15 and over having: no schooling and incomplete primary 15.6%; completed primary 35.7%; some secondary 34.0%; complete secondary 11.1%; some postsecondary through advanced degree 3.6%.

Distribution of urban household income (1996)

avg. per capita income by quintile (avg. Y 4,845 [U.S.$583])

first quintile	second quintile	third quintile	fourth quintile	fifth quintile
Y 2,801	Y 3,780	Y 4,580	Y 5,599	Y 8,039

Quality of working life. Average workweek (1998): 40 hours. Annual rate per 100,000 workers for (1997)[9]: injury or accident 0.7; industrial illness, n.a.; death 1.4. Funds for pensions and social welfare relief (2001): Y 26,668,000,000.
Access to services. Percentage of population having access to electricity (2000) 98.6%. Percentage of total (urban, rural) population with safe public water supply (2002) 83.6% (94.0%, 73.0%). Sewage system (1999): total (urban, rural) households with flush apparatus 20.7% (50.0%, 4.3%), with pit latrines 69.3% (33.6%, 86.7%), with no latrine 5.3% (7.8%, 4.1%).
Social participation. Eligible voters participating in last national election: n.a. Population participating in voluntary work: n.a. Trade union membership in total labour force (2002): c. 18%. Practicing religious population in total affiliated population: n.a.
Social deviance. Annual reported arrest rate per 100,000 population (1986) for: property violation 20.7; infringing personal rights 7.2; disruption of social administration 3.3; endangering public security 1.0[10].
Material well-being. Urban households possessing (number per household; 2003): bicycles 1.4; colour televisions 1.3; washing machines 0.9; refrigerators 0.9; cameras 0.5. Rural families possessing (number per household; 2003): bicycles 1.2; colour televisions 0.7; washing machines 0.2; refrigerators 0.1; cameras 0.02.

National economy

Gross national product (2004): U.S.$1,676,846,000,000 (U.S.$1,290 per capita).

Structure of gross domestic product and labour force

	2002 in value Y '000,000	% of total value	labour force ('000)	% of labour force
Agriculture	1,611,730	15.4	324,870	43.1
Mining	}		5,580	0.7
Manufacturing	} 4,653,570	44.4	83,070	11.0
Public utilities	}		2,900	0.4
Construction	700,500	6.7	38,930	5.2
Transp. and commun.	624,090	6.0	20,840	2.8
Trade	821,530	7.8	49,690	6.6
Finance	...	...	4,580	0.6
Pub. admin.	...	...	10,750	1.4
Services	2,067,640	19.7	33,150	4.4
Other			179,240[11]	23.8[11]
TOTAL	10,479,060	100.0	753,600	100.0

Budget (2003). Revenue: Y 2,171,525,000,000 (tax revenue 92.2%, of which VAT 33.3%, corporate income taxes 13.4%, business tax 13.1%, consumption tax 5.4%; nontax revenue 7.8%). Expenditures: Y 2,464,995,000,000 (economic development 30.1%; social, cultural, and educational development 26.2%; administration 19.0%; debt payment 12.0%; defense 7.7%; other 5.0%).
Public debt (external, outstanding; 2003): U.S.$85,570,000,000.
Tourism (2003): receipts from visitors U.S.$17,406,000,000; expenditures by nationals abroad U.S.$15,187,000,000.

Retail and catering enterprises (1996)

	no. of enterprises	no. of employees	annual wage as a % of all wages	annual gross output value (Y '000,000)
Retail trade	13,963,162	31,892,181	...	...
Food, beverage, and tobacco	5,177,416	10,738,924	...	241,350
Articles for daily use	3,242,769	8,614,944	...	88,470
Textile goods, garments, shoes, and hats	2,018,136	4,030,888	...	125,250
Sundry goods for daily use	799,486	1,670,984	...	...
Hardware, electrical appliances, and chemicals	583,466	1,828,788	...	...
Books and newspapers	140,856	365,424	...	23,110
Medicines and medical appliances	123,534	405,424	...	57,980
Other	1,877,499	4,236,805	...	...
Catering trade	2,587,730	7,753,108	...	...
Restaurants	1,181,732	4,321,824	...	...
Fast-food eateries	397,561	1,049,829	...	...
Other	1,008,437	2,381,455	...	...

Production (metric tons except as noted). Agriculture, forestry, fishing (2004): grains—rice 186,730,000, corn (maize) 131,860,000, wheat 91,330,265, barley 3,200,000, sorghum 3,107,500, millet 2,200,800; oilseeds—soybeans 17,-750,340, peanuts (groundnuts) 14,075,000, rapeseed 11,900,010, sunflower seeds 1,880,000; fruits and nuts—watermelons 68,300,000, apples 20,503,000, cantaloupes 14,338,000, pears 10,120,000, bananas 6,220,000; other—sweet potatoes 106,197,100, sugarcane 93,200,000, potatoes 75,048,000, cabbage 32,601,000, tomatoes 30,142,040, cucumbers 25,558,000, onions 18,035,000, seed cotton 18,000,000, eggplants 16,529,300, chillies and peppers 12,028,000, garlic 10,578,000, tobacco leaves 2,405,000, tea 821,000, silkworm cocoons

(2003) 667,000; livestock (number of live animals) 472,896,000 pigs, 183,363,000 goats, 157,330,000 sheep, 106,540,000 cattle, 22,809,000 water buffalo, 8,499,000 asses, 7,902,000 horses, 3,974,750,000 chickens, 660,360,000 ducks; roundwood (2003) 236,107,000 cu m; fish catch (2002) 44,320,000, of which aquaculture 27,767,000. Mining and quarrying (2003): metal content of mine output—zinc 2,030,000, lead 955,000, manganese 920,000, copper 610,000, tin 102,000, antimony 100,000, tungsten 50,000, silver 2,400, gold 205; metal ores—iron ore 261,000,000, bauxite 13,000,000, vanadium 35,000; nonmetals—salt 34,377,000, soda ash 11,336,000, gypsum 6,850,000, magnesite 3,700,000, barite 3,500,000, fluorspar 2,650,000, talc 2,600,000, asbestos 350,000. Manufacturing (value added in U.S.$'000,000; 2001): electrical machinery 41,240; food products, beverages, and tobacco products 37,842; industrial chemicals 30,757; textiles and wearing apparel 25,077; transportation equipment 19,738; nonelectrical machinery 19,433; iron and steel 18,487; cement, bricks, and tiles 10,601; rubber and plastic products 9,585; fabricated metal products 8,618; nonferrous base metals 7,142; paper and paper products 5,737; wood products and furniture, excluding metal furniture, 3,752. Distribution of industrial production (percentage of total value of output by sector; 2001): state-operated enterprises 26.8%; urban collectives 16.6%; rural collectives 23.2%; privately operated enterprises 33.4%. Retail sales (percentage of total sales by sector; 2001): state-operated enterprises 25.3%; collectives 29.8%; privately operated enterprises 44.9%.

Manufacturing and mining enterprises (1996)

	no. of enter- prises	no. of employees[12]	annual wages as a % of avg. of all wages	annual gross output value (Y '000,000)
Manufacturing				
Machinery, transport equipment, and metal manufactures, of which,	23,032	21,560	...	880,886
Metal products	2,641	1,810,000	...	23,593
Industrial equipment	8,875	7,020,000	...	183,951
Transport equipment	4,303	3,540,000	...	187,581
Electronic goods	1,579	1,630,000	...	70,046
Measuring equipment	1,179	820,000	...	14,738
Textiles	4,031	6,340,000	...	161,949
Garments	1,177	1,680,000	...	11,359
Foodstuffs, of which,	18,191	4,710,000	...	383,264
Food processing	14,520	3,170,000	...	196,393
Beverages	3,367	1,210,000	...	70,368
Tobacco manufactures	304	330,000	...	116,503
Chemicals, of which,	10,707	8,140,000	...	537,768
Pharmaceuticals	2,044	1,020,000	...	53,749
Plastics	1,667	1,050,000	...	15,167
Secondary forest products (including paper and stationery)	3,664	2,310,000	...	51,238
Primary forest products	877	1,140,000	...	16,750
Mining				
Nonferrous and ferrous metals	1,163	810,000	...	22,711
Crude petroleum	71	1,250,000	...	149,525
Coal	2,011	5,050,000	...	105,946

Energy production (consumption): electricity (kW-hr; 2004) 2,187,000,000,000 ([2002] 1,921,508,000,000); hard coal (metric tons; 2003) 1,315,200,000 ([2002] 1,313,900,000); crude petroleum (barrels; 2003) 1,248,000,000 ([2002] 1,670,-000,000); petroleum products (metric tons; 2002) 158,179,000 (171,734,000); natural gas (cu m; 2002) 40,278,000,000 (37,985,000,000).

Financial aggregates[13]

	1998	1999	2000	2001	2002	2003	2004
Exchange rate, Y per:							
U.S. dollar	8.28	8.28	8.28	8.28	8.28	8.28	8.28
£	13.77	13.38	12.35	12.00	13.34	14.77	15.99
SDR	11.66	11.36	10.78	10.40	11.25	12.30	12.85
International reserves (U.S.$)							
Total (excl. gold; '000,000)	149,188	157,728	168,278	215,605	291,128	408,151	614,500
SDRs ('000,000)	676	741	798	851	998	1,102	1,247
Reserve pos. in IMF ('000,000)	3,553	2,312	1,905	2,590	3,723	3,798	3,320
Foreign exchange	144,959	154,675	165,574	212,165	286,407	403,251	609,932
Gold ('000,000 fine troy oz)	12.7	12.7	12.7	16.1	19.3	19.3	19.3
% world reserves	1.4	1.3	1.3	1.7	2.1	2.1	2.1
Interest and prices							
Central bank discount (%)	4.59	3.24	3.24	3.24	2.70	2.70	3.33
Govt. bond yield (%)	...	...	...	...	...	...	...
Industrial share prices	...	...	...	...	...	...	...
Balance of payments (U.S.$'000,000)							
Balance of visible trade, of which:	+46,614	+35,982	+34,474	+34,017	+44,167	+44,652	...
Imports, f.o.b.	-136,915	-158,734	-214,657	-232,058	-281,484	-393,618	...
Exports, f.o.b.	183,529	194,716	249,131	266,075	325,651	438,270	...
Balance of invisibles	-15,142	-20,540	-13,956	-16,616	-8,745	+1,223	...
Balance of payments, current account	+31,472	+21,115	+20,518	+17,401	+35,422	+45,875	...

Household income and expenditure. Average household size (2001) 3.5; rural households (2003) 4.1, urban households (2003) 3.0. Average annual per capita disposable income of household (2003): rural households Y 2,622 (U.S.$317), urban households Y 8,472 (U.S.$1,024). Sources of income (2003): rural households—income from household businesses 75.7%, wages 19.1%, transfers 3.7%, other 1.5%; urban households—wages 70.7%, transfers 23.3%, business income 4.5%, other 2.1%. Expenditure: rural (urban) households—food 45.6% (37.1%), housing 15.9% (10.7%), education and recreation 12.1% (14.4%), transportation and communications 8.4% (11.1%), clothing 5.7% (9.8%), medicine and medical service 6.0% (7.1%), household furnishings 4.2% (6.3%).

Population economically active (2002): total 753,600,000; activity rate of total population 58.5% (participation rates: over age 15 [2001] 77.7%; female [2001] 37.8%; registered unemployed in urban areas [December 2004] 4.2%). Urban employed workforce (2001): 239,400,000; by sector: state enterprises 76,400,000, collectives 28,130,000, self-employment or privately run enterprises 134,870,000. Rural employed workforce 490,850,000.

Price and earnings indexes (2000 = 100)

	1998	1999	2000	2001	2002	2003	2004
Consumer price index	98.9	100.3	100.0	100.5	99.7	100.9	104.8
Monthly earnings index[14]	80.7	89.1	100.0	111.7	125.7	...	...

Land use as % of total land area (2000): in temporary crops 14.7%, in permanent crops 1.2%, in pasture 42.9%; overall forest area 17.5%.

Foreign trade[15]

Balance of trade (current prices)

	1998	1999	2000	2001	2002	2003
U.S.$'000,000	+46,614	+35,982	+34,474	+34,017	+44,167	+44,652
% of total	14.5%	10.2%	7.4%	6.8%	7.3%	5.4%

Imports (2002): U.S.$295,170,000,000 (machinery and apparatus 46.4%, of which transistors/microcircuits 11.9%; telecommunications equipment 4.8%; artificial resins and plastic materials 5.3%; iron and steel 4.6%; textile yarn, fabrics, and made-up articles 4.5%; crude petroleum 4.3%). *Major import sources* (2004): Japan 16.8%; Taiwan 11.5%; South Korea 11.1%; United States 8.0%; Germany 5.4%.
Exports (2002): U.S.$325,596,000,000 (machinery and apparatus 39.0%, of which computers and related units 11.1%, telecommunications equipment and related parts 9.8%; wearing apparel 12.7%; textile yarn, fabrics, and made-up articles 6.4%; toys, games, and sporting goods 3.9%). *Major export destinations* (2004): United States 21.1%; Hong Kong 17.0%; Japan 12.4%; South Korea 4.7%; Germany 4.0%.

Transport and communications

Transport. Railroads (2003): route length 45,360 mi, 73,000 km; passenger-mi 297,550,000,000, passenger-km 478,860,000,000; short ton-mi cargo 1,094,030,-000,000, metric ton-km cargo 1,724,670,000,000. Roads (2002): total length 1,096,856 mi, 1,765,222 km (paved, n.a.). Vehicles (2001): passenger cars 9,939,600; trucks and buses 7,652,400. Air transport (2003): passenger-mi 78,491,000,000, passenger-km 126,320,000,000; short ton-mi cargo 3,670,-000,000, metric ton-km cargo 5,790,000,000; airports (1996) with scheduled flights 113.

Communications

Medium	date	unit	number	units per 1,000 persons
Daily newspapers	2003	circulation	88,657,000	69
Radio	2000	receivers	428,000,000	339
Television	2000	receivers	448,000,000	350
Telephones	2004	main lines	312,443,000	238
Cellular telephones	2004	subscribers	334,824,000	255
Personal computers	2004	units	52,990,000	40
Internet	2004	users	94,000,000	72

Education and health

Literacy (2000): total population age 15 and over literate 90.9%; males literate 95.1%; females literate 86.5%.

Education (2003)

	schools	teachers	students	student/ teacher ratio
Primary (age 7–13)	425,846	5,703,000	116,897,000	20.5
Secondary (age 13–17)	79,490	4,537,000	85,832,000	18.9
Secondary specialized	3,065	199,000	5,024,000	25.2
Voc., teacher tr.	6,843	289,000	5,282,000	18.3
Higher	1,552	725,000	11,086,000	15.3

Health (2004): physicians 1,892,000 (1 per 687 persons); hospital beds 3,004,-000 (1 per 432 persons); infant mortality rate per 1,000 live births (2004) 25.3.
Food (2002): daily per capita caloric intake 2,951 (vegetable products 79%, animal products 21%); 125% of FAO recommended minimum requirement.

Military

Total active duty personnel (2004): 2,255,000 (army 71.0%, navy 11.3%, air force 17.7%). *Military expenditure as percentage of GDP* (2003): 2.3%; per capita expenditure U.S.$26.

[1]As of March 2003; 36 seats are allotted to Hong Kong and 12 to Macau. [2]Names of the provinces, autonomous regions, and municipalities are stated in conventional form, followed by Pinyin transliteration; names of capitals are stated in conventional form or Wade-Giles transliteration, followed by Pinyin transliteration. [3]Data for Taiwan, Quemoy, and Matsu (parts of Fukien province occupied by Taiwan); Hong Kong (which reverted to China from British administration on July 1, 1997) and Macau (which reverted to China from Portuguese administration on Dec. 20, 1999) are excluded. [4]Estimated figures. [5]July 1. [6]Excluding Hong Kong and Macau. [7]January 1. [8]Based on urban sample population. [9]Reported cases. [10]Excludes arrests for anti-Communist activities. [11]Includes 7,700,000 registered unemployed; remainder mostly activities not defined. [12]In state-owned and collective-owned industries only. [13]All data are for end of period. [14]Manufacturing sector only. [15]Imports f.o.b. in balance of trade and c.i.f. in commodities and trading partners.

Internet resource for further information:
• **Embassy of The People's Republic of China** http://www.china-embassy.org
• **China Statistical Information Net** http://www.stats.gov.cn/english

Colombia

Official name: República de Colombia (Republic of Colombia).
Form of government: unitary, multiparty republic with two legislative houses (Senate [102]; House of Representatives [166[1]]).
Head of state and government: President.
Capital: Bogotá.
Official language: Spanish.
Official religion: none.
Monetary unit: 1 peso (Col$) = 100 centavos; valuation (Sept. 1, 2005) 1 U.S.$ = Col$2,295; 1 £ = Col$4,225.

Area and population

Departments	Capitals	area sq mi	area sq km	population 2005 projection[2]
Antioquia	Medellín	24,445	63,912	5,761,175
Atlántico	Barranquilla	1,308	3,388	2,370,753
Bolívar	Cartagena	10,030	25,978	2,231,163
Boyacá	Tunja	8,953	23,189	1,413,064
Caldas	Manizales	3,046	7,888	1,172,510
Caquetá	Florencia	34,349	88,965	465,078
Cauca	Popayán	11,316	29,308	1,367,496
Cesar	Valledupar	8,844	22,905	1,053,123
Chocó	Quibdó	17,965	46,530	416,318
Córdoba	Montería	9,660	25,020	1,396,764
Cundinamarca	Bogotá, D.C.	8,735	22,623	2,340,894
Huila	Neiva	7,680	19,890	996,617
La Guajira	Riohacha	8,049	20,848	526,148
Magdalena	Santa Marta	8,953	23,188	1,406,126
Meta	Villavicencio	33,064	85,635	772,853
Nariño	Pasto	12,845	33,268	1,775,973
Norte de Santander	Cúcuta	8,362	21,658	1,494,219
Orinoquía-Amazonía[3]	...	186,519	483,083	1,371,986
Quindío	Armenia	712	1,845	612,719
Risaralda	Pereira	1,598	4,140	1,025,539
San Andrés y Providencia	San Andrés	17	44	83,403
Santander	Bucaramanga	11,790	30,537	2,086,649
Sucre	Sincelejo	4,215	10,917	870,219
Tolima	Ibagué	9,097	23,562	1,316,053
Valle del Cauca	Cali	8,548	22,140	4,532,378
Capital District				
Bogotá		613	1,587	7,185,889
TOTAL		440,762[4]	1,141,568[4]	46,045,109[5]

Demography

Population (2005): 42,954,000[6].
Density (2005): persons per sq mi 97.5, persons per sq km 37.6.
Urban-rural (2003): urban 76.5%; rural 23.5%.
Sex distribution (2003): male 49.08%; female 50.92%.
Age breakdown (2003): under 15, 31.3%; 15–29, 25.8%; 30–44, 22.8%; 45–59, 12.8%; 60–74, 5.8%; 75 and over, 1.5%.
Population projection: (2010) 46,109,000; (2020) 52,199,000.
Ethnic composition (2000): mestizo 47.3%; mulatto 23.0%; white 20.0%; black 6.0%; black-Amerindian 1.0%; Amerindian/other 2.7%.
Religious affiliation (2000): Roman Catholic 96.1%; other 3.9%.
Major cities (2003): Bogotá, D.C., 6,850,205; Cali 2,287,819; Medellín 1,955,753; Barranquilla 1,329,579; Cartagena 902,688.

Vital statistics

Birth rate per 1,000 population (2004): 21.2 (world avg. 21.1).
Death rate per 1,000 population (2004): 5.6 (world avg. 9.0).
Natural increase rate per 1,000 population (2004): 15.6 (world avg. 12.1).
Total fertility rate (avg. births per childbearing woman; 2004): 2.6.
Life expectancy at birth (2004): male 67.6 years; female 75.4 years.
Major causes of death per 100,000 population (1997): violence and suicides 85.6; malignant neoplasms (cancers) 84.8; ischemic heart disease 71.4; cerebrovascular diseases 44.8; accidents 43.6.

National economy

Budget (2003–04). Revenue: Col$39,951,400,000,000 (tax revenue 92.0%, nontax revenue 8.0%). Expenditures: Col$53,934,600,000,000 (transfers 53.1%, debt service 19.0%, other 27.9%).
Public debt (external, outstanding; 2003): U.S.$22,816,000,000.
Population economically active (2003): total 20,408,000[7]; activity rate 47.2% (participation rates: ages 12–55, 48.1%; female 42.6%; unemployed [2004] 13.6%).

Price index (2000 = 100)

	1998	1999	2000	2001	2002	2003	2004
Consumer price index	82.6	91.6	100.0	108.0	114.8	123.0	130.3

Production (metric tons except as noted). Agriculture, forestry, fishing (2004): sugarcane 37,100,000, potatoes 2,959,380, plantains 2,950,000, rice 2,663,239, cassava 2,218,112, bananas 1,550,000, corn 1,458,434, coffee 678,000; livestock (number of live animals) 25,250,000 cattle, 2,720,000 horses, 2,310,000 pigs; roundwood (2003) 9,958,513 cu m; fish catch (2003) 157,794. Mining and quarrying (2003): nickel (metal content) 70,844; gold 46,515 kg; emeralds 8,963,000 carats. Manufacturing (value added in Col$'000,000,000; 2002): processed food 6,599; chemicals 5,077; beverages 3,154; petroleum products 2,829; cement, bricks, and ceramics 2,163; clothing 1,765; paper products 1,582; plastic products 1,341.[8] Energy production (consumption): electricity (kW-hr;

2002) 45,242,000,000 (44,632,000,000); coal (metric tons; 2002) 43,900,000 (3,950,000); crude petroleum (barrels; 2003) 206,000,000 ([2002] 105,000,000); petroleum products (metric tons; 2002) 13,668,000 (9,130,000); natural gas (cu m; 2002) 8,805,000,000 (8,805,000,000).
Gross national product (2004): U.S.$90,626,000,000 (U.S.$2,000 per capita).

Structure of gross domestic product and labour force

	2004 in value Col$'000,000	2004 % of total value	2003 labour force	2003 % of labour force
Agriculture	29,541,116	11.5	3,941,000	19.4
Mining	17,343,664	6.8	191,000	0.9
Manufacturing	36,838,341	14.4	2,654,000	13.1
Construction	13,391,667	5.2	998,000	4.9
Public utilities	11,625,842	4.5	79,000	0.4
Transp. and commun.	18,773,366	7.3	1,271,000	6.3
Trade	28,030,192	11.0	4,971,000	24.4
Finance	37,368,127	14.6	1,087,000	5.3
Pub. admin., defense } Services	52,658,281	20.6	4,578,000	22.5
Other	10,413,777[9]	4.1[9]	575,000	2.8
TOTAL	255,984,373	100.0	20,345,000	100.0

Land use as % of total land area (2000): in temporary crops 2.7%, in permanent crops 1.7%, in pasture 39.4%; overall forest area 47.8%.
Household income and expenditure (2002). Average household size 4.9; sources of income: wages 42.6%, self-employment 38.9%; expenditure (1992): food 34.2%, transportation 18.5%, housing 7.8%, health care 6.4%.
Tourism (2003): receipts U.S.$816,000,000; expenditures U.S.$1,026,000,000.

Foreign trade[10]

Balance of trade (current prices)

	1999	2000	2001	2002	2003	2004
U.S.$'000,000	+1,626	+2,160	+333	+78	+105	+1,104
% of total	7.5%	8.9%	1.4%	0.3%	0.4%	3.4%

Imports (2004): U.S.$16,745,000,000 (machinery and equipment 43.7%, chemicals and chemical products 27.1%, base metals 6.4%). *Major import sources:* U.S. 28.9%; Venezuela 6.7%; Mexico 6.2%; Brazil 5.8%; Germany 3.9%.
Exports (2004): U.S.$16,730,000,000 (crude and refined petroleum 25.3%, coal 11.1%, chemicals and chemical products 10.4%, textiles and clothing 8.2%, machinery and equipment 7.4%, food, beverages, and tobacco 7.3%, coffee 5.7%). *Major export destinations:* U.S. 39.4%; EU 14.0%; Venezuela 9.7%; Mexico 3.1%; Japan 1.6%.

Transport and communications

Transport. Railroads (2003): route length 1,980 mi, 3,185 km; passenger-km (1999) negligible; metric ton-km cargo (1999) 473,000,000. Roads (1999): total length 71,400 mi, 114,912 km (paved 14%). Vehicles (1999): cars 762,000; trucks 672,000. Air transport (2003): passenger-km 8,713,500,000; metric ton-km cargo 645,800,000; airports (1998) 43.

Communications

Medium	date	unit	number	units per 1,000 persons
Daily newspapers	2002	circulation	1,110,000[11]	27[11]
Radio	2001	receivers	25,968,000	549
Television	2002	receivers	13,241,000	303
Telephones	2004	main lines	8,768,000	195
Cellular telephones	2004	subscribers	10,401,000	232
Personal computers	2004	units	2,996,000	67
Internet	2004	users	3,585,700	80

Education and health

Educational attainment (1985). Percentage of population age 25 and over having: no schooling 15.3%; primary education 50.1%; secondary 25.4%; higher 6.8%; not stated 2.4%. *Literacy* (2002): population age 15 and over literate 92.1%; males literate 92.1%; females literate 92.2%.

Education (2003)

	schools	teachers	students	student/ teacher ratio
Primary (age 6–10)	33,957	190,961	5,207,772	27.3
Secondary (age 11–16)	12,293	168,587	3,603,949	21.4
Higher[12]	266	75,568	673,353	8.9

Health (2003): physicians 57,000 (1 per 729 persons); hospital beds 49,000 (1 per 850 persons); infant mortality rate (2004) 21.7.
Food (2002): daily per capita caloric intake 2,585 (vegetable products 84%, animal products 16%); 111% of FAO recommended minimum requirement.

Military

Total active duty personnel (2004): 207,000 (army 86.0%, navy 10.6%, air force 3.4%); U.S. troops (August 2004) 400. *Military expenditure as percentage of GDP* (2003): 4.4%; per capita expenditure U.S.$84.

---

[1]Two seats are occupied by representatives from indigenous communities. [2]Projection based on 1993 census. [3]Geographic designation for eight political entities in eastern Colombia elevated to departmental status in the early 1990s. [4]Detail does not add to total given because of rounding. [5]De jure estimates. [6]De facto estimate per U.S. Bureau of the Census International Database. [7]Includes ages 11 and under. [8]Illegal cocaine production (2004) 430 metric tons. [9]Import duties and VAT, less imputed bank service charges and less subsidies. [10]Import figures are f.o.b. in balance of trade and c.i.f. in commodities and trading partners. [11]Circulation for 10 newspapers only. [12]1996.

Internet resources for further information:
• National Administration Department of Statistics http://www.dane.gov.co

Comoros[1]

Official name: L'Union des Comores (French); Udzima wa Komori (Comorian); (Union of the Comoros).
Form of government: republic[2] with one legislative house (Assembly of the Union [33[3]]).
Head of state and government: President assisted by Vice Presidents.
Capital: Moroni.
Official languages: Comorian (Shikomor); Arabic; French.
Official religion: Islam.
Monetary unit: 1 Comorian franc[4] (CF) = 100 centimes; valuation (Sept. 1, 2005) 1 U.S.$ = CF 392.08; 1 £ = CF 721.93.

Indian Ocean

Area and population		area		population
				2003
Autonomous islands	Capitals	sq mi	sq km	census[5]
Mwali (Mohéli)	Fomboni	112	290	35,400
Ngazidja (Grande Comore)	Moroni	443	1,148	295,700
Nzwani (Anjouan)	Mutsamudu	164	424	259,100
TOTAL		719	1,862	590,200

Demography

Population (2005): 614,000[6].
Density (2005): persons per sq mi 854.0, persons per sq km 329.8.
Urban-rural (2003): urban 35.0%; rural 65.0%.
Sex distribution (2004): male 49.61%; female 50.39%.
Age breakdown (2004): under 15, 42.8%; 15–29, 27.1%; 30–44, 17.3%; 45–59, 8.1%; 60–74, 3.9%; 75 and over, 0.8%.
Population projection: (2010) 684,000; (2020) 850,000.
Doubling time: 23 years.
Ethnic composition (2000): Comorian (a mixture of Bantu, Arab, Malay, and Malagasy peoples) 97.1%; Makua 1.6%; French 0.4%; Arab 0.1%; other 0.8%.
Religious affiliation (2000): Sunnī Muslim 98.0%; Christian 1.2%; other 0.8%.
Major cities (2002): Moroni (2003) 41,557 (urban agglomeration [2003] 53,000); Mutsamudu 21,558; Domoni 13,254; Fomboni 13,053.

Vital statistics

Birth rate per 1,000 population (2004): 38.0 (world avg. 21.1).
Death rate per 1,000 population (2004): 8.6 (world avg. 9.0).
Natural increase rate per 1,000 population (2004): 29.4 (world avg. 12.1).
Total fertility rate (avg. births per childbearing woman; 2004): 5.1.
Marriage rate per 1,000 population: n.a.[7]
Divorce rate per 1,000 population: n.a.
Life expectancy at birth (2004): male 59.3 years; female 63.9 years.
Major causes of death per 100,000 population: n.a.; however, major diseases include malaria (afflicts 80–90% of the adult population), tuberculosis, leprosy, and kwashiorkor (a nutritional deficiency disease).

National economy

Budget (2002). Revenue: CF 22,433,000,000 (tax revenue 60.5%, of which taxes on international trade 39.3%, income and profit taxes 12.9%, sales tax 7.1%; grants 25.7%; nontax revenue 13.8%). Expenditures: CF 29,250,000,000 (current expenditures 70.1%, of which wages 23.7%, goods and services 22.1%, technical assistance 9.9%, interest on debt 5.5%, transfers 3.5%; development expenditures 29.9%).
Production (metric tons except as noted). Agriculture, forestry, fishing (2004): coconuts 77,000, bananas 60,000, cassava 55,000, rice 17,000, taro 9,000, corn (maize) 4,000, cloves 3,000, vanilla 110, ylang-ylang essence (2002) 40; other export crops grown in small quantities include coffee, cinnamon, and tuberoses; livestock (number of live animals; 2004) 115,000 goats, 50,000 cattle, 21,000 sheep; roundwood (2003) 8,650; fish catch (2002) 12,200. Mining and quarrying: sand, gravel, and crushed stone from coral mining for local construction. Manufacturing: products of small-scale industries include processed vanilla and ylang-ylang, cement, handicrafts, soaps, soft drinks, woodwork, and clothing. Energy production (consumption): electricity (kW-hr; 2002) 19,000,000 (19,000,000); coal, none (none); crude petroleum, none (none); petroleum products (metric tons; 2002) none (27,000); natural gas, none (none).
Population economically active (2000): total 156,000; activity rate of total population 28.4% (participation rates: [1991] ages 10 years and over, 57.8%; female 40.0%; unemployed [2002] 32%).

Price index (2000 = 100)						
	1998	1999	2000	2001	2002	2003
Consumer price index	92.2	95.4	100.0	104.6	109.3	114.0

Tourism: receipts from visitors (2002) U.S.$11,000,000; expenditures by nationals abroad (1998) U.S.$3,000,000.
Household income and expenditure. Average household size (1995) 6.3[8]; average annual income per household (1995) CF 188,985 (U.S.$505)[8]; sources of income: n.a.; expenditure (1993)[9]: food and beverages 67.3%, clothing and footwear 11.6%, tobacco and cigarettes 4.1%, energy 3.8%, health 3.2%, education 2.5%, transportation 2.2%, other 5.3%.

Gross national product (2004): U.S.$328,000,000 (U.S.$530 per capita).

Structure of gross domestic product and labour force				
	2002		1980	
	in value CF '000,000	% of total value	labour force[10]	% of labour force[10]
Agriculture, fishing	53,000	41.1	53,063	53.3
Mining	...	...	62	0.1
Manufacturing	5,400	4.2	3,946	4.0
Construction	7,837	6.1	3,267	3.3
Public utilities	2,000	1.5	129	0.1
Transportation and communications	6,652	5.2	2,118	2.1
Trade, restaurants, hotels	33,000	25.6	1,873	1.9
Finance, insurance	5,800	4.5	237	0.2
Public admin., defense	17,949	13.9	2,435	2.5
Services	692	0.5	4,646	4.7
Other	-3,350[11]	-2.6[11]	27,687[12]	27.8[12]
TOTAL	128,980	100.0	99,463	100.0

Public debt (external, outstanding; 2002): U.S.$239,900,000.
Land use as % of total land area (2000)[13]: in temporary crops c. 36%, in permanent crops c. 22%, in pasture c. 7%; overall forest area c. 4%.

Foreign trade[14]

Balance of trade (current prices)						
	1997	1998	1999	2000	2001	2002
CF '000,000,000	-23.6	-19.6	-20.7	-16.7	-18.6	-21.6
% of total	81.8%	78.8%	70.9%	57.0%	50.5%	48.0%

Imports (2002): CF 33,220,000,000 (petroleum products 18.0%, rice 12.4%, meat 7.1%, iron and steel 3.5%, cement 3.3%, unspecified 55.7%). *Major import sources* (2003): France 32.1%; Japan 13.9%; South Africa 10.4%; United Arab Emirates 5.6%; Kenya 5.5%.
Exports (2002): CF 11,662,000,000 (vanilla 61.6%, cloves 24.1%, ylang-ylang 11.6%). *Major export destinations* (2003): France 46.1%; Germany 18.8%; United States 11.4%; Madagascar 5.8%; Singapore 4.3%.

Transport and communications

Transport. Railroads: none. Roads (1999): total length 550 mi, 880 km (paved 77%). Vehicles (1996): passenger cars 9,100; trucks and buses 4,950. Air transport (1996): passenger-mi 1,900,000, passenger-km 3,000,000; short ton-mi cargo, n.a., metric ton-mi cargo, n.a.; airports (2002) with scheduled flights 4.

Communications				units per 1,000
Medium	date	unit	number	persons
Daily newspapers	1997	circulation	0	0
Radio	1997	receivers	90,000	170
Television	1997	receivers	1,000	1.8
Telephones	2003	main lines	13,200	17
Cellular telephones	2003	subscribers	2,000	2.5
Personal computers	2004	units	5,000	6.3
Internet	2004	users	8,000	10

Education and health

Educational attainment (1980). Percentage of population age 25 and over having: no formal schooling 56.7%; Qur'anic school education 8.3%; primary 3.6%; secondary 2.0%; higher 0.2%; not specified 29.2%. *Literacy* (2003): total population age 15 and over literate 56.4%; males literate 63.6%; females literate 49.3%.

Education (1998)	schools	teachers	students	student/ teacher ratio
Primary (age 7–12)	348	2,381	82,789	34.8
Secondary (age 13–19)	...	591	28,599	48.4
Higher	...	67	649	9.7

Health (2004): physicians 48 (1 per 12,417 persons); hospital beds (1995) 1,450[15] (1 per 342[15] persons); infant mortality rate per 1,000 live births (2004) 77.2.
Food (2002): daily per capita caloric intake 1,754 (vegetable products 95%, animal products 5%); 75% of FAO recommended minimum requirement.

Military

Total active duty personnel (2004): the Comoros have a small standing army excluding a 500-member police force and 500-member defense force; France provides training for military personnel. *Military expenditure as percentage of GNP:* n.a.

---

[1]Excludes Mayotte, an overseas possession of France, unless otherwise indicated. [2]In actuality, a loose union of semiautonomous islands. [3]Includes 15 nonelected seats. [4]Formerly pegged to the French franc and since Jan. 1, 2002, to the euro at the rate of €1 = CF 491.97. [5]Preliminary. [6]Excludes Comorians living abroad in France or Mayotte. [7]In the early 1990s, 20% of adult men had more than one wife. [8]Based on sample survey of 2,004 households on all three islands. [9]Weights of consumer price index components for Moroni. [10]The wage labour force was very small in 1995; total of less than 7,000 including government employees, and less than 2,000 excluding them. [11]Less imputed bank service charge. [12]Not adequately defined. [13]Includes Mayotte. [14]Imports c.i.f.; exports f.o.b. [15]Estimated figure.

Internet resources for further information:
• **Indian Ocean Commission http://www.coi-info.org**
• **UN Development Programme http://www.km.undp.org**
• **La Banque de France: La Zone Franc http://www.banque-france.fr/fr/eurosys/zonefr/zonefr.htm**

Congo, Democratic Republic of the

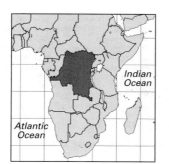

Official name: République Democratique du Congo (Democratic Republic of the Congo).
Form of government: transitional regime[1] with two legislative bodies (Senate [120]; National Assembly [500]).
Head of state and government: President assisted by Vice Presidents[1].
Capital: Kinshasa.
Official languages: French; English.
Official religion: none.
Monetary unit: Congo franc (FC)[2]; valuation (Sept. 1, 2005) 1 U.S.$ = FC 472.50; 1 £ = FC 869.99.

Area and population

Provinces	Capitals	area sq mi	area sq km	population 1998 estimate
Bandundu	Bandundu	114,154	295,658	5,201,000
Bas-Congo	Matadi	20,819	53,920	2,835,000
Equateur	Mbandaka	155,712	403,292	4,820,000
Kasai-Occidental	Kananga	59,746	154,742	3,337,000
Kasai-Oriental	Mbuji-Mayi	65,754	170,302	3,830,000
Katanga	Lubumbashi	191,845	496,877	4,125,000
Maniema	Kindu	51,062	132,250	1,246,787
Nord-Kivu	Goma	22,967	59,483	3,564,434
Orientale	Kisangani	194,302	503,239	5,566,000
Sud-Kivu	Bukavu	25,147	65,130	2,837,779
City				
Kinshasa	—	3,848	9,965	4,787,000
TOTAL		905,354[3]	2,344,858	42,150,000

Demography

Population (2005): 57,549,000.
Density (2005): persons per sq mi 63.6, persons per sq km 24.5.
Urban-rural (2003): urban 31.6%; rural 68.4%.
Sex distribution (2002): male 49.38%; female 50.62%.
Age breakdown (2002): under 15, 48.3%; 15–29, 27.2%; 30–44, 13.6%; 45–59, 6.9%; 60–74, 3.2%; 75 and over, 0.8%.
Population projection: (2010) 67,129,000; (2020) 90,022,000.
Ethnic composition (1983): Luba 18.0%; Kongo 16.1%; Mongo 13.5%; Rwanda 10.3%; Azande 6.1%; Bangi and Ngale 5.8%; Rundi 3.8%; Teke 2.7%; Boa 2.3%; Chokwe 1.8%; Lugbara 1.6%; Banda 1.4%; other 16.6%.
Religious affiliation (2004): Roman Catholic c. 50%; Protestant c. 20%; Kimbanguist (indigenous Christian) c. 10%; Muslim c. 10%; traditional beliefs and syncretic sects c. 10%.
Major cities (1994): Kinshasa 4,655,313; Lubumbashi 851,381; Mbuji-Mayi 806,475; Kolwezi 417,800; Kisangani 417,517; Kananga 393,030.

Vital statistics

Birth rate per 1,000 population (2004): 44.4 (world avg. 21.1).
Death rate per 1,000 population (2004): 13.8 (world avg. 9.0).
Natural increase rate per 1,000 population (2004): 30.6 (world avg. 12.1).
Total fertility rate (avg. births per childbearing woman; 2004): 6.6.
Life expectancy at birth (2004): male 49.3 years; female 52.2 years.
Adult population (ages 15–49) *living with HIV* (beginning of 2004): 4.2% (world avg. 1.1%).

National economy

Budget (2003). Revenue: FC 223,323,000,000,000 (tax revenue 54.4%, of which taxes on international trade 32.5%; grants 20.8%; petroleum revenue 16.3%; other nontax revenue 8.5%). Expenditures: FC 312,270,000,000,000 (current expenditure 79.5%, of which interest on debt 25.3%; wages and salaries 18.3%; capital expenditure 19.8%; other 0.7%).
Public debt (external, outstanding; 2003): U.S.$10,077,000,000.
Production (metric tons except as noted). Agriculture, forestry, fishing (2004): cassava 14,950,000, sugarcane 1,787,300, plantains 1,250,000, corn (maize) 1,155,030, oil palm fruit 1,150,000, peanuts (groundnuts) 363,850, yams 330,000, rice 315,130, bananas 315,000, sweet potatoes 224,450, papayas 211,000, mangoes 200,000, pineapples 193,000, oranges 180,000, dried beans 109,340, coffee 33,000, seed cotton 30,000, natural rubber 7,000; livestock (number of live animals) 4,004,000 goats, 953,000 pigs; roundwood (2003) 72,170,264 cu m; fish catch (2003) 220,000. Mining and quarrying (2003–04): copper (metal content) 10,451; cobalt (metal content) 3,735; tantalum 25[4]; silver 35,500 kg[4]; diamonds 27,000,000 carats[4]. Manufacturing (2001): butter 2,052,000[5]; explosives 246,000[5]; cement 201,000[5]; steel 159,000[5]; sugar 73,000[5]; soap 15,000; printed fabrics 3,600,000 sq m; cotton fabrics 2,353,000 sq m; beer 1,550,000 hectolitres; soft drinks 640,000 hectolitres. Energy production (consumption): electricity (kW-hr; 2003–04) 6,221,000,000 ([2002] 4,670,000,000); coal (metric tons; 2002) 97,000 (134,000); crude petroleum (barrels; 2003–04) 9,600,000 ([2001] 780,000); petroleum products (metric tons; 2002) none (276,000); natural gas, none (none).
Household income and expenditure. Average household size (1998) 2.3; expenditure (1995)[6]: food 61.4%, housing and energy 13.9%, clothing and footwear 4.8%, other 19.9%.
Gross national product (2004): U.S.$6,538,000,000 (U.S.$120 per capita).

Structure of gross domestic product and labour force

	2001 in value FC '000,000	2001 % of total value	2002 labour force	2002 % of labour force
Agriculture	824,300	56.3	13,340,000	62.3
Mining	142,000	9.7		
Manufacturing	57,100	3.9		
Construction	64,400	4.4		
Public utilities	11,700	0.8		
Transp. and commun.	39,500	2.7	8,086,000	37.7
Trade	218,200	14.9		
Pub. admin., defense	26,400	1.8		
Finance and services	60,200	4.1		
Other	20,200[7]	1.4[7]		
TOTAL	1,464,000	100.0	21,426,000	100.0

Population economically active (2000): total 20,686,000; activity rate 42.6% (participation rates: over age 10, n.a.; female, n.a.; unemployed, n.a.).

Price index (2000 = 100)

	1998	1999	2000	2001	2002	2003	2004
Consumer price index	4.0	15.4	100.0	413.7	571.3	644.6	670.9

Tourism (1998): receipts U.S.$2,000,000; expenditures (1997) U.S.$7,000,000.
Land use as % of total land area (2000): in temporary crops 3.0%, in permanent crops 0.5%, in pasture 6.6%; overall forest area 59.6%.

Foreign trade

Balance of trade (current prices)

	1999	2000	2001	2002	2003	2004
U.S.$'000,000	+516	+217	+73	−17	−156	−243
% of total	36.0%	13.8%	4.3%	0.8%	5.5%	6.3%

Imports (2004): U.S.$2,056,000,000 (aid-related imports 14.9%, other imports 85.1%). *Major import sources:* South Africa 18.5%; Belgium 15.6%; France 10.9%; U.S. 6.2%; Germany 5.9%; Kenya 4.9%.
Exports (2004): U.S.$1,813,000,000 (diamonds 47.3%, crude petroleum 19.9%, cobalt 15.0%, copper 3.3%, coffee 0.9%, gold 0.7%). *Major export destinations:* Belgium 42.5%; Finland 17.8%; Zimbabwe 12.2%; U.S. 9.2%; China 6.5%.

Transport and communications

Transport. Railroads (2002): length 3,641 km; passenger-km 160,000,000; metric ton-km cargo 429,000,000. Roads (1999): total length 157,000 km (paved c. 2%). Vehicles (1996): passenger cars 787,000; trucks and buses 598,000. Air transport (1999): passenger-km 263,000,000; metric ton-km cargo 39,000,000; airports (1997) with scheduled flights 22.

Communications

Medium	date	unit	number	units per 1,000 persons
Daily newspapers	1998	circulation	136,000	2.8
Radio	2001	receivers	19,688,000	386
Television	1997	receivers	6,478,000	135
Telephones	2002	main lines	10,000	0.2
Cellular telephones	2003	subscribers	1,000,000	19
Personal computers	1999	units	500,000	10.2
Internet	2002	users	50,000	0.9

Education and health

Educational attainment: n.a. Literacy (2002–03): percentage of total population age 15 and over literate 65.6%; males literate 79.8%; females literate 51.9%.

Education (1998)

	schools	teachers	students	student/ teacher ratio
Primary (age 6–11)	17,585	154,618	4,022,411	26.0
Secondary (age 12–17) } Voc., teacher tr.	6,007	89,461	1,234,528	13.8
Higher	...	3,788	60,341	15.9

Health: physicians (1996) 3,129 (1 per 14,494 persons); hospital beds, n.a.; infant mortality rate per 1,000 live births (2004) 92.6.
Food (2002): daily per capita caloric intake 1,599 (vegetable products 98%, animal products 2%); 72% of FAO recommended minimum requirement.

Military

Total active duty personnel (2004): 64,800 (army 92.6%, air force 4.6%, navy 2.8%); UN peacekeepers (April 2005): 15,800 troops. *Military expenditure as percentage of GDP:* n.a.

---

[1]Per transitional constitution promulgated April 2004. Transitional government to end pending approval of new constitution by referendum on Dec. 18, 2005, and legislative and executive elections in mid-2006. [2]The Congo franc (FC) replaced the new zaïre (NZ) at a rate of FC 1 to NZ 100,000 on July 1, 1998. [3]Detail does not add to total given because of rounding. [4]2003. [5]2000. [6]Weights of consumer price index components. [7]Import duties.

Internet resources for further information:
• **Permanent Mission of the Democratic Republic of the Congo**
  http://www.un.int/drcongo
• **Central Bank of the Democratic Republic of the Congo**
  http://www.bcc.cd/go.html

Congo, Republic of the

Official name: République du Congo (Republic of the Congo).
Form of government: republic with two legislative houses (Senate [66[1]]; National Assembly [137[1]]).
Chief of state and government: President.
Capital: Brazzaville.
Official language: French[2].
Official religion: none.
Monetary unit: 1 CFA franc (CFAF) = 100 centimes; valuation (Sept. 1, 2005) 1 U.S.$ = CFAF 522.78; 1 £ = CFAF 962.57[3].

Area and population

Regions	Capitals	area sq mi	area sq km	population 2005 estimate[4]
Bouenza	Madingou	4,733	12,258	229,820
Cuvette	Owando	18,861	48,850	135,767
Cuvette-Ouest	Ewo	10,039	26,000	55,765
Kouilou	Pointe-Noire	5,270	13,650	80,951
Lékoumou	Sibiti	8,089	20,950	81,672
Likouala	Impfondo	25,500	66,044	84,513
Niari	Dolisie	10,007	25,918	105,147
Plateaux	Djambala	14,826	38,400	170,978
Pool	Kinkala	13,110	33,955	362,357
Sangha	Ouesso	21,542	55,795	46,727
Communes				
Brazzaville	—	39	100	1,174,005
Dolisie	—	7	18	106,262
Mossendjo	—	2	5	18,209
Nkayi	—	3	8	56,686
Ouesso	—	2	5	24,322
Pointe-Noire	—	17	44	663,359
TOTAL		132,047	342,000	3,396,540

Demography

Population (2005): 3,602,000[5].
Density (2005): persons per sq mi 27.3, persons per sq km 10.5.
Urban-rural (2003): urban 53.5%; rural 46.5%.
Sex distribution (2004): male 49.62%; female 50.38%.
Age breakdown (2004): under 15, 46.6%; 15–29, 26.8%; 30–44, 14.9%; 45–59, 7.3%; 60–74, 3.5%; 75 and over, 0.9%.
Population projection: (2010) 4,124,000; (2020) 5,445,000.
Doubling time: 24 years.
Ethnic composition (2000): Kongo 21.2%; Yombe 11.5%; Teke 10.7%; Kougni 8.0%; Mboshi 5.4%; Ngala 4.2%; Sundi 4.0%; other 35.0%.
Religious affiliation (2000): Roman Catholic 49.3%; Protestant 17.0%; African Christian 12.6%; unaffiliated Christian 11.9%; traditional beliefs 4.8%; other 4.4%.
Major cities (1992): Brazzaville (urban agglomeration; 2003) 1,080,000; Pointe-Noire (1996) 455,131; Dolisie 83,605; Nkayi 42,465; Mossendjo 16,405.

Vital statistics

Birth rate per 1,000 population (2004): 43.4 (world avg. 21.1).
Death rate per 1,000 population (2004): 13.7 (world avg. 9.0).
Natural increase rate per 1,000 population (2004): 29.7 (world avg. 12.1).
Total fertility rate (avg. births per childbearing woman; 2004): 6.2.
Life expectancy at birth (2004): male 50.7 years; female 52.8 years.
Adult population (ages 15–49) *living with HIV* (beginning of 2004): 4.9% (world avg. 1.1%).

National economy

Budget (2003). Revenue: CFAF 613,500,000,000 (petroleum revenue 68.7%; nonpetroleum receipts 29.7%, of which taxes 21.8%; grants 1.6%). Expenditures: CFAF 606,100,000,000 (current expenditure 77.7%, of which transfers 21.6%, wages and salaries 19.9%, interest 19.5%; capital expenditure 22.3%).
Public debt (external, outstanding; 2003): U.S.$4,426,000,000.
Household income and expenditure. Average household size (2000) 5.9.
Gross national product (2004): U.S.$2,974,000,000 (U.S.$770 per capita).

Structure of gross domestic product and labour force

	2003 in value CFAF '000,000	2003 % of total value	1991 labour force	1991 % of labour force
Agriculture, forestry, fishing	128,000	6.3	471,000	59.1
Petroleum	1,003,400	49.2		
Manufacturing, mining	131,900	6.5	101,000	12.7
Construction	89,400	4.4		
Public utilities	19,700	1.0		
Trade	180,600	8.8		
Transp. and commun.	137,400	6.7	225,000	28.2
Pub. admin., defense	148,400	7.3		
Services	124,900	6.1		
Other	76,300[6]	3.7[6]	—	—
TOTAL	2,040,000	100.0	797,000	100.0

Production (metric tons except as noted). Agriculture, forestry, fishing (2004): cassava 880,000, sugarcane 460,000, oil palm fruit 90,000, bananas 85,000, plantains 71,000, mangoes 25,000, peanuts (groundnuts) 24,000, coffee 1,700, cacao beans 1,260, rubber 1,200; livestock (number of live animals) 294,000 goats, 123,000 cattle, 97,000 sheep; roundwood (2003) 2,453,000 cu m; fish

catch (2002) 43,000. Mining and quarrying (2003): gold 30 kg; diamonds, no reported production[7]. Manufacturing (2001): residual fuel oil 206,000[8]; refined sugar 71,814; distillate fuel oils 62,000[8]; gasoline 40,000[8]; aviation gas 38,000[8]; wheat flour 35,000; kerosene 21,000[8]; soap 1,620[8]; cigarettes 4,000,000 cartons; beer 610,000 hectolitres; nonalcoholic drinks 349,000 hectolitres; veneer sheets 12,000 cu m. Energy production (consumption): electricity (kW-hr; 2002) 399,000,000 (763,000,000); crude petroleum (barrels; 2003) 81,800,000 ([2002] 6,300,000); petroleum products (metric tons; 2002) 409,000 (181,000); natural gas (cu m; 2002) 127,000,000 (127,000,000).
Population economically active (2000): total 1,232,000; activity rate of total population 35.7% (participation rates [1984]: ages 15–64, 54.0%; female [1997] 43.4%; unemployed, n.a.).

Price index (2000 = 100)

	1998	1999	2000	2001	2002	2003	2004
Consumer price index	95.7	100.9	100.0	100.1	104.7	103.8	106.3

Land use as % of total land area (2000): in temporary crops 0.5%, in permanent crops 0.1%, in pasture 29.3%, overall forest area 64.6%.
Tourism (2003): receipts U.S.$20,000,000; expenditures U.S.$53,000,000.

Foreign trade

Balance of trade (current prices)

	1998	1999	2000	2001	2002	2003
CFAF '000,000,000	+478.5	+636.2	+1,319.7	+1,007.1	+1,075.1	+1,003.8
% of total	42.1%	49.7%	60.9%	50.2%	52.2%	51.5%

Imports (2003): CFAF 471,800,000,000 (non-petroleum sector 67.9%; government 17.2%; petroleum sector 14.9%). *Major import sources* (1999): France c. 23%; U.S. c. 8%; Italy c. 8%; Hong Kong c. 5%; Belgium c. 4%.
Exports (2003): CFAF 1,475,600,000,000 (crude petroleum 75.2%, wood and wood products 12.0%, sugar 0.9%). *Major export destinations* (1999): Taiwan c. 32%; U.S. c. 23%; South Korea c. 15%; Germany c. 7%; China c. 3%.

Transport and communications

Transport. Railroads: (1998) length 894 km; passenger-km 242,000,000; metric ton-km cargo 135,000,000. Roads (2001): total length 17,244 km (paved 7%). Vehicles (1997): passenger cars 37,240; trucks and buses 15,500. Air transport: n.a.; airports (1998) with scheduled flights 10.

Communications

Medium	date	unit	number	units per 1,000 persons
Daily newspapers	2000	circulation	10,300	3.0
Radio	2000	receivers	403,300	109
Television	2000	receivers	114,000	13
Telephones	2003	main lines	7,000	2.0
Cellular telephones	2004	subscribers	442,200	116
Personal computers	2004	units	17,000	4.5
Internet	2004	users	45,000	12

Education and health

Educational attainment (1984). Percentage of population age 25 and over having: no formal schooling 58.7%; primary education 21.4%; secondary education 16.9%; postsecondary 3.0%. *Literacy* (2002): total population age 15 and over literate 82.8%; males literate 88.9%; females literate 77.1%.

Education (1998)

	schools	teachers	students	student/ teacher ratio
Primary (age 6–13)	1,168	4,515	270,451	59.9
Secondary (age 14–18)	...	5,094	114,450	22.5
Voc., teacher tr.[9]	...	1,746	23,606	13.5
Higher	...	1,341[9]	16,862	12.4

Health: physicians (1995) 632 (1 per 4,083 persons); hospital beds (1989) 4,817 (1 per 446 persons); infant mortality rate per 1,000 live births (2004) 89.5.
Food (2002): daily per capita caloric intake 2,162 (vegetable products 94%, animal products 6%); 97% of FAO recommended minimum requirement.

Military

Total active duty personnel (2004): 10,000 (army 80.0%, navy 8.0%, air force 12.0%). *Military expenditure as percentage of GDP* (2003): 1.4%; per capita expenditure U.S.$14.

---

[1]Includes vacant seats. [2]"Functional" national languages are Lingala and Monokutuba. [3]Formerly pegged to the French franc and since Jan. 1, 2002, to the euro at a rate of €1 = CFAF 655.96. [4]January 1st projection of the Congolese statistical office. [5]Estimate of U.S. Bureau of the Census International Database. [6]Import duties. [7]Annual volume of large-scale diamond smuggling as of July 2004 equaled 5,200,000 carats. [8]2000. [9]1996–97.

Internet resources for further information:
• La Banque de France: La Zone Franc
  http://www.banque-france.fr/fr/eurosys/zonefr/zonefr.htm

Costa Rica

Official name: República de Costa Rica (Republic of Costa Rica).
Form of government: unitary multiparty republic with one legislative house (Legislative Assembly [57]).
Head of state and government: President.
Capital: San José.
Official language: Spanish.
Official religion: Roman Catholicism.
Monetary unit: 1 Costa Rican colón (₡) = 100 céntimos; valuation (Sept. 1, 2005) 1 U.S.$ = ₡484.60; 1 £ = ₡892.27.

Area and population

Provinces	Capitals	area sq mi	area sq km	population 2004[1] estimate
Alajuela	Alajuela	3,766	9,753	783,116
Cartago	Cartago	1,207	3,125	469,982
Guanacaste	Liberia	3,915	10,141	288,448
Heredia	Heredia	1,026	2,657	386,259
Limón	Limón	3,547	9,188	376,209
Puntarenas	Puntarenas	4,354	11,277	393,226
San José	San José	1,915	4,959	1,462,517
TOTAL		19,730	51,100	4,159,757

Demography

Population (2005): 4,221,000.
Density (2005): persons per sq mi 213.9, persons per sq km 82.6.
Urban-rural (2003): urban 60.6%; rural 39.4%.
Sex distribution (2004): male 50.52%; female 49.48%.
Age breakdown (2004): under 15, 29.5%; 15–29, 27.4%; 30–44, 21.7%; 45–59, 13.4%; 60–74, 5.9%; 75 and over, 2.1%.
Population projection: (2010) 4,538,000; (2020) 5,095,000.
Doubling time: 48 years.
Ethnic composition (2000): white 77.0%; mestizo 17.0%; black/mulatto 3.0%; East Asian (mostly Chinese) 2.0%; Amerindian 1.0%.
Religious affiliation (2000): Roman Catholic 91.0%; Protestant 8.1%, of which Pentecostal 5.5%; other 0.9%.
Major cities (2000): San José 309,672[2] (urban agglomeration 983,000[3]); Limón 60,298[4]; Alajuela 42,889[4]; San Isidro de El General 41,221[4]; Cartago 39,958[5]; Liberia 39,242[4].

Vital statistics

Birth rate per 1,000 population (2004): 19.0 (world avg. 21.1); (2003) legitimate 44.4%; illegitimate 55.6%.
Death rate per 1,000 population (2004): 4.3 (world avg. 9.0).
Natural increase rate per 1,000 population (2004): 14.7 (world avg. 12.1).
Total fertility rate (avg. births per childbearing woman; 2004): 2.3.
Marriage rate per 1,000 population (2004): 6.0.
Divorce rate per 1,000 population (1998): 2.2.
Life expectancy at birth (2004): male 74.1 years; female 79.3 years.
Major causes of death per 100,000 population (2002): diseases of the circulatory system 123.2; malignant neoplasms (cancers) 112.3; accidents and violence 45.4; communicable diseases 22.5.

National economy

Budget (2002). Revenue: ₡808,802,000,000 (taxes on goods and services 63.5%, income tax 22.9%, import duties 7.0%, other 6.6%). Expenditures: ₡1,068,-113,500,000 (current expenditures 91.6%, of which transfers 30.1%, wages 29.5%, interest on debt 24.3%; development expenditures 8.4%).
Public debt (external, outstanding; 2003): U.S.$3,622,000,000.
Gross national product (2004): U.S.$18,969,000,000 (U.S.$4,670 per capita).

Structure of gross domestic product and labour force

	2002 in value ₡'000,000	2002 % of total value	2003 labour force	2003 % of labour force
Agriculture, forestry, fishing	462,705	7.6	260,734	14.8
Mining	9,193	0.2	2,486	0.1
Manufacturing	1,182,910	19.5	244,710	13.9
Construction	255,213	4.2	121,861	6.9
Public utilities	147,646	2.4	22,567	1.3
Transp. and commun.	479,346	7.9	96,683	5.5
Trade, restaurants	1,069,110	17.6	438,964	25.0
Finance, real estate	799,075	13.2	145,327	8.3
Public administration	238,403	3.9	79,222	4.5
Services	1,066,068	17.6	312,444	17.8
Other	348,513[6]	5.8[6]	32,580[7]	1.9[7]
TOTAL	6,058,182	100.0[8]	1,757,578	100.0

Production (metric tons except as noted). Agriculture, forestry, fishing (2004): sugarcane 3,945,000, bananas 1,863,000, pineapples 725,000, oil palm fruit 700,000, oranges 367,000, rice 222,000, cantaloupes/other melons 215,000, green coffee 126,000, potatoes 80,000, cassava 71,000; livestock (number of live animals) 1,080,900 cattle, 500,000 pigs, 18,500,000 chickens; roundwood (2003) 5,140,781 cu m; fish catch (2002) 33,000. Mining and quarrying (2003): limestone 920,000; gold 110 kg. Manufacturing (value added in U.S.$'000,000; 2001): food products 777; beverages 211; paints, soaps, and pharmaceuticals 148; plastic products 111; paper and paper products 100; bricks, tiles, and cement 93; industrial chemicals 72. Energy production (consumption): elec-

---

tricity (kW-hr; 2002) 7,473,000,000 (7,055,000,000); coal, none (none); crude petroleum (barrels; 2002) none (3,500,000); petroleum products (metric tons; 2002) 393,000 (1,635,000); natural gas, none (none).
Population economically active (2003): total 1,757,578; activity rate of total population 43.0% (participation rates: ages 12–59, 59.4%; female 35.4%; unemployed [July 2003] 6.7%[9]).

Price and earnings indexes (2000 = 100)

	1998	1999	2000	2001	2002	2003	2004
Consumer price index	81.9	90.1	100.0	111.2	121.4	132.9	149.2
Monthly earnings index	81.1	89.6	100.0	124.2	...	...	...

Tourism (2003): receipts U.S.$1,293,000,000; expenditures U.S.$353,000,000.
Household income and expenditure. Average household size (2004) 3.8; average annual household income (2004) ₡3,267,648 (U.S.$7,125); sources of income (1987–88): wages and salaries 61.0%, self-employment 22.6%, transfers 9.6%; expenditure (1987–88): food and beverages 39.1%, housing and energy 12.1%, transportation 11.6%, household furnishings 10.9%.
Land use as % of total land area (2000): in temporary crops 4.4%, in permanent crops 5.9%, in pasture 45.8%; overall forest area 38.5%.

Foreign trade[10]

Balance of trade (current prices)[11]

	1999	2000	2001	2002	2003	2004
U.S.$'000,000	+308	−539	−1,548	−1,944	−1,561	−1,971
% of total	2.4%	4.4%	13.4%	16.4%	11.3%	13.5%

Imports (2002): U.S.$6,894,000,000 (machinery and apparatus 35.7%, of which electronic microcircuits 12.8%; chemicals and chemical products 13.8%; mineral fuels 6.7%; food 6.4%). *Major import sources* (2003): U.S. 33.2%; Japan 4.2%; Mexico 4.1%; Venezuela 3.4%; Israel 2.9%.
Exports (2002): U.S.$4,950,000,000 (food 30.2%, of which bananas 9.7%; machinery and apparatus 28.5%, of which office machine/computer parts 18.1%; wearing apparel 8.0%). *Major export destinations* (2003): U.S. 25.1%; The Netherlands 6.9%; U.K. 5.0%; Mexico 4.1%; China 3.9%.

Transport and communications

Transport. Railroads[12]. Roads (2002): total length 21,936 mi, 35,303 km (paved 12%). Vehicles (2002): passenger cars 367,832; trucks and buses 204,206. Air transport (2003)[13]: passenger-mi 1,028,000,000, passenger-km 1,654,000,000; short-ton mi cargo 6,175,000, metric ton-km cargo 9,735,000; airports (1996) 14.

Communications

Medium	date	unit	number	units per 1,000 persons
Daily newspapers	2004	circulation	275,000	65
Radio	2000	receivers	3,200,000	816
Television	2000	receivers	907,000	231
Telephones	2004	main lines	1,343,200	316
Cellular telephones	2004	subscribers	923,100	217
Personal computers	2004	units	1,014,000	239
Internet	2004	users	1,000,000	235

Education and health

Educational attainment (2004). Percentage of population age 5 and over having: no formal schooling 9.9%; incomplete primary education 23.3%; complete primary 24.5%; incomplete secondary 18.2%; complete secondary 8.5%; higher 12.7%; other/unknown 2.9%. *Literacy* (2002): total population age 15 and over literate 95.8%; males literate 95.7%; females literate 95.9%.

Education (1999)

	schools	teachers	students	student/ teacher ratio
Primary (age 7–12)	3,768	20,185	535,057	26.5
Secondary (age 13–17)	468	11,891	235,425	19.8
Higher	52	...	59,947	...

Health (2004): physicians 6,600 (1 per 644 persons); hospital beds (2003) 6,000 (1 per 700 persons); infant mortality rate per 1,000 live births 10.3.
Food (2002): daily per capita caloric intake 2,876 (vegetable products 80%, animal products 20%); 128% of FAO recommended minimum requirement.

Military

Paramilitary expenditure as percentage of GDP (2003): 0.6%; per capita expenditure U.S.$24. The army was officially abolished in 1948. Paramilitary (police) forces had 8,400 members in 2002.

---

[1]July 1. [2]Population of San José canton. [3]2001 estimate. [4]District population. [5]Population of three districts. [6]Taxes less subsidies and imputed bank service charges. [7]Includes 7,866 not adequately defined and 22,093 unemployed, not previously employed. [8]Detail does not add to total given because of rounding. [9]Ages 12 and over. [10]Imports c.i.f.; exports f.o.b. [11]Includes goods imported for reassembly and reexported. [12]National rail service was not in regular service from 1995 through 2000. [13]Lacsa (Costa Rican Airlines) only.

Internet resources for further information:
- **Central Bank of Costa Rica: Economic Indicators** http://websiec.bccr.fi.cr
- **Government of Costa Rica** http://www.casapres.go.cr
- **National Institute of Statistics and the Census** http://www.inec.go.cr

Côte d'Ivoire

Atlantic Ocean

Gulf of Guinea

Official name: République de Côte d'Ivoire (Republic of Côte d'Ivoire [Ivory Coast][1]).
Form of government: transitional regime[2] with one legislative house (National Assembly [223])[3].
Chief of state and government: Interim Prime Minister assisted by interim President[2].
De facto capital: Abidjan.
Official language: French.
Official religion: none.
Monetary unit: 1 CFA franc (CFAF) = 100 centimes; valuation (Sept. 1, 2005) 1 U.S.$ = CFAF 522.78; 1 £ = CFAF 962.57[4].

Area and population		area		population
Regions	Capitals	sq mi	sq km	2002 estimate
Agnebi	Agboville	3,510	9,080	720,900
Bafing	Touba	3,370	8,720	178,400
Bas-Sassandra	San-Pédro	9,960	25,800	443,200
Denguélé	Odienné	7,950	20,600	277,000
Dix-huit Montagnes	Man	6,410	16,600	1,125,800
Fromager	Gagnoa	2,660	6,900	679,900
Haut-Sassandra	Daloa	5,870	15,200	1,186,600
Lacs	Yamoussoukro	3,450	8,940	597,500
Lagunes	Abidjan	5,480	14,200	4,210,200
Marahoué	Bouaflé	3,280	8,500	651,700
Moyen-Cavally	Guiglo	5,460	14,150	443,200
Moyen-Comoé	Abengourou	2,660	6,900	488,200
N'zi-Comoé	Dimbokro	7,550	19,560	909,800
Savanes	Korhogo	15,570	40,323	1,215,100
Sud-Bandama	Divo	4,110	10,650	826,300
Sud-Comoé	Aboisso	2,410	6,250	536,500
Vallée du Bandama	Bouaké	11,020	28,530	1,335,500
Worodougou	Séguéla	8,460	21,900	400,200
Zanzan	Bondoukou	14,670	38,000	839,000
TOTAL		123,863[5]	320,803	17,065,000

Demography

Population (2005): 17,298,000.
Density (2005): persons per sq mi 139.7, persons per sq km 53.9.
Urban-rural (2003): urban 44.9%; rural 55.1%.
Sex distribution (2002): male 50.28%; female 49.72%.
Age breakdown (2002): under 15, 45.6%; 15–29, 28.7%; 30–44, 14.4%; 45–59, 7.6%; 60–74, 3.0%; 75 and over, 0.7%.
Population projection: (2010) 19,093,000; (2020) 22,650,000.
Doubling time: 58 years.
Ethnolinguistic composition (1998)[6]: Akan 42.1%; Mande 26.5%; other 31.4%.
Religious affiliation (1998): Muslim 38.6%; Christian 30.4%; nonreligious 16.7%; animist 11.9%; other 2.4%.
Major cities (2003): Abidjan (agglomeration) 4,113,600; Bouaké 600,000; Yamoussoukro 185,600; Daloa 135,000; Korhogo 115,000.

Vital statistics

Birth rate per 1,000 population (2004): 35.9 (world avg. 21.1).
Death rate per 1,000 population (2004): 15.0 (world avg. 9.0).
Natural increase rate per 1,000 population (2004): 20.9 (world avg. 12.1).
Total fertility rate (avg. births per childbearing woman; 2004): 4.7.
Life expectancy at birth (2004): male 45.9 years; female 51.1 years.
Adult population (ages 15–49) *living with HIV* (2004[7]): 7.0% (world avg. 1.1%).

National economy

Budget (2003). Revenue: CFAF 1,379,500,000,000 (tax revenue 86.4%; nontax revenue 11.2%; grants 2.4%). Expenditures: CFAF 1,631,100,000,000 (wages and salaries 33.1%; debt service 13.3%; capital expenditure 12.0%; other 41.6%).
Production (metric tons except as noted). Agriculture, forestry, fishing (2004): yams 3,000,000, cassava 1,700,000, plantains 1,420,000, oil palm fruit 1,400,000, cacao beans 1,000,000, sugarcane 930,000, rice 820,000, corn (maize) 625,000, taro 370,000, cotton seed 320,000, bananas 270,000, pineapples 225,000, rubber 123,000, coffee 120,000; livestock (number of live animals) 1,523,000 sheep, 1,192,000 goats, 1,111,000 cattle; roundwood (2003) 11,615,380 cu m; fish catch (2003) 68,903. Mining and quarrying (2003): gold 1,313 kg; diamonds 230,000 carats. Manufacturing (value added in CFAF '000,000,000; 1997): food 156.6, of which cocoa and chocolate 72.4, vegetable oils 62.7; chemicals 60.2; wood products 55.9; refined petroleum 46.0; textiles 37.9; tobacco 27.6. Energy production (consumption): electricity (kW-hr; 2002) 4,788,000,000 (3,223,000,000); crude petroleum (barrels; 2002) 5,500,000 (22,000,000); petroleum products (metric tons; 2002) 2,643,000 (1,010,000); natural gas (cu m; 2003) 1,457,000,000 (1,303,000,000).
Tourism: receipts (2002) U.S.$50,000,000; expenditures (2001) U.S.$192,000,000.
Population economically active (2000): total 6,531,000; activity rate of total population 40.9% (participation rates [1994]: over ages 10, 64.3%; female 33.0%; unemployed [1996] 38.8%).

Price index (2000 = 100)							
	1998	1999	2000	2001	2002	2003	2004
Consumer price index	96.8	97.6	100.0	104.3	107.5	111.1	112.7

Household income and expenditure. Average household size (2002) 8.1; expenditure (1996)[8]: food 32.2%, housing and energy 13.9%, hotels and restaurants 12.3%, transportation 9.6%, clothing 7.4%, household equipment 5.7%.
Gross national product (2004): U.S.$13,414,000,000 (U.S.$770 per capita).

Structure of gross domestic product and labour force				
	2002			
	in value CFAF '000,000,000	% of total value	labour force	% of labour force
Agriculture	2,048.1	25.1	3,127,000	47.0
Mining	45.5	0.6		
Manufacturing	1,412.1	17.3		
Public utilities	179.0	2.2		
Construction	212.0	2.6		
Transp. and commun.	503.1	6.2	3,524,000	53.0
Trade	1,075.6	13.2		
Public admin., defense	1,063.4	13.0		
Services	1,059.6	13.0		
Other (customs receipts)	568.5	7.0		
TOTAL	8,166.9	100.0[5]	6,651,000	100.0

Public debt (external, outstanding; 2003): U.S.$9,701,000,000.
Land use as % of total land area (2000): in temporary crops 9.7%, in permanent crops 13.8%, in pasture 40.9%; overall forest area 22.4%.

Foreign trade[9]

Balance of trade (current prices)						
	1998	1999	2000	2001	2002	2003
CFAF '000,000,000	+1,015	+1,167	+1,058	+1,123	+1,965	+1,467
% of total	23.0%	25.5%	23.6%	24.1%	36.5%	27.5%

Imports (2002): CFAF 1,811,500,000,000 (crude and refined petroleum 20.6%, machinery and transport equipment 20.2%, food products 20.1%, chemicals and chemical products 17.2%). *Major import sources* (2003): France 34.6%; Nigeria 15.3%; U.K. 7.4%; China 3.7%; The Netherlands 3.5%.
Exports (2002): CFAF 3,465,400,000,000 (cocoa beans and products 44.3%, crude petroleum and petroleum products 11.3%, machinery and transport equipment 8.9%, wood and wood products 5.1%, coffee 2.4%). *Major export destinations* (2003): France 17.9%; The Netherlands 16.7%; U.S. 6.7%; Spain 5.3%; Italy 3.2%; U.K. 2.9%.

Transport and communications

Transport. Railroads (1999): route length (2002) 639 km; passenger-km 93,100,000; metric ton-km cargo 537,600,000. Roads (1999): total length 50,400 km (paved 9.7%). Vehicles (1999): passenger cars 109,600; trucks and buses 54,100. Air transport (1999): passenger-km 381,000,000; metric ton-km cargo, n.a.; airports (2004) 7.

Communications				units per 1,000 persons
Medium	date	unit	number	
Daily newspapers	2000	circulation	1,440,000	91
Radio	2001	receivers	3,053,000	185
Television	2002	receivers	1,007,000	61
Telephones	2003	main lines	238,000	14
Cellular telephones	2004	subscribers	1,531,800	91
Personal computers	2004	units	262,000	16
Internet	2004	users	300,000	18

Education and health

Educational attainment (1988). Percentage of population age 6 and over having: no formal schooling 60.0%; Qur'anic school 3.6%; primary education 24.8%; secondary 10.7%; higher 0.9%. *Literacy* (2003): percentage of population age 15 and over literate 50.9%; males 57.9%; females 43.6%.

Education (2001–02)	schools	teachers	students	student/teacher ratio
Primary (age 7–12)	7,599[10]	40,529[10]	2,113,836	...
Secondary (age 13–19)	147[10]	15,959[10]	682,461	...
Vocational[11]	...	1,424	11,037	7.8
Higher	7[11]	1,657[11]	87,565[12]	...

Health: physicians (2001) 1,113 (1 per 14,297 persons); hospital beds (2001) 5,981 (1 per 2,660 persons); infant mortality rate (2004) 92.5.
Food (2002): daily per capita caloric intake 2,631 (vegetable products 96%, animal products 4%); 114% of FAO recommended minimum requirement.

Military

Total active duty personnel: [13]. *Military expenditure as percentage of GDP* (2003): 1.5%; per capita expenditure U.S.$13.

[1]Since 1986, Côte d'Ivoire has requested that the French form of the country's name be used as the official protocol version in all languages. [2]Expect transitional government from December 2005 to October 2006. [3]Côte d'Ivoire has been split between a government-controlled south and a rebel-held north from September 2002 through early December 2005. [4]Formerly pegged to the French franc and since Jan. 1, 2002, to the euro at the rate of €1 = CFAF 655.96. [5]Detail does not add to total given because of rounding. [6]Local population only; in 1998 foreigners constituted 26% of the population and two-thirds of all foreigners were from Burkina Faso. [7]January 1. [8]Weights of consumer price index components. [9]Imports are f.o.b. in balance of trade and c.i.f. for commodities and trading partners. [10]1996–97. [11]1994–95. [12]Universities of Abobo-Adjamé and Cocody only. [13]New national army to be created pending final resolution of 2002–03 civil war. Peacekeeping troops (June 2005): UN 5,800; French 4,000.

Internet resources for further information:
• **La Banque de France: La Zone Franc**
  http://www.banque-france.fr/fr/eurosys/zonefr/zonefr.htm

Croatia

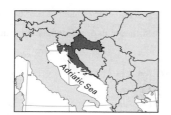

Official name: Republika Hrvatska (Republic of Croatia).
Form of government: multiparty republic with one legislative house (House of Representatives [1521])[2].
Head of state: President.
Head of government: Prime Minister.
Capital: Zagreb.
Official language: Croatian (Serbo-Croatian).
Official religion: none.
Monetary unit: 1 kuna (HrK; plural kune) = 100 lipa; valuation (Sept. 1, 2005) 1 U.S.$ = HrK 5.93; 1 £ = HrK 10.93.

Area and population		population			area	population
Counties	area sq km	2001 census	Counties		sq km	2001 census
Bjelovar-Bilogora	2,640	133,084	Sisak-Moslavina		4,468	185,387
Dubrovnik-Neretva	1,781	122,870	Slavonski Brod-Posavina		2,030	176,765
Istria	2,813	206,344	Split-Dalmatia		4,540	463,676
Karlovac	3,626	141,787	Varaždin		1,262	184,769
Koprivnica-Križevci	1,748	124,467	Virovitica-Podravina		2,024	93,389
Krapina-Zagorje	1,229	142,432	Vukovar-Srijem		2,454	204,768
Lika-Senj	5,353	53,677	Zadar		3,646	162,045
Medimurje	729	118,426	Zagreb		3,060	309,696
Osijek-Baranja	4,155	330,506	**City**			
Požega-Slavonia	1,823	85,831	Zagreb		641	779,145
Primorje-Gorski kotar	3,588	305,505	TOTAL		56,594	4,437,460
Šibenik-Knin	2,984	112,891				

Demography

Population (2005): 4,440,000.
Density (2005): persons per sq mi 203.2, persons per sq km 78.5.
Urban-rural (2003): urban 59.0%; rural 41.0%.
Sex distribution (2004): male 48.01%; female 51.99%.
Age breakdown (2004): under 15, 16.6%; 15–29, 20.5%; 30–44, 20.6%; 45–59, 21.0%; 60–74, 14.9%; 75 and over, 6.4%.
Population projection: (2010) 4,432,000; (2020) 4,373,000.
Ethnic composition (2001): Croat 89.6%; Serb 4.5%; Bosniac 0.5%; Italian 0.4%; Hungarian 0.4%; other 4.6%.
Religious affiliation (2000): Christian 95.2%, of which Roman Catholic 88.5%, Eastern Orthodox 5.6%, Protestant 0.6%; Sunnī Muslim 2.3%; nonreligious/atheist 2.5%.
Major cities (2001): Zagreb 691,724; Split 175,140; Rijeka 143,800; Osijek 90,411; Zadar 69,556.

Vital statistics

Birth rate per 1,000 population (2004): 9.5 (world avg. 21.1); (2002) legitimate 90.4%; illegitimate 9.6%.
Death rate per 1,000 population (2004): 11.3 (world avg. 9.0).
Natural increase rate per 1,000 population (2004): –1.8 (world avg. 12.1).
Total fertility rate (avg. births per childbearing woman; 2004): 1.4.
Marriage rate per 1,000 population (2004): 5.0.
Divorce rate per 1,000 population (2004): 1.1.
Life expectancy at birth (2004): male 70.2 years; female 78.3 years.
Major causes of death per 100,000 population (2003): diseases of the circulatory system 499.6; malignant neoplasms (cancers) 214.3; accidents, violence, and poisoning 57.7; diseases of the respiratory system 46.1; diseases of the digestive system 42.7.

National economy

Budget (2003). Revenue: HrK 78,534,000,000 (tax revenue 92.6%, of which VAT 35.8%, social contributions 34.9%, excise taxes 10.8%; nontax revenue 7.4%). Expenditures: HrK 79,762,500,000 (social security and welfare 42.2%; education 8.6%; public order 6.5%; defense 5.2%).
Population economically active (2004): total 1,836,000; activity rate 40.8% (participation rates: ages 15–64, 58.9%; female 45.3%; unemployed 13.8%).

Price and earnings indexes (2000 = 100)							
	1998	1999	2000	2001	2002	2003	2004
Consumer price index	91.8	95.0	100.0	104.8	106.5	106.7	110.7
Annual earnings index	80.6	91.9	100.0	106.5	111.8	118.4	125.4

Production (metric tons except as noted). Agriculture, forestry, fishing (2004): corn (maize) 2,100,000, sugar beets 1,000,000, wheat 850,000, potatoes 528,000, grapes 350,000, barley 180,000, soybeans 110,000, cabbage 110,000, tomatoes 71,400, sunflower seed 65,000, apples 58,000, plums 30,000; livestock (number of live animals) 1,300,000 pigs, 528,000 sheep, 438,000 cattle, 10,800,000 chickens; roundwood (2003) 3,847,000 cu m; fish catch (2002) 30,000. Mining and quarrying (2002): gypsum 145,000; ornamental stone 1,128,000 sq m. Manufacturing (value added in U.S.$'000,000; 1996): food products 895; transport equipment 425; electrical machinery 362; textiles 285; wearing apparel 260. Energy production (consumption): electricity (kW-hr; 2003) 13,247,000,000 (15,810,000,000); hard coal (metric tons; 2002) negligible (872,000); lignite (metric tons; 2002) none (93,000); crude petroleum (barrels; 2002) 7,400,000 (35,000,000); petroleum products (metric tons; 2002) 4,589,000 (3,826,000); natural gas (cu m; 2003) 2,190,000,000 ([2002] 2,826,000,000).

Gross national product (2004): U.S.$29,700,000,000 (U.S.$6,590 per capita).

Structure of gross domestic product and labour force				
	2001		2004	
	in value HrK '000,000	% of total value	labour force	% of labour force
Agriculture, forestry	12,482	7.5	269,000	14.7
Mining			8,000	0.4
Manufacturing	33,858	20.4	304,000	16.6
Public utilities			27,000	1.5
Construction	6,832	4.1	130,000	7.1
Transp. and commun.	13,821	8.3	104,000	5.7
Trade, restaurants	20,716	12.5	301,000	16.4
Finance, real estate	21,260	12.8	98,000	5.3
Pub. admin., defense	30,090	18.2	106,000	5.8
Services			234,000	12.7
Other	26,579[3]	16.0[3]	253,000[4]	13.8[4]
TOTAL	165,640[5]	100.0[5]	1,836,000[5]	100.0

Public debt (external, outstanding; 2003): U.S.$10,062,000,000.
Household income and expenditure. Average household size (2001) 3.0; income per household HrK 64,288 (U.S.$8,700); sources: wages 42.8%, self-employment 22.5%, pension 20.6%, other 14.1%; expenditure (2002): food and non-alcoholic beverages 32.2%, housing and energy 13.7%, transportation 11.1%, clothing 8.9%, recreation and culture 6.4%, household furnishings 5.5%, communications 4.8%, other 17.4%.
Tourism (2003): receipts U.S.$6,376,000,000; expenditures U.S.$672,000,000.
Land use as % of total land area (2000): in temporary crops 26.1%, in permanent crops 2.3%, in pasture 28.1%; overall forest area 31.9%.

Foreign trade[6]

Balance of trade (current prices)						
	1999	2000	2001	2002	2003	2004
U.S.$'000,000	–3,299	–3,204	–4,012	–5,649	–7,908	–6,602
% of total	27.3%	26.0%	29.7%	36.1%	38.5%	33.1%

Imports (2001): U.S.$9,044,000,000 (machinery and transport equipment 33.2%, chemical products 11.5%, base and fabricated metals 10.1%, crude and refined petroleum 9.2%). *Major import sources* (2003): Italy 18.2%; Germany 15.6%; Slovenia 7.4%; Austria 6.6%; France 5.3%.
Exports (2001): U.S.$4,659,000,000 (machinery and transport equipment 29.4%, chemical and chemical products 10.6%, clothing 10.5%, crude petroleum and petroleum products 7.4%, food 6.9%). *Major export destinations* (2003): Italy 26.4%; Bosnia and Herzegovina 14.5%; Germany 11.9%; Slovenia 8.3%; Austria 7.8%.

Transport and communications

Transport. Railroads (2003): length 2,726 km; passenger-km 1,163,000,000; metric ton-km cargo 2,487,000,000. Roads (2002): total length 28,344 km ([2001] paved 82%). Vehicles (2003): passenger cars 1,293,421; trucks and buses 143,123. Air transport (2004)[7]: passenger-km 1,014,000,000; metric ton-km cargo 1,989,000; airports (2001) 4.

Communications				units per 1,000
Medium	date	unit	number	persons
Daily newspapers	2004	circulation	382,000	85
Radio	2000	receivers	1,120,000	252
Television	2000	receivers	1,693,000	380
Telephones	2003	main lines	1,700,000	389
Cellular telephones	2003	subscribers	2,553,000	584
Personal computers	2004	units	842,000	191
Internet	2004	users	1,303,000	295

Education and health

Educational attainment (2001). Percentage of population age 15 and over having: no schooling or unknown 3.5%; incomplete primary education 15.8%; primary 21.7%; secondary 47.1%; postsecondary and higher 11.9%. *Literacy* (1999): population age 15 and over literate 98.2%; males 99.3%; females 97.1%.

Education (2003–04)				student/
	schools	teachers	students	teacher ratio
Primary (age 7–14)	2,138	28,335	393,421	13.9
Secondary (age 15–18)	665	20,073	195,340	9.7
Higher[8]	89	7,622	100,297	13.2

Health (2003): physicians 10,820 (1 per 410 persons); hospital beds 24,927 (1 per 178 persons); infant mortality rate per 1,000 live births (2004) 7.0.
Food (2002): daily per capita caloric intake 2,799 (vegetable products 81%, animal products 19%); 110% of FAO recommended minimum requirement.

Military

Total active duty personnel (2004): 20,800 (army 67.5%, navy 12.0%, air force and air defense 11.1%, headquarters staff 9.4%). *Military expenditure as percentage of GDP* (2003): 2.1%; per capita expenditure U.S.$134.

---

[1]Includes 6 seats representing Croatians abroad and 2 seats for minorities. [2]A constitutional amendment in March 2001 abolished the former upper house (House of Counties). [3]Import and turnover taxes less imputed bank service charges. [4]Unemployed. [5]Detail does not add to total given because of rounding. [6]Imports f.o.b. in balance of trade and c.i.f. for commodities and trading partners. [7]Croatia Airlines only. [8]2001–02.

Internet resources for further information:
• **Croatian Bureau of Statistics http://www.dzs.hr/defaulte.htm**
• **Ministry of Foreign Affairs http://www.mfa.hr/MVP.asp?pcpid=1612**

Cuba

Official name: República de Cuba (Republic of Cuba).
Form of government: unitary socialist republic with one legislative house (National Assembly of the People's Power [609]).
Head of state and government: President.
Capital: Havana.
Official language: Spanish.
Official religion: none.
Monetary unit: 1 Cuban peso (CUP) = 100 centavos; valuation (Sept. 1, 2005) 1 U.S.\$ = CUP 21.00[1]; 1 £ = CUP 38.68[1].

Area and population

Provinces	Capitals	area[2] sq mi	area[2] sq km	population 2003 estimate
Camagüey	Camagüey	6,174	15,990	786,400
Ciego de Ávila	Ciego de Ávila	2,668	6,910	415,300
Cienfuegos	Cienfuegos	1,613	4,178	398,000
Ciudad de la Habana	—	281	727	2,200,400
Granma	Bayamo	3,232	8,372	828,100
Guantánamo	Guantánamo	2,388	6,186	510,300
Holguín	Holguín	3,591	9,301	1,027,800
La Habana[3]	Havana	2,213	5,731	719,900
Las Tunas	Las Tunas	2,544	6,589	529,200
Matanzas	Matanzas	4,625	11,978	674,600
Pinar del Río	Pinar del Río	4,218	10,925	730,400
Sancti Spíritus	Sancti Spíritus	2,604	6,744	462,800
Santiago de Cuba	Santiago de Cuba	2,382	6,170	1,042,100
Villa Clara	Santa Clara	3,345	8,662	818,200
Special municipality				
Isla de la Juventud	Nueva Gerona	926	2,398	86,600
TOTAL		42,803[4]	110,860[4]	11,230,100

Demography

Population (2005): 11,269,000.
Density (2005): persons per sq mi 263.3, persons per sq km 101.7.
Urban-rural (2003): urban 75.6%; rural 24.4%.
Sex distribution (2003): male 50.02%; female 49.98%.
Age breakdown (2003): under 15, 20.5%; 15–29, 21.2%; 30–44, 27.7%; 45–59, 16.5%; 60–74, 9.9%; 75 and over, 4.2%.
Population projection: (2010) 11,379,000; (2020) 11,432,000.
Ethnic composition (1994): mixed 51.0%; white 37.0%; black 11.0%; other 1.0%.
Religious affiliation (2000): Roman Catholic (including some Santería) *c.* 38%; Protestant *c.* 5%; other (mostly nonreligious and Santería) *c.* 57%.
Major cities (2000): Havana (2004; agglomeration) 2,300,000; Santiago de Cuba 411,100; Camagüey 304,500; Holguín 263,300; Guantánamo 222,300; Santa Clara 216,000.

Vital statistics

Birth rate per 1,000 population (2003): 12.2 (world avg. 21.1).
Death rate per 1,000 population (2003): 7.0 (world avg. 9.0).
Natural increase rate per 1,000 population (2003): 5.2 (world avg. 12.1).
Total fertility rate (avg. births per childbearing woman; 2003): 1.6.
Marriage rate per 1,000 population (2003): 4.9.
Divorce rate per 1,000 population (2003): 3.2.
Life expectancy at birth (2003): male 74.6 years; female 79.2 years.
Major causes of death per 100,000 population (2002): malignant neoplasms (cancers) 162.7; ischemic heart disease 139.9; cerebrovascular disease 74.9; communicable diseases 61.8; accidents 41.6; suicide and violence 21.7.

National economy

Budget (2003). Revenue: CUP 17,250,000,000. Expenditures: CUP 18,324,000,000 (education 17.5%, social security contributions 11.5%, health 11.1%, housing and community services 5.1%, general administration 3.3%, other 51.5%).
Production (metric tons except as noted). Agriculture, forestry, fishing (2004): sugarcane 24,000,000, plantains 800,000, rice 716,000, cassava 685,000, tomatoes 645,000, oranges 500,000, sweet potatoes 490,000, pumpkins, squash, and gourds 490,000, corn (maize) 370,000, tobacco leaves 34,494; livestock (number of live animals) 4,050,000 cattle, 3,200,000 sheep, 1,700,000 pigs, 23,500,000 chickens; roundwood (2003) 3,597,000 cu m; fish catch (2003) 41,466. Mining and quarrying (2003): nickel (metal content) 74,018; cobalt (metal content) 3,982. Manufacturing (2002): asbestos-cement tile 4,400,000; cement 1,345,500; tobacco products (2002) 340,000; steel 335,000; soft drinks (2002) 3,091,000 hectolitres; beer 2,409,200 hectolitres. Energy production (consumption): electricity (kW-hr; 2003) 15,811,000,000 (14,620,000,000); coal (metric tons; 2002) none (26,000); crude petroleum (barrels; 2003) 26,000,000 ([2002] 33,000,000); petroleum products (metric tons; 2002) 1,590,000 (3,902,000); natural gas (cu m; 2003) 653,000,000 ([2002] 585,000,000).
Population economically active (2002): total 4,300,000; activity rate 38.2% (participation rates: over age 14, 45.4%[5]; female 37.7%[5]; unemployed [2004] 2.5%).

Price and earnings indexes (2000 = 100)

	1996	1997	1998	1999	2000	2001	2002
Consumer price index	90.1	91.8	94.4	97.2	100.0	...	...
Monthly earnings index	89.7	90.6	91.5	96.2	100.0	104.7	112.4

Gross domestic product (2003): U.S.\$32,307,000,000 (U.S.\$2,880 per capita).

Structure of gross domestic product and labour force

	2003 in value CUP '000[6]	2003 % of total value[6]	2002 labour force[5]	2002 % of labour force[5]
Agriculture	1,923,900	6.8	1,064,600	26.5
Mining	478,000	1.7	28,300	0.7
Manufacturing	4,671,800	16.5	564,100	14.0
Public utilities	611,500	2.1	51,200	1.3
Construction	1,636,700	5.8	176,400	4.4
Transp. and commun.	2,712,400	9.6	201,700	5.0
Finance, insurance	2,186,000	7.7	54,200	1.3
Trade	8,163,800	28.7	507,900	12.6
Public administration	} 5,625,400	} 19.8	1,375,700	34.2
Services				
Other	383,600[7]	1.3[7]	—	—
TOTAL	28,393,100	100.0	4,024,100	100.0

Public debt (external, outstanding; 2004): U.S.\$12,000,000,000.
Household income and expenditure. Average household size (2000) 3.6; average annual income per household, n.a.; sources of income, n.a.
Tourism (2003): U.S.\$1,265,000,000; expenditures by nationals abroad, n.a.
Land use as % of total land area (2000): in temporary crops 33.1%, in permanent crops 7.6%, in pasture 20.0%; overall forest area 21.4%.

Foreign trade[8]

Balance of trade (current prices)

	1999	2000	2001
U.S.\$'000,000	−2,896	−3,167	−3,178
% of total	49.2%	48.6%	48.9%

Imports (2001): U.S.\$4,838,700,000 (machinery and transport equipment 25.5%, of which motor vehicles and parts 5.0%; food and live animals 15.7%, of which cereals 6.5%; refined petroleum 13.1%; crude petroleum 6.6%). *Major import sources* (2004): Spain 15.4%; Venezuela 13.7%; U.S. 11.5%; China 8.0%; Canada 6.6%; Italy 6.5%.
Exports (2001): U.S.\$1,660,600,000 (raw sugar 32.6%; nickel [all forms] 27.8%; raw tobacco and tobacco products 15.8%; fresh and frozen fish 4.6%; medicinal and pharmaceutical products 2.4%). *Major export destinations* (2004): The Netherlands 23.5%; Canada 21.9%; China 8.3%; Russia 7.8%; Spain 6.6%.

Transport and communications

Transport. Railroads (2003)[9]: length 2,651 mi, 4,226 km; (2001) passenger-km 1,766,600; metric ton-km cargo 806,900,000. Roads (1999): total length 37,815 mi, 60,858 km (paved 49%). Vehicles (1998): passenger cars 172,574; trucks and buses 185,495. Air transport (2003)[10]: passenger-km 2,044,000,000; metric ton-km cargo 40,933,000; airports with scheduled flights (1999) 14.

Communications

Medium	date	unit	number	units per 1,000 persons
Daily newspapers	2001	circulation	1,317,000	118
Radio	2001	receivers	2,091,000	185
Television	2001	receivers	2,801,000	251
Telephones	2004	main lines	768,200	68
Cellular telephones	2004	subscribers	75,800	6.7
Personal computers	2004	units	300,000	27
Internet	2004	users	150,000	13

Education and health

Educational attainment: n.a. *Literacy* (2004): total population age 15 and over literate 96.9%; males 97.0%; females 96.8%.

Education (2002–03)

	schools	teachers	students	student/ teacher ratio
Primary (age 6–11)	9,397	86,641	925,335	10.9
Secondary (age 12–17)	2,032	80,372	938,047	11.7
Voc., teacher tr.	...	27,267[11]	244,253[11]	9.0[11]
Higher	64	24,199	235,997	9.8

Health (2003): physicians 67,417 (1 per 167 persons); hospital beds 69,534 (1 per 161 persons); infant mortality rate per 1,000 live births 6.3.
Food (2002): daily per capita caloric intake 3,152 (vegetable products 88%, animal products 12%); 136% of FAO recommended minimum requirement.

Military

Total active duty personnel (2004): 49,000 (army 77.6%, navy 6.1%, air force 16.3%); U.S. military forces at Naval Base Guantanamo Bay (2004) 2,255.
Military expenditure as percentage of GDP (2003): 4.0%; per capita expenditure: U.S.\$107.

[1]Unofficial rate for domestic use; official rate for international transactions is 1 U.S.\$ = CUP 1.00; 1 £ = CUP 1.84. [2]Geographic areas: island of Cuba 40,520 sq mi (104,945 sq km); Isla de la Juventud 850 sq mi (2,200 sq km); numerous adjacent cays (administratively a part of provinces or the Isla de la Juventud) 1,434 sq mi (3,715 sq km). [3]Province bordering Ciudad de la Habana on the east, south, and west. [4]Detail does not add to total given because of rounding. [5]Employed persons only. [6]At constant 1997 prices. [7]Import duties. [8]Imports are f.o.b. in trading partners and c.i.f. for balance of trade and commodities. [9]Cuban Railways only; length of railways exclusively for the transport of sugar equals 4,811 mi (7,742 km). [10]Cubana airline only. [11]1995–96.

Internet resources for further information:
- Oficina Nacional de Estadísticas
  http://www.cubagob.cu/otras_info/estadisticas.htm
- Naciones Unidas en Cuba
  http://www.onu.org.cu/uunn/homepage/index2.html

Cyprus

Island of Cyprus

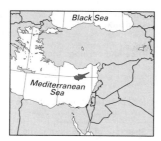

Area: 3,572 sq mi, 9,251 sq km.
Population (2005): 968,000[1].

Two de facto states currently exist on the island of Cyprus: the Republic of Cyprus (ROC), predominantly Greek in character, occupying the southern two-thirds of the island, which is the original and still the internationally recognized de jure government of the whole island; and the Turkish Republic of Northern Cyprus (TRNC), proclaimed unilaterally Nov. 15, 1983, on territory originally secured for the Turkish Cypriot population by the July 20, 1974, intervention of Turkey. Only Turkey recognizes the TRNC, and the two ethnic communities have failed to reestablish a single state. Provision of separate data below does not imply recognition of either state's claims but is necessitated by the lack of unified data.

Republic of Cyprus

Official name: Kipriakí Dhimokratía (Greek); Kıbrıs Cumhuriyeti (Turkish) (Republic of Cyprus).
Form of government: unitary multiparty republic with a unicameral legislature (House of Representatives [80[2]]).
Head of state and government: President.
Capital: Lefkosia (Nicosia).
Official languages: Greek; Turkish.
Monetary unit: 1 Cyprus pound (£C) = 100 cents; valuation (Sept. 1, 2005) 1 £C = U.S.$2.19 = £1.19.

Demography

Area[3]: 2,276 sq mi, 5,896 sq km.
Population (2005): 747,000[4].
Urban-rural (2003): urban 69.2%; rural 30.8%.
Age breakdown (2004): under 15, 21.4%; 15–29, 22.9%; 30–44, 21.0%; 45–59, 18.9%; 60–74, 11.0%; 75 and over, 4.7%.
Ethnic composition (2000): Greek Cypriot 91.8%; Armenian 3.3%; Arab 2.9%, of which Lebanese 2.5%; British 1.4%; other 0.6%.
Religious affiliation (2001): Greek Orthodox 94.8%; Roman Catholic 2.1%, of which Maronite 0.6%; Anglican 1.0%; Muslim 0.6%; other 1.5%.
Urban areas (2004): Lefkosia 219,200[5]; Limassol 172,500; Larnaca 77,000.

Vital statistics

Birth rate per 1,000 population (2004): 12.7 (world avg. 21.1).
Death rate per 1,000 population (2004): 7.6 (world avg. 9.0).
Natural increase rate per 1,000 population (2004): 5.1 (world avg. 12.1).
Life expectancy at birth (2002–03): male 77.0 years; female 81.4 years.

National economy

Budget (2003). Revenue: £C 2,402,800,000 (indirect taxes 43.5%, direct taxes 24.2%, social security contributions 13.4%). Expenditures: £C 2,824,300,000 (current expenditures 89.2%, development expenditures 10.8%).
Tourism (2003): receipts U.S.$2,015,000,000; expenditures U.S.$631,000,000.
Household expenditure (2000): housing and energy 21.3%, food and beverages 20.0%, transportation and communications 19.2%.
Gross national product (2004): U.S.$13,633,000,000 (U.S.$17,580 per capita).

Structure of gross domestic product and labour force

| | 2003 | | | |
	in value £C '000,000	% of total value	labour force	% of labour force
Agriculture, fishing	258.8	3.9	17,000	5.0
Mining	21.6	0.3	500	0.1
Manufacturing	575.5	8.8	35,900	10.5
Construction	504.1	7.7	34,900	10.2
Public utilities	147.9	2.3	3,600	1.1
Transportation and communications	549.6	8.4	17,300	5.1
Trade	1,282.5	19.5	88,000	25.8
Finance, insurance	1,326.1	20.2	38,800	11.4
Pub. admin., defense	624.5	9.5	24,400	7.1
Services	907.9	13.8	63,900	18.7
Other	365.3[6]	5.6[6]	16,900[7]	5.0[7]
TOTAL	6,563.8	100.0	341,200	100.0

Production. Agriculture (in '000 metric tons; 2004): potatoes 116.0, barley 94.0, grapes 80.8, oranges 35.0, grapefruit 30.0, olives 27.5. Manufacturing (value added in U.S.$'000,000; 2001): food products 186; cement, bricks, and ceramics 93; beverages 84; tobacco products 77; fabricated metal products 59. Energy production: electricity (kW-hr; 2003) 4,044,000,000.

Foreign trade[8]

Imports (2003): £C 2,314,200,000 (consumer goods 27.6%; capital goods 11.1%; transportation equipment 9.9%; for reexport 9.5%). *Major import sources:* Russia 36.2%; Greece 6.4%; U.K. 5.3%; Germany 5.2%; Italy 5.1%.

Exports (2003): £C 476,800,000 (reexports 47.1%[9]; domestic exports 43.2%, of which pharmaceuticals 8.1%, citrus fruit 4.0%; ships' stores 9.7%). *Major export destinations:* U.K. 24.4%; France 11.0%; Germany 7.2%; Greece 6.4%; Poland 3.7%.

Transport and communications

Transport. Roads (2002): total length 11,593 km (paved 62%). Vehicles (2002): cars 287,622; trucks and buses 119,539. Air transport (2003)[10]: passenger-km 3,352,000,000; metric ton-km cargo 43,055,000; airports (2000) 2.

Communications

Medium	date	unit	number	units per 1,000 persons
Television	2001	receivers	127,000	181
Telephones	2004	main lines	418,400	518
Cellular telephones	2004	subscribers	640,500	794
Personal computers	2004	units	249,000	309
Internet	2004	users	298,000	369

Education and health

Educational attainment (2001). Percentage of population age 15 and over having: no formal schooling 2.1%; incomplete primary 6.4%; complete primary 20.6%; secondary 48.3%; higher education 22.3%; not stated 0.3%.

Education (2000–01)

	schools	teachers	students	student/ teacher ratio
Primary (age 6–11)	367	3,756	63,387	16.9
Secondary (age 12–17)	123	4,724	59,526	12.6
Vocational	11	597	4,497	7.5
Higher	32	1,077	11,934	11.1

Health (2003): physicians 1,879 (1 per 384 persons); hospital beds 3,083 (1 per 234 persons); infant mortality rate per 1,000 live births (2003) 4.1.

Internet resources for further information:
• **Central Bank of Cyprus http://www.centralbank.gov.cy**
• **Rep. of Cyprus Statistical Service http://www.mof.gov.cy/mof/cystat/ statistics.nsf/index_en/index_en?OpenDocument**

Turkish Republic of Northern Cyprus

Official name: Kuzey Kıbrıs Türk Cumhuriyeti (Turkish) (Turkish Republic of Northern Cyprus).
Capital: Lefkoşa (Nicosia).
Official language: Turkish.
Monetary unit: 1 new Turkish lira (YTL) = 100 kurush; valuation (Sept. 1, 2005) 1 U.S.$ = YTL 1.34; 1 £ = YTL 2.46; 1 YTL = 1,000,000 (old) TL.
Population (2005): 221,000[1] (Lefkoşa 39,176[11]; Gazimağusa [Famagusta] 27,637[11]; Girne [Kyrenia] 14,205[11]).
Ethnic composition (1996): Turkish Cypriot/Turkish 96.4%; other 3.6%.

Structure of gross domestic product and labour force

| | 2002 | | | |
	in value TL '000,000,000	% of total value	labour force	% of labour force
Agriculture and fishing	125,668.9	9.3	14,632	15.6
Mining and manufacturing	82,002.3	6.0	7,510	7.9
Construction	62,013.0	4.6	15,786	16.7
Public utilities	75,574.2	5.5	1,381	1.4
Transportation and communications	185,264.8	13.6	8,310	8.8
Trade, restaurants	215,553.6	15.9	10,520	11.1
Pub. admin.	227,867.1	16.8	18,084	19.1
Finance, real estate	131,384.2	9.7	2,397	2.5
Services	138,860.1	10.2	14,494	15.3
Other	113,513.4[12]	8.4[12]	1,535[13]	1.6[13]
TOTAL	1,357,701.6	100.0	94,649	100.0

Budget (2003). Revenue: U.S.$691,400,000 (loans 25.6%, indirect taxes 16.6%, direct taxes 16.4%, foreign aid 15.9%). Expenditures: U.S.$691,400,000 (wages 27.8%, social transfers 21.7%, investments 11.4%, defense 6.7%).
Imports[8] (2003): U.S.$477,800,000 (machinery and transport equipment 29.6%, food 12.2%). *Major import sources:* Turkey 62.6%; U.K. 10.3%.
Exports[8] (2003): U.S.$50,800,000 (citrus fruits 35.1%, clothing 20.1%). *Major export destinations:* Turkey 45.1%; U.K. 23.4%.

Education (2003–04)

	schools	teachers	students	student/ teacher ratio
Primary (age 7–11)	95	1,257	16,073	12.8
Secondary (age 12–17)	50	1,608	16,491	10.3
Vocational	13	440	2,260	5.1
Higher	6	884[14]	30,605	24.8[14]

Health (2003): physicians 554 (1 per 390 persons); hospital beds 1,236 (1 per 175 persons); infant mortality rate per 1,000 live births (1999) 3.7.

Internet resources for further information:
• **Turkish Republic of Northern Cyprus Public Information Office http://www.trncpio.org/ingilizce/ingilizcesayfa.htm**

[1]Includes roughly 80,000 "settlers" from Turkey and 38,000 Turkish military in the TRNC; excludes 3,300 British military in the Sovereign Base Areas (SBA) in the ROC and 850 UN peacekeeping forces. [2]Twenty-four seats reserved for Turkish Cypriots are not occupied. [3]Area includes 99 sq mi (256 sq km) of British military SBA and *c.* 107 sq mi (*c.* 278 sq km) of the UN Buffer Zone. [4]Excludes British and UN military forces. [5]ROC only. [6]Import duties and taxes less imputed bank service charges. [7]Includes 3,200 unemployed. [8]Imports c.i.f.; exports f.o.b. [9]Mainly cigarettes, vehicles, and consumer electronics. [10]Cyprus Airways. [11]1996 census. [12]Import duties. [13]Unemployed. [14]1998–99.

Czech Republic

Official name: Česká Republika (Czech Republic).
Form of government: unitary multiparty republic with two legislative houses (Senate [81]; Chamber of Deputies [200]).
Chief of state: President.
Head of government: Prime Minister.
Capital: Prague.
Official language: Czech.
Official religion: none.
Monetary unit: 1 koruna (Kč) = 100 halura; valuation (Sept. 1, 2005)
1 U.S.$ = Kč 23.24;
1 £ = Kč 42.79.

Area and population

Regions[1]	area sq km	population 2004 estimate	Regions[1]	area sq km	population 2004 estimate
Brno	7,067	1,122,570	Pardubice	4,519	505,486
Budejovice	10,056	625,541	Plzeň	7,560	550,113
Hradec Králové	4,757	547,563	Střed	11,014	1,135,795
Jihlava	6,925	517,511	Ústí	5,335	820,868
Karlovy Vary	3,315	304,249	Zlín	3,965	591,866
Liberec	3,163	427,722	**Capital city**		
Olomouc	5,139	636,313	Prague (Praha)	496	1,165,581
Ostrava	5,555	1,260,277	TOTAL	78,866	10,211,455

Demography

Population (2005): 10,235,000.
Density (2005): persons per sq mi 336.1, persons per sq km 129.8.
Urban-rural (2003): urban 74.3%; rural 25.7%.
Sex distribution (2004): male 48.72%; female 51.28%.
Age breakdown (2004): under 15, 14.9%; 15–29, 22.1%; 30–44, 21.3%; 45–59, 22.0%; 60–74, 13.6%; 75 and over, 6.1%.
Population projection: (2010) 10,260,000; (2020) 10,260,000.
Ethnic composition (2001): Czech 90.4%; Moravian 3.7%; Slovak 1.9%; Polish 0.5%; German 0.4%; Silesian 0.1%; Rom (Gypsy) 0.1%; other 2.9%.
Religious affiliation (2000): Catholic 43.8%, of which Roman Catholic 40.4%, Hussite Church of the Czech Republic 2.2%; nonreligious 31.9%; atheist 5.0%; Protestant 3.1%; Orthodox Christian 0.6%; Jewish 0.1%; other (mostly unaffiliated Christian) 15.5%.
Major cities (2004): Prague 1,165,581; Brno 369,559; Ostrava 313,088; Plzeň 164,180; Olomouc 101,268.

Vital statistics

Birth rate per 1,000 population (2004): 9.6 (world avg. 21.1); (2003) legitimate 71.5%; illegitimate 28.5%.
Death rate per 1,000 population (2004): 10.5 (world avg. 9.0).
Natural increase rate per 1,000 population (2004): –0.9 (world avg. 12.1).
Total fertility rate (avg. births per childbearing woman; 2003): 1.2.
Marriage rate per 1,000 population (2004): 5.0.
Divorce rate per 1,000 population (2004): 3.2.
Life expectancy at birth (2003): male 72.0 years; female 78.5 years.
Major causes of death per 100,000 population (2003): diseases of the circulatory system 569.2; malignant neoplasms (cancers) 287.8; accidents, poisoning, and violence 71.5; diseases of the respiratory system 51.8; diseases of the digestive system 45.2.

National economy

Budget (2003). Revenue: Kč 985,436,000,000 (tax revenue 90.8%, of which social security contributions 36.5%, value-added tax 16.7%, personal income tax 12.5%, corporate tax 11.8%, excise tax 8.5%; nontax revenue 8.0%; grants 1.2%). Expenditures: Kč 1,115,642,000,000 (social security and welfare 31.0%; health 15.0%; education 10.0%; police 4.8%; defense 4.1%).
Production (metric tons except as noted). Agriculture, forestry, fishing (2004): cereals 8,326,000 (of which wheat 4,693,000, barley 2,286,000, corn [maize] 538,000), sugar beets 3,367,000, potatoes 1,076,000, rapeseed 910,000; livestock (number of live animals) 3,309,000 pigs, 1,427,000 cattle; roundwood (2003) 14,541,000 cu m; fish catch (2002) 24,000. Mining and quarrying (2004): kaolin 4,100,000; feldspar 400,000. Manufacturing (value added in U.S.$'000,000; 1999): fabricated metal products 1,208; nonelectrical machinery and apparatus 1,202; food products 1,126; motor vehicles and parts (1997) 965; electrical machinery and apparatus 767; cement, bricks, and ceramics 649; iron and steel 452; basic chemicals 450; beverages 392; glass and glass products 385. Energy production (consumption): electricity (kW-hr; 2003) 83,227,000,000 (41,791,000,000); hard coal (metric tons; 2002) 14,500,000 (10,200,000); lignite (metric tons; 2002) 48,900,000 (46,900,000); crude petroleum (barrels; 2002) 1,800,000 (46,000,000); petroleum products (metric tons; 2002) 4,465,000 (6,057,000); natural gas (cu m; 2002) 162,000,000 (9,254,000,000).
Tourism (2003): receipts from visitors U.S.$3,556,000,000; expenditures by nationals abroad U.S.$1,934,000,000.
Household income and expenditure. Average household size (2004) 2.5; disposable income per capita of household (2004) Kč 102,217 (U.S.$4,560); sources of income (2004): wages and salaries 66.7%, transfer payments 20.6%, self-employment 8.8%, other 3.9%; expenditure (2004): food and non-alcoholic beverages 16.5%, housing and utilities 15.1%, transportation and communications 12.2%, recreation 8.5%, household furnishings 5.1%.

Population economically active (2004): total 5,137,800; activity rate of total population 50.3% (participation rates: ages 15–64 [2002] 70.9%; female 44.1%; unemployed [July 2003–June 2004] 9.8%).

Price and earnings indexes (2000 = 100)

	1998	1999	2000	2001	2002	2003	2004
Consumer price index	94.2	96.2	100.0	104.7	106.6	106.7	109.7
Annual earnings index	86.7	94.0	100.0	108.7	116.5	124.3	132.5

Public debt (external, outstanding; 2003): U.S.$8,558,000,000.
Gross national product (2004): U.S.$93,155,000,000 (U.S.$9,150 per capita).

Structure of gross domestic product and labour force

	2002 in value Kč '000,000	2002 % of total value	2004 labour force	2004 % of labour force
Agriculture, forestry	77,600	3.4	207,500	4.0
Mining	[2]	[2]	58,800	1.2
Manufacturing	671,700[2]	29.5[2]	1,279,000	24.9
Construction	138,600	6.1	440,400	8.6
Public utilities	[2]	[2]	75,400	1.5
Transportation and communications	189,200	8.3	366,300	7.1
Trade, hotels	354,400	15.6	811,700	15.8
Finance, real estate	350,400	15.4	366,700	7.1
Pub. admin., defense	326,900	14.4	324,100	6.3
Services			782,500	15.2
Other	166,900[3]	7.3[3]	425,400[4]	8.3[4]
TOTAL	2,275,600[5]	100.0	5,137,800	100.0

Land use as % of total land area (2000): in temporary crops 39.9%, in permanent crops 3.1%, in pasture 12.4%; overall forest area 34.1%.

Foreign trade

Balance of trade (current prices)

	1998	1999	2000	2001	2002	2003
Kč '000,000	–76,319	–64,413	–120,825	–116,685	–74,455	–69,396
% of total	4.3%	3.4%	5.1%	4.4%	2.9%	2.5%

Imports (2003): Kč 1,440,733,000,000 (machinery and apparatus 23.5%; chemicals and chemical products 10.6%; motor vehicles 9.7%; base metals 6.4%; fabricated metals 4.5%). *Major import sources:* Germany 32.6%; Italy 5.3%; China 5.2%; Slovakia 5.2%; France 4.9%.
Exports (2003): Kč 1,371,337,000,000 (machinery and apparatus 27.7%, of which office machinery and computers 6.3%; motor vehicles 16.2%; fabricated metals 6.7%; base metals 5.6%; chemicals and chemical products 5.4%). *Major export destinations:* Germany 37.1%; Slovakia 8.0%; Austria 6.3%; United Kingdom 5.4%; Poland 4.8%.

Transport and communications

Transport. Railroads (2004): length (2001) 9,444 km; passenger-km 6,590,000,000; metric ton-km cargo 15,091,000,000. Roads (2002): total length 127,204 km (paved 100%). Vehicles (2002): passenger cars 3,647,067; trucks and buses 344,774. Air transport: passenger-km (2004) 8,815,000,000; metric ton-km (2001) 29,209,000; airports (2001) with scheduled flights 2.

Communications

Medium	date	unit	number	units per 1,000 persons
Daily newspapers	2004	circulation	1,861,000	182
Television	2000	receivers	3,289,000	341
Telephones	2004	main lines	3,450,000	337
Cellular telephones	2004	subscribers	10,771,000	1,053
Personal computers	2004	units	2,450,000	240
Internet	2004	users	4,800,000	469

Education and health

Educational attainment (2001). Percentage of population age 15 and over having: no formal schooling 0.2%; primary education 21.6%; secondary 68.7%; higher 9.5%. *Literacy* (2001): 99.8%.

Education (2003–04)

	schools	teachers	students	student/ teacher ratio
Primary (age 6–14)	3,870	65,615	956,324	14.6
Secondary (age 15–18)	344	12,175	142,167	11.7
Voc., teacher tr.	1,344	31,874	399,524	12.5
Higher	193	17,458	264,123	15.1

Health (2003): physicians 44,106 (1 per 230 persons); hospital beds 66,492 (1 per 153 persons); infant mortality rate per 1,000 live births (2003) 3.9.
Food (2002): daily per capita caloric intake 3,171 (vegetable products 73%, animal products 27%); 128% of FAO recommended minimum requirement.

Military

Total active duty personnel (2004): 45,000 (army 81.3%, air force 14.9%, ministry of defense 3.8%). *Military expenditure as percentage of GDP* (2003): 2.2%; per capita expenditure: U.S.$181.

---

[1]New local government structure as of November 2000 elections. [2]Manufacturing includes Mining and Public utilities. [3]Taxes less subsidies and imputed bank charges. [4]Includes 5,000 activities not defined and 420,400 unemployed. [5]Detail does not add to total given because of rounding.

Internet resources for further information:
• Czech Statistical Office http://www.czso.cz

Denmark

Official name: Kongeriget Danmark (Kingdom of Denmark).
Form of government: parliamentary state and constitutional monarchy with one legislative house (Folketing [179]).
Chief of state: Danish Monarch.
Head of government: Prime Minister.
Capital: Copenhagen.
Official language: Danish.
Official religion: Evangelical Lutheran.
Monetary unit: 1 Danish krone (Dkr; plural kroner) = 100 øre; valuation (Sept. 1, 2005) 1 U.S.$ = Dkr 5.94; 1 £ = Dkr 10.94.

Area and population[1]

Counties	Capitals	area sq mi	area sq km	population 2005[2] estimate
Århus	Århus	1,761	4,561	657,671
Frederiksborg	Hillerød	520	1,347	375,705
Fyn	Odense	1,346	3,486	476,580
København	Copenhagen	204	528	618,237
Nordjylland	Ålborg	2,383	6,173	495,068
Ribe	Ribe	1,209	3,132	224,454
Ringkøbing	Ringkøbing	1,874	4,854	274,574
Roskilde	Roskilde	344	891	239,049
Sønderjylland	Åbenrå	1,521	3,939	252,980
Storstrøm	Nykøbing Falster	1,312	3,398	262,144
Vejle	Vejle	1,157	2,997	358,055
Vestsjælland	Sorø	1,152	2,984	304,761
Viborg	Viborg	1,592	4,123	234,434
Municipalities				
Bornholm	Rønne	227	589	43,445
Copenhagen (København)	—	34	88	502,362
Frederiksberg	—	3	9	91,886
TOTAL		16,640[3]	43,098[3]	5,411,405

Demography

Population (2005): 5,416,000.
Density (2005): persons per sq mi 325.5, persons per sq km 125.7.
Urban-rural (2004): urban 85.4%; rural 14.6%.
Sex distribution (2005[2]): male 49.47%; female 50.53%.
Age breakdown (2005[2]): under 15, 18.8%; 15–29, 17.4%; 30–44, 22.2%; 45–59, 20.7%; 60–74, 13.9%; 75 and over, 7.0%.
Population projection: (2010) 5,459,000; (2020) 5,530,000.
Ethnic composition (2005[2])[4]: Danish 95.1%; Asian 1.3%, of which Turkish 0.6%, Iraqi 0.4%; residents of pre-1992 Yugoslavia 0.5%; Norwegian 0.3%; German 0.3%; English 0.2%; Somali 0.2%; Swedish 0.2%; other 1.9%.
Religious affiliation (2000): Christian 91.6%, nearly all of which are Evangelical Lutheran; Muslim 1.3%; nonreligious 5.4%; other 1.7%.
Major urban areas (2004[2]): Greater Copenhagen 1,086,762; Århus 228,547; Odense 145,554; Ålborg 121,549; Esbjerg 72,550.

Vital statistics

Birth rate per 1,000 population (2004): 11.9 (world avg. 21.1).
Death rate per 1,000 population (2004): 10.3 (world avg. 9.0).
Natural increase rate per 1,000 population (2004): 1.6 (world avg. 12.1).
Total fertility rate (avg. births per childbearing woman; 2004): 1.8.
Marriage rate per 1,000 population (2004): 7.0.
Divorce rate per 1,000 population (2004): 2.9.
Life expectancy at birth (2003): male 74.9 years; female 79.5 years.
Major causes of death per 100,000 population (2001): diseases of the circulatory system 394.7; malignant neoplasms (cancers) 298.2.

National economy

Budget (2004)[5]. Revenue: Dkr 531,792,000,000 (current revenue 98.1%, of which tax revenue 84.0%; capital revenue 1.9%). Expenditures: Dkr 501,053,000,000 (health and social protection 41.4%, education 11.7%, economic affairs 7.0%, foreign affairs 6.7%, defense 4.7%, public order 2.5%).
National debt (end of year; 2004): Dkr 688,500,000,000.
Tourism (2004): receipts U.S.$5,781,000,000; expenditures U.S.$7,744,000,000.
Population economically active (2004): total 2,854,100; activity rate of total population 52.9% (participation rates: ages 16–66, 76.6%; female 49.2%; unemployed 5.2%).

Price and earnings indexes (2000 = 100)

	1998	1999	2000	2001	2002	2003	2004
Consumer price index	99.3	97.2	100.0	102.4	104.8	107.0	108.3
Hourly earnings index[5]	...	96.2	100.0	104.0	112.9	116.0	...

Household income and expenditure. Average household size (2004) 2.2; annual disposable income per household (2002) Dkr 275,980 (U.S.$34,956).
Production (in Dkr '000,000 except as noted). Agriculture, forestry, fishing (value added; 2003): meat 18,655 (of which pork 15,130, beef 2,094), milk 11,279, cereals 7,727 (of which barley 3,706, wheat 3,585), flowers and plants 2,591, furs 2,345; livestock (number of live animals; 2004) 13,233,235 pigs, 1,645,764 cattle; roundwood (2003) 1,626,941 cu m; fish catch (2004) 984,037 metric tons. Mining and quarrying (2003): sand and gravel 27,600,000 cu m; chalk 1,900,000 metric tons. Manufacturing (value of sales in U.S.$'000,000; 2004): food products 19,899; nonelectrical machinery and apparatus 10,558; fabricated metals 7,257; computer and telecommunications equipment 6,201;

pharmaceuticals 5,375; printing and publishing 4,508. Energy production (consumption): electricity (kW-hr; 2003) 43,752,000,000 (31,680,000,000); coal (metric tons; 2003) none (9,450,000); crude petroleum (barrels; 2004) 148,000,000 ([2003] 69,000,000); petroleum products (metric tons; 2002) 7,890,000 (6,759,000); natural gas (cu m; 2004) 4,578,000,000 ([2003] 4,231,000,000).
Gross national product (2004): U.S.$219,422,000,000 (U.S.$40,650 per capita).

Structure of gross domestic product and labour force

	2004 in value Dkr '000,000	2004 % of total value	2004 labour force	2004 % of labour force
Agriculture, fishing	28,013	2.3	94,300	3.3
Mining	36,859	3.0		
Manufacturing	175,931	14.2	417,900	14.7
Construction	65,383	5.3	166,700	5.8
Public utilities	26,454	2.1	14,600	0.5
Transp. and commun.	108,909	8.8	171,400	6.0
Trade, restaurants	173,535	14.0	488,900	17.1
Finance, real estate	318,360	25.8	369,300	12.9
Pub. admin., defense } Services	345,847	28.0	969,400	34.0
Other	–43,139[6]	–3.5[6]	161,600[7]	5.7[7]
TOTAL	1,236,151[3]	100.0	2,854,100	100.0

Land use as % of total land area (2000): in temporary crops 53.8%, in permanent crops 0.2%, in pasture 8.4%; overall forest area 10.7%.

Foreign trade[8]

Balance of trade (current prices)

	1998	1999	2000	2001	2002	2003	2004
Dkr '000,000	+16,717	+41,330	+49,368	+57,638	+58,044	+59,571	+53,043
% of total	2.6%	6.2%	6.4%	7.3%	7.0%	7.5%	6.2%

Imports (2004): Dkr 399,042,700,000 (machinery and apparatus [including parts] 24.7%; food, beverages, and tobacco 11.6%; transport equipment and parts 11.3%; chemical products 8.3%; clothing, textiles, and footwear 7.4%; fuels 5.3%). *Major import sources:* Germany 22.0%; Sweden 13.4%; The Netherlands 6.8%; U.K. 6.1%; Norway 4.7%.
Exports (2004): Dkr 453,642,000,000 (machinery and apparatus 23.2%; food, beverages, and tobacco 21.8%; chemical products 10.9%, of which pharmaceuticals 7.5%; fuels 8.4%, of which petroleum products 7.2%; furniture 3.6%). *Major export destinations:* Germany 17.9%; Sweden 12.9%; U.K. 8.7%; U.S. 5.8%; The Netherlands 5.5%; Norway 5.4%.

Transport and communications

Transport. Railroads (2004[2]): route length 2,785 km; passenger-km (2003) 5,893,000,000; metric ton-km cargo (2003) 2,013,000,000. Roads (2004[2]): total length 72,075 km (paved 100%). Vehicles (2005[2]): passenger cars 1,915,821; trucks and buses 623,365. Air transport (2003)[9]: passenger-km 6,976,677,000; metric ton-km cargo 169,851,000; airports with scheduled flights 10.

Communications

Medium	date	unit	number	units per 1,000 persons
Daily newspapers	2004	circulation	1,328,000	246
Radio	2000	receivers	7,200,000	1,349
Television	2000	receivers	4,310,000	807
Telephones	2004	main lines	3,475,000	647
Cellular telephones	2004	subscribers	5,165,500	961
Personal computers	2004	units	3,543,000	659
Internet	2004	users	3,762,500	700

Education and health

Educational attainment (2004). Percentage of population age 25–69 having: completed lower secondary or not stated 30.3%; completed upper secondary or vocational 43.9%; undergraduate 19.6%; graduate 6.2%. *Literacy:* 100%.

Education (2003)

	schools	teachers[10]	students	student/ teacher ratio
Primary/lower secondary (age 7–15)	2,690	58,500	705,974	...
Upper secondary (age 16–18)	152	11,000	68,313	...
Vocational	157	12,000	172,225	...
Higher	162	8,000	183,694	...

Health: physicians (2002) 19,600 (1 per 274 persons); hospital beds (2002) 22,225 (1 per 242 persons); infant mortality rate per 1,000 live births (2004) 4.0.
Food (2002): daily per capita caloric intake 3,439 (vegetable products 61.9%, animal products 38.1%); 128% of FAO recommended minimum requirement.

Military

Total active duty personnel (2004): 21,180 (army 59.0%, air force 19.8%, navy 18.0%, other 3.2%). *Military expenditure as percentage of GDP* (2003): 1.5%; per capita expenditure U.S.$618.

---

[1]Excludes the Faroe Islands and Greenland. [2]January 1. [3]Detail does not add to total given because of rounding. [4]Based on nationality. [5]Central government only. [6]Imputed bank service charges. [7]Includes 13,900 not adequately defined and 147,700 unemployed. [8]Imports c.i.f., exports f.o.b. [9]Danish share of Scandinavian Airlines System (scheduled air service only) and Maersk Air. [10]1993–94.

Internet resources for further information:
• Statistics Denmark http://www.dst.dk/yearbook
• StatBank Denmark http://www.statbank.dk

Djibouti

Official name: Jumhūrīyah Jībūtī (Arabic); République de Djibouti (French) (Republic of Djibouti).
Form of government: multiparty republic with one legislative house (National Assembly [65]).
Head of state and government: President.
Capital: Djibouti.
Official languages: Arabic; French.
Official religion: none.
Monetary unit: 1 Djibouti franc (DF) = 100 centimes; valuation (Sept. 1, 2005) 1 U.S.$ = DF 177.72; 1 £ = DF 327.22.

Area and population

Regions[2]	Capitals	area[1] sq mi	area[1] sq km	population 2004 estimate
'Alī Sabīḥ (Ali-Sabieh)	'Alī Sabīḥ	850	2,200	...
Arta	Arta	700	1,800	...
Dikhil	Dikhil	2,775	7,200	...
Obock	Obock	1,800	4,700	...
Tadjoura (Tadjourah)	Tadjoura	2,750	7,100	...
City				
Djibouti	—	75	200	...
TOTAL		8,950	23,200	466,900

Demography

Population (2005): 477,000.
Density (2005): persons per sq mi 53.3, persons per sq km 20.6.
Urban-rural (2003): urban 83.7%; rural 16.3%.
Sex distribution (2004): male 51.36%; female 48.64%.
Age breakdown (2004): under 15, 43.2%; 15–29, 28.1%; 30–44, 13.2%; 45–59, 9.9%; 60–74, 4.9%; 75 and over, 0.7%.
Population projection: (2010) 526,000; (2020) 627,000.
Doubling time: 33 years.
Ethnic composition (2000): Somali 46.0%; Afar 35.4%; Arab 11.0%; mixed African and European 3.0%; French 1.6%; other/unspecified 3.0%.
Religious affiliation (1995): Sunnī Muslim 97.2%; Christian 2.8%, of which Roman Catholic 2.2%, Orthodox 0.5%, Protestant 0.1%.
Major city and towns (1991): Djibouti 350,000[3]; 'Alī Sabīḥ 8,000; Tadjoura 7,500; Dikhil 6,500.

Vital statistics

Birth rate per 1,000 population (2004): 40.4 (world avg. 21.1).
Death rate per 1,000 population (2004): 19.4 (world avg. 9.0).
Natural increase rate per 1,000 population (2004): 21.0 (world avg. 12.1).
Total fertility rate (avg. births per childbearing woman; 2004): 5.5.
Life expectancy at birth (2004): male 41.8 years; female 44.4 years.
Major causes of death (percentage of total deaths [infants and children to age 10, district of Djibouti only]; 1984): diarrhea and acute dehydration 16.0%; malnutrition 16.0%; poisoning 11.0%; tuberculosis 6.0%; acute respiratory disease 6.0%; malaria 6.0%; anemia 6.0%; heart disease 2.0%; kidney disease 1.0%; other ailments 19.0%; no diagnosis 11.0%.

National economy

Budget (2002). Revenue: DF 30,947,000,000 (tax revenue 71.6%, of which indirect taxes 37.0%, direct taxes 31.7%; nontax revenue 8.3%; grants 20.1%). Expenditures: DF 34,660,000,000 (current expenditures 88.7%, of which general administration 33.1%, defense 13.0%, transfers 12.7%, education 11.4%, health 4.6%; capital expenditures 11.3%).
Tourism (1998): receipts from visitors U.S.$4,000,000; expenditures by nationals abroad U.S.$4,000,000.
Production (metric tons except as noted). Agriculture, forestry, fishing (2004): vegetables and melons 24,460 (of which tomatoes 1,100, onions 110, eggplant 33), lemons and limes 1,800, tropical fruit 1,100; livestock (number of live animals) 512,000 goats, 466,000 sheep, 297,000 cattle, 69,000 camels, 8,700 asses; roundwood, n.a.; fish catch (2002) 350. Mining and quarrying: mineral production limited to locally used construction materials and evaporated salt (2003) 163,000. Manufacturing (2000): structural detail, n.a.; main products include furniture, nonalcoholic beverages, meat and hides, light electro-mechanical goods, and mineral water. Energy production (consumption): electricity (kW-hr; 2004) 271,000,000 (224,000,000); coal, none (none); crude petroleum, none (none); petroleum products (metric tons; 2002) none (117,000); natural gas, none (none); geothermal, wind, and solar resources are substantial but largely undeveloped.
Population economically active (1991): total 282,000; activity rate of total population, n.a. (participation rates: ages 15–64, n.a.; female 40.8%; unemployed [2000] c. 50%).

Price index (2000 = 100)

	1999[4]	2000	2001	2002
Consumer price index	97.7	100.0	101.3	102.6

Household income and expenditure. Average household size (2000) 5.3; income per household: n.a.; sources of income: n.a.; expenditure (1999)[5]: food 36.2%, housing and energy 18.1%, tobacco and related products 14.4%, transportation 8.8%, household furnishings 7.7%.
Gross national product (2004): U.S.$739,000,000 (U.S.$1,030 per capita).

Structure of gross domestic product and labour force

	2003 in value DF '000,000[6]	2003 % of total value[6]	1991 labour force	1991 % of labour force
Agriculture	3,445	3.5	212,000	75.2
Mining				
Manufacturing	3,334	3.4	31,000	11.0
Construction	6,778	7.0		
Public utilities	5,556	5.7		
Transp. and commun.	26,779	27.5		
Trade	15,557	16.0		
Finance	13,223	13.6	39,000	13.8
Pub. admin., defense	20,890	21.4		
Services	1,889	1.9		
Other	—	—	...	...
TOTAL	97,451	100.0	282,000	100.0

Public debt (external, outstanding; 2003): U.S.$363,300,000.
Land use as % of total land area (2000): in temporary crops, negligible, in permanent crops, negligible, in pasture 56.1%; overall forest area 0.3%.

Foreign trade

Balance of trade (current prices)[7]

	1997	1998	1999	2000	2001	2002
U.S.$'000,000	−161.4	−180.5	−182.5	−194.9	−178.7	−200.5
% of total	65.3%	60.4%	56.9%	56.4%	54.1%	54.6%

Imports (1999): U.S.$152,700,000[8] (food and beverages 25.0%; machinery and electric appliances 12.5%; khat 12.2%; petroleum products 10.9%; transport equipment 10.3%). *Major import sources* (2003): Saudi Arabia 20.2%; Ethiopia 11.2%; China 9.5%; France 6.7%; U.K. 5.2%.
Exports (2001): U.S.$10,200,000[8] (aircraft parts 24.5%; hides and skins of cattle, sheep, goats, and camels 20.6%; unspecified special transactions 8.8%; leather 7.8%; live animals 6.9%). *Major export destinations* (2003): Somalia 61.4%; Yemen 21.7%; Pakistan 6.0%; Ethiopia 4.8%; Ireland 1.0%.

Transport and communications

Transport. Railroads (2003): length 62 mi, 100 km[9]; (1999) passenger-mi 50,331,000, passenger-km 81,000,000; short ton-mile cargo 165,347,000, metric ton-km cargo 266,100,000. Roads (1999): total length 1,796 mi, 2,890 km (paved 13%). Vehicles (1996): passenger cars 9,200; trucks and buses 2,040. Air transport (2002): passengers handled 168,221; metric tons of freight handled 8,636; airports (2000) with scheduled flights 1.

Communications

Medium	date	unit	number	units per 1,000 persons
Daily newspapers	1995	circulation	500	0.8
Radio	1997	receivers	52,000	84
Television	2000	receivers	45,000	104
Telephones	2004	main lines	11,100	16
Cellular telephones	2003	subscribers	23,000	34
Personal computers	2004	units	21,000	31
Internet	2004	users	11,400	13

Education and health

Educational attainment: n.a. *Literacy* (2003): percentage of population age 15 and over literate 68.0%; males literate 78.2%; females literate 58.6%.

Education (2000–01)

	schools	teachers	students	student/ teacher ratio
Primary (age 6–11)	73	1,127	37,938	33.7
Secondary (age 12–18)	26[10]	628[11]	16,121	...
Voc., teacher tr.				
Higher	1[10]	13[10]	478	...

Health: physicians (2004) 86 (1 per 5,429 persons); hospital beds[12] (1999) 1,159 (1 per 368 persons); infant mortality rate per 1,000 live births (2004) 105.5.
Food (2002): daily per capita caloric intake 2,220 (vegetable products 87%, animal products 13%); 96% of FAO recommended minimum requirement.

Military

Total active duty personnel (2004): 9,850[13] (army 81.3%, navy 2.0%, air force 2.5%, paramilitary 14.2%). Foreign troops: French (August 2004) 2,850; U.S. and coalition military personnel at Camp Lemonier (mid-2004) 1,400; German sailors and soldiers (mid-2004) 900. *Military expenditure as percentage of GDP* (2003): 3.9%; per capita expenditure U.S.$53.

---

[1]Areas are estimated. [2]New administrative division structure as of July 2002. [3]2005 estimate. [4]March 1 through October 31 only. [5]Weights of consumer price index components for Djibouti city only. [6]At factor cost. [7]Includes trade with Ethiopia (via rail) comprising c. 20% of all imports and c. 75% of all exports. [8]Excludes Ethiopian trade via rail. [9]Djibouti portion of 485 mi (781 km) Chemins de Fer Djibouti-Ethiopien linking Djibouti city and Addis Ababa, Ethiopia. [10]1991. [11]1995–96. [12]Public health facilities only. [13]Excluding foreign troops.

Internet resources for further information:
- **Banque Centrale de Djibouti**
  http://www.banque-centrale.dj
- **Ministère de l'Economie**
  http://www.ministere-finances.dj

Dominica

Atlantic Ocean

Caribbean Sea

Official name: Commonwealth of Dominica.
Form of government: multiparty republic with one legislative house (House of Assembly [31[1]]).
Chief of state: President.
Head of government: Prime Minister.
Capital: Roseau.
Official language: English.
Official religion: none.
Monetary unit: 1 East Caribbean dollar (EC$) = 100 cents; valuation (Sept. 1, 2005) 1 U.S.$ = EC$2.70; 1 £ = EC$4.97.

Area and population	area		population
Parishes	sq mi	sq km	2001 census
St. Andrew	69.3	179.6	10,240
St. David	49.0	126.8	6,758
St. George	20.7	53.5	19,825
St. John	22.5	58.5	5,327
St. Joseph	46.4	120.1	5,765
St. Luke	4.3	11.1	1,571
St. Mark	3.8	9.9	1,907
St. Patrick	32.6	84.4	8,383
St. Paul	26.0	67.4	8,397
St. Peter	10.7	27.7	1,452
TOTAL	285.3[2]	739.0[2]	71,474[3]

Demography

Population (2005): 69,000.
Density (2005)[2]: persons per sq mi 237.9, persons per sq km 92.0.
Urban-rural (2003): urban 72.0%; rural 28.0%.
Sex distribution (2004): male 50.33%; female 49.67%.
Age breakdown (2004): under 15, 27.3%; 15–29, 24.2%; 30–44, 26.9%; 45–59, 11.2%; 60–74, 7.0%; 75 and over, 3.4%.
Population projection: (2010) 70,000; (2020) 75,000.
Doubling time: 74 years.
Ethnic composition (2000): black 88.3%; mulatto 7.3%; black-Amerindian 1.7%; British expatriates 1.0%; Indo-Pakistani 1.0%; other 0.7%.
Religious affiliation (1991): Roman Catholic 70.1%; six largest Protestant groups 17.2%, of which Seventh-day Adventist 4.6%, Pentecostal 4.3%, Methodist 4.2%; other 8.9%; nonreligious 2.9%; unknown 0.9%.
Major towns (1991): Roseau 20,200[4]; Portsmouth 3,621; Marigot 2,919; Atkinson 2,518; Mahaut 2,372.

Vital statistics

Birth rate per 1,000 population (2004): 16.3 (world avg. 21.1); (1991) legitimate 24.1%; illegitimate 75.9%.
Death rate per 1,000 population (2004): 6.9 (world avg. 9.0).
Natural increase rate per 1,000 population (2004): 9.4 (world avg. 12.1).
Total fertility rate (avg. births per childbearing woman; 2004): 2.0.
Marriage rate per 1,000 population (1999): 4.7.
Divorce rate per 1,000 population (1998): 0.9.
Life expectancy at birth (2004): male 71.5 years; female 77.4 years.
Major causes of death per 100,000 population (1997): diseases of the circulatory system 293.8; malignant neoplasms (cancers) 160.0; diabetes mellitus 75.4; infectious and parasitic diseases 56.7; accidents, poisoning, and violence 43.9.

National economy

Budget (2002). Revenue: EC$224,700,000 (tax revenue 72.1%, of which taxes on international trade and transactions 38.0%, income taxes 18.5%; nontax revenue 16.5%; grants 11.4%). Expenditures: EC$258,600,000 (current expenditures 89.5%, of which wages 47.9%, debt payment 15.3%, transfers 14.7%; development expenditures 10.5%).
Tourism: receipts from visitors (2003) U.S.$51,000,000; expenditures by nationals abroad U.S.$9,000,000.
Gross national product (2004): U.S.$261,000,000 (U.S.$3,650 per capita).

Structure of gross domestic product and labour force	2003		1997	
	in value EC$'000,000[5]	% of total value[5]	labour force	% of labour force
Agriculture	103.8	14.7	6,100	18.2
Mining	4.6	0.7	...	...
Manufacturing	45.5	6.4	2,250	6.7
Construction	45.9	6.5	2,150	6.4
Public utilities	34.4	4.9	280	0.8
Transportation and communications	76.1	10.7	1,500	4.5
Trade, hotels, restaurants	90.3	12.8	5,030	15.1
Finance, real estate	88.9	12.6	1,390	4.2
Services	10.9	1.5	4,370	13.1
Pub. admin., defense	127.6	18.0	1,530	4.6
Other	79.4[6]	11.2[6]	8,820[7]	26.4[7]
TOTAL	707.4	100.0	33,420	100.0

Land use as % of total land area (2000): in temporary crops *c.* 7%, in permanent crops *c.* 19%, in pasture *c.* 3%; overall forest area *c.* 61%.
Public debt (external, outstanding; 2002): U.S.$178,300,000.

Population economically active (1997): total 33,420; activity rate of total population 45.8% (participation rates: over age 14, 65.6%; female 45.8%; unemployed 23.1%).

Price index (2000 = 100)							
	1998	1999	2000	2001	2002	2003	2004
Consumer price index	98.0	99.2	100.0	101.5	101.8	103.3	105.7

Household income and expenditure. Average household size (1991) 3.6; income per household: n.a.; sources of income: n.a.; expenditure (2001)[8]: food 32.9%, transportation and communications 19.4%, housing 11.2%, household furnishings 9.4%, clothing and footwear 8.2%, energy 5.9%.
Production (metric tons except as noted). Agriculture, forestry, fishing (2004): bananas 29,000, root crops 26,720 (of which taro 11,200, yams 8,000, yautia 4,550, sweet potatoes 1,850), grapefruit and pomelos 17,000, coconuts 11,500, oranges 7,200, plantains 5,700, sugarcane 4,400; livestock (number of live animals; 2004) 13,400 cattle, 9,700 goats, 7,600 sheep; roundwood, n.a.; fish catch (2002) 1,217. Mining and quarrying: pumice, limestone, and sand and gravel are quarried primarily for local consumption. Manufacturing (value of production in EC$'000; 2001): toilet and laundry soap 18,815; toothpaste 10,063; crude coconut oil 1,758; other products include fruit juices, beer, garments, bottled spring water, and cardboard boxes. Energy production (consumption): electricity (kW-hr; 2003) 78,000,000 ([2002] 85,000,000); coal, none (none); crude petroleum, none (none); petroleum products (metric tons; 2002) none (39,000); natural gas, none (none).

Foreign trade[9]

Balance of trade (current prices)						
	1998	1999	2000	2001	2002	2003
EC$'000,000	−196.8	−233.6	−251.6	−253.7	−216.6	−228.3
% of total	36.6%	44.4%	46.3%	51.4%	48.1%	52.2%

Imports (2000): EC$397,700,000 (food and beverages 19.3%; machinery and apparatus 17.7%; refined petroleum 8.6%; road vehicles 8.3%). *Major import sources* (2003): Japan 21.6%; U.S. 15.1%; China 14.8%; Trinidad and Tobago 12.0%; South Korea 7.7%.
Exports (2000): EC$147,300,000 (agricultural exports 37.5%, of which bananas 25.9%; coconut-based soaps 25.0%; perfumery and cosmetics 13.7%). *Major export destinations* (2003): Japan 27.1%; U.K. 16.4%; Jamaica 15.1%; U.S. 6.6%; Antigua and Barbuda 6.2%.

Transport and communications

Transport. Railroads: none. Roads (1999): total length 485 mi, 780 km (paved 50%). Vehicles (1998): passenger cars 8,700; trucks and buses 3,400. Air transport: (1997) passenger arrivals and departures 74,100; (1997) cargo unloaded 575 metric tons, cargo loaded 363 metric tons; airports (1996) with scheduled flights 2.

Communications				units per 1,000
Medium	date	unit	number	persons
Radio	1997	receivers	46,000	608
Television	2000	receivers	15,700	220
Telephones	2004	main lines	21,000	295
Cellular telephones	2004	subscribers	41,800	589
Personal computers	2004	units	9,000	127
Internet	2004	users	18,500	261

Education and health

Educational attainment (1991). Percentage of population age 25 and over having: no formal schooling 4.2%; primary education 78.4%; secondary 11.0%; higher vocational 2.3%; university 2.8%; other/unknown 1.3%. *Literacy* (1996): total population age 15 and over literate, 94.0%.

Education (1997–98)	schools	teachers	students	student/ teacher ratio
Primary	63	587	13,636	23.2
Secondary	15	293	5,455	18.6
Higher[10]	2	34	484	14.2

Health (2004): physicians 38 (1 per 1,824 persons); hospital beds (2002) 270 (1 per 257 persons); infant mortality rate per 1,000 live births 14.8.
Food (2002): daily per capita caloric intake 2,763 (vegetable products 76%, animal products 24%); 114% of FAO recommended minimum requirement.

Military

Total active duty personnel (2003): none[11].

[1]Includes 22 seats that are elective (including speaker if elected from outside of the House of Assembly) and 9 seats that are nonelective (including appointees of the president and the attorney general serving ex officio). [2]Total area of Dominica per more recent survey is 290 sq mi (750 sq km). [3]Reported total; summed total is 69,625. [4]2004. [5]At current prices. [6]Taxes less imputed banking service charges and subsidies. [7]Includes 7,720 unemployed and 1,100 unclassified by economic activity. [8]Weights of consumer price index components. [9]Imports c.i.f.; exports f.o.b. [10]1992–93. [11]300-member police force includes a coast guard unit.

Internet resources for further information:
• **Eastern Caribbean Central Bank**
  http://www.eccb-centralbank.org

Dominican Republic

Official name: República Dominicana (Dominican Republic).
Form of government: multiparty republic with two legislative houses (Senate [32]; Chamber of Deputies [150]).
Head of state and government: President.
Capital: Santo Domingo.
Official language: Spanish.
Official religion: none[1].
Monetary unit: 1 Dominican peso (RD$) = 100 centavos; valuation (Sept. 1, 2005) 1 U.S.$ = RD$29.25; 1 £ = RD$53.86.

Area and population

Provinces	area sq km	population 2002 final census	Provinces	area sq km	population 2002 final census
Azua	2,532	208,857	Peravia	998	169,865
Baoruco	1,283	91,480	Puerto Plata	1,857	312,706
Barahona	1,739	179,239	Salcedo	440	96,356
Dajabón	1,021	62,046	Samaná	854	91,875
Duarte	1,605	283,805	San Cristóbal	1,265	532,880
El Seíbo (El Seybo)	1,786	89,261	San José de Ocoa[2]	650	62,368
Elías Piña	1,424	63,879	San Juan	3,571	241,105
Espaillat	838	225,091	San Pedro de Macorís	1,255	301,744
Hato Mayor	1,329	87,631	Sánchez Ramírez	1,196	151,179
Independencia	2,008	50,833	Santiago	2,836	908,250
La Altagracia	3,010	182,020	Santiago Rodríguez	1,112	59,629
La Romana	654	219,812	Santo Domingo[3]	1,296	1,817,754
La Vega	2,286	385,101	Valverde	823	158,293
María Trinidad Sánchez	1,271	135,727			
Monseñor Nouel	992	167,618	**National District**		
Monte Cristi	1,925	111,014	Santo Domingo (city)	104	913,540
Monte Plata	2,633	180,376	TOTAL	48,671[4, 5]	8,562,541
Pedernales	2,077	21,207			

Demography

Population (2005): 8,895,000.
Density (2005): persons per sq mi 473.3, persons per sq km 182.8.
Urban-rural (2002): urban 63.6%; rural 36.4%.
Sex distribution (2002): male 49.81%; female 50.19%.
Age breakdown (2002): under 15, 34.0%; 15–29, 27.0%; 30–44, 20.0%; 45–59, 11.0%; 60–74, 5.8%; 75 and over, 2.2%.
Population projection: (2010) 9,522,000; (2020) 10,676,000.
Doubling time: 38 years.
Ethnic composition (2000): mulatto 69.5%; white 17.0%; local black 9.4%; Haitian black 2.4%; other/unknown 1.7%.
Religious affiliation (2000): Roman Catholic 88.6%; Protestant 4.2%; other Christian 2.4%; other 4.8%.
Major urban centres (2004): Santo Domingo 1,817,754; Santiago 505,600; La Romana 171,500; San Francisco de Macorís 152,600; San Cristóbal 120,200.

Vital statistics

Birth rate per 1,000 population (2004): 23.9 (world avg. 21.1).
Death rate per 1,000 population (2004): 5.7 (world avg. 9.0).
Natural increase rate per 1,000 population (2004): 18.2 (world avg. 12.1).
Total fertility rate (avg. births per childbearing woman; 2004): 2.9.
Marriage rate per 1,000 population (2001): 2.9.
Divorce rate per 1,000 population (2001): 1.0.
Life expectancy at birth (2004): male 69.7 years; female 72.8 years.
Major causes of death per 100,000 population (1998): diseases of the circulatory system 318; accidents and violence 126; malignant neoplasms (cancers) 115.

National economy

Budget (2004). Revenue: RD$126,245,100,000 (tax revenue 92.9%, of which taxes on goods and services 42.4%, import duties 25.1%, income taxes 19.3%; nontax revenue 7.1%). Expenditures: RD$133,161,500,000 (current expenditures 79.7%; development expenditures 20.3%).
Public debt (external, outstanding; 2003): U.S.$5,077,000,000.
Gross national product (2004): U.S.$18,443,000,000 (U.S.$2,080 per capita).

Structure of gross domestic product and labour force

	2004 in value RD$'000[6]	% of total value	labour force	% of labour force
Agriculture	842,500	11.7	511,613	13.8
Mining	115,200	1.6	8,003	0.2
Manufacturing	1,116,900[7]	15.5[7]	525,289	14.2
Construction	775,400	10.7	206,683	5.6
Public utilities	131,100	1.8	28,707	0.8
Transp. and commun.	1,254,900	17.4	243,863	6.6
Trade, restaurants	1,330,300	18.4	923,896	25.0
Finance, real estate	552,400	7.7	71,435	1.9
Pub. admin., defense	580,000	8.0	172,242	4.6
Services	521,000	7.2	776,574	21.0
Other			233,499	6.3
TOTAL	7,219,700	100.0	3,701,804	100.0

Household income and expenditure (1998). Average household size (2002) 3.9; average annual household income RD$131,647 (U.S.$8,623); sources of income: wages and salaries 31.7%, self-employment 28.9%, non-monetary income 22.6%, transfers 11.9%; expenditure: housing and energy 20.8%, food, beverages, and tobacco 20.8%, transportation 10.0%, clothing 4.9%.
Production (metric tons except as noted). Agriculture, forestry, fishing (2004): sugarcane 5,255,833, rice 639,785, bananas 480,000, plantains 192,500, cacao beans 45,000, coffee 45,000; livestock (number of live animals) 2,165,000 cattle, 578,000 pigs, 47,000,000 chickens; roundwood (2003) 562,300 cu m; fish catch (2003) 18,097. Mining (2003): nickel (metal content) 45,400; gold, none[8]. Manufacturing (2004)[9]: cement 2,636,274; refined sugar 124,029; beer 2,040,380 hectolitres; rum 546,610 hectolitres. Energy production (consumption): electricity (kW-hr; 2002) 11,510,000,000 (11,510,000,000); coal (metric tons; 2002) none (233,000); crude petroleum (barrels; 2002) none (15,000,000); petroleum products (metric tons; 2002) 1,461,000 (5,797,000); natural gas, none (none).
Tourism (2003): receipts U.S.$3,110,000,000; expenditures U.S.$260,000,000.
Population economically active (2004): total 3,701,804; activity rate of total population 43.1% (participation rates: ages 10 and over, 55.1%; female 38.7%; unemployed 18.4%).

Price and earnings indexes (2000 = 100)

	1998	1999	2000	2001	2002	2003	2004
Consumer price index	87.2	92.8	100.0	108.9	114.6	146.0	221.2
Hourly earnings index	85.4	93.1	100.0	106.1	107.9	127.4	141.0

Land use as % of total land area (2000): in temporary crops 22.7%, in permanent crops 10.3%, in pasture 43.4%; overall forest area 28.4%.

Foreign trade[7]

Balance of trade (current prices)

	1998	1999	2000	2001	2002	2003	2004
U.S.$'000,000	–2,616	–2,905	–3,741	–3,503	–3,673	–2,156	–2,095
% of total	20.8%	22.0%	24.6%	24.9%	26.2%	16.5%	15.4%

Imports (2004): U.S.$7,844,600,000 (imports for free zones 31.5%, refined petroleum 13.9%, crude petroleum 7.4%, food 7.0%, machinery and apparatus 5.1%). *Major import sources* (2003): U.S. 52.1%; Mexico 4.7%; Colombia 4.2%; Spain 3.1%; Chile 3.0%.
Exports (2004): U.S.$5,749,900,000 (reexports of free zones 76.8%, ferronickel 6.8%, ships' stores 4.1%, raw sugar 1.3%, cacao and cocoa 1.0%). *Major export destinations* (2003): U.S. 83.8%; U.K. 1.5%; Haiti 1.5%.

Transport and communications

Transport. Railroads (2003)[10]: route length 1,083 mi, 1,743 km. Roads (1999): total length 7,829 mi, 12,600 km (paved 49%). Vehicles (1998): passenger cars 353,177; trucks and buses 200,347. Air transport (1999): passenger-km 4,900,000; metric ton-km cargo (2003) 200,000; airports (2002) 6.

Communications

Medium	date	unit	number	units per 1,000 persons
Daily newspapers	2001	circulation	226,500	27
Radio	2001	receivers	1,518,200	181
Television	2001	receivers	813,600	97
Telephones	2004	main lines	936,200	107
Cellular telephones	2004	subscribers	2,534,100	288
Internet	2004	users	800,000	91

Education and health

Educational attainment (2002). Percentage of population age 5 and older having: no formal education or unknown 1.9%, incomplete/complete primary education 59.4%, secondary 25.8%, undergraduate 12.3%, graduate 0.6%.
Literacy (2003): total population age 15 and over literate 84.7%; males literate 84.6%; females literate 84.8%.

Education (2002–03)

	schools	teachers	students	student/teacher ratio
Primary (age 6–13)	4,001[11]	35,867	1,374,624	38.3
Secondary (age 14–17)	...	24,723	658,164	26.6
Voc., teacher tr.				
Higher	...	11,111	286,957	25.8

Health: physicians (2000) 16,530 (1 per 500 persons); hospital beds (2003) 9,395 (1 per 920 persons); infant mortality rate per 1,000 live births (2004) 30.5.
Food (2002): daily per capita caloric intake 2,347 (vegetable products 85%, animal products 15%); 104% of FAO recommended minimum requirement.

Military

Total active duty personnel (2004): 24,500 (army 61.2%, navy 16.3%, air force 22.4%). *Military expenditure as percentage of GDP* (2003): 1.0%; per capita expenditure U.S.$19.

---

[1]Roman Catholicism is the state religion per concordat with Vatican City. [2]Created in 2001 from part of Peravia province. [3]Created in 2001 from part of the National District. [4]Detail does not add to total given because of rounding. [5]Mainland total is 48,512 sq km and offshore islands total is 159 sq km. [6]At prices of 1970. [7]Includes a free-zone sector for reexport (significantly of ready-made garments but also cigars and footwear, with a value in 2004 [in prices of 1970] of RD$195,700,000 and representing 2.7% of the GDP). [8]The mining of gold was suspended in 1999 and was expected to resume in early 2005. [9]Excludes free-zone sector employing (2002) 162,000. [10]Includes 762 mi (1,226 km) of track that is privately owned and serves the sugar industry only. [11]1994–95.

Internet resources for further information:
• Banco Central de la República Dominicana http://www.bancentral.gov.do
• Oficina Nacional de Estadística http://www.one.gov.do

East Timor[1]

Official name: Repúblika Demokrátika Timor Lorosa'e (Tetum); República Democrática de Timor-Leste (Portuguese) (Democratic Republic of Timor-Leste)[1].
Form of government: republic with one legislative body (National Parliament [88]).
Chief of state: President.
Head of government: Prime Minister.
Capital: Dili.
Official languages: Tetum; Portuguese[2].
Official religion: none.
Monetary unit: 1 United States dollar (U.S.$) = 100 centavos[3] (100 U.S. cents); valuation (Sept. 1, 2005) 1 U.S.$ = £0.54.

Area and population		area		population
				2004
Districts	Capitals	sq mi	sq km	census[4]
Aileu	Aileu	281	729	36,889
Ainaro	Ainaro	308	797	53,629
Ambeno (Ocussi) exclave	Pante Macassar	315	815	58,521
Baucau (Baukau)	Baucau	577	1,494	104,571
Bobonaro	Maliana	528	1,368	82,385
Cova Lima	Suai	473	1,226	55,941
Dili	Dili	144	372	167,777
Ermera	Ermera	288	746	103,169
Lautem	Los Palos	657	1,702	57,453
Liquiça	Liquiça	210	543	55,058
Manatuto	Manatuto	659	1,706	38,580
Manufahi	Same	512	1,325	44,235
Viqueque	Viqueque	688	1,781	66,434
TOTAL		5,639[5]	14,604	924,642

Demography

Population (2005): 975,000.
Density (2005): persons per sq mi 172.9, persons per sq km 66.8.
Urban-rural (2003): urban 7.6%; rural 92.4%.
Sex distribution (2004): male 50.59%; female 49.41%.
Age breakdown (2004): under 15, 37.8%; 15–29, 27.6%; 30–44, 18.9%; 45–59, 10.8%; 60–74, 4.1%; 75 and over, 0.8%.
Population projection: (2010) 1,292,000; (2020) 1,780,000.
Doubling time: 33 years.
Ethnic composition (1999): East Timorese c. 80%; other (nearly all Indonesian, and particularly West Timorese) c. 20%.
Religious affiliation (2000): Roman Catholic c. 87%; Protestant c. 5%; Muslim c. 3%; traditional beliefs c. 3%; other c. 2%.
Major cities (2000): Dili 48,200; Dare 17,100; Baucau 14,200; Maliana 12,300; Ermera 12,000.

Vital statistics

Birth rate per 1,000 population (2004): 27.5 (world avg. 21.1).
Death rate per 1,000 population (2004): 6.4 (world avg. 9.0).
Natural increase rate per 1,000 population (2004): 21.1 (world avg. 12.1).
Total fertility rate (avg. births per childbearing woman; 2004): 3.7.
Marriage rate per 1,000 population (1997–98): 0.4.
Divorce rate per 1,000 population (1997–98): 0.1.
Life expectancy at birth (2004): male 63.3 years; female 67.9 years.
Major causes of death per 100,000 population (2002): n.a.[6]

National economy

Budget (2004–05). Revenue: U.S.$98,000,000 (oil and gas revenue 45.1%; grants 31.4%; domestic revenue 23.5%, of which tax revenue 19.4%, nontax revenue 4.1%). Expenditures: U.S.$75,100,000 (current expenditure 86.4%, of which goods and services 48.9%, wages and salaries 37.5%; capital expenditure 13.6%).
Public debt (external, outstanding; 2001): n.a.
Production (metric tons except as noted). Agriculture, forestry, fishing (2004): corn (maize) 70,200, rice 65,400, cassava 41,500, sweet potatoes 26,000, coffee 14,000, coconuts 14,000, peanuts (groundnuts) 4,000, candlenut (1997) 1,055, spices 425; livestock (number of live animals; 2004) 346,000 pigs, 170,000 cattle, 70,000 buffalo, 2,100,000 chickens; roundwood, n.a.; sandalwood exports were formerly more significant; fish catch (2002) 350. Mining and quarrying (2001): commercial quantities of marble are exported. Manufacturing (2001): principally the production of textiles, garments, handicrafts, bottled water, and processed coffee. Energy production (consumption): electricity (kW-hr; 1998) 40,000,000 (n.a.); coal, n.a. (n.a.); crude petroleum, n.a. (n.a.); petroleum products, n.a. (n.a.); natural gas, n.a. (n.a.).
Household income and expenditure. Average household size (2004) 4.7; average annual income per household, n.a.[7]; sources of income, n.a.; expenditure, n.a.
Population economically active (2001): total 232,000[8]; activity rate of total population 28%[8] (participation rates: ages 15–64, 57%[8]; female, n.a.; unemployed, n.a.).

Price index (2000 = 100)					
	2000	2001	2002	2003	2004[9]
Consumer price index[8]	100.0	113.5	118.9	127.4	130.9

Gross national product (2004): U.S.$506,000,000 (U.S.$550 per capita).

Structure of gross domestic product and labour force				
	2003		2001	
	in value U.S.$'000,000	% of total value	labour force	% of labour force
Agriculture	104.0	30.5	...	73.2
Mining	3.8	1.1	...	
Manufacturing	11.0	3.2	...	
Public utilities	3.2	0.9	...	4.8
Construction	55.9	16.4	...	
Transp. and commun.	27.5	8.1	...	
Trade, hotels	29.9	8.8	...	
Finance, insurance	23.8	7.0	...	
Services	2.3	0.7	...	22.0
Pub. admin., defense	79.9	23.4	...	
Other			...	
TOTAL	341.2[5]	100.0[5]	...	100.0

Tourism: receipts, n.a.; expenditures, n.a.; available beds for tourists (1998) 580.
Land use as % of total land area (2000): in temporary crops 4.7%, in permanent crops 0.7%, in pasture 10.1%; overall forest area 34.3%.

Foreign trade

Balance of trade (current prices)[10]					
	2000	2001	2002	2003	2004
U.S.$'000,000	−235	−264	−245	−196	−139
% of total	95.6%	97.1%	95.3%	93.3%	90.8%

Imports (2004): U.S.$146,100,000 (mineral fuels and oils 25.2%; vehicles and vehicle parts 10.1%; electrical machinery and equipment 6.7%; cereals 5.6%). *Major import sources:* Indonesia 42.8%; Australia 17.1%; Singapore 11.2%; Vietnam 3.6%; Portugal 3.0%.
Exports (2004): U.S.$6,972,000[10] (coffee 86.1%; unspecified 13.9%). *Major export destinations:* Australia 41.7%; Japan 22.8%; Portugal 13.0%; U.S. 4.1%.

Transport and communications

Transport. Railroads: none. Roads (December 1999): total length 879 mi (1,414 km)[11]. Vehicles (1998): passenger cars 3,156; trucks and buses 7,140. Air transport: airports (2001) with scheduled flights 2.

Communications				units per 1,000
Medium	date	unit	number	persons
Daily newspaper	2002	circulation	1,500	1.8
Television	2002[12]	receivers	...	...
Telephones	1996	main lines	6,600	8.0
Internet	2004	users	1,000	1.1

Education and health

Educational attainment (2002). Percentage of population age 15 and over having: no formal education 54.3%, some primary education 14.4%, complete primary 6.2%, lower secondary 10.4%, upper secondary and higher 14.7%.
Literacy (2002): percentage of population age 15 and over literate 58.6%; males literate 65%; females literate 52%.

Education (2003)				student/
	schools	teachers	students	teacher ratio
Primary (age 7–12)	...	4,080	183,600[13]	45.0[13]
Lower secondary (age 13–15)	...	1,103	38,180	34.6
Upper secondary (age 16–18)	...	...	...	...
Higher[14]	1	...	4,500	...

Health: physicians (2002) 47 (1 per 17,355 persons); hospital beds (1999) 560 (1 per 1,277 persons); infant mortality rate per 1,000 live births (2004) 48.9.
Food (2002)[15]: daily per capita caloric intake 2,806 (vegetable products 89%, animal products 11%); 130% of FAO recommended minimum requirement.

Military

Total active duty personnel (2004): 1,250 (army 100%); UN peacekeeping troops were withdrawn May 2005. *Military expenditure as percentage of GDP* (2003): 1.3%; per capita expenditure U.S.$5.

---

[1]Per U.S. Board on Geographic Names: conventional short-form name is East Timor, conventional long-form name is Democratic Republic of Timor-Leste. [2]Indonesian and English are "working" languages. [3]Minor currency coins introduced in November 2003 at par with U.S. coins; the U.S. dollar is the official currency. [4]Preliminary. [5]Detail does not add to total given because of rounding. [6]The health sector faces immense difficulties; malaria is endemic and prevalence rates for tuberculosis and leprosy are 2.4% and 1.2%, respectively. [7]Minimum annual wage (1999) U.S.$276; average public administration wage (2003) U.S.$1,500. [8]Estimated figures. [9]April. [10]Excludes reexports. [11]57% of paved roads were in poor or damaged condition in late 1999; gravel roads were not usable for most vehicles. [12]Locally produced television service commenced in May 2002. [13]Rounded figures. [14]2001. [15]Based on FAO guidelines for Indonesia.

Internet resources for further information:
• **Banking and Payments Authority of Timor-Leste**
  http://www.bancocentral.tl/en
• **National Statistics Directorate**
  http://dne.mopf.gov.tp

Ecuador

Official name: República del Ecuador (Republic of Ecuador).
Form of government: unitary multiparty republic with one legislative house (National Congress [125]).
Head of state and government: President.
Capital: Quito.
Official language: Spanish[1].
Official religion: none.
Monetary unit[2]: 1 dollar (U.S.$); valuation (Sept. 1, 2005) 1 U.S.$ = £ 0.54.

Area and population

Regions Provinces	area sq km	population 2001 census	Regions Provinces	area sq km	population 2001 census
Amazonica			Insular		
Morona-Santiago	33,930	115,412	Galápagos	8,010	18,640
Napo	} 25,690	79,139	Sierra		
Orellana		86,493	Azuay	8,125	599,546
Pastaza	29,774	61,779	Bolívar	3,940	169,370
Sucumbíos	18,327	128,995	Cañar	3,122	206,981
Zamora-Chinchipe	23,111	76,601	Carchi	3,605	152,939
Costa			Chimborazo	6,569	403,632
El Oro	5,850	525,763	Cotopaxi	6,072	349,540
Esmeraldas	15,239	385,223	Imbabura	4,559	344,044
Guayas	20,503	3,309,034	Loja	11,026	404,835
Los Ríos	7,175	650,178	Pichincha	12,915	2,388,817
Manabí	18,879	1,186,025	Tungurahua	3,335	441,034
			TOTAL	272,045[3]	12,156,608[4]

Demography

Population (2005): 13,364,000.
Density (2005): persons per sq mi 127.2, persons per sq km 49.1.
Urban-rural (2003): urban 61.8%; rural 38.2%.
Sex distribution (2003): male 49.99%; female 50.01%.
Age breakdown (2003): under 15, 34.4%; 15–29, 28.6%; 30–44, 19.1%; 45–59, 10.9%; 60–74, 5.1%; 75 and over, 1.9%.
Doubling time: 37 years.
Population projection: (2010) 14,245,000; (2020) 16,178,000.
Ethnic composition (2000): mestizo 42.0%; Amerindian 40.8%; white 10.6%; black 5.0%; other 1.6%.
Religious affiliation (2000): Roman Catholic 94.1%; Protestant 1.9%; other 4.0%.
Major cities (2001): Guayaquil 1,985,379; Quito 1,399,378; Cuenca 277,374; Machala 204,578; Santo Domingo de los Colorados 200,421; Manta 183,166.

Vital statistics

Birth rate per 1,000 population (2004): 23.2 (world avg. 21.1).
Death rate per 1,000 population (2004): 4.2 (world avg. 9.0).
Natural increase rate per 1,000 population (2004): 19.0 (world avg. 12.1).
Total fertility rate (avg. births per childbearing woman; 2004): 2.8.
Marriage rate per 1,000 population (2003): 5.0.
Divorce rate per 1,000 population (2003): 0.8.
Life expectancy at birth (2004): male 73.2 years; female 79.0 years.
Major causes of death per 100,000 population (2002): diseases of the circulatory system 153.1; malignant neoplasms (cancers) 82.3; communicable diseases 76.1; accidents 46.7.

National economy

Budget (2002). Revenue: U.S.$4,526,000,000 (nonpetroleum revenue 72.4%, of which value-added tax 33.8%, income tax 14.8%; petroleum revenue 27.6%). Expenditures: U.S.$4,694,000,000 (current expenditure 73.9%; capital expenditure 26.1%).
Public debt (external, outstanding; 2003): U.S.$11,371,000,000.
Production (metric tons except as noted). Agriculture, forestry, fishing (2004): bananas 5,900,000, sugarcane 5,400,000, oil palm fruit 1,600,000, rice 1,100,000, plantains 652,000, corn (maize) 651,000, potatoes 400,000; livestock (live animals) 5,125,850 cattle, 3,063,000 pigs, 2,880,000 sheep, 535,000 horses, 147,000,000 chickens; roundwood (2003) 6,262,517 cu m; fish catch (2003) 397,864. Mining and quarrying (2003): limestone 6,280,000; gold 3,020 kg. Manufacturing (value added in U.S.$'000; 2004): food products 1,380; textiles and wearing apparel 552; wood and wood products 304; beverages 206; paper and paper products 144; chemicals and chemical products 143. Energy production (consumption): electricity (kW-hr; 2002) 11,884,000,000 (11,942,-000,000); crude petroleum (barrels; 2004) 191,000,000 ([2002] 58,000,000); petroleum products (metric tons; 2002) 7,298,000 (6,457,000); natural gas (cu m; 2002) 141,000,000 (141,000,000).
Population economically active (2001): total 4,124,185; activity rate of total population 49.6% (participation rates: ages 15 and over, 72.8%; female 42.3%; unemployed [April 2004–March 2005] 11.0%).

Price and earnings indexes (2000 = 100)

	1998	1999	2000	2001	2002	2003	2004
Consumer price index	33.5	51.0	100.0	137.7	154.9	167.1	171.7
Monthly earnings index	172.0	108.5	100.0	147.6	170.2	...	...

Household income and expenditure (2003)[5]. Average household size 4.2; average annual income per household U.S.$8,161; sources of income: wages 47.0%, self-employment 25.6%, transfer payments 15.7%, rent 11.7%; expenditure: food, beverages, and tobacco 23.8%, housing and energy 19.1%, transportation and communications 12.9%, restaurants and hotels 10.4%, clothing 8.1%.
Gross national product (2004): U.S.$28,783,000,000 (U.S.$2,178 per capita).

Structure of gross domestic product and labour force

	2004 in value U.S.$'000	2004 % of total value	2001 labour force	2001 % of labour force
Agriculture	2,160,425	7.1	391,300	9.5
Crude petroleum, nat. gas	4,953,607	16.4 }	18,300	0.4
Other mining	123,009	0.4		
Manufacturing	1,518,713	5.0	610,600	14.8
Construction	2,252,217	7.4	234,900	5.7
Public utilities	482,025	1.6	27,800	0.7
Transp. and commun.	4,859,754	16.0	244,600	5.9
Trade	4,496,341	14.8	1,184,900	28.7
Finance, real estate	3,225,521	10.7	191,700	4.6
Pub. admin., defense	1,539,976	5.1	159,900	3.9
Services	2,286,347	7.6	511,700	12.4
Other	2,383,569	7.9	548,300[6]	13.3[6]
TOTAL	30,281,504	100.0	4,124,000	100.0[7]

Land use as % of total land area (2000): in temporary crops 5.8%, in permanent crops 4.9%, in pasture 18.4%; overall forest area 38.1%.
Tourism (2003): receipts U.S.$406,000,000; expenditures U.S.$354,000,000.

Foreign trade[8]

Balance of trade (current prices)

	1999	2000	2001	2002	2003	2004
U.S.$'000,000	+1,714	+1,526	−258	−917	−33	+383
% of total	23.8%	18.3%	2.7%	8.3%	0.3%	2.6%

Imports (2004): U.S.$7,861,063,760 ([2002] machinery and apparatus 26.3%; chemicals and chemical products 16.2%; base metals and fabricated metal products 10.4%; food and live animals 7.5%; mineral fuels and lubricants 4.5%). *Major import sources:* U.S. 20.7%; Colombia 14.6%; Venezuela 6.8%; Brazil 6.1%; Chile 5.3%.
Exports (2004): U.S.$7,655,394,960 (mineral fuels and lubricants 55.3%, of which crude petroleum 50.9%; food 26.5%, of which bananas and plantains 13.4%, fish and crustaceans 10.1%; cut flowers 4.5%). *Major export destinations:* U.S. 42.9%; Peru 7.9%; Italy 4.6%; Colombia 3.9%; Germany 2.5%.

Transport and communications

Transport. Railroads (2003): route length 966 km; passenger-km (2000) 5,000,000; metric ton-km cargo (2000) less than 500,000. Roads (2002): total length 43,197 km (paved 19%). Vehicles (2001): passenger cars 529,359; trucks and buses 63,660. Air transport (2001)[9]: passenger-km 901,000,000; metric ton-km cargo 14,344,000.

Communications

Medium	date	unit	number	units per 1,000 persons
Daily newspapers	2001	circulation	1,219,400	96
Radio	2001	receivers	5,130,000	422
Television	2002	receivers	3,034,000	237
Telephones	2004	main lines	1,612,300	122
Cellular telephones	2004	subscribers	4,544,200	344
Personal computers	2004	units	724,000	55
Internet	2004	users	624,600	47

Education and health

Educational attainment (1990). Percentage of population age 25 and over having: no formal schooling 2.2%; incomplete primary and complete primary education 54.3%; secondary 28.0%; postsecondary 15.5%. *Literacy* (2003): total population age 15 and over literate 92.5%; males 94.0%; females 91.0%.

Education (2002–03)

	schools	teachers	students	student/teacher ratio
Primary (age 6–12)	17,367[10]	83,736	1,987,465	23.7
Secondary (age 12–18)	} ...	73,284	972,777	13.3
Vocational				
Higher	...	12,856[11]	115,554[12]	...

Health: physicians (2002) 20,592 (1 per 627 persons); hospital beds (2003) 19,975 (1 per 655 persons); infant mortality rate (2004) 24.5.
Food (2002): daily per capita caloric intake 2,754 (vegetable products 82%, animal products 18%); 120% of FAO recommended minimum requirement.

Military

Total active duty personnel (2004): 46,500 (army 79.6%, navy 11.8%, air force 8.6%); U.S. troops (2004) 290. *Military expenditure as percentage of GDP* (2003): 2.4%; per capita expenditure U.S.$49.

[1]Quechua and Shuar are also official languages for the indigenous peoples. [2]The United States dollar was formally adopted as the national currency on Sept. 9, 2000; the pegged value of the Sucre (S/.), the former national currency, to the U.S. dollar was S/. 25,000 = 1 U.S.$. [3]Includes 2,289 sq km in nondelimited areas. [4]Total includes 72,588 persons in nondelimited areas. [5]Based on a survey of urban households only. [6]Unemployed. [7]Detail does not add to total given because of rounding. [8]Import figures are f.o.b. in balance of trade and c.i.f. for commodities and trading partners. [9]Ecuatoriana and TAME airlines. [10]1996–97. [11]1990–91. [12]2000.

Internet resources for further information:
• **Instituto Nacional de Estadística y Censos** http://www.inec.gov.ec
• **Banco Central del Ecuador** http://www.bce.fin.ec

Egypt

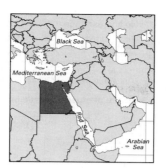

Official name: Jumhūrīah Miṣr al-ʿArabīyah (Arab Republic of Egypt).
Form of government: republic with one legislative house (People's Assembly [454[1]]).
Chief of state: President.
Head of government: Prime Minister.
Capital: Cairo.
Official language: Arabic.
Official religion: Islam.
Monetary unit: 1 Egyptian pound (£E) = 100 piastres; valuation (Sept. 1, 2005) 1 U.S.\$ = £E 5.77; 1 £ = £E 10.62.

Area and population

Regions Governorates	area sq km	population 2004 estimate	Regions Governorates	area sq km	population 2004 estimate
Frontier			Upper Egypt		
Al-Baḥr al-Aḥmar	203,685	182,526	Aswān	679	1,098,870
Janūb Sīnāʾ	33,140	63,834	Asyūṭ	1,553	3,351,057
Maṭrūḥ	212,112	262,210	Banī Suwayf	1,322	2,208,082
Shamāl Sīnāʾ	27,574	302,077	Al-Fayyūm	1,827	2,371,780
Al-Wādī al-Jadīd	376,505	166,211	Al-Jīzah	85,153	5,535,498
Lower Egypt			Al-Minyā	2,262	3,960,656
Al-Buḥayrah	10,130	4,604,443	Qinā	1,851	2,876,746
Ad-Daqahlīyah	3,471	4,839,359	Sawhāj	1,547	3,730,894
Dumyāṭ	589	1,056,324	Urban		
Al-Gharbīyah	1,942	3,859,378	Būr Saʿīd		
Al-Ismāʿīlīyah (Ismailia)	1,442	844,091	(Port Said)	72	529,684
Kafr ash-Shaykh	3,437	2,541,124	Al-Iskandarīyah (Alexandria)	2,679	3,755,901
Al-Minūfīyah	1,532	3,171,058	Al-Qāhirah (Cairo)	214	7,629,866
Al-Qalyūbīyah	1,001	3,804,188	As-Suways (Suez)	17,840	478,553
Ash-Sharqīyah	4,180	5,009,690	Al-Uqṣur (Luxor)	55	414,389
			TOTAL	997,739[2]	70,548,718[3]

Demography

Population (2005): 70,457,000[4].
Density (2005): persons per sq mi 182.9, persons per sq km 70.6.
Urban-rural (2003): urban 42.1%; rural 57.9%.
Sex distribution (2004): male 50.45%; female 49.55%.
Age breakdown (2004): under 15, 33.4%; 15–29, 28.1%; 30–44, 19.6%; 45–59, 12.1%; 60–74, 5.6%; 75 and over, 1.2%.
Population projection: (2010) 76,751,000; (2020) 88,531,000.
Doubling time: 38 years.
Ethnic composition (2000): Egyptian Arab 84.1%; Sudanese Arab 5.5%; Arabized Berber 2.0%; Bedouin 2.0%; Rom (Gypsy) 1.6%; other 4.8%.
Religious affiliation (2000): Muslim 84.4%[5]; Christian 15.1%, of which Orthodox 13.6%, Protestant 0.8%, Roman Catholic 0.3%; nonreligious 0.5%.
Major cities ('000; 1996): Cairo 6,789 (10,834[6]); Alexandria 3,328; Al-Jīzah 2,222; Shubrā al-Khaymah 871; Port Said 470; Suez 418.

Vital statistics

Birth rate per 1,000 population (2004): 23.8 (world avg. 21.1).
Death rate per 1,000 population (2004): 5.3 (world avg. 9.0).
Natural increase rate per 1,000 population (2004): 18.5 (world avg. 12.1).
Total fertility rate (avg. births per childbearing woman; 2004): 3.0.
Life expectancy at birth (2004): male 68.2 years; female 73.3 years.

National economy

Budget (2003–04). Revenue: £E 116,490,000,000 (income and profits taxes 28.3%, sales taxes 19.4%, customs duties 13.0%, Suez Canal fees 4.4%, petroleum revenue 3.5%). Expenditures: £E 159,600,000,000 (current expenditure 76.6%; capital expenditure 23.4%).
Public debt (external, outstanding; 2003): U.S.\$27,266,000,000.
Population economically active (2001): total 19,253,000; activity rate 30.0% (participation rates: ages 15–64, 46.9%; female 21.9%; unemployed [2003–04] 9.5%).

Price index (2000 = 100)

	1998	1999	2000	2001	2002	2003	2004
Consumer price index	94.5	97.4	100.0	102.3	105.1	109.8	122.2

Production ('000; metric tons except as noted). Agriculture, forestry, fishing (2004): sugarcane 16,335, wheat 7,178, tomatoes 6,780, rice 6,150, corn (maize) 5,800, sugar beets 2,860, potatoes 1,950, oranges 1,750, grapes 1,104, dates 1,100, seed cotton 740; livestock ('000; number of live animals) 5,110 sheep, 3,900 cattle, 3,650 buffalo; roundwood (2003) 16,905,059 cu m; fish catch (2002) 801. Mining and quarrying (2003): iron ore 2,500; salt 2,400; gypsum 2,000; phosphate rock 1,500; kaolin 260. Manufacturing (value added in U.S.\$'000,000; 1998): chemicals (all forms) 1,535; food products 958; textiles 828; bricks, cement, ceramics 683; iron and steel 365. Energy production (consumption): electricity ('000,000 kW-hr; 2002–03) 88,854 (74,356); coal ('000 metric tons; 2002) 48 (1,350); crude petroleum ('000 barrels; 2004) 217,300 ([2002] 234,000); petroleum products ('000 metric tons; 2002) 32,220 (25,972); natural gas ('000,000 cu m; 2002) 26,034 (26,034).
Household income and expenditure. Average household size (2000) 4.7; average annual income per household: n.a.; sources of income: n.a.; expenditure: n.a.
Tourism (2003): receipts U.S.\$4,584,000,000; expenditures U.S.\$1,321,000,000.

Gross national product (2004): U.S.\$91,129,000,000 (U.S.\$1,310 per capita).

Structure of gross domestic product and labour force

	2003–04[7] in value £E '000,000	2003–04[7] % of total value	2002 labour force	2002 % of labour force
Agriculture	70,319.0	15.8	4,921,600	24.8
Mining (petroleum)	} 133,696.3	30.0	47,200	0.2
Manufacturing			2,087,700	10.5
Construction	17,880.0	4.0	1,329,200	6.7
Public utilities	8,690.0	2.0	242,300	1.2
Transp. and commun.	42,362.6[8]	9.5[8]	1,136,600	5.7
Trade, hotels	62,250.9	14.0	2,684,100	13.5
Finance	50,568.4	11.4	568,000	2.9
Pub. admin., defense	45,195.4	10.2	1,947,000	9.8
Services	14,210.0	3.2	2,996,000	15.1
Other	—	—	1,917,200[9]	9.6[9]
TOTAL	445,172.6	100.0[2]	19,876,800[2]	100.0

Land use as % of total land area (2000): in temporary crops 2.8%, in permanent crops 0.5%, in pasture, n.a.; overall forest area 0.1%.

Foreign trade[10]

Balance of trade (current prices)

	1998–99	1999–2000	2000–01	2001–02	2002–03	2003–04
U.S.\$'000,000	−12,563	−11,472	−9,363	−7,516	−6,615	−7,834
% of total	58.6%	47.3%	39.8%	34.5%	28.7%	27.3%

Imports (2004): U.S.\$12,866,000,000 (machinery and apparatus 15.9%; vegetable products 11.4%; metal products 10.0%; chemicals and chemical products 9.1%). *Major import sources* (2003): U.S. 13.4%; Germany 7.3%; Italy 6.9%; France 6.5%; China 4.7%.
Exports (2004): U.S.\$7,701,000,000 (petroleum 40.0%, of which crude petroleum 5.2%; finished goods 27.2%; semi-manufactured goods 14.1%; raw cotton 6.3%). *Major export destinations* (2003): U.S. 13.6%; Italy 12.5%; U.K. 8.1%; France 4.8%; Germany 4.8%.

Transport and communications

Transport. Railroads (2002–03): length 9,432 km; passenger-km 46,185,000,000; metric ton-km cargo 3,844,000,000. Roads (1999): length 64,000 km (paved 78%). Vehicles (2002): passenger cars 1,847,000; trucks and buses 650,000. Inland water (2002–03): Suez Canal, number of transits 14,200; metric ton cargo 450,000,000. Air transport (2004)[11]: passenger-km 9,782,000,000; metric ton-km cargo 248,534,000; airports (1998) 11.

Communications

Medium	date	unit	number	units per 1,000 persons
Daily newspapers	2000	circulation	2,780,000	43
Radio	2000	receivers	21,900,000	418
Television	2002	receivers	15,206,000	229
Telephones	2004	main lines	9,464,100	135
Cellular telephones	2004	subscribers	7,643,000	109
Personal computers	2004	units	2,300,000	33
Internet	2004	users	3,900,000	56

Education and health

Educational attainment (2000)[12]. Percentage of population ages 15–49 having no formal schooling/incomplete primary education, n.a.; complete primary c. 23%; complete secondary c. 37%[13]; higher, n.a. *Literacy* (2001): total population age 15 and over literate 56.1%; males 67.2%; females 44.8%.

Education (2002–03)

	schools	teachers	students	student/ teacher ratio
Primary (age 6–15)[14, 15]	24,198	533,831	11,433,939	21.4
Secondary (age 16–18)[14]	1,942	91,458	1,249,706	13.7
Vocational	1,959	151,792	2,214,152	14.6
Higher	293	...	1,239,441	...

Health (2005): physicians 157,000 (1 per 448 persons); hospital beds 170,000 (1 per 414 persons); infant mortality rate (2004) 33.9.
Food (2002): daily per capita caloric intake 3,338 (vegetable products 92%, animal products 8%); 133% of FAO recommended minimum requirement.

Military

Total active duty personnel (2004): 450,000 (army 71.1%, navy 4.4%, air force [including air defense] 24.5%). *Military expenditure as percentage of GDP* (2003): 2.5%; per capita expenditure U.S.\$25.

---

[1]Includes 10 nonelective seats. [2]Detail does not add to total given because of rounding. [3]January 1; includes 1,900,229 Egyptians temporarily abroad. [4]De facto population. [5]Nearly all Sunnī; Shīʿī comprise less than 1% of population. [6]2003 urban agglomeration. [7]At factor cost. [8]Transportation includes earnings from traffic on the Suez Canal. [9]Including 1,865,500 unemployed not previously employed. [10]Imports c.i.f.; exports f.o.b. [11]EgyptAir only. [12]Based on survey of 16,957 households. [13]Ages 20–49. [14]Data exclude 1,090,022 primary and 278,134 secondary students in the Al-Azhar education system. [15]Includes preparatory; excludes an estimated 55,602 (primarily female) students in public one-classroom schools.

Internet resources for further information:
• Egypt State Information Service http://www.sis.gov.eg
• Central Bank of Egypt http://www.cbe.org.eg

El Salvador

Official name: República de El
Salvador (Republic of El Salvador).
Form of government: republic with
one legislative house (Legislative
Assembly [84]).
Chief of state and government:
President.
Capital: San Salvador.
Official language: Spanish.
Official religion: none[1].
Monetary unit: 1 dollar (U.S.$)[2] = 100
cents; valuation (Sept. 1, 2005)
1 U.S.$ = £0.54.

Area and population

Departments	Capitals	area sq mi	area sq km	population 2004 estimate
Ahuachapán	Ahuachapán	479	1,240	347,357
Cabañas	Sensuntepeque	426	1,104	156,162
Chalatenango	Chalatenango	779	2,017	201,912
Cuscatlán	Cojutepeque	292	757	210,596
La Libertad	Nueva San Salvador	638	1,653	764,349
La Paz	Zacatecoluca	474	1,228	312,943
La Unión	La Unión	801	2,074	299,727
Morazán	San Francisco	559	1,447	177,768
San Miguel	San Miguel	802	2,077	522,057
San Salvador	San Salvador	342	886	2,159,793
San Vicente	San Vicente	456	1,181	168,953
Santa Ana	Santa Ana	781	2,023	595,212
Sonsonate	Sonsonate	473	1,226	494,678
Usulután	Usulután	822	2,130	345,901
TOTAL		8,124	21,042[3]	6,757,408

Demography

Population (2005): 6,881,000.
Density (2005): persons per sq mi 847.0, persons per sq km 327.0.
Urban-rural (2004): urban 59.7%; rural 40.3%.
Sex distribution (2004): male 47.81%; female 52.19%.
Age breakdown (2005): under 15, 34.0%; 15–29, 28.9%; 30–44, 19.1%; 45–59, 10.5%; 60–74, 5.6%; 75 and over 1.9%.
Population projection: (2010) 7,461,000; (2020) 8,550,000.
Doubling time: 37 years.
Ethnic composition (2000): mestizo 88.3%; Amerindian 9.1%, of which Pipil 4.0%; white 1.6%; other/unknown 1.0%.
Religious affiliation (2000): Roman Catholic 78.7%; Independent Christian (mostly Pentecostal) 9.7%; Protestant 7.2%; other/nonreligious 4.4%.
Major cities (2000): San Salvador 479,600 (urban agglomeration [2004] 2,143,338); Soyapango 285,300[4]; Mejicanos 172,500[4]; Santa Ana 164,500; San Miguel 159,700.

Vital statistics

Birth rate per 1,000 population (2004): 24.8 (world avg. 21.1); (1998) legitimate 27.2%; illegitimate 72.8%.
Death rate per 1,000 population (2004): 5.9 (world avg. 9.0).
Natural increase rate per 1,000 population (2004): 18.9 (world avg. 12.1).
Total fertility rate (avg. births per childbearing woman; 2004): 2.8.
Marriage rate per 1,000 population (2003): 3.8.
Divorce rate per 1,000 population (2003): 0.6.
Life expectancy at birth (2004): male 67.9 years; female 74.0 years.
Major causes of death per 100,000 population (1998)[5]: accidents and violence 118; diseases of the circulatory system 89; diseases of the respiratory system 60; malignant neoplasms (cancers) 58; ill-defined conditions 116.

National economy

Budget. Revenue (2004): U.S.$2,095,900,000 (VAT 45.4%, individual income taxes 25.5%, nontax revenue 10.9%, import duties 8.4%, other 9.8%). Expenditures: U.S.$2,273,100,000 (education 20.1%, defense and public security 13.0%, public health and welfare 10.1%, public works 5.4%, other 51.4%).
Production (metric tons except as noted). Agriculture, forestry, fishing (2004): sugarcane 5,280,400, corn (maize) 648,045, sorghum 147,631, dry beans 84,300, coffee 78,510, plantains 75,709, yautia 52,000, tobacco 1,100; livestock (number of live animals) 1,259,209 cattle, 188,025 pigs; roundwood (2003) 4,829,082 cu m; fish catch (2003) 35,410. Mining and quarrying (2003): limestone 1,190,000. Manufacturing (value added in U.S.$'000,000; 2004): food products 875; textiles and wearing apparel 262; chemicals and chemical products 262; refined petroleum 234; beverages 217; printing and publishing 167. Energy production (consumption): electricity (kW-hr; 2004) 4,253,000,000 (4,635,000,000); coal (metric tons; 2003) none (900); crude petroleum (barrels; 2002) none (6,900,000); petroleum products (metric tons; 2002) 887,000 (1,788,000); natural gas, none (none).
Household income and expenditure. Average household size (2004) 4.1; average income per household (2004) U.S.$5,016; expenditure (June 2005)[6]: food, beverages, and tobacco 36.4%, housing and energy 16.8%, transportation and communications 10.2%, household furnishings 8.4%.
Land use as % of total land area (2000): in temporary crops 30.9%, in permanent crops 12.1%, in pasture 38.3%; overall forest area 5.8%.
Population economically active (2003): total 2,707,300; activity rate of total population 40.8% (participation rates: ages 15–64, 64.4%; female 40.3%; unemployed [2004] 6.8%).

Price and earnings indexes (2000 = 100)

	1998	1999	2000	2001	2002	2003	2004
Consumer price index	97.3	97.8	100.0	103.8	105.7	107.9	112.7
Hourly earnings index[7]	101.8	105.8	100.0	...	...	...	...

Public debt (external, outstanding; 2003): U.S.$5,213,000,000.
Gross national product (2004): U.S.$15,613,000,000 (U.S.$2,350 per capita).

Structure of gross domestic product and labour force

	2004 in value U.S.$'000,000	% of total value	labour force	% of labour force
Agriculture	1,390	8.8	483,129	17.8
Mining	80	0.5	1,827	0.1
Manufacturing	3,550	22.4	423,418	15.6
Construction	670	4.2	162,755	6.0
Public utilities	270	1.7	10,319	0.4
Transp. and commun.	1,540	9.7	125,805	4.6
Trade	3,020	19.1	739,510	27.3
Finance, real estate	2,580	16.3	103,103	3.8
Public admin., defense	1,060	6.7	98,395	3.6
Services	1,170	7.4	378,102	14.0
Other	500[8]	3.2[8]	183,874[9]	6.8[9]
TOTAL	15,824[3]	100.0	2,710,237	100.0

Tourism (2003): receipts U.S.$226,000,000; expenditures U.S.$160,000,000.

Foreign trade[10]

Balance of trade (current prices)

	1999	2000	2001	2002	2003	2004
U.S.$'000,000	−1,585	−2,006	−2,163	−2,190	−2,626	−2,974
% of total	24.0%	25.4%	27.4%	26.8%	29.6%	31.1%

Imports (2004): U.S.$6,268,754,000 (imports for reexport 22.0%; machinery and apparatus 12.3%; food 11.3%; petroleum [all forms] 10.2%; chemicals and chemical products 9.6%). *Major import sources:* U.S. 46.3%; Guatemala 8.1%; Costa Rica 2.8%; Honduras 2.5%; Japan 2.1%.
Exports (2004): U.S.$3,295,258,000 (reexports [mostly clothing] 55.2%; yarn, fabrics, made-up articles 6.8%; chemicals and chemical products 4.8%; coffee 3.8%). *Major export destinations:* U.S. 65.4%; Guatemala 11.7%; Honduras 6.3%; Nicaragua 3.9%; Costa Rica 3.0%.

Transport and communications

Transport. Railroads (2003): operational route length 283 km; (2000) passenger-km 10,700,000; metric ton-km cargo 13,100,000. Roads (2002): total length 11,458 km (paved 23%). Vehicles (2000): passenger cars 148,000; trucks and buses 250,800. Air transport (2004)[11]: passenger-km 4,112,000,000; metric ton-km cargo 5,000,000; airports (2003) with scheduled flights 2.

Communications

Medium	date	unit	number	units per 1,000 persons
Daily newspapers	2001	circulation	179,300	28
Radio	2001	receivers	3,060,200	478
Television	2001	receivers	1,286,800	201
Telephones	2004	main lines	887,800	134
Cellular telephones	2004	subscribers	1,832,600	277
Personal computers	2004	units	297,000	45
Internet	2004	users	587,500	89

Education and health

Educational attainment (2002)[12]. Percentage of population over age 15 having: no formal schooling to incomplete primary education 39.9%; complete primary 32.4%; secondary 18.7%; higher technical and vocational 2.4%; higher 6.5%; other/unknown 0.1%. *Literacy* (2004): total population age 10 and over literate 84.5%; males literate 87.0%; females literate 82.3%.

Education (2000)

	schools	teachers	students	student/ teacher ratio
Primary (age 7–15)	5,090	26,209	1,212,622	46.3
Secondary (age 16–18)	...	9,255[13]	147,867	15.5[13]
Higher	...	7,501	114,675	15.3

Health (2003): physicians 4,100 (1 per 1,620 persons); hospital beds 4,625 (1 per 1,436 persons); infant mortality rate per 1,000 live births (2004) 25.4.
Food (2002): daily per capita caloric intake 2,584 (vegetable products 87%, animal products 13%); 113% of FAO recommended minimum requirement.

Military

Total active duty personnel (2004): 15,500 (army 89.4%, navy 4.5%, air force 6.1%). *Military expenditure as percentage of GDP* (2003): 0.7%; per capita expenditure U.S.$16.

---

[1]Roman Catholicism, although not official, enjoys special recognition in the constitution. [2]The U.S. dollar was legal tender in El Salvador from Jan. 1, 2001 (along with the colón) at a pegged rate of 1 U.S.$ = ₡8.75; the colón was hardly used by mid-2004. [3]Detail does not add to total given because of rounding. [4]Within San Salvador urban agglomeration. [5]Projected rates based on about 78% of total deaths. [6]Weights of consumer price index components. [7]Manufacturing only. [8]Import duties and VAT less imputed bank service charges. [9]Unemployed. [10]Imports c.i.f., exports f.o.b. (including assembled components for reexport). [11]TACA International Airlines only. [12]Economically active population only. [13]1996.

Internet resources for further information:
• Banco Central de Reserva de El Salvador http://www.bcr.gob.sv
• Dirección General de Estadística y Censos http://www.digestyc.gob.sv

Equatorial Guinea

Official name: República de Guinea Ecuatorial (Spanish); République du Guinée Équatoriale (French) (Republic of Equatorial Guinea).
Form of government: republic with one legislative house (House of Representatives of the People [100]).
Chief of state: President.
Head of government: Prime Minister.
Capital: Malabo[1].
Official languages: Spanish; French.
Official religion: none.
Monetary unit: 1 CFA franc (CFAF) = 100 centimes; valuation (Sept. 1, 2005) 1 U.S.$ = CFAF 522.78; 1 £ = CFAF 962.57[2].

Area and population

Regions Provinces	Capitals	area sq mi	area sq km	population 1994 census
Insular		785[3]	2,034	90,500
Annobón	Palé	7	17	2,800
Bioko Norte	Malabo	300	776	75,100
Bioko Sur	Luba	479	1,241	12,600
Continental		10,045[3]	26,017	315,600
Centro-Sur	Evinayong	3,834	9,931	60,300
Kie-Ntem	Ebebiyin	1,522	3,943	92,800
Litoral[4]	Bata	2,573	6,665	100,000
Wele-Nzas	Mongomo	2,115	5,478	62,500
TOTAL		10,831[3]	28,051	406,200[3]

Demography

Population (2005): 504,000.
Density (2005): persons per sq mi 46.5, persons per sq km 18.0.
Urban-rural (2003): urban 48.1%; rural 51.9%.
Sex distribution (2004): male 48.79%; female 51.21%.
Age breakdown (2004): under 15, 42.1%; 15–29, 27.3%; 30–44, 16.4%; 45–59, 8.3%; 60–74, 4.8%; 75 and over, 1.1%.
Population projection: (2010) 563,000; (2020) 693,000.
Doubling time: 32 years.
Ethnic composition (2000): Fang 56.6%; migrant labourers from Nigeria 12.5%, of which Yoruba 8.0%, Igbo 4.0%; Bubi 10.0%; Seke 2.9%; Spaniard 2.8%; other 15.2%.
Religious affiliation (2000): Roman Catholic 80.1%; Muslim 4.0%; African Christian 3.7%; Protestant 3.1%; other 9.1%.
Major cities (2003): Malabo 92,900; Bata 66,800; Mbini 11,600; Ebebiyin 9,100; Luba 6,800.

Vital statistics

Birth rate per 1,000 population (2004): 36.4 (world avg. 21.1).
Death rate per 1,000 population (2004): 15.0 (world avg. 9.0).
Natural increase rate per 1,000 population (2004): 21.5 (world avg. 12.1).
Total fertility rate (avg. births per childbearing woman; 2004): 4.7.
Life expectancy at birth (2004): male 48.1 years; female 51.9 years.
Major causes of death per 100,000 population: n.a.; however, major diseases include malaria (about 24% of total mortality), respiratory infections (about 12% of mortality), cholera, leprosy, trypanosomiasis (sleeping sickness), and waterborne (especially gastrointestinal) diseases.

National economy

Budget (2004). Revenue: CFAF 870,537,000,000 (oil revenue 91.8%, of which royalties 51.3%; non-oil revenue 8.1%, of which tax revenue 6.6%, nontax revenue 1.5%; grants 0.1%). Expenditures: CFAF 542,221,000,000 (capital expenditure 66.2%; current expenditure 17.5%; net lending 16.3%).
Public debt (external, outstanding; 2004): U.S.$115,100,000.
Gross domestic product (at current market prices; 2004): U.S.$4,483,000,000[5] (U.S.$9,110[5] per capita).

Structure of gross domestic product and labour force

	2002 in value CFAF '000,000	2002 % of total value	1997 labour force	1997 % of labour force
Agriculture, fishing	41,900	2.8	...	...
Forestry	31,800	2.1	...	...
Crude petroleum	1,291,600	86.9	...	...
Manufacturing	1,600	0.1	...	...
Construction	32,200	2.2	...	...
Public utilities	5,200	0.4	...	...
Transportation and communications	4,900	0.3	...	...
Trade	24,600	1.7	...	...
Finance, real estate	7,200	0.5	...	...
Pub. admin., defense	31,100	2.1	...	...
Services	8,900	0.6	...	...
Other	4,700[6]	0.3[6]	...	...
TOTAL	1,485,500[3]	100.0	177,000	100.0

Production (metric tons except as noted). Agriculture, forestry, fishing (2004): roots and tubers 105,000 (of which cassava 45,000, sweet potatoes 36,000), oil palm fruit 35,000, plantains 31,000, bananas 20,000, coconuts 6,000, coffee 3,500, cacao beans 2,422; livestock (number of live animals) 37,600 sheep, 9,000 goats, 6,100 pigs, 5,050 cattle; roundwood (2003) 811,000 cu m, of which saw logs and veneer logs 364,000; fish catch (2002) 3,500. Mining and quarrying: gold (2003) 500 kg. Manufacturing (2002): methanol 719,000; processed timber (2001) 31,000 cu m. Energy production (consumption): electricity (kW-hr; 2003) 69,000,000 (36,000,000); coal, none (none); crude petroleum (barrels; 2004) 124,000,000 ([2002] negligible); petroleum products (metric tons; 2002) none (55,000); natural gas (cu m; 2002) 1,050,000,000 (n.a.).
Population economically active (1997): total 177,000; activity rate of total population 40.0% (participation rates: ages 15–64, 74.7%; female 35.4%; unemployed, n.a.).

Price index (2000 = 100)

	1998	1999	2000	2001	2002	2003
Consumer price index	95.0	95.5	100.0	108.8	117.0	125.6

Household income and expenditure. Average household size, n.a.; income per household: n.a.; sources of income: n.a.; expenditure (2000)[7]: food and beverages 60.4%, clothing 14.7%, household furnishings 8.6%.
Tourism: tourism is a government priority but remains undeveloped.
Land use as % of total land area (2000): in temporary crops 4.6%, in permanent crops 3.6%, in pasture 3.7%; overall forest area 62.5%.

Foreign trade[8]

Balance of trade (current prices)

	2000	2001	2002	2003	2004
CFAF '000,000,000	+420.2	+503.0	+373.8	+835.0	+1,036.4
% of total	32.6%	26.2%	15.2%	34.9%	26.4%

Imports (2004): CFAF 1,442,900,000,000 (for petroleum sector 76.7%; for public sector 17.4%; petroleum products 2.7%). *Major import sources* (2003): U.S. 30.6%; U.K. 16.0%; France 15.0%; Côte d'Ivoire 11.9%; Spain 8.2%; Italy 5.3%.
Exports (2004): CFAF 2,479,300,000,000 (petroleum [including gas] 98.4%; timber 1.1%; cocoa beans 0.1%). *Major export destinations* (2003): U.S. 33.2%; Spain 25.4%; China 14.2%; Canada 12.7%; Italy 6.3%; France 3.6%.

Transport and communications

Transport. Railroads: none. Roads (1999): total length 1,790 mi, 2,880 km (paved 13%). Vehicles (1994): passenger cars 6,500; trucks and buses 4,000. Air transport (1998): passenger-km 4,000,000; metric ton-km cargo, n.a.; airports (2003) with scheduled flights 3.

Communications

Medium	date	unit	number	units per 1,000 persons
Daily newspapers	1996	circulation	2,000	4.9
Radio	1997	receivers	180,000	428
Television	1997	receivers	4,000	9.8
Telephones	2003	main lines	9,600	18
Cellular telephones	2004	units	55,500	110
Personal computers	2004	units	7,000	3.3
Internet	2004	users	5,000	9.9

Education and health

Educational attainment: n.a. Literacy (2001): percentage of total population age 15 and over literate 84.2%; males literate 92.8%; females literate 76.0%.

Education (1998)

	schools	teachers	students	student/ teacher ratio
Primary (age 6–11)	483	1,322	78,390[9]	56.7
Secondary (age 12–17)	...	763	19,748[9]	24.6
Voc., teacher tr.	...	...	1,425[9]	...
Higher	...	...	1,003[10]	...

Health: physicians (2004) 101 (1 per 5,020 persons); hospital beds (1990) 992 (1 per 350 persons); infant mortality rate per 1,000 live births (2004) 93.2.

Military

Total active duty personnel (2004): 1,320 (army 83.3%, navy 9.1%, air force 7.6%). *Military expenditure as percentage of GDP* (2003): 0.2%; per capita expenditure U.S.$12.

[1]Construction work on new capital complex in Malabo suburbs under way in late 2003. [2]Formerly pegged to the French franc and since Jan. 1, 2002, to the euro at the rate of CFAF 655.96 = €1. [3]Detail does not add to total given because of rounding. [4]Includes three islets in Corisco Bay. [5]Estimated figure. [6]Import duties. [7]Weights of consumer price index components. [8]Imports c.i.f.; exports f.o.b. [9]2001–02. [10]1999–2000.

Internet resources for further information:
• La Banque de France: La Zone Franc
  http://www.banque-france.fr/fr/eurosys/zonefr/zonefr.htm
• Ministerio de Planificación, Desarrollo Económico e Inversiones Públicas
  http://www.dgecnstat-ge.org

Eritrea

Official name: State of Eritrea.
Form of government: transitional
  regime with one interim
  legislative body (Transitional
  National Assembly [150][1]).
Head of state and government:
  President.
Capital: Asmara.
Official language: none.
Official religion: none.
Monetary unit: 1 nakfa (Nfa) = 100
  cents; valuation (Sept. 1, 2005)
  1 U.S.$ = Nfa 13.79; 1 £ = Nfa 25.39.

Area and population

Regions	Capitals	area[2] sq mi	area[2] sq km	population 2002 estimate[3]
Anseba	Keren	8,960	23,200	580,700
Debub	Mendefera	3,090	8,000	1,018,000
Debub-Keih-Bahri	Asseb (Aseb)	10,660	27,600	274,800
Gash-Barka	Barentu	12,820	33,200	747,200
Maekel	Asmara (Asmera)	500	1,300	727,800
Semien-Keih-Bahri	Massawa (Mitsiwa)	10,730	27,800	569,000
TOTAL		46,760	121,100	3,917,500

Demography

Population (2005): 4,670,000[4].
Density (2005)[5]: persons per sq mi 119.7, persons per sq km 46.2.
Urban-rural (2003): urban 19.9%; rural 80.1%.
Sex distribution (2003): male 49.75%; female 50.25%.
Age breakdown (2003): under 15, 44.7%; 15–29, 27.2%; 30–44, 14.1%; 45–59,
  8.7%; 60–74, 4.3%; 75 and over, 1.0%.
Population projection[4]: (2010) 5,278,000; (2020) 6,590,000.
Doubling time: 28 years.
Ethnolinguistic composition (2004): Tigrinya (Tigray) 50.0%; Tigré 31.4%;
  Afar 5.0%; Saho 5.0%; Beja 2.5%; Bilen 2.1%; other 4.0%.
Religious affiliation (2000): Christian 50.5%, of which Eritrean Orthodox
  46.1%; Muslim 44.7%; other 4.8%.
Major cities (2002): Asmara 500,600; Keren 74,800; Asseb (2003) 56,300;
  Mendefera 25,700; Dek'emhare 25,400.

Vital statistics

Birth rate per 1,000 population (2004): 35.2 (world avg. 21.1).
Death rate per 1,000 population (2004): 10.1 (world avg. 9.0).
Natural increase rate per 1,000 population (2004): 25.1 (world avg. 12.1).
Total fertility rate (avg. births per childbearing woman; 2004): 5.3.
Marriage rate per 1,000 population (1992): 6.8.
Divorce rate per 1,000 population: n.a.
Life expectancy at birth (2004): male 56.5 years; female 59.5 years.
Major causes of death per 100,000 population: n.a.; morbidity (principal caus-
  es of illness) arises mainly in malaria and other infectious diseases, parasitic
  infections, malnutrition, diarrheal diseases, and dysenteries.

National economy

Budget (2002). Revenue: Nfa 3,409,800,000 (tax revenue 45.1%, of which
  import duties 18.1%, sales tax 10.8%, corporate tax 9.9%; grants 32.8%; nontax revenue 21.2%; extraordinary revenue 0.9%). Expenditures: Nfa
  6,138,200,000 (defense 34.3%, health 9.6%, humanitarian assistance 7.9%,
  education 7.6%, transportation, construction, and communications 6.5%,
  debt service 5.7%).
Production (metric tons except as noted). Agriculture, forestry, fishing (2004):
  roots and tubers 85,000, sorghum 56,743, pulses 25,000, oilseeds 18,000, barley 16,864, potatoes 16,000, millet 11,554, wheat 7,199, chickpeas 4,700, vetch-
  es 4,500; livestock (number of live animals; 2004) 2,100,000 sheep, 1,930,000
  cattle, 1,700,000 goats, 75,000 camels, 1,370,000 chickens; roundwood (2003)
  1,265,924; fish catch (2003) 6,689. Mining and quarrying (2003): salt 117,000;
  marble and granite are quarried, as are sand and aggregate (gravel) for construction. Manufacturing (value added in U.S.$'000,000; 2001): beverages 17;
  food products 6; tobacco products 5; furniture 4; leather products and shoes
  3; printing and publishing 3. Energy production (consumption): electricity
  (kW-hr; 2002) 264,000,000 (264,000,000); crude petroleum, none (none);
  petroleum products (metric tons; 2002) n.a. (205,000); natural gas, none
  (none).
Gross national product (2004): U.S.$806,000,000 (U.S.$180 per capita).

Structure of gross domestic product

	2002 in value Nfa '000,000	% of total value
Agriculture	941.3	10.4
Manufacturing	942.4	10.4
Mining		
Public utilities	100.8	1.1
Construction	954.0	10.6
Transp. and commun.	1,071.3	11.9
Trade	1,672.4	18.5
Finance	448.0	5.0
Pub. admin., defense	1,387.6	15.4
Services	528.0	5.8
Other	985.4[6]	10.9[6]
TOTAL	9,031.2	100.0

Public debt (external, outstanding; 2003): U.S.$605,000,000.
Household income and expenditure (1996–97). Average household size (2002)
  4.8; average annual disposable income per household[7]: Nfa 10,967 (U.S.
  $1,707); sources of income[7]: wages and salaries 34.0%, transfers 29.3%, rent
  19.8%, self-employment 16.9%; expenditure[7]: food 36.2%, housing 30.2%,
  clothing and footwear 9.3%, energy 6.8%, household furnishings 4.6%, transportation and communications 4.1%.
Population economically active (1996): 1,649,000; activity rate of total population 41.4%.

Price index (2000 = 100)

	1997	1998	1999	2000	2001	2002
Consumer price index	70.3	76.9	83.4	100.0	114.6	134.0[8]

Tourism (2002): receipts from visitors U.S.$73,000,000.
Land use as % of total land area (2000): in temporary crops 5.0%, in permanent crops 0.03%, in pasture 69.0%; overall forest area 13.5%.

Foreign trade[9]

Balance of trade (current prices)

	1997	1998	1999	2000	2001	2002
U.S.$'000,000	−441	−499	−481	−309	−404	−486
% of total	80.4%	89.9%	90.2%	89.2%	91.4%	82.4%

Imports (2002): U.S.$538,000,000 (food and live animals 28.4%, of which cere-
  als [all forms] 13.6%, raw sugar 7.9%; machinery and apparatus 17.5%; road
  vehicles 11.5%; chemicals and chemical products 6.6%; iron and steel 6.2%).
  Major import sources: United Arab Emirates 17.3%; Saudi Arabia 14.7%;
  Italy 14.2%; Germany 4.0%; Belgium 3.8%.
Exports (2002): U.S.$52,000,000 (raw sugar 60.8%; synthetic woven fabrics
  4.4%; vegetables and fruits 3.3%; fish 2.9%; sesame 2.7%). *Major export destinations:* The Sudan 82.7%; Italy 4.9%; Djibouti 2.1%; Germany 1.1%.

Transport and communications

Transport. Railroads (2003): part of the 190-mi (306-km) rail line that formerly connected Massawa and Agordat is under reconstruction; the 73-mi
  (118-km) section between Massawa and Asmara was reopened in 2003.
  Roads (1999): total length 2,491 mi, 4,010 km (paved 22%). Vehicles (1996):
  automobiles 5,940, trucks and buses, n.a. Air transport (2001)[10]: passenger
  arrivals 39,266, passenger departures 46,448; freight loaded 202 metric tons,
  freight unloaded 1,548 metric tons; airports (2000) with scheduled flights 2.

Communications

Medium	date	unit	number	units per 1,000 persons
Daily newspapers	2000	circulation	104,000	28
Radio	2001	receivers	1,763,000	464
Television	2002	receivers	215,000	50
Telephones	2004	main lines	39,300	9.1
Cellular telephones	2004	subscribers	20,000	4.7
Personal computers	2004	units	15,000	3.5
Internet	2004	users	50,000	12

Education and health

Educational attainment (2002). Percentage of population age 6 and over having: no formal education or unknown 47.3%, incomplete primary education
  to complete primary 39.4%, incomplete secondary 8.3%, secondary 3.3%,
  higher 1.7%. *Literacy* (2003): total population age 15 and over literate 58.6%;
  males 69.9%; females 47.6%.

Education (2001–02)

	schools	teachers	students	student/ teacher ratio
Primary (age 7–12)	695	6,706	330,278	49.3
Secondary (age 13–18)	196	2,671	151,065	56.6
Voc., teacher tr.	12	174	1,992	11.4
Higher[11]	1	198	3,096	15.6

Health (2000): physicians 173 (1 per 21,457 persons); hospital beds 3,126 (1 per
  1,187 persons); infant mortality rate per 1,000 live births (2004) 48.5.
Food (2002): daily per capita caloric intake 1,513 (vegetable 95%, animal products 5%); 65% of FAO recommended minimum requirement.

Military

Total active duty personnel (2004): 201,750 (army 99.1%, navy 0.7%, air force
  0.2%). UN peacekeeping force along Eritrean-Ethiopian border (June 2005)
  3,100 troops. *Military expenditure as percentage of GDP* (2003): 19.4%; per
  capita expenditure U.S.$33.

---

[1]New constitution adopted in May 1997 was still not implemented in mid-2005.
[2]Approximate figures. The published total area is 46,774 sq mi (121,144 sq km); water
area is 7,776 sq mi (20,140 sq km). [3]Unofficial figures. [4]Estimate of the U.S. Bureau of
the Census International Database (April 2005 release). [5]Based on land area only.
[6]Including indirect taxes less subsidies. [7]Data taken from a 1996–97 survey of the 12
largest urban centres in the country. [8]Estimate. [9]Imports c.i.f.; exports f.o.b. [10]Asmara
airport only. [11]1997–98.

Internet resources for further information:
• **Eritrea: Interim Poverty Reduction Strategy Paper**
  http://www.er.undp.org/docs/i-prsp-er.pdf
• **Eritrea Demographic and Health Survey 2002**
  http://www.measuredhs.com/pubs/
  pdftoc.cfm?ID=405&PgName=country.cfm0ctry_id=12

Estonia

Official name: Eesti Vabariik (Republic of Estonia).
Form of government: unitary multiparty republic with a single legislative body (Riigikogu[1] [101]).
Chief of state: President.
Head of government: Prime Minister.
Capital: Tallinn.
Official language: Estonian.
Official religion: none.
Monetary unit: 1 kroon (EEK) = 100 senti; valuation (Sept. 1, 2005)
1 U.S.$ = EEK 12.47;
1 £ = EEK 22.96.

Area and population		area		population
				2004
Counties	Capitals	sq mi	sq km	estimate[2]
Harju	Tallinn	1,672	4,332	521,410
Hiiu	Kärdla	395	1,023	10,289
Ida-Viru	Jõhvi	1,299	3,364	174,809
Järva	Paide	1,013	2,623	38,255
Jõgeva	Jõgeva	1,005	2,604	37,647
Lääne	Haapsalu	920	2,383	28,101
Lääne-Viru	Rakvere	1,338	3,465	66,743
Pärnu	Pärnu	1,856	4,806	89,660
Põlva	Põlva	836	2,165	31,954
Rapla	Rapla	1,151	2,980	37,093
Saare	Kuressaare	1,128	2,922	35,356
Tartu	Tartu	1,156	2,993	148,872
Valga	Valga	789	2,044	35,059
Viljandi	Viljandi	1,321	3,422	56,854
Võru	Võru	890	2,305	38,967
TOTAL		16,769[3, 4, 5]	43,431[3, 4, 5]	1,351,069

Demography

Population (2005): 1,345,000.
Density (2005)[3]: persons per sq mi 77.0, persons per sq km 29.7.
Urban-rural (2003): urban 69.4%; rural 30.6%.
Sex distribution (2004[2]): male 46.07%; female 53.93%.
Age breakdown (2004): under 15, 16.0%; 15–29, 22.3%; 30–44, 20.7%; 45–59, 19.3%; 60–74, 15.3%; 75 and over, 6.4%.
Population projection: (2010) 1,323,000; (2020) 1,286,000.
Ethnic composition (2000): Estonian 67.9%; Russian 25.6%; Ukrainian 2.1%; Belarusian 1.3%; Finnish 0.9%; other 2.2%.
Religious affiliation (2000): Christian 63.5%, of which unaffiliated Christian 25.6%, Protestant 17.2%, Orthodox 16.5%, independent Christian 3.3%; nonreligious 25.1%; atheist 10.9%; other 0.5%.
Major cities (2003): Tallinn 400,378; Tartu 101,169; Narva 67,752[2]; Kohtla-Järve 46,765[2]; Pärnu 44,781[2].

Vital statistics

Birth rate per 1,000 population (2004): 10.4 (world avg. 21.1); (2003) legitimate 42.2%; illegitimate 57.8%.
Death rate per 1,000 population (2004): 13.2 (world avg. 9.0).
Natural increase rate per 1,000 population (2004): −2.8 (world avg. 12.1).
Total fertility rate (avg. births per childbearing woman; 2003): 1.4.
Marriage rate per 1,000 population (2004): 4.2.
Divorce rate per 1,000 population (2004): 3.1.
Life expectancy at birth (2003): male 66.0 years; female 76.9 years.
Major causes of death per 100,000 population (2003): diseases of the circulatory system 735.3; malignant neoplasms (cancers) 247.6; accidents, poisoning, and violence 135.7; diseases of the digestive system 47.4.

National economy

Budget (2003). Revenue: EEK 48,412,600,000 (tax revenue 85.4%, of which social security contributions 29.5%, value-added taxes 23.1%, personal income taxes 18.2%, excise taxes 8.6%; nontax revenue 11.5%; grants 3.1%). Expenditures: EEK 45,346,400,000 (current expenditure 89.9%, of which social benefits 30.2%; capital expenditure 8.5%; other 1.6%).
Public debt (external, outstanding; 2003): U.S.$560,000,000.
Production (metric tons except as noted). Agriculture, forestry, fishing (2004): barley 289,500, wheat 184,700, potatoes 178,900, oats 75,200, rapeseed 73,000, rye 19,700; livestock (number of live animals) 344,600 pigs, 257,200 cattle; roundwood (2003) 10,200,000 cu m; fish catch (2002) 101,452. Mining and quarrying (2002): oil shale 12,400,000; peat 1,518,600. Manufacturing (value added in U.S.$'000,000; 2001): food products 113; wood products (excluding furniture) 105; furniture 67; fabricated metal products 66; textiles 62; printing and publishing 53. Energy production (consumption): electricity (kW-hr; 2004) 10,347,000,000 (6,326,000,000); hard coal (metric tons; 2002) none (61,000); lignite (metric tons; 2002) 12,400,000 (13,000,000); crude petroleum, none (none); petroleum products (metric tons; 2002) none (799,000); natural gas (cu m; 2002) none (710,000,000).
Population economically active (2003): total 660,500; activity rate of total population 48.7% (participation rates: ages 15–64, 69.8%; female 49.0%; unemployed [July 2003–June 2004] 9.7%).

Price and earnings indexes (2000 = 100)						
	1998	1999	2000	2001	2002	2003	2004
Consumer price index	93.1	96.1	100.0	105.7	109.5	111.0	114.4
Annual earnings index	83.9	90.4	100.0	112.9	…	…	…

Household income and expenditure (2002). Average household size (2000) 2.2; average disposable income per household (1998) EEK 53,049 (U.S.$3,769); sources of income: wages and salaries 64.5%, transfers 25.0%, self-employment 5.2%, other 5.3%; expenditure: food and beverages 32.6%, housing 15.7%, transportation and communications 13.1%, clothing and footwear 6.2%.
Gross national product (2004): U.S.$9,435,000,000 (U.S.$7,010 per capita).

Structure of gross domestic product and labour force				
	2003			
	in value EEK '000,000	% of total value	labour force	% of labour force
Agriculture, fishing, forestry	4,992.4	4.0	36,700	5.6
Mining	1,097.8	0.9	5,700	0.9
Manufacturing	20,029.9	15.9	134,200	20.3
Public utilities	3,170.8	2.5	10,200	1.5
Construction	7,392.8	5.9	42,900	6.5
Trade, restaurants	15,765.9	12.5	98,200	14.9
Transp. and commun.	16,969.1	13.5	56,200	8.5
Finance, real estate	23,620.1	18.8	52,000	7.9
Pub. admin., defense	5,514.3	4.4	34,500	5.2
Services	14,412.8	11.4	123,700	18.7
Other	12,866.8[6]	10.2[6]	66,200[7]	10.0[7]
TOTAL	125,832.7	100.0	660,500	100.0

Tourism (2003): receipts U.S.$674,000,000; expenditures U.S.$321,000,000.
Land use as % of total land area (2000): in temporary crops 26.5%, in permanent crops 0.3%, in pasture 7.1%; overall forest area 48.7%.

Foreign trade[8]

Balance of trade (current prices)						
	1999	2000	2001	2002	2003	2004
EEK '000,000	−17,070	−18,985	−17,241	−22,609	−27,179	−31,152
% of total	16.5%	15.1%	13.0%	16.6%	17.9%	17.3%

Imports (2004): EEK 105,429,000,000 (electrical and nonelectrical machinery 28.6%, vehicles and transport equipment 12.1%, chemicals and chemical products 6.9%, textiles and apparel 6.8%). *Major import sources:* Finland 22.1%; Germany 12.9%; Sweden 9.7%; Russia 9.2%; Lithuania 5.3%; Latvia 4.7%.
Exports (2004): EEK 74,277,000,000 (electrical and nonelectrical machinery 27.2%, wood and paper products 15.7%, textiles and apparel 9.0%, household furnishings 8.5%). *Major export destinations:* Finland 23.1%; Sweden 15.3%; Germany 8.4%; Latvia 7.9%; Russia 5.6%; Lithuania 4.4%.

Transport and communications

Transport. Railroads (2003): route length 967 km; passenger-km 182,000,000; metric ton-km cargo 9,670,000,000. Roads (2003): total length 53,640 km (paved 20%). Vehicles (2003): passenger cars 434,000; trucks and buses 88,800. Air transport (2004)[9]: passenger-km 634,000,000; metric ton-km cargo 1,357,000; airports (2001) 1.

Communications				units per 1,000
Medium	date	unit	number	persons
Daily newspapers	2004	circulation	257,000	192
Radio	2001	receivers	1,590,000	1,136
Television	2002	receivers	702,000	502
Telephones	2004	main lines	444,000	340
Cellular telephones	2004	subscribers	1,255,700	960
Personal computers	2004	units	1,242,000	950
Internet	2004	users	670,000	512

Education and health

Education (2002–03)				student/
	schools	teachers	students	teacher ratio
Primary (age 7–12) } Secondary (age 13–17) }	592	15,762[10]	200,500	13.5[10]
Vocational	79	1,279[10]	28,100	24.1[10]
Higher[11]	14	…	46,801	

Health (2003): physicians 4,277 (1 per 316 persons); hospital beds 8,017 (1 per 169 persons); infant mortality rate per 1,000 live births 7.0.
Food (2002): daily per capita caloric intake 3,002 (vegetable products 73%, animal products 27%); 117% of FAO recommended minimum requirement.

Military

Total active duty personnel (2004): 4,980 (army 89.4%, navy 6.7%, air force 3.9%). *Military expenditure as a percentage of GDP* (2003): 1.9%; per capita expenditure U.S.$126.

[1]Official legislation bans translation of parliament's name. [2]As of January 1. [3]Based on area used by Estonian government to calculate population densities. [4]Total area including the Estonian portion of Lake Peipus (590 sq mi [1,529 sq km]), Lake Võrtsjärv, and Muuga harbour is 17,462 sq mi (45,227 sq km). [5]Total includes 1,596 sq mi (4,133 sq km) of Baltic Sea islands. [6]Includes net taxes (EEK 14,557,700,000) less imputed bank service charges (EEK 1,690,900,000). [7]Unemployed. [8]Imports c.i.f.; exports f.o.b. [9]Estonian Air. [10]2000–01. [11]Universities only.

Internet resources for further information:
• **Statistical Office of Estonia** http://www.stat.ee
• **Bank of Estonia** http://www.bankofestonia.info

Ethiopia

Official name: Federal Democratic
Republic of Ethiopia.
Form of government: federal republic
with two legislative houses (House
of the Federation [112]; House of
People's Representatives [547]).
Chief of state: President.
Head of government: Prime Minister.
Capital: Addis Ababa.
Official language: none[1].
Official religion: none.
Monetary unit: 1 birr (Br) = 100 cents;
valuation (Sept. 1, 2005) 1 U.S.$ =
Br 8.71; 1 £ = Br 16.05.

Area and population		area		population
				2000
Regional states	Capitals	sq mi	sq km	estimate
Afar	Aysaita	37,339	96,708	1,216,000
Amara (Amhara)	Bahir Dar	60,603	156,960	16,294,000
Binshangul				
Gumuz	Asosa	19,401	50,248	537,000
Gambela	Gambela	9,795	25,369	211,000
Harer Zuriya	Harer (Harar)	144	374	160,000
Oromiya	Addis Ababa	136,538	353,632	22,354,000
Southern Nations,				
Nationalities				
and Peoples'	Awasa	43,524	112,727	12,513,000
Sumale (Somali)	Jijiga	107,820	279,252	3,698,000
Tigray	Mekele	19,415	50,286	3,694,000
Cities				
Addis Ababa	...	211	546	2,495,000
Dire Dawa	...	396	1,025	318,000
TOTAL		435,186	1,127,127	63,490,000

Demography

Population (2005): 73,053,000.
Density (2005): persons per sq mi 167.9, persons per sq km 64.8.
Urban-rural (2003–04): urban 15.8%; rural 84.2%.
Sex distribution (2002): male 50.14%; female 49.86%.
Age breakdown (2002): under 15, 44.9%; 15–29, 28.0%; 30–44, 14.5%; 45–59,
8.2%; 60–74, 3.7%; 75 and over, 0.7%.
Population projection: (2010) 81,754,000; (2020) 99,279,000.
Doubling time: 29 years.
Ethnolinguistic composition (2000)[2]: Oromo 35.8%; Amharic 31.0%; Tigrinya
6.1%; Gurage 4.9%; Sidamo 3.8%; Welaita 2.1%; Somali 1.4%; Afar 0.9%;
other 14.0%.
Religious affiliation (2000)[2]: Ethiopian Orthodox 50.1%; Muslim 29.9%;
Protestant 15.8%; Roman Catholic 0.8%; other 3.4%.
Major cities (1999): Addis Ababa 2,424,000; Dire Dawa 208,456; Nazret
163,533; Gonder 142,328; Dese 123,558.

Vital statistics

Birth rate per 1,000 population (2004): 39.3 (world avg. 21.1).
Death rate per 1,000 population (2004): 15.3 (world avg. 9.0).
Natural increase rate per 1,000 population (2004): 24.0 (world avg. 12.1).
Total fertility rate (avg. births per childbearing woman; 2004): 5.4.
Life expectancy at birth (2004): male 47.5 years; female 49.9 years.
Adult population (ages 15–49) *living with HIV* (beginning of 2004): 4.4%
(world avg. 1.1%).

National economy

Budget (2002–03). Revenue: Br 15,702,000,000 (tax revenue 52.5%, of which
import duties 22.7%, income and profit tax 18.3%, sales tax 10.6%; grants
29.0%; nontax revenue 18.5%). Expenditures: Br 19,840,000,000 (current
expenditure 68.2%, of which defense 11.8%, education 11.5%, debt payment
6.1%, public order and security 4.0%; capital expenditure 31.8%).
Public debt (external, outstanding; 2003): U.S.$6,906,000,000.
Tourism (2003): receipts U.S.$114,000,000; expenditures U.S.$50,000,000.
Gross national product (2004): U.S.$7,747,000,000 (U.S.$110 per capita).

Structure of gross domestic product and labour force				
	2002–03		1995[3]	
	in value Br '000,000[4]	% of total value	labour force	% of labour force
Agriculture	6,687	39.5	21,605,317	87.8
Mining	102	0.6	16,540	0.1
Manufacturing	1,137	6.7	384,955	1.6
Construction	502	3.0	61,232	0.2
Public utilities	271	1.6	17,066	0.1
Transp. and commun.	1,221	7.2	103,154	0.4
Trade, hotels	1,528	9.0	935,937	3.8
Finance, real estate	1,259	7.4	19,451	0.1
Pub. admin., defense	2,617	15.4	1,252,224	5.1
Services	1,617	9.5 }		
Other	—	—	210,184[5]	0.9[5]
TOTAL	16,941	100.0[6]	24,606,060	100.0[6]

Production (metric tons except as noted). Agriculture, forestry, fishing (2004):
corn (maize) 2,743,881, sugarcane 2,454,276, sorghum 1,784,282, wheat
1,618,093, barley 1,087,374, dry broad beans 426,892, potatoes 400,000, sweet
potatoes 360,000, yams 310,000, millet 305,101, coffee 259,980, seed cotton
64,750, sesame seed 61,462; Ethiopia is one of the world's leading producers
of beeswax, honey, and khat; livestock (number of live animals) 38,102,688

cattle, 16,575,520 sheep, 9,626,000 goats, 5,537,880 horses, mules, and asses,
468,390 camels; roundwood (2003) 94,061,392 cu m; fish catch (2003) 9,213.
Mining and quarrying (2002–03): rock salt 61,000; tantalum 37,000 kg; niobium 6,100 kg; gold 5,300 kg. Manufacturing (value added in U.S.$'000,000;
2001): food products 143; beverages 95; nonmetallic mineral products 38; textiles 32; leather products 23. Energy production (consumption): electricity
(kW-hr; 2002) 2,050,000,000 (2,050,000,000); crude petroleum (barrels; 2002)
none (5,600,000); petroleum products (metric tons; 2002) 619,000 (1,716,000).
Land use as % of total land area (2000): in temporary crops 10.0%, in permanent crops 0.7%, in pasture 20.0%; overall forest area 4.2%.
Population economically active (1999): total 27,272,000; activity rate of
total population 49.7% (participation rates: ages 15–64, 68.4%; female
45.5%; unemployed [2000] 8%).

Price index (2000 = 100)						
	1999	2000	2001	2002	2003	2004
Consumer price index	99.3	100.0	91.8	93.3	109.8	113.4

Household income and expenditure (1999–2000). Average household size
(2002) 5.2; sources of income[7]: self-employment 70.9% (of which agricul-
ture-based 57.6%), wages and salaries 10.9%, salvaging 6.6%, rent 3.9%,
other 7.7%; expenditure[7]: food and beverages 52.8%, housing and energy
14.4%, household operations 13.9%, clothing and footwear 7.9%.

Foreign trade[8]

Balance of trade (current prices)			
	2001–02	2002–03	2003–04
U.S.$'000,000	−1,243	−1,374	−1,987
% of total	57.9%	58.7%	62.3%

Imports (2003–04): U.S.$2,587,400,000 ([2002] machinery and apparatus
20.2%, chemicals and chemical products 12.8%, road vehicles 12.0%, refined
petroleum 11.7%, iron and steel 6.4%). *Major import sources* (2003): Saudi
Arabia 23.7%; U.S. 16.7%; China 6.2%; Switzerland 5.0%; Italy 4.0%.
Exports (2003–04): U.S.$600,700,000 (coffee 37.2%, khat 14.7%, sesame seeds
13.8%, nonmonetary gold 8.1%, leather 7.5%). *Major export destinations*
(2003): Djibouti 13.4%; Germany 11.4%; Saudi Arabia 7.0%; Japan 6.8%;
Italy 6.5%.

Transport and communications

Transport. Railroads (2003): length 781 km[9]; (1998–99) passenger-km
151,000,000[10]; (1998–99) metric ton-km cargo 90,000,000[10]. Roads (2002):
total length 33,297 km (paved 12%). Vehicles (2002): passenger cars 67,614;
trucks and buses 52,169. Air transport (2003)[11]: passenger-km 3,573,000,000;
metric ton-km cargo 93,000,000; airports (1997) 31.

Communications				units per 1,000
Medium	date	unit	number	persons
Daily newspapers	1997	circulation	86,000	1.5
Radio	2002	receivers	15,200,000	224
Television	2002	receivers	682,000	10
Telephones	2003	main lines	435,000	6.3
Cellular telephones	2003	subscribers	97,800	1.4
Personal computers	2003	units	150,000	2.2
Internet	2003	users	75,000	1.1

Education and health

Educational attainment (2000)[2]. Percentage of population age 15 and over having: no formal schooling 63.8%; incomplete primary education 21.6%; primary 2.6%; incomplete secondary 8.1%; secondary 2.5%; post-secondary
1.4%. *Literacy* (2003): total population age 15 and over literate 42.7%; males
50.3%; females 35.1%.

Education (1999–2000)				student/
	schools	teachers	students	teacher ratio
Primary (age 7–12)	11,490	115,777	6,462,503	55.8
Secondary (age 13–18)	410	13,154	571,719	43.5
Voc., teacher tr.	62	1,309	12,551	9.6
Higher	6	1,779	40,894	23.0

Health (2003–04): physicians 1,764 (1 per 39,954 persons); hospital beds 13,384
(1 per 5,266 persons); infant mortality rate (2004) 96.9.
Food (2002): daily per capita caloric intake 1,857 (vegetable products 95%,
animal products 5%); 80% of FAO recommended minimum requirement.

Military

Total active duty personnel (2004): 182,500 (army 98.6%, air force 1.4%); UN
peacekeeping personnel along Ethiopian-Eritrean border (June 2005): 3,100
troops. *Military expenditure as percentage of GDP* (2003): 4.3%; per capita
expenditure U.S.$5.

[1]Amharic is the "working" language. [2]Based on the national Ethiopian Demographic
and Health Survey, comprising 14,072 households. [3]For ages 10 and up. [4]At 1980–81 factor cost. [5]First-time job seekers. [6]Detail does not add to total given because of rounding. [7]Based on the national Household Income and Expenditure Survey, comprising
17,332 households. [8]Imports c.i.f.; exports f.o.b. [9]Length of Ethiopian segment of Addis
Ababa–Djibouti railroad. [10]Includes Djibouti part of Addis Ababa–Djibouti railroad.
[11]Ethiopian Airlines only.

Internet resources for further information:
• **Ethiopian Embassy (Washington, D.C.)** http://www.ethiopianembassy.org
• **National Bank of Ethiopia** http://www.nbe.gov.et

Faroe Islands[1]

Official name: Føroyar (Faroese);
  Færøerne (Danish) (Faroe Islands).
Political status: self-governing region
  of the Danish realm with a single
  legislative body (Lagting [32]).
Chief of state: Danish Monarch
  represented by High Commissioner.
Head of home government: Prime
  Minister.
Capital: Tórshavn (Thorshavn).
Official languages: Faroese; Danish.
Official religion: Evangelical Lutheran.
Monetary unit: 1 Danish krone[2]
  (Dkr) = 100 øre; valuation (Sept. 1,
  2005) 1 U.S.$ = Dkr 5.94;
  1£ = Dkr 10.94.

Area and population

Districts	Capitals	area		population
		sq mi	sq km	2004[3] estimate
Klaksvík	Klaksvík	4.9	12.7	5,293
Nordhara Eysturoy (Østerø Nordre)	Eidhi	48.4	125.4	1,617
Nordhoy (Norderøernes)	...	88.1	228.1	717
Sandoy (Sandø)	Húsavík	48.1	124.7	1,496
Streymoy (Strømø)	Vestmanna	145.6	377.0	3,337
Sudhuroy (Suderø)	Tvøroyri	64.4	166.8	5,074
Sydhra Eysturoy (Østerø Søndre)	Runavík	62.1	160.9	9,121
Tórshavn (Thorshavn)	Tórshavn	5.9	15.3	18,684
Vágar (Vágø)	Midvágs	72.6	187.9	2,875
TOTAL		540.1	1,398.8	48,214

Demography

Population (2005): 48,400.
Density (2005): persons per sq mi 89.6, persons per sq km 34.6.
Urban-rural (2003): urban 38.8%; rural 61.2%.
Sex distribution (2005[3]): male 51.98%; female 48.02%.
Age breakdown (2003[3]): under 15, 23.6%; 15–29, 19.4%; 30–44, 20.9%; 45–59, 18.4%; 60–74, 11.3%; 75 and over, 6.4%.
Population projection: (2010) 50,000; (2020) 52,000.
Ethnic composition (2000): Faroese 97.0%; Danish 2.5%; other Scandinavian 0.4%; other 0.1%.
Religious affiliation (1995): Evangelical Lutheran Church of Denmark 80.8%; Plymouth Brethren 10.1%; Roman Catholic 0.2%; other (mostly nonreligious) 8.9%.
Major municipalities (2005[3]): Tórshavn 19,351; Klaksvík 4,904; Runavík 3,645; Tvøroyri 1,835.

Vital statistics

Birth rate per 1,000 population (2004): 13.9 (world avg. 21.1); (1998) legitimate 62.0%; illegitimate 38.0%.
Death rate per 1,000 population (2004): 8.7 (world avg. 9.0).
Natural increase rate per 1,000 population (2004): 5.2 (world avg. 12.1).
Total fertility rate (avg. births per childbearing woman; 2003): 2.5.
Marriage rate per 1,000 population (2003): 4.8.
Divorce rate per 1,000 population (2003): 1.2.
Life expectancy at birth (2004): male 75.6 years; female 82.5 years.
Major causes of death per 100,000 population (1999): diseases of the circulatory system 339.2; malignant neoplasms (cancers) 257.2; diseases of the respiratory system 48.8; accidents 39.9; other 166.3, of which suicide 2.2.

National economy

Budget (2002). Revenue: Dkr 3,762,060,000 (income taxes 44.5%, customs and excise duties 32.9%, transfers from the Danish government 16.7%). Expenditures: Dkr 3,586,220,000 (health and social welfare 46.6%, education 17.6%, debt service 10.5%, agriculture, fishing, and commerce 4.1%).
Gross national product (at current market prices; 2002): U.S.$1,290,000,000 (U.S.$27,270 per capita).

Structure of gross domestic product and labour force

	2001		2003	
	in value Dkr '000,000	% of total value	labour force	% of labour force
Agriculture	57	0.7	...	...
Mining	497	5.8	...	...
Fishing[4]	1,865	21.7	} 9,000	33.3
Manufacturing[5]	290	3.4		
Construction	471	5.5	...	...
Public utilities	186	2.2	...	...
Transp. and commun.	711	8.3	...	...
Trade, hotels	959	11.2	...	...
Finance and real estate	1,205	14.0	...	...
Pub. admin., defense	1,800	20.9	9,000	33.4
Services	305	3.5	...	...
Other	250	2.9	9,000	33.3
TOTAL	8,598[6]	100.0[6]	27,000	100.0

Production (metric tons except as noted). Agriculture, forestry, fishing (2004): potatoes 1,500, other vegetables, grass, hay, and silage are produced; livestock (number of live animals) 68,100 sheep, 2,000 cattle; fish catch (2003) 613,075 (of which blue whiting 322,592, cod 58,029, saithe [pollock] 50,851, capelin 50,468, haddock 30,053, herring 28,369, prawns, shrimps, and other

crustaceans 14,125, mackerel 12,299). Mining and quarrying: negligible[7]. Manufacturing (value added in Dkr '000,000; 1999): processed fish 393; all other manufacturing 351; important products include handicrafts and woolen textiles and clothing. Energy production (consumption): electricity (kW-hr; 2004) 249,000,000 ([2002] 195,000,000); coal, none (none); crude petroleum, none (none); petroleum products (metric tons; 2002) none (213,000); natural gas, none (none).
Population economically active (2003): total 27,000; activity rate of total population *c.* 56% (participation rates: ages 15–64, n.a.; female [1997] *c.* 46%; unemployed [2004] *c.* 3%).

Price and earnings indexes (2000 = 100)

	1998	1999	2000	2001	2002	2003	2004
Consumer price index	91.7	95.8	100.0	107.6	108.1	109.5	110.2
Hourly wage index	93.8	95.5	100.0	...	...	...	...

Public debt (external, outstanding; 2002): U.S.$297,000,000[8].
Household income and expenditure. Average household size: n.a.; average annual income per household: n.a.; sources of income: n.a.; expenditure (1998)[9]: food and beverages 25.1%, transportation and communications 17.7%, housing 12.5%, recreation 11.9%, energy 7.7%.
Land use as % of total land area (1997): in temporary crops *c.* 2%, in permanent crops, n.a., in pasture *c.* 93%; overall forest area, negligible.

Foreign trade

Balance of trade (current prices)

	1999	2000	2001	2002	2003	2004
Dkr '000,000	−38	−485	+123	+339	−952	−70
% of total	0.6%	6.0%	1.5%	4.2%	10.8%	0.9%

Imports (2004): Dkr 3,738,000,000 (goods for household consumption 29.0%; goods for industries 18.4%; fuels, lubricants, and electrical equipment 14.2%). *Major import sources:* Denmark 32.9%; Norway 18.4%; Germany 7.5%; Sweden 7.0%; United Kingdom 5.3%.
Exports (2004): Dkr 3,668,000,000 (chilled and frozen fish 64.3%; salted fish 14.8%; dried fish 9.9%; smoked, canned, and other conserved fish 5.3%). *Major export destinations:* United Kingdom 25.7%; Denmark 19.4%; Spain 10.1%; France and Monaco 8.3%; Norway 7.7%; Germany 5.2%.

Transport and communications

Transport. Railroads: none. Roads (2001): total length 288 mi, 464 km (paved, n.a.). Vehicles (2004): passenger cars 17,420; trucks, vans, and buses 4,212. Air transport (2003): passenger arrivals 79,791, passenger departures 80,065; airports with scheduled flights 1.

Communications

Medium	date	unit	number	units per 1,000 persons
Daily newspapers	1996	circulation	6,000	136
Radio	2000	receivers	102,000	2,222
Television	2000	receivers	46,800	1,022
Telephones	2004	main lines	24,000	495
Cellular telephones	2004	subscribers	41,300	854
Internet	2002	users	25,000	524

Education and health

Educational attainment: n.a. *Literacy:* n.a.

Education (2001–02)

	schools	teachers	students	student/ teacher ratio
Primary (age 6–14)	38	...	5,579	...
Secondary (age 15–17)	23	...	2,019	...
Voc., teacher tr.	11	...	2,195[10]	...
Higher[11]	1	19	173	9.1

Health (2001): physicians 90 (1 per 518 persons); hospital beds (2003) 290 (1 per 166 persons); infant mortality rate per 1,000 live births (2004) 6.4.
Food: n.a.

Military

Defense responsibility lies with Denmark.

---

[1]English-language alternative spelling is Faeroe Islands. [2]The local currency, the Faroese króna (Fkr), is equivalent to the Danish krone. Banknotes used are Faroese or Danish; coins are Danish. [3]January 1. [4]Fishing includes fish processing. [5]Manufacturing excludes fish processing. [6]Detail does not add to total given because of rounding. [7]The maritime boundary demarcation agreement between the Shetland Islands (U.K.) and the Faroes in 1999 has allowed for the still unsuccessful exploration for deep-sea petroleum as of May 2005. [8]Includes corporate debt. [9]Weights of consumer price index. [10]1996–97. [11]University of the Faroe Islands.

Internet resources for further information:
• **Faroe Islands in Figures**
  http://www.hagstova.fo
• **Governmental Bank of the Faroe Islands**
  http://landsbank.fo
• **Danmarks Statistik**
  http://www.dst.dk/HomeUK.aspx

Fiji

Official name: Republic of the
Fiji Islands[1].
Form of government: multiparty
republic with two legislative
houses (Senate [32[2]]; House of
Representatives [72]).
Chief of state: President.
Head of government: Prime Minister.
Capital: Suva.
Official languages: [3].
Official religion: none.
Monetary unit: 1 Fiji dollar
(F$) = 100 cents; valuation (Sept. 1,
2005) 1 U.S.$ = F$1.69; 1 £ = F$3.11.

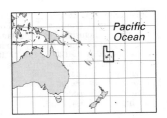

Pacific
Ocean

Area and population

Divisions Provinces	Capitals	area sq mi	area sq km	population 1996 census
Central	Suva			
Naitasiri	—	643	1,666	126,641
Namosi	—	220	570	5,742
Rewa	—	105	272	101,547
Serua	—	320	830	15,461
Tailevu	—	369	955	48,216
Eastern	Levuka			
Kadavu	—	185	478	9,535
Lau	—	188	487	12,211
Lomaiviti	—	159	411	16,214
Rotuma	—	18	46	2,810
Northern	Labasa			
Bua	—	532	1,379	14,988
Cakaudrove	—	1,087	2,816	44,321
Macuata	—	774	2,004	80,207
Western	Lautoka			
Ba	—	1,017	2,634	212,197
Nadroga-Navosa	—	921	2,385	54,083
Ra	—	518	1,341	30,904
TOTAL		7,055[4]	18,272[4]	775,077

Demography

Population (2005): 846,000.
Density (2005): persons per sq mi 119.9, persons per sq km 46.3.
Urban-rural (2003): urban 51.7%; rural 48.3%.
Sex distribution (2003): male 50.21%; female 49.79%.
Age breakdown (2003): under 15, 32.1%; 15–29, 28.8%; 30–44, 19.9%; 45–59, 12.8%; 60–74, 5.6%; 75 and over, 0.8%.
Population projection: (2010) 876,000; (2020) 918,000.
Doubling time: 41 years.
Ethnic composition (2004): Fijian 54.3%; Indian 38.2%; other 7.5%.
Religious affiliation (2000): Christian 56.8%, of which Protestant 37.1%, independent Christian 8.5%, Roman Catholic 8.4%; Hindu 33.3%; Muslim 6.9%; nonreligious 1.3%; Sikh 0.7%; other 1.0%.
Major cities (1996; "urban centres"): Suva (2003) 210,472; Lautoka 42,917; Nadi 30,791; Labasa 24,187; Nausori 21,645.

Vital statistics

Birth rate per 1,000 population (2004): 22.9 (world avg. 21.1).
Death rate per 1,000 population (2004): 5.7 (world avg. 9.0).
Natural increase rate per 1,000 population (2004): 17.2 (world avg. 12.1).
Total fertility rate (avg. births per childbearing woman; 2004): 2.8.
Life expectancy at birth (2004): male 66.7 years; female 71.8 years.
Major causes of death per 100,000 population (2001): diseases of the circulatory system 330.0; diseases of the respiratory system 50.2; infectious and parasitic diseases 45.8; malignant neoplasms (cancers) 38.0; accidents and violence 31.7.

National economy

Budget (2004). Revenue: F$1,172,100,000 (indirect taxes 59.7%, direct taxes 28.5%, non-tax revenue 11.4%, other 0.4%). Expenditures: F$1,479,100,000 (current expenditures 79.8%, of which charges on public debt 18.8%; capital expenditures 13.9%; other 6.3%).
Public debt (external, outstanding; 2002): U.S.$165,400,000.
Production (metric tons except as noted). Agriculture, forestry, fishing (2004): sugarcane 3,000,000, coconuts 140,000, taro 38,000, cassava 33,000, rice 15,000, bananas 6,500, ginger 3,300; livestock (number of live animals) 310,000 cattle, 250,000 goats, 139,000 pigs; roundwood (2003) 383,000 cu m; fish catch (2003) 34,685. Mining and quarrying (2003): gold 3,517 kg; silver 1,247 kg. Manufacturing (value added in F$'000,000; 2001): food products 94.6; textiles and clothing 92.4; beverages and tobacco 88.3; chemicals and chemical products 43.0. Energy production (consumption): electricity (kW-hr; 2002) 520,000,000 (520,000,000); coal (metric tons; 2002) none (15,000); petroleum products (metric tons; 2002) none (412,000).
Tourism: receipts from visitors (2003) U.S.$349,000,000; expenditures by nationals abroad (2003) U.S.$63,000,000.
Population economically active (1996): total 297,770; activity rate of total population 38.4% (participation rates: ages 15–64, 60.6%; female 32.8%; unemployed [2002] 14.1%).

Price and earnings indexes (2000 = 100)

	1998	1999	2000	2001	2002	2003	2004
Consumer price index	97.0	98.9	100.0	104.3	105.1	109.6	112.8
Earnings index	94.6	99.0	100.0	104.3	105.2	109.5	…

Gross national product (2004): U.S.$2,281,000,000 (U.S.$2,690 per capita).

Structure of gross domestic product and labour force

	2002 in value F$'000	2002 % of total value	1996 labour force	1996 % of labour force
Agriculture	546,831	15.9	132,676	44.6
Mining	32,293	0.9	2,507	0.8
Manufacturing	493,837	14.3	29,043	9.8
Construction	159,762	4.6	10,639	3.6
Public utilities	99,367	2.9	2,107	0.7
Transp. and commun.	517,708	15.0	16,722	5.6
Trade, hotels	581,321	16.9	32,175	10.8
Finance, real estate	437,193	12.7	7,812	2.6
Pub. admin., defense	687,180	20.0	15,854	5.3
Services			28,766	9.7
Other	−112,587[5]	−3.3[5]	19,469[6]	6.5[6]
TOTAL	3,442,905	100.0[4]	297,770	100.0

Household income and expenditure (2002)[7]. Average household size 4.7; average annual income per household F$15,757 (U.S.$12,784); sources of income: wages and salaries 64.3%, transfers 8.4%, self-employment 7.2%; expenditure: food, beverages, and tobacco 31.2%, housing and energy 18.5%, transportation and communications 17.9%, education 4.5%.
Land use as % of total land area (2000): in temporary crops 10.9%, in permanent crops 4.7%, in pasture 9.6%; overall forest area 44.6%.

Foreign trade[8, 9]

Balance of trade (current prices)

	1999	2000	2001	2002	2003	2004
F$'000,000	−623	−513	−584	−758	−941	−1,029
% of total	20.4%	17.1%	19.3%	24.1%	27.0%	30.8%

Imports (2004): F$2,204,689,000 (machinery and apparatus 16.2%, mineral fuels 14.9%, textiles and clothing 10.9%, transport equipment 8.6%, chemicals and chemical products 7.2%). *Major import sources:* Australia 34.0%; New Zealand 20.2%; Singapore 12.5%; Japan 4.5%; U.S. 3.7%.
Exports (2004): F$1,175,185,000 (clothing 21.8%, reexports [mostly petroleum products] 18.5%, sugar 15.2%, gold 7.5%, fish 7.2%). *Major export destinations:* Australia 30.0%; U.S. 22.5%; U.K. 13.0%; Singapore 8.4%; New Zealand 5.1%.

Transport and communications

Transport. Railroads (2003)[10]: length 371 mi, 597 km. Roads (1999): total length 2,140 mi, 3,440 km (paved 49%). Vehicles (2003): passenger cars 75,268; trucks and buses 40,044. Air transport (2003–04)[11]: passenger-km 2,389,000,000; metric ton-km cargo 74,769,000; airports (1997) 13.

Communications

Medium	date	unit	number	units per 1,000 persons
Daily newspapers	2001	circulation	49,000	60
Radio	2001	receivers	555,200	681
Television	2001	receivers	94,600	116
Telephones	2003	main lines	102,000	124
Cellular telephones	2003	subscribers	109,900	133
Personal computers	2004	units	44,000	52
Internet	2004	users	61,000	72

Education and health

Educational attainment (1996): Percentage of population age 25 and over having: no formal schooling 4.4%; some education 22.3%; incomplete secondary 47.7%; complete secondary 17.0%; some higher 6.7%; university degree 1.9%. *Literacy* (2003): total population age 15 and over literate 93.7%; males 95.5%; females 91.9%.

Education (2003)

	schools	teachers	students	student/teacher ratio
Primary (age 5–15)	712	5,127	142,781	27.8
Secondary (age 16–19)	157	3,935	68,178	17.3
Voc., teacher tr.	64	1,023[12]	9,706	…
Higher[13]	1	355[14]	15,393[15]	11.3[14]

Health: physicians (2003) 373 (1 per 2,229 persons); hospital beds (1999) 2,097 (1 per 385 persons); infant mortality rate per 1,000 live births (2004) 13.0.
Food (2002): daily per capita caloric intake 2,894 (vegetable products 84%, animal products 16%); 127% of FAO recommended minimum requirement.

Military

Total active duty personnel (2004): 3,500 (army 91.4%, navy 8.6%, air force, none). *Military expenditure as percentage of GDP* (2003): 1.6%; per capita expenditure U.S.$44.

---

[1]The long-form name in Fijian is Kai Vakarairai ni Fiji. [2]All seats are nonelected. [3]English, Fijian, and Hindustani (Fijian Hindi) have equal status per 1998 constitution. [4]Detail does not add to total given because of rounding. [5]Less imputed bank service charges. [6]Includes 2,204 not stated and 17,265 unemployed. [7]Based on a survey of 3,015 urban households. [8]Imports c.i.f.; exports f.o.b. [9]All export data include reexports. [10]Owned by the Fiji Sugar Corporation. [11]Air Pacific only. [12]2002. [13]University of the South Pacific only. [14]2000. [15]Includes distance learning and 5,232 non-Fijian students.

Internet resources for further information:
• **Fiji Islands Bureau of Statistics**
　http://www.statsfiji.gov.fj
• **Reserve Bank of Fiji http://www.reservebank.gov.fj**

Finland

Official names[1]: Suomen Tasavalta
(Finnish); Republiken Finland
(Swedish) (Republic of Finland).
Form of government: multiparty
republic with one legislative house
(Parliament [200]).
Chief of state: President.
Head of government: Prime Minister.
Capital: Helsinki.
Official languages: none[1].
Official religion: none.
Monetary unit: 1 euro (€) = 100
cents; valuation (Sept. 1, 2005)
1 U.S.$ = €0.80; 1 £ = €1.47[2].

Area and population

Provinces	Capitals	area sq mi	area sq km	population 2004[3] estimate
Eastern Finland	Mikkeli	23,444	60,720	582,781
Lapland	Rovaniemi	38,203	98,946	186,917
Oulu	Oulu	23,773	61,572	458,504
Southern Finland	Hämeenlinna	13,273	34,378	2,116,914
Western Finland	Turku	31,265	80,976	1,848,269
Autonomous Territory				
Åland (Ahvenanmaa)[4]	Mariehamn (Maarianhamina)	599	1,552	26,347
TOTAL		130,559[5, 6]	338,145[5, 6]	5,219,732

Demography

Population (2005): 5,244,000.
Density (2005)[7]: persons per sq mi 44.6, persons per sq km 17.2.
Urban-rural (2003): urban 60.9%; rural 39.1%.
Sex distribution (2005[3]): male 48.93%; female 51.07%.
Age breakdown (2005[3]): under 15, 17.5%; 15–29, 18.7%; 30–44, 19.9%; 45–59, 22.8%; 60–74, 13.8%; 75 and over, 7.3%.
Population projection: (2010) 5,304,000; (2020) 5,406,000.
Ethnic composition (2000): Finnish 91.9%; Swedish 5.9%; Karelian 0.8%; Russian 0.2%; other 1.2%.
Religious affiliation (2005[3]): Evangelical Lutheran 83.8%; Finnish (Greek) Orthodox 1.1%; nonreligious 14.0%; other 1.1%.
Major cities (2005[3]): Helsinki 559,046 (urban agglomeration [2003] 1,075,000); Espoo 227,472[8]; Tampere 202,932; Vantaa 185,429[8]; Turku 174,824; Oulu 127,226.

Vital statistics

Birth rate per 1,000 population (2004): 11.0 (world avg. 21.1); legitimate 59.2%; illegitimate 40.8%.
Death rate per 1,000 population (2004): 9.1 (world avg. 9.0).
Natural increase rate per 1,000 population (2004): 1.9 (world avg. 12.1).
Total fertility rate (avg. births per childbearing woman; 2003): 1.8.
Marriage rate per 1,000 population (2004): 5.6.
Divorce rate per 1,000 population (2004): 2.5.
Life expectancy at birth (2004): male 75.3 years; female 82.3 years.
Major causes of death per 100,000 population (2002): diseases of the circulatory system 406.4, of which ischemic heart disease 244.8, cerebrovascular diseases 93.0; malignant neoplasms (cancers) 202.3; accidents and violence 78.4; diseases of the respiratory system 74.3.

National economy

Budget (2004). Revenue: €37,065,000,000 (income and property taxes 34.8%, value-added taxes 29.0%, excise duties 12.2%). Expenditures: €37,065,000,-000 (social security and health 25.3%, education 16.3%, interest on state debt 7.5%, agriculture and forestry 7.2%, defense 5.6%).
Production (metric tons except as noted). Agriculture, forestry, fishing (2003): silage 6,670,200, barley 1,697,400, oats 1,294,500, sugar beets 892,300, potatoes 617,400, spring wheat 561,300; livestock (number of live animals; 2004) 1,365,000 pigs, 969,000 cattle, 201,000 reindeer; roundwood (2003) 53,779,000 cu m; fish catch (2002) 144,808. Mining and quarrying (2003): chromite (concentrate) 340,000; zinc (metal content) 38,900; gold 5,600 kg. Manufacturing (value added in €'000,000; 2002): telephone apparatus 5,581; paper and paper products 4,269; nonelectrical machinery and apparatus 3,191; food products 1,676; printing and publishing 1,658; wood and wood products (including metal furniture) 1,646. Energy production (consumption): electricity (kW-hr; 2002) 74,899,000,000 (86,824,000,000); hard coal (metric tons; 2002) none (6,620,000); crude petroleum (barrels; 2002) none (82,000,000); petroleum products (metric tons; 2002) 12,341,000 (9,751,000); natural gas (cu m; 2002) none (4,392,000,000).
Population economically active (2003): total 2,600,000; activity rate of total population 49.8% (participation rates: ages 15–64, 74.1%; female 48.0%; unemployed [October 2003–September 2004] 9.3%).

Price and earnings indexes (2000 = 100)

	1998	1999	2000	2001	2002	2003	2004
Consumer price index	95.6	96.7	100.0	102.6	104.2	105.1	105.3
Hourly earnings index	93.6	96.1	100.0	104.5	108.2	112.6	...

Household income and expenditure (2002). Average household size 2.1; disposable income per household €29,718 (U.S.$28,084); sources of gross income (2000): wages and salaries 55.4%, transfer payments 24.3%, other 20.3%; expenditure: housing and energy 28.7%, transportation and communications 18.0%, food, beverages, and tobacco 16.0%.

Gross national product (2004): U.S.$171,024,000,000 (U.S.$32,790 per capita).

Structure of gross domestic product and labour force

	2003 in value €'000,000	2003 % of total value	2003 labour force	2003 % of labour force
Agriculture, fishing, forestry	4,276	3.0	120,000	4.6
Mining	373	0.3	5,000	0.2
Manufacturing	28,465	20.0	445,000	17.1
Public utilities	2,850	2.0	20,000	0.8
Construction	6,698	4.7	151,000	5.8
Transp. and commun.	13,557	9.5	173,000	6.7
Trade, restaurants	14,983	10.5	363,000	14.0
Finance, real estate	26,969	18.9	313,000	12.0
Pub. admin., defense	23,270	16.3	118,000	4.5
Services	4,646	3.3	649,000	25.0
Other	16,431[9]	11.5[9]	243,000[10]	9.3[10]
TOTAL	142,518	100.0	2,600,000	100.0

Public debt (2001): U.S.$52,850,000,000.
Tourism (in U.S.$'000,000; 2003): receipts 1,894; expenditures 2,907.
Land use as % of total land area (2000): in temporary crops 7.2%, in permanent crops 0.03%, in pasture 0.07%; overall forest area 72.0%.

Foreign trade[11]

Balance of trade (current prices)

	1999	2000	2001	2002	2003	2004
€'000,000	+9,554	+12,647	+11,910	+11,634	+9,603	+8,520
% of total	13.9%	14.7%	14.3%	14.0%	11.5%	9.6%

Imports (2003): €36,775,000,000 (electrical machinery and apparatus 15.7%; nonelectrical machinery and apparatus 13.3%; mineral fuels 12.2%; automobiles and bicycles 9.2%). *Major import sources* (2004): Germany 14.7%; Russia 13.2%; Sweden 10.9%; China 4.9%; U.S. 4.6%; France 4.6%; U.K. 4.5%.
Exports (2003): €46,378,000,000 (electrical machinery and apparatus 23.3%, of which telecommunications equipment 16.6%; paper and paper products 17.3%; nonelectrical machinery and apparatus 11.1%; wood and wood products [excluding furniture] 5.4%). *Major export destinations* (2004): Sweden 11.0%; Germany 10.7%; Russia 8.9%; U.K. 7.1%; U.S. 6.4%; The Netherlands 5.1%.

Transport and communications

Transport. Railroads (2004): route length 5,741 km; passenger-km 3,400,000,-000; metric ton-km cargo 10,100,000,000. Roads (2004[3, 12]): total length 78,197 km (paved 65%). Vehicles (2003): passenger cars 2,274,577; trucks and buses 260,465. Air transport (2004)[13]: passenger-km 15,453,000,000; metric ton-km cargo 327,274,000; airports (2001) 27.

Communications

Medium	date	unit	number	units per 1,000 persons
Daily newspapers	2004	circulation	2,255,000	431
Radio	2000	receivers	8,400,000	1,623
Television	2000	receivers	3,580,000	692
Telephones	2004	main lines	2,368,000	454
Cellular telephones	2004	subscribers	4,988,000	956
Personal computers	2004	units	2,515,000	482
Internet	2004	users	3,286,000	630

Education and health

Educational attainment (end of 2002). Percentage of population age 25 and over having: incomplete upper-secondary education 36.6%; complete upper secondary or vocational 35.4%; higher 28.0%. *Literacy:* virtually 100%.

Education (2003)

	schools	teachers[14]	students	student/ teacher ratio
Primary/lower secondary (age 7–15)	3,808	43,783	597,414	...
Upper secondary (age 16–18)	440	7,480	121,816	...
Voc. (incl. higher)	340	19,698	304,688	...
Higher[15]	20	7,728	169,864	...

Health (2003): physicians 16,633 (1 per 313 persons); hospital beds 37,656 (1 per 138 persons); infant mortality rate per 1,000 live births 3.1.
Food (2002): daily per capita caloric intake 3,100 (vegetable products 62%, animal products 38%); 114% of FAO recommended minimum requirement.

Military

Total active duty personnel (2004): 27,000 (army 71.1%, navy 18.5%, air force 10.4%). *Military expenditure as percentage of GDP* (2003): 1.4%; per capita expenditure U.S.$441.

[1]Finnish and Swedish are national (not official) languages. [2]The Finnish markka (Fmk) was the former monetary unit; on Jan. 1, 2002, Fmk 5.95 = €1. [3]January 1. [4]Has increased autonomy in relationship to Finland from 1993. [5]Detail does not add to total given because of rounding. [6]Total includes land area of 117,558 sq mi (304,473 sq km) and inland water area of 13,001 sq mi (33,672 sq km). [7]Based on land area only. [8]Within Helsinki urban agglomeration. [9]Taxes less subsidies and imputed bank service charges. [10]Includes 235,000 unemployed persons not previously employed and 8,000 not adequately defined. [11]Imports c.i.f., exports f.o.b. [12]Excludes Åland Islands. [13]Finnair. [14]2002. [15]Universities only.

Internet resources for further information:
• **Embassy of Finland (Washington, D.C.)** http://www.finland.org
• **Statistics Finland** http://www.stat.fi/index_en.html

France

Official name: République Française (French Republic).
Form of government: republic with two legislative houses (Parliament; Senate [321], National Assembly [577]).
Chief of state: President.
Head of government: Prime Minister.
Capital: Paris.
Official language: French.
Official religion: none.
Monetary unit: 1 euro (€) = 100 cents; valuation (Sept. 1, 2005) 1 U.S.$ = €0.80; 1 £ = €1.47[1].

Area and population

Regions / Departments	Capitals	area sq mi	area sq km	population 2003[2] estimate
Alsace	Strasbourg			1,775,390
Bas-Rhin	Strasbourg	1,836	4,755	1,052,698
Haut-Rhin	Colmar	1,361	3,525	722,692
Aquitaine	Bordeaux			2,988,395
Dordogne	Périgueux	3,498	9,060	392,291
Gironde	Bordeaux	3,861	10,000	1,330,683
Landes	Mont-de-Marsan	3,569	9,243	341,254
Lot-et-Garonne	Agen	2,070	5,361	309,993
Pyrénées-Atlantiques	Pau	2,952	7,645	614,174
Auvergne	Clermont-Ferrand			1,314,476
Allier	Moulins	2,834	7,340	342,307
Cantal	Aurillac	2,211	5,726	148,359
Haute-Loire	Le Puy-en-Velay	1,922	4,977	213,993
Puy-de-Dôme	Clermont-Ferrand	3,077	7,970	609,817
Basse-Normandie	Caen			1,436,134
Calvados	Caen	2,142	5,548	659,893
Manche	Saint-Lô	2,293	5,938	484,967
Orne	Alençon	2,356	6,103	291,274
Bourgogne (Burgundy)	Dijon			1,612,397
Côte-d'Or	Dijon	3,383	8,763	510,334
Nièvre	Nevers	2,632	6,817	222,298
Saône-et-Loire	Mâcon	3,311	8,575	543,848
Yonne	Auxerre	2,868	7,427	335,917
Bretagne (Brittany)	Rennes			2,977,932
Côtes-d'Armor	Saint-Brieuc	2,656	6,878	553,969
Finistère	Quimper	2,600	6,733	863,798
Ille-et-Vilaine	Rennes	2,616	6,775	894,625
Morbihan	Vannes	2,634	6,823	665,540
Centre	Orléans			2,466,617
Cher	Bourges	2,793	7,235	312,277
Eure-et-Loir	Chartres	2,270	5,880	412,094
Indre	Châteauroux	2,622	6,791	230,954
Indre-et-Loire	Tours	2,366	6,127	563,062
Loir-et-Cher	Blois	2,449	6,343	318,853
Loiret	Orléans	2,616	6,775	629,377
Champagne-Ardenne	Châlons su Marne			1,336,741
Ardennes	Charleville-Mézières	2,019	5,229	288,806
Aube	Troyes	2,318	6,004	293,925
Haute-Marne	Chaumont	2,398	6,211	190,983
Marne	Châlons-en-Champagne	3,151	8,162	563,027
Corse[3] (Corsica)	Ajaccio			265,999
Corse-du-Sud	Ajaccio	1,550	4,014	121,371
Haute-Corse	Bastia	1,802	4,666	144,628
Franche-Comté	Besançon			1,130,532
Doubs	Besançon	2,021	5,234	505,557
Haute-Saône	Vesoul	2,070	5,360	232,283
Jura	Lons-le-Saunier	1,930	4,999	253,309
Territoire de Belfort	Belfort	235	609	139,383
Haute-Normandie	Rouen			1,787,319
Eure	Évreux	2,332	6,040	550,056
Seine-Maritime	Rouen	2,424	6,278	1,237,263
Île-de-France	Paris			11,131,412
Essonne	Évry	696	1,804	1,153,434
Hauts-de-Seine	Nanterre	68	176	1,470,706
Paris	Paris	40	105	2,147,274
Seine-et-Marne	Melun	2,284	5,915	1,232,467
Seine-Saint-Denis	Bobigny	91	236	1,396,122
Val-de-Marne	Créteil	95	245	1,239,352
Val-d'Oise	Pontoise	481	1,246	1,121,614
Yvelines	Versailles	882	2,284	1,370,443
Languedoc-Roussillon	Montpellier			2,401,838
Aude	Carcassonne	2,370	6,139	321,734
Gard	Nîmes	2,260	5,853	648,522
Hérault	Montpellier	2,356	6,101	945,901
Lozère	Mende	1,995	5,167	74,234
Pyrénées-Orientales	Perpignan	1,589	4,116	411,447
Limousin	Limoges			710,645
Corrèze	Tulle	2,261	5,857	234,144
Creuse	Guéret	2,149	5,565	122,713
Haute-Vienne	Limoges	2,131	5,520	353,788
Lorraine	Metz			2,319,109
Meurthe-et-Moselle	Nancy	2,024	5,241	718,250
Meuse	Bar-le-Duc	2,400	6,216	191,728
Moselle	Metz	2,400	6,216	1,027,854
Vosges	Épinal	2,268	5,874	381,277
Midi-Pyrénées	Toulouse			2,637,957
Ariège	Foix	1,888	4,890	139,612
Aveyron	Rodez	3,373	8,736	266,940
Gers	Auch	2,416	6,257	175,055
Haute-Garonne	Toulouse	2,436	6,309	1,102,919
Haute-Pyrénées	Tarbes	1,724	4,464	224,053
Lot	Cahors	2,014	5,217	164,413
Tarn	Albi	2,223	5,758	350,477
Tarn-et-Garonne	Montauban	1,435	3,718	214,488
Nord-Pas-de-Calais	Lille			4,013,107
Nord	Lille	2,217	5,742	2,561,800
Pas-de-Calais	Arras	2,576	6,671	1,451,307

Area and population (continued)

Regions / Departments	Capitals	area sq mi	area sq km	population 2003[2] estimate
Pays de la Loire	Nantes			3,312,473
Loire-Atlantique	Nantes	2,631	6,815	1,174,120
Maine-et-Loire	Angers	2,767	7,166	745,486
Mayenne	Laval	1,998	5,175	290,780
Sarthe	Le Mans	2,396	6,206	536,857
Vendée	La Roche-sur-Yon	2,595	6,720	565,230
Picardie (Picardy)	Amiens			1,869,386
Aisne	Laon	2,845	7,369	535,326
Oise	Beauvais	2,263	5,860	776,999
Somme	Amiens	2,382	6,170	557,061
Poitou-Charentes	Poitiers			1,668,337
Charente	Angoulême	2,300	5,956	341,275
Charente-Maritime	La Rochelle	2,650	6,864	576,855
Deux-Sèvres	Niort	2,316	5,999	347,652
Vienne	Poitiers	2,699	6,990	402,555
Provence-Alpes–Côte d'Azur	Marseille			4,665,051
Alpes-de-Haute-Provence	Digne	2,674	6,925	144,508
Alpes-Maritimes	Nice	1,660	4,299	1,045,970
Bouches-du-Rhône	Marseille	1,964	5,087	1,883,645
Hautes-Alpes	Gap	2,142	5,549	126,810
Var	Toulon	2,306	5,973	946,305
Vaucluse	Avignon	1,377	3,567	517,810
Rhône-Alpes	Lyon			5,813,733
Ain	Bourg-en-Bresse	2,225	5,762	539,006
Ardèche	Privas	2,135	5,529	294,933
Drôme	Valence	2,521	6,530	452,652
Haute-Savoie	Annecy	1,694	4,388	663,810
Isère	Grenoble	2,869	7,431	1,128,755
Loire	Saint-Étienne	1,846	4,781	726,613
Rhône	Lyon	1,254	3,249	1,621,718
Savoie	Chambéry	2,327	6,028	386,246
TOTAL		210,026	543,965	59,634,980

Demography

Population (2005): 60,733,000.
Density (2005): persons per sq mi 289.2, persons per sq km 111.6.
Urban-rural (2003): urban 76.3%; rural 23.7%.
Sex distribution (2004): male 48.78%; female 51.22%.
Age breakdown (2004): under 15, 18.6%; 15–29, 19.1%; 30–44, 21.5%; 45–59, 20.1%; 60–74, 12.7%; 75 and over, 8.0%.
Population projection: (2010) 61,797,000; (2020) 63,903,000.
Ethnic composition (2000): French 76.9%; Algerian and Moroccan Berber 2.2%; Italian 1.9%; Portuguese 1.5%; Moroccan Arab 1.5%; Fleming 1.4%; Algerian Arab 1.3%; Basque 1.3%; Jewish 1.2%; German 1.2%; Vietnamese 1.0%; Catalan 0.5%; other 8.1%.
Religious affiliation (2000): Roman Catholic 82.3%; Muslim 7.1%; atheist 4.4%; Protestant 3.7%; Orthodox 1.1%; Jewish 1.0%; other 0.4%.
Major cities (1999): Paris 2,125,246 (metropolitan area 9,644,507); Marseille 798,430 (1,349,772); Lyon 445,452 (1,348,832); Toulouse 390,350 (761,090); Nice 342,738 (888,784); Nantes 270,251 (544,932); Strasbourg 264,115 (427,245); Montpellier 225,392 (287,981); Bordeaux 215,363 (753,931); Rennes 206,229 (272,263); Le Havre 190,905 (248,547); Reims 187,206 (215,581); Lille 184,493 (1,000,900); Saint-Étienne 180,210 (291,960); Toulon 160,639 (519,640).
Households (1999). Average household size 2.4; 1 person 31.0%, 2 persons 31.1%, 3 persons 16.2%, 4 persons 13.8%, 5 persons or more 7.9%. Family households (1999): 15,942,369 (67.0%); nonfamily 7,865,703 (33.0%).
Immigration (2000): immigrants admitted 53,879 (from Africa 56.0%, of which Algerian 16.9%; from Europe 23.1%; from Asia 12.4%).

Vital statistics

Birth rate per 1,000 population (2004): 12.7 (world avg. 21.1); (2003) legitimate 54.8%; illegitimate 45.2%.
Death rate per 1,000 population (2004): 8.4 (world avg. 9.0).
Natural increase rate per 1,000 population (2004): 4.3 (world avg. 12.1).
Total fertility rate (avg. births per childbearing woman; 2004): 1.9.
Marriage rate per 1,000 population (2004): 4.3.
Divorce rate per 1,000 population (2002): 2.2.
Life expectancy at birth (2004): male 76.7 years; female 83.8 years.
Major causes of death per 100,000 population (2001): malignant neoplasms (cancers) 185.0; diseases of the circulatory system 163.8; accidents and violence 55.6; diseases of the respiratory system 32.3; diseases of the digestive system 29.7; endocrine, metabolic, and nutritional disorders 20.5.

Social indicators

Educational attainment (2002). Percentage of population age 25–64 with no formal schooling through lower-secondary education 35%, upper secondary/higher vocational 41%, university 24%.
Quality of working life. Average workweek (2004): 37.4 hours. Annual rate per 100,000 workers for (1999): injury or accident 4,432 (deaths 0.1%); accidents in transit to work (1994) 708 (deaths 68.3). Average days lost to labour stoppages per 1,000 workers (2003): 15. Trade union membership (2003): 1,900,000 (c. 8% of labour force).
Access to services. Proportion of dwellings having: central heating (1997) 86.1%; piped water (2002) 99.0%; indoor plumbing (1992) 95.8%.
Social participation. Eligible voters participating in last (June 2002) national election: 64.4%. Population over 15 years of age participating in voluntary associations (1997): 28.0%.
Social deviance. Offense rate per 100,000 population (1998) for: murder 1.6, rape 13.4, other assault 583.8; theft (including burglary and housebreaking) 6,107.6. Incidence per 100,000 in general population of: homicide (2001) 0.8; suicide (2001) 16.1.
Leisure (2003). Participation rate for population age 15 and over for selected leisure activities: attending a movie 52%; visiting a historic monument 46%; cycling 38%; attending an exposition 37%; swimming 30%; visiting a museum 29%; attending a concert 25%; playing *pétanque* or billiards 22%.

Material well-being (2002). Households possessing: automobile 79%; colour television 94%; VCR (2001) 70%; microcomputer (2004) 45%; washing machine 91%; microwave 68%; dishwasher (2001) 39%.

National economy

Gross national product (2004)[4]: U.S.$1,858,731,000,000 (U.S.$30,090 per capita).

Structure of gross domestic product and labour force

| | 2003 | | 2001 | |
	in value €'000,000[5]	% of total value[5]	labour force[6]	% of labour force[6]
Agriculture	36,400	2.9	348,200	1.6
Mining	...	...	49,500	0.2
Manufacturing	244,400	19.4	3,919,800	17.6
Construction	53,500	4.3	1,256,000	5.6
Public utilities	35,400	2.8	210,100	0.9
Transp. and commun.	56,100	4.5	1,563,100	7.0
Trade, hotels	129,000	10.2	3,659,300	16.4
Finance, real estate	407,600	32.4	3,542,600	15.9
Pub. admin., defense	112,400	8.9	2,353,700	10.6
Services	219,000	17.4	4,955,400	22.2
Other	−35,300[7]	−2.8[7]	441,700[8]	2.0[8]
TOTAL	1,258,600[9]	100.0	22,302,800[9]	100.0

Budget (2004). Revenue: €330,140,000,000 (value-added taxes 47.1%, direct taxes 38.3%, other taxes 14.6%). Expenditures: €355,470,000,000 (current civil expenditure 86.0%; military expenditure 8.7%; development expenditure 5.3%).
Public debt (end of 2003): U.S.$1,014,000,000,000.

Manufacturing enterprises (1995)

	no. of enter-prises[10]	no. of employees	annual salaries as a % of avg. of all salaries[10]	annual value added (F '000,000)
Food products	55,197	545,900	87	208,065
Transport equipment	4,293	508,700	108	167,357
Electrical machinery	15,620	433,600	118	156,221
Iron and steel	27,847	403,800	96	131,376
Mechanical equipment	32,134	390,300	104	127,637
Petroleum refineries	180	46,200	174	117,041
Printing, publishing	30,359	231,900	125	83,083
Textiles and wearing apparel	29,701	281,500	78	63,633
Rubber products	5,875	204,200	94	57,758
Chemical products	1,442	102,100	128	51,146
Paper and paper products	1,916	101,500	102	38,585
Metal products	442	43,700	103	28,115
Glass products	1,536	52,400	104	16,638
Footwear	4,236	55,400	75	12,970

Production (metric tons except as noted). Agriculture, forestry, fishing (2004): wheat 39,705,000, sugar beets 30,554,000, corn (maize) 16,391,000, barley 11,040,000, grapes 7,542,000, potatoes 7,254,000, rapeseed 3,969,000, apples 2,217,000, triticale 1,824,000, dry peas 1,617,000, sunflower seeds 1,467,000, tomatoes 809,000, carrots 703,000, oats 598,000, lettuce 463,000, dry onions 446,000, green peas 441,000, cauliflower 413,000, string beans 374,000; livestock (number of live animals) 19,320,000 cattle, 15,004,000 pigs, 9,151,000 sheep, 200,000,000 chickens; roundwood (2003) 36,850,000 cu m; fish catch (2003) 877,995. Mining and quarrying (2003): gypsum 3,500,000; kaolin 323,000; potash (2002) 139,000; gold 1,470 kg. Manufacturing (value added in U.S.$'000,000; 2000[11]): motor vehicles, trailers, and motor vehicle parts 17,157; pharmaceuticals, soaps, and paints 16,360; fabricated metal products 12,996; general purpose machinery 7,064; basic chemicals 6,378; aircraft and spacecraft 6,045; plastic products 6,014; publishing 5,184; medical, measuring, and testing appliances 4,765; telecommunications equipment 4,615.

Financial aggregates

	1999	2000	2001	2002	2003	2004
Exchange rate, € per:						
U.S. dollar	1.00	1.07	1.13	0.95	0.79	0.73
£	1.62	1.60	1.65	1.43	1.41	1.42
SDR	1.37	1.40	1.43	1.30	1.18	1.14
International reserves (U.S.$)						
Total (excl. gold; '000,000)	39,701	37,039	31,749	28,365	30,186	35,314
SDRs ('000,000)	347	402	492	622	761	875
Reserve pos. in IMF ('000,000)	5,241	4,522	4,894	5,778	6,303	5,363
Foreign exchange	33,933	32,114	26,363	21,965	23,122	29,077
Gold ('000,000 fine troy oz)	97.24	97.25	97.25	97.25	97.25	95.98
% world reserves	10.1	10.2	10.3	10.5	10.7	10.7
Interest and prices						
Central bank discount (%)	...	...	...	...	...	...
Govt. bond yield (%)	4.69	5.45	5.05	4.93	4.18	4.15
Industrial share prices						
(2000 = 100)	74.0	100.0	80.1	60.4	...	...
Balance of payments (U.S.$'000,000)						
Balance of visible trade	+17,990	−3,620	+2,840	+6,920	+1,040	−7,950
Imports, f.o.b.	282,060	301,820	291,780	300,740	360,830	429,070
Exports, f.o.b.	300,050	298,200	294,620	307,660	361,870	421,120
Balance of invisibles	+23,520	+22,200	+25,920	+4,080	+10,760	+3,120
Balance of payments, current account	+41,510	+18,580	+28,760	+11,000	+11,800	−4,830

Retail trade enterprises (1995)[2]

	no. of enter-prises	no. of employees	weekly wages as a % of all wages	annual turnover (F '000,000)
Large food stores	4,373	385,402	...	617,222
Clothing stores	51,873	195,535	...	126,504
Pharmacies	22,301	126,508	...	121,980
Small food stores	64,565	163,474	...	110,928
butcher shops	21,548	59,962	...	36,732
Furniture stores	7,179	53,080	...	54,390
Electrical and electronics stores	10,990	55,560	...	43,995

Energy production (consumption): electricity (kW-hr; 2002) 560,212,000,000 (483,312,000,000); hard coal (metric tons; 2002) 1,920,000[12] (18,890,000); lignite (metric tons; 2002) 147,000 (184,000); crude petroleum (barrels; 2004) 8,500,000 ([2002] 597,000,000[13]); petroleum products (metric tons; 2002) 71,019,000 (74,283,000[13]); natural gas (cu m; 2003) 2,832,000,000 (43,736,-000,000).
Population economically active (2003): total 27,125,000; activity rate of total population 45.3% (participation rates: ages 15–64, 69.3%; female 45.9%; unemployed [October 2003–September 2004] 9.9%).

Price and earnings indexes (2000 = 100)

	1998	1999	2000	2001	2002	2003	2004
Consumer price index	97.8	98.3	100.0	101.7	103.6	105.8	108.1
Earnings index	93.6	95.7	100.0	104.5	108.4	112.8	116.1

Household income and expenditure. Average household size (2004) 2.3; average disposable income per household (2001) €26,570 (U.S.$23,776); sources of income (1995): wages and salaries 70.0%, self-employment 24.4%, social security 5.6%; expenditure (2001): housing and energy 23.4%, transportation 15.2%, food and nonalcoholic beverages 14.4%, recreation 8.9%, restaurants and hotels 7.6%.
Tourism (in U.S.$'000,000; 2003): receipts U.S.$37,038; expenditures U.S.$23,576.
Land use as % of total land area (2000): in temporary crops 33.5%, in permanent crops 2.1%, in pasture 18.4%; overall forest area 27.9%.

Foreign trade[14]

Balance of trade (current prices)

	1998	1999	2000	2001	2002	2003
U.S.$'000,000,000	+14.6	+9.4	−8.7	−4.3	+1.1	−3.9
% of total	2.5%	1.7%	1.4%	0.7%	0.2%	0.5%

Imports (2002)[15]: U.S.$303,800,000,000 (machinery and apparatus 24.2%; transport equipment 13.5%; chemicals and chemical products 12.9%; petroleum [all forms] 9.2%; food 7.0%). *Major import sources:* Germany 17.2%; Italy 9.0%; U.S. 8.0%; U.K. 7.3%; Spain 7.2%; Belgium 6.6%; The Netherlands 4.7%; China 3.5%; Japan 3.2%; Switzerland 2.2%; Ireland 2.0%.
Exports (2002)[15]: U.S.$304,900,000,000 (machinery and apparatus 23.2%; transport equipment 20.5%, of which road vehicles 14.0%, aircraft and spacecraft 5.6%; chemicals and chemical products 14.9%, of which pharmaceuticals 4.9%; food 7.9%; iron and steel 3.2%; perfumes, cosmetics, and toiletries 2.9%). *Major export destinations:* Germany 14.5%; U.K. 10.3%; Spain 9.7%; Italy 9.1%; U.S. 8.1%; Belgium 7.2%; The Netherlands 4.0%; Switzerland 3.2%; Japan 1.7%; Portugal 1.5%.

Transport and communications

Transport. Railroads (2002): route length 32,008 km; passenger-km 73,540,-000,000; metric ton-km cargo 50,040,000,000. Roads (2002): total length 893,100 km (paved 100%). Vehicles (2002): passenger cars 29,160,000; trucks and buses 5,903,081. Air transport (2004)[16]: passenger-km 168,998,000,000; metric ton-km cargo 10,078,000,000; airports (1996) 61.

Communications

Medium	date	unit	number	units per 1,000 persons
Daily newspapers	2004	circulation	7,934,000	131
Radio	2000	receivers	55,900,000	950
Television	2000	receivers	37,000,000	628
Telephones	2004	main lines	33,870,200	560
Cellular telephones	2004	subscribers	44,552,000	737
Personal computers	2004	units	29,410,000	482
Internet	2005	users	25,600,000	422

Education and health

Education (2000–01)

	schools	teachers	students	student/teacher ratio
Primary (age 6–10)	39,131[17]	211,192	3,839,770	18.2
Secondary (age 11–18) Voc., teacher tr.	11,052[17]	483,493	5,399,433	11.2
Higher[18]	...	46,196	1,400,393	30.3

Health (2004): physicians 196,000 (1 per 306 persons); hospital beds (2001) 477,000 (1 per 126 persons); infant mortality rate 4.1.
Food (2002): daily per capita caloric intake 3,654 (vegetable products 63%, animal products 37%); 145% of FAO recommended minimum requirement.

Military

Total active duty personnel (2004): 259,050 (army 52.9%, navy 17.1%, air force 24.7%, unallocated 5.3%). *Military expenditure as percentage of GDP* (2003): 2.6%; per capita expenditure U.S.$756.

[1]The French franc was the former monetary unit; on Jan. 1, 2002, F 6.56 = €1. [2]January 1. [3]Commonly referred to as a region but officially a territorial collectivity. [4]Includes the overseas departments of French Guiana, Guadeloupe, Martinique, and Réunion. [5]At constant prices of 1995. [6]Paid employees only; excludes 2,140,300 non-salaried workers and 3,369,500 unemployed. [7]Less imputed bank service charges. [8]Private households with employed persons. [9]Detail does not add to total given because of rounding. [10]1991. [11]Data unavailable for production of food, beverages, and tobacco products. [12]Last coal-producing mine closed in April 2004. [13]Consumption data includes Monaco. [14]Imports c.i.f.; exports f.o.b. [15]Includes Monaco. [16]Air France–KLM only. [17]1996–97. [18]Universities only.

Internet resources for further information:
• INSEE http://www.insee.fr/en/home/home_page.asp

French Guiana

Official name: Département de la Guyane française (Department of French Guiana).
Political status: overseas department of France with two legislative houses (General Council [19]; Regional Council [31]).
Chief of state: President of France.
Heads of government: Prefect (for France); President of the General Council (for French Guiana); President of the Regional Council (for French Guiana).
Capital: Cayenne.
Official language: French.
Official religion: none.
Monetary unit: 1 euro (€) = 100 cents; valuation (Sept. 1, 2005) 1 U.S.$ = €0.80; 1 £ = €1.47[1].

Area and population		area		population
				1999
Arrondissements	**Capitals**	sq mi	sq km	census
Cayenne	Cayenne	17,727	45,913	119,660
Saint-Laurent-du-Maroni	Saint-Laurent-du-Maroni	14,526	37,621	37,553
TOTAL		32,253	83,534	157,213

Demography

Population (2005): 192,000.
Density (2005): persons per sq mi 6.0, persons per sq km 2.3.
Urban-rural (2003): urban 75.4%; rural 24.6%.
Sex distribution (2002): male 49.71%; female 50.29%.
Age breakdown (1999): under 15, 34.0%; 15–29, 24.2%; 30–44, 23.3%; 45–59, 12.5%; 60–74, 4.3%; 75 and over, 1.7%.
Population projection: (2010) 215,000; (2020) 261,000.
Doubling time: 28 years.
Ethnic composition (2000): Guianese Mulatto 37.9%; French 8.0%; Haitian 8.0%; Surinamese 6.0%; Antillean 5.0%; Chinese 5.0%; Brazilian 4.9%; East Indian 4.0%; other (other West Indian, Hmong, other South American) 21.2%.
Religious affiliation (2000): Christian 84.6%, of which Roman Catholic 80.0%, Protestant 3.9%; Chinese folk-religionist 3.6%; Spiritist 3.5%; nonreligious/atheist 3.0%; traditional beliefs 1.9%; Hindu 1.6%; Muslim 0.9%; other 0.9%.
Major cities (1999)[2]: Cayenne (2003) 60,500 (urban agglomeration 84,181); Saint-Laurent-du-Maroni 19,211; Kourou 19,107; Matoury 18,032[3]; Rémire-Montjoly 15,555[3].

Vital statistics

Birth rate per 1,000 population (2003): 29.3 (world avg. 21.1); (2001) legitimate 16.1%; illegitimate 83.9%.
Death rate per 1,000 population (2003): 4.1 (world avg. 9.0).
Natural increase rate per 1,000 population (2003): 25.2 (world avg. 12.1).
Total fertility rate (avg. births per childbearing woman; 2004): 3.1.
Marriage rate per 1,000 population (2002): 3.0.
Divorce rate per 1,000 population (2001): 0.7.
Life expectancy at birth (2004): male 73.6 years; female 80.4 years.
Major causes of death per 100,000 population (1999): diseases of the circulatory system *c.* 100; violence and accidents *c.* 71; malignant neoplasms (cancers) *c.* 54[4]; infectious and parasitic diseases *c.* 33, of which HIV/AIDS *c.* 16; diseases of the digestive system *c.* 16; endocrine and metabolic disorders *c.* 16.

National economy

Budget (2002). Revenue: €145,000,000 (direct taxes 33.1%, indirect taxes 31.7%, revenue from French central government 20.7%). Expenditures: €145,000,000 (current expenditures 83.4%, capital expenditures 16.6%).
Production (metric tons except as noted). Agriculture, forestry, fishing (2004): rice 23,500, cassava 10,400, cabbages 6,350, sugarcane 5,350, bananas 4,500, taro 4,100, tomatoes 3,770; livestock (number of live animals) 10,500 pigs, 9,200 cattle; roundwood (2003) 149,170 cu m; fish catch (2003) 5,565. Mining and quarrying (2002): stone, sand, and gravel 3,000; gold 2,971 kg; tantalum 1,500 kg. Manufacturing (2001): pork 1,245; chicken meat 560; finished wood products 3,172 cu m[5]; rum (2000) 3,072 hectolitres; other products include leather goods, clothing, rosewood essence, yogurt, and beer. Number of satellites launched from the Kourou Space Centre (2003): 8[6]. Energy production (consumption): electricity (kW-hr; 2002) 477,000,000 (477,000,000); coal, none (none); crude petroleum, none (none); petroleum products (metric tons; 2002) none (312,000); natural gas, none (none).
Household income and expenditure. Average household size (1999) 3.3; income per household (2000) €30,542 (U.S.$28,139); sources of income (2000): wages and salaries 55.4%, self-employment 17.6%, transfer payments 14.4%; expenditure (2005)[7]: food and beverages 21.7%, housing and energy 20.8%, transportation and communications 15.4%, restaurants and hotels 7.9%, household furnishings 7.3%, clothing and footwear 6.4%.
Land use as % of total land area (2000): in temporary crops 0.14%, in permanent crops 0.05%, in pasture 0.08%; overall forest area 89.9%.
Gross national product (2003): U.S.$1,610,000,000 (U.S.$9,040 per capita).

Structure of gross domestic product and labour force

	2000		2002	
	in value €'000,000	% of total value	labour force[8]	% of labour force[8]
Agriculture, forestry, fishing	81	5.1	1,024	2.1
Mining	30	1.9	409	0.8
Manufacturing	158	9.9	1,053	2.1
Construction	147	9.2	2,583	5.2
Public utilities	22	1.4	644	1.3
Finance, real estate[9]	379	23.8	830	1.7
Transp. and commun.	−165	−10.4	2,134	4.3
Trade, restaurants, hotels	245	15.4	4,815	9.8
Pub. admin., defense	256	16.1	9,758	19.8
Services	439	27.6	14,975	30.4
Other	—	—	11,095	22.5
TOTAL	1,592	100.0	49,320	100.0

Population economically active (1999): total 62,634; activity rate of total population 39.9% (participation rates: ages 15–59, 65.0%; female 43.8%; unemployed [2004] 26.3%).

Price and earnings indexes (2000 = 100)

	1998	1999	2000	2001	2002	2003	2004
Consumer price index	98.4	98.6	100.0	101.6	103.1	105.2	106.4
Monthly earnings index[10, 11]	...	99.4	100.0	101.6	102.6	102.6	103.9

Tourism (2002): receipts U.S.$45,000,000; expenditures, n.a.

Foreign trade

Balance of trade (current prices)

	1999	2000	2001	2002	2003	2004
€'000,000	−421	−499	−515	−514	−524	−581
% of total	68.2%	67.3%	66.3%	66.6%	70.2%	76.3%

Imports (2004): €672,000,000 (machinery and apparatus 18.3%, transportation equipment 16.7%, food products, beverages, and tobacco 13.1%, mineral fuels [mostly refined petroleum] 10.7%, chemicals and chemical products 9.7%). *Major import sources:* France 47.2%; Trinidad and Tobago 9.4%; Japan 2.3%; Martinique 1.8%; U.S. 1.5%.
Exports (2004): €91,000,000 (nonferrous metals [nearly all gold] 49.7%, live animals and food products [mostly fish, shrimp, and rice] 13.3%, transportation equipment [mostly parts for air and space vehicles] 9.9%, machinery and apparatus 9.9%). *Major export destinations:* France 62.0%; Switzerland 17.1%; Martinique 5.9%; Guadeloupe 3.3%; Italy 2.7%.

Transport and communications

Transport. Railroads: none. Roads (1996): total length 774 mi, 1,245 km (paved, n.a.). Vehicles (1999): passenger cars 32,900; trucks and buses 11,900. Air transport (2004): passengers carried 400,921; cargo carried 4,400 metric tons; airports (2004) with scheduled flights 1.

Communications				units per 1,000
Medium	date	unit	number	persons
Daily newspapers	1996	circulation	2,000	14
Radio	1997	receivers	104,000	702
Television	1998	receivers	37,000	202
Telephones	2001	main lines	51,000	301
Cellular telephones	2002	subscribers	87,300	499
Personal computers	1999	units	23,000	145
Internet	2002	users	25,000	143

Education and health

Educational attainment (1999). Percentage of population age 20 and over having: no formal education through lower secondary education 57.3%; vocational 17.5%; upper secondary 9.3%; incomplete higher 5.6%; completed higher 6.7%; other 3.6%. *Literacy:* n.a.

Education (2001–02)	schools	teachers	students	student/ teacher ratio
Primary (age 6–11)	92	1,871	22,051	11.8
Secondary (age 12–18)	36	1,919	21,439	11.2
Higher[12]	1	194	637	3.3

Health (2003): physicians 319 (1 per 570 persons); hospital beds 764 (1 per 238 persons); infant mortality rate per 1,000 live births (2004) 12.5.
Food (1992): daily per capita caloric intake 2,900 (vegetable products 70%, animal products 30%); 128% of FAO recommended minimum requirement.

Military

Total active duty personnel (2004): French troops 3,100.

[1]The French franc (F) was replaced by the euro (on Jan. 1, 2002, F 6.56 = €1). [2]Commune population. [3]Within Cayenne urban agglomeration. [4]Excludes breast and lung neoplasms (cancers). [5]1996. [6]In 2004 the European Space Agency accounted for 26% of GDP and employed 8,300. [7]Weights of consumer price index components. [8]Employed only. [9]Includes insurance. [10]Index based on end-of-year figures. [11]Based on minimum-level wage in public administration. [12]Université des Antilles et de la Guyane, Cayenne campus.

Internet resources for further information:
• Chambre de Commerce et l'Industrie: Guyane http://www.guyane.cci.fr

French Polynesia

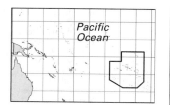

Pacific Ocean

Official name: Polynésie française (French); Polynesia Farani (Tahitian) (French Polynesia).
Political status: overseas country[1] (France) with one legislative house (Assembly [57]).
Chief of state: President of France represented by High Commissioner.
Head of government: President.
Capital: Papeete.
Official languages: French; Tahitian.
Official religion: none.
Monetary unit: 1 Franc de la Comptoirs française du pacifique (CFPF) = 100 centimes; valuation (Sept. 1, 2005)[2]
1 U.S.$ = CFPF 95.04;
1 £ = CFPF 174.99.

Area and population

Administrative subdivisions	Capitals	area		population
		sq mi	sq km	2002 census
Austral (Tubuai) Islands	Mataura	57	148	6,386
Leeward Islands	Uturoa	156	404	30,221
Marquesas Archipelago	Taiohae	405	1,049	8,712
Tuamotu–Gambier Islands	Papeete	280	726	15,973
Windward Islands	Papeete	461	1,194	184,224
TOTAL		1,544[3]	4,000[3]	245,516

Demography

Population (2005): 255,000.
Density (2005)[4]: persons per sq mi 187.6, persons per sq km 72.4.
Urban-rural (2003): urban 52.1%; rural 47.9%.
Sex distribution (2004): male 51.66%; female 48.34%.
Age breakdown (2004): under 15, 27.5%; 15–29, 27.5%; 30–44, 22.7%; 45–59, 13.7%; 60–74, 6.8%; 75 and over, 1.8%.
Population projection: (2010) 272,000; (2020) 305,000.
Doubling time: 54 years.
Ethnic composition (2000): Polynesian 58.4%, of which Tahitian 41.0%, Tuamotuan 8.5%; mixed European–Polynesian 17.0%; Han Chinese 11.3%; French 11.0%; other 2.3%.
Religious affiliation (2000): Protestant (mostly Evangelical Church of French Polynesia [Presbyterian]) c. 39%; Roman Catholic c. 35%; other affiliated Christian (including Mormon and Jehovah's Witness) c. 11%; unaffiliated Christian c. 3%; Chinese folk-religionist c. 8%; nonreligious c. 4%.
Major communes (2002): Faaa 28,339[5]; Papeete 26,181 (urban agglomeration 124,864); Punaauia 23,706[5]; Moorea-Maiao 14,550; Pirae 14,499[5].

Vital statistics

Birth rate per 1,000 population (2004): 17.7 (world avg. 21.1); (2000) legitimate 29.9%; illegitimate 70.1%.
Death rate per 1,000 population (2004): 4.5 (world avg. 9.0).
Natural increase rate per 1,000 population (2004): 13.2 (world avg. 12.1).
Total fertility rate (avg. births per childbearing woman; 2004): 2.1.
Marriage rate per 1,000 population (2004): 4.5.
Life expectancy at birth (2004): male 73.3 years; female 78.2 years.
Major causes of death per 100,000 population (2002): diseases of the circulatory system 113; malignant neoplasms (cancers) 102; accidents, suicide, and violence 54; respiratory diseases 46; diseases of the digestive system 13.

National economy

Budget (2001). Revenue: CFPF 108,036,000,000 (indirect taxes 55.1%, direct taxes and nontax revenue 44.9%). Expenditures: CFPF 140,709,000,000 (current expenditure 68.1%, capital expenditure 31.9%).
Public debt (external, outstanding; 1999): U.S.$542,000,000.
Production (metric tons except as noted). Agriculture, forestry, fishing (2004): coconuts 86,800, copra (2003) 9,400, roots and tubers 5,300, cassava 4,300, pineapples 3,400, sugarcane 3,100, tomatoes 1,200, watermelon 1,000, cucumbers 900, bananas 800, vanilla 35; livestock (number of live animals) 27,500 pigs, 16,500 goats, 11,000 cattle; roundwood, n.a.; fish catch (2002) 15,543; export production of black pearls (2004) 9,015 kg. Mining and quarrying: phosphate deposits were not mined in 2005. Manufacturing (2001): copra (metric tons sold) 8,262; coconut oil 5,000; other manufactures include *monoï* oil (primarily refined coconut and sandalwood oils), beer, printed cloth, and sandals. Energy production (consumption): electricity (kW-hr; 2003) 491,000,000 ([2002] 520,000,000); coal, none (none); crude petroleum, none (none); petroleum products (metric tons; 2002) none (228,000); natural gas, none (none).
Population economically active (2002): total 99,498; activity rate of total population 40.6% (participation rates: ages 15–64, 61.7%; female 40.0%; unemployed 11.7%).

Price and earnings indexes (2000 = 100)

	1998	1999	2000	2001	2002	2003	2004
Consumer price index	98.2	99.0	100.0	101.0	103.9	104.3	104.8
Earnings index[6]	93.1	97.0	100.0	102.0	105.2	106.0	...

Tourism (2003): receipts from visitors U.S.$398,000,000; expenditures by nationals abroad, n.a.
Gross national product (2003): U.S.$4,710,000,000 (U.S.$19,250 per capita).

Structure of gross domestic product and labour force

	1997		1996	
	in value CFPF '000,000	% of total value	labour force	% of labour force
Agriculture, fishing	15,534	4.1	10,888	12.5
Manufacturing[7]	26,360	7.0	6,424	7.4
Construction	20,104	5.3	4,777	5.5
Public utilities[7]	12,221	3.2	459	0.5
Transp. and commun.	27,832	7.4	3,788	4.4
Trade	81,854	21.6	9,357	10.7
Finance, real estate	...[8]	...[8]	1,865	2.1
Pub. admin., defense	97,238	25.7	13,475	15.5
Services	97,360[8]	25.7[8]	23,514	27.0
Other	...	...	12,574[9]	14.4[9]
TOTAL	378,503	100.0	87,121	100.0

Household income and expenditure. Average household size (2002) 4.0; average annual income per household, n.a.; sources of income (1993): salaries 61.9%, self-employment 21.5%, transfer payments 16.6%; expenditure (2000–01): food and beverages 21.9%, housing 19.2%, transportation 16.7%, hotel and cafe expenditures 7.7%, culture and recreation 6.9%, household furnishings 5.8%.
Land use as % of total land area (2000): in temporary crops 0.8%, in permanent crops 5.5%, in pasture 5.5%; overall forest area 28.7%.

Foreign trade[10]

Balance of trade (current prices)

	1999	2000	2001	2002	2003	2004
CFPF '000,000	−78,463	−97,343	−116,892	−140,667	−151,179	−124,485
% of total	64.8%	67.5%	75.8%	75.2%	82.1%	78.0%

Imports (2004): CFPF 142,080,900,000 (machinery and apparatus 17.9%; vehicles and transport equipment 10.7%; mineral fuels 7.9%). *Major import sources:* France 34.5%; U.S. 9.3%; Australia 9.1%; New Zealand 7.8%; China 5.0%.
Exports (2004): CFPF 17,596,300,000 (pearl products 67.3%, of which black cultured pearls 62.3%; *noni*[11] fruit 7.4%; fish 2.2%; coconut oil 1.7%; vanilla 1.4%; *monoï* oil 0.9%). *Major export destinations:* Japan 30.7%; Hong Kong 21.4%; U.S. 15.6%; France 14.3%; Thailand 6.3%.

Transport and communications

Transport. Railroads: none. Roads (1996): total length 549 mi, 884 km (paved 44%). Motor vehicles: passenger cars (1996) 47,300; trucks and buses (1993) 15,300. Air transport (2004)[12]: passenger-km 3,392,000,000; metric ton-km 71,397,000; airports (1994) with scheduled flights 17.

Communications

Medium	date	unit	number	units per 1,000 persons
Daily newspapers	1996	circulation	24,000	110
Radio	1997	receivers	128,000	574
Television	2000	receivers	44,500	189
Telephones	2003	main lines	53,500	214
Cellular telephones	2003	subscribers	90,000	367
Personal computers	2004	units	78,000	315
Internet	2004	users	61,000	246

Education and health

Educational attainment (2002). Percentage of population age 25 and over having: no formal schooling 4.9%; less than lower-secondary education 46.2%; lower secondary 10.9%; upper secondary 11.7%; vocational 15.8%; higher 10.5%. *Literacy* (2000): total population age 15 and over literate, almost 100%.

Education (1998–99)

	schools	teachers	students	student/ teacher ratio
Primary (age 6–10)[13]	255	2,751	...	...
Secondary (age 11–17) } Vocational	82	2,059	30,473	14.8
Higher[14]	1	54	1,600	29.6

Health: physicians (2002) 429 (1 per 568 persons); hospital beds (2003) 971 (1 per 256 persons); infant mortality rate per 1,000 live births (2004) 8.6.
Food (2002): daily per capita caloric intake 2,880 (vegetable products 69%, animal products 31%); 126% of FAO recommended minimum.

Military

Total active duty personnel (2004): 2,400 French military personnel. *Military expenditure as percentage of GDP:* n.a.

[1]Status change to "overseas country" in effect from Feb. 27, 2004. [2]Pegged to the euro on Jan. 1, 2002, at the rate of €1 = CFPF 119.25. [3]Approximate total area including inland water; total land area is 1,359 sq mi (3,521 sq km). [4]Based on land area. [5]Part of Papeete urban agglomeration. [6]Guaranteed minimum wage. [7]The manufacture of energy-generating products is included in Public utilities. [8]Services includes Finance, real estate. [9]Includes not adequately defined and unemployed. [10]Imports c.i.f.; exports f.o.b. [11]Fruit known locally as *nono*; also known as Indian mulberry. [12]Air Tahiti Nui only. [13]Includes preprimary. [14]University of French Polynesia only; 2000–01.

Internet resources for further information:
• Institut de la Statistique de la Polynésie Francaise
  http://www.ispf.pf

Gabon

Official name: République Gabonaise (Gabonese Republic).
Form of government: unitary multiparty republic with a Parliament comprising two legislative houses (Senate [91]; National Assembly [120]).
Chief of state: President.
Head of government: Prime Minister.
Capital: Libreville.
Official language: French.
Official religion: none.
Monetary unit: 1 CFA franc (CFAF) = 100 centimes; valuation (Sept. 1, 2005) 1 U.S.$ = CFAF 522.78; 1 £ = CFAF 962.57[1].

Area and population

Provinces	Capitals	area sq mi	area sq km	population 2002 estimate
Estuaire	Libreville	8,008	20,740	597,200
Haut-Ogooué	Franceville	14,111	36,547	134,500
Moyen-Ogooué	Lambaréné	7,156	18,535	54,600
Ngounié	Mouila	14,575	37,750	100,300
Nyanga	Tchibanga	8,218	21,285	50,800
Ogooué-Ivindo	Makokou	17,790	46,075	63,000
Ogooué-Lolo	Koulamoutou	9,799	25,380	56,600
Ogooué-Maritime	Port-Gentil	8,838	22,890	126,200
Woleu-Ntem	Oyem	14,851	38,465	125,400
TOTAL		103,347[2]	267,667	1,308,600

Demography

Population (2005): 1,384,000[3].
Density (2005): persons per sq mi 13.4, persons per sq km 5.2.
Urban-rural (2003): urban 83.8%; rural 16.2%.
Sex distribution (2003): male 49.59%; female 50.41%.
Age breakdown (2003): under 15, 42.3%; 15–29, 26.3%; 30–44, 16.6%; 45–59, 8.7%; 60–74, 4.8%; 75 and over, 1.3%.
Population projection: (2010) 1,498,000; (2020) 1,709,000.
Doubling time: 28 years.
Ethnic composition (2000): Fang 28.6%; Punu 10.2%; Nzebi 8.9%; French 6.7%; Mpongwe 4.1%; Teke 4.0%; other 37.5%.
Religious affiliation (2000): Christian 90.6%, of which Roman Catholic 56.8%, Protestant 17.8%, independent Christian 13.7%; Muslim 4.6%; traditional beliefs 3.1%; other 1.7%.
Major urban areas (2003): Libreville 661,600; Port-Gentil 116,200; Franceville 41,300; Lambaréné 9,000.

Vital statistics

Birth rate per 1,000 population (2004): 36.5 (world avg. 21.1).
Death rate per 1,000 population (2004): 11.8 (world avg. 9.0).
Natural increase rate per 1,000 population (2004): 24.7 (world avg. 12.1).
Total fertility rate (avg. births per childbearing woman; 2004): 4.8.
Life expectancy at birth (2004): male 54.0 years; female 57.1 years.
Adult population (ages 15–49) *living with HIV* (January 1, 2004): 8.1% (world avg. 1.1%).

National economy

Budget (2004). Revenue: CFAF 1,113,600,000,000 (oil revenues 53.9%; taxes on international trade 18.0%; corporate tax 7.7%; value-added tax 7.2%; income tax 5.5%; other revenues 7.7%). Expenditures: CFAF 827,100,000,000 (current expenditure 75.9%, of which wages and salaries 27.4%; service on public debt 18.2%, transfers 15.2%; capital expenditure 19.4%; other expenditure 4.7%).
Public debt (external, outstanding; 2003): U.S.$3,395,000,000.
Tourism: receipts from visitors (2001) U.S.$7,000,000; expenditures by nationals abroad (2002) U.S.$219,000,000.
Gross national product (2004): U.S.$5,415,000,000 (U.S.$3,940 per capita).

Structure of gross domestic product and labour force

	2004 in value CFAF '000,000	2004 % of total value	1993 labour force	1993 % of labour force
Agriculture, forestry, fishing	214,600	5.6	128,332	34.0
Crude petroleum	1,654,700	43.3	2,824	0.8
Other mining	66,300	1.7	3,299	0.9
Manufacturing	188,600	4.9	16,805	4.5
Construction	81,200	2.1	9,610	2.6
Public utilities	51,300	1.4	2,834	0.8
Transp. and commun.	206,600	5.4	15,775	4.2
Trade, restaurants	238,300	6.2	40,719	10.8
Finance, real estate	62,700	1.7	4,841	1.3
Services	475,200	12.5	32,977	8.8
Pub. admin., defense	308,600	8.1	48,208	12.8
Other	270,000[4]	7.1[4]	69,720[5]	18.5[5]
TOTAL	3,818,000[2]	100.0	375,944	100.0

Production (metric tons except as noted). Agriculture, forestry, fishing (2004): plantains 270,000, sugarcane 235,000, cassava 230,000, yams 155,000, taro 59,000, oil palm fruit 32,000, corn (maize) 31,000, peanuts (groundnuts) 20,000, bananas 12,000, natural rubber 11,000; livestock (number of live animals) 300,000 rabbits, 212,000 pigs, 195,000 sheep; roundwood (2003)

3,106,710 cu m; fish catch (2003) 44,775. Mining and quarrying (2004): manganese ore 2,460,000; gold 70 kg[6]. Manufacturing (value added in CFAF '000,000,000; 2004): agricultural products 48.0; wood products (excluding furniture) 31.3; refined petroleum products 18.1. Energy production (consumption): electricity (kW-hr; 2004) 1,364,000,000 ([2002] 1,513,000,000); crude petroleum (barrels; 2004) 97,000,000 ([2002] 6,000,000); petroleum products (metric tons; 2004) 707,000 ([2002] 609,000); natural gas (cu m; 2002) 820,000,000 (820,000,000).
Population economically active (1993): total 375,944; activity rate of total population 37.2% (participation rates: over age 9, 52.5%; female 44.5%; unemployed [2003] c. 21%).

Price index (2000 = 100)

	1998	1999	2000	2001	2002	2003	2004
Consumer price index	100.2	99.5	100.0	102.1	102.3	104.4	104.9

Household income and expenditure. Average household size (2002) 5.0; average annual income per household (2004)[7] CFAF 1,730,000 (U.S.$3,275); sources of income: n.a.; expenditure (2004)[7]: food 85.3%, transportation and communications 3.6%, clothing 1.8%, housing 1.4%.
Land use as % of total land area (2000): in temporary crops 1.3%, in permanent crops 0.7%, in pasture 18.1%; overall forest area 84.7%.

Foreign trade

Balance of trade (current prices)

	1998	1999	2000	2001	2002	2003
CFAF '000,000,000	+439	+978	+1,796	+1,295	+1,141	+1,240
% of total	24.3%	46.6%	61.2%	51.0%	46.2%	50.7%

Imports (2003): CFAF 602,000,000,000 (for petroleum sector 27.9%, other unspecified 72.1%). *Major import sources:* France c. 50%; U.S. c. 5%; U.K. c. 5%; The Netherlands c. 4%; Cameroon c. 4%.
Exports (2003): CFAF 1,842,000,000,000 (crude petroleum and petroleum products 80.5%, wood 10.2%, manganese ore and concentrate 4.8%). *Major export destinations:* U.S. c. 52%; France c. 9%; China c. 8%; Japan c. 4%; Trinidad and Tobago c. 3%.

Transport and communications

Transport. Railroads (2004): route length 506 mi, 814 km; (2002) passenger-km 97,500,000; (2002) metric ton-km cargo carried 1,553,000,000. Roads (2000): total length 5,260 mi, 8,464 km (paved 10%). Vehicles (1997): passenger cars 24,750; trucks and buses 16,490. Air transport (2000): passenger-km 1,204,000,000; metric ton-km cargo, n.a.; airports (1997) 17.

Communications

Medium	date	unit	number	units per 1,000 persons
Daily newspapers	2001	circulation	38,900	30
Radio	2001	receivers	649,800	501
Television	2002	receivers	400,000	308
Telephones	2004	main lines	38,700	29
Cellular telephones	2004	subscribers	489,400	362
Personal computers	2004	units	50,000	37
Internet	2004	users	40,000	30

Education and health

Educational attainment (2000)[8]: no formal schooling 6.2%; incomplete primary and complete primary education 32.7%; lower secondary 41.3%; upper secondary 14.2%; higher 5.6%. *Literacy* (2000): total population age 15 and over literate 71%; males literate 80%; females literate 62%.

Education (2002–03)

	schools	teachers	students	student/ teacher ratio
Primary	1,175[9]	7,764	279,816	36.0
Secondary	881[10]	2,504	97,604	...
Voc., teacher tr.	111[10]		7,587	...
Higher[11]	2[10]	585[9]	7,473[9]	12.8[9]

Health (2003–04): physicians 270 (1 per 5,006 persons); hospital beds 4,460 (1 per 303 persons); infant mortality rate per 1,000 live births (2004) 56.1.
Food (2002): daily per capita caloric intake 2,637 (vegetable products 87%, animal products 13%); 112% of FAO recommended minimum requirement.

Military

Total active duty personnel (2004): 4,700 (army 68.1%, navy 10.6%, air force 21.3%); French troops (2003) 800. *Military expenditure as percentage of GDP* (2003): 0.2%; per capita expenditure U.S.$11.

[1]Formerly pegged to the French franc and since Jan. 1, 2002, to the euro at the rate of 1 € = CFAF 655.96. [2]Detail does not add to total given because of rounding. [3]Not based on disputed December 2003 preliminary census results totaling 1,520,911. [4]Indirect taxes. [5]Includes 67,612 unemployed. [6]Excludes about 400 kg of illegally mined gold smuggled out of Gabon. Uranium mining ceased in 1999. [7]Figures based on a national sample survey of 529 households. [8]Figures based on a national sample survey of people ages 15–59 from 6,203 households. [9]1998. [10]1995–96. [11]Universities only.

Internet resources for further information:
- **Direction Generale de la Statistique et des Etudes Economiques**
  http://www.stat-gabon.ga/Home/Index1.htm
- **La Banque de France: La Zone Franc**
  http://www.banque-france.fr/fr/eurosys/zonefr/zonefr.htm

Gambia, The

Atlantic Ocean

Gulf of Guinea

Official name: The Republic of The Gambia.
Form of government: multiparty republic with one legislative house (National Assembly [53[1]]).
Head of state and government: President.
Capital: Banjul.
Official language: English.
Official religion: none.
Monetary unit: 1 dalasi (D) = 100 butut; valuation (Sept. 1, 2005) 1 U.S.$ = D 27.85; 1 £ = D 51.28.

Area and population

Divisions	Capitals	area		population
		sq mi	sq km	2003 census[2]
Basse	Basse	799	2,069	183,033
Brikama	Brikama	681	1,764	392,987
Janjanbureh	Janjanbureh	494	1,280	106,799
Kanifing[3, 4]	Kanifing	29	76	322,410
Kerewan	Kerewan	871	2,256	172,806
Kuntaur	Kuntaur	623	1,614	79,098
Mansakonko	Mansakonko	625	1,618	72,546
City				
Banjul[4]	—	5	12	34,828
TOTAL		4,127[5]	10,689[5]	1,364,507

Demography

Population (2005): 1,517,000.
Density (2005)[6]: persons per sq mi 456.2, persons per sq km 176.1.
Urban-rural (2003): urban 26.1%; rural 73.9%.
Sex distribution (2004): male 49.95%; female 50.05%.
Age breakdown (2004): under 15, 44.5%; 15–29, 26.7%; 30–44, 15.6%; 45–59, 8.8%; 60–74, 3.6%; 75 and over, 0.8%.
Population projection: (2010) 1,706,000; (2020) 2,070,000.
Doubling time: 25 years.
Ethnic composition (2000): Malinke 36.9%; Wolof 14.4%; Fulani 13.6%; Soninke 7.3%; Tukulor 6.7%; Diola 4.3%; other 16.8%.
Religious affiliation (2000): Muslim 86.9%; traditional beliefs 7.8%; Christian 3.6%, of which Roman Catholic 2.4%; other 1.7%.
Major cities/urban areas (2003): Kanifing 322,410[3]; Brikama 63,000; Banjul 34,828 (Greater Banjul 523,589[4]).

Vital statistics

Birth rate per 1,000 population (2004): 40.4 (world avg. 21.1).
Death rate per 1,000 population (2004): 12.8 (world avg. 9.0).
Natural increase rate per 1,000 population (2004): 27.6 (world avg. 12.1).
Total fertility rate (avg. births per childbearing woman; 2004): 5.5.
Marriage rate per 1,000 population: n.a.
Life expectancy at birth (2004): male 51.6 years; female 55.3 years.
Major causes of death per 100,000 population: n.a.; however, major infectious diseases include malaria, gastroenteritis and dysentery, pneumonia and bronchitis, measles, schistosomiasis, and whooping cough.

National economy

Budget (2003). Revenue: D 1,776,300,000 (tax revenue 77.2%, of which taxes on international trade 40.7%, corporate taxes 13.8%; grants 11.7%; nontax revenue 11.1%). Expenditures: D 2,327,900,000 (current expenditure 72.2%, of which interest payments 26.3%; capital expenditure 27.8%).
Production (metric tons except as noted). Agriculture, forestry, fishing (2004): millet 90,000, peanuts (groundnuts) 73,000, oil palm fruit 35,000, corn (maize) 25,000, sorghum 25,000, paddy rice 22,000, fresh vegetables 9,000, cassava 7,500, pulses (mostly beans) 3,200; livestock (number of live animals) 328,000 cattle, 265,000 goats, 147,000 sheep; roundwood (2003) 741,594 cu m; fish catch (2002) 45,769, of which Atlantic Ocean 43,269, inland water 2,500. Mining and quarrying: sand, clay, and gravel are excavated for local use. Manufacturing (value added in U.S.$; 1995): food products and beverages 6,000,000; textiles, clothing, and footwear 750,000; wood products 550,000. Construction: n.a. Energy production (consumption): electricity (kW-hr; 2003) 161,000,000 ([2002] 140,000,000); coal, none (none); crude petroleum, none (none); petroleum products (metric tons; 2002) none (92,000); natural gas, none (none).
Population economically active (1993): total 345,381; activity rate of total population 33.3% (participation rates: age 9 and over, 48.9%; female 40.0%; unemployed, n.a.).

Price and earnings indexes (2000 = 100)

	1998	1999	2000	2001	2002	2003	2004
Consumer price index	97.7	99.8	100.0	108.1	113.4	132.7	151.6
Daily earnings index[7]	100.0	100.0	100.0	100.0	106.0	132.5	...

Tourism (2000): receipts from visitors U.S.$48,000,000; expenditures by nationals abroad (1997) U.S.$16,000,000.
Household income and expenditure. Average household size (2000) 7.9; income per household: n.a.; sources of income: n.a.; expenditure (1991)[8]: food and beverages 58.0%, clothing and footwear 17.5%, energy and water 5.4%, housing 5.1%, education, health, transportation and communications, recreation, and other 14.0%.

Public debt (external, outstanding; 2003): U.S.$561,000,000.
Gross national product (at current market prices; 2004): U.S.$414,000,000 (U.S.$290 per capita).

Structure of gross domestic product and labour force

	2003		1993	
	in value D '000,000	% of total value	labour force	% of labour force
Agriculture	3,054.8	29.7	181,752	52.6
Mining	9	9	398	0.1
Manufacturing	485.4	4.7	21,682	6.3
Construction	665.1[9]	6.5[9]	9,679	2.8
Public utilities	123.7	1.2	1,858	0.5
Transp. and commun.	1,740.8	16.9	14,203	4.1
Trade	1,624.1	15.8	54,728	15.8
Finance	567.1	5.5	2,415	0.7
Public administration	712.9	6.9	} 41,254	11.9
Services	344.8	3.4		
Other	956.6[10]	9.3[10]	17,412[11]	5.0[11]
TOTAL	10,275.2[12]	100.0[12]	345,381	100.0[12]

Land use as % of total land area (2000): in temporary crops 23.0%, in permanent crops 0.5%, in pasture 45.9%; overall forest area 48.1%.

Foreign trade[13]

Balance of trade (current prices)

	1998	1999	2000	2001	2002	2003
U.S.$'000,000	−78.9	−68.7	−63.3	−43.1	−49.1	−51.8
% of total	23.2%	21.5%	20.0%	17.5%	18.0%	20.3%

Imports (2002): U.S.$160,100,000[14] (food and live animals 23.5%; machinery and transport equipment 17.0%; petroleum products 10.6%). *Major import sources:* EU 31.0%; China 22.3%; Senegal 9.2%.
Exports (2002): U.S.$111,000,000 (reexports 70.4%; peanuts [groundnuts] 21.6%; fruits and vegetables 3.7%; fish and fish products 2.6%). *Major export destinations:* EU 76.6%; Asian countries 16.7%.

Transport and communications

Transport. Railroads: none. Roads (1999): total length 1,678 mi, 2,700 km (paved 35%). Vehicles (1997): passenger cars 7,267; trucks and buses (1996) 9,000. Air transport (2001)[15]: passenger arrivals 300,000, passenger departures 300,000; cargo loaded and unloaded 2,700 metric tons; airports (2000) with scheduled flights 1.

Communications

Medium	date	unit	number	units per 1,000 persons
Daily newspapers	2000	circulation	39,400	30
Radio	2000	receivers	520,000	396
Television	2000	receivers	3,940	3.0
Telephones	2002	main lines	38,400	29
Cellular telephones	2004	subscribers	175,000	120
Personal computers	2004	units	23,000	16
Internet	2004	users	49,000	34

Education and health

Educational attainment: n.a. *Literacy* (2003): total population age 15 and over literate 40.1%; males literate 47.4%; females literate 33.1%.

Education (1998–99)

	schools	teachers	students	student/ teacher ratio
Primary (age 8–14)	331	4,572	150,403	32.9
Secondary (age 15–21)[16]	85	1,936	46,769	24.2
Postsecondary	4	155[17]	1,082[17]	7.0[17]

Health (2000): physicians 105 (1 per 12,977 persons); hospital beds 1,140 (1 per 1,199 persons); infant mortality rate per 1,000 live births (2004) 74.5.
Food (2002): daily per capita caloric intake 2,273 (vegetable products 94%, animal products 6%); 96% of FAO recommended minimum requirement.

Military

Total active duty personnel (2004): 800 (army 100%). *Military expenditure as percentage of GDP* (2003): 0.5%; per capita expenditure U.S.$1.

[1]Includes 5 nonelective seats. [2]Preliminary. [3]Kanifing includes the urban areas of Serekunda and Bakau. [4]Kanifing and Banjul make up most of Greater Banjul. [5]Includes inland water area of 802 sq mi (2,077 sq km). [6]Based on land area only. [7]Minimum wage. [8]Low-income population in Banjul and Kanifing only; weights of consumer price index components. [9]Construction includes Mining. [10]Indirect taxes. [11]Not adequately defined. [12]Detail does not add to total given because of rounding. [13]Imports c.i.f.; exports f.o.b. [14]Imports for reexport constitute 36.0% of total. [15]Yumdum International Airport at Banjul. [16]Includes teacher training and vocational. [17]1994.

Internet resources for further information:
• **Central Statistics Department**
  http://www.csd.gm

Georgia

Official name: Sak'art'velo (Georgia).
Form of government: unitary multiparty republic with a single legislative body (Parliament [235]).
Head of state and government: President, assisted by Prime Minister.
Capital: Tbilisi.
Official language: Georgian[1].
Official religion: none[2].
Monetary unit: 1 Georgian lari = 100 tetri; valuation (Sept. 1, 2005) 1 U.S.$ = 1.79 lari; 1 £ = 3.30 lari.

Area and population

Autonomous republics	area sq km	population 2002 census[3]	Regions	area sq km	population 2002 census[3]
Abkhazia[4]	8,640	…[5]	Racha-Lechkhumi & Kvemo Svaneti	4,990	50,969
Ajaria (Adjara)	2,880	376,016	Samegrelo & Zemo Svaneti	7,440	466,100
Regions			Samtskhe-Javakheti	6,413	207,598
Guria	2,032	143,357	Shida Kartli[6]	5,729[6]	314,039[7]
Imereti	6,475	699,666	**City**		
Kakheti	11,311	407,182	Tbilisi (T'bilisi)	1,384	1,081,679
Kvemo Kartli	6,072	497,530	TOTAL	70,152	4,369,579[3]
Mtskheta-Mtianeti	6,786	125,443			

Demography

Population (2005): 4,496,000[8].
Density (2005): persons per sq mi 166.0, persons per sq km 64.1.
Urban-rural (2004)[9]: urban 52.2%; rural 47.8%.
Sex distribution (2004)[9]: male 47.25%; female 52.75%.
Age breakdown (2004)[9]: under 15, 18.6%; 15–29, 24.5%; 30–44, 21.2%; 45–59, 17.7%; 60 and over, 18.0%.
Population projection[8]: (2010) 4,308,000; (2020) 4,067,000.
Ethnic composition (2002)[9]: Georgian 83.8%; Azerbaijani 6.5%; Armenian 5.7%; Russian 1.5%; Ossetian 0.9%; other 1.6%.
Religious affiliation (2002): Christian 88.6%, of which Georgian Orthodox 83.9%, Armenian Apostolic 3.9%, Catholic 0.8%; Muslim 9.9%; other (mostly nonreligious) 1.5%.
Major cities (2002): Tbilisi 1,081,679; K'ut'aisi 185,965; Bat'umi 121,806; Rust'avi 116,348; Sokhumi (1994) 112,000.

Vital statistics

Birth rate per 1,000 population (2003)[9]: 10.6 (world avg. 21.1); legitimate 55.4%; illegitimate 44.6%.
Death rate per 1,000 population (2003)[9]: 10.6 (world avg. 9.0).
Natural increase rate per 1,000 population (2003)[9]: 0.0 (world avg. 12.1).
Total fertility rate (avg. births per childbearing woman; 2003): 1.4.
Marriage rate per 1,000 population (2003)[9]: 2.8.
Divorce rate per 1,000 population (2003)[9]: 0.4.
Life expectancy at birth (2004): male 72.4 years; female 79.4 years.
Major causes of death per 100,000 population (2003)[9]: diseases of the circulatory system 698.2; malignant neoplasms (cancers) 131.2; diseases of the digestive system 51.4; diseases of the respiratory system 39.3.

National economy

Budget (2003). Revenue: 1,320,600,000 lari (tax revenue 89.9%, of which value-added tax 30.8%, income tax 11.6%, taxes on corporate profits 7.7%, excise tax 7.6%; nontax revenue 6.5%; grants 3.6%). Expenditures: 1,609,900,000 lari (social security and welfare 21.3%, general public service 18.7%, education 10.2%, public order 7.1%, defense 3.8%).
Public debt (external, outstanding; 2003): U.S.$1,564,000,000.
Population economically active (2002): total 2,104,200[9]; activity rate of total population 48.3% (participation rates: ages 15–64 [male], 15–59 [female] 71.8%; female 47.3%; unemployed [2004] 12.6%).

Price and earnings indexes (2000 = 100)

	1998	1999	2000	2001	2002	2003	2004
Consumer price index	80.6	96.1	100.0	104.6	110.5	115.8	122.3
Monthly earnings index	…	93.4	100.0	130.8	157.0	174.1	…

Production (metric tons except as noted). Agriculture, forestry, fishing (2004): potatoes 419,527, corn (maize) 410,613, wheat 185,834, grapes 180,000, melons 109,574, apples 76,343, barley 61,351, sunflower seeds 22,279, tea 20,000; livestock (number of live animals) 1,250,672 cattle, 804,935 sheep and goats; fish catch (2001) 1,910. Mining and quarrying (2003): manganese ore 173,700. Manufacturing (value of production in '000,000 lari; 2003): food products and beverages 401.4, transport equipment 128.3, basic metals 120.2, nonmetallic mineral products 75.6. Energy production (consumption): electricity (kW-hr; 2002) 7,357,000,000 (7,809,000,000); crude petroleum (barrels; 2002) 540,000 (210,000); petroleum products (metric tons; 2003) 19,000 ([2002] 514,000); natural gas (cu m; 2003) 18,000,000 ([2002] 810,000,000).
Tourism (U.S.$'000,000; 2003): receipts 147; expenditures 132.
Household income and expenditure. Average household size (2002) 3.7; average annual income per household (2004) 3,635 lari (U.S.$1,896); sources of income (2003): wages and salaries 21.0%, remittances 13.5%, self-employment 11.0%, agricultural income 11.0%, non-cash income 25.0%, other 18.5%; expenditure (2003): food, beverages, and tobacco 40.0%, transportation 8.0%, energy 7.0%, health 5.0%, clothing and footwear 5.0%.

Gross national product (2004): U.S.$4,683,000,000 (U.S.$1,040 per capita).

Structure of net material product and labour force

	2004		2003	
	in value '000,000 lari	% of total value	labour force[9]	% of labour force[9]
Agriculture	1,622.1	16.3	995,600	48.6
Mining	80.2	0.8	2,800	0.1
Manufacturing	1,298.8	13.0	88,800	4.3
Public utilities	317.6	3.2	19,800	1.0
Construction	621.4	6.2	40,100	2.0
Transp. and commun.	1,357.7	13.6	76,900	3.7
Trade, restaurants	1,584.8	15.9	215,100	10.5
Finance, real estate	724.8	7.3	42,100	2.0
Pub. admin., defense	573.8	5.8	91,400	4.5
Services	1,028.8	10.3	237,600	11.6
Other	760.0[10]	7.6[10]	239,400[11]	11.7[11]
TOTAL	9,969.8[12]	100.0	2,049,600	100.0

Land use as % of total land area (2000): in temporary crops 11.4%, in permanent crops 3.9%, in pasture 27.9%; overall forest area 43.7%.

Foreign trade[13]

Balance of trade (current prices)

	1998	1999	2000	2001	2002	2003
U.S.$'000,000	…	−348	−385	−433	−448	−676
% of total	…	42.2%	37.3%	40.5%	39.3%	42.1%

Imports (2003): U.S.$1,141,052,000 (mineral fuels 18.6%; food products and beverages 17.4%; machinery and apparatus 17.1%; base metals 13.0%; chemicals and chemical products 10.6%; transport equipment 8.3%). *Major import sources:* Russia 14.1%; U.K. 12.8%; Turkey 9.8%; Azerbaijan 8.2%; U.S. 8.0%; Germany 7.2%; Ukraine 7.0%.
Exports (2003): U.S.$465,303,000 (food and beverages [including wine] 35.4%; iron and steel 24.5%; mineral fuels 12.0%; transportation equipment 10.4%). *Major export destinations:* Russia 18.0%; Turkey 17.7%; Turkmenistan 12.6%; Switzerland 7.1%; Armenia 6.6%; Ukraine 6.5%; U.K. 6.0%.

Transport and communications

Transport. Railroads (2004): 1,612 km; passenger-km (2003) 396,000,000; metric ton-km cargo (2002) 5,057,500,000. Roads (2003): 20,247 km (paved [2002] 93.5%). Vehicles (2003): passenger cars 255,200; trucks and buses 68,600. Air transport (2003): passenger-km 400,000,000; metric ton-km cargo (2001) 3,000,000; airports with scheduled flights 1.

Communications

Medium	date	unit	number	units per 1,000 persons
Daily newspapers	2001	circulation	23,100	5
Radio	2001	receivers	2,623,100	568
Television	2002	receivers	1,856,000	357
Telephones	2004	main lines	596,000	132
Cellular telephones	2004	subscribers	800,400	177
Personal computers	2003	units	172,000	38
Internet	2004	users	175,600	35

Education and health

Educational attainment (2002)[9]. Percentage of population age 25 and over having: no formal education *c.* 2%; primary education *c.* 10%; secondary *c.* 61%; higher *c.* 27%. *Literacy* (1999): virtually 100%.

Education (2003–04)

	schools	teachers	students	student/ teacher ratio
Primary (age 6–9)	765[14]	15,823[14]	230,918	…
Secondary (age 10–16)	150	54,804[14]	441,008	…
Voc., teacher tr.	78	1,507	9,300	6.2
Higher	176	27,357[15]	153,254	…

Food (2002): daily per capita caloric intake 2,354 (vegetable products 82%, animal products 18%); 92% of FAO recommended minimum requirement.
Health (2003): physicians 20,936 (1 per 218 persons); hospital beds 18,200 (1 per 250 persons); infant mortality rate per 1,000 live births 26.3.

Military

Total active duty personnel (2004): 17,770[16] (army 48.5%, centrally controlled staff 32.6%, navy 11.3%, air force 7.6%).[17] *Military expenditure as percentage of GDP* (2003): 1.1%; per capita expenditure U.S.$9.

---

[1]Locally Abkhazian, in Abkhazia. [2]Special recognition is given to the Georgian Orthodox Church. [3]Excludes Abkhazia and South Ossetia; alternate census total is 4,371,534. [4]Abkhazia has had de facto autonomy from Georgia since 1993. Its final status was unresolved in June 2005. [5]2002 population estimate is 180,000. [6]Includes the 1,506-sq-mi (3,900-sq-km) area of the autonomous region (from 1992) of South Ossetia; the final status of South Ossetia was unresolved in June 2005. [7]Excludes 2002 population estimate for South Ossetia equaling 50,000. [8]Includes Abkhazia (177,000) and South Ossetia (48,000). [9]Excludes Abkhazia and South Ossetia. [10]Taxes on products less subsidies and less imputed bank service charges. [11]Including 235,900 unemployed. [12]Detail does not add to total given because of rounding. [13]Imports c.i.f.; exports f.o.b. [14]Excludes private institutions. [15]2002–03. [16]Excluding 11,700 paramilitary troops. [17]Foreign troops (June 2005): about 3,000 Russian troops (scheduled to be withdrawn by 2008); 118 UN peacekeeping troops.

Internet resources for further information:
- **National Bank of Georgia**
  http://www.nbg.gov.ge/NBG_New/home_nf1.htm
- **State Department for Statistics of Georgia**
  http://www.statistics.ge/bottom_eng.htm

Germany

Official name: Bundesrepublik Deutschland (Federal Republic of Germany).
Form of government: federal multiparty republic with two legislative houses (Federal Council [69]; Federal Diet [614]).
Chief of state: President.
Head of government: Chancellor.
Capital: Berlin, some ministries remain in Bonn.
Official language: German.
Official religion: none.
Monetary unit: 1 euro (€) = 100 cents; valuation (Sept. 1, 2005) 1 U.S.$ = €0.80; 1 £ = €1.47[1].

Area and population

States[2] Administrative districts	Capitals	area		population 2004[3] estimate
		sq mi	sq km	
Baden-Württemberg	Stuttgart	13,804[4]	35,752	10,692,556
Freiburg	Freiburg im Breisgau	3,613	9,357	2,178,813
Karlsruhe	Karlsruhe	2,671	6,919	2,722,550
Stuttgart	Stuttgart	4,076	10,558	3,994,612
Tübingen	Tübingen	3,443	8,918	1,796,581
Bavaria	Munich	27,240	70,550	12,423,386
Mittelfranken	Ansbach	2,798	7,246	1,706,615
Niederbayern	Landshut	3,988	10,330	1,194,472
Oberbayern	Munich	6,768	17,530	4,195,673
Oberfranken	Bayreuth	2,792	7,230	1,109,674
Oberpfalz	Regensburg	3,742	9,691	1,089,826
Schwaben	Augsburg	3,858	9,992	1,782,386
Unterfranken	Würzburg	3,294	8,531	1,344,740
Berlin	—	344	892	3,388,477
Brandenburg	Potsdam	11,381	29,476	2,574,521
Bremen	Bremen	156	404	663,129
Hamburg	Hamburg	292	755	1,734,083
Hessen	Wiesbaden	8,152	21,114	6,089,428
Darmstadt	Darmstadt	2,874	7,444	3,762,995
Giessen	Giessen	2,078	5,381	1,065,467
Kassel	Kassel	3,200	8,289	1,260,966
Lower Saxony	Hannover	18,385	47,616	7,993,415
Mecklenburg-West Pomerania	Schwerin	8,947	23,173	1,732,226
North Rhine-Westphalia	Düsseldorf	13,159[4]	34,082[4]	18,079,686
Arnsberg	Arnsberg	3,090	8,002	3,786,638
Cologne (Köln)	Cologne (Köln)	2,843	7,364	4,350,368
Detmold	Detmold	2,517	6,518	2,071,803
Düsseldorf	Düsseldorf	2,042	5,290	5,245,132
Münster	Münster	2,666	6,906	2,625,745
Rhineland-Palatinate	Mainz	7,663	19,846	4,058,682
Saarland	Saarbrücken	992	2,568	1,061,376
Saxony	Dresden	7,109	18,413[4]	4,321,437
Chemnitz	Chemnitz	2,354	6,097	1,568,153
Dresden	Dresden	3,062	7,931	1,674,343
Leipzig	Leipzig	1,693	4,386	1,078,941
Saxony-Anhalt	Magdeburg	7,895[4]	20,447	2,522,941
Schleswig-Holstein	Kiel	6,085	15,761	2,823,171
Thuringia	Erfurt	6,244	16,172	2,373,157
TOTAL		137,847[4]	357,023[4]	82,531,671

Demography

Population (2005): 82,443,000.
Density (2005): persons per sq mi 598.1, persons per sq km 230.9.
Urban-rural (2003): urban 88.1%; rural 11.9%.
Population projection: (2010) 82,455,000; (2020) 82,038,000.
Major cities (2002; *urban agglomerations*[5]): Berlin 3,388,434[6]; Hamburg 1,726,363 (2,664,000); Munich 1,227,958 (2,291,000); Cologne 967,940 (3,050,000); Frankfurt am Main 641,076 (3,681,000); Essen 591,889 (6,531,000[7]); Dortmund 589,240 (6,531,000[7]); Stuttgart 587,152 (2,672,000); Düsseldorf 570,765 (3,233,000); Bremen 540,950 (880,000); Hannover 516,415 (1,283,000); Duisburg 512,030 (6,531,000[7]); Leipzig 493,052; Nuremberg (Nürnberg) 491,307 (1,189,000).

Other principal cities (2002)

	population		population		population
Aachen	245,778	Heidelberg	141,509	Neuss	150,957
Augsburg	257,836	Herne	174,018	Oberhausen	221,619
Bielefeld	323,373	Karlsruhe	279,578	Oldenburg	155,908
Bochum	390,087	Kassel	194,748	Osnabrück	164,195
Bonn	306,016	Kiel	232,242	Paderborn	140,869
Braunschweig	245,516	Krefeld	239,559	Potsdam	130,435
Chemnitz	255,798	Leverkusen	160,829	Recklinghausen	124,587
Darmstadt	138,457	Lübeck	213,496	Regensburg	127,198
Dresden	478,631	Ludwigshafen		Rostock	198,964
Erfurt	200,126	am Rhein	162,458	Saarbrücken	182,858
Freiburg		Magdeburg	229,755	Solingen	165,032
im Breisgau	208,294	Mainz	185,293	Wiesbaden	271,076
Gelsenkirchen	276,740	Mannheim	308,385	Wuppertal	364,784
Göttingen	123,822	Mönchengladbach	262,963	Würzburg	129,915
Hagen	202,060	Mülheim			
Halle	243,045	an der Ruhr	172,332		
Hamm	183,805	Münster	267,197		

Sex distribution (2004[3]): male 48.90%; female 51.10%.
Ethnic composition (by nationality; 2000): German 88.2%; Turkish 3.4% (including Kurdish 0.7%); Italian 1.0%; Greek 0.7%; Serb 0.6%; Russian 0.6%; Polish 0.4%; other 5.1%.
Households (2004). Number of households 39,122,000; average household size 2.1; 1 person 37.2%, 2 persons 34.1%, 3 persons 13.8%, 4 persons 10.8%, 5 or more persons 4.1%.

Age breakdown (2004): under 15, 14.6%; 15–29, 17.1%; 30–44, 23.9%; 45–59, 19.6%; 60–74, 16.9%; 75 and over, 7.9%.
Religious affiliation (2000): Christian 75.8%, of which Protestant 35.6% (including Lutheran 33.9%), Roman Catholic 33.5%, Orthodox 0.9%, independent Christian 0.9%, other Christian 4.9%; Muslim 4.4%; Jewish 0.1%; nonreligious 17.2%; atheist 2.2%; other 0.3%.

Vital statistics

Birth rate per 1,000 population (2004): 8.5 (world avg. 21.1); legitimate 72.0%; illegitimate 28.0%.
Death rate per 1,000 population (2004): 10.4 (world avg. 9.0).
Natural increase rate per 1,000 population (2004): –1.9 (world avg. 12.1).
Total fertility rate (avg. births per childbearing woman; 2004): 1.4.
Marriage rate per 1,000 population (2003): 4.6.
Divorce rate per 1,000 population (2003): 2.6.
Life expectancy at birth (2004): male 75.6 years; female 81.7 years.
Major causes of death per 100,000 population (2003): diseases of the circulatory system 384.0; malignant neoplasms (cancers) 253.6; diseases of the respiratory system 70.3; diseases of the digestive system 51.2; accidents, poisoning, and violence 38.8.

Social indicators

Educational attainment (2002). Percentage of population age 25–64 having: no formal schooling through lower secondary 17%; upper secondary/higher vocational 60%; university 23%.
Quality of working life. Average workweek (2002): 37.9 hours. Annual rate per 100,000 workers (2000) for: injuries or accidents at work 3,928; deaths, including commuting accidents, 5.1. Proportion of labour force insured for damages of income loss resulting from: injury, virtually 100%; permanent disability, virtually 100%; death, virtually 100%. Average days lost to labour stoppages per 1,000 workers (2000): 0.3.
Access to services. Proportion of dwellings (2002) having: electricity, virtually 100%; piped water supply, virtually 100%; flush sewage disposal (1993) 98.4%; public fire protection, virtually 100%.
Social participation. Eligible voters participating in last (September 2005) national election 77.7%. Trade union membership in total workforce (2003): c. 18%. Practicing religious population: 5% of Protestants (in 1994) and 15% of Roman Catholics (in 2003) "regularly" attend religious services.
Social deviance (2000). Offense rate per 100,000 population for: murder and manslaughter 3.8; sexual abuse 37.0, of which rape and forcible sexual assault 11.7, child molestation 10.2; assault and battery 153.2; theft 754.2.
Leisure. Favourite leisure activities include playing football (soccer; registered participants, 2003) 6,274,021, as well as watching television, going to the cinema, attending theatrical and musical performances, and visiting museums.
Material well-being (2003). Households possessing: automobile 76.9%; telephone 98.7%; mobile telephone 72.5%; refrigerator 98.8%; television 94.4%; DVD player 27.1%; washing machine 93.5%; clothes dryer 36.5%; personal computer 61.4%; dishwasher 56.6%; microwave oven 62.7%; high-speed Internet access 23.4%.

National economy

Budget (general government; 2002). Revenue: €949,500,000,000 (tax revenue 50.6%, of which taxes on goods and services 23.2%, individual income taxes 21.9%; social security contributions 38.7%; nontax revenue 8.0%; other 2.7%). Expenditures: €1,023,900,000,000 (social protection 46.2%; health 13.2%; education 8.6%; economic affairs 8.2%; public debt transactions 6.4%; defense 2.5%).
Total public debt (2004): U.S.$1,732,000,000,000.
Production (metric tons except as noted; 2004). Agriculture, forestry, fishing: cereal grains 51,097,000 (of which wheat 25,427,000, sugar beets 27,159,000, potatoes 13,044,000, rapeseed 5,277,000, apples 1,592,000, grapes 1,120,000, cabbages 825,000, hops 29,000; livestock (number of live animals; 2004) 26,495,000 pigs, 13,386,000 cattle, 2,170,000 sheep, 110,000,000 chickens; roundwood (2004) 54,505,000 cu m; fish catch (metric tons; 2002) 224,451. Mining and quarrying (metric tons; 2003): potash (potassium oxide content) 3,563,000; feldspar 500,000. Manufacturing (value added in U.S.$'000,000; 2000): transportation equipment 52,270, of which motor vehicles 28,005, motor vehicle parts 14,978; nonelectrical machinery and apparatus 51,363; electrical machinery and electronics 43,671, of which electricity distribution and control apparatus 18,362; fabricated metal products 34,248; food and food products 23,740; printing and publishing 18,981; paints, soaps, and pharmaceuticals 18,803; industrial chemicals 17,682; professional and scientific equipment 14,759, of which medical, measuring, and testing appliances 12,949; plastic products 14,024; cement, bricks, and ceramics 10,836.

Manufacturing enterprises (2000)

	no. of enterprises	no. of employees	wages as a % of avg. of all wages	annual value added (€'000,000)
Manufacturing	40,052	6,424,000	100.0	600,009
of which				
Machinery (electrical and nonelectrical)	7,996	1,480,000	110.0	119,652
Transport equipment	1,239	967,000	117.8	90,538
Chemical products	1,282	481,000	119.9	68,313
Fabricated metals	7,211	855,000	95.4	63,945
Food and beverages	5,448	599,000	68.2	48,538
Refined petroleum, coke	48	23,000	130.9	30,453
Publishing and printing	2,679	274,000	105.5	27,594
Rubber and plastic products	2,708	359,000	85.5	26,022
Wood and wood products	3,688	329,000	79.7	21,427
Glass and ceramics	2,203	248,000	88.1	20,847
Professional and scientific equipment	1,930	224,000	100.0	17,930
Radio and television	514	161,000	115.4	17,269

Energy production (consumption): electricity (kW-hr; 2003) 532,000,000,000 ([2002] 576,538,000,000); hard coal (metric tons; 2002) 29,200,000 (63,300,000); lignite (metric tons; 2002) 181,800,000 (182,800,000); crude petroleum (barrels; 2003) 30,003,000 ([2002] 784,000,000); petroleum products (metric tons; 2002) 96,925,000 (101,633,000); natural gas (cu m; 2002) 24,486,000,000 (95,519,000,000).

Gross national product (at current market prices; 2004): U.S.$2,488,974,000,000 (U.S.$30,120 per capita).

Structure of gross domestic product and labour force

	2002		2003	
	in value €'000,000	% of total value	labour force	% of labour force
Agriculture	21,950	1.0	895,000	2.2
Public utilities	42,370	2.0	287,000	0.7
Mining			128,000	0.3
Manufacturing	432,930	20.5	8,243,000	20.5
Construction	87,210	4.1	2,607,000	6.5
Transp. and commun.	119,310	5.7	2,001,000	5.0
Trade, restaurants	245,690	11.7	6,296,000	15.7
Finance, real estate	589,970	28.0	4,572,000	11.4
Services	424,150	20.1	8,144,000	20.3
Pub. admin., defense			2,973,000	7.4
Other	144,620[8]	6.9[8]	4,051,000[9]	10.1[9]
TOTAL	2,108,200	100.0	40,195,000[4]	100.0[4]

Household income and expenditure. Average annual disposable income per household (2003) €33,840 (U.S.$38,194); sources of take-home income (1997): wages 77.6%, self-employment 12.0%, transfer payments 10.4%; expenditure (2003): housing and energy 32.5%, transportation 14.4%, food, beverages, and tobacco 14.0%, recreation and culture 11.8%, household furnishings 5.7%, clothing and footwear 5.0%, restaurants and hotels 4.3%.

Financial aggregates[10]

	1998	1999	2000	2001	2002	2003	2004
Exchange rate, DM per[11]:							
U.S. dollar	1.67	1.00	1.07	1.13	0.95	0.79	0.73
£	2.78	1.62	1.60	1.64	1.53	1.41	1.41
SDR	2.36	1.37	1.40	1.43	1.30	1.18	1.14
International reserves (U.S.$)							
Total (excl. gold; '000,000)	74,024	61,039	56,890	51,404	51,171	50,694	48.823
SDRs ('000,000)	1,868	1,959	1,763	1,793	1,980	1,942	2,061
Reserve pos. in IMF ('000,000)	8,023	6,419	5,460	5,901	6,695	7,656	6,863
Foreign exchange	64,133	52,661	49,667	43,710	42,495	41,095	39,899
Gold ('000,000 fine troy oz)	118.98	111.52	111.52	111.13	110.79	110.58	110.38
% world reserves	12.31	11.53	11.71	11.79	11.91	12.11	12.26
Interest and prices							
Central bank discount (%)	2.5	…	…	…	…	…	…
Govt. bond yield (%)	4.4	4.3	5.2	4.7	4.6	3.8	3.8
Industrial share prices (2000 = 100)[12]	77.3	80.1	100.0	76.2	57.6	45.5	55.8
Balance of payments (U.S.$'000,000,000)							
Balance of visible trade	+76.91	+69.64	+57.21	+89.20	+127.83	+147.93	+191.78
Imports, f.o.b.	465.71	472.28	491.90	480.48	488.79	604.51	717.92
Exports, f.o.b.	542.62	541.92	549.11	569.68	616.62	752.44	909.70
Balance of invisibles	−88.56	−95.19	−86.81	−86.13	−82.19	−96.48	−87.48
Balance of payments, current account	−11.65	−25.55	−29.60	+3.07	+45.64	+51.45	+104.30

Tourism (2003): receipts U.S.$23,002,000,000; expenditures U.S.$64,628,000,000.

Service enterprises (1991)

	no. of enterprises	no. of employees	weekly wages as a % of all wages	annual turnover (DM '000,000)
Gas	151	37,000	…	42,228
Water	183	40,000	…	3,443
Electrical power	462	296,000	…	147,076
Transport				
air	133	57,390	…	20,270
buses	6,054	192,869	…	12,586
rail	1	416,199	…	14,697
shipping	1,449	9,076	…	
Communications				
press	2,452	240,075	…	31,096
Postal services	…	652,573	…	68,346
Hotels and restaurants	135,141	652,251	…	60,257
Wholesale trade	…	1,214,000	…	1,015,984
Retail trade	152,629	2,241,000	…	605,755

Population economically active (2003): total 40,195,000; activity rate of total population 48.7% (participation rates: ages 15–64, 72.2%; female 44.5%; unemployed [July 2003–June 2004] 11.6%).

Price and earnings indexes (2000 = 100)

	1998	1999	2000	2001	2002	2003	2004
Consumer price index	98.0	98.6	100.0	102.0	103.4	104.5	106.2
Hourly earnings index	…	97.8	100.0	102.5	104.8	107.6	…

Land use as % of total land area (2000): in temporary crops 33.8%, in permanent crops 0.6%, in pasture 14.5%; overall forest area 30.7%.

Foreign trade[13]

Balance of trade (current prices)

	1999	2000	2001	2002	2003	2004
€'000,000	+65,211	+59,129	+95,494	+132,788	+129,921	+156,081
% of total	6.8%	5.2%	8.1%	11.4%	10.8%	11.9%

Imports (2002): €522,062,000,000 (machinery and equipment 22.6%, of which televisions, telecommunications equipment, and electronic components 6.0%, office machinery and computers 5.3%; transport equipment 14.3%, of which road vehicles 10.2%; chemicals and chemical products 10.6%; crude petroleum and natural gas 6.0%; food products and beverages 5.0%; base metals 4.8%; wearing apparel 3.1%). *Major import sources* (2004): France 9.0%; The Netherlands 8.3%; U.S. 7.0%; Italy 6.1%; U.K. 5.9%; China 5.6%; Belgium 4.9%; Austria 4.2%; Switzerland 3.7%; Japan 3.7%.

Exports (2002): €648,306,000,000 (machinery and equipment 26.3%, of which nonelectrical machinery 14.1%, televisions, telecommunications equipment, and electronic components 4.8%; transport equipment 23.4%, of which road vehicles 19.1%; chemicals and chemical products 11.8%; base metals 4.5%; medical and precision instruments and watches and clocks 4.0%). *Major export destinations* (2004): France 10.3%; U.S. 8.8%; U.K. 8.3%; Italy 7.1%; The Netherlands 6.2%; Belgium 5.6%; Austria 5.4%; Spain 5.0%; Switzerland 3.8%; China 2.9%.

Transport and communications

Transport. Railroads (2001): length 53,222 mi, 85,653 km; (2002) passenger-mi 44,002,000,000, passenger-km 70,814,000,000; (2002) short ton-mi cargo 49,326,000,000, metric ton-km cargo 72,014,000,000. Roads (2002): total length 143,400 mi, 230,800 km (paved 99%). Vehicles (2004): passenger cars 45,022,900; trucks and buses 2,586,300. Air transport (2004)[14]: passenger-km 179,781,000,000; metric ton-km cargo 8,103,205,000; airports (1997) 35.

Communications

Medium	date	unit	number	units per 1,000 persons
Daily newspapers	2004	circulation	22,095,000	268
Radio	2000	receivers	77,900,000	948
Television	2002	receivers	54,533,000	661
Telephones	2004	main lines	54,550,000	661
Cellular telephones	2004	subscribers	71,316,000	864
Personal computers	2004	units	46,300,000	561
Internet	2004	users	41,263,000	500

Education and health

Health: physicians (2003) 304,000 (1 per 271 persons); hospital beds (2003) 541,901 (1 per 152 persons); infant mortality rate per 1,000 live births (2004) 4.2.

Education (2003–04)

	schools	teachers	students	student/teacher ratio
Primary (age 6–10)[15]	16,992	164,664[16]	3,146,900	20.6[16]
Secondary (age 10–19)[15]	16,801	380,188[16]	6,080,300	16.0[16]
Voc., teacher tr.	8,812	114,892[16]	2,725,500	27.0[16]
Higher	365	166,100	2,019,831	12.2

Food (2002): daily per capita caloric intake 3,496 (vegetable products 69%, animal products 31%); 131% of FAO recommended minimum requirement.

Military

Total active duty personnel (2004): 284,500 (army 67.3%, navy 9.0%, air force 23.7%); German peacekeeping troops abroad (May 2004) 7,700; U.S. troops in Germany (December 2004) 74,745; British troops (August 2004) 22,000; French troops (August 2004) 3,200; Dutch troops (August 2004) 2,600. *Military expenditure as percentage of GDP* (2003): 1.4%; per capita expenditure U.S.$421.

[1]The Deutsche Mark (DM) was the former monetary unit; on Jan. 1, 2002, DM 1.96 = €1. [2]State names used in this table are English conventional. [3]January 1. [4]Detail does not add to total given because of rounding. [5]2000 estimate. [6]2002 city population estimate coextensive with urban agglomeration. [7]Part of the Rhine-Ruhr North urban agglomeration. [8]Taxes less subsidies and imputed bank service charges. [9]Unemployed. [10]End-of-period figures. [11]Beginning in 1999 exchange rates expressed in euros (€). [12]Period averages. [13]Imports c.i.f.; exports f.o.b. [14]Lufthansa Group, Condor, Eurowings, Air Berlin, Germanwings, LTU, and Hapag-Lloyd only. [15]Excludes 3,479 *Sonderschulen* for students with physical and mental disabilities. [16]2000–01.

Internet resources for further information:
• **Federal Statistical Office of Germany (in English)**
  http://www.destatis.de/e_home.htm

Ghana

Official name: Republic of Ghana.
Form of government: unitary multiparty republic with one legislative house (House of Parliament [230]).
Head of state and government: President.
Capital: Accra.
Official language: English.
Official religion: none.
Monetary unit: 1 cedi (₵) = 100 pesewas; valuation (Sept. 1, 2005) 1 U.S.$ = ₵9,065; 1 £ = ₵16,691.

Atlantic Ocean

Gulf of Guinea

Area and population

Regions	Capitals	area sq mi	area sq km	population 2000 census
Ashanti	Kumasi	9,417	24,389	3,600,358
Brong-Ahafo	Sunyani	15,273	39,557	1,798,058
Central	Cape Coast	3,794	9,826	1,593,888
Eastern	Koforidua	7,461	19,323	2,101,650
Greater Accra	Accra	1,253	3,245	2,903,753
Northern	Tamale	27,175	70,384	1,805,428
Upper East	Bolgatanga	3,414	8,842	919,549
Upper West	Wa	7,134	18,476	575,579
Volta	Ho	7,942	20,570	1,630,254
Western	Sekondi-Takoradi	9,236	23,921	1,916,748
TOTAL		92,098[1]	238,533	18,845,265[2]

Demography

Population (2005): 21,946,000.
Density (2005): persons per sq mi 238.3, persons per sq km 92.0.
Urban-rural (2003): urban 45.4%; rural 54.6%.
Sex distribution (2003): male 49.80%; female 50.20%.
Age breakdown (2000): under 15, 41.2%; 15–29, 28.3%; 30–44, 17.3%; 45–59, 7.9%; 60–74, 4.3%; 75 and over, 1.0%.
Population projection: (2010) 24,258,000; (2020) 28,684,000.
Doubling time: 32 years.
Ethnic composition (2000): Akan 41.6%; Mossi 23.0%; Ewe 10.0%; Ga-Adangme 7.2%; Gurma 3.4%; Nzima 1.8%; Yoruba 1.6%; other 11.4%.
Religious affiliation (2000): Christian 55.4%, of which Protestant 16.6%, African Christian 14.4%, Roman Catholic 9.5%; traditional beliefs 24.4%; Muslim 19.7%; other 0.5%.
Major cities (2002[3]): Accra (2003) 1,847,432; Kumasi 627,600; Tamale 269,200; Tema 237,700; Obuasi 122,600.

Vital statistics

Birth rate per 1,000 population (2004): 31.8 (world avg. 21.1).
Death rate per 1,000 population (2004): 10.1 (world avg. 9.0).
Natural increase rate per 1,000 population (2004): 21.7 (world avg. 12.1).
Total fertility rate (avg. births per childbearing woman; 2004): 4.2.
Life expectancy at birth (2004): male 57.4 years; female 58.9 years.
Major causes of death per 100,000 population (2002): communicable diseases (excluding HIV/AIDS; significantly malaria) 458; cardiovascular diseases 159; HIV/AIDS 147; accidents and violence 83; malignant neoplasms (cancers) 61.

National economy

Budget (2004). Revenue: ₵23,938,360,000,000 (tax revenue 74.6%, of which value-added tax 18.1%, trade tax 16.7%, petroleum tax 13.0%, corporate tax 9.8%, income tax 9.2%; grants 20.6%; nontax revenue 4.8%). Expenditures: ₵26,229,460,000,000 (current expenditure 62.1%, capital expenditure 37.9%).
Public debt (external, outstanding; 2004): U.S.$6,426,770,000.
Household income and expenditure (1999). Average household size (2003) 3.9[4]; mean annual household income[5] ₵2,267,000 (U.S.$849); sources of income[5]: income from agriculture 37.0%, other self-employment 31.3%, wages and salaries 22.8%, remittances 4.8%; expenditure[5]: food and nonalcoholic beverages 53.6%, clothing and footwear 10.0%, household operations 8.8%, education 6.1%, transportation and communications 5.6%.
Gross national product (2004): U.S.$8,090,000,000 (U.S.$380 per capita).

Structure of gross domestic product and labour force

	2004 in value ₵'000,000[6]	2004 % of total value	1999 labour force[7, 8]	1999 % of labour force
Agriculture	2,256,600	36.4	3,778,000	50.5
Mining	322,900	5.2	48,000	0.6
Manufacturing	561,400	9.1	798,000	10.7
Construction	502,600	8.1	97,000	1.3
Public utilities	156,000	2.5	14,000	0.2
Transp. and commun.	305,100	4.9	150,000	2.0
Trade, hotels	428,500	6.9	1,257,000	16.8
Finance, real estate	267,400	4.3	52,000	0.7
Pub. admin., defense	667,100	10.8	673,000	9.0
Services	170,500	2.7		
Other	565,500[9]	9.1[9]	613,000[10]	8.2[10]
TOTAL	6,203,600	100.0	7,480,000	100.0

Production (metric tons except as noted). Agriculture, forestry, fishing (2004): cassava 9,738,812, yams 3,892,259, plantains 2,380,858, taro 1,800,000, corn (maize) 1,157,621, oil palm fruit 1,070,000, cacao 736,000, sorghum 399,300, peanuts (groundnuts) 389,649, coconuts 315,000, oranges 300,000, chilies and peppers 270,000, rice 241,807, tomatoes 200,000; livestock (number of live

animals) 3,595,600 goats, 3,111,500 sheep, 1,365,000 cattle, 29,500,000 chickens; roundwood 22,078,000 cu m; fish catch (2003) 390,756. Mining and quarrying (2003): bauxite 495,000; manganese (metal content) 480,000; gold 2,208,750 troy oz[11]; gem diamonds 724,000 carats. Manufacturing (value added in ₵'000,000,000; 1993): tobacco 71.5; footwear 60.4; chemical products 40.3; beverages 36.2; metal products 35.1; petroleum products 32.1. Energy production (consumption): electricity (kW-hr; 2002) 8,201,000,000 (8,514,000,000); coal (metric tons; 2002) none (4,000); crude petroleum (barrels; 2002) 73,000 (13,000,000); petroleum products (metric tons; 2002) 1,194,000 (1,617,000); natural gas, none (none).
Population economically active (1999): total 9,680,000; activity rate of total population 53.5% (participation rates: ages 15–64, 79.9%; female 52.7%; unemployed [2001] 20.3%).
Tourism (2003): receipts U.S.$414,000,000; expenditures U.S.$138,000,000.

Price and earnings indexes (2000 = 100)

	1998	1999	2000	2001	2002	2003	2004
Consumer price index	71.1	79.9	100.0	132.9	152.6	193.3	217.7
Monthly earnings index[12]	69.0	69.0	100.0	131.0	170.2	219.0	266.7

Land use as % of total land area (2000): in temporary crops 15.9%, in permanent crops 9.7%, in pasture 36.7%; overall forest area 27.8%.

Foreign trade

Balance of trade (current prices)

	1997	1998	1999	2000	2001	2002
U.S.$'000,000	−638	−806	−1,073	−840	−1,101	−692
% of total	17.6%	16.2%	23.4%	17.8%	22.8%	14.6%

Imports (2004): U.S.$4,297,270,000 (crude and refined petroleum 18.0%, non-petroleum imports 82.0%). Major import sources (2004): Nigeria 12.8%; China 10.1%; U.K. 7.0%; U.S. 6.7%; France 5.3%.
Exports (2004): U.S.$2,784,650,000 (cocoa beans and products 38.5%, gold 30.2%, sawn wood 7.6%). Major export destinations (2004): The Netherlands 11.1%; U.K. 10.9%; France 6.9%; U.S. 6.0%; Belgium 4.8%.

Transport and communications

Transport. Railroads (2004): route length 592 mi, 953 km; (2001) passenger-km 62,000,000; (2001) metric ton-km cargo 220,000,000. Roads (1999): total length 28,692 mi, 46,176 km (paved 18.4%). Vehicles (2002): passenger cars 463,000; trucks and buses 56,000. Air transport (2003)[13]: passenger-km 906,000,000; metric ton-km cargo 16,630,000; airports (1996) with scheduled flights 1.

Communications

Medium	date	unit	number	units per 1,000 persons
Daily newspapers	2001	circulation	281,300	14
Radio	2001	receivers	14,300,000	710
Television	2001	receivers	2,371,000	118
Telephones	2004	main lines	313,300	15
Cellular telephones	2004	subscribers	1,695,000	79
Personal computers	2004	units	112,000	5.2
Internet	2004	users	368,000	17.2

Education and health

Educational attainment (2003)[4]. Percentage of population age 25 and over having: no formal schooling or unknown 41.8%; incomplete primary education 9.6%; primary 3.6%; incomplete secondary 35.0%; secondary 5.4%; higher 4.6%. Literacy (2003): total population age 15 and over literate 74.8%; males literate 82.7%; females literate 67.1%.

Education (2003–04)

	schools[14]	teachers	students	student/teacher ratio
Primary (age 6–12)	13,115	82,833	2,678,912	32.3
Secondary (age 13–20)	6,906	67,946	1,276,670	18.8
Voc., teacher tr.	...	959	18,672	19.5
Higher	...	3,933	69,968	17.8

Health: physicians (2002) 975 (1 per 21,086 persons); hospital beds (2001) 18,448 (1 per 1,089 persons); infant mortality rate per 1,000 live births (2004) 57.7.
Food (2002): daily per capita caloric intake 2,667 (vegetable products 95%, animal products 5%); 116% of FAO recommended minimum requirement.

Military

Total active duty personnel (2004): 7,000 (army 71.4%, navy 14.3%, air force 14.3%). Military expenditure as percentage of GDP (2003): 0.7%; per capita expenditure U.S.$2.

---

[1]Detail does not add to total given because of rounding. [2]Alternate census total is 18,912,079; unknown if this total is final or unadjusted. [3]January 1. [4]Based on the Ghana Demographic and Health Survey of 6,251 households. [5]Based on the Ghana Living Standards Survey of 5,998 households. [6]In constant prices of 1993. [7]Ages 15–64 only. [8]Derived figures calculated from percentages. [9]Indirect taxes. [10]Unemployed. [11]Legal production only. [12]Minimum wage, for December only. [13]Ghana Airways only, which subsequently ceased operations in July 2004. [14]1998–99.

Internet resources for further information:
• Bank of Ghana http://www.bog.gov.gh

Greece

Official name: Ellinikí Dhimokratía (Hellenic Republic).
Form of government: unitary multiparty republic with one legislative house (Greek Chamber of Deputies [300]).
Chief of state: President.
Head of government: Prime Minister.
Capital: Athens.
Official language: Greek.
Official religion: [1].
Monetary unit: 1 euro (€) = 100 cents; valuation (Sept. 1, 2005) 1 U.S.$ = €0.80; 1 £ = €1.47[2].

Area and population

Regions[3]	Principal cities	area sq mi	area sq km	population 2001 census
Insular				
Aegean Islands	Mitilíni	3,519	9,113	508,807
Crete	Iráklion	3,218	8,336	601,131
Ionian Islands	Kérkira	891	2,307	212,984
Mainland				
Central Greece and Euboea	Lamía	8,147	21,100	829,758
Epirus	Ioánnina	3,553	9,203	353,820
Greater Athens	Athens	1,470	3,808	3,761,810
Macedonia	Thessaloníki	13,195	34,174	2,424,765
Peloponnese	Pátrai	8,278	21,440	1,155,019
Thessaly	Lárisa	5,378	13,930	753,888
Thrace	Alexandroúpolis	3,312	8,578	362,038
TOTAL		50,949[4]	131,957[4]	10,964,020[5]

Demography

Population (2005): 11,088,000.
Density (2005): persons per sq mi 217.6, persons per sq km 84.0.
Urban-rural (2003): urban 60.8%; rural 39.2%.
Sex distribution (2004): male 49.12%; female 50.88%.
Age breakdown (2004): under 15, 14.5%; 15–29, 19.8%; 30–44, 22.6%; 45–59, 19.3%; 60–74, 15.9%; 75 and over, 7.9%.
Population projection: (2010) 11,246,000; (2020) 11,392,000.
Ethnic composition (2000)[6]: Greek 90.4%; Macedonian 1.8%; Albanian 1.5%; Turkish 1.4%; Pomak 0.9%; Rom (Gypsy) 0.9%; other 3.1%.
Religious affiliation (2000): Christian 94.7%, of which Eastern Orthodox 91.3%; Muslim 3.3%; nonreligious 1.7%; other 0.3%.
Major cities (2001): Athens 745,514 (urban agglomeration 3,120,000); Thessaloníki 363,987 (urban agglomeration [2000] 789,000); Piraeus (Piraiévs) 175,697[7]; Pátrai 163,446; Peristérion 137,918[7]; Iráklion 137,711.

Vital statistics

Birth rate per 1,000 population (2004): 9.7 (world avg. 21.1); (2003) legitimate 95.2%; illegitimate 4.8%.
Death rate per 1,000 population (2004): 10.1 (world avg. 9.0).
Natural increase rate per 1,000 population (2004): –0.4 (world avg. 12.1).
Total fertility rate (avg. births per childbearing woman; 2004): 1.3.
Marriage rate per 1,000 population (2001): 5.7.
Life expectancy at birth (2004): male 76.4 years; female 81.6 years.
Major causes of death per 100,000 population (2003): diseases of the circulatory system 326.5; malignant neoplasms (cancers) 160.5; diseases of the respiratory system 46.0; accidents, poisoning, and violence 32.5; diseases of the digestive system 16.2.

National economy

Budget (2003). Revenue: €41,050,000,000 (tax revenue 92.7%, of which VAT 35.9%, income taxes 29.6%; nontax revenue 7.3%). Expenditures: €48,410,000,000 (wages and salaries 50.4%; interest payments 19.3%; operating expenditure 12.7%; health and social insurance 11.8%).
Public debt (2001): U.S.$116,870,000,000.
Production (metric tons except as noted). Agriculture, forestry, fishing (2004): sugar beets 2,300,000, corn (maize) 2,300,000, olives 2,300,000, wheat 1,800,000, tomatoes 1,800,000, grapes 1,300,000, seed cotton 1,100,000, peaches and nectarines 955,000, oranges 930,000, potatoes 850,000, apples 288,000, barley 220,000, tobacco 121,000; livestock (number of live animals) 9,042,000 sheep, 5,362,000 goats; roundwood (2004) 1,672,856 cu m; fish catch (2002) 176,911. Mining and quarrying (2003): bauxite 2,418,000; crude magnesite 500,000; marble 200,000 cu m. Manufacturing (value added in Dr '000,000,000; 2000): food products and beverages 799; textiles and clothing 349; cement, bricks, and ceramics 298; chemicals and chemical products 279; basic metals 263; refined petroleum 247. Energy production (consumption): electricity (kW-hr; 2002) 54,760,000,000 (57,656,000,000); hard coal (metric tons; 2002) none (964,000); lignite (metric tons; 2002) 70,500,000 (68,700,000); crude petroleum (barrels; 2003) 1,030,000 ([2002] 135,000,000); petroleum products (metric tons; 2002) 19,540,000 (77,390,000); natural gas (cu m; 2002) 51,000,000 (2,147,000,000).
Land use as % of total land area (2000): in temporary crops 21.3%, in permanent crops 8.6%, in pasture 36.3%; overall forest area 27.9%.
Household income and expenditure. Average household size (2000) 3.0; income per family (1998–99) Dr 6,429,000 (U.S.$21,390); sources of income (1998–99): wages and salaries 35.7%, transfer payments 16.7%, self-employment 14.9%, other 32.7%; expenditure (1999): food and beverages 24.9%, transportation and communications 14.3%, cafe/hotel expenditures 9.4%, housing 8.1%, household furnishings 7.3%.
Gross national product (2004): U.S.$183,917,000,000 (U.S.$16,610 per capita).

Structure of gross domestic product and labour force

	2002 in value €'000,000	% of total value	labour force	% of labour force
Agriculture	8,985	6.4	623,800	14.3
Mining	873	0.6	18,900	0.4
Manufacturing	15,055	10.7	540,800	12.4
Construction	10,390	7.4	293,900	6.7
Public utilities	2,296	1.6	33,700	0.8
Transp. and commun.	10,939	7.7	243,500	5.6
Trade, restaurants	25,971	18.4	947,300	21.7
Finance, real estate	27,196	19.2	324,300	7.4
Pub. admin., defense	9,279	6.6	922,700	21.1
Services	17,604	12.4	420,100[9]	9.6[9]
Other	12,766[8]	9.0[8]		
TOTAL	141,354	100.0	4,369,000	100.0

Population economically active (2002): total 4,369,000; activity rate of total population 42.1% (participation rates: ages 15–64, 63.1%; female 40.4%; unemployed [April 2003–March 2004] 9.6%).

Price index (2000 = 100)

	1998	1999	2000	2001	2002	2003	2004
Consumer price index	94.5	96.9	100.0	103.4	107.1	110.9	114.1

Tourism (2003): receipts U.S.$10,766,000,000; expenditures U.S.$2,431,000,000.

Foreign trade[10]

Balance of trade (current prices)

	1999	2000	2001	2002	2003	2004
U.S.$'000,000	–18,244	–18,852	–20,444	–20,849	–31,180	–36,563
% of total	46.5%	46.2%	51.9%	50.3%	54.2%	54.9%

Imports (2000): U.S.$29,816,000,000 (machinery and apparatus 18.6%, chemicals and chemical products 11.5%, crude petroleum 10.1%, road vehicles 9.5%, food products 9.1%, ships and boats 5.2%). *Major import sources* (2003): Germany 12.5%; Italy 12.2%; France 6.6%; Russia 6.1%; South Korea 5.4%.
Exports (2000): U.S.$10,964,000,000 (food 14.6%, of which fruits and nuts 6.0%; clothing and apparel 12.8%; refined petroleum 12.5%; machinery and apparatus 9.8%; aluminum 4.2%). *Major export destinations* (2003): Germany 12.6%; Italy 10.5%; U.K. 7.1%; U.S. 6.5%; Bulgaria 6.2%.

Transport and communications

Transport. Railroads (2000): route length 2,299 km; passenger-km 1,629,000,000; metric ton-km cargo 427,000,000. Roads (1999): total length 117,000 km (paved 92%). Vehicles (2001): passenger cars 3,423,704; trucks and buses 1,112,926. Air transport (2004)[11]: passenger-km 9,177,000,000; metric ton-km cargo 56,356,000; airports (1997) 36.

Communications

Medium	date	unit	number	units per 1,000 persons
Daily newspapers	2000	circulation	1,530,000	140
Radio	2000	receivers	5,220,000	478
Television	2000	receivers	5,330,000	488
Telephones	2004	main lines	5,157,500	470
Cellular telephones	2004	subscribers	11,044,200	1,006
Personal computers	2004	units	1,476,000	150
Internet	2004	users	1,955,000	178

Education and health

Educational attainment (2001). Percentage of population age 25 and over having: no formal schooling/preprimary 12.7%; primary education 34.3%; lower secondary 8.5%; upper secondary 25.7%; postsecondary 3.4%; incomplete and complete higher 15.4%. *Literacy* (2001): total population age 15 and over literate 97.3%; males 98.5%; females 96.1%.

Education (2002–03)

	schools	teachers	students	student/ teacher ratio
Primary (age 6–12)	6,018	52,788	647,642	12.3
Secondary (age 12–18)	3,162	58,114	576,613	9.9
Voc., teacher tr.	684	17,457	154,139	8.8
Higher[12]	19	10,438	175,597	16.8

Health: physicians (2001) 46,325[13] (1 per 221 persons); hospital beds (2000) 49,804[13] (1 per 205 persons); infant mortality rate (2004) 5.6.
Food (2002): daily per capita caloric intake 3,721 (vegetable products 78%, animal products 22%); 149% of FAO recommended minimum requirement.

Military

Total active duty personnel (2004): 170,800 (army 69.1%, navy 11.9%, air force 19.0%). *Military expenditure as percentage of GDP* (2003): 4.1%; per capita expenditure U.S.$646.

[1]The autocephalous Greek Orthodox Church has special recognition per the constitution. [2]The drachma (Dr) was the former monetary unit; on Jan. 1, 2002, Dr 340.75 = €1. [3]Created for planning and economic development; local administration is based on 50 departments, 4 prefectures, and 1 autonomous self-governing monastic region (Mount Athos). [4]Detail does not add to total given because of statistical discrepancy. [5]De facto figure; de jure total equals 10,215,539. [6]Unofficial source; government states there are no ethnic divisions in Greece. [7]Within Athens urban agglomeration. [8]Taxes less imputed bank service charges and subsidies. [9]Unemployed. [10]Imports c.i.f.; exports f.o.b. [11]Olympic Airways and Aegean Airlines only. [12]Universities only. [13]Derived figure based on pre-2001 census de jure population.

Internet resources for further information:
• Bank of Greece http://www.bankofgreece.gr/en

Greenland

Official name: Kalaallit Nunaat
  (Greenlandic); Grønland (Danish)
  (Greenland).
Political status: integral part of the
  Danish realm with one legislative
  house (Parliament [31]).
Chief of state: Danish Monarch.
Heads of government: High
  Commissioner (for Denmark);
  Prime Minister (for Greenland).
Capital: Nuuk (Godthåb).
Official languages: Greenlandic; Danish.
Official religion: Evangelical Lutheran
  (Lutheran Church of Greenland).
Monetary unit: 1 Danish krone
  (Dkr) = 100 øre; valuation (Sept. 1,
  2005) 1 U.S.$ = Dkr 5.94;
  1 £ = Dkr 10.94.

ATLANTIC
OCEAN

Area and population	area[1]	population
Counties		2003[2]
Communes	sq km	estimate
Avanersuaq (Nordgrønland)	225,500	859
Qaanaaq (Thule)	225,500	859
Kitaa (Vestgrønland)	623,000	52,020
Aasiaat (Egedesminde)	600	3,367
Ilulissat (Jakobshavn)	36,400	5,007
Ivittuut (Ivigtut)	100	178
Kangaatsiaq (Kangâtsiaq)	38,700	1,516
Maniitsoq (Sukkertoppen)	62,600	3,681
Nanortalik	18,000	2,468
Narsaq (Narssaq)	28,900	2,047
Nuuk (Godthåb)	88,200	14,265
Paamiut (Frederikshåb)	27,100	2,019
Qaqortoq (Julianehåb)	4,100	3,406
Qasigiannguit (Christianshåb)	13,400	1,422
Qeqertarsuaq (Godhavn)	9,700	1,059
Sisimiut (Holsteinsborg)	34,400	6,024
Upernavik	186,300	2,906
Uummannaq (Umanaq)	74,500	2,655
Tunu (Østgrønland)	459,900	3,548
Ammassalik	232,100	3,007
Illoqqortoormiit (Scoresbysund)	227,800	541
NON–COUNTY/COMMUNE AREA	857,600	249
TOTAL	2,166,000	56,676

Demography

Population (2005): 57,100.
Density[3] (2005): persons per sq mi 0.36, persons per sq km 0.14.
Urban-rural (2003): urban (town) 82.4%; rural (settlement) 17.6%.
Sex distribution (2005[2]): male 53.22%; female 46.78%.
Age breakdown (2005[2]): under 15, 25.1%; 15–29, 20.8%; 30–44, 26.1%; 45–59,
  18.5%; 60–74, 8.0%; 75 and over, 1.5%.
Population projection: (2010) 57,000; (2020) 58,000.
Doubling time: 83 years.
Ethnic composition (2000): Greenland Eskimo 79.1%; Danish 13.6%; other
  7.3%.
Religious affiliation (2000): Protestant 69.2%, of which Evangelical Lutheran
  64.2%, Pentecostal 2.8%; other Christian 27.4%; other/nonreligious 3.4%.
Major towns (2005): Nuuk (Godthåb) 14,501; Sisimiut (Holsteinsborg) 5,350;
  Ilulissat (Jakobshavn) 4,533; Qaqortoq (Julianehåb) 3,144; Aasiaat
  (Egedesminde) 3,100.

Vital statistics

Birth rate per 1,000 population (2004): 16.0 (world avg. 21.1); (1993) legitimate
  29.2%; illegitimate 70.8%.
Death rate per 1,000 population (2004): 7.7 (world avg. 9.0).
Natural increase rate per 1,000 population (2004): 8.3 (world avg. 12.1).
Total fertility rate (avg. births per childbearing woman; 2004): 2.4.
Marriage rate per 1,000 population (1999): 4.5.
Life expectancy at birth (2004): male 65.8 years; female 73.0 years.
Major causes of death per 100,000 population (1996–98): diseases of the cir-
  culatory system 187.5; malignant neoplasms (cancers) 181.5; violence 95.8;
  infectious and parasitic diseases 64.9; suicides 63.7; diseases of the respirato-
  ry system 51.8; accidents 46.4.

National economy

Budget (2003). Revenue: Dkr 7,718,000,000 (block grant from Danish government 47.6%; income tax 31.8%; import duties 7.7%; other 12.9%).
  Expenditures (2003): Dkr 7,426,000,000 (social welfare 24.2%, education
  17.1%, health 11.7%, defense 3.5%, public order 2.8%).
Public debt (2000): U.S.$53,000,000.
Tourism (2004): number of overnight stays at hotels 190,755, of which visitors
  from within Greenland 95,512, from Denmark 64,777, from the U.S. 7,720.
Production (metric tons except as noted). Fishing, animal products: fish catch
  (2003) 340,200 (by local boats 196,500, of which prawn 98,900, halibut 28,900,
  cod 8,500, crab 6,900; by foreign boats 143,700); livestock (number of live
  animals; 2003) 19,259 sheep, 3,100 reindeer; animal products (value of external sales in Dkr '000; 1998) sealskins 31,044, polar bear skins 579. Mining: [4].
  Manufacturing: principally handicrafts and fish processing. Energy production (consumption): electricity (kW-hr; 2003) 310,000,000 (238,000,000); coal,
  none (none); crude petroleum (barrels; 2002) none (none); petroleum products (metric tons; 2002) none (184,000); natural gas, none (none).
Gross national product (2003): U.S.$1,412,000,000 (U.S.$24,870 per capita).

Structure of gross domestic product and labour force

	2003		2001	
	in value Dkr '000,000	% of total value	labour force[5]	% of labour force[5]
Agriculture, fishing, hunting, trapping	...	...	2,005	7.3
Mining	...	...	20	0.1
Manufacturing	...	...	3,037	11.1
Public utilities	...	...	475	1.7
Construction	...	...	1,927	7.0
Transp. and commun.	...	...	2,228	8.1
Trade, restaurants	...	...	2,460	9.0
Finance, real estate	...	...	1,282	4.7
Public administration	...	...	12,911	47.0
Services	...	...	1,076	3.9
Other	...	...	25	0.1
TOTAL	9,546	100.0	27,446	100.0

Population economically active (2002): total 31,506; activity rate of total population 55.7% (participation rates: ages 15–62, 83.2%; female 45.7%; unemployed [2003] 7.4%).

Price index (2000 = 100)							
	1998	1999	2000	2001	2002	2003	2004
Consumer price index	97.6	98.3	100.0	103.0	107.2	109.0	112.0

Household income and expenditure. Average household size (2004) 2.5; disposable income per household (2002) Dkr 243,287 (U.S.$30,815); sources of
  income: n.a.; expenditure (1994): food, beverages, and tobacco 41.6%, housing and energy 22.4%, transportation and communications 10.2%, recreation
  6.4%.
Land use as % of total land area (2000): in temporary crops, negligible, in permanent crops, none, in pasture 0.6%; overall forest area, negligible.

Foreign trade

Balance of trade (current prices)						
	1999	2000	2001	2002	2003	2004
Dkr '000,000	−924	−742	−460	−668	−746	−994
% of total	19.3%	14.4%	9.3%	12.3%	14.0%	17.9%

Imports (2004): Dkr 3,279,000,000 (goods for trades and industries 21.4%;
  food, beverages, and tobacco products 21.2%; mineral fuels 13.6%; goods for
  construction industry 12.6%; machinery 6.7%; transport equipment 2.4%).
  Major import sources: Denmark 59.2%; Sweden 14.1%; U.S. 2.0%; Norway
  2.0%; China 1.8%.
Exports (2004): Dkr 2,285,000,000 (marine products 86.8%, of which shrimp
  50.6%, halibut 19.9%, cod 3.1%; leather and fur products 1.0%). *Major
  export destinations:* Denmark 88.0%; Spain 5.7%; U.S. 1.6%; Iceland 1.0%.

Transport and communications

Transport. Railroads: none. Roads (1998): total length 93 mi, 150 km (paved
  60%). Vehicles (2003): passenger cars 2,974; trucks and buses 1,474. Air transport (2001)[6]: passenger-mi 131,100,000, passenger-km 211,000,000; short ton-
  mi cargo 16,400,000; metric ton-km cargo 24,000,000; airports (1998) with
  scheduled flights 18.

Communications				units per 1,000
Medium	date	unit	number	persons
Daily newspapers	1996	circulation	1,000	18
Radio	1997	receivers	27,000	482
Television	1997	receivers	22,000	393
Telephones	2003	main lines	25,200	444
Cellular telephones	2003	subscribers	30,300	534
Internet	2003	users	10,210	180

Education and health

Educational attainment (2002). Two-thirds of labour force has no formal education. *Literacy* (1999): total population age 15 and over literate: virtually
  100%.

Education (2001–02)	schools	teachers	students	student/ teacher ratio
Primary (age 6–15)				
Secondary (age 15–19)	87	1,191	11,368	9.5
Voc., teacher tr.				
Higher[7]	1	14	100	7.1

Health: physicians (2003) 91 (1 per 624 persons); hospital beds (2001) 406 (1
  per 139 persons); infant mortality rate per 1,000 live births (2004) 16.3.

Military

Total active duty personnel. Denmark is responsible for Greenland's defense.
  Greenlanders are not liable for military service. U.S. troops (2004): 122.

[1]Areas of counties and non-county are approximate and add to rounded total of 2,166,000
sq km. Surveyed ice-free area is 410,449 sq km (158,475 sq mi) and permanent ice area
is 1,755,637 sq km (677,855 sq mi), making the total surveyed area 2,166,086 sq km
(836,330 sq mi). [2]January 1. [3]Population density calculated with reference to ice-free
area only. [4]Greenland's first gold mine officially opened in August 2004. [5]Employed persons only. [6]Air Greenland A/S only. [7]University of Greenland only.

Internet resources for further information:
• Statistics Greenland http://www.statgreen.gl/english
• Danmarks Statistik http://www.dst.dk/yearbook

Grenada

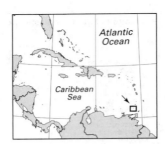

Official name: Grenada.
Form of government: constitutional monarchy with two legislative houses (Senate [13]; House of Representatives [15[1]]).
Chief of state: British Monarch represented by Governor-General.
Head of government: Prime Minister.
Capital: St. George's.
Official language: English.
Official religion: none.
Monetary unit: 1 East Caribbean dollar (EC$) = 100 cents; valuation (Sept. 1, 2005) 1 U.S.$ = EC$2.70; 1 £ = EC$4.97.

Area and population

Local councils	Principal towns	area sq mi	area sq km	population 2001 census[2]
Carriacou	Hillsborough	10	26 }	6,063
Petite Martinique	…	3	8	
St. Andrew	Grenville	38	99	24,661
St. David	St. David's	17	44	11,476
St. George	…	25[3]	65[3]	31,651
St. John	Gouyave	14	35	8,557
St. Mark	Victoria	10	25	3,955
St. Patrick	Sauteurs	16	42	10,624
Town				
St. George's	—	3	3	3,908
TOTAL		133	344	100,895

Demography

Population (2005): 103,000.
Density (2005): persons per sq mi 774.4, persons per sq km 299.4.
Urban-rural (2004): urban 41.5%; rural 58.5%.
Sex distribution (2001): male 49.55%; female 50.45%.
Age breakdown (2001): under 15, 35.1%; 15–29, 28.1%; 30–44, 17.6%; 45–59, 9.0%; 60 and over, 10.2%.
Population projection: (2010) 106,000; (2020) 112,000.
Doubling time: 46 years.
Ethnic composition (2000): black 51.7%; mixed 40.0%; Indo-Pakistani 4.0%; white 0.9%; other 3.4%.
Religious affiliation (2000): Roman Catholic 56.0%; Protestant 35.7%, of which Anglican 15.4%, the significant portion of the remainder being Pentecostal and Seventh-day Adventist; Spiritist 1.2%; Hindu 0.7%; other 6.4%.
Major localities (2001): St. George's 3,908 (urban agglomeration 35,559); Gouyave 3,100[4]; Grenville 2,300[4]; Victoria 2,100[4].

Vital statistics

Birth rate per 1,000 population (2004): 22.6 (world avg. 21.1).
Death rate per 1,000 population (2004): 7.3 (world avg. 9.0).
Natural increase rate per 1,000 population (2004): 15.3 (world avg. 12.1).
Total fertility rate (avg. births per childbearing woman; 2004): 2.4.
Marriage rate per 1,000 population (2001): 5.0.
Divorce rate per 1,000 population (2001): 1.1.
Life expectancy at birth (2004): male 62.7 years; female 66.3 years.
Major causes of death per 100,000 population (2002): diseases of the circulatory system 413; malignant neoplasms (cancers) 178; diabetes mellitus 63; diseases of the respiratory system 25.

National economy

Budget (2004). Revenue: EC$392,700,000 (tax revenue 71%, of which tax on international trade 43%, general sales taxes 13%, income taxes 11%; grants 23%; nontax revenue 6%). Expenditures: EC$417,000,000 (current expenditure 75%, of which wages 35%, debt service 15%, transfers 13%; capital expenditure 25%).
Public debt (external, outstanding; 2004): U.S.$330,000,000.
Tourism (2004): receipts from visitors U.S.$92,000,000; expenditures by nationals abroad (2003) U.S.$8,000,000.
Gross national product (at current market prices; 2004): U.S.$397,000,000 (U.S.$3,760 per capita).

Structure of gross domestic product and labour force

	2004 in value EC$'000,000	2004 % of total value	1998 labour force	1998 % of labour force
Agriculture	81.3	8.5	4,794	11.7
Quarrying	5.4	0.6	58	0.1
Manufacturing	52.8	5.5	2,579	6.3
Construction	102.9	10.7	5,163	12.6
Public utilities	60.8	6.3	505	1.2
Transp. and commun.	210.9	22.0	2,043	5.0
Trade, restaurants	180.5	18.8	8,298	20.2
Finance, real estate	151.5	15.8	1,312	3.2
Pub. admin., defense	185.6	19.3	1,879	4.6
Services	26.1	2.7	6,837	16.7
Other	−97.8[5]	−10.2[5]	7,547[6]	18.4[6]
TOTAL	960.0	100.0	41,015	100.0

Production (metric tons except as noted). Agriculture, forestry, fishing (2004): sugarcane 7,200, coconuts 6,500, bananas 4,100, roots and tubers 3,200, nut-

meg 2,747[7], grapefruit 2,000, mangoes 1,900, avocados 1,500, cacao 1,000, oranges 900, plantains 740, other crops include cinnamon, cloves, and pimiento; livestock (number of live animals) 13,200 sheep, 7,200 goats, 5,850 pigs; roundwood, n.a.; fish catch (2003) 2,544. Mining and quarrying: excavation of limestone, sand, and gravel for local use. Manufacturing (value of production in EC$'000; 1997): wheat flour 13,390; soft drinks 9,798; beer 7,072; animal feed 5,852; rum 5,497; toilet paper 4,237; malt 4,192; stout 3,835; cigarettes 1,053. Energy production (consumption): electricity (kW-hr; 2003) 166,000,000 ([2002] 153,000,000); coal, none (none); crude petroleum, none (none); petroleum products (metric tons; 2002) none (75,000); natural gas, none (none).
Household income and expenditure. Average household size (2001) 3.3; income per household (1988) EC$7,097 (U.S.$2,629); sources of income: n.a.; expenditure (2001)[8]: food, beverages, and tobacco 38.6%, transportation and communications 15.7%, housing 10.2%, clothing and footwear 9.8%.
Population economically active (1998): total 41,015; activity rate of total population c. 46% (participation rate: ages 15–64, c. 78%; female 43.5%; unemployed [2002] 12.2%).

Price index (2000 = 100)

	1999	2000	2001	2002	2003	2004
Consumer price index	97.9	100.0	101.7	102.7	105.0	107.4

Land use as % of total land area (2000): in temporary crops c. 3%, in permanent crops c. 29%, in pasture c. 3%; overall forest area c. 15%.

Foreign trade[9]

Balance of trade (current prices)

	1999	2000	2001	2002	2003	2004
U.S.$'000,000	−109.8	−137.4	−132.8	−139.6	−180.9	−200.7
% of total	42.4%	45.3%	51.1%	62.8%	66.5%	74.1%

Imports (2004): U.S.$263,100,000 (food and live animals 21.2%, machinery and transport equipment 17.9%, mineral fuels 9.6%, chemicals and chemical products 6.7%). *Major import sources:* U.S. 27.7%; Trinidad and Tobago 25.4%; U.K. 5.2%.
Exports (2004): U.S.$31,000,000 (domestic exports 78.7%, of which nutmeg 31.6%, fish 9.7%, flour 8.7%, paper products 6.8%, cocoa beans 6.5%; reexports 21.3%). *Major export destinations:* Saint Lucia 11.8%; U.S. 11.6%; The Netherlands 8.1%; Antigua and Barbuda 8.0%; Germany 7.7%.

Transport and communications

Transport. Railroads: none. Roads (1999): total length 646 mi, 1,040 km (paved 61%). Vehicles (2000): passenger cars 15,500; trucks and buses 3,900. Air transport (2001)[10]: passengers 331,000; cargo 2,747 metric tons; airports (1998) with scheduled flights 2.

Communications

Medium	date	unit	number	units per 1,000 persons
Radio	2001	receivers	60,250	597
Television	2001	receivers	37,850	375
Telephones	2004	main lines	32,700	318
Cellular telephones	2004	subscribers	43,300	421
Personal computers	2004	units	16,000	155
Internet	2004	users	8,000	777

Education and health

Educational attainment (2001). Percentage of population age 18 and over having: no formal schooling or unknown 7.6%; primary education 65.1%; secondary 21.7%; higher 5.6%, of which university 1.5%. *Literacy* (2004): total population age 15 and over literate 98.0%.

Education (2002–03)

	schools	teachers	students	student/ teacher ratio
Primary (age 5–11)	62	888	16,598	18.7
Secondary (age 12–16)	20	696	13,808	19.8
Vocational	…	44	1,052	23.9
Higher[11, 12]	1	66	651	9.9

Health (2003): physicians 127 (1 per 803 persons); hospital beds 330 (1 per 309 persons); infant mortality rate per 1,000 live births (2004) 14.6.
Food (2002): daily per capita caloric intake 2,932 (vegetable products 74%, animal products 26%); 121% of FAO recommended minimum requirement.

Military

Total active duty personnel (2001) [13]. *Military expenditure as percentage of GDP:* n.a.; per capita expenditure, n.a.

[1]Excludes the speaker, who may be elected from outside its elected membership. [2]Preliminary noninstitutional figures; another 2001 census total equals 101,306. [3]St. George local council includes St. George's town. [4]1991. [5]Less imputed bank service charges. [6]Includes 1,321 activities not adequately defined and 6,226 unemployed. [7]Hurricane Ivan, which struck Grenada in September 2004, destroyed much of the nutmeg and cacao fields; it is estimated that it will take a decade to regrow the nutmeg groves. [8]Weights of consumer price index components. [9]Imports are f.o.b. in balance of trade and c.i.f. for commodities and trading partners. [10]Point Salines airport. [11]1994–95. [12]Excludes Grenada Teachers' College. [13]A 755-member police force includes an 80-member paramilitary unit and a 40-member coast guard unit.

Internet resources for further information:
• **Eastern Caribbean Central Bank** http://www.eccb-centralbank.org
• **Caricom Statistics**
  http://www.caricomstats.org

Guadeloupe

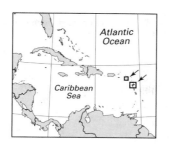

Official name: Département de la Guadeloupe (Department of Guadeloupe).
Political status: overseas department (France) with two legislative houses (General Council [42]; Regional Council [41]).
Chief of state: President of France.
Heads of government: Commissioner of the Republic (for France); President of the General Council (for Guadeloupe); President of the Regional Council (for Guadeloupe).
Capital: Basse-Terre.
Official language: French.
Official religion: none.
Monetary unit: 1 euro (€) = 100 centimes; valuation (Sept. 1, 2005) 1 U.S.$ = €0.80; 1 £ = €1.47[1].

Area and population		area		population
				1999
Arrondissements	Capitals	sq mi	sq km	census
Basse-Terre[2]	Basse-Terre	330	855	175,691
Pointe-à-Pitre[3]	Pointe-à-Pitre	299	775	210,875
Saint-Martin–Saint-Barthélemy[4, 5]	Marigot	29	74	35,930
TOTAL		658	1,705[6]	422,496

Demography

Population (2005): 448,000.
Density (2005): persons per sq mi 680.9, persons per sq km 262.8.
Urban-rural (2003): urban 99.7%; rural 0.3%.
Sex distribution (2004): male 49.24%; female 50.76%.
Age breakdown (2004): under 15, 24.4%; 15–29, 23.0%; 30–44, 26.1%; 45–59, 14.2%; 60–74, 8.3%; 75 and over, 4.0%.
Population projection: (2010) 462,000; (2020) 480,000.
Doubling time: 72 years.
Ethnic composition (2000): Creole (mulatto) 76.7%; black 10.0%; Guadeloupe mestizo (French–East Asian) 10.0%; white 2.0%; other 1.3%.
Religious affiliation (1995): Roman Catholic 81.1%; Jehovah's Witness 4.8%; Protestant 4.7%; other 9.4%.
Major communes (1999): Les Abymes 63,054[7]; Saint-Martin (Marigot) 29,078; Le Gosier 25,360[7]; Pointe-à-Pitre 20,948 (urban agglomeration 171,773); Basse-Terre 12,410 (urban agglomeration 54,076).

Vital statistics

Birth rate per 1,000 population (2004): 15.8 (world avg. 21.1); (1999) legitimate 34.7%; illegitimate 65.3%.
Death rate per 1,000 population (2004): 6.0 (world avg. 9.0).
Natural increase rate per 1,000 population (2004): 9.7 (world avg. 12.1).
Total fertility rate (avg. births per childbearing woman; 2004): 1.9.
Marriage rate per 1,000 population (2002): 4.1.
Divorce rate per 1,000 population (2001): 2.9.
Life expectancy at birth (2004): male 74.6 years; female 81.0 years.
Major causes of death per 100,000 population (1996): diseases of the circulatory system 183.7; malignant neoplasms (cancers) 134.8; accidents, violence, and poisoning 68.1; diseases of the respiratory system 32.1; diseases of the digestive system 31.4; endocrine and metabolic diseases 26.2; infectious and parasitic diseases 23.8.

National economy

Budget (2004). Revenue: €312,400,000 (direct tax revenues 46.7%; transfers from France 36.9%; loans 16.0%; other 0.4%). Expenditures: €312,400,000 (current expenditures 62.3%, capital [development] expenditures 37.7%).
Public debt: n.a.
Production (metric tons except as noted). Agriculture, forestry, fishing (2004): sugarcane 800,000, bananas 123,000, yams 10,750, plantains 9,000, sweet potatoes 4,210, melons 4,070, pineapples 3,500, tomatoes 3,070, eggplant 180; livestock (number of live animals) 73,500 cattle, 45,000 goats; roundwood (2004) 15,300 cu m; fish catch (2002) 10,100. Mining and quarrying (2002): pumice 210,000. Manufacturing (2002): cement 284,000; raw sugar 51,726; rum 67,151 hectolitres; other products include clothing, wooden furniture and posts, and metalware. Energy production (consumption): electricity (kW-hr; 2003) 1,386,000,000 ([2002] 1,160,000,000); coal, none (none); crude petroleum, none (none); petroleum products (metric tons; 2002) none (523,000); natural gas, none (none).
Land use as % of total land area (2000): in temporary crops c. 11%, in permanent crops c. 4%, in pasture c. 14%; overall forest area c. 48%.
Population economically active (1999): total 191,362; activity rate of total population 45.3% (participation rates: ages 15–59, 70.6%; female 49.1%; unemployed [2003] 24.1%).

Price and earnings indexes (2000 = 100)							
	1998	1999	2000	2001	2002	2003	2004
Consumer price index	99.6	100.0	100.0	102.6	105.0	107.1	108.6
Monthly earnings index	...	...	...	...	...	...	...

Gross national product (at current market prices; 2003): U.S.$6,190,000,000 (U.S.$14,090 per capita).

Structure of gross domestic product and labour force				
	2002[8]		1998	
	in value U.S.$'000,000	% of total value	labour force	% of labour force
Agriculture	370	7.4	8,200	4.5
Mining, manufacturing	405	8.1	7,900	4.3
Public utilities			...	...
Construction	372	7.4	13,000	7.1
Transp. and commun.	356	7.1	4,200	2.3
Trade, hotels	906	18.0	20,700	11.4
Finance, real estate			3,500	1.9
Pub. admin., defense	2,611	52.0	43,400	23.8
Services			24,400	13.4
Other			56,900[9]	31.2[9]
TOTAL	5,020	100.0	182,200	100.0[6]

Household income and expenditure. Average household size (1999) 2.9; disposable income per household (2000) €25,441 (U.S.$23,439); sources of income (2000): wages and salaries 81.5%, transfer payments 17.2%, property 1.3%; expenditure (1994–95): housing 26.2%, food and beverages 21.4%, transportation and communications 14.1%, household durables 6.0%, culture and leisure 4.2%.
Tourism (2003): receipts from visitors U.S.$421,000,000; expenditures, n.a.

Foreign trade

Balance of trade (current prices)						
€'000,000	1998	1999	2000	2001	2002	2003
	–9,996[10]	–1,431	–1,666	–1,666	–1,635	–1,690
% of total	88.2%	83.4%	86.2%	83.1%	84.9%	83.7%

Imports (2001): €1,835,000,000 (food and agriculture products 19.8%, consumer goods 18.6%, machinery and equipment 15.8%). *Major import sources* (1998): France 63.4%; Germany 4.4%; Italy 3.5%; Martinique 3.4%; U.S. 2.9%.
Exports (2001): €169,000,000 (food and agricultural products 58.4% [including bananas, sugar, rum, melons, eggplant, and flowers]). *Major export destinations* (1998): France 68.5%; Martinique 9.4%; Italy 4.8%; Belgium-Luxembourg 3.3%; French Guiana 3.0%.

Transport and communications

Transport. Railroads: none. Roads (1998): total length 1,988 mi, 3,415 km (paved [1986] 80%). Vehicles (2001): passenger cars 117,700; trucks and buses 31,400. Air transport (2002): passenger arrivals and departures 1,807,400; cargo handled 16,179 metric tons, cargo unloaded 5,204 metric tons; airports (1997) with scheduled flights 7.

Communications				units
Medium	date	unit	number	per 1,000 persons
Daily newspapers	1995	circulation	35,000	81
Radio	1997	receivers	113,000	258
Television	1999	receivers	118,000	262
Telephones	2001	main lines	210,000	457
Cellular telephones	2002	subscribers	323,500	697
Personal computers	2001	units	100,000	217
Internet	2002	users	50,000	115

Education and health

Educational attainment (1999). Percentage of population age 20 and over having: no formal education through lower secondary education 59.5%; upper secondary 10.1%; vocational 16.6%; incomplete higher 4.8%; complete higher 5.0%; other 4.0%. *Literacy* (1992): total population age 15 and over literate 225,400 (90.1%); males literate 108,700 (89.7%); females literate 116,700 (90.5%).

Education (1998–99)				student/
	schools	teachers	students	teacher ratio
Primary (age 6–10)	348	2,936	40,042	13.6
Secondary (age 11–17)	85	3,392	51,491	15.2
Vocational				
Higher[11]	1	...	10,919	...

Health (2003): physicians 924 (1 per 477 persons); hospital beds 2,428 (1 per 181 persons); infant mortality rate per 1,000 live births (2004) 8.8.
Food (1995): daily per capita caloric intake 2,732 (vegetable products 75%, animal products 25%); 129% of FAO recommended minimum requirement.

Military

Total active duty personnel (2004): French troops in Antilles (Guadeloupe and Martinique) 4,100.

[1]French franc replaced by euro as of Jan. 1, 2002. [2]Comprises Basse-Terre 325 sq mi (842 sq km), pop. 172,693, and Îles des Saintes 5 sq mi (13 sq km), pop. 2,998. [3]Comprises Grande-Terre 230 sq mi (596 sq km), pop. 196,767; Marie-Galante 61 sq mi (158 sq km), pop. 12,488; La Désirade 8 sq mi (21 sq km), pop. 1,620; and the uninhabited Îles de la Petite-Terre. [4]Comprises the French part of Saint-Martin 21 sq mi (53 sq km), pop. 29,078; Saint-Barthélemy 8 sq mi (21 sq km), pop. 6,852; and the small, uninhabited island of Tintamarre. [5]Saint-Martin and Saint-Barthélemy are expected to have new administrative statuses ("territorial collectivities") by 2006. [6]Detail does not add to total given because of rounding. [7]Within Pointe-à-Pitre urban agglomeration. [8]Derived figures from UN source. [9]Includes 55,900 unemployed. [10]In millions of French francs (F). [11]University of Antilles-French Guiana, Guadeloupe campus.

Internet resources for further information:
• INSEE Guadeloupe
  http://www.insee.fr/fr/insee_regions/guadeloupe/home/home_page.asp

Guam

Official name: Teritorion Guam
(Chamorro); Territory of Guam
(English).
Political status: self-governing,
organized, unincorporated territory
of the United States with one
legislative house (Guam Legislature
[15]).
Chief of state: President of the
United States.
Head of government: Governor.
Capital: Hagåtña (Agana).
Official languages: Chamorro; English.
Official religion: none.
Monetary unit: 1 United States dollar
(U.S.$) = 100 cents; valuation
(Sept. 1, 2005) 1 U.S.$ = £0.54.

Area and population		land area		population[1]
Election Districts		sq mi	sq km	2000 census
Agat		11	29	5,656
Asan		6	16	2,090
Barrigada		9	23	8,652
Chalan Pago-Ordot		6	16	5,923
Dededo		30	78	42,980
Hagåtña (Agana)		1	3	1,100
Hagåtña Heights		1	3	3,940
Inarajan		19	49	3,052
Mangilao		10	26	13,313
Merizo		6	16	2,163
Mongmong-Toto-Maite		2	5	5,845
Piti		7	18	1,666
Santa Rita		16	42	7,500
Sinajana		1	3	2,853
Talofofo		17	44	3,215
Tamuning		6	16	18,012
Umatac		6	16	887
Yigo		35	91	19,474
Yona		20	52	6,484
TOTAL		209	541[2]	154,805

Demography

Population (2005): 170,000.
Density (2005)[3]: persons per sq mi 813.4, persons per sq km 314.2.
Urban-rural (2003): urban 93.7%; rural 6.3%.
Sex distribution (2004): male 51.00%; female 49.00%.
Age breakdown (2004): under 15, 29.8%; 15–29, 22.8%; 30–44, 23.0%; 45–59, 15.3%; 60–74, 7.0%; 75 and over, 2.1%.
Population projection: (2010) 182,000; (2020) 206,000.
Doubling time: 47 years.
Ethnic composition (2000): Pacific Islander 44.6%, of which Chamorro 37.0%; Asian 32.5%, of which Filipino 26.3%, Korean 2.5%; white 6.8%; black 1.0%; mixed 13.9%; other 1.2%.
Religious affiliation (2000): Roman Catholic 79.0%; Protestant 9.9%; other Christian 5.2%; nonreligious 1.7%; Buddhist 1.3%; other 2.9%.
Major populated places (2000): Tamuning 10,833; Mangilao 7,794; Yigo 6,391; Astumbo 5,207; Hagåtña 1,122.

Vital statistics

Birth rate per 1,000 population (2004): 19.3 (world avg. 21.1); legitimate 42.8%; illegitimate 57.2%.
Death rate per 1,000 population (2004): 4.4 (world avg. 9.0).
Natural increase rate per 1,000 population (2004): 14.9 (world avg. 12.1).
Total fertility rate (avg. births per childbearing woman; 2004): 2.6.
Marriage rate per 1,000 population (2003): 8.2.
Divorce rate per 1,000 population (2002): 3.0.
Life expectancy at birth (2004): male 75.1 years; female 81.3 years.
Major causes of death per 100,000 population (2002): diseases of the heart 130.4; malignant neoplasms (cancers) 77.0; cerebrovascular disease 32.3; accidents 22.3; suicide 13.7; pneumonia 13.7.

National economy

Budget (2002). Revenue: U.S.$319,629,000 (local taxes 82.0%, federal contributions 16.7%, other 1.3%). Expenditures: U.S.$313,002,000 (education 47.2%, public order 19.4%, health 5.4%, social protection 3.2%).
Production (metric tons except as noted). Agriculture, forestry, fishing (2004): coconuts 53,000, watermelons 2,400, roots and tubers 2,350, cucumbers 390; livestock (number of live animals) 205,000 poultry, 5,100 pigs, 680 goats; roundwood, n.a.; fish catch (metric tons; 2002) 464, value of aquaculture production (1996) U.S.$1,442,000. Mining and quarrying: sand and gravel. Manufacturing (value of sales in U.S.$'000; 2002): food processing 26,733; printing and publishing 7,382; fabricated metal products 4,052. Energy production (consumption): electricity (kW-hr; 2002) 1,745,000,000 (1,745,000,000); petroleum products (metric tons; 2002) none (1,333,000).
Household income and expenditure. Average household size (2003) 3.7; average annual income per household U.S.$41,196; sources of income: n.a.; expenditure: n.a.
Land use as % of total land area (2000): in temporary crops c. 9%, in permanent crops c. 16%, in pasture c. 15%; overall forest area c. 38%.
Gross domestic product (at current market prices; 2002): U.S.$2,463,000,000 (U.S.$15,440 per capita).

Structure of gross domestic product and labour force

	1995		2002	
	in value U.S.$'000,000	% of total value	labour force[4]	% of labour force[4]
Agriculture	5	5	290	0.5
Manufacturing	5	5	1,570	2.8
Construction	379.0	12.5	3,420	6.1
Trade	622.9	20.6	12,690	22.7
Transp. and commun.	5	5	4,590	8.2
Finance	5	5	2,450	4.4
Pub. admin. (local)	513.3	16.9	13,280	23.7
Pub. admin., defense (federal)	452.7	14.9	3,220	5.7
Services	486.9	16.1	14,510	25.9
Other	575.4[5]	19.0[5]	—	—
TOTAL	3,030.2	100.0	56,020	100.0

Population economically active (2002): total 62,050[6]; activity rate of total population c. 39% (participation rates: over age 15, 62.4%; female 45.9%; unemployed [March 2004] 7.7%).

Price and earnings indexes (2000 = 100)							
	1998	1999	2000	2001	2002	2003	2004
Consumer price index	96.3	98.0	100.0	98.7	99.3	102.5	110.2
Weekly earnings index[7]	93.9	91.9	100.0	92.6	92.0	98.7	…

Tourism (1999): receipts from visitors U.S.$1,908,000,000.

Foreign trade

Balance of trade (current prices)						
	1997[8]	1998[8]	1999[8]	2000	2001[8]	2002
U.S.$'000,000	−545	−480	−485	…	−442	−352
% of total	78%	73%	74%	…	78%	83%

Imports (2001): c. U.S.$503,000,000[9], [10] (1999; food products and nonalcoholic beverages c. 32%; leather products including footwear c. 20%; motor vehicles and parts c. 12%; clothing c. 8%). *Major import sources:* significantly U.S. and Japan.
Exports (2001): U.S.$60,800,000 (food products 52.2%, of which fish 51.4%; petroleum and natural gas products 6.2%; perfumes and colognes 6.0%; tobacco products 5.8%). *Major export destinations:* Japan 50.0%; Palau 9.4%; Federated States of Micronesia 9.1%; Hong Kong 7.4%; Taiwan 4.7%.

Transport and communications

Transport. Railroads: none. Roads (1999): total length 550 mi, 885 km (paved 76%). Vehicles (2004): passenger cars 62,007; trucks and buses 25,319. Air transport (2004)[11]: passenger-km 4,167,000,000; metric ton-km cargo 60,246,000; airports with scheduled flights 1.

Communications				units per 1,000
Medium	date	unit	number	persons
Daily newspapers	1996	circulation	28,000	178
Radio	1997	receivers	221,000	1,400
Television	1997	receivers	106,000	668
Telephones	2002	main lines	76,425	478
Cellular telephones	2001	subscribers	32,600	207
Internet	2002	users	50,000	313

Education and health

Educational attainment (2000). Percentage of population age 25 and over having: no formal schooling to some secondary education 23.7%; completed secondary 31.9%; some higher 24.5%; undergraduate 15.3%; advanced degree 4.6%. *Literacy:* virtually 100%.

Education (2000–01)	schools	teachers	students	student/ teacher ratio
Primary (age 5–10)	24	1,063	17,001	16.0
Secondary (age 11–18)	11	1,010	18,217	18.0
Higher[12]	1	…	2,923	…

Health: physicians (2005) 93[13] (1 per 1,828 persons); hospital beds (2000) 225 (1 per 689 persons); infant mortality rate per 1,000 live births (2004) 7.2.

Military

Total active duty U.S. personnel (end of 2004): 3,237 (army 1.2%; navy 41.4%; air force 57.4%).

---

[1]Includes active-duty military personnel, U.S. Department of Defense employees, their dependents, and Guamanian nationals. [2]Detail does not add to total given because of rounding. [3]Based on land area; total area per most recent survey including area designated as inland water equals 217 sq mi (561 sq km). [4]Payroll employment only; excludes proprietors, the self-employed, unpaid family workers, and military personnel. [5]Other includes Agriculture, Manufacturing, Transportation and communications, and Finance. [6]For civilian labour force only including unemployed. [7]Private sector only. [8]Estimated figures. [9]The estimated 1999 import total is based on a projection of summed figures for four months only (January, April, July, and October). [10]Excludes petroleum imports for transshipment. [11]Continental Micronesia only. [12]University of Guam only; 2004–05. [13]Members of Guam Medical Society only.

Internet resources for further information:
• **U.S. Office of Insular Affairs http://www.pacificweb.org**

Guatemala

Official name: República de Guatemala (Republic of Guatemala).
Form of government: republic with one legislative house (Congress of the Republic [158]).
Head of state and government: President.
Capital: Guatemala City.
Official language: Spanish.
Official religion: none.
Monetary unit: 1 quetzal (Q) = 100 centavos; valuation (Sept. 1, 2005) 1 U.S.$ = Q 7.60; 1 £ = Q 13.99.

Area and population

Departments	Capitals	area sq mi	area sq km	population 2002 census
Alta Verapaz	Cobán	3,695	9,569	776,246
Baja Verapaz	Salamá	1,198	3,104	215,915
Chimaltenango	Chimaltenango	757	1,960	446,133
Chiquimula	Chiquimula	912	2,361	302,485
El Progreso	Guastatoya (Progreso)	737	1,910	139,490
Escuintla	Escuintla	1,682	4,356	538,746
Guatemala	Guatemala City	856	2,218	2,541,581
Huehuetenango	Huehuetenango	2,813	7,285	846,544
Izabal	Puerto Barrios	3,468	8,981	314,306
Jalapa	Jalapa	792	2,050	242,926
Jutiapa	Jutiapa	1,235	3,199	389,085
Petén	Flores	12,987	33,635	366,735
Quetzaltenango	Quetzaltenango	810	2,098	624,716
Quiché	Santa Cruz del Quiché	3,927	10,172	655,510
Retalhuleu	Retalhuleu	712	1,844	241,411
Sacatepéquez	Antigua Guatemala	178	462	248,019
San Marcos	San Marcos	1,468	3,802	794,951
Santa Rosa	Cuilapa	1,134	2,936	301,370
Sololá	Sololá	405	1,050	307,661
Suchitepéquez	Mazatenango	930	2,409	403,945
Totonicapán	Totonicapán	403	1,043	339,254
Zacapa	Zacapa	1,032	2,673	200,167
TOTAL		42,130[1]	109,117	11,237,196

Demography

Population (2005): 12,599,000.
Density (2005): persons per sq mi 299.1, persons per sq km 115.5.
Urban-rural (2004): urban 46.8%; rural 53.2%.
Sex distribution (2003): male 50.67%; female 49.33%.
Age breakdown (2003): under 15, 42.9%; 15–29, 27.8%; 30–44, 15.6%; 45–59, 8.7%; 60–74, 4.0%; 75 and over, 1.0%.
Population projection: (2010) 14,213,000; (2020) 17,527,000.
Ethnic composition (2000): mestizo 63.7%; Amerindian (virtually all Mayan) 33.1%; black 2.0%; white 1.0%; other 0.2%.
Religious affiliation (2000): Roman Catholic 73%; Protestant 11%; indigenous Christian 8%; unaffiliated Christian 4%; nonreligious/other 4%.
Major cities (2002)[2]: Guatemala City 942,348 (urban agglomeration [2001] 3,366,000); Mixco 277,400[3]; Villa Nueva 187,700[3]; Quetzaltenango 106,700; Escuintla 65,400.

Vital statistics

Birth rate per 1,000 population (2003): 31.3 (world avg. 21.1).
Death rate per 1,000 population (2003): 5.6 (world avg. 9.0).
Natural increase rate per 1,000 population (2003): 25.7 (world avg. 12.1).
Total fertility rate (avg. births per childbearing woman; 2004): 4.2.
Marriage rate per 1,000 population (2003): 4.3.
Life expectancy at birth (2004): male 63.6 years; female 69.5 years.
Major causes of death per 100,000 population (2002): communicable diseases 339.0; diseases of the circulatory system 80.0; accidents and violence 71.0; malignant neoplasms (cancers) 44.0.

National economy

Budget (2004). Revenue: Q 23,462,100,000 (tax revenue 93.7%, of which VAT 44.7%, income tax 14.0%; nontax revenue 5.0%; grants 1.3%). Expenditures: Q 25,542,200,000 (current expenditures 68.5%; capital expenditures 31.5%).
Public debt (external, outstanding; 2004): U.S.$3,843,900,000.
Tourism (2003): receipts from visitors U.S.$621,000,000; expenditures by nationals abroad U.S.$312,000,000.
Production (metric tons except as noted). Agriculture, forestry, fishing (2004): sugarcane 18,000,000, corn (maize) 1,072,310, bananas 1,000,000, oil palm fruit 580,000, plantains 268,000, coffee 216,600, cardamom and nutmeg 19,000; livestock (number of live animals) 2,540,000 cattle, 780,000 pigs, 27,000,000 chickens; roundwood 16,413,542 cu m; fish catch (2003) 24,134. Mining and quarrying (2003): gypsum 66,981; gold 4,550 kg; marble 10,000 cu m. Manufacturing (value added in Q '000,000; 2004)[4]: food products 213; beverages 93; textiles 68; wearing apparel 53; fabricated metal products 41. Energy production (consumption): electricity (kW-hr; 2004) 7,096,000,000 ([2002] 7,916,000,000); crude petroleum (barrels; 2004) 9,000,000 ([2002] 4,300,000); petroleum products (metric tons; 2002) 603,000 (3,099,000); natural gas (cu m; 2002) 11,000,000 (11,000,000).
Household income and expenditure. Average household size (2002) 4.4; income per household (1989) Q 4,306 (U.S.$1,529); sources of income: n.a.; expenditure (2000)[5]: food and beverages 32.9%, household furnishings 14.7%, clothing 11.8%, recreation and culture 9.2%, health 7.3%.
Gross national product (at current market prices; 2004): U.S.$26,945,000,000 (U.S.$2,130 per capita).

Structure of gross domestic product and labour force

	2004 in value Q '000,000[4]	2004 % of total value	2002 labour force	2002 % of labour force
Agriculture	1,275.2	22.9	1,844,265	38.7
Mining	27.9	0.5	11,279	0.2
Manufacturing	704.1	12.7	716,633	15.0
Construction	72.8	1.3	213,007	4.5
Public utilities	247.0	4.4	12,673	0.3
Transp. and commun.	631.9	11.4	103,917	2.2
Trade	1,387.3	24.9	1,050,499	22.0
Finance, real estate	534.9	9.6 }	31,513	0.7
Pub. admin., defense	350.7	6.3 }		
Services	334.6	6.0	601,831	12.6
Other	—	—	183,767	3.9
TOTAL	5,566.4	100.0	4,769,384	100.0[1]

Population economically active (1998–99): total 3,981,893; activity rate of total population 35.0% (participation rates: ages 15–64, 50.5%; female 22.6%; unemployed [2003] 7.5%).

Price and earnings indexes (2000 = 100)

	1998	1999	2000	2001	2002	2003	2004
Consumer price index	90.0	94.4	100.0	107.6	116.3	122.6	131.7
Annual earnings index	79.8	89.4	100.0	110.2	121.3	129.3	...

Land use as % of total land area (2000): in temporary crops 12.5%, in permanent crops 5.0%, in pasture 24.0%; overall forest area 26.3%.

Foreign trade[6]

Balance of trade (current prices)

	1999	2000	2001	2002	2003	2004
U.S.$'000,000	−1,613	−1,728	−2,768	−3,349	−3,474	−4,249
% of total	25.2%	24.3%	35.9%	42.9%	41.1%	42.0%

Imports (2004): U.S.$7,811,560,400 (machinery and apparatus 16.7%; mineral fuels 15.0%; chemicals and chemical products 13.6%; road vehicles 11.1%). *Major import sources:* U.S. 40.9%; Mexico 8.2%; El Salvador 5.6%; Panama 5.1%; Costa Rica 4.1%.
Exports (2004): U.S.$2,931,777,400 (chemical products 17.7%[7]; coffee 11.2%; bananas 7.8%; sugar 6.4%; crude petroleum 6.1%; cardamom 2.5%). *Major export destinations:* U.S. 29.3%; El Salvador 18.6%; Honduras 11.9%; Costa Rica 6.2%; Nicaragua 6.0%.

Transport and communications

Transport. Railroads (2004): route length 886 km[8]. Roads (2002): total length 14,044 km (paved 39%). Vehicles (1999): passenger cars 578,733; trucks and buses 53,236. Air transport (1999): passenger-km 341,700,000; metric ton-km cargo (2003) 200,000; airports (1996) 2.

Communications

Medium	date	unit	number	units per 1,000 persons
Daily newspapers	2001	circulation	377,300	33
Radio	2001	receivers	903,300	79
Television	2001	receivers	697,500	61
Telephones	2004	main lines	1,132,000	89
Cellular telephones	2004	subscribers	3,168,300	250
Personal computers	2004	units	231,000	18
Internet	2004	users	756,000	60

Education and health

Educational attainment (1994). Percentage of population age 25 and over having: no formal schooling 45.2%; incomplete primary education 20.8%; complete primary 18.0%; some secondary 4.8%; secondary 7.2%; higher 4.0%. *Literacy* (2004): total population age 15 and over literate 71.2%; males literate 78.5%; females literate 63.9%.

Education (2002–03)

	schools[9]	teachers	students	student/ teacher ratio
Primary (age 7–12)	17,905	68,901	2,075,694	30.1
Secondary (age 13–18)	3,118	44,435	608,420	13.7
Higher	1,462	4,033	111,739	27.7

Health (2003): physicians 11,700 (1 per 1,053 persons); hospital beds 6,118 (1 per 1,961 persons); infant mortality rate per 1,000 live births (2004) 33.1.
Food (2002): daily per capita caloric intake 2,219 (vegetable products 91%, animal products 9%); 101% of FAO recommended minimum.

Military

Total active duty personnel (2004): 29,200 (army 92.5%, navy 5.1%, air force 2.4%). *Military expenditure as percentage of GDP* (2003): 0.5%; per capita expenditure U.S.$10.

---

[1]Detail does not add to total given because of rounding. [2]Urban populations of municipios. [3]Within Guatemala City urban agglomeration. [4]At prices of 1958. [5]Weights of consumer price index components. [6]Import figures are f.o.b. in balance of trade and c.i.f. for commodities and trading partners. [7]Data for 2002. [8]Mostly inoperable in 2003; no passenger service is available. [9]1999–2000.

Internet resources for further information:
• Banco de Guatemala http://www.banguat.gob.gt
• Instituto Nacional de Estadistica http://www.segeplan.gob.gt/ine/index.htm

Guernsey[1]

Atlantic Ocean

Official name: Bailiwick of Guernsey.
Political status: crown dependency (United Kingdom) with one legislative house (States of Deliberation [51[2, 3, 4]]).
Chief of state: British Monarch represented by Lieutenant Governor.
Head of government: Chief Minister[5] assisted by the Policy Council.
Capital: St. Peter Port.
Official language: English.
Official religion: n.a.
Monetary unit: 1 Guernsey pound[6] = 100 pence; valuation (Sept. 1, 2005) 1 Guernsey pound = U.S.$1.84.

Area and population	area		population
	sq mi	sq km	2001 census
Parishes of Guernsey			
Castel	3.9	10.1	8,975
Forest	1.6	4.1	1,549
St. Andrew	1.7	4.5	2,409
St. Martin	2.8	7.3	6,267
St. Peter (St. Pierre du Bois)	2.4	6.2	2,188
St. Peter Port	2.6	6.6	16,488
St. Sampson	2.3	6.0	8,592
St. Saviour	2.4	6.3	2,696
Torteval	1.2	3.1	973
Vale	3.4	8.8	9,573
Dependencies of Guernsey			
Alderney	3.1	7.9	2,294
Brechou	0.1	0.3	0
Herm[7]	0.5	1.3	95
Jethou[7]	0.1	0.2	2
Lihou	0.1	0.2	0
Little Sark	0.4	1.0	591
Sark (Great Sark)	1.6	4.2	
TOTAL	30.2	78.1	62,692

Demography

Population (2005)[8]: 63,600.
Density (2005)[8]: persons per sq mi 2,106.0, persons per sq km 814.3.
Urban-rural (2003)[8, 9]: urban 30.5%; rural 69.5%.
Sex distribution (2001): male 48.72%; female 51.28%.
Age breakdown (2001): under 15, 17.2%; 15–29, 18.8%; 30–44, 23.2%; 45–59, 20.0%; 60–74, 13.4%; 75 and over, 7.4%.
Population projection[8]: (2010) 64,000; (2020) 65,000.
Population by place of birth (2001): Guernsey 64.3%; United Kingdom 27.4%; Portugal 1.9%; Jersey 0.7%; Ireland 0.7%; Alderney 0.2%; Sark 0.1%; other Europe 3.2%; other 1.5%.
Religious affiliation (2000)[8, 9]: Protestant 51.0%, of which Anglican 44.1%; unaffiliated Christian 20.1%; Roman Catholic 14.6%; nonreligious 12.4%; other 1.9%.
Major cities (2001)[10]: St. Peter Port 16,488; Vale 9,573; Castel 8,975; St. Sampson 8,592; St. Martin 6,267.

Vital statistics

Birth rate per 1,000 population (2004): 9.2 (world avg. 21.1); (2000) legitimate 65.2%, illegitimate 34.8%.
Death rate per 1,000 population (2004): 9.9 (world avg. 9.0).
Natural increase rate per 1,000 population (2004): –0.7 (world avg. 12.1).
Total fertility rate (avg. births per childbearing woman; 2004): 1.4.
Marriage rate per 1,000 population (2000): 5.7.
Divorce rate per 1,000 population (2000): 2.9.
Life expectancy at birth (2003): male 77.0 years; female 83.1 years.
Major causes of death per 100,000 population (1993): diseases of the circulatory system 423.5; malignant neoplasms (cancers) 288.0; diseases of the respiratory system 133.8; endocrine and metabolic disorders 25.4; accidents, poisoning, and violence 22.0; diseases of the digestive system 11.8.

National economy

Budget (2003). Revenue: £287,969,000 (income tax 83.0%, customs duties and excise taxes 5.3%, document duties 4.7%, automobile taxes 1.9%, company fees 1.7%). Expenditures: £254,390,000 (health 24.7%, social security and welfare 21.7%, education 20.5%, advisers and finance 6.9%, law and order 5.9%).
Production (metric tons except as noted). Agriculture, forestry, fishing (1999): tomatoes 2,449[11], flowers 1,154,000 boxes, of which roses 288,000 boxes, freesia 184,000 boxes, carnations 161,000 boxes; livestock (number of live animals) 3,262 cattle; roundwood, n.a.; fish catch (2001)[8, 9]: 4,414, of which crustaceans 2,169 (sea spiders and crabs 1,988), mollusks 1,456 (abalones, winkles, and conch 523), marine fish 789. Mining and quarrying: n.a. Manufacturing (value of exports in £'000,000; 1998): flowers 34.0. Energy production (consumption): electricity (kW-hr; 1999–2000), n.a. (273,013,000).
Population economically active (2001): total 32,631; activity rate of total population 54.6% (participation rates: ages 15–64, 79.1%; female 45.2%; unemployed 1.0%).

Retail price index (March 2000 = 100)						
	2000	2001	2002	2003	2004	2005
Retail price index[12]	100.0	102.9	106.8	111.4	115.0	118.6

Gross national product (at current market prices; 2004): U.S.$2,727,550,000 (U.S.$43,090 per capita).

Structure of gross domestic product and labour force				
	2004			
	in value £'000	% of total value	labour force	% of labour force
Horticulture, fishing	24,835	1.8	1,125	3.6
Mining	—	—	—	—
Manufacturing	37,834	2.7	1,383	4.4
Construction	116,994	8.2	3,214	10.2
Public utilities	15,476	1.1	423	1.3
Transp. and commun.	28,590	2.0	1,892	6.0
Trade, hotels	197,551	13.9	6,512	20.6
Finance, real estate, insurance, international business	580,845	40.9	9,167	29.1
Pub. admin., defense	89,195	6.3	2,637	8.4
Services	179,264	12.6	5,058	16.0
Other	148,416	10.5	126	0.4
TOTAL	1,419,000	100.0	31,537	100.0

Public debt: n.a.
Household income and expenditure. Average household size (2001) 2.6; expenditure (1998–99): housing 21.6%, food 12.7%, household furnishings and services 11.2%, recreation services 9.2%, transportation 8.5%, recreation products 6.3%, clothing and footwear 5.6%, food away from home 5.5%.
Tourism (1996): receipts U.S.$275,000,000.
Land use as % of total land area (1999): in temporary crops, n.a., in permanent crops, n.a., in pasture *c.* 37%; overall forest area *c.* 3%.

Foreign trade

Imports (1998): petroleum products are important. *Major import sources* (1998): mostly United Kingdom.
Exports (1998): £93,000,000[13] (manufactured goods *c.* 51%, of which electronic components *c.* 18%, printed products *c.* 10%; agricultural products *c.* 42%, of which flowers *c.* 25%, plants *c.* 10%; fish, crustaceans, and mollusks *c.* 7%). *Major export destinations* (1998): mostly United Kingdom.

Transport and communications

Transport. Railroads: n.a. Vehicles (2004): passenger cars 40,268; trucks and buses 7,673. Air transport (2001)[14]: passenger arrivals 429,076, passenger departures 430,254; cargo loaded 969 metric tons, cargo unloaded 3,557 metric tons; airports (1999) with scheduled flights 2[15].

Communications				units per 1,000
Medium	date	unit	number	persons
Daily newspapers	1998	circulation	15,784	260
Telephones	2002	main lines	55,000	874
Cellular telephones	2002	subscribers	37,000	588
Internet	2002	users	30,000	536

Education and health

Educational attainment: n.a. *Literacy* (2002): virtually 100%.

Education (2000)	schools	teachers	students	student/ teacher ratio
Primary (age 5–10)	22[16]	253	4,977	19.9
Secondary (age 11–16)	8[16]	295	3,900	13.2
Higher	1	...	211[17]	...

Health: physicians (1999) 93 (1 per 654 persons); hospital beds (2004) *c.* 310[18] (1 per 204 persons); infant mortality rate per 1,000 live births (2004) 4.8.
Food (2002)[19]: daily per capita caloric intake 3,412 (vegetable products 69%, animal products 31%); 135% of FAO recommended minimum requirement.

Military

Total active duty personnel: n.a.[20]

[1]Data excludes Alderney and Sark unless otherwise noted. [2]The States of Deliberation was reorganized in 2004. [3]Includes 4 ex officio members with voting rights and 2 representatives from Alderney. [4]Alderney and Sark have their own parliaments. The States of Alderney has 12 elected members; the parliament of Sark consists of 40 *tenants* or landowners and 12 elected deputies. [5]The first chief minister was elected by the States of Deliberation in May 2004. [6]Equivalent in value to pound sterling (£). [7]Populated islets that are directly administered by Guernsey. [8]Includes Alderney, Sark, and other dependencies. [9]Includes Jersey. [10]Population of parishes. [11]1998. [12]March. [13]Excluding administrative and financial services; financial services accounted for 66% of the export economy in 2002. [14]Guernsey airport. [15]Includes one airport on Alderney. [16]1992. [17]1999. [18]Princess Elizabeth and King Edward VII hospitals only. [19]Data for the United Kingdom. [20]The United Kingdom is responsible for defense.

Internet resources for further information:
• **The States of Guernsey**
  http://www.gov.gg/ccm/portal

Guinea

Official name: République de Guinée (Republic of Guinea).
Form of government: unitary multiparty republic with one legislative house (National Assembly [114 seats]).
Head of state and government: President assisted by the Prime Minister.
Capital: Conakry.
Official language: French.
Official religion: none.
Monetary unit: 1 Guinean franc (GF) = 100 cauris; valuation (Sept. 1, 2005) 1 U.S.\$ = GF 3,775; 1 £ = GF 6,951.

Area and population		area		population
Regions	Capitals	sq mi	sq km	1996[1] census
Boké	Boké	12,041	31,186	760,119
Conakry	Conakry	174	450	1,092,936
Faranah	Faranah	13,738	35,581	602,845
Kankan	Kankan	27,855	72,145	1,011,644
Kindia	Kindia	11,148	28,873	928,312
Labé	Labé	8,830	22,869	799,545
Mamou	Mamou	6,592	17,074	612,218
Nzérékoré	Nzérékoré	14,540	37,658	1,348,787
TOTAL		94,918	245,836	7,156,406

Demography

Population (2005): 9,402,000.
Density (2005): persons per sq mi 99.1, persons per sq km 38.2.
Urban-rural (2004): urban 29.6%; rural 70.4%.
Sex distribution (2003): male 49.95%; female 50.05%.
Age breakdown (2003): under 15, 44.5%; 15–29, 26.4%; 30–44, 15.4%; 45–59, 8.7%; 60–74, 4.1%; 75 and over, 0.9%.
Population projection: (2010) 10,485,000; (2020) 13,371,000.
Doubling time: 26 years.
Ethnic composition (1996): Fulani 38.6%; Malinke 23.2%; Susu 11.0%; Kisi 6.0%; Kpelle 4.6%; other 16.6%.
Religious affiliation (2000): Muslim 67.3%; Christian 4.0%; other 28.7%.
Major cities (2004): Conakry 1,851,800; Kankan 113,900; Labé (2001) 64,500; Kindia (2001) 56,000; Nzérékoré (2001) 55,000.

Vital statistics

Birth rate per 1,000 population (2004): 42.3 (world avg. 21.1).
Death rate per 1,000 population (2004): 15.8 (world avg. 9.0).
Natural increase rate per 1,000 population (2004): 26.5 (world avg. 12.1).
Total fertility rate (avg. births per childbearing woman; 2004): 5.9.
Life expectancy at birth (2004): male 48.1 years; female 50.5 years.

National economy

Budget (2004). Revenue: GF 1,000,030,000,000 (current revenue 93.6%, of which value-added tax 40.3%, tax on trade 18.2%, mining sector revenue 17.1%, income tax 11.8%, nontax revenue 6.2%; grants 6.4%). Expenditures: GF 1,295,790,000,000 (current expenditure 71.2%, of which wages and salaries 21.2%, interest on debt 9.0%; capital expenditure 28.8%).
Production (metric tons except as noted). Agriculture, forestry, fishing (2004): cassava 1,350,000, rice 900,000, oil palm fruit 830,000, plantains 430,000, peanuts (groundnuts) 300,000, sugarcane 280,000, corn (maize) 260,000, mangoes 164,000, bananas 150,000, fonio 135,000, coffee 20,500; livestock (number of live animals) 3,285,000 cattle, 1,278,000 goats, 1,070,000 sheep, 14,000,000 chickens; roundwood 12,286,474 cu m; fish catch (2003) 118,845. Mining and quarrying (2004): bauxite 16,371,000; alumina 887,000; gold 16,320 kg; diamonds 627,900 carats. Manufacturing (2004): cement 313,500; paints 3,165. Energy production (consumption): electricity (kW-hr; 2004) 661,000,000 ([2002] 798,000,000); crude petroleum (barrels; 2003) none (3,100,000); petroleum products (metric tons; 2002) none (378,000).
Household income and expenditure (1994–95). Average household size (2002) 6.6; average annual household income[2] GF 1,905,899 (U.S.\$1,952); sources of income[2]: agriculture 49.3%, self-employment 22.2%, wages and salaries 15.7%; expenditure[2]: food 50.0%; housing 14.0%; health 12.3%; transportation and communications 8.4%; clothing 6.3%.
Gross national product (2004): U.S.\$3,681,000,000 (U.S.\$460 per capita).

Structure of gross domestic product and labour force				
	2004		1996	
	in value GF '000,000,000	% of total value	labour force	% of labour force
Agriculture, forestry, fishing	1,879.3	22.8	2,433,480	74.2
Mining	1,186.5	14.4	34,975	1.1
Manufacturing	283.7	3.5	90,885	2.8
Construction	849.1	10.3	60,526	1.9
Public utilities	71.8	0.9	4,690	0.1
Transp. and commun.	506.0	6.2	77,070	2.4
Trade, hotels	1,968.1	23.9	373,709	11.4
Finance, real estate	...	...	3,440	0.1
Pub. admin., defense	365.9	4.5	63,192	1.9
Services	571.2	6.9	132,045	4.0
Other	545.1[3]	6.6[3]	4,822	0.1
TOTAL	8,226.7	100.0	3,278,834	100.0

Public debt (external, outstanding; 2003): U.S.\$3,154,000,000.

Population economically active (2000): total 4,047,000; activity rate of total population 49.9% (participation rates: n.a.; female, n.a.; unemployed, n.a.).

Price index (2000 = 100)							
	1998	1999	2000	2001	2002	2003	2004
Consumer price index	89.5	93.5	100.0	105.4	108.4	122.4	141.4

Tourism: receipts (2002) U.S.\$43,000,000; expenditures (2003) U.S.\$26,000,000.
Land use as % of total land area (2000): in temporary crops 3.6%, in permanent crops 2.4%, in pasture 43.5%; overall forest area 28.2%.

Foreign trade

Balance of trade (current prices)						
	1998	1999	2000	2001	2002	2003
U.S.\$'000,000	+121.0	+54.0	+79.2	+169.2	+40.1	−35.0
% of total	9.6%	4.4%	6.3%	13.1%	2.9%	2.8%

Imports (2004): U.S.\$569,320,000 (machinery and apparatus 28.0%, food 20.6%, refined petroleum 18.9%). *Major import sources:* France 14.6%; China 9.6%; The Netherlands 6.8%; Belgium 6.0%; U.S. 5.9%; Italy 5.0%.
Exports (2004): U.S.\$772,820,000 (bauxite 39.0%, alumina 20.3%, gold 18.9%, diamonds 6.5%, cotton 5.6%, fish 4.5%, coffee 3.1%). *Major export destinations:* South Korea 15.6%; Russia 13.1%; Spain 12.3%; Ireland 9.1%; U.S. 7.5%; Germany 6.2%; France 5.9%.

Transport and communications

Transport. Railroads (2004): route length (mostly for bauxite transport) 520 mi, 837 km; passenger-km, n.a.[4]; metric ton-km cargo (1993) 710,000,000. Roads (2003): total length 34,585 km (paved 6.9%). Vehicles (2003): passenger cars 47,524; trucks and buses 26,467. Air transport (1999): passenger-km 94,000,000; metric ton-km cargo 10,000,000; airports (2000) 1.

Communications				units per 1,000 persons
Medium	date	unit	number	
Daily newspapers	1988	circulation	13,000	2.0
Radio	2001	receivers	448,100	52
Television	2001	receivers	379,100	44
Telephones	2003	main lines	26,200	3.4
Cellular telephones	2003	subscribers	111,500	14
Personal computers	2004	units	44,000	5.5
Internet	2004	users	46,000	5.8

Education and health

Educational attainment of those age 25 and over having attended school (1999)[5]: none or unknown 81.4%; primary 7.8%; secondary 6.8%; higher 4.0%. *Literacy* (2000): percentage of total population age 15 and over literate 41.0%; males literate 55.0%; females literate 27.0%.

Education (2002–03)				student/ teacher ratio
	schools	teachers	students	
Primary (age 7–12)	5,765	23,859	1,073,458	45.0
Secondary (age 13–18)	557	8,409	301,491	35.9
Voc., teacher tr.	41	...	7,172	...
Higher	7	860	16,361	19.0

Health: physicians (2003) 493 (1 per 18,262 persons); hospital beds (2004) 2,990 (1 per 3,078 persons); infant mortality rate per 1,000 live births (2004) 92.8.
Food (2002): daily per capita caloric intake 2,409 (vegetable products 96%, animal products 4%); 104% of FAO recommended minimum requirement.

Military

Total active duty personnel (2004): 9,700 (army 87.7%, navy 4.1%, air force 8.2%). *Military expenditure as percentage of GDP* (2003): 1.9%; per capita expenditure U.S.\$8.

[1]December 1. [2]Based on the national Enquête Intégrale sur les Conditions de Vie des Ménages avec Module Budget et Consommation, comprising 4,416 households. [3]Indirect taxes and import duties. [4]Passenger service has been limited and irregular since the late 1980s. [5]Based on the national Enquête Démographique et de Santé, comprising 5,090 households.

Internet resources for further information:
• **National Statistics Directorate**
  http://www.stat-guinee.org
• **Official site of Guinea**
  http://www.guinee.gov.gn

Guinea-Bissau

Official name: República da Guiné-Bissau (Republic of Guinea-Bissau).
Form of government: transitional regime[1] with one legislative house (National People's Assembly [102]).
Head of state and government: President assisted by the Prime Minister.
Capital: Bissau.
Official language: Portuguese.
Official religion: none.
Monetary unit: 1 CFA franc[2] (CFAF) = 100 centimes; valuation (Sept. 1, 2005) 1 U.S.$ = CFAF 522.78; 1 £ = CFAF 962.57.

Area and population		area		population
				2004
Regions	Chief towns	sq mi	sq km	estimate[3]
Bafatá	Bafatá	2,309	5,981	182,959
Biombo	Quinhámel	324	840	63,835
Bolama	Bolama	1,013	2,624	27,959
Cacheu	Cacheu	1,998	5,175	164,676
Gabú	Gabú	3,533	9,150	178,318
Oio	Bissorã	2,086	5,403	179,048
Quinara	Fulacunda	1,212	3,138	52,134
Tombali	Catió	1,443	3,736	91,930
Autonomous sector				
Bissau	—	30	78	354,983
TOTAL		13,948[4]	36,125[4]	1,295,841[5]

Demography

Population (2005): 1,413,000.
Density (2005)[6]: persons per sq mi 130.1, persons per sq km 50.2.
Urban-rural (2003): urban 34.0%; rural 66.0%.
Sex distribution (2004): male 48.50%; female 51.50%.
Age breakdown (2004): under 15, 41.7%; 15–29, 28.1%; 30–44, 16.0%; 45–59, 9.4%; 60–74, 4.1%; 75 and over, 0.7%.
Population projection: (2010) 1,564,000; (2020) 1,892,000.
Doubling time: 33 years.
Ethnic composition (1996): Balante 30%; Fulani 20%; Mandyako 14%; Malinke 13%; Pepel 7%; nonindigenous Cape Verdean mulatto 2%; other 14%.
Religious affiliation (2000): traditional beliefs 45.2%; Muslim 39.9%; Christian 13.2%, of which Roman Catholic 9.9%; other 1.7%.
Major cities (1997): Bissau 200,000 (urban agglomeration [2003] 336,000); Bafatá 15,000; Cacheu 14,000; Gabú 10,000.

Vital statistics

Birth rate per 1,000 population (2004): 38.0 (world avg. 21.1).
Death rate per 1,000 population (2004): 16.9 (world avg. 9.0).
Natural increase rate per 1,000 population (2004): 21.1 (world avg. 12.1).
Total fertility rate (avg. births per childbearing woman; 2004): 5.0.
Marriage rate per 1,000 population: n.a.
Divorce rate per 1,000 population: n.a.
Life expectancy at birth (2004): male 44.6 years; female 48.4 years.
Major causes of death per 100,000 population (2002): diseases of the circulatory system 165, HIV/AIDS 126, accidents, poisoning, and violence 114, malignant neoplasms (cancers) 66, chronic respiratory diseases 41.

National economy

Budget (2003). Revenue: CFAF 32,200,000,000 (tax revenue 39.4%, of which taxes on international trade 13.5%, general sales tax 11.3%; grants 32.9%; nontax revenue 27.7%, of which fishing licenses 23.3%). Expenditures: CFAF 51,506,000,000 (current expenditures 66.0%, of which wages and salaries 21.2%, scheduled external interest payments 12.7%; capital expenditures 34.0%).
Public debt (external, outstanding; 2003): U.S.$712,000,000.
Production (metric tons except as noted). Agriculture, forestry, fishing (2004): rice 127,000, cashew nuts 81,000, oil palm fruit 80,000, roots and tubers 68,000, coconuts 45,500, plantains 39,000, corn (maize) 27,000, millet 22,000, peanuts (groundnuts) 20,000, seed cotton 4,500; livestock (number of live animals) 520,000 cattle, 360,000 pigs, 330,000 goats, 290,000 sheep; roundwood (2004) 592,000 cu m; fish catch (2002) 5,000. Mining and quarrying: extraction of construction materials only. Manufacturing (2001): processed wood 11,800; wood products 4,700; dried and smoked fish 3,600; soap 2,600; vegetable oils 36,000 hectolitres; distilled liquor 11,000 hectolitres. Energy production (consumption): electricity (kW-hr; 2002) 60,000,000 (60,000,000); coal, none (none); crude petroleum, none (none); petroleum products (metric tons; 2002) none (91,000); natural gas, none (none).
Tourism (2002): receipts from visitors U.S.$2,000,000; expenditures by nationals abroad U.S.$5,000,000.
Population economically active (1995): total 491,000; activity rate of total population 45.8% (participation rates: over age 10, 65.5%; female 39.9%; unemployed, n.a.).

Price and earnings indexes (2000 = 100)							
	1998	1999	2000	2001	2002	2003	2004
Consumer price index	94.0	92.1	100.0	103.2	106.6	102.9	103.8
Monthly earnings index	...	...	...	...	...	...	...

Household income and expenditure. Average household size (1996) 6.9; income per household: n.a.; sources of income: n.a.; expenditure (2001–02)[7, 8]: food and nonalcoholic beverages 59.7%, housing and energy 13.6%, clothing and footwear 7.6%, transport and communications 6.5%, household furnishings 4.4%.
Gross national product (at current market prices; 2004): U.S.$250,000,000 (U.S.$160 per capita).

Structure of gross domestic product and labour force				
	2003		1995	
	in value CFAF '000,000[9]	% of total value[9]	labour force	% of labour force
Agriculture	77,872	57.1	373,000	76.0
Mining				
Manufacturing	14,287	10.5	20,000	4.1
Public utilities				
Construction	3,249	2.4		
Transportation and communications	5,889	4.3		
Trade	23,296	17.1	98,000	20.0
Finance, services	541	0.4		
Pub. admin., defense	11,130	8.2		
TOTAL	136,263[10]	100.0	491,000	100.0[10]

Land use as % of total land area (2000): in temporary crops 10.7%, in permanent crops 8.8%, in pasture 38.4%; overall forest area 60.5%.

Foreign trade[11]

Balance of trade (current prices)						
	1998	1999	2000	2001	2002	2003
U.S.$'000,000	−38.9	−30.8	−24.2	−45.2	−31.8	−23.6
% of total	42.9%	23.1%	16.3%	31.1%	22.9%	15.9%

Imports (2003): U.S.$85,800,000 (foodstuffs 30.1%, of which rice 21.2%; petroleum products 10.1%; construction material 8.4%; equipment and machinery 7.0%; beverages and tobacco 6.4%; transport equipment 5.7%). *Major import sources:* Senegal 21.7%; Portugal 21.2%; India 17.0%; China 4.2%; The Netherlands 3.6%; Italy 3.5%.
Exports (2003): U.S.$62,200,000 (cashew nuts 89.5%; cotton 1.4%; wood products 1.4%). *Major export destinations:* India 62.2%; Thailand 23.5%; Portugal 2.9%; Guinea 0.9%.

Transport and communications

Transport. Railroads: none. Roads (2003): total length 1,710 mi, 2,755 km (paved 28%). Vehicles (1996): passenger cars 7,120; trucks and buses 5,640. Air transport (1998): passenger-mi 6,200,000, passenger-km 10,000,000; short ton-mi cargo, n.a., metric ton-km cargo, n.a.; airports (1997) with scheduled flights 2.

Communications				units per 1,000
Medium	date	unit	number	persons
Daily newspapers	2000	circulation	6,390	5.0
Radio	2001	receivers	56,200	178
Television	2001	receivers	47,000	36
Telephones	2003	main lines	10,600	8.2
Cellular telephones	2003	subscribers	1,300	1.0
Internet	2004	users	26,000	20

Education and health

Educational attainment: n.a. *Literacy* (2001): total population age 15 and over literate 39.6%; males literate 55.2%; females literate 24.7%.

Education (1999)				student/
	schools	teachers	students	teacher ratio
Primary (age 7–13)	759	4,306	149,530	...
Secondary (age 13–18)		1,913	25,034[12]	...

Health: physicians (2003) 250 (1 per 5,546 persons); hospital beds (2001) 1,448 (1 per 902 persons); infant mortality rate per 1,000 live births (2004) 109.0.
Food (2002): daily per capita caloric intake 2,024 (vegetable products 93%, animal products 7%); 88% of FAO recommended minimum requirement.

Military

Total active duty personnel (2004): 9,250 (army 73.5%, navy 3.8%, air force 1.1%, paramilitary [gendarmerie] 21.6%). *Military expenditure as percentage of GNP* (2003): 4.1%; per capita expenditure U.S.$7.

---

[1]Legal ambiguity persists in December 2005. A constitution adopted by the National Assembly in 2001 has been neither promulgated nor vetoed by the President. [2]Formerly pegged to the French franc and since Jan. 1, 2002, to the euro at the rate of €1 = CFAF 655.96. [3]Projection based on 1991 census. [4]Includes water area of about 3,089 sq mi (8,000 sq km). [5]Reported total is 1,295,841; sum total is 1,295,842. [6]Based on land area of 10,859 sq mi (28,125 sq km). [7]Bissau only. [8]Weights of consumer price index components. [9]At factor costs. [10]Detail does not add to total given because of rounding. [11]Imports c.i.f.; exports f.o.b. [12]UNESCO estimate.

Internet resources for further information:
• La Banque de France: La Zone Franc
  http://www.banque-france.fr/fr/eurosys/zonefr/zonefr.htm
• National Institute of Statistics and Census
  http://www.stat-guineabissau.com

Guyana

Official name: Co-operative Republic of Guyana.
Form of government: unitary multiparty republic with one legislative house (National Assembly [65[1]]).
Head of state and government: President.
Capital: Georgetown.
Official language: English.
Official religion: none.
Monetary unit: 1 Guyana dollar (G$) = 100 cents; valuation (Sept. 1, 2005) 1 U.S.$ = G$190.00; 1 £ = G$349.84.

Area and population

Administrative regions	Capitals	area sq mi	area sq km	population 2002 preliminary census
Region 1 (Barima-Waini)	Mabaruma	7,853	20,339	23,204
Region 2 (Pomeroon-Supenaam)	Anna Regina	2,392	6,195	48,411
Region 3 (Essequibo Islands–West Demerara)	Vreed en Hoop	1,450	3,755	101,920
Region 4 (Demerara-Mahaica)	Paradise	862	2,233	309,059
Region 5 (Mahaica-Berbice)	Fort Wellington	1,610	4,170	52,321
Region 6 (East Berbice–Corentyne)	New Amsterdam	13,998	36,255	122,849
Region 7 (Cuyuni-Mazaruni)	Bartica	18,229	47,213	15,935
Region 8 (Potaro-Siparuni)	Mahdia	7,742	20,052	9,211
Region 9 (Upper Takutu–Upper Essequibo)	Lethem	22,313	57,790	19,365
Region 10 (Upper Demerara–Berbice)	Linden	6,595	17,081	39,766
TOTAL		83,044[2]	215,083[2]	742,041[3]

Demography

Population (2005): 751,000.
Density (2005)[4]: persons per sq mi 9.9, persons per sq km 3.8.
Urban-rural (2003): urban 37.6%; rural 62.4%.
Sex distribution (2004): male 50.15%; female 49.85%.
Age breakdown (2004): under 15, 26.7%; 15–29, 30.4%; 30–44, 22.6%; 45–59, 12.9%; 60–74, 5.5%; 75 and over, 1.9%.
Population projection: (2010) 751,000; (2020) 725,000.
Doubling time: 69 years.
Ethnic composition (2000): East Indian 45.9%; local black 32.4%; mulatto 11.4%; Amerindian 7.7%, of which detribalized 1.7%; Portuguese 1.3%; Chinese 0.6%; British 0.4%; other 0.3%.
Religious affiliation (2000): Christian 51.0%, of which Protestant 28.5% (including Anglican 8.9%), Roman Catholic 10.1%, unaffiliated Christian 7.6%; Hindu 32.5%; Muslim 8.1%; traditional beliefs 2.2%; Spiritist 2.0%; other 4.2%.
Major cities (2002): Georgetown 137,330 (urban agglomeration [2003] 231,000); Linden 29,572; New Amsterdam (1997) 25,000; Corriverton (1997) 24,000.

Vital statistics

Birth rate per 1,000 population (2004): 18.6 (world avg. 21.1).
Death rate per 1,000 population (2004): 8.4 (world avg. 9.0).
Natural increase rate per 1,000 population (2004): 10.2 (world avg. 12.1).
Total fertility rate (avg. births per childbearing woman; 2004): 2.1.
Life expectancy at birth (2004): male 62.5 years; female 67.8 years.
Major causes of death per 100,000 population (2002): diseases of the circulatory system 323, of which cerebrovascular disease 115, ischemic heart diseases 104; HIV/AIDS 179; accidents and violence 89; malignant neoplasms (cancers) 55; diabetes mellitus 40.

National economy

Budget (2002): Revenue: G$47,249,700,000 (tax revenue 85.8%, of which income taxes 39.7%, consumption taxes 31.0%, import duties 9.8%; nontax revenue 8.5%; grants 5.7%). Expenditures: G$60,367,800,000 (current expenditure 74.0%, of which wages and salaries 26.2%, interest payments 11.9%, transfers 3.9%; development expenditure 26.0%).
Production (metric tons except as noted). Agriculture, forestry, fishing (2004): rice 501,500, raw sugar 325,000, coconuts 45,000, cassava (manioc) 29,000, plantains 17,000, bananas 17,000, mangoes 12,000, oranges 5,000, pineapples 4,500; livestock (number of live animals) 130,000 sheep, 110,000 cattle, 21,300,000 chickens; roundwood 1,158,000 cu m; fish catch 51,492, of which shrimps and prawns 14,800. Mining and quarrying (2003): bauxite 1,716,000; gold 357,000 troy oz; diamonds 413,000 carats. Manufacturing (2003): flour 34,657; rum 120,000 hectolitres; beer and stout 84,300 hectolitres; soft drinks 4,198,000 cases; pharmaceuticals 9,680,000 tablets; garments 3,356,000 units. Energy production (consumption): electricity (kW-hr; 2002) 924,000,000 (924,000,000); coal, none (none); crude petroleum, none (none); petroleum products (metric tons; 2002) none (524,000); natural gas, none (none).
Population economically active (1997): total 263,807; activity rate of total population 33.9% (participation rates: ages 15–64 [1992] 59.5%; female 35.2%; unemployed, n.a.).

Price and earnings indexes (2000 = 100)

	1998	1999	2000	2001	2002	2003	2004
Consumer price index	87.6	94.2	100.0	102.6	108.1	114.6	119.9
Earnings index	...	...	...	...	...	...	...

Gross national product (2004): U.S.$765,000,000 (U.S.$990 per capita).

Structure of gross domestic product and labour force

	2003 in value G$'000,000	2003 % of total value	1997 labour force	1997 % of labour force
Sugar	18,448	12.8		
Other agriculture	17,015	11.8	66,789	25.3
Fishing, forestry	10,800	7.5		
Mining	15,930	11.1	7,299	2.8
Manufacturing	3,874	2.7	27,869	10.6
Public utilities			2,547	0.9
Construction	6,199	4.3	16,545	6.3
Transp. and commun.	11,502	8.0	20,154	7.6
Trade	4,996	3.5	44,653	16.9
Finance, real estate	9,487	6.6	12,219	4.6
Pub. admin., defense	22,800	15.8	15,219	5.8
Services	2,201	1.5	22,558	8.6
Other	20,803[5]	14.4[5]	27,955[6]	10.6[6]
TOTAL	144,064	100.0	263,807	100.0

Public debt (external, outstanding; 2004): U.S.$1,079,000,000.
Household income and expenditure. Average household size (2002) 4.0.
Tourism (2003): receipts from visitors U.S.$39,000,000; expenditures by nationals abroad U.S.$31,000,000.
Land use as % of total area (2000): in temporary crops 2.4%, in permanent crops 0.2%, in pasture 6.2%; overall forest area 78.5%.

Foreign trade[7]

Balance of trade (current prices)

	1999	2000	2001	2002	2003	2004
U.S.$'000,000	−25.2	−80.2	−93.8	−68.2	−58.9	−69.0
% of total	2.3%	7.4%	8.7%	6.4%	5.4%	5.6%

Imports (2004): U.S.$647,000,000 (fuels and lubricants 26.2%, consumer goods 23.9%, capital goods 21.0%). *Major import sources* (2001)[8]: U.S. 24%; Netherlands Antilles 17%; Chile 16%; Trinidad and Tobago 13%; U.K. 6%.
Exports (2004): U.S.$578,000,000 (gold 25.1%, sugar 23.6%, shrimp 10.1%, rice 9.5%, timber 7.8%, bauxite 7.3%). *Major export destinations* (2001)[8]: U.S. 22%; Canada 20%; U.K. 12%; Netherlands Antilles 12%; Belgium 5%.

Transport and communications

Transport. Railroads: [9]. Roads (1999): total length 4,952 mi, 7,970 km (paved 7%). Vehicles (2001): passenger cars 61,300; trucks and buses 15,500. Air transport (2001)[10]: passenger-mi 109,000,000, passenger-km 174,800,000; short ton-mi cargo 1,015,000, metric ton-km cargo 1,600,000; airports (2000) with scheduled flights 1[11].

Communications

Medium	date	unit	number	units per 1,000 persons
Daily newspapers	1996	circulation	42,000	54
Radio	1997	receivers	420,000	539
Television	1999	receivers	60,000	77
Telephones	2004	main lines	102,700	134
Cellular telephones	2004	subscribers	143,900	188
Personal computers	2004	units	27,000	35
Internet	2004	users	145,000	189

Education and health

Educational attainment (1992). Percentage of employed persons[12] having: no formal schooling 1.6%; incomplete primary education 9.3%; complete primary 54.7%; secondary 30.0%; higher 4.4%. *Literacy* (2002): total population age 15 and over literate 98.7%; males literate 99.0%; females literate 98.3%.

Education (1999–2000)

	schools	teachers	students	student/teacher ratio
Primary (age 6–11)	428	3,951	105,800	26.8
Secondary (age 12–17)	109	2,764	50,459	18.3
Voc., teacher tr.	7	512	6,266	12.2
Higher	1	371	7,496	20.2

Health: physicians (2004) 366 (1 per 2,055 persons); hospital beds (2002) 3,274 (1 per 229 persons); infant mortality rate per 1,000 live births (2004) 34.1.
Food (2002): daily per capita caloric intake 2,692 (vegetable products 84%, animal products 16%); 119% of FAO recommended minimum requirement.

Military

Total active duty personnel (2004): 1,600 (army 87.5%, navy 6.3%, air force 6.2%). *Military expenditure as percentage of GDP* (2003): 0.7%; per capita expenditure U.S.$8.

---

[1]Includes 12 indirectly elected seats. [2]Includes inland water area equaling *c.* 7,000 sq mi (*c.* 18,000 sq km). [3]Summed total; reported total equals 749,190. [4]Based on land area only. [5]Indirect taxes less subsidies. [6]Includes 23,960 unemployed. [7]Imports are f.o.b. in balance of trade and commodities and c.i.f. for trading partners. [8]Estimated figures. [9]No public railways. [10]Scheduled traffic only. [11]International only; domestic air service is provided on a charter basis. [12]Based on 245,500 persons.

Internet resources for further information:
• **Bank of Guyana**
   http://www.bankofguyana.org.gy
• **UNDP Common Country Assessment**
   http://www.undp.org.gy/ccassess.pdf

Haiti

Official name: Repiblik Dayti (Haitian Creole); République d'Haïti (French) (Republic of Haiti).
Form of government: interim regime with two legislative houses (Senate [27[1]]; Chamber of Deputies [83[1]]).
Chief of state: President.
Head of government: Prime Minister.
Capital: Port-au-Prince.
Official languages: Haitian Creole; French.
Official religions: [2].
Monetary unit: 1 gourde (G) = 100 centimes; valuation (Sept. 1, 2005) 1 U.S.$ = G 41.40; 1 £ = G 76.23.

Area and population		area		population
				2003 preliminary
Departements	**Capitals**	sq mi	sq km	census[7]
Artibonite	Gonaïves	1,924	4,984	1,070,397
Centre	Hinche	1,419	3,675	565,043
Grand'Anse[3] Nippes[3] }	Jérémie	1,278	3,310	603,894
Nord	Cap-Haïtien	813	2,106	773,546
Nord-Est	Fort-Liberté	697	1,805	300,493
Nord-Ouest	Port-de-Paix	840	2,176	445,080
Ouest	Port-au-Prince	1,864	4,827	3,093,699
Sud	Les Cayes	1,079	2,794	627,311
Sud-Est	Jacmel	781	2,023	449,585
TOTAL		10,695	27,700	7,929,048

Demography

Population (2005): 8,528,000.
Density (2005): persons per sq mi 797.4, persons per sq km 307.9.
Urban-rural (2003): urban 37.5%; rural 62.5%.
Sex distribution (2003): male 48.35%; female 51.65%.
Age breakdown (2003): under 15, 42.7%; 15–29, 29.3%; 30–44, 14.2%; 45–59, 8.2%; 60–74, 4.5%; 75 and over, 1.1%.
Population projection[4]: (2010) 9,145,000; (2020) 10,328,000.
Ethnic composition (2000): black 94.2%; mulatto 5.4%; other 0.4%.
Religious affiliation (2000): Roman Catholic 71%[4]; Protestant 17%; independent Christian 5%; other 7%.
Major cities (1999): Port-au-Prince 990,558 (metropolitan area [2003] 1,977,036); Carrefour 336,222[5]; Delmas 284,079[5]; Cap-Haïtien 113,555; Pétion-Ville (1997) 76,155[5].

Vital statistics

Birth rate per 1,000 population (2004): 36.7 (world avg. 21.1).
Death rate per 1,000 population (2004): 12.5 (world avg. 9.0).
Natural increase rate per 1,000 population (2004): 24.2 (world avg. 12.1).
Total fertility rate (avg. births per childbearing woman; 2004): 5.1.
Life expectancy at birth (2004): male 51.3 years; female 54.0 years.
Adult population (ages 15–49) *living with HIV* (2004[6]): 5.6% (world avg. 1.1%).

National economy

Budget (2003–04)[7]. Revenue: G 12,473,800,000 (customs duties 28.3%; sales tax 27.7%; individual taxes on income and profits 22.3%). Expenditures: G 17,164,900,000 (current expenditure 78.7%, of which wages 24.1%, transfers 6.0%, interest on public debt 5.0%; capital expenditure 21.3%).
Production (metric tons except as noted). Agriculture, forestry, fishing (2004): sugarcane 1,080,000, cassava (manioc) 330,000, bananas 290,000, plantains 280,000, mangoes 260,000, yams 197,000, corn (maize) 180,000, sweet potatoes 170,000, rice 102,000, coffee 28,000, sisal 5,500, cacao 4,400; livestock (number of live animals) 1,900,000 goats, 1,456,000 cattle, 1,000,000 pigs, 500,000 horses; roundwood 2,231,557 cu m; fish catch (2003) 5,000. Mining and quarrying (2002): sand 2,000,000 cu m. Manufacturing (value added in G '000,000; 2002[8]): food and beverages 484.5; textiles, wearing apparel, and footwear 195.7; chemical and rubber products 63.8; tobacco products 38.2. Energy production (consumption): electricity (kW-hr; 2002) 632,000,000 (632,000,000); petroleum products (metric tons; 2002) none (529,000).
Public debt (external, outstanding; 2003–04): U.S.$1,263,900,000.
Gross national product (at current market prices; 2004): U.S.$3,380,000,000 (U.S.$390 per capita).

Structure of gross domestic product and labour force					
	2002–03			1990	
	in value G '000,000[8]	% of total value		labour force[9]	% of labour force[9]
Agriculture, forestry	3,336.8	25.7		1,535,444	57.3
Mining	14.1	0.1		24,012	0.9
Manufacturing	1,003.5	7.7		151,387	5.6
Construction	969.4	7.5		28,001	1.0
Public utilities	62.9	0.5		2,577	0.1
Transp. and commun.	774.7	6.0		20,691	0.8
Trade, restaurants	3,509.1	27.0		352,970	13.2
Finance, real estate	1,019.6	7.8		5,057	0.2
Services	1,380.5	10.6		155,347	5.8
Pub. admin., defense }					
Other	921.0[10]	7.1[10]		403,654[11]	15.1[11]
TOTAL	12,991.6	100.0		2,679,140	100.0

Population economically active (2002): total *c.* 4,100,000; activity rate of total population *c.* 55% (participation rates: ages 15–64 [1990] 64.8%; female [1996] 43.0%; unemployed unofficially [2003] *c.* 70%).

Price and earnings indexes (2000 = 100)							
	1998	1999	2000	2001	2002	2003	2004
Consumer price index	80.9	87.9	100.0	114.2	125.4	174.7	214.5
Daily earnings index[12]	100.0	100.0	100.0	100.0	100.0	194.4	194.4

Household income and expenditure. Average household size (2000)[13] 4.7; expenditure (1996)[14]: food, beverages, and tobacco 49.4%, housing and energy 9.1%, transportation 8.7%, clothing and footwear 8.5%.
Tourism: receipts from visitors (2003) U.S.$93,000,000; expenditures by nationals abroad (1998) U.S.$37,000,000.
Land use as % of total land area (2000): in temporary crops 28.3%, in permanent crops 11.6%, in pasture 17.8%; overall forest area 3.2%.

Foreign trade[15]

Balance of trade (current prices)					
	1998	1999	2000	2001	2002	2003
U.S.$'000,000	−527.3	−674.2	−755.0	−750.2	−706.0	−783.6
% of total	47.2%	49.5%	53.2%	58.8%	56.3%	54.1%

Imports (2003): U.S.$1,115,800,000 (food and live animals 24.0%, basic manufactures 22.4%, petroleum and derivatives 17.6%, machinery and transport equipment 14.8%, chemicals and chemical products 4.7%). *Major import sources* (2004): U.S. 52.9%; Dominican Republic 6.0%; Japan 2.9%.
Exports (2003): U.S.$333,160,000 (reexports to U.S. 83.5%, of which clothing and apparel 82.1%; cacao 1.8%; essential oils 1.5%; mangoes 1.4%; coffee 1.1%). *Major export destinations* (2004): U.S. 81.8%; Dominican Republic 7.2%; Canada 4.2%.

Transport and communications

Transport. Railroad: none. Roads (1999): total length 2,585 mi, 4,160 km (paved 24%). Vehicles (1996): passenger cars 32,000; trucks and buses 21,000. Air transport (2000)[16]: passenger arrivals and departures 924,000; cargo unloaded and loaded 15,300 metric tons; airports (1997) with scheduled flights 2.

Communications				units per 1,000
Medium	date	unit	number	persons
Daily newspapers	2001	circulation	24,200	3.0
Radio	2001	receivers	145,000	18
Television	2001	receivers	48,300	6.0
Telephones	2004	main lines	140,000	17
Cellular telephones	2004	subscribers	400,000	47
Internet	2003	users	149,200	18

Education and health

Educational attainment (2000)[10]. Percentage of population age 25 and over having: no formal schooling or unknown 46.1%; incomplete primary education 28.9%; primary 5.3%; incomplete secondary 15.6%; secondary 1.8%; higher 2.3%. *Literacy* (2003): total population age 15 and over literate (52.9%); males literate (54.8%); females literate (51.2%).

Education (1994–95)				student/
	schools	teachers	students	teacher ratio
Primary (age 6–12)	10,071	30,205	1,110,398	36.8
Secondary (age 13–18) }	1,038	15,275	195,418	12.8
Voc., teacher tr.				
Higher[17, 18]	2	899	12,348	13.7

Health: physicians (1999) 1,910 (1 per 4,000 persons); hospital beds (2000) 6,431 (1 per 1,234 persons); infant mortality rate per 1,000 live births (2004) 75.2.
Food (2002): daily per capita caloric intake 2,086 (vegetable products 93%, animal products 7%); 92% of FAO recommended minimum requirement.

Military

Total active duty personnel: [19, 20].

[1]Stopped functioning effectively in early 2004. [2]Roman Catholicism has special recognition per concordat with the Vatican; voodoo became officially sanctioned per governmental decree of April 2003. [2]Preliminary. [3]Formally created from eastern Grand'Anse in late 2003. [4]About 80% of all Roman Catholics also practice voodoo. [5]Within Port-au-Prince metropolitan area. [6]Beginning of year. [7]Does not include projects financed with loans and grants. [8]At prices of 1986–87. [9]The 2002 labour force equaled *c.* 4,100,000, of which formal sector equaled *c.* 110,000 (including 35,000 government employees). [10]Import duties less imputed bank service charges. [11]Includes 63,975 not adequately defined and 339,679 officially unemployed. [12]Standard minimum wage rate. [13]Based on a national sample survey of 44,573 people in 9,595 households. [14]Weights of consumer price index components. [15]Includes reexports. [16]Port-au-Prince Airport only. [17]Port-au-Prince universities only. [18]2000–01. [19]The Haitian army was disbanded in 1995. The national police force had 5,000 personnel in mid-2005. [20]UN peacekeeping troops (August 2005) 6,264.

Internet resources for further information:
• Embassy of Haiti (Washington, D.C.) http://www.haiti.org
• Banque de la République d'Haïti http://www.brh.net

Honduras

Official name: República de Honduras (Republic of Honduras).
Form of government: multiparty republic with one legislative house (National Congress [128]).
Head of state and government: President.
Capital: Tegucigalpa.
Official language: Spanish.
Official religion: none.
Monetary unit: 1 Honduran lempira (L) = 100 centavos; valuation (Sept. 1, 2005) 1 U.S.$ = L 18.86; 1 £ = L 34.73.

Area and population

Departments	Administrative centres	area sq mi	area sq km	population 2001 census
Atlántida	La Ceiba	1,688	4,372	344,099
Choluteca	Choluteca	1,515	3,923	390,805
Colón	Trujillo	1,683	4,360	246,708
Comayagua	Comayagua	3,185	8,249	352,881
Copán	Santa Rosa de Copán	1,978	5,124	288,766
Cortés	San Pedro Sula	1,252	3,242	1,202,510
El Paraíso	Yuscarán	2,892	7,489	350,054
Francisco Morazán	Tegucigalpa	3,328	8,619	1,180,676
Gracias a Dios	Puerto Lempira	6,563	16,997	67,384
Intibucá	La Esperanza	1,206	3,123	179,862
Islas de la Bahía	Roatán	91	236	38,073
La Paz	La Paz	975	2,525	156,560
Lempira	Gracias	1,632	4,228	250,067
Ocotepeque	Nueva Ocotepeque	629	1,630	108,029
Olancho	Juticalpa	9,230	23,905	419,561
Santa Bárbara	Santa Bárbara	1,940	5,024	342,054
Valle	Nacaome	643	1,665	151,841
Yoro	Yoro	3,004	7,781	465,414
TOTAL		43,433[1]	112,492	6,535,344[2]

Demography

Population (2005): 7,187,000.
Density (2005): persons per sq mi 165.5, persons per sq km 63.9.
Urban-rural (2004): urban 48.1%; rural 51.9%.
Sex distribution (2001): male 49.44%; female 50.56%.
Age breakdown (2002): under 15, 41.9%; 15–29, 29.1%; 30–44, 15.3%; 45–59, 8.3%; 60–74, 4.1%; 75 and over, 1.3%.
Population projection: (2010) 7,965,000; (2020) 9,385,000.
Doubling time: 28 years.
Ethnic composition (2000): mestizo 86.6%; Amerindian 5.5%; black (including Black Carib) 4.3%; white 2.3%; other 1.3%.
Religious affiliation (1995): Roman Catholic 83.2%; Protestant 9.1% (significantly Pentecostal); other 7.7%.
Major cities (2004): Tegucigalpa 879,200; San Pedro Sula 538,100; Choloma 162,700; La Ceiba 144,000; El Progreso 104,000.

Vital statistics

Birth rate per 1,000 population (2004): 29.8 (world avg. 21.1).
Death rate per 1,000 population (2004): 5.2 (world avg. 9.0).
Natural increase rate per 1,000 population (2004): 24.6 (world avg. 12.1).
Total fertility rate (avg. births per childbearing woman; 2004): 3.8.
Life expectancy at birth (2004): male 67.7 years; female 71.0 years.
Major causes of death (percent of total; 2000–02): diseases of the circulatory system 23.6%; accidents and violence 21.3%; malignant neoplasms (cancers) 12.2%; diseases of the respiratory system 10.9%.

National economy

Budget (2003). Revenue: L 23,627,800,000 (tax revenue 91.7%, of which indirect taxes 67.7%, direct taxes 24.0%; nontax revenue 8.3%). Expenditures: L 30,116,600,000 (current expenditure 78.0%; capital expenditure 22.0%).
Public debt (external, outstanding; 2004): U.S.$5,081,000,000.
Production (metric tons except as noted). Agriculture, forestry, fishing (2004): sugarcane 5,362,753, oil palm fruit 1,135,000, bananas 965,066, corn (maize) 514,152, plantains 260,000, cantaloupes 198,000, coffee 178,140, oranges 167,226, pineapples 61,814; livestock (number of live animals) 1,800,000 cattle, 478,000 pigs, 18,700,000 chickens; roundwood 9,500,212 cu m; fish catch (2003) 10,800. Mining and quarrying (2003): gypsum 60,000; zinc (metal content) 46,500; silver 48,000 kg; gold 5,000 kg. Manufacturing (value added in L '000,000; 1996): food products 1,937; wearing apparel 1,266[3]; beverages 700; nonmetallic mineral products 504; wood products 326. Energy production (consumption): electricity (kW-hr; 2004) 5,220,000,000 (5,220,000,000); coal (metric tons; 2002) none (141,000); crude petroleum (barrels) none (n.a.); petroleum products (metric tons; 2002) none (1,636,000); natural gas (cu m) none (n.a.).
Tourism (2003): receipts from visitors U.S.$337,000,000; expenditures by nationals abroad U.S.$138,000,000.
Population economically active (2001): total 2,438,000; activity rate of total population 38.5% (participation rates: ages 15–64, 64.5%; female 35.7%; unemployed [2004] unofficially 28.5%).

Price index (2000 = 100)

	1998	1999	2000	2001	2002	2003	2004
Consumer price index	80.7	90.0	100.0	109.6	118.0	127.1	137.5

Gross national product (at current market prices; 2004): U.S.$7,321,000,000 (U.S.$1,030 per capita).

Structure of gross domestic product and labour force

	2004 in value L '000,000	2004 % of total value	2004 labour force	2004 % of labour force
Agriculture	16,101	11.7	851,100	34.9
Mining	2,127	1.5	6,400	0.3
Manufacturing	24,765	18.1	385,500	15.8
Construction	5,143	3.7	143,500	5.9
Public utilities	5,860	4.3	10,000	0.4
Transp. and commun.	7,229	5.3	82,800	3.4
Trade, hotels	15,176	11.1	514,500	21.1
Finance, real estate	20,234	14.8	69,500	2.8
Public admin., defense	9,070	6.6	375,600	15.4
Services	15,301	11.2		
Other	16,082[4]	11.7[4]	...	...
TOTAL	137,089[1]	100.0	2,439,000[1, 5]	100.0[5]

Household income and expenditure (2003). Average household size 5.0; average annual income per household L 85,020 (U.S.$4,902); sources of income: wages and salaries 40%, self-employment 35%, transfer payments 8%, other 17%; expenditure: n.a.
Land use as % of total land area (2000): in temporary crops 9.5%, in permanent crops 3.2%, in pasture 13.5%; overall forest area 48.1%.

Foreign trade[6]

Balance of trade (current prices)

	1999	2000	2001	2002	2003	2004
U.S.$'000,000	−1,292	−1,233	−1,395	−1,442	−1,675	−2,098
% of total	34.7%	30.0%	33.7%	34.6%	37.7%	39.9%

Imports (2004): U.S.$3,921,800,000 (machinery and electrical equipment 22.0%, mineral fuels and lubricants 16.2%, food products and live animals 15.0%, chemicals and chemical products 12.9%, fabricated metal products 7.4%, transportation equipment 6.2%). *Major import sources:* U.S. 34.6%; Guatemala 7.7%; El Salvador 5.0%; Costa Rica 4.9%; Mexico 4.7%.
Exports (2004): U.S.$1,533,900,000 (coffee 16.4%, bananas 13.6%, shrimp 10.5%, gold 4.8%, African palm oil 3.5%, soaps and detergents 3.0%). *Major export destinations:* U.S. 41.5%; El Salvador 10.9%; Guatemala 7.3%; Germany 5.9%; Belgium 4.2%.

Transport and communications

Transport. Railroads (2004): serviceable lines 158 mi (255 km); most tracks are out of use but not dismantled. Roads (2004): total length 8,525 mi, 13,720 km (paved 22%). Vehicles (2002): passenger cars 277,960; trucks and buses 70,950. Air transport (1995)[7]: passenger-km 341,000,000; metric ton-km cargo 33,000,000; airports (1996) with scheduled flights 8.

Communications

Medium	date	unit	number	units per 1,000 persons
Daily newspapers	2001	circulation	359,200	55
Radio	2001	receivers	2,697,000	413
Television	2002	receivers	809,000	119
Telephones	2004	main lines	371,400	53
Cellular telephones	2004	subscribers	707,201	101
Personal computers	2004	units	110,000	15
Internet	2004	users	203,958	29

Education and health

Educational attainment (1988). Percentage of population age 10 and over having: no formal schooling 33.4%; primary education 50.1%; secondary education 13.4%; higher 3.1%. *Literacy* (2003): total population age 15 and over literate 76.2%; males literate 76.1%; females literate 76.3%.

Education (2003)

	schools	teachers	students	student/ teacher ratio
Primary (age 6–14)	11,115	42,788	1,589,074	37.1
Secondary (age 15–17) Voc., teacher tr.	871	16,435	151,790	9.2
Higher[8]	21	5,997	110,996	18.5

Health: physicians (2000) 5,287 (1 per 1,201 persons); hospital beds (2003) 5,069 (1 per 1,353 persons); infant mortality rate (2004) 27.1.
Food (2002): daily per capita caloric intake 2,356 (vegetable products 86%, animal products 14%); 104% of FAO recommended minimum.

Military

Total active duty personnel (2004): 12,000 (army 69.2%, navy 11.7%, air force 19.1%); U.S. troops (end of December 2004) 446. *Military expenditure as percentage of GDP* (2003): 0.4%; per capita expenditure U.S.$8.

---

[1]Detail does not add to total given because of rounding. [2]Census population adjusted for underenumeration; unadjusted census figure is 6,071,200. [3]Important product of the maquiladora sector; garment assembly employed 110,000 in 2001. [4]Indirect taxes less subsidies. [5]Does not include unemployed. [6]Import figures are f.o.b. in balance of trade and c.i.f. in commodities and trading partners. [7]Sol Air, Honduras' first airline in nearly a decade, began operations in mid-2002. [8]2004.

Internet resources for further information:
• Banco Central de Honduras http://www.bch.hn
• Instituto Nacional de Estadística http://www.ine-hn.org

Hong Kong

Official name: Xianggang Tebie Xingzhengqu (Chinese); Hong Kong Special Administrative Region (English).
Political status: special administrative region of China with one legislative house (Legislative Council [60[1]]).
Chief of state: President of China.
Head of government: Chief Executive.
Government offices: Central & Western District (within the historic capital area of Victoria), Hong Kong Island.
Official languages: Chinese; English.
Official religion: none.
Monetary unit: 1 Hong Kong dollar (HK$) = 100 cents; valuation (Sept. 1, 2005) 1 U.S.$ = HK$7.77; 1 £ = HK$14.30.

Area and population	area		population
Geographic areas	sq mi	sq km	2001 census
Hong Kong Island	31	81	1,335,469
Kowloon	18	47	2,023,979
New Territories (mainland)	288	747	3,256,379
New Territories (islands[2])	88	227	86,667
Marine	—	—	5,895
TOTAL	425	1,102	6,708,389

Demography

Population (2005): 6,926,000.
Density (2005): persons per sq mi 16,296, persons per sq km 6,285.
Urban-rural (2003): urban 100.0%.
Sex distribution (2004): male 48.17%; female 51.83%.
Age breakdown (2004): under 15, 15.1%; 15–29, 20.1%; 30–44, 28.0%; 45–59, 21.6%; 60–74, 10.3%; 75 and over, 4.9%.
Population projection: (2010) 7,188,000; (2020) 7,802,000.
Ethnic composition (2003): Chinese 95%; other 5%.
Religious affiliation (1994): Buddhist and Taoist 73.8%; Christian 8.4%, of which Protestant 4.3%, Roman Catholic 4.1%; New Religionist 3.2%; Muslim 0.8%; Hindu 0.2%; nonreligious/atheist 13.5%; other 0.1%.

Vital statistics

Birth rate per 1,000 population (2004): 7.0 (world avg. 21.1).
Death rate per 1,000 population (2004): 5.3 (world avg. 9.0).
Natural increase rate per 1,000 population (2004): 1.7 (world avg. 12.1).
Total fertility rate (avg. births per childbearing woman; 2004): 0.9.
Marriage rate per 1,000 population (2004): 6.0.
Life expectancy at birth (2004): male 78.6 years; female 84.6 years.
Major causes of death per 100,000 population (2003): malignant neoplasms (cancers) 175.0; diseases of the circulatory system 126.7; diseases of the respiratory system 87.1; accidents and violence 28.6.

National economy

Budget (2003–04). Revenue: HK$203,837,000,000 (earnings and profits taxes 38.3%; indirect taxes 22.6%, of which property taxes 5.5%; capital revenue 15.5%; other 23.6%). Expenditures: HK$279,183,000,000 (education 20.7%; health 12.4%; social welfare 12.2%; housing 10.0%; police 7.6%; economic services 5.6%).
Gross national product (2004): U.S.$169,200,000,000 (U.S.$24,600 per capita).

Structure of gross domestic product and labour force				
	2002		2003	
	in value HK$'000,000[3]	% of total value[3]	labour force	% of labour force
Agriculture	997	0.1	7,800	0.2
Mining	179	—	500	—
Manufacturing	59,107	4.5	294,800	8.4
Construction	60,677	4.6	328,400	9.4
Public utilities	41,030	3.1	16,500	0.5
Transp. and commun.	133,498	10.1	370,500	10.6
Trade	341,835	25.8	1,081,700	30.9
Finance, insurance, and real estate	292,640	22.1	495,900	14.1
Pub. admin., defense, and services	264,266	20.0	881,200	25.2
Other	129,531[4]	9.8[4]	23,400[5]	0.7[5]
TOTAL	1,323,650[6]	100.0[6]	3,500,900[6]	100.0

Production (metric tons except as noted). Agriculture, forestry, fishing (2003): vegetables 27,700, fruits 940, field crops 380, eggs 808,000 units; livestock (number of live animals) 390,900 pigs, 10,154,000 chickens; roundwood, n.a.; fish catch 141,670. Manufacturing (value added in HK$'000,000; 2003): publishing and printed materials 11,384; textiles 6,038; food 5,136; wearing apparel 4,625; electronic parts and components 3,315; transport equipment 2,918; machinery and equipment 2,847; chemicals and chemical products 1,955. Construction (2004)[7]: residential 953,000 sq m; nonresidential 685,000 sq m. Energy production (consumption): electricity (kW-hr; 2002) 34,312,000,000 (42,328,000,000); hard coal (metric tons; 2002) none (8,718,000); petroleum products (metric tons; 2002) none (4,124,000).
Tourism: receipts (2003) U.S.$7,106,000,000; expenditures (2001) U.S.$12,494,-000,000.

Population economically active (2003): total 3,500,900; activity rate of total population 51.7% (participation rates: 15–64, 70.2%; female 43.9%; unemployed [November 2003–November 2004] 7.0%).

Price index (2000 = 100)							
	1998	1999	2000	2001	2002	2003	2004
Consumer price index	108.2	103.9	100.0	98.4	95.4	92.9	92.5

Household income and expenditure. Average household size (2004) 3.1; median annual income per household (2001) HK$224,500 (U.S.$28,800); sources of income: n.a.; expenditure (2001): housing and energy 22.2%, clothing and footwear 15.2%, food and nonalcoholic beverages 13.5%, household furnishings 12.6%, transportation 11.0%.
Land use as % of total land area (2000): in temporary and permanent crops 5.4%, in pasture 29.3%[8]; overall forest area 18.0%.

Foreign trade[9]

Balance of trade (current prices)						
	1999	2000	2001	2002	2003	2004
HK$'000,000	–43,718	–85,273	–87,208	–58,902	–63,400	–92,000
% of total	1.6%	2.6%	2.9%	1.9%	1.8%	2.2%

Imports (2004): HK$2,111,100,000,000 (consumer goods 29.9%, capital goods 26.8%, foodstuffs 2.8%, mineral fuels and lubricants 2.3%). *Major import sources:* China 43.5%; Japan 12.1%; Taiwan 7.3%; U.S. 5.3%; Singapore 5.3%.
Exports (2004): HK$2,019,100,000,000 (reexports 93.8%, of which consumer goods 33.6%, capital goods 26.6%; domestic exports 6.2%, of which clothing accessories and apparel 3.1%). *Major export destinations*[10]: China 44.0%; U.S. 16.9%; Japan 5.3%; U.K. 3.3%; Germany 3.1%.

Transport and communications

Transport. Railroads (2003): route length 40 mi, 64 km[11]; (2002) passenger-km 4,540,000,000[12]; metric ton-km cargo, n.a. Roads (2003): total length 1,196 mi, 1,924 km (paved 100%). Vehicles (2003): passenger cars 357,000; trucks and buses 137,000. Air transport (2004)[13]: passenger-km 63,238,000,000; metric ton-km cargo 7,094,000,000; airports (2003) with scheduled flights 1.

Communications				units per 1,000 persons
Medium	date	unit	number	
Daily newspapers	2000	circulation	5,280,000	792
Radio	2000	receivers	4,560,000	684
Television	2003	receivers	3,467,000	507
Telephones	2004	main lines	3,779,700	531
Cellular telephones	2004	subscribers	8,148,700	1,145
Personal computers	2004	units	4,187,000	589
Internet	2004	users	3,479,700	489

Education and health

Educational attainment (2004). Percentage of population age 15 and over having: no formal schooling 6.8%; primary education 19.7%; secondary 46.7%; matriculation 5.2%; nondegree higher 7.4%; higher degree 14.1%.
Literacy (2000): total population age 15 and over literate 93.5%; males literate 96.5%; females literate 90.2%.

Education (2004–05)	schools	teachers	students	student/teacher ratio
Primary (age 6–11)	759	23,805	447,137	19.1
Secondary (age 12–18)	519	26,865	474,054	18.0
Vocational	1	1,021	59,270	...
Higher	24	5,515	101,190	18.3

Health (2003): physicians 10,884[14] (1 per 625 persons); hospital beds 35,378 (1 per 192 persons); infant mortality rate per 1,000 live births (2004) 2.5.
Food (2001): daily per capita caloric intake 3,104 (vegetable products 68%, animal products 32%); 136% of FAO recommended minimum requirement.

Military

Total active duty personnel (2003): 4,000 troops of Chinese military (including elements of army, navy, and air force) intervene in local matters only at the request of the Hong Kong government; Hong Kong residents are exempted from military service.

[1]Thirty seats are directly elected by ordinary voters, and the remaining 30 are elected by special interest groups. [2]Primarily Lantau. [3]At constant prices of 2000. [4]Includes ownership of premises, taxes on production, and imports less adjustment for financial intermediation services. [5]Unemployed not previously employed. [6]Detail does not add to total given because of rounding. [7]Usable floor area only. [8]Represents grassland that may not be grazed. [9]Imports are c.i.f., exports f.o.b. [10]Includes reexports and domestic exports. [11]Combined length of East Rail and West Rail; West Rail was inaugurated in December 2003. [12]East Rail only. [13]Cathay Pacific and Dragonair only. [14]Registered personnel; all may not be present and working in the country.

Internet resources for further information:
• **Census and Statistics Department** http://www.info.gov.hk/censtatd

Hungary

Official name: Magyar Köztársaság
(Republic of Hungary).
Form of government: unitary multi-
party republic with one legislative
house (National Assembly [386]).
Chief of state: President.
Head of government: Prime Minister.
Capital: Budapest.
Official language: Hungarian.
Official religion: none.
Monetary unit: 1 forint (Ft) = 100
filler; valuation (Sept. 1, 2005)
1 U.S.$ = Ft 194.15;
1 £ = Ft 357.47.

Area and population		area		population
				2004[1]
Counties	Capitals	sq mi	sq km	estimate
Bács-Kiskun	Kecskemét	3,261	8,445	542,000
Baranya	Pécs	1,710	4,430	402,000
Békés	Békéscsaba	2,174	5,631	393,000
Borsod-Abaúj-Zemplén	Miskolc	2,798	7,247	738,000
Csongrád	Szeged	1,646	4,263	426,000
Fejér	Székesfehérvár	1,683	4,359	428,000
Győr-Moson-Sopron	Győr	1,579	4,089	440,000
Hajdú-Bihar	Debrecen	2,398	6,211	550,000
Heves	Eger	1,404	3,637	324,000
Jász-Nagykun-Szolnok	Szolnok	2,155	5,582	413,000
Komárom-Esztergom	Tatabánya	875	2,265	316,000
Nógrád	Salgótarján	982	2,544	218,000
Pest	Budapest[2]	2,468	6,393	1,123,000
Somogy	Kaposvár	2,331	6,036	334,000
Szabolcs-Szatmár-Bereg	Nyíregyháza	2,292	5,937	583,000
Tolna	Szekszárd	1,430	3,703	247,000
Vas	Szombathely	1,288	3,336	267,000
Veszprém	Veszprém	1,781	4,613	368,000
Zala	Zalaegerszeg	1,461	3,784	297,000
Capital city				
Budapest[2]		203	525	1,708,000
TOTAL		35,919	93,030	10,117,000

Demography

Population (2005): 10,078,000.
Density (2005): persons per sq mi 280.6, persons per sq km 108.3.
Urban-rural (2004): urban 64.8%; rural 35.2%.
Sex distribution (2005): male 47.47%; female 52.53%.
Age breakdown (2004): under 15, 15.9%; 15–29, 21.9%; 30–44, 19.8%; 45–59, 21.4%; 60–74, 14.5%; 75 and over, 6.5%.
Population projection: (2010) 9,949,000; (2020) 9,698,000.
Ethnic composition (2000): Hungarian 84.4%; Rom (Gypsy) 5.3%; Ruthenian 2.9%; German 2.4%; Romanian 1.0%; Slovak 0.9%; Jewish 0.6%; other 2.5%.
Religious affiliation (1998): Roman Catholic 57.8%; Reformed 17.7%; Lutheran 3.9%; Jewish 0.2%; nonreligious 18.5%; other/unknown 1.9%.
Major cities (2004[1]): Budapest 1,708,000; Debrecen 205,000; Miskolc 178,000; Szeged 163,000; Pécs 158,000; Győr 129,000.

Vital statistics

Birth rate per 1,000 population (2004): 9.4 (world avg. 21.1); (2002) legitimate 68.7%; illegitimate 31.3%.
Death rate per 1,000 population (2004): 13.1 (world avg. 9.0).
Natural increase rate per 1,000 population (2004): –3.7 (world avg. 12.1).
Total fertility rate (avg. births per childbearing woman; 2004): 1.3.
Marriage rate per 1,000 population (2004): 4.3.
Life expectancy at birth (2004): male 68.6 years; female 76.9 years.
Major causes of death per 100,000 population (2003): heart diseases *c.* 392; malignant neoplasms (cancers) *c.* 329; cerebrovascular diseases *c.* 183; arteriosclerosis *c.* 68; accidents *c.* 68; liver diseases *c.* 62.

National economy

Budget (2002). Revenue: Ft 6,338,100,000,000 (social contributions 34.1%, taxes on goods and services 32.1%, personal income taxes 15.1%). Expenditures: Ft 7,781,600,000,000 (social protection 30.2%, public debt 8.8%, transport 8.1%, health 5.8%, education 5.2%, defense 3.0%).
Production (metric tons except as noted). Agriculture, forestry, fishing (2004): corn (maize) 8,317,000, wheat 6,020,000, sugar beets 3,130,000, barley 1,423,000, sunflower seeds 1,198,000, apples 680,000, grapes 650,000; live-stock (number of live animals) 4,913,000 pigs, 1,296,000 sheep, 739,000 cattle; roundwood 5,660,000 cu m; fish catch (2003) 18,406. Mining and quarrying (2002): bauxite 720,000. Manufacturing (value added in U.S.$'000,000; 2000): electrical machinery and apparatus 1,309; motor vehicles and parts 1,105; food products 1,001; chemicals and chemical products 870; nonelectrical machinery and apparatus 711; fabricated metal products 448. Energy production (consumption): electricity (kW-hr; 2003) 34,282,000,000 (43,188,-000,000); hard coal (metric tons; 2003) 672,000 ([2002] 836,000); lignite (metric tons; 2003) 11,984,000 (14,619,000); crude petroleum (barrels; 2003) 7,586,000 ([2002] 40,400,000); petroleum products (metric tons; 2002) 6,190,000 (6,020,000); natural gas (cu m; 2003) 3,087,000,000 (14,558,000,000).
Public debt (external, outstanding; 2003): U.S.$14,751,000,000.
Tourism (U.S.$'000,000; 2003): receipts 3,440; expenditures 2,027.
Population economically active (2003): total 4,166,400; activity rate of total population 41.1% (participation rates: ages 15–64, 60.6%; female 45.6%; unemployed [October 2003–September 2004] 6.0%).

Price and earnings indexes (2000 = 100)							
	1998	1999	2000	2001	2002	2003	2004
Consumer price index	82.8	91.1	100.0	109.2	115.0	120.3	128.5
Annual earnings index	79.1	88.7	100.0	113.2	130.2	146.7	159.1

Gross national product (2004): U.S.$83,315,000,000 (U.S.$8,270 per capita).

Structure of gross domestic product and labour force				
	2003			
	in value Ft '000,000	% of total value	labour force	% of labour force
Agriculture, forestry	531,100	2.9	215,200	5.2
Mining	37,200	0.2	12,800	0.3
Manufacturing	3,595,700	19.4	925,500	22.2
Construction	844,800	4.5	299,400	7.2
Public utilities	478,200	2.6	68,200	1.6
Transp. and commun.	1,293,500	7.0	303,200	7.3
Trade, restaurants	2,110,400	11.4	692,500	16.6
Finance, real estate	3,394,900	18.3	338,700	8.1
Public administration, defense	1,509,200	8.1	295,400	7.1
Services	2,381,900	12.8	771,000	18.5
Other	2,391,500[3]	12.9[3]	244,500[4]	5.9[4]
TOTAL	18,568,300[5]	100.0[5]	4,166,400	100.0

Household income and expenditure. Average household size (2002) 2.5; income per household[6] (2001) Ft 2,898,000 (U.S.$10,300); sources of income (2001): wages 48.3%, transfers 25.7%, self-employment 16.3%; expenditure (2002): food products 28.8%, housing and energy 17.6%, transportation and communications 16.5%, recreation 7.0%.
Land use as % of total land area (2000): in temporary crops 50.0%, in permanent crops 2.2%, in pasture 11.4%; overall forest area 19.9%.

Foreign trade[7]

Balance of trade (current prices)						
	1999	2000	2001	2002	2003	2004
Ft '000,000,000	–707	–1,121	–917	–830	–1,134	–970
% of total	5.6%	6.6%	4.5%	4.5%	5.6%	4.2%

Imports (2002): Ft 9,704,000,000,000 (electrical machinery 17.0%, nonelectrical machinery 14.6%, road vehicles 8.1%, mineral fuels 7.0%, telecommunications equipment 6.2%). *Major import sources* (2004): Germany 28.8%; Austria 8.2%; Russia 5.7%; Italy 5.4%; The Netherlands 4.9%.
Exports (2002): Ft 8,874,000,000,000 (telecommunications equipment 15.5%, electrical machinery 11.2%, power-generating machinery 10.9%, road vehicles 8.7%, office machines and computers 7.1%). *Major export destinations* (2004): Germany 31.0%; Austria 6.7%; France 5.6%; Italy 5.6%; U.K. 5.0%.

Transport and communications

Transport. Railroads (2003): route length 7,898 km; passenger-km (2004) 10,544,000,000; metric ton-km cargo 8,878,000,000. Roads (2002): total length 159,568 km (paved 44%). Vehicles (2003): passenger cars 2,777,000; trucks and buses 395,000. Air transport (2004)[8]: passenger-km 4,270,000,000; metric ton-km cargo 23,400,000; airports with scheduled flights 1.

Communications				units per 1,000
Medium	date	unit	number	persons
Daily newspapers	2004	circulation	1,820,000	181
Radio	2000	receivers	7,050,000	690
Television	2000	receivers	4,460,000	437
Telephones	2004	main lines	3,577,300	364
Cellular telephones	2004	subscribers	8,727,200	888
Personal computers	2004	units	1,476,000	150
Internet	2004	users	2,700,000	275

Education and health

Educational attainment (2002). Population age 25–64 having: no formal schooling through lower-secondary education 29%; upper secondary/higher vocational 57%; university 14%.

Education (2004–05)				student/
	schools	teachers	students	teacher ratio
Primary (age 6–13)	3,690	87,116	890,600	10.2
Secondary (age 14–17)	1,653	38,572	529,000	13.7
Vocational	642	9,690	135,300	14.0
Higher	69	23,787	421,500	17.7

Health (2004): physicians 38,877 (1 per 260 persons); hospital beds 79,610 (1 per 127 persons); infant mortality rate per 1,000 live births 6.6.
Food (2002): daily per capita caloric intake 3,483 (vegetable products 67%, animal products 33%); 132% of FAO recommended minimum requirement.

Military

Total active duty personnel (2004): 32,300 (army 74.1%, air force 23.2%, headquarters staff 2.6%). *Military expenditure as percentage of GDP* (2003): 1.8%; per capita expenditure U.S.$150.

[1]January 1. [2]Budapest acts as the capital of Pest county even though it is administratively not part of Pest county. [3]Net taxes less imputed bank service charges. [4]Unemployed. [5]Detail does not add to total given because of rounding. [6]Adjusted disposable income including government transfers. [7]Imports c.i.f.; exports f.o.b. [8]Malév Hungarian Airlines only.

Internet resources for further information:
• Hungarian Central Statistical Office http://portal.ksh.hu

Iceland

Official name: Lýdhveldidh Ísland (Republic of Iceland).
Form of government: unitary multiparty republic with one legislative house (Althingi [63]).
Chief of state: President.
Head of government: Prime Minister.
Capital: Reykjavík.
Official language: Icelandic.
Official religion: Evangelical Lutheran.
Monetary unit: 1 króna (ISK) = 100 aurar; valuation (Sept. 1, 2005) 1 U.S.\$ = ISK 61.21; 1 £ = ISK 112.69.

Area and population

Constituencies[1]	Principal centres	area sq mi	area sq km	population 2005[2] estimate
Austurland	Egilsstadhir	8,773	22,721	12,430
Höfudhborgarsvædhi[3]	Reykjavík	410	1,062	184,244
Nordhurland eystra	Akureyri	8,482	21,968	26,893
Nordhurland vestra	Saudhárkrókur	4,918	12,737	8,988
Sudhurland	Selfoss	9,469	24,526	21,790
Sudhurnes	Keflavík	320	829	17,110
Vestfirdhir	Ísafjördhur	3,633	9,409	7,700
Vesturland	Borgarnes	3,689	9,554	14,422
Unallocated area	—	47	122	0
TOTAL		39,741	102,928	293,577

Demography

Population (2005): 295,000.
Density (2005)[4]: persons per sq mi 32.1, persons per sq km 12.4.
Urban-rural (2005[2]): urban 94.0%; rural 6.0%.
Sex distribution (2005[2]): male 50.13%; female 49.87%.
Age breakdown (2005[2]): under 15, 22.3%; 15–29, 21.8%; 30–44, 21.5%; 45–59, 18.6%; 60–74, 10.2%; 75 and over, 5.6%.
Population projection: (2010) 306,000; (2020) 327,000.
Doubling time: 82 years.
Ethnic composition (2004)[5]: Icelandic 96.4%; European 2.5%, of which Polish 0.6%, Nordic 0.5%; Asian 0.7%; other 0.4%.
Religious affiliation (2004): Evangelical Lutheran 85.5%; other Lutheran 2.1%; Roman Catholic 2.0%; other Christian 4.2%; other and not specified 6.2%.
Major cities (2005[2]): Reykjavík 113,848 (urban area 184,244); Kópavogur 25,803[6]; Hafnarfjördhur 22,000[6]; Akureyri 16,475; Gardhabær 9,053[6].

Vital statistics

Birth rate per 1,000 population (2004): 14.4 (world avg. 21.1); legitimate 36.3%; illegitimate 63.7%.
Death rate per 1,000 population (2004): 6.2 (world avg. 9.0).
Natural increase rate per 1,000 population (2004): 8.2 (world avg. 12.1).
Total fertility rate (avg. births per childbearing woman; 2004): 2.0.
Marriage rate per 1,000 population (2004): 5.0.
Divorce rate per 1,000 population (2004): 1.9.
Life expectancy at birth (2001–04): male 78.8 years; female 82.6 years.
Major causes of death per 100,000 population (2002): diseases of the circulatory system 219.8, of which ischemic heart diseases 119.4, cerebrovascular disease 46.2; malignant neoplasms (cancers) 167.8; diseases of the nervous system 45.8; diseases of the respiratory system 41.9; accidents and violence 38.8.

National economy

Budget (2004). Revenue: ISK 279,425,000,000 (tax revenue 90.3%, of which value-added tax 30.8%, individual income tax 26.4%, social security contribution 10.4%; nontax revenue 9.7%). Expenditures: ISK 273,035,000,000 (social security and health 40.4%, education 11.8%, social affairs 8.4%, interest payment 5.5%).
Public debt (2003): U.S.\$3,333,000,000.
Production (metric tons except as noted). Agriculture, forestry, fishing (2003): potatoes 7,090, cereals 4,337, tomatoes 1,074, hay 2,287,936 cu m; livestock (number of live animals) 463,006 sheep, 71,412 horses, 66,035 cattle; fish catch (value in ISK '000,000; 2004) 67,975, of which cod 27,979, haddock 7,660, redfish 6,356, herring 4,550, capelin 4,540, halibut 4,136, shrimp 2,015. Mining and quarrying (2004): diatomite 28,000. Manufacturing (value of sales in ISK '000,000; 2004): food products and beverages (mainly preserved and processed fish) 179,749; base metals 42,067; chemicals and chemical products 20,504; printing and publishing 18,918; cement, bricks, and ceramics 13,755; fabricated metal products 13,438. Energy production (consumption): electricity (kW-hr; 2002) 8,423,000,000 (8,423,000,000); coal (metric tons; 2002) none (98,000); crude petroleum, none (none); petroleum products (metric tons; 2002) none (581,000); natural gas, none (none).
Land use as % of total land area (2000): in temporary crops 0.07%, in permanent crops, none, in pasture 22.7%; overall forest area 0.3%.
Population economically active (2004): total 161,100; activity rate of total population 54.9% (participation rates: ages 16–74, 82.3%; female 47.1%; unemployed [May 2004–April 2005] 2.8%).

Price and earnings indexes (2000 = 100)

	1998	1999	2000	2001	2002	2003	2004
Consumer price index	92.1	95.1	100.0	106.4	111.9	114.2	117.4
Annual earnings index	87.8	94.0	100.0	108.5	117.0	123.6	129.3

Gross national product (2004): U.S.\$11,199,000,000 (U.S.\$38,620 per capita).

Structure of gross domestic product and labour force

	2003 in value ISK '000,000	2003 % of total value	2003 labour force	2003 % of labour force
Agriculture	11,322	1.4	5,700	3.5
Fishing	63,594	8.0	5,100	3.1
Fish processing			5,400	3.3
Manufacturing, mining	67,189	8.4	16,300	10.0
Construction	61,905	7.8	10,880	6.7
Public utilities	26,420	3.3	1,600	1.0
Transp. and commun.	57,567	7.2	9,700	6.0
Trade, restaurants	93,801	11.8	26,000	16.0
Finance, real estate	187,374	23.5	20,500	12.6
Services			47,600	29.3
Public administration	156,852	19.7	8,200	5.1
Other	71,463	8.9	5,500	3.4
TOTAL	797,487	100.0	162,400	100.0

Household income and expenditure. Average household size (2002) 2.8; annual employment income per household (2003) ISK 2,428,000 (U.S.\$31,700); sources of income (2001): wages and salaries 78.6%, pension 10.3%, self-employment 2.0%, other 9.1%; expenditure (2004): housing and energy 18.0%, transportation and communications 16.5%, food 13.2%, recreation, education, and culture 12.0%, expenditures in cafes and hotels 7.2%.
Tourism (2004): receipts U.S.\$372,000,000; expenditures U.S.\$691,000,000.

Foreign trade[7]

Balance of trade (current prices)

	1999	2000	2001	2002	2003	2004
ISK '000,000	−22,382	−37,480	−5,936	+14,082	−15,900	−36,548
% of total	7.2%	11.2%	1.5%	3.6%	4.2%	8.3%

Imports (2004): ISK 260,431,100,000 (machinery and apparatus 22.8%; transport equipment 14.7%; chemicals and chemical products 9.5%; crude petroleum and petroleum products 8.5%; food products 8.2%). *Major import sources:* Germany 12.6%; U.S. 10.1%; Norway 9.6%; Denmark 7.6%; U.K. 6.8%; Sweden 6.2%; The Netherlands 5.7%.
Exports (2004): ISK 202,373,600,000 (marine products 60.2%, of which cod 23.7%, shrimp 5.8%, haddock 5.0%, capelin 4.6%; aluminum 18.0%; medicinal products 4.4%). *Major export destinations:* U.K. 19.0%; Germany 17.7%; The Netherlands 10.7%; U.S. 9.3%; Spain 6.9%.

Transport and communications

Transport. Railroads: none. Roads (2004[2]): total length 8,080 mi, 13,004 km (paved c. 33%). Vehicles (2004[2]): passenger cars 166,869; trucks and buses 22,944. Air transport (2004)[8]: passenger-mi 2,258,700,000, passenger-km 3,635,000,000; short ton-mi cargo 81,010,000, metric ton-km cargo 118,272,000; airports (1996) with scheduled flights 24.

Communications

Medium	date	unit	number	units per 1,000 persons
Daily newspapers	2001	circulation	95,775	336
Radio	2001	receivers	308,100	1,081
Television	2000	receivers	143,000	509
Telephones	2004	main lines	190,500	651
Cellular telephones	2004	subscribers	291,400	996
Personal computers	2004	units	138,000	472
Internet	2004	users	225,600	771

Education and health

Educational attainment (2002): Percentage of population ages 25–64 having primary and some secondary education 34.4%; secondary 45.7%; higher 19.9%. *Literacy:* virtually 100%.

Education (2004)

	schools	teachers	students	student/ teacher ratio
Primary/lower secondary (age 7–15)	178	4,045	44,511	11.0
Upper secondary (age 16–19)	36[9]	1,597	22,629	14.2
Higher	11[9]	1,536	18,243	11.9

Health: physicians (2003) 1,047 (1 per 276 persons); hospital beds (2002) 2,432 (1 per 118 persons); infant mortality rate per 1,000 live births (2004) 2.8.
Food (2002): daily per capita caloric intake 3,250 (vegetable products 58%, animal products 42%); 122% of FAO recommended minimum requirement.

Military

Total active duty personnel (2003): 130 coast guard personnel; NATO-sponsored U.S.-manned Iceland Defense Force (December 2004): 1,400. *Coast guard expenditure as percentage of GDP* (2003): 0.4%; per capita expenditure U.S.\$114.

---

[1]Constituencies are electoral districts. Actual local administration is based on towns or rural districts. [2]January 1. [3]In English, Capital Region. [4]Population density calculated with reference to 9,191 sq mi (23,805 sq km) area free of glaciers (comprising 4,603 sq mi [11,922 sq km]), lava fields or wasteland (comprising 24,918 sq mi [64,538 sq km]), and lakes (comprising 1,064 sq mi [2,757 sq km]). [5]By citizenship. [6]Within Reykjavík urban area. [7]Imports f.o.b. in balance of trade and c.i.f. in commodities and trading partners. [8]Icelandair only. [9]2002.

Internet resources for further information:
• **Statistics Iceland http://www.statice.is**
• **Central Bank of Iceland http://www.sedlabanki.is**

India

Official name: Bharat (Hindi);
Republic of India (English).
Form of government: multiparty federal
republic with two legislative houses
(Council of States [245[1]]; House of
the People [545[2]]).
Chief of state: President.
Head of government: Prime Minister.
Capital: New Delhi.
Official languages: Hindi; English.
Official religion: none.
Monetary unit: 1 Indian rupee
(Re, plural Rs) = 100 paise; valuation
(Sept. 1, 2005) 1 U.S.$ = Rs 43.87;
1 £ = Rs 80.77.

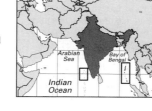

Oriya 3.32%; Punjabi 2.76%; Assamese 1.55%; Bhili/Bhilodi 0.66%; Santhali 0.62%; Kashmiri 0.47%[12]; Gondi 0.25%; Sindhi 0.25%; Nepali 0.25%; Konkani 0.21%; Tulu 0.18%; Kurukh 0.17%; Manipuri 0.15%; Bodo 0.14%; Khandeshi 0.12%; other 3.26%. Hindi (66.00%) and English (19.00%) are also spoken as lingua francas (second languages).
Religious affiliation (2000): Hindu 73.72%; Muslim 11.96%, of which Sunnī 8.97%, Shī'ī 2.99%; Christian 6.08%, of which Independent 2.99%, Protestant 1.47%, Roman Catholic 1.35%, Orthodox 0.27%; traditional beliefs 3.39%; Sikh 2.16%; Buddhist 0.71%; Jain 0.40%; Bahā'ī 0.12%; Zoroastrian (Parsi) 0.02%; other 1.44%.
Households (2001). Total number of households 191,963,935. Average household size 5.4. Type of household: permanent 51.8%; semipermanent 30.0%; temporary 18.2%. Average number of rooms per household 2.2; 1 room 38.4%, 2 rooms 30.0%, 3 rooms 14.3%, 4 rooms 7.5%, 5 rooms 2.9%, 6 or more rooms 3.7%, unspecified number of rooms 3.2%.

Area and population

States	Capitals	area sq mi	area sq km	population 2001 census
Andhra Pradesh	Hyderabad	106,204	275,068	76,210,007
Arunachal Pradesh	Itanagar	32,333	83,743	1,097,968
Assam	Dispur	30,285	78,438	26,655,528
Bihar	Patna	38,301	99,200	82,998,509
Chhattisgarh	Raipur	52,199	135,194	20,833,803
Goa	Panaji	1,429	3,702	1,347,668
Gujarat	Gandhinagar	75,685	196,024	50,671,017
Haryana	Chandigarh	17,070	44,212	21,144,564
Himachal Pradesh	Shimla	21,495	55,673	6,077,900
Jammu and Kashmir	Srinagar	39,146	101,387	10,143,700
Jharkhand	Ranchi	28,833	74,677	26,945,829
Karnataka	Bangalore	74,051	191,791	52,850,562
Kerala	Thiruvananthapuram (Trivandrum)	15,005	38,863	31,841,374
Madhya Pradesh	Bhopal	119,016	308,252	60,348,023
Maharashtra	Mumbai (Bombay)	118,800	307,690	96,878,627
Manipur	Imphal	8,621	22,327	2,166,788
Meghalaya	Shillong	8,660	22,429	2,318,822
Mizoram	Aizawl	8,139	21,081	888,573
Nagaland	Kohima	6,401	16,579	1,990,036
Orissa	Bhubaneshwar	60,119	155,707	36,804,660
Punjab	Chandigarh	19,445	50,362	24,358,999
Rajasthan	Jaipur	132,139	342,239	56,507,188
Sikkim	Gangtok	2,740	7,096	540,851
Tamil Nadu	Chennai (Madras)	50,216	130,058	62,405,679
Tripura	Agartala	4,049	10,486	3,199,203
Uttar Pradesh	Lucknow	93,933	243,286	166,197,921
Uttaranchal	Dehra Dun	19,739	51,125	8,489,349
West Bengal	Kolkata (Calcutta)	34,267	88,752	80,176,197
Union Territories				
Andaman and Nicobar Islands	Port Blair	3,185	8,249	356,152
Chandigarh	Chandigarh	44	114	900,635
Dadra and Nagar Haveli	Silvassa	190	491	220,490
Daman and Diu	Daman	43	112	158,204
Lakshadweep	Kavaratti	12	32	60,650
Pondicherry	Pondicherry	190	492	974,345
National Capital Territory				
Delhi[3]	Delhi	573	1,483	13,850,507
TOTAL		1,222,559[4, 5]	3,166,414[4]	1,028,610,328

Demography

Population (2005): 1,103,371,000.
Density (2005)[4]: persons per sq mi 902.5, persons per sq km 348.5.
Urban-rural (2003): urban 28.3%; rural 71.7%.
Sex distribution (2004): male 51.60%; female 48.40%.
Age breakdown (2004): under 15, 31.7%; 15–29, 27.9%; 30–44, 20.3%; 45–59, 12.7%; 60–74, 5.8%; 75 and over, 1.6%.
Population projection: (2010) 1,183,293,000; (2020) 1,332,032,000.
Doubling time: 49 years.
Major cities (2001; *urban agglomerations*[6], 2001): Greater Mumbai (Greater Bombay) 11,978,450 (16,368,084); Delhi 9,879,172 (12,791,458); Kolkata (Calcutta) 4,580,546 (13,216,546); Chennai (Madras) 4,343,645 (6,424,624); Bangalore 4,301,326 (5,686,844); Hyderabad 3,637,483 (5,533,640); Ahmadabad 3,520,085 (4,519,278); Kanpur 2,551,337 (2,690,486); Pune (Poona) 2,538,473 (3,755,525); Surat 2,433,835 (2,811,466); Jaipur 2,322,575 (2,324,-319); New Delhi[7] 302,363.

Other principal cities (2001)

	population		population		population
Agra	1,275,134	Jabalpur	932,484	Shambajinagar	
Allahabad		Jodhpur	851,051	(Aurangabad)	873,311
(Prayag Raj)	975,393	Kalyan-Dombivali[8]	1,193,512	Sholapur (Solapur)	872,478
Amritsar	966,862	Lucknow	2,185,927	Srinagar	898,440
Bareilly	718,395	Ludhiana	1,398,467	Thane (Thana)[8]	1,262,551
Bhopal	1,437,354	Madurai	928,869	Thiruvanan-	
Chandigarh	808,515	Meerut	1,068,772	thapuram	
Coimbatore	930,882	Mysore	755,379	(Trivandrum)	744,983
Faridabad	1,055,938	Nagpur	2,052,066	Tiruchirappalli	752,066
Ghaziabad	968,256	Nashik (Nasik)	1,077,236	Vadodara (Baroda)	1,306,227
Guwahati	809,895	Patna	1,366,444	Varanasi	
Gwalior	827,026	Pimpri-		(Benares)	1,091,918
Howrah (Haora)[9]	1,007,532	Chinchwad[10]	1,012,472	Vijayawada	851,282
Hubli-Dharwad	786,195	Rajkot	967,476	Vishakhapatnam	982,904
Indore	1,474,968	Ranchi	847,093		

Linguistic composition (1991)[11]: Hindi 27.58% (including associated languages and dialects, 38.58%); Bengali 8.22%; Telugu 7.80%; Marathi 7.38%; Tamil 6.26%; Urdu 5.13%; Gujarati 4.81%; Kannada 3.87%; Malayalam 3.59%;

Vital statistics

Birth rate per 1,000 population (2004): 22.8 (world avg. 21.1).
Death rate per 1,000 population (2004): 8.4 (world avg. 9.0).
Natural increase rate per 1,000 population (2004): 14.4 (world avg. 12.1).
Total fertility rate (avg. births per childbearing woman; 2004): 2.8.
Life expectancy at birth (2004): male 63.3 years; female 64.8 years.
Major causes of death per 100,000 population (2002): infectious and parasitic diseases 420, of which HIV/AIDS 34; diseases of the circulatory system 268, of which ischemic heart disease 146; accidents, homicide, and other violence 100; malignant neoplasms (cancers) 71; chronic respiratory diseases 58.

Social indicators

Educational attainment (2001). Percentage of population age 25 and over having: no formal schooling 48.1%; incomplete primary education 9.0%; complete primary 22.1%; secondary 13.7%; higher 7.1%.

Distribution of expenditure (1999–2000)[13]

percentage of household expenditure by decile/quintile									
1	2	3	4	5	6	7	8	9	10 (highest)
3.9	5.0	—12.3—		—16.0—		—21.2—		14.8	28.5

Quality of working life. Average workweek (2001): c. 46 hours[14]. Rate of fatal injuries per 100,000 employees (2001) 36[14]. Agricultural workers in servitude to creditors (early 1990s) 10–20%.
Access to services (2001). Percentage of total (urban, rural) households having access to: electricity for lighting purposes (2003) 61.5% (90.8%, 51.6%); kerosene for lighting purposes 36.9% (8.3%, 46.6%), water closets 18.0% (46.1%, 7.1%), pit latrines 11.5% (14.6%, 10.3%), no latrines 63.6% (26.3%, 78.1%), closed drainage for waste water 12.5% (34.5%, 3.9%), open drainage for waste water 33.9% (43.4%, 30.3%), no drainage for waste water 53.6% (22.1%, 65.8%). Type of fuel used for cooking in households (2003): firewood 61.1% (20.0%, 74.9%), LPG (liquefied petroleum gas) 20.8% (55.4%, 9.1%), cow dung 7.4% (1.8%, 9.3%), kerosene 4.7% (13.0%, 1.9%), coal 1.5% (3.3%, 0.9%), other 4.6% (6.6%, 3.9%). Source of drinking water: hand pump or tube well 41.3% (21.3%, 48.9%), piped water 36.7% (68.7%, 24.3%), well 18.2% (7.7%, 22.2%), river, canal, spring, public tank, pond, or lake 2.7% (0.7%, 3.5%).
Social participation. Eligible voters participating in April/May 2004 national election: 58.1%. Trade union membership (1998): c. 16,000,000 (primarily in the public sector).
Social deviance (2003)[14]. Offense rate per 100,000 population for: murder 3.1; rape 1.5; dacoity (gang robbery) 0.5; theft 23.0; riots 5.4. Rate of suicide per 100,000 population (2002): 11.2, in Kerala 30.8.
Material well-being (2001). Total (urban, rural) households possessing: television receivers 31.6% (64.3%, 18.9%), telephones 9.1% (23.0%, 3.8%), scooters, motorcycles, or mopeds 11.7% (24.7%, 6.7%), cars, jeeps, or vans 2.5% (5.6%, 1.3%). Households availing banking services 35.5% (49.5%, 30.1%).

National economy

Gross national product (at current market prices; 2004): U.S.$674,580,000,000 (U.S.$620 per capita).

Structure of gross domestic product and labour force

	2003–04 in value Rs '000,000,000[16]	2003–04 % of total value	1999–2000 labour force	1999–2000 % of labour force
Agriculture, forestry	5,604.8	22.2	190,940,000	52.6
Mining	658.5	2.6	2,260,000	0.6
Manufacturing	3,977.1	15.8	40,790,000	11.2
Construction	1,550.6	6.1	14,950,000	4.1
Public utilities	524.7	2.1	1,150,000	0.3
Transp. and commun.	5,703.4	22.6	13,650,000	3.8
Trade, restaurants			37,540,000	10.3
Finance, real estate	3,496.7	13.9	4,620,000	1.3
Pub. admin., defense	3,723.0	14.8	30,840,000	8.5
Services			26,580,000[17]	7.3[17]
TOTAL	25,238[5]	100.0[5]	363,330,000[5]	100.0

Budget (2002). Revenue[18]: Rs 3,088,200,000,000 (tax revenue 76.4%, of which excise taxes 29.5%, taxes on income and profits 29.4%; nontax revenue 23.1%; other 0.5%). Expenditures: Rs 4,239,100,000,000 (general public services 61.0%, of which public debt payments 26.8%; economic affairs 15.3%; defense 15.2%; education 2.5%; health 1.7%).
Public debt (external, outstanding; 2003): U.S.$92,822,000,000.
Production (in '000 metric tons except as noted). Agriculture, forestry, fishing (2004): cereals 317,960 (of which rice 129,000, wheat 72,060, corn [maize] 14,000, millet 9,400, sorghum 7,530), sugarcane 244,800, fruits 48,983 (of which

bananas 16,820, mangoes 10,800, oranges 3,100, apples 1,470, lemons and limes 1,420, pineapples 1,300, oilseeds 22,064 (of which rapeseed 6,800, peanuts [groundnuts] 6,500, soybeans 5,500, sunflower seeds 1,250, castor beans 805, sesame 680), pulses (2002) 10,760 (of which chickpeas [2002] 5,320, dry beans [2002] 3,000, pigeon peas [2002] 2,440), coconuts 9,500, seed cotton 9,000, eggplants 8,200, jute 1,900, tea 850, natural rubber 762, tobacco 598, garlic 500, cashews 460, betel 400, coffee 275, ginger 230, pepper 51; livestock (number of live animals; 2004) 185,500,000 cattle, 120,000,000 goats, 97,700,000 water buffalo, 62,500,000 sheep, 14,300,000 pigs, 635,000 camels; roundwood 322,667,444 cu m, of which fuelwood 303,839,000 cu m, industrial roundwood 18,828,000; fish catch (metric tons; 2003) 5,904,584, of which freshwater fish 2,717,782, marine fish 2,447,228, crustaceans 586,704. Mining and quarrying (2003): limestone 120,000; iron ore 54,400[19]; bauxite 10,002; chromium 1,800; barite 700; manganese 620[19]; zinc 162[19]; lead 33.1[19]; copper 28.4[19]; mica 1.6; gold (2002–03) 2,873 kg; gem diamonds 16,000 carats. Manufacturing (value added in U.S.$'000,000; 2000): industrial chemicals 4,274; food products 3,723; paints, soaps, varnishes, drugs, and medicines 3,500; textiles 3,498; iron and steel 2,989; nonelectrical machinery and apparatus 2,457; cements, bricks, and tiles 1,988; refined petroleum 1,870; motor vehicles and parts 1,744.

Manufacturing enterprises (1995–96)[20]

	no. of factories	no. of persons engaged	avg. wages as a % of avg. of all wages	annual value added (Rs '000,000)[21]
Chemicals and chemical products,	9,206	758,500	140.3	237,093
of which synthetic fibres	395	97,100	183.8	68,420
fertilizers/pesticides	753	104,500	217.4	59,521
drugs and medicine	2,542	204,600	129.3	40,050
Transport equipment,	6,120	838,600	142.7	120,207
of which motor vehicles	3,758	392,400	162.4	77,240
Textiles	16,228	1,579,400	80.2	99,855
Iron and steel	3,519	507,700	152.9	97,274
Nonelectrical machinery/apparatus	9,075	548,400	137.2	92,762
Food products,	22,878	1,285,900	60.4	92,163
of which refined sugar	1,285	341,000	92.0	28,125
Electrical machinery/apparatus,	5,472	443,700	149.4	84,320
of which industrial machinery	2,048	165,600	190.8	35,717
Refined petroleum	161	31,100	349.3	52,778
Bricks, cement, plaster products	10,067	394,500	70.3	49,413
Nonferrous basic metals	3,301	228,700	124.3	42,252
Fabricated metal products	7,984	277,700	98.6	32,565
Paper and paper products	2,742	175,200	99.5	26,380
Wearing apparel	3,463	263,700	55.0	23,485

Energy production (consumption): electricity (kW-hr; 2002) 596,543,000,000 (597,888,000,000); hard coal (metric tons; 2003) 348,432,000 ([2002] 361,500,000); lignite (metric tons; 2003) 26,004,000 ([2002] 25,010,000); crude petroleum (barrels; 2002) 250,000,000 (874,000,000); petroleum products (metric tons; 2002) 81,700,000 (78,200,000); natural gas (cu m; 2002) 26,293,000,000 (26,293,000,000).

Financial aggregates[22]

	1998	1999	2000	2001	2002	2003	2004
Exchange rate, Rs per:							
U.S. dollar	42.48	43.49	46.75	48.18	48.03	45.61	43.59
£	70.67	70.30	69.76	69.88	77.41	81.40	84.19
SDR	59.81	59.69	60.91	60.55	65.30	67.77	67.69
International reserves (U.S.$)							
Total (excl. gold; '000,000)	27,341	32,667	37,902	45,870	67,665	98,938	126,593
SDRs ('000,000)	83	4	2	5	7	3	5
Reserve pos. in IMF ('000,000)	300	671	637	614	665	1,318	1,424
Foreign exchange ('000,000)	26,958	31,992	37,264	45,251	66,994	97,617	125,164
Gold ('000,000 fine troy oz)	11.487	11.502	11.502	11.502	11.502	11.502	11.502
% world reserves	1.2	1.2	1.2	1.2	1.2	1.2	1.3
Interest and prices							
Central bank discount (%)	9.00	8.00	8.00	6.50	6.25	6.00	6.00
Advance (prime) rate (%)	13.5	12.5	12.3	12.1	11.9	11.5	10.9
Industrial share prices (2000 = 100)	72.4	89.9	100.0	75.5	70.7	117.6	138.6
Balance of payments (U.S.$'000,000)							
Balance of visible trade	−10,752	−8,679	−10,640	−6,418	−3,559	−8,870	...
Imports, f.o.b.	44,828	45,556	53,887	51,211	54,700	68,208	...
Exports, f.o.b.	34,076	36,877	43,247	44,793	51,141	59,338	...
Balance of invisibles	+3,849	+5,451	+5,938	+7,669	+10,523	+15,588	...
Balance of payments, current account	−6,903	−3,228	−4,702	+1,251	+6,964	+6,718	...

Land use as % of total land area (2000): in temporary crops 54.4%, in permanent crops 2.7%, in pasture 3.7%; overall forest area 21.6%.
Population economically active (2001): total 402,512,190; activity rate of total population 39.1% (participation rates: ages 15–64, n.a.; female 31.6%; unemployed 10.4%).

Price and earnings indexes (2000 = 100)

	1998	1999	2000	2001	2002	2003	2004
Consumer price index	91.9	96.1	100.0	103.7	108.2	112.4	116.6
Monthly earnings index	...	...	...	...	...	...	...

Household income and expenditure. Average household size (2003) 4.9; sources of income: n.a.; expenditure (2003): food and nonalcoholic beverages 50.0%, housing and energy 11.2%, clothing and footwear 7.8%, health 6.7%, transportation 4.1%, tobacco and intoxicants 2.3%.
Service enterprises (net value added in Rs '000,000,000; 1998–99): wholesale and retail trade 1,562; finance, real estate, and insurance 1,310; transport and storage 804; community, social, and personal services 763; construction 545.
Tourism: receipts from visitors (2003) U.S.$3,533,000,000; expenditures by nationals abroad (2002) U.S.$3,449,000,000.

Foreign trade[23]

Balance of trade (current prices)

	1999–2000	2000–01	2001–02	2002–03	2003–04	2004–05
U.S.$'000,000	−12,848	−5,976	−7,587	−8,693	−14,307	−27,819
% of total	14.9%	6.3%	8.0%	7.6%	10.1%	14.9%

Imports (2004–05): U.S.$107,066,100,000 (crude petroleum and petroleum products 27.9%; gold and silver 10.1%; electronic goods [including computer software] 9.7%; precious and semiprecious stones 8.8%; nonelectrical machinery and apparatus 6.1%; organic and inorganic chemicals 5.0%). Major import sources: China 6.3%; U.S. 5.9%; Switzerland 5.4%; U.A.E. 4.3%; Belgium 4.3%; Australia 3.3%; U.K. 3.2%; South Korea 3.0%; Japan 2.8%.
Exports (2004–05): U.S.$79,247,000,000 (engineering goods 20.7%; gems and jewelry 17.3%; chemicals and chemical products 15.0%; food and agricultural products 10.1%; petroleum products 8.6%; ready-made garments 7.6%; cotton yarn, fabrics, and thread 4.0%). Major export destinations: U.S. 16.7%; U.A.E. 9.0%; China 5.8%; Singapore 4.8%; Hong Kong 4.6%; U.K. 4.5%; Germany 3.3%; Belgium 3.1%; Italy 2.7%; Japan 2.5%.

Transport and communications

Transport. Railroads (2002): route length 89,879 mi, 144,647 km; passenger-mi 581,625,000,000[24], passenger-km 936,037,000,000[24]; short ton-mi cargo 370,711,000,000[25], metric ton-km cargo 541,783,000,000[25]. Roads (2002): total length 2,062,727 mi, 3,319,644 km (paved 46%). Vehicles (2001): passenger cars 7,058,000; trucks and buses 3,582,000. Air transport (2003): passenger-mi 19,355,000,000, passenger-km 31,149,000,000; short ton-mi cargo 367,900,000, metric ton-km cargo 579,900,000; airports (2002) with scheduled flights 96.

Communications

Medium	date	unit	number	units per 1,000 persons
Daily newspapers	2003	circulation	72,939,000	68
Radio	2000	receivers	123,000,000	121
Television	2001	receivers	85,800,000	83
Telephones	2004	main lines	43,960,000	41
Cellular telephones	2004	subscribers	47,300,000	44
Personal computers	2004	units	13,030,000	12
Internet	2004	users	35,000,000	32

Education and health

Literacy (2001): percentage of total population age 15 and over literate 64.8%; males literate 75.3%; females literate 53.7%.

Education (2001–02)

	schools	teachers	students	student/ teacher ratio
Primary (age 6–10)	664,041	1,928,075	113,883,060	59.0
Secondary (age 11–17)	311,061	2,486,715	64,882,041	26.1
Higher	42,057	758,706	10,453,229	13.8

Health (2001): physicians 555,000 (1 per 1,853 persons); hospital beds 903,000 (1 per 1,139 persons); infant mortality rate per 1,000 live births (2004) 57.9.
Food (2002): daily per capita caloric intake 2,458 (vegetable products 92%, animal products 8%); 111% of FAO recommended minimum requirement.

Military

Total active duty personnel (2004): 1,325,000 (army 83.0%, navy 4.2%, air force 12.8%); personnel in paramilitary forces 1,089,700. Military expenditure as percentage of GDP (2003): 2.1%; per capita expenditure U.S.$12.

[1]Council of States can have a maximum of 250 members; a maximum of 12 of these members may be nominated by the President. [2]Includes 2 nonelective seats. [3]Bill of 2003 changing the status of Delhi to full statehood not implemented as of early 2005. [4]Excludes 46,660 sq mi (120,849 sq km) of territory claimed by India as part of Jammu and Kashmir but occupied by Pakistan or China; inland water constitutes 9.6% of total area of India (including all of Indian-claimed Jammu and Kashmir). [5]Detail does not add to total given because of rounding. [6]Preliminary figures. [7]Within Delhi urban agglomeration. [8]Within Greater Mumbai urban agglomeration. [9]Within Kolkata urban agglomeration. [10]Within Pune urban agglomeration. [11]Mother tongue unless otherwise noted. [12]1981. [13]Detail does not add to total given because of gross rounding. [14]Data apply to the workers employed in the "organized sector" only (27.8 million in 2001, of which 19.1 million were employed in the public sector and 8.7 million were employed in the private sector); few legal protections exist for the more than 370 million workers in the "unorganized sector." [15]Crimes reported to National Crime Records Bureau by police authorities of state governments. [16]At factor cost. [17]Unemployed. [18]Central government only. [19]Metal content. [20]Establishments with at least 10 workers on any workday and all establishments employing 20 or more workers. [21]In factor values. [22]End-of-period. [23]Fiscal year beginning April 1. [24]Includes Indian Railways and 15 regional railways. [25]Includes Indian Railways and 9 regional railways.

Internet resources for further information:
- **India Image: Directory of Government Web Sites http://www.nic.in**
- **Census of India http://www.censusindia.net**
- **Reserve Bank of India http://www.rbi.org.in**
- **Union Budget and Economic Survey http://www.indiabudget.nic.in**

Indonesia

Official name: Republik Indonesia (Republic of Indonesia).
Form of government: multiparty republic with two legislative houses (Regional Representatives Council [128]; House of Representatives [550]).
Head of state and government: President.
Capital: Jakarta.
Official language: Indonesian.
Official religion: monotheism.
Monetary unit: 1 Indonesian rupiah (Rp) = 100 sen; valuation (Sept. 1, 2005) 1 U.S.$ = Rp 10,350; 1 £ = Rp 19,057.

Area and population

Island(s) Provinces	area sq km	population 2000 census[1]	Island(s) Provinces	area sq km	population 2000 census[1]
Bali and the Lesser			Central Kalimantan	153,564	1,857,000
Sunda Islands	73,137	11,112,702	East Kalimantan	230,277	2,455,120
Bali	5,633	3,151,162	South Kalimantan	43,546	2,985,240
East Nusa Tenggara	47,351	3,952,279	West Kalimantan	146,807	4,034,198
West Nusa Tenggara	20,153	4,009,261	Maluku (Moluccas)[2]	77,870	1,990,598
Celebes (Sulawesi)[2]	191,671	14,946,488	Maluku	46,975	1,205,539
Central Sulawesi	63,678	2,218,435	North Maluku	30,895	785,059
Gorontalo	12,215	835,044	Papua (Irian)[2,7]	365,466	2,220,934
North Sulawesi	15,273	2,012,098	Sumatra[2]	480,847	43,309,707
South Sulawesi[3]	21,344	8,059,627[4]	Aceh[8]	51,937	3,930,905
Southeast Sulawesi	62,365	1,821,284	Bangka-Belitung	16,171	900,197
West Sulawesi[3]	16,796	[4]	Bengkulu	19,789	1,567,432
Java[2]	127,569	121,352,608	Jambi	53,437	2,413,846
Banten	8,651	8,098,780	Lampung	35,384	6,741,439
Central Java	32,549	31,228,940	North Sumatra	73,587	11,649,655
East Java	47,922	34,783,640	Riau[9]	94,560	4,957,627
Jakarta[5]	664	8,389,443	Riau Islands[9]		
West Java	34,597	35,729,537	South Sumatra	93,083	6,899,675
Yogyakarta	3,186	3,122,268	West Sumatra	42,899	4,248,931
Kalimantan[2,6]	574,194	11,331,558	TOTAL	1,890,754	206,264,595

Demography

Population (2005): 222,781,000.
Density (2005): persons per sq mi 305.2, persons per sq km 117.8.
Urban-rural (2003): urban 45.6%; rural 54.4%.
Sex distribution (2003): male 50.00%; female 50.00%.
Age breakdown (2000): under 15, 30.4%; 15–29, 29.3%; 30–44, 21.8%; 45–59, 11.3%; 60–74, 5.8%; 75 and over, 1.4%.
Population projection: (2010) 235,755,000; (2020) 255,853,000.
Ethnic composition (2000): Javanese 36.4%; Sundanese 13.7%; Malay 9.4%; Madurese 7.2%; Han Chinese 4.0%; Minangkabau 3.6%; other 25.7%.
Religious affiliation (2000): Muslim 76.5%; Christian 13.1%, of which Protestant 5.7%, independent Christian 4.0%, Roman Catholic 2.7%; Hindu 3.4%; traditional beliefs 2.5%; nonreligious 1.9%; other 2.6%.
Major cities (2000): Jakarta 8,347,083 (urban agglomeration [2003] 12,300,000); Surabaya 2,599,796; Bandung 2,136,260; Medan 1,904,273; Bekasi 1,663,802; Palembang 1,451,419; Semarang 1,348,803; Tangerang 1,325,854.

Vital statistics

Birth rate per 1,000 population (2004): 21.1 (world avg. 21.1).
Death rate per 1,000 population (2004): 6.3 (world avg. 9.0).
Total fertility rate (avg. births per childbearing woman; 2004): 2.5.
Marriage rate per 1,000 population (2003): 7.7.
Life expectancy at birth (2004): male 66.8 years; female 71.8 years.

National economy

Budget (2003). Revenue: Rp 341,094,000,000,000 (tax revenue 70.8%, of which income tax 33.7%, VAT 22.5%; nontax revenue 29.2%, of which revenue from petroleum 12.5%). Expenditures: Rp 374,764,000,000,000 (current expenditure 50.5%; regional expenditure 32.2%; developmental expenditure 17.3%).
Public debt (external, outstanding; end of March 2005): U.S.$80,833,000,000.
Population economically active (2004): total 103,973,387; activity rate 46.7% (participation rates: over age 15, 67.5%; unemployed 9.9%).

Price index (2000 = 100)

	1998	1999	2000	2001	2002	2003	2004
Consumer price index	80.0	96.4	100.0	111.5	124.7	133.0	141.3

Household income and expenditure. Average household size (2003) 3.8.
Production (metric tons except as noted). Agriculture, forestry, fishing (2004): oil palm fruit 60,400,000, rice 54,088,468, sugarcane 24,600,000, cassava 19,424,707, corn (maize) 11,225,243, natural rubber 2,765,636; livestock (number of live animals) 13,441,700 goats, 11,107,986 cattle, 8,245,330 sheep; roundwood 109,060,284 cu m; fish catch (2003) 4,675,100. Mining and quarrying (2003): bauxite 1,262,600; copper (metal content) 1,005,837; nickel (metal content) 143,000; silver 285,206 kg; gold 141,019 kg. Manufacturing (value added in U.S.$'000,000; 2001): textiles, clothing, and footwear 3,028; food products 2,971; chemicals and chemical products 2,737; transport equipment 2,360; wood products (including metal furniture) 2,353; tobacco products 2,124. Energy production (consumption): electricity (kW-hr; 2003) 110,200,000,000 (92,350,000,000); coal (metric tons; 2003–04) 119,200,000

([2002] 28,000,000); crude petroleum (barrels; 2003–04) 443,000,000 ([2003] 432,000,000); petroleum products (metric tons; 2002) 44,776,000 (50,235,000); natural gas (cu m; 2003) 88,936,000,000 (55,300,000,000).
Gross national product (2004): U.S.$248,007,000,000 (U.S.$1,140 per capita).

Structure of gross domestic product and labour force

	2004–05 in value Rp '000,000,000	2004–05 % of total value	2004 labour force	2004 % of labour force
Agriculture	361,514	15.0	40,608,019	39.0
Mining	214,908	8.9	1,034,716	1.0
Manufacturing	678,024	28.2	11,070,498	10.6
Public utilities	23,633	1.0	228,297	0.2
Construction	142,722	5.9	4,540,102	4.4
Transp. and commun.	147,709	6.2	5,480,527	5.3
Trade	388,738	16.2	19,119,156	18.4
Finance, real estate	200,928	8.4	1,125,056	1.1
Public admin., defense	124,300	5.2 }	10,515,665	10.1
Services	120,272	5.0		
Other	—	—	10,251,351[10]	9.9[10]
TOTAL	2,402,748	100.0	103,973,387	100.0

Tourism (2003): receipts U.S.$4,002,000,000; expenditures U.S.$3,082,000,000.
Land use as % of total land area (2000): in temporary crops 11.3%, in permanent crops 7.2%, in pasture 6.2%; overall forest area 58.0%.

Foreign trade[11]

Balance of trade (current prices)

	1999	2000	2001	2002	2003	2004
U.S.$'000,000	+17,922	+21,808	+19,827	+21,854	+21,864	+19,185
% of total	21.2%	20.0%	20.9%	22.2%	20.6%	15.6%

Imports (2004–05): U.S.$62,638,000,000 (petroleum products and natural gas 21.7%, machinery and apparatus 17.2%, chemicals and chemical products 10.6%, base metals 9.0%, transport equipment 6.0%). *Major import sources* (2004): Japan 19.3%; China 11.0%; Singapore 9.2%; Thailand 6.8%; Malaysia 6.5%.
Exports (2004–05): U.S.$79,589,000,000 (petroleum products and natural gas 21.9%, machinery and apparatus 13.9%, textiles 10.3%, base metals 6.5%, rubber products 5.6%, wood products 4.0%). *Major export destinations* (2004): Japan 21.8%; U.S. 13.5%; China 7.5%; Singapore 7.4%; South Korea 5.9%.

Transport and communications

Transport. Railroads (2004): route length 6,458 km; passenger-km 15,077,000,000; metric ton-km cargo 4,698,000,000. Roads (2002): length 368,362 km (paved 58%). Vehicles (2003): passenger cars 3,602,000; trucks and buses (2002) 2,579,620. Air transport (2004): passenger-km 28,012,000,000; metric ton-km cargo 248,000,000; airports (1996) 81.

Communications

Medium	date	unit	number	units per 1,000 persons
Daily newspapers	2004	circulation	4,866,000	22
Radio	2001	receivers	33,690,000	159
Television	2001	receivers	32,420,000	153
Telephones	2004	main lines	9,990,000	45
Cellular phones	2004	subscribers	30,000,000	136
Personal computers	2004	units	3,022,000	14
Internet	2004	users	14,508,000	66

Education and health

Educational attainment (2000). Percentage of population age 15 and over having: no schooling or incomplete primary education 23.9%; primary and some secondary 53.8%; complete secondary 17.9%; some higher 2.2%; complete higher 2.2%. *Literacy* (2002): total population age 15 and over literate 87.9%; males literate 92.5%; females literate 83.4%.

Education (2002–03)

	schools[12]	teachers	students	student/ teacher ratio
Primary (age 7–12)	146,052	1,431,486	29,050,834	20.3
Secondary (age 13–18)	28,954	967,539	13,772,782	14.2
Voc., teacher tr.	4,943	147,559	2,099,753	14.2
Higher	1,924	233,359	3,441,429	14.7

Health (2001): physicians 21,467 (1 per 9,871 persons); hospital beds 124,834 (1 per 1,697 persons); infant mortality rate per 1,000 live births (2004) 36.8.
Food (2003): daily per capita caloric intake 3,046 (vegetable products 97%, animal products 3%); 141% of FAO recommended minimum.

Military

Total active duty personnel (2004): 302,000 (army 77.2%, navy 14.9%, air force 7.9%). *Military expenditure as percentage of GDP* (2003): 1.5%; per capita expenditure U.S.$15.

[1]Adjusted figure. [2]Includes area and population of nearby islands. [3]West Sulawesi province formally created from part of South Sulawesi in October 2004. [4]South Sulawesi includes West Sulawesi. [5]Formally a metropolitan district. [6]Kalimantan is the name of the Indonesian part of the island of Borneo. [7]West Irian Jaya, the former westernmost part of Papua, was formally split off from the rest of Papua in February 2003. [8]Formally an autonomous province. [9]Riau Islands formally separated from Riau in July 2004. [10]Unemployed. [11]Imports are c.i.f. in balance of trade and commodities and f.o.b. in trading partners. [12]Schools under the Ministry of National Education only.

Internet resources for further information:
• Central Bureau of Statistics http://www.bps.go.id

Iran

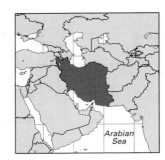

Official name: Jomhūrī-ye Eslamī-ye Irān (Islamic Republic of Iran).
Form of government: unitary Islamic republic with one legislative house (Islamic Consultative Assembly [290]).
Supreme political/religious authority: Leader.
Head of state and government: President.
Capital: Tehrān.
Official language: Farsī (Persian).
Official religion: Islam.
Monetary unit: 1 rial (Rls);
valuation (Sept. 1, 2005)
1 U.S.$ = Rls 9,008; 1 £ = Rls 16,586.

Area and population

Provinces	area sq km	population 2004[1] estimate	Provinces	area sq km	population 2004[1] estimate
Ardabīl	17,881	1,247,202	Khūzestān	63,213	4,277,998
Āzārbāyjān-e Gharbī	37,463	2,896,657	Kohgīlūyeh va		
Āzārbāyjān-e Sharqī	45,481	3,482,672	Būyer Ahmad	15,563	674,113
Būshehr	23,168	808,482	Kordestān	28,817	1,546,256
Chahār Mahāll va			Lorestān	28,392	1,739,644
Bakhtīārī	16,201	832,945	Markazī	29,406	1,344,920
Esfahān	128,811	4,395,645	Māzandarān	23,833	2,796,120
Fārs	121,825	4,323,626	Qazvīn	15,491	1,133,547
Gilan	13,952	2,389,195	Qom	11,237	1,038,424
Golestān	20,893	1,613,691	Semnān	96,816	578,910
Hamadān	19,547	1,732,080	Sīstān va		
Hormozgān	71,193	1,284,925	Balūchestān	178,431	2,219,393
Īlam	20,150	538,877	Tehrān	19,196	11,931,656
Kermān	181,714	2,380,682	Yazd	107,027	940,802
Kermānshāh	24,641	1,921,284	Zanjān	21,841	963,434
Khorāsān[2]	247,622	6,444,320	TOTAL	1,629,807[3, 4]	67,477,500

Demography

Population: (2005): 69,515,000.
Density (2005)[5]: persons per sq mi 109.2, persons per sq km 42.2.
Urban-rural (2003): urban 66.7%; rural 33.3%.
Sex distribution (2004): male 50.97%; female 49.03%.
Age breakdown (2004): under 15, 28.2%; 15–29, 34.8%; 30–44, 19.9%; 45–59, 10.4%; 60–74, 5.0%; 75 and over, 1.7%.
Population projection: (2010) 74,283,000; (2020) 85,036,000.
Ethnic composition (2000): Persian 34.9%; Azerbaijani 15.9%; Kurd 13.0%; Lurī 7.2%; Gīlaki 5.1%; Mazāndarānī 5.1%; Afghan 2.8%; Arab 2.5%; other 13.5%.
Religious affiliation (2000): Muslim 95.6% (Shīʿī 90.1%, Sunnī 5.5%); Zoroastrian 2.8%; Christian 0.5%; other 1.1%.
Major cities (1996): Tehrān 6,758,845; Mashhad 1,887,405; Esfahān 1,266,072; Tabriz 1,191,043; Shīrāz 1,053,025; Karaj 940,968; Ahvāz 804,980.

Vital statistics

Birth rate per 1,000 population (2004): 17.1 (world avg. 21.1).
Death rate per 1,000 population (2004): 5.6 (world avg. 9.0).
Natural increase rate per 1,000 population (2004): 11.5 (world avg. 12.1).
Total fertility rate (avg. births per childbearing woman; 2004): 1.9.
Marriage rate per 1,000 population (2003–04): 10.2.
Life expectancy at birth (2004): male 68.3 years; female 71.1 years.
Major causes of death per 100,000 population (2002): diseases of the circulatory system 232; accidents and violence 104; infectious diseases 69; malignant neoplasms (cancers) 65; chronic respiratory diseases 23.

National economy

Budget (2003–04). Revenue: Rls 305,735,000,000,000 (petroleum and natural gas revenue 60.4%; taxes 21.3%, of which import duties 7.2%, corporate 6.7%; other 18.3%). Expenditures: Rls 307,521,000,000,000 (current expenditure 59.1%; development expenditures 18.8%; net lending 3.0%; other 19.1%).
Public debt (external, outstanding; 2003): U.S.$8,209,000,000.
Tourism (2003): receipts U.S.$1,777,000,000; expenditures U.S.$4,190,000,000.
Gross national product (2004): U.S.$153,984,000,000 (U.S.$2,300 per capita).

Structure of gross domestic product and labour force

	2003–04 in value Rls '000,000,000	2003–04 % of total value	1996 labour force	1996 % of labour force
Agriculture, forestry	127,578	11.7	3,357,263	21.0
Petroleum	252,144	23.0	119,884	0.7
Other mining	6,491	0.6		
Manufacturing	123,139	11.2	2,551,962	15.9
Construction	51,892	4.7	1,650,481	10.3
Public utilities	18,420	1.7	150,631	0.9
Transportation and communications	83,119	7.6	972,792	6.1
Trade, restaurants	131,849	12.0	1,927,067	12.0
Finance, real estate	175,693	16.0	301,962	1.9
Pub. admin., defense	122,496	11.2	1,618,100	10.1
Services	29,029	2.7	1,664,402	10.4
Other	−26,136[6]	−2.4[6]	1,712,028[7]	10.7[7]
TOTAL	1,095,717	100.0	16,026,572	100.0

Production (metric tons except as noted). Agriculture, forestry, fishing (2004): wheat 14,000,000, sugarcane 6,500,000, sugar beets 6,050,000, tomatoes 4,200,000, potatoes 4,180,000, rice 3,400,000, grapes 2,800,000, barley 2,700,000, apples 2,400,000, oranges 1,900,000, corn (maize) 1,500,000, dates 880,000, pistachios 275,000; livestock (number of live animals) 54,000,000 sheep, 26,300,000 goats, 9,150,000 cattle; roundwood (2004) 844,414 cu m; fish catch (2001–02) 399,000. Mining and quarrying (2001): iron ore 7,200,000[8]; chromite 250,000; copper ore 161,000[8]; zinc 120,000[8]; manganese 50,000[8]. Manufacturing (value added in U.S.$'000,000; 2000): basic chemicals 5,871; motor vehicles and parts 5,091; iron and steel 4,199; refined petroleum products 3,997; food products 3,485; nonmetallic mineral products 3,443. Energy production (consumption): electricity (kW-hr; 2004–05) 158,951,000,000 ([2002–03] 136,231,000,000); coal (metric tons; 2002) 1,400,000 (1,825,000); crude petroleum (barrels; 2004) 1,374,000,000 ([2002] 502,000,000); petroleum products (metric tons; 2002) 64,708,000 (55,401,000); natural gas (cu m; 2002) 69,928,000,000 (74,757,000,000).
Population economically active (2002–03): total 19,819,000; activity rate of total population 30.0% (participation rates: ages 15–64 [1996] 44.1%; female [1996] 12.7%; unemployed [April 1–September 30, 2004] 10.9%).

Price and earnings indexes (2000–01 = 100)

	1999–2000	2000–01	2001–02	2002–03	2003–04	2004–05
Consumer price index	88.8	100.0	111.4	129.0	149.1	171.8
Daily earnings index[9]	90.3	100.0	109.7	129.3	159.7	...

Household income and expenditure (2003–04). Average household size (2000) 4.6; annual average income per urban household Rls 39,202,427 (U.S.$4,704); sources of urban income: wages 34.1%, self-employment 27.7%, other 38.2%; expenditure: housing and energy 31.7%, food, beverages, and tobacco 26.0%, transportation and communications 11.9%.
Land use as % of total land area (2000): in temporary crops 8.8%, in permanent crops 1.2%, in pasture 26.9%; overall forest area 4.5%.

Foreign trade[10]

Balance of trade (current prices)

	1999–2000	2000–01	2001–02	2002–03	2003–04	2004–05
U.S.$'000,000	+7,597	+13,375	+5,775	+6,201	+4,430	+7,764
% of total	22.0%	30.7%	13.7%	12.3%	7.0%	9.6%

Imports (2002): U.S.$20,336,000,000 (nonelectrical machinery and apparatus 22.1%, road vehicles 15.4%, chemicals and chemical products 11.1%, iron and steel 8.0%, food products 7.2%, gold 7.1%). *Major import sources* (2003): Germany 11.7%; France 9.2%; China 9.0%; Italy 8.6%; Switzerland 7.3%.
Exports (2002): U.S.$28,356,000,000 (crude and refined petroleum 85.4%, carpets 1.9%, nuts 1.7%). *Major export destinations* (2003): Japan 23.0%; China 10.2%; Italy 6.6%; Taiwan 6.4%; South Korea 5.0%.

Transport and communications

Transport. Railroads (2003–04): route length 4,515 mi, 7,266 km; (2001–02) passenger-km 8,043,000,000; (2001–02) metric ton-km cargo 14,613,000,000. Roads (2002–03)[11]: length 50,525 mi, 81,313 km (paved 100%). Vehicles (2000–01): passenger cars 1,351,800; trucks and buses 384,900. Air transport (2004)[12]: passenger-km 8,325,000,000; metric ton-km cargo 45,811,000; airports (1996) 19.

Communications

Medium	date	unit	number	units per 1,000 persons
Daily newspapers	2000	circulation	1,780,000	28
Radio	2000	receivers	17,900,000	281
Television	2002	receivers	11,331,500	173
Telephones	2003	main lines	14,571,100	220
Cellular telephones	2004	subscribers	4,300,000	62
Personal computers	2004	units	7,347,000	105
Internet	2004	users	4,800,000	70

Education and health

Educational attainment: n.a. *Literacy* (2002): total population age 15 and over literate 77.1%; males literate 83.5%; females literate 70.4%.

Education (2003–04)

	schools	teachers	students	student/ teacher ratio
Primary (age 7–11)	67,800	294,098	6,647,917	22.6
Secondary (age 12–18)	51,097	355,074	8,596,308	24.2
Higher	...	...	1,892,119	...

Health (2003–04): physicians 19,482[13] (1 per 3,413 persons); hospital beds 111,552 (1 per 596 persons); infant mortality rate (2004) 42.9.
Food (2002): daily per capita caloric intake 3,085 (vegetable products 91%, animal products 9%); 128% of FAO recommended minimum requirement.

Military

Total active duty personnel (2004): 540,000 (revolutionary guard corps 22.2%, army 64.9%, navy 3.3%, air force 9.6%). *Military expenditure as percentage of GDP* (2003): 3.8%[14]; per capita expenditure U.S.$75[14].

[1]Official projection made in 2002. [2]Formally split into 3 new provinces in September 2004. [3]Land area only; estimated total area is 1,648,200 sq km. [4]Detail does not add to total given because of rounding. [5]Based on total area. [6]Less imputed bank service charges. [7]Includes 1,455,000 unemployed. [8]Metal content. [9]Construction sector only. [10]Imports f.o.b. in balance of trade and c.i.f. in commodities and trading partners. [11]Roads maintained by Ministry of Roads and Transportation only. [12]Iran Air. [13]Excludes private sector physicians. [14]Includes public order.

Internet resources for further information:
• **Statistical Centre of Iran** http://www.sci.org.ir/english/default.htm
• **Central Bank of Iran** http://www.cbi.ir

Iraq

Official name: Al-Jumhūrīyah al-ʿIrāqīyah (Republic of Iraq).
Form of government[1]: transitional regime with one legislative body (National Council [100[2]]).
Head of state and government[1]: President assisted by Prime Minister.
Capital: Baghdad.
Official languages: Arabic; Kurdish.
Official religion: Islam.
Monetary unit[3]: 1 (new) Iraqi dinar (ID); valuation (Sept. 1, 2005) 1 U.S.$ = (new) ID 1,470; 1 £ = (new) ID 2,706.

Area and population

Governorates	Capitals	area sq mi	area sq km	population 2004 estimate
Al-Anbār	Ar-Ramādī	53,208	137,808	1,328,776
Bābil	Al-Hillah	2,163	5,603	1,493,718
Baghdād	Baghdad	1,572	4,071	6,554,126
Al-Baṣrah	Al-Baṣrah	7,363	19,070	1,797,821
Dahūk	Dahūk	2,530	6,553	472,238
Dhī Qār	An-Nāṣirīyah	4,981	12,900	1,472,405
Diyālā	Baʿqūbah	6,828	17,685	1,418,455
Irbīl	Irbīl	5,820	15,074	1,392,093
Karbalāʾ	Karbalāʾ	1,944	5,034	787,072
Maysān	Al-ʿAmārah	6,205	16,072	762,872
Al-Muthannā	As-Samāwah	19,977	51,740	554,994
An-Najaf	An-Najaf	11,129	28,824	978,400
Nīnawā	Mosul	14,410	37,323	2,554,270
Al-Qādisiyah	Ad-Dīwānīyah	3,148	8,153	911,641
Salāh ad-Dīn	Tikrīt	9,407	24,363	1,119,369
As-Sulaymānīyah	As-Sulaymānīyah	6,573	17,023	1,715,585
At-Taʾmīm	Karkūk (Kirkūk)	3,737	9,679	854,470
Wāsiṭ	Al-Kūt	6,623	17,153	971,280
TOTAL		167,618	434,128	27,139,585

Demography

Population (2005): 27,818,000.
Density (2005): persons per sq mi 166.0, persons per sq km 64.1.
Urban-rural (2004): urban 65.0%; rural 35.0%.
Sex distribution (2001): male 50.57%; female 49.43%.
Age breakdown (2004)[4]: under 15, 39.5%; 15–29, 29.8%; 30–44, 16.6%; 45–59, 9.2%; 60–74, 3.8%; 75 and over, 1.1%.
Population projection: (2010) 31,470,000; (2020) 39,197,000.
Doubling time: 26 years.
Ethnic composition (2000): Arab 64.7%; Kurd 23.0%; Azerbaijani 5.6%; Turkmen 1.2%; Persian 1.1%; other 4.4%.
Religious affiliation (2000): Shīʿī Muslim 62.0%; Sunnī Muslim 34.0%; Christian (primarily Chaldean rite and Syrian rite Catholic and Nestorian) 3.2%; other (primarily Yazīdī syncretist) 0.8%.
Major cities (2003)[5]: Baghdad 5,750,000; Mosul 1,800,000; Al-Baṣrah 1,400,000; Irbīl 850,000; Karkūk 750,000.

Vital statistics

Birth rate per 1,000 population (2004): 33.1 (world avg. 21.1).
Death rate per 1,000 population (2004): 5.7 (world avg. 9.0).
Natural increase rate per 1,000 population (2004): 27.4 (world avg. 12.1).
Total fertility rate (avg. births per childbearing woman; 2004): 4.4.
Marriage rate per 1,000 population (2000): 7.3.
Divorce rate per 1,000 population (2000): 1.3.
Life expectancy at birth (2004): male 67.1 years; female 69.5 years.
Major causes of death per 100,000 population (2002): communicable diseases 377, diseases of the circulatory system 187, accidents and violence 115, malignant neoplasms (cancers) 54.

National economy

Budget (2004). Revenue: ID 30,018,000,000,000 (petroleum revenue 87%; other 13%). Expenditures: ID 45,243,000,000,000 (operating expenditure 82%; development expenditure 18%).
Public debt (external, outstanding; 2004): U.S.$125,000,000,000.
Production (metric tons except as noted). Agriculture, forestry, fishing (2002): wheat 800,000, dates 650,000, potatoes 625,000, tomatoes 500,000, barley 500,000, watermelons 380,000, oranges 270,000, grapes 265,000, cucumbers 215,000; livestock (number of live animals) 6,200,000 sheep, 1,400,000 cattle; roundwood (2004) 114,364 cu m; fish catch (2003) 21,600. Mining and quarrying (2003): phosphate rock 10,000. Manufacturing (value added in U.S.$'000,000; 1995): refined petroleum 143; bricks, tiles, and cement 103; food products 59; industrial chemicals 52; metal products 27. Energy production (consumption): electricity (kW-hr; 2004) 32,600,000,000 (33,700,000,000); coal, none (none); crude petroleum (barrels; 2004) 718,000,000 ([2002] 193,000,000); petroleum products (metric tons; 2002) 24,178,000 (20,709,000); natural gas (cu m; 2003) 4,000,000,000 ([2002] 5,141,000,000).
Population economically active (1997)[6]: total 4,757,000; activity rate of total population 24.8% (participation rates: ages 15–59, 42.9%; female 10.5%; unemployed [2004] 28%).

Price index (December 2002 = 100)

	2002[7]	2003[7]	2004[8]
Consumer price index	100.0	146.9	150.0

Household income and expenditure (2004). Average household size 6.4; median annual household income ID 2,230,000 (U.S.$1,517); sources of income: n.a.; expenditure (1993)[9]: food *c.* 62%, housing *c.* 12%, clothing *c.* 10%.
Gross national product (2003): U.S.$14,100,000,000 (U.S.$540 per capita).

Structure of gross domestic product

	2003 in value ID '000,000	2003 % of total value	2000 labour force	2000 % of labour force
Agriculture	2,582,601	10.5	...	...
Crude petroleum	20,349,772	82.5	...	...
Other mining	22,633	0.1	...	...
Manufacturing	514,297	2.1	...	...
Public utilities	26,405	0.1	...	...
Construction	220,915	0.9	...	...
Transp. and commun.	2,745,802	11.1	...	...
Trade	2,426,115	9.8	...	...
Finance, real estate	386,986	1.6	...	...
Pub. admin., defense	325,323	1.3	...	...
Services	526,722	2.1	...	...
Other	−5,464,492[10]	−22.1[10]	...	...
TOTAL	24,663,079	100.0	6,339,000	100.0

Tourism (2001): receipts U.S.$14,500,000; expenditures U.S.$30,600,000.
Land use as % of total land area (2000): in temporary crops 12.5%, in permanent crops 0.8%, in pasture 9.1%; overall forest area 1.8%.

Foreign trade[11]

Balance of trade (current prices)

	1998	1999	2000	2001	2002	2003
U.S.$'000,000	+1,705	+2,491	+5,867	−248	+419	+153
% of total	13.0%	11.4%	18.6%	1.0%	2.1%	0.8%

Imports (2003): U.S.$9,933,000,000 (UN oil-for-food program 65.7%, capital goods 17.0%, consumer goods 11.4%). *Major import sources* (2004): Turkey 25.0%; U.S. 11.1%; Jordan 10.0%; Vietnam 7.7%; Germany 5.6%.
Exports (2003): U.S.$10,086,000,000 (crude petroleum 82.8%; food and live animals 5.0%). *Major export destinations* (2004): U.S. 55.8%; Spain 8.0%; Japan 7.3%; Italy 6.5%; Canada 5.8%.

Transport and communications

Transport. Railroads (2004): route length 2,200 km; passenger-km (1999) 499,600,000; metric ton-km cargo (1999) 830,200,000. Roads (2002): total length 45,550 km (paved 84%). Vehicles (2001): passenger cars 754,066; trucks and buses 372,241. Air transport: [12].

Communications

Medium	date	unit	number	units per 1,000 persons
Daily newspapers	2001	circulation	472,000	19
Radio	2001	receivers	5,510,000	222
Television	2001	receivers	2,060,000	83
Telephones	2003	main lines	675,000	26
Cellular telephones	2002	subscribers	20,000	1.0
Personal computers	2002	units	212,000	8.3
Internet	2002	users	25,000	1.0

Education and health

Educational attainment (2004)[4]. Percentage of population age 25 and over having: no formal schooling 28%; incomplete primary education 12%; primary 36%; secondary 9%; higher 15%. *Literacy* (2003): total population age 15 and over literate 40.4%; males 55.9%; females 24.4%.

Education (2002–03)

	schools[13]	teachers	students	student/ teacher ratio
Primary (age 6–11)	8,333	220,366	4,280,602	19.4
Secondary (age 12–17)	2,822	78,848	1,414,775	17.9
Voc., teacher tr.	303	5,242	62,841	12.0
Higher	11	14,743[14]	317,993[14]	21.6[14]

Health (2003): physicians 16,594 (1 per 1,587 persons); hospital beds 34,505 (1 per 763 persons); infant mortality rate per 1,000 live births (2004) 52.7.
Food (2000): daily per capita caloric intake 2,197 (vegetable products 96%, animal products 4%); 91% of FAO recommended minimum requirement.

Military

Total active duty personnel (July 2005): 77,300; U.S./allied coalition forces (July 2005): 138,000/23,000. *Military expenditure as percentage of GDP:* n.a.

---

[1]As of Dec. 7, 2005; elections based on constitution adopted on Oct. 15, 2005, were held on Dec. 15, 2005, for the permanent 275-seat Council of Representatives of Iraq. [2]All seats are nonelected. [3]The (new) Iraqi dinar (ID) introduced on Oct. 15, 2003, replaced the (old) Iraqi dinar at a rate of 1 to 1. [4]Based on the Iraq Living Conditions Survey, which comprised 21,668 households and was conducted between March and August 2004. [5]Unofficial estimate(s). [6]Excludes Kurdish Autonomous Region. [7]December. [8]July. [9]Weights of consumer price index components. [10]Less imputed bank service charges and less indirect taxes. [11]Imports are c.i.f. in balance of trade and commodities and f.o.b. in trading partners. [12]Iraqi Airways resumed international flights in September 2004 after 14 years of being grounded by war and sanctions. [13]1997–98. [14]2001–02.

Internet resources for further information:
• **Central Bank of Iraq**
   http://www.cbiraq.org/cb1.htm

Ireland

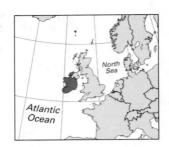

Official name: Éire (Irish); Ireland[1] (English).
Form of government: unitary multi-party republic with two legislative houses (Senate [60[2]]; House of Representatives [166]).
Chief of state: President.
Head of government: Prime Minister.
Capital: Dublin.
Official languages: Irish; English.
Official religion: none.
Monetary unit: 1 euro (€) = 100 cents; valuation (Sept. 1, 2005) 1 U.S.$ = €0.80; 1 £ = €1.47[3].

Area and population

Provinces Counties/County Boroughs (C.B.)	area sq km	population 2002 census	Provinces Counties/County Boroughs (C.B.)	area sq km	population 2002 census
Connaught (Connacht)	17,711	464,296	Westmeath	1,840	71,858
Galway	6,098	143,245	Wexford	2,367	116,596
Galway C.B.	51	65,832	Wicklow	2,027	114,676
Leitrim	1,590	25,799	Munster	24,674	1,100,614
Mayo	5,586	117,446	Clare	3,450	103,277
Roscommon	2,548	53,774	Cork	7,460	324,767
Sligo	1,838	58,200	Cork C.B.	40	123,062
Leinster	19,801[4]	2,105,579	Kerry	4,807	132,527
Carlow	897	46,014	Limerick	2,735	121,281
Dublin C.B.	118	495,781	Limerick C.B.	21	54,023
Dun Laoghaire-Rathdown	126	191,792	Tipperary North Riding	2,046	61,010
Fingal	455	196,413	Tipperary South Riding	2,258	79,121
Kildare	1,695	163,944	Waterford	1,816	56,952
Kilkenny	2,073	80,339	Waterford C.B.	41	44,594
Laoighis	1,720	58,774	Ulster (part of)	8,088	246,714
Longford	1,091	31,068	Cavan	1,932	56,546
Louth	826	101,821	Donegal	4,861	137,575
Meath	2,342	134,005	Monaghan	1,295	52,593
Offaly	2,001	63,663	TOTAL	70,273[4,5]	3,917,203
South Dublin	224	238,835			

Demography

Population (2005): 4,152,000.
Density (2005): persons per sq mi 153.0, persons per sq km 59.1.
Urban-rural (2003): urban 59.9%; rural 40.1%.
Sex distribution (2005): male 49.85%; female 50.15%.
Age breakdown (2005): under 15, 20.7%; 15–29, 23.9%; 30–44, 22.5%; 45–59, 17.6%; 60–74, 10.4%; 75 and over, 4.9%.
Population projection: (2010) 4,354,000; (2020) 4,753,000.
Ethnic composition (2000): Irish 95.0%; British 1.7%, of which English 1.4%; Ulster Irish 1.0%; U.S. white 0.8%; other 1.5%.
Religious affiliation (2002): Roman Catholic 88.4%; Church of Ireland (Anglican) 3.0%; other Christian 1.6%; nonreligious 3.5%; other 3.5%.
Major cities (2002): Dublin 495,781 (urban agglomeration 1,004,600); Cork 123,062; Galway 65,832; Limerick 54,023; Waterford 44,594.

Vital statistics

Birth rate per 1,000 population (2004): 15.3 (world avg. 21.1); legitimate 67.7%; illegitimate 32.3%.
Death rate per 1,000 population (2004): 7.0 (world avg. 9.0).
Natural increase rate per 1,000 population (2004): 8.3 (world avg. 12.1).
Marriage rate per 1,000 population (2004): 5.1.
Total fertility rate (avg. births per childbearing woman; 2004): 1.9.
Life expectancy at birth (2002): male 75.1 years; female 80.3 years.
Major causes of death per 100,000 population (2003): diseases of the circulatory system 275.3; malignant neoplasms (cancers) 189.7; diseases of the respiratory system 111.0; accidents and violence 34.0.

National economy

Budget (2000). Revenue: £Ir 21,741,000,000 (income taxes 33.0%, value-added tax 27.0%, excise taxes 15.4%). Expenditures: £Ir 19,297,000,000 (social welfare 27.9%, health 20.9%, education 14.9%, debt service 10.5%).
Total public debt (2003): U.S.$42,530,500,000.
Gross national product (2004): U.S.$137,761,000,000 (U.S.$34,280 per capita).

Structure of gross domestic product and labour force

	2001 in value €'000,000	2001 % of total value	2004[6] labour force	2004[6] % of labour force
Agriculture	3,546.8	3.1	117,000	6.1
Mining	644.5	0.6	} 300,600	} 15.6
Manufacturing	33,865.4	29.6		
Public utilities	1,316.0	1.1		
Construction	7,477.2	6.5	206,000	10.7
Transp. and commun.	5,667.3	5.0	113,200	5.9
Trade, hotels	13,110.0	11.5	368,000	19.2
Pub. admin., defense	4,013.9	3.5	89,500	4.7
Services	12,476.8	10.9	404,900	21.1
Finance	20,792.9	18.2	237,000	12.3
Other	11,568.0[7]	10.1[7]	84,200[8]	4.4[8]
TOTAL	114,479.0[4]	100.0[4]	1,920,400	100.0

Tourism (2003): receipts U.S.$3,862,000,000; expenditures U.S.$4,736,000,000.
Production (metric tons except as noted). Agriculture, forestry, fishing (2004): sugar beets 1,500,000, barley 1,159,000, wheat 849,000, potatoes 500,000, oats

134,000; livestock (number of live animals) 7,044,100 cattle, 4,850,100 sheep, 1,731,600 pigs; roundwood (2004) 2,499,306 cu m; fish catch (2003) 328,751. Mining and quarrying (2003): zinc ore 419,041[9]; lead ore 50,339[9]. Manufacturing (gross value added in €'000,000; 2001): chemicals and chemical products 12,370; electrical and optical equipment 7,293; food, beverages, and tobacco 6,902; paper products, printing, and publishing 3,250. Energy production (consumption): electricity (kW-hr; 2002) 25,194,000,000 (25,697,000,000); coal (metric tons; 2002) none (2,770,000); crude petroleum (barrels; 2002) none (23,300,000); petroleum products (metric tons; 2002) 3,124,000 (7,167,000); natural gas (cu m; 2002) 792,000,000 (4,386,000,000).
Population economically active (2002): total 1,827,100; activity rate 46.6% (participation rates: ages 15–64 [2004] 68.1%; female [2004] 41.7%; unemployed [October 2003–September 2004] 4.5%).

Price and earnings indexes (2000 = 100)

	1998	1999	2000	2001	2002	2003	2004
Consumer price index	93.2	94.7	100.0	104.9	109.8	113.6	116.1
Weekly earnings index	88.5	93.7	100.0	109.1	115.2	122.6	128.7

Household income and expenditure. Average household size (2002) 2.9; average annual disposable income per household (1999–2000): £Ir 22,589 (U.S.$28,800); expenditure (1999–2000): food 20.3%, transportation 16.4%, housing and energy 13.4%.
Land use as % of total land area (2000): in temporary crops 15.2%, in permanent crops 0.03%, in pasture 48.6%; overall forest area 9.6%.

Foreign trade[10]

Balance of trade (current prices)

	1999	2000	2001	2002	2003	2004
€'000,000	+22,629	+27,980	+35,306	+38,415	+34,211	+33,266
% of total	20.3%	20.0%	23.5%	25.0%	26.3%	24.6%

Imports (2002): €55,277,000,000 (machinery 42.0%, of which office machines and parts 15.5%, electronic microcircuits 12.4%; chemicals and chemical products 12.3%; road vehicles 6.0%; food 5.6%). Major import sources: U.K. 36.1%; U.S. 15.3%; Germany 6.4%; France 4.0%; Japan 3.6%.
Exports (2002): €93,692,000,000 (organic chemicals 18.8%; office machines and parts 18.5%; medicinal and pharmaceutical products 16.7%; electronic microcircuits 8.6%). Major export destinations: U.K. 24.0%; U.S. 17.6%; Belgium 14.4%; Germany 7.2%; France 5.0%.

Transport and communications

Transport. Railroads (2001): route length 1,947 km; passenger-km 1,515,303,000; metric ton-km cargo 515,754,000. Roads (2002): length 95,736 km (paved 100%). Vehicles (2000): passenger cars 1,269,245; trucks and buses 188,814. Air transport (2004)[11]: passenger-km 11,291,000,000; metric ton-km cargo 124,156,000; airports (1996) 9.

Communications

Medium	date	unit	number	units per 1,000 persons
Daily newspapers	2004	circulation	742,000	183
Radio	2000	receivers	2,660,000	695
Television	2002	receivers	2,707,000	694
Telephones	2004	main lines	2,019,100	505
Cellular telephones	2004	subscribers	3,780,000	945
Personal computers	2002	units	2,011,000	503
Internet	2004	users	1,079,700	270

Education and health

Educational attainment (2002). Percentage of population ages 25–64 having: no formal schooling through lower secondary 40%; upper secondary/higher vocational 35%; university 25%.

Education (2002–03)

	schools	teachers	students	student/ teacher ratio
Primary (age 6–11)	3,318	24,700	448,754	18.2
Secondary (age 12–18)	410	12,447	189,093	15.2
Voc., teacher tr.	336	9,615	150,138	15.6
Higher	55	5,644[12]	137,323	19.0[12]

Health: physicians (2003) 10,270 (1 per 389 persons); hospital beds (2002) 13,020[13] (1 per 306 persons); infant mortality rate per 1,000 live births (2004) 4.9.
Food (2002): daily per capita caloric intake 3,656 (vegetable products 69%, animal products 31%); 146% of FAO recommended minimum requirement.

Military

Total active duty personnel (2004): 10,460 (army 81.3%, navy 10.5%, air force 8.2%). Military expenditure as percentage of GDP (2003): 0.7%; per capita expenditure U.S.$247.

---

[1]As provided by the constitution; the 1948 Republic of Ireland Act provides precedent for this longer formulation of the official name but, per official sources, "has not changed the usage *Ireland* as the name of the state in the English language." [2]Includes 11 nonelective seats. [3]The Irish pound was the former monetary unit; on Jan. 1, 2002, 1 £Ir = €1.27. [4]Detail does not add to total given because of rounding. [5]27,133 sq mi. [6]March–May. [7]Taxes less subsidies and less statistical discrepancy. [8]Unemployed. [9]Metal content. [10]Imports c.i.f.; exports f.o.b. [11]Aer Lingus only. [12]1998–99. [13]Publicly funded acute hospitals only.

Internet resources for further information:
• **Central Statistics Office (Ireland)** http://www.cso.ie
• **Central Bank of Ireland** http://www.centralbank.ie

Isle of Man

Official name: Isle of Man[1].
Political status: crown dependency (United Kingdom) with two legislative bodies[2] (Legislative Council [11[3]]; House of Keys [24]).
Chief of state: British Monarch represented by Lieutenant-Governor.
Head of government: Chief Minister assisted by the Council of Ministers.
Capital: Douglas.
Official language: English.
Official religion: none.
Monetary unit: 1 Manx pound (£M)[4] = 100 new pence; valuation (Sept. 1, 2005) 1 £M = U.S.$1.84.

Area and population

	area	population		area	population
	sq km	2001 census		sq km	2001 census
Towns			**Parishes** (cont.)		
Castletown	2.3	3,100	Ballaugh	23.6	868
Douglas	10.1	25,347	Braddan	42.6	2,665
Peel	1.7	3,785	Bride	21.7	408
Ramsey	3.7	7,322	German	45.3	1,010
			Jurby	17.7	677
Villages			Lezayre	62.3	1,134
Laxey	2.4	1,725	Lonan	35.2	1,393
Onchan	24.7	8,803	Malew	47.1	2,262
Port Erin	2.6	3,369	Marown	26.7	1,879
Port St. Mary	1.4	1,941	Maughold	34.5	941
			Michael	33.9	1,431
Parishes			Patrick	42.2	1,305
Andreas	31.1	1,152	Rushen	24.6	1,504
Arbory	17.7	1,714	Santon	16.9	580
			TOTAL	572.0[5]	76,315

Demography

Population (2005): 78,000.
Density (2005): persons per sq mi 352.9, persons per sq km 136.4.
Urban-rural (2001): urban 72.6%; rural 27.4%.
Sex distribution (2001): male 48.97%; female 51.03%.
Age breakdown (2001): under 15, 17.9%; 15–29, 17.5%; 30–44, 22.6%; 45–59, 20.1%; 60–74, 13.6%; 75 and over, 8.3%.
Population projection: (2010) 80,000; (2020) 84,000.
Population by place of birth (2001): Isle of Man 48.0%; United Kingdom 45.2%, of which England 38.2%, Scotland 3.5%, Northern Ireland 2.3%, Wales 1.2%; Ireland 2.3%; other Europe 1.0%; other 3.5%.
Religious affiliation (2000): Christian 63.7%, of which Anglican 40.5%, Methodist 9.9%, Roman Catholic 8.2%; other (mostly nonreligious) 36.3%.
Major towns (2001): Douglas 25,347; Onchan 8,803; Ramsey 7,322; Peel 3,785; Port Erin 3,369.

Vital statistics

Birth rate per 1,000 population (2004): 11.1 (world avg. 21.1); (2003) legitimate 61.6%; illegitimate 38.4%.
Death rate per 1,000 population (2004): 10.3 (world avg. 9.0).
Natural increase rate per 1,000 population (2004): 0.8 (world avg. 12.1).
Total fertility rate (avg. births per childbearing woman; 2005): 1.7.
Marriage rate per 1,000 population (2003): 5.4.
Divorce rate per 1,000 population (2002): 5.2.
Life expectancy at birth (2005): male 75.0 years; female 81.9 years.
Major causes of death per 100,000 population (2002): diseases of the circulatory system 495.6, of which ischemic heart diseases 264.1, cerebrovascular disease 132.7; malignant neoplasms (cancers) 278.3; diseases of the respiratory system 106.7.

National economy

Budget (2003–04). Revenue: £462,615,000 (customs duties and excise taxes 66.2%; income taxes 33.1%, of which resident 29.0%, nonresident 4.1%; nontax revenue 0.7%). Expenditures: £425,083,000 (health and social security 39.6%; education 18.8%; transportation 7.6%; home affairs 6.4%; tourism and recreation 5.6%).
Public debt: n.a.
Production. Agriculture, forestry, fishing: main crops include hay, oats, barley, wheat, and orchard crops; livestock (number of live animals; 2002) 171,000 sheep, 34,000 cattle; fish catch (value of principal catch in £; 2004): 2,828,618, of which scallops 1,741,614, queen scallops 449,022, crab 323,842. Mining and quarrying: sand and gravel. Manufacturing (value added in U.S.$; 2001–02): electrical and nonelectrical machinery/apparatus, textiles, other 76,100,000; food and beverages 21,900,000. Energy production (consumption): electricity (kW-hr; 2001–02), n.a. (345,000,000); crude petroleum, none (n.a.); petroleum products, n.a. (n.a.); natural gas, none (n.a.).
Household income and expenditure. Average household size (2001) 2.4; income per household (1981–82)[6, 7] £7,479 (U.S.$13,721); sources of income (1981–82)[6, 7]: wages and salaries 64.1%, transfer payments 16.9%, interest and dividends 11.2%, self-employment 6.6%; expenditure (1981–82)[6, 7]: food and beverages 31.0%, transportation 14.9%, energy 11.0%, housing 7.9%, clothing and footwear 7.0%.
Gross national product (at current market prices; 2003–04): U.S.$2,490,000,000 (U.S.$32,185 per capita).

Structure of gross domestic product and labour force

	2002–03		2001	
	in value £'000[8]	% of total value[8]	labour force	% of labour force
Agriculture, fishing	17,808	1.5	543	1.4
Mining	} 98,883	8.0	3,185	8.0
Manufacturing				
Construction	134,631	11.0	2,512	6.3
Public utilities	23,842	1.9	515	1.3
Transp. and commun.	79,780	6.5	3,331	8.4
Trade, hotels	140,253	11.4	7,231	18.2
Finance, real estate, insurance	539,996[9]	43.9[9]	} 8,959	22.6
International business	275,091[9]	22.4[9]		
Pub. admin., defense	63,202	5.1	3,105	7.8
Services	53,747	4.4	9,669	24.4
Other	−197,821[10]	−16.1[10]	635[11]	1.6[11]
TOTAL	1,229,414[12]	100.0	39,685	100.0

Population economically active (2001): total 39,685; activity rate of total population 52.0% (participation rates: ages 16–64, 78.9%; female 45.4%; registered unemployed [2004] 1.0%).

Price and earnings indexes (2000 = 100)

	1998	1999	2000	2001	2002	2003	2004
Retail price index[13]	...	...	100.0	102.5	104.1	107.0	112.9
Weekly earnings index[13]	93.3	97.6	100.0	106.6	112.3	120.4	123.3

Tourism (2004): receipts from visitors U.S.$83,720,000; expenditures by nationals abroad, n.a.; number of tourists 240,958.
Land use as % of total land area (2000): in temporary crops 8.1%, in permanent crops 0.7%, in pasture 71.5%; overall forest area, n.a.

Foreign trade[14]

Imports: n.a. *Major import sources:* mostly the United Kingdom.
Exports: traditional exports include scallops, herring, beef, lambs, and tweeds. *Major export destinations:* mostly the United Kingdom.

Transport and communications

Transport. Railroads (2003): route length 38 mi, 61 km[15]. Roads (2003): total length, 500 mi, 800 km (paved virtually 100%). Vehicles (2003): passenger cars 50,596; trucks and buses 11,637. Air transport (1998)[16]: passenger-mi 526,161,000, passenger-km 846,775,000; short ton-mi cargo 115,000, metric ton-km cargo 168,000; airports (2001) with scheduled flights 1.

Communications

Medium	date	unit	number	units per 1,000 persons
Daily newspapers	2001	circulation	—[17]	—
Television	2000	receivers	28,600	355
Telephones	2001	main lines	56,000	741
Cellular telephones	2001	subscribers	32,000	424

Education and health

Educational attainment: n.a. *Literacy:* n.a.

Education (2003)

	schools	teachers	students	student/ teacher ratio
Primary (age 5–10)	35	...	6,744	...
Secondary (age 11–16)	5	...	5,566	...
Higher	1	...	8,300[18]	...

Health: physicians (2003) 143 (1 per 540 persons); hospital beds (1998) 505 (1 per 143 persons); infant mortality rate per 1,000 live births (2002–03) 4.5.
Food (2002)[19]: daily per capita caloric intake 3,412 (vegetable products 69%, animal products 31%); 135% of FAO recommended minimum requirement.

Military

Total active duty personnel: [20].

[1]Ellan Vannin in Manx Gaelic. [2]Collective name is Tynwald. [3]Includes 3 nonelected seats. [4]Equivalent in value to pound sterling (£). [5]220.9 sq mi. [6]Fiscal year ending March 31. [7]Based on survey of 259 households; "high income" and "pensioner" households are excluded. [8]At factor cost. [9]The Isle of Man is an international finance centre with 57 banks and 33,351 registered companies in 2003; more than U.S.$47,000,000,000 is deposited in the island. [10]Ownership of dwellings less adjustments. [11]Unemployed. [12]Detail does not add to total given because of rounding. [13]June. [14]Because of the customs union between the Isle of Man and the U.K. since 1980, there are no customs controls on the movement of goods between the Isle of Man and the U.K. [15]Length of three tourist (novel) railways operating in summer. [16]Manx Airlines. [17]Isle of Man has 3 weekly newspapers and 1 biweekly newspaper. [18]Enrollees at Isle of Man College. [19]Data for United Kingdom. [20]The United Kingdom is responsible for defense.

Internet resources for further information:
• **Isle of Man Government**
  http://www.gov.im
• **Isle of Man Finance**
  http://www.isleofman.com/finance/index.htm

Israel

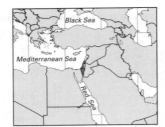

Official name: Medinat Yisra'el (Hebrew); Isrā'īl (Arabic) (State of Israel).
Form of government: multiparty republic with one legislative house (Knesset [120]).
Chief of state: President.
Head of government: Prime Minister.
Capital: Jerusalem is the proclaimed capital and actual seat of government; international recognition of its capital status has largely been withheld.
Official languages: Hebrew; Arabic.
Official religion: none.
Monetary unit: 1 New (Israeli) sheqel (NIS) = 100 agorot; valuation (Sept. 1, 2005) 1 U.S.$ = NIS 4.49; 1 £ = NIS 8.27.

Area and population

Districts	Capitals	area[1] sq mi	area[1] sq km	population 2005[2] estimate[3]
Central (Ha Merkaz)	Ramla	493	1,276	1,610,900
Haifa (Hefa)	Haifa	333	863	852,600
Jerusalem (Yerushalayim)	Jerusalem	252	652	829,800
Northern (Ha Zafon)	Tiberias	1,729	4,478	1,165,800
Southern (Ha Darom)	Beersheba	5,494	14,231	985,200
Tel Aviv	Tel Aviv–Yafo	66	171	1,177,300
TOTAL		8,367	21,671	6,621,600[3]

Demography

Population (2005): 6,677,000[4].
Density (2005)[4]: persons per sq mi 798.0, persons per sq km 308.1.
Urban-rural (2003): urban 91.6%; rural 8.4%.
Sex distribution (2003): male 49.36%; female 50.64%.
Age breakdown (2003): under 15, 28.4%; 15–29, 24.7%; 30–44, 18.8%; 45–59, 15.3%; 60–74, 8.4%; 75 and over, 4.4%.
Population projection: (2010) 7,304,000; (2020) 8,687,000.
Ethnic composition (2004[2]): Jewish 76.2%; Arab and other 23.8%.
Religious affiliation (2004[2]): Jewish 76.2%; Muslim (mostly Sunnī) 15.7%; Christian 2.1%; Druze 1.6%; other 4.4%.
Major cities (2005[2]): Jerusalem 704,900; Tel Aviv–Yafo 371,000 (metro area [2001[2]] 2,785,749); Haifa 269,300 (metro area [2001[2]] 942,021); Rishon LeZiyyon 217,500; Ashdod 196,800.

Vital statistics

Birth rate per 1,000 population (2003): 21.7 (world avg. 21.1); (2000; Jewish population only) legitimate 97.2%; illegitimate 2.8%.
Death rate per 1,000 population (2003): 5.7 (world avg. 9.0).
Natural increase rate per 1,000 population (2003): 16.0 (world avg. 12.1).
Total fertility rate (avg. births per childbearing woman; 2003): 3.0.
Marriage rate per 1,000 population (2002): 6.2.
Divorce rate per 1,000 population (2002): 1.7.
Life expectancy at birth (2002): male 77.5 years; female 81.5 years.
Major causes of death per 100,000 population (1998): diseases of the circulatory system 222; malignant neoplasms (cancers) 149; accidents and violence 43; diseases of the respiratory system 40; diabetes mellitus 39.

National economy

Budget (2003). Revenue: NIS 205,703,000,000 (tax revenue 75.4%, of which income tax 35.4%, value-added tax 27.7%; nontax revenue 18.0%; grants 6.6%). Expenditures: NIS 220,903,000,000 (defense 21.2%; social security and welfare 19.5%; interest on loans 15.1%; education 14.6%; health 7.2%).
Public debt (2004): U.S.$121,839,000,000.
Gross national product (2004): U.S.$118,124,000,000 (U.S.$17,380 per capita).

Structure of net domestic product and labour force

	2001 in value NIS '000,000	2001 % of total value	2003 labour force	2003 % of labour force
Agriculture	7,351	1.5	42,500	1.6
Mining	} 72,727	14.8	3,400	0.1
Manufacturing			376,500	14.4
Construction	21,321	4.3	129,000	4.9
Public utilities	8,170	1.7	18,000	0.7
Transp. and commun.	33,789	6.9	152,100	5.8
Trade, hotels	43,038	8.8	406,500	15.6
Finance, real estate	132,718	27.0	374,900	14.4
Public admin., defense	36,417	7.4	126,500	4.8
Services	82,454	16.8	684,100	26.2
Other	53,513[5]	10.9[5]	296,500[6]	11.4[6]
TOTAL	491,498	100.0[7]	2,610,100[7]	100.0[7]

Production (metric tons except as noted). Agriculture, forestry, fishing (2004): potatoes 570,777, tomatoes 405,000, grapefruit and pomelos 235,000, wheat 165,635, oranges 146,000, apples 125,000, grapes 95,000, olives 50,000; livestock (number of live animals) 400,000 cattle, 390,000 sheep; roundwood (2004) 27,000 cu m; fish catch (2003) 24,831. Mining and quarrying (2003): phosphate rock 3,210,000, potash 1,960,000. Manufacturing (value added in U.S.$'000,000; 2000): electronic components 2,243; medical, measuring, and testing appliances 2,103; fabricated metals 1,686; food products 1,681; telecommunications equipment 1,615; transport equipment 956; chemicals

and chemical products 914. Energy production (consumption): electricity (kW-hr; 2002) 45,393,000,000 (44,006,000,000); hard coal (metric tons; 2002) none (12,500,000); lignite (metric tons; 2002) 458,000 (458,000); crude petroleum (barrels; 2002) 36,000 (71,900,000); petroleum products (metric tons; 2002) 9,919,000 (11,547,000); natural gas (cu m; 2002) 5,900,000 (5,900,000).
Population economically active (2003): total 2,610,100; activity rate 39.0% (participation rates: ages 15–64, 61.7%; female 46.3%; unemployed [October 2003–September 2004] 10.6%).

Price and earnings indexes (2000 = 100)

	1998	1999	2000	2001	2002	2003	2004
Consumer price index	94.0	98.9	100.0	101.1	106.8	107.6	107.1
Daily earnings index	87.1	94.1	100.0	108.6	109.7	111.9	114.5

Household income and expenditure (2002). Average household size 3.4; net annual income per household (2001) NIS 136,332 (U.S.$28,285); sources of income (2000)[8]: salaries and wages 67.5%, self-employment 11.5%; expenditure (2001): housing 22.6%, transport and communications 20.1%, food and beverages 17.0%, education 13.4%, health 4.9%.
Tourism (2003): receipts U.S.$2,039,000,000; expenditures U.S.$2,550,000,000.
Land use as % of total land area (2000): in temporary crops 16.4%, in permanent crops 4.2%, in pasture 6.9%; overall forest area 6.4%.

Foreign trade[9]

Balance of trade (current prices)

	1999	2000	2001	2002	2003	2004
U.S.$'000,000	−4,238	−2,870	−3,047	−3,694	−2,240	−1,888
% of total	7.6%	4.4%	5.2%	6.3%	3.6%	2.5%

Imports (2002): U.S.$33,106,000,000 (machinery and apparatus 23.7%; diamonds 21.7%; chemicals and chemical products 9.6%; crude petroleum and refined petroleum 7.7%; road vehicles 5.7%). *Major import sources:* U.S. 18.5%; Belgium 9.1%; Germany 7.1%; U.K. 6.7%; Switzerland 6.3%.
Exports (2002): U.S.$29,511,000,000 (cut diamonds 28.2%; telecommunications equipment 9.2%; rough diamonds 6.5%; organic chemicals 3.9%; electronic microcircuits 3.6%; aircraft parts 3.6%). *Major export destinations:* U.S. 40.2%; Belgium 6.3%; Hong Kong 4.7%; U.K. 3.9%; Germany 3.5%.

Transport and communications

Transport. Railroads (2003): route length 615 km; passenger-km 1,278,000,000, metric ton-km cargo 1,112,000,000. Roads (2002): total length 16,903 km (paved 100%). Vehicles (2003): passenger cars 1,520,571; trucks and buses 349,148. Air transport (2004)[10]: passenger-km 14,364,000,000; metric ton-km cargo 863,324,000; airports (1999) with scheduled flights 7.

Communications

Medium	date	unit	number	units per 1,000 persons
Daily newspapers	2000	circulation	1,770,000	290
Radio	2000	receivers	3,210,000	526
Television	2000	receivers	2,040,000	335
Telephones	2004	main lines	3,000,000	437
Cellular telephones	2004	subscribers	7,187,500	1,005
Personal computers	2004	units	5,037,000	734
Internet	2004	users	3,200,000	466

Education and health

Educational attainment (2001). Percentage of population age 15 and over having: no formal schooling 3.1%; primary 1.7%; secondary 56.7%; postsecondary, vocational, and higher 38.5%. *Literacy* (2001): 96.9%.

Education (2002–03)

	schools	teachers	students	student/teacher ratio
Primary (age 6–13)	2,178	60,600	758,798	12.5
Secondary (age 14–17)[11]	1,768	75,938	451,027	5.9
Voc., teacher tr.	180	...	138,361	...
Higher	7	10,171	219,763	21.6

Health (2002): physicians 21,800[12] (1 per 291 persons); hospital beds 40,116 (1 per 158 persons); infant mortality rate per 1,000 live births 11.3.
Food (2002): daily per capita caloric intake 3,666 (vegetable products 78%, animal products 22%); 143% of FAO recommended minimum.

Military

Total active duty personnel (2004): 168,000 (army 74.4%, navy 4.8%, air force 20.8%). *Military expenditure as percentage of GDP* (2003): 9.1%[13]; per capita expenditure U.S.$1,553.

[1]Excludes the West Bank (2,278 sq mi [5,900 sq km]), the Gaza Strip (140 sq mi [363 sq km]), the Sea of Galilee (63 sq mi [164 sq km]), and the Dead Sea (120 sq mi [310 sq km]); includes the Golan Heights (446 sq mi [1,154 sq km]) and East Jerusalem (27 sq mi [70 sq km]). [2]January 1. [3]Includes the population of the Golan Heights (37,800) and East Jerusalem; excludes the Jewish population of the West Bank and the Gaza Strip (242,400) and 200,000–300,000 foreign workers. [4]Excludes mid-year Jewish population of West Bank (246,000). [5]Taxes on products less imputed bank service charges, subsidies, and statistical discrepancy. [6]Includes 16,600 not adequately classified and 279,900 unemployed. [7]Detail does not add to total given because of rounding. [8]Money income only. [9]Imports f.o.b. in balance of trade and c.i.f. in commodities and trading partners (c.i.f. data exclude military goods). [10]El Al only. [11]Includes intermediate schools. [12]Full-time doctors only. [13]1/5 of which is military aid from the U.S.

Internet resources for further information:
- **Central Bureau of Statistics (Israel) http://www.cbs.gov.il/engindex.htm**
- **Bank of Israel http://www.bankisrael.gov.il/firsteng.htm**

Italy

Official name: Repubblica Italiana (Italian Republic).
Form of government: republic with two legislative houses (Senate [321[1]]; Chamber of Deputies [630]).
Chief of state: President.
Head of government: Prime Minister.
Capital: Rome.
Official language: Italian.
Official religion: none.
Monetary unit: 1 euro (€) = 100 cents; valuation (Sept. 1, 2005)
1 U.S.$ = €0.80; 1 £ = €1.47[2].

Area and population

Regions Provinces	Capitals	area sq mi	area sq km	population 2003[3] estimate
Abruzzo	L'Aquila	4,168	10,794	1,273,284
Chieti	Chieti	999	2,587	383,058
L'Aquila	L'Aquila	1,944	5,034	298,082
Pescara	Pescara	473	1,225	302,983
Teramo	Teramo	752	1,948	289,161
Basilicata	Potenza	3,858	9,992	596,821
Matera	Matera	1,331	3,447	204,108
Potenza	Potenza	2,527	6,545	392,713
Calabria	Catanzaro	5,823	15,080	2,007,392
Catanzaro	Catanzaro	924	2,392	368,856
Cosenza	Cosenza	2,568	6,650	733,142
Crotone	Crotone	662	1,716	172,735
Reggio di Calabria	Reggio di Calabria	1,229	3,183	562,692
Vibo Valentia	Vibo Valentia	440	1,139	169,967
Campania	Naples	5,249	13,595	5,725,098
Avellino	Avellino	1,078	2,792	432,115
Benevento	Benevento	800	2,071	286,611
Caserta	Caserta	1,019	2,639	854,956
Napoli	Naples	452	1,171	3,075,660
Salerno	Salerno	1,900	4,922	1,075,756
Emilia-Romagna	Bologna	8,542	22,123	4,030,220
Bologna	Bologna	1,429	3,702	926,637
Ferrara	Ferrara	1,016	2,632	344,025
Forlì-Cesena	Forlì	969	2,510	362,245
Modena	Modena	1,039	2,690	643,043
Parma	Parma	1,332	3,449	396,782
Piacenza	Piacenza	1,000	2,589	267,274
Ravenna	Ravenna	718	1,859	351,193
Reggio nell'Emilia	Reggio nell'Emilia	885	2,292	462,637
Rimini	Rimini	154	400	276,384
Friuli-Venezia Giulia	Trieste	3,029	7,845	1,191,588
Gorizia	Gorizia	180	467	138,463
Pordenone	Pordenone	878	2,273	290,229
Trieste	Trieste	82	212	240,638
Udine	Udine	1,889	4,893	522,258
Lazio	Rome	6,642	17,203	5,145,805
Frosinone	Frosinone	1,251	3,239	485,041
Latina	Latina	869	2,251	497,415
Rieti	Rieti	1,061	2,749	148,547
Roma	Rome	2,066	5,352	3,723,649
Viterbo	Viterbo	1,395	3,612	291,153
Liguria	Genoa	2,092	5,418	1,572,197
Genova	Genoa	709	1,836	873,604
Imperia	Imperia	446	1,155	205,998
La Spezia	La Spezia	341	882	215,707
Savona	Savona	596	1,545	276,888
Lombardy	Milan	9,211	23,857	9,108,645
Bergamo	Bergamo	1,051	2,722	986,924
Brescia	Brescia	1,846	4,782	1,126,249
Como	Como	497	1,288	543,546
Cremona	Cremona	684	1,771	338,690
Lecco	Lecco	315	816	315,183
Lodi	Lodi	302	783	201,554
Mantova	Mantova	903	2,339	381,330
Milano	Milan	765	1,980	3,721,428
Pavia	Pavia	1,145	2,965	497,233
Sondrio	Sondrio	1,240	3,212	177,568
Varese	Varese	463	1,199	818,940
Marche	Ancona	3,743	9,693	1,484,601
Ancona	Ancona	749	1,940	452,175
Ascoli Piceno	Ascoli Piceno	806	2,087	372,407
Macerata	Macerata	1,071	2,774	305,080
Pesaro e Urbino	Pesaro	1,117	2,892	354,939
Molise	Campobasso	1,713	4,438	321,047
Campobasso	Campobasso	1,123	2,909	231,017
Isernia	Isernia	590	1,529	90,030
Piedmont	Turin	9,807[4]	25,399	4,231,334
Alessandria	Alessandria	1,375	3,560	418,203
Asti	Asti	583	1,511	209,116
Biella	Biella	352	913	187,962
Cuneo	Cuneo	2,665	6,903	561,729
Novara	Novara	530	1,373	345,952
Torino	Turin	2,637	6,830	2,172,226
Verbano-Cusio-Ossola	Verbania	858	2,221	159,636
Vercelli	Vercelli	806	2,088	176,510
Puglia	Bari	7,470	19,348	4,023,957
Bari	Bari	1,980	5,129	1,564,122
Brindisi	Brindisi	710	1,838	400,974
Foggia	Foggia	2,774	7,185	688,902
Lecce	Lecce	1,065	2,759	790,572
Taranto	Taranto	941	2,437	579,387
Sardinia	Cagliari	9,301[4]	24,090	1,637,639
Cagliari	Cagliari	1,764	4,570	543,310[5]
Carbonia-Iglesias[6]	Carbonia, Iglesias	577	1,495	131,890[5]
Medio Campidano[6]	Sanluri	585	1,516	105,400[5]
Nuoro	Nuoro	1,519	3,934	164,260[5]
Ogliastra[6]	Lanusei; Tortolì	716	1,854	58,389[5]
Olbia-Tempio[6]	Olbia; Tempio	1,312	3,399	138,334[5]
Oristano	Oristano	1,174	3,040	167,971[5]

Area and population (continued)

		area sq mi	area sq km	population 2003[3] estimate
Sassari	Sassari	1,653	4,282	322,326[5]
Sicily	Palermo	9,926	25,709	4,972,124
Agrigento	Agrigento	1,175	3,042	450,034
Caltanissetta	Caltanissetta	822	2,128	272,167
Catania	Catania	1,371	3,552	1,058,162
Enna	Enna	989	2,562	176,496
Messina	Messina	1,254	3,248	659,513
Palermo	Palermo	1,927	4,992	1,236,799
Ragusa	Ragusa	623	1,614	296,744
Siracusa	Siracusa	814	2,109	396,517
Trapani	Trapani	951	2,462	425,692
Trentino-Alto Adige	Bolzano	5,258	13,618	950,495
Bolzano-Bozen	Bolzano	2,857	7,400	467,338
Trento	Trento	2,401	6,218	483,157
Tuscany	Florence	8,877	22,992[4]	3,516,296
Arezzo	Arezzo	1,248	3,232	326,172
Firenze	Florence	1,365	3,536	935,883
Grosseto	Grosseto	1,739	4,504	212,001
Livorno	Livorno	468	1,213	327,472
Lucca	Lucca	684	1,773	373,820
Massa-Carrara	Massa-Carrara	447	1,157	197,562
Pisa	Pisa	945	2,448	386,466
Pistoia	Pistoia	373	965	271,443
Prato	Prato	133	344	231,207
Siena	Siena	1,475	3,821	254,270
Umbria	Perugia	3,265	8,456	834,210
Perugia	Perugia	2,446	6,334	613,004
Terni	Terni	819	2,122	221,206
Valle d'Aosta	Aosta	1,259	3,262	120,909
Veneto	Venice	7,090	18,364	4,577,408
Belluno	Belluno	1,420	3,678	210,503
Padova	Padova	827	2,142	857,660
Rovigo	Rovigo	691	1,789	242,608
Treviso	Treviso	956	2,477	808,076
Venezia	Venice	950	2,460	813,294
Verona	Verona	1,195	3,096	838,221
Vicenza	Vicenza	1,051	2,722	807,046
TOTAL		116,324[4, 7]	301,277[4, 7]	57,321,070

Demography

Population (2005): 57,989,000.
Density (2005): persons per sq mi 498.4, persons per sq km 192.4.
Urban-rural (2003): urban 67.4%; rural 32.6%.
Sex distribution (2005[3]): male 48.54%; female 51.46%.
Age breakdown (2003): under 15, 14.2%; 15–29, 18.0%; 30–44, 23.5%; 45–59, 19.3%; 60–74, 16.3%; 75 and over, 8.7%.
Population projection: (2010) 58,325,000; (2020) 58,145,000.
Ethnolinguistic composition (2000): Italian 96.0%; North African Arab 0.9%; Italo-Albanian 0.8%; Albanian 0.5%; German 0.4%; Austrian 0.4%; other 1.0%.
Religious affiliation (2000): Roman Catholic 79.6%; nonreligious 13.2%; Muslim 1.2%; other 6.0%.
Major cities and urban agglomerations (2005[3]/2000): Rome 2,553,873 (2,649,000); Milan 1,299,439 (4,251,000); Naples 995,171 (3,012,000); Turin 902,255 (1,294,000); Palermo 675,084; Genoa 605,084 (890,000); Bologna 374,425; Florence 368,059 (778,000); Bari 328,458; Catania 305,773; Venice 271,251; Verona 259,068; Messina (2004) 248,616; Padua (2004) 208,938.
National origin (1991): Italian 99.3%; foreign-born 0.7%, of which European 0.3%, African 0.2%, Asian 0.1%, other 0.1%.
Households. Average household size (2005[3]) 2.5; composition of households (2001): 1 person 24.9%, 2 persons 27.1%, 3 persons 21.6%, 4 persons 19.0%, 5 or more persons 7.4%. Family households (1991): 15,538,335 (73.8%); non-family 5,527,105 (26.2%), of which one-person 19.5%.
Immigration (1997): immigrants 162,857, from Europe 41.1%, of which EU countries 14.2%; Africa 25.5%; Asia 19.0%; Western Hemisphere 14.0%.

Vital statistics

Birth rate per 1,000 population (2005[3]): 9.6 (world avg. 21.1); (2003) legitimate 86.3%; illegitimate 13.7%.
Death rate per 1,000 population (2005[3]): 9.5 (world avg. 9.0).
Natural increase rate per 1,000 population (2005[3]): 0.1 (world avg. 12.1).
Total fertility rate (avg. births per childbearing woman; 2005[3]): 1.3.
Marriage rate per 1,000 population (2004): 4.3.
Divorce rate per 1,000 population (2003): 0.7.
Life expectancy at birth (2004): male 77.3 years; female 83.1 years.
Major causes of death per 100,000 population (2003): diseases of the circulatory system 429.5; malignant neoplasms 282.9; diseases of the respiratory system 73.0; accidents and violence 45.5; diseases of the digestive system 42.9.

Social indicators

Educational attainment (2002). Percentage of labour force ages 25 to 64 having: no formal schooling through lower secondary education 55.6%; completed upper secondary 34.0%; completed higher 10.4%.
Quality of working life. Average workweek (2001): 39.3 hours. Annual rate per 100,000 workers (2000) for: nonfatal injury 4,030; fatal injury 7. Percentage of labour force insured for damages or income loss (1992) resulting from: injury 100%; permanent disability 100%; death 100%. Number of working days lost to labour stoppages per 1,000 workers (1996): 97.
Material well-being. Rate per 1,000 of population possessing (1995): telephone 434; automobile 550; television 436.
Social participation. Eligible voters participating in last national election (May 13, 2001): 81.2%. Trade union membership in total workforce (2004): c. 30%.
Social deviance (2000). Offense rate per 100,000 population for: murder 1.3; rape 4.1; theft, including burglary and housebreaking 2,466; drug trafficking 61.1; suicide 6.3[8].
Access to services (2002). Nearly 100% of dwellings have access to electricity, a safe water supply, and toilet facilities.

Leisure (1998). Favourite leisure activities (as percentage of household spending on culture): cinema 21.8%; sporting events 14.6%; theatre 13.8%.

National economy

Gross national product (at current market prices; 2004): U.S.$1,503,562,000,000 (U.S.$26,120 per capita).

Structure of gross domestic product and labour force

	2003			
	in value €'000,000[9]	% of total value[9]	labour force[3]	% of labour force[3]
Agriculture	32,067	2.7	1,075,000	4.4
Mining	4,949	0.4	59,000	0.2
Manufacturing	221,642	18.8	4,990,000	20.6
Construction	59,806	5.1	1,809,000	7.5
Public utilities	26,829	2.3	161,000	0.7
Transportation and communications	87,547	7.4	1,162,000	4.8
Trade	193,760	16.4	4,483,000	18.5
Finance	318,205	27.0	2,393,000	9.9
Pub. admin., defense	65,754	5.6	1,934,000	8.0
Services	169,404	14.4	4,050,000	16.7
Other	—	—	2,113,000[10]	8.7[10]
TOTAL	1,179,963	100.0[4]	24,229,000	100.0

Budget (2000). Revenue: €444,502,000,000 (social security contributions 32.5%, individual income taxes 28.6%, taxes on goods and services 15.9%, corporate income tax 5.9%). Expenditures: €462,352,000,000 (social benefits 41.9%, interest payments 16.0%, grants to general government units 14.9%).
Public debt (2002): U.S.$1,333,669,000,000.

Financial aggregates

	1999	2000	2001	2002	2003	2004
Exchange rate, € per:						
U.S. dollar	1.00	1.07	1.13	0.95	0.79	0.73
£	1.61	1.60	1.65	1.54	1.41	1.42
SDR	1.37	1.40	1.43	1.30	1.18	1.14
International reserves (U.S.$)						
Total (excl. gold; '000,000)	22,422	25,567	24,419	28,603	30,366	27,859
SDRs ('000,000)	168	238	297	108	156	145
Reserve pos. in IMF ('000,000)	3,546	2,906	3,217	3,907	4,154	3,703
Foreign exchange ('000,000)	18,708	22,423	20,905	24,588	26,056	24,011
Gold ('000,000 fine troy oz)	78.83	78.83	78.83	78.83	78.83	78.83
% world reserves	8.2	8.3	8.4	8.5	8.6	8.8
Interest and prices						
Central bank discount (%)	...	...	...	...	...	...
Govt. bond yield (%)	4.04	5.29	4.64	4.48	3.36	3.34
Industrial share prices (2000 = 100)	77.0	100.0	81.1	64.3	58.1	66.8
Balance of payments (U.S.$'000,000)						
Balance of visible trade	+23,436	+9,548	+15,539	+13,412	+11,477	+10,911
Imports, f.o.b.	−212,420	−230,925	−229,392	−239,206	−286,641	−341,255
Exports, f.o.b.	235,856	240,473	244,931	252,618	298,118	352,166
Balance of invisibles	−15,325	−15,329	−16,191	−22,781	−30,833	−26,048
Balance of payments, current account	+8,111	−5,781	−652	−9,369	−19,406	−15,137

Tourism (2003): receipts U.S.$31,222,000,000; expenditures U.S.$20,528,000,000.

Manufacturing, mining, and construction enterprises (1995)

	no. of enterprises	no. of employees[11]	hourly wages as a % of avg. of all wages	annual value added (Lit '000,000,000)
Manufacturing				
Metal products	5,780	360,979	...	36,249
Machinery (nonelectrical)	4,503	379,027	...	35,221
Industrial chemicals	1,206	180,836	...	27,505
Electrical machinery	2,962	303,439	...	26,306
Food products	2,549	224,025	...	22,878
Transport equipment	1,122	275,077	...	22,642
Printing, publishing[12]	2,086	148,757	...	16,150
Pottery, ceramics, and glass	2,128	149,586	...	14,361
Textiles[13]	3,514	215,387	...	14,335
Rubber and plastic products	1,836	123,119	...	12,711
Wearing apparel	2,436	114,059	...	7,279
Paper and paper products[12]	...	...	...	...
Petroleum and gas	108	22,566	...	4,221
Mining and quarrying	340	20,013	...	5,991
Construction	6,228	1,564,100	...	94,887

Production (metric tons except as noted). Agriculture, forestry, fishing (2004): corn (maize) 10,983,080, sugar beets 10,100,000, grapes 8,691,970, wheat 8,628,758, tomatoes 7,496,997, olives 3,300,000, apples 2,069,243, oranges 2,064,099, potatoes 1,809,097, peaches and nectarines 1,672,609, rice 1,496,000, barley 1,166,877, pears 833,400, lettuce 830,580; livestock (number of live animals) 9,223,000 pigs, 8,000,000 sheep, 6,727,000 cattle, 100,000,000 chickens; roundwood 8,697,393 cu m; fish catch (2003) 295,694. Mining and quarrying (2003): limestone 120,000,000; marble 5,600,000; feldspar 2,500,000; pumice 600,000. Manufacturing (value added in U.S.$'000,000; 2000): non-electrical machinery and apparatus 25,935; fabricated metal products 22,934; food products 13,468; paints, soaps, pharmaceuticals 10,594; bricks, cement, ceramics 8,418; textiles 8,165; wearing apparel 7,524; motor vehicles and parts 7,254; plastic products 6,627; furniture 5,924; footwear and leather products 5,592; telecommunications equipment 5,374.
Energy production (consumption): electricity (kW-hr; 2004) 299,700,000,000 ([2002] 335,873,000,000); hard coal (metric tons; 2002) 163,000 (20,000,000); lignite (metric tons; 2003) 10,000 ([2002] 10,000); crude petroleum (barrels; 2003) 30,000,000 ([2002] 593,000,000); petroleum products (metric tons; 2002) 86,578,000 (83,836,000); natural gas (cu m; 2004) 12,527,000,000 ([2002] 70,483,000,000).

Population economically active (2003): total 24,229,000; activity rate of total population 42.2% (participation rates: ages 15–64, 61.6%; female 39.1%; unemployed [2004] 8.6%).

Price and earnings indexes (2000 = 100)

	1998	1999	2000	2001	2002	2003	2004
Consumer price index	95.9	97.5	100.0	102.8	105.3	108.1	110.5
Earnings index	95.8	98.0	100.0	101.8	104.5	107.2	110.5

Household income and expenditure. Average household size (2005[3]) 2.5; average annual disposable income per household (2000): c. €28,100 (c. U.S.$25,900); sources of income (1996): salaries and wages 38.8%, property income and self-employment 38.5%, transfer payments 22.0%; expenditure (2005[3]): housing and energy 30.1%, food and beverages 19.0%, transportation and communications 16.3%, clothing 6.6%, household operations 6.3%.
Land use as % of total land area (2000): in temporary crops 28.2%, in permanent crops 9.7%, in pasture 15.1%; overall forest area 34.0%.

Foreign trade[14]

Balance of trade (current prices)

	1998	1999	2000	2001	2002	2003	2004
U.S.$'000,000	+27,300	+14,941	+1,757	+8,263	+7,376	+1,826	−2,065
% of total	5.9%	3.3%	0.4%	1.7%	1.5%	0.3%	0.3%

Imports (2004): U.S.$350,391,000,000 (transport equipment 14.2%, chemical products 13.5%, electrical equipment 13.1%, fuels 10.4%, fabricated metals 10.4%). *Major import sources:* Germany 18.1%; France 10.7%; The Netherlands 5.8%; Spain 4.7%; Belgium 4.4%; U.K. 4.3%; China 4.1%.
Exports (2004): U.S.$348,513,000,000 (machinery and apparatus 20.4%, transport equipment 11.2%, chemical products 9.7%, fabricated metals 9.6%, textiles and wearing apparel 9.2%, electrical equipment 9.1%). *Major export destinations:* Germany 13.7%; France 12.1%; U.S. 8.0%; Spain 7.3%; U.K. 6.9%; Switzerland 4.1%.

Transport and communications

Transport. Railroads: (2004) length 19,319 km; (2002) passenger-km 45,818,000,000; (2002) metric ton-km cargo 23,000,000,000. Roads (1999): total length 479,688 km (paved 100%). Vehicles (2002): passenger cars 33,706,153; trucks and buses 3,843,415. Air transport (2004)[15]: passenger-km 31,394,000,000; metric ton-km cargo 1,392,705,000; airports (1997) 34.

Communications

Medium	date	unit	number	units per 1,000 persons
Daily newspapers	2004	circulation	7,737,000	134
Radio	2001	receivers	50,036,000	878
Television	2001	receivers	28,153,000	494
Telephones	2004	main lines	25,957,000	448
Cellular telephones	2004	subscribers	62,750,000	1,083
Personal computers	2004	units	18,150,000	313
Internet	2004	users	28,870,000	498

Education and health

Literacy (2003): total population age 15 and over literate 98.6%; males literate 99.0%; females literate 98.3%.

Education (2002–03)

	schools	teachers	students	student/ teacher ratio
Primary (age 6–10)	18,575	256,650	2,778,877	10.8
Secondary (age 11–18)	7,883	263,563	3,829,583	14.5
Voc., teacher tr. }	6,527	164,614	698,717	4.2
Higher		87,215	1,913,352	21.9

Health: physicians (2002) 353,692 (1 per 162 persons); hospital beds (2003) 237,216 (1 per 243 persons); infant mortality rate (2004) 6.1.
Food (2002): daily per capita caloric intake 3,671 (vegetable products 74%, animal products 26%); 146% of FAO recommended minimum requirement.

Military

Total active duty personnel (2004): 198,000 (army 58.6%, navy 17.2%, air force 24.2%); U.S. military forces (December 2004) 12,500. *Military expenditure as percentage of GDP* (2003): 1.9%; per capita expenditure U.S.$478.

---

[1]Includes 6 nonelective seats in mid-2005 (4 presidential appointees and 2 former presidents serving ex officio). [2]The Italian lira (Lit) was the former monetary unit; on Jan. 1, 2002, Lit 1,936 = €1. [3]January 1. [4]Detail does not add to total given because of rounding. [5]2001 census figures. [6]Established May 2005. [7]The total area for Italy, per 2003 survey, is 116,346 sq mi (301,336 sq km). [8]1996. [9]At factor cost. [10]Including 2,096,000 unemployed. [11]Total number of persons engaged. [12]Printing, publishing includes Paper and paper products. [13]1993. [14]Imports are c.i.f. in balance of trade and commodities and f.o.b. in trading partners. [15]Alitalia and Alitalia Express only.

Internet resources for further information:
• **National Statistical Institute** http://www.istat.it
• **Banca d'Italia** http://www.bancaditalia.it

Jamaica

Official name: Jamaica.
Form of government: constitutional monarchy[1] with two legislative houses (Senate [21]; House of Representatives [60]).
Chief of state: British Monarch represented by Governor-General.
Head of government: Prime Minister.
Capital: Kingston.
Official language: English.
Official religion: none.
Monetary unit: 1 Jamaica dollar (J$) = 100 cents; valuation (Sept. 1, 2005) 1 U.S.$ = J$62.53; 1 £ = J$115.12.

Area and population		area		population
				2001
Parishes	Capitals	sq mi	sq km	census[2]
Clarendon	May Pen	462	1,196	237,025
Hanover	Lucea	174	450	67,037
Kingston	[3]	9	22	96,052
Manchester	Mandeville	320	830	185,801
Portland	Port Antonio	314	814	80,205
Saint Andrew	[3]	166	431	555,827
Saint Ann	Saint Ann's Bay	468	1,213	166,762
Saint Catherine	Spanish Town	460	1,192	482,308
Saint Elizabeth	Black River	468	1,212	146,404
Saint James	Montego Bay	230	595	175,127
Saint Mary	Port Maria	236	611	111,466
Saint Thomas	Morant Bay	287	743	91,604
Trelawny	Falmouth	338	875	73,066
Westmoreland	Savanna-la-Mar	312	807	138,947
TOTAL		4,244	10,991	2,607,631

Demography

Population (2005): 2,736,000.
Density (2005): persons per sq mi 644.7, persons per sq km 248.9.
Urban-rural (2001): urban 52.0%; rural 48.0%.
Sex distribution (2001): male 49.22%; female 50.78%.
Age breakdown (2002): under 15, 32.3%; 15–29, 25.9%; 30–44, 20.6%; 45–59, 11.0%; 60–74, 6.8%; 75 and over, 3.4%.
Population projection: (2010) 2,843,000; (2020) 3,034,000.
Doubling time: 55 years.
Ethnic composition (2001): black 91.6%; mixed race 6.2%; East Indian 0.9%; Chinese 0.2%; white 0.2%; other/unknown 0.9%.
Religious affiliation (2001): Protestant 61.2%, of which Church of God 23.8%[4], Seventh-day Adventist 10.8%, Pentecostal 9.5%; Roman Catholic 2.6%; other Christian 1.7%; Rastafarian 0.9%; nonreligious 20.9%; other 12.7%.
Major cities (2001): Kingston 96,052[5] (metro area 579,137); Portmore 161,658[6]; Spanish Town 131,515; Montego Bay 96,488; May Pen 57,334.

Vital statistics

Birth rate per 1,000 population (2004): 17.6 (world avg. 21.1).
Death rate per 1,000 population (2004): 6.0 (world avg. 9.0).
Natural increase rate per 1,000 population (2004): 11.6 (world avg. 12.1).
Total fertility rate (avg. births per childbearing woman; 2003): 2.0.
Marriage rate per 1,000 population (1999): 10.4.
Divorce rate per 1,000 population (1999): 0.4.
Life expectancy at birth (2003): male 73.8 years; female 78.0 years.
Major causes of death per 100,000 population (2002): circulatory diseases 321, of which cerebrovascular disease 135; malignant neoplasms (cancers) 130; communicable diseases 106; diabetes 81.

National economy

Budget (2002). Revenue: J$131,282,000,000 (tax revenue 78.6%, of which taxes on goods and services 33.8%, income taxes 29.7%, customs duties 7.7%; nontax revenue 17.5%; social contributions 3.9%). Expenditures: J$158,407,-000,000 (public debt 38.1%; education 14.6%; public order 8.2%; health 7.1%; defense 1.9%).
Public debt (external, outstanding; 2003): U.S.$4,516,000,000.
Production (metric tons except as noted). Agriculture, forestry, fishing (2004): sugarcane 2,100,000, citrus fruits 222,500, vegetables and melons 196,504, coconuts 170,000, yams 148,000, bananas 125,000, cabbages 28,500, plantains 21,000, tomatoes 19,300, coffee 2,700; livestock (number of live animals) 440,000 goats, 430,000 cattle, 150,000 pigs; roundwood (2003) 859,519 cu m; fish catch (2001) 10,212. Mining and quarrying (2004): bauxite 13,351,000; alumina 4,024,000; gypsum 162,000[7]. Manufacturing (2004): cement 807,869,000; animal feeds (2001) 385,000; sugar 181,402; flour (2001) 130,000; molasses 78,884; beer 765,220 hectolitres; rum [and other distilled spirits] 247,770 hectolitres; cigarettes 1,024,933,000[7] units. Energy production (consumption): electricity (kW-hr; 2002) 6,934,000,000 (6,934,000,000); coal (metric tons; 2002) none (88,000); crude petroleum (barrels; 2002) none (8,041,000); petroleum products (metric tons; 2002) 1,100,000 (3,363,000).
Population economically active (April 2005): total 1,193,000; activity rate of total population 44.9% (participation rates: ages 14 and over 64.0%; female 44.4%; unemployed 12.2%).

Price index (2000 = 100)							
	1998	1999	2000	2001	2002	2003	2004
Consumer price index	87.3	92.4	100.0	107.0	114.6	126.4	143.6

Gross national product (2004): U.S.$7,738,000,000 (U.S.$2,900 per capita).

Structure of gross domestic product and labour force				
	2003			
	in value J$'000,000	% of total value	labour force	% of labour force
Agriculture	24,251	5.2	188,000	17.1
Mining	20,154	4.3	4,000	0.4
Manufacturing	59,105	12.6	68,000	6.2
Construction	43,766	9.3	90,000	8.2
Public utilities	17,192	3.7	6,000	0.5
Transp. and commun.	56,539	12.0	64,000	5.9
Trade	88,496	18.8	210,000	19.1
Finance, real estate	62,702	13.3	66,000	6.0
Pub. admin., defense	54,643	11.6	} 257,000	23.4
Services	33,616	7.1		
Other	9,976[8]	2.1[8]	145,300[9]	13.2[9]
TOTAL	470,440	100.0	1,098,300	100.0

Household income and expenditure. Average household size (2001) 3.5; average annual income per household: n.a.; sources of income (1989): wages and salaries 66.1%, self-employment 19.3%, transfers 14.6%; expenditure (1988)[10]: food and beverages 55.6%, housing 7.9%, fuel and other household supplies 7.4%, health care 7.0%, transportation 6.4%.
Tourism (2003): receipts U.S.$1,621,000,000; expenditures U.S.$269,000,000.
Land use as % of total land area (2000): in temporary crops 16.1%, in permanent crops 10.2%, in pasture 21.1%; overall forest area 30.0%.

Foreign trade[11]

Balance of trade (current prices)				
	2001	2002	2003	2004
U.S.$'000,000	−1,618	−1,870	−1,942	−1,940
% of total	35.7%	41.7%	41.2%	37.9%

Imports (2004): U.S.$3,911,000,000 (mineral fuels 23.2%, machinery and transport equipment 22.4%, manufactured goods 14.3%, food 13.4%, chemicals 10.3%). *Major import sources* (2003): U.S. 44.4%; Caricom 12.8%; Latin American countries 10.6%; EU 10.5%, of which U.K. 4.1%.
Exports (2004): U.S.$1,411,000,000 (alumina 51.9%, nontraditional exports [including chemical products and mineral fuels] 17.9%, free zone exports [mostly wearing apparel] 8.0%, refined sugar 6.2%, bauxite 5.0%). *Major export destinations* (2003): U.S. 28.8%; Canada 16.1%; U.K. 12.8%; Norway 3.7%.

Transport and communications

Transport. Railroads (2004): route length 125 mi, 201 km[12]. Roads (1999): total length 11,620 mi, 18,700 km (paved 70%). Vehicles (2000–01): passenger cars 168,179, trucks and buses 62,634. Air transport (2004)[13]: passenger-km 5,060,000,000; metric ton-km cargo 37,698,000; airports (2000) 4.

Communications				units per 1,000 persons
Medium	date	unit	number	
Daily newspapers	2004	circulation	45,000[14]	17[14]
Radio	2000	receivers	2,030,000	784
Television	2000	receivers	502,000	194
Telephones	2004	main lines	500,000	187
Cellular telephones	2004	subscribers	2,200,000	822
Personal computers	2004	units	166,000	62
Internet	2004	users	1,067,000	399

Education and health

Educational attainment (2001). Percentage of population age 15 and over having: no formal schooling 0.9%; primary education 25.5%; secondary 55.5%; higher 12.3%, of which university 4.2%; other/unknown 5.8%. *Literacy* (2000): population age 15 and over literate 88%; males 83%; females 91%.

Education (2000–01)				student/
	schools	teachers	students	teacher ratio
Primary (age 6–11)[15]	788[16]	10,215	334,735	32.8
Secondary (age 12–16)	135	9,077	174,094	19.2
Voc., teacher tr.	17	1,083	17,768	16.4
Higher[17]	1	418	8,191	19.6

Health (2000)[18]: physicians 435 (1 per 5,988 persons); hospital beds (2003) 3,711 (1 per 714 persons); infant mortality rate (2003) 13.3.
Food (2002): daily per capita caloric intake 2,685 (vegetable products 85%, animal products 15%); 120% of FAO recommended minimum requirement.

Military

Total active duty personnel (2004): 2,830 (army 88.3%, coast guard 6.7%, air force 5.0%). *Military expenditure as percentage of GDP* (2003): 0.7%; per capita expenditure U.S.$19.

[1]Jamaica is to become a republic by 2007 per announcement of prime minister in September 2003. [2]Final adjusted figure. [3]The parishes of Kingston and Saint Andrew are jointly administered from the Half Way Tree section of Saint Andrew. [4]Includes numerous denominations. [5]City of Kingston is coextensive with Kingston parish. [6]Includes adjoining rural area of Hellshire per 2001 defined census boundaries. [7]2003. [8]Value-added taxes less imputed bank service charges. [9]Includes 4,300 not adequately defined and 141,000 unemployed. [10]Weights of consumer price index components. [11]Imports f.o.b. in balance of trade and c.i.f. in commodities and trading partners. [12]Inoperable since 1992 except for 57-mi (92-km) section leased to a mining operator. [13]Air Jamaica only. [14]*Jamaica Gleaner* only. [15]Includes lower-secondary students at all-age schools. [16]1991–92. [17]1996–97. [18]Public health only.

Internet resources for further information:
• **Statistical Institute of Jamaica http://www.statinja.com/stats.html**
• **Bank of Jamaica http://www.boj.org.jm**

Japan

Official name: Nihon (Japan).
Form of government: constitutional monarchy with a national Diet consisting of two legislative houses (House of Councillors [242]; House of Representatives [480]).
Symbol of state: Emperor.
Head of government: Prime Minister.
Capital: Tokyo.
Official language: Japanese.
Official religion: none.
Monetary unit: 1 yen (¥) = 100 sen; valuation (Sept. 1, 2005) 1 U.S.$ = ¥109.71; 1 £ = ¥201.99.

Area and population

Regions Prefectures	Capitals	area sq mi	area sq km	population 2004[1] estimate
Chūbu		25,786	66,786	21,767,000
Aichi	Nagoya	1,991	5,156	7,192,000
Fukui	Fukui	1,617	4,189	825,000
Gifu	Gifu	4,092	10,598	2,110,000
Ishikawa	Kanazawa	1,616	4,185	1,179,000
Nagano	Nagano	5,245	13,585	2,211,000
Niigata	Niigata	4,858	12,582	2,452,000
Shizuoka	Shizuoka	3,003	7,779	3,795,000
Toyama	Toyama	1,640	4,247	1,117,000
Yamanashi	Kōfu	1,724	4,465	886,000
Chūgoku		12,322	31,913	7,692,000
Hiroshima	Hiroshima	3,273	8,477	2,878,000
Okayama	Okayama	2,746	7,112	1,952,000
Shimane	Matsue	2,590	6,707	749,000
Tottori	Tottori	1,354	3,507	609,000
Yamaguchi	Yamaguchi	2,359	6,110	1,504,000
Hokkaidō		32,221	83,453	5,644,000
Hokkaidō	Sapporo	32,221	83,453	5,644,000
Kantō		12,518	32,422	41,231,000
Chiba	Chiba	1,991	5,156	6,039,000
Gumma	Maebashi	2,457	6,363	2,033,000
Ibaraki	Mito	2,354	6,096	2,989,000
Kanagawa	Yokohama	932	2,415	8,732,000
Saitama	Saitama	1,466	3,797	7,047,000
Tochigi	Utsunomiya	2,474	6,408	2,013,000
Tokyo-to	Tokyo	844	2,187	12,378,000
Kinki		12,783	33,108	22,756,000
Hyōgo	Kōbe	3,240	8,392	5,587,000
Kyōto-fu	Kyōto	1,781	4,613	2,638,000
Mie	Tsu	2,230	5,776	1,864,000
Nara	Nara	1,425	3,691	1,431,000
Ōsaka-fu	Ōsaka	731	1,893	8,814,000
Shiga	Ōtsu	1,551	4,017	1,372,000
Wakayama	Wakayama	1,825	4,726	1,050,000
Kyūshū		17,157	44,436	14,780,000
Fukuoka	Fukuoka	1,919	4,971	5,058,000
Kagoshima	Kagoshima	3,547	9,187	1,769,000
Kumamoto	Kumamoto	2,859	7,404	1,852,000
Miyazaki	Miyazaki	2,986	7,734	1,162,000
Nagasaki	Nagasaki	1,580	4,092	1,495,000
Ōita-ken	Ōita	2,447	6,338	1,215,000
Okinawa	Naha	877	2,271	1,359,000
Saga	Saga	942	2,439	870,000
Shikoku		7,259	18,802	4,111,000
Ehime	Matsuyama	2,192	5,676	1,477,000
Kagawa	Takamatsu	724	1,876	1,018,000
Kōchi	Kōchi	2,743	7,105	803,000
Tokushima	Tokushima	1,600	4,145	813,000
Tohoku		25,825	66,886	9,706,000
Akita	Akita	4,483	11,612	1,159,000
Aomori	Aomori	3,709	9,606	1,452,000
Fukushima	Fukushima	5,321	13,782	2,106,000
Iwate	Morioka	5,899	15,278	1,395,000
Miyagi	Sendai	2,813	7,285	2,371,000
Yamagata	Yamagata	3,600	9,323	1,223,000
TOTAL		145,898[2]	377,873[2]	127,687,000

Demography

Population (2005): 128,085,000[3].
Density (2005): persons per sq mi 877.8, persons per sq km 338.9.
Urban-rural (2003): urban 65.4%; rural 34.6%.
Sex distribution (2004): male 48.79%; female 51.21%.
Age breakdown (2004): under 15, 13.9%; 15–29, 18.2%; 30–44, 20.7%; 45–59, 21.0%; 60–74, 17.6%; 75 and over, 8.6%.
Population projection[3]: (2010) 128,457,000; (2020) 126,713,000.
Doubling time: not applicable; doubling time exceeds 100 years.
Composition by nationality (2002): Japanese 98.7%; Korean 0.5%; Chinese 0.3%; other 0.5%.
Immigration/Emigration: Permanent immigrants/registered aliens in Japan (end of 2003) 1,915,000, from North and South Korea 32.1%, Taiwan, Hong Kong, and China 24.1%, Brazil 14.4%, Philippines 9.7%, Peru 2.8%, United States 2.5%, other 14.4%. Japanese living abroad (October 2003) 911,000, in the U.S. 36.4%, in China 8.5%, in Brazil 7.8%, in the U.K. 5.6%, other 41.7%.
Major cities (2002): Tokyo 8,025,538; Yokohama 3,433,612; Osaka 2,484,326; Nagoya 2,109,681; Sapporo 1,822,992; Kōbe 1,478,380; Kyōto 1,387,264; Fukuoka 1,302,454; Kawasaki 1,245,780; Hiroshima 1,113,786; Saitama 1,029,327; Kita-Kyūshū 999,806; Sendai 986,713.

Other principal cities (2002)

	population		population		population
Akashi	291,649	Kagoshima	544,840	Nishinomiya	436,877
Akita	319,926	Kakogawa	265,393	Ōita	437,699
Amagasaki	463,256	Kanazawa	439,892	Okayama	621,809
Aomori	297,292	Kashiwa	326,097	Okazaki	336,169
Asahikawa	361,372	Kasugai	288,208	Ōtsu	291,322
Chiba	880,164	Kawagoe	325,373	Sagamihara	600,386
Fujisawa	382,038	Kawaguchi	463,879	Sakai	787,833
Fukui	249,656	Kōchi	326,490	Shimonoseki	246,924
Fukushima	288,926	Koriyama	330,776	Shizuoka	468,775
Fukuyama	381,098	Koshigaya	308,413	Suita	342,112
Funabashi	551,918	Kumamoto	653,835	Takamatsu	333,387
Gifu	401,269	Kurashiki	432,938	Takasaki	241,672
Hachinohe	243,880	Machida	384,572	Takatsuki	353,362
Hachiōji	521,359	Maebashi	283,005	Tokorozawa	330,020
Hakodate	284,690	Matsudo	464,224	Tokushima	262,286
Hamamatsu	573,504	Matsuyama	473,039	Toyama	321,049
Higashi-Ōsaka	496,747	Mito	246,095	Toyohashi	356,794
Himeji	475,892	Miyazaki	305,270	Toyonaka	387,869
Hirakata	401,753	Morioka	281,182	Toyota	342,835
Hiratsuka	252,982	Nagano	359,045	Utsunomiya	443,404
Ibaraki	257,577	Nagasaki	419,901	Wakayama	391,008
Ichihara	280,313	Naha	303,146	Yamagata	250,316
Ichikawa	447,686	Nara	364,411	Yao	268,012
Ichinomiya	277,473	Neyagawa	248,464	Yokkaichi	288,319
Iwaki	363,526	Niigata	514,678	Yokosuka	434,613

Religious affiliation (1995): Shintō and related religions 93.1%[4]; Buddhism 69.6%; Christian 1.2%; other 8.1%.
Households (2000). Total households 46,782,000; average household size 2.7; composition of households 1 person 27.6%, 2 persons 25.1%, 3 persons 18.8%, 4 persons 16.9%, 5 persons 6.8%, 6 or more persons 4.8%. Family households 33,769,000 (72.2%); nonfamily 13,013,000 (27.8%).

Type of household (1998)

Total number of occupied dwelling units: 43,922,000

	number of dwellings	percentage of total
by kind of dwelling		
exclusively for living	41,744,000	95.0
mixed use	124,000	0.3
combined with nondwelling	2,054,000	4.7
detached house	23,469,000	56.2
apartment building	16,420,000	39.3
tenement (substandard or overcrowded building)	1,735,000	4.2
other	120,000	0.3
by legal tenure of householder		
owned	26,468,000	60.3
rented	16,730,000	38.1
other	724,000	1.6
by kind of amenities		
flush toilet	36,461	83.0
bathroom	41,919	95.4
by year of construction		
prior to 1945	1,647,000	3.8
1945–70	8,077,000	18.9
1971–80	11,492,000	26.8
1981–90	11,973,000	28.0
1991–98 (Sept.)	9,650,000	22.5

Mobility (2002). Percentage of total population moving: within a prefecture 2.5%; between prefectures 2.1%.

Vital statistics

Birth rate per 1,000 population (2004): 8.8 (world avg. 21.1).
Death rate per 1,000 population (2004): 8.2 (world avg. 9.0).
Natural increase rate per 1,000 population (2004): 0.6 (world avg. 12.1).
Total fertility rate (avg. births per childbearing woman; 2004): 1.3.
Marriage rate per 1,000 population (2004): 5.7; average age at first marriage, men 29.6 years, women 27.8 years.
Divorce rate per 1,000 population (2004): 2.2.
Life expectancy at birth (2004): male 78.6 years; female 85.6 years.
Major causes of death per 100,000 population (2001): circulatory diseases 329.2, of which cerebrovascular disease 103.6; malignant neoplasms (cancers) 236.2; pneumonia and bronchitis 78.8; accidents and adverse effects 63.8, of which suicide 23.1; nephritis, nephrotic syndrome, and nephrosis 13.9; cirrhosis of the liver 12.5; diabetes mellitus 9.5.

Social indicators

Educational attainment (2002). Percentage of population ages 25–64 having: no formal schooling through lower-secondary education 16%; upper secondary/higher vocational 47%; university 36%.

Distribution of income (2000)

percentage of average household income by quintile

1	2	3	4	5 (highest)
11.2	15.3	18.7	23.0	31.7

Quality of working life. Average hours worked per month (2002): 153.1. Annual rate of industrial deaths per 100,000 workers (2001): 2.7. Proportion of labour force insured for damages or income loss resulting from injury, permanent disability, and death (2001): 65.4%. Average man-days lost to labour stoppages per 1,000,000 workdays (1998): 6.8. Average duration of journey to work (1996): 19.0 minutes. Rate per 1,000 workers of discouraged workers (unemployed no longer seeking work: 1997): 89.4.

Access to services. Proportion of households having access to: safe public water supply (end of 1997) 96.1%; public sewage system (2004) *c.* 65%.
Social participation. Eligible voters participating in last national election (September 2005): 67%. Adult population working as volunteers in previous year (1996): 25.3%. Trade union membership in total workforce (2002): 20.2%.
Social deviance (2001). Offense rate per 100,000 population for: homicide 0.6; robbery 1.2; larceny and theft 14.2. Incidence in general population of: alcoholism per 100,000 population, n.a.; drug and substance abuse 0.1. Rate of suicide per 100,000 population: 23.1.

Leisure/use of personal time

Discretionary daily activities (1996)
(Population age 10 years and over)

	weekly average hrs./min.
Total discretionary daily time	6:12
of which	
Hobbies and amusements	0:36
Sports	0:13
Learning (except schoolwork)	0:12
Social activities	0:04
Associations	0:27
Radio, television, newspapers, and magazines	2:59
Rest and relaxation	1:15
Other activities	0:20

Major leisure activities (1996)
(Population age 15 years and over)

	percentage of participation		
	male	female	total
Sports	81.7	70.5	76.1
Light gymnastics	25.9	30.6	28.3
Swimming	24.6	20.9	22.8
Bowling	33.7	24.6	29.2
Learning (except schoolwork)	30.7	30.6	30.6
Travel (1991)			
Domestic	72.7	68.3	70.4
Foreign	10.4	7.6	9.0

Material well-being (2003). Households possessing: automobile (2002) 84.4%; air conditioner (2002) 87.2%; personal computer 78.2%; cellular phone 93.9%; Internet connection 56.5%.

National economy

Gross national product (at current market prices; 2004): U.S.$4,749,910,000,-000 (U.S.$37,180 per capita).

Structure of gross domestic product and labour force

	2002		2003	
	in value ¥'000,000,000	% of total value	labour force	% of labour force
Agriculture, fishing	6,613	1.3	2,930,000	4.4
Mining	623	0.1	50,000	0.1
Manufacturing	102,299	20.5	11,780,000	17.7
Construction	34,318	6.9	6,040,000	9.1
Public utilities	14,135	2.8	320,000	0.5
Transportation and communications	31,546	6.3	4,960,000	7.4
Trade	68,482	13.7	14,830,000	22.2
Finance	102,343	20.5	2,320,000	3.5
Pub. admin., defense	46,040	9.2	2,270,000	3.4
Services	113,363	22.8	17,050,000	25.6
Other	−21,660[5]	−4.3[5]	4,110,000[6]	6.2[6]
TOTAL	498,102	100.0[7]	66,660,000	100.0[7]

Budget (2002–03). Revenue: ¥81,230,000,000,000 (government bonds 36.9%; income tax 19.5%; corporation tax 13.8%; value-added tax 12.1%; stamp and customs duties 3.9%). Expenditures: ¥81,230,000,000,000 (social security 22.5%; debt service 20.5%; public works 10.3%; national defense 6.1%).
Public debt (March 2004): U.S.$6,740,000,000,000.

Financial aggregates

	1998	1999	2000	2001	2002	2003	2004
Exchange rate[8], ¥ per:							
U.S. dollar	115.60	102.20	114.90	131.80	119.90	107.10	104.12
£	192.10	165.20	171.45	191.16	193.25	191.14	201.10
SDR	162.77	140.27	149.70	165.64	163.01	159.15	161.70
International reserves (U.S.$)							
Total (excl. gold; '000,000)	215,471	286,916	354,902	395,155	461,186	663,289	833,891
SDRs ('000,000)	2,663	2,656	2,437	2,377	2,524	2,766	2,839
Reserve pos. in IMF ('000,000)	9,593	6,552	5,253	5,051	7,203	7,733	6,789
Foreign exchange ('000,000)	203,215	277,708	347,212	387,727	451,458	652,790	824,264
Gold ('000,000 fine troy oz)	24.23	24.23	24.55	24.60	24.60	24.60	24.60
% world reserves	2.5	2.6	2.6	2.6	2.6	2.7	2.7
Interest and prices							
Central bank discount (%)[8]	0.50	0.50	0.50	0.10	0.10	0.10	0.10
Govt. bond yield (%)	1.10	1.77	1.75	1.33	1.25	1.01	1.50
Industrial share prices (2000 = 100)	76.2	89.6	100.0	77.3	62.7	59.4	72.3
Balance of payments (U.S.$'000,000,000)							
Balance of visible trade	+122.39	+123.32	+116.72	+70.21	+93.83	+106.40	+132.13
Imports, f.o.b.	251.66	280.37	342.80	313.38	301.75	342.72	406.87
Exports, f.o.b.	374.04	403.69	459.51	383.59	395.58	449.12	539.00
Balance of invisibles	−1.69	−16.45	+0.16	+19.07	+18.62	+29.82	+39.93
Balance of payments, current account	+120.70	+106.87	+116.88	+89.28	+112.45	+136.22	+172.06

Manufacturing and mining enterprises (2002)

	no. of establishments	avg. no. of persons engaged	annual wages as a % of avg. of all mfg. wages	annual value added (¥'000,000,000)
Electrical machinery	42,164	1,829,000	112.1	13,293
Food, beverages, and tobacco	66,507	1,488,000	70.1	7,888
Transport equipment	25,756	1,026,000	125.3	9,174
Chemical products	9,099	495,000	136.6	8,479
Nonelectrical machinery	73,782	1,168,000	112.9	7,176
Fabricated metal products	81,544	856,000	93.3	5,920
Printing and publishing	57,364	697,000	120.9	5,598
Ceramic, stone, and clay	28,148	413,000	104.6	2,702
Plastic products	28,120	472,000	90.7	4,265
Iron and steel	7,662	264,000	117.0	2,297
Paper and paper products	15,271	286,000	103.9	1,930
Apparel products	51,078	487,000	51.5	1,612
Precision instruments	11,793	250,000	103.4	2,426
Nonferrous metal products	5,830	181,000	111.6	1,380
Rubber products	7,798	161,000	85.1	1,560
Textiles	35,611	246,000	85.3	1,303
Furniture and fixtures	33,349	220,000	76.8	1,395
Lumber and wood products	22,055	192,000	82.7	900
Petroleum and coal products	1,379	38,000	161.9	883
Leather products	9,871	65,000	65.2	312
Mining and quarrying	3,764	47,000	101.3	839

Energy production (consumption): electricity (kW-hr; 2002) 1,097,167,000,000 (1,097,167,000,000); coal (metric tons; 2002) 3,320,000 (160,800,000); crude petroleum (barrels; 2002) 2,100,000 (1,469,000,000); petroleum products (metric tons; 2002) 178,424,000, of which (by volume [1998]) diesel 32.8%, heavy fuel oil 21.7%, gasoline 21.7%, kerosene and jet fuel 12.0% (189,562,000); natural gas (cu m; 2002) 2,744,000,000 (79,127,000,000). Composition of energy supply by source (2002): crude oil and petroleum products 49.7%, coal 19.5%, natural gas 13.5%, nuclear power 11.6%, hydroelectric power 3.2%, solar power and other new energy supplies 2.4%, geothermal 0.1%. Domestic energy demand by end use (1998): mining and manufacturing 46.3%, residential and commercial 26.3%, transportation 25.2%, other 2.2%.
Population economically active (2003): total 66,660,000; activity rate of total population 52.2% (participation rates: ages 15–64, 72.3%; female 41.0%; unemployed [October 2004–September 2004] 4.9%).

Price and earnings indexes (2000 = 100)

	1998	1999	2000	2001	2002	2003	2004
Consumer price index	101.0	100.7	100.0	99.3	98.4	98.1	98.1
Monthly earnings index	99.5	99.8	100.0	99.5	97.9	97.9	97.9

Household income and expenditure (2002). Average household size 2.7; average annual income per household ¥6,338,000 (U.S.$51,400); sources of income (1994): wages and salaries 59.0%, transfer payments 20.5%, self-employment 12.8%, other 7.3%; expenditure (2002): food 23.3%, transportation and communications 12.0%, recreation 10.1%, fuel, light, and water charges 6.9%, housing 6.5%, clothing and footwear 4.7%, education 4.2%, medical care 3.8%, furniture and household utensils 3.4%.
Tourism (2003): receipts from visitors U.S.$8,848,000,000; expenditures by nationals abroad U.S.$28,959,000,000.

Retail and wholesale trade and services (2002)

	no. of establishments	avg. no. of employees	annual sales (¥'000,000,000)
Retail trade	1,300,043	7,974,000	135,125
Food and beverages	466,590	3,162,000	41,238
Grocery	36,469	755,000	15,080
Liquors	65,098	194,000	3,785
General merchandise	4,995	542,000	17,318
Department stores	2,029	523,000	16,938
Motor vehicles and bicycles	89,091	556,000	16,217
Furniture and home furnishings	120,743	535,000	11,884
Apparel and accessories	185,939	720,000	10,980
Gasoline service stations	65,261	425,000	11,137
Books and stationery	59,327	703,000	4,839
Wholesale trade	379,547	4,004,000	413,547
Machinery and equipment	97,730	1,167,000	146,500
Motor vehicles and parts	18,218	189,000	16,487
General machinery except electrical	34,970	334,000	24,277
General merchandise	1,156	40,000	48,129
Farm, livestock, and fishery products	38,300	413,000	40,267
Food and beverages	83,597	919,000	43,983
Minerals and metals	17,106	202,000	43,859
Building materials	86,803	767,000	91,132
Textiles, apparel, and accessories	31,281	328,000	20,889
Chemicals	16,006	168,000	21,266
Drugs and toilet goods	18,730	247,000	21,575

Production (metric tons except as noted). Agriculture, forestry, fishing (2004): rice 10,912,000, sugar beets 4,656,000, potatoes 2,839,000, cabbages 2,300,000, sugarcane 1,350,000, onions 1,125,000, sweet potatoes 1,009,000, apples 881,100, wheat 860,000, tomatoes 740,000, cucumbers 700,000, carrots 660,000, lettuce 550,000, watermelons 480,000, eggplant 400,000, pears 393,400, spinach 310,000, soybeans 280,000, cantaloupes 260,000, barley 240,000, persimmons 232,500, pumpkins 230,000, taro 210,000, grapes 205,800, strawberries 205,000, yams 180,000, peaches 151,900, peppers 150,000, cauliflower 125,000, tea 95,000, plums 90,000; livestock (number of live animals) 9,724,000 pigs, 4,478,000 cattle, 286,000,000 chickens; roundwood (2004) 15,285,419 cu m; fish catch (2003) 5,455,828, of which scallops 602,489, squid 433,040, cod 269,156, crabs 33,081. Mining and quarrying (2003): limestone 163,565,000; silica sand 4,699,000; dolomite 3,579,000; pyrophyllite 600,000; zinc 44,574; lead 5,660; copper (2001) 744; silver 78,862 kg; gold 8,143 kg. Manufacturing (value added in U.S.$'000,000; 2001): machinery and apparatus 219,275, of which electronics, televisions, and radios 66,937, special purpose machinery 43,111, general purpose machinery 39,650, other electrical equipment 39,597; transportation equipment 99,874, of which automobile parts 43,711, automobiles 40,761; food and food products 77,264; paints, soaps, and pharmaceuticals 64,423; fabricated metal products 61,673; printing and publishing 53,609; rubber products and plastic products 43,677, of which plastic products 33,122; industrial chemicals 27,704; iron and steel 26,939; cement, bricks, and ceramics 26,738; paper and paper products 23,612; textiles, wearing apparel, and footwear 19,799; professional and scientific equipment and watches 19,774; beverages 19,736. Construction (value in ¥'000,000; 2001): residential 42,700,000; nonresidential 28,271,000.

Land use as % of total land area (2000): in temporary crops 12.3%, in permanent crops 1.0%, in pasture 1.1%; overall forest area 64.0%.

Foreign trade[9]

Balance of trade (current prices)

	1999	2000	2001	2002	2003	2004
¥'000,000,000	+12,279	+10,716	+6,564	+9,931	+10,230	+12,023
% of total	14.8%	11.6%	7.2%	10.5%	10.3%	10.9%

Imports (2001): ¥42,415,500,000,000 (machinery and apparatus 28.5%, of which computers and office machinery 6.5%; crude and refined petroleum 13.3%; food products 12.4%, chemicals and chemical products 7.3%; apparel and clothing accessories 5.5%). *Major import sources:* U.S. 18.1%; China 16.6%; South Korea 4.9%; Indonesia 4.3%; Australia 4.1%; Taiwan 4.1%; Malaysia 3.7%; U.A.E. 3.7%; Germany 3.6%; Saudi Arabia 3.5%.

Exports (2001): ¥48,979,200,000,000 (machinery and apparatus 44.4%, of which electronic microcircuits 7.4%, computers and office machinery 5.8%; road vehicles and parts 18.6%; base and fabricated metals 5.9%; precision instruments 5.4%). *Major export destinations:* U.S. 30.0%; China 7.7%; South Korea 6.3%; Taiwan 6.0%; Hong Kong 5.8%; Germany 3.9%; Singapore 3.6%; U.K. 3.0%; Thailand 2.9%; The Netherlands 2.8%.

Trade by commodity group (2001)

		imports		exports	
SITC group		U.S.$'000,000	%	U.S.$'000,000	%
00	Food and live animals	38,583	11.0	2,608	0.6
01	Beverages and tobacco	4,479	1.3		
02	Crude materials, excluding fuels	22,485[10]	6.4[10]	3,349[10]	0.8[10]
03	Mineral fuels, lubricants, and related materials	70,424	20.2	...	...
04	Animal and vegetable oils, fats, and waxes	10	10	10	10
05	Chemicals and related products, n.e.s.	24,961	7.2	29,662	7.4
06	Basic manufactures	25,872	7.4	44,825	11.1
07	Machinery and transport equipment	95,143	27.2	269,888	66.9
08	Miscellaneous manufactured articles	54,905	15.7	36,226	9.0
09	Goods not classified by kind	12,448	3.6	16,806	4.2
	TOTAL	349,300	100.0	403,364	100.0

Direction of trade (2001)

	imports		exports	
	U.S.$'000,000	%	U.S.$'000,000	%
Africa	4,931	1.4	4,311	1.1
Asia	192,798	55.2	174,136	43.2
South America	9,119	2.6	4,891	1.2
North America and Central America	71,584	20.5	140,641	34.9
United States	63,758	18.3	122,549	30.4
other North and Central America	7,826	2.2	18,092	4.5
Europe	53,659	15.4	69,037	17.1
EU	44,594	12.8	64,469	16.0
Russia	4,062	1.2	1,439	0.4
other Europe	5,003	1.4	3,129	0.7
Oceania	17,209	4.9	10,348	2.6
TOTAL	349,300	100.0	403,364	100.0[7]

Transport and communications

Transport. Railroads (2001): length 14,698 mi, 23,654 km; passengers carried 21,700,000,000; (2003) passenger-mi 237,385,000,000, passenger-km 382,035,000,000; short ton-mi cargo 15,200,000,000, metric ton-km cargo 22,193,000,000. Roads (2002): total length 765,600 mi, 1,232,000 km (paved 82%). Vehicles (2003): passenger cars 55,288,000; trucks and buses 17,247,000. Air transport (2000): passengers carried 205,106,000; (2003) passenger-km 97,632,000,000, passenger-km 157,123,000,000; short ton-mi cargo 6,712,000,000, metric ton-km cargo 9,800,000,000; airports (1996) with scheduled flights 73.
Urban transport (2000)[11]: passengers carried 57,719,000, of which by rail 34,020,000, by road 19,466,000, by subway 4,233,000.

Distribution of traffic (2001)

	cargo carried ('000,000 tons)	% of national total	passengers carried ('000,000)	% of national total
Road	5,578	90.6	64,590	74.7
Rail (intercity)	59	1.0	21,720	25.1
Inland water	520	8.4	112	0.1
Air	1	0.0	95	0.1
TOTAL	6,158	100.0	86,517	100.0

Communications

Medium	date	unit	number	units per 1,000 persons
Daily newspapers	2004	circulation	70,364,000	550
Radio	2000	receivers	121,000,000	956
Television	2002	receivers	99,852,000	785
Telephones	2004	main lines	58,788,000	460
Cellular telephones	2004	subscribers	91,473,900	716
Personal computers	2004	units	69,200,000	542
Internet	2004	users	75,000,000	589

Radio and television broadcasting (2001): total radio stations 1,586, of which commercial 707; total television stations 15,088, of which commercial 8,299. Commercial broadcasting hours (by percentage of programs; 2001): reports—radio 12.6%, television 21.4%; education—radio 2.4%, television 12.1%; culture—radio 13.5%, television 24.8%; entertainment—radio 69.0%, television 39.2%. Advertisements (daily average; 2001): radio 158, television 431.

Other communications media (2001)

Print	titles	Cinema	titles
Books (new)	71,073	Feature films	640
of which		Domestic	293
Social sciences	14,648	Foreign	347
Fiction	12,119		
Arts	10,199		traffic
Engineering	7,709		('000)
Natural sciences	5,385	Post	
History	5,148	Postal offices	24,773
Philosophy	2,967	Mail	26,216,000
Magazines/journals	4,447	Domestic	25,578,000
Weekly	145	International	638,000
Monthly	2,793	Parcels	411,000,000
		Domestic	387,000,000
		International	24,000,000

Education and health

Literacy: total population age 15 and over literate, virtually 100%.

Education (2002)

	schools	teachers	students	student/teacher ratio
Primary (age 6–11)	23,316	410,505	7,239,000	17.6
Secondary (age 12–17)	16,427	516,325	7,792,000	15.1
Higher	1,289	174,006	3,110,349	17.9

Health (2002): physicians 260,500 (1 per 489 persons); dentists 91,783 (1 per 1,388 persons); nurses 1,096,967 (1 per 116 persons); pharmacists 212,720 (1 per 583 persons); midwives (2000) 24,511 (1 per 5,176 persons); hospital beds 1,642,593 (1 per 78 persons); infant mortality rate per 1,000 live births (2004) 2.8.

Food (2002): daily per capita caloric intake 2,761 (vegetable products 79%, animal products 21%); 118% of FAO recommended minimum requirement.

Military

Total active duty personnel (2004): 239,900 (army 61.8%, navy 18.5%, air force 19.0%); U.S. troops (December 2004) 36,000. *Military expenditure as percentage of GDP* (2003): 1.0%[12]; per capita expenditure U.S.$335.

[1]Population as of October 1 from projection made in January 2002 based on 2000 census. [2]Regional prefecture areas do not sum to total given because of particular excluded inland water areas; total area per more recent 2003 survey equals 145,908 sq mi (377,899 sq km). [3]Based on UN *World Population Prospects* (2004 revision). [4]Many Japanese practice both Shintōism and Buddhism. [5]Import duties and statistical discrepancy less imputed bank service charges and consumption taxes. [6]Includes 610,000 not adequately defined and 3,500,000 unemployed. [7]Detail does not add to total given because of rounding. [8]End of period. [9]Imports c.i.f.; exports f.o.b. [10]Crude materials and vegetable oils, fats, and waxes. [11]Tokyo, Nagoya, and Ōsaka metropolis traffic range only. [12]Excludes military pensions.

Internet resources for further information:
- Bank of Japan http://www.boj.or.jp/en/index.htm
- Statistics Bureau and Statistics Center (Japan) http://www.stat.go.jp/english/index.htm

Jersey

Official name: Bailiwick of Jersey.
Political status: crown dependency (United Kingdom) with one legislative house (States of Jersey [58][1]).
Chief of state: British Monarch represented by Lieutenant Governor.
Head of government: Chief Minister[2] assisted by the Council of Ministers.
Capital: Saint Helier.
Official language: English[3].
Official religion: none.
Monetary unit: 1 Jersey pound (£J) = 100 pence; valuation (Sept. 1, 2005) 1 Jersey pound = U.S.$1.84; at par with the British pound.

Area and population	area		population
Parishes	sq mi	sq km	2001 census
Grouville	3.0	7.8	4,702
St. Brelade	4.9	12.8	10,134
St. Clement	1.6	4.2	8,196
St. Helier	4.1	10.6	28,310
St. John	3.4	8.7	2,618
St. Lawrence	3.7	9.5	4,702
St. Martin	3.8	9.9	3,628
St. Mary	2.5	6.5	1,591
St. Ouen	5.8	15.0	3,803
St. Peter	4.5	11.6	4,293
St. Saviour	3.6	9.3	12,491
Trinity	4.7	12.3	2,718
TOTAL	45.6	118.2	87,186

Demography

Population (2005): 87,800.
Density (2005): persons per sq mi 1,925.4, persons per sq km 742.8.
Urban-rural (2001)[4]: urban 28.9%, rural 71.1%.
Sex distribution (2004): male 49.19%; female 50.81%.
Age breakdown (2004): under 15, 17.7%; 15–29, 15.0%; 30–44, 25.7%; 45–59, 21.3%; 60–74, 13.4%; 75 and over, 6.9%.
Population projection: (2010) 88,000; (2020) 89,000.
Population by place of birth (2001): Jersey 52.6%; United Kingdom, Guernsey, or Isle of Man 35.8%; Portugal 5.9%; France 1.2%; other 4.5%.
Religious affiliation (2000)[4]: Christian 86.0%, of which Anglican 44.1%, Roman Catholic 14.6%, other Protestant 6.9%, unaffiliated Christian 20.1%; nonreligious/atheist 13.4%; other 0.6%.
Major cities (2001)[5]: St. Helier 28,310; St. Saviour 12,491; St. Brelade 10,134.

Vital statistics

Birth rate per 1,000 population (2004): 11.1 (world avg. 21.1).
Death rate per 1,000 population (2004): 8.5 (world avg. 9.0).
Natural increase rate per 1,000 population (2004): 2.6 (world avg. 12.1).
Total fertility rate (avg. births per childbearing woman; 2004): 1.6.
Marriage rate per 1,000 population (2001): 7.6.
Divorce rate per 1,000 population (2001): 3.2.
Life expectancy at birth (2004): male 76.6 years; female 81.7 years.
Major causes of death per 100,000 population (2000): diseases of the circulatory system c. 328, malignant neoplasms (cancers) c. 255, diseases of the respiratory system c. 136, accidents and violence c. 35, diseases of the digestive system c. 35.

National economy

Budget (2001). Revenue: £400,085,000 (income tax 86.8%, import duties 8.7%, interest payment 1.5%, other 3.0%). Expenditures: £369,138,000 (current expenditure 79.3%, of which health 25.7%, education 19.0%, social security 18.2%, public services 5.1%; capital expenditure 20.7%).
Production. Agriculture, forestry, fishing (value of export crops in £'000; 2002): potatoes 23,194, tomatoes 7,707, cauliflower 267, other fruits and vegetables 1,881, flowers 982; livestock (number of live animals; 2001) 4,552 mature dairy cattle; roundwood, none; fish catch (value of catch in £'000; 2003): 6,100, of which lobsters 2,665, brown crabs 810, scallops 628, oysters 607, spider crab 350. Mining and quarrying: n.a. Manufacturing: light industry, mainly electrical goods, textiles, and clothing. Energy production (consumption): electricity (kW-hr; 2001) 153,000,000 (567,000,000); crude petroleum, none (n.a.); petroleum products, n.a. (n.a.); natural gas, none (n.a.).
Gross national product (at current market prices; 2004): U.S.$5,568,700,000 (U.S.$63,530 per capita).

Structure of gross domestic product and labour force	2003			
	in value £J '000,000	% of total value	labour force	% of labour force
Agriculture, fishing	49	1.6	2,140	4.0
Mining	...	...	4,690	8.8
Construction	163	5.2		
Manufacturing	66	2.1	2,120	4.0
Public utilities	36	1.1	540	1.0
Transp. and commun.	130	4.2	1,450	2.7
Trade, hotels, restaurants	321	10.3	14,690	27.5
Finance, real estate[6]	2,143	68.4		
Pub. admin., defense	222	7.1	27,750	52.0
Services	...	...		
TOTAL	3,131[7, 8]	100.0	53,380	100.0

Household income and expenditure. Average household size (2001) 2.4; average annual income of workers (2001) £22,700 (U.S.$35,200); sources of income: n.a.; expenditure (1998–99)[9]: housing 20.1%, recreation 16.5%, transportation 12.8%, household furnishings 11.6%, food 11.5%, alcoholic beverages 6.0%, clothing and footwear 5.5%.
Population economically active (2001): total 48,105; activity rate of total population 55.2% (participation rates: ages 15–64 [male], 15–59 [female] 81.7%; female 44.1%; unemployed [June 2004] 0.9%).

Price index (2000 = 100)[10]							
	1999	2000	2001	2002	2003	2004	2005
Consumer price index	96.2	100.0	103.9	108.3	112.9	118.3	122.6

Public debt: none.
Tourism (2003): receipts U.S.$348,000,000; expenditures by nationals abroad, n.a.; number of visitors for at least one night 378,900.
Land use as % of total land area (1997): in temporary and permanent crops c. 29%, in pasture c. 22%; overall forest area c. 6%.

Foreign trade

Imports: [11]. *Major import sources* (2001): mostly the United Kingdom.
Exports: [11]; agricultural and marine exports (2001): £40,626,000 (potatoes 67.4%, greenhouse tomatoes 19.1%, flowers 3.3%, zucchini 3.0%, crustaceans 2.0%, mollusks 2.0%). *Major export destinations:* mostly the United Kingdom.

Transport and communications

Transport. Railroads: none. Roads (1995): total length 346 mi, 557 km (paved 100%). Vehicles (2002): passenger cars 74,007; trucks and buses 12,957. Air transport (2004)[12]: passenger-mi 1,229,000,000, passenger-km 1,978,000,000; short ton-mi cargo 250,000, metric ton-km cargo 394,000; airports (2002) with scheduled flights 1.

Communications				units per 1,000 persons
Medium	date	unit	number	
Daily newspapers	2002	circulation	22,897	262
Telephones	2003	main lines	73,200	836
Cellular telephones	2003	subscribers	79,200	904
Internet	2001	users	8,000	92

Education and health

Educational attainment (2001). Percentage of male population (16–64), female population (16–59) having: no formal degree 34.1%; primary education, n.a.; secondary, n.a.; undergraduate 7.1%; graduate (advanced degree) 4.1%.
Literacy (2002): 100.0%.

Education (2002)	schools	teachers	students	student/ teacher ratio
Primary (age 5–10)	21	...	7,386	...
Secondary (age 11–16)	10	...	5,715	...
Voc., teacher tr.	...	...	...	...
Higher[13]	1	...	582	...

Health: physicians (2001) 174 (1 per 500 persons); hospital beds (1995) 651 (1 per 130 persons); infant mortality rate per 1,000 live births (2004) 5.3.
Food: daily per capita caloric intake, n.a.

Military

Total active duty personnel (2004): none; defense is the responsibility of the United Kingdom.

[1]Includes 53 elected officials and 5 ex officio members (3 of the 5 ex officio members have voting rights). [2]The first chief minister of Jersey was elected in December 2005. [3]Until the 1960s French was an official language of Jersey and is still used by the court and legal professions; Jerriais, a Norman-French dialect, is spoken by a small number of residents. [4]Includes Guernsey. [5]Population of parishes. [6]Jersey is an international finance centre with 59 banks in 2002 and 2,829 registered companies; more than U.S.$209,000,000,000 is deposited in the island. [7]Detail does not add to total given because of rounding. [8]A second measurement of GDP for 2003 equals £J 2,610,000,000. [9]Weights of retail price index components. [10]June. [11]Customs ceased recording imports and exports as of 1980. [12]Flybe only. [13]2001; Highlands College.

Internet resources for further information:
• **States of Jersey: Statistics**
  http://www.gov.je/statistics

Jordan

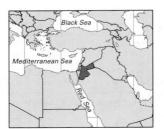

Official name: Al-Mamlakah al-Urdunnīyah al-Hāshimīyah (Al-Urdun) (Hashemite Kingdom of Jordan).
Form of government: constitutional monarchy with two legislative houses (Senate [55[1]]; House of Representatives [110]).
Head of state and government: King assisted by Prime Minister.
Capital: Amman.
Official language: Arabic.
Official religion: Islam.
Monetary unit: 1 Jordan dinar (JD) = 1,000 fils; valuation (Sept. 1, 2005) JD 1.00 = U.S.$1.41 = £0.77.

Area and population		area		population
				2004
Governorates	**Capitals**	sq mi	sq km	census[2]
'Ajlūn	'Ajlūn	159	412	118,496
'Amman	Amman	3,178	8,231	1,939,405
Al-'Aqabah	Al-'Aqabah	2,542	6,583	101,736
Al-Balqā'	Aṣ-Ṣalt	415	1,076	344,985
Irbid	Irbid	626	1,621	925,736
Jarash	Jarash	155	402	153,650
Al-Karak	Al-Karak	1,242	3,217	204,135
Ma'ān	Ma'ān	12,804	33,163	92,672
Mādabā	Mādabā	775	2,008	129,792
Al-Mafraq	Al-Mafraq	10,207	26,435	240,515
Aṭ-Ṭafīlah	Aṭ-Ṭafīlah	816	2,114	75,290
Az-Zarqā'	Az-Zarqā'	1,575	4,080	774,569
TOTAL		34,495[3]	89,342	5,100,981

Demography

Population (2005): 5,182,000[4].
Density (2005): persons per sq mi 150.2, persons per sq km 58.0.
Urban-rural (2003): urban 78.7%; rural 21.3%.
Sex distribution (2004): male 51.55%; female 48.45%.
Age breakdown (2002): under 15, 36.6%; 15–29, 30.4%; 30–44, 19.8%; 45–59, 8.0%; 60–74, 4.3%; 75 and over, 0.9%.
Population projection: (2010) 5,759,000; (2020) 6,866,000.
Doubling time: 28 years.
Ethnic composition (2000): Arab 97.8%, of which Jordanian 32.4%, Palestinian 32.2%, Iraqi 14.0%, Bedouin 12.8%; Circassian 1.2%; other 1.0%.
Religious affiliation (2000): Sunnī Muslim 93.5%; Christian 4.1%; other 2.4%.
Major cities (1994): Amman 969,598; Az-Zarqā' 350,849; Irbid 208,329; Ar-Ruṣayfah 137,247; Wādī Essier 89,104; Al-'Aqabah 62,773.

Vital statistics

Birth rate per 1,000 population (2004): 28.1 (world avg. 21.1).
Death rate per 1,000 population (2004): 3.2 (world avg. 9.0).
Natural increase rate per 1,000 population (2004): 24.9 (world avg. 12.1).
Total fertility rate (avg. births per childbearing woman; 2003): 3.7.
Marriage rate per 1,000 population (2004): 10.0.
Divorce rate per 1,000 population (2004): 1.8.
Life expectancy at birth (2003): male 70.6 years; female 72.4 years.
Major causes of death per 100,000 population: n.a.

National economy

Budget (2003). Revenue: JD 2,511,000,000 (tax revenue 43.1%, of which sales tax 23.7%, custom duties 8.0%, income and profits taxes 7.8%; nontax revenue 32.9%, of which licenses and fees 11.2%; foreign grants 24.0%). Expenditures: JD 2,678,000,000 (current expenditure 76.8%, of which defense 23.5%, social security and other transfers 21.7%, wages 15.6%, interest payments 10.1%; capital expenditure 23.2%).
Public debt (external, outstanding; 2003): U.S.$7,173,000,000.
Production (metric tons except as noted). Agriculture, forestry, fishing (2004): tomatoes 415,600, citrus fruits 147,300, olives 120,000, potatoes 120,000, cucumbers 100,000, watermelons 95,000, eggplants 52,000, cauliflower 51,000, bananas 51,000, wheat 50,000, apples 42,000; livestock (number of live animals) 1,475,000 sheep, 530,000 goats; roundwood 257,302 cu m; fish catch (2003) 1,131. Mining and quarrying (2003): phosphate ore 6,763,000; potash 1,961,000. Manufacturing (value added in U.S.$'000,000; 2000): chemicals and chemical products 236; tobacco products 184; bricks, cement, ceramics 168; food products 132; refined petroleum 90; beverages 82. Energy production (consumption): electricity (kW-hr; 2002) 7,341,000,000 (7,341,000,000); crude petroleum (barrels; 2002) 14,400 (28,800,000); petroleum products (metric tons; 2002) 3,749,000 (4,698,000); natural gas (cu m; 2002) 223,000,000 (223,000,000).
Land use as % of total land area (2000): in temporary crops 2.7%, in permanent crops 1.8%, in pasture 8.9%; overall forest area 1.0%.
Tourism (2003): receipts U.S.$815,000,000; expenditures U.S.$377,000,000.
Population economically active (2003): total 1,293,000; activity rate of total population 23.6% (participation rates: over age 15, 37.9%; female 14.9%; unemployed 14.5%).

Price and earnings indexes (2000 = 100)							
	1998	1999	2000	2001	2002	2003	2004
Consumer price index	98.7	99.3	100.0	101.8	103.6	105.3	108.9
Daily earnings index	...	...	...	...	...	...	...

Gross national product (2004): U.S.$11,629,000,000 (U.S.$2,140 per capita).

Structure of gross domestic product and labour force				
	2003			
	in value JD '000,000	% of total value	labour force	% of labour force
Agriculture	147	2.1	39,000	3.0
Mining	194	2.8	14,000	1.1
Manufacturing	954	13.6	137,000	10.6
Construction	265	3.8	71,000	5.5
Public utilities	157	2.2	18,000	1.4
Transp. and commun.	1,050	15.0	110,000	8.5
Trade, hotels	668	9.6	224,000	17.3
Pub. admin., defense	1,161	16.6	184,000	14.2
Finance, real estate	1,478	21.1	59,000	4.5
Services			246,000	19.1
Other	917[5]	13.1[5]	191,000[6]	14.8[6]
TOTAL	6,991	100.0[3]	1,293,000	100.0

Household income and expenditure. Average household size (2004) 5.3; income per household (1997) JD 5,464 (U.S.$7,700); sources of income (1997): wages and salaries 52.4%, rent and property income 24.5%, transfer payments 12.8%, self-employment 10.3%; expenditure (1997): food and beverages 44.3%, housing and energy 23.5%, transportation 8.2%, clothing and footwear 6.2%, education 4.5%, health care 2.5%.

Foreign trade[7]

Balance of trade (current prices)						
	1998	1999	2000	2001	2002	2003
JD '000,000	−1,436	−1,336	−1,913	−1,827	−1,635	−1,887
% of total	36.0%	34.0%	41.5%	36.0%	29.4%	30.2%

Imports (2003): JD 4,072,000,000 (food products 15.5%; machinery and apparatus 13.4%; crude petroleum 11.5%; chemicals and chemical products 10.9%; transport equipment 9.2%). *Major import sources:* Saudi Arabia 11.3%; Germany 7.9%; China 7.9%; United States 6.8%; Iraq 6.5%.
Exports (2003): JD 2,185,000,000 (domestic exports 76.7%, of which clothing 20.5%, chemicals and chemical products 17.8% [including medicines and pharmaceuticals 6.0%], potash 6.6%, vegetables 4.6%, phosphates 4.2%; reexports 23.3%). *Major export destinations*[8]: United States 29.0%; Iraq 13.4%; India 8.4%; Saudi Arabia 6.5%; Israel 4.1%.

Transport and communications

Transport. Railroads (2003): length 788 km; passenger-km 2,100,000; metric ton-km cargo 348,000,000. Roads (2002): total length 7,301 km (paved [2000] 69%). Vehicles (2001): passenger cars 245,357; trucks and buses 110,920. Air transport (2004)[9]: passenger-km 5,327,000,000; metric ton-km cargo 253,853,000; airports (1999) 3.

Communications				units per 1,000
Medium	date	unit	number	persons
Daily newspapers	2000	circulation	383,000	77
Radio	2000	receivers	1,850,000	372
Television	2002	receivers	138,900	177
Telephones	2004	main lines	617,300	110
Cellular telephones	2004	subscribers	1,594,500	284
Personal computers	2004	units	300,000	53
Internet	2004	users	600,000	107

Education and health

Educational attainment (2003). Percentage of population age 15 and over having: no formal schooling 9.9%; primary education 54.8%; secondary 17.8%; postsecondary and vocational 8.1%; higher 9.4%. *Literacy* (2003): percentage of population age 15 and over literate 90.1%; males literate 94.9%; females literate 85.1%.

Education (2002–03)				student/
	schools[10]	teachers	students	teacher ratio
Primary (age 6–14)	2,708	55,900	1,222,400	21.9
Secondary (age 15–17)	912	15,200	179,800	11.8
Voc., teacher tr.[10]	214	3,026	43,861	14.5
Higher[10]	22	6,036	153,965	25.5

Health: physicians (2001) 10,623 (1 per 448 persons); hospital beds (2001) 8,982 (1 per 577 persons); infant mortality rate per 1,000 live births (2003) 22.0.
Food (2002): daily per capita caloric intake 2,673 (vegetable products 91%, animal products 9%); 109% of FAO recommended minimum requirement.

Military

Total active duty personnel (2004): 100,500 (army 84.6%, navy 0.5%, air force 14.9%). *Military expenditure as percentage of GDP* (2003): 8.9%[11]; per capita expenditure U.S.$173[11].

---

[1]Appointed by king. [2]Preliminary. [3]Detail does not add to total given because of rounding. [4]Based on 2004 preliminary census results. [5]Net taxes on products less imputed bank service charges. [6]Including 4,000 not adequately defined and 187,000 unemployed. [7]Imports c.i.f.; exports f.o.b. [8]Domestic exports only. [9]Royal Jordanian airlines only. [10]2001. [11]Includes security expenditures.

Internet resources for further information:
• Dept. of Statistics http://www.dos.gov.jo
• Central Bank of Jordan http://www.cbj.gov.jo

Kazakhstan

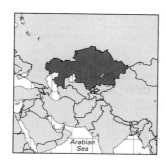

Official name: Qazaqstan Respūblīkasy (Republic of Kazakhstan).
Form of government: unitary republic with a Parliament consisting of two chambers (Senate [39[1]] and Assembly [77]).
Head of state and government: President assisted by Prime Minister.
Capital: Astana[2].
Official language: Kazakh[3].
Official religion: none.
Monetary unit: 1 tenge (T) = 100 tiyn; valuation (Sept. 1, 2005) 1 U.S.$ = 135.13 tenge; 1 £ = 248.80 tenge.

Area and population

Provinces	Capitals	area sq mi	area sq km	population 2001[4] estimate
Almaty	Taldykorgan	86,450	223,900	1,561,800
Aqmola	Kokshetau	56,450	146,200	810,300
Aqtöbe	Aqtöbe	116,050	300,600	672,600
Atyraū	Atyraū	45,800	118,600	447,100
Batys Qazaqstan	Oral	58,400	151,300	604,400
Mangghystaū	Aqtaū	63,950	165,600	323,700
Ongtüstik Qazaqstan	Shymkent	45,300	117,300	2,025,400
Pavlodar	Pavlodar	48,200	124,800	776,800
Qaraghandy	Qaraghandy	165,250	428,000	1,381,600
Qostanay	Qostanay	75,700	196,000	972,300
Qyzylorda[5]	Qyzylorda	87,250	226,000	605,500
Shyghys Qazaqstan	Öskemen	109,400	283,300	1,504,300
Soltüstik Qazaqstan	Petropavlovsk	37,850	98,000	706,400
Zhambyl	Taraz	55,700	144,300	985,700
Cities				
Almaty[6]	—	100	300	1,139,900
Astana[2]	—	250	700	324,100
TOTAL		1,052,100	2,724,900	14,841,900

Demography

Population (2005): 15,186,000.
Density (2005): persons per sq mi 14.4, persons per sq km 5.6.
Urban-rural (2003): urban 55.8%; rural 44.2%.
Sex distribution (2003): male 48.35%; female 51.65%.
Age breakdown (2003): under 15, 25.3%; 15–29, 27.8%; 30–44, 21.3%; 45–59, 14.4%; 60–74, 8.9%; 75 and over, 2.3%.
Population projection: (2010) 15,460,000; (2020) 15,977,000.
Ethnic composition (1999): Kazakh 53.4%; Russian 30.0%; Ukrainian 3.7%; Uzbek 2.5%; German 2.4%; Tatar 1.7%; other 6.3%.
Religious affiliation (2000): Muslim (mostly Sunnī) 42.7%; nonreligious 29.3%; Christian 16.7%, of which Orthodox 8.6%; atheist 10.9%; other 0.4%.
Major cities (1999): Almaty[6] 1,130,068; Qaraghandy (Karaganda) 436,900; Shymkent (Chimkent) 360,100; Taraz 330,100; Astana 319,318[2].

Vital statistics

Birth rate per 1,000 population (2003): 15.3 (world avg. 21.1); (2000) legitimate 76.1%, illegitimate 23.9%.
Death rate per 1,000 population (2003): 9.7 (world avg. 9.0).
Natural increase rate per 1,000 population (2003): 5.6 (world avg. 12.1).
Total fertility rate (avg. births per childbearing woman; 2003): 1.9.
Life expectancy at birth (2003): male 65.6 years; female 71.3 years.
Major causes of death per 100,000 population (2002): cardiovascular diseases 623; accidents, poisoning, and violence 157; malignant neoplasms (cancers) 154; diseases of the respiratory system 51.

National economy

Budget (2004). Revenue: 1,441,000,000,000 tenge (tax revenue 90.7%, of which corporate income taxes 33.8%, VAT 16.9%, social security 11.7%, petroleum taxes 10.0%, personal income taxes 6.9%; nontax revenue 9.3%). Expenditures: 1,289,300,000,000 tenge (social security 21.1%; education 14.8%; health 10.2%; public order 9.2%; transportation and communications 8.1%).
Public debt (external, outstanding; 2003): U.S.$3,546,000,000.
Population economically active (2003): total 7,657,300; activity rate of total population 51.2% (participation rates: ages 15–64, 76.9%; female 49.1%; unemployed [April 2004–March 2005] 8.3%).

Price and earnings indexes (2000 = 100)

	1998	1999	2000	2001	2002	2003	2004
Consumer price index	81.6	88.4	100.0	108.4	114.7	122.1	130.5
Monthly earnings index	70.1	80.7	100.0	125.6	147.5	168.8	205.3

Production (metric tons except as noted). Agriculture, forestry, fishing (2004): wheat 9,942,300, potatoes 2,243,300, barley 1,534,000, tomatoes 480,000, cotton 467,100, sugar beets 397,900, corn (maize) 300,000; livestock (number of live animals) 10,789,300 sheep, 4,871,000 cattle, 1,457,800 goats, 24,700,000 chickens; roundwood 300,800 cu m; fish catch (2003) 23,107. Mining and quarrying (2002): iron ore 15,423,000, bauxite 4,376,600, chromite 2,369,400; copper (metal content) 473,100; zinc (metal content) 392,400; silver 892,100 kg; gold 22,402 kg. Manufacturing (value of production in '000,000 tenge; 2004): base metals 600,000; food and food products 356,000; coke, refined petroleum products, and nuclear fuel 134,000; machinery and apparatus 124,000; cement, bricks, and ceramics 71,000. Energy production (consumption): electricity (kW-hr; 2004) 66,820,000,000 ([2003] 66,210,000,000); hard coal (metric tons; 2004) 86,800,000 ([2002] 56,600,000); lignite (metric tons; 2002) 3,000,000 (2,800,000); crude petroleum (barrels; 2004) 438,000,000 ([2003]

69,000,000); petroleum products (metric tons; 2002) 8,782,000 (7,876,000); natural gas (cu m; 2004) 21,855,000,000 ([2002] 11,281,000,000).
Gross national product (2004): U.S.$33,780,000,000 (U.S.$2,260 per capita).

Structure of gross domestic product and labour force

	2003 in value '000,000 tenge	2003 % of total value	2003 labour force	2003 % of labour force
Agriculture	324,600	7.3	2,462,600	32.2
Mining	}		181,700	2.4
Manufacturing	1,310,500	29.4	506,400	6.6
Public utilities	}		167,300	2.2
Construction	275,600	6.2	329,500	4.3
Transp. and commun.	536,300	12.1	503,900	6.6
Trade	539,200	12.1	1,085,300	14.2
Finance			260,600	3.4
Pub. admin., defense	} 1,463,600[7]	32.9[7]	318,200	4.2
Services			1,169,800	15.3
Other	}		672,100	8.8
TOTAL	4,449,800	100.0	7,657,300[8]	100.0[8]

Household income and expenditure. Average household size (1999) 3.6; sources of income (2001): salaries and wages 72.1%, social benefits 9.2%; expenditure (2001): food and beverages 56.0%, housing 11.7%.
Land use as % of total land area (2000): in temporary crops 8.0%, in permanent crops 0.05%, in pasture 68.6%; overall forest area 4.5%.
Tourism (2003): receipts U.S.$564,000,000; expenditures U.S.$669,000,000.

Foreign trade[9]

Balance of trade (current prices)

	1999	2000	2001	2002	2003	2004
U.S.$'000,000	+2,217	+3,772	+2,193	+3,086	+4,518	+7,312
% of total	23.3%	27.2%	14.5%	19.0%	21.2%	22.2%

Imports (2003): U.S.$8,408,700,000 (machinery and apparatus 25.6%; transportation equipment 14.5%; mineral fuels and lubricants 12.0%; base metals 11.8%; chemicals and chemical products 10.8%). *Major import sources:* Russia 39.0%; Germany 8.7%; China 6.2%; U.S. 5.6%; Ukraine 3.9%.
Exports (2003): U.S.$12,926,700,000 (mineral fuels 64.3%; base metals 20.4%; agricultural products [mostly cereals] 5.1%; chemicals and chemical products 3.4%). *Major export destinations:* Bermuda 17.0%; Russia 15.2%; Switzerland 13.0%; China 12.8%; Italy 7.8%.

Transport and communications

Transport. Railroads: route length (2004) 13,700 km; passenger-km (2003) 10,686,000,000; metric ton-km cargo (2003) 147,672,000,000. Roads (2002): total length 82,980 km (paved 94%). Vehicles (2003): passenger cars 1,148,754; trucks and buses 322,718. Air transport (2003): passenger-km 2,654,000,000; metric ton-km cargo 94,000,000; airports (1999) 20.

Communications

Medium	date	unit	number	units per 1,000 persons
Daily newspapers	1996	circulation	500,000	32
Radio	2001	receivers	6,186,000	411
Television	2001	receivers	5,440,000	361
Telephones	2004	main lines	2,500,000	165
Cellular telephones	2004	subscribers	2,758,900	182
Internet	2004	users	400,000	26

Education and health

Educational attainment (1999). Population age 25 and over having: no formal schooling or some primary education 9.1%; primary education 23.1%; secondary and some postsecondary 57.8%; higher 10.0%. *Literacy* (2002): percentage of total population age 15 and over literate 99.4%; males literate 99.7%; females literate 99.2%.

Education (2002–03)

	schools	teachers	students	student/ teacher ratio
Primary (age 7–13)	} 8,334	60,509	1,120,005	18.5
Secondary (age 14–17)		170,190	1,976,390	11.6
Voc., teacher tr.	335	5,893	90,778	15.4
Higher	177	37,602	603,072	16.0

Health (2003): physicians 54,600 (1 per 274 persons); hospital beds 114,800 (1 per 130 persons); infant mortality rate per 1,000 live births (2003) 31.9.
Food (2002): daily per capita caloric intake 2,677 (vegetable products 74%, animal products 26%); 105% of FAO minimum requirement.

Military

Total active duty personnel (2004): 65,800[10] (army 71.1%, air force 28.9%).
Military expenditure as percentage of GDP (2003): 1.1%; per capita expenditure U.S.$21.

[1]Includes 7 nonelective seats. [2]City of Akmola (Kazakh: Aqmola; capital replacing Almaty) was renamed Astana on May 6, 1998. [3]Russian has equal status with Kazakh at state-owned organizations and bodies of local government. [4]January 1. [5]Includes an area of 6,000 sq km (2,300 sq mi) enclosing the Bayqongyr (Baykonur) space launch facilities and the city of Bayqongyr (formerly Leninsk) leased to Russia in 1995 for a period of 20 years. [6]Formerly known as Alma-Ata. [7]Import duties less imputed bank service charges. [8]Detail does not add to total given because of rounding. [9]Imports c.i.f.; exports f.o.b. [10]34,000 paramilitary (primarily state border protection forces and internal security troops) are excluded.

Internet resources for further information:
• **National Bank of Kazakhstan** http://www.nationalbank.kz
• **Agency of Statistics of Kazakhstan**
   http://www.stat.kz/stat/index.aspx?sl=news&l=en

Kenya

Official name: Jamhuri ya Kenya (Swahili); Republic of Kenya (English).
Form of government: unitary multiparty republic with one legislative house (National Assembly [224[1]]).
Head of state and government: President.
Capital: Nairobi.
Official languages: Swahili; English.
Official religion: none.
Monetary unit: 1 Kenya shilling[2] (K Sh) = 100 cents; valuation (Sept. 1, 2005) 1 U.S.$ = K Sh 74.90; 1 £ = K Sh 137.91.

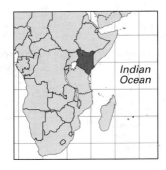

Indian Ocean

Area and population		area		population
				1999
Provinces	**Provincial headquarters**	sq mi	sq km	census[3]
Central	Nyeri	5,087	13,176	3,724,159
Coast	Mombasa	32,279	83,603	2,487,264
Eastern	Embu	61,734	159,891	4,631,779
North Eastern	Garissa	48,997	126,902	962,143
Nyanza	Kisumu	6,240	16,162	4,392,196
Rift Valley	Nakuru	67,131	173,868	6,987,036
Western	Kakamega	3,228	8,360	3,358,776
Special area				
Nairobi	—	264	684	2,143,254
TOTAL		224,961[4, 5]	582,646[5]	28,686,607

Demography

Population (2005): 33,830,000.
Density (2005): persons per sq mi 150.4, persons per sq km 58.1.
Urban-rural (2003): urban 39.4%; rural 60.6%.
Sex distribution (2004): male 50.16%; female 49.84%.
Age breakdown (2004): under 15, 42.4%; 15–29, 31.5%; 30–44, 15.1%; 45–59, 7.3%; 60–74, 3.0%; 75 and over, 0.7%.
Population projection: (2010) 38,383,000; (2020) 46,249,000.
Doubling time: 28 years.
Ethnic composition (2004): Kikuyu c. 21%; Luhya c. 14%; Luo c. 13%; Kalenjin c. 11%; Kamba c. 11%; Gusii c. 6%; Meru c. 5%; other c. 19%.
Religious affiliation (2000): Christian 79.3%, of which Roman Catholic 22.0%, African Christian 20.8%, Protestant 20.1%; Muslim 7.3%; other 13.4%.
Major cities (1999)[6]: Nairobi 2,143,354; Mombasa 665,018; Kisumu 322,734; Nakuru 219,366; Eldoret 167,016; Machacos 144,109.

Vital statistics

Birth rate per 1,000 population (2004): 40.2 (world avg. 21.1).
Death rate per 1,000 population (2004): 15.2 (world avg. 9.0).
Natural increase rate per 1,000 population (2004): 25.0 (world avg. 12.1).
Total fertility rate (avg. births per childbearing woman; 2004): 5.0.
Life expectancy at birth (2004): male 48.1 years; female 46.3 years.
Adult population (ages 15–49) *living with HIV* (2004[7]): 6.7% (world avg. 1.1%).

National economy

Budget (2001–02). Revenue: K Sh 206,665,600,000 (tax revenue 86.6%, of which income and profit taxes 29.0%, value-added tax 27.2%, import duties 15.3%; nontax revenue 13.4%). Expenditures: K Sh 235,832,000,000 (recurrent expenditure 80.4%, of which administration 29.7%, education 22.2%, defense 6.1%, health 6.0%; development expenditure 19.6%).
Public debt (external, outstanding; 2003): U.S.$5,704,000,000.
Production (metric tons except as noted). Agriculture, forestry, fishing (2004): sugarcane 4,660,995, corn (maize) 2,138,425, potatoes 1,000,000, plantains 830,000, cassava 630,000, pineapples 600,000, sweet potatoes 580,000, dry beans 400,000, wheat 300,000, tea 295,000, cabbages 270,000, tomatoes 260,000, bananas 210,000, sorghum 120,000, mangoes 118,000, papayas 86,000, avocados 70,000, coffee 64,500; cut flowers (2002): largest supplier to EU (25% of total market); livestock (number of live animals) 12,000,000 cattle, 12,000,000 goats, 10,000,000 sheep; roundwood 22,211,617 cu m; fish catch (2003) 120,534, of which freshwater fish 113,627. Mining and quarrying (2003): soda ash 352,560; fluorite 95,278; salt 19,000. Manufacturing (value added in U.S.$'000,000; 2000): food and food products 457; beverages and tobacco products 152; chemicals and chemical products 98; textiles and wearing apparel 80; fabricated metal products 76. Energy production (consumption): electricity (kW-hr; 2002) 4,678,000,000 (4,900,000,000); coal (metric tons; 2002) none (99,000); crude petroleum (barrels; 2002) none (10,900,000); petroleum products (metric tons; 2002) 1,549,000 (2,228,000); natural gas, none (none).
Household income and expenditure. Average household size (2003) 4.4; average annual income per household: n.a.; sources of income: n.a.; expenditure (1993–94): food 42.4%, housing and energy 24.1%, clothing and footwear 9.1%, transportation 6.4%, other 18.0%.
Population economically active (2001): total 12,952,000; activity rate of total population 42.1% (participation rates [1998–99]: ages 15–64, 73.6%; female [1997] 46.1%; unemployed [1998–99] 14.6%).

Price index (2000 = 100)							
	1998	1999	2000	2001	2002	2003	2004
Consumer price index	86.0	90.9	100.0	105.7	107.8	118.4	132.2

Gross national product (2004): U.S.$14,987,000,000 (U.S.$460 per capita).

Structure of gross domestic product and labour force				
	2003		2001	
	in value K Sh '000,000	% of total value	labour force	% of labour force
Agriculture	152,546	14.0	312,500[8]	2.4[8]
Mining	1,619	0.1	5,200[8]	—[8]
Manufacturing	131,614	12.1	216,600[8]	1.7[8]
Construction	43,870	4.0	76,800[8]	0.6[8]
Public utilities	12,591	1.2	21,400[8]	0.2[8]
Transp. and commun.	84,666	7.8	84,300[8]	0.7[8]
Trade	250,333	22.9	156,900[8]	1.2[8]
Finance	135,905	12.4	83,800[8]	0.6[8]
Pub. admin., defense	129,263	11.8	} 719,600[8]	5.6[8]
Services	60,512	5.5		
Other	88,722[9]	8.1[9]	11,274,900[10]	87.0[10]
TOTAL	1,091,640[4]	100.0[4]	12,952,000	100.0

Tourism (2003): receipts from visitors U.S.$359,000,000; expenditures by nationals abroad U.S.$127,000,000.
Land use as % of total land area (2000): in temporary crops 7.9%, in permanent crops 1.0%, in pasture 37.4%; overall forest area 30.0%.

Foreign trade[11]

Balance of trade (current prices)						
	1999	2000	2001	2002	2003	2004
K Sh '000,000	−76,246	−104,430	−98,070	−118,675	−92,893	−151,032
% of total	23.8%	28.3%	24.3%	27.2%	19.1%	25.7%

Imports (2002): K Sh 277,275,000,000 (crude petroleum and petroleum products 22.8%, machinery and transport equipment 19.3%, chemicals and chemical products 14.1%). *Major import sources* (2001): U.S. 16.4%; U.A.E. 10.7%; Saudi Arabia 7.8%; South Africa 7.1%; U.K. 7.1%.
Exports (2002): K Sh 158,600,000,000 (tea 21.4%, horticultural products [mostly cut flowers] 13.8%, petroleum products 7.6%, coffee 4.1%, other [including nontraditional fruits and vegetables, iron and steel, and fish] 53.1%). *Major export destinations* (2001): Uganda 17.4%; U.K. 12.5%; The Netherlands 6.5%; Pakistan 6.1%; U.S. 5.6%.

Transport and communications

Transport. Railroads (2000): route length 1,678 mi, 2,700 km; passenger-mi 187,600,000; passenger-km 302,000,000; short ton-mi cargo 967,000,000, metric ton-km cargo 1,557,000,000. Roads (2000): total length 39,730 mi, 63,942 km (paved 12%). Vehicles (2000): passenger cars 244,836; trucks and buses 96,726. Air transport (2004)[12]: passenger-mi 3,283,000,000, passenger-km 5,283,000,000; short ton-mi cargo 122,700,000, metric ton-km cargo 193,430,000; airports (1997) with scheduled flights 11.

Communications				units per 1,000
Medium	date	unit	number	persons
Daily newspapers	2000	circulation	303,000	10
Radio	2001	receivers	6,801,000	221
Television	2000	receivers	758,000	25
Telephones	2004	main lines	299,300	9.2
Cellular telephones	2004	subscribers	2,546,200	79
Personal computers	2004	units	441,000	14
Internet	2004	users	1,500,000	46

Education and health

Educational attainment (1998–99). Percentage of population age 6 and over having: no formal schooling 16.4%; primary education 59.0%; secondary 19.7%; university 1.1%; other/unknown 3.8% *Literacy* (2002): total population over age 15 literate 84.3%; males literate 90.0%; females literate 78.5%.

Education (2003)				student/
	schools	teachers	students	teacher ratio
Primary (age 5–11)	19,496	178,580	5,882,625	32.9
Secondary (age 12–17)	3,999	46,445	862,907	18.6
Voc., teacher tr.	32	...	53,854	...
Higher[13]	23	...	67,556	...

Health (2002): physicians 4,740 (1 per 6,623 persons); hospital beds 60,657 (1 per 515 persons); infant mortality rate per 1,000 live births (2004): 63.6.
Food (2002): daily per capita caloric intake 2,090 (vegetable products 88%, animal products 12%); 90% of FAO recommended minimum requirement.

Military

Total active duty personnel (2004): 24,120 (army 82.9%, navy 6.7%, air force 10.4%). *Military expenditure as percentage of GDP* (2003): 1.7%; per capita expenditure U.S.$8.

---

[1]Includes 14 nonelective seats. [2]Kenya pound (K£) as a unit of account equals 20 K Sh. [3]Preliminary. [4]Detail does not add to total given because of rounding. [5]Includes water area of 4,336 sq mi (11,230 sq km). [6]Population of urban core(s). [7]January 1. [8]Formally employed only. [9]Indirect taxes less subsidies and less imputed bank service charges. [10]Includes informally employed, small-scale farmers and pastoralists, unemployed, self-employed, and unpaid family workers. [11]Import figures are c.i.f. [12]Kenya Airways only. [13]Universities only.

Internet resources for further information:
• Central Bank of Kenya http://www.centralbank.go.ke
• Central Bureau of Statistics http://www.cbs.go.ke

Kiribati

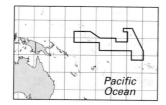

Official name: Republic of Kiribati.
Form of government: unitary republic with a unicameral legislature (House of Assembly [42[1]]).
Head of state and government: President.
Seats of government: islets of Bairiki (executive), Ambo (legislative), Betio (judicial) on South Tarawa.
Official language: English.
Official religion: none.
Monetary unit: 1 Australian dollar ($A) = 100 cents; valuation (Sept. 1, 2005) 1 U.S.$ = $A 1.31; 1 £ = $A 2.41.

Pacific Ocean

Area and population

Island Groups Islands	Capitals	area[2] sq mi	area[2] sq km	population 2000 census
Gilberts Group		110.2[3]	285.5[3]	78,158
Abaiang	Tuarabu	6.8	17.5	5,794
Abemama	Kariatebike	10.6	27.4	3,142
Aranuka	Takaeang	4.5	11.6	966
Arorae	Roreti	3.7	9.5	1,225
Banaba	Anteeren	2.4	6.3	276
Beru	Taubukinberu	6.8	17.7	2,732
Butaritari	Butaritari	5.2	13.5	3,464
Kuria	Tabontebike	6.0	15.5	961
Maiana	Tebangetua	6.4	16.7	2,048
Makin	Makin	3.1	7.9	1,691
Marakei	Rawannawi	5.4	14.1	2,544
Nikunau	Rungata	7.4	19.1	1,733
Nonouti	Teuabu	7.7	19.9	3,176
Onotoa	Buariki	6.0	15.6	1,668
Tabiteuea, North	Utiroa	10.0	25.8	3,365
Tabiteuea, South	Buariki	4.6	11.9	1,217
Tamana	Bakaka	1.8	4.7	962
Tarawa, North	Abaokoro	5.9	15.3	4,477
Tarawa, South	Bairiki	6.1	15.8	36,717
Line and Phoenix Group		202.7[3]	525.0[3]	6,336
Northern Line		166.7	431.7	6,275
Kiritimati (Christmas)	London	150.0	388.4	3,431
Tabuaeran (Fanning)	Paelau	13.0	33.7	1,757
Teraina (Washington)	Washington	3.7	9.6	1,087
Southern Line and Phoenix Group		36.1	93.4	61
Kanton (Canton) in Phoenix Group	Kanton	3.6	9.2	61
TOTAL		312.9	810.5	84,494

Demography

Population (2005): 95,300.
Density (2005)[4]: persons per sq mi 340.4, persons per sq km 131.3.
Urban-rural (2003): urban 47.3%; rural 52.7%.
Sex distribution (2004): male 49.65%; female 50.35%.
Age breakdown (2004): under 15, 39.3%; 15–29, 26.7%; 30–44, 18.6%; 45–59, 10.2%; 60–74, 4.3%; 75 and over, 0.9%.
Population projection: (2010) 107,000; (2020) 134,000.
Doubling time: 31 years.
Ethnic composition (2000): Micronesian 98.8%; Polynesian 0.7%; European 0.2%; other 0.3%.
Religious affiliation (2000): Roman Catholic 54.6%; Kiribati Protestant (Congregational) 37.0%; Mormon 2.7%; Bahā'ī 2.4%; other Protestant 2.3%; other/nonreligious 1.0%.
Major city (2000): Tarawa (urban area) 36,717.

Vital statistics

Birth rate per 1,000 population (2004): 31.0 (world avg. 21.1).
Death rate per 1,000 population (2004): 8.5 (world avg. 9.0).
Natural increase rate per 1,000 population (2004): 22.5 (world avg. 12.1).
Total fertility rate (avg. births per childbearing woman; 2003): 4.3.
Life expectancy at birth (2004): male 58.3 years; female 64.4 years.
Major causes of death per 100,000 population (2002): diseases of the circulatory system 80.0; diseases of the digestive system 67.5; infectious and parasitic diseases 65.2; endocrine and metabolic disorders 52.6; diseases of the respiratory system 40.0.

National economy

Budget (2000). Revenue: $A 107,800,000 (nontax revenue 59.5%, tax revenue 22.9%, grants 17.6%). Expenditures: $A 90,000,000 (current expenditures 87.2%, capital expenditures 12.8%).
Tourism: receipts from visitors (2001) U.S.$3,200,000; expenditures by nationals abroad (1999) U.S.$2,000,000.
Land use as % of total land area (2000): in temporary crops *c.* 3%, in permanent crops *c.* 51%, in pasture, none; overall forest area *c.* 38%.
Production (metric tons except as noted). Agriculture, forestry, fishing (2004): coconuts 103,000, roots and tubers 9,800 (of which taro 2,000), fresh vegetables 5,900, bananas 5,000, tropical fruit 1,300, seaweed (2003) 489; livestock (number of live animals) 12,200 pigs, 460,000 chickens; fish catch (2003) 32,043. Mining and quarrying: none. Manufacturing: limited production of processed fish, baked goods, clothing, and handicrafts. Energy production (consumption): electricity (kW-hr; 2002) 13,000,000 (13,000,000); petroleum products (metric tons; 2002) none (10,000).
Gross national product (2004): U.S.$95,000,000 (U.S.$970 per capita).

Structure of gross domestic product and labour force

	2002 in value $A '000[5]	2002 % of total value[5]	2000 labour force	2000 % of labour force
Agriculture, fishing	11,605	11.8	30,966[6]	71.7[6]
Mining	—	—	—	—
Manufacturing	695	0.7	150	0.4
Construction	7,224	7.4	346	0.8
Public utilities	1,000	1.0	187	0.4
Transp. and commun.	9,834	10.0	944	2.2
Trade	11,632	11.8	1,181	2.7
Finance	5,360	5.5	317	0.7
Pub. admin., defense	34,640	35.3	5,821	13.5
Services	16,223[7]	16.5[7]	2,649	6.1
Other			644[8]	1.5[8]
TOTAL	98,213	100.0	43,205	100.0

Public debt (external, outstanding; 2000): U.S.$8,500,000.
Population economically active (1995): total 38,407; activity rate of total population 49.5% (participation rates: over age 15, 84.0%; female 47.8%; unemployed [2000] 1.5%).

Price index (2000 = 100)

	1997	1998	1999	2000	2001	2002	2003
Consumer price index	91.1	94.5	96.2	100.0	106.0	109.4	110.9

Household income and expenditure. Average household size (1995) 6.5; expenditure (1996)[9]: food 45.0%, nonalcoholic beverages 10.0%, transportation 8.0%, energy 8.0%, education 8.0%.

Foreign trade[10]

Balance of trade (current prices)

	1997	1998	1999	2000	2001	2002
$A '000,000	−44.1	−42.6	−49.7	−61.7	−70.2	−72.9
% of total	72.3%	69.6%	63.8%	83.3%	80.1%	86.0%

Imports (2001): $A 78,900,000 (food and beverages 27.2%; machinery and apparatus 17.1%; mineral fuels 14.3%; transport equipment 11.5%). *Major import sources:* Australia 26.5%; Poland 15.7%; Fiji 14.8%; United States 9.5%; Japan 8.0%.
Exports (2001): $A 8,700,000 (domestic exports 82.9%, of which aquarium fish 27.9%, copra 22.8%, trepang 11.9%, lobster 5.8%, seaweed 4.8%; reexports 17.1%). *Major export destinations:* Japan 45.8%; Thailand 24.8%; South Korea 10.7%; Bangladesh 5.5%; Brazil 3.0%.

Transport and communications

Transport. Roads (1999): total length 416 mi, 670 km (paved [1996] 5%). Vehicles (2001)[11]: passenger cars 397; trucks and buses 210. Air transport: n.a.[12]; airports 9.

Communications

Medium	date	unit	number	units per 1,000 persons
Radio	2000	receivers	32,600	386
Television	2001	receivers	3,100	35
Telephones	2002	main lines	4,500	51
Cellular telephones	2002	subscribers	500	5.7
Personal computers	2001	units	2,000	25
Internet	2002	users	2,000	23

Education and health

Educational attainment (1995). Percentage of population age 25 and over having: no schooling 7.8%; primary education 68.5%; secondary or higher 23.7%.
Literacy (1998): population age 15 and over literate 92%; males literate 94%; females literate 91%.

Education (2001)

	schools	teachers	students	student/ teacher ratio
Primary (age 6–13)	88	627	16,096	25.7
Secondary (age 14–18)	19	324	5,743	17.7
Voc., teacher tr.	2	39	1,501	38.5
Higher[13]	—	—	—	—

Health (2004): physicians 20 (1 per 4,455 persons); hospital beds 140 (1 per 680 persons); infant mortality rate per 1,000 live births 49.9.
Food (2002): daily per capita caloric intake 2,859 (vegetable products 88%, animal products 12%); 125% of FAO recommended minimum requirement.

Military

Total active duty personnel (2004): none; defense assistance is provided by Australia and New Zealand.

[1]Includes two nonelective members. [2]Includes uninhabited islands in Southern Line and Phoenix Group. [3]Detail does not add to total given because of rounding. [4]Based on inhabited island areas (280 sq mi [726 sq km]) only. [5]At current factor cost. [6]Includes 30,712 persons engaged in "village work" (subsistence agriculture or fishing). [7]Indirect taxes less subsidies and less imputed bank service charges. [8]Unemployed. [9]Weights of consumer price index components. [10]Imports c.i.f.; exports f.o.b. [11]Registered vehicles in South Tarawa only. [12]Air Kiribati international service ended in 2004. [13]129 students overseas in 2001.

Internet resources for further information:
• **Key Indicators of Developing Asian and Pacific Countries**
  http://www.adb.org/Documents/Books/Key_Indicators/2005
• **Kiribati Statistics Office**
  http://www.spc.int/prism/Country/KI/Stats

Korea, North

Official name: Chosŏn Minjujuŭi In'min Konghwaguk (Democratic People's Republic of Korea).
Form of government: unitary single-party republic with one legislative house (Supreme People's Assembly [687]).
Head of state and government: Chairman of the National Defense Commission[1].
Capital: P'yŏngyang.
Official language: Korean.
Official religion: none.
Monetary unit: 1 won = 100 chŏn; valuation (Sept. 1, 2005) 1 U.S.$ = 900 won; 1 £ = 1,657 won.

Area and population

Provinces	Capitals	area sq mi	area sq km	population 1993 census
Chagang-do	Kanggye	6,551	16,968	1,152,733
Kangwŏn-do	Wŏnsan	4,306[2]	11,152[2]	1,304,481[2]
North Hamgyŏng (Hamgyŏng-pukto)	Ch'ŏngjin	6,784[3]	17,570[3]	2,060,725[3]
North Hwanghae (Hwanghae-pukto)	Sariwŏn	3,576	9,262	1,846,493
North P'yŏngan (P'yŏngan-pukto)	Sinŭiju	4,656	12,059	2,437,442[4]
South Hamgyŏng (Hamgyŏng-namdo)	Hamhŭng	7,324	18,970	2,732,232
South Hwanghae (Hwanghae-namdo)	Haeju	3,090	8,002	2,010,953
South P'yŏngan (P'yŏngan-namdo)	P'yŏngsan	4,761	12,330	3,597,557
Yanggang-do	Hyesan	5,528	14,317	638,474
Special administrative regions				
Kaesŏng (industrial region)[5]	...	2	2	2
Kŭmgang-san (tourist region)[5]	...	2	2	2
Sinŭiju (trade zone)[5]	—	51	132	4
Special cities				
Najin Sŏnbong	—	3	3	3
P'yŏngyang	—	772	2,000	2,741,260
TOTAL		**47,399**	**122,762**	**20,522,350**

Demography

Population (2005): 22,488,000.
Density (2005): persons per sq mi 474.4, persons per sq km 183.2.
Urban-rural (2003): urban 61.1%; rural 38.9%.
Sex distribution (2003): male 50.10%; female 49.90%.
Age breakdown (2000): under 15, 25.6%; 15–29, 24.5%; 30–44, 24.7%; 45–59, 14.4%; 60–74, 9.0%; 75 and over, 1.8%.
Population projection: (2010) 22,907,000; (2020) 23,722,000.
Doubling time: 71 years.
Ethnic composition (1999): Korean 99.8%; Chinese 0.2%.
Religious affiliation (2000): nonreligious 55.6%; atheist 15.6%; Ch'ŏndogyo 12.9%; traditional beliefs 12.3%; Christian 2.1%; Buddhist 1.5%.
Major cities (1993): P'yŏngyang (2001) 3,164,000[6]; Namp'o (2000) 1,022,000[6]; Hamhŭng 709,730; Ch'ŏngjin 582,480; Kaesŏng 334,433; Sinŭiju 326,011.

Vital statistics

Birth rate per 1,000 population (2004): 16.8 (world avg. 21.1).
Death rate per 1,000 population (2004): 7.0 (world avg. 9.0).
Natural increase rate per 1,000 population (2004): 9.8 (world avg. 12.1).
Total fertility rate (avg. births per childbearing woman; 2004): 2.2.
Marriage rate per 1,000 population (1987): 9.3.
Divorce rate per 1,000 population (1987): 0.2.
Life expectancy at birth (2004): male 68.4 years; female 73.9 years.
Major causes of death per 100,000 population (2002): diseases of the circulatory system 288; malignant neoplasms (cancers) 90; diseases of the respiratory system 62; injuries, violence, and accidents 62.

National economy

Budget (1999). Revenue: 19,801,000,000 won (turnover tax and profits from state enterprises). Expenditures: 20,018,200,000 won (1994; national economy 67.8%, social and cultural affairs 19.0%, defense 11.6%).
Population economically active (1997)[7]: total 11,898,000; activity rate of total population 55.8% (participation rates [1988–93]: ages 15–64, 49.5%; female [2002] 43.3%; unemployed [2000] 24.1%).
Production (metric tons except as noted). Agriculture, forestry, fishing (2004): rice 2,370,000, potatoes 2,052,000, corn (maize) 1,727,000, cabbages 680,000, apples 660,000, soybeans 360,000, sweet potatoes 350,000, wheat 175,000, pears 134,500, peaches and nectarines 122,000, garlic 90,000, pumpkins, squash, and gourds 89,000, onions 86,400, tomatoes 71,000, cucumbers and gherkins 66,000, barley 64,000, tobacco leaves 64,000, rye 60,000; livestock (number of live animals) 3,194,000 pigs, 2,736,000 goats, 566,000 cattle, 171,000 sheep; roundwood 7,237,495 cu m; fish catch (2003) 205,000. Mining and quarrying (2003): iron ore (metal content) 1,260,000; magnesite 1,000,000; phosphate rock 300,000; zinc (metal content) 100,000; lead (metal content) 60,000; sulfur 42,000; copper (metal content) 13,000; silver 40; gold 2,000 kg. Manufacturing (2002): cement 53,200,000; crude steel 10,400,000; pig iron (1999) 6,600,000; chemical fertilizers 5,000,000; coke (2001) 3,100,000; steel semimanufactures (1994) 2,700,000; textile fabrics 100,000,000 sq m. Energy production (consumption): electricity (kW-hr; 2002) 34,342,000,000 (34,342,-000,000); hard coal (metric tons; 2002) 39,500,000 (41,175,000); lignite (metric tons; 2002) 11,200,000 (11,200,000); crude petroleum (barrels; 2002) none (19,000,000); petroleum products (metric tons; 2002) 2,552,000 (3,913,000).

Household income and expenditure. Average household size (1999) 4.6.
Public debt (external, outstanding; 1999): U.S.$12,000,000,000.
Gross national product (2004): U.S.$20,752,000,000 (U.S.$930 per capita).

Structure of gross domestic product and labour force

	2004 in value '000,000,000 won	2004 % of total value	1997 labour force	1997 % of labour force
Agriculture	5,961	27.2	3,853,000	32.4
Mining	1,820	8.3		
Manufacturing	4,042	18.5		
Construction	1,896	8.7		
Public utilities	995	4.5		
Transp. and commun.	...	...		
Trade	...	...	8,045,000	67.6
Finance	...	...		
Pub. admin., defense	5,017	22.9		
Services	2,156	9.9		
Other	...	...		
TOTAL	**21,887**	**100.0**	**11,898,000**	**100.0**

Land use as % of total land area (2000): in temporary crops 20.8%, in permanent crops 2.5%, in pasture 0.4%; overall forest area 68.2%.

Foreign trade

Balance of trade (current prices)

	1998	1999	2000	2001	2002	2003
U.S.$'000,000	−320	−540	−961	−1,021	−889	−983
% of total	22.2%	29.8%	40.1%	38.2%	30.6%	31.6%

Imports (2002): U.S.$1,895,600,000 ([8]food, beverages, and other agricultural products 19.3%, mineral fuels and lubricants 15.5%, machinery and apparatus 15.4%, textiles and clothing 10.4%). *Major import sources:* China 30.7%; South Korea 19.5%; India 12.2%; Thailand 11.3%; Germany 9.2%.
Exports (2002): U.S.$1,006,600,000 ([8]live animals and agricultural products 39.3%, textiles and wearing apparel 16.7%, machinery and apparatus 11.6%, mineral fuels and lubricants 9.5%). *Major export destinations:* South Korea 27.0%; China 26.9%; Japan 23.3%; Thailand 4.4%; Bangladesh 3.2%.

Transport and communications

Transport. Railroads (2004): length 5,235 km. Roads (2004): total length 15,649 mi, 25,185 km (paved *c.* 12%). Vehicles (1990): passenger cars 248,000. Air transport (1997): passenger-mi 177,712,000, passenger-km 286,000,000; short ton-mi cargo 18,600,000; metric ton-km cargo 30,000,000; airports (2001) with scheduled flights 1.

Communications

Medium	date	unit	number	units per 1,000 persons
Daily newspapers	2001	circulation	4,578,000	208
Radio	2001	receivers	3,390,000	154
Television	2001	receivers	1,299,000	59
Telephones	2001	main lines	1,100,000	50

Education and health

Educational attainment (1987–88). Percentage of population age 16 and over having attended or graduated from postsecondary-level school: 13.7%.
Literacy (1997): 95%.

Education (1988)

	schools[9]	teachers	students	student/teacher ratio
Primary (age 6–9)	4,886	59,000	1,543,000	26.2
Secondary (age 10–15)	4,772	111,000	2,468,000	22.2
Voc., teacher tr.	...	4,000	...	...
Higher	300	23,000	325,000	14.1

Health (2002): physicians 70,870 (1 per 313 persons); hospital beds 292,340 (1 per 76 persons); infant mortality rate per 1,000 live births (2004) 24.8.
Food (2002): daily per capita caloric intake 2,142 (vegetable products 94%, animal products 6%); 92% of FAO recommended minimum requirement.

Military

Total active duty personnel (2004): 1,106,000 (army 85.9%, navy 4.2%, air force 9.9%). *Military expenditure as percentage of GNP* (2003): 7.3%; per capita expenditure U.S.$72.

[1]Position in effect from Sept. 5, 1998, is the declared "highest office of state." It is defined as an enhanced military post with revised constitutional powers. [2]Kangwŏn-do includes Kaesŏng and Kŭmgang-san special administrative regions. [3]North Hamgyŏng includes Najin Sŏnbong. [4]North P'yŏngan includes Sinŭiju special administrative region. [5]Established in 2002. [6]Urban agglomeration. [7]The Democratic People's Republic of Korea categorizes economically active as including students in higher education, retirees, and heads of households, as well as those in the civilian labour force. [8]Data for commodities exclude trade with South Korea. [9]2000.

Internet resources for further information:
• **Digital KOTRA: North Korean Economy**
  http://crm.kotra.or.kr/eng/index.php3
• **Ministry of Unification**
  http://www.unikorea.go.kr

Korea, South

Official name: Taehan Min'guk
(Republic of Korea).
Form of government: unitary multiparty
republic with one legislative house
(National Assembly [299]).
Head of state and government:
President, assisted by Prime Minister.
Capital: Seoul.
Official language: Korean.
Official religion: none.
Monetary unit: 1 won (W) = 100 chon;
valuation (Sept. 1, 2005)
1 U.S.$ = W 1,027; 1 £ = W 1,890.

Area and population

Provinces	area sq km	population 2000 census	Metropolitan cities	area sq km	population 2000 census
Cheju	1,848	513,260	Inch'ŏn	987	2,475,139
Kangwŏn	16,613	1,487,011	Kwangju	501	1,352,797
Kyŏnggi	10,131	8,984,134	Pusan	763	3,662,884
North Chŏlla	8,051	1,890,669	Sŏul (Seoul)	605	9,895,217
North Ch'ungch'ŏng	7,432	1,466,567	Taegu	886	2,480,578
North Kyŏngsang	19,025	2,724,931	Taejŏn	540	1,368,207
South Chŏlla	12,046	1,996,456	Ulsan	1,057	1,014,428
South Ch'ungch'ŏng	8,598	1,845,321			
South Kyŏngsang	10,518	2,978,502	TOTAL	99,601	46,136,101

Demography

Population (2005): 48,294,000.
Density (2005): persons per sq mi 1,255.8, persons per sq km 484.9.
Urban-rural (2003): urban 80.3%; rural 19.7%.
Sex distribution (2004): male 50.39%; female 49.61%.
Age breakdown (2004): under 15, 19.6%; 15–29, 22.8%; 30–44, 26.8%; 45–59, 18.1%; 60–74, 9.9%; 75 and over, 2.8%.
Population projection: (2010) 49,220,000; (2020) 49,956,000.
Ethnic composition (2000): Korean 97.7%; Japanese 2.0%; U.S. white 0.1%; Han Chinese 0.1%; other 0.1%.
Religious affiliation (2000): Christian *c.* 41%, of which Protestant *c.* 17%, independent Christian *c.* 14%, Roman Catholic *c.* 7%; traditional beliefs *c.* 16%; Buddhist *c.* 15%; New Religionist *c.* 15%; Confucianist *c.* 11%; other *c.* 2%.
Major cities (2003): Seoul 10,280,523; Pusan 3,747,369; Inch'ŏn 2,596,102; Taegu 2,540,647; Taejŏn 1,424,844.

Vital statistics

Birth rate per 1,000 population (2004): 9.8 (world avg. 21.1).
Death rate per 1,000 population (2004): 5.1 (world avg. 9.0).
Natural increase rate per 1,000 population (2004): 4.7 (world avg. 12.1).
Total fertility rate (avg. births per childbearing woman; 2004): 1.2.
Marriage rate per 1,000 population (2004): 6.4.
Divorce rate per 1,000 population (2004): 2.9.
Life expectancy at birth (2003): male 71.7 years; female 79.3 years.
Major causes of death per 100,000 population (2004): malignant neoplasms (cancers) 133.8; diseases of the circulatory system 120.4; accidents, poisoning, and violence 63.0; diseases of the respiratory system 29.4.

National economy

Budget (2002). Revenue: W 105,876,700,000,000 (tax revenue 88.6%, of which income and profits taxes 34.3%, value-added tax 30.2%; nontax revenue 11.4%). Expenditures: W 105,876,700,000,000 (economic services 25.9%, education 17.4%, defense 16.2%, social services 13.1%).
Public debt (external, outstanding; 2003): U.S.$158,870,000,000.
Production (metric tons except as noted). Agriculture, forestry, fishing (2004): rice 6,800,000, cabbages 2,800,000, watermelons 760,000, onions 745,000, tangerines, mandarins, satsuma 620,000, potatoes 550,000, cucumbers and gherkins 440,000, grapes 360,000, apples 350,000; livestock (number of live animals) 9,100,000 pigs, 2,096,000 cattle, 97,000,000 chickens; roundwood 4,136,202 cu m; fish catch (2003) 2,035,337. Mining and quarrying (2003): feldspar 477,000; iron ore (metal content) 161,000. Manufacturing (value added in U.S.$'000,000; 2001): electrical machinery and apparatus 31,583, of which televisions, radios, telecommunications equipment, and electronic parts 25,223; transportation equipment 26,027, of which automobiles 12,660, ship and boat construction 6,050, automobile parts 5,938; chemicals and chemical products 16,296, of which paints, soaps, and pharmaceuticals 8,040, industrial chemicals 7,131; textiles, wearing apparel, and footwear 11,646, of which textiles 6,878; nonelectrical machinery 11,591; food and food products 9,383; iron and steel 8,802; fabricated metal products 6,920; office, accounting, and computing machinery 5,560. Energy production (consumption): electricity (kW-hr; 2002) 336,237,000,000 (336,237,000,000); coal (metric tons; 2004) 3,247,000 ([2002] 75,950,000); crude petroleum (barrels; 2002) none (788,000,000); petroleum products (metric tons; 2002) 86,481,000 (62,938,000); natural gas (cu m; 2002) none (23,931,000,000).
Tourism (2003): receipts U.S.$5,256,000,000; expenditures U.S.$9,988,000,000.
Household income and expenditure (2001). Average household size 3.5; annual income per household W 31,501,200 (U.S.$24,400); sources of income: wages 84.2%, other 15.8%; expenditure: food and beverages 26.3%, transportation and communications 16.3%, education 11.3%.
Gross national product (at current market prices; 2004): U.S.$673,036,000,000 (U.S.$13,980 per capita).

Structure of gross domestic product and labour force

	2003 in value W '000,000,000[1]	2003 % of total value[1]	2000 labour force	2000 % of labour force
Agriculture	22,833.3	3.2	2,288,000	10.4
Mining	2,136.9	0.3	18,000	0.1
Manufacturing	169,113.8	23.4	4,244,000	19.3
Construction	61,021.3	8.4	1,583,000	7.2
Public utilities	17,338.1	2.4	63,000	0.3
Transp. and commun.	47,467.7	6.6	1,260,000	5.7
Trade	62,071.4	8.6	5,943,000	27.1
Finance	139,240.9	19.3	2,089,000	9.5
Pub. admin., defense	38,704.8	5.4	753,000	3.4
Services	76,603.6	10.6	2,798,000	12.8
Other	84,814.2[2]	11.8[2]	911,000[3]	4.2[3]
TOTAL	721,346.0	100.0	21,950,000	100.0

Population economically active (2003): total 22,846,000; activity rate 48.3% (participation rates: ages 15–64, 65.3%; female 41.0%; unemployed [2004] 3.5%).

Price and earnings indexes (2000 = 100)

	1998	1999	2000	2001	2002	2003	2004
Consumer price index	97.0	97.8	100.0	104.1	106.9	110.7	114.7
Monthly earnings index	91.0	92.1	100.0	105.8	118.5	128.7	140.9

Land use as % of total land area (2000): in temporary crops 17.4%, in permanent crops 2.0%, in pasture 0.5%; overall forest area 63.3%.

Foreign trade[4]

Balance of trade (current prices)

	1999	2000	2001	2002	2003	2004
U.S.$'000,000	+23,934	+11,787	+9,341	+10,345	+14,990	+29,382
% of total	9.1%	3.5%	3.2%	3.3%	4.0%	6.1%

Imports (2003): U.S.$178,827,000,000 (electric and electronic products 17.5%, nonelectrical machinery and transport equipment 17.5%, crude petroleum 12.9%, chemicals and chemical products 9.2%, food and live animals 4.7%). *Major import sources:* Japan 20.3%; U.S. 13.9%; China 12.3%; Saudi Arabia 5.2%; Germany 3.8%.
Exports (2003): U.S.$193,817,000,000 (machinery and apparatus 44.7%, transport equipment 17.8%, chemicals and chemical products 9.2%, textile yarn, fabrics 5.6%). *Major export destinations:* China 18.1%; U.S. 17.7%; Japan 8.9%; Hong Kong 7.6%; Taiwan 3.6%.

Transport and communications

Transport. Railroads (2003): length (2001) 6,819 km; passenger-km 28,379,200,000; metric ton-km cargo 11,057,000,000. Roads (2001): total length 91,396 km (paved 77%). Vehicles (2002): passenger cars 9,750,238; trucks and buses 4,179,959. Air transport (2004)[5]: passenger-km 65,611,-000,000; metric ton-km cargo 11,209,000,000; airports (1996) with scheduled flights 14.

Communications

Medium	date	unit	number	units per 1,000 persons
Daily newspapers	2000	circulation	18,500,000	393
Radio	2000	receivers	48,600,000	1,033
Television	2000	receivers	17,100,000	364
Telephones	2004	main lines	26,058,100	542
Cellular telephones	2004	subscribers	36,586,100	761
Personal computers	2004	units	26,201,000	545
Internet	2004	users	31,580,000	657

Education and health

Educational attainment (2002). Percentage of population ages 25–64 having: no formal schooling through lower secondary 29%; upper secondary/higher vocational 45%; university 26%. *Literacy* (2001): total population age 15 and over literate 97.9%; males 99.2%; females 96.6%.

Education (2003–04)

	schools[6]	teachers	students	student/ teacher ratio
Primary (age 6–13)	13,739	139,057	4,185,330	30.1
Secondary (age 14–19)	4,739	168,464	3,099,216	18.4
Voc., teacher tr.	169	37,699	546,401	14.5
Higher	162[7]	172,572	3,223,431	18.7

Health (2002): physicians 78,592 (1 per 606 persons); hospital beds 316,015 (1 per 151 persons); infant mortality rate (2003) 7.3.
Food (2002): daily per capita caloric intake 3,058 (vegetable products 84%, animal products 16%); 130% of FAO recommended minimum.

Military

Total active duty personnel (2004): 686,000 (army 81.6%, navy 9.2%, air force 9.2%); U.S. military forces (December 2004): 36,050. *Military expenditure as percentage of GDP* (2003): 2.5%; per capita expenditure U.S.$311.

[1]At current prices. [2]Taxes on products less subsidies. [3]Includes 22,000 inadequately defined and 889,000 unemployed. [4]Imports c.i.f.; exports f.o.b. [5]Asiana and Korean Air only. [6]2001. [7]Excludes graduate schools.

Internet resources for further information:
• **National Statistical Office http://www.nso.go.kr/eng**

Kuwait

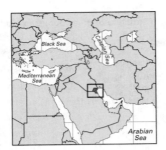

Official name: Dawlat al-Kuwayt (State of Kuwait).
Form of government: constitutional monarchy with one legislative body (National Assembly [50[1]]).
Head of state and government: Emir assisted by the Prime Minister[2].
Capital: Kuwait (city)[3].
Official language: Arabic.
Official religion: Islam.
Monetary unit: 1 Kuwaiti dinar (KD) = 1,000 fils; valuation (Sept. 1, 2005) 1 KD = U.S.$3.42 = £1.86.

Area and population		area		population
				2001
Governorates	Capitals	sq mi	sq km	estimate
Al-Aḥmadī	Al-Aḥmadī	1,977	5,120	364,484
Al-'Āṣimah	Kuwait (city)	77	200	388,532
Al-Farwānīyah	Al-Farwānīyah	73	190	572,252
Al-Jahrā'	Al-Jahrā'	4,336	11,230	282,353
Ḥawallī	Ḥawallī	69	178	488,294
Mubārak al-Kabīr	...			144,981
Islands[4]	—	347	900	...
TOTAL		6,880[5]	17,818	2,240,896[6]

Demography

Population (2005): 2,847,000.
Density (2005): persons per sq mi 413.8, persons per sq km 159.8.
Urban-rural (2003): urban 96.3%; rural 3.7%.
Sex distribution (2003): male 60.31%; female 39.69%.
Age breakdown (2003): under 15, 27.9%; 15–29, 31.8%; 30–44, 23.9%; 45–59, 12.1%; 60–74, 3.7%; 75 and over, 0.6%.
Population projection: (2010) 3,228,000; (2020) 3,918,000.
Doubling time: 36 years.
Ethnic composition (2000): Arab 74%, of which Kuwaiti 30%, Palestinian 17%, Jordanian 10%; Bedouin 9%; Kurd 10%; Indo-Pakistani 8%; Persian 4%; other 4%.
Religious affiliation (2000): Muslim 83%, of which Sunnī 58%, Shī'ī 25%; Christian 13%, of which Eastern-rite Catholic 9%; Hindu 3%; other 1%.
Major cities (1995): As-Sālimīyah 130,215; Qalīb ash-Shuyūkh 102,178; Ḥawallī 82,238; Kuwait (city) 28,859 (urban agglomeration [2003] 1,222,000).

Vital statistics

Birth rate per 1,000 population (2004): 21.9 (world avg. 21.1).
Death rate per 1,000 population (2004): 2.4 (world avg. 9.0).
Natural increase rate per 1,000 population (2004): 19.5 (world avg. 12.1).
Total fertility rate (avg. births per childbearing woman; 2004): 3.0.
Marriage rate per 1,000 population (2002): 5.1.
Divorce rate per 1,000 population (2002): 2.6.
Life expectancy at birth (2004): male 75.9 years; female 77.9 years.
Major causes of death per 100,000 population (2002): circulatory diseases 74; accidents and violence 28; cancers 22; diabetes mellitus 10; respiratory diseases 4.

National economy

Budget[7] (2003–04). Revenue: KD 3,397,000,000 (oil revenue 87.5%). Expenditures: KD 5,666,000,000 (wages 32.4%, defense 18.5%, social security and welfare 14.8%, health 14.8%, economic development 8.5%, education 6.0%).
Public debt (external, outstanding; 2003): U.S.$510,000,000.
Tourism (2003): receipts from visitors U.S.$117,000,000; expenditures by nationals abroad U.S.$3,349,000,000.
Gross national product (2004): U.S.$43,052,000,000 (U.S.$17,970 per capita).

Structure of gross domestic product and labour force				
	2003			
	in value KD '000,000	% of total value	labour force	% of labour force
Agriculture	65.8	0.5	24,500	1.7
Mining (petroleum sector)	5,794.0[8]	46.6[8]	7,100	0.5
Manufacturing	897.3[8]	7.2[8]	88,500	6.0
Construction	285.3	2.3	109,800	7.5
Public utilities	300.8	2.4	9,200	0.6
Transp. and commun.	633.0	5.1	45,000	3.1
Trade, hotels	791.5	6.4	231,300	15.8
Finance and business services	1,385.8	11.1	63,900	4.4
Pub. admin., defense Services	2,744.1	22.1	769,000	52.4
Other	−456.3[9]	−3.7[9]	117,800[10]	8.0[10]
TOTAL	12,441.3	100.0	1,466,092[5]	100.0

Production (metric tons except as noted). Agriculture, forestry, fishing (2004): tomatoes 36,000, potatoes 33,000, cucumbers and gherkins 32,300, eggplants 16,000, cauliflower 11,500, dates 10,500, garlic 450; livestock (number of live animals) 900,000 sheep, 150,000 goats, 25,000 cattle, 4,950 camels; fish catch (2003) 5,900. Mining and quarrying (2004): sulfur 730,000; lime 40,000. Manufacturing (value added in U.S.$'000,000; 2001): refined petroleum products 1,221; food products 164; cement, bricks, and tiles 126; textiles and wearing apparel 113; fabricated metal products 95. Energy production (consumption): electricity (kW-hr; 2002) 37,422,000,000 (37,422,000,000); coal, none (none); crude petroleum (barrels; 2004) 832,000,000 ([2002]

320,000,000); petroleum products (metric tons; 2002) 30,843,000 (4,859,000); natural gas (cu m; 2002) 9,983,000,000 (9,983,000,000).
Population economically active (2003): total 1,466,092, of which Kuwaiti 19.1%, non-Kuwaiti 80.9%; activity rate of total population 57.6% (participation rates: ages 15 and over, 75.1%; female [2002] 25.7%; unemployed [2004] 2.2%).

Price and earnings indexes (2000 = 100)							
	1998	1999	2000	2001	2002	2003	2004
Consumer price index	95.4	98.2	100.0	101.7	103.1	104.1	105.3
Earnings index	...	...	...	...	...	...	...

Household income and expenditure. Average household size (2002) 5.0; sources of income (1986): wages and salaries 53.8%, self-employment 20.8%, other 25.4%; expenditure (2000)[11]: housing energy 26.7%, food 18.3%, transportation and communications 16.1%, household furnishings 14.7%, clothing and footwear 8.9%.
Land use as % of total land area (2000): in temporary crops 0.6%, in permanent crops 0.1%, in pasture 7.6%; overall forest area 0.3%.

Foreign trade[12]

Balance of trade (current prices)						
	1999	2000	2001	2002	2003	2004
KD '000,000	+1,385	+3,767	+2,556	+1,931	+2,888	+4,928
% of total	23.0%	46.2%	34.6%	26.1%	30.6%	41.1%

Imports (2003): KD 3,217,000,000 (machinery and apparatus 24.0%, transport equipment 20.5%, food 14.0%, chemicals and chemical products 8.7%). *Major import sources:* U.S. 11.1%; Japan 10.7%; Germany 9.5%; Saudi Arabia 6.6%; Italy 5.5%; China 5.3%.
Exports (2003): KD 6,162,000,000 (crude petroleum and petroleum products 91.9%, ethylene products 3.0%, reexports 2.5%). *Major export destinations:* Japan 22.1%; South Korea 13.1%; U.S. 12.0%; Taiwan 10.7%; Singapore 10.2%.

Transport and communications

Transport. Railroads: none. Roads (1999): total length 2,765 mi, 4,450 km (paved 81%). Vehicles (2001): passenger cars 715,185; trucks and buses 116,371. Air transport (2003–04): passenger-mi 4,151,373,000, passenger-km 6,681,000,000; short ton-mi cargo 153,094,000, metric ton-km cargo 223,514,000; airports (2003) with scheduled flights 1.

Communications				units per 1,000
Medium	date	unit	number	persons
Daily newspapers[13]	2001	circulation	390,000	172
Radio	2001	receivers	1,412,000	624
Television	2001	receivers	1,091,000	482
Telephones	2004	main lines	497,000	188
Cellular telephones	2004	subscribers	2,000,000	755
Personal computers	2004	units	450,000	170
Internet	2004	users	600,000	226

Education and health

Educational attainment (1988). Percentage of population age 25 and over having: no formal schooling 44.8%; primary education 8.6%; some secondary 15.1%; complete secondary 15.1%; higher 16.4%. *Literacy* (2003): total population age 15 and over literate 82.9%; males literate 84.7%; females literate 81.0%.

Education (2000–01)				student/
	schools	teachers	students	teacher ratio
Primary (age 6–9)[14, 15]	349	17,385	193,582	11.1
Secondary (age 10–17)[14]	117	9,234	76,221	8.3
Voc., teacher tr.[14]	40	1,107	2,997	2.7
Higher[16]	1	918	17,447	19.0

Health (2002): physicians 3,780 (1 per 625 persons); hospital beds 5,200 (1 per 455 persons); infant mortality rate per 1,000 live births (2004) 10.3.
Food (2002): daily per capita caloric intake 3,010 (vegetable products 83%, animal products 17%); 124% of FAO recommended minimum requirement.

Military

Total active duty personnel (2004): 15,500[17] (army 71.0%, navy 12.9%, air force 16.1%); U.S. troops (May 2005) 15,000. *Military expenditure as percentage of GDP* (2003): 9.0%; per capita expenditure U.S.$1,521.

---

[1]Excludes 15 cabinet ministers not elected to National Assembly serving ex officio. [2]As of July 13, 2003, the office of prime minister became separated from the role of emir for the first time since independence in 1961. [3]Officially Al-Kuwayt; Kuwait is variant. [4]Būbiyān Island 333 sq mi (863 sq km) and Warbah Island 14 sq mi (37 sq km). [5]Detail does not add to total given because of rounding. [6]Sum of governorate populations. Actual mid-year est. pop. is 2,243,080. [7]Preliminary. [8]Manufacturing includes petroleum products; Mining (petroleum sector) excludes petroleum products. [9]Includes import duties less imputed bank service charges. [10]Unclassified. [11]Weights of consumer price index components. [12]Imports c.i.f.; exports f.o.b. [13]Refers to the circulation of the six largest daily newspapers only. [14]Government schools only; private education: 112 schools, 7,324 teachers, 128,204 students. [15]Includes intermediate. [16]University only. [17]Up to 3,700 personnel (all army) are foreign.

Internet resources for further information:
• **Central Bank of Kuwait** http://www.cbk.gov.kw
• **Ministry of Planning** http://www.mop.gov.kw/MopWebSite/english/default.asp

Kyrgyzstan

Official name: Kyrgyz Respublikasy (Kyrgyz); Respublika Kirgizstan (Russian) (Kyrgyz Republic).
Form of government: unitary multiparty republic with one legislative house (Supreme Council [75][1]).
Head of state and government: President assisted by Prime Minister.
Capital: Bishkek.
Official languages: Kyrgyz; Russian.
Official religion: none.
Monetary unit: 1 som (K.S.) = 100 tyiyn; valuation (Sept. 1, 2005) 1 U.S.$ = K.S. 40.95; 1 £ = K.S. 75.40.

Area and population		area		population
				1999
Provinces	**Capitals**	sq mi	sq km	census
Batken	Batken	6,573	17,024	382,426
Chüy (Chu)	Tokmok	7,214	18,684	770,811
Jalal-Abad	Jalal-Abad			
(Dzhalal-Abad)	(Dzhalal-Abad)	12,992	33,648	869,259
Naryn	Naryn	18,035	46,710	249,115
Osh	Osh	11,261	29,165	1,175,998
Talas	Talas	4,419	11,446	199,872
Ysyk-Köl	Ysyk-Köl			
(Issyk-Kul)	(Issyk-Kul)	16,646	43,114	413,149
City				
Bishkek (Frunze)	—	49	127	762,308
TOTAL		77,199[2, 3]	199,945[2, 3]	4,822,938

Demography

Population (2005): 5,146,000.
Density (2005): persons per sq mi 67.1, persons per sq km 25.9.
Urban-rural (2003): urban 33.9%; rural 66.1%.
Sex distribution (2004): male 49.03%; female 50.97%.
Age breakdown (2004): under 15, 32.3%; 15–29, 29.3%; 30–44, 18.9%; 45–59, 11.3%; 60–74, 6.1%; 75 and over, 2.1%.
Population projection: (2010) 5,509,000; (2020) 6,314,000.
Doubling time: 48 years.
Ethnic composition (1999): Kyrgyz 64.9%; Uzbek 13.8%; Russian 12.5%; Hui 1.1%; Ukrainian 1.0%; Uighur 1.0%; other 5.7%.
Religious affiliation (1997): Muslim (mostly Sunnī) 75.0%; Christian 6.7%, of which Russian Orthodox 5.6%; other (mostly nonreligious) 18.3%.
Major cities (1999): Bishkek 750,327; Osh 208,520; Jalal-Abad 70,401; Tokmok 59,409; Kara-Köl 47,159.

Vital statistics

Birth rate per 1,000 population (2004): 21.6 (world avg. 21.1); (1994) legitimate 83.2%; illegitimate 16.8%.
Death rate per 1,000 population (2004): 6.9 (world avg. 9.0).
Natural increase rate per 1,000 population (2004): 14.7 (world avg. 12.1).
Total fertility rate (avg. births per childbearing woman; 2004): 2.7.
Marriage rate per 1,000 population (2002): 6.3.
Life expectancy at birth (2003): male 64.5 years; female 72.2 years.
Major causes of death per 100,000 population (1999): diseases of the circulatory system 285.6; diseases of the respiratory system 84.2; malignant neoplasms (cancers) 59.9; accidents, poisoning, and violence 45.4.

National economy

Budget (2001). Revenue: K.S. 12,544,000,000 (tax revenue 73.2%, of which VAT 33.6%, taxes on income 16.0%, excise taxes 8.8%, other taxes 14.8%; nontax revenue 21.3%; grants 5.5%). Expenditures: K.S. 13,133,000,000 (education 21.7%; general public services 16.0%; social security 10.8%; health 10.5%; defense 7.5%).
Public debt (external, outstanding; 2003): U.S.$1,588,000,000.
Land use as % of total land area (2000): in temporary crops 7.1%, in permanent crops 0.3%, in pasture 48.4%; overall forest area 5.2%.
Population economically active (2002): total 2,116,000; activity rate of total population 42.5% (participation rates: ages 15–64, 68.7%; female 44.0%; unemployed [2003] 9.0%).

Price and earnings indexes (2000 = 100)							
	1998	1999	2000	2001	2002	2003	2004
Consumer price index	62.0	84.3	100.0	106.9	109.2	113.0	122.7
Average earnings index	71.2	82.1	100.0	118.2	136.9	161.6	186.6

Production (metric tons except as noted). Agriculture, forestry, fishing (2004): mixed grasses and legumes 3,000,000, potatoes 1,362,500, wheat 998,200, sugar beets 642,400, corn (maize) 452,900, seed cotton 121,700, tobacco leaves 13,000; livestock (number of live animals) 3,030,000 sheep, 1,003,400 cattle, 361,141 horses; roundwood 26,000 cu m; fish catch (2002) 48. Mining and quarrying (2002): mercury 250; antimony 150; gold 18,000 kg. Manufacturing (value of production in K.S. '000,000; 2004): base metals and fabricated metal products 24,330; food and tobacco products 6,811; cement, bricks, and ceramics 3,574; electrical machinery and optical equipment 1,402. Energy production (consumption): electricity (kW-hr; 2002) 11,922,000,000 (11,245,000,000); hard coal (metric tons; 2002) 108,000 (889,000); lignite (metric tons; 2002) 351,000 (350,000); crude petroleum (barrels; 2002) 560,000 (840,000); petroleum products (metric tons; 2002) 110,000 (357,000); natural gas (cu m; 2002) 30,000,000 (886,000,000).

Household income and expenditure. Average household size (1999) 4.3; income per capita of household (2003) K.S. 9,270 (U.S.$212); sources of income (1999): wages and salaries 29.2%, self-employment 25.6%, other 45.2%; expenditure (1990): food and clothing 48.0%, health care 13.1%, housing 5.9%.
Gross national product (2004): U.S.$2,050,000,000 (U.S.$400 per capita).

Structure of gross domestic product and labour force				
	2003		2002	
	in value K.S. '000,000	% of total value	labour force[4]	% of labour force[4]
Agriculture	29,380.3	35.2	951,900	52.7
Mining	376.6	0.4	6,500	0.3
Manufacturing	11,384.5	13.6	111,900	6.2
Public utilities	3,267.0	3.9	21,800	1.2
Construction	2,383.4	2.9	45,600	2.5
Transp. and commun.	4,225.0	5.1	68,000	3.7
Trade	13,367.0	16.0	217,000	12.1
Finance	2,744.2	3.3	38,300	2.1
Public admin., defense	3,989.5	4.8	66,300	3.7
Services	4,798.4	5.8	279,800	15.5
Other	7,504.9[5]	9.0[5]	—	—
TOTAL	83,420.8	100.0	1,807,100	100.0

Tourism (2003): receipts from visitors U.S.$48,000,000; expenditures by nationals abroad U.S.$17,000,000.

Foreign trade[6]

Balance of trade (current prices)						
	1998	1999	2000	2001	2002	2003
U.S.$'000,000	−220.7	−88.6	+4.0	+39.9	−54.0	−82.7
% of total	17.1%	8.7%	0.4%	4.3%	5.1%	6.5%

Imports (2001): U.S.$467,200,000 (petroleum and natural gas 22.6%, machinery and apparatus 21.0%, food products 11.7%, chemicals and chemical products 9.5%). *Major import sources:* Russia 18.2%; Kazakhstan 17.5%; Uzbekistan 14.3%; China 10.4%; United States 5.7%.
Exports (2001): U.S.$476,200,000 (nonferrous metals [significantly gold] 51.7%, machinery and apparatus 12.0%, electricity 9.8%, agricultural products [significantly tobacco] 9.5%). *Major export destinations:* Switzerland 26.1%; Germany 19.8%; Russia 13.5%; Uzbekistan 10.1%; Kazakhstan 8.2%.

Transport and communications

Transport. Railroads (2000): length 424 km; passenger-km (2002) 43,000,000; metric ton-km cargo (2000) 348,000,000. Roads (1999): total length 18,500 km (paved 91%). Vehicles (2002): passenger cars 188,711; trucks and buses, n.a. Air transport (2004)[7]: passenger-km 190,808,000; metric ton-km cargo 1,551,000; airports with scheduled flights 2.

Communications				units per 1,000
Medium	date	unit	number	persons
Daily newspapers	2000	circulation	73,000	15
Radio	2000	receivers	542,000	111
Television	2000	receivers	239,000	49
Telephones	2003	main lines	396,200	76
Cellular phones	2004	subscribers	300,000	58
Personal computers	2004	units	87,000	17
Internet	2004	users	263,000	50

Education and health

Educational attainment (1999). Percentage of population age 15 and over having: primary education 6.3%; some secondary 18.3%; completed secondary 50.0%; some postsecondary 14.9%; higher 10.5%. *Literacy* (1999): total population age 15 and over literate 97.5%; males 98.5%; females 96.5%.

Education (1999–2000)				student/
	schools	teachers	students	teacher ratio
Primary (age 6–13)	1,985	19,200	466,200	24.3
Secondary (age 14–17)	1,474[8]	36,600	633,900	17.3
Voc., teacher tr.	53[8]	5,100	52,200	10.2
Higher	23	8,400	159,200	19.0

Health: physicians (2001) 13,379 (1 per 366 persons); hospital beds (2003) 26,600 (1 per 188 persons); infant mortality rate (2004) 25.7.
Food (2002): daily per capita caloric intake 2,999 (vegetable products 80%, animal products 20%); 117% of FAO recommended minimum.

Military

Total active duty personnel (2004): 12,500 (army 68.0%, air force 32.0%)[9].
Military expenditure as percentage of GDP (2003): 2.9%; per capita expenditure U.S.$11.

[1]Former bicameral parliament was replaced by the unicameral Supreme Council per elections of February 2005. [2]Area of Kyrgyzstan prior to border demarcation agreement signed with China in September 2004; approximate post-2004 area figure is 198,500 sq km (76,641 sq m). [3]Detail does not add to total given because of statistical discrepancy. [4]Employed only. [5]Taxes on products. [6]Imports are f.o.b. in balance of trade and c.i.f. for commodities and trading partners. [7]Kyrghyzstan Airlines only. [8]1993–94. [9]U.S. troops (July 2005) 1,000; Russian troops (July 2005) 500.

Internet resources for further information:
• **National Statistical Committee of the Kyrgyz Republic**
 http://www.stat.kg/English/index.html
• **National Bank of Kyrgyz Republic**
 http://www.nbkr.kg/web/interfeis.builder_frame?language=ENG

Laos

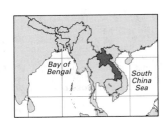

Official name: Sathalanalat Paxathipatai Paxaxôn Lao (Lao People's Democratic Republic).
Form of government: unitary single-party people's republic with one legislative house (National Assembly [109]).
Chief of state: President.
Head of government: Prime Minister.
Capital: Vientiane (Viangchan).
Official language: Lao.
Official religion: none.
Monetary unit: 1 kip (KN) = 100 at; valuation (Sept. 1, 2005) 1 U.S.$ = KN 10,400; 1 £ = KN 19,149.

Area and population		area		population
				1996
Provinces	Capitals	sq mi	sq km	estimate
Attapu	Attapu	3,985	10,320	87,700
Bokèo	Houayxay	2,392	6,196	114,900
Bolikhamxai	Pakxan	5,739	14,863	164,900
Champasak	Pakxé	5,952	15,415	503,300
Houaphan	Xam Nua	6,371	16,500	247,300
Khammouan	Thakhek	6,299	16,315	275,400
Louangnamtha	Louangnamtha	3,600	9,325	115,200
Louangphrabang	Louangphrabang	6,516	16,875	367,200
Oudomxay	Xay	5,934	15,370	211,300
Phôngsali	Phôngsali	6,282	16,270	153,400
Salavan	Salavan	4,128	10,691	258,300
Savannakhét	Savannakhét	8,407	21,774	674,900
Viangchan	Muang Phôn-Hông	6,149	15,927	286,800
Xaignabouli	Xaignabouli	6,328	16,389	293,300
Xékong	Thong	2,959	7,665	64,200
Xiangkhoang	Phônsavan	6,131	15,880	201,200
Municipality				
Viangchan	Vientiane (Viangchan)	1,514	3,920	531,800
Special zone				
Xaisomboun	Ban Mouang Cha	2,743	7,105	54,200
TOTAL		91,429	236,800	4,605,300

Demography

Population (2005): 5,924,000[1].
Density (2005): persons per sq mi 64.8, persons per sq km 25.0.
Urban-rural (2003): urban 20.7%; rural 79.3%.
Sex distribution (2003): male 49.40%; female 50.60%.
Age breakdown (2000): under 15, 42.8%; 15–29, 27.0%; 30–44, 16.3%; 45–59, 8.3%; 60–74, 4.6%; 75 and over, 1.0%.
Population projection: (2010) 6,604,000; (2020) 8,014,000.
Ethnic composition (2000): Lao-Lum (Lao) 53.0%; Lao-Theung (Mon-Khmer) 23.0%; Lao-Tai (Tai) 13.0%; Lao-Soung (Miao [Hmong] and Man [Yao]) 10.0%; other (ethnic Chinese or Vietnamese) 1.0%.
Religious affiliation (2000): Buddhist 48.8%; traditional beliefs 41.7%; nonreligious 4.3%; Christian 2.1%; other 3.1%.
Major cities (2003): Vientiane 194,200 (urban agglomeration 716,380); Savannakhét 58,200; Pakxé 50,100; Xam Nua 40,700; Muang Khammouan 27,300; Louangphrabang 26,400.

Vital statistics

Birth rate per 1,000 population (2004): 36.5 (world avg. 21.1).
Death rate per 1,000 population (2004): 12.1 (world avg. 9.0).
Natural increase rate per 1,000 population (2004): 24.4 (world avg. 12.1).
Total fertility rate (avg. births per childbearing woman; 2004): 4.9.
Life expectancy at birth (2004): male 52.7 years; female 56.8 years.
Major causes of death per 100,000 population (2002): communicable diseases 673; cardiovascular diseases 210; injuries, accidents, and violence 112; malignant neoplasms (cancers) 73; chronic respiratory diseases 58.

National economy

Budget (2003–04). Revenue: KN 3,282,000,000,000 (tax revenue 72.5%, of which sales tax 18.9%, excise tax 13.6%; grants 14.2%; nontax revenue 13.3%). Expenditures: KN 4,261,000,000,000 (capital expenditure 51.1%, of which foreign-financed 34.2%; current expenditure 48.9%).
Public debt (external, outstanding; 2003): U.S.$2,801,000,000.
Tourism (2003): receipts from visitors U.S.$87,000,000; expenditures by nationals abroad (2001) U.S.$100,000.
Population economically active (2000): total 2,625,000; activity rate of total population c. 50% (participation rates: ages 15–64, n.a.; female c. 47%; unemployed [1997] 5.7%).

Price index (2000 = 100)							
	1998	1999	2000	2001	2002	2003	2004
Consumer price index	35.0	79.9	100.0	107.8	119.3	137.7	152.2

Production (metric tons except as noted). Agriculture, forestry, fishing (2004): rice 2,529,000, sugarcane 223,300, corn (maize) 203,500, sweet potatoes 194,000, cassava 55,500, bananas 46,000, pineapples 36,000, potatoes 36,000, tobacco 33,000, oranges 28,000, coffee 23,100, peanuts (groundnuts) 16,500, ramie 1,700; livestock (number of live animals) 1,728,600 pigs, 1,248,800 cattle, 1,111,500 water buffalo, 14,000,000 chickens; roundwood 6,320,214 cu m; fish catch (2003) 29,800. Mining and quarrying (2004): gypsum 102,000; tin (metal content) 340; gold 4,400 kg. Manufacturing (value added in

U.S.$'000,000; 1999): food and food products 22; wearing apparel 14; tobacco products 8; glass and glass products 5. Energy production (consumption): electricity (kW-hr; 2002) 1,290,000,000 (733,000,000); hard coal (metric tons; 2002) 290,000 (290,000); crude petroleum, none (none); petroleum products (metric tons; 2002) none (128,000); natural gas, none (none).
Gross national product (2004): U.S.$2,239,000,000 (U.S.$390 per capita).

Structure of gross domestic product and labour force				
	2003		2002	
	in value KN '000,000	% of total value	labour force	% of labour force
Agriculture	10,828,834	48.1	2,113,000	76.1
Manufacturing	4,276,550	19.0		
Mining	378,238	1.7		
Construction	508,363	2.2		
Public utilities	619,398	2.7		
Transp. and commun.	1,408,139	6.2	663,000	23.9
Trade	2,291,722	10.2		
Finance	99,487	0.4		
Pub. admin., defense	804,925	3.6		
Services	1,080,569	4.8		
Other	239,882[2]	1.1[2]		
TOTAL	22,536,107	100.0	2,776,000	100.0

Household income and expenditure. Average household size (2002) 6.2; average annual income per household (1995) KN 3,710 (U.S.$371); sources of income: n.a.; expenditure[3]: food and nonalcoholic beverages 46.2%, transportation and communications 17.9%, household furnishings 8.1%, alcoholic beverages and tobacco 6.4%, clothing and footwear 4.9%.
Land use as % of total land area (2000): in temporary crops 3.8%, in permanent crops 0.4%, in pasture 3.8%; overall forest area 54.4%.

Foreign trade[4]

Balance of trade (current prices)						
	1999	2000	2001	2002	2003	2004
U.S.$'000,000	−212	−218	−209	−230	−217	−145
% of total	23.7%	23.7%	23.9%	25.3%	21.3%	16.7%

Imports (2002): U.S.$570,000,000 (consumption goods 49.1%, construction and electrical equipment 12.5%, materials for garment assembly 11.0%, mineral fuels 10.2%). *Major import sources* (2001): Thailand 52.0%; Vietnam 26.5%; China 5.7%; Singapore 3.3%; Japan 1.5%.
Exports (2002): U.S.$340,000,000 (garments 30.8%, electricity 30.4%, wood products [mostly logs and timber] 27.5%, coffee 5.0%). *Major export destinations* (2001): Vietnam 41.5%; Thailand 14.8%; France 6.1%; Germany 4.6%; Belgium 2.2%.

Transport and communications

Transport. Railroads: none. Roads (1999): total length 13,494 mi, 21,716 km (paved 45%). Vehicles (1996): passenger cars 16,320; trucks and buses 4,200. Air transport (2000): passenger-km 85,000,000; metric ton-km cargo, n.a.; airports (1996) with scheduled flights 11.

Communications				units per 1,000
Medium	date	unit	number	persons
Daily newspapers[5]	2004	circulation	22,000	3.8
Radio	2001	receivers	800,000	148
Television	2001	receivers	281,000	52
Telephones	2004	main lines	75,000	13
Cellular telephones	2004	subscribers	204,200	35
Personal computers	2004	units	22,000	3.8
Internet	2004	users	20,900	3.6

Education and health

Educational attainment (1985). Percentage of population age 6 and over having: no schooling 49.3%; primary 41.2%; secondary 9.1%; higher 0.4%.
Literacy (2003): total population age 15 and over literate 67.2%; males literate 78.0%; females literate 56.6%.

Education (2002–03)				student/
	schools[6]	teachers	students	teacher ratio
Primary (age 6–10)	7,896	28,571	875,300	30.6
Secondary (age 11–16)	...	13,421	348,309	26.0
Voc., teacher tr.	...	350	5,053	14.4
Higher	...	1,794	28,117	15.7

Health (2002): physicians 5,203 (1 per 1,063 persons); hospital beds 5,144 (1 per 1,075 persons); infant mortality rate (2004) 87.1.
Food (2002): daily per capita caloric intake 2,312 (vegetable products 93%, animal products 7%); 104% of FAO recommended minimum requirement.

Military

Total active duty personnel (2004): 29,100 (army 88.0%, air force 12.0%). *Military expenditure as percentage of GDP* (2003): 2.0%; per capita expenditure U.S.$7.

[1]Estimate of *UN World Population Prospects* (2004 revision). March 2005 preliminary census total equals 5,609,997. [2]Indirect taxes less subsidies. [3]Weights of consumer price index components used in 2004; date of weights is unknown. [4]Imports c.i.f.; exports f.o.b. [5]Refers to the circulation of the four largest daily newspapers only. [6]1996–97.

Internet resources for further information:
• **Asian Development Bank: Key Indicators 2005** http://www.adb.org
• **Vietnam Ministry of Trade: Laos website** http://www1.mot.gov.vn/Laowebsite/English/gioithieuAP.asp

Latvia

Official name: Latvijas Republika (Republic of Latvia).
Form of government: unitary multiparty republic with a single legislative body (Parliament, or Saeima [100]).
Chief of state: President.
Head of government: Prime Minister.
Capital: Riga.
Official language: Latvian.
Official religion: none.
Monetary unit: 1 lats (Ls; plural lati) = 100 santimi; valuation (Sept. 1, 2005) 1 U.S.$ = Ls 0.55; 1 £ = Ls 1.02.

Area and population

Cities	area sq km	population 2002[1] estimate	Districts	area sq km	population 2002[1] estimate
Daugavpils	72	113,409	Jelgava	1,604	37,086
Jelgava	60	65,927	Krāslava	2,285	36,203
Jūrmala	100	55,328	Kuldīga	2,502	37,584
Liepāja	60	87,505	Liepāja	3,594	46,170
Rēzekne	17	38,054	Limbaži	2,602	39,920
Riga	307	747,157	Ludza	2,569	34,380
Ventspils	46	44,004	Madona	3,346	45,717
			Ogre	1,840	63,028
Districts			Preiļi	2,041	41,041
Aizkraukle	2,565	41,546	Rēzekne	2,655	43,012
Alūksne	2,243	26,020	Rīga (Riga)	3,059	145,261
Balvi	2,386	29,843	Saldus	2,182	38,311
Bauska	1,882	52,517	Talsi	2,751	48,959
Cēsis	3,067	59,914	Tukums	2,447	55,050
Daugavpils	2,525	42,193	Valka	2,437	33,597
Dobele	1,633	39,791	Valmiera	2,365	59,593
Gulbene	1,877	27,937	Ventspils	2,472	14,529
Jēkabpils	2,998	55,182	TOTAL	64,589	2,345,768

Demography

Population (2005): 2,299,000.
Density (2005): persons per sq mi 92.2, persons per sq km 35.6.
Urban-rural (2003): urban 66.2%; rural 33.8%.
Sex distribution (2004): male 46.10%; female 53.90%.
Age breakdown (2004): under 15, 15.0%; 15–29, 22.3%; 30–44, 22.1%; 45–59, 18.9%; 60–74, 15.6%; 75 and over, 6.1%.
Population projection: (2010) 2,233,000; (2020) 2,115,000.
Ethnic composition (2004): Latvian 58.6%; Russian 28.8%; Belarusian 3.9%; Ukrainian 2.6%; Polish 2.5%; Lithuanian 1.4%; other 2.2%.
Religious affiliation (2000): Christian 67.0%, of which Protestant (mostly Lutheran) 21.8%, Roman Catholic 21.6%, Orthodox 19.0%; Jewish 0.6%; Muslim 0.4%; nonreligious 26.0%; atheist 6.0%.
Major cities (2002[1]): Riga 747,157; Daugavpils 113,409; Liepāja 87,505; Jelgava 65,927; Jūrmala 55,328.

Vital statistics

Birth rate per 1,000 population (2004): 8.8 (world avg. 21.1); legitimate 54.7%; illegitimate 45.3%.
Death rate per 1,000 population (2004): 13.9 (world avg. 9.0).
Natural increase rate per 1,000 population (2004): –5.1 (world avg. 12.1).
Total fertility rate (avg. births per childbearing woman; 2004): 1.2.
Marriage rate per 1,000 population (2004): 4.5.
Divorce rate per 1,000 population (2004): 2.3.
Life expectancy at birth (2003): male 65.9 years; female 76.9 years.
Major causes of death per 100,000 population (2002): diseases of the circulatory system 777.8; malignant neoplasms (cancers) 245.0; accidents, poisoning, and violence 156.8, of which suicide 28.7; diseases of the digestive system 43.1.

National economy

Budget (2001). Revenue: Ls 1,244,100,000 (social security contributions 35.3%, value-added taxes 28.2%, income taxes 14.3%, excises 13.0%, nontax revenue 9.2%). Expenditures: Ls 1,399,800,000 (social security and welfare 40.7%, health 11.0%, police 7.0%, education 6.3%, defense 3.1%).
Public debt (external, outstanding; 2003): U.S.$1,238,000,000.
Production (metric tons except as noted). Agriculture, forestry, fishing (2004): grasses for forage and silage 14,000,000, potatoes 628,000, wheat 530,000, sugar beets 506,000, barley 275,000, rye 100,000; livestock (number of live animals) 444,400 pigs, 378,600 cattle; roundwood 12,419,987 cu m; fish catch 125,900. Mining and quarrying (2003): peat 1,076,142. Manufacturing (value added in U.S.$'000,000; 2001): food and food products 222; wood and wood products (excl. furniture) 216; beverages 70; printing and publishing 55; wearing apparel 51; fabricated metal products 49. Energy production (consumption): electricity (kW-hr; 2004) 4,680,000,000 (6,786,000,000); coal (metric tons; 2004) none (98,000); crude petroleum[2], none (none); petroleum products[2] (metric tons; 2002) none (997,000); natural gas (cu m; 2004) none (1,663,000,000).
Household income and expenditure. Average household size (2004) 2.5; annual disposable income per household (2002) Ls 2,076 (U.S.$3,460); sources of income (1998): wages and salaries 55.8%, pensions and transfers 25.7%; expenditure (2001–02): food, beverages, and tobacco 40.0%, transportation and communications 15.0%, housing and energy 14.0%.
Tourism (in U.S.$'000,000; 2003): receipts 222; expenditures 328.
Gross national product (2004): U.S.$12,570,000,000 (U.S.$5,460 per capita).

Structure of gross domestic product and labour force

	2003 in value Ls '000,000	% of total value	labour force	% of labour force
Agriculture, forestry	235.3	4.0	139,000	12.3
Mining and quarrying	7.9	0.1	2,500	0.2
Manufacturing	773.5	13.2	174,000	15.4
Public utilities	175.1	3.0	21,500	1.9
Construction	316.7	5.4	74,000	6.6
Transp. and commun.	752.6	12.8	95,000	8.4
Trade, restaurants	1,124.7	19.2	177,000	15.7
Finance, real estate	795.0	13.5	58,000	5.1
Pub. admin., defense	337.0	5.7	67,000	6.0
Services	671.3	11.4	199,000	17.7
Other	683.0[3]	11.6[3]	119,000[4]	10.6[4]
TOTAL	5,872.2[5]	100.0[5]	1,126,000	100.0[5]

Population economically active (2003): total 1,126,000; activity rate of total population 48.3% (participation rates: ages 15–64, 69.2%; female 48.6%; unemployed [July 2003–June 2004] 10.6%).

Price and earnings indexes (2000 = 100)

	1998	1999	2000	2001	2002	2003	2004
Consumer price index	95.2	97.4	100.0	102.5	104.5	107.5	114.2
Annual earnings index	93.3	97.0	100.0	104.9	111.5	121.6	133.5

Land use as % of total land area (2000): in temporary crops 29.7%, in permanent crops 0.5%, in pasture 9.8%; overall forest area 47.1%.

Foreign trade[6]

Balance of trade (current prices)

	1999	2000	2001	2002	2003	2004
Ls '000,000	–716	–803	–945	–1,088	–1,338	–1,629
% of total	26.2%	26.2%	27.4%	27.9%	28.8%	27.8%

Imports (2002): Ls 2,497,000,000 (machinery and apparatus 21.3%, chemicals and chemical products 10.5%, transport vehicles 9.8%, mineral fuels 9.7%). *Major import sources:* Germany 17.2%; Lithuania 9.8%; Russia 8.8%; Finland 8.0%; Sweden 6.4%.
Exports (2002): Ls 1,409,000,000 (wood and wood products [mostly sawn wood] 33.6%, base and fabricated metals [mostly iron and steel] 13.2%, textiles and clothing 12.8%). *Major export destinations:* Germany 15.5%; U.K. 14.6%; Sweden 10.5%; Lithuania 8.4%; Estonia 6.0%.

Transport and communications

Transport. Railroads (2004): length 2,270 km; passenger-km 811,000,000; metric-km cargo 18,618,000,000. Roads (1999): total length 73,227 km (paved 39%). Vehicles (2004): passenger cars 686,100; trucks and buses 118,300. Air transport (2004)[7]: passenger-km 566,043,000; metric ton-km cargo 934,000; airports with scheduled flights (2001) 2.

Communications

Medium	date	unit	number	units per 1,000 persons
Daily newspapers	2000	circulation	586,000	247
Radio	2000	receivers	1,650,000	695
Television	2002	receivers	1,955,000	850
Telephones	2004	main lines	631,000	276
Cellular telephones	2004	subscribers	1,536,700	672
Personal computers	2004	units	501,000	219
Internet	2004	users	810,000	354

Education and health

Educational attainment (2000). Percentage of population age 15 and over having: some and complete primary education 8.5%; lower secondary 26.5%; upper secondary 51.1%; higher 13.9%. *Literacy* (2000): 99.8%.

Education (2002–03)

	schools[8]	teachers	students	student/ teacher ratio
Primary	1,074	7,544	103,359	13.7
Secondary		21,101	236,949	11.2
Vocational	...	3,666	39,123	10.7
Higher	33	5,360	118,944	22.2

Health (2004): physicians 8,100 (1 per 285 persons); hospital beds 18,000 (1 per 128 persons); infant mortality rate per 1,000 live births (2004) 9.4.
Food (2002): daily per capita caloric intake 2,938 (vegetable products 72%, animal products 28%); 115% of FAO recommended minimum requirement.

Military

Total active duty personnel (2004): 4,880[9] (army 82.0%, navy 12.7%, air force 5.3%). *Military expenditure as percentage of GDP* (2003): 1.7%; per capita expenditure U.S.$81.

---

[1]January 1. [2]Shipments of Russian crude and refined petroleum through Latvia have declined significantly since 2002. [3]Indirect taxes less subsidies. [4]Unemployed. [5]Detail does not add to total given because of rounding. [6]Imports c.i.f.; exports f.o.b. [7]AirBaltic only. [8]2000–01. [9]Excludes 3,200 border guards classified as paramilitary.

Internet resources for further information:
• Bank of Latvia http://www.bank.lv/eng/info/jaunzin
• Central Statistical Bureau of Latvia http://www.csb.lv/avidus.cfm

Lebanon

Official name: Al-Jumhūrīyah al-Lubnānīyah (Lebanese Republic).
Form of government: unitary multiparty republic with one legislative house (National Assembly [128])[1].
Chief of state: President.
Head of government: Prime Minister.
Capital: Beirut.
Official language: Arabic.
Official religion: none.
Monetary unit: 1 Lebanese pound[2] (£L) = 100 piastres; valuation (Sept. 1, 2005) 1 U.S.$ = £L 1,508; 1 £ = £L 2,776.

Area and population		area		population
				1996
Governorates	Capitals	sq mi	sq km	estimate
Al-Biqā'	Zahlah	1,653	4,280	399,890
Al-Janūb	Sidon (Saydā)	364	943	283,056
An-Nabaṭīyah	An-Nabaṭīyah	408	1,058	205,412
Ash-Shamāl	Tripoli (Ṭarābulus)	765	1,981	670,609
Bayrūt	Beirut (Bayrūt)	7	18	407,403
Jabal Lubnān	B'abdā	753	1,950	1,145,458
WATER AREA		66	170	—
TOTAL		4,016	10,400	3,111,828

Demography

Population (2005): 3,577,000[3].
Density (2005): persons per sq mi 890.7, persons per sq km 343.9.
Urban-rural (2003): urban 87.5%; rural 12.5%.
Sex distribution (2004): male 49.77%; female 50.23%.
Age breakdown (2004): under 15, 27.3%; 15–29, 27.8%; 30–44, 20.8%; 45–59, 13.2%; 60–74, 8.6%; 75 and over, 2.3%.
Population projection: (2010) 3,773,000; (2020) 4,140,000.
Doubling time: 54 years.
Ethnic composition (2000): Arab 84.5%, of which Lebanese 71.2%, Palestinian 12.1%; Armenian 6.8%; Kurd 6.1%; other 2.6%.
Religious affiliation (1995): Muslim 55.3%, of which Shī'ī 34.0%, Sunnī 21.3%; Christian 37.6%, of which Catholic 25.1% (Maronite 19.0%, Greek Catholic or Melchite 4.6%), Orthodox 11.7% (Greek Orthodox 6.0%, Armenian Apostolic 5.2%), Protestant 0.5%; Druze 7.1%.
Major cities (2003): Beirut 1,171,000 (urban agglomeration [2001] 2,115,000); Tripoli 212,900; Sidon 149,000; Tyre (Ṣūr) 117,100; An-Nabaṭīyah 89,400.

Vital statistics

Birth rate per 1,000 population (2004): 19.3 (world avg. 21.1).
Death rate per 1,000 population (2004): 6.3 (world avg. 9.0).
Natural increase rate per 1,000 population (2004): 13.0 (world avg. 12.1).
Total fertility rate (avg. births per childbearing woman; 2004): 2.0.
Marriage rate per 1,000 population (2004): 8.5.
Divorce rate per 1,000 population (2004): 1.2.
Life expectancy at birth (2004): male 69.9 years; female 74.9 years.
Major causes of death per 100,000 population (2002): cardiovascular diseases 305; injuries, accidents, and violence 87; malignant neoplasms (cancers) 67; communicable diseases 64; chronic respiratory diseases 33.

National economy

Budget (2004). Revenue: £L 7,075,000,000,000 (tax revenue 73.1%, of which VAT revenues 24.9%, customs and excise revenues 22.8%; nontax revenue 26.9%). Expenditures: £L 8,306,000,000,000 (general expenditures 51.6%; interest expenditures 48.4%, of which domestic 27.0%, foreign 21.4%).
Public debt (external, outstanding; July 2005): U.S.$18,373,000,000.
Gross national product (2004): U.S.$22,668,000,000 (U.S.$4,980 per capita).

Structure of gross domestic product and labour force					
	2002			1995	
	in value £L '000,000,000	% of total value		labour force	% of labour force
Agriculture	2,665	9.9	}	143,900	14.0
Mining	—	—			
Manufacturing	2,607	9.7			
Construction	650	2.4	}	277,600	27.0
Public utilities	1,760	6.6			
Transp. and commun.	827	3.1			
Trade	8,649	32.2	}		
Finance	3,675	13.7			
Real estate and business services	1,151	4.3	}	606,500	59.0
Services	2,764	10.3			
Pub. admin., defense	2,090	7.8			
TOTAL	26,838	100.0		1,028,000	100.0

Production (metric tons except as noted). Agriculture, forestry, fishing (2004): potatoes 350,000, tomatoes 218,000, oranges 190,000, olives 180,000, cucumbers and gherkins 160,000, apples 140,000, wheat 120,000, grapes 110,000, lemons and limes 83,000; livestock (number of live animals) 430,000 goats, 350,000 sheep, 90,000 cattle, 35,000,000 chickens; roundwood 88,732 cu m; fish catch (2003) 3,898. Mining and quarrying (2003): lime 14,000; salt 3,500; gypsum 1,700. Manufacturing (value added in U.S.$'000,000; 1998) food and food products 345; cement, bricks, and ceramics 212; wood and wood products 188, of which furniture (including metal furniture) 135; fabricated metal products 185; textiles, wearing

apparel, and footwear 147, of which wearing apparel 91; paints, soaps, and pharmaceuticals 94. Energy production (consumption): electricity (kW-hr; 2004–05) 10,457,000,000 ([2002] 10,192,000,000); coal (metric tons; 2002) none (200,000); crude petroleum (barrels; 2002) none (none); petroleum products (metric tons; 2002) none (4,697,000); natural gas (cu m; 2002) none (none).
Population economically active (1997): total 1,362,000; activity rate of total population 34.0% (participation rates: ages 15–64, 49.2%; female 21.6%; unemployed [2001] 18%).

Price index (2000 = 100)					
	1999	2000	2001	2002	2003
Consumer price index	100.1	100.0	99.5	98.9	98.9

Household income and expenditure. Average household size (2004) 4.3; average annual income per household (1994)[4] £L 2,400,000 (U.S.$1,430); sources of income: n.a.; expenditure (1997)[5]: food, beverages, and tobacco 34.6%, education 13.4%, transportation and communications 11.3%, health 8.8%, housing and energy 8.8%, household furnishings 7.9%.
Tourism (2003): receipts from visitors U.S.$1,016,000,000.
Land use as % of total land area (2000): in temporary crops 18.6%, in permanent crops 13.9%, in pasture 1.6%; overall forest area 3.5%.

Foreign trade[6]

Balance of trade (current prices)					
	1999	2000	2001	2002	2003	2004
U.S.$'000,000	−5,530	−5,514	−6,423	−5,399	−5,647	−7,650
% of total	80.3%	79.4%	78.7%	72.1%	64.9%	68.3%

Imports (2004): U.S.$9,397,000,000 (mineral products 22.0%, electrical equipment 11.8%, food and live animals 10.4%, transportation equipment 9.0%, chemicals and chemical products 8.8%). *Major import sources:* Italy 9.9%; Germany 7.8%; France 7.8%; China 7.6%; U.S. 5.9%.
Exports (2004): U.S.$1,747,000,000 (precious metal jewelry and stones [significantly gold and pearls] 16.4%, electrical equipment 15.7%, base metals 13.0%, chemicals and chemical products 8.5%, food and beverages 8.5%). *Major export destinations:* Iraq 14.6%; Switzerland 10.7%; Syria 8.3%; U.A.E. 7.7%; Turkey 7.3%.

Transport and communications

Transport. Railroads: [7]. Roads (1999): total length 7,300 km (paved 85%). Vehicles (1997): passenger cars 1,299,398; trucks and buses 85,242. Air transport (2004)[8]: passenger-km 2,197,000,000; metric ton-km cargo 84,900,000; airports (1999) 1.

Communications				units per 1,000 persons
Medium	date	unit	number	
Daily newspapers	2004	circulation	215,000	61
Radio	2000	receivers	2,460,000	687
Television	2001	receivers	1,154,000	336
Telephones	2004	main lines	630,000	178
Cellular telephones	2004	subscribers	888,000	251
Personal computers	2004	units	400,000	113
Internet	2004	users	600,000	169

Education and health

Educational attainment (2004). Percentage of population age 4 and over having: no formal education or unknown 13.7%; incomplete primary education 3.2%; primary 54.2%; secondary/vocational 15.5%; upper vocational 1.7%; higher 11.7%. *Literacy* (2003): total population age 15 and over literate 87.4%; males literate 93.1%; females literate 82.2%.

Education (2002–03)				student/ teacher ratio
	schools	teachers	students	
Primary (age 5–9)	2,160[9]	26,428	449,311	17.0
Secondary (age 10–16)	...	34,613	303,940	8.8
Voc., teacher tr.	275[10]	11,595	46,271	4.0
Higher	20[9]	11,196	144,050	12.9

Health: physicians (2002) 9,748 (1 per 356 persons); hospital beds (2001) 10,302 (1 per 333 persons); infant mortality rate per 1,000 live births (2004) 25.5.
Food (2002): daily per capita caloric intake 3,196 (vegetable products 83%, animal products 17%); 129% of FAO recommended minimum.

Military

Total active duty personnel (2004): 72,100 (army 97.1%, navy 1.5%, air force 1.4%). UN peacekeeping troops (July 2005) 2,000; Syrian troops ended 29-year presence in April 2005. *Military expenditure as percentage of GDP* (2003): 4.3%; per capita expenditure: U.S.$223.

---

[1]The current legislature was elected between May and June 2005; one-half of its membership is Christian and one-half Muslim/Druze. [2]Pegged to the U.S. dollar from February 2002. [3]Excludes about 300,000 unnaturalized Palestinian refugees. [4]ESCWA estimate for Beirut only. [5]Weights of consumer price index components. [6]Imports are c.i.f. [7]Only short sections of the 250-mi (401-km) network was usable in 2004. [8]For Middle East Airlines and Trans-Mediterranean Airways. [9]1996–97. [10]1994–95.

Internet resources for further information:
• **Central Administration for Statistics**
  http://www.cas.gov.lb
• **Central Bank of Lebanon**
  http://www.bdl.gov.lb

Lesotho

Official name: Lesotho (Sotho); Kingdom of Lesotho (English).
Form of government: constitutional monarchy with 2 legislative houses (Senate [33[1]]; National Assembly [120]).
Chief of state: King.
Head of government: Prime Minister.
Capital: Maseru.
Official languages: Sotho; English.
Official religion: Christianity.
Monetary unit: 1 loti (plural maloti [M]) = 100 lisente; valuation (Sept. 1, 2005) 1 U.S.$ = M 6.27; 1 £ = M 11.54.

Area and population

Districts	Capitals	area		population
		sq mi	sq km	2001 census[2]
Berea	Teyateyaneng	858	2,222	300,557
Butha-Buthe	Butha-Buthe	682	1,767	126,948
Leribe	Hlotse	1,092	2,828	362,339
Mafeteng	Mafeteng	818	2,119	238,946
Maseru	Maseru	1,652	4,279	477,599
Mohale's Hoek	Mohale's Hoek	1,363	3,530	206,842
Mokhotlong	Mokhotlong	1,573	4,075	89,705
Qacha's Nek	Qacha's Nek	907	2,349	80,323
Quthing	Quthing	1,126	2,916	140,641
Thaba-Tseka	Thaba-Tseka	1,649	4,270	133,680
TOTAL		11,720	30,355	2,157,580

Demography

Population (2005): 2,031,000[3].
Density (2005): persons per sq mi 173.3, persons per sq km 66.9.
Urban-rural (2001)[2]: urban 12.0%; rural 88.0%.
Sex distribution (2001)[2]: male 49.44%; female 50.56%.
Age breakdown (2001)[2]: under 15, 35.8%; 15–29, 31.2%; 30–44, 14.7%; 45–59, 10.0%; 60–74, 6.0%; 75 and over, 2.1%; unknown 0.2%.
Population projection[3]: (2010) 1,983,000; (2020) 1,878,000.
Doubling time: not applicable.
Ethnic composition (2000): Sotho 80.3%; Zulu 14.4%; other 5.3%.
Religious affiliation (2000): Christian 91.0%, of which Roman Catholic 37.5%, unaffiliated Christian 23.9%, Protestant (mostly Presbyterian and Anglican) 17.7%, independent Christian 11.8%; traditional beliefs 7.7%; other 1.3%.
Major urban centres (1996): Maseru 137,837 (urban agglomeration [2001] 271,000); Teyateyaneng 48,869; Maputsoe 27,951; Hlotse 23,122; Mafeteng 20,804.

Vital statistics

Birth rate per 1,000 population (2004): 25.7 (world avg. 21.1).
Death rate per 1,000 population (2004): 28.3 (world avg. 9.0).
Natural increase rate per 1,000 population (2004): –2.6 (world avg. 12.1).
Total fertility rate (avg. births per childbearing woman; 2004): 3.4.
Life expectancy at birth (2001): male 45.1 years; female 54.2 years.
Adult population (ages 15–49) *living with HIV* (2004[4]): 28.9% (world avg. 1.1%).

National economy

Budget (2000–01). Revenue: M 2,752,200,000 (customs receipts 40.9%, grants and nontax revenue 29.4%, income tax 11.4%, sales tax 10.2%). Expenditures: M 2,897,900,000 (personal emoluments 31.8%, capital expenditure 17.8%, subsidies and transfers 9.6%, interest payments 9.0%).
Public debt (external, outstanding; 2003): U.S.$676,000,000.
Production (metric tons except as noted). Agriculture, forestry, fishing (2004): corn (maize) 150,000, potatoes 90,000, wheat 51,000, sorghum 46,000, vegetables 18,000, fruit 13,000, dry beans 8,000; livestock (number of live animals) 850,000 sheep, 650,000 goats, 540,000 cattle, 154,000 asses, 100,000 horses; roundwood 2,046,594 cu m; fish catch (2003) 32. Mining and quarrying (2004): diamonds 4,000 carats. Manufacturing (value of manufactured exports; U.S.$'000,000; 2001): men's pants 53.5[5]; footwear 35.8; colour television receivers 26.6; undergarments 21.6[5]. Energy production (consumption): electricity (kW-hr; 2003) 350,000,000 (360,000,000); coal, none (none); crude petroleum, none (none); petroleum products (metric tons; 2003) none (100,000); natural gas, none (none).
Tourism (2002): receipts from visitors U.S.$20,000,000; expenditures by nationals abroad U.S.$14,000,000.
Population economically active (1996): total 573,064; activity rate of total population 29.2% (participation rates: ages 15–64, 49.9%; female 33.5%; unemployed [2005] c. 50%).

Price index (2000 = 100)

	1998	1999	2000	2001	2002	2003	2004
Consumer price index	86.7	94.2	100.0	106.9	119.3	129.0	135.5

Household income and expenditure. Average household size (2001) 4.9; average annual income per household: n.a.; sources of income: n.a.; expenditure (1989): food 48.0%, clothing 16.4%, household durable goods 11.9%, housing and energy 10.1%, transportation 4.7%.
Gross national product (at current market prices; 2004): U.S.$1,336,000,000 (U.S.$740 per capita).

Structure of gross domestic product and labour force

	2003		1996	
	in value M '000,000	% of total value	labour force	% of labour force
Agriculture	1,308	16.1	105,250	18.4
Mining	12	0.1	102,037[6]	17.8[6]
Manufacturing	1,433	17.6	21,087	3.7
Construction	1,215	14.9	19,202	3.4
Public utilities	361	4.4	2,486	0.4
Transp. and commun.	331	4.1	14,690	2.6
Trade	918	11.3	14,891	2.6
Finance	770	9.5	3,829	0.7
Pub. admin., defense	534	6.6	} 130,684	22.8
Services	768	9.4		
Other	495[7]	6.1[7]	158,908[8]	27.7[8]
TOTAL	8,144[9]	100.0[9]	573,064[10]	100.0[9, 10]

Land use as % of total land area (2000): in temporary crops 10.9%, in permanent crops 0.1%, in pasture 65.9%; overall forest area 0.5%.

Foreign trade[11]

Balance of trade (current prices)

	1998	1999	2000	2001	2002	2003
M '000,000	–3,590	–3,707	–3,582	–3,398	–4,018	–4,138
% of total	61.8%	63.7%	55.0%	41.2%	34.9%	36.8%

Imports (2001): M 5,824,000,000 (1999; food products 15.3%, unspecified commodities 84.7%). *Major import sources* (2001): Customs Union of Southern Africa (mostly South Africa) 82.8%; Asian countries 14.9%.
Exports (2001): M 2,426,000,000 (manufactured goods [mostly clothing] 74.7%, machinery and transport equipment 10.5%, beverages 3.6%, wool 2.5%). *Major export destinations:* North America (mostly the United States) 62.8%; Customs Union of Southern Africa (mostly South Africa) 37.0%.

Transport and communications

Transport. Railroads (2001): length 1.6 mi, 2.6 km. Roads (1999): total length 3,691 mi, 5,940 km (paved 18%). Vehicles (1996): passenger cars 12,610; trucks and buses 25,000. Air transport (1999): passenger-km, negligible (less than 500,000); metric ton-km cargo, negligible; airports (1997) with scheduled flights 1.

Communications

Medium	date	unit	number	units per 1,000 persons
Daily newspapers	2000	circulation	14,300	8
Radio	2000	receivers	94,600	53
Television	2002	receivers	63,000	35
Telephones	2004	main lines	37,200	21
Cellular telephones	2004	subscribers	159,000	88
Internet	2004	users	43,000	24

Education and health

Educational attainment (1986–87). Percentage of population age 10 and over having: no formal education 22.9%; primary 52.8%; secondary 23.2%; higher 0.6%. *Literacy* (2000–04): total population age 15 and over literate 81.4%; males literate 73.7%; females literate 90.3%.

Education (2002)

	schools	teachers	students	student/ teacher ratio
Primary (age 6–12)	1,333	8,908	418,668	47.0
Secondary (age 13–17)	224	3,384	81,130	24.0
Vocational	8	172	1,859	10.8
Higher	1	436[12]	6,273	8.0

Health (2003): physicians 140 (1 per 16,298 persons); hospital beds 1,025 (1 per 2,226 persons); infant mortality rate per 1,000 live births (2004) 90.3.
Food (2002): daily per capita caloric intake 2,638 (vegetable products 96%, animal products 4%); 116% of FAO recommended minimum requirement.

Military

Total active duty personnel (2004): 2,000 (army 100%). *Military expenditure as percentage of GDP* (2003): 2.6%; per capita expenditure U.S.$14.

[1]All seats are nonelective. [2]De jure figure including absentee miners working in South Africa. [3]De facto figure(s). [4]January 1. [5]Many textile plants in Lesotho closed in early 2005. [6]Includes 94,190 mine workers in South Africa; the number of mine workers in South Africa in early 2004 equaled 61,500. [7]Indirect taxes less imputed bank service charges. [8]Includes 101,599 not adequately defined and military personnel and 57,309 unemployed, not previously employed. [9]Detail does not add to total given because of rounding. [10]Includes 132,609 workers outside Lesotho (nearly all in South Africa). [11]Import figures are f.o.b. in balance of trade and c.i.f. in commodities and trading partners. [12]1998.

Internet resources for further information:
• **Central Bank of Lesotho** http://www.centralbank.org.ls
• **Kingdom of Lesotho Bureau of Statistics** http://www.bos.gov.ls

Liberia

Official name: Republic of Liberia.
Form of government: transitional regime[1] with one legislative body (Legislative Assembly [76]).
Head of state and government: Chairman[1].
Capital: Monrovia.
Official language: English.
Official religion: none.
Monetary unit: 1 Liberian dollar (L$) = 100 cents; valuation (Sept. 1, 2005) 1 U.S.$ = L$56.00; 1 £ = L$103.11.

Area and population		area		population
				1999
Counties	**Capitals**	sq mi	sq km	estimate
Bomi	Tubmanburg	755	1,955	114,316
Bong	Gbarnga	3,127	8,099	299,825
Gbarpolu	Bopulu	2,982	7,723	2
Grand Bassa	Buchanan	3,382	8,759	215,338
Grand Cape Mount	Robertsport	2,250	5,827	120,141
Grand Gedeh	Zwedru	6,575[3]	17,029[3]	94,497[3]
Grand Kru	Barclayville	4	4	39,062
Lofa	Voinjama	4,493	11,367	351,492[2]
Margibi	Kakata	1,260	3,263	219,417
Maryland	Harper	2,066[4]	5,351[4]	71,977
Montserrado	Bensonville	1,058	2,740	843,783
Nimba	Sanniquellie	4,650	12,043	338,887
River Gee	Fish Town	3	3	3
Rivercess	Rivercess City	1,693	4,385	38,167
Sinoe	Greenville	3,959	10,254	79,241
TOTAL		38,250[5]	99,067[5,6]	2,826,143

Demography

Population (2005): 2,900,000.
Density (2005)[5]: persons per sq mi 76.8, persons per sq km 29.7.
Urban-rural (2003): urban 46.7%; rural 53.3%.
Sex distribution (2002): male 49.47%; female 50.53%.
Age breakdown (2001): under 15, 43.2%; 15–29, 27.0%; 30–44, 15.1%; 45–59, 9.4%; 60–74, 4.2%; 75 and over, 1.1%.
Population projection: (2010) 3,531,000; (2020) 4,318,000.
Doubling time: 33 years.
Ethnic composition (2000): Kpelle 18.9%; Bassa 13.1%; Grebo 10.3%; Gio (Dan) 7.4%; Kru 6.9%; Mano 7.4%; Loma 5.3%; Kissi 3.8%; Krahn 3.7%; Americo-Liberians 2.4%[7]; other 22.1%.
Religious affiliation (2000): traditional beliefs 42.9%; Christian 39.3%, of which independent Christian 13.7%, Protestant 10.9%, unaffiliated Christian 9.7%, Roman Catholic 3.9%; Muslim 16.0%; other 1.8%.
Major cities (2003): Monrovia 550,200; Zwedru 35,300; Buchanan 27,300; Yekepa 22,900; Harper 20,000.

Vital statistics

Birth rate per 1,000 population (2004): 46.0 (world avg. 21.1).
Death rate per 1,000 population (2004): 24.7 (world avg. 9.0).
Natural increase rate per 1,000 population (2004): 21.3 (world avg. 12.1).
Total fertility rate (avg. births per childbearing woman; 2004): 6.2.
Marriage rate per 1,000 population: n.a.
Divorce rate per 1,000 population: n.a.
Life expectancy at birth (2004): male 36.1 years; female 40.3 years.
Adult population (ages 15–49) *living with HIV* (2004[8]): 5.9% (world avg. 1.1%).

National economy

Budget (2004). Revenue: U.S.$69,200,000 (tax revenue 90.5%, of which import duties 33.2%, income and profit taxes 26.0%, maritime revenue 19.5%, taxes on goods and services 11.6%; nontax revenue 8.1%; grants 1.4%). Expenditures: U.S.$69,700,000 (current expenditures 85.9%, of which goods and services 36.9%, wages 35.0%, interest on debt 3.7%; development expenditures [including national security] 14.1%).
Public debt (external, outstanding; December 2004): U.S.$3,010,100,000.
Population economically active (1997): total 1,183,000; activity rate 51.4% (participation rates: ages 10–64 [1994] 64.0%; female 39.5%; unemployed [2004] c. 80%).

Price earning index (2000 = 100)							
	1998	1999	2000	2001	2002	2003	2004
Consumer price index	90.0	95.0	100.0	112.2	128.1	141.3	152.4

Production (metric tons except as noted). Agriculture, forestry, fishing (2004): cassava 490,000, sugarcane 255,000, oil palm fruit 174,000, natural rubber 115,000, rice 110,000, bananas 110,000, plantains 42,000, taro 25,500 yams 20,000, peanuts (groundnuts) 4,800, coffee 3,200, cacao beans 1,500; livestock (number of live animals) 220,000 goats, 210,000 sheep, 130,000 pigs, 5,000,000 chickens; roundwood 5,912,817 cu m; fish catch (2003) 11,300. Mining and quarrying (2003): diamonds[9] 40,000 carats. Manufacturing (value of sales in U.S.$'000; 2003): cement 5,323; carbonated beverages 3,226; beer 2,627; candles 412; bleach 79. International maritime licensing (fees earned; 2004): more than U.S.$15,000,000. Energy production (consumption): electricity (kW-hr; 2002) 540,000,000 (540,000,000); coal, none (none); crude petroleum, none (none); petroleum products (metric tons; 2002) negligible (143,000); natural gas, none (none).

Household income and expenditure. Average household size (1983) 4.3; income per household: n.a.; sources of income: n.a.; expenditure (1998)[10]: food 34.4%, housing 14.9%, clothing 13.8%, household furnishings 6.1%, beverages and tobacco 5.7%, energy 5.0%.
Gross national product (2004): U.S.$391,000,000 (U.S.$110 per capita).

Structure of gross domestic product and labour force				
	2004		2002	
	in value U.S.$'000,000	% of total value	labour force	% of labour force
Agriculture	171.3	34.8		
Rubber	84.0	17.1	823,000	66.6
Timber	58.2	11.8		
Mining	0.4	0.1		
Manufacturing	46.3	9.4		
Construction	10.9	2.2		
Public utilities	4.0	0.8		
Transp. and commun.	36.8	7.5	412,000	33.4
Trade	32.5	6.6		
Finance	14.1	2.9		
Pub. admin., defense	14.3	2.9		
Services	19.2	3.9		
Other	...	...		
TOTAL	492.1[6]	100.0	1,235,000	100.0

Land use as % of total land area (2000): in temporary crops 3.9%, in permanent crops 2.2%, in pasture 20.8%; overall forest area 31.3%.

Foreign trade

Balance of trade (current prices)					
	2000	2001	2002[11]	2003[11]	2004[11]
U.S.$'000,000	−25.5	−27.1	+21.1	−31.1	−164.3
% of total	9.6%	9.6%	6.8%	12.5%	44.2%

Imports (2004): U.S.$268,100,000 (donor and foreign-direct-investment-related 39.6%; petroleum and petroleum products 24.7%; rice 10.3%). *Major import sources:* South Korea 38.1%; Japan 21.9%; Singapore 12.6%; Croatia 4.8%.
Exports (2004): U.S.$103,800,000 (rubber 90.0%; cocoa beans 3.4%). *Major export destinations:* U.S. 61.4%; Belgium 29.5%; China 5.3%; France 1.6%.

Transport and communications

Transport. Railroads (2004)[12]: route length 304 mi, 490 km; (1998) short ton-mi cargo 534,000,000, metric ton-km cargo 860,000,000. Roads (1999): total length 6,600 mi, 10,600 km (paved 6%). Vehicles (1998): passenger cars 17,400; trucks and buses 10,700. Air transport: n.a.; airports (2000) with scheduled flights 2.

Communications				units
				per 1,000
Medium	date	unit	number	persons
Daily newspapers	2001	circulation	33,100	12
Radio	2001	receivers	755,700	274
Television	2001	receivers	69,000	25
Telephones	2001	main lines	7,000	2.5
Internet	2002	users	1,000	0.4

Education and health

Educational attainment, n.a. *Literacy* (2003): total population age 15 and over literate 57.5%; males literate 73.3%; females literate 41.6%.

Education (2000)				student/
	schools	teachers	students	teacher ratio
Primary (age 6–12)	2,405	16,000	507,000	31.7
Secondary (age 13–18)	1,162	10,000	115,000	11.5
Higher	...	300	13,000	43.3

Health (2001): physicians 24 (1 per 116,667 persons); hospital beds 2,751 (1 per 1,003 persons); infant mortality rate per 1,000 live births (2004) 168.4.
Food (2002): daily per capita caloric intake 1,900 (vegetable products 97%, animal products 3%); 82% of FAO recommended minimum requirement.

Military

Total active duty personnel: [13]; UN peacekeeping troops (July 2005) 14,700.
Military expenditure as percentage of GDP (2003): c. 11%; per capita expenditure U.S.$16.

---

[1]Transitional government established in October 2003 to be replaced in January 2006 by an elected transitional government that includes a president, a 30-member Senate, and a 64-member National Transitional Legislative Assembly. [2]Gbarpolu (created late 2000) included with Lofa. [3]River Gee (created mid-2000) included with Grand Gedeh. [4]Grand Kru included with Maryland. [5]Total area per more recent survey is 37,743 sq mi (97,754 sq km). [6]Detail does not add to total given because of rounding. [7]Descendants of freed U.S. slaves. [8]January 1. [9]The UN in May 2001 placed a ban on the export of rough diamonds from Liberia; this ban has subsequently been extended at least through the end of 2005. [10]Weights of consumer price index components. [11]Estimated figures. [12]Almost the entire railroad network has been rendered inoperable through years of civil war. [13]Planned size of new national army is 2,000 per official announcement of July 2005.

Internet resources for further information:
• **Central Bank of Liberia**
  http://www.cbl.org.lr

Libya

Official name: Al-Jamāhīrīyah al-ʿArabīyah al-Lībīyah ash-Shaʿbīyah al-Ishtirākīyah al-ʿUẓmā (Socialist People's Libyan Arab Jamahiriya).
Form of government: authoritarian with one policy-making body (General People's Congress [760]).
Chief of state: Muammar al-Qaddafi (de facto)[1]; Secretary of General People's Congress (de jure).
Head of government: Secretary of the General People's Committee (prime minister).
Capital: Tripoli[2].
Official language: Arabic.
Official religion: Islam.
Monetary unit: 1 Libyan dinar (LD) = 1,000 dirhams; valuation (Sept. 1, 2005) 1 U.S.$ = LD 1.32; 1 £ = LD 2.44.

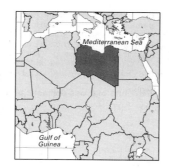

Area and population		area		population
Administrative regions[3]	**Capitals**	sq mi	sq km	1995 census[4]
Banghāzī	Banghāzī	...	...	665,615
Al-Bāṭin	...	...	...	151,240
Fazzān	...	...	...	314,029
Al-Jabal al-Akhḍar	Al-Baydāʾ	...	...	381,165
Al-Jabal al-Gharbī	Gharyān	...	...	316,970
Al-Jufrah	...	...	...	39,335
Miṣrātah (Misurata)	...	...	...	488,573
Najghaza	...	...	...	244,553
Sofuljin	...	...	...	76,401
Ṭarābulus	Tripoli (Ṭarābulus)	...	...	1,313,996
Al-Wāḥah	...	...	...	62,056
Al-Wasṭa	...	...	...	240,574
Az-Zāwiyah	Az-Zāwiyah	...	...	517,395
TOTAL		679,362	1,759,540	4,811,902

Demography

Population (2005): 5,853,000.
Density (2005): persons per sq mi 8.6, persons per sq km 3.3.
Urban-rural (2003): urban 86.3%; rural 13.7%.
Sex distribution (2004): male 51.33%; female 48.67%.
Age breakdown (2004): under 15, 34.2%; 15–29, 30.7%; 30–44, 20.6%; 45–59, 8.6%; 60–74, 4.5%; 75 and over, 1.4%.
Population projection: (2010) 6,439,000; (2020) 7,538,000.
Doubling time: 29 years.
Ethnic composition (2000): Arab 87.1%, of which Libyan 57.2%, Bedouin 13.8%, Egyptian 7.7%, Sudanese 3.5%, Tunisian 2.9%; Berber 6.8%, of which Arabized 4.2%; other 6.1%.
Religious affiliation (2000): Muslim (nearly all Sunnī) 96.1%; Orthodox 1.9%; Roman Catholic 0.8%; other 1.2%.
Major cities (1995): Tripoli 1,140,000 (urban agglomeration [2003] 2,006,000); Banghāzī 650,000 (urban agglomeration [2000] 829,000); Miṣrātah 280,000; Surt 150,000.

Vital statistics

Birth rate per 1,000 population (2004): 27.2 (world avg. 21.1).
Death rate per 1,000 population (2004): 3.5 (world avg. 9.0).
Natural increase rate per 1,000 population (2004): 23.7 (world avg. 12.1).
Total fertility rate (avg. births per childbearing woman; 2004): 3.4.
Life expectancy at birth (2004): male 74.1 years; female 78.6 years.
Major causes of death per 100,000 population (2002): diseases of the circulatory system 185, of which ischemic heart disease 98; infectious and parasitic diseases 72; malignant neoplasms (cancers) 44; accidents, injuries, and violence 43; chronic respiratory diseases 16.

National economy

Budget (2001). Revenue: LD 5,998,800,000 (oil revenues 60.1%, other 39.9%). Expenditures: LD 5,625,600,000 (current expenditures 63.9%, development expenditures 27.3%, extraordinary expenditures 8.8%).
Public debt (external outstanding; 2004): U.S.$3,900,000,000.
Production (metric tons except as noted). Agriculture, forestry, fishing (2004): watermelons 240,000, potatoes 195,000, tomatoes 190,000, dry onions 182,000, olives 180,000, dates 150,000, wheat 125,000, barley 80,000; livestock (number of live animals) 4,500,000 sheep, 1,265,000 goats, 130,000 cattle, 47,000 camels, 25,000,000 chickens; roundwood 652,000 cu m; fish catch (2003) 33,666. Mining and quarrying (2004): lime 250,000; gypsum 175,000; salt 40,000. Manufacturing (value of production in LD '000,000; 1996): base metals 212, electrical equipment 208, petrochemicals 175, food products 79, cement and other building materials 68. Energy production (consumption): electricity (kW-hr; 2002) 21,470,000,000 (21,470,000,000); coal (metric tons; 2002) none (4,000); crude petroleum (barrels; 2004) 573,000,000 ([2002] 143,000,000); petroleum products (metric tons; 2002) 14,829,000 (8,675,000); natural gas (cu m; 2002) 5,851,000,000 (5,044,000,000).
Household income and expenditure. Average household size (2000) 6.3; income per household: n.a.; sources of income: n.a.; expenditure: n.a.
Tourism: receipts (2003) U.S.$79,000,000; expenditures (2002) U.S.$548,000,000.

Population economically active (1996): total 1,224,000; activity rate of total population 26.1% (participation rates [1993]: ages 10 and over, 35.2%; female 9.8%; unemployed [2000] 30.0%).

Price index (2000 = 100)							
	1998	1999	2000	2001	2002	2003	2004[5]
Consumer price index	100.4	103.0	100.0	91.2	81.3	79.2	75.8

Gross national product (2004): U.S.$25,257,000,000 (U.S.$4,450 per capita).

Structure of gross domestic product and labour force				
	2003		1996	
	in value LD '000,000[6]	% of total value	labour force	% of labour force
Agriculture	1,376	4.9	219,500	17.9
Petroleum and natural gas[7]	15,782	56.3	31,000	2.5
Other mining	383	1.4		
Manufacturing[8]	765	2.7	128,500	10.5
Construction	1,327	4.7	171,000	14.0
Public utilities	303	1.1	35,500	2.9
Transp. and commun.	1,530	5.5	104,000	8.5
Trade	2,205	7.9	73,000	6.0
Finance, insurance	974	3.5	22,000	1.8
Pub. admin., defense	3,362	12.0	439,500	35.9
Services				
TOTAL	28,007	100.0	1,224,000	100.0

Land use as % of total land area (2000): in temporary crops 1.0%, in permanent crops 0.2%, in pasture 7.6%; overall forest area 0.2%.

Foreign trade

Balance of trade (current prices)					
	1999	2000	2001	2002	2003
U.S.$'000,000	+4,091	+9,379	+6,160	+2,443	+7,464
% of total	30.1%	53.2%	39.0%	14.2%	34.1%

Imports (2003): U.S.$7,200,000,000 (machinery and transport equipment 48.0%; food and live animals 13.4%; chemicals and chemical products 5.3%). *Major import sources:* Europe 71.8%, of which Italy 18.4%, Germany 8.9%, U.K. 5.4%; Arab countries 10.1%; Japan 8.7%.
Exports (2003): U.S.$14,664,000,000 (hydrocarbons [mostly crude petroleum] 96.7%; remainder 3.3%). *Major export destinations:* Europe 89.9%, of which Italy 39.6%, Germany 14.7%, Spain 14.7%, Turkey 7.7%; Arab countries 4.6%.

Transport and communications

Transport. Railroads: none. Roads (1999): total length 83,200 km (paved 57%). Vehicles (1996): passenger cars 809,514; trucks and buses 357,528. Air transport (2001): passenger-km 410,000,000; metric ton-km cargo 259,000; airports with scheduled flights, n.a.

Communications				units per 1,000 persons
Medium	**date**	**unit**	**number**	
Daily newspapers	2000	circulation	78,600	14
Radio	2000	receivers	1,430,000	259
Television	2000	receivers	717,000	133
Telephones	2003	main lines	750,000	136
Cellular telephones	2003	subscribers	100,000	18
Personal computers	2002	units	130,000	23
Internet	2004	users	205,000	36

Education and health

Educational attainment (1984). Percentage of population age 25 and over having: no formal schooling (illiterate) 59.7%; incomplete primary education 15.4%; complete primary 8.5%; some secondary 5.2%; secondary 8.5%; higher 2.7%. *Literacy* (2003): percentage of total population age 15 and over literate 82.5%; males literate 92.3%; females literate 71.8%.

Education (2002–03)				student/ teacher ratio
	schools	teachers	students	
Primary (age 6–12)	2,733[9]	122,020[10]	743,997	...
Secondary (age 13–18)	...	17,668[10]	619,940	...
Voc., teacher tr.	480[10]	...	178,052	...
Higher	13[10]	15,711	375,028	23.9

Health (2002): physicians 6,635 (1 per 827 persons); hospital beds 21,400 (1 per 256 persons); infant mortality rate per 1,000 live births (2004) 25.7.
Food (2002): daily per capita caloric intake 3,320 (vegetable products 90%, animal products 10%); 141% of FAO recommended minimum requirement.

Military

Total active duty personnel (2004): 76,000 (army 59.2%, navy 10.5%, air force 30.3%). *Military expenditure as percentage of GDP* (2003): 2.0%; per capita expenditure U.S.$86.

[1]No formal titled office exists. [2]Policy-making body (General People's Congress) may meet in Surt or Tripoli. [3]Libya was divided into 34 administrative entities as of 2001; area and population details are unavailable. [4]Preliminary. [5]July. [6]At current factor cost. [7]Includes refined petroleum. [8]Excludes refined petroleum. [9]1994–95. [10]1995–96.

Internet resources for further information:
• **Central Bank of Libya**
  http://www.cbl-ly.com/eindex.htm

Liechtenstein

Official name: Fürstentum Liechtenstein (Principality of Liechtenstein).
Form of government: constitutional monarchy with one legislative house (Diet [25]).
Chief of state: Prince.
Head of government: Head of the government.
Capital: Vaduz.
Official language: German.
Official religion: none.
Monetary unit: 1 Swiss franc (Sw F) = 100 centimes; valuation (Sept. 1, 2005) 1 U.S.$ = Sw F 1.23; 1 £ = Sw F 2.26.

Area and population	area		population
Regions			2005[1]
Communes	sq mi	sq km	estimate
Oberland (Upland)	48.3	125.2	22,738
Balzers	7.6	19.6	4,423
Planken	2.0	5.3	368
Schaan	10.3	26.8	5,752
Triesen	10.2	26.4	4,578
Triesenberg	11.5	29.8	2,564
Vaduz	6.7	17.3	5,053
Unterland (Lowland)	13.4[2]	34.8	11,862
Eschen	4.0	10.3	3,996
Gamprin	2.4	6.1	1,414
Mauren	2.9	7.5	3,634
Ruggell	2.9	7.4	1,872
Schellenberg	1.4	3.5	946
TOTAL	61.8[2]	160.0	34,600

Demography

Population (2005): 34,800.
Density (2005): persons per sq mi 563.1, persons per sq km 217.5.
Urban-rural (2003): urban 21.6%; rural 78.4%.
Sex distribution (2005[1]): male 49.28%; female 50.72%.
Age breakdown (2003[1]): under 15, 17.0%; 15–29, 20.2%; 30–44, 25.9%; 45–59, 21.2%; 60–74, 10.8%; 75 and over, 4.9%.
Population projection: (2010) 36,000; (2020) 38,000.
Ethnic composition (2005[1]): Liechtensteiner 65.7%; Swiss 10.4%; Austrian 5.9%; Italian 3.5%; German 3.4%; Turkish 2.6%; other 8.5%.
Religious affiliation (2000): Christian 87.9%, of which Roman Catholic 78.4%, Protestant 8.3%, Orthodox 1.1%; Muslim 4.8%; unknown 4.1%; nonreligious 2.8%; other 0.4%.
Major cities (2005[1]): Schaan 5,752; Vaduz 5,053; Triesen 4,578; Balzers 4,423; Eschen 3,996.

Vital statistics

Birth rate per 1,000 population (2005[1]): 11.0 (world avg. 21.1); (1997) legitimate 86.0%; illegitimate 14.0%.
Death rate per 1,000 population (2003): 6.3 (world avg. 9.0).
Natural increase rate per 1,000 population (2003): 3.9 (world avg. 12.1).
Total fertility rate (avg. births per childbearing woman; 2004): 1.5.
Marriage rate per 1,000 population (2003): 8.3.
Divorce rate per 1,000 population (1994): 1.4.
Life expectancy at birth (2004): male 75.8 years; female 83.0 years.
Major causes of death per 100,000 population (2003): diseases of the circulatory system 233.3; malignant neoplasms (cancers) 148.7; diseases of the respiratory system 61.2; old age 32.1; accidents, poisonings, and acts of violence 14.6; diseases of the digestive tract 8.7.

National economy

Budget (2003). Revenue: Sw F 1,077,400,000 (current revenue 73.7%, of which taxes and duties 55.6%, investment income 12.8%, charges and fees 3.8%, real estate capital-gains taxes and death and estate taxes 1.5%; capital revenue 26.3%). Expenditures: Sw F 1,052,900,000 (current expenditure 70.8%, of which financial affairs 19.9%, social welfare 16.0%, education 11.2%, general administration 7.5%, public safety 4.1%, transportation 3.0%; capital expenditure 29.2%).
Public debt: none.
Tourism (2004): 161,128 tourist overnight stays; receipts from visitors, n.a.; expenditures by nationals abroad, n.a.
Population economically active (2004[1]): total 15,642[3]; activity rate of total population 45.6% (participation rates: age 15 and over, 55.6%; female 41.4%; unemployed [2003] 2.2%).

Price and earnings indexes (2000 = 100)						
	1999	2000	2001	2002	2003	2004[4]
Consumer price index[5]	98.5	100.0	101.0	101.6	102.3	103.0
Earnings index	…	…	…	…	…	…

Household income and expenditure. Average household size (2003) 2.5; income per household: n.a.; sources of income: n.a.; expenditure: n.a.
Production (metric tons except as noted). Agriculture, forestry, fishing (2004): grapes 150; significantly market gardening, other crops include cereals and apples; livestock (number of live animals) 6,000 cattle, 3,000 pigs, 2,900 sheep; commercial timber (2002) 22,000 cu m; fish catch, n.a. Mining and quarrying: n.a. Manufacturing (2004): small-scale precision manufacturing includes

optical lenses, electron microscopes, electronic equipment, and high-vacuum pumps; metal manufacturing, construction machinery, and ceramics are important; dairy products and wine are also produced. Energy production (consumption): electricity (kW-hr; 2002) 81,000,000 ([2003] 330,000,000); coal (metric tons; 2003) none (13); petroleum products (metric tons; 2003) none (50,000); natural gas (cu m; 2003) none (n.a.).
Gross national product (2001): U.S.$2,241,000,000 (U.S.$67,510 per capita).

Structure of gross domestic product and labour force				
	2001		2004[1]	
	in value Sw F '000,000[6]	% of total value[6]	labour force	% of labour force
Agriculture			386	1.3
Mining			47	0.2
Manufacturing			10,340	35.6
Construction	1,892	45.0	2,485	8.6
Public utilities			201	0.7
Transportation and communications			1,020	3.5
Trade, public accommodation			3,116	10.7
Finance, insurance, real estate	1,262	30.0	4,447	15.3
Consulting, trust management			2,123	7.3
Pub. admin., defense	1,051	25.0	1,466	5.0
Services			3,424	11.8
TOTAL	4,205	100.0	29,055[7]	100.0

Land use as % of total land area (2000): in temporary crops *c.* 25%, in permanent crops *c.* 1%, in pasture *c.* 31%; overall forest area *c.* 47%.

Foreign trade[8, 9]

Balance of trade (current prices)						
	1998	1999	2000	2001	2002	2003
Sw F '000,000	+2,394	+1,632	+1,576	+1,514	+1,453	+1,395
% of total	49.1%	39.5%	35.1%	33.7%	34.8%	32.1%

Imports (2003): Sw F 1,476,000,000 (machinery and apparatus 33.2%, fabricated metals 11.4%, glass [all forms] and ceramics 9.2%, chemicals and chemical products 4.5%). *Major direct import sources:* Germany 40.4%; Austria 32.5%; Italy 6.9%; France 2.8%; U.S. 2.7%.
Exports (2003): Sw F 2,871,000,000 (machinery and apparatus [mostly electronic products and precision tools] 33.9%, fabricated metals 14.8%, transport equipment and parts 10.7%, glass and ceramic products [including lead crystal and specialized dental products] 9.1%). *Major direct export destinations:* Germany 21.7%; U.S. 17.3%; France 11.6%; Austria 9.8%; Italy 7.6%.

Transport and communications

Transport. Railroads (1998): length 11.5 mi, 18.5 km; passenger and cargo traffic, n.a. Roads (1999): total length 201 mi, 323 km. Vehicles (2004[1]): passenger cars 23,524; trucks and buses 2,560. Air transport: the nearest scheduled airport service is through Zürich, Switzerland.

Communications				units per 1,000
Medium	date	unit	number	persons
Daily newspapers	1998	circulation	17,900	565
Radio	1997	receivers	21,000	658
Television	2001	receivers	15,600	469
Telephones	2002	main lines	19,900	583
Cellular telephones	2002	subscribers	11,400	333
Internet	2002	users	20,000	585

Education and health

Educational attainment (1990). Percentage of population not of preschool age or in compulsory education having: no formal schooling 0.3%; primary and lower secondary education 39.3%; higher secondary and vocational 47.6%; some postsecondary 7.4%; university 4.2%; other and unknown 1.1%.
Literacy: virtually 100%.

Education (2002–03)				student/
	schools	teachers	students	teacher ratio
Primary (age 7–12)	14[10]	242	2,218	9.2
Secondary (age 13–19)	9[10]	162[10]	2,028	…
Vocational	2[11]	309[11]	1,227	…
Higher	…	…	440	…

Health: physicians (2005) *c.* 70 (1 per 497 persons); hospital beds (1997) 108 (1 per 288 persons); infant mortality rate per 1,000 live births (2004) 4.8.
Food (2002)[4]: daily per capita caloric intake 3,526 (vegetable products 66%, animal products 34%); 131% of FAO recommended minimum requirement.

Military

Total active duty personnel: none; Liechtenstein has had no standing army since 1868; defense is the responsibility of Switzerland. *Military expenditure as percentage of GDP:* none.

[1]January 1. [2]Detail does not add to total given because of rounding. [3]Employed within Liechtenstein only (including 9,670 Liechtensteiners resident in Liechtenstein and 5,972 other nationalities resident in Liechtenstein); 13,413 inward commuters are excluded along with 1,182 outward commuters. [4]Data from January through November only. [5]Figures are derived from statistics for Switzerland. [6]Figures are derived from percentages. [7]Employed within Liechtenstein only plus inward commuters. [8]Excludes trade with Switzerland and transshipments through Switzerland. [9]Liechtenstein has formed a customs union with Switzerland since 1923. [10]1998–99. [11]1997–98.

Internet resources for further information:
• **Liechtenstein Government Portal**
  http://www.llv.li/en/amtsstellen/llv-avw-home.htm

Lithuania

Official name: Lietuvos Respublika (Republic of Lithuania).
Form of government: unitary multi-party republic with a single legislative body, the Seimas (141).
Head of state: President.
Head of government: Prime Minister.
Capital: Vilnius.
Official language: Lithuanian.
Official religion: none.
Monetary unit: 1 litas (LTL) = 100 centai; valuation (Sept. 1, 2005) 1 U.S.$ = LTL 2.75; 1 £ = LTL 5.07[1].

Area and population		area		population
				2005[2]
Provinces	Capitals	sq mi	sq km	estimate
Alytus	Alytus	2,095	5,425	182,851
Kaunas	Kaunas	3,112	8,060	685,723
Klaipėda	Klaipėda	2,011	5,209	382,179
Marijampolė	Marijampolė	1,723	4,463	185,419
Panevėžys	Panevėžys	3,043	7,881	292,376
Šiauliai	Šiauliai	3,297	8,540	360,755
Tauragė	Tauragė	1,703	4,411	131,481
Telšiai	Telšiai	1,680	4,350	177,008
Utena	Utena	2,780	7,201	178,977
Vilnius	Vilnius	3,768	9,760	848,555
TOTAL		25,212	65,300	3,425,324

Demography

Population (2005): 3,413,000.
Density (2005): persons per sq mi 135.4, persons per sq km 52.3.
Urban-rural (2003): urban 66.7%; rural 33.3%.
Sex distribution (2004): male 46.67%; female 53.33%.
Age breakdown (2005[2]): under 15, 17.1%; 15–29, 21.9%; 30–44, 22.4%; 45–59, 18.4%; 60–74, 14.2%; 75 and over, 6.0%.
Population projection: (2010) 3,331,000; (2020) 3,189,000.
Ethnic composition (2001): Lithuanian 83.5%; Polish 6.7%; Russian 6.3%; Belarusian 1.2%; Ukrainian 0.7%; other 1.6%.
Religious affiliation (2001): Roman Catholic 79.0%; nonreligious 9.5%; Orthodox 4.8%, of which Old Believers 0.8%; Protestant 1.0%; unknown 5.4%; other 0.3%.
Major cities (2005[2]): Vilnius 541,278; Kaunas 364,059; Klaipėda 188,767; Šiauliai 130,020; Panevėžys 116,247; Alytus 69,859.

Vital statistics

Birth rate per 1,000 population (2004): 8.8 (world avg. 21.1); (2001) legitimate 74.6%; illegitimate 25.4%.
Death rate per 1,000 population (2004): 12.0 (world avg. 9.0).
Natural increase rate per 1,000 population (2004): –3.2 (world avg. 12.1).
Total fertility rate (avg. births per childbearing woman; 2004): 1.3.
Marriage rate per 1,000 population (2004): 5.6.
Divorce rate per 1,000 population (2004): 3.2.
Life expectancy at birth (2004): male 66.4 years; female 77.8 years.
Major causes of death per 100,000 population (2001): diseases of the circulatory system 628.2; malignant neoplasms (cancers) 223.9; accidents, injury, homicide 145.8, of which suicide 46.6.

National economy

Budget (2002). Revenue: LTL 15,112,000,000 (tax revenue 92.5%, of which value-added tax 25.2%, individual income tax 23.6%, social security tax 22.7%, excise tax 10.6%; nontax revenue 7.5%). Expenditures: LTL 15,907,000,000 (current expenditure 90.0%, of which social security and welfare 28.0%, wages 23.2%; capital expenditure 10.0%).
Gross national product (2004): U.S.$19,727,000,000 (U.S.$5,740 per capita).

Structure of gross national product and labour force				
	2003			
	in value LTL '000,000[3]	% of total value	labour force	% of labour force
Agriculture, forestry	3,119	5.6	257,000	15.6
Mining	279	0.5	5,100	0.3
Manufacturing	9,970	17.9	264,600	16.1
Construction	3,453	6.2	107,100	6.5
Public utilities	2,339	4.2	27,800	1.7
Transp. and commun.	6,740	12.1	92,200	5.6
Trade, restaurants	9,748	17.5	244,100	14.9
Finance, real estate	6,071	10.9	70,300	4.3
Pub. admin., defense	2,729	4.9	74,900	4.6
Services	6,016	10.8	295,000	18.0
Other	5,236[4]	9.4[4]	203,800[5]	12.4[5]
TOTAL	55,700	100.0	1,641,900	100.0

Production (metric tons except as noted). Agriculture, forestry, fishing (2004): wheat 1,315,000, potatoes 1,021,400, barley 970,000, sugar beets 904,900, triticale 234,000, rapeseed 204,500, rye 180,000, cabbages 150,000, oats 115,000, carrots 90,000, flax fibre 5,800; livestock (number of live animals) 1,057,400 pigs, 812,100 cattle; roundwood (2004) 6,120,000 cu m; fish catch (2003) 159,561. Mining and quarrying (2003): limestone 944,600; peat 366,900. Manufacturing (value of production in LTL '000,000; 2000): food and beverages 4,952; refined petroleum products 4,303; wearing apparel 2,034; textiles 1,248; chemicals and chemical products 1,231; wood and wood products (excluding furniture) 1,164. Energy production (consumption): elec-

tricity (kW-hr; 2004) 18,912,000,000 ([2002] 11,235,000,000); coal (metric tons; 2002) none (211,000); crude petroleum (barrels; 2002) 3,200,000 (47,000,000); petroleum products (metric tons; 2002) 6,144,000 (2,132,000); natural gas (cu m; 2002) none (2,617,000,000).
Public debt (external outstanding; 2003): U.S.$2,107,000,000.
Population economically active (2003): total 1,641,900; activity rate of total population 47.5% (participation rates: ages 15–64, 65.7%; female 49.3%; registered unemployed [July 2003–June 2004] 9.6%).

Price and earnings indexes (2000 = 100)							
	1998	1999	2000	2001	2002	2003	2004
Consumer price index	98.3	99.0	100.0	101.3	101.6	100.4	101.6
Annual earnings index	95.2	100.7	100.0	100.9	103.0	106.5	122.1

Household income and expenditure. Average household size (2000) 2.7; average annual per capita disposable household income (2004): LTL 5,950 (U.S.$2,139); sources of income (2001): wages and salaries 53.6%, transfers 24.2%, self-employment 11.3%; expenditure (2001): food and beverages 42.4%, housing and energy 13.6%, transportation and communications 11.8%, clothing and footwear 6.5%.
Land use as % of total land area (2000): in temporary crops 45.3%, in permanent crops 0.9%, in pasture 7.7%; overall forest area 31.9%.
Tourism (2003): receipts from visitors U.S.$638,000,000; expenditures by nationals abroad U.S.$471,000,000.

Foreign trade[6]

Balance of trade (current prices)						
	1999	2000	2001	2002	2003	2004
LTL '000,000	–7,323	–6,588	–7,081	–7,940	–8,124	–8,565
% of total	23.4%	17.8%	16.2%	16.4%	15.5%	14.2%

Imports (2002): LTL 28,220,000,000 (mineral fuels [mostly crude petroleum] 17.8%, machinery and apparatus 17.5%, transport equipment 16.4%, chemicals and chemical products 8.7%, textiles and clothing 7.9%). *Major import sources:* Russia 21.4%; Germany 17.2%; Italy 4.9%; Poland 4.8%; France 3.9%.
Exports (2002): LTL 20,280,000,000 (mineral fuels [mostly refined petroleum] 19.0%, transport equipment [mostly auto components] 15.9%, textiles and clothing 15.0%, agricultural and food products 10.8%, machinery and apparatus 9.9%). *Major export destinations:* United Kingdom 13.5%; Russia 12.1%; Germany 10.3%; Latvia 9.6%; Denmark 5.0%.

Transport and communications

Transport. Railroads (2004): route length 1,100 mi, 1,782 km; passenger-mi 275,000,000, passenger-km 443,000,000; short ton-mi cargo 7,231,000,000, metric ton-km cargo 11,637,000,000. Roads (2004): total length 49,290 mi, 79,331 km (paved 88%). Vehicles (2004): passenger cars 1,315,914; trucks and buses 115,661. Air transport (2004): passenger-mi 557,000,000; passenger-km 896,000,000; short ton-mi cargo 5,600,000, metric ton-km cargo 9,000,000; airports with scheduled flights (2001) 3.

Communications				units per 1,000
Medium	date	unit	number	persons
Daily newspapers	1996	circulation	344,000	93
Radio	2000	receivers	1,750,000	500
Television	2002	receivers	1,704,500	487
Telephones	2004	main lines	820,000	238
Cellular telephones	2004	subscribers	3,421,500	993
Personal computers	2004	units	533,000	155
Internet	2004	users	968,000	281

Education and health

Educational attainment (2001). Percentage of population age 10 and over having: no schooling and incomplete primary education 5.1%; complete primary 20.8%; incomplete and complete secondary 42.2%; postsecondary 31.9%, of which university 12.6%. *Literacy* (2000): total population age 15 and over literate 99.6%.

Education (2002–03)	schools	teachers	students	student/ teacher ratio
Primary (age 7–10)[7] Secondary (age 11–18)	2,172	50,200	594,300	11.8
Voc., teacher tr.	82	4,700	44,400	9.4
Higher	70	14,200	168,200	11.8

Health (2004[2]): physicians 13,682 (1 per 252 persons); hospital beds 29,990 (1 per 115 persons); infant mortality rate per 1,000 live births (2004) 7.9.
Food (2002): daily per capita caloric intake 3,324 (vegetable products 74%, animal products 26%); 130% of FAO recommended minimum requirement.

Military

Total active duty personnel (2004): 13,500[8] (army 85.9%, navy 5.2%, air force 8.9%). *Military expenditure as percentage of GDP* (2003): 1.6%; per capita expenditure U.S.$87.

[1]Pegged to the euro from February 2002, at the rate of 1€ = LTL 3.45. [2]January 1. [3]Derived figures based on published percentages. [4]Taxes less imputed bank service charges and less subsidies. [5]Unemployed. [6]Imports c.i.f.; exports f.o.b. [7]Excludes special education. [8]Excludes 14,600 in paramilitary.

Internet resources for further information:
• **Lithuanian Department of Statistics http://www.std.lt**
• **Bank of Lithuania http://www.lbank.lt/eng/default.htm**

Luxembourg

Official name: Groussherzogtum Lëtzebuerg (Luxembourgian); Grand-Duché de Luxembourg (French); Grossherzogtum Luxemburg (German) (Grand Duchy of Luxembourg).
Form of government: constitutional monarchy with two legislative houses (Council of State [21][1]; Chamber of Deputies [60]).
Chief of state: Grand Duke.
Head of government: Prime Minister.
Capital: Luxembourg.
Official language: none[2].
Official religion: none.
Monetary unit: 1 € (euro) = 100 cents; valuation (Sept. 1, 2005) 1 U.S.$ = €0.80; 1 £ = €1.47[3].

Area and population

Districts	Principal cities	area sq mi	area sq km	population 2001 preliminary census
Diekirch	Ettelbruck	447	1,157	67,487
Grevenmacher	Echternach	203	525	51,960
Luxembourg	Luxembourg	349	904	320,317
TOTAL		999	2,586	439,764

Demography

Population (2005): 457,000.
Density (2005): persons per sq mi 457.5, persons per sq km 176.7.
Urban-rural (2003): urban 91.9%; rural 8.1%.
Sex distribution (2005[4]): male 49.39%; female 50.61%.
Age breakdown (2005[4]): under 15, 18.7%; 15–29, 17.9%; 30–44, 24.7%; 45–59, 19.8%; 60–74, 12.6%; 75 and over, 6.3%.
Population projection: (2010) 479,000; (2020) 523,000.
Ethnic composition (nationality; 2003): Luxembourger 61.9%; Portuguese 13.5%; French 4.8%; Italian 4.2%; Belgian 3.5%; German 2.3%; English 1.0%; other 8.8%.
Religious affiliation (2000): Roman Catholic 90.6%; Protestant 2.1%; other Christian 1.1%; Muslim 1.0%; nonreligious 3.7%; other 1.5%.
Major cities (2001)[5]: Luxembourg 76,688; Esch-sur-Alzette 27,146; Dudelange 17,320; Differdange 10,248; Schifflange 7,849.

Vital statistics

Birth rate per 1,000 population (2004): 12.0 (world avg. 21.1); (2002) legitimate 76.8%; illegitimate 23.2%.
Death rate per 1,000 population (2004): 7.9 (world avg. 9.0).
Natural increase rate per 1,000 population (2004): 4.1 (world avg. 12.1).
Total fertility rate (avg. births per childbearing woman; 2004): 1.7.
Marriage rate per 1,000 population (2004): 4.4.
Life expectancy at birth (2000–02): male 74.9 years; female 81.0 years.
Major causes of death per 100,000 population (2003): diseases of the circulatory system 350.0; malignant neoplasms (cancers) 218.9.

National economy

Budget (2002). Revenue: €5,977,200,000 (direct taxes 47.4%, indirect taxes 38.5%, other 14.1%). Expenditures: €5,976,100,000 (current expenditure 85.7%, development expenditure 14.3%).
Public debt (2004): negligible.
Production (metric tons except as noted). Agriculture, forestry, fishing (2004): corn (maize) 184,000, wheat 80,000, barley 53,000, potatoes 22,000, grapes 17,000, rapeseed 16,000; livestock (number of live animals) 186,725 cattle, 84,611 pigs; roundwood (2004) 277,180 cu m. Mining and quarrying (2003): limited quantities of limestone and slate. Manufacturing (value added in €'000,000; 2003): base metals 402; rubber and plastic products 371; fabricated metal products 272; nonelectrical machinery and apparatus 270; cement, bricks, and ceramics 253. Energy production (consumption): electricity (kW-hr; 2004) 3,741,000,000[6] ([2002] 4,683,000,000); coal (metric tons; 2002) none (127,000); crude petroleum, none (none); petroleum products (metric tons; 2002) none (2,051,000); natural gas (cu m; 2002) none (1,228,700,000).
Gross national product (2004): U.S.$25,302,000,000 (U.S.$56,230 per capita).

Structure of gross domestic product and labour force

	2003 in value €'000,000	% of total value	labour force	% of labour force
Agriculture	130.3	0.6	3,900	1.3
Mining	31.6	0.1	300	0.1
Manufacturing	2,506.8	11.8	32,700	10.9
Construction	1,539.0	7.2	28,500	9.5
Public utilities	301.5	1.4	1,600	0.5
Transp. and commun.	2,372.4	11.2	24,500	8.1
Trade, restaurants	3,004.1	14.1	54,800	18.2
Finance[7], insurance	8,220.6	38.7	33,300	11.0
Real estate	4,516.2	21.2	48,400	16.1
Pub. admin., defense	1,378.6	6.5	15,300	5.1
Services	2,723.8	12.8	50,300	16.7
Other	−5,464.3[8]	−25.7[8]	7,600	2.5
TOTAL	21,260.7[9]	100.0[9]	301,100[9, 10]	100.0

Population economically active (2003): total 195,144[11]; activity rate of total population 43.2% (participation rates: ages 15–64, 64.1%; female 41.5%; unemployed [July 2003–June 2004] 4.1%).

Price and earnings indexes (2000 = 100)

	1998	1999	2000	2001	2002	2003	2004
Consumer price index	96.0	96.9	100.0	102.7	104.8	106.9	109.3
Hourly earnings index[12]	...	97.4	100.0	100.6	104.8	...	...

Household income and expenditure. Average household size (2001) 2.5; income per household (2002) €61,800 (U.S.$55,600); sources of income (1992): wages and salaries 67.1%, transfer payments 28.1%, self-employment 4.8%; expenditure (2002): food, beverages, and tobacco 21.0%, housing 20.7%, transportation and communications 19.3%, entertainment and education 8.6%, household goods and furniture 8.3%, clothing and footwear 5.3%.
Land use as % of total land area (2000): in temporary crops 23.6%, in permanent crops 0.5%, in pasture 25.2%; overall forest area 34.3%.
Tourism (2003): receipts from visitors U.S.$2,793,000,000; expenditures U.S.$2,389,000,000.

Foreign trade[13]

Balance of trade (current prices)

	1999	2000	2001	2002	2003	2004
€'000,000	−2,967	−3,032	−3,253	−3,270	−3,227	−3,640
% of total	16.7%	15.0%	15.2%	15.4%	15.4%	15.7%

Imports (2003): €12,067,000,000 (machinery and apparatus 18.3%, transport equipment 13.0%, base and fabricated metals 11.5%, chemicals and chemical products 10.2%). *Major import sources:* Belgium 35.2%; Germany 28.1%; France 14.1%; The Netherlands 5.5%; Italy 2.4%.
Exports (2003): €8,840,000,000 (base and fabricated metals [mostly iron and steel] 26.7%, machinery and apparatus 19.6%, chemicals and chemical products 7.5%, transport equipment 6.6%, plastics, rubber products, and other diverse manufactures 30.6%). *Major export destinations:* Germany 26.5%; France 20.1%; Belgium 12.4%; U.K. 6.0%; Italy 5.9%.

Transport and communications

Transport. Railroads (2004): route length 275 km; passenger-km 266,000,000; metric ton-km cargo 600,000,000. Roads (2000): total length 5,210 km (paved 100%). Vehicles (2004): passenger cars 293,398; trucks and buses 24,557. Air transport (2004)[14]: passenger-km 572,582,000; metric ton-km cargo 257,000; airports with scheduled flights 1.

Communications

Medium	date	unit	number	units per 1,000 persons
Daily newspapers	2004	circulation	115,000	253
Radio	2000	receivers	300,000	685
Television	2000	receivers	170,000	391
Telephones	2003	main lines	360,100	798
Cellular telephones	2003	subscribers	539,000	1,194
Personal computers	2004	units	296,000	645
Internet	2004	users	270,800	590

Education and health

Educational attainment (2002). Percentage of population age 25–64 having: no formal schooling through lower-secondary education 38%; upper secondary/higher vocational 43%; university 19%. *Literacy* (2001): virtually 100% literate.

Education (2003–04)

	schools	teachers	students	student/ teacher ratio
Primary (age 6–11)	...	3,002	32,456	10.8
Secondary (age 12–18)	...	3,359	10,316	...
Voc., teacher tr.	...		22,204	...
Higher	5	...	2,849[15]	...

Health (2004): physicians 1,591 (1 per 285 persons); hospital beds 3,045 (1 per 149 persons); infant mortality rate per 1,000 live births 4.0.
Food (1995): daily per capita caloric intake 3,530 (vegetable products 68%, animal products 32%); 134% of FAO recommended minimum.

Military

Total active duty personnel (2004): 900 (army 100.0%). *Military expenditure as percentage of GDP* (2003): 0.9%; per capita expenditure U.S.$513.

[1]Has limited legislative authority. [2]Luxembourgian is the national language, German is the lingua franca, and French is used for most official purposes. [3]The Luxembourg franc was the former monetary unit; on Jan. 1, 2002, Lux F 40.34 = €1. [4]January 1. [5]Populations of localities (comparable to cities proper or towns proper). [6]Excludes December. [7]In early 2005 total banking assets (at 161 banks) exceeded U.S.$725,000,000,000. [8]Imputed bank service charges. [9]Detail does not add to total given because of rounding. [10]Includes c. 111,000 Luxembourgers, c. 84,000 resident foreigners, and c. 106,000 workers from neighbouring countries. [11]Luxembourgers and resident foreigners only. [12]Manufacturing only. [13]Imports c.i.f.; exports f.o.b. [14]Luxair only. [15]Excludes 6,723 students at foreign universities.

Internet resources for further information:
• STATEC: Luxembourg in Figures http://statec.gouvernement.lu/html_en

Macau

South China Sea

Official name: Aomen Tebie Xingzhengqu (Chinese); Região Administrativa Especial de Macau (Portuguese) (Macau Special Administrative Region).
Political status: special administrative region (China[1]) with one legislative house (Legislative Council [29[2]]).
Chief of state: President of China.
Head of government: Chief Executive.
Capital: Macau.
Official languages: Chinese; Portuguese.
Official religion: none.
Monetary unit: 1 pataca (MOP) = 100 avos; valuation (Sept. 1, 2005)
1 U.S.$ = MOP 8.00; 1 £ = MOP 14.73.

Area and population

Geographic areas	area		population
	sq mi	sq km	2001 census
Macau peninsula	3.4	8.8	388,647
Islands	5.4	14.0	44,690
Coloane	2.9	7.6	2,904
Taipa	2.5	6.4	41,786
Marine	—	—	1,898
Embankment[3]	1.8	4.7	
TOTAL	10.6	27.5	435,235

Demography

Population (2005): 470,000.
Density (2005): persons per sq mi 44,340, persons per sq km 17,091.
Urban-rural (2004): urban, virtually 100%[4].
Sex distribution (2005[5]): male 47.97%; female 52.03%.
Age breakdown (2005[5]): under 15, 17.1%; 15–29, 23.2%; 30–44, 26.8%; 45–59, 22.3%; 60–74, 6.8%; 75 and over, 3.8%.
Population projection: (2010) 486,000; (2020) 520,000.
Doubling time: over 100 years.
Nationality (2001)[6]: Chinese 95.2%; Portuguese 2.0%; Filipino 1.2%; other 1.6%.
Religious affiliation (1998): nonreligious 60.8%; Buddhist 16.7%; other 22.5%.
Major city (2005[5]): Macau 465,333.

Vital statistics

Birth rate per 1,000 population (2005[5]): 7.1 (world avg. 21.1); (2004) legitimate 82.7%; illegitimate 17.3%.
Death rate per 1,000 population (2005[5]): 3.3 (world avg. 9.0).
Natural increase rate per 1,000 population (2005[5]): 3.8 (world avg. 12.1).
Total fertility rate (avg. births per childbearing woman; 2004): 0.9.
Marriage rate per 1,000 population (2004): 3.8.
Divorce rate per 1,000 population (2004): 1.0.
Life expectancy at birth (2000–03): male 77.4 years; female 82.0 years.
Major causes of death per 100,000 population (2004): malignant neoplasms (cancers) 102.5; diseases of the circulatory system 96.1; diseases of the respiratory system 52.2; accidents, poisoning, and violence 26.0; ill-defined conditions 14.2; diseases of the digestive system 11.2.

National economy

Budget (2003). Revenue: MOP 14,120,000,000 (revenue from gambling tax 74.9%; property income tax 6.2%; stamp duties 3.5%). Expenditures: MOP 15,713,000,000 (current expenditure 55.6%; specific accounts 27.1%; capital expenditure 17.3%).
Tourism: receipts from visitors (2003) U.S.$5,303,000,000; expenditures by nationals abroad (1999) U.S.$131,000,000.
Land use as % of total land area (2000): "green area" 22.4%.
Gross national product (at current market prices; 2003): U.S.$7,700,000,000 (U.S.$16,600 per capita).

Structure of gross domestic product and labour force

	2003			
	in value MOP '000,000[7]	% of total value	labour force	% of labour force
Agriculture, fishing	...	...	600	0.3
Mining, quarrying	—	—		
Manufacturing	4,005	6.3	37,100	17.2
Construction	2,543	4.0	16,300	7.6
Public utilities	1,716	2.7	1,300	0.6
Transportation and communications	3,496	5.5	14,200	6.6
Trade, hotels	7,628	12.0	54,900	25.5
Finance	12,331	19.4	18,700	8.4
Public administration	5,339	8.4	17,800	8.3
Services	6,229	9.8	42,000	19.5
Gaming activities	22,756	35.8	...	...
Other	−2,670[8]	−4.2[8]	13,200[9]	6.1[9]
TOTAL	63,564[10]	100.0[10]	215,500	100.0[10]

Production (metric tons except as noted). Agriculture, forestry, fishing (2003): eggs 1,100,000; livestock (number of live animals) 700,000 chickens; roundwood, n.a.; fish catch 1,500. Quarrying (value added in MOP '000; 2003): 17,139. Manufacturing (value added in MOP '000,000; 2003): wearing apparel 1,942; textiles 448; printing and publishing 111; food products 93; chemicals 73; footwear 64. Energy production (consumption): electricity (kW-hr; 2004)

1,893,000,000 ([2002] 1,904,000,000); petroleum products (metric tons; 2002) none (589,000).
Public debt (long-term, external; 2003): U.S.$2,700,000,000.
Population economically active (2003): total 215,500; activity rate of total population 49.9% (participation rates: ages 14–64, 66.2%; female 46.6%; unemployed [July 2004–June 2005] 4.3%).

Price and earnings indexes (2000 = 100)

	1998	1999	2000	2001	2002	2003	2004
Consumer price index	105.0	101.6	100.0	98.0	95.4	93.9	94.9
Monthly earnings index	104.7	102.0	100.0	96.5	96.9	99.6	107.1

Household income and expenditure (2002–03). Average household size (2002) 2.8; annual income per household MOP 183,648 (U.S.$22,862); sources of income: n.a.; expenditure[11]: food and nonalcoholic beverages 31.4%, housing and energy 29.9%, education, health, and other services 19.2%, transportation and communications 9.8%, clothing and footwear 5.3%, household durable goods 3.2%.

Foreign trade[12]

Balance of trade (current prices)

	1999	2000	2001	2002	2003	2004
MOP '000,000	+1,280	+2,283	−697	−1,398	−1,849	−5,343
% of total	3.8%	5.9%	1.9%	3.6%	4.3%	10.6%

Imports (2004): MOP 27,904,000,000 (consumer goods 39.3%; capital goods 17.2%; mineral fuels 7.7%). *Major import sources:* China 44.4%; EU 12.5%; Hong Kong 10.6%; Japan 9.6%; Taiwan 4.9%.
Exports (2004): MOP 22,561,000,000 (domestic exports 76.8%, of which machine-knitted clothing 38.6%, machine-woven clothing 30.1%, footwear 3.6%; reexports 23.2%). *Major export destinations:* United States 48.7%; EU 21.6%, of which Germany 8.3%; China 13.9%; Hong Kong 7.6%.

Transport and communications

Transport. Railroads: none. Roads (2004): total length 225 mi, 362 km (paved 100%). Vehicles (2004[5]): passenger cars 59,556; trucks and buses 4,517. Air transport (2004)[13]: passenger-mi 1,321,738,000, passenger-km 2,127,136,000; short ton-mi cargo 73,707,000, metric ton-km cargo 107,610,000.

Communications

Medium	date	unit	number	units per 1,000 persons
Daily newspapers	2003	circulation	169,000	380
Radio	2001	receivers	218,800	504
Television	2001	receivers	122,900	283
Telephones	2004	main lines	173,900	381
Cellular telephones	2004	subscribers	432,400	946
Personal computers	2004	units	130,000	285
Internet	2004	users	150,000	328

Education and health

Educational attainment (2001). Population age 25 and over having: no formal schooling 7.6%; incomplete primary education 13.6%; completed primary 26.6%; some secondary 23.9%; completed secondary and post-secondary 28.3%. *Literacy* (2003): percentage of population age 15 and over literate 94.5%; males literate 97.2%; females literate 92.0%.

Education (2003–04)

	schools	teachers	students	student/ teacher ratio
Primary (age 6–11)	85	1,638	39,278	24.0
Secondary (age 12–18)	60	2,139	43,251	20.2
Voc., teacher tr.	4	132	2,349	17.8
Higher	12	1,104	13,680	12.4

Health (2004): physicians 1,006 (1 per 454 persons); hospital beds 966 (1 per 473 persons); infant mortality rate per 1,000 live births (2004) 3.0.
Food (1998): daily per capita caloric intake 2,471 (vegetable products 76%, animal products 24%); 108% of FAO recommended minimum requirement.

Military

Total active duty personnel (2004): up to 1,000 Chinese troops; Macau residents are prohibited from entering military service. *Military expenditure as percentage of GDP:* n.a.

[1]Macau reverted to Chinese sovereignty on Dec. 20, 1999. [2]Includes 12 directly elected seats, 7 seats appointed by the chief executive, and 10 seats appointed by business and special-interest groups. [3]Landfill linking Coloane and Taipa. [4]About 0.5% of Macau's population live on sampans and other vessels. [5]January 1. [6]Resident population. [7]Values are derived from estimated percentages by sector. [8]Less imputed bank service charge. [9]Includes 300 in activities undefined and 12,900 unemployed. [10]Detail does not add to total given because of rounding. [11]Weights of consumer price index components. [12]Includes reexports. [13]Air Macau only.

Internet resources for further information:
- **Macau Census and Statistics Service**
  http://www.dsec.gov.mo/e_index.html
- **Monetary Authority of Macao**
  http://www.amcm.gov.mo

Macedonia

Official name[1]: Republika Makedonija (Macedonian); Republika e Maqedonisë (Albanian) (Republic of Macedonia).
Form of government: unitary multiparty republic with a unicameral legislature (Assembly [120]).
Head of state: President.
Head of government: Prime Minister.
Capital: Skopje.
Official languages[2]: Macedonian; Albanian.
Official religion: none.
Monetary unit: denar (MKD); valuation (Sept. 1, 2005) 1 U.S.$ = MKD 49.42; 1 £ = MKD 90.99.

Area and population

Former administrative districts[3]	area sq km	population 1994 census	Former administrative districts[3]	area sq km	population 1994 census
Berovo	806	19,737	Negotino	734	23,094
Bitola	1,798	106,012	Ohrid	1,069	60,841
Brod	924	10,912	Prilep	1,675	93,248
Debar	274	26,449	Probištip	326	16,373
Delčevo	589	25,052	Radoviš	735	30,378
Demir Hisar	443	10,321	Resen	739	17,467
Gevgelija	757	34,767	Skopje	1,818	541,280
Gostivar	1,341	108,189	Štip	815	50,531
Kavadarci	1,132	41,801	Struga	507	62,305
Kičevo	854	53,044	Strumica	952	89,759
Kočani	570	48,105	Sveti Nikole	649	21,391
Kratovo	376	10,855	Tetovo	1,080	174,748
Kriva Palanka	720	25,112	Titov Veles	1,536	65,523
Kruševo	239	11,981	Valandovo	331	12,049
Kumanovo	1,212	126,543	Vinica	432	19,010
			TOTAL	25,713[4]	1,936,877[5]

Demography

Population (2005): 2,034,000.
Density (2005): persons per sq mi 204.9, persons per sq km 79.1.
Urban-rural (2003): urban 59.5%; rural 40.5%.
Sex distribution (2004): male 49.97%; female 50.03%.
Age breakdown (2004): under 15, 20.9%; 15–29, 23.9%; 30–44, 21.8%; 45–59, 18.4%; 60–74, 11.5%; 75 and over, 3.5%.
Population projection: (2010) 2,046,000; (2020) 2,057,000.
Ethnic composition (2002): Macedonian 64.2%; Albanian 25.2%; Turkish 3.9%; Rom (Gypsy) 2.7%; Serbian 1.8%; Bosniac 0.8%; other 1.4%.
Religious affiliation (2000): Orthodox 59.3%; Sunnī Muslim 28.3%; Roman Catholic 3.5%; nonreligious 6.6%; other 2.3%.
Major cities (1994): Skopje 440,577; Bitola 75,386; Prilep 67,371; Kumanovo 66,237; Tetovo 50,376.

Vital statistics

Birth rate per 1,000 population (2004): 13.2 (world avg. 21.1); legitimate 87.7%; illegitimate 12.3%.
Death rate per 1,000 population (2004): 8.8 (world avg. 9.0).
Natural increase rate per 1,000 population (2004): 4.4 (world avg. 12.1).
Total fertility rate (avg. births per childbearing woman; 2004): 1.6.
Marriage rate per 1,000 population (2004): 6.9.
Life expectancy at birth (2004): male 71.0 years; female 76.1 years.
Major causes of death per 100,000 population (2003): diseases of the circulatory system 599.1; malignant neoplasms 165.1; diseases of the respiratory system 41.6; accidents, violence, and poisoning 32.9; diabetes mellitus 31.6.

National economy

Budget (2002). Revenue: MKD 53,089,000,000 (tax revenue 94.2%, of which value-added tax 33.7%, excise taxes 20.6%, income and profit tax 19.6%, import duties 10.0%; nontax revenue 5.8%). Expenditure: MKD 59,979,-000,000 (wages and salaries 29.5%, pensions 26.1%, interest 6.1%).
Public debt (external, outstanding; 2003): U.S.$1,438,000,000.
Production (metric tons except as noted). Agriculture, forestry, fishing (2004): wheat 358,351, grapes 247,673, potatoes 199,000, corn (maize) 146,105, tomatoes 116,837, tobacco leaves 21,140; livestock (number of live animals) 1,432,369 sheep, 255,000 cattle; roundwood 812,000 cu m; fish catch (2003) 1,648. Mining and quarrying (2003): copper 15,000[6]; lead 5,000[6]; zinc 4,000[6]; silver 10,000 kg. Manufacturing (value added in U.S.$'000,000; 1999) food products 224; textiles 100; glass and glass products 63; iron and steel 61; basic chemicals 46; paper and paper products 40. Energy production (consumption): electricity (kW-hr; 2002) 6,090,000,000 (6,881,000,000); hard coal (metric tons; 2002) none (4,000); lignite (metric tons; 2002) 7,580,000 (7,280,000); crude petroleum (barrels; 2002) none (3,900,000); petroleum products (metric tons; 2002) 524,000 (721,000); natural gas (cu m; 2002) none (89,000,000).
Household income and expenditure. Average household size (2002) 3.6; income per household (2000) U.S.$3,798; sources of income (2000): wages and salaries 54.2%, transfer payments 22.6%, savings 3.2%, other 20.0%; expenditure: food 38.4%, transportation and communications 9.7%, fuel and lighting 8.2%, beverages and tobacco 7.6%.
Tourism (2003): receipts from visitors U.S.$57,000,000; expenditures by nationals abroad U.S.$48,000,000.
Gross national product (at current market prices; 2004): U.S.$4,855,000,000 (U.S.$2,350 per capita).

Structure of gross domestic product and labour force

	2003			
	in value MKD '000,000	% of total value	labour force	% of labour force
Agriculture	29,727	11.7	120,132	13.9
Mining	989	0.4	2,498	0.3
Manufacturing	39,651	15.6	131,307	15.2
Construction	13,537	5.3	35,874	4.2
Public utilities	11,778	4.7	15,176	1.8
Transp. and commun.	21,062	8.3	30,642	3.6
Trade	33,875	13.4	75,273	8.7
Finance	14,563	5.8	17,904	2.1
Pub. admin., defense	16,984	6.7	34,744	4.0
Services	24,836	9.8	80,020	9.3
Other	46,459[7]	18.3[7]	317,405[8]	36.9[8]
TOTAL	253,461	100.0	860,975	100.0

Population economically active (2003): total 860,975; activity rate 42.3% (participation rates: ages 15–64, 61.3%; female 39.7%; unemployed 36.7%).

Price and earnings indexes (2000 = 100)

	1998	1999	2000	2001	2002	2003	2004
Consumer price index	95.0	93.8	100.0	105.2	107.6	108.8	108.4
Annual earnings index	92.1	94.7	100.0	103.6	110.7	116.0	120.5

Land use as % of total land area (2000): in temporary crops 21.8%, in permanent crops 1.7%, in pasture 25.0%; overall forest area 35.6%.

Foreign trade[9]

Balance of trade (current prices)

	1999	2000	2001	2002	2003	2004
U.S.$'000,000	−585	−771	−536	−880	−937	−1,214
% of total	19.7%	22.6%	18.8%	28.3%	25.6%	26.8%

Imports (2002): U.S.$1,995,000,000 (machinery and transport equipment 20.4%, mineral fuels 13.2%, food and live animals 12.4%, chemicals and chemical products 10.6%). *Major import sources*: Germany 13.0%; Greece 9.7%; Russia 8.7%; Serbia and Montenegro 8.4%; Bulgaria 7.2%.
Exports (2002): U.S.$1,115,000,000 (clothing and accessories 30.0%, iron and steel 14.0%, tobacco [all forms] 6.8%, food and live animals 6.7%, chemicals and chemical products 6.2%). *Major export destinations* (2004): Serbia and Montenegro 20.8%; Germany 18.9%; Greece 13.7%; Italy 8.0%; Croatia 4.8%.

Transport and communications

Transport. Railroads (2002): route length 434 mi, 699 km; passenger-km 98,000,000; metric ton-km cargo 334,000,000. Roads (2000): length 7,782 mi, 12,522 km (paved 58%). Vehicles (2002): passenger cars 307,600; trucks and buses 33,000. Air transport (2004)[10]: passenger-km 275,000,000; metric ton-km cargo 131,000; airports (2002) with scheduled flights 2.

Communications

Medium	date	unit	number	units per 1,000 persons
Daily newspapers	2000	circulation	89,400	44
Radio	2000	receivers	415,000	205
Television	2000	receivers	571,000	282
Telephones	2002	main lines	560,000	271
Cellular telephones	2002	subscribers	365,300	177
Personal computers	2004	units	140,000	68
Internet	2004	users	159,000	77

Education and health

Educational attainment (2002). Percentage of population age 15 and over having: less than full primary education 18.1%; primary 35.0%; secondary 36.9%; postsecondary and higher 10.0%. *Literacy* (2002): total population age 10 and over literate 96.4%.

Education (2003–04)

	schools	teachers	students	student/ teacher ratio
Primary (age 7–14)	1,056	14,030	230,602	16.4
Secondary (age 15–18)	96	5,863	93,791	16.0
Higher[11]	31	1,495	40,246	26.9

Health (2001): physicians 4,459 (1 per 452 persons); hospital beds 10,045 (1 per 201 persons); infant mortality rate per 1,000 live births (2004) 11.0.
Food (2002): daily per capita caloric intake 2,655 (vegetable products 78%, animal products 22%); 105% of FAO recommended minimum requirement.

Military

Total active duty personnel (2004): 10,890 (army 89.6%, air force 10.4%). *Military expenditure as percentage of GDP* (2003): 2.5%; per capita expenditure U.S.$57.

[1]Member of the United Nations under the name The Former Yugoslav Republic of Macedonia (FYROM). [2]Albanian was made an official language in June 2002. [3]Local government was enlarged to 123 municipalities in 1996 and then reduced to 84 municipalities by 2004. [4]Total includes 280 sq km of inland water not distributed by district. [5]2002 census population: 2,022,547. [6]Metal content. [7]Rent and taxes on production less imputed bank service charges. [8]Includes 315,868 unemployed. [9]Imports c.i.f.; exports f.o.b. [10]Macedonian Airlines. [11]2000–01.

Internet resources for further information:
• **National Bank of the Republic of Macedonia** http://www.nbrm.gov.mk
• **State Statistical Office** http://www.stat.gov.mk/english/glavna_eng.asp

Madagascar

Indian Ocean

Official name: Repoblikan'i Madagasikara (Malagasy); République de Madagascar (French) (Republic of Madagascar).
Form of government: federal[1] multiparty republic with two legislative houses (Senate [90]; National Assembly [160]).
Heads of state and government: President assisted by Prime Minister.
Capital: Antananarivo.
Official languages: [2].
Official religion: none.
Monetary unit: 1 ariary[3] (MGA) = 5 iraimbilanja; valuation (Sept. 1, 2005) 1 U.S.$ = MGA 2,010; 1 £ = MGA 3,701.

Area and population		area		population
				2001
Autonomous provinces[1]	Capitals	sq mi	sq km	estimate
Antananarivo	Antananarivo	22,503	58,283	4,580,788
Antsiranana	Antsiranana	16,624	43,056	1,188,425
Fianarantsoa	Fianarantsoa	39,527	102,373	3,366,291
Mahajanga	Mahajanga	57,924	150,023	1,733,917
Toamasina	Toamasina	27,765	71,911	2,593,063
Toliara	Toliara	62,319	161,405	2,229,550
TOTAL		226,662	587,051	15,692,034

Demography

Population (2005): 18,606,000.
Density (2005): persons per sq mi 82.1, persons per sq km 31.7.
Urban-rural (2004): urban 30.7%; rural 69.3%.
Sex distribution (2000): male 49.70%; female 50.30%.
Age breakdown (2000): under 15, 45.0%; 15–29, 26.5%; 30–44, 15.8%; 45–59, 7.9%; 60–74, 3.8%; 75 and over, 1.0%.
Population projection: (2010) 21,151,000; (2020) 26,584,000.
Doubling time: 23 years.
Ethnic composition (2000): Malagasy 95.9%, of which Merina 24.0%, Betsimisaraka 13.4%, Betsileo 11.3%, Tsimihety 7.0%, Sakalava 5.9%; Makua 1.1%; French 0.6%; Comorian 0.5%; Reunionese 0.4%; other 1.5%.
Religious affiliation (2000): Christian 49.5%, of which Protestant 22.7%, Roman Catholic 20.3%; traditional beliefs 48.0%; Muslim 1.9%; other 0.6%.
Major cities (2001): Antananarivo 1,403,449; Toamasina 179,045; Antsirabe 160,356; Fianarantsoa 144,225; Mahajanga 135,660.

Vital statistics

Birth rate per 1,000 population (2004): 41.1 (world avg. 21.1).
Death rate per 1,000 population (2004): 11.6 (world avg. 9.0).
Natural increase rate per 1,000 population (2004): 29.5 (world avg. 12.1).
Total fertility rate (avg. births per childbearing woman; 2004): 5.7.
Life expectancy at birth (2004): male 54.2 years; female 59.0 years.
Major causes of death per 100,000 population: n.a.

National economy

Budget (2004). Revenue: MGA 1,653,000,000,000 (tax revenue 53.7%, of which import duties 26.9%, VAT 10.5%; grants 40.6%; nontax revenue 5.7%). Expenditures: MGA 2,045,000,000,000 (current expenditure 50.2%; capital expenditure 49.8%).
Public debt (external, outstanding; 2004): U.S.$5,142,000,000.
Production (metric tons except as noted). Agriculture, forestry, fishing (2004): paddy rice 3,030,000, sugarcane 2,459,705, cassava 2,191,420, sweet potatoes 542,230, corn (maize) 349,646, bananas 290,000, potatoes 280,500, mangoes 210,000, taro 200,000, coffee 65,000, peanuts (groundnuts) 39,170, cloves (whole and stem) 15,500, vanilla 6,000; livestock (number of live animals) 10,500,000 cattle, 1,600,000 pigs, 1,200,000 goats; roundwood 10,866,866 cu m; fish catch (2003) 140,838, of which crustaceans 22,266. Mining and quarrying (2003): chromite ore 33,000; graphite 2,000; sapphires 6,000 kg; gold 10 kg (illegally smuggled, c. 2,000 kg). Manufacturing (2004): raw sugar 67,917; cement 51,882; soap 15,915; cigarettes 4,139[4]; beer 692,000 hectolitres; fuel oil 247,000 cu m; gasoline 128,000 cu m; shoes 873,000[4] pairs. Energy production (consumption): electricity (kW-hr; 2002) 840,000,000 (840,000,000); coal (metric tons; 2002) none (10,000); crude petroleum (barrels; 2002) none (3,400,000); petroleum products (metric tons; 2002) 319,000 (599,000); natural gas, none (none).
Population economically active (2002): total 8,481,000; activity rate of total population 50.7% (participation rates: ages 15–64, 83.2%; female 49.5%; unemployed 4.5%).

Price and earnings indexes (2000 = 100)							
	1998	1999	2000	2001	2002	2003	2004
Consumer price index[5]	81.2	89.3	100.0	106.9	124.0	122.5	139.4
Annual earnings index	...	...	...	...	...	...	...

Land use as % of total land area (2000): in temporary crops 5.0%, in permanent crops 1.0%, in pasture 41.3%; overall forest area 20.2%.
Tourism (2003): receipts from visitors U.S.$76,000,000; expenditures by nationals abroad U.S.$64,000,000.
Gross national product (at current market prices; 2004): U.S.$5,181,000,000 (U.S.$300 per capita).

Structure of gross domestic product and labour force				
	2004		2002	
	in value FMG '000,000,000	% of total value	labour force	% of labour force
Agriculture	9,857	26.2	6,316,000	74.5
Manufacturing			449,000	5.3
Mining	5,456	14.5	14,000	0.2
Public utilities			19,000	0.2
Construction	794	2.1	60,000	0.7
Transp. and commun.	5,796	15.4	117,000	1.4
Trade, hotels	4,316	11.5	468,000	5.5
Finance	324	0.9	6,000	0.1
Services	5,644	15.0	443,000	5.2
Pub. admin., defense	2,281	6.0	206,000	2.4
Other	3,184[6]	8.4[6]	383,000[7]	4.5[7]
TOTAL	37,651[8]	100.0	8,481,000	100.0

Household income and expenditure. Average household size (1993) 4.6[9]; expenditure (2000)[10]: food, beverages, and tobacco 50.1%, housing and energy 18.2%, transportation 8.0%, clothing 7.0%, household furnishings 4.6%.

Foreign trade[11]

Balance of trade						
	1999	2000	2001	2002	2003	2004
SDR[12] '000,000	−122.3	−78.5	+11.6	−36.4	−135.9	−303.2
% of total	12.6%	5.9%	0.8%	4.6%	9.2%	19.0%

Imports (2004): SDR 1,119,600,000[12] (machinery and apparatus 22.0%, consumer goods 13.3%, petroleum [all forms] 13.0%, other [mostly imports for EPZ[13]] 30.2%). *Major import sources:* France 16.8%; China 11.3%; Hong Kong 6.5%; Iran 6.3%; South Africa 5.5%.
Exports (2004): SDR 646,400,000[12] (EPZ[13] exports [mostly textiles and clothing] 52.0%, vanilla 13.0%, shellfish 5.2%, cloves 3.0%). *Major export destinations:* U.S. 35.5%; France 30.5%; Germany 7.0%; Mauritius 4.6%; Italy 3.4%.

Transport and communications

Transport. Railroads: route length (2003) 560 mi, 901 km[14]; (2000) passenger-km 24,471,000; (2000) metric ton-km cargo 27,200,000. Roads (1999): total length 30,968 mi, 49,827 km (paved 12%). Vehicles (1998): passenger cars 64,000; trucks and buses 9,100. Air transport (2004)[15]: passenger-km 911,000,000; metric ton-km cargo 12,657,000.

Communications				
				units per 1,000
Medium	date	unit	number	persons
Daily newspapers	2001	circulation	83,300	5.0
Radio	2001	receivers	3,600,100	216
Television	2002	receivers	410,000	25
Telephones	2003	main lines	59,600	3.6
Cellular telephones	2004	subscribers	333,900	18
Personal computers	2004	users	91,000	5.0
Internet	2004	users	90,000	5.0

Education and health

Educational attainment (1993). Percentage of population age 10 and over having: no formal schooling 33.7%; primary education 47.0%; general secondary 17.0%; technical secondary 0.8%; higher 1.5%. *Literacy* (2003): percentage of total population age 15 and over literate 68.9%; males literate 75.5%; females literate 62.5%.

Education (2002–03)				
	schools	teachers	students	student/ teacher ratio
Primary (age 6–13)	19,961[16]	55,309	2,856,480	51.6
Secondary (age 14–18)	...	19,471	436,211	22.4
Voc., teacher tr.	...	...	12,691[17]	...
Higher	6[17]	1,857	32,593	17.6

Health (2004): physicians 1,861 (1 per 9,998 persons); hospital beds 9,303 (1 per 2,000 persons); infant mortality rate 78.5.
Food (2002): daily per capita caloric intake 2,005 (vegetable products 91%, animal products 9%); 88% of FAO recommended minimum requirement.

Military

Total active duty personnel (2004): 13,500 (army 92.6%, navy 3.7%, air force 3.7%). *Military expenditure as percentage of GDP* (2003): 1.5%; per capita expenditure U.S.$5.

[1]Each of the six autonomous provinces is adopting its own statutory laws per article 2 of the 1998 constitution. [2]The 1998 constitution identifies Malagasy as the "national" language, although neither Malagasy nor French, the languages of the two official texts of the constitution, is itself "official." [3]The ariary (MGA), the precolonial currency of Madagascar, officially replaced the Malagasy franc (FMG) in August 2003 at a rate of 1 MGA = FMG 5; both currencies circulated through the end of 2004. [4]2000. [5]Antananarivo only. [6]Indirect taxes less subsidies and less imputed bank charges. [7]Unemployed. [8]Detail does not add to total given because of rounding. [9]Malagasy households only. [10]Weights of consumer price index components. [11]Imports are f.o.b. in balance of trade and c.i.f. for commodities and trading partners. [12]SDRs (Special Drawing Rights) are reserve assets created by the IMF and used by governments to settle their international indebtedness. [13]Export-processing zones. [14]Railroad infrastructure was either inoperable or in poor condition in June 2003. [15]Air Madagascar. [16]2003–04. [17]1998–99.

Internet resources for further information:
• Institut National de la Statistique
  http://www.cite.mg/instat/index.htm

Malawi

Indian Ocean

Official name: Republic of Malawi.
Form of government: multiparty republic with one legislative house (National Assembly [193]).
Head of state and government: President.
Capital: Lilongwe[1].
Official language: none.
Official religion: none.
Monetary unit: 1 Malawi kwacha (MK) = 100 tambala; valuation (Sept. 1, 2005) 1 U.S.$ = MK 124.17; 1 £ = MK 228.63.

Area and population

Regions Districts	Capitals	area sq mi	area sq km	population 2004 estimate[2]
Central	Lilongwe	13,742	35,592	4,992,753
Dedza	Dedza	1,399	3,624	582,289
Dowa	Dowa	1,174	3,041	469,924
Kasungu	Kasungu	3,042	7,878	589,019
Lilongwe	Lilongwe	2,378	6,159	1,720,784
Mchinji	Mchinji	1,296	3,356	395,171
Nkhotakota	Nkhotakota	1,644	4,259	275,213
Ntcheu	Ntcheu	1,322	3,424	443,474
Ntchisi	Ntchisi	639	1,655	207,997
Salima	Salima	848	2,196	308,882
Northern	Mzuzu	10,398	26,931	1,427,807
Chitipa	Chitipa	1,656	4,288	152,691
Karonga	Karonga	1,295	3,355	230,026
Likoma	Likoma	7	18	9,856
Mzimba	Mzimba	4,027	10,430	701,269
Nkhata Bay	Nkhata Bay	1,572	4,071	187,906
Rumphi	Rumphi	1,841	4,769	146,059
Southern	Blantyre	12,260	31,753	5,517,374
Balaka	Balaka	847	2,193	295,623
Blantyre	Blantyre	777	2,012	1,027,808
Chikwawa	Chikwawa	1,836	4,755	425,080
Chiradzulu	Chiradzulu	296	767	273,893
Machinga	Machinga	1,456	3,771	417,594
Mangochi	Mangochi	2,422	6,273	711,179
Mulanje	Mulanje	794	2,056	506,598
Mwanza	Mwanza	886	2,295	162,739
Nsanje	Nsanje	750	1,942	223,278
Phalombe	Phalombe	538	1,394	280,043
Thyolo	Thyolo	662	1,715	539,610
Zomba	Zomba	996	2,580	653,929
TOTAL LAND AREA		36,400	94,276	
INLAND WATER		9,347	24,208	
TOTAL		45,747	118,484	11,937,934

Demography

Population (2005): 12,707,000.
Density (2005)[3]: persons per sq mi 349.1, persons per sq km 134.8.
Urban-rural (2003): urban 16.3%; rural 83.7%.
Sex distribution (2002): male 49.20%; female 50.80%.
Age breakdown (2001): under 15, 44.4%; 15–29, 30.4%; 30–44, 13.5%; 45–59, 7.2%; 60–74, 3.7%; 75 and over, 0.8%.
Population projection: (2010) 14,309,000; (2020) 17,974,000.
Doubling time: 29 years.
Ethnic composition (2000): Chewa 34.7%; Maravi 12.2%; Ngoni 9.0%; Yao 7.9%; Tumbuka 7.9%; Lomwe 7.7%; Ngonde 3.5%; other 17.1%.
Religious affiliation (2000): Protestant 38.5%; Roman Catholic 24.7%; Muslim 14.8%; traditional beliefs 7.8%; other 14.2%.
Major cities (2004)[2]: Blantyre 678,381; Lilongwe 632,867; Mzuzu 126,885; Zomba 95,797; Karonga (1998) 27,811.

Vital statistics

Birth rate per 1,000 population (2004): 43.8 (world avg. 21.1).
Death rate per 1,000 population (2004): 19.9 (world avg. 9.0).
Natural increase rate per 1,000 population (2004): 23.9 (world avg. 12.1).
Total fertility rate (avg. births per childbearing woman; 2004): 6.0.
Life expectancy at birth (2004): male 41.4 years; female 41.0 years.
Adult population (ages 15–49) *living with HIV* (2004[4]): 14.2% (world avg. 1.1%).

National economy

Budget (2004). Revenue: MK 68,359,000,000 (tax revenue 62.1%, of which surtax 27.0%, income and profit tax 25.9%, import tax 9.2%; grants 30.4%; nontax revenue 7.5%). Expenditures: MK 94,826,000,000 (current expenditure 83.3%; capital expenditure 16.7%).
Public debt (external, outstanding; June 2005): U.S.$3,100,000,000.
Production (metric tons except as noted). Agriculture, forestry, fishing (2004): cassava 2,559,319, sugarcane 2,100,000, potatoes 1,784,749, corn (maize) 1,733,125, plantains 200,000, peanuts (groundnuts) 161,162, bananas 93,000, tobacco leaves 69,500, tea 45,000, coffee 3,900; livestock (number of live animals) 1,700,000 goats, 750,000 cattle, 456,300 pigs; roundwood 5,621,655 cu m; fish catch (2003) 53,543. Mining and quarrying (2003): limestone 35,000; gemstones 20,000 kg. Manufacturing (value added in U.S.$'000,000; 2001): food products 62; beverages 28; chemicals and chemical products 11; wearing apparel 7. Energy production (consumption): electricity (kW-hr; 2002) 893,000,000 (891,000,000); hard coal (metric tons; 2003) 14,000 ([2002] 18,000); lignite (metric tons; 2003) 60,000 (n.a.); petroleum products (metric tons; 2002) none (212,000).
Land use as % of total land area (2000): in temporary crops 22.3%, in permanent crops 1.5%, in pasture 19.7%; overall forest area 27.2%.

Population economically active (1998): total 4,509,290; activity rate 45.4% (participation rates: ages 15–64, 76.5%; female 50.2%).

Price index (2000 = 100)

	1998	1999	2000	2001	2002	2003	2004
Consumer price index	53.3	77.2	100.0	122.7	140.8	154.3	171.6

Gross national product (2004): U.S.$1,922,000,000 (U.S.$170 per capita).

Structure of gross domestic product and labour force

	2004 in value MK '000,000[5]	2004 % of total value[5]	1998 labour force	1998 % of labour force
Agriculture	5,469	39.1	3,765,827	83.6
Mining	129	0.9	2,499	0.1
Manufacturing	1,603	11.4	118,483	2.6
Construction	391	2.8	73,402	1.6
Public utilities	204	1.5	7,319	0.2
Transp. and commun.	744	5.3	32,623	0.7
Trade	2,996	21.4	257,389	5.7
Finance	1,445	10.3	13,957	0.3
Public administration	1,230	8.8	101,433	2.2
Services	303	2.2	85,996	1.9
Other	−516[6]	−3.7[6]	50,362[7]	1.1[7]
TOTAL	14,002[8]	100.0	4,509,290	100.0

Household income and expenditure. Average household size (2002) 4.3; income per household: n.a.; sources of income: n.a.; expenditure (2001)[9]: food 55.5%, clothing and footwear 11.7%, housing 9.6%, household goods 8.4%.
Tourism (2003): receipts U.S.$33,000,000; expenditures U.S.$38,000,000.

Foreign trade[10]

Balance of trade (current prices)

	1999	2000	2001	2002	2003	2004
MK '000,000	−9,788	−8,658	−7,663	−22,240	−24,978	−48,927
% of total	19.7%	15.5%	10.7%	26.1%	19.5%	31.7%

Imports (2001): MK 39,480,000,000 (machinery and apparatus 17.8%; refined petroleum products 16.1%; chemicals and chemical products 13.2%; road vehicles 10.5%; food 5.5%). *Major import sources* (2004): South Africa 40.4%; India 7.9%; Tanzania 4.9%; Zambia 4.4%; U.S. 3.6%.
Exports (2003): MK 43,349,000,000 (tobacco 52.0%; sugar 14.9%; tea 7.4%; reexports 2.0%). *Major export destinations* (2004): South Africa 13.4%; U.S. 12.2%; Germany 11.9%; Egypt 8.6%; U.K. 6.8%.

Transport and communications

Transport. Railroads (2004): route length 495 mi, 797 km; (2002) passenger-km 42,323,000; (2002) metric ton-km cargo 64,036,000. Roads (1999): total length 17,647 mi, 28,400 km (paved 19%). Vehicles (2001): passenger cars 22,500; trucks and buses 57,600. Air transport (2004)[11]: passenger-km 145,849,000; metric ton-km cargo 1,232,000; airports (1998) 5.

Communications

Medium	date	unit	number	units per 1,000 persons
Daily newspapers	1996	circulation	22,000[12]	2.3[12]
Radio	2001	receivers	5,758,400	499
Television	2001	receivers	46,160	4.0
Telephones	2004	main lines	93,000	7.4
Cellular telephones	2004	subscribers	222,100	18
Personal computers	2004	units	20,000	1.6
Internet	2004	users	46,100	3.7

Education and health

Educational attainment (1998). Percentage of population age 25 and over having: no formal education 40.9%; primary education 48.7%; secondary 9.7%; university 0.7%. *Literacy* (2003): total population age 15 and over literate 62.7%; males literate 76.1%; females literate 49.8%.

Education (2003)

	schools	teachers	students	student/teacher ratio
Primary (age 6–13)	3,160[13]	32,875	3,112,513	94.7
Secondary (age 14–18)	...	7,076	131,100	18.5
Voc., teacher tr.[14]	...	224	2,525	11.3
Higher	6	654	4,757	7.3

Health: physicians (2003) 137 (1 per 88,418 persons); hospital beds (1998) 14,200 (1 per 746 persons); infant mortality rate per 1,000 live births (2004) 97.9.
Food (2002): daily per capita caloric intake 2,155 (vegetable products 97%, animal products 3%); 93% of FAO recommended minimum requirement.

Military

Total active duty personnel (2004): 5,300 (army 100%). *Military expenditure as percentage of GDP* (2003): 0.8%; per capita expenditure U.S.$1.

[1]Judiciary meets in Blantyre. [2]Official projections based on 1998 census. [3]Based on land area. [4]Beginning of year. [5]At factor cost in constant prices of 1994. [6]Less imputed bank service charges. [7]Unemployed. [8]Detail does not add to total given because of rounding. [9]Weights of consumer price index components. [10]Imports c.i.f.; exports f.o.b. [11]Air Malawi only. [12]Circulation for one newspaper only. [13]1997. [14]1995–96.

Internet resources for further information:
• **National Statistical Office of Malawi** http://www.nso.malawi.net
• **Reserve Bank of Malawi** http://www.rbm.mw

Malaysia

Official name: Malaysia.
Form of government: federal
  constitutional monarchy with two
  legislative houses (Senate [70[1]];
  House of Representatives [219]).
Chief of state: Yang di-Pertuan Agong
  (Paramount Ruler).
Head of government: Prime Minister.
Capitals: Kuala Lumpur/Putrajaya[2].
Official language: Malay.
Official religion: Islam.
Monetary unit: 1 ringgit, or Malaysian
  dollar (RM) = 100 cents; valuation[3]
  (Sept. 1, 2005) 1 U.S.$ = RM 3.76;
  1 £ = RM 6.92.

Indian
Ocean

Area and population

Regions States	Capitals	area sq mi	area sq km	population 2000 census
East Malaysia				
Sabah	Kota Kinabalu	28,425	73,619	2,603,485
Sarawak	Kuching	48,050	124,450	2,071,506
West Malaysia (Peninsular Malaysia)				
Johor	Johor Bahru	7,331	18,987	2,740,625
Kedah	Alor Setar	3,639	9,425	1,649,756
Kelantan	Kota Baharu	5,801	15,024	1,313,014
Melaka	Melaka	638	1,652	635,791
Negeri Sembilan	Seremban	2,565	6,644	859,924
Pahang	Kuantan	13,886	35,965	1,288,376
Perak	Ipoh	8,110	21,005	2,051,236
Perlis	Kangar	307	795	204,450
Pulau Pinang	George Town	398	1,031	1,313,449
Selangor	Shah Alam	3,054	7,910	4,188,876[4]
Terengganu	Kuala Terengganu	5,002	12,955	898,825
Federal Territories				
Kuala Lumpur	—	94	243	1,379,310
Labuan	—	36	92	76,067
Putrajaya	—	19	50	[4]
TOTAL		127,355	329,847	23,274,690

Demography

Population (2005): 26,130,000.
Density (2005): persons per sq mi 205.2, persons per sq km 79.2.
Urban-rural (2003): urban 63.9%; rural 36.1%.
Sex distribution (2004): male 50.29%; female 49.71%.
Age breakdown (2004): under 15, 33.3%; 15–29, 26.4%; 30–44, 20.6%; 45–59, 12.8%; 60–74, 5.5%; 75 and over, 1.4%.
Population projection: (2010) 28,382,000; (2020) 32,446,000.
Ethnic composition (2000): Malay and other indigenous 61.3%; Chinese 24.5%; Indian 7.2%; other nonindigenous 1.1%; noncitizen 5.9%.
Religious affiliation (2000): Muslim 60.4%; Buddhist 19.2%; Christian 9.1%; Hindu 6.3%; Chinese folk religionist 2.6%; other 2.4%.
Major cities (2000[5]): Kuala Lumpur 1,297,526; Ipoh 566,211; Klang 563,173; Petaling Jaya 438,084; Johor Bahru 384,613.

Vital statistics

Birth rate per 1,000 population (2004): 21.3 (world avg. 21.1).
Death rate per 1,000 population (2004): 4.6 (world avg. 9.0).
Natural increase rate per 1,000 population (2004): 16.7 (world avg. 12.1).
Total fertility rate (avg. births per childbearing woman; 2004): 3.1.
Life expectancy at birth (2004): male 70.4 years; female 76.2 years.
Major causes of death per 100,000 population (2002): diseases of the circulatory system 149; infectious and parasitic diseases 101; malignant neoplasms (cancers) 83; accidents and violence 43; chronic respiratory diseases 40.

National economy

Budget (2001). Revenue: RM 79,567,000,000 (income tax 52.9%, nontax revenue 25.1%, taxes on goods and services 16.9%, taxes on international trade 5.1%). Expenditures: RM 63,757,000,000 (education 22.6%, interest payments 15.1%, defense and internal security 13.0%, social security 8.7%, health 7.3%, transport 2.1%, agriculture 2.1%).
Public debt (external, outstanding; 2003): U.S.$25,517,000,000.
Population economically active (2000): total 9,616,000; activity rate 41.3% (participation rates: ages 15–64, 65.5%; female 34.7%; unemployed [October 2003–September 2004] 3.5%).

Price index (2000 = 100)

	1998	1999	2000	2001	2002	2003	2004
Consumer price index	95.9	98.5	100.0	101.4	103.3	104.3	105.9

Production (metric tons except as noted). Agriculture, forestry, fishing (2004): oil palm fruit 69,881,000, rice 2,183,664, rubber 1,190,000, coconuts 710,000, bananas 530,000, cocoa beans 33,423, pepper 22,000; livestock (number of live animals) 2,100,000 pigs, 750,000 cattle; roundwood 21,284,279 cu m; fish catch (2003) 1,454,244. Mining and quarrying (2003): iron ore 597,000; tin (metal content) 3,359; struverite 2,619; gold 4,739 kg. Manufacturing (value added in U.S.$'000,000; 2000): electronic products 4,962; refined petroleum products 2,492; telecommunications equipment 2,062; food products 1,982; basic chemicals 1,602; computers/office equipment 1,488. Energy production (consumption): electricity (kW-hr; 2003) 84,024,000,000[6] ([2002] 77,501,-000,000); coal (metric tons; 2003) 168,000 ([2002] 5,250,000); crude petroleum (barrels; 2004) 279,000,000[7] ([2002] 181,000,000); petroleum products

(metric tons; 2002) 20,219,000 (21,408,000); natural gas (cu m; 2003) 51,808,000,000 ([2002] 28,017,000,000).
Gross national product (2004): U.S.$117,132,000,000 (U.S.$4,650 per capita).

Structure of gross domestic product and labour force

	2003–04 in value RM '000,000	2003–04 % of total value	2002 labour force	2002 % of labour force
Agriculture	42,594	9.8	1,422,000	14.4
Mining	50,053	11.5	29,000	0.3
Manufacturing	137,390	31.6	2,071,000	20.9
Construction	14,910	3.4	907,000	9.2
Public utilities	13,707	3.2	48,000	0.5
Transp. and commun.	28,833	6.6	496,000	5.0
Trade	56,965	13.1	2,118,000	21.4
Finance	49,155	11.3	639,000	6.5
Pub. admin., defense	31,272	7.2	1,822,000	18.4
Services	27,627	6.4		
Other	−18,139[8]	−4.1[8]	334,000	3.4
TOTAL	434,367	100.0	9,886,000	100.0

Household income and expenditure. Average household size (2000) 4.5; annual income per household (1999) RM 32,784 (U.S.$8,627); sources of income: n.a.; expenditure (1998–99): food at home 22.2%, housing and energy c. 21%, food away from home 10.9%.
Tourism (2003): receipts U.S.$5,901,000,000; expenditures U.S.$2,846,000,000.
Land use as % of total land area (2000): in temporary crops 5.5%, in permanent crops 17.6%, in pasture 0.9%; overall forest area 58.7%.

Foreign trade[9]

Balance of trade (current prices)

	1999	2000	2001	2002	2003	2004
RM '000,000	+73,080	+61,810	+53,729	+50,970	+66,200	+77,696
% of total	12.8%	9.0%	8.7%	7.7%	9.6%	8.8%

Imports (2002): RM 303,510,000,000 (microcircuits, transistors, and valves 29.2%; computers/office machines 6.9%; telecommunications equipment 4.3%; other electrical machinery 6.6%). *Major import sources:* Japan 17.8%; U.S. 16.4%; Singapore 12.0%; China 7.8%; Taiwan 5.6%.
Exports (2002): RM 354,480,000,000 (microcircuits, transistors, and valves 20.5%; computers/office machines 18.4%; telecommunications equipment 5.4%; fixed vegetable oils 3.9%; crude petroleum 3.3%). *Major export destinations:* U.S. 20.2%; Singapore 17.1%; Japan 11.2%; Hong Kong 5.7%; China 5.6%.

Transport and communications

Transport. Railroads (2000): route length 2,227 km; passenger-km 1,241,000,-000[10]; metric ton-km cargo 918,000,000[10]. Roads (2000): total length 66,445 km (paved 76%). Vehicles (2002): passenger cars 5,069,412; trucks and buses 764,306. Air transport (2004)[11]: passenger-km 35,298,000,000; metric ton-km cargo 2,068,000,000; airports (1997) 39.

Communications

Medium	date	unit	number	units per 1,000 persons
Daily newspapers	2000	circulation	3,672,000	158
Radio	2000	receivers	9,762,000	420
Television	2002	receivers	5,103,000	210
Telephones	2004	main lines	4,446,300	179
Cellular telephones	2004	subscribers	14,611,900	587
Personal computers	2004	units	4,900,000	197
Internet	2004	users	9,878,200	397

Education and health

Educational attainment (1996). Percentage of population age 25 and over having: no formal schooling 16.7%; primary education 33.7%; secondary 42.8%; higher 6.8%. *Literacy* (2000): total population age 15 and over literate 87.5%; males literate 91.4%; females literate 83.4%.

Education (2002–03)

	schools	teachers	students	student/ teacher ratio
Primary (age 7–12)	7,231[12]	159,041	3,009,009	18.9
Secondary (age 13–19)	1,561[12]	123,171	2,158,820	17.5
Voc., teacher tr.	80[13]	6,665	141,242	21.2
Higher	55[12]	34,955	632,309	18.1

Health (2002): physicians 17,442 (1 per 1,406 persons); hospital beds (2001) 41,927 (1 per 570 persons); infant mortality rate (2004) 5.9.
Food (2002): daily per capita caloric intake 2,881 (vegetable products 82%, animal products 18%); 129% of FAO recommended minimum.

Military

Total active duty personnel (2004): 110,000 (army 72.8%, navy 13.6%, air force 13.6%). *Military expenditure as percentage of GDP* (2003): 2.8%; per capita expenditure U.S.$115.

[1]Includes 44 appointees of the Paramount Ruler; the remaining 26 are indirectly elected. [2]The transfer of government offices to the new federal administrative centre at Putrajaya is occurring between 1999 and 2012. [3]Peg to the U.S. dollar ended in July 2005. [4]Selangor includes population data for Putrajaya. [5]Preliminary. [6]Excludes Sabah and Sarawak. [7]Sabah and Sarawak only. [8]Net of import duties less imputed bank service charges. [9]Imports c.i.f.; exports f.o.b. [10]Peninsular Malaysia and Singapore. [11]Malaysia Airlines and Air Asia only. [12]2000. [13]1999.

Internet resources for further information:
• **Department of Statistics** http://www.statistics.gov.my
• **Central Bank of Malaysia** http://www.bnm.gov.my/

Maldives

Official name: Dhivehi Raajjeyge
Jumhooriyyaa (Republic of Maldives).
Form of government: republic[1] with one
legislative house (Majlis[2] [42[3]]).
Head of state and government:
President[1].
Capital: Male.
Official language: Divehi.
Official religion: Islam.
Monetary unit: 1 Maldivian rufiyaa
(Rf) = 100 laari; valuation (Sept. 1,
2005) 1 U.S.$ = Rf 12.80;
1 £ = Rf 23.57.

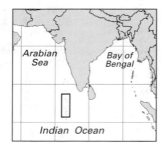

Arabian Sea | *Bay of Bengal* | *Indian Ocean*

Area and population[4]

Administrative atolls	Capitals	area sq mi	area sq km	population 2000 census
North Thiladhunmathi (Haa-Alifu)	Dhidhdhoo	...	...	14,161
South Thiladhunmathi (Haa-Dhaalu)	Nolhivaranfaru	...	...	16,956
North Miladhunmadulu (Shaviyani)	Farukolhu-funadhoo	...	...	11,406
South Miladhunmadulu (Noonu)	Manadhoo	...	...	10,429
North Maalhosmadulu (Raa)	Ugoofaaru	...	...	14,486
South Maalhosmadulu (Baa)	Eydhafushi	...	...	9,612
Faadhippolhu (Lhaviyani)	Naifaru	...	...	9,385
Male (Kaafu)	Thulusdhoo	...	...	13,474
Ari Atoll Uthuru Gofi (Alifu)	Rasdhoo	...	...	5,518
Ari Atoll Dhekunu Gofi (Alifu)	Mahibadhoo	...	...	7,803
Felidhu Atoll (Vaavu)	Felidhoo	...	...	1,753
Mulakatholhu (Meemu)	Muli	...	...	5,084
North Nilandhe Atoll (Faafu)	Magoodhoo	...	...	3,827
South Nilandhe Atoll (Dhaalu)	Kudahuvadhoo	...	...	5,067
Kolhumadulu (Thaa)	Veymandoo	...	...	9,305
Hadhdhunmathi (Laamu)	Hithadhoo	...	...	11,588
North Huvadhu Atoll (Gaafu-Alifu)	Viligili	...	...	8,249
South Huvadhu Atoll (Gaafu-Dhaalu)	Thinadhoo	...	...	11,886
Foammulah (Gnyaviyani)	Foahmulah	...	...	7,528
Addu Atoll (Seenu)	Hithadhoo	...	...	18,515
Capital island				
Male (Maale)		...	...	74,069
TOTAL		115	298	270,101

Demography

Population (2005): 294,000.
Density (2005): persons per sq mi 2,557, persons per sq km 986.6.
Urban-rural (2003): urban 28.8%; rural 71.2%.
Sex distribution (2003): male 50.73%; female 49.27%.
Age breakdown (2003): under 15, 36.1%; 15–29, 31.7%; 30–44, 18.0%; 45–59, 7.9%; 60–74, 5.2%; 75 and over, 1.1%.
Population projection: (2010) 318,000; (2020) 368,000.
Doubling time: 23 years.
Ethnic composition (2000): Maldivian 98.5%; Sinhalese 0.7%; other 0.8%.
Religious affiliation: virtually 100% Sunnī Muslim.
Major city (2000): Male 74,069.

Vital statistics

Birth rate per 1,000 population (2003): 35.7 (world avg. 21.1).
Death rate per 1,000 population (2003): 6.0 (world avg. 9.0).
Natural increase rate per 1,000 population (2003): 29.7 (world avg. 12.1).
Total fertility rate (avg. births per childbearing woman; 2003): 5.3.
Marriage rate per 1,000 population (2003): 10.8.
Divorce rate per 1,000 population (2003): 4.0.
Life expectancy at birth (2003): male 62.0 years; female 64.6 years.
Major causes of death per 100,000 population (2002): communicable diseases 251; ischemic heart diseases 91; malignant neoplasms (cancers) 54; cerebrovascular diseases 49; accidents, violence, and suicide 44; chronic respiratory diseases 43.

National economy

Budget (2003). Revenue: Rf 3,061,800,000 (nontax revenue 54.8%; tax revenue 40.3%, of which import duties 25.6%; grants 4.9%). Expenditures: Rf 3,529,200,000 (general public services 33.6%, of which defense 13.6%; education 20.3%; health 10.6%; transportation and communications 12.3%; debt service 3.8%).
Public debt (external, outstanding; January 2005): U.S.$310,100,000.
Production (metric tons except as noted). Agriculture, forestry, fishing (2004): coconuts 35,000, bananas 3,500, roots and tubers 7,700, taro 350, sweet potatoes 200; fish catch 158,600. Mining and quarrying: coral for construction materials. Manufacturing: details, n.a.; however, major industries include boat building and repairing, coir yarn and mat weaving, coconut and fish processing, lacquerwork, garment manufacturing, and handicrafts. Energy production (consumption): electricity (kW-hr; 2002) 126,000,000 (126,000,000); petroleum products (metric tons; 2002) none (336,000).
Tourism (2003): receipts from visitors U.S.$402,000,000; expenditures by nationals abroad U.S.$46,000,000.
Population economically active (2000): total 87,987; activity rate of total population 32.6% (participation rates: ages 15–64, 55.7%; female 33.7%; unemployed [2001] 2.0%).

Price index (2000 = 100)

	1998	1999	2000	2001	2002	2003	2004
Consumer price index	98.3	101.2	100.0	100.7	101.6	98.7	105.0

Household income and expenditure (2002–03)[5]. Average household size 6.7; average annual income per household Rf 188,743 (U.S.$14,746); sources of income: self-employment 34.5%, wages and salaries 31.5%, rent 13.4%, transfers 8.7%; expenditure: housing and energy 35.8%, food, beverages, and tobacco 29.9%, transportation and communications 7.8%, health 5.2%, clothing and footwear 4.3%, household operations 4.2%.
Gross national product (2004): U.S.$752,000,000 (U.S.$2,510 per capita).

Structure of gross domestic product and labour force

	2003 in value Rf '000,000[6]	2003 % of total value	2000 labour force	2000 % of labour force
Agriculture[7]	694	8.3	11,789	13.4
Mining	46	0.5	473	0.5
Manufacturing	630	7.5	11,081	12.6
Public utilities	273	3.3	1,132	1.3
Construction	275	3.3	3,691	4.2
Transp. and commun.	1,079	12.9	7,873	9.0
Trade	308	3.7	15,606	17.7
Tourism (resorts)	2,482	29.6	...	...
Finance, real estate	1,048	12.5	1,690	1.9
Pub. admin., defense	907	10.8	} 18,089	20.6
Services	144	1.7		
Other	496	5.9	16,563	18.8
TOTAL	8,382	100.0	87,987	100.0

Land use as % of total land area (2000): in temporary crops *c.* 13%, in permanent crops *c.* 17%, in pasture *c.* 3%; overall forest area *c.* 3%.

Foreign trade[8, 9]

Balance of trade (current prices)

	1999	2000	2001	2002	2003	2004
U.S.$'000,000	–310.7	–279.9	–283.3	–259.4	–318.8	–472.0
% of total	62.9%	56.3%	56.2%	49.5%	51.2%	57.7%

Imports (2004): U.S.$644,700,000 (consumer goods 37.2%, of which food products 17.3%; petroleum products 14.4%; construction-related goods 13.3%). *Major import sources:* Singapore 25.1%; Sri Lanka 10.7%; U.A.E. 10.4%; India 10.2%; Malaysia 7.6%.
Exports (2004): U.S.$172,700,000 (domestic exports 70.9%, of which fish 50.6% [including frozen fish 33.2%, canned fish 7.7%], garments 18.4%; reexports [mostly jet fuel] 29.1%). *Major export destinations:* U.S. 26.5%; Thailand 23.5%; Sri Lanka 12.3%; Japan 11.7%; U.K. 9.8%.

Transport and communications

Transport. Railroads: none. Roads: total length, n.a. Vehicles: passenger cars (2005[10]) 2,939; trucks and buses (2003) 1,422. Air transport (2001): passenger-km 385,000,000; airports (1997) with scheduled flights 5.

Communications

Medium	date	unit	number	units per 1,000 persons
Daily newspapers	1996	circulation	5,000	19
Radio	2000[10]	receivers	29,700	109
Television	2000	receivers	10,900	40
Telephones	2005[10]	main lines	31,900	109
Cellular telephones	2005[10]	subscribers	129,100	439
Personal computers	2004	units	36,000	124
Internet	2004	users	19,000	66

Education and health

Educational attainment (2000). Population age 25 and over 71,937; percentage with university education 0.4%. *Literacy* (2003): total population age 15 and over literate 97.4%; males literate 97.4%; females literate 97.3%.

Education (2003)

	schools	teachers	students	student/teacher ratio
Primary (age 6–11)	231	2,216	66,169	29.9
Secondary (age 11–18)	106	1,530	26,967	17.6
Voc., teacher tr.	...	38	1,328	34.9
Higher[11]	1	138	6,898	50.0

Health (2004): physicians 302 (1 per 959 persons); hospital beds 760 (1 per 381 persons); infant mortality rate per 1,000 live births (2004) 15.0.
Food (2002): daily per capita caloric intake 2,548 (vegetable products 76%, animal products 24%); 115% of FAO recommended minimum requirement.

Military

Total active duty personnel (2004): n.a.; the national security service (paramilitary police force) includes an air element and coast guard. *Military expenditure as percentage of GDP* (2004): 5.5%; per capita expenditure U.S.$142.

[1]Constitutional reforms, including the formation of an office of prime minister, the legalization of political parties, and the abolition of the power of the president to name eight members to the Majlis, were expected to be implemented post-2005. [2]Also known or translated as People's Majlis, Citizens' Council, or Citizens' Assembly. [3]Excludes eight nonelective seats. [4]Maldives is divided into 20 administrative districts corresponding to atoll groups; arrangement shown here is from north to south. Total area figures are pre-December 2004 (or pre-Indian Ocean tsunami). [5]Data taken from the Household Income and Expenditure Survey 2002–03, comprising 834 households in both Male and the atolls. [6]At 1995 prices. [7]Primarily fishing. [8]Imports c.i.f.; exports f.o.b. [9]Exports include reexports. [10]June. [11]Maldives College of Higher Education.

Internet resources for further information:
• **Ministry of Planning and National Development**
  http://www.planning.gov.mv
• **Maldives Monetary Authority** http://www.mma.gov.mv

Mali

Official name: République du Mali (Republic of Mali).
Form of government: multiparty republic with one legislative house (National Assembly [147]).
Chief of state: President.
Head of government: Prime Minister.
Capital: Bamako.
Official language: French.
Official religion: none.
Monetary unit: 1 CFA franc (CFAF) = 100 centimes; valuation (Sept. 1, 2005) 1 U.S.$ = CFAF 522.78; 1 £ = CFAF 962.57[1].

Area and population

Regions	Capitals	area sq mi	area sq km	population 1998 census
Gao	Gao	65,858	170,572	495,178
Kayes	Kayes	46,233	119,743	1,424,657
Kidal	Kidal	58,467	151,430	65,524
Koulikoro	Koulikoro	37,007	95,848	1,620,811
Mopti	Mopti	30,509	79,017	1,405,370
Ségou	Ségou	25,028	64,821	1,652,594
Sikasso	Sikasso	27,135	70,280	1,839,747
Tombouctou	Tombouctou (Timbuktu)	191,743	496,611	496,312
District				
Bamako	Bamako	97	252	1,178,977
TOTAL		482,077	1,248,574	10,179,170[2]

Demography

Population (2005): 11,415,000.
Density (2005): persons per sq mi 23.7, persons per sq km 9.1.
Urban-rural (1998): urban 26.9%; rural 73.1%.
Sex distribution (2004): male 49.48%; female 50.52%.
Age breakdown (2004): under 15, 48.0%; 15–29, 27.7%; 30–44, 12.7%; 45–59, 6.7%; 60–74, 4.1%; 75 and over, 0.8%.
Population projection: (2010) 13,060,000; (2020) 17,543,000.
Doubling time: 21 years.
Ethnic composition (2000): Bambara 30.6%; Senufo 10.5%; Fula Macina (Niafunke) 9.6%; Soninke 7.4%; Tuareg 7.0%; Maninka 6.6%; Songhai 6.3%; Dogon 4.3%; Bobo 3.5%; other 14.2%.
Religious affiliation (2000): Muslim c. 82%; traditional beliefs c. 16%; Christian c. 2%.
Major cities (1998): Bamako 1,016,167; Sikasso 113,803; Ségou 90,898; Mopti 79,840; Gao 54,903.

Vital statistics

Birth rate per 1,000 population (2004): 50.3 (world avg. 21.1).
Death rate per 1,000 population (2004): 17.6 (world avg. 9.0).
Natural increase rate per 1,000 population (2004): 32.8 (world avg. 12.1).
Total fertility rate (avg. births per childbearing woman; 2004): 7.5.
Life expectancy at birth (2004): male 46.3 years; female 50.34 years.
Major causes of death per 100,000 population (2002): infectious and parasitic diseases 1,487, of which HIV/AIDS 97; diseases of the circulatory system 135; accidents and injuries 120; malignant neoplasms (cancers) 54; chronic respiratory diseases 36.

National economy

Budget (2002). Revenue: CFAF 379,400,000,000 (tax revenue 82.7%, nontax revenue 17.3%). Expenditures: CFAF 601,500,000,000 (current expenditure 46.7%, of which wages and salaries 14.9%, education 4.9%, interest on public debt 3.5%; capital expenditure 53.3%).
Public debt (external, outstanding; 2003): U.S.$2,910,000,000.
Tourism (2002): receipts from visitors U.S.$104,000,000; expenditures by nationals abroad U.S.$36,000,000.
Population economically active (2001): total 5,895,000; activity rate of total population 53.7% (participation rates: ages 15–64, n.a.; female, n.a.; unemployed, n.a.).

Price index (2000 = 100)

	1998	1999	2000	2001	2002	2003	2004
Consumer price index	101.9	100.7	100.0	105.2	110.5	109.0	105.6

Production (metric tons except as noted). Agriculture, forestry, fishing (2004): rice 870,000, millet 815,000, sorghum 650,000, seed cotton 600,000, corn (maize) 365,000, sugarcane 350,000, peanuts (groundnuts) 156,000, sweet potatoes 74,500; livestock (number of live animals) 12,036,000 goats, 8,364,000 sheep, 7,500,000 cattle, 720,000 asses, 472,000 camels, 172,000 horses; roundwood (2004) 5,378,031 cu m; fish catch (2003) 101,008. Mining and quarrying (2003): salt 6,000; gold 45,535 kg[3]. Manufacturing (2000): sugar 29,100; soap 10,097[4]; cement 10,000; soft drinks 68,609 hectolitres[4]; beer 41,690 hectolitres[4]; shoes 111,000 pairs[4]; cigarettes [1999] 51,400 cartons. Energy production (consumption): electricity (kW-hr; 2002) 417,000,000 (417,000,000); coal, none (none); crude petroleum, none (none); petroleum products (metric tons; 2002) none (180,000); natural gas, none (none).
Household income and expenditure. Average household size (2000) 5.6; average annual income per household: n.a.; sources of income: n.a.; expenditure: n.a.
Gross national product (2004): U.S.$4,335,000,000 (U.S.$360 per capita).

Structure of gross domestic product and labour force

	2002 in value CFAF '000,000	2002 % of total value	2001 labour force	2001 % of labour force
Agriculture	799,200	33.9	4,580,000	77.7
Mining	251,300	10.6		
Manufacturing	162,200	6.9		
Construction	119,200	5.1		
Public utilities	36,700	1.6		
Transp. and commun.	281,400	11.9	1,315,000	22.3
Trade	158,400	6.7		
Finance				
Pub. admin., defense	250,200	10.6		
Services	97,200	4.1	...	...
Other	203,500[5]	8.6[5]	...	...
TOTAL	2,359,300	100.0	5,895,000	100.0

Land use as % of total land area (2000): in temporary crops 3.8%, in permanent crops, negligible, in pasture 24.6%; overall forest area 10.8%.

Foreign trade

Balance of trade (current prices)

	1999	2000	2001	2002	2003	2004
CFAF '000,000,000	−21.2	−33.4	−7.0	+113.4	−35.1	−16.0
% of total	2.9%	4.1%	0.7%	10.2%	3.2%	1.5%

Imports (2004): CFAF 558,300,000,000 (machinery and apparatus 39.0%, petroleum products 21.0%, food products 13.2%). *Major import sources* (2003)[6]: African countries c. 50%, of which Senegal c. 8%, Côte d'Ivoire c. 7%; France c. 15%; Germany c. 4%.
Exports (2004): CFAF 542,300,000,000 (gold 50.0%, raw cotton and cotton products 36.1%). *Major export destinations* (2003)[7]: Thailand c. 14%; China c. 12%; India c. 8%; Italy c. 8%; Bangladesh c. 6%.

Transport and communications

Transport. Railroads (1999): route length 453 mi, 729 km; passenger-mi 130,000,000, passenger-km 210,000,000; short ton-mi cargo 165,000,000, metric ton-km cargo 241,000,000. Roads (1999): total length 9,383 mi, 15,100 km (paved 12%). Vehicles (2001): passenger cars 18,900; trucks and buses 31,700. Air transport (2001)[8]: passenger-km 130,000,000; metric ton-km cargo, n.a.; airports (1999) 9.

Communications

Medium	date	unit	number	units per 1,000 persons
Daily newspapers	1997	circulation	45,000	4.6
Radio	2001	receivers	1,976,000	180
Television	2002	receivers	376,200	33
Telephones	2004	main lines	74,900	6.8
Cellular phones	2004	subscribers	400,000	36
Personal computers	2004	units	42,000	3.8
Internet	2004	users	50,000	4.5

Education and health

Educational attainment: n.a. *Literacy* (2000): percentage of total population age 15 and over literate 41.5%; males literate 48.9%; females literate 34.4%.

Education (2000–01)

	schools	teachers	students	student/ teacher ratio
Primary (age 6–14)	2,871	14,962	1,115,563	74.5
Secondary (age 15–17)	...	...	257,574	...
Vocational	...	...	47,883	...
Higher	...	1,312	28,000	21.3

Health: physicians (2000) 529 (1 per 19,040 persons); hospital beds (1998) 2,412 (1 per 4,168 persons); infant mortality rate per 1,000 live births (2004) 111.2.
Food (2002): daily per capita caloric intake 2,174 (vegetable products 90%, animal products 10%); 93% of FAO recommended minimum requirement.

Military

Total active duty personnel (2004): 7,350 (army 100.0%). *Military expenditure as percentage of GDP* (2003): 1.9%; per capita expenditure U.S.$8.

[1]Formerly pegged to the French franc, and since Jan. 1, 2002, to the euro at the rate of €1 = CFAF 655.96. [2]Excludes 772,006 Malians living abroad. [3]Excludes artisanal production of c. 2,000 kg. [4]1995. [5]Import taxes. [6]Estimated figures. [7]Estimated figures based on c. 1/4th of total exports. [8]Represents 1/11 of the traffic of the defunct (from 2002) Air Afrique. Mali did not have a national airline as of early 2005.

Internet resources for further information:
- La Banque de France: La Zone Franc
  http://www.banque-france.fr/fr/eurosys/zonefr/page2_2004.htm
- Direction Nationale de la Statistique et de l'Informatique
  http://www.dnsi.gov.ml/permanent.htm

Malta

Official name: Repubblikka ta' Malta (Maltese); Republic of Malta (English).
Form of government: unitary multiparty republic with one legislative house (House of Representatives [65]).
Chief of state: President.
Head of government: Prime Minister.
Capital: Valletta.
Official languages: Maltese; English.
Official religion: Roman Catholicism.
Monetary unit: 1 Maltese lira (Lm) = 100 cents = 1,000 mils; valuation (Sept. 1, 2005)
1 U.S.$ = Lm 0.34; 1 £ = Lm 0.63.

Area and population	area		population
Islands/statistical districts[2]	sq mi	sq km	2004[1] estimate
Comino	1.4	3.5	4
Gozo	25.2	65.2	31,613
Malta	95.1[3]	246.4	368,250
Northern District	28.5	73.7	49,395
Northern Harbour	9.3	24.1	122,913
South Eastern District	19.2	49.7	55,199
Southern Harbour	10.1	26.1	85,629
Western District	28.1	72.8	55,114
TOTAL	121.7	315.1	399,867[4]

Demography

Population (2005): 404,000.
Density (2005): persons per sq mi 3,311, persons per sq km 1,283.
Urban-rural (2003): urban 91.7%; rural 8.3%.
Sex distribution (2004[1]): male 49.54%; female 50.46%.
Age breakdown (2004[1]): under 15, 18.2%; 15–29, 22.1%; 30–44, 20.0%; 45–59, 22.3%; 60–74, 12.1%; 75 and over, 5.3%.
Population projection: (2010) 422,000; (2020) 455,000.
Ethnic composition (2000): Maltese 93.8%; British 2.1%; Arab 2.0%; Italian 1.5%; other 0.6%.
Religious affiliation (2000): Roman Catholic 94.5%; unaffiliated Christian 2.7%; Protestant 0.8%; Muslim 0.5%; nonreligious 1.0%; other 0.5%.
Major localities (2004[1]): Birkirkara 22,435; Qormi 18,547; Mosta 18,070; Zabbar 15,134; Valletta 7,137 (urban agglomeration [2003] 83,000).

Vital statistics

Birth rate per 1,000 population (2003): 10.1 (world avg. 21.1); legitimate 83.2%; illegitimate 16.8%.
Death rate per 1,000 population (2003): 7.9 (world avg. 9.0).
Natural increase rate per 1,000 population (2003): 2.2 (world avg. 12.1).
Total fertility rate (avg. births per childbearing woman; 2004): 1.4.
Marriage rate per 1,000 population (2003): 6.1.
Life expectancy at birth (2004): male 76.4 years; female 80.4 years.
Major causes of death per 100,000 population (2002): diseases of the circulatory system 335.4; malignant neoplasms (cancers) 185.6; diseases of the respiratory system 88.0; accidents, poisonings, and violence 31.4; endocrine and metabolic diseases 26.3; diseases of the digestive system 26.3.

National economy

Budget (2001). Revenue: Lm 797,400,000 (social security 22.5%; income tax 20.9%; value-added tax 14.4%; grants and loans 13.6%). Expenditures: Lm 766,700,000 (recurrent expenditures 80.2%, of which social security 24.1%, education 6.1%; capital expenditure 10.5%; public debt service 9.3%).
Public debt (2004): U.S.$878,700,000[5].
Production (metric tons except where noted). Agriculture, forestry, fishing (2004): potatoes 23,000, melons 12,800, wheat 9,500, tomatoes 9,000, onions 8,100, cabbages 2,900, barley 2,200; livestock (number of live animals) 73,100 pigs, 17,900 cattle, 14,900 sheep; roundwood, n.a.; fish catch (2003) 1,070. Quarrying (2004): limestone 1,200,000 cu m, small quantities of salt. Manufacturing (value added in Lm '000,000; 1998): telecommunications equipment and electronics 149; food products 69; wearing apparel 63; beverages 55; printing and publishing 52. Energy production (consumption): electricity (kW-hr; 2002) 1,951,000,000 (1,951,000,000); coal (metric tons; 2002) none (326,000); crude petroleum none (none); petroleum products (metric tons; 2002) none (722,000); natural gas, none (none).
Population economically active (2003): total 159,638; activity rate of total population 39.9% (participation rates: ages 15–59, 60.8%; female 31.3%; unemployed 7.6%).

Price and earnings indexes (2000 = 100)	1998	1999	2000	2001	2002	2003	2004
Consumer price index	95.6	97.7	100.0	102.9	105.2	105.7	108.7
Earnings index	92.2	95.8	100.0	104.5	111.1	121.3	...

Household income and expenditure. Average household size (2001) 3.1; average annual income per household (2000) Lm 7,945 (U.S.$18,155); sources of income (1993): wages and salaries 63.8%, professional and unincorporated enterprises 19.3%, rents, dividends, and interest 16.9%; expenditure (2000): food and beverages 36.6%, transportation and communications 23.4%, recreation, entertainment, and education 9.4%, household furnishings and operations 7.6%.
Tourism (2003): receipts from visitors U.S.$696,000,000; expenditures by nationals abroad U.S.$215,000,000.

Gross national product (2004): U.S.$4,913,000,000 (U.S.$12,250 per capita).

Structure of gross domestic product and labour force				
	2002		2003	
	in value Lm '000	% of total value	labour force	% of labour force
Agriculture	39,297	2.3	2,488	1.6
Manufacturing	326,468	19.4	28,117	17.6
Mining	48,315	2.9	...	...
Construction			11,214	7.0
Public utilities	6	6	4,116	2.6
Transp. and commun.	88,704	5.3	11,309	7.1
Trade	155,319	9.3	33,990	21.3
Finance, real estate	132,182	7.9	12,612	7.9
Pub. admin., defense	464,349[6]	27.6[6]	13,248	8.3
Services	170,235	10.1	27,799	17.4
Other	255,575[7]	15.2[7]	14,745[8]	9.2[8]
TOTAL	1,680,644	100.0	159,638	100.0

Land use as % of total land area (2000): in temporary crops *c.* 25%, in permanent crops *c.* 3%, in pasture, n.a.; overall forest area, negligible.

Foreign trade[9]

Balance of trade (current prices)	1999	2000	2001	2002	2003	2004
Lm '000,000	−345.1	−420.0	−345.7	−266.4	−351.3	−407.6
% of total	17.9%	16.4%	16.4%	12.2%	15.9%	18.3%

Imports (2004): Lm 1,316,900,000 (machinery and transport equipment 47.4%, food 9.2%, chemicals and chemical products 8.4%, mineral fuels 8.0%). *Major import sources:* Italy 17.9%; France 17.7%; U.K. 9.6%; Germany 9.1%; Singapore 6.9%.
Exports (2004): Lm 909,300,000 (machinery and transport equipment [mostly electronic microcircuits] 63.9%, basic manufactures 18.8%, refined petroleum 4.4%). *Major export destinations:* Singapore 15.2%; U.S. 11.6%; France 10.9%; U.K. 10.0%; Germany 8.9%.

Transport and communications

Transport. Railroads: none. Roads (2002): total length 1,380 mi, 2,222 km (paved 90%). Vehicles (2005[10]): passenger cars 207,055; trucks and buses 45,054. Air transport (2004)[11]: passenger-km 2,653,000,000; metric ton-km cargo 10,672,000; airports (1999) with scheduled flights 1.

Communications				units per 1,000 persons
Medium	date	unit	number	
Daily newspapers	1996	circulation	54,000	145
Radio	1997	receivers	255,000	680
Television	2000	receivers	217,000	556
Telephones	2004	main lines	210,700	525
Cellular telephones	2004	subscribers	308,400	769
Personal computers	2004	units	126,000	318
Internet	2004	users	301,000	760

Education and health

Educational attainment (2001). Percentage of population age 15 and over having: no formal schooling 4.3%; primary education 34.4%; general secondary 37.6%; vocational secondary 5.7%; some postsecondary 11.8%; undergraduate 5.4%; graduate 0.8%. *Literacy* (2000): total population age 15 and over literate 279,000 (92.1%).

Education (2002–03)	schools[12]	teachers	students	student/ teacher ratio
Primary (age 5–10)	111	1,745	31,710	18.2
Secondary (age 11–17)	59	3,289	35,229	10.7
Voc., teacher tr.	22	551	2,327	4.2
Higher	...	579	8,946	15.5

Health (2002): physicians 1,084 (1 per 365 persons); hospital beds 1,932 (1 per 205 persons); infant mortality rate per 1,000 live births (2003) 4.0.
Food (2002): daily per capita caloric intake 3,587 (vegetable products 73%, animal products 27%); 145% of FAO recommended minimum requirement.

Military

Total active duty personnel (2004): 2,140 (armed forces includes air and marine elements). *Military expenditure as percentage of GDP* (2003): 0.8%[13]; per capita expenditure U.S.$100[13].

[1]January 1. [2]Actual local administration in 2003 was based on 3 regions divided into 68 local councils. [3]Detail does not add to total given because of rounding. [4]Includes foreign workers and foreign residents (11,000 persons as of Jan. 1, 2004). [5]Government guaranteed debt. [6]Pub. admin., defense includes Public utilities. [7]Indirect taxes less subsidies. [8]Includes 2,149 not adequately defined and 12,596 unemployed. [9]Imports c.i.f.; exports f.o.b. [10]June 30. [11]Air Malta only. [12]1995–96. [13]Excludes expenditure on military pensions.

Internet resources for further information:
• **National Statistics Office** http://www.nso.gov.mt
• **Central Bank of Malta**
  http://www.centralbankmalta.com

Marshall Islands

Official name: Majōl (Marshallese);
Republic of the Marshall Islands
(English).
Form of government: unitary republic
with two legislative houses (Council
of Iroij [12][1]; Nitijela [33]).
Head of state and government:
President.
Capital: Majuro[2].
Official languages: Marshallese
(Kajin-Majōl); English.
Official religion: none.
Monetary unit: 1 U.S. dollar
(U.S.$) = 100 cents; valuation
(Sept. 1, 2005) 1 U.S.$ = £0.54.

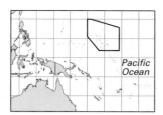
Pacific
Ocean

Area and population	area		population
Atolls/Islands[3]	sq mi	sq km	1999 census
Ailinglaplap	5.67	14.69	1,959
Ailuk	2.07	5.36	514
Arno	5.00	12.95	2,069
Aur	2.17	5.62	537
Bikini	2.32	6.01	13
Ebon	2.22	5.75	902
Enewetak	2.26	5.85	853
Jabat	0.22	0.57	95
Jaluit	4.38	11.34	1,669
Kili	0.36	0.93	774
Kwajalein	6.33	16.39	10,903
Lae	0.56	1.45	322
Lib	0.36	0.93	147
Likiep	3.96	10.26	527
Majuro	3.75	9.71	23,682
Maloelap	3.79	9.82	856
Mejit	0.72	1.86	416
Mili	6.15	15.93	1,032
Namorik	1.07	2.77	772
Namu	2.42	6.27	903
Rongelap	3.07	7.95	19
Ujae	0.72	1.86	440
Ujelang	0.67	1.74	0
Utirik	0.94	2.43	433
Wotho	1.67	4.33	145
Wotje	3.16	8.18	866
Other atolls	4.04	10.46	0
TOTAL	70.05[4]	181.43[4, 5]	50,848

Demography

Population (2005): 56,300.
Density (2005): persons per sq mi 804.3, persons per sq km 311.0.
Urban-rural (2004): urban 65.0%; rural 35.0%.
Sex distribution (2004): male 51.10%; female 48.90%.
Age breakdown (2003): under 15, 39.2%; 15–29, 30.7%; 30–44, 16.4%; 45–59, 9.6%; 60–74, 3.1%; 75 and over, 1.0%.
Population projection: (2010) 61,000; (2020) 72,000.
Doubling time: 24 years.
Ethnic composition (nationality; 2000): Marshallese 88.5%; U.S. white 6.5%; other Pacific Islanders and East Asians 5.0%.
Religious affiliation (1999): Protestant 80.6%, of which Assemblies of God 25.8% (remainder is significantly United Church of Christ); Roman Catholic 8.4%; other 11.0%.
Major towns (1999): Majuro[2] 19,300; Ebeye 9,300; Laura 2,300; Ajeltake 1,200; Enewetak 820.

Vital statistics

Birth rate per 1,000 population (2004): 33.9 (world avg. 21.1).
Death rate per 1,000 population (2004): 4.9 (world avg. 9.0).
Natural increase rate per 1,000 population (2004): 29.0 (world avg. 12.1).
Total fertility rate (avg. births per childbearing woman; 2004): 4.0.
Life expectancy at birth (2004): male 67.8 years; female 71.7 years.
Major causes of death per 100,000 population (2003–04; registered deaths only): sepsis/septicemia 83.7; malignant neoplasms (cancers) 41.9; myocardial infarction 27.3; pneumonia 25.5; suicide 23.7.

National economy

Budget (2002). Revenue: U.S.$83,600,000 (U.S. government grants 70.3%, tax revenue 22.2%, nontax revenue 7.5%). Expenditures: U.S.$74,000,000 (current expenditure 79.3%, capital expenditure 20.7%).
Public debt (external, outstanding; 2004): U.S.$90,000,000.
Production (metric tons except as noted). Agriculture, forestry, fishing (value of production for household consumption in U.S.$'000; 1999): fish 3,920; pork 1,496; breadfruit 646; chickens 591; coconuts 434; taro 166; bananas 108; fish catch (2003) 38,375, of which skipjack 23,427. Mining and quarrying: for local construction only. Manufacturing (2003): copra 3,885; coconut oil and processed (chilled or frozen) fish are important products; the manufacture of handicrafts and personal items (clothing, mats, boats, etc.) by individuals is also significant. Energy production (consumption): electricity (kW-hr; 2002) 79,764,000 (79,764,000); coal, none (none); petroleum products, n.a. (n.a.).
Household income and expenditure (2002)[6]. Average household size 7.7; annual median income per household (1999) U.S.$6,840; sources of income: wages and salaries 89.3%, rent and investments 2.4%, social security 2.2%; expenditure: food 24.3%, transportation 14.0%, housing and energy 13.1%, education and communication 6.9%, home furnishings 3.7%.

Gross national product (2004): U.S.$142,000,000 (U.S.$2,710 per capita).

Structure of gross domestic product and labour force				
	2001		1999	
	in value U.S.$'000	% of total value	labour force	% of labour force
Agriculture	10,296.1	10.4	2,114	14.4
Mining	291.4	0.3	—	—
Manufacturing	4,489.5	4.5	761	5.2
Public utilities	3,402.2	3.4	258	1.8
Construction	11,314.1	11.4	848	5.8
Transp. and commun.	5,044.8	5.1	763	5.2
Trade, restaurants, hotels	16,937.3	17.1	788	5.4
Finance, insurance, real estate	15,458.2	15.6	559	3.8
Public administration, services	31,043.6	31.3	3,803	25.9
Other	896.7[7]	0.9[7]	4,783[8]	32.6[8]
TOTAL	99,173.8[5]	100.0	14,677	100.0[5]

Population economically active (1999): total 14,677; activity rate of total population 28.9% (participation rates: ages 15–64, 52.1%; female 34.1%; unemployed [2000] 30.9%).

Price index (2000 = 100)[9]							
	1997	1998	1999	2000	2001	2002	2003
Consumer price index	106.5	103.3	98.8	100.0	98.7	100.0	99.7

Tourism (2002): receipts U.S.$4,000,000; expenditures, n.a.
Land use as % of total land area (2000): in temporary crops c. 17%, in permanent crops c. 39%, in pasture c. 22%; overall forest area, n.a.

Foreign trade[10]

Balance of trade (current prices)						
	1995	1996	1997	1998	1999	2000
U.S.$'000,000	−52.0	−53.6	−45.2	−61.5	−61.2	−60.9
% of total	53.0%	58.6%	58.9%	84.1%	79.9%	80.8%

Imports (2000): U.S.$68,200,000 (mineral fuels and lubricants 43.6%; machinery and transport equipment 16.9%; food, beverages, and tobacco 10.9%). *Major import sources:* U.S. 61.4%; Japan 5.1%; Australia 2.0%; Hong Kong 1.9%; Taiwan 1.3%.
Exports (2000): U.S.$7,300,000 (chilled and frozen fish, n.a.; copra cake 16.2%; crude coconut oil 14.7%; aquarium fish 6.2%). *Major export destinations:* U.S. c. 71%; other c. 29%.

Transport and communications

Transport. Roads (2002): only Majuro and Kwajalein have paved roads (40.0 mi, 64.5 km). Vehicles (2002): passenger cars 1,910; trucks and buses 193. Air transport (2004)[11]: passenger-km 38,128,000; metric ton-km cargo 453,000; airports (2002) 32.

Communications				
Medium	date	unit	number	units per 1,000 persons
Telephones	2003	main lines	4,500	83
Cellular telephones	2003	subscribers	600	11
Personal computers	2004	units	5,000	90
Internet	2004	users	2,000	36

Education and health

Educational attainment (1999). Percentage of population age 25 and over having: no formal schooling 3.1%; elementary education 35.5%; secondary 46.5%; some higher 12.3%; undergraduate degree 1.7%; advanced degree 0.9%. *Literacy* (2000): total population age 15 and over literate 92.0%; males literate 92.0%; females literate 92.0%.

Education (2002–03)				
	schools	teachers	students	student/teacher ratio
Primary (age 6–14)	100	703	10,957	15.6
Secondary (age 15–18)	17	202	3,147	15.6
Higher	2	...	3,330	...

Health: physicians (2003–04) 32 (1 per 1,717 persons); hospital beds (2002) 140 (1 per 380 persons); infant mortality rate per 1,000 live births (2004) 30.5.

Military

The United States provides for the defense of the Republic of the Marshall Islands under the 1984 and 2003 compacts of free association.

[1]Council of Iroij is an advisory body only. [2]Local name of town is DUD (an acronym for Delap [Woja], Uliga, and Djarrit [Rita]—three small islands now merged by landfill). [3]Four districts centred at Majuro, Ebeye, Wotje, and Jaluit make up the local government structure. [4]Land area only; excludes lagoon area of 4,507 sq mi (11,673 sq km). [5]Detail does not add to total given because of rounding. [6]Based on the 2002 Household Income and Expenditure Survey, comprising 5,074 respondents in 657 households. [7]Import duties less imputed bank service charges. [8]Includes 4,536 unemployed and 247 undistributed employees. [9]As of midyear. [10]Imports c.i.f.; exports f.o.b. [11]Air Marshall Islands only.

Internet resources for further information:
• **Secretariat of the Pacific Community: PRISM**
  http://www.spc.org.nc/prism/country/country.html
• **U.S. Office of Insular Affairs http://www.pacificweb.org**

Martinique

Official name: Département de la Martinique (Department of Martinique).
Political status: overseas department (France) with two legislative houses (General Council [45]; Regional Council [41]).
Chief of state: President of France.
Heads of government: Prefect (for France); President of the General Council (for Martinique); President of the Regional Council (for Martinique).
Capital: Fort-de-France.
Official language: French.
Official religion: none.
Monetary unit: 1 euro (€) = 100 cents; valuation (Sept. 1, 2005) 1 U.S.$ = €0.80; 1 £ = €1.47[1].

Area and population

Arrondissements	Capitals	area sq mi	area sq km	population 1999 census
Fort-de-France	Fort-de-France	66	171	166,139
La Trinité	La Trinité	131	338	85,006
Le Marin	Le Marin	158	409	106,818
Saint-Pierre	Saint-Pierre	81	210	23,464
TOTAL		436	1,128	381,427

Demography

Population (2005): 396,000.
Density (2005): persons per sq mi 908.3, persons per sq km 351.1.
Urban-rural (2003): urban 95.7%; rural 4.3%.
Sex distribution (2002[2]): male 47.16%; female 52.84%.
Age breakdown (2001): under 15, 23.1%; 15–29, 23.3%; 30–44, 26.3%; 45–59, 13.8%; 60–74, 9.1%; 75 and over, 4.4%.
Population projection: (2010) 401,000; (2020) 405,000.
Doubling time: 85 years.
Ethnic composition (2000): mixed race (black/white/Asian) 93.4%; French (metropolitan and Martinique white) 3.0%; East Indian 1.9%; other 1.7%.
Religious affiliation (2000): Roman Catholic 86.0%; Protestant 5.6% (mostly Seventh-day Adventist); other Christian 5.4%; other 3.0%.
Major communes (2003): Fort-de-France 96,400; Le Lamentin 36,400; Schoelcher 21,400; Le Robert (1999) 21,201; Sainte-Marie 20,600.

Vital statistics

Birth rate per 1,000 population (2004): 14.6 (world avg. 21.1); (1997) legitimate 31.8%; illegitimate 68.2%.
Death rate per 1,000 population (2004): 6.4 (world avg. 9.0).
Natural increase rate per 1,000 population (2004): 8.2 (world avg. 12.1).
Total fertility rate (avg. births per childbearing woman; 2004): 1.8.
Marriage rate per 1,000 population (2002): 3.9.
Divorce rate per 1,000 population (2001): 1.2.
Life expectancy at birth (2004): male 79.4 years; female 78.4 years.
Major causes of death per 100,000 population (1999): diseases of the circulatory system 219.8; malignant neoplasms (cancers) 151.6; accidents, poisoning, and violence 52.3; diseases of the respiratory system 43.2; endocrine and metabolic disorders 35.4; diseases of the digestive system 29.4.

National economy

Budget (1999). Revenue: F 1,298,000,000 (general receipts from French central government and local administrative bodies 45.0%; tax receipts 34.0%, of which indirect taxes 19.5%, direct taxes 14.5%). Expenditures: F 1,298,000,000 (health and social assistance 42.0%; wages and salaries 16.7%; other administrative services 7.2%; debt amortization 5.0%).
Public debt (1994): U.S.$186,700,000.
Production (metric tons except as noted). Agriculture, forestry, fishing (2004): bananas 300,000, sugarcane 193,000, roots and tubers 21,300, pineapples 18,000, plantains 18,000, yams 7,500, tomatoes 6,700, lettuce 5,000, cucumbers and gherkins 4,000, melons 2,700, sweet potatoes 1,200, coconuts 1,150; livestock (number of live animals) 25,000 cattle, 20,000 pigs, 18,000 sheep, 13,500 goats; roundwood 12,000 cu m; fish catch (2003) 6,200. Mining and quarrying (2003): salt 200,000, pumice 130,000. Manufacturing (2004): cement 224,090; sugar 4,140; rum 81,091 hectolitres; other products include clothing, fabricated metals, and yawls and sails. Energy production (consumption): electricity (kW-hr; 2002) 1,180,000,000 (1,180,000,000); coal, none (none); crude petroleum (barrels; 2002) none (6,500,000); petroleum products (metric tons; 2002) 801,000 (606,000); natural gas, none (none).
Household income and expenditure. Average household size (1999) 3.0; annual net income per household (1997) €29,516 (U.S.$33,174); sources of income (2000): wages and salaries 54.7%, inheritance or endowment 14.0%, self-employment 12.7%, other 18.6%; expenditure (1993): food and beverages 32.1%, transportation and communications 20.7%, housing and energy 10.6%, household durable goods 9.4%, clothing and footwear 8.0%.
Tourism (2003): receipts from visitors U.S.$247,000,000; number of visitors 722,000.
Population economically active (1999): total 173,950; activity rate of total population 45.6% (participation rates: ages 15–59, 71.6%; female 50.3%; unemployed [November 2004] 24.1%).

Price and earnings indexes (2000 = 100)

	1998	1999	2000	2001	2002	2003	2004
Consumer price index	98.6	99.0	100.0	102.1	104.3	106.4	108.6
Monthly earnings index[6]	99.5	99.5	100.0	...	...	...	...

Gross national product (2003): U.S.$5,780,000,000 (U.S.$14,730 per capita).

Structure of gross domestic product and labour force

	2001 in value €'000	2001 % of total value	1999 labour force	1999 % of labour force
Agriculture, fishing	307,835	5.6	8,384	4.8
Mining	40,884	0.8 }	7,732	4.4
Manufacturing	212,490	3.9		
Construction	391,642	7.2	7,070	4.1
Public utilities	67,017	1.2	1,326	0.8
Transp. and commun.	341,724	6.2	4,783	2.7
Trade, restaurants, hotels	947,777	17.3	16,530	9.5
Finance, real estate, insurance	1,447,214	26.4	12,317	7.1
Pub. admin., defense	610,731	11.2	19,927	11.5
Services	1,370,843	25.0	37,998	21.8
Other	−264,430[3]	−4.8[3]	57,883[4]	33.3[4]
TOTAL	5,473,726[5]	100.0	173,950	100.0

Land use as % of total land area (2000): in temporary crops *c.* 10%, in permanent crops *c.* 9%, in pasture *c.* 11%; overall forest area *c.* 44%.

Foreign trade[7]

Balance of trade (current prices)

€'000,000	1999	2000	2001	2002	2003	2004
€'000,000	−1,355	−1,448	−1,576	−1,530	...	−1,661
% of total	72.2%	71.1%	71.8%	70.2%	...	73.5%

Imports (2002): €1,855,000,000 (products for agricultural industry and food 18.5%, automobiles 12.2%, mineral fuels 9.7%, chemicals and chemical products 7.9%). *Major import sources:* France 64.5%; Venezuela 5.9%; Netherlands Antilles 3.8%; Germany 3.3%; Italy 2.7%.
Exports (2002): €325,000,000 (agricultural products [significantly bananas] 42.8%, refined petroleum 20.0%, processed foods and beverages [significantly rum] 19.1%). *Major export destinations:* France 68.9%; Guadeloupe 19.1%; French Guiana 4.0%.

Transport and communications

Transport. Railroads: none. Roads (2000): total length 1,308 mi, 2,105 km (paved [1988] 75%). Vehicles (1998): passenger cars 147,589; trucks and buses 35,615. Air transport (2001): passenger arrivals 706,929, passenger departures 701,597; cargo loaded 5,656 metric tons; cargo unloaded 9,303 metric tons; airports (2000) 1.

Communications

Medium	date	unit	number	units per 1,000 persons
Daily newspapers	1996	circulation	30,000	79
Radio	1997	receivers	82,000	213
Television	1999	receivers	62,000	161
Telephones	2001	main lines	172,192	417
Cellular telephones	2002	subscribers	319,900	790
Personal computers	2001	units	52,000	130
Internet	2002	users	40,000	103

Education and health

Educational attainment (1999). Percentage of population age 20 and over having: unknown, or no formal education through lower secondary education 63.6%; vocational 16.7%; upper secondary 9.2%; incomplete higher 5.0%; complete higher 5.5%. *Literacy* (2003): percentage of total population age 15 and over literate 97.7%; males literate 97.4%; females literate 98.1%.

Education (2004–05)

	schools[8]	teachers	students	student/teacher ratio
Primary (age 6–11)	273	1,971[8]	49,615	...
Secondary (age 12–18)	77	2,024[8]	38,568	...
Vocational	14	896[9]	12,095	...
Higher	...	3,190[8]	12,000[10]	...

Health (2003[2]): physicians 909 (1 per 430 persons); hospital beds 2,338 (1 per 167 persons); infant mortality rate per 1,000 live births (2004) 7.3.
Food (1998): daily per capita caloric intake 2,865 (vegetable products 75%, animal products 25%); 118% of FAO recommended minimum requirement.

Military

Total active duty personnel (2004): 4,100 French troops (including troops stationed in Guadeloupe).

---

[1]The French franc was the former monetary unit; on Jan. 1, 2002, F 6.56 = €1. [2]January 1. [3]Unattributed charges. [4]Includes 910 activities not defined and 56,973 unemployed. [5]Detail does not add to total given because of rounding. [6]Based on minimum-level wage of public employees. [7]Imports c.i.f.; exports f.o.b. [8]2002–03. [9]1995–96. [10]Total enrollment of the University of the Antilles and French Guiana at 7 sites.

Internet resources for further information:
• **INSEE: Martinique http://www.insee.fr/fr/insee_regions/Martinique**
• **Martinique Chamber of Commerce and Industry http://www.martinique.cci.fr**

Mauritania

Official name: Al-Jumhūrīyah
al-Islāmīyah al-Mūrītānīyah (Arabic)
(Islamic Republic of Mauritania).
Form of government: military regime[1].
Head of state and government:
Chairman of MCJD[2] assisted by the
Prime Minister.
Capital: Nouakchott.
Official language: Arabic[3].
Official religion: Islam.
Monetary unit: 1 ouguiya (UM) =
5 khoums; valuation (Sept. 1, 2005)
1 U.S.$ = UM 268.17;
1 £ = UM 493.77.

Area and population

Regions	Capitals	area sq mi	area sq km	population 2000 census
El-'Açâba	Kiffa	14,100	36,600	242,265
Adrar	Atar	83,100	215,300	69,542
Brakna	Aleg	13,000	33,800	247,006
Dakhlet Nouadhibou	Nouadhibou	8,600	22,300	79,516
Gorgol	Kaédi	5,300	13,600	242,711
Guidimaka	Sélibaby	4,000	10,300	177,707
Hodh ech-Chargui	Néma	70,600	182,700	281,600
Hodh el-Gharbi	'Ayoûn el-'Atroûs	20,600	53,400	212,156
Inchiri	Akjoujt	18,100	46,800	11,500
Tagant	Tidjikdja	36,800	95,200	76,620
Tiris Zemmour	Zouérate	97,600	252,900	41,121
Trarza	Rosso	25,800	66,800	268,220
Capital District				
Nouakchott	Nouakchott	400	1,000	558,195
TOTAL		398,000	1,030,700	2,508,159

Demography

Population (2005): 3,069,000.
Density (2005): persons per sq mi 7.7, persons per sq km 3.0.
Urban-rural (2003): urban 61.8%; rural 38.2%.
Sex distribution (2004): male 49.49%; female 50.51%.
Age breakdown (2004): under 15, 45.9%; 15–29, 26.9%; 30–44, 15.6%; 45–59, 7.9%; 60–74, 3.2%; 75 and over, 0.5%.
Population projection: (2010) 3,520,000; (2020) 4,473,000.
Doubling time: 24 years.
Ethnic composition (2003)[4]: black African-Arab-Berber (Black Moor) 40%; Arab-Berber (White Moor) 30%; black African (mostly Wolof, Tukulor, Soninke, and Fulani) 30%.
Religious affiliation (2000): Sunnī Muslim 99.1%; traditional beliefs 0.5%; Christian 0.3%; other 0.1%.
Major cities (2000): Nouakchott 558,195; Nouadhibou 72,337; Rosso 48,922; Boghé 37,531; Adel Bagrou 36,007.

Vital statistics

Birth rate per 1,000 population (2004): 41.8 (world avg. 21.1).
Death rate per 1,000 population (2004): 12.7 (world avg. 9.0).
Natural increase rate per 1,000 population (2004): 29.1 (world avg. 12.1).
Total fertility rate (avg. births per childbearing woman; 2004): 6.0.
Life expectancy at birth (2004): male 50.2 years; female 54.6 years.

National economy

Budget (2002). Revenue: UM 101,000,000,000 (fishing royalties 51.2%; tax revenue 38.7%, of which taxes on goods and services 19.3%, income taxes 12.0%, import taxes 6.2%; revenue from public enterprises 4.8%; capital revenue 2.3%; other 3.0%). Expenditures: UM 84,400,000,000 (current expenditure 62.1%, of which goods and services 25.6%, wages and salaries 15.4%, interest on public debt 9.8%, defense 5.8%; capital expenditure 37.9%).
Land use as % of total land area (2000): in temporary crops 0.5%, in permanent crops 0.01%, in pasture 38.3%; overall forest area 0.3%.
Production (metric tons except as noted). Agriculture, forestry, fishing (2004): rice 77,000, sorghum 68,000, dates 24,000, dry beans 10,000, peas 10,000, cowpeas 7,500; livestock (number of live animals) 8,850,000 sheep, 5,600,000 goats, 1,600,000 cattle, 1,300,000 camels, 1,587,039 cu m; fish catch (2001) 83,596, of which octopuses 20,308[5]. Mining and quarrying (gross weight; 2003): iron ore 10,600,000; gypsum 100,000. Manufacturing (value added in U.S.$'000,000; 1997): food, beverages, and tobacco products 5.2; machinery, transport equipment, and fabricated metals 3.8; bricks, tiles, and cement 1.6. Energy production (consumption): electricity (kW-hr; 2002) 165,000,000 (165,000,000); coal (metric tons; 2002) none (6,000); crude petroleum (barrels; 2002) none[6] (7,200,000); petroleum products (metric tons; 2002) 863,000 (964,000); natural gas, none (none).
Population economically active (2000)[7]: total 651,767; activity rate of total population 26.0% (participation rates: over age 9, 38.1%; female 28%; registered unemployed 3.8%).

Price and earnings indexes (2000 = 100)

	1998	1999	2000	2001	2002	2003	2004
Consumer price index[8]	93.1	96.8	100.0	104.7	108.8	114.4	126.3
Hourly earnings index[9]	100.0	100.0	100.0	100.0	100.0	...	...

Household income and expenditure. Average household size (2000): 5.3; expenditure (1990): food and beverages 73.1%, clothing and footwear 8.1%, energy and water 7.7%, transportation and communications 2.0%.

Gross national product (2004): U.S.$1,210,000,000 (U.S.$420 per capita).

Structure of gross domestic product and labour force

	2002 in value UM '000,000	2002 % of total value	2000 labour force[7]	2000 % of labour force[7]
Agriculture, livestock, fishing	50,436	18.7	314,306	48.2
Mining	29,521	11.0	5,769	0.9
Manufacturing	21,490	8.0	30,156	4.6
Public utilities	[10]	[10]	2,837	0.4
Construction	20,253	7.5	15,562	2.4
Transp. and commun.	29,233	10.9	17,916	2.8
Trade	47,965	17.8	108,532	16.7
Finance			2,011	0.3
Services	14,340[10]	5.3[10]	98,720	15.1
Pub. admin., defense	29,465	11.0		
Other	26,353[11]	9.8[11]	55,958[12]	8.6[12]
TOTAL	269,056	100.0	651,767	100.0

Public debt (external, outstanding; 2003): U.S.$2,084,000,000.
Tourism (1999): receipts U.S.$28,000,000; expenditures U.S.$55,000,000.

Foreign trade

Balance of trade (current prices)

	1998	1999	2000	2001	2002
U.S.$'000,000	+1.9	+22.6	+8.5	−33.7	−87.7
% of total	0.3%	3.5%	1.2%	4.7%	11.7%

Imports (2002): U.S.$418,000,000 (capital goods 26.0%; petroleum products 25.8%; food products 12.8%; vehicles and parts 9.3%; construction materials 9.1%). *Major import sources:* France 20.8%; Belgium-Luxembourg 8.8%; Spain 6.7%; Germany 5.6%; Italy 4.2%.
Exports (2002): U.S.$330,300,000 (iron ore 55.6%; fish 43.4%, of which cephalopods 29.0%). *Major export destinations:* Italy 14.8%; France 14.4%; Spain 12.1%; Germany 10.8%; Belgium-Luxembourg 10.3%; Japan 6.4%.

Transport and communications

Transport. Railroads (2000): route length 446 mi, 717 km; passenger-km, negligible; (2000) metric ton-km cargo 7,766,000,000. Roads (1999): total length 4,900 mi, 7,891 km (paved 26%). Vehicles (2001): passenger cars 12,200; trucks and buses 18,200. Air transport: n.a.; airports (1997) with scheduled flights 9.

Communications

Medium	date	unit	number	units per 1,000 persons
Daily newspapers	1996	circulation	1,000	0.4
Radio	1997	receivers	360,000	147
Television	1999	receivers	247,000	100
Telephones	2003	main lines	38,200	14
Cellular telephones	2004	subscribers	522,400	175
Personal computers	2004	units	42,000	14
Internet	2004	users	14,000	4.7

Education and health

Educational attainment (2000). Percentage of population age 6 and over having: no formal schooling 43.9%; no formal schooling but literate 2.5%; Islamic schooling 18.4%; primary education 23.2%; lower secondary 5.3%; upper secondary 4.6%; higher technical 0.4%; higher 1.7%. Literacy (2000): percentage of total population age 10 and over literate 52.5%; males literate 60.1%; females literate 45.3%.

Education (2002–03)

	schools	teachers	students	student/ teacher ratio
Primary (age 6–11)	2,676[13]	9,606	394,401	41.1
Secondary (age 12–17)	...	2,980	81,278	27.3
Voc., teacher tr.	...	257	3,129	12.2
Higher	...	353	9,198	26.1

Health: physicians (1998) c. 250 (1 per 10,000 persons); hospital beds (1994) c. 1,800 (1 per 1,250 persons); infant mortality rate per 1,000 live births (2004) 72.4.
Food (2002): daily per capita caloric intake 2,772 (vegetable products 83%, animal products 17%); 120% of FAO recommended minimum requirement.

Military

Total active duty personnel (2004): 15,750 (army 95.2%, navy 3.2%, air force 1.6%). *Military expenditure as percentage of GDP* (2003): 1.6%; per capita expenditure U.S.$6.

[1]From August 2005 for a maximum of 2 years. [2]Military Council for Justice and Democracy. [3]The 1991 constitution names Arabic as the official language and the following as national languages: Arabic, Fulani, Soninke, and Wolof. [4]Estimated figures. [5]Fish catch (2002) including foreign fishing vessels equals 672,643 metric tons. [6]Offshore crude petroleum production is expected to begin in 2006. [7]Excludes 122,647 unemployed, not previously employed. [8]Nouakchott only. [9]Minimum wage. [10]Public utilities included with Services. [11]Indirect taxes. [12]Not adequately defined. [13]1998–99.

Internet resources for further information:
• **Office National de la Statistique**
  http://www.ons.mr

Mauritius

Official name: Republic of Mauritius.
Form of government: republic with
one legislative house (National
Assembly [70[1]]).
Chief of state: President.
Head of government: Prime Minister.
Capital: Port Louis.
Official language: English.
Official religion: none.
Monetary unit: 1 Mauritian rupee
(Mau Re; plural Mau Rs) = 100 cents;
valuation (Sept. 1, 2005) 1 U.S.$ =
Mau Rs 29.52; 1 £ = Mau Rs 54.35.

Indian
Ocean

Area and population		area		population
Islands Districts/Dependencies	Administrative Centres	sq mi	sq km	2004 estimate
Mauritius		720	1,865[2]	1,196,696
Black River	Tamarin	100	259	67,235
Flacq	Centre de Flacq	115	298	133,798
Grand Port	Mahébourg	100	260	111,424
Moka	Moka	89	231	78,577
Pamplemousses	Pamplemousses	69	179	129,631
Plaines Wilhems	Rose Hill	78	203	372,711
Port Louis	Port Louis	17	43	130,439
Rivière du Rempart	Poudre d'Or	57	148	104,166
Savanne	Souillac	95	245	68,715
Mauritian dependencies				
Agalega[3]	...	27	70	289
Cargados Carajos Shoals (Saint Brandon)[3]	—	0.4	1	0
Rodrigues[4]	Port Mathurin	40	104	36,690
TOTAL		788[2]	2,040	1,233,675

Demography

Population (2005): 1,245,000.
Density (2005): persons per sq mi 1,580, persons per sq km 610.3.
Urban-rural (2004): urban 42.3%; rural 57.7%.
Sex distribution (2004): male 49.47%; female 50.53%.
Age breakdown (2004): under 15, 24.8%; 15–29, 25.1%; 30–44, 23.6%; 45–59, 17.0%; 60–74, 6.9%; 75 and over, 2.6%.
Population projection: (2010) 1,298,000; (2020) 1,384,000.
Doubling time: 73 years.
Ethnic composition (2000): Indo-Pakistani 67.0%; Creole (mixed Caucasian, Indo-Pakistani, and African) 27.4%; Chinese 3.0%; other 2.6%.
Religious affiliation (2000)[5]: Hindu 49.6%; Christian 32.2%, of which Roman Catholic 23.6%; Muslim 16.6%; Buddhist 0.4%; other 1.2%.
Major urban areas (2000)[5]: Port Louis 144,303; Beau Bassin-Rose Hill 103,872; Vacoas-Phoenix 100,066; Curepipe 78,920; Quatre Bornes 75,884.

Vital statistics

Birth rate per 1,000 population (2004): 15.6[6] (world avg. 21.1).
Death rate per 1,000 population (2004): 6.9[6] (world avg. 9.0).
Natural increase rate per 1,000 population (2004): 8.7[6] (world avg. 12.1).
Total fertility rate (avg. births per childbearing woman; 2004): 1.8[6].
Marriage rate per 1,000 population (2004): 9.2[6].
Divorce rate per 1,000 population (2004): 0.9[6].
Life expectancy at birth (2004)[6]: male 68.7 years; female 75.6 years.
Major causes of death per 100,000 population (2004)[6]: diseases of the circulatory system 348.7; malignant neoplasms (cancers) 78.5; diseases of the respiratory system 53.8; endocrine and metabolic disorders 45.8.

National economy

Budget (2003–04). Revenue: Mau Rs 33,594,000,000 (tax revenue 86.8%, of which taxes on goods and services 46.2%, import duties 22.0%, income tax 13.9%; nontax revenue 11.4%; grants 1.8%). Expenditures: Mau Rs 42,382,000,000 (social security 18.6%; government services 17.0%; interest on debt 15.5%; education 14.5%; economic services 10.1%; health 8.9%).
Tourism (2003): receipts from visitors U.S.$683,000,000; expenditures by nationals abroad U.S.$216,000,000.
Public debt (external, outstanding; 2003): U.S.$928,000,000.
Gross national product (2003): U.S.$5,730,000,000 (U.S.$4,640 per capita).

Structure of gross domestic product and labour force				
	2004			
	in value Mau Rs '000,000	% of total value	labour force[7]	% of labour force[7]
Agriculture	9,444	5.4	23,111	7.8
Mining	87	0.1	217	0.1
Manufacturing	31,850	18.2	101,715	34.4
Construction	8,775	5.0	15,333	5.2
Public utilities	3,597	2.1	2,932	1.0
Transp. and commun.	19,883	11.4	17,801	6.0
Trade	28,014	16.1	36,633	12.4
Finance	29,271	16.8	19,888	6.7
Pub. admin., defense	22,769	13.0	72,196	24.5
Services	5,390	3.1	5,591	1.9
Other	15,388[8]	8.8[8]	—	—
TOTAL	174,468	100.0	295,417[9]	100.0[9]

Production (metric tons except as noted). Agriculture, forestry, fishing (2004): sugarcane 5,200,000, vegetables 18,500, tomatoes 13,200, roots and tubers 13,110, potatoes 12,300, bananas 12,100, cabbages 6,300, carrots 5,000,

pineapples 4,600, onions 4,000; livestock (number of live animals) 93,000 goats, 28,000 cattle; roundwood 13,400 cu m; fish catch (2003) 9,449. Manufacturing (value added in Mau Rs '000,000; 2002): apparel 10,851; food products 3,631; beverages and tobacco 2,297; nonmetallic mineral products 1,709; textiles 1,626; chemical products 1,037; printing and publishing 965. Energy production (consumption): electricity (kW-hr; 2002) 1,974,000,000 (1,974,000,000); coal (metric tons; 2002) none (315,000); petroleum products (metric tons; 2002) none (741,000).
Population economically active (2004): total 549,600; activity rate of total population 44.5% (participation rates: ages 15 and over, 59.2%; female 35.0%; unemployed 8.5%).

Price and earnings indexes (2000 = 100)							
	1998	1999	2000	2001	2002	2003	2004
Consumer price index	89.8	96.0	100.0	105.4	112.1	116.5	122.0
Daily earnings index[10]	92.6	95.2	100.0	...	...	...	...

Household income and expenditure. Average household size (2000) 4.2; annual income per household (2001–02) Mau Rs 170,784 (U.S.$5,780); sources of income (1990): salaries and wages 48.4%, self-employment 41.2%, transfers 10.4%; expenditure (2001–02): food and nonalcoholic beverages 31.9%, transportation 12.7%, housing and energy 9.4%, alcohol and tobacco 9.1%.
Land use as % of total land area (2000): in temporary crops c. 49%, in permanent crops c. 3%, in pasture c. 3%; overall forest area c. 8%.

Foreign trade[11]

Balance of trade (current prices)						
	1999	2000	2001	2002	2003	2004
Mau Rs '000,000	−16,604	−14,046	−10,429	−10,995	−12,265	−21,354
% of total	17.2%	14.7%	9.9%	9.3%	10.2%	16.2%

Imports (2004): Mau Rs 76,577,000,000 (machinery and apparatus 17.4%; food and live animals 15.6%; fabrics and yarn 12.0%; refined petroleum 11.5%; transport equipment 6.2%). *Major import sources:* South Africa 11.2%; China 9.2%; India 9.1%; France 8.9%; Japan 4.0%.
Exports (2004): Mau Rs 55,223,000,000 (domestic exports 79.6%, of which clothing 42.0%, sugar 17.7%, fabric, yarn, and made-up articles 2.8%; reexports 16.4%; ships' stores and bunkers 4.0%). *Major export destinations:* U.K. 31.8%; France 16.5%; U.S. 14.2%; Madagascar 4.9%; Italy 3.9%.

Transport and communications

Transport. Railroads: none. Roads (2004): total length 1,255 mi, 2,020 km (paved 98%). Vehicles (2004): passenger cars 75,707; trucks and buses 13,685. Air transport (2004)[12]: passenger-km 5,742,891,000; metric ton-km cargo 219,624,000; airports (1998) with scheduled flights 1.

Communications				units per 1,000
Medium	date	unit	number	persons
Daily newspapers	2004	circulation	60,000	49
Radio	2000	receivers	450,000	379
Television	2004	receivers	260,300	211
Telephones	2004	main lines	353,808	287
Cellular telephones	2004	subscribers	547,831	444
Personal computers	2004	units	344,000	279
Internet	2004	users	180,000	146

Education and health

Educational attainment (2000). Percentage of population age 25 and over having: no formal education 12.3%; primary 44.1%; lower secondary 23.2%; upper secondary/some higher 17.3%; complete higher 2.6%; unknown 0.5%.
Literacy (2000): percentage of total population age 12 and over literate 85.1%; males literate 88.7%; females literate 81.6%.

Education (2004)				student/
	schools	teachers	students	teacher ratio
Primary (age 5–12)	289	5,741	126,226	22
Secondary (age 12–20)	176	5,938	105,988	17.8
Voc., teacher tr.	12	380[13]	7,061	15.7[13]
Higher	5	461[14]	14,232	13.9[14]

Health (2004): physicians 1,303 (1 per 947 persons); hospital beds 3,677 (1 per 335 persons); infant mortality rate per 1,000 live births 14.4[6].
Food (2002): daily per capita caloric intake 2,955 (vegetable products 86%, animal products 14%); 130% of FAO recommended minimum requirement.

Military

Total active duty personnel (2004): none; a 2,000-person paramilitary force includes a coast guard unit. *Paramilitary expenditure as percentage of GDP* (2003): 0.2%; per capita expenditure U.S.$9.

---

[1]Includes 8 "bonus" seats designated by the electoral commission to balance the representation of ethnic communities. [2]Detail does not add to total given because of rounding. [3]Administered directly from Port Louis. [4]Local autonomy status granted by Mauritius in November 2001. [5]Based on census. [6]Excludes Agalega. [7]Employed persons in large establishments only; March. [8]Indirect taxes less imputed bank service charges. [9]Total labour force equals 549,600 and includes 45,100 unemployed. [10]Manufacturing sector; March data only. [11]Imports c.i.f.; exports f.o.b. [12]Air Mauritius. [13]2002. [14]1998.

Internet resources for further information:
• **Central Statistical Office** http://statsmauritius.gov.mu
• **Bank of Mauritius** http://bom.intnet.mu

Mayotte

Official name: Collectivité Départementale de Mayotte[1] (Departmental Collectivity of Mayotte).
Political status: overseas dependency of France[2] with one legislative house (General Council [19]).
Chief of state: President of France.
Head of government: President of the General Council[3].
Capital: Mamoudzou.
Official language: French.
Official religion: none.
Monetary unit: 1 euro (€) = 100 cents; valuation (Sept. 1, 2005) 1 U.S.$ = €0.80; 1 £ = €1.47[4].

Indian
Ocean

Area and population		area		population
Islands				2002
Communes	Capitals	sq mi	sq km	census
Grande Terre				
Acoua	Acoua	4.9	12.6	4,605
Bandraboua	Bandraboua	12.5	32.4	7,501
Bandrele	Bandrele	14.1	36.5	5,537
Boueni	Boueni	5.4	14.1	5,151
Chiconi	Chiconi	3.2	8.3	6,167
Chirongui	Chirongui	10.9	28.3	5,696
Dembeni	Dembeni	15.0	38.8	7,825
Kani-Keli	Kani-Keli	7.9	20.5	4,336
Koungou	Koungou	11.0	28.4	15,383
Mamoudzou	Mamoudzou	16.2	41.9	45,485
M'tsangamouji	M'tsangamouji	8.4	21.8	5,382
M'tzamboro	M'tzamboro	5.3	13.7	7,068
Ouangani	Ouangani	7.3	19.0	5,569
Sada	Sada	4.3	11.2	6,963
Tsingoni	Tsingoni	13.4	34.8	7,779
Petite Terre				
Dzaoudzi-				
Labattoir	Dzaoudzi	2.6	6.7	12,308
Pamandzi	Pamandzi	1.7	4.3	7,510
TOTAL		144.1[5]	373.3[5]	160,265[6]

Demography

Population (2005): 181,000.
Density (2005): persons per sq mi 1,257, persons per sq km 484.0.
Urban-rural: n.a.
Sex distribution (2002): male 50.10%; female 49.90%.
Age breakdown (2002): under 15, 42.0%; 15–29, 29.0%; 30–44, 17.0%; 45–59, 7.0%; 60 and over, 5.0%.
Population projection: (2010) 216,000; (2020) 292,000.
Doubling time: 21 years.
Place of birth (2002): Mayotte (including 2–4% for metropolitan France) 65.6%[7]; nearby islands of the Comoros 33.1%[7]; other 1.3%.
Ethnic composition (2000): Comorian (Mauri, Mahorais) 92.3%; Swahili 3.2%; white (French) 1.8%; Makua 1.0%; other 1.7%.
Religious affiliation (2000): Sunnī Muslim 96.5%; Christian, principally Roman Catholic, 2.2%; other 1.3%.
Major communes (2002): Mamoudzou 45,485; Koungou 15,383; Dzaoudzi 12,308.

Vital statistics

Birth rate per 1,000 population (2004): 42.2 (world avg. 21.1).
Death rate per 1,000 population (2004): 8.1 (world avg. 9.0).
Natural increase rate per 1,000 population (2004): 34.1 (world avg. 12.1).
Total fertility rate (avg. births per childbearing woman; 2004): 6.0.
Marriage rate per 1,000 population: n.a.
Divorce rate per 1,000 population: n.a.
Life expectancy at birth (2004): male 58.9; female 63.2.

National economy

Budget (1997)[8]. Revenue: F 1,022,400,000 (current revenue 76.7%, development revenue 23.3%). Expenditures: F 964,200,000 (current expenditure 75.2%, development expenditure 24.8%).
Production (metric tons except as noted). Agriculture, forestry, fishing (2000): bananas 30,200[9], cassava 10,000[9], ylang-ylang 17,600 kg, vanilla 2,300 kg, cinnamon 2,300 kg; livestock (number of live animals; 1997) 25,000 goats, 17,000 cattle, 2,000 sheep; roundwood, n.a.; fish catch (1999) 1,502. Mining and quarrying: negligible. Manufacturing: mostly processing of agricultural products and materials used in housing construction (including siding and roofing materials, joinery, and latticework). Energy production (consumption): electricity (kW-hr; 2002) 107,000,000 ([2004] 123,000,000); coal, none (none); crude petroleum, none (none); petroleum products, none (n.a.); natural gas, none (none).
Tourism (number of visitors; 2004): 32,000; receipts (2003) U.S.$13,900,000.
Population economically active (2002): total 44,558; activity rate of total population 27.8% (participation rates: ages 15–60, 50.0%; female 38.6%; unemployed 29.3%).

Price index (2000 = 100)							
	1998	1999	2000	2001	2002	2003	2004
Consumer price index	99.5	100.4	100.0	100.3	103.2	104.3	104.9

Gross national product (2002): U.S.$444,000,000 (U.S.$2,780 per capita).

Structure of gross domestic product and labour force				
	1997		2002	
	in value U.S.$'000	% of total value	labour force	% of labour force
Agriculture, forestry, and fishing	...	...	3,229	7.2
Mining	...	...	...	...
Manufacturing	...	...	1,105	2.5
Construction	...	...	5,614	12.6
Public utilities	...	...	519	1.2
Transp. and commun.	...	...	2,007	4.5
Trade	...	...	5,435	12.2
Finance, insurance	...	...	145	0.3
Pub. admin., defense	...	...	} 13,460	30.2
Services	...	...		
Other	...	...	13,044[10]	29.3[10]
TOTAL	154,900	100.0	44,558	100.0

Household income and expenditure. Average household size (1997) 4.6; average annual income per household (1995) F 32,400 (U.S.$6,491); expenditure (1995): food 34.3%, transport and communications 12.7%, clothing and footwear 10.0%, housing 10.0%.
Land use as % of total land area (2000): in temporary crops, n.a., in permanent crops, n.a., in pasture, n.a.; overall forest area, n.a.
Public debt (1997): U.S.$74,600,000.

Foreign trade

Balance of trade (current prices)						
	1999	2000	2001	2002	2003	2004
€'000,000	−126.7	−147.8	−176.5	−175.7	−180.1	−209.1
% of total	96.2%	96.2%	95.7%	93.3%	95.3%	96.6%

Imports (2004): €212,865,000 (food products 25.4%; transport equipment 16.3%; machinery and apparatus 15.8%; mineral fuels 9.0%; metals and metal products 8.7%). *Major import sources* (2003): France 55.1%; South Africa 4.8%; Thailand 3.5%; China 3.2%.
Exports (2004): €3,736,000 (fish 14.7%; ylang-ylang 6.7%; vanilla 0.1%; unspecified commodities 78.5%). *Major export destinations* (2003): France 61.4%; Comoros 25.0%; Réunion 6.8%.

Transport and communications

Transport. Railroads: none. Roads (1998): total length 145 mi, 233 km (paved 77%). Vehicles (1998): 8,213. Air transport (2004): passenger arrivals and departures 166,121; cargo unloaded and loaded 1,143 metric tons; airports (2002) with scheduled flights 1.

Communications				units per 1,000
Medium	date	unit	number	persons
Daily newspapers[11]	1998	circulation	...	...
Radio	1996	receivers	50,000	427
Television	1999	receivers	3,500	30
Telephones	2003	main lines	10,000	60
Cellular telephones	2003	subscribers	36,000	230
Internet	2003	users	5,000	30

Education and health

Educational attainment (2002). Percentage of population age 15 and over having: no formal education *c.* 46%; primary education *c.* 25%; lower secondary *c.* 16%; upper secondary *c.* 8%; higher *c.* 5%. *Literacy* (1997): total population age 15 and over literate 63,053 (86.1%).

Education (2001–02)				student/
	schools	teachers	students	teacher ratio
Primary (age 6–11)	112	555[12]	28,591	38.9[12]
Secondary (age 12–18)	14	246[12]	15,626	16.2[12]
Voc., teacher tr.	2[9]	...	1,733	...
Higher	—	—	—	—

Health (1997): physicians 57 (1 per 2,304 persons); hospital beds 186 (1 per 706 persons); infant mortality rate per 1,000 live births (2004) 64.2.

Military

Total active duty personnel (2004): n.a.; a detachment of the French Foreign Legion is stationed at Dzaoudzi.

[1]Mahoré or Maore in Shimaoré, the local Swahili-based language. [2]Final status of Mayotte has not yet been determined; it is claimed by Comoros as an integral part of that country. [3]From April 2004 executive authority in Mayotte is with the President of the General Council; the position of prefect (France's representative in Mayotte) is to be phased out by 2007. [4]The French franc was the former monetary unit; on Jan. 1, 2002, F 6.56 = €1. [5]Revised area as of 2002 census equals 144.5 sq mi (374.2 sq km). [6]Including about 45,000 illegal residents, of which nearly all are Comorians from adjacent islands. [7]Nearly all ethnic Comorian (a mixture of Bantu, Arab, and Malagasy peoples). [8]Mayotte is largely dependent on French aid. [9]1997. [10]Unemployed. [11]One weekly newspaper has a total circulation of 15,000. [12]1992–93.

Internet resources for further information:
• Ministère de l'Outre-Mer http://www.outre-mer.gouv.fr
• INSEE: Mayotte
  http://www.insee.fr/fr/insee_regions/reunion/zoom/Mayotte

Mexico

Official name: Estados Unidos
  Mexicanos (United Mexican States).
Form of government: federal republic
  with two legislative houses (Senate
  [128]; Chamber of Deputies [500]).
Head of state and government:
  President.
Capital: Mexico City.
Official language: Spanish.
Official religion: none.
Monetary unit: 1 Mexican
  peso (Mex$) = 100 centavos;
  valuation (Sept. 1, 2005)
  1 U.S.$ = Mex$10.68;
  1 £ = Mex$19.66.

Area and population

States	Capitals	area sq mi	area sq km	population 2000 census
Aguascalientes	Aguascalientes	2,112	5,471	944,285
Baja California	Mexicali	26,997	69,921	2,487,367
Baja California Sur	La Paz	28,369	73,475	424,041
Campeche	Campeche	19,619	50,812	690,689
Chiapas	Tuxtla Gutiérrez	28,653	74,211	3,920,892
Chihuahua	Chihuahua	94,571	244,938	3,052,907
Coahuila de Zaragoza	Saltillo	57,908	149,982	2,298,070
Colima	Colima	2,004	5,191	542,627
Durango	Durango	47,560	123,181	1,448,661
Guanajuato	Guanajuato	11,773	30,491	4,663,032
Guerrero	Chilpancingo	24,819	64,281	3,079,649
Hidalgo	Pachuca	8,036	20,813	2,235,591
Jalisco	Guadalajara	31,211	80,836	6,322,002
México	Toluca	8,245	21,355	13,096,686
Michoacán de Ocampo	Morelia	23,138	59,928	3,985,667
Morelos	Cuernavaca	1,911	4,950	1,555,296
Nayarit	Tepic	10,417	26,979	920,185
Nuevo León	Monterrey	25,067	64,924	3,834,141
Oaxaca	Oaxaca	36,275	93,952	3,438,765
Puebla	Puebla	13,090	33,902	5,076,686
Querétaro de Arteaga	Querétaro	4,420	11,449	1,404,306
Quintana Roo	Chetumal	19,387	50,212	874,963
San Luis Potosí	San Luis Potosí	24,351	63,068	2,299,360
Sinaloa	Culiacán	22,521	58,328	2,536,844
Sonora	Hermosillo	70,291	182,052	2,216,969
Tabasco	Villahermosa	9,756	25,267	1,891,829
Tamaulipas	Ciudad Victoria	30,650	79,384	2,753,222
Tlaxcala	Tlaxcala	1,551	4,016	962,646
Veracruz–Llare	Xalapa (Jalapa)	27,683	71,699	6,908,975
Yucatán	Mérida	14,827	38,402	1,658,210
Zacatecas	Zacatecas	28,283	73,252	1,353,610
Federal District				
Distrito Federal	—	571	1,479	8,605,239
CONTINENTAL AREA		756,066[1]	1,958,201[1]	
LAND		736,950	1,908,690	
WATER		19,116	49,511	
INSULAR AREA[2]		1,980	5,127	
TOTAL		758,450[3]	1,964,375[3]	97,483,412

Demography

Population (2005): 107,029,000.
Density (2005): persons per sq mi 141.1, persons per sq km 54.5.
Urban-rural (2003): urban 75.5%; rural 24.5%.
Sex distribution (2004): male 48.90%; female 51.10%.
Age breakdown (2000): under 15, 34.3%; 15–29, 28.5%; 30–44, 19.5%; 45–59,
  10.5%; 60–74, 5.3%; 75 and over, 1.9%.
Population projection: (2010) 113,271,000; (2020) 124,652,000.
Doubling time: 49 years.
Ethnic composition (2000): mestizo 64.3%; Amerindian 18.0%, of which
  detribalized 10.5%; Mexican white 15.0%; Arab 1.0%; Mexican black 0.5%;
  Spaniard 0.3%; U.S. white 0.2%; other 0.7%.
Religious affiliation (2000): Christian 96.3%, of which Roman Catholic 87.0%,
  Protestant 3.2%, independent Christian 2.7%, unaffiliated Christian 1.4%,
  other Christian (mostly Mormon and Jehovah's Witness) 2.0%; Muslim 0.3%;
  nonreligious 3.1%; other 0.3%.
Major cities (2000): Mexico City 8,605,239 (urban agglomeration [2003]
  18,660,000); Guadalajara 1,646,183 (urban agglomeration 3,697,000); Puebla
  1,271,673 (urban agglomeration 1,888,000); Ciudad Netzahualcóyotl 1,225,-
  083; Juárez 1,187,275; Tijuana 1,148,681; Monterrey 1,110,909 (urban agglomeration 3,267,000); León 1,020,818; Mérida 662,530; Chihuahua 657,876.
Place of birth (1990): 93.1% native-born; 6.9% foreign-born and unknown.
Households. Total households (2000) 21,954,733; distribution by size (2000): 1
  person 6.0%, 2 persons 12.3%, 3 persons 17.2%, 4 persons 21.8%, 5 persons
  17.7%, 6 persons 10.9%, 7 or more persons 14.1%.
Emigration (2000): legal immigrants into the United States 173,900.

Vital statistics

Birth rate per 1,000 population (2004): 18.8 (world avg. 21.1).
Death rate per 1,000 population (2004): 4.5 (world avg. 9.0).
Natural increase rate per 1,000 population (2004): 14.3 (world avg. 12.1).
Total fertility rate (avg. births per childbearing woman; 2004): 2.2.
Marriage rate per 1,000 population (2003): 5.6.
Divorce rate per 1,000 population (2003): 0.6.
Life expectancy at birth (2004): male 72.7 years; female 77.6 years.
Major causes of death per 100,000 population (2001): diseases of the circula-
  tory system 98.5; diabetes mellitus 62.2; malignant neoplasms (cancers) 58.3;

accidents and violence 51.3; diseases of the digestive system 42.3; diseases
of the respiratory system 36.9.

Social indicators

Access to services (2000). Proportion of dwellings having: electricity 94.8%;
  piped water supply 83.3%; drained sewage 76.2%.
Educational attainment (2000). Population age 15 and over having: no primary education 10.3%; some primary 18.1%; completed primary 19.4%; incomplete secondary 5.3%; complete secondary 19.1%; some higher 16.8%; higher 11.0%.

Distribution of income (2000)

percentage of household income by decile

1	2	3	4	5	6	7	8	9	10 (highest)
0.4	1.5	2.4	3.4	4.7	6.2	8.1	11.0	16.7	45.6

Quality of working life. Average workweek (2004): 43.5 hours[4]. Annual rate
  per 100,000 insured workers for (2004): injury 2,922; death 11. Labour stoppages (2001): 35, involving 23,234 workers.
Social participation. Eligible voters participating in last national election (July
  2003): 41.7%. Trade union membership in total workforce (2000): formal sector only, less than 20%; both formal and informal sectors, c. 17%. Practicing
  religious population (1995–97): percentage of adult population attending
  church services at least once per week 46%.
Social deviance (1991). Criminal cases tried by local authorities per 100,000
  population for: murder 60.3; rape 22.4; other assault 301.0; theft 703.8.
  Incidence per 100,000 in general population of: alcoholism (2000) 7.6; drug
  and substance abuse 26.6; suicide (2001) 3.1.

National economy

Gross national product (2004): U.S.$703,080,000,000 (U.S.$6,770 per capita).

Structure of gross domestic product and labour force

	2002 in value Mex$'000,000	2002 % of total value	2001 labour force	2001 % of labour force
Agriculture	225,879	3.7	7,074,400	17.8
Mining	75,501	1.2	127,200	0.3
Manufacturing	1,060,438	17.2	7,373,000	18.6
Construction	275,293	4.5	2,396,900	6.0
Public utilities	76,342	1.2	194,900	0.5
Transp. and commun.	628,129	10.2	1,776,700	4.5
Trade	1,163,226	18.9	10,821,400	27.3
Finance	710,099	11.5	1,504,600	3.8
Pub. admin., defense }	1,483,433	24.1	1,682,100	4.2
Services			5,910,200	14.9
Other	454,490[5]	7.4[5]	821,400[6]	2.1[6]
TOTAL	6,152,829[7]	100.0[7]	39,682,800	100.0

Budget (2001). Revenue: Mex$939,114,500,000 (income tax 30.4%, VAT
  22.2%, royalties 21.7%, excise tax 11.8%, import duties 3.1%, other 10.8%).
  Expenditures: Mex$996,950,600,000 (current expenditure 63.4%, of which
  social security and welfare 41.8%, interest on public debt 16.7%; capital
  expenditure 36.6%).
Public debt (external, outstanding; 2003): U.S.$77,473,000,000.
Tourism (2003): receipts from visitors U.S.$9,457,000,000; expenditures by
  nationals abroad U.S.$6,253,000,000.

Manufacturing (2000)

	no. of enter-prises[8]	no. of employees ('000)	yearly wages as a % of avg. of all wages	value added (U.S.$'000,000)
Manufacturing	266,033	1,476,309	100.0	60,760
Transport equipment	...	105,429	105.4	9,439
Food	91,894	247,869	91.5	8,883
Chemicals and chemical products	7,321	131,530	165.7	8,726
Beverages	...	110,074	92.9	5,422
Nonmetallic mineral products	24,397	46,520	99.4	3,580
Electrical machinery	...	132,335	93.0	3,484
Iron and steel	401	34,591	135.3	2,891
Nonelectrical machinery	...	49,374	105.1	2,254
Paper and paper products	15,022	51,860	91.9	2,243
Rubber and plastic	...	85,470	103.8	2,031
Metal products	...	60,180	83.2	1,691
Automobile parts	...	49,737	102.4	1,585
Tobacco	...	4,337	169.3	1,104
Nonferrous metals	...	19,627	95.1	1,093

Production (metric tons except as noted). Agriculture, forestry, fishing (2004):
  sugarcane 45,126,500, corn (maize) 20,000,000, sorghum 6,300,000, oranges
  3,969,810, wheat 2,500,000, tomatoes 2,148,130, bananas 2,026,610, chilies and
  green peppers 1,853,610, lemons and limes 1,824,890, mangoes 1,503,010, dry
  beans 1,400,160, barley 1,109,420, avocados 1,040,390, watermelons 970,055,
  coconuts 959,000, papayas 955,694, pineapples 720,900, blue agave (2002)
  c. 650,000, coffee (green) 310,861, cauliflower 215,000, safflower seeds
  212,765, vanilla 189; livestock (number of live animals) 31,476,600 cattle,
  14,000,000 pigs, 8,991,752 goats, 8,100,000 ducks, 6,819,770 sheep, 6,260,000
  horses, 4,806,000 mules, 3,260,000 asses, 425,000,000 chickens; roundwood 45,688,734 cu m; fish catch (2003) 1,523,675. Mining and
  quarrying (2003): bismuth 1,064[9] [world rank: 1]; fluorite 756,000 [world rank:
  2]; celestite 130,329 [world rank: 2]; silver 2,568,877 kg[9] [world rank: 2]; cadmium 1,616[9] [world rank: 4]; lead 139,348[9] [world rank: 5]; gypsum 6,986,491
  [world rank: 6]; zinc 413,991[9] [world rank: 6]; sulfur 1,630,000 [world rank:
  9]; copper 355,653[9] [world rank: 11]; iron ore 6,759,000[9]; gold 20,406 kg.
  Manufacturing (value added in U.S.$'000,000; 2000): motor vehicles and parts
  10,718; food products 8,883; paints, soaps, pharmaceuticals 7,044; beverages

5,422; bricks, cement, ceramics 3,580; iron and steel 2,891; paper and paper products 2,243; basic chemicals 1,682; fabricated metal products 1,518.
Household income and expenditure. Average household size (2000) 4.4; income per household (2000) Mex$15,762 (U.S.$1,667); sources of income (2000): wages and salaries 63.4%, property and entrepreneurship 23.6%, transfer payments 10.0%, other 2.9%; expenditure (2000): food, beverages, and tobacco 29.9%, transportation and communications 17.8%, education 17.3%, housing (includes household furnishings) 16.5%, clothing and footwear 5.8%.

Trade and service enterprises (1998)

	no. of establish-ments	no. of employees	yearly wage as a % of avg. of all wages	annual income (Mex$'000,000)[8]
Trade	1,497,828	3,790,764	...	565,728,373
Wholesale	110,180	864,569	...	249,597,035
Retail	1,387,648	2,926,195	...	316,131,338
Boutiques (excluding food products)	536,900	1,192,597	...	108,507,889
Food and tobacco speciality stores	768,799	1,234,656	...	65,305,180
Automobile, tire, and auto parts dealers	41,236	164,493	...	47,888,576
Supermarkets and grocery stores	24,697	254,497	...	48,769,283
Gasoline stations	4,345	53,610	...	32,517,091
Services[8]	711,843	2,766,750	...	200,001,682
Professional services	130,475	652,148	...	53,533,318
Transp. and travel agencies	9,967	62,767	...	11,858,406
Lodging	9,913	151,445	...	8,960,922
Automotive repair	112,293	252,950	...	7,263,560
Educational services (private)	20,622	247,086	...	10,815,238
Medical and social assistance	79,748	203,348	...	7,497,794
Amusement services (cinemas and theatres)	4,855	65,608	...	9,845,129
Recreation[8]	20,973	65,936	...	3,065,672
Other[8]	248,245	937,780	...	83,259,134

Energy production (consumption): electricity (kW-hr; 2003) 263,488,000,000 ([2002] 235,360,000,000); hard coal (metric tons; 2002) 1,746,000 (1,774,000); lignite (metric tons; 2002) 9,238,000 (12,360,000); crude petroleum (barrels; 2004) 1,249,000,000 ([2002] 498,000,000); petroleum products (metric tons; 2002) 73,086,000 (80,875,000); natural gas (cu m; 2003) 47,377,000,000 ([2002] 40,473,000,000).
Population economically active (2003): total 41,515,700; activity rate of total population 40.4% (participation rates: ages 15–64, 61.2%; female 34.3%; unemployed 3.0%).

Price and earnings indexes (2000 = 100)

	1998	1999	2000	2001	2002	2003	2004
Consumer price index	78.3	91.3	100.0	106.4	111.7	116.8	122.3
Monthly earnings index	93.0	94.4	100.0	106.7	108.7	110.0	110.2

Financial aggregates

	1998	1999	2000	2001	2002	2003	2004
Exchange rate[10], Mex$ per:							
U.S. dollar	9.87	9.51	9.57	9.14	10.31	11.24	11.26
£	16.41	15.38	14.28	13.26	16.62	20.05	21.75
SDR	13.89	13.06	12.47	11.49	14.02	16.70	17.49
International reserves (U.S.$)							
Total (excl. gold; '000,000)	31,799	31,782	35,509	44,741	50,594	58,956	64,141
SDRs ('000,000)	337	790	366	356	392	433	465
Reserve pos. in IMF ('000,000)	—	—	—	—	308	782	898
Foreign exchange	31,461	30,992	35,142	44,384	49,895	57,740	62,778
Gold ('000,000 fine troy oz)	0.22	0.16	0.25	0.23	0.23	0.17	0.14
% world reserves	0.03	0.02	0.02	0.02	0.02	0.02	0.02
Interest and prices							
Treasury bill rate	24.76	21.41	15.24	11.31	7.09	6.23	6.82
Balance of payments (U.S.$'000,000)							
Balance of visible trade, of which:	−7,834	−5,613	−8,337	−9,617	−7,633	−5,780	−8,811
Imports, f.o.b.	−125,373	−141,975	−174,458	−168,397	−168,679	−170,546	−196,810
Exports, f.o.b.	117,539	136,362	166,121	158,780	161,046	164,766	187,999
Balance of invisibles	−8,183	−8,318	−10,283	−7,725	−5,375	−699	+1,402
Balance of payments, current account	−16,017	−13,931	−18,620	−17,352	−13,008	−6,479	−7,409

Land use as % of total land area (2000): in temporary crops 13.0%, in permanent crops 1.3%, in pasture 41.9%; overall forest area 28.9%.

Foreign trade

Balance of trade (current prices)

	1999	2000	2001	2002	2003	2004
U.S.$'000,000	−5,613	−8,337	−9,617	−7,633	−5,780	−8,530
% of total	2.0%	2.4%	2.9%	2.3%	1.7%	2.2%

Imports (2004): U.S.$197,156,000,000 (non-maquiladora sector 65.3%, of which machinery and apparatus 18.3%, transport and communications equipment 10.9%, chemicals and chemical products 6.6%, processed food, beverages, and tobacco 4.0%, iron and steel 3.7%; maquiladora sector 34.7%, of which electrical machinery, apparatus, and electronics 14.8%, nonelectrical machinery and apparatus 6.7%, rubber and plastic products 2.9%). *Major import sources:* U.S. 56.2%; China 7.3%; Japan 5.4%; Germany 3.6%; Canada 2.7%; South Korea 2.7%; Brazil 2.2%.
Exports (2004): U.S.$188,626,000,000 (non-maquiladora sector 53.6%, of which road vehicles and parts 13.5%, crude petroleum 11.3%, machinery and apparatus 8.6%; maquiladora sector 46.4%, of which electrical machinery,

apparatus, and electronics 21.7%, nonelectrical machinery and apparatus 11.3%, textiles and clothing 3.4%). *Major export destinations:* U.S. 87.6%; Canada 1.7%; Spain 1.1%; Germany 0.9%; Japan 0.6%; Brazil 0.5%; China 0.5%.

Trade by commodity group (2002)

SITC group	imports U.S.$'000,000	%	exports U.S.$'000,000	%
00 Food and live animals	8,132	4.8	6,015	3.7
01 Beverages and tobacco	11	11	1,974	1.2
02 Crude materials, excluding fuels	4,667	2.8	1,594	1.0
03 Mineral fuels, lubricants, and related materials	4,564	2.7	14,318	8.9
04 Animal and vegetable oils, fats, and waxes	11	11	12	12
05 Chemicals and related products, n.e.s.	15,342	9.1	5,512	3.4
06 Basic manufactures	27,360	16.2	13,230	8.2
07 Machinery and transport equipment	86,094	51.0	94,740	59.0
08 Miscellaneous manufactured articles	20,138	11.9	23,058	14.4
09 Goods not classified by kind	1,475	0.9	12	12
TOTAL	168,650	100.0	160,670	100.0

Direction of trade (2002)

	imports U.S.$'000,000	%	exports U.S.$'000,000	%
Western Hemisphere	117,721	69.8	152,268	94.8
United States	106,901	63.4	143,151	89.1
Latin America and the Caribbean	6,340	3.8	6,308	3.9
Canada	4,480	2.6	2,809	1.8
Europe	17,914	10.6	5,729	3.6
EU	16,443	9.7	5,216	3.3
Other Europe	1,471	0.9	513	0.3
Asia	31,479	18.7	2,443	1.5
Japan	9,349	5.6	469	0.3
China	6,274	3.7	456	0.3
Other Asia	15,856	9.4	1,518	0.9
Africa	388	0.2	53	—
Other	1,149	0.7	177	0.1
TOTAL	168,651	100.0	160,670	100.0

Transport and communications

Transport. Railroads (2003): route length 16,563 mi, 26,655 km; passenger-km 67,000,000; metric ton-km cargo 54,813,000,000. Roads (2004): total length 216,994 mi, 349,219 km (paved 34%). Vehicles (2003): passenger cars 14,006,708; trucks and buses 6,810,560. Air transport (2004)[13]: passenger-km 30,614,000,000; metric ton-km cargo 187,273,000; airports (2001) 85.

Communications

Medium	date	unit	number	units per 1,000 persons
Daily newspapers	2000	circulation	9,580,000	98
Radio	2000	receivers	32,300,000	330
Television	2000	receivers	27,700,000	283
Telephones	2004	main lines	18,073,200	172
Cellular telephones	2004	subscribers	38,451,100	366
Personal computers	2004	units	11,210,000	107
Internet	2004	users	14,036,500	134

Education and health

Literacy (2000): total population age 15 and over literate 91.4%; males literate 93.4%; females literate 89.5%.

Education (2001–02)

	schools	teachers	students	student/teacher ratio
Primary (age 6–12)	99,230	609,654	14,843,400	24.3
Secondary (age 12–18)	39,691	536,579	8,600,700	16.0
Voc., teacher tr.[14]	6,610	63,674	883,000	13.9
Higher	4,183	216,804	2,147,100	9.9

Health (2002): physicians 140,286 (1 per 734 persons); hospital beds 76,529 (1 per 1,346 persons); infant mortality rate per 1,000 live births (2003) 12.6.
Food (2002): daily per capita caloric intake 3,145 (vegetable products 81%, animal products 19%); 135% of FAO recommended minimum requirement.

Military

Total active duty personnel (2004): 192,770 (army 74.7%, navy 19.2%, air force 6.1%). *Military expenditure as percentage of GDP* (2003): 0.5%[15]; per capita expenditure U.S.$28[15].

[1]Continental area per more recent survey equals 756,470 sq mi (1,959,248 sq km). [2]Uninhabited (nearly all Pacific) islands directly administered by federal government. [3]Total area based on more recent survey figure for continental area. [4]Hours actually worked. [5]Taxes less subsidies and less imputed bank service charge. [6]Includes 678,500 unemployed. [7]Detail does not add to total given because of rounding. [8]1993. [9]Metal content. [10]End of year. [11]Together categories 01 and 04 equal U.S.$878,000,000 and 0.6%. [12]Together categories 04 and 09 equal U.S.$229,000,000 and 0.2%. [13]AeroMexico, Aviacsa, and Mexicana only. [14]1996–97. [15]Excludes military pensions.

Internet resources for further information:
• **National Institute of Statistics, Geography, and Informatics**
  http://www.inegi.gob.mx/inegi/default.asp
• **Banco de México**
  http://www.banxico.org.mx/siteBanxicoINGLES/index.html

Micronesia, Federated States of

Pacific
Ocean

Official name: Federated States of Micronesia.
Form of government: federal nonparty republic in free association with the United States with one legislative house (Congress [14])[1].
Head of state and government: President.
Capital: Palikir, on Pohnpei.
Official language: none.
Official religion: none.
Monetary unit: 1 U.S. dollar (U.S.$) = 100 cents; valuation (Sept. 1, 2005) 1 U.S.$ = £0.54.

Area and population

States Major Islands	Capitals	area sq mi	area sq km	population 2000 census
Chuuk (Truk)	Weno (Moen)	49.1	127.2	53,595
Chuuk Islands		...	...	40,465
Kosrae	Lelu	42.3	109.6	7,686
Kosrae Island		42.3	109.6	7,686
Pohnpei (Ponape)	Kolonia	133.3	345.2	34,486
Pohnpei Island		129.0	334.1	32,178
Yap	Colonia	45.9	118.9	11,241
Yap Island		38.7	100.2	7,391
TOTAL		270.8[2]	701.4[2]	107,008

Demography

Population (2005): 113,000.
Density (2005): persons per sq mi 417.0, persons per sq km 161.2.
Urban-rural (2003): urban 29.3%; rural 70.7%.
Sex distribution (2003): male 50.50%; female 49.50%.
Age breakdown (2000): under 15, 40.3%; 15–29, 28.4%; 30–44, 16.9%; 45–59, 9.1%; 60–74, 3.9%; 75 and over, 1.4%.
Population projection: (2010) 117,000; (2020) 120,000.
Doubling time: 34 years.
Ethnic composition (2000): Chuukese/Mortlockese 33.6%; Pohnpeian 24.9%; Yapese 10.6%; Kosraean 5.2%; U.S. white 4.5%; Asian 1.3%; other 19.9%.
Religious affiliation (2000): Roman Catholic 52.7%; Protestant 41.7%, of which Congregational 40.1%; Mormon 1.0%; other/unknown 4.6%.
Major towns (2000): Weno, in Chuuk state 13,900; Tol, in Chuuk state 9,500; Palikir, on Pohnpei 6,227; Kolonia, on Pohnpei 5,681; Colonia, on Yap 3,350.

Vital statistics

Birth rate per 1,000 population (2004): 25.8 (world avg. 21.1); (1998) legitimate 75.6%; illegitimate 24.4%.
Death rate per 1,000 population (2004): 5.0 (world avg. 9.0).
Natural increase rate per 1,000 population (2004): 20.8 (world avg. 12.1).
Total fertility rate (avg. births per childbearing woman; 2004): 3.4.
Life expectancy at birth (2004): male 67.7 years; female 71.3 years.
Major causes of death per 100,000 population (2002): communicable diseases 242; diseases of the circulatory system 202; malignant neoplasms (cancers) 52; diseases of the respiratory system 46; homicide, suicide, and accidents 39; diabetes mellitus 24.

National economy

Budget (2002–03). Revenue: U.S.$163,700,000 (external grants 70.4%, tax revenue 17.4%, nontax revenue [including fishing access revenue] 12.2%). Expenditures: U.S.$159,600,000 (current expenditures 81.9%, capital expenditure 18.1%).
Public debt (external, outstanding; 2002–03): U.S.$53,100,000.
Population economically active (2000): total 37,414; activity rate of total population 35.0% (participation rates: ages 15–64, 60.7%; female 42.9%; unemployed 22.0%).

Price and earnings indexes (2000 = 100)

	1999	2000	2001	2002	2003
Price index	98.0	100.0	101.3	101.1	100.9
Earnings index	97.9	100.0	102.5	104.2	105.5

Production (metric tons except as noted). Agriculture, forestry, fishing (2004): coconuts 140,000, cassava 11,800, sweet potatoes 3,000, bananas 2,000; livestock (number of live animals) 32,000 pigs, 13,900 cattle, 4,000 goats; roundwood, n.a.; fish catch (2002) 20,400, of which skipjack tuna 14,000, yellowfin tuna 3,900. Mining and quarrying: quarrying of sand and aggregate for local construction only. Manufacturing: n.a.; however, copra and coconut oil, traditionally important products, are being displaced by garment production; the manufacture of handicrafts and personal items (clothing, mats, boats, etc.) by individuals is also important. Energy production (consumption): electricity (kW-hr; 2002) 192,000,000 (179,000,000); coal, none (none); crude petroleum, none (none); petroleum products, none (n.a.); natural gas, none (none).
Household income and expenditure. Average household size (2000) 6.7; annual income per household U.S.$8,944 (median income: U.S.$4,618); sources of income (1994): wages and salaries 51.8%, operating surplus 23.0%, social security 2.1%; expenditure (2000)[3]: food 40.2%, alcohol, tobacco, sakau, and betel nut 9.8%, energy 6.4%, clothing and footwear 3.0%.

Land use as % of total land area (2000): in temporary crops *c.* 6%, in permanent crops *c.* 46%, in pasture *c.* 16%; overall forest area *c.* 22%.
Gross national product (at current market prices; 2004): U.S.$252,000,000 (U.S.$1,990 per capita).

Structure of gross domestic product and labour force

	1996 in value U.S.$'000,000	1996 % of total value	2000 labour force	2000 % of labour force
Agriculture and fishing[4]	34.7	19.1	15,216	40.7
Mining	0.7	0.4	} 1,164	3.1
Manufacturing	2.6	1.4		
Construction	1.9	1.0	781	2.1
Public utilities	2.0	1.1	360	1.0
Transp. and commun.	8.5	4.7	806	2.1
Finance	5.5	3.0	726	1.9
Services	5.7	3.1	1,445	3.9
Trade, hotels	43.6	24.0	2,540	6.8
Public administration	76.5	42.1	6,137	16.4
Other	...	...	8,239[5]	22.0[5]
TOTAL	181.6[2]	100.0[2]	37,414	100.0

Tourism (2003): receipts from visitors U.S.$17,000,000; expenditures by nationals abroad U.S.$6,000,000.

Foreign trade

Balance of trade (current prices)

	1997[6]	1998[6]	1999[6]	2000[7]	2001[7]	2002[7]
U.S.$'000,000	−40.9	−80.2	−60.3	−90.0	−95.4	−89.9
% of total	95.6%	91.5%	43.4%	72.8%	72.2%	75.7%

Imports (2002): U.S.$104,300,000 (food and beverages 32.5%, industrial supplies 19.4%, machinery and transport equipment 17.0%, mineral fuels 14.2%). *Major import sources:* United States 41.8%; Guam 20.2%; Japan 10.6%; Australia 8.3%; Taiwan 4.8%.
Exports (2002): U.S.$14,400,000 (marine products [mostly fish] 63.3%, garment products 24.9%, betel nuts 6.1%, kava 1.7%, copra 1.5%). *Major export destinations:* United States 25.5%; Japan 18.7%; Guam 7.9%; Northern Marianas 3.4%; unspecified 44.0%.[8]

Transport and communications

Transport. Railroads: none. Roads (1999): total length 149 mi, 240 km (paved 18%). Vehicles (1998): passenger cars 2,044; trucks and buses 354. Air transport: n.a.; airports (1997) with scheduled flights 4.

Communications

Medium	date	unit	number	units per 1,000 persons
Radio	2001	receivers	7,740	71
Television	2001	receivers	2,180	20
Telephones	2001	main lines	10,000	93
Cellular telephones	2002	subscribers	1,800	150
Internet	2003	users	10,500	93

Education and health

Educational attainment (2000). Percentage of population age 25 and over having: no formal schooling 12.3%; primary education 37.0%; some secondary 18.3%; secondary 12.9%; some college 18.4%. *Literacy* (2000): total population age 10 and over literate 72,140 (92.4%); males literate 36,528 (92.9%); females literate 35,612 (91.9%).

Education (2001–02)

	schools	teachers	students	student/ teacher ratio
Elementary (age 6–12)	171[9]	917[10]	26,440	...
Secondary (age 13–18)	24[9]	234[10]	7,446	...
College[11]	1	92	4,352	47.3

Health: physicians (2001) 61 (1 per 1,788 persons); hospital beds (2000) 333 (1 per 323 persons); infant mortality rate per 1,000 live births (2004) 31.3.
Food: daily per capita caloric intake, n.a.

Military

External security is provided by the United States[1].

---

[1]The compact of free association (from 1986) between the United States and the Federated States of Micronesia (FSM) was renewed in 2003 for another 20 years. Terms of the new compact included a cut in U.S. grants after 2004. [2]Detail does not add to total given because of rounding. [3]Weights of consumer price index components. [4]Includes subsistence farming and fishing. [5]Unemployed. [6]Based on imports f.o.b. [7]Based on imports c.i.f. [8]Value of fishing services (in 2002) for foreign licenses and transshipment fees was U.S.$13,954,000. [9]1997–98. [10]1998–99. [11]Data refers to the 1999–2000 school year at the five campuses of the College of Micronesia-FSM.

Internet resources for further information:
• Division of Statistics
  http://www.spc.int/prism/country/FM/stats
• Asian Development Bank: Key Indicators 2005
  http://www.adb.org/Documents/Books/Key_Indicators/2005/pdf/FSM.pdf

Moldova

Official name: Republica Moldova (Republic of Moldova).
Form of government: unitary parliamentary republic with a single legislative body (Parliament [101]).
Head of state: President.
Head of government: Prime Minister.
Capital: Chişinău.
Official language: Romanian[1].
Official religion: none.
Monetary unit: 1 Moldovan leu (plural lei) = 100 bani; valuation (Sept. 1, 2005) 1 U.S.$ = 12.48 Moldovan lei; 1 £ = 22.98 Moldovan lei.

Population (2004 census[2])[3]

Districts[4]	population	Districts[4]	population	Districts[4]	population
Anenii-Noi	81,719	Floreşti	89,406	Străşeni	88,937
Basarabeasca	28,978	Glodeni	60,968	Taraclia	43,151
Briceni	77,978	Hînceşti	119,765	Teleneşti	70,022
Cahul	119,201	Ialoveni	97,759	Ungheni	110,750
Călăraşi	75,167	Leova	51,161		
Cantemir	60,008	Nisporeni	64,945	**Municipalities[4]**	
Căuşeni	90,616	Ocniţa	56,706	Bălţi	127,673
Cimişlia	60,936	Orhei	116,296	Chişinău	716,530
Crivleni	72,259	Rezina	48,112		
Donduşeni	46,437	Rîşcani	69,415	**Autonomous Region**	
Drochia	87,083	Sîngerei	87,158	Găgăuzia	155,781
Dubăsari (rural)	34,004	Şoldăneşti	42,216		
Edineţ	81,384	Soroca	95,015	**Disputed Territory[5]**	
Făleşti	89,915	Ştefan-Vodă	70,620	Transnistria (Stînga Nistrului)	611,200[3]
				TOTAL	3,999,271[6]

Demography

Population (2005): 4,206,000[7].
Density (2005): persons per sq mi 321.9, persons per sq km 124.3.
Urban-rural (2004)[8]: urban 38.6%; rural 61.4%.
Sex distribution (2004)[8]: male 48.18%; female 51.82%.
Age breakdown (2001): under 15, 22.4%; 15–29, 25.5%; 30–44, 21.1%; 45–59, 16.6%; 60–74, 11.0%; 75 and over, 3.4%.
Population projection[7]: (2010) 4,160,000; (2020) 4,054,000.
Ethnic composition (2000): Moldovan 48.2%; Ukrainian 13.8%; Russian 12.9%; Bulgarian 8.2%; Rom (Gypsy) 6.2%; Gagauz 4.2%; other 6.5%.
Religious affiliation (2000): Christian 68.8%, of which Orthodox 44.5%, independent Christian 15.3%, Protestant 1.8%, Roman Catholic 1.7%; Muslim 5.5%; Jewish 1.1%; nonreligious 20.4%; atheist 4.2%.
Major cities (2003)[7]: Chişinău 662,400; Tiraspol 185,000; Bălţi 145,900; Tighina 125,000; Râbniţa 62,000.

Vital statistics

Birth rate per 1,000 population (2004): 14.8 (world avg. 21.1); (1995) legitimate 87.7%; illegitimate 12.3%.
Death rate per 1,000 population (2004): 12.8 (world avg. 9.0).
Natural increase rate per 1,000 population (2004): 2.0 (world avg. 12.1).
Total fertility rate (avg. births per childbearing woman; 2004): 1.8.
Marriage rate per 1,000 population (2002): 6.0.
Life expectancy at birth (2004): male 60.9 years; female 69.4 years.
Major causes of death per 100,000 population (2002)[8]: circulatory diseases 559.0; digestive system diseases 93.8; accidents and violence 83.9; cancers 66.0.

National economy

Budget (2003). Revenue: 9,310,000,000 lei (tax revenue 81.6%, of which value-added tax 30.0%, social fund contributions 21.2%, excise taxes 9.5%, personal income tax 6.7%, profits tax 6.2%, duties and customs taxes 5.1%; nontax and extra budgetary revenue 18.4%). Expenditures: 9,129,000,000 lei (current expenditures 96.3%, of which social fund expenditures 24.8%, education 20.2%, health care 11.7%, interest payments 6.4%; capital expenditure 3.7%).
Production (metric tons except as noted). Agriculture, forestry, fishing (2004): corn (maize) 1,840,000, sugar beets 907,000, wheat 690,000, grapes 600,000, apples 338,000, sunflower seeds 331,000, potatoes 318,000, barley 260,000, tobacco leaves 10,200; livestock (number of live animals) 817,000 sheep, 446,000 pigs, 373,000 cattle; roundwood 56,800 cu m; fish catch (2003) 343. Mining and quarrying (2002): sand and gravel 300,000; gypsum 32,000. Manufacturing (value of production in '000,000 lei; 2004)[8]: alcoholic beverages 4,013, of which wine 3,098; food products 3,461, of which dairy products 624; non-metallic mineral products 1,273, of which glass products 536; tobacco products 410. Energy production (consumption): electricity (kW-hr; 2002) 3,233,000,000 (5,835,000,000); coal (metric tons; 2002) none (152,000); crude petroleum (barrels) none (none); petroleum products (metric tons; 2002) none (513,000); natural gas (cu m; 2002) none (2,460,000,000).
Tourism (2003): receipts from visitors U.S.$58,000,000; expenditures by nationals abroad U.S.$97,000,000.
Population economically active (2004)[8]: total 1,432,500; activity rate of total de facto population 39.6% (participation rates: ages 15–64 [2002] 61.3%; female [2001] 50.4%; unemployed [2004] 8.1%).

Price and earnings indexes (2000 = 100)

	1998	1999	2000	2001	2002	2003	2004
Consumer price index	52.2	76.2	100.0	109.8	115.6	129.2	145.3
Earnings index	61.4	74.7	100.0	133.3	169.5	218.4	270.6

Gross national product (2004): U.S.$2,563,000,000 (U.S.$710 per capita).

Structure of gross domestic product and labour force

	2004		2003	
	in value '000,000 lei[8]	% of total value[8]	labour force[8]	% of labour force[8]
Agriculture	5,833	18.2	583,200	39.6
Mining	105	0.3	1,400	0.1
Manufacturing	4,602	14.4	136,700	9.3
Public utilities	524	1.6	26,400	1.8
Construction	1,314	4.1	53,200	3.6
Transp. and commun.	3,692	11.6	67,600	4.6
Trade, hotels	3,392	10.6	175,700	11.9
Finance	...	...	36,300	2.5
Pub. admin., defense	...	...	65,600	4.5
Services	8,609	26.9	209,700	14.2
Other	3,921[9]	12.3[9]	117,600[10]	8.0[10]
TOTAL	31,992	100.0	1,473,600[11]	100.0[11]

Public debt (external, outstanding; end of 2004): U.S.$678,080,000.
Household income and expenditure. Average household size (2002) 3.3; annual average income per household (2002) U.S.$1,200; sources of income (1994): wages and salaries 41.2%, social benefits 15.3%, agricultural income 10.4%, other 33.1%; expenditure (2001): food and drink 40.4%, housing 13.5%, utilities 10.5%, transportation 8.9%, clothing 7.6%, health 3.9%.
Land use as % of total land area (2000): in temporary crops 55.1%, in permanent crops 10.7%, in pasture 11.7%; overall forest area 9.9%.

Foreign trade

Balance of trade (current prices)

	1999	2000	2001	2002	2003	2004
U.S.$'000,000	−122	−305	−325	−395	−613	−788
% of total	11.7%	24.4%	22.2%	23.5%	27.9%	28.5%

Imports (2004): U.S.$1,774,000,000 (mineral fuels 21.7%; machinery and apparatus 13.5%; chemicals and chemical products 9.1%; textiles and wearing apparel 8.6%). *Major import sources:* Ukraine 24.6%; Russia 12.2%; Romania 9.3%; Germany 8.5%; Italy 7.4%.
Exports (2004): U.S.$986,000,000 (processed food, beverages [significantly wine], and tobacco products 35.1%; textiles and wearing apparel 17.3%; vegetables, fruits, seeds, and nuts 12.2%). *Major export destinations:* Russia 35.8%; Italy 13.9%; Romania 10.0%; Germany 7.3%; Ukraine 6.6%.

Transport and communications

Transport. Railroads (2004): length 1,138 km; passenger-km (2002) 355,000,000; metric ton-km cargo (2002) 2,748,000,000. Roads (2002): total length 12,719 km (paved 86%). Vehicles (2002): passenger cars 268,882; trucks and buses 62,054. Air transport (2004)[12]: passenger-km 262,404,000; metric ton-km cargo 598,000; airports (2001) 1.

Communications

Medium	date	unit	number	units per 1,000 persons
Daily newspapers	2004	circulation	75,000	18
Radio	2001	receivers	3,229,000	758
Television	2001	receivers	1,261,000	296
Telephones	2004	main lines	863,400	205
Cellular telephones	2004	subscribers	787,000	187
Personal computers	2004	units	112,000	27
Internet	2004	users	406,000	96

Education and health

Educational attainment: n.a. *Literacy* (2003): total population age 15 and over literate 99.1%; males 99.6%; females 98.7%.

Education (2003–04)

	schools	teachers	students	student/ teacher ratio
Primary (age 7–13)	119	} 42,600	17,200	...
Secondary (age 14–17)	1,457		561,600	...
Voc., teacher tr.	83	2,200	22,800	10.4
Higher	100	7,700	122,700	15.9

Health: physicians (2002) 12,800 (1 per 332 persons); hospital beds (2003) 28,348 (1 per 149 persons); infant mortality rate per 1,000 live births (2004) 41.0.
Food (2002): daily per capita caloric intake 2,806 (vegetable products 84%, animal products 16%); 110% of FAO recommended minimum requirement.

Military

Total active duty personnel (2004): 6,809 (army 81.0%, air force 15.4%, headquarters staff 3.6%). Opposition forces (excluding Russian troops) in Transnistria (2004) c. 7,500; Russian troops in Transnistria (2005) c. 1,500.
Military expenditure as percentage of GDP (2003): 0.4%; per capita expenditure U.S.$2.

[1]Officially designated Moldovan per constitution. [2]De facto figures. [3]Population for the Disputed Territory (Transnistria) is a 2003 estimate. [4]New administrative scheme implemented in 2003. [5]Breakaway area from 1991 also known as Transdniester or Dubăsari. [6]Summed total of 2004 census and 2003 estimate for Transnistria. Total population including 259,554 Moldovans abroad (at 2004 census) equals 4,258,825. [7]Estimate(s) of *UN World Population Prospects (2004 revision).* [8]Excludes Transnistria. [9]Import and production taxes less imputed bank service charges. [10]Includes unemployed. [11]Detail does not add to total given because of rounding. [12]Air Moldova only.

Internet resources for further information:
• **Department for Statistics and Sociology http://www.statistica.md**
• **Moldovan Economic Trends http://www.met.dnt.md**

Monaco

Official name: Principauté de Monaco (Principality of Monaco).
Form of government: constitutional monarchy with one legislative body (National Council [24]).
Chief of state: Prince.
Head of government[1]: Minister of State assisted by the Council of Government.
Capital: [2].
Official language: French.
Official religion: Roman Catholicism.
Monetary unit: 1 euro[3] (€) = 100 centimes; valuation (Sept. 1, 2005) 1 U.S.$ = €0.80; 1 £ = €1.47.

Area and population		area		population
				2000
Quarters	Capitals[2]	sq mi	sq km	census
Fontvieille	—	0.13	0.33	3,292
La Condamine	—	0.23	0.61	12,187
Monaco-Ville	—	0.07	0.19	1,034
Monte-Carlo	—	0.32	0.82	15,507
TOTAL		0.75[4]	1.95[4]	32,020

Demography

Population (2005): 32,700.
Density (2005): persons per sq mi 43,026, persons per sq km 16,599.
Urban-rural (2003): urban 100%; rural 0%.
Sex distribution (2000): male 48.54%; female 51.46%.
Age breakdown (2000): under 15, 13.2%; 15–29, 13.4%; 30–44, 22.1%; 45–59, 22.4%; 60–74, 17.4%; 75 and over, 11.5%.
Population projection: (2010) 33,000; (2020) 35,000.
Doubling time: not applicable.
Ethnic composition (2000): French 45.8%; Ligurian (Genoan) 17.2%; Monegasque 16.9%; British 4.5%; Jewish 1.7%; other 13.9%.
Religious affiliation (2000): Christian 93.2%, of which Roman Catholic 89.3%; Jewish 1.7%; nonreligious and other 5.1%.

Vital statistics

Birth rate per 1,000 population (2004): 9.4 (world avg. 21.1).
Death rate per 1,000 population (2004): 12.7 (world avg. 9.0).
Natural increase rate per 1,000 population (2004): –3.3 (world avg. 12.1).
Total fertility rate (avg. births per childbearing woman; 2004): 1.8.
Marriage rate per 1,000 population (2002): 5.4.
Divorce rate per 1,000 population (2002): 2.1.
Life expectancy at birth (2004): male 75.5 years; female 83.5 years.
Major causes of death per 100,000 population: n.a.; however, principal causes are those of a developed country with an older population.

National economy

Budget (2001). Revenue: €624,254,804 (value-added taxes c. 50%[5], state-run monopolies c. 20%). Expenditures: €621,041,725 (current expenditure 65.5%, capital expenditure 34.5%).
Public debt: n.a.
Production. Agriculture, forestry, fishing: some horticulture and greenhouse cultivation; no agriculture as such. Mining and quarrying: none. Manufacturing (value of sales in €'000,000; 2003): chemicals, cosmetics, perfumery, and pharmaceuticals 374; plastic products 229; light electronics and precision instruments 76; paper and card manufactures 41; textiles 33. Energy production (consumption): electricity (kW-hr; 2001), n.a. (475,000,000 [imported from France]); coal, none (n.a.); crude petroleum, none (n.a.); natural gas, none (n.a.).
Gross national product (2003): U.S.$1,010,000,000 (U.S.$29,360 per capita)[6].

Labour force		
	2000	
	labour force	% of labour force
Agriculture	20	0.2
Manufacturing	599	4.7
Public utilities, communications	206	1.6
Construction, real estate	874	6.9
Transportation	499	3.9
Trade, hotels	2,591	20.4
Finance	1,114	8.8
Public administration	1,815	14.3
Services	4,288	33.8
Other	694	5.5
TOTAL	12,700[7]	100.0[8]

Population economically active (2000): total 12,700[7]; activity rate of total population 39.7% (participation rates: ages 17–64, 61.1%; female 39.8%; unemployed, n.a.).

Price and earnings indexes (2000 = 100)							
	1998	1999	2000	2001	2002	2003	2004
Consumer price index[9]	97.8	98.3	100.0	101.7	103.6	105.8	108.1
Earnings index[9]	93.6	95.7	100.0	104.5	108.4	112.8	116.1

Household income and expenditure. Average household size (1998) 2.2; average annual income per household: n.a.; sources of income: n.a.; expenditure: n.a.
Tourism (2003): 2,203 hotel rooms; 234,600 overnight stays; 3 casinos run by the state attract 400,000 visitors annually.
Land use as % of total land area (2000): public gardens c. 20%.

Foreign trade[10]

Balance of trade (current prices)						
	1999	2000	2001	2002	2003	2004
€'000,000	–54	+20	+9	–79	+107	+16
% of total	6.4%	2.1%	1.1%	8.3%	11.4%	1.5%

Imports (2004): €512,000,000 (consumer goods and parts for industrial production [including pharmaceuticals, perfumes, clothing, publishing] 25.0%, food products 16.5%, transport equipment and parts 15.2%). *Major import sources:* Italy 32.8%; Belgium 9.9%; Madagascar 6.6%; Germany 6.3%; China 5.7%.
Exports (2004): €528,000,000 (rubber and plastic products, glass, construction materials, organic chemicals, and paper and paper products 40.7%; products of automobile industry 18.3%; pharmaceuticals, perfumes, clothing, publishing 15.0%). *Major export destinations:* Germany 20.7%; Italy 18.5%; Spain 11.7%; U.K. 7.1%; Switzerland 3.4%.

Transport and communications

Transport. Railroads (2001): length 1.1 mi, 1.7 km; passengers 2,171,100; cargo 3,357 tons. Roads (2001): total length 31 mi, 50 km (paved 100%). Vehicles (1997): passenger cars 21,120; trucks and buses 2,770. Air transport: airports with scheduled flights, none[11, 12].

Communications				units per 1,000
Medium	date	unit	number	persons
Daily newspapers	1999	circulation	10,000	300
Radio	1997	receivers	34,000	1,030
Television	1997	receivers	25,000	758
Telephones	2003	main lines	33,500	1,028
Cellular telephones	2003	subscribers	15,100	463
Internet	2003	users	16,000	491

Education and health

Education (2002–03)				student/
	schools	teachers	students	teacher ratio
Primary (age 6–10)	7	...	1,899	...
Secondary (age 11–17)	4	...	3,140	...
Higher	1	53	650	12.3

Educational attainment (2000). Percentage of population age 17 and over having: primary/lower secondary education 24.7%; upper secondary 27.6%; vocational 12.7%; university 35.0%. *Literacy:* virtually 100%.
Health (2002): physicians 156 (1 per 207 persons); hospital beds 521 (1 per 62 persons); infant mortality rate per 1,000 live births (2004) 5.5.
Food: daily per capita caloric intake, n.a.; assuming consumption patterns similar to France (2002) 3,654 (vegetable products 63%, animal products 37%); 145% of FAO recommended minimum requirement.

Military

Defense responsibility lies with France according to the terms of the Versailles Treaty of 1919.

[1]Under the authority of the prince. [2]The principality is a single administrative unit, and no separate area within it is distinguished as capital. [3]French franc (F) replaced by euro on Jan. 1, 2002. [4]0.76 sq mi (1.97 sq km) per most recent survey. [5]On hotels, banks, and the industrial sector. [6]Monaco does not publish national income figures. In 2003 trade, hotels, and restaurants accounted for c. 42% of national revenue and banking and financial activities c. 14%. [7]Includes 3,925 Monegasque workers, 2,900 resident French workers, 5,863 other resident workers, and 12 non-residents; excludes c. 25,000 non-resident foreign workers (mostly French). [8]Detail does not add to total given because of rounding. [9]The index is for France. [10]Excludes trade with France; Monaco has participated in a customs union with France since 1963. [11]Fixed-wing service is provided at Nice, France; helicopter service is available at Fontvieille. [12]Charter service of Monacair (2004): passenger-km 414,000; metric ton-km cargo, none.

Internet resources for further information:
• La Principauté de Monaco
  http://www.gouv.mc
• Monaco—Monte-Carlo
  http://www.monte-carlo.mc

Mongolia

Official name: Mongol Uls
(Mongolia).
Form of government: unitary multiparty
republic with one legislative house
(State Great Hural [76]).
Chief of state: President.
Head of government: Prime Minister.
Capital: Ulaanbaatar (Ulan Bator).
Official language: Khalkha Mongolian.
Official religion: none.
Monetary unit: 1 tugrik (Tug) = 100
möngö; valuation (Sept. 1, 2005)
1 U.S.\$ = Tug 1,207; 1 £ = Tug 2,222.

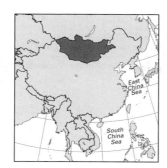

Area and population		area[1]		population
Provinces	Capitals	sq mi	sq km	2004[2] estimate
Arhangay	Tsetserleg	21,400	55,300	96,100
Bayan-Ölgiy	Ölgiy	17,600	45,700	100,800
Bayanhongor	Bayanhongor	44,800	116,000	83,200
Bulgan	Bulgan	18,800	48,700	62,800
Darhan-Uul	Darhan	1,270	3,280	86,500
Dornod	Choybalsan	47,700	123,600	74,400
Dornogovĭ	Saynshand	42,300	109,500	52,100
Dundgovĭ	Mandalgovi	28,800	74,700	50,500
Dzavhan	Uliastay	31,900	82,500	82,900
Govĭ-Altay	Altay	54,600	141,400	61,400
Govĭ-Sümber	Choyr	2,140	5,540	12,200
Hentiy	Öndörhaan	31,000	80,300	71,100
Hovd	Hovd	29,400	76,100	87,500
Hövsgöl	Mörön	38,800	100,600	121,500
Ömnögovĭ	Dalandzadgad	63,900	165,400	46,700
Orhon	Erdenet	320	840	75,100
Övörhangay	Arvayheer	24,300	62,900	113,200
Selenge	Sühbaatar	15,900	41,200	101,800
Sühbaatar	Baruun-Urt	31,800	82,300	56,400
Töv	Dzüünmod	28,600	74,000	92,500
Uvs	Ulaangom	26,900	69,600	81,900
Autonomous municipality				
Ulaanbaatar	—	1,800	4,700	893,400
TOTAL	...	603,930[3]	1,564,160	2,504,000

Demography

Population (2005): 2,550,000.
Density (2005): persons per sq mi 4.2, persons per sq km 1.6.
Urban-rural (2005[2]): urban 59.1%; rural 40.9%.
Sex distribution (2005[2]): male 49.60%; female 50.40%.
Age breakdown (2002): under 15, 32.7%; 15–29, 31.4%; 30–44, 21.2%; 45–59, 9.2%; 60–69, 3.4%; 70 and over, 2.1%.
Population projection: (2010) 2,711,000; (2020) 3,024,000.
Doubling time: 60 years.
Ethnic composition (2000): Khalkha Mongol 81.5%; Kazakh 4.3%; Dörbed Mongol 2.8%; Bayad 2.1%; Buryat Mongol 1.7%; Dariganga Mongol 1.3%; Zakhchin 1.3%; Tuvan (Uriankhai) 1.1%; other 3.9%.
Religious affiliation (2000): traditional beliefs (Shamanism) c. 31%; Buddhist (Lamaism) c. 22%; Muslim c. 5%; Christian c. 1%; nonreligious/atheist c. 40%; other 1%.
Major cities (2000): Ulaanbaatar (Ulan Bator [2005[2]]) 942,747; Erdenet 68,310; Darhan 65,791; Choybalsan 41,714; Ulaangom 26,319.

Vital statistics

Birth rate per 1,000 population (2005[2]): 18.1 (world avg. 21.1); legitimate (2001) 82.2%; illegitimate (2001) 17.8%.
Death rate per 1,000 population (2005[2]): 6.5 (world avg. 9.0).
Natural increase rate per 1,000 population (2005[2]): 11.6 (world avg. 12.1).
Total fertility rate (avg. births per childbearing woman; 2004): 2.3.
Marriage rate per 1,000 population (2005[2]): 4.4.
Life expectancy at birth (2005[2]): male 61.6 years; female 67.8 years.
Major causes of death per 100,000 population (2003): diseases of the circulatory system 244.1; malignant neoplasms (cancers) 121.6; accidents 84.0; diseases of the digestive system 49.0; diseases of the respiratory system 34.2.

National economy

Budget (2003). Revenue: Tug 553,900,000,000 (taxes 76.0%, of which VAT 34.3%, income tax 17.6%, social security contributions 11.8%; nontax revenue 24.0%). Expenditures: Tug 615,800,000,000 (education, health, social services 47.4%; wages 19.0%; capital investment 14.7%; interest 2.9%).
Public debt (external; 2003): U.S.\$1,138,000,000.
Tourism (2003): receipts U.S.\$143,000,000; expenditures U.S.\$108,000,000.
Population economically active (2004[2]): total 959,800; activity rate of total population 38.8% (participation rates: age 16–59, 63.8%; female 49.6%; unemployed [2005[2]] 3.6%).

Price index (2000 = 100)							
	1998	1999	2000	2001	2002	2003	2004
Consumer price index	83.3	89.6	100.0	106.3	107.3	112.8	122.0

Production (metric tons except as noted). Agriculture, forestry, fishing (2005[2]): hay 850,500, potatoes 80,200, vegetables 49,000; livestock (number of live animals) 12,238,000 goats, 11,686,400 sheep, 2,005,300 horses, 1,841,600 cattle, 256,600 camels; roundwood (2004) 631,000 cu m; fish catch (2003) 130. Mining and quarrying (2003): fluorspar 275,000; copper (metal content) 130,270; molybdenum (metal content) 1,793; gold 11,100 kg. Manufacturing (value

added by manufacturing in Tug '000,000; 2001): textiles 82,486; food and beverages 81,319; clothing and apparel 23,007; printing 6,380; nonmetallic mineral products 6,088; chemicals 4,849; wood products 2,694; leather and footwear 1,573. Energy production (consumption): electricity (kW-hr; 2002) 3,112,000,000 (3,263,000,000); hard coal (metric tons; 2002) 922,000 (922,000); lignite (metric tons; 2002) 4,746,000 (4,746,000); petroleum products (metric tons; 2002) none (466,000).
Gross national product (2004): U.S.\$1,484,000,000 (U.S.\$590 per capita).

Structure of gross domestic product and labour force				
	2004		2005[2]	
	in value Tug '000,000,000	% of total value	labour force	% of labour force
Agriculture	385.7	21.3	381,800	38.7
Mining	312.8	17.3	33,500	3.4
Manufacturing	96.4	5.3	57,300	5.8
Construction	47.0	2.6	39,200	4.0
Public utilities	53.6	3.0	23,400	2.4
Transp. and commun.	229.1	12.7	42,200	4.3
Trade	445.5	24.6	162,100	16.4
Finance, real estate	14.6	0.8	27,100	2.7
Public admin., defense	68.2	3.8	46,200	4.7
Services	...	...	137,900	14.0
Other	155.2	8.6	35,600[4]	3.6[4]
TOTAL	1,808.0[3]	100.0	986,100	100.0

Household income and expenditure (2001): Average household size (2005[2]) 4.2; annual income per household (2001) Tug 1,226,000 (U.S.\$1,100); sources of income (2001): wages 29.2%, self-employment 28.6%, transfer payments 8.0%, other 34.2%; expenditure (2001): food 42.5%, clothing 16.2%, transportation and communications 7.8%, education 7.1%, housing 6.8%, health care 1.7%.
Land use as % of total land area (2000): in temporary crops 0.7%, in permanent crops, negligible, in pasture 82.5%; overall forest area 6.8%.

Foreign trade[5]

Balance of trade (current prices)						
	1999	2000	2001	2002	2003	2004
U.S.\$'000,000	−58.6	−78.7	−116.2	−158.1	−185.1	−158.3
% of total	6.1%	6.8%	10.0%	13.6%	13.1%	8.5%

Imports (2004): U.S.\$1,011,600,000 (mineral fuels 22.9%; machinery and apparatus 19.9%; food and agricultural products 15.5%; transportation equipment 10.3%). *Major import sources:* Russia 31.0%; China 23.1%; Japan 8.4%; South Korea 6.7%; U.S. 3.7%.
Exports (2004): U.S.\$853,300,000 (2001: copper concentrate 28.1%, gold 14.3%, cashmere [all forms] 13.4%, fluorspar 3.8%). *Major export destinations:* China 50.7%; U.S. 26.3%; Canada 5.3%; U.K. 4.3%.

Transport and communications

Transport. Railroads (2005[2]): length 1,815 km; passenger-km 2,555,700,000; metric ton-km cargo 9,168,500,000. Roads (2004): total length 49,256 km (paved 18%). Vehicles (2005[2]): passenger cars 79,700; trucks and buses 36,000. Air transport (2004)[6]: passenger-km 692,602,000; metric ton-km cargo 6,528,000; airports (2001) with scheduled flights 1.

Communications				units per 1,000
Medium	date	unit	number	persons
Daily newspapers	2004	circulation	50,000	20
Radio	2000	receivers	368,000	154
Television	2003	receivers	220,000	88
Telephones	2005[2]	main lines	154,600	61
Cellular telephones	2005[2]	subscribers	466,566	183
Personal computers	2004	units	312,000	124
Internet	2004	users	200,000	79

Education and health

Educational attainment (2000). Percentage of population age 10 and over having: no formal education 11.6%; primary education 23.5%; secondary 46.1%; vocational secondary 11.2%; higher 7.6%. *Literacy* (2003): percentage of total population age 15 and over literate 97.8%; males 98.0%; females 97.5%.

Education (2003–04)				student/
	schools	teachers	students	teacher ratio
Primary (age 6–12)	72	7,200	232,400	32.3
Secondary (age 13–16)	614	13,600	305,000	22.4
Vocational (age 16–18)	32	642[7]	21,500	...
Higher	183	5,366[7]	108,500	...

Health (2005[2]): physicians 6,590 (1 per 384 persons); hospital beds 18,400 (1 per 138 persons); infant mortality rate per 1,000 live births 22.2.
Food (2002): daily per capita caloric intake 2,249 (vegetable products 60%, animal products 40%); 93% of FAO recommended minimum.

Military

Total active duty personnel (2004): 8,600 (army 87.2%, air force 9.3%, unspecified 3.5%). *Military expenditure as percentage of GDP* (2003): 1.4%; per capita expenditure U.S.\$6.

[1]Rounded figures. [2]January 1. [3]Detail does not add to total given because of rounding. [4]Unemployed. [5]Imports c.i.f.; exports f.o.b. [6]Mongolian Airlines (MIAT) only. [7]2002–03.

Internet resources for further information:
• **National Statistical Office of Mongolia http://www.nso.mn/eng/index.php**
• **Bank of Mongolia http://www.mongolbank.mn**

Morocco

Official name: Al-Mamlakah al-Maghrībīyah (Kingdom of Morocco).
Form of government: constitutional monarchy with two legislative houses (House of Councillors [270[1]]; House of Representatives [325]).
Chief of state and head of government: King assisted by Prime Minister.
Capital: Rabat.
Official language: Arabic.
Official religion: Islam.
Monetary unit: 1 Moroccan dirham (DH) = 100 Moroccan francs; valuation (Sept. 1, 2005)
1 U.S.$ = DH 8.80; 1 £ = DH 16.20.

Population[2]

Regions	Administrative centres	population 2004 census
Chaouia-Ouardigha	Settat	1,655,660
Doukkala-Abda	Safi	1,984,039
Fès-Boulemane	Fès	1,573,055
Gharb-Chrarda-Béni Hsen	Kénitra	1,859,540
Grand Casablanca	Casablanca	3,631,061
Guelmim-Es Semara	Guelmim	462,410
Laâyoune-Bojador-Sakia El-Hamra	Laâyoune	256,152
Marrakech-Tensift-El Haouz	Marrakech	3,102,652
Meknès-Tafilalt	Meknès	2,141,527
Oriental	Oujda	1,918,094
Oued Eddahab-Lagouira	Dakhla	99,367
Rabat-Salé-Zemmour-Zaër	Rabat	2,366,494
Sous-Massa-Draâ	Agadir	3,113,653
Tadla-Azilal	Béni Mellal	1,450,519
Tangier-Tetouan	Tangier	2,470,372
Taza-Al Hoceïma-Taounate	Al-Hoceïma	1,807,113
TOTAL		29,891,708

Demography

Area[2]: 274,461 sq mi, 710,850 sq km.
Population (2005)[2]: 30,230,000[3].
Density (2005)[2]: persons per sq mi 110.1, persons per sq km 42.5.
Urban-rural (2004): urban 55.1%; rural 44.9%.
Sex distribution (2003): male 49.76%; female 50.24%.
Age breakdown (2003): under 15, 30.2%; 15–29, 30.3%; 30–44, 20.7%; 45–59, 11.2%; 60–74, 6.0%; 75 and over, 1.6%.
Population projection[2]: (2010) 32,368,000; (2020) 36,669,000.
Doubling time: 48 years.
Ethnic composition (2000): Berber c. 45%, of which Arabized c. 24%; Arab c. 44%; Moors originally from Mauritania c. 10%; other c. 1%.
Religious affiliation (2000): Muslim (mostly Sunnī) 98.3%; Christian 0.6%; other 1.1%.
Major urban areas (2003): Casablanca 3,353,000; Rabat-Salé (2000) 1,616,000; Fès 1,053,000; Marrakech (2000) 822,000; Tangier 681,444; Agadir 550,200.

Vital statistics

Birth rate per 1,000 population (2004): 20.1 (world avg. 21.1).
Death rate per 1,000 population (2004): 5.5 (world avg. 9.0).
Natural increase rate per 1,000 population (2004): 14.6 (world avg. 12.1).
Total fertility rate (avg. births per childbearing woman; 2004): 2.8.
Life expectancy at birth (2002): male 67.5 years; female 72.1 years.
Major causes of death per 100,000 population (2002): diseases of the circulatory system 201, of which ischemic heart disease 100; infectious and parasitic diseases 120; malignant neoplasms (cancers) 41; accidents and injuries 40; chronic respiratory disease 23.

National economy

Budget. Revenue (2003): DH 102,482,000,000 (value-added tax 25.5%; individual income tax 17.2%; excise taxes 15.2%; corporate taxes 14.2%; international trade 12.2%; stamp tax 5.2%). Expenditures (2003): DH 128,113,-000,000 (current expenditure 76.8%, of which wages 42.1%, debt payment 13.5%; capital expenditure 17.1%; transfers to local governments 6.1%).
Public debt (external, outstanding; 2003): U.S.$15,224,000,000.
Population economically active (2002)[4]: total 10,482,000; activity rate 35.4% (participation rates: ages 15–59, 54.5%; female 24.8%; unemployed [2003] 11.9%).

Price index (2000 = 100)

	1998	1999	2000	2001	2002	2003	2004
Consumer price index	97.5	98.1	100.0	100.6	103.4	104.6	106.2

Production (metric tons except as noted). Agriculture, forestry, fishing (2004): wheat 5,539,840, sugar beets 4,560,000, barley 2,760,340, potatoes 1,440,000, tomatoes 1,201,230, oranges 719,300, olives 470,000; livestock (number of live animals) 17,026,300 sheep, 5,358,600 goats, 2,728,800 cattle, 980,000 asses; roundwood 885,000 cu m; fish catch (2003) 914,253, of which sardines 659,208. Mining and quarrying (2003): phosphate rock 22,877,000; barite 356,394; zinc (metal content) 70,000; lead (metal content) 38,000; silver (including smelter bullion) 200,528 kg. Manufacturing (value added in U.S.$'000,000; 2001): food products 778; tobacco products 635; wearing apparel 565; bricks, pottery, and cement 456; basic chemicals 358. Energy production (consumption): electricity (kW-hr; 2002) 15,050,000,000 (16,607,000,000); coal (metric tons; 2002)

16,000 (5,227,000); crude petroleum (barrels; 2002) 91,000 (53,000,000); petroleum products (metric tons; 2002) 5,937,000 (7,457,000); natural gas (cu m; 2002) 51,000,000 (51,000,000).
Gross national product (2004): U.S.$46,518,000,000 (U.S.$1,520 per capita).

Structure of gross domestic product and labour force

	2003		2002	
	in value DH '000,000	% of total value	labour force	% of labour force
Agriculture	70,427	16.8	3,951,000	38.1
Mining	6,634[5]	1.6[5]		
Manufacturing	69,569[5]	16.6[5]	1,231,000	11.9
Public utilities	28,019[5]	6.7[5]		
Construction	19,462	4.7	646,000	6.2
Transp. and commun.	29,860	7.1	332,000	3.2
Pub. admin., defense	66,569	15.9	503,000	4.8
Trade			1,180,000	11.4
Finance, real estate	127,935	30.6	1,330,000	12.8
Services				
Other			1,206,000[6]	11.6[6]
TOTAL	418,655	100.0	10,379,000	100.0

Tourism (2003): receipts U.S.$2,856,000,000; expenditures U.S.$485,000,000.
Household income and expenditure. Average household size (2004) 5.3; expenditure (1994)[7]: food 45.2%, housing 12.5%, transportation 7.6%.
Land use as % of total land area (2000): in temporary crops 19.6%, in permanent crops 2.2%, in pasture 47.1%; overall forest area 6.8%.

Foreign trade[8]

Balance of trade (current prices)

	1999	2000	2001	2002	2003	2004
DH '000,000	−32,314	−43,700	−44,051	−44,021	−52,183	−69,932
% of total	18.0%	21.7%	21.4%	20.3%	23.7%	28.8%

Imports (2004): DH 156,297,000,000 (machinery and apparatus 22.0%; mineral fuels 16.7%, of which crude petroleum 9.3%; food and beverages 8.3%; cotton fabric and fibres 4.9%). *Major import sources:* France 17.9%; Spain 12.0%; Italy 6.6%; Germany 6.0%; China 4.2%.
Exports (2004)[9]: DH 86,365,000,000 (garments 21.6%; food, beverages, and tobacco products 15.7%; knitwear 8.8%; phosphoric acid 7.6%; machinery and apparatus 7.6%; phosphate 4.6%). *Major export destinations:* France 33.1%; Spain 17.4%; U.K. 7.7%; Italy 4.7%; U.S. 4.1%.

Transport and communications

Transport. Railroads (2003): route length 1,907 km; passenger-km 2,374,000,-000; metric ton-km cargo 5,146,000,000. Roads (2002): total length 57,694 km (paved 56%). Vehicles: passenger cars (2002) 1,326,108; trucks and buses (2000) 415,700. Air transport (2004)[10]: passenger-km 7,328,000,000; metric ton-km cargo 62,568,000; airports (2002) 15.

Communications

Medium	date	unit	number	units per 1,000 persons
Daily newspapers	2000	circulation	740,000	26
Radio	2000	receivers	6,920,000	243
Television	2000	receivers	4,720,000	166
Telephones	2004	main lines	1,308,600	44
Cellular telephones	2004	subscribers	9,336,900	312
Personal computers	2004	units	620,000	21
Internet	2004	users	3,500,000	117

Education and health

Educational attainment: n.a. *Literacy* (2000): total population over age 15 literate 48.9%; males literate 61.1%; females literate 35.1%.

Education (2002–03)

	schools[11]	teachers	students	student/ teacher ratio
Primary (age 7–12)	6,565	135,199	4,101,157	30.3
Secondary (age 13–17)	1,664	87,887	1,679,077	19.1
Vocational	69	...	143,692	...
Higher	68	10,064	276,018	27.4

Health (2003): physicians 16,307 (1 per 1,804 persons); hospital beds 26,257 (1 per 1,120 persons); infant mortality rate (2004) 43.3.
Food (2002): daily per capita caloric intake 3,052 (vegetable products 92%, animal products 8%); 126% of FAO recommended minimum requirement.

Military

Total active duty personnel (2004): 196,300 (army 89.1%, navy 4.0%, air force 6.9%). *Military expenditure as percentage of GDP* (2003): 4.2%; per capita expenditure U.S.$63.

[1]All seats indirectly elected: 162 by regional councils; 108 by industry, agriculture, and trade unions. [2]Includes Western Sahara, annexure of Morocco whose unresolved political status (from 1991) is to be decided by an internationally sponsored referendum; Western Sahara area: 97,344 sq mi, 252,120 sq km; Western Sahara population (2005 est.) 341,000. [3]Another 170,000 Western Saharan refugees live in camps near Tindouf, Alg. [4]Estimated figures. [5]Public utilities includes crude petroleum and refined petroleum. [6]Including 1,203,000 unemployed. [7]Weights of consumer price index components. [8]Imports c.i.f.; exports f.o.b. [9]Cannabis is an important illegal export; estimated production (2003) 47,400 metric tons. [10]Royal Air Maroc only. [11]1999–2000.

Internet resources for further information:
• **Royaume du Maroc: Direction de la statistique**
  http://www.statistic-hcp.ma
• **Bank al-Maghrib http://www.bkam.ma**

Mozambique

Official name: República de Moçambique (Republic of Mozambique).
Form of government: multiparty republic with a single legislative house (Assembly of the Republic [250]).
Head of state and government: President.
Capital: Maputo.
Official language: Portuguese.
Official religion: none.
Monetary unit: 1 metical (Mt; plural meticais) = 100 centavos; valuation (Sept. 1, 2005) 1 U.S.$ = Mt 24,458; 1 £ = Mt 45,033.

Area and population		area		population
Provinces	Capitals	sq mi	sq km	2002 estimate
Cabo Delgado	Pemba	31,902	82,625	1,525,634
Gaza	Xai-Xai	29,231	75,709	1,266,431
Inhambane	Inhambane	26,492	68,615	1,326,848
Manica	Chimoio	23,807	61,661	1,207,332
Maputo	Maputo	9,944	25,756	1,003,992
Nampula	Nampula	31,508	81,606	3,410,141
Niassa	Lichinga	49,828	129,055	916,672
Sofala	Beira	26,262	68,018	1,516,166
Tete	Tete	38,890	100,724	1,388,205
Zambézia	Quelimane	40,544	105,008	3,476,484
City				
Maputo	—	232	602	1,044,618
TOTAL LAND AREA		308,642[1]	799,379	
INLAND WATER		5,019	13,000	
TOTAL		313,661	812,379	18,082,523

Demography

Population (2005): 19,407,000.
Density (2005): persons per sq mi 61.9, persons per sq km 23.9.
Urban-rural (2003): urban 35.6%; rural 64.4%.
Sex distribution (2004): male 49.00%; female 51.00%.
Age breakdown (2004): under 15, 43.5%; 15–29, 26.5%; 30–44, 16.5%; 45–59, 9.0%; 60–74, 3.8%; 75 and over, 0.7%.
Population projection: (2010) 20,673,000; (2020) 22,710,000.
Doubling time: 44 years.
Ethnic composition (2000): Makuana 15.3%; Makua 14.5%; Tsonga 8.6%; Sena 8.0%; Lomwe 7.1%; Tswa 5.7%; Chwabo 5.5%; other 35.3%.
Religious affiliation (2000): traditional beliefs 50.4%; Christian 38.4%, of which Roman Catholic 15.8%, Protestant 8.9%; Muslim 10.5%.
Major cities (1997): Maputo 989,386; Matola 440,927; Beira 412,588; Nampula 314,965; Chimoio 177,608.

Vital statistics

Birth rate per 1,000 population (2004): 36.5 (world avg. 21.1).
Death rate per 1,000 population (2004): 20.6 (world avg. 9.0).
Natural increase rate per 1,000 population (2004): 15.9 (world avg. 12.1).
Total fertility rate (avg. births per childbearing woman; 2004): 4.8.
Life expectancy at birth (2004): male 40.3 years; female 41.4 years.
Adult population (ages 15–49) *living with HIV* (2004[2]): 12.2% (world avg. 1.1%).

National economy

Budget (2002). Revenue: Mt 22,077,000,000,000 (tax revenue 48.1%, of which VAT 20.8%, taxes on international trade 8.4%, personal income tax 5.9%; grants 45.1%; nontax revenue 6.8%). Expenditures: Mt 29,032,000,000,000 (current expenditures 46.4%; capital expenditures 41.8%; net lending 11.8%).
Public debt (external, outstanding; 2003): U.S.$2,992,000,000.
Production (metric tons except as noted). Agriculture, forestry, fishing (2004): cassava 6,150,000, corn (maize) 1,248,000, sugarcane 400,000, sorghum 314,000, coconuts 265,000, rice 201,000, peanuts (groundnuts) 110,000, bananas 90,000, cashews 58,000, tobacco 12,000; livestock (number of live animals) 1,320,000 cattle, 392,000 goats, 28,000,000 chickens; roundwood 18,043,000 cu m; fish catch (2002) 36,462. Mining and quarrying (2003): limestone 1,348,000; bauxite 11,800; tantalite 188,695 kg; gold 63 kg[3]. Manufacturing (value added in Mt '000,000,000; 2002): aluminum 13,547; beverages 2,130; food products 1,789; paper and paper products 1,449; textiles 596. Energy production (consumption): electricity (kW-hr; 2002) 12,713,000,000 (7,446,000,000); coal (metric tons; 2003) 36,700 ([2002] 8,000); crude petroleum, none (none); petroleum products (metric tons; 2002) none (436,000); natural gas (cu m; 2003) 2,500,000 ([2002] 2,400,000).
Household income and expenditure. Average family size (1997) 4.1; income per household: n.a.; source of income (1992–93)[4]: wages and salaries 51.6%, self-employment 12.5%, barter 11.5%, private farming 7.7%; expenditure (1998)[4]: food, beverages, and tobacco 63.5%, firewood and furniture 17.0%, transportation and communications 4.6%, clothing and footwear 4.6%, education and recreation 2.7%.
Population economically active (2002): total 9,696,000; activity rate 55.3% (participation rates: over age 15, n.a.; female [1996] 46.3%; unemployed, n.a.).

Price index (2000 = 100)							
	1998	1999	2000	2001	2002	2003	2004
Consumer price index	86.2	88.7	100.0	109.0	127.4	144.4	160.5

Gross national product (2004): U.S.$4,710,000,000 (U.S.$250 per capita).

Structure of gross domestic product and labour force				
	2003		2002	
	in value Mt '000,000,000	% of total value	labour force	% of labour force
Agriculture	32,869	15.9	7,837,000	80.8
Mining	817	0.4		
Manufacturing	37,121	18.0		
Construction	28,758	13.9		
Public utilities	6,852	3.3		
Transp. and commun.	22,117	10.7	1,859,000	19.2
Finance	8,604	4.2		
Trade	41,960	20.3		
Pub. admin., defense	15,568	7.5		
Services	11,832	5.7		
Other	...	...	...	...
TOTAL	206,497[1]	100.0[1]	9,696,000	100.0

Tourism (2003): receipts from visitors U.S.$98,000,000; expenditures by nationals abroad U.S.$140,000,000.
Land use as % of total land area (2000): in temporary crops 5.0%, in permanent crops 0.3%, in pasture 56.1%; overall forest area 39.0%.

Foreign trade[5]

Balance of trade (current prices)						
	1999	2000	2001	2002	2003	2004
U.S.$'000,000	−806	−682	−271	−667	−604	−346
% of total	58.7%	48.4%	15.7%	29.2%	22.4%	10.3%

Imports (2003): U.S.$1,753,000,000 (mineral fuels 16.5%; machinery and apparatus 16.2%; food products 12.3%, of which cereals 7.2%; transport equipment 9.0%). *Major import sources:* South Africa 37.3%; Australia 12.1%; U.S. 5.9%; India 4.2%; Portugal 3.6%.
Exports (2003): U.S.$1,044,000,000 (aluminum 54.4%; electricity 10.9%; prawns 7.3%; cotton 3.1%; tobacco 2.1%). *Major export destinations:* Belgium 43.5%; South Africa 16.2%; Spain 6.7%; Portugal 3.7%; Malawi 3.1%.

Transport and communications

Transport. Railroads (2002): route length 1,940 mi, 3,123 km; (2001) passenger-km 142,000,000; (2001) metric ton-km cargo 774,500,000. Roads (1999): total length 18,890 mi, 30,400 km (paved 19%). Vehicles (2001): passenger cars 81,600; trucks and buses 76,000. Air transport (2004)[6]: passenger-km 388,412,000; metric ton-km cargo 5,490,000; airports (1997) with scheduled flights 7.

Communications				units per 1,000 persons
Medium	date	unit	number	
Daily newspapers	2000	circulation	53,000	3.0
Radio	2000	receivers	778,000	44
Television	2002	receivers	257,600	14
Telephones	2002	main lines	83,700	4.6
Cellular telephones	2004	subscribers	708,000	37
Personal computers	2004	units	112,000	5.9
Internet	2004	users	138,000	7.3

Education and health

Educational attainment (1997). Percentage of population age 15 and over having: no formal schooling 78.4%; primary education 18.4%; secondary 2.0%; technical 0.4%; higher 0.2%; other/unknown 0.6%. *Literacy* (2000): percentage of total population age 15 and over literate 43.8%; males literate 59.9%; females literate 28.4%.

Education (2001–02)				student/ teacher ratio
	schools	teachers	students	
Primary (age 7–12)	6,263[7]	38,762	2,555,975	65.9
Secondary (age 13–18)	75[8]	13,916	381,619	27.4
Voc., teacher tr.	25[8]	862	20,880	24.2
Higher[8]	3	954	7,156	7.5

Health: physicians (2000) 435 (1 per 40,847 persons); hospital beds (1997) 12,630 (1 per 1,210 persons); infant mortality rate per 1,000 live births (2004) 132.0.
Food (2002): daily per capita caloric intake 2,079 (vegetable products 98%, animal products 2%); 89% of FAO recommended minimum requirement.

Military

Total active duty personnel (2004): c. 10,700 (army c. 89%, navy c. 2%, air force c. 9%). *Military expenditure as percentage of GDP* (2003): 1.3%; per capita expenditure U.S.$3.

[1]Detail does not add to total given because of rounding. [2]Beginning of year. [3]Official figures; unofficial artisanal production is 360–480 kg per year. [4]Weights of consumer price index components. [5]Imports are f.o.b. in balance of trade and c.i.f. for commodities and trading partners. [6]LAM (Linhas Aéreas de Moçambique) only. [7]1998. [8]1997.

Internet resources for further information:
• **Instituto Nacional de Estatística** http://www.ine.gov.mz
• **Banco de Moçambique** http://www.bancomoc.mz

Myanmar (Burma)

Official name: Pyidaungzu Myanma
Nainngngandaw (Union of Myanmar).
Form of government: military regime.
Head of state and government:
Chairman of the State Peace and
Development Council, assisted by
Prime Minister.
Capital: Yangôn (Rangoon)[1].
Official language: Burmese.
Official religion: none.
Monetary unit: 1 Myanmar kyat
(K) = 100 pyas; valuation[2] (Sept. 1,
2005) 1 U.S.$ = K 6.42; 1 £ = K 11.82.

Area and population

Divisions	Capitals	area sq mi	area sq km	population 1994 estimate
Irrawaddy (Ayeyarwady)	Bassein (Pathein)	13,567	35,138	6,107,000
Magwe (Magway)	Magwe (Magway)	17,305	44,820	4,067,000
Mandalay	Mandalay	14,295	37,024	5,823,000
Pegu (Bago)	Pegu (Bago)	15,214	39,404	4,607,000
Sagaing	Sagaing	36,535	94,625	4,889,000
Tenasserim (Tanintharyi)	Tavoy (Dawei)	16,735	43,343	1,187,000
Yangôn	Yangôn (Rangoon)	3,927	10,171	5,037,000
States				
Chin	Hakha	13,907	36,019	438,000
Kachin	Myitkyinā	34,379	89,041	1,135,000
Karen (Kayin)	Pa-an (Hpa-an)	11,731	30,383	1,323,000
Kayah	Loi-kaw	4,530	11,733	228,000
Mon	Moulmein (Mawlamyine)	4,748	12,297	2,183,000
Rakhine (Arakan)	Sittwe (Akyab)	14,200	36,778	2,482,000
Shan	Taunggyi	60,155	155,801	4,416,000
TOTAL		261,228	676,577	43,922,000

Demography

Population (2005): 46,997,000.
Density (2005): persons per sq mi 179.9, persons per sq km 69.5.
Urban-rural (2004): urban 30.0%; rural 70.0%.
Sex distribution (2003): male 49.60%; female 50.40%.
Age breakdown (2002): under 15, 28.5%; 15–29, 30.8%; 30–44, 22.0%; 45–59, 11.4%; 60 and over, 5.7%.
Population projection: (2010) 48,844,000; (2020) 51,709,000.
Doubling time: 58 years.
Ethnic composition (2000): Burman 55.9%; Karen 9.5%; Shan 6.5%; Han Chinese 2.5%; Mon 2.3%; Yangbye 2.2%; Kachin 1.5%; other 19.6%.
Religious affiliation (2000): Buddhist 72.7%; Christian 8.3%; Muslim 2.4%; Hindu 2.0%; traditional beliefs 12.6%; other 2.0%.
Major cities (2004 est.): Yangôn (Rangoon) 4,455,500; Mandalay 1,176,900; Moulmein (Mawlamyine) 405,800; Bassein (Pathein) 215,600; Pegu (Bago) 200,900.

Vital statistics

Birth rate per 1,000 population (2004): 23.2 (world avg. 21.1).
Death rate per 1,000 population (2004): 11.2 (world avg. 9.0).
Natural increase rate per 1,000 population (2004): 12.0 (world avg. 12.1).
Total fertility rate (avg. births per childbearing woman; 2004): 2.8.
Life expectancy at birth (2004): male 57.5 years; female 63.6 years.
Major causes of death per 100,000 population (2002): infectious and parasitic diseases 477; cardiovascular diseases 258; injuries, accidents, and violence 92; malignant neoplasms (cancers) 74; chronic respiratory diseases 57.

National economy

Budget (2000–01). Revenue: K 134,550,000,000 (revenue from taxes 56.4%, of which taxes on goods and services 32.8%, taxes on income 19.4%; nontax revenue 43.4%; foreign grants 0.2%). Expenditures: K 221,255,000,000 (defense 28.7%; agriculture and forestry 17.4%; education 14.2%; public works and housing 9.2%).
Public debt (external, outstanding; 2003): U.S.$5,857,000,000.
Tourism (2003): receipts from visitors U.S.$58,000,000; expenditures by nationals abroad U.S.$32,000,000.
Production (metric tons except as noted). Agriculture, forestry, fishing (2004): rice 22,000,000, sugarcane 6,368,000, dry beans 1,550,000, onions 738,000, peanuts (groundnuts) 715,000, corn (maize) 600,000, sesame seeds 550,000, plantains 530,000, pigeon peas 500,000, sunflower seeds 350,000, chickpeas 230,000, betel nuts 57,000, natural rubber 36,000, opium poppy (2003) 810; livestock (number of live animals) 11,939,000 cattle, 5,217,000 pigs, 2,650,000 buffalo; roundwood 39,815,200 cu m; fish catch (2003) 1,349,169. Mining and quarrying (2003): copper (metal content) 27,900; jade 11,000,000 kg; rubies, sapphires, and spinel (2003–04) 4,700,000 carats. Manufacturing (value added in U.S.$'000,000; 2000): tobacco products 1,320; paints, soaps, and pharmaceuticals (1998) 300; transportation equipment 183; non-electrical machinery 147; iron and steel 129; food and food products, n.a.; refined petroleum, n.a.; cement, bricks, and ceramics, n.a. Energy production (consumption): electricity (kW-hr; 2002) 6,614,000,000 (6,614,000,000); hard coal (metric tons; 2002) 50,000 (50,000); lignite (metric tons; 2003) 57,000 (57,000); crude petroleum (barrels; 2002) 3,500,000 (7,500,000); petroleum products (metric tons; 2002) 909,000 (1,530,000); natural gas (cu m; 2002) 6,483,000,000 (1,199,000,000).
Household income and expenditure. Average household size (2000) 4.8; average annual income per household: n.a.; sources of income: n.a.; expenditure (1994)[3]: food and beverages 67.1%, fuel and lighting 6.6%, transportation 4.0%, charitable contributions 3.1%, medical care 3.1%.

Gross national product (2003): U.S.$58,064,000,000 (U.S.$1,170 per capita).

Structure of gross domestic product and labour force

	2002–03 in value K '000,000	2002–03 % of total value	1997–98 labour force[4]	1997–98 % of labour force[4]
Agriculture	3,019,693	54.6	12,093,000	65.9
Mining	24,409	0.5	121,000	0.7
Manufacturing	508,737	9.2	1,666,000	9.1
Construction	182,455	3.3	400,000	2.2
Public utilities	4,540	0.1	26,000	0.1
Transp. and commun.	344,149	6.2	495,000	2.7
Trade	1,304,516	23.6	1,781,000	9.7
Finance	4,189	0.1	} 1,485,000	} 8.1
Public administration	49,775	0.9		
Services	84,537	1.5	270,000	1.5
TOTAL	5,527,000	100.0	18,337,000	100.0

Population economically active (1999): total 23,700,000; activity rate of total population 57.1% (participation rates: ages 15–64, n.a.; female, n.a.; unemployed [2004] 5.2%).

Price index (2000 = 100)

	1998	1999	2000	2001	2002	2003	2004
Consumer price index	84.6	100.1	100.0	121.1	190.2	259.8	271.6

Land use as % of total land area (2000): in temporary crops 15.1%, in permanent crops 0.9%, in pasture 0.5%; overall forest area 52.3%.

Foreign trade[5]

Balance of trade (current prices)[6]

	1997–98	1998–99	1999–2000	2000–01	2001–02	2002–03
K '000,000	−7,919	−10,116	−7,318	−2,638	−1,346	+5,045
% of total	38.0%	42.8%	29.0%	9.7%	3.5%	14.5%

Imports (2002–03[6]): K 14,910,000,000 (basic manufactures 27.4%, machinery and transport equipment 23.9%, mineral fuels 14.1%, chemicals and chemical products 11.8%). *Major import sources* (2004): China 28.3%; Singapore 20.6%; Thailand 19.1%; South Korea 5.8%; Malaysia 4.4%.
Exports (2002–03[6]): K 19,955,000,000 (mineral fuels [mostly natural gas] 29.6%; food 19.0%, of which pulses and beans 8.8%; garments c. 14%; teak and other hardwood 9.4%). *Major export destinations* (2004): Thailand 37.0%; India 14.0%; China 6.2%; Japan 5.1%; United Kingdom 4.0%.

Transport and communications

Transport. Railroads (2004): route length 3,955 km; passenger-km 4,163,000,000; metric ton-km cargo 885,000,000. Roads (1996): total length 28,200 km (paved 12%). Vehicles: passenger cars (2003) 183,000; trucks and buses (2001) 98,900. Air transport (2004): passenger-km 187,600,000; metric ton-km cargo 208,000,000; airports (1996) 19.

Communications

Medium	date	unit	number	units per 1,000 persons
Daily newspapers	2002	circulation	455,000	10
Radio	2001	receivers	2,772,000	66
Television	2003	receivers	322,200	7.0
Telephones	2004	main lines	424,900	9.1
Cellular telephones	2004	subscribers	92,000	2.0
Personal computers	2004	units	325,000	7.0
Internet	2004	users	63,700	1.4

Education and health

Educational attainment: n.a. *Literacy* (2002): total population age 15 and over literate 85.3%; males literate 89.2%; females literate 81.4%.

Education (2002–03)

	schools	teachers	students	student/ teacher ratio
Primary (age 5–9)	36,010	149,001	4,889,325	32.8
Secondary (age 10–15) } Voc., teacher tr.	3,068	73,062	2,382,608	32.6
Higher	923[7]	17,089[7]	555,060[8]	...

Health (2003–04): physicians 17,564 (1 per 2,635 persons); hospital beds 34,654 (1 per 1,335 persons); infant mortality rate per 1,000 live births (2004) 81.0.
Food (2002): daily per capita caloric intake 2,937 (vegetable products 95%, animal products 5%); 136% of FAO recommended minimum requirement.

Military

Total active duty personnel (2004): 485,000 (army 72.2%, navy 2.7%, air force 3.1%, paramilitary [people's militia and people's police] 22.0%). *Military expenditure as percentage of GDP* (2003): n.a.

---

[1]Early-stage movement of the capital to Pyinmana was acknowledged in November 2005. [2]The kyat is pegged to the Special Drawing Right of the International Monetary Fund at 1 SDR = K 8.51 and is not freely traded internationally; the unofficial (but tolerated) black market rate in September 2005 was about 1 U.S.$ = K 1,205. [3]Yangôn only. [4]Employed only. [5]Imports c.i.f.; exports f.o.b. [6]Fiscal year beginning April 1. [7]1997–98. [8]2001–02.

Internet resources for further information:
• **Key Indicators of Developing Asian and Pacific Countries**
  http://www.adb.org/Documents/Books/Key_Indicators/2005/default.asp
• **Asia-Pacific Development Center on Disability**
  http://www.apcdproject.org/countryprofile/myanmar/myanmar_intro.html

Namibia

Official name: Republic of Namibia.
Form of government: republic with two legislative houses (National Council [26]; National Assembly [72[1]]).
Head of state and government: President.
Capital: Windhoek.
Official language: English.
Official religion: none.
Monetary unit: 1 Namibian dollar (N$) = 100 cents; valuation (Sept. 1, 2005) 1 U.S.$ = N$6.27; 1 £ = N$11.54.

Area and population

Regions	Largest towns	area sq mi	area sq km	population 2001 census
Erongo	Walvis Bay	24,602	63,720	107,629
Hardap	Rehoboth	42,428	109,888	67,998
Karas	Keetmanshoop	62,288	161,324	69,677
Khomas	Windhoek	14,210	36,805	250,305
Kunene	Khorixas	55,697	144,255	68,224
Liambezi (Caprivi)	Katima Mulilo	7,541	19,532	79,852
Ohangwena	Oshikango	4,086	10,582	227,728
Okavango	Rundu	16,763	43,417	201,093
Omaheke	Gobabis	32,715	84,732	67,496
Omusati	Ongandjera	5,266	13,638	228,364
Oshana	Oshakati	2,042	5,290	161,977
Oshikoto	Tsumeb	10,273	26,607	160,788
Otjozondjupa	Otjiwarongo	40,667	105,328	135,723
TOTAL		318,580[2]	825,118	1,826,854

Demography

Population (2005): 2,031,000.
Density (2005): persons per sq mi 6.4, persons per sq km 2.5.
Urban-rural (2003): urban 32.4%; rural 67.6%.
Sex distribution (2001): male 48.73%; female 51.27%.
Age breakdown (2004): under 15, 39.1%; 15–29, 30.5%; 30–44, 15.7%; 45–59, 9.2%; 60–74, 4.4%; 75 and over, 1.1%.
Population projection: (2010) 2,077,000; (2020) 2,087,000.
Doubling time: 80 years.
Ethnic composition (2000): Ovambo 34.4%; mixed race (black/white) 14.5%; Kavango 9.1%; Afrikaner 8.1%; San (Bushmen) and Bergdama 7.0%; Herero 5.5%; Nama 4.4%; Kwambi 3.7%; German 2.8%; other 10.5%.
Religious affiliation (2000): Protestant (mostly Lutheran) 47.5%; Roman Catholic 17.7%; African Christian 10.8%; traditional beliefs 6.0%; other 18.0%.
Major cities (2001): Windhoek 216,000[3]; Walvis Bay 40,849; Swakopmund 25,442[4]; Rehoboth 21,782; Rundu 19,597.

Vital statistics

Birth rate per 1,000 population (2004): 26.3 (world avg. 21.1).
Death rate per 1,000 population (2004): 17.6 (world avg. 9.0).
Natural increase rate per 1,000 population (2004): 8.7 (world avg. 12.1).
Total fertility rate (avg. births per childbearing woman; 2004): 3.3.
Life expectancy at birth (2004): male 45.2 years; female 44.4 years.
Adult population (ages 15–49) living with HIV (2004[5]): 21.3% (world avg. 1.1%).

National economy

Budget (2003–04). Revenue: N$10,836,000,000 (tax revenue 90.3%, of which taxes on income and profits 34.7%, customs duties and excise tax 28.0%, VAT 23.5%; nontax revenue 8.9%; other 0.8%). Expenditures: N$11,843,000,000 (current expenditure 87.5%; development expenditure 12.5%).
Public debt (external, outstanding 2003–04): U.S.$252,300,000[6].
Production (metric tons except as noted). Agriculture, forestry, fishing (2004): roots and tubers 295,000, millet 51,000, corn (maize) 33,000, fruits 23,000 (of which grapes 8,500), vegetables 16,000, pulses 9,000, wheat 8,000; livestock (number of live animals) 2,900,000 sheep, 2,500,000 cattle, 2,100,000 goats; roundwood, n.a.; fish catch (2003) 636,346. Mining and quarrying (2004): salt 697,914; fluorspar 79,349; zinc (metal content) 60,500; copper (metal content) 19,500; lead (metal content) 18,782; uranium oxide 2,401; silver 45,100 kg; gold 2,425 kg; gem diamonds 1,481,000 carats. Manufacturing (value added in N$'000,000; 2003): food and food products 2,645 (of which fish processing 899, meat processing 147); other manufactures, which include fur products (from Karakul sheep), textiles, carved wood products, and refined metals 892. Energy production (consumption): electricity (kW-hr; 2003) 1,460,000,000 (2,370,000,000); coal, none (none); crude petroleum, none (none); petroleum products, none (n.a.); natural gas, none (none).
Household income and expenditure. Average household size (2001) 5.1; average annual income per household, n.a.; sources of income (1992): wages and salaries 69.0%, income from property 25.6%, transfer payments 5.4%; expenditure: n.a.
Population economically active (2000): total 652,483; activity rate of total population c. 34% (participation rates: ages 15–69, c. 60%; female c. 51%; unemployed 33.8%).

Price index (2000 = 100)

	1998	1999	2000	2001	2002	2003	2004
Consumer price index	84.5	91.7	100.0	109.5	122.0	130.7	135.8

Gross national product (2004): U.S.$4,813,000,000 (U.S.$2,370 per capita).

Structure of gross domestic product and labour force

	2003 in value N$'000,000	2003 % of total value	2000 labour force	2000 % of labour force
Agriculture, fishing	3,123	9.7	134,259	20.6
Diamond mining	1,807	5.6	3,868	0.6
Other mining	377	1.2		
Manufacturing	3,537	10.9	22,922	3.5
Construction	880	2.7	21,788	3.3
Public utilities	766	2.4	4,193	0.6
Transp. and commun.	2,301	7.1	14,308	2.2
Trade, hotels	4,339	13.4	46,579	7.1
Finance, real estate	4,138	12.8	44,251	6.8
Services	267	0.8	112,172	17.2
Public administration and defense	7,104	22.0	24,419	3.7
Other	3,670[7]	11.4[7]	223,726[8]	34.3[8]
TOTAL	32,309	100.0	652,483[2]	100.0[2]

Tourism (2003): receipts U.S.$333,000,000; expenditures U.S.$74,000,000.
Land use as % of total land area (2000): in temporary crops 1.0%, in permanent crops, negligible, in pasture 46.2%; overall forest area 9.8%.

Foreign trade[9]

Balance of trade (current prices)

	1998	1999	2000	2001	2002	2003
N$'000,000	−1,580	−1,249	+48	−1,711	−2,183	−3,493
% of total	10.6%	7.9%	0.3%	8.0%	8.8%	15.6%

Imports (2003): N$13,500,800,000 (machinery and apparatus 21.5%; food, beverages, and tobacco 16.0%; transport equipment 15.1%; chemicals, plastic, medicinal products, and rubber 14.5%). Major import sources: South Africa 80.5%; Germany 2.3%; Switzerland 2.3%; Spain 1.4%; China 1.3%.
Exports (2003): N$9,450,600,000 (diamonds 40.9%; fish 17.8%; other minerals [mainly gold, zinc, copper, lead, and silver] 14.6%; meat [mostly beef] and meat preparations 6.3%). Major export destinations: South Africa 31.5%; Angola 24.9%; Spain 12.8%; U.K. 10.4%; U.S. 2.7%.

Transport and communications

Transport. Railroads: route length (2004) 1,480 mi, 2,382 km; (1995–96) passenger-km 48,300,000; (1995–96) metric ton-km 1,082,000,000. Roads (2002): total length 26,245 mi, 42,237 km (paved 13%). Vehicles (2002): passenger cars 82,580; trucks and buses 81,002. Air transport (2004)[10]: passenger-km 911,000,000; metric ton-km cargo 56,475,000; airports (1997) 11.

Communications

Medium	date	unit	number	units per 1,000 persons
Daily newspapers	2000	circulation	34,700	19
Radio	2000	receivers	258,000	141
Television	2000	receivers	69,400	38
Telephones	2004	main lines	127,900	64
Cellular telephones	2004	subscribers	286,100	142
Personal computers	2004	units	220,000	109
Internet	2004	users	75,000	37

Education and health

Educational attainment (1991). Percentage of population age 25 and over having: no formal schooling 35.1%; primary education 31.9%; secondary 28.5%; higher 4.5%. Literacy (2000): total population age 15 and over literate 830,200 (82.1%); males literate 416,000 (82.9%); females literate 414,200 (81.2%).

Education (2002–03)

	schools	teachers	students	student/ teacher ratio
Primary (age 6–12)	1,362[11]	14,330	404,783	28.2
Secondary (age 13–19)	114[12]	5,869	138,099	23.5
Higher	24[12]	931	13,536	14.5

Health (2000): physicians 244[13] (1 per 7,500 persons); hospital beds 6,739[13] (1 per 271 persons); infant mortality rate per 1,000 live births (2004) 49.8.
Food (2002): daily per capita caloric intake 2,278 (vegetable products 84%, animal products 16%); 100% of FAO recommended minimum requirement.

Military

Total active duty personnel (2004): 9,000 (army 100.0%). Military expenditure as percentage of GDP (2003): n.a.

---

[1]An additional 6 non-voting members may be appointed. [2]Detail does not add to total given because of rounding. [3]Urban agglomeration. [4]Population of constituency (second-order administrative subdivision). [5]Beginning of year. [6]Excludes government-guaranteed debt. [7]Taxes less imputed bank service charges and less subsidies. [8]Includes 220,634 unemployed. [9]Imports are f.o.b. in balance of trade and c.i.f. for commodities and trading partners. [10]Air Namibia only. [11]1998. [12]1994. [13]Public sector only.

Internet resources for further information:
• Bank of Namibia http://www.bon.com.na
• Central Bureau of Statistics http://www.npc.gov.na/cbs/index.htm

Nauru

Pacific
Ocean

Official name: Naoero (Nauruan[1])
　(Republic of Nauru).
Form of government: republic with one
　legislative house (Parliament [18]).
Head of state and government:
　President.
Capital: [2].
Official language: none[1].
Official religion: none.
Monetary unit: 1 Australian dollar
　($A) = 100 cents; valuation (Sept. 1,
　2005) 1 U.S.$ = $A 1.31;
　1 £ = $A 2.41.

Area and population	area		population
Districts	sq mi	sq km	1992 census[3]
Aiwo	0.4	1.1	1,072
Anabar	0.6	1.5	320
Anetan	0.4	1.0	427
Anibare	1.2	3.1	165
Baitsi	0.5	1.2	450
Boe	0.2	0.5	750
Buada	1.0	2.6	661
Denigomodu	0.3	0.9	2,548
Ewa	0.5	1.2	355
Ijuw	0.4	1.1	206
Meneng	1.2	3.1	1,269
Nibok	0.6	1.6	577
Uaboe	0.3	0.8	447
Yaren	0.6	1.5	672
TOTAL	8.2	21.2	9,919

Demography

Population (2005): 10,200.
Density (2005): persons per sq mi 1,244, persons per sq km 481.1.
Urban-rural (2003): urban 100%.
Sex distribution (2004): male 50.17%; female 49.83%.
Age breakdown (2004): under 15, 38.2%; 15–29, 28.9%; 30–44, 18.0%; 45–59,
　11.5%; 60–74, 3.1%; 75 and over, 0.3%.
Population projection: (2010) 11,000; (2020) 12,000.
Doubling time: 35 years.
Ethnic composition (2000): Nauruan 48.0%; Kiribertese (Gilbertese) 19.3%;
　Chinese 13.0%; Tuvaluan 6.9%; Australian white 6.2%; other 6.6%.
Religious affiliation (1995): Protestant 53.5%, of which Congregational 35.3%,
　Pentecostal 4.8%; Roman Catholic 27.5%; other 19.0%.
Major cities: none; population of Yaren district (1996) 700.

Vital statistics

Birth rate per 1,000 population (2002): 21.8 (world avg. 21.1); legitimate, n.a.;
　illegitimate, n.a.
Death rate per 1,000 population (2002): 7.5 (world avg. 9.0).
Natural increase rate per 1,000 population (2002): 14.3 (world avg. 12.1).
Total fertility rate (avg. births per childbearing woman; 2004): 3.3.
Marriage rate per 1,000 population (1995): 5.3.
Divorce rate per 1,000 population: n.a.
Life expectancy at birth (2004): male 58.8 years; female 66.1 years.
Major causes of death per 100,000 population (2003): diabetes mellitus 159.0;
　diseases of the respiratory system 149.0; diseases of the circulatory system
　119.2; neoplasms 79.5; accidents 79.5.

National economy

Budget (1999). Revenue: $A 38,700,000[4]. Expenditures: $A 37,200,000.
Public debt: [5].
Tourism: receipts from visitors, virtually none; expenditures by nationals
　abroad, n.a.
Gross national product (at current market prices; 2003): U.S.$48,900,000
　(U.S.$3,740 per capita).

Distribution of gross domestic product and labour force	2001		1997	
	in value U.S.$'000,000[6]	% of total value[7]	labour force[8, 9, 10]	% of labour force
Agriculture	11.0	18.0	...	...
Mining (phosphate) }				
Public utilities }	0.5	1.0	528	24.7
Manufacturing	0.5	1.0	...	...
Construction	2.0	3.0	...	...
Transportation and communications	8.0	13.0	...	...
Trade, hotels	9.5	16.0	137	6.4
Finance[11] }			33	1.6
Services }			...	...
Pub. admin. }	28.5	48.0	1,238	58.0
Other }			198	9.3
TOTAL	60.0	100.0	2,134	100.0

Production (metric tons except as noted). Agriculture, forestry, fishing (2004):
coconuts 1,600, vegetables 450, tropical fruit (including mangoes) 275;
almonds, figs, and pandanus are also cultivated, but most foodstuffs and beverages (including water) are imported; livestock (number of live animals)
2,800 pigs, 5,000 chickens; roundwood, none; fish catch (2002) 21. Mining and
quarrying (2004): phosphate rock (gross weight including basic slag and

guano) 22,000. Manufacturing: none; virtually all consumer manufactures are
imported. Energy production (consumption): electricity (kW-hr; 2002)
30,000,000 (30,000,000); coal, none (none); crude petroleum, none (none);
petroleum products (metric tons; 2002) none (45,000); natural gas, none
(none).
Population economically active (1992): 2,453[9, 12]; activity rate of total population 35.9% (participation rates: over age 15, 67.9%; female 43.5%; unemployed 18.2%).

Price index (2000 = 100)	2000	2001	2002	2003
Implicit GDP deflator	100.0	107.2	114.2	119.9

Household income and expenditure. Average household size (1992) 10.0[9];
income per household: n.a.; sources of income: n.a.; expenditure: n.a.
Land use as % of total land area (2000): in temporary crops, n.a., in permanent crops, n.a., in pasture, n.a.; overall forest area, n.a.

Foreign trade[13]

Balance of trade (current prices)			
	2000	2001	2002
$A '000,000	+1.7	−15.5	−29.4
% of total	1.8%	−23.6%	−47.0%

Imports (1999): *c.* $A 31,000,000 (agricultural products 6.5%, of which food
4.5%; remainder 93.5%). *Major import sources* (2002): Australia 60.3%;
United States 10.3%; Ireland 7.7%; Malaysia 5.8%; United Kingdom 2.6%.
Exports (1999): *c.* $A 62,000,000 (phosphate, virtually 100%[14]). *Major export
destinations* (2002): India 46.3%; South Korea 18.4%; Australia 10.6%; New
Zealand 7.8%; U.S. 2.8%.

Transport and communications

Transport. Railroads (2001): length 3 mi, 5 km; passenger traffic, n.a.; metric
ton-km cargo, n.a. Roads (2001): total length 19 mi, 30 km (paved 79%).
Vehicles (1989): passenger cars, trucks, and buses 1,448. Air transport: passenger-mi (2001) 178,000,000, passenger-km (2001) 287,000,000; short ton-mi
cargo (1996) 15,000,000, metric ton-km cargo (1996) 24,000,000; airports
(2001) with scheduled flights 1.

Communications				units per 1,000
Medium	date	unit	number	persons
Daily newspapers	—	circulation	...	...
Radio	1997	receivers	7,000	609
Television	1997	receivers	500	48
Telephones	2001	main lines	1,900	160
Cellular telephones	2001	subscribers	1,500	130
Internet	2001	users	300	26

Education and health

Educational attainment (1992)[9]. Percentage of population age 5 and over having: primary education or less 77.4%; secondary education 12.9%; higher
4.1%; not stated 5.6%. *Literacy* (1999): total population age 15 and over literate 99%.

Education (2003)[9]	schools	teachers	students	student/ teacher ratio
Primary (age 6–13)	9	63	1,375	21.8
Secondary (age 14–17)	2	34	645	19.0
Vocational	2	4	31	7.8

Health (2003): physicians 5 (1 per 2,016 persons); hospital beds 60 (1 per 168
persons); infant mortality rate per 1,000 live births (2004) 10.1.
Food (2002)[15]: daily per capita caloric intake 2,952 (vegetable products 70%,
animal products 30%); 129% of FAO recommended minimum requirement.

Military

Total active duty personnel (2004): Nauru does not have any military establishment. The defense is assured by Australia, but no formal agreement exists.

---

[1]Nauruan is the national language; English is the language of business and government. [2]Government offices are located in Yaren district. [3]Preliminary. [4]Largely from
phosphate exports. [5]Official admission of near bankruptcy made by president of Nauru
to UN General Assembly in October 2005. Actual financial situation of country is
unknown by its government. [6]Derived figures based on published percentages.
[7]Percentages are rounded figures. [8]Employed only. [9]Nauruan only. [10]Most non-Nauruans
are phosphate industry contract workers. [11]400 offshore banks were registered in Nauru
in mid-2001, but by November 2004 all were closed down. [12]Excludes activity not stated. [13]Imports c.i.f.; exports f.o.b. [14]Phosphate deposits were nearly exhausted by 2004.
[15]Data for Oceania.

Internet resources for further information:
• **Nauru Bureau of Statistics**
　http://www.spc.int/prism/country/nr/stats

Nepal

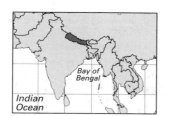

Official name: Nepal Adhirajya (Kingdom of Nepal).
Form of government: monarchy backed by military[1].
Head of state and government: King[1].
Capital: Kathmandu.
Official language: Nepali.
Official religion: Hinduism.
Monetary unit: 1 Nepalese rupee (NRs) = 100 paisa (pice); valuation (Sept. 1, 2005) 1 U.S.$ = NRs 70.18; 1 £ = NRs 129.23.

Area and population

Development regions	Capitals	area		population 2001 census[2]
		sq mi	sq km	
Eastern	Dhankuta	10,987	28,456	5,344,476
Central	Kathmandu	10,583	27,410	8,031,629
Western	Pokhara	11,351	29,398	4,571,013
Mid-western	Surkhet	16,362	42,378	3,012,975
Far-western	Dipayal	7,544	19,539	2,191,330
TOTAL		56,827	147,181	23,151,423

Demography

Population (2005): 27,133,000.
Density (2005): persons per sq mi 477.5, persons per sq km 184.4.
Urban-rural (2003): urban 15.0%; rural 85.0%.
Sex distribution (2004): male 49.96%; female 50.04%.
Age breakdown (2001): under 15, 39.3%; 15–29, 27.0%; 30–44, 17.1%; 45–59, 10.1%; 60–74, 5.2%; 75 and over, 1.3%.
Population projection: (2010) 29,891,000; (2020) 35,679,000.
Doubling time: 32 years.
Ethnic composition (2000): Nepalese 55.8%; Maithili 10.8%; Bhojpuri 7.9%; Tharu 4.4%; Tamang 3.6%; Newar 3.0%; Awadhi 2.7%; Magar 2.5%; Gurkha 1.7%; other 7.6%.
Religious affiliation (2001): Hindu 80.6%; Buddhist 10.7%; Muslim 4.2%; Kirat (local traditional belief) 3.6%; Christian 0.5%; other 0.4%.
Major cities (2001): Kathmandu 671,846; Biratnagar 166,674; Lalitpur 162,991; Pokhara 156,312; Birganj 112,484.

Vital statistics

Birth rate per 1,000 population (2004): 31.3 (world avg. 21.1).
Death rate per 1,000 population (2004): 9.2 (world avg. 9.0).
Natural increase rate per 1,000 population (2004): 22.1 (world avg. 12.1).
Total fertility rate (avg. births per childbearing woman; 2004): 3.7.
Life expectancy at birth (2004): male 61.8 years; female 62.5 years.
Major causes of death per 100,000 population (2002): infectious and parasitic diseases 472; diseases of the circulatory system 203, of which ischemic heart disease 95; accidents and injuries 86; malignant neoplasms (cancers) 63.

National economy

Budget (2001). Revenue: NRs 48,596,000,000 (taxes on goods and services 34.1%, taxes on international trade 28.1%, income taxes 19.0%, state property revenues 1.9%, other 16.9%). Expenditures: NRs 74,289,000,000 (current expenditure 59.3%, of which education 14.0%, defense 7.8%, health 2.8%; development expenditure 40.7%, of which economic services 25.7%).
Public debt (external, outstanding; 2003): U.S.$3,176,000,000.
Production (metric tons except as noted). Agriculture, forestry, fishing (2004): rice 4,300,000, sugarcane 2,305,326, potatoes 1,643,357, corn (maize) 1,590,097, wheat 1,387,191, oil seeds 160,328 (of which mustard seed 132,865), lentils 158,671; livestock (number of live animals) 6,979,875 goats, 6,966,436 cattle, 3,952,654 buffalo, 935,076 pigs, 824,187 sheep; roundwood (2003) 13,961,766 cu m; fish catch (2003) 36,568. Mining and quarrying (2004): limestone 388,109; salt 4,000; talc 3,435. Manufacturing (value added in U.S.$'000,000; 1996): textiles 99; tobacco products 46; beverages 35; food products 30; wearing apparel 24. Energy production (consumption): electricity (kW-hr; 2002) 1,433,000,000 (1,532,000,000); coal (metric tons; 2002) 16,000 (496,000); crude petroleum, none (none); petroleum products (metric tons; 2002) none (776,000); natural gas, none (none).
Tourism (2003): receipts from visitors U.S.$199,000,000; expenditures by nationals abroad U.S.$81,000,000.
Gross national product (at current market prices; 2004): U.S.$6,538,000,000 (U.S.$260 per capita).

Structure of gross domestic product and labour force

	2002–03		1998–99	
	in value NRs '000,000	% of total value	labour force[3]	% of labour force[3]
Agriculture	170,073	37.5	7,203,000	76.1
Mining	2,188	0.5	8,000	0.1
Manufacturing	34,337	7.6	552,000	5.8
Construction	45,014	9.9	344,000	3.7
Public utilities	9,345	2.0	26,000	0.3
Transp. and commun.	38,030	8.4	135,000	1.4
Trade	44,046	9.7	522,000	5.5
Finance	47,553	10.5	51,000	0.5
Services	43,708	9.6	614,000	6.5
Other	19,404[4]	4.3[4]	8,000	0.1
TOTAL	453,698	100.0	9,463,000	100.0

Population economically active (1998–99): total 11,628,000[5]; activity rate of total population 60.9% (participation rates: ages 15 years and over, 85.8%; female 50.9%; unemployed [2001] 5.1%).

Price and earnings indexes (2000 = 100)

	1998	1999	2000	2001	2002	2003	2004
Consumer price index	90.8	97.6	100.0	102.7	105.8	111.8	115.0
Monthly earnings index[6]	85.1	85.1	100.0	100.0	100.0	...	...

Household income and expenditure (2003–04). Average household size 5.3; income per household NRs 80,111 (U.S.$1,084); sources of income: self-employment 47%, wages and salaries 28%, other 25%; expenditure: food and beverages 59.0%, housing 9.5%, education 2.8%, other 28.7%.
Land use as % of total land area (2000): in temporary crops 21.3%, in permanent crops 0.6%, in pasture 12.3%; overall forest area 27.3%.

Foreign trade[7]

Balance of trade (current prices)

	1999	2000	2001	2002	2003	2004
NRs '000,000	−55,969	−54,569	−55,141	−66,368	−83,089	−82,001
% of total	40.5%	32.3%	33.3%	42.9%	45.2%	42.4%

Imports (2000–01): NRs 115,687,000,000 (basic manufactures [including fabrics, yarns, and made-up articles] 35.6%, machinery and transport equipment 19.9%, chemicals and chemical products 11.2%, mineral fuels [mostly refined petroleum] 9.7%). Major import sources (2004): India 43.0%; China 10.0%; U.A.E. 10.0%; Saudi Arabia 4.4%; Singapore 4.0%.
Exports (2000–01): NRs 55,654,000,000 (ready-made garments 23.6%, carpets 15.4%, pashminas[8] 12.4%, vegetable ghee 6.4%). Major export destinations (2004): India 48.8%; U.S. 22.3%; Germany 8.5%; U.K. 2.8%; France 2.2%.

Transport and communications

Transport. Railroads (2002): route length 59 km; passengers carried 1,600,000; freight handled 22,000 metric tons. Roads (2002): total length 16,834 km (paved 28%). Vehicles (2003): passenger cars 66,395; trucks and buses 40,267. Air transport: passenger-km (2001) 1,135,000,000; metric ton-km cargo (2000) 108,000,000; airports (1996) with scheduled flights 24.

Communications

Medium	date	unit	number	units per 1,000 persons
Daily newspapers	2000	circulation	272,000	12
Radio	2000	receivers	883,000	39
Television	2003	receivers	193,000	8.0
Telephones	2004	main lines	400,200	16
Cellular telephones	2004	subscribers	104,600	7.0
Personal computers	2004	units	118,000	4.6
Internet	2004	users	175,000	6.8

Education and health

Educational attainment (2001). Percentage of population age 6 and over having: no formal schooling 8.7%; primary education 41.9%; incomplete secondary 30.6%; complete secondary and higher 17.6%; unknown 1.2%.
Literacy (2001): total population age 15 and over literate c. 53%; males literate c. 60%; females literate c. 43%.

Education (2002–03)

	schools[9]	teachers	students	student/ teacher ratio
Primary (age 6–10)	25,927	110,173	3,928,684	35.7
Secondary (age 11–15) }	11,639	50,913	1,806,355	35.5
Vocational		1,615	15,708	9.7
Higher[9]	2	6,313	149,060	23.6

Health (2002–03): physicians 1,259 (1 per 20,480 persons); hospital beds 5,250[10] (1 per 4,911 persons); infant mortality rate per 1,000 live births (2004) 64.4.
Food (2002): daily per capita caloric intake 2,453 (vegetable products 93%, animal products 7%); 112% of FAO recommended minimum requirement.

Military

Total active duty personnel (2004): 69,000 (army 100.0%). Military expenditure as percentage of GDP (2003): 1.6%; per capita expenditure U.S.$4.

[1]Most constitutional liberties suspended from February 2005. [2]Final figures adjusted for undercount. [3]Employed only; excludes 1,987,000 workers age 5–14. [4]Includes indirect taxes less imputed bank service charges and less subsidies. [5]Per 1998–99 Nepal labour force survey. [6]Ending fiscal year; minimum monthly wage rates for unskilled industrial workers. [7]Imports c.i.f.; exports f.o.b. [8]Fine shawls made of cashmere or cashmere-silk blend. [9]2000. [10]Public-sector only.

Internet resources for further information:
• Central Bank of Nepal http://www.nrb.org.np
• Central Bureau of Statistics http://www.cbs.gov.np

Netherlands, The

North Sea

Official name: Koninkrijk der Nederlanden (Kingdom of The Netherlands).
Form of government: constitutional monarchy with a parliament (States General) comprising two legislative houses (First Chamber [75]; Second Chamber [150]).
Chief of state: Monarch.
Head of government: Prime Minister.
Seat of government: The Hague.
Capital: Amsterdam.
Official language: Dutch.
Official religion: none.
Monetary unit: 1 euro (€) = 100 cents; valuation (Sept. 1, 2005) 1 U.S.$ = €0.80; 1 £ = €1.47[1].

Area and population

Provinces	Capitals	area sq mi	area sq km	population 2004[2] estimate
Drenthe	Assen	1,035	2,680	482,415
Flevoland	Lelystad	931	2,412	359,904
Friesland	Leeuwarden	2,217	5,741	642,066
Gelderland	Arnhem	1,983	5,137	1,966,929
Groningen	Groningen	1,146	2,968	574,384
Limburg	Maastricht	853	2,209	1,139,335
Noord-Brabant	's-Hertogenbosch	1,962	5,082	2,406,994
Noord-Holland	Haarlem	1,567	4,059	2,587,265
Overijssel	Zwolle	1,321	3,421	1,105,512
Utrecht	Utrecht	556	1,439	1,162,258
Zeeland	Middelburg	1,133	2,934	379,028
Zuid-Holland	The Hague	1,331	3,446	3,451,942
TOTAL		16,034[3, 4]	41,528[4]	16,258,032

Demography

Population (2005): 16,306,000.
Density (2005)[5]: persons per sq mi 1,250, persons per sq km 482.7.
Urban-rural (2001): urban 89.6%; rural 10.4%.
Sex distribution (2004[2]): male 49.49%; female 50.51%.
Age breakdown (2004[2]): under 15, 18.6%; 15–29, 18.1%; 30–44, 23.8%; 45–59, 20.8%; 60–74, 12.5%; 75 and over, 6.2%.
Population projection: (2010) 16,500,000; (2020) 16,800,000.
Ethnic composition (by place of origin [including 2nd generation]; 2004[2]): Netherlander 81.0%; German 2.5%; Indonesian 2.4%; Turkish 2.2%; Surinamese 2.0%; Moroccan 1.9%; Netherlands Antillean/Aruban 0.8%; other 7.2%[6].
Religious affiliation (1999[2]): Roman Catholic 31.0%; Reformed (NHK) 14.0%; other Reformed 7.0%; Muslim 4.5%; Hindu 0.5%; nonreligious and other 43.0%.
Major urban agglomerations (2000[2]): Amsterdam 1,002,868; Rotterdam 989,956; The Hague 610,245; Utrecht 366,186; Eindhoven 302,274.

Vital statistics

Birth rate per 1,000 population (2003): 12.4 (world avg. 21.1); legitimate 72.8%; illegitimate 27.2%.
Death rate per 1,000 population (2003): 8.7 (world avg. 9.0).
Total fertility rate (avg. births per childbearing woman; 2003): 1.7.
Marriage rate per 1,000 population (2004): 4.7.
Life expectancy at birth (2003): male 76.2 years; female 80.9 years.
Major causes of death per 100,000 population (2000): diseases of the circulatory system 310.1; malignant neoplasms (cancers) 237.9; diseases of the respiratory system 92.5; accidents and violence 32.6.

National economy

Budget (2002). Revenue: €181,463,000,000 (social security taxes 35.3%, value-added and excise taxes 27.7%, income and corporate taxes 26.1%, property taxes 3.0%). Expenditures: €187,736,000,000 (social security and welfare 35.3%, health 10.1%, economic affairs 4.7%, defense 3.8%, education 2.3%).
Public debt (2003): U.S.$289,377,000,000.
Production (metric tons except as noted). Agriculture, forestry, fishing (2004): potatoes 7,488,000, sugar beets 6,292,000, wheat 1,225,000, onions 808,000, tomatoes 645,000, apples 436,000, carrots 430,000, barley 288,000, flowering bulbs and tubers 59,300 acres (24,000 hectares), of which tulips 27,200 acres (11,000 hectares), cut flowers/plants under glass 13,100 acres (5,300 hectares); livestock (number of live animals) 11,097,000 pigs, 3,767,000 cattle, 1,236,000 sheep; roundwood (2002) 839,000 cu m; fish catch (2001) 570,226. Manufacturing (value added in €'000,000; 2002): food, beverages, and tobacco 12,936; chemicals and chemical products 7,542; printing and publishing 5,743; electric/electronic machinery 5,050; nonelectrical machinery 4,822; fabricated metal products 4,744. Energy production (consumption): electricity (kW-hr; 2004) 98,484,000,000 ([2002] 112,363,000,000); coal (metric tons; 2002) negligible (13,466,000); crude petroleum (barrels; 2004) 14,500,000 ([2002] 331,034,000); petroleum products (metric tons; 2002) 63,560,000 (32,756,000); natural gas (cu m; 2004) 88,147,000,000 ([2002] 52,682,000,000).
Household income and expenditure. Average household size (2004) 2.3; disposable income per household (2000) €26,653 (U.S.$24,521); sources of income (1996): wages 48.4%, transfers 28.5%, self-employment 11.3%; expenditure (2000): housing and energy 23.2%, food and beverages 14.2%, transportation and communications 11.7%, textiles and clothing 6.4%.
Gross national product (2004): U.S.$515,148,000,000 (U.S.$31,700 per capita).

Structure of gross domestic product and labour force

	2003 in value €'000,000	2003 % of total value	2002 labour force[7]	2002 % of labour force[7]
Agriculture	10,235	2.4	230,000	2.8
Mining	11,042	2.6	11,000	0.1
Manufacturing	60,590	14.4	1,087,000	13.2
Construction	24,251	5.8	485,000	5.9
Public utilities	7,657	1.8	38,000	0.5
Transp. and commun.	29,961	7.1	458,000	5.6
Trade	59,591	14.2	1,580,000	19.2
Finance, real estate	112,219	26.7	1,268,000	15.4
Pub. admin., defense	50,155	11.9	559,000	6.8
Services	54,918	13.1	2,042,000	24.9
Other	...	...	453,000[8]	5.5[8]
TOTAL	420,619	100.0	8,213,000[3]	100.0[3]

Population economically active (2003): total 8,370,000; activity rate of total population c. 52% (participation rates: ages 15–64, 75.9%; female 44.1%; unemployed [2004] 6.3%).

Price and earnings indexes (2000 = 100)

	1998	1999	2000	2001	2002	2003	2004
Consumer price index	95.4	97.5	100.0	104.5	108.2	110.4	111.8
Hourly earnings index	93.7	96.4	100.0	104.2	108.0	110.8	112.7

Tourism (2003): receipts U.S.$9,162,000,000; expenditures U.S.$14,609,000,000.
Land use as % of total land area (2000): in temporary crops 26.9%, in permanent crops 1.0%, in pasture 29.9%; overall forest area 11.1%.

Foreign trade[9]

Balance of trade (current prices)

	1998	1999	2000	2001	2002	2003
€'000,000	+26,926[10]	+11,931	+11,444	+23,669	+30,229	+22,730
% of total	4.5%	3.3%	2.5%	5.2%	6.9%	5.2%

Imports (2003): €204,494,000,000 (chemicals and chemical products 12.0%, computers and related equipment 11.6%, mineral fuels 10.4%, food 8.8%, road vehicles 6.6%). Major import sources: Germany 20.0%; Belgium-Luxembourg 11.3%; U.S. 7.8%; U.K. 7.2%; France 5.5%.
Exports (2003): €232,422,000,000 (chemicals and chemical products 16.7%, food 12.6%, computers and related equipment 10.5%, mineral fuels 8.3%). Major export destinations: Germany 24.4%; Belgium-Luxembourg 11.9%; U.K. 10.3%; France 10.0%; Italy 6.0%.

Transport and communications

Transport. Railroads (2003): length 2,806 km; passenger-km 14,392,000,000; metric ton-km cargo 4,293,000,000. Roads (2003): total length 119,437 km (paved 90%). Vehicles (2003): passenger cars 6,855,000; trucks and buses 929,000. Air transport (2001)[11]: passenger-km 57,848,000,000; metric ton-km cargo 4,464,000,000; airports (1996) 6.

Communications

Medium	date	unit	number	units per 1,000 persons
Daily newspapers	2004	circulation	4,712,000	289
Radio	2000	receivers	15,600,000	980
Television	2000	receivers	8,570,000	538
Telephones	2004	main lines	7,861,000	484
Cellular telephones	2004	subscribers	14,821,000	913
Personal computers	2004	units	11,110	685
Internet	2004	users	10,000,000	616

Education and health

Educational attainment (2001). Percentage of population ages 15–64 having: primary education 14.1%; lower secondary 9.3%; upper secondary/vocational 54.3%; tertiary vocational 15.1%; university 6.9%; unknown 0.3%.

Education (2002–03)[12]

	schools	teachers	students	student/ teacher ratio
Primary (age 6–12)	7,610	...	1,602,050	...
Secondary (age 12–18)	692	...	913,670	...
Vocational[13]	59	...	325,950	...
Higher[14]	13	...	180,550	...

Health (2000): physicians 27,161 (1 per 586 persons); hospital beds 90,747 (1 per 175 persons); infant mortality rate per 1,000 live births (2003) 5.2.
Food (2002): daily per capita caloric intake 3,352 (vegetable products 66%, animal products 34%); 125% of FAO recommended minimum requirement.

Military

Total active duty personnel (2004): 53,130 (army 43.6%, navy 22.8%, air force 20.8%, paramilitary[15] 12.8%). *Military expenditure as percentage of GDP* (2003): 1.6%; per capita expenditure U.S.$505.

---

[1]The Netherlands guilder (f.) was the former monetary unit; on Jan. 1, 2002, f. 2.20 = €1. [2]January 1. [3]Detail does not add to total given because of rounding. [4]Includes inland water area totaling 1,380 sq mi (3,574 sq km) and coastal water totaling 1,610 sq mi (4,171 sq km). [5]Based on land area only (13,044 sq mi [33,783 sq km]). [6]Includes Netherlander-EU country 4.7%. [7]Ages 15–64 only. [8]Includes 261,000 registered unemployed. [9]Imports c.i.f.; exports f.o.b. [10]In guilders. [11]KLM only. [12]Public schools only. [13]Colleges only. [14]Universities. [15]Military constabulary.

Internet resources for further information:
• **Statistics Netherlands** http://www.cbs.nl/en-GB/default.htm

Netherlands Antilles

Official name: Nederlandse Antillen (Netherlands Antilles).
Political status: nonmetropolitan territory of The Netherlands with one legislative house (States of the Netherlands Antilles [22])[1].
Chief of state: Dutch Monarch represented by Governor.
Head of government: Prime Minister.
Capital: Willemstad.
Official language: Dutch.
Official religion: none.
Monetary unit: 1 Netherlands Antillean guilder (NA f.) = 100 cents; valuation (Sept. 1, 2005)
1 U.S.$ = NA f. 1.79;
1 £ = NA f. 3.30.

Area and population

Island councils	Capitals	area sq mi	area sq km	population 2004 estimate
Leeward Islands				
Bonaire	Kralendijk	111	288	10,185
Curaçao	Willemstad	171	444	133,644
Windward Islands				
Saba	The Bottom	5	13	1,424
Sint Eustatius, or Statia	Oranjestad	8	21	2,498
Sint Maarten (Dutch part only)	Philipsburg	13	34	33,119
TOTAL		308	800	180,870

Demography

Population (2005): 183,000.
Density (2005): persons per sq mi 594.2, persons per sq km 228.8.
Urban-rural (2003): urban 69.7%; rural 30.3%.
Sex distribution (2004): male 46.66%; female 53.34%.
Age breakdown (2004): under 15, 23.3%; 15–29, 17.6%; 30–44, 25.4%; 45–59, 20.1%; 60–74, 9.8%; 75 and over, 3.8%.
Population projection: (2010) 188,000; (2020) 198,000.
Ethnic composition (2000): local black-other (Antillean Creole) 81.1%; Dutch 5.3%; Surinamese 2.9%; other (significantly West Indian black) 10.7%.
Religious affiliation (2001): Roman Catholic 72.0%; Protestant 16.0%; Spiritist 0.9%; Buddhist 0.5%; Jewish 0.4%; Bahā'ī 0.3%; Hindu 0.2%; Muslim 0.2%; other/unknown 9.5%.
Major cities (2001): Willemstad (urban agglomeration) 125,000; Kralendijk 7,900; Philipsburg 6,300.

Vital statistics

Birth rate per 1,000 population (2003): 14.2 (world avg. 21.1); (1988)[2] legitimate 51.6%; illegitimate 48.4%.
Death rate per 1,000 population (2003): 7.7 (world avg. 9.0).
Natural increase rate per 1,000 population (2003): 6.5 (world avg. 12.1).
Total fertility rate (avg. births per childbearing woman; 2004): 2.0.
Marriage rate per 1,000 population (2003): 4.2.
Divorce rate per 1,000 population (2003): 3.1.
Life expectancy at birth (2004): male 73.4 years; female 78.0 years.
Major causes of death per 100,000 population (1993): infectious and parasitic diseases/diseases of the respiratory system 209.0; diseases of the circulatory system 180.2; malignant neoplasms (cancers) 117.7.

National economy

Budget (2002). Revenue: NA f. 616,500,000 (tax revenue 86.5%, of which sales tax 40.6%, import duties 20.6%, excise on gasoline 12.7%; nontax revenue 11.7%; grants 1.8%). Expenditures: NA f. 669,000,000 (current expenditures 94.7%, of which transfers 32.0%, wages 31.1%, interest payments 16.1%, goods and services 12.9%; development expenditures 5.3%).
Production (metric tons except as noted). Agriculture, forestry, fishing: [3]; livestock (number of live animals; 2004) 13,500 goats, 9,000 sheep, 2,600 asses, 135,000 chickens; roundwood, n.a.; fish catch (2002) 12,901. Mining and quarrying (2002): salt 500,000, sulfur by-product 30,000. Manufacturing (2000): residual fuel oil 5,112,000; gas-diesel oils 2,525,000; asphalt 1,022; other manufactures include electronic parts, cigarettes, textiles, rum, and Curaçao liqueur. Energy production (consumption): electricity (kW-hr; 2002) 1,000,000,000 (1,000,000,000); coal, none (none); crude petroleum (barrels; 2002) none (108,000,000); petroleum products (metric tons; 2002) 10,712,000 (694,000); natural gas, none (none).
Land use as % of total land area (2000): in temporary crops 10.0%, in permanent crops, n.a., in pasture, n.a.; overall forest area c. 1%.
Tourism (2002): receipts from visitors U.S.$792,000,000[2, 4]; expenditures by nationals abroad (2000) U.S.$339,000,000.
Household income and expenditure. Average household size (2003) 2.9; income per household: n.a.; sources of income: n.a.; expenditure (1996)[5, 6]: housing 26.5%, transportation and communications 19.9%, food 14.7%, household furnishings 8.8%, recreation and education 8.2%, clothing and footwear 7.5%.
Gross national product (at current market prices; 2003): U.S.$2,910,000,000 (U.S.$13,160 per capita).

Structure of gross domestic product and labour force

	2003 in value NA f. '000,000	2003 % of total value	2001 labour force	2001 % of labour force
Agriculture, forestry	36.7	0.7	441	0.5
Mining			131	0.2
Manufacturing	268.0	5.0	4,619	5.7
Construction	204.9	3.8	5,335	6.5
Public utilities	198.8	3.7	1,131	1.4
Transp. and commun.	433.6	8.1	5,410	6.6
Trade, hotels, restaurants	948.8	17.7	19,002	23.3
Finance, real estate, insurance	1,655.8	30.8	10,103	12.4
Pub. admin., defense	348.9	6.5	5,997	7.3
Services	742.7	13.8	15,961	19.6
Other	529.27[7]	9.97[7]	13,428[8]	16.58[8]
TOTAL	5,367.69[9]	100.0	81,558	100.0

Population economically active (2001): total 81,558; activity rate of total population 46.5% (participation rates: ages 15–64, 68.7%; female 49.0%; unemployed [2003] 15.3%).

Price index (2000 = 100)

	1998	1999	2000	2001	2002	2003	2004
Consumer price index	94.2	94.5	100.0	101.8	102.2	104.3	105.7

Public debt (external outstanding; 2004): U.S.$477,900,000.

Foreign trade[10]

Balance of trade (current prices)

	2000	2001	2002
U.S.$'000,000	−845	−410	−569
% of total	17.4%	7.8%	14.3%

Imports (2002): U.S.$2,268,500,000 (crude petroleum 59.7%, refined petroleum 8.7%, food 6.4%, electrical machinery and apparatus 4.0%). *Major import sources* (2004): Venezuela 51.1%; United States 21.9%; The Netherlands 5.0%.
Exports (2002): U.S.$1,699,200,000 (refined petroleum 94.7%, food 1.2%, furniture and parts 0.8%). *Major export destinations* (2004): United States 20.4%; Panama 11.2%; Guatemala 8.8%; Haiti 7.1%; The Bahamas 5.6%.

Transport and communications

Transport. Railroads: none. Roads (2003): total length 373 mi, 600 km (paved 50%). Vehicles (1999): passenger cars 74,840; trucks and buses 17,415. Air transport (2001)[11]: passenger arrivals and departures 2,131,000; freight loaded and unloaded 18,900 metric tons; airports (2000) with scheduled flights 5.

Communications

Medium	date	unit	number	units per 1,000 persons
Daily newspapers	1996	circulation	70,000	341
Radio	1997	receivers	217,000	1,039
Television	1997	receivers	69,000	330
Telephones	2001	main lines	81,000	372
Cellular telephones	1998	subscribers	16,000	77
Internet	1999	users	2,000	9.3

Education and health

Educational attainment (2001). Percentage of population 25 and over having: no formal schooling 0.8%; primary education 24.2%; lower secondary 42.8%; upper secondary 16.8%; higher 11.4%; unknown 4.0%. *Literacy* (2001): total population age 15 and over literate 111,083 (96.3%); males literate 50,980 (96.7%); females literate 60,103 (96.1%).

Education (1999–2000)

	schools	teachers	students	student/ teacher ratio
Primary (age 6–12)	90	1,139[12]	23,205	21.1[12]
Secondary (age 12–17)	22	46[12]	8,112	18.2[12]
Voc., teacher tr.	32	853[12]	7,576	9.7[12]
Higher	2	123	825	6.7

Health (2001): physicians 333 (1 per 520 persons); hospital beds 1,343 (1 per 129 persons); infant mortality rate per 1,000 live births (2004) 10.4.
Food (2002): daily per capita caloric intake 2,554 (vegetable products 73%, animal products 27%); 106% of FAO recommended minimum requirement.

Military

Total active duty personnel (2004): 1,000 Dutch naval personnel in Netherlands Antilles and Aruba.

---

[1]The Netherlands Antilles is to be dissolved as of July 1, 2007, per an official announcement in November 2005. Curaçao and Sint Maarten are to become separate overseas territories within The Netherlands. Bonaire, Saba, and Sint Eustatius will probably be directly administered from The Hague. [2]Excludes Sint Eustatius. [3]Mostly tomatoes, beans, cucumbers, gherkins, melons, and lettuce grown on hydroponic farms; aloes grown for export, divi-divi pods, and sour orange fruit are nonhydroponic crops. [4]Excludes Saba. [5]Curaçao only. [6]Weights of consumer price index components. [7]Taxes less subsidies. [8]Includes 11,876 unemployed. [9]Detail does not add to total given because of rounding. [10]Imports c.i.f.; exports f.o.b. [11]Curaçao and Sint Maarten airports. [12]1996–97.

Internet resources for further information:
• **Central Bank of the Netherlands Antilles http://www.centralbank.an**
• **Central Bureau of Statistics http://www.cbs.an**

New Caledonia

Official name: Nouvelle-Calédonie (New Caledonia).
Political status[1]: overseas country (France) with one legislative house (Congress[2] [54]).
Chief of state: President of France represented by High Commissioner.
Head of government: President.
Capital: Nouméa.
Official language: none[3].
Official religion: none.
Monetary unit: 1 franc of the Comptoirs français du Pacifique (CFPF) = 100 centimes; valuation (Sept. 1, 2005)[4]
1 U.S.$ = CFPF 95.04;
1 £ = CFPF 174.99.

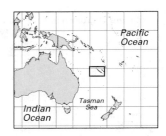

Area and population		area		population
Provinces Island(s)	Capitals	sq mi	sq km	2004 census
Loyauté (Loyalty)	Wé	765	1,981	22,080
Lifou		466	1,207	10,320
Maré		248	642	7,401
Ouvéa		51	132	4,359
Nord (Northern)	Koné	3,305	8,561	44,474
Belep		27	70	930
New Caledonia (part)		3,278	8,491	43,544
Sud (Southern)	Nouméa	3,102	8,033	164,235
New Caledonia (part)		3,043	7,881	162,395
Pins		59	152	1,840
TOTAL		7,172	18,575	230,789

Demography

Population (2005): 237,000.
Density (2005): persons per sq mi 33.0, persons per sq km 12.8.
Urban-rural (2003): urban 61.2%; rural 38.8%.
Sex distribution (2004): male 50.30%; female 49.70%.
Age breakdown (2004): under 15, 29.4%; 15–29, 25.2%; 30–44, 21.8%; 45–59, 14.0%; 60–74, 7.7%; 75 and over, 1.9%.
Population projection: (2010) 257,000; (2020) 296,000.
Doubling time: 55 years.
Ethnic composition (1996): Melanesian 45.3%, of which local (Kanak) 44.1%; Vanuatuan 1.2%; European 34.1%; Wallisian or Futunan 9.0%; Indonesian 2.6%; Tahitian 2.6%; Vietnamese 1.4%; other 5.0%.
Religious affiliation (2000): Roman Catholic 54.2%; Protestant 14.0%; Muslim 2.7%; other Christian 2.1%; other 27.0%.
Major cities (2004): Nouméa 91,386 (urban agglomeration 146,245); Mont-Dore 24,195[5]; Dumbéa 18,602[5]; Païta 12,062[5]; Poindimié 4,824.

Vital statistics

Birth rate per 1,000 population (2004): 17.6 (world avg. 21.1); (2003) legitimate 32.3%; illegitimate 67.7%.
Death rate per 1,000 population (2004): 4.8 (world avg. 9.0).
Natural increase rate per 1,000 population (2004): 12.8 (world avg. 12.1).
Total fertility rate (avg. births per childbearing woman; 2004): 2.4.
Marriage rate per 1,000 population (2003): 4.0.
Divorce rate per 1,000 population (2003): 1.1.
Life expectancy at birth (2003): male 71.3 years; female 77.2 years.
Major causes of death per 100,000 population (2002): malignant neoplasms (cancers) 135.6; diseases of the circulatory system 119.2; accidents, poisonings, and violence 77.6; diseases of the respiratory system 45.2; infectious and parasitic diseases 20.6.

National economy

Budget (2001). Revenue: $A 1,184,000,000[6] (tax revenue 74.7%, nontax revenue 25.3%). Expenditures: $A 1,156,000,000[6] (current expenditure 90.1%, development expenditure 9.9%).
Production (metric tons except as noted). Agriculture, forestry, fishing (2004): coconuts 16,000, yams 11,000, vegetables 4,000, corn (maize) 3,800, sweet potatoes 3,000, fruit 3,000; livestock (number of live animals) 110,000 cattle, 25,500 pigs, 510,000 chickens; roundwood 4,800 cu m; fish catch (2002) 5,299, of which tuna 2,020, shrimp 1,815, sea cucumbers 450. Mining and quarrying (metric tons): nickel ore (2003) 7,000,000, of which nickel content 112,000; cobalt 900 (recovered). Manufacturing (metric tons; 2003): cement 100,000; ferronickel (metal content) 50,666; nickel matte (metal content) 10,857; other manufactures include beer, copra cake, and soap. Energy production (consumption): electricity (kW-hr; 2002) 1,729,000,000 (1,729,000,000); coal (metric tons; 2002) none (115,000); crude petroleum, none (none); petroleum products (metric tons; 2002) none (478,000); natural gas, none (none).
Population economically active (1996): total 80,589; activity rate of total population 40.9% (participation rates: over age 14, 57.3%; female 39.7%; unemployed [2001] 16.0%).

Price and earnings indexes (December 2000 = 100)							
	1998	1999	2000	2001	2002	2003	2004
Consumer price index	97.7	97.8	100.0	102.3	103.8	104.8	105.7
Earnings index[7]	98.4	98.9	100.0	127.5	127.5	131.9	...

Public debt (external, outstanding; 1998): U.S.$79,000,000.
Gross national product (at current market prices; 2003): U.S.$3,740,000,000 (U.S.$16,360 per capita).

Structure of gross domestic product and labour force				
	2001			
	in value CFPF '000,000,000	% of total value	labour force[8]	% of labour force[8]
Agriculture	78.5	17.0	2,490	4.0
Mining	} 78.5	} 17.0	1,772	2.9
Public utilities				
Manufacturing	5.0	1.0	} 5,720	9.3
Construction	9.5	2.0	7,031	11.4
Transp. and commun.	55.5	12.0	2,861	4.6
Trade	55.5	12.0	9,799	15.9
Finance			5,461	8.9
Services	} 175.5	} 38.0	11,165	18.1
Pub. admin., defense			...	...
Other			15,348[9]	24.9[9]
TOTAL	461.0[10]	100.0[10]	61,647	100.0

Household income and expenditure. Average household size (2002) 3.9; average annual income per household (1991) CFPF 3,361,233 (U.S.$32,879)[11]; sources of income (1991): wages and salaries 68.2%, transfer payments 13.7%, other 18.1%; expenditure (1991): food and beverages 25.9%, housing 20.4%, transportation and communications 16.1%, recreation 4.8%.
Tourism: receipts from visitors (2001) U.S.$93,000,000.
Land use as % of total land area (2000): in temporary crops 0.4%, in permanent crops 0.3%, in pasture 11.8%; overall forest area 20.4%.

Foreign trade[12]

Balance of trade (current prices)						
	1999	2000	2001	2002	2003	2004
CFPF '000,000	–60,500	–41,312	–63,824	–64,764	–81,112	–58,203
% of total	36.6%	20.8%	34.6%	34.2%	32.9%	22.8%

Imports (2004): CFPF 156,767,000,000 (machinery and apparatus 20.9%, transportation equipment 17.6%, food 13.9%, mineral products [mostly coal and refined petroleum] 12.5%, chemicals and chemical products 7.8%). *Major import sources:* EU 55.0%, of which France 40.3%; Singapore 10.9%; Australia 9.1%; New Zealand 4.9%.
Exports (2004): CFPF 98,564,000,000 (ferronickel 60.6%, nickel ore 16.1%, nickel matte 14.3%, shrimp 2.3%). *Major export destinations* (2003): EU 25.7%, of which France 15.4%; Japan 21.7%; Taiwan 12.9%; South Korea 11.9%; Australia 6.0%.

Transport and communications

Transport. Railroads: none. Roads (2000): total length 3,375 mi, 5,432 km (paved [1993] 52%). Vehicles: passenger cars (2002) 92,600; trucks and buses (1997) 23,000. Air transport (2004)[13]: passenger-km 1,267,131,000, metric ton-km cargo 20,390,000; airports with scheduled flights 11.

Communications				units per 1,000 persons
Medium	date	unit	number	
Daily newspapers	2000	circulation	18,000	84
Radio	1997	receivers	107,000	533
Television	2000	receivers	106,000	493
Telephones	2004	main lines	53,300	230
Cellular telephones	2004	subscribers	116,400	502
Internet	2004	users	70,000	302

Education and health

Educational attainment (1996). Percentage of population age 14 and over having: no formal schooling 5.7%; primary education 28.9%; lower secondary 30.2%; upper secondary 24.6%; higher 10.5%. *Literacy:* n.a.

Education (2001)				student/ teacher ratio
	schools	teachers	students	
Primary (age 6–10)	289	1,837	36,996	20.1
Secondary (age 11–17) } Vocational	64	2,371	29,036	12.2
Higher	4[14]	55[15]	2,069[15]	37.6[15]

Health (2002): physicians 476 (1 per 471 persons); hospital beds 766 (1 per 292 persons); infant mortality rate per 1,000 live births (2004) 7.9.
Food (2002): daily per capita caloric intake 2,809 (vegetable products 75%, animal products 25%); 123% of FAO recommended minimum requirement.

Military

Total active duty personnel (2004): 2,700 French troops. *Military expenditure as percentage of GDP:* n.a.

---

[1]The Nouméa Accord granting New Caledonia limited autonomy was signed in May 1998; a referendum on independence is scheduled for 2014. [2]Operates in association with 3 provincial assemblies. [3]Kanak languages and French have special recognition per Nouméa Accord. [4]Pegged to the euro on January 1, 2002, at €1 = CFPF 119.25. [5]Within Nouméa urban agglomeration. [6]Australian dollars. [7]Based on minimum hourly wage. [8]Excludes civil servants and self-employed. [9]Includes 5,488 not adequately defined and 9,860 unemployed. [10]Detail does not add to total given because of gross rounding. [11]Includes both monetary (92%) and nonmonetary income (8%). [12]Imports c.i.f.; exports f.o.b. [13]Air Calédonie only. [14]1996. [15]2000.

Internet resources for further information:
• **Ministère de l'Outre-Mer**
　http://www.outre-mer.gouv.fr
• **Institut de la statistique et des études économiques Nouvelle-Calédonie**
　http://www.isee.nc

New Zealand

Official name: New Zealand (English); Aotearoa (Māori).
Form of government: constitutional monarchy with one legislative house (House of Representatives [121[1]]).
Chief of state: British Monarch, represented by Governor-General.
Head of government: Prime Minister.
Capital: Wellington.
Official languages: English; Māori.
Official religion: none.
Monetary unit: 1 New Zealand dollar ($NZ) = 100 cents; valuation (Sept. 1, 2005) 1 U.S.$ = $NZ 1.42; 1 £ = $NZ 2.61.

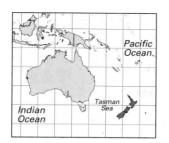

Area and population	area		population
Islands			2005
Regional Councils	sq mi	sq km	estimate
North Island	44,702	115,777	3,116,100
Auckland	...	...	1,337,000
Bay of Plenty	...	...	260,300
Gisborne[2]	...	...	44,700
Hawkes Bay	...	...	149,400
Manawatu-Wanganui	...	...	226,100
Northland	...	...	148,600
Taranaki	...	...	105,000
Waikato	...	...	384,700
Wellington	...	...	460,300
South Island	58,384	151,215	981,400
Canterbury	...	...	526,300
Marlborough[2]	...	...	42,700
Nelson[2]	...	...	45,700
Otago	...	...	196,600
Southland	...	...	93,000
Tasman[2]	...	...	46,600
West Coast	...	...	30,500
Offshore islands	1,368	3,542	760
TOTAL	104,454	270,534	4,098,260

Demography

Population (2005): 4,096,000.
Density (2005): persons per sq mi 39.2, persons per sq km 15.1.
Urban-rural (2002): urban 86.0%; rural 14.0%.
Sex distribution (2001): male 49.07%; female 50.93%.
Age breakdown (2001): under 15, 22.5%; 15–29, 20.4%; 30–44, 23.0%; 45–59, 18.0%; 60–74, 10.7%; 75 and over, 5.4%.
Population projection[3]: (2010) 4,258,000; (2020) 4,564,000.
Ethnic composition (2001): European 73.8%; Māori (local Polynesian) 13.5%; Asian 6.1%; other Pacific Peoples (mostly other Polynesian) 6.0%; other 0.6%.
Religious affiliation (2001): Christian 55.2%, of which Anglican 15.3%, Roman Catholic 12.7%, Presbyterian 11.3%; nonreligious 26.9%; Buddhist 1.1%; Hindu 1.0%; other religions/not specified 15.8%.
Major urban areas (2001): Auckland 1,074,513; Wellington 339,750; Christchurch 334,107; Hamilton 166,128; Dunedin 107,088.

Vital statistics

Birth rate per 1,000 population (2003): 14.1 (world avg. 21.1); (2001) legitimate 56.3%; illegitimate 43.7%.
Death rate per 1,000 population (2003): 7.5 (world avg. 9.0).
Natural increase rate per 1,000 population (2003): 6.6 (world avg. 12.1).
Total fertility rate (avg. births per childbearing woman; 2003): 2.0.
Marriage rate per 1,000 population (2001): 5.1.
Life expectancy at birth (2003): male 75.3 years; female 81.4 years.
Major causes of death per 100,000 population (2001): diseases of the circulatory system 273.5; malignant neoplasms (cancers) 201.0; diseases of the respiratory system 52.4; accidents, suicide, homicide, and other violence 35.4.

National economy

Budget (2000–01). Revenue: $NZ 37,156,000,000 (income taxes 59.4%, taxes on goods and services 34.4%, nontax revenue 6.2%). Expenditures: $NZ 37,019,000,000 (social welfare 37.0%, health 19.0%, education 17.6%).
Production (metric tons except as noted). Agriculture, forestry, fishing (2004): apples 500,000, potatoes 500,000, barley 380,000, wheat 287,000, corn (maize) 170,000; livestock (number of live animals) 40,049,000 sheep, 9,540,000 cattle, 390,000 pigs; roundwood 21,399,000 cu m; fish catch (2001) 637,000. Mining and quarrying (2003): limestone 4,877,000; iron-sand concentrate 1,947,000; gold 9,305 kg. Manufacturing (value of sales in $NZ '000,000; 2003–04[4]): food products 4,456; machinery and apparatus 1,515; wood products (excluding furniture) 1,157; fabricated metals 1,130; printing and publishing 724. Energy production (consumption): electricity (kW-hr; 2002) 40,296,000,000 (40,296,000,000); hard coal (metric tons; 2002) 4,421,000 (2,445,000); lignite (metric tons; 2002) 218,000 (265,000); crude petroleum (barrels; 2002) 11,085,000 (39,408,000); petroleum products (metric tons; 2002) 5,334,000 (5,667,000); natural gas (cu m; 2002) 5,531,000,000 (5,531,000,000).
Household income and expenditure. Average household size (1998) 2.8; annual income per household[5] (2000–01) $NZ 53,076 (U.S.$24,403); sources of income (1998): wages and salaries 65.8%, transfer payments 15.2%, self-employment 9.8%, other 9.2%; expenditure (2000–01): housing 23.9%, food 16.5%, transportation 15.9%, household goods 12.8%, clothing 3.2%.
Gross national product (2004): U.S.$82,465,000,000 (U.S.$20,310 per capita).

Structure of gross domestic product and labour force

	2003–04		2003	
	in value $NZ '000,000[6]	% of total value	labour force	% of labour force
Agriculture	} 8,954	7.4	156,600	7.8
Mining			3,300	0.2
Manufacturing	18,479	15.3	278,700	13.8
Construction	5,600	4.6	138,600	6.9
Public utilities	2,492	2.1	8,500	0.4
Transp. and commun.	12,298	10.2	111,000	5.5
Trade, hotels	19,335	16.0	442,500	22.0
Finance, real estate	29,130	24.1	250,900	12.4
Pub. admin., defense	4,999	4.1	110,600	5.5
Services	14,900	12.3	417,100	20.7
Other	4,781	3.9	97,100[7]	4.8[7]
TOTAL	120,968	100.0	2,014,900	100.0

Population economically active (2003): total 2,014,900; activity rate 50.3% (participation rates: ages 15–64, 74.5%; female 45.7%; unemployed [2004] 3.9%).

Price and earnings indexes (2000 = 100)

	1998	1999	2000	2001	2002	2003	2004
Consumer price index	97.6	97.4	100.0	102.6	105.4	107.2	109.7
Weekly earnings index[8]	95.4	98.4	100.0	102.7	...	...	...

Tourism (2003): receipts U.S.$3,974,000,000; expenditures U.S.$1,781,000,000.
Land use as % of total land area (2000): in temporary crops 5.6%, in permanent crops 6.9%, in pasture 51.7%; overall forest area 29.7%.

Foreign trade[9]

Balance of trade (current prices)

	1999	2000	2001	2002	2003	2004
$NZ '000,000	−1,896	+347	+2,987	+698	−1,464	−1,967
% of total	3.9%	0.6%	4.8%	1.1%	2.5%	3.1%

Imports (2003): $NZ 32,161,000,000 (machinery and apparatus 21.9%, vehicles and parts 15.5%, crude and refined petroleum 9.1%, plastics 4.0%). *Major import sources:* Australia 22.6%; U.S. 12.6%; Japan 12.1%; China 8.4%; Germany 5.3%.
Exports (2003): $NZ 29,291,000,000 (dairy products 16.1%, beef and sheep meat 13.1%, wood and paper products 8.1%, machinery and apparatus 4.6%, fish and fish products 4.1%, fruits and nuts 3.5%). *Major export destinations:* Australia 20.7%; U.S. 14.9%; Japan 11.5%; China 5.0%; U.K. 4.6%.

Transport and communications

Transport. Railroads (2003): route length 3,898 km; passenger-km, n.a.; metric ton-km cargo 1999–2000[10]) 4,040,000,000. Roads (2002–03)[11]: total length 92,494 km (paved 64%). Vehicles (2001–02)[11]: passenger cars 1,988,522; trucks and buses 380,297. Air transport[12] (2004): passenger-km 24,710,000,000; metric ton-km cargo 748,833,000; airports (1997) 36.

Communications

Medium	date	unit	number	units per 1,000 persons
Daily newspapers	2004	circulation	738,000	181
Radio	2000	receivers	3,850,000	997
Television	2000	receivers	2,010,000	522
Telephones	2004	main lines	1,800,500	461
Cellular telephones	2004	subscribers	3,027,000	775
Personal computers	2004	units	1,924,000	493
Internet	2004	users	3,200,000	819

Education and health

Educational attainment (2001). Percentage of population ages 25–64 having: no formal schooling to incomplete secondary 26%; secondary 36%; vocational and some undergraduate 24%; completed undergraduate 14%.
Literacy: virtually 100.0%.

Education (1999)

	schools	teachers	students	student/ teacher ratio
Primary (age 5–12)[13]	2,366	25,832	478,065	18.5
Secondary (age 13–17)	335	15,401	226,164	14.7
Voc., teacher tr.	29	5,428	111,855	20.6
Higher[14]	7	5,008	105,996	21.2

Health (2002): physicians 8,403 (1 per 469 persons); hospital beds 23,825 (1 per 165 persons); infant mortality rate per 1,000 live births (2003) 6.1.
Food (2002): daily per capita caloric intake 3,210 (vegetable products 67%, animal products 33%); 122% of FAO recommended minimum requirement.

Military

Total active duty personnel (2004): 8,610 (army 51.4%, air force 25.6%, navy 23.0%). *Military expenditure as percentage of GDP* (2003): 1.1%; per capita expenditure U.S.$213.

[1]Includes seven elected seats allocated to Māoris. [2]Reorganized as a unitary authority that is administered by a district council with regional powers. [3]Official government projections of December 2004. [4]At end of 1997 constant prices. [5]Gross income. [6]Constant 1995–96 prices. [7]Mostly unemployed. [8]Excluding overtime. [9]Import figures are f.o.b. in balance of trade and c.i.f. in commodities and trading partners. [10]Data for fiscal year. [11]Figure at end of June of fiscal year. [12]Air New Zealand only. [13]Includes composite schools that provide both primary and secondary education. [14]Universities only.

Internet resources for further information:
• **Statistics New Zealand/Te Tari Tatau http://www.stats.govt.nz/default.htm**
• **Reserve Bank of New Zealand http://www.rbnz.govt.nz**

Nicaragua

Official name: República de Nicaragua (Republic of Nicaragua).
Form of government: unitary multiparty republic with one legislative house (National Assembly [92[1]]).
Head of state and government: President.
Capital: Managua.
Official language: Spanish.
Official religion: none.
Monetary unit: 1 córdoba oro (C$) = 100 centavos;
valuation (Sept. 1, 2005)
1 U.S.$ = C$16.37; 1 £ = C$30.14.

Area and population

Departments	Capitals	area[2] sq mi	sq km	population 2004 estimate[3]
Boaco	Boaco	1,613	4,177	173,444
Carazo	Jinotepe	417	1,081	182,640
Chinandega	Chinandega	1,862	4,822	452,190
Chontales	Juigalpa	2,502	6,481	186,672
Estelí	Estelí	861	2,230	220,521
Granada	Granada	402	1,040	196,275
Jinotega	Jinotega	3,714	9,620	305,818
León	León	2,107	5,457	402,710
Madriz	Somoto	659	1,708	137,111
Managua	Managua	1,338	3,465	1,413,257
Masaya	Masaya	236	611	324,855
Matagalpa	Matagalpa	2,627	6,804	497,931
Nueva Segovia	Ocotal	1,194	3,093	217,444
Río San Juan	San Carlos	2,912	7,541	97,825
Rivas	Rivas	835	2,162	172,119
Autonomous regions				
North Atlantic	Puerto Cabezas	12,549	32,501	256,440
South Atlantic	Bluefields	10,636	27,546	389,240
TOTAL LAND AREA		46,464	120,340[4]	
INLAND WATER		3,874	10,034	
TOTAL		50,337[4]	130,373[4]	5,626,492

Demography

Population (2005): 5,487,000[5].
Density (2005)[6]: persons per sq mi 118.1, persons per sq km 45.6.
Urban-rural (2004): urban 58.6%; rural 41.4%.
Sex distribution (2004): male 49.81%; female 50.19%.
Age breakdown (2003): under 15, 38.8%; 15–29, 30.4%; 30–44, 17.5%; 45–59, 8.6%; 60–74, 3.7%; 75 and over, 0.9%.
Population projection: (2010) 6,066,000; (2020) 7,179,000.
Doubling time: 33 years.
Ethnic composition (2000): mestizo (Spanish/Indian) 63.1%; white 14.0%; black 8.0%; multiple ethnicities 5.0%; other 9.9%.
Religious affiliation (2000): Roman Catholic 80.6%; Protestant 11.0%; independent Christian 2.8%; other Christian 1.8%; Spiritist 1.4%; other 2.3%.
Major cities (1995): Managua (urban agglomeration, 2003) 1,098,000; León 123,865; Chinandega 97,387; Masaya 88,971; Granada 71,783; Estelí 71,550.

Vital statistics

Birth rate per 1,000 population (2004): 25.5 (world avg. 21.1).
Death rate per 1,000 population (2004): 4.5 (world avg. 9.0).
Natural increase rate per 1,000 population (2004): 21.0 (world avg. 12.1).
Total fertility rate (avg. births per childbearing woman; 2004): 2.9.
Life expectancy at birth (2004): male 68.0 years; female 72.2 years.
Major causes of death per 100,000 population (2000)[7]: diseases of the circulatory system 63; malignant neoplasms 30; accidents, injuries, and violence 20; diseases of the respiratory system 18; infectious and parasitic diseases 15.

National economy

Budget (2004). Revenue: C$12,250,700,000 (tax revenue 96.3%, of which sales tax 38.2%, import duties 27.8%, tax on income and profits 25.9%; nontax revenue 3.7%). Expenditures: C$16,697,800,000 (current expenditure 58.4%, development expenditure 41.6%).
Public debt (external, outstanding; July 2005): U.S.$5,280,000,000.
Production (metric tons except as noted). Agriculture, forestry, fishing (2004): sugarcane 4,090,910, corn (maize) 521,943, rice 241,701, dry beans 223,679, cassava 117,300, sorghum 113,954, peanuts (groundnuts) 99,545, oranges 75,000, coffee 70,909, bananas 61,091; livestock (number of live animals) 3,400,000 cattle, 450,000 pigs; roundwood 5,999,111 cu m; fish catch (2004–05) 25,430, of which crustaceans 13,930. Mining and quarrying (2004–05): gold 123,600 troy oz. Manufacturing (value added in C$'000,000; 2003[8]): food 1,917; textiles and wearing apparel 969; beverages 713; wood products (incl. furniture) 503. Energy production (consumption): electricity (kW-hr; 2002) 2,554,000,000 (2,562,000,000); coal, none (none); crude petroleum (barrels; 2002) none (6,025,000); petroleum products (metric tons; 2002) 775,000 (1,167,000); natural gas, none (none).
Tourism (2003): receipts from visitors U.S.$151,000,000; expenditures by nationals abroad U.S.$75,000,000.
Land use as % of total land area (2000): in temporary crops 15.9%, in permanent crops 1.9%, in pasture 39.7%; overall forest area 27.0%.
Population economically active (2001): total 1,900,400; activity rate of total population 36.5% (participation rates: ages 15–64 [2000] 64.1%; female 30.8%; officially unemployed [2003] 7.8%).

Price index (2000 = 100)

	1998	1999	2000	2001	2002	2003	2004
Consumer price index	80.6	89.6	100.0	107.4	111.6	117.4	127.3

Gross national product (2004): U.S.$4,452,000,000 (U.S.$790 per capita).

Structure of gross domestic product and labour force

	2004 in value C$'000	2004 % of total value	2003 labour force	2003 % of labour force
Agriculture, forestry	12,388,100	17.1	595,800	28.1
Mining	736,200	1.0	4,600	0.2
Manufacturing	12,995,500	17.9	259,400	12.3
Construction	4,342,700	6.0	74,000	3.5
Public utilities	1,694,000	2.3	12,700	0.6
Transp. and commun.	3,967,200	5.5	74,800	3.5
Trade, restaurants	9,967,100	13.7	457,000	21.6
Finance, real estate	9,044,800	12.5	52,100	2.5
Pub. admin., defense	7,737,000	10.6	422,400	19.9
Services	4,935,500	6.8		
Other	4,795,100[9]	6.6[9]	164,700[10]	7.8[10]
TOTAL	72,603,300[4]	100.0	2,117,600[4]	100.0

Household income and expenditure. Average household size (2002) 5.6; expenditure (1999)[11]: food and beverages 41.8%, education 9.8%, housing 9.8%, transportation 8.5%.

Foreign trade[12]

Balance of trade (current prices)

	1999	2000	2001	2002	2003	2004
U.S.$'000,000	−1,152	−1,010	−1,028	−1,038	−1,116	−1,266
% of total	51.3%	44.0%	46.6%	48.1%	48.0%	45.6%

Imports (2003): U.S.$1,887,000,000 (nondurable consumer goods 25.9%; mineral fuels 17.4%; capital goods for industry 11.8%; durable consumer goods 7.5%). *Major import sources:* U.S. 24.7%; Venezuela 9.7%; Costa Rica 9.0%; Mexico 8.4%; Guatemala 7.3%.
Exports (2003): U.S.$605,000,000 (non-marine food products 44.6%, of which coffee 14.1%, meat 13.5%; lobster 6.0%; gold 5.8%; shrimp 5.5%). *Major export destinations:* U.S. 33.4%; El Salvador 17.3%; Costa Rica 8.1%; Honduras 7.2%; Mexico 4.6%.

Transport and communications

Transport. Railroads: [13]. Roads (2002): total length 18,709 km (paved 11%). Vehicles (2002): passenger cars 83,168; trucks and buses 121,796. Air transport (2000): passenger-km 72,200,000; metric ton-km cargo (2003) 200,000; airports (1997) with scheduled flights 10.

Communications

Medium	date	unit	number	units per 1,000 persons
Daily newspapers	2000	circulation	152,000	30
Radio	2000	receivers	1,370,000	270
Television	2003	receivers	648,000	123
Telephones	2004	main lines	214,500	40
Cellular telephones	2004	subscribers	738,600	137
Personal computers	2004	units	200,000	37
Internet	2004	users	125,000	23

Education and health

Educational attainment (1995). Percentage of population age 25 and over having: no formal schooling 30.6%; no formal schooling (literate) 3.9%; primary education 39.2%; secondary 17.0%; technical 3.1%; incomplete undergraduate 2.2%; complete undergraduate 4.0%. *Literacy* (2003): total population age 15 and over literate 67.5%; males literate 67.2%; females literate 67.8%.

Education (2002)

	schools	teachers	students	student/ teacher ratio
Primary (age 7–12)	8,251	21,020[14]	923,391	...
Secondary (age 13–18)	1,249	5,970[14]	364,012	...
Higher	108[15]	3,840[15]	...	14.6[15]

Health (2003): physicians 2,076 (1 per 2,538 persons); hospital beds 5,030 (1 per 1,047 persons); infant mortality rate (2004) 30.2.
Food (2002): daily per capita caloric intake 2,298 (vegetable products 92%, animal products 8%); 102% of FAO recommended minimum requirement.

Military

Total active duty personnel (2004): 14,000 (army 85.7%, navy 5.7%, air force 8.6%). *Military expenditure as percentage of GDP* (2003): 0.9%; per capita expenditure U.S.$7.

[1]Includes 2 unsuccessful 2001 presidential candidates meeting special conditions. [2]Lakes and lagoons are excluded from the areas of departments and autonomous regions. [3]Official projection based on 1995 census. [4]Detail does not add to total given because of rounding. [5]Estimate of *UN World Population Prospects (2004 revision)*. [6]Based on land area. [7]Estimates. [8]At prices of 1994. [9]Taxes less imputed bank service charges. [10]Represents unemployed. [11]Weights of consumer price index components. [12]Imports f.o.b. in balance of trade and c.i.f. in commodities and trading partners. [13]Public railroad service ended in January 1994; private rail service (2004) 4 mi (6 km). [14]1996. [15]2000.

Internet resources for further information:
• **Central Bank of Nicaragua** http://www.bcn.gob.ni/english
• **Instituto Nacional de Estadísticas y Censos** http://www.inec.gob.ni

Niger

Official name: République du Niger (Republic of Niger).
Form of government: multiparty republic with one legislative house (National Assembly [113]).
Head of state and government: President, assisted by Prime Minister.
Capital: Niamey.
Official language: French.
Official religion: none.
Monetary unit: 1 CFA franc (CFAF) = 100 centimes; valuation (Sept. 1, 2005) 1 U.S.$ = CFAF 522.78; 1 £ = CFAF 962.57[1].

Atlantic Ocean

Gulf of Guinea

Area and population		area		population
				2001
Departments	Capitals	sq mi	sq km	census
Agadez	Agadez	242,117	627,080	313,274
Diffa	Diffa	56,764	147,017	329,658
Dosso	Dosso	12,255	31,740	1,479,095
Maradi	Maradi	15,143	39,219	2,202,035
Tahoua	Tahoua	41,080	106,397	1,908,100
Tillabéri	Tillabéri	35,336	91,521	1,858,342
Zinder	Zinder	56,437	146,170	2,024,898
City				
Niamey	Niamey	155	402	674,950
TOTAL		459,286[2]	1,189,546	10,790,352

Demography

Population (2005): 12,163,000.
Density (2005): persons per sq mi 26.5, persons per sq km 10.2.
Urban-rural (2003): urban 22.2%; rural 77.8%.
Sex distribution (2004): male 51.19%; female 48.81%.
Age breakdown (2004): under 15, 46.8%; 15–29, 26.2%; 30–44, 14.8%; 45–59, 8.1%; 60–74, 3.6%; 75 and over, 0.5%.
Population projection: (2010) 14,054,000; (2020) 18,457,000.
Doubling time: 23 years.
Ethnolinguistic composition (2000): Zerma- (Djerma-) Songhai 25.7%; Tazarawa 14.9%; Fulani (Peul) 11.1%; Hausa 6.6%; other 41.7%.
Religious affiliation (2000): Sunnī Muslim 90.7%; traditional beliefs 8.7%; Christian 0.5%; other 0.1%.
Major cities (2001): Niamey 674,950 (urban agglomeration [2003] 890,000); Zinder 170,574; Maradi 147,038; Agadez 76,957; Tahoua 72,446; Arlit 67,398.

Vital statistics

Birth rate per 1,000 population (2004): 51.4 (world avg. 21.1).
Death rate per 1,000 population (2004): 21.4 (world avg. 9.0).
Natural increase rate per 1,000 population (2004): 30.0 (world avg. 12.1).
Total fertility rate (avg. births per childbearing woman; 2004): 7.6.
Marriage rate per 1,000 population: n.a.
Divorce rate per 1,000 population: n.a.
Life expectancy at birth (2004): male 43.3 years; female 43.2 years.
Major causes of death: n.a.; however, among selected major causes of infectious disease registered at medical facilities were malaria, measles, diarrhea, meningitis, pneumonia, diphtheria, tetanus, viral hepatitis, and poliomyelitis; malnutrition and shortages of trained medical personnel are widespread.

National economy

Budget (2003). Revenue: CFAF 221,281,000,000 (taxes 69.3%, external aid and gifts 29.2%, nontax revenue 1.5%). Expenditures: CFAF 272,200,000,000 (current expenditures 57.6%, of which education 10.9%, defense and public order 8.4%, interest 6.4%, health 3.8%; development expenditures 42.4%).
Public debt (external, outstanding; 2003): U.S.$1,900,000,000.
Tourism (2003): receipts from visitors U.S.$34,000,000; expenditures by nationals abroad U.S.$21,000,000.
Gross national product (2004): U.S.$2,836,000,000 (U.S.$230 per capita).

Structure of gross domestic product and labour force				
	2003		1988	
	in value CFAF '000,000	% of total value	labour force[3]	% of labour force[3]
Agriculture	632,800	39.9	1,764,049	76.2
Mining	96,500	6.1	5,295	0.2
Manufacturing	104,200	6.6	65,793	2.8
Construction	30,900	1.9	13,742	0.6
Public utilities	34,500	2.2	1,778	0.1
Transp. and commun.	77,900	4.9	14,764	0.6
Trade and finance	294,000	18.5	210,354	9.1
Pub. admin., defense	121,000	7.6	59,271	2.6
Services	156,600	9.9	63,991	2.8
Other	39,300[4]	2.5[4]	116,657	5.0
TOTAL	1,587,500[2]	100.0[2]	2,315,694	100.0

Production (metric tons except as noted). Agriculture, forestry, fishing (2004): millet 2,500,000, sorghum 580,000, cowpeas 549,035, onions 270,000, sugarcane 220,000, peanuts (groundnuts) 209,369, cassava 100,000, tomatoes 100,000, rice 76,500, tobacco leaf 1,000; livestock (number of live animals) 6,900,000 goats, 4,500,000 sheep, 2,260,000 cattle, 580,000 asses, 420,000 camels, 106,000 horses; roundwood 9,006,806 cu m; fish catch (2002) 23,520. Mining and quarrying: uranium (2004) 3,282; salt (2003) 3,000. Manufacturing

(value added in CFAF '000,000; 1998): paper and paper products 3,171; food 1,697; soaps and other chemical products 1,547; textiles 784. Energy production (consumption): electricity (kW-hr; 2002) 243,000,000 (458,000,000); coal (metric tons; 2002) 178,000 (178,000); crude petroleum, none (none); petroleum products (metric tons; 2002) none (233,000); natural gas, none (none).
Population economically active (1988)[3]: total 2,315,694; activity rate of total population 31.9% (participation rates: ages 15–64, 55.2%; female 20.4%).

Price index (2000 = 100)							
	1998	1999	2000	2001	2002	2003	2004
Consumer price index	99.5	97.2	100.0	104.0	106.7	105.0	105.3

Household income and expenditure. Average household size (2002) 6.4; income per household: n.a.; expenditure (1996)[5]: food, beverages, and tobacco products 45.1%, housing and energy 13.9%, transportation 12.1%, household furnishings 7.7%, clothing and footwear 5.8%.
Land use as % of total land area (2000): in temporary crops 3.5%, in permanent crops 0.01%, in pasture 9.5%; overall forest area 1.0%.

Foreign trade

Balance of trade (current prices)						
	1999	2000	2001	2002	2003	2004
CFAF '000,000	−26,200	−33,900	−43,300	−63,800	−72,400	−86,200
% of total	6.9%	7.8%	9.8%	14.1%	15.1%	17.6%

Imports (2003): CFAF 275,700,000,000 (food products 28.6%, capital goods 26.3%, petroleum products 11.5%, intermediate goods 6.7%). *Major import sources:* France 17.1%; Côte d'Ivoire 15.0%; Nigeria 8.1%; Japan 4.6%.
Exports (2003): CFAF 203,300,000,000 (uranium 32.2%, reexports 17.9%, cattle 17.5%, onions 7.7%, cowpeas 5.3%). *Major export destinations:* France 37.1%; Nigeria 33.6%; Japan 17.2%; Spain 3.8%.

Transport and communications

Transport. Railroads: none. Roads (2000): total length 8,700 mi, 14,000 km (paved 26%). Vehicles (1999): passenger cars 26,000; trucks and buses 35,600. Air transport: n.a.; airports (1999) with scheduled flights 6.

Communications				
Medium	date	unit	number	units per 1,000 persons
Daily newspapers	1996	circulation	2,000	0.2
Radio	2000	receivers	1,270,000	121
Television	2000	receivers	388,000	37
Telephones	2004	main lines	24,100	1.9
Cellular telephones	2004	subscribers	148,300	12
Personal computers	2004	units	9,000	0.7
Internet	2004	users	24,000	1.9

Education and health

Educational attainment (1988). Percentage of population age 25 and over having: no formal schooling 85.0%; Qur'ānic education 11.2%; primary education 2.5%; secondary 1.1%; higher 0.2%. *Literacy* (2001): total population age 15 and over literate 16.5%; males literate 24.4%; females literate 8.9%.

Education (2001–02)				
	schools	teachers	students	student/ teacher ratio
Primary (age 7–12)	5,970	18,441	760,987	41.3
Secondary (age 13–19)	242	3,634	100,140	27.6
Voc., teacher tr.[6]	...	215	2,145	10.0
Higher[7]	2	355	5,569	15.7

Health: physicians (1997) 324 (1 per 28,171 persons); hospital beds, n.a.; infant mortality rate per 1,000 live births (2004) 121.0.
Food (2002): daily per capita caloric intake 2,130 (vegetable products 95%, animal products 5%); 91% of FAO recommended minimum requirement.

Military

Total active duty personnel (2004): 5,300 (army 98.1%, air force 1.9%). *Military expenditure as percentage of GDP* (2003): 1.2%; per capita expenditure U.S.$2.

[1]Formerly pegged to the French franc and since Jan. 1, 2002, to the euro at the rate of 1€ = CFAF 655.96. [2]Detail does not add to total given because of rounding. [3]Excluding nomadic population. [4]Import taxes and duties. [5]Weights of consumer price index components. [6]1996–97. [7]Université de Niamey and École Nationale d'Administration du Niger only; 1997–98.

Internet resources for further information:
- Niger Profile
  http://www.nigerembassyusa.org/profile.html
- La Banque de France: La Zone Franc
  http://www.banque-france.fr/fr/eurosys/zonefr/zonefr.htm

Nigeria

Official name: Federal Republic of
Nigeria.
Form of government: federal republic
with two legislative bodies (Senate
[109]; House of Representatives
[360]).
Head of state and government: President.
Capital: Abuja.
Official language: English.
Official religion: none.
Monetary unit: 1 Nigerian naira
(₦) = 100 kobo; valuation (Sept. 1,
2005) 1 U.S.$ = ₦133.75;
1 £ = ₦246.27.

Area and population

States[1]	area sq km	population 1995 estimate	States[1]	area sq km	population 1995 estimate
Abia	6,320	2,569,362[2]	Kebbi	36,800	2,305,768
Adamawa	36,917	2,374,892	Kogi	29,833	2,346,936
Akwa Ibom	7,081	2,638,413	Kwara	36,825	1,751,464
Anambra	4,844	3,094,783	Lagos	3,345	6,357,253
Bauchi	45,837	4,801,569[3]	Nassarawa	27,117	[6]
Bayelsa	10,773	[4]	Niger	76,363	2,775,526
Benue	34,059	3,108,754	Ogun	16,762	2,614,747
Borno	70,898	2,903,238	Ondo	14,606	4,343,230[5]
Cross River	20,156	2,085,926	Osun	9,251	2,463,185
Delta	17,698	2,873,711	Oyo	28,454	3,900,803
Ebonyi	5,670	[2]	Plateau	30,913	3,671,498[6]
Edo	17,802	2,414,919	Rivers	11,077	4,454,337[4]
Ekiti	6,353	[5]	Sokoto	25,973	4,911,118[7]
Enugu	7,161	3,534,633[2]	Taraba	54,473	1,655,443
Gombe	18,768	[3]	Yobe	45,502	1,578,172
Imo	5,530	2,779,028	Zamfara	39,762	[7]
Jigawa	23,154	3,164,134			
Kaduna	46,053	4,438,007	**Federal Capital**		
Kano	20,131	6,297,165	**Territory**		
Katsina	24,192	4,336,363	Abuja	7,315	423,391
			TOTAL	923,768	98,967,768

Demography

Population (2005): 131,530,000.
Density (2005): persons per sq mi 368.8, persons per sq km 142.4.
Urban-rural (2003): urban 46.7%; rural 53.3%.
Sex distribution (2004): male 50.57%; female 49.43%.
Age breakdown (2004): under 15, 42.4%; 15–29, 28.0%; 30–44, 15.7%; 45–59,
9.0%; 60–74, 4.2%; 75 and over, 0.7%.
Population projection: (2010) 145,991,000; (2020) 175,798,000.
Doubling time: 29 years.
Ethnic composition (2000): Yoruba 17.5%; Hausa 17.2%; Igbo (Ibo) 13.3%;
Fulani 10.7%; Ibibio 4.1%; Kanuri 3.6%; Egba 2.9%; Tiv 2.6%; Bura 1.1%;
Nupe 1.0%; Edo 1.0%; other 25.0%.
Religious affiliation (2000): Christian 45.9%, of which independent Christian
15.0%, Anglican 13.0%, other Protestant 9.0%, Roman Catholic 8.0%;
Muslim 43.9%; traditional beliefs 9.8%; other 0.4%.
Major cities (2002): Lagos 8,030,000; Kano 3,250,000; Ibadan 3,080,000; Kaduna
1,460,000; Benin City 1,050,000; Port Harcourt 1,050,000; Maiduguri 971,700;
Zaria 898,900; Aba 784,500; Ilorin 756,400; Jos 742,100.

Vital statistics

Birth rate per 1,000 population (2004): 40.9 (world avg. 21.1).
Death rate per 1,000 population (2004): 17.4 (world avg. 9.0).
Natural increase rate per 1,000 population (2004): 23.5 (world avg. 12.1).
Total fertility rate (avg. births per childbearing woman; 2004): 5.6.
Life expectancy at birth (2004): male 46.0 years; female 47.0 years.
Adult population (ages 15–49) *living with HIV* (2004[8]): 5.4% (world avg. 1.1%).

National economy

Budget (2003). Revenue: ₦2,752,107,000,000 (nontax revenue 62.6%, of which
crude oil export proceeds 35.1%, crude oil sales to domestic refineries 14.0%;
tax revenue 37.4%, of which oil profits tax 15.9%, tax on international trade
8.5%). Expenditures: ₦2,853,918,000,000 (state and local governments
40.5%, current expenditure 32.0%, Nigerian National Petroleum Corporation
[NNPC] 15.8%, capital expenditure 8.8%).
Production (metric tons except as noted). Agriculture, forestry, fishing (2004):
cassava 38,179,000, yams 26,587,000, sorghum 8,028,000, millet 6,282,000, corn
(maize) 4,779,000, taro 4,027,000, rice 3,542,000, peanuts (groundnuts)
2,937,000, sweet potatoes 2,516,000, cowpeas 2,317,000, plantains 2,103,000,
cocoa beans 366,000, sesame seeds 76,000; livestock 28,000,000 goats,
23,000,000 sheep, 15,200,000 cattle, 6,610,500 pigs; roundwood 70,270,440 cu
m; fish catch (2002) 481,056. Mining and quarrying (2003): limestone
2,200,000; marble 70,000. Manufacturing (value added in ₦'000,000; 1995):
food and beverages 25,415; textiles 16,193; chemical products 11,181; machinery and transport equipment 5,639; paper products 2,828. Energy production (consumption): electricity (kW-hr; 2002) 18,125,000,000 (18,125,-
000,000); coal (metric tons; 2002) 62,000 (62,000); crude petroleum (barrels;
2004) 904,000,000 ([2002] 79,000,000); petroleum products (metric tons; 2002)
4,596,000 (11,753,000); natural gas (cu m; 2002) 14,347,000,000 (6,426,-
000,000).
Household income and expenditure. Avg. household size (2002) 4.9; annual
income per household (1992–93) ₦15,000 (U.S.$760); sources of income: n.a.;
expenditures: n.a.

Gross national product (2004): U.S.$53,983,000,000 (U.S.$390 per capita).

Structure of gross domestic product and labour force

	2003 in value ₦'000,000	2003 % of total value	1986 labour force	1986 % of labour force
Agriculture	1,940,587	25.7	13,259,000	43.1
Mining	3,297,206[9]	43.7[9]	6,800	0.1
Manufacturing	293,083	3.9	1,263,700	4.1
Construction	44,753	0.6	545,600	1.8
Public utilities	5,153	0.1	130,400	0.4
Transp. and commun.	243,015	3.2	1,111,900	3.6
Trade, hotels	1,050,928	13.9	7,417,400	24.1
Finance	346,696	4.6	120,100	0.4
Pub. admin., defense	50,812	0.7 }	4,902,100	15.9
Services	87,907	1.2 }		
Other	185,123[10]	2.4[10]	2,008,500[11]	6.5[11]
TOTAL	7,545,263	100.0	30,765,500	100.0

Public debt (external, outstanding; 2003): U.S.$31,563,000,000.
Population economically active (1993–94): total 29,000,000; activity rate 31.0%
(participation rates: ages 15–59, 64.4%; female 44.0%; officially unemployed
[March 2003] 10.8%).

Price index (2000 = 100)

	1998	1999	2000	2001	2002	2003	2004
Consumer price index	83.3	87.3	100.0	113.0	127.5	145.4	167.2

Tourism (2002): receipts U.S.$263,000,000; expenditures U.S.$950,000,000.
Land use as % of total land area (2000): in temporary crops 31.0%, in permanent crops 2.9%, in pasture 43.0%; overall forest area 14.8%.

Foreign trade[12]

Balance of trade (current prices)

	1999	2000	2001	2002	2003	2004
U.S.$'000,000	+5,268	+12,254	+5,675	+7,560	+9,034	+16,984
% of total	23.5%	41.3%	19.7%	33.4%	29.4%	37.5%

Imports (2003): U.S.$10,853,000,000 ([2000] machinery and apparatus 21.1%;
chemicals and chemical products 20.1%; food 18.9%, of which cereals 7.1%;
road vehicles 10.4%; iron and steel 6.2%). *Major import sources* (2003):
China 13.6%; U.K. 9.3%; France 8.0%; U.S. 7.8%; The Netherlands 6.5%;
Germany 5.9%; South Korea 5.8%.
Exports (2003): U.S.$19,887,000,000 (crude petroleum 99.7%, remainder
0.3%). *Major export destinations* (2003): U.S. 40.2%; Spain 8.3%; Brazil
5.3%; France 5.0%; Indonesia 4.6%; Japan 4.1%; India 4.0%.

Transport and communications

Transport. Railroads (2000): length 3,505 km; passenger-km 179,000,000[13];
metric ton-km cargo 120,000,000[13]. Roads (1999): total length 62,598 km
(paved 19%). Vehicles (1996): passenger cars 773,000; trucks and buses, n.a.
Air transport[14] (2002): passenger-km 892,720,000; metric ton-km cargo
10,783,000; airports (1998) 12.

Communications

Medium	date	unit	number	units per 1,000 persons
Daily newspapers	2000	circulation	2,770,000	24
Radio	2000	receivers	23,000,000	200
Television	2000	receivers	7,840,000	68
Telephones	2004	main lines	1,027,500	8.1
Cellular telephones	2004	subscribers	9,147,200	72
Personal computers	2004	units	867,000	6.8
Internet	2004	users	1,769,700	14

Education and health

Literacy (2002): total population age 15 and over literate 40,700,000 (64.1%);
males literate 22,600,000 (62.3%); females literate 18,100,000 (56.2%).

Education (2002)

	schools	teachers	students	student/ teacher ratio
Primary (age 6–12)	49,343	537,741	29,575,790	55.0
Secondary (age 12–17)	10,000	187,126	7,485,072	40.0
Higher	158	...	1,249,776	...

Health (2002): physicians 25,914 (1 per 4,722 persons); hospital beds 54,872 (1
per 2,230 persons); infant mortality rate per 1,000 live births (2004) 100.4.
Food (2002): daily per capita caloric intake 2,726 (vegetable products 97%,
animal products 3%); 116% of FAO recommended minimum requirement.

Military

Total active duty personnel (2004): 78,500 (army 79.0%, navy 8.9%, air force
12.1%). *Military expenditure as percentage of GDP* (2003): 1.2%; per capita
expenditure U.S.$5.

---

[1]In October 1996 six new states were created: Bayelsa, Ebonyi, Ekiti, Gombe,
Nassarawa, and Zamfara. [2]Ebonyi is included partly in Abia and partly in Enugu.
[3]Bauchi includes Gombe. [4]Rivers includes Bayelsa. [5]Ondo includes Ekiti. [6]Plateau
includes Nassarawa. [7]Sokoto includes Zamfara. [8]January 1. [9]Includes ₦3,291,115
(43.6%) from petroleum and natural gas. [10]Indirect taxes less subsidies. [11]Includes
1,263,000 unemployed. [12]Imports c.i.f.; exports f.o.b. [13]1997. [14]Nigeria Airways only.

Internet resources for further information:
• **Information on corporate Nigeria http://www.nigeriabusinessinfo.com**
• **Central Bank of Nigeria http://www.cenbank.org**

Northern Mariana Islands

Pacific Ocean

Official name: Commonwealth of the Northern Mariana Islands.
Political status: self-governing commonwealth in association with the United States, having two legislative houses (Senate [9]; House of Representatives [18])[1].
Chief of state: President of the United States.
Head of government: Governor.
Seat of government: on Saipan[2].
Official languages: Chamorro, Carolinian, and English.
Official religion: none.
Monetary unit: 1 dollar (U.S.$) = 100 cents; valuation (Sept. 1, 2005) 1 U.S.$ = £0.54.

Area and population

Municipal councils	Major villages	area sq mi	area sq km	population 2000 census
Northern Islands[3]	...	55.3	143.2	6
Rota (island)	Songsong	32.8	85.0	3,283
Saipan (island)	San Antonio	46.5	120.4	62,392
Tinian[4]	San Jose	41.9	108.5	3,540
TOTAL		176.5[5]	457.1[5]	69,221

Demography

Population (2005): 80,400.
Density (2005): persons per sq mi 456.8, persons per sq km 175.9.
Urban-rural (2002)[6]: urban 90.0%; rural 10.0%.
Sex distribution (2000): male 46.21%; female 53.79%.
Age breakdown (2000): under 15, 22.5%; 15–29, 31.8%; 30–44, 32.3%; 45–59, 10.7%; 60–74, 2.3%; 75 and over, 0.4%.
Population projection: (2010) 91,000; (2020) 109,000.
Doubling time: 40 years.
Ethnic composition (2000)[7]: Filipino 26.2%; Chinese 22.1%; Chamorro 21.3%; Carolinian 3.8%; other Asian 7.5%; other Pacific Islander 6.6%; white 1.8%; multiethnic and other 10.7%.
Religious affiliation (2000): Christian 88.9%, of which Roman Catholic 72.7%, independent Christian 7.0%, Protestant 6.8%; Buddhist 5.3%; other 5.8%.
Major villages (2000)[6, 8]: San Antonio 4,741; Garapan 3,588; Susupe 2,083; Capital Hill 1,498; Songsong (on Rota) 1,411; San Jose (on Tinian) 1,361.

Vital statistics

Birth rate per 1,000 population (2004): 19.8 (world avg. 21.1).
Death rate per 1,000 population (2004): 2.3 (world avg. 9.0).
Natural increase rate per 1,000 population (2004): 17.5 (world avg. 12.1).
Total fertility rate (avg. births per childbearing woman; 2004): 1.3.
Life expectancy at birth (2004): male 73.1 years; female 78.4 years.
Major causes of death per 100,000 population (1998): heart diseases 51; malignant neoplasms (cancers) 40; cerebrovascular disease 22; perinatal conditions 20; accidents 18.

National economy

Budget (2002). Revenue: U.S.$199,713,000 (tax revenue 83.5%, of which income tax 28.5%, corporate tax 24.3%, excise tax 9.4%; nontax revenue 16.5%). Expenditures: U.S.$212,089,000 (2001; health 20.4%, education 20.1%, general government 15.0%, social services 12.0%, public safety 9.3%).
Public debt (external, outstanding): n.a.
Gross domestic product (2004): U.S.$557,000,000 (U.S.$8,040 per capita).

Structure of labour force

	2000 labour force	2000 % of labour force
Agriculture, forestry, and fishing	623	1.4
Mining and quarrying	—	—
Manufacturing	17,398	39.1
Construction	2,785	6.2
Public utilities	} 1,449	3.3
Transp. and commun.		
Trade, restaurants	9,570	21.5
Finance, insurance, and real estate	1,013	2.3
Pub. admin., defense	2,583	5.8
Services	7,332	16.5
Other	1,718	3.9
TOTAL	44,471	100.0

Production (metric tons except as noted). Agriculture, forestry, fishing (2002): bananas 98, cucumbers 97, sweet potatoes 78, cabbages 76, taro 73, eggplant 45, yams 45; livestock (number of live animals) 2,242 pigs, 1,319 cattle, 14,190 chickens; roundwood, n.a.; fish catch (2003) 163. Mining and quarrying: negligible amount of quarrying for building material. Manufacturing (value of sales in U.S.$'000,000; 2002): garments 639; bricks, tiles, and cement 12; printing and related activities 5; food products 3. Energy production (consumption): electricity, n.a. (n.a.); coal, none (none); crude petroleum, none (none); petroleum products, n.a. (n.a.); natural gas, none (none).
Tourism (2002): receipts from visitors U.S.$225,000,000; expenditures by nationals abroad, n.a.

Population economically active (2000): total 44,471; activity rate of total population 64.2% (participation rates: ages 16 and over, 84.1%; female 54.2%; unemployed [July 2003] 4.6%).

Price index (2000 = 100)

	1998	1999	2000	2001	2002	2003
Consumer price index	96.9	98.0	100.0	99.2	99.3	98.3

Household income and expenditure. Average household size (2000) 3.7; average income per household (2000) U.S.$37,015; sources of income (1994): wages 83.9%, interest and rental 7.2%, self-employment 7.2%, transfer payments 1.7%.
Land use as % of total land area (2000): in temporary crops *c.* 13%, in permanent crops *c.* 4%, in pasture *c.* 11%; overall forest area *c.* 30%.

Foreign trade

Balance of trade (current prices)

	2002	2003	2004
U.S.$'000,000	...	...	...
% of total			

Imports (1997): U.S.$836,200,000 (clothing and accessories 37.0%, foodstuffs 9.6%, petroleum and petroleum products 8.2%, transport equipment and parts 5.0%, construction materials 4.2%). *Major import sources:* Guam 35.6%, Hong Kong 24.0%, Japan 14.1%, South Korea 9.6%, United States 7.6%.
Exports (2004): U.S.$811,000,000[9] (garments and accessories 99.5%; remainder 0.5%). *Major export destinations:* nearly all to the United States.

Transport and communications

Transport. Railroads: none. Roads (2003): total length *c.* 225 mi, *c.* 360 km (paved, nearly 100%). Vehicles (2002): passenger cars 11,983; trucks and buses 4,858. Air transport (1999)[10]: aircraft landings 23,853; boarding passengers 562,364; airports (2002) with scheduled flights 2[11].

Communications

Medium	date	unit	number	units per 1,000 persons
Radio	2000	receivers	10,684	153
Television	1999	receivers	4,100	59
Telephones	2001	main lines	25,306	352
Cellular telephones	2000	subscribers	3,000	57
Personal computers	...	units	...	...
Internet	...	users	...	...

Education and health

Educational attainment (2000). Percentage of population age 25 and over having: primary education 14.1%; some secondary 17.5%; completed secondary 35.8%; some postsecondary 12.0%; completed undergraduate or higher 20.6%. *Literacy* (2000): *c.* 100%.

Education (2001–02)

	schools	teachers	students	student/teacher ratio
Primary (age 6–11) }	37	728	13,323	18.3
Secondary (age 12–17) }				
Higher[12]	1	504	2,383	4.7

Health (2004): physicians 40[13] (1 per 1,956 persons); hospital beds 86[13] (1 per 885 persons); infant mortality rate per 1,000 live births 7.3.
Food: n.a.

Military

The United States is responsible for military defense; headquarters of the U.S. Pacific Command are in Hawaii.

[1]Residents elect a nonvoting representative to U.S. Congress. [2]Executive and legislative branches meet at Capital Hill; the judiciary meets at Susupe. [3]Comprises the islands of Agrihan, Pagan, and Alamagan, as well as seven other uninhabited islands. [4]Comprises Tinian island and Aguijan island. [5]Area measured at high tide; at low tide, total dry land area is 184.0 square mi (476.6 square km). [6]All of Saipan was designated an urban area in 2002. [7]Includes aliens. [8]All villages are unincorporated census designated places. [9]To U.S. only. [10]Saipan International Airport only. [11]International flights are regularly scheduled at Saipan and at Rota; Tinian has nonscheduled domestic service. Additional domestic airports mainly handle charter flights. [12]Northern Marianas College; 2000–01. [13]Saipan Commonwealth Health Center only.

Internet resources for further information:
• **Bank of Hawaii: Economics Research Center**
  http://www.boh.com/econ/512_803.asp#2
• **CNMI: Economic Policy, Planning, and Statistics Office**
  http://www.spc.int/prism/country/mh/stats/Index.htm

Norway

Official name: Kongeriket Norge (Kingdom of Norway).
Form of government: constitutional monarchy with one legislative house (Parliament [169]).
Chief of state: King.
Head of government: Prime Minister.
Capital: Oslo.
Official language: Norwegian.
Official religion: Evangelical Lutheran.
Monetary unit: 1 Norwegian krone (NKr) = 100 øre; valuation (Sept. 1, 2005) 1 U.S.$ = NKr 6.21; 1 £ = NKr 11.44.

Area and population

Mainland counties	area[1] sq km	population 2004[2] estimate	Mainland counties	area[1] sq km	population 2004[2] estimate
Akershus	4,918	488,618	Sør–Trøndelag	18,848	270,266
Aust-Agder	9,157	103,374	Telemark	15,299	166,124
Buskerud	14,910	242,331	Troms	25,877	152,628
Finnmark	48,618	73,210	Vest-Agder	7,276	160,127
Hedmark	27,397	188,326	Vestfold	2,224	219,480
Hordaland	15,460	445,059	SUBTOTAL	323,802[3]	4,577,457
Møre og Romsdal	15,121	244,570			
Nord-Trøndelag	22,412	127,973	**Overseas Arctic**		
Nordland	38,456	237,057	**territories**		
Oppland	25,192	183,690	Jan Mayen	377[4]	18
Oslo	454	521,886	Svalbard	61,020[3, 4]	2,706
Østfold	4,182	256,668	SUBTOTAL	61,397	2,724
Rogaland	9,378	388,848	TOTAL	385,199	4,580,181
Sogn og Fjordane	18,623	107,222			

Demography

Population (2005): 4,617,000.
Density (2005)[5]: persons per sq mi 36.4, persons per sq km 14.0.
Urban-rural (2003): urban 78.6%; rural 21.4%.
Sex distribution (2003[2]): male 49.56%; female 50.44%.
Age breakdown (2003[2]): under 15, 20.0%; 15–29, 18.7%; 30–44, 22.4%; 45–59, 19.7%; 60–74, 11.4%; 75 and over, 7.8%.
Population projection: (2010) 4,735,000; (2020) 4,989,000.
Ethnic composition (2000): Norwegian 93.8%; Vietnamese 2.4%; Swedish 0.5%; Punjabi 0.4%; Urdu 0.3%; U.S. white 0.3%; Lapp 0.3%; Danish 0.3%; other 1.7%.
Major cities (2003[2])[6]: Oslo 517,401 (urban agglomeration 795,000); Bergen 235,423; Trondheim 152,699; Stavanger 111,007; Bærum 102,529.

Vital statistics

Birth rate per 1,000 population (2003): 12.4 (world avg. 21.1); (2004) legitimate 48.6%; illegitimate 51.4%.
Death rate per 1,000 population (2003): 9.3 (world avg. 9.0).
Natural increase rate per 1,000 population (2003): 3.1 (world avg. 12.1).
Total fertility rate (avg. births per childbearing woman; 2004): 1.8.
Marriage rate per 1,000 population (2003): 4.9.
Divorce rate per 1,000 population (2003): 2.4.
Life expectancy at birth (2003): male 77.0 years; female 81.9 years.
Major causes of death per 100,000 population (2003): circulatory diseases 365.2; malignant neoplasms (cancers) 235.6; respiratory diseases 86.6; violence 54.1.

National economy

Budget (2002). Revenue: NKr 827,365,000,000 (tax on income 37.7%, social security taxes 18.2%, value-added taxes 16.2%). Expenditures: NKr 674,750,000,000 (social security and welfare 39.3%, health 16.6%, education 13.2%, general public service 11.2%).
Production (metric tons except as noted). Agriculture, forestry, fishing (2003): barley 584,000, oats 344,000, potatoes 341,000, wheat 334,000; livestock (number of live animals) 2,422,000 sheep, 955,000 cattle; roundwood (2002) 8,649,000 cu m; fish catch 2,544,692, of which herring 561,858, capelin 249,124, cod 217,462[7], pollock 212,209. Mining and quarrying (2003): ilmenite concentrate 800,000, iron ore (metal content) 350,000, cobalt 4,556. Manufacturing (value added in U.S.$'000,000; 2001): food products 2,353; ships and oil platforms 1,543; nonelectrical machinery 1,257; publishing 1,092; base non-ferrous metals 940; fabricated metal products 898; paper and paper products 788. Energy production (consumption): electricity (kW-hr; 2004) 110,400,-000,000 ([2002] 120,893,000,000); coal (metric tons; 2003) 2,950,000[8] (1,300,000); crude petroleum (barrels; 2004) 1,085,000,000 ([2002] 95,000,-000); petroleum products (metric tons; 2002) 16,467,000 (7,317,000); natural gas (cu m; 2004) 80,672,000,000 ([2002] 7,091,000,000).
Household income and expenditure. Average household size (2001) 2.3; annual income (excluding taxes) per household (2002) NKr 333,500 (U.S.$41,772); expenditure (2001–03): housing 20.1%, transportation 17.3%, recreation and culture 12.6%, food 10.3%, household furnishings 7.0%.
Population economically active (2003): total 2,373,000; activity rate of total population 52.0% (participation rates: ages 15–64, 79.3%; female 47.0%; unemployed [October 2003–September 2004] 4.3%).

Price and earnings indexes (2000 = 100)

	1998	1999	2000	2001	2002	2003	2004
Consumer price index	94.8	97.0	100.0	103.0	104.3	106.9	107.4
Monthly earnings index	91.3	96.1	100.0	104.5	110.0	115.2	…

Gross national product (2004): U.S.$238,398,000,000 (U.S.$52,030 per capita).

Structure of gross domestic product and labour force

	2003 in value NKr '000,000	2003 % of total value	2004 labour force	2004 % of labour force
Agriculture, fishing	19,549	1.2	79,000	3.3
Mining	3,127	0.2	3,000	0.1
Crude petroleum and natural gas	273,954	17.4	30,000	1.3
Manufacturing	141,711	9.0	264,000	11.1
Construction	65,315	4.2	160,000	6.7
Public utilities	40,027	2.5	16,000	0.7
Transp. and commun.	133,188	8.5	149,000	6.3
Trade, hotels	153,439	9.8	415,000	17.4
Finance	191,010	12.2	271,000	11.4
Pub. admin., defense	72,211	4.6	144,000	6.0
Services	336,145	21.4	742,000	31.2
Other	140,641[9]	9.0[9]	107,000[10]	4.5[10]
TOTAL	1,570,317	100.0	2,382,000[11]	100.0

Public debt (2003): U.S.$79,880,000,000.
Tourism (2003): receipts U.S.$2,541,000,000; expenditures U.S.$6,408,000,000.
Land use as % of total land area (2000): in temporary crops 2.9%, in permanent crops, n.a., in pasture 0.5%; overall forest area 28.9%.

Foreign trade[12]

Balance of trade (current prices)

	1999	2000	2001	2002	2003	2004
NKr '000,000	+88,495	+226,962	+235,907	+196,702	+199,649	+226,591
% of total	14.2%	27.3%	28.5%	26.2%	26.1%	26.0%

Imports (2003): NKr 283,247,300,000 (machinery and transport equipment 38.5%, of which road vehicles 9.6%, ships 2.1%; chemicals and chemical products 10.1%; metals and metal products 8.5%; food products 5.9%; petroleum products 2.8%). *Major import sources:* Sweden 16.1%; Germany 13.3%; Denmark 7.9%; U.K. 7.2%; U.S. 5.1%.
Exports (2003): NKr 482,896,300,000 (crude petroleum 42.7%; natural gas 12.9%; machinery and transport equipment 11.3%; metals and metal products 8.4%; fish 5.2%). *Major export destinations:* U.K. 21.3%; Germany 13.0%; The Netherlands 9.6%; France 8.2%; Sweden 7.4%.

Transport and communications

Transport. Railroads (2001): route length 4,178 km; passenger-km 2,536,000,-000; metric ton-km cargo 2,451,000,000. Roads (2004[2]): total length 91,910 km (paved [2002] 78%). Vehicles (2003): passenger cars 1,933,660; trucks and buses 441,056. Air transport (2004)[13]: passenger-km 13,229,000,000; metric ton-km cargo 177,522,000; airports (1996) 50.

Communications

Medium	date	unit	number	units per 1,000 persons
Daily newspapers	2000	circulation	2,620,000	585
Radio	2000	receivers	4,110,000	915
Television	2000	receivers	3,000,000	669
Telephones	2003	main lines	3,268,100	714
Cellular telephones	2003	subscribers	4,163,400	909
Personal computers	2004	units	2,630,000	578
Internet	2004	users	1,792,000	394

Education and health

Educational attainment (2000). Percentage of population age 16 and over having: primary and lower secondary education 21.5%; higher secondary 55.0%; higher 21.3%; unknown 2.2%. *Literacy* (2000): virtually 100% literate.

Education (2001–02)

	schools	teachers	students	student/ teacher ratio
Primary (age 7–12)	3,248	44,925	599,468	13.3
Secondary (age 13–18) and vocational[14]	696	20,567	220,328	10.7
Higher	71	11,090	197,614	17.8

Health: physicians (2003) 12,322 (1 per 370 persons); hospital beds (2003[2]) 22,662 (1 per 201 persons); infant mortality rate (2003) 3.4.
Food (2001): daily per capita caloric intake 3,382 (vegetable products 67%, animal products 33%); 126% of FAO recommended minimum requirement.

Military

Total active duty personnel (2004): 26,600 (army 55.3%, navy 22.9%, air force 18.8%, other 3.0%). *Military expenditure as percentage of GDP* (2003): 2.0%; per capita expenditure U.S.$961.

---

[1]Excludes areas of the uninhabited overseas Antarctic territories of Bouvet Island (58 sq km) and Peter I Island (249 sq km). [2]January 1. [3]Includes area of freshwater lakes. [4]Includes area of glaciers. [5]Population density calculated with reference to 328,657 sq km area free of mainland freshwater lakes (19,522 sq km), Svalbard freshwater lakes (395 sq km), Svalbard glaciers (36,500 sq km), and Jan Mayen glaciers (125 sq km). [6]Population of municipalities. [7]Norwegian catches on quotas bought from other countries are included. [8]Production is in Svalbard. [9]Includes taxes less imputed bank service charges and statistical discrepancy. [10]Includes 106,000 unemployed. [11]Detail does not add to total given because of rounding. [12]Imports c.i.f.; exports f.o.b. [13]SAS (Norwegian part), Braathens, Norwegian, and Widerøe only. [14]2000–01.

Internet resources for further information:
• **Statistics Norway** http://www.ssb.no/www-open/english

Oman

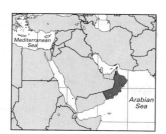

Official name: Salṭanat ʿUmān (Sultanate of Oman).
Form of government: monarchy with two advisory bodies (Council of State [57[1]]; Consultative Council [83]).
Head of state and government: Sultan.
Capital: Muscat.
Official language: Arabic.
Official religion: Islam.
Monetary unit: 1 rial Omani (RO) = 1,000 baizas; valuation (Sept. 1, 2005) 1 RO = U.S.$2.60 = £1.41.

Area and population		area[2]		population
Regions	**Capitals**	sq mi	sq km	2003 census[3]
Al-Bāṭinah	Ar-Rustāq; Ṣuḥār	4,850	12,500	653,505
Ad-Dākhilīyah	Nizwā; Samāʾil	12,300	31,900	267,140
Ash-Sharqīyah	Ibrā; Ṣūr	14,200	36,800	313,761
Al-Wusṭā	Haymāʾ	30,750	79,700	22,983
Az-Ẓāhirah	Al-Buraymī; ʿIbrī	17,000	44,000	207,015
Governorates				
Masqaṭ	Muscat (Masqaṭ)	1,350	3,500	632,073
Musandam	Khaṣab	700	1,800	28,378
Ẓufār (Dhofar)	Salālah	38,350	99,300	215,960
TOTAL		119,500	309,500	2,340,815

Demography

Population (2005): 2,409,000.
Density (2005): persons per sq mi 20.2, persons per sq km 7.8.
Urban-rural (2003): urban 77.6%; rural 22.4%.
Sex distribution (2003): male 56.10%; female 43.90%.
Age breakdown (2003): under 15, 33.8%; 15–29, 32.3%; 30–44, 20.8%; 45–59, 8.9%; 60–74, 3.2%; 75 and over 1.0%.
Population projection: (2010) 2,667,000; (2020) 3,269,000.
Doubling time: 33 years.
Ethnic composition (2000): Omani Arab 48.1%; Indo-Pakistani 31.7%, of which Balochi 15.0%, Bengali 4.4%, Tamil 2.5%; other Arab 7.2%; Persian 2.8%; Zanzibari (blacks originally from Zanzibar) 2.5%; other 7.7%.
Religious affiliation (2000): Muslim 87.4%, of which Ibāḍiyah Muslim c. 75% (principal minorities are Sunnī Muslim and Shīʿī Muslim); Hindu 5.7%; Christian 4.9%; Buddhist 0.8%; other 1.2%.
Major cities (2003): As-Sīb 223,267[4]; Salālah 156,587; Maṭraḥ 154,316[4]; Bawshar 149,506[4]; Ṣuḥār 104,057; Muscat 24,769 (urban agglomeration [2003] 638,000).

Vital statistics

Birth rate per 1,000 population (2004): 24.0 (world avg. 21.1).
Death rate per 1,000 population (2004): 2.6 (world avg. 9.0).
Natural increase rate per 1,000 population (2004): 21.4 (world avg. 12.1).
Total fertility rate (avg. births per childbearing woman; 2004): 3.2.
Life expectancy at birth (2004): male 73.2 years; female 75.4 years.
Major causes of death per 100,000 population: n.a.; however, the main causes of hospital deaths in 1995 were diseases of the circulatory system 34.1%, infectious diseases 11.1%, malignant neoplasms (cancers) 9.4%, perinatal problems 7.2%, diseases of the respiratory system 6.3%.

National economy

Budget (2004). Revenue: RO 2,925,000,000 (oil revenue 72.8%; other 27.2%). Expenditures: RO 3,425,000,000 (current expenditure 71.3%, of which civil ministries 36.7%, defense 28.4%, interest paid on loans 2.3%; capital expenditure 26.6%; other 2.1%).
Public debt (external, outstanding; 2003): U.S.$1,480,000,000.
Gross national product (2003): U.S.$19,877,000,000 (U.S.$7,830 per capita).

Structure of gross national product and labour force				
	2003			
	in value RO '000,000	% of total value	labour force[5]	% of labour force[5]
Agriculture, fishing	164.9	2.0	58,114	7.9
Oil and natural gas	3,470.2[6]	41.8[6]	} 20,115	2.7
Other mining	14.2	0.2		
Manufacturing	685.1[6]	8.2[6]	59,492	8.1
Construction	189.0	2.3	118,257	16.0
Public utilities	105.5	1.3	4,045	0.5
Transp. and commun.	582.1	7.0	27,674	3.8
Trade, restaurants, hotels	1,038.2	12.5	109,157	14.8
Finance, real estate	673.8	8.1	25,200	3.4
Pub. admin., defense	803.1	9.7	162,742	22.1
Services	750.8	9.0	137,420	18.7
Other	−174.5[7]	−2.1[7]	14,408	2.0
TOTAL	8,302.4	100.0	736,624	100.0

Tourism (2003): receipts U.S.$219,000,000; expenditures U.S.$577,000,000.
Household income and expenditure. Average household size (2002) 6.7; expenditure (1995): housing and utilities 27.9%, food, beverages, and tobacco 26.4%, transportation 19.8%, clothing and shoes 7.9%, household goods and furniture 6.2%, education, health services, entertainment, and other 11.8%.
Production (metric tons except as noted). Agriculture, forestry, fishing (2004): dates 238,000, tomatoes 43,000, bananas 33,000, watermelons 27,000, dry onions 18,000, potatoes 15,500, mangoes 11,000, papayas 2,515, tobacco leaves 1,270; livestock (number of live animals) 1,050,000 goats, 370,000 sheep, 330,000 cattle, 122,000 camels; roundwood, n.a.; fish catch (2002)

142,670. Mining and quarrying (2004): marble 140,000; gypsum 60,000; chromite (gross weight) 18,575. Manufacturing (value added in U.S.$'000,000; 2001): petroleum products 1,012; nonmetallic mineral products 124; food products 106; chemicals and chemical products 45; fabricated metals 40; furniture 36. Energy production (consumption): electricity (kW-hr; 2002) 14,160,000,000 (14,160,000,000); crude petroleum (barrels; 2003) 285,000,000 (22,000,000); petroleum products (metric tons; 2002) 4,354,000 (3,661,000); natural gas (cu m; 2002) 17,188,000,000 (8,013,000,000).
Population economically active (2003)[5]: total 736,624; activity rate of total population 31.5% (participation rates: over age 15, n.a.; female 15.4%; unemployed, n.a.).

Price index (2000 = 100)							
	1998	1999	2000	2001	2002	2003	2004
Consumer price index	100.7	101.2	100.0	98.9	98.3	97.9	98.2

Land use as % of total land area (2000): in temporary crops 0.1%, in permanent crops 0.1%, in pasture 3.2%; overall forest area, negligible.

Foreign trade[8]

Balance of trade (current prices)						
	1998	1999	2000	2001	2002	2003
RO '000,000	+118	+1,130	+2,586	+2,216	+2,129	+2,147
% of total	2.9%	25.5%	42.3%	35.2%	33.0%	31.4%

Imports (2003): RO 2,527,000,000 (machinery and apparatus 28.4%; manufactured goods 15.4%; motor vehicles and parts 13.4%; food and live animals 11.4%; chemicals and chemical products 7.5%). *Major import sources:* United Arab Emirates 21.6%; Japan 17.1%; United States 6.2%; United Kingdom 5.7%; Germany 4.4%; India 4.4%.
Exports (2003): RO 4,487,000,000 (domestic exports 86.6%, of which crude and refined petroleum 66.5%, natural gas 13.3%, live animals and animal products 1.4%, base and fabricated [mostly copper] metals 0.9%; reexports 13.4%, of which motor vehicles and parts 7.5%, beverages and tobacco products 1.8%). *Major export destinations*[9]: United Arab Emirates 32.7%; Iran 18.3%; Saudi Arabia 8.4%; United States 3.6%; Yemen 2.6%.

Transport and communications

Transport. Railroads: none. Roads (1999): total length 20,518 mi, 33,020 km (paved 24%). Vehicles (2002): passenger cars 390,000; trucks and buses 140,200. Air transport (2004)[10]: passenger-mi 933,000,000, passenger-km 1,501,000,000; short ton-mi cargo 5,882,000, metric ton-km cargo 9,273,000; airports (1999) with scheduled flights 6.

Communications				units per 1,000 persons
Medium	date	unit	number	
Daily newspapers	1996	circulation	63,000	28
Radio	2000	receivers	1,490,000	621
Television	2002	receivers	1,382,500	553
Telephones	2004	main lines	240,300	82
Cellular telephones	2004	subscribers	805,000	274
Personal computers	2004	units	118,000	40
Internet	2004	users	245,000	83

Education and health

Educational attainment (2003). Percentage of population age 10 and over having: no formal schooling (illiterate) 15.9%; no formal schooling (literate) 22.3%; primary 35.3%; secondary 17.0%; higher technical 3.3%; higher undergraduate 5.2%; higher graduate 0.7%; other 0.3%. *Literacy* (2003): percentage of total population age 15 and over literate 75.8%; males literate 83.0%; females literate 67.2%.

Education (2001–02)	schools	teachers	students	student/ teacher ratio
Primary (age 6–14)	2941[11]	8,417	236,904	28.1
Secondary (age 15–17)[12]	674[13]	13,096	266,923	20.4
Voc., teacher tr.	15	1,072	16,472	15.4
Higher[14]	1	918	11,834	12.9

Health (2002): physicians 3,536 (1 per 713 persons); hospital beds 5,168 (1 per 488 persons); infant mortality rate per 1,000 live births (2004) 10.3.

Military

Total active duty personnel (2004): 41,700 (army 60.0%, navy 10.1%, air force 9.8%, royal household/foreign troops 20.1%). *Military expenditure as percentage of GDP* (2003): 12.2%; per capita expenditure U.S.$1,127.

[1]All seats are nonelected. [2]Approximate; no comprehensive survey of surface area has ever been carried out in Oman. [3]Final figures. [4]Within Muscat urban agglomeration. [5]Employed only; includes 424,178 expatriate workers and 312,446 Omani workers. [6]Manufacturing includes petroleum products; Oil and natural gas excludes petroleum products. [7]Includes import taxes less bank service charges. [8]Imports are f.o.b. in balance of trade and c.i.f. for commodities and trading partners. [9]Excludes petroleum and natural gas; includes reexports. [10]Oman Air only. [11]2000–01. [12]Includes preparatory. [13]1998–99. [14]University only.

Internet resources for further information:
• **Ministry of National Economy**
  http://www.moneoman.gov.om/english.htm
• **Central Bank of Oman**
  http://www.cbo-oman.org/pub_annual.htm

Pakistan

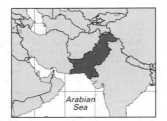

Official name: Islam-i Jamhuriya-e Pakistan (Islamic Republic of Pakistan).
Form of government: military-backed constitutional regime with two legislative houses (Senate [100]; National Assembly [342]).
Chiefs of state and government: President[1] assisted by Prime Minister.
Capital: Islamabad.
Official language: Urdu.
Official religion: Islam.
Monetary unit: 1 Pakistan rupee (PRs) = 100 paisa; valuation (Sept. 1, 2005) 1 U.S.$ = PRs 59.72; 1 £ = PRs 109.95.

Area and population		area[2]		population
Provinces	Capitals	sq mi	sq km	2003 estimate[3]
Balochistan	Quetta	134,051	347,190	7,450,000
North-West Frontier	Peshawar	28,773	74,521	20,170,000
Punjab	Lahore	79,284	205,345	82,710,000
Sindh	Karachi	54,407	140,914	34,240,000
Federally Administered Tribal Areas	...		10,509	27,220	3,420,000
Federal Capital Area				
Islamabad	...	350	906	1,040,000
TOTAL		307,374	796,096	149,030,000

Demography

Population (2005)[3]: 153,960,000.
Density (2005)[2, 3]: persons per sq mi 500.9, persons per sq km 193.4.
Urban-rural (2002)[3, 4]: urban 38.0%; rural 62.0%.
Sex distribution (2004)[3, 4]: male 52.04%; female 47.96%.
Age breakdown (2003): under 15, 42.2%; 15–29, 27.9%; 30–44, 15.2%; 45–59, 9.3%; 60–74, 4.3%; 75 and over, 1.1%.
Population projection[3]: (2010) 169,153,000; (2020) 204,184,000.
Doubling time: 30 years.
Ethnic composition (2000): Punjabi 52.6%; Pashtun 13.2%; Sindhi 11.7%; Urdu-speaking muhajirs 7.5%; Balochi 4.3%; other 10.7%.
Religious affiliation (2000): Muslim 96.1%[5]; Christian 2.5%; Hindu 1.2%; others (including Ahmadiyah) 0.2%.
Major cities (1998): Karachi 9,339,023; Lahore 5,143,495; Faisalabad 2,008,861; Rawalpindi 1,409,768; Multan 1,197,384; Hyderabad 1,166,894; Gujranwala 1,132,509; Peshawar 982,816; Quetta 565,137; Islamabad 529,180.

Vital statistics

Birth rate per 1,000 population (2003): 32.0 (world avg. 21.1).
Death rate per 1,000 population (2003): 8.9 (world avg. 9.0).
Natural increase rate per 1,000 population (2003): 23.1 (world avg. 12.1).
Total fertility rate (avg. births per childbearing woman; 2003): 4.4.
Life expectancy at birth (2003): male 61.3 years; female 63.1 years.
Major cause of death (percentage of total deaths; 1987): malaria 18.2%; childhood diseases 12.1%; diseases of digestive system 9.8%; diseases of respiratory system 9.2%; infection of intestinal tract 7.7%.

National economy

Budget (2001–02). Revenue: PRs 632,799,000,000 (sales tax 26.9%, nontax receipts 26.0%, income taxes 22.4%, customs duties 8.0%, excise taxes 7.4%). Expenditures: PRs 773,289,000,000 (public-debt service 41.4%, defense 19.6%, development 16.1%, general administration 6.6%).
Public debt (external, outstanding; 2004–05): U.S.$34,874,000,000.
Production (metric tons except as noted). Agriculture, forestry, fishing (2004): sugarcane 53,419,000, wheat 19,767,000, rice 7,486,500, seed cotton 7,350,000, corn (maize) 2,775,000, potatoes 1,854,700, onions 1,657,900, chickpeas 548,000; livestock (number of live animals) 54,700,000 goats, 25,500,000 buffalo, 24,700,000 sheep, 23,800,000 cattle, 800,000 camels, 160,000,000 chickens; roundwood 28,277,956 cu m; fish catch (2003) 564,743. Mining and quarrying (2003): limestone 12,000,000; rock salt 1,700,000; gypsum 397,000; silica sand 175,000; chromite 13,000. Manufacturing (2003–04): cement 12,957,000; urea 4,432,000; refined sugar 4,021,000; cotton yarn 1,935,000; vegetable ghee 957,000; jute textiles (2002–03) 93,800; cotton textiles 664,600,000 sq m; cigarettes 55,180,000,000 units; tires 1,900,000 units; bicycles 664,000 units. Energy production (consumption): electricity (kW-hr; 2003) 75,270,-000,000 (52,660,000,000); coal (metric tons; 2002) 3,180,000 (4,130,000); crude petroleum (barrels; 2004) 22,000,000 (133,000,000); petroleum products (metric tons; 2002) 7,900,000 (18,000,000); natural gas (cu m; 2002) 22,996,000,000 (22,996,000,000).
Land use as % of total land area (2000): in temporary crops 27.6%, in permanent crops 0.9%, in pasture 6.5%; overall forest area 3.1%.
Population economically active (2001–02): total 42,388,000; activity rate of total population 29.6% (participation rates: ages 15–64, 51.6%; female 16.1%; unemployed [2004] 8.3%).

Price index (2000 = 100)							
	1998	1999	2000	2001	2002	2003	2004
Consumer price index	92.0	95.8	100.0	103.1	106.5	109.6	117.8

Gross national product (2004): U.S.$90,663,000,000 (U.S.$600 per capita).

Structure of gross domestic product and labour force				
	2003–04		2001–02	
	in value PRs '000,000	% of total value	labour force	% of labour force
Agriculture	1,174,586	21.5	16,366,000	38.6
Mining	84,539	1.6	26,000	0.1
Manufacturing	869,896	15.9	5,380,000	12.7
Construction	129,996	2.4	2,353,000	5.6
Public utilities	166,356	3.1	313,000	0.7
Transp. and commun.	656,957	12.0	2,295,000	5.4
Trade	897,097	16.4	5,776,000	13.6
Finance	142,533	2.6	346,000	0.8
Pub. admin., defense	325,305	6.0	}	
Services	641,056	11.7	6,027,000	14.2
Other	369,742[6]	6.8[6]	3,506,000[7]	8.3[7]
TOTAL	5,458,063	100.0	42,388,000	100.0

Household income and expenditure (1998–99). Average household size (2003) 6.8; income per household PRs 81,444 (U.S.$441); sources of income: self-employment 40.9%, wages and salaries 32.3%, transfer payments 11.3%, other 15.5%; expenditure: food 49.1%, housing 20.9%, clothing 7.8%, education 3.6%, transportation and communications 3.3%, recreation 0.2%.
Tourism (2003): receipts U.S.$120,000,000; expenditures U.S.$924,000,000.

Foreign trade[8]

Balance of trade (current prices)						
	1999–2000	2000–01	2001–02	2002–03	2003–04	2004–05
U.S.$'000,000	−1,412	−1,269	−360	−359	−1,279	−4,515
% of total	7.9%	6.6%	1.9%	1.6%	4.9%	13.5%

Imports (2004–05): U.S.$20,598,000,000 (machinery and apparatus 22.5%; chemicals and chemical products 13.7%; crude petroleum 10.4%; refined petroleum 9.4%; food and oils 6.8%; road motor vehicles 5.2%). *Major import sources* (2004): China 10.7%; U.S. 9.8%; U.A.E. 9.4%; Saudi Arabia 9.2%; Japan 6.7%.
Exports (2004–05): U.S.$14,391,000,000 (textiles 58.8%, of which woven cotton fabric 12.9%, knitwear 11.3%, bedding 10.1%, ready-made garments 7.5%, cotton yarn 7.3%; rice 6.5%; leather products 3.7%; petroleum products 3.4%). *Major export destinations:* U.S. 20.7%; U.A.E. 10.8%; U.K. 6.9%; Germany 5.0%; Saudi Arabia 4.5%.

Transport and communications

Transport. Railroads (2002–03): route length 7,791 km; passenger-km (2004–05) 17,879,920,000; metric ton-km cargo (2002–03) 5,604,720,000. Roads (2004–05): total length 161,406 mi, 259,758 km (paved 63%). Vehicles (2003): passenger cars 1,377,165; trucks and buses 341,840. Air transport (2002–03): passenger-km 11,203,364; metric ton-km cargo 357,300,000; airports (1997) 35.

Communications				units per 1,000
Medium	date	unit	number	persons
Daily newspapers	2004	circulation	7,818,000	51
Radio	2000	receivers	14,700,000	121
Television	2003	receivers	22,447,500	150
Telephones	2004	main lines	4,880,000	32
Cellular telephones	2004	subscribers	5,020,000	33
Personal computers	2001	units	600,000	4.1
Internet	2004	users	2,000,000	13

Education and health

Educational attainment (1990). Percentage of population age 25 and over having: no formal schooling 73.8%; some primary education 9.7%; secondary 14.0%; postsecondary 2.5%. *Literacy* (2004–05): total population age 15 and over literate 53.0%; males literate 65.0%; females literate 40.0%.

Education (2000–01)				student/
	schools	teachers	students	teacher ratio
Primary (age 5–9)	165,700	373,900	20,999,000	56.2
Secondary (age 10–14)	31,600	320,100	6,576,000	20.5
Voc., teacher tr.	580	7,062	75,000	10.6
Higher	1,187	41,673	1,067,999	25.6

Health (2004): physicians 113,206 (1 per 1,347 persons); hospital beds 99,908 (1 per 1,527 persons); infant mortality rate per 1,000 live births (2003) 76.6.
Food (2002): daily per capita caloric intake 2,419 (vegetable products 82%, animal products 18%); 105% of FAO recommended minimum.

Military

Total active duty personnel (2004): 619,000[9] (army 88.8%, navy 3.9%, air force 7.3%). *Military expenditure as percentage of GDP* (2003): 4.4%; per capita expenditure U.S.$24.

[1]Military leader (from October 1999) who was sworn in as president in June 2001. [2]Excludes 32,494-sq-mi (84,159-sq-km) area of Pakistani-administered Jammu and Kashmir (comprising both Azad Kashmir [AK] and the Northern Areas [NA]). [3]Excludes Afghan refugees (2005; 950,000) and the populations of AK (2005; 3,250,000) and NA (2005; 1,100,000). [4]Excludes Federally Administered Tribal Areas. [5]Mostly Sunnī, with Shīʿī comprising about 17% of total population. [6]Taxes less subsidies. [7]Unemployed. [8]Import figures are f.o.b. in balance of trade and c.i.f. for commodities and trading partners. [9]Excludes c. 290,000 in paramilitary (mostly national guard and frontier corps).

Internet resources for further information:
• **Economic Survey, Ministry of Finance**
  http://www.finance.gov.pk/survey/home.htm
• **Statistics Division: Government of Pakistan** http://www.statpak.gov.pk

Palau

Official name: Belu'u er a Belau (Palauan); Republic of Palau (English).
Form of government: nonparty republic with two legislative houses (Senate [9]; House of Delegates [16]).
Head of state and government: President.
Capital: Koror (acting)[1].
Official languages[2]: Palauan; English.
Official religion: none.
Monetary unit: 1 U.S. dollar (U.S.$) = 100 cents; valuation (Sept. 1, 2005) 1 U.S.$ = £0.54.

Pacific Ocean

Area and population

States	area sq mi	area sq km	population 2000 census
Aimeliik	20	52	272
Airai	17	44	2,104
Angaur	3	8	188
Hatobohel	1	3	23
Kayangel	1	3	138
Koror	7	18	13,303
Melekeok	11	28	239
Ngaraard	14	36	638
Ngarchelong	4	10	267
Ngardmau	18	47	286
Ngatpang	18	47	367
Ngchesar	16	41	280
Ngeremlengui	25	65	221
Ngiwal	10	26	193
Peleliu	5	13	571
Sonsorol	1	3	39
Other			
Rock Islands	18	47	—
TOTAL	188[3]	488[3]	19,129

Demography

Population (2005): 21,100.
Density (2005): persons per sq mi 112.2, persons per sq km 43.2.
Urban-rural (2003): urban 68.6%; rural 31.4%.
Sex distribution (2000): male 54.63%; female 45.37%.
Age breakdown (2000): under 15, 23.9%; 15–29, 24.2%; 30–44, 29.9%; 45–59, 14.2%; 60–74, 5.5%; 75 and over, 2.3%.
Population projection: (2010) 23,000; (2020) 29,000.
Doubling time: 58 years.
Ethnic composition (2000): Palauan 69.9%; Asian 25.5%; other Micronesian 2.5%; other 2.1%.
Religious affiliation (2000): Roman Catholic 41.6%; Protestant 23.3%; Modekngei (marginal Christian sect) 8.8%; other Christian 6.8%; other 19.5%.
Major city (2000): Koror 13,303.

Vital statistics

Birth rate per 1,000 population (2004): 18.7 (world avg. 21.1).
Death rate per 1,000 population (2004): 6.9 (world avg. 9.0).
Natural increase rate per 1,000 population (2004): 11.8 (world avg. 12.1).
Total fertility rate (avg. births per childbearing woman; 2004): 2.5.
Life expectancy at birth (2004): male 66.7 years; female 73.2 years.
Major causes of death per 100,000 population (1999): diseases of the circulatory system 227.4; malignant and benign neoplasms (cancers) 119.1; accidents, poisoning, and violence 92.1; endocrine, nutritional, metabolic, and immunity disorders 59.6; diseases of the respiratory system 43.3; diseases of the digestive system 21.7; diseases of the genitourinary system 21.7; infectious and parasitic diseases 16.2.

National economy

Budget (2002). Revenue: U.S.$70,058,000 (grants from the U.S. 49.4%; tax revenue 36.0%; nontax revenue 14.6%). Expenditures: U.S.$79,691,000 (current expenditure 74.6%, of which wages and salaries 38.1%; capital expenditure 25.4%).
Public debt (external, outstanding; 2000): U.S.$20,000,000.
Production (metric tons except as noted). Agriculture, forestry, fishing (value of sales in U.S.$; 2001): eggs (2003) 638,750, fruit and vegetables (including cabbages, cucumbers, eggplants, bean sprouts, bananas, watermelons, and papayas) 337,354, root crops (taro, cassava, sweet potatoes) 26,906; livestock (number of live animals; 2001) 702 pigs, 21,189 poultry; roundwood, n.a.; fish catch (2001; pounds) 593,473, of which sturgeon and unicorn fish 101,613, parrot fish 57,516, rabbit fish 25,613, groupers 23,835, emperor fish 20,586, crabs 17,347, wrasses 14,315, tuna and mackerel 13,366. Mining and quarrying: n.a. Manufacturing: includes handicrafts and small items. Energy production (consumption): electricity (kW-hr; 2002) 166,000,000 (166,000,000); coal, none (none); crude petroleum, none (none); petroleum products (metric tons; 2002) none (76,000); natural gas, none (none).
Tourism (2002): receipts from visitors U.S.$59,000,000.
Land use as % of total land area (2000): in temporary crops c. 9%, in permanent crops c. 4%, in pasture c. 7%; overall forest area c. 76%.
Population economically active (2000): total 9,607; activity rate of total population 50.2% (participation rates: over age 15, 67.5%; female 38.1%; unemployed 2.3%).

Price index (June 2000 = 100)

	2000	2001	2002	2003	2004
Consumer price index[4]	100.0	102.0	100.5	100.1	104.8

Gross national product (at current market prices; 2004): U.S.$137,000,000 (U.S.$6,870 per capita).

Structure of gross domestic product and labour force

	2002 in value U.S.$'000	2002 % of total value	2000 labour force	2000 % of labour force
Agriculture, fisheries	1,300	1.2	} 668	7.0
Mining	1,800	1.6		
Manufacturing	800	0.7	65	0.7
Public utilities	3,300	3.0	5	5
Construction	13,100	12.0	1,232	12.8
Transportation and communications	5,500	5.0	499[5]	5.2[5]
Trade	33,200	30.3	2,873	29.9
Finance, real estate	6,900	6.3	354	3.7
Public administration, defense	31,900	29.1	1,166	12.1
Services	7,500	6.8	2,526	26.3
Other	4,205[6]	3.8[6]	224[7]	2.3[7]
TOTAL	109,505	100.0[3]	9,607	100.0

Household income and expenditure. Average household size (2000) 5.7; annual average income per household (2000) U.S.$19,975; sources of income (1989): wages 63.7%, social security 12.0%, self-employment 7.4%, retirement 5.5%, interest, dividend, or net rental 4.3%, remittance 4.1%, public assistance 1.0%, other 2.0%; expenditure (1997): food 42.2%, beverages and tobacco 14.8%, entertainment 13.1%, transportation 6.4%, clothing 5.7%, household goods 2.7%, other 15.1%.

Foreign trade

Balance of trade (current prices)

	1998	1999	2000	2001	2002	2003
U.S.$'000	−54,800	−92,400	−111,500	−86,700	−77,200	−76,400
% of total	71.2%	79.8%	82.0%	82.8%	81.1%	65.3%

Imports (2001): U.S.$95,700,000 (machinery and transport equipment 24.2%; food and live animals 15.2%; mineral fuels and lubricants 10.4%; beverages and tobacco products 8.3%; chemicals and chemical products 7.4%). *Major import sources* (2003): South Korea 56.4%; Japan 18.7%; Germany 11.3%; Indonesia 3.6%; Australia 3.0%.
Exports (2001): U.S.$9,000,000 (mostly high-grade tuna and garments). *Major export destinations* (2003): Japan 86.7%; Vietnam 5.9%; Zambia 4.6%.

Transport and communications

Transport. Railroads: none. Roads (2004): total length 38 mi, 61 km (paved 59%). Vehicles (2001): passenger cars and trucks 4,452. Air transport (2001): passenger arrivals 64,143, passenger departures 61,472; airports (1997) with scheduled flights 1.

Communications

Medium	date	unit	number	units per 1,000 persons
Radio	1997	receivers	12,000	663.0
Television	1997	receivers	11,000	606.0
Telephones	1994	main lines	2,615	160.0

Education and health

Educational attainment (2000). Percentage of population age 25 and over having: no formal schooling 3.1%; completed primary 11.5%; some secondary 7.9%; completed secondary 48.9%; some postsecondary 18.6%; higher 10.0%. *Literacy* (1997): total population age 15 and over literate 99.9%.

Education (2001–02)

	schools	teachers	students	student/ teacher ratio
Primary (age 6–13)	23	235	3,033	12.9
Secondary (age 14–18)	6	132	1,168	8.8
Higher[8]	1	25	598	23.9

Health: physicians (1998) 20 (1 per 906 persons); hospital beds (1990) 70 (1 per 200 persons); infant mortality rate per 1,000 live births (2004) 16.2.
Food: daily per capita caloric intake, n.a.

Military

The United States is responsible for the external security of Palau, as specified in the Compact of Free Association of Oct. 1, 1994.

[1]New capital buildings at Melekeok on Babelthuap are scheduled to be completed in 2006. [2]Sonsorolese-Tobian is also, according to official sources, considered an official language. [3]Detail does not add to total given because of rounding. [4]As of June. [5]Transportation and communications includes Public utilities. [6]Includes import duties less imputed bank service charges. [7]Unemployed. [8]Palau Community College.

Internet resources for further information:
• **Department of the Interior: Office of Insular Affairs**
  http://www.pacificweb.org
• **Palau Office of Planning and Statistics**
  http://www.palaugov.net/stats

Panama

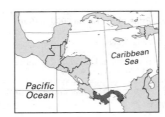

Official name: República de Panamá (Republic of Panama).
Form of government: multiparty republic with one legislative house (Legislative Assembly [78]).
Head of state and government: President assisted by Vice Presidents.
Capital: Panama City.
Official language: Spanish.
Official religion: none.
Monetary unit: 1 balboa (B) = 100 cents; valuation (Sept. 1, 2005)
1 U.S.$ = B 1.00; 1 £ = B 1.84.

Area and population

Provinces	Capitals	area sq mi	area sq km	population 2004 estimate
Bocas del Toro	Bocas del Toro	1,793	4,644	103,072
Chiriquí	David	2,528	6,547	400,321
Coclé	Penonomé	1,911	4,950	221,514
Colón	Colón	1,880	4,868	227,592
Darién	La Palma	4,593	11,897	43,828
Herrera	Chitré	902	2,336	109,371
Los Santos	Las Tablas	1,469	3,805	88,606
Panamá	Panama City	4,506	11,671	1,580,940
Veraguas	Santiago	4,104	10,630	222,382
Indigenous districts[1]				
Emberá	Unión Chocó	1,693	4,384	9,269
Kuna Yala (San Blas)	El Porvenir	904	2,341	36,487
Ngöbe Buglé	Quebrada Guabo	2,690	6,968	128,978
TOTAL		28,973	75,040[2]	3,172,360

Demography

Population (2005): 3,140,000[3].
Density (2005): persons per sq mi 108.4, persons per sq km 41.8.
Urban-rural (2003): urban 57.1%; rural 42.9%.
Sex distribution (2002): male 50.48%; female 49.52%.
Age breakdown (2002): under 15, 31.3%; 15–29, 26.9%; 30–44, 21.4%; 45–59, 12.2%; 60–74, 6.1%; 75 and over, 2.1%.
Population projection: (2010) 3,393,000; (2020) 3,877,000.
Doubling time: 42 years.
Ethnic composition (2000): mestizo 58.1%; black and mulatto 14.0%; white 8.6%; Amerindian 6.7%; Asian 5.5%; other 7.1%.
Religious affiliation (2000): Christian 88.2%, of which Roman Catholic 70.6%, Protestant 10.9%; Muslim 4.4%; Bahā'ī 1.2%; nonreligious 2.5%; other 3.7%.
Major cities (2000): Panama City 415,964 (urban agglomeration [2001] 1,202,000); San Miguelito 293,745[4]; David 77,734[5]; Arraiján 63,753[5]; La Chorrera 55,871.

Vital statistics

Birth rate per 1,000 population (2004): 21.9 (world avg. 21.1); (2003) legitimate 19.7%; illegitimate 80.3%.
Death rate per 1,000 population (2004): 5.2 (world avg. 9.0).
Natural increase rate per 1,000 population (2004): 16.7 (world avg. 12.1).
Total fertility rate (avg. births per childbearing woman; 2004): 2.7.
Marriage rate per 1,000 population (2004): 3.2.
Divorce rate per 1,000 population (2004): 0.8.
Life expectancy at birth (2004): male 72.7 years; female 78.0 years.
Major causes of death per 100,000 population (2002): diseases of the circulatory system 108.8; malignant neoplasms (cancers) 64.5; accidents and violence 39.3; diseases of the respiratory system 34.9.

National economy

Budget (2002). Revenue: B 2,067,000,000 (tax revenue 50.8%, of which income taxes 21.9%, taxes on domestic transactions 17.4%, taxes on foreign trade 8.9%; other current revenue 44.8%, of which revenue from Panama Canal 7.4%; development revenue 4.4%). Expenditures: B 2,305,000,000 (current expenditure 85.6%; development expenditure 14.4%).
Public debt (external, outstanding; 2003): U.S.$6,563,000,000.
Production (metric tons except as noted). Agriculture, forestry, fishing (2004): sugarcane 1,650,000, bananas 525,000, rice 296,000, plantains 129,000, corn (maize) 80,000, watermelons 40,000, cantaloupes and other melons 39,500, coffee 8,700, tobacco 2,300; livestock (number of live animals) 1,550,000 cattle, 315,000 pigs, 178,000 horses; roundwood 1,372,137 cu m; fish catch (2002) 305,081. Mining and quarrying (2003): limestone 270,000; marine salt 23,000. Manufacturing (value added in U.S.$'000,000; 2001): food and food products 428; beverages 82; cement, bricks, and ceramics 59; printing and publishing 55; paper and paper products 37. Energy production (consumption): electricity (kW-hr; 2002) 5,076,000,000 (5,062,000,000); coal (metric tons; 2002) none (60,000); crude petroleum (barrels; 2002) none (9,400,000); petroleum products (metric tons; 2002) 814,000 (1,352,000); natural gas (cu m; 2002) none (62,800,000).
Tourism (2003): receipts from visitors U.S.$585,000,000; expenditures by nationals abroad U.S.$208,000,000.
Population economically active (2003)[6]: total 1,250,874; activity rate of total population 40.1%[7] (participation rates: ages 15–64, 67.1%, female 37.1%, unemployed 12.8%).

Price index (2000 = 100)

	1998	1999	2000	2001	2002	2003	2004
Consumer price index	97.3	98.5	100.0	100.3	101.3	102.7	103.0

Gross national product (2004): U.S.$13,468,000,000 (U.S.$4,450 per capita).

Structure of gross domestic product and labour force

	2003 in value B '000,000[8]	% of total value[8]	labour force	% of labour force
Agriculture, fishing	918	7.5	188,864	15.1
Mining	112	0.9	1,024	0.1
Manufacturing	983	8.1	96,603	7.7
Construction	517	4.2	79,636	6.4
Public utilities	388	3.2	8,796	0.7
Transp. and commun.	2,048	16.8	85,811	6.9
Trade, restaurants	1,964	16.1	247,564	19.8
Finance, real estate	2,886	23.7	66,167	5.3
Pub. admin.	1,201	9.8	73,791	5.9
Services	691	5.7	231,268	18.5
Other	489[9]	4.0[9]	171,360[10]	13.7[10]
TOTAL	12,196[2]	100.0	1,250,884	100.0[2]

Household income and expenditure. Average household size (2000) 4.2; average annual income per household (1990) B 5,450 (U.S.$5,450).
Land use as % of total land area (2000): in temporary crops 7.3%, in permanent crops 2.0%, in pasture 20.2%; overall forest area 38.6%.

Foreign trade[11, 12]

Balance of trade (current prices)

	1999	2000	2001	2002	2003	2004
B '000,000	−2,781	−2,626	−2,177	−2,276	−2,323	−2,650
% of total	66.2%	62.8%	57.4%	60.0%	59.3%	58.4%

Imports (2003): B 3,122,000,000 (machinery and apparatus 18.7%; mineral fuels 13.0%; chemicals and chemical products 12.4%; transport equipment 11.1%). Major import sources: U.S. 34.4%; Colón Free Zone 12.5%; Japan 6.2%; Costa Rica 4.8%; Colombia 3.9%.
Exports (2003): B 799,000,000 (marine products 42.3%, of which tuna 16.4%, shrimp and lobster 9.6%, salmon 7.0%; bananas 13.2%; melons 5.9%; cattle 2.3%). Major export destinations: U.S. 50.4%; Sweden 6.0%; Spain 5.7%; Costa Rica 4.2%; Portugal 3.4%.

Transport and communications

Transport. Railroads (2000): route length 354 km; (2002) passenger km 35,693,000,000[13]; (2002) metric ton-km cargo 20,665,000,000[13]. Roads (2000): total length 7,235 mi, 11,643 km (paved [1999] 35%). Vehicles (2002): passenger cars 224,504; trucks and buses 90,618. Panama Canal traffic (2003–04): oceangoing transits 12,518; cargo 203,415,000 metric tons. Air transport (2004)[14]: passenger-km 4,100,000,000; metric ton-km cargo 34,461,000; airports (1996) 10.

Communications

Medium	date	unit	number	units per 1,000 persons
Daily newspapers	2000	circulation	183,000	62
Radio	2000	receivers	884,000	300
Television	2002	receivers	553,900	191
Telephones	2004	main lines	376,100	119
Cellular telephones	2004	subscribers	855,900	270
Personal computers	2004	units	130,000	41
Internet	2004	users	300,000	95

Education and health

Educational attainment (2000). Percentage of population age 25 and over having: no formal schooling 8.9%; primary 36.4%; secondary 33.9%; undergraduate 14.4%; graduate 1.5%; other/unknown 4.9%. Literacy (2000): total population age 15 and over literate 91.3%; males 92.5%; females 91.3%.

Education (1997)

	schools	teachers	students	student/ teacher ratio
Primary (age 6–11)	2,866	15,058	377,898	25.1
Secondary (age 12–17) } Voc., teacher tr. }	417	12,450	223,155	17.9
Higher	14	6,409	95,341	14.9

Health (2000): physicians 3,798 (1 per 776 persons); hospital beds 7,553 (1 per 390 persons); infant mortality rate per 1,000 live births (2004) 14.9.
Food (2002): daily per capita caloric intake 2,272 (vegetable products 76%, animal products 24%); 98% of FAO recommended minimum requirement.

Military

Total active duty personnel (2004): none[15]; Paramilitary expenditure as percentage of GDP (2003): 0.9%; per capita expenditure U.S.$33.

---

[1]Province-level indigenous districts only. [2]Detail does not add to total given because of rounding. [3]Estimate of U.S. Bureau of the Census, International Data Base announced April 2005. [4]District adjacent to Panama City within Panama City urban agglomeration. [5]Population of cabecera. [6]Per August 2003 labour force survey. [7]Estimated figure. [8]At purchaser's prices of 1996. [9]Taxes less imputed bank service charges and less subsidies. [10]Includes 170,351 unemployed. [11]Imports c.i.f.; exports f.o.b. [12]Excludes Colón Free Zone (2003 imports c.i.f. B 4,039,000,000; 2003 reexports f.o.b. B 4,543,000,000, of which machinery and apparatus 24.1%, textiles and clothing 23.6%). [13]Data for 76-km Panama Canal Railway, which reopened in 2001. [14]COPA only. [15]Military abolished 1990; 11,800-member paramilitary includes air and maritime units.

Internet resources for further information:
• Contraloría General de la República Panamá
  http://www.contraloria.gob.pa/index.htm

Papua New Guinea

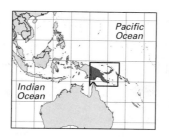

Official name: Independent State of Papua New Guinea.
Form of government: constitutional monarchy with one legislative house (National Parliament [109]).
Chief of state: British Monarch represented by Governor-General.
Head of government: Prime Minister.
Capital: Port Moresby.
Official language: English[1].
Official religion: none.
Monetary unit: 1 Papua New Guinea kina (K) = 100 toea; valuation (Sept. 1, 2005) 1 U.S.$ = K 3.02; 1 £ = K 5.56.

Area and population

Provinces	Administrative centres	area sq mi	area sq km	population 2000 census
Central	Port Moresby	11,400	29,500	183,983
East New Britain	Rabaul	6,000	15,500	220,133
East Sepik	Wewak	16,550	42,800	343,181
Eastern Highlands	Goroka	4,300	11,200	432,972
Enga	Wabag	4,950	12,800	295,031
Gulf	Kerema	13,300	34,500	106,898
Madang	Madang	11,200	29,000	365,106
Manus	Lorengau	800	2,100	43,387
Milne Bay	Alotau	5,400	14,000	210,412
Morobe	Lae	13,300	34,500	539,404
National Capital District	Port Moresby	100	240	254,158
New Ireland	Kavieng	3,700	9,600	118,350
Oro (Northern)	Popondetta	8,800	22,800	133,065
Sandaun (West Sepik)	Vanimo	14,000	36,300	185,741
Simbu (Chimbu)	Kundiawa	2,350	6,100	259,703
Southern Highlands	Mendi	9,200	23,800	546,265
West New Britain	Kimbe	8,100	21,000	184,508
Western	Daru	38,350	99,300	153,304
Western Highlands	Mount Hagen	3,300	8,500	440,025
Autonomous region				
Bougainville[2]	Buka	3,600	9,300	175,160
TOTAL		178,704[3]	462,840	5,190,786

Demography

Population (2005): 5,887,000.
Density (2005): persons per sq mi 32.9, persons per sq km 12.7.
Urban-rural (2003): urban 13.2%; rural 86.8%.
Sex distribution (2000): male 51.87%; female 48.13%.
Age breakdown (2000): under 15, 38.8%; 15–29, 28.7%; 30–44, 17.1%; 45–59, 9.7%; 60–74, 4.7%; 75 and over, 1.0%.
Population projection: (2010) 6,450,000; (2020) 7,602,000.
Doubling time: 30 years.
Ethnic composition (1983)[4]: New Guinea Papuan 84.0%; New Guinea Melanesian 15.0%; other 1.0%.
Religious affiliation (2000): Christian 95.1%, of which non-Anglican Protestant 56.6%, Roman Catholic 30.0%, Anglican 6.7%; traditional beliefs 3.6%; Baha'í 0.8%; other 0.5%.
Major cities (2000): Port Moresby (2003) 274,872; Lae 78,038; Madang 27,394; Wewak 19,724; Goroka 18,618.

Vital statistics

Birth rate per 1,000 population (2004): 30.5 (world avg. 21.1).
Death rate per 1,000 population (2004): 7.5 (world avg. 9.0).
Natural increase rate per 1,000 population (2004): 23.0 (world avg. 12.1).
Total fertility rate (avg. births per childbearing woman; 2004): 4.0.
Life expectancy at birth (2004): male 62.4 years; female 66.8 years.
Major causes of death per 100,000 population (2002): communicable diseases (including significantly malaria) 436; cardiovascular diseases 153; malignant neoplasms (cancers) 50; chronic respiratory diseases (including significantly pneumonia) 36.

National economy

Budget (2004). Revenue: K 3,939,500,000 (tax revenue 81.7%, of which corporate tax 27.2%, income tax 21.0%, excise tax 8.3%, VAT 8.0%; grants 12.2%; nontax revenue 6.1%). Expenditures: K 3,705,500,000 (current expenditure 75.6%, of which transfer to provincial governments 18.1%, interest payments 10.1%; development expenditure 24.4%).
Production (metric tons except as noted). Agriculture, forestry, fishing (2004): oil palm fruit 1,250,000, bananas 870,000, coconuts 650,000, sweet potatoes 520,000, sugarcane 442,000, yams 280,000, taro 256,000, cassava 120,000, coffee 60,000, cacao 42,500, tea 9,000, natural rubber 4,000; livestock (number of live animals) 1,700,000 pigs, 3,900,000 chickens; roundwood 7,241,000 cu m; fish catch (2003) 187,900. Mining and quarrying (2003): copper (metal content) 204,000; silver 73,000 kg; gold 70,000 kg. Manufacturing (value of exports in U.S.$'000; 2003): palm oil 115,000; coconut oil 16,100; rubber 3,500; copra 1,800. Energy production (consumption): electricity (kW-hr; 2002) 1,390,000,000 (1,390,000,000); coal (metric tons; 2000) none (1,000); crude petroleum (barrels; 2002) 29,000,000 (660,000); natural gas (cu m; 2002) 85,000,000 (85,000,000); petroleum products (metric tons; 2002) 49,000 (713,000).
Land use as % of total land area (2000): in temporary crops 0.5%, in permanent crops 1.4%, in pasture 0.4%; overall forest area 67.6%.
Gross national product (2004): U.S.$3,262,000,000 (U.S.$580 per capita).

Structure of gross domestic product and labour force

	2003 in value K '000,000	2003 % of total value	2000 labour force	2000 % of labour force
Agriculture, fishing	3,356	27.5	1,696,271	70.3
Mining	3,062	25.1	9,282	0.4
Manufacturing	1,109	9.1	25,557	1.1
Construction	588	4.8	48,312	2.0
Public utilities	158	1.3	2,208	0.1
Transp. and commun.	581	4.8	24,513	1.0
Trade	1,170	9.6	357,581	14.8
Finance	496	4.1	31,129	1.3
Pub. admin., defense	1,495	12.3	32,043	1.3
Services			86,391	3.6
Other	189[5]	1.5[5]	100,070	4.1
TOTAL	12,204	100.0[3]	2,413,357	100.0

Public debt (external, outstanding; June 2005): U.S.$1,264,000,000.
Population economically active (2000): total 2,413,357; activity rate 46.5% (participation rates: ages 15–64, 73.2%; female 47.9%; unemployed 2.8%).

Price index (2000 = 100)

	1998	1999	2000	2001	2002	2003	2004
Consumer price index	75.3	86.5	100.0	109.3	122.2	140.2	143.1

Tourism (2001): receipts U.S.$101,000,000; expenditures U.S.$38,000,000.

Foreign trade[6]

Balance of trade (current prices)

	1999	2000	2001	2002	2003	2004
U.S.$'000,000	+823	+987	+775	+545	+1,094	+1,130
% of total	29.4%	35.3%	31.6%	20.7%	30.3%	27.3%

Imports (2000): U.S.$1,035,000,000 (petroleum products c. 22%; food c. 16%; transport equipment c. 14%; nonelectrical machinery c. 12%; chemicals and chemical products c. 7%). *Major import sources* (2004): Australia 57.3%; U.S. 8.4%; Singapore 6.2%; Japan 4.6%; New Zealand 3.4%.
Exports (2004): U.S.$2,635,000,000 (gold 33.8%; crude petroleum 20.1%; copper 18.8%; palm oil 5.3%; logs 4.3%). *Major export destinations* (2004): Australia 45.6%; Japan 10.8%; Germany 7.1%; South Korea 6.1%; China 4.9%.

Transport and communications

Transport. Railroads: none. Roads (1999): total length 19,600 km (paved 4%). Vehicles (2000): passenger cars 24,900; trucks and buses 87,800. Air transport (2001): passenger-km 1,110,000,000; metric ton-km cargo 124,000,000; airports (1999) with scheduled flights 42.

Communications

Medium	date	unit	number	units per 1,000 persons
Daily newspapers	2000	circulation	72,600	14
Radio	2000	receivers	446,000	86
Television	2000	receivers	88,200	17
Telephones	2002	main lines	62,000	11
Cellular telephones	2002	subscribers	15,000	2.7
Personal computers	2004	units	367,000	64
Internet	2004	users	170,000	29

Education and health

Educational attainment (1990). Percentage of population age 25 and over having: no formal schooling 82.6%; some primary education 8.2%; completed primary 5.0%; some secondary 4.2%. *Literacy* (2002): total population age 15 and over literate 64.6%; males literate 71.1%; females literate 57.7%.

Education (2002–03)

	schools	teachers	students	student/ teacher ratio
Primary (age 7–12)	2,790[7]	18,630	660,425	35.4
Secondary (age 13–16)	159[8]	7,058	168,052	23.8
Voc., teacher tr.	128[8]	1,111	16,599	14.9
Higher	3[8]	815[7]	9,220[8]	...

Health: physicians (2000) 275 (1 per 19,269 persons); hospital beds (1993) 14,119 (1 per 294 persons); infant mortality rate (2004) 53.2.
Food (2001): daily per capita caloric intake 2,193 (vegetable products 91%, animal products 9%); 96% of FAO recommended minimum.

Military

Total active duty personnel (2004): 3,100 (army 80.6%, maritime element [coastal patrol] 12.9%, air force 6.5%). *Military expenditure as percentage of GDP* (2003): 0.6%; per capita expenditure U.S.$3.

---

[1]The national languages are English, Tok Pisin (English Creole), and Motu. [2]Bougainville formally attained autonomy within Papua New Guinea on June 15, 2005. A referendum on possible future independence is to be held in 10 to 15 years. [3]Detail does not add to total given because of rounding. [4]Papua New Guinea has about 1,200 ethnic communities, more than half of which number less than 1,000 people. New Guinea Papuans are predominantly descendants of original arrivals; New Guinea Melanesians are more racially mixed with other Pacific peoples. [5]Import duties less imputed bank service charges and less subsidies. [6]Imports f.o.b. in balance of trade and trading partners and c.i.f. in commodities. [7]1999. [8]1997.

Internet resources for further information:
• Bank of Papua New Guinea http://www.bankpng.gov.pg
• National Statistical Office of Papua New Guinea http://www.nso.gov.pg

Paraguay

Official name: República del Paraguay
(Spanish); Tetã Paraguáype
(Guaraní) (Republic of Paraguay).
Form of government: multiparty
republic with two legislative
houses (Senate [45]; Chamber of
Deputies [80]).
Head of state and government:
President.
Capital: Asunción.
Official languages: Spanish; Guaraní.
Official religion: none[1].
Monetary unit: 1 Paraguayan Guaraní
(₲) = 100 céntimos; valuation
(Sept. 1, 2005) 1 U.S.$ = ₲6,115;
1 £ = ₲11,259.

Area and population

Regions Departments	Capitals	area sq mi	area sq km	population 2002 census
Occidental		95,338	246,925	142,501
Alto Paraguay	Fuerte Olimpo	31,795	82,349	15,008
Boquerón	Filadelfia	35,393	91,669	45,617
Presidente Hayes	Pozo Colorado	28,150	72,907	81,876
Oriental		61,710	159,827	5,063,600
Alto Paraná	Ciudad del Este	5,751	14,895	563,042
Amambay	Pedro Juan Caballero	4,994	12,933	113,888
Asunción[2]	—	45	117	513,399
Caaguazú	Coronel Oviedo	4,430	11,474	448,983
Caazapá	Caazapá	3,666	9,496	139,241
Canindeyú	Salto del Guairá	5,663	14,667	140,551
Central	Asunción	952	2,465	1,363,399
Concepción	Concepción	6,970	18,051	180,277
Cordillera	Caacupé	1,910	4,948	234,805
Guairá	Villarrica	1,485	3,846	176,933
Itapúa	Encarnación	6,380	16,525	463,410
Misiones	San Juan Bautista	3,690	9,556	103,633
Ñeembucú	Pilar	4,690	12,147	76,738
Paraguarí	Paraguarí	3,361	8,705	226,514
San Pedro	San Pedro	7,723	20,002	318,787
TOTAL		157,048	406,752	5,206,101[3]

Demography

Population (2005): 5,905,000.
Density (2005): persons per sq mi 37.6, persons per sq km 14.5.
Urban-rural (2002): urban 56.7%; rural 43.3%.
Sex distribution (2002): male 50.42%; female 49.58%.
Age breakdown (2002): under 15, 37.1%; 15–29, 27.3%; 30–44, 17.9%; 45–59,
10.6%; 60–74, 5.1%; 75 and over, 2.0%.
Population projection: (2010) 6,609,000; (2020) 8,010,000.
Ethnic composition (2000): mixed (white/Amerindian) 85.6%; white 9.3%, of
which German 4.4%, Latin American 3.4%; Amerindian 1.8%; other 3.3%.
Religious affiliation (2002): Roman Catholic 89.6%; Protestant (including all
Evangelicals) 6.2%; nonreligious/atheist 1.1%; other 3.1%.
Major urban areas (2002): Asunción 513,399[4]; Ciudad del Este 223,350;
Encarnación 69,769; Pedro Juan Caballero 64,153; Caaguazú 50,329.

Vital statistics

Birth rate per 1,000 population (2004): 29.8 (world avg. 21.1).
Death rate per 1,000 population (2004): 4.6 (world avg. 9.0).
Natural increase rate per 1,000 population (2004): 25.2 (world avg. 12.1).
Total fertility rate (avg. births per childbearing woman; 2004): 4.0.
Marriage rate per 1,000 population (2002): 3.0[5].
Life expectancy at birth (2004): male 72.1 years; female 77.3 years.
Major causes of death per 100,000 population (2001)[6]: diseases of the circula-
tory system 114; malignant neoplasms (cancers) 67; accidents 55; diseases of
the respiratory system 32; infectious and parasitic diseases 22.

National economy

Budget (2002): Revenue: ₲5,048,300,000,000 (tax revenue 64.2%, of which
taxes on goods and services 38.9%, customs duties 10.3%, income taxes 8.9%,
social security 6.1%; nontax revenue including grants 35.8%). Expenditures:
₲6,072,900,000,000 (current expenditure 78.6%; capital expenditure 21.4%).
Public debt (external, outstanding; 2003): U.S.$2,224,000,000.
Population economically active (2002): total 1,980,492; activity rate 38.4% (participation rates: ages 15–64, 61.4%; female 32.1%; unemployed [2003] 8.1%).

Price index (2000 = 100)

	1998	1999	2000	2001	2002	2003	2004
Consumer price index	86.0	91.8	100.0	107.3	118.5	135.4	139.0

Production (metric tons except as noted). Agriculture, forestry, fishing (2004):
cassava 5,500,000, sugarcane 3,637,000, soybeans 3,583,680, corn (maize)
1,120,000, wheat 715,000, seed cotton 330,000, oranges 200,075, sweet potatoes 166,932, bananas 44,031; livestock (number of live animals) 9,622,340
cattle, 1,650,000 pigs, 17,000,000 chickens; roundwood 9,987,627 cu m; fish
catch (2002) 25,000. Mining and quarrying (2002): hydraulic cement 650,000;
kaolin 66,700; gypsum 4,300. Manufacturing (value added in constant prices
of 1982, ₲'000,000; 2001): food products 61,056; wood products (excluding
furniture) 21,695; beverages 18,589; handicrafts 10,440; textiles 8,412; printing and publishing 8,387; leather and hides 8,249; nonmetal products 5,391;
plastics 4,428; petroleum products 3,208. Energy production (consumption):

electricity (kW-hr; 2002) 48,251,000,000 (6,481,000,000); crude petroleum
(barrels; 2002) none (704,000); petroleum products (metric tons; 2002)
105,000 (1,245,000).
Gross national product (2004): U.S.$6,752,000,000 (U.S.$1,170 per capita).

Structure of gross domestic product and labour force

	2002 in value ₲'000,000,000	2002 % of total value	2002 labour force	2002 % of labour force
Agriculture	7,546.6	23.6	531,570	26.8
Mining	87.9	0.3	1,995	0.1
Manufacturing	4,475.0	14.0	213,573	10.8
Construction	1,432.8	4.5	141,816	7.2
Public utilities	2,041.8	6.4	8,640	0.4
Transp. and commun.	1,679.6	5.2	85,628	4.3
Trade	8,189.4	25.6	416,953	21.1
Finance, real estate	7	7	68,133	3.4
Pub. admin., defense	1,570.9	4.9	86,882	4.4
Services	7	7	370,279	18.7
Other	4,952.9[7]	15.5[7]	55,023	2.8
TOTAL	31,976.9	100.0	1,980,492	100.0

Household income and expenditure. Average household size (2002) 4.7.
Tourism (2003): receipts U.S.$64,000,000; expenditures U.S.$57,000,000.
Land use as % of total land area (2000): in temporary crops 7.2%, in perma-
nent crops 0.2%, in pasture 54.6%; overall forest area 58.8%.

Foreign trade[8]

Balance of trade (current prices)

	1999	2000	2001	2002	2003	2004
U.S.$'000,000	−984	−1,181	−999	−560	−624	−1,026
% of total	39.9%	40.4%	33.5%	22.8%	20.1%	24.0%

Imports (2002): U.S.$1,672,000,000 (machinery and apparatus 21.6%, chemi-
cals and chemical products 17.4%, refined petroleum 14.3%, transport equipment 6.0%, food products 5.6%). *Major import sources:* Brazil 30.6%;
Argentina 20.6%; China 12.6%; U.S. 5.0%; Japan 4.0%.
Exports (2002): U.S.$951,000,000[9] (soybeans 35.8%, processed meats 7.6%,
soybean oil 7.5%, leather and leather products 6.1%, wood manufactures
5.9%). *Major export destinations:* Brazil 37.1%; Uruguay 17.4%; Cayman
Islands 8.2%; Chile 5.2%; U.S. 3.9%.

Transport and communications

Transport. Railroads (2004): route length 441 km; (1998) passenger-km
3,000,000; (1998) metric ton-km cargo 5,500,000. Roads (1999): total length
29,500 km (paved 51%). Vehicles (2002): passenger cars 274,186; trucks
189,115. Air transport (2004)[10]: passenger-km 433,368,000; metric ton-km
cargo, none; airports (1998) 5.

Communications

Medium	date	unit	number	units per 1,000 persons
Daily newspapers	2000	circulation	227,000	43
Radio	2000	receivers	961,000	182
Television	2000	receivers	1,150,000	218
Telephones	2003	main lines	273,200	46
Cellular telephones	2004	subscribers	1,767,800	293
Personal computers	2004	units	356,000	59
Internet	2004	users	150,000	25

Education and health

Educational attainment (2002). Percentage of population age 15 and over having: no formal schooling 5.0%; primary education 55.0%; secondary 33.5%;
higher 5.3%; not stated 1.2%. *Literacy* (2002): percentage of total population
age 15 and over literate 92.9%; males 93.9%; females 91.9%.

Education (1999)

	schools	teachers	students	student/ teacher ratio
Primary (age 7–12)	7,456	59,423[11]	1,036,700	15.7[11]
Secondary (age 13–18)[12]	1,844	21,052	260,500	12.3
Higher	111	1,135	57,292	…

Health: physicians (2000) 4,726 (1 per 1,119 persons); hospital beds (2002)
5,834 (1 per 945 persons); infant mortality rate per 1,000 live births (2004)
26.7.
Food (2001): daily per capita caloric intake 2,576 (vegetable products 78%,
animal products 22%); 112% of FAO recommended minimum requirement.

Military

Total active duty personnel (2004): 10,100 (army 75.2%, navy 13.9%, air force
10.9%). *Military expenditure as percentage of GDP* (2003): 0.9%; per capita
expenditure U.S.$10.

[1]Roman Catholicism, although not official, enjoys special recognition in the 1992 constitution. [2]Asunción is the capital city, not a department. [3]Preliminary figure; adjusted
final total equals 5,542,886. [4]2003 urban agglomeration population equals 1,639,000.
[5]Civil Registry records only. [6]Projected rates based on about 71% of total deaths. [7]Other
includes Services and Finance, real estate. [8]Imports f.o.b. in balance of trade and c.i.f.
in commodities and trading partners. [9]Excludes value of hydroelectricity exports to
Brazil and Argentina. [10]Transportes Aéreos del Mercosur only. [11]1998. [12]Includes vocational and teacher training.

Internet resources for further information:
• **Banco Central del Paraguay** http://www.bcp.gov.py
• **Dirección General Estadística, Encuestas y Censos**
http://www.dgeec.gov.py/index.htm

Peru

Official name: República del Perú (Spanish) (Republic of Peru).
Form of government: unitary multiparty republic with one legislative house (Congress [120]).
Head of state and government: President, assisted by Prime Minister.
Capital: Lima.
Official languages: Spanish; Quechua (locally); Aymara (locally).
Official religion: Roman Catholicism.
Monetary unit: 1 nuevo sol (S/.) = 100 céntimos; valuation (Sept. 1, 2005) 1 U.S.$ = S/. 3.28; 1 £ = S/. 6.03.

Area and population

Regions	area sq km	population 2003 estimate	Regions	area sq km	population 2003 estimate
Amazonas	39,249	435,556	Lambayeque	14,213	1,131,467
Ancash	35,915	1,123,410	Lima	34,802	7,880,039
Apurímac	20,896	470,719	Loreto	368,852	919,505
Arequipa	63,345	1,113,916	Madre de Dios	85,301	102,174
Ayacucho	43,815	561,029	Moquegua	15,734	160,232
Cajamarca	33,318	1,515,827	Pasco	25,320	270,987
Callao	147	799,530	Piura	35,892	1,660,952
Cusco	71,986	1,223,248	Puno	71,999[1]	1,280,555
Huancavelica	22,131	451,508	San Martin	51,253	767,890
Huánuco	36,849	822,804	Tacna	16,076	301,960
Ica	21,328	698,437	Tumbes	4,669	206,578
Junín	44,197	1,260,773	Ucayali	102,411	460,557
La Libertad	25,500	1,528,448	TOTAL	1,285,198[1]	27,148,101

Demography

Population (2005): 27,968,000.
Density (2005): persons per sq mi 56.4, persons per sq km 21.8.
Urban-rural (2003): urban 73.5%; rural 26.5%.
Sex distribution (2003): male 50.35%; female 49.65%.
Age breakdown (2003): under 15, 32.6%; 15–29, 27.2%; 30–44, 20.8%; 45–59, 11.9%; 60–74, 6.0%; 75 and over, 1.5%.
Population projection: (2010) 30,063,000; (2020) 34,250,000.
Doubling time: 47 years.
Ethnic composition (2000): Quechua 47.0%; mestizo 31.9%; white 12.0%; Aymara 5.4%; Japanese 0.5%; other 3.2%.
Religious affiliation (2000): Christian 97.2%, of which Roman Catholic 86.2%, Protestant 5.2%, disaffiliated or unaffiliated Christian 3.1%, independent Christian 1.6%; nonreligious 1.2%; traditional beliefs 0.6%; other 1.0%.
Major cities (2000): metropolitan Lima 7,496,831; Arequipa 762,000; Trujillo 652,000; Chiclayo 517,000; Iquitos 367,000.

Vital statistics

Birth rate per 1,000 population (2004): 21.3 (world avg. 21.1).
Death rate per 1,000 population (2004): 6.3 (world avg. 9.0).
Natural increase rate per 1,000 population (2004): 15.0 (world avg. 12.1).
Total fertility rate (avg. births per childbearing woman; 2004): 2.6.
Life expectancy at birth (2004): male 67.5 years; female 71.0 years.
Major causes of death per 100,000 population (2000): diseases of the circulatory system 54.2; malignant neoplasms (cancers) 52.8; respiratory diseases 45.8; accidents, poisoning, and violence 35.2; infectious diseases 24.5.

National economy

Budget (2004). Revenue: S/. 35,381,000,000 (tax revenue 88.0%, nontax revenue 12.0%). Expenditures: S/. 34,165,000,000 (current expenditure 87.4%, capital expenditure 12.6%).
Public debt (external, outstanding; 2003): U.S.$22,072,000,000.
Tourism (2003): receipts U.S.$923,000,000; expenditures U.S.$620,000,000.
Production (metric tons except as noted). Agriculture, forestry, fishing (2004): sugarcane 7,950,000, alfalfa 5,626,000, potatoes 2,996,000, rice 1,817,000, plantains 1,660,000, corn (maize) 1,181,000, cassava 961,000; livestock (number of live animals) 14,050,000 sheep, 5,050,000 cattle, 4,400,000 llamas and alpacas; roundwood 10,486,832 cu m; fish catch (2003) 6,089,660. Mining and quarrying (2003): iron ore 3,540,700[2]; zinc 1,171,000[2]; copper 625,300[2]; lead 283,200[2]; silver 2,611[2]; gold 172,900 kg. Manufacturing (value in S/. '000,000; 2003): food and food products 10,016; textiles and wearing apparel 4,330; base and fabricated metals 4,052; chemicals and chemical products 3,447; paper and paper products 2,026. Energy production (consumption): electricity (kW-hr; 2002) 24,266,000,000 (24,266,000,000); coal (metric tons; 2002) 22,000 (910,000); crude petroleum (barrels; 2002) 36,800,000 (58,900,000); petroleum products (metric tons; 2002) 8,626,000 (7,369,000); natural gas (cu m; 2002) 907,000,000 (907,000,000).
Population economically active (2002)[3]: total 12,892,000; activity rate of total population 48.2% (participation rates: ages 15–64, 72.6%; female 42.0%; urban unemployed [2003] 9.4%).

Price and earnings indexes (2000 = 100)

	1998	1999	2000	2001	2002	2003	2004
Consumer price index	93.1	96.4	100.0	102.0	102.2	104.5	108.3
Monthly earnings index[4]	94.6	95.8	100.0	100.8	...	...	...

Gross national product (at current market prices; 2004): U.S.$65,043,000,000 (U.S.$2,360 per capita).

Structure of gross domestic product and labour force

	2003 in value S/. '000	2003 % of total value	2001 labour force[5]	2001 % of labour force[5]
Agriculture	14,550,851	6.9	667,800	8.1
Mining	12,703,862	6.0	45,900	0.6
Manufacturing	30,065,053	14.3	956,400	11.6
Construction	11,475,391	5.4	341,300	4.1
Public utilities	4,679,672	2.2	20,400	0.2
Transp. and commun.	16,819,022	8.0	641,000	7.7
Trade[6]	36,803,250	17.5	2,718,300	32.9
Finance, real estate	35,747,416	17.0	390,500	4.7
Pub. admin., defense	15,978,318	7.6	298,100	3.6
Services	13,278,078	6.3	1,540,200	18.6
Other	18,646,510[7]	8.8[7]	651,500[8]	7.9[8]
TOTAL	210,747,423	100.0	8,271,400	100.0

Household income and expenditure. Average household size (2001) 4.5; income per household (1988) U.S.$2,173; sources of income (1991): self-employment 67.1%, wages 23.3%, transfers 7.6%; expenditure (1990): food 29.4%, recreation and education 13.2%, household durables 10.1%.
Land use as % of total land area (2000): in temporary crops 2.9%, in permanent crops 0.4%, in pasture 21.2%; overall forest area 50.9%.

Foreign trade

Balance of trade (current prices)

	1999	2000	2001	2002	2003	2004
U.S.$'000,000	−655	−411	−195	+292	+836	+2,793
% of total	5.1%	2.9%	1.4%	1.9%	4.8%	12.4%

Imports (2004): U.S.$9,824,000,000 (consumer goods 20.1%, mineral fuels and lubricants 17.9%, capital goods for industry 16.8%, food products 7.3%). *Major import sources:* U.S. 19.9%; China 7.9%; Colombia 7.6%; Brazil 6.6%; Ecuador 6.6%; Venezuela 6.6%.
Exports (2004): U.S.$12,617,000,000 (copper 19.4%, gold 18.8%, clothing and textiles 8.7%, fishmeal 7.6%, processed agricultural and livestock products 6.3%, crude and refined petroleum 5.1%, zinc 4.6%). *Major export destinations:* U.S. 29.1%; China 9.9%; U.K. 9.2%; Chile 5.1%; Japan 4.4%.

Transport and communications

Transport. Railroads (2003): length 2,123 km; (2002) passenger-km 98,000,000; (2002) metric ton-km cargo 1,008,000,000. Roads (2003): total length 78,672 km (paved 13%). Vehicles (2003): passenger cars 812,978; trucks and buses 444,392. Air transport (2003): passenger-km 2,443,100,000; metric ton-km cargo 114,300,000; airports (1996) 27.

Communications

Medium	date	unit	number	units per 1,000 persons
Daily newspapers	1996	circulation	2,000,000	84
Radio	1997	receivers	7,080,000	273
Television	2002	receivers	4,592,400	172
Telephones	2004	main lines	2,049,800	74
Cellular telephones	2004	subscribers	4,092,600	149
Personal computers	2004	units	2,689,000	98
Internet	2004	users	3,220,000	117

Education and health

Educational attainment (1993). Percentage of population age 15 and over having: no formal schooling 12.3%; less than primary education 0.3%; primary 31.5%; secondary 35.5%; higher 20.4%. *Literacy* (2000): total population age 15 and over literate 89.9%; males 94.7%; females 85.3%.

Education (2002)

	schools	teachers	students	student/teacher ratio
Primary (age 6–11)	33,734	177,257	4,219,800	23.8
Secondary (age 12–16)	9,168	139,349	2,302,099	16.5
Higher[9]	2,161	57,874	1,495,957	25.8

Health (2002): physicians 32,619 (1 per 821 persons); hospital beds 43,074 (1 per 621 persons); infant mortality rate per 1,000 live births (2004) 33.0.
Food (2001): daily per capita caloric intake 2,610 (vegetable products 87%, animal products 13%); 111% of FAO recommended minimum requirement.

Military

Total active duty personnel (2004): 80,000 (army 50.0%, navy 31.3%, air force 18.7%). *Military expenditure as percentage of GDP* (2003): 1.3%; per capita expenditure U.S.$29.

[1]Includes the 4,996 sq km area of the Peruvian part of Lake Titicaca. [2]Metal content. [3]Official estimate. [4]Private sector only, Lima metropolitan area. [5]Excludes rural areas. [6]Trade includes hotels and restaurants. [7]Other includes import duties and other taxes on products. [8]Unemployed. [9]2000.

Internet resources for further information:
• Instituto Nacional de Estadística e Informática (Spanish)
  http://www.inei.gob.pe
• Banco Central de Reserva del Peru
  http://www.bcrp.gob.pe

Philippines

Official name: Republika ng Pilipinas (Pilipino); Republic of the Philippines (English).
Form of government: unitary republic with two legislative houses (Senate [24]; House of Representatives [236]).
Chief of state and head of government: President.
Capital: Quezon City/Manila[1].
Official languages: Pilipino; English.
Official religion: none.
Monetary unit: 1 Philippine peso (P) = 100 centavos; valuation (Sept. 1, 2005) 1 U.S.$ = P 56.05; 1 £ = P 103.21.

Area and population

Regions	Capitals	area sq mi	area sq km	population 2000 census
Bicol	Legaspi	6,963	18,035	4,674,855
Cagayan Valley	Tuguegarao	11,641	30,149	2,813,159
CALABARZON[2]	Quezon City[3]	6,198	16,052	9,320,629
Caraga	Butuan	7,461	19,324	2,095,367
Central Luzon	San Fernando	7,559	19,579	8,204,742
Central Visayas	Cebu	6,016	15,582	5,701,064
Cordillera Administrative	Baguio	6,465	16,745	1,365,220
Davao[4]	Davao	10,491	27,172	5,189,335
Eastern Visayas	Tacloban	8,490	21,988	3,610,355
Ilocos	San Fernando	4,950	12,821	4,200,478
MIMAROPA[2]	Quezon City[3]	11,274	29,199	2,299,229
National Capital	Manila	244	633	9,932,560
Northern Mindanao	Cagayan de Oro	6,030	15,617	2,747,585
SOCCSKSARGEN[4]	Cotabato	6,135	15,890	2,598,210
Western Visayas	Iloilo	7,783	20,158	6,208,733
Zamboanga Peninsula[4]	Zamboanga	7,009	18,154	3,091,208
Autonomous region				
Muslim Mindanao	Sultan Kudarat	7,412	19,196	2,412,159
TOTAL		122,121	316,294[5]	76,498,735[6]

Demography

Population (2005): 84,191,000.
Density (2005): persons per sq mi 689.4, persons per sq km 266.2.
Urban-rural (2003): urban 61.0%; rural 39.0%.
Sex distribution (2003): male 50.30%; female 49.70%.
Age breakdown (2002): under 15, 35.1%; 15–29, 28.1%; 30–44, 19.3%; 45–59, 11.2%; 60–74, 5.0%; 75 and over, 1.3%.
Population projection: (2010) 91,280,000; (2020) 104,680,000.
Ethnic composition (2000): Tagalog 20.9%; Visayan (Cebu) 19.0%; Ilocano 11.1%; Hiligaynon (Visaya) 9.4%; Waray-Waray (Binisaya) 4.7%; Central Bikol (Naga) 4.6%; Filipino mestizo 3.5%; Pampango 3.1%; other 23.7%.
Religious affiliation (2000): Roman Catholic 81.0%; Protestant 6.6%; Muslim 5.1%; indigenous Christian 4.3%; other Christian 0.7%; traditional beliefs 0.2%; other/unknown 2.1%.
Major cities (2000): Quezon City 2,173,831; Manila 1,581,082 (Metro Manila [2003] 10,352,249); Caloocan 1,177,604; Davao 1,147,116; Cebu 718,821.

Vital statistics

Birth rate per 1,000 population (2004): 24.6 (world avg. 21.1).
Death rate per 1,000 population (2004): 5.7 (world avg. 9.0).
Natural increase rate per 1,000 population (2004): 18.9 (world avg. 12.1).
Total fertility rate (avg. births per childbearing woman; 2004): 3.1.
Life expectancy at birth (2004): male 67.5 years; female 72.8 years.
Marriage rate per 1,000 population (2002): 7.3.
Major causes of death per 100,000 population (2001): circulatory diseases 143.7; respiratory diseases 65.1; malignant neoplasms (cancers) 48.4; tuberculosis 35.0; accidents and violence 34.3.

National economy

Budget (2004). Revenue: P 675,898,000,000 (income taxes 41.3%, international duties 16.7%, sales tax 13.9%, nontax revenues 11.8%). Expenditures: P 856,129,000,000 (debt service 31.7%, economic affairs 18.2%, education 15.6%, public order 6.2%, defense 5.1%).
Public debt (external, outstanding; 2003): U.S.$36,221,000,000.
Production (metric tons except as noted). Agriculture, forestry, fishing (2004): sugarcane 28,000,000, rice 14,496,800, coconuts 14,344,920, bananas 5,638,060, corn (maize) 5,413,390, pineapples 1,759,290; livestock (number of live animals) 12,561,690 pigs, 6,300,000 goats, 3,269,980 buffalo, 122,010,000 chickens; roundwood 15,861,593 cu m; fish catch (2003) 2,164,000. Mining and quarrying (2003): nickel 27,000[7]; copper 20,414[7]; chromite 2,600; gold 37,840 kg[7]. Manufacturing (gross value added in P '000,000; 2001): food products 361,217; electrical machinery 95,592; petroleum and coal products 73,280; chemicals 58,487; beverages and tobacco 49,933. Energy production (consumption): electricity (kW-hr; 2004) 55,958,000,000 (44,861,000,000); hard coal (metric tons; 2004) 2,726,000 (8,993,000); crude petroleum (barrels; 2004) 1,000,000 (816,000,000); petroleum products (metric tons; 2002) 13,049,000 (15,265,000); natural gas (cu m; 2002) 370,000,000 (370,000,000).
Household income and expenditure (2000). Average household size (2002) 5.0; income per family (2003) P 148,616 (U.S.$2,742); sources of income: wages 52.1%, self-employment 25.1%, receipts from abroad 11.1%; expenditure: food, beverages and tobacco 45.4%, housing 14.2%, transportation 6.8%.
Gross national product (at current market prices; 2004): U.S.$92,212,000,000 (U.S.$1,090 per capita).

Structure of gross domestic product and labour force

	2004 in value P '000,000	2004 % of total value	2004 labour force	2004 % of labour force
Agriculture, fishing	742,112	15.3	11,444,000	31.9
Mining	53,032	1.1	114,000	0.3
Manufacturing	1,116,163	23.1	3,056,000	8.5
Construction	217,699	4.5	1,654,000	4.6
Public utilities	155,346	3.2	110,000	0.3
Transp. and commun.	370,228	7.6	2,464,000	6.9
Trade	680,762	14.1	6,706,000	18.7
Finances	508,886	10.5	1,039,000	2.9
Pub. admin., defense	393,503	8.1	1,414,000	4.0
Services	605,719	12.5	3,621,000	10.1
Others	—	—	4,208,000[8]	11.8[8]
TOTAL	4,843,450	100.0	35,830,000	100.0

Population economically active (2004): total 35,830,000; activity rate *c.* 42% (participation rates: ages 15 and over 67.1%; female *c.* 37%; unemployed [July 2004–June 2005] 10.6%).

Price index (2000 = 100)

	1998	1999	2000	2001	2002	2003	2004
Consumer price index	90.8	96.2	100.0	106.8	110.0	113.8	120.6

Tourism (2003): receipts U.S.$1,522,700,000; expenditures U.S.$632,000,000.
Land use as % of total land area (2000): in temporary crops 18.9%, in permanent crops 16.8%, in pasture 4.3%; overall forest area 19.4%.

Foreign trade

Balance of trade (current prices)

	2000	2001	2002	2003	2004
U.S.$'000,000	+3,714	−910	−221	−1,275	−1,160
% of total	5.1%	1.4%	0.3%	1.7%	1.2%

Imports (2004): U.S.$47,865,000,000 (machinery and transport equipment 34.7%, mineral fuels 10.9%, chemicals and chemical products 7.4%, food 5.9%). *Major import sources:* Japan 20.6%; U.S. 16.0%; Singapore 8.4%; China 7.4%; Taiwan 7.3%.
Exports (2004): U.S.$46,705,000,000 (electronic microcircuits and office machines 57.1%, apparel and clothing accessories 4.6%, coconut oil 1.2%). *Major export destinations:* U.S. 17.4%; Japan 15.8%; China 11.4%; Hong Kong 8.3%; Singapore 7.7%; The Netherlands 6.0%.

Transport and communications

Transport. Railroads (2004): route length 897 km; passenger-km 83,400,000; metric ton-km cargo (2000) 660,000,000. Roads (2003): total length 200,037 km (paved 10%). Vehicles (2004): passenger cars 939,607; trucks and buses 302,980. Air transport (2004)[9]: passenger-km 13,326,644,000; metric ton-km cargo 278,214,000; airports (1996) with scheduled flights 21.

Communications

Medium	date	unit	number	units per 1,000 persons
Daily newspapers	2000	circulation	6,300,000	82
Radio	2000	receivers	12,400,000	161
Television	2003	receivers	14,770,000	182
Telephones	2004	main lines	3,437,500	42
Cellular telephones	2004	subscribers	32,935,900	398
Personal computers	2004	units	3,684,000	45
Internet	2004	users	4,400,000	53

Education and health

Educational attainment (2000). Percentage of population age 25 and over having: no formal schooling 3.8%; primary education 38.5%; incomplete secondary 12.5%; complete secondary 17.2%; technical 5.9%; incomplete undergraduate 11.8%; complete undergraduate 7.3%; graduate 0.7%; unknown 2.3%. *Literacy* (2002): total population age 15 and over literate 92.6%.

Education (2002–03)

	schools	teachers	students	student/ teacher ratio
Primary (age 7–12)	37,506[10]	371,384	12,970,635	34.9
Secondary (age 13–16)	5,784[10]	163,646	6,069,063	37.1
Higher	1,626	109,979	2,427,211	22.1

Health: physicians (2004) 93,862 (1 per 880 persons); hospital beds (2003) 85,040 (1 per 954 persons); infant mortality rate per 1,000 live births (2004) 24.2.
Food (2002): daily per capita caloric intake 2,379 (vegetable products 84%, animal products 16%); 105% of FAO recommended minimum.

Military

Total active duty personnel (2004): 106,000 (army 62.3%, navy 22.6%, air force 15.1%). *Military expenditure as percentage of GDP* (2003): 0.9%; per capita expenditure U.S.$9.

---

[1]Additional offices/ministries are located in other suburbs of Metro Manila. [2]Created 2002. [3]Located outside of region. [4]Officially renamed in 2001. [5]Sum of regional areas; actual reported total is *c.* 300,000 sq km. [6]Includes foreign-service employees stationed abroad. [7]Metal content. [8]Unemployed. [9]Philippines Airlines only. [10]2003–04.

Internet resources for further information:
• National Statistics Office http://www.census.gov.ph

Poland

Official name: Rzeczpospolita Polska (Republic of Poland).
Form of government: unitary multiparty republic with two legislative houses (Senate [100]; Diet [460]).
Chief of state: President.
Head of government: Prime Minister.
Capital: Warsaw.
Official language: Polish.
Official religion: none[1].
Monetary unit: 1 zloty (Zł) = 100 groszy; valuation (Sept. 1, 2005) 1 U.S.$ = Zł 3.16; 1 £ = Zł 5.81.

Area and population

Provinces[3]	Capitals	area sq mi	area sq km	population 2003[2] estimate
Dolnośląskie	Wrocław	7,702	19,948	2,902,400
Kujawsko-pomorskie	Bydgoszcz/Toruń	6,938	17,970	2,068,400
Łódzkie	Łódź	7,034	18,219	2,603,700
Lubelskie	Lublin	9,697	25,114	2,194,900
Lubuskie	Gorzów Wielkopolski/ Zielona Góra	5,399	13,984	1,008,000
Małopolskie	Kraków	5,847	15,144	3,245,900
Mazowieckie	Warsaw (Warszawa)	13,744	35,598	5,128,400
Opolskie	Opole	3,634	9,412	1,059,400
Podkarpackie	Rzeszów	6,921	17,926	2,096,100
Podlaskie	Białystok	7,792	20,180	1,206,700
Pomorskie	Gdańsk	7,063	18,293	2,184,400
Śląskie	Katowice	4,747	12,294	4,726,000
Świętokrzyskie	Kielce	4,507	11,672	1,294,200
Warmińsko-Mazurskie	Olsztyn	9,345	24,203	1,428,200
Wielkopolskie	Poznań	11,516	29,826	3,355,200
Zachodniopomorskie	Szczecin	8,843	22,902	1,697,200
TOTAL		120,728[4]	312,685	38,199,100

Demography

Population (2005): 38,164,000.
Density (2005): persons per sq mi 316.1, persons per sq km 122.1.
Urban-rural (2003): urban 61.9%; rural 38.1%.
Sex distribution (2004): male 48.40%; female 51.60%.
Age breakdown (2002): under 15, 18.3%; 15–29, 24.6%; 30–44, 20.6%; 45–59, 20.1%; 60–74, 11.5%; 75 and over, 4.5%.
Population projection: (2010) 37,763,000; (2020) 37,102,000.
Ethnic composition (2000): Polish 90.0%; Ukrainian 4.0%; German 4.0%; Belarusian 0.5%; Kashubian 0.4%; other 1.1%.
Religious affiliation (end of 2003): Roman Catholic 89.8%; other Catholic 0.3%; Polish Orthodox 1.3%; Protestant 0.4%; Jehovah's Witness 0.3%; other (mostly nonreligious) 7.9%.
Major cities (2002): Warsaw 1,671,670 (urban agglom.; 2001) 2,282,000; Łódź 789,318; Kraków 758,544; Wrocław 640,367; Poznań 578,886; Gdańsk 461,334.

Vital statistics

Birth rate per 1,000 population (2004): 9.3 (world avg. 21.1); (2003) legitimate 84.2%; illegitimate 15.8%.
Death rate per 1,000 population (2004): 9.5 (world avg. 9.0).
Natural increase rate per 1,000 population (2004): –0.2 (world avg. 12.1).
Total fertility rate (avg. births per childbearing woman; 2004): 1.2.
Marriage rate per 1,000 population (2004): 5.0.
Divorce rate per 1,000 population (2004): 1.5.
Life expectancy at birth (2004): male 70.7 years; female 79.2 years.
Major causes of death per 100,000 population (2001): diseases of the circulatory system 449.8; malignant neoplasms (cancers) 228.3; accidents, poisoning, and violence 64.8; diseases of the respiratory system 40.8.

National economy

Budget (2002). Revenue: Zł 143,022,000,000 (value-added tax 40.0%, income tax 27.3%, excise tax 21.9%, nontax revenue 10.8%). Expenditures: Zł 182,922,000,000 (social security and welfare 25.2%, public debt 13.1%, education 12.2%, defense 5.1%).
Gross national product (2004): U.S.$232,398,000,000 (U.S.$6,090 per capita).

Structure of gross domestic product and labour force

	2001 in value Zł '000,000	2001 % of total value	2003 labour force	2003 % of labour force
Agriculture	24,731.9	3.2	2,508,000	14.8
Mining	15,283.4	2.0	247,000	1.5
Manufacturing	118,590.1	15.6	2,592,000	15.3
Public utilities	24,213.6	3.2	250,000	1.5
Construction	48,194.5	6.3	803,000	4.7
Transp. and commun.	48,191.9	6.3	823,000	4.9
Trade, restaurants	142,645.0	18.7	2,191,000	12.9
Finance, real estate	100,687.2	13.2	975,000	5.8
Pub. admin., defense	45,155.9	5.9	853,000	5.0
Services	88,401.2	11.6	2,373,000	14.0
Other	105,261.5[5]	13.8[5]	3,329,000[6]	19.6[6]
TOTAL	761,356.2	100.0[4]	16,945,000[4]	100.0

Production (metric tons except as noted). Agriculture, forestry, fishing (2004): potatoes 13,349,932, sugar beets 11,471,800, wheat 9,450,486, rye 4,129,078, sour cherries 205,000, currants 192,000; livestock (number of live animals) 18,100,000 pigs, 5,277,000 cattle; roundwood 32,634,000 cu m; fish catch (2001) 261,376. Mining and quarrying (2002): sulfur 1,620,000; copper ore

(metal content of concentrate) 503,000; silver (recoverable metal content) 1,229. Manufacturing (value added in Zł '000,000; 1999): food products 13,764; beverages 13,582; transport equipment 10,596; nonelectrical machinery 7,542; electrical machinery 7,506. Energy production (consumption): electricity ('000,000 kW-hr; 2004) 150,708 ([2002] 137,058); hard coal ('000 metric tons; 2004) 101,000 ([2002] 82,300); lignite ('000 metric tons; 2004) 61,100 ([2002] 58,200); crude petroleum (barrels; 2002) 5,400,000 (131,000,000); petroleum products (metric tons; 2002) 15,090,000 (16,279,000); natural gas (cu m; 2004) 5,675,000,000 ([2002] 12,064,000,000).
Public debt (external, outstanding; 2003): U.S.$34,964,000,000.
Population economically active (2003): total 16,945,000; activity rate of total population 44.4% (participation rates: 15–64, 64.4%; female 46.0%; unemployed [2004] 19.6%).

Price and earnings indexes (2000 = 100)

	1998	1999	2000	2001	2002	2003	2004
Consumer price index	84.6	90.8	100.0	105.5	107.5	108.3	110.9
Annual earnings index	83.1	90.6	100.0	106.9	111.0	114.2	119.8

Household income and expenditure. Average household size (2002) 2.9; average annual income (2002) Zł 25,600 (U.S.$6,400); sources of income (2001): wages 46.7%, transfers 33.8%, self-employment 13.9%; expenditure (2001): food, beverages, and tobacco 28.0%, housing and energy 25.6%, transportation and communications 14.6%, recreation 6.6%.
Tourism (2003): receipts U.S.$4,069,000,000; expenditures U.S.$2,801,000,000.
Land use as % of total land area (2000): in temporary crops 46.0%, in permanent crops 1.1%, in pasture 13.4%, overall forest area 29.7%.

Foreign trade[7]

Balance of trade (current prices)

	1999	2000	2001	2002	2003	2004
Zł '000,000	–73,656	–75,163	–58,138	–57,478	–56,189	–52,557
% of total	25.3%	21.4%	16.4%	14.7%	11.9%	8.8%

Imports (2001): Zł 206,253,000,000 (machinery and apparatus 26.1%, chemicals and chemical products 13.9%, road vehicles 7.8%, crude petroleum 5.7%, food 5.3%, textile yarn and fabrics 5.2%). *Major import sources* (2004): Germany 24.4%; Italy 7.9%; Russia 7.2%; France 6.7%; China 4.6%.
Exports (2001): Zł 148,115,000,000 (machinery and apparatus 20.4%, road vehicles 8.9%, food 7.1%, furniture and furniture parts 6.9%, chemicals and chemical products 5.9%, apparel and clothing accessories 5.4%, ships and boats 5.2%). *Major export destinations* (2004): Germany 30.0%; Italy 6.1%; France 6.0%; U.K. 5.4%; The Netherlands 4.3%.

Transport and communications

Transport. Railroads (2002): length 22,981 km; (2003) passenger-km 19,638,000,000; (2002) metric ton-km cargo 47,756,000. Roads (2003): total length 423,997 km (paved 70%). Vehicles (2003): passenger cars 11,243,827; trucks and buses 2,274,531. Air transport (2004)[8]: passenger-km 6,821,000,000; metric ton-km cargo 86,329,000; airports (1997) 8.

Communications

Medium	date	unit	number	units per 1,000 persons
Daily newspapers	2000	circulation	4,170,000	108
Radio	2000	receivers	20,200,000	523
Television	2000	receivers	15,500,000	400
Telephones	2003	main lines	12,300,000	319
Cellular telephones	2004	subscribers	23,096,100	599
Personal computers	2004	units	7,362,000	191
Internet	2004	users	9,000,000	233

Education and health

Educational attainment (2002). Percentage of population age 13 and over having: no formal schooling/incomplete primary education 5.6%; complete primary 29.8%; secondary/vocational 51.5%; postsecondary 3.2%; university 9.9%, of which doctorate 0.3%. *Literacy* (2000): 99.8%.

Education (2000–01)

	schools	teachers	students	student/teacher ratio
Primary (age 7–12)	16,766	226,400	3,220,600	14.2
Secondary (age 13–18)	8,587	115,700	2,114,100	18.3
Voc., teacher tr.	8,251	89,700	1,527,900	17.0
Higher	310	79,900	1,584,800	19.8

Health (2002[9]): physicians 86,608 (1 per 446 persons); hospital beds 188,038 (1 per 205 persons); infant mortality rate per 1,000 live births (2004) 6.8.
Food (2001): daily per capita caloric intake 3,397 (vegetable products 75%, animal products 25%); 130% of FAO recommended minimum requirement.

Military

Total active duty personnel (2004): 141,500 (army 62.9%, navy 10.1%, air force 21.2%, centrally controlled staff 5.8%). *Military expenditure as percentage of GDP* (2003): 2.0%; per capita expenditure U.S.$107.

[1]Roman Catholicism has special recognition per 1997 concordat with Vatican City. [2]March 31. [3]Administrative organization effective from Jan. 1, 1999. [4]Detail does not add to total given because of rounding. [5]Taxes less subsidies. [6]Unemployed. [7]Imports c.i.f.; exports f.o.b. [8]LOT only. [9]January 1.

Internet resources for further information:
• **Polish Official Statistics**
  http://www.stat.gov.pl/english/index.htm

Portugal

Official name: República Portuguesa (Portuguese Republic).
Form of government: republic with one legislative house (Assembly of the Republic [230]).
Chief of state: President.
Head of government: Prime Minister.
Capital: Lisbon.
Official language: Portuguese[1].
Official religion: none.
Monetary unit: 1 euro (€) = 100 cents; valuation (Sept. 1, 2005) 1 U.S.$ = €0.80; 1 £ = €1.47[2].

Area and population		area[3, 4]		population
		sq mi	sq km	2003 estimate
Continental Portugal				9,991,654
Regions	**Principal cities**			
Alentejo	Évora	12,080	31,280	767,549
Algarve	Faro	1,920	4,970	405,380
Centre (Centro)	Coimbra	11,030	28,570	2,366,691
Lisbon and Tagus Valley (Lisboa e Vale do Tejo)	Lisbon	1,140	2,950	2,740,237
North (Norte)	Porto	8,220	21,280	3,711,797
Insular Portugal				483,031
Autonomous regions				
Azores (Açores)	Ponta Delgado	897	2,322	240,024
Madeira	Funchal	303	785	243,007
TOTAL		35,580[5]	92,152[5]	10,474,685

Demography

Population (2005): 10,513,000[6].
Density (2005): persons per sq mi 295.5, persons per sq km 114.1.
Urban-rural (2003): urban 54.6%; rural 45.4%.
Sex distribution (2001): male 48.34%; female 51.66%.
Age breakdown (2000): under 15, 17.1%; 15–29, 23.0%; 30–44, 21.5%; 45–59, 17.8%; 60–74, 14.5%; 75 and over, 6.1%.
Population projection[6]: (2010) 10,643,000; (2020) 10,744,000.
Ethnic composition (2000): Portuguese 91.9%; mixed race people from Angola, Mozambique, and Cape Verde 1.6%; Brazilian 1.4%; Marrano 1.2%; other European 1.2%; Han Chinese 0.9%; other 1.8%.
Religious affiliation (2000): Christian 92.4%, of which Roman Catholic 87.4%, independent Christian 2.7%, Protestant 1.3%, other Christian 1.0%; nonreligious/atheist 6.5%; Buddhist 0.6%; other 0.5%.
Major cities (2001)[6]: Lisbon 564,657 (urban agglom. [2005] 1,977,000); Porto 263,131 (urban agglom. [2005] 1,303,000); Braga 164,192; Coimbra 148,443; Funchal 103,961.

Vital statistics

Birth rate per 1,000 population (2004): 10.4 (world avg. 21.1).
Death rate per 1,000 population (2004): 9.7 (world avg. 9.0).
Natural increase rate per 1,000 population (2004): 0.7 (world avg. 12.1).
Total fertility rate (avg. births per childbearing woman; 2004): 1.5.
Marriage rate per 1,000 population (2004): 4.7.
Divorce rate per 1,000 population (2004): 2.2.
Life expectancy at birth (2003–04): male 74.5 years; females 81.0 years.
Major causes of death per 100,000 population (2000): circulatory diseases 396.6; malignant neoplasms (cancers) 207.6; respiratory diseases 99.5; accidents and violence 46.1.

National economy

Budget (2004). Revenue: €59,636,000,000 (social contributions 30.9%, indirect taxes 28.4%, direct taxes 21.0%). Expenditures: €63,511,000,000 (current expenditure 90.0%, development expenditure 10.0%).
Public debt (2001): U.S.$61,224,180,000.
Production (metric tons except as noted). Agriculture, forestry, fishing (2002): potatoes 1,200,000, tomatoes 994,000, grapes 900,000, corn (maize) 851,000, sugar beets 600,000, wheat 387,000, olives 320,000, apples 240,000, oranges 220,000, cork (2004) 120,000; livestock (number of live animals) 5,478,000 sheep, 2,389,000 pigs, 1,399,000 cattle; roundwood 8,742,000 cu m; fish catch (2003) 212,949. Mining and quarrying (2003): marble 800,000; copper (metal content) 77,581; tungsten (metal content) 715; silver 21,100 kg. Manufacturing (value added in U.S.$'000,000; 2000): food products and beverages 1,992; wearing apparel and footwear 1,750; cement, bricks, and ceramics 1,464; textiles 1,254; wood and cork products (incl. metal furniture) 1,252; transport equipment 1,156. Energy production (consumption): electricity (kW-hr; 2002) 46,096,000,000 (47,995,000,000); coal (metric tons; 2002) none (5,668,000); crude petroleum (barrels; 2002) none (86,100,000); petroleum products (metric tons; 2002) 10,577,000 (12,841,000); natural gas (cu m; 2002) none (3,254,000,000).
Tourism (2003): receipts U.S.$6,937,000,000; expenditures U.S.$2,703,000,000.
Population economically active (2003): total 5,470,000; activity rate of total population 52.4% (participation rates: ages 15–64, 73.0%; female 45.9%; unemployed [2004] 6.7%).

Price index (2000 = 100)							
	1998	1999	2000	2001	2002	2003	2004
Consumer price index	95.0	97.2	100.0	104.4	108.1	111.6	114.3

Gross national product (at current market prices; 2004): U.S.$149,790,000,000 (U.S.$14,350 per capita).

Structure of gross domestic product and labour force				
	2002		2003	
	in value €'000	% of total value	labour force	% of labour force
Agriculture	4,083,800	3.2	642,100	11.7
Mining			14,300	0.3
Manufacturing	20,958,200	16.2	1,018,800	18.6
Construction	8,450,800	6.5	583,600	10.7
Public utilities	3,151,400	2.4	36,100	0.7
Trade, hotels	19,816,900	15.3	1,034,200	18.9
Finance	13,920,600	10.8	349,100	6.4
Transp. and commun.	7,171,900	5.5	213,700	3.9
Services			894,800	16.4
Pub. admin., defense	38,982,000	30.1	339,100	6.2
Other	12,864,200[7]	9.9[7]	344,200[8]	6.3[8]
TOTAL	129,399,800	100.0[5]	5,470,000	100.0[5]

Household income and expenditure. Average household size (1999) 3.1; sources of income (1995): wages and salaries 44.4%, self-employment 23.4%, transfers 22.2%; expenditure (1994–95): food 23.9%, housing 20.6%, transportation and communications 18.9%.
Land use as % of total land area (2000): in temporary crops 21.7%, in permanent crops 7.8%, in pasture 15.7%; overall forest area 40.1%.

Foreign trade[9]

Balance of trade (current prices)						
	1999	2000	2001	2002	2003	2004
€'000,000	−13,790	−16,184	−16,731	−14,342	−9,044	−13,011
% of total	22.5%	24.3%	23.4%	20.3%	14.3%	20.6%

Imports (2002): €42,485,000,000 (machinery and apparatus 21.0%; road vehicles 12.5%; chemicals and chemical products 10.6%; food products 10.3%; mineral fuels and lubricants 9.7%). *Major import sources:* Spain 28.9%; Germany 14.9%; France 10.2%; Italy 6.7%; U.K. 5.2%.
Exports (2002): €28,143,000,000 (machinery and apparatus 19.0%; road vehicles 16.1%; apparel and clothing accessories 10.6%; fabrics and made-up articles 6.6%; chemicals and chemical products 5.5%; footwear 5.4%). *Major export destinations:* Spain 20.5%; Germany 18.1%; France 13.3%; U.K. 10.5%; U.S. 5.6%.

Transport and communications

Transport. Railroads (2004): route length 2,850 km; (2001) passenger-km 3,899,000,000; (2001) metric ton-km cargo 2,498,000,000. Roads (2002): total length 72,600 km (paved [1999] 86%). Vehicles (2001): passenger cars 4,416,557; trucks and buses 352,659. Air transport (2004)[10]: passenger-km 16,937,000,000; metric ton-km cargo 239,205,000; airports (2000) 16.

Communications				units per 1,000 persons
Medium	date	unit	number	
Daily newspapers	2000	circulation	324,000	32
Radio	2000	receivers	3,080,000	304
Television	2000	receivers	6,380,000	630
Telephones	2004	main lines	4,237,700	421
Cellular telephones	2004	subscribers	10,300,000	1,023
Personal computers	2004	units	1,402,000	139
Internet	2004	users	2,951,000	295

Education and health

Educational attainment (1991). Percentage of population age 25 and over having: no formal schooling 16.1%; some primary education 61.5%; some secondary 10.6%; postsecondary 3.5%. *Literacy* (2000): total population age 15 and over literate 92.2%; males literate 94.8%; females literate 90.0%.

Education (1998–99)				
	schools	teachers	students	student/ teacher ratio
Primary (age 5–11)				
Secondary (age 12–19)	12,635	145,513	1,563,700	10.7
Vocational	215	6,895	80,130[11]	...
Higher	282	16,192[11]	346,034	...

Health (2001): physicians 33,536 (1 per 310 persons); hospital beds 38,802 (1 per 268 persons); infant mortality rate per 1,000 live births (2004) 3.8.
Food (2002): daily per capita caloric intake 3,741 (vegetable products 71%, animal products 29%); 153% of FAO recommended minimum requirement.

Military

Total active duty personnel (2004): 44,900 (army 59.5%, navy 24.4%, air force 16.1%); U.S. troops (August 2004) 1,000. *Military expenditure as percentage of GDP* (2003): 2.1%; per capita expenditure U.S.$302.

[1]Mirandese, spoken in the vicinity of Miranda do Douro, has official linguistic rights. [2]The escudo was the former monetary unit; on Jan. 1, 2002, Esc 200.48 = €1. [3]Includes new areas based on regional boundaries changed in c. 2001. [4]Regional figures are rounded. [5]Detail does not add to total given because of rounding. [6]De jure figures. [7]Includes imputed bank service charges. [8]Includes 1,900 inadequately defined and 342,300 unemployed. [9]Imports c.i.f.; exports f.o.b. [10]TAP, Air Luxor, Portugalia, and SATA domestic and international airlines. [11]1996–97.

Internet resources for further information:
• Instituto Nacional de Estatística http://www.ine.pt/index_eng.htm
• Banco de Portugal http://www.bportugal.pt/default_e.htm

Puerto Rico

Atlantic
Ocean

Caribbean
Sea

Official name: Estado Libre Asociado
de Puerto Rico (Spanish);
Commonwealth of Puerto Rico.
Political status: self-governing
commonwealth in association with the
United States, having two legislative
houses (Senate [27[1]]; House of
Representatives [51[1]]).
Chief of state: President of the
United States.
Head of government: Governor.
Capital: San Juan.
Official languages: Spanish; English.
Monetary unit: 1 U.S. dollar
(U.S.$) = 100 cents; valuation (Sept. 1,
2005) 1 £ = U.S.$1.84.

Population (2004 estimate)

Municipalities	population	Municipalities	population	Municipalities	population
Adjuntas	18,970	Fajardo	41,860	Naguabo	24,082
Aguada	43,948	Florida	13,655	Naranjito	30,235
Aguadilla	66,277	Guánica	22,456	Orocovis	24,660
Agunas Buenas	30,137	Guayama	45,097	Patillas	20,301
Aibonito	26,938	Guayanilla	23,510	Peñuelas	28,037
Añasco	29,292	Guaynabo	102,169	Ponce	185,744
Arecibo	102,117	Gurabo	39,371	Quebradillas	26,713
Arroyo	19,176	Hatillo	40,879	Rincón	15,577
Barceloneta	22,725	Hormigueros	17,032	Río Grande	54,423
Barranquitas	29,914	Humacao	60,161	Sabana Grande	26,878
Bayamón	225,121	Isabela	46,060	Salinas	31,943
Cabo Rojo	49,584	Jayuya	17,858	San Germán	37,732
Caguas	142,556	Juana Díaz	52,143	San Juan	433,319
Camuy	37,261	Juncos	38,287	San Lorenzo	42,806
Canóvanas	45,369	Lajas	27,170	San Sebastián	45,857
Carolina	187,767	Lares	36,108	Santa Isabel	22,376
Cataño	27,763	Las Marías	11,612	Toa Alta	70,950
Cayey	47,563	Las Piedras	36,603	Toa Baja	95,432
Ceiba	18,254	Loíza	33,509	Trujillo Alto	80,431
Ciales	20,326	Luquillo	20,329	Utuado	35,437
Cidra	45,054	Manatí	47,501	Vega Alta	38,911
Coamo	38,729	Maricao	6,519	Vega Baja	63,710
Comerío	19,854	Maunabo	12,854	Vieques	9,253
Corozal	38,004	Mayagüez	97,350	Villalba	29,277
Culebra	1,972	Moca	41,841	Yabucoa	40,061
Dorado	34,995	Morovis	31,430	Yauco	47,680
				TOTAL	3,894,855

Demography

Area: 3,515 sq mi, 9,104 sq km.
Population (2005): 3,911,000.
Density (2005): persons per sq mi 1,113, persons per sq km 429.6.
Urban-rural (2003): urban 96.7%; rural 3.3%.
Sex distribution (2004[2]): male 48.05%; female 51.95%.
Age breakdown (2004[2]): under 15, 22.2%; 15–29, 22.6%; 30–44, 20.3%; 45–59, 18.1%; 60–74, 11.5%; 75 and over, 5.3%.
Population projection: (2010) 3,985,000; (2020) 4,076,000.
Ethnic composition (2000): local white 72.1%; black 15.0%; mulatto 10.0%; U.S. white 2.2%; other 0.7%.
Religious affiliation (2000): Roman Catholic 74.8%; Protestant 13.3%; independent Christian 6.3%; marginal Christian 2.5%; nonreligious 1.6%; other 1.5%.
Major metropolitan areas (2002): San Juan 2,541,914; Aguadilla 319,743; Ponce 266,276; San Germán 139,190; Yauco 120,158.

Vital statistics

Birth rate per 1,000 population (2004): 13.8 (world avg. 21.1).
Death rate per 1,000 population (2004): 7.4 (world avg. 9.0).
Natural increase rate per 1,000 population (2004): 6.4 (world avg. 12.1).
Total fertility rate (avg. births per childbearing woman; 2004): 1.9.
Marriage rate per 1,000 population (2003): 6.5.
Divorce rate per 1,000 population (2003): 4.7.
Life expectancy at birth (2004): male 73.5 years; female 81.7 years.
Major causes of death per 100,000 population (2003): circulatory diseases 219.4; malignant neoplasms (cancers) 125.3; diabetes mellitus 65.9; accidents 27.4; violence and suicide 26.6; pneumonia and influenza 26.4.

National economy

Budget. Revenue (2002): U.S.$10,556,400,000 (tax revenue 62.6%, of which income taxes 46.5%, excise taxes 14.1%; federal grants 19.0%; nontax revenue 18.4%). Expenditures: U.S.$10,556,400,000 (2001: welfare 22.3%; education 22.3%; public safety 15.7%; debt service 9.8%; health 9.2%).
Public debt (outstanding; December 2004): U.S.$39,420,000,000.
Production (in metric tons except as noted). Agriculture, forestry, fishing (2004): sugarcane (2002) 320,000, plantains 105,000, bananas 52,400, pineapples 19,100, oranges 18,000, pumpkins, squash, and gourds 14,300, mangoes 12,150, coffee 10,000; livestock (number of live animals) 420,000 cattle, 100,000 pigs; roundwood, n.a.; fish catch (2003) 2,919. Mining (value of production in U.S.$'000; 2002): crushed stone 38. Manufacturing (value added in U.S.$'000; 2001): chemicals, pharmaceuticals, and allied products 17,365; nonelectrical machinery 3,320; professional and scientific equipment 1,874; electrical machinery 1,739; beverages 1,455. Energy production (consumption): electricity (kW-hr; 2004) 24,100,000,000 (20,260,000,000); coal (metric tons; 2002) none (176,000); crude petroleum (barrels; 2004) none (81,000,000); petroleum products (metric tons; 2002) 3,001,000 (6,610,000).

Gross national product (2004): U.S.$50,320,000,000 (U.S.$12,920 per capita).

Structure of gross domestic product and labour force

	2002–03		2003	
	in value U.S.$'000,000	% of total value	labour force	% of labour force
Agriculture	203,000	0.3	24,000	1.7
Manufacturing	31,297,300	42.1	139,000	10.0
Mining	1,759,800	2.4	1,000	0.1
Construction			87,000	6.3
Public utilities	5,145,000	6.9	13,000	0.9
Transp. and commun.			43,000	3.1
Trade	8,622,500	11.6	258,000	18.5
Finance, real estate	12,731,600	17.1	43,000	3.1
Pub. admin., defense	7,146,800	9.6		
Services	7,390,800	9.9	617,000	44.3
Other	65,600[3]	–0.1[3]	167,000[4]	12.0[4]
TOTAL	74,362,400	100.0[5]	1,393,000[5]	100.0

Population economically active (July 2004): total 1,400,400; activity rate 35.9% (participation rates: ages 16 and over, 46.3%; female [2002] 42.6%; unemployed [2004] 10.6%).

Price index (2000 = 100)

	1998	1999	2000	2001	2002	2003	2004
Consumer price index	89.9	94.6	100.0	107.0	113.6	122.4	137.1

Household income and expenditure (2002). Average family size 3.6; average income per family (2004) U.S.$37,990; sources of income: wages and salaries 56.3%, transfers 29.5%, self-employment 6.4%, rent 5.2%, other 2.6%; expenditure (1999): food and beverages 18.8%, health care 17.8%, transportation 12.8%, housing 12.1%, household furnishings 11.6%.
Tourism (2003): receipts U.S.$2,676,600,000; expenditures U.S.$985,000,000.
Land use as % of total land area (2000): in temporary crops 3.9%, in permanent crops 5.5%, in pasture 23.7%; overall forest area 25.8%.

Foreign trade

Balance of trade (current prices)[2]

	1999	2000	2001	2002	2003	2004
U.S.$'000,000	+9,600	+11,500	+17,800	+18,200	+21,500	+16,200
% of total	15.9%	17.6%	23.4%	23.9%	24.2%	17.2%

Imports (2002–03): U.S.$33,800,000,000 (chemicals 44.8%, electronics 10.2%, transport equipment 7.0%, food and beverages 6.7%, refined petroleum 6.0%). *Major import sources:* U.S. 48.9%; Ireland 20.7%; Japan 3.9%.
Exports (2002–03): U.S.$55,200,000,000 (pharmaceutical and chemical products 71.8%, electronic and electrical products 12.5%). *Major export destinations:* U.S. 86.4%; The Netherlands 2.1%; Belgium 2.0%.

Transport and communications

Transport. Railroads (2004)[6]: length 59 mi, 96 km. Roads (2004): total length 15,738 mi, 25,328 km (paved 93%). Vehicles: passenger cars (2001) 2,064,100; trucks and buses (1999) 306,600. Air transport (2001): passenger arrivals and departures 9,396,306; cargo loaded and unloaded 215,603 metric tons[7]; airports (1998) with scheduled flights 7.

Communications

Medium	date	unit	number	units per 1,000 persons
Daily newspapers	2000	circulation	481,000	126
Radio	2000	receivers	2,830,000	742
Television	2000	receivers	1,290,000	338
Telephones	2002	main lines	1,329,500	344
Cellular telephones	2001	subscribers	1,211,100	315
Internet	2002	users	600,000	155

Education and health

Educational attainment (2000). Percentage of population age 25 and over having: no formal schooling to secondary education 25.4%; some upper secondary to some higher 56.3%; undergraduate or graduate degree 18.3%.
Literacy (2002): total population age 15 and over literate 94.1%.

Education (2000–01)

	schools	teachers	students	student/ teacher ratio
Primary (age 5–12)	1,129[8]	24,663	516,458	20.9
Secondary (age 13–18)	363[8]	12,208	260,346	21.3
Higher	45[9]	9,045[9]	236,734	...

Health: physicians (2001) 7,623 (1 per 504 persons); hospital beds (2002) 12,351 (1 per 312 persons); infant mortality rate (2004) 8.4.

Military

Total active duty U.S. personnel (December 2004): 282[10].

[1]Number of members per constitution. Excludes additional seats allotted to either the Senate or House of Representatives to meet ⅓ total representation requirements for minority parties per constitution. [2]For fiscal year ending June 30. [3]Statistical discrepancy. [4]Unemployed. [5]Detail does not add to total given because of rounding. [6]Privately owned railway for sugarcane transport only. [7]Luis Muñoz Marín International Airport only. [8]Public schools only. [9]1985–86. [10]The U.S. naval base at Ceiba was closed in March 2004.

Internet resources for further information:
• **Junta de Planificación** http://www.jp.gobierno.pr
• **Government Development Bank for Puerto Rico** http://www.gdb-pur.com/homeEng.htm

Qatar

Official name: Dawlat Qatar (State of Qatar).
Form of government: constitutional emirate[1].
Heads of state and government: Emir assisted by Prime Minister.
Capital: Doha.
Official language: Arabic.
Official religion: Islam.
Monetary unit: 1 riyal (QR) = 100 dirhams; valuation (Sept. 1, 2005) 1 U.S.$ = QR 3.64; 1 £ = QR 6.70.

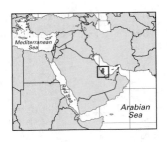

Area and population

Municipalities	Capitals	area sq mi	area sq km	population 2004 census
Ad-Dawhah (Doha)	—	51	132	339,847
Al-Ghuwayriyah	Al-Ghuwayriyah	240	622	2,159
Jarayan al-Batinah	Jarayan al-Batinah	1,434[2]	3,715[2]	6,678
Al-Jumayliyah	Al-Jumayliyah	991[3]	2,565[3]	10,303
Al-Khawr	Al-Khawr	385	996	31,547
Ar-Rayyan	Ar-Rayyan	343	889	272,860
Ash-Shamal	Madinat ash-Shamal	348	901	4,915
Umm Sa'id	Umm Sa'id	2	2	12,674
Umm Salal	Umm Salal Muhammad	190	493	31,605
Al-Wakrah	Al-Wakrah	430[2]	1,114[2]	31,441
TOTAL		4,412	11,427	744,029

Demography

Population (2005): 773,000.
Density (2005): persons per sq mi 175.2, persons per sq km 67.6.
Urban-rural (2003): urban 92.0%; rural 8.0%.
Sex distribution (2004): male 66.72%; female 33.28%.
Age breakdown (2004): under 15, 22.5%; 15–29, 25.0%; 30–44, 34.4%; 45–59, 15.6%; 60–74, 2.2%; 75 and over, 0.3%.
Population projection: (2010) 869,000; (2020) 1,007,000.
Doubling time: 63 years.
Ethnic composition (2000): Arab 52.5%, of which Palestinian 13.4%, Qatari 13.3%, Lebanese 10.4%, Syrian 9.4%; Persian 16.5%; Indo-Pakistani 15.2%; black African 9.5%; other 6.3%.
Religious affiliation (2000): Muslim *c.* 83%, of which Sunni *c.* 73%, Shi'i *c.* 10%; Christian *c.* 10%, of which Roman Catholic *c.* 6%; Hindu *c.* 3%; nonreligious *c.* 2%; other *c.* 2%.
Major cities (2004): Ad-Dawhah (Doha) 339,847; Ar-Rayyan 272,860; Al-Wakrah (1997) 20,205; Umm Salal (1997) 15,935.

Vital statistics

Birth rate per 1,000 population (2004): 15.6 (world avg. 21.1).
Death rate per 1,000 population (2004): 4.5 (world avg. 9.0).
Natural increase rate per 1,000 population (2004): 11.1 (world avg. 12.1).
Total fertility rate (avg. births per childbearing woman; 2004): 2.9.
Marriage rate per 1,000 population (2004): 3.4.
Divorce rate per 1,000 population (2004): 1.1.
Life expectancy at birth (2004): male 70.9 years; female 76.0 years.
Major causes of death per 100,000 population (2002)[4]: diseases of the circulatory system 95; accidents and violence 74; malignant neoplasms (cancers) 45; endocrine, metabolic, and nutritional disorders 32; diseases of the respiratory system 21; ill-defined conditions 73.

National economy

Budget (2003–04). Revenue: QR 29,155,000,000 (oil and natural gas revenue 67.5%, investment income 23.5%, other 9.0%). Expenditures: QR 23,212,000,000 (current expenditure 73.6%, of which wages and salaries 26.0%; capital expenditure 26.4%).
Production (metric tons except as noted). Agriculture, forestry, fishing (2002): dates 16,500, tomatoes 11,000, pumpkin and squash 8,500, barley 4,650, dry onions 4,000, melons 3,450, watermelons 1,400; livestock (number of live animals; 2002) 200,000 sheep, 179,000 goats, 50,000 camels, 15,000 cattle; roundwood, n.a.; fish catch (2003) 11,000. Mining and quarrying (2002): limestone 900,000; sulfur 221,000; gypsum, sand and gravel, and clay are also produced. Manufacturing (value added in QR '000,000; 2002): chemicals, chemical products, and petroleum products 1,464; textiles, wearing apparel, and leather products 1,126; paper products, printing, and publishing 430; base metals 166. Energy production (consumption): electricity (kW-hr; 2002) 10,511,000,000 (10,511,000,000); coal, none (n.a.); crude petroleum (barrels; 2004) 276,000,000 ([2002] 23,900,000); petroleum products (metric tons; 2002) 8,317,000 (3,158,000); natural gas (cu m; 2002) 29,300,000,000 (11,629,000,000).
Tourism (2003): receipts from visitors U.S.$369,000,000; expenditures by nationals abroad U.S.$471,000,000.
Population economically active (1997): total 280,122; activity rate of total population 53.7% (participation rates: ages 15–64, 73.6%; female 13.5%; unemployed [2001] 2.7%).

Price index (2000 = 100)

	1998	1999	2000	2001	2002	2003	2004
Consumer price index	96.3	98.3	100.0	101.4	101.7	104.0	111.1

Gross national product (2004): U.S.$29,300,000,000 (U.S.$37,690 per capita).

Structure of gross domestic product and labour force

	2003 in value QR '000,000	2003 % of total value	2001 labour force	2001 % of labour force
Agriculture, fishing	260	0.4	7,074	2.2
Oil, natural gas	42,350	59.8	13,138	4.1
Manufacturing	3,960	5.6	41,041	12.7
Construction	2,850	4.0	59,286	18.4
Public utilities	980	1.4	4,951	1.5
Transp. and commun.	2,360	3.3	9,860	3.1
Trade	4,030	5.7	42,612	13.2
Finance	5,348	7.6	10,132	3.0
Pub. admin., defense	8,850	12.5	43,785	13.6
Services	1,210	1.7	76,082	23.6
Other	−1,370	−2.0	14,945[5]	4.6[5]
TOTAL	70,828	100.0	322,906	100.0

Household income and expenditure. Average household size (2002) 7.1; income per household: n.a.; sources of income, n.a.; expenditure (2001): housing 17.8%, food 16.5%, transportation 15.8%, household furnishings 8.6%, clothing and footwear 7.1%, education 5.5%, communications 5.5%.
Land use as % of total land area (2000): in temporary crops 1.6%, in permanent crops 0.3%, in pasture 4.5%; overall forest area 0.1%.

Foreign trade[6]

Balance of trade (current prices)

	2000	2001	2002	2003	2004
U.S.$'000,000	+8,664	+7,485	+7,327	+9,024	+13,275
% of total	59.7%	52.5%	50.1%	50.9%	55.1%

Imports (2002): U.S.$4,052,000,000 (machinery and apparatus 30.7%, of which general industrial machinery 9.0%, specialized machinery 6.4%; road vehicles 13.3%; food and live animals 10.4%; chemicals and chemical products 6.8%). *Major import sources* (2004): France 26.7%; U.S. 9.6%; Saudi Arabia 9.5%; U.A.E. 6.3%; Germany 5.3%; Japan 5.2%; U.K. 5.1%.
Exports (2002): U.S.$8,231,000,000 (liquefied natural gas 42.6%; crude petroleum 35.0%; refined petroleum 6.7%; iron and steel 2.8%). *Major export destinations* (2004): Japan 42.2%; South Korea 15.9%; Singapore 9.2%; India 5.4%; United Arab Emirates 2.9%.

Transport and communications

Transport. Railroads: none. Roads (1999): total length 764 mi, 1,230 km (paved 90%). Vehicles (2002): passenger cars 230,155; trucks and buses 118,685. Air transport (2004)[7]: passenger-km 12,171,615,000; metric ton-km cargo 469,190,000; airports (2002) with scheduled flights 1.

Communications

Medium	date	unit	number	units per 1,000 persons
Daily newspapers	2004	circulation	95,000[8]	126
Radio	1997	receivers	250,000	432
Television	1998	receivers	490,000	846
Telephones	2004	main lines	190,900	308
Cellular telephones	2004	subscribers	490,300	792
Personal computers	2004	units	133,000	215
Internet	2004	users	165,000	267

Education and health

Educational attainment (2004). Percentage of population age 10 and over having: no formal education 34.8%, of which illiterate 10.2%; primary 13.0%; preparatory (lower secondary) 16.2%; secondary 20.0%; postsecondary 15.9%; other 0.1%. *Literacy* (2001): total population age 15 and over literate 81.7%; males literate 80.8%; females literate 83.7%.

Education (2001)[9]

	schools	teachers	students	student/teacher ratio
Primary (age 6–11)	113	3,445	37,923	11.0
Secondary (age 12–17)	102	3,296	32,624	9.9
Vocational	5	109	778	7.1
Higher	1	669	9,915	14.8

Health (2002): physicians 1,518 (1 per 399 persons); hospital beds 1,357 (1 per 447 persons); infant mortality rate per 1,000 live births (2004) 19.3.

Military

Total active duty personnel (2004): 12,400 (army 68.6%, navy 14.5%, air force 16.9%); U.S. troops (August 2004) 6,600. *Military expenditure as percentage of GDP* (2003): 9.9%; per capita expenditure U.S.$2,646.

---

[1]Constitution came into force on June 9, 2005. [2]Umm Sa'id municipality created in 2004 from parts of Jarayan al-Batinah and Al-Wakrah municipalities. [3]Includes the area of the unpopulated and formerly disputed (with Bahrain) Hawar Islands. The International Court of Justice awarded Hawar to Bahrain in 2001. Qatar was awarded jurisdiction over some nearby islets. [4]Projected rates based on about 42% of total deaths. [5]Including 12,615 unemployed. [6]Import figures are f.o.b. in balance of trade and c.i.f. in commodities and trading partners. [7]Qatar Airways. [8]For top four dailies excluding *The Peninsula*. [9]Public schools only; number of students in private schools (2001–02) 41,344, of which primary 26,456, preparatory 9,072, secondary 5,816.

Internet resources for further information:
• **Qatar: The Planning Council http://www.planning.gov.qa**
• **Qatar National Bank http://www.qnb.com.qa/publications**

Réunion

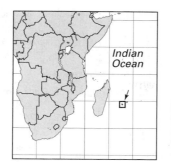

Indian Ocean

Official name: Département de la Réunion (Department of Réunion).
Political status: overseas department (France) with two legislative houses (General Council [49]; Regional Council [45]).
Chief of state: President of France.
Heads of government: Prefect (for France); President of General Council (for Réunion); President of Regional Council (for Réunion).
Capital: Saint-Denis.
Official language: French.
Official religion: none.
Monetary unit: 1 euro (€) = 100 cents; valuation (Sept. 1, 2005) 1 U.S.$ = €0.80; 1 £ = €1.47[1].

Area and population		area		population
				1999
Arrondissements	Capitals	sq mi	sq km	census
Saint-Benoît	Saint-Benoît	285	737	101,804
Saint-Denis	Saint-Denis	163	421	236,599
Saint-Paul	Saint-Paul	180	467	138,551
Saint-Pierre	Saint-Pierre	341	883	229,346
TOTAL		968[2, 3]	2,507[2, 3]	706,300

Demography

Population (2005): 780,000.
Density (2005): persons per sq mi 805.8, persons per sq km 311.1.
Urban-rural (2003): urban 91.5%; rural 8.5%.
Sex distribution (2004[4]): male 49.12%; female 50.88%.
Age breakdown (1999): under 15, 27.0%; 15–29, 24.8%; 30–44, 24.4%; 45–59, 13.8%; 60–74, 7.2%; 75 and over, 2.8%.
Population projection: (2010) 834,000; (2020) 927,000.
Doubling time: 52 years.
Ethnic composition (2000): mixed race (black-white-South Asian) 42.6%; local white 25.6%; South Asian 23.0%, of which Tamil 20.0%; Chinese 3.4%; East African 3.4%; Malagasy 1.4%; other 0.6%.
Religious affiliation (2000): Christian 87.8%, of which Roman Catholic 81.8%, Pentecostal 4.2%; Hindu 4.5%; Muslim 4.2%; nonreligious 1.7%; other 1.8%.
Major cities (2004): Saint-Denis 133,600[5] (agglomeration [2003] 178,000); Saint-Paul 92,500[5]; Saint-Pierre 74,000[5] (agglomeration 140,600); Le Tampon 66,600[5, 6]; Saint-Louis (1999) 43,519[5].

Vital statistics

Birth rate per 1,000 population (2003): 19.0 (world avg. 21.1); legitimate *c.* 37%; illegitimate *c.* 63%.
Death rate per 1,000 population (2003): 5.3 (world avg. 9.0).
Natural increase rate per 1,000 population (2003): 13.7 (world avg. 12.1).
Total fertility rate (avg. births per childbearing woman; 2003): 2.4.
Marriage rate per 1,000 population (2003): 4.2.
Divorce rate per 1,000 population (2003): 1.1.
Life expectancy at birth (2003): male 71.3 years; female 79.8 years.
Major causes of death per 100,000 population (2000): diseases of the circulatory system 162.8; malignant neoplasms (cancers) 112.4; accidents, suicide, and violence 54.7; diseases of the respiratory system 33.1.

National economy

Budget (2002). Revenue: €696,000,000 (receipts from the French central government and local administrative bodies 49.9%, indirect taxes 19.9%, subsidies 11.2%, loans 8.8%, direct taxes 7.6%). Expenditures: €696,000,000 (current expenditures 67.2%, development expenditures 32.8%).
Public debt (external, outstanding): n.a.
Tourism (2003): receipts U.S.$351,400,000; expenditures, n.a.
Gross national product (2003): U.S.$10,900,000,000 (U.S.$14,390 per capita).

Structure of gross domestic product and labour force					
	2000		1999		
	in value €'000,000	% of total value	labour force	% of labour force	
Agriculture, fishing	431	5.5	9,562	3.2	
Manufacturing, mining	303	3.8	13,424	4.5	
Public utilities	628	8.0			
Construction			11,003	3.7	
Transp. and commun.	478	6.1	5,494	1.8	
Trade, restaurants	1,015	12.9	24,658	8.3	
Finance, real estate, business services	1,485	18.8	16,076	5.4	
Pub. admin., defense	1,075	13.6	39,052	13.1	
Services	2,777	35.2	54,408	18.3	
Other	−308[7]	−3.9[7]	124,203[8]	41.7[8]	
TOTAL	7,884	100.0	297,880	100.0	

Production (metric tons except as noted). Agriculture, forestry, fishing (2004): sugarcane 2,000,000, corn (maize) 17,000, pineapples 10,000, onions 6,000, cauliflower 5,300, cabbages 5,000, tomatoes 4,000, carrots 3,800, potatoes 3,700, eggplants 3,200, pimento 800, ginger 200, vanilla 35, tobacco 20, geranium essence (1998) 6.3; livestock (number of live animals) 79,000 pigs, 37,000 goats, 30,000 cattle; roundwood 36,100 cu m; fish catch (2003) 2,844. Mining and quarrying: gravel and sand for local use. Manufacturing (value added in

F '000,000; 1997): food and beverages 1,019, of which meat and milk products 268; construction materials (mostly cement) 394; fabricated metals 258; printing and publishing 192. Energy production (consumption): electricity (kW-hr; 2002) 1,613,000,000 (1,613,000,000); petroleum products (metric tons; 2002) none (739,000).
Population economically active (1999): total 297,880; activity rate of total population 42.2% (participation rates: ages 15–64, 63.9%; female 44.8%; unemployed [2003] 32.9%).

Price and earnings indexes (2000 = 100)							
	1998	1999	2000	2001	2002	2003	2004
Consumer price index	97.8	98.3	100.0	101.6	103.6	105.8	108.0
Monthly earnings index[9, 10]	97.5	98.8	100.0	101.0	102.4	103.1	…

Household income and expenditure. Average household size (1999) 3.3; average annual income per household (1997) F 136,800 (U.S.$23,438); sources of income (1997): wages and salaries and self-employment 41.8%, transfer payments 41.3%, other 16.9%; expenditure (2001): housing and energy 24.0%, transportation and communications 20.0%, food and beverages 17.0%, recreation and culture 10.0%.
Land use as % of total land area (2000): in temporary crops *c.* 14%, in permanent crops *c.* 2%, in pasture *c.* 5%; overall forest area *c.* 28%.

Foreign trade

Balance of trade (current prices)					
	1999	2000	2001	2002	2003	2004
€'000,000	−2,220	−2,495	−2,627	−2,711	−3,000	−2,917
% of total	85.2%	84.6%	85.2%	86.0%	86.3%	85.4%

Imports (2003): €3,238,000,000 (transport equipment 18.5%, of which automobiles 12.4%; food and agricultural products 14.8%; chemicals and chemical products 11.1%; machinery and equipment 10.6%; mineral fuels 5.9%).
Major import sources (2002): France *c.* 59%; U.S. *c.* 6%; Germany *c.* 4%; Australia *c.* 3%.
Exports (2003): €238,000,000 (food products 70.0%, of which sugar 49.6%; machinery and apparatus 12.1%; transportation equipment and parts 5.7%).
Major export destinations (2002): France *c.* 65%; Japan *c.* 7%; Mayotte *c.* 5%; Madagascar *c.* 3%.

Transport and communications

Transport. Railroads: [11]. Roads (2001): total length 754 mi, 1,214 km (paved [1991] 79%). Vehicles (1999): passenger cars 190,300; trucks and buses 44,300. Air transport (2004)[12]: passenger-km 2,234,972,000; metric ton-km cargo 45,498,000; airports (2001) with scheduled flights 2.

Communications				units per 1,000
Medium	date	unit	number	persons
Daily newspapers	1996	circulation	83,000	123
Radio	1997	receivers	173,000	252
Television	1998	receivers	130,000	186
Telephones	2001	main lines	300,000	410
Cellular telephones	2002	subscribers	489,800	659
Personal computers	1999	units	32,000	45
Internet	2002	users	150,000	202

Education and health

Educational attainment (1999). Percentage of population age 25 and over having: no formal schooling through incomplete secondary education 83.0%; complete secondary 7.4%; some higher 3.9%; complete higher 5.7%. *Literacy* (2003): total population age 15 and over literate 88.9%; males literate 87.0%; females literate 90.8%.

Education (2003–04)				student/
	schools	teachers	students	teacher ratio
Primary (age 6–10)	532	6,148	121,789	19.8
Secondary (age 11–17)	120	8,051	101,522	12.6
Higher[13]	1	343[14]	10,759	…

Health: physicians (2004[4]) 1,791 (1 per 424 persons); hospital beds (2003[4]) 2,027 (1 per 369 persons); infant mortality rate per 1,000 live births (2003) 6.2.
Food (2004): daily per capita caloric intake, n.a.

Military

Total active duty personnel (2004): 3,600 French troops[15].

[1]The French franc (F) was the former monetary unit; on Jan. 1, 2002, F 6.56 = €1. [2]Detail does not add to total given because of rounding. [3]Excludes the French overseas territory of French Southern and Antarctic Territories (FSAT), which has been administered from Réunion since January 2001. FSAT comprises numerous, not permanently inhabited, archipelagos as well as other remote islands in the South Indian Ocean and the French-claimed part of Antarctica. [4]January 1. [5]Population of commune. [6]Within Saint-Pierre agglomeration. [7]Less imputed bank service charges. [8]Unemployed. [9]Indexes refer to December. [10]Minimum salary in public administration. [11]No public railways; railways in use are for sugar industry. [12]Air Austral only. [13]University only. [14]2001–02. [15]Includes troops stationed on Mayotte.

Internet resources for further information:
• **INSEE: Réunion**
  http://www.insee.fr/fr/insee_regions/reunion/home/home_page.asp
• **Ministère de l'Outre-mer (Paris) http://www.outre-mer.gouv.fr**

Romania

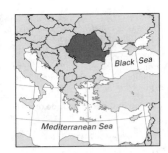

Official name: România (Romania).
Form of government: unitary republic with two legislative houses (Senate [137]; Assembly of Deputies [332[1]]).
Chief of state: President.
Head of government: Prime Minister.
Capital: Bucharest.
Official language: Romanian.
Official religion: none.
Monetary unit: 1 (new) leu[2] (plural lei [RON]) = 100 bani; valuation (Sept. 1, 2005) 1 U.S.$ = RON 2.80; 1 £ = RON 5.15.

Area and population

Counties	area sq km	population 2002 census	Counties	area sq km	population 2002 census
Alba	6,242	382,747	Iaşi	5,476	816,910
Arad	7,754	461,791	Ilfov	1,583	300,123
Argeş	6,826	652,625	Maramureş	6,304	510,110
Bacău	6,621	706,623	Mehedinţi	4,933	306,732
Bihor	7,544	600,246	Mureş	6,714	580,851
Bistriţa-Năsăud	5,355	311,657	Neamţ	5,896	554,516
Botoşani	4,986	452,834	Olt	5,498	489,274
Brăila	4,766	373,174	Prahova	4,716	829,945
Braşov	5,363	589,028	Sălaj	3,864	248,015
Buzău	6,103	496,214	Satu Mare	4,418	367,281
Călăraşi	5,088	324,617	Sibiu	5,432	421,724
Caraş-Severin	8,520	333,219	Suceava	8,553	688,435
Cluj	6,674	702,755	Teleorman	5,790	436,025
Constanţa	7,071	715,151	Timiş	8,697	677,926
Covasna	3,710	222,449	Tulcea	8,499	256,492
Dâmboviţa	4,054	541,763	Vâlcea	5,765	413,247
Dolj	7,414	734,231	Vaslui	5,318	455,049
Galaţi	4,466	619,556	Vrancea	4,857	387,632
Giurgiu	3,526	297,859	**Municipality**		
Gorj	5,602	387,308	Bucharest	238	1,926,334
Harghita	6,639	326,222	**TOTAL**	238,391	21,680,974
Hunedoara	7,063	485,712			
Ialomiţa	4,453	296,572			

Demography

Population (2005): 21,602,000.
Density (2005): persons per sq mi 234.7, persons per sq km 90.6.
Urban-rural (2002): urban 53.3%; rural 46.7%.
Sex distribution (2002): male 48.83%; female 51.17%.
Age breakdown (2002): under 15, 17.3%; 15–29, 23.6%; 30–44, 21.1%; 45–59, 18.8%; 60–74, 14.3%; 75 and over, 4.9%.
Population projection: (2010) 21,239,000; (2020) 20,265,000.
Ethnic composition (2002): Romanian 89.5%; Hungarian 6.6%; Roma (Gypsy) 2.5%; other 1.4%.
Religious affiliation (2002): Romanian Orthodox 86.7%; Protestant 6.4%; Roman Catholic 4.7%; Greek Orthodox 0.9%; Muslim 0.3%; other 1.0%.
Major cities (2002): Bucharest 1,934,449; Constanţa 312,010; Timişoara 308,765; Iaşi 303,714; Craiova 300,487; Cluj-Napoca 297,014.

Vital statistics

Birth rate per 1,000 population (2002): 9.7 (world avg. 21.1).
Death rate per 1,000 population (2002): 12.4 (world avg. 9.0).
Natural increase rate per 1,000 population (2002): −2.7 (world avg. 12.1).
Total fertility rate (avg. births per childbearing woman; 2002): 1.3.
Marriage rate per 1,000 population (2002): 5.9.
Life expectancy at birth (2002): male 67.4 years; female 74.8 years.
Major causes of death per 100,000 population (2002): circulatory disease 771.9; malignant neoplasms (cancers) 199.2; diseases of the digestive system 74.4; respiratory disease 70.7.

National economy

Budget ('000,000 [old] lei; 2001). Revenue: 146,937,400 (value-added tax 35.2%, excise tax 18.6%, personal income tax 16.6%, nontax revenue 6.5%). Expenditures: 137,565,000 (economic affairs 23.8%, social security and welfare 17.2%, public order 14.5%, defense 12.8%).
Public debt (external, outstanding; 2003): U.S.$11,730,000,000.
Population economically active (2003): total 9,914,300; activity rate 45.6% (participation rates: ages 15–64, 62.4%; female 44.9%; unemployed [October 2003–September 2004] 6.9%.

Price and earnings indexes (2000 = 100)

	1998	1999	2000	2001	2002	2003	2004
Consumer price index	47.1	68.6	100.0	134.5	164.8	190.0	212.5
Annual earnings index	48.0	71.5	100.0	138.9	178.6	224.0	274.5

Household income and expenditure. Average household size (2000) 3.1.
Production (metric tons). Agriculture (2003): corn (maize) 9,577,000, potatoes 3,947,000, wheat 2,496,000, grapes 1,078,000, plums 910,000, apples 811,000, sugar beets 764,000; livestock (number of live animals) 7,312,000 sheep, 5,058,000 pigs, 2,878,000 cattle; roundwood (2002) 15,154,000 cu m; fish catch (2001) 18,455. Mining (2003): iron (metal content) 79,000; zinc 23,464[3]; copper 21,317[3]; lead 18,102[3]. Manufacturing (value added in U.S.$'000,000; 2001): food products 2,006; textiles and wearing apparel 811; wood and wood products (incl. metal furniture) 704; beverages 494; chemicals and chemical products 442; transport equipment 437; nonelectrical machinery 407. Energy

production (consumption): electricity (kW-hr; 2004) 57,036,000,000 ([2002] 52,081,000,000); hard coal (metric tons; 2002) 13,000 (3,470,000); lignite (metric tons; 2004) 31,600,000 ([2002] 30,800,000); crude petroleum (barrels; 2004) 41,000,000 ([2002] 89,000,000); petroleum products (metric tons; 2002) 11,583,000 (8,531,000); natural gas (cu m; 2004) 12,564,000,000 ([2002] 15,538,000,000).
Gross national product (2004): U.S.$63,910,000,000 (U.S.$2,920 per capita).

Structure of gross domestic product and labour force

	2002 in value '000,000,000 (old) lei	2002 % of total value	2003 labour force	2003 % of labour force
Agriculture	171,131	11.3	3,292,400	33.2
Mining	}		138,200	1.4
Manufacturing	428,859	28.4	1,999,100	20.2
Public utilities	}		187,100	1.9
Construction	84,265	5.6	425,900	4.3
Transp. and commun.	150,399	9.9	461,400	4.7
Trade	168,948	11.2	980,700	9.9
Finance	236,912	15.7	232,800	2.3
Pub. admin.	53,191	3.5	529,900	5.3
Services	73,479	4.9	975,200	9.8
Other	145,433[4]	9.6[4]	691,800[5]	7.0[5]
TOTAL	1,512,617	100.0[6]	9,914,300[6]	100.0

Tourism (2002): receipts U.S.$612,000,000; expenditures U.S.$396,000,000.
Land use as % of total land area (2000): in temporary crops 40.7%, in permanent crops 2.3%, in pasture 21.5%; overall forest area 28.0%.

Foreign trade[7]

Balance of trade (current prices)

	1999	2000	2001	2002	2003	2004
U.S.$'000,000	−1,087	−1,683	−2,973	−2,611	−4,537	−6,664
% of total	6.0%	7.5%	11.5%	8.6%	11.4%	12.4%

Imports (2002): U.S.$17,862,000,000 (textiles 16.4%, nonelectrical machinery and apparatus 12.0%, petroleum and petroleum products 11.1%, electrical machinery and telecommunications equipment 11.0%, chemicals and chemical products 8.4%). *Major import sources:* Italy 20.7%; Germany 14.9%; Russia 7.1%; France 6.4%; U.K. 3.8%.
Exports (2002): U.S.$13,876,000,000 (apparel and clothing accessories 25.3%, electrical machinery and telecommunications equipment 10.3%, footwear 8.4%, petroleum products 7.9%, iron and steel 7.0%, nonelectrical machinery and apparatus 5.3%). *Major export destinations:* Italy 25.0%; Germany 15.6%; France 7.6%; U.K. 5.8%; Turkey 4.2%.

Transport and communications

Transport. Railroads (2000): length 11,385 km; (2002) passenger-km 8,502,000,000; (2002) metric ton-km cargo 15,218,000,000. Roads (2003): length 198,817 km (paved 30%). Vehicles (2003): cars 3,087,628; trucks and buses 556,123. Air transport (2002): passenger-km 1,908,000,000; metric ton-km cargo 8,664,000; airports (2001) 8.

Communications

Medium	date	unit	number	units per 1,000 persons
Daily newspapers	2000	circulation	6,560,000	300
Radio	2000	receivers	7,310,000	334
Television	2003	receivers	15,150,000	697
Telephones	2004	main lines	4,389,100	197
Cellular telephones	2004	subscribers	10,215,400	459
Personal computers	2004	units	2,450,000	110
Internet	2004	users	4,500,000	202

Education and health

Educational attainment (2002). Percentage of population age 10 and over having: no formal schooling 5.5%; primary education 20.1%; lower secondary 27.6%; upper secondary/vocational 36.7%; higher vocational 3.0%; university 7.1%. *Literacy* (2002): total population age 15 and over literate 97.3%; males 98.4%; females 96.3%.

Education (2002–03)

	schools	teachers	students	student/ teacher ratio
Primary (age 6–9)	12,456	154,197	2,198,312	14.3
Secondary (age 10–17)	1,388	60,988	740,404	12.1
Voc., teacher tr.	163	7,559	332,070	43.9
Higher	125	29,619	596,297	20.1

Health: physicians (2003) 41,547 (1 per 525 persons); hospital beds (2002) 162,588 (1 per 133 persons); infant mortality rate (2002) 17.3.

Military

Total active duty personnel (2004): 97,200 (army 67.9%, navy 7.4%, air force 14.4%, centrally controlled units 10.3%). *Military expenditure as percentage of GDP* (2003): 2.4%; per capita expenditure U.S.$62.

[1]Includes 18 elective seats for minority parties. [2]The leu was redenominated on July 1, 2005. As of this date 10,000 (old) leu = 1 (new) leu. [3]Metal content of concentrate. [4]Taxes and customs duties less imputed bank charges and less subsidies. [5]Unemployed. [6]Detail does not add to total given because of rounding. [7]Imports f.o.b. in balance of trade and c.i.f. in commodities and trading partners.

Internet resources for further information:
• **Embassy of Romania (Washington, D.C.)** http://www.roembus.org
• **National Institute of Statistics** http://www.insse.ro/indexe.htm
• **National Bank of Romania** http://www.bnro.ro/def_en.htm

Russia

Official name: Rossiyskaya Federatsiya (Russian Federation).
Form of government: federal multiparty republic with a bicameral legislative body (Federal Assembly comprising the Federation Council [178] and the State Duma [450]).
Head of state: President.
Head of government: Prime Minister.
Capital: Moscow.
Official language: Russian.
Official religion: none.
Monetary unit: 1 ruble (Rub) = 100 kopecks; valuation (Sept. 1, 2005)
1 U.S.$ = Rub 28.28;
1 £ = Rub 52.07.

Area and population

Federal districts	Capitals	area sq mi	area sq km	population 2002 census
Central	Moscow (Moskva)	251,200	650,700	38,000,651
Belgorod (region)	Belgorod	10,500	27,100	1,511,620
Bryansk (region)	Bryansk	13,500	34,900	1,378,941
Ivanovo (region)	Ivanovo	8,400	21,800	1,148,329
Kaluga (region)	Kaluga	11,500	29,900	1,041,641
Kostroma (region)	Kostroma	23,200	60,100	736,641
Kursk (region)	Kursk	11,500	29,800	1,235,091
Lipetsk (region)	Lipetsk	9,300	24,100	1,213,499
Moscow (city)		400	1,000	10,382,754
Moskva (Moscow; region)	Moscow (Moskva)	17,800	46,000[1]	6,618,538
Oryol (region)	Oryol	9,500	24,700	860,262
Ryazan (region)	Ryazan	15,300	39,600	1,227,910
Smolensk (region)	Smolensk	19,200	49,800	1,049,574
Tambov (region)	Tambov	13,200	34,300	1,178,443
Tula (region)	Tula	9,900	25,700	1,675,758
Tver (region)	Tver	32,500	84,100	1,471,459
Vladimir (region)	Vladimir	11,200	29,000	1,523,990
Voronezh (region)	Voronezh	20,200	52,400	2,378,803
Yaroslavl (region)	Yaroslavl	14,100	36,400	1,367,398
Far Eastern	Khabarovsk	2,400,000	6,215,900	6,692,865
Amur (region)	Blagoveshchensk	140,400	363,700	902,844
Chukot (autonomous district)	Anadyr	284,800	737,700	53,824
Kamchatka (region)	Petropavlovsk-Kamchatsky	66,000	170,800	333,644
Khabarovsk (territory)	Khabarovsk	304,500	788,600	1,436,570
Koryak (autonomous district)	Palana	116,400	301,500	25,157
Magadan (region)	Magadan	178,100	461,400	182,726
Primorye (territory)	Vladivostok	64,100	165,900	2,071,210
Sakha (republic)	Yakutsk	1,198,200	3,103,200	949,280
Sakhalin (region)	Yuzhno-Sakhalinsk	33,600	87,100	546,695
Yevreyskaya (autonomous region)	Birobidzhan	13,900	36,000	190,915
Northwest	St. Petersburg	648,000	1,677,900	13,974,466
Arkhangelsk (region)	Arkhangelsk	158,700	411,000	1,294,993
Kaliningrad (region)	Kaliningrad	5,800	15,100	955,281
Kareliya (republic)	Petrozavodsk	66,600	172,400	716,281
Komi (republic)	Syktyvkar	160,600	415,900	1,018,674
Leningrad (region)	St. Petersburg	32,600	84,500[2]	1,669,205
Murmansk (region)	Murmansk	55,900	144,900	892,534
Nenets (autonomous district)	Naryan-Mar	68,100	176,400	41,546
Novgorod (region)	Novgorod	21,400	55,300	694,355
Pskov (region)	Pskov	21,400	55,300	760,810
St. Petersburg (city)		600	1,400	4,661,219
Vologda (region)	Vologda	56,300	145,700	1,269,568
Siberia	Novosibirsk	1,974,800	5,114,800	20,062,938
Agin Buryat (autonomous district)	Aginskoye	7,300	19,000	72,213
Altay (republic)	Gorno-Altaysk	35,700	92,600	202,947
Altay (territory)	Barnaul	65,300	169,100	2,607,426
Buryatiya (republic)	Ulan-Ude	135,600	351,300	981,238
Chita (region)	Chita	159,300	412,500	1,083,133
Evenk (autonomous district)	Tyra	296,400	767,600	17,697
Irkutsk (region)	Irkutsk	287,900	745,500	2,446,378
Kemerovo (region)	Kemerovo	36,900	95,500	2,899,142
Khakassia (republic)	Abakan	23,900	61,900	546,072
Krasnoyarsk (territory)	Krasnoyarsk	274,100	710,000	2,908,559
Novosibirsk (region)	Novosibirsk	68,800	178,200	2,692,251
Omsk (region)	Omsk	53,900	139,700	2,079,220
Taymyr (Dolgano-Nenets) (autonomous district)	Dudinka	332,900	862,100	39,786
Tomsk (region)	Tomsk	122,400	316,900	1,046,039
Tuva (republic)	Kyzyl-Orda	65,800	170,500	305,510
Ust-Ordyn Buryat	Ust-Ordinsky	8,600	22,400	135,327
Southern	Rostov-na-Donu	227,300	589,200	22,907,141
Adygeya (republic)	Maykop	2,900	7,600	447,109
Astrakhan (region)	Astrakhan	17,000	44,100	1,005,276
Chechnia (republic)	Grozny	6,010	15,700	1,103,686
Dagestan (republic)	Makhachkala	19,400	50,300	2,576,531
Ingushetiya (republic)	Magas	1,390	3,600	467,294
Kabardino-Balkariya (republic)	Nalchik	4,800	12,500	901,494
Kalmykiya (republic)	Elista	29,400	76,100	292,410
Karachayevo-Cherkessia (republic)	Cherkessk	5,400	14,100	439,470
Krasnodar (territory)	Krasnodar	29,300	76,000	5,125,221
Rostov (region)	Rostov-na-Donu	38,900	100,800	4,404,013
Severnaya Osetiya–Alania (republic)	Vladikavkaz	3,100	8,000	710,275
Stavropol (territory)	Stavropol	25,700	66,500	2,735,139
Volgograd (region)	Volgograd	44,000	113,900	2,699,223
Urals	Yekaterinburg	690,600	1,788,900	12,373,926
Chelyabinsk (region)	Chelyabinsk	33,900	87,900	3,603,339
Khanty-Mansi (autonomous district)	Khanty-Mansiysk	202,000	523,100	1,432,817
Kurgan (region)	Kurgan	27,400	71,000	1,019,532
Sverdlovsk (region)	Sverdlovsk	75,200	194,800	4,486,214
Tyumen (region)	Tyumen	62,400	161,800	1,325,018
Yamalo-Nenets (autonomous district)	Salekhard	289,700	750,300	507,006

Area and population (continued)

		area sq mi	area sq km	population 2002 census
Volga	Nizhny Novgorod	400,900	1,038,300[4]	31,154,744
Bashkortostan (republic)	Ufa	55,400	143,600	4,104,336
Chuvashiya (republic)	Cheboksary	7,100	18,300	1,313,754
Kirov (region)	Kirov	46,600	120,800	1,503,529
Mari-El (republic)	Toshkar-Ola	9,000	23,200	727,979
Mordoviya (republic)	Saransk	10,100	26,200	888,766
Nizhny Novgorod (region)	Nizhny Novgorod	29,700	76,900	3,524,028
Orenburg (region)	Orenburg	47,900	124,000	2,179,551
Penza (region)	Penza	16,700	43,200	1,452,941
Perm (territory)[3]	Perm	62,000	160,600	2,819,421
Samara (region)	Samara	20,700	53,600	3,239,737
Saratov (region)	Saratov	38,700	100,200	2,668,310
Tatarstan (republic)	Kazan	26,300	68,000	3,779,265
Udmurtia (republic)	Izhevsk	16,300	42,100	1,570,316
Ulyanovsk (Simbirsk; region)	Simbirsk	14,400	37,300	1,382,811
TOTAL		6,592,800	17,075,400[4]	145,166,731

Demography

Population (2005): 143,420,000.
Density (2005): persons per sq mi 21.8, persons per sq km 8.4.
Urban-rural (2004): urban 73.4%; rural 26.6%.
Sex distribution (2004): male 46.49%; female 53.51%.
Age breakdown (2004): under 15, 15.7%; 15–29, 24.5%; 30–44, 22.1%; 45–59, 19.9%; 60 and over 17.8%.
Population projection: (2010) 140,771,000; (2020) 134,386,000.
Ethnic composition (2002): Russian 79.82%; Tatar 3.83%; Ukrainian 2.03%; Bashkir 1.15%; Chuvash 1.13%; Chechen 0.94%; Armenian 0.78%; Mordvin 0.58%; Belarusian 0.56%; Avar 0.52%; Kazakh 0.45%; Udmurt 0.44%; Azerbaijani 0.43%; Mari 0.42%; German 0.41%; Kabardinian 0.36%; Ossetian 0.35%; Dargin 0.35%; Buryat 0.31%; Sakha 0.31%; other 4.83%.
Religious affiliation (2000): Christian 57.4%, of which Orthodox 49.7%, Protestant 6.2%, Roman Catholic 1.0%, other Christian 0.5%; Muslim 7.6%; traditional beliefs 0.8%; Jewish 0.7%; Hindu 0.5%; Buddhist 0.4%; nonreligious 27.4%; atheist 5.2%.
Major cities (2002): Moscow 10,101,500; St. Petersburg 4,669,400; Novosibirsk 1,425,600; Nizhny Novgorod 1,311,200; Yekaterinburg 1,293,000; Samara 1,158,100; Omsk 1,133,900; Kazan 1,105,300; Chelyabinsk 1,078,300; Rostov-na-Donu 1,070,200; Ufa 1,042,400; Volgograd 1,012,800.

Other principal cities (2002)

	population		population		population
Astrakhan	506,400	Lipetsk	506,900	Simbirsk (Ulyanovsk)	635,600
Barnaul	603,500	Naberezhnye Chelny	510,000	Tolyatti	701,900
Irkutsk	593,400	Novokuznetsk	550,100	Tomsk	487,700
Izhevsk	632,100	Orenburg	548,800	Tula	472,300
Kemerovo	485,000	Penza	518,200	Tyumen	510,700
Khabarovsk	582,700	Perm	1,000,100	Vladivostok	591,800
Krasnodar	644,800	Ryazan	521,700	Voronezh	848,700
Krasnoyarsk	911,700	Saratov	873,500	Yaroslavl	613,200

Migration (2004): immigrants 119,157; emigrants 79,795.
Refugees (2002): 828,784, of which from Kazakhstan 301,137, Uzbekistan 106,299, Tajikistan 86,041, Georgia 62,868.
Households (1999). Total households 52,116,000; average household size 2.8; distribution by size (1995): 1 person 19.2%; 2 persons 26.2%; 3 persons 22.6%; 4 persons 20.5%; 5 persons or more 11.5%.

Vital statistics

Birth rate per 1,000 population (2004): 10.5 (world avg. 21.1); (2001) legitimate 70.5%; illegitimate 29.5%.
Death rate per 1,000 population (2004): 15.9 (world avg. 9.0).
Natural increase rate per 1,000 population (2004): –5.4 (world avg. 12.1).
Total fertility rate (avg. births per childbearing woman; 2004): 1.3.
Marriage rate per 1,000 population (2004): 6.8.
Divorce rate per 1,000 population (2004): 4.4.
Life expectancy at birth (2003): male 58.8 years; female 72.0 years.
Major causes of death per 100,000 population (2004): circulatory diseases 892; accidents, poisoning, and violence 221, of which suicide 34, transport accidents 29, murder 27; malignant neoplasms (cancers) 201; respiratory diseases 64; digestive diseases 59; infectious and parasitic diseases 25.

Social indicators

Educational attainment (2002). Percentage of population age 15 and over having: no formal schooling 2.1%; primary education 7.7%; some secondary 18.1%; complete secondary/basic vocational 53.0%; incomplete higher 3.1%; complete higher 16.0%, of which advanced degrees 0.3%.
Quality of working life (2004). Average workweek: 40 hours. Annual rate per 100,000 workers of: injury or accident 340; industrial illness (2002) 22.2; death 12.9. Average days lost to labour strikes per 1,000 employees (1999): 35.7.
Social participation. Eligible voters participating in last national election (2003): 55.7%. Trade union membership in total workforce, n.a.
Social deviance. Offense rate per 100,000 population (2002) for: murder 22.5; rape 5.6; serious injury 40.7; larceny-theft 761.5. Incidence per 100,000 population (2000) of: alcoholism (1992) 1,727.5; substance abuse 25.6; suicide 39.2.
Material well-being (2002). Durable goods possessed per 100 households: automobiles 27; personal computers 7; television receivers 126; refrigerators and freezers 113; washing machines 93; VCRs 50; motorcycles 26; bicycles 71.

National economy

Public debt (external, outstanding; 2002): U.S.$98,264,000,000.
Budget (2004). Revenue: Rub 5,427,300,000,000 (tax revenue 91.0%, of which VAT 19.7%, corporate taxes 16.0%, import duties 15.8%, individual income tax 10.6%, excise tax 4.5%; nontax revenue 9.0%). Expenditures: Rub 4,665,400,000,000 (social and cultural services 31.4%, defense 9.2%, energy and construction 8.4%, law enforcement 8.2%).

Gross national product (2004): U.S.$487,335,000,000 (U.S.$3,410 per capita).

Structure of gross domestic product and labour force

	2004		2003	
	in value Rub '000,000	% of total value	labour force	% of labour force
Agriculture, forestry, fishing	929,100	5.5	6,651,000	9.2
Mining	1,144,500	6.8	1,109,000	1.5
Manufacturing	2,694,800	16.1	13,166,000	18.2
Public utilities	526,100	3.1	2,193,000	3.0
Construction	897,400	5.4	4,316,000	6.0
Transp. and commun.	1,485,500	8.9	5,957,000	8.3
Trade, restaurants, hotels	3,311,300	19.8	11,024,000	15.3
Finance, real estate	2,059,300	12.3	4,530,000	6.3
Services	1,097,200	6.6	12,915,000	17.9
Pub. admin., defense	774,000	4.6	4,622,000	6.4
Other	1,832,400[5]	10.9[5]	5,729,000[6]	7.9[6]
TOTAL	16,751,500[4]	100.0	72,212,000	100.0

Production (metric tons except as noted). Agriculture, forestry, fishing (2004): wheat 45,412,712, potatoes 35,914,240, sugar beets 21,848,320, barley 17,179,740, oats 4,954,780, sunflower seeds 4,800,710, cabbages 4,067,680, corn (maize) 3,515,690, rye 2,871,870, apples 2,030,000, tomatoes 2,017,860, carrots 1,762,040, onions 1,673,420; livestock (number of live animals) 24,935,140 cattle, 15,979,833 pigs, 14,669,420 sheep; roundwood 182,000,000 cu m; fish catch (2003) 3,281,248. Mining and quarrying (2002): iron ore 84,236,000; copper (metal content) 695,000; nickel (metal content) 310,000; zinc (metal content) 130,000; chrome ore (marketable) 70,000; vanadium 8,000; antimony (metal content; 2001) 4,500; molybdenum 2,900; silver 400,000 kg; gold 158,000 kg; platinum 34,000 kg; gem diamonds 11,500,000 carats. Manufacturing (value added in U.S.$'000,000; 2002): basic chemicals 18,612; food 5,522; iron and steel 3,829; nonferrous base metals 3,467; motor vehicles and parts 2,693; bricks, cement, ceramics 2,515; general purpose machinery 2,182; beverages 2,058; special purpose machinery 2,044; fabricated metal 1,964; refined petroleum 1,872; paper products 1,289; paints, soaps, pharmaceuticals 1,273; tobacco products 956; wood products (excluding furniture) 619.

Financial aggregates

	1999	2000	2001	2002	2003	2004
Exchange rate[7], Rub per:						
U.S. dollar	27.00	28.16	30.14	31.78	29.45	27.75
£	43.64	42.02	43.72	51.22	52.56	53.60
SDR	37.06	36.69	37.88	43.21	43.77	43.09
International reserves (U.S.$)						
Total (excl. gold; '000,000)	8,457	24,264	32,542	44,054	73,175	120,809
SDRs ('000,000)	0.6	0.5	2.9	1.2	0.7	0.9
Reserve pos. in IMF ('000,000)	1.3	1.2	1.4	1.6	2.1	2.8
Foreign exchange ('000,000)	8,455	24,263	32,538	44,051	73,172	120,805
Gold ('000,000 fine troy oz)	13.33	12.36	13.60	12.46	12.55	12.44
% world reserves	1.4	1.3	1.4	1.3	1.4	1.4
Balance of payments (U.S.$'000,000)						
Balance of visible trade	+36,012	+60,172	+48,120	+46,335	+59,859	+87,145
Imports, f.o.b.	−39,537	−44,862	−53,764	−60,966	−76,070	−96,307
Exports, f.o.b.	75,549	105,034	101,884	107,301	135,929	183,452
Balance of invisibles	−11,401	−13,332	−14,325	−17,219	−24,449	−27,210
Balance of payments, current account	+24,611	+46,840	+33,795	+29,116	+35,410	+59,935

Energy production (consumption): electricity (kW-hr; 2004) 930,744,000,000 (894,300,000,000); hard coal (metric tons; 2004) 209,900,000 ([2002] 147,100,000); lignite (metric tons; 2004) 70,300,000 ([2002] 77,000,000); crude petroleum (barrels; 2004) 3,292,000,000 ([2002] 1,391,000,000); petroleum products (metric tons; 2002) 170,333,000 (94,473,000); natural gas (cu m; 2004) 633,000,000,000 ([2003] 405,800,000,000).
Population economically active (2003): total 72,212,000; activity rate of total population 50.1% (participation rates: ages 15–64, 69.6%; female 48.6%; unemployed [July 2004–June 2005] 7.9%).

Price and earnings indexes (2000 = 100)

	1998	1999	2000	2001	2002	2003	2004
Consumer price index	44.6	82.8	100.0	121.5	140.6	159.8	177.2
Monthly earnings index	...	...	100.0	145.7	196.1	247.3	307.3

Land use as % of total land area (2000): in temporary crops 7.4%, in permanent crops 0.1%, in pasture 5.4%; overall forest area 50.4%.
Household income and expenditure. Average household size (2002) 2.8; income per household: Rub 52,400 (U.S.$1,692); sources of income (2002): wages 66.2%, pensions and stipends 14.9%, income from entrepreneurial activities 12.0%, property income 4.9%, other 2.0%; expenditure (2002): food 41.7%, clothing 13.3%, housing 6.2%, furniture and household appliances 5.7%, alcohol and tobacco 3.2%, transportation 2.7%.
Tourism (2003): receipts U.S.$4,502,000,000; expenditures U.S.$12,880,000,000.

Foreign trade[8]

Balance of trade (current prices)

	1999	2000	2001	2002	2003	2004
U.S.$'000,000	+42,607	+69,214	+58,087	+60,538	+76,309	+106,053
% of total	41.3%	50.5%	40.9%	39.6%	40.0%	41.2%

Imports (2004): U.S.$75,581,000,000 ([9]machinery, apparatus, and professional equipment 41.6%; food, beverages, and tobacco 18.5%; chemicals and chemical products 16.5%; nonferrous metals and iron and steel 7.4%). *Major import sources:* Germany 14.0%; Belarus 8.6%; Ukraine 8.1%; China 6.3%; Japan 5.2%; Kazakhstan 4.6%; U.S. 4.2%; Italy 4.2%; France 3.1%.
Exports (2004): U.S.$181,634,000,000 ([9]fuels and lubricants 58.2%, of which crude petroleum 32.3%, natural gas 12.3%, refined petroleum 11.2%; non-

ferrous metals and iron and steel 16.8%; machinery, apparatus, and professional goods 7.2%; chemicals and chemical products 6.4%; wood and paper products 4.0%). *Major export destinations:* The Netherlands 8.4%; Germany 7.3%; Italy 6.7%; Belarus 6.1%; Ukraine 5.9%; China 5.6%; Switzerland 4.3%; U.S. 3.6%; U.K. 3.1%; Poland 3.1%.

Trade by commodity group (2001)[10]

	imports		exports	
SITC group	U.S.$'000,000	%	U.S.$'000,000	%
0 Food and live animals	6,705	16.1	1,212	1.2
3 Mineral fuels, lubricants	1,013	2.4	53,478	53.9
5 Chemicals, related products	5,023	12.1	4,802	4.8
67 Iron and steel	1,471	3.5	5,582	5.6
68 Nonferrous metals	372	0.9	6,765	6.8
74 General industrial machinery	2,467	5.9	1,283	1.3
76 Telecommunications, incl. parts	1,433	3.5	—	—
78 Road vehicles	1,869	4.5	826	0.8
TOTAL (all groups)	41,528		99,197	

Direction of trade (2001)

	imports		exports	
	U.S.$'000,000	%	U.S.$'000,000	%
Africa	405	1.0	942	0.9
Americas	5,433	13.1	6,875	6.9
United States	3,208	7.7	2,876	2.9
Asia (excl. former U.S.S.R.)	5,401	13.0	15,772	15.9
China	1,617	3.9	3,878	3.9
Asia (former U.S.S.R. only)	2,833	6.8	47,449	4.8
Europe	23,058	55.5	58,598	59.1
EU	15,282	36.8	33,295	33.6
Eastern Europe	2,218	5.3	11,279	11.4
Europe (former U.S.S.R. only)	4,552	11.0	11,150	11.2
Oceania	177	0.4	20	—
TOTAL	41,528[11]		99,198[11]	

Transport and communications

Transport. Railroads (2002): length 139,000 km; passenger-km 152,900,000,000; metric ton-km cargo (2003) 1,664,300,000,000. Roads (2004): total length 601,000 km (paved 91%). Vehicles (2000): passenger cars 20,247,800; trucks and buses (1999) 5,021,000. Air transport (2004)[12]: passenger-km 49,491,153,000; metric ton-km cargo 1,198,687,000; airports (1998) 75.

Distribution of traffic (2000)

	cargo carried ('000,000 tons)	% of national total	passengers carried ('000,000)	% of national total
Intercity transport			23,502	54.5
Road	550	21.5	22,033	51.1
Rail	1,046	40.9	1,419	3.3
Sea and river	134	5.2	27	0.1
Air	0.8	...	23	...
Pipeline	829	32.4	—	—
Urban transport	—	—	19,628	45.5
TOTAL	2,559.8	100.0	43,130	100.0

Communications

Medium	date	unit	number	units per 1,000 persons
Daily newspapers	2004	circulation	15,075,000[13]	105
Radio	2000	receivers	61,100,000	418
Television	2000	receivers	61,500,000	421
Telephones	2003	main lines	36,993,000	256
Cellular telephones	2004	subscribers	74,420,000	517
Personal computers	2004	units	19,010,000	132
Internet	2004	users	16,000,000	111

Education and health

Education (2004–05)

	schools	teachers	students	student/ teacher ratio
Primary (age 6–13) Secondary (age 14–17)	64,908	1,633,000	16,631,000	10.2
Voc., teacher tr.	2,637	137,100	2,504,000	18.3
Higher	1,071	364,300	6,884,000	18.9

Health (2003)[7]: physicians 686,000 (1 per 211 persons); hospital beds 1,597,000 (1 per 91 persons); infant mortality rate per 1,000 live births (2004) 11.5.
Food (2002): daily per capita caloric intake 3,072 (vegetable products 78%, animal products 22%); 120% of FAO recommended minimum requirement.

Military

Total active duty personnel (2004): 1,212,700 (army 29.7%, navy 12.8%, air force 15.2%, strategic deterrent forces 8.2%, paramilitary 34.1%[14]). *Military expenditure as percentage of GDP* (2003): 4.3%; per capita expenditure U.S.$128.

[1]Remainder of combined Moscow city and Moskva region areas (47,000 sq km less 1,000 sq km). [2]Remainder of combined Leningrad (region) and St. Petersburg (city) areas (85,900 sq km less 1,400 sq km). [3]On Dec. 1, 2005, Komi-Permyak (autonomous district) merged with Perm (region) to form Perm (territory). [4]Detail does not add to total given because of gross rounding. [5]Net taxes on products less imputed bank service charges. [6]Includes 5,716,000 unemployed. [7]End of period. [8]Imports c.i.f.; exports f.o.b. including trade with Belarus unless otherwise indicated. [9]Excludes trade with Belarus. [10]Selected commodities only. [11]Includes unspecified. [12]Scheduled traffic of Aeroflot and 12 other airlines only. [13]Refers to top 20 dailies only. [14]Includes railway troops, special construction troops, federal border guards, interior troops, and other federal guard units.

Internet resources for further information:
• **Russian Statistical Agency** http://www.gks.ru/eng/default.asp

Rwanda

Official name: Republika y'u Rwanda (Rwanda); République Rwandaise (French); Republic of Rwanda (English).
Form of government: multiparty republic with two legislative bodies (Senate [26]; Chamber of Deputies [80]).
Head of state and government: President assisted by Prime Minister.
Capital: Kigali.
Official languages: Rwanda; French; English.
Official religion: none.
Monetary unit: 1 Rwanda franc (RF); valuation (Sept. 1, 2005) 1 U.S.$ = RF 542.75; 1 £ = RF 999.3.

Area and population		area		population
Provinces	Capitals	sq mi	sq km	2002 final census
Butare	Butare	714	1,849	725,914
Byumba	Byumba	668	1,730	707,786
Cyangugu	Cyangugu	900	2,330	607,495
Gikongoro	Gikongoro	845	2,188	489,729
Gisenyi	Gisenyi	828	2,145	864,377
Gitarama	Gitarama	845	2,188	856,488
Kibungo	Kibungo	1,256	3,253	702,248
Kibuye	Kibuye	516	1,336	469,016
Kigali (city)	—	43	112	603,049
Kigali Ngali	Masaka	1,210	3,133	789,330
Ruhengeri	Ruhengeri	680	1,762	891,498
Umutara	Nyagatare	1,665	4,312	421,623
TOTAL		10,169[1, 2]	26,338[2]	8,128,553

Demography

Population (2005): 8,574,000.
Density (2005)[3]: persons per sq mi 878.7, persons per sq km 339.3.
Urban-rural (2002): urban 16.9%; rural 83.1%.
Sex distribution (2002): male 47.73%; female 52.27%.
Age breakdown (2002): under 15, 43.8%; 15–29, 30.1%; 30–44, 14.7%; 45–59, 7.1%; 60–74, 3.3%; 75 and over, 1.0%.
Population projection: (2010) 9,605,000; (2020) 11,718,000.
Doubling time: 29 years.
Ethnic composition (2002): Hutu 85%; Tutsi 14%; Twa 1%.
Religious affiliation (2002): Roman Catholic 49.5%; Protestant 39.4%, of which Seventh-day Adventist 12.2%; other Christian 4.5%; Muslim 1.8%[4]; nonreligious 3.6%; other 1.2%.
Major cities (2002): Kigali (2003) 656,153; Gitarama 84,669; Butare 77,449; Ruhengeri 71,511; Gisenyi 67,766.

Vital statistics

Birth rate per 1,000 population (2004): 40.7 (world avg. 21.1).
Death rate per 1,000 population (2004): 16.5 (world avg. 9.0).
Natural increase rate per 1,000 population (2004): 24.2 (world avg. 12.1).
Total fertility rate (avg. births per childbearing woman; 2004): 5.5.
Life expectancy at birth (2004): male 45.6 years; female 47.7 years.
Adult population (ages 15–49) *living with HIV* (2005[5]): 5.1% (world avg. 1.1%).

National economy

Budget (2003). Revenue: RF 195,500,000,000 (grants 37.4%; taxes on goods and services 29.4%; income tax 18.0%; import and export duties 11.3%; nontax revenue 3.9%). Expenditures: RF 217,800,000,000 (current expenditures 74.7%, of which wages 20.2%, defense 11.2%, education 9.6%, debt payment 5.4%, health 3.4%; capital expenditure 25.3%).
Public debt (external, outstanding; 2003): U.S.$1,418,000,000.
Production (metric tons except as noted). Agriculture, forestry, fishing (2004): plantains 2,469,741, potatoes 1,072,772, cassava 912,108, sweet potatoes 908,306, beans 198,224, sorghum 163,772, corn (maize) 88,209, coffee 20,017, tea 14,493; livestock (number of live animals) 1,003,721 cattle, 760,000 goats, 260,000 sheep, 180,000 pigs; roundwood 5,495,000 cu m; fish catch (2003) 7,400. Mining and quarrying (2004): cassiterite (tin content) 300; niobium 63,000 kg; tantalum 40,000 kg; gold (2003) 2 kg. Manufacturing (value added in RF '000,000; 2002): food products, beverages, and tobacco products 61,073; cement, bricks, and ceramics 4,326; chemicals and chemical products 3,201; wood and wood products (including furniture) 2,486. Energy production (consumption): electricity (kW-hr; 2003) 178,000,000 (244,300,000); petroleum products (metric tons; 2002) none (176,000); natural gas (cu m; 2002) 333,000 (333,000).
Population economically active (2002): total 3,418,047; activity rate of total population 42.0% (participation rates: ages 6 and over, 52.1%; female 55.2%; officially unemployed 0.9%).

Price index (2000 = 100)							
	1998	1999	2000	2001	2002	2003	2004
Consumer price index	98.2	95.9	100.0	103.0	105.3	112.8	126.3

Land use as % of total land area (2000): in temporary crops 36.5%, in permanent crops 10.1%, in pasture 22.1%; overall forest area 12.4%.

Household income and expenditure. Average household size (2002) 4.5; average annual income per household, n.a.; sources of income: n.a.; expenditure: n.a.
Gross national product (2004): U.S.$1,875,000,000 (U.S.$220 per capita).

Structure of gross domestic product and labour force				
	2003		2002	
	in value RF '000,000	% of total value	labour force	% of labour force
Agriculture	373,900	41.3	2,951,492	86.2
Mining	5,700	0.6	5,274	0.2
Manufacturing	80,300	8.9	43,053	1.3
Construction	103,100	11.4	42,180	1.2
Public utilities	3,600	0.4	2,482	0.1
Transp. and commun.	61,700	6.8	30,255	0.9
Trade	91,700	10.1	94,175	2.8
Finance	...	...	10,920	0.3
Pub. admin., defense	64,800	7.2	25,668	0.7
Services	} 120,400	} 13.3	155,980	4.6
Other			56,568	1.7
TOTAL	905,300[1]	100.0	3,418,047	100.0

Tourism: receipts (2002) U.S.$31,000,000; expenditures U.S.$24,000,000.

Foreign trade

Balance of trade (current prices)						
	1998	1999	2000	2001	2002	2003
U.S.$'000,000	−168.5	−186.7	−168.6	−147.4	−167.4	−181.0
% of total	56.8%	60.0%	55.0%	44.9%	55.4%	59.0%

Imports (2003): U.S.$244,000,000 (capital goods 25.1%, intermediate goods 22.0%, energy products 16.7%, food 11.6%). *Major import sources* (2002): Kenya 21.9%; Germany 8.4%; Belgium 7.9%; Israel 4.3%; U.S. 3.5%.
Exports (2003): U.S.$63,000,000 (tea 35.7%, coffee 23.8%, cassiterite 7.1%, hides and skins 6.0%, other [mostly niobium and tantalum] 27.4%). *Major export destinations* (2002): Indonesia 30.8%; Germany 14.6%; Hong Kong 8.9%; South Africa 5.5%.

Transport and communications

Transport. Railroads: none. Roads (1999): total length 7,460 mi, 12,000 km (paved 8%). Vehicles (1996): passenger cars 13,000; trucks 17,100. Air transport (2000)[6]: passengers embarked and disembarked 101,000; cargo loaded and unloaded 4,300 metric tons; airports (2002) with scheduled flights 2.

Communications				units
Medium	date	unit	number	per 1,000 persons
Daily newspapers	1995	circulation	500	0.1
Radio	2002	receivers	3,898,000	477
Television	2002	receivers	22,900	11.0
Telephones	2002	main lines	23,200	2.8
Cellular telephones	2004	subscribers	150,000	18
Personal computers	2002	units	16,300	2.0
Internet	2004	users	38,000	4.5

Education and health

Educational attainment: n.a. *Literacy* (2003): percentage of total population age 15 and over literate 70.4%; males literate 76.3%; females literate 64.7%.

Education (2002–03)	schools	teachers	students	student/ teacher ratio
Primary (age 7–15)	1,710[7]	27,319	1,636,563	59.9
Secondary (age 16–19)[8]	...	7,058	189,153	26.8
Higher	...	1,348	20,393	15.1

Health: physicians (2005[6]) 450 (1 per 19,054 persons); hospital beds, n.a.; infant mortality rate per 1,000 live births (2004) 92.7.
Food (2002): daily per capita caloric intake 2,084 (vegetable products 97%, animal products 3%); 90% of FAO recommended minimum requirement.

Military

Total active duty personnel (2004): 51,000 (army 78.4%, navy 2.0%, national police 19.6%). *Military expenditure as percentage of GDP* (2003): 2.8%; per capita expenditure U.S.$6.

---

[1]Detail does not add to total given because of rounding. [2]Includes Lake Kivu (Rwandan part) area of 411 sq mi (1,065 sq km). [3]Based on land area (9,758 sq mi [25,273 sq km]). [4]Official figure per 2002 census; unofficial figure equals c. 15%. [5]Beginning of year. [6]Kigali airport only. [7]1991–92. [8]Includes vocational and teacher training.

Internet resources for further information:
• **Ministry of Finance and Economic Planning**
  http://www.minecofin.gov.rw
• **Banque Nationale du Rwanda**
  http://www.bnr.rw

Saint Kitts and Nevis

Official name: Federation of Saint Kitts and Nevis[1].
Form of government: constitutional monarchy with one legislative house (National Assembly [15[2]]).
Chief of state: British Monarch represented by Governor-General.
Head of government: Prime Minister.
Capital: Basseterre.
Official language: English.
Official religion: none.
Monetary unit: 1 Eastern Caribbean dollar (EC$) = 100 cents; valuation (Sept. 1, 2005) 1 U.S.$ = EC$2.70; 1 £ = EC$4.97.

Area and population		area		population
				2001
Islands	**Capitals**	sq mi	sq km	census[3]
Nevis[4]	Charlestown	36.0	93.2	11,181
St. Kitts	Basseterre	68.0	176.2	34,703
TOTAL		104.0	269.4	45,884

Demography

Population (2005): 46,600.
Density (2005): persons per sq mi 448.1, persons per sq km 173.0.
Urban-rural (2002): urban 34.5%; rural 65.5%.
Sex distribution (2001): male 49.70%; female 50.30%.
Age breakdown (2000): under 15, 30.3%; 15–29, 24.9%; 30–44, 22.2%; 45–59, 11.2%; 60–74, 7.1%; 75 and over, 4.3%.
Population projection: (2010) 48,000; (2020) 53,000.
Doubling time: 72 years.
Ethnic composition (2000): black 90.4%; mulatto 5.0%; Indo-Pakistani 3.0%; white 1.0%; other/unspecified 0.6%.
Religious affiliation (1995): Protestant 84.6%, of which Anglican 25.2%, Methodist 25.2%, Pentecostal 8.4%, Moravian 7.6%; Roman Catholic 6.7%; Hindu 1.5%; other 7.2%.
Major towns (2001): Basseterre 13,033; Charlestown 1,820.

Vital statistics

Birth rate per 1,000 population (2004): 18.3 (world avg. 21.1).
Death rate per 1,000 population (2004): 8.7 (world avg. 9.0).
Natural increase rate per 1,000 population (2004): 9.6 (world avg. 12.1).
Total fertility rate (avg. births per childbearing woman; 2004): 2.4.
Marriage rate per 1,000 population (2001): 7.1.
Divorce rate per 1,000 population (2002): 0.5.
Life expectancy at birth (2004): male 69.0 years; female 74.9 years.
Major causes of death per 100,000 population (2002): diseases of the circulatory system 404.9; malignant neoplasms (cancers) 110.4; communicable diseases 104.6; accidents, violence, and poisoning 42.9.

National economy

Budget (2003). Revenue: EC$329,700,000 (tax revenue 70.9%, of which taxes on international trade 36.2%, taxes on income and profits 19.4%, taxes on domestic goods and services 13.7%; nontax revenue 26.5%; grants/other 2.6%). Expenditures: EC$409,500,000 (current expenditure 81.3%; development expenditure 15.3%; net lending 3.4%).
Production (metric tons except as noted). Agriculture, forestry, fishing (2004): sugarcane 193,000[5], tropical fruit 1,300, coconuts 1,000, roots and tubers 700, pulses 210, potatoes 160, sweet potatoes 150, tomatoes 100, cabbages 80, onions 60; sea island cotton is grown on Nevis; livestock (number of live animals) 14,400 goats, 14,000 sheep, 4,300 cattle, 4,000 pigs; roundwood, n.a.; fish catch (2001) 291. Mining and quarrying: excavation of sand for local use. Manufacturing (2001): raw sugar 20,193; carbonated beverages (1995) 45,000 hectolitres; beer (1995) 20,000 hectolitres; other manufactures include electronic components, garments, footwear, and batik. Energy production (consumption): electricity (kW-hr; 2002) 110,000,000 (110,000,000); coal, none (none); crude petroleum, none (none); petroleum products (metric tons; 2002) none (37,000); natural gas, none (none).
Gross national product (2004): U.S.$357,000,000 (U.S.$7,600 per capita).

Structure of gross domestic product and labour force				
	2003		1994	
	in value EC$'000,000	% of total value	labour force[6]	% of labour force[6]
Sugarcane	5.0	0.5	1,525[7]	9.2[7]
Other agriculture, forestry, fisheries	19.6	2.0	914	5.5
Mining	2.3	0.2	29	0.2
Manufacturing	76.7	7.8	1,290[8]	7.8[8]
Construction	129.8	13.2	1,745	10.5
Public utilities	23.7	2.4	416	2.5
Transp. and commun.	111.5	11.3	534	3.2
Trade, restaurants	160.6	16.3	3,367	20.3
Finance, real estate	155.1	15.8	3,708[9]	22.3[9]
Pub. admin., defense	156.5	15.9	2,738	16.5
Services	36.2	3.7	[9]	[9]
Other	107.4[10]	10.9[10]	342	2.1
TOTAL	984.4	100.0	16,608	100.0[11]

Household income and expenditure. Average household size (2001) 2.9; average annual income per wage earner (1994) EC$9,940 (U.S.$3,681); sources of income: n.a.; expenditure (2001)[12]: food, beverages, and tobacco 28.8%, education 19.3%, health 14.1%, housing 13.0%, clothing and footwear 9.3%, fuel and light 4.4%, household furnishings 3.7%, transportation 2.1%, other 5.3%.
Public debt (external, outstanding; 2002): U.S.$252,200,000.
Population economically active (1991): total 16,880[6]; activity rate of total population 41.6%[6] (participation rates: ages 15–64, 70.5%; female 44.4%[6]; unemployed [1997] 4.5%).

Price and earnings indexes (2000 = 100)							
	1998	1999	2000	2001	2002	2003	2004
Consumer price index	94.3	97.9	100.0	102.1	104.2	106.6	108.4
Earnings index	...	...	...	...	...	...	...

Land use as % of total land area (2000): in temporary crops *c.* 19%, in permanent crops *c.* 3%, in pasture *c.* 6%; overall forest area *c.* 11%.
Tourism: receipts from visitors (2003) U.S.$61,000,000; expenditures by nationals abroad (2003) U.S.$8,000,000.

Foreign trade[13]

Balance of trade (current prices)					
	1998	1999	2000	2001	2002
U.S.$'000,000	–86.6	–90.2	–121.2	–111.6	–113.2
% of total	49.4%	50.1%	54.1%	50.3%	46.8%

Imports (2001): U.S.$189,200,000 (machinery and apparatus 22.4%; food 14.4%; fabricated metals 7.9%; chemicals and chemical products 6.9%; refined petroleum 6.4%). *Major import sources* (2002): United States 41.5%; Trinidad and Tobago 16.2%; Canada 9.8%; United Kingdom 6.9%; Japan 4.0%.
Exports (2001): U.S.$31,000,000 (electrical switches, relays, and fuses 56.1%; raw sugar 21.0%; telecommunications equipment [parts] 3.2%). *Major export destinations* (2002): United States 66.6%; United Kingdom 7.6%; Canada 6.8%; Portugal 6.0%; Germany 2.9%.

Transport and communications

Transport. Railroads (2000)[14]: length 36 mi, 58 km. Roads (2001): total length 197 mi, 318 km (paved 44%). Vehicles (2001): passenger cars 5,826; trucks and buses 2,989. Air transport (2001)[15]: passenger arrivals 135,237; passenger departures 134,937; cargo handled 1,802; airports (1998) with scheduled flights 2.

Communications				units per 1,000
Medium	date	unit	number	persons
Radio	1997	receivers	28,000	701
Television	1997	receivers	10,000	264
Telephones	2002	main lines	23,500	500
Cellular telephones	2004	units	10,000	217
Personal computers	2004	units	11,000	239
Internet	2004	users	40,000	870

Education and health

Educational attainment (1991). Percentage of population age 25 and over having: no formal schooling 1.6%; primary education 45.9%; secondary 38.4%; higher 8.9%; other or not stated 5.2%. *Literacy* (1990): total population age 15 and over literate 25,500 (90.0%); males literate 13,100 (90.0%); females literate 12,400 (90.0%).

Education (2001–02)				student/
	schools	teachers	students	teacher ratio
Primary (age 5–12)[16]	24	301	5,608	18.6
Secondary (age 13–17)[16]	7	389	4,445	11.4
Higher[17]	1	51	394	7.7

Health (2001): physicians 49 (1 per 936 persons); hospital beds 178 (1 per 258 persons); infant mortality rate per 1,000 live births (2004) 14.9.
Food (2001): daily per capita caloric intake 2,997 (vegetable products 74%, animal products 26%); 124% of FAO recommended minimum requirement.

Military

Total active duty personnel: the defense force includes coast guard and police units. *Military expenditure as percentage of GDP:* n.a.

[1]Both Saint Christopher and Nevis and the Federation of Saint Christopher and Nevis are officially acceptable, variant, short- and long-form names of the country. [2]Includes 4 nonelective seats. [3]Preliminary figures. [4]Nevis has full internal self-government. The Nevis legislature is subordinate to the National Assembly only with regard to external affairs and defense. [5]Sugarcane production ended in July 2005. [6]Employed persons only. [7]Includes sugar manufacturing. [8]Excludes sugar manufacturing. [9]Finance, real estate includes Services. [10]Taxes less subsidies and less imputed bank service charges. [11]Detail does not add to total given because of rounding. [12]Weights of consumer price index components. [13]Imports f.o.b. in balance of trade and c.i.f. in commodities and trading partners. [14]Light railway serving the sugar industry on Saint Kitts. [15]Saint Kitts airport only. [16]Public schools only. [17]1992–93.

Internet resources for further information:
• **Official Web site of the Government of St. Kitts & Nevis**
  http://www.stkittsnevis.net/index2.html
• **Eastern Caribbean Central Bank**
  http://www.eccb-centralbank.org

Saint Lucia

Official name: Saint Lucia.
Form of government: constitutional monarchy with a Parliament consisting of two legislative chambers (Senate [11]; House of Assembly [17[1]]).
Chief of state: British Monarch represented by Governor-General.
Head of government: Prime Minister.
Capital: Castries.
Official language: English.
Official religion: none.
Monetary unit: 1 Eastern Caribbean dollar (EC$) = 100 cents; valuation (Sept. 1, 2005) 1 U.S.$ = EC$2.70; 1 £ = EC$4.97.

Area and population

Districts	Capitals	area		population
		sq mi	sq km	2001 census[2]
Anse-la-Raye	Anse-la-Raye }	18	47	6,060
Canaries	Canaries }			1,788
Castries	Castries	31	79	64,344
Choiseul	Choiseul	12	31	6,128
Dennery	Dennery	27	70	12,767
Gros Islet	Gros Islet	39	101	20,872
Laborie	Laborie	15	38	7,363
Micoud	Micoud	30	78	16,041
Soufrière	Soufrière	19	51	7,656
Vieux Fort	Vieux Fort	17	44	14,754
TOTAL		238[3]	617[3]	157,773[4]

Demography

Population (2005): 161,000.
Density (2005): persons per sq mi 676.5, persons per sq km 260.9.
Urban-rural (2003): urban 30.5%; rural 69.5%.
Sex distribution (2001): male 48.92%; female 51.08%.
Age breakdown (2001): under 15, 31.2%; 15–29, 27.4%; 30–44, 20.6%; 45–59, 10.7%; 60 and over, 10.1%.
Population projection: (2010) 168,000; (2020) 180,000.
Doubling time: 46 years.
Ethnic composition (2000): black 50%; mulatto 44%; East Indian 3%; white 1%; other 2%.
Religious affiliation (2001): Roman Catholic 67.5%; Protestant 22.0%, of which Seventh-day Adventist 8.4%, Pentecostal 5.6%; Rastafarian 2.1%; nonreligious 4.5%; other/unknown 3.9%.
Major towns (2001): Castries 13,191 (urban area 37,549); Vieux Fort (2002) 4,700; Micoud (2002) 3,700; Soufrière (2002) 3,400.

Vital statistics

Birth rate per 1,000 population (2004): 20.5 (world avg. 21.1); (2002) legitimate 14.0%; illegitimate 86.0%.
Death rate per 1,000 population (2004): 5.2 (world avg. 9.0).
Natural increase rate per 1,000 population (2004): 15.3 (world avg. 12.1).
Total fertility rate (avg. births per childbearing woman; 2004): 2.3.
Marriage rate per 1,000 population (2002): 3.0.
Divorce rate per 1,000 population (2002): 0.3.
Life expectancy at birth (2004): male 69.8 years; female 77.2 years.
Major causes of death per 100,000 population (2002): diseases of the circulatory system 192.7, of which cerebrovascular diseases 75.9; malignant neoplasms (cancers) 101.8; diabetes mellitus 77.4; communicable diseases 39.4.

National economy

Budget (2002). Revenue: EC$505,700,000 (tax revenue 81.6%, of which consumption duties on imported goods 42.5%, taxes on income and profits 21.3%, goods and services 16.5%; nontax revenue 12.7%; grants 5.7%). Expenditures: EC$543,600,000 (current expenditures 74.6%; development expenditures and net lending 25.4%).
Public debt (external, outstanding; 2003): U.S.$337,100,000.
Production (metric tons except as noted). Agriculture, forestry, fishing (2004): bananas 120,000, mangoes 28,000, coconuts 14,000, yams 4,500, grapefruit 2,973, tropical fruit 2,800, plantains 1,300, cassava 1,000, vegetables 1,000, oranges 600; livestock (number of live animals) 14,950 pigs, 12,500 sheep, 12,400 cattle, 9,800 goats; roundwood, n.a.; fish catch (2003) 1,462. Mining and quarrying: excavation of sand for local construction and pumice. Manufacturing (value of production in EC$'000; 2003): beverages and tobacco products (2002) 51,017, of which rum, other alcoholic beverages, and tobacco products 43,286; electrical products 20,846; paper products and cardboard boxes 15,125; textiles 7,900; copra 1,308. Energy production (consumption): electricity (kW-hr; 2002) 270,000,000 (270,000,000); coal, none (none); crude petroleum, none (none); petroleum products (metric tons; 2002) none (123,000); natural gas, none (none).
Population economically active (2002): total 74,949; activity rate of total population 47.0% (participation rates: ages 15 and over, 66.8%; female [2000] 47.2%; unemployed [2003] 22.3%).

Price index (2000 = 100)

	1998	1999	2000	2001	2002	2003	2004
Consumer price index	93.2	96.3	100.0	100.1	101.7	102.7	107.4

Gross national product (at current market prices; 2004): U.S.$706,000,000 (U.S.$4,310 per capita).

Structure of gross domestic product and labour force

	2003		2000	
	in value EC$'000,000[5]	% of total value[5]	labour force	% of labour force
Agriculture, fishing	84.1	4.4	13,195	17.4
Mining	6.0	0.3	...	...
Manufacturing	78.1	4.1	6,200	8.1
Construction	116.8	6.1	5,995	7.9
Public utilities	85.0	4.5	685	0.9
Transportation and communications	342.2	17.9	4,095	5.4
Trade, restaurants	428.7	22.4	17,930	23.6
Finance, real estate	269.7	14.1	2,290	3.0
Pub. admin., defense	241.5	12.6	7,530	9.9
Services	82.9	4.3	4,700	6.2
Other	177.5[6]	9.3[6]	13,385[7]	17.6[7]
TOTAL	1,912.5	100.0	76,005	100.0

Household income and expenditure. Average household size (2001) 3.2; income per household: n.a.; sources of income: n.a.; expenditure: n.a.
Land use as % of total land area (2000): in temporary crops *c.* 7%, in permanent crops *c.* 23%, in pasture *c.* 3%; overall forest area *c.* 15%.
Tourism (2003): receipts from visitors U.S.$282,000,000; expenditures by nationals abroad U.S.$34,000,000.

Foreign trade

Balance of trade (current prices)

	1998	1999	2000	2001	2002	2003
U.S.$'000,000	−224.7	−251.1	−259.6	−218.0	−222.2	−286.4
% of total	61.5%	67.3%	71.0%	66.8%	66.9%	68.4%

Imports (2002): U.S.$277,100,000 (food and beverages 26.2%; machinery and apparatus 23.5%; manufactured goods 17.3%; chemicals and chemical products 9.0%; refined petroleum 8.7%). *Major import sources:* United States 38.0%; Trinidad and Tobago 14.6%; United Kingdom 9.5%; Japan 3.3%; Canada 3.1%.
Exports (2002): U.S.$54,900,000 (bananas 49.9%; beer and ale 15.9%; clothing 3.2%; electrical and electronic components 3.2%). *Major export destinations:* United Kingdom 37.6%; United States 20.3%; Trinidad and Tobago 11.8%; Barbados 9.7%; Dominica 5.3%.

Transport and communications

Transport. Railroads: none. Roads (1999): total length 750 mi, 1,210 km (paved 5%). Vehicles (2001): passenger cars 22,453; trucks and buses 8,972. Air transport (2001)[8]: passenger arrivals and departures 679,000; cargo unloaded and loaded 3,500 metric tons; airports (2000) with scheduled flights 2.

Communications

Medium	date	unit	number	units per 1,000 persons
Radio	1997	receivers	100,000	668
Television	1997	receivers	40,000	267
Telephones	2002	main lines	51,100	320
Cellular telephones	2004	subscribers	93,000	620
Personal computers	2004	units	26,000	173
Internet	2004	users	55,000	367

Education and health

Educational attainment (2000). Percentage of population age 15 and over having: no formal schooling 6.5%; primary education 56.2%; secondary 27.5%; higher vocational 4.5%; university 2.7%; other/unknown 2.6%. *Literacy* (2000): 90.2%.

Education (2000–01)

	schools	teachers	students	student/ teacher ratio
Primary (age 5–11)	82	1,052	28,618	27.2
Secondary (age 12–16)	18	678	12,865	19.0
Higher	...	127	1,403	11.0

Health (2002): physicians 92 (1 per 1,740 persons); hospital beds 285 (1 per 562 persons); infant mortality rate per 1,000 live births (2004) 14.0.
Food (2001): daily per capita caloric intake 2,849 (vegetable products 72%, animal products 28%); 118% of FAO recommended minimum requirement.

Military

Total active duty personnel (2000): [9].

---

[1]Represents elected seats only. Attorney general and speaker serve ex officio. [2]Preliminary. [3]Total includes the uninhabited 30 sq mi (78 sq km) Central Forest Reserve. [4]Total adjusted pop. (including institutionalized individuals but excluding visitors) equals 158,361. [5]At current prices. [6]Taxes less subsidies and less imputed bank service charges. [7]Includes 12,535 unemployed. [8]Combined data for both Castries and Vieux Fort airports. [9]The 300-member police force includes a specially trained paramilitary unit and a coast guard unit.

Internet resources for further information:
• **Saint Lucian Government Statistics Department**
  http://www.stats.gov.lc
• **Eastern Caribbean Central Bank**
  http://www.eccb-centralbank.org

Saint Vincent and the Grenadines

Official name: Saint Vincent and the Grenadines.
Form of government: constitutional monarchy with one legislative house (House of Assembly [22[1]]).
Chief of state: British Monarch represented by Governor-General.
Head of government: Prime Minister.
Capital: Kingstown.
Official language: English.
Official religion: none.
Monetary unit: 1 Eastern Caribbean dollar (EC$) = 100 cents; valuation (Sept. 1, 2005) 1 U.S.$ = EC$2.70; 1 £ = EC$4.97.

Area and population	area		population
Census Divisions[3]	sq mi	sq km	2003[2] estimate
Island of Saint Vincent			
Barrouallie	14.2	36.8	5,313
Bridgetown	7.2	18.6	6,593
Calliaqua	11.8	30.6	22,084
Chateaubelair	30.9	80.0	5,915
Colonarie	13.4	34.7	7,286
Georgetown	22.2	57.5	6,794
Kingstown (city)	1.9	4.9	13,477
Kingstown (suburbs)	6.4	16.6	12,670
Layou	11.1	28.7	6,164
Marriaqua	9.4	24.3	8,028
Sandy Bay	5.3	13.7	2,728
Saint Vincent Grenadines			
Northern Grenadines	9.0	23.3	5,492
Southern Grenadines	7.5	19.4	3,491
TOTAL	150.3	389.3[4]	106,035

Demography

Population (2005): 119,000.
Density (2005): persons per sq mi 791.7, persons per sq km 305.7.
Urban-rural (2003): urban 58.3%; rural 41.7%.
Sex distribution (2000): male 49.90%; female 50.10%.
Age breakdown (1999): under 15, 31.3%; 15–29, 31.2%; 30–44, 19.6%; 45–59, 9.4%; 60–74, 5.9%; 75 and over, 2.6%.
Population projection: (2010) 122,000; (2020) 125,000.
Doubling time: 61 years.
Ethnic composition (1999): black 65.5%; mulatto 23.5%; Indo-Pakistani 5.5%; white 3.5%; black-Amerindian 2.0%.
Religious affiliation (2000): Protestant 47.0%; unaffiliated Christian 20.3%; independent Christian 11.7%; Roman Catholic 8.8%; Hindu 3.4%; Spiritist 1.8%; Muslim 1.5%; nonreligious 2.3%; other 3.2%.
Major cities (2002): Kingstown 17,400; Georgetown 1,600; Byera 1,300; Barrouallie 1,300.

Vital statistics

Birth rate per 1,000 population (2002): 17.6 (world avg. 21.1); (1999) legitimate 17.9%; illegitimate 82.1%.
Death rate per 1,000 population (2002): 6.9 (world avg. 9.0).
Natural increase rate per 1,000 population (2002): 10.7 (world avg. 12.1).
Total fertility rate (avg. births per childbearing woman; 2004): 1.9.
Marriage rate per 1,000 population (2002): 4.5.
Divorce rate per 1,000 population (2002): 0.4.
Life expectancy at birth (2004): male 71.5 years; female 75.2 years.
Major causes of death per 100,000 population (2002): diseases of the circulatory system 229.9; malignant neoplasms (cancers) 106.9; diabetes mellitus 82.0; diseases of the respiratory system 57.0; infectious and parasitic diseases 54.4.

National economy

Budget (2002). Revenue: EC$312,000,000 (current revenue 80.8%, of which taxes on international trade and transactions 38.8%, income tax 25.6%, taxes on goods and services 15.7%; grants 5.1%; nontax revenue 13.8%; capital revenue 0.3%). Expenditures: EC$348,000,000 (current expenditure 81.3%, development expenditure 18.7%).
Public debt (external, outstanding; 2003): U.S.$192,400,000.
Production (metric tons except as noted). Agriculture, forestry, fishing (2004): bananas 45,000, sugarcane 18,000, roots and tubers (mainly eddoes and dasheens[5]) 9,800, plantains 3,500, coconuts 2,550, yams 2,200, oranges 1,600, sweet potatoes 1,225, ginger (2002) 510, nutmegs (2002) 285; soursops, guavas, mangoes, and papayas are also grown; livestock (number of live animals) 12,000 sheep, 9,150 pigs, 7,000 goats, 5,000 cattle; roundwood, n.a.; fish catch (2003) 4,782. Mining and quarrying: sand and gravel for local use. Manufacturing (value added in EC$'000,000; 2000): beverages and tobacco products 17.4; food 15.6; paper products and publishing 3.6; textiles, clothing, and footwear 3.3. Energy production (consumption): electricity (kW-hr; 2002) 108,000,000 (108,000,000); coal, none (none); crude petroleum, none (none); petroleum products (metric tons; 2002) none (60,000).
Tourism (2003): receipts from visitors U.S.$85,000,000; expenditures by nationals abroad U.S.$11,000,000.
Land use as % of total land area (2000): in temporary crops c. 18%, in permanent crops c. 18%, in pasture c. 5%; overall forest area c. 15%.

Gross national product (2004): U.S.$396,000,000 (U.S.$3,650 per capita).

Structure of gross domestic product and labour force				
	2003		1991	
	in value EC$'000,000	% of total value	labour force	% of labour force
Agriculture, forestry, fishing	75.1	7.4	8,377	20.1
Mining	2.0	0.2	98	0.2
Manufacturing	54.9	5.4	2,822	6.8
Construction	101.9	10.0	3,535	8.5
Public utilities	52.8	5.2	586	1.4
Transp. and commun.	167.1	16.5	2,279	5.5
Trade, restaurants	174.9	17.2	6,544	15.7
Finance, real estate	81.2	8.0	1,418	3.4
Pub. admin., defense	161.7	15.9	} 7,696	18.5
Services	17.0	1.7		
Other	126.9[6]	12.5[6]	8,327[7]	20.0[7]
TOTAL	1,015.5	100.0	41,682	100.0[4]

Population economically active (1991): total 41,682; activity rate of total population 39.1% (participation rates: ages 15–64, 67.5%; female 35.9%; unemployed [2001] more than 20%).

Price and earnings indexes (2000 = 100)							
	1998	1999	2000	2001	2002	2003	2004
Consumer price index	98.8	99.8	100.0	100.8	101.6	101.9	104.9
Daily earnings index	...	...	...	...	...	...	...

Household income and expenditure. Average household size (1991) 3.9; income per household (1988) EC$4,579 (U.S.$1,696); sources of income: n.a.; expenditure[8]: food and beverages 59.8%; clothing and footwear 7.7%; housing 6.3%; energy 6.2%.

Foreign trade[9]

Balance of trade (current prices)						
	1999	2000	2001	2002	2003	2004
U.S.$'000,000	−152.4	−115.6	−144.4	−139.2	−162.2	−190.4
% of total	61.0%	54.9%	63.5%	63.9%	68.0%	71.8%

Imports (2002): U.S.$178,500,000 (machinery and transport equipment 23.4%; food products 22.1%; chemicals and chemical products 9.9%; mineral fuels 8.6%). *Major import sources:* U.S. 40.4%; Caricom countries 28.4%, of which Trinidad and Tobago 20.7%, Barbados 4.0%; U.K. 8.4%; Japan 3.5%.
Exports (2002): U.S.$39,300,000 (domestic exports 92.2%, of which bananas 40.4%, packaged flour 11.5%, packaged rice 10.7%, eddoes and dasheens[5] 5.2%; reexports 7.8%). *Major export destinations:* Caricom countries 50.9%, of which Barbados 10.6%, Trinidad and Tobago 9.0%, St. Lucia 8.3%; U.K. 38.8%; U.S. 5.0%.

Transport and communications

Transport. Railroads: none. Roads (2003): total length 515 mi, 829 km (paved 70%). Vehicles (2003): passenger cars 11,679; trucks and buses 4,499. Air transport (2000): passenger arrivals 132,445; passenger departures 134,012; airports (1998) with scheduled flights 5.

Communications				units per 1,000
Medium	date	unit	number	persons
Radio	1995	receivers	65,000	591
Television	1995	receivers	17,700	161
Telephones	2004	main lines	19,000	157
Cellular telephones	2004	subscribers	57,000	471
Personal computers	2004	units	16,000	132
Internet	2004	users	8,000	66

Education and health

Educational attainment (1991). Percentage of employed population[10] having: no formal schooling 0.1%; primary education 69.1%; secondary 23.8%; higher vocational 3.5%; university 2.6%; other/unknown 0.9%. *Literacy* (1998): total population age 15 and over literate c. 82%.

Education (2000)	schools	teachers	students	student/ teacher ratio
Primary (age 5–11)	60	987	20,530	20.8
Secondary (age 12–18)	21	406	7,939	19.6
Voc., teacher tr.	4	48	904	18.8

Health: physicians (1998) 59 (1 per 1,883 persons); hospital beds (2000) 209 (1 per 535 persons); infant mortality rate per 1,000 live births (2004) 15.2.
Food (2001): daily per capita caloric intake 2,609 (vegetable products 83%, animal products 17%); 108% of FAO recommended minimum requirement.

Military

Total active duty personnel (2004): no regular military forces; the paramilitary includes coast guard and police units.

[1]Includes 7 nonelective seats. [2]January 1. [3]For statistical purposes and the election of legislative representatives only. [4]Detail does not add to total given because of rounding. [5]Varieties of taro roots. [6]Indirect taxes less subsidies and less imputed bank service charges. [7]Unemployed. [8]Based on 1981 (current) weights of consumer price index components. [9]Imports c.i.f.; exports f.o.b. [10]33,440 persons.

Internet resources for further information:
• **Eastern Caribbean Central Bank** http://www.eccb-centralbank.org
• **Embassy of St. Vincent & the Grenadines** http://www.embsvg.com/Default.asp

Samoa[1]

Pacific Ocean

Official name: Malo Sa'oloto Tuto'atasi o Samoa (Samoan); Independent State of Samoa (English).
Form of government: constitutional monarchy[2] with one legislative house (Legislative Assembly [49]).
Chief of state: Head of State.
Head of government: Prime Minister.
Capital: Apia.
Official languages: Samoan; English.
Official religion: none.
Monetary unit: 1 tala (SA$[3], plural tala) = 100 sene; valuation (Sept. 1, 2005) 1 U.S.$ = SA$2.70; 1 £ = SA$4.97.

Area and population

Islands Districts	Largest towns	area sq mi	area sq km	population 2001 census
Savai'i	Matavai	649[4]	1,682	46,010
Fa'aseleleaga		103	266	12,949
Gaga'emauga		86	223	7,108
Gaga'ifomauga		141	365	4,770
Palauli		202	523	8,984
Satupa'itea		49	127	5,556
Vaisigano		69	178	6,643
Upolu[5]	Apia	444	1,150	130,700
A'ana[5]		75	193	20,167
Aiga-i-le-Tai		10	27	4,508
Atua[5]		159	413	21,168
Tuamasaga		185	479	83,191
Vaa-o-Fonoti		15	38	1,666
TOTAL		1,093	2,831[4]	176,710

Demography

Population (2005): 185,000.
Density (2005): persons per sq mi 169.3, persons per sq km 65.3.
Urban-rural (2003): urban 22.3%; rural 77.7%.
Sex distribution (2001): male 52.09%; female 47.91%.
Age breakdown (2001): under 15, 40.8%; 15–29, 25.6%; 30–44, 17.9%; 45–59, 9.2%; 60–74, 5.0%; 75 and over, 1.5%.
Population projection: (2010) 189,000; (2020) 190,000.
Doubling time: 31 years.
Ethnic composition (1997): Samoan (Polynesian) 92.6%; Euronesian (European and Polynesian) 7.0%; European 0.4%.
Religious affiliation (2001): Congregational 34.8%; Roman Catholic 19.6%; Methodist 15.0%; Mormon 12.7%; Assemblies of God 6.6%; other Christian 9.6%; other/unknown 1.7%.
Major towns (2001): Apia 38,836 (urban agglomeration 60,734); Vaitele 5,200[6]; Faleasi'u 3,209; Vailele 3,175[6]; Le'auva'a 2,828.

Vital statistics

Birth rate per 1,000 population (2003): 28.6 (world avg. 21.1).
Death rate per 1,000 population (2003): 5.5 (world avg. 9.0).
Natural increase rate per 1,000 population (2003): 23.1 (world avg. 12.1).
Total fertility rate (avg. births per childbearing woman; 2003): 4.1.
Marriage rate per 1,000 population: n.a.
Divorce rate per 1,000 population: n.a.
Life expectancy at birth (2004): male 67.6 years; female 73.3 years.
Major causes of death per 100,000 population (2002): cerebrovascular diseases 24.3; septicemia 19.2; congestive heart failure 15.8; pneumonia 15.8; myocardial infarction 13.6.

National economy

Budget (2003–04). Revenue: SA$317,700,000 (tax revenue 69.2%, of which VAT 24.2%, excise taxes 18.7%, income tax 13.4%; grants 22.4%; nontax revenue 8.4%). Expenditures: SA$326,600,000 (current expenditure 62.6%, of which general services 21.6%, education 15.6%, health 11.5%; development expenditure 26.5%; net lending 10.9%).
Production (metric tons except as noted). Agriculture, forestry, fishing (2004): coconuts 140,000, bananas 21,500, taro 17,000, pineapples 4,600, mangoes 4,000, papayas 3,600, yams 2,600, avocados 1,000, cacao beans 500; livestock (number of live animals) 201,000 pigs, 29,000 cattle, 450,000 chickens; roundwood 131,000 cu m; fish catch (2003) 10,267. Mining and quarrying: n.a. Manufacturing (value of manufactured exports in SA$'000; January 1–November 30, 2004): noni[7] juice 4,350; beer 3,920; coconut cream 2,390; wearing apparel 1,980; coconut oil (January 1–October 31, 2004) 750. Energy production (consumption): electricity (kW-hr; 2002) 105,000,000 (105,000,-000); coal, none (n.a.); crude petroleum, none (none); petroleum products (metric tons; 2002) none (47,000).
Tourism: receipts from visitors (2003) U.S.$53,000,000; expenditures by nationals abroad (1999) U.S.$4,000,000.
Household income and expenditure. Average household size (2001) 7.7; income per household: n.a.; sources of income (1997): wages and salaries 44%, other 56%; expenditure (2002)[8]: food 50.3%, transportation and communications 14.4%, alcohol and tobacco products 12.2%, household furnishings and operation 11.1%.
Population economically active (2001): total 52,900; activity rate of total population 30.0% (participation rates: ages 15 and over, 50.7%; female 30.6%; unemployed 4.9%).

Price and earnings indexes (2000 = 100)

	1998	1999	2000	2001	2002	2003	2004
Consumer price index	98.8	99.0	100.0	103.8	112.2	112.3	130.7
Earnings index	...	...	...	...	...	...	...

Public debt (external, outstanding; 2003–04): U.S.$171,400,000.
Gross national product (2004): U.S.$333,000,000 (U.S.$1,860 per capita).

Structure of gross domestic product and labour force

	2004 in value SA$'000	2004 % of total value	2001 labour force	2001 % of labour force
Agriculture	146,459	14.1	20,600	38.9
Mining	...	...		
Manufacturing	153,639	14.7		
Construction	85,680	8.2		
Public utilities	45,305	4.4		
Transp. and commun.	128,670	12.3	29,400	55.6
Trade, hotels, restaurants	225,520	21.6		
Finance	99,629	9.6		
Pub. admin., defense	76,484	7.3		
Services	96,943	9.3		
Other	−15,975[9]	−1.5[9]	2,900	5.5
TOTAL	1,042,354	100.0	52,900	100.0

Land use as % of total land area (2000): in temporary crops 20.8%, in permanent crops 24.0%, in pasture 0.7%; overall forest area 37.2%.

Foreign trade[10]

Balance of trade (current prices)

	1999	2000	2001	2002	2003	2004
SA$'000,000	−293.6	−303.9	−396.1	−407.9	−362.7	−435.1
% of total	72.9%	77.2%	79.0%	81.5%	80.4%	86.8%

Imports (2001–02): SA$465,000,000 (petroleum products 10.2%, imports for government 5.2%, unspecified 84.6%). *Major import sources:* New Zealand 34.4%; Australia 26.6%; U.S. 11.8%; Fiji 8.7%; Japan 6.6%.
Exports (2001–02): SA$49,500,000 (fresh fish 66.9%, garments 11.5%, beer 6.7%, coconut cream 6.6%). *Major export destinations:* American Samoa 52.3%; U.S. 32.2%; New Zealand 6.8%; Germany 3.4%; Australia 2.7%.

Transport and communications

Transport. Railroads: none. Roads (1999): total length 491 mi, 790 km (paved 42%). Vehicles (1998): passenger cars 2,904; trucks and buses 2,500. Air transport (2004)[11]: passenger-km 326,090,000; metric ton-km cargo 2,709,000; airports (1997) with scheduled flights 3.

Communications

Medium	date	unit	number	units per 1,000 persons
Radio	1997	receivers	178,000	1,035
Television	2001	receivers	26,000	147
Telephones	2003	main lines	13,300	73
Cellular telephones	2003	subscribers	10,500	58
Personal computers	2002	units	1,000	6.7
Internet	2004	users	6,000	33

Education and health

Educational attainment (2001). Percentage of population age 15 and over having: no formal schooling 0.6%; incomplete/complete primary education c. 30%; incomplete/complete secondary c. 57%; postsecondary 10.3%, of which university 3.0%; other 2.1%. *Literacy* (2003): total population over age 15 literate 99.7%; males literate 99.6%; females literate 99.7%.

Education (2002–03)

	schools	teachers	students	student/ teacher ratio
Primary (age 5–11)	155[12]	1,121	30,164	26.9
Secondary (age 12–18)	...	1,074	22,941	21.4
Higher[13]	...	140	1,179	8.4

Health (1998): physicians 57 (1 per 3,007 persons); hospital beds 476 (1 per 360 persons); infant mortality rate per 1,000 live births (2004) 28.7.
Food (2002): daily per capita caloric intake 2,945 (vegetable products 70%, animal products 30%); (1992) 124% of FAO recommended minimum requirement.

Military

No military forces are maintained; informal defense ties exist with New Zealand per 1962 Treaty of Friendship.

[1]In 1997 the short-form name of the country was officially changed from Western Samoa to Samoa. [2]According to the constitution, the current Head of State, paramount chief HH Malietoa Tanumafili II, will hold office for life. Upon his death, the monarchy will functionally cease, and future Heads of State will be elected by the Legislative Assembly. [3]Symbol of the monetary unit was changed from WS$ to SA$ in 1997. [4]Detail does not add to total given because of rounding. [5]Includes area and any population of off-shore islets. [6]Within Apia urban agglomeration. [7]Fruit known locally as *nonu;* also known as Indian mulberry. [8]Weights of consumer price index components. [9]Less imputed bank service charges. [10]Imports c.i.f.; exports f.o.b. [11]Polynesian Airlines only. [12]1996. [13]2001–02.

Internet resources for further information:
• **Central Bank of Samoa** http://www.cbs.gov.ws
• **Samoa Statistical Services Division**
   http://www.spc.org.nc/prism/Country/WS/stats/index.html

San Marino

Official name: Serenissima Repubblica di San Marino (Most Serene Republic of San Marino).
Form of government: unitary multiparty republic with one legislative house (Great and General Council [60]).
Head of state and government: Captains-Regent (2).
Capital: San Marino.
Official language: Italian.
Official religion: none.
Monetary unit: 1 euro (€) = 100 cents; valuation (Sept. 1, 2005) 1 U.S.$ = €0.80; 1 £ = €1.47[1].

Area and population

Castles	Capitals	area sq mi	area sq km	population 2003[2] estimate
Acquaviva	Acquaviva	1.88	4.86	1,602
Borgo Maggiore	Borgo Maggiore	3.48	9.01	5,916
Chiesanuova	Chiesanuova	2.11	5.46	969
Città	San Marino	2.74	7.09	4,483
Domagnano	Domagnano	2.56	6.62	2,651
Faetano	Faetano	2.99	7.75	1,050
Fiorentino	Fiorentino	2.53	6.57	2,031
Montegiardino	Montegiardino	1.28	3.31	786
Serravalle/Dogano	Serravalle	4.07	10.53	9,265
TOTAL		23.63[3]	61.20	28,753

Demography

Population (2005): 30,100.
Density (2005): persons per sq mi 1,274, persons per sq km 491.8.
Urban-rural (2003): urban 88.7%; rural 11.3%.
Sex distribution (2004): male 49.02%; female 50.98%.
Age breakdown (2003[2]): under 15, 14.1%; 15–29, 16.6%; 30–44, 27.3%; 45–59, 19.7%; 60–74, 14.2%; 75 and over, 8.1%.
Population projection: (2010) 32,000; (2020) 35,000.
Ethnic composition (2003[2]): Sammarinesi 85.7%; Italian 13.0%; other 1.3%.
Religious affiliation (2000): Roman Catholic 88.7%; other Christian 3.5%; non-religious 5.1%; other 2.7%.
Major cities (2000): Serravalle/Dogano 8,547; San Marino 4,439; Borgo Maggiore 2,394[4]; Murata 1,549[4]; Domagnano 1,048[4].

Vital statistics

Birth rate per 1,000 population (2004): 10.3 (world avg. 21.1).
Death rate per 1,000 population (2004): 6.2 (world avg. 9.0).
Natural increase rate per 1,000 population (2004): 4.1 (world avg. 12.1).
Total fertility rate (avg. births per childbearing woman; 2004): 1.3.
Marriage rate per 1,000 population (2004): 7.0.
Divorce rate per 1,000 population (2004): 2.1.
Life expectancy at birth (2004): male 78.6 years; female 85.0 years.
Major causes of death per 100,000 population (1998–2002): disease of the circulatory system 339.0; malignant neoplasms (cancers) 225.3; diseases of the respiratory system 31.0; accidents, violence, and suicide 29.5.

National economy

Budget (2003). Revenue: €288,000,000 (direct taxes 34.7%; import taxes 33.0%; nontax revenue 22.0%). Expenditures: €272,400,000 (current expenditures 92.0%; capital expenditures 8.0%).
Public debt (2003): U.S.$52,900,000.
Tourism: number of tourist arrivals (2003) 2,882,207; receipts from visitors (1994) U.S.$252,500,000; expenditures by nationals abroad, n.a.
Population economically active (2003): total 20,236[5]; activity rate of total population 69.3%[6] (participation rates: ages 15–64 [2002] 72.1%[6]; female 41.5%[6]; unemployed [2004[2]] 3.9%).

Price and earnings indexes (2000 = 100)

	1997	1998	1999	2000	2001	2002	2003
Consumer price index	94.3	96.3	98.3	100.0	102.8	105.3	108.0
Annual earnings index	...	...	...	...	...	...	...

Household income and expenditure. Total number of households (2003[2]) 11,723; average household size (2003[2]) 2.5; income per household: n.a.; sources of income: n.a.; expenditure (1991)[7]: food, beverages, and tobacco 22.1%, housing, fuel, and electrical energy 20.9%, transportation and communications 17.6%, clothing and footwear 8.0%, furniture, appliances, and goods and services for the home 7.2%, education 7.1%.
Production (metric tons except as noted). Agriculture, forestry, fishing: small amounts of wheat, grapes, and barley; livestock (number of live animals; 1998) 831 cattle, 748 pigs. Quarrying: building stone is an important export product. Manufacturing (1998): processed meats 324,073 kg, of which beef 226,570 kg, pork 87,764 kg, veal 7,803 kg; cheese 61,563 kg; butter 12,658 kg; milk 1,167,620 litres; yogurt 5,131 litres; other major products include electrical appliances, musical instruments, printing ink, paint, cosmetics, furniture, floor tiles, gold and silver jewelry, clothing, and postage stamps. Energy production (consumption): all electrical power is imported via electrical grid from Italy (consumption [2001] 193,000,000); coal, none (n.a.); crude petroleum, none (n.a.); petroleum products, none (n.a.); natural gas, none ([2001] 51,000,000).

Gross national product (at current market prices; 2004): U.S.$1,110,000,000 (U.S.$39,830 per capita).

Structure of gross domestic product and labour force

	2001 in value €'000,000[8]	2001 % of total value[8]	2003 labour force[5]	2003 % of labour force[5]
Agriculture	27	3.0	31	0.2
Manufacturing	182	20.0	6,070	29.9
Construction	46	5.0	} 1,363	} 6.7
Public utilities	} 27	} 3.0		
Mining			...	...
Transp. and commun.	64	7.0	380	1.9
Trade	155	17.0	2,650	13.1
Finance and insurance			660	3.3
Services	} 410	} 45.0	2,059	10.2
Pub. admin., defense			4,136[9]	20.4[9]
Other			2,887[10]	14.3[10]
TOTAL	911	100.0	20,236	100.0

Land use as % of total land area (2000): in temporary crops, permanent crops, pasture, or forest c. 65%[11].

Foreign trade[12]

Balance of trade (current prices)

	1997	1998	1999	2000	2001	2002
U.S.$'000,000	−34.0	−17.9	−28.0	−53.3	−54.4	−91.0
% of total	1.0%	0.5%	0.8%	1.5%	1.8%	2.8%

Imports (2002): U.S.$1,657,000,000 (manufactured goods of all kinds, petroleum products, natural gas, electricity, and gold). *Major import source:* Italy[13].
Exports (2002): U.S.$1,566,000,000 (goods include electronics, postage stamps, leather products, ceramics, wine, wood products, and building stone). *Major export destination:* Italy[13].

Transport and communications

Transport. Railroads: none (nearest rail terminal is at Rimini, Italy, 17 mi [27 km] northeast). Roads (2001): total length 156 mi, 252 km. Vehicles (2002): passenger cars 28,470; trucks and buses 2,748. Air transport: airports with scheduled flights, none; there is, however, a heliport that provides passenger and cargo service between San Marino and Rimini, Italy, during the summer months.

Communications

Medium	date	unit	number	units per 1,000 persons
Daily newspapers	1998	circulation	2,000	77
Radio	1998	receivers	16,000	610
Television	1998	receivers	9,055	358
Telephones	2003	main lines	20,700	766
Cellular telephones	2003	subscribers	16,900	626
Internet	2003	users	14,500	536

Education and health

Educational attainment (2003[2]). Percentage of population age 14 and over having: basic literacy or primary education 41.0%; some secondary 25.0%; secondary 27.0%; higher degree 7.0%. *Literacy* (2001): total population age 15 and over literate 98.7%; males literate 98.9%; females literate 98.4%.

Education (2002–03)

	schools	teachers	students	student/teacher ratio
Primary (age 6–10)	14	242	1,343	5.4
Secondary (age 11–18)[14]	7	227	2,162	8.7
Higher	1	27	950	35.6

Health (2002): physicians 117 (1 per 230 persons); hospital beds 134 (1 per 191 persons); infant mortality rate per 1,000 live births (2004) 3.4.
Food (2002)[15]: daily per capita caloric intake 3,671 (vegetable products 74%, animal products 26%); 146% of FAO recommended minimum requirement.

Military

Total active duty personnel (2004): [16]. *Military expenditure as percentage of GDP:* n.a.

[1]Italian lira replaced by euro (€) from Jan. 1, 2002, at a conversion rate of Lit 1,936 = €1. [2]January 1. [3]Detail does not add to total given because of rounding. [4]1997. [5]Includes about 4,400 cross-border workers. [6]Percentage includes cross-border workers. [7]Weighting coefficients for component expenditures are those of the 1991 official Italian consumer price index for the North-Central region of Italy. [8]All figures are rounded estimates. [9]Includes 778 employees of public corporations. [10]Includes 619 unemployed and 2,268 self-employed. [11]Includes rock outcrops. [12]A customs union with Italy has existed since 1862. [13]In the late 1990s Italy accounted for 87% of all foreign trade. [14]Includes vocational schools. [15]Figures are for Italy. [16]Defense is the responsibility of Italy; a small voluntary military force performs ceremonial duties and provides limited assistance to police.

Internet resources for further information:
• **Office of Economic Planning: Data Processing and Statistics**
  http://www.upeceds.sm/eng

São Tomé and Príncipe

Official name: República democrática
de São Tomé e Príncipe (Democratic
Republic of São Tomé and Príncipe).
Form of government: multiparty
republic with one legislative house
(National Assembly [55]).
Chief of state: President.
Head of government: Prime Minister.
Capital: São Tomé.
Official language: Portuguese.
Official religion: none.
Monetary unit: 1 dobra (Db) = 100
cêntimos; valuation (Sept. 1, 2005)
1 U.S.$ = Db 7,955; 1 £ = Db 14,647.

Atlantic
Ocean

Area and population

Island	Capitals	area sq mi	area sq km	population 2001 census
Districts				
São Tomé		332	859	131,633
Aqua Grande	São Tomé	7	17	51,886
Cantagalo	Santana	46	119	13,258
Caué	São João Angolares	103	267	5,501
Lemba	Neves	88	229	10,696
Lobata	Guadalupe	41	105	15,187
Mé-Zóchi	Trindade	47	122	35,105
Autonomous Island				
Príncipe (Pagué)	Santo António	55	142	5,966
TOTAL		386[1]	1,001	137,599

Demography

Population (2005): 157,000.
Density (2005): persons per sq mi 406.7, persons per sq km 156.8.
Urban-rural (2001): urban 47.7%; rural 52.3%.
Sex distribution (2001): male 49.59%, female 50.41%.
Age breakdown (2001): under 15, 42.1%; 15–29, 30.3%; 30–44, 14.5%; 45–59,
6.9%; 60–74, 4.7%; 75 and over, 1.5%.
Population projection: (2010) 174,000; (2020) 209,000.
Doubling time: 20 years.
Ethnic composition (2000): black-white admixture 79.5%; Fang 10.0%; ango-
lares (descendants of former Angolan slaves) 7.6%; Portuguese 1.9%; other
1.0%.
Religious affiliation (2001): Roman Catholic, about 70.3%; Protestant 7.1%;
nonreligious 19.5%; other 3.1%.
Major cities (2001): São Tomé 3,666[2] (urban agglomeration 49,957); Neves
3,603[2]; São João Angolares 1,870[2]; Trindade 1,041[2]; Guadalupe 948[2].

Vital statistics

Birth rate per 1,000 population (2004): 41.4 (world avg. 21.1).
Death rate per 1,000 population (2004): 6.9 (world avg. 9.0).
Natural increase rate per 1,000 population (2004): 34.5 (world avg. 12.1).
Total fertility rate (avg. births per childbearing woman; 2004): 5.8.
Marriage rate per 1,000 population: n.a.
Divorce rate per 1,000 population: n.a.
Life expectancy at birth (2004): male 65.1 years; female 68.2 years.
Major causes of death per 100,000 population (1987): malaria 160.6; direct
obstetric causes 76.7; pneumonia 74.0; influenza 61.5; anemias 47.3; hyper-
tensive disease 32.1.

National economy

Budget (2003). Revenue: Db 280,900,000,000 (grants 48.8%; taxes 40.7%, of
which consumption taxes 14.0%, income and profit taxes 11.7%, import
taxes 11.0%; nontax revenue 9.3%; other [petroleum revenue] 1.2%).
Expenditures: Db 361,900,000,000 (current expenditure 47.2%; capital
expenditure 45.1%; other 7.7%).
Public debt (external, outstanding; 2002): U.S.$307,900,000.
Production (metric tons except as noted). Agriculture, forestry, fishing (2004):
oil palm fruit 40,000, coconuts 28,500, taro 28,000, bananas 27,900, vegetables 6,500, cassava 5,800, cacao 3,500, fruits (other than melon) 2,900, corn
(maize) 2,500, cinnamon 30, coffee 20; livestock (number of live animals)
5,000 goats, 4,600 cattle, 2,800 sheep, 2,500 pigs; roundwood 9,000 cu m; fish
catch (2001) 3,500, principally marine fish and shellfish. Mining and quarrying: some quarrying to support local construction industry. Manufacturing
(value in Db; 1995): beer 880,000; clothing 679,000; lumber 369,000; bakery
products 350,000; palm oil 228,000; soap 133,000; ceramics 87,000. Energy
production (consumption): electricity (kW-hr; 2002) 18,000,000 (18,000,000);
coal, none (none); crude petroleum, none (none); petroleum products (metric tons; 2002) none (30,000); natural gas, none (none).
Household income and expenditure. Average family size (2001) 3.5; income per
household: n.a.; sources of income: n.a.; expenditure (1995)[3]: food 71.9%,
housing and energy 10.2%, transportation and communications 6.4%, clothing and other items 5.3%, household durable goods 2.8%, education and
health 1.7%.
Tourism (2002): receipts from visitors U.S.$10,000,000; expenditures by nation-
als abroad U.S.$600,000.
Population economically active (2001)[4]: total 42,937; activity rate of total population 31.2% (participation rates: ages 10 and over 43.7%; female 33.8%;
unemployed [2002] 17.9%).

Price index (2000 = 100)

	1997	1998	1999	2000	2001	2002	2003
Consumer price index	55.9	79.1	89.1	100.0	109.2	120.2	132.1

Gross national product (2004): U.S.$60,000,000 (U.S.$370 per capita).

Structure of gross domestic product and labour force

	2003 in value Db '000,000	2003 % of total value	2001 labour force[4]	2001 % of labour force[4]
Agriculture, fishing	94,500	17.0	13,518	31.5
Mining	...	...	...	...
Manufacturing	24,700	4.4	2,893	6.7
Public utilities				
Construction	56,500	10.1	4,403	10.2
Transp. and commun.	150,000	26.9	792	1.8
Trade			8,787	20.5
Finance	59,100	10.6	...	...
Pub. admin., defense	156,800	28.2	3,307	7.7
Services	15,300	2.7	9,237	21.5
TOTAL	556,900	100.0[1]	42,937	100.0[1]

Land use as % of total land area (2000): in temporary crops 6.3%, in permanent crops 46.9%, in pasture 1.0%; overall forest area 28.3%.

Foreign trade

Balance of trade (current prices)

	1998	1999	2000	2001	2002	2003
U.S.$'000,000	–12.1	–18.0	–19.7	–20.7	–20.5	–21.1
% of total	56.3%	69.8%	75.5%	73.7%	67.0%	61.9%

Imports (2003): U.S.$27,500,000 (investment goods 42.2%, food and other agri-
cultural products 35.3%, petroleum products 16.7%). *Major import sources:*
Portugal c. 61%; Belgium c. 13%; Angola c. 9%; France c. 4%.
Exports (2003): U.S.$6,400,000 (cocoa beans 86.0%; remainder 14.0%). *Major
export destinations:* The Netherlands c. 42%; Belgium c. 25%; Portugal c.
19%; Angola c. 3%.

Transport and communications

Transport. Railroads: none. Roads (1999): total length 199 mi, 320 km (paved
68%). Vehicles (1996): passenger cars 4,040; trucks and buses 1,540. Air
transport (2001): passenger-km 7,000,000; short ton-km cargo, n.a.; airports
(2000) 2.

Communications

Medium	date	unit	number	units per 1,000 persons
Radio	1997	receivers	38,000	272
Television	1997	receivers	23,000	163
Telephones	2003	main lines	7,000	46
Cellular telephones	2003	subscribers	4,800	32
Internet	2004	users	20,000	122

Education and health

Educational attainment (2001). Percentage of population age 25 and over having: no formal schooling 0.3%; primary education 41.4%; lower secondary
25.0%; upper secondary/vocational 8.8%; higher 1.9%; unknown 22.6%.
Literacy (1991): total population age 15 and over literate 73.0%; males literate 85.0%; females literate 62.0%.

Education (1998)

	schools	teachers[5]	students	student/ teacher ratio
Primary (age 6–13)	71	638	20,287	34.1[5]
Secondary (age 14–18)[6]	11	415	11,814	29.6[5]
Voc., teacher tr.	...	...	...	...
Higher	...	...	...	...

Health: physicians (1996) 61 (1 per 2,147 persons); hospital beds (1991) 532
(1 per 211 persons); infant mortality rate per 1,000 live births (2004) 44.6.
Food (2002): daily per capita caloric intake 2,460 (vegetable products 96%,
animal products 4%); 105% of FAO recommended minimum requirement.

Military

Total active duty personnel (2004): tiny force with army, coast guard, and presidential guard branches. *Military expenditure as percentage of GDP* (2004):
0.8%; per capita expenditure U.S.$5.

[1]Detail does not add to total given because of rounding. [2]City proper population.
[3]Weights based on CPI components. [4]Employed only. [5]1997. [6]Includes vocational.

Internet resources for further information:
• **Instituto Nacional de Estatística**
  http://www.ine.st/home.html
• **UN Development Programme: Human Development Indicators (2003)**
  http://www.undp.org/hdr2003/indicator/cty_f_STP.html

Saudi Arabia

Official name: Al-Mamlakah al-'Arabīyah as-Sa'ūdīyah (Kingdom of Saudi Arabia).
Form of government: monarchy[1].
Heads of state and government: King.
Capital: Riyadh.
Official language: Arabic.
Official religion: Islam.
Monetary unit: 1 Saudi riyal (SRls) = 100 halalah; valuation (Sept. 1, 2005) 1 U.S.$ = SRls 3.75; 1 £ = SRls 6.91.

Area and population		area		population
Geographic Regions				2004
Administrative Regions	Capitals	sq mi	sq km	census[2]
Al-Gharbīyah (Western)		121,637	315,039	7,687,786
Al-Bāhah	Al-Bāhah	3,830	9,921	377,739
Al-Madīnah al-Munawwarah	Medina (Al-Madīnah)	58,684	151,990	1,512,076
Makkah al-Mukarramah	Mecca (Makkah)	59,123	153,128	5,797,971
Al-Janūbīyah (Southern)		91,844	237,875	3,293,964
'Asīr	Abha	29,611	76,693	1,688,368
Jīzān	Jīzān	4,506	11,671	1,186,139
Najrān	Najrān	57,727	149,511	419,457
Ash-Shamālīyah (Northern)		138,256	358,081	1,332,479
Al-Hudūd ash-Shamālīyah (Northern Borders)	'Ar'ar	43,165	111,797	279,286
Al-Jawf	Sakākah	38,692	100,212	361,676
Tabūk	Tabūk	56,399	146,072	691,517
Ash-Sharqīyah (Eastern)		259,662	672,522	3,360,157
Ash-Sharqīyah (Eastern)	Ad-Dammām	259,662	672,522	3,360,157
Al-Wūsṭā (Central)		218,601	566,173	6,999,152
Hā'il	Hā'il	40,111	103,887	527,033
Al-Qaṣīm	Buraydah	22,412	58,046	1,016,756
Ar-Riyāḍ	Riyadh (Ar-Riyāḍ)	156,078	404,240	5,455,363
TOTAL		830,000	2,149,690	22,673,538

Demography

Population (2005): 23,230,000[3].
Density (2005): persons per sq mi 28.0, persons per sq km 10.8.
Urban-rural (2003): urban 87.7%; rural 12.3%.
Sex distribution (2004): male 55.38%; female 44.62%.
Age breakdown (2003): under 15, 39.7%; 15–29, 26.9%; 30–44, 21.7%; 45–59, 8.0%; 60–74, 2.9%; 75 and over, 0.8%.
Population projection: (2010) 26,230,000; (2020) 33,440,000.
Doubling time: 26 years.
Ethnic composition (2000): Arab 88.1%, of which Saudi Arab 74.2%, Bedouin 3.9%, Gulf Arab 3.0%; Indo-Pakistani 5.5%; African black 1.5%; Filipino 1.0%; other 3.9%.
Religious affiliation (2000): Muslim *c.* 94%, of which Sunnī *c.* 84%, Shī'ī *c.* 10%; Christian *c.* 3.5%, of which Roman Catholic *c.* 3%; Hindu *c.* 1%; nonreligious/other *c.* 1.5%.
Major cities (2004): Riyadh 4,087,152; Jiddah 2,801,481; Mecca 1,294,106; Medina 918,889; Ad-Dammām 744,321.

Vital statistics

Birth rate per 1,000 population (2004): 29.7 (world avg. 21.1).
Death rate per 1,000 population (2004): 2.7 (world avg. 9.0).
Natural increase rate per 1,000 population (2004): 27.0 (world avg. 12.1).
Total fertility rate (avg. births per childbearing woman; 2004): 4.1.
Life expectancy at birth (2004): male 73.3 years; female 77.3 years.
Major causes of death per 100,000 population: n.a.

National economy

Budget (2004). Revenue: SRls 200,000,000,000 (oil revenues 72.5%). Expenditures: SRls 230,000,000,000 (defense and security 34.1%, human resource development 24.3%, public administration, municipal transfers, and subsidies 21.7%, health and social development 7.7%).
Production (metric tons except as noted). Agriculture, forestry, fishing (2004): wheat 2,358,000, alfalfa 2,000,000, dates 900,540, tomatoes 440,033, potatoes 320,897, watermelons 294,843, cantaloupes 245,564, sorghum 243,746, barley 138,432, grapes 101,653, dry onions 97,173; livestock (number of live animals) 7,000,000 sheep, 2,200,000 goats, 341,958 cattle, 260,000 camels; roundwood, n.a.; fish catch (2003) 52,929. Mining and quarrying (2003): gypsum 450,000; silver 13,000 kg; gold 8,769 kg. Manufacturing (value added in U.S.$'000,000; 1998): industrial chemicals 3,349; refined petroleum 1,806; cement, bricks, and tiles 1,505; fabricated metal products 1,129; food products 990; iron and steel 615. Energy production (consumption): electricity (kW-hr; 2002) 145,631,000,000 (145,631,000,000); coal, none (none); crude petroleum (barrels; 2004) 3,219,000,000 ([2002] 620,000,000); petroleum products (metric tons; 2002) 88,996,000 (56,760,000); natural gas (cu m; 2002) 55,401,000,000 (55,401,000,000).
Population economically active (2003): total 7,437,400, of which 3,833,000 Saudi workers and 3,604,400 foreign nationals; activity rate of total population 32.8% (participation rates: ages 15–64, *c.* 54%; female, n.a.; unemployed [end of 2002] 5.3%).

Price and earnings indexes (2000 = 100)							
	1998	1999	2000	2001	2002	2003	2004
Consumer price index	102.5	101.1	100.0	98.9	99.1	99.7	100.2
Earnings index	...	...	...	...	...	...	...

Gross national product (2004): U.S.$242,180,000,000 (U.S.$10,430 per capita).

Structure of gross domestic product and labour force				
	2003			
	in value SRls '000,000	% of total value	labour force	% of labour force
Agriculture	36,454	4.5	577,300	7.8
Petroleum and natural gas[4]	296,842	37.2	100,100	1.3
Other mining	2,785	0.4	14,400	0.2
Manufacturing[5]	81,001	10.2	645,900	8.7
Construction	46,283	5.8	1,084,300	14.6
Public utilities	9,870	1.2	99,900	1.3
Transp. and commun.	33,224	4.2	307,900	4.1
Trade	53,856	6.8	1,064,200	14.3
Finance, real estate	85,843	10.8	366,800	4.9
Pub. admin., defense	132,702	16.6	929,100	12.5
Services	25,114	3.2	} 2,247,500	30.2
Other	−6,800[6]	−0.9[6]		
TOTAL	797,174	100.0	7,437,400[7]	100.0[7, 8]

Household income and expenditure. Average household size (2002) 6.1; income per household: n.a.; sources of income: n.a.; expenditure (1998–99): food and nonalcoholic beverages 37.3%, transportation 18.9%, housing and energy 15.7%, household furnishings 9.7%.
National debt (domestic only; end of 2004): *c.* U.S.$150,000,000,000.
Tourism (in U.S.$'000,000; 2002): receipts 3,418; expenditures (2003) 4,165.
Land use as % of total land area (2000): in temporary crops 1.7%, in permanent crops 0.1%, in pasture 79.1%; overall forest area 0.7%.

Foreign trade[9]

Balance of trade (current prices)						
	1999	2000	2001	2002	2003	2004
SRls '000,000,000	+85.2	+177.3	+138.0	+150.6	+211.2	+304.5
% of total	28.9%	43.9%	37.1%	38.3%	43.3%	47.7%

Imports (2001): SRls 116,930,000,000 (transport equipment 21.3%, of which road vehicles 16.5%; machinery and apparatus 20.6%, of which general industrial machinery 5.7%; food and live animals 13.5%; chemicals and chemical products 9.6%; iron and steel 4.0%). *Major import sources* (2003): U.S. 15.0%; Japan 10.3%; Germany 8.9%; U.K. 5.9%; China 5.9%.
Exports (2001): SRls 274,085,000,000 (crude petroleum 72.8%; refined petroleum 16.0%; organic chemicals 3.6%; polyethylene 1.6%). *Major export destinations* (2004): U.S. 18.5%; Japan 15.2%; South Korea 10.1%; China 5.7%; Singapore 4.1%.

Transport and communications

Transport. Railroads (2004): route length 1,392 km; (2001) passenger-km 267,000,000; (2001) metric ton-km cargo 856,000,000. Roads (2003): total length 167,857 km (paved 100%). Vehicles (1996): passenger cars 1,744,000; trucks and buses 1,192,000. Air transport (2004)[10]: passenger-km 22,557,069,000; metric ton-km cargo 956,687,000; airports (2002) with scheduled flights 25.

Communications				units per 1,000
Medium	date	unit	number	persons
Daily newspapers[11]	2004	circulation	1,093,000	48
Radio	2000	receivers	7,180,000	326
Television	2003	receivers	5,851,200	265
Telephones	2004	main lines	3,695,100	163
Cellular telephones	2004	subscribers	9,175,800	405
Personal computers	2004	units	8,476,000	374
Internet	2004	users	1,586,000	70

Education and health

Educational attainment (2000). Percentage of Saudi (non-Saudi) population age 10 and over who: are illiterate 19.9% (12.1%), are literate/have primary education 39.5% (40.6%), have some/completed secondary education 34.2% (36.0%), have at least begun university education 6.4% (11.3%).

Education (2003)				student/
	schools	teachers	students	teacher ratio
Primary (age 6–12)	12,880	198,181	2,342,214	11.8
Secondary (age 13–18)	10,584	165,523	1,949,471	11.8
Vocational	86	6,121	70,755	11.6
Higher	...	10,673	525,344	49.2

Health (2003): physicians 34,595 (1 per 638 persons); hospital beds 48,042 (1 per 460 persons); infant mortality rate per 1,000 live births (2004) 13.7.
Food (2002): daily per capita caloric intake 2,844 (vegetable products 86%, animal products 14%); 118% of FAO recommended minimum requirement.

Military

Total active duty personnel (2004): 124,500[12] (army 60.2%, navy 12.4%, air force 14.5%, air defense forces 12.9%). U.S. troops (August 2004) 1,600.
Military expenditure as percentage of GDP (2003): 8.7%; per capita expenditure U.S.$850.

[1]Assisted by the Consultative Council consisting of 150 appointed members. [2]Preliminary figures. [3]Expatriates constitute 23% of total population. [4]Excludes refined petroleum. [5]Includes refined petroleum. [6]Other equals import duties less imputed bank service charges. [7]Includes 3,604,400 (48.5%) foreign workers. [8]Detail does not add to total given because of rounding. [9]Imports c.i.f., exports f.o.b. [10]Saudi Arabian Airlines only. [11]Circulation of top 10 dailies only. [12]Excludes 75,000 in national guard and 15,500 paramilitary.

Internet resources for further information:
• Ministry of Information http://www.saudinf.com

Senegal

Official name: République du Sénégal (Republic of Senegal).
Form of government: multiparty republic with one legislative house (National Assembly [120]).
Head of state and government: President assisted by Prime Minister.
Capital: Dakar[1].
Official language: French.
Official religion: none.
Monetary unit: 1 CFA franc (CFAF) = 100 centimes; valuation (Sept. 1, 2005) 1 U.S.$ = CFAF 522.78; 1 £ = CFAF 962.57[2].

Atlantic Ocean
Gulf of Guinea

Area and population

Regions	Capitals	area sq mi	area sq km	population 2002 census[3]
Dakar	Dakar	212	550	2,267,356
Diourbel	Diourbel	1,683	4,359	1,049,954
Fatick	Fatick	3,064	7,935	613,000
Kaolack	Kaolack	6,181	16,010	1,066,375
Kolda	Kolda	8,112	21,011	847,243
Louga	Louga	11,270	29,188	677,533
Matam	Matam	9,685	25,083	423,041
Saint-Louis	Saint-Louis	7,353	19,044	688,767
Tambacounda	Tambacounda	23,012	59,602	605,695
Thiès	Thiès	2,549	6,601	1,290,265
Ziguinchor	Ziguinchor	2,834	7,339	437,986
TOTAL		75,955	196,722	9,967,215

Demography

Population (2005): 11,706,000.
Density (2005): persons per sq mi 154.1, persons per sq km 59.5.
Urban-rural (2003): urban 49.6%; rural 50.4%.
Sex distribution (2002): male 49.08%; female 50.92%.
Age breakdown (2003): under 15, 43.7%; 15–29, 28.1%; 30–44, 15.7%; 45–59, 8.0%; 60–74, 3.6%; 75 and over, 0.9%.
Population projection: (2010) 13,109,000; (2020) 15,816,000.
Doubling time: 29 years.
Ethnic composition (2000): Wolof 34.6%; Peul (Fulani) and Tukulor 27.1%; Serer 12.0%; Malinke (Mandingo) 9.7%; other 16.6%.
Religious affiliation (2000): Muslim 87.6%; traditional beliefs 6.2%; Christian 5.5%, of which Roman Catholic 4.7%; other 0.7%.
Major cities (2002)[3]: Dakar 1,983,093[4]; Thiès 237,849; Kaolack 172,305; Saint-Louis 154,555; Mbour 153,503; Ziguinchor 153,269.

Vital statistics

Birth rate per 1,000 population (2004): 34.1 (world avg. 21.1).
Death rate per 1,000 population (2004): 9.8 (world avg. 9.0).
Natural increase rate per 1,000 population (2004): 24.3 (world avg. 12.1).
Total fertility rate (avg. births per childbearing woman; 2004): 4.6.
Life expectancy at birth (2004): male 57.1 years; female 60.1 years.
Major causes of death: n.a.; major diseases are malaria, tetanus, meningitis, and tuberculosis.

National economy

Budget (2002). Revenue: CFAF 713,900,000,000 (tax revenue 85.7%; grants 9.6%; nontax revenue 4.7%). Expenditures: CFAF 738,100,000,000 (current expenditures 62.6%, of which wages 27.0%, education 21.2%, health 5.7%, interest payment 3.8%; development expenditure 37.4%).
Public debt (external, outstanding; 2003): U.S.$3,983,000,000.
Production (metric tons except as noted). Agriculture, forestry, fishing (2004): sugarcane 850,000, peanuts (groundnuts) 465,000, corn (maize) 422,623, watermelons 398,549, millet 379,166, paddy rice 264,500, cassava 180,000, sorghum 132,400, oil palm fruit 70,000; livestock (number of live animals) 4,700,000 sheep, 4,000,000 goats, 3,100,000 cattle, 504,500 horses; roundwood 6,036,939 cu m; fish catch (2003) 448,174. Mining and quarrying (2004): phosphate 1,576,000; salt 240,000. Manufacturing (value added in U.S.$'000,000; 2000): food and food products 60; industrial chemicals 35; refined petroleum products 30; cement, bricks, and ceramics 30; paints, soaps, and pharmaceuticals 22. Energy production (consumption): electricity (kW-hr; 2002) 1,495,000,000 (1,495,000,000); coal, none (none); crude petroleum (barrels; 2002) none (6,780,000); petroleum products (metric tons; 2002) 907,000 (1,195,000); natural gas (cu m; 2002) 897,000 (897,000).
Population economically active (2001): total 4,294,000; activity rate of total population 44.6% (participation rates: ages 15–64, n.a.; female, n.a.; unemployed c. 48%).

Price and earnings indexes (2000 = 100)

	1998	1999	2000	2001	2002	2003	2004
Consumer price index	98.5	99.3	100.0	103.1	105.4	105.3	105.9
Hourly earnings index	...	...	...	...	...	...	...

Household income and expenditure. Average household size (2002) 8.7.
Tourism: receipts (2003) U.S.$184,000,000; expenditures (2002) U.S.$43,000,000.
Gross national product (at current market prices; 2004): U.S.$6,967,000,000 (U.S.$670 per capita).

Structure of gross domestic product and labour force

	2003 in value CFAF '000,000,000	2003 % of total value	1991 labour force	1991 % of labour force
Agriculture	568.2	15.2	1,789,467	65.3
Mining	46.0	1.2	1,998	0.1
Manufacturing	446.3	12.0	161,124	5.9
Public utilities	84.5	2.3	...	...
Construction	172.9	4.7	60,935	2.2
Transp. and commun.	265.9	7.1	58,081	2.1
Trade, hotels	679.9	18.2	378,241	13.8
Finance			4,623	0.2
Services	1,005.2	27.0	...	...
Pub. admin., defense			268,721	9.8
Other	460.8[5]	12.3[5]	16,286	0.6
TOTAL	3,729.7	100.0	2,739,476	100.0

Land use as % of total land area (2000): in temporary crops 12.3%, in permanent crops 0.2%, in pasture 29.3%; overall forest area 32.2%.

Foreign trade

Balance of trade (current prices)

	1999	2000	2001	2002	2003	2004
CFAF '000,000,000	−201	−254	−312	−375	−470	−533
% of total	13.5%	15.4%	17.5%	20.1%	24.3%	25.6%

Imports (2003): CFAF 1,200,000,000,000 (food and live animals 27.4%, of which rice 10.5%; mineral fuels and lubricants 19.3%, of which crude petroleum 13.3%; capital goods 17.5%). *Major import sources:* France 24.9%; Asian countries 16.5%; Nigeria 12.2%; Spain 4.3%; United States 3.6%.
Exports (2001): CFAF 575,000,000,000 (fresh fish 16.1%; refined petroleum 15.5%; fresh crustaceans and mollusks 12.0%; bunkers and ships' stores 12.0%; phosphorous pentoxide and phosphoric acids 9.5%; peanut [groundnut] oil 9.1%). *Major export destinations* (2003): African countries 37.3%, of which Mali 9.5%, Côte d'Ivoire 5.4%; Asian countries 16.5%; France 12.2%; Italy 8.5%.

Transport and communications

Transport. Railroads (2002): route length 563 mi, 906 km; passenger-km 105,000,000; metric ton-km cargo 345,000,000. Roads (2000): total length 9,061 mi, 14,583 km (paved 29%). Vehicles (2001): passenger cars 193,000; trucks and buses 79,000. Air transport (2003)[6]: passenger-km 388,000,000; metric ton-km cargo, none; airports (1996) with scheduled flights 7.

Communications

Medium	date	unit	number	units per 1,000 persons
Daily newspapers	2000	circulation	47,000	5.0
Radio	2001	receivers	1,254,400	128
Television	2003	receivers	869,000	78
Telephones	2003	main lines	228,800	22
Cellular telephones	2004	subscribers	1,028,100	99
Personal computers	2004	units	242,000	23
Internet	2004	users	482,000	47

Education and health

Educational attainment: n.a. *Literacy* (2003): percentage of total population age 15 and over literate 40.2%; males literate 49.9%; females literate 30.8%.

Education (2002–03)

	schools	teachers	students	student/ teacher ratio
Primary (age 6–12)	5,670	29,216	1,287,093	44.1
Secondary (age 13–18)	579	7,601	306,026	40.3
Vocational[7]	12	384	4,425	11.5
Higher[8]	2	963	22,157	23.0

Health: physicians (1996) 649 (1 per 13,162 persons); hospital beds (1998) 3,582 (1 per 2,500 persons); infant mortality rate per 1,000 live births (2004) 55.3.
Food (2002): daily per capita caloric intake 2,279 (vegetable products 91%, animal products 9%); 95% of FAO recommended minimum requirement.

Military

Total active duty personnel (2004): 13,620 (army 87.4%, navy 7.0%, air force 5.6%); French troops (August 2004) 1,100. *Military expenditure as percentage of GDP* (2003): 1.5%; per capita expenditure U.S.$8.

[1]Movement of capital out of Dakar was officially approved July 2005; future capital location was undecided. [2]Formerly pegged to the French franc and since Jan. 1, 2002, to the euro at the rate of 1€ = CFAF 656.96. [3]Preliminary. [4]Includes urban departments of Pikine (pop. 768,826) and Guédiawaye (pop. 258,370), adjacent to Dakar department (pop. 955,897). [5]Taxes and duties on imports. [6]Air Sénégal International only. [7]1999–2000. [8]Universities only; 2000–01.

Internet resources for further information:
- **République du Sénégal: Site officiel du Gouvernement**
  http://www.gouv.sn
- **La Banque de France: La Zone Franc**
  http://www.banque-france.fr/fr/eurosys/zonefr/zonefr.htm
- **Situation Economique et Sociale du Senegal**
  http://www.ansd.org/donnees/analyse/pdf/
  situation%20%C3%A9conomique.pdf

Serbia and Montenegro

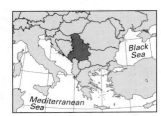

Official name: Srbija i Crna Gora
(Serbia and Montenegro[1]).
Form of government: state union
("loose confederation") with one
legislative house (Parliament [126]).
Head of state and government: President
assisted by Council of Ministers.
Administrative centre: Belgrade[2].
Official language: none.
Official religion: none.
Monetary unit: 1 Serbian dinar[3] = 100
paras; valuation (Sept. 1, 2005)
1 U.S.$ = 67.62 Serbian dinars;
1 £ = 124.50 Serbian dinars.

Area and population

Republics	Major cities	area sq mi	area sq km	population 2002–03 data[4]
Montenegro (Crna Gora)	Podgorica	5,333	13,812	620,145[4]
Serbia (Srbija)	Belgrade	29,913	77,474	7,479,437[4]
Central Serbia	Belgrade	21,609	55,968	5,454,950
Vojvodina	Novi Sad	8,304	21,506	2,024,487
UN interim-admin. province[5]				
Kosovo (Kosova)	Priština	4,203	10,887	1,900,000[4]
TOTAL		39,449	102,173	9,999,582[4]

Demography

Population (2005): 9,960,000.
Density (2005): persons per sq mi 252.5, persons per sq km 97.5.
Urban-rural (2003): urban 52.0%; rural 48.0%.
Sex distribution (2003): male 49.19%; female 50.81%.
Age breakdown (2003): under 15, 18.6%; 15–29, 22.5%; 30–44, 20.5%; 45–59, 19.0%; 60–74, 13.9%; 75 and over, 5.5%.
Population projection: (2010) 9,935,000; (2020) 9,799,000.
Ethnic composition (2000): Serb 62.1%; Albanian 17.1%; Montenegrin 4.3%; Hungarian 4.3%; Croat 3.1%; Bosniac 1.8%; Rom (Gypsy) 1.4%; Slovak 0.9%; Romanian 0.8%; other 4.2%.
Religious affiliation (2000): Christian 67.8%, of which Orthodox 56.8%, Roman Catholic 5.1%; Muslim 16.2%; nonreligious/atheist 15.9%; other 0.1%.
Major cities (2002): Belgrade 1,120,092; Novi Sad 191,405; Niš 173,724; Priština 165,844[6]; Kragujevac 146,373; Podgorica 139,724[6].

Vital statistics

Birth rate per 1,000 population (2004)[7]: 10.9 (world avg. 21.1).
Death rate per 1,000 population (2004)[7]: 13.5 (world avg. 9.0).
Natural increase rate per 1,000 population (2004)[7]: –2.6 (world avg. 12.1).
Total fertility rate (avg. births per childbearing woman; 2004): 1.7.
Life expectancy at birth (2004): male 71.9 years; female 77.1 years.
Major causes of death per 100,000 population (2003)[7]: diseases of the circulatory system 549.5; malignant neoplasms (cancers) 183.3; accidents, violence, and poisoning 37.6; diseases of the respiratory system 36.1.

National economy

Budget (2004)[8]. Revenue: 633,000,000,000 Serbian dinars (tax revenue 91.0%, of which VAT 27.0%, social security tax 26.2%, income tax 12.9%, excise tax 12.3%; nontax revenue 9.0%). Expenditure: 637,100,000,000 Serbian dinars (transfers 48.6%, wages 22.7%, other 28.7%).
Public debt (external, outstanding; 2004): U.S.$12,918,000,000.
Production[7] (metric tons except as noted). Agriculture, forestry, fishing (2004): corn (maize) 6,287,000, wheat 2,746,000, sugar beets 2,643,034, potatoes 1,098,000, plums 561,000, grapes 490,000, sunflower seeds 428,589, raspberries 90,000; livestock (number of live animals) 3,463,000 pigs, 1,838,000 sheep, 1,276,000 cattle; roundwood 3,520,000 cu m; fish catch (2003) 1,055. Mining and quarrying (2003): bauxite 540,000; copper (metal content of ore) 22,000; lead (metal content of ore) 2,000. Manufacturing (value added in '000,000 Yugoslav new dinars; 2002): food products and beverages 65,222; chemicals and chemical products 21,951; fabricated metal products 13,658; cement, bricks, and ceramics 12,213; textiles, wearing apparel, and footwear 11,108; nonelectrical machinery 10,929. Energy production (consumption): electricity (kW-hr; 2004) 37,152,000,000[7] ([2002] 37,822,000,000); hard coal (metric tons; 2002) 112,000 (267,000); lignite (metric tons; 2004) 44,196,000 ([2002] 35,900,000); crude petroleum (barrels; 2004) 4,800,000[7] ([2002] 19,000,000); petroleum products (metric tons; 2002) 2,200,000 (3,029,000); natural gas (cu m; 2002) 844,000,000 (2,703,000,000).
Population economically active (2002)[7, 9]: total 2,241,241; activity rate 27.8% (participation rates: over age 15, 33.8%; female 41.8%; unemployed [2004] 31.7%[10]).

Price and earnings indexes (2000 = 100)

	1998	1999	2000	2001	2002	2003	2004
Consumer price index	37.2	53.9	100.0	189.2	220.4	241.2	267.2
Monthly earnings index[7]	...	50.6	100.0	214.3	355.3	443.8	...

Household income and expenditure (2002)[7]. Average household size 2.9; income per household 206,267 Yugoslav new dinars (U.S.$3,370); sources of income: wages and salaries 50.4%, transfers 27.3%, self-employment 8.8%; expenditure: food 46.2%, housing, n.a., energy 11.9%, clothing and footwear 8.3%, transportation and communications 8.2%.

Gross national product (2004)[7]: U.S.$21,715,000,000 (U.S.$2,620 per capita).

Structure of gross material product and labour force[7]

	2002 in value '000,000 Yugoslav new dinars	% of total value	labour force[9]	% of labour force
Agriculture	143,621	18.8	159,516	7.1
Mining	18,104	2.4	54,152	2.4
Manufacturing	222,187	29.2	576,176	25.7
Construction	43,970	5.8	140,477	6.3
Public utilities	42,067	5.5	53,743	2.4
Transp. and commun.	101,009	13.2	138,067	6.2
Trade, restaurants	163,225	21.4	418,453	18.7
Finance, real estate	24,926	3.3	72,122	3.2
Pub. admin., defense	...	...	184,258	8.2
Services	2,933	0.4	425,988	19.0
Other	—	—	18,289	0.8
TOTAL	762,042	100.0	2,241,241	100.0

Land use as % of total land area (2000): in temporary crops 33.4%, in permanent crops 3.2%, in pasture 18.1%; overall forest area 28.3%.
Tourism (2003): receipts from visitors U.S.$201,000,000; expenditures, n.a.

Foreign trade

Balance of trade (current prices)

	1999	2000	2001	2002	2003	2004
U.S.$'000,000	–1,620	–1,772	–2,540	–3,539	–5,302	–7,047
% of total	32.6%	36.3%	42.5%	46.0%	50.0%	47.5%

Imports (2003): U.S.$7,952,000,000 (machinery and transport equipment 28.5%; mineral fuels 15.2%, of which crude petroleum 7.9%; chemical products 13.4%; food 7.1%). *Major import sources:* Germany 13.6%; Russia 13.0%; Italy 10.1%; China 4.1%; Slovenia 3.7%.
Exports (2003): U.S.$2,650,000,000 (food 18.8%, of which raspberries 4.3%; machinery and transport equipment 9.6%; chemical products 9.3%; aluminum 5.4%). *Major export destinations:* Bosnia and Herzegovina 15.0%; Italy 13.5%; Germany 10.9%; Macedonia 8.3%; Switzerland 6.1%.

Transport and communications

Transport. Railroads (2002)[7]: length 4,058 km; passenger-km 1,146,000,000; metric ton-km cargo 2,319,000,000. Roads (2002)[7]: total length 45,290 km (paved 62%). Vehicles (2001): passenger cars 1,481,400; trucks and buses 330,500. Air transport (2004)[11]: passenger-km 1,285,717,000; metric ton-km cargo 56,218,000; airports (2000) 5.

Communications

Medium	date	unit	number	units per 1,000 persons
Daily newspapers	2000	circulation	1,130,000	107
Radio	2000	receivers	3,130,000	297
Television	2000	receivers	2,980,000	282
Telephones	2004	main lines	2,685,400	243
Cellular telephones	2004	subscribers	4,729,600	338
Personal computers	2004	units	389,000	27
Internet	2004	users	1,200,000	79

Education and health

Educational attainment (1991). Percentage of population age 15 and over having: less than full primary education 33.5%; primary 25.0%; secondary 32.2%; postsecondary and higher 9.3%. *Literacy* (2002): total population age 15 and over literate 96.4%; males literate 98.9%; females literate 94.1%.

Education (2002–03)[7]

	schools	teachers	students	student/teacher ratio
Primary (age 7–14)	4,063	49,212	751,772	15.3
Secondary (age 15–18)	534	28,711	336,937	11.7
Higher	150	11,320	207,082	18.3

Health (2002): physicians 21,455[7] (1 per 378 persons); hospital beds 50,702[7] (1 per 157 persons); infant mortality rate per 1,000 live births (2004)[7] 7.5.
Food (2002): daily per capita caloric intake 2,678 (vegetable products 65%, animal products 35%); 105% of FAO recommended minimum.

Military

Total active duty personnel (2004)[12]: 65,300 (army 84.2%, air force 10.0%, navy 5.8%). *Military expenditure as percentage of GDP* (2003)[7]: 3.0%; per capita expenditure U.S.$79.

[1]Replaced Yugoslavia per effective date of new constitution (Feb. 4, 2003). [2]Principal executive and legislative bodies meet in Belgrade; the principal judicial body meets in Podgorica. [3]Replaced Yugoslav new dinar on Feb. 4, 2003, at rate of 1 to 1. Montenegro and Kosovo (Kosova) use the euro adopted on Jan. 1, 2002. [4]Summed total for 2003 de jure census (for Montenegro), 2002 census (for Serbia), and 2003 estimate (for Kosovo [Kosova]). [5]From June 1999. [6]2003. [7]Excludes Kosovo. [8]Consolidated general government. [9]Employed only. [10]Excludes Kosovo and Montenegro. [11]JAT Airways and Montenegro Airlines only. [12]More than 17,000 troops from 36 NATO and non-NATO countries were deployed in Kosovo in September 2005.

Internet resources for further information:
• **Serbia and Montenegro Statistical Office**
http://www.szs.sv.gov.yu/english.htm
• **National Bank of Serbia** http://www.nbs.yu/english/index.htm
• **Central Bank of Montenegro** http://www.cb-mn.org/lijevoE.htm
• **Statistical Office of Kosovo** http://www.sok-kosovo.org

Seychelles

Official name: Repiblik Sesel (Creole);
Republic of Seychelles (English);
République des Seychelles (French).
Form of government: multiparty
republic with one legislative house
(National Assembly [34]).
Head of state and government:
President.
Capital: Victoria.
Official languages: none[1].
Official religion: none.
Monetary unit: 1 Seychelles rupee
(SR) = 100 cents; valuation (Sept. 1,
2005) 1 U.S.$ = SR 5.50;
1 £ = SR 10.13.

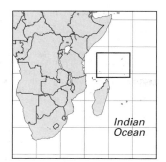

Indian
Ocean

Area and population

Island Groups[2]	Capital	area		population
		sq mi	sq km	2001 estimate
Central (Granitic) group				
La Digue and satellites	—	6	15	2,100
Mahé and satellites	Victoria	59	153	72,100
Praslin and satellites	—	15	40	6,500
Silhouette	—	8	20	500
Other islands	—	2	4	0
Outer (Coralline) islands	—	86	223	0
TOTAL		176	455	81,200[3]

Demography

Population (2005): 82,800.
Density (2005): persons per sq mi 470.5, persons per sq km 182.0.
Urban-rural (2003): urban 49.9%; rural 50.1%.
Sex distribution (2003): male 49.40%; female 50.60%.
Age breakdown (2003): under 15, 25.5%; 15–29, 26.3%; 30–44, 25.0%; 45–59, 12.8%; 60–74, 7.1%; 75 and over, 3.3%.
Population projection: (2010) 85,000; (2020) 88,000.
Doubling time: 70 years.
Ethnic composition (2000): Seychellois Creole (mixture of Asian, African, and European) 93.2%; British 3.0%; French 1.8%; Chinese 0.5%; Indian 0.3%; other unspecified 1.2%.
Religious affiliation (2000): Roman Catholic 90.4%; Anglican 6.7%; Hindu 0.6%; other (mostly nonreligious) 2.3%.
Major towns: Victoria (2004) 25,500; Anse Royale (2002) 3,700.

Vital statistics

Birth rate per 1,000 population (2003): 18.1 (world avg. 21.1); (1998) legitimate 24.7%; illegitimate 75.3%.
Death rate per 1,000 population (2003): 8.1 (world avg. 9.0).
Natural increase rate per 1,000 population (2003): 10.0 (world avg. 12.1).
Total fertility rate (avg. births per childbearing woman; 2003): 2.1.
Marriage rate per 1,000 population (2003): 4.4.
Divorce rate per 1,000 population (2003): 1.5.
Life expectancy at birth (2003): male 66.2 years; female 76.1 years.
Major causes of death per 100,000 population (2002): diseases of the circulatory system 306.7; malignant neoplasms (cancers) 122.0; diseases of the respiratory system 66.5; diseases of the digestive system 37.0.

National economy

Budget (2002). Revenue: SR 1,487,000,000 (tax revenue 70.0%, of which customs taxes and duties 23.7%, sales tax 18.9%, tax on income and profit 16.9%; nontax revenue 28.3%; grants 1.7%). Expenditures: SR 2,061,000,000 (current expenditure 82.0%, of which debt service 15.4%, education 7.6%, health 6.7%; capital expenditure 16.0%; net lending 2.0%).
Tourism (2002): receipts from visitors U.S.$161,000,000; expenditures by nationals abroad U.S.$34,000,000.
Land use as % of total land area (2000): in temporary crops c. 2%, in permanent crops c. 13%, in pasture, n.a.; overall forest area c. 67%.
Gross national product (2004): U.S.$685,000,000 (U.S.$8,090 per capita).

Structure of gross domestic product and labour force

	2003		1997	
	in value SR '000,000[4]	% of total value[4]	labour force	% of labour force
Agriculture, fishing	100.5	2.6	1,885	5.0
Manufacturing	623.2	16.4	2,715	7.3
Construction, mining	342.5	9.0	2,392	6.4
Public utilities	78.7	2.1	714	1.9
Trade, hotels	} 1,856.7[5]	} 48.9[5]	6,000	16.0
Transportation and communications			3,551	9.5
Finance	204.9	5.4	967	2.6
Pub. admin., defense	488.8	12.9	} 12,815	} 34.3
Services	101.9	2.7		
Other	...	...	6,370[6]	17.0[6]
TOTAL	3,797.2	100.0	37,409	100.0

Production (metric tons except as noted). Agriculture, forestry, fishing (2004): coconuts 3,200, bananas 1,970, tea 225, cinnamon 200; livestock (number of live animals) 18,500 pigs, 5,150 goats, 1,400 cattle, 330,000 chickens; roundwood, n.a.; fish catch (2003) 85,785. Mining and quarrying (2004): gravel and crushed rock 213,000. Manufacturing (2003): canned tuna 36,436; animal feed (2002) 18,565; copra (2002) 262; tea 261; soft drinks 80,940 hectolitres; beer

and stout 65,190 hectolitres; fruit juices 39,460 hectolitres; cigarettes 50,000,000 units. Energy production (consumption): electricity (kW-hr; 2002) 219,000,000 (219,000,000); coal, none (n.a.); crude petroleum, none (n.a.); petroleum products (metric tons; 2002) none (174,000); natural gas, none (n.a.).
Population economically active (1997): total 37,409; activity rate of total population 49.3% (participation rates: ages 15–62, 77.8%; female 47.6%; unemployed [1999] 11.5%).

Price index (2000 = 100)

	1998	1999	2000	2001	2002	2003	2004
Consumer price index	88.5	94.1	100.0	106.0	106.2	109.7	113.9

Public debt (2004): U.S.$860,000,000.
Household income and expenditure. Average household size (2002) 4.0; average annual income per household, n.a.; sources of income (1997): wages and salaries 77.2%, self-employment 3.8%, transfer payments 3.2%; expenditure (2001)[7]: food 25.5%, housing and energy 14.8%, beverages 13.3% (of which alcoholic 10.7%), clothing and footwear 6.7%, transportation 5.8%, recreation 5.5%.

Foreign trade[8]

Balance of trade (current prices)

	1999	2000	2001	2002	2003	2004
SR '000,000	−1,542	−841	−1,513	−1,046	−747	−1,730
% of total	49.9%	27.5%	37.5%	29.5%	20.1%	46.2%

Imports (2003): SR 2,231,000,000 (food and beverages 31.0%, of which fish, crustaceans, and mollusks 16.1%; mineral fuels 16.1%; machinery 12.3%; base and fabricated metals 8.1%; transport equipment 5.7%). *Major import sources:* Saudi Arabia 15.7%; South Africa 12.6%; Italy 10.6%; France 10.4%; Spain 10.4%; U.K. 7.7%.
Exports (2003): SR 1,484,000,000 (domestic exports 76.9%, of which canned tuna 69.0%, other processed fish 1.8%, fresh and frozen fish 1.9%; reexports 23.1%, of which petroleum products 19.8%). *Major export destinations* (2002)[9]: United Kingdom 39.2%; France 32.0%; Italy 14.5%; Germany 7.5%.

Transport and communications

Transport. Railroads: none. Roads (2003): total length 285 mi, 458 km (paved 96%). Vehicles (2002): passenger cars 6,923; trucks and buses 2,551. Air transport (2004)[10]: passenger-km 1,097,107,000; metric ton-km cargo 22,600,000; airports (2002) with scheduled flights 2.

Communications

Medium	date	unit	number	units per 1,000 persons
Daily newspapers	1996	circulation	3,000	46
Radio	1997	receivers	42,000	560
Television	2000	receivers	16,000	203
Telephones	2004	main lines	21,200	262
Cellular telephones	2004	subscribers	49,200	608
Personal computers	2004	units	15,000	185
Internet	2004	users	20,000	247

Education and health

Educational attainment (2003). Percentage of population age 12 and over having: less than primary or primary education 23.2%; secondary 73.4%; higher 3.4%. *Literacy* (2002): total population age 12 and over literate 91.0%; males literate 90.0%; females literate 92.0%.

Education (2003)

	schools	teachers	students	student/ teacher ratio
Primary (age 6–15)	26	675	9,477	14.0
Secondary (age 16–18)	12	552	7,551	13.7
Voc., teacher tr.	11	193	1,652	8.6

Health (2003): physicians 107 (1 per 774 persons); hospital beds 419 (1 per 198 persons); infant mortality rate per 1,000 live births 16.0.
Food (2002): daily per capita caloric intake 2,465 (vegetable products 83%, animal products 17%); 105% of FAO recommended minimum requirement.

Military

Total active duty personnel (2004): 450 (army 100%[11]). *Military expenditure as percentage of GDP* (2003): 1.7%; per capita expenditure U.S.$147.

[1]Creole, English, and French are all national languages per 1993 constitution. [2]The Seychelles are administratively divided into 25 districts. [3]2002 preliminary census total equals 81,177. [4]At current prices. [5]Includes import duties. [6]Includes 2,560 not adequately defined and 3,810 unemployed. [7]Weights of consumer price index components. [8]Imports c.i.f.; exports f.o.b. [9]Domestic exports only. [10]Air Seychelles only. [11]The coast guard forms part of the army.

Internet resources for further information:
• **Seychelles in Figures** http://www.seychelles.net/misdstat
• **Central Bank of Seychelles** http://www.cbs.sc

Sierra Leone

Official name: Republic of
Sierra Leone.
Form of government: republic with one
legislative body (Parliament [124[1]]).
Head of state and government:
President.
Capital: Freetown.
Official language: English.
Official religion: none.
Monetary unit: 1 leone (Le) = 100
cents; valuation (Sept. 1, 2005)
1 U.S.$ = Le 2,902; 1 £ = Le 5,344.

Area and population

Provinces/Area Districts	Capitals	area sq mi	area sq km	population 2004 census[2]
Eastern Province	Kenema	6,005	15,553	1,187,532
Kailahun	Kailahun	1,490	3,859	358,259
Kenema	Kenema	2,337	6,053	487,755
Kono	Sefadu	2,178	5,641	341,518
Northern Province	Makeni	13,875	35,936	1,718,240
Bombali	Makeni	3,083	7,985	406,012
Kambia	Kambia	1,200	3,108	276,989
Koinadugu	Kabala	4,680	12,121	234,330
Port Loko	Port Loko	2,208	5,719	455,025
Tonkolili	Magburaka	2,704	7,003	345,884
Southern Province	Bo	7,604	19,694	1,106,602
Bo	Bo	2,015	5,219	472,919
Bonthe	Bonthe	1,339	3,468	139,832
Moyamba	Moyamba	2,665	6,902	259,617
Pujehun	Pujehun	1,585	4,105	234,234
Western Area	Freetown	215	557	950,924
TOTAL		27,699	71,740	4,963,298

Demography

Population (2005): 5,018,000.
Density (2005): persons per sq mi 181.2, persons per sq km 69.9.
Urban-rural (2000): urban 36.6%; rural 63.4%.
Sex distribution (2004): male 48.61%; female 51.39%.
Age breakdown (2003): under 15, 41.7%; 15–29, 27.1%; 30–44, 16.7%; 45–59, 8.0%; 60–74, 4.3%; 75 and over, 2.2%.
Population projection: (2010) 5,570,000; (2020) 7,030,000.
Doubling time: 30 years.
Ethnic composition (2000): Mende 26.0%; Temne 24.6%; Limba 7.1%; Kuranko 5.5%; Kono 4.2%; Fulani 3.8%; Bullom-Sherbro 3.5%; other 25.3%.
Religious affiliation (2000): Sunnī Muslim 45.9%; traditional beliefs 40.4%; Christian 11.4%; other 2.3%.
Major cities (2004): Freetown 786,900[3]; Bo 167,144; Kenema 137,696; Koidu 87,789; Makeni 85,017.

Vital statistics

Birth rate per 1,000 population (2004): 46.5 (world avg. 21.1).
Death rate per 1,000 population (2004): 23.7 (world avg. 9.0).
Natural increase rate per 1,000 population (2004): 22.8 (world avg. 12.1).
Total fertility rate (avg. births per childbearing woman; 2004): 6.2.
Life expectancy at birth (2004): male 37.6 years; female 41.8 years.
Major causes of death per 100,000 population: n.a.; however, the major diseases are malaria, tuberculosis, leprosy, measles, tetanus, and diarrhea.

National economy

Budget (2002). Revenue: Le 239,425,000,000 (customs duties and excise taxes 64.0%, income tax 25.1%, other 10.9%). Expenditures: Le 701,834,000,000 (recurrent expenditures 65.1%, of which wages and salaries 18.8%, goods and services 12.9%, defense and security 12.9%, debt service 9.4%; capital expenditures 34.9%).
Gross national product (2004): U.S.$1,113,000,000 (U.S.$200 per capita).

Structure of gross domestic product and labour force

	2001 in value Le '000,000	2001 % of total value	2002 labour force	2002 % of labour force
Agriculture	857,128	48.8	1,083,000	61.2
Mining	298,205	17.0		
Manufacturing	44,638	2.5		
Construction	36,717	2.1		
Public utilities	5,242	0.3		
Transp. and commun.	92,066	5.2		
Trade[4]	97,459	5.5	688,000	38.8
Finance	87,793	5.0		
Pub. admin., defense	68,069	3.9		
Services	79,118	4.5		
Other	88,770[5]	5.1[5]		
TOTAL	1,755,205	100.0[6]	1,771,000	100.0

Production (metric tons except as noted). Agriculture, forestry, fishing (2004): cassava 390,000, rice 265,000, oil palm fruit 195,000, pulses 56,000, plantains 30,000, sugarcane 28,000, sweet potatoes 26,000, sorghum 21,000, coffee 18,000, peanuts (groundnuts) 16,000, tomatoes 15,000, cacao beans 11,000, millet 10,000, mangoes 6,500; livestock (number of live animals) 400,000 cattle, 375,000 sheep, 220,000 goats, 52,000 pigs; roundwood 5,526,720 cu m; fish catch (2003) 82,923. Mining and quarrying (2003): rutile, none[7]; diamonds 506,819 carats. Manufacturing (value added in Le '000,000; 1993): food 36,117; chemicals 10,560; earthenware 1,844; printing and publishing 1,171;

metal products 1,073; furniture 647. Energy production (consumption): electricity (kW-hr; 2002) 257,000,000 (257,000,000); crude petroleum (barrels; 2002) none (1,907,000); petroleum products (metric tons; 2002) 190,000 (152,000).
Household income and expenditure. Average household size (2004) 6.1; average annual income per household, n.a.
Public debt (external, outstanding; 2003): U.S.$1,420,000,000.
Population economically active (2002): total 1,771,000; activity rate of total population 36.7% (participation rates [1991]: ages 10–64, 53.3%; female [2001] 32.4%; unemployed [registered; 1992] 10.6%).

Price index (2000 = 100)

	1998	1999	2000	2001	2002	2003	2004
Consumer price index	75.2	100.8	100.0	102.1	98.7	106.2	121.3

Tourism (2003): receipts U.S.$60,000,000; expenditures U.S.$37,000,000.
Land use as % of total land area (2000): in temporary crops 6.8%, in permanent crops 0.8%, in pasture 30.7%; overall forest area 14.7%.

Foreign trade[8]

Balance of trade (current prices)

	1999	2000	2001	2002	2003	2004
Le '000,000	−142,509	−287,868	−313,608	−452,826	−490,166	−400,959
% of total	86.3%	84.3%	73.0%	68.9%	53.0%	34.9%

Imports (2002): Le 554,837,500,000 (food and live animals 26.7%; fuels 19.6%; machinery and transport equipment 18.9%; chemicals and chemical products 6.9%). *Major import sources* (2001): U.K. 25.3%; The Netherlands 10.1%; U.S. 7.9%; Germany 6.3%; Italy 5.6%.
Exports (2002): Le 102,011,900,000 (diamonds 85.7%; cacao 2.5%; rutile, none[7]; reexports 4.8%). *Major export destinations* (2001): Belgium 40.6%; U.S. 9.1%; U.K. 8.5%; Germany 7.8%; Japan 5.6%.

Transport and communications

Transport. Railroads (2002)[9]: length 52 mi, 84 km. Roads (1999): total length 7,270 mi, 11,700 km (paved 11%). Vehicles (2003): passenger cars 17,439; trucks and buses 12,428. Air transport (2001): passenger-km 73,000,000; metric ton-km cargo, n.a.; airports (2003) with scheduled flights 1.

Communications

Medium	date	unit	number	units per 1,000 persons
Daily newspapers	2000	circulation	17,700	4.0
Radio	2000	receivers	1,140,000	259
Television	2000	receivers	57,400	13
Telephones	2002	main lines	24,000	4.8
Cellular telephones	2003	subscribers	113,200	23
Personal computers	1999	units	100	—
Internet	2004	users	10,000	1.9

Education and health

Educational attainment, n.a. *Literacy* (1995): total population age 15 and over literate 791,000 (31.4%); males 555,000 (45.4%); females 236,000 (18.2%).

Education (2000–01)

	schools	teachers	students	student/ teacher ratio
Primary (age 5–11)	2,704	14,932	554,308	37.1
Secondary (age 12–18)	495	5,264	70,900[10]	16.4[10]
Voc., teacher tr.	44[10]	1,321	9,660	7.3
Higher[11]	2	257	2,571	10.0

Health: physicians (1996) 339 (1 per 13,696 persons); hospital beds (1998) 3,364 (1 per 1,250 persons); infant mortality rate per 1,000 live births (2004) 163.8.
Food (2002): daily per capita caloric intake 1,936 (vegetable products 96%, animal products 4%); 84% of FAO recommended minimum requirement.

Military

Total active duty personnel (2004): c. 12,500 (army c. 98%, navy c. 2%, air force, none); UN peacekeeping troops (August 2005) 3,200. *Military expenditure as percentage of GDP* (2003): 1.7%; per capita expenditure U.S.$4.

[1]Includes 12 paramount chiefs elected to represent each of the provincial districts. [2]Provisional figures. [3]Urban population of Western Area. [4]Includes hotels. [5]Import duties less imputed bank service charges. [6]Detail does not add to total given because of rounding. [7]Production at world's richest deposit was resumed in early 2005 after being halted in 1995 because of the civil war. [8]Imports c.i.f.; exports f.o.b. [9]Marampa Mineral Railway; there are no passenger railways. [10]1992–93. [11]1990–91.

Internet resources for further information:
• **Sierra Leone Annual Statistical Digest, 2004**
  http://www.statistics-sierra-leone.org/annual_statistical_digests.htm
• **Bank of Sierra Leone**
  http://www.bankofsierraleone-centralbank.org

Singapore

Official name: Hsin-chia-p'o
Kung-ho-kuo (Mandarin Chinese);
Republik Singapura (Malay);
Singapore Kudiyarasu (Tamil);
Republic of Singapore (English).
Form of government: unitary multiparty
republic with one legislative house
(Parliament [90[1]]).
Chief of state: President[2].
Head of state government: Prime
Minister[3].
Capital: Singapore.
Official languages: Chinese; Malay;
Tamil; English.
Official religion: none.
Monetary unit: 1 Singapore dollar
(S$) = 100 cents; valuation (Sept. 1,
2005) 1 U.S.$ = S$1.68; 1 £ = S$3.09.

Population (2004 estimate)	
De facto population	4,240,300[4]
De jure population	3,486,900[5]

Demography

Area: 269.9 sq mi, 699.0 sq km.
Population (2005): 4,291,000.
Density (2005): persons per sq mi 15,898, persons per sq km 6,139.
Urban-rural: urban 100.0%.
Sex distribution (2004)[6]: male 49.69%; female 50.31%.
Age breakdown (2004)[6]: under 15, 20.2%; 15–29, 20.1%; 30–44, 27.0%; 45–59, 21.1%; 60–74, 8.6%; 75 and over, 3.0%.
Population projection: (2010) 4,555,000; (2020) 4,948,000.
Ethnic composition (2003)[6]: Chinese 76.3%; Malay 13.8%; Indian 8.3%; other 1.6%.
Religious affiliation (2000)[6]: Buddhist 42.5%; Muslim 14.9%; Christian 14.6%; Taoist 8.5%; Hindu 4.0%; traditional beliefs 0.6%; nonreligious 14.9%.

Vital statistics

Birth rate per 1,000 population (2004)[6]: 10.1 (world avg. 21.1).
Death rate per 1,000 population (2004)[6]: 4.3 (world avg. 9.0).
Natural increase rate per 1,000 population (2004)[6]: 5.8 (world avg. 12.1).
Total fertility rate (avg. births per childbearing woman; 2004)[6]: 1.2.
Marriage rate per 1,000 population (2004)[6]: 6.4.
Life expectancy at birth (2004)[6]: male 77.4 years; female 81.3 years.
Major causes of death per 100,000 population (2003)[6]: malignant neoplasms (cancers) 120.8; heart diseases 116.9; pneumonia 68.1; cerebrovascular diseases 45.2; accidents and violence 30.8.

National economy

Budget (2003). Revenue: S$24,659,200,000 (income tax 42.2%, nontax revenue 14.6%, goods and services tax 11.0%, customs and excise duties 7.3%, motor vehicle taxes 5.3%). Expenditures: S$27,189,300,000 (security 34.0%, development expenditure 29.3%, education 17.9%, health 6.1%, trade and industry 1.9%).
Public debt (2004): U.S.$110,000,000,000.
Production (metric tons except as noted). Agriculture, forestry, fishing (2004): vegetables and fruits 5,150, orchids and other ornamental plants are cultivated for export; livestock (number of live animals) 250,000 pigs, 2,000,000 chickens; fish catch[7] (2003) 2,085. Quarrying: limestone, n.a.[8]. Manufacturing (value added in S$'000,000; 2004): pharmaceuticals 8,980; semiconductors 7,332; professional and scientific equipment 7,099; refined petroleum and petrochemicals 5,298; computer-related electronics 4,094; other electronics 3,504; ships, oil platforms, and related products 2,187; aircraft and spacecraft 1,877; printing 1,312; food and food products, beverages, and tobacco products 1,059. Energy production (consumption): electricity (kW-hr; 2004) 36,888,000,000 ([2002] 35,404,000,000); crude petroleum (barrels; 2002) none (298,000,000); petroleum products (metric tons; 2002) 27,987,000 (10,877,000); natural gas (cu m; 2002) none (4,411,000,000).
Household income and expenditure. Average household size (2002) 4.2; income per household (2000) S$59,316 (U.S.$34,406); sources of income: n.a.; expenditure (1998): food 23.7%, transportation and communications 22.8%, housing costs and furnishings 21.6%, education 6.9%, clothing and footwear 4.1%, health 3.3%, other 17.6%.
Gross national product (2004): U.S.$104,994,000,000 (U.S.$24,220 per capita).

Structure of gross domestic product and labour force				
	2004		2003	
	in value S$'000,000	% of total value	labour force[6]	% of labour force[6]
Agriculture } Quarrying	192	0.1	5,000 1,000	0.2 —
Manufacturing	48,961	27.1	364,800	17.0
Construction	7,672	4.3	114,500	5.3
Public utilities	2,962	1.6	10,000	0.5
Transp. and commun.	19,525	10.8	216,000	10.0
Trade	28,730	15.9	424,900	19.8
Finance, real estate	48,157	26.7	347,700	16.2
Pub. admin., defense } Services	20,685	11.5	148,000 400,000	6.9 18.6
Other	3,671[9]	2.0[9]	118,400[10]	5.5[10]
TOTAL	180,554[11]	100.0	2,151,100[11]	100.0

Population economically active (2000): total 2,192,278; activity rate of total population 54.6% (participation rates: ages 15–64, 73.4%; female 39.6%; unemployed [2004] 4.0%).

Price and earnings indexes (2000 = 100)							
	1998	1999	2000	2001	2002	2003	2004
Consumer price index	98.6	98.7	100.0	101.0	100.6	101.1	102.8
Monthly earnings index	89.5	91.9	100.0	102.3	...	...	...

Tourism (2003): receipts from visitors U.S.$3,998,000,000; expenditures by nationals abroad U.S.$4,925,000,000.
Land use as % of total land area (2000): in temporary and permanent crops 1.4%, in pasture, n.a.; overall forest area 3.3%.

Foreign trade[12]

Balance of trade (current prices)						
	1999	2000	2001	2002	2003	2004
S$'000,000	+6,147	+5,651	+10,335	+15,590	+28,285	+26,582
% of total	1.6%	1.2%	2.4%	5.8%	6.0%	4.6%

Imports (2003): S$222,811,000,000 (electronic valves [including integrated circuits and semiconductors] 21.7%; crude and refined petroleum 13.5%; computers and related parts 11.2%; chemicals and chemical products 6.7%; telecommunications equipment 4.0%). *Major import sources:* Malaysia 16.8%; U.S. 13.9%; Japan 12.0%; China 8.7%; Taiwan 5.1%; Thailand 4.3%.
Exports (2003): S$251,096,000,000 (electronic valves 20.9%; computers and related parts 17.9%; chemicals and chemical products 11.8%, of which organic chemicals 6.4%; crude and refined petroleum 10.9%; telecommunications equipment 4.6%). *Major export destinations:* Malaysia 15.8%; U.S. 13.3%; Hong Kong 10.0%; China 7.0%; Japan 6.7%; Taiwan 4.8%; Thailand 4.3%.

Transport and communications

Transport. Railroads (2003): length 131 km. Roads (2003): total length 3,144 km (paved 99%). Vehicles (2003): passenger cars 424,712; trucks and buses 138,538. Air transport (2003): passenger-km 65,376,000,000; metric ton-km cargo 6,683,000,000; airports (2003) 1.

Communications				
Medium	date	unit	number	units per 1,000 persons
Daily newspapers	2000	circulation	1,197,301	298
Radio	2000	receivers	2,700,000	672
Television	2000	receivers	1,220,000	304
Telephones	2004	main lines	1,864,000	432
Cellular telephones	2004	subscribers	3,860,600	895
Personal computers	2004	units	3,939,000	913
Internet	2004	users	2,421,800	561

Education and health

Educational attainment (2000)[6]. Percentage of population age 15 and over having: no schooling 19.6%; primary education 23.1%; secondary 39.5%; postsecondary 17.8%. *Literacy* (2004)[6]: total population age 15 and over literate 94.6%.

Education (2003)				
	schools[13]	teachers	students	student/ teacher ratio
Primary (age 6–11)	201	12,025	299,939	24.9
Secondary (age 12–18)	180	10,830	206,426	19.1
Voc., teacher tr.	10	1,956	23,708	12.1
Higher[13]	8	7,318	111,538	15.2

Health (2003): physicians 6,292 (1 per 670[6] persons); hospital beds 11,855 (1 per 290[6] persons); infant mortality rate per 1,000 live births (2004) 2.0.
Food (1988–90): daily per capita caloric intake 3,121 (vegetable products 76%, animal products 24%); 136% of FAO recommended minimum requirement.

Military

Total active duty personnel (2004): 72,500 (army 69.0%, navy 12.4%, air force 18.6%). *Military expenditure as percentage of GDP* (2003): 5.1%; per capita expenditure U.S.$1,123.

[1]Includes 6 nonelective seats. [2]Title per constitution is Head of State. [3]Has principal executive authority per constitution. [4]The de facto population figure (as of the 2000 census) includes citizens (2,973,091), noncitizens with permanent residency status (290,118), and temporary residents (754,524). [5]The de jure population figure excludes temporary residents. [6]Based on de jure population. [7]Aquarium fish farming is also an important economic pursuit. [8]The last granite quarry closed in 1999. [9]Taxes less imputed bank service charges. [10]Includes 116,400 unemployed. [11]Detail does not add to total given because of rounding. [12]Imports c.i.f., exports f.o.b. [13]2000.

Internet resources for further information:
• **Statistics Singapore** http://www.singstat.gov.sg
• **Monetary Authority of Singapore**
  http://www.mas.gov.sg/masmcm/bin/pt1home.htm

Slovakia

Official name: Slovenská Republika (Slovak Republic).
Form of government: unitary multiparty republic with one legislative house (National Council [150]).
Chief of state: President.
Head of government: Prime Minister.
Capital: Bratislava.
Official language: Slovak.
Official religion: none.
Monetary unit: 1 Slovak koruna (Sk) = 100 halura; valuation (Sept. 1, 2005) 1 U.S.$ = Sk 30.63; 1 £ = Sk 56.40.

Area and population		area		population
				2001
Regions	Capitals	sq mi	sq km	census
Banská Bystrica	Banská Bystrica	3,651	9,455	662,121
Bratislava	Bratislava	793	2,053	599,015
Košice	Košice	2,607	6,753	766,012
Nitra	Nitra	2,449	6,343	713,422
Prešov	Prešov	3,472	8,993	789,968
Trenčín	Trenčín	1,738	4,501	605,582
Trnava	Trnava	1,602	4,148	551,003
Žilina	Žilina	2,621	6,788	692,332
TOTAL		18,933	49,035[1]	5,379,455[2]

Demography

Population (2005): 5,384,000.
Density (2005): persons per sq mi 284.4, persons per sq km 109.8.
Urban-rural (2003): urban 57.4%; rural 42.6%.
Sex distribution (2005[3]): male 48.53%; female 51.47%.
Age breakdown (2005[3]): under 15, 17.1%; 15–29, 24.9%; 30–44, 21.5%; 45–59, 20.5%; 60–74, 11.2%; 75 and over, 4.8%.
Population projection: (2010) 5,401,000; (2020) 5,417,000.
Ethnic composition (2001): Slovak 85.8%; Hungarian 9.7%; Rom (Gypsy) 1.7%; Czech 0.8%; Ruthenian and Ukrainian 0.7%; other 1.3%.
Religious affiliation (2001): Roman Catholic 68.9%; Protestant 9.2%, of which Slovak Evangelical 6.9%, Reformed Christian 2.0%; Greek Catholic 4.1%; Eastern Orthodox 0.9%; nonreligious and other 16.9%.
Major cities (2001): Bratislava 428,672; Košice 236,093; Prešov 92,786; Nitra 87,285; Žilina 85,400; Banská Bystrica 83,056.

Vital statistics

Birth rate per 1,000 population (2005[3]): 10.0 (world avg. 21.1); (2001) legitimate 80.2%; illegitimate 19.8%.
Death rate per 1,000 population (2005[3]): 9.6 (world avg. 9.0).
Natural increase rate per 1,000 population (2005[3]): 0.4 (world avg. 12.1).
Total fertility rate (avg. births per childbearing woman; 2005[3]): 1.2.
Marriage rate per 1,000 population (2005[3]): 5.2.
Divorce rate per 1,000 population (2005[3]): 2.0.
Life expectancy at birth (2005[3]): male 70.3 years; female 77.8 years.
Major causes of death per 100,000 population (2001): diseases of the circulatory system 533.4; malignant neoplasms (cancers) 220.6; accidents and violence 56.5; diseases of the respiratory system 50.7; diseases of the digestive system 48.4.

National economy

Budget (2002). Revenue: Sk 391,800,000,000 (tax revenue 88.1%, of which social security contribution 35.6%, value-added tax 21.0%, income tax 11.9%; nontax revenue 11.9%). Expenditures: Sk 459,300,000,000 (current expenditures 88.9%, of which social welfare 26.5%, wages 14.4%, health 11.7%, debt service 8.3%; investment 11.1%).
Production (metric tons except as noted). Agriculture, forestry, fishing (2004): wheat 1,764,846, sugar beets 1,598,773, barley 915,903, corn [maize] 862,435, potatoes 381,891, rapeseed 262,660, sunflower seeds 196,350, rye 124,340; livestock (number of live animals) 1,149,282 pigs, 540,146 cattle, 321,227 sheep; roundwood 7,240,000 cu m; fish catch (2003) 1,646. Mining and quarrying (2002): iron ore (metal content) 175,000; gold 77 kg. Manufacturing (value added in Sk '000,000; 2004): base and fabricated metals 54,558; transportation equipment 26,251; electrical equipment 26,146; food products 23,621; machinery and apparatus 21,935; mineral and nuclear fuels 19,511. Energy production (consumption): electricity (kW-hr; 2003) 31,150,000,000 (28,890,000,000); hard coal (metric tons; 2002) none (4,730,000); lignite (metric tons; 2002) 3,400,000 (4,050,000); crude petroleum (barrels; 2002) 320,000 (41,000,000); petroleum products (metric tons; 2002) 5,014,000 (2,756,000); natural gas (cu m; 2003) 190,000,000 (6,800,000,000).
Population economically active (2003): total 2,628,800[4]; activity rate of total population 48.7%[4] (participation rates: ages 15–64, 69.9%[4]; female 45.8[4]%; unemployed [April 2004–March 2005] 17.7%).

Price and earnings indexes (2000 = 100)							
	1998	1999	2000	2001	2002	2003	2004
Consumer price index	80.7	89.3	100.0	107.3	110.9	120.4	129.5
Annual earnings index	87.5	93.9	100.0	108.2	118.2	125.7	138.5

Household income and expenditure. Average household size (2002) 3.2; gross income per household (2001) Sk 89,352 (U.S.$1,848); sources of income

(2004): wages and salaries 62.5%, transfer payments 30.7%; expenditure (2004): food, beverages, and tobacco 24.1%, housing and energy 21.2%, transportation and communications 9.0%, recreation and culture 5.8%.
Public debt (external, outstanding; 2005[3]): U.S.$6,645,900,000.
Gross national product (2004): U.S.$34,907,000,000 (U.S.$6,480 per capita).

Structure of gross domestic product and labour force				
	2003			
	in value Sk '000,000	% of total value	labour force[5]	% of labour force[5]
Agriculture	43,800	3.6	125,300	4.8
Mining	6,100	0.5	18,700	0.7
Manufacturing	233,400	19.4	570,000	21.7
Construction	59,200	4.9	194,900	7.4
Public utilities	56,800	4.7	45,400	1.7
Transp. and commun.	114,200	9.5	149,400	5.7
Trade	154,400	12.9	349,500	13.3
Finance			152,300	5.8
Pub. admin., defense	442,000	36.8	159,700	6.1
Services			396,800	15.1
Other	91,300[6]	7.6[6]	462,000[7]	17.6[7]
TOTAL	1,201,200	100.0[1]	2,624,000	100.0[1]

Tourism: receipts from visitors (2002) U.S.$865,000,000; expenditure by nationals abroad U.S.$573,000,000.
Land use as % of total land area (2000): in temporary crops 30.2%, in permanent crops 2.6%, in pasture 18.0%; overall forest area 45.3%.

Foreign trade

Balance of trade (current prices)						
	1998	1999	2000	2001	2002	2003
U.S.$'000,000	−2,353	−1,093	−904	−2,135	−2,117	−635
% of total	9.9%	5.1%	3.7%	7.8%	6.9%	1.4%

Imports (2002): U.S.$16,502,000,000 (machinery and apparatus 25.6%, mineral fuels 14.6%, transport equipment 12.8%, base and fabricated metals 8.9%). *Major import sources:* Germany 22.6%; Czech Republic 15.2%; Russia 12.5%; Italy 6.9%; France 4.4%.
Exports (2002): U.S.$14,385,000,000 (transport equipment [mostly road vehicles] 21.2%, machinery and apparatus 18.8%, base and fabricated metals [mostly iron and steel] 14.3%, mineral fuels 7.2%). *Major export destinations:* Germany 26.0%; Czech Republic 15.2%; Italy 10.7%; Austria 7.7%; Hungary 5.5%; Poland 5.3%.

Transport and communications

Transport. Railroads (2004): length 3,660 km; passenger-km 2,228,000,000; metric ton-km cargo 9,702,000,000. Roads (2004): total length 17,780 km (paved, n.a.). Vehicles (2005[3]): passenger cars 1,337,425; trucks and buses 179,412. Air transport (2004)[8]: passenger-km 39,645,000; metric ton-km cargo 218,000; airports (2002) with scheduled flights 2.

Communications				units per 1,000
Medium	date	unit	number	persons
Daily newspapers	2004	circulation	480,000	89
Radio	2000	receivers	5,200,000	965
Television	2003	receivers	2,200,000	409
Telephones	2005[3]	main lines	1,250,415	232
Cellular telephones	2005[3]	subscribers	4,275,164	794
Personal computers	2004	units	1,593,000	296
Internet	2004	users	2,276,000	423

Education and health

Educational attainment (1991). Percentage of adult population having: incomplete primary education 0.7%; primary and incomplete secondary 37.9%; complete secondary 50.9%; higher 9.5%; unknown 1.0%. *Literacy* (2001): total population age 15 and over literate virtually 100%.

Education (2004)				student/
	schools	teachers	students	teacher ratio
Primary (age 6–14)	2,342	35,984	555,335	15.4
Secondary (age 15–18)	234	7,543	99,738	13.2
Voc., teacher tr.	262	8,274	87,533	10.6
Higher	24	3,573	108,608	30.4

Health (2004[3]): physicians 18,760 (1 per 286 persons); hospital beds 52,363 (1 per 103 persons); infant mortality rate per 1,000 live births (2005[3]) 6.8.
Food (2002): daily per capita caloric intake 2,889 (vegetable products 72%, animal products 28%); 117% of FAO recommended minimum requirement.

Military

Total active duty personnel (2004): 20,195 (army 63.7%, air force 25.5%, headquarters staff 10.8%). *Military expenditure as percentage of GDP* (2003): 1.9%; per capita expenditure U.S.$116[9].

---

[1]Detail does not add to total given because of rounding. [2]De jure figure; 2001 de facto census total equals 5,193,376. [3]January 1. [4]Data for fourth quarter. [5]Excludes persons on child-care leave and conscripts. [6]Bank service charges and indirect taxes. [7]Including 459,200 unemployed. [8]Slovak Airlines only. [9]Excludes expenditures for military pensions.

Internet resources for further information:
• **National Bank of Slovakia** http://www.nbs.sk
• **Statistical Office of the Slovak Republic** http://www.statistics.sk/webdata/english/index2_a.htm

Slovenia

Official name: Republika Slovenija (Republic of Slovenia).
Form of government: unitary multiparty republic with two legislative houses (National Council [40]; National Assembly [90]).
Head of state: President.
Head of government: Prime Minister.
Capital: Ljubljana.
Official language: Slovene.
Official religion: none.
Monetary unit: 1 Slovene tolar (SIT; plural tolarjev) = 100 stotin; valuation (Sept. 1, 2005) 1 U.S.$ = SIT 191.05; 1 £ = SIT 239.72.

Area and population

Statistical regions[1]	Principal cities	area sq mi	area sq km	population 2002 census
Gorenjska	Kranj	825	2,137	195,885
Goriška	Nova Gorica	898	2,325	118,511
Jugovzhodna Slovenija	Novo Mesto	653	1,690	136,474
Koroška	Ravne na Koroškem	401	1,041	73,296
Notranjsko-kraška	Postojna	562	1,456	50,243
Obalno Kraško	Koper	403	1,044	102,070
Osrednjeslovenska	Ljubljana	1,367	3,540	488,364
Podravska	Maribor	838	2,170	310,743
Pomurska	Murska Sobota	516	1,337	120,875
Savinjska	Celje	920	2,384	253,574
Spodnjeposavska	Krško	342	885	68,565
Zasavska	Trbovlje	102	264	45,436
TOTAL		7,827	20,273	1,964,036

Demography

Population (2005): 1,999,000.
Density (2005): persons per sq mi 255.4, persons per sq km 98.6.
Urban-rural (2003): urban 50.8%; rural 49.2%.
Sex distribution (2004): male 48.93%; female 51.07%.
Age breakdown (2004): under 15, 14.5%; 15–29, 21.2%; 30–44, 22.6%; 45–59, 21.2%; 60–74, 14.4%; 75 and over, 6.1%.
Population projection: (2010) 2,010,000; (2020) 2,016,000.
Ethnic composition (2002)[2]: Slovene 91.2%; Serb 2.2%; Croat 2.0%; Bosniac (ethnic Muslim) 1.8%; other 2.8%.
Religious affiliation (2000): Christian 92.1%, of which Roman Catholic 83.5%, unaffiliated Christian 4.7%, Protestant 1.6%, Orthodox 0.6%; nonreligious/atheist 7.8%; other 0.1%.
Major cities (2002): Ljubljana 258,873; Maribor 93,847; Celje 37,834; Kranj 35,587; Velenje 26,742.

Vital statistics

Birth rate per 1,000 population (2004): 9.0 (world avg. 21.1); legitimate 55.2%; illegitimate 44.8%.
Death rate per 1,000 population (2004): 9.3 (world avg. 9.0).
Natural increase rate per 1,000 population (2004): –0.3 (world avg. 12.1).
Total fertility rate (avg. births per childbearing woman; 2004): 1.3.
Marriage rate per 1,000 population (2004): 3.3.
Divorce rate per 1,000 population (2004): 1.2.
Life expectancy at birth (2004): male 73.5 years; female 81.1 years.
Major causes of death per 100,000 population (2002): diseases of the circulatory system 359.2; malignant neoplasms (cancers) 253.7; accidents and violence 74.6; diseases of the respiratory system 70.5.

National economy

Budget (2003). Revenue: SIT 2,376,000,000,000 (2002; tax revenue 91.7%, of which social security contributions 32.7%, taxes on goods and services 32.3%, personal income tax 19.0%; nontax revenue 8.3%). Expenditures: SIT 2,454,000,000,000 (2002; current expenditures 90.8%, of which wages 45.9%, transfers 44.9%; development expenditures 9.2%).
Production (metric tons except as noted). Agriculture, forestry, fishing (2004): silage 1,460,339, corn (maize) 357,621, apples 230,000, sugar beets 213,092, potatoes 171,475, wheat 146,829, grapes 134,792, hops 1,500; livestock (number of live animals) 620,506 pigs, 450,226 cattle; roundwood 2,551,000 cu m; fish catch (2003) 1,281. Mining and quarrying (2002): dimension stone 105,000. Manufacturing (value added in SIT '000,000; 2003): chemicals and chemical products 199,562; fabricated metal products 165,692; nonelectrical machinery 133,091; food and food products and beverages 129,762; electrical machinery and apparatus 116,602; wood and wood products (including furniture) 110,743. Energy production (consumption): electricity (kW-hr; 2003) 13,064,000,000 (12,588,000,000); hard coal (metric tons; 2002) none (570,000); lignite (metric tons; 2003) 4,854,000 (5,358,000); crude petroleum (barrels; 2002) 7,330 (none); petroleum products (metric tons; 2002) none (2,210,000); natural gas (cu m; 2003) 4,900,000 (1,114,000,000).
Land use as % of total land area (2000): in temporary crops 8.6%, in permanent crops 1.5%, in pasture 15.6%, overall forest area 55.0%.
Household income and expenditure (2001). Average household size (2002) 2.8; income per household SIT 3,090,000 (U.S.$12,800); sources of income: wages 60.0%, transfers 26.6%; expenditure: transportation and communications 25.8%, food and beverages 17.8%, housing 10.4%, recreation 9.3%.
Gross national product (at current market prices; 2004): U.S.$32,000,000,000 (U.S.$16,250 per capita).

Structure of gross domestic product and labour force

	2003 in value SIT '000,000	% of total value	labour force[3]	% of labour force[3]
Agriculture, forestry	132,888	2.3	75,000	7.8
Mining	27,048	0.5	6,000	0.6
Manufacturing	1,365,106	23.7	264,000	27.5
Construction	290,819	5.1	52,000	5.4
Public utilities	148,407	2.6	9,000	0.9
Transp. and commun.	363,183	6.3	59,000	6.2
Trade, restaurants	707,794	12.3	154,000	16.1
Finance, real estate	1,030,887	17.9	75,000	7.8
Pub. admin., defense	333,153	5.8	50,000	5.2
Services	709,457	12.3	146,000	15.2
Other	638,426[4]	11.1[4]	69,000[5]	7.2[5]
TOTAL	5,747,168	100.0[6]	959,000	100.0[6]

Public debt (external, outstanding; 2004): U.S.$5,155,000,000.
Population economically active (2003): total 959,000; activity rate 48.1% (participation rates: ages 15–64, 66.9%; female 45.9%; unemployed [October 2003–September 2004] 10.8%).

Price and earnings indexes (2000 = 100)

	1998	1999	2000	2001	2002	2003	2004
Consumer price index	86.6	91.9	100.0	108.5	116.6	123.1	127.5
Annual earnings index	82.5	90.4	100.0	111.9	122.9	132.1	139.6

Tourism (2003): receipts from visitors U.S.$1,342,000,000; expenditures by nationals abroad U.S.$756,000,000.

Foreign trade[7]

Balance of trade (current prices)

€'000,000	2000	2001	2002	2003	2004
	–1,492	–998	–612	–952	–1,360
% of total	7.3%	4.6%	2.7%	4.0%	5.1%

Imports (2003): €12,237,000,000 (machinery and transport equipment 34.4%, of which road vehicles 11.1%; chemicals and chemical products 13.3%; mineral fuels 7.7%; food products 5.1%). *Major import sources:* Germany 19.3%; Italy 18.3%; France 10.1%; Austria 8.6%; Croatia 3.6%.
Exports (2003): €11,285,000,000 (machinery and transport equipment 36.5%, of which electrical machinery and apparatus 11.6%, road vehicles 11.4%; chemicals and chemical products 13.8%, of which medicines and pharmaceuticals 7.0%; furniture and parts 6.9%). *Major export destinations:* Germany 23.1%; Italy 13.1%; Croatia 8.9%; Austria 7.3%; France 5.7%.

Transport and communications

Transport. Railroads (2004): length 764 mi, 1,229 km; passenger-km 764,-000,000; metric ton-km cargo 3,466,000,000. Roads (2003): total length 12,524 mi, 20,155 km (paved 81%). Vehicles (2004): passenger cars 910,723; trucks and buses 63,243. Air transport (2004): passenger-km 896,000,000; metric ton-km cargo 3,201,000; airports (2003) with scheduled flights 3.

Communications

Medium	date	unit	number	units per 1,000 persons
Daily newspapers	2000	circulation	334,000	171
Radio	2000	receivers	792,000	405
Television	2002	receivers	732,000	366
Telephones	2003	main lines	812,300	407
Cellular telephones	2003	subscribers	1,739,100	871
Personal computers	2004	units	704,000	355
Internet	2004	users	950,000	480

Education and health

Educational attainment (2002). Percentage of population age 15 and over having: no formal schooling 0.7%; incomplete and complete primary education 32.2%; secondary 54.1%; some higher 5.1%; undergraduate 6.9%; advanced degree 1.0%. *Literacy* (2001): 99.6%.

Education (2002–03)

	schools	teachers	students	student/teacher ratio
Primary (age 7–14)	811	15,625	175,211	11.2
Secondary (age 15–18)	143	8,482	103,538	12.2
Higher	49	3,056[8]	87,205	18.9[8]

Health (2002): physicians 4,636 (1 per 430 persons); hospital beds 10,147 (1 per 197 persons); infant mortality rate per 1,000 live births (2004) 3.7.

Military

Total active duty personnel (2004): 6,550 (army 100%). *Military expenditure as percentage of GNP* (2003): 1.5%; per capita expenditure U.S.$209.

---

[1]Actual first-order administration is based on 193 municipalities. [2]Prorating 8.9% of population not responding to census questionnaire. [3]June. [4]Import taxes less imputed bank service charges. [5]Includes 63,000 unemployed and 6,000 not distributed. [6]Detail does not add to total given because of rounding. [7]Imports c.i.f.; exports f.o.b. [8]2001–02.

Internet resources for further information:
• **Statistical Office of the Republic of Slovenia**
  http://www.stat.si/eng/index.asp
• **Bank of Slovenia** http://www.bsi.si

Solomon Islands

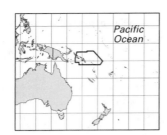

Official name: Solomon Islands.
Form of government: constitutional
  monarchy[1] with one legislative house
  (National Parliament [50]).
Chief of state: British Monarch
  represented by Governor-General.
Head of government: Prime Minister.
Capital: Honiara.
Official language: English.
Official religion: none.
Monetary unit: 1 Solomon Islands
  dollar (SI$) = 100 cents; valuation
  (Sept. 1, 2005) 1 U.S.$ = SI$7.30;
  1 £ = SI$13.44.

Area and population		area		population
				1999
Provinces	Capitals	sq mi	sq km	census
Central Islands	Tulagi	237	615	21,577
Choiseul	Taro	1,481	3,837	20,008
Guadalcanal	Honiara	2,060	5,336	60,275
Isabel	Buala	1,597	4,136	20,421
Makira-Ulawa	Kira Kira	1,231	3,188	31,006
Malaita	Auki	1,631	4,225	122,620
Rennell and Bellona	Tigoa	259	671	2,377
Temotu	Santa Cruz	334	865	18,912
Western	Gizo	2,114	5,475	62,739
Capital Territory				
Honiara	—	8	22	49,107
TOTAL		10,954[2]	28,370	409,042

Demography

Population (2005): 471,000.
Density (2005): persons per sq mi 43.0, persons per sq km 16.6.
Urban-rural (2003): urban 16.5%; rural 83.5%.
Sex distribution (2004): male 51.64%; female 48.36%.
Age breakdown (2003): under 15, 42.9%; 15–29, 29.2%; 30–44, 15.5%; 45–59,
  7.6%; 60–74, 3.8%; 75 and over, 1.0%.
Population projection: (2010) 530,000; (2020) 645,000.
Doubling time: 25 years.
Ethnic composition (2002): Melanesian 93.0%; Polynesian 4.0%; Micronesian
  1.5%; other 1.5%.
Religious affiliation (2000): Christian 90.8%, of which Protestant 74.0% (includ-
  ing Church of Melanesia [Anglican] 38.2%), Roman Catholic 10.8%; tradi-
  tional beliefs 3.1%; other 6.1%.
Major cities (2002): Honiara (on Guadalcanal) 52,900; Noro (on Guadalcanal)
  3,482; Gizo (in the New Georgia Islands) 2,960; Auki (on Malaita) 1,606.

Vital statistics

Birth rate per 1,000 population (2004): 31.6 (world avg. 21.1).
Death rate per 1,000 population (2004): 4.0 (world avg. 9.0).
Natural increase rate per 1,000 population (2004): 27.6 (world avg. 12.1).
Total fertility rate (avg. births per childbearing woman; 2004): 4.2.
Marriage rate per 1,000 population: n.a.
Life expectancy at birth (2004): male 69.9 years; female 75.0 years.
Major causes of death per 100,000 population (2004): n.a.; however, about 20%
  of the population has malaria, one of the world's highest rates.

National economy

Budget (2003). Revenue: SI$681,300,000 (tax revenue 48.9%, of which inter-
  national trade tax 19.3%, sales tax 16.4%, income tax 13.2%; grants 45.4%;
  nontax revenue 5.7%). Expenditures: SI$670,900,000 (current expenditure
  60.2%, of which wages 24.4%, goods and services 13.2%, interest 7.4%; capital expenditure 39.8%).
Tourism (2002): receipts from visitors U.S.$1,000,000; expenditures by nation-
  als abroad U.S.$6,000,000.
Land use as % of total land area (2000): in temporary crops 0.6%, in permanent crops 2.0%, in pasture 1.4%; overall forest area 88.8%.
Gross national product (at current market prices; 2004): U.S.$260,000,000
  (U.S.$550 per capita).

Structure of gross domestic product and labour force				
	2003		1993	
	in value SI$'000[3]	% of total value[3]	labour force[4]	% of labour force[4]
Agriculture	123,500	31.9	7,426	21.8
Mining	—	—	4,348	12.8
Manufacturing	16,100	4.2		
Construction	3,200	0.8	1,187	3.5
Public utilities	15,800	4.1	387	1.1
Transportation and communications	11,800	3.0	1,878	5.5
Trade	68,100	17.6	4,641	13.6
Finance	29,100	7.5	1,183	3.5
Pub. admin., defense	119,700	30.9	4,261	12.5
Services			8,750	25.7
Other	...	...	...	...
TOTAL	387,300	100.0	34,061	100.0

Household income and expenditure. Average household size (2002) 6.6; average annual income per household[5] (1991) U.S.$2,387; sources of income: n.a.;
  expenditure (1992)[6]: food 46.8%, housing 11.0%, household operations
  10.9%, transportation 9.9%, recreation and health 7.9%.

Population economically active (1999)[7]: total 85,124; activity rate of total population 21.0% (participation rates: ages 14 and over, n.a.; female 32.2%;
  unemployed 32.5%).

Price index (2000 = 100)							
	1998	1999	2000	2001	2002	2003	2004
Consumer price index	86.5	93.4	100.0	106.9	117.7	129.5	138.7

Production (metric tons except as noted). Agriculture, forestry, fishing (2004):
  coconuts 330,000, oil palm fruit 155,000, sweet potatoes 86,000, taro 40,000,
  yams 29,000, cacao beans 4,000; livestock (number of live animals) 69,000
  pigs, 13,500 cattle, 230,000 chickens; roundwood 692,000 cu m; fish catch
  (2003) 39,849. Mining and quarrying (2000): gold 338 kg[8]. Manufacturing
  (2002): vegetable oils and fats 50,000, palm oil 34,000, coconut oil 15,000,
  dried coconut (2003) 15,000. Energy production (consumption): electricity
  (kW-hr; 2002) 32,000,000 (32,000,000); coal, none (n.a.); petroleum products
  (metric tons; 2002) none (56,000); natural gas, none (n.a.).
Public debt (external, outstanding; 2002): U.S.$150,200,000.

Foreign trade[9]

Balance of trade (current prices)						
	1999	2000	2001	2002	2003	2004
SI$'000,000	+69.0	−167.7	−229.5	−27.1	−82.5	−14.6
% of total	6.0%	19.3%	31.6%	3.3%	6.9%	1.0%

Imports (2003): SI$639,500,000 (food, beverages, and tobacco 23.6%, crude
  petroleum 17.3%, machinery and transport equipment 12.7%, construction
  materials 10.7%, unspecified 32.9%). *Major import sources:* Australia 28.0%;
  Singapore 23.2%; New Zealand 5.2%; Fiji 4.6%; Papua New Guinea 4.4%.
Exports (2003): SI$557,000,000 (timber 66.6%, fish products 16.7%, cacao
  beans 9.6%, palm oil, none, gold[8], none). *Major export destinations:* China
  25.8%; Japan 17.9%; South Korea 15.2%; Philippines 9.9%; Thailand 6.2%;
  Singapore 5.6%.

Transport and communications

Transport. Railroads: none. Roads (1999): total length 1,360 km (paved 2.5%).
  Vehicles (1993): passenger cars 2,052; trucks and buses 2,574. Air transport
  (2004)[10]: passenger-km 76,733,000; metric ton-km cargo 2,259,000; airports
  (1997) with scheduled flights 21.

Communications				units per 1,000
Medium	date	unit	number	persons
Radio	1997	receivers	57,000	141
Television	2000	receivers	9,570	23
Telephones	2003	main lines	6,200	13
Cellular telephones	2003	subscribers	1,500	3.1
Personal computers	2004	units	20,000	41
Internet	2004	users	3,000	6.1

Education and health

Educational attainment (1986)[11]. Percentage of population age 25 and over
  having: no schooling 44.4%; primary education 46.2%; secondary 6.8%; higher 2.6%. *Literacy* (1999): total population age 15 and over literate 181,000
  (76%); males 102,500 (83%); females 78,500 (68%).

Education (2002)				student/
	schools	teachers	students	teacher ratio
Primary (age 6–11)	520[12]	2,510[12]	82,330	...
Secondary (age 12–16)	23[12]	618[12]	21,700	...
Voc., teacher tr.[13]	1	...	9,560	...
Higher[13]				

Health: physicians (2003) 53 (1 per 8,491 persons); hospital beds (1999) 881 (1
  per 459 persons); infant mortality rate per 1,000 live births (2004) 22.1.
Food (2002): daily per capita caloric intake 2,265 (vegetable products 92%,
  animal products 8%); 99% of FAO recommended minimum requirement.

Military

Total active duty personnel (2005): none; an Australian-led multinational
  regional intervention force (from mid-2003) maintains civil and political
  order.

[1]In mid-2003 the Solomon Islands now-established government requested regional assistance in order to restore law and order. [2]Detail does not add to total given because
of rounding. [3]At 1992 factor cost. [4]Persons employed in the monetary sector only.
[5]Public-service earnings. [6]Retail price index components. [7]Total includes 57,472
employed in the monetary sector and 27,652 unemployed; activity rate, female participation, and unemployment rates are based on this total. [8]Production at the country's
only gold mine was suspended from 2000 through mid-2005 because of lawlessness
(from 2000–2003) followed by a slow return to normalcy. [9]Imports c.i.f.; exports f.o.b.
[10]Solomon Airlines only. [11]Indigenous population only. [12]1994. [13]Vocational and teacher
training are carried out at the College of Higher Education.

Internet resources for further information:
• **Central Bank of Solomon Islands**
  http://www.cbsi.com.sb
• **Solomon Islands Statistics**
  http://www.spc.int/prism/country/SB/stats

Somalia[1]

Official name: Soomaaliya (Somali) (Somalia).
Form of government: transitional regime[2] with one legislative body (Transitional Federal Assembly [275[3]]).
Head of state and government: President assisted by Prime Minister[2].
Capital: Mogadishu.
Official languages: Somali; Arabic.
Official religion: Islam.
Monetary unit: 1 Somali shilling (So.Sh.) = 100 cents; valuation (Sept. 1, 2005) 1 U.S.$ = So.Sh. 2,728[4]; 1 £ = So.Sh. 4,908.

Area and population		area		population
Regions	Principal cities	sq mi	sq km	1980 estimate
Bakool[5]	Xuddur	10,000	27,000	148,700
Banaadir	Mogadishu (Muqdisho)	400	1,000	520,100
Bari[6]	Boosaaso	27,000	70,000	222,300
Bay[5]	Baydhabo	15,000	39,000	451,000
Galguduud	Dhuusamarreeb	17,000	43,000	255,900
Gedo[5]	Garbahaarrey	12,000	32,000	235,000
Hiiraan	Beledweyne	13,000	34,000	219,300
Jubbada Dhexe[5]	Bu'aale	9,000	23,000	147,800
Jubbada Hoose[5]	Kismaayo	24,000	61,000	272,400
Mudug[6]	Gaalkacyo	27,000	70,000	311,200
Nugaal[6]	Garoowe	19,000	50,000	112,200
Sanaag[7]	Ceerigaabo	21,000	54,000	216,500
Shabeellaha Dhexe	Jawhar	8,000	22,000	352,000
Shabeellaha Hoose[5]	Marka	10,000	25,000	570,700
Togdheer[7]	Burao	16,000	41,000	383,900
Woqooyi Galbeed[7]	Hargeysa	17,000	45,000	655,000
TOTAL		246,000[8]	637,000	5,074,000

Demography

Population (2005): 8,228,000[9].
Density (2005): persons per sq mi 33.4, persons per sq km 12.9.
Urban-rural (2003): urban 34.8%; rural 63.2%.
Sex distribution (2002): male 51.47%; female 48.53%.
Age breakdown (2002): under 15, 46.4%; 15–29, 26.4%; 30–44, 16.3%; 45–59, 8.1%; 60–74, 2.4%; 75 and over, 0.4%.
Population projection: (2010) 9,590,000; (2020) 12,336,000.
Doubling time: 24 years.
Ethnic composition (2000): Somali 92.4%; Arab 2.2%; Afar 1.3%; other 4.1%.
Religious affiliation (2000): Sunnī Muslim 98.3%; Christian 1.4%, of which Orthodox 1.3%; other 0.3%.
Major cities (1990): Mogadishu 1,212,000[10]; Hargeysa (1997) 300,000; Kismaayo 90,000; Berbera 70,000; Marka 62,000.

Vital statistics

Birth rate per 1,000 population (2004): 46.0 (world avg. 21.1).
Death rate per 1,000 population (2004): 17.3 (world avg. 9.0).
Natural increase rate per 1,000 population (2004): 28.7 (world avg. 12.1).
Total fertility rate (avg. births per childbearing woman; 2004): 6.9.
Life expectancy at birth (2004): male 46.0 years; female 49.5 years.
Major causes of death as percentage of all deaths (2001–02): sickness 61.1%; old age 19.0%; accidents 11.0%, of which land mines 3.6%; war-related 4.3%; pregnancy/childbirth-related 4.0%.

National economy

Budget (1991). Revenue: So.Sh. 151,453,000,000 (domestic revenue sources [principally indirect taxes and import duties] 60.4%; external grants and transfers 39.6%). Expenditures: So.Sh. 141,141,000,000 (general services 46.9%; economic and social services 31.2%; debt service 7.0%).
Production (metric tons except as noted). Agriculture, forestry, fishing (2003): sugarcane 200,000, corn (maize) 164,000, sorghum 121,000, cassava 85,000, bananas 35,000, sesame seed 25,000, pulses 16,000, dates 11,000, oranges 8,000, lemons and limes 8,000, grapefruit 6,000, watermelon 6,000, sweet potatoes 6,000, other tree/bush products include khat, frankincense, and myrrh; livestock (number of live animals) 13,100,000 sheep, 12,700,000 goats, 7,000,000 camels, 5,350,000 cattle; roundwood 10,576,453 cu m; fish catch (2003) 18,000. Mining and quarrying (2004): gypsum 1,500; salt 1,000; garnet and opal are mined in Somaliland. Manufacturing (value added in So.Sh. '000,000; 1988): food 794; cigarettes and matches 562; hides and skins 420; paper and printing 328; plastics 320; chemicals 202; beverages 144. Energy production (consumption): electricity (kW-hr; 2002) 282,000,000 (282,000,000); coal, none (none); crude petroleum, none (none); petroleum products (metric tons; 2002) n.a. (n.a.); natural gas, none (none).
Population economically active (2001–02): total 3,906,000; activity rate of total population 52.6% (participation rates: ages 15–64, 56.4%; female, n.a.; unemployed 47.4%).

Price index (2000 = 100)							
	1998	1999	2000	2001	2002	2003	2004
Consumer price index	...	...	100.0	...	...	...	...

Household income and expenditure (2001–02). Average household size 5.8; income per household: U.S.$226; sources of income: self-employment 50%, remittances 22.5%, wages 14%, rent/aid 13.5%; expenditure (1983)[11]: food and tobacco 62.3%, housing 15.3%, clothing 5.6%, energy 4.3%, other 12.5%.
Gross national product (2004): U.S.$1,900,000,000 (U.S.$240 per capita).

Structure of gross domestic product and labour force				
	2001		2001–02	
	in value U.S.$'000,000	% of total value	labour force	% of labour force
Agriculture	630	63.0	2,617,000	67.0
Mining	10	1.0		
Public utilities				
Manufacturing	30	3.0	469,000	12.0
Construction	50	5.0		
Transp. and commun.	90	9.0		
Trade, restaurants	100	10.0		
Finance			820,000	21.0
Pub. admin., defense	90	9.0		
Services				
TOTAL	1,000	100.0	3,906,000	100.0

Public debt (external, outstanding; 2003): U.S.$1,936,000,000.
Tourism: n.a.
Land use as % of total land area (2000): in temporary crops 1.7%, in permanent crops 0.04%, in pasture 68.5%; overall forest area 12.0%.

Foreign trade[12]

Balance of trade (current prices)						
	1998	1999	2000	2001	2002	2003
U.S.$'000,000	−118	−105	−166	−267	−257	−302
% of total	31.6%	21.6%	32.8%	60.3%	57.0%	61.4%

Imports (2003): U.S.$397,000,000 (agricultural products 26.5%, of which cereals 6.4%; unspecified 73.5%). *Major import sources* (2004): Djibouti 31%; Kenya 14%; India 10%; Brazil 6%; Oman 5%.
Exports (2003): U.S.$95,000,000 (agricultural products 45.1%, of which goats and sheep 25.6%, bovines 7.8%; unspecified 54.9%). *Major export destinations* (2004): Thailand 29%; United Arab Emirates 24%; Yemen 15%; India 8%; Oman 6%.

Transport and communications

Transport. Railroads: none. Roads (2003): total length 13,650 mi, 22,000 km (paved 12%). Vehicles: passenger cars, n.a.; trucks and buses, n.a.; Air transport (2003)[13]: passenger arrivals 50,096, passenger departures 41,979; cargo unloaded 3,817 metric tons, cargo loaded 152 metric tons; airports (2004) with scheduled flights, n.a.

Communications				units per 1,000 persons
Medium	date	unit	number	
Daily newspapers	2000	circulation	7,250	1.0
Radio	2002	receivers	760,000	98
Television	2003	receivers	107,900	14
Telephones	2002	main lines	100,000	13
Cellular telephones	2002	subscribers	35,000	4.4
Personal computers	2002	units	6,200	0.8
Internet	2002	users	89,000	11

Education and health

Educational attainment: n.a. *Literacy* (2002): percentage of total population age 15 and over literate 19.2%; males literate 25.1%; females literate 13.1%.

Education (1989–90)				student/
	schools	teachers	students	teacher ratio
Primary (age 6–14)	1,125	8,208	377,000	20.9
Secondary (age 15–18)	82	2,109	44,000	20.3
Voc., teacher tr.	21	498	10,400	9.7
Higher[14]	1	549	4,640	8.5

Health (1997): physicians 265 (1 per 25,032 persons); hospital beds 2,786 (1 per 2,381 persons); infant mortality rate per 1,000 live births (2004) 118.5.
Food (2000): daily per capita caloric intake 1,628 (vegetable products 62%, animal products 38%); 70% of FAO recommended minimum requirement.

Military

Total active duty personnel: no national army from 1991. *Military expenditure as percentage of GDP* (2004): n.a.

[1]Proclamation of the "Republic of Somaliland" in May 1991 on territory corresponding to the former British Somaliland (which unified with the former Italian Trust Territory of Somalia to form Somalia in 1960) had not received international recognition as of mid-December 2005. This entity represented about a quarter of Somalia's territory. [2] "New transitional government" from October 2004 lacked effective control in mid-December 2005. [3]Planned number; the Transitional Federal Assembly was not functioning as an actual legislative body in December 2005. [4]1 U.S.$ equaled about 18,000 So.Sh. on the black market in September 2003. [5]Part of "autonomous region" of Southwestern Somalia from April 2002; status of this "autonomous region" is unclear in late 2005. [6]Part of "autonomous region" of Puntland from 1998. [7]Part of "Republic of Somaliland" from 1991. [8]Detail does not add to total given because of rounding. [9]Estimate of *UN World Population Prospects (2004 revision).* [10]Estimated urban agglomeration, 2003. [11]Mogadishu only. [12]Imports c.i.f.; exports f.o.b. [13]Four Somaliland airports only. [14]1991.

Internet resources for further information:
• **World Bank and UNDP Survey on Somalia**
  http://www.so.undp.org/socecon.htm

South Africa

Official name: Republic of South
Africa (English).
Form of government: multiparty
republic with two legislative houses
(National Council of Provinces [90];
National Assembly [400]).
Head of state and government:
President.
Capitals (de facto): Pretoria[1]
(executive); Bloemfontein[2]
(judicial); Cape Town (legislative).
Official languages: [3].
Official religion: none.
Monetary unit: 1 rand (R) = 100 cents;
valuation (Sept. 1, 2005)
1 U.S.$ = R 6.27; 1 £ = R 11.54.

Area and population

Provinces	Capitals	area sq mi	area sq km	population 2005 estimate
Eastern Cape	Bisho	65,475	169,580	7,039,300
Free State	Bloemfontein	49,993	129,480	2,953,100
Gauteng	Johannesburg	6,568	17,010	9,018,000
KwaZulu–Natal	Pietermaritzburg	35,560	92,100	9,651,100
Limpopo	Polokwane	47,842	123,910	5,635,000
Mpumalanga	Nelspruit	30,691	79,490	3,219,900
North West	Mafikeng/Mmabatho	44,911	116,320	3,823,900
Northern Cape	Kimberley	139,703	361,830	902,300
Western Cape	Cape Town	49,950	129,370	4,645,600
TOTAL		470,693[4]	1,219,090[4]	46,888,200

Demography

Population (2005): 46,888,000.
Density (2005)[5]: persons per sq mi 99.5, persons per sq km 38.4.
Urban-rural (2003): urban 56.9%; rural 43.1%.
Sex distribution (2004): male 49.34%; female 50.66%.
Age breakdown (2001): under 15, 32.0%; 15–29, 29.5%; 30–44, 20.2%; 45–59, 11.0%; 60–74, 5.5%; 75 and over, 1.8%.
Population projection: (2010) 47,271,000; (2020) 47,549,000.
Ethnic composition (2001): black 78.4%, of which Zulu 23.8%, Xhosa 17.6%, Pedi 9.4%, Tswana 8.2%, Sotho 7.9%, Tsonga 4.4%, Swazi 2.7%, other black 4.4%; white 9.6%; Coloured 8.9%; Asian 2.5%; other 0.6%.
Religious affiliation (2000): Christian 83.1%, of which black independent churches 39.1%, Protestant 31.8%, Roman Catholic 7.1%; traditional beliefs 8.4%; Hindu 2.4%; Muslim 2.4%; nonreligious 2.4%; other 1.3%.
Major urban agglomerations (2005): Johannesburg 3,288,000; Cape Town 3,103,000; Ekurhuleni (East Rand) 3,043,000; Durban 2,643,000; Tshwane (Pretoria) 1,282,000.

Vital statistics

Birth rate per 1,000 population (2004): 19.1[6] (world avg. 21.1).
Death rate per 1,000 population (2004): 20.4[6] (world avg. 9.0).
Natural increase rate per 1,000 population (2004): –1.3[6] (world avg. 12.1).
Marriage rate per 1,000 population (2002): 3.9.
Divorce rate per 1,000 population (2002): 0.7.
Total fertility rate (avg. births per childbearing woman; 2004): 2.8.
Life expectancy at birth (2004): male 45.5 years; female 48.9 years.
Adult population (ages 15–49) *living with HIV* (2004[7]): 21.5% (world avg. 1.1%).

National economy

Budget (2004–05). Revenue: R 337,960,000,000 (personal income taxes 32.1%, value-added taxes 27.7%, company income taxes 21.2%). Expenditures: R 370,113,000,000 (transfer to provinces 44.3%, debt payments 13.2%, police and prisons 8.9%, defense 5.2%, education 3.1%, health 2.4%).
Public debt (external, outstanding; 2003): U.S.$9,120,000,000.
Production (in metric tons except as noted). Agriculture, forestry, fishing (2004): sugarcane 19,094,760, corn (maize) 9,737,000, wheat 1,761,000, grapes 1,682,951, potatoes 1,574,458, oranges 1,150,045, grapefruits 233,420; livestock (number of live animals) 29,100,100 sheep, 13,512,000 cattle, 6,372,000 goats; roundwood 33,159,400 cu m; fish catch (2003) 822,854 metric tons. Mining and quarrying (value of export sales in U.S.$'000,000,000; 2003): gold 4.3; platinum-group metals 3.4; coal 1.8; rough diamond production 1.4; ferrous metals 0.6. Manufacturing (value added in U.S.$'000,000; 1999): food products 2,225; iron and steel 2,225; transport equipment 2,100; fabricated metals 1,400; electrical machinery 1,325; refined petroleum 1,325; nonferrous base metals 1,200. Energy production (consumption)[8]: electricity (kW-hr; 2002) 231,833,000,000 (236,924,000,000); coal (metric tons; 2004) 247,900,000 ([2002] 161,977,000); crude petroleum (barrels; 2004) 4,800,000 ([2002] 209,000,000); petroleum products (metric tons; 2002) 26,180,000 (18,931,000); natural gas (cu m; 2002) 2,371,000,000 (2,371,000,000).
Population economically active (2003): total 16,192,000; activity rate of total population c. 36% (participation rates: ages 15–64, 54.4%; female 46.7%; unemployed [September 2003–March 2004] 18.1%).

Price and earnings indexes (2000 = 100)

	1998	1999	2000	2001	2002	2003	2004
Consumer price index	90.3	94.9	100.0	105.7	115.4	122.1	123.8
Monthly earnings index[9]	87.9	92.9	100.0	108.6	...	...	...

Household income and expenditure. Average household size (2001) 3.8; average annual disposable income per household (1996)[10] R 47,600 (U.S.$11,070);

expenditure (1998): food, beverages, and tobacco 31.3%; transportation 14.3%; housing 9.3%; household furnishings and operation 8.9%.
Gross national product (2004): U.S.$165,542,000,000 (U.S.$3,630 per capita).

Structure of gross domestic product and labour force

	2004 in value R '000,000	2004 % of total value	2003 labour force	2003 % of labour force
Agriculture	41,323	3.0	1,197,000	7.4
Mining	87,058	6.3	503,000	3.1
Manufacturing	246,467	17.9	1,634,000	10.1
Construction	29,190	2.1	626,000	3.9
Public utilities	28,239	2.1	86,000	0.5
Transp. and commun.	120,095	8.7	563,000	3.5
Trade	172,667	12.6	2,451,000	15.1
Finance, real estate	247,514	18.0	1,079,000	6.7
Pub. admin., defense	180,976	13.2 }	3,469,000	21.4
Services	76,880	5.6 }		
Other	144,067[11]	10.5[11]	4,581,000[12]	28.3[12]
TOTAL	1,374,476	100.0	16,192,000[13]	100.0

Tourism (2003): receipts U.S.$4,270,000,000; expenditures U.S.$2,452,000,000.
Land use as % of total land area (2000): in temporary crops 12.1%, in permanent crops 0.8%, in pasture 68.7%; overall forest area 7.3%.

Foreign trade[14]

Balance of trade (current prices)

	1999	2000	2001	2002	2003	2004
U.S.$'000,000	+4,008	+4,698	+5,255	+4,756	+3,285	–115
% of total	7.6%	7.9%	9.2%	8.1%	4.4%	0.1%

Imports (2002): U.S.$26,212,000,000 (nonelectrical machinery 13.5%, chemicals and chemical products 11.8%, crude petroleum 10.7%, road vehicles 6.3%, telecommunications equipment 6.2%). *Major import sources:* Germany 15.6%; U.S. 11.8%; U.K. 9.0%; Japan 6.9%; China 5.2%.
Exports (2002): U.S.$23,064,000,000[15] (gold c. 13%, platinum-group metals c. 11%, iron and steel 10.5%, road vehicles 10.4%, coal c. 10%, food 8.2%, diamonds 6.7%). *Major export destinations:* U.K. 10.9%; U.S. 10.6%; Germany 8.2%; Japan 6.5%; The Netherlands 5.2%.

Transport and communications

Transport. Railroads: route length (2001) 20,384 km; passenger-km 3,930,000,000; metric ton-km cargo 106,786,000,000. Roads (2000): length 362,099 km (paved 20%). Vehicles (2002): passenger cars 4,135,037; trucks and buses 2,202,032. Air transport (2004)[16]: passenger-km 23,080,000,000; metric ton-km cargo 917,107,000; airport (1996) 24.

Communications

Medium	date	unit	number	units per 1,000 persons
Daily newspapers	2000	circulation	1,590,000	32
Radio	2000	receivers	16,800,000	338
Television	2002	receivers	8,018,000	177
Telephones	2002	main lines	4,844,000	107
Cellular telephones	2004	subscribers	19,500,000	431
Personal computers	2004	units	3,740,000	83
Internet	2004	users	3,566,000	79

Education and health

Educational attainment (2000). Percentage of population age 20 and over having: no formal schooling 17.9%; some primary education 16.0%; complete primary/some secondary 37.2%; complete secondary 20.4%; higher 8.5%.
Literacy (2000): total population age 15 and over literate 85.3%; males 86.0%; females 84.6%.

Education (2000)

	schools	teachers	students	student/ teacher ratio
Primary (age 6–12)	17,213	183,639	6,266,223	34.1
Secondary (age 13–17)[17]	10,547	177,084	5,588,866	31.6
Higher[18]	21	...	169,604	...

Health: physicians (end of 2002) 30,153 (1 per 1,519 persons); hospital beds (1998) 144,363 (1 per 290 persons); infant mortality rate (2004) 57.3.
Food (2002): daily per capita caloric intake 2,956 (vegetable products 88%, animal products 12%); 121% of FAO recommended minimum.

Military

Total active duty personnel (2004): 55,750 (army 64.6%, navy 8.1%, air force 16.6%, national defense force 10.7%). *Military expenditure as percentage of GDP* (2003): 1.6%; per capita expenditure U.S.$56.

[1]Name of larger municipality including Pretoria is Tshwane. [2]Name of larger municipality including Bloemfontein is Mangaung. [3]Afrikaans; English; Ndebele; Pedi (North Sotho); Sotho (South Sotho); Swazi; Tsonga; Tswana (West Sotho); Venda; Xhosa; Zulu. [4]Area of provincial South Africa; total area including Prince Edward Islands equals 471,011 sq mi (1,219,912 sq km). [5]Based on total area. [6]Estimate from the U.S. Bureau of the Census, International Database. [7]January 1. [8]2002 data include Botswana, Lesotho, Namibia, and Swaziland. [9]Manufacturing sector only. [10]Estimated figures. [11]Taxes on products less subsidies on products. [12]Includes 11,000 not adequately defined and 4,570,000 unemployed. [13]Detail does not add to total given because of rounding. [14]Imports f.o.b. in balance of trade and c.i.f. in commodities and trading partners. [15]Total reported in International Trade Statistical Yearbook (2002) may be incomplete. [16]SAA only. [17]Includes combined and intermediate. [18]Universities only.

Internet resources for further information:
• **South African Reserve Bank** http://www.reservebank.co.za
• **Statistics South Africa** http://www.statssa.gov.za

Spain

Official name: Reino de España
(Kingdom of Spain).
Form of government: constitutional
monarchy with two legislative
houses (Senate [259[1]]; Congress of
Deputies [350]).
Chief of state: King.
Head of government: Prime Minister.
Capital: Madrid.
Official languages: Castilian Spanish[2].
Official religion: none.
Monetary unit: 1 euro (€) = 100
céntimos; valuation (Sept. 1, 2005)
1 U.S.$ = €0.80; 1 £ = €1.47[3].

Area and population		area		population
				2004[4]
Autonomous communities	Capitals	sq mi	sq km	estimate
Andalucía	Seville	33,821	87,597	7,687,518
Aragón	Zaragoza	18,425	47,720	1,249,584
Asturias	Oviedo	4,094	10,604	1,073,761
Baleares (Balearic Islands)	Palma de Mallorca	1,927	4,992	955,045
Canarias (Canary Islands)	Santa Cruz de Tenerife	2,876	7,447	1,915,540
Cantabria	Santander	2,054	5,321	554,784
Castilla-La Mancha	Toledo	30,681	79,463	1,848,881
Castilla y León	Valladolid	36,380	94,223	2,493,918
Cataluña	Barcelona	12,399	32,114	6,813,319
Extremadura	Mérida	16,075	41,634	1,075,286
Galicia	Santiago	11,419	29,574	2,750,985
La Rioja	Logroño	1,948	5,045	293,553
Madrid	Madrid	3,100	8,028	5,804,829
Murcia	Murcia	4,368	11,313	1,294,694
Navarra	Pamplona	4,012	10,391	584,734
País Vasco	Vitoria (Gasteiz)	2,793	7,234	2,115,279
Valenciana	Valencia	8,979	23,255	4,543,304
Autonomous cities				
Ceuta	—	7	19	74,654
Melilla	—	5	13	68,016
TOTAL		195,363	505,988[5]	43,197,684

Demography

Population (2005): 44,079,000.
Density (2005): persons per sq mi 225.6, persons per sq km 87.1.
Urban-rural (2002): urban 77.8%; rural 22.2%.
Sex distribution (2004): male 49.27%; female 50.73%.
Age breakdown (2004): under 15, 14.5%; 15–29, 21.0%; 30–44, 24.4%; 45–59, 18.4%; 60–74, 13.9%; 75 and over, 7.8%.
Population projection: (2010) 46,415,000; (2020) 49,779,000.
Ethnic composition (2000): Spaniard 44.9%; Catalonian 28.0%; Galician 8.2%; Basque 5.5%; Aragonese 5.0%; Rom (Gypsy) 2.0%; other 6.4%.
Religious affiliation (2000): Roman Catholic 92.0%; Muslim 0.5%; Protestant 0.3%; other 7.2%.
Major cities (2004): Madrid 3,099,834; Barcelona 1,578,546; Valencia 785,732; Seville 704,203; Zaragoza 638,799.

Vital statistics

Birth rate per 1,000 population (2004): 10.6 (world avg. 21.1).
Death rate per 1,000 population (2004): 8.7 (world avg. 9.0).
Natural increase rate per 1,000 population (2004): 1.9 (world avg. 12.1).
Total fertility rate (avg. births per childbearing woman; 2004): 1.3.
Life expectancy at birth (2003): male 77.2 years; female 83.7 years.
Major causes of death per 100,000 population (2002): circulatory diseases 304.5; malignant neoplasms (cancers) 236.7; respiratory diseases 100.3; accidents, poisonings, and violence 37.8; diseases of the nervous system 30.3.

National economy

Budget (2002). Revenue: €108,824,300,000 (direct taxes 46.6%, of which income tax 27.2%; indirect taxes 41.8%, of which value-added tax on products 27.8%; other taxes 11.6%). Expenditures: €112,586,900,000 (public debt 15.7%; health 9.8%; pensions 5.7%; defense 5.6%; public works 4.8%).
Tourism (2004): receipts U.S.$29,297,000,000; expenditures U.S.$7,870,000,000.
Gross national product (2004): U.S.$875,817,000,000 (U.S.$21,210 per capita).

Structure of gross domestic product and labour force				
	2001		2003	
	in value €'000,000[6]	% of total value[6]	labour force	% of labour force
Agriculture	21,000	3.2	942,100	5.0
Mining	2,740	0.4	63,300	0.3
Manufacturing	106,770	16.4	2,960,500	15.7
Public utilities	13,230	2.1	99,600	0.5
Construction	53,670	8.2	1,984,600	10.6
Transp. and commun.	53,220	8.2	1,026,900	5.5
Trade and hotels	116,610	17.9	3,681,200	19.6
Finance, real estate	123,340	18.9	1,769,000	9.4
Services	87,840	13.5	3,069,400	16.3
Pub. admin., defense	37,220	5.7	1,096,800	5.8
Other	36,000[7]	5.5[7]	2,128,500[8]	11.3[8]
TOTAL	651,640	100.0	18,821,900	100.0

Land use as % of total land area (2000): in temporary crops 26.5%, in permanent crops 9.9%, in pasture 22.9%; overall forest area 28.8%.
Production (metric tons except as noted). Agriculture, forestry, fishing (2003): alfalfa 12,843,000, barley 8,698,000, olives 7,290,900, grapes 6,863,000, sugar beets 6,484,000, wheat 6,290,000, corn (maize) 4,339,000, tomatoes 3,849,000,

potatoes 2,790,000; livestock (number of live animals) 24,055,676 pigs, 23,485,948 sheep, 6,548,379 cattle; roundwood 16,105,000 cu m; fish catch (2001) 1,289,081. Mining and quarrying (metal content in metric tons; 2003): zinc 44,660; gold 5,362 kg. Manufacturing (value added in €'000,000; 2001): transport equipment 35,774; petroleum products 26,242; food products 14,771; chemical products 14,137; plastics 11,893; pharmaceutical products 10,050; furniture 9,653; alcoholic beverages 9,195. Energy production (consumption): electricity (kW-hr; 2002) 246,000,000,000 (251,400,000,000); hard coal (metric tons; 2002) 9,752,000 (33,653,000); lignite (metric tons; 2002) 12,282,000 (12,588,000); crude petroleum (barrels; 2003) 2,701,000 ([2002] 424,000,000); petroleum products (metric tons; 2002) 48,983,000 (52,606,000); natural gas (cu m; 2002) 536,782,000 (21,559,000,000).
Public debt (December 2004): U.S.$416,742,000,000.
Population economically active (2003)[9]: total 18,815,300; activity rate of total population 46.4% (participation rates: ages 16–64, 68.5%; female 40.5%; unemployed [January–October 2004] 10.9%).

Price and earnings indexes (2000 = 100)							
	1998	1999	2000	2001	2002	2003	2004
Consumer price index	94.5	96.7	100.0	103.6	106.8	110.0	113.2
Earnings index	95.3	97.7	100.0	103.8	108.1	112.7	118.8

Household income and expenditure (2004). Average household size (2001) 2.9; income per household €22,688 (U.S.$28,170); expenditure: housing 26.3%; food 18.6%, household expenses 7.4%, clothing/footwear 6.4%.

Foreign trade[10]

Balance of trade (current prices)						
	1999	2000	2001	2002	2003	2004
€'000,000	−32,523	−43,039	−43,019	−41,975	−46,280	−60,673
% of total	9.5%	14.9%	14.3%	13.8%	14.4%	17.2%

Imports (2002): €175,268,000,000 (road vehicles 15.9%; nonelectrical machinery 12.1%; crude and refined petroleum 10.8%; chemicals and chemical products 10.4%; electrical machinery 8.5%). *Major import sources* (2002): France 16.4%; Germany 16.2%; Italy 9.1%; The Netherlands, Belgium, and Luxembourg 7.1%; U.K. 6.5%.
Exports (2002): €133,293,000,000 (road vehicles 22.7%; food 15.4%, of which fruits and vegetables 6.5%; machinery 15.1%; chemicals and chemical products 8.7%). *Major export destinations* (2002): France 19.0%; Germany 11.5%; Portugal 10.2%; U.K. 9.6%; Italy 9.4%.

Transport and communications

Transport. Railroads (2001): route length 13,832 km; passenger-km 19,190,000,000; metric ton-km cargo 12,216,000,000. Roads (2003): length 677,646 km (paved 99%). Vehicles (2004): cars 19,541,918; trucks, vans, and buses 4,474,996. Air transport (2004)[11]: passenger-km 52,992,000,000; metric ton-km cargo 1,182,922,000; airports (1997) with scheduled flights 25.

Communications				units per 1,000
Medium	date	unit	number	persons
Daily newspapers	2004	circulation	4,240,000	97
Radio	2000	receivers	13,500,000	333
Television	2000	receivers	24,000,000	591
Telephones	2004	main lines	17,752,000	432
Cellular telephones	2004	subscribers	38,622,600	939
Personal computers	2004	units	10,957,000	266
Internet	2004	users	13,000,000	316

Education and health

Educational attainment (2001). Percentage of population age 16 and over having: no formal schooling 15.4%; primary education 23.1%; secondary 48.0%; undergraduate degree 6.6%; graduate degree 6.9%. *Literacy* (2001): total population age 15 and over literate 97.7%; males 96.9%; females 98.6%.

Education (2001–02)				student/
	schools	teachers	students	teacher ratio
Primary (age 6–11)	8,547	170,691	2,475,027	14.5
Secondary (age 12–18)[12]	4,319	264,464	3,116,895	11.8
Higher	1,774	98,567	1,508,116	15.3

Health: physicians (2003) 190,665 (1 per 223 persons); hospital beds (2001) 160,815 (1 per 254 persons); infant mortality rate (2004) 3.5.
Food (2002): daily per capita caloric intake 3,371 (vegetable products 72%, animal products 28%); 137% of FAO recommended minimum requirement.

Military

Total active duty personnel (2004): 150,700 (army 63.4%, navy 15.2%, air force 15.1%, other 6.3%). *Military expenditure as percentage of GDP* (2003): 1.2%; per capita expenditure U.S.$226.

[1]Includes 51 indirectly elected seats. [2]The constitution states that "Castilian is the Spanish official language of the State," but that "all other Spanish languages (including Euskera [Basque], Catalan, and Galician) will also be official in the corresponding Autonomous Communities." [3]The peseta (Pta) was the former monetary unit; on Jan. 1, 2002, Ptas 166.33 = €1. [4]January 1. [5]Detail does not add to total given due to North African islets not listed equaling 0.66 sq km in area. [6]At current prices. [7]Taxes less subsidies and less imputed bank service charges. [8]Unemployed. [9]Excludes conscripts. [10]Imports are f.o.b. in balance of trade. [11]Combined total of Iberia, Air Europa, Air Nostrum, Binter Canarias, Spanair, and regional airlines. [12]Includes vocational.

Internet resources for further information:
• Banco de España http://www.bde.es
• National Institute of Statistics http://www.ine.es/en/welcome_en.htm

Sri Lanka

Official name: Śri Lanka Prajatantrika Samajavadi Janarajaya (Sinhala); Ilangai Jananayaka Socialisa Kudiarasu (Tamil) (Democratic Socialist Republic of Sri Lanka).
Form of government: unitary multiparty republic with one legislative house (Parliament [225]).
Head of state and government: President assisted by Prime Minister.
Capitals: Colombo (executive and judicial); Sri Jayewardenepura Kotte (Colombo suburb; legislative).
Official languages: Sinhala; Tamil.
Official religion: none.
Monetary unit: 1 Sri Lanka rupee (SL Rs) = 100 cents; valuation (Sept. 1, 2005) 1 U.S.$ = SL Rs 101.33; 1 £ = SL Rs 186.57.

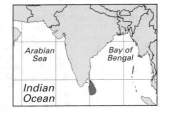

Area and population		area		population
Districts	**Capitals**	sq mi	sq km	2004 estimate
Amparai	Amparai	1,705	4,415	613,000
Anuradhapura	Anuradhapura	2,772	7,179	773,000
Badulla	Badulla	1,105	2,861	813,000
Batticaloa	Batticaloa	1,102	2,854	544,000
Colombo	Colombo	270	699	2,342,000
Galle	Galle	638	1,652	1,020,000
Gampaha	Gampaha	536	1,387	2,099,000
Hambantota	Hambantota	1,007	2,609	538,000
Jaffna	Jaffna	396	1,025	596,000
Kalutara	Kalutara	617	1,598	1,085,000
Kandy	Kandy	749	1,940	1,325,000
Kegalle	Kegalle	654	1,693	791,000
Kilinochchi	Kilinochchi	494	1,279	143,000
Kurunegala	Kurunegala	1,859	4,816	1,486,000
Mannar	Mannar	771	1,996	97,000
Matale	Matale	770	1,993	459,000
Matara	Matara	495	1,283	788,000
Monaragala	Monaragala	2,177	5,639	410,000
Mullaitivu	Mullaitivu	1,010	2,617	144,000
Nuwara Eliya	Nuwara Eliya	672	1,741	722,000
Polonnaruwa	Polonnaruwa	1,271	3,293	372,000
Puttalam	Puttalam	1,186	3,072	728,000
Ratnapura	Ratnapura	1,264	3,275	1,049,000
Trincomalee	Trincomalee	1,053	2,727	383,000
Vavuniya	Vavuniya	759	1,967	142,000
TOTAL		25,332	65,610	19,462,000[1]

Demography

Population (2005): 20,743,000[2].
Density (2005): persons per sq mi 818.8, persons per sq km 316.2.
Urban-rural (2003): urban 21.0%; rural 79.0%.
Sex distribution (2003–04)[3]: male 47.70%; female 52.30%.
Age breakdown (2001): under 15, 27.9%; 15–29, 27.1%; 30–44, 22.7%; 45–59, 13.6%; 60–74, 7.0%; 75 and over, 1.7%.
Population projection: (2010) 21,557,000; (2020) 22,902,000.
Ethnic composition (2000): Sinhalese 72.4%; Tamil 17.8%; Sri Lankan Moor 7.4%; other 2.4%.
Religious affiliation (2001): Buddhist 76.7%; Muslim 8.5%; Hindu 7.9%; Christian 6.8%; other 0.1%.
Major cities (2001): Colombo 642,163; Dehiwala–Mount Lavinia 209,787; Moratuwa 177,190; Negombo 121,933; Sri Jayewardenepura Kotte 115,826.

Vital statistics

Birth rate per 1,000 population (2003): 18.9 (world avg. 21.1).
Death rate per 1,000 population (2003): 5.9 (world avg. 9.0).
Natural increase rate per 1,000 population (2003): 13.0 (world avg. 12.1).
Total fertility rate (avg. births per childbearing woman; 2003): 1.9.
Life expectancy at birth (2003): male 70.1 years; female 75.3 years.
Major causes of death per 100,000 population (2002): diseases of the circulatory system 252; communicable diseases 103; malignant neoplasms (cancers) 101; respiratory diseases 82; injuries, accidents, and violence 81.

National economy

Budget (2003). Revenue: SL Rs 281,166,000,000 (VAT 34.6%, excises 18.1%, nontax revenue 17.6%, income taxes 14.0%). Expenditures: SL Rs 417,672,-000,000 (interest payments 30.0%, civil administration 18.4%, defense 14.8%).
Public debt (external, outstanding; 2004): U.S.$9,106,000,000.
Tourism (2003): receipts U.S.$424,000,000; expenditures U.S.$279,000,000.
Production (metric tons except as noted). Agriculture, forestry, fishing (2004): rice 2,509,800, coconuts 1,950,000, sugarcane 1,000,000, plantains 610,000, tea 303,000, natural rubber 92,000; livestock (number of live animals) 1,150,000 cattle, 415,000 goats, 280,000 buffalo; roundwood 6,340,385 cu m; fish catch (2003) 279,110. Mining and quarrying (2003): graphite 3,387; sapphires 773,547 carats; diamonds, n.a. Manufacturing (value added in SL Rs '000,000; 2004): textiles and apparel 91,308; food, beverages, and tobacco 72,636; petrochemicals 26,179. Energy production (consumption): electricity (kW-hr; 2004–05) 8,178,000,000 ([2004] 6,638,000,000); coal (metric tons; 2002) none (1,000); crude petroleum (barrels; 2002) none (16,000,000); petroleum products (metric tons; 2002) 2,077,000 (3,274,000).
Gross national product (2004): U.S.$19,618,000,000 (U.S.$1,010 per capita).

Structure of gross domestic product and labour force				
	2004		2003	
	in value SL Rs '000,000	% of total value	labour force	% of labour force
Agriculture	320,201	15.8	2,380,900	31.2
Mining	35,965	1.8	120,100	1.6
Public utilities	27,668	1.4		
Manufacturing	275,630	13.6	1,106,900	14.5
Construction	142,430	7.0	397,200	5.2
Transp. and commun.	255,654	12.6	375,700	4.9
Trade, hotels, restaurants	369,727	18.2	987,700	12.9
Finance, real estate	177,893	8.8	216,800	2.8
Pub. admin., defense	97,485	4.8	560,400	7.3
Services	95,288	4.7	543,800	7.1
Other	231,500[4]	11.4[4]	954,300[5]	12.5[5]
TOTAL	2,029,441	100.0[6]	7,643,200[6]	100.0

Land use as % of total land area (2000): in temporary crops 13.8%, in permanent crops 15.7%, in pasture 6.8%; overall forest area 30.0%.
Population economically active: total (2000) 6,708,620[3]; activity rate 42.0% (participation rates: ages 15–59, 60.6%; female 33.8%; unemployed [2004] 8.3%).

Price and earnings indexes (2000 = 100)							
	1998	1999	2000	2001	2002	2003	2004
Consumer price index	90.0	94.2	100.0	114.2	125.1	133.0	143.0
Minimum wage index	95.3	97.7	100.0	104.9	112.7	120.5	123.3

Household income and expenditure. Average household size (2003–04)[3] 4.3; income per household (2002) SL Rs 124,620 (U.S.$1,303)[7]; sources of income (2000): wages 48.5%, property income and self-employment 41.8%, transfers 9.7%; expenditure (1995–97)[8]: food, beverages, and tobacco 71.2%, housing and energy 13.1%.

Foreign trade[9]

Balance of trade (current prices)					
	1999	2000	2001	2002	2003	2004
SL Rs '000,000	−90,316	−64,970	−102,591	−134,641	−149,101	−227,171
% of total	12.2%	7.2%	10.6%	13.0%	13.1%	16.3%

Imports (2004): SL Rs 811,138,000,000 (textiles [mostly yarns and fabrics] 18.9%; petroleum and natural gas 15.1%; machinery and equipment 10.7%; foods 7.5%). *Major import sources:* India 18.0%; Singapore 8.7%; Hong Kong 7.7%; China 5.7%; Iran 5.2%; Japan 5.1%.
Exports (2004): SL Rs 583,967,000,000 (clothing and accessories 48.8%; tea 12.8%; precious and semiprecious stones 6.1%; rubber products 4.9%). *Major export destinations:* U.S. 32.4%; U.K. 13.5%; India 6.8%; Belgium-Luxembourg 5.1%; Germany 4.7%.

Transport and communications

Transport. Railroads (2004): route length 1,449 km; passenger-km 4,684,-000,000; metric ton-km cargo 134,000,000. Roads (2003): total length 97,286 km (paved 81%). Vehicles (2002): passenger cars 253,447; trucks and buses 396,615. Air transport (2004)[10]: passenger-km 8,310,070; metric ton-km cargo 289,671,000; airports (2001) 1.

Communications				units per 1,000 persons
Medium	date	unit	number	
Daily newspapers	2002	circulation	493,000	24
Radio	2000	receivers	3,870,000	208
Television	2003	receivers	2,386,100	117
Telephones	2004	main lines	991,200	48
Cellular telephones	2004	subscribers	2,211,200	107
Personal computers	2004	units	530,000	26
Internet	2004	users	280,000	14

Education and health

Educational attainment: n.a. Literacy (2003–04)[3]: percentage of population age 5 and over literate 93.0%; males literate 94.9%; females literate 91.3%.

Education (2002–03)				student/ teacher ratio
	schools	teachers	students	
Primary (age 5–10)	10,475	194,931	4,096,886	21.0
Secondary (age 11–17)				
Voc., teacher tr.	36	535	18,074	33.8
Higher	13	3,386	59,734	17.6

Health (2004): physicians 8,749 (1 per 2,351 persons); hospital beds 60,328 (1 per 341 persons); infant mortality rate (2003) 11.2.
Food (2002): daily per capita caloric intake 2,385 (vegetable products 93%, animal products 7%); 107% of FAO recommended minimum.

Military

Total active duty personnel (2004): 151,000 (army 78.2%, navy 9.9%, air force 11.9%). Military expenditure as percentage of GDP (2003): 2.7%; per capita expenditure U.S.$24.

[1]De facto figure. [2]De jure figure. [3]Excludes Northern and Eastern provinces. [4]Indirect taxes less subsidies. [5]Mainly unemployed. [6]Detail does not add to total given because of rounding. [7]Monetary income accounts for 81.1% of total income. [8]Weights of consumer price index components. [9]Imports c.i.f.; exports f.o.b. [10]SriLankan Airlines only.

Internet resources for further information:
• Central Bank of Sri Lanka http://www.centralbanklanka.org
• Department of Census and Statistics http://www.statistics.gov.lk

Sudan, The

Official name: Jumhūrīyat as-Sūdān (Republic of the Sudan).
Form of government: military regime with two legislative bodies (Council of States [50[1]]; National Assembly [450[2]])[3].
Head of state and government: President assisted by Vice Presidents[3].
Capitals: Khartoum (executive); Omdurman (legislative).
Official languages[4]: Arabic; English.
Official religion: [5].
Monetary unit: 1 Sudanese dinar (Sd); valuation (Sept. 1, 2005)
1 U.S.$ = Sd 242.28; 1 £ = Sd 446.11.

Area and population[2]

States[6]	area sq km	population 2000 estimate	States[6]	area sq km	population 2000 estimate
Bahr el-Ghazal[7]	...	2,256,942	Red Sea	...	709,637
Blue Nile	...	633,129	River Nile	...	895,893
Equatoria	...	1,234,486	Sinnar	...	1,132,758
Gedaref	...	1,414,531	Southern Darfur	...	2,708,007
Gezira	...	3,310,928	Southern Kordofan	...	1,066,117
Kassalā	...	1,433,730	Upper Nile	...	1,342,943
Khartoum	...	4,740,290	Western Darfur	...	1,531,682
Northern	...	578,376	Western Kordofan	...	1,078,330
Northern Darfur	...	1,409,894	White Nile	...	1,431,701
Northern Kordofan	...	1,439,930	TOTAL	2,503,890[8]	30,349,304[9, 10]

Demography

Population (2005): 36,233,000.
Density (2005): persons per sq mi 37.5, persons per sq km 14.5.
Urban-rural (2003): urban 38.9%; rural 61.1%.
Sex distribution (2001): male 50.64%; female 49.36%.
Age breakdown (2001): under 15, 44.6%; 15–29, 27.6%; 30–44, 15.6%; 45–59, 8.4%; 60–74, 3.3%; 75 and over, 0.5%.
Population projection: (2010) 40,254,000; (2020) 47,536,000.
Doubling time: 27 years.
Ethnic composition (2003): black *c.* 52%; Arab *c.* 39%; Beja *c.* 6%; foreigners *c.* 2%; other *c.* 1%.
Religious affiliation (2000): Sunnī Muslim 70.3%; Christian 16.7%, of which Roman Catholic *c.* 8%, Anglican *c.* 6%; traditional beliefs 11.9%; other 1.1%.
Major cities (1993): Omdurman 1,271,403; Khartoum 947,483[11]; Khartoum North 700,887; Port Sudan 308,195; Kassalā 234,622.

Vital statistics

Birth rate per 1,000 population (2004): 35.8 (world avg. 21.1).
Death rate per 1,000 population (2004): 9.4 (world avg. 9.0).
Natural increase rate per 1,000 population (2004): 26.4 (world avg. 12.1).
Total fertility rate (avg. births per childbearing woman; 2004): 5.0.
Life expectancy at birth (2004): male 57.0 years; female 59.4 years.
Major causes of death per 100,000 population: n.a.

National economy

Budget (2001). Revenue: Sd 365,200,000,000 (tax revenue 51.5%, of which custom duties 21.3%, VAT 10.3%; nontax revenue 48.5%). Expenditures: Sd 418,800,000,000 (current expenditure 81.9%, of which wages 31.4%; development expenditure 18.1%).
Public debt (external, outstanding; 2003): U.S.$9,570,000,000.
Production (metric tons except as noted). Agriculture, forestry, fishing (2004): sugarcane 5,500,000, sorghum 2,600,000, peanuts (groundnuts) 1,200,000, millet 784,000, wheat 332,000, dates 330,000, sesame seeds 325,000, seed cotton 265,000, tea 173,000, gum arabic (2002) 15,700; livestock (number of live animals) 48,000,000 sheep, 42,000,000 goats, 38,325,000 cattle, 3,300,000 camels; roundwood 19,654,776 cu m; fish catch (2003) 58,000. Mining and quarrying (2003): salt 84,000; gold 5,000 kg. Manufacturing (value of exports in U.S.$'000,000; 2003): benzene 75,860; animal hides and skins 18,649; propane and butane 15,598; molasses 8,645; sugar 6,995. Energy production (consumption): electricity (kW-hr; 2002) 2,897,000,000 (2,897,000,000); coal, none (none); crude petroleum (barrels; 2004) 125,000,000 ([2002] 22,600,000); petroleum products (metric tons; 2002) 2,651,000 (2,409,000); natural gas, none (none).
Gross national product (2004): U.S.$18,152,000,000 (U.S.$530 per capita).

Structure of gross domestic product and labour force

	2003 in value Sd '000,000,000	2003 % of total value	2000 labour force[12]	2000 % of labour force[12]
Agriculture	2,030.8	45.6	7,454,000	61.1
Mining	426.5	9.6		
Manufacturing	365.1	8.2		
Construction	208.3	4.7		
Public utilities	73.2	1.7		
Transportation and communications			4,753,000	38.9
Trade, hotels	1,090.4	24.5		
Finance				
Services				
Pub. admin., defense	255.6	5.7		
Other	—	—		
TOTAL	4,449.9	100.0	12,207,000	100.0

Population economically active (2000): total 12,207,000[12]; activity rate of total population 37.8% (participation rates: n.a.; female 29.9%; unemployed [2002] *c.* 19%).

Price and earnings indexes (2000 = 100)

	1998	1999	2000	2001	2002	2003	2004
Consumer price index	81.6	94.6	100.0	107.2	116.2	125.2	135.8
Earnings index	...	...	...	...	...	...	...

Household income and expenditure. Average household size (2002): 6.1; income per household: n.a.; expenditure: n.a.
Tourism (2003): receipts from visitors U.S.$118,000,000; expenditures by nationals abroad U.S.$119,000,000.
Land use as % of total land area (2000): in temporary crops 6.8%, in permanent crops 0.2%, in pasture 49.3%; overall forest area 25.9%.

Foreign trade[13]

Balance of trade (current prices)

	1999	2000	2001	2002	2003	2004
U.S.$'000,000	−635	+254	+113	−497	−340	−297
% of total	28.8%	7.6%	3.4%	11.3%	6.3%	3.8%

Imports (2004): U.S.$4,075,000,000 (machinery and equipment 31.1%; manufactured goods 25.8%; foodstuffs 13.5%, of which wheat and wheat flour 7.9%; transport equipment 12.6%). *Major import sources:* China 13.0%; Saudi Arabia 11.6%; U.A.E. 5.9%; India 4.8%; Germany 4.5%; Japan 4.1%.
Exports (2004): U.S.$3,778,000,000 (crude petroleum 78.3%; sesame seeds 4.7%; refined petroleum 3.8%; sheep and goats 3.7%; cotton 2.5%; gum arabic 1.6%). *Major export destinations* (2004): China 66.9%; Japan 10.6%; Saudi Arabia 4.3%; U.A.E. 2.4%.

Transport and communications

Transport. Railroads: route length (2004) 5,995 km; (2001) passenger-km 78,000,000; metric ton-km cargo 1,250,000,000. Roads (1999): total length 11,900 km (paved 36%). Vehicles (2001): passenger cars 46,000; trucks and buses 60,500. Air transport (2001): passenger-km 652,000,000; metric ton-km cargo 54,542,000; airports (1997) with scheduled flights 3.

Communications

Medium	date	unit	number	units per 1,000 persons
Daily newspapers	2000	circulation	912,000	26
Radio	2001	receivers	16,642,000	461
Television	2002	receivers	12,661,000	386
Telephones	2004	main lines	1,028,000	30
Cellular telephones	2004	subscribers	1,048,600	30
Personal computers	2004	units	606,000	18
Internet	2004	users	1,140,000	33.0

Education and health

Educational attainment: n.a. *Literacy* (2003): total population age 15 and over literate 60.9%; males 71.6%; females 50.4%.

Education (1999–2000)

	schools	teachers	students	student/ teacher ratio
Primary (age 7–12)	11,923	117,151	3,137,494	26.8
Secondary (age 13–18)	1,694	21,114	401,424	19.0
Vocational[14]	...	761	26,421	34.7
Higher[15]	19	1,417[14]	200,538	

Health: physicians (2000) 4,973 (1 per 6,616 persons); hospital beds (1998) 36,419 (1 per 909 persons); infant mortality rate (2004) 64.1.
Food (2002): daily per capita caloric intake 2,228 (vegetable products 80%, animal products 20%); 95% of FAO recommended minimum.

Military

Total active duty personnel (2004): 104,800 (army 95.4%, navy 1.7%, air force 2.9%); UN peacekeeping troops in Darfur (August 2005): 1,700. *Military expenditure as percentage of GDP* (2003): 2.4%; per capita expenditure U.S.$11.

[1]Excludes two observers with no voting rights. [2]All appointed. [3]Comprehensive peace agreement ending 21-year-long war in southern Sudan signed Jan. 9, 2005; interim constitution from July 9, 2005, to be effective for 6 years. [4]Arabic and English are both designated official working languages per 2005 interim constitution. [5]Islamic law and custom are applicable to Muslims only. [6]Names listed below are English-language variants; six states of the Southern Sudan are excluded (an interim legislature for Southern Sudan was inaugurated at Juba in September 2005). [7]Includes Western Bahr el-Ghazal and Northern Bahr el-Ghazal. [8]Including *c.* 130,000 sq km of inland water area. [9]Summary total; actual total per official source is 31,081,000. [10]Population estimates are unavailable for six states in southern Sudan experiencing civil war between 1983 and 2004. [11]Population of 2003 urban agglomeration (including Omdurman and Khartoum North) is 4,286,000. [12]FAO estimate. [13]Imports c.i.f.; exports f.o.b. [14]1996–97. [15]Universities only.

Internet resources for further information:
• **Bank of Sudan**
  http://www.bankofsudan.org
• **The Sudan Government's official website**
  http://www.sudan.gov.sd/english.htm

Suriname

Caribbean Sea · Atlantic Ocean · Pacific Ocean

Official name: Republiek Suriname (Republic of Suriname).
Form of government: multiparty republic with one legislative house (National Assembly [51]).
Head of state and government: President.
Capital: Paramaribo.
Official language: Dutch.
Official religion: none.
Monetary unit: 1 Suriname dollar (SRD)[1] = 100 cents; valuation (Sept. 1, 2005) 1 U.S.$ = SRD 2.74; 1 £ = SRD 5.05.

Area and population

Districts	Capitals	area sq mi	area sq km	population 2004 census
Brokopondo	Brokopondo	2,843	7,364	13,299
Commewijne	Nieuw Amsterdam	908	2,353	24,657
Coronie	Totness	1,507	3,902	2,809
Marowijne	Albina	1,786	4,627	16,641
Nickerie	Nieuw Nickerie	2,067	5,353	36,611
Para	Onverwacht	2,082	5,393	18,958
Saramacca	Groningen	1,404	3,636	16,135
Sipaliwini	[2]	50,412	130,566	28,202
Wanica	Lelydorp	171	443	86,072
Town district				
Paramaribo	Paramaribo	71	183	243,640
TOTAL		63,251[3]	163,820[3]	487,024[4]

Demography

Population (2005): 493,000.
Density (2005): persons per sq mi 7.8, persons per sq km 3.0.
Urban-rural (2003): urban 76.1%; rural 23.9%.
Sex distribution (2004): male 50.40%; female 49.60%.
Age breakdown (2004): under 15, 29.4%; 15–29, 25.6%; 30–44, 22.1%; 45–59, 12.3%; 60 and over, 8.6%; unknown 2.0%.
Population projection: (2010) 507,000; (2020) 525,000.
Doubling time: 58 years.
Ethnic composition (1999): Indo-Pakistani 37.0%; Suriname Creole 31.0%; Javanese 15.0%; Bush Negro 10.0%; Amerindian 2.5%; Chinese 2.0%; white 1.0%; other 1.5%.
Religious affiliation (2000): Christian 50.4%, of which Roman Catholic 22.3%, Protestant (mostly Moravian) 17.1%, unaffiliated/other Christian 11.0%; Hindu 17.8%; Muslim 13.9%; nonreligious 4.8%; Spiritists (including followers of Voodoo) 3.5%; traditional beliefs 1.7%; other 7.7%.
Major cities (1996/1997): Paramaribo 222,800 (urban agglomeration 289,000); Lelydorp 15,600; Nieuw Nickerie 11,100; Mungo (Moengo) 6,800; Meerzorg 6,600.

Vital statistics

Birth rate per 1,000 population (2004): 18.9 (world avg. 21.1).
Death rate per 1,000 population (2004): 7.0 (world avg. 9.0).
Natural increase rate per 1,000 population (2004): 11.9 (world avg. 12.1).
Total fertility rate (avg. births per childbearing woman; 2004): 2.4.
Marriage rate per 1,000 population (2000): 5.3.
Divorce rate per 1,000 population (2000): 0.9.
Life expectancy at birth (2004): male 66.8 years; female 71.6 years.
Major causes of death per 100,000 population (2002): diseases of the circulatory system 265; communicable diseases 172; malignant neoplasms (cancers) 87; injuries 76; diabetes mellitus 32.

National economy

Budget (2003). Revenue: SRD 919,600,000 (indirect taxes 46.7%; direct taxes 33.5%; nontax revenue 13.0%; grants 6.8%). Expenditures: SRD 922,800,000 (current expenditures 88.2%, of which wages and salaries 44.0%, transfers 15.1%, interest 7.1%; capital expenditures 10.7%; net lending 1.1%).
Public debt (external, outstanding; 2004): U.S.$235,620,000.
Production (metric tons except as noted). Agriculture, forestry, fishing (2004): rice 195,000, sugarcane 120,000, bananas 43,000, oranges 13,037, plantains 11,843, coconuts 9,000, cassava 4,300; livestock (number of live animals) 137,000 cattle, 24,500 pigs, 3,800,000 chickens; roundwood (2004) 207,408 cu m; fish catch (2001) 18,915, of which shrimp 7,390. Mining and quarrying (2003): bauxite 4,215,000; alumina 2,004,000; gold 300 kg[5]. Manufacturing (value of production at factor cost in Sf; 1993): food products 992,000,000; beverages 558,000,000; tobacco 369,000,000; chemical products 291,000,000; pottery and earthenware 258,000,000; wood products 180,000,000. Energy production (consumption): electricity (kW-hr; 2002) 1,921,000,000 (1,921,000,000); coal, none (none); crude petroleum (barrels; 2002) 3,800,000 (3,300,000); petroleum products (metric tons; 2002) 374,000 (558,000); natural gas, none (none).
Population economically active (1999): total 85,878[6]; activity rate of total population 34.6%[6] (participation rates: ages 15–59, 55.0%[6]; female 36.9%[6]; unemployed [2000] 17%).

Price and earnings indexes (2000 = 100)

	1997	1998	1999	2000	2001	2002	2003
Consumer price index	26.5	31.5	62.7	100.0	138.6	160.1	196.9
Earnings index	...	...	...	...	...	...	...

Gross national product (2004): U.S.$997,000,000 (U.S.$2,250 per capita).

Structure of gross domestic product and labour force

	2002 in value Sf '000,000	2002 % of total value	1999 labour force[7]	1999 % of labour force
Agriculture, forestry	213,060	9.5	4,456	5.3
Mining	153,158	6.9	1,727	2.0
Manufacturing	103,122	4.6	2,863	3.4
Construction	61,983	2.8	4,953	5.8
Public utilities	57,922	2.6	1,000	1.2
Transp. and commun.	149,602	6.7	5,817	6.9
Trade, hotels	242,144	10.8	17,262	20.4
Finance, real estate	253,068	11.3	4,544	5.4
Pub. admin., defense	377,678	16.9	27,305	32.2
Services	45,508	2.0		
Informal sector[7]	332,270	14.9	...	...
Other	244,884[8]	11.0[8]	14,719[9]	17.4[9]
TOTAL	2,234,399	100.0	84,646	100.0

Household income and expenditure. Average household size (2002) 5.3; income per household: n.a.; sources of income: n.a.; expenditure: n.a.
Tourism (2003): receipts from visitors U.S.$4,000,000; expenditures by nationals abroad U.S.$6,000,000.
Land use as % of total land area (2000): in temporary crops 0.4%, in permanent crops 0.06%, in pasture 0.1%; overall forest area 90.5%.

Foreign trade[10]

Balance of trade (current prices)

	1999	2000	2001	2002	2003
U.S.$'000,000	−56.5	−13.0	−7.5	+27.4	−65.4
% of total	5.5%	1.2%	0.8%	2.7%	4.9%

Imports (2003): U.S.$703,900,000 (machinery and transport equipment 34.0%, mineral fuels 13.8%, food products 12.0%, chemicals and chemical products 8.8%). *Major import sources:* U.S. 30.1%; The Netherlands 17.8%; Trinidad and Tobago 11.9%; China 6.9%; Japan 6.1%.
Exports (2003): U.S.$638,500,000 (alumina 52.6%, gold 22.0%, shrimp and fish 5.8%, crude petroleum 5.4%, rice 2.2%). *Major export destinations:* U.S. 21.0%; Norway 16.5%; France 9.1%; Trinidad and Tobago 6.4%; Iceland 4.2%; The Netherlands 3.7%.

Transport and communications

Transport. Railroads (1997)[11]: length 187 mi, 301 km; passengers, not applicable; cargo, n.a. Roads (2002): total length 2,791 mi, 4,492 km (paved 26%). Vehicles (2000): passenger cars 61,365; trucks and buses 23,220. Air transport (1998): passenger-km 1,072,000,000; metric ton-km cargo 127,000,000; airports with scheduled flights 1.

Communications

Medium	date	unit	number	units per 1,000 persons
Daily newspapers	1996	circulation	50,000	122
Radio	1997	receivers	300,000	728
Television	2000	receivers	109,000	253
Telephones	2004	main lines	81,300	185
Cellular telephones	2004	subscribers	212,800	485
Personal computers	2001	units	20,000	45
Internet	2004	users	30,000	68

Education and health

Educational attainment: n.a. *Literacy* (2001): total population age 15 and over literate 92.2%; males literate 93.6%; females literate 90.7%.

Education (2002–03)

	schools	teachers	students	student/ teacher ratio
Primary (age 6–11)	304[12]	3,324	64,659	19.5
Secondary (age 12–18)	104[12]	1,334	23,034	17.3
Voc., teacher tr.	...	1,380	17,966	13.0
Higher[13]	1	286	3,081	10.8

Health: physicians (2000) 191 (1 per 2,411 persons); hospital beds (1998) 1,449 (1 per 288 persons); infant mortality rate per 1,000 live births (2004) 24.2.
Food (2002): daily per capita caloric intake 2,652 (vegetable products 87%, animal products 13%); 117% of FAO recommended minimum requirement.

Military

Total active duty personnel (2004): 1,840[14] (army 76.1%, navy 13.0%, air force 10.9%). *Military expenditure as percentage of GDP* (2003): 0.7%; per capita expenditure U.S.$16.

---

[1]The Suriname dollar (SRD) replaced the Suriname guilder (Sf) on Jan. 1, 2004, at a rate of 1 SRD = Sf1,000. [2]No capital; administered from Paramaribo. [3]Area excludes 6,809 sq mi (17,635 sq km) of territory disputed with Guyana. [4]Other undefined census totals are 492,829 and 446,430. [5]Recorded production; unrecorded production may be as high as 30,000 kg. [6]Based on total population of 248,448 (probably Paramariba only). [7]Smuggling or unregulated activities in such areas as gold mining and tree removal. [8]Taxes on products less imputed bank service charges and less subsidies. [9]Includes 11,812 unemployed. [10]Imports c.i.f.; exports f.o.b. [11]There are no public railways operating in Suriname. [12]1995–96. [13]Anton de Kom University of Suriname; 2001–02. [14]All services are part of the army.

Internet resources for further information:
• **Suriname Statistical Yearbook**
  http://www.suriname.nu/101alg/statis01.html
• **General Bureau of Statistics**
  http://www.statistics-suriname.org

Swaziland

Official name: Umbuso weSwatini (Swazi); Kingdom of Swaziland (English).
Form of government: monarchy[1] with two legislative houses (Senate [30[2]]; House of Assembly [65[3]]).
Head of state and government: King, assisted by Prime Minister.
Capitals: Mbabane (administrative and judicial); Lozitha and Ludzidzini (royal); Lobamba (legislative).
Official languages: Swati (Swazi); English.
Official religion: none.
Monetary unit: 1 lilangeni[4] (plural emalangeni [E]) = 100 cents; valuation (Sept. 1, 2005) 1 U.S.$ = E 6.27; 1 £ = E 11.54.

Area and population

Districts	Capitals	area sq mi	area sq km	population 1997 census
Hhohho	Mbabane	1,378	3,569	269,826
Lubombo	Siteki	2,296	5,947	201,696
Manzini	Manzini	1,571	4,068	292,100
Shiselweni	Nhlangano	1,459	3,780	217,100
TOTAL		6,704	17,364	980,722[5]

Demography

Population (2005): 1,032,000.
Density (2005): persons per sq mi 153.9; persons per sq km 59.4.
Urban-rural (2003): urban 23.5%; rural 76.5%.
Sex distribution (2004): male 48.63%; female 51.37%.
Age breakdown (2004): under 15, 41.4%; 15–29, 31.5%; 30–44, 13.9%; 45–59, 8.0%; 60–74, 4.1%; 75 and over, 1.1%.
Population projection: (2010) 1,010,000; (2020) 983,000.
Ethnic composition (2000): Swazi 82.3%; Zulu 9.6%; Tsonga 2.3%; Afrikaner 1.4%; mixed (black-white) 1.0%; other 3.4%.
Religious affiliation (2000): Christian 67.5%, of which African indigenous 45.6%, Protestant 15.2%, Roman Catholic 5.4%; traditional beliefs 12.2%; other (mostly unaffiliated Christian) 20.3%.
Major cities (1997): Mbabane 57,992; Manzini 25,571 (urban agglomeration 78,734); Big Bend 9,374; Mhlume 7,661; Malkerns 7,400.

Vital statistics

Birth rate per 1,000 population (2004): 28.6 (world avg. 21.1).
Death rate per 1,000 population (2004): 27.6 (world avg. 9.0).
Natural increase rate per 1,000 population (2004): 1.1 (world avg. 12.1).
Total fertility rate (avg. births per childbearing woman; 2004): 3.7.
Life expectancy at birth (2004): male 33.1 years; female 35.2 years.
Adult population (ages 15–49) *living with HIV* (2004[6]): 38.8% (world avg. 1.1%).

National economy

Budget (2003–04). Revenue: E 3,947,000,000 (receipts from Customs Union of Southern Africa 47.6%, sales tax 14.3%, individual income tax 11.9%, company tax 7.9%, grants 6.7%). Expenditures: E 4,392,000,000 (general administration 34.9%, education 17.1%, police 14.2%, transportation and communications 11.1%, health 5.0%).
Gross national product (2004): U.S.$1,859,000,000 (U.S.$1,660 per capita).

Structure of gross domestic product and labour force

	2001 in value E '000	2001 % of total value	2001 labour force[7]	2001 % of labour force[7]
Agriculture	1,055,100	9.6	195,098[8]	49.8[8]
Mining	24,900	0.2	620	0.1
Manufacturing	2,757,100	25.1	19,898	5.1
Construction	452,000	4.1	5,779	1.5
Public utilities	111,700	1.0	1,409	0.3
Transp. and commun.	391,300	3.6	} 12,509	3.2
Trade	689,200	6.3		
Finance	326,200	3.0	7,492	1.9
Pub. admin., defense	1,367,900	12.5	} 25,323	6.5
Services	82,600	0.8		
Other	3,713,000[9]	33.8[9]	123,872[10]	31.6[10]
TOTAL	10,971,000	100.0	392,000	100.0

Population economically active (2001): total 392,000; activity rate of total population 39.3% (participation rates: ages 15 and over, n.a.; female n.a.; unemployed [2003] 29.8%).

Price and earnings indexes (2000 = 100)

	1998	1999	2000	2001	2002	2003	2004
Consumer price index	85.9	91.0	100.0	107.7	120.2	129.0	133.5
Weekly earnings index	95.0	96.7	100.0	102.9	106.4	109.4	...

Public debt (external, outstanding; 2003): U.S.$346,000,000.
Land use as % of total land area (2000): in temporary crops 10.3%, in permanent crops 0.7%, in pasture 69.8%; overall forest area 30.3%.
Production (metric tons except as noted). Agriculture, forestry, fishing (2004): sugarcane 4,500,000, corn (maize) 70,000, grapefruit and pomelo 37,000, oranges 36,000, pineapples 32,000, seed cotton 6,500; livestock

(number of live animals) 580,000 cattle, 273,576 goats; roundwood 890,000 cu m; fish catch (2003) 70. Mining and quarrying (2004): stone 300,000 cu m. Manufacturing (value of exports in U.S.$'000; 2001): food, beverages, and tobacco 255,000; chemicals and chemical products 152,000; textiles 97,600; paper and paper products 77,300; fabricated metal products 42,000. Energy production (consumption): electricity (kW-hr; 2003) 390,000,000 (1,160,000,000); coal (metric tons; 2003) 372,000 (372,000); crude petroleum, none (none).
Household income and expenditure. Average household size (2002) 6.3; average annual income per household (2002) c. U.S.$1,540; sources of income, n.a.; expenditure (1996)[11]: food 24.5%, housing 15.9%, household furnishings and operation 13.2%, clothing and footwear 11.0%, transportation and communications 8.2%, education 6.1%.
Tourism: receipts (2003) U.S.$13,000,000; expenditures (2002) U.S.$33,000,000.

Foreign trade[12]

Balance of trade (current prices)

	1997	1998	1999	2000	2001	2002
U.S.$'000,000	−104	−106	−131	−136	−73	−79
% of total	5.1%	5.2%	6.5%	7.0%	4.3%	4.0%

Imports (2001): U.S.$832,000,000 (food and live animals 15.6%, machinery and apparatus 13.6%, chemicals and chemical products 13.2%, road vehicles 9.5%, refined petroleum 9.2%). *Major import sources:* South Africa 94.5%; Hong Kong 1.0%; Japan 0.9%.
Exports (2001): U.S.$678,000,000 (soft drink [including sugar and fruit juice] concentrates c. 38%, sugar c. 14%, apparel and clothing accessories c. 12%, wood pulp c. 9%). *Major export destinations:* South Africa 78.0%; Mozambique 4.6%; U.S. 4.0%.

Transport and communications

Transport. Railroads (2001): route length 187 mi, 301 km; passenger-km, n.a.[13]; metric ton-km cargo 700,000,000. Roads (2002): total length 2,233 mi, 3,594 km (paved [1996] 29%). Vehicles (2003): passenger cars 44,113; trucks and buses 47,761. Air transport: (2000) passenger-km 68,000,000; metric ton-km cargo, n.a.; airports (1997) with scheduled flights 1.

Communications

Medium	date	unit	number	units per 1,000 persons
Daily newspapers	2000	circulation	27,100	26
Radio	2000	receivers	169,000	162
Television	2000	receivers	124,000	110
Telephones	2003	main lines	46,200	44
Cellular telephones	2004	subscribers	113,000	104
Personal computers	2004	units	36,000	33
Internet	2004	users	36,000	33

Education and health

Educational attainment (1986). Percentage of population age 25 and over having: no formal schooling 42.1%; some primary education 23.9%; complete primary 10.5%; some secondary 19.2%; complete secondary and higher 4.3%.
Literacy (2000): total population age 15 and over literate 79.6%; males literate 80.8%; females literate 78.6%.

Education (2001)

	schools	teachers	students	student/ teacher ratio
Primary (age 6–13)	541	6,594	212,064	32.2
Secondary (age 14–18)	182	3,647	61,335	16.8
Voc., teacher tr.	5	...	1,822	...
Higher	1	...	3,692	...

Health (2000): physicians 184 (1 per 5,560 persons); hospital beds 1,570[14] (1 per 665 persons); infant mortality rate per 1,000 live births (2004) 73.9.
Food (2002): daily per capita caloric intake 2,322 (vegetable products 87%, animal products 13%); 100% of FAO recommended minimum requirement.

Military

Total active duty personnel (2003): c. 3,500 troops. *Military expenditure as percentage of GDP* (2004): 1.4%; per capita expenditure U.S.$39.

---

[1]Disputed constitution signed by the King on July 26, 2005. [2]Includes 20 nonelective seats. [3]Includes 10 nonelective seats. [4]The lilangeni is at par with the South African rand. [5]Final results, includes 51,005 residents abroad. [6]January 1. [7]Formally employed only (except for Agriculture and Other). [8]Includes informally employed (mostly in Agriculture). [9]Includes indirect taxes less imputed bank service charges and subsidies. [10]Unemployed. [11]Weights of consumer price index components. [12]Imports f.o.b. in balance of trade and c.i.f. in commodities and trading partners. [13]Scheduled passenger train service was terminated in January 2001. [14]Excludes National Psychiatric Hospital.

Internet resources for further information:
• **Central Bank of Swaziland**
  http://www.centralbank.org.sz
• **Swaziland Government**
  http://www.gov.sz

Sweden

Official name: Konungariket Sverige
(Kingdom of Sweden).
Form of government: constitutional
monarchy and parliamentary
state with one legislative house
(Parliament [349]).
Chief of state: King.
Head of government: Prime Minister.
Capital: Stockholm.
Official language: Swedish.
Official religion: none.
Monetary unit: 1 Swedish krona (SKr)
= 100 öre; valuation (Sept. 1, 2005)
1 U.S.$ = SKr 7.39; 1 £ = SKr 13.62.

Area and population

Counties	area sq km	population 2005[1] estimate	Counties	area sq km	population 2005[1] estimate
Blekinge	3,055	150,335	Södermanland	6,607	261,070
Dalarna	30,404	276,042	Stockholm	6,789	1,872,900
Gävleborg	19,756	276,599	Uppsala	7,206	302,564
Gotland	3,184	57,661	Värmland	19,388	273,547
Halland	5,719	283,788	Västerbotten	59,284	256,875
Jämtland	54,100	127,424	Västernorrland	23,107	244,195
Jönköping	11,253	329,297	Västmanland	6,614	261,005
Kalmar	11,694	234,496	Västra Götaland	25,389	1,521,895
Kronoberg	9,429	178,285	TOTAL LAND AND		
Norrbotten	106,012	252,585	SMALL LAKES AREA	441,348[2]	
Örebro	9,343	273,920	4 LARGE LAKES	8,926[2]	
Östergötland	11,646	415,990	OTHER UNDISTRIBUTED	21	
Skåne	11,369	1,160,919	TOTAL	450,295	9,011,392

Demography

Population (2005): 9,024,000.
Density (2004)[3]: persons per sq mi 57.0, persons per sq km 22.0.
Urban-rural (2003): urban 83.4%; rural 16.6%.
Sex distribution (2005[1]): male 49.56%; female 50.44%.
Age breakdown (2005[1]): under 15, 17.6%; 15–29, 18.2%; 30–44, 20.9%; 45–59, 20.1%; 60–74, 14.4%; 75 and over, 8.8%.
Population projection: (2010) 9,220,000; (2020) 9,643,000.
Ethnic composition (2002[1])[4]: Swedish 88.5%; other European 6.9%, of which Finnish 2.2%, Serb/Montenegrin 0.8%, Bosniac 0.6%; Asian 3.0%, of which Iranian 0.6%; African 0.6%; other 1.0%.
Religious affiliation (1999): Church of Sweden 86.5% (about 30% nonpracticing); Muslim 2.3%; Roman Catholic 1.8%; Pentecostal 1.1%; other 8.3%.
Major cities (2005[1]): Stockholm 765,044; Göteborg 481,410; Malmö 269,142; Uppsala 182,076; Linköping 136,912; Västerås 131,014.

Vital statistics

Birth rate per 1,000 population (2004): 11.2 (world avg. 21.1); legitimate (2003) 44.0%; illegitimate 56.0%.
Death rate per 1,000 population (2004): 10.0 (world avg. 9.0).
Natural increase rate per 1,000 population (2004): 1.2 (world avg. 12.1).
Total fertility rate (avg. births per childbearing woman; 2003): 1.7.
Marriage rate per 1,000 population (2004): 4.8.
Divorce rate per 1,000 population (2004): 2.2.
Life expectancy at birth (2004): male 78.4 years; female 82.7 years.
Major causes of death per 100,000 population (2001): heart disease 323.8; malignant neoplasms (cancers) 243.0; cerebrovascular disease 112.3.

National economy

Budget (2004). Revenue: SKr 693,058,000,000 (value-added and excise taxes 45.1%, social security 38.6%, income and capital gains taxes 6.6%, property taxes 5.3%). Expenditures: SKr 756,190,000,000 (health and social affairs 44.3%, debt service 6.4%, defense 6.0%, education 5.8%).
Public debt (2004[1]): U.S.$170,915,000,000.
Production (metric tons except as noted). Agriculture, forestry, fishing (2004): sugar beets 2,484,400, wheat 2,412,300, barley 1,691,900, potatoes 979,100, oats 925,300, triticale 270,200, rapeseed 227,500; livestock (number of live animals) 1,903,000 pigs, 1,605,400 cattle, 450,000 sheep, (2003) 238,819 reindeer; roundwood 67,300,000 cu m; fish catch (2003) 286,875. Mining and quarrying (2004): iron ore 22,300,000; zinc (metal content) 160,600; copper (metal content) 85,500; silver (metal content) 292,600 kg. Manufacturing (value added in U.S.$'000,000; 1999): telecommunications equipment, electronics 9,200; nonelectrical machinery and apparatus 6,100; road vehicles 6,000; paper and paper products 5,950; fabricated metals 4,050; printing and publishing 3,500; food products 3,450. Energy production (consumption): electricity (kW-hr; 2002) 146,057,000,000 (151,413,000,000); coal (metric tons; 2002) none (3,020,000); crude petroleum (barrels; 2002) none (137,000,000); petroleum products (metric tons; 2002) 16,349,000 (12,069,000); natural gas (cu m; 2002) none (930,000,000).
Household income and expenditure (2002). Average household size 2.1; average annual disposable income per household SKr 247,300 (U.S.$25,398); sources of gross income: wages and salaries 61.2%, transfer payments 29.6%; expenditure (2003): housing 22.8%, transportation and communications 16.5%, recreation and culture 12.0%, food 11.3%, energy 6.6%.
Land use as % of total land area (2000): in temporary crops 6.6%, in permanent crops 0.01%, in pasture 10.9%; overall forest area 65.9%.
Gross national product (at current market prices; 2004): U.S.$321,401,000,000 (U.S.$35,770 per capita).

Structure of gross domestic product and labour force

| | 2004 | | 2003 | |
	in value SKr '000,000	% of total value	labour force	% of labour force
Agriculture	40,579	1.6	89,000	2.0
Mining	6,559	0.3		
Manufacturing	465,701	18.3	723,000	16.2
Public utilities	63,927	2.5		
Construction	102,375	4.0	239,000	5.4
Transp. and commun.	166,190	6.5	802,000	18.0
Trade	266,745	10.5		
Finance, real estate	541,223	21.3	593,000	13.3
Pub. admin., defense	481,481	18.9	243,000	5.5
Services	140,803	5.5	1,541,000	34.6
Other	267,267[5]	10.5[5]	221,000[6]	5.0[6]
TOTAL	2,542,850	100.0[7]	4,450,000[7]	100.0

Population economically active (2003): total 4,450,000; activity rate of total population 49.6% (participation rates: ages 16–64, 78.1%; female 48.0%; unemployed [July 2004–June 2005] 5.6%).

Price and earnings indexes (2000 = 100)

	1998	1999	2000	2001	2002	2003	2004
Consumer price index	98.7	99.1	100.0	102.4	104.6	106.6	107.0
Hourly earnings index	95.0	96.7	100.0	102.9	106.4	109.4	112.3

Tourism (2003): receipts U.S.$5,304,000,000; expenditures U.S.$8,296,000,000.

Foreign trade[8]

Balance of trade (current prices)

	1999	2000	2001	2002	2003	2004
SKr '000,000	+132,700	+127,700	+127,900	+145,800	+150,635	+167,600
% of total	10.5%	8.7%	8.9%	10.2%	10.1%	10.2%

Imports (2003): SKr 673,263,000,000 (electrical machinery and apparatus 16.5%; nonelectrical machinery and apparatus 11.3%; chemicals and chemical products 11.0%; road vehicles 10.8%; crude and refined petroleum 7.7%). *Major import sources:* Germany 18.7%; Denmark 9.0%; U.K. 8.0%; Norway 8.0%; The Netherlands 6.8%.
Exports (2003): SKr 823,898,000,000 (nonelectrical machinery and apparatus 15.6%; road vehicles 13.8%; telecommunications equipment, electronics 13.6%; paper and paper products 8.1%; medicines and pharmaceuticals 6.5%; iron and steel 5.1%). *Major export destinations:* U.S. 11.5%; Germany 10.0%; Norway 8.4%; U.K. 7.8%; Denmark 6.4%.

Transport and communications

Transport. Railroads (2004): length 7,134 mi, 11,481 km; (2001) passenger-km 8,791,000,000; metric ton-km cargo (2003) 20,141,000,000. Roads (2004[1]): total length 263,030 mi, 423,307 km (public 51.6%). Vehicles (2004[1]): passenger cars 4,075,414; trucks and buses 435,303. Air transport (2004)[9]: passenger-km 10,824,000,000; metric ton-km cargo 256,356,000; airports (2001) 49.

Communications

Medium	date	unit	number	units per 1,000 persons
Daily newspapers	2004	circulation	4,312,000	480
Radio	2000	receivers	8,270,000	932
Television	2003	receivers	8,644,700	965
Telephones	2003	main lines	6,873,000	767
Cellular telephones	2004	subscribers	9,302,000	1,035
Personal computers	2004	units	6,861,000	763
Internet	2004	users	6,800,000	756

Education and health

Educational attainment (2002[1]). Percentage of population age 16–74 having: lower secondary education 27%; incomplete or complete upper secondary education 45%; up to 3 years postsecondary 12%; 3 years or more postsecondary 14%; unknown 2%. *Literacy* (2004): virtually 100%.

Education (2002–03)

	schools[10]	teachers	students	student/ teacher ratio
Primary (age 7–12)	5,048	69,256	774,888	11.2
Secondary (age 13–18)		72,132	917,978	12.7
Higher	64	36,413	414,657	11.4

Health (2003): physicians 26,400 (1 per 339 persons); hospital beds 27,332 (1 per 328 persons); infant mortality rate per 1,000 live births 3.1.
Food (2002): daily per capita caloric intake 3,185 (vegetable 66%, animal 34%); 118% of FAO recommended minimum requirement.

Military

Total active duty personnel (2004): 27,600 (army 50.0%, navy 28.6%, air force 21.4%). *Military expenditure as percentage of GDP* (2003): 1.8%; per capita expenditure U.S.$597.

---

[1]January 1. [2]Area of small lakes equals 31,034 sq km; total inland water area including 4 large lakes equals 39,960 sq km. [3]Density based on land area only (410,335 sq km). [4]By place of birth. [5]Taxes less subsidies and less imputed bank service charges. [6]Includes 217,000 unemployed. [7]Detail does not add to total given because of rounding. [8]Imports c.i.f.; exports f.o.b. [9]Includes SAS international and domestic traffic applicable to Sweden. [10]1999–2000.

Internet resources for further information:
• **Statistics Sweden** http://www.scb.se/indexeng.asp

Switzerland

Official name: Confédération Suisse (French); Schweizerische Eidgenossenschaft (German); Confederazione Svizzera (Italian) (Swiss Confederation)[1].
Form of government: federal state with two legislative houses (Council of States [46]; National Council [200]).
Head of state and government: President of the Federal Council.
Capitals: Bern (administrative); Lausanne (judicial).
Official languages: French; German; Italian; Romansh (locally).
Official religion: none.
Monetary unit: 1 Swiss Franc (Sw F) = 100 centimes; valuation (Sept. 1, 2005) 1 U.S.\$ = Sw F 1.23; 1 £ = Sw F 2.26.

Area and population

Cantons	area sq km	population 2003[2] estimate	Cantons	area sq km	population 2003[2] estimate
Aargau	1,404	556,229	Nidwalden[3]	276	38,897
Appenzell Ausser-Rhoden[3]	243	53,189	Obwalden[3]	491	32,999
			Sankt Gallen	2,026	455,193
Appenzell Inner-Rhoden[3]	172	14,995	Schaffhausen	298	73,916
Basel-Landschaft[3]	518	263,194	Schwyz	908	133,358
Basel-Stadt[3]	37	186,871	Solothurn	791	246,504
Bern	5,959	950,209	Thurgau	991	229,882
Fribourg	1,671	242,679	Ticino	2,812	314,563
Genève	282	419,254	Uri	1,077	35,246
Glarus	685	38,380	Valais	5,224	281,020
Graubünden	7,105	186,105	Vaud	3,212	631,999
Jura	838	69,196	Zug	239	102,247
Luzern	1,493	352,311	Zürich	1,729	1,242,488
Neuchâtel	803	166,949	TOTAL	41,284	7,317,873[4]

Demography

Population (2005): 7,519,000.
Density (2005): persons per sq mi 471.7, persons per sq km 182.1.
Urban-rural (2003): urban 67.5%; rural 32.5%.
Sex distribution (2004[2]): male 48.91%; female 51.09%.
Age breakdown (2004[2]): under 15, 15.5%; 15–29, 18.0%; 30–44, 24.1%; 45–59, 20.4%; 60–74, 13.5%; 75 and over, 7.5%.
Population projection: (2010) 7,761,000; (2020) 8,269,000.
National composition (2001[2]): Swiss 80.2%; former Yugoslav 4.8%; Italian 4.5%; Portuguese 1.9%; German 1.5%; Spanish 1.2%; other 5.9%.
Religious affiliation (2000): Roman Catholic 41.8%; Protestant 35.2%; Muslim 4.3%; Orthodox 1.8%; Jewish 0.2%; nonreligious 11.1%; other 5.6%.
Major urban agglomerations (2004): Zürich 1,081,664; Geneva 484,455; Basel 484,104; Bern 342,887; Lausanne 304,759; Luzern 197,527.

Vital statistics

Birth rate per 1,000 population (2004): 9.9 (world avg. 21.1); (2003) legitimate 87.6%; illegitimate 12.4%.
Death rate per 1,000 population (2004): 8.1 (world avg. 9.0).
Natural increase rate per 1,000 population (2004): 1.8 (world avg. 12.1).
Total fertility rate (avg. births per childbearing woman; 2004): 1.4.
Marriage rate per 1,000 population (2004): 5.3.
Divorce rate per 1,000 population (2004): 2.4.
Life expectancy at birth (2004): male 78.6 years; female 83.7 years.
Major causes of death per 100,000 population (2000): diseases of the circulatory system 345.5; malignant neoplasms (cancers) 221.6; diseases of the respiratory system 64.2; accidents, suicide, violence 51.9.

National economy

Budget (2001)[5]. Revenue: Sw F 130,882,000,000 (taxes on individual income and wealth 33.2%, taxes on consumption 18.5%, corporation and capital gains tax 10.8%). Expenditures: Sw F 129,966,000,000 (social security 18.6%, education 18.5%, health 13.0%, transportation and communications 10.8%, defense 4.1%).
Public debt (end of year; 2003): U.S.\$112,000,000,000.
Production (metric tons except as noted). Agriculture, forestry, fishing (2004): cow's milk (2003) 3,906,000, sugar beets 1,340,000, potatoes 492,000, wheat 456,000, barley 230,000, apples 230,000, grapes 145,000; livestock (number of live animals) 1,570,178 cattle, 1,536,000 pigs; roundwood 4,713,000 cu m; fish catch (2003) 1,815. Mining (2003): salt 300,000.[6] Manufacturing (value added in Sw F '000,000; 2002): chemicals and chemical products 14,771; professional and scientific equipment 10,892; food products, beverages, and tobacco 8,907; fabricated metal products 7,883. Energy production (consumption)[7]: electricity (kW-hr; 2002) 66,649,000,000 (62,141,000,000); coal (metric tons; 2002) none (168,000); crude petroleum (barrels; 2002) none (35,200,000); petroleum products (metric tons; 2002) 4,749,000 (10,731,000); natural gas (cu m; 2002) none (2,964,000,000).
Household income and expenditure. Average household size (2002) 2.4; average gross income per household (2001) Sw F 105,564 (U.S.\$62,553); sources of income (2001): work 62.9%, transfers 22.2%; expenditure (2002): housing and energy 23.6%, health 14.3%, food and nonalcoholic beverages 10.9%, recreation 8.5%, transportation 8.0%.

Gross national product (2004): U.S.\$356,052,000,000 (U.S.\$48,230 per capita).

Structure of gross domestic product and labour force

	2002 in value Sw F '000,000	2002 % of total value	2003 labour force[8]	2003 % of labour force[8]
Agriculture	5,778	1.3	165,000	4.0
Manufacturing	82,958	19.3		
Mining	769	0.2	662,000	16.1
Public utilities	10,341	2.4		
Construction	23,827	5.5	247,000	6.0
Transp. and commun.	26,655	6.2	241,000	5.9
Trade, restaurants	67,179	15.6	718,000	17.4
Finance, insurance	105,676	24.5	675,000	16.4
Pub. admin., defense	45,616	10.6	218,000	5.3
Services	67,740	15.7	1,019,000	24.7
Other	-5,475[9]	-1.3[9]	174,000	4.2
TOTAL	431,064	100.0	4,119,000	100.0

Population economically active (2002): total 4,180,000[10]; activity rate of total population 56.2% (participation rates: ages 15–64, 81.3%; female 44.5%; unemployed [2004] 4.3%).

Price and earnings indexes (2000 = 100)

	1998	1999	2000	2001	2002	2003	2004
Consumer price index	97.7	98.5	100.0	101.0	101.6	102.3	103.1
Annual earnings index	99.4	99.6	100.0	102.4	...	...	...

Tourism (2003): receipts U.S.\$9,325,000,000; expenditures U.S.\$7,461,000,000.
Land use as % of total land area (2000): in temporary crops 10.4%, in permanent crops 0.6%, in pasture 28.9%; overall forest area 30.3%.

Foreign trade[11]

Balance of trade (current prices)

	1999	2000	2001	2002	2003	2004
Sw F '000,000	+1,030	-2,066	+1,665	+7,255	+6,900	+9,312
% of total	0.5%	0.8%	0.6%	2.9%	2.7%	3.4%

Imports (2002): Sw F 123,125,000,000 (chemical products 22.1%, machinery 21.1%, vehicles 10.4%, food products 8.0%). *Major import sources* (2003): Germany 33.3%; Italy 11.1%; France 11.1%; U.S. 4.4%; U.K. 4.0%.
Exports (2002): Sw F 130,380,000,000 (chemicals and chemical products 34.4%, machinery 24.3%, precision instruments, watches, jewelry 17.3%, fabricated metals 7.5%). *Major export destinations* (2003): Germany 21.2%; U.S. 10.6%; France 8.8%; Italy 8.4%; U.K. 4.8%; Japan 3.9%.

Transport and communications

Transport. Railroads: length (2000) 3,145 mi, 5,062 km; (2003) passenger-km 15,400,000,000; metric ton-km cargo (2000) 9,112,000,000. Roads (2003): total length 44,254 mi, 71,220 km. Vehicles (2004): passenger cars 3,811,351; trucks and buses 298,193. Air transport (2004)[12]: passenger-km 21,303,000,000; metric ton-km cargo 1,156,000,000; airports (1996) with scheduled flights 5.

Communications

Medium	date	unit	number	units per 1,000 persons
Daily newspapers	2000	circulation	2,650,000	369
Radio	2000	receivers	7,200,000	1,002
Television	2003	receivers	4,090,000	552
Telephones	2004	main lines	5,250,000	733
Cellular telephones	2004	subscribers	6,275,000	876
Personal computers	2004	units	6,105,000	852
Internet	2004	users	4,700,000	656

Education and health

Educational attainment (2004). Percentage of resident Swiss and resident alien population age 25–64 having: compulsory education 18.9%; secondary 54.1%; higher 27.0%.

Education (2001–02)

	schools	teachers	students	student/teacher ratio
Primary (age 7–12)	...	39,363	536,423	13.6
Secondary (age 13–18)	...	36,767	375,424	10.2
Vocational	...	11,239	174,893	15.6
Higher	...	28,019	170,086	6.1

Health (2002): physicians 25,921 (1 per 281 persons); hospital beds 43,964 (1 per 167 persons); infant mortality rate per 1,000 live births (2003) 4.3.
Food (2002): daily per capita caloric intake 3,526 (vegetable products 66%, animal products 34%); 131% of FAO recommended minimum.

Military

Total active duty personnel (2004): 4,400[13]. Military expenditure as percentage of GDP (2003): 1.0%; per capita expenditure U.S.\$446.

[1]Long-form name in Romansh is Confederaziun Svizra. [2]January 1. [3]Demicanton; functions as a full canton. [4]Includes 1,484,800 resident aliens. [5]Consolidated central government. [6]Worked and unworked gemstone exports (2002): U.S.\$740,000,000. [7]Includes Liechtenstein. [8]Excludes border and seasonal workers. [9]Taxes less subsidies and less imputed bank charges. [10]Includes 1,050,000 foreign workers. [11]Imports c.i.f.; exports f.o.b. [12]Swiss International Air Lines only. [13]Excludes 170,000 reservists and 26,000 air force personnel to be mobilized as needed; the 120,000-member civil defense forces are not part of the armed forces.

Internet resources for further information:
• **Embassy of Switzerland (Washington, D.C.)** http://www.swissemb.org
• **Swiss Federal Statistical Office** http://www.statistik.admin.ch

Syria

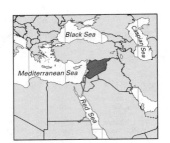

Official name: Al-Jumhūrīyah al-ʿArabīyah as-Sūrīyah (Syrian Arab Republic).
Form of government: unitary multiparty republic with one legislative house (People's Council [250]).
Head of state and government: President.
Capital: Damascus.
Official language: Arabic.
Official religion: none[1].
Monetary unit: 1 Syrian pound (LS) = 100 piastres; valuation (Sept. 1, 2005) 1 U.S.$ = LS 52.21; 1 £ = LS 96.13.

Area and population

Governorates	Capitals	area sq mi	area sq km	population 2002 estimate
Darʿā	Darʿā	1,440	3,730	780,000
Dayr az-Zawr	Dayr az-Zawr	12,765	33,060	919,000
Dimashq	Damascus	6,962	18,032	2,235,000
Halab	Aleppo	7,143	18,500	3,719,000
Hamāh	Hamāh	3,430	8,883	1,335,000
Al-Hasakah	Al-Hasakah	9,009	23,334	1,265,000
Hims	Homs (Hims)	16,302	42,223	1,490,000
Idlib	Idlib	2,354	6,097	1,120,000
Al-Lādhiqīyah	Latakia	887	2,297	876,000
Al-Qunaytirah	Al-Qunaytirah (abandoned)	719[2]	1,861[2]	66,000
Ar-Raqqah	Ar-Raqqah	7,574	19,616	691,000
As-Suwaydāʾ	As-Suwaydāʾ	2,143	5,550	307,000
Tartūs	Tartūs	730	1,892	674,000
Municipality				
Damascus	—	41	105	1,653,000
TOTAL		71,498[2, 3]	185,180[2]	17,130,000

Demography

Population (2005): 17,794,000.
Density (2005): persons per sq mi 248.9, persons per sq km 96.1.
Urban-rural (2003): urban 50.1%; rural 49.9%.
Sex distribution (2003): male 51.20%; female 48.80%.
Age breakdown (2001): under 15, 40.4%; 15–29, 30.1%; 30–44, 15.6%; 45–59, 8.8%; 60 and over, 5.1%.
Population projection: (2010) 19,901,000; (2020) 23,831,000.
Doubling time: 29 years.
Ethnic composition (2000): Syrian Arab 74.9%; Bedouin Arab 7.4%; Kurd 7.3%; Palestinian Arab 3.9%; Armenian 2.7%; other 3.8%.
Religious affiliation (2000): Muslim c. 86%, of which Sunnī c. 74%, ʿAlawite (Shīʿī) c. 11%; Christian c. 8%, of which Orthodox c. 5%, Roman Catholic c. 2%; Druze c. 3%; nonreligious/atheist c. 3%.
Major cities (2004): Aleppo 1,975,200; Damascus 1,614,500; Homs (Hims) 800,400; Latakia 468,700; Hamāh 366,800.

Vital statistics

Birth rate per 1,000 population (2004): 28.9 (world avg. 21.1).
Death rate per 1,000 population (2004): 5.0 (world avg. 9.0).
Natural increase rate per 1,000 population (2004): 23.9 (world avg. 12.1).
Total fertility rate (avg. births per childbearing woman; 2004): 3.6.
Marriage rate per 1,000 population (2001)[4]: 9.5.
Divorce rate per 1,000 population (2001)[4]: 0.8.
Life expectancy at birth (2004): male 68.5 years; female 71.0 years.
Major causes of death per 100,000 population: n.a.

National economy

Budget (2003). Revenue: LS 321,700,000,000 (petroleum royalties and taxes 50.1%, nontax revenues 13.1%, income tax 12.0%, taxes on international trade 9.0%). Expenditures: LS 350,600,000,000 (current expenditures 56.4%, capital [development] expenditures 43.6%).
Public debt (external, outstanding; 2003): U.S.$15,848,000,000.
Gross national product (2004): U.S.$21,125,000,000 (U.S.$1,190 per capita).

Structure of gross domestic product and labour force

	2003 in value LS '000,000	2003 % of total value	2002 labour force	2002 % of labour force
Agriculture	258,391	24.6	1,461,855	26.8
Mining	200,351	19.0	}	
Manufacturing	36,741	3.5	} 661,446	12.1
Public utilities	13,237	1.3	}	
Construction	36,063	3.4	634,271	11.6
Transp. and commun.	131,072	12.5	264,881	4.9
Trade, restaurants, hotels	174,685	16.6	724,420	13.3
Finance, real estate	34,957	3.3	61,140	1.1
Pub. admin.	105,865	10.1	} 1,013,744	18.6
Services	27,918	2.6	}	
Other	32,708[5]	3.1[5]	637,805[6]	11.7[6]
TOTAL	1,051,988	100.0	5,459,562	100.0[3]

Production (metric tons except as noted). Agriculture, forestry, fishing (2004): wheat 4,537,459, sugar beets 1,250,000, seed cotton 1,022,769, olives 950,000, tomatoes 920,000, watermelons 620,000, barley 515,000, potatoes 500,000, oranges 427,000, grapes 300,000, apples 215,000, eggplants 132,000, almonds 130,000; livestock (number of live animals) 15,300,000 sheep, 1,018,000 goats, 940,000 cattle; roundwood 50,400 cu m; fish catch (2003) 8,911. Mining and

quarrying (2003): phosphate rock 2,401,000; gypsum 380,000; salt 128,000. Manufacturing (value added in LS '000,000; 2002): food, beverages, and tobacco 23,788; textiles and wearing apparel 20,344; fabricated metal products 15,462; cement, bricks, and tiles 11,194. Energy production (consumption): electricity (kW-hr; 2003) 29,533,000,000 (28,264,000,000); coal, none (none); crude petroleum (barrels; 2004) 168,000,000 ([2002] 88,000,000); petroleum products (metric tons; 2002) 12,435,000 ([2004] 12,090,000); natural gas (cu m; 2004) 8,117,000,000 ([2002] 5,766,000,000).
Population economically active (2002): total 5,459,562; activity rate of total population 31.9% (participation rates: ages 15–64, 54.9%; female 21.4%; unemployed [2003] 12.1%).

Price and earnings indexes (2000 = 100)

	1998	1999	2000	2001	2002	2003	2004
Consumer price index	108.0	104.0	100.0	103.4	102.9	108.8	113.7
Earnings index[7]	...	89.5	100.0	122.3	142.6	150.7	...

Average household size (2003): 5.6; income per household: n.a.; sources of income (2003–04)[8]: wages 49.2%, self-employment 39.8%; expenditure: n.a.
Tourism (2003): receipts U.S.$1,147,000,000; expenditures (2002) U.S.$760,000,000.
Land use as % of total land area (2000): in temporary crops 24.7%, in permanent crops 4.4%, in pasture 45.5%; overall forest area 2.5%.

Foreign trade[9]

Balance of trade (current prices)

	2000	2001	2002	2003
LS '000,000	+28,655	+22,405	+56,795	+28,271
% of total	7.1%	4.8%	10.8%	5.6%

Imports (2003): LS 236,768,000,000 (machinery and equipment 18.3%, foodstuffs 17.7%, chemicals and chemical products 14.9%, base and fabricated metals 14.6%). *Major import sources* (2002): U.S. 7%; Italy 7%; Germany 6%; Ukraine 6%; China 6%; South Korea 6%; Turkey 5%.
Exports (2003): LS 265,039,000,000 (crude petroleum 62.5%, refined petroleum 8.8%, textiles 4.2%, live animals and meat 4.2%, fruits and vegetables 3.8%). *Major export destinations* (2002): Italy 33%; France 14%; Turkey 8%; Saudi Arabia 8%; Spain 3%.

Transport and communications

Transport. Railroads (2004): route length 2,711 km; passenger-km (2003) 525,357,000; metric ton-km cargo (2002) 1,812,000,000[10]. Roads (2002): total length 45,697 km (paved 14%). Vehicles (2003): passenger cars 206,130; trucks and buses 855,193. Air transport (2001): passenger-km 1,626,950; metric ton-km cargo 15,357,000; airports with scheduled flights 5.

Communications

Medium	date	unit	number	units per 1,000 persons
Daily newspapers	2000	circulation	326,000	20
Radio	2000	receivers	4,500,000	276
Television	2003	receivers	3,093,200	182
Telephones	2004	main lines	2,660,000	153
Cellular telephones	2004	units	2,345,000	135
Personal computers	2004	units	600,000	34
Internet	2004	users	800,000	46

Education and health

Educational attainment (2003–04)[8]. Percentage of population having: no formal education (illiterate) 14.3%; no formal education (literate) 9.9%; primary education 45.8%; secondary 22.5%; incomplete higher 3.9%; higher 3.6%. *Literacy* (2003): percentage of population age 15 and over literate 76.9%; males literate 89.7%; females literate 64.0%.

Education (2002–03)

	schools	teachers	students	student/teacher ratio
Primary (age 6–11)	11,482[11]	204,264	2,984,834	14.6
Secondary (age 12–18)	2,911[11]	26,273	1,162,613	44.3
Voc., teacher tr.	595	14,597	121,744	8.3
Higher[11]	4	8,702	201,689	23.2

Health (2003): physicians 25,147 (1 per 699 persons); hospital beds 26,202 (1 per 671 persons); infant mortality rate (2004) 30.6.
Food (2002): daily per capita caloric intake 3,038 (vegetable products 86%, animal products 14%); 123% of FAO recommended minimum.

Military

Total active duty personnel (2004): 296,800[12] (army 67.4%, navy 2.5%, air force 11.8%, air defense 18.3%); Syria's 29-year military presence in Lebanon ended in April 2005. UN peacekeeping troops in Golan Heights (August 2005) 1,000. *Military expenditure as percentage of GDP* (2003): 7.1%; per capita expenditure U.S.$390.

---

[1]Islam is required to be the religion of the head of state and is the basis of the legal system. [2]Includes territory in the Golan Heights recognized internationally as part of Syria. [3]Detail does not add to total given because of rounding. [4]Syrian Arabs only. [5]Import duties less imputed bank service charges. [6]Unemployed. [7]Public administration only. [8]Based on the Household Income and Expenditure Survey with a survey population of 124,525. [9]Imports c.i.f.; exports f.o.b. [10]Chemins de Fer Syriens only. [11]2000. [12]Excludes 108,000 in paramilitary.

Internet resources for further information:
• **Ministry of Economy and Foreign Trade**
  http://www.syrecon.org/right_frame1.html

Taiwan

Official name: Chung-hua Min-kuo (Republic of China).
Form of government: multiparty republic with one legislative body (Legislative Yuan [225])[1].
Chief of state: President.
Head of government: Premier.
Capital: Taipei.
Official language: Mandarin Chinese.
Official religion: none.
Monetary unit: 1 New Taiwan dollar (NT$) = 100 cents; valuation (Sept. 1, 2005) 1 U.S.$ = NT$32.53; 1 £ = NT$59.89.

Area and population

Taiwan area Counties	area sq km	population 2005[2] estimate	Special Municipalities	area sq km	population 2005[2] estimate
Chang-hua	1,074	1,316,762	Kao-hsiung	154	1,512,677
Chia-i	1,902	557,903	Taipei	272	2,622,472
Hsin-chu	1,428	467,246	**Municipalities**		
Hua-lien	4,628	349,149	Chia-i	60	270,341
I-lan	2,144	462,286	Chi-lung	133	392,337
Kao-hsiung	2,793	1,238,925	Hsin-chu	104	386,950
Miao-li	1,820	560,643	T'ai-chung	163	1,021,292
Nan-t'ou	4,106	538,413	T'ai-nan	176	754,917
P'eng-hu	127	91,808			
P'ing-tung	2,776	900,199	**Non-Taiwan area**		
T'ai-chung	2,051	1,527,040	**Counties**		
T'ai-nan	2,016	1,105,674	Kinmen		
T'ai-pei	2,052	3,708,099	(Quemoy)	153	64,456
T'ai-tung	3,515	240,373	Lienchiang		
T'ao-yüan	1,221	1,853,029	(Matsu)	29	9,359
Yün-lin	1,291	736,772	**TOTAL**	36,188	22,689,122

Demography

Population (2005)[3]: 22,726,000.
Density (2004)[3]: persons per sq mi 1,626, persons per sq km 628.0.
Urban-rural (2000)[4]: urban 80%; rural 20%.
Sex distribution (2003)[3]: male 50.98%; female 49.02%.
Age breakdown (2002)[3]: under 15, 20.8%; 15–29, 24.9%; 30–44, 25.3%; 45–59, 16.7%; 60–74, 9.1%; 75 and over, 3.2%.
Population projection: (2010) 23,137,000; (2020) 23,931,000.
Ethnic composition (2003): Taiwanese c. 84%; mainland Chinese c. 14%; indigenous tribal peoples c. 2%, of which Ami 0.6%.
Religious affiliation (1997)[5, 6]: Buddhism 22.4%; Taoism 20.7%; I-kuan Tao 4.3%; Protestant 1.6%; Roman Catholic 1.4%; other Christian 0.3%; Muslim 0.2%; Bahā'ī 0.1%; other (mostly Christian folk-religionists) 49.0%.
Major cities (2005[2]): Taipei 2,622,472; Kao-hsiung 1,512,677; T'ai-chung 1,021,292; T'ai-nan 754,917; Chi-lung 392,337.

Vital statistics

Birth rate per 1,000 population (2004): 9.6 (world avg. 21.1).
Death rate per 1,000 population (2004): 6.0 (world avg. 9.0).
Natural increase rate per 1,000 population (2004): 3.6 (world avg. 12.1).
Total fertility rate (avg. births per childbearing woman; 2003): 1.2.
Marriage rate per 1,000 population (2004): 5.8.
Divorce rate per 1,000 population (2004): 2.8.
Life expectancy at birth (2003): male 73.4 years; female 79.1 years.
Major causes of death per 100,000 population (2003)[4]: malignant neoplasms 156.0; cerebrovascular diseases 55.0; heart disease 52.2; accidents and suicide 50.5; diabetes 44.4; liver diseases 23.0; pneumonia 22.6; kidney diseases 19.1.

National economy

Budget (2002[7]). Revenue: NT$1,782,000,000,000 (tax revenue 66.8%, of which income taxes 22.0%, business tax 12.0%; income from public enterprises 14.6%). Expenditures: NT$2,139,000,000,000 (current expenditure 77.1%; capital expenditure 22.9%).
Population economically active (2003): total 10,076,000; activity rate of total population 44.8% (participation rates: ages 15–64, 63.9%; female 41.4%; unemployed [2004] 4.4%).

Price and earnings indexes (2000 = 100)

	1998	1999	2000	2001	2002	2003	2004
Consumer price index	98.6	98.8	100.0	100.0	99.8	99.5	101.1
Monthly earnings index[8]	93.5	96.9	100.0	98.7	98.7	101.3	103.9

Production (metric tons except as noted). Agriculture, forestry, fishing (2003): sugarcane 1,696,000, rice 1,338,000, citrus fruits 529,080, pineapples 447,807, bananas 223,061, sweet potatoes 200,000; livestock (number of live animals) 6,778,799 pigs, 155,565 goats, 148,870 cattle; timber (2000) 21,134 cu m; fish catch (2003) 1,498,983. Mining and quarrying (2000): marble 17,800,000. Manufacturing (value added in NT$'000,000,000; 2003): electronic parts and components 452; computers, telecommunications, video electronics 232; refined petroleum products 223; base chemicals 180; base metals 180; transport equipment 159. Energy production (consumption): electricity (kW-hr; 2003) 173,810,000,000 (159,380,000,000); coal (metric tons; 2002)[9] (50,600,000); crude petroleum (barrels; 2003) 292,000 (327,000,000); natural gas (cu m; 2002) 850,000,000 (8,127,000,000).
Tourism (2003): receipts from visitors U.S.$2,913,000,000; expenditures by nationals abroad U.S.$6,480,000,000.

Gross national product (2003): U.S.$295,895,000,000 (U.S.$13,160 per capita).

Structure of gross domestic product and labour force

	2003			
	in value NT$'000,000	% of total value	labour force[10]	% of labour force[10]
Agriculture	177,556	1.8	696,000	6.9
Mining	36,625	0.4	8,000	0.1
Manufacturing	2,519,343	25.6	2,590,000	25.7
Construction	221,035	2.2	702,000	7.0
Public utilities	218,360	2.2	35,000	0.3
Transp. and commun.	675,170	6.9	484,000	4.8
Trade, restaurants	1,955,766	19.8	2,283,000	22.6
Finance, real estate	2,356,552	23.9	727,000	7.2
Pub. admin., defense	1,067,571	10.8	369,000	3.7
Services	1,041,369	10.6	1,680,000	16.7
Other	-412,956[11]	-4.2[11]	502,000[12]	5.0[12]
TOTAL	9,856,391	100.0	10,076,000	100.0

Household income and expenditure (2003). Average household size (March 2005) 3.2; income per household NT$1,064,825 (U.S.$30,672); sources of income: wages and salaries 57.8%, self-employment 16.0%, transfers 15.7%; expenditure: rent, fuel, and power 24.0%, food 22.2%, education and recreation 13.1%, health care 12.7%, transportation 12.1%.
Land use as % of total land area (2001): in temporary crops 16.1%, in permanent crops 6.6%, in pasture 0.3%; overall forest area 58.1%.

Foreign trade[13]

Balance of trade (current prices)

	1999	2000	2001	2002	2003	2004
U.S.$'000,000	+10,901	+8,310	+15,629	+18,050	+16,931	+6,124
% of total	4.7%	2.8%	6.8%	7.4%	6.2%	1.8%

Imports (2004): U.S.$167,890,000,000 (electronic machinery 18.2%, mineral fuels 12.8%, metals and metal products 11.0%, nonelectrical machinery 10.5%, chemicals 10.5%, precision instruments, clocks, watches, and musical instruments 7.5%). *Major import sources:* Japan 26.0%; U.S. 12.9%; China 9.9%; South Korea 6.9%; Germany 3.5%.
Exports (2004): U.S.$174,014,000,000 (nonelectrical machinery, electrical machinery, and electronics 50.5%, metal products 10.5%, textile products 7.2%, plastic articles 7.2%). *Major export destinations:* China 19.5%; Hong Kong 17.1%; U.S. 16.2%; Japan 7.6%; Singapore 3.6%.

Transport and communications

Transport. Railroads (2003)[14]: route length 1,117 km; passenger-km 8,726,000,000, metric ton-km cargo 846,000,000. Roads (2003): total length 37,342 km (paved, n.a.). Vehicles (2003): passenger cars 5,169,733; trucks and buses 911,408. Air transport (2004)[15]: passenger-km 54,684,000,000; metric ton-km cargo 11,262,000,000; airports (1996) 13.

Communications

Medium	date	unit	number	units per 1,000 persons
Radio	1996	receivers	8,620,000	402
Television	1999	receivers	9,200,000	418
Telephones	2004	main lines	13,529,900	594
Cellular telephones	2004	subscribers	22,760,100	1,000
Personal computers	2004	units	11,924,000	524
Internet	2004	users	12,210,000	536

Education and health

Educational attainment (2003). Percentage of population age 15 and over having: no formal schooling 4.6%; primary 19.8%; lower and upper higher vocational 23.7%; secondary 26.8%; some college 12.0%; higher 13.1%. *Literacy* (1999): population age 15 and over literate 16,414,896 (94.6%); males 8,641,549 (97.6%); females 7,773,347 (91.4%).

Education (2003–04)

	schools	teachers	students	student/ teacher ratio
Primary (age 6–12)	2,638	103,793	1,912,791	18.4
Secondary (age 13–18) Vocational	1,192	97,738	1,745,073	17.9
Higher	158	47,472	1,202,091	25.3

Health (2003): physicians 32,390 (1 per 697 persons); hospital beds 137,400 (1 per 164 persons); infant mortality rate per 1,000 live births 5.3.

Military

Total active duty personnel (2003): 290,000 (army 69.0%, navy 15.5%, air force 15.5%). *Military expenditure as percentage of GDP* (2003): 2.5%; per capita expenditure U.S.$312.

[1]The National Assembly became a nonstanding body with limited specialized authority per April 2000 amendment; the Legislative Yuan is the formal lawmaking body. [2]January 1. [3]Includes Quemoy and Matsu groups. [4]For Taiwan area only, excluding Quemoy and Matsu groups. [5]Formal subscribers to religious beliefs. [6]Almost all Taiwanese adults engage in religious practices stemming from one or a combination of traditional folk religions. [7]General government. [8]In manufacturing. [9]Coal production ceased in 2000. [10]Civilian persons only. [11]Import duties, VAT, and other producers less imputed bank service charges. [12]Unemployed. [13]Imports c.i.f.; exports f.o.b. [14]Taiwan Railway Administration only. [15]China Airlines, EVA, and Transasia airlines only.

Internet resources for further information:
• Directorate-General of Budget, Accounting and Statistics (Taiwan)
  http://eng.dgbas.gov.tw/mp.asp?mp=2
• Taiwan Yearbook 2004
  http://www.gio.gov.tw/taiwan-website/5-gp/yearbook

Tajikistan

Official name: Jumhurii Tojikistan (Republic of Tajikistan).
Form of government: parliamentary republic with two legislative houses (National Assembly [33[1]]; Assembly of Representatives [63]).
Chief of state: President.
Head of government: Prime Minister.
Capital: Dushanbe.
Official language: Tajik (Tojik).
Official religion: none.
Monetary unit: 1 somoni[2] = 100 dinars; valuation (Sept. 26, 2005)
1 U.S.$ = 3.19 somoni;
1 £ = 5.65 somoni.

Area and population		area		population
		sq mi	sq km	2005 estimate[3]
Oblasts	**Capitals**			
Khatlon (Qŭrghonteppa)	Qŭrghonteppa	9,600	24,800	2,404,100
Sughd	Khujand	9,800	25,400	2,027,800
Autonomous oblast				
Kŭhistoni Badakhshon (Gorno-Badakhshan)	Khorugh	24,800	64,200	217,900
City				
Dushanbe	—	40	100	631,700
No oblast administration	—	11,050	28,600	1,498,900
TOTAL		55,300[4, 5]	143,100[4]	6,780,400

Demography

Population (2005): 6,849,000.
Density (2005): persons per sq mi 123.9, persons per sq km 47.9.
Urban-rural (2003): urban 24.7%; rural 75.3%.
Sex distribution (2000): male 50.30%; female 49.70%.
Age breakdown (2000): under 15, 39.4%; 15–29, 27.7%; 30–44, 18.4%; 45–59, 7.6%; 60–74, 5.4%; 75 and over, 1.5%.
Population projection: (2010) 7,360,000; (2020) 8,648,000.
Doubling time: 31 years.
Ethnic composition (2000): Tajik 80.0%; Uzbek 15.3%; Russian 1.1%; Tatar 0.3%; other 3.3%.
Religious affiliation (2000): Sunnī Muslim 78.6%; Shīʿī Muslim 5.0%; Christian 2.1%, of which crypto-Christian 1.8%; nonreligious 12.0%; atheist 1.9%; other 0.4%.
Major cities (2002): Dushanbe 575,900; Khujand 147,400; Kulyab 79,500; Kurgan-Tyube 61,200; Ura-Tyube 51,700.

Vital statistics

Birth rate per 1,000 population (2004): 26.8 (world avg. 21.1); (1994) legitimate 90.8%; illegitimate 9.2%.
Death rate per 1,000 population (2004): 4.4 (world avg. 9.0).
Natural increase rate per 1,000 population (2004): 22.4 (world avg. 12.1).
Total fertility rate (avg. births per childbearing woman; 2004): 4.1.
Marriage rate per 1,000 population (2004): 7.1.
Divorce rate per 1,000 population (2004): 0.4.
Life expectancy at birth (2004): male 61.5 years; female 67.6 years.
Major causes of death per 100,000 population (1999): diseases of the circulatory system 211.5; diseases of the respiratory system 56.3; infectious and parasitic diseases 31.6; violence, poisoning, and accidents 28.3; malignant neoplasms (cancers) 27.9; diseases of the digestive system 19.0.

National economy

Budget (2004). Revenue: 1,104,000,000 somoni (tax revenue 84.6%, of which value-added tax 31.6%, payroll tax 10.9%, customs duties 8.9%, taxes on aluminum and cotton 7.9%; nontax revenue 11.7%; grants 3.7%). Expenditures: 1,273,000,000 somoni (current expenditures 60.6%; capital expenditures 39.4%).
Public debt (external, outstanding; 2003): U.S.$926,000,000.
Production (metric tons except as noted). Agriculture, forestry, fishing (2004): wheat 672,000, raw seed cotton 558,313, potatoes 535,000, tomatoes 225,000, onions 190,000; livestock (number of live animals) 1,608,000 sheep, 1,143,500 cattle, 850,000 goats; roundwood, n.a.; fish catch (2003) 158. Mining and quarrying (2002): antimony (metal content) 3,000; gold 5,000 kg. Manufacturing (value of production in '000,000 somoni[6]; 2001): nonferrous metals (nearly all aluminum) 442,000; food 138,000; textiles 104,000; grain mill products 51,000; basic chemicals 10,000. Energy production (consumption): electricity (kW-hr; 2002) 15,241,000,000 (16,462,000,000); coal (metric tons; 2002) 29,000 (131,000); crude petroleum (barrels; 2002) 117,000 (88,000); petroleum products (metric tons; 2002) none (977,000); natural gas (cu m; 2002) 29,000,000 (749,000,000).
Tourism (2003): receipts from visitors U.S.$2,000,000; expenditures by nationals abroad U.S.$2,000,000.
Population economically active (2003): total 1,932,000; activity rate of total population 29.1% (participation rates: ages 15–62 [male], 15–57 [female] 51.7%; female [1996] 46.5%; unofficially unemployed c. 40%).

Price and earnings indexes (2000 = 100)							
	1998	1999	2000	2001	2002	2003	2004
Consumer price index	64.0	80.6	100.0	137.0	150.7	176.3	206.3
Monthly earnings index	58.9	74.6	100.0	150.9	...	...	...

Gross national product (2004): U.S.$1,779,000,000 (U.S.$280 per capita).

Structure of gross domestic product and labour force				
	2002		2003	
	in value '000,000 somoni	% of total value	labour force	% of labour force
Agriculture	731.6	21.9	1,275,000	66.0
Mining	} 86.1	} 2.6	...	...
Public utilities			31,000	1.6
Construction				
Manufacturing	634.5	19.0	115,000	6.0
Transp. and commun.	119.9	3.6	454,000	2.3
Trade	676.6	20.2	88,000	4.6
Finance	} 759.1	} 22.7	28,000	1.4
Pub. admin., defense			296,000	15.3
Services				
Other	336.6[7]	10.0[7]	54,000[8]	2.8[8]
TOTAL	3,344.6[9]	100.0	1,932,000	100.0

Land use as % of total land area (2000): in temporary crops 6.6%, in permanent crops 0.9%, in pasture 24.9%; overall forest area 2.8%.
Household income and expenditure. Average household size (2002) 5.6; (1995) income per household 18,744 Tajik rubles[2] (U.S.$114); sources of income (1995): wages and salaries 34.5%, self-employment 34.0%, borrowing 2.4%, pension 2.0%, other 27.1%; expenditure: food 81.5%, clothing 10.2%, transport 2.5%, fuel 2.1%, other 3.7%.

Foreign trade

Balance of trade (current prices)					
	2000	2001	2002	2003	2004
U.S.$'000,000	−26.6	−125.4	−125.2	−204.6	−332.0
% of total	1.5%	8.8%	8.2%	11.4%	15.4%

Imports (2004): U.S.$1,247,000,000 (alumina 26.8%, petroleum products 8.2%, electricity 5.3%, grain and flour 4.3%, natural gas 2.7%, unspecified 52.7%). *Major import sources* (2003): Russia 20.2%; Uzbekistan 15.1%; Kazakhstan 10.9%; Ukraine 7.1%; Azerbaijan 7.1%.
Exports (2004): U.S.$915,000,000 (aluminum 62.6%, cotton fibre 17.7%, electricity 6.6%). *Major export destinations* (2003): The Netherlands 25.4%; Turkey 24.4%; Latvia 9.9%; Switzerland 9.7%; Uzbekistan 8.5%.

Transport and communications

Transport. Railroads (2001): length 299 mi, 482 km; passenger-km 32,000,000; metric ton-km cargo 1,248,000,000. Roads (2000): total length 17,254 mi, 27,767 km (paved [1996] 83%). Vehicles (1996): passenger cars 680,000; trucks and buses 8,190. Air transport (2003)[10]: passenger-km 906,000,000; metric ton-km cargo 6,785,000; airports (2002) 2.

Communications				units per 1,000
Medium	date	unit	number	persons
Daily newspapers	2000	circulation	123,000	20
Radio	2000	receivers	870,000	141
Television	2003	receivers	2,350,000	357
Telephones	2003	main lines	242,100	37
Cellular phones	2003	subscribers	47,600	7.3
Personal computers	...	units	...	...
Internet	2004	users	5,000	0.8

Education and health

Educational attainment (1989). Percentage of population age 25 and over having: primary education or no formal schooling 16.3%; some secondary 21.1%; completed secondary and some postsecondary 55.1%; higher 7.5%. *Literacy* (2001): percentage of total population age 15 and over literate 99.3%; males literate 98.9%; females literate 99.6%.

Education (2002–03)				student/
	schools	teachers	students	teacher ratio
Primary (age 6–13)	662	31,080	694,930	22.4
Secondary (age 14–17)	3,011[11]	51,685	922,795	17.9
Voc., teacher tr.	50	3,228	25,546	7.9
Higher	33	6,472	97,466	15.1

Health (2002): physicians 13,393 (1 per 472 persons); hospital beds 40,387 (1 per 157 persons); infant mortality rate per 1,000 live births (2003) 50.0.
Food (2002): daily per capita caloric intake 1,828 (vegetable products 91%, animal products 9%); 71% of FAO recommended minimum requirement.

Military

Total active duty personnel (2004): 7,600 (army 100%); Russian troops (October 2005) 6,000. *Military expenditure as percentage of GDP* (2003): 2.2%; per capita expenditure U.S.$15.

[1]Eight members are appointed by the President. [2]The somoni (equal to 1,000 Tajik rubles) was introduced on Oct. 30, 2000. [3]January 1. [4]Includes c. 400 sq mi (c. 1,035 sq km) ceded to China in May 2002. [5]Detail does not add to total given because of gross rounding. [6]At 1998 constant prices. [7]Indirect taxes less subsidies. [8]Including 47,000 unemployed. [9]Detail does not add to total given because of rounding. [10]Tajikistan Airlines only. [11]Excludes special education.

Internet resources for further information:
• **State Statistical Committee: Database**
  http://www.stat.tj/english/database.htm

Tanzania

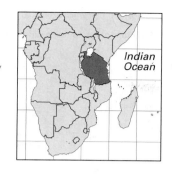

Official name: Jamhuri ya Muungano wa Tanzania (Swahili); United Republic of Tanzania (English).
Form of government: unitary multiparty republic with one legislative house (National Assembly [324[1]]).
Head of state and government: President.
Capital: Dar es Salaam (acting)[2].
Official languages: Swahili; English.
Official religion: none.
Monetary unit: 1 Tanzania shilling (T Sh) = 100 cents; valuation (Sept. 1, 2005) 1 U.S.$ = T Sh 1,138; 1 £ = T Sh 2,095.

Area and population

Administrative regions	area sq km	population 2002 census	Administrative regions	area sq km	population 2002 census
Mainland Tanzania (Tanganyika)			Rukwa	68,635	1,141,743
Arusha	36,486	1,292,973	Ruvuma	63,498	1,117,166
Dar es Salaam	1,393	2,497,940	Shinyanga	50,781	2,805,580
Dodoma	41,311	1,698,996	Singida	49,341	1,090,758
Iringa	56,864	1,495,333	Tabora	76,151	1,717,908
Kagera	28,388	2,033,888	Tanga	26,808	1,642,015
Kigoma	37,037	1,679,109	**Autonomous territory**		
Kilimanjaro	13,309	1,381,149	Zanzibar and Pemba[3]		
Lindi	66,046	791,306	Pemba	906	362,166
Manyara	45,820	1,040,461	Zanzibar	1,554	622,459
Mara	19,566	1,368,602	TOTAL LAND AREA	883,749	
Mbeya	60,350	2,070,046	INLAND WATER	59,050	
Morogoro	70,799	1,759,809	TOTAL	942,799[4]	34,569,232
Mtwara	16,707	1,128,523			
Mwanza	19,592	2,942,148			
Pwani (Coast)	32,407	889,154			

Demography

Population (2005): 36,766,000.
Density (2005)[5]: persons per sq mi 107.5, persons per sq km 41.5.
Urban-rural (2002): urban 23.0%; rural 77.0%.
Sex distribution (2002): male 48.92%; female 51.08%.
Age breakdown (2002): under 15, 44.3%; 15–29, 27.7%; 30–44, 15.3%; 45–59, 7.1%; 60–74, 4.1%; 75 and over, 1.5%.
Population projection: (2010) 40,382,000; (2020) 48,824,000.
Doubling time: 32 years.
Ethnolinguistic composition (2000): 130 different Bantu tribes 95%, of which Sukuma 9.5%; Hehe and Bena 4.5%; Gogo 4.4%; Haya 4.2%; Nyamwezi 3.6%; Makonde 3.3%; Chagga 3.0%; Ha 2.9%; other 5%.
Religious affiliation (2004): Muslim c. 35%; traditional beliefs c. 35%; Christian c. 30%; Zanzibar only is 98% Muslim.
Major urban areas (2002): Dar es Salaam 2,336,055; Arusha 270,485; Mbeya 230,318; Mwanza 209,806; Morogoro 206,868; Zanzibar 205,870.

Vital statistics

Birth rate per 1,000 population (2004): 38.6 (world avg. 21.1).
Death rate per 1,000 population (2004): 17.0 (world avg. 9.0).
Natural increase rate per 1,000 population (2004): 21.6 (world avg. 12.1).
Total fertility rate (avg. births per childbearing woman; 2004): 5.2.
Life expectancy at birth (2004): male 44.2 years; female 45.6 years.
Adult population (ages 15–49) *living with HIV* (2004[6]): 8.8% (world avg. 1.1%).

National economy

Budget (2003–04). Revenue: T Sh 1,447,500,000,000 (VAT 34.2%, income tax 24.9%, excise tax 15.0%, import duties 9.0%). Expenditures: T Sh 2,531,-500,000 (current expenditure 74.5%, of which wages 18.3%, education 17.7%, health 8.4%, interest payments on debt 4.8%; capital expenditure 25.5%).
Tourism (2003): receipts U.S.$450,000,000; expenditures U.S.$353,000,000.
Gross national product (2004)[7]: U.S.$11,560,000,000 (U.S.$330 per capita).

Structure of gross domestic product and labour force

	2003 in value T Sh '000,000	2003 % of total value	2001 labour force	2001 % of labour force
Agriculture	4,417,900	41.3	13,890,100	77.9
Mining	191,200	1.8	29,200	0.2
Manufacturing	711,000	6.6	245,400	1.4
Construction	546,200	5.1	151,700	0.9
Public utilities	157,000	1.5	14,700	0.1
Transp. and commun.	454,000	4.2	111,600	0.6
Trade	1,153,300	10.8	1,263,000	7.1
Finance	564,300	5.3	26,500	0.1
Pub. admin., defense	869,300	8.1	1,182,700	6.6
Services	929,800	8.7		
Other	698,400[8]	6.5[8]	912,800[9]	5.1[9]
TOTAL	10,692,400	100.0[10]	17,827,600[10]	100.0

Public debt (external, outstanding; 2004): U.S.$6,233,000,000.
Production (metric tons except as noted). Agriculture (2004): cassava 6,890,000, corn (maize) 2,800,000, sweet potatoes 970,000, sorghum 650,000, rice 647,000, seed cotton 330,000, mangoes 195,000, bananas 150,400, cashew nuts 100,000, pineapples 77,500, coffee 57,000, dry onions 55,000, tea 25,500, tobacco leaves 24,500; livestock (number of live animals) 17,800,000 cattle,

12,550,000 goats, 3,521,000 sheep; roundwood 23,819,209 cu m; fish catch (2001) 336,200. Mining and quarrying (2003): gold 48,018 kg; garnets 5,911 kg; tanzanites 4,490 kg; sapphires 1,338 kg; diamonds 236,582 carats. Manufacturing (value added in U.S.$'000,000; 1999): beverages 39; food products 33; tobacco products 28; paper and paper products 22; bricks, tiles, and cement 22. Energy production (consumption): electricity (kW-hr; 2002) 2,994,000,000 (2,994,000,000); coal (metric tons; 2002) 83,000 (83,000); crude petroleum (barrels; 2002) none (negligible); petroleum products (metric tons; 2002) none (940,000); natural gas, none (none).
Population economically active (2001): total 17,827,600; activity rate c. 53% (participation rates: over age 9, 77.7%; female 51.0%; unemployed [2000–01] 12.9%).

Price index (2000 = 100)

	1998	1999	2000	2001	2002	2003	2004
Consumer price index	87.5	94.4	100.0	105.1	106.2	109.9	114.4

Household income and expenditure. Average household size (2002) 4.9; annual income per household (2000–01)[7]: TSh 1,055,000 (U.S.$1,310); sources of income (2000–01)[7]: agricultural income 51.4%, self-employment 20.6%, wages and salaries 12.0%, transfer payments 7.8%; expenditure (2001)[11]: food 55.9%, transportation 9.7%, energy 8.5%, beverages and tobacco 6.9%, clothing and footwear 6.4%.
Land use as % of total land area (2000): in temporary crops 4.5%, in permanent crops 1.1%, in pasture 39.6%; overall forest area 43.9%.

Foreign trade[12]

Balance of trade (current prices)

	1999	2000	2001	2002	2003	2004
T Sh '000,000,000	–649	–537	–626	–547	–823	–1,257
% of total	44.1%	33.6%	31.5%	24.4%	37.7%	30.2%

Imports (2002): T Sh 1,601,000,000,000 (consumer goods 31.0%, of which food products 8.8%; machinery and apparatus 22.2%; transport equipment 13.2%; crude and refined petroleum 11.8%). *Major import sources:* South Africa 11.4%; Japan 8.4%; India 6.5%; Russia 6.1%; U.A.E. 5.9%; U.K. 5.7%.
Exports (2002): T Sh 846,000,000,000 (minerals [mostly gold, significantly diamonds and other gemstones] 42.4%; cashews 5.8%; tobacco 5.6%; coffee 4.0%; tea 3.4%; other [significantly fish products] 38.8%). *Major export destinations:* U.K. 18.5%; France 17.4%; Japan 11.0%; India 7.3%; The Netherlands 6.2%.

Transport and communications

Transport. Railroads (2001): length 3,690 km; passenger-km 471,000,000[13]; metric ton-km cargo 1,380,000,000[13]. Roads (2003): length 78,891 km (paved 8.6%). Vehicles (1999): passenger cars 33,900; trucks and buses 98,800. Air transport (2004)[14]: passenger-km 222,000,000; metric ton-km 2,107,000; airports (1999) with scheduled flights 11.

Communications

Medium	date	unit	number	units per 1,000 persons
Daily newspapers	2004	circulation	105,000[15]	2.9
Radio	2000	receivers	9,130,000	281
Television	2000	receivers	650,000	20
Telephones	2003	main lines	149,100	4.2
Cellular telephones	2004	subscribers	1,640,000	44
Personal computers	2004	units	278,000	7.4
Internet	2004	users	333,000	8.8

Education and health

Educational attainment: n.a. *Literacy* (2001): percentage of population age 15 and over literate 76.0%; males 84.5%; females 67.9%.

Education (1998)[7]

	schools	teachers	students	student/ teacher ratio
Primary (age 7–13)	11,339	106,329	4,042,568	38.0
Secondary (age 14–19)	491[16]	11,691	226,903	19.4
Teacher training	40[16]	1,062	9,136	8.6
Higher	...	2,064	18,867	9.1

Health: physicians (2002) 822 (1 per 42,085 persons); hospital beds (1993) 26,820 (1 per 1,000 persons); infant mortality rate (2004) 100.6.
Food (2002): daily per capita caloric intake 1,975 (vegetable products 94%, animal products 6%); 85% of FAO recommended minimum requirement.

Military

Total active duty personnel (2004): 27,000 (army 85.2%, navy 3.7%, air force 11.1%). *Military expenditure as percentage of GDP* (2003): 2.1%[16]; per capita expenditure U.S.$6[17].

---

[1]Includes 232 directly elected seats, 75 seats reserved for women, 5 seats indirectly elected, 10 appointed by the President, and 1 each for the Attorney General and the Speaker. [2]Only the legislature meets in Dodoma, the longtime planned capital. [3]Has local internal government structure; Zanzibar has 3 administrative regions, Pemba has 2. [4]A recent survey indicates a total area of 945,090 sq km (364,901 sq mi). [5]Based on land area only. [6]January 1. [7]Mainland Tanzania only. [8]Net taxes less imputed bank service charge. [9]Unemployed. [10]Detail does not add to total given because of rounding. [11]Weights of consumer price index components. [12]Imports f.o.b. in balance of trade and c.i.f. in commodities and trading partners. [13]Tanzanian Railways only. [14]Air Tanzania only. [15]Circulation for eight newspapers only. [16]1994. [17]Includes police.

Internet resources for further information:
• Bank of Tanzania http://www.bot-tz.org

Thailand

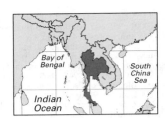

Official name: Muang Thai, or Prathet Thai (Kingdom of Thailand).
Form of government: constitutional monarchy with two legislative houses (Senate [200]; House of Representatives [500]).
Chief of state: King.
Head of government: Prime Minister.
Capital: Bangkok.
Official language: Thai.
Official religion: Buddhism.
Monetary unit: 1 Thai baht (B) = 100 stangs; valuation (Sept. 1, 2005) 1 U.S.$ = B 41.10; 1 £ = B 75.67.

Area and population	area		population
Regions[1]	sq mi	sq km	2002 estimate
Bangkok and vicinities	2,997	7,762	9,668,854
Eastern	14,094	36,503	4,300,513
Northeastern	65,195	168,855	21,609,185
Northern	65,500	169,644	12,152,502
Southern	27,303	70,715	8,415,908
Sub-central	6,407	16,594	3,002,544
Western	16,621	43,047	3,650,366
TOTAL	198,117	513,120	62,799,872

Demography

Population (2005): 64,186,000.
Density (2005): persons per sq mi 324.0, persons per sq km 125.1.
Urban-rural (2003): urban 31.9%; rural 68.1%.
Sex distribution (2004): male 49.81%; female 50.19%.
Age breakdown (2003): under 15, 24.5%; 15–29, 26.5%; 30–44, 23.7%; 45–59, 15.7%; 60–74, 7.8%; 75 and over, 1.8%.
Population projection: (2010) 66,303,000; (2020) 69,466,000.
Doubling time: 97 years.
Ethnic composition (2000): Tai peoples 81.4%, of which Thai (Siamese) 34.9%; Lao 26.5%; Han Chinese 10.6%; Malay 3.7%; Khmer 1.9%; other 2.4%.
Religious affiliation (2000): Buddhist 85.3%; Muslim 6.8%; Christian 2.2%, of which independent Christian 1.3%; traditional beliefs 2.1%; nonreligious 2.0%; other 1.6%.
Major cities (2000)[2]: Bangkok 6,320,174; Samut Prakan 378,694; Nonthaburi 291,307; Udon Thani 220,493; Nakhon Ratchasima 204,391.

Vital statistics

Birth rate per 1,000 population (2004): 14.1 (world avg. 21.1).
Death rate per 1,000 population (2004): 6.9 (world avg. 9.0).
Natural increase rate per 1,000 population (2004): 7.2 (world avg. 12.1).
Total fertility rate (avg. births per childbearing woman; 2004): 1.6.
Marriage rate per 1,000 population (2000): 5.4.
Divorce rate per 1,000 population (2000): 1.1.
Life expectancy at birth (2004): male 69.3 years; female 74.1 years.
Major causes of death per 100,000 population (2000): malignant neoplasms (cancers) 63.4; accidents, homicide, and poisonings 60.6; diseases of the circulatory system 52.6; infectious and parasitic diseases 51.7.

National economy

Budget (2001–02). Revenue: B 903,550,000,000 (tax revenue 90.3%, of which income taxes 28.7%, VAT 26.1%, taxes on international trade 11.5%, consumption tax 10.8%; nontax revenue 9.7%). Expenditures: B 1,023,000,000,000 (education 21.8%; defense 7.5%; agriculture 7.4%; health 7.1%; social security 6.9%; public order 5.5%).
Public debt (external, outstanding; 2003): U.S.$17,764,000,000.
Production (metric tons except as noted). Agriculture, forestry, fishing (2004): sugarcane 67,900,000, rice 26,948,000, cassava 20,400,000, oil palm fruit 4,600,-000, corn (maize) 4,094,000, natural rubber 3,030,000, pineapples 1,900,000, bananas 1,900,000, mangoes 1,700,000, coconuts 1,450,000, tobacco 80,000; livestock (number of live animals) 7,159,000 pigs, 5,000,000 cattle, 2,000,000 buffalo, 170,000,000 chickens; roundwood (2004) 27,785,000 cu m; fish catch (2001) 3,605,544, of which mollusks 224,222. Mining and quarrying (2003): gypsum 7,291,000; dolomite 865,708; feldspar 824,990; zinc [metal content] 37,000; gemstones (significantly rubies and sapphires) 716,000 carats. Manufacturing (value added in U.S.$'000,000; 2000) textiles and wearing apparel 1,905; electronics 1,817; food products 1,311; motor vehicles 1,245; office machines and computers 1,045. Energy production (consumption): electricity (kW-hr; 2002) 115,513,000,000 (118,061,000,000); hard coal (metric tons; 2002) negligible (5,530,000); lignite (metric tons; 2004) 20,700,000 ([2002] 19,500,000); crude petroleum (barrels; 2004) 52,000,000 ([2002] 289,000,000); petroleum products (metric tons; 2002) 36,373,000 (31,367,000); natural gas (cu m; 2002) 19,223,000,000 (26,488,000,000).
Tourism (2003): receipts from visitors U.S.$7,822,000,000; expenditures by nationals abroad U.S.$3,495,000,000.
Population economically active (2003): total 35,311,000; activity rate of total population 55.1% (participation rates: over age 14, 73.0%; female 45.0%; unemployed [February 2004–January 2005] 2.1%).

Price and earnings indexes (2000 = 100)							
	1998	1999	2000	2001	2002	2003	2004
Consumer price index	98.2	98.5	100.0	101.6	102.3	104.1	107.0
Average earnings index	99.6	99.8	100.0	101.0	100.2	102.5	...

Gross national product (2004): U.S.$158,703,000,000 (U.S.$2,540 per capita).

Structure of gross domestic product and labour force				
	2004		2003	
	in value B '000,000	% of total value	labour force[3]	% of labour force[3]
Agriculture	649,000	9.9	15,561,000	44.9
Mining	174,200	2.6	40,000	0.1
Manufacturing	2,312,900	35.2	5,086,000	14.7
Construction	204,600	3.1	1,614,000	4.7
Public utilities	207,200	3.1	105,000	0.3
Transp. and commun.	509,100	7.7	988,000	2.8
Trade	1,305,500	19.9	7,160,000	20.6
Finance	430,000	6.5	846,000	2.4
Pub. admin., defense	293,400	4.5	903,000	2.6
Services	490,100	7.5	2,351,000	6.8
Other			23,000	0.1
TOTAL	6,576,000	100.0	34,677,000	100.0

Household income and expenditure. Average household size (2002) 3.5; average annual income per household (2002) B 164,832 (U.S.$3,837); sources of income (2000): wages and salaries 42.4%, self-employment 28.1%, transfer payments 8.3%, income in-kind 18.4%; expenditure (2000): food and nonalcoholic beverages 37.1%, housing 25.5%, transportation and communications 17.1%, medical and personal care 6.2%.
Land use as % of total land area (2000): in temporary crops 29.4%, in permanent crops 6.5%, in pasture 1.6%; overall forest area 28.9%.

Foreign trade[4]

Balance of trade (current prices)						
	1999	2000	2001	2002	2003	2004
U.S.$'000,000	+14,013	+11,700	+8,582	+9,775	+11,175	+11,124
% of total	14.1%	9.4%	7.3%	7.9%	7.7%	6.1%

Imports (2001): U.S.$62,057,000,000 (electrical machinery 22.1%, of which electronic components and parts 10.9%; nonelectrical machinery 17.4%, of which computers and parts 6.3%; chemicals and chemical products 10.3%; crude petroleum 9.3%). *Major import sources* (2004): Japan 23.6%; China 8.6%; U.S. 7.6%; Malaysia 5.8%; Singapore 4.4%.
Exports (2001): U.S.$65,113,000,000 (food products 14.9%, of which fish, crustaceans, and mollusks 6.2%; computers and parts 12.3%; microcircuits and other electronics 7.2%; chemicals and chemical products 5.7%; garments and clothing accessories 5.6%). *Major export destinations* (2004): U.S. 15.9%; Japan 13.9%; China 7.3%; Singapore 7.2%; Malaysia 5.4%.

Transport and communications

Transport. Railroads (2000): route length 4,041 km; passenger-km 10,040,-000,000; metric ton-km cargo 3,347,000,000. Roads (2001): total length 53,436 km (paved 98.5%). Vehicles (2002): passenger cars 2,281,000; trucks and buses 4,145,000. Air transport (2004)[5]: passenger-km 51,780,000,000; metric ton-km cargo 1,875,000,000; airports (1996) 25.

Communications				units per 1,000 persons
Medium	date	unit	number	
Daily newspapers	2000	circulation	3,990,000	64
Radio	2000	receivers	14,700,000	235
Television	2003	receivers	18,980,000	300
Telephones	2004	main lines	6,724,000	106
Cellular telephones	2004	subscribers	28,000,000	441
Personal computers	2004	units	3,716,000	59
Internet	2004	users	6,970,000	110

Education and health

Educational attainment (2000). Percentage of population age 6 and over having: no formal schooling 8.5%; primary education 59.0%; lower secondary 12.5%; upper secondary 11.2%; some higher 2.2%; undergraduate 5.2%; advanced degree 0.4%; other/unknown 1.0%. *Literacy* (2000): 95.5%.

Education (2002–03)	schools	teachers	students	student/ teacher ratio
Primary (age 7–12)	34,001[6]	295,484	6,109,642	20.7
Secondary (age 13–18)	2,318[7]	194,298	4,754,611	24.5
Voc., teacher tr.	679[7]	21,500	610,943	28.4
Higher	102[7]	65,548	2,205,581	33.6

Health (2001): physicians 18,531 (1 per 3,395 persons); hospital beds 141,380 (1 per 445 persons); infant mortality rate (2003) 7.2.
Food (2002): daily per capita caloric intake 2,467 (vegetable products 88%, animal products 12%); 111% of FAO recommended minimum requirement.

Military

Total active duty personnel (2004): 306,600 (army 62.0%, navy 23.0%, air force 15.0%). *Military expenditure as percentage of GDP* (2003): 1.3%; per capita expenditure U.S.$29.

---

[1]Actual local administration is based on 76 provinces. [2]Preliminary census figures. [3]Employed only. [4]Import figures are f.o.b. in balance of trade and c.i.f. for commodities and trading partners. [5]Thai and Bangkok airways. [6]1995–96. [7]1993.

Internet resources for further information:
• **National Statistical Office Thailand**
  http://www.nso.go.th
• **Bank of Thailand**
  http://www.bot.or.th

Togo

Official name: République Togolaise (Togolese Republic).
Form of government: multiparty republic[1] with one legislative body (National Assembly [81]).
Chief of state: President.
Head of government: Prime Minister.
Capital: Lomé.
Official language: French.
Official religion: none.
Monetary unit: 1 CFA franc (CFAF) = 100 centimes; valuation (Sept. 1, 2005) 1 U.S.$ = CFAF 522.78; 1 £ = CFAF 962.57[2].

Population

Regions Prefectures	population 2005[3] estimate	Regions Prefectures	population 2005[3] estimate
Centrale	510,446	Haho	194,917
Blitta	111,997	Kloto	192,763
Sotouboua	141,073	Moyen-Mono	75,382
Tchamba	83,997	Ogou	264,915
Tchaoudjo	173,379	Wawa	162,610
De la Kara	689,210[4]	Des Savanes	628,904[4]
Assoli	53,845	Kpendjal	120,612
Bassar	108,766	Oti	138,919
Binah	67,844	Tandjouaré	92,613
Dankpen	77,536	Tône	276,761
Doufelgou	87,228	Maritime	2,196,857
Kéran	73,229	Avé	91,536
Kozah	220,763	Golfe[5]	1,224,425
Des Plateaux	1,201,810[4]	Lacs	234,762
Agou	88,305	Vo	225,070
Amou	100,151	Yoto	159,380
Danyi	43,076	Zio	261,684
Est-Mono	79,690	TOTAL	5,227,227

Demography

Area: 21,925 sq mi, 56,785 sq km.
Population (2005): 5,400,000.
Density (2005): persons per sq mi 246.3, persons per sq km 95.1.
Urban-rural (2004): urban 34.5%; rural 65.5%.
Sex distribution (2004): male 49.55%; female 50.45%.
Age breakdown (2001): under 15, 45.6%; 15–29, 28.1%; 30–44, 14.8%; 45–59, 7.5%; 60–74, 3.3%; 75 and over, 0.7%.
Population projection: (2010) 6,185,000; (2020) 8,000,000.
Doubling time: 26 years.
Ethnic composition (2000): Ewe 22.2%; Kabre 13.4%; Wachi 10.0%; Mina 5.6%; Kotokoli 5.6%; Bimoba 5.2%; Losso 4.0%; Gurma 3.4%; Lamba 3.2%; Adja 3.0%; other 24.4%.
Religious affiliation (2000): Christian 37.8%, of which Roman Catholic 24.3%; traditional beliefs 37.7%; Muslim 18.9%; other 5.6%.
Major cities (2003): Lomé 676,400 (urban agglomeration 749,700); Sokodé 84,200; Kpalimé 75,200; Atakpamé 64,300; Kara 49,800.

Vital statistics

Birth rate per 1,000 population (2004): 37.3 (world avg. 21.1).
Death rate per 1,000 population (2004): 10.2 (world avg. 9.0).
Natural increase rate per 1,000 population (2004): 27.1 (world avg. 12.1).
Total fertility rate (avg. births per childbearing woman; 2004): 5.1.
Life expectancy at birth (2004): male 54.6 years; female 58.7 years.
Adult population (ages 15–49) *living with HIV* (2004[3]): 4.1% (world avg. 1.1%).

National economy

Budget (2004). Revenue: CFAF 170,700,000,000 (tax revenue 85.1%, of which taxes on international trade 37.1%; grants 7.6%; nontax revenue 7.3%). Expenditures: CFAF 167,000,000,000 (current expenditure 85.9%, capital expenditure 14.1%).
Public debt (external, outstanding; 2003): U.S.$1,489,000,000.
Production (metric tons except as noted). Agriculture, forestry, fishing (2004): cassava 725,000, yams 570,000, corn (maize) 485,000, seed cotton 185,000, sorghum 180,000, oil palm fruit 115,000, rice 68,100, coffee 13,500, cacao beans 8,500; livestock (number of live animals) 1,850,000 sheep, 1,480,000 goats, 320,000 pigs, 279,000 cattle; roundwood 5,914,769 cu m; fish catch (2003) 27,485. Mining and quarrying: limestone 2,400,000; phosphate rock 1,115,000. Manufacturing (value added in CFAF '000,000; 1998): food products, beverages, and tobacco manufactures 41,400; metallic goods 12,000; nonmetallic manufactures 8,500; textiles, clothing, and leather 4,900; wood products 4,700; paper, printing, and publishing 4,600; chemicals 3,600. Energy production (consumption): electricity (kW-hr; 2002) 122,000,000 (577,000,-000); petroleum products (metric tons; 2002) none (434,000).
Population economically active (2000): total 1,913,000; activity rate of total population 38.1% (participation rates: over age 15, 70.7%; female 39.9%; unemployed [1996] c. 11.5%).

Price index (2000 = 100)							
	1998	1999	2000	2001	2002	2003	2004
Consumer price index	98.2	98.1	100.0	103.9	107.1	106.1	106.5

Gross national product (at current market prices; 2004): U.S.$1,868,000,000 (U.S.$380 per capita).

Structure of gross domestic product and labour force

	2004		2000	
	in value CFAF '000,000,000	% of total value	labour force	% of labour force
Agriculture	404.3	37.3	1,142,000	59.7
Mining	35.5	3.3		
Manufacturing	96.5	8.9		
Construction	27.1	2.5		
Public utilities	51.6	4.8		
Transp. and commun.	54.6	5.0	771,000	40.3
Trade	123.1	11.3		
Finance	103.9	9.6		
Pub. admin., defense	...	...		
Services	102.8	9.5		
Other	84.5[6]	7.8[6]	...	...
TOTAL	1,083.9	100.0[6]	1,913,000	100.0

Household income and expenditure. Average household size (2002) 6.0; expenditure (1987): food and beverages 45.9%, services 20.5%, household durable goods 13.9%, clothing 11.4%, housing 5.9%.
Land use as % of total land area (2000): in temporary crops 46.1%, in permanent crops 2.2%, in pasture 18.4%; overall forest area 9.4%.
Tourism (2002): receipts U.S.$13,000,000; expenditures U.S.$5,000,000.

Foreign trade[7]

Balance of trade (current prices)						
	1999	2000	2001	2002	2003	2004
U.S.$'000,000	−97.9	−122.8	−158.8	−151.4	−156.7	−136.1
% of total	11.1%	14.5%	18.2%	15.1%	11.6%	8.9%

Imports (2002): U.S.$405,300,000 (food 16.1%, of which cereals 9.7%; refined petroleum 14.8%; machinery and apparatus 10.8%; chemicals and chemical products 10.5%; cement, bricks, and tiles 9.1%; road vehicles 8.2%; iron and steel 7.6%). *Major import sources:* France 20.4%; Côte d'Ivoire 6.3%; Canada 5.8%; Germany 5.1%; Belgium 5.1%.
Exports (2002): U.S.$250,600,000 (cement 26.5%; phosphates 16.6%; food 16.6%; cotton 15.9%; iron and steel 7.4%). *Major export destinations:* Ghana 21.5%; Benin 13.2%; Burkina Faso 13.0%; Niger 4.6%; Australia 3.7%.

Transport and communications

Transport. Railroads (2004): route length 568 km; (1999) passenger-km 370,000; metric ton-km cargo 92,374,000. Roads (1999): total length 7,520 km (paved 32%). Vehicles (1997[3]): passenger cars 79,200; trucks and buses 34,240. Air transport (2001): passenger-km 130,000,000; metric ton-km cargo, n.a.; airports (1998) 2.

Communications				units
Medium	date	unit	number	per 1,000 persons
Daily newspapers	2000	circulation	20,100	4.0
Radio	2000	receivers	1,330,000	265
Television	2003	receivers	667,800	123
Telephones	2003	main lines	60,600	12
Cellular telephones	2003	subscribers	220,000	44
Personal computers	2004	units	171,000	31
Internet	2004	users	221,000	40

Education and health

Educational attainment, n.a. *Literacy* (2003): total population age 15 and over literate 60.9%; males 75.4%; females 46.9%.

Education (2002–03)	schools	teachers	students	student/ teacher ratio
Primary (age 6–11)	4,701[8]	27,504	975,063	35.5
Secondary (age 12–18)	...	9,001	334,864	37.2
Vocational	...			
Higher[8, 9]	1	384	15,028	39.1

Health: physicians (2004) 265 (1 per 20,969 persons); hospital beds (1998) 6,250 (1 per 761 persons); infant mortality rate (2004) 63.8.
Food (2002): daily per capita caloric intake 2,345 (vegetable products 97%, animal products 3%); 102% of FAO recommended minimum requirement.

Military

Total active duty personnel (2004): 8,550 (army 94.7%, navy 2.3%, air force 3.0%). *Military expenditure as percentage of GDP* (2003): 1.6%; per capita expenditure U.S.$6.

---

[1]International observers considered the April 2005 presidential elections to be deeply flawed. [2]Formerly pegged to the French franc and since Jan. 1, 2002, to the euro at the rate of €1 = CFAF 655.96. [3]January 1. [4]Detail does not add to total given because of rounding. [5]Golfe prefecture includes Lomé. [6]Import duties and taxes. [7]Import figures are f.o.b. in balance of trade and c.i.f. for commodities and trading partners. [8]1998. [9]University only.

Internet resources for further information:
- **Banque Centrale des Etats de l'Afrique de l'Ouest**
  http://www.bceao.int
- **La Banque de France: La Zone Franc**
  http://www.banque-france.fr/fr/eurosys/zonefr/zonefr.htm

Tonga

Pacific Ocean

Official name: Pule'anga Fakatu'i 'o Tonga (Tongan); Kingdom of Tonga (English).
Form of government: hereditary constitutional monarchy with one legislative house (Legislative Assembly [30[1]]).
Head of state and government: King assisted by Privy Council.
Capital: Nuku'alofa.
Official languages: Tongan; English.
Official religion: none.
Monetary unit: 1 pa'anga (T$) = 100 seniti; valuation (Sept. 1, 2005) 1 U.S.$ = T$1.93; 1 £ = T$3.55.

Area and population		area		population
				1996
Divisions[2]	Principal towns	sq mi	sq km	census
'Eua[3]	'Ohonua	33.7	87.4	4,934
Ha'apai[4]	Pangai	42.5	110.0	8,138
Niuas[5]	Hihifo	27.7	71.7	2,018
Tongatapu[3]	Nuku'alofa	100.6	260.5	66,979
Vava'u[4]	Neiafu	46.0	119.2	15,715
TOTAL LAND AREA		278.1[6]	720.3[6]	
INLAND WATER		11.4	29.6	
TOTAL		289.5	749.9	97,784

Demography

Population (2005): 98,600.
Density (2005)[7]: persons per sq mi 354.5, persons per sq km 136.9.
Urban-rural (2003): urban 33.4%; rural 66.6%.
Sex distribution (2002): male 50.93%; female 49.07%.
Age breakdown (1996): under 15, 39.1%; 15–29, 28.0%; 30–44, 15.1%; 45–59, 10.0%; 60–74, 6.0%; 75 and over, 1.8%.
Population projection: (2010) 99,000; (2020) 99,000.
Doubling time: 36 years.
Ethnic composition (2000): Tongan 95.2%; mixed-race (Euronesian) 0.7%; British or Australian expatriates 0.5%; other 3.6%.
Religious affiliation (2000): Christian 92.9%, of which Protestant (incl. Anglican) 55.6%, independent Christian 20.5%, Mormon c. 14%; Bahā'ī 6.7%; other 0.4%.
Major towns (2002): Nuku'alofa (on Tongatapu) 24,300[8]; Mu'a (on Tongatapu) 4,200; Neiafu (on Vava'u) 4,100; Haveloloto (on Tongatapu) 3,200; Pangai (in the Ha'apai Group) 1,700.

Vital statistics

Birth rate per 1,000 population (2004): 24.9 (world avg. 21.1).
Death rate per 1,000 population (2004): 5.5 (world avg. 9.0).
Natural increase rate per 1,000 population (2004): 19.4 (world avg. 12.1).
Total fertility rate (avg. births per childbearing woman; 2004): 3.0.
Marriage rate per 1,000 population (2000): 7.4.
Divorce rate per 1,000 population (2000): 1.1.
Life expectancy at birth (2004): male 66.7 years; female 71.8 years.
Major causes of death per 100,000 population (2002): circulatory diseases 190.1; malignant neoplasms (cancers) 77.2; respiratory diseases 49.5; endocrine, nutritional, and metabolic disorders 43.6.

National economy

Budget (2002–03). Revenue: T$96,200,000 (foreign-trade taxes 52.6%, government services revenue 18.1%, direct taxes 12.5%, indirect taxes 10.2%). Expenditures: T$98,600,000 (education 16.6%, general administration 13.6%, public debt 11.2%, law and order 11.2%, health 10.2%, social security 7.8%).
Production (metric tons except as noted). Agriculture, forestry, fishing (2004): coconuts 58,000, pumpkins, squash, and gourds 20,000, cassava 9,000, sweet potatoes 6,000, yams 4,400, plantains 3,000, vanilla 130; livestock (number of live animals) 81,000 pigs, 12,500 goats, 11,400 horses, 11,250 cattle, 300,000 chickens; roundwood 2,100 cu m; fish catch (2003) 4,435. Mining and quarrying: coral and sand for local use. Manufacturing (output in T$'000,000; 1996): food products and beverages 8,203; paper products 1,055; chemical products 964; metal products 889; textile and wearing apparel 742; nonmetallic products 715. Energy production (consumption): electricity (kW-hr; 2002) 36,000,000 (36,000,000); crude petroleum, none (none); petroleum products (metric tons; 2002) n.a. (35,000).
Gross national product (2004): U.S.$186,000,000 (U.S.$1,830 per capita).

Structure of gross domestic product and labour force				
	2002–03		1996	
	in value T$'000	% of total value	labour force	% of labour force
Agriculture	85,370	23.6	9,953	29.3
Mining	1,144	0.3	43	0.1
Manufacturing	12,449	3.4	6,710	19.8
Construction	25,909	7.2	500	1.5
Public utilities	5,270	1.5	504	1.5
Transp. and commun.	22,617	6.3	1,209	3.6
Trade	46,035	12.8	2,506	7.4
Finance	33,118	9.2	657	1.9
Pub. admin., defense	44,740	12.4	3,701	10.9
Services	28,684	7.9	3,623	10.7
Other	55,637[9]	15.4[9]	4,502	13.3
TOTAL	360,973	100.0	33,908	100.0

Population economically active (1996): total 33,908; activity rate 35.3% (participation rates: ages 15–64, 60.4%; female 36.0%; unemployed [2002–03] 5.2%).

Price index (2000 = 100)							
	1998	1999	2000	2001	2002	2003	2004
Consumer price index	90.0	94.1	100.0	108.3	119.5	133.4	148.1

Public debt (external, outstanding; 2004): U.S.$82,000,000.
Household income and expenditure (2000–01). Average household size 5.5; cash income per household[10]: T$12,871 (U.S.$6,511); sources of cash income[10]: wages and salaries 35.6%, remittances from overseas 19.7%, sales of own produce 16.1%, other 28.6%; cash expenditure: food and nonalcoholic beverages 44.6%, transportation 15.0%, household furnishings and operation 8.4%, alcoholic beverages and tobacco 5.7%, housing 3.5%, education 2.1%.
Tourism: receipts (2003) U.S.$15,000,000; expenditures (2002) U.S.$3,000,000.
Land use as % of total land area (2000): in temporary crops c. 24%, in permanent crops c. 43%, in pasture c. 6%; overall forest area c. 5%.

Foreign trade[11]

Balance of trade (current prices)						
	1998–99	1999–2000	2000–01	2001–02	2002–03	2003–04
U.S.$'000,000	−43.5	−43.0	−49.9	−44.0	−58.0	−70.5
% of total	64.3%	65.5%	67.6%	55.1%	61.7%	71.3%

Imports (2003–04): U.S.$97,600,000 (food and beverages 30.2%, mineral fuels and chemical products 25.8%, machinery and transport equipment 15.2%). *Major import sources:* New Zealand 39.3%; Australia 22.5%; Fiji 17.7%; U.S. 8.4%.
Exports (2003–04): U.S.$18,900,000 (squash 36.6%, fish 32.5%, vanilla beans 14.0%, root crops 3.9%). *Major export destinations:* Japan 39.8%; U.S. 26.6%; New Zealand 6.5%.

Transport and communications

Transport. Railroads: none. Roads (1999): total length 680 km (paved 27%). Vehicles (2000): passenger cars 4,800, commercial vehicles 4,400. Air transport (2000): passenger-km 13,000,000; metric ton-km cargo, n.a.; airports (1996) with scheduled flights 6.

Communications				units per 1,000
Medium	date	unit	number	persons
Daily newspapers	2000	circulation	12,300	123
Radio	1997	receivers	61,000	619
Television	1997	receivers	2,000	21
Telephones	2002	main lines	11,200	113
Cellular telephones	2002	subscribers	3,400	34
Personal computers	2004	units	5,000	48
Internet	2004	users	3,000	29

Education and health

Educational attainment (1996). Percentage of population age 25 and over having: primary education 26%; lower secondary 58%; upper secondary 8%; higher 6%; not stated 2%. *Literacy* (2000): 98.8%.

Education (1999)				student/
	schools	teachers	students	teacher ratio
Primary (age 6–11)	117	745	16,206	21.8
Secondary (age 12–18)	39	961	13,987	14.6
Voc., teacher tr.	5	67	755	11.3
Higher[12]	1	19	226	11.9

Health (2004): physicians (2003) 32[13] (1 per 3,072 persons); hospital beds 296 (1 per 332 persons); infant mortality rate per 1,000 live births 13.0.
Food (1992): daily per capita caloric intake 2,946 (vegetable products 82%, animal products 18%); 129% of FAO recommended minimum requirement.

Military

Total active duty personnel (2005): 400-member force includes air and coast guard elements. Tonga has defense cooperation agreements with both Australia and New Zealand. *Military expenditure as percentage of GDP:* n.a.

[1]Includes 12 nonelective seats and 9 nobles elected by the 33 hereditary nobles of Tonga. [2]Divisions have no administrative functions; 3 island councils constitute the local administrative framework (including a combined islands council for 'Eua, Niuas, and Tongatapu. [3]'Eua and Tongatapu together constitutes Tongatapu island group. [4]Also the name of an island group. [5]Also known as Niuatoputapu island group. [6]Total includes 27.6 sq mi (71.5 sq km) of uninhabited islands. [7]Based on land area. [8]Population of urban agglomeration (2003) is 35,000. [9]Net indirect taxes less imputed bank service charges. [10]Noncash annual income equals T$5,734 (U.S.$2,901). [11]Imports f.o.b. in balance of trade and c.i.f. in commodities and trading partners. [12]1992. [13]Government only.

Internet resources for further information:
• **Government of Tonga Statistics**
  http://www.spc.int/prism/Country/TO/stats
• **National Reserve Bank of Tonga**
  http://www.reservebank.to

Trinidad and Tobago

Official name: Republic of Trinidad and Tobago.
Form of government: multiparty republic with two legislative houses (Senate [31]; House of Representatives [36[1]]).
Chief of state: President.
Head of government: Prime Minister.
Capital: Port of Spain.
Official language: English.
Official religion: none.
Monetary unit: 1 Trinidad and Tobago dollar (TT$) = 100 cents; valuation (Sept. 1, 2005) 1 U.S.$ = TT$6.27; 1 £ = TT$11.55.

Area and population

	area[2]	population		area[2]	population
	sq km	2000 census		sq km	2000 census
Trinidad	4,827	1,208,282	**Cities**		
Counties			Port of Spain	12	49,031
Couva/Tabaquite/			San Fernando	19	55,419
Talparo	723	162,779	**Boroughs**		
Diego Martin	126	105,720	Arima	12	32,278
Mayaro/Rio Claro	814	33,480	Chaguanas	59	67,433
Penal/Debe	246	83,609	Point Fortin	25	19,056
Princes Town	620	91,947	**Tobago[3]**	300	54,084
San Juan/Laventille	239	157,295	TOTAL	5,127	1,262,366
Sangre Grande	927	64,343			
Siparia	495	81,917			
Tunapuna/Piarco	510	203,975			

Demography

Population (2005): 1,298,000.
Density (2005): persons per sq mi 655.6, persons per sq km 253.1.
Urban-rural (2003): urban 75.4%; rural 24.6%.
Sex distribution (2001): male 51.22%; female 48.78%.
Age breakdown (2001): under 15, 24.3%; 15–29, 27.1%; 30–44, 22.5%; 45–59, 15.5%; 60–74, 7.7%; 75 and over, 2.9%.
Population projection: (2010) 1,316,000; (2020) 1,337,000.
Ethnic composition (2000): black 39.2%; East Indian 38.6%; mixed 16.3%; Chinese 1.6%; white 1.0%; other/not stated 3.3%.
Religious affiliation (2000): Christian 64.6%, of which Roman Catholic 30.7%, Protestant (including Anglican) 25.7%, independent Christian 3.2%; Hindu 22.8%; Muslim 6.8%; nonreligious 2.2%; Spiritist 1.5%; other 2.1%.
Major cities (2000): Chaguanas 67,433; San Fernando 55,149; Port of Spain 49,031; Arima 32,278; Point Fortin 19,056.

Vital statistics

Birth rate per 1,000 population (2004): 12.7 (world avg. 21.1).
Death rate per 1,000 population (2004): 10.2 (world avg. 9.0).
Natural increase rate per 1,000 population (2004): 2.5 (world avg. 12.1).
Total fertility rate (avg. births per childbearing woman; 2004): 1.8.
Marriage rate per 1,000 population (1999): 5.9.
Divorce rate per 1,000 population (1999): 1.1.
Life expectancy at birth (2004): male 65.5 years; female 68.0 years.
Major causes of death per 100,000 population (1998): diseases of the circulatory system 302.8; endocrine and metabolic disorders 142.3; malignant neoplasms (cancers) 96.7; accidents, violence, and homicide 49.6.

National economy

Budget (2003–04). Revenue: TT$20,630,000,000 (petroleum sector 37.0%; individual income tax 15.9%; VAT 14.6%; company income tax 11.2%). Expenditures: TT$19,120,000,000 (current expenditures 91.5%; development expenditures 8.5%).
Production (metric tons except as noted). Agriculture, forestry, fishing (2004): sugarcane 680,000, coconuts 18,000, oranges 5,100, rice 3,000, pigeon peas 2,900, cocoa 1,300, coffee 540, nutmeg 155; livestock (number of live animals) 78,000 pigs, 59,000 goats, 28,200,000 chickens; roundwood 94,856 cu m; fish catch (2003) 9,740. Mining and quarrying (2003): natural asphalt 16,200. Manufacturing (2004): anhydrous ammonia 4,714,400; methanol 3,418,400; iron and steel billets 790,000; cement (2003) 766,000; urea 621,200; steel wire rods 616,000; refined sugar (2003) 18,200; beer and stout (2000) 524,000 hectolitres; rum (2000) 146,000 hectolitres. Energy production (consumption): electricity (kW-hr; 2002) 5,643,000,000 (5,643,000,000); crude petroleum (barrels; 2004) 45,100,000 ([2002] 55,400,000); petroleum products (metric tons; 2002) 7,527,000 (1,229,000); natural gas (cu m; 2004) 30,273,000,000 ([2002] 18,043,000,000).
Household income and expenditure. Average household size[4] 3.8; average income per household[4] TT$53,015 (U.S.$8,484); expenditure (1993): food, beverages, and tobacco 25.5%, housing 21.6%, transportation 15.2%, household furnishings 14.3%, clothing and footwear 10.4%.
Tourism (2002): receipts from visitors U.S.$224,000,000; expenditures by nationals abroad U.S.$186,000,000.
Land use as % of total land area (2000): in temporary crops 14.6%, in permanent crops 9.2%, in pasture 2.1%; overall forest area 50.5%.
Gross national product (at current market prices; 2004): U.S.$11,360,000,000 (U.S.$8,580 per capita).

Structure of gross domestic product and labour force

	2002			
	in value TT$'000,000	% of total value	labour force	% of labour force
Agriculture	800	0.9	36,100	6.2
Crude petroleum	11,693	13.7		
Asphalt	3,815	4.5	73,800	12.6
Manufacturing[5]	15,812	18.5		
Construction	5,952	7.0	68,900	11.8
Public utilities			6,600	1.1
Transp. and commun.	12,377	14.5	41,900	7.1
Trade	15,433	18.0	94,600	16.1
Finance, real estate	14,437	16.9	43,800	7.5
Pub. admin., defense	7,187	8.4	158,100	27.0
Services				
Other	−2,002[6]	−2.3[6]	62,300[7]	10.6[7]
TOTAL	85,503[8]	100.0[8]	586,200[8]	100.0

Population economically active (2002): total 586,200; activity rate of total population *c.* 45% (participation rates: ages 15–64, 66.9%; female 39.1%; unemployed [April 2003–March 2004] 10.3%).

Price and earnings indexes (2000 = 100)

	1998	1999	2000	2001	2002	2003	2004
Consumer price index	93.4	96.6	100.0	105.5	109.9	114.1	118.3
Weekly earnings index[9]	77.7	80.2	100.0	99.2	...	...	...

Public debt (external, outstanding; 2003): U.S.$1,751,000,000.

Foreign trade[10]

Balance of trade (current prices)

	1999	2000	2001	2002	2003	2004
TT$'000,000	+398	+6,082	+7,363	+1,189	+8,099	+9,544
% of total	1.1%	12.7%	13.1%	2.5%	14.2%	13.5%

Imports (2001): TT$24,510,000,000 (crude petroleum 19.3%, general industrial machinery 16.1%, floating docks 9.3%, food products 7.5%, refined petroleum 4.1%). *Major import sources:* United States 34.4%; Venezuela 11.1%; Brazil 5.1%; United Kingdom 4.9%; Panama 4.6%.
Exports (2001): TT$31,873,000,000 (refined petroleum 29.4%, floating docks 12.6%, crude petroleum 9.3%, anhydrous ammonia 8.5%, iron and steel 5.7%, methanol 5.0%). *Major export destinations:* United States 42.3%; Mexico 7.4%; Jamaica 7.0%; Barbados 5.5%; France 3.9%.

Transport and communications

Transport. Railroads: none. Roads (1999): total length 8,320 km (paved 51%). Vehicles (2000): passenger cars 246,977; trucks and buses 52,627. Air transport (2004)[11]: passenger-km 3,014,000,000; metric ton-km cargo 41,791,000; airports (2000) with scheduled flights 2.

Communications

Medium	date	unit	number	units per 1,000 persons
Daily newspapers	2001	circulation	191,000	151
Radio	2000	receivers	672,000	532
Television	2000	receivers	429,000	340
Telephones	2004	main lines	321,300	246
Cellular telephones	2004	subscribers	647,900	496
Personal computers	2004	units	137,000	105
Internet	2004	users	160,000	122

Education and health

Educational attainment (2000). Percentage of population age 15 and over having: no formal schooling 2.5%; primary education 35.4%; secondary 52.0%; university 4.6%; other/not stated 5.5%. *Literacy* (2000): total population age 15 and over literate 93.8%; males 95.5%; females 92.1%.

Education (2002–03)

	schools	teachers	students	student/ teacher ratio
Primary (age 5–11)	481[12]	7,623	141,036	18.5
Secondary (age 12–16)	...	5,555	105,330	19.0
Voc., teacher tr.	...	145	2,550	17.6
Higher	...	969	12,316	12.7

Health (2001): physicians 1,234 (1 per 1,027 persons); hospital beds 4,339 (1 per 292 persons); infant mortality rate (2004) 26.5.
Food (2002): daily per capita caloric intake 2,732 (vegetable products 84%, animal products 16%); 113% of FAO recommended minimum requirement.

Military

Total active duty personnel (2004): 2,700 (army 74.1%, coast guard 25.9%). *Military expenditure as percentage of GNP* (2003): 0.3%; per capita expenditure U.S.$22.

---

[1]Excludes speaker, who may be elected from outside the House of Representatives. [2]Area figures for counties are estimated. [3]Semiautonomous island. [4]Approximately 2002; exact date of information is unknown. [5]Includes petroleum refining and petrochemicals. [6]Net of VAT less imputed bank service charges. [7]Includes 61,100 unemployed. [8]Detail does not add to total given because of rounding. [9]Manufacturing only. [10]Imports c.i.f.; exports f.o.b. [11]BWIA only. [12]1999–2000.

Internet resources for further information:
• **Central Bank of Trinidad and Tobago**
  http://www.central-bank.org.tt
• **Central Statistical Office http://www.cso.gov.tt**

Tunisia

Official name: Al-Jumhūrīyah
at-Tūnisīyah (Republic of Tunisia).
Form of government: multiparty
republic[1] with two legislative houses
(Chamber of Councilors [126[2]];
Chamber of Deputies [189]).
Chief of state: President.
Head of government: Prime Minister.
Capital: Tunis.
Official language: Arabic.
Official religion: Islam.
Monetary unit: 1 dinar (D) = 1,000
millimes; valuation (Sept. 1, 2005)
1 U.S.$ = D 1.30; 1 £ = D 2.39.

Area and population

Governorates	Capitals	area sq mi	area sq km	population 2004 census
Al-Ariānah	Al-Ariānah	192	498	422,246
Bājah	Bājah	1,374	3,558	304,501
Banzart	Bizerte (Banzart)	1,423	3,685	524,128
Bin ʿArūs	Bin ʿArūs	294	761	505,773
Jundūbah	Jundūbah	1,198	3,102	416,608
Al-Kāf	Al-Kāf	1,917	4,965	258,790
Madanīn	Madanīn	3,316	8,588	432,503
Al-Mahdīyah	Al-Mahdīyah	1,145	2,966	377,853
Manūbah	Manūbah	409	1,060	335,912
Al-Munastīr	Al-Munastīr	393	1,019	455,590
Nābul	Nābul	1,076	2,788	693,890
Qābis	Qābis	2,770	7,175	342,630
Qafṣah	Qafṣah	3,471	8,990	323,709
Al-Qaṣrayn	Al-Qaṣrayn	3,114	8,066	412,278
Al-Qayrawān	Al-Qayrawān	2,592	6,712	546,209
Qibilī	Qibilī	8,527	22,084	143,218
Ṣafāqis	Ṣafāqis	2,913	7,545	855,256
Sīdī Bū Zayd	Sīdī Bū Zayd	2,700	6,994	395,506
Siliānah	Siliānah	1,788	4,631	233,985
Sūsah	Sūsah	1,012	2,621	544,413
Tatāuīn	Tatāuīn	15,015	38,889	143,524
Tawzar	Tawzar	1,822	4,719	97,526
Tūnis	Tunis (Tūnis)	134	346	983,861
Zaghwān	Zaghwān	1,069	2,768	160,963
TOTAL		63,170[3]	163,610[3]	9,910,872

Demography

Population (2005): 10,038,000.
Density (2005): persons per sq mi 158.9, persons per sq km 61.4.
Urban-rural (2004): urban 64.9%; rural 35.1%.
Sex distribution (2004): male 50.10%; female 49.90%.
Age breakdown (2004): under 15, 26.0%; 15–29, 29.9%; 30–44, 22.7%; 45–59, 12.2%; 60–74, 7.0%; 75 and over, 2.2%.
Population projection: (2010) 10,544,000; (2020) 11,509,000.
Doubling time: 66 years.
Ethnic composition (2000): Tunisian Arab 67.2%; Bedouin Arab 26.6%; Algerian Arab 2.4%; Berber 1.4%; other 2.4%.
Religious affiliation (2000): Sunnī Muslim 98.9%; Christian 0.5%; other 0.6%.
Major cities (2004): Tunis 728,453 (urban agglomeration [2003] 1,996,000); Ṣafāqis 265,131; Al-Ariānah 240,749[4]; Sūsah 173,047; Ettadhamen 118,487[4].

Vital statistics

Birth rate per 1,000 population (2004): 15.7 (world avg. 21.1).
Death rate per 1,000 population (2004): 5.1 (world avg. 9.0).
Natural increase rate per 1,000 population (2004): 10.6 (world avg. 12.1).
Total fertility rate (avg. births per childbearing woman; 2004): 1.8.
Marriage rate per 1,000 population (2001): 6.4.
Divorce rate per 1,000 population (1999): 0.1.
Life expectancy at birth (2004): male 73.0 years; female 76.4 years.
Major causes of death per 100,000 population (2002): cardiovascular diseases 267; accidents, injuries, and violence 62; malignant neoplasms (cancers) 57.

National economy

Budget (2002). Revenue: D 11,533,000,000 (tax revenue 91.5%, of which goods and services 34.4%, income tax 22.1%, social security 18.9%, import duties 9.9%; nontax revenue 8.5%). Expenditures: D 11,533,000,000 (current expenditure 79.8%, of which interest on public debt 8.5%; development expenditure 20.2%).
Production (metric tons except as noted). Agriculture, forestry, fishing (2004): wheat 1,719,000, olives 1,400,000, tomatoes 970,000, barley 618,000, potatoes 375,000, onions 355,000, grapes 127,000, dates 122,000, apples 121,000; livestock (live animals) 6,850,000 sheep, 1,400,000 goats, 760,000 cattle, 231,000 camels; roundwood 2,351,308 cu m; fish catch 109,600. Mining and quarrying: phosphate rock 8,051,000; iron ore 244,000; zinc (metal content) 29,011. Manufacturing (value added in U.S.$'000,000; 2002): wearing apparel 887; food products 514; chemicals and chemical products 386; electrical machinery 280; refined petroleum (2001) 277; textiles 251. Energy production (consumption): electricity (kW-hr; 2004) 12,455,000,000 (10,854,000,000); coal (metric tons; 2002) none (1,000); crude petroleum (barrels; 2004) 26,000,000 ([2002] 14,000,000); petroleum products (metric tons; 2004) 1,791,000 (3,091,000); natural gas (cu m; 2004) 2,299,000,000 (3,521,000,000).
Household income and expenditure (2000). Average household size (2002) 4.7; income per household D 6,450 (U.S.$4,640); expenditure: food and beverages 38.0%, housing and energy 21.5%, household durables 11.1%, health and personal care 10.0%, transportation 9.7%, recreation 8.7%, other 1.0%.

Gross national product (2004): U.S.$26,301,000,000 (U.S.$2,630 per capita).

Structure of gross domestic product and labour force

	2004 in value D '000	2004 % of total value	2002 labour force	2002 % of labour force
Agriculture	4,418,300	12.6	709,000	21.0
Mining	213,900	0.6		
Public utilities	1,507,200	4.3	1,144,400	33.9
Manufacturing	6,237,300	17.8		
Construction	1,786,300	5.1		
Transp. and commun.	3,201,200	9.1		
Trade	9,552,200	27.2	1,522,300	45.1
Finance				
Pub. admin., defense	4,670,200	13.3		
Services	132,200	0.4		
Other	3,385,200[5]	9.6[5]	...	...
TOTAL	35,104,000	100.0	3,375,700	100.0

Population economically active (2003): total 3,460,500; activity rate of total population *c.* 35% (participation rates: age 15 and over 48.2%; female 25.5%; unemployed [2004] 13.9%).

Price and earnings indexes (2000 = 100)

	1998	1999	2000	2001	2002	2003	2004
Consumer price index	94.6	97.2	100.0	102.0	104.8	107.6	111.5
Hourly earnings index[6]	92.8	97.0	100.0	104.2	107.7	111.9	...

Public debt (external, outstanding; 2004): U.S.$13,516,000,000.
Tourism (2004): receipts U.S.$1,838,600,000; expenditures U.S.$300,000,000.
Land use as % of total land area (2000): in temporary crops 18.4%, in permanent crops 13.7%, in pasture 26.3%; overall forest area 3.1%.

Foreign trade[7]

Balance of trade (current prices)

	1999	2000	2001	2002	2003	2004
D '000,000	−3,104	−3,733	−4,161	−3,762	−3,696	−3,910
% of total	18.2%	18.9%	17.9%	16.2%	15.2%	14.0%

Imports (2004): D 15,965,100,000 (textiles 18.8%, electrical machinery 11.9%, crude and refined petroleum 9.6%, motor vehicles 7.3%, iron and steel 6.0%, food products 5.2%). *Major import sources:* France 24.9%; Italy 18.9%; Germany 8.4%; Spain 5.3%; Libya 3.3%.
Exports (2004): D 12,054,900,000 (textiles 37.2%, electrical machinery 13.9%, crude and refined petroleum 9.5%, olive oil 5.9%, leather products 5.2%, phosphates and phosphate derivatives 4.9%). *Major export destinations:* France 33.1%; Italy 25.3%; Germany 9.2%; Spain 6.1%; Libya 3.6%.

Transport and communications

Transport. Railroads (2004): route length 2,153 km; passenger-km 1,294,000,000; metric ton-km cargo 2,081,000,000. Roads (2001): total length 18,997 km (paved 65%). Vehicles (2002): passenger cars 585,194; trucks and buses 278,680. Air transport (2004)[8]: passenger-km 2,919,000,000; metric ton-km cargo 20,312,000; airports (1998) 5.

Communications

Medium	date	unit	number	units per 1,000 persons
Daily newspapers	2000	circulation	180,000	19
Radio	1997	receivers	2,060,000	224
Television	2003	receivers	2,036,800	207
Telephones	2004	main lines	1,203,500	121
Cellular telephones	2004	subscribers	3,735,700	376
Personal computers	2004	units	472,000	47
Internet	2004	users	835,000	84

Education and health

Educational attainment (2004). Percentage of population age 10 and over having: no formal schooling 23.1%; primary education 37.0%; secondary 32.0%; higher 7.9%. *Literacy* (2004): total population age 10 and over literate 77.1%; males literate 85.2%; females literate 69.0%.

Education (2004–05)

	schools	teachers	students	student/ teacher ratio
Primary (age 6–11)	4,552	59,252	1,184,301	20.0
Secondary (age 12–18)	1,459	67,503	1,136,657	16.8
Higher	175	16,671	311,569	18.7

Health (2004): physicians (2003) 8,189 (1 per 1,202 persons); hospital beds 17,269 (1 per 576 persons); infant mortality rate per 1,000 live births 25.8.
Food (2002): daily per capita caloric intake 3,238 (vegetable products 89%, animal products 11%); 135% of FAO recommended minimum requirement.

Military

Total active duty personnel (2004): 35,000 (army 77.1%, navy 12.9%, air force 10.0%). *Military expenditure as percentage of GDP* (2003): 1.6%; per capita expenditure U.S.$41.

[1]A single party dominates the political system in practice. [2]Statutory number; 41 seats are nonelective. [3]Total includes 3,506 sq mi (9,080 sq km) of saline lakes that are not distributed by governorate. [4]Within Tunis urban agglomeration. [5]Indirect taxes less subsidies and less imputed bank service charges. [6]Minimum wage for 40-hour workweek. [7]Imports c.i.f.; exports f.o.b. [8]Tunis Air only.

Internet resources for further information:
• **Central Bank of Tunisia** http://www.bct.gov.tn/english/index.html
• **National Statistics Institute (French only)** http://www.ins.nat.tn

Turkey

Official name: Türkiye Cumhuriyeti (Republic of Turkey).
Form of government: multiparty republic with one legislative house (Turkish Grand National Assembly [550]).
Chief of state: President.
Head of government: Prime Minister.
Capital: Ankara.
Official language: Turkish.
Official religion: none.
Monetary unit: 1 New Turkish lira (YTL)[1] = 100 kurush; valuation (Sept. 1, 2005) 1 U.S.$ = YTL 1.34; 1 £ = YTL 2.46.

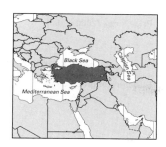

Area and population

Geographic regions[2]	Largest cities	area sq mi	area sq km	population 2004 estimate
Aegean	İzmir	34,748	89,997	9,393,000
Black Sea	Samsun	44,881	116,240	8,417,000
Central Anatolia	Ankara	72,607	188,052	12,174,000
East Anatolia	Malatya	57,876	149,899	6,402,000
Marmara	Istanbul	28,196	73,028	18,929,000
Mediterranean	Adana	34,687	89,838	9,321,000
South Eastern Anatolia	Gaziantep	29,540	76,509	7,158,000
TOTAL		302,535	783,562[3]	71,789,000[3]

Demography

Population (2005): 72,083,000.
Density (2005): persons per sq mi 238.3, persons per sq km 92.0.
Urban-rural (2004): urban 61.2%; rural 38.8%.
Sex distribution (2004): male 50.45%; female 49.55%.
Age breakdown (2004): under 15, 29.2%; 15–29, 27.5%; 30–44, 21.7%; 45–59, 13.3%; 60–74, 6.7%; 75 and over, 1.6%.
Population projection: (2010) 76,926,000; (2020) 85,490,000.
Doubling time: 52 years.
Ethnic composition (2000): Turk 65.1%; Kurd 18.9%; Crimean Tatar 7.2%; Arab 1.8%; Azerbaijani 1.0%; Yoruk 1.0%; other 5.0%.
Religious affiliation (2000): Muslim 97.2%, of which Sunnī c. 67%, Shīʿī c. 30% (including nonorthodox Alevi c. 26%); Christian (mostly Eastern Orthodox) 0.6%; other 2.2%.
Major urban agglomerations (2001): Istanbul 10,243,000; Ankara 4,611,000; İzmir 3,437,000; Bursa (2000) 1,166,000; Adana (2000) 1,091,000.

Vital statistics

Birth rate per 1,000 population (2004): 20.6 (world avg. 21.1).
Death rate per 1,000 population (2004): 7.1 (world avg. 9.0).
Natural increase rate per 1,000 population (2004): 13.5 (world avg. 12.1).
Total fertility rate (avg. births per childbearing woman; 2004): 2.4.
Marriage rate per 1,000 population (2003): 6.8.
Divorce rate per 1,000 population (2003): 0.7.
Life expectancy at birth (2004): male 66.6 years; female 71.2 years.
Major causes of death per 100,000 population (2003)[4]: diseases of the circulatory system 340; malignant neoplasms (cancers) 91; accidents and violence 24; infectious and parasitic diseases 21; ill-defined conditions 68.

National economy

Budget (2003). Revenue: TL 100,238,122,000,000,000 (tax revenue 84.1%, of which tax on income 27.7%; nontax revenue 14.0%; grants 1.9%). Expenditures: TL 140,053,981,000,000,000 (interest payments 41.8%; personnel 21.6%; investments 5.1%).
Production (in '000 metric tons except as noted). Agriculture, forestry, fishing (2004): wheat 21,000, sugar beets 13,965, barley 9,000, tomatoes 8,000, potatoes 4,800, watermelons 4,300, grapes 3,600, corn (maize) 3,000, seed cotton 2,570, apples 2,300, olives 1,800, cucumbers 1,780, oranges 1,280, eggplants 935, chickpeas 650, lentils 560, hazelnuts 425, peaches 370, apricots 300, figs 280, cherries 265, tobacco 160, tea 154, garlic 125, attar of roses (1993) 800 kg; livestock (number of live animals) 25,000,000 sheep, 9,800,000 cattle, (2003) 256,000 angora goats; roundwood 15,810,000 cu m; fish catch (2003) 508. Mining (2003): refined borates 436; chromite 282; copper ore (metal content) 45. Manufacturing (value added in U.S.$'000,000; 2000): textiles 16,289; refined petroleum 4,839; food products 4,111; chemicals and chemical products 3,805; motor vehicles 2,177; nonelectrical machinery 2,020. Energy production (consumption): electricity (kW-hr; 2004) 149,184,000,000 ([2002] 132,553,000,000); hard coal (metric tons; 2004) 2,840,000 ([2002] 13,800,000); lignite (metric tons; 2004) 39,300,000 ([2002] 51,500,000); crude petroleum (barrels; 2004) 16,300,000 ([2002] 191,000,000); petroleum products (metric tons; 2002) 22,430,000 (25,672,000); natural gas (cu m; 2002) 389,000,000 (17,567,000,000).
Tourism (2003): receipts from visitors U.S.$13,203,000,000; expenditures by nationals abroad U.S.$2,113,000,000.
Population economically active (2004): total[5] 24,457,000; activity rate of total population[5] 34.1% (participation rates: over age 14[5], 49.2%; female[5] 26.6%; unemployed 10.3%).

Price and earnings indexes (2000 = 100)

	1998	1999	2000	2001	2002	2003	2004
Consumer price index	39.2	64.6	100.0	154.4	223.8	280.4	304.6
Annual earnings index	...	...	...	...	...	...	...

Gross national product (2004): U.S.$268,741,000,000 (U.S.$3,750 per capita).

Structure of gross domestic product and labour force

	2003–04 in value YTL '000	2003–04 % of total value	2003 labour force	2003 % of labour force
Agriculture	46,192,181	11.4	7,165,000	30.3
Mining	4,714,194	1.2	83,000	0.4
Manufacturing	82,854,031	20.4	3,664,000	15.5
Construction	14,043,042	3.5	965,000	4.1
Public utilities	14,003,577	3.5	100,000	0.4
Transp. and commun.	58,529,894	14.4	1,022,000	4.3
Trade	83,091,418	20.5	4,052,000	17.1
Finance, real estate	19,075,356	4.7	738,000	3.1
Pub. admin., defense	40,882,526	10.1	1,177,000	5.0
Services	34,823,354	8.6	2,181,000	9.2
Other	7,615,993[6]	1.9[6]	2,496,000[7]	10.6[7]
TOTAL	405,825,566	100.0[3]	23,641,000[3]	100.0

Public debt (external, outstanding; 2003): U.S.$64,758,000,000.
Household income and expenditure (1994). Average household size (2002) 4.5; income per household TL 165,089,000 (U.S.$5,576); expenditure: food, tobacco, and café expenditures 38.5%, housing 22.8%, clothing 9.0%.
Land use as % of total land area (2000): in temporary crops 31.4%, in permanent crops 3.3%, in pasture 16.1%; overall forest area 13.3%.

Foreign trade[8]

Balance of trade (current prices)

	1999	2000	2001	2002	2003	2004
U.S.$'000,000	−14,084	−26,782	−10,065	−15,450	−21,856	−34,324
% of total	20.9%	32.5%	13.8%	17.8%	18.9%	21.4%

Imports (2003): U.S.$68,734,000,000 (chemicals and chemical products 16.2%; nonelectrical machinery 11.9%; crude petroleum and natural gas 11.3%; motor vehicles 9.3%; electrical machinery 9.1%; iron and steel 6.8%). *Major import sources:* Germany 13.7%; Italy 7.9%; Russia 7.9%; France 6.0%; U.S. 5.0%; U.K. 5.0%.
Exports (2003): U.S.$46,878,000,000 (textiles, apparel, and clothing accessories 20.3%; vehicles 11.2%; electrical and electronic machinery 7.4%; nonelectrical machinery 6.3%; iron and steel 6.2%; raw and prepared fruits and vegetables 5.3%). *Major export destinations:* Germany 15.9%; U.S. 8.0%; U.K. 7.8%; Italy 6.8%; France 6.0%.

Transport and communications

Transport. Railroads (2003): length 5,388 mi, 8,671 km; passenger-km 5,893,000,000; metric ton-km cargo 8,271,000,000. Roads (2002): total length 220,267 mi, 354,421 km (paved 42%). Vehicles (2003): passenger cars 4,677,765; trucks and buses 1,713,605. Air transport (2004)[9]: passenger-km 18,594,000,000; metric ton-km cargo 394,317,000; airports (1996) 26.

Communications

Medium	date	unit	number	units per 1,000 persons
Daily newspapers	2000	circulation	7,480,000	111
Radio	2001	receivers	32,195,000	470
Television	2002	receivers	29,440,000	423
Telephones	2004	main lines	19,125,000	265
Cellular telephones	2004	subscribers	34,707,500	480
Personal computers	2004	units	3,703,000	51
Internet	2004	users	10,220,000	141

Education and health

Educational attainment (2002). Percentage of population age 25–64 having: no formal schooling through lower-secondary education 75%; upper secondary/higher vocational 16%; university 9%. *Literacy* (2003): total population age 15 and over literate 88.3%; males literate 95.3%; females literate 79.9%.

Education (2000)

	schools	teachers	students	student/ teacher ratio
Primary (age 6–10)	36,072	345,015	10,480,700	30.4
Secondary (age 11–16)	2,747	73,418	1,487,400	20.3
Voc., teacher tr.	3,544	71,665	875,200	12.2
Higher	1,273	67,880	1,607,400	23.7

Health: physicians (2002) 95,190 (1 per 721 persons); hospital beds (2003) 180,797 (1 per 391 persons); infant mortality rate (2004) 37.4.
Food (2002): daily per capita caloric intake 3,357 (vegetable products 91%, animal products 9%); 133% of FAO recommended minimum requirement.

Military

Total active duty personnel (2004): 514,850 (army 78.1%, navy 10.2%, air force 11.7%)[10]. *Military expenditure as percentage of GDP* (2003): 4.9%; per capita expenditure U.S.$146.

---

[1]New Turkish lira (YTL) introduced Jan. 1, 2005; 1 YTL = TL 1,000,000. [2]Administratively divided into 81 provinces as of 2004. [3]Detail does not add to total given because of rounding. [4]Projected rates based on about 37% of total deaths. [5]Second quarter; civilian population only. [6]Import duties less imputed bank service charges. [7]Includes 2,493,000 unemployed. [8]Imports c.i.f.; exports f.o.b. [9]Turkish Airlines only. [10]Turkish troops in Turkish Republic of Northern Cyprus (August 2004) 36,000.

Internet resources for further information:
• **Ministry of Foreign Affairs** http://www.mfa.gov.tr
• **Central Bank of Turkey** http://www.tcmb.gov.tr
• **State Institute of Statistics** http://www.die.gov.tr

Turkmenistan

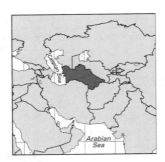

Official name: Türkmenistan (Turkmenistan).
Form of government: unitary single-party republic with one legislative body (Majlis [Parliament; 50]).
Head of state and government: President assisted by the People's Council[1].
Capital: Ashgabat (formerly Ashkhabad).
Official language: Turkmen.
Official religion: none.
Monetary unit: manat; valuation (Sept. 1, 2005) 1 U.S.$ = 5,148 manat; 1 £ = 9,479 manat.

Area and population

Provinces	Capitals	area sq mi	area sq km	population 2001 estimate
Ahal	Ashgabat	37,500[2]	97,100[2]	767,700
Balkan	Balkanabat	53,500	138,600	468,900
Daşoguz	Daşoguz	28,100	72,700	1,165,000
Lebap	Türkmenabat (Chärjew)	36,000	93,200	1,130,700
Mary	Mary	33,400	86,400	1,251,300
City				
Ashgabat	—	[2]	[2]	695,300
TOTAL		188,500	488,100[3]	5,478,900

Demography

Population (2005): 4,833,000[4].
Density (2005): persons per sq mi 25.6, persons per sq km 9.9.
Urban-rural (2003): urban 45.3%; rural 54.7%.
Sex distribution (2001): male 49.44%; female 50.56%.
Age breakdown (2001): under 15, 37.9%; 15–29, 27.9%; 30–44, 23.7%; 45–59, 6.5%; 60–74, 3.5%; 75 and over, 0.5%.
Population projection[4]: (2010) 5,163,000; (2020) 5,811,000.
Doubling time: 37 years.
Ethnic composition (2000): Turkmen 79.2%; Uzbek 9.0%; Russian 3.0%; Kazakh 2.5%; Tatar 1.1%; other 5.2%.
Religious affiliation (2000): Muslim (mostly Sunnī) 87.2%; Russian Orthodox 1.7%; nonreligious 9.0%; other 2.1%.
Major cities (1999): Ashgabat (2002) 743,000; Türkmenabat 203,000; Daşoguz 165,000; Mary 123,000; Balkanabat 108,000.

Vital statistics

Birth rate per 1,000 population (2004): 27.8 (world avg. 21.1); (1998) legitimate 96.2%; illegitimate 3.8%.
Death rate per 1,000 population (2004): 8.8 (world avg. 9.0).
Natural increase rate per 1,000 population (2004): 19.0 (world avg. 12.1).
Total fertility rate (avg. births per childbearing woman; 2004): 3.5.
Marriage rate per 1,000 population (1998): 5.4.
Divorce rate per 1,000 population (1994): 1.5.
Life expectancy at birth (2004): male 57.9 years; female 64.9 years.
Major causes of death per 100,000 population (1998): diseases of the circulatory system 314.6; diseases of the respiratory system 101.1; infectious and parasitic diseases 99.1; accidents, poisoning, and violence 59.3; malignant neoplasms (cancers) 43.9; diseases of the digestive system 30.2.

National economy

Budget (1999)[5]. Revenue: 3,693,100,000,000 manat (value-added tax 25.6%, pension and social security fund 22.5%, repayments of scheduled gas 13.0%, excise tax 10.2%, personal income tax 6.1%). Expenditures: 3,894,300,000,000 manat (education 26.9%, pension and social security 15.6%, defense and security 14.9%, health 14.1%, agriculture 5.7%).
Public debt (external, outstanding; 2001): between U.S.$2,400,000,000 and U.S.$5,000,000,000.
Production (metric tons except as noted). Agriculture, forestry, fishing (2004): wheat 2,600,000, seed cotton 2,200,000, tomatoes 250,000, watermelons 230,000, grapes 180,000; livestock (number of live animals) 13,150,000 sheep, 2,000,000 cattle, 750,000 goats, 7,000,000 chickens; roundwood 3,400 cu m; fish catch (2003) 14,543. Mining and quarrying (2002): iodine 200,000, gypsum 100,000, sodium sulfate 60,000, sulfur 9,000. Manufacturing (2003): residual fuel oils (1998) 2,214; distillate fuel (gas-diesel oil) 1,750; motor spirits (1998) 693; wheat flour 503; cement 239; nitrogenous fertilizers 103. Energy production (consumption): electricity (kW-hr; 2004) 11,410,000,000 ([2002] 10,190,000,000); crude petroleum (barrels; 2002) 68,900,000 (48,300,000); petroleum products (metric tons; 2002) 5,984,000 (3,293,000); natural gas (cu m; 2004) 58,570,000,000 ([2002] 14,421,000,000).
Household income and expenditure. Average household size (2002) 5.7; income per household: n.a.; sources of income (1998): wages and salaries 70.6%, pensions and grants 20.9%, self-employment (mainly agricultural income) 2.3%, nonwage income of workers 1.1%; expenditure (1998): food 45.2%, clothing and footwear 16.8%, furniture 13.3%, transportation 7.6%, health 7.0%.
Tourism: receipts from visitors (1998) U.S.$192,000,000; expenditures (1997) U.S.$125,000,000.
Population economically active (2000): total 1,950,000; activity rate of total population 42.0% (participation rates [1996]: ages 16–59 [male], 16–54 [female] 73.0%; female 42.7%; unemployed [2003] 2.6%).

Price index (2000 = 100)

	1997	1998	1999	2000	2001	2002	2003
Consumer price index	64.2	75.0	92.6	100.0	111.6	121.4	128.2

Gross national product (2004): U.S.$6,615,000,000 (U.S.$1,340 per capita).

Structure of gross domestic product and labour force

	2001 in value '000,000 manat	2001 % of total value	1998 labour force	1998 % of labour force
Agriculture	8,327,600	23.5	892,400	48.5
Mining	}	}	226,800	12.3
Manufacturing	12,996,700	36.7	48,300	2.6
Public utilities	}	}		
Construction	2,136,800	6.0	108,200	5.9
Transp. and commun.	1,919,200	5.4	90,700	4.9
Trade	2,363,900	6.7	115,800	6.4
Finance	422,000	1.2	12,600	0.7
Public administration, defense	912,800	2.6	28,800	1.6
Services	}	}	284,900	15.5
Other	6,333,800	17.9	30,200	1.6
TOTAL	35,412,800	100.0	1,838,700	100.0

Land use as % of total land area (2000): in temporary crops 3.7%, in permanent crops 0.1%, in pasture 65.3%; overall forest area 8.0%.

Foreign trade[6]

Balance of trade (current prices)

	1998	1999	2000	2001	2002	2003
U.S.$'000,000	−414	−291	+721	+271	+737	+1,270
% of total	25.8%	10.9%	16.8%	5.5%	14.8%	20.6%

Imports (2003): U.S.$2,450,000,000 (machinery and transport equipment 45.9%, basic manufactures 19.9%, chemicals and chemical products 11.1%, food products 5.3%). *Major import sources* (2004): Russia 14%; Ukraine 14%; U.S. 11%; U.A.E. 8%; Turkey 8%; Germany 7%.
Exports (2003): U.S.$3,720,000,000 (natural gas 49.7%, petrochemicals 18.3%, crude petroleum 8.9%, cotton fibre 3.2%, cotton yarn 2.2%). *Major export destinations* (2004): Ukraine 50%; Iran 17%; Italy 5%; Turkey 5%; U.A.E. 3%.

Transport and communications

Transport. Railroads (2004): length 1,516 mi, 2,440 km; (1999) passenger-km 701,000,000; (1999) metric ton-km cargo 7,337,000,000. Roads (2001): total length 22,000 km (paved 82%). Vehicles (1995): passenger cars 220,000; trucks and buses 58,200. Air transport (2001)[7]: passenger-km 1,631,000,000; metric ton-km cargo 35,000,000; airports (2002) with scheduled flights 1.

Communications

Medium	date	unit	number	units per 1,000 persons
Radio	2000	receivers	1,190,000	256
Television	2003	receivers	855,000	182
Telephones	2003	main lines	376,100	77
Cellular phones	2002	subscribers	8,200	1.7
Internet	2004	users	36,000	7.3

Education and health

Educational attainment: n.a. *Literacy* (2002): total population age 15 and over literate 98.8%; males literate 99.3%; females literate 98.3%.

Education (1994–95)

	schools	teachers	students	student/ teacher ratio
Primary (age 6–13)	}			
Secondary (age 14–17)	1,900	72,900	940,600	12.9
Voc., teacher tr.	78	…	26,000	…
Higher	15	…	29,435[8]	…

Health: physicians (1998) 12,691 (1 per 345 persons); hospital beds (1995) 46,000 (1 per 97 persons); infant mortality rate per 1,000 live births (2004) 73.1.
Food (2002): daily per capita caloric intake 2,742 (vegetable products 85%, animal products 15%); 107% of FAO recommended minimum requirement.

Military

Total active duty personnel (2004): 26,000 (army 80.8%, navy 2.7%, air force 16.5%). *Military expenditure as percentage of GDP* (2003): 1.2%; per capita expenditure U.S.$74.

---

[1]Hybrid body with a number of legislative powers that is a branch of state power per August 2003 constitutional amendment. [2]Ahal includes Ashgabat. [3]Detail does not add to total given because of rounding. [4]Estimate of *UN World Population Prospects (2004 revision);* official Turkmen estimates are significantly higher. [5]Budget statistics are unreliable because the government spends large amounts of extra-budgetary funds. [6]Import data in balance of trade is c.i.f. [7]Turkmenavia only. [8]1995–96.

Internet resources for further information:
• **Interstate Statistical Committee of the Commonwealth of Independent States** http://www.cisstat.com/eng/macro0.htm
• **Asia Development Bank: Turkmenistan** http://www.adb.org/Turkmenistan/default.asp

Tuvalu

Official name: Tuvalu.
Form of government: constitutional monarchy with one legislative house (Parliament [15]).
Chief of state: British Monarch, represented by Governor-General.
Head of government: Prime Minister.
Capital: government offices are at Vaiaku, Fongafale islet, of Funafuti atoll.
Official language: none.
Official religion: none.
Monetary units[1]: 1 Tuvalu dollar = 1 Australian dollar ($T = $A) = 100 Tuvalu and Australian cents; valuation (Sept. 1, 2005) 1 U.S.$ = $A 1.31; 1 £ = $A 2.41.

Pacific Ocean

Area and population

Islands[2]	Capitals	area sq mi	area sq km	population 2002 census
Funafuti	Fongafale	1.08	2.79	4,492
Nanumaga	Tonga	1.07	2.78	589
Nanumea	Lolua	1.49	3.87	664
Niulakita	—	0.16	0.42	35
Niutao	Kua	0.98	2.53	663
Nui	Tanrake	1.09	2.83	548
Nukufetau	Savave	1.15	2.99	586
Nukulaelae	Fangaua	0.70	1.82	393
Vaitupu	Asau	2.16	5.60	1,591
TOTAL		9.90[3, 4]	25.63[3]	9,561

Demography

Population (2005): 9,700.
Density (2005): persons per sq mi 979.8, persons per sq km 378.9.
Urban-rural (2004): urban 55.2%; rural 44.8%.
Sex distribution (2002): male 49.46%; female 50.54%.
Age breakdown (2002): under 15, 36.2%; 15–29, 21.2%; 30–44, 20.2%; 45–59, 13.8%; 60–74, 6.8%; 75 and over, 1.8%.
Population projection: (2010) 11,000; (2020) 12,000.
Doubling time: 49 years.
Ethnic composition (2000): Tuvaluan (Polynesian) 96.3%; mixed (Pacific Islander/European/Asian) 1.0%; Micronesian 1.0%; European 0.5%; other 1.2%.
Religious affiliation (1995): Church of Tuvalu (Congregational) 85.4%; Seventh-day Adventist 3.6%; Roman Catholic 1.4%; Jehovah's Witness 1.1%; Bahā'ī 1.0%; other 7.5%.
Major locality (2002): Fongafale islet of Funafuti atoll 4,492.

Vital statistics

Birth rate per 1,000 population (2004): 21.6 (world avg. 21.1); (2003) legitimate 91.9%; illegitimate 8.1%.
Death rate per 1,000 population (2004): 7.2 (world avg. 9.0).
Natural increase rate per 1,000 population (2004): 14.4 (world avg. 12.1).
Total fertility rate (avg. births per childbearing woman; 2004): 3.0.
Life expectancy at birth (2004): male 65.5 years; female 70.0 years.
Number of deaths (2002): diseases of the circulatory system 35, of which ischemic heart diseases 11, cerebrovascular diseases 11; malignant neoplasms (cancers) 9; injuries 7; diseases of the respiratory system 7.

National economy

Budget (2004). Revenue: $A 20,679,618 (direct taxes 27.9%, indirect taxes 2.8%, other 69.3%). Expenditures: $A 21,093,370.
Public debt (external; 2002): U.S.$5,000,000.
Gross national product (2004): U.S.$21,800,000 (U.S.$2,100 per capita).

Structure of gross domestic product and labour force

	2002 in value $A '000	2002 % of total value	1991 labour force	1991 % of labour force
Agriculture, fishing, forestry	4,565	16.9	4,020	68.0
Mining	237	0.9	—	—
Manufacturing	1,016	3.8	60	1.0
Construction	1,370	5.1	240	4.0
Public utilities	1,433	5.3	—	—
Transp. and commun.	3,429	12.7	60	1.0
Trade, hotels, and restaurants	3,700	13.7	240	4.0
Finance	4,055	15.0	—	—
Pub. admin., defense	7,188	26.7	} 1,290	22.0
Services	1,794	6.7		
Other	–1,841[5]	–6.8[5]	...	...
TOTAL	26,945[4]	100.0	5,910	100.0

Production (metric tons except as noted). Agriculture[6], forestry, fishing (2004): coconuts 1,600, vegetables 530, tropical fruit 465, bananas 270, roots and tubers 140, other agricultural products include breadfruit, pulaka (taro), pandanus fruit, sweet potatoes, and pawpaws; livestock (number of live animals) 13,500 pigs, 15,000 ducks, 45,000 chickens; roundwood, n.a.; fish catch (2003) 1,500. Mining and quarrying: n.a. Manufacturing: tiny amounts of copra, handicrafts, and garments. Overseas employment (2000) of Tuvaluan seafarers contributes about U.S.$5,000,000 annually to the Tuvalu economy.

Energy production (consumption): electricity (kW-hr; 1995) 3,000,000 (n.a.); coal, none (none); crude petroleum, none (none); petroleum products, none (none); natural gas, none (none).
Tourism (1998): receipts from visitors U.S.$200,000; expenditures by nationals abroad, n.a.
Population economically active (2002): total 3,237[7]; activity rate of total population 33.9% (participation rates: ages 15 and over, 53.0%; female 42.4%; unemployed 6.5%).

Price index (2000 = 100)

	1998	1999	2000	2001	2002	2003	2004
Consumer price index	112.4	96.2	100.0	101.5	106.7	110.2	113.3

Household income and expenditure (1994). Average household size (2002): 6.1; average annual net income per household: $A 5,527 (U.S.$4,044); sources of income: cash economy only 47.0%, agriculture and other 31.7%, overseas remittances 21.3%; expenditure: food and nonalcoholic beverages 48.7%, housing and household operations 11.5%, energy 8.9%, transportation 8.2%, recreation 5.8%, alcohol and tobacco 4.8%, household furnishings 4.3%.
Land use as % of total land area (2000): in temporary crops, n.a., in permanent crops, n.a., in pasture, n.a.; overall forest area, n.a.[8]

Foreign trade

Balance of trade (current prices)

	1998	1999	2000	2001	2002	2003
$A '000	–15,495	–12,289	–8,866	–6,737	–20,110	–23,896
% of total	96.8%	97.2%	99.6%	99.1%	97.6%	98.8%

Imports (2003): $A 24,043,441 (food products including live animals 23.2%, machinery and apparatus 15.9%, mineral fuels 12.9%, transport equipment 10.2%, base and fabricated metals 6.7%). *Major import sources:* Australia 36.2%; Fiji 32.4%; New Zealand 12.0%; Japan 6.6%; China 3.5%.
Exports (2003): $A 147,000 (primarily copra, stamps, and handicrafts). *Major export destinations* (2002): Fiji 58.9%; Australia 22.3%; New Zealand 11.4%; Japan 5.7%.

Transport and communications

Transport. Railroads: none. Roads (2000): total length 28 km (paved, none). Vehicles (2003): passenger cars 102; trucks and buses 33. Air transport: n.a.; airports (2001) 1.

Communications

Medium	date	unit	number	units per 1,000 persons
Radio	2002	receivers	14,970	1,568
Television	1996	receivers	100	13
Telephones	2003	main lines	3,350	350
Internet	2002	users	1,250	131

Education and health

Educational attainment (2002). Percentage of population age 15 and over having: no formal education through incomplete primary education 22.2%; primary 54.3%; secondary 14.2%; higher 9.3%. *Literacy* (2002): total population literate 92%.

Education (2004)

	schools	teachers	students	student/ teacher ratio
Primary (age 5–11)	9[9]	84	2,010	23.9
Secondary (age 12–18)	2	52	629	12.1
Vocational	1	...	60[9]	...
Higher[10]	1	...	270	...

Health (2003): physicians 4 (1 per 2,393 persons); hospital beds (2001) 56 (1 per 170 persons); infant mortality rate per 1,000 live births (2004) 20.7.

Military

Total active duty personnel (2004): none; Tuvalu has nonformal security arrangements with Australia and New Zealand.

[1]The value of the Tuvalu dollar is pegged to the value of the Australian dollar, which is also legal currency in Tuvalu. [2]Local government councils have been established on all islands except Niulakita. [3]Another survey puts the area at 9.4 sq mi (24.4 sq km). [4]Detail does not add to total given because of rounding. [5]Indirect taxes less subsidies and less imputed bank service charges. [6]Because of poor soil quality, only limited subsistence agriculture is possible on the islands. [7]Total number of wage earners, unpaid workers, and subsistence workers. [8]Coconut trees occupy c. 77% of land area. [9]2000. [10]University of the South Pacific Tuvalu campus.

Internet resources for further information:
• **United Nations Development Programme, Common Country Assessments**
   http://www.undp.org.fj/CCAs.htm
• **Secretariat of Pacific Community**
   http://www.spc.int/prism/country/tv/tv_index.html

Uganda

Indian Ocean

Official name: Republic of Uganda.
Form of government: nonparty republic with one legislative house (Parliament [305[1]]).
Head of state and government: President.
Capital: Kampala.
Official languages: English; Swahili[2].
Official religion: none.
Monetary unit: 1 Uganda shilling (U Sh) = 100 cents; valuation (Sept. 1, 2005) 1 U.S.$ = U Sh 1,834; 1 £ = U Sh 3,377.

Area and population

Geographic regions[3]	Principal cities	area sq mi	area sq km	population 2002 census[4]
Central	Kampala	23,749	61,510	6,683,887
Eastern	Jinja	15,426	39,953	6,301,677
Northern	Gulu	32,687	84,658	5,345,964
Western	Mbarara	21,204	54,917	6,417,449
TOTAL		93,065[5, 6]	241,038[5]	24,748,977

Demography

Population (2005): 27,269,000.
Density (2005)[7]: persons per sq mi 358.4, persons per sq km 138.4.
Urban-rural (2002): urban 12.3%; rural 87.7%.
Sex distribution (2002): male 48.81%; female 51.19%.
Age breakdown (2002): under 15, 49.3%; 15–29, 27.3%; 30–44, 13.4%; 45–59, 5.6%; 60–74, 3.3%; 75 and over, 1.1%.
Population projection: (2010) 32,500,000; (2020) 47,134,000.
Doubling time: 21 years.
Ethnolinguistic composition (2002): Ganda 17.3%; Nkole 9.8%; Soga 8.6%; Kiga 7.0%; Teso 6.6%; Lango 6.2%; Acholi 4.8%; Gisu 4.7%.
Religious affiliation (2002): Christian 85.3%, of which Roman Catholic 41.9%, Anglican 35.9%, Pentecostal 4.6%, Seventh-day Adventist 1.5%; Muslim 12.1%; traditional beliefs 1.0%; nonreligious 0.9%; other 0.7%.
Major cities (2002): Kampala 1,208,544[8]; Gulu 119,430; Lira 80,879; Jinja 71,213; Mbale 71,130.

Vital statistics

Birth rate per 1,000 population (2004): 47.5 (world avg. 21.1).
Death rate per 1,000 population (2004): 13.4 (world avg. 9.0).
Natural increase rate per 1,000 population (2004): 34.1 (world avg. 12.1).
Total fertility rate (avg. births per childbearing woman; 2004): 6.8.
Life expectancy at birth (2004): male 49.8 years; female 51.1 years.
Adult population (ages 15–49) *living with HIV* (2004[9]): 4.1% (world avg. 1.1%).

National economy

Budget (2001–02). Revenue: U Sh 1,977,500,000,000 (tax revenue 58.4%, of which VAT 19.9%, excise taxes 18.3%, income taxes 14.3%, tax on international trade 5.9%; grants 36.6%; nontax revenue 5.0%). Expenditures: U Sh 2,565,000,000,000 (current expenditures 55.8%, of which public administration 14.3%, education 14.1%, defense 8.2%, health 6.4%, public order 4.5%; capital expenditures 44.2%).
Production (metric tons except as noted). Agriculture, forestry, fishing (2004): plantains 9,900,000, cassava 5,500,000, sweet potatoes 2,650,000, sugarcane 1,600,000, corn (maize) 1,350,000, millet 700,000, potatoes 573,000, sorghum 420,000, coffee 186,000, rice 140,000, tea 36,000, tobacco 33,000; livestock (number of live animals) 7,700,000 goats, 6,100,000 cattle, 1,600,000 sheep, 1,300,000 pigs, 24,000,000 chickens; roundwood 39,409,604 cu m; fish catch (2003) 239,931. Mining and quarrying (2002): cobalt 436; columbite-tantalite (ore and concentrate) 4,200 kg. Manufacturing (2002): cement 506,000; sugar 168,000; soap 92,200; metal products (2001) 77,049; wheat flour 52,700; footwear 978,000 pairs; beer 989,000 hectolitres; soft drinks 956,000 hectolitres. Energy production (consumption): electricity (kW-hr; 2002) 1,675,000,000 (1,510,000,000); coal, none (none); crude petroleum, none (none); petroleum products (metric tons; 2002) none (470,000); natural gas, none (none).
Tourism (2003): receipts from visitors U.S.$189,000,000; expenditures by nationals abroad (1999) U.S.$141,000,000.
Gross national product (2004): U.S.$6,911,000,000 (U.S.$270 per capita).

Structure of gross domestic product and labour force

	2003–04 in value U Sh '000,000	2003–04 % of total value	2002 labour force	2002 % of labour force
Agriculture	4,009,330	30.3	9,493,000	79.1
Mining	92,240	0.7		
Manufacturing	1,090,129	8.2		
Construction	1,211,934	9.1		
Public utilities	166,087	1.3		
Transp. and commun.	835,955	6.3	2,502,000	20.9
Trade	1,711,644	12.9		
Pub. admin., defense	537,242	4.1		
Finance	2,466,898	18.6		
Services				
Other	1,120,201[10]	8.5[10]		
TOTAL	13,241,662[6]	100.0	11,995,000	100.0

Population economically active (2002): total 11,995,000; activity rate of total population 48.5% (participation rates [2001]: ages 15–64, 78.9%; female 35.2%; officially unemployed [2002–03] 3.2%).

Price index (2000 = 100)

	1998	1999	2000	2001	2002	2003	2004
Consumer price index	91.4	97.3	100.0	102.0	101.7	109.6	113.3

Public debt (external, outstanding; 2003): U.S.$4,168,000,000.
Household income and expenditure (1999–2000)[11]. Average household size (2002) 4.7; income per household U Sh 141,000 (U.S.$91[12]); sources of income: wages and self-employment 78.0%, transfers 13.0%, rent 9.0%; expenditure: food and beverages 51.0%, rent, energy, and services 17.0%, education 7.0%, household durable goods 6.0%, transportation 5.0%, health 4.0%.
Land use as % of total land area (2000): in temporary crops 25.7%, in permanent crops 10.7%, in pasture 25.9%; overall forest area 21.0%.

Foreign trade[13]

Balance of trade (current prices)

	1999–2000	2000–01	2001–02	2002–03	2003–04	2004–05
U.S.$'000,000	−462.2	−483.0	−529.8	−622.6	−674.0	−830.1
% of total	33.4%	34.5%	35.9%	38.0%	34.2%	34.1%

Imports (2004): U.S.$1,735,100,000 (machinery and transport equipment 28.4%, food, beverages, and tobacco products 15.9%, chemicals and chemical products 11.2%, refined petroleum 10.1%). *Major import sources:* Kenya 22.6%; South Africa 8.5%; Japan 7.1%; India 6.9%; China 5.8%; U.S. 5.6%.
Exports (2004): U.S.$654,800,000 (coffee 18.8%, fish and fish products 15.6%, gold 11.2%[14], tobacco 6.1%, cotton 6.0%, tea 5.4%). *Major export destinations:* EU 36.9%, of which The Netherlands 7.4%; African countries 34.4%, of which Kenya 9.8%; Switzerland 9.0%; U.A.E. 4.1%.

Transport and communications

Transport. Railroads (2000): route length 1,241 km; passenger-km[15]; metric ton-km cargo (2003) 212,616,000. Roads (2003): total length 70,746 km (paved 23%). Vehicles (2003): passenger cars 56,837; trucks and buses 85,222. Air transport (2001): passenger-km 235,000,000; metric ton-km cargo, n.a.; airports (2002) 1.

Communications

Medium	date	unit	number	units per 1,000 persons
Daily newspapers	2000	circulation	45,900	2.0
Radio	2000	receivers	2,920,000	127
Television	2002	receivers	442,800	18
Telephones	2004	main lines	71,600	2.7
Cellular telephones	2004	subscribers	1,165,000	44
Personal computers	2004	units	121,000	4.5
Internet	2004	users	200,000	7.5

Education and health

Educational attainment (2002). Percentage of population age 25 and over having: no formal schooling 34.4%; incomplete primary education 36.0%; complete primary 11.1%; incomplete secondary 12.0%; complete secondary (some higher) 1.8%; complete higher (incl. vocational) 4.7%. *Literacy* (2002): population age 10 and over literate 68%; males literate 76%; females literate 61%.

Education (2001)

	schools	teachers	students	student/ teacher ratio
Primary (age 5–11)	12,280	127,038	6,900,916	54.3
Secondary (age 12–15)	2,400	30,425	539,786	17.7
Voc., teacher tr.[16, 17]	...	2,094	38,500	18.4
Higher[18]	2	1,134[19]	30,243	12.6[19]

Health (2002): physicians 1,175 (1 per 21,055 persons); hospital beds 25,628 (1 per 966 persons); infant mortality rate per 1,000 live births (2004) 69.5.
Food (2002): daily per capita caloric intake 2,410 (vegetable products 94%, animal products 6%); 103% of FAO recommended minimum requirement.

Military

Total active duty personnel (2004): c. 45,000 (army 100%). *Military expenditure as percentage of GDP* (2003): 2.3%; per capita expenditure U.S.$6.

[1]Includes 10 ex officio members (ministers who are not elected to Parliament). [2]Swahili became official in September 2005. [3]Actual local administration in 2005 is based on 56 districts and one city; Kampala city has special administrative status as of September 2005. [4]Revised preliminary. [5]Includes water area of 16,984 sq mi (43,989 sq km); Uganda's portion of Lake Victoria comprises 11,954 sq mi (30,960 sq km). [6]Detail does not add to total given because of rounding. [7]Based on land area only. [8]Urban agglomeration. [9]Beginning of year. [10]Indirect taxes. [11]Based on nationally representative household survey. [12]The household income for urban areas is U Sh 302,900 (U.S.$195). [13]Imports f.o.b. in balance of trade and c.i.f. in commodities and trade partners. [14]Most gold exports are reexports from the Democratic Republic of the Congo. [15]Uganda has had no railway passenger service from 1997 through mid-2005. [16]Public sector only. [17]1998. [18]State universities only. [19]1999.

Internet resources for further information:
• Bank of Uganda http://www.bou.or.ug

Ukraine

Official name: Ukrayina (Ukraine).
Form of government: unitary multiparty republic with a single legislative body (Supreme Council [450]).
Head of state: President.
Head of government: Prime Minister.
Capital: Kiev (Kyyiv).
Official language: Ukrainian.
Official religion: none.
Monetary unit: hryvnya (pl. hryvnyas); (Sept. 1, 2005) 1 U.S.\$ = 5.00 hryvnyas; 1 £ = 9.20 hryvnyas.

Price and earnings indexes (2000 = 100)

	1998	1999	2000	2001	2002	2003	2004
Consumer price index	68.7	78.0	100.0	113.1	114.0	126.6	...
Monthly earnings index	66.7	77.1	100.0	135.2	163.6	200.9	256.2

Gross national product (2004): U.S.\$60,297,000,000 (U.S.\$1,260 per capita).

Structure of gross domestic product and labour force

	2003			
	in value '000,000 hryvnyas	% of total value	labour force	% of labour force
Agriculture	29,059	10.9	3,882,500	17.2
Mining	10,854	4.1	769,500	3.4
Manufacturing	49,702	18.6	3,607,400	16.0
Public utilities	12,270	4.6	723,600	3.2
Construction	10,268	3.8	1,047,300	4.6
Transp. and commun.	35,092	13.1	1,494,200	6.6
Trade	31,622	11.8	3,070,500	13.6
Finance			854,700	3.8
Pub. admin., defense }	65,630	24.6	1,188,000	5.3
Services			3,915,500	17.3
Other	22,847[3]	8.5[3]	2,061,000[4]	9.1[4]
TOTAL	267,344	100.0	22,614,200	100.0[5]

Household income and expenditure (2004). Average household size 2.6; income per household 8,705 hryvnyas (U.S.\$1,637); sources of income: wages and salaries 42.3%, subsidies and pensions 38.5%, profit and mixed income 16.5%, property income 2.7%; expenditures: food and beverages 61.7%, consumer goods 30.9%, housing 7.4%.
Tourism (2003): receipts U.S.\$935,000,000; expenditures U.S.\$789,000,000.
Land use as % of total land area (2000): in temporary crops 56.2%, in permanent crops 1.6%, in pasture 13.7%; overall forest area 16.5%.

Foreign trade

Balance of trade (current prices)

	1999	2000	2001	2002	2003	2004
U.S.\$'000,000	+244	+779	+198	+710	+518	+3,676
% of total	0.9%	2.5%	0.6%	1.9%	1.1%	6.0%

Imports (2004): U.S.\$28,996,000,000 (crude petroleum 16.7%, machinery 16.3%, chemicals and chemical products 12.6%, natural gas 12.4%, transportation equipment 8.6%). *Major import sources:* Russia 40.7%; Germany 9.4%; Turkmenistan 6.7%; Poland 3.3%; Italy 2.8%; U.S. 2.6%.
Exports (2004): U.S.\$32,672,000,000 (ferrous and nonferrous metals 39.9%, food and raw materials 10.6%, machinery 9.3%, chemicals and chemical products 9.9%, transportation equipment 6.2%). *Major export destinations:* Russia 18.0%; Germany 5.8%; Turkey 5.7%; Italy 5.0%; U.S. 4.6%.

Transport and communications

Transport. Railroads (2004): length 22,473 km; passenger-km 51,800,000,000; metric ton-km cargo 233,600,000,000. Roads (2003): total length 169,739 km (paved 97%). Vehicles (2003): passenger cars 5,524,494; trucks and buses 1,113,615. Air transport (2004): passenger-km 3,288,000,000; metric ton-km cargo 20,868,000; airports (1999) with scheduled flights 12.

Communications

Medium	date	unit	number	units per 1,000 persons
Daily newspapers	2000	circulation	4,970,000	101
Radio	2000	receivers	43,800,000	889
Television	2000	receivers	22,500,000	456
Telephones	2004	main lines	12,142,000	257
Cellular telephones	2004	subscribers	13,735,000	290
Personal computers	2004	units	1,327,000	28
Internet	2004	users	3,750,000	79

Demography

Population (2005): 47,075,000.
Density (2005): persons per sq mi 202.0, persons per sq km 78.0.
Urban-rural (2005[1]): urban 67.8%; rural 32.2%.
Sex distribution (2004): male 46.22%; female 53.78%.
Age breakdown (2003): under 15, 16.3%; 15–29, 22.6%; 30–44, 21.7%; 45–59, 18.7%; 60–74, 15.0%; 75 and over, 5.7%.
Population projection: (2010) 44,692,000; (2020) 40,115,000.
Ethnic composition (2001): Ukrainian 77.8%; Russian 17.3%; Belarusian 0.6%; Moldovan 0.5%; Crimean Tatar 0.5%; other 3.3%.
Religious affiliation (2000): Orthodox 53%, of which Ukrainian Orthodox (Russian patriarchy) 38%, Ukrainian Orthodox (Kiev patriarchy) 10%, Ukrainian Autocephalous Orthodox 4%; independent Christian 16%; Ukrainian-rite Catholic 9%; Protestant 3%; Latin-rite Catholic 2%; Muslim 2%; nonreligious/atheist 15%[2].
Major cities (2003): Kiev (2003) 2,621,700; Kharkiv 1,470,000; Dnipropetrovsk 1,064,000; Odessa 1,029,000; Donetsk 1,016,000; Zaporizhzhya 814,000.

Vital statistics

Birth rate per 1,000 population (2004): 9.0 (world avg. 21.1); legitimate 79.6%; illegitimate 20.4%.
Death rate per 1,000 population (2004): 16.1 (world avg. 9.0).
Natural increase rate per 1,000 population (2004): –7.1 (world avg. 12.1).
Total fertility rate (avg. births per childbearing woman; 2004): 1.1.
Marriage rate per 1,000 population (2004): 5.9.
Divorce rate per 1,000 population (2004): 3.7.
Life expectancy at birth (2004): male 63.4 years; female 74.5 years.
Major causes of death per 100,000 population (2002): diseases of the circulatory system 799.7, of which ischemic heart disease 517.0, cerebrovascular disease 184.6; malignant neoplasms (cancers) 166.9; accidents and violence 153.5; diseases of the respiratory system 56.7.

National economy

Budget (2003). Revenue: 54,986,700,000 hryvnyas (tax revenue 64.9%, of which tax on profits of enterprises 23.8%, VAT 22.9%, excise tax 9.3%; nontax revenue 28.6%; other 6.5%). Expenditures: 56,010,900,000 hryvnyas (2001: social security 43.2%; economy 8.2%; debt payment 6.7%; education 6.2%; public order 6.1%; defense 5.8%; health 1.9%).
Public debt (external; July 2005): U.S.\$11,633,000,000.
Production (metric tons except as noted). Agriculture, forestry, fishing (2004): potatoes 20,755,000, wheat 17,517,700, sugar beets 16,502,000, barley 11,068,800, corn (maize) 8,793,100, sunflower seeds 3,052,000, rye 1,592,300, tomatoes 1,200,000, oats 1,006,100; livestock (number of live animals) 7,712,100 cattle, 7,321,500 pigs, 1,859,000 sheep and goats; roundwood 14,861,800 cu m; fish catch (2003) 222,349. Mining and quarrying (2002): iron ore (2003) 62,952,000; manganese (metal content) 940,000; ilmenite concentrate 670,000. Manufacturing (value of production in '000,000,000 hryvnyas; 2003): base and fabricated metals 57.3; food and beverages 48.9; machinery and apparatus 34.8; coke and refined petroleum 21.5; chemicals and chemical products 18.6. Energy production (consumption): electricity (kW-hr; 2004) 181,174,000,000 ([2002] 170,619,000,000); hard coal (metric tons; 2004) 64,600,000 ([2003] 97,900,000); lignite (metric tons; 2004) 456,000 ([2002] 759,000); crude petroleum (barrels; 2004) 31,700,000 ([2003] 111,000,000); petroleum products (barrels; 2002) 19,048,000 (11,473,000); natural gas (cu m; 2004) 17,755,000,000 ([2003] 76,089,-500,000).
Population economically active (2003): total 22,614,200; activity rate of total population c. 47% (participation rates: ages 15–64, 65.8%; female 48.9%; unemployed [2004] 8.6%).

Education and health

Educational attainment: n.a. *Literacy* (2003): percentage of total population age 15 and over literate 99.7%; males literate 99.8%; females literate 99.6%.

Education (2004–05)

	schools	teachers	students	student/ teacher ratio
Primary (age 6–13) }	21,700	547,000	5,731,000	10.5
Secondary (age 14–17)				
Voc., teacher tr.	1,011	...	507,300	...
Higher	966	...	2,575,200	...

Health (2004): physicians 223,000 (1 per 212 persons); hospital beds 451,000 (1 per 105 persons); infant mortality rate per 1,000 live births 9.4.
Food (2002): daily per capita caloric intake 3,054 (vegetable products 79%, animal products 21%); 119% of FAO recommended minimum requirement.

Military

Total active duty personnel (2005): 272,500 (army 45.9%, air force/air defense 18.0%, navy 5.0%, paramilitary 31.1%[6]); Russian naval forces (August 2005) 1,100. *Military expenditure as percentage of GDP* (2003): 2.9%; per capita expenditure U.S.\$30.

[1]October 1. [2]Jewish 0.4%. [3]Net indirect taxes and taxes on production less subsidies and less imputed bank service charges. [4]Unemployed. [5]Detail does not add to total given because of rounding. [6]Includes internal security troops and border/coastal guards.

Area and population

Provinces	area sq km	population 2004[1] estimate	Provinces	area sq km	population 2004[1] estimate
Cherkasy	20,900	1,346,850	Rivne	20,047	1,158,114
Chernihiv	31,865	1,174,299	Sumy	23,834	1,231,551
Chernivtsi	8,097	909,202	Ternopil	13,823	1,114,471
Dnipropetrovsk	31,974	3,453,646	Vinnytsya	26,513	1,707,513
Donetsk	26,517	4,635,012	Volyn	20,144	1,042,045
Ivano-Frankivsk	13,928	1,390,155	Zakarpatska	12,777	1,246,164
Kharkiv	31,415	2,832,206	Zaporizhzhya	27,180	1,865,420
Kherson	28,461	1,130,190	Zhytomyr	29,832	1,334,786
Khmelnytsky	20,645	1,378,183	**Autonomous republic**		
Kirovohrad	24,588	1,072,371	Crimea (Krym)	26,081	1,986,669
Kyyiv (Kiev)	28,131	1,768,886	**Cities**		
Luhansk	26,684	2,417,105	Kiev	839	2,675,111
Lviv	21,833	2,580,166	Sevastopol	864	378,934
Mykolayiv	24,598	1,222,737	TOTAL	603,628	47,015,251
Odessa	33,310	2,404,786			
Poltava	28,748	1,558,679			

Internet resources for further information:

- **National Bank of Ukraine** http://www.bank.gov.ua/ENGL/Of_publ/index.htm
- **The State Statistics Committee of Ukraine** http://www.ukrstat.gov.ua

United Arab Emirates

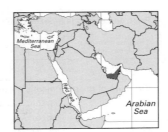

Official name: Al-Imārāt al-ʿArabīyah al-Muttaḥidah (United Arab Emirates).
Form of government: federation of seven emirates with one advisory body (Federal National Council [40[1]]).
Chief of state: President.
Head of government: Prime Minister.
Capital: Abu Dhabi.
Official language: Arabic.
Official religion: Islam.
Monetary unit: 1 U.A.E. dirham (Dh) = 100 fils; valuation (Sept. 1, 2005) 1 U.S.$ = Dh 3.67; 1 £ = Dh 6.76.

Area and population		area[2]		population
				2003
Emirates	**Capitals**	sq mi	sq km	estimate
Abū Ẓaby (Abu Dhabi)	Abu Dhabi	28,210	73,060	1,591,000
ʿAjmān (Ajman)	ʿAjmān	100	260	235,000
Dubayy (Dubai)	Dubai	1,510	3,900	1,204,000
Al-Fujayrah (Fujairah)	Al-Fujayrah	500	1,300	118,000
Raʾs al-Khaymah (Ras al-Khaimah)	Raʾs al-Khaymah	660	1,700	195,000
Ash-Shāriqah (Sharjah)	Sharjah	1,000	2,600	636,000
Umm al-Qaywayn (Umm al-Qaiwain)	Umm al-Qaywayn	300	780	62,000
TOTAL		32,280	83,600	4,041,000

Demography

Population (2005): 4,690,000.
Density (2005): persons per sq mi 145.3, persons per sq km 56.1.
Urban-rural (2003): urban 85.1%; rural 14.9%.
Sex distribution (2004): male 67.80%; female 32.20%.
Age breakdown (2004): under 15, 25.3%; 15–29, 29.2%; 30–44, 34.2%; 45–59, 9.7%; 60–74, 1.3%; 75 and over, 0.3%.
Population projection: (2010) 5,252,000; (2020) 6,409,000.
Doubling time: 51 years.
Ethnic composition (2000): Arab 48.1%, of which U.A.E. Arab 12.2%, U.A.E Bedouin 9.4%, Egyptian Arab 6.2%, Omani Arab 4.1%, Saudi Arab 4.0%; South Asian 35.7%, of which Pashtun 7.1%, Balochi 7.1%, Malayali 7.1%; Persian 5.0%; Filipino 3.4%; white 2.4%; other 5.4%.
Religious affiliation (2000): Muslim 76% (Sunnī 63%, Shīʿī 13%); Christian 11%, of which Roman Catholic 5%, Orthodox 3%; Hindu 7%; other 6%.
Major cities (2003): Dubai 1,171,000; Abu Dhabi 552,000; Sharjah 519,000; Al-ʿAyn 348,000; ʿAjmān 225,000; Raʾs al-Khaymah 102,000.

Vital statistics

Birth rate per 1,000 population (2003): 15.1 (world avg. 21.1).
Death rate per 1,000 population (2003): 1.5 (world avg. 9.0).
Natural increase rate per 1,000 population (2003): 13.6 (world avg. 12.1).
Total fertility rate (avg. births per childbearing woman; 2003): 2.5.
Marriage rate per 1,000 population (2003): 3.0.
Divorce rate per 1,000 population (2003): 0.8.
Life expectancy at birth (2004): male 72.5 years; female 77.6 years.
Major causes of death per 100,000 population (1998): cardiovascular diseases 44.1; accidents and poisoning 31.1; malignant neoplasms (cancers) 15.3; congenital anomalies 9.4.

National economy

Budget (2004). Revenue: Dh 110,574,000,000 (hydrocarbons revenue 66.3%, investment income 12.6%, fees and charges 5.7%). Expenditures: Dh 93,384,000,000 (current expenditures 85.2%, capital [development] expenditure 14.8%).
Gross national product (2004): U.S.$85,700,000,000 (U.S.$20,000 per capita).

Structure of gross domestic product and labour force				
	2003			
	in value Dh '000,000[3]	% of total value[3]	labour force	% of labour force
Agriculture	9,359	3.2	168,262	7.7
Crude petroleum, nat. gas	93,369	31.9	28,073	1.3
Quarrying	765	0.3	4,838	0.2
Manufacturing	40,100	13.7	297,834	13.6
Construction	18,791	6.4	362,251	16.5
Public utilities	5,513	1.9	33,140	1.5
Transp. and commun.	23,629	8.1	133,913	6.1
Trade	32,119	11.0	527,607	24.1
Finance, real estate	39,599	13.5	89,279	4.1
Pub. admin., defense	29,272	10.0	248,592	11.3
Services	6,644	2.3	297,509	13.6
Other	–6,039[4]	–2.1[4]	—	—
TOTAL	293,121	100.0[5]	2,191,298	100.0

Public debt: n.a.
Tourism (2003): receipts U.S.$1,439,000,000; expenditure U.S.$3,959,000,000.
Production (metric tons except as noted). Agriculture, forestry, fishing (2004): dates 760,000, tomatoes 240,000, eggplants 20,000, pumpkins and squash 20,000, onions 15,944, cabbages 15,000, cucumbers and gherkins 15,000, lemons and limes 11,269, cantaloupes and watermelons 10,000, mangoes 4,255; livestock (number of live animals) 1,450,000 goats, 590,000 sheep, 250,000 camels, 115,000 cattle, 13,000,000 chickens; roundwood, n.a.; fish

catch (2003) 95,150. Mining and quarrying (2003): gypsum 100,000; lime 50,000; chromite 10,000. Manufacturing (value added in Dh '000,000; 2002): chemical products (including refined petroleum) 18,467; textiles and wearing apparel 4,281; fabricated metal products and machinery 3,695; food, beverages, and tobacco 2,673; cement, bricks, and tiles 2,508. Energy production (consumption): electricity (kW-hr; 2002) 41,750,000,000 (41,750,000,000); crude petroleum (barrels; 2004) 809,000,000 (157,000,000); petroleum products (metric tons; 2002) 29,741,000 (6,614,000); natural gas (cu m; 2002) 44,071,000,000 (36,958,000,000).
Population economically active (2003): total 2,191,000; activity rate of total population 54.2% (participation rates: over age 14, 72.6%; female [2001] 11.7%; unemployed [2001] 1.8%).

Price and earnings indexes (2000 = 100)							
	1998	1999	2000	2001	2002	2003	2004
Consumer price index	96.5	98.4	100.0	102.8	105.8	109.1	114.2
Wages and services index	...	...	100.0	117.0	125.2	130.9	...

Household income and expenditure. Average household size (2002) 6.5; income per household: n.a.; sources of income: n.a.; expenditure (1996): rent, fuel, and light 36.1%, transportation and communications 14.9%, food 14.4%, education, recreation, and entertainment 10.3%, durable household goods 7.4%, clothing 6.7%.
Land use as % of total land area (2000): in temporary crops 0.7%, in permanent crops 2.2%, in pasture 3.6%; overall forest area 3.8%.

Foreign trade

Balance of trade (current prices)[6]						
	1999	2000	2001	2002	2003	2004
Dh '000,000,000	+17.5	+54.5	+42.2	+53.7	+78.3	+104.9
% of total	7.0%	17.5%	13.3%	16.3%	18.9%	20.8%

Imports (2001): Dh 120,600,000,000[7] (machinery and transport equipment 37.6%, food 23.2%, textiles 13.9%, basic manufactures 8.4%, chemicals 6.3%, optical and medical equipment 2.8%). *Major import sources* (2004): China 9.2%; India 8.4%; Japan 6.7%; Germany 6.6%; U.S. 6.4%; France 6.4%; Switzerland 5.5%.
Exports (2001): Dh 176,900,000,000 (domestic exports 71.1%, of which crude petroleum 36.7%, natural gas 7.1%, refined petroleum products 4.6%, nonmonetary gold 4.4%; reexports 28.9%). *Major export destinations* (2004): Japan 26.1%; South Korea 10.5%; Iran 4.4%; Thailand 3.7%; Singapore 3.4%.

Transport and communications

Transport. Railroads: none. Roads (1999): total length 676 mi, 1,088 km (paved 100%). Vehicles (2001): passenger cars 794,100; trucks and buses 477,900. Air transport (2004)[8]: passenger-mi 30,291,000,000, passenger-km 48,749,000,000; short ton-mi cargo 2,225,000,000, metric ton-km cargo 3,507,745,000; airports (2001) with scheduled flights 6.

Communications				units per 1,000
Medium	date	unit	number	persons
Daily newspapers	2000	circulation	507,000	156
Radio	2000	receivers	1,030,000	318
Television	2000	receivers	948,000	292
Telephones	2004	main lines	1,187,700	273
Cellular telephones	2004	subscribers	3,683,100	847
Personal computers	2002	units	450,000	141
Internet	2004	users	1,384,800	319

Education and health

Educational attainment (1995). Percentage of population age 10 and over having: no formal schooling 47.6%; primary education 27.8%; secondary 16.0%; higher 8.6%. *Literacy* (2002): total population age 15 and over literate 77.3%; males literate 75.6%; females literate 80.7%.

Education (2002–03)	schools	teachers	students	student/teacher ratio
Primary (age 6–11)	...	16,323	248,370	15.2
Secondary (age 12–18)	...	19,848	271,767	13.7
Vocational	...	230	1,724	7.5
Higher	49	2,948[10]	68,182	21.5[10]

Health: physicians (2001) 5,825 (1 per 599 persons); hospital beds (1999) 7,448 (1 per 394 persons); infant mortality rate per 1,000 live births (2003) 8.0.
Food (2002): daily per capita caloric intake 3,225 (vegetable products 77%, animal products 23%); 133% of FAO recommended minimum requirement.

Military

Total active duty personnel (2005): 50,500 (army 87.1%, navy 5.0%, air force 7.9%); U.S. Air Force personnel (August 2005) 1,300. *Military expenditure as percentage of GDP* (2003): 3.1%; per capita expenditure U.S.$622.

[1]All seats are appointed. [2]Approximate figures. [3]At current prices. [4]Less imputed bank service charges. [5]Detail does not add to total given because of rounding. [6]For all Emirates. [7]For Emirates of Abu Dhabi, Dubai, and Sharjah only. [8]Emirates Air only. [9]1996–97. [10]2001–02.

Internet resources for further information:
• **United Arab Emirates Ministry of Planning**
  http://www.uae.gov.ae/mop/E_home.htm
• **Central Bank of the United Arab Emirates** http://www.cbuae.gov.ae

United Kingdom

Official name: United Kingdom of Great Britain and Northern Ireland.
Form of government: constitutional monarchy with two legislative houses (House of Lords [703[1]]; House of Commons [646]).
Chief of state: Sovereign.
Head of government: Prime Minister.
Capital: London.
Official language: English; both English and Welsh in Wales.
Official religion: [2].
Monetary unit: 1 pound sterling (£) = 100 new pence; valuation (Sept. 1, 2005) 1 £ = U.S.$1.84; 1 U.S.$ = £0.54.

Religious affiliation (2001): Christian 71.6%, of which Anglican 29.0%, Roman Catholic 11.0%; Muslim 2.7%; Hindu 1.0%; Sikh 0.6%; Jewish 0.5%; nonreligious 15.5%; other 8.1%.
Major cities (2001; urban agglomeration [2000]): Greater London 7,172,091; Manchester 392,819 ([2001] 2,482,328); Birmingham 977,087 (2,272,000); Leeds 715,402 (1,433,000); Newcastle 259,536 (1,026,000); Liverpool 439,473 (951,000); Glasgow 629,501; Sheffield 513,234; Bradford 467,665; Edinburgh 452,194; Bristol 380,615; Wakefield 315,172; Cardiff 305,353; Coventry 300,848; Doncaster 286,865; Sunderland 280,807; Belfast 277,391.
Mobility (1991)[6]. Population living in the same residence as 1990: 90.1%; different residence, same country (of Great Britain) 8.1%; different residence, different country of Great Britain 1.2%; from outside Great Britain 0.6%.
Households (2002)[6]. Average household size 2.4; 1 person 29%, couple 29%, couple with 1–2 children 19%, couple with 3 or more children 10%, single parent with children 9%, other 4%.
Immigration (2002): permanent residents 386,000, from Australia 9.6%, Bangladesh, India, and Sri Lanka 7.5%, South Africa 6.2%, New Zealand 2.8%, United States 2.6%, Pakistan 1.8%, Canada 1.8%, other 67.7%, of which EU 21.8%.

Vital statistics

Birth rate per 1,000 population (2004): 12.0 (world avg. 21.1); legitimate 57.7%; illegitimate 42.3%.
Death rate per 1,000 population (2004): 9.8 (world avg. 9.0).
Natural increase rate per 1,000 population (2004): 2.2 (world avg. 12.1).
Total fertility rate (avg. births per childbearing woman; 2004): 1.7.
Marriage rate per 1,000 population (2003): 5.1.
Divorce rate per 1,000 population (2003): 2.8.
Life expectancy at birth (2003): male 76.2 years; female 80.7 years.
Major causes of death per 100,000 population (2004)[7]: diseases of the circulatory system 320.8, of which ischemic heart disease 154.9, cerebrovascular disease 88.6; malignant neoplasms (cancers) 225.5; diseases of the respiratory system 116.2, of which pneumonia 51.4; diseases of the digestive system 41.8; diseases of the genitourinary system 15.8; diseases of the endocrine system 12.6, of which diabetes mellitus 9.8; suicide 5.8.

Social indicators

Educational attainment (1999). Percentage of population age 25–64 having: up to lower secondary education only 38%; completed secondary 37%; higher 25%, of which at least some university 17%.

Distribution of disposable income (2000–01)

percentage of household income by quintile

1	2	3	4	5 (highest)
8.8	12.0	17.4	26.1	35.7

Quality of working life (2004). Average full-time workweek (hours): male 40.8, female 37.5. Annual rate per 100,000 workers for (2000–01)[6]: injury or accident 2,778.6; death 5.0. Proportion of labour force (employed persons) insured for damages or income loss resulting from: injury 100%; permanent disability 100%; death 100%. Average days lost to labour stoppages per 1,000 employee workdays (2003): 19.
Access to services (2004). Proportion of households having access to: bath or shower 100%; toilet 100%.
Social participation. Eligible voters participating in last national election (May 2005): 61.3%. Population age 16 and over participating in voluntary work (2001)[6]: 39%. Trade union membership in total workforce (2001) 29.1%.
Social deviance (2003–04)[7]. Offense rate per 100,000 population for: theft and handling stolen goods 3,801.1; vandalism 2,020.4; violence against the person 1,601.8; burglary 1,371.9; fraud and forgery 532.8; drug offenses 236.5; robbery 124.4.
Leisure (1994). Favourite leisure activities (hours weekly): watching television 17.1; listening to radio 10.3; reading 8.8, of which books 3.8, newspapers 3.3; gardening 2.1.
Material well-being (2001). Households possessing: automobile 74.0%, telephone 94.0%, television receiver (2000) 98.3%, refrigerator/freezer 95.0%, washing machine 93.0%, central heating 92.0%, video recorder 90.0%.

National economy

Budget (2003–04). Revenue: £410,165,000,000 (production and import taxes 35.6%, income tax 35.5%, social security contributions 17.2%). Expenditures: £467,209,000,000 (social protection 37.8%, health 16.2%, education 11.9%, defense 6.6%).
Gross national product (at current market prices; 2004): U.S.$2,016,393,000,000 (U.S.$33,940 per capita).

Population (2001 census)

Countries	population		population		population
England	49,138,831	Nottingham	266,988	Scotland	5,062,011
Counties		Peterborough	156,061	**Unitary Districts**	
Bedfordshire	381,572	Plymouth	240,720	Aberdeen City	212,125
Buckinghamshire	479,026	Poole	138,288	Aberdeenshire	226,871
Cambridgeshire	552,658	Portsmouth	186,701	Angus	108,400
Cheshire	673,788	Reading	143,096	Argyll and Bute	91,306
Cornwall (incl.		Redcar and		City of Edinburgh	448,624
Isles of Scilly)	501,267	Cleveland	139,132	Clackmannanshire	48,077
Cumbria	487,607	Rutland	34,563	Dumfries and	
Derbyshire	734,585	Slough	119,067	Galloway	147,765
Devon	704,493	South		Dundee City	145,663
Dorset	390,980	Gloucestershire	245,641	East Ayrshire	120,235
Durham	493,470	Southampton	217,445	East Dumbarton-	
East Sussex	492,324	Southend-on-Sea	160,257	shire	108,243
Essex	1,310,835	Stockton-on-Tees	178,408	East Lothian	90,088
Gloucestershire	564,559	Stoke-on-Trent	240,636	East Renfrewshire	89,311
Hampshire	1,240,103	Swindon	180,051	Eilean Siar[5]	26,502
Hertfordshire	1,033,977	Telford and		Falkirk	145,191
Isle of Wight[3]	132,731	Wrekin	158,325	Fife	349,429
Kent	1,329,718	Thurrock	143,128	Glasgow City	577,869
Lancashire	1,134,974	Torbay	129,706	Highland	208,914
Leicestershire	609,578	Warrington	191,080	Inverclyde	84,203
Lincolnshire	646,645	West Berkshire	144,483	Midlothian	80,941
Norfolk	796,728	Windsor and		Moray	86,940
North Yorkshire	569,660	Maidenhead	133,626	North Ayrshire	135,817
Northamptonshire	629,676	Wokingham	150,229	North Lanarkshire	321,067
Northumberland	307,190	York	181,094	Orkney Islands	19,245
Nottinghamshire	748,510	**Metropolitan**		Perth and Kinross	134,949
Oxfordshire	605,488	**Counties/Greater**		Renfrewshire	172,867
Shropshire	283,173	**London**		Scottish Borders	106,764
Somerset	498,093	Greater London[4]	7,172,091	Shetland Islands	21,988
Staffordshire	806,744	Greater		South Ayrshire	112,097
Suffolk	668,553	Manchester	2,482,328	South Lanarkshire	302,216
Surrey	1,059,015	Merseyside	1,362,026	Stirling	86,212
Warwickshire	505,860	South Yorkshire	1,266,338	West Dumbarton-	
West Sussex	753,614	Tyne and Wear	1,075,938	shire	93,378
Wiltshire	432,973	West Midlands	2,555,592	West Lothian	158,714
Worcestershire	542,107	West Yorkshire	2,079,211		
Unitary Districts				Northern Ireland	1,685,267
Bath and		Wales	2,903,085	**Districts**	
NE Somerset	169,040	**Unitary Districts**		Antrim	48,366
Blackburn with		Blaenau Gwent	70,064	Ards	73,244
Darwen	137,470	Bridgend	128,645	Armagh	54,263
Blackpool	142,283	Caerphilly	169,519	Ballymena	58,610
Bournemouth	163,444	Cardiff	305,353	Ballymoney	26,894
Bracknell Forest	109,617	Carmarthenshire	172,842	Banbridge	41,392
Brighton and		Ceredigion	74,941	Belfast	277,391
Hove	247,817	Conwy	109,596	Carrickfergus	37,659
Bristol	380,615	Denbighshire	93,065	Castlereagh	66,488
Darlington	97,838	Flintshire	148,594	Coleraine	56,315
Derby	221,708	Gwynedd	116,843	Cookstown	32,581
East Riding of		Isle of Anglesey	66,829	Craigavon	80,671
Yorkshire	314,113	Merthyr Tydfil	55,981	Derry	105,066
Halton	118,208	Monmouthshire	84,885	Down	63,828
Hartlepool	88,611	Neath and		Dungannon	47,735
Herefordshire	174,871	Port Talbot	134,468	Fermanagh	57,527
Kingston upon		Newport	137,011	Larne	30,832
Hull	243,589	Pembrokeshire	114,131	Limavady	32,422
Leicester	279,921	Powys	126,354	Lisburn	108,694
Luton	184,371	Rhondda, Cynon,		Magherafelt	39,780
Medway	249,488	Taff	231,946	Moyle	15,933
Middlesbrough	134,855	Swansea	223,301	Newry and Mourne	87,058
Milton Keynes	207,057	Torfaen	90,949	Newtownabbey	79,995
NE Lincolnshire	157,979	The Vale of		North Down	76,323
North Lincolnshire	152,849	Glamorgan	119,292	Omagh	47,952
North Somerset	188,564	Wrexham	128,476	Strabane	38,248
			TOTAL		58,789,194

Demography

Population (2005): 60,020,000.
Area: 93,635 sq mi, 242,514 sq km, of which England 50,302 sq mi, 130,281 sq km; Wales 8,004 sq mi, 20,732 sq km; Scotland 30,087 sq mi, 77,925 sq km; Northern Ireland 5,242 sq mi, 13,576 sq km.
Density (2005): persons per sq mi 641.0, persons per sq km 247.5.
Urban-rural (2003): urban 89.1%; rural 10.9%.
Age breakdown (2003): under 15, 18.3%; 15–29, 18.9%; 30–44, 22.7%; 45–59, 19.2%; 60–74, 13.3%; 75 and over, 7.6%.
Ethnic composition (2002–03): white 89.2%; black 2.0%, of which Caribbean origin 1.0%, African origin 0.9%; Asian Indian 1.7%; Pakistani 1.2%; Bangladeshi 0.5%; Chinese 0.3%; other and not stated 5.1%.
Population projection: (2010) 61,170,000; (2020) 63,587,000.
Sex distribution (2003): male 48.88%; female 51.12%.

Structure of gross domestic product and labour force

	2003		2004	
	in value £'000,000	% of total value	labour force[8]	% of labour force[8]
Agriculture	9,476	0.9	420,000	1.4
Mining[9]	27,500	2.5	} 3,654,000	12.0
Manufacturing	152,803	13.9		
Construction	61,538	5.6	2,111,000	7.0
Public utilities	14,924	1.3	203,000	0.7
Transp. and commun.	75,634	6.9	1,813,000	6.0
Trade, hotels, restaurants	156,852	14.3	7,040,000	23.2
Finance, real estate	294,758	26.8	5,828,000	19.2
Pub. admin., defense	50,489	4.6	} 9,255,000	30.5
Services	177,467	16.1		
Other	78,454[10]	7.1[10]	—	—
TOTAL	1,099,896[11]	100.0	30,325,000[11]	100.0

Total national debt (2003–04): £480,673,000,000 (U.S.$857,857,000,000).
Land use as % of total land area (2000): in temporary crops 24.4%, in permanent crops 0.2%, in pasture 45.8%; overall forest area 11.6%.
Tourism (2004–05): receipts from visitors U.S.$26,806,000,000; expenditures by nationals abroad U.S.$61,084,000,000.
Production (metric tons except as noted). Agriculture, forestry, fishing (2004): wheat 15,706,000, sugar beets 7,600,000, potatoes 6,000,000, barley 5,860,000, rapeseed 1,612,000, peas 678,000, oats 652,000, carrots 650,000, onions 380,000, cabbages 233,500, apples 125,000; livestock (number of live animals) 35,500,000 sheep, 10,504,000 cattle, 5,038,000 pigs; roundwood 8,100,389 cu m; fish catch (2003) 635,486. Mining and quarrying (2003): sand and gravel 91,000,000; limestone and dolomite 12,950,000; chalk 8,500,000; china clay (kaolin) 2,097,000. Manufacturing (value added in £'000,000; 2003): food, beverages, and tobacco 22,232; paper products, printing, and publishing 20,343; transport equipment 18,133; electrical and optical equipment 16,874; chemicals and chemical products 15,409; base metals and fabricated metal products 15,210; machinery and equipment 12,022; rubber and plastic products 7,914.

Financial aggregates

	1998	1999	2000	2001	2002	2003	2004
Exchange rate (end of year)							
U.S. dollar per £	1.66	1.62	1.49	1.45	1.61	1.78	1.93
SDRs per £	1.18	1.18	1.15	1.15	1.19	1.20	1.24
International reserves (U.S.$)							
Total (excl. gold; '000,000,000)	32.21	35.87	43.89	37.28	39.36	41.85	45.34
SDRs ('000,000,000)	0.47	0.51	0.33	0.29	0.36	0.38	0.33
Reserve pos. in IMF ('000,000)	4.38	5.28	4.28	5.05	6.21	6.32	5.53
Foreign exchange	27.36	30.08	39.28	31.94	32.79	35.15	39.48
Gold ('000,000 fine troy oz)	23.00	20.55	15.67	11.42	10.09	10.07	10.04
% world reserves	2.4	2.1	1.6	1.2	1.1	1.1	1.1
Interest and prices							
Central bank discount (%)	...	...	...	...	...	...	...
Govt. bond yield (%) long term	5.45	4.70	4.68	4.78	4.83	4.64	4.77
Industrial share prices (1995 = 100)	150.5	...	...	...	...	...	...
Balance of payments (U.S.$'000,000,000,000)							
Balance of visible trade	−36.13	−47.02	−49.85	−58.48	−70.84	−78.24	−107.30
Imports, f.o.b.	−307.85	−315.90	−334.23	−332.14	−350.69	−386.51	−456.92
Exports, f.o.b.	271.72	268.88	284.38	273.66	279.85	308.27	349.62
Balance of invisibles	+29.50	+7.73	+13.17	+26.63	+46.27	+50.74	+65.42
Balance of payments, current account	−6.63	−39.29	−36.68	−31.85	−24.57	−27.50	−41.88

Manufacturing, mining, and construction enterprises (2001)

	no. of enterprises	no. of employees	annual costs as a % of avg. of employment costs	annual value added (£'000,000)
Manufacturing				
Food, beverages, and tobacco	7,706	515,000	86.6	20,370
Paper and paper products; printing and publishing	32,493	475,000	101.5	19,444
Chemical products	3,864	251,000	138.8	14,850
Metal manufacturing	31,629	487,000	92.3	15,269
Machinery and equipment	13,650	355,000	104.3	11,696
Mineral products (nonmetallic)	5,439	134,000	93.7	4,852
Electrical and optical equipment	16,141	475,000	118.3	16,070
Transport equipment	5,665	390,000	120.0	17,411
Rubber and plastics	7,021	233,000	92.3	7,632
Textiles	11,310	210,000	66.5	5,147
Wood and wood products	8,444	89,000	68.2	2,345
Other manufacturing	20,155	229,000	76.8	6,452
Mining				
Extraction of coal, mineral oil, and natural gas	444	39,000	...	20,629
Extraction of minerals other than fuels	1,224	33,000	...	1,798
Construction	192,000	1,367,000	...	47,969

Retail trade and service enterprises (2001)

	no. of enterprises	no. of employees	weekly wage as a % of all wages	annual turnover (£'000,000)
Food, beverages, and tobacco	27,074	993,000	...	85,534
of which				
meats	8,485	46,000	...	2,216
Household goods,	23,553	319,000	...	29,151
of which				
electronics, appliances	7,157	101,000	...	10,821
furniture	10,592	119,000	...	8,784
Clothing and footwear	17,869	446,000	...	25,963
Pharmaceuticals and cosmetics	6,915	110,000	...	9,543
Business services,	534,956	4,273,000	...	265,631
of which				
real estate	30,779	79,000	...	32,779
Transp. and commun.	81,154	1,621,000	...	181,669
Hotels, restaurants	118,988	1,792,000	...	49,902
Social services,	35,622	1,026	...	16,233
of which				
health	9,683	453,000	...	7,575

Energy production (consumption): electricity (kW-hr; 2004) 419,088,000,000 ([2003] 337,400,000,000); hard coal (metric tons; 2004) 25,100,000 (61,500,-000); crude petroleum (barrels; 2004) 652,900,000 ([2002] 582,100,000); petroleum products (metric tons; 2002) 79,200,000 (66,626,000); natural gas (cu m; 2004) 113,434,000,000 (110,102,000,000).
Population economically active (2003): total 29,595,000; activity rate of total population 49.7% (participation rates: ages 16–64 [male], 16–59 [female] 78.8%; female 45.5%; unemployed [October 2004–September 2005] 2.8%).

Price and earnings indexes (2000 = 100)

	1998	1999	2000	2001	2002	2003	2004
Consumer price index	95.7	97.2	100.0	101.8	103.5	106.5	109.7
Monthly earnings index	91.3	95.7	100.0	104.4	108.1	111.8	116.7

Household income and expenditure (2002–03). Average household size 2.4; average annual disposable income per household £23,483 (U.S.$37,850); sources of income: wages and salaries 67.7%, social security benefits 14.9%, income from self-employment 8.1%, dividends and interest 7.2%; expenditure (2004): housing 18.7%, transportation 14.2%, recreation and culture 12.3%, expenditures in cafés and hotels 12.0%, food and beverages 9.2%, clothing and footwear 6.0%.

Foreign trade

Balance of trade (current prices)

	1998	1999	2000	2001	2002	2003
£'000,000	−21,813	−29,051	−32,976	−40,648	−46,675	−47,290
% of total	6.2%	8.0%	8.1%	9.7%	11.1%	11.2%

Imports (2003): £235,136,000,000 (machinery and apparatus 26.6%, of which radios, televisions, and electronics 18.5%; transport equipment 16.4%, of which motor vehicles and parts 12.7%, aircraft and other transport equipment 3.7%; chemicals and chemical products 11.1%, of which pharmaceuticals 3.5%, basic chemicals 2.6%; food, beverages, and tobacco 9.0%; petroleum and petroleum products 4.5%). *Major import sources* (2004): Germany 13.7%; U.S. 9.2%; France 7.8%; The Netherlands 7.1%; Belgium-Luxembourg 5.4%; Italy 4.7%; China 4.3%; Ireland 4.0%; Spain 3.5%; Norway 3.5%; Japan 3.3%.
Exports (2003): £187,846,000,000 (machinery and apparatus 29.1%, of which radios, televisions, and electronics 16.2%, nonelectrical machinery 12.9%; chemicals and chemical products 16.6%, of which pharmaceuticals 6.3%; transport equipment 13.2%, of which motor vehicles and parts 9.3%, aircraft and other transport equipment 3.9%; crude petroleum and petroleum products 7.8%; food, beverages, and tobacco 5.8%). *Major export destinations* (2004): U.S. 15.1%; Germany 11.3%; France 9.7%; Ireland 7.3%; The Netherlands 6.3%; Belgium-Luxembourg 5.5%; Spain 4.7%; Italy 4.4%; Sweden 2.3%; Japan 2.0%; Canada 1.8%.

Transport and communications

Transport. Railroads (2003–04): length (2004) 10,734 mi, 17,274 km; passenger-mi 26,112,000,000, passenger-km 42,024,000,000; ton-mi cargo[6] 12,945,-000,000, metric ton-km cargo[6] 18,900,000,000. Roads (2003): total length 244,156 mi, 392,931 km (paved 100%). Vehicles (2004)[6]: passenger cars 25,754,000, trucks and buses 3,334,000. Air transport (2003)[12]: passenger-mi 102,405,700,000, passenger-km 164,806,300,000; short ton-mi cargo 3,552,-800,000, metric ton-km cargo 5,187,000,000; airports (2001) 150[13].

Communications

Medium	date	unit	number	units per 1,000 persons
Daily newspapers	2004	circulation	17,485,000	292
Radio	2000	receivers	84,500,000	1,432
Television	2003	receivers	56,576,300	950
Telephones	2004	main lines	33,700,000	564
Cellular telephones	2004	subscribers	61,100,000	1,002
Personal computers	2004	units	35,890,000	600
Internet	2004	users	37,600,000	629

Education and health

Literacy (2004): total population literate, virtually 100%.

Education (2003–04)[14]

	schools	teachers	students	student/ teacher ratio
Primary (age 5–10)	22,509	226,200	4,953,900	21.9
Secondary (age 11–19)	4,255	244,600	4,014,100	16.4
Voc., teacher tr.	...	157,751[15]	5,301,751[15]	33.6[15]
Higher	149	120,800[15]	2,374,900[15]	19.7[15]

Health: physicians (2004) 129,260 (1 per 462 persons); hospital beds (2003) 236,370 (1 per 252 persons); infant mortality rate per 1,000 live births (2004) 5.1.
Food (2002): daily per capita caloric intake 3,412 (vegetable products 69%, animal products 31%); 135% of FAO recommended minimum requirement.

Military

Total active duty personnel (2004): 207,630 (army 56.5%, navy 19.6%, air force 23.4%; strategic forces 0.5%); U.S. troops (December 2004) 11,300. *Military expenditure as percentage of GDP* (2003): 2.8%; per capita expenditure U.S.$858.

[1]As of July 2004 including 91 hereditary peers, 586 life peers, and 26 bishops. [2]Church of England "established" (protected by the state but not "official"); Church of Scotland "national" (exclusive jurisdiction in spiritual matters per Church of Scotland Act 1921); no established church in Northern Ireland or Wales. [3]Only unitary district with county status. [4]Has administrative authority from July 2000. [5]Formerly Western Isles. [6]Great Britain only. [7]England and Wales only. [8]Number of workforce jobs by sector as of March 2004. [9]Includes petroleum extraction. [10]VAT and other taxes less subsidies and less imputed bank service charges. [11]Detail does not add to total given because of rounding. [12]U.K.-based airlines only. [13]Estimate. [14]Public sector only. [15]2002–03.

Internet resources for further information:
• Office for National Statistics http://www.statistics.gov.uk

United States

Official name: United States of America.
Form of government: federal republic with two legislative houses (Senate [100]; House of Representatives [435[1]]).
Head of state and government: President.
Capital: Washington, D.C.
Official language: none.
Official religion: none.
Monetary unit: 1 dollar (U.S.$) = 100 cents; valuation (Sept. 1, 2005) 1 U.S.$ = €0.80; 1 U.S.$ = £0.54.

Area and population

States	Capitals	area sq mi	area sq km	population 2004 estimate
Alabama	Montgomery	51,700	133,902	4,530,182
Alaska	Juneau	589,194	1,526,005	655,435
Arizona	Phoenix	113,999	295,256	5,743,834
Arkansas	Little Rock	53,178	137,730	2,752,629
California	Sacramento	158,633	410,858	35,893,799
Colorado	Denver	104,094	269,602	4,601,403
Connecticut	Hartford	5,006	12,966	3,503,604
Delaware	Dover	2,026	5,247	830,364
Florida	Tallahassee	58,599	151,771	17,397,161
Georgia	Atlanta	58,922	152,607	8,829,383
Hawaii	Honolulu	6,461	16,734	1,262,840
Idaho	Boise	83,570	216,445	1,393,262
Illinois	Springfield	57,915	149,999	12,713,634
Indiana	Indianapolis	36,418	94,322	6,237,569
Iowa	Des Moines	56,271	145,741	2,954,451
Kansas	Topeka	82,277	213,096	2,735,502
Kentucky	Frankfort	40,409	104,659	4,145,922
Louisiana	Baton Rouge	47,716	123,584	4,515,770
Maine	Augusta	33,126	85,795	1,317,253
Maryland	Annapolis	10,454	27,076	5,558,058
Massachusetts	Boston	8,263	21,401	6,416,505
Michigan	Lansing	96,716	250,493	10,112,620
Minnesota	St. Paul	86,939	225,171	5,100,958
Mississippi	Jackson	47,692	123,522	2,902,966
Missouri	Jefferson City	69,704	180,533	5,754,618
Montana	Helena	147,042	380,837	926,865
Nebraska	Lincoln	77,353	200,343	1,747,214
Nevada	Carson City	110,561	286,352	2,334,771
New Hampshire	Concord	9,282	24,040	1,299,500
New Jersey	Trenton	7,813	20,236	8,698,879
New Mexico	Santa Fe	121,590	314,917	1,903,289
New York	Albany	53,097	137,521	19,227,088
North Carolina	Raleigh	52,671	136,417	8,541,221
North Dakota	Bismarck	70,700	183,112	634,366
Ohio	Columbus	44,825	116,096	11,459,011
Oklahoma	Oklahoma City	69,898	181,035	3,523,553
Oregon	Salem	97,047	251,351	3,594,586
Pennsylvania	Harrisburg	46,056	119,284	12,406,292
Rhode Island	Providence	1,223	3,168	1,080,632
South Carolina	Columbia	31,118	80,595	4,198,068
South Dakota	Pierre	77,117	199,732	770,883
Tennessee	Nashville	42,143	109,150	5,900,962
Texas	Austin	266,853	691,146	22,490,022
Utah	Salt Lake City	84,899	219,887	2,389,039
Vermont	Montpelier	9,615	24,903	621,394
Virginia	Richmond	40,600	105,154	7,459,827
Washington	Olympia	68,097	176,370	6,203,788
West Virginia	Charleston	24,230	62,755	1,815,354
Wisconsin	Madison	65,498	169,639	5,509,026
Wyoming	Cheyenne	97,813	253,334	506,529
District				
District of Columbia	—	68	176	553,523
TOTAL		3,676,487[2, 3]	9,522,057[2, 3]	293,655,404[4]

Demography

Population (2005): 296,748,000.
Density (2004)[5]: persons per sq mi 83.9, persons per sq km 32.4.
Urban-rural (2000): urban 79.0%; rural 21.0%.
Sex distribution (2004): male 49.22%; female 50.78%.
Age breakdown (2004): under 15, 20.7%; 15–29, 20.9%; 30–44, 22.0%; 45–59, 19.8%; 60–74, 10.6%; 75 and over, 6.0%.
Population projection: (2010) 310,720,000; (2020) 336,766,000.
Doubling time: not applicable; doubling time exceeds 100 years.
Population by race and Hispanic[6] origin (2003): non-Hispanic white 67.9%; Hispanic 13.7%; non-Hispanic black 12.2%; Asian and Pacific Islander 4.1%; American Indian and Eskimo 1.1%.
Religious affiliation (2000): Christian 84.7%, of which independent Christian 24.7%, Protestant 21.1%, Roman Catholic 18.2%, unaffiliated Christian 15.8%, Orthodox 1.8%, other Christian (primarily Mormon and Jehovah's Witness) 3.1%; Jewish 2.0%; Muslim 1.5%; Buddhist 0.9%; Hindu 0.4%; nonreligious 9.0%; atheist 0.4%; New Religionists 0.3%; Bahā'ī 0.3%; traditional beliefs 0.2%; other 0.3%.
Mobility (2000). Population living in the same residence as in 1999: 84.0%; different residence, same county 9.0%; different county, same state 3.0%; different state 3.0%; moved from abroad 1.0%.
Households (2004). Total households 113,146,000 (married-couple families 58,109,000 [51.4%]). Average household size (2004) 2.6; 1 person 26.4%, 2 persons 33.9%, 3 persons 16.2%, 4 persons 14.6%, 5 or more persons 8.9%. Family households: 77,010,000 (68.1%); nonfamily 36,136,000 (31.9%), of which 1-person 82.6%.
Place of birth (2000): native-born 245,708,000 (89.6%); foreign-born 28,379,000 (10.4%), of which Mexico 7,841,000, the Philippines 1,222,000, China and Hong Kong 1,067,000, India 1,007,000, Cuba 952,000, Vietnam 863,000, El Salvador 765,000, South Korea 701,000.

Components of population change (2000–03)[7]

States	Net change in population	Percentage change	Births	Deaths	Net domestic/ international migration
Alabama	53,652	1.2	198,297	149,646	6,723
Alaska	21,887	3.5	32,190	10,102	−117
Arizona	450,179	8.8	278,744	136,492	306,247
Arkansas	52,316	2.0	122,012	92,026	22,760
California	1,612,800	4.8	1,701,252	756,758	660,643
Colorado	248,691	5.8	217,234	93,256	122,281
Connecticut	77,788	2.3	137,197	97,971	41,354
Delaware	33,891	4.3	35,263	23,141	22,308
Florida	1,036,248	6.5	675,642	543,406	889,862
Georgia	498,198	6.1	438,289	212,673	267,059
Hawaii	46,071	3.8	59,044	29,180	16,797
Idaho	72,376	5.6	66,337	32,085	36,648
Illinois	233,974	1.9	598,234	347,071	−20,773
Indiana	115,137	1.9	277,808	181,651	21,305
Iowa	17,680	0.6	121,048	91,168	−10,393
Kansas	34,693	1.3	125,734	80,523	−10,108
Kentucky	75,618	1.9	177,581	130,520	30,493
Louisiana	27,376	0.6	219,361	135,991	−55,144
Maine	30,805	2.4	43,434	40,920	28,848
Maryland	212,424	4.0	241,352	144,272	111,121
Massachusetts	84,325	1.3	265,871	185,556	5,832
Michigan	141,505	1.4	428,261	285,979	3,918
Minnesota	139,890	2.8	216,100	122,759	46,271
Mississippi	36,625	1.3	141,826	92,710	−11,761
Missouri	107,801	1.9	245,375	180,689	33,355
Montana	15,426	1.7	35,234	27,673	7,907
Nebraska	28,026	1.6	80,474	50,477	−979
Nevada	242,897	12.2	102,521	53,711	190,642
New Hampshire	51,901	4.2	47,194	32,188	37,082
New Jersey	224,049	2.7	370,057	240,899	99,345
New Mexico	55,568	3.1	87,305	45,302	13,805
New York	213,294	1.1	835,326	515,916	−108,872
North Carolina	360,797	4.5	386,343	235,328	210,546
North Dakota	−8,363	−1.3	24,648	19,620	−13,288
Ohio	82,655	0.7	493,802	354,822	−53,041
Oklahoma	60,878	1.8	162,253	115,649	15,639
Oregon	138,164	4.0	145,101	100,483	95,743
Pennsylvania	84,401	0.7	464,646	424,782	52,463
Rhode Island	27,845	2.7	40,114	31,964	20,573
South Carolina	135,304	3.4	182,193	122,447	77,775
South Dakota	9,465	1.3	33,914	22,917	−1,114
Tennessee	152,486	2.7	255,980	181,364	78,473
Texas	1,266,716	6.1	1,190,484	475,020	546,729
Utah	118,269	5.3	154,257	42,133	3,623
Vermont	10,280	1.7	20,066	16,774	7,514
Virginia	307,847	4.3	321,525	184,285	168,252
Washington	237,304	4.0	255,338	144,509	128,164
West Virginia	2,004	0.1	66,283	68,098	4,504
Wisconsin	108,595	2.0	220,988	153,446	44,586
Wyoming	7,460	1.5	20,306	13,398	700
District					
District of Columbia	−8,675	−1.5	25,698	19,520	−14,898
TOTAL/RATE	9,386,543	3.3	13,085,536	7,889,270	4,190,277

Major cities (2004): New York 8,104,079; Los Angeles 3,845,541; Chicago 2,862,244; Houston 2,012,626; Philadelphia 1,470,151; Phoenix 1,418,041; San Diego 1,263,756; San Antonio 1,236,249; Dallas 1,210,393; San Jose 904,522.

Other principal cities (2004)

	population		population		population
Akron	212,179	Garland (Tex.)	217,176	Norfolk	237,835
Albuquerque	484,246	Glendale (Ariz.)	235,591	Oakland	397,976
Anaheim	333,776	Glendale (Calif.)	201,326	Oklahoma City	528,042
Anchorage	272,687	Greensboro	231,543	Omaha	409,416
Arlington (Tex.)	359,467	Hialeah (Fla.)	224,522	Pittsburgh	322,450
Atlanta	419,122	Honolulu	377,260	Plano (Tex.)	245,411
Austin	681,804	Indianapolis	784,242	Portland (Ore.)	533,492
Bakersfield	283,936	Jacksonville	777,704	Raleigh	326,653
Baltimore	636,251	Jersey City	239,079	Riverside	288,384
Baton Rouge	224,097	Kansas City (Mo.)	444,387	Rochester	212,481
Birmingham	233,149	Las Vegas	534,847	Sacramento	454,330
Boston	569,165	Lexington (Ky.)	266,358	St. Louis	343,279
Buffalo	282,864	Lincoln	236,146	St. Paul	276,963
Chandler (Ariz.)	223,991	Long Beach	476,564	St. Petersburg	249,090
Charlotte	594,359	Louisville–		San Francisco	744,230
Chesapeake (Va.)	214,725	Jefferson county	556,332	Santa Ana	342,715
Cincinnati	314,154	Lubbock	207,852	Scottsdale	221,792
Cleveland	458,684	Madison	220,332	Seattle	571,480
Colorado Springs	369,363	Memphis	671,929	Stockton	279,888
Columbus	730,008	Mesa (Ariz.)	437,454	Tampa	321,772
Corpus Christi	281,196	Miami	379,724	Toledo	304,973
Denver	556,835	Milwaukee	583,624	Tucson	512,023
Detroit	900,198	Minneapolis	373,943	Tulsa	383,764
El Paso	592,099	Modesto	206,769	Virginia Beach	440,098
Fort Wayne	219,351	Montgomery	200,983	Washington, D.C.	553,523
Fort Worth	603,337	Nashville	546,719	Wichita	353,823
Fremont (Calif.)	202,373	New Orleans	462,269		
Fresno	457,719	Newark	280,451		

Immigration (2002): permanent immigrants admitted 1,063,700, from Mexico 20.6%, India 6.7%, China 5.8%, Africa 5.7%, the Philippines 4.8%, Vietnam 3.1%, El Salvador 2.9%, Cuba 2.7%, Bosnia and Herzegovina 2.4%, Haiti 2.1%, Dominican Republic 2.0%, South Korea 1.9%, Jamaica 1.4%, other 37.9%. Refugees (end of 2003) 452,548. Asylum seekers (end of 2000): 386,330.

Vital statistics

Birth rate per 1,000 population (2004): 14.0 (world avg. 21.1); legitimate 64.3%; illegitimate 35.7%.
Death rate per 1,000 population (2004): 8.1 (world avg. 9.0).
Natural increase rate per 1,000 population (2004): 5.9 (world avg. 12.1).
Marriage rate per 1,000 population (2004): 7.6; median age at first marriage (1991): men 26.3 years, women 24.1 years.

Divorce rate per 1,000 population (2004): 3.7.
Total fertility rate (avg. births per childbearing woman; 2004): 2.1.
Life expectancy at birth (2003): white male 75.4 years, black and other male (1996) 68.9 years; white female 80.5 years, black and other female 76.1 (1996) years.

Vital statistics (2002)

States	Live births	Birth rate per 1,000 population	Death rate per 1,000 population	Infant mortality rate per 1,000 live births[8]	Abortion rate per 1,000 live births	Life expectancy[9]
Alabama	58,967	13.9	10.3	8.6	208	73.6
Alaska	9,938	15.4	4.7	6.3	—	
Arizona	87,837	16.1	7.8	6.7	122	76.1
Arkansas	37,437	13.8	10.5	8.6	142	74.3
California	529,357	15.1	6.7	5.1	—	75.9
Colorado	68,418	15.2	6.5	6.5	113	77.0
Connecticut	42,001	12.1	8.7	5.6	321	76.9
Delaware	11,090	13.7	8.5	7.6	405	74.8
Florida	205,579	12.3	10.0	6.9	428	75.8
Georgia	133,300	15.6	7.6	8.4	256	73.6
Hawaii	17,477	14.0	7.1	5.2	224	78.2
Idaho	20,970	15.6	7.4	6.8	40	76.9
Illinois	180,622	14.3	8.5	7.0	260	74.9
Indiana	85,081	13.8	9.0	8.3	129	75.4
Iowa	37,559	12.8	9.5	5.2	166	77.3
Kansas	39,412	14.5	9.2	7.2	299	76.8
Kentucky	54,233	13.3	10.1	6.3	65	74.4
Louisiana	64,872	14.5	9.4	10.0	161	73.0
Maine	13,559	10.5	9.8	5.8	171	73.1
Maryland	73,323	13.4	8.1	8.7	185	76.4
Massachusetts	80,645	12.5	8.9	4.3	313	74.8
Michigan	129,967	12.9	8.7	7.7	225	75.0
Minnesota	68,025	13.6	7.7	4.9	209	77.8
Mississippi	41,518	14.5	10.0	9.2	87	73.0
Missouri	75,251	13.3	9.9	7.2	109	75.3
Montana	11,049	12.1	9.4	4.3	203	76.2
Nebraska	25,383	14.7	9.1	6.7	149	76.9
Nevada	32,571	15.0	7.8	6.3	306	74.2
New Hampshire	14,442	11.3	7.8	6.0	—	76.7
New Jersey	114,751	13.4	8.6	5.0	286	75.4
New Mexico	27,753	15.0	7.7	6.0	183	75.7
New York	251,415	13.1	8.3	6.0	509	74.7
North Carolina	117,335	14.1	8.7	8.5	249	74.5
North Dakota	7,757	12.2	9.3	4.9	157	77.6
Ohio	148,720	13.0	9.6	7.5	241	75.3
Oklahoma	50,387	14.4	10.2	8.2	129	75.1
Oregon	45,192	12.8	8.8	5.5	291	76.4
Pennsylvania	142,850	11.6	10.6	6.9	249	75.4
Rhode Island	12,894	12.1	9.6	4.6	430	76.5
South Carolina	54,570	13.3	9.2	8.4	122	73.5
South Dakota	10,698	14.1	9.1	7.7	77	76.9
Tennessee	77,482	13.4	9.8	8.5	230	74.3
Texas	372,450	17.1	7.3	6.1	215	75.1
Utah	49,182	21.2	5.7	5.1	72	77.7
Vermont	6,387	10.4	8.2	4.6	256	76.5
Virginia	99,672	13.7	7.8	7.1	251	75.2
Washington	79,028	13.0	7.5	5.4	318	76.8
West Virginia	20,712	11.5	11.7	6.5	99	74.3
Wisconsin	68,560	12.6	8.6	5.9	153	76.9
Wyoming	6,550	13.1	8.4	9.2	…	76.2
District						
District of Columbia	7,498	13.1	10.2	11.0	735	68.0
TOTAL/RATE	4,021,726	13.9	8.5	6.6	246	75.8

Major causes of death per 100,000 population (2003): cardiovascular diseases 310.1, of which ischemic heart disease 164.8, cerebrovascular diseases 54.3, atherosclerosis 4.5; malignant neoplasms (cancers) 190.7; diseases of the respiratory system 80.9, of which pneumonia 22.3; accidents and adverse effects 36.3, of which motor-vehicle accidents 15.2; diabetes mellitus 25.4; suicide 10.5; chronic liver disease and cirrhosis 9.4; AIDS 4.7.
Morbidity rates of infectious diseases per 100,000 population (2003): chlamydia 301.8; gonorrhea 115.2; AIDS 15.2; salmonellosis 15.0; syphilis 11.8; shigellosis 8.1; lyme disease 7.3; chicken pox 7.2; pertussis 4.0; hepatitis A (infectious) 2.6; hepatitis B (serum) 2.6.

Leading cause of death by age group (2003)

	Number of deaths			Total death rate per 100,000 population	Percentage of all deaths
	Total	Male[10]	Female[10]		
All ages[11]	2,443,930	1,177,578	1,225,773	854.0	100.0
1 to 4 years	4,911	2,824	2,155	31.1	0.20
Accidents	1,679	1,109	739	10.6	0.07
Congenital anomalies	514	246	221	3.3	0.02
Malignant neoplasms	383	233	187	2.4	0.02
Homicide	342	221	139	2.2	0.01
Diseases of the heart	186	…	…	1.2	0.01
5 to 14 years	6,930	4,401	3,012	16.9	0.28
Accidents	2,561	1,876	1,134	6.3	0.10
Malignant neoplasms	1,060	569	445	2.6	0.04
Congenital anomalies	370	…	…	0.9	0.02
Homicide	310	221	139	0.8	0.01
Suicide	255	244	63	0.6	0.01
15 to 24 years	33,022	23,071	8,236	80.1	1.35
Accidents	14,966	10,476	3,669	36.3	0.61
Homicide	5,148	4,191	732	12.5	0.21
Suicide	3,921	3,419	569	9.5	0.16
Malignant neoplasms	1,628	1,022	691	4.0	0.07
Diseases of the heart	1,083	…	…	2.6	0.04
25 to 44 years	128,924	85,187	45,062	153.0	5.28
Accidents	27,844	20,626	6,790	33.1	1.14
Malignant neoplasms	19,041	9,198	11,238	22.6	0.78
Diseases of the heart	16,283	…	…	19.3	0.67
Suicide	11,251	9,044	2,297	13.4	0.46
Homicide	7,367	5,613	1,693	8.7	0.30

Leading cause of death by age group (2003) (continued)

	Number of deaths			Total death rate per 100,000 population	Percentage of all deaths
	Total	Male[10]	Female[10]		
45 to 64 years	437,058	243,719	157,468	636.1	17.88
Malignant neoplasms	144,936	72,642	64,397	211.0	5.93
Diseases of the heart	101,713	72,979	34,119	148.0	4.16
Accidents	23,669	14,520	5,934	34.5	0.97
Diabetes mellitus	16,326	7,764	6,376	23.8	0.66
Cerebrovascular diseases	15,971	…	…	23.2	0.65
65 and over	1,804,131	802,369	997,366	5,022.8	73.8
Diseases of the heart	564,204	285,900	361,933	1,570.8	23.09
Malignant neoplasms	387,475	202,358	190,008	1,078.7	15.85
Cerebrovascular diseases	138,397	54,200	93,845	385.3	5.66
Lower respiratory diseases	109,199	…	…	304.0	4.47
Alzheimer's disease	62,707	…	…	174.6	2.57

Incidence of chronic health conditions per 1,000 population (1996): arthritis 126.8; chronic sinusitis 125.0; deformities or orthopedic impairments 111.2; hypertension 106.8; hay fever 89.4; hearing impairment 83.1; heart conditions 77.9; asthma 55.0; chronic bronchitis 53.4; migraine 43.5.

Social indicators

Educational attainment (2003). Percentage of population age 25 and over having: primary and incomplete secondary 15.4%; secondary 32.0%; some post-secondary 25.4%; 4-year higher degree 17.9%; advanced degree 9.3%. Number of earned degrees (2002): bachelor's degree 1,292,000; master's degree 482,000; doctor's degree 44,000; first-professional degrees (in fields such as medicine, theology, and law) 81,000.

Distribution of income (2003)

percentage of disposable family income by quintile

1	2	3	4	5 (highest)
3.4	8.7	14.7	23.4	49.8

Quality of working life (2003). Average workweek: 39.0 hours. Annual death rate per 100,000 workers (2003): 2.5; leading causes of occupational deaths (2003): transportation incidents 24%, falls 12%, assaults/violent acts 11%, struck by object 10%. Annual occupational injury rate per 100,000 workers (2002): 2.4. Average duration of journey to work (2004): 24.7 minutes (private automobile 87.8%, of which drive alone 77.7%, carpool 10.1%; take public transportation 4.6%; walk 2.4%; work at home 3.8%; other 1.4%). Rate per 1,000 employed workers of discouraged workers (unemployed no longer seeking work; 2000): 1.8.
Access to services (2003). Proportion of occupied dwellings having access to: electricity 100.0%; safe public water supply 100.0%; public sewage collection (1995) 77.0%; septic tanks (1995) 22.8%.
Social participation. Eligible voters participating in last presidential election (2004): 60.7%. Population age 18 and over participating in voluntary work (1999): 66.0%. Trade-union membership in total workforce (2003): 14.3%.
Social deviance (2002). Offense rate per 100,000 population for: murder 5.6; rape 33.0; robbery 145.9; aggravated assault 310.1; motor-vehicle theft 432.1; burglary and housebreaking 746.2; larceny-theft 2,445.8; drug-abuse violation 587.1; drunkenness 149.1. Estimated drug and substance users (population age 12 and over; 2002)[12]: cigarettes 26.0%; binge alcohol[13] 22.9%; marijuana and hashish 6.2%; cocaine 0.9%; hallucinogens 0.5%; heroin 0.1%. Rate per 100,000 population of suicide (2003): 12.0.
Leisure (2002). Favourite leisure activities (percentage of total population age 18 and over that undertook activity at least once in the previous year): movie 60.0%, exercise program 55.0%, gardening 47.0%, home improvement 42.0%, amusement park 42.0%, sports events 35.0%, charity work 29.0%.
Material well-being (2002). Occupied dwellings with householder possessing: automobile 95.6%; telephone 95.5%; television receiver 99.0%; video and DVD players 91.2%; personal computers 56.1%; washing machine 80.1%; clothes dryer 75.9%; air conditioner 75.6%; cable television 69.4%.
Recreational expenditures (2001): U.S.$593,900,000,000 (television and radio receivers, computers, and video equipment 17.8%; golfing, bowling, and other participatory activities 12.3%; nondurable toys and sports equipment 11.2%; sports supplies 10.2%; magazines and newspapers 5.9%; books and maps 5.9%; spectator amusements 4.9%, of which theatre and opera 1.7%, spectator sports 1.7%, movies 1.5%; flowers, seeds, and potted plants 3.1%; other 28.7%).

National economy

Budget (2004). Revenue: U.S.$1,880,100,000,000 (individual income tax 43.0%, social-insurance taxes and contributions 39.0%, corporation income tax 10.1%, excise taxes 3.7%, customs duties 1.1%). Expenditures: U.S.$2,292,-215,000,000 (social security and medicare 36.0%, defense 19.9%, interest on debt 6.7%, other 37.4%).
Total outstanding national debt (December 2005): U.S.$8,097,000,000,000, of which debt held by the public U.S.$4,714,000,000,000, intragovernment holdings U.S.$3,383,000,000,000.

Manufacturing, mining, and construction enterprises (2002)

	no. of enterprises	no. of employees	hourly wages as a % of all wages[14]	value added (U.S.$'000,000)
Manufacturing				
Chemical and related products	13,107	790.2	131.0	226,615
Transportation equipment	12,264	1,646,400	137.2	227,675
Electric and electronic machinery	6,420	500,600	100.9	73,644
Computers	15,698	1,302,000	…	223,718
Machinery, except electrical	28,129	1,163,900	113.2	131,103
Food and related products	26,374	1,507,900	90.1	193,224

Manufacturing, mining, and construction enterprises (2002) (continued)

	no. of enter-prises	no. of employees	hourly wages as a % of all wages[14]	value added (U.S.$'000,000)
Manufacturing (continued)				
Fabricated metal products	60,602	1,557,100	100.4	138,793
Printing and publishing	37,168	718,100	104.0	60,483
Rubber and plastic products	15,305	939,900	92.2	86,558
Paper and related products	5,463	475,800	118.0	73,036
Primary metals	5,952	489,000	119.9	53,111
Lumber and wood	16,912	535,200	85.4	33,130
Stone, clay, and glass products[14]	16,537	524,000	102.9	43,900
Petroleum and coal products	2,278	105,900	162.1	47,346
Furniture and fixtures	21,824	571,000	84.6	39,849
Textile-mill products	7,333	190,300	79.8	31,694
Apparel and related products	12,516	352,200	66.3	24,809
Beverages and tobacco products	2,997	157,300	127.4	77,735
Leather and leather products	1,515	45,700	72.6	3,500
Miscellaneous manufacturing industries	31,886	746,800	85.1	29,100[14]
Mining				
Oil and gas extraction	8,000	123,000	128.9	84,600
Coal mining	1,400	59,000	137.6	13,200
Nonmetallic, except fuels	4,800	105,000	110.8	14,900
Metal mining	400	20,000	137.4	8,570
Construction				
Special trade contractors	437,986	4,265,000	130.4	453,737
General contractors and operative builders	223,114	1,753,000	124.3	531,162
Heavy construction contractors	36,647	925,000	121.5	155,468

Gross national product (2003): U.S.$11,031,600,000,000 (U.S.$37,898 per capita).

Structure of gross domestic product and labour force

	2003			
	in value U.S.$'000,000,000	% of total value	labour force[15]	% of labour force[15]
Agriculture	113.9	1.0	2,275,000	1.6
Mining	130.3	1.2	525,000	0.4
Manufacturing	1,402.3	12.7	16,902,000	11.5
Construction	501.3	4.6	10,138,000	6.9
Public utilities	222.2	2.0	1,193,000	0.8
Transp. and commun.	813.1	7.4	9,445,000	6.4
Trade	1,705.7[16]	15.5[16]	29,727,000[16]	20.3[16]
Finance, real estate	2,250.3	20.5	23,627,000	16.1
Public administration, defense	1,399.9	12.7	6,243,000	4.3
Services	2,465.1	22.4	37,662,000	25.7
Other	...	...	8,774,000[17]	6.0[17]
TOTAL	11,004.0[3]	100.0	146,510,000[3]	100.0

Gross domestic product

(in U.S.$'000,000,000)

	1999	2000	2001	2002	2003
Gross domestic product	9,274.3	9,824.6	10,082.2	10,480.8	10,987.9
By type of expenditure					
Personal consumption expenditures	6,246.5	6,683.7	6,987.0	7,385.3	7,757.4
Durable goods	755.9	803.9	835.9	911.3	941.6
Nondurable goods	1,830.1	1,972.9	2,041.3	2,086.0	2,209.7
Services	3,660.5	3,906.9	4,109.9	4,388.0	4,606.2
Gross private domestic investment	1,636.7	1,755.4	1,586.0	1,589.2	1,670.6
Fixed investment	1,577.2	1,691.8	1,646.3	1,583.9	1,673.0
Changes in business inventories	59.5	63.6	-60.3	5.4	-2.4
Net exports of goods and services	-249.9	-365.5	-348.9	-426.3	-495.0
Exports	989.3	1,101.1	1,034.1	1,006.8	1,048.9
Imports	1,239.2	1,466.6	1,383.0	1,433.1	1,543.8
Government purchases of goods and services	1,641.0	1,751.0	1,858.0	1,932.5	2,054.8
Federal	565.0	589.2	628.1	679.5	757.2
State and local	1,076.0	1,161.8	1,229.9	1,253.1	1,297.6
By major type of product					
Goods output	3,473.4	3,651.0	3,593.7	3,456.2	3,579.8
Durable goods	1,649.6	1,735.0	1,611.4	1,582.8	1,633.6
Nondurable goods	1,823.8	1,915.9	1,982.3	1,873.4	1,946.2
Services	4,947.1	5,259.2	5,535.1	6,049.8	6,377.7
Structures	853.8	914.5	953.3	974.8	1,030.4
National income (incl. capital consumption adjustment)	...	...	8,979.8	9,229.3	9,660.9
By type of income					
Compensation of employees	...	...	5,942.1	6,091.2	6,321.1
Proprietors' income	...	...	771.9	768.4	810.2
Rental income of persons	...	...	167.4	152.9	131.7
Corporate profits	...	...	767.3	886.3	1,031.8
Net interest	...	...	566.3	520.9	528.5
By industry division (incl. capital consumption adjustment)					
Agriculture, forestry, fishing	93.8	98	103	98.6	112.0
Mining and construction	492	557.2	578.2	570.5	606.7
Manufacturing	1,373.1	1,426.2	1,346.0	1,351.6	1,392.8
Durable	820.4	865.3	788	786.1	810.1
Nondurable	552.7	560.9	558	565.5	582.7
Transportation	287.4	301.6	295.1	294.9	310.6
Communications	439.3	458.3	474.8	484.0	536.1
Public utilities	185.4	189.3	195.1	201.6	212.7
Wholesale and retail trade	1,213.2	1,254.1	1,290.7	1,388.7	1,435.1
Finance, insurance, real estate	1,798.4	1,931.0	2,028.0	2,125.7	2,228.5
Services	2,244.6	2,398.4	2,530.3	2,638.5	2,763.4
Government and government enterprise	1,141.2	1,202.7	1,259.6	1,326.7	1,390.0

Business activity (1997): number of businesses 23,645,000 (sole proprietorships 72.6%, active corporations 19.9%, active partnerships 7.5%), of which services 10,114,000, wholesaling and retailing 4,455,000; business receipts

U.S.$18,057,000,000,000 (active corporations 88.0%, sole proprietorships 4.8%, active partnerships 7.2%), of which wholesaling and retailing U.S.$5,136,-000,000,000, services U.S.$2,130,000,000,000; net profit U.S.$1,270,000,000,000 (active corporations 72.0%, sole proprietorships 14.7%, partnerships 13.3%), of which services U.S.$203,000,000,000, wholesaling and retailing U.S.$10,-000,000,000. New business starts and business failures (1995): total number of new business starts 168,158; total failures 71,194, of which commercial service 21,850, retail trade 12,952; failure rate per 10,000 concerns 90.0; current liabilities of failed concerns U.S.$37,507,000,000; average liability U.S.$526,830. Business expenditures for new plant and equipment (1995): total U.S.$594,-465,000,000, of which trade, services, and communications U.S.$244,-829,000,000, manufacturing businesses U.S.$172,308,000,000 (durable goods 53.0%, nondurable goods 47.0%), public utilities U.S.$42,816,000,000, transportation U.S.$37,021,000,000, mining and construction U.S.$35,985,000.

Components of gross domestic product (2004)

States	Gross state product (U.S.$'000,-000,000)	Personal income (U.S.$'000,-000,000)	Disposable personal income (U.S.$'000,-000,000)	Per capita disposable personal income (U.S.$)
Alabama	139.8	125.2	114.0	27,630
Alaska	34.0	22.3	20.4	34,678
Arizona	200.0	164.3	148.7	28,609
Arkansas	80.9	70.8	64.5	25,724
California	1,550.8	1,262.5	1,113.1	35,172
Colorado	201.2	166.2	148.5	36,109
Connecticut	185.8	159.4	135.9	45,506
Delaware	54.3	29.5	26.1	35,559
Florida	599.1	512.0	497.0	31,460
Georgia	343.1	265.5	237.4	30,074
Hawaii	50.3	41.2	36.8	32,606
Idaho	43.6	37.4	34.0	26,839
Illinois	521.9	441.5	393.2	34,725
Indiana	227.6	187.6	168.9	30,070
Iowa	111.1	91.5	83.2	30,970
Kansas	98.9	84.8	76.5	31,003
Kentucky	136.4	112.6	101.1	27,151
Louisiana	152.9	122.9	112.6	27,219
Maine	43.3	39.5	35.5	29,973
Maryland	228.0	220.3	191.9	39,629
Massachusetts	317.8	270.1	234.2	42,102
Michigan	372.2	324.1	291.7	32,052
Minnesota	223.8	184.5	162.7	36,173
Mississippi	76.2	70.8	65.5	24,379
Missouri	203.3	175.6	158.4	30,516
Montana	27.5	25.6	23.3	27,666
Nebraska	68.2	56.4	51.1	32,276
Nevada	100.3	78.9	70.8	33,793
New Hampshire	51.9	47.7	43.1	36,676
New Jersey	416.1	362.2	316.8	41,636
New Mexico	61.0	49.8	45.2	26,154
New York	896.7	737.0	633.0	38,333
North Carolina	336.4	250.3	224.2	29,333
North Dakota	21.6	18.6	17.0	29,247
Ohio	419.9	356.8	317.9	31,135
Oklahoma	107.6	98.0	88.9	27,819
Oregon	128.1	110.0	97.5	30,584
Pennsylvania	468.1	412.6	367.9	33,257
Rhode Island	41.7	36.9	32.9	34,180
South Carolina	136.1	114.0	103.6	27,153
South Dakota	29.4	23.6	22.0	30,617
Tennessee	217.6	175.9	162.4	29,806
Texas	884.1	690.4	633.7	30,697
Utah	82.6	64.4	58.2	26,946
Vermont	21.9	19.7	17.8	31,737
Virginia	329.3	269.9	236.9	36,175
Washington	261.5	217.2	197.6	35,017
West Virginia	49.4	46.6	42.6	25,681
Wisconsin	211.6	176.6	157.0	32,063
Wyoming	24.0	17.3	15.7	34,199
District				
District of Columbia	76.7	28.8	25.2	52,101
TOTAL/AVERAGE	11,665.6	9,667.3	8,654.1	29,472

Retail and wholesale trade and services (2002)

	no. of establish-ments	no. of employees	hourly wage as a % of all wages[14]	annual sales or receipts (U.S.$'000,000)
Retail trade	1,111,583	15,029,000	68.7	3,171,000
Automotive dealers	122,692	1,884,000	93.5	812,000
Food stores	149,802	2,896,000	68.8	488,000
General merchandise group stores	39,846	2,549,000	74.7	451,000
Eating and drinking places	484,000	8,012,000	50.0[18, 19]	333,500
Building materials, hardware, garden supply, and mobile home dealers	94,100	1,249,000	74.2	299,900
Gasoline service stations	119,600[14]	937,000[14]	93.5	244,800
Apparel and accessory stores	149,318	1,425,000	67.8	170,000
Drugstores and proprietary stores	79,360	1,043,000	79.8	183,000
Furniture, home furnishings, equipment stores	65,088	554,000	92.2	94,000
Electronics and appliances	46,724	418,000	75.1	88,000
Sporting goods, book and music stores	63,033	633,000	92.1	78,000
Liquor stores	28,600	136,000	...	27,200
Wholesale trade	438,900	6,142,000	110.1	2,742,300
Durable goods	288,286	3,565,000	114.9	1,334,100
Professional and commercial equipment	43,100	777,000	136.6	249,400
Machinery, equipment, and supplies	72,100	797,000	115.9	223,300
Electrical goods	37,800	569,000	117.5	204,400
Motor vehicles, automotive equipment	27,600	387,000	101.8	215,400
Computers and software	...	...	...	113,500

Retail and wholesale trade and services (2002) (continued)

	no. of establishments	no. of employees	hourly wage as a % of all wages[14]	annual sales or receipts (U.S.$'000,000)
Metals and minerals, except petroleum	11,300	166,000	109.1	89,800
Lumber and other construction materials	15,500	185,000	101.8	77,900
Hardware, plumbing, heating equipment and supplies	21,300	248,000	106.4	66,100
Furniture and home furnishings	14,500	166,000	100.8	43,600
Miscellaneous durable goods	39,600	347,000	89.6	164,200
Nondurable goods	153,524	2,470,000	97.3	1,408,200
Groceries and related products	39,200	871,000	101.5	402,700
Petroleum and products	10,400	129,000	93.8	181,100
Drugs, drug proprietaries, and druggists' sundries	7,200	235,000	142.6	233,200
Farm-products raw materials	9,300	91,000	79.2	111,300
Apparel and accessories	19,500	212,000	97.6	91,100
Paper and paper products	14,400	226,000	104.9	76,700
Beer, wine, and distilled alcoholic beverages	4,600	161,000	115.0	79,800
Chemicals and allied products	15,800	164,000	119.7	60,400
Miscellaneous nondurable goods	35,100	420,000	84.0	185,000
Services	11,958,000	61,289,000	101.6	2,151,500
Health	712,000	15,347,000	107.1	1,234,000
Business, except computer services	276,000	8,345,000	100.9	414,000
Computer and data-processing services	100,000[14]	1,171,000[14]	168.4	172,138
Legal services	177,000	1,110,000	145.3	184,305
Automotive repair, services, garages	164,000	871,000	86.7	88,612
Management and public relations	48,000	2,879,000	139.6	121,511
Hotels and motels	60,196	1,753,000	70.1	463,000
Amusement and recreation	66,000	1,334,000	76.4	74,000
Professional, scientific, and technical services	747,000	7,509,000	...	896,000
Personal services	192,000	1,217,000	72.2	73,000
Motion pictures	23,000	334,000	111.4	77,000

Production. Agriculture, forestry, fishing (value of production/catch in U.S.$'000,000 except as noted; 2004): corn (maize) 23,033, soybeans 16,098, wheat 7,192, cotton lint 5,300, grapes 2,879, potatoes 2,564, almonds 2,052, apples 1,758, tobacco 1,752, rice 1,676, strawberries 1,471, tomatoes 1,342, lettuce 1,176, mushrooms 920, cottonseed 874, onions 863, sorghum 839, peanuts (groundnuts) 834, barley 694, broccoli 677, sweet corn 619; livestock (number of live animals) 94,888,000 cattle, 60,444,000 pigs, 6,105,000 sheep, 5,400,000 horses, 1,960,000 chickens; roundwood 293,951,000 cu m; fish and shellfish catch (2002) 3,092, of which fish 1,359 (including salmon 155, Alaska pollack 204), shellfish 1,706 (including shrimp 461, crabs 398). Mining (metal content in metric tons except as noted; 2003): iron 44,500,000; copper 1,120,000; zinc 738,000; lead 449,000; molybdenum 33,600; silver 1,240,000 kg; gold 277,000 kg; helium 122,000,000 cu m. Quarrying (metric tons; 2003): crushed stone 1,530,000,000; sand and gravel 1,160,000,000; portland cement 88,100,000; common salt 41,100,000; clay 40,030,000; phosphate rock 35,000,000; lime 17,900,000; gypsum 16,700,000. Manufacturing (value added in U.S.$'000,000; 2001): transportation equipment 227,675, of which motor vehicle parts 74,532, aerospace products and parts 71,839, motor vehicles 54,173; chemicals and chemical products 226,615, of which pharmaceuticals and medicine 91,697; computers and electronic products 223,718, navigational, measuring, medical, and scientific equipment 60,035, communications equipment 50,757, computers and related components 34,394; food and food products 193,224; fabricated metal products 138,793; nonelectrical machinery 131,103; beverages and tobacco products 77,735; paper and paper products 73,036; plastic products 69,475; printing and publishing 60,483; general electrical equipment 56,304; cement, bricks, and ceramics 53,195; nonferrous metals 53,111; refined petroleum and coke 47,346; furniture 39,849; wood and wood products 33,130; textiles 31,694; wearing apparel 24,809. Construction (completed; 2003): private U.S.$690,019,000,000, of which residential U.S.$476,143,000,000, nonresidential U.S.$213,876,000,000; public U.S.$202,882,000,000.

Energy production (consumption): electricity (kW-hr; 2002) 3,058,452,000,000 (3,880,352,000,000); hard coal (metric tons; 2002) 917,911,000 (896,996,000); lignite (metric tons; 2002) 74,806,000 (74,667,000); crude petroleum (barrels; 2002) 2,078,000,000 (5,600,000,000); petroleum products (metric tons; 2002) 756,313,000 (784,690,000); natural gas (cu m; 2002) 559,907,000,000 (673,226,000,000). Domestic production of energy by source (2002): coal 31.6%, natural gas 27.2%, crude petroleum 16.6%, nuclear power 11.3%, renewable energy 8.1%, other 5.2%.

Energy consumption by source (2002): petroleum and petroleum products 40.0%, natural gas 23.6%, coal 22.7%, nuclear electric power 8.3%, hydroelectric and thermal 5.4%; by end use: industrial 33.4%, residential and commercial 39.4%, transportation 27.2%.

Energy consumption by source and by state (2001)

('000,000,000,000 Btu)

States	Petroleum	Natural gas[20]	Coal	Hydroelectric power	Nuclear electric power
Alabama	539	342	845	85	317
Alaska	292	413	16	14	0.0
Arizona	524	245	424	80	300
Arkansas	378	232	274	26	154
California	3,604	2,514	68	256	347
Colorado	462	385	400	13	0.0
Connecticut	439	149	40	3	161
Delaware	147	52	38	0.0	0.0
Florida	1,990	570	726	2	330
Georgia	1,034	363	772	21	352
Hawaii	240	2	18	1	0.0
Idaho	155	82	11	74	0.0
Illinois	1,304	971	994	2	965

Energy consumption by source and by state (2001) (continued)

('000,000,000,000 Btu)

States	Petroleum	Natural gas[20]	Coal	Hydroelectric power	Nuclear electric power
Indiana	837	514	1,567	6	0.0
Iowa	401	225	445	9	40
Kansas	391	274	355	0.3	108
Kentucky	704	217	1,011	39	0.0
Louisiana	1,491	1,340	240	7	181
Maine	233	101	8	27	0.0
Maryland	568	191	317	12	143
Massachusetts	762	364	109	0.0	54
Michigan	1,042	929	797	4	279
Minnesota	674	345	353	9	123
Mississippi	486	341	198	0.0	104
Missouri	719	289	716	9	88
Montana	168	67	184	67	0.0
Nebraska	218	124	228	11	91
Nevada	250	181	189	26	0.0
New Hampshire	178	25	40	10	91
New Jersey	1,246	586	112	−1[21]	318
New Mexico	251	262	297	2	0.0
New York	1,713	1,206	315	225	422
North Carolina	950	216	757	26	395
North Dakota	138	63	420	14	0.0
Ohio	1,305	836	1,343	5	162
Oklahoma	588	548	377	23	0.0
Oregon	368	236	43	291	0.0
Pennsylvania	1,454	669	1,379	11	770
Rhode Island	100	99	[22]	0.1	0.0
South Carolina	470	147	414	2	521
South Dakota	112	37	44	35	0.0
Tennessee	708	265	688	63	299
Texas	5,521	4,435	1,493	12	399
Utah	261	168	390	5	0.0
Vermont	89	8	[22]	9	44
Virginia	911	247	482	−13[21]	269
Washington	843	323	100	557	86
West Virginia	215	152	872	10	0.0
Wisconsin	668	363	405	21	120
Wyoming	157	104	500	9	0.0
District					
District of Columbia	34	31	[22]	0.0	0.0
TOTAL	38,332	22,848	21,814	2,118	8,033

Household income[23] level by selected characteristics (2004)

Characteristics	Number of households ('000)	Number ('000) Under $15,000	$15,000–$34,999	$35,000–$74,999	$75,000 and over	Median income ($)
Total/Average	113,146	17,361	28,109	38,334	29,342	44,389
Age of householder						
15 to 24 years	6,686	1,714	2,320	2,063	589	27,586
25 to 34 years	19,255	2,196	4,832	7,654	4,573	45,485
35 to 44 years	23,226	2,192	4,427	8,455	8,152	56,785
45 to 54 years	23,370	2,379	4,030	7,834	9,127	61,111
55 to 64 years	17,476	2,365	3,883	5,834	5,394	50,400
65 years and over	23,133	6,513	8,618	5,603	2,339	24,509
Size of household						
One person	29,858	10,132	10,402	7,212	2,112	22,480
Two persons	37,247	3,732	9,784	13,651	10,080	47,031
Three persons	18,347	1,676	3,312	6,793	6,566	57,876
Four persons	16,506	1,066	2,589	5,779	7,072	65,869
Five persons	7,230	488	1,249	2,618	2,875	62,475
Six persons	2,552	166	506	886	994	57,087
Seven or more persons	1,435	104	262	541	528	58,688
Educational attainment of householder						
Total[24]	106,461	15,647	25,787	35,369	29,658	45,996
Less than 9th grade	6,355	2,443	2,372	1,252	288	19,541
Some high school	9,217	3,120	3,572	1,876	649	22,476
High school graduate	32,206	5,373	9,710	11,485	5,638	37,378
Some college, no degree	18,744	2,181	4,610	7,047	4,906	47,390
Associate degree	9,405	799	2,010	3,662	2,934	54,004
Bachelor's degree	19,595	1,216	2,776	6,438	9,165	68,626
Master's degree	7,714	388	815	2,359	4,152	80,282
Professional degree	1,767	62	135	375	1,195	100,000
Doctorate degree	1,459	62	100	348	949	100,000

Household income and expenditure (2002). Average household size 2.6; median annual income per household U.S.$42,409, of which median Asian (including Hispanic) household U.S.$52,626, median white (including Hispanic) household U.S.$45,086, median non-Hispanic household (2001) U.S.$46,305, median Hispanic[6] household U.S.$33,103, median black (including Hispanic) household U.S.$29,026; sources of personal income (2003): wages and salaries 55.4%, self-employment 9.2%, transfer payments 6.5%, other 28.9%; consumption expenditure: housing 19.2%, transportation 19.1%, food at home 7.6%, fuel and utilities 6.6%, health 5.8%, food away from home 5.6%, recreation 5.1%, wearing apparel 4.3%, household furnishings 3.7%, education 1.8%, other 21.2%.

Financial aggregates

	1999	2000	2001	2002	2003	2004	2005[25]
Exchange rate, U.S.$ per:							
£[26]	1.62	1.52	1.44	1.50	1.63	1.79	1.77
SDR[26]	1.37	1.32	1.27	1.29	1.40	1.48	1.47
International reserves (U.S.$)[27]							
Total (excl. gold; '000,000,000)	60.50	56.60	57.63	67.96	74.89	75.89	60.23
SDRs ('000,000,000)	10.35	10.54	10.78	12.17	12.64	13.63	8.24
Reserve pos. in IMF ('000,000,000)	17.97	14.82	17.87	21.98	22.53	19.54	13.25
Foreign exchange ('000,000,000)	32.18	31.24	29.98	33.82	39.72	42.72	38.74

Financial aggregates (continued)

	1999	2000	2001	2002	2003	2004	2005[25]
Gold ('000,000 fine troy oz)	261.67	261.61	262.00	262.00	261.55	261.59	261.50
% world reserves	27.13	27.52	27.83	28.16	28.60	...	...
Interest and prices							
Central bank discount (%)[27]	5.00	6.00	1.25	0.75	2.00	3.2	4.6
Govt. bond yield (%)[26]	5.64	6.03	5.02	4.61	4.02	4.27	4.20
Industrial share prices[26] (2000 = 100)	92.1	100.0	78.9	65.3	62.9	73.7	80.5
Balance of payments (U.S.$'000,000,000)							
Balance of visible trade	−343.72	−449.79	−424.09	−479.41	−544.30	−661.93	...
Imports, f.o.b.	−1,029.99	−1,224.43	−1,145.93	−1,164.75	−1,260.71	−1,472.96	...
Exports, f.o.b.	686.27	774.63	721.84	685.34	716.41	811.03	...
Balance of invisibles	+46.87	+36.46	+38.39	+5.47	+13.64	+6.14	...
Balance of payments, current account	−296.85	−413.44	−385.70	−473.94	−530.66	−668.07	...

Average employee earnings

	average hourly earnings in U.S.$		average weekly earnings in U.S.$	
	2002	2003	2002	2003
Manufacturing				
Durable goods	16.02	16.46	652.97	671.53
Lumber and wood products	12.33	12.71	492.00	513.92
Furniture and fixtures	12.61	12.98	494.01	505.23
Nonmetallic mineral products	15.40	15.77	646.91	665.11
Primary metal industries	17.68	18.13	749.32	767.63
Fabricated metal products	14.68	15.01	596.38	610.33
Machinery, except electrical	15.92	16.30	645.55	664.79
Electrical equipment and appliances	13.98	14.35	560.24	582.68
Transportation equipment	20.64	21.25	877.87	890.32
Computer and electronic products	16.20	16.68	642.87	674.68
Miscellaneous manufacturing	12.91	13.30	499.13	510.69
Nondurable goods	14.15	14.63	566.84	582.65
Food and kindred products	12.55	12.80	496.91	502.65
Tobacco manufactures	17.73	17.96	698.39	702.75
Textile mill products	11.73	12.00	476.52	480.00
Apparel and other textile products	9.10	9.58	333.66	340.22
Paper and allied products	16.85	17.32	705.62	719.21
Printing and publishing	14.93	15.37	503.05	587.42
Chemicals and allied products	17.97	18.52	759.53	784.56
Petroleum and coal products	23.04	23.64	990.88	1,052.97
Rubber and miscellaneous plastics products	13.55	14.18	662.70	634.70
Leather and leather products	11.00	11.67	412.99	458.26
Nonmanufacturing				
Mining	17.19	17.58	741.97	766.83
Utilities	23.96	24.76	979.09	1,016.94
Construction	18.52	18.95	711.82	727.11
Transportation and warehousing	15.76	16.25	579.75	597.79
Wholesale trade	16.98	17.36	644.38	657.12
Retail trade	11.67	11.90	360.81	367.28
Finance, insurance, and real estate	16.17	17.13	575.51	608.87
Leisure and hospitality services	8.58	8.76	221.25	224.25
Education and health services	15.21	15.64	492.74	505.76
Professional and business services	15.94	16.04	574.66	586.68
Information services	20.20	21.01	738.17	761.13
Other services	13.72	13.84	439.76	434.49

Median household income[28]

(in current 2004 U.S.$)

States	1999	2000	2001	2002	2003	2004
Alabama	36,251	35,424	35,160	37,603	37,225	38,111
Alaska	51,396	52,847	57,363	52,774	51,837	54,627
Arizona	36,995	39,783	42,704	39,734	41,166	42,590
Arkansas	29,682	29,697	33,339	32,387	32,002	33,948
California	43,629	46,816	47,262	47,437	49,300	49,894
Colorado	48,177	48,240	49,397	48,294	49,940	51,022
Connecticut	50,593	50,172	53,347	53,387	54,965	55,970
Delaware	46,628	50,365	49,602	49,650	49,019	50,152
Florida	35,831	38,856	36,421	38,024	38,972	40,171
Georgia	39,425	41,901	42,576	42,939	42,438	43,217
Hawaii	44,504	51,546	47,439	47,303	51,834	53,123
Idaho	35,800	37,611	38,241	37,715	42,372	42,519
Illinois	46,330	46,064	46,171	42,710	45,153	45,787
Indiana	40,838	40,865	40,379	41,047	42,425	43,003
Iowa	41,098	40,991	40,976	41,049	41,384	43,042
Kansas	37,348	41,059	41,415	42,619	44,232	43,725
Kentucky	33,738	36,265	38,437	36,762	36,936	37,396
Louisiana	32,654	30,718	33,322	34,008	33,507	35,523
Maine	38,862	37,266	36,612	36,853	37,113	39,395
Maryland	52,205	54,535	53,530	56,407	52,314	56,763
Massachusetts	44,005	46,753	52,253	49,855	50,955	52,354
Michigan	46,089	45,512	45,047	42,715	45,022	44,476
Minnesota	47,038	54,251	52,681	54,622	52,823	55,914
Mississippi	32,478	34,299	30,161	30,882	32,728	33,659
Missouri	41,383	45,097	41,339	42,776	43,762	43,988
Montana	31,038	32,777	32,126	34,835	34,108	35,201
Nebraska	38,626	41,750	43,611	42,796	43,974	44,623
Nevada	41,461	45,758	45,403	44,958	45,184	46,984
New Hampshire	46,055	50,926	51,331	55,321	55,567	57,352
New Jersey	49,734	50,405	51,771	54,568	56,045	56,772
New Mexico	32,574	35,093	33,124	35,457	35,105	37,587
New York	39,989	40,744	42,114	41,966	42,788	44,228
North Carolina	37,254	38,317	38,162	36,415	37,279	39,000
North Dakota	32,663	35,996	35,793	36,200	40,410	39,594
Ohio	39,489	42,962	41,785	42,684	43,520	44,160
Oklahoma	32,683	32,432	35,609	36,458	35,902	38,281

Median household income[28] (continued)

(in current 2004 U.S.$)

States	1999	2000	2001	2002	2003	2004
Oregon	40,619	42,499	41,273	41,802	41,638	42,617
Pennsylvania	37,758	42,176	43,499	42,498	42,933	44,286
Rhode Island	42,719	42,197	45,723	42,417	44,711	46,199
South Carolina	36,462	37,570	37,736	37,812	38,479	39,326
South Dakota	35,828	36,475	39,671	37,873	39,522	40,518
Tennessee	36,522	34,096	35,783	37,030	37,523	38,550
Texas	38,688	38,609	40,860	40,149	39,271	41,275
Utah	46,050	47,550	47,342	47,861	49,275	50,614
Vermont	41,584	39,594	40,794	42,999	43,261	45,692
Virginia	45,693	47,163	50,241	49,631	54,783	53,275
Washington	45,473	42,525	42,490	45,183	47,508	48,688
West Virginia	29,297	29,411	29,673	29,359	32,763	32,589
Wisconsin	45,667	45,088	45,346	45,903	46,269	47,220
Wyoming	37,248	39,629	39,719	39,763	42,555	43,641
District						
District of Columbia	38,670	41,222	41,169	39,070	45,044	...
U.S. AVERAGE	40,696	41,990	42,228	42,409	43,318	44,473

Average annual expenditure of "consumer units" (households, plus individuals sharing households or budgets; 2001): total U.S.$39,518, of which housing U.S.$13,011, transportation U.S.$7,633, food U.S.$5,321, pensions and social security U.S.$3,326, health care U.S.$2,182, clothing U.S.$1,743, other U.S.$6,302.

Selected household characteristics (2004). Total number of households 113,146,000, of which (family households by race) white 83.1%, black 12.5%, other 4.4%; (by tenure) owned 78,574,000 (69.4%), rented 34,572,000 (30.6%); family households 77,010,000, of which married couple 75.5%, female householder 18.2%, male householder 6.3%; nonfamily households 36,136,000, of which female living alone 47.6%, male living alone 35.0%, other 17.4%.

Population economically active (2003): total 146,510,000 (civilian population only); activity rate of total population 50.4% (participation rates: age 16–64, 74.6%; female 46.6%; unemployed [February 2004–January 2005] 5.5%).

Price and earnings indexes (2000 = 100)

	1998	1999	2000	2001	2002	2003	2004
Consumer price index	94.7	96.7	100.0	102.8	104.5	106.8	109.7
Hourly earnings index	93.9	96.7	100.0	103.1	106.8	109.9	112.7

Tourism (2003): receipts from visitors U.S.$65,054,000,000; expenditures by nationals abroad U.S.$59,664,000,000; number of foreign visitors 41,212,000 ([2002] 12,968,000 from Canada, 9,807,000 from Mexico, 10,131,000 from Europe); number of nationals traveling abroad 56,175,000 ([2002] 16,810,000 to Mexico, 16,161,000 to Canada).

Land use as % of total land area (2000): in temporary crops 19.3%, in permanent crops 0.2%, in pasture 25.5%; overall forest area 24.7%.

Foreign trade

Balance of trade (current prices)

	1999	2000	2001	2002	2003	2004
U.S.$'000,000,000	−328.8	−436.1	−411.9	−468.3	−549.4	−652.0
% of total	19.1%	21.8%	22.0%	25.3%	27.8%	28.5%

Imports (2004): U.S.$1,471,000,000,000 (motor vehicles and parts 12.6%; crude petroleum 9.7%; chemicals and chemical products 7.8%; nonelectrical machinery 6.6%; computers and office equipment 6.5%; electrical machinery 6.4%, of which televisions and electronic components 2.6%; wearing apparel 5.1%; iron and steel 1.9%; footwear 1.2%). *Major import sources:* Canada 17.4%; China 13.4%; Mexico 10.6%; Japan 8.8%; Germany 5.3%; United Kingdom 3.2%; South Korea 3.1%; Taiwan 2.4%; France 2.2%; Italy 1.9%; Malaysia 1.9%; Ireland 1.9%.

Exports (2004): U.S.$819,000,000,000 (chemicals and related products 14.7%; electrical machinery 8.6%; motor vehicles 8.5%; agricultural commodities 6.0%; airplanes 5.6%; power generating machinery 4.2%; telecommunications equipment 4.2%; computers and office equipment 3.9%; general industrial machinery 3.8%; scientific and precision equipment 3.8%; specialized industrial machinery 1.7%). *Major export destinations:* Canada 23.2%; Mexico 13.5%; Japan 6.6%; United Kingdom 4.4%; China 4.2%; Germany 3.8%; South Korea 3.2%; The Netherlands 2.9%; Taiwan 2.7%; France 2.6%; Singapore 2.4%; Belgium 2.1%.

Trade by commodity group (2004)

SITC Group	imports U.S.$'000,000	%	exports U.S.$'000,000	%
00 Food and live animals	51,489	3.5	43,642	5.3
01 Beverages and tobacco	13,429	0.9	4,662	0.6
02 Crude materials, excluding fuels	28,459	1.9	36,072	4.4
03 Mineral fuels, lubricants, and related materials	216,337	14.7	18,544	2.3
04 Animal and vegetable oils, fat, and waxes	2,397	0.2	1,957	0.2
05 Chemicals and related products, n.e.s.	115,065	7.8	106,965	13.1
06 Basic manufactures	180,009	12.2	66,976	8.2
07 Machinery and transport equipment	609,150	41.4	426,721	52.0
08 Miscellaneous manufactured articles	254,425	17.3	82,834	10.1
09 Goods not classified by kind	...	...	30,807[29]	3.8[29]
TOTAL	1,470,760	100.0[3]	819,180	100.0

Direction of trade (2004)

	imports U.S.$'000,000	%	exports U.S.$'000,000	%
Africa	35,900	2.4	8,600	1.0
Nigeria	16,248	1.1	1,554	0.2
South Africa	5,945	0.4	3,179	0.4
Americas	532,500	36.2	377,500	46.1
Brazil	21,200	1.4	13,900	1.7
Canada	255,900	17.4	190,200	23.2
Caribbean countries	10,900	0.7	12,300	1.5
Central America	14,700	1.0	10,600	1.3
Mexico	155,800	10.6	110,800	13.5
Venezuela	25,000	1.7	4,767	0.6
Asia	570,700	38.8	224,900	27.5
China	196,700	13.4	34,700	4.2
Israel	14,551	1.0	9,169	1.1
Japan	129,600	8.8	54,400	6.6
Saudi Arabia	20,900	1.4	5,257	0.6
Singapore	15,300	1.0	19,600	2.4
South Korea	46,200	3.1	26,300	3.2
Europe	321,400	21.9	193,300	23.6
France	31,800	2.2	21,200	2.6
Germany	77,200	5.3	31,400	3.8
Italy	28,100	1.9	10,685	1.3
Russia	11,891	0.8	2,961	0.4
United Kingdom	46,400	3.2	36,000	4.4
Oceania	10,200	0.7	14,700	1.8
Australia	7,546	0.5	14,300	1.7
TOTAL	1,470,700	100.0	819,000	100.0

Transport and communications

Transport. Railroads (2003): route length 99,126 mi, 159,528 km, of which Amtrak operates 22,677 mi, 36,495 km; (1999) passenger-mi 13,402,000,000, passenger-km 21,568,000,000; (1997) short ton-mi cargo 1,421,000,000,000, metric ton-km cargo 2,075,000,000,000. Roads (2003): total length 3,974,100 mi, 6,395,705 km (paved 91%). Vehicles (2002): passenger cars 135,921,000; trucks and buses 93,700,000. Merchant marine (1999): vessels (1,000 gross tons and over) 579; total deadweight tonnage 16,747,000. Navigable channels 26,000 mi, 41,843 km; oil pipeline length 160,868 mi, 258,892 km; gas pipeline[30] (2002) 1,411,380 mi, 2,271,400 km. Air transport (2004): passenger-mi 709,539,000,000, passenger-km 1,141,896,000,000; short ton-mi cargo (2002) 54,302,000,000, metric ton-km cargo (2002) 87,390,000,000; localities (1996) with scheduled flights 834[31]. Certified route passenger/cargo air carriers (1992) 77; operating revenue (U.S.$'000,000; 1991) 74,942, of which domestic 56,119, international 18,823; operating expenses 76,669, of which domestic 56,596, international 20,073.

Intercity passenger and freight traffic by mode of transportation (2002)

	cargo traffic ('000,000,000 ton-mi)	% of nat'l total	passenger traffic ('000,000,000 passenger-mi)	% of nat'l total
Rail	1,558	41.7	15	0.6
Road	1,051	28.2	1,980	79.2
Inland water	494	13.2	—	—
Air	15	0.4	504	20.2
Petroleum pipeline	616	16.5	—	—
TOTAL	3,734	100.0	2,499	100.0

Communications

Medium	date	unit	number	units per 1,000 persons
Daily newspapers	2003	circulation	55,186,000	190
Radio	2000	receivers	598,000,000	2,118
Television	2002	receivers	254,000,000	881
Telephones	2004	main lines	177,947,000	599
Cellular telephones	2004	subscribers	181,105,100	610
Personal computers	2004	units	220,000,000	741
Internet	2004	users	185,000,000	623

Other communications media (2002)

Print	titles		titles
Books (new)	120,106	Engineering	265
of which		Fine and applied arts	145
Agriculture	888	General interest	181
Art	4,483	History	151
Biography	5,052	Home economics	90
Business	4,571	Industrial arts	106
Education	3,658	Journalism and commun.	90
Fiction	15,133	Labour and industrial	
General works	1,470	relations	70
History	6,827	Law	273
Home economics	2,161	Library and information	
Juvenile	9,545	sciences	118
Language	2,420	Literature and language	158
Law	2,206	Mathematics and science	238
Literature	3,946	Medicine	182
Medicine	5,949	Philosophy and religion	130
Music	1,615	Physical education and	
Philosophy, psychology	6,012	recreation	151
Poetry, drama	2,812	Political science	136
Religion	6,664	Psychology	138
Science	7,043	Sociology and anthropology	149
Sociology, economics	13,829	Zoology	94
Sports, recreation	3,569		
Technology	7,926	**Cinema**	
Travel	2,327	Feature films[3]	478
Periodicals[18]	3,731		
of which			(pieces of mail)
Agriculture	153		
Business and economics	262	**Post**	
Chemistry and physics	170	Mail	202,822,000,000
Children's periodicals	78	Domestic	201,248,000,000
Education	203	International	1,574,000

Education and health

Literacy: n.a.

Education (2004–05)

	schools	teachers	students	student/ teacher ratio
Primary (age 5–13)[32]	...	} 3,369,000	38,412,000	} 17.3
Secondary and vocational (age 14–17)	...		16,203,000	
Higher, including teacher-training colleges	4,064[18]	1,012,000	16,680,000	15.1

Food (2002): daily per capita caloric intake 3,774 (vegetable products 72.3%, animal products 27.7%); 143% of FAO recommended minimum requirement. Per capita consumption of major food groups (kilograms annually; 2002): milk 261.8; fresh vegetables 127.7; cereal products 112.5; fresh fruits 110.9; red meat 73.1; potatoes 64.4; poultry products 49.8; sugar 32.9; fats and oils 27.8; fish and shellfish 21.3.

Health: doctors of medicine (2002) 853,200[33] (1 per 346 persons), of which office-based practice 516,200 (including specialties in internal medicine 18.7%, general and family practice 13.9%, pediatrics 8.9%, other specialty 7.9%, obstetrics and gynecology 6.3%, anesthesiology 5.6%, psychiatry 4.9%, general surgery 4.8%, orthopedic surgery 3.5%, cardiovascular diseases 3.3%, emergency medicine 3.3%, ophthalmology 3.1%, diagnostic radiology 3.1%); doctors of osteopathy 49,200; nurses (2003) 2,449,000 (1 per 118 persons); dentists (2003) 188,000 (1 per 1,547 persons); hospital beds (2002) 976,000 (1 per 295 persons), of which nonfederal 94.9% (community hospitals 84.1%, psychiatric 8.7%, long-term general and special 1.8%), federal 5.1%; infant mortality rate per 1,000 live births (2004) 6.6.

Military

Total active duty personnel (2004): 1,433,600 (army 35.0%, navy 26.3%, air force 26.5%, marines 12.2%). *Total reserve duty personnel* (2004): national guard 460,050 (army 76.4%, air force 23.6%); ready reserves 680,700 (army 47.6%, navy 22.5%, air force 16.4%, marines 13.5%); standby reserves 21,500 (army 3.3%, navy 11.6%, air force 81.9%, marines 3.2%). *Total special operations forces* (2004): active 31,496; reserve 11,247. *Military expenditure as percentage of GDP* (2003): 3.8%; per capita expenditure U.S.$1,424. *Security assistance to the world* (2002): U.S.$7,209,000,000, for underwriting the purchase of U.S. weapons 50.6%, of which Israel 28.3%, Egypt 18.0%, Jordan 1.0%; for economic support 30.5%, of which Israel 10.0%, Egypt 9.1%, Jordan 2.1%; for the Andean Counterdrug Initiative 9.2%; for nonproliferation, antiterrorism, and de-mining 4.3%; for international narcotics and law enforcement 3.0%; for peacekeeping operations 1.9%.

[1]Excludes 4 nonvoting delegates from the District of Columbia, the U.S. Virgin Islands, American Samoa, and Guam; a nonvoting resident commissioner from Puerto Rico; and a nonvoting resident representative from the Northern Mariana Islands. [2]Total area (excluding 42,241 sq mi [109,404 sq km] of coastal water and 75,372 sq mi [195,213 sq km] of territorial water) equals 3,676,487 sq mi (9,522,057 sq km), of which land area equals 3,537,439 sq mi (9,161,925 sq km), inland water area equals 78,797 sq mi (204,083 sq km), and Great Lakes water area equals 60,251 sq mi (156,049 sq km). [3]Detail does not add to total given because of rounding. [4]Excludes 251,113 military personnel overseas; adjusted 2000 census total announced December 2002 equaled 284,683,782. [5]Based on land area only. [6]Persons of Hispanic origin may be of any race. [7]April 1, 2000, to July 1, 2003. [8]2004. [9]1989–91. [10]Age breakdown by causes is for 2000. [11]Includes deaths with age not known. [12]Current users. [13]Drinking 5 or more drinks on the same occasion on at least one day in the past 30 days per survey. [14]2000. [15]Excludes military personnel overseas. [16]Trade includes hotels and restaurants. [17]Unemployed. [18]1999. [19]Excludes tips. [20]Includes supplemental gaseous fuels. [21]Minus sign indicates when amount of energy expended exceeds amount consumed. [22]Less than 0.5 trillion Btu. [23]Gross income from all sources, including transfer payments to individuals. [24]Householder 25 years old or older. [25]September. [26]Period average. [27]End-of-period. [28]In 2004 current dollars in conjunction with annually revised U.S. Bureau of Labor Statistics experimental Consumer Price Index (or CPI-U-RS deflator). [29]Includes special transactions and gold nonmonetary exchange operations. [30]Excludes service pipelines. [31]Includes 292 localities in Alaska. [32]Primary includes kindergarten. [33]768,500 professionally active.

Internet resources for further information:
- **U.S. Census Bureau**
  http://www.census.gov
- **Statistical Abstract of the United States**
  http://www.census.gov/prod/www/statistical-abstract-us.html

Uruguay

Official name: República Oriental del Uruguay (Oriental Republic of Uruguay).
Form of government: republic with two legislative houses (Senate [31][1]; Chamber of Representatives [99]).
Head of state and government: President.
Capital: Montevideo.
Official language: Spanish.
Official religion: none.
Monetary unit: 1 peso uruguayo ($U) = 100 centesimos; valuation (Sept. 1, 2005) 1 U.S.$ = $U 24.19; 1 £ = $U 44.53.

Area and population

Departments	area sq km	population 2004 census	Departments	area sq km	population 2004 census
Artigas	11,928	78,019	Río Negro	9,282	53,989
Canelones	4,536	485,240	Rivera	9,370	104,921
Cerro Largo	13,648	86,564	Rocha	10,551	69,937
Colonia	6,106	119,266	Salto	14,163	123,120
Durazno	11,643	58,859	San José	4,992	103,104
Flores	5,144	25,104	Soriano	9,008	84,563
Florida	10,417	68,181	Tacuarembó	15,438	90,489
Lavalleja	10,016	60,925	Treinta y Tres	9,529	49,318
Maldonado	4,793	140,192	TOTAL LAND AREA	175,016	
Montevideo	530	1,325,968	INLAND WATER	1,199	
Paysandú	13,922	113,244	TOTAL	176,215	3,241,003

Demography

Population (2005): 3,256,000.
Density (2005): persons per sq mi 47.9, persons per sq km 18.5.
Urban-rural (2004): urban 91.8%; rural 8.2%.
Sex distribution (2004): male 48.30%; female 51.70%.
Age breakdown (2004): under 15, 23.9%; 15–29, 22.9%; 30–44, 19.5%; 45–59, 16.0%; 60–74, 11.8%; 75 and over, 5.9%.
Population projection: (2010) 3,307,000; (2020) 3,413,000.
Ethnic composition (2000): white (mostly Spanish, Italian, or mixed Spanish-Italian) 94.5%; mestizo 3.1%; mulatto 2.0%; other 0.4%.
Religious affiliation (2000): Roman Catholic 78.2%[2]; Protestant 3.3%; other Christian 5.3%; Jewish 1.2%; atheist 6.3%; other 5.7%.
Major cities (2004): Montevideo 1,269,552; Salto 99,072; Paysandú 73,272; Las Piedras 69,222; Rivera 64,426.

Vital statistics

Birth rate per 1,000 population (2004): 15.4 (world avg. 21.1); (2001) legitimate 44.7%; illegitimate 55.3%.
Death rate per 1,000 population (2004): 9.9 (world avg. 9.0).
Natural increase rate per 1,000 population (2004): 5.5 (world avg. 12.1).
Total fertility rate (avg. births per childbearing woman; 2004): 2.1.
Marriage rate per 1,000 population (2003): 4.2.
Divorce rate per 1,000 population (2003): 2.0.
Life expectancy at birth (2004): male 71.7 years; female 78.9 years.
Major causes of death per 100,000 population (2002): diseases of the circulatory system 310.5; malignant neoplasms 229.8; accidents 33.0.

National economy

Budget (2004). Revenue: $U 77,574,000,000 (tax revenue 84.9%, of which taxes on goods and services 49.5%, income and profit taxes 19.9%, property taxes 9.5%; nontax revenue 10.6%; grants 3.9%; other 0.6%). Expenditures: $U 88,510,000,000 (social security and welfare 19.0%, general public services 15.2%, education 13.4%, health 7.4%, public order 6.1%, defense 4.9%).
Public debt (external, outstanding; June 2005): U.S.$6,678,000,000.
Production (metric tons except as noted). Agriculture, forestry, fishing (2004): rice 1,262,600, wheat 532,600, barley 406,500, soybeans 377,000, corn (maize) 223,000, sugarcane 181,500, sunflower seeds 177,000, grapes 147,057, potatoes 136,345, oranges 124,091; livestock (number of live animals) 11,700,000 cattle, 9,508,000 sheep; roundwood 6,399,152 cu m; fish catch (2003) 116,911. Mining and quarrying (2003): limestone 1,300,000; gypsum 1,130,000; gold 55,620 troy oz. Manufacturing (value added in $U '000,000; 2001): food products and beverages 8,558; refined petroleum products 6,963; chemicals and chemical products 2,412; tobacco products 2,272; textiles and wearing apparel 1,540; publishing 1,150. Energy production (consumption): electricity (kW-hr; 2004) 5,753,000,000 ([2003] 5,980,000,000); coal (metric tons; 2004) none (1,000); crude petroleum (barrels; 2002) none (9,400,000); petroleum products (metric tons; 2002) 1,181,000 (1,205,000); natural gas (cu m; 2003) none (65,000,000).
Household income and expenditure. Avg. household size (2004) 3.1; avg. annual income per household (2003) $U 151,416 (U.S.$5,368); expenditure: n.a.
Population economically active (2003): total 1,269,500[3]; activity rate 46.9% (participation rates: ages 14–64, 72.4%; female 45.0%; unemployed [October 2004–September 2005] 12.2%).

Price and earnings indexes (2000 = 100)

	1998	1999	2000	2001	2002	2003	2004
Consumer price index	90.3	95.5	100.0	104.4	118.9	142.0	155.0
Monthly earnings index	90.1	96.7	100.0	104.1	105.1	110.6	120.7

Gross national product (at current market prices; 2004): U.S.$13,414,000,000 (U.S.$3,950 per capita).

Structure of gross domestic product and labour force

	2004 in value $U '000,000	2004 % of total value	2003 labour force[3,4]	2003 % of labour force[3,4]
Agriculture	44,459	11.7	46,900	3.8
Mining	806	0.2	1,200	0.1
Manufacturing	80,191	21.1	151,100[5]	12.2[5]
Construction	13,127	3.5	69,600	5.6
Public utilities	16,896	4.5	[5]	[5]
Transp. and commun.	36,555	9.6	61,100	4.9
Trade	49,236	13.0	225,400	18.2
Finance	81,735	21.6	91,000	7.3
Pub. admin., defense	30,717	8.1	91,200	7.4
Services	35,337	9.3	294,300	23.7
Other	−9,742[6]	−2.6[6]	208,500[7]	16.8[7]
TOTAL	379,317	100.0	1,240,500[8]	100.0

Tourism (2003): receipts U.S.$318,100,000; expenditures U.S.$168,800,000.
Land use as % of total land area (2000): in temporary crops 7.4%, in permanent crops 0.2%, in pasture 77.4%; overall forest area 7.4%.

Foreign trade[9]

Balance of trade (current prices)

	1999	2000	2001	2002	2003	2004
U.S.$'000,000	−1,115	−1,171	−1,003	−103	−16	+200
% of total	19.9%	20.3%	19.6%	2.7%	0.4%	3.3%

Imports (2004): U.S.$3,118,631,000 (crude and refined petroleum 24.1%; chemicals and chemical products 16.0%; machinery and appliances 14.1%; food, beverages, and tobacco 8.5%; plastic products 6.2%). *Major import sources:* Argentina 22.2%; Brazil 21.7%; Russia 11.0%; United States 7.1%; China 5.5%; Nigeria 4.9%.
Exports (2004): U.S.$2,918,240,000 (beef 20.6%; hides and leather goods 9.5%; textiles and wearing apparel 8.1%; dairy products and eggs 7.0%; rice 6.2%; fish and crustaceans 4.2%). *Major export destinations:* United States 19.8%; Brazil 16.5%; Argentina 7.6%; Germany 5.2%; Mexico 4.0%.

Transport and communications

Transport. Railroads (2003): track length 2,993 km; passenger-km (2000) 9,000,000; metric ton-km cargo (2000) 239,000,000. Roads (2004): length 8,732 km (paved 40%). Vehicles (2004): passenger cars 524,145; trucks and buses 56,895. Air transport (2003): passenger-km 1,028,800,000; metric ton-km cargo 23,200,000; airports (1997) 1.

Communications

Medium	date	unit	number	units per 1,000 persons
Daily newspapers	2000	circulation	973,000	293
Radio	2000	receivers	2,000,000	603
Television	2000	receivers	1,760,000	536
Telephones	2004	main lines	996,701	307
Cellular telephones	2004	subscribers	599,768	185
Personal computers	2004	units	430,000	132
Internet	2004	users	680,000	210

Education and health

Educational attainment (2002). Percentage of population age 25 and over having: incomplete primary education 9.8%; primary 33.6%; some secondary 17.2%; complete secondary 22.2%; higher 17.2%. *Literacy* (2003): population age 15 and over literate 98.0%; males 97.6%; females 98.4%.

Education (2004)

	schools	teachers	students	student/ teacher ratio
Primary (age 6–11)	2,398	20,170	355,568	17.6
Secondary (age 12–17)	413[10]	25,168[10]	225,388	9.1[10]
Vocational, teacher tr.	124	8,160[11]	89,392	8.0[11]
Higher	9	11,165[10]	86,615	7.8[10]

Health (2003): physicians 13,071 (1 per 248 persons); hospital beds 6,661 (1 per 486 persons); infant mortality rate per 1,000 live births (2004) 13.2.
Food (2002): daily per capita caloric intake 2,828 (vegetable products 70%, animal products 30%); 106% of FAO recommended minimum.

Military

Total active duty personnel (2004): 24,000 (army 63.3%, navy 23.8%, air force 12.9%). *Military expenditure as percentage of GDP* (2003): 1.6%; per capita expenditure U.S.$54.

---

[1]Includes the vice president, who serves as ex officio presiding officer. [2]About 30–40% of Roman Catholics are estimated to be nonreligious. [3]Urban areas only. [4]Excludes military conscripts. [5]Manufacturing includes Public utilities. [6]Includes indirect taxes less imputed bank service charges. [7]Unemployed. [8]Detail does not add to total given because of rounding. [9]Import figures are c.i.f. [10]2003. [11]2002.

Internet resources for further information:
• **Instituto Nacional de Estadística—Uruguay http://www.ine.gub.uy**
• **Banco Central del Uruguay http://www.bcu.gub.uy**

Uzbekistan

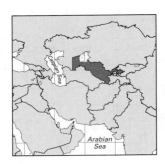

Official name: Ŭzbekiston Respublikasi (Republic of Uzbekistan).
Form of government: republic[1] with two legislative bodies (Senate [100[2]]; Legislative Chamber [120]).
Chief of state: President.
Head of government: Prime Minister.
Capital: Tashkent (Toshkent).
Official language: Uzbek.
Official religion: none.
Monetary unit: sum (plural sumy); valuation (Sept. 1, 2005) 1 U.S.$ = 1,133 sumy; 1 £ = 2,086 sumy.

Area and population

Autonomous republic	Administrative centres	area sq mi	area sq km	population 2002 estimate[3]
Qoraqalpoghiston	Nuqus	63,700	164,900	1,633,900
Provinces				
Andijon	Andijon	1,600	4,200	2,286,000
Buxoro	Bukhara (Buxoro)	15,200	39,400	1,534,900
Farghona	Fergana (Farghona)	2,700	7,100	2,761,300
Jizzakh	Jizzakh	7,900	20,500	1,026,000
Khorazm	Urganch	2,400	6,300	1,402,600
Namangan	Namangan	3,100	7,900	2,049,900
Nawoiy	Nawoiy	42,800	110,800	877,100
Qashqadaryo	Qarshi	11,000	28,400	2,302,000
Samarqand	Samarkand (Samarqand)	6,300	16,400	2,749,100
Sirdaryo	Guliston	2,000	5,100	670,800
Surkhondaryo	Termiz	8,000	20,800	1,846,400
Tashkent (Toshkent)	Tashkent (Toshkent)	6,000[4]	15,600[4]	4,986,800[4]
City				
Tashkent (Toshkent)	—	4	4	4
TOTAL		172,700	447,400	26,126,800

Demography

Population (2005): 26,593,000.
Density (2005): persons per sq mi 154.0, persons per sq km 59.4.
Urban-rural (2003): urban 36.6%; rural 63.4%.
Sex distribution (2001): male 49.55%; female 50.45%.
Age breakdown (2001): under 15, 36.4%; 15–29, 28.6%; 30–44, 19.6%; 45–59, 8.5%; 60–74, 5.4%; 75 and over, 1.5%.
Population projection: (2010) 28,578,000; (2020) 32,515,000.
Doubling time: 45 years.
Ethnic composition (2000): Uzbek 78.3%; Tajik 4.7%; Kazakh 4.1%; Tatar 3.3%; Russian 2.5%; Karakalpak 2.1%; other 5.0%.
Religious affiliation (2000): Muslim (mostly Sunnī) 76.2%; Russian Orthodox 0.8%; Jewish 0.2%; nonreligious 18.1%; other 4.7%.
Major cities (1999): Tashkent 2,142,700; Namangan 376,600; Samarkand 362,300; Andijon 323,900; Bukhara 237,900.

Vital statistics

Birth rate per 1,000 population (2004): 21.3 (world avg. 21.1).
Death rate per 1,000 population (2004): 5.8 (world avg. 9.0).
Natural increase rate per 1,000 population (2004): 15.5 (world avg. 12.1).
Total fertility rate (avg. births per childbearing woman; 2004): 2.4.
Marriage rate per 1,000 population (2001): 6.8.
Life expectancy at birth (2004): male 67.0 years; female 73.0 years.
Major causes of death per 100,000 population (2000): diseases of the circulatory system 288.7; diseases of the respiratory system 63.5; accidents, poisoning, and violence 43.2; cancers 38.8; diseases of the digestive system 30.6; infectious and parasitic diseases 20.7; diseases of the nervous system 10.5.

National economy

Budget (1999). Revenue: 611,897,000,000 sumy (taxes on income and profits 30.5%, value-added tax 27.3%, excise taxes 22.8%, property and land taxes 12.1%, other 7.3%). Expenditures: 654,259,000,000 sumy (social and cultural affairs 36.7%, investments 18.7%, national economy 10.4%, transfers 10.4%, administration 2.2%, interest on debt 1.9%, other 19.2%).
Household income and expenditure (1995). Average household size (2002) 5.5; income per household 35,165 sumy (U.S.$1,040); sources of income: wages and salaries 63.0%, subsidies, grants, and nonwage income 34.9%, other 2.1%; expenditure: food and beverages 71%, clothing and footwear 14%, recreation 6%, household durables 4%, housing 3%.
Public debt (external, outstanding; 2003): U.S.$4,250,000,000.
Tourism (2003): receipts U.S.$48,000,000.
Production (metric tons except as noted). Agriculture, forestry, fishing (2004): wheat 4,476,000, seed cotton 3,540,000, tomatoes 1,100,000, cabbages 900,000, potatoes 830,000, fruit (except grapes) and berries 764,500, grapes 500,000, rice 279,000; livestock (number of live animals) 8,800,000 sheep, 5,400,000 cattle, 900,000 goats, 15,000,000 chickens; roundwood 24,980 cu m; fish catch (2003) 2,000. Mining and quarrying (2002): copper (metal content) 65,000; gold 80,000 kg. Manufacturing (metric tons except as noted; 2001): cement (2003) 3,900,000; gas-diesel oils (distillate fuel) 1,786,000; motor fuel (2000) 1,709,000; residual fuel oils 1,550,000; cotton fibre (1998) 1,138,000; mineral fertilizer 712,000; steel 453,000; television sets 26,000 units; cigarettes 6,976,000,000 units. Energy production (consumption): electricity (kW-hr; 2002) 49,600,000,000 (50,927,000,000); lignite (metric tons; 2002) 2,467,000 (2,407,000); crude petroleum (barrels; 2002) 27,600,000 (27,600,000); petroleum products (metric tons; 2002) 5,657,000 (5,386,000); natural gas (cu m; 2003) 58,062,000,000 (51,599,000,000).

Gross national product (2004): U.S.$11,860,000,000 (U.S.$460 per capita).

Structure of gross domestic product and labour force

	2002 in value '000,000 sumy	2002 % of total value	2000 labour force	2000 % of labour force
Agriculture	2,244,241	30.1	3,083,000	34.3
Manufacturing, mining, and public utilities	1,079,273	14.5	1,145,000	12.7
Construction	365,163	4.9	676,000	7.5
Transp. and commun.	612,868	8.2	382,000	4.3
Trade	735,202	9.9	754,000	8.4
Finance	278,744	3.7		
Pub. admin., defense	242,398	3.3	2,042,000	22.7
Services	994,218	13.3		
Other	898,127[5]	12.1[5]	901,000[6]	10.0[6]
TOTAL	7,450,234	100.0	8,983,000	100.0[7]

Population economically active (2001): total 9,136,000; activity rate of total population 36.5% (participation rates: ages 16–59 [male], 16–54 [female] 70.4%; female [1994] 43.0%; unemployed [official rate, 2002] 0.4%).

Price index (2000 = 100)

	2000	2001	2002	2003	2004
Consumer price index	100.0	127.4	162.6	179.3	182.2

Land use as % of total land area (2000): in temporary crops 10.8%, in permanent crops 0.8%, in pasture 55.0%; overall forest area 4.8%.

Foreign trade[8]

Balance of trade (current prices)

	1999	2000	2001	2002	2003	2004
U.S.$'000,000	+125.1	+317.3	+33.5	+276.4	+760.8	+1,037.0
% of total	2.0%	5.1%	0.5%	4.8%	11.4%	12.0%

Imports (2002): U.S.$2,712,000,000 (machinery and metalworking products 48.9%, food products 21.3%, other 29.8%). *Major import sources* (2004): Russia 26.4%; South Korea 10.8%; Germany 9.4%; China 8.3%; Kazakhstan 6.0%; Turkey 6.0%.
Exports (2002): U.S.$2,988,400,000 ([2000] cotton fibre 27.5%, energy products [including natural gas and crude petroleum] 10.3%, base metals [significantly gold] 6.6%, food products 5.4%). *Major export destinations* (2004): Russia 21.2%; China 14.0%; Ukraine 7.0%; Turkey 6.3%; Tajikistan 5.8%; Kazakhstan 3.9%.

Transport and communications

Transport. Railroads (2000): length 3,950 km; (2001) passenger-km 2,000,000; (2001) metric ton-km cargo 16,000,000. Roads (1999): total length 81,600 km (paved 87%). Vehicles (1994): passenger cars 865,300; buses 14,500. Air transport (2004)[9]: passenger-km 4,550,000,000; metric ton-km cargo 115,566,000; airports (1998) with scheduled flights 9.

Communications

Medium	date	unit	number	units per 1,000 persons
Daily newspapers	2000	circulation	74,200	3.0
Television	2003	receivers	7,230,000	280
Telephones	2003	main lines	1,717,100	67
Cellular telephones	2004	subscribers	544,100	21
Internet	2004	users	880,000	33

Education and health

Educational attainment: n.a. *Literacy* (2002): percentage of total population age 15 and over literate 99.3%; male 99.6%; female 98.9%.

Education (1995–96)

	schools	teachers	students	student/ teacher ratio
Primary (age 6–13) Secondary (age 14–17)	9,300	413,000	5,090,000	12.3
Voc., teacher tr.[10]	248	22,164[11]	240,100	...
Higher[11]	55	...	272,300	...

Health: physicians (2001) 73,041 (1 per 343 persons); hospital beds (1995) 192,000 (1 per 120 persons); infant mortality rate per 1,000 live births (2004) 36.0.
Food (2002): daily per capita caloric intake 2,241 (vegetable products 82%, animal products 18%); 88% of FAO recommended minimum requirement.

Military

Total active duty personnel (2004): c. 52,500 (army 76.2%, air force 23.8%); all U.S. troops withdrawn by November 2005. *Military expenditure as percentage of GDP* (2003): 0.5%; per capita expenditure U.S.$3.

---

[1]Operates as a single-party republic; opposition parties were barred from December 2004–January 2005 elections. [2]Includes 16 nonelected seats. [3]Unofficial figures; 2005 estimate for country is not based on these estimates. [4]Tashkent province includes Tashkent city. [5]Indirect taxes less subsidies. [6]Includes 863,000 persons on forced leave and 38,000 unemployed. [7]Detail does not add to total given because of rounding. [8]Imports c.i.f., exports f.o.b. [9]Uzbekistan Airways. [10]1998. [11]1992–93.

Internet resources for further information:
• **Center for Economic Research** http://cer.uz
• **Republic of Uzbekistan** http://www.gov.uz/en

Vanuatu

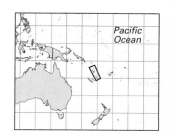

Official name: Ripablik blong Vanuatu
(Bislama); République de Vanuatu
(French); Republic of Vanuatu
(English).
Form of government: republic with a
single legislative house (Parliament
[52]).
Chief of state: President.
Head of government: Prime Minister.
Capital: Vila.
Official languages: Bislama; French;
English.
Official religion: none.
Monetary unit: vatu (VT); valuation
(Sept. 1, 2005) 1 U.S.$ = VT 111.70;
1 £ = VT 205.67.

Area and population		area		population
Provinces	Capitals	sq mi	sq km	2001 estimate
Malampa	Lakatoro	1,073	2,779	33,627
Penama	Longana	463	1,198	27,560
Sanma	Luganville	1,640	4,248	38,282
Shefa	Vila	562	1,455	57,307
Tafea	Isangel	628	1,627	30,518
Torba	Sola	341	882	8,150
TOTAL		4,707	12,190[1]	195,444

Demography

Population (2005): 211,000.
Density (2005): persons per sq mi 44.8, persons per sq km 17.3.
Urban-rural (2003): urban 22.8%; rural 77.2%.
Sex distribution (2003): male 51.40%; female 48.60%.
Age breakdown (1999): under 15, 42.2%; 15–29, 26.9%; 30–44, 17.0%; 45–59, 8.8%; 60–74, 3.7%; 75 and over, 1.4%.
Population projection: (2010) 232,000; (2020) 273,000.
Doubling time: 45 years.
Ethnic composition (1999): Ni-Vanuatu (Melanesian) 98.7%; European and other Pacific Islanders 1.3%.
Religious affiliation (2000): Christian 89.3%, of which Protestant 53.7%, Anglican 18.2%, Roman Catholic 15.5%; Custom (traditional beliefs) 3.5%; Bahā'ī 2.9%; other 4.3%.
Major towns (2003): Vila (Port-Vila) 33,987; Luganville (1999) 10,738.

Vital statistics

Birth rate per 1,000 population (2004): 23.7 (world avg. 21.1).
Death rate per 1,000 population (2004): 8.0 (world avg. 9.0).
Natural increase rate per 1,000 population (2004): 15.7 (world avg. 12.1).
Total fertility rate (avg. births per childbearing woman; 2004): 2.9.
Marriage rate per 1,000 population: n.a.
Divorce rate per 1,000 population: n.a.
Life expectancy at birth (2004): male 60.6 years; female 63.6 years.
Major causes of death per 100,000 population (2002): cardiovascular diseases 194.5; infectious and parasitic diseases 112.6; diseases of the respiratory system 65.3; malignant neoplasms (cancers) 50.3; diseases of the digestive system 26.1.

National economy

Budget (2004). Revenue: VT 8,129,700,000 (tax revenue 81.4%, of which taxes on goods and services 49.1%, tax on international trade 31.0%; nontax revenue 10.1%; foreign grants 8.4%). Expenditures: VT 7,685,800,000 (wages and salaries 53.0%; goods and services 19.9%; transfers 15.1%; interest payments 4.8%; other [including technical assistance] 7.2%).
Public debt (external, outstanding; 2004): U.S.$78,970,000.
Production (metric tons except as noted). Agriculture, forestry, fishing (2004): coconuts 240,000, roots and tubers 42,500, bananas 14,300, peanuts (groundnuts) 2,450, cacao beans 2,000, kava 825, corn (maize) 700; livestock (number of live animals) 150,000 cattle, 62,000 pigs, 12,000 goats, 340,000 chickens; roundwood 119,000 cu m; fish catch (2003) 31,329. Mining and quarrying: small quantities of coral-reef limestone, crushed stone, sand, and gravel. Manufacturing (value added in VT '000,000; 1995): food, beverages, and tobacco 645; wood products 423; fabricated metal products 377; paper products 125; chemical, rubber, plastic, and nonmetallic products 84; textiles, clothing, and leather 54. Energy production (consumption): electricity (kW-hr; 2004) 43,000,000 (43,000,000); coal, none (none); crude petroleum, none (none); petroleum products (metric tons; 2002) none (28,000); natural gas, none (none).
Land use as % of total land area (2000): in temporary crops 2.5%, in permanent crops 7.4%, in pasture 3.4%; overall forest area 36.7%.
Population economically active (1999): total 76,370; activity rate of total population 40.9% (participation rates: ages 15–64, 75.1%; female 44.9%; unemployed [2000] 1.7%).

Price index (2000 = 100)							
	1998	1999	2000	2001	2002	2003	2004
Consumer price index	95.7	97.6	100.0	103.7	105.7	108.9	110.4

Gross national product (2004): U.S.$287,000,000 (U.S.$1,340 per capita).

Structure of gross domestic product and labour force				
	2003		1999	
	in value VT '000,000	% of total value	labour force	% of labour force
Agriculture	5,051	15.0	58,690[2]	76.8[2]
Mining	...	...	3	—
Manufacturing	1,209	3.6	810	1.1
Construction	1,089	3.2	1,494	2.0
Public utilities	683	2.0	107	0.1
Transportation and communications	4,261	12.6	1,570	2.1
Trade, restaurants	12,648	37.5	4,070	5.3
Finance	4,758	14.1	738	1.0
Pub. admin., defense	4,960	14.7	2,513	3.3
Services	752	2.2	5,117	6.7
Other	−1,683[3]	−5.0[3]	1,258[4]	1.6[4]
TOTAL	33,728	100.0[1]	76,370	100.0

Household income and expenditure. Average household size (1999) 5.6; income per household, n.a.; sources of income (1985): wages and salaries 59.0%, self-employment 33.7%; expenditure (1990)[5, 6]: food and nonalcoholic beverages 30.5%, housing and energy 20.7%, transportation 13.2%, health and recreation 12.3%, tobacco and alcohol 10.4%.
Tourism (2003): receipts from visitors U.S.$52,000,000; expenditures by nationals abroad U.S.$12,000,000.

Foreign trade[7]

Balance of trade (current prices)							
	1998	1999	2000	2001	2002	2003	2004
VT '000,000	−7,634	−9,281	−8,335	−10,223	−9,843	−9,451	−10,138
% of total	46.9%	58.2%	53.5%	63.8%	65.5%	59.2%	54.9%

Imports (2004): VT 14,303,000,000 (machinery and transport equipment 21.4%, food and live animals 19.3%, mineral fuels 13.1%, chemicals and chemical products 10.9%). *Major import sources:* Australia 42.5%; New Zealand 13.0%; Fiji 8.6%; Singapore 6.2%; Japan 4.3%.
Exports (2004): VT 4,264,000,000 (domestic exports 79.5%, of which coconut oil 24.1%, copra 10.5%, kava 10.3%, beef 6.7%, timber 5.8%; reexports 20.5%). *Major export destinations*[8]: EC 44.9%; Australia 12.1%; Japan 6.8%; New Caledonia 4.6%; Singapore 2.9%.

Transport and communications

Transport. Railroads: none. Roads (1999): total length 665 mi, 1,070 km (paved 24%). Vehicles (2001): passenger cars 2,600; trucks and buses 4,400. Air transport (2001)[9]: passenger-mi 131,755,000, passenger-km 212,039,000; short ton-mi cargo 1,301,000, metric ton-km 1,899,000; airports (1996) with scheduled flights 29.

Communications				units per 1,000 persons
Medium	date	unit	number	
Daily newspapers	2004	circulation	3,000	14
Radio	1997	receivers	62,000	350
Television	2000	receivers	2,280	12
Telephones	2004	main lines	6,800	33
Cellular telephones	2004	subscribers	10,500	51
Personal computers	2004	units	3,000	14
Internet	2004	users	7,500	36

Education and health

Educational attainment (1999). Percentage of population age 15 and over having: no formal schooling 18.0%; incomplete primary education 20.6%; completed primary 35.5%; some secondary 12.2%; completed secondary 8.5%; higher 5.2%, of which university 1.3%. *Literacy* (1998): total population age 15 and over literate 64%.

Education (2004)	schools	teachers	students	student/ teacher ratio
Primary (age 6–11)	272[10]	1,947	38,960	20.0
Secondary (age 11–18)	27[10]	692	10,591	15.3
Voc., teacher tr.	...	80[11]	3,246	...
Higher	...	27[11]	2,639	...

Health (2004): physicians 29 (1 per 7,138 persons); hospital beds (2003) 397 (1 per 511 persons); infant mortality rate per 1,000 live births 56.6.
Food (2002): daily per capita caloric intake 2,587 (vegetable products 86%, animal products 14%); 113% of FAO recommended minimum requirement.

Military

Total active duty personnel (2004): none; in 2001 Vanuatu had a paramilitary force of about 300.

---

[1]Detail does not add to total given because of rounding. [2]Mostly not stated, which are significantly subsistence workers. [3]Less imputed bank service charges. [4]Unemployed. [5]Vila and Luganville only. [6]Weights of consumer price index components. [7]Imports c.i.f.; exports f.o.b. [8]Destination of domestic exports only. [9]Air Vanuatu only. [10]1992. [11]2003.

Internet resources for further information:
• Vanuatu Statistics Office http://www.vanuatustatistics.gov.vu
• Secretariat of the Pacific Community
   http://www.spc.int/prism/country/vu/vu_index.html
• Reserve Bank of Vanuatu
   http://www.rbv.gov.vu

Venezuela

Official name: República Bolivariana de Venezuela (Bolivarian Republic of Venezuela).
Form of government: federal multiparty republic with a unicameral legislature (National Assembly [167]).
Head of state and government: President.
Capital: Caracas.
Official language: Spanish[1].
Official religion: none.
Monetary unit: 1 bolívar (B, plural Bs) = 100 céntimos; valuation (Sept. 1, 2005) 1 U.S.$ = Bs 2,541; 1 £ = Bs 4,678.

Area and population		area		population
				2001
States	Capitals	sq mi	sq km	census[2]
Amazonas	Puerto Ayacucho	69,554	180,145	70,464
Anzoátegui	Barcelona	16,700	43,300	1,222,225
Apure	San Fernando de Apure	29,500	76,500	377,756
Aragua	Maracay	2,708	7,014	1,449,616
Barinas	Barinas	13,600	35,200	624,508
Bolívar	Ciudad Bolívar	91,900	238,000	1,214,846
Carabobo	Valencia	1,795	4,650	1,932,168
Cojedes	San Carlos	5,700	14,800	253,105
Delta Amacuro	Tucupita	15,500	40,200	97,987
Falcón	Coro	9,600	24,800	763,188
Guárico	San Juan de Los Morros	25,091	64,986	627,086
Lara	Barquisimeto	7,600	19,800	1,556,415
Mérida	Mérida	4,400	11,300	715,268
Miranda	Los Teques	3,070	7,950	2,330,872
Monagas	Maturín	11,200	28,900	712,626
Nueva Esparta	La Asunción	440	1,150	373,851
Portuguesa	Guanare	5,900	15,200	725,740
Sucre	Cumaná	4,600	11,800	786,483
Táchira	San Cristóbal	4,300	11,100	992,669
Trujillo	Trujillo	2,900	7,400	608,563
Vargas	La Guaira	578	1,497	298,109
Yaracuy	San Felipe	2,700	7,100	499,049
Zulia	Maracaibo	24,400	63,100	2,983,679
Other federal entities				
Dependencias Federales	—	50	120	1,651
Distrito Capital	Caracas	167	433	1,836,286
TOTAL		353,841[3]	916,445	23,054,210

Demography

Population (2005): 26,749,000.
Density (2005): persons per sq mi 75.6, persons per sq km 29.2.
Urban-rural (2003): urban 87.7%; rural 12.3%.
Sex distribution (2001): male 49.46%; female 50.54%.
Age breakdown (2001): under 15, 33.1%; 15–29, 27.5%; 30–44, 20.7%; 45–59, 11.7%; 60–74, 5.1%; 75 and over, 1.9%.
Population projection: (2010) 29,076,000; (2020) 33,450,000.
Ethnic composition (2000): mestizo 63.7%; local white 20.0%; local black 10.0%; other white 3.3%; Amerindian 1.3%; other 1.7%.
Religious affiliation (2000): Roman Catholic 89.5%; Protestant 2.0%; other Christian 1.4%; Spiritist 1.1%; nonreligious/atheist 2.2%; other 3.8%.
Major cities (2001): Caracas 1,836,000[2] (urban agglomeration 3,177,000); Maracaibo 1,609,000[2]; Valencia 1,196,000[2]; Barquisimeto 811,000[2]; Ciudad Guayana 629,000[2].

Vital statistics

Birth rate per 1,000 population (2004): 22.3 (world avg. 21.1).
Death rate per 1,000 population (2004): 5.0 (world avg. 9.0).
Total fertility rate (avg. births per childbearing woman; 2004): 2.7.
Marriage rate per 1,000 population (2004): 2.8.
Life expectancy at birth (2004): male 71.0 years; female 77.3 years.
Major causes of death per 100,000 population (2000): circulatory diseases 131.2; cancers 62.3; accidents 33.1; violence 26.2; diabetes mellitus 24.5.

National economy

Budget (2004). Revenue: Bs 67,433,000,000,000 (ordinary income 67.3%, of which petroleum royalties 25.8%, VAT 23.7%; extraordinary income 32.7%). Expenditures: Bs 61,604,000,000,000 (ordinary expenditure 83.4%; extraordinary expenditure 16.6%, of which debt amortization 7.2%).
Public debt (external, outstanding; 2003): U.S.$24,491,000,000.
Production (metric tons except as noted). Agriculture, forestry, fishing (2004): sugarcane 9,832,005, corn (maize) 2,068,464, rice 989,478, sorghum 612,450, bananas 549,628, cassava 525,687, plantains 428,450, potatoes 336,894; livestock (number of live animals) 16,231,616 cattle, 3,046,915 pigs, 1,301,863 goats, 110,000,000 chickens; roundwood 5,082,092 cu m; fish catch (2003) 524,449. Mining and quarrying (2003): iron ore 17,954,000; bauxite 5,446,000; gold 8,190 kg; diamonds 34,790 carats. Manufacturing (value added in U.S.$'000,000; 1998): chemicals 7,217; food products 4,639; ferrous and nonferrous metals 4,382; metal products 2,458; pottery, china, and glass products 1,089; paper products 579. Energy production (consumption): electricity (kW-hr; 2003) 87,400,000,000 (81,300,000,000); coal (metric tons; 2003) 7,120,000 (54,000); crude petroleum (barrels; 2004) 1,082,000,000 ([2002] 301,000,000); petroleum products (metric tons; 2002) 54,687,000 (22,116,000); natural gas (cu m; 2003) 29,733,000 (29,733,000).
Tourism (2003): receipts U.S.$323,000,000; expenditures U.S.$859,000,000.
Land use as % of total land area (2000): in temporary crops 2.9%, in permanent crops 0.9%, in pasture 20.7%; overall forest area 56.1%.

Gross national product (2004): U.S.$104,958,000,000 (U.S.$4,020 per capita).

Structure of gross domestic product and labour force				
	2003		2002	
	in value Bs '000,000,000	% of total value	labour force	% of labour force
Agriculture	5,813	4.2	949,000	8.2
Petroleum and natural gas	29,568	21.5 }	47,300	0.4
Mining	1,038	0.8 }		
Manufacturing[4]	15,921	11.6	1,150,300	10.0
Construction	4,607	3.4	775,800	6.7
Public utilities	2,233	1.6	51,400	0.4
Transp. and commun.	11,503	8.4	703,600	6.1
Trade	18,212	13.3	2,585,300	22.4
Finance	18,226	13.3	481,800	4.2
Pub. admin., defense	6,500	4.7 }	2,932,700	25.5
Services	19,705	14.3 }		
Other	4,043	2.9	1,844,400[5]	16.0[5]
TOTAL	137,368[3]	100.0	11,521,500[3, 6]	100.0[3, 6]

Population economically active (2002): total 11,673,915; activity rate 46.4% (participation rates: ages 15–64, 72.1%; female 39.6%; unemployed [July 2003–June 2004] 16.7%).

Price and earnings indexes (2000 = 100)						
	1998	1999	2000	2001	2002	2003	2004
Consumer price index	69.6	86.1	100.0	112.5	137.8	180.6	219.9
Annual earnings index	...	82.7	100.0	120.2	130.3	141.4	172.6

Household income and expenditure. Average household size (2002) 4.9; expenditure (2001): food and nonalcoholic beverages 31.7%, expenditures in cafés and hotels 13.5%, housing and energy 12.2%, transport 9.8%.

Foreign trade

Balance of trade (current prices)						
	1999	2000	2001	2002	2003	2004
U.S.$'000,000	+6,522	+16,364	+8,869	+13,939	+16,483	+21,430
% of total	19.4%	35.9%	21.2%	36.2%	43.5%	38.2%

Imports (2003): U.S.$16,435,000,000 (nonelectrical machinery 16.5%, chemicals and chemical products 14.1%, road vehicles 14.0%, electrical machinery 9.8%). *Major import sources* (2004): U.S. 33.1%; Colombia 11.4%; Brazil 8.1%; Mexico 4.8%; Germany 3.5%.
Exports (2003): U.S.$27,170,000,000 (crude petroleum 58.3%, refined petroleum 23.6%, iron and steel 3.1%, aluminum 3.0%). *Major export destinations* (2004): U.S. 55.0%; Netherlands Antilles 4.7%; Dominican Republic 2.8%; Canada 2.3%; Colombia 2.0%.

Transport and communications

Transport. Railroads (1996): length (2004) 682 km; passenger-km, n.a.; metric ton-km cargo 54,474,000. Roads (2002): total length 96,155 km (paved 34%). Vehicles (2001): passenger cars 1,372,000; trucks and buses 1,107,900. Air transport (2003): passenger-km 2,042,800,000; metric ton-km cargo 2,000,000; airports (1997) with scheduled flights 20.

Communications				units per 1,000 persons
Medium	date	unit	number	
Daily newspapers	2000	circulation	5,000,000	206
Radio	2000	receivers	7,140,000	294
Television	2000	receivers	4,490,000	185
Telephones	2004	main lines	3,346,500	128
Cellular telephones	2004	subscribers	8,421,000	322
Personal computers	2004	units	2,145,000	82
Internet	2004	users	2,312,700	88

Education and health

Educational attainment (1993). Percentage of population age 25 and over having: no formal schooling 8.0%; primary education or less 43.7%; some secondary and secondary 38.3%; postsecondary 10.0%. *Literacy* (2002): total population age 15 and over literate 93.1%; males 93.5%; females 92.7%.

Education (1998–99)				student/
	schools	teachers[7]	students	teacher ratio
Primary (age 7–12)	17,372	186,658	4,299,671	...
Secondary (age 13–17)[8]	2,524	61,761	400,794	...
Higher	99[9]	43,833[9]	717,192	12.6[10]

Health (2001): physicians 48,000 (1 per 518 persons); public hospital beds (2000) 40,675 (1 per 620 persons); infant mortality rate (2004) 17.2.
Food (2002): daily per capita caloric intake 2,337 (vegetable products 83%, animal products 17%); 95% of FAO recommended minimum.

Military

Total active duty personnel (2005): 82,300 (army 41.3%, navy 22.2%, air force 8.5%, national guard 28.0%). *Military expenditure as percentage of GDP* (2003): 1.3%; per capita expenditure U.S.$44.

[1]31 indigenous Indian languages were also made official in May 2002. [2]Preliminary unadjusted census results. [3]Detail does not add to total given because of rounding. [4]Includes refined petroleum. [5]Mostly unemployed. [6]Excludes military personnel. [7]1997–98. [8]Includes vocational and teacher training. [9]1990–91. [10]1991–92.

Internet resources for further information:
• Banco Central de Venezuela http://www.bcv.org.ve/EnglishVersion/Index.asp
• Instituto Nacional de Estadística http://www.ine.gov.ve

Vietnam

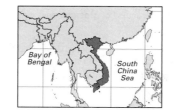

Official name: Cong Hoa Xa Hoi Chu Nghia Viet Nam (Socialist Republic of Vietnam).
Form of government: socialist republic with one legislative house (National Assembly [498]).
Head of state: President.
Head of government: Prime Minister.
Capital: Hanoi.
Official language: Vietnamese.
Official religion: none.
Monetary unit: 1 dong (D) = 10 hao = 100 xu; valuation (Sept. 1, 2005) 1 U.S.$ = D 15,879; 1 £ = D 29,237.

Area and population		area		population
Economic regions[1]	Principal cities	sq mi	sq km	2004 estimate
Central Highlands	Buon Ma Thuot	21,033	54,475	4,657,300
Mekong River Delta	Long Xuyen	15,333	39,712	17,098,900
North Central Coast	Hue	19,885	51,501	10,547,900
North East	Thai Nguyen	25,223	65,327	9,258,000
North West	Hoa Binh	13,760	35,637	2,523,600
Red River Delta	Hanoi	5,710	14,789	17,860,700
South Central Coast	Da Nang	12,767	33,067	6,973,700
South East	Ho Chi Minh City	13,410	34,733	13,149,700
TOTAL		127,121[2]	329,241[2]	82,069,800[3]

Demography

Population (2005): 82,628,000.
Density (2005): persons per sq mi 650.0, persons per sq km 251.0.
Urban-rural (2004): urban 26.3%; rural 73.7%.
Sex distribution (2004): male 49.15%; female 50.85%.
Age breakdown (2003): under 15, 30.2%; 15–29, 29.4%; 30–44, 21.8%; 45–59, 10.8%; 60–74, 5.7%; 75 and over, 2.0%.
Population projection: (2010) 86,860,000; (2020) 95,294,000.
Doubling time: 63 years.
Ethnic composition (1999): Vietnamese 86.2%; Tho (Tay) 1.9%; Montagnards 1.7%; Thai 1.7%; Muong 1.5%; Khmer 1.4%; Nung 1.1%; Miao (Hmong) 1.0%; Dao 0.8%; other 2.7%.
Religious affiliation (2000): Buddhist 49.2%; New-Religionist 11.3%; traditional beliefs 8.5%; Christian 8.3%, of which Roman Catholic 6.7%; Chinese folk-religionist 1.0%; Muslim 0.7%; nonreligious 13.4%; atheist 7.0%; other 0.6%.
Major cities (2004): Ho Chi Minh City 3,452,100 (5,030,000[2]); Hanoi 1,420,400 (4,147,000[2]); Haiphong 591,100 (1,817,000[2]); Da Nang 459,400; Bien Hoa 384,400.

Vital statistics

Birth rate per 1,000 population (2004): 17.2 (world avg. 21.1).
Death rate per 1,000 population (2004): 6.2 (world avg. 9.0).
Natural increase rate per 1,000 population (2004): 11.0 (world avg. 12.1).
Total fertility rate (avg. births per childbearing woman; 2004): 2.0.
Life expectancy at birth (2004): male 67.6 years; female 73.3 years.

National economy

Budget (2003). Revenue: D 123,700,000,000,000 (tax revenue 77.9%, of which corporate income taxes 24.6%, VAT 23.2%, taxes on trade 18.7%; nontax revenues 20.5%; grants 1.6%). Expenditures: D 148,400,000,000,000 (current expenditures 64.6%, of which social services 27.9%, economic services 5.3%, interest payment 4.5%; capital expenditures 35.4%).
Public debt (external, outstanding; 2004): U.S.$15,400,000,000.
Gross national product (2004): U.S.$45,082,000,000 (U.S.$550 per capita).

Structure of gross domestic product and labour force				
	2004			
	in value D '000,000,000	% of total value	labour force	% of labour force
Agriculture, forestry, fishing	155,144	21.8	24,430,700	58.8
Public utilities	23,890	3.3		
Mining	72,492	10.2	5,293,600	12.7
Manufacturing	144,924	20.3		
Construction	44,558	6.2	1,922,900	4.6
Transp. and commun.	30,402	4.3	1,202,200	2.9
Trade and restaurants	119,889	16.8	5,522,300	13.3
Finance, insurance	44,041	6.2		
Pub. admin., defense	19,061	2.7	3,214,600	7.7
Services, other	58,670	8.2		
TOTAL	713,071	100.0	41,586,300	100.0

Tourism (2002): receipts from visitors U.S.$177,536,000[3]; expenditures by nationals abroad, n.a.
Production (metric tons except as noted). Agriculture, forestry, fishing (2004): rice 36,117,800, sugarcane 15,879,600, cassava 5,687,800, corn (maize) 3,453,600, sweet potatoes 1,535,700, bananas 1,353,800, coconuts 930,600, coffee 834,600, cashews 825,696, oranges 538,000, groundnuts (peanuts) 451,100, pineapples 422,200, natural rubber 400,100, tea 108,422, black pepper 95,700, pimento 78,500; livestock (number of live animals) 75,000,000 ducks, 26,143,728 pigs, 4,907,910 cattle, 2,869,802 buffalo; roundwood 30,597,040 cu m, of which fuelwood 26,414,040 cu m, industrial roundwood 4,183,000 cu m; fish catch 1,724,200, of which marine fish 1,288,900. Mining and quarrying (2004): phosphate rock (gross weight) 800,000; tin (metal content) 3,500.

Manufacturing (value added in U.S.$'000,000; 2000): food products 736; cement, bricks, and pottery 418; wearing apparel 376; beverages 359; footwear 308; tobacco products 228; paints, soaps, and pharmaceuticals 206. Energy production (consumption): electricity (kW-hr; 2004) 46,049,000,000 ([2002] 3,122,000,000); coal (metric tons; 2004) 26,800,000 ([2002] 8,710,000); crude petroleum (barrels; 2004) 142,800,000 ([2002] negligible); petroleum products (metric tons; 2002) 265,000 (9,592,000); natural gas (cu m; 2004) 6,250,000,000 ([2002] 2,064,000,000).
Population economically active (2003): total 41,900,000; activity rate 51.8% (participation rates [2001]: ages 15 and over 70.5%; female c. 49%; urban unemployed [2004] 5.6%).

Price and earnings indexes (2000 = 100)							
	1998	1999	2000	2001	2002	2003	2004
Consumer price index	97.7	101.7	100.0	99.6	103.4	106.6	114.9
Earnings index	...	...	...	...	...	...	...

Household income and expenditure. Average household size (2002) 5.0; income per household (1990)[4] D 577,008 (U.S.$93); sources of income: n.a.; expenditure (1990): food 62.4%, clothing 5.0%, household goods 4.6%, education 2.9%, housing 2.5%.
Land use as % of total land area (2000): in temporary crops 18.7%, in permanent crops 5.4%, in pasture 2.0%; overall forest area 30.2%.

Foreign trade[5]

Balance of trade (current prices)					
	2000	2001	2002	2003	2004
U.S.$'000,000	−1,154	−1,189	−3,027	−5,107	−5,450
% of total	3.8%	4.4%	8.3%	11.2%	9.3%

Imports (2002): U.S.$19,733,000,000 (machinery equipment [including aircraft] 19.2%; petroleum products 10.2%; garment material and leather 8.7%; iron and steel 6.8%; fertilizers 2.7%; motorcycles 2.1%). *Major import sources* (2004): China 13.9%; Taiwan 11.6%; Singapore 11.3%; Japan 11.1%; South Korea 10.4%.
Exports (2002): U.S.$16,706,000,000 (crude petroleum 19.6%; garments 16.5%; fish, crustaceans, and mollusks 12.1%; footwear 11.2%; rice 4.3%; electronic products 2.9%). *Major export destinations* (2004): U.S. 18.8%; Japan 13.2%; China 10.3%; Australia 6.9%; Singapore 5.2%; Germany 4.0%.

Transport and communications

Transport. Railroads (2004): route length 1,616 mi, 2,600 km; passenger-km 4,378,000,000; metric ton-km cargo 2,790,800,000. Roads (2003): total length 78,320 mi, 126,045 km (paved 40.4%). Vehicles (2003): passenger cars, trucks, and buses 600,000. Air transport (2004)[6]: passenger-km 8,518,293,000; metric ton-km cargo 216,527,000; airports (1997) with scheduled flights 12.

Communications				units per 1,000
Medium	date	unit	number	persons
Daily newspapers[7]	2003	circulation	1,530,000	19
Radio	2000	receivers	8,520,000	109
Television	2003	receivers	15,937,800	197
Telephones	2004	main lines	10,124,900	124
Cellular telephones	2004	subscribers	4,960,000	61
Personal computers	2004	units	1,044,000	13
Internet	2004	users	5,870,000	72

Education and health

Educational attainment (1989). Percentage of population age 25 and over having: no formal education (illiterate) 16.6%; incomplete and complete primary 69.8%; incomplete and complete secondary 10.6%; higher 2.6%; unknown 0.4%. *Literacy* (2002): percentage of population age 15 and over literate 90.3%; males 93.9%; females 86.9%.

Education (2004–05)				student/
	schools	teachers	students	teacher ratio
Primary (age 7–12)	15,552	362,400	8,346,000	23.0
Secondary (age 13–18)	11,265	408,600	9,159,400	22.4
Vocational	285	13,900	465,300	33.5
Higher	230	47,600	1,319,800	27.7

Health (2004): physicians 50,100 (1 per 1,632 persons); hospital beds 196,300 (1 per 417 persons); infant mortality rate 26.8.
Food (2002): daily per capita caloric intake 2,566 (vegetable products 88%, animal products 12%); 119% of FAO recommended minimum requirement.

Military

Total active duty personnel (2004): 484,000 (army 85.1%, navy 8.7%, air force 6.2%). *Military expenditure as percentage of GDP* (2003): 8.2%[8]; per capita expenditure U.S.$40.

[1]Eight economic regions are divided into 59 provinces and 5 municipalities as of the administrative reorganization of late 2003. [2]Projection of 2005 urban agglomeration. [3]Accommodation establishment revenue only. [4]Wage workers and government officials only. [5]Imports c.i.f.; exports f.o.b. [6]Vietnam Airlines only. [7]Refers to the circulation of the top ten dailies only. [8]Excludes extra-budgetary funding.

Internet resources for further information:
• **Ministry of Foreign Affairs** http://www.mofa.gov.vn
• **General Statistics Office of Vietnam** http://www.gso.gov.vn

Virgin Islands (U.S.)

Official name: Virgin Islands of the United States.
Political status: organized unincorporated territory of the United States with one legislative house (Senate [15]).
Chief of state: President of the United States.
Head of government: Governor.
Capital: Charlotte Amalie.
Official language: English.
Official religion: none.
Monetary unit: 1 U.S. dollar (U.S.$) = 100 cents; valuation (Sept. 1, 2005) 1 £ = U.S.$1.84.

Area and population

Islands[1]	Principal towns	area sq mi	area sq km	population 2002 estimate
St. Croix	Christiansted	84	218	53,898
St. John	Cruz Bay[2]	20	52	4,306
St. Thomas	Charlotte Amalie	32	83	51,822
TOTAL		136	353	110,026[3]

Demography

Population (2005): 109,000.
Density (2005): persons per sq mi 801.5, persons per sq km 309.7.
Urban-rural (2000): urban 92.6%; rural 7.4%.
Sex distribution (2001): male 46.81%; female 53.19%.
Age breakdown (2001): under 15, 26.0%; 15–29, 19.8%; 30–44, 20.7%; 45–59, 19.9%; 60–74, 10.9%; 75 and over, 2.7%.
Population projection: (2010) 108,000; (2020) 107,000.
Doubling time: 82 years.
Ethnic composition (2000): black 61.1%; U.S. white 15.0%; Puerto Rican 12.0%; French Creole (from Martinique and Guadeloupe) 9.0%; British 1.0%; other 1.9%.
Religious affiliation (2000): Christian 96.3%, of which Protestant 51.0% (including Anglican 13.0%), Roman Catholic 27.5%, independent Christian 12.2%; nonreligious 2.2%; other 1.5%.
Major towns (2000): Charlotte Amalie 11,004 (urban agglomeration 18,914); Christiansted 2,637; Frederiksted 732.

Vital statistics

Birth rate per 1,000 population (2004): 14.5 (world avg. 21.1); (1998) legitimate 30.2%[4]; illegitimate 69.8%.
Death rate per 1,000 population (2004): 6.1 (world avg. 9.0).
Natural increase rate per 1,000 population (2004): 8.4 (world avg. 12.1).
Total fertility rate (avg. births per childbearing woman; 2004): 2.2.
Life expectancy at birth (2004): male 74.9 years; female 82.8 years.
Major causes of death per 100,000 population (2002): malignant neoplasms (cancers) 114.6; diseases of the heart 110.9; cerebrovascular diseases 46.1; accidents 31.6; communicable diseases 27.5; diabetes mellitus 25.6.

National economy

Budget. Revenue (2002): U.S.$580,200,000 (personal income tax 54.7%, gross receipts tax 16.5%, property tax 7.9%). Expenditures (2002): U.S.$573,000,-000 (direct federal expenditures 100.0%).
Production. Agriculture, forestry, fishing (value of sales in U.S.$'000; 2002): ornamental plants and other nursery products 799, livestock and livestock products 775 (notably cattle and calves and hogs and pigs), vegetables 340 (notably tomatoes and cucumbers), fruits and nuts 131 (notably mangoes, bananas, papayas, and avocados); livestock (number of live animals; 2004) 8,000 cattle, 4,000 goats, 3,200 sheep, 2,600 hogs and pigs, 35,000 chickens; roundwood, n.a.; fish catch (2003) 1,492. Mining and quarrying: sand and crushed stone for local use. Manufacturing (U.S.$'000[5]; 2002): beverages and tobacco products 44,766; stone, clay, and glass products 32,939; computer and electronic products 22,875; chemicals and chemical products 16,989. Energy production (consumption) (kW-hr; 2002) 1,100,000,000 (1,100,-000,000); coal (metric tons; 2002) none (290,000); crude petroleum (barrels; 2002) none (149,000,000); petroleum products (metric tons; 2002) 18,801,000 (1,588,000); natural gas, none (none).
Tourism (2003): receipts from visitors U.S.$1,271,000,000; expenditures by nationals abroad, n.a.
Household income and expenditure. Average household size (2000) 2.6; average annual income per household (2000) U.S.$34,991; sources of income (1999): wages and salaries 73.9%, transfers 10.0%, self-employment 8.8%, interest, dividends, and rents 5.7%; expenditures (2001)[6]: housing 38.8%, food and beverages 12.5%, transportation 11.1%, education and communications 7.1%, health 5.8%.
Population economically active (2002)[7]: total 49,440; activity rate of total population 45.4% (participation rates: over age 15, 65.2%[8]; female 49.9%[8]; unemployed 9.4%[9]).

Price and earnings indexes (2001 = 100)

	2001	2002	2003	2004
Consumer price index	100.0	102.1	104.4	107.1
Annual earnings index[10]	100.0	104.4	106.0	109.4

Gross domestic product (at current market prices; 2004): U.S.$2,622,000,000 (U.S.$24,100 per capita).

Structure of gross domestic product and labour force

	2003 in value U.S.$'000,000	2003 % of total value	2000 labour force[11]	2000 % of labour force[11]
Agriculture, fishing	...	...	} 324	0.6
Mining	...	...		
Manufacturing	189	7.5	2,754	5.4
Construction	142	5.6	4,900	9.6
Public utilities	...	...	} 4,252	8.3
Transp. and commun.	...	...		
Trade, hotels, restaurants	648	25.7	} 27,074	53.2
Services	555	22.0		
Finance, insurance, real estate	...	...	2,330	4.6
Pub. admin., defense	584	23.2	4,931	9.7
Other	404	16.0	4,368[12]	8.6[12]
TOTAL	2,522[13]	100.0	50,933	100.0

Public debt (1999): U.S.$1,200,000,000.
Land use as % of total land area (2000): in temporary crops *c.* 12%, in permanent crops *c.* 3%, in pasture *c.* 15%; overall forest area *c.* 41%.

Foreign trade

Balance of trade (current prices)

	1998	1999	2000	2001	2002	2003
U.S.$'000,000	−120.3	−99.4	−149.5	−374.5	−336.9	−9.6
% of total	2.2%	1.5%	1.4%	4.2%	3.8%	0.1%

Imports (2003): U.S.$5,570,400,000 (foreign crude petroleum 80.3%, other [significantly manufactured goods] 19.7%). *Major import sources:* United States 10.9%; other countries 89.1%.
Exports (2003): U.S.$5,560,800,000 (refined petroleum 93.1%, unspecified [significantly rum and watches] 6.9%). *Major export destinations:* United States 93.2%; other countries 6.8%.

Transport and communications

Transport. Railroads: none. Roads (2003): total length 781 mi, 1,257 km (paved 95%). Vehicles (1993): passenger cars 51,000; trucks and buses 13,300. Cruise ships (2004): passenger arrivals 1,964,700. Air transport (2003)[14]: passenger arrivals 598,907; airports (1999) with scheduled flights 2.

Communications

Medium	date	unit	number	units per 1,000 persons
Daily newspapers	2000	circulation	43,000	364
Radio	1997	receivers	107,000	987
Television	2000	receivers	64,700	594
Telephones	2003	main lines	68,961	634
Cellular telephones	2001	subscribers	41,000	375
Internet	2003	users	30,000	276

Education and health

Educational attainment (2000). Percentage of population age 25 and over having: no formal schooling through lower secondary education 18.5%; incomplete upper secondary 21.0%; completed secondary 26.0%; incomplete undergraduate degree 17.8%; completed undergraduate degree 10.4%; graduate degree 6.3%. *Literacy:* n.a.

Education (2000)

	schools	teachers	students	student/ teacher ratio
Primary (age 5–12) } Secondary (age 12–18) }	289	1,511	25,620	17.0
Higher	1	266	3,107	11.7

Health: physicians (2002) 161 (1 per 675 persons); hospital beds (2001) 349[15] (1 per 311 persons); infant mortality rate per 1,000 live births (2004) 8.2.
Food: daily per capita caloric intake, n.a.

Military

Total active duty personnel (2004): no domestic military force is maintained; the United States is responsible for defense and external security.

[1]May be administered by officials assigned by the governor. [2]Census designated place. [3]De jure figure. [4]Percentage of legitimate births may be an underestimation due to the common practice of consensual marriage. [5]Figures are for value of sales. [6]Weights of consumer price index components. [7]Excludes armed forces. [8]2000. [9]2003. [10]Average gross pay. [11]Excludes 109 members of armed forces. [12]Unemployed. [13]Tourism in 2003 accounts for more than 60% of gross domestic product. [14]St. Croix and St. Thomas airports. [15]Main hospitals on St. Thomas and St. Croix only.

Internet resources for further information:
• **Office of Insular Affairs**
  http://www.pacificweb.org
• **U.S. Census Bureau: Economic Census of Outlying Areas**
  http://www.census.gov/csd/oat

Yemen

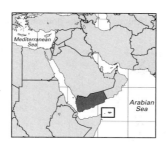

Official name: Al-Jumhūrīyah al-Yamanīyah (Republic of Yemen).
Form of government: multiparty republic with two legislative houses (Consultative Council [111 nonelected seats]; House of Representatives [301]).
Head of state: President.
Head of government: Prime Minister.
Capital: Sanaa.
Official language: Arabic.
Official religion: Islam.
Monetary unit: 1 Yemeni Rial (YRls) = 100 fils; valuation (Sept. 1, 2005) 1 U.S.$ = YRls 192.66; 1 £ = YRls 354.74.

Area and population

Governorates	Capitals	area sq mi	area sq km	population 2004 census
Abyān	Zinjibār	...	...	438,656
ʿAdan[1]	Aden	...	...	590,413
ʿAmrān[1]	ʿAmrān	...	...	872,789
Al-Baydāʾ	Al-Baydāʾ	...	...	571,778
Al-Ḍāliʿ[1]	Al-Ḍāliʿ	...	...	470,460
Dhamār	Dhamār	...	...	1,339,229
Ḥaḍramawt	Al-Mukallā	...	...	1,029,462
Ḥajjah	Ḥajjah	...	...	1,480,897
Al-Ḥudaydah	Al-Ḥudaydah	...	...	2,161,379
Ibb	Ibb	...	...	2,137,546
Al-Jawf	Al-Jawf	...	...	451,426
Lahij	Lahij	...	...	727,203
Al-Mahrah	Al-Ghaydah	...	...	89,093
Al-Maḥwīt	Al-Maḥwīt	...	...	495,865
Maʾrib[2]	Maʾrib	...	...	241,690
Raymah[2]	...	...	...	395,076
Saʿdah	Saʿdah	...	...	693,217
Sanʿāʾ	Sanaa	...	...	918,379
Shabwah	ʿAtāq	...	...	466,889
Taʿizz	Taʿizz	...	...	2,402,569
City				
Sanaa	—	...	...	1,747,627
TOTAL		214,300[3]	555,000[3]	19,721,643

Demography

Population (2005): 20,043,000.
Density (2005)[4]: persons per sq mi 93.5, persons per sq km 36.1.
Urban-rural (2003): urban 25.6%; rural 74.4%.
Sex distribution (2004): male 52.99%; female 47.01%.
Age breakdown (2003): under 15, 46.8%; 15–29, 29.0%; 30–44, 12.8%; 45–59, 7.3%; 60–74, 3.1%; 75 and over, 1.0%.
Population projection: (2010) 23,414,000; (2020) 31,279,000.
Doubling time: 21 years.
Ethnic composition (2000): Arab 92.8%; Somali 3.7%; black 1.1%; Indo-Pakistani 1.0%; other 1.4%.
Religious affiliation (2000): Muslim 98.9%, of which Sunnī c. 60%, Shīʿī c. 40%; Hindu 0.7%; Christian 0.2%; other 0.2%.
Major cities (2004): Sanaa 1,747,627; Aden 580,000; Taʿizz (2001) 450,000; Al-Ḥudaydah (2001) 425,000; Al-Mukallā (2001) 165,000.

Vital statistics

Birth rate per 1,000 population (2004): 43.2 (world avg. 21.1).
Death rate per 1,000 population (2004): 8.8 (world avg. 9.0).
Total fertility rate (avg. births per childbearing woman; 2004): 6.7.
Life expectancy at birth (2004): male 59.5 years; female 63.3 years.

National economy

Budget (2004). Revenue: YRls 804,200,000,000 (tax revenue 94.0%, of which oil revenue 72.0%; nontax revenue 5.8%; grants 0.2%). Expenditures: YRls 626,300,000,000 (transfers and subsidies 36.0%; wages and salaries 25.5%; defense 16.8%; interest on debt 8.9%).
Public debt (external, outstanding; 2003): U.S.$4,747,000,000.
Population economically active (1999): total 4,090,680; activity rate of total population c. 24% (participation rates: ages 15–64, 47.8%; female 23.7%; unemployed [2002] 11.5%).

Price index (2000 = 100)

	1998	1999	2000	2001	2002	2003	2004
Consumer price index	88.0	95.6	100.0	111.9	125.6	139.2	156.6

Production (metric tons except as noted). Agriculture, forestry, fishing (2004): sorghum 263,428, potatoes 213,197, onions 203,474, tomatoes 200,438, grapes 169,000, oranges 166,000, wheat 105,273, bananas 99,000, papayas 73,800; livestock (number of live animals) 7,300,000 goats, 6,600,000 sheep, 1,400,000 cattle, 500,000 asses, 277,000 camels, 34,800,000 chickens; roundwood 352,768 cu m; fish catch (2003) 159,000. Mining and quarrying (2004): salt 120,000; gypsum 44,000. Manufacturing (value added in YRls '000,000; 2004): food, beverages, and tobacco 42,342; nonmetallic mineral products 13,209; chemicals and chemical products 9,884; paper products 5,222; fabricated metal products 4,622; clothing, textiles, and leather 2,502; wood products 2,012. Energy production (consumption): electricity (kW-hr; 2003) 4,094,000,000 ([2002] 3,094,000,000); coal, none (none); crude petroleum (barrels; 2004) 155,000,000 ([2003] 28,500,000); petroleum products (metric tons; 2002) 4,199,000 (3,899,000); natural gas (cu m; 2004) 28,000,000,000[5] ([5]).
Gross national product (2004): U.S.$11,218,000,000 (U.S.$570 per capita).

Structure of gross domestic product and labour force

	2004 in value YRls '000,000	2004 % of total value	2003 labour force	2003 % of labour force
Agriculture[6]	330,440	12.9	2,195,000	54.2
Crude pet., natural gas	793,661	31.1	18,700	0.5
Mining	3,133	0.1		
Manufacturing	142,196	5.6	152,000	3.7
Public utilities	24,134	0.9	13,400	0.3
Construction	157,398	6.2	280,000	6.9
Transp. and commun.	287,294	11.3	140,000	3.5
Trade, restaurants	343,528	13.5	504,000	12.4
Finance, real estate	190,324	7.5	33,000	0.8
Pub. admin., defense	250,864	9.8	448,000	11.1
Services	35,768	1.4	268,000	6.6
Other	−6,746	−0.3	...	...
TOTAL	2,551,994	100.0	4,052,000[7]	100.0

Household income and expenditure. Average household size (2002) 7.1; income per household (1998) YRls 29,035 (U.S.$217); expenditures (1999)[8]: food and nonalcoholic beverages 43.8%, tobacco and khat (qat) 14.8%, housing and energy 13.3%, transportation 4.3%.
Tourism (2003): receipts U.S.$139,000,000; expenditures U.S.$77,000,000.
Land use as % of total land area (2000): in temporary crops 2.9%, in permanent crops 0.2%, in pasture 30.4%; overall forest area 0.9%.

Foreign trade[9]

Balance of trade (current prices)

	1999	2000	2001	2002	2003	2004
YRls '000,000	+67,261	+283,826	+153,108	+72,920	+10,779	+17,063
% of total	9.7%	27.4%	15.5%	6.6%	0.8%	1.1%

Imports (2004): YRls 736,533,100,000 (food and live animals 27.4%, of which cereals and related products 11.4%; machinery and apparatus 19.5%; crude and refined petroleum 12.1%; chemicals and chemical products 10.3%). *Major import sources:* U.A.E. 16.7%; Saudi Arabia 8.8%; China 6.4%; Kuwait 6.2%; U.S. 4.7%.
Exports (2004): YRls 753,595,992,000 (crude and refined petroleum 91.3%; fish and fish products 2.4%; vegetables and fruits 0.8%). *Major export destinations:* Thailand 29.0%; China 28.7%; India 13.2%; Singapore 4.7%; South Korea 3.2%.

Transport and communications

Transport. Railroads: none. Roads (2001)[10]: total length 17,973 km (paved 54%). Vehicles (2001): passenger cars 354,048; trucks and buses (2000) 454,584. Air transport (2001): passenger-km 1,580,000,000; metric ton-km cargo (2000) 32,000,000; airports (1998) with scheduled flights 12.

Communications

Medium	date	unit	number	units per 1,000 persons
Daily newspapers	2000	circulation	270,000	15
Radio	2000	receivers	1,170,000	65
Television	2003	receivers	5,812,100	308
Telephones	2004	main lines	798,100	41
Cellular telephones	2004	subscribers	1,072,000	55
Personal computers	2004	units	300,000	15
Internet	2004	users	180,000	9.3

Education and health

Educational attainment (1998). Percentage of population age 10 and over having: no formal schooling 49.5%; reading and writing ability 32.2%; primary education 11.0%; secondary education 4.6%; higher 2.7%. *Literacy* (2003): percentage of total population age 15 and over literate 50.3%; males literate 70.5%; females literate 30.1%.

Education (2003–04)

	schools	teachers	students	student/ teacher ratio
Primary (age 7–12)	11,013[11]	113,812[11]	3,995,000	29.9[11]
Secondary (age 13–18)	3,463	14,063[11]	575,000	34.6[11]
Voc., teacher tr.[12]	...	1,406	9,233	6.6
Higher	7	3,429[11]	193,250[12]	53.7[11]

Health (2001): physicians 4,384 (1 per 4,052 persons); hospital beds 12,272 (1 per 1,448 persons); infant mortality rate (2004) 63.3.
Food (2002): daily per capita caloric intake 2,038 (vegetable products 93%, animal products 7%); 84% of FAO recommended minimum requirement.

Military

Total active duty personnel (2004): 66,700 (army 90.0%, navy 2.5%, air force 7.5%). *Military expenditure as percentage of GDP* (2003): 7.1%; per capita expenditure U.S.$43.

---

[1]Created in 1998 from parts of three other governorates. [2]Approved in 2004 from parts of two other governorates. [3]Estimated total area. A survey to demarcate the official boundary with Saudi Arabia was begun in June 2000 and was to be completed in mid-2006. [4]Based on the total area estimate of 214,300 sq mi (555,000 sq km). [5]Virtually all natural gas was flared or reinjected for field pressure maintenance. [6]Khat's (or qat's) agricultural and nonagricultural contribution to GDP is about 10% of total GDP; khat cultivation employs nearly 15% of the labour force. [7]Detail does not add to total given because of rounding. [8]Weights of consumer price index components. [9]Imports c.i.f.; exports f.o.b. [10]Excludes unimproved roads and all roads in Adan governorate. [11]2001–02. [12]2002–03.

Internet resources for further information:
• Central Bank of Yemen http://www.centralbank.gov.ye
• National Information Center http://www.nic.gov.ye/English%20site

Zambia

Official name: Republic of Zambia.
Form of government: multiparty
republic with one legislative house
(National Assembly [158[1]]).
Head of state and government:
President.
Capital: Lusaka.
Official language: English.
Official religion: none[2].
Monetary unit: 1 Zambian kwacha
(K) = 100 ngwee; valuation (Sept. 1,
2005) 1 U.S.$ = K 4,600;
1 £ = K 8,470.

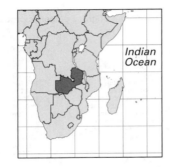

Area and population

Provinces	Capitals	area sq mi	area sq km	population 2000 census
Central	Kabwe	36,446	94,394	1,012,257
Copperbelt	Ndola	12,096	31,328	1,581,221
Eastern	Chipata	26,682	69,106	1,306,173
Luapula	Mansa	19,524	50,567	775,353
Lusaka	Lusaka	8,454	21,896	1,391,329
North-Western	Solwezi	48,582	125,827	583,350
Northern	Kasama	57,076	147,826	1,258,696
Southern	Livingstone	32,928	85,283	1,212,124
Western	Mongu	48,798	126,386	765,088
TOTAL		290,585[3]	752,612[3]	9,885,591

Demography

Population (2005): 11,262,000.
Density (2005): persons per sq mi 38.8, persons per sq km 15.0.
Urban-rural (2003): urban 35.7%; rural 64.3%.
Sex distribution (2000): male 50.04%; female 49.96%.
Age breakdown (2000): under 15, 47.0%; 15–29, 30.0%; 30–44, 12.9%; 45–59,
5.9%; 60–74, 3.4%; 75 and over, 0.8%.
Population projection: (2010) 12,497,000; (2020) 15,105,000.
Doubling time: 33 years.
Ethnic composition (2000): Bemba 18.0%; Tonga 12.7%; Chewa 7.2%; Lozi
5.6%; Tumbuka 4.2%; other 52.3%.
Religious affiliation (2000): Christian 82.4%, of which Roman Catholic 29.7%,
Protestant (including Anglican) 28.2%, independent Christian 15.2%, unaf-
filiated Christian 5.5%; traditional beliefs 14.3%; Bahā'ī 1.8%; Muslim 1.1%;
other 0.4%.
Major cities (2000): Lusaka 1,084,703 (urban agglomeration [2003] 1,394,000);
Ndola 374,757; Kitwe 363,734; Kabwe 176,758; Chingola 147,448.

Vital statistics

Birth rate per 1,000 population (2004): 41.8 (world avg. 21.1).
Death rate per 1,000 population (2004): 20.5 (world avg. 9.0).
Natural increase rate per 1,000 population (2004): 21.3 (world avg. 12.1).
Total fertility rate (avg. births per childbearing woman; 2004): 5.6.
Life expectancy at birth (2004): male 39.1 years; female 39.6 years.
Adult population (ages 15–49) *living with HIV* (2004[4]): 16.5% (world avg. 1.1%).

National economy

Budget (2003). Revenue: K 5,104,000,000,000 (tax revenue 69.5%, of which
income tax 31.5%, value-added tax 28.3%, excise taxes 9.4%; grants 27.9%;
nontax revenue 2.6%). Expenditures: K 6,338,000,000,000 (current expenditures 63.2%, of which wages 27.3%, interest payment 12.5%, transfers 10.2%;
capital expenditures 36.8%).
Public debt (external, outstanding; 2003): U.S.$5,043,000,000.
Production (metric tons except as noted). Agriculture, forestry, fishing (2004):
sugarcane 1,800,000, corn (maize) 1,161,000, cassava 950,000, wheat 135,000,
seed cotton 62,000, sweet potatoes 53,000, peanuts (groundnuts) 42,000, sunflower seeds 10,000, tobacco 4,800, fresh-cut flowers (value of sales; 2000)
U.S.$21,000,000; livestock (number of live animals) 2,600,000 cattle, 1,270,000
goats, 340,000 pigs, 30,000,000 chickens; roundwood 8,053,000 cu m; fish catch
(2003) 65,000. Mining and quarrying (2003): copper (metal content) 349,000;
cobalt (metal content) 11,300; amethyst 1,000,000 kg; emeralds 2,000 kg[5].
Manufacturing (2001): cement 350,000; refined copper (2003) 349,800; vegetable oils 11,800; refined cobalt (2003) 3,200. Energy production (consumption): electricity (kW-hr; 2002) 9,109,000,000 (6,452,000,000); coal (metric
tons; 2002) 210,000 (136,000); crude petroleum (barrels; 2002) none
(3,500,000); petroleum products (metric tons; 2002) 426,000 (485,000); natural gas, none (none).
Household income and expenditure. Average household size (2002) 5.1.
Tourism (2003): receipts from visitors U.S.$149,000,000; expenditures by
nationals abroad U.S.$77,000,000.
Population economically active (1996): total 3,507,000; activity rate of total
population 36.1% (participation rates: ages 15–64, 54.5%; female 30.3%;
unemployed [2000] 12.9%).

Price and earnings indexes (2000 = 100)

	1998	1999	2000	2001	2002	2003	2004
Consumer price index	62.6	79.3	100.0	121.4	148.4	180.1	212.5
Earnings index	...	...	...	...	...	...	...

Gross national product (at current market prices; 2004): U.S.$4,748,000,000
(U.S.$450 per capita).

Structure of gross domestic product and labour force

	2002 in value K '000,000,000	2002 % of total value	1990 labour force	1990 % of labour force
Agriculture	3,247	20.0	1,872,000	68.9
Mining	575	3.5	56,800	2.1
Manufacturing	1,694	10.4	50,900	1.9
Construction	1,068	6.6	29,100	1.1
Public utilities	488	3.0	8,900	0.3
Transp. and commun.	1,056	6.5	25,600	0.9
Trade	3,411	21.0	30,700	1.1
Finance	2,534	15.6	24,200	0.9
Pub. admin., defense } Services	1,414	8.7	111,600	4.1
Other	773[6]	4.7[6]	506,100	18.6
TOTAL	16,260	100.0	2,716,000[3]	100.0[3]

Land use as % of total land area (2000): in temporary crops 7.1%, in permanent crops 0.03%, in pasture 40.4%; overall forest area 42.0%.

Foreign trade

Balance of trade (current prices)

	1998	1999	2000	2001	2002	2003
U.S.$'000,000	−155	−115	−232	−369	−323	−271
% of total	8.7%	7.1%	13.5%	17.3%	14.8%	10.8%

Imports (2002): U.S.$1,253,000,000 (nonelectrical machinery and equipment
21.6%, chemicals and chemical products 14.9%, printed matter 11.3%, road
vehicles 8.8%, cereals [all forms] 8.0%). *Major import sources:* South Africa
51.2%; U.K. 12.3%; Zimbabwe 7.8%; India 3.6%; Japan 3.2%.
Exports (2002): U.S.$930,000,000 (refined copper 50.0%, other base metals
[including cobalt] 8.9%, food and live animals 7.3%, manufactures of base
metals 5.8%). *Major export destinations:* U.K. 42.3%; South Africa 23.0%;
Tanzania 7.6%; Switzerland 6.1%; Democratic Republic of the Congo 4.3%.

Transport and communications

Transport. Railroads (1998): length (2004)[7] 1,350 mi, 2,173 km; passenger-km
586,000,000; metric ton-km cargo 702,000,000. Roads (2001): total length
56,820 mi, 91,440 km (paved 22%). Vehicles (1996): passenger cars 157,000;
trucks and buses 81,000. Air transport (2004)[8]: passenger-km 19,366,000; metric ton-km cargo, none; airports (1998) 4.

Communications

Medium	date	unit	number	units per 1,000 persons
Daily newspapers	2000	circulation	125,000	12
Radio	2000	receivers	1,510,000	145
Television	2000	receivers	1,400,000	134
Telephones	2003	main lines	88,400	7.9
Cellular telephones	2004	subscribers	300,000	28
Personal computers	2004	units	113,000	10
Internet	2004	users	231,000	21

Education and health

Educational attainment (2001–02)[9]. Percentage of population age 15 and over
having: no formal schooling 14.4%; some primary education 33.4%; completed primary 19.7%; some secondary 22.0%; completed secondary 5.9%;
higher 4.3%; unknown 0.3%. *Literacy* (2002): population age 15 and over literate 79.1%; males literate 86.3%; females literate 73.8%.

Education (2002–03)

	schools	teachers	students	student/ teacher ratio
Primary (age 7–13)	4,221[10]	40,488	1,731,579	42.8
Secondary (age 14–18)	246[11]	9,725	345,442	35.5
Voc., teacher tr.	4[11]	150	6,000	40.0
Higher	2[11]	640[11]	24,553[12]	...

Health: physicians (1995) 647 (1 per 14,492 persons); hospital beds (1989)
22,461 (1 per 349 persons); infant mortality rate per 1,000 live births (2004)
89.7.
Food (2002): daily per capita caloric intake 1,927 (vegetable products 95%,
animal products 5%); 83% of FAO recommended minimum requirement.

Military

Total active duty personnel (2005): 15,100 (army 89.4%; navy, none; air force
10.6%). *Military expenditure as percentage of GDP* (2003): 0.6%; per capita
expenditure U.S.$3.

---

[1]Includes 8 nonelective seats. [2]In 1996 Zambia was declared a Christian nation per the
preamble of a constitutional amendment. [3]Detail does not add to total given because
of rounding. [4]Beginning of year. [5]In 1999 legal and illegal exports of emeralds were
estimated to equal U.S.$20,000,000 (about 20% of world total). [6]Import duties less
imputed bank service charges. [7]Includes 891 km of the Tanzania-Zambia Railway
Authority. [8]Zambian Airways Limited only. [9]Based on a sample survey of 19,531 persons. [10]1998. [11]1996. [12]2000–01.

Internet resources for further information:
• **Zambian Department of Census and Statistics**
  http://www.zamstats.gov.zm
• **Bank of Zambia**
  http://www.boz.zm

Zimbabwe

Official name: Republic of Zimbabwe.
Form of government: multiparty republic with two legislative houses (Senate [66[1]]; House of Assembly [150[2]]).
Head of state and government: President.
Capital: Harare.
Official language: English.
Official religion: none.
Monetary unit: 1 Zimbabwe dollar (Z$) = 100 cents; valuation (Sept. 1, 2005) 1 U.S.$ = Z$24,521; 1 £ = Z$45,149.

Area and population		area		population
				2002 preliminary
Provinces	**Capitals**	sq mi	sq km	census
Bulawayo	—	185	479	676,787
Harare	—	337	872	1,903,510
Manicaland	Mutare	14,077	36,459	1,566,889
Mashonaland Central	Bindura	10,945	28,347	998,265
Mashonaland East	Marondera	12,444	32,230	1,125,355
Mashonaland West	Chinhoyi	22,178	57,441	1,222,583
Masvingo	Masvingo	21,840	56,566	1,318,705
Matabeleland North	Lupane	28,967	75,025	701,359
Matabeleland South	Gwanda	20,916	54,172	654,879
Midlands	Gweru	18,983	49,166	1,466,331
TOTAL		150,872	390,757	11,634,663

Demography

Population (2005): 12,161,000[3].
Density (2005): persons per sq mi 80.6, persons per sq km 31.1.
Urban-rural (2003): urban 34.9%; rural 65.1%.
Sex distribution (2003): male 49.57%; female 50.43%.
Age breakdown (2003): under 15, 39.7%; 15–29, 32.6%; 30–44, 15.1%; 45–59, 7.3%; 60–74, 4.1%; 75 and over, 1.2%.
Population projection: (2010) 12,516,000; (2020) 12,902,000.
Doubling time: not applicable; doubling time exceeds 100 years.
Ethnic composition (2003): Shona 71%; Ndebele 16%; other African 11%; white 1%; mixed race/Asian 1%.
Religious affiliation (2000): Christian 67.5%, of which independent Christian 36.4%, Protestant (including Anglican) 13.5%, Roman Catholic 8.7%, unaffiliated Christian 8.2%; traditional beliefs 30.1%; other 2.4%.
Major cities (2002): Harare 1,444,534; Bulawayo 676,787; Chitungwiza 321,782; Mutare (1992) 131,808; Gweru (1992) 124,735.

Vital statistics

Birth rate per 1,000 population (2004): 28.4 (world avg. 21.1).
Death rate per 1,000 population (2004): 22.0 (world avg. 9.0).
Natural increase rate per 1,000 population (2004): 6.4 (world avg. 12.1).
Total fertility rate (avg. births per childbearing woman; 2004): 3.2.
Life expectancy at birth (2004): male 40.1 years; female 38.0 years.
Adult population (ages 15–49) *living with HIV* (2004[4]): 24.6% (world avg. 1.1%).

National economy

Budget (2002). Revenue: Z$300,385,000,000 (tax revenue 93.5%, of which income tax 53.0%, sales tax 24.1%, customs duties 9.0%, excise tax 6.2%; nontax revenue 6.5%). Expenditures: Z$351,321,000,000 (current expenditures 91.3%, of which goods and services 61.5%, transfer payments 15.7%, interest payments 14.1%; development expenditure 7.2%; net lending 1.5%).
Population economically active (1999): total 4,963,259; activity rate of total population c. 43% (participation rates: over age 14, 72.2%; female 48.2%; unemployed [2005] c. 75%).

Price and earnings indexes (2000 = 100)							
	1998	1999	2000	2001	2002	2003	2004
Consumer price index	40.5	64.2	100.0	176.7	424.3	2,255.8	8,625.8
Earnings index	...	...	...	...	...	...	...

Production (metric tons except as noted). Agriculture, forestry, fishing (2004): sugarcane 4,100,000, corn (maize) 1,000,000, seed cotton 265,000, cassava 190,000, peanuts (groundnuts) 125,000, oranges 93,000, bananas 85,000, soybeans 84,000, tobacco 80,000, sorghum 80,000, wheat 80,000, tea 22,000, coffee 9,000; livestock (number of live animals) 5,400,000 cattle, 2,970,000 goats, 610,000 sheep, 112,000 asses; roundwood 9,107,600 cu m; fish catch (2003) 13,000. Mining and quarrying (2003): chromite 637,099; asbestos 147,000; granite 47,007; nickel (metal content) 11,600; gold 12,564 kg; platinum-group metals (palladium, platinum, rhodium, ruthenium, and iridium) 8,418 kg. Manufacturing (value added in U.S.$'000,000; 1998): beverages 171; foodstuffs 148; textiles 99; iron and steel 86; fabricated metal products 64; cement, bricks, and tiles 63; tobacco products 51. Energy production (consumption): electricity (kW-hr; 2002) 8,598,000,000 (12,593,000,000); coal (metric tons; 2002) 3,690,000 (3,727,000); crude petroleum, none (none); petroleum products (metric tons; 2002) none (938,000); natural gas, none (none).
Public debt (external, outstanding; 2003): U.S.$3,367,000,000.
Household income and expenditure. Average household size (2002) 4.4; income per household (1992) Z$1,689 (U.S.$332); expenditure (1995)[5]: food 33.6%, housing 17.3%, beverages and tobacco 16.0%, household durable goods 7.5%, clothing and footwear 6.9%, transportation 6.6%, education 4.5%.

Gross national product (2002): U.S.$6,165,000,000 (U.S.$480 per capita).

Structure of gross domestic product and labour force				
	1999		2002	
	in value Z$'000,000[6]	% of total value[6]	labour force	% of labour force
Agriculture	35,812	19.4	2,800,000	56.4
Mining	3,380	1.8	50,000	1.0
Manufacturing	30,538	16.5	378,000	7.6
Construction	5,132	2.8	106,000	2.1
Public utilities	5,171	2.8	10,000	0.2
Transp. and commun.	11,373	6.2	102,000	2.1
Trade, restaurants	36,261	19.7	333,000	6.7
Finance, real estate	26,917	14.6	121,000	2.4
Pub. admin., defense	22,913	12.4	578,000	11.7
Services	8,273	4.5		
Other	-1,357[7]	-0.7[7]	485,000[8]	9.8[8]
TOTAL	184,413	100.0	4,963,000	100.0

Tourism: receipts (2003) U.S.$44,000,000; expenditures (1998) U.S.$131,000,000.
Land use as % of total land area (2000): in temporary crops 8.3%, in permanent crops 0.3%, in pasture 44.5%; overall forest area 49.2%.

Foreign trade

Balance of trade (current prices)						
	1998	1999	2000	2001	2002	2003
U.S.$'000,000	-95	+249	+293	-217	-525	-402
% of total	2.4%	6.9%	7.1%	6.4%	15.8%	14.1%

Imports (2003): U.S.$1,627,000,000 (machinery and transport equipment 21.0%, chemicals and chemical products 20.2%, emergency food supply 17.3%, fuel and electricity 14.0%). *Major import sources* (2002): South Africa 47.7%; Democratic Republic of the Congo 5.7%; Mozambique 5.3%; Germany 3.1%; U.K. 3.1%.
Exports (2003): U.S.$1,225,000,000 (tobacco 26.2%, gold 11.2%, horticultural products [including cut flowers] 9.6%, ferroalloys 8.6%, nickel 6.4%, platinum 5.6%, sugar 4.5%). *Major export destinations* (2002): South Africa 16.4%; Japan 9.5%; Switzerland 8.2%; U.K. 7.9%; Germany 7.5%; Zambia 6.2%; Spain 5.1%.

Transport and communications

Transport. Railroads (2004): route length 3,077 km; (1998) passenger-km 408,223,000; (2000) metric ton-km cargo 3,326,000. Roads (2002): total length 97,267 km (paved 19%). Vehicles (2002): passenger cars 570,866; trucks and buses 84,456. Air transport (2004)[9]: passenger-km 575,944,000; metric ton-km cargo 17,449,000; airports (1997) with scheduled flights 7.

Communications				units per 1,000
Medium	date	unit	number	persons
Daily newspapers	2000	circulation	205,000	18
Radio	2000	receivers	4,110,000	362
Television	2003	receivers	672,300	56
Telephones	2004	main lines	317,000	25
Cellular telephones	2004	subscribers	397,500	31
Personal computers	2004	units	1,000,000	77
Internet	2004	users	820,000	63

Education and health

Educational attainment (1992). Percentage of population age 25 and over having: no formal schooling 22.3%; primary 54.3%; secondary 13.1%; higher 3.4%. *Literacy* (2001): percentage of total population age 15 and over literate 89.3%; males literate 93.3%; females literate 85.5%.

Education (2003–04)				student/
	schools	teachers	students	teacher ratio
Primary (age 7–13)	4,706[10]	61,251	2,361,588	38.6
Secondary (age 14–19)	1,530[10]	33,964	758,229	22.3
Voc., teacher tr.[11]	25	1,479	27,431	18.5
Higher[12]	28[11]	3,581[10]	46,492[10]	13.0[10]

Health: physicians (2002) 736 (1 per 16,205 persons); hospital beds (1996) 22,975 (1 per 501 persons); infant mortality rate (2004) 53.0.
Food (2002): daily per capita caloric intake 1,943 (vegetable products 92%, animal products 8%); 81% of FAO recommended minimum requirement.

Military

Total active duty personnel (2005): 29,000 (army 86.2%, air force 13.8%). *Military expenditure as percentage of GDP* (2003): 2.1%; per capita expenditure U.S.$15.

[1]Includes 6 presidential appointees and 10 traditional chiefs. [2]Includes 20 presidential appointees and 10 traditional chiefs. [3]De facto estimate; 3 to 4 million people have left Zimbabwe since 1999. [4]January 1. [5]Weights of consumer price index components. [6]At factor cost. [7]Less imputed bank service charges. [8]Includes 187,000 not adequately defined and 298,000 unemployed. [9]Air Zimbabwe only. [10]1998. [11]1992. [12]Includes postsecondary vocational and teacher training at the higher level.

Internet resources for further information:
• Reserve Bank of Zimbabwe http://www.rbz.co.zw

Comparative National Statistics

World and regional summaries

region/bloc	area: square miles	area: square kilometres	population: total	per sq mi	per sq km	population projection, 2020	total ('000,000 U.S.$), 2003	GNP per capita (U.S.$), 2003	% agriculture, 2000	% industry, 2000	% services, 2000	growth rate, 1990–99	total ('000)	% male	% female
World	52,429,502	135,791,667	6,418,916,367	122.4	47.3	7,503,260,267	35,988,170	5,547	4	28	68	2.5	2,828,551	60.2	39.8
Africa	11,682,118	30,256,320	879,227,300	75.3	29.1	1,179,452,800	603,612	723	16	30	53	2.5	321,761	60.2	39.8
Central Africa	2,552,967	6,612,155	105,706,000	41.4	16.0	156,497,000	34,250	350	17	36	21	1.3	38,800	57.6	42.4
East Africa	2,471,068	6,399,920	277,707,800	112.4	43.4	383,839,000	67,022	260	28	17	54	2.9	114,915	52.9	47.1
North Africa	3,288,574	8,517,370	185,665,000	56.5	21.8	232,407,000	268,393	1,464	16	33	51	3.3	56,141	75.5	24.5
Southern Africa	1,032,545	2,674,283	53,747,000	52.1	20.1	54,168,000	139,903	2,663	3	28	68	1.3	21,488	60.6	39.4
West Africa	2,336,964	6,052,592	256,401,500	109.7	42.4	352,418,000	94,045	386	31	30	38	3.0	90,417	60.9	39.1
Americas	16,300,080	42,217,014	884,488,400	54.3	21.0	1,032,621,500	14,859,793	17,217	2	23	75	3.0	395,502	58.3	41.7
Anglo-America[2]	8,368,034	21,673,109	329,103,800	39.3	15.2	373,328,300	12,977,141	40,201	1	22	76	3.0	165,111	54.2	45.8
Canada	3,855,103	9,984,670	32,227,000	8.4	3.2	36,428,000	756,899	23,930	3	27	70	2.8	16,224	54.3	45.7
United States	3,676,487	9,522,057	296,750,000	80.7	31.2	336,766,000	10,946,358	37,610	1	22	77	3.0	148,850	54.2	45.8
Latin America	7,932,046	20,543,905	555,384,600	70.0	27.0	659,293,200	1,882,652	3,485	7	29	64	3.4	230,391	61.2	38.8
Caribbean	90,706	234,922	39,154,100	431.7	166.7	43,604,700	160,328	4,195	5	33	56	2.8	15,932	61.2	38.8
Central America	201,594	522,129	39,806,000	197.5	76.2	52,006,000	80,524	2,088	17	21	63	4.4	13,248	67.1	32.9
Mexico	758,449	1,964,375	107,029,000	141.1	54.5	124,652,000	649,166	6,230	4	27	69	2.8	40,300	66.4	33.6
South America	6,881,297	17,822,479	369,395,500	53.7	20.7	439,030,500	992,634	2,763	8	30	63	3.6	160,911	59.4	40.6
Andean Group	2,111,952	5,469,933	136,188,000	64.5	24.9	165,463,000	344,865	2,616	9	32	59	3.8	56,750	60.2	39.8
Brazil	3,287,612	8,514,877	184,016,000	56.0	21.6	216,384,000	483,234	2,710	8	31	60	3.0	83,387	58.8	41.2
Other South America	1,481,733	3,837,669	49,191,500	33.2	12.8	57,183,500	164,535	3,349	5	24	70	4.8	20,774	59.7	40.3
Asia	12,263,750	31,762,951	3,891,415,000	317.3	122.5	4,525,993,000	9,288,291	2,445	8	35	57	3.7	1,751,066	61.6	38.4
Eastern Asia	4,546,180	11,774,596	1,535,908,000	337.9	130.4	1,647,199,000	6,873,627	4,517	4	36	59	3.1	860,729	55.8	44.2
China	3,696,100	9,572,900	1,304,369,000	352.9	136.3	1,411,531,000	1,420,626	1,100	18	49	33	10.8	745,715	55.3	44.7
Japan	145,908	377,899	128,085,000	877.9	338.9	126,713,000	4,402,612	34,510	2	33	66	1.4	67,705	59.4	40.6
South Korea	38,456	99,601	48,294,000	1,255.8	484.9	49,956,000	575,903	12,020	6	49	45	5.7	22,501	59.7	40.3
Other Eastern Asia	665,716	1,724,196	55,160,000	82.9	32.0	58,999,000	474,466	8,665	1	22	73	5.5	24,808	60.1	39.9
South Asia	1,933,355	5,007,370	1,467,780,000	759.2	293.1	1,811,159,000	728,920	516	28	23	48	5.5	530,171	71.0	29.0
India	1,222,559	3,166,414	1,103,371,000	902.5	348.5	1,332,032,000	564,695	530	28	24	48	5.9	398,363	72.0	28.0
Pakistan	307,374	796,096	153,960,000	500.9	193.4	204,184,000	69,692	470	24	18	58	3.5	48,238	75.2	24.8
Other South Asia	403,422	1,044,860	210,449,000	521.7	201.4	274,943,000	94,533	477	35	28	36	4.9	83,570	63.7	36.3
Southeast Asia	1,735,428	4,494,736	551,794,000	318.0	122.8	642,110,000	755,045	1,404	21	30	49	5.3	247,704	58.5	41.5
Southwest Asia	4,048,787	10,486,249	335,933,000	83.0	32.0	425,525,000	931,873	2,850	10	36	52	2.8	112,462	68.8	31.2
Central Asia	1,545,231	4,002,000	58,607,000	37.9	14.6	69,265,000	46,009	825	16	25	58	-4.3	23,445	54.3	45.7
Gulf Cooperation Council	993,350	2,572,755	34,664,000	34.9	13.5	48,938,000	360,438	10,513	4	51	45	2.2	11,300	85.6	14.4
Iran	636,374	1,648,200	69,515,000	109.2	42.2	85,036,000	134,295	2,000	21	30	50	3.4	22,788	70.5	29.5
Other Southwest Asia	873,832	2,263,294	173,147,000	198.2	76.5	222,286,000	391,132	2,323	11	28	57	4.0	54,929	70.9	29.1
Europe	8,895,898	23,040,396	730,498,100	82.1	31.7	725,949,000	10,715,397	14,684	3	27	70	1.3	345,442	54.9	45.1
European Union (EU)	1,534,320	3,973,872	460,353,000	300.0	115.8	473,790,000	9,638,144	21,082	2	27	71	1.8	212,021	56.5	43.5
France	210,026	543,965	60,733,000	289.2	111.7	63,903,000	1,480,379	24,770	3	22	75	1.5	26,345	54.6	45.4
Germany	137,847	357,023	82,443,000	598.1	230.9	82,038,000	2,083,706	25,250	1	31	68	1.4	40,464	56.3	43.7
Italy	116,346	301,336	57,989,000	498.4	192.4	58,145,000	1,239,226	21,560	3	31	67	1.4	23,838	61.7	38.3
Spain	195,379	506,030	44,079,000	225.6	87.1	49,779,000	738,746	16,990	3	24	73	2.3	18,661	60.5	39.5
United Kingdom	93,635	242,514	60,020,000	641.0	247.5	63,587,000	1,683,884	28,350	1	26	73	2.5	29,558	54.5	45.5
Other EU	781,087	2,023,004	155,089,000	198.6	76.7	156,338,000	2,412,203	15,610	3	25	72	2.4	73,155	55.4	44.6
Other Western Europe[3]	205,512	532,271	12,909,100	62.8	24.3	14,093,000	508,064	40,694	2	29	67	1.7	6,761	54.5	45.5
Eastern Europe	7,156,066	18,534,253	257,236,000	36.0	13.9	238,066,000	569,189	2,186	7	32	61	-3.2	126,660	52.2	47.8
Russia	6,592,800	17,075,400	143,420,000	21.8	8.4	134,386,000	378,129	2,610	7	35	59	-6.0	71,319	51.5	48.5
Ukraine	233,062	603,628	47,075,000	202.0	78.0	40,115,000	46,307	970	11	30	59	-10.8	22,847	51.1	48.9
Other Eastern Europe	330,204	855,225	66,741,000	202.1	78.0	63,565,000	144,753	2,135	7	30	62	1.3	32,494	54.7	45.3
Oceania	3,287,656	8,514,986	33,287,567	10.1	3.9	39,243,967	513,414	15,848	4	21	74	3.9	14,780	55.3	44.7
Australia	2,969,978	7,692,208	20,345,000	6.9	2.6	23,537,000	430,793	21,650	3	22	76	4.1	9,498	55.6	44.4
Pacific Ocean Islands	317,678	822,778	12,942,567	40.7	15.7	15,706,967	82,621	6,611	9	21	64	2.9	5,282	54.8	45.2

[1]Refers only to the outstanding long-term external public and publicly guaranteed debt of the 137 countries that report under the World Bank's Debtor Reporting System (DRS). [2]Anglo-America includes Canada, the United States, Greenland, Bermuda, and St. Pierre and Miquelon. [3]Other Western Europe includes Andorra, Faroe Islands, Gibraltar, Guernsey, Iceland, Isle of Man, Jersey, Liechtenstein,

Africa

Americas

Asia

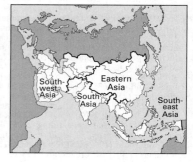

economic indicators							social indicators								region/bloc
pop. per 1,000 ha of arable land, 2002	electricity consumption (kW-hr per capita), 2002	trade ('000,000 U.S.$), 2001–03			debt ('000,000 U.S.$), 1999[1]		life expectancy (years), 2003		health			food (% FAO recommended minimum), 2002	literacy (%) (latest)		
		imports (c.i.f.)	exports (f.o.b.)	balance	total	% of GNP	male	female	pop. per doctor (latest)	infant mortality per 1,000 births, 2003	pop. having safe water (%), 2000		male	female	
4,387	2,584	6,930,434	6,744,616	−185,818	1,464,107	24.0	65.5	69.5	730	39.6	82	119	84.0	70.8	World
4,434	597	128,896	140,874	+11,978	236,331	48.0	51.0	53.2	2,560	78.1	64	103	69.6	52.0	Africa
4,365	124	8,854	16,653	+7,799	34,588	134.3	45.7	49.1	12,890	102.1	46	82	79.5	60.0	Central Africa
5,667	163	19,575	9,904	−9,671	45,902	77.9	45.1	46.5	13,620	93.6	50	86	69.5	53.6	East Africa
4,591	941	39,602	41,639	+2,037	87,534	44.0	66.4	70.4	890	42.6	87	123	69.2	45.8	North Africa
3,161	4,715	38,442	36,089	−2,353	10,458	7.7	44.1	45.3	1,610	64.1	85	119	84.8	84.4	Southern Africa
3,876	150	22,423	36,590	+14,167	57,849	79.6	49.2	50.6	6,260	81.7	65	110	62.7	44.7	West Africa
2,328	6,423	2,138,514	1,595,412	−543,102	398,042	20.6	71.0	77.3	520	18.8	91	135	91.5	90.2	Americas
1,441	13,951	1,528,316	976,367	−551,949	—	—	74.6	80.4	370	6.6	100	158	95.7	95.3	Anglo-America[2]
686	18,541	222,241	252,418	+30,177	—	—	76.4	83.4	540	5.0	100	135	96.6	96.6	Canada
1,637	13,456	1,305,092	723,609	−581,483	—	—	74.4	80.1	360	6.8	100	143	95.7	95.3	United States
3,692	1,961	610,198	619,045	+8,847	398,042	20.6	68.9	75.4	690	26.1	86	120	89.0	87.1	Latin America
7,532	1,865	134,133	113,899	−20,234	10,091	26.6	67.1	71.4	380	29.3	79	99	82.5	82.1	Caribbean
6,969	841	25,355	11,344	−14,011	24,967	41.2	66.9	70.9	950	29.5	88	107	78.2	72.3	Central America
4,153	2,280	168,651	160,670	−7,981	87,531	18.6	71.9	77.6	810	17.4	88	135	93.1	89.1	Mexico
3,253	2,000	120,755	158,917	+38,162	275,453	20.2	68.4	75.7	710	27.9	86	120	89.7	88.6	South America
9,110	1,665	56,520	68,915	+12,395	87,634	26.6	68.9	75.0	830	26.5	86	108	92.7	90.1	Andean Group
2,986	2,183	49,735	60,632	+10,897	95,233	27.5	67.2	75.3	770	31.8	87	128	85.5	85.4	Brazil
1,358	2,241	14,500	29,640	+15,140	92,586	30.4	71.5	78.9	410	17.7	82	123	96.6	96.4	Other South America
7,318	1,437	1,799,979	2,028,586	+228,607	595,398	20.9	66.6	69.7	970	41.8	81	117	82.5	65.2	Asia
9,736	2,363	1,179,486	1,321,391	+141,905	166,210	12.1	70.9	74.6	610	23.4	78	123	93.3	80.4	Eastern Asia
9,005	1,484	295,170	325,596	+30,426	108,163	11.1	70.1	73.3	620	26.4	75	125	92.3	77.4	China
28,837	8,613	383,452	471,996	+88,544	—	—	78.4	85.3	530	3.0	97	118	100.0	100.0	Japan
28,282	7,058	149,572	160,855	+11,283	57,231	14.2	71.7	79.3	740	7.3	92	130	99.2	96.4	South Korea
6,672	4,535	351,292	362,945	+11,653	816	94.7	71.3	76.9	500	14.1	94	92	97.5	90.9	Other Eastern Asia
6,864	415	91,054	75,813	−15,241	139,322	24.4	62.3	63.7	2,100	63.4	85	107	65.8	39.4	South Asia
6,490	463	61,118	52,471	−8,647	82,380	18.5	62.9	64.4	1,920	59.6	84	111	68.6	42.1	India
6,805	469	13,013	11,910	−1,103	28,514	48.5	61.3	63.2	1,840	76.6	90	105	57.6	27.8	Pakistan
9,923	127	16,923	11,432	−5,491	28,428	41.3	60.0	60.3	5,080	73.7	85	85	56.7	33.4	Other South Asia
8,406	791	353,337	410,291	+56,954	186,531	37.6	66.1	71.0	3,120	36.2	78	123	92.9	85.8	Southeast Asia
3,508	2,726	176,101	221,090	+44,989	103,335	25.5	66.4	70.5	610	43.1	85	117	88.0	72.9	Southwest Asia
1,876	2,627	12,654	15,806	+3,152	9,819	25.1	62.0	68.7	330	55.9	82	94	98.8	96.4	Central Asia
8,843	8,695	79,974	121,229	+41,255	1,768	12.8	68.5	72.2	620	39.3	95	120	82.9	69.9	Gulf Cooperation Council
4,455	2,075	20,336	28,356	+8,020	6,184	5.6	68.0	70.7	1,200	44.2	92	128	83.7	70.0	Iran
3,868	1,826	63,138	55,700	−7,438	85,563	35.5	66.9	70.8	690	39.1	82	119	87.0	66.8	Other Southwest Asia
2,534	6,174	2,932,353	3,068,534	+136,181	232,295	28.0	70.0	78.3	300	9.2	98	130	99.4	98.5	Europe
4,422	6,685	2,667,945	2,727,170	+59,225	—	—	74.8	81.3	290	5.2	100	136	99.4	98.9	European Union (EU)
3,223	8,123	362,398	357,881	−4,517	—	—	75.6	83.1	330	4.4	100	145	98.9	98.7	France
6,997	6,989	601,761	748,531	+146,770	—	—	75.5	81.6	290	4.2	100	131	100.0	100.0	Germany
6,935	5,840	242,744	251,003	+8,259	—	—	76.5	82.5	180	6.2	100	146	98.9	98.1	Italy
3,054	6,154	165,920	125,872	−40,048	—	—	75.7	83.1	240	3.6	99	137	98.6	96.8	Spain
10,296	6,614	399,478	320,057	−79,421	—	—	75.7	80.7	720	5.3	100	135	100.0	100.0	United Kingdom
3,436	6,454	895,644	923,825	+28,181	—	—	72.8	79.7	320	6.2	100	131	99.4	98.9	Other EU
9,474	15,454	125,857	153,411	+27,554	—	—	77.2	82.6	480	4.2	100	130	100.0	100.0	Other Western Europe[3]
1,427	4,794	138,550	187,954	+49,404	232,295	28.0	61.3	72.7	290	16.4	95	119	99.4	97.6	Eastern Europe
1,177	6,062	52,410	125,960	+73,550	120,375	32.1	58.5	71.9	240	13.3	99	120	99.8	99.2	Russia
1,481	3,525	16,976	17,927	+951	10,027	26.7	61.1	72.2	330	20.8	98	119	99.5	97.4	Ukraine
2,496	2,966	69,164	44,066	−25,098	101,893	24.4	67.2	74.8	370	20.1	84	118	98.5	94.4	Other Eastern Europe
564	8,414	91,999	85,427	−6,572	2,042	33.7	73.4	79.1	480	15.0	87	119	94.7	91.9	Oceania
407	11,299	69,260	66,366	−2,894	—	—	77.0	83.1	400	4.8	100	115	99.5	99.5	Australia
1,498	3,878	22,738	19,061	−3,677	2,042	33.7	67.7	72.7	770	31.3	67	128	87.9	80.6	Pacific Ocean Islands

Monaco, Norway, San Marino, and Switzerland.

Europe

Eastern Europe

Oceania

Government and international organizations

This table summarizes principal facts about the governments of the countries of the world, their branches and organs, the topmost layers of local government constituting each country's chief administrative subdivisions, and the participation of their central governments in the principal intergovernmental organizations of the world.

In this table "date of independence" may refer to a variety of circumstances. In the case of the newest countries, those that attained full independence after World War II, the date given is usually just what is implied by the heading—the date when the country, within its present borders, attained full sovereignty over both its internal and external affairs. In the case of longer established countries, the choice of a single date may be somewhat more complicated, and grounds for the use of several different dates often exist. The reader should refer to appropriate Britannica articles on national histories and relevant historical acts.

The date of the current, or last, constitution is in some ways a less complicated question, but governments sometimes do not, upon taking power, either adhere to existing constitutional forms or trouble to terminate the previous document and legitimize themselves by the installation of new constitutional forms. Often, however, the desire to legitimize extraconstitutional political activity by associating it with existing forms of long precedent leads to partial or incomplete modification, suspension, or abrogation of a constitution, so that the actual day-to-day conduct of government may be largely unrelat-

ed to the provisions of a constitution still theoretically in force. When a date in this column is given in italics, it refers to a document that has been suspended, abolished by extraconstitutional action, or modified extensively.

The characterizations adopted under "type of government" represent a compromise between the forms provided for by the national constitution and the more pragmatic language that a political scientist might adopt to describe these same systems. For an explanation of the application of these terms in the Britannica World Data, see the Glossary at page 501.

The positions denoted by the terms "chief of state" and "head of government" are usually those identified with those functions by the constitution. The duties of the chief of state may range from largely ceremonial responsibilities, with little or no authority over the day-to-day conduct of government, to complete executive authority as the effective head of government. In certain countries, an individual outside the constitutional structure may exercise the powers of both positions.

Membership in the legislative house(s) of each country as given here includes all elected or appointed members, as well as ex officio members (those who by virtue of some other office or title are members of the body), whether voting or nonvoting. The legislature of a country with a unicameral system is shown as the upper house in this table.

The number of administrative subdivisions for each country is listed down to the second level. In some instances, planning or statistical sub-

Government and international organizations

country	date of independence[a]	date of current or last constitution[b]	type of government	executive branch[c]		legislative branch[d]		admin. subdivisions		seaward claims	
				chief of state	head of government	upper house (members)	lower house (members)	first-order (number)	second-order (number)	territorial (nautical miles)	fishing/ economic (nautical miles)
Afghanistan	Aug. 19, 1919	Jan. 26, 2004	Islamic republic	————president————		102	249	34	...	—	2
Albania	Nov. 28, 1912	Nov. 28, 1998	republic	president	prime minister	140	—	12	36	12	2
Algeria	July 5, 1962	Dec. 7, 1996[3]	republic	president	prime minister	144	389	48	553	12	4
American Samoa	—	July 1, 1967	territory (U.S.)	U.S. president	governor	18	20[5]	—	5[6]	12	200
Andorra	Dec. 6, 1288	May 4, 1993	parl. coprincipality	[7]	head of govt.	28	—	7	...		
Angola	Nov. 11, 1975	Aug. 27, 1992	republic	————president[8]————		220	—	18	163	12	200
Antigua and Barbuda	Nov. 1, 1981	Nov. 1, 1981	constitutional monarchy	British monarch	prime minister	17	17[9]	30	—	12[10]	200[10]
Argentina	July 9, 1816	Aug. 24, 1994[11]	federal republic	————president[12]————		72	257	24	820	12	200
Armenia	Sept. 23, 1991	July 5, 1995	republic	president	prime minister	131	—	11	929	—	—
Aruba		Jan. 1, 1986	overseas territory (Neth.)	Dutch monarch	[13]	21	—	...	...	12	200
Australia	Jan. 1, 1901	Jan. 1, 1901	federal parl. state[15]	British monarch	prime minister	76	150	8	664[16]	12	200
Austria	Oct. 30, 1918	Oct. 1, 1920[17]	federal state	president	chancellor	64	183	9	99	—	—
Azerbaijan	Aug. 30, 1991	Aug. 24, 2002[18]	republic	————president[8]————		125[19]	—	67	...	...	...
Bahamas, The	July 10, 1973	July 10, 1973	constitutional monarchy	British monarch	prime minister	16	40	32	80	12	200
Bahrain	Aug. 15, 1971	Feb. 14, 2002	constitutional monarchy	monarch	prime minister	40	40	5	50	12	20
Bangladesh	March 26, 1971	Dec. 16, 1972	republic	president	prime minister	300	—	7[21]	64	12	200
Barbados	Nov. 30, 1966	Nov. 30, 1966	constitutional monarchy	British monarch	prime minister	21	30	—	—	12	200
Belarus	Aug. 25, 1991	Nov. 27, 1996[22]	republic	————president[8]————		64[19]	110[19]	7	118	—	—
Belgium	Oct. 4, 1830	Feb. 17, 1994	fed. const. monarchy	monarch	prime minister	71[23]	150	24	43	12	25
Belize	Sept. 21, 1981	Sept. 21, 1981	constitutional monarchy	British monarch	prime minister	8	29	26	...	12[27]	200
Benin	Aug. 1, 1960	Dec. 2, 1990	republic	————president————		83	—	12	77	200	200
Bermuda		June 8, 1968	overseas territory (U.K.)	British monarch	[28]	11	36	11	—	12	200
Bhutan	March 24, 1910	—	[29]	monarch	prime minister	152	—	20	201	—	—
Bolivia	Aug. 6, 1825	Feb. 2, 1967	republic	————president————		27	130	9	112	—	—
Bosnia and Herzegovina	March 3, 1992	Dec. 14, 1995[30]	emerging fed. republic	[31]	chairman CM	15	42	3	...	...	...
Botswana	Sept. 30, 1966	Sept. 30, 1966	republic	————president————		15[32]	63	16	28	—	—
Brazil	Sept. 7, 1822	Oct. 5, 1988[17]	federal republic	————president————		81	513	27	5,562	12	200
Brunei	Jan. 1, 1984	Sept. 29, 1959[33]	monarchy (sultanate)	————sultan————		29[32]	—	4	38	12	200
Bulgaria	Oct. 5, 1908	July 12, 1991	republic	president	prime minister	240	—	28	263	12	200
Burkina Faso	Aug. 5, 1960	June 11, 1991	republic	president	prime minister	90[32]	111	45	382	—	—
Burundi	July 1, 1962	Feb. 28, 2005[34]	republic	————president[35]————		54[19]	100[19]	17	125	—	—
Cambodia	Nov. 9, 1953	March 4, 1999[36]	constitutional monarchy	king	prime minister	61	123	24	185	12	200
Cameroon	Jan. 1, 1960	Jan. 18, 1996	republic	president	prime minister	180	—	10	58	...	...
Canada	July 1, 1867	April 17, 1982	federal parl. state[15]	Canadian GG[37]	prime minister	105	308	13	...	12	200
Cape Verde	July 5, 1975	Sept. 25, 1992	republic	president	prime minister	72	—	22	...	12[10]	200[10]
Central African Republic	Aug. 13, 1960	Dec. 5, 2004[34]	republic	president	prime minister	105	—	17	71	—	—
Chad	Aug. 11, 1960	April 14, 1996	republic	president	prime minister	155	—	...	...	—	—
Chile	Sept. 18, 1810	Sept. 17, 2005	republic	————president————		38	120	13	51	12	200
China	1523 BC	Dec. 4, 1982	people's republic	president	premier SC	2,980	—	31	345	12	200
Colombia	July 20, 1810	July 6, 1991	republic	————president————		102	166	33	1,105	12	200
Comoros	July 6, 1975	June 5, 2002[38]	republic[39]	————president[35]————		33	—	3	...	12[10]	200[10]
Congo, Dem. Rep. of the	June 30, 1960	April 4, 2004[40]	transitional regime	————president[35]————		120	500	11	...	12	...
Congo, Rep. of the	Aug. 15, 1960	Aug. 10, 2002	republic	————president————		66[19]	137[19]	16	93	200	2
Costa Rica	Sept. 15, 1821	Nov. 9, 1949	republic	————president————		57	—	7	81	12	200
Côte d'Ivoire	Aug. 7, 1960	Aug. 23, 2000	transitional regime	——interim prime minister[41, 42]——		223	—	19	58	12	200
Croatia	June 25, 1991	Dec. 22, 1990	republic	president	prime minister	152	—	21	124	12	...
Cuba	May 20, 1902	Feb. 24, 1976	socialist republic	————president————		609	—	15	169	12	200
Cyprus[44]	Aug. 16, 1960	Aug. 16, 1960	republic	————president————		56[45]	—	...	647	12	...
Czech Republic	Jan. 1, 1993	Jan. 1, 1993	republic	president	prime minister	81	200	14	82	—	—
Denmark	c. 800	June 5, 1953	constitutional monarchy	monarch	prime minister	179	—	16	270	12	200
Djibouti	June 27, 1977	Sept. 15, 1992	republic	————president————		65	—	6	...	12	200
Dominica	Nov. 3, 1978	Nov. 3, 1978	republic	president	prime minister	31	—	37	...	12	200
Dominican Republic	Feb. 27, 1844	Nov. 28, 1966	republic	————president————		32	150	32	161	6	200
East Timor	May 20, 2002	May 20, 2002	republic	president	prime minister	88	—	13	65	12	200
Ecuador	May 24, 1822	Aug. 10, 1998	republic	————president————		125	—	22	219	200	200
Egypt	Feb. 28, 1922	Sept. 11, 1971	republic	president	prime minister	454	—	27	186	12[46]	...
El Salvador	Jan. 30, 1841	Dec. 20, 1983	republic	————president————		84	—	14	262	200	200
Equatorial Guinea	Oct. 12, 1968	Nov. 17, 1991	republic	president	prime minister	100	—	7	18	12	200
Eritrea	May 24, 1993	[47]	transitional regime	————president————		150	—	6	...	12	48
Estonia	Feb. 24, 1918	July 3, 1992	republic	president	prime minister	101	—	15	249	12[49]	49

divisions may be substituted when administrative subdivisions do not exist.

Finally, in the second half of the table are listed the memberships each country maintains in the principal international intergovernmental organizations of the world. This part of the table may also be utilized to provide a complete membership list for each of these organizations as of Dec. 1, 2005.

Notes for the column headings

a. The date may also be either that of the organization of the present form of government or the inception of the present administrative structure (federation, confederation, union, etc.).

b. Constitutions whose dates are in italic type had been wholly or substantially suspended or abolished as of late 2005.

c. For abbreviations used in this column see the list on the facing page.

d. When a legislative body has been adjourned or otherwise suspended, figures in parentheses indicate the number of members in the legislative body as provided for in constitution or law.

e. 15 nations with judicial representation in ICJ in 2005.

f. 18 nations with judicial representation in ICC in 2005 (ICC entered into force in July 2002; 100 countries had ratified or acceded to the ICC statute by November 2005).

International organizations, conventions

AC — Arctic Council
ACP — African, Caribbean, and Pacific (Cotonou Agreement) states
ADB — Asian Development Bank
APEC — Asia-Pacific Economic Co-operation
ASEAN — Association of Southeast Asian Nations
ATs — Antarctic Treaty signatories
AU — African Union
CARICOM — Caribbean Community and Common Market
ECOWAS — Economic Community of West African States
EU — The European Union

FAO — Food and Agriculture Org.
FZ — The Franc Zone
GCC — Gulf Cooperation Council
I-ADB — Inter-American Development Bank
IAEA — International Atomic Energy Agency
IBRD — International Bank for Reconstruction and Development
ICAO — International Civil Aviation Org.
ICC — International Criminal Court
ICJ — International Court of Justice
IDA — International Development Association
IDB — Islamic Development Bank
ILO — International Labour Org.
IMF — International Monetary Fund
IMO — International Maritime Org.
ITU — International Telecommunication Union
LAS — League of Arab States (Arab League)
OAS — Organization of American States
OPEC — Organization of the Petroleum Exporting Countries
PC — Pacific Community

UNCTAD — United Nations Conference on Trade and Development
UNESCO — United Nations Educational, Scientific and Cultural Org.
UNIDO — United Nations Industrial Development Org.
WHO — World Health Org.
WIPO — World Intellectual Property Org.
WTO — World Trade Org.

Abbreviations used in the executive-branch column

CM — Council of Ministers
FC — Federal Council
GC — General Council
GG — Governor-General
GPC — General People's Committee
MCJD — Military Council for Justice and Democracy
NDC — National Defense Commission
NTG — National Transitional Government
PC — People's Council
Pc — Policy Council
SC — State Council
SPDC — State Peace and Development Council

United Nations (date of admission)	UN organs* and affiliated intergovernmental organizations — UNCTAD*	ICJ*e	FAO	IAEA	IBRD	ICAO	ICCf	IDA	ILO	IMF	IMO	ITU	UNESCO	UNIDO	WHO	WIPO	WTO	The Commonwealth	AC	ASEAN	ATs	AU	EU	GCC	LAS	OAS	PC	ACP	ADB	APEC	CARICOM	ECOWAS	FZ	I-ADB	IDB	OPEC	country
1946	•		•	•	•	•		•	•	•		•	•	•	•	•	1												•						•		Afghanistan
1955	•		•	•	•	•		•	•	•		•	•	•	•	•	1					•				•									•		Albania
1962	•		•	•	•	•		•	•	•	•	•	•	•	•	•	1					•			•			•							•	•	Algeria
—	•					•					•	•		•	•		1																				American Samoa
1993	•										•	•		•	•		1																				Andorra
1976	•		•	•	•	•		•	•	•	•	•	•	•	•	•	•					•						•							•		Angola
1981	•		•	•	•	•		•	•	•	•	•	•	•	•	•	•	•								•		•			•				•		Antigua and Barbuda
1945	•		•	•	•	•		•	•	•	•	•	•	•	•	•	•				•		•				•			•				•			Argentina
1992	•		•	•	•	•		•	•	•		•	•	•	•	•	1											•						•	•		Armenia
—						•							•	14																							Aruba
1945	•		•	•	•	•		•	•	•	•	•	•	•	•	•	•				•		•				•	•		•	•						Australia
1955	•		•	•	•	•		•	•	•	•	•	•	•	•	•	•				•		•				•			•				•			Austria
1992	•		•	•	•	•		•	•	•		•	•	•	•	•	1												•					•	•		Azerbaijan
1973	•		•		•	•		•	•	•	•	•	•	•	•	•	1	•								•		•			•			•			Bahamas, The
1971	•		•		•	•		•	•	•	•	•	•	•	•	•	•							•	•			•						•			Bahrain
1974	•		•	•	•	•		•	•	•	•	•	•	•	•	•	•	•										•	•						•		Bangladesh
1966	•		•	•	•	•		•	•	•	•	•	•	•	•	•	•	•								•		•			•			•			Barbados
1945	•		•	•	•	•		•	•	•	•	•	•	•	•	•	1																				Belarus
1945	•		•	•	•	•		•	•	•	•	•	•	•	•	•	•				•		•							•				•			Belgium
1981	•		•		•	•		•	•	•	•	•	•	•	•	•	•	•								•		•			•			•			Belize
1960	•		•	•	•	•		•	•	•		•	•	•	•	•	•					•						•				•	•		•		Benin
—														14																							Bermuda
1971	•		•	•	•	•		•	•	•		•	•	•	•	•	1												•								Bhutan
1945	•		•	•	•	•	•	•	•	•	•	•	•	•	•	•	•									•			•					•			Bolivia
1992	•		•	•	•	•		•	•	•	•	•	•	•	•	•	1																		•		Bosnia and Herzegovina
1966	•		•	•	•	•		•	•	•	•	•	•	•	•	•	•	•				•						•							•		Botswana
1945	•		•	•	•	•	•	•	•	•	•	•	•	•	•	•	•				•					•			•	•				•			Brazil
1984	•		•		•	•		•	•	•	•	•	•	•	•	•	•	•		•								•	•	•					•		Brunei
1955	•		•	•	•	•		•	•	•	•	•	•	•	•	•	•				•		•							•							Bulgaria
1960	•		•	•	•	•		•	•	•		•	•	•	•	•	•					•						•				•	•		•		Burkina Faso
1962	•		•	•	•	•		•	•	•		•	•	•	•	•	•					•						•						•	•		Burundi
1955	•		•	•	•	•		•	•	•	•	•	•	•	•	•	•			•								•	•					•			Cambodia
1960	•		•	•	•	•		•	•	•	•	•	•	•	•	•	•					•						•				•	•	•	•		Cameroon
1945	•		•	•	•	•		•	•	•	•	•	•	•	•	•	•	•	•		•					•	•		•	•				•		Canada
1975	•		•		•	•		•	•	•	•	•	•	•	•	•	1					•						•				•			•		Cape Verde
1960	•		•	•	•	•		•	•	•		•	•	•	•	•	•					•						•				•	•		•		Central African Republic
1960	•		•	•	•	•		•	•	•		•	•	•	•	•	•					•						•				•	•		•		Chad
1945	•		•	•	•	•		•	•	•	•	•	•	•	•	•	•				•		•				•	•		•	•				•		Chile
1945	•		•	•	•	•		•	•	•	•	•	•	•	•	•	•				•							•		•	•				•		China
1945	•		•	•	•	•		•	•	•	•	•	•	•	•	•	•					•				•			•					•			Colombia
1975	•		•		•	•		•	•	•	•	•	•	•	•	•						•			•			•							•		Comoros
1960	•		•	•	•	•		•	•	•		•	•	•	•	•	•					•						•				•			•		Congo, Dem. Rep. of the
1960	•		•	•	•	•		•	•	•		•	•	•	•	•	•					•						•				•	•		•		Congo, Rep. of the
1945	•		•	•	•	•		•	•	•	•	•	•	•	•	•	•									•			•					•			Costa Rica
1960	•		•	•	•	•		•	•	•		•	•	•	•	•	•					•						•				•	•	•	•		Côte d'Ivoire
1992	•		•	•	•	•		•	•	•	•	•	•	•	•	•	•																				Croatia
1945	•		•	•	•	•		•	•	•	•	•	•	•	•	•	•					•															Cuba
1960	•		•	•	•	•	•	•	•	•	•	•	•	•	•	•	•	•					•					43	•			•					Cyprus[44]
1993	•		•	•	•	•		•	•	•	•	•	•	•	•	•	•					•	•						•								Czech Republic
1945	•		•	•	•	•		•	•	•	•	•	•	•	•	•	•		•		•		•											•			Denmark
1977	•		•		•	•		•	•	•	•	•	•	•	•	•		•				•			•			•							•		Djibouti
1978	•		•		•	•		•	•	•	•	•	•	•	•	•	•	•								•		•			•			•			Dominica
1945	•		•	•	•	•		•	•	•	•	•	•	•	•	•	•									•		•						•			Dominican Republic
2002	•		•		•	•		•	•	•		•	•		•														•								East Timor
1945	•		•	•	•	•		•	•	•	•	•	•	•	•	•	•				•						•			•					•		Ecuador
1945	•	•	•	•	•	•		•	•	•	•	•	•	•	•	•	•					•			•			•							•		Egypt
1945	•	•	•	•	•	•		•	•	•	•	•	•	•	•	•	•									•		•						•			El Salvador
1968	•	•	•	•	•	•		•	•	•		•	•	•	•	•	1					•						•				•	•		•	•	Equatorial Guinea
1993	•	•	•	•	•	•		•	•	•		•	•	•	•	•						•						•							•		Eritrea
1991	•	•	•	•	•	•		•	•	•		•	•	•	•	•	•				•	•														Estonia

Government and international organizations (continued)

country	date of independence[a]	date of current or last constitution[b]	type of government	executive branch[c] chief of state	head of government	legislative branch[d] upper house (members)	lower house (members)	admin. subdivisions first-order (number)	second-order (number)	seaward claims territorial (nautical miles)	fishing/economic (nautical miles)
Ethiopia	c. 1000 BC	Aug. 22, 1995	federal republic	president	prime minister	112	547	11	57	—	—
Faroe Islands		April 1, 1948	ext. terr. (Den.)	Danish monarch	[50]	32	—	—	49	...	200[51]
Fiji	Oct. 10, 1970	July 27, 1998	republic	president	prime minister	32	72	4	15	12[10]	200[10]
Finland	Dec. 6, 1917	March 1, 2000	republic	president	prime minister	200	—	6	20	12[52]	49
France	August 843	Oct. 4, 1958[17]	republic	president	prime minister	321	577	22	96	12	200
French Guiana	—	Feb. 28, 1983	overseas dept. (Fr.)	French president	[53]	19	31	2	22	12	200
French Polynesia		Feb. 27, 2004	overseas country (Fr.)	French president[54]	president	57	—	5	48	12	200
Gabon	Aug. 17, 1960	March 26, 1991	republic	president	prime minister	91	120	9	37	12	200
Gambia, The	Feb. 18, 1965	Jan. 16, 1997	republic	president		53	—	8	45	12	200
Gaza Strip	—	May 4, 1994[55]	interim authority	president[56]	prime minister[56]	89	—	5	...	...	...
Georgia	April 9, 1991	Feb. 6, 2004	republic	president[8]		235	—	12	75	...	...
Germany	May 5, 1955	May 23, 1949	federal republic	president	chancellor	69	614	16	22	12[51]	...
Ghana	March 6, 1957	Jan. 7, 1993	republic	president		230	—	10	110	12	200
Greece	Feb. 3, 1830	April 6, 2001[58]	republic	president	prime minister	300	—	55	1,033	6/10	2
Greenland		May 1, 1979	ext. terr. (Den.)	Danish monarch	[50]	31	—	18	...	3	200
Grenada	Feb. 7, 1974	Feb. 7, 1974	constitutional monarchy	British monarch	prime minister	13	15	9	...	12	200
Guadeloupe	—	Feb. 28, 1983	overseas dept. (Fr.)	French president	[53]	42	41	3	34	12	200
Guam	—	Aug. 1, 1950	territory (U.S.)	U.S. president	governor	15	—	—	—	12	200
Guatemala	Sept. 15, 1821	Jan. 14, 1986	republic	president		158	—	22	331	12	200
Guernsey	—	Jan. 1, 1949[17]	crown dependency (U.K.)	British monarch[59]	chief minister Pc	51[60]	—	3	...	3	12
Guinea	Oct. 2, 1958	November 2001[36]	republic	president[8]		114	—	8	34	12	200
Guinea-Bissau	Sept. 10, 1974	[61]	transitional regime	president	prime minister	102	—	9	37	12	200
Guyana	May 26, 1966	Oct. 6, 1980	cooperative republic	president		65	—	10	71	12	200
Haiti	Jan. 1, 1804	March 29, 1987	transitional regime	president	prime minister	27[62]	83[62]	10	41	12	200
Honduras	Nov. 5, 1838	Jan. 20, 1982	republic	president		128	—	18	298	12	200
Hong Kong	—	July 1, 1997	[63]	Chinese president	chief executive	60	—	—	—	12	2
Hungary	Nov. 16, 1918	Aug. 20, 1949[64]	republic	president	prime minister	386	—	20	274[65]	12	200
Iceland	June 17, 1944	June 17, 1944	republic	president	prime minister	63	—	8	101	12	200
India	Aug. 15, 1947	Jan. 26, 1950	federal republic	president	prime minister	245	545	35	593	12	200
Indonesia	Aug. 17, 1945	Aug. 17, 1945	republic	president		128	550	33	66	12[10]	200[10]
Iran	Oct. 7, 1906	Dec. 2–3, 1979	Islamic republic	president[67]		290	—	30	316	12	50[68]
Iraq	Oct. 3, 1932	Oct. 15, 2005	interim authority[69]	president[8, 69]		275[69]	—	18	...	12	2
Ireland	Dec. 6, 1921	Dec. 29, 1937	republic	president	prime minister	60	166	34	86	12	200
Isle of Man	—	[70]	crown dependency (U.K.)	British monarch[59]	chief minister CM	11	24	24	—	12[71]	...
Israel	May 14, 1948	June 1950[17]	republic	president	prime minister	120	—	6	15	12	2
Italy	March 17, 1861	Jan. 1, 1948	republic	president	prime minister	321	630	20	107	12	2
Jamaica	Aug. 6, 1962	Aug. 6, 1962	constitutional monarchy	British monarch	prime minister	21	60	13	—	12	200
Japan	c. 660 BC	May 3, 1947	constitutional monarchy		[72]	242	480	47	3,230	12[73]	200
Jersey	—	Jan. 1, 1949[17]	crown dependency (U.K.)	British monarch[59]	chief minister CM	58	—	12	—	12	...
Jordan	May 25, 1946	Jan. 8, 1952	constitutional monarchy	king[8]		55	110	12	...	3	2
Kazakhstan	Dec. 16, 1991	Sept. 6, 1995	republic	president[8]		39	77	16	160	—	—
Kenya	Dec. 12, 1963	Dec. 12, 1963	republic	president		224	—	8	72	12	200
Kiribati	July 12, 1979	July 12, 1979	republic	president		42	—	...	...	12[10]	200[10]
Korea, North	Sept. 9, 1948	Sept. 5, 1998[74]	socialist republic	chairman NDC		687	—	14	152	12	200
Korea, South	Aug. 15, 1948	Feb. 25, 1988	republic	president[8]		299	—	16	165[75]	12	200
Kuwait	June 19, 1961	Nov. 16, 1962	const. mon. (emirate)	emir[8]		50[76]	—	6	...	12	2
Kyrgyzstan	Aug. 31, 1991	May 5, 1993	republic	president[8]		75[19]	—	8	54[77]	—	—
Laos	Oct. 23, 1953	Aug. 15, 1991	people's republic	president	prime minister	109	—	18	133	—	—
Latvia	Nov. 18, 1918	Nov. 7, 1922	republic	president	prime minister	100	—	33	70	12	78
Lebanon	Nov. 26, 1941	Sept. 21, 1990	republic	president	prime minister	128	—	6	26	12	2
Lesotho	Oct. 4, 1966	April 2, 1993	constitutional monarchy	king	prime minister	33[32]	120	10	129	—	—
Liberia	July 26, 1847	Aug. 18, 2003[79]	transitional regime	chairman NTG[80]		76[80]	—	15	...	200	2
Libya	Dec. 24, 1951	March 2, 1977	[81]	leader[82]	sec. GPC	760	—	...	...	12	2
Liechtenstein	July 12, 1806	March 16, 2003	constitutional monarchy	prince	head of govt.	25	—	11	—	—	—
Lithuania	Feb. 16, 1918	Nov. 6, 1992	republic	president	prime minister	141	—	10	60	12	...
Luxembourg	May 10, 1867	Oct. 17, 1868	constitutional monarchy	grand duke	prime minister	21[32]	60	3	12	—	—
Macau	—	Dec. 20, 1999	[63]	Chinese president	chief executive	29	—	...	...	—	—
Macedonia	Nov. 17, 1991	Nov. 16, 2001[83]	republic	president	prime minister	120	—	84	...	—	—
Madagascar	June 26, 1960	April 8, 1998	federal republic	president[8]		90	160	6	111	12	200
Malawi	July 6, 1964	May 18, 1994	republic	president		193	—	3	27	—	—
Malaysia	Aug. 31, 1957	Aug. 31, 1957	fed. const. monarchy	paramount ruler	prime minister	70	219	16	137	12	200
Maldives	July 26, 1965	Jan. 1, 1998	republic	president		42[76]	—	21	...	12[10]	200
Mali	Sept. 22, 1960	Feb. 25, 1992	republic	president	prime minister	147	—	9	49	—	—
Malta	Sept. 21, 1964	Dec. 13, 1974	republic	president	prime minister	65	—	3	68	12	25
Marshall Islands	Dec. 22, 1990	May 1, 1979	republic	president		12[32]	33	4	—	12[10]	200
Martinique	—	Feb. 28, 1983	overseas dept. (Fr.)	French president	[53]	45	41	4	34	12	200
Mauritania	Nov. 28, 1960	July 21, 1991	military regime	chairman MCJD[8]		(56)	(81)	13	53	12	200
Mauritius	March 12, 1968	March 12, 1992	republic	president	prime minister	70	—	11	130	12	200
Mayotte	—	July 11, 2001	dept. collectivity (Fr.)	French president	president GC	19	—	17	—	12	200
Mexico	Sept. 16, 1810	Feb. 5, 1917	federal republic	president		128	500	32	2,445	12	200
Micronesia	Dec. 22, 1990	Jan. 1, 1981	federal republic	president		14	—	4	74	12	200
Moldova	Aug. 27, 1991	Aug. 27, 1994	parliamentary republic	president	prime minister	101	—	1	35	—	—
Monaco	Feb. 2, 1861	April 12, 2002[36]	constitutional monarchy	prince	min. of state[84]	24	—	—	—	12	2
Mongolia	March 13, 1921	Feb. 12, 1992	republic	president	prime minister	76	—	22	340	—	—
Morocco	March 2, 1956	Oct. 7, 1996	constitutional monarchy	king[8]		270	325	16[85]	71[85]	12	200
Mozambique	June 25, 1975	Nov. 16, 2004	republic	president		250	—	11	112	12	200
Myanmar (Burma)	Jan. 4, 1948	Jan. 4, 1974	military regime	chairman SPDC[8]		(492)	—	14	64	12	200
Namibia	March 21, 1990	March 21, 1990	republic	president		26	72[76]	13	114	12	200
Nauru	Jan. 31, 1968	Jan. 31, 1968	republic	president		18	—	—	—	12	200
Nepal	Nov. 13, 1769	Nov. 9, 1990	monarchy[86]	king		(60)	(205)	5[87]	75	—	—
Netherlands, The	March 30, 1814	Feb. 17, 1983	constitutional monarchy	monarch	prime minister	75	150	12	496	12	25
Netherlands Antilles	—	Dec. 29, 1954	overseas territory (Neth.)	Dutch monarch	[13]	22	—	5	—	12	200
New Caledonia	—	March 19, 2003	overseas country (Fr.)	French president[88]	president	54	—	3	33	12	200
New Zealand	Sept. 26, 1907	June 30, 1852[17]	constitutional monarchy	British monarch	prime minister	121	—	17	...	12	200
Nicaragua	April 30, 1838	Jan. 9, 1987	republic	president		92	—	17	151	12	200

membership in international organizations																																					country
United Nations (date of admission)	UN organs★ and affiliated intergovernmental organizations																	The Commonwealth	regional multipurpose										economic										
	UNCTAD★	ICJ★e	FAO	IAEA	IBRD	ICAO	ICCf	IDA	ILO	IMF	IMO	ITU	UNESCO	UNIDO	WHO	WIPO	WTO		AC	ASEAN	ATs	AU	EU	GCC	LAS	OAS	PC	ACP	ADB	APEC	CARICOM	ECOWAS	FZ	I-ADB	IDB	OPEC	
1945	•		•	•	•	•		•	•	•	•	•	•	•	•	•	1					•						•									Ethiopia
—											14								•																		Faroe Islands
1970	•		•		•	•		•	•	•	•	•	•	•	•	•	•	•									•	•	•								Fiji
1955	•		•	•	•	•	•	•	•	•	•	•	•	•	•	•	•		•		•		•						•					•			Finland
1945	•	•	•	•	•	•	•	•	•	•	•	•	•	•	•	•	•				•		•				•		•				•	•			France
—												•																					•				French Guiana
—												•															•						•				French Polynesia
1960	•		•	•	•	•		•	•	•	•	•	•	•	•	•	•					•						•					•		•		Gabon
1965	•		•		•	•		•	•	•	•	•	•	•	•	•	•	•				•						•				•			•		Gambia, The
—																									•57										•57		Gaza Strip
1992	•		•	•	•	•		•	•	•	•	•	•	•	•	•	•																				Georgia
1973	•	•	•	•	•	•	•	•	•	•	•	•	•	•	•	•	•				•		•						•					•			Germany
1957	•		•	•	•	•	•	•	•	•	•	•	•	•	•	•	•	•				•						•				•					Ghana
1945	•		•	•	•	•		•	•	•	•	•	•	•	•	•	•				•		•														Greece
—																			•																		Greenland
1974	•		•		•	•		•	•	•	•	•	•	•	•	•	•	•								•		•			•						Grenada
—												•																					•				Guadeloupe
—												•															•										Guam
1945	•		•	•	•	•		•	•	•	•	•	•	•	•	•	•				•					•								•			Guatemala
—												•																									Guernsey
1958	•		•		•	•		•	•	•	•	•	•	•	•	•	•					•						•				•			•		Guinea
1974	•		•		•	•		•	•	•	•	•	•	•	•	•	•					•						•				•	•		•		Guinea-Bissau
1966	•		•		•	•		•	•	•	•	•	•	•	•	•	•	•								•		•			•			•			Guyana
1945	•		•	•	•	•		•	•	•	•	•	•	•	•	•	•									•		•			43			•			Haiti
1945	•		•	•	•	•		•	•	•	•	•	•	•	•	•	•									•								•			Honduras
—										•	14						•												•	•							Hong Kong
1955	•		•	•	•	•		•	•	•	•	•	•	•	•	•	•				•		•														Hungary
1946	•		•	•	•	•		•	•	•	•	•	•		•	•	•		•																		Iceland
1945	•		•	•	•	•		•	•	•	•	•	•	•	•	•	•	•			•								•								India
1950	•		•	•	•	•		•	•	•	•	•	•	•	•	•	•			•									•	•					•	•	Indonesia
1945	•		•	•	•	•		•	•	•	•	•	•	•	•	•	1																		•	•	Iran
1945	•		•	•	•	•		•	•	•	•	•	•	•	•	•	1								•										•	•	Iraq
1955	•		•	•	•	•	•	•	•	•	•	•	•	•	•	•	•						•														Ireland
—												•																									Isle of Man
1949	•		•	•	•	•		•	•	•	•	•	•	•	•	•	•																	•			Israel
1955	•		•	•	•	•	•	•	•	•	•	•	•	•	•	•	•				•		•						•					•			Italy
1962	•		•	•	•	•		•	•	•	•	•	•	•	•	•	•	•								•		•			•			•			Jamaica
1956	•	•	•	•	•	•		•	•	•	•	•	•	•	•	•	•				•								•	•				•			Japan
—												•																									Jersey
1955	•	•	•	•	•	•		•	•	•	•	•	•	•	•	•	•								•										•		Jordan
1992	•		•	•	•	•		•	•	•	•	•	•	•	•	•	1												•						•		Kazakhstan
1963	•		•	•	•	•		•	•	•	•	•	•	•	•	•	•	•				•						•									Kenya
1999	•		•		•	•		•	•	•	•	•	•		•			•									•	•	•								Kiribati
1991	•		•			•					•	•	•	•	•	•					•																Korea, North
1991	•		•	•	•	•	•	•	•	•	•	•	•	•	•	•	•				•								•	•				•			Korea, South
1963	•		•	•	•	•		•	•	•	•	•	•	•	•	•	•							•	•										•	•	Kuwait
1992	•		•	•	•	•		•	•	•		•	•	•	•	•	•												•						•		Kyrgyzstan
1955	•		•		•	•		•	•	•		•	•	•	•	•	1			•									•								Laos
1991	•		•	•	•	•	•	•	•	•	•	•	•		•	•	•						•														Latvia
1945	•		•	•	•	•		•	•	•	•	•	•	•	•	•	1								•										•		Lebanon
1966	•		•		•	•		•	•	•		•	•	•	•	•	•	•				•						•									Lesotho
1945	•		•	•	•	•		•	•	•	•	•	•	•	•	•						•						•				•					Liberia
1955	•		•	•	•	•		•	•	•	•	•	•	•	•	•	1					•			•										•	•	Libya
1990	•			•								•				•	•																				Liechtenstein
1991	•		•	•	•	•			•	•	•	•	•	•	•	•	•						•														Lithuania
1945	•		•	•	•	•		•	•	•	•	•	•	•	•	•	•						•						•								Luxembourg
—										•	14		14				•																				Macau
1993	•		•	•	•	•		•	•	•	•	•	•	•	•	•	•																				Macedonia
1960	•	•	•	•	•	•		•	•	•	•	•	•	•	•	•	•					•						•									Madagascar
1964	•		•		•	•		•	•	•	•	•	•	•	•	•	•	•				•						•									Malawi
1957	•		•	•	•	•		•	•	•	•	•	•	•	•	•	•	•		•									•	•					•		Malaysia
1965	•		•		•	•		•		•	•	•	•	•	•	•	•	•											•						•		Maldives
1960	•		•	•	•	•	•	•	•	•		•	•	•	•	•	•					•						•				•	•		•		Mali
1964	•		•	•	•	•			•	•	•	•	•	•	•	•	•	•					•														Malta
1991	•		•	•	•	•		•		•	•	•	•		•												•	•	•								Marshall Islands
—												•																					•				Martinique
1961	•		•	•	•	•		•	•	•	•	•	•	•	•	•	•					•			•			•							•		Mauritania
1968	•		•	•	•	•		•	•	•	•	•	•	•	•	•	•	•				•						•									Mauritius
—												•																					•				Mayotte
1945	•		•	•	•	•		•	•	•	•	•	•	•	•	•	•									•				•				•			Mexico
1991	•		•		•	•		•		•		•	•		•												•	•	•								Micronesia
1992	•		•	•	•	•		•	•	•	•	•	•	•	•	•	•																				Moldova
1993	•		•	•		•					•	•	•	•	•	•																	•				Monaco
1961	•		•	•	•	•		•	•	•	•	•	•	•	•	•	•												•								Mongolia
1956	•		•	•	•	•		•	•	•	•	•	•	•	•	•	•								•										•		Morocco
1975	•		•		•	•		•	•	•	•	•	•	•	•	•	•	•				•						•							•		Mozambique
1948	•		•	•	•	•		•	•	•	•	•	•	•	•	•	•			•									•								Myanmar (Burma)
1990	•		•	•	•	•			•	•	•	•	•	•	•	•	•	•				•						•									Namibia
1999	•		•			•						•	•		•			•									•	•	•								Nauru
1955	•		•		•	•		•	•	•	•	•	•	•	•	•	•												•								Nepal
1945	•	•	•	•	•	•		•	•	•	•	•	•	•	•	•	•				•		•						•					•			Netherlands, The
—										•			14																								Netherlands Antilles
—												•															•						•				New Caledonia
1945	•		•	•	•	•		•	•	•	•	•	•	•	•	•	•	•			•						•		•	•							New Zealand
1945	•		•	•	•	•		•	•	•	•	•	•	•	•	•	•									•								•			Nicaragua

Government and international organizations (continued)

country	date of independence[a]	date of current or last constitution[b]	type of government	executive branch[c] chief of state	head of government	legislative branch[d] upper house (members)	lower house (members)	admin. subdivisions first-order (number)	second-order (number)	seaward claims territorial (nautical miles)	fishing/economic (nautical miles)
Niger	Aug. 3, 1960	Aug. 9, 1999	republic	—president[8]		113	—	8	39	—	—
Nigeria	Oct. 1, 1960	May 5, 1999	federal republic	—president		109	360	37	774	12	200
Northern Mariana Is.	—	Jan. 9, 1978	commonwealth (U.S.)	U.S. president	governor	9	18	4	—	12	200
Norway	June 7, 1905	May 17, 1814	constitutional monarchy	king	prime minister	169		19	433	4	200
Oman	Dec. 20, 1951	Nov. 6, 1996[89]	monarchy (sultanate)	—sultan—		90		8	60	12	200
Pakistan	Aug. 14, 1947	Aug. 14, 1973	republic	—president[8]		100	342	8	27	12	200
Palau	Oct. 1, 1994	Jan. 1, 1981	republic	—president—		9	16	16	—	3	200
Panama	Nov. 3, 1903	May 20, 1983[36]	republic	—president[35]		78	—	12	75	12	200
Papua New Guinea	Sept. 16, 1975	Sept. 16, 1975	constitutional monarchy	British monarch	prime minister	109	—	20	267	3/12	200[10]
Paraguay	May 14, 1811	June 22, 1992	republic	—president		45	80	18	235	—	—
Peru	July 28, 1821	Dec. 29, 1993	republic	—president[8]		120	—	25	194	200	200
Philippines	July 4, 1946	Feb. 11, 1987	republic	—president		24	236	17	91	92	200[10]
Poland	Nov. 10, 1918	Oct. 17, 1997	republic	president	prime minister	100	460	16	308	12	...
Portugal	c. 1140	April 25, 1976	republic	president	prime minister	230	—	7	20	12	200
Puerto Rico	—	July 25, 1952	commonwealth (U.S.)	U.S. president	governor	27[93]	51[93]	78	—	12	200
Qatar	Sept. 3, 1971	June 9, 2005	constitutional emirate	—emir[8]		35[32]	—	10	—	12	...
Réunion	—	Feb. 28, 1983	overseas dept. (Fr.)	French president	53	49	45	4	25	12	200
Romania	May 21, 1877	Oct. 29, 2003	republic	president	prime minister	137	332	42	2,686	12[46]	200[46]
Russia	Dec. 8, 1991	Dec. 24, 1993	federal republic	president	prime minister	178	450	7	88	12	200
Rwanda	July 1, 1962	June 4, 2003	republic	—president[8]		26	80	12	94	—	—
St. Kitts and Nevis	Sept. 19, 1983	Sept. 19, 1983	constitutional monarchy	British monarch	prime minister	15	—	1	—	12	200
St. Lucia	Feb. 22, 1979	Feb. 22, 1979	constitutional monarchy	British monarch	prime minister	11	17[9]	10	—	12	200
St. Vincent	Oct. 27, 1979	Oct. 27, 1979	constitutional monarchy	British monarch	prime minister	22	—	...	—	12	200
Samoa	Jan. 1, 1962	Oct. 28, 1960	95	head of state		49	—	11	—	12	200
San Marino	855	Oct. 8, 1600	republic	—captains-regent (2)—		60	—	9	—	—	—
São Tomé and Príncipe	July 12, 1975	Sept. 10, 1990	republic	president	prime minister	55	—	1	6	12[10]	200[10]
Saudi Arabia	Sept. 23, 1932	96	monarchy	—king—		150	—	13	178	12	2
Senegal	Aug. 20, 1960	Jan. 7, 2001	republic	—president[8]		120	—	11	34	12[46]	200[46]
Serbia and Montenegro	Dec. 1, 1918	Feb. 4, 2003	state union[97]	—president CM—		126	—	2[98]	46[98]	12	...
Seychelles	June 29, 1976	June 21, 1993	republic	—president—		34	—	25	—	12	200
Sierra Leone	April 27, 1961	Oct. 1, 1991	republic	—president		124	—	13	166	12	200
Singapore	Aug. 9, 1965	June 3, 1959[17]	republic	president	prime minister	90	—	5[99]	—	3	...
Slovakia	Jan. 1, 1993	Jan. 1, 1993	republic	president	prime minister	150	—	8	79	—	—
Slovenia	June 25, 1991	Dec. 23, 1991	republic	president	prime minister	40	90	12[100]	193	...	...
Solomon Islands	July 7, 1978	July 7, 1978	constitutional monarchy	British monarch	prime minister	50	—	10	...	12[10]	200[10]
Somalia	July 1, 1960	March 12, 2004[101]	102	—president[8, 102]		275[102]	—	4	...	200	200
South Africa	May 31, 1910	June 30, 1997	republic	—president—		90	400	9	360	12	200
Spain	1492	Dec. 29, 1978	constitutional monarchy	king	prime minister	259	350	19	50	12	200[103]
Sri Lanka	Feb. 4, 1948	Sept. 7, 1978	republic	—president[8]		225	—	25	324	12	200
Sudan, The	Jan. 1, 1956	July 9, 2005[104]	military regime	—president[35]		50[105]	450	2	26	12	2
Suriname	Nov. 25, 1975	Nov. 25, 1987	republic	—president—		51	—	10	62	12	200
Swaziland	Sept. 6, 1968	July 26, 2005[106]	monarchy	—king[8]		30[32]	65[32]	4	55	—	—
Sweden	before 836	Jan. 1, 1975	constitutional monarchy	king	prime minister	349	—	21	288	12	20
Switzerland	Sept. 22, 1499	Jan. 1, 2000	federal state	—president FC—		46	200	26	181	—	—
Syria	April 17, 1946	March 14, 1973	republic	—president—		250	—	14	60	35	2
Taiwan	—	Dec. 25, 1947[17]	republic	president	premier	225	—	2	25	24	200
Tajikistan	Sept. 9, 1991	Nov. 6, 1994	republic	president	prime minister	33	63	4	62	—	—
Tanzania	Dec. 9, 1961	April 25, 1977	republic	—president—		324	—	1	26	12	200
Thailand	1350	Oct. 11, 1997	constitutional monarchy	king	prime minister	200	500	76	795	12	200
Togo	April 27, 1960	Sept. 27, 1992	republic	president	prime minister	81	—	5	30	30	200
Tonga	June 4, 1970	Nov. 4, 1875	107	—monarch—		30	—	3	...	12	200
Trinidad and Tobago	Aug. 31, 1962	July 27, 1976	republic	president	prime minister	31	36	15	...	12[10]	200[10]
Tunisia	March 20, 1956	June 1, 2002[36]	republic	president	prime minister	126	189	24	264	12	...
Turkey	Oct. 29, 1923	Nov. 7, 1982	republic	president	prime minister	550	—	81	923	12[108]	200[109]
Turkmenistan	Oct. 27, 1991	Aug. 15, 2003[36]	republic	—president PC—		50	—	6	...	—	—
Tuvalu	Oct. 1, 1978	Oct. 1, 1986	constitutional monarchy	British monarch	prime minister	15	—	8	—	12[10]	200[10]
Uganda	Oct. 9, 1962	Oct. 8, 1995	republic	—president—		305	—	57	160	—	—
Ukraine	Aug. 24, 1991	June 28, 1996	republic	president	prime minister	450	—	27	490	12	200
United Arab Emirates	Dec. 2, 1971	Dec. 2, 1971	federation of emirates	president	prime minister	40[32]	—	7	—	12	200
United Kingdom	Dec. 6, 1921	110	constitutional monarchy	monarch	prime minister	703	646	3	468	12[71]	200
United States	July 4, 1776	March 4, 1789	federal republic	—president—		100	435	51	3,141	12	200
Uruguay	Aug. 25, 1828	Feb. 15, 1967	republic	—president—		31	99	19	...	12	200
Uzbekistan	Aug. 31, 1991	Dec. 8, 1992	republic	—president[8]		100	120	14	227[111]	—	—
Vanuatu	July 30, 1980	July 30, 1980	republic	president	prime minister	52	—	6	...	12[10]	200[10]
Venezuela	July 5, 1811	Dec. 20, 1999	federal republic	—president—		167	—	25	336	12	200
Vietnam	Sept. 2, 1945	April 15, 1992	socialist republic	president	prime minister	498	—	8	64	12	200
Virgin Islands (U.S.)	—	July 22, 1954	territory (U.S.)	U.S. president	governor	15	—	...	...	12	200
West Bank	—	May 4, 1994[55]	interim authority	president[56]	prime minister[56]	89	—	11	...	—	—
Western Sahara	—	—	annexure of Morocco			—	—	...	...	12	200
Yemen	December 1918	Sept. 29, 1994	republic	president	prime minister	111[32]	301	21	...	12	200
Zambia	Oct. 24, 1964	May 28, 1996[3]	republic	—president—		158	—	9	72	—	—
Zimbabwe	April 18, 1980	April 18, 1980	republic	—president—		66	150	10	63	—	—

[1]Observer. [2]Territorial sea claim. [3]Date president signed new constitution. [4]Varies between 32 and 52 nautical miles. [5]Excludes nonvoting delegate from Swains Island. [6]Comprises 3 districts and 2 islands. [7]President of France and Bishop of Urgell, Spain. [8]Assisted by the prime minister. [9]Excludes possible ex officio members. [10]Measured from claimed archipelagic baselines. [11]Promulgation date of significant amendments to July 9, 1853, constitution. [12]Assisted by the cabinet chief (ministerial coordinator). [13]Executive responsibilities divided between (for The Netherlands) the governor and (locally) the prime minister. [14]Associate member. [15]Formally a constitutional monarchy. [16]Number of 6 different kinds of Local Government Areas in 1999. [17]Evolving body of constitutional law. [18]Date of referendum approving significant constitutional amendments. [19]Statutory number of seats. [20]Defined by equidistant line. [21]Includes the Chittagong Hill Tracts, a tribal region formally established in 1999. [22]Per nondemocratic national referendum of Nov. 24, 1996, amending the constitution. [23]Excludes children of the monarch serving ex officio from age 18. [24]3 autonomous regions/3 linguistic communities; 10 provinces. [25]Defined by coordinates of points. [26]6 districts; 8 town boards. [27]3 nautical miles from the mouth of the Sarstoon River (southern boundary with Guatemala) to Ranguana Caye. [28]Executive responsibilities divided between (for the U.K.) the governor and (locally) the premier. [29]Resembles a constitutional monarchy without a formal constitution. [30]Date of international treaty confirming the existence of a single state under the final international authority of the high representative. [31]Tripartite presidency. [32]Body with limited or no legislative authority. [33]Some sections of the constitution have been suspended since 1962, others since 1984. [34]Date constitution approved by referendum. [35]Assisted by vice presidents. [36]Date of significant amendments. [37]Governor-general can exercise all the powers of the reigning monarch of the Commonwealth. [38]Effective date of new government. [39]In actuality, a loose union of semiautonomous islands. [40]Transitional constitution promulgated. [41]Assisted by president. [42]To assume most executive powers of war-torn country from December 2005 to October 2006. [43]Suspended membership. [44]Republic of Cyprus only. [45]24 seats reserved for Turkish Cypriots are not occupied. [46]Zone defined by geographic coordinates. [47]Constitution adopted in May 1997 had not been promulgated by November 2005. [48]Partially delimited by Eritrean–Yemeni arbitration. [49]Defined by coordinates in some parts of the Gulf of Finland. [50]Executive responsibilities divided between (for Denmark) the high commissioner and (locally) the prime minister. [51]Or agreed boundaries or median line. [52]3 nautical miles in the Gulf of Finland. [53]Executive responsibilities divided among (for France) the prefect and (locally) the president of the General Council and the president of the Regional Council. [54]Represented by high commissioner. [55]Date of agreement providing for Palestinian self-rule. [56]Of Palestinian

membership in international organizations																																					country
United Nations (date of admission)	UN organs★ and affiliated intergovernmental organizations																	The Commonwealth	regional multipurpose									economic									
	UNCTAD★	ICJ★[e]	FAO	IAEA	IBRD	ICAO	ICC[f]	IDA	ILO	IMF	IMO	ITU	UNESCO	UNIDO	WHO	WIPO	WTO		AC	ASEAN	ATs	AU	EU	GCC	LAS	OAS	PC	ACP	ADB	APEC	CARICOM	ECOWAS	FZ	I-ADB	IDB	OPEC	
1960	●		●	●	●	●		●	●	●		●	●	●	●	●	●					●						●				●	●		●		Niger
1960	●		●	●	●	●		●	●	●	●	●	●	●	●	●	●	●				●						●				●				●	Nigeria
—																											●										Northern Mariana Is.
1945	●		●	●	●	●		●	●	●	●	●	●	●	●	●	●		●		●								●					●			Norway
1971	●		●		●	●		●	●	●	●	●	●	●	●	●	●							●	●										●		Oman
1947	●		●	●	●	●		●	●	●	●	●	●	●	●	●	●	●											●						●		Pakistan
1994	●		●		●	●		●		●			●		●												●	●	●								Palau
1945	●		●	●	●	●		●	●	●	●	●	●	●	●	●	●									●								●			Panama
1975	●		●		●	●		●	●	●	●	●	●	●	●	●	●	●			●						●	●	●	●							Papua New Guinea
1945	●		●	●	●	●		●	●	●	●	●	●	●	●	●	●									●								●			Paraguay
1945	●		●	●	●	●		●	●	●	●	●	●	●	●	●	●				●					●				●				●			Peru
1945	●		●	●	●	●		●	●	●	●	●	●	●	●	●	●			●									●	●							Philippines
1945	●		●	●	●	●		●	●	●	●	●	●	●	●	●	●				●		●														Poland
1955	●		●	●	●	●		●	●	●	●	●	●	●	●	●	●						●						●					●			Portugal
—											●			14																							Puerto Rico
1971	●		●	●	●	●			●	●	●	●	●	●	●	●	●							●	●										●	●	Qatar
—											●																						●				Réunion
1955	●		●	●	●	●			●	●	●	●	●	●	●	●	●				●																Romania
1991	●	●		●	●	●		●	●	●	●	●	●	●	●	●	1		●		●									●							Russia
1962	●		●		●	●		●	●	●		●	●	●	●	●	●					●						●									Rwanda
1983	●		●		●	●		●	●	●	●		●	●	●	●	●	●								●		●			●						St. Kitts and Nevis
1979	●		●		●	●		●	●	●	●	●	●	●	●	●	●	●								●		●			●						St. Lucia
1980	●		●		●	●		●	●	●	●	●	●	●	●	●	●	●								●		●			●						St. Vincent
1976	●		●		●	●	●	●	●	●	●	●	●		●	●	1	●									●	●	●								Samoa
1992	●		●		●	●			●	●	●	●	●		●	●																					San Marino
1975	●		●		●	●		●	●	●	●	●	●	●	●	●	1					●						●									São Tomé and Príncipe
1945	●		●	●	●	●		●	●	●	●	●	●	●	●	●	1							●	●										●	●	Saudi Arabia
1960	●		●	●	●	●		●	●	●	●	●	●	●	●	●	●					●						●				●	●		●		Senegal
1945	●		●	●	●	●		●	●	●	●	●	●	●	●	●	1																				Serbia and Montenegro
1976	●		●	●	●	●			●	●	●	●	●	●	●	●	1	●				●						●									Seychelles
1961	●	●	●	●	●	●		●	●	●	●	●	●	●	●	●	●	●				●						●				●			●		Sierra Leone
1965	●			●	●	●		●	●	●	●	●			●	●	●	●		●									●	●							Singapore
1993	●	●	●	●	●	●		●	●	●	●	●	●	●	●	●	●				●		●														Slovakia
1992	●		●	●	●	●		●	●	●	●	●	●	●	●	●	●						●											●			Slovenia
1978	●		●		●	●		●	●	●	●	●	●		●		●	●									●	●	●								Solomon Islands
1960	●		●		●	●		●	●	●	●	●	●	●	●	●						●			●			●							●		Somalia
1945	●		●	●	●	●	●	●	●	●	●	●	●	●	●	●	●	●			●	●						●									South Africa
1955	●		●	●	●	●		●	●	●	●	●	●	●	●	●	●				●		●						●					●			Spain
1955	●		●	●	●	●		●	●	●	●	●	●	●	●	●	●	●											●								Sri Lanka
1956	●		●	●	●	●		●	●	●	●	●	●	●	●	●	1					●			●			●							●		Sudan, The
1975	●		●		●	●			●	●	●	●	●	●	●	●	●									●		●			●			●	●		Suriname
1968	●		●		●	●		●	●	●		●	●	●	●	●	●	●				●						●									Swaziland
1946	●		●	●	●	●		●	●	●	●	●	●	●	●	●	●		●		●		●						●					●			Sweden
2002	●		●	●	●	●		●	●	●	●	●	●	●	●	●	●				●								●					●			Switzerland
1945	●		●	●	●	●		●	●	●	●	●	●	●	●	●									●										●		Syria
—																	●												●	●							Taiwan
1992	●		●	●	●	●		●	●	●		●	●	●	●	●	1												●						●		Tajikistan
1961	●		●	●	●	●		●	●	●	●	●	●	●	●	●	●	●				●						●									Tanzania
1946	●		●	●	●	●		●	●	●	●	●	●	●	●	●	●			●									●	●							Thailand
1960	●		●	●	●	●		●	●	●	●	●	●	●	●	●	●					●						●				●	●		●		Togo
1999	●		●		●	●		●		●	●	●	●	●	●	●	1	●									●	●	●								Tonga
1962	●		●		●	●	●	●	●	●	●	●	●	●	●	●	●	●								●		●			●			●			Trinidad and Tobago
1956	●		●	●	●	●		●	●	●	●	●	●	●	●	●	●					●			●										●		Tunisia
1945	●		●	●	●	●		●	●	●	●	●	●	●	●	●	●				●								●						●		Turkey
1992	●		●		●	●			●	●	●	●	●	●	●	●													●						●		Turkmenistan
2000	●		●								●	●	●		●			●									●	●	●								Tuvalu
1962	●		●	●	●	●		●	●	●		●	●	●	●	●	●	●				●						●							●		Uganda
1945	●		●	●	●	●		●	●	●	●	●	●	●	●	●	1				●																Ukraine
1971	●		●	●	●	●		●	●	●	●	●	●	●	●	●	●							●	●										●	●	United Arab Emirates
1945	●	●	●	●	●	●	●	●	●	●	●	●	●	●	●	●	●	●			●		●						●					●			United Kingdom
1945	●	●	●	●	●	●		●	●	●	●	●	●		●	●	●		●		●					●	●		●	●				●			United States
1945	●		●	●	●	●			●	●	●	●	●	●	●	●	●				●					●								●			Uruguay
1992	●		●	●	●	●		●	●	●		●	●	●	●	●	1												●						●		Uzbekistan
1981	●		●		●	●		●	●	●	●	●	●	●	●		1	●									●	●	●								Vanuatu
1945	●	●	●	●	●	●			●	●	●	●	●	●	●	●	●				●					●								●		●	Venezuela
1977	●		●	●	●	●		●	●	●	●	●	●	●	●	●	1			●									●	●							Vietnam
—											●																										Virgin Islands (U.S.)
—																									● [57]										● [57]		West Bank
—																						112															Western Sahara
1947	●		●	●	●	●		●	●	●	●	●	●	●	●	●	1								●										●		Yemen
1964	●		●	●	●	●		●	●	●		●	●	●	●	●	●	●				●						●									Zambia
1980	●		●	●	●	●		●	●	●	●	●	●	●	●	●	●	113				●						●									Zimbabwe

Authority. [57]As Palestine. [58]Date parliament approved constitutional amendments for 78 articles. [59]Represented by the lieutenant governor. [60]Excludes two crown officers having no voting rights. [61]Legal ambiguity persists in December 2005. The 2001 constitution approved by the National Assembly has neither been promulgated nor vetoed by the president. [62]Stopped functioning effectively in early 2004. [63]Special administrative region (China). [64]Has been significantly amended. [65]Number of towns. [66]Increased from 268 districts in 2001 to *c.* 440 districts in 2003. [67]Shares coexecutive authority with spiritual leader. [68]Sea of Oman only; median line boundaries in Persian Gulf. [69]As of Dec. 7, 2005. [70]Based on evolving body of statutes and common law in both the United Kingdom and the Isle of Man. [71]Median line boundary between the Isle of Man and the United Kingdom. [72]The emperor is the symbol of state. [73]3 nautical miles in 5 straits. [74]Essentially 1992 constitution with new preamble. [75]Number of cities and counties. [76]Elected seats only. [77]Number of non-district towns and districts. [78]Limits established by international agreements with Estonia, Lithuania, and Sweden. [79]Date of peace accord laying framework for transitional government. [80]Until January 2006. [81]Formally a *jamahiriya* or "state of the masses"; in practice, an authoritarian state. [82]De facto chief of state. [83]Date parliament adopted significant constitutional amendments. [84]Under prince's authority. [85]Includes Western Sahara annexure. [86]Backed by military from February 2005. [87]Development regions. [88]Represented by high commissioner. [89]Basic law promulgated by sultan. [90]Has 2 consultative bodies with advisory authority only. [91]79 provinces; 116 chartered cities. [92]Rectangle defined by coordinates; claim extends beyond 12 mi. [93]Excludes additional seats for both houses of the legislature to meet ⅓ total representation requirements for minority parties per constitution. [94]14 towns; 92 districts. [95]Mixed political system approximating a constitutional monarchy. [96]Royal decrees from March 1, 1992, created first written rules of governance. [97]"Loose confederation." [98]Excludes Kosovo. [99]Represents districts that function as quasi-governmental bodies. [100]Statistical regions. [101]Approval date of federal transitional charter. [102]No effective central government in December 2005. [103]Atlantic Ocean only. [104]Transitional constitution. [105]Excludes nonvoting members. [106]Date disputed constitution ratified by king. [107]Hereditary constitutional monarchy. [108]Black Sea and Mediterranean Sea; 6 nautical miles in Aegean Sea. [109]In the Black Sea only. [110]Based on evolving body of statutes and common law. [111]Number of cities and districts. [112]Membership held by the Saharawi Arab Democratic Republic. [113]Officially withdrew from the Commonwealth in December 2003.

Area and population

This table provides the area and particular populations for each of the countries of the world and for all but the smallest political dependencies having a permanent civilian population. The data represent the latest published and unpublished data for both the surveyed area of the countries and their populations, the latter as of a single recent year (2005), as of a recent census to provide the fullest comparison of certain demographic measures that are not always available between successive national censuses, and as of decade population estimates over a seventy year (1950–2020) span. The 2005 midyear estimates (as a population estimate by decade) are based on a combination of national sources (both print and online), the United Nations' *World Population Prospects: The 2004 Revision,* the U.S. Bureau of the Census International Data Base, databases of other international organizations, and *Encyclopædia Britannica*'s own estimates.

One principal point to bear in mind when studying these statistics is that all of them, whatever degree of precision may be implied by the exactness of the numbers, are estimates—all of varying, and some of suspect, accuracy—even when they *contain* a very full enumeration. The United States—which has a long tradition both of census taking and of the use of the most sophisticated analytical tools in processing the data—is unable to determine within 1.2% (the estimated 2000 undercount) its total population nationally. And that is an *average* underenumeration. In states and larger cities, where enumeration of particular populations, including illegal, is more difficult, the accuracy of the enumerated count may be off as much as 3.1% at a state level (in New Mexico, for instance) and by a greater percent for a single city. The high accuracy attained by census operations in China may approach 0.25% of rigorously maintained civil population registers. Other national census operations not so based, however, are inherently less accurate. For example, Ethiopia's first-ever census in 1984 resulted in figures that were 30% or more above prevailing estimates; Nigeria's 1991 census corrected decades of miscounts and was well below prevailing estimates. An undercount of 2–8% is more typical, but even census operations offering results of 30% or more above or below prevailing estimates can still represent well-founded benchmarks from which future planning may proceed. The editors have tried to take account of the range of variation and accuracy in published data, but it is difficult to establish a value for many sources of inaccuracy unless some country or agency has made a conscientious effort to establish both the relative accuracy (precision) of its estimate and the absolute magnitude of the quantity it is trying to measure—for example, the number of people in Cambodia who died at the hands of the Khmer Rouge. If a figure of 2,000,000 is adopted, what is its accuracy: ± 1%, 10%, 50%? Are the original data documentary or evidentiary, complete or incomplete, analytically biased or unbiased, in good agreement with other published data?

Many similar problems exist and in endless variations: What is the extent of eastern European immigration to western Europe in search of jobs? How many registered and unregistered refugees from Afghanistan, The Sudan, or Burundi are there in surrounding countries? How many undocumented aliens are there in the United Kingdom, Japan, or the United States? How many Tamils have left Sri Lanka as a result of civil unrest in their homeland? How many Amerindians exist (remain, preserving their original language and a mode of life unassimilated by the larger national culture) in the countries of South America?

Area and population

country	area			population (latest estimate)					population (recent census)				
	square miles	square kilometres	rank	total midyear 2005	rank	density		% annual growth rate 2000–05	census year	total	male (%)	female (%)	urban (%)
						per sq mi	per sq km						
Afghanistan	249,347	645,807	41	23,867,000	45	95.7	37.0	3.3	1979	13,051,358[1]	51.4	48.6	15.1
Albania	11,082	28,703	142	3,130,000	132	282.4	109.0	0.4	2001	3,069,275	49.9	50.1	42.2
Algeria	919,595	2,381,741	11	32,854,000	35	35.7	13.8	1.5	1998	29,272,343	50.6	49.4	80.8
American Samoa	77	200	206	63,900	206	829.9	319.5	2.1	2000	57,291	51.1	48.9	46.6[2]
Andorra	179	464	193	74,800	203	417.9	161.2	2.0	2003[3, 4]	67,159	51.8	48.2	92.0[2]
Angola	481,354	1,246,700	24	11,827,000	69	24.6	9.5	2.5	1970	5,673,046	52.1	47.9	14.2
Antigua and Barbuda	171	442	196	77,800	202	455.0	176.0	0.9	2001	72,309[5]	48.3	51.7	37.1[6]
Argentina	1,073,400	2,780,092	8	38,592,000	30	36.0	13.9	1.0	2001	36,260,130	48.7	51.3	88.3[6]
Armenia	11,484	29,743	141	2,983,000	134	259.8	100.3	−0.4	2001	3,002,594	46.9	53.1	64.8
Aruba	75	193	207	97,400	196	1,298.7	504.7	1.4	2000	90,506	48.0	52.0	50.5[2]
Australia	2,969,978	7,692,208	6	20,345,000	52	6.9	2.6	1.2	2001	18,972,350	49.3	50.7	91.2[6]
Austria	32,383	83,871	114	8,168,000	91	252.3	97.4	0.4	2001	8,032,926	48.4	51.6	66.8
Azerbaijan	33,400	86,600	113	8,381,000	89	250.9	96.8	0.8	1999	7,953,438	48.8	51.2	56.9[7]
Bahamas, The	5,382	13,939	159	323,000	176	60.0	23.2	1.4	2000	303,611	48.7	51.3	88.4[2]
Bahrain	278	720	186	715,000	162	2,571.9	993.1	2.3	2001	650,604	57.4	42.6	88.4
Bangladesh	56,977	147,570	93	137,636,000	8	2,415.6	932.7	1.4	2001	123,151,246[8]	50.9	49.1	23.4
Barbados	166	430	197	270,000	180	1,626.5	627.9	0.3	2000	250,010[9]	48.0	52.0	50.0[2]
Belarus	80,153	207,595	85	9,776,000	81	122.0	47.1	−0.5	1999	10,045,237	47.0	53.0	69.3
Belgium	11,787	30,528	139	10,432,000	76	885.0	341.7	0.3	1996[3, 4]	10,143,047	48.9	51.1	96.8
Belize	8,867	22,965	150	291,000	179	32.8	12.7	3.1	2000	240,204	50.5	49.5	47.7
Benin	43,484	112,622	101	7,649,000	94	175.9	67.9	2.9	2002	6,769,914	48.5	51.5	38.9
Bermuda	21	54	213	65,400	205	3,114.3	1,211.1	0.7	2000[10]	62,059	48.0	52.0	100.0
Bhutan	14,824	38,394	135	776,000	159	52.3	20.2	2.8	...	...	50.5[2]	49.5[2]	21.0[2]
Bolivia	424,164	1,098,581	28	8,858,000	86	20.9	8.1	1.7	2001	8,274,325	49.8	50.2	62.4
Bosnia and Herzegovina	19,772	51,209	127	3,853,000	126	194.9	75.2	0.4	1991	4,377,033	49.9	50.1	39.6
Botswana	224,848	582,356	47	1,765,000	146	7.8	3.3	0.1	2001	1,680,863	48.4	51.6	51.5
Brazil	3,287,612	8,514,877	5	184,016,000	5	56.0	21.6	1.5	2000	169,872,856	49.2	50.8	81.2
Brunei	2,226	5,765	168	364,000	174	163.5	63.1	2.4	2001	332,844	50.8	49.2	72.8[6]
Bulgaria	42,858	111,002	103	7,740,000	93	180.6	69.7	−0.6	2001	7,928,901	48.7	51.3	69.0
Burkina Faso	103,456	267,950	75	13,492,000	62	130.4	50.4	3.6	1996	10,312,609	48.2	51.8	15.0[2]
Burundi	10,740	27,816	145	7,795,000	92	725.8	280.2	3.3	1990[10]	5,292,793	48.6	51.4	6.3
Cambodia	69,898	181,035	89	13,327,000	64	190.7	73.6	1.7	1998	11,437,656	48.2	51.8	20.9
Cameroon	183,569	475,442	53	16,988,000	58	92.5	35.7	2.2	1987	10,516,232	49.0	51.0	38.3
Canada	3,855,103	9,984,670	2	32,227,000	36	8.4	3.2	1.0	2001	30,007,094[8]	49.0[8]	51.0[8]	78.9[6]
Cape Verde	1,557	4,033	170	476,000	167	305.7	118.0	1.8	2000	434,625	48.5	51.5	53.4
Central African Republic	240,324	622,436	43	4,038,000	124	16.8	6.5	1.3	1988	2,688,426	49.1	50.9	36.5
Chad	495,755	1,284,000	21	9,657,000	82	19.5	7.5	3.0	1993	6,279,931	47.9	52.1	21.4
Chile	291,930	756,096	38	16,295,000	60	55.8	21.6	1.1	2002	15,116,435	49.3	50.7	86.6
China	3,696,100	9,572,900	3	1,304,369,000	1	352.9	136.3	0.6	2000	1,265,830,000	51.6	48.4	36.2
Colombia	440,762	1,141,568	26	42,954,000	29	97.5	37.6	1.6	1993	33,109,840	49.2	50.8	72.0[15]
Comoros	719	1,862	176	614,000	163	854.0	329.8	2.2	1991	446,817	49.5	50.5	28.5
Congo, Dem. Rep. of the	905,354	2,344,858	12	57,549,000	23	63.6	24.5	2.8	1984	29,671,407	49.2	50.8	29.1[15]
Congo, Rep. of the	132,047	342,000	64	3,602,000	127	27.3	10.5	3.0	1984[10]	1,909,248	48.7	51.3	52.0
Costa Rica	19,730	51,100	128	4,221,000	120	213.9	82.6	1.5	2000	3,810,179	49.9	50.1	59.0
Côte d'Ivoire	123,863	320,803	68	17,298,000	57	139.7	53.9	2.1	1998	15,366,672	51.0	49.0	43.6[2]
Croatia	21,851	56,594	126	4,440,000	118	203.2	78.5	0.3	2001	4,437,460	48.1	51.9	58.1[6]
Cuba	42,804	110,860	104	11,269,000	72	263.3	101.7	0.3	1993	10,904,466	50.3	49.7	74.4
Cyprus[17]	3,572	9,251	165	968,000	156	271.0	104.6	1.4	2001[18]	689,565	49.1	50.9'	68.8
Czech Republic	30,450	78,866	117	10,235,000	77	336.1	129.8	−0.1	2001	10,230,060	48.7	51.3	74.6
Denmark	16,640	43,098	132	5,416,000	106	325.5	125.7	0.3	2003[3]	5,383,507	49.5	50.5	85.3
Djibouti	8,950	23,200	149	477,000	166	53.3	20.6	2.0	1983	273,974	51.9	48.1	82.8[15]
Dominica	290	750	184	69,000	204	237.9	92.0	−0.7	2001	71,239	51.0	49.0	71.4[6]
Dominican Republic	18,792	48,671	130	8,895,000	85	73.3	182.8	1.5	2002	8,562,541	49.8	50.2	63.6
East Timor	5,639	14,604	158	975,000	155	172.9	66.8	6.2	2004	924,642	50.6	49.4	8.4[20]
Ecuador	105,037	272,045	73	13,364,000	63	127.2	49.1	1.3	2001	12,156,608	49.5	50.5	61.0[22]

Still, much information is accurate, well founded, and updated regularly. The sources of these data are censuses; national population registers (cumulated periodically); registration of migration, births, deaths, and so on; sample surveys to establish demographic conditions; and the like.

The statistics provided for area and population by country are ranked, and the population densities based on those values are also provided. The population densities, for purposes of comparison within this table, are calculated on the bases of the 2005 midyear population estimate as shown and of total area of the country. Elsewhere in individual country presentations the reader may find densities calculated on more specific population figures and more specialized area bases: land area for Finland (because of its many lakes) or ice-free area for Greenland (most of which is ice cap). The data in this section conclude with the estimated average annual growth rate for the country (including both natural growth and net migration) during the five-year period 2000–2005.

In the section containing census data, information supplied includes the census total (usually de facto, the population actually present, rather than de jure, the population legally resident, who might be anywhere); the male-female breakdown; the proportion that is urban (usually according to the country's own definition); and finally an analysis of the age structure of the population by 15-year age groups. This last analysis may be particularly useful in distinguishing the type of population being recorded—young, fast-growing nations show a high proportion of people under 30 (many countries in sub-Saharan Africa and the Middle East have about 40% of their population under 15 years), while other nations (for example, Sweden, which suffered no age-group losses in World War II) exhibit quite uniform proportions.

Finally, a section is provided giving the population of each country at 10-year intervals from 1950 to 2020 based on sources cited earlier. The projections for 2010 and 2020 represent the best fit of available data through the autumn of 2005. The evidence of the last 30 years with respect to similar estimates published about 1970, however, shows how cloudy is the glass through which these numbers are read. In 1970 no respectable Western analyst would have imagined proposing that mainland China could achieve the degree of birth control that it apparently has since then; on the other hand, even the Chinese admit that their methods have been somewhat Draconian and that they have already seen some backlash in terms of higher birth rates among those who have so far postponed larger families. How much is "some" by 2010? Compound that problem with all the social, economic, political, and biological factors (including the impact of AIDS) that can affect 217 countries' populations, and the difficulty facing the prospective compiler of such projections may be appreciated.

Specific data about the vital rates affecting the data in this table may be found in great detail in both the country statistical boxes in "The Nations of the World" section and in the Vital statistics, marriage, family table, beginning at page 770.

Percentages in this table for male and female population will always total 100.0, but percentages by age group may not, for reasons such as nonresponse on census forms, "don't know" responses (which are common in countries with poor birth registration systems), and the like.

0–14	15–29	30–44	45–59	60–74	75 and over	1950	1960	1970	1980	1990	2000	2010 projection	2020 projection	country
44.5	26.9	15.8	8.6	3.6	0.6	8,151	9,966	12,596	15,209	14,606	20,259	28,926	38,981	Afghanistan
29.3	24.1	21.2	14.2	8.7	2.5	1,215	1,611	2,136	2,671	3,289	3,062	3,216	3,420	Albania
36.2	30.6	17.7	8.9	5.1	1.5	8,753	10,800	13,746	18,811	25,291	30,463	35,420	40,624	Algeria
38.8	25.5	19.4	10.8	4.5	1.0	19	20	27	32	47	58	71	86	American Samoa
15.1	18.0	29.1	20.5	11.1	6.2	6	8	19	33	53	68	78	82	Andorra
41.7	23.2	17.0	7.4	3.8	1.0	4,118	4,797	5,606	6,741	8,291	10,443	13,262	16,157	Angola
26.4	25.4	23.9	13.9	——10.4——		46	55	66	69	63	75	80	84	Antigua and Barbuda
28.3	25.0	18.6	14.7	9.3	4.1	17,150	20,616	23,962	28,094	32,581	36,784	40,519	44,247	Argentina
24.8	24.9	21.8	13.6	12.1	2.8	1,355	1,869	2,520	3,115	3,377	3,043	2,967	3,017	Armenia
23.2	19.4	28.0	18.2	8.6	2.6	51	57	61	60	63	91	102	111	Aruba
20.6[6]	21.1[6]	22.9[6]	18.7[6]	10.9[6]	5.8[6]	8,219	10,315	12,552	14,471	17,065	19,153	21,401	23,537	Australia
16.9	18.6	24.9	18.6	13.8	7.2	6,935	7,047	7,467	7,549	7,678	8,012	8,232	8,304	Austria
31.8	25.6	24.1	9.5	7.6	1.4	2,896	3,895	5,172	6,165	7,166	8,049	8,710	9,350	Azerbaijan
29.6	25.8	24.2	12.6	5.9	1.9	79	110	170	210	255	301	344	385	Bahamas, The
27.9	27.5	29.6	11.0	3.2	0.8	110	149	210	334	503	638	778	895	Bahrain
35.9	31.5	17.6	9.9	4.0	1.1	45,646	54,622	67,403	88,077	109,897	128,100	150,491	175,954	Bangladesh
21.8	22.5	24.4	16.0	——15.3——		211	231	239	249	257	266	273	278	Barbados
19.5	21.8	23.4	16.4	——18.9——		7,745	8,190	9,040	9,650	10,186	10,005	9,504	8,958	Belarus
17.9	20.0	23.0	17.7	15.0	6.4	8,639	9,153	9,690	9,859	9,967	10,251	10,511	10,589	Belgium
41.0	27.7	17.4	8.1	——5.8——		68	90	120	146	189	250	326	393	Belize
46.8	——47.7——			——5.5——		1,673	2,055	2,620	3,444	4,676	6,628	8,731	10,886	Benin
19.1	18.4	27.9	19.6	10.9	4.1	39	44	53	55	58	63	67	70	Bermuda
40.2[2]	26.0[2]	17.4[2]	10.1[2]	5.2[2]	1.1[2]	...	...	...	519	675	866	1,059		Bhutan
38.6	27.4	17.0	10.0	5.2	1.8	2,766	3,434	4,346	5,441	6,574	8,153	9,499	10,747	Bolivia
23.5[11]	26.3[11]	22.6[11]	16.9[11]	8.9[11]	2.7[11]	2,661	3,180	3,564	3,914	4,308	3,781	3,875	3,768	Bosnia and Herzegovina
40.2[6]	31.2[6]	14.8[6]	7.7[6]	4.4[6]	1.7[6]	449	572	750	1,049	1,429	1,754	1,729	1,671	Botswana
29.6	28.2	21.1	12.5	6.5	2.1	53,975	72,742	95,989	121,615	145,946	171,062	195,954	216,384	Brazil
30.8[6]	27.0[6]	25.4[6]	12.5[6]	3.5[6]	0.8[6]	45	83	128	185	258	324	403	478	Brunei
15.0[12]	21.3[12]	20.4[12]	20.9[12]	16.1[12]	6.3[12]	7,251	7,867	8,490	8,862	8,718	7,973	7,459	6,871	Bulgaria
47.9[13]	26.8[13]	12.9[13]	7.6[13]	3.9[13]	0.9[13]	4,376	4,866	5,304	6,315	8,336	11,309	15,667	20,915	Burkina Faso
46.4	25.3	15.4	7.0	4.0	1.7	2,363	2,815	3,522	4,300	5,505	6,621	9,281	12,266	Burundi
42.8	26.1	17.2	8.5	4.3	1.1	4,471	5,761	7,395	6,869	9,355	12,224	14,574	17,442	Cambodia
46.4	24.5	14.6	8.7	4.1	1.6	4,888	5,609	6,727	8,746	11,779	15,234	18,780	22,463	Cameroon
18.3[14]	20.3[14]	23.5[14]	20.7[14]	11.3[14]	5.9[14]	13,737	17,909	21,717	24,516	27,701	30,689	33,668	36,428	Canada
43.6[2]	24.8[2]	17.1[2]	5.8[2]	6.3[2]	2.4[2]	146	196	267	289	355	435	523	630	Cape Verde
43.2	27.5	15.0	9.2	4.1	0.8	1,314	1,530	1,871	2,329	3,000	3,777	4,333	4,960	Central African Republic
48.1	24.6	14.7	7.2	4.2	1.3	2,608	3,042	3,730	4,542	6,023	8,316	11,170	14,839	Chad
25.7	24.3	23.6	15.0	8.3	3.1	6,082	7,643	9,570	11,174	13,179	15,412	17,134	18,639	Chile
22.9	25.4	25.6	15.7	8.2	2.2	562,580	650,661	820,403	984,736	1,148,364	1,268,853	1,342,723	1,411,531	China
34.5	28.5	20.1	10.0	4.3	1.6	11,592	15,953	21,430	26,583	32,859	39,686	46,109	52,199	Colombia
47.6[11]	27.0[11]	13.1[11]	7.7[11]	3.5[11]	1.0[11]	148	183	236	334	429	549	684	850	Comoros
47.3[15]	25.9[15]	14.1[15]	8.1[15]	3.8[15]	0.8[15]	12,184	15,451	20,543	27,996	37,764	50,052	67,129	90,022	Congo, Dem. Rep. of the
44.7	27.2	13.3	9.1	4.6	0.7	826	1,002	1,272	1,674	2,265	3,102	4,124	5,445	Congo, Rep. of the
31.9	27.1	21.7	11.4	5.7	2.2	862	1,236	1,758	2,302	3,051	3,925	4,538	5,095	Costa Rica
46.5[16]	27.5[16]	14.9[16]	7.6[16]	3.0[16]	0.5[16]	2,860	3,576	5,504	8,376	11,981	15,563	19,093	22,650	Côte d'Ivoire
17.1	20.4	21.4	19.5	16.3	5.3	3,837	4,036	4,205	4,383	4,508	4,381	4,432	4,373	Croatia
22.3	29.4	21.3	14.8	8.4	3.9	5,850	6,976	8,483	9,645	10,537	11,125	11,379	11,432	Cuba
21.5[19]	22.6[19]	22.0[19]	17.8[19]	11.2[19]	4.9[19]	494	573	615	658	751	902	1,018	1,116	Cyprus[17]
16.3	23.5	20.1	21.8	12.8	5.5	8,925	9,539	9,805	10,326	10,363	10,273	10,260	10,260	Czech Republic
18.8	17.9	22.3	20.9	13.1	7.0	4,271	4,581	4,929	5,123	5,140	5,337	5,459	5,530	Denmark
39.4	32.9	16.9	7.4	2.8	0.6	60	78	158	279	366	431	526	627	Djibouti
32.7	28.4	17.2	9.5	——12.2——		51	60	70	75	73	72	70	75	Dominica
34.0	27.0	20.0	11.0	5.8	2.2	2,353	3,231	4,424	5,718	7,090	8,265	9,522	10,676	Dominican Republic
41.1[21]	28.9[21]	15.0[21]	10.0[21]	4.3[21]	0.7[21]	433	501	604	581	740	722	1,292	1,780	East Timor
34.0[22]	28.0[22]	19.0[22]	10.0[22]	6.0[22]	3.0[22]	3,370	4,416	5,939	7,920	10,318	12,505	14,245	16,178	Ecuador

Area and population (continued)

country	area square miles	area square kilometres	rank	population (latest estimate) total midyear 2005	rank	density per sq mi	density per sq km	% annual growth rate 2000–05	census year	total	male (%)	female (%)	urban (%)
Egypt	385,229	997,739	30	70,457,000	17	182.9	70.6	1.8	1996	59,312,914	51.2	48.8	42.6
El Salvador	8,124	21,042	151	6,881,000	98	847.0	327.0	1.8	1992	5,118,599	48.6	51.4	50.4
Equatorial Guinea	10,831	28,051	144	504,000	164	46.5	18.0	2.3	1983	300,060	48.8	51.2	28.2
Eritrea	46,774	121,144	99	4,670,000	115	99.8	38.5	1.4	1984	2,703,998	49.9	50.1	15.1
Estonia	17,462	45,227	131	1,345,000	151	77.0	29.7	–0.4	2000	1,370,052	46.1	53.9	69.2
Ethiopia	435,186	1,127,127	27	73,053,000	15	167.9	64.8	2.5	1994	53,477,265	50.3	49.7	14.4[15]
Faroe Islands	540	1,399	178	48,400	210	89.6	34.6	1.1	2003[3, 4]	47,704	51.9	48.1	38.6
Fiji	7,055	18,272	155	846,000	157	119.9	46.3	0.9	1996	775,077	50.8	49.2	46.4
Finland	130,559	338,145	65	5,244,000	109	40.2	15.5	0.3	2003[3, 4]	5,206,295	48.9	51.1	83.3
France	210,026	543,965	49	60,733,000	20	289.2	111.6	0.6	1999	58,518,748	48.6	51.4	75.5
French Guiana	32,253	83,534	116	192,000	184	6.0	2.3	3.2	1999	157,274	50.4	49.6	77.8[7]
French Polynesia	1,544	4,000	171	255,000	181	163.2	63.0	1.6	2002	245,405	51.4	48.6	52.1[24]
Gabon	103,347	267,667	76	1,384,000	150	13.4	5.2	1.7	1993	1,011,710	49.3	50.7	73.2
Gambia, The	4,127	10,689	163	1,517,000	147	367.6	141.9	2.9	2003	1,364,507	49.6	50.4	26.1[24]
Gaza Strip	140	363	200	1,481,000[26]	148	10,578.6	4,079.9	5.3	1997	1,001,569	50.7	49.3	95.9
Georgia	27,086	70,152	121	4,496,000[27]	117	166.0	64.1	–0.7	2002	4,371,534[28]	47.2	52.8	52.3
Germany	137,847	357,023	63	82,443,000	14	598.1	230.9	0.1	2003[3]	82,536,700	48.9	51.1	88.1[24]
Ghana	92,098	238,533	81	21,946,000	49	238.3	92.0	2.2	2000	18,845,265	49.5	50.5	43.9[2]
Greece	50,949	131,957	96	11,088,000	74	217.6	84.0	0.3	2001	10,964,020	49.5	50.5	72.8
Greenland	836,330	2,166,086	13	57,100	208	0.07	0.03	0.3	2003[3, 4]	56,676	53.4	46.6	82.2
Grenada	133	344	202	103,000	194	774.4	299.4	0.5	2001	101,306	49.6	50.4	38.4
Guadeloupe	658	1,705	177	448,000	171	680.9	262.8	0.9	1999	422,496	48.1	51.9	99.7[7]
Guam	217	561	191	170,000	188	783.4	303.0	1.9	2000	154,805	51.1	48.9	93.2[2]
Guatemala	42,130	109,117	105	12,599,000	66	299.1	115.5	2.4	1994	8,331,874	49.3	50.7	35.0
Guernsey	30	78	211	63,600	207	2,120	815.4	0.4	2001	59,807	48.7	51.3	28.9[6, 29]
Guinea	94,918	245,836	78	9,402,000	83	99.1	38.2	2.2	1996	7,165,750	48.8	51.2	26.0
Guinea-Bissau	13,948	36,125	137	1,413,000	149	101.3	39.1	2.0	1991	983,367	48.4	51.6	20.3[11]
Guyana	83,044	215,083	84	751,000	161	9.0	3.5	0.2	2002	749,190	49.3	50.7	37.6[24]
Haiti	10,695	27,700	146	8,528,000	88	797.4	307.9	1.4	2003	7,929,048	48.3	51.7	37.5[24]
Honduras	43,433	112,492	102	7,187,000	96	165.5	63.9	2.5	2001	6,535,344	49.4	50.6	44.8
Hong Kong	425	1,102	180	6,926,000	97	16,296.5	6,284.9	0.8	2001	6,708,389	49.0	51.0	100.0
Hungary	35,919	93,030	110	10,078,000	78	280.6	108.3	–0.3	2001	10,198,135	47.6	52.4	64.3
Iceland	39,741	102,928	106	295,000	177	7.4	2.9	0.9	2003[3, 4]	288,471	50.0	50.0	93.8
India	1,222,559	3,166,414	7	1,103,371,000	2	902.5	348.5	1.6	2001	1,028,610,328	51.7	48.3	27.8
Indonesia	730,024	1,890,754	16	222,781,000	4	305.2	117.8	1.3	2000	206,264,595	50.1	49.9	42.0
Iran	636,374	1,648,200	18	69,515,000	18	109.2	42.2	0.9	1996	60,055,488	50.8	49.2	61.3
Iraq	167,618	434,128	58	27,818,000	39	166.0	64.1	2.9	1997	21,941,050	49.7	50.3	67.9
Ireland	27,133	70,273	122	4,152,000	122	153.0	59.1	1.8	2002	3,917,203	49.7	50.3	59.6
Isle of Man	221	572	190	78,000	201	352.9	136.4	0.6	2001[10]	76,315	49.0	51.0	72.6
Israel[32, 33]	8,367	21,671	152	6,677,000	100	798.0	308.1	1.8	1995[10, 34]	5,548,523	49.3	50.7	92.9[15]
Italy	116,346	301,336	72	57,989,000	22	498.4	192.4	0.4	2001	56,995,744	48.4	51.6	67.3
Jamaica	4,244	10,991	162	2,736,000	137	644.7	248.9	0.9	2001	2,607,632	49.2	50.8	52.0
Japan	145,908	377,899	62	128,085,000	10	877.8	338.9	0.2	2000	126,925,843	48.9	51.1	78.7
Jersey	46	118	210	87,800	198	1,908.7	744.1	0.2	2001	87,186	48.7	51.3	28.9[6, 29]
Jordan	34,495	89,342	112	5,182,000	110	150.2	58.0	2.2	1994	4,139,458	52.2	47.8	78.3
Kazakhstan	1,052,090	2,724,900	9	15,186,000	61	14.4	5.6	0.2	1999	14,953,126	48.2	51.8	55.9
Kenya	224,961	582,646	46	33,830,000	34	150.4	58.1	2.4	1999	28,686,607	49.5	50.5	32.2[7]
Kiribati	313	811	182	95,300	197	304.5	117.5	1.8	2000	84,494	49.3	50.7	43.5
Korea, North	47,399	122,762	98	22,488,000	48	474.4	183.2	0.6	1993	21,213,378	48.7	51.3	58.9
Korea, South	38,456	99,601	108	48,294,000	24	1,255.8	484.9	0.5	2000	45,985,289	50.2	49.8	79.7
Kuwait	6,880	17,818	156	2,847,000	136	413.8	159.8	4.9	1995	1,575,570	58.5	41.5	97.0[15]
Kyrgyzstan	76,641	198,500	86	5,146,000	111	67.1	25.9	1.2	1999	4,822,938	49.4	50.6	34.8
Laos	91,429	236,800	83	5,924,000	101	64.8	25.0	2.3	1995	4,581,258	49.5	50.5	20.7[15]
Latvia	24,938	64,589	124	2,299,000	141	92.2	35.6	–0.6	2000	2,377,383	46.1	53.9	68.1
Lebanon	4,016	10,400	164	3,577,000	128	890.7	343.9	1.0	1997	4,005,025[35]	50.2[35]	49.8[35]	85.0[15]
Lesotho	11,720	30,355	140	2,031,000	143	173.3	66.9	–0.1	2001[10]	2,157,580	49.4	50.6	12.0
Liberia	37,743	97,754	109	2,900,000	135	76.8	29.7	1.5	1984	2,101,628	50.6	49.4	38.8
Libya	679,362	1,759,540	17	5,853,000	104	8.6	3.3	2.0	1995[10]	4,404,986	50.8	49.2	85.3[15]
Liechtenstein	62	160	209	34,800	212	561.3	217.5	1.3	2003[3, 4]	33,863	49.1	50.9	21.6[24]
Lithuania	25,212	65,300	123	3,413,000	129	135.4	52.3	–0.5	2001	3,483,972	46.8	53.2	66.9
Luxembourg	999	2,586	173	457,000	170	457.5	176.7	0.9	2001	439,539	49.3	50.7	91.9[6]
Macau	10.6	27.5	214	470,000	169	44,339.6	17,090.9	1.8	2001	435,235	48.0	52.0	98.9[6]
Macedonia	9,928	25,713	148	2,034,000	142	204.9	79.1	0.2	2002	2,022,547	50.2	49.8	59.5[24]
Madagascar	226,662	587,051	45	18,606,000	55	82.1	31.7	2.8	1993	12,238,914	49.7	50.3	22.9
Malawi	45,747	118,484	100	12,707,000	65	277.8	107.2	2.5	1998	9,933,868	49.0	51.0	14.0
Malaysia	127,355	329,847	66	26,130,000	44	205.2	79.2	2.4	2000	23,274,690	50.9	49.1	62.0
Maldives	115	298	204	294,000	178	2,556.5	986.6	1.6	2000	270,101	50.8	49.2	27.4
Mali	482,077	1,248,574	23	11,415,000	71	23.7	9.1	2.5	1998	9,790,492	49.5	50.5	26.9
Malta	122	315	203	404,000	172	3,311.5	1,282.5	0.7	1995	378,132	49.4	50.6	89.4[15]
Marshall Islands	70	181	208	56,300	209	804.3	311.0	1.7	1999	50,848	51.2	48.8	65.2
Martinique	436	1,128	179	396,000	173	908.3	351.1	0.5	1999	381,427	47.4	52.6	97.3
Mauritania	398,000	1,030,700	29	3,069,000	133	7.7	3.0	3.0	2000	2,508,159	49.5	50.5	57.7[2]
Mauritius	788	2,040	175	1,245,000	153	1,579.9	610.3	1.0	2000[10]	1,179,137	49.5	50.5	42.7[2]
Mayotte	144	374	199	181,000	187	1,256.9	484.0	4.2	2002	160,265	50.1	49.9	...
Mexico	758,449	1,964,375	15	107,029,000	11	141.1	54.5	1.4	2000	97,483,412	48.8	51.2	74.6
Micronesia	271	701	187	113,000	192	417.0	161.2	1.1	2000	107,008	50.6	49.4	28.3[2]
Moldova	13,068	33,845	138	4,206,000	121	321.9	124.3	–0.3	2004	3,388,071[37]	48.2[37]	51.8[37]	61.4[37]
Monaco	0.76	1.97	217	32,700	213	43,026.3	16,599.0	0.4	2000	32,020	48.5	51.5	100.0
Mongolia	603,909	1,564,116	19	2,550,000	139	4.2	1.6	1.3	2000	2,373,500	49.6	50.4	58.6
Morocco[39]	177,117	458,730	55	29,889,000	37	168.8	65.2	1.4	2004	29,891,708[40]	49.9[21, 40]	50.1[21, 40]	55.1[40]
Mozambique	313,661	812,379	35	19,407,000	54	61.9	23.9	1.8	1997	16,099,246	47.9	52.1	28.6
Myanmar (Burma)	261,228	676,577	40	46,997,000	26	179.9	69.5	1.0	1983	35,307,913	49.6	50.4	24.0
Namibia	318,580	825,118	34	2,031,000	143	6.4	2.5	1.3	2001	1,826,854	48.7	51.3	31.4[6]
Nauru	8.2	21.2	216	10,200	216	1,243.9	481.1	0.3	2002	10,065	51.2[41]	48.8[41]	100.0
Nepal	56,827	147,181	94	27,133,000	41	477.5	184.4	2.1	2001	23,151,423	49.9	50.1	14.2

age distribution (%)						population (by decade, '000s)								country
0–14	15–29	30–44	45–59	60–74	75 and over	1950	1960	1970	1980	1990	2000	2010 projection	2020 projection	
37.7	27.6	18.6	10.4	5.0	0.7	20,461	26,085	33,329	40,546	51,959	64,590	76,751	88,531	Egypt
38.7	28.7	16.0	9.2	5.4	1.9	1,951	2,578	3,598	4,586	5,110	6,280	7,461	8,550	El Salvador
41.7	25.1	15.7	11.2	5.3	1.0	226	254	294	219	353	449	563	693	Equatorial Guinea
46.1	23.0	15.9	8.9	4.4	1.6	1,402	1,615	2,160	2,569	2,996	4,357	5,278	6,590	Eritrea
18.1	21.4	20.8	18.6	15.6	5.5	1,096	1,211	1,360	1,477	1,569	1,370	1,323	1,286	Estonia
46.1[23]	26.0[23]	15.1[23]	8.3[23]	3.8[23]	0.7[23]	20,175	24,169	29,469	36,036	48,197	64,690	81,754	99,279	Ethiopia
23.6	19.4	20.9	18.4	11.3	6.4	31	35	39	43	48	46	50	52	Faroe Islands
35.4	27.4	20.7	11.4	4.2	0.9	289	394	520	634	737	810	876	918	Fiji
17.8	18.6	20.6	22.5	13.6	6.9	4,009	4,430	4,606	4,800	4,986	5,176	5,304	5,406	Finland
17.9	20.2	21.9	18.7	13.6	7.7	41,736	45,684	50,770	53,880	56,710	58,969	61,797	63,903	France
34.0	24.2	23.3	12.5	4.3	1.7	27	33	49	68	116	164	215	261	French Guiana
29.9	26.0	23.5	13.3	5.9	1.4	62	84	117	151	197	235	272	305	French Polynesia
33.8[25]	23.7[25]	17.0[25]	17.4[25]	6.9[25]	1.2[25]	469	486	529	696	957	1,272	1,498	1,709	Gabon
44.9[24]	26.4[24]	15.5[24]	8.8[24]	3.6[24]	0.8[24]	294	355	469	652	936	1,316	1,706	2,070	Gambia, The
50.2	25.7	13.7	6.0	3.5	0.9	245	308	370	456	630	1,145	1,889	2,621	Gaza Strip
21.0	22.8	21.9	15.6	14.6	4.1	3,527	4,159	4,707	5,073	5,439	4,654	4,320	4,079	Georgia
14.9[24]	17.0[24]	24.3[24]	19.3[24]	16.9[24]	7.6[24]	68,377	72,674	77,709	78,275	79,365	82,203	82,455	82,038	Germany
41.2[2]	28.3[2]	17.3[2]	7.9[2]	4.3[2]	1.0[2]	5,297	6,958	8,789	11,016	15,399	19,658	24,258	28,684	Ghana
15.2	22.0	22.3	18.0	16.5	6.0	7,566	8,327	8,793	9,643	10,161	10,917	11,246	11,392	Greece
26.2	19.7	27.9	17.4	7.5	1.3	23	32	46	50	56	56	57	58	Greenland
35.1	28.1	17.6	9.0	——10.2——		76	90	95	89	95	100	106	112	Grenada
23.6	22.4	24.3	15.7	9.3	4.7	206	265	320	327	386	428	462	480	Guadeloupe
30.5	24.1	23.3	13.9	6.7	1.5	60	67	85	107	134	155	182	206	Guam
44.0	26.1	15.8	8.3	——5.8——		3,146	4,139	5,418	7,012	8,894	11,166	14,213	17,527	Guatemala
17.2	18.8	23.2	20.0	13.4	7.4	44	45	51	53	61	62	64	65	Guernsey
44.1[13]	26.5[13]	15.9[13]	9.0[13]	3.9[13]	0.6[13]	2,758	3,248	4,008	4,798	6,217	8,434	10,485	13,371	Guinea
43.9[11]	26.5[11]	16.1[11]	8.8[11]	3.7[11]	1.0[11]	573	617	620	789	996	1,278	1,564	1,892	Guinea-Bissau
27.6[30]	31.0[30]	21.3[30]	12.8[30]	5.4[30]	1.9[30]	423	569	709	761	729	744	751	725	Guyana
42.7[24]	29.3[24]	14.2[24]	8.2[24]	4.5[24]	1.1[24]	3,261	3,803	4,520	5,453	6,867	7,939	9,145	10,328	Haiti
42.2[6]	29.1[6]	15.1[6]	8.3[6]	4.1[6]	1.2[6]	1,431	1,952	2,761	3,402	4,792	6,355	7,965	9,385	Honduras
16.5	21.6	29.0	18.0	10.6	4.3	2,237	3,075	3,959	5,063	5,688	6,665	7,188	7,802	Hong Kong
16.6	22.2	19.8	21.0	14.3	6.1	9,338	9,984	10,337	10,707	10,374	10,211	9,949	9,698	Hungary
22.9	22.1	21.9	17.8	9.9	5.4	143	176	204	228	255	281	306	327	Iceland
33.1[6]	27.8[6]	19.9[6]	12.1[6]	5.6[6]	1.5[6]	357,561	442,344	554,911	688,856	849,415	1,021,084	1,183,293	1,332,032	India
30.4	29.3	21.8	11.3	5.8	1.4	79,538	95,931	119,936	150,072	181,414	209,174	235,755	255,853	Indonesia
44.3	26.6	15.1	8.2	4.8	0.8	16,913	21,704	28,805	39,330	56,674	66,365	74,283	85,036	Iran
43.8[31]	30.2[31]	14.5[31]	6.9[31]	3.6[31]	1.0[31]	5,340	7,332	9,440	13,300	17,890	24,095	31,470	39,197	Iraq
21.1	24.4	22.1	17.3	10.2	4.9	2,969	2,834	2,954	3,401	3,515	3,801	4,354	4,753	Ireland
17.9	17.5	22.6	20.1	13.6	8.3	55	49	52	64	69	76	80	84	Isle of Man
29.2	25.0	19.6	13.1	9.1	4.0	1,258	2,114	2,958	3,862	4,613	6,098	7,304	8,687	Israel[32, 33]
14.1[6]	18.9[6]	23.8[6]	19.0[6]	16.0[6]	8.2[6]	47,104	50,200	53,822	56,434	56,719	56,967	58,325	58,145	Italy
32.4	25.9	20.6	11.0	6.8	3.3	1,385	1,632	1,944	2,229	2,348	2,615	2,843	3,034	Jamaica
14.6	20.3	19.5	22.2	16.3	7.1	83,625	94,096	104,331	116,807	123,537	127,034	128,457	126,713	Japan
16.9	18.4	25.9	19.7	12.6	6.5	57	63	71	76	84	87	88	89	Jersey
41.3	31.8	14.6	8.1	3.4	0.8	472	896	1,623	2,225	3,254	4,659	5,759	6,866	Jordan
28.7	25.7	22.1	12.9	——10.6——		6,693	9,982	13,106	14,967	16,398	15,032	15,460	15,977	Kazakhstan
44.1[7]	31.3[7]	13.8[7]	6.7[7]	3.3[7]	0.8[7]	6,121	8,157	11,247	16,331	23,358	29,986	38,383	46,249	Kenya
40.1	25.2	19.8	9.7	——5.2——		33	41	49	58	71	87	107	134	Kiribati
29.5[25]	31.9[25]	21.3[25]	11.0[25]	5.0[25]	1.2[25]	10,815	11,430	14,397	17,196	19,690	21,862	22,907	23,722	Korea, North
21.0	25.3	26.7	15.8	8.9	2.3	21,147	25,012	32,241	38,124	42,869	47,008	49,220	49,956	Korea, South
30.0	28.4	30.0	9.2	——2.4——		145	292	748	1,358	2,141	2,236	3,228	3,918	Kuwait
36.2[7]	27.3[7]	18.6[7]	8.9[7]	7.2[7]	1.8[7]	1,739	2,171	2,964	3,623	4,382	4,851	5,509	6,314	Kyrgyzstan
45.4[15]	26.5[15]	14.9[15]	8.1[15]	4.2[15]	1.0[15]	1,755	2,177	2,713	3,205	4,132	5,279	6,604	8,014	Laos
18.1	21.2	21.4	18.3	15.7	5.3	1,949	2,121	2,359	2,512	2,713	2,373	2,233	2,115	Latvia
28.0[35]	30.0[35]	19.8[35]	12.4[35]	——9.8[35]——		1,443	1,888	2,390	2,698	2,741	3,398	3,773	4,140	Lebanon
36.0[36]	31.2	14.7	10.0	6.0	2.1	726	859	1,067	1,344	1,722	2,038	1,983	1,878	Lesotho
43.2	28.2	14.7	7.7	4.4	1.8	824	1,055	1,397	1,849	2,117	2,694	3,531	4,318	Liberia
45.4[15]	26.4[15]	14.7[15]	9.1[15]	3.7[15]	0.6[15]	1,029	1,349	1,986	3,043	4,334	5,306	6,439	7,538	Libya
17.0	20.2	25.9	21.2	10.8	4.9	14	16	21	26	29	33	36	38	Liechtenstein
19.5	21.2	22.8	17.2	14.2	5.1	2,553	2,765	3,138	3,436	3,698	3,500	3,331	3,189	Lithuania
18.9	18.6	25.5	18.4	12.9	5.7	296	314	339	364	382	436	479	523	Luxembourg
21.7	22.2	29.1	17.5	6.6	2.9	205	186	261	256	352	431	486	520	Macau
21.1	23.8	22.0	18.1	11.7	3.3	1,230	1,392	1,568	1,795	1,909	2,010	2,046	2,057	Macedonia
44.7	27.7	15.6	7.2	3.9	0.9	4,230	5,368	6,931	9,066	12,045	16,195	21,151	26,584	Madagascar
43.7	28.7	14.8	7.3	4.2	1.3	2,817	3,450	4,489	6,129	9,287	11,258	14,309	17,974	Malawi
33.0[2]	28.3[2]	21.0[2]	11.6[2]	4.9[2]	1.2[2]	6,110	8,140	10,853	13,763	17,845	23,259	28,382	32,446	Malaysia
40.9	28.6	17.2	7.2	5.1	1.0	79	92	115	155	215	271	318	368	Maldives
46.3	25.0	14.9	8.2	4.5	1.1	3,688	4,504	5,569	6,775	8,084	10,072	13,060	17,543	Mali
21.9	20.9	22.5	18.8	11.6	4.3	312	329	326	364	360	390	422	455	Malta
42.9	28.7	16.7	8.2	2.6	0.9	11	15	22	31	44	52	61	72	Marshall Islands
22.0	21.0	24.4	16.0	11.1	5.5	222	282	325	326	360	386	401	405	Martinique
43.9	27.0	15.9	7.7	4.3	1.2	825	1,001	1,262	1,609	2,030	2,645	3,520	4,473	Mauritania
25.2	26.0	24.8	14.9	6.8	2.3	479	662	829	966	1,059	1,187	1,298	1,384	Mauritius
42.0	29.0	17.0	7.0	——5.0——		17	25	35	52	89	147	216	292	Mayotte
34.3	28.5	19.5	10.5	5.3	1.9	27,737	36,940	50,611	68,046	84,296	100,088	113,271	124,652	Mexico
40.3	28.4	16.9	9.1	3.9	1.4	32	45	61	73	96	107	117	120	Micronesia
20.6[20, 38]	26.4[20, 38]	20.6[20, 38]	18.3[20, 38]	10.4[20, 38]	3.7[20, 38]	2,341	3,004	3,595	4,010	4,364	4,275	4,160	4,054	Moldova
13.2	13.4	22.1	22.4	17.4	11.5	18	21	24	27	30	32	33	35	Monaco
35.8	30.2	20.5	8.3	——5.2——		747	931	1,248	1,663	2,086	2,390	2,711	3,024	Mongolia
31.1[21, 40]	29.7[21, 40]	20.4[21, 40]	12.0[21, 40]	5.3[21, 40]	1.5[21, 40]	8,953	11,626	15,310	19,527	24,696	27,934	31,939	36,042	Morocco[39]
44.8	27.6	15.1	8.0	3.7	0.8	6,250	7,472	9,304	12,103	12,656	17,768	20,673	22,710	Mozambique
38.6	28.7	15.5	10.9	5.2	1.1	19,488	22,836	27,386	33,373	39,655	44,702	48,844	51,709	Myanmar (Burma)
42.7[6]	28.6[6]	15.5[6]	7.9[6]	3.9[6]	1.4[6]	464	591	765	1,058	1,471	1,906	2,077	2,087	Namibia
41.8[41]	25.0[41]	20.7[41]	8.2[41]	——2.8[41]——		3	4	7	8	9	10	11	12	Nauru
39.3	27.0	17.1	10.1	5.2	1.3	8,643	10,070	12,155	15,159	19,114	24,431	29,891	35,679	Nepal

Area and population   (continued)

country	area			population (latest estimate)					population (recent census)				
	square miles	square kilo-metres	rank	total midyear 2005	rank	density per sq mi	density per sq km	% annual growth rate 2000–05	census year	total	male (%)	female (%)	urban (%)
Netherlands, The	16,034	41,528	133	16,306,000	59	1,017.0	392.7	0.5	2001	15,985,538	49.5	50.5	89.6[6]
Netherlands Antilles	308	800	183	183,000	186	594.2	228.8	0.4	2001	175,653	47.0	53.0	69.3[6]
New Caledonia	7,172	18,575	154	237,000	182	33.0	12.8	2.0	1996	196,836	51.2	48.8	60.4
New Zealand	104,454	270,534	74	4,096,000	123	39.2	15.1	1.2	2001	3,912,000[42]	49.1[42]	50.9[42]	85.9[6]
Nicaragua	50,337	130,373	97	5,487,000	105	109.0	42.1	2.0	1995	4,357,099	49.3	50.7	54.4
Niger	459,286	1,189,546	22	12,163,000	67	26.5	10.2	3.0	2001	10,790,352	49.9	50.1	16.2
Nigeria	356,669	923,768	32	131,530,000	9	368.8	142.4	2.3	1991	88,514,501	50.3	49.7	35.0[43]
Northern Mariana Islands	176	457	194	80,400	200	456.8	175.9	2.9	2000	69,221	46.2	53.8	90.1
Norway	148,726[44]	385,199[44]	61	4,617,000	116	31.0	12.0	0.6	2001	4,520,947	49.6	50.4	76.5
Oman	119,500	309,500	71	2,409,000	140	20.2	7.8	1.6	2003	2,340,815	56.1	43.9	71.5
Pakistan[46]	307,374	796,096	36	153,960,000	6	500.9	193.4	1.9	1998	130,579,571	52.0	48.0	33.3
Palau	188	488	192	21,100	215	112.2	43.2	1.9	2000	19,129	54.6	45.4	69.5
Panama	28,973	75,040	118	3,140,000	131	108.4	41.8	1.7	2000	2,839,177	50.5	49.5	56.3
Papua New Guinea	178,704	462,840	54	5,887,000	103	32.9	12.7	2.1	2000	5,130,365	51.9	48.1	13.2[22]
Paraguay	157,048	406,752	59	5,905,000	102	37.6	14.5	2.2	2002	5,163,198	50.4	49.6	56.7
Peru	496,218	1,285,198	20	27,968,000	38	56.4	21.8	1.5	1993	22,639,443	49.7	50.3	70.1
Philippines	122,121[47]	316,294[47]	69	84,191,000	12	689.4	266.2	1.9	2000	76,504,077	50.4	49.6	58.5[2]
Poland	120,728	312,685	70	38,164,000	31	316.1	122.1	-0.2	2002	38,230,100	48.4	51.6	61.8
Portugal	35,580	92,152	111	10,513,000	75	295.5	114.1	0.3	2001	10,356,117[10]	48.3[10]	51.7[10]	65.8[6]
Puerto Rico	3,515	9,104	166	3,911,000	125	1,112.7	429.6	0.5	2000	3,808,610	48.1	51.9	94.6[2]
Qatar	4,412	11,427	161	773,000	160	175.2	67.6	4.6	2004	744,029	66.7	33.3	92.0[24]
Réunion	968	2,507	174	780,000	158	805.8	311.1	1.6	1999	706,300	49.1	50.9	82.7
Romania	92,043	238,391	82	21,602,000	50	234.7	90.6	-0.4	2002	21,680,974	48.7	51.3	52.7
Russia	6,592,800	17,075,400	1	143,420,000	7	21.8	8.4	-0.5	2002	145,164,000	46.6	53.3	73.3
Rwanda	10,169	26,338	147	8,574,000	87	843.2	325.5	2.1	2002	8,128,553	47.7	52.3	16.9
St. Kitts and Nevis	104	269	205	46,600	211	448.1	173.2	0.4	2001	46,111	49.7	50.3	34.2[6]
St. Lucia	238	617	189	161,000	189	676.5	260.9	0.9	2001	151,156	48.9	51.1	38.0[6]
St. Vincent and the Grenadines	150	389	198	119,000	191	793.3	305.9	0.5	1991	106,499	49.9	50.1	24.6
Samoa	1,093	2,831	172	185,000	185	169.3	65.3	0.9	2001	176,710	52.1	47.9	22.0
San Marino	24	61	212	30,100	214	1,254.2	493.4	2.4	2003[3,4]	28,753	48.9	51.1	88.7[24]
São Tomé and Príncipe	386	1,001	181	157,000	190	406.7	156.8	2.3	2001	137,599	49.6	50.4	47.7[6]
Saudi Arabia	830,000	2,149,690	14	23,230,000	46	28.0	10.8	2.9	2004	22,673,538	55.4	44.6	87.7[24]
Senegal	75,955	196,722	87	11,706,000	70	154.1	59.5	2.5	2002	9,956,202	49.1	50.9	49.6[24]
Serbia and Montenegro	39,449	102,173	107	9,960,000	80	252.5	97.5	-0.2	2002	7,498,001[49]	48.6[49]	51.4[49]	56.4[49]
Seychelles	176	455	195	82,800	199	470.5	182.0	0.4	2002	81,177	49.8	50.2	64.6[6]
Sierra Leone	27,699	71,740	119	5,018,000	112	181.2	69.9	1.9	2004	4,963,298	48.6	51.4	38.8[24]
Singapore	270	699	188	4,291,000[52]	119	15,892.6	6,138.8	1.3	2000[10]	3,263,209	50.0	50.0	100.0
Slovakia	18,933	49,035	129	5,384,000	108	284.4	109.8	-0.1	2001	5,379,455	48.6	51.4	55.0
Slovenia	7,827	20,273	153	1,999,000	145	255.4	98.6	0.1	2002	1,964,036	48.8	51.2	50.8
Solomon Islands	10,954	28,370	143	471,000	168	43.0	16.6	2.5	1999	409,042	51.7	48.3	15.6
Somalia	246,000	637,000	42	8,228,000	90	33.4	12.9	3.2	1975	4,089,203	50.1	49.9	25.4
South Africa	471,011	1,219,912	25	46,888,000	27	99.5	38.4	1.0	2001	44,819,778	47.8	52.2	57.7[6]
Spain	195,379	506,030	51	44,079,000	28	225.6	87.1	1.8	2001	40,847,371	49.0	51.0	77.8[6]
Sri Lanka	25,332	65,610	122	20,743,000	51	818.8	316.2	0.9	2001	16,864,544[53]	49.5[53]	50.5[53]	14.6[53]
Sudan, The	966,757	2,503,890	10	36,233,000	33	37.5	14.5	1.9	1993	24,940,683	50.2	49.8	31.3[15]
Suriname	63,251	163,820	91	493,000	165	7.8	3.0	1.4	2004	487,024	50.4	49.6	76.1[24]
Swaziland	6,704	17,364	157	1,032,000	154	153.9	59.4	0.2	1997	929,718	47.3	52.7	23.1
Sweden	173,860	450,295	56	9,024,000	84	51.9	20.0	0.3	2003[3,4]	8,940,788	49.5	50.5	84.0
Switzerland	15,940	41,284	134	7,519,000	95	471.7	182.1	0.8	2000[56]	7,288,010	49.0	51.0	68.0
Syria	71,498	185,180	88	17,794,000	56	248.9	96.1	2.4	1994	13,782,315	51.1	48.9	52.2[15]
Taiwan	13,972	36,188	136	22,726,000	47	1,626.5	628.0	0.5	2000[10]	22,300,929	51.1	48.9	80.0[2]
Tajikistan	55,300	143,100	95	6,849,000	99	123.9	47.9	2.1	2000	6,127,493	50.3	49.7	26.6
Tanzania	364,901	945,090	31	36,766,000	32	100.8	38.9	2.1	2002	34,569,232	48.9	51.1	23.0
Thailand	198,117	513,120	50	64,186,000	19	324.0	125.1	0.7	2000	60,617,200	49.2	50.8	31.1
Togo	21,925	56,785	125	5,400,000	107	246.3	95.1	2.8	1981	2,719,567	48.7	51.3	15.2
Tonga	290	750	185	98,600	195	340.0	131.5	0.1	1996[10]	97,784	50.7	49.3	32.1
Trinidad and Tobago	1,980	5,128	169	1,298,000	152	655.6	253.1	0.5	2000	1,262,366	50.1	49.9	74.1[2]
Tunisia	63,170	163,610	92	10,038,000	79	158.9	61.4	1.0	2004	9,910,872	50.1	49.9	64.9
Turkey	302,535	783,562	37	72,083,000	16	238.3	92.0	1.3	2000	67,803,927	50.7	49.3	65.0
Turkmenistan	188,500	488,100	52	4,833,000	113	25.6	9.9	1.4	1995	4,483,251	49.6	50.4	46.0
Tuvalu	9.9	25.6	215	9,700	217	979.8	378.9	0.6	2002	9,561	49.5	50.5	47.0
Uganda	93,065	241,038	80	27,269,000	40	293.0	113.1	3.2	2002	24,442,084	48.8	51.2	12.3
Ukraine	233,062	603,628	44	47,075,000	25	202.0	78.0	-0.9	2001	48,457,102	46.3	53.7	67.2
United Arab Emirates	32,280	83,600	115	4,690,000	114	145.3	56.1	7.6	1995	2,411,041	66.6	33.4	77.3
United Kingdom	93,635	242,514	79	60,020,000	21	641.0	247.5	0.4	2001	58,789,194	48.6	51.4	89.5[6]
United States	3,676,487[59]	9,522,057[59]	4	296,748,000	3	80.7	31.2	1.0	2000	281,421,906	49.1	50.9	79.0
Uruguay	68,037	176,215	90	3,256,000	130	47.9	18.5	0.3	2004	3,241,003	48.3	51.7	91.8
Uzbekistan	172,700	447,400	57	26,593,000	43	154.0	59.4	1.5	1989	19,905,158	49.3	50.7	40.7
Vanuatu	4,707	12,190	160	211,000	183	44.8	17.3	2.0	1999	186,678	51.3	48.7	21.5
Venezuela	353,841	916,445	33	26,749,000	42	75.6	29.2	1.8	2001	23,054,210	49.5	50.5	87.2[6]
Vietnam	127,121	329,241	67	82,628,000	13	650.0	251.0	1.3	1999	76,323,173	49.1	50.9	23.7
Virgin Islands (U.S.)	136	352	201	109,000	193	801.5	309.7	0.0	2000	108,612	47.8	52.2	92.6[2]
West Bank[60]	2,270	5,900	167	2,632,000[61,62]	138[61]	1,159.5[61]	446.1[61]	3.5[61]	1997[63]	1,600,100[63]	50.9[63]	49.1[63]	60.9[63]
Western Sahara	97,344	252,120	77	341,000	175	3.5	1.4	2.6	...	...	...	...	...
Yemen	214,300	555,000	48	20,043,000	53	93.5	36.1	3.1	2004	19,721,643	53.0	47.0	25.6[24]
Zambia	290,585	752,612	39	11,262,000	73	38.8	15.0	2.2	2000	9,885,591	50.0	50.0	34.7
Zimbabwe	150,872	390,757	60	12,161,000	68	80.6	31.1	0.7	2002	11,634,663	48.4	51.6	34.9[24]

[1]Settled population only. [2]2000 estimate. [3]Civil register not a census. [4]Beginning of year. [5]Preliminary, variant figure. [6]2001 estimate. [7]1999 estimate. [8]Unadjusted for undercount. [9]Preliminary figure. [10]Data are for de jure population. [11]1991 estimate. [12]Beginning of 2002 estimate based on 2001 census. [13]1996 estimate. [14]2003 estimate based on adjusted 2001 census. [15]1995 estimate. [16]1998 estimate. [17]Data are for the island of Cyprus (excepting census information). [18]Republic of Cyprus only. [19]End of 2001 estimate based on 2001 census. [20]2004 estimate. [21]2005 projection. [22]Rounded percentage of 2001 census. [23]1994 estimate. [24]2003 estimate. [25]1993 estimate. [26]Official Palestinian estimate. Mid-2005 population based on an unofficial demographic survey released in January 2005 equals 1,086,000. [27]Includes Abkhazia and South Ossetia. [28]Excludes about 230,000 people in Abkhazia and South Ossetia. [29]Combined percentage for Guernsey and Jersey. [30]2002 estimate. [31]1997 estimate. [32]Area figures exclude the West Bank and the Gaza Strip. [33]Population figures (unless otherwise indicated) exclude Israelis in the West Bank and the Gaza Strip. [34]Census data include Israelis in the West Bank and the Gaza Strip. [35]Derived figure from sample survey. [36]Includes unknown. [37]De facto population excluding Transnistria. [38]Includes Moldovans abroad and the population of Transnistria. [39]Excludes Western Sahara, an annexure of Morocco, unless otherwise indicated. [40]Includes Western Sahara. [41]1992 census. [42]End of 2001

age distribution (%)						population (by decade, '000s)								country
0–14	15–29	30–44	45–59	60–74	75 and over	1950	1960	1970	1980	1990	2000	2010 projection	2020 projection	
18.6	18.8	24.3	20.0	12.2	6.1	10,090	11,494	13,020	14,150	14,952	15,926	16,500	16,800	Netherlands, The
24.2	18.2	25.5	19.0	9.4	3.7	112	136	163	174	188	179	188	198	Netherlands Antilles
30.7	27.2	21.3	13.3	5.9	1.6	65	78	105	143	171	215	257	296	New Caledonia
22.5[42]	20.4[42]	23.0[42]	18.0[42]	10.7[42]	5.4[42]	1,909	2,377	2,820	3,144	3,452	3,850	4,258	4,564	New Zealand
45.1	27.5	15.0	7.2	3.7	1.4	1,190	1,617	2,228	3,067	3,960	4,959	6,066	7,179	Nicaragua
47.8[6]	26.5[6]	14.2[6]	7.9[6]	3.1[6]	0.5[6]	3,271	3,913	4,841	6,119	7,945	10,516	14,054	18,457	Niger
45.5[11]	26.0[11]	15.3[11]	8.8[11]	3.8[11]	0.6[11]	32,769	40,866	51,857	68,447	90,557	117,608	145,991	175,798	Nigeria
22.5	31.8	32.3	10.7	2.3	0.4	6	9	12	17	44	70	91	109	Northern Mariana Islands
20.0[45]	18.8[45]	22.4[45]	19.6[45]	11.4[45]	7.8[45]	3,265	3,581	3,877	4,086	4,241	4,491	4,735	4,989	Norway
33.8	32.3	20.8	8.9	3.2	1.0	456	565	747	1,187	1,843	2,225	2,667	3,269	Oman
43.2	26.9	15.6	8.8	4.3	1.2	39,448	50,387	65,706	85,219	109,710	139,960	169,153	204,184	Pakistan[46]
23.9	24.2	29.9	14.2	5.5	2.3	7	9	12	13	15	19	23	29	Palau
32.0	26.8	20.6	12.0	6.1	2.5	893	1,148	1,531	1,956	2,390	2,889	3,393	3,877	Panama
38.8[2]	28.7[2]	17.1[2]	9.7[2]	4.7[2]	1.0[2]	1,798	2,080	2,554	3,241	4,114	5,299	6,450	7,602	Papua New Guinea
37.1	27.3	17.9	10.6	5.1	2.0	1,488	1,842	2,350	3,114	4,219	5,289	6,609	8,010	Paraguay
37.0	28.6	17.7	9.8	——7.0——		7,632	9,931	13,193	17,324	21,753	25,952	30,063	34,250	Peru
37.0	27.6	19.1	10.3	4.7	1.3	20,988	27,561	36,850	48,286	60,937	76,803	91,280	104,680	Philippines
18.3[48]	24.6[48]	20.6[48]	20.1[48]	11.5[48]	4.9[48]	24,824	29,561	32,526	35,578	38,057	38,454	37,763	37,102	Poland
17.0[6]	22.5[6]	21.7[6]	18.1[6]	14.4[6]	6.3[6]	8,443	9,037	9,044	9,778	9,923	10,336	10,643	10,744	Portugal
23.8	23.3	20.4	17.1	10.6	4.8	2,218	2,358	2,722	3,210	3,537	3,816	3,985	4,076	Puerto Rico
22.5	25.0	34.4	15.6	2.2	0.3	47	59	151	229	423	617	869	1,007	Qatar
27.0	24.8	24.4	13.8	7.2	2.8	244	338	447	507	601	722	834	927	Réunion
17.6	23.4	21.0	18.7	14.4	4.9	16,311	18,407	20,253	22,201	23,207	22,072	21,239	20,265	Romania
16.7[30]	23.4[30]	22.4[30]	18.7[30]	14.0[30]	4.8[30]	101,937	119,632	130,245	139,039	147,974	146,732	140,771	134,386	Russia
43.8	30.1	14.7	7.1	3.3	1.0	2,162	2,887	3,776	5,197	7,096	7,718	9,605	11,718	Rwanda
30.7[2]	26.5[2]	21.1[2]	10.8[2]	——10.9[2]——		49	51	46	44	41	46	48	53	St. Kitts and Nevis
31.2	27.4	20.6	10.7	——10.1——		83	90	104	118	138	154	168	180	St. Lucia
37.2	29.5	16.1	8.3	6.4	2.5	67	81	90	100	109	116	122	125	St. Vincent and the Grenadines
40.8	25.6	17.9	9.2	5.0	1.5	82	110	142	155	161	177	189	190	Samoa
14.1	16.6	27.3	19.7	14.2	8.1	13	15	19	21	23	27	32	35	San Marino
42.1	30.3	14.5	6.9	4.7	1.5	60	64	74	94	117	140	174	209	São Tomé and Príncipe
38.3[20]	29.8[20]	22.7[20]	5.7[20]	2.7[20]	0.8[20]	3,201	4,075	5,745	9,604	16,379	20,160	26,230	33,440	Saudi Arabia
42.4	28.5	15.8	8.6	3.9	0.8	2,654	3,270	4,318	5,776	7,844	10,324	13,109	15,816	Senegal
15.8[49]	20.3[49]	20.1[49]	21.2[49]	17.3[49]	5.3[49]	7,131	8,050	8,691	9,522	10,156	10,038	9,935	9,799	Serbia and Montenegro
25.5[50]	26.3[50]	25.0[50]	12.8[50]	7.1[50]	3.3[50]	34	42	54	63	70	81	85	88	Seychelles
41.7[51]	27.1[51]	16.7[51]	8.0[51]	4.3[51]	2.2[51]	1,944	2,256	2,697	3,236	4,078	4,556	5,570	7,030	Sierra Leone
21.5	21.2	28.4	18.2	8.2	2.5	1,022	1,646	2,075	2,414	3,047	4,018	4,555	4,948	Singapore
18.9	25.1	21.5	18.9	11.0	4.6	3,463	4,145	4,528	4,976	5,256	5,401	5,401	5,417	Slovakia
15.3	21.5	22.7	20.5	14.4	5.6	1,467	1,580	1,727	1,901	1,998	1,990	2,010	2,016	Slovenia
44.6[7]	29.0[7]	14.3[7]	7.5[7]	3.7[7]	0.9[7]	107	126	163	232	315	416	530	645	Solomon Islands
45.6	24.9	15.5	7.4	——5.4——		2,264	2,820	3,601	6,487	6,674	7,012	9,590	12,336	Somalia
32.0	29.5	20.2	11.0	5.5	1.8	13,683	17,396	22,657	29,140	37,450	44,510	47,271	47,549	South Africa
14.5	22.4	23.7	17.8	14.2	7.4	27,868	30,303	33,779	37,636	38,798	40,264	46,415	49,779	Spain
26.0[54]	27.5[54]	22.3[54]	14.5[54]	7.3[54]	2.4[54]	7,782	10,066	12,734	15,235	17,786	19,848	21,557	22,902	Sri Lanka
43.0	27.0	16.4	9.3	3.7	0.6	9,190	11,513	14,699	19,970	26,066	32,902	40,254	47,536	Sudan, The
30.0[55]	26.1[55]	22.5[55]	12.6[55]	——8.8[55]——		215	290	372	356	402	461	507	525	Suriname
44.3	28.6	14.4	7.7	3.4	1.6	273	353	454	616	865	1,023	1,010	983	Swaziland
18.0	18.1	20.8	20.6	13.6	8.9	7,014	7,480	8,042	8,310	8,559	8,872	9,220	9,643	Sweden
17.1[57]	18.0[57]	24.3[57]	20.1[57]	13.2[57]	7.3[57]	4,694	5,362	6,187	6,319	6,834	7,209	7,761	8,269	Switzerland
44.8	28.3	14.7	7.2	——5.0——		3,495	4,533	6,258	8,774	12,436	15,837	19,901	23,831	Syria
21.2	25.5	25.4	15.9	9.0	3.0	7,619	10,668	14,583	17,642	20,279	22,185	23,137	23,931	Taiwan
39.4	27.7	18.4	7.6	5.4	1.5	1,532	2,082	2,942	3,953	5,303	6,188	7,360	8,648	Tajikistan
44.3	27.7	15.3	7.1	4.1	1.5	7,935	10,260	13,807	18,715	25,138	33,065	40,382	48,824	Tanzania
24.1	25.6	25.9	15.0	7.5	1.9	20,041	27,513	37,091	47,026	55,197	61,863	66,303	69,466	Thailand
49.8	24.8	13.1	6.8	3.3	2.0	1,172	1,456	1,964	2,481	3,505	4,712	6,185	8,000	Togo
39.1	28.0	15.1	10.0	6.0	1.8	50	65	80	92	96	98	99	99	Tonga
25.5[58]	27.5[58]	22.6[58]	14.5[58]	7.2[58]	2.7[58]	668	828	941	1,082	1,235	1,263	1,316	1,337	Trinidad and Tobago
26.0[20]	29.9[20]	22.7[20]	12.2[20]	7.0[20]	2.2[20]	3,517	4,149	5,099	6,443	8,154	9,564	10,544	11,509	Tunisia
29.1[2]	28.8[2]	21.5[2]	11.8[2]	6.8[2]	2.0[2]	21,122	28,217	35,758	44,439	56,098	67,418	76,926	85,490	Turkey
40.1[15]	27.1[15]	18.8[15]	7.9[15]	4.9[15]	1.2[15]	1,211	1,594	2,189	2,861	3,668	4,502	5,163	5,811	Turkmenistan
36.2	21.2	20.2	13.8	6.8	1.8	5	5	6	8	9	9	11	12	Tuvalu
49.3	27.3	13.4	5.6	3.3	1.1	5,522	7,262	9,728	12,297	17,074	23,249	32,500	47,134	Uganda
17.0[22]	22.0[22]	21.0[22]	18.5[22]	15.5[22]	6.0[22]	36,906	42,783	47,317	50,034	51,892	49,235	44,692	40,115	Ukraine
26.3	29.2	33.2	9.6	1.4	0.3	70	90	223	1,042	1,844	3,247	5,252	6,409	United Arab Emirates
18.9	18.8	22.6	18.9	13.3	7.5	50,290	52,372	55,632	56,330	57,237	58,886	61,170	63,587	United Kingdom
21.4	20.8	23.3	18.2	10.4	5.9	152,271	180,671	204,879	227,726	249,806	282,402	310,720	336,766	United States
23.9	22.9	19.5	16.0	11.8	5.9	2,194	2,531	2,824	2,920	3,106	3,205	3,307	3,413	Uruguay
40.8	28.4	15.0	9.3	4.7	1.8	6,314	8,559	11,973	15,952	20,515	24,724	28,578	32,515	Uzbekistan
42.2	26.9	17.0	8.8	3.7	1.4	48	64	86	117	149	191	232	273	Vanuatu
33.1	27.5	20.7	11.7	5.1	1.9	5,094	7,579	10,721	15,091	19,735	24,418	29,076	33,450	Venezuela
33.1	28.5	21.2	9.2	6.0	2.0	27,367	33,648	42,898	53,005	66,074	77,635	86,860	95,294	Vietnam
26.1	19.4	21.2	20.5	9.8	3.0	27	32	63	100	104	109	108	107	Virgin Islands (U.S.)
45.0[63]	27.7[63]	15.1[63]	6.6[63]	4.2[63]	1.4[63]	...	...	608[61]	733[61]	1,011[61]	2,211[61]	3,011[61]	3,747[61]	West Bank[60]
...	...	...	...	...	...	14	33	76	151	218	300	429	627	Western Sahara
46.4[21]	28.6[21]	13.7[21]	7.6[21]	3.0[21]	0.7[21]	4,316	5,223	6,337	8,197	12,086	17,238	23,414	31,279	Yemen
47.0[2]	30.0[2]	12.9[2]	5.9[2]	3.4[2]	0.8[2]	2,553	3,254	4,252	5,700	7,942	10,117	12,497	15,105	Zambia
40.0[30]	32.3[30]	15.2[30]	7.4[30]	4.0[30]	1.1[30]	2,853	4,011	5,515	7,170	10,153	11,751	12,516	12,902	Zimbabwe

estimate based on 2001 adjusted census figures (including residents temporarily abroad). [43]1990 estimate. [44]Includes Svalbard and Jan Mayen. [45]Mean figures for 2002. [46]Excludes Afghan refugees (January 2005; c. 950,000) and the area and population (2005; 4.35 million) of Pakistan-occupied Jammu and Kashmir. [47]Sum of regional ("administrative subdivision") areas; actual total area may be different. [48]Percentages derived from 2002 census population graph. [49]Excludes Montenegro and Kosovo (Kosova). [50]2003 estimate based on 2002 census. [51]Based on 2003 pilot census of 142,550 individuals. [52]De facto population. [53]Excludes 7 districts experiencing civil war whose 2001 estimated population equaled 1,867,711. [54]2001 estimate for entire country. [55]Excludes unknown accounting for 2.0% of total population. [56]Includes resident aliens; excludes seasonal workers. [57]Beginning of 2002 estimate based on 2000 census. [58]Based on known census population by age of 1,114,772. [59]Includes inland water area of 78,797 sq mi (204,083 sq km) and Great Lakes water area of 60,251 sq mi (156,049 sq km); excludes coastal water area of 42,241 sq mi (109,404 sq km) and territorial water area of 75,372 sq mi (195,213 sq km). [60]Excludes East Jerusalem. [61]Based on official Palestinian estimate; Israeli Jews living in the West Bank are included. [62]Mid-2005 estimated Palestinian Arab population only based on an unofficial demographic survey released in January 2005 equals 1,371,000. [63]Census total not adjusted for undercount; excludes Israeli Jews.

Major cities and national capitals

The following table lists the principal cities or municipalities (those exceeding 100,000 in population [75,000 for Anglo-America, Australia, and the United Kingdom]) of the countries of the world, together with figures for each national capital (indicated by a ★), regardless of size.

Most of the populations given refer to a so-called city proper, that is, a legally defined, incorporated, or chartered area defined by administrative boundaries and by national or state law. In some instances, where cities proper do not exist or are not strictly demarcated, populations of locally defined urban areas may be used. In a few cases, data refer to the municipality, or commune, similar to the medieval city-state in that the city is governed together with its immediately adjoining, economically dependent areas, whether urban or rural in nature. Some countries define no other demographic or legal entities within such communes or municipalities, but many identify a centre, seat, head (cabecera), or locality that corresponds to the most densely populated, compact, contiguous core of the municipality. Figures referring to municipalities or communes may be given (identified by the abbreviation "MU"), even though the country itself may define a smaller, more closely knit city proper.

Populations for urban agglomerations as defined by the United Nations are occasionally inset beneath the populations of cities proper. Specifically that is when the urban agglomeration populations are at least three times the size of cities proper.

For certain countries, more than one form of the name of the city is given, usually to permit recognition of recent place-name changes or of forms of the place-name likely to be encountered in press stories if the title of the city's entry in the Encyclopædia Britannica is spelled according to a different romanization or spelling policy.

Chinese names for China are usually given in their Pinyin spelling, the official Chinese system encountered in official documents and maps. For Taiwan, the Wade-Giles spelling of place-names is used.

Sources for this data were often national censuses and statistical abstracts of the countries concerned, supplemented by Internet sources.

Internet sources for further information
- City Population: http://www.citypopulation.de/cities.html
- The World Gazetteer: http://www.gazetteer.de/st/stata.htm

Major cities and national capitals

country / city	population
Afghanistan (2003 est.)	
Herāt	254,800
★ Kabul	700,000[1]
agglomeration	2,799,300
Kandahār	
(Qandahār)	323,900
Mazār-e Sharīf	187,700
Albania (2001)	
★ Tiranë	354,304
Algeria (2004 est.)	
★ Algiers	1,790,700
Annaba	410,700
Batna	285,800
Béchar	154,400
Bejaïa	173,300
Biskra (Beskra)	201,500
Blida (el-Boulaida)	180,400
Bordj Bou Arreridj	151,500
Constantine	
(Qacentina)	544,700
Djelfa	181,800
Ech-Cheliff (el-Asnam)	157,800
El-Eulma	123,900
El-Wad	123,500
Ghilizane	122,900
Guelma	128,100
Jijel	124,900
Khenchela	125,000
Médéa	145,600
Mostaganem	146,600
Oran (Wahran)	772,900
Saïda	130,600
Sétif (Stif)	249,700
Sidi bel Abbès	212,400
Skikda	179,500
Souq Ahras	136,600
Tébessa (Tbessa)	180,600
Tihert	171,300
Tlemcen (Tilimsen)	141,600
Wargla (Ouargla)	139,900
American Samoa (2000)	
★ Fagatogo (legislative and judicial)	2,096[2]
★ Utulei (executive)	807[2]
Andorra (2002)	
★ Andorra la Vella	20,787
Angola (2004 est.)	
Huambo	173,600
★ Luanda	2,783,000
Antigua and Barbuda (2004)	
★ Saint John's	23,600
Argentina (2001)	
Almirante Brown	513,777
Avellaneda	329,638
Bahía Blanca	280,729
Belén de Escobar	172,494
Berazategui	287,642
★ Buenos Aires	2,768,772
agglomeration	11,453,725
Caseros	335,578
Catamarca	140,556
Comodoro Rivadavia	135,813
Concordia	137,046

country / city	population
Córdoba	1,267,774
Corrientes	314,247
Esteban Echeverría	243,715
Ezeiza	118,080
Florencio Varela	343,238
Formosa	198,146
General San Martín	405,122
Godoy Cruz	182,555
Hurlingham	171,724
Ituzaingo	157,769
José Carlos Paz	229,760
La Plata	553,002
La Rioja	143,921
Lanús	452,513
Las Heras	168,410
Lomas de Zamora	590,667
Mar del Plata	541,857
Mendoza	110,716
Merlo	468,734
Moreno	379,801
Morón	309,086
Neuquén	201,729
Paraná	235,931
Pilar	228,724
Posadas	253,389
Quilmes	518,723
Resistencia	274,001
Río Cuarto	144,140
Rosario	906,004
Salta	462,668
San Fernando	147,409
San Isidro	293,213
San Juan	115,556
San Justo (La Matanza)	1,253,858
San Luis	152,918
San Miguel	253,133
San Miguel de Tucumán	535,883
San Nicolás de los Arroyos	125,308
San Rafael	104,782
San Salvador de Jujuy	230,999
Santa Fe	368,369
Santiago del Estero	230,424
Tandil	100,869
Tigre	295,561
Vicente López	273,802
Villa Krause	102,099
Villa Nueva	222,951
Armenia (2002 est.)	
Gyumri (Kumayri; Leninakan)	210,100
★ Yerevan	1,246,100
Aruba (2000)	
★ Oranjestad	26,355
Australia (2001)[3]	
Adelaide	1,002,127
Brisbane	1,508,161
Cairns	98,981
★ Canberra	339,727
Geelong	130,194
Gold Coast	421,557
Gosford	255,429
Hobart	126,048
Melbourne	3,160,171
Newcastle	279,975
Perth	1,176,542

country / city	population
Sunshine Coast	169,931
Sydney	3,502,301
Toowoomba	89,338
Townsville	119,504
Wollongong	228,846
Austria (2001)	
Graz	226,244
Innsbruck	113,392
Linz	183,504
Salzburg	142,662
★ Vienna	1,550,123
Azerbaijan (2001 est.)	
★ Baku (Baky)	1,817,900
Gäncä (Gyandzha)	301,400
Sumqayit (Sumgait)	288,400
Bahamas, The (2000)	
★ Nassau	210,832[4]
Bahrain (2001)	
★ Al-Manāmah	143,035
Bangladesh (2001)	
Barisal	202,242
Bogra	150,138
Brahmanbaria	131,334
Chittagong	2,199,500
Comilla	168,378
★ Dhaka (Dacca)	5,644,235
Dinajpur	157,303
Jamalpur	116,764
Jessore	178,273
Khulna	811,490
Kotwali	285,308
Madhabdi	126,736
Mymensingh	225,811
Naogaon	123,101
Narayanganj	241,694
Nawabganj (Nowabganj)	153,252
Pabna	116,371
Rajshahi	402,646
Rangpur	251,699
Saidpur	110,151
Shailakupa	317,881
Sirajganj	127,147
Tangail	128,543
Tongi	295,883
Barbados (1990)	
★ Bridgetown	6,070
agglomeration	140,000[5]
Belarus (2004 est.)	
Babruysk	228,100
Baranavichy	176,600
Barysaw	155,700
Brest	294,400
Homyel	497,200
Hrodna	315,500
Mahilyow	365,400
Mazyr	109,400
★ Minsk	1,682,900
Orsha	123,800
Pinsk	136,200
Salihorsk	101,900
Vitsyebsk	355,200
Belgium (2002 est.)	
Antwerp	448,709
Brugge (Bruges)	116,836

country / city	population
★ Brussels	136,730
agglomeration	978,384
Charleroi	200,578
Ghent	226,220
Liège (Luik)	185,131
Namur	105,393
Schaerbeek	107,736
Belize (2004 est.)	
★ Belmopan	12,300
Benin (2000 est.)	
★ Cotonou (official)	650,660
Djougou	134,099[6]
Parakou	144,627
★ Porto-Novo (de facto)	232,756
Bermuda (2000)	
★ Hamilton	969
Bhutan (2002 est.)	
★ Thimphu	45,000
Bolivia (2001)	
Cochabamba	516,683
El Alto	647,350
★ La Paz (administrative)	789,585
Oruro	201,230
Potosí	132,966
Quillacollo	119,961
Santa Cruz	1,116,059
★ Sucre (judicial)	193,873
Tarija	135,783
Bosnia and Herzegovina (2003 est.)	
Banja Luka	170,000
★ Sarajevo	380,000
Botswana (2001)	
★ Gaborone	186,007
Brazil (2003 est.)	
Águas Lindas de Goiás	131,900
Alagoinhas	116,000
Alvorada	196,200
Americana	191,000
Ananindeua	436,100
Anápolis	290,000
Angra dos Reis	124,200
Aparecida de Goiânia	384,100
Apucarana	103,900
Aracaju	479,800
Araçatuba	169,400
Araguaina	112,500
Arapiraca	157,800
Araraquara	180,400
Araras	102,700
Atibaia	103,600
Barbacena	107,600
Barra Mansa	167,300
Barreiras	108,500
Barretos	101,400
Barueri	232,200
Bauru	327,100
Belém	1,333,500
Belford Roxo	457,200
Belo Horizonte	2,305,800
Betim	338,900
Blumenau	256,100

country / city	population
Boa Vista	217,200
Botucatu	109,200
Bragança Paulista	118,000
★ Brasília	2,094,100
Cabo (de Santo Agostinho)	141,500
Cabo Frio	119,800
Cachoeirinha	113,500
Cachoeiro de Itapemirim	164,000
Camaçari	168,500
Camaragibe	137,700
Campina Grande	347,200
Campinas	990,100
Campo Grande	697,800
Campos dos Goytacazes	372,600
Canoas	317,400
Carapicuíba	363,400
Cariacica	327,800
Caruaru	228,000
Cascavel	243,700
Castanhal	130,300
Catanduva	108,800
Caucaia	249,800
Caxias	104,900
Caxias do Sul	353,000
Chapecó	144,600
Colombo	194,200
Conselheiro Lafaiete	103,600
Contagem	560,300
Cotia	161,800
Criciúma	159,700
Cubatão	112,900
Cuiabá	501,000
Curitiba	1,671,200
Diadema	373,000
Divinópolis	187,700
Dourados	158,000
Duque de Caxias	805,400
Embu	223,600
Feira de Santana	452,300
Ferraz	155,300
Florianópolis	358,200
Fortaleza	2,256,200
Foz do Iguaçu	277,400
Franca	298,700
Francisco Morato	148,900
Franco de Rocha	106,900
Garanhuns	107,300
Goiânia	1,138,600
Governador Valadares	241,000
Gravataí	226,600
Guarapuava	147,000
Guaratinguetá	102,600
Guarujá	281,500
Guarulhos	1,135,500
Hortolândia	173,100
Ibirité	149,200
Ilhéus	161,800
Imperatriz	219,500
Indaiatuba	158,700
Ipatinga	220,800
Itaboraí	190,500
Itabuna	194,600
Itajaí	150,200
Itapecerica da Serra	141,800
Itapetininga	118,700
Itapevi	179,200
Itaquaquecetuba	306,200
Itu	131,900
Jaboatão	596,900
Jacareí	191,500

country city	population
Jandira	100,800
Jaraguá do Sul	104,900
Jaú	112,500
Jequié	131,000
João Pessoa	628,800
Joinville	445,900
Juàzeiro	144,000
Juàzeiro do Norte	213,600
Juiz de Fora	474,600
Jundiaí	310,000
Lages	157,800
Lauro de Freitas	121,400
Limeira	250,500
Londrina	453,000
Luziânia	147,900
Macaé	137,200
Macapá	304,500
Maceió	847,700
Magé	206,100
Manaus	1,517,500
Marabá	145,300
Maracanaú	186,100
Marília	200,400
Maringá	298,600
Mauá	384,500
Mesquita	174,000
Mogi Guaçu	122,900
Moji das Cruzes	318,200
Montes Claros	305,700
Mossoró	205,300
Natal	744,800
Nilópolis	152,400
Niterói	466,600
Nossa Senhora de Socorro	151,000
Nova Friburgo	153,600
Nova Iguaçu	792,200
Novo Hamburgo	241,200
Olinda	368,600
Osasco	678,600
Palhoça	108,000
Palmas	168,200
Paranaguá	130,600
Parnaíba	129,500
Parnamirim	125,700
Passo Fundo	171,800
Patos de Minas	117,100
Paulista	277,900
Pelotas	308,700
Petrolina	179,400
Petrópolis	279,700
Pindamonhangaba	126,100
Pinhais	109,000
Piracicaba	332,400
Poá	100,600
Poços de Caldas	138,400
Ponta Grossa	279,400
Porto Alegre	1,353,300
Porto Velho	289,500
Pouso Alegre	104,800
Praia Grande	215,200
Presidente Prudente	192,400
Queimados	129,100
Recife	1,461,300
Resende	101,800
Ribeirão das Neves	276,900
Ribeirão Pires	110,500
Ribeirão Preto	525,500
Rio Branco	245,500
Rio Claro	172,500
Rio de Janeiro	5,974,100
Rio Grande	183,400
Rio Verde	113,500
Rondonópolis	149,500
Sabará	120,400
Salvador	2,555,400
Santa Bárbara d'Oeste	175,500
Santa Luzia	198,700
Santa Maria	241,100
Santa Rita	106,200
Santarém	190,300
Santo André	659,300
Santos	415,900
São Bernardo do Campo	732,200
São Caetano do Sul	137,300
São Carlos	193,600
São Gonçalo	925,400
São João de Meriti	456,800
São José	182,600
São José do Rio Prêto	359,600
São José dos Campos	562,200
São José dos Pinhais	204,600
São Leopoldo	200,800
São Luís	889,100
São Paulo	10,041,500
São Vicente	314,200
Sapucaia do Sul	127,300
Serra	350,000

country city	population
Sete Lagoas	193,100
Sobral	141,900
Sorocaba	521,500
Sumaré	210,900
Susano (Suzano)	242,300
Taboão da Serra	209,200
Taubaté	240,600
Teixeira de Freitas	104,900
Teófilo Otoni	102,200
Teresina	711,700
Teresopolis	119,700
Timon	119,000
Uberaba	257,500
Uberlândia	529,300
Uruguaiana	122,200
Valparaíso de Goiás	107,000
Varginha	110,300
Várzea Grande	227,400
Várzea Paulista	100,200
Viamão	225,000
Vila Velha	369,300
Vitória	302,600
Vitória da Conquista	235,400
Volta Redonda	248,700
Brunei (2001)	
★ Bandar Seri Begawan	27,285
Bulgaria (2001)	
Burgas	193,316
Dobrich	100,379
Pleven	122,149
Plovdiv	340,638
Ruse	162,128
Sliven	100,695
★ Sofia	1,096,389
Stara Zagora	143,989
Varna	314,539
Burkina Faso (1996)	
Bobo Dioulasso	309,711
★ Ouagadougou	709,736
Burundi (2001 est.)	
★ Bujumbura	346,000
Cambodia (2001 est.)	
★ Phnom Penh	1,109,000
Cameroon (1992)	
Bafoussam	147,580
Bamenda	160,493
Douala	1,048,915
Garoua	203,799
Maroua	162,479
Nkongsamba	107,211
★ Yaoundé	903,649
Canada (2001)	
Abbotsford	115,463
Barrie	103,710
Brampton	325,428
Brantford	86,417
Burlington	150,836
Burnaby	193,954
Calgary	878,866
Cambridge	110,372
Cape Breton[7]	105,968
Chatham-Kent	107,341
Coquitlam	112,890
Delta[7]	96,950
Edmonton	666,104
Gatineau	102,898
Greater Sudbury	155,219
Guelph	106,170
Halifax[7]	359,111
Hamilton	490,268
Kamloops	77,281
Kelowna	96,288
Kingston	114,195
Kitchener	190,399
Langley[7]	86,896
Laval	343,005
London	336,539
Longueuil	128,016
Markham	208,615
Mississauga	612,925
Montreal	1,039,534
Montréal-Nord	83,600
Niagara Falls	78,815
North Vancouver[7]	82,310
Oakville	144,738
Oshawa	139,051
★ Ottawa	774,072
Pickering	87,139
Quebec	169,076
Regina	178,225
Richmond	164,345
Richmond Hill	132,030
Saanich[7]	103,654

country city	population
Saint Catharines	129,170
Saint-Hubert	75,912
Saint John's	99,182
Saint-Laurent	77,391
Saskatoon	196,811
Sherbrooke	75,916
Surrey	347,825
Thunder Bay	109,016
Toronto	2,481,494
Vancouver	545,671
Vaughan	182,022
Waterloo	86,543
Whitby	87,413
Windsor	208,402
Winnipeg	619,544
Cape Verde (2000)	
★ Praia	94,757
Central African Republic (1995 est.)	
★ Bangui	553,000
Chad (1993; MU)	
Abéché	187,936
Bongor	196,713
Doba	185,461
Moundou	282,103
★ N'Djamena	530,965
Sarh	193,753
Chile (2002)	
Antofagasta	295,792
Arica	175,441
Calama	136,600
Chillán	148,015
Concepción	373,400
Copiapó	125,983
Coquimbo	154,316
Curicó	100,506
Iquique	214,586
La Serena	147,815
Los Angeles	123,445
Osorno	132,245
Puente Alto	492,603
Puerto Montt	155,895
Punta Arenas	116,005
Quilpué	126,893
Rancagua	206,971
San Bernardo	241,138
★ Santiago	200,792
(administrative)	
agglomeration	4,658,687
Talca	193,755
Talcahuano	248,964
Temuco	232,528
Valdívia	129,952
★ Valparaíso	
(legislative)	275,141
Viña del Mar	286,931
China (2003 est.)[8]	
Acheng	242,973
Aksu	251,345
Altay	118,042
Anda	180,795[9]
Ankang	197,129
Anlu	107,323
Anning	146,183
Anqing	384,701
Anqiu	157,925
Anshan	1,286,513
Anshun	218,975
Anyang	570,773
Baicheng	275,403
Baise	126,893
Baishan	261,098
Baiyin	282,471
Baoding	666,068
Baoji	496,113
Baoshan	114,247
Baotou	1,166,634
Bazhong	198,167
Bazhou	132,496
Bei'an	242,251
Beihai	240,640
★ Beijing (Peking)	7,699,297
Beiliu	154,313
Beining	108,405
Beipiao	203,192
Bengbu	533,323
Benxi	834,176
Bijie	159,126
Binzhou	237,910
Botou	109,746
Bozhou	257,213
Cangzhou	371,431
Cenxi	121,712
Changchun	2,283,765
Changde	437,039

country city	population
Changge	127,774
Changji	217,398
Changle	148,047
Changning	146,520
Changsha	1,562,204
Changshu	451,712
Changyi	126,860
Changzhi	484,235
Changzhou	891,942
Chaohu	312,679
Chaoyang (Guangdong)	791,746
Chaoyang (Liaoning)	314,943
Chaozhou	311,249
Chengde	329,970
Chengdu	2,663,971
Chenghai	303,418
Chenzhou	293,703
Chibi	162,143
Chifeng	492,054
Chizhou	121,996
Chongqing (Chungking)	4,239,742
Chuxiong	136,067
Chuzhou	211,430
Cixi	148,240
Conghua	143,052
Da'an	157,409
Dachuan	200,785[9]
Dafeng	153,147[9]
Dali	195,846
Dalian	2,181,583
Dandong	602,028
Dangyang	120,806
Danjiangkou	157,727
Danyang	223,674
Danzhou	224,787
Daqing	879,288
Dashiqiao	199,597
Datong	1,028,730
Daye	142,297
Dazhou	217,376
Dehui	159,332
Dengzhou	131,004
Dexing	109,373
Deyang	274,722
Dezhou	360,981
Dingzhou	123,096
Donggang	115,081
Dongguan	562,741
Dongsheng	113,436[9]
Dongtai	349,901
Dongyang	119,666
Dongying	539,645
Dujiangyan	159,140
Dunhua	264,662
Duyun	165,447
Emeishan	133,894
Enping	164,929[9]
Enshi	132,680
Erdos	144,793
Ezhou	305,560
Fangchenggang	128,832
Fanyu	345,275[9]
Feicheng	321,827
Fengcheng (Guangdong)	173,112[9]
Fengcheng (Jiangxi)	282,090
Fengnan	121,767[9]
Foshan	431,120
Fu'an	100,793[9]
Fuding	216,035
Fujin	155,886
Fuqing	293,110
Fushun	1,243,612
Fuxin	690,355
Fuyang (Anhui)	387,315
Fuyang (Zhejiang)	109,387
Fuzhou	1,387,266
Gaizhou	238,440
Ganzhou	319,673
Gao'an	167,126
Gaomi	218,832
Gaoming	122,847
Gaoyao	114,331
Gaoyou	155,462
Gaozhou	317,132
Gejiu	218,652
Genhe	173,189[9]
Gongyi	139,167
Gongzhuling	376,516
Guanghan	132,293
Guangshui	154,716
Guangyuan	287,295
Guangzhou (Canton)	4,653,131
Guichi	103,860[9]
Guigang	224,755
Guilin	534,861
Guiping	161,216
Guixi	110,037

country city	population
Guiyang	1,372,600
Gujiao	125,591
Haicheng	282,981
Haikou	533,960
Hailar	209,294[9]
Hailin	243,563
Hailun	170,303
Haimen	363,648
Haining	133,971
Haiyang	119,446
Hami	237,042
Hancheng	121,256
Hanchuan	171,827[9]
Handan	1,097,802
Hangzhou	2,059,774
Hanzhong	236,024
Harbin	2,735,095
Hebi	331,501
Hechi	113,361
Hechuan	263,211
Hefei	1,170,014
Hegang	593,052
Heihe	123,297
Helong	134,074
Hengshui	233,674
Hengyang	640,502
Heshan	150,679
Heyuan	243,640
Heze	339,792
Hezhou	122,532
Hohhot	826,354
Honghu	201,421[9]
Hongjiang	127,018
Hongta	110,048[9]
Houma	119,166
Huadian	200,833
Huadu	195,921[9]
Huai'an (Jiangsu)	747,873
Huaibei	629,333
Huaihua	217,755
Huainan	877,752
Huaiyin	320,841[9]
Huanggang	201,206
Huangshan	150,845
Huangshi	598,822
Huazhou	200,670
Huichun	141,562
Huixian	104,505
Huiyang	228,887
Huizhou	354,500
Hulin	154,845
Huludao	492,278
Huzhou	351,539
Jiamusi	590,276
Ji'an (Jiangxi)	215,865
Jiande	111,039
Jiangdu	235,191
Jiangjin	360,835
Jiangmen	362,357
Jiangyan	149,706[9]
Jiangyin	294,654
Jiangyou	233,530
Jianyang (Fujian)	114,692
Jianyang (Sichuan)	161,496[9]
Jiaohe	170,359
Jiaonan	270,852
Jiaozhou	267,385
Jiaozuo	576,686
Jiaxing	312,846
Jiayuguan	139,067
Jieshou	106,253
Jieyang	358,176
Jilin	1,242,280
Jimo	258,992
Jinan	2,345,969
Jinchang	148,345
Jincheng	200,659[9]
Jingdezhen	335,492
Jinghong	150,178
Jingjiang	216,104
Jingmen	389,557
Jingzhou	619,170
Jinhua	274,267
Jining (Inner Mongolia)	227,191
Jining (Shandong)	507,020
Jinjiang	296,433
Jintan	151,745
Jinzhong	262,414
Jinzhou	702,914
Jishou	132,406
Jiujiang	411,532
Jiuquan	121,975
Jiutai	197,779
Jixi	757,640
Jiyuan	241,406[9]
Jurong	139,146
Kaifeng	594,887
Kaili	163,366
Kaiping	281,924
Kaiyuan (Liaoning)	141,103

Major cities and national capitals (continued)

country / city	population
Kaiyuan (*Yunnan*)	108,668
Karamay	237,918
Kashgar (Kashi)	229,408
Korla	231,369
Kuitun	162,744
Kunming	1,597,768
Kunshan	312,370
Laiwu	416,656
Laixi	160,269
Laiyang	204,000
Laizhou	215,247
Langfang	277,856
Langzhong	238,500
Lanxi	114,959
Lanzhou	1,576,446
Laohekou	165,771
Lechang	177,572[9]
Leiyang	163,278[9]
Leizhou	251,383
Lengshuijiang	176,182[9]
Leping	138,677
Leqing	103,118[9]
Leshan	422,194
Lhasa	129,490
Lianjiang	263,767
Lianyuan	145,329
Lianyungang	536,210
Liaocheng	349,634
Liaoyang	586,882
Liaoyuan	388,364
Liling	140,755
Linchuan	275,230
Linfen	323,671
Lingbao	120,293
Lingyuan	146,756
Linhai	138,794
Linhe	211,506
Linjiang	115,198
Linqing	143,203[9]
Linxia	108,464
Linxiang	111,163
Linyi	679,225
Linzhou	130,055
Lishui	120,592
Liu'an	315,337
Liupanshui	392,783
Liuyang	137,836
Liuzhou	830,515
Liyang	340,743
Longhai	164,716
Longjing	142,732
Longkou	235,994
Longyan	299,192
Loudi	244,728
Lufeng	434,589
Luoding	362,696
Luohe	328,594
Luoyang	1,059,818
Luzhou	404,626
Ma'anshan	443,484
Macheng	175,322[9]
Manzhouli	153,571
Maoming	455,140
Meihekou	261,377
Meishan	140,920
Meizhou	236,424
Mianyang	466,777
Mianzhu	101,157
Miluo	109,282
Mingguang	125,222
Mishan	159,115
Mudanjiang	660,662
Muling	139,871
Nan'an	108,684[9]
Nanchang	1,419,813
Nanchong	508,859
Nanhai	374,363
Nanjing (Nanking)	2,966,047
Nankang	113,543
Nanning	1,031,672
Nanping	272,795
Nantong	564,713
Nanyang	531,220
Nehe	135,382
Neijiang	334,592
Ning'an	147,881
Ningbao	1,045,048
Ningguo	112,785
Panjin	495,174
Panshi	165,101[9]
Panzhihua	507,387
Penglai	115,022
Pengzhou	126,028
Pingdingshan	686,984
Pingdu	243,689
Pinghu	111,183
Pingliang	142,299
Pingxiang	357,785
Pizhou	352,380
Pulandian	166,331[9]
Puning	607,247
Putian	145,051[9]
Puyang	328,449
Qianjiang	314,489
Qidong	254,354
Qilin	210,230[9]
Qingdao	1,930,150
Qingyuan	204,793
Qingzhen	114,026
Qingzhou	196,467
Qinhuangdao	549,118
Qinzhou	193,081
Qiongshan	163,163
Qiqihar (Tsitsihar)	1,125,311
Qitaihe	318,850
Qixia	117,605
Quanzhou	497,723
Qufu	194,053
Qujing	230,129
Quzhou	151,122[9]
Renqiu	158,242[9]
Rizhao	370,306
Rongcheng	261,482
Rugao	316,619
Rui'an	164,563[9]
Rushan	159,179
Ruzhou	107,390
Sanhe	131,214
Sanmenxia	213,604
Sanming	279,538
Sanshui	168,676
Sanya	161,869[9]
Shanghai	10,030,788
Shangqiu	800,157
Shangrao	168,263[9]
Shangyu	141,622
Shangzhi	246,646
Shangzhou	150,384
Shantou	1,201,184
Shanwei	233,450
Shaoguan	463,272
Shaowu	135,616
Shaoxing	347,342
Shaoyang	351,418
Shengzhou	101,649
Shenyang	3,995,531
Shenzhen	1,120,394
Shihezi	352,489
Shijiazhuang	1,970,956
Shishou	158,427
Shiyan	404,809
Shizuishan	322,211
Shouguang	217,903
Shuangcheng	172,936[9]
Shuangliao	141,355
Shuangyashan	436,642
Shulan	212,968
Shunde	648,301
Shuozhou	158,838
Sihui	132,657
Siping	508,533
Songyuan	315,135
Songzi	157,271
Suihua	286,044
Suining	271,461
Suizhou	349,149
Suqian	234,816
Suzhou (*Anhui*)	316,173
Suzhou (*Jiangsu*)	1,215,967
Tai'an	641,239
Taicang	119,862[9]
Taishan	241,356
Taixing	323,540
Taiyuan	1,970,304
Taizhou (*Jiangsu*)	312,210
Taizhou (*Zhejiang*)	281,045
Tangshan	1,498,175
Taonan	153,474
Tengzhou	412,776
Tianchang	167,508[9]
Tianjin (Tientsin)	4,933,106
Tianmen	388,559
Tianshui	480,638
Tiefa	165,956[9]
Tieli	278,768
Tieling	333,008
Tongcheng	104,584
Tongchuan	312,225
Tonghua	392,845
Tongliao	327,008
Tongling	322,960
Tongren	106,937
Tongxiang	117,999
Tongzhou	375,904
Tumen	104,132
Ulanhot	208,643
Ürümqi	1,401,990
Wafangdian	318,793
Weifang	718,772
Weihai	392,947
Weihui	104,257
Weinan	239,542
Wendeng	219,278
Wenling	169,979
Wenzhou	573,469
Wuchang	232,412
Wuchuan	275,845
Wudalianchi	157,547[9]
Wuhai	351,856
Wuhan	4,593,410
Wuhu	567,015
Wujiang	223,322
Wujin	193,775
Wuwei	199,370
Wuxi	1,318,726
Wuxian	176,694[9]
Wuxue	155,855
Wuzhong	112,468
Wuzhou	261,868
Xiamen (Amoy)	963,019
Xi'an (Sian)	2,657,900
Xiangcheng	152,366
Xiangfan	835,170
Xiangtan	561,706
Xiangxiang	115,670
Xianning	222,624
Xiantao	433,034
Xianyang	540,838
Xiaogan	243,816
Xiaoshan	220,815[9]
Xiaoyi	134,150
Xichang	174,781[9]
Xilinhot	121,472
Xingcheng	126,119
Xinghua	263,038
Xingning	300,766
Xingping	114,723
Xingtai	489,715
Xingyang	103,366
Xingyi	118,874
Xinhui	237,675
Xining	654,574
Xinmin	134,802
Xintai	352,171
Xinxiang	647,868
Xinyang	410,393
Xinyi (*Guangdong*)	280,028
Xinyi (*Jiangsu*)	206,602
Xinyu	289,104
Xinzheng	154,539
Xinzhou	143,840[9]
Xishan	171,316[9]
Xuancheng	236,680
Xuanwei	131,150
Xuanzhou	136,914[9]
Xuchang	305,454
Xuzhou	1,210,841
Ya'an	133,263
Yakeshi	386,327
Yan'an	158,038
Yancheng	419,265
Yangchun	213,862
Yangjiang	314,339
Yangquan	487,332
Yangzhou	548,204
Yanji	348,317
Yantai	991,905
Yanzhou	220,768
Yibin	312,462
Yichang	653,040
Yicheng	121,338
Yichun (*Heilongjiang*)	800,649
Yichun (*Jiangxi*)	231,070
Yima	123,228
Yinchuan	535,743
Yingcheng	134,284
Yingde	214,978
Yingkou	528,961
Yingtan	124,632
Yining	258,640
Yixing	297,304
Yiyang	320,675
Yizheng	192,533
Yizhou	101,582
Yong'an	130,689[9]
Yongcheng	147,231
Yongchuan	244,797
Yongzhou	295,690
Yuanjiang	147,395
Yuanping	110,303
Yuci	243,948[9]
Yueyang	522,769
Yuhang	152,429[9]
Yulin (*Guangxi*)	202,413
Yulin (*Shaanxi*)	130,008
Yumen	106,812
Yuncheng	204,080
Yunfu	208,887
Yushu	171,692[9]
Yuxi	126,635
Yuyao	162,722
Yuzhou	148,159
Zaoyang	223,453
Zaozhuang	733,080
Zengcheng	226,776
Zhalantin	152,797
Zhangjiagang	354,935
Zhangjiajie	128,240
Zhangjiakou	688,297
Zhangqiu	227,712
Zhangshu	127,961
Zhangye	158,235
Zhangzhou	356,825
Zhanjiang	719,681
Zhaodong	264,125
Zhaoqing	352,490
Zhaotong	114,996
Zhaoyuan	163,259
Zhengzhou	1,770,828
Zhenjiang	536,137
Zhijiang	132,703
Zhongshan	581,571
Zhongxiang	207,768
Zhoukou	221,767
Zhoushan	253,327
Zhuanghe	161,223[9]
Zhucheng	239,308
Zhuhai	460,937
Zhuji	137,511
Zhumadian	227,088
Zhuozhou	152,480
Zhuzhou	580,450
Zibo	1,519,276
Zigong	485,962
Zixing	125,124
Ziyang	145,665[9]
Zoucheng	352,049
Zunyi	378,602
Colombia (2003 est.)	
Armenia	303,939
Barrancabermeja	187,142
Barranquilla	1,329,579
Bello	372,857
★ Bogotá	6,850,205
Bucaramanga	553,046
Buenaventura	235,054
Buga	115,627
Cali	2,287,819
Cartagena	902,688
Cartago	131,927
Cúcuta	682,671
Dos Quebradas	172,684
Envigado	153,911
Florencia	123,038
Floridablanca	242,016
Girardot	123,637
Giron	102,048
Ibagué	412,820
Itagüí	263,808
Maicao	122,435
Manizales	351,878
Medellín	1,955,753
Montería	264,252
Neiva	335,248
Palmira	241,113
Pasto	365,121
Pereira	420,415
Popayán	212,359
Santa Marta	406,231
Sincelejo	247,211
Soacha	298,138
Sogamoso	120,161
Soledad	326,067
Tuluá	161,057
Tunja	115,127
Valledupar	292,760
Villavicencio	305,476
Comoros (1995 est.)	
★ Moroni	34,168
Congo, Dem. Rep. of the (1994 est.)	
Boma	135,284
Bukavu	201,569
Butembo	109,406
Goma	109,094
Kalemi	101,309
Kananga	393,030
Kikwit	182,142
★ Kinshasa	4,655,313
Kisangani	417,517
Kolwezi	417,810
Likasi	299,118
Lubumbashi	851,381
Matadi	172,730
Mbandaka	169,841
Mbuji-Mayi	806,475
Mwene-Ditu	137,459
Tshikapa	180,860
Uvira	115,590
Congo, Rep. of the (1996)	
★ Brazzaville	856,410
Pointe-Noire	455,131
Costa Rica (2000)	
★ San José	309,762[10]
Côte d'Ivoire (1998)	
★ Abidjan	2,877,948
Bouaké	461,618
Daloa	173,107
Gagnoa	107,124
Korhogo	142,093
Man	116,657
San Pédro	131,800
Yamoussoukro	110,013
Croatia (2001)	
Rijeka	143,800
Split	175,140
★ Zagreb	691,724
Cuba (2000 est.)	
Bayamo	152,000
Camagüey	304,500
Ciego de Avila	114,600
Cienfuegos	153,300
Guantánamo	222,300
★ Havana	2,175,900[11]
Holguín	263,300
Las Tunas	141,300
Manzanillo	109,300
Matanzas	128,600
Pinar del Río	146,100
Sancti Spíritus	105,700
Santa Clara	216,000
Santiago de Cuba	411,100
Cyprus (2001)	
★ Lefkosia (Nicosia)	47,832[12]
agglomeration	200,686[12]
Czech Republic (2003 est.)	
Brno	370,505
Olomouc	101,624
Ostrava	314,102
Plzeň	163,791
★ Prague	1,161,938
Denmark (2003 est.)	
Ålborg	121,100
Århus	222,599
★ Copenhagen	501,285
Odense	145,374
Djibouti (2004 est.)	
★ Djibouti	465,300
Dominica (2004 est.)	
★ Roseau	20,200
Dominican Republic (2004 est.)	
La Romana	171,500
La Vega	123,400
Puerto Plata	135,600
San Cristóbal	120,200
San Francisco de Macorís	132,700
San Pedro de Macorís	152,600
Santiago	505,600
★ Santo Domingo	1,817,754[13]
East Timor (2004 est.)	
★ Dili	51,700
Ecuador (2001)	
Ambato	154,095
Cuenca	277,374
Duran	174,531
Guayaquil	1,985,379
Ibarra	108,535
Loja	118,532
Machala	204,578
Manta	183,105
Milagro	113,440
Portoviejo	171,847
Quevedo	120,379
★ Quito	1,399,378
Riobamba	124,807
Santo Domingo	199,827
Egypt (1996)	
Alexandria	3,328,196
Al-'Arîsh	100,447

country / city	population
Aswān	219,017
Asyūṭ	343,498
Banhā	145,792
Banī Suwayf	172,032
Bilbays	113,608
Būr Saʿīd (Port Said)	469,533
★ Cairo	6,789,479
Damanhūr	212,203
Al-Fayyūm	260,964
Al-Ismāʿīlīyah	254,477
Al-Jīzah (Giza)	2,221,868
Kafr ad-Dawwar	231,978
Kafr ash-Shaykh	124,819
Al-Maḥallah al-Kubrā	395,402
Mallawī	119,283
Al-Manṣūrah	369,621
Al-Minyā	201,360
Mīt Ghamr	101,801
Qinā	171,275
Sawhāj	170,125
Shibīn al-Kawm	159,909
Shubrā al-Khaymah	870,716
As-Suways (Suez)	417,610
Ṭanṭā	371,010
Al-Uqṣur (Luxor)	360,503
Az-Zaqāzīq	267,351
El Salvador (2000 est.)	
Apopa	139,800[14]
Ilopango	115,400[14]
Mejicanos	172,500[14]
Nueva San Salvador	136,900
San Miguel	159,700
★ San Salvador	479,600
Santa Ana	164,500
Soyapango	285,300[14]
Equatorial Guinea (2003 est.)	
★ Malabo	92,900
Eritrea (2002 est.)	
★ Asmara	500,600
Estonia (2003 est.)	
★ Tallinn	400,378
Tartu	101,169
Ethiopia (1994)	
★ Addis Ababa	2,112,737
Dire Dawa	164,851
Gonder	112,249
Harer (Harar)	131,139
Jima	106,842
Nazret	127,842
Faroe Islands (2002 est.)	
★ Tórshavn	18,070
Fiji (1996)	
★ Suva	77,366
Finland (2003 est.)	
Espoo	221,097
★ Helsinki	559,716
Oulu	124,588
Tampere	199,823
Turku	174,618
Vantaa	181,890
France (1999)	
Aix-en-Provence	134,222
Amiens	135,501
Angers	151,279
Besançon	117,304
Bordeaux	215,118
Boulogne-Billancourt	106,367
Brest	149,634
Caen	113,987
Clermont-Ferrand	137,140
Dijon	149,867
Grenoble	153,317
Le Havre	190,651
Le Mans	146,105
Lille	182,228
Limoges	133,960
Lyon	445,257
Marseille	797,486
Metz	123,776
Montpellier	225,392
Mulhouse	110,359
Nancy	103,605
Nantes	268,695
Nice	342,738
Nîmes	133,424
Orléans	112,833
★ Paris	2,123,261
agglomeration	9,608,000[9]

country / city	population
Perpignan	105,115
Reims	187,206
Rennes	206,229
Rouen	106,035
Saint-Étienne	179,755
Strasbourg	263,940
Toulon	159,389
Toulouse	390,413
Tours	132,820
Villeurbanne	124,215
French Guiana (1999)	
★ Cayenne	50,594
French Polynesia (2002)	
★ Papeete	26,181
agglomeration	124,864
Gabon (1993)	
★ Libreville	362,386
Gambia, The (2003)	
★ Banjul	34,828
agglomeration	523,589
Gaza Strip (2003 est.)	
★ Gaza (Ghazzah; acting administrative centre)	460,899
Jabālyah	159,003
Khān Yūnus	161,880
Rafah	121,223
Georgia (2002)	
Baṭʿumi (Batumi)	121,800
Kʿutʿaisi (Kutaisi)	186,000
Rustʿavi (Rustavi)	116,400
★ Tbilisi	1,081,700
Germany (2002 est.)	
Aachen	245,778
Augsburg	257,836
Bergisch Gladbach	105,569
★ Berlin	3,388,434
Bielefeld	323,373
Bochum	390,087
Bonn	306,016
Bottrop	120,780
Braunschweig	245,516
Bremen	540,950
Bremerhaven	118,701
Chemnitz	255,798
Cologne (Köln)	967,940
Cottbus	105,954
Darmstadt	138,457
Dortmund	589,240
Dresden	478,631
Duisburg	512,030
Düsseldorf	570,765
Erfurt	200,126
Erlangen	101,919
Essen	591,889
Frankfurt am Main	641,076
Freiburg im Breisgau	208,294
Fürth	111,257
Gelsenkirchen	276,740
Gera	109,926
Göttingen	123,822
Hagen	202,060
Halle	243,045
Hamburg	1,726,363
Hamm	183,805
Hannover	516,415
Heidelberg	141,509
Heilbronn	120,163
Herne	174,018
Hildesheim	103,717
Ingolstadt	117,311
Jena	101,157
Karlsruhe	279,578
Kassel	194,748
Kiel	232,242
Koblenz	107,730
Krefeld	239,559
Leipzig	493,052
Leverkusen	160,829
Lübeck	213,496
Ludwigshafen	162,458
Magdeburg	229,755
Mainz	185,293
Mannheim	308,385
Moers	107,421
Mönchengladbach	262,963
Mülheim an der Ruhr	172,332
Munich (München)	1,227,958
Münster	267,197
Neuss	150,957

country / city	population
Nürnberg	491,307
Oberhausen	221,619
Offenbach am Main	118,429
Oldenburg	155,908
Osnabrück	164,195
Paderborn	140,869
Pforzheim	118,002
Potsdam	130,435
Recklinghausen	124,587
Regensburg	127,198
Remscheid	118,753
Reutlingen	111,338
Rostock	198,964
Saarbrücken	182,858
Salzgitter	111,696
Siegen	108,397
Solingen	165,032
Stuttgart	587,152
Trier	100,024
Ulm	118,347
Wiesbaden	271,076
Witten	103,158
Wolfsburg	121,887
Wuppertal	364,784
Würzburg	129,915
Zwickau	101,726
Ghana (2001 est.)	
★ Accra	1,551,200
Kumasi	610,600
Obuasi	118,000
Tamale	259,200
Tema	225,900
Greece (2001)	
★ Athens	745,514
agglomeration	3,187,734
Iráklion	133,012
Kallithéa	109,609[15]
Larissa	124,786
Pátrai (Patras)	161,114
Peristérion	137,918[15]
Piraiévs (Piraeus)	175,697[15]
Thessaloníki	363,987
Greenland (2003 est.)	
★ Nuuk (Godthåb)	14,265
Grenada (2001)	
★ Saint George's	3,908
agglomeration	31,651
Guadeloupe (1999)	
★ Basse-Terre	12,410
Guam (2000)	
★ Hagåtña (Agana)	1,122
agglomeration	140,000[5]
Guatemala (2002)	
★ Guatemala City	942,348
Mixco	277,400
Quetzaltenango	106,700
Villa Nueva	187,700
Guernsey (2001)	
★ St. Peter Port	16,488
Guinea (2004 est.)	
★ Conakry	1,851,800
Kankan	113,900
Guinea-Bissau (2004 est.)	
★ Bissau	305,700
Guyana (2002)	
★ Georgetown	137,330
Haiti (1997 est.)	
Cap-Haïtien	107,026
Carrefour	306,074
Delmas	257,247
★ Port-au-Prince	917,112
Honduras (2001)	
Choloma	108,260
La Ceiba	114,584
San Pedro Sula	439,086
★ Tegucigalpa	769,061
Hong Kong (2001)	
★ Hong Kong	6,708,389
Hungary (2001)	
★ Budapest	1,775,203
Debrecen	211,034
Győr	129,412
Kecskemét	107,749
Miskolc	184,125

country / city	population
Nyíregyháza	118,795
Pécs	162,498
Szeged	168,372
Székesfehérvár	106,346
Iceland (2003 est.)	
★ Reykjavík	112,490
India (2001)	
Abohar	124,303
Achalpur	107,364
Adilabad	108,233
Adityapur	119,221
Adoni	155,969
Agartala	189,300
Agra	1,259,979
Ahmadabad	3,515,361
Ahmadnagar	307,455
Aizawl	229,700
Ajmer	485,197
Akola	399,978
Alandur	146,154
Alappuzha (Alleppey)	177,079
Aligarh	667,732
Allahabad (Prayag Raj)	990,298
Alwal	106,424
Alwar	260,245
Ambala	139,222
Ambala Sadar	106,378
Ambarnath	203,795
Ambattur	302,492
Amravati	549,370
Amritsar	975,695
Amroha	164,890
Anand	130,462
Anantapur	220,951
Ara (Arrah)	203,395
Asansol	486,304
Ashoknagar Kalyangarh	111,475
Avadi	230,913
Azamgarh	104,943
Bahadurgarh	119,839
Baharampur	160,168
Bahraich	168,376
Baidyabati	108,231
Baleshwar	106,032
Ballia	102,226
Bally	261,575
Balurghat	135,516
Banda	134,832
Bangalore	4,292,223
Bangaon	102,115
Bankura	128,811
Bansberia	104,453
Baranagar (Barahanagar)	250,615
Barasat	231,515
Barddhaman (Burdwan)	285,871
Bareilly	699,830
Barrackpore	144,331
Barshi	104,786
Basirhat	113,120
Basti	106,985
Batala	126,646
Bathinda (Bhatinda)	217,389
Beawar	123,701
Belgaum	399,600
Bellary	317,000
Bettiah	116,692
Bhadravati	160,392
Bhadreswar	105,944
Bhagalpur	340,349
Bhalswa Jahangir Pur	151,427
Bharatpur	204,456
Bharuch (Broach)	148,391
Bhatpara	441,956
Bhavnagar	510,958
Bhilainagar	553,837
Bhilwara	280,185
Bhimavaram	137,327
Bhind	153,768
Bhiwandi	598,703
Bhiwani	169,424
Bhopal	1,443,875
Bhubaneshwar	647,302
Bhusawal	172,366
Bid (Bhir)	138,091
Bidar	172,298
Bidhan Nagar	167,848
Bihar Sharif	231,972
Bijapur	245,946
Bikaner	529,007
Bilaspur	265,178
Bokaro (Bokaro Steel City)	394,173
Bommanahalli	201,220
Botad	100,059
Brahmapur	289,724

country / city	population
Budaun	148,138
Bulandshahr	176,256
Burhanpur	194,360
Byatarayanapura	180,931
Champdani	103,232
Chandannagar	162,166
Chandawsi	103,757
Chandigarh	808,796
Chandrapur	297,612
Chapra	178,835
Chennai (Madras)	4,216,268
Chhindwara	122,309
Chikmagalur	101,022
Chitradurga	122,594
Chittoor	152,966
Coimbatore	923,085
Cuddalore	158,569
Cuddapah	125,725
Cuttack	535,139
Dallo Pura	132,628
Damoh	112,160
Darbhanga	266,834
Darjiling	107,530
Dasarahalli	263,636
Davanagere	363,780
Dehra Dun	447,808
Dehri	119,207
Delhi	9,817,439
Delhi Cantonment	124,452
Deoli	119,432
Deoria	104,222
Dewas	230,658
Dhanbad	198,963
Dharmavaram	103,400
Dhule (Dhulia)	341,473
Dibrugarh	122,523
Dimapur	107,382
Dinapur Nizamat	130,339
Dindigul	196,619
Dum Dum	101,319
Durg	231,182
Durgapur	492,996
Eluru	189,772
Erode	151,184
Etah	107,098
Etawah	211,460
Faizabad	144,924
Faridabad	1,054,981
Farrukhabad-cum-Fatehgarh	227,876
Fatehpur	151,757
Fīrozabad	278,801
Gadag-Betigeri	154,849
Gajuwaka	258,944
Gandhinagar	195,891
Ganganagar	210,788
Gaya	383,197
Ghatlodiya	106,259
Ghaziabad	968,521
Godhra	121,852
Gonda	122,164
Gondia	120,878
Gorakhpur	624,570
Gudivada	112,245
Gulbarga	427,929
Guna	137,132
Guntakal	117,403
Guntur	514,707
Gurgaon	173,542
Guwahati (Gauhati)	808,021
Gwalior	826,919
Habra	127,695
Hajipur	119,276
Haldia	170,695
Haldwani-cum-Kathgodam	129,140
Halisahar	124,479
Hanumangarh	129,654
Haora (Howrah)	1,008,704
Hapur	211,987
Hardoi	112,474
Haridwar (Hardwar)	175,010
Hassan	117,386
Hathras	123,243
Hazaribag	127,243
Hindupur	125,056
Hisar (Hissar)	256,810
Hoshiarpur	148,243
Hospet	163,284
Hubli-Dharwad	786,018
Hugli-Chunchura	170,201
Hyderabad	3,449,878
Ichalkaranji	257,572
Imphal	217,300
Indore	1,597,441
Ingraj Bazar (English Bazar)	161,148
Jabalpur	951,469
Jagadhri	101,300
Jaipur	2,324,319

Major cities and national capitals (continued)

country / city	population
Jalandhar (Jullundur)	701,223
Jalgaon	368,579
Jalna	235,529
Jalpaiguri	100,212
Jammu	378,431
Jamnagar	447,734
Jamshedpur	570,349
Jamuria	129,456
Jaunpur	159,996
Jetpur Navagadh	104,311
Jhansi	383,248
Jhunjhunun	100,476
Jind	136,089
Jodhpur	846,408
Junagadh	168,686
Kaithal	117,226
Kakinada	289,920
Kalol	100,021
Kalyan-Dombivali	1,193,266
Kamarhati	314,334
Kanchipuram	152,984
Kanchrapara	126,118
Kanpur	2,532,138
Kapra	159,176
Karawal Nagar	148,549
Karimnagar	203,819
Karnal	210,476
Katihar	175,169
Khammam	158,022
Khandwa	171,976
Khanna	103,059
Kharagpur	207,984
Khardaha	116,252
Kirari Suleman Nagar	153,874
Kishangarh	116,156
Kochi (Cochin)	596,473
Kolar	113,299
Kolhapur	485,183
Kolkata (Calcutta)	4,580,544
Kollam (Quilon)	361,441
Korba	315,695
Kota	695,899
Kozhikode (Calicut)	436,527
Krishnanagar	139,170
Krishnarajapura	187,453
Kukatpalle	290,591
Kulti-Barakar	290,057
Kumbakonam	140,021
Kurnool	267,739
Lakhimpur	120,566
Lalbahadur Nagar (L.B. Nagar)	261,987
Lalitpur	111,810
Latur	299,828
Loni	120,659
Lucknow	2,207,340
Ludhiana	1,395,053
Machilipatnam (Masulipatam)	183,370
Madhyamgram	155,503
Madurai	922,913
Mahadevapura	135,597
Mahbubnagar	130,849
Maheshtala	389,214
Malegaon	409,190
Malerkotla	106,802
Malkajgiri	175,000
Mandsaur	116,483
Mandya	131,211
Mangalore	398,745
Mango	166,091
Mathura	298,827
Maunath Bhanjan	210,071
Medinipur (Midnapore)	153,349
Meerut	1,074,229
Mira-Bhayandar	520,301
Mirzapur-cum-Vindhyachal	205,264
Modinagar	112,918
Moga	124,624
Moradabad	641,240
Morena	150,890
Motihari	101,506
Mumbai (Bombay)	11,914,398
Munger (Monghyr)	187,311
Murwara (Katni)	186,738
Muzaffarnagar	316,452
Muzaffarpur	305,465
Mysore	742,261
Nabadwip	115,036
Nadiad	192,799
Nagaon	107,471
Nagercoil	208,149
Nagpur	2,051,320
Naihati	215,432
Nala Sopara	184,664
Nalgonda	110,651
Nanded-Waghala	430,598
Nandyal	151,771
Nangloi Jat	150,371
Nashik (Nasik)	1,076,967
Navghar-Manikpur	116,700
Navi Mumbai (New Mumbai)	703,947
Navsari	134,009
Neemuch	107,496
Nellore	378,947
★ New Delhi	294,783
Neyveli	128,133
Nizamabad	286,956
Noida	293,908
North Barrackpore	123,523
North Dum Dum	220,032
Ongole	149,589
Orai	139,444
Ozhukarai	217,263
Palakkad	130,736
Palanpur	110,383
Pali	187,571
Pallavaram	143,984
Palwal	100,528
Panchkula	140,992
Panihati	348,379
Panipat	261,665
Panvel	104,031
Parbhani	259,170
Patan	112,038
Pathankot	159,559
Patiala	302,870
Patna	1,376,950
Pilibhit	124,082
Pimpri-Chinchwad	1,006,417
Pondicherry	220,749
Porbandar	133,083
Port Blair	100,186
Proddatur	164,932
Pudukkottai	108,947
Pune	2,540,069
Puri	157,610
Purnia (Purnea)	171,235
Puruliya	113,766
Quthbullapur	225,816
Rae Bareli	169,285
Raichur	205,634
Raiganj	165,222
Raigarh	110,987
Raipur	605,131
Raj Nandgaon	143,727
Rajahmundry	313,347
Rajapalaiyam	121,982
Rajarhat Gopalpur	271,781
Rajendranagar	143,184
Rajkot	966,642
Rajpur Sonanpur	336,390
Ramagundam	235,540
Rampur	281,549
Ranchi	846,454
Raniganj	122,891
Ratlam	221,267
Raurkela	224,601
Raurkela Township	206,566
Rewa	183,232
Rewari	100,946
Rishra	113,259
Robertson Pet	141,294
Rohtak	286,773
S.A.S. Nagar (Mohali)	123,284
Sagar	232,321
Saharanpur	452,925
Saharsa	124,015
Salem	693,236
Sambalpur	154,164
Sambhal	182,930
Sangli-Miraj	436,639
Santipur	138,195
Sasaram	131,142
Satara	108,043
Satna	225,468
Secunderabad	204,182
Serampore	197,955
Serilingampalle	150,525
Shahjahanpur	297,932
Shambajinagar (Aurangābād)	872,667
Shantipur	138,200
Shiliguri (Siliguri)	470,275
Shillong	132,876
Shimla	142,161
Shimoga	274,105
Shivapuri	146,859
Sholapur (Solapur)	873,037
Sikandarabad (Secundarabad) Cantonment	204,182
Sikar	184,904
Silchar	142,393
Singrauli	185,580
Sirsa	160,129
Sitapur	151,827
Siwan	108,172
Solapur	873,037
Sonipat (Sonepat)	216,213
South Dum Dum	392,150
Srikakulam	109,666
Srinagar	894,940
Sultan Pur Majra	163,716
Sultanpur	100,085
Surat	2,433,787
Surendranagar Dudhrej	156,417
Tadepalligudem	102,303
Tambaram	137,609
Tenali	149,839
Thane (Thana)	1,261,517
Thanesar	120,072
Thanjavur	215,725
Thiruvananthapuram (Trivandrum)	744,739
Thoothukkudi (Tuticorin)	216,058
Thrissur (Trissur)	317,474
Tiruchchirappalli	746,062
Tirunelveli	411,298
Tirupati	227,657
Tirupper (Tiruppur)	346,551
Tiruvannamalai	130,301
Tiruvottiyur	211,678
Titagarh	124,198
Tonk	135,663
Tumkur	248,592
Udaipur	389,317
Udupi	113,039
Ujjain	429,933
Ulhasnagar	472,943
Uluberia	202,095
Unnao	144,917
Uppal Kalan	118,259
Uttarpara-Kotrung	150,204
Vadodara (Baroda)	1,306,035
Varanasi (Benares)	1,100,748
Vejalpur	113,304
Vellore	177,413
Veraval	141,207
Vidisha	125,457
Vijayawada	825,436
Virar	118,945
Vishakhapatnam	969,608
Vizianagaram	174,324
Warangal	528,570
Wardha	111,070
Yamunanagar	189,587
Yavatmal (Yeotmal)	122,906
Indonesia (2000)[16]	
Ambon	186,911
Balikpapan	409,023
Banda Aceh	154,767
Bandar Lampung	457,927[17]
Bandung	2,136,260
Banjarbaru	123,979
Banjarmasin	527,415
Batam	437,358
Bekasi	1,663,802
Bengkulu	279,753
Binjai	213,725
Bitung	140,270
Blitar	119,372
Bogor	750,819
Cianjur	114,335[17]
Cibinong	101,317[17]
Cilacap	206,928[17]
Cilegon-Merak	294,936
Cimahi	344,607[17]
Ciomas	187,379[17]
Ciparay	111,467[17]
Ciputat	270,815[17]
Cirebon	272,263
Citeurup	105,079[17]
Denpasar	532,440
Depok (*West Java*)	1,143,403
Depok (*Yogyakarta*)	106,825[17]
Dumai	173,188
Gorontalo	134,931
★ Jakarta	8,347,083
Jambi	417,507
Jayapura	155,548
Jember	218,529[17]
Karawang (Krawang)	145,041[17]
Kediri	244,519
Kendari	200,474
Klaten	103,327[17]
Kupang	237,271
Lhokseumawe	109,569[17]
Madiun	163,956
Magelang	117,531
Malang	756,982
Manado	372,887
Mataram	315,738
Medan	1,904,273
Metro	118,448
Mojokerto	108,938
Padang	713,242
Palangkaraya	158,770
Palembang	1,451,419
Palu	263,826
Pangkalpinang	125,319
Parepare	108,258
Pasuruan	168,323
Pekalongan	262,272
Pekanbaru	585,440
Pemalang	103,540[17]
Pematang Siantar	241,480
Percut	129,036[17]
Pondokgede	263,152[17]
Pontianak	464,534
Probolinggo	191,522
Purwokerto	202,452[17]
Salatiga	151,438
Samarinda	521,619
Semarang	1,348,803
Serang	122,429[17]
Sukabumi	252,420
Surabaya	2,599,796
Surakarta	490,214
Taman	106,975[17]
Tangerang	1,325,854
Tanjung Balai	132,385
Tanjung Karang	742,749
Tarakan	116,995
Tasikmalaya	179,766[17]
Tebingtinggi	124,979
Tegal	236,900
Ternate	152,097
Ujung Pandang	1,100,019
Waru	124,282[17]
Yogyakarta	396,711
Iran (1996)	
Ābādān	206,073
Ahvāz	804,980
Āmol	159,092
Andīmeshk	106,923
Arāk	380,755
Ardabīl	340,386
Bābol	158,346
Bandar ʿAbbās	273,578
Bandar-e Būshehr (Būshehr)	143,641
Bīrjand	127,608
Bojnūrd	134,835
Borūjerd	217,804
Būkān	120,020
Dezfūl	202,639
Emāmshahr (Shāhrūd)	104,765
Eṣfahān (Isfahan)	1,266,072
Gonbad-e Kavus	111,253
Gorgān	188,710
Hamadān	401,281
Īlām	126,346
Islāmshahr (Eslāmshahr)	265,450
Karaj	940,968
Kāshān	201,372
Kermān	384,991
Kermānshāh (Bākhtarān)	692,986
Khomeynīshahr	165,888
Khorramābād	272,815
Khorramshahr	105,636
Khvoy (Khoy)	148,944
Mahābād	107,799
Malāyer	144,373
Marāgheh	132,318
Marv Dasht	103,579
Mashhad (Meshed)	1,887,405
Masjed-e Soleymān	116,882
Najafābād	178,498
Neyshābūr	158,847
Orūmīyeh	435,200
Qāʾemshahr	143,286
Qarchak	142,690
Qazvīn	291,117
Qods	138,278
Qom	777,677
Rasht	417,748
Sabzevār	170,738
Sanandaj	277,808
Saqqez	115,394
Sārī	195,882
Sāveh	111,245
Shahr-e Kord	100,477
Shīrāz	1,053,025
Sīrjān	135,024
Tabrīz	1,191,043
★ Tehrān	6,758,845
Vārāmīn	107,233
Yazd	326,776
Zābol	100,888
Zāhedān	419,518
Zanjān	286,295
Iraq (1997 est.)	
Al-ʿAmārah	362,000
★ Baghdad	5,423,964
Baʿqūbah	312,000
Al-Baṣrah	725,000
Dīwanīyah	467,000
Al-Fallūjah	284,500[18]
Al-Ḥillah	573,000
Irbīl	700,000
Karbalāʾ	380,000
Karkūk	525,000
Al-Kūfah	123,500[18]
Al-Kūt	420,000
Mosul	925,000
An-Najaf	410,000
An-Nāṣirīyah	587,000
Ar-Ramādī	470,000
Sāmarrā	214,100[18]
As-Samāwah	131,900[18]
As-Sulaymānīyah	525,000
Tall ʿAfar	167,800[18]
Az-Zubayr	180,900[18]
Ireland (2002)	
Cork	123,062[19]
★ Dublin	495,781[19]
Isle of Man (2001)	
★ Douglas	25,347
Israel (2003 est.)	
Ashdod	187,500
Ashqelon	103,200
Bat Yam	133,900
Beersheba (Beʾer Shevaʿ)	181,500
Bene Beraq	138,900
Haifa (Ḥefa)	270,800
Ḥolon	165,800
★ Jerusalem (Yerushalayim, Al-Quds)	680,400
Netanya	164,800
Petaḥ Tiqwa	172,600
Ramat Gan	126,600
Rishon LeẔiyyon	211,600
Tel Aviv–Yafo	360,400
Italy (2001)[20]	
Ancona	100,507
Bari	316,532
Bergamo	113,143
Bologna	371,217
Brescia	187,567
Cagliari	164,249
Catania	313,110
Ferrara	130,992
Florence (Firenze)	356,118
Foggia	155,203
Forlì	108,335
Genoa (Genova)	610,307
Latina	107,898
Livorno	156,274
Messina	252,026
Milan (Milano)	1,256,211
Modena	175,502
Monza	120,204
Naples (Napoli)	1,004,500
Novara	100,910
Padua (Padova)	204,870
Palermo	686,722
Parma	163,457
Perugia	149,125
Pescara	116,286
Prato	172,499
Ravenna	134,631
Reggio di Calabria	180,353
Reggio nell'Emilia	141,877
Rimini	128,656
★ Rome (Roma)	2,546,804
Salerno	138,188
Sassari	120,729
Siracusa (Syracuse)	123,657
Taranto	202,033
Terni	105,018
Trento	104,946
Trieste	211,184
Turin (Torino)	865,263
Venice (Venezia)	271,073
Verona	253,208
Vicenza	107,223
Jamaica (2001)	
★ Kingston	96,052
agglomeration	575,000[5]
Spanish Town	131,515

country / city	population
Japan (2000)	
Abiko	127,718
Ageo	212,949
Aizuwakamatsu	118,126
Akashi	293,117
Akishima	106,547
Akita	317,625
Amagasaki	466,187
Anjō	158,826
Aomori	297,859
Asahikawa	359,536
Asaka	119,716
Ashikaga	163,136
Atsugi	217,369
Beppu	125,518
Chiba	887,164
Chigasaki	220,809
Chōfu	204,759
Daitō	129,011
Ebetsu	123,875
Ebina	117,510
Fuchu	226,769
Fuji	234,187
Fujieda	128,477
Fujimi	103,228
Fujinomiya	120,233
Fujisawa	379,185
Fukaya	103,533
Fukui	252,274
Fukuoka	1,341,470
Fukushima	291,121
Fukuyama	378,789
Funabashi	550,074
Gifu	402,751
Habikino	119,254
Hachinohe	241,920
Hachiōji	536,046
Hadano	168,142
Hagi	140,458
Hakodate	287,637
Hamamatsu	582,095
Handa	110,819
Higashi-Hiroshima	123,418
Higashi-Kurume	113,300
Higashi-Murayama	113,264
Higashi-Ōsaka	515,094
Hikone	107,864
Himeji	478,309
Hino	167,934
Hirakata	402,563
Hiratsuka	254,633
Hirosaki	177,086
Hiroshima	1,126,239
Hitachi	193,353
Hitachinaka	151,666
Hōfu	104,658
Hoya	102,713
Ibaraki	260,648
Ichihara	278,218
Ichikawa	448,642
Ichinomiya	273,711
Iida	107,378
Ikeda	101,601
Ikoma	112,858
Imabari	117,931
Inazawa	100,273
Iruma	147,905
Ise	100,144
Isesaki	125,762
Ishinomaki	119,796
Itami	192,152
Iwaki	360,138
Iwakuni	105,765
Iwatsuki	109,278
Izumi	172,975
Joetsu	134,763
Kadoma	135,669
Kagoshima	552,098
Kakamigahara	131,990
Kakogawa	266,170
Kamagaya	102,579
Kamakura	167,583
Kanazawa	456,438
Kariya	132,060
Kashihara	125,016
Kashiwa	327,851
Kasuga	105,146
Kasugai	287,623
Kasukabe	203,375
Kawachinagano	121,012
Kawagoe	330,766
Kawaguchi	460,027
Kawanishi	153,762
Kawasaki	1,249,905
Kiryū	115,435
Kisarazu	122,766
Kishiwada	200,104
Kita-Kyūshū	1,011,471
Kitami	112,040
Kobe	1,493,398
Kochi	330,654
Kodaira	178,562
Kofu	196,155
Koganei	111,665
Kokubunji	111,310
Komaki	143,117
Komatsu	108,615
Koriyama	334,824
Koshigaya	308,307
Kumagaya	156,192
Kumamoto	662,012
Kurashiki	430,291
Kure	203,159
Kurume	236,543
Kusatsu	115,450
Kushiro	191,739
Kuwana	108,417
Kyōto	1,467,785
Machida	377,494
Maebashi	284,155
Matsubara	132,560
Matsudo	464,841
Matsue	152,616
Matsumoto	208,970
Matsuyama	473,379
Matsuzaka	123,733
Minōh	124,905
Misato	131,056
Mishima	110,522
Mitaka	171,601
Mito	246,739
Miyakonojō	131,918
Miyazaki	305,755
Moriguchi	152,032
Morioka	288,843
Muroran	103,278
Musashino	135,775
Nagano	360,112
Nagaoka	193,414
Nagareyama	150,520
Nagasaki	423,167
Nagoya	2,171,557
Naha	301,032
Nara	366,185
Narashino	154,040
Neyagawa	250,806
Niigata	501,431
Niihama	125,539
Niiza	149,516
Nishinomiya	438,105
Nishio	100,804
Nobeoka	124,762
Noda	119,941
Numazu	207,558
Obihiro	173,030
Odawara	200,173
Ōgaki	150,238
Ōita	436,470
Okayama	626,642
Okazaki	336,583
Okinawa	119,699
Ōme	141,307
Ōmiya	456,271
Ōmuta	138,635
Ōsaka	2,598,774
Ōta	147,897
Ōtaru	150,687
Ōtsu	288,240
Oyama	155,198
Saga	167,972
Sagamihara	605,561
Sakai	792,018
Sakata	101,300
Sakura	170,931
Sanda	111,734
Sapporo	1,822,368
Sasebo	240,838
Sayama	161,467
Sendai	1,008,130
Seto	131,650
Shimizu	236,818
Shimonoseki	252,389
Shizuoka	469,695
Sōka	225,018
Suita	347,929
Suzuka	186,138
Tachikawa	164,634
Tajimi	104,134
Takamatsu	332,865
Takaoka	172,171
Takarazuka	213,037
Takasaki	239,904
Takatsuki	357,438
Tama	145,859
Toda	108,092
Tokorozawa	330,100
Tokushima	268,218
Tokuyama	108,700
★ Tokyo	8,134,688
Tomakomai	172,086
Tondabayashi	126,551
Tottori	150,439
Toyama	325,700
Toyohashi	364,856
Toyokawa	117,356
Toyonaka	391,726
Toyota	351,101
Tsu	163,246
Tsuchiura	134,710
Tsukuba	165,978
Tsuruoka	165,968
Ube	174,427
Ueda	125,344
Uji	189,113
Urasoe	102,746
Urawa	484,845
Urayasu	133,012
Utsunomiya	443,508
Wakayama	386,551
Yachiyo	168,848
Yaizu	118,247
Yamagata	255,369
Yamaguchi	140,447
Yamato	212,761
Yao	274,777
Yatsushiro	106,145
Yokkaichi	291,105
Yokohama	3,426,651
Yokosuka	428,645
Yonago	135,800
Zama	125,683
Jersey (2001)	
★ St. Helier	28,310
Jordan (2000 est.)	
★ Amman	1,147,447
Irbid	247,275
Ar-Ruṣayfah	218,211
Az-Zarqā'	428,623
Kazakhstan (1999)	
Almaty (Alma-Ata)	1,129,400
Aqtaū (Aktau; Shevchenko)	143,400
Aqtöbe (Aktyubinsk)	253,100
★ Astana (Aqmola; Tselinograd)	313,000
Atyraū (Guryev)	142,500
Ekibastuz	127,200
Kökshetaū (Kokchetav)	123,400
Oral (Uralsk)	195,500
Öskemen (Ust-Kamenogorsk)	311,000
Pavlodar	300,500
Petropavl (Petropavlovsk)	203,500
Qaraghandy (Karaganda)	436,900
Qostanay (Kustanay)	221,400
Qyzylord (Kzyl-Orda)	157,400
Rŭdny	109,500
Semey (Semipalatinsk)	269,600
Shymkent (Shimkent; Chimkent)	360,100
Taraz (Auliye-Ata; Dzhambul)	330,100
Temirtaū	170,500
Kenya (1999)	
Eldoret	167,016
Kisumu	322,734
Machakos	144,109
Meru	126,427
Mombasa	665,018
★ Nairobi	2,143,354
Nakuru	219,366
Kiribati (2000)	
★ Bairiki (agglomeration)	36,717
Korea, North (1993)	
Anju	186,000[21]
Ch'ŏngjin	582,480
Haeju	229,172
Hamhŭng-Hungnam	709,730
Hŭich'ŏn	163,000[21]
Hyesan	178,020
Kaesŏng	334,433
Kanggye	223,410
Kimch'aek (Songjin)	179,000[21]
Kusŏng	177,000[21]
Namp'o	731,448
P'yŏngsŏng	272,934
★ P'yŏngyang	2,741,260
Sariwŏn	254,146
Sinp'o	158,000[21]
Sinŭiju	326,011
Sunch'ŏn	356,000[21]
Tanch'ŏn	284,000[21]
Tŏkch'ŏn	217,000[21]
Wŏnsan	300,148
Korea, South (2003 est.)	
Andong	179,587
Ansan	637,660
Ansŏng	149,233
Anyang	597,656
Asan	193,188
Ch'angwŏn	517,577
Chech'ŏn	143,655
Cheju (Jeju)	290,664
Chinhae	141,936
Chinju	340,816
Ch'ŏnan	445,485
Ch'ŏngju	626,069
Chŏng-ŭp	139,876
Chŏnju	626,069
Ch'unch'ŏn	253,532
Ch'ungju	212,875
Hanam	127,935
Hwasŏng	231,347
Ich'ŏn	190,641
Iksan (Iri)	332,545
Inch'ŏn (Incheon)	2,596,102
Kangnŭng	230,714
Kimch'ŏn	147,760
Kimhae	393,936
Kimje	111,462
Kimp'o	196,193
Kōje	183,897
Kongju	133,012
Koyang	840,345
Kumi	354,746
Kunp'o	269,889
Kunsan	273,086
Kuri	193,850
Kwangju (Kwangju)	1,401,525
Kwangju (Kyŏnggi)	177,593
Kwangmyŏng	341,617
Kwangyang	138,102
Kyŏngju	285,900
Kyŏngsan	221,196
Masan	434,996
Miryang	120,808
Mokp'o	245,315
Naju	103,452
Namwon	100,677
Namyangju	394,202
Nonsan	138,013
Osan	116,624
P'aju	237,341
P'ohang	513,424
Poryŏng	113,671
Puch'ŏn	821,081
Pusan (Busan)	3,747,369
P'yŏngt'aek	362,507
Sach'ŏn	117,427
Sangju	119,283
★ Seoul (Sŏul)	10,280,523
Shihŭng	359,072
Sŏngnam	946,445
Sŏsan	148,697
Sunch'ŏn	271,636
Suwŏn	1,023,875
Taegu	2,540,647
Taejŏn	1,424,844
Tonghae	103,039
Tongyŏng	134,581
Ŭijŏngbu	380,521
Ŭiwang	133,967
Ulsan	1,070,271
Wŏnju	277,987
Yangsan	208,304
Yŏngch'ŏn	116,523
Yongin	529,300
Yŏngju	126,303
Yŏsu	316,143
Kuwait (1995)	
★ Kuwait (Al-Kuwayt)	28,859
agglomeration	888,000[22]
Qalīb ash-Shuyūkh	102,178
As-Sālimīyah	130,215
Kyrgyzstan (1999 est.)	
★ Bishkek	750,327
Osh	208,520
Laos (2003 est.)	
★ Vientiane (Viangchan)	194,200
agglomeration	716,000
Latvia (2002 est.)	
Daugavpils	113,400
★ Rīga	747,157
Lebanon (2003 est.)	
★ Beirut (Bayrūt)	1,171,000
Tripoli (Ṭarābulus)	212,900
Lesotho (1996 est.)	
★ Maseru	160,100
Liberia (2002 est.)	
★ Monrovia	543,000
Libya (2003 est.)	
Banghāzī	446,250
Miṣrātah	121,669
★ Tripoli (Ṭarābulus)	591,060
agglomeration	2,006,000
Liechtenstein (2002 est.)	
★ Vaduz	4,949
Lithuania (2004 est.)	
Kaunas	368,917
Klaipėda	190,098
Panevėžys	117,606
Šiauliai	131,184
★ Vilnius	553,038
Luxembourg (2001)	
★ Luxembourg	76,688
Macau (2001)	
★ Macau	435,235
Macedonia (2002; MU)	
Kumanovo	103,205
★ Skopje (Skopije)	467,257
Madagascar (2001 est.)	
★ Antananarivo	1,403,449
Antsirabe	160,356
Fianarantsoa	144,225
Mahajanga	135,660
Toamasina	179,045
Toliara	101,661
Malawi (2003 est.)	
★ Blantyre (judicial)	646,235
★ Lilongwe (executive; legislative)	597,619
Mzuzu	119,592
Malaysia (2000)	
Alor Setar	114,949
Ampang	126,459
George Town (Pinang)	180,573
Ipoh	566,211
Johor Bahru	384,613
Klang	563,173
Kota Bharu	233,673
Kota Kinabalu	145,000[23]
★ Kuala Lumpur	1,297,526
Kuala Terengganu	250,528
Kuantan	283,041
Kuching	152,310[23]
Miri	140,000[23]
Petaling Jaya	438,084
★ Putrajaya (partly completed in 2004)	...
Sandakan	220,000[23]
Selayang Baru	170,000[23]
Seremban	246,441
Shah Alam	319,612
Sibu	155,000[23]
Sungai Petani	170,000[23]
Taiping	183,320
Tawau	145,000[23]
Maldives (2000)	
★ Male	74,069
Mali (1998)	
★ Bamako	1,016,167
Sikasso	113,803
Malta (2002 est.)	
★ Valletta	7,199
agglomeration	83,000[5]
Marshall Is. (2004 est.)	
★ Majuro	20,800
Martinique (1999)	
★ Fort-de-France	94,049
Mauritania (2000)	
★ Nouakchott	558,195
Mauritius (2000)	
Beau Bassin-Rose Hill	103,872
★ Port Louis	144,303
Vacoas-Phoenix	100,066
Mayotte (2002; MU)	
★ Mamoudzou	45,485

Major cities and national capitals (continued)

country city	population
Mexico (2000)	
Acapulco	620,656
Aguascalientes	594,092
Atizapán de Zaragoza (Ciudad López Mateos)	467,544
Boca del Río	123,891
Buenavista	193,707
Campeche	190,813
Cancún	397,191
Celaya	277,750
Chalco	125,027
Chetumal	121,602
Chihuahua	657,876
Chilpancingo	142,746
Chimalhuacán	482,530
Ciudad Acuña (Acuña)	108,159
Ciudad Apodaca (Apodaca)	270,369
Ciudad del Carmen	126,024
Ciudad Madero	182,325
Ciudad Obregón	250,790
Ciudad Santa Catarina (Santa Catarina)	225,976
Ciudad Valles	105,721
Ciudad Victoria (Victoria)	249,029
Coacalco	252,291
Coatzacoalcos	225,973
Colima	119,639
Córdoba	133,807
Cuautitlán Izcalli	433,830
Cuautla Morelos	136,932
Cuernavaca	327,162
Culiacán	540,823
Durango	427,135
Ecatepec (de Morelos)	1,621,827
Ensenada	223,492
General Escobedo	230,556
Gómez Palacio	210,113
Guadalajara	1,646,183
Guadalupe	669,842
Hermosillo	545,928
Heroica Nogales (Nogales)	156,854
Huixquilucan	107,951
Iguala	104,759
Irapuato	319,148
Ixtapaluca	235,827
Jiutepec	142,459
Juárez (Ciudad Juárez)	1,187,275
La Paz	162,954
León	1,020,818
Los Mochis	200,906
Los Reyes la Paz	211,298
Matamoros	376,279
Mazatlán	327,989
Mérida	662,530
Metepec	158,605
Mexicali	549,873
★ Mexico City	8,605,239
Minatitlán	109,193
Monclova	192,554
Monterrey	1,110,909
Morelia	549,996
Naucalpan	835,053
Nezahualcóyotl	1,225,083
Nicolás Romero	216,192
Nuevo Laredo	308,828
Oaxaca	251,846
Orizaba	118,552
Pachuca	231,602
Piedras Negras	126,386
Poza Rica de Hidalgo	151,441
Puebla	1,271,673
Puerta Vallarta	151,432
Querétaro	536,463
Reynosa	403,718
Salamanca	137,000
Saltillo	562,587
San Cristóbal de las Casas	112,442
San Francisco Coacalco	252,291
San Luis Potosí	629,208
San Luis Río Colorado	126,645
San Nicolás de los Garzas	496,879
San Pablo de las Salinas	146,560
San Pedro Garza García	125,945
Soledad de Graciano Sanchez	169,574
Tampico	295,442
Tapachula	179,839

country city	population
Tehuacán	204,598
Tepic	265,817
Texcoco (de Mora)	101,711
Tijuana	1,148,681
Tlalnepantla	714,735
Tlaquepaque	458,674
Toluca	435,125
Tonala	315,278
Torreón	502,964
Tuxtla Gutiérrez	424,579
Uruapan	225,816
Valle de Chalco (Xico)	322,784
Veracruz	411,582
Villahermosa	330,846
Xalapa (Jalapa Enríquez)	373,075
Xico	322,784
Zacatecas	113,947
Zamora de Hidalgo	122,881
Zapopan	910,690
Micronesia (2000)	
★ Palikir	6,227
Moldova (2003 est.)	
Bălți (Beltsy)	145,900
★ Chişinău (Kishinyov)	662,400
Tighina (Bendery)	125,000
Tiraspol	185,000
Monaco (2000)	
★ Monaco	32,020
Mongolia (2000)	
★ Ulaanbaatar (Ulan Bator)	760,077
Morocco (1994)	
Agadir	524,564
Beni-Mellal	140,212
Casablanca	2,770,560
El-Jadida	119,083
Fès	769,014
Kenitra	292,627
Khouribga	152,090
Ksar el-Kebir	107,065
Marrakech	672,506
Meknès	443,214
Mohammedia	170,063
Nador	112,450
Oujda	351,878
★ Rabat	623,457
Safi	262,276
Salé	504,420
Tangier	497,147
Temara	126,303
Tétouan	277,516
Mozambique (1997)	
Beira	412,588
Chimoio	177,608
★ Maputo	989,386
Matola	440,927
Mocuba	124,650
Nacala	164,309
Nampula	314,965
Quelimane	153,187
Tete	104,832
Xai-Xai	103,251
Myanmar (Burma) (2004 est.)	
Bassein (Pathein)	215,600
Henzada	122,700
Lashio	133,600
Mandalay	1,176,900
Maymyo	113,900
Meiktila	161,000
Mergui	148,200
Monywa	163,400
Moulmein (Mawlamyine)	405,800
Myingyan	128,600
Pakokku	112,500
Pegu (Bago)	200,900
Pyay (Prome, Pye)	131,200
Sittwe (Akyab)	161,400
Taunggyi	151,400
Tavoy (Dawei)	139,900
Thaton	104,800
★ Yangôn (Rangoon)	4,454,500
Namibia (2001 est.)	
★ Windhoek	220,000
Nauru (1992)	
★ Yaren	672
Nepal (2001; MU)	
Biratnagar	166,674
Birganj	112,484

country city	population
★ Kathmandu	671,846
Lalitpur (Patan)	162,991
Pokhara	156,312
Netherlands, The (2003 est.)	
Almere	164,943
Amersfoort	131,164
★ Amsterdam (capital)	735,080
Apeldoorn	155,779
Arnhem	141,728
Breda	164,378
Dordrecht	119,970
Ede	104,801
Eindhoven	206,138
Emmen	108,226
Enschede	152,255
Groningen	177,145
Haarlem	147,596
Haarlemmermeer	123,164
Leiden	117,682
Maastricht	122,004
Nijmegen	156,197
Rotterdam	599,472
's-Hertogenbosch	132,696
★ The Hague (seat of government)	463,841
Tilburg	198,028
Utrecht	265,107
Zaanstad	139,457
Zoetermeer	112,632
Zwolle	109,916
Netherlands Antilles (2001 est.)	
★ Willemstad	125,000
New Caledonia (1996)	
★ Nouméa	76,293
New Zealand (2003 est.)[24]	
Auckland	406,000
Christchurch	358,000
Dunedin	113,600
Hamilton	150,400
Manukau	358,000
North Shore	244,200
Waitakere	191,000
★ Wellington	178,000
Nicaragua (1995)	
León	123,865
★ Managua	864,201
Niger (2001)	
Maradi	147,038
★ Niamey	674,950
Zinder	170,574
Nigeria (1991)	
Aba	500,183
Abeokuta	352,735
★ Abuja	420,000[22]
Ado-Ekiti	156,122
Akure	239,124
Awka	104,682
Bauchi	206,537
Benin City	762,719
Bida	111,245
Calabar	310,839
Damaturu	141,897
Ede	142,363
Effon-Alaiye	158,977
Enugu	407,756
Gboko	101,281
Gombe	163,604
Gusau	132,393
Ibadan	1,835,300
Ife	186,856
Ijebu-Ode	124,313
Ikare	103,843
Ikire	111,435
Ikorodu	184,674
Ikot Ekpene	119,402
Ilawe-Ekiti	104,049
Ilesha	139,445
Ilorin	532,089
Ise	108,136
Iseyin	170,936
Iwo	125,645
Jimeta	141,724
Jos	510,300
Kaduna	993,642
Kano	2,166,554
Katsina	259,315
★ Lagos	5,195,247
agglomeration	13,400,000[22]
Maiduguri	618,278
Makurdi	151,515

country city	population
Minna	189,191
Mubi	128,900
Nnewi	121,065
Ogbomosho	433,030
Okene	312,775
Okpogho	105,127
Ondo	146,051
Onitsha	350,280
Oshogbo	250,951
Owerri	119,711
Owo	157,181
Oyo	369,894
Port Harcourt	703,421
Sagamu	127,513
Sango Otta	103,332
Sapele	109,576
Sokoto	329,639
Suleja	105,075
Ugep	134,773
Umuahia	147,167
Warri	363,382
Zaria	612,257
Northern Mariana Is. (2000)	
★ Saipan	62,392
Norway (2003 est.; MU)	
Bærum	102,529
Bergen	235,423
★ Oslo	517,401
Stavanger	111,007
Trondheim	152,699
Oman (2003)	
As-Sïb	223,267
Bawshar	149,506
Matrah	154,316
★ Muscat	56,410
agglomeration	631,033
Salālah	156,587
Şuḥār	104,057
Pakistan (1998)	
Abbottabad	105,999[25]
Bahawalnagar	109,642
Bahawalpur	403,408[25]
Burewala	149,857
Chiniot	169,282
Chishtian Mandi	101,659
Daska	101,500
Dera Ghazi Khan	188,149
Faisalabad (Lyallpur)	1,977,246
Gojra	114,967
Gujranwala	1,124,799
Gujrat	250,121
Hafizabad	130,216
Hyderabad	1,151,274[25]
★ Islamabad	524,500
Jacobabad	137,773
Jaranwala	103,308
Jhang Sadar	292,214
Jhelum	145,847
Kamoke	150,984
Karachi	9,269,265[25]
Kasur	241,649
Khairpur	102,188
Khanewal	132,962
Khanpur	117,764
Kohat	125,271[25]
Lahore	5,063,499[25]
Larkana	270,366
Mardan	244,511[25]
Mingaora	174,469
Mirpur Khas	184,465
Multan	1,182,441[25]
Muridike	108,578
Muzaffargarh	121,641
Nawabshah	183,110
Okara	200,901
Pakpattan	107,791
Peshawar	988,055[25]
Quetta	560,307
Rahimyar Khan	228,479
Rawalpindi	1,406,214[25]
Sadiqabad	141,509
Sahiwal	207,388
Sargodha	455,360[25]
Shekhupura	271,875
Shikarpur	133,259
Sialkot	417,597[25]
Sukkur	329,176
Tando Adam	103,363
Wah	198,431[25]
Palau (2000)	
★ Koror (de facto)	13,303
★ Melekeok (complex under construction)	239

country city	population
Panama (2000)	
★ Panama City	469,307
San Miguelito	293,745[26]
Papua New Guinea (2000)	
★ Port Moresby (National Capital District)	254,158
Paraguay (2002)	
★ Asunción	513,399
Capiatá	154,469
Ciudad del Este	223,350
Fernando de la Mora	114,332
Lambaré	119,984
Luque	170,433
San Lorenzo	202,745
Peru (1998 est.)	
Arequipa	710,103
Ayacucho	118,960
Cajamarca	108,009
Chiclayo	469,200
Chimbote	298,800
Chincha Alta	130,000
Cusco	278,590
Huancayo	305,039
Húanuco	129,688
Ica	194,820
Iquitos	334,013
Juliaca	180,000
Lima agglomeration	7,899,000[27]
Ate	324,799
Callao	407,904
Carabayllo	115,000
Chorrillos	238,739
Comas	434,690
El Agustino	159,707
Independencia	191,151
La Victoría	213,239
★ Lima	316,322
Los Olivos	281,115
Lurigancho	110,347
Puente Piedra	131,000
Rímac	190,836
San Borja	109,233
San Juan de Lurigancho	652,681
San Juan de Miraflores	329,023
San Martin de Porras	411,000
San Miguel	126,825
Santa Anita	131,519
Santiago de Surco	224,866
Ventanilla	105,824
Villa el Salvador	296,000
Villa Maria del Triunfo	301,505
Piura	308,155
Pucallpa	220,866
Puno	101,578
Sullana	170,000
Tacna	215,683
Trujillo	603,657
Philippines (2000)	
Angeles	263,971
Antipolo	200,000[23]
Bacolod	429,076
Bacoor	305,699
Baguio	252,386
Baliuag	119,675
Biñan	201,186
Binangonan	187,691
Butuan	120,000[23]
Cagayan de Oro	461,877
Cainta	242,511
Calamba	160,000[23]
Cebu	718,821
Cotabato	163,849
Dagupan	130,328
Dasmariñas	250,000[23]
Davao	700,000[23]
Dumaguete	102,265
General Mariano Alvarez	112,446
General Santos	250,000[23]
Iloilo	365,820
Kalookan (Caloocan)	1,177,604
Lapu-Lapu	217,019
Las Piñas	472,780
Lucena	196,075
Makati	444,867
Malabon	338,855
Malolos	175,291
Mandaluyong	278,474
Mandaue	259,728
★ Manila	1,581,082
Metro Manila	9,932,560

country city	population
Marawi	131,090
Marikina	391,170
Meycauayan	163,037
Muntinlupa	379,310
Naga	137,810
Navotas	230,403
Olongapo	194,260
Parañaque	449,811
Pasay	354,908
Pasig	505,058
★ Quezon City	2,173,831
San Fernando	221,857
San Juan del Monte	117,680
San Pablo	105,000[23]
San Pedro	231,403
Santa Rosa	185,633
Tacloban	178,639
Tagig	467,375
Taytay	198,183
Valenzuela	485,433
Zamboanga	135,000[23]
Poland (2002)	
Białystok	291,383
Bielsko-Biała	178,028
Bydgoszcz	373,804
Bytom	193,546
Chorzów	117,430
Częstochowa	251,436
Dąbrowa Górnicza	132,236
Elbląg	128,134
Gdańsk	461,334
Gdynia	253,458
Gliwice	203,814
Gorzów Wielkopolski	125,914
Grudziadz	100,376
Kalisz	109,498
Katowice	327,222
Kielce	212,429
Koszalin	108,709
Kraków	758,544
Legnica	107,100
Łódź	789,318
Lublin	357,110
Olsztyn	173,102
Opole	129,946
Płock	128,361
Poznań	578,886
Radom	229,699
Ruda Śląska	150,595
Rybnik	142,731
Rzeszów	160,376
Sosnowiec	232,622
Szczecin	415,399
Tarnów	119,913
Toruń	211,243
Tychy	132,816
Wałbrzych	130,268
★ Warsaw (Warszawa)	1,671,670
Włocławek	121,229
Wrocław	640,367
Zabrze	195,293
Zielona Góra	118,293
Portugal (2001)	
Amadora	151,486
Braga	112,039
Coimbra	104,489
Funchal	103,961
★ Lisbon	564,657
agglomeration	1,962,000[5]
Porto	263,131
Puerto Rico (2000)	
Bayamón	203,499[24]
Carolina	168,164[24]
Ponce	155,038[24]
★ San Juan	421,958[24]
agglomeration	2,332,000[5]
Qatar (2004)	
★ Doha	338,760
Ar-Rayyān	272,583
Réunion (1999)	
★ Saint-Denis	131,557
Romania (2002)	
Arad	172,824
Bacău	175,921
Baia Mare	137,976
Botoşani	115,344
Brăila	216,929
Braşov	283,901
★ Bucharest	1,921,751
Buzău	133,116
Cluj-Napoca	318,027
Constanţa	310,526
Craiova	302,622
Drobeta-Turnu Severin	104,035

country city	population
Focşani	103,219
Galaţi	298,584
Iaşi	321,580
Oradea	206,527
Piatra Neamţ	105,499
Piteşti	168,756
Ploieşti	232,452
Râmnicu Vâlcea	107,656
Satu Mare	115,630
Sibiu	155,045
Suceava	106,138
Timişoara	317,651
Târgu Mureş	149,577
Russia (2002)	
Abakan	165,200
Achinsk	118,700
Almetyevsk	140,500
Angarsk	247,100
Arkhangelsk	355,500
Armavir	193,900
Arzamas	109,500
Astrakhan	506,400
Balakovo	200,600
Balashikha	148,200
Barnaul	603,500
Bataisk	107,300
Belgorod	337,600
Berezniki	173,500
Biysk	218,600
Blagoveshchensk	218,800
Bratsk	259,200
Bryansk	431,600
Cheboksary	440,800
Chelyabinsk	1,078,300
Cherepovets	312,200
Cherkessk	116,400
Chita	317,800
Derbent	100,800
Dimitrovgrad	130,900
Dzerzhinsk	261,400
Elektrostal	146,100
Elista	104,300
Engels	193,800
Glazov	100,900
Grozny (Dzhokhar)	223,000
Irkutsk	593,400
Ivanovo	432,200
Izhevsk	632,100
Kaliningrad	430,300
Kaluga	335,100
Kamensk-Uralsky	186,300
Kamyshin	128,100
Kansk	103,100
Kazan	1,105,300
Kemerovo	485,000
Khabarovsk	582,700
Khasavyurt	122,000
Khimki	141,300
Kirov	457,400
Kiselyovsk	106,400
Kislovodsk	129,800
Kolomna	150,100
Kolpino	161,900
Komsomolsk-na-Amure	281,000
Korolyov (Kaliningrad)	143,100
Kostroma	279,400
Kovrov	155,600
Krasnodar	644,800
Krasnoyarsk	911,700
Kurgan	345,700
Kursk	412,600
Kyzyl	104,100
Leninsk-Kuznetsky	112,300
Lipetsk	506,000
Lyubertsy	156,900
Magadan	101,100
Magnitogorsk	419,100
Makhachkala	466,800
Maykop	162,400
Mezhdurechensk	102,000
Miass	158,500
★ Moscow	10,101,500
Murmansk	336,700
Murom	126,800
Mytishchi	159,200
Naberezhnye Chelny (Brezhnev)	510,000
Nakhodka	149,300
Nalchik	273,900
Nazran	126,700
Nefteyugansk	107,800
Nevinnomyssk	132,100
Nikolo-Beryozovka (Neftekamsk)	122,300
Nizhnekamsk	225,500
Nizhnevartovsk	239,000
Nizhny Novgorod (Gorky)	1,311,200

country city	population
Nizhny Tagil	390,600
Noginsk	118,000
Norilsk	135,100
Novgorod	217,200
Novocheboksarsk	125,900
Novocherkassk	170,900
Novokuybyshevsk	113,000
Novokuznetsk	550,100
Novomoskovsk	134,000
Novorossiysk	231,900
Novoshakhtinsk	101,200
Novosibirsk	1,425,600
Novotroitsk	106,200
Obninsk	105,800
Odintsovo	134,700
Oktyabrsky	108,700
Omsk	1,133,900
Orekhovo-Zuyevo	122,300
Orenburg	548,800
Orsk	250,600
Oryol	333,600
Penza	518,200
Perm	1,000,100
Pervouralsk	132,800
Petropavlovsk-Kamchatsky	198,200
Petrozavodsk	266,200
Podolsk	181,500
Prokopyevsk	224,600
Pskov	202,700
Pyatigorsk	140,300
Rostov-na-Donu	1,070,200
Rubtsovsk	163,100
Ryazan	521,700
Rybinsk (Andropov)	222,800
Saint Petersburg (Leningrad)	4,669,400
Salavat	158,500
Samara (Kuybyshev)	1,158,100
Saransk	304,900
Sarapul	103,200
Saratov	873,500
Sergiev Posad (Zagorsk)	113,800
Serov	100,300
Serpukhov	131,200
Severodvinsk	201,500
Seversk	115,700
Shakhty	220,400
Shchyolkovo	113,700
Simbirsk (Ulyanovsk)	635,600
Smolensk	325,500
Sochi	328,800
Solikamsk	102,800
Stary Oskol	216,000
Stavropol	354,600
Sterlitamak	264,400
Surgut	285,500
Syktyvkar	230,000
Syzran	187,800
Taganrog	282,300
Tambov	294,300
Tolyatti	701,900
Tomsk	487,700
Tula	472,300
Tver (Kalinin)	409,400
Tyumen	510,700
Ufa	1,042,400
Ukhta	103,500
Ulan-Ude	359,400
Usolye-Sibirskoye	103,500
Ussuriysk	157,800
Ust-Ilimsk	100,600
Velikiye Luki	105,000
Vladikavkaz (Ordzhonikidze)	315,100
Vladimir	316,300
Vladivostok	591,800
Volgodonsk	166,500
Volgograd	1,012,800
Vologda	292,800
Volzhsky	310,700
Voronezh	848,700
Votkinsk	101,700
Yakutsk	209,500
Yaroslavl	613,200
Yekaterinburg (Sverdlovsk)	1,293,000
Yelets	116,700
Yoshkar-Ola	256,800
Yuzhno-Sakhalinsk	174,700
Zelenodolsk	100,100
Zelenograd	215,900
Zheleznodorozhny	104,100
Zhukovsky	101,900
Zlatoust	194,800
Rwanda (2002)	
★ Kigali	608,141

country city	population
St. Kitts and Nevis (2001)	
★ Basseterre	13,220
St. Lucia (2001)	
★ Castries	12,439
agglomeration	37,549
St. Vincent and the Grenadines (2000 est.)	
★ Kingstown	16,209
Samoa (2001)	
★ Apia	38,836
San Marino (2003 est.)	
★ San Marino	4,483
São Tomé and Príncipe (2001)	
★ São Tomé	51,886
Saudi Arabia (1992)	
Abhā	112,316
'Ar'ar	108,055
Buraydah	248,636
Ad-Dammām	482,321
Hafar al-Bāţin	137,793
Hā'il	176,757
Al-Hufūf	225,847
Jiddah	2,046,251
Al-Jubayl	140,828
Khamīs Mushayţ	217,870
Al-Kharj	152,071
Al-Khubar	141,683
Mecca (Makkah)	965,697
Medina (Al-Madīnah)	608,295
Al-Mubarraz	219,123
★ Riyadh (Ar-Riyāḏ)	2,776,096
Tabūk	292,555
Aţ-Ţā'if	416,121
Ath-Thuqbah	125,650
Yanbu' al-Baḥr	119,819
Senegal (2001 est.)	
★ Dakar	919,683
Diourbel	112,950
Kaolack	243,209
Mbour	148,985
Rufisque	165,274
Saint-Louis	154,496
Thiès	273,599
Ziguinchor	216,971
Serbia and Montenegro (2002)	
★ Belgrade (executive and legislative)	1,120,092
Kragujevac	146,373
Niš	173,724
Novi Sad	191,405
★ Podgorica (judicial)	139,100[5]
Priština	165,844[5]
Prizren	107,614[5]
Seychelles (1997)	
★ Victoria	24,701[28]
Sierra Leone (2004 est.)	
★ Freetown	1,070,200
Koidu	115,700
Makeni	115,600
Singapore (2002 est.)	
★ Singapore	4,171,300[29]
Slovakia (2001)	
★ Bratislava	428,672
Košice	236,093
Slovenia (2002)	
★ Ljubljana	258,873
Solomon Islands (2000 est.)	
★ Honiara	50,100
Somalia (2003 est.)	
★ Mogadishu	...
agglomeration	1,212,000
South Africa (1996)[28, 30]	
Alberton	147,948
Benoni	365,467
★ Bloemfontein (de facto judicial)	333,769
Boksburg	260,905
Botshabelo	177,971
Brakpan	171,359
★ Cape Town (de facto legislative)	2,415,408
Carletonville	164,367

country city	population
Durban	2,117,650
East London	212,323
Johannesburg	1,480,530
Kimberley	170,432
Klerksdorp	137,318
Krugersdorp	203,168
Mdantsane	182,998
Midrand	126,400
Newcastle	219,682
Paarl	140,376
Pietermaritzburg	378,126
Port Elizabeth	749,921
Potchefstroom	101,682
★ Pretoria (de facto executive)	1,104,479
Rustenburg	104,537
Somerset West	112,489
Soweto	1,098,094
Springs	160,795
Tembisa	282,272
Uitenhage	192,120
Vanderbijlpark	253,335
Vereeniging	346,780
Verwoerdburg	114,575
Welkom	203,296
Westonaria	113,932
Witbank	167,183
Spain (2001)	
Albacete	148,934
Alcalá de Henares	176,434
Alcorcón	153,100
Algeciras	101,468
Alicante (Alacant)	284,580
Almería	166,328
Badajoz	133,519
Badalona	205,836
Barcelona	1,503,884
Bilbao	349,972
Burgos	166,187
Cádiz	133,363
Cartagena	184,686
Castellón de la Plana (Castelló de la Plana)	147,667
Córdoba	308,072
Coruña, A (Coruña, La)	236,379
Donostia–San Sebastián	178,377
Dos Hermanas	101,988
Elche (Elx)	194,767
Fuenlabrada	182,705
Getafe	151,479
Gijón	266,419
Granada	240,661
Hospitalet (de Llobregat)	239,019
Huelva	142,284
Jaén	112,590
Jerez de la Frontera	183,273
Laguna, La	128,822
Leganés	173,584
León	130,916
Lleida (Lérida)	112,199
Logroño	133,058
★ Madrid	2,938,723
Málaga	524,414
Marbella	100,036
Mataró	106,358
Móstoles	196,524
Murcia	370,745
Ourense (Orense)	107,510
Oviedo	201,154
Palma (de Mallorca)	333,801
Palmas de Gran Canaria, Las	354,863
Pamplona (Iruña)	183,964
Sabadell	183,788
Salamanca	156,368
Santa Coloma de Gramanet	112,992
Santa Cruz de Tenerife	188,477
Santander	180,717
Sevilla (Seville)	684,633
Tarragona	113,129
Terrassa (Tarrasa)	173,775
Valencia (València)	738,441
Valladolid	316,580
Vigo	280,186
Vitoria–Gasteiz	216,852
Zaragoza (Saragossa)	614,905
Sri Lanka (2001)[24]	
★ Colombo (administrative)	642,163
Dehiwala-Mount Lavinia	209,787

Major cities and national capitals   (continued)

country city	population
Jaffna	145,600[31]
Kandy	110,049
Moratuwa	177,190
Negombo	121,933
★ Sri Jayawardenepura Kotte (legislative and judicial)	115,826
Sudan, The (1993)	
Al-Fāshir	141,884
Juba	125,000[1]
Kassalā	234,622
★ Khartoum (executive)	947,483
Khartoum North	700,887
Kūstī	173,599
Nyala	227,183
★ Omdurman (legislative)	1,271,403
Port Sudan	308,195
Al-Qaḍārif	191,164
Al-Ubayyiḍ	229,425
Wad Madanī	211,362
Suriname (2004 est.)	
★ Paramaribo	218,500
Swaziland (1997)	
★ Lobamba (legislative)	...
★ Lozitha (royal)	...
★ Ludzidzini (royal)	...
★ Mbabane (administrative)	57,992
Sweden (2003 est.; MU)	
Göteborg	474,921
Helsingborg	119,406
Jönköping	118,581
Linköping	135,066
Lund	100,402
Malmö	265,481
Norrköping	123,303
Örebro	125,520
★ Stockholm	758,148
Umeå	106,525
Uppsala	179,673
Västerås	128,902
Switzerland (2003 est.)	
Basel (Bâle)	165,031
★ Bern (Berne) (administrative)	122,707
Geneva (Genève)	177,535
★ Lausanne (judicial)	116,332
Zürich	342,518
Syria (2004 est.)	
Aleppo (Halab)	1,975,200
★ Damascus (Dimashq)	1,614,500
Darʿā	103,300
Dayr az-Zawr	239,800
Dūmā	104,600
Hamāh	366,800
Ál-Ḥasakah	211,300
Homs (Ḥimṣ)	800,400
Jaramānah	192,800
Latakia (al-Ladhiqiyah)	468,700
Al-Qāmishlī	210,300
Ar-Raqqah	229,100
Tarṭūs	162,300
Aṭ-Ṭawrah	102,100
Taiwan (2002 est.)	
Chang-hua	232,156
Chi-lung (Keelung)	391,450
Chia-i	267,906
Chung-ho	403,510
Chung-li	334,683
Feng-shan	323,799
Feng-yüan	162,115
Hsi-chih	167,224
Hsin-chu	378,797
Hsin-chuang	380,334
Hsin-tien	275,467
Hua-lien	107,525
Kao-hsiung	1,509,510
Lu-chou	173,209
Nan-t'ou	105,061
Pa-te	167,085
Pan-ch-'iao (T'ai-pei-hsien)	535,476
P'ing-chen	196,408
P'ing-tung	215,584
San-chu'ung	384,217
Shu-lin	157,913
T'ai-chung	996,706
T'ai-nan	745,081

country city	population
T'ai-p'ing	168,892
T'ai-tung	110,899
★ Taipei (T'ai-pei)	2,641,856
Ta-li	178,998
T'ao-yuan	347,160
Tou-liu	102,460
T'u-ch'eng	234,125
Yung-ho	230,660
Yung-k'ang	200,719
Tajikistan (2002 est.)	
★ Dushanbe	575,900
Khujand (Khudzhand; Leninabad)	147,400
Tanzania (2002)	
Arusha	270,485
★ Dar es Salaam (acting)	2,336,055
Dodoma (future capital)	149,180
Kigoma	130,142
Mbeya	230,218
Morogoro	206,868
Moshi	143,799
Musoma	103,497
Mwanza	209,806
Tabora	127,887
Tanga	179,400
Zanzibar	205,870
Thailand (2000)	
★ Bangkok (Krung Thep)	6,320,174
Chiang Mai	167,776
Chon Buri	182,641
Hat Yai	185,557
Khlong Luang	103,282
Khon Kaen	141,034
Lampang	147,812
Nakhon Pathom	120,657
Nakhon Ratchasima	204,391
Nakhon Si Thammarat	118,764
Nonthaburi	291,307
Pak Kret	141,788
Phra Pradaeng	166,828
Rayong	106,585
Samut Prakan	378,694
Si Racha	141,334
Surat Thani	111,276
Thanya Buri	113,818
Ubon Ratchathani	106,552
Udon Thani	220,493
Togo (2003 est.)	
★ Lomé	676,400
Tonga (1996)	
★ Nuku'alofa	22,400
Trinidad and Tobago (2000)	
★ Port of Spain	49,031
Tunisia (2004 est.)	
Aryānah	217,600
Bizerte (Banzart)	112,800
Ettadhamen	197,400
Qābis	110,000
Al-Qayrawān (Kairouan)	116,000
Ṣafāqis (Sfax)	273,300
Sūsah	156,600
★ Tunis	695,500
Turkey (2000)	
Adana	1,130,710
Adıyaman	178,538
Afyon	128,516
Aksaray	129,949
★ Ankara	3,203,362
Antakya (Hatay)	144,910
Antalya	603,190
Aydın	143,267
Balıkesir	215,436
Batman	246,678
Bursa	1,194,687
Ceyhan	108,602
Çorlu	141,525
Çorum	161,321
Denizli	275,480
Diyarbakır	545,983
Edirne	119,298
Elazığ	266,495
Erzincan	107,175
Erzurum	361,235
Eskişehir	482,793
Gaziantep	853,513

country city	population
Gebze	253,487
İçel (Mersin)	537,842
İnegöl	105,959
İskenderun	159,149
Isparta	148,496
Istanbul	8,803,468
İzmir	2,232,265
Kahramanmaraş (Maraş)	326,198
Karabük	100,749
Karaman	105,384
Kayseri	536,392
Kırıkkale	205,078
Kızıltepe	113,143
Kocaeli (İzmit)	195,699
Konya	742,690
Kütahya	166,665
Malatya	381,081
Manisa	214,345
Nazilli	105,665
Ordu	112,525
Osmaniye	173,977
Sakarya (Adapazarı)	283,752
Samsun	363,180
Sivas	251,776
Siverek	126,820
Sultanbeyli	175,700
Tarsus	216,382
Tekirdağ	107,191
Tokat	113,100
Trabzon	214,949
Urfa (Şanlıurfa)	385,588
Uşak	137,001
Van	284,464
Viranşehir	121,382
Zonguldak	104,276
Turkmenistan (2004 est.)	
★ Ashgabat	773,400
Balkanabat (Nebitdag)	101,600
Daşoguz	163,100
Mary	129,200
Türkmenabat (Chärjew)	242,000
Tuvalu (2002)	
★ Funafuti	4,492
Uganda (2002)	
Gulu	113,144
★ Kampala	1,208,544
Ukraine (2001)	
Alchevsk	119,193
Berdyansk	121,692
Bila Tserkva	200,131
Cherkasy	295,414
Chernihiv	304,994
Chernivtsi	240,621
Dniprodzerzhynsk	255,841
Dnipropetrovsk	1,065,008
Donetsk	1,016,194
Horlivka	292,250
Ivano-Frankivsk	218,359
Kerch	157,007
Kharkiv	1,470,902
Kherson	328,360
Khmelnytskyy	253,994
★ Kiev	2,611,327
Kirovohrad	254,103
Kramatorsk	181,025
Kremenchuk	234,073
Kryvyy Rih	668,980
Luhansk	463,097
Lutsk	208,816
Lviv	732,818
Lysychansk	115,229
Makiyivka	389,589
Mariupol	492,176
Melitopol	160,657
Mykolayiv	514,136
Nikopol	136,280
Odesa	1,029,049
Pavlohrad	118,816
Poltava	317,998
Rivne	248,813
Sevastopol	342,451
Simferopol	343,644
Slov'yansk	124,829
Sumy	293,141
Syeverodonetsk	119,940
Ternopil	227,755
Uzhhorod	117,317
Vinnytsya	356,665
Yenakiyeve	103,997
Yevpatoriya	105,915
Zaporizhzhya	815,256
Zhytomyr	284,236

country city	population
United Arab Emirates (2003 est.)	
★ Abu Dhabi	552,000
ʿAjmān	225,000
Al-ʿAyn	348,000
Dubai	1,171,000
Raʾs al-Khaymah	102,000
Sharjah	519,000
United Kingdom (2001)	
England[32]	
Barnsley	218,062
Birmingham	977,091
Blackburn with Darwen	137,471
Blackpool	142,284
Bolton	261,035
Bournemouth	163,441
Bracknell Forest	109,506
Bradford	467,668
Brighton and Hove	247,820
Bristol	380,615
Bury	180,612
Calderdale	192,396
Cambridge	108,879
Canterbury	135,287
Carlisle	100,734
Chester	118,207
Coventry	300,844
Darlington	97,872
Derby	221,716
Doncaster	286,865
Dudley	305,164
Durham	87,725
Exeter	111,078
Gateshead	191,151
Gloucester	109,888
Halton	118,215
Kingston upon Hull	243,595
Kirklees	388,576
Knowsley	150,468
Lancaster	133,914
Leeds	715,404
Leicester	279,923
Lincoln	85,616
Liverpool	439,476
★ London (Greater London)	7,172,091[33]
Luton	184,390
Manchester	392,819
Milton Keynes	207,063
Newcastle upon Tyne	259,573
North Tyneside	191,663
Norwich	121,553
Nottingham	266,995
Oldham	217,393
Oxford	134,248
Peterborough	156,060
Plymouth	240,718
Poole	138,299
Portsmouth	186,704
Reading	143,124
Rochdale	205,233
Rotherham	248,176
St. Albans	128,982
St. Helens	176,845
Salford	216,119
Sandwell	282,901
Sefton	282,956
Sheffield	513,234
Slough	119,070
Solihull	199,521
South Tyneside	152,785
Southampton	217,478
Southend	160,256
Stockport	284,544
Stockton-on-Tees	178,405
Stoke-on-Trent	240,643
Sunderland	280,807
Swindon	180,061
Tameside	213,045
Thurrock	143,042
Torbay	129,702
Trafford	210,135
Wakefield	315,173
Walsall	253,502
Warrington	191,084
Wigan	301,417
Winchester	107,213
Windsor and Maidenhead	133,606
Wirral	312,289
Wolverhampton	236,573
Worcester	93,358
York	181,131

country city	population
Northern Ireland[34]	
Belfast	277,391
Craigavon	80,671
Derry (Londonderry)	105,066
Lisburn	108,694
Newtonabbey	79,993
Scotland[35]	
Aberdeen	184,788
Dundee	145,663
Edinburgh	448,624
Glasgow	577,869
Wales[36]	
Cardiff	305,340
Conwy	109,597
Neath Port Talbot	134,471
Newport	137,017
Rhondda, Cynon, Taff	231,952
Swansea	223,293
Torfaen	90,967
Wrexham	128,477
United States (2003 est.)	
Abilene (Texas)	114,889
Akron (Ohio)	212,215
Albany (Ga.)	76,202
Albany (N.Y.)	93,919
Albuquerque (N.M.)	471,856
Alexandria (Va.)	128,923
Alhambra (Calif.)	87,754
Allentown (Pa.)	105,958
Amarillo (Texas)	178,612
Anaheim (Calif.)	332,361
Anchorage (Alaska)	270,951
Ann Arbor (Mich.)	114,498
Antioch (Calif.)	101,124
Arden-Arcade (Calif.)[37]	96,025[38]
Arlington (Texas)	355,007
Arlington (Va.)[37]	187,873
Arlington Heights (Ill.)	75,784
Arvada (Colo.)	101,972
Athens (Ga.)	102,498
Atlanta (Ga.)	423,019
Augusta (Ga.)	193,316
Aurora (Colo.)	290,418
Aurora (Ill.)	162,184
Austin (Texas)	672,011
Bakersfield (Calif.)	271,035
Baldwin Park (Calif.)	78,747
Baltimore (Md.)	628,670
Baton Rouge (La.)	225,090
Beaumont (Texas)	112,434
Beaverton (Ore.)	80,520
Bellevue (Wash.)	112,344
Berkeley (Calif.)	102,049
Billings (Mont.)	95,220
Birmingham (Ala.)	236,620
Bloomington (Minn.)	83,080
Boca Raton (Fla.)	78,449
Boise (Idaho)	190,117
Boston (Mass.)	581,616
Boulder (Colo.)	93,051
Brandon (Fla.)[37]	77,895[38]
Brick Township (N.J.)[37]	76,119[38]
Bridgeport (Conn.)	139,664
Brockton (Mass.)	95,090
Broken Arrow (Okla.)	83,607
Brownsville (Texas)	156,178
Buena Park (Calif.)	78,934
Buffalo (N.Y.)	285,018
Burbank (Calif.)	103,359
Cambridge (Mass.)	101,587
Camden (N.J.)	80,089
Canton (Mich.)[37]	76,366[38]
Canton (Ohio)	79,255
Cape Coral (Fla.)	118,737
Carlsbad (Calif.)	87,372
Carrollton (Texas)	116,714
Carson (Calif.)	93,747
Cary (N.C.)	99,824
Cedar Rapids (Iowa)	122,542
Centennial (Colo.)	98,586
Chandler (Ariz.)	211,299
Charleston (S.C.)	101,024
Charlotte (N.C.)	584,658
Chattanooga (Tenn.)	154,887
Cheektowaga (N.Y.)[37]	79,988[38]
Chesapeake (Va.)	210,834
Chicago (Ill.)	2,869,121
Chula Vista (Calif.)	199,060
Cicero (Ill.)	83,029
Cincinnati (Ohio)	317,361
Citrus Heights (Calif.)	88,515
Clarksville (Tenn.)	107,953
Clearwater (Fla.)	108,272
Cleveland (Ohio)	461,324

country city	population
Clifton (*N.J.*)	79,823
Clinton Township (*Mich.*)[37]	95,648[38]
Clovis (*Calif.*)	78,558
Colorado Springs (*Colo.*)	370,448
Columbia (*Md.*)[37]	88,254[38]
Columbia (*Mo.*)	88,553
Columbia (*S.C.*)	117,357
Columbus (*Ga.*)	185,702
Columbus (*Ohio*)	728,432
Compton (*Calif.*)	95,835
Concord (*Calif.*)	124,977
Coral Springs (*Fla.*)	127,005
Corona (*Calif.*)	142,454
Corpus Christi (*Texas*)	279,208
Costa Mesa (*Calif.*)	109,563
Cranston (*R.I.*)	81,679
Dallas (*Texas*)	1,208,318
Daly City (*Calif.*)	100,819
Danbury (*Conn.*)	77,353
Davenport (*Iowa*)	97,512
Davie (*Fla.*)	80,364
Dayton (*Ohio*)	161,696
Dearborn (*Mich.*)	96,670
Decatur (*Ill.*)	79,285
Deltona (*Fla.*)	76,597
Denton (*Texas*)	93,435
Denver (*Colo.*)	557,478
Des Moines (*Iowa*)	195,093
Detroit (*Mich.*)	911,402
Dover Township (*N.J.*)[37]	86,327[38]
Downey (*Calif.*)	110,360
Duluth (*Minn.*)	85,734
Durham (*N.C.*)	198,376
East Los Angeles (*Calif.*)[37]	124,283[38]
Edison Township (*N.J.*)	100,138
El Cajon (*Calif.*)	95,159
El Monte (*Calif.*)	121,740
El Paso (*Texas*)	584,113
Elgin (*Ill.*)	97,117
Elizabeth (*N.J.*)	123,215
Elk Grove (*Calif.*)	82,499
Erie (*Pa.*)	101,373
Escondido (*Calif.*)	136,093
Eugene (*Ore.*)	142,185
Evansville (*Ind.*)	117,881
Everett (*Wash.*)	96,643
Fairfield (*Calif.*)	102,762
Fall River (*Mass.*)	92,760
Fargo (*N.D.*)	91,484
Farmington Hills (*Mich.*)	80,874
Fayetteville (*N.C.*)	124,372
Federal Way (*Wash.*)	81,711
Flint (*Mich.*)	120,292
Fontana (*Calif.*)	151,903
Fort Collins (*Colo.*)	125,740
Fort Lauderdale (*Fla.*)	162,917
Fort Smith (*Ark.*)	81,562
Fort Wayne (*Ind.*)	219,495
Fort Worth (*Texas*)	585,122
Fremont (*Calif.*)	204,525
Fresno (*Calif.*)	451,455
Fullerton (*Calif.*)	131,249
Gainesville (*Fla.*)	109,146
Garden Grove (*Calif.*)	167,029
Garland (*Texas*)	218,027
Gary (*Ind.*)	99,961
Gilbert (*Ariz.*)	145,250
Glendale (*Ariz.*)	232,838
Glendale (*Calif.*)	200,499
Grand Prairie (*Texas*)	136,671
Grand Rapids (*Mich.*)	195,601
Greeley (*Colo.*)	83,414
Green Bay (*Wis.*)	101,467
Greensboro (*N.C.*)	229,110
Gresham (*Ore.*)	95,816
Hammond (*Ind.*)	80,547
Hampton (*Va.*)	146,878
Hartford (*Conn.*)	124,387
Hawthorne (*Calif.*)	86,173
Hayward (*Calif.*)	141,336
Henderson (*Nev.*)	214,852
Hialeah (*Fla.*)	226,401
High Point (*N.C.*)	91,543
Hillsboro (*Ore.*)	77,709
Hollywood (*Fla.*)	143,408
Honolulu (*Hawaii*)[37]	380,149
Houston (*Texas*)	2,009,690
Huntington Beach (*Calif.*)	194,248
Huntsville (*Ala.*)	164,237
Independence (*Mo.*)	112,079
Indianapolis (*Ind.*)	783,438
Inglewood (*Calif.*)	115,208
Irvine (*Calif.*)	170,561
Irving (*Texas*)	194,455
Jackson (*Miss.*)	179,599
Jacksonville (*Fla.*)	773,781
Jersey City (*N.J.*)	239,097
Joliet (*Ill.*)	123,570
Kalamazoo (*Mich.*)	75,312
Kansas City (*Kan.*)	145,757
Kansas City (*Mo.*)	442,768
Kendall (*Fla.*)[37]	75,226[38]
Kenosha (*Wis.*)	92,871
Kent (*Wash.*)	81,567
Killeen (*Texas*)	96,159
Knoxville (*Tenn.*)	173,278
Lafayette (*La.*)	111,667
Lake Forest (*Calif.*)	76,738
Lakeland (*Fla.*)	87,860
Lakewood (*Calif.*)	81,300
Lakewood (*Colo.*)	142,474
Lancaster (*Calif.*)	125,896
Lansing (*Mich.*)	118,379
Laredo (*Texas*)	197,488
Las Cruces (*N.M.*)	76,990
Las Vegas (*Nev.*)	517,017
Lawrence (*Kan.*)	82,120
Lawton (*Okla.*)	91,730
Lee's Summit (*Mo.*)	77,052
Lewisville (*Texas*)	87,127
Lexington (*Ky.*)	266,798
Lincoln (*Neb.*)	235,594
Little Rock (*Ark.*)	184,053
Livermore (*Calif.*)	77,744
Livonia (*Mich.*)	99,487
Long Beach (*Calif.*)	475,460
Longmont (*Colo.*)	79,556
Los Angeles (*Calif.*)	3,819,951
Louisville (*Ky.*)	248,762
Lowell (*Mass.*)	104,351
Lubbock (*Texas*)	206,481
Lynn (*Mass.*)	89,571
McAllen (*Texas*)	116,501
McKinney (*Texas*)	79,958
Macon (*Ga.*)	95,267
Madison (*Wis.*)	218,432
Manchester (*N.H.*)	108,871
Memphis (*Tenn.*)	645,978
Mesa (*Ariz.*)	432,376
Mesquite (*Texas*)	129,270
Metairie (*La.*)[37]	146,136[38]
Miami (*Fla.*)	376,815
Miami Beach (*Fla.*)	89,312
Midland (*Texas*)	96,573
Milwaukee (*Wis.*)	586,941
Minneapolis (*Minn.*)	373,188
Miramar (*Fla.*)	96,646
Mission Viejo (*Calif.*)	95,831
Mobile (*Ala.*)	193,464
Modesto (*Calif.*)	206,872
Montgomery (*Ala.*)	200,123
Moreno Valley (*Calif.*)	157,063
Murfreesboro (*Tenn.*)	78,074
Napa (*Calif.*)	75,560
Naperville (*Ill.*)	137,894
Nashua (*N.H.*)	87,285
Nashville (*Tenn.*)	544,765
New Bedford (*Mass.*)	94,112
New Haven (*Conn.*)	124,512
New Orleans (*La.*)	469,032
New York City (*N.Y.*)	8,085,742
Newark (*N.J.*)	277,911
Newport Beach (*Calif.*)	78,043
Newport News (*Va.*)	181,647
Newton (*Mass.*)	84,323
Norfolk (*Va.*)	241,727
Norman (*Okla.*)	99,197
North Charleston (*S.C.*)	81,577
North Las Vegas (*Nev.*)	144,502
Norwalk (*Calif.*)	107,155
Norwalk (*Conn.*)	84,170
Oakland (*Calif.*)	398,844
Oceanside (*Calif.*)	167,082
Odessa (*Texas*)	91,113
Ogden (*Utah*)	78,293
Oklahoma City (*Okla.*)	523,303
Olathe (*Kan.*)	105,274
Omaha (*Neb.*)	404,267
Ontario (*Calif.*)	167,402
Orange (*Calif.*)	132,197
Orem (*Utah*)	87,599
Orlando (*Fla.*)	199,336
Overland Park (*Kan.*)	160,368
Oxnard (*Calif.*)	180,872
Palm Bay (*Fla.*)	85,076
Palmdale (*Calif.*)	127,759
Paradise (*Nev.*)[37]	186,070[38]
Parma (*Ohio*)	83,861
Pasadena (*Calif.*)	141,114
Pasadena (*Texas*)	144,413
Paterson (*N.J.*)	150,782
Pembroke Pines (*Fla.*)	148,927
Peoria (*Ariz.*)	127,580
Peoria (*Ill.*)	112,907
Philadelphia (*Pa.*)	1,479,339
Phoenix (*Ariz.*)	1,388,416
Pittsburgh (*Pa.*)	325,337
Plano (*Texas*)	241,991
Plantation (*Fla.*)	84,929
Pomona (*Calif.*)	154,147
Pompano Beach (*Fla.*)	88,064
Port St. Lucie (*Fla.*)	105,507
Portland (*Ore.*)	538,544
Portsmouth (*Va.*)	99,617
Providence (*R.I.*)	176,365
Provo (*Utah*)	105,410
Pueblo (*Colo.*)	103,648
Quincy (*Mass.*)	89,059
Racine (*Wis.*)	80,266
Raleigh (*N.C.*)	316,802
Rancho Cucamonga (*Calif.*)	151,640
Reading (*Pa.*)	80,305
Redding (*Calif.*)	87,579
Reno (*Nev.*)	193,882
Rialto (*Calif.*)	98,091
Richardson (*Texas*)	99,536
Richmond (*Calif.*)	102,327
Richmond (*Va.*)	194,729
Riverside (*Calif.*)	281,514
Roanoke (*Va.*)	92,863
Rochester (*Minn.*)	92,507
Rochester (*N.Y.*)	215,093
Rockford (*Ill.*)	151,725
Roseville (*Calif.*)	98,359
Roswell (*Ga.*)	78,229
Round Rock (*Texas*)	77,946
Sacramento (*Calif.*)	445,335
St. Louis (*Mo.*)	332,223
St. Paul (*Minn.*)	280,404
St. Petersburg (*Fla.*)	247,610
Salem (*Ore.*)	142,914
Salinas (*Calif.*)	147,840
Salt Lake City (*Utah*)	179,894
San Angelo (*Texas*)	87,922
San Antonio (*Texas*)	1,214,725
San Bernardino (*Calif.*)	195,357
San Buenaventura (Ventura) (*Calif.*)	104,140
San Diego (*Calif.*)	1,266,753
San Francisco (*Calif.*)	751,682
San Jose (*Calif.*)	898,349
San Leandro (*Calif.*)	80,139
San Mateo (*Calif.*)	91,157
Sandy (*Utah*)	89,319
Sandy Springs (*Ga.*)[37]	85,781[38]
Santa Ana (*Calif.*)	342,510
Santa Barbara (*Calif.*)	88,251
Santa Clara (*Calif.*)	102,095
Santa Clarita (*Calif.*)	162,742
Santa Maria (*Calif.*)	81,944
Santa Monica (*Calif.*)	87,162
Santa Rosa (*Calif.*)	153,386
Savannah (*Ga.*)	127,573
Scottsdale (*Ariz.*)	217,989
Seattle (*Wash.*)	569,101
Shreveport (*La.*)	198,364
Silver Spring (*Md.*)[37]	76,540[38]
Simi Valley (*Calif.*)	117,115
Sioux City (*Iowa*)	83,876
Sioux Falls (*S.D.*)	133,834
Somerville (*Mass.*)	76,296
South Bend (*Ind.*)	105,540
South Gate (*Calif.*)	98,966
Southfield (*Mich.*)	77,488
Sparks (*Nev.*)	77,295
Spokane (*Wash.*)	196,624
Spring Valley (*Nev.*)[37]	117,390[38]
Springfield (*Ill.*)	113,586
Springfield (*Mass.*)	152,157
Springfield (*Mo.*)	150,867
Stamford (*Conn.*)	120,107
Sterling Heights (*Mich.*)	126,182
Stockton (*Calif.*)	271,466
Sunnyvale (*Calif.*)	128,549
Sunrise (*Fla.*)	89,136
Sunrise Manor (*Nev.*)[37]	156,120[38]
Syracuse (*N.Y.*)	144,001
Tacoma (*Wash.*)	196,790
Tallahassee (*Fla.*)	153,938
Tampa (*Fla.*)	317,647
Temecula (*Calif.*)	76,836
Tempe (*Ariz.*)	158,880
Thornton (*Colo.*)	96,584
Thousand Oaks (*Calif.*)	124,102
Toledo (*Ohio*)	308,973
Topeka (*Kan.*)	122,008
Torrance (*Calif.*)	142,621
Trenton (*N.J.*)	85,314
Troy (*Mich.*)	81,071
Tucson (*Ariz.*)	507,658
Tulsa (*Okla.*)	387,807
Tuscaloosa (*Ala.*)	79,294
Tyler (*Texas*)	88,318
Vacaville (*Calif.*)	94,129
Vallejo (*Calif.*)	119,708
Vancouver (*Wash.*)	151,654
Virginia Beach (*Va.*)	439,467
Visalia (*Calif.*)	100,612
Vista (*Calif.*)	91,813
Waco (*Texas*)	116,887
Warren (*Mich.*)	136,016
Warwick (*R.I.*)	87,365
★ Washington, D.C.	563,384
Waukegan (*Ill.*)	91,452
Waterbury (*Conn.*)	108,130
West Covina (*Calif.*)	108,251
West Jordan (*Utah*)	84,701
West Palm Beach (*Fla.*)	88,932
West Valley City (*Utah*)	111,687
Westland (*Mich.*)	85,707
Westminster (*Calif.*)	89,493
Westminster (*Colo.*)	103,391
Whittier (*Calif.*)	85,368
Wichita (*Kan.*)	354,617
Wichita Falls (*Texas*)	102,340
Wilmington (*N.C.*)	91,137
Winston-Salem (*N.C.*)	190,299
Worcester (*Mass.*)	175,706
Yakima (*Wash.*)	80,223
Yonkers (*N.Y.*)	197,388
Youngstown (*Ohio*)	79,271
Yuma (*Ariz.*)	81,605
Uruguay (1996)	
★ Montevideo	1,378,707
Uzbekistan (1999 est.)	
Andijon (Andizhan)	323,900
Angren	128,600
Buxoro (Bukhara)	237,900
Chirchiq (Chirchik)	145,600
Farghona (Fergana)	182,800
Jizzakh (Dzhizak)	126,400
Margilon (Margilan)	143,600
Namangan	376,600
Nawoiy (Navoi)	117,600
Nuqus (Nukus)	199,000
Olmaliq (Almalyk)	115,100
Qarshi (Karshi)	197,600
Qoqon (Kokand)	192,500
Samarqand (Samarkand)	362,300
★ Tashkent (Toshkent)	2,142,700
Termiz	111,500
Urganch (Urgench)	139,100
Vanuatu (1999)	
★ Vila	29,356
Venezuela (2001)	
Acarigua	137,000
Barcelona	328,000
Barinas	229,000
Barquisimeto	811,000
Baruta	192,000
Cabimas	210,000
Calabozo	102,000
★ Caracas	1,836,000
Carúpano	112,000
Catia la Mar	112,000
Ciudad Bolívar	287,000
Ciudad Guayana	629,000
Ciudad Ojeda	114,000
Coro	159,000
Cumaná	263,000
El Tigre	146,000
Guacara	142,000
Guanare	111,000
Guarenas	186,000
Guatire	129,000
La Victoria	104,000
Los Teques	175,000
Maracaibo	1,609,000
Maracay	394,000
Maturín	325,000
Mérida	196,000
Ocumare del Tuy	104,000
Petare	369,000
Puerto Cabello	154,000
Puerto La Cruz	199,000
Punto Fijo	117,000
San Cristóbal	234,000
Santa Teresa	125,000
Turmero	306,000
Valencia	1,196,000
Valera	113,000
Vietnam (2004 est.)	
Bac Lieu	104,400
Bien Hoa	384,400
Buon Me Thuot	139,900
Ca Mau	107,400
Cam Pha	146,600
Cam Ranh	145,700
Can Tho	255,100
Da Lat	128,900
Da Nang	459,400
Haiphong	591,100
★ Hanoi	1,420,400
Hoa Binh	100,100
Ho Chi Minh City (Saigon)	3,452,100
Hong Gai	145,900
Hue	277,100
Long Xuyen	157,200
My Tho	121,200
Nam Dinh	192,200
Nha Trang	274,800
Phan Thiet	146,000
Pleiku (Play Cu)	109,100
Qui Nhon	203,300
Rach Gia	207,600
Soc Trang	111,500
Thai Nguyen	132,600
Thanh Hoa	107,900
Vinh Long	101,100
Vung Tau	195,400
Virgin Islands (U.S.) (2000)	
★ Charlotte Amalie	11,004
West Bank (2003 est.)	
Hebron (Al-Khalīl)	154,714
Nābulus	126,884
★ Rām Allāh (Ramallah) (acting administrative centre)	23,663
Western Sahara (1998 est.)	
Laayoune (El Aaiún)	164,000[39]
Yemen (2001 est.)	
Aden	509,886
Dhamār	120,000
Al-Ḥudaydah	425,000
Ibb	140,000
Al-Mukallā	165,000
★ Ṣan‘ā’	1,590,624
Ta‘izz	450,000
Zambia (2000)	
Chingola	147,400
Kabwe	176,758
Kitwe	363,700
Luanshya	115,600
★ Lusaka	1,084,703
Mufulira	122,300
Ndola	374,757
Zimbabwe (2002)	
Bulawayo	676,787
Chitungwiza	321,782
Epworth	113,884
Gweru	137,000[11]
★ Harare	1,444,534
Mutare	153,000[11]

[26]Urban districts adjacent to Panama City. [27]2003 estimate; populations of cities within the Lima agglomeration are 1997 estimates. [28]Urban agglomeration(s). [29]De facto figure; de jure figure equals 3,378,300. [30]A new municipal system is being created throughout South Africa from 2000. [31]1997 estimate; 2001 census enumeration was not conducted because of the civil war. [32]Officially designated cities and metropolitan boroughs of England after the local government reorganization of 1995–98. [33]32 borough counties, not listed separately, constitute Greater London. [34]Cities and borough councils of Northern Ireland with more than 75,000 population. [35]Cities of Scotland after the local government reorganization of 1994–95. Borough councils do not exist in Scotland. [36]Cities and boroughs in Wales with more than 75,000 population after the local government reorganization of 1994–96. [37]Unincorporated place. [38]2000 census. [39]Urban population of Laayoune and northern Western Sahara.

Language

This table presents estimated data on the principal language communities of the countries of the world. The countries, and the principal languages (occasionally, language families) represented in each, are listed alphabetically. A bullet (●) indicates those languages that are official in each country. The sum of the estimates equals the 2003 population of the country given in the "Area and population" table.

The estimates represent, so far as national data collection systems permit, the distribution of mother tongues (a mother tongue being the language spoken first and, usually, most fluently by an individual). Many countries do not collect any official data whatever on language use, and published estimates not based on census or survey data usually span a substantial range of uncertainty. The editors have adopted the best-founded distribution in the published literature (indicating uncertainty by the degree of rounding shown) but have also adjusted or interpolated using data not part of the base estimate(s). Such adjustments have not been made to account for large-scale refugee movements, as these are of a temporary nature.

A variety of approaches have been used to approximate mother-tongue distribution when census data were unavailable. Some countries collect data on ethnic or "national" groups only; for such countries ethnic distribution often had to be assumed to conform roughly to the distribution of language communities. This approach, however, should be viewed with caution, because a minority population is not always free to educate its children in its own language and because better economic opportunities often draw minority group members into the majority-language community. For some countries, a given individual may be visible in national statistics only as a passport-holder of a foreign country, however long he may remain resident. Such persons, often guest workers, have sometimes had to be assumed to be speakers of the principal language of their home country. For other countries, the language mosaic may be so complex, the language communities so minute in size, scholarly study so inadequate, or the census base so obsolete that it was possible only to assign percentages to entire groups, or families, of related languages, despite their mutual unintelligibility (Papuan and Melanesian languages in Papua New Guinea, for instance). For some countries in the Americas, so few speakers of any single indigenous language remain that it was necessary to combine these groups as *Amerindian* so as to give a fair impression of their aggregate size within their respective countries.

No systematic attempt has been made to account for populations that may legitimately be described as bilingual, unless the country itself collects data on that basis, as does Bolivia or the Comoros, for example. Where a nonindigenous official or excolonial language constitutes a lingua franca of the country, however, speakers of the language as a second tongue are shown in italics, even though very few may speak it as a mother tongue. Lingua franca figures that are both italicized and indented are not included in population totals. No comprehensive effort has been made to distinguish between dialect communities *usually* classified as belonging to the same language, though such distinctions were possible for some countries—*e.g.*, between French and Occitan (the dialect of southern France) or among the various dialects of Chinese.

In giving the names of Bantu languages, grammatical particles specific to a language's autonym (name for itself) have been omitted (the form *Rwanda* is used here, for example, rather than *kinyaRwanda* and *Tswana* instead of *seTswana*). Parenthetical alternatives are given for a number of languages that differ markedly from the name of the people speaking them (such as Kurukh, spoken by the Oraon tribes of India) or that may be combined with other groups sometimes distinguishable in national data but appearing here under the name of the largest member—*e.g.*, "Tamil (and other Indian languages)" combining data on South Asian Indian populations in Singapore. The term *creole* as used here refers to distinguishable dialectal communities related to a national, official, or former colonial language (such as the French creole that survives in Mauritius from the end of French rule in 1810).

Internet resources for further information:
- *Ethnologue* (14th ed.; Summer Institute of Linguistics) http://www.ethnologue.com
- Joshua Project 2000—People's List (Christian interfaith missionary database identifying some 2,000 ethnolinguistic groups) http://www.ad2000.org/peoples/index.htm
- U.S. Census Bureau: http://www.census.gov/ftp/pub/ipc/www/idbconf.html (especially tables 57 and 59)

Language

Major languages by country	Number of speakers	Major languages by country	Number of speakers	Major languages by country	Number of speakers	Major languages by country	Number of speakers	Major languages by country	Number of speakers
Afghanistan[1]		**Antigua and Barbuda**		**Azerbaijan**		Spanish	85,000	Japanese	677,000
Indo-Aryan languages		● English	76,800	Armenian	163,000	Spanish (lingua franca)	149,000	● Portuguese	174,226,000
Pashai	178,000	English/English Creole	72,000	● Azerbaijani (Azeri)	7,326,000			Other	1,655,000
Iranian languages		Other	4,200	Lezgi (Lezgian)	184,000	**Benin[1]**		**Brunei**	
Balochi	266,000	**Argentina**		Russian	249,000	Adja	782,000	Chinese	32,000
● Dari (Persian)		Amerindian languages	109,000	Other	317,000	Aizo (Ouidah)	606,000	English	10,400
Chahar Aimak	810,000	Italian	647,000	**Bahamas, The**		Bariba	606,000	English-Chinese	7,300
Hazara	2,530,000	● Spanish	35,682,000	● English	...	Dendi	154,000	● Malay	159,000
Tajik	5,859,000	Other	408,000	English/English Creole	282,000	Djougou	209,000	Malay-Chinese	3,100
Nuristani group	222,000	**Armenia**		French (Haitian)		Fon	2,799,000	Malay-Chinese-	
Pamir group	178,000	● Armenian	2,853,000	Creole	32,000	● French	661,000	English	13,500
● Pashto	15,046,000	Azerbaijani (Azeri)	80,000	**Bahrain[2]**		Fula (Fulani)	397,000	Malay-English	101,000
Turkic languages		Other	128,000	● Arabic	459,000	Somba (Ditamari)	463,000	Other	18,700
Turkmen	555,000	**Aruba**		English	...	Yoruba (Nago)	859,000	**Bulgaria[1]**	
Uzbek	2,530,000	● Dutch	4,800	Other	215,000	Other	165,000	● Bulgarian	6,480,000
Other	544,000	English	8,700	**Bangladesh[1]**		**Bermuda**		Macedonian	191,000
Albania[1]		Papiamento	71,500	● Bengali	130,078,000	● English	64,000	Romany	286,000
● Albanian	3,102,000	Spanish	6,800	Chakma	496,000	Portuguese	6,100	Turkish	734,000
Greek	59,000	Other	1,000	English	3,503,000	**Bhutan[1]**		Other	95,000
Macedonian	4,600	**Australia**		Garo	124,000	Assamese	104,000	**Burkina Faso[4]**	
Other	900	Aboriginal languages	53,000	Khasi	103,000	● Dzongkha (Bhutia)	343,000	Dogon	44,000
Algeria		Arabic	194,000	Marma (Magh)	258,000	Nepali (Hindi)	239,000	French	44,000
● Arabic	27,346,000	Cantonese	227,000	Mro	41,000	**Bolivia**		● French (lingua franca)	5,419,000
Berber	4,454,000	Dutch	48,000	Santhali	93,000	● Aymara	278,000	Fula (Fulani)	1,272,000
English	...	● English	16,141,000	Tripuri	93,000	Guaraní	10,000	Gur (Voltaic) languages	
French	6,243,000	English (lingua		Other	1,824,000	● Quechua	700,000	Bwamu	288,000
American Samoa		franca)	19,189,000	**Barbados**		● Spanish	3,583,000	Gouin (Cerma)	77,000
● English	1,900	French	47,000	Bajan (English		Spanish-Amerindian		Grusi (Gurunsi) group	
English (lingua		German	115,000	Creole)	259,000	(multilingual),	3,943,000	Ko	22,000
franca)	60,000	Greek	310,000	● English	...	of which		Lyele	321,000
● Samoan	56,000	Hungarian	31,000	Other	13,000	Spanish-Aymara	1,699,000	Nuni	155,000
Tongan	1,900	Indonesian Malay	31,000	**Belarus**		Spanish-Guaraní	31,000	Sissala	11,000
Other	1,900	Italian	439,000	● Belarusian	6,488,000	Spanish-		Lobi	254,000
Andorra[2]		Macedonian	82,000	Polish	49,000	Quechua	2,224,000	Moore (Mossi) group	
● Catalan (Andorran)	22,000	Maltese	53,000	● Russian	3,155,000	Other	72,000	Dagara	409,100
French	5,000	Mandarin	105,000	Ukrainian	129,000	**Bosnia and Herzegovina[1]**		Gurma	752,000
Portuguese	7,000	Pilipino (Filipino)	81,000	Other	59,000	● Bosnian	1,637,000	Kusaal	22,000
Spanish	29,000	Polish	73,000	**Belgium[2, 3]**		● Croatian	630,000	Moore (Mossi)	6,636,000
Other	4,000	Portuguese	28,000	Arabic	161,000	● Serbian	1,153,000	Senufo group	
Angola[1]		Russian	36,000	● Dutch (Flemish;		Other	300,000	Minianka	—
Ambo (Ovambo)	255,000	Serbo-Croatian	122,000	Netherlandic)	6,128,000	**Botswana[1]**		Senufo	188,000
Chokwe	457,000	Spanish	104,000	● French (Walloon)	3,376,000	● English (lingua franca)	665,000	Kru languages	
Herero	74,000	Turkish	51,000	● German	101,000	Khoekhoe (Hottentot)	41,000	Seme (Siamou)	22,000
Kongo	1,423,000	Vietnamese	160,000	Italian	252,000	Ndebele	21,000	Mande languages	
Luchazi	255,000	Other/not stated	1,352,000	Spanish	50,000	San (Bushman)	58,000	Bobo	299,000
Luimbe-Nkangala	584,000	**Austria**		Turkish	91,000	Shona	207,000	Busansi (Bisa)	476,000
Lunda	127,000	Czech	19,000	Other	181,000	Tswana	1,255,000	Dyula (Jula)	343,000
Luvale (Lwena)	382,000	● German	7,409,000	**Belize**		Tswana (lingua		Marka	221,000
Mbundu	127,000	Hungarian	34,000	● English	136,000	franca)	1,330,000	Samo	310,000
Mbundu	2,325,000	Polish	19,000	English Creole (lingua		Other	81,000	Tamashek (Tuareg)	122,000
Nyaneka-Nkhumbi	584,000	Romanian	17,000	franca)	202,000	**Brazil[1]**		Other	940,000
Ovimbundu		Serbo-Croatian	175,000	Garifuna (Black Carib)	18,000	Amerindian languages	183,000	**Burundi[1]**	
(Umbundu)	4,003,000	Slovene	30,000	German	4,300	German	978,000	● French	285,000
● Portuguese	3,822,000	Turkish	122,000	Mayan languages	26,000	Italian	752,000	● Rundi	3,015,000
Other	170,000	Other	229,000					Hutu	2,542,000

Major languages by country	Number of speakers
Tutsi	447,000
Twa	31,000
Other[5]	61,000
Cambodia[1]	
Cham	308,000
Chinese	403,000
● Khmer	11,629,000
Vietnamese	722,000
Other[6]	64,000
Cameroon[1]	
Chadic languages	
Buwal	307,000
Hausa	194,000
Kotoko	174,000
Mandara (Wandala)	889,000
Masana (Masa)	623,000
● English	*7,868,000*
● French	*4,700,000*
Niger-Congo languages	
Adamawa-Ubangi languages	
Chamba	378,000
Gbaya (Baya)	194,000
Mbum	204,000
Atlantic languages	
Fula (Fulani)	1,512,000
Benue-Congo languages	
Bamileke (Medumba)-Widikum (Mogha-mo)-Bamum (Mum)	2,922,000
Basa (Bassa)	174,000
Duala	1,717,000
Fang (Pangwe)-Beti-Bulu	3,096,000
Ibibio (Efik)	20,000
Igbo	82,000
Jukun	102,000
Lundu	429,000
Maka	777,000
Tikar	1,165,000
Tiv	409,000
Wute	51,000
Saharan languages	
Kanuri	51,000
Semitic languages	
Arabic	153,000
Other	123,000
Canada	
● English	18,703,000
● French	7,349,000
English-French	119,000
English-other	276,000
French-other	40,000
English-French-other	10,000
Arabic	164,000
Chinese	793,000
Cree	85,000
Dutch	148,000
Eskimo (Inuktitut) languages	30,000
German	499,000
Greek	135,000
Italian	537,000
Pilipino (Filipino)	149,000
Polish	236,000
Portuguese	234,000
Punjābī	224,000
Spanish	236,000
Ukrainian	180,000
Vietnamese	118,000
Other	1,327,000
Cape Verde	
Crioulo (Portuguese Creole)	438,000
● Portuguese	...
Central African Republic	
Banda	858,000
● French	*942,000*
Gbaya (Baya)	869,000
Mandjia	544,000
Mbum	230,000
Ngbaka	283,000
Nzakara	63,000
● Sango (lingua franca)	*3,244,000*
Sara	241,000
Zande (Azande)	73,000
Other	523,000
Chad[1]	
● Arabic	1,140,000
Bagirmi	143,000
Fitri-Batha	428,000
● French	*2,774,000*
Fula (Fulani)	230,000
Gorane	581,000
Hadjarai	614,000
Kanem-Bornu	833,000
Lac-Iro	55,000
Mayo-Kebbi	1,063,000
Ouaddai	811,000
Sara	2,554,000
Tandjile	603,000
Other	197,000
Chile[1]	
Araucanian (Mapuche)	1,421,000
Aymara	81,000
Rapa Nui	35,000
● Spanish	13,740,000
China[1]	
Achang	31,000
Bulang (Blang)	92,000
Ch'iang (Qiang)	225,000
Chinese (Han)	1,185,204,000
Cantonese (Yüeh [Yue])	*51,093,000*
Hakka	*28,612,000*
Hsiang (Xiang)	*39,853,000*
Kan (Gan)	*22,481,000*
● Mandarin	*918,652,000*
Min	*39,853,000*
Wu	*84,814,000*
Ching-p'o (Jingpo)	133,000
Chuang (Zhuang)	17,607,000
Daghur (Daur)	133,000
Evenk (Ewenki)	31,000
Gelo	501,000
Hani (Woni)	1,431,000
Hui	9,772,000
Kazak	1,267,000
Korean	2,187,000
Kyrgyz	164,000
Lahu	470,000
Li	1,267,000
Lisu	654,000
Manchu	11,169,000
Maonan	82,000
Miao	8,410,000
Mongol	5,467,000
Mulam	184,000
Na-hsi (Naxi)	317,000
Nu	31,000
Pai (Bai)	1,809,000
Pumi	31,000
Puyi (Chung-chia)	2,892,000
Salar	102,000
She	715,000
Shui	388,000
Sibo (Xibe)	194,000
Tai (Dai)	1,165,000
Tajik	41,000
Tibetan	5,222,000
Tu (Monguor)	215,000
T'u-chia (Tujia)	6,489,000
Tung (Dong)	2,861,000
Tung-hsiang (Dongxiang)	429,000
Uighur	8,206,000
Wa (Va)	399,000
Yao	2,422,000
Yi	7,470,000
Other	1,012,000
Colombia[1]	
Amerindian languages	352,000
Arawakan	39,000
Cariban	29,000
Chibchan	176,000
Other	107,000
English Creole	49,000
● Spanish	40,910,000
Comoros	
● Arabic	...
● Comorian	374,000
Comorian-French	65,000
Comorian-Malagasy	28,000
Comorian-Arabic	8,600
Comorian-Swahili	2,600
Comorian-French-other	20,000
● French	*104,000*
Other	2,600
Congo, Dem. Rep. of the[1]	
Boa	1,239,000
Chokwe	965,000
● English	...
● French	*4,062,000*
Kongo	8,470,000
Kongo (lingua franca)	*16,250,000*
Lingala (lingua franca)	*36,562,000*
Luba	9,486,000
Lugbara	853,000
Mongo	7,109,000
Ngala and Bangi	3,047,000
Rundi	2,031,000
Rwanda	5,423,000
Swahili (lingua franca)	*25,390,000*
Teke	1,442,000
Zande (Azande)	3,219,000
Other	9,486,000
Congo, Rep. of the[1]	
Bobangi	39,000
● French	*1,960,000*
Kongo	1,908,000
Kota	39,000
Lingala (lingua franca)	...
Maka	65,000
Mbete	183,000
Mboshi	431,000
Monokutuba (lingua franca)	*2,221,000*
Punu	118,000
Sango	105,000
Teke	640,000
Other	196,000
Costa Rica	
Chibchan languages	12,500
Bribrí	8,000
Cabécar	4,600
Chinese	8,000
English Creole	83,000
● Spanish	4,044,000
Other	11,000
Côte d'Ivoire[1]	
Akan (including Baule and Anyi)	4,996,000
● French	*8,326,000*
Gur ([Voltaic] including Senufo and Lobi)	1,946,000
Kru (including Bete)	1,748,000
Malinke (including Dyula and Bambara)	1,905,000
Southern Mande (including Dan and Guro)	1,280,000
Other (non-Ivoirian population)	4,756,000
Croatia	
● Serbo-Croatian (Croatian)	4,252,000
Other	176,000
Cuba	
● Spanish	11,295,000
Cyprus (island)[1]	
● Greek	685,000
● Turkish	203,000
Other	32,000
Czech Republic[1]	
Bulgarian	3,000
● Czech	8,282,000
German	48,000
Greek	3,000
Hungarian	20,000
Moravian	1,313,000
Polish	60,000
Romanian	1,000
Romany	33,000
Russian	5,000
Ruthenian	2,000
Silesian	44,000
Slovak	312,000
Ukrainian	8,000
Other	70,000
Denmark[2]	
Arabic	39,000
● Danish	5,102,000
English	20,000
German	26,000
South Slavic languages	39,000
Turkish	47,000
Other	120,000
Djibouti[1]	
Afar	162,000
● Arabic	51,000
● French	*71,000*
Somali	203,000
Gadaboursi	...
Issa	...
Issaq	...
Other	41,000
Dominica	
● English	...
English Creole	69,700
French Creole	*63,000*
Dominican Republic	
French (Haitian) Creole	176,000
● Spanish	8,540,000
East Timor	
Portuguese	80,000
Tetum (Tetun)	608,000
Other	310,000
Ecuador	
Quechuan (and other Amerindian languages)	915,000
● Spanish	12,088,000
Egypt[1]	
● Arabic	67,367,000
Other	818,000
El Salvador	
● Spanish	6,515,000
Equatorial Guinea[1]	
Bubi	51,000
Fang	401,000
● French	...
Krio (English Creole)	...
● Spanish	...
Other	41,000
Eritrea	
Cushitic languages	
Afar	180,000
Bilin	130,000
Hadareb (Beja)	160,000
Saho	120,000
Nilotic languages	
Kunama	110,000
Nara	90,000
Semitic languages	
Arabic (Rashaida)	10,000
Tigré	1,310,000
Tigrinya	2,031,000
Estonia[1]	
Belarusian	20,000
● Estonian	883,000
Finnish	12,000
Russian	380,000
Ukrainian	34,000
Other	25,000
Ethiopia[1]	
Afar	1,205,000
Agew (Awngi)	607,000
Amharic	18,668,000
Berta	149,000
Gedeo	548,000
Gumuz	129,000
Gurage	2,708,000
Hadya–Libida	1,085,000
Kaffa	717,000
Kambata	797,000
Kimant	199,000
Oromo (Oromifa)	20,291,000
Sidamo	2,161,000
Somali	3,973,000
Tigrinya	3,764,000
Walaita	3,883,000
Other	5,705,000
Faroe Islands	
● Danish	...
● Faroese	48,000
Fiji[1]	
● English	*172,000*
Fijian	420,000
Hindi	361,000
Other	45,000
Finland	
Finnish	4,820,000
Russian	26,000
Sami (Lapp)	2,000
Swedish	295,000
Other	68,000
France	
Arabic[7]	1,514,000
English[7]	81,000
● French[7, 8, 9]	55,974,000
Basque	*102,000*
Breton	*813,000*
Catalan (Rousillonais)	*264,000*
Corsican	*81,000*
Dutch (Flemish)	*91,000*
German (Alsatian)	*1,016,000*
Occitan	*711,000*
Italian[7]	264,000
Polish[7]	51,000
Portuguese[7]	691,000
Spanish[7]	224,000
Turkish[7]	213,000
Other[7]	762,000
French Guiana	
Amerindian languages	3,200
● French	...
French/French Creoles	167,000
Other	7,600
French Polynesia[10]	
Chinese	13,600
● French	197,000
Polynesian languages	271,000
● Tahitian	...
Other	48,000
Gabon[1]	
Fang	476,000
● French	*1,108,000*
Kota	44,000
Mbete	188,000
Mpongwe (Myene)	199,000
Punu, Sira, Nzebi	222,000
Teke	22,000
Other	177,000
Gambia, The[1]	
● English	...
Gambians	
Aku (Krio)	8,300
Atlantic languages	
Diola (Jola)	131,000
Fula (Fulani)	230,000
Manjak	23,000
Serer	34,000
Wolof	179,000
Mande languages	
Bambara	10,000
Malinke	486,000
Soninke	109,000
Other	18,000
non-Gambians	196,000
Gaza Strip	
Arabic	1,297,000
Hebrew	6,800
Georgia	
Abkhaz	88,000
Armenian	343,000
Azerbaijani (Azeri)	274,000
● Georgian (Kartuli)	3,514,000
Ossetian	118,000
Russian	441,000
Other	157,000
Germany[2]	
● German	75,429,000
Greek	362,000
Italian	613,000
Kurdish	*402,000*
Polish	281,000
South Slavic languages	1,196,000
Turkish	2,120,000
Other	2,603,000
Ghana[1]	
Akan	10,732,000
● English	*1,436,000*
Ewe	2,431,000
Ga-Adangme	1,593,000
Gurma	681,000
Hausa (lingua franca)	*12,262,000*
Mole-Dagbani (Moore)	3,238,000
Yoruba	272,000
Other	1,520,000
Greece	
● Greek	10,834,000
Turkish	104,000
Other	63,000
Greenland[2]	
● Danish	7,100
● Greenlandic	50,000
Grenada	
● English	...
English/English Creole	102,000
Guadeloupe	
● French	...
French/French Creole	414,000
Other	21,000
Guam	
Asian languages	10,800
● Chamorro	34,000
● English	59,000
English (lingua franca)	*153,000*
Philippine languages	34,000
Other Pacific Island languages	10,500
Guatemala	
Garífuna (Black Carib)	26,000
Mayan languages	3,416,000
Cakchiquel	873,000
Kekchí	471,000
Mam	265,000
Quiché	985,000
● Spanish	6,311,000
Guernsey	
● English	63,000
Norman French	...
Guinea[1]	
Atlantic languages	
Basari-Konyagi	102,000
Fula (Fulani)	3,269,000
Kissi	511,000
Other	261,000
● French	*795,000*
Mande languages	
Kpelle	397,000
Loma	193,000
Malinke	1,964,000
Susu	931,000
Yalunka	250,000
Other	590,000
Other	11,400
Guinea-Bissau[1]	
Balante	411,000
Crioulo (Portuguese Creole)	*601,000*
Ejamat	32,000
French	*137,000*
Fula (Fulani)	295,000
Malinke	179,000
Mandyako	148,000
Mankanya	53,000
Pepel	137,000
● Portuguese	*148,000*
Other	106,000
Guyana	
Amerindian languages	
Arawakan	11,000
Cariban	17,000
● English	...
English/English Creoles	750,000

Language (continued)

Major languages by country	Number of speakers
Haiti	
● French	*1,535,000*
● Haitian (French) Creole	7,528,000
Honduras	
English Creole	13,000
Garifuna (Black Carib)	86,000
Miskito	12,000
● Spanish	6,611,000
Other	82,000
Hong Kong	
Chinese	
● Cantonese	6,059,000
Cantonese (lingua franca)	*6,549,000*
Chiu Chau	98,000
Fukien (Min)	130,000
Hakka	114,000
Putonghua (Mandarin)	76,000
Putonghua (lingua franca)	*1,239,000*
Sze Yap	27,000
● English	151,000
English (lingua franca)	*2,156,000*
Japanese	14,000
Pilipino (Filipino)	7,000
Other	164,000
Hungary	
German	40,000
● Hungarian	9,984,000
Romanian	10,000
Romany	51,000
Serbo-Croatian	20,000
Slovak	10,000
Other	20,000
Iceland[2]	
● Icelandic	278,000
Other	12,000
India	
Afro-Asiatic languages	
Arabic	32,000
Austroasiatic languages	
Ho	1,198,000
Kharia	284,000
Khasi	1,146,000
Korku	589,000
Munda	526,000
Mundari	1,083,000
Santhali	6,568,000
Savara (Sora)	347,000
Other Austroasiatic	200,000
Dravidian languages	
Gondi	2,680,000
Kannada	41,239,000
Khond	273,000
Koya	336,000
Kui	809,000
Kurukh (Oraon)	1,797,000
Malayalam	38,254,000
Tamil	66,745,000
Telugu	83,129,000
Tulu	1,955,000
Other Dravidian	694,000
English	221,000
● English (lingua franca)	*202,831,000*
Indo-Iranian (Indo-Aryan) languages	
Assamese	16,468,000
Bengali	87,638,000
Bhili (Bhilodi)	7,020,000
Barel	*586,000*
Bhilali	*586,000*
Gujarati	51,212,000
Halabi	673,000
● Hindi	424,684,000
Awadhi	*610,000*
Baghelkhandi	*1,745,000*
Bagri	*746,000*
Banjari	*1,114,000*
Bhojpuri	*29,090,000*
Bundelkhandi	*2,091,000*
Chhattisgarhi	*13,336,000*
Dhundhari	*1,219,000*
Garhwali	*2,354,000*
Harauti	*1,555,000*
Haryanvi	*452,000*
Hindi	*293,936,000*
Kangri	*620,000*
Khortha (Khotta)	*1,324,000*
Kumauni	*2,165,000*
Lamani (Banjari)	*2,585,000*
Magahi (Magadhi)	*13,305,000*
Maithili	*9,784,000*
Malvi	*3,741,000*
Mandeali	*557,000*
Marwari	*5,885,000*
Mewari	*2,659,000*
Nagpuri	*977,000*
Nimadi	*1,787,000*
Pahari	*2,743,000*
Rajasthani	*16,784,000*
Sadani (Sadri)	*1,976,000*
Surgujia	*1,314,000*
Surjapuri	*462,000*
Other Hindi dialects	*7,766,000*
Hindi (lingua franca)	*703,078,000*
Kashmiri	4,960,000
Khandeshi	1,230,000
Konkani	2,218,000
Lahnda	32,000
Marathi	78,673,000
Nepali (Gorkhali)	2,617,000
Oriya	35,333,000
Punjabi	29,437,000
Sanskrit	63,000
Sindhi	2,669,000
Kachchhi	*715,000*
Urdu	54,659,000
Sino-Tibetan languages	
Adi	200,000
Angami	126,000
Ao	221,000
Bodo/Boro	1,534,000
Dimasa	116,000
Garo	851,000
Karbi/Makir	462,000
Konyak	179,000
Lotha	105,000
Lushai (Mizo)	683,000
Manipuri (Meithei)	1,597,000
Miri/Mishing	494,000
Nissi/Dafla	221,000
Rabha	179,000
Sema	210,000
Tangkhul	126,000
Thado	137,000
Tripuri	872,000
Kokbarak	*652,000*
Other Sino-Tibetan languages	1,902,000
Other	5,560,000
Indonesia	
Balinese	3,655,000
Banjarese	3,844,000
Batak	4,884,000
Buginese	4,842,000
● Indonesian (Malay)	26,627,000
Javanese	86,697,000
Madurese	9,516,000
Minangkabau	5,189,000
Sundanese	34,673,000
Other	39,956,000
Iran[1]	
Armenian	317,000
Iranian languages	
Bakhtyari (Luri)	1,110,000
Balochi	1,511,000
● Farsi (Persian)	30,232,000
Farsi (lingua franca)	*54,843,000*
Gilaki	3,498,000
Kurdish	6,044,000
Luri	2,864,000
Mazandarani	2,388,000
Other	1,437,000
Semitic languages	
Arabic	1,427,000
Other	159,000
Turkic languages	
Afshari	750,000
Azerbaijani (Azeri)	11,138,000
Qashqa'i	845,000
Shahsavani	402,000
Turkish (mostly Pishagchi, Bayat, and Qajar)	476,000
Turkmen	1,036,000
Other	137,000
Other	486,000
Iraq[1]	
● Arabic	19,026,000
Assyrian	207,000
Azerbaijani (Azeri)	424,000
Kurdish	4,678,000
Persian	207,000
Other	141,000
Ireland	
● English	3,751,000
● Irish[11]	62,000
Irish	*1,571,000*
Isle of Man	
● English	77,000
Israel[12]	
● Arabic	1,165,000
● Hebrew	4,079,000
Russian	583,000
Other	646,000
Italy[1]	
Albanian	117,000
Catalan	29,000
French	302,000
German	302,000
Greek	39,000
● Italian	52,956,000
Rhaetian	722,000
Friulian	702,000
Ladin	20,000
Romany	107,000
Sardinian	1,492,000
Slovene	117,000
Other	127,000
Jamaica	
● English	…
English/English Creoles	2,492,000
Hindī and other Indian languages	51,000
Other	101,000
Japan[2]	
Ainu[1]	15,000
Chinese	241,000
English	80,000
● Japanese	126,406,000
Korean	663,000
Philippine languages	90,000
Other	50,000
Jersey	
● English	82,200
French	…
Norman French	*5,500*
Jordan[1]	
● Arabic	5,287,000
Armenian	54,000
Kabardian (Circassian)	54,000
Kazakhstan[1]	
Azerbaijani (Azeri)	89,000
Belarusian	149,000
German	456,000
● Kazakh	6,800,000
Korean	89,000
Russian	5,135,000
Tatar	288,000
Uighur	169,000
Ukrainian	734,000
Uzbek	337,000
Other	545,000
Kenya[1]	
Arabic	83,000
Bantu languages	
Bajun (Rajun)	73,000
Basuba	125,000
Embu	375,000
Gusii (Kisii)	1,949,000
Kamba	3,565,000
Kikuyu	6,609,000
Kuria	188,000
Luhya	4,378,000
Mbere	125,000
Meru	1,731,000
Nyika (Mijikenda)	1,512,000
Pokomo	83,000
Swahili	10,000
● Swahili (lingua franca)	*20,849,000*
Taita	313,000
Cushitic languages	
Oromo languages	
Boran	146,000
Gabbra	63,000
Gurreh	167,000
Orma	63,000
Somali languages	
Degodia	198,000
Ogaden	52,000
Somali	323,000
● English (lingua franca)	*2,815,000*
Nilotic languages	
Kalenjin	3,409,000
Luo	4,034,000
Masai	500,000
Sambur	156,000
Teso	271,000
Turkana	427,000
Other	709,000
Kiribati[1]	
● English	*22,000*
Kiribati (Gilbertese)	87,000
Tuvaluan (Ellice)	500
Other	600
Korea, North[1]	
Chinese	31,000
● Korean	22,435,000
Korea, South[1]	
Chinese	51,000
● Korean	47,874,000
Kuwait	
● Arabic	1,900,000
Other	539,000
Kyrgyzstan[1]	
Azerbaijani (Azeri)	21,000
German	31,000
Kazakh	52,000
● Kyrgyz	3,021,000
● Russian	817,000
Tajik	41,000
Tatar	62,000
Ukrainian	83,000
Uzbek	714,000
Other	217,000
Laos[1]	
● Lao-Lum (Lao)	3,004,000
Lao-Soung (Miao [Hmong] and Man [Yao])	569,000
Lao-Tai (Tai)	733,000
Lao-Theung (Mon-Khmer)	1,301,000
Other[13]	52,000
Latvia[1]	
Belarusian	87,000
● Latvian	1,298,000
Lithuanian	29,000
Polish	48,000
Russian	755,000
Ukrainian	69,000
Other	39,000
Lebanon[1]	
● Arabic	3,468,000
Armenian	219,000
French	*896,000*
Other	42,000
Lesotho[1]	
● English	*429,000*
● Sotho	1,533,000
Zulu	270,000
Liberia[1]	
Atlantic (Mel) languages	
Gola	137,000
Kissi	137,000
● English	*661,000*
Krio (English Creole)	*2,939,000*
Kru languages	
Bassa	462,000
Belle	21,000
De (Dewoin, Dey)	11,000
Grebo	294,000
Krahn	126,000
Kru (Krumen)	241,000
Mande (Northern) languages	
Gbandi	95,000
Kpelle	640,000
Loma	189,000
Malinke (Mandingo)	168,000
Mende	21,000
Vai	116,000
Mande (Southern) languages	
Gio (Dan)	262,000
Mano	231,000
Other	168,000
Libya	
● Arabic	5,334,000
Berber	54,000
Other[14]	163,000
Liechtenstein[2]	
● German	30,000
Italian	1,100
Other	3,200
Lithuania[1]	
Belarusian	43,000
● Lithuanian	2,907,000
Polish	235,000
Russian	220,000
Ukrainian	23,000
Other	24,000
Luxembourg[2]	
Belgian	11,000
Dutch	2,800
English	3,500
French	13,500
German	7,800
Italian	14,200
Luxemburgian	197,000
Portuguese	182,200
Other	21,300
Macau	
Chinese	
● Cantonese (Yüeh [Yue])	381,000
Mandarin	5,000
Other Chinese languages	40,000
English	2,000
● Portuguese	10,000
Other	5,000
Macedonia[1]	
Albanian	470,000
● Macedonian	1,368,000
Romany	46,000
Serbo-Croatian	41,000
Turkish	82,000
Vlach	9,000
Other	39,000
Madagascar[1]	
French	*2,464,000*
Malagasy	16,435,000
Other	171,000
Malawi[1]	
Chewa (Maravi)	6,802,000
● English	*606,000*
Lomwe	2,144,000
Ngoni	746,000
Yao	1,538,000
Other	393,000
Malaysia	
Bajau	163,000
Chinese	1,464,000
Chinese-others	824,000
Dusun	260,000
English	130,000
English-others	282,000
English (lingua franca)	*7,700,000*
Iban	597,000
Iban-others	98,000
● Malay	10,877,000
Malay-others	3,861,000
Tamil	976,000
Tamil-others	11,000
Other	5,683,000
Maldives	
● Divehi (Maldivian)	285,000
Mali[1]	
Afro-Asiatic languages	
Berber languages	
Tamashek (Tuareg)	848,000
Semitic languages	
Arabic (Mauri)	185,000
● French	*1,195,000*
Niger-Congo languages	
Atlantic languages	
Dogon	467,000
Fula (Fulani) and Tukulor	1,619,000
Gur (Voltaic) languages	
Bwa (Bobo)	283,000
Moore (Mossi)	44,000
Senufo and Minianka	1,391,000
Mande languages	
Bambara	3,705,000
Bambara (lingua franca)	*9,236,000*
Bobo Fing	11,000
Dyula (Jula)	337,000
Malinke, Khasonke, and Wasulunka	771,000
Samo (Duun)	76,000
Soninke	1,021,000
Nilo-Saharan languages	
Songhai	837,000
Other	33,000
Malta[1]	
● English	14,000
English (lingua franca)	*99,000*
● Maltese	380,000
Other	5,200
Marshall Islands[2]	
● English	*56,000*
● Marshallese	55,000
Other	1,700
Martinique	
● French	…
French/French Creole	380,000
Other	13,300
Mauritania[1]	
● Arabic	…
French	*274,000*
Fula (Fulani)	30,000
Hassānīyah Arabic	2,199,000
Soninke	71,000
Tukulor	142,000
Wolof	182,000
Zenaga	30,000
Other	41,000
Mauritius	
Bhojpuri	233,000
Bhojpuri-other	26,000
Chinese	4,000
● English	2,000
French	42,000
French Creole	754,000
French Creole-other	108,000
Hindi	16,000
Marathi	8,000
Tamil	9,000
Telugu	7,000
Urdu	8,000
Other	3,000
Mayotte[15]	
● Arabic	…
● French	68,000
Mahorais (local dialect of Comorian Swahili)	140,000
Other Comorian Swahili dialects	62,000
Malagasy	54,000
Other	10,000
Mexico	
Amerindian languages	7,278,000
Amuzgo	50,000
Aztec (Nahuatl)	1,744,000
Chatino	49,000
Chinantec	159,000

Major languages by country	Number of speakers
Chocho	1,200
Chol	194,000
Chontal	53,000
Cora	20,000
Cuicatec	16,000
Huastec	180,000
Huave	17,000
Huichol	38,000
Kanjobal	11,000
Mame	11,000
Mayo	44,000
Mazahua	172,000
Mazatec	254,000
Mixe	139,000
Mixtec	538,000
Otomí	360,000
Popoluca	66,000
Purépecha (Tarasco)	143,000
Tarahumara	92,000
Tepehua	11,000
Tepehuan	31,000
Tlapanec	123,000
Tojolabal	46,000
Totonac	287,000
Trique	25,000
Tzeltal	344,000
Tzotzil	362,000
Yaqui	16,000
Yucatec (Mayan)	948,000
Zapotec	533,000
Zoque	64,000
Other	496,000
● Spanish	85,871,000
Spanish-Amerindian languages	*5,987,000*
Micronesia	
Chuukese (Trukese)/Mortlockese	56,000
English	1,500
Kosraean	7,700
Pohnpeian	28,000
Polynesian languages	1,600
Woleaian	4,700
Yapese	6,000
Other	1,400
Moldova	
Bulgarian	70,000
Gagauz	139,000
● Romanian (Moldovan)	2,646,000
Russian	985,000
Ukrainian	368,000
Other	60,000
Monaco[2]	
English	2,100
● French	13,600
Italian	5,200
Monegasque	5,200
Other	6,300
Mongolia[1]	
Bayad	49,000
Buryat	43,000
Darhat	18,000
Dariganga	35,000
Dörbet	68,000
Dzakhchin	27,000
Kazakh	147,000
● Khalkha (Mongolian)	1,962,000
Khalkha (lingua franca)	*2,232,000*
Ould	10,000
Torgut	13,000
Tuvan (Uryankhai)	25,000
Other	98,000
Morocco	
● Arabic	19,390,000
Berber	9,845,000
French	*11,905,000*
Other	600,000
Mozambique	
Bantu languages	
Chuabo	1,167,000
Lomwe	1,410,000
Makua	4,883,000
Sena	1,303,000
Tsonga (Changana)	2,120,000
Other Bantu languages	6,128,000
● Portuguese	1,206,000
Portuguese (lingua franca)	*7,363,000*
Other	350,000
Myanmar (Burma)[1]	
● Burmese	29,312,000
Burmese (lingua franca)	*34,017,000*
Chin	927,000
Kachin (Ching-p'o)	581,000
Karen	2,648,000
Kayah	173,000
Mon	1,029,000
Rakhine (Arakanese)	1,915,000
Shan	3,595,000
Other	2,332,000
Namibia	
Afrikaans	183,000
Caprivi	90,000
● English	15,000
English (lingua franca)	*370,000*
German	17,000
Herero	154,000
Kavango (Okavango)	187,000
Nama	240,000
Ovambo (Ambo [Kwanyama])	976,000
San (Bushman)	37,000
Tswana	8,700
Other	18,500
Nauru	
Chinese	1,100
English	1,000
English (lingua franca)	*11,000*
Kiribati (Gilbertese)	2,200
Nauruan	7,300
Tuvaluan (Ellice)	1,100
Nepal	
Austroasiatic (Munda) languages	
Santhali	39,000
English	*7,147,000*
Indo-Aryan languages	
Bengali	39,000
Bhojpuri	1,801,000
Dhanwar	29,000
Hindi	225,000
Hindi (Awadhi dialect)	490,000
Maithili	2,869,000
● Nepali (Eastern Pahari)	12,169,000
Rajbansi	108,000
Tharu	1,302,000
Urdu	264,000
Tibeto-Burman languages	
Bhutia (Sherpa)	157,000
Chepang	29,000
Gurung	294,000
Limbu	333,000
Magar	558,000
Newari	901,000
Rai and Kiranti	578,000
Tamang	1,185,000
Thakali	9,800
Thami	20,000
Other	773,000
Netherlands, The[2]	
Arabic	133,000
● Dutch	15,556,000
Dutch and Frisian	*613,000*
Turkish	105,000
Other	444,000
Netherlands Antilles	
● Dutch	...
English	14,000
Papiamento	145,000
Other	10,000
New Caledonia[1]	
● French	75,000
Indonesian	5,000
Melanesian languages	99,000
Polynesian languages	26,000
Vietnamese	3,100
Other	12,000
New Zealand	
● English	3,483,000
English-Māori	155,000
● Māori	15,000
Other	349,000
Nicaragua	
English Creole	31,000
Misumalpan languages	
Miskito	90,000
Sumo	9,000
● Spanish	5,350,000
Other	2,300
Niger[1]	
Atlantic languages	
Fula (Fulani)	1,106,000
Berber languages	
Tamashek (Tuareg)	1,185,000
Chadic languages	
Hausa	6,029,000
Hausa (lingua franca)	*8,016,000*
● French	*1,694,000*
Gur (Voltaic) languages	
Gurma	34,000
Saharan languages	
Kanuri	508,000
Teda (Tubu)	45,000
Semitic languages	
Arabic	34,000
Songhai and Zerma	2,416,000
Other	23,000
Nigeria[1]	
Arabic	305,000
Bura	1,932,000
Edo	4,271,000
● English/English Creole (lingua franca)	*56,943,000*
Fula (Fulani)	14,134,000
Hausa	26,743,000
Hausa (lingua franca)	*63,044,000*
Ibibio	7,016,000
Igbo (Ibo)	22,574,000
Ijo (Ijaw)	2,237,000
Kanuri	5,186,000
Nupe	1,525,000
Tiv	2,847,000
Yoruba	26,743,000
Other	9,762,000
Northern Mariana Islands	
● Carolinian	3,100
● Chamorro	16,000
Chinese	16,900
● English	8,000
English (lingua franca)	*66,000*
Philippine languages	17,600
Other Pacific Island languages	3,900
Other	6,700
Norway[2]	
Danish	18,000
English	24,000
● Norwegian	4,411,000
Swedish	13,000
Other	102,000
Oman	
● Arabic (Omani)	2,012,000
Other	609,000
Pakistan	
Balochi	4,484,000
Brahui	1,821,000
English (lingua franca)	*16,842,000*
Pashto	19,579,000
Punjabi	
Hindko	3,621,000
Punjabi	71,778,000
Sindhi	
Saraiki	14,642,000
Sindhi	17,537,000
● Urdu	11,326,000
Other	4,242,000
Palau	
Chinese	300
● English	600
English (lingua franca)	*20,000*
● Palauan	17,000
Philippine languages	2,000
Other	700
Panama	
Amerindian languages	
Bokotá	5,500
Chibchan	
Guaymí (Ngöbe Buglé)	166,000
Kuna	63,000
Teribe	3,000
Chocó	
Emberá	20,000
Wounaan	3,000
Arabic	18,000
Chinese	9,000
English	...
English Creoles	436,000
● Spanish	2,393,000
Papua New Guinea[1]	
● English	*159,000*
Melanesian languages	1,121,000
Motu	*181,000*
Papuan languages	4,349,000
Tok Pisin (English Creole)	*3,624,000*
Other	113,000
Paraguay	
German	51,000
● Guaraní	2,267,000
Guaraní-Spanish	2,739,000
Portuguese	174,000
● Spanish	369,000
Other	41,000
Peru	
Amerindian languages	
● Aymara	624,000
● Quechua	4,465,000
Other	190,000
● Spanish	21,657,000
Other	212,000
Philippines	
Aklanon	595,000
Bantoanon	74,000
Bicol	4,614,000
Bilaan	43,000
Bontoc	64,000
Butuanon	85,000
Cebuano	18,882,000
Chavacano	500,000
Chinese	74,000
Davaweno (Mansaka)	553,000
● English (lingua franca)	*42,207,000*
Hiligaynon	7,389,000
Ibaloi (Nabaloi)	138,000
Ibanag	298,000
Ifugao	223,000
Ilocano	7,559,000
Ilongot	117,000
Kalinga	138,000
Kankanai	308,000
Kinaray-a (Hamtikanon)	510,000
Maguindanao	1,180,000
Manobo	542,000
Maranao	1,031,000
Masbateño	564,000
Palawano	85,000
Pampango	2,424,000
Pangasinan	1,467,000
● Pilipino (Filipino; Tagalog)	23,761,000
Romblon	255,000
Samal	510,000
Sambal	213,000
Subanon	330,000
Surigaonon	595,000
Tau Sug	936,000
Tboli	106,000
Tinggian	74,000
Tiruray	74,000
Waray-Waray	3,094,000
Yakan	160,000
Other	1,595,000
Poland	
Belarusian	190,000
German	500,000
● Polish	37,704,000
Ukrainian	230,000
Portugal[2]	
● Portuguese	10,079,000
Other	102,000
Puerto Rico	
● English	543,000
● Spanish	3,297,000
Other	39,000
Qatar[2]	
● Arabic	250,000
Other[16]	376,000
Réunion	
Chinese	21,000
Comorian	21,000
● French	*232,000*
French Creole	697,000
Malagasy	11,000
Tamil	*148,000*
Other	11,000
Romania[1]	
Bulgarian	8,000
Czech	4,000
German	64,000
Hungarian	1,427,000
Polish	4,000
● Romanian	19,346,000
Romany (Tigani)	540,000
Russian	43,000
Serbo-Croatian	26,000
Slovak	22,000
Tatar	22,000
Turkish	43,000
Ukrainian	64,000
Other	43,000
Russia[1]	
Adyghian	119,000
Armenian	713,000
Avar	604,000
Azerbaijani (Azeri)	336,000
Bashkir	1,375,000
Belarusian	972,000
Buryat	453,000
Chechen	898,000
Chuvash	1,722,000
Dargin	353,000
Georgian (Kartuli)	132,000
German	788,000
Ingush	253,000
Kabardian	367,000
Kalmyk	166,000
Karachay	150,000
Kazakh	569,000
Komi-Permyak	147,000
Komi-Zyryan	354,000
Kumyk	286,000
Lak	117,000
Lezgi (Lezgian)	295,000
Mari	66,000
Mordvin	723,000
Ossetian	463,000
Romanian	95,000
Romany	130,000
● Russian	118,000,000
Tabasaran	97,000
Tatar	5,519,000
Tuvan	198,000
Udmurt	713,000
Ukrainian	3,446,000
Uzbek	127,000
Yakut	441,000
Other	3,836,000
Rwanda	
● English	...
● French	*576,000*
● Rwanda	8,387,000
St. Kitts and Nevis	
● English	...
English/English Creole	46,400
St. Lucia	
● English	32,000
English/French Creole	130,000
St. Vincent and the Grenadines	
● English	...
English/English Creole	112,000
Other	1,000
Samoa	
● English	1,000
● Samoan	85,000
Samoan-English	93,000
San Marino[1]	
● Italian (Romagnolo)	29,000
São Tomé and Príncipe	
Crioulo (Portuguese Creole)	124,000
English	...
French	1,000
● Portuguese	...
Other	17,000
Saudi Arabia[1]	
● Arabic	22,809,000
Other	1,199,000
Senegal	
● French	*3,547,000*
Senegalese	
Bambara	91,000
Diola	497,000
Fula (Fulani)-Tukulor	2,199,000
Malinke (Mandingo)	375,000
Serer	1,267,000
Soninke	132,000
Wolof	4,865,000
Wolof (lingua franca)	*8,108,000*
Other	446,000
non-Senegalese	223,000
Serbia and Montenegro[1]	
Albanian	1,738,000
Hungarian	346,000
Macedonian	49,000
Romanian	40,000
Romany	148,000
● Serbo-Croatian (Serbian)	7,920,000
Serbo-Croatian (lingua franca)	*9,974,000*
Slovak	69,000
Vlach	20,000
Other	198,000
Seychelles	
English	3,000
English (lingua franca)	*29,000*
French	1,000
French (lingua franca)	*78,000*
Seselwa (French Creole)	75,000
Other	3,000
Sierra Leone[1]	
Atlantic languages	
Bullom-Sherbro	190,000
Fula (Fulani)	190,000
Kissi	114,000
Limba	418,000
Temne	1,578,000
● English	*475,000*
Krio (English Creole [lingua franca])	*4,182,000*
Mande languages	
Kono-Vai	257,000
Kuranko	171,000
Mende	1,720,000
Susu	76,000
Yalunka	171,000
Other	86,000
Singapore[1]	
Chinese	3,253,000
● English	*1,585,000*
● Malay	589,000
● Mandarin Chinese	*1,837,000*
● Tamil (and other Indian languages)	335,000
Other	56,000
Slovakia[1]	
Czech, Moravian, and Silesian	59,000
German	5,000
Hungarian	569,000

Language (continued)

Major languages by country	Number of speakers
Polish	3,000
Romany	90,000
Ruthenian, Ukrainian, and Russian	35,000
● Slovak	4,626,000
Other	15,000
Slovenia	
Hungarian	9,000
Serbo-Croatian	156,000
● Slovene	1,732,000
Other	74,000
Solomon Islands[1]	
● English	*9,000*
Melanesian languages	385,000
Papuan languages	39,000
Polynesian languages	16,000
Solomon Island Pidgin (English Creole)	*157,000*
Other	10,000
Somalia[1]	
● Arabic	...
English	...
● Somali	7,892,000
Other	133,000
South Africa	
● Afrikaans	5,961,000
● English	3,675,000
Nguni	
● Ndebele	717,000
● Swazi	1,210,000
● Xhosa	7,888,000
● Zulu	10,667,000
Sotho	
● North Sotho (Pedi)	4,213,000
● South Sotho	3,540,000
● Tswana (Western Sotho)	3,675,000
● Tsonga	1,972,000
● Venda	1,031,000
Other	224,000
Spain	
Basque (Euskera)	641,000
● Castilian Spanish	30,373,000
Catalan (Català)	6,886,000
Galician (Gallego)	2,604,000
Other	305,000
Sri Lanka	
English	10,000
English-Sinhala	1,051,000
English-Sinhala-Tamil	684,000
English-Tamil	218,000
● Sinhala	11,510,000
Sinhala-Tamil	1,785,000
● Tamil	3,748,000
Other	60,000
Sudan, The[1]	
● Arabic	18,818,000
Arabic (lingua franca)	*22,816,000*
Bari	934,000
Beja	2,434,000
Dinka	4,400,000
● English	...
Fur	782,000
Lotuko	565,000
Nubian languages	3,086,000
Nuer	1,869,000
Shilluk	652,000
Zande (Azande)	1,032,000
Other	3,542,000
Suriname	
● Dutch	*111,000*
English/English Creole	*415,000*
Sranantonga	172,000
Sranantonga-other	172,000
Other (mostly Hindi, Javanese, and Saramacca)	91,000
Swaziland[1]	
● English	*50,000*
● Swazi	976,000
Zulu	20,000
Other	81,000
Sweden[2]	
Arabic	69,000
Danish	41,000
English	32,000
Finnish	211,000
German	46,000
Iranian languages[1]	50,000
Norwegian	47,000
Polish	39,000
South Slavic languages[1]	117,000
Spanish	57,000
● Swedish	8,021,000
Turkish	29,000
Other	199,000
Switzerland	
● French	1,410,000
● German	4,669,000
● Italian	562,000
Romansch	41,000
Other	654,000
Syria[1]	
● Arabic	15,829,000
Kurdish	1,585,000
Other	173,000
Taiwan	
Austronesian languages	
Ami	140,000
Atayal	91,000
Bunun	43,000
Paiwan	69,000
Puyuma	10,000
Rukai	11,000
Saisiyat	6,000
Tsou	7,000
Yami	4,000
Chinese languages	
Hakka	2,481,000
● Mandarin	4,535,000
Min (South Fukien)	15,049,000
Other	122,000
Tajikistan	
Russian	633,000
● Tajik (Tojik)	4,066,000
Uzbek	1,515,000
Other	322,000
Tanzania[1]	
Chaga (Chagga), Pare	1,719,000
● English	*3,775,000*
Gogo	1,381,000
Ha	1,202,000
Haya	2,066,000
Hehet	2,414,000
Iramba	1,003,000
Luguru	1,719,000
Luo	288,000
Makonde	2,066,000
Masai	348,000
Ngoni	467,000
Nyakusa	1,898,000
Nyamwesi (Sukuma)	7,401,000
Shambala	1,500,000
● Swahili	3,100,000
Swahili (lingua franca)	*31,790,000*
Tatoga	258,000
Yao	854,000
Other	5,394,000
Thailand[1]	
Chinese	7,764,000
Karen	226,000
Malay	2,328,000
Mon-Khmer languages	
Khmer	810,000
Kuy	687,000
Other	226,000
Tai languages	
Lao	17,221,000
● Thai (Siamese)	33,662,000
Other	441,000
Other	656,000
Togo[1]	
Atlantic (Mel) languages	
Fula (Fulani)	74,000
Benue-Congo languages	
Ana (Ana-Ife)	136,000
Nago	14,000
Yoruba	11,000
Chadic languages	
Hausa	15,000
● French	*2,704,000*
Gur (Voltaic) languages	
Basari	95,000
Chakossi (Akan)	64,000
Chamba	53,000
Dye (Gangam)	51,000
Gurma	184,000
Kabre	748,000
Konkomba	77,000
Kotokoli (Tem)	313,000
Moba	292,000
Moore (Mossi)	14,000
Namba (Lamba)	166,000
Naudemba (Losso)	223,000
Tamberma	30,000
Yanga	16,000
Kwa languages	
Adele	11,000
Adja (Aja)	170,000
Ahlo	10,000
Akposo	145,000
Ane (Basila)	307,000
Anlo	4,300
Anyaga	11,000
Ewe	1,259,000
Fon	54,000
Hwe	6,500
Kebu	63,000
Kpessi	4,300
Peda-Hula (Pla)	22,000
Watyi (Ouatchi)	559,000
Other	229,000
Tonga	
● English	*31,000*
● Tongan	100,000
Other	2,000
Trinidad and Tobago	
● English	...
English Creole[17]	37,000
Hindi	45,000
Trinidad English	1,195,000
● Other	3,000
Tunisia	
● Arabic	6,911,000
Arabic-French	2,596,000
Arabic-French-English	309,000
Arabic-other	10,000
Other-no Arabic	31,000
Other	31,000
Turkey[1]	
Arabic	967,000
Kurdish[18]	7,482,000
● Turkish	61,825,000
Other	323,000
Turkmenistan[1]	
Armenian	37,000
Azerbaijani (Azeri)	40,000
Balochi	40,000
Kazakh	96,000
Russian	328,000
Tatar	40,000
● Turkmen	3,731,000
Ukrainian	25,000
Uzbek	446,000
Other	85,000
Tuvalu	
English	...
Kiribati (Gilbertese)	800
Tuvaluan (Ellice)	9,400
Uganda[1]	
Bantu languages	
Amba	98,000
Ganda (Luganda)	4,603,000
Gisu (Masaba)	1,145,000
Gwere	415,000
Kiga (Chiga)	2,127,000
Konjo	556,000
Nkole (Nyankole and Hororo)	2,727,000
Nyole	349,000
Nyoro	753,000
Ruli	109,000
Rundi	153,000
Rwanda	818,000
Samia	338,000
Soga	2,094,000
● Swahili	...
Swahili (lingua franca)	*8,944,000*
Toro	742,000
Central Sudanic languages	
Lugbara	1,200,000
Madi	196,000
Ndo	251,000
● English	*2,727,000*
Nilotic languages	
Acholi	1,124,000
Alur	600,000
Kakwa	131,000
Karamojong	535,000
Kumam	175,000
Lango	1,494,000
Padhola	382,000
Sebei (Kupsabiny)	164,000
Teso	1,527,000
Other (mostly Gujarati and Hindi)	633,000
Ukraine	
Belarusian	145,000
Bulgarian	154,000
Hungarian	145,000
Polish	29,000
Romanian	318,000
Russian	15,714,000
● Ukrainian	30,937,000
Other	414,000
United Arab Emirates[2]	
● Arabic	1,606,000
Other[16]	2,212,000
United Kingdom	
● English	57,559,000
Scots-Gaelic	79,000
Welsh	565,000
Other	961,000
United States	
Amharic	42,000
Arabic	683,000
Armenian	225,000
Bengali	53,000
Cajun	42,000
Chinese (including Formosan)	2,247,000
Czech	117,000
Danish	42,000
Dutch	180,000
English	239,407,000
English (lingua franca)	*282,724,000*
Finnish	64,000
French	2,150,000
French Creole (mostly Haitian)	233,000
German	1,537,000
Greek	406,000
Gujarati	262,000
Hebrew	217,000
Hindi (including Urdu)	645,000
Hungarian	131,000
Ilocano	53,000
Italian	1,121,000
Japanese	531,000
Korean	994,000
Kru (Gullah)	85,000
Lithuanian	74,000
Malayalam	42,000
Miao (Hmong)	187,000
Mon-Khmer (mostly Cambodian)	202,000
Navajo	198,000
Norwegian	106,000
Pennsylvania Dutch	106,000
Persian	347,000
Polish	742,000
Portuguese	627,000
Punjābī	64,000
Romanian	85,000
Russian	785,000
Samoan	42,000
Serbo-Croatian	260,000
Slovak	106,000
Spanish	31,230,000
Swedish	95,000
Syriac	42,000
Tagalog	1,361,000
Tai (including Laotian)	300,000
Turkish	53,000
Ukrainian	127,000
Vietnamese	1,122,000
Yiddish	199,000
Other	858,000
Uruguay	
● Spanish	3,235,700
Other	114,000
Uzbekistan[1]	
Kazakh	1,046,000
Russian	1,542,000
Tajik	1,232,000
Tatar	414,000
● Uzbek	19,429,000
Other	1,977,000
Vanuatu[19]	
● Bislama (English Creole)	116,000
● English	58,000
● French	29,000
Other	1,900
Venezuela	
Amerindian languages	
Goajiro	170,000
Warrau (Warao)	21,000
Other	160,000
● Spanish	24,795,000
Other	553,000
Vietnam[1]	
Bahnar	177,000
Cham	125,000
Chinese (Hoa)	1,142,000
French	*395,000*
Hre	125,000
Jarai	312,000
Khmer	1,132,000
Koho	114,000
Man (Mien, or Yao)	602,000
Miao (Meo, or Hmong)	716,000
Mnong	83,000
Muong	1,162,000
Nung	903,000
Rade (Rhadé)	249,000
Roglai	96,000
San Chay (Cao Lan)	146,000
San Diu	125,000
Sedang	125,000
Stieng	62,000
Tai	1,329,000
Tho (Tay)	1,515,000
● Vietnamese	70,972,000
Other	168,000
Virgin Islands (U.S.)	
● English	91,000
French	2,800
Spanish	15,000
Other	2,800
West Bank[20]	
Arabic	2,275,000
Hebrew	192,000
Western Sahara	
Arabic	262,000
Yemen[1]	
● Arabic	19,930,000
Other	80,000
Zambia[21]	
Bemba group	
Bemba	3,217,000
Bemba (lingua franca)	*5,643,000*
Bisa	124,000
Lala	260,000
Lamba	237,000
Other	451,000
● English	124,000
English (lingua franca)	*2,032,000*
Lozi (Barotse) group	
Lozi (Barotse)	688,000
Other	124,000
Mambwe group	
Lungu	79,000
Mambwe	124,000
Mwanga (Winawanga)	148,000
Other	11,000
North-Western group	
Kaonde	248,000
Lunda	214,000
Luvale (Luena)	192,000
Other	293,000
Nyanja (Maravi) group	
Chewa	621,000
Ngoni	181,000
Nsenga	463,000
Nyanja (Maravi)	847,000
Nyanja (lingua franca)	*2,822,000*
Other	68,000
Tonga (Ila-Tonga) group	
Ila	102,000
Lenje	169,000
Tonga	1,185,000
Other	135,000
Tumbuka group	
Senga	79,000
Tumbuka	316,000
Other	11,000
Other	102,000
Zimbabwe	
● English	258,000
English (lingua franca)	*5,477,000*
Ndebele (Nguni)	1,902,000
Nyanja	269,000
Shona	8,453,000
Other	837,000

[1]Figures given represent ethnolinguistic groups. [2]Data refer to nationality (usually resident aliens holding foreign passports). [3]Data are partly based on place of residence. [4]Majority of population speak Moore (language of the Mossi); Dyula is language of commerce. [5]Swahili also spoken. [6]English and French also spoken. [7]Based on "nationality" at 1982 census. [8]Includes naturalized citizens. [9]French is the universal language throughout France; traditional dialects and minority languages are retained regionally in the approximate numbers shown, however. [10]Data reflect multilingualism; 2000 population estimate is 233,000. [11]Refers to Irish speakers in Gaeltacht areas. [12]Includes the population of the Golan Heights and East Jerusalem; excludes the Israeli population in the West Bank and Gaza Strip. [13]English and French also spoken. [14]English and Italian also spoken. [15]Data reflect ability to speak the language, not mother tongue; 2003 population estimate is 160,000. [16]Mostly Pakistanis, Indians, and Iranians. [17]Spoken on Tobago only. [18]Other estimates of the Kurdish population range from 6 percent to 20–25 percent. [19]Data reflect multilingualism; 2000 population is 190,000. [20]Excludes East Jerusalem. [21]Groups are officially defined geographic divisions; elements comprising them are named by language.

Religion

The following table presents statistics on religious affiliation for each of the countries of the world. An assessment was made for each country of the available data on distribution of religious communities within the total population; the best available figures, whether originating as census data, membership figures of the churches concerned, or estimates by external analysts in the absence of reliable local data, were applied as percentages to the estimated 2001 midyear population of the country to obtain the data shown below.

Several concepts govern the nature of the available data, each useful separately but none the basis of any standard of international practice in the collection of such data. The word "affiliation" was used above to describe the nature of the relationship joining the religious bodies named and the populations shown. This term implies some sort of formal, usually documentary, connection between the religion and the individual (a baptismal certificate, a child being assigned the religion of its parents on a census form, maintenance of one's name on the tax rolls of a state religion, etc.) but says nothing about the nature of the individual's personal religious practice, in that the individual may have lapsed, never been confirmed as an adult, joined another religion, or may have joined an organization that is formally atheist.

The user of these statistics should be careful to note that not only does the nature of the affiliation (with an organized religion) differ greatly from country to country, but the social context of religious practice does also. A country in which a single religion has long been predominant will often show more than 90% of its population to be *affiliated*, while in actual fact, no more than 10% may actually *practice* that religion on a regular basis. Such a situation often leads to undercounting of minority religions (where someone [head of household, communicant, child] is counted at all), blurring of distinctions seen to be significant elsewhere (a Hindu country may not distinguish Protestant [or even Christian] denominations; a Christian country may not distinguish among its Muslim or Buddhist citizens), or double-counting in countries where an individual may conscientiously practice more than one "religion" at a time.

Until 1989 communist countries had for long consciously attempted to ignore, suppress, or render invisible religious practice within their borders. Countries with large numbers of adherents of traditional, often animist, religions and belief systems usually have little or no formal methodology for defining the nature of local religious practice. On the other hand, countries with strong missionary traditions, or good census organizations, or few religious sensitivities may have very good, detailed, and meaningful data.

The most comprehensive works available are DAVID B. BARRETT (ed.), *World Christian Encyclopedia* (2001); and PETER BRIERLEY, *World Churches Handbook* (1997).

Religion

Religious affiliation	2001 population	Religious affiliation	2001 population	Religious affiliation	2001 population	Religious affiliation	2001 population	Religious affiliation	2001 population
Afghanistan		**Azerbaijan**		Roman Catholic	710,000	**Central African Republic**		**Cuba**	
Sunnī Muslim	23,090,000	Shīʿī Muslim	5,299,000	other	350,000	Roman Catholic	660,000	Roman Catholic	4,420,000
Shīʿī Muslim	2,310,000	Sunnī Muslim	2,271,000	**Botswana**		Muslim	560,000	Protestant	270,000
other	490,000	other	535,000	African Christian	490,000	traditional beliefs	550,000	other (mostly Santeria)	6,500,000
				Protestant	170,000	Protestant	520,000		
Albania		**Bahamas, The**		Roman Catholic	60,000	other	1,290,000	**Cyprus**	
Muslim	1,200,000	Protestant	135,000	other (mostly				Greek Orthodox	630,000
Roman Catholic	520,000	Roman Catholic	50,000	traditional beliefs)	870,000	**Chad**		Muslim (mostly Sunnī)	200,000
Albanian Orthodox	320,000	Anglican	32,000			Muslim	4,690,000	other (mostly	
other	1,050,000	other	77,000	**Brazil**		Roman Catholic	1,770,000	Christian)	40,000
				Roman Catholic		Protestant	1,250,000		
Algeria		**Bahrain**		(including syncretic		traditional beliefs	640,000	**Czech Republic**	
Sunnī Muslim	30,550,000	Shīʿī Muslim	420,000	Afro-Catholic cults		other	350,000	Roman Catholic	4,010,000
Ibāḍīyah Muslim	180,000	Sunnī Muslim	140,000	having Spiritist				Evangelical Church of	
other	90,000	other	140,000	beliefs and rituals)	124,470,000	**Chile**		Czech Brethren	200,000
				Evangelical Protestant	39,850,000	Roman Catholic	11,810,000	Czechoslovak Hussite	180,000
American Samoa		**Bangladesh**		other	7,800,000	Evangelical		Silesian Evangelical	30,000
Congregational	23,800	Muslim	112,660,000			Protestant	1,910,000	Eastern Orthodox	20,000
Roman Catholic	11,300	Hindu	16,260,000	**Brunei**		other	1,690,000	atheist and	
other	23,400	other	2,360,000	Muslim	222,000			nonreligious	4,100,000
				other	121,000	**China**		other	1,730,000
Andorra		**Barbados**				nonreligious	661,390,000		
Roman Catholic	60,000	Anglican	89,000	**Bulgaria**		Chinese folk-		**Denmark**	
other	7,000	Protestant	80,000	Bulgarian Orthodox	5,690,000	religionist	256,260,000	Evangelical Lutheran	4,600,000
		Roman Catholic	12,000	Muslim (mostly		atheist	152,990,000	Muslim	120,000
Angola		other	88,000	Sunnī)	940,000	Buddhist	108,110,000	other	640,000
Roman Catholic	6,440,000			other	1,320,000	Christian	76,540,000		
Protestant	1,550,000	**Belarus**				Muslim	18,360,000	**Djibouti**	
African Christian	710,000	Belarusian		**Burkina Faso**		traditional beliefs	1,280,000	Sunnī Muslim	434,000
other	1,660,000	Orthodox	3,151,000	Muslim	5,960,000			other	27,000
		Roman Catholic	1,772,000	traditional beliefs	4,180,000	**Colombia**			
Antigua and Barbuda		other	5,062,000	Christian	2,040,000	Roman Catholic	39,590,000	**Dominica**	
Protestant	30,000			other	80,000	other	3,480,000	Roman Catholic	50,000
Anglican	23,000	**Belgium**						Protestant	12,000
Roman Catholic	8,000	Roman Catholic	8,310,000	**Burundi**		**Comoros**		other	10,000
other	10,000	nonreligious	600,000	Roman Catholic	4,050,000	Sunnī Muslim	555,000		
		other	1,360,000	nonreligious	1,160,000	other	11,000	**Dominican Republic**	
Argentina				other (mostly				Roman Catholic	7,110,000
Roman Catholic	29,920,000	**Belize**		Protestant)	1,020,000	**Congo, Dem. Rep. of the**		Protestant	560,000
Protestant	2,040,000	Roman Catholic	143,000			Roman Catholic	21,990,000	other	1,020,000
Muslim	730,000	Protestant	67,000	**Cambodia**		Protestant	16,950,000		
Jewish	500,000	Anglican	17,000	Buddhist	10,780,000	African Christian	7,170,000	**East Timor**	
nonreligious	880,000	other	20,000	Chinese folk-religionist	600,000	traditional beliefs	5,740,000	Roman Catholic	780,000
other	3,430,000			traditional beliefs	550,000	Muslim	750,000	Protestant	50,000
		Benin		Muslim	290,000	other	1,040,000	Muslim	30,000
Armenia		Voodoo		other	500,000			other	40,000
Armenian Apostolic		(traditional beliefs)	3,390,000			**Congo, Rep. of the**			
(Orthodox)	2,454,000	Roman Catholic	1,370,000	**Cameroon**		Roman Catholic	1,430,000	**Ecuador**	
other	1,353,000	Muslim	1,320,000	Roman Catholic	4,180,000	Protestant	490,000	Roman Catholic	11,910,000
		other	500,000	traditional beliefs	3,750,000	African Christian	360,000	Protestant	440,000
Aruba				Muslim	3,350,000	other	610,000	other	530,000
Roman Catholic	80,000	**Bermuda**		Protestant	3,270,000				
other	18,000	Anglican	23,700	other	1,250,000	**Costa Rica**		**Egypt**	
		Methodist	10,400			Roman Catholic	3,380,000	Sunnī Muslim	58,060,000
Australia		Roman Catholic	8,800	**Canada**		Protestant	360,000	Coptic Orthodox[1]	6,520,000
Roman Catholic	5,230,000	other	20,900	Roman Catholic	14,010,000	other	190,000	other	660,000
Anglican	4,260,000			Protestant	8,620,000				
Uniting Church	1,460,000	**Bhutan**		Anglican	2,490,000	**Côte d'Ivoire**		**El Salvador**	
Presbyterian	740,000	Lamaistic Buddhist	510,000	Eastern Orthodox	440,000	Muslim	6,340,000	Roman Catholic	4,880,000
other Protestant	1,400,000	Hindu	140,000	Jewish	360,000	Roman Catholic	3,400,000	Protestant	1,070,000
Orthodox	540,000	other	40,000	Muslim	290,000	traditional beliefs	2,790,000	other	290,000
nonreligious	3,220,000			Buddhist	190,000	nonreligious	2,220,000		
other	2,510,000	**Bolivia**		Hindu	180,000	Protestant	870,000	**Equatorial Guinea**	
		Roman Catholic	7,540,000	Sikh	170,000	other	770,000	Roman Catholic	390,000
Austria		Protestant	770,000	nonreligious	3,880,000			other	110,000
Roman Catholic	6,060,000	other	210,000	other	380,000	**Croatia**			
Protestant (mostly						Roman Catholic	3,890,000	**Eritrea**	
Lutheran)	430,000	**Bosnia and Herzegovina**		**Cape Verde**		Serbian Orthodox	250,000	Eritrean Orthodox	1,980,000
atheist and		Sunnī Muslim	1,690,000	Roman Catholic	370,000	Sunnī Muslim	100,000	Muslim	1,920,000
nonreligious	690,000	Serbian Orthodox	1,180,000	other	35,000	Protestant	30,000	other	400,000
other	890,000					other	130,000		

Religion   (continued)

Religious affiliation	2001 population
Estonia	
Estonian Orthodox	277,000
Evangelical Lutheran	187,000
other	899,000
Ethiopia	
Ethiopian Orthodox	33,110,000
other Christian	7,090,000
Muslim (mostly Sunnī)	21,710,000
traditional beliefs	3,180,000
other	820,000
Faroe Islands	
Evangelical Lutheran	38,000
other	9,000
Fiji	
Christian (mostly Methodist and Roman Catholic)	437,000
Hindu	316,000
Muslim	65,000
other	9,000
Finland	
Evangelical Lutheran	4,420,000
other	770,000
France	
Roman Catholic	38,690,000
nonreligious	9,230,000
Muslim	4,180,000
atheist	2,380,000
Protestant	720,000
Jewish	590,000
other	3,290,000
French Guiana	
Roman Catholic	91,000
other	77,000
French Polynesia	
Protestant	119,000
Roman Catholic	94,000
other	25,000
Gabon	
Roman Catholic	690,000
Protestant	220,000
African Christian	170,000
other	160,000
Gambia, The	
Muslim (mostly Sunnī)	1,340,000
other	70,000
Gaza Strip	
Muslim (mostly Sunnī)	1,190,000
other	20,000
Georgia	
Georgian Orthodox	1,828,000
Sunnī Muslim	549,000
Armenian Apostolic (Orthodox)	279,000
Russian Orthodox	133,000
other (mostly nonreligious)	2,200,000
Germany	
Protestant (mostly Evangelical Lutheran)	29,330,000
Roman Catholic	27,590,000
Muslim	3,660,000
atheist	1,800,000
other (mostly nonreligious)	20,020,000
Ghana	
traditional beliefs	4,860,000
Muslim	3,910,000
Protestant	3,310,000
African Christian	2,870,000
Roman Catholic	1,890,000
other	3,050,000
Greece	
Greek Orthodox	10,010,000
Muslim	360,000
other	500,000
Greenland	
Evangelical Lutheran	36,500
other	19,800
Grenada	
Roman Catholic	54,000
Anglican	14,000
other	34,000

Religious affiliation	2001 population
Guadeloupe	
Roman Catholic	350,000
other	82,000
Guam	
Roman Catholic	118,000
Protestant	19,000
other	21,000
Guatemala	
Roman Catholic	8,880,000
Evangelical Protestant	2,540,000
other	270,000
Guernsey	
Anglican	42,000
other	22,000
Guinea	
Muslim	6,470,000
Christian	760,000
other	380,000
Guinea-Bissau	
traditional beliefs	590,000
Muslim	530,000
Christian	170,000
other	20,000
Guyana	
Hindu	264,000
Protestant	145,000
Roman Catholic	89,000
Muslim	70,000
Anglican	67,000
other	142,000
Haiti	
Roman Catholic	4,770,000
Protestant	1,590,000
other	610,000
Honduras	
Roman Catholic	5,740,000
Evangelical Protestant	690,000
other	200,000
Hong Kong	
Buddhist and Taoist	4,970,000
Protestant	290,000
Roman Catholic	280,000
other	1,200,000
Hungary	
Roman Catholic	6,120,000
Protestant	2,470,000
nonreligious	750,000
other	850,000
Iceland	
Evangelical Lutheran	260,000
other	20,000
India	
Hindu	759,350,000
Sunnī Muslim	92,380,000
traditional beliefs	34,930,000
Shī'ī Muslim	30,790,000
independent	30,750,000
Sikh	22,290,000
Protestant	15,130,000
Roman Catholic	13,940,000
Buddhist	7,290,000
Jain	4,160,000
atheist	1,670,000
Bahā'ī	1,190,000
Zoroastrian (Parsi)	210,000
nonreligious	12,910,000
other	3,000,000
Indonesia	
Muslim	185,060,000
Protestant	12,820,000
Roman Catholic	7,600,000
Hindu	3,880,000
Buddhist	2,190,000
other	660,000
Iran	
Shī'ī Muslim	57,180,000
Sunnī Muslim	3,460,000
Zoroastrian	1,780,000
Bahā'ī	430,000
Christian	340,000
other	250,000
Iraq	
Shī'ī Muslim	13,890,000
Sunnī Muslim	8,510,000
Christian	750,000
other	180,000

Religious affiliation	2001 population
Ireland	
Roman Catholic	3,500,000
other	320,000
Isle of Man	
Anglican	30,000
Methodist	7,000
Roman Catholic	6,000
other	31,000
Israel	
Jewish[2]	4,960,000
Muslim (mostly Sunnī)	930,000
other	360,000
Italy	
Roman Catholic	46,260,000
nonreligious and atheist	9,600,000
Muslim	680,000
other	1,350,000
Jamaica	
Protestant	1,020,000
Roman Catholic	270,000
Anglican	100,000
other	1,230,000
Japan	
Shintoist[3]	118,270,000
Buddhist[3]	88,490,000
Christian	1,470,000
other	10,250,000
Jersey	
Anglican	55,000
Roman Catholic	21,000
other	14,000
Jordan	
Sunnī Muslim	4,800,000
Christian	210,000
other	120,000
Kazakhstan	
Muslim (mostly Sunnī)	6,988,000
Russian Orthodox	1,216,000
Protestant	318,000
other (mostly nonreligious)	6,345,000
Kenya	
Roman Catholic	6,780,000
African Christian	6,400,000
Protestant	6,170,000
traditional beliefs	3,540,000
Anglican	2,900,000
Muslim	2,240,000
Orthodox	720,000
other	2,030,000
Kiribati	
Roman Catholic	50,000
Congregational	36,000
other	9,000
Korea, North	
atheist and nonreligious	15,000,000
traditional beliefs	3,430,000
Ch'ŏndogyo	3,050,000
other	480,000
Korea, South	
nonreligious	23,490,000
Buddhist	11,040,000
Protestant	9,370,000
Roman Catholic	3,160,000
Confucian	230,000
Wonbulgyo	90,000
other	290,000
Kuwait	
Sunnī Muslim	1,020,000
Shī'ī Muslim	680,000
other Muslim	230,000
other (mostly Christian and Hindu)	340,000
Kyrgyzstan	
Muslim (mostly Sunnī)	3,701,000
Russian Orthodox	276,000
other (mostly nonreligious)	958,000
Laos	
Buddhist	2,750,000
traditional beliefs	2,350,000
other	540,000

Religious affiliation	2001 population
Latvia	
Roman Catholic	350,000
Evangelical Lutheran	345,000
Russian Orthodox	181,000
other (mostly nonreligious)	1,482,000
Lebanon	
Shī'ī Muslim	1,230,000
Sunnī Muslim	770,000
Maronite Catholic	690,000
Druze	260,000
Greek Orthodox	220,000
Armenian Apostolic (Orthodox)	190,000
Greek Catholic (Melchite)	170,000
other	110,000
Lesotho	
Roman Catholic	820,000
Protestant	280,000
African Christian	260,000
traditional beliefs	170,000
Anglican	100,000
other	550,000
Liberia	
traditional beliefs	1,390,000
Christian	1,270,000
Muslim	520,000
other	60,000
Libya	
Sunnī Muslim	5,040,000
other	200,000
Liechtenstein	
Roman Catholic	26,000
other	7,000
Lithuania	
Roman Catholic	2,660,000
Russian Orthodox	90,000
other (mostly nonreligious)	940,000
Luxembourg	
Roman Catholic	400,000
other	40,000
Macau	
nonreligious	271,000
Buddhist	75,000
other	100,000
Macedonia	
Serbian (Macedonian) Orthodox	1,210,000
Sunnī Muslim	580,000
other	260,000
Madagascar	
traditional beliefs	7,670,000
Roman Catholic	3,250,000
Protestant	3,630,000
other	1,420,000
Malawi	
Roman Catholic	2,600,000
Protestant	2,070,000
African Christian	1,770,000
Muslim	1,560,000
traditional beliefs	820,000
other	1,730,000
Malaysia	
Muslim	10,770,000
Chinese folk-religionist	5,450,000
Christian	1,880,000
Hindu	1,660,000
Buddhist	1,500,000
other	1,350,000
Maldives	
Sunnī Muslim	273,000
other	2,000
Mali	
Muslim	9,010,000
traditional beliefs	1,760,000
Christian	220,000
other	10,000
Malta	
Roman Catholic	363,000
other	21,000
Marshall Islands	
Protestant	32,800
Roman Catholic	3,700
other	15,700

Religious affiliation	2001 population
Martinique	
Roman Catholic	336,000
other	52,000
Mauritania	
Sunnī Muslim	2,720,000
other	20,000
Mauritius	
Hindu	610,000
Roman Catholic	330,000
Muslim	190,000
other	70,000
Mayotte	
Sunnī Muslim	153,000
Christian	5,000
Mexico	
Roman Catholic	90,370,000
Protestant	3,820,000
other Christian	1,820,000
other (mostly nonreligious)	3,970,000
Micronesia	
Roman Catholic	63,600
Protestant	40,100
other	14,200
Moldova	
Romanian Orthodox	1,263,000
Russian (Moldovan) Orthodox	342,000
other (mostly nonreligious)	2,007,000
Monaco	
Roman Catholic	28,000
other	4,000
Mongolia	
Tantric Buddhist (Lamaist)	2,340,000
Muslim	100,000
Morocco	
Muslim (mostly Sunnī)	28,730,000
other	500,000
Mozambique	
traditional beliefs	9,750,000
Roman Catholic	3,060,000
Muslim	2,040,000
Protestant	1,720,000
African Christian	1,400,000
other	1,400,000
Myanmar (Burma)	
Buddhist	37,560,000
Christian	2,060,000
Muslim	1,610,000
traditional beliefs	480,000
Hindu	210,000
other	70,000
Namibia	
Protestant (mostly Lutheran)	850,000
Roman Catholic	320,000
African Christian	200,000
other	430,000
Nauru	
Protestant	6,100
Roman Catholic	3,300
other	2,700
Nepal	
Hindu	19,180,000
traditional beliefs	2,350,000
Buddhist	2,050,000
Muslim	970,000
Christian	600,000
other	140,000
Netherlands, The	
Roman Catholic	4,950,000
Dutch Reformed Church (NHK)	2,240,000
Reformed Churches	1,120,000
Muslim	720,000
nonreligious	6,550,000
other	400,000
Netherlands Antilles	
Roman Catholic	152,000
other	54,000
New Caledonia	
Roman Catholic	132,000
Protestant	31,300
other	52,200

Religious affiliation	2001 population
New Zealand	
Anglican	674,000
Roman Catholic	505,000
Presbyterian	489,000
Methodist	130,000
Baptist	57,000
Mormon	44,000
Ratana	39,000
nonreligious	954,000
other	969,000
Nicaragua	
Roman Catholic	3,590,000
Protestant	810,000
other (mostly nonreligious)	520,000
Niger	
Sunnī Muslim	9,390,000
traditional beliefs	900,000
other	70,000
Nigeria	
Muslim	55,600,000
traditional beliefs	12,500,000
Christian	58,100,000
other	500,000
Northern Mariana Islands	
Roman Catholic	53,600
other	19,700
Norway	
Evangelical Lutheran (Church of Norway)	3,990,000
other	530,000
Oman	
Ibāḍīyah Muslim	1,840,000
Sunnī Muslim	350,000
Hindu	190,000
Christian	100,000
other	20,000
Pakistan	
Sunnī Muslim	113,950,000
Shīʿī Muslim	25,010,000
Christian	3,560,000
Hindu	1,730,000
other	370,000
Palau	
Roman Catholic	7,600
Modekne	5,200
Protestant	4,900
other	2,100
Panama	
Roman Catholic	2,330,000
Protestant	420,000
other	150,000
Papua New Guinea	
Protestant	3,180,000
Roman Catholic	1,500,000
Anglican	210,000
other	420,000
Paraguay	
Roman Catholic	4,990,000
Protestant	280,000
other	370,000
Peru	
Roman Catholic	23,170,000
Protestant	1,730,000
other (mostly nonreligious)	1,190,000
Philippines	
Roman Catholic	63,530,000
Protestant	4,160,000
Muslim	3,500,000
Aglipayan	2,010,000
Church of Christ (Iglesia ni Cristo)	1,790,000
other	1,620,000
Poland	
Roman Catholic	35,050,000
Polish Orthodox	550,000
other (mostly nonreligious)	3,050,000
Portugal	
Roman Catholic	9,520,000
other	810,000

Religious affiliation	2001 population
Puerto Rico	
Roman Catholic	2,480,000
Protestant	1,080,000
other	270,000
Qatar	
Muslim (mostly Sunnī)	490,000
Christian	60,000
other	40,000
Réunion	
Roman Catholic	599,000
Hindu	33,000
other	102,000
Romania	
Romanian Orthodox	19,460,000
Roman Catholic	1,140,000
other	1,810,000
Russia	
Russian Orthodox	23,580,000
Muslim	10,980,000
Protestant	1,320,000
Jewish	590,000
other (mostly nonreligious)	107,960,000
Rwanda	
Roman Catholic	3,730,000
Protestant	1,530,000
traditional beliefs	660,000
Muslim	580,000
Anglican	570,000
other	260,000
St. Kitts and Nevis	
Anglican	10,000
Methodist	10,000
other	15,000
Pentecostal	7,000
other	12,000
St. Lucia	
Roman Catholic	125,000
Protestant	20,000
other	13,000
St. Vincent and the Grenadines	
Anglican	20,000
Pentecostal	17,000
Methodist	12,000
Roman Catholic	12,000
other	52,000
Samoa	
Mormon	46,200
Congregational	44,000
Roman Catholic	38,100
Methodist	21,800
other	29,100
San Marino	
Roman Catholic	24,000
other	3,000
São Tomé and Príncipe	
Roman Catholic	111,000
African Christian	16,000
other	20,000
Saudi Arabia	
Sunnī Muslim	20,490,000
Shīʿī Muslim	840,000
Christian	840,000
Hindu	250,000
other	330,000
Senegal	
Sunnī Muslim	9,010,000
traditional beliefs	640,000
Roman Catholic	480,000
other	160,000
Serbia and Montenegro	
Serbian Orthodox	6,680,000
Sunnī Muslim	2,030,000
Roman Catholic	620,000
other (mostly nonreligious)	1,350,000
Seychelles	
Roman Catholic	69,800
other	10,800
Sierra Leone	
Sunnī Muslim	2,490,000

Religious affiliation	2001 population
traditional beliefs	2,190,000
Christian	620,000
other	130,000
Singapore	
Buddhist and Taoist	1,695,000
Muslim	495,000
Christian	485,000
Hindu	133,000
nonreligious	493,000
other	21,000
Slovakia	
Roman Catholic	3,270,000
Slovak Evangelical	340,000
other (mostly nonreligious)	1,800,000
Slovenia	
Roman Catholic	1,650,000
other	340,000
Solomon Islands	
Protestant	173,000
Anglican	149,000
Roman Catholic	83,000
other	75,000
Somalia	
Sunnī Muslim	7,364,000
other	125,000
South Africa	
Christian	36,220,000
independents	17,040,000
Protestant	13,860,000
Roman Catholic	3,090,000
traditional beliefs	3,660,000
Hindu	1,050,000
Muslim	1,050,000
Bahāʾī	260,000
Jewish	170,000
nonreligious	1,050,000
other	130,000
Spain	
Roman Catholic	36,920,000
Muslim	200,000
other (mostly nonreligious)	3,010,000
Sri Lanka	
Buddhist	13,270,000
Hindu	2,190,000
Muslim	1,750,000
Roman Catholic	1,300,000
other	900,000
Sudan, The	
Sunnī Muslim	25,360,000
Christian	6,020,000
traditional beliefs	4,300,000
other	390,000
Suriname	
Hindu	119,000
Roman Catholic	91,000
Muslim	85,000
Protestant	71,000
other	68,000
Swaziland	
African Christian	480,000
Protestant	160,000
traditional beliefs	120,000
other	340,000
Sweden	
Church of Sweden (Lutheran)	7,690,000
other	1,200,000
Switzerland	
Roman Catholic	3,330,000
Protestant	2,890,000
other	1,000,000
Syria	
Sunnī Muslim	12,380,000
Shīʿī Muslim	2,010,000
Christian	920,000
Druze	500,000
other	920,000
Taiwan	
nonreligious	10,670,000
Buddhist	5,100,000
Taoist	4,040,000

Religious affiliation	2001 population
I Kuan Tao	990,000
Protestant	440,000
Roman Catholic	320,000
Tien Te Chiao	210,000
Tien Ti Chiao	190,000
Confucianism (Li)	150,000
Hsuan Yuan Chiao	140,000
Muslim	50,000
Shinto (Tenrikyo)	20,000
Bahāʾī	20,000
Tajikistan	
Sunnī Muslim	4,920,000
Shīʿī Muslim	310,000
Russian Orthodox	90,000
atheist	120,000
other (mostly nonreligious)	820,000
Tanzania	
Christian	18,260,000
Muslim	11,520,000
traditional beliefs	5,830,000
other	620,000
Thailand	
Buddhist	57,920,000
Muslim	2,850,000
Christian	440,000
other	40,000
Togo	
traditional beliefs	1,940,000
Roman Catholic	1,250,000
Sunnī Muslim	970,000
Protestant	530,000
other	450,000
Tonga	
Free Wesleyan	44,000
Roman Catholic	16,000
other	41,000
Trinidad and Tobago	
Roman Catholic	380,000
Hindu	308,000
Protestant	244,000
Anglican	142,000
Muslim	76,000
other	149,000
Tunisia	
Sunnī Muslim	9,720,000
other	104,000
Turkey	
Muslim (mostly Sunnī)	64,360,000
nonreligious	1,340,000
other	530,000
Turkmenistan	
Muslim (mostly Sunnī)	4,752,000
Russian Orthodox	129,000
other (mostly nonreligious)	581,000
Tuvalu	
Congregational	9,400
other	1,600
Uganda	
Roman Catholic	10,050,000
Anglican	9,450,000
Muslim (mostly Sunnī)	1,250,000
traditional beliefs	1,050,000
other	2,190,000
Ukraine	
Ukrainian Orthodox (Russian patriarchy)	9,491,000
Ukrainian Orthodox (Kiev patriarchy)	4,746,000
Ukrainian Autocephalous Orthodox	332,000
Ukrainian Catholic (Uniate)	3,417,000
Protestant	1,736,000
Roman Catholic	576,000
Jewish	423,000
other (mostly nonreligious)	28,044,000
United Arab Emirates	
Sunnī Muslim	2,490,000
Shīʿī Muslim	500,000
other	120,000
United Kingdom	
Christian	49,510,000

Religious affiliation	2001 population
Anglican	26,140,000
Roman Catholic	5,590,000
Protestant	5,020,000
Eastern Orthodox	370,000
other Christian	12,390,000
Muslim	1,220,000
Hindu	440,000
Jewish	310,000
Sikh	240,000
other (mostly nonreligious and atheist)	8,240,000
United States	
Christian (professing)	242,011,000
Christian (affiliated)	196,929,000
independent	80,639,000
Protestant	66,287,000
Roman Catholic	59,542,000
Eastern Orthodox	5,915,000
Anglican	2,464,000
other Christian	10,348,000
multi-affiliated Christians	−28,266,000
Christian (unaffiliated)	45,082,000
non-Christian	44,056,000
nonreligious	25,745,000
Jewish	5,771,000
Muslim	4,242,000
Buddhist	2,515,000
atheist	1,181,000
Hindu	1,059,000
New-Religionist	832,000
Bahāʾī	773,000
Ethnic religionist	447,000
Sikh	240,000
Chinese folk-religionist	80,000
other	1,171,000
Uruguay	
Roman Catholic	2,590,000
Protestant	150,000
Mormon	50,000
Jewish	30,000
other	480,000
Uzbekistan	
Muslim (mostly Sunnī)	19,156,000
Russian Orthodox	195,000
other (mostly nonreligious)	5,804,000
Vanuatu	
Presbyterian	70,000
Roman Catholic	28,000
Anglican	27,000
other	69,000
Venezuela	
Roman Catholic	22,050,000
other	2,590,000
Vietnam	
Buddhist	53,290,000
Roman Catholic	6,180,000
New-Religionist	
Cao Dai	2,810,000
Hoa Hao	1,690,000
other	16,500,000
Virgin Islands (U.S.)	
Protestant	56,000
Roman Catholic	41,000
other	24,000
West Bank	
Muslim (mostly Sunnī)	1,860,000
Jewish[4]	230,000
Christian and other	180,000
Western Sahara	
Sunnī Muslim	250,000
other	1,000
Yemen	
Muslim (mostly Sunnī)	18,050,000
other	20,000
Zambia	
traditional beliefs	2,640,000
Protestant	2,240,000
Roman Catholic	1,650,000
other	3,240,000
Zimbabwe	
African Christian	4,580,000
traditional beliefs	3,430,000
Protestant	1,400,000
Roman Catholic	1,090,000
other	870,000

[1]Official 1986 census figure is 5.9 percent.　[2]Includes the Golan Heights and East Jerusalem; excludes the West Bank and Gaza Strip.　[3]Many Japanese practice both Shintoism and Buddhism.
[4]Excludes East Jerusalem.

Vital statistics, marriage, family

This table provides some of the basic measures of the factors that influence the size, direction, and rates of population change within a country. The accuracy of these data depends on the effectiveness of each respective national system for registering vital and civil events (birth, death, marriage, etc.) and on the sophistication of the analysis that can be brought to bear upon the data so compiled.

Data on birth rates, for example, depend not only on the completeness of registration of births in a particular country but also on the conditions under which those data are collected: Do all births take place in a hospital? Are the births reported comparably in all parts of the country? Are the records of the births tabulated at a central location in a timely way with an effort to eliminate inconsistent reporting of birth events, perinatal mortality, etc.? Similar difficulties attach to death rates but with the added need to identify "cause of death." Even in a developed country such identifications are often left to nonmedical personnel, and in a developing country with, say, only one physician for every 10,000 population, there will be too few physicians to perform autopsies to assess accurately the cause of death after the fact and also too few to provide ongoing care at a level where records would permit inference about cause of death based on prior condition or diagnosis.

Calculating natural increase, which at its most basic is simply the difference between the birth and death rates, may be affected by the differing degrees of completeness of birth and death registration for a given country. The total fertility rate may be understood as the average number of children that would be borne per woman if all childbearing women lived to the end of their childbearing years and bore children at each age at the average rate for that age. Calculating a meaningful fertility rate requires analysis of changing age structure of the female population over time,

changing mortality rates among mothers and their infants, and changing medical practice at births, each improvement of natural survivorship or medical support leading to greater numbers of live-born children and greater numbers of children who survive their first year (the basis for measurement of infant mortality, another basic indicator of demographic conditions and trends within a population).

As indicated above, data for causes of death are not only particularly difficult to obtain, since many countries are not well equipped to collect the data, but also difficult to assess, as their accuracy may be suspect and their meaning may be subject to varying interpretation. Take the case of a citizen of a less developed country who dies of what is clearly a lung infection: Was the death complicated by chronic malnutrition, itself complicated by a parasitic infestation, these last two together so weakening the subject that he died of an infection that he might have survived had his general health been better? Similarly, in a developed country: Someone may die from what is identified in an autopsy as a cerebrovascular accident, but if that accident occurred in a vascular system that was weakened by diabetes, what was the actual cause of death? Statistics on causes of death seek to identify the "underlying" cause (that which sets the final train of events leading to death in motion) but often must settle for the most proximate cause or symptom. Even this kind of analysis may be misleading for those charged with interpreting the data with a view to ordering health-care priorities for a particular country. The eight groups of causes of death utilized here include most, but not all, of the detailed causes classified by the World Health Organization and would not, thus, aggregate to the country's crude death rate for the same year. Among the lesser causes excluded by the present classification are: benign neoplasms; anemias; mental disorders; kidney and genito-urinary diseases not classifi-

Vital statistics, marriage, family

country	vital rates						causes of death (rate per 100,000 population)								
	year	birth rate per 1,000 population	death rate per 1,000 population	infant mortality rate per 1,000 live births	rate of natural increase per 1,000 population	total fertility rate	year	infectious and parasitic diseases	malignant neoplasms (cancers)	endocrine and metabolic disorders	diseases of the nervous system	diseases of the circulatory system	diseases of the respiratory system	diseases of the digestive system	accidents, poisoning, and violence
Afghanistan	2004	47.3	21.1	166	26.2	6.8	...	...	...	...	...	...	...	...	...
Albania	2004	15.1	5.0	16.8	10.1	2.1	2003	3.0	95.5	5.9	17.9	288.5	32.9	10.1	39.2
Algeria	2004	17.8	9.0	32.2	12.1	2.0	...	...	...	...	...	...	...	...	...
American Samoa	2004	24.5	3.4	9.5	12.1	3.4	2002	...	62.0	48.0	...	147.0	18.0	...	72.0
Andorra	2003	10.0	3.1	4.1	6.9	1.3	2002	14.0	223.0	20.0	66.0	269.0	72.0	43.0	56.0
Angola	2004	45.1	25.9	192.5	19.2	6.3	...	...	...	...	...	...	...	...	...
Antigua and Barbuda	2004	17.7	5.6	20.2	12.1	2.3	1999	11.3	111.0	53.0	14.8	296.0	93.0	28.4	52.0
Argentina	2003	17.5	7.6	16.2	9.9	2.3	2002	37.2	155.8	25.7	15.5	272.6	73.3	30.9	44.2
Armenia	2004	11.2	8.1	12.0	3.1	1.3	2003	9.1	135.7	53.2	8.7	443.8	48.6	33.5	32.3
Aruba	2003	12.3	5.2	6.1	7.1	1.8	2002	24.6	126.4	28.3	4.8	181.1	26.4	13.0	45.3
Australia	2003	12.6	7.3	4.8	5.3	1.8	2002	8.5	190.4	16.9	34.8	225.6	47.3	34.8	39.2
Austria	2003	9.5	9.6	4.5	-0.1	1.4	2003	2.0	238.1	22.3	33.5	432.2	50.9	44.6	53.7
Azerbaijan	2004	16.1	6.1	9.8	10.0	1.8	2002	16.8	77.2	17.2	19.3	345.5	38.7	66.5	22.4
Bahamas, The	2004	18.2	8.8	25.7	9.4	2.2	2000	9.2	73.8	37.5	12.2	145.0	26.3	29.3	71.8
Bahrain	2004	18.5	4.0	17.9	14.5	2.7	2003	11.9	39.3	24.4	5.9	86.6	20.7	13.8	26.5
Bangladesh	2004	30.0	8.5	64.3	21.5	3.2	2001	44.5	...	...	...	49.8	57.6	...	43.0
Barbados	2004	13.0	8.8	12.2	4.2	1.6	2000	38.3	123.3	70.2	18.8	219.6	46.6	25.2	15.0
Belarus	2004	10.5	14.1	7.7	-3.6	1.4	2003	10.8	171.2	7.6	14.9	693.5	45.0	28.4	161.6
Belgium	2003	10.7	10.2	4.8	0.5	1.6	1997	13.1	294.1	22.8	57.8	388.4	78.9	44.4	54.3
Belize	2004	29.9	5.6	26.3	24.3	3.8	2000	39.1	107.2	42.4	9.6	248.8	50.0	18.8	77.0
Benin	2004	40.2	12.7	82.9	27.5	5.4	...	...	...	...	...	...	...	...	...
Bermuda	2004	11.8	7.5	8.8	4.3	1.9	2000	14.5	117.6	37.1	16.1	336.8	67.7	27.4	37.1
Bhutan	2002	34.9	8.7	55.0	26.2	4.9	...	...	...	...	...	...	...	...	...
Bolivia	2004	24.7	7.8	54.6	16.9	3.1	2000	...	73.5	...	...	370.3	...	...	109.7
Bosnia and Herzegovina	2003	9.2	8.3	7.7	0.9	1.2	2003	6.1	149.8	25.2	6.4	441.0	22.7	21.1	24.7
Botswana	2004	24.0	28.9	55.6	-4.9	3.0	...	...	...	...	...	...	...	...	...
Brazil	2004	17.3	6.1	30.7	11.2	2.0	2000	26.2	70.1	27.9	10.5	153.4	52.0	25.3	62.5
Brunei	2004	19.3	3.4	13.1	15.9	2.3	...	...	...	...	...	...	...	...	...
Bulgaria	2004	9.0	14.2	11.6	-5.2	1.3	2003	7.7	201.8	25.8	12.2	967.3	36.3	44.3	51.6
Burkina Faso	2004	46.3	16.2	94.4	29.8	6.6	...	...	...	...	...	...	...	...	...
Burundi	2004	42.6	14.1	65.6	28.5	6.7	...	...	...	...	...	...	...	...	...
Cambodia	2004	27.0	9.2	73.0	17.8	3.5	...	...	...	...	...	...	...	...	...
Cameroon	2004	34.7	13.8	66.2	20.9	4.6	...	...	...	...	...	...	...	...	...
Canada	2004	10.4	7.3	4.8	3.1	1.6	2002	10.1	207.5	27.8	30.7	240.6	56.6	26.5	44.1
Cape Verde	2004	26.1	6.7	49.1	19.4	3.6	...	...	...	...	...	...	...	...	...
Central African Republic	2004	34.8	18.9	89.0	15.9	4.6	...	...	...	...	...	...	...	...	...
Chad	2004	46.6	17.0	94.7	29.6	6.4	...	...	...	...	...	...	...	...	...
Chile	2004	15.8	5.7	9.1	10.1	2.1	2001	13.0	130.5	20.3	12.3	154.3	55.3	41.2	52.0
China	2004	13.0	6.9	25.3	6.1	1.7	2002[3]	16.7	119.7	17.2	5.4	162.5	78.1	17.1	43.5
Colombia	2004	21.2	5.6	21.7	15.6	2.6	1999	16.4	63.5	22.1	5.1	121.0	41.3	17.0	104.5
Comoros	2004	38.0	8.6	77.2	29.4	5.1	...	...	...	...	...	...	...	...	...
Congo, Dem. Rep. of the	2004	44.4	13.8	92.6	30.6	6.6	...	...	...	...	...	...	...	...	...
Congo, Rep. of the	2004	43.4	13.7	89.5	29.7	6.2	...	...	...	...	...	...	...	...	...
Costa Rica	2004	19.0	4.3	10.3	14.7	2.3	2002	9.4	112.3	14.0	8.8	123.2	31.0	26.0	45.4
Côte d'Ivoire	2004	35.9	15.0	92.5	20.9	4.7	...	...	...	...	...	...	...	...	...
Croatia	2004	9.5	11.3	7.0	-1.8	1.4	2002	12.8	276.1	21.0	11.2	499.6	41.1	42.7	57.7
Cuba	2003	12.2	7.0	6.3	3.2	1.6	2001	6.7	149.7	15.6	9.7	295.4	88.5	26.4	51.8
Cyprus	2004	12.7	7.6	3.7	5.1	2.0	...	...	...	...	...	...	...	...	...
Czech Republic	2004	9.6	10.6	3.8	-0.9	1.2	2002	3.2	283.0	13.2	17.9	563.4	46.5	43.7	67.4
Denmark	2004	11.9	10.3	4.0	1.6	1.8	2001	8.7	298.2	34.4	20.8	394.7	105.6	54.1	64.6

able under the main groups; maternal deaths (for which data *are* provided, however, in the "Health services" table); diseases of the skin and musculoskeletal systems; congenital and perinatal conditions; and general senility and other ill-defined (ill-diagnosed) conditions, a kind of "other" category.

Expectation of life is probably the most accurate single measure of the quality of life in a given society. It summarizes in a single number all of the natural and social stresses that operate upon individuals in that society. The number may range from as few as 40 years of life in the least developed countries to as much as 80 years for women in the most developed nations. The lost potential in the years separating those two numbers is prodigious, regardless of how the loss arises—wars and civil violence, poor public health services, or poor individual health practice in matters of nutrition, exercise, stress management, and so on.

Data on marriages and marriage rates probably are less meaningful in terms of international comparisons than some of the measures mentioned above because the number, timing, and kinds of social relationships that substitute for marriage depend on many kinds of social variables—income, degree of social control, heterogeneity of the society (race, class, language communities), or level of development of civil administration (if one must travel for a day or more to obtain a legal civil ceremony, one may forgo it). Nevertheless, the data for a single country say specific things about local practice in terms of the age at which a man or woman typically marries, and the overall rate will at least define the number of legal civil marriages, though it cannot say anything about other, less formal arrangements (here the figure for the legitimacy rate for children in the next section may identify some of the societies in which economics or social constraints may operate to limit the number of marriages that are actually confirmed on

civil registers). The available data usually include both first marriages and remarriages after annulment, divorce, widowhood, or the like.

The data for families provide information about the average size of a family unit (individuals related by blood or civil register) and the average number of children under a specified age (set here at 15 to provide a consistent measure of social minority internationally, though legal minority depends on the laws of each country). When well-defined family data are not collected as part of a country's national census or vital statistics surveys, data for households have been substituted on the assumption that most households worldwide represent families in some conventional sense. But increasing numbers of households worldwide are composed of unrelated individuals (unmarried heterosexual couples, aged [or younger] groups sharing limited [often fixed] incomes for reasons of economy, or homosexual couples). Such arrangements do not yet represent great numbers overall. Increasing numbers of census programs, however, even in developing countries, are making more adequate provision for distinguishing these nontraditional, often nonfamily households.

Internet resources for further information:
- World Health Organization Mortality Database (World)
  http://www3.who.int/whosis/mort/table1_process.cfm
- Pan American Health Organization (the Americas)
  http://www.paho.org
- National Center for Health Statistics (U.S.)
  http://www.cdc.gov/nchs
- U.S. Census Bureau: International Data Base (World)
  http://www.census.gov/ipc/www/idbprint.html

expectation of life at birth (latest year)		nuptiality, family, and family planning															country
		marriages			age at marriage (latest)						families (F), households (H) (latest)						
		year	total number	rate per 1,000 popu- lation	groom (percent)			bride (percent)			families (households)		children		induced abortions		
male	female				19 and under	20–29	30 and over	19 and under	20–29	30 and over	total ('000)	size	number under age 15	percent legiti- mate	number	ratio per 100 live births	
42.3	42.7	...	...	...	...	...	...	...	...	...	H 2,774	H 8.0	H 2.8[1]	...	...	...	Afghanistan
72.1	78.6	2003	27,342	8.7	1.5	80.4	18.1	24.0	71.4	4.6	F 729	F 4.2	F 1.6	...	22,600	39.0	Albania
71.2	74.3	2002	218,620	7.0	0.7	67.1	32.2	29.8	61.4	8.8	H 5,072	H 6.2	H 3.0	...	...	...	Algeria
72.1	79.4	2000	300	4.7	...	...	...	...	...	...	H 9	H 6.0	H 2.7	71.7	...	...	American Samoa
80.6	86.6	2003	268	3.7	...	...	...	...	...	...	...	...	...	...	...	...	Andorra
36.1	37.2	...	...	...	...	...	...	...	...	...	H 2,787	H 5.0	...	...	...	...	Angola
69.3	74.1	2001	1,787	23.6	1.2	38.4	60.4	2.8	53.1	44.1	H 24	H 3.1	H 1.2	25.7	...	...	Antigua and Barbuda
71.7	79.4	2002	122,343	3.2	5.6	71.5	22.9	26.0	58.6	15.4	H 10,106	H 3.6	H 1.0	67.5	...	...	Argentina
69.9	75.8	2001	12,302	4.8	0.9	72.3	26.8	16.9	73.3	9.8	H 841	H 4.5	H 1.8	88.2	9,372	29.1	Armenia
75.6	82.5	2002	649	6.9	...	...	...	...	...	...	H 29	H 3.1	...	56.0	...	...	Aruba
77.3	83.1	2002	105,435	5.4	0.5	43.7	55.8	2.5	53.9	43.6	H 7,488	H 2.6	H 0.6	70.1	84,460	33.6	Australia
76.0	81.8	2002	36,570	4.5	1.2	36.1	62.7	3.9	49.5	46.6	H 3,337	H 2.4	H 0.5	64.7	2,380	3.0	Austria
69.6	75.2	2002	41,661	5.1	1.0	66.2	32.8	22.0	65.0	13.0	H 1,740	H 4.7	H 1.7	93.6	16,606	15.0	Azerbaijan
62.2	69.1	2001	1,787	5.8	0.6	41.6	57.8	4.6	50.6	44.8	H 87	H 3.5	...	43.2	...	...	Bahamas, The
71.5	76.5	2002	4,909	7.8	1.6	66.9	31.5	20.5	64.4	15.1	H 109	H 6.2	H 2.2	100.0	17[2]	0.1[2]	Bahrain
61.8	61.6	1998	1,154,000	9.2	...	...	...	...	...	...	H 25,673	H 5.2	...	...	...	...	Bangladesh
70.4	74.4	2000	3,516	13.1	0.1	40.2	59.7	1.4	53.6	44.9	H 97	H 2.8	H 1.5	26.9	723	19.6	Barbados
62.8	74.7	2002	66,652	6.7	3.6	68.6	27.8	17.8	61.0	21.2	H 3,210	H 3.1	H 0.8	82.2	101,402	111.0	Belarus
75.9	81.7	2002	40,434	3.9	0.5	51.3	48.2	3.1	61.2	35.7	F 4,319	F 2.4	F 0.5	88.7	14,775	13.9	Belgium
66.5	70.6	2003	1,713	6.3	7.1	56.4	36.5	24.9	51.5	23.6	H 55	H 5.0	H 2.2	40.3	990	15.1	Belize
51.2	53.4	...	...	...	...	...	...	...	...	...	H 1,068	H 6.4	...	...	...	...	Benin
75.5	79.7	2002	970	15.1	0.2	22.0	77.8	0.9	32.2	66.9	H 28	H 2.3	H 0.5	62.3	92	11.0	Bermuda
62.0	64.0	...	...	...	...	...	...	...	...	...	H 147	H 4.6	...	...	...	...	Bhutan
62.5	67.9	...	...	...	...	...	...	...	...	...	H 1,923	H 4.3	H 1.6	80.9	...	...	Bolivia
65.0	70.0	2003	20,733	5.4	13.3	61.8	24.9	15.7	63.7	20.6	H 1,203	H 3.4	H 1.1	88.7	...	...	Bosnia and Herzegovina
34.0	34.4	...	...	...	...	...	...	...	...	...	H 414	H 4.2	H 2.0	28.8	...	...	Botswana
67.5	75.1	2000	710,121	4.1	4.2	60.3	35.5	21.3	55.3	23.4	F 48,514	F 3.5	H 1.2	...	...	...	Brazil
72.1	77.1	2002	2,336	6.7	6.2	65.1	28.7	19.6	63.4	17.0	H 57	H 6.1	H 2.0	99.6	...	...	Brunei
68.9	76.0	2002	29,218	3.7	1.5	64.6	33.9	11.0	69.2	19.8	H 2,913	H 2.7	...	71.8	50,824	76.4	Bulgaria
46.6	49.5	...	...	...	...	...	...	...	...	...	H 1,759	H 6.8	...	...	...	...	Burkina Faso
49.2	50.4	...	...	...	...	...	...	...	...	...	H 1,398	H 5.0	...	...	...	...	Burundi
56.6	60.6	...	...	...	...	...	...	...	...	...	H 2,418	H 5.7	...	...	...	...	Cambodia
50.5	50.9	...	...	...	...	...	...	...	...	...	H 2,880	H 5.5	...	...	...	...	Cameroon
76.6	83.5	2004	146,377	4.7	0.7	43.4	55.9	2.5	52.9	44.6	H 12,021	H 2.6	H 0.6	72.3	105,154	32.0	Canada
66.8	73.5	1994	1,200	3.2	...	...	...	...	...	...	H 95	H 4.7	...	28.9	...	...	Cape Verde
43.1	43.5	...	...	...	...	...	...	...	...	...	H 646	H 6.1	...	...	...	...	Central African Republic
45.3	48.6	...	...	...	...	...	...	...	...	...	H 1,574	H 5.0	...	...	...	...	Chad
73.1	79.8	2002	60,971	3.9	2.9	54.6	42.5	11.9	62.2	25.9	H 4,141	H 3.6	...	61.9	...	...	Chile
70.4	73.7	2002	7,800,000	6.1	...	...	...	...	...	...	H 348[4]	H 3.7	H 1.1	...	6,340,000	37.1	China
67.6	75.4	...	...	...	...	...	...	...	...	...	H 8,835	H 4.9	F 2.5	75.2	...	...	Colombia
59.3	63.9	...	...	...	...	...	...	...	...	...	H 94	H 6.3	...	...	...	...	Comoros
49.3	52.2	...	...	...	...	...	...	...	...	...	H 18,326	H 2.3	...	...	...	...	Congo, Dem. Rep. of the
50.7	52.8	...	...	...	...	...	...	...	...	...	H 326	H 4.7	H 2.0	...	...	...	Congo, Rep. of the
74.1	79.3	2001	23,790	6.1	5.6	54.8	39.6	21.0	51.7	27.3	H 960	H 4.3	...	50.3	...	...	Costa Rica
45.9	51.1	...	...	...	...	...	...	...	...	...	H 2,027	H 8.1	...	...	...	...	Côte d'Ivoire
70.2	78.3	2002	22,806	5.1	0.9	61.6	37.5	9.9	65.3	24.8	H 1,877	H 2.3	H 0.6	92.7	6,191	15.4	Croatia
74.6	79.8	2002	56,876	5.1	2.7	39.9	57.4	13.0	42.3	44.7	F 3,121	F 3.6	H 1.6	...	76,293	53.2	Cuba
77.0	81.4	2002	10,284	12.9	0.7	45.5	53.8	4.6	58.8	36.6	H 233	H 3.0	H 1.1	99.6	...	...	Cyprus
72.0	78.5	2002	52,732	5.2	0.8	58.4	40.8	3.7	70.3	26.0	H 3,828	H 2.6	...	71.5	31,142	33.6	Czech Republic
74.9	79.5	2002	37,210	6.9	0.6	29.7	69.7	2.3	40.7	57.0	H 2,467	H 2.2	...	53.5	15,567	24.1	Denmark

Vital statistics, marriage, family (continued)

country	vital rates						causes of death (rate per 100,000 population)								
	year	birth rate per 1,000 population	death rate per 1,000 population	infant mortality rate per 1,000 live births	rate of natural increase per 1,000 population	total fertility rate	year	infectious and parasitic diseases	malignant neoplasms (cancers)	endocrine and metabolic disorders	diseases of the nervous system	diseases of the circulatory system	diseases of the respiratory system	diseases of the digestive system	accidents, poisoning, and violence
Djibouti	2004	40.4	19.4	105.5	21.0	5.5	1999	18.3	154.2	90.2	9.2	283.7	66.7	26.1	36.6
Dominica	2004	16.3	6.9	14.8	9.4	2.0	1999	18.3	154.2	90.2	9.2	283.7	66.7	26.1	36.6
Dominican Republic	2004	23.9	5.7	30.5	18.2	2.9	1998	30.6	38.0	15.9	4.7	102.7	19.0	17.2	42.1
East Timor	2004	27.5	6.4	48.9	21.1	3.7									
Ecuador	2004[1]	23.2	4.2	24.5	19.0	2.8	2000	26.8	53.0	30.6	8.0	98.5	36.2	22.6	64.1
Egypt	2004	23.8	5.3	33.9	18.5	3.0	2000	32.3	25.7	11.5	5.4	230.3	49.5	48.6	26.3
El Salvador	2004	24.8	9.0	25.4	18.9	2.8	1999	32.8	44.4	19.5	12.3	88.3	40.5	25.8	118
Equatorial Guinea	2004	36.4	15.0	93.2	21.5	4.7									
Eritrea	2004	35.2	10.1	48.5	25.1	5.3									
Estonia	2004	10.4	13.2	7.0	-2.8	1.4	2003	9.1	247.6	11.3	17.0	735.3	42.7	47.4	135.7
Ethiopia	2004	39.3	15.3	94.2	24.0	5.4									
Faroe Islands	2004	13.9	8.7	6.4	5.2	2.5	1999	4.1	257.2	16.8	...	339.2	48.8	20.1	39.9
Fiji	2004	22.9	5.7	13.0	17.2	2.8	2001	45.8	38.0	23.7	0.5	330.0	50.2	14.1	31.7
Finland	2004	11.0	9.1	3.1	1.9	1.8	2002	7.3	202.3	12.3	41.6	406.4	74.3	39.1	78.4
France	2004	12.7	8.4	4.1	4.3	1.9	2001	17.9	185.0	20.5	33.8	272.8	32.3	29.7	55.6
French Guiana	2004	29.3	4.1	12.5	25.2	3.1	1989	61.7	58.1	16.3	10.9	114.3	20.9	13.6	98.0
French Polynesia	2004	17.7	4.5	8.6	13.2	2.1	2002	12.0	103.0	16.0	11.0	113.0	46.0	13.0	54.0
Gabon	2004	36.5	f1.8	56.1	24.7	4.8		...	...	...	...	...	...	...	...
Gambia, The	2004	40.4	12.8	74.5	27.6	5.5									
Gaza Strip	2004	40.6	4.0	23.5	36.6	6.0									
Georgia	2004	10.6	10.6	26.3	0.0	1.4	2001	7.4	85.1	13.7	1.5	569.5	18.9	25.4	25.4
Germany	2004	8.5	10.4	4.2	-1.9	1.4	2001	12.6	251.8	29.6	20.2	475.1	58.9	49.6	41.5
Ghana	2004	31.8	10.1	57.7	21.7	4.2									
Greece	2004	9.7	10.1	5.6	-0.4	1.3	2001	5.9	230.3	9.3	11.7	486.2	66.3	22.8	41.5
Greenland	2004	16.0	7.7	16.3	8.3	2.4	1996–98	64.9	181.5	3.9[5]	1.8[5]	187.5	51.8	5.7[5]	110.1
Grenada	2004	22.6	7.3	14.6	15.3	2.4	1996	18.3	125.2	89.5	11.2	235.1	38.7	18.3	43.8
Guadeloupe	2004	15.8	6.0	8.8	9.7	1.9	1996	23.8	134.8	26.2	...	183.7	32.1	31.4	68.1
Guam	2004	19.3	4.4	7.6	14.9	2.6	2002	1.7	77.0	28.5	6.9	162.7	32.6	16.9	69.7
Guatemala	2004	31.3	5.6	33.1	25.7	4.2	1999	59.3	44.9	48.2	8.9	74.7	110.8	33.5	71.6
Guernsey	2004	9.2	9.9	4.8	-0.7	1.4	1996	5.3	282.3	15.9	15.9	441.1	150.0	49.4	24.7
Guinea	2004	42.3	15.8	92.8	26.5	5.9									
Guinea-Bissau	2004	38.0	16.9	109.0	21.1	5.0									
Guyana	2004	18.6	8.4	34.1	10.2	2.1	1996	41.4	40.7	79.6	9.8	190.8	40.0	29.7	64.8
Haiti	2004	36.7	12.5	75.2	24.2	5.1									
Honduras	2004	29.8	5.2	27.1	24.6	3.8									
Hong Kong	2004	7.0	5.3	2.5	1.7	0.9	2003	10.8	175.0	13.1	4.1	126.8	87.1	21.5	28.6
Hungary	2004	9.4	13.1	6.6	-3.7	1.3	2002	1.9	325.2	24.8	16.8	668.1	46.3	90.5	94.0
Iceland	2004	14.4	6.2	2.8	8.2	2.0	2001	5.9	169.0	11.8	26.8	237.6	49.5	16.4	45.6
India	2004	22.8	8.4	57.9	14.4	2.8	2002	...	71.0	...	...	268.0	58.0	...	100.0
Indonesia	2004	21.1	6.3	36.8	14.8	2.5									
Iran	2004	17.1	5.6	42.9	11.5	1.9	2002	67.0	65.0	18.0	29.0	232.0	23.0	41.0	104.0
Iraq	2004	33.1	5.7	52.7	27.4	4.4	2002	...	54.0	...	...	187.0	...	...	115.0
Ireland	2004	15.3	7.0	4.9	8.3	1.9	2003	4.7	189.7	37.0	8.3	275.3	111.0	11.3	34.0
Isle of Man	2004	11.1	10.3	4.5	0.8	1.7	2003	—	278.3	14.3	29.8	495.6	106.7	54.4	47.9
Israel	2004	21.7	5.7	11.0	16.0	3.0	1999	18.2	141.1	46.2	16.8	190.6	43.9	21.1	35.3
Italy	2005	9.6	9.5	6.1	0.1	1.3	2003	6.4	282.9	30.7	24.1	429.5	73.0	42.9	45.5
Jamaica	2004	17.6	6.0	12.9	11.6	2.0	2002	12.0	130.0	81.0	13.0	321.0	61.0	43.0	38.0
Japan	2004	8.8	8.2	2.8	0.6	1.3	2002	15.6	239.0	13.8	8.2	237.8	107.1	30.2	57.5
Jersey	2004	11.1	8.5	5.3	2.6	1.6	2000–03	...	255.0	...	...	328.0	136.0	48.0	35.0
Jordan	2004	28.1	3.2	20.9	24.9	3.7									
Kazakhstan	2003	15.3	9.7	31.9	5.6	1.9	2002	28.3	118.1	10.1	8.1	472.5	61.3	39.3	129.6
Kenya	2004	40.2	15.2	63.6	25.0	5.0		...	...	...	...	...	...	...	...
Kiribati	2004	31.0	8.5	49.9	22.5	4.3									
Korea, North	2004	16.8	7.0	24.8	9.8	2.2									
Korea, South	2004	9.8	5.1	6.8	4.7	1.2	2004	10.7	135.1	25.6	8.5	120.4	29.4	25.0	63.0
Kuwait	2004	21.9	2.4	10.3	19.5	3.0	2002	5.0	22.4	11.0	3.3	72.3	9.3	4.7	27.2
Kyrgyzstan	2004	21.6	6.9	25.7	14.7	2.7	2002	7.6	60.5	6.5	11.8	338.4	83.6	42.3	26.1
Laos	2004	36.5	12.1	87.1	24.4	4.9	2002	...	73.0	...	...	210.0	58.0	...	112.0
Latvia	2004	8.3	13.9	9.4	-5.1	1.2	2002	13.2	245.0	11.6	16.8	777.8	36.4	43.1	156.8
Lebanon	2004	19.3	6.3	25.5	13.0	2.0	2002	...	67.0	...	...	305.0	33.0	...	87.0
Lesotho	2004	25.7	28.3	90.3	2.6	3.4									
Liberia	2004	46.0	24.7	168.0	21.3	6.2									
Libya	2004	27.2	3.5	25.7	23.7	3.4									
Liechtenstein	2004	11.0	6.3	4.8	3.9	1.5	2003	5.8	148.7	...	...	233.3	32.1	8.7	26.3
Lithuania	2004	8.8	12.0	7.9	-3.2	1.3	2002	13.7	227.3	9.8	10.5	644.8	46.6	43.6	153.0
Luxembourg	2004	12.0	7.9	4.0	4.1	1.7	2002	12.5	205.3	17.0	25.8	322.2	80.9	36.8	67.5
Macau	2005	7.1	3.3	3.0	3.8	0.9	2003	9.3	115.0	2.3	...	98.8	33.9	2.8	66.3
Macedonia	2004	13.2	8.8	11.0	4.4	1.6	2003	14.8	165.1	31.1	32.4	599.1	41.6	17.9	32.9
Madagascar	2004	41.1	9.0	78.5	29.5	5.7									
Malawi	2004	43.8	19.9	97.9	23.9	6.0									
Malaysia	2004	21.3	4.6	5.9	16.7	3.1	1997	17.6	20.1	4.2	3.1	56.5	20.3	8.3	33.0
Maldives	2003	35.7	6.0	15.0	29.7	5.3									
Mali	2004	50.3	17.6	111.2	32.8	7.5									
Malta	2003	10.0	7.9	4.0	2.1	1.5	2002	4.5	185.6	26.3	12.6	335.4	88.0	26.3	31.4
Marshall Islands	2004	33.9	4.9	30.5	29.0	4.0	1993	169.9	68.4	...	—	155.1	105.1	63.3	36.7
Martinique	2004	14.6	6.4	7.3	8.2	1.8	1996	21.9	150.1	27.7	...	206.6	36.3	27.2	47.2
Mauritania	2004	41.8	12.7	72.4	29.1	6.0									
Mauritius	2004	15.6	6.9	14.4	8.7	1.8	2003	8.5	78.9	45.0	10.4	357.9	60.0	34.8	38.9
Mayotte	2004	42.2	8.1	64.2	34.1	6.0									
Mexico	2004	18.8	4.5	12.6	14.3	2.2	2001	18.2	58.3	62.2	7.4	98.5	36.9	42.3	51.3
Micronesia	2004	25.8	5.0	31.3	20.8	3.4	2002	...	52.0	24.0	...	202.0	46.0	...	39.0
Moldova	2004	14.8	12.8	41.0	2.0	1.8	2002	15.4	109.1	8.3	8.5	539.0	61.2	90.5	81.0
Monaco	2004	9.4	12.7	5.5	-3.3	1.8									
Mongolia	2005	18.1	6.5	22.2	11.6	2.3	2003	33[6]	121.6	3[6]	14[6]	244.1	34.2	49.0	84.0
Morocco	2004	20.1	5.5	43.3	14.6	2.8	2002	120.0	41.0	...	...	201.0	23.0	...	40.0

expectation of life at birth (latest year) male	female	marriages year	total number	rate per 1,000 population	groom (percent) 19 and under	20–29	30 and over	bride (percent) 19 and under	20–29	30 and over	families (households) total ('000)	size	children number under age 15	percent legitimate	induced abortions number	ratio per 100 live births	country
41.8	44.4	1999	3,808	6.1	...	...	...	...	...	...	H 98	H 5.6	...	96.8	...	...	Djibouti
71.5	77.4	1999	339	4.7	—	37.0	63.0	2.7	56.2	41.1	H 19	H 3.6	H 2.2	24.1	...	...	Dominica
69.7	72.8	2001	24,470	2.9	...	...	...	...	...	...	H 2,195	H 3.9	...	32.8	31,068	17.3	Dominican Republic
63.3	67.9	...									H 197	H 4.7	...	...	...	...	East Timor
73.2	79.0	2002	66,208	5.6	11.7	60.0	28.3	28.4	53.2	18.4	H 2,876	H 4.5	...	67.9	...	...	Ecuador
68.2	73.3	1999	525,412	3.1	2.9	58.8	38.3	10.4	56.3	33.3	H 14,476	H 4.6	H 2.1	100.0	10[2]	2	Egypt
67.9	74.0	2002	25,996	4.0	3.9	50.7	45.4	13.4	52.9	33.7	H 1,467	H 4.3	...	27.2	...	...	El Salvador
48.1	51.9	...									H	H 4.5	...	...	...	...	Equatorial Guinea
56.5	59.5	1992	23,000	6.8							H 792	H 5.0	...	...	...	...	Eritrea
66.0	76.9	2002	5,853	4.3	1.3	49.8	48.9	7.1	57.3	35.6	H 567	H 2.4	H 0.8	42.2	10,074	71.7	Estonia
47.5	49.9	1999	630,290	9.1	...	...	...	...	...	...	H 12,874	H 5.2	...	...	...	...	Ethiopia
75.6	82.5	2003	229	4.8	...	...	...	...	...	...	F 14	F 3.0	F 0.9	62.0	...	...	Faroe Islands
66.7	71.8	1998	8,058	10.1	...	...	...	...	...	...	F 137	F 6.0	F 2.5	82.7	...	...	Fiji
75.3	82.3	2002	26,969	5.2	0.9	40.0	59.1	2.9	49.3	47.8	H 2,373	H 2.2	...	59.2	10,709	19.0	Finland
76.7	83.8	2002	280,600	4.6	0.1	44.9	55.0	1.2	57.4	41.4	H 24,643	H 2.4	H 1.0	54.8	205,600	27.0	France
73.6	80.4	2002	522	3.0	0.6	26.8	72.6	4.2	41.6	54.2	H 33	H 3.4	H 1.2	16.1	388	16.8	French Guiana
73.3	78.2	2004	1,148	4.5	...	...	...	...	...	...	H 55	H 4.4	H 1.7	29.9	...	...	French Polynesia
54.0	57.1	...									H 260	H 5.0	...	...	...	...	Gabon
51.6	55.3	...									H 154	H 8.6	...	...	...	...	Gambia, The
70.3	72.9	...											...	...	...	...	Gaza Strip
72.4	79.4	2001	13,336	2.7	5.8	58.0	36.2	21.9	59.9	18.2	H 1,225	H 4.0	H 1.1	55.4	13,908	29.8	Georgia
75.6	81.7	2002	391,967	4.8	0.7	44.6	54.7	3.7	56.3	40.0	H 38,720	H 2.1	H 0.3	72.0	128,030	17.7	Germany
57.4	58.9	...									H 4,463	H 4.9	H 2.2	...	...	...	Ghana
76.4	81.6	2001	58,491	5.3	0.8	46.3	52.9	7.0	65.4	27.6	H 3,600	H 2.9	H 0.7	95.2	12,289	12.1	Greece
65.8	73.0	1999	250	4.5	1.1	44.6	54.3	2.7	59.6	37.7	F 31	F 1.8	F 0.5	29.2	821	87.3	Greenland
62.7	66.3	2001	509	5.0	0.3	28.6	71.1	2.6	40.1	57.3	H 29	H 3.3	...	18.1	...	...	Grenada
74.6	81.0	2002	1,809	4.1	—	25.9	74.1	1.9	41.2	56.9	H 146	H 2.9	H 0.9	34.7	561	8.7	Guadeloupe
75.1	81.3	2002	1,288	8.0	3.0	55.5	41.5	9.2	59.3	31.5	H 44	H 3.7	H 1.3	42.8	...	...	Guam
63.6	69.5	1999	60,922	5.5	18.1	55.9	26.0	41.0	40.8	18.2	H 2,600	H 4.5	...	34.8	...	...	Guatemala
77.0	83.1	2000	343	5.7	...	...	...	...	...	...	H 21	H 2.6	H 0.5	65.2	...	...	Guernsey
48.1	50.5	...									H 1,161	H 6.6	...	...	...	...	Guinea
44.6	48.4	...									H 179	H 7.0	H 2.8	11.3	...	...	Guinea-Bissau
62.5	67.8	...									H 196	H 4.5	H 2.1	...	...	...	Guyana
51.3	54.0	...									H 1,732	H 4.7	H 1.8	...	...	...	Haiti
67.7	71.0	...									H 1,520	H 4.4	H 2.8	...	...	...	Honduras
78.6	84.6	2002	32,070	4.7	0.6	41.5	57.9	3.1	62.5	34.4	H 2,158	H 3.1	...	94.5	20,235	42.0	Hong Kong
68.6	76.9	2004	43,500	4.3	1.2	58.0	40.8	5.7	67.8	26.5	F 4,104	F 2.5	F 0.8	68.7	56,075	57.9	Hungary
78.8	82.6	2002	1,619	5.6	0.2	34.0	65.8	1.7	44.4	53.9	H 104	H 2.8	H 1.3	36.3	951	23.0	Iceland
63.3	64.8	...									H 194,736	H 5.4	H 2.4	...	723,142	2.8	India
66.8	71.8	2003	1,588,000	7.7							H 53,972	H 3.9	...	...	...	...	Indonesia
68.3	71.1	2002	650,960	9.9	...	...	...	...	...	...	H 14,456	H 4.5	H 2.2	100	...	...	Iran
67.1	69.5	2000	171,134	7.3							H 3,965	H 6.4	H 4.1	...	...	...	Iraq
75.1	80.3	2003	20,302	5.1	0.7	62.2	37.1	1.6	74.7	23.7	H 1,328	H 3.0	H 1.3	67.7	6,320	10.3	Ireland
75.0	81.9	2002	430	5.6	0.2	33.7	66.1	1.7	45.4	47.1	H 29,377	H 2.4	...	61.6	152	17.6	Isle of Man
77.5	81.5	2002	39,718	6.0	3.4	69.3	27.3	18.3	68.2	13.5	H 1,856	H 3.6	H 1.1	97.2	20,069	13.8	Israel
77.3	83.1	2002	265,635	4.6	0.4	47.6	52.0	3.3	41.2	55.5	F 21,488	F 2.7	F 0.5	86.3	126,124	23.6	Italy
73.8	78.0	1999	26,871	10.4							H 753	H 3.5	H 1.4	14.9	...	...	Jamaica
78.6	85.6	2002	757,331	5.9	1.5	55.2	43.3	3.1	67.2	29.7	H 48,105	H 2.6	...	99.0	319,831	28.5	Japan
76.6	81.7	2001	660	7.6							H 36	H 2.4	H 0.4	88.1	296	28.0	Jersey
70.6	72.4	2002	46,873	8.8	2.8	66.7	30.5	33.0	56.6	10.4	H 919	H 5.8	H 3.4	100	...	...	Jordan
65.6	71.3	2002	98,986	6.7	4.9	71.4	23.7	21.7	63.4	14.9	H 3,984	H 4.0	H 1.4	86.6	135,000	61.2	Kazakhstan
48.1	46.3	...									H 6,848	H 4.6	H 2.7	...	...	...	Kenya
50.3	64.4	...									H 13	H 6.5	H 2.5	...	...	...	Kiribati
68.4	73.9	...									H 4,565	H 4.6	H 1.7	...	...	...	Korea, North
71.8	79.4	2002	306,573	6.4	0.6	52.8	46.6	2.2	72.5	25.3	H 14,852	H 3.2	H 1.0	99.5	...	...	Korea, South
75.9	77.9	2002	11,973	6.4	3.9	64.0	32.1	26.3	54.4	19.3	H 472	H 5.0	H 1.6	100.0	19[2]	...	Kuwait
64.5	72.2	2002	31,240	6.3	2.5	73.2	24.3	22.3	66.0	11.7	H 1,145	H 4.4	H 1.9	83.2	23,390	23.8	Kyrgyzstan
52.7	56.8	...									H 891	H 6.2	...	...	...	...	Laos
65.9	76.9	2002	9,738	4.2	1.6	56.6	41.8	6.7	61.4	31.9	H 925	H 2.5	H 0.8	54.7	13,700	67.4	Latvia
69.9	74.9	2004	30,400	8.5	...	...	...	...	...	...	H 727	H 4.7	H 2.2	...	...	...	Lebanon
45.1	54.2	...									H 433	H 5.0	H 2.0	...	...	...	Lesotho
36.1	40.3	...									H 474	H 5.0	...	...	...	...	Liberia
74.1	78.6	2002	33,323	5.9							H 794	H 6.3	F 2.9	...	...	...	Libya
75.8	83.0	2002	173	5.1	—	54.5	44.5	0.0	66.3	29.2	H 14	H 2.5	H 0.7	86.0	...	...	Liechtenstein
66.4	77.8	2002	16,151	4.7	2.4	64.2	33.4	11.1	66.0	22.9	H 1,357	H 2.5	H 0.8	74.6	12,495	41.6	Lithuania
74.9	81.0	2003	2,001	4.5	0.4	34.7	64.9	2.5	47.0	50.5	H 174	H 2.6	H 0.5	75.0	...	...	Luxembourg
77.4	82.0	2003	1,309	3.8	1.5	43.2	55.3	4.0	62.3	33.7	H 156	H 2.8	H 0.9	99.3	...	...	Macau
71.0	76.1	2004	14,073	6.9	3.3	72.1	24.6	19.8	67.9	12.3	H 561	H 3.6	H 1.3	87.7	11,407	38.9	Macedonia
54.2	59.0	...									H 3,182	H 5.0	H 2.0	...	...	...	Madagascar
41.4	41.0	...									H 2,426	H 4.3	...	...	...	...	Malawi
70.4	76.2	...									H 5,176	H 4.7	...	...	...	...	Malaysia
62.0	64.6	2003	3,120	10.8	13.7	58.2	29.1	...	...	...	H 43	H 6.5	...	...	...	...	Maldives
46.3	50.3	...									H 1,757	H 6.0	...	...	...	...	Mali
76.4	80.4	2002	2,240	5.6	1.0	66.3	32.7	5.4	42.8	51.8	H 132	H 3.0	H 1.2	83.2	47	1.2	Malta
67.8	71.7	...									H 7	H 7.7	...	...	...	...	Marshall Islands
79.4	78.4	2002	1,524	3.9	0.1	23.8	76.1	0.3	37.5	62.2	H 127	H 3.0	H 0.8	31.8	2,900	42.9	Martinique
50.2	54.6	...									H 487	H 5.5	...	...	...	...	Mauritania
68.7	75.6	2003	10,484	8.7	1.3	54.7	44.0	15.9	59.5	24.6	F 310	F 3.9	F 2.0	72.8	...	...	Mauritius
58.9	63.2	...									H 19	H 4.9	H 2.3	89.2	...	...	Mayotte
72.7	77.6	2002	570,060	5.5	13.6	62.9	23.5	30.6	54.2	15.2	H 24,682	H 4.1	H 2.0	72.5	3,281	0.1	Mexico
67.7	71.3	...									H 18	H 6.7	...	...	...	...	Micronesia
60.9	69.4	2002	21,685	6.1	7.1	68.2	24.7	18.3	69.7	12.0	H 1,348	H 3.3	H 1.1	87.7	15,739	44.1	Moldova
75.5	83.5	2002	173	5.4	...	...	...	...	...	...	H 14	H 2.2	H 0.3	96.8	...	...	Monaco
61.6	67.8	2004	13,514	4.4	3.8	73.1	23.1	9.5	73.8	16.7	F 555	F 4.4	...	...	12,870	25.9	Mongolia
67.5	72.1	...									H 5,390	H 5.5	H 2.5	...	...	...	Morocco

Vital statistics, marriage, family (continued)

country	vital rates						causes of death (rate per 100,000 population)								
	year	birth rate per 1,000 population	death rate per 1,000 population	infant mortality rate per 1,000 live births	rate of natural increase per 1,000 population	total fertility rate	year	infectious and parasitic diseases	malignant neoplasms (cancers)	endocrine and metabolic disorders	diseases of the nervous system	diseases of the circulatory system	diseases of the respiratory system	diseases of the digestive system	accidents, poisoning, and violence
Mozambique	2004	36.5	20.6	132.0	15.9	4.8	2002	477.0	74.0	...	...	258.0	57.0	...	92.0
Myanmar (Burma)	2004	23.2	11.2	81.0	12.0	2.8									
Namibia	2004	26.3	17.6	49.8	8.7	3.3									
Nauru	2004	25.6	7.0	10.2	18.6	3.3	2003	...	79.5	159.0	...	119.2	149.0	...	79.5
Nepal	2004	32.0	9.7	68.8	22.3	4.3									
Netherlands, The	2003	12.4	8.7	5.2	3.0	1.7	2003	11.7	235.5	28.1	22.7	289.3	87.8	36.1	33.4
Netherlands Antilles	2004	14.2	7.7	10.4	6.5	2.0	1995[7]	16.7	149.0	61.7	9.9	71.6	40.8	21.4	47.6
New Caledonia	2004	17.6	4.8	7.9	12.8	2.4	2001	20.4	128.8	8.8	9.3	132.9	57.4	15.8	69.9
New Zealand	2004	13.9	7.0	5.6	6.9	1.8	2000	4.6	201.8	26.7	21.2	289.3	54.4	19.1	42.8
Nicaragua	2004	25.5	4.5	30.2	21.0	2.9	2000	15.0	31.9	17.4	5.9	66.9	18.4	16.6	39.4
Niger	2004	51.4	21.4	121.0	30.0	7.6									
Nigeria	2004	40.9	17.4	100.4	23.5	5.6									
Northern Mariana Islands	2004	19.8	2.3	7.3	17.5	1.3	2000[8]	...	...	...	...	...	...	...	30.8
Norway	2004	11.9	9.5	3.7	2.4	1.8	2003	11.5[9]	235.6	18.6[9]	22.8	365.2	86.6	27.0[9]	54.1
Oman	2004	24.0	2.6	10.3	21.4	3.2									
Pakistan	2004	31.2	8.7	74.4	22.5	4.3									
Palau	2004	18.7	6.9	6.2	11.8	2.5	1993	43.6	136.9	...	...	192.9	43.6	...	112.0
Panama	2004	21.9	5.2	14.9	16.7	2.7	2002	31.0	64.5	19.4	4.1	108.8	34.9	11.2	39.3
Papua New Guinea	2004	30.5	7.5	53.2	23.0	4.0									
Paraguay	2004	29.8	4.6	26.7	25.2	4.0	2000	16.8	43.1	20.9	2.7	80.5	24.1	11.8	38.2
Peru	2004	21.3	6.3	33.0	15.0	2.6	2000	24.5	52.8	13.9	5.9	54.2	45.8	22.5	35.2
Philippines	2004	24.6	5.7	24.2	18.9	3.1	1998	65.8	43.3	19.5	6.5	133.3	76.8	22.3	41.0
Poland	2004	9.3	6.8	9.5	-0.2	1.2	2002	6.2	227.2	14.6	10.2	438.5	40.2	38.3	62.6
Portugal	2004	10.4	9.7	3.8	0.7	1.5	2002	19.7	215.5	48.2	19.6	396.7	89.5	44.3	55.8
Puerto Rico	2004	13.8	7.4	8.4	6.4	1.9	2000	40.4	123.4	76.0	32.3	218.3	74.4	40.9	63.4
Qatar	2004	15.0	4.5	19.3	11.1	2.9	1995	6.9	24.5	11.2	4.7	69.4	7.9	6.5	34.3
Réunion	2003	19.0	5.3	6.2	13.7	2.4	2000	14.9[10]	112.4	22.5[10]	16.0[10]	162.8	33.1	48.4	54.7
Romania	2002	9.7	12.4	27.3	-2.7	1.3	2002	15.1	198.0	9.0	7.7	771.9	70.7	74.4	67.1
Russia	2004	10.5	15.9	11.5	-5.4	1.3	2002	25.2	199.9	16.9	20.2	892.4	137.8	103.0	231.5
Rwanda	2004	40.7	16.5	92.7	24.2	5.5									
St. Kitts and Nevis	2004	18.3	8.7	14.9	9.6	2.4	1995	57.8	108.0	55.3	20.1	482.4	65.3	50.3	45.2
St. Lucia	2004	20.5	5.2	14.0	15.3	2.3	2001	19.0	91.2	89.4	13.9	173.7	43.1	17.7	50.1
St. Vincent and the Grenadines	2002	17.6	6.9	18.1	10.7	2.0	1999	10.6	131.7	122.8	10.6	239.5	65.4	23.0	40.6
Samoa	2003	28.6	5.5	26.0	23.1	4.1	2002	89.0	54.0	39.0	8.0	222.0	43.0	29.0	35.0
San Marino	2004	10.3	6.2	3.4	4.1	1.3	1998–2002	...	225.3	2.2	...	339.0	31.0	12.6	29.5
São Tomé and Príncipe	2004	41.4	6.9	44.6	34.5	5.8									
Saudi Arabia	2004	29.7	2.7	13.7	27.0	4.1									
Senegal	2004	34.1	9.8	55.3	24.3	4.6									
Serbia and Montenegro	2004	10.9	13.5	7.5	-2.6	1.7	2003	9.0	183.3	31.2	12.6	549.5	36.1	30.4	37.6
Seychelles	2004	18.1	8.1	16.0	10.0	2.1	2002	43.3[6]	122.0	16.2[6]	16.2[6]	306.7	66.5	37.0	43.3[6]
Sierra Leone	2004	46.5	23.7	163.8	22.8	6.2									
Singapore	2004	10.1	4.3	2.0	5.8	1.7	2001	6.4	100.1	14.6	2.8	129.3	51.9	6.8	19.2
Slovakia	2004	10.0	9.6	6.8	0.4	1.2	2001	3.5	220.6	14.9	8.6	533.4	50.7	48.4	56.5
Slovenia	2004	9.0	9.3	3.7	-0.3	1.3	2003	5.4	258.1	36.3	13.6	368.5	79.0	63.6	71.5
Solomon Islands	2004	31.6	4.0	22.1	27.6	4.2									
Somalia	2004	46.0	17.3	118.5	28.7	6.9									
South Africa	2004	19.1	20.4	57.3	-1.3	2.8	1996	92.9	65.2	29.5	14.7	149.8	67.0	20.3	131.3
Spain	2004	10.6	9.0	3.5	1.6	1.3	2002	16.0	236.7	23.5	30.3	304.5	100.3	20.9	37.8
Sri Lanka	2003	18.9	5.9	11.2	13.0	1.9	1996	...	17.2	...	32.4	123.8	55.5	...	127.5
Sudan, The	2004	35.8	9.4	64.1	26.4	5.0									
Suriname	2004	18.9	7.0	24.2	11.9	2.4	1992	55.6	47.8	30.2	7.5	135.0	28.0	22.2	50.2
Swaziland	2004	28.6	27.6	73.9	1.1	3.7									
Sweden	2004	11.2	10.0	3.1	1.2	1.7	2001	12.4	243.0	25.3	24.0	479.9	68.3	33.0	53.3
Switzerland	2004	9.9	8.1	4.3	1.8	1.4	2000	9.9	221.6	25.0	31.8	345.5	64.2	33.1	51.9
Syria	2004	28.9	5.0	30.6	23.9	3.6									
Taiwan	2004	9.6	6.0	5.3	3.6	1.2	2003	...	160.5	40.6	...	164.8	34.8	23.6	52.7
Tajikistan	2004	26.8	4.1	49.0	22.4	3.0	2001	30.5	28.3	6.8	7.8	186.3	58.3	20.3	25.8
Tanzania	2004	38.6	17.0	100.6	21.6	5.2									
Thailand	2003	11.8	6.1	7.2	5.7	1.8	2000	51.7	63.4	13.0	17.3	52.6	34.1	14.6	60.6
Togo	2004	37.3	10.2	63.8	27.1	5.1									
Tonga	2004	24.9	5.5	13.0	19.4	3.0	2002	16.3[11]	77.2	43.6	6.1[11]	190.1	49.5	18.3[11]	4.1[11]
Trinidad and Tobago	2004	12.7	10.2	26.5	2.5	1.8	1998	13.6	96.7	142.3	11.9	302.8	47.4	26.4	49.6
Tunisia	2004	15.7	5.1	25.8	10.6	1.8	2002	...	57.0	...	...	267.0	...	...	62.0
Turkey	2004	20.6	7.1	37.4	13.5	2.4	2003	21.0	91.0	15.0	2.0	340.0	11.0	14.0	24.0
Turkmenistan	2004	27.8	8.8	73.1	19.0	3.5	1998	99.1	43.9	9.2	5.8	314.6	101.1	30.2	59.3
Tuvalu	2004	21.6	7.2	20.7	14.4	3.0	2002	...	...	...	...	35.0	7.0	...	...
Uganda	2004	47.5	13.4	69.5	34.1	6.8									
Ukraine	2004	9.0	16.1	9.4	-7.1	1.1	2002	24.4	166.9	7.2	11.2	799.7	56.7	48.4	153.5
United Arab Emirates	2004	18.7	4.1	15.1	14.6	3.0	1998	...	15.3	...	...	44.1	...	...	31.1
United Kingdom	2004	10.9	10.2	5.2	0.7	1.7	2003	8.6	229.0	13.5	28.1	346.2	126.2	42.0	34.3
United States	2004	14.1	8.3	7.3	5.8	2.1	2000	20.9	195.9	33.4	32.2	333.4	81.8	29.8	53.6
Uruguay	2004	14.4	9.1	12.3	5.3	2.0	2000	20.1	228.3	26.9	27.6	319.6	76.8	38.8	64.1
Uzbekistan	2004	26.1	8.0	71.3	18.1	3.0	2000	20.7	38.8	9.9	10.5	288.7	63.5	30.6	43.2
Vanuatu	2004	23.7	8.0	56.6	15.7	2.9	1994[12]	25.0	29.2	9.1	5.5	39.0	30.4	9.7	9.1
Venezuela	2004	19.3	4.9	23.0	14.4	2.3	2000	24.5	62.3	29.9	7.5	131.2	25.9	18.2	82.5
Vietnam	2004	17.2	6.2	26.8	11.0	2.0									
Virgin Islands (U.S.)	2004	14.5	6.1	9.3	8.4	2.2	2000	17.4	121.1	40.5	19.3	246.8	19.3	24.9	26.7
West Bank	2004	33.2	4.1	20.2	29.1	4.5									
Western Sahara	2000	45.1	16.1	133.6	29.0	6.6									
Yemen	2004	43.2	8.8	63.3	34.4	6.7									
Zambia	2004	41.8	20.5	89.7	21.3	5.6									
Zimbabwe	2004	28.4	22.0	53.0	6.4	3.2	1990	64.7	28.4	4.9	9.4	40.8	39.5	12.1	44.9

expectation of life at birth (latest year)		nuptiality, family, and family planning															country
		marriages			age at marriage (latest)						families (F), households (H) (latest)						
		year	total number	rate per 1,000 population	groom (percent)			bride (percent)			families (households)		children		induced abortions		
male	female				19 and under	20–29	30 and over	19 and under	20–29	30 and over	total ('000)	size	number under age 15	percent legitimate	number	ratio per 100 live births	
40.3	41.4	...	...	...	...	...	...	...	...	...	F 4,270	F 4.2	F 2.0	73.1	...	...	Mozambique
57.5	63.6	...	...	...	...	...	...	...	...	...	H 10,434	H 4.7	...	...	...	...	Myanmar (Burma)
45.2	44.4	...	...	...	...	...	...	...	...	...	H 357	H 5.3	...	...	...	...	Namibia
58.8	66.1	1995	57	5.3	...	...	...	...	...	...	H 1	H 8.0	H 2.6	...	...	...	Nauru
59.7	59.1	...	...	...	...	...	...	...	...	...	H 4,250	H 5.5	H 2.3	...	...	...	Nepal
76.2	80.9	2002	83,970	4.7	0.4	32.8	66.8	2.6	48.5	48.9	H 7,041	H 2.3	H 0.4	72.8	29,450	14.6	Netherlands, The
73.4	78.0	2003	748	4.3							H 62	H 2.9	H 2.1	51.6			Netherlands Antilles
71.3	77.2	2002	905	4.2	0.4	40.0	59.6	2.9	55.1	42.0	H 58	H 3.9	...	32.3	1,466	33.7	New Caledonia
76.7	81.2	2004	21,000	5.3	1.1	39.6	59.3	3.1	48.5	48.4	H 1,382	H 2.9	H 0.7	56.1	18,511	33.0	New Zealand
68.0	72.2	2002	21,039	4.1	...	...	...	...	...	...	H 967	H 5.6	...	...	...	...	Nicaragua
43.3	43.2	...	...	...	...	...	...	...	...	...	H 1,836	H 6.4	...	...	...	...	Niger
46.0	47.0	...	...	...	...	...	...	...	...	...	H 24,554	H 4.9	...	...	...	...	Nigeria
73.1	78.4	...	...	...	...	...	...	...	...	...	H 19	H 3.7	H 1.5	40.2	...	...	Northern Mariana Islands
76.6	82.0	2003	24,069	4.9	0.5	33.0	66.5	2.4	48.6	49.0	H 1,981	H 2.3	...	48.6	14,071	24.6	Norway
73.2	75.4	...	...	...	...	...	...	...	...	...	H 379	H 6.7	...	...	...	...	Oman
61.7	63.6	...	...	...	...	...	...	...	...	...	H 20,971	H 7.0	...	...	...	...	Pakistan
66.7	73.2	...	...	...	...	...	...	...	...	...	H	H 4.9	...	...	44	...	Palau
72.7	78.0	2002	9,392	3.1	1.8	46.5	51.7	8.2	53.9	37.9	H 715	H 4.2	H 1.5	19.7	11	0.02	Panama
62.4	66.8	...	...	...	...	...	...	...	...	...	H 1,138	H 4.8	...	...	...	...	Papua New Guinea
72.1	77.3	2002	17,400	3.0	4.2	64.8	31.0	30.4	50.2	19.4	H 1,368	H 4.1	H 1.9	68.7	...	...	Paraguay
67.5	71.0	1998	60,730	2.4	...	...	...	...	...	...	H 5,855	H 4.5	...	57.8	...	...	Peru
67.5	72.8	2002	583,167	7.3	4.0	63.7	32.3	14.8	64.1	21.1	F 15,967	F 5.0	F 2.4	93.9	2,315	...	Philippines
70.7	79.2	2002	191,935	5.0	3.1	76.1	20.8	13.5	73.3	13.2	F 13,132	F 2.9	F 0.9	84.2	188	0.05	Poland
74.5	81.0	2002	56,457	5.4	1.9	64.9	33.2	8.7	67.7	23.6	H 3,568	H 2.9	H 0.8	85.5	388	0.3	Portugal
73.5	81.7	2002	25,645	6.6	5.6	54.2	40.2	17.1	52.2	30.7	H 1,278	H 3.0	H 1.0	59.6	...	...	Puerto Rico
70.9	76.0	2001	2,104	3.4	1.5	64.8	33.7	17.5	66.7	15.8	H 87	H 7.1	...	...	8[2]	...	Qatar
71.3	79.8	2001	3,334	4.5	0.6	45.7	53.7	6.2	56.3	37.5	H 203	H 3.3	...	37.0	4,302	31.7	Réunion
67.4	74.8	2002	129,018	5.9	1.2	68.0	30.8	15.8	65.5	18.7	H 7,320	H 3.0	...	...	246,708	118	Romania
58.8	72.0	2002	1,019,200	7.1	6.5	64.5	29.0	28.5	47.7	23.8	H 52,000	H 2.8	H 0.8	70.5	1,944,500	139	Russia
45.6	47.7	...	...	...	...	...	...	...	...	...	H 1,509	H 4.7	H 2.3	94.9	...	...	Rwanda
69.0	74.9	2001	325	7.1	9.8	42.5	47.7	15.6	50.8	33.6	H 23	H 2.0	H 1.4	19.2	...	...	St. Kitts and Nevis
69.8	77.2	2002	472	3.0	0.6	37.1	62.3	2.4	48.9	48.7	H 49	H 3.2	H 2.0	14.0	...	...	St. Lucia
71.5	75.2	2002	509	4.5	1.0	37.0	62.0	4.8	46.3	48.9	H 27	H 3.9	H 2.0	17.9	...	...	St. Vincent and the Grenadines
67.6	73.3	1998	935	4.6	0.5	51.0	48.5	8.0	65.0	27.0	F 24	F 7.5	F 3.8	43.5	...	...	Samoa
78.6	85.0	2000	193	7.2	0.5	43.5	56.0	1.0	67.8	31.2	H 11	H 2.5	H 0.4	95.2	...	...	San Marino
65.1	68.2	...	...	...	...	...	...	...	...	...	F 39	F 3.5	...	...	...	...	São Tomé and Príncipe
73.3	77.7	2002	90,982	...	...	...	...	...	...	...	H 3,611	H 6.1	...	100.0	5[2]	...	Saudi Arabia
57.1	60.1	...	...	...	...	...	...	...	...	...	H 1,157	H 8.7	...	...	...	...	Senegal
71.9	77.1	2004	57,165	5.7	1.8	60.8	37.4	14.3	64.5	21.2	H 2,550	H 4.2	H 0.9	...	58,739	45.7	Serbia and Montenegro
61.2	76.1	2001	790	9.7	0.9	27.2	71.9	3.3	42.3	54.4	H 21	H 3.9	H 1.9	24.7	146	9.0	Seychelles
37.6	41.8	...	...	...	...	...	...	...	...	...	H 750	H 6.6	...	...	...	...	Sierra Leone
77.4	81.3	2002	23,198	5.6	0.7	52.6	46.7	3.2	71.9	24.9	H 1,001	H 4.2	H 1.3	...	12,749	31.2	Singapore
70.3	77.8	2005	28,000	5.2	2.3	68.9	28.8	10.0	74.0	16.0	H 1,681	H 3.2	...	80.2	17,382	34.2	Slovakia
73.5	81.1	2004	7,064	3.3	0.4	50.0	49.6	2.7	66.0	31.3	H 685	H 2.9	...	55.2	7,327	41.9	Slovenia
69.9	75.0	...	...	...	...	...	...	...	...	...	H 67	H 6.6	...	...	...	...	Solomon Islands
46.0	49.5	...	...	...	...	...	...	...	...	...	H	H 4.9	...	...	...	...	Somalia
45.5	48.9	2002	175,000	3.9	0.2	33.2	66.6	2.0	49.9	48.1	H 11,400	H 4.0	...	75.9	82,686	10.8	South Africa
77.2	83.7	2001	206,254	5.1	0.7	56.7	42.6	3.1	70.0	26.9	F 13,860	F 2.9	...	89.5	79,188	18.1	Spain
70.1	75.3	2002	190,618	9.5	1.3	64.3	34.4	16.7	67.1	16.2	H 4,741	H 4.0	...	96.3	...	...	Sri Lanka
57.0	59.4	...	...	...	...	...	...	...	...	...	H 5,362	H 6.1	...	...	...	...	Sudan, The
66.8	71.6	2000	2,267	4.9	1.5	45.3	53.2	16.8	46.1	37.1	H 91	H 5.3	...	...	...	...	Suriname
33.1	35.2	...	...	...	...	...	...	...	...	...	H 164	H 6.3	...	...	...	...	Swaziland
78.4	82.7	2002	38,012	4.3	1.1	27.2	71.7	0.9	35.2	63.9	H 4,320	H 2.1	H 0.5	44.0	34,374	34.7	Sweden
78.6	83.7	2002	40,213	5.5	0.5	33.3	66.2	2.6	49.7	47.7	H 3,035	H 2.4	H 0.4	87.6	11,792	16.3	Switzerland
68.5	71.0	2002	174,449	9.5	...	...	...	...	...	...	F 3,527	F 4.8	F 2.4	...	...	...	Syria
73.4	79.1	2003	171,483	7.6	1.5	62.3	36.2	6.0	77.7	16.3	H 6,925	H 3.3	H 1.0	96.4	42,282	14.9	Taiwan
61.5	67.6	1999	21,600	3.5	10.7	80.6	8.7	49.6	45.7	4.7	H 1,145	H 5.6	H 2.7	93.0	28,500	13.2	Tajikistan
44.2	45.6	...	...	...	...	...	...	...	...	...	H 6,996	H 4.9	H 2.3	...	...	...	Tanzania
69.9	74.9	2000	354,198	5.4	...	...	...	...	...	...	H 15,889	H 3.9	...	...	...	...	Thailand
54.6	58.7	...	...	...	...	...	...	...	...	...	H 812	H 6.0	...	...	...	...	Togo
66.7	71.8	2002	747	7.4	8.3	63.5	28.2	22.6	59.0	18.4	F 18	F 5.5	F 2.7	80.6	...	...	Tonga
65.5	68.0	1999	7,600	5.9	4.3	54.9	40.8	20.0	52.8	27.2	H 347	H 3.8	H 1.3	...	...	—	Trinidad and Tobago
73.0	76.4	2001	61,800	6.4	...	43.3	56.7	13.2	65.8	21.0	H 2,091	H 4.7	H 1.9	99.8	19,000	10.6	Tunisia
66.6	71.2	2001	453,213	6.8	4.5	75.3	20.2	26.6	63.1	10.3	H 14,820	H 4.5	...	...	...	...	Turkey
57.9	64.9	1998	25,000	5.4	3.0	87.4	9.6	16.1	77.1	6.8	H 850	H 5.7	H 2.4	96.2	32,000	28.8	Turkmenistan
65.5	70.0	...	...	...	...	...	...	...	...	...	H 1.6	H 6.1	H 2.2	82.2	...	...	Tuvalu
49.8	51.1	...	...	...	...	...	...	...	...	...	H 5,255	H 4.7	...	...	...	...	Uganda
63.4	74.5	2002	317,228	6.6	4.4	66.0	29.6	23.5	54.9	21.6	H 17,609	H 2.8	H 0.8	89.2	434,223	113	Ukraine
72.5	77.6	2003	12,100	3.0	...	...	...	...	...	...	H 582	H 6.5	...	...	66[2]	...	United Arab Emirates
75.8	80.8	2001	305,912	5.1	0.8	38.2	61.0	2.9	48.5	48.6	H 24,410	H 2.5	H 1.7	63.2	207,907	27.9	United Kingdom
74.6	80.4	2002	2,254,000	7.8	4.3	51.8	43.9	10.9	55.8	35.3	H 109,000	H 2.6	F 1.0	67.2	857,475	24.5	United States
72.7	79.2	2002	14,073	4.2	2.6	51.5	45.9	11.1	55.4	33.5	H 994	H 3.4	H 0.9	73.8	...	...	Uruguay
60.7	67.7	2001	170,101	6.8	5.2	84.9	9.9	36.7	57.8	5.5	H 4,616	H 5.5	H 2.4	95.8	54,900	10.4	Uzbekistan
60.6	63.6	...	...	...	...	...	...	...	...	...	H 28	H 5.1	H 2.2	...	113	2.4	Vanuatu
71.0	77.3	2002	73,183	2.9	5.8	56.2	38.0	19.3	55.4	25.3	H 5,185	H 4.9	H 2.2	47.0	...	...	Venezuela
67.6	73.3	2002	964,701	12.1	...	...	...	...	...	...	H 16,386	H 5.0	H 1.9	...	1,000,000	59.0	Vietnam
74.9	82.8	1993	3,646	35.1	0.4	33.6	66.0	1.9	45.9	52.2	H 41	H 2.6	H 1.0	30.2	...	...	Virgin Islands (U.S.)
71.1	74.7	2002[13]	22,611	...	9.3	72.9	17.8	56.2	37.9	5.9	...	...	...	...	...	...	West Bank
48.7	51.3	...	...	...	...	...	...	...	...	...	...	...	...	...	...	...	Western Sahara
59.5	63.3	...	...	...	...	...	...	...	...	...	H 2,729	H 7.1	...	...	...	...	Yemen
39.1	39.6	...	...	...	...	...	...	...	...	...	H 2,116	H 5.1	H 2.1	...	...	...	Zambia
40.1	38.0	...	...	...	...	...	...	...	...	...	H 2,644	H 4.4	H 1.1	95.8	...	...	Zimbabwe

[1]Excludes nomadic tribes. [2]Abortions performed abroad. [3]Based on urban sample population. [4]Millions of households. [5]1995. [6]1994. [7]Includes Aruba. [8]Natural causes of death: 177.7 per 100,000 population. [9]2001. [10]1993. [11]1992. [12]Reported to the Ministry of Health. [13]Includes Gaza Strip.

National product and accounts

This table furnishes, for most of the countries of the world, breakdowns of (1) gross national product (GNP)—its global and per capita values, and purchasing power parity (PPP), (2) growth rates (1990–99) and principal industrial and accounting components of gross domestic product (GDP), and (3) principal elements of each country's balance of payments, including international goods trade, invisibles, external public debt outstanding, and tourism payments.

Measures of national output. The two most commonly used measures of national output are GDP and GNP. Each of these measures represents an aggregate value of goods and services produced by a specific country. The GDP, the more basic of these, is a measure of the total value of goods and services produced entirely within a given country. The GNP, the more comprehensive value, is composed of both domestic production (GDP) and the net income from current (short-term) transactions with other countries. When the income received from other countries is greater than payments to them, a country's GNP is greater than its GDP. In theory, if all national accounts could be equilibrated, the global summation of GDP would equal GNP.

In the first section of the table, data are provided for the nominal and real GNP. ("Nominal" refers to value in current prices for the year indicated and is distinguished from a "real" valuation, which is one adjusted to eliminate the effect of recent inflation [most often] or, occasionally, of deflation between two given dates.) Both the total and per capita values of this product are denominated in U.S. dollars for ease of comparison, as is a new value for GNP per capita adjusted for purchasing power parity.

The latter is a concept that provides a better approximation of the ability of equivalent values of two (or more) national currencies to purchase comparable quantities of goods and services in their respective domestic markets and may differ substantially from two otherwise equal GNP per capita values based solely on currency exchange rates. Beside these are given figures for average annual growth of total and per capita real GNP. GNP per capita provides a rough measure of annual national income per person, but values should be compared cautiously, as they are subject to a number of distortions, notably of exchange rate, but also of purchasing power parity and in the existence of elements of national production that do not enter the monetary economy in such a way as to be visible to fiscal authorities (e.g., food, clothing, or housing produced and consumed within families or communal groups or services exchanged). For reasons of comparability, the majority of the data in this section are taken from the World Bank's *The World Bank Atlas* (annual).

The internal structure of the national product. GDP/GNP values allow comparison of the relative size of national economies, but further information is provided when these aggregates are analyzed according to their industrial sectors of origin, component kinds of expenditure, and cost components.

The distribution of GDP for ten industrial sectors, usually compiled from national sources, is aggregated into three major industrial groups:

1. The primary sector, composed of agriculture (including forestry and fishing) and mineral production (including fossil fuels).

National product and accounts

country	gross national product (GNP), 1999 nominal ('000,000 U.S.$)	per capita nominal (U.S.$)	per capita purchasing power parity (PPP; U.S.$)	gross domestic product (GDP), 1990–99 average annual growth rates, 1990–99 real GDP (%)	popu-lation (%)	real GDP per capita (%)	origin of gross domestic product (GDP) by economic sector, 1998 (%) primary agri-culture	mining	secondary manu-factur-ing	con-struc-tion	public utili-ties	tertiary transp., commu-nications	trade	finan-cial svcs.	other svcs.	govern-ment	other
Afghanistan	5,666[1]	250[1]	...	...	...	...	...	...	...	...	...	...	...	...	...	...	...
Albania	3,146	930	3,240	3.4	0.6	2.8	54	2	12[2]	13	2	3	——————18——————				—
Algeria	46,548	1,550	4,840	1.7	2.2	−0.5	11	23	10	11	—	—————— 24 ——————		13			8
American Samoa	253[1]	4,300[1]	...	...	...	...	...	...	...	...	...	...	...	...	...	...	...
Andorra	850[3]	13,100[3]	...	...	...	...	...	...	...	...	...	...	...	...	...	...	...
Angola	3,276	270	1,100	−0.5	2.3	−2.8	13	45	6	6	—	——18——		——11——			1
Antigua and Barbuda	606	8,990	9,870	3.8	1.1	2.7	3	1	2	10	3	17	19	14	6	15	10
Argentina	296,097	7,550	11,940	4.9	1.3	3.6	5[3]	2[3]	20[3]	6[3]	2[3]	6[3]	14[3]	18[3]	——24[3]——		3[3]
Armenia	1,878	490	2,360	−3.1	0.8	−3.9	31	2	22[2]	9	2	5	9	——— 25 ———			−1
Aruba	1,728[4,5]	18,700[4,5]	...	...	...	...	...	...	...	...	...	...	...	...	...	...	...
Australia	397,345	20,950	23,850	4.1	1.2	2.9	3	4	13	6	2	8	10	16	33	4	1
Austria	205,743	25,430	24,600	1.9	0.5	1.4	3	1	24	7	3	8	19	18	6	10	1
Azerbaijan	3,705	460	2,450	−9.5	1.2	−10.7	20[3]	2	25[2,3]	14[3]	2	10[3]	——————31[3]——————				−1
Bahamas, The	3,288[3]	11,830[3]	...	...	...	...	16	15[6]	17[6]	6[6]	2[6]	11[6]	11[6]	19[6]	5[6]	19[6]	−6[6]
Bahrain	4,909[4]	7,640[4]	...	...	...	...	1[7]	17[7]	22[7]	6[7]	2[7]	9[7]	11[7]	18[7]	5[7]	19[7]	−10[7]
Bangladesh	41,071	370	1,530	4.7	1.6	3.1	23	1	18	7	1	10	15	11	11	2	1
Barbados	2,294	8,600	14,010	1.8	0.3	1.5	6	1	10	8	4	8	35	———17———		12	−1
Belarus	26,299	2,620	6,880	−3.1	−0.2	−2.9	13	8	36[8]	7	4	12	12	———16———			—
Belgium	252,051	24,650	25,710	1.7	0.3	1.4	1[3]	—	21[3]	5[3]	2[3]	8[3]	12[3]	14[3]	7[3]	24[3]	6[3]
Belize	673	2,730	4,750	3.2	2.5	0.7	18	1	13	5	2	12	15	8	6	6	14
Benin	2,320	380	920	5.0	3.2	1.8	38[3]	8	9[3,8]	4[3]	1[3]	7[3]	18[3]	9[3]	——7[3]——		7[3]
Bermuda	2,128[3]	34,950[3]	...	...	...	...	...	...	...	...	...	...	...	...	...	...	...
Bhutan	399	510	1,260	6.1	2.7	3.4	38	2	12	11	11	8	7	5	——9——		−3
Bolivia	8,092	990	2,300	4.2	2.4	1.8	15	11	18	5	1	12	9	13	6	10	—
Bosnia and Herzegovina	4,706	1,210	...	...	...	...	12	...	24	6	3	9	19	4	14	8	—
Botswana	5,139	3,240	6,540	3.8	2.0	1.8	3	36	5	6	2	4	18	8	4	14	—
Brazil	730,424	4,350	6,840	3.0	1.5	1.5	7[3]	13	19[3]	9[3]	3[3]	5[3]	7[3]	20[3]	11[3]	13[3]	5[3]
Brunei	7,209[4]	22,280[4]	...	...	...	...	3	8	37[8]	7	1	4	10	9	——33——		−4
Bulgaria	11,572	1,410	5,070	−2.8	−0.7	−2.1	19	1	17	3	4	7	7	2	——29——		11
Burkina Faso	2,602	240	960	4.2	2.8	1.4	30	8	20[8]	5	1	4	12	——22——			6
Burundi	823	120	570	−3.9	1.1	−5.0	46	19	9	5	9	4	4	——2——		18	11
Cambodia	3,023	260	1,350	5.2	3.3	1.9	51	—	6	7	1	4	15	5	7	3	1
Cameroon	8,798	600	1,490	1.3	2.8	−1.5	41	5	10	4	1	——————35——————					4
Canada	614,003	20,140	25,440	2.8	1.1	1.7	2	4	18	6	3	8	12	16	24	6	1
Cape Verde	569	1,330	4,450	4.6	1.4	3.2	12	—	10	9	—	18	19	12	7	14	−1
Central African Republic	1,035	290	1,150	2.0	2.3	−0.3	49	4	8	4	1	2	12	——6——		6	8
Chad	1,555	210	840	2.5	3.4	−0.9	37	1	12	2	1	——24——		——9——		11	3
Chile	69,602	4,630	8,410	7.1	1.5	5.6	7	9	15	5	2	9	18	17	6	2	10
China	979,894	780	3,550	10.8	1.3	9.5	18	2	42[2]	7	2	6	8	——18——			1
Colombia	90,007	2,170	5,580	3.3	1.9	1.4	14	4	14	5	...	8	12	——34——		9	—
Comoros	189	350	1,430	−0.1	3.0	−3.1	40	...	4	6	1	5	25	3	1	13	2
Congo, Dem. Rep. of the	5,433[4]	110[4]	...	...	...	...	58[7]	47	67	27	27	37	17[7]	——67——		17	17
Congo, Rep. of the	1,571	550	540	−0.8	2.5	−3.3	11[7]	33[7]	8[7]	27	17	12[7]	9[7]	——87——		13[7]	37[7]
Costa Rica	12,828	3,570	7,880	5.0	2.0	3.0	15	8	19[8]	2	3	6	21	12	8	14	—
Côte d'Ivoire	10,387	670	1,540	3.6	3.0	0.6	28	2	20[2]	5	2	8	15	——12——		8	4
Croatia	20,222	4,530	7,260	0.4	−0.6	1.0	7	8	24[8]	6	3	8	12	13	——14——		13
Cuba	18,600[5]	1,700[5]	...	...	...	...	7[3]	2[3]	37[3]	5[3]	2[3]	4[3]	21[3]	2[3]	——19[3]——		2[3]
Cyprus[10]	9,086	11,950	19,080	4.2	1.4	2.8	4	—	11	8	2	9	20	19	10	14	3
Czech Republic	51,623	5,020	12,840	0.9	−0.0	0.9	4	2	32[2]	7	2	9	12	17	——13——		6
Denmark	170,685	32,050	25,600	2.4	0.4	2.0	4[3]	—	20[3]	6[3]	2[3]	10[3]	13[3]	19[3]	6[3]	22[3]	−3[3]
Djibouti	511	790	...	−3.0	2.1	−5.1	3	—	5	8	5	17	16	10	5	20	11
Dominica	238	3,260	5,040	2.4	0.6	1.8	20	1	9	8	5	17	14	14	1	19	−8
Dominican Republic	16,130	1,920	5,210	5.7	1.8	3.9	12	2	17	12	2	12	20	9	8	8	−2
East Timor	113[4,5]	130[4,5]	...	...	...	...	...	...	...	...	...	...	...	...	...	...	...
Ecuador	16,841	1,360	2,820	2.1	2.1	0.0	17[3]	15[3]	15[3]	2[3]	1[3]	9[3]	15[3]	12[3]	6[3]	7[3]	13

2. The secondary sector, composed of manufacturing, construction, and public utilities.
3. The tertiary sector, which includes transportation and communications, trade (wholesale and retail), restaurants and hotels, financial services (including banking, real estate, insurance, and business services), other services (community, social, and personal), and government services.

The category "other" contains adjustments such as import duties and bank service charges that are not distributed by sector.

There are three major domestic components of GDP expenditure: private consumption (analyzed in greater detail in the "Household budgets and consumption" table), government spending, and gross domestic investment. The fourth, nondomestic, component of GDP expenditure is net foreign trade; values are given for both exports (a positive value) and imports (a negative value, representing obligations to other countries). The sum of these five percentages, excluding statistical discrepancies and rounding, should be 100% of the GDP.

Balance of payments (external account transactions). The external account records the sum (net) of all economic transactions of a current nature between one country and the rest of the world. The account shows a country's net of overseas receipts and obligations, including not only the trade of goods and merchandise but also such invisible items as services, interest and dividends, short- and long-term investments, tourism, transfers to or from overseas residents, etc. Each transaction gives rise either to a foreign claim for payment, recorded as a deficit (*e.g.*, from imports, capital outflows), or a foreign obligation to pay, recorded as a surplus (*e.g.*, from exports, capital inflows) or a domestic claim on another country. Any international transaction automatically creates a deficit in the balance of payments of one country and a surplus in that of another. Values are given in U.S. dollars for comparability.

External public debt. Because the majority of the world's countries are in the less developed bloc, and because their principal financial concern is often external debt and its service, data are given for outstanding external public and publicly guaranteed long-term debt rather than for total public debt, which is the major concern in the developed countries. For comparability, the data are given in U.S. dollars. The data presented in the table come from the World Bank's *Global Development Finance* (formerly *World Debt Tables*).

Tourist trade. Net income or expenditure from tourism (in U.S. dollars for comparability) is often a significant element in a country's balance of payments. Receipts from foreign nationals reflect payments for goods and services from foreign currency resources by tourists in the given country. Expenditures by nationals abroad are also payments for goods and services, but in this case made by the residents of the given country as tourists abroad. The majority of the data in this section are compiled by the World Tourism Organization.

gross domestic product (GDP) by type of expenditure, 1998 (%)					external public debt outstanding (long-term, disbursed only), 1999							balance of payments, 1999 (current external transactions; '000,000 U.S.$)			tourist trade, 1997 ('000,000 U.S.$)		country
consumption		gross domestic invest-ment	foreign trade		total ('000,000 U.S.$)	creditors (%)		debt service				net transfers		current balance of payments	receipts from foreign nationals	expendi-tures by nationals abroad	
private	govern-ment		exports	imports		offi-cial	private	total ('000,000 U.S.$)	repayment (%)		goods, merchan-dise	invisibles					
									princi-pal	inter-est							
...	...	...	...	...	...	...	...	...	...	...	...	...	...	1	1	Afghanistan
...	...	...	...	...	849.1	70.7	29.3	27.1	28.4	71.6	−663.0	507.6	−155.4	27	5	Albania
51	17	27	28	−23	25,913	71.3	28.7	4,885	64.7	35.3	3,360	−3,340	20	20	64	Algeria
...	...	...	...	...										10	...	American Samoa
...	...	...	...	...										...	...	Andorra
...	...	...	...	...	9,248	39.6	60.4	1,099	89.6	10.4	1,463.5[4]	−3,323.1[4]	−1,857.6[4]	9	73	Angola
58	22	32	73	−84							−321.3[4]	232.7[4]	−88.6[4]	260	26	Antigua and Barbuda
71		20	10	−13	84,568	24.8	75.2	12,170	48.1	51.9	−770	−11,676	−12,446	5,069	2,680	Argentina
103	11	19	19	−53	681.9	100.0	—	39.8	64.6	35.4	−474.0	167.0	−307.1	7	41	Armenia
73	13	11	2		...	...	...	...	...	...	−591.7	258.5	−333.2	666	130	Aruba
59	18	24	20	−22							−9,730	−13,340	−23,070	9,026	6,129	Australia
55	20	26	44	−45							−3,649	−2,098	−5,747	12,393	10,992	Austria
78[3]	12[3]	38[3]	28[3]	−55[3]	493.3	91.1	8.9	49.8	81.5	18.5	−408.2	−191.5	−599.7	159	72	Azerbaijan
66[7]	15[7]	23[7]	54[7]	−58[7]	...	...	...	...	...	...	−1,428.2	756.3	−671.9	1,416	250	Bahamas, The
51	21	18	78	−68	...	...	...	...	...	...	672.1	−1,012.5	−340.4	260	129	Bahrain
78	14	13	19	−23	16,962	99.4	0.6	675	72.3	27.7	−1,962.1	1,670.6	−291.5	59	170	Bangladesh
59	21	20	58	−57	359.1	75.4	24.6	84.2	64.4	35.6	−691.7	565.9	−125.8	717	74	Barbados
58	20	27	60	−65	851	52.8	47.2	141	64.5	35.5	−570.0	376.3	−193.7	25	114	Belarus
54	21	21	76	−72	...	...	...	...	...	...	6,642	6,732	13,374	5,275	8,275	Belgium
65	17	27	52	−61	294.6	73.6	26.4	40.2	59.6	40.4	−128.8	51.4	−77.4	87	30	Belize
81	9	18	27	−35	1,472	99.8	0.2	56	64.3	35.7	−158.3[4]	6.8[4]	−151.5[4]	31	7	Benin
...	...	...	...	...										474	148	Bermuda
36[1]	29[1]	44[1]	34[1]	−44[1]	181.8	100.0	—	6.9	71.0	29.0	−24.8[4]	−21.7[4]	−46.5[4]	6	...	Bhutan
75	14	23	20	−32	3,864	99.4	0.6	257	57.0	43.0	−488.0	−67.8	−555.8	170	172	Bolivia
100		38	35	−73	1,826	92.6	7.4	388	64.3	35.7	−2,072.0	1,284.6	−787.4	15	...	Bosnia and Herzegovina
28	29	28	56	−41	442.3	95.2	4.8	82.5	74.7	25.3	674.5	−157.7	516.8	184	140	Botswana
64	18	21	7	−10	95,233	33.8	66.2	24,374	72.1	27.9	−1,261	−24,139	−25,400	2,595	6,583	Brazil
...	...	...	...	...							175[4]	1,910[4]	2,085[4]	39	...	Brunei
72	15	14	44	−45	7,602	32.8	67.2	632	49.5	50.5	−1,081.0	396.3	−684.7	368	222	Bulgaria
81	10	24	15	−30	1,295	99.7	0.3	53	69.8	30.2	−184.5	−38.6	−223.1	39	32	Burkina Faso
96	12	3	8	−19	1,050	99.9	0.1	20	70.0	30.0	−42.3	15.3	−27.0	1	10	Burundi
96[1]	7[1]	16[1]	28[1]	−46[1]	2,136	100.0	—	28	51.8	48.2	−209.5	143.5	−66.0	143	12	Cambodia
71	9	18	26	−27	7,614	95.2	4.8	346	47.8	52.2	112.4	−343.7	−231.3	39	107	Cameroon
59	20	20	41	−40	...	...	...	...	...	...	22,756	−25,029	−2,273	8,770	11,304	Canada
68	23	40	25	−57	265.1	95.7	4.3	21.6	84.7	15.3	−185.6[4]	127.6[4]	−58.0[4]	15	17	Cape Verde
84	12	14	16	−25	830.1	96.1	3.9	11.9	60.9	39.1	−8.3[4]	−79.1[4]	−87.4[4]	5	39	Central African Republic
90	10	15	18	−33	1,045	98.5	1.5	27	61.1	38.9	−50.3[4]	−155.8[4]	−206.1[4]	9	24	Chad
67	11	26	25	−29	5,655	37.1	62.9	780	60.1	39.9	1,664	−1,744	−80	1,021	946	Chile
46	12	38	4		108,163	46.6	53.4	15,668	68.2	31.8	36,207	−20,540	15,667	12,074	10,166	China
68	19	20	15	−22	19,434	39.6	60.4	4,775	65.5	34.5	1,776	−1,837	−61	955	958	Colombia
91[1]	15[1]	19[1]	20[1]	−45[1]	179.9	100.0	—	7.1	87.3	12.7	−35.6[4]	40.8[4]	5.2[4]	26	8	Comoros
81[7]	5[7]	9[7]	28[7]	−23[7]	8,188	93.8	6.2	...	...	...	830[1]	−1,375[1]	−515[1]	2	7	Congo, Dem. Rep. of the
46	16	26	67	−55	3,932	80.1	19.9	—	—	—	644.1	−885.7	−241.6	3	36	Congo, Rep. of the
56	16	28	50	−50	3,186	64.0	36.0	475	70.3	29.7	659.6	−1,309.1	−649.5	719	358	Costa Rica
64	11	19	44	−37	9,699	74.8	28.2	992	53.8	46.2	1,832.3[4]	−2,144.9[4]	−312.6[4]	88	282	Côte d'Ivoire
59[1]	29[1]	22[1]	42[1]	−52[1]	5,433	26.3	73.7	667	47.1	52.9	−3,298.7	1,776.5	−1,522.2	2,529	521	Croatia
71[1]	24[1]	7[1]	16[1]	−18[1]	...	...	...	...	...	...	1,338			Cuba
64	19	25	44	−52	...	...	...	...	...	...	−2,309.2	2,075.5	−233.7	1,639	278	Cyprus[10]
52	19	30	60	−61	13,440	8.6	91.4	2,470	62.5	37.5	−1,902	870	−1,032	3,647	2,380	Czech Republic
51	26	21	35	−33	...	...	...	...	...	...	6,689	−3,725	2,964	3,156	4,128	Denmark
79	24	15	45	−64	252.7	100.0	—	3.0	68.3	31.7	−179.7[4]	165.3[4]	−14.4[4]	4	5	Djibouti
58[3]	21[3]	34[3]	51[3]	−63[3]	89.0	100.0	—	9.3	75.3	23.7	−58.4	29.0	−29.4	37	7	Dominica
75	8	26	47	−56	3,665	80.5	19.5	331	52.3	47.7	−2,904.4	2,475.2	−429.2	2,107	242	Dominican Republic
...	...	...	...	...										...	...	East Timor
70	12	25	25	−32	12,756	42.7	57.3	1,382	45.2	54.8	1,655	−700	955	290	227	Ecuador

National product and accounts   (continued)

country	gross national product (GNP), 1999: nominal ('000,000 U.S.$)	per capita: nominal (U.S.$)	per capita: purchasing power parity (PPP; U.S.$)	GDP 1990–99 avg. annual growth: real GDP (%)	population (%)	real GDP per capita (%)	primary: agriculture	primary: mining	secondary: manufacturing	secondary: construction	secondary: public utilities	tertiary: transp., communications	tertiary: trade	tertiary: financial svcs.	tertiary: other svcs.	tertiary: government	other
Egypt	86,544	1,380	3,460	4.6	2.2	2.4	16[3]	8	27[3,8]	5[3]	2[3]	11[3]	19[3]	6[3]	— 7[3] —		7[3]
El Salvador	11,806	1,920	4,260	4.6	1.8	2.8	12	—	22	4	2	8	19	12	7	14	—
Equatorial Guinea	516	1,170	3,910	18.9	2.6	16.3	22	61	—	3	1	1	4	1	2	5	—
Eritrea	779	200	1,040	5.6	3.4	2.2	15	—	13	11	1	9	20	4	1	17	9
Estonia	4,906	3,400	8,190	-1.2	-0.9	-0.3	6	1	14	5	3	12	18	13	14	4	10
Ethiopia	6,524	100	620	5.3	2.9	2.4	46	8	7[8]	3	2	6	9	7	8	13	-1
Faroe Islands	976[4]	24,620[4]	...	...	...	...	...	...	...	...	...	...	...	...	...	...	...
Fiji	1,848	2,310	4,780	2.2	1.0	1.2	16	3	15	5	5	14	16	14	— 20 —		-8
Finland	127,764	27,730	22,600	2.4	0.4	2.0	4	—	22	4	2	8	11	11	9	16	13
France	1,453,211	24,170	23,020	1.5	0.4	1.1	3[3]	1[3]	22[3]	5[3]	3[3]	6[3]	14[3,11]	5[3]	18[3,11]	19[3]	6[3]
French Guiana	1,543[7]	10,580[7]	...	...	...	...	...	...	...	...	...	...	...	...	...	...	...
French Polynesia	3,908	16,930	22,200	1.6	1.7	-0.1	...	...	...	...	...	...	...	...	...	...	...
Gabon	3,987	3,300	5,280	1.8	1.2	0.6	7[3]	43[3]	6[3]	4[3]	1[3]	5[3]	8[3]	— 11[3] —		9[3]	6[3]
Gambia, The	415	330	1,550	3.0	3.6	-0.6	24	—	5	5	2	14	17	7	5	9	12
Gaza Strip	1,368[4,5]	1,320[4,5]	...				13	—	10	8	2	5	15	23	8	16	—
Georgia	3,362	620	2,540	...	...	...	32	2	13[2]	4	2	11	11	11	— 13 —		5
Germany	2,103,804	26,620	23,510	1.4	0.4	1.0	1	2	25[2]	5	2	— 17 —		30	— 21 —		1
Ghana	7,451	400	1,850	4.1	2.5	1.6	36	5	9	9	3	4	7	4	3	10	10
Greece	127,648	12,110	15,800	2.5	0.7	1.8	14[3]	1[3]	14[3]	6[3]	2[3]	7[3]	14[3]	3[3]	11[3]	19[3]	9[3]
Greenland	1,142[3]	20,380[3]	...	...	...	...	...	...	...	...	...	...	...	...	...	...	...
Grenada	334	3,440	6,300	2.9	0.7	2.2	9[3]	1[3]	7[3]	7[3]	5[3]	24[3]	20[3]	14[3]	3[3]	16[3]	-6[3]
Guadeloupe	3,706[5,7]	9,200[5,7]	...	...	...	...	...	...	...	...	...	...	...	...	...	...	...
Guam	3,301[4,5]	20,660[4,5]	...	...	...	...	...	...	...	...	...	...	...	...	...	...	...
Guatemala	18,625	1,680	3,630	4.2	2.7	1.5	23	1	14	2	3	9	25	10	6	8	-1
Guernsey[12]	1,902	29,810	...	...	...	...	...	...	...	...	...	...	...	...	...	...	...
Guinea	3,556	490	1,870	3.9	2.4	1.5	21	16	4	9	1	6	— 28 —		9	4	2
Guinea-Bissau	194	160	630	0.7	2.6	-1.9	62	2	9[2]	3	2	2	19	— 1 —		3	1
Guyana	651	760	3,330	5.6	0.4	5.2	29	14	9[13]	5	13	6	4	6	1	11	15
Haiti	3,584	460	1,470	-2.1	1.3	-3.4	30	—	7	12	1	2	13	8	5	18	4
Honduras	4,829	760	2,270	3.6	3.3	0.3	19	2	19	5	2	5	12	17	11	6	-1
Hong Kong	165,122	24,570	22,570	3.7	1.8	1.9	—		6	8	3	9	23	24	— 19 —		10
Hungary	46,751	4,640	11,050	1.1	-0.3	1.4	6[3]	8	20[3,8]	4[3]	3[3]	9[3]	10[3]	16[3]	13[3]	6[3]	13[3]
Iceland	8,197	29,540	27,210	2.7	0.9	1.8	9[3]	—	13[3]	6[3]	3[3]	6[3]	10[3]	15[3]	5[3]	14[3]	18[3]
India	441,834	440	2,230	5.9	1.8	4.1	25	2	15	4	2	7	14	10	6	5	10
Indonesia	125,043	600	2,660	4.6	1.6	3.0	19	13	26	5	1	5	15	8	3	4	1
Iran	113,729	1,810	5,520	3.4	1.5	1.9	20	12	16	4	2	8	17	10	2	10	-1
Iraq	11,500[1,5]	600[1,5]	...	...	...	...	8[1]	14	38[1,14]	14	14	— 18[1] —		— 31[1] —		5[1]	—
Ireland	80,559	21,470	22,460	6.8	0.7	6.1	2[3]	—	12[3]	7[3]	3[3]	10[3]	12[3]	59[3]	4[3]	6[3]	-15[3]
Isle of Man	1,319[4,5]	18,270[4,5]	...	...	...	...	...	...	...	...	...	...	...	...	...	...	...
Israel	99,574	16,310	18,070	5.2	2.9	2.3	2[3]	2	19[2,3]	7	2	6[3]	12[3]	30[3]	— 28[3] —		-6[3]
Italy	1,162,910	20,170	22,000	1.4	0.2	1.2	3[1]	4[1]	16[1]	5[1]	6[1]	6[1]	19[1]	5[1]	13[1]	22[1]	1[1]
Jamaica	6,311	2,430	3,390	0.4	1.0	-0.6	7	5	14	10	2	11	23	12	3	12	1
Japan	4,054,545	32,030	25,170	1.4	0.3	1.1	2[3]	—	24[3]	10[3]	3[3]	7[3]	12[3]	19[3]	20[3]	8[3]	-5[3]
Jersey	2,670[1,5]	30,940[1,5]	...	...	...	...	...	...	...	...	...	...	...	...	...	...	...
Jordan	7,717	1,630	3,880	5.4	4.3	1.1	3	3	12	4	2	14	11	16	5	18	12
Kazakhstan	18,732	1,250	4,790	-6.1	-1.2	-4.9	8	2	22[2]	4	2	11	17	— 37 —			1
Kenya	10,696	360	1,010	2.3	2.6	-0.3	30[1]	—	10[1]	5[1]	11	8[1]	19[1]	18[1]	— 8[1] —		—
Kiribati	81	910	740[3]	3.6	2.6	1.0	12[1]	—	1[1]	3[1]	2[1]	12[1]	19[1]	6[1]	3[1]	33[1]	9[1]
Korea, North	17,700[3]	740[3]	...	...	...	...	...	...	...	...	...	...	...	...	...	...	...
Korea, South	397,910	8,490	15,530	5.7	1.0	4.7	5	—	31	10	2	7	11	20	8	8	-2
Kuwait	35,152[3]	22,110[3]	...	...	...	...	—	31	12	3	—	6	10	14	— 26 —		-2
Kyrgyzstan	1,465	300	2,420	-5.4	1.0	-6.4	41	2	17[2]	3	2	8	12	3	1	3	8
Laos	1,476	290	1,430	6.5	2.7	3.8	52	—	17	3	2	6	12	3	1	3	1
Latvia	5,913	2,430	6,220	-4.7	-1.0	-3.7	8[1]	8	19[1,8]	4[1]	5[1]	— 51[1] —					13[1]
Lebanon	15,796	3,700	...	7.0	1.3	5.7	...	...	...	...	...	...	...	...	...	...	...
Lesotho	1,158	550	2,350	4.3	2.2	2.1	12[1]	—	14[1]	18[1]	3[1]	3[1]	10[1]	8[1]	1[1]	18[1]	13[1]
Liberia	1,174[1]	490[1]	...	...	...	...	78	2	5	2	—	5	3	3	2	2	-2
Libya	32,663[4,5]	6,700[4,5]	...	...	...	...	...	...	...	...	...	...	...	...	...	...	...
Liechtenstein	714[1,5]	23,000[1,5]	...	...	...	...	...	...	...	...	...	...	...	...	...	...	...
Lithuania	9,751	2,640	6,490	-4.0	-0.1	-3.9	9	8	17[8]	8	4	9	16	9	11	6	11
Luxembourg	18,545	42,930	41,230	5.2	1.4	3.8	1	—	17	7	1	— 24 —		45	— 19 —		-14
Macau	6,161	14,200	16,940	3.7	3.0	0.7	...	...	...	...	...	...	...	...	...	...	...
Macedonia	3,348	1,660	4,590	-0.7	0.8	-1.5	10	8	22[8]	6	3	6	13	6	— 19 —		15
Madagascar	3,712	250	790	1.8	3.0	-1.2	33	8	— 12[8] —			42				5	8
Malawi	1,961	180	570	2.0	1.1	0.9	36	1	13	2	1	4	25	9	2	10	-3
Malaysia	76,944	3,390	7,640	7.4	2.7	4.7	9	8	28	4	3	8	16	13	— 16 —		-5
Maldives	322	1,200	...	6.3	2.4	3.9	16	2	7[13]	11	13	7	20	— 29 —			8
Mali	2,577	240	740	3.7	2.6	1.1	44	6	9	5	—	5	— 16 —		7	4	4
Malta	3,492	9,210	...	5.0	0.8	4.2	2	15	19	3[15]	7	6	10	17	9	14	13
Marshall Islands	99	1,950	...	...	...	...	15[3]	—	2[3]	7[3]	2[3]	7[3]	18[3]	15[3]	— 30[3] —		4[3]
Martinique	4,271[3,5]	11,320[3,5]	...	...	...	...	...	...	...	...	...	...	...	...	...	...	...
Mauritania	1,001	390	1,550	4.3	3.0	1.3	22[3]	10[3]	10[3]	— 9[3] —		8[3]	15[3]	— 7[3] —		10[3]	9[3]
Mauritius	4,157	3,540	8,950	5.1	1.2	3.9	7	—	21	5	2	10	15	14	5	9	12
Mayotte	486[4]	3,700[4]	...	...	...	...	...	...	...	...	...	...	...	...	...	...	...
Mexico	428,877	4,440	8,070	2.8	1.8	1.0	5	1	21	5	1	11	20	14	— 23 —		-1
Micronesia	212	1,830	...	-0.2	1.6	-1.8	19[1]	—	1[1]	1[1]	1[1]	5[1]	24[1]	3[1]	3[1]	42[1]	1[1]
Moldova	1,481	410	2,100	-11.0	-0.2	-10.8	21	8	17[8]	4	2	4	7	6	— 12 —		27
Monaco	793[1,5]	25,000[1,5]	...	...	...	...	...	...	...	...	...	...	...	...	...	...	...
Mongolia	927	390	1,610	0.8	1.4	-0.6	33	8	24[8]	3	—	7	19	— 14 —			
Morocco	33,715	1,190	3,320	2.1	1.7	0.4	15[3]	2[3]	18[3]	5[3]	9[3]	6[3]	19[3]	— 13[3] —			13[3]
Mozambique	3,804	220	810	6.9	3.1	3.8	32	—	8	8	1	11	23	—	12	3	2
Myanmar (Burma)	55,700[3,5]	1,190[3,5]	...	...	...	...	53	—	6	2	—	5	30	— 9 —			2
Namibia	3,211	4,890	5,580	3.2	2.4	0.8	9[3]	12[3]	12[3]	3[3]	3[3]	4[3]	9[3]	8[3]	3[3]	23[3]	14[3]
Nauru	128[4]	11,540[4]	...	...	...	...	...	...	...	...	...	...	...	...	...	...	...
Nepal	5,173	220	1,280	4.8	2.5	2.3	38	1	9	10	2	8	11	10	— 9 —		2

consumption private	consumption government	gross domestic investment	foreign trade exports	foreign trade imports	external public debt total ('000,000 U.S.$)	creditors (%) official	creditors (%) private	debt service total ('000,000 U.S.$)	repayment (%) principal	repayment (%) interest	net transfers goods, merchandise	net transfers invisibles	current balance of payments	tourist receipts from foreign nationals	tourist expenditures by nationals abroad	country
74	10	22	17	−23	25,998	97.9	2.1	1,478	56.8	43.2	−9,928	8,293	−1,635	3,727	1,347	Egypt
86	10	17	23	−36	2,649	91.8	8.2	254	54.3	45.7	−1,358.9	1,117.0	−241	75	75	El Salvador
...	...	...	102	−173	207.9	93.7	6.3	1.7	58.8	41.2	26.5[4]	−400.1[4]	−373.6[4]	2	8	Equatorial Guinea
...	...	...	...	...	253.8	100.0	—	3.9	16.7	83.3	−498.9[4]	323.5[4]	−175.4[4]	75	...	Eritrea
59	22	29	78	−88	205.5	81.8	18.2	61.2	80.5	19.5	−877.5	582.9	−294.6	465	118	Estonia
79	14	18	16	−26	5,360	97.6	2.4	147	62.6	37.4	−797.1	480.9	−316.2	36	40	Ethiopia
...	...	...	...	...	...	...	...	...	...	...	51.6[4]	102.4[4]	154.0[4]	...	...	Faroe Islands
72	18	12	67	−69	120.7	100.0	...	29.2	75.3	24.7	−115.6	128.3	12.7	297	53	Fiji
39	21	19	50	−30	...	...	...	...	...	...	11,655	−4,067	7,588	1,963	2,270	Finland
54	24	19	26	−23	...	...	...	...	...	...	19,390	17,190	36,580	28,009	16,576	France
...	...	...	...	...	...	...	...	...	...	...	...	...	...	...	...	French Guiana
...	...	...	...	...	...	...	...	...	...	...	...	...	...	359	...	French Polynesia
40[3]	11[3]	26[3]	64[3]	−42[3]	3,290	96.1	3.9	487	52.6	47.4	202.5[3]	34.6[3]	237.1[3]	7	178	Gabon
76	17	18	51	−62	425.4	100.0	—	16.6	67.2	32.8	−69.0[4]	52.7[4]	−16.3[4]	32	16	Gambia, The
...	...	...	...	...	...	...	...	...	...	...	...	...	...	...	...	Gaza Strip
...	...	...	...	...	1,308	99.8	0.2	80	48.1	51.9	−533.9	335.5	−198.4	416	228	Georgia
57	19	22	29	−27	...	...	...	...	...	...	72,000	−91,310	−19,310	16,509	46,200	Germany
77	10	25	34	−47	5,647	91.2	8.8	391	68.3	31.7	−1,111.5	345.5	−766.0	266	22	Ghana
71	15	21	18	−25	...	...	...	...	...	...	−17,947	12,845	−5,102	3,771	1,325	Greece
...	...	...	...	...	...	...	...	...	...	...	...	...	...	...	...	Greenland
61	18	44	53	−76	122.2	93.9	6.1	6.4	73.4	26.6	−133.4[4]	43.9[4]	−89.5[4]	61	5	Grenada
...	...	...	...	...	...	...	...	...	...	...	...	...	...	499	...	Guadeloupe
...	...	...	...	...	...	...	...	...	...	...	...	...	...	...	...	Guam
87	6	16	19	−27	3,129	80.0	20.0	313	58.5	41.5	1,445.1	−2,471.0	−1,025.9	325	119	Guatemala
...	...	...	...	...	...	...	...	...	...	...	...	...	...	...	...	Guernsey[12]
77	7	17	22	−23	3,057	99.1	0.9	114	61.4	38.6	94.5	−246.1	−151.6	5	23	Guinea
100	9	11	15	−35	837.1	99.9	0.1	8.6	44.2	55.8	−14.4	−12.6	−27.0	...	...	Guinea-Bissau
43[3]	20[3]	43[3]	78[3]	−84[3]	1,238	96.6	3.4	74	52.7	47.3	−25	−50	−75	39	22	Guyana
— 103 —		13	13	−29	1,049	100.0	—	43	65.1	34.9	−469.7	410.1	−59.6	97	37	Haiti
67	10	30	44	−51	4,231	96.7	3.3	296	59.3	40.7	−709.1	172.3	−536.8	146	62	Honduras
61	9	30	127	−127	...	...	...	...	...	...	−3,159	14,635	11,476	9,242	...	Hong Kong
62	11	29	51	−53	16,064	14.0	86.0	3,282	69.5	30.5	−2,189	83	−2,106	2,582	1,153	Hungary
62	21	22	35	−39	...	...	...	...	...	...	−308	−292	−600	173	324	Iceland
66	13	23	12	−13	82,380	71.1	28.9	8,221	62.7	37.3	−8,029	5,245	−2,784	3,152	1,342	India
53	4	35	40	−33	72,554	75.5	24.5	9,192	59.5	40.5	20,644	−14,859	5,785	5,437	2,436	Indonesia
65	13	22	8	−8	6,184	59.4	40.6	2,971	86.6	13.4	6,215	−1,488	4,727	327	253	Iran
...	...	...	...	...	...	...	...	...	...	...	...	...	...	13	...	Iraq
51	13	24	84	−72	...	...	...	...	...	...	24,178	−23,583	595	3,189	2,223	Ireland
...	...	...	...	...	...	...	...	...	...	...	...	...	...	...	...	Isle of Man
61	30	20	32	−43	...	...	...	...	...	...	−4,408	2,527	−1,881	2,741	3,570	Israel
60	18	20	24	−22	...	...	...	...	...	...	20,383	−14,079	6,304	29,714	16,631	Italy
67	18	29	43	−56	2,905	77.5	22.5	648	52.3	47.7	−1,137.7	882.0	−255.7	1,131	181	Jamaica
61	10	26	11	−9	...	...	...	...	...	...	123,320	−16,450	106,870	4,326	33,041	Japan
...	...	...	...	...	...	...	...	...	...	...	...	...	...	...	...	Jersey
70	27	25	49	−70	7,546	83.2	16.8	559	52.6	47.4	−1,460.1	1,865.0	404.9	774	398	Jordan
75	11	18	32	−37	2,995	77.0	23.0	629	71.7	28.3	343.7	−514.7	−171.0	289	445	Kazakhstan
74	16	17	25	−32	5,385	90.2	9.8	533	78.9	21.1	−829.2	840.2	11.0	377	194	Kenya
...	...	...	...	...	...	...	...	...	...	...	−31.6[1]	29.3[1]	−2.3[1]	2	4	Kiribati
...	...	...	...	...	...	...	...	...	...	...	...	...	...	...	...	Korea, North
55	11	21	48	−35	57,231	27.1	72.9	23,000	81.4	18.6	28,371	−3,894	24,477	5,116	6,262	Korea, South
56	31	14	45	−47	...	...	...	...	...	...	5,571	−509	5,062	188	2,558	Kuwait
88	18	16	36	−58	1,130.4	97.2	2.8	16.5	8.2	91.8	−84.4	−168.9	−253.3	7	4	Kyrgyzstan
...	...	...	...	...	2,471	100.0	—	29	69.0	31.0	−189.5	68.4	−121.1	73	21	Laos
64	26	23	48	−61	864.8	70.2	29.8	41.4	50.7	49.3	−1,027	380	−647	192	326	Latvia
...	...	...	...	...	5,568	16.4	83.6	653	45.6	54.4	...	...	...	1,000	...	Lebanon
116	20	46	27	−109	661.8	91.6	8.4	44.6	55.8	44.2	−606.7	385.9	−220.8	20	8	Lesotho
...	...	...	...	...	1,062	80.7	19.3	—	—	—	−118.5[4]	76.6[4]	−41.9[4]	...	...	Liberia
55[3]	27[3]	12[3]	29[3]	−23[3]	...	...	...	...	...	...	2,974	−838	2,136	6	215	Libya
...	...	...	...	...	...	...	...	...	...	...	...	...	...	...	...	Liechtenstein
63	25	24	47	−59	1,891.5	34.2	65.8	166.7	54.3	45.7	−1,404.6	210.6	−1,194.0	399	290	Lithuania
46	17	21	116	−99	...	...	...	...	...	...	−2,449	3,761	1,312	297	...	Luxembourg
40	11	18	76	−46	...	...	...	...	...	...	...	...	...	2,947	153	Macau
74	18	23	43	−58	1,135	75.4	24.6	377	85.0	15.0	−420.3	108.6	−311.7	14	27	Macedonia
89	7	12	21	−30	4,023	99.1	0.9	147	46.9	53.1	−154[4]	−147[4]	−301[4]	73	48	Madagascar
85	14	14	30	−42	2,596	99.3	0.7	44	62.5	37.5	−93.0[1]	−0.3[1]	−92.7[1]	7	17	Malawi
42	10	27	114	−93	18,929	24.2	75.8	2,278	52.3	47.7	22,648	−10,042	12,606	2,703	2,478	Malaysia
...	...	...	...	...	192.5	84.9	15.1	16.7	73.7	26.3	−262.6	192.6	−70.0	286	38	Maldives
70	14	24	24	−33	2,798	100.0	—	85	75.3	24.7	9.7[3]	−187.7[3]	−178.0[3]	26	42	Mali
62	20	23	88	−94	...	...	...	...	...	...	−571.4	449.0	−112.4	664	191	Malta
...	...	...	...	...	...	...	...	...	...	...	−35.8[3]	52.2[3]	16.4[3]	3	...	Marshall Islands
...	...	...	...	...	...	...	...	...	...	...	...	...	...	400	...	Martinique
69[3]	20[3]	17[3]	42[3]	−49[3]	2,138	99.1	0.9	88	68.2	31.8	40.0[4]	37.2[4]	77.2[4]	11	24	Mauritania
63	12	25	67	−67	1,155	45.8	54.2	161	62.4	37.6	−547.2	494.9	52.4	475	177	Mauritius
...	...	...	...	...	...	...	...	...	...	...	...	...	...	...	...	Mayotte
68	9	24	31	−33	87,531	24.9	75.1	16,015	61.4	38.6	−5,581	−8,585	−14,166	7,594	3,892	Mexico
...	...	...	...	...	...	...	...	...	...	...	−52.0[3]	115.8[3]	63.8[3]	...	...	Micronesia
71	24	30	— −25 —		722	82.5	17.5	98	55.1	44.9	−128.0	83.3	−44.7	4	...	Moldova
...	...	...	...	...	...	...	...	...	...	...	...	...	...	...	...	Monaco
65[3]	16[3]	23[3]	1[3]	−5[3]	816.3	97.4	2.6	20.9	57.2	42.8	−56.4	−55.8	−112.2	22	21	Mongolia
65	18	22	22	−26	17,284	75.9	24.1	2,985	64.6	35.4	−2,448	2,277	−171	1,443	315	Morocco
88	9	23	12	−32	4,625	99.7	0.3	68	47.8	52.2	−491.0[4]	61.7[4]	−429.3[4]	...	...	Mozambique
— 89 —		12	0	−1	5,333	90.1	9.9	88	72.7	27.3	−1,035.2	669.5	−365.7	34	25	Myanmar (Burma)
55[3]	31[3]	20[3]	53[3]	−58[3]	...	...	...	...	...	...	−172.6[4]	334.4[4]	161.8[4]	336	99	Namibia
...	...	...	...	...	...	...	...	...	...	...	...	...	...	...	...	Nauru
81	9	21	24	−35	2,910	99.3	0.7	99	69.7	30.3	−880.7	891.3	10.6	119	103	Nepal

National product and accounts (continued)

country	gross national product (GNP), 1999 nominal ('000,000 U.S.$)	per capita nominal (U.S.$)	per capita purchasing power parity (PPP; U.S.$)	GDP 1990–99 avg annual growth real GDP (%)	popu-lation (%)	real GDP per capita (%)	agri-culture	mining	manu-factur-ing	con-struc-tion	public util-ities	transp., commu-nications	trade	finan-cial svcs.	other svcs.	govern-ment	other
Netherlands, The	397,384	25,140	24,410	2.7	0.6	2.1	3	2	17	5	2	7	15	26	11	12	—
Netherlands Antilles	2,400[3,5]	11,500[3,5]	...				17	—	77	77	47	13[7]	25[7]	17[7]	9[7]	18[7]	-17
New Caledonia	3,169	15,160	21,130	1.4	2.2	-0.8	2[3]	4[3]	11[3]	5[3]	2[3]	7[3]	23[3]	—20[3]—		25[3]	-13
New Zealand	53,299	13,990	17,630	3.0	1.2	1.8	7	1	17	3	3	11	15	22	—22—		1
Nicaragua	2,012	410	2,060	3.3	2.9	0.4	28	2	21	5	3	5	18	7	4	8	-1
Niger	1,974	190	740	1.8	2.8	-1.0	37[3]	4[3]	7[3]	2[3]	2[3]	6[3]	17[3]	—21[3]—			4[3]
Nigeria	31,600	260	770	2.4	2.9	-0.5	37	26	5	1	—	3	16	5	1	1	5
Northern Mariana Is.	665	9,600	...				...	...	...	...	...	...	...	...	...	...	...
Norway	149,280	33,470	28,140	3.8	0.6	3.2	2	11	12	4	2	9	10	17	5	16	12
Oman	13,135[4]	5,950[4]	...				2[1]	43[1]	4[1]	2[1]	1[1]	6[1]	13[1]	8[1]	8[1]	12[1]	1[1]
Pakistan	62,915	470	1,860	3.5	2.5	1.0	24	—	15	3	4	9	15	8	7	7	8
Palau	129[4,5]	7,140[4,5]	...				5	—	1	8		16	27	12	7	22	2
Panama	8,657	3,080	5,450	4.3	1.9	2.4	8	—	10	4	4	13	21	25	6	10	-1
Papua New Guinea	3,834	810	2,260	4.9	2.6	2.3	24	26	9	6	1	5	9	1	—13—		6
Paraguay	8,374	1,560	4,380	2.5	2.7	-0.2	28	—	14	5	6	5	23	3	10	6	—
Peru	53,705	2,130	4,480	5.0	1.8	3.2	6[3]	2[3]	19[3]	11[3]	1[3]	4[3]	16[3]	14[3]	13[3]	7[3]	7[3]
Philippines	77,967	1,050	3,990	3.2	2.3	0.9	17	1	22	6	3	5	14	12	11	10	-1
Poland	157,429	4,070	8,390	4.6	0.2	4.4	5	3	22	8	3	6	21	15	3	13	1
Portugal	110,175	11,030	15,860	2.4	0.1	2.3	...	...	...	...	...	...	...	...	...	...	...
Puerto Rico	25,380[3]	7,010[3]	...				1[1]	15	41[1]	21,15	16	8[1,16]	14[1]	13[1]	11[1]	11[1]	-1[1]
Qatar	6,473[4]	11,600[4]	...				1[3]	38[3]	7[3]	7[3]	1[3]	4[3]	8[3]	10[3]	—24[3]—		...
Réunion	5,680[3]	8,260[3]	...				...	...	...	...	...	...	...	...	...	...	...
Romania	33,034	1,470	5,970	-0.9	-0.4	-0.5	19[1]	2	34[1,2]	7[1]	2	9[1]	10[1]	—17[1]—			4[1]
Russia	328,995	2,250	6,990	-6.0	-0.1	-5.9	7	2	33[2]	8	2	—23—		14	9	6	—
Rwanda	2,041	250	880	-2.7	0.3	-3.0	44	—	13	7	—	4	11	—15—		7	-1
St. Kitts	259	6,330	10,400	4.2	-0.7	4.9	6[1]	—	11[1]	12[1]	2[1]	16[1]	23[1]	16[1]	4[1]	18[1]	-8[1]
St. Lucia	590	3,820	5,200	2.4	1.5	0.9	7	—	5	6	4	15	23	15	3	13	9
St. Vincent	301	2,640	4,990	3.3	0.7	2.6	9	—	6	12	5	17	15	8	2	15	11
Samoa	181	1,070	4,070	2.0	0.6	1.4	17[3]	...	19[3]	5[3]	2[3]	11[3]	17[3]	11[3]	7[3]	9[3]	2[3]
San Marino	883[3,5]	34,330[3,5]	...				...	...	...	...	...	...	...	...	...	...	...
São Tomé and Príncipe	40	270	...	1.1	2.0	-0.9	23[3]	—	4[3]	15[3]		—19[3]—		8[3]	9[3]	22[3]	—
Saudi Arabia	139,365	6,900	11,050	2.2	3.3	-1.1	6[1]	36[1]	9[1]	9[1]		6[1]	7[1]	5[1]	3[1]	17[1]	2[1]
Senegal	4,685	500	1,400	3.7	3.1	0.6	18	5	13[5]	5	2	12	—21—		20	9	—
Serbia and Montenegro	13,742[4]	1,290[4]	...				20	8	36[8]	6	3	12	19	—5—			-1
Seychelles	520	6,500	...	2.9	1.6	1.3	3	—	14	9	3	15	24	10	2	13	7
Sierra Leone	653	130	440	-4.9	2.1	-7.0	39[7]	17[7]	9[7]	2[7]	—	9[7]	14[7]	2[7]	2[7]	3[7]	4[7]
Singapore	95,429	24,150	22,310	6.6	1.9	4.7	—	—	24	9	2	14	19	28	—11—		-7
Slovakia	20,318	3,770	10,430	1.8	0.2	1.6	4	1	23	5	3	8	—22—		—29—		5
Slovenia	19,862	10,000	16,050	2.4	-0.1	2.5	4[3]	1[3]	25[3]	5[3]	3[3]	7[3]	13[3]	14[3]	12[3]	5[3]	11[3]
Solomon Islands	320	750	2,050	3.7	3.4	0.3	48[1]	—	3[1]	7[1]	2[1]	6[1]	9[1]	4[1]	—21[1]—		—
Somalia	706[1]	110[1]	...				...	...	...	...	...	...	...	...	...	...	—
South Africa	133,569	3,170	8,710	1.2	1.4	-0.2	4	7	19	3	3	10	13	18	—23—		—
Spain	583,082	14,800	17,850	2.3	0.3	2.0	4[1]	2	24[1,2]	8[1]	2	—59[1]—					5[1]
Sri Lanka	15,578	820	3,230	5.3	1.3	4.0	19	2	15	7	1	10	19	—13—			5
Sudan, The	9,435	330	...				41	—	9	6	1	6	20	—14—			3
Suriname	684[4]	1,660[4]	...				12[1]	11[1]	13[1]	3[1]	9[1]	15[1]	12[1]	14[1]	—13[1]—		-2[1]
Swaziland	1,379	1,350	4,380	2.3	2.5	-0.2	12	1	27	4	2	4	7	4	1	15	23
Sweden	236,940	26,750	22,510	1.6	0.4	1.2	2[1]	—	20[1]	5[1]	3[1]	6[1]	11[1]	23[1]	4[1]	19[1]	7[1]
Switzerland	273,856	38,380	28,760	0.6	0.7	-0.1	...	...	...	...	...	...	...	...	...	...	...
Syria	15,172	970	3,450	5.5	2.8	2.7	28[1]	7[1]	4[1]	4[1]	1[1]	11[1]	26[1]	5[1]	2[1]	10[1]	—
Taiwan	297,953[4]	13,900[4]	...				3	—	27	4	2	7	17	23	10	10	-3
Tajikistan	1,749	280	...				20	—	28[2]	2	2	—18—		—22—			10
Tanzania	8,515	260	500	3.0	3.1	-0.1	43[3]	1[3]	6[3]	4[3]	2[3]	5[3]	12[3]	12[3]	2[3]	7[3]	6[3]
Thailand	121,051	2,010	5,950	4.9	1.1	3.8	14	2	28	5	3	8	14	—26—			-5
Togo	1,398	310	1,380	2.7	3.2	-0.5	42	6	9	3	3	5	17	—8—		7	5
Tonga	172	1,732	...	1.1	0.4	0.7	32	—	3	5	2	7	11	10	—18—		12
Trinidad and Tobago	6,142	4,750	7,690	2.5	0.5	2.0	2	21	8	10	—	—18—		12	17	9	3
Tunisia	19,757	2,090	5,700	4.5	1.6	2.9	12	1	18	5	5	8	—24—			14	13
Turkey	186,490	2,900	6,440	3.7	1.5	2.2	17	1	19	6	2	14	20	—13—		9	-1
Turkmenistan	3,205	670	3,340	-6.6	3.0	-9.6	25	2	30[2]	12	2	10	5	—13—			5
Tuvalu	7[1]	650[1]	...				22[7]	2[7]	3[7]	14[7]	2[7]	4[7]	14[7]	10[7]	—28[7]—		12[1]
Uganda	6,794	320	1,160	7.1	3.1	4.0	41[1]	—	7[1]	7[1]	1[1]	4[1]	12[1]	7[1]	5[1]	4[1]	12[1]
Ukraine	41,991	840	3,360	-10.8	-0.5	-10.3	11	2	25[2]	5	2	13	8	—25—			13
United Arab Emirates	48,673[4]	17,870[4]	...				2[1]	35[1]	9[1]	9[1]	1[1]	6[1]	13[1]	13[1]	2[1]	11[1]	-11[1]
United Kingdom	1,403,843	23,500	22,220	2.5	0.4	2.1	1	2	18	5	2	7	13	23	4	15	10
United States	8,879,500	31,910	31,910	3.0	1.0	2.0	2[3]	1[3]	17[3]	4[3]	3[3]	6[3]	17[3]	19[3]	20[3]	13[3]	—
Uruguay	20,604	6,220	8,750	3.7	0.7	3.0	11	—	20	4	4	10	14	21	—15—		1
Uzbekistan	17,613	720	2,230	-1.2	1.9	-3.1	26	2	15[2]	8	2	6	8	—21—			16
Vanuatu	227	1,180	2,880	2.3	3.1	-0.8	23	—	5	5	2	7	34	7	—17—		—
Venezuela	87,313	3,680	5,420	1.7	2.2	-0.5	5	12	16	7	2	10	18	16	9	6	-1
Vietnam	28,733	370	1,860	8.0	1.8	6.2	26	8	—33[8]—			4	19	7	—12—		-1
Virgin Islands (U.S.)	2,666[3]	18,290[3]	...				...	...	...	...	...	...	...	...	...	...	...
West Bank	2,758[4,5]	1,680[4,5]	...				7	2	17[2]	11	2	17	14	11	19[17]	10	13
Western Sahara	605[5,18]	300[5,18]	...				...	...	...	...	...	...	...	...	...	...	...
Yemen	6,080	360	730	3.5	3.9	-0.4	24	17	10	4	2	7	14	6	2	14	—
Zambia	3,222	330	720	-0.4	2.0	-2.4	17	6	11	5	4	6	19	16	—9—		7
Zimbabwe	6,302	530	2,690	1.9	1.3	0.6	14[7]	5[7]	18[7]	2[7]	3[7]	5[7]	18[7]	9[7]	11[7]	4[7]	11[7]

private	govern-ment	gross domestic invest-ment	exports	imports	total ('000,000 U.S.$)	offi-cial	private	total ('000,000 U.S.$)	princi-pal	inter-est	goods, merchan-dise	invisibles	current balance of payments	receipts from foreign nationals	expendi-tures by nationals abroad	country
59	14	20	55	−49	...	...	...	...	...	...	17,940	−704	17,236	6,219	10,232	Netherlands, The
67[7]	28[7]	19[7]	72[7]	−85[7]	...	...	...	...	...	...	−1,064[4]	1,008[4]	−56[4]	576	243	Netherlands Antilles
...	...	...	...	...	...	...	...	...	...	...	...	...	...	110	...	New Caledonia
65	15	19	31	−30	...	...	...	...	...	...	−435	−3,161	3,596	2,093	1,451	New Zealand
94	14	34	36	−78	5,799	93.3	6.7	137	43.1	56.9	−1,133.2	481.0	−652.2	74	65	Nicaragua
82[3]	16[3]	12[3]	19[3]	−29[3]	1,424	100.0	—	19	52.6	47.7	−17.6[5]	−134.1[5]	−151.7[5]	18	24	Niger
64	14	29	32	−38	22,423	74.3	25.7	835	67.2	32.8	4,288	−3,782	506	118	1,816	Nigeria
...	...	...	...	...	...	...	...	...	...	...	...	...	...	672	...	Northern Mariana Is.
50	22	28	37	−37	...	...	...	...	...	...	10,119	−4,105	6,014	2,226	4,496	Norway
55	24	23	37	−39	1,768	37.4	62.6	711	82.3	17.7	2,918	−3,110	−192	108	47	Oman
72	12	17	16	−17	28,514	92.5	7.5	1,597	63.1	36.9	−1,874[4]	—[4]	−1,874[4]	117	364	Pakistan
...	...	...	...	...	...	...	...	...	...	...	...	...	...	227[7]	...	Palau
58	16	33	90	−97	5,678	23.6	76.4	619	45.7	54.3	−1,415.0	39.0	−1,376.0	374	164	Panama
55[7]	16[7]	18[7]	49[7]	−37[7]	1,517	95.6	4.4	160	66.9	33.1	856.0	−761.3	94.7	72	81	Papua New Guinea
86	8	23	28	−45	1,672	96.7	3.3	183	62.3	37.7	−334.4	270.8	−63.6	753	195	Paraguay
72	9	24	12	−17	20,709	79.7	20.3	1,957	41.3	58.7	−616	−1,206	−1,822	805	485	Peru
73	13	20	51	−58	33,568	63.8	36.2	5,097	68.1	31.9	4,958	2,952	7,910	2,831	1,936	Philippines
63	16	27	25	−32	33,151	75.6	24.4	2,162	39.1	60.9	−15,072	2,585	−12,487	8,679	6,900	Poland
66	20	26	28	−40	...	...	...	...	...	...	−13,766	4,137	−9,629	4,277	2,164	Portugal
...	...	...	...	...	...	...	...	...	...	...	...	...	...	2,046	869	Puerto Rico
...	...	...	...	...	...	...	...	...	...	...	...	...	...	...	...	Qatar
...	...	...	...	...	...	...	...	...	...	...	...	...	...	249	...	Réunion
76	15	18	26	−34	5,985	64.4	35.6	2,754	85.7	14.3	−1,092	−205	−1,297	526	783	Romania
58	19	15	31	−23	120,375	59.1	40.9	4,470	42.9	57.1	36,130	−11,482	24,648	6,900	10,113	Russia
94	9	16	6	−24	1,162	99.9	0.1	20	60.0	40.0	−140.6	138.1	−2.5	...	...	Rwanda
76[1]	18[1]	24[1]	44[1]	−63[1]	131.7	73.4	26.6	16.9	54.4	45.6	...	...	...	72	6	St. Kitts
69	15	19	65	−68	125.6	88.5	11.5	16.4	63.4	36.8	−201.2[4]	160.2[4]	−41.0[4]	282	29	St. Lucia
74	19	32	47	−72	159.8	63.2	36.8	12.6	49.2	50.8	−119.4[4]	75.1[4]	−44.3[4]	70	7	St. Vincent
...	...	...	...	...	156.5	100.0	—	4.8	70.8	29.2	−97.5	78.7	18.8	41	5	Samoa
66[1]	12[1]	17[1]	234[1]	−229[1]	...	...	...	...	...	...	22.6[1]	−11.9[1]	10.7[1]	...	...	San Marino
...	...	...	...	...	232.2	100.0	—	3.9	64.1	35.9	−12.1[4]	3.6[4]	−8.5[4]	2	1	São Tomé and Príncipe
41	32	21	36	−31	...	...	...	...	...	...	25,039	−24,627	412	1,420	...	Saudi Arabia
76	10	20	32	−38	3,111	99.7	0.3	179	68.2	31.8	−284.3[4]	174.6[4]	−109.7[4]	160	77	Senegal
...	...	...	...	...	7,416	44.4	55.6	...	...	...	...	...	...	41	...	Serbia and Montenegro
51	27	37	65	−81	132.2	81.6	18.4	23.4	76.3	23.7	−232.4	118.4	−114.0	122	30	Seychelles
81	11	4	14	−10	938	99.4	0.6	7	57.1	42.9	−126.7[7]	0.2[7]	−126.5[7]	57	2	Sierra Leone
39	10	33	—18—		...	...	...	...	...	...	11,303	9,951	21,254	6,843	3,224	Singapore
50	22	39	64	−75	4,457	29.6	70.4	639	67.9	32.1	−1,109	−46	−1,155	546	439	Slovakia
56	21	25	57	−58	...	...	...	...	...	...	−1,245.2	462.8	−782.4	1,188	544	Slovenia
...	...	...	...	...	120.4	97.2	2.8	5.5	72.7	27.3	54.5	−33.1	21.5	7	9	Solomon Islands
...	...	...	...	...	1,859	98.2	1.8	—	—	—	...	...	...	...	...	Somalia
63	20	16	26	−25	9,148	—	100.0	3,162	78.5	21.5	4,150	−4,683	−533	2,297	1,947	South Africa
62	16	22	29	−28	...	...	...	...	...	...	−30,339	16,623	−13,716	26,651	4,467	Spain
71	10	25	36	−42	8,182	92.6	7.4	401	64.1	35.9	−707.4	214.4	−493.0	212	180	Sri Lanka
91	4	18	6	−19	8,852	84.8	15.2	12	45.8	54.2	−475.9	11.1	−464.8	4	34	Sudan, The
...	...	...	...	...	...	...	...	...	...	...	−27.2[4]	−127.7[4]	−154.9[4]	17	4	Suriname
63	25	34	76	−99	205.5	100.0	—	29.0	64.3	35.7	−110.8	128.0	17.2	40	37	Swaziland
50	27	17	44	−38	...	...	...	...	...	...	15,714	−9,732	5,982	3,572	6,579	Sweden
60	15	21	40	−36	...	...	...	...	...	...	723	28,476	29,199	7,902	6,904	Switzerland
69	11	20	30	−31	16,142	93.3	6.7	206	61.7	38.3	216	−15	201	1,035	545	Syria
61	14	22	49	−47	...	...	...	...	...	...	10,531[4]	−6,803[4]	3,728[4]	3,402	6,500	Taiwan
...	...	...	...	...	594.9	90.7	9.3	22.6	88.7	11.3	−38[3]	−36[3]	−74[3]	...	...	Tajikistan
85	8	15	19	−28	6,595	96.7	3.3	150	59.3	40.7	−876.0	69.1	−806.9	392	407	Tanzania
50	10	24	56	−40	31,011	71.3	28.7	4,255	60.0	40.0	14,013	1,585	12,428	7,048	1,888	Thailand
81	11	14	34	−40	1,263	100.0	—	26	65.4	34.6	−98.0	−29.1	−127.1	13	19	Togo
...	...	...	...	...	63.5	98.0	2.0	4.3	81.4	18.6	−67.1[4]	47.8[4]	−19.3[4]	14	3	Tonga
62	16	26	48	−54	1,485	46.3	53.7	401	74.1	25.9	−740.8[4]	97.3[4]	−643.5[4]	108	75	Trinidad and Tobago
60	16	28	42	−46	9,487	67.5	32.5	1,359	63.8	36.2	−2,141	1,698	−443	1,423	160	Tunisia
67	12	24	24	−27	50,095	25.8	74.2	8,559	64.0	36.0	−10,443	9,083	−1,360	8,088	1,716	Turkey
...	...	...	...	...	1,678	23.7	76.3	449	86.2	13.8	−523.0[4]	−411.5[4]	−934.5[4]	74	125	Turkmenistan
...	...	...	...	...	...	...	...	...	...	...	...	...	...	0.3	...	Tuvalu
83[3]	10[3]	15[3]	12[3]	−21[3]	3,564	98.0	2.0	126	65.1	34.9	−596.4	45.6	−550.8	135	137	Uganda
59	23	21	40	−43	10,027	61.5	38.5	1,277	62.4	37.6	244	1,414	1,658	270	305	Ukraine
45[1]	16[1]	26[1]	77[1]	−65[1]	...	...	...	...	...	...	8,254[3]	...	6,701[3]	535	...	United Arab Emirates
65	18	18	27	−28	...	...	...	...	...	...	−42,350	26,370	−15,980	20,039	27,710	United Kingdom
67	15	20	11	−13	...	...	...	...	...	...	−343,260	11,780	−331,480	73,268	51,220	United States
71	14	16	22	−22	5,108	42.1	57.9	917	61.6	38.4	−868.4	263.4	−605.0	759	264	Uruguay
...	...	...	...	...	3,421	54.8	45.2	461	65.7	34.3	171[4]	−210[4]	−39[4]	19	...	Uzbekistan
49[5]	27[5]	34[5]	47[5]	−57[5]	63.4	100.0	—	1.6	53.1	46.9	−51.5	48.4	−3.1	51	5	Vanuatu
73	8	20	20	−20	25,216	18.9	81.1	4,148	54.6	45.4	7,606	−3,917	3,689	1,086	2,381	Venezuela
71	7	29	42	−49	20,529	82.2	17.8	1,347	75.8	24.2	−981[4]	−86[4]	−1,067[4]	88	...	Vietnam
...	...	...	...	...	...	...	...	...	...	...	...	...	...	601	...	Virgin Islands (U.S.)
...	...	...	...	...	...	...	...	...	...	...	...	...	...	...	...	West Bank
...	...	...	...	...	...	...	...	...	...	...	...	...	...	...	...	Western Sahara
61[3]	16[3]	28[3]	43[3]	−48[3]	3,729	95.3	4.7	100	46.0	54.0	357.9	219.2	577.1	69	81	Yemen
79	16	14	29	−38	4,498	99.3	0.7	416	69.5	30.5	−148[4]	−121[4]	−269[4]	75	59	Zambia
70[3]	17[3]	20[3]	38[3]	−46[3]	3,211	88.7	11.3	480	71.6	28.4	79[4]	−423[4]	−344[4]	230	118	Zimbabwe

[1]1996. [2]Manufacturing includes mining and public utilities. [3]1997. [4]1998. [5]Gross domestic product (GDP). [6]1994. [7]1995. [8]Manufacturing includes mining. [9]Mining includes public utilities. [10]Republic of Cyprus only. [11]Services includes hotels. [12]Excludes Alderney and Sark. [13]Manufacturing includes public utilities. [14]Manufacturing includes mining, construction, and public utilities. [15]Construction includes mining. [16]Transportation, communications includes public utilities. [17]Services includes transportation, communications. [18]1991.

Employment and labour

This table provides international comparisons of the world's national labour forces—giving their size; composition by demographic component and employment status; and structure by industry.

The table focuses on the concept of "economically active population," which the International Labour Organisation (ILO) defines as persons of all ages who are either employed or looking for work. In general, the economically active population does not include students, persons occupied solely in domestic duties, retired persons, persons living entirely on their own means, and persons wholly dependent on others. Persons engaged in illegal economic activities—smugglers, prostitutes, drug dealers, bootleggers, black marketeers, and others—also fall outside the purview of the ILO definition. Countries differ markedly in their treatment, as part of the labour force, of such groups as members of the armed forces, inmates of institutions, the unemployed (both persons seeking their first job and those previously employed), seasonal and international migrant workers, and persons engaged in informal, subsistence, or part-time economic activities. Some countries include all or most of these groups among the economically active, while others may treat the same groups as inactive.

Three principal structural comparisons of the economically active total are given in the first part of the table: (1) participation rate, or the proportion of the economically active who possess some particular characteristic, is given for women and for those of working age (usually ages 15 to 64), (2) activity rate, the proportion of the total population who are economically active, is given for both sexes and as a total, and (3) employment status, grouped as employers and self-employed; employees; family workers (usually unpaid); and others (excluding unemployed).

Each of these measures indicates certain characteristics in a given national labour market; none should be interpreted in isolation, however, as the meaning of each is influenced by a variety of factors—demographic structure and change, social or religious customs, educational opportunity, sexual differentiation in employment patterns, degree of technological development, and the like. Participation and activity rates, for example, may be high in a particular country because it possesses an older population with few children, hence a higher proportion of working age, or because, despite a young population with many below working age, the economy attracts eligible immigrant workers, themselves almost exclusively of working age. At the same time, low activity and participation rates might be characteristic of a country having a young population with poor employment possibilities or of a country with a good job market distorted by the presence of large numbers of "guest" or contract workers who are not part of the domestic labour force. An illiterate woman in a strongly sex-differentiated labour force is likely to begin and end as a family or

Employment and labour

country	year	total ('000)	participation rate (%) female	participation rate (%) ages 15–64	activity rate (%) total	activity rate (%) male	activity rate (%) female	employment status (%) employers, self-employed	employment status (%) employees	employment status (%) unpaid family workers	employment status (%) other	agriculture, forestry, fishing number ('000)	agriculture, forestry, fishing % of econ. active	manufacturing; mining, quarrying; public utilities number ('000)	manufacturing; mining, quarrying; public utilities % of econ. active
Afghanistan	1994	5,557	9.0	49.1[1]	29.4	54.2[1]	4.9[1]	52.2[1]	33.8[1]	14.0[1]	—	4,276[2]	76.9[2]	299[2]	5.4[2]
Albania	2002	1,318	43.7	65.9	42.4	48.8	36.2	...	...	...	...	767[4,5]	72.2[4,5]	56[4,5]	5.3[4,5]
Algeria	2000	8,154	12.2	48.4[6,7]	27.0	47.0	6.6	16.8[8]	61.7[8]	2.6[8]	18.9[8]	898	11.0	721	8.8
American Samoa	2000	17.7	41.5	52.0[10]	30.8	35.3	26.2	3.4	96.4	0.2	—	0.5	2.9	5.9	33.4
Andorra	2000	34	45.6[11]	72.6	...	...	...	...	...	...	...	0.1	0.4	1.0	3.0
Angola	1996	4,581	37.3	65.1[12]	40.0	50.8	29.5	...	...	...	...	3,170	69.2	528[13]	11.5[13]
Antigua and Barbuda	1991	26.8	45.6	69.7	45.1	50.9	39.6	12.1	82.8	0.7	4.4	1.0	3.9	1.9	7.3
Argentina	2001	15,265	40.9	57.2[16]	42.1	51.1	33.5	21.3	68.6	2.4	1.4	911	6.0	1,374	9.0
Armenia	2003	1,232	49.5	72.1[15]	49.5[5]	54.5[5]	44.9[5]	5.0	84.9	...	15.2	509	41.3	139[17]	11.3[17]
Aruba	2000	45.0	46.6	70.9	49.8	55.4	44.6	2.6[20]	96.8[20]	0.5[20]	0.1[20]	0.2	0.5	3.0	6.7
Australia	2003	10,067	44.8	74.2	50.6	56.3	45.0	13.1	86.5	0.4	...	395	3.9	1,282	12.7
Austria	2003	3,967	44.6	71.8	49.2	56.2	42.6	10.6	87.3	2.1	—	215	5.4	808	20.4
Azerbaijan	2003	3,801	47.8	...	46.0	48.9	43.2	...	...	...	...	1,500	39.5	252	6.6
Bahamas, The	2000	154	47.5	76.6	50.9	54.8	47.1	11.6[22]	85.1[22]	0.3[22]	3.0[22]	5.1	3.3	8.3	5.4
Bahrain	2001	308	21.7	65.7[23]	47.4	64.6	24.1	3.6	96.3	0.1	...	4	1.5	55	18.0
Bangladesh	1999–2000	60,291	37.8	73.8	47.3	56.3	37.5	35.3	12.6	33.7	18.4	36,217	60.1	4,799	8.0
Barbados	2002[24]	143	48.5	68.2[23]	52.7	56.5	49.2	14.0	85.6	0.1	0.5	5.2	3.6	10.9	7.6
Belarus	2003	4,446	53.4	69.7[25]	45.5	45.2	45.7	...	...	...	...	493	11.1	987	22.2
Belgium	2002	4,402	43.0	64.8	42.6	49.6	35.9	14.7[25]	82.1[25]	3.2[25]	...	72	1.6	823	18.7
Belize	2002	94.2	32.8	57.3	35.9	48.4	23.4	31.5[25]	65.0[25]	3.4[25]	0.1[25]	19.1	20.3	7.5	8.0
Benin	1992[26]	2,085	42.6	73.4	43.0	50.6	35.7	58.4	5.3	30.5	5.8	1,148	55.0	162	7.8
Bermuda	2000	37.9	48.3	84.8[27]	61.0	65.8	56.7	10.0	89.6	0.2	0.3	0.6[28]	1.5[28]	1.6[29]	4.2[29]
Bhutan	...	...	...	...	...	...	...	...	...	...	...	...	...	...	...
Bolivia	2000	3,637	44.6	71.8	46.2	52.1	40.5	42.2	49.6	7.8	0.4	1,415	38.9	436	12.0
Bosnia and Herzegovina	2001	1,038	...	...	57.6	71.8	43.1	...	...	...	...	21[25]	2.0[25]	224[25]	21.6[25]
Botswana	2001[24]	588	43.8	57.6	35.0	40.6	29.7	15.9	82.7	1.3	0.1	55	9.9	56	10.0
Brazil	2000	77,467	39.9	69.1[7]	45.6	55.7	35.8	26.3[22]	62.3[22]	7.7[22]	3.7[22]	12,119	15.6	9,320	12.0
Brunei	2001	158	41.2	66.6[30]	45.2	52.5	37.7	4.6[30]	95.0[30]	0.4[30]	...[30]	2.0	1.3	19.0	12.1
Bulgaria	2003[24,31]	3,283	46.8	60.9	47.0	52.0	42.4	13.1	84.7	1.9	0.3	286	8.7	778	23.7
Burkina Faso	1996	5,076	48.2	70.0[32]	49.2	52.9	46.0	2.6[20]	96.8[20]	0.5[20]	0.1[20]	4,514	88.9	78	1.5
Burundi	1990	2,780	52.6	91.4	52.5	51.2	53.8	62.8	5.1	30.3	1.8	2,574	92.6	37	1.3
Cambodia	1998	5,119	51.6	79.0	44.8	44.9	44.6	41.2[33]	12.9[33]	45.7[33]	0.2[33]	4,480[34]	70.0[34]	572[34]	8.9[34]
Cameroon	1991	4,740	33.2	58.9[12]	40.0	53.9	26.3	60.2[22]	14.6[22]	18.0[22]	7.1[22]	...	...	...	...
Canada	2004	17,269	46.6	65.9[23]	54.1	58.3	49.9	15.1[35]	84.7[35]	0.2[35]	...[35]	334	1.9	2,712	15.7
Cape Verde	2000	175	39.0	75.7[36]	40.6	42.6	38.9	24.7[22]	53.7[22]	2.0[22]	19.6[22]	29.9[22]	24.8[22]	6.8[22]	5.7[22]
Central African Republic	1988	1,187	46.8	78.3	48.2	52.2	44.3	75.3	8.0	8.1	8.6	881	74.2	31	2.6
Chad	1993	2,294	48.4	71.1[23]	37.0	39.5	34.7	...	...	...	...	1,903	83.0	37	1.6
Chile	2003[24]	6,128	34.3	58.8	38.7	51.3	26.3	29.7	68.2	2.0	—	796	13.0	966	15.8
China	2002	753,600	37.8[5]	77.7[5,10]	58.5	61.8[22]	53.7[22]	...	...	...	...	324,870	43.1	91,550	12.1
Colombia	2003[24]	20,408	42.6	48.1[38]	47.2	56.1	38.9	43.9	49.8	6.0	0.3	3,941[39]	19.4[39]	2,924[39]	14.4[39]
Comoros	1996	252	38.9	59.2	37.2	44.8	29.3	...	...	...	...	...	...	...	...
Congo, Dem. Rep. of the	1996	14,082	35.0	47.9[12]	31.1	40.9	21.6	...	...	...	...	...	...	...	...
Congo, Rep. of the	1984	563	45.6	54.0	29.5	33.0	26.2	64.3	31.4	1.2	3.1	294	52.2	50	8.8
Costa Rica	2003	1,758	35.4	59.4[40]	43.0	56.3	30.1	27.9	69.5	2.6	—	261	14.8	270	15.3
Côte d'Ivoire	1988	4,263	32.3	66.6	39.4	52.2	26.0	...	...	...	...	2,628	61.6	100	2.3
Croatia	2004	1,836	45.3	58.9	40.8	46.5	35.6	20.5[35]	75.9[35]	3.6[35]	—	269	14.7	339	18.5
Cuba	2002[24]	4,024	37.7	45.4[23]	35.8	44.7	27.0	...	...	...	...	1,065	26.5	644	16.0
Cyprus[41]	2003	341	44.7	70.6	49.6	56.7	42.9	20.2	76.3	3.5	—	17	5.0	40	11.7
Czech Republic	2004	5,138	44.1	70.9[34]	50.3	57.7	43.3	16.1	82.7	0.7	0.5	208	4.0	1,413	27.5
Denmark	2002	2,893	46.9	77.8[42]	53.9	57.9	49.9	8.2	91.0	0.8	...	102	3.5	468	16.2
Djibouti	...	...	...	...	...	...	...	...	...	...	...	...	...	...	...
Dominica	1997	33.4	45.8	65.6[23]	45.8	49.4	42.1	31.9	65.6	1.9	0.6	6.1	18.3	2.5	7.6
Dominican Republic	2002	3,702	38.7	55.1[23]	43.1	52.0	33.9	42.9[33]	55.2[33]	1.9[33]	—[33]	512	13.8	562	15.2
East Timor	2001	250[4,23]	31.6[4,23]	56.0[4,23]	31.4[4,23]	42.7[4,23]	20.0[4,23]	61.0	17.4	21.2	0.4	...	73.2[4]	...	4.8[4,43]
Ecuador	2003[44]	3,992	41.1	70.4	46.6	55.4	37.9	34.3	61.3	4.4	—	349	8.7	578	14.5
Egypt	2001[24]	19,253	21.9	46.9	30.0	45.8	13.5	29.4[34]	60.2[34]	10.4[34]	—[34]	4,922[34]	24.8[34]	2,377[34]	12.0[34]
El Salvador	2003	2,707	40.3	64.4	40.8	51.1	31.4	32.6	53.5	8.7	5.2	516	19.1	477	17.6
Equatorial Guinea	1983	103	35.7	66.7	39.2	52.5	26.9	29.0	16.0	29.9	25.1	59.4	57.9	1.8	1.8
Eritrea	...	...	...	...	...	...	...	...	...	...	...	...	...	...	...
Estonia	2003	661	49.0	69.8	48.7	53.9	44.3	8.5	91.1	0.4	—	37	5.6	150	22.7

traditional agricultural worker. Loss of working-age men to war, civil violence, or emigration for job opportunities may also affect the structure of a particular labour market.

The distribution of the economically active population by employment status reveals that a large percentage of economically active persons in some less developed countries falls under the heading "employers, self-employed." This occurs because the countries involved have poor, largely agrarian economies in which the average worker is a farmer who tills his own small plot of land. In countries with well-developed economies, "employees" will usually constitute the largest portion of the economically active.

Caution should be exercised when using the economically active data to make intercountry comparisons, as countries often differ in their choices of classification schemes, definitions, and coverage of groups and in their methods of collection and tabulation of data. The population base containing the economically active population, for example, may range, in developing countries, from age 9 or 10 with no upper limit to, in developed countries, age 18 or 19 upward to a usual retirement age of from 55 to 65, with sometimes a different range for each sex. Data on female labour-force participation, in particular, often lack comparability. In many less developed countries, particularly those dominated by the Islamic faith,

a cultural bias favouring traditional roles for women results in the undercounting of economically active women. In other less developed countries, particularly those in which subsistence workers are deemed economically active, the role of women may be overstated.

The second major section of the table provides data on the distribution by economic (also conventionally called industrial) sector of the economically active population. The data usually include such groups as unpaid family workers, members of the armed forces, and the unemployed, the last distributed by industry as far as possible.

The categorization of industrial sectors is based on the divisions listed in the *International Standard Industrial Classification of All Economic Activities*. The "other" category includes persons whose activities were not adequately defined and the unemployed who were not distributable by industrial sector.

A substantial part of the data presented in this table is summarized from the online database of the ILO, which compiles its statistics both from official publications and from information submitted directly by national census and labour authorities. The editors have supplemented and updated ILO statistical data with information from Britannica's holdings of relevant official publications.

construction		transportation, communications		trade, hotels, restaurants		finance, real estate		public administration, defense		services		other		country
number ('000)	% of econ. active	number ('000)	% of econ. active	number ('000)	% of econ. active	number ('000)	% of econ. active	number ('000)	% of econ. active	number ('000)	% of econ. active	number ('000)	% of econ. active	
81[2]	1.5[2]	140[2]	2.5[2]	421[2]	7.6[2]	[3]	[3]	[3]	[3]	929[2,3]	16.7[2,3]	214[2]	3.9[2]	Afghanistan
13[4,5]	1.2[4,5]	24[4,5]	2.3[4,5]	55[4,5]	5.2[4,5]	[3]	[3]	[3]	[3]	147[3,4,5]	15.9[3,4,5]	...[4,5]	...[4,5]	Albania
669	8.2	9	9	9	9	9	9	1,773	21.7	1,665[9]	20.5[9]	2,428	29.8	Algeria
1.1	6.0	1.0	5.9	1.8	10.1	0.3	1.8	1.6	8.8	4.6	25.7	0.9	5.4	American Samoa
5.7	16.6	...	...	12.5	36.2	1.4	4.1	4.4	12.7	6.6	19.1	2.7	7.9	Andorra
[13]	[13]	[14]	[14]	[14]	[14]	[14]	[14]	[14]	[14]	883[14]	19.3[14]	—	—	Angola
3.1	11.6	2.4	9.0	8.5	31.9	1.5	5.4	[15]	[15]	6.4[15]	23.9[15]	1.9	7.0	Antigua and Barbuda
639	4.1	718	4.7	2,213	14.5	898	5.9	969	6.3	2,762	18.1	4,781	31.3	Argentina
37	3.0	42	3.4	105	8.5	38[18]	3.1[18]	37	3.0	193	15.7	132[19]	10.7[19]	Armenia
3.9	8.7	2.9	6.5	14.8	33.0	5.2	11.7	3.5	7.9	8.0	18.0	3.2[19]	7.1[19]	Aruba
786	7.8	622	6.2	2,574	25.6	1,537	15.3	566	5.6	2,144	21.3	162	1.6	Australia
363	9.2	247	6.2	861	21.7	460	11.6	241	6.1	759	19.1	13	0.3	Austria
180	4.7	179	4.7	630	16.6	111	2.9	330	8.7	566	14.9	542[21]	14.2[21]	Azerbaijan
17.0	11.0	10.8	7.0	46.9	30.4	15.9	10.3	13.1	8.5	29.3	19.2	7.8[19]	5.0[19]	Bahamas, The
26	8.6	14	4.5	48	15.5	25	8.1	52	17.0	61	19.9	22[19]	7.0[19]	Bahrain
1,144	1.9	2,672	4.4	7,045	11.7	415	0.7	[15]	[15]	5,775[15]	9.6[15]	2,224[19]	3.7[19]	Bangladesh
13.2	9.3	4.7	3.3	33.8	23.7	10.9	7.6	[15]	[15]	49.5[15]	34.7[15]	14.5	10.2	Barbados
231	5.2	265	5.9	257	5.8	57	1.3	84	1.9	1,033	23.2	1,039	23.4	Belarus
276	6.3	327	7.4	777	17.7	553	12.6	406	9.2	1,038	23.6	130	3.0	Belgium
7.1	7.5	3.1	3.3	22.9	24.3	3.1	3.3	[15]	[15]	20.0[15]	21.3[15]	11.3[19]	12.0[19]	Belize
52	2.5	53	2.5	433	20.7	3	0.1	[15]	[15]	165[15]	7.9[15]	71	3.4	Benin
3.8	10.0	2.8	7.5	9.1	23.9	6.4	17.0	2.5	6.6	6.8	17.9	4.3	11.2	Bermuda
...	...	...	...	...	...	...	...	...	...	...	...	...	...	Bhutan
240	6.6	156	4.3	724	19.9	120	3.3	80	2.2	324	8.9	142	3.9	Bolivia
36[25]	3.5[25]	45[25]	4.3[25]	91[25]	8.8[25]	42[25]	4.1[25]	73[25]	7.0[25]	96[25]	9.3[25]	409[21,25]	39.4[21,25]	Bosnia and Herzegovina
59	10.5	53	2.7	74	13.2	30	5.4	70	12.5	86	15.5	113[19]	20.3[19]	Botswana
4,568	5.9	3,319	4.3	13,971	18.0	4,586	5.9	3,523	4.6	13,383	17.3	12,676	16.4	Brazil
12.3	7.8	4.8	3.0	20.0	12.7	8.2	5.2	[15]	[15]	79.9[15]	50.7[15]	11.3[21]	7.2[21]	Brunei
151	4.6	215	6.6	552	16.8	146	4.5	230	7.0	474	14.4	451	13.7	Bulgaria
21	0.4	21	0.4	225	4.4	13	0.3	...	...	104	2.0	100	2.0	Burkina Faso
20	0.7	9	0.3	26	0.9	2.0	0.1	[15]	[15]	85[15]	3.1[15]	27[19]	1.0[19]	Burundi
100[34]	1.6[34]	175[34]	2.7[34]	661[34]	10.3[34]	16[34]	0.3[34]	144[34]	2.2[34]	252[34]	3.9[34]	—[34]	—[34]	Cambodia
...	...	...	...	...	...	...	...	...	...	...	...	...	...	Cameroon
984	5.7	800	4.6	3,514	20.4	2,634	15.3	820	4.7	4,222	24.5	1,249[21]	7.2[21]	Canada
22.7[22]	18.8[22]	6.1[22]	5.1[22]	12.7[22]	10.6[22]	0.8[22]	0.7[22]	[15]	[15]	17.4[15,22]	14.4[15,22]	24.1[22]	20.0[22]	Cape Verde
6	0.5	7	0.6	92	7.8	0.7	0.1	[15]	[15]	70[15]	5.9[15]	100[19]	8.5[19]	Central African Republic
11	0.5	13	0.6	212	9.2	1	—	62	2.7	46	2.0	9	0.4	Chad
493	8.0	519	8.5	1,145	18.7	494	8.1	[15]	[15]	1,643[15]	26.8[15]	71[37]	1.2[37]	Chile
38,930	5.2	20,840	2.8	49,690	6.6	4,580	0.6	10,750	1.4	33,150	4.4	179,240	3.8	China
998[39]	4.9[39]	1,271[39]	6.2[39]	4,971[39]	24.4[39]	1,087[39]	5.3[39]	[15]	[15]	4,578[15,39]	2.5[15,39]	575[19,39]	2.8[19,39]	Colombia
...	...	...	...	...	...	...	...	...	...	...	...	...	...	Comoros
...	...	...	...	...	...	...	...	...	...	...	...	...	...	Congo, Dem. Rep. of the
25	4.5	29	5.1	67	11.8	3	0.5	[15]	[15]	85[15]	15.1[15]	10	2.0	Congo, Rep. of the
122	6.9	97	5.5	439	25.0	145	8.3	79	4.5	312	17.8	33	1.9	Costa Rica
85	2.0	118	2.8	530	12.4	[3]	[3]	[3]	[3]	591[3]	13.9[3]	210[21]	4.9[21]	Côte d'Ivoire
130	7.1	104	5.7	301	16.4	98	5.3	106	5.8	234	12.7	253	13.8	Croatia
176	4.4	202	5.0	508	12.6	54	1.3	[15]	[15]	1,376[15]	34.2[15]	—	—	Cuba
35	10.2	17	5.1	88	25.8	39	11.4	24	7.2	64	18.7	17[19]	4.8[19]	Cyprus[41]
440	8.6	366	7.1	812	15.8	367	7.1	324	6.3	782	15.2	425[21]	8.3[21]	Czech Republic
173	6.0	179	6.2	495	17.1	376	13.0	[15]	[15]	974[15]	33.7[15]	125[19]	4.3[19]	Denmark
...	...	...	...	...	...	...	...	...	...	...	...	...	...	Djibouti
2.2	6.4	1.5	4.5	5.0	15.1	1.4	4.2	1.5	4.6	4.4	13.1	8.8[19]	26.3[19]	Dominica
207	5.6	244	6.6	924	25.0	71	1.9	172	4.7	777	21.0	233	6.3	Dominican Republic
...	...[4,43]	...	...	...	...	...	...	...	...	...	...	...	22.0[4]	East Timor
271	6.8	248	6.2	1,198	30.0	228	5.7	192	4.8	736	18.4	192[37]	4.8[37]	Ecuador
1,329[34]	6.7[34]	1,137[34]	5.7[34]	2,684[34]	13.5[34]	568[34]	2.9[34]	1,947[34]	9.8[34]	2,996[34]	15.1[34]	1,917[34]	9.6[34]	Egypt
195	7.2	121	4.5	747	27.6	116	4.3	107	4.0	400	14.8	27	1.0	El Salvador
1.9	1.9	1.8	1.7	3.1	3.0	0.4	0.4	[15]	[15]	8.4[15]	8.2[15]	25.8[19]	25.2[19]	Equatorial Guinea
...	...	...	...	...	...	...	...	...	...	...	...	...	...	Eritrea
43	6.5	56	8.5	98	14.9	52	7.9	35	5.2	124	18.7	66[21]	10.0[21]	Estonia

Employment and labour   (continued)

country	year	economically active population											distribution by economic sector			
		total ('000)	participation rate (%)		activity rate (%)			employment status (%)				agriculture, forestry, fishing		manufacturing; mining, quarrying; public utilities	
			female	ages 15–64	total	male	female	employers, self-employed	employees	unpaid family workers	other	number ('000)	% of econ. active	number ('000)	% of econ. active
Ethiopia	1999	27,272	45.5	68.4	49.7	54.9	44.7	...	...	...	...	21,605[11]	87.8[11]	419[11]	1.7[11]
Faroe Islands	2003	27	...	...	56.0	...	...	...	...	...	...	...	...	...	...
Fiji	1996	298	32.8	60.6	38.4	50.8	25.6	...	...	...	...	133	44.6	34	11.3
Finland	2003	2,600	48.0	74.1	49.8	52.9	46.8	12.3	86.4	0.4	0.9	120	4.6	470	18.1
France	2003	27,125	45.9	69.3	45.3	50.4	40.5	10.2[45]	77.4[45]	—	12.4[45]	1,057[4]	4.3[4]	4,249[4]	17.4[4]
French Guiana	1999	62.6	43.8	65.0[7]	39.9	44.6	35.3	15.2[46]	84.8	[46]	—	2.9	4.5	3.5	5.6
French Polynesia	2002	99.5	40.0	61.7	40.6	47.5	33.4	...	...	...	...	10.9[47]	12.5[47]	6.9[47]	7.9[47]
Gabon	1993	376	44.5	52.5[32]	37.2	41.9	32.7	...	...	...	...	128	34.1	26	6.9
Gambia, The	1993	345	40.0	48.9[32]	33.3	39.9	26.6	...	...	...	...	182	52.6	24	6.9
Gaza Strip	2003	254	12.1	37.6[23]	19.0	33.0	4.7	26.7	61.8	11.5	—	30	11.7	16[48]	6.2[48]
Georgia	2000[49]	2,104	47.3	71.8[50]	48.3	54.1	43.1	64.4	35.4	...	0.2	989	46.9	117	5.6
Germany	2003	40,195	44.5	72.2	48.7	55.3	42.4	10.4	88.6	1.1	—	1,064	2.6	9,631	24.0
Ghana	1999	9,680	52.7	79.9	53.5	52.5	54.3	68.8	13.8	17.2	0.2	3,778[51]	50.5[51]	860[51]	11.5[51]
Greece	2002	4,369	40.4	63.1	42.1	51.9	33.0	32.0	60.2	7.8	—	624	14.3	593	13.6
Greenland	2002	31.5	45.7	83.2[52]	55.7	56.7	54.5	...	...	...	...	2.0[4,5]	7.3[4,5]	3.5[4,5]	12.9[4,5]
Grenada	1998	41.0	43.5	78.0[53]	46.0[53]	50.0[53]	41.0[53]	22.9	71.3	1.1	4.7	4.8	11.7	3.1	7.7
Guadeloupe	1999	191	49.1	70.6[7]	45.3	47.9	42.9	18.2	80.5	1.3	—	8.2[6]	4.5[6]	7.9[6]	4.3[6]
Guam	2002[24]	62.1	45.9	62.4[10]	39.0[53]	41.0[53]	37.0[53]	4.2[54]	95.5[54]	0.3[54]	—[54]	0.3[55]	0.5[55]	1.6[55,56]	2.8[55,56]
Guatemala	1998–99	3,982	22.6	50.5	35.0	53.7	15.9	32.7[57]	47.6[57]	16.2[57]	3.5[57]	1,844[34]	38.7[34]	741[34]	15.5[34]
Guernsey	2001[58]	32.6	45.2	79.1	54.6	61.4	48.1	12.8	87.2	—	—	1.5	4.5	2.3	6.9
Guinea	1990	3,067	47.4	...	49.0[53]	52.0[53]	46.0[53]	...	...	...	...	...	...	...	...
Guinea-Bissau	1995	491	39.9	65.5[12]	45.8	55.9	36.0	...	...	...	...	373	76.0	20[13]	4.1[13]
Guyana	1997	263.8	35.2	61.8[2]	38.8[2]	51.9[2]	26.0[2]	...	...	...	...	66.8	25.3	37.7	14.3
Haiti	1990	2,679	40.0	64.8	41.1	50.3	32.3	59.1	16.5	10.4	14.0	1,535	57.3	178	6.6
Honduras	2001[24,59]	2,438	35.7	64.5	38.5	50.6	26.8	39.7[25]	46.8[25]	13.0[25]	0.5[25]	775	31.8	391	16.0
Hong Kong	2003[24]	3,501	43.9	70.2	51.7	59.9	44.0	12.0	87.3	0.7	—	8	0.2	312	8.9
Hungary	2003	4,166	45.6	60.6	41.1	47.1	35.8	12.6	86.7	0.5	0.2	226	5.4	1,069	25.7
Iceland	2003	162.4	47.4	82.2[60]	56.1	59.1	53.2	16.3[34]	83.4[34]	0.3[34]	—[34]	10.8	6.7	23.3	14.3
India	2001	402,512	31.6	...	39.1	51.8	24.3	48.0[61,62]	10.3[61,63]	31.6[61,64]	10.1[61]	190,940[61]	52.6[61]	44,200[61]	12.2[61]
Indonesia	2002[24]	91,647	36.1	58.3[7]	39.6	50.7	28.5	46.3	27.3	17.6	8.8	40,633	44.3	12,920	14.1
Iran	1996	16,027	12.7	44.1	26.7	45.8	6.9	39.3	51.7	5.5	3.5	3,357	20.9	2,822	17.6
Iraq	1997	4,757[65]	10.5[65]	42.9[7,65]	24.8[65]	44.7[65]	5.2[65]	...	...	...	...	477[66]	11.6[66]	439[66]	10.6[66]
Ireland	2004	1,876	41.7	68.1	47.1	55.3	39.1	16.7	82.3	1.0	—	117	6.2	306	16.3
Isle of Man	2001	39.7	45.4	78.9[27]	52.0	58.0	46.3	14.6	85.4	—	—	0.5	1.4	3.7	9.3
Israel	2003[24]	2,610	46.3	61.7	39.0	42.4	35.7	11.4	86.2	0.4	2.0	42	1.6	398	15.2
Italy	2003	24,229	39.1	61.6	42.2	52.8	32.1	22.2	72.8	4.1	0.9	1,075	4.4	5,210	21.5
Jamaica	2003[24]	1,098	44.3	66.0[67]	41.6	47.4	36.1	35.7	62.3	1.3	0.4	188	17.1	78	7.1
Japan	2003	66,660	41.0	72.3	52.2	63.2	41.8	10.4	84.5	4.7	0.4	2,930	4.4	12,150	18.2
Jersey	2001	48.1	46.0	81.7[68]	55.2	61.2	49.5	11.9	88.1	—	—	2.1[35]	4.0[35]	2.7[35]	5.0[35]
Jordan	2003	1,293	14.9	37.9[23]	23.6	39.6	7.1	18.6	80.7	0.5	0.2	39	3.0	169	13.1
Kazakhstan	2003	7,657	49.1	76.9	51.2	...	...	37.4	60.5	1.0	1.1	2,463	32.1	855	11.2
Kenya	1998–99	12,300	46.1[20]	73.6	42.1[5]	...	...	...	...	...	...	...	...	...	...
Kiribati	1995	40.6	47.8	84.0[23]	49.5	52.1	46.8	...	...	...	...	31.0[54,69]	71.7[54,69]	0.3[54]	0.8[54]
Korea, North	1985	9,084	46.0	75.3	44.6	48.6	40.6	...	...	...	...	...	...	...	...
Korea, South	2003	22,846	41.0	65.3	48.3	56.5	39.9	27.1	66.2	6.7	—	1,955	8.6	4,409	19.3
Kuwait	2002	1,364	25.7	74.4[23]	56.4	69.3	36.6	2.2[11]	97.8[11]	—[11]	—[11]	22	1.6	100	7.3
Kyrgyzstan	2002	2,116	44.0	68.7	42.5[53]	48.4[53]	36.8[53]	42.5	42.7	10.6	4.2	952[4]	52.7[4]	140[4]	7.7[4]
Laos	1995	2,166	56.4	83.3	47.3	46.2	52.8	...	...	...	...	...	...	...	...
Latvia	2003	1,126	48.6	69.2	48.3	53.9	43.5	9.3	87.0	3.7	—	139	12.3	198	17.6
Lebanon	1997	1,362	21.6	49.3	34.0	55.2	14.2	...	...	...	...	132[71]	19.1[71]	131[71]	18.9[71]
Lesotho	1996	573	33.5	49.9	29.2	39.5	19.3	...	...	...	...	105	18.4	126	21.9
Liberia	1984	704	41.0	56.3	33.5	39.1	27.8	59.1	21.6	14.4	5.0	481	68.3	31	4.4
Libya	1996	1,224	9.8	37.1[12,30]	26.1	42.9[30]	4.9[30]	...	...	...	...	219	17.9	195	15.9
Liechtenstein	2004	15.6[73]	41.4[73]	55.6[23,73]	45.6[73]	54.3[73]	37.2[73]	...	...	...	...	0.4[74]	1.3[74]	10.6[74]	36.4[74]
Lithuania	2003[24]	1,642	49.3	65.7	47.5	51.6	44.0	16.9	79.6	3.5	—	257	15.6	298	18.1
Luxembourg	2003	195[75]	41.5[75]	64.1[75]	43.2[75]	51.2[75]	35.4[75]	8.6[5,75]	85.6[5,75]	1.7[5,75]	4.1[5,75]	4[76]	1.3[76]	35[76]	11.5[76]
Macau	2003[24]	215.5	46.6	66.2[67]	49.9	55.9	44.4	9.4	89.0	1.6	—	0.6	0.3	38.4	17.8
Macedonia	2003	861	39.7	61.3	42.3	51.1	33.6	15.8	72.7	11.4	—	120	13.9	149	17.3
Madagascar	2003	8,481	49.5	83.2	50.7	51.6	49.8	43.7	15.0	40.6	0.7	6,316	74.5	482	5.7
Malawi	1998	4,509	50.2	76.5	45.4	46.1	44.7	84.6	12.9	2.5	—	3,766	83.6	128	2.8
Malaysia	2000	9,616	34.7	65.5	41.3	52.7	29.4	21.1[77]	71.4[77]	7.5[77]	—	1,422[34]	14.4[34]	2,148[34]	21.7[34]
Maldives	2000	88.0	33.7	55.7	32.6	42.5	22.4	51.6	23.8	2.0	22.6	11.8	13.4	12.7	14.4
Mali	1987	3,438	37.4	67.4	44.7	57.2	32.7	35.4	5.2	57.6	1.8	2,803	81.5	191	5.6
Malta	2003	159.6	31.3	60.8[7]	39.9	55.3	24.8	14.2	85.1	...	0.7	2.5	1.6	32.2	20.2
Marshall Islands	1999	14.7	34.1	52.1	28.9	37.2	20.1	28.8[78]	71.2[79]	...	...	2.1	14.4	1.0	6.9
Martinique	1999	174.0	50.3	71.6[7]	45.6	47.8	43.7	14.4	84.9	0.7	—	8.4	4.8	9.1	5.2
Mauritania	2000[80]	652	28.0	38.1[32]	26.0	37.8	14.4	57.1	23.3	12.4	7.2	314	48.2	39	5.9
Mauritius	2000	514	33.6	62.7	43.3	58.0	28.9	15.8	83.0	0.9	0.3	53	10.3	139	27.1
Mayotte	2002	44.6	38.6	50.0[36,53]	27.8	...	...	26.1[20]	71.9[20]	2.0[20]	—[20]	3.2	7.2	1.6	3.6
Mexico	2003	41,516	34.3	61.2	40.4	54.8	26.9	28.6[34]	62.3[34]	9.1[34]	—[34]	7,074[5]	17.8[5]	7,695[5]	19.4[5]
Micronesia	2000	37.4	42.9	60.7	35.0	39.4	30.4	...	...	...	...	15.2	40.7	1.5	4.1
Moldova	2003	1,474	50.4	61.3[34]	40.8	42.3	39.5	33.5	64.0	2.4	0.1	583	39.6	164	11.2
Monaco	2000[81]	12.7	39.8	61.1[82]	39.7	49.2	30.7	17.4[22]	75.1[22]	0.3[22]	7.2[22]	0.02	0.2	0.8	6.3
Mongolia	2004	960	49.6	63.8[84]	38.8	39.9	37.7	32.5[54]	41.3[54]	25.3[54]	0.9[54]	388	40.4	109	11.4
Morocco	2002	10,482[53]	24.8[53]	54.5[7,53]	35.4[53]	53.5[53]	17.5[53]	...	...	...	...	3,951	38.1	1,231	11.9
Mozambique	1996	9,318	46.3	83.2[12]	56.3	61.1	51.5	...	...	...	...	7,360	79.0	987[43]	10.6[43]
Myanmar (Burma)	1997–98[4,24]	18,337	...	...	...	...	...	...	...	...	...	12,093	65.9	1,831	9.9
Namibia	2000	652	51.5[53]	59.7[53,84]	34.2[53]	33.2[53]	35.3[53]	32.5	62.2	3.3	2.0	134	20.6	31	4.7
Nauru	1992[86]	2.5	43.5	67.9[23]	35.9	40.1	31.5	...	...	...	...	...	...	0.5[4,20]	24.7[4,20]
Nepal	1998–99[87]	11,628	50.9	85.8[23]	60.9	61.2	60.5	40.7	16.0	43.3	...	7,203	61.9	585	5.0
Netherlands, The	2003	8,370	44.1	75.9	51.7[53]	58.4[53]	45.1[53]	10.7	88.7	0.6	—	230[34,88]	2.8[34,88]	1,136[34,88]	13.8[34,88]
Netherlands Antilles	2001	81.6	49.0	68.7	46.5	50.4	42.9	9.0[54]	87.8[54]	0.5[54]	2.7[54]	0.4	0.5	5.9	7.2
New Caledonia	1996	80.6	39.7	68.2[89]	40.9	48.2	33.3	15.9	83.8	0.3	—	4.7	5.8	8.2	10.1
New Zealand	2003[24]	2,015	45.7	74.5	50.3	55.5	45.2	18.6	80.7	0.7	—	157	7.8	290	14.4
Nicaragua	2001	1,900	30.8	61.7[25]	36.5	50.8	22.4	...	...	...	...	596[35]	28.1[35]	277[35]	13.1[35]

construction number ('000)	construction % of econ. active	transportation, communications number ('000)	transportation, communications % of econ. active	trade, hotels, restaurants number ('000)	trade, hotels, restaurants % of econ. active	finance, real estate number ('000)	finance, real estate % of econ. active	public administration, defense number ('000)	public administration, defense % of econ. active	services number ('000)	services % of econ. active	other number ('000)	other % of econ. active	country
61[11]	0.2[11]	103[11]	0.4[11]	936[11]	3.8[11]	19[11]	0.1[11]	11, 15	11, 15	1,252[11,15]	5.1[11,15]	210[11,37]	0.9[11,37]	Ethiopia
...	...	...	...	...	...	...	...	...	...	...	...	...	...	Faroe Islands
11	3.6	17	5.6	32	10.8	8	2.6	16	5.3	29	9.7	19[19]	6.5[19]	Fiji
151	5.8	173	6.7	363	14.0	313	12.0	118	4.5	649	25.0	243[19]	9.3[19]	Finland
1,576[4]	6.4[4]	1,051[4]	4.3[4]	3,234[4]	13.2[4]	4,088[4]	16.7[4]	2,581[4]	10.5[4]	6,530[4]	26.7[4]	117[4]	0.5[4]	France
3.3	5.3	1.6	2.6	4.6	7.3	5.0	8.0	10.3	16.4	12.2	19.5	19.2	30.7	French Guiana
4.8[47]	5.5[47]	3.8[47]	4.4[47]	9.4[47]	10.7[47]	1.9[47]	2.1[47]	13.5[47]	15.5[47]	23.5[47]	27.0[47]	12.6[19,47]	14.4[19,47]	French Polynesia
10	2.6	16	4.2	40	10.8	5	1.3	48	12.8	33	8.8	70[19]	18.5[19]	Gabon
10	2.8	14	4.1	55	15.8	2	0.7	15	15	41[15]	11.9[15]	17	5.0	Gambia, The
18	7.0	9	3.5	29	11.4	3	3	3	3	70[3,48]	27.5[3,48]	83[19]	32.7[19]	Gaza Strip
34	1.6	78	3.7	231	11.0	28	1.3	109	5.2	253	12.0	265	12.6	Georgia
3,230	8.0	2,192	5.5	7,029	17.5	4,957	12.3	15	15	11,835[15]	29.4[15]	258[37]	0.6[37]	Germany
97[51]	1.3[51]	150[51]	2.0[51]	1,257[51]	16.8[51]	52[51]	0.7[51]	15	15	673[15,51]	9.0[15,51]	613[21,51]	8.2[21,51]	Ghana
294	6.7	244	5.6	947	21.7	324	7.4	294	6.7	628	14.4	421	9.6	Greece
1.9[4,5]	7.0[4,5]	2.2[4,5]	8.1[4,5]	2.5[4,5]	9.0[4,5]	1.3[4,5]	4.7[4,5]	12.9[4,5]	47.0[4,5]	1.1[4,5]	3.9[4,5]	—[4,5]	0.1[4,5]	Greenland
5.2	12.6	2.0	5.0	8.3	20.2	1.3	3.2	1.9	4.6	6.9	16.7	7.5[19]	18.4[19]	Grenada
13.0[6]	7.1[6]	4.2[6]	2.3[6]	20.7[6]	11.4[6]	3.5[6]	1.9[6]	43.4[6]	23.8[6]	24.4[6]	13.4[6]	56.9[6,19]	31.2[6,19]	Guadeloupe
3.4[55]	6.1[55]	4.6[55,56]	8.2[55,56]	12.7[55]	22.7[55]	2.5[55]	4.4[55]	16.5[55]	29.5[55]	14.5[55]	25.9[55]	—	—	Guam
213[34]	4.5[34]	104[34]	2.2[34]	1,050[34]	22.0[34]	32[34]	0.7[34]	15	15	602[15,34]	12.6[15,34]	184[34]	3.9[34]	Guatemala
2.9	9.0	1.2	3.8	7.5	22.8	8.6	26.4	1.9	5.8	6.2	19.1	0.5[19]	1.7[19]	Guernsey
...	...	...	...	...	...	...	...	...	...	...	...	...	...	Guinea
13	13	14	14	14	14	14	14	14	14	98[14]	20.0[14]	—	—	Guinea-Bissau
16.5	6.3	20.2	7.6	44.7	16.9	12.2	4.6	15.2	5.8	22.6	8.6	28.0[19]	10.6[19]	Guyana
28	1.0	21	0.8	353	13.2	5	0.2	15	15	155[15]	5.8[15]	404[19]	15.1[19]	Haiti
135	5.5	79	3.2	574	23.6	69	2.8	15	15	395[15]	16.2[15]	21[37]	0.9[37]	Honduras
328	9.4	371	10.6	1,082	30.9	496	14.2	15	15	881[15]	25.2[15]	23[37]	0.7[37]	Hong Kong
318	7.6	311	7.5	729	17.5	350	8.4	314	7.5	789	18.9	60	1.4	Hungary
10.8	6.7	9.7	6.0	26.0	16.0	20.5	12.6	8.2	5.0	47.6	29.3	5.5[21]	3.4[21]	Iceland
14,950[61]	4.1[61]	13,650[61]	3.8[61]	37,540[61]	10.3[61]	4,620[61]	1.3[61]	15	15	30,840[15,61]	8.5[15,61]	26,580[21,61]	7.3[21,61]	India
4,274	4.7	4,673	5.1	17,795	19.4	992	1.1	15	15	10,360[15]	11.3[15]	—	—	Indonesia
1,650	10.3	973	6.1	1,927	12.0	302	1.9	1,618	10.1	1,631	10.2	1,747[19]	10.9[19]	Iran
461[66]	11.2[66]	266[66]	6.4[66]	282[66]	6.8[66]	42[66]	1.0[66]	15, 66	15, 66	2,160[15,66]	52.3[15,66]	—	—	Iraq
191	10.2	112	6.0	366	19.5	227	12.1	92	4.9	382	20.4	82[21]	4.4[21]	Ireland
2.5	6.3	3.3	8.4	7.2	18.2	9.0	22.6	3.1	7.8	9.7	24.4	0.6[21]	1.6[21]	Isle of Man
129	4.9	152	5.8	406	15.6	375	14.4	127	4.8	684	26.2	297[19]	11.4[19]	Israel
1,809	7.5	1,162	4.8	4,483	18.5	2,393	9.9	1,934	8.0	4,050	16.7	2,113[19]	8.7[19]	Italy
90	8.2	64	5.9	210	19.1	66	6.0	15	15	257[15]	23.4[15]	145[19]	13.2[19]	Jamaica
6,040	9.1	4,960	7.4	14,830	22.2	2,320	3.5	2,270	3.4	17,050	25.6	4,110	6.2	Japan
4.7[35]	8.8[35]	1.4[35]	2.7[35]	14.7[35]	27.5[35]	3	3	3	3	27.8[3,35]	52.0[3,35]	—	—	Jersey
71	5.5	110	8.5	224	17.3	59	4.5	184	14.2	246	19.1	191[19]	14.8[19]	Jordan
329	4.3	504	6.6	1,085	14.2	261	3.4	318	4.1	1,170	15.3	672[21]	8.8[21]	Kazakhstan
...	...	...	...	...	...	...	...	...	...	...	...	...	...	Kenya
0.3[54]	0.8[54]	0.9[54]	2.2[54]	1.2[54]	2.7[54]	0.3[54]	0.7[54]	5.8[54]	13.5[54]	2.6[54]	6.1[54]	0.6[21,54]	1.5[21,54]	Kiribati
...	...	...	...	...	...	...	...	...	...	...	...	...	...	Korea, North
1,898	8.3	1,358	5.9	6,046	26.5	2,535	11.1	802	3.5	3,724	16.3	119	0.5	Korea, South
108	7.9	43	3.2	220	16.1	59	4.3	15	15	720[15]	52.8[15]	92[70]	6.7[70]	Kuwait
46[4]	2.5[4]	68[4]	3.7[4]	217[4]	12.1[4]	38[4]	2.1[4]	66[4]	3.7[4]	280[4]	15.5[4]	—	—	Kyrgyzstan
...	...	...	...	...	...	...	...	...	...	...	...	...	...	Laos
74	6.6	95	8.4	177	15.7	58	5.1	67	6.0	199	17.7	119[21]	10.6[21]	Latvia
43[71]	6.2[71]	48[71]	7.0[71]	115[71]	16.5[71]	24[71]	3.5[71]	15	15	200[15,71]	28.8[15,71]	—	—	Lebanon
19	3.4	15	2.6	15	2.6	4	0.7	15	15	131[15]	22.8[15]	159[72]	27.7[72]	Lesotho
4	0.6	14	2.0	47	6.7	3	3	3	3	63[3]	9.0[3]	64[19]	9.1[19]	Liberia
171	14.0	104	8.5	73	6.0	22	1.8	15	15	440[15]	35.9[15]	—	—	Libya
2.5[74]	8.6[74]	1.0[74]	3.5[74]	3.1[74]	10.7[74]	4.4[74]	15.3[74]	1.5[74]	5.0[74]	3.4[74]	11.8[74]	2.1[74]	7.3[74]	Liechtenstein
107	6.5	92	5.6	244	14.9	70	4.3	75	4.6	295	18.0	204[21]	12.4[21]	Lithuania
29[76]	9.5[76]	24[76]	8.1[76]	55[76]	18.2[76]	82[76]	27.1[76]	15[76]	5.1[76]	50[76]	16.7[76]	8[76]	2.5[76]	Luxembourg
16.3	7.6	14.2	6.6	54.9	25.5	18.1	8.4	17.8	8.3	42.0	19.5	13.2[19]	6.1[19]	Macau
36	4.2	31	3.6	75	8.7	18	2.1	35	4.0	80	9.3	317[19]	36.9[19]	Macedonia
61	0.7	117	1.4	468	5.5	6	0.1	206	2.4	443	5.2	383[21]	4.5[21]	Madagascar
73	1.6	33	0.7	257	5.7	14	0.3	101	2.2	86	1.9	50	1.1	Malawi
907[34]	9.2[34]	496[34]	5.0[34]	2,118[34]	21.4[34]	639[34]	6.5[34]	15	15	1,822[15,34]	18.4[15,34]	334[21,34]	3.4[21,34]	Malaysia
3.7	4.2	7.9	8.9	15.6	17.7	1.7	1.9	15	15	18.1[15]	20.6[15]	16.6[21]	18.8[21]	Maldives
13	0.4	6	0.2	159	4.6	0.3	—	75	2.2	84	2.4	107	3.1	Mali
11.2	7.0	11.3	7.1	34.0	21.3	12.6	7.9	13.2	8.3	27.8	17.4	14.7[19]	9.2[19]	Malta
0.8	5.8	0.8	5.2	0.8	5.4	0.6	3.8	15	15	3.8[15]	25.9[15]	4.8[21]	32.6[21]	Marshall Islands
7.1	4.1	4.8	2.7	16.5	9.5	12.3	7.1	19.9	11.5	38.0	21.8	57.9[19]	33.3[19]	Martinique
16	2.4	18	2.7	109	16.7	2	0.3	15	15	99[15]	15.1[15]	56	8.6	Mauritania
44	8.5	31	6.0	82	16.0	21	4.2	30	5.8	65	12.6	49[19]	9.5[19]	Mauritius
5.6	12.6	2.0	4.5	5.4	12.2	0.1	0.3	15	15	13.5[15]	30.2[15]	13.1[21]	29.3[21]	Mayotte
2,397[5]	6.0[5]	1,777[5]	4.5[5]	10,821[5]	27.3[5]	1,505[5]	3.8[5]	1,682[5]	4.2[5]	5,910[5]	14.9[5]	821[5]	2.1[5]	Mexico
0.8	2.1	0.8	2.2	2.6	6.8	0.7	1.9	6.1	16.4	1.5	3.9	8.2[21]	22.0[21]	Micronesia
53	3.6	68	4.6	176	11.9	36	2.5	66	4.5	210	14.2	117[21]	7.9[21]	Moldova
83	83	0.5	3.9	2.6	20.4	2.0[83]	15.7[83]	1.8	14.3	4.3	33.8	0.7	5.5	Monaco
35	3.7	40	4.1	153	15.9	22	2.3	45	4.7	135	14.1	33[21]	3.5[21]	Mongolia
646	6.2	332	3.2	1,180	11.4	85	85	503	4.8	1,330[85]	12.8[85]	1,206[19]	11.6[19]	Morocco
43	43	14	14	14	14	14	14	14	14	97[14]	10.4[14]	—	—	Mozambique
400	2.2	495	2.7	1,781	9.7	...	...	15	15	1,485[15]	8.1[15]	270	1.5	Myanmar (Burma)
22	3.3	14	2.2	47	7.1	44	6.8	24	3.7	112	17.2	224[19]	34.3[19]	Namibia
...	...	...	...	0.1[4,20]	6.4[4,20]	—[4,20]	1.6[4,20]	1.2[4,20]	58.0[4,20]	...	...	0.2[4,20]	9.3[4,20]	Nauru
344	3.0	135	1.2	522	4.5	51	0.4	70	0.6	544	4.7	2,173	18.7	Nepal
485[34,88]	5.9[34,88]	458[34,88]	5.6[34,88]	1,580[34,88]	19.2[34,88]	1,268[34,88]	15.4[34,88]	559[34,88]	6.8[34,88]	2,042[34,88]	24.9[34,88]	453[19,34,88]	5.5[19,34,88]	Netherlands, The
5.3	6.5	5.4	6.6	19.0	23.3	10.1	12.4	6.0	7.4	16.0	19.6	13.4[19]	16.5[19]	Netherlands Antilles
6.9	8.5	3.7	4.6	11.3	14.0	4.8	6.0	9.6	12.0	14.3	17.8	17.1[19]	21.2[19]	New Caledonia
139	6.9	111	5.5	442	22.0	251	12.4	111	5.5	417	20.7	97[19]	4.8[19]	New Zealand
74[35]	3.5[35]	75[35]	3.5[35]	457[35]	21.6[35]	52[35]	2.5[35]	15	15	422[15,35]	19.9[15,35]	165[21,35]	7.8[21,35]	Nicaragua

Employment and labour (continued)

country	year	economically active population										distribution by economic sector			
		total ('000)	participation rate (%)		activity rate (%)			employment status (%)				agriculture, forestry, fishing		manufacturing; mining, quarrying; public utilities	
			female	ages 15–64	total	male	female	employers, self-employed	employees	unpaid family workers	other	number ('000)	% of econ. active	number ('000)	% of econ. active
Niger	1988[90]	2,316	20.4	55.2	31.9	51.1	13.0	51.4	5.0	40.3	3.3	1,764	76.2	73	3.1
Nigeria	1986[24]	30,766	33.3	58.8	31.1	41.1	20.9	64.6	18.8	10.7	5.9	13,259	43.1	1,401	4.6
Northern Mariana Islands	2000	44.5	54.2	84.1[10]	64.2	63.7	64.7	1.0	98.9	0.1	—	0.6	1.4	17.4[55]	39.1[55]
Norway	2003	2,373	47.0	79.3	52.0	55.6	48.4	7.0	92.5	0.3	0.2	83	3.5	327	13.8
Oman	2003[4]	737	15.4	…	31.5	47.4	11.1	11.4[54, 91]	87.8[54, 91]	…[54, 91]	0.8[54, 91]	58	7.9	84	11.4
Pakistan	2001–02[24]	42,388	16.1	51.6	29.6	48.0	9.9	39.3	39.9	20.8	—	16,366	38.6	5,719	13.5
Palau	2000	9.6	38.1	67.5[10]	50.2	56.9	42.2	1.1	98.5	0.4	—	0.7[28]	7.0[28]	0.1[17, 29]	0.7[17, 29]
Panama	2003[92]	1,251	37.1	67.1	40.1[53]	50.0[53]	30.1[53]	31.7	64.9	3.4	—	189	15.1	106	8.5
Papua New Guinea	2000[93]	2,413	47.9	73.2	46.5	46.7	46.3	…	…	…	…	1,696	70.3	37	1.5
Paraguay	2002	1,980	32.1	61.4	38.4	51.7	24.8	44.6	47.6	5.4	1.4	532	26.8	224	11.3
Peru	2002	12,892[53]	42.0[53]	72.6[53]	48.2[53]	56.2[53]	40.2[53]	38.8[35, 94, 95]	51.1[35, 94, 95]	3.8[35, 94, 95]	6.3[35, 94, 95]	2,693[77]	32.5[77]	1,091[77]	13.2[77]
Philippines	2004	35,830	37.4[53]	67.1[23]	41.5[53]	52.0[53]	31.0[53]	36.0	52.8	11.2	—	11,444	31.9	3,280	9.2
Poland	2003	16,945	46.0	64.4	44.4	49.5	39.6	21.7	73.0	5.3	—	2,508	14.8	3,089	18.2
Portugal	2003[24]	5,470	45.9	73.0	52.4	58.5	46.6	24.9	73.1	1.6	0.4	642	11.7	1,069	19.5
Puerto Rico	2002	1,356	42.6	54.3[27]	35.1[53]	42.0[53]	28.8[53]	14.3	85.1	0.6	—	23	1.7	152	11.2
Qatar	1997	280	13.5	73.6	53.7	70.8	21.0	1.2	98.7	—	0.1	7.1[5]	2.2[5]	59.1[5]	18.3[5]
Réunion	1999	298	44.8	63.9	42.2	47.3	37.2	…	…	…	…	10	3.2	13[17]	4.5[17]
Romania	2003	9,914	44.9	62.4	45.6	51.5	40.0	22.5	62.5	14.8	0.2	3,292	33.2	2,324	23.4
Russia	2003	72,212	48.6	69.6	50.1	55.3	45.5	6.9	92.6	0.1	0.4	6,651	9.2	16,468	22.8
Rwanda	2002	3,418	55.2	52.1[98]	42.0	39.4	44.4	75.6	7.4	14.9	2.1	2,951	86.3	51	1.5
St. Kitts and Nevis	1991	16.9[4]	44.4[4]	70.5[4]	41.6[4]	47.1[4]	36.3[4]	14.8[4]	81.9[4]	1.0[4]	2.3[4]	2.4[4, 45]	14.7[4, 45]	1.7[4, 45]	10.5[4, 45]
St. Lucia	2000	76.0	47.2	74.0[53]	48.6[53]	52.3[53]	45.1[53]	33.1	64.1	0.9	1.9	13.2	17.4	6.9	9.1
St. Vincent	1991	41.7	35.9	67.5	39.1	50.3	28.0	18.2	59.6	2.1	20.1	8.4	20.1	3.5	8.4
Samoa	2001	52.9	30.6	50.7[23]	30.0	39.9	19.1	…	…	…	…	26.8[4, 30]	63.0[4, 30]	1.9[4, 30]	4.5[4, 30]
San Marino	2003	20.0[99]	41.6	78.3[25]	66.2	79.2	53.8	11.5	88.5	—	—	0.1	0.4	6.3	31.5
São Tomé and Príncipe	2001	42.9[4]	33.8	43.7[32]	31.2	41.7	20.9	47.5	49.3	2.2	1.0	13.5	31.5	2.9	6.7
Saudi Arabia	2003	7,437	…	54.3	32.8	…	…	…	…	…	…	577	7.8	860	11.6
Senegal	1995	3,508	38.3	62.1[12]	42.2	52.0	32	…	…	…	…	2,719	77.5	259[13]	7.4[13]
Serbia and Montenegro[100]	2002	2,241[4]	41.8	33.8[10]	27.8	33.2	22.6	…	…	…	…	160	7.1	684	30.5
Seychelles	1997	37.4	47.6	77.8[52]	49.3	52.2	46.5	13.7	79.1	3.1	4.1	1.9	5.0	3.4	9.2
Sierra Leone	1995	1,648	31.7	54.1[12]	36.5	50.9	22.7	…	…	…	…	964	58.5	319[13]	19.4[13]
Singapore	2000	2,192	39.6	73.4	54.6	60.8[6]	42.6[6]	12.8[35, 101]	86.5[35, 101]	0.7[35, 101]	—[35, 101]	5[35, 101]	0.2[35, 101]	376[35, 101]	17.5[35, 101]
Slovakia	2003[24]	2,629	45.8	69.9	48.7	54.2	43.4	9.6	90.0	0.1	0.3	125	4.8	634	24.2
Slovenia	2003	959	45.9	66.9	48.1	53.2	43.1	9.8	86.0	4.2	—	75	7.8	279	29.1
Solomon Islands	1999	57.5[102]	27.1[102]	23.0[16, 102]	14.1[102]	19.8[102]	7.9[102]	—	33.9[103]	66.1[104]	—	7.4[77, 105]	21.8[77, 105]	4.7[77, 105]	13.9[77, 105]
Somalia	2001–02	3,906	…	56.4	52.6	…	…	…	…	…	…	2,617[28]	67.0[28]	469[29, 106]	12.0[29, 106]
South Africa	2003	16,192	46.7	54.4	36.4[53]	40.0[53]	33.0[53]	18.2	80.7	1.0	0.1	1,197	7.4	2,223	13.7
Spain	2003	18,815[24]	40.5[24]	68.5[24, 27]	46.4[24]	56.3[24]	36.9[24]	16.3[24]	81.4[24]	1.6[24]	0.7[24]	942	5.0	3,123	16.6
Sri Lanka	2000	6,709[107]	33.8[107]	60.6[7, 107]	42.0[107]	56.7[107]	27.8[107]	32.3[35]	58.2[35]	9.5[35]	—[35]	2,381[35]	31.2[35]	1,227[35]	16.1[35]
Sudan, The	1996	7,983[108]	30.6[108]	51.4[108]	33.7[108]	47.2[108]	20.4[108]	…	…	…	…	…	…	…	…
Suriname	1999[109]	85.9	36.9	55.0[7]	34.6	43.9	25.3	16.3[6]	71.7[6]	1.2[6]	1.8[6]	4.4	5.3	10.0	11.9
Swaziland	2001	392.0	39.3	60.5[12, 47]	42.3[47]	55.0[47]	30.6[47]	…	…	…	…	195.1	49.8[110]	21.9	8.2
Sweden	2003	4,450	48.0	78.1[27]	49.6	52.0	47.2	9.3	90.3	0.3	0.1	89	2.0	723	16.2
Switzerland	2002	4,180	44.5	81.3	56.2	62.9	49.7	15.1[35]	82.5[35]	2.4[35]	—[35]	165[35]	4.0[35]	662[35]	16.1[35]
Syria	2002[24]	5,460	21.4	54.9	31.9	48.9	14.0	27.7[54]	55.5[54]	16.8[54]	—[54]	1,462	26.8	661	12.1
Taiwan	2003[24]	10,076	41.4	63.9	44.8	51.5	37.8	20.7	72.1	7.2	—	696	6.9	2,633	26.1
Tajikistan	2003	1,932	46.5[47]	51.7[112]	29.1	32.5[47]	28.2[47]	…	…	…	…	1,275	66.0	115	6.0
Tanzania	2001	17,828	51.0	77.7[32]	53.0[53]	52.7[53]	53.3[53]	8.3	6.9	3.8	81.0	13,890	77.9	289	1.6
Thailand	2003	35,311	45.0	73.0[23]	55.1	60.9	49.4	34.8	40.5	24.6	0.1	15,561[4, 113]	44.9[4, 113]	5,231[4, 113]	15.1[4, 113]
Togo	1995	1,575	35.4	57.1[12]	38.1	49.7	26.7	…	…	…	…	1,059	67.2	183[13]	11.6[13]
Tonga	1996	33.9	36.0	60.4	35.3	44.6	25.8	33.7[22]	45.4[22]	16.8[22]	4.1[22]	10.0	29.3	7.3	21.4
Trinidad and Tobago	2002	586	39.1	66.9	45.3[53]	55.8[53]	35.1[53]	20.8	77.3	1.0	0.9	36	6.2	80	13.7
Tunisia	2003	3,460	25.5	48.2[23]	35.2	52.3	18.0	…	…	…	…	510[57]	21.6[57]	418[57]	17.7[57]
Turkey	2003	23,641	27.7	51.1	33.2[53]	47.6[53]	18.6[53]	29.8	50.6	19.6	—	7,165	30.3	3,847	16.3
Turkmenistan	1996	1,680	40.0	71.9[114]	36.1	43.9	28.5	…	…	…	…	892[4, 6]	48.5[4, 6]	227[4, 6]	12.3[4, 6]
Tuvalu	2002	3.2[115]	42.4	53.0[23]	33.9	39.4	28.4	…	…	…	…	…	…	…	…
Uganda	1996	9,636	39.9	68.9[12]	44.0	53.2	34.8	42.0[34]	15.0[34]	39.0[34]	4.0[34]	7,440	77.2	637[13]	6.6[13]
Ukraine	2003	22,614	48.9	65.8	47.4[53]	52.5[53]	43.1[53]	10.9	87.6	1.5	—	3,883	17.2	5,101	22.6
United Arab Emirates	2003	2,191	11.7[11]	72.6[23]	54.2	73.4[11]	19.4[11]	…	…	…	…	168	7.7	364	16.6
United Kingdom	2003	29,595	45.5	78.8[68]	49.7	55.5	44.2	11.9	87.5	0.3	0.3	420[116]	1.4[116]	3,857[116]	12.8[116]
United States	2003[24]	146,510	46.6	74.6[27]	50.4	54.7	46.2	7.5	92.4	0.1	—	2,275	1.6	18,620	12.7
Uruguay	2003[117]	1,269	45.0	72.4[67]	46.9	54.4	40.1	28.5[24]	70.2[24]	1.3[24]	—[24]	47[24]	3.8[24]	152[24]	12.3[24]
Uzbekistan	2001	9,136	…	70.4[114]	36.5	…	…	…	…	…	…	3,083	34.3	1,145	12.7
Vanuatu	1999	76.4	44.9	75.1	40.9	44.0	37.7	…	…	…	…	58.7[118]	76.8[118]	0.9	1.2
Venezuela	2002	11,674	39.6	72.1	46.4	55.7	37.0	28.0[5]	68.0[5]	0.5[5]	3.5[5]	949[24]	8.2[24]	1,249[24]	10.8[24]
Vietnam	2003	41,900	48.5[53]	…	51.8	53.9	49.7	41.4	21.9	35.9	0.8	23,100	55.1	4,900	11.7
Virgin Islands (U.S.)	2000	51.0	49.9	65.2[10]	47.0	49.3	44.8	10.8	88.7	0.5	—	0.3	0.6	2.8[55]	5.4[55]
West Bank	2003	555	16.2[121]	42.3[23]	23.6	36.3[121]	7.2[121]	33.3	55.3	11.4	—	93[121]	11.6[121]	75[121]	9.5[121]
Western Sahara	…	…	…	…	…	…	…	…	…	…	…	…	…	…	…
Yemen	1999	4,091	23.7	47.8	24.2[53]	36.2[53]	11.7[53]	33.2	41.6	0.3	24.9	1,959	48.0	165	4.0
Zambia	1996	3,507	30.3	54.5	36.1	50.9	21.7	…	…	…	…	2,322	66.2	428[43]	12.2[43]
Zimbabwe	1999	4,963	48.2	72.2[23]	42.6	44.6	40.6	45.0	40.0	15.0	—	2,800	56.4	438	8.8

[1]1979. [2]1992–93. [3]Services includes finance, real estate and public administration, defense. [4]Employed persons only. [5]2001. [6]1998. [7]Ages 15–59. [8]1987. [9]Services includes transportation, communications; trade, hotels, restaurants; and finance, real estate. [10]Over age 15. [11]1995. [12]Over age 10. [13]Manufacturing; mining, quarrying; public utilities includes construction. [14]Services includes transportation, communications; trade, hotels, restaurants; finance, real estate; and public administration, defense. [15]Services includes public administration, defense. [16]Over age 13. [17]Excludes public utilities. [18]Includes public utilities. [19]Mostly unemployed. [20]1997. [21]Unemployed. [22]1990. [23]Over age 14. [24]Excludes some or all classes or elements of the military. [25]1999. [26]Based on census. [27]Ages 16–64. [28]Includes mining, quarrying. [29]Excludes mining, quarrying. [30]1991. [31]Based on July labour force survey. [32]Over age 9. [33]2004. [34]2002. [35]2003. [36]Ages 15–60. [37]Unemployed, not previously employed. [38]Ages 12–55. [39]Excludes ages 11 and under. [40]Ages 12–59. [41]Republic of Cyprus only. [42]Ages 16–66. [43]Manufacturing; mining, quarrying; public utilities includes construction. [44]Urban population only. [45]1994. [46]Employers, self-employed includes unpaid family workers. [47]1996. [48]Services includes public utilities. [49]Excludes Abkhazia and South Ossetia. [50]Ages 15–64 (male) and 15–59 (female). [51]Based on economically active population age 15–64 of 7,480,000. [52]Ages 15–62. [53]Estimate calculated in part from a secondary source (often for total population calculated from the U.S. Bureau of the Census International Database). [54]2000. [55]Payroll employment only; excludes proprietors, the self-employed, and unpaid family workers. [56]Transportation, communications includes public utilities. [57]1989. [58]Excludes Alderney and Sark. [59]Excludes the departments of Islas de la Bahía and Gracias a Dios. [60]Ages 16–74. [61]1999–2000. [62]Self-employed only. [63]Workers receiving periodic wages or salaries. [64]Not self-employed agricultural/other labourers in rural areas and casual labourers in urban areas. [65]Excludes Kurdish Autonomous Region. [66]1988. [67]Ages 14–64. [68]Ages 16–64 (male) and 16–59 (female). [69]Nearly all "village work" (subsistence fishing and

construction number ('000)	construction % of econ. active	transportation, communications number ('000)	transportation, communications % of econ. active	trade, hotels, restaurants number ('000)	trade, hotels, restaurants % of econ. active	finance, real estate number ('000)	finance, real estate % of econ. active	public administration, defense number ('000)	public administration, defense % of econ. active	services number ('000)	services % of econ. active	other number ('000)	other % of econ. active	country
14	0.6	15	0.6	209	9.0	2	0.1	15	15	123[15]	5.3[15]	117	5.0	Niger
546	1.8	1,112	3.6	7,417	24.1	120	0.4	15	15	4,902[15]	15.9[15]	2,009[19]	6.5[19]	Nigeria
2.8	6.3	1.4[55]	3.3[55]	9.6	21.5	1.0	2.3	2.6	5.8	7.3	16.5	1.7[19]	3.9[19]	Northern Mariana Islands
159	6.7	149	6.3	407	17.2	272	11.5	149	6.3	720	30.3	107	4.5	Norway
118	16.0	28	3.8	109	14.8	25	3.4	163	22.1	137	18.6	14	2.0	Oman
2,353	5.6	2,295	5.4	5,776	13.6	346	0.8	15	15	6,027[15]	14.2[15]	3,506[21]	8.3[21]	Pakistan
1.2	12.8	0.5[18]	5.2[18]	2.9	29.9	0.4	3.7	1.2	12.1	2.5	26.3	0.2[21]	2.3[21]	Palau
80	6.4	86	6.9	248	19.8	66	5.3	74	5.9	231	18.5	171[19]	13.7[19]	Panama
48	2.0	25	1.0	358	14.8	31	1.3	32	1.3	86	3.6	100[19]	4.1[19]	Papua New Guinea
142	7.2	86	4.3	417	21.1	68	3.4	87	4.4	370	18.7	55	2.8	Paraguay
308[77]	3.7[77]	364[77]	4.4[77]	1,352[77]	16.3[77]	197[77]	2.4[77]	15	15	2,287[15, 77]	27.6[15, 77]	—	—	Peru
1,654	4.6	2,464	6.9	6,706	18.7	1,039	2.9	1,414	3.9	3,621	10.1	4,209[19]	11.8[19]	Philippines
803	4.7	823	4.9	2,191	12.9	975	5.8	853	5.0	2,373	14.0	3,329[21]	19.6[21]	Poland
584	10.7	214	3.9	1,034	18.9	349	6.4	339	6.2	895	16.4	342[21]	6.3[21]	Portugal
85	6.3	42	3.1	250[96]	18.4[96]	44	3.2	15	15	595[15, 97]	43.9[15, 97]	166[21]	12.2[21]	Puerto Rico
59.3[5]	18.4[5]	9.9[5]	3.1[5]	42.6[5]	13.2[5]	10.1[5]	3.1[5]	43.8[5]	13.6[5]	76.1[5]	23.6[5]	14.9[5, 19]	4.6[5, 19]	Qatar
11[18]	3.7[18]	5	1.8	25	8.3	16	5.4	39	13.1	54	18.3	124[21]	41.7[21]	Réunion
426	4.3	461	4.7	981	9.9	233	2.3	530	5.3	975	9.8	692[21]	7.0[21]	Romania
4,316	6.0	5,957	8.3	11,024	15.3	4,530	6.3	4,622	6.4	12,915	17.9	5,729[19]	7.9[19]	Russia
42	1.2	30	0.9	94	2.8	11	0.3	26	0.7	156	4.6	57[19]	1.7[19]	Rwanda
1.7[4, 45]	10.5[4, 45]	0.5[4, 45]	3.2[4, 45]	3.4[4, 45]	20.3[4, 45]	85	85	2.7[4, 45]	16.5[4, 45]	3.7[4, 45, 85]	22.4[4, 45, 85]	0.3[4, 45]	2.1[4, 45]	St. Kitts and Nevis
6.0	7.9	4.1	5.4	17.9	23.6	2.3	3.0	7.5	9.9	4.7	6.2	13.4[19]	17.6[19]	St. Lucia
3.5	8.5	2.3	5.5	6.5	15.7	1.4	3.4	15	15	7.7[15]	18.5[15]	8.3[21]	20.0[21]	St. Vincent
2.0[4, 30]	4.8[4, 30]	1.9[4, 30]	4.5[4, 30]	1.9[4, 30]	4.4[4, 30]	1.4	3.2	15	15	6.6[4, 15, 30]	15.6[4, 15, 30]	—	—	Samoa
1.7	8.4	0.5	2.4	3.2	16.1	0.7	3.4	2.1	10.6	4.8	24.0	0.7[21]	3.2[21]	San Marino
4.4	10.2	0.8	1.8	8.8	20.5	...	...	3.3	7.7	9.2	21.5	—	—	São Tomé and Príncipe
1,084	14.6	308	4.1	1,064	14.3	367	4.9	929	12.5	2,248	30.2	—	—	Saudi Arabia
13	13	14	14	14	14	14	14	14	14	530[14]	15.1[14]	—	—	Senegal
140	6.3	138	6.2	418	18.7	72	3.2	184	8.2	426	19.0	18	0.8	Serbia and Montenegro[100]
2.4	6.4	3.6	9.5	6.0	16.0	1.0	2.6	15	15	12.8[15]	34.3[15]	6.4[19]	17.0[19]	Seychelles
13	13	14	14	14	14	14	14	14	14	365[14]	22.1[14]	—	—	Sierra Leone
115[35, 101]	5.3[35, 101]	216[35, 101]	10.0[35, 101]	425[35, 101]	19.8[35, 101]	348[35, 101]	16.2[35, 101]	148[35, 101]	6.9[35, 101]	400[35, 101]	18.6[35, 101]	116[19, 35, 101]	5.4[19, 35, 101]	Singapore
195	7.4	149	5.7	349	13.3	152	5.8	160	6.1	397	15.1	462[19]	17.6[19]	Slovakia
52	5.4	59	6.2	154	16.1	75	7.8	50	5.2	146	15.2	69[19]	7.2[19]	Slovenia
1.2[77, 105]	3.5[77, 105]	1.9[77, 105]	5.5[77, 105]	4.6[77, 105]	13.6[77, 105]	1.2[77, 105]	3.5[77, 105]	4.3[77, 105]	12.5[77, 105]	8.8[77, 105]	25.7[77, 105]	—	—	Solomon Islands
...	...	14	14	15	14	14	14	14	14	82[14]	21.0[14]	—	—	Somalia
626	3.9	563	3.5	2,451	15.1	1,079	6.7	15	15	3,469[15]	21.4[15]	4,581[19]	28.3[19]	South Africa
1,985	10.5	1,027	5.5	3,681	19.6	1,769	9.4	1,097	5.8	3,069	16.3	2,128[19]	11.3[19]	Spain
397[35]	5.2[35]	376[35]	4.9[35]	988[35]	12.9[35]	217[35]	2.8[35]	560[35]	7.3[35]	544[35]	7.1[35]	954[19, 35]	12.5[19, 35]	Sri Lanka
...	...	...	...	...	...	...	...	...	...	...	...	...	...	Sudan, The
5.0	5.9	5.8	6.9	17.3	20.4	4.5	5.4	15	15	27.3[15]	32.3[15]	14.7[19]	17.4[19]	Suriname
5.8	1.5	111	111	12.5[111]	3.2[111]	7.5	1.9	15	15	25.3[15]	6.5[15]	123.9	31.6	Swaziland
239	5.4	111	111	802[111]	18.0[111]	593	13.3	243	5.5	1,541	34.6	221	5.0	Sweden
247[35]	6.0[35]	241[35]	5.9[35]	718[35]	17.4[35]	675[35]	16.4[35]	218[35]	5.3[35]	1,019[35]	24.7[35]	175[35]	4.2[35]	Switzerland
634	11.6	265	4.9	724	13.3	61	1.1	15	15	1,014[15]	18.6[15]	638[21]	11.7[21]	Syria
702	7.0	484	4.8	2,283	22.7	727	7.2	369	3.7	1,680	16.7	503[21]	5.0[21]	Taiwan
31	1.6	45	2.3	88	4.6	...	...	28	1.4	296	15.3	54[19]	2.8[19]	Tajikistan
152	0.9	112	0.6	1,263	7.1	26	0.1	15	15	1,183[15]	6.6[15]	913[21]	5.1[21]	Tanzania
1,614[4, 113]	4.7[4, 113]	988[4, 113]	2.8[4, 113]	7,160[4, 113]	20.6[4, 113]	846[4, 113]	2.4[4, 113]	903[4, 113]	2.6[4, 113]	2,351[4, 113]	6.8[4, 113]	234[4, 113]	0.1[4, 113]	Thailand
13	13	14	14	14	14	14	14	14	14	331[14]	21.0[14]	—	—	Togo
0.5	1.5`	1.2	3.6	2.5	7.4	0.7	1.9	3.7	10.9	3.6	10.7	4.5	13.3	Tonga
69	11.8	42	7.1	95	16.1	44	7.5	15	15	158[15]	27.0[15]	62[19]	10.6[19]	Trinidad and Tobago
248[57]	10.5[57]	96[57]	4.1[57]	217[57]	9.2[57]	15[57]	0.7[57]	15	15	444[15, 57]	18.8[15, 57]	412[19, 57]	17.5[19, 57]	Tunisia
965	4.1	1,022	4.3	4,052	17.1	738	3.1	1,177	5.0	2,181	9.2	2,496[19]	10.6[19]	Turkey
108[4, 6]	5.9[4, 6]	914[4, 6]	4.9[4, 6]	116[4, 6]	6.3[4, 6]	13[4, 6]	0.7[4, 6]	294[4, 6]	1.6[4, 6]	334[4, 6]	18.2[4, 6]	29	1.6	Turkmenistan
...	...	...	...	...	...	...	...	...	...	...	...	...	...	Tuvalu
13	13	14	14	14	14	14	14	14	14	1,559[14]	16.2[14]	—	—	Uganda
1,047	4.6	1,494	6.6	3,071	13.6	855	3.8	1,188	5.3	3,915	17.3	2,060	9.1	Ukraine
362	16.5	134	6.1	528	24.1	89	4.1	248	11.3	298	13.6	—	—	United Arab Emirates
2,111[116]	7.0[116]	1,813[116]	6.0[116]	7,040[116]	23.2[116]	5,828[116]	19.2[116]	15	15	9,255[15, 116]	30.5[15, 116]	—	—	United Kingdom
10,138	6.9	9,445	6.4	29,727	20.3	23,627	16.1	6,243	4.3	37,662	25.7	8,774[21]	6.0[21]	United States
70[24]	5.6[24]	61[24]	4.9[24]	225[24]	18.2[24]	91[24]	7.3[24]	91[24]	7.4[24]	294[24]	23.7[24]	209[21, 24]	16.8[21, 24]	Uruguay
676	7.5	382	4.3	754	8.4	3	3	3	3	2,042[23]	22.7[23]	901	10.0	Uzbekistan
1.5	2.0	1.6	2.1	4.1	5.3	0.7	1.0	2.5	3.3	5.1	6.7	1.3[21]	1.6[21]	Vanuatu
776[24]	6.7[24]	704[24]	6.1[24]	2,585[24]	22.4[24]	482[24]	4.2[24]	15	15	2,933[15, 24]	25.5[15, 24]	1,844[19, 24]	16.0[19, 24]	Venezuela
119	119	119	119	119	119	119	119	119	119	13,200[119]	31.5[119]	700[21]	1.7[21]	Vietnam
4.9	9.6	4.2[55]	8.3[55]	120	120	2.3	4.6	4.9	9.7	27.1[120]	53.0[120]	4.5[19]	8.8[19]	Virgin Islands (U.S.)
78[121]	9.8[121]	34[121]	4.3[121]	119[121]	14.9[121]	13[121]	1.7[121]	71[121]	9.0[121]	101[121]	12.8[121]	210[19, 121]	26.4[19, 121]	West Bank
...	...	...	...	...	...	...	...	...	...	...	...	...	...	Western Sahara
238	5.8	123	3.0	437	10.7	30	0.7	358	8.7	310	7.6	470[19]	11.5[19]	Yemen
43	43	14	14	14	14	14	14	14	14	757[14]	21.6[14]	—	—	Zambia
106	2.1	102	2.1	333	6.7	121	2.4	15	15	579[15]	11.7[15]	485[19]	9.8[19]	Zimbabwe

agriculture). [70]Unspecified. [71]1986. [72]Includes not adequately defined, military personnel, and unemployed not previously employed. [73]Employed within Liechtenstein only, excluding inward commuters. [74]Employed within Liechtenstein only, including inward commuters. [75]Includes resident foreigners; excludes workers from neighbouring countries. [76]Includes resident foreigners and workers from neighbouring countries. [77]1993. [78]Self-employed and unpaid family workers. [79]Includes employers. [80]Excludes 123,000 unemployed, not previously employed. [81]Includes resident foreign workers; excludes c. 25,000 nonresident foreign workers (mostly French). [82]Ages 17–64. [83]Finance, real estate includes construction. [84]Ages 16–59. [85]Services includes finance, real estate. [86]Nauruan population only. [87]Includes 1,987,000 workers age 5–14. [88]Ages 15–64 only. [89]Ages 20–69. [90]Excludes nomadic population. [91]Omanis only. [92]August labour force survey. [93]De facto population. [94]Metropolitan Lima only. [95]Third quarter. [96]Excludes hotels. [97]Includes hotels. [98]Over age 5. [99]All data include cross border workers. [100]Excludes Kosovo. [101]De jure population. [102]Paid workers only. [103]Paid workers as percent of all workers. [104]Unpaid workers as percent of all workers. [105]Employees of monetary sector only. [106]Includes construction. [107]Excludes Northern and Eastern provinces. [108]Official estimate. [109]Paramaribo only. [110]Represents informally foreigners; excludes workers (mostly in agriculture). [111]Trade, hotels, restaurants includes transportation, communications. [112]Ages 15–62 (male) and 15–57 (female). [113]Over age 12. [114]Ages 16–59 (male) and 16–54 (female). [115]Total of wage earners, unpaid workers, and subsistence workers. [116]March 2004; number of workforce jobs in sector. [117]Urban areas only. [118]Includes not stated (mostly subsistence workers). [119]Services includes construction; transportation, communications; trade, hotels, restaurants; finance, real estate; and public administration, defense. [120]Services includes trade, hotels, restaurants. [121]Includes the Gaza Strip.

Crops and livestock

This table provides comparative data for selected categories of agricultural production for the countries of the world. The data are taken mainly from the United Nations Food and Agriculture Organization's (FAO's) annual *Production Yearbook* and the online FAOSTAT statistics database (http://apps.fao.org/default.htm).

The FAO depends largely on questionnaires supplied to each country for its statistics, but, where no official or semiofficial responses are returned, the FAO makes estimates, using incomplete, unofficial, or other similarly limited data. And, although the FAO provides standardized guidelines upon which many nations have organized their data collection systems and methods, persistent, often traditional, variations in standards of coverage, methodology, and reporting periods reduce the comparability of statistics that *can* be supplied on such forms. FAO data are based on calendar-year periods; that is, data for any particular crop refer to the calendar year in which the harvest (or the bulk of the harvest) occurred.

In spite of the often tragic food shortages in a number of countries in recent years, worldwide agricultural production is probably more often underreported than overreported. Many countries do not report complete domestic production. Some countries, for example, report only crops that are sold commercially and ignore subsistence crops produced for family or communal consumption, or barter; others may limit reporting to production for export only, to holdings above a certain size, or represent a sampling only.

Methodological problems attach to much smaller elements of the agricultural whole, however. The FAO's cereals statistics relate, ideally, to weight or volume of crops harvested for dry grain (excluding cereal crops used for grazing, harvested for hay, or harvested green for food, feed, or silage). Some countries, however, collect the basic data they report to the FAO on sown or cultivated areas instead and calculate production statistics from estimates of yield. Millet and sorghum, which in many European and North American countries are used primarily as livestock or poultry feed, may be reportable by such countries as animal fodder only, while elsewhere many nations use the same grains for human consumption and report them as cereals. Statistics for tropical fruits are frequently not compiled by producing countries, and coverage is not uniform, with some countries reporting only commercial fruits and others including those consumed for

Crops and livestock

country	grains production ('000 metric tons) 1989–91 average	grains production 2001	grains yield (kg/hectare) 1989–91 average	grains yield 2001	roots and tubers[a] production ('000 metric tons) 1989–91 average	roots and tubers production 2001	roots and tubers yield (kg/hectare) 1989–91 average	roots and tubers yield 2001	pulses[b] production ('000 metric tons) 1989–91 average	pulses production 2001	pulses yield (kg/hectare) 1989–91 average	pulses yield 2001	fruits[c] production ('000 metric tons) 1989–91 average	fruits production 2001	vegetables[d] production ('000 metric tons) 1989–91 average	vegetables production 2001
Afghanistan	2,754	2,046	1,200	978	217	230	16,291	16,429	32	50	913	1,351	644	615	466	652
Albania	792	581	2,609	2,609	88	180	8,409	14,400	20	32	729	922	153	132	377	653
Algeria	2,481	2,502	854	856	962	1,200	8,862	16,000	49	26	477	376	1,026	1,440	1,867	2,565
American Samoa	...	...	...	...	2	2	3,721	3,361	...	...	...	...	1	1	...	...
Andorra	...	...	...	...	...	...	...	...	...	...	...	...	...	...	...	...
Angola	298	585	338	638	1,815	3,504	4,220	6,295	35	75	273	375	414	450	250	271
Antigua and Barbuda	...	—	1,921	1,607	—	—	5,171	4,811	1	—	1,199	676	9	8	2	2
Argentina	19,988	38,372	2,343	3,387	2,279	2,555	18,183	23,018	249	329	1,105	1,140	5,915	7,781	2,802	3,163
Armenia	284[1]	374	1,642[1]	1,858	385[1]	364	12,564[1]	11,459	4[1]	3	1,876[1]	1,655	266[1]	202	485[1]	430
Aruba	...	...	...	...	...	...	...	...	...	...	...	...	...	...	...	...
Australia	21,390	36,487	1,665	2,032	1,127	1,256	28,301	29,658	1,530	2,597	1,025	1,190	2,345	3,139	1,504	1,950
Austria	5,115	4,538	5,443	5,516	810	695	24,907	26,604	119	69	3,555	2,411	946	1,090	455	613
Azerbaijan	1,162[1]	1,994	1,788[1]	2,648	153[1]	575	8,190[1]	10,419	13[1]	21	2,129[1]	2,901	800[1]	548	548[1]	1,198
Bahamas, The	1	—	1,522	2,171	1	1	6,900	8,357	1	1	1,261	1,254	12	25	27	22
Bahrain	—	—	—	—	—	—	14,629	11,000	—	—	836	1,091	14	22	10	10
Bangladesh	28,032	41,176	2,530	3,484	1,643	3,311	9,744	11,655	512	381	699	768	1,329	1,360	1,332	1,804
Barbados	2	2	2,656	2,500	6	7	9,271	9,024	...	...	...	...	3	3	7	12
Belarus	6,771[1]	4,823	2,602[1]	1,859	9,623[1]	8,700	12,967[1]	12,000	172[1]	227	1,619[1]	987	561[1]	271	972[1]	1,505
Belgium[2]	2,236	2,430	6,094	7,585	1,838	2,497	37,421	39,016	18	10	4,062	3,607	372	742	1,438	1,771
Belize	28	48	1,640	1,979	4	4	21,838	20,263	3	4	763	818	134	363	5	6
Benin	566	878	860	1,043	2,102	4,627	9,354	10,863	60	92	552	673	180	223	211	239
Bermuda	...	...	...	...	1	1	20,985	20,735	633	3,559	1,584	1,358	—	—	3	3
Bhutan	102	159	1,089	1,456	52	56	9,910	10,750	2	2	800	800	64	65	9	10
Bolivia	845	1,279	1,363	1,725	1,155	1,524	5,935	7,558	30	33	1,079	1,030	853	1,342	383	588
Bosnia and Herzegovina	963[1]	1,031	3,560[1]	2,781	300[1]	320	7,838[1]	8,000	18[1]	13	1,121[1]	1,054	122[1]	81	550[1]	649
Botswana	60	22	306	117	7	13	5,385	7,222	18	17	562	515	11	2	17	17
Brazil	37,702	56,329	1,868	3,095	27,229	27,595	12,567	14,053	2,471	2,464	473	702	30,472	31,732	5,605	7,062
Brunei	1	—	1,793	1,667	1	2	3,344	4,286	...	...	...	...	5	5	8	9
Bulgaria	8,872	5,238	4,121	2,544	495	450	11,987	8,491	89	25	1,021	756	1,576	703	1,792	1,439
Burkina Faso	1,975	2,796	717	867	70	86	5,968	8,641	56	59	742	801	71	73	229	229
Burundi	296	272	1,362	1,311	1,420	1,616	6,800	7,033	335	284	1,020	946	1,638	1,633	210	250
Cambodia	2,591	4,273	1,431	2,083	105	176	5,366	7,799	13	17	500	631	239	325	472	470
Cameroon	890	1,441	1,181	1,801	2,370	2,795	7,700	6,267	72	176	534	725	1,876	2,453	499	831
Canada	52,915	44,251	2,470	2,417	2,903	4,030	24,683	24,589	34	16	524	443	752	785	2,020	2,304
Cape Verde	10	21	287	429	18	9	9,099	7,890	9	3	184	86	15	15	7	16
Central African Republic	103	195	939	1,289	816	1,023	3,551	3,571	16	31	941	1,069	202	260	60	83
Chad	677	1,156	576	501	628	697	4,692	4,741	37	56	722	693	109	113	74	95
Chile	2,997	3,116	3,862	4,936	858	1,218	14,315	18,957	131	105	1,156	1,748	2,596	4,295	1,943	2,579
China	390,171	404,126	4,192	4,904	141,074	184,588	14,960	17,512	4,575	4,588	1,354	1,587	21,900	67,767	128,265	302,271
Colombia	4,090	3,731	2,471	3,268	4,342	5,281	11,973	13,040	167	169	691	1,118	5,024	6,666	1,433	1,955
Comoros	19	20	1,289	1,306	59	68	4,843	4,945	7	14	833	992	54	60	5	6
Congo, Dem. Rep. of the	1,471	1,590	799	782	19,477	16,125	7,913	7,961	204	160	602	534	3,321	1,741	513	426
Congo, Rep. of the	11	8	722	783	719	904	6,708	8,830	6	8	704	772	132	221	38	40
Costa Rica	262	322	2,775	3,957	172	284	20,840	16,637	...	...	...	...	2,121	3,494	118	384
Côte d'Ivoire	1,225	1,808	874	1,228	4,365	5,308	5,683	5,501	8	8	667	667	1,611	2,029	450	563
Croatia	2,562[1]	3,018	4,124[1]	4,469	517[1]	634	8,078[1]	9,900	22[1]	14	1,942[1]	1,166	538[1]	541	269[1]	466
Cuba	547	556	2,346	2,635	666	890	4,398	7,236	13	25	260	455	1,424	1,268	509	407
Cyprus	107	125	1,901	2,443	187	123	22,329	18,653	2	1	967	1,377	369	283	125	147
Czech Republic	6,629[3]	7,432	4,057[3]	4,569	1,652[3]	1,590	18,819[3]	29,285	176[3]	95	2,379[3]	2,374	496[3]	428	539[3]	464
Denmark	9,211	9,358	5,887	6,039	1,394	1,600	36,010	42,105	481	182	4,303	2,933	88	89	304	309
Djibouti	—	—	1,524	1,625	...	...	...	...	...	...	...	...	1	3	22	24
Dominica	—	—	1,354	1,308	29	27	9,292	9,286	—	—	410	417	97	72	6	6
Dominican Republic	531	763	3,951	4,179	243	278	7,085	7,629	98	54	937	880	1,560	1,363	245	395
East Timor[4]	...	...	...	...	...	...	...	2,531	...	...	...	...	...	1	...	...
Ecuador	1,422	2,084	1,718	2,257	500	1,059	6,596	9,529	40	39	489	552	4,446	9,344	369	414
Egypt	12,672	19,464	5,551	7,269	1,904	2,157	21,762	24,316	542	513	2,951	2,980	4,456	7,282	8,923	14,118
El Salvador	785	751	1,840	1,888	38	88	15,090	17,050	55	74	802	870	290	272	146	148
Equatorial Guinea	...	...	...	...	89	105	3,070	2,853	...	...	...	...	32	51	...	...
Eritrea	156[3]	197	523[3]	665	124[3]	125	3,180[3]	3,205	42[3]	56	561[3]	610	43[3]	4	30[3]	28
Estonia	638[1]	570	1,687[1]	1,747	590[1]	400	13,730[1]	13,841	11[1]	8	1,487[1]	1,453	331[1]	29	761[1]	44

subsistence as well. Figures on wild fruits and berries are seldom included in national reports at all. FAO vegetable statistics include vegetables and melons grown for human consumption only. Some countries do not make this distinction in their reports, and some exclude the production of kitchen gardens and small family plots, although in certain countries, such small-scale production may account for 20 to 40 percent of total output.

Livestock statistics may be distorted by the timing of country reports. Ireland, for example, takes a livestock enumeration in December that is reported the following year and that appears low against data for otherwise comparable countries because of the slaughter and export of animals at the close of the grazing season. It balances this, however, with a June enumeration, when numbers tend to be high. Milk production as defined by the FAO includes whole fresh milk, excluding milk sucked by young animals but including amounts fed by farmers or ranchers to livestock, but national practices vary. Certain countries do not distinguish between milk cows and other cattle, so that yield per dairy cow must be estimated. Some countries do not report egg production statistics (here given of metric tons), and external estimates must be based on the numbers of chickens and reported or assumed egg-laying rates. Other countries report egg production by number, and this must be converted to weight, using conversion factors specific to the makeup by species of national poultry flocks.

Metric system units used in the table may be converted to English system units as follow:

metric tons × 1.1023 = short tons
kilograms × 2.2046 = pounds
kilograms per hectare × 0.8922 = pounds per acre.

The notes that follow, keyed by references in the table headings, provide further definitional information.

a. Includes such crops as potatoes and cassava.
b. Includes beans and peas harvested for dry grain only. Does not include green beans and green peas.
c. Excludes melons.
d. Includes melons, green beans, and green peas.
e. From cows only.
f. From chickens only.

livestock														country
cattle		sheep		hogs		chickens		milk[e]		yield		eggs[f]		
stock ('000 head)		stock ('000 head)		stock ('000 head)		stock ('000 head)		production ('000 metric tons)		(kg/animal)		production (metric tons)		
1989–91 average	2001	1989–91 average	2001	1989–91 average	2001	1989–91 average	2001	1989–91 average	2001	1989–91 average	2001	1989–91 average	2001	
1,600	2,000	14,173	11,000	...	...	7,073	6,000	507	1,200	633	1,200	14,000	18,000	Afghanistan
657	690	1,645	1,941	183	81	4,864	4,000	403	815	1,384	1,701	15,000	21,000	Albania
1,366	1,600	17,301	19,300	5	6	73,000	110,000	595	1,150	940	1,278	122,000	145,000	Algeria
—	—	—	—	11	11	34	...	—	—	800	800	...	...	American Samoa
...	...	...	...	...	...	...	...	...	...	...	...	...	...	Andorra
3,117	4,150	240	350	802	800	6,117	7,000	151	195	483	483	4,000	4,000	Angola
16	14	12	12	2	2	87	...	6	6	935	968	...	...	Antigua and Barbuda
52,633	50,669	28,139	13,500	2,533	4,200	67,000	110,000	6,375	9,600	2,621	3,918	298,000	325,000	Argentina
522[1]	520	858[1]	497	130[1]	69	27,330[1]	4,000	393[1]	450	1,516[1]	1,699	12,028[1]	19,000	Armenia
...	...	1	—	1	—	50	—	...	...	...	...	...	...	Aruba
23,086	30,500	165,046	120,000	2,617	2,433	56,000	96,000	6,514	11,398	3,945	5,167	178,000	149,000	Australia
2,546	2,118	284	358	3,762	3,427	14,000	11,000	3,344	3,340	3,805	4,703	94,000	97,000	Austria
1,726[1]	2,098	4,714[1]	5,560	84[1]	19	211,340[1]	14,000	811[1]	1,018	1,115[1]	1,015	35,282[1]	29,000	Azerbaijan
1	1	7	6	5	5	1,733	4,000	1	1	1,000	1,000	...	1,000	Bahamas, The
13	11	20	18	...	...	1,000	...	19	14	2,602	1,970	3,000	3,000	Bahrain
23,173	24,000	871	1,132	...	...	90,253	140,000	741	763	206	206	57,000	133,000	Bangladesh
32	21	40	41	29	33	3,437	4,000	14	8	1,784	1,688	2,000	1,000	Barbados
6,216[1]	4,084	325[1]	130	4,397[1]	3,431	486,430[1]	32,000	5,660[1]	4,300	2,573[1]	2,337	195,283[1]	190,000	Belarus
3,264	3,106	174	155	6,439	7,349	33,000	38,000	3,875	3,700	4,313	5,498	168,000	197,000	Belgium[2]
57	57	4	3	26	24	987	1,000	7	7	1,159	1,050	1,000	2,000	Belize
1,029	1,550	869	645	479	470	23,333	23,000	15	21	130	116	17,000	17,000	Benin
1	1	...	...	1	1	75	...	1	1	2,901	3,857	...	...	Bermuda
382	355	49	58	69	75	250	...	29	29	257	257	...	...	Bhutan
5,542	6,576	7,573	8,752	2,160	2,800	23,697	74,000	113	232	1,399	1,657	47,000	37,000	Bolivia
633[1]	440	700[1]	640	300[1]	330	5,167[1]	5,000	383[1]	460	733[1]	1,637	15,333[1]	15,000	Bosnia and Herzegovina
2,250	1,700	317	370	16	7	2,080	4,000	113	102	350	350	2,000	3,000	Botswana
147,797	176,000	20,061	15,000	33,643	29,424	557,282	1,006,000	15,004	22,580	780	1,407	1,244,000	1,538,000	Brazil
2	2	...	...	17	6	2,254	5,000	...	...	...	...	3,000	4,000	Brunei
1,548	635	8,226	2,286	4,219	1,144	34,161	15,000	1,999	1,290	3,370	3,000	129,000	81,000	Bulgaria
3,938	4,800	5,048	6,782	507	622	17,027	22,000	101	163	156	172	15,000	18,000	Burkina Faso
431	315	352	230	92	70	4,000	5,000	33	19	350	350	3,000	3,000	Burundi
2,178	2,924	...	...	1,601	2,118	9,000	15,000	17	21	170	170	9,000	12,000	Cambodia
4,660	5,900	3,290	3,800	1,288	1,350	17,333	30,000	116	125	500	500	12,000	14,000	Cameroon
11,165	13,700	595	840	10,505	12,600	110,000	158,000	7,915	8,170	5,800	7,192	319,000	363,000	Canada
18	22	6	8	104	200	1,000	...	2	5	447	638	1,000	2,000	Cape Verde
2,529	3,273	134	220	434	680	3,000	4,000	46	62	224	264	1,000	1,000	Central African Republic
4,298	5,900	1,926	2,400	14	22	3,950	5,000	116	159	270	270	4,000	4,000	Chad
3,402	3,566	4,803	4,200	1,144	2,500	32,000	78,000	1,353	2,200	1,559	1,375	96,000	110,000	Chile
79,284	106,175	112,299	133,160	360,543	454,420	2,127,000	3,771,000	4,411	9,570	1,562	1,902	6,701,000	19,884,000	China
24,383	27,000	2,547	2,300	2,627	2,750	58,000	110,000	4,017	5,980	963	1,000	237,000	355,000	Colombia
45	52	16	21	...	...	392	440	4	4	500	500	1,000	1,000	Comoros
1,466	761	930	911	1,034	1,000	25,000	21,000	8	5	851	825	8,000	7,000	Congo, Dem. Rep. of the
65	93	104	96	45	46	2,000	2,000	1	1	500	500	1,000	1,000	Congo, Rep. of the
2,181	1,220	2	...	270	430	14,000	17,000	431	730	1,308	1,327	19,000	39,000	Costa Rica
1,101	1,476	1,137	1,451	361	336	24,333	29,000	18	22	150	146	13,000	18,000	Côte d'Ivoire
566[1]	417	503[1]	539	1,264[1]	1,234	9,828[1]	11,000	643[1]	616	1,903[1]	2,404	47,731[1]	46,000	Croatia
4,822	4,038	385	310	2,567	2,700	27,876	13,000	995	614	1,782	1,163	...	68,000	Cuba
50	54	300	246	281	418	3,000	3,000	...	...	4,746	6,004	8,000	11,000	Cyprus
2,337[3]	1,520	225[3]	90	4,335[3]	3,594	255,743[3]	15,000	3,294[3]	2,736	4,015[3]	5,658	155,163[3]	188,000	Czech Republic
2,227	1,923	164	145	9,390	12,125	16,000	22,000	4,710	4,660	3,832	...	83,000	77,000	Denmark
188	270	433	465	...	...	...	...	7	8	350	350	...	...	Djibouti
14	13	7	8	4	5	31,000	47,000	7	6	902	910	120	...	Dominica
2,283	2,160	115	106	543	566	31,227	...	345	410	1,701	1,356	35,000	65,000	Dominican Republic
69	175	...	...	...	...	...	...	98	140	...	...	...	...	East Timor[4]
4,351	5,578	1,417	1,976	2,213	2,392	52,000	138,000	1,529	2,192	2,092	2,125	51,000	57,000	Ecuador
2,771	3,810	3,310	4,545	24	30	38,000	88,000	974	1,679	890	1,112	144,000	200,000	Egypt
1,213	13,292	5	5	305	150	52,000	8,000	292	395	1,083	790	46,000	53,000	El Salvador
5	5	35	38	5	6	228	...	...	...	...	...	...	...	Equatorial Guinea
1,279[3]	2,200	1,515[3]	1,570	...	...	2,750[3]	1,000	303[3]	52	192[3]	196	37,950[3]	2,000	Eritrea
595[1]	260	116[1]	29	588[1]	300	3,965[1]	2,000	833[1]	687	3,374[1]	7,516	24,071[1]	17,000	Estonia

Crops and livestock (continued)

country	grains production ('000 metric tons) 1989–91 avg	grains production 2001	grains yield (kg/hectare) 1989–91 avg	grains yield 2001	roots and tubers[a] production ('000 metric tons) 1989–91 avg	roots and tubers production 2001	roots and tubers yield (kg/hectare) 1989–91 avg	roots and tubers yield 2001	pulses[b] production ('000 metric tons) 1989–91 avg	pulses production 2001	pulses yield (kg/hectare) 1989–91 avg	pulses yield 2001	fruits[c] production ('000 metric tons) 1989–91 avg	fruits production 2001	vegetables[d] production ('000 metric tons) 1989–91 avg	vegetables production 2001
Ethiopia	5,760[3]	8,732	1,143[3]	1,172	3,770[3]	4,305	6,912[3]	7,334	638[3]	1,050	743[3]	848	228[3]	220	666[3]	574
Faroe Islands	...	...	...	...	1	2	13,663	13,636	14	12	2,549	2,167	...	...	...	...
Fiji	30	17	2,289	2,487	36	85	3,739	10,872	...	...	773	1,000	13	15	9	18
Finland	3,845	3,670	3,360	3,165	845	750	20,656	25,000	...	...	...	...	22	32	205	251
France	57,683	60,477	6,240	6,751	5,213	6,536	29,853	40,346	3,310	1,890	4,735	3,900	10,561	11,169	7,628	7,805
French Guiana	22	20	4,199	2,601	32	14	10,178	5,906	...	...	...	...	7	15	9	25
French Polynesia	...	...	...	...	11	12	12,667	12,778	...	...	...	...	8	7	7	7
Gabon	23	27	1,599	1,636	378	447	5,424	5,721	...	...	639	667	268	294	30	35
Gambia, The	99	190	1,078	1,286	6	8	3,000	3,000	4	6	267	275	4	4	8	9
Gaza Strip	1	1	510	529	23	35	22,624	21,875	...	...	...	...	168	137	140	158
Georgia	457[1]	545	1,927[1]	1,676	252[1]	380	11,259[1]	10,270	8[1]	9	656[1]	929	800[1]	494	402[1]	463
Germany	37,910	50,056	5,534	7,078	14,057	10,903	27,747	38,965	337	634	2,770	3,448	4,752	5,376	2,864	2,447
Ghana	1,155	1,711	1,076	1,309	6,608	13,972	8,143	11,983	16	15	102	100	1,147	2,385	414	635
Greece	5,491	3,876	3,727	3,165	1,052	882	19,880	19,300	51	41	1,512	1,682	4,005	3,962	4,070	4,206
Greenland	...	...	...	...	...	...	...	...	...	...	...	...	...	...	...	...
Grenada	—	—	1,036	1,000	4	4	5,214	5,322	1	1	1,080	1,149	26	18	2	3
Guadeloupe	...	...	...	...	20	20	9,649	11,681	—	...	577	2,600	129	137	24	35
Guam	...	...	2,000	2,000	2	2	14,904	14,904	...	...	...	...	2	2	4	5
Guatemala	1,413	1,199	1,950	1,825	169	243	13,507	16,547	135	129	945	849	988	1,578	603	949
Guernsey	...	...	...	...	...	...	...	...	...	...	...	...	...	...	...	...
Guinea	632	1,103	1,052	1,312	578	1,251	7,320	6,448	60	55	857	846	840	990	432	476
Guinea-Bissau	165	166	1,556	1,312	69	99	6,911	7,857	2	2	960	622	62	74	21	25
Guyana	218	544	3,197	3,897	35	44	10,027	10,233	1	2	612	630	49	51	10	10
Haiti	405	363	996	827	770	755	3,785	4,000	100	70	655	658	1,005	969	277	199
Honduras	664	599	1,403	1,439	30	38	8,836	7,891	71	59	746	775	1,399	958	197	281
Hong Kong	—	—	1,667	—	...	...	22,000	33,333	...	...	...	...	4	4	116	55
Hungary	14,603	14,881	5,160	4,862	1,230	800	16,713	17,778	347	100	2,249	4,656	2,184	1,848	1,937	1,629
Iceland	...	...	...	...	11	10	9,159	12,250	8	19	4,798	4,524	—	...	2	4
India	195,478	230,611	1,911	2,318	21,280	33,200	15,906	19,015	13,604	11,271	571	586	27,138	48,571	48,971	68,059
Indonesia[4]	51,258	59,186	3,814	3,920	19,270	19,194	11,522	12,181	666	901	1,393	1,603	5,497	7,870	4,336	6,738
Iran	12,973	11,909	1,365	1,536	2,387	3,000	17,384	20,000	398	439	584	489	7,088	10,467	7,743	10,760
Iraq	2,541	1,207	927	460	196	150	15,980	6,250	19	29	995	890	1,457	1,215	2,855	1,908
Ireland	1,950	2,156	6,374	7,606	577	400	25,060	28,571	...	...	...	...	2	24	235	200
Isle of Man	...	...	...	...	...	...	...	...	...	...	...	...	...	...	...	...
Israel	331	272	2,968	2,901	209	393	32,359	31,799	9	13	1,334	1,809	1,715	1,259	1,143	1,599
Italy	17,921	20,067	4,005	4,737	2,340	1,998	19,637	24,117	221	121	1,430	1,543	17,569	18,377	14,436	14,943
Jamaica	3	2	1,232	1,180	225	229	12,534	16,777	6	5	898	1,093	383	414	108	172
Japan	13,946	12,270	5,645	6,184	5,539	4,480	25,459	25,839	145	104	1,670	1,830	4,837	4,285	14,455	12,564
Jersey	...	...	...	...	...	...	...	...	...	...	...	...	...	...	...	...
Jordan	105	65	1,040	1,103	59	91	23,167	26,000	6	2	690	547	247	221	709	851
Kazakhstan	22,519[1]	16,353	1,056[1]	1,239	2,302[1]	1,600	9,929[1]	9,756	97[1]	37	739[1]	1,000	160[1]	159	1,051[1]	2,278
Kenya	2,893	3,166	1,567	1,662	1,536	1,995	8,200	7,824	219	230	312	329	888	983	629	649
Kiribati	...	...	...	...	7	9	7,449	8,113	...	...	...	...	5	6	4	6
Korea, North	7,201	3,854	4,507	3,026	1,051	2,232	13,414	9,935	325	290	922	853	1,304	1,350	4,344	3,811
Korea, South	8,412	7,791	5,891	6,662	939	1,003	21,133	26,814	45	28	1,134	1,034	2,019	2,700	9,729	12,303
Kuwait	1	4	4,143	2,198	1	32	19,530	41,256	...	...	...	...	2	12	92	151
Kyrgyzstan	1,420	1,804	2,379	2,874	327[1]	1,056	11,330	15,761	...	...	...	...	101	202	334	824
Laos	1,443	2,319	2,244	3,018	246	224	8,150	7,475	12	15	780	967	130	180	89	290
Latvia	1,093	938	1,752	2,200	1,161[1]	706	13,181	13,519	6[1]	3	1,576[1]	1,432	73[1]	64	256	129
Lebanon	80	96	1,955	2,424	249	271	18,708	20,008	28	43	1,631	2,095	1,223	1,312	798	1,324
Lesotho	170	398	805	1,517	47	90	15,553	16,667	9	14	481	586	18	13	24	18
Liberia	191	183	1,035	1,278	422	504	7,253	6,802	3	4	517	636	111	166	73	76
Libya	284	218	680	637	141	210	7,891	7,000	12	20	1,126	1,405	307	381	706	906
Liechtenstein	...	...	...	...	...	...	...	...	...	...	...	...	...	...	...	...
Lithuania	2,323[1]	2,293	1,934[1]	2,704	1,316[1]	1,300	11,148[1]	12,683	34[1]	107	1,438[1]	2,830	145[1]	138	306[1]	325
Luxembourg[2]	...	...	...	...	...	...	...	...	...	...	...	...	...	...	...	...
Macau	...	...	...	...	...	...	...	...	...	...	...	...	...	...	...	...
Macedonia	583	487	2,453	2,291	127[1]	176	9,526	12,571	29[1]	27	2,589	2,546	342[1]	310	463[1]	524
Madagascar	2,541	2,460	1,943	1,761	3,160	3,152	6,359	6,155	67	99	883	909	790	854	328	344
Malawi	1,560	2,658	1,104	1,623	506	2,900	4,294	8,170	234	229	560	526	485	511	252	256
Malaysia	1,886	2,282	2,710	3,172	497	459	9,683	9,107	...	...	633	778	1,126	1,082	334	496
Maldives	—	—	1,125	1,000	7	8	4,537	4,578	...	...	...	...	9	9	20	28
Mali	2,114	2,866	907	1,159	23	155	4,721	14,390	40	111	172	406	15	34	307	328
Malta	8	12	3,422	4,000	17	27	13,181	15,112	1	1	2,336	2,556	14	7	52	67
Marshall Islands	...	...	...	...	...	...	...	...	...	...	...	...	...	...	...	...
Martinique	...	...	...	...	23	22	10,917	10,866	...	1	...	...	273	349	24	32
Mauritania	131	201	831	791	6	6	1,933	2,115	28	34	385	330	12	24	11	14
Mauritius	2	1	3,885	4,769	19	16	18,659	19,159	...	...	...	...	8	11	43	93
Mayotte	...	...	...	...	...	...	...	...	...	...	...	...	...	...	...	...
Mexico	23,553	29,737	2,350	2,817	1,302	1,771	15,957	23,235	1,412	1,411	704	747	9,430	13,236	6,604	9,451
Micronesia	...	...	...	...	...	...	...	...	...	...	...	...	...	...	...	...
Moldova	2,275[1]	2,086	2,981[1]	2,518	504[1]	425	7,796[1]	10,630	104[1]	62	1,492[1]	1,247	1,562[1]	743	737[1]	564
Monaco	...	...	...	...	...	...	...	...	...	...	...	...	...	...	...	...
Mongolia	719	160	1,104	813	128	64	10,613	7,303	3	1	708	833	—	...	42	42
Morocco	7,456	4,607	1,346	895	975	1,086	17,001	17,952	386	183	791	523	2,310	2,179	2,946	3,697
Mozambique	629	1,674	404	821	4,122	5,460	4,322	5,811	87	130	301	342	368	260	197	115
Myanmar (Burma)	14,111	21,230	2,738	2,999	212	473	8,579	10,072	434	1,945	648	777	957	1,284	2,027	3,475
Namibia	103	107	482	388	212	255	8,610	8,500	8	8	1,097	1,133	10	16	9	11
Nauru	...	...	...	...	...	...	...	...	...	...	...	...	...	...	...	...
Nepal	5,680	7,172	1,885	2,164	826	1,419	7,398	9,272	168	226	597	791	457	488	962	1,648
Netherlands, The	1,327	1,732	6,909	7,744	6,947	7,700	40,168	45,562	85	14	4,109	4,531	507	713	3,470	3,536
Netherlands Antilles	...	...	...	...	...	...	...	...	...	...	...	...	...	...	...	...
New Caledonia	1	2	1,837	3,736	21	21	6,023	5,778	—	...	393	600	4	3	5	4
New Zealand	783	883	4,870	6,467	277	516	30,899	46,071	62	52	2,941	3,826	806	955	576	1,058
Nicaragua	453	770	1,483	1,813	77	84	11,790	10,195	69	124	621	654	303	261	35	32

livestock														country
cattle stock ('000 head)		sheep stock ('000 head)		hogs stock ('000 head)		chickens stock ('000 head)		milk[e] production ('000 metric tons)		yield (kg/animal)		eggs[f] production (metric tons)		
1989–91 average	2001	1989–91 average	2001	1989–91 average	2001	1989–91 average	2001	1989–91 average	2001	1989–91 average	2001	1989–91 average	2001	
29,450[3]	35,500	10,860[3]	22,500	20[3]	25	27,225[3]	56,000	755[3]	970	199[3]	204	28,413[3]	76,000	Ethiopia
2	2	67	68	...	...	...	...	...	...	...	...	...	...	Faroe Islands
274	340	—	7	88	137	3,000	4,000	58	52	1,705	1,798	2,000	4,000	Fiji
1,352	1,025	59	100	1,322	1,300	6,000	6,000	2,712	2,500	5,666	6,452	73,000	60,000	Finland
21,407	20,281	11,196	10,000	11,999	14,635	198,306	230,000	26,334	24,890	4,797	5,641	903,000	1,047,000	France
15	9	4	3	9	10	202	...	—	—	1,222	583	...	...	French Guiana
8	11	—	—	33	37	100	...	2	1	2,207	2,000	1,000	2,000	French Polynesia
31	35	161	198	169	213	2,217	3,000	1	2	250	250	2,000	2,000	Gabon
331	327	143	106	14	14	1,000	1,000	6	8	175	175	1,000	1,000	Gambia, The
3	3	24	24	...	...	3,000	4,000	7	8	4,000	4,000	5,000	8,000	Gaza Strip
1,046[1]	1,180	1,159[1]	545	525[1]	443	11,786[1]	8,000	387[1]	660	773[1]	1,021	14,800[1]	24,000	Georgia
20,048	14,227	3,824	2,140	33,350	25,767	116,263	108,000	30,976	28,300	4,931	6,256	989,000	890,000	Germany
1,159	1,430	2,199	2,743	495	324	9,682	20,000	22	34	130	130	10,000	22,000	Ghana
651	585	8,684	9,000	1,002	905	27,213	28,000	622	770	2,523	4,529	123,000	120,000	Greece
...	...	21	22	...	...	...	...	...	...	...	...	...	...	Greenland
4	4	12	13	3	5	260	...	—	1	797	800	1,000	1,000	Grenada
70	85	4	3	35	19	311	...	1	...	506	500	1,000	2,000	Guadeloupe
...	...	...	...	4	55	170	...	...	...	...	...	...	1,000	Guam
2,055	2,540	432	552	602	1,450	14,633	35,000	251	270	680	712	68,000	109,000	Guatemala
...	...	...	...	...	...	...	...	...	...	...	...	...	...	Guernsey
1,501	3,128	429	892	24	98	8,000	12,000	42	72	185	185	8,000	12,000	Guinea
407	515	239	285	290	350	1,000	1,000	12	13	170	170	1,000	1,000	Guinea-Bissau
165	100	129	130	42	20	2,000	12,000	19	30	840	1,911	1,000	7,000	Guyana
1,067	1,450	120	152	330	1,000	5,167	6,000	40	42	250	250	4,000	4,000	Haiti
2,412	1,860	10	14	589	480	9,436	18,000	346	594	911	1,001	28,000	43,000	Honduras
2	25	—	—	296	110	5,678	3,000	2	—	2,190	2,273	1,000	...	Hong Kong
1,619	783	2,050	1,129	7,996	4,834	50,950	31,000	2,733	2,143	4,977	6,036	254,000	156,000	Hungary
75	71	540	465	36	44	450	...	112	108	3,509	4,000	3,000	3,000	Iceland
202,533	221,900	48,708	58,200	12,000	17,500	294,000	413,000	22,259	35,000	731	946	1,161,000	1,906,000	India
10,391	11,200	6,008	7,427	7,228	5,897	577,000	751,000	348	550	1,176	1,585	366,000	600,000	Indonesia[4]
7,382	8,738	44,754	53,000	—	—	162,000	260,000	2,480	4,000	1,014	1,250	310,000	600,000	Iran
1,366	1,400	8,127	6,780	—	—	63,000	23,000	297	319	730	750	64,000	14,000	Iraq
5,923	6,408	5,523	5,130	1,125	1,732	9,000	11,000	5,355	5,416	3,967	4,374	33,000	37,000	Ireland
...	...	...	...	...	...	...	...	...	...	...	...	...	...	Isle of Man
340	390	383	389	122	150	23,000	30,000	964	1,211	8,783	10,093	105,000	85,000	Israel
8,541	7,068	11,088	11,089	9,150	8,329	138,000	100,000	10,926	11,900	3,733	5,535	687,000	707,000	Italy
382	400	2	1	192	180	7,167	11,000	51	53	1,000	1,000	26,000	28,000	Jamaica
4,772	4,564	30	11	11,673	9,785	338,000	297,000	8,169	8,450	5,825	6,654	2,446,000	2,526,000	Japan
...	...	...	...	...	...	...	...	...	...	...	...	...	...	Jersey
38	68	1,660	1,850	...	...	14,000	24,000	60	163	2,425	3,468	32,000	46,000	Jordan
9,336[1]	4,282	33,651[1]	8,939	2,610[1]	1,076	516,830[1]	20,000	5,335[1]	3,700	1,481[1]	1,850	177,300[1]	90,000	Kazakhstan
13,442	13,500	9,241	6,500	125	315	24,667	32,000	2,280	1,800	499	450	41,000	50,000	Kenya
...	...	...	...	9	13	259	...	...	...	...	...	...	...	Kiribati
986	575	496	189	5,793	3,137	21,000	17,000	88	90	2,379	2,308	146,000	120,000	Korea, North
2,149	1,951	3	1	4,792	8,720	70,336	102,000	1,752	2,339	5,944	9,064	399,000	460,000	Korea, South
15	18	197	630	...	...	17,000	32,000	21	40	3,226	5,672	6,000	22,000	Kuwait
1,125	988	8,269	4,160	258	117	98,640	3,000	926	1,100	1,854	2,200	22,196	11,000	Kyrgyzstan
853	1,150	...	...	1,397	1,500	8,165	14,000	5	6	200	200	4,000	10,000	Laos
1,068[1]	388	154[1]	29	865[1]	394	61,970	3,000	1,211[1]	855	2,675	4,181	25,096	27,000	Latvia
65	79	221	380	46	64	23,000	32,000	94	205	2,826	3,254	35,000	42,000	Lebanon
550	540	1,450	730	62	60	967	2,000	24	24	290	250	1,000	2,000	Lesotho
38	36	222	210	123	130	38,000	4,000	1	1	130	130	4,000	4,000	Liberia
238	220	5,100	5,100	...	...	15,867	25,000	99	135	1,197	1,205	34,000	59,000	Libya
6	6	3	3	3	3	...	...	13	12	4,645	4,444	...	...	Liechtenstein
1,761[1]	752	52[1]	12	1,579[1]	856	10,860[1]	6,000	2,128[1]	1,810	2,915[1]	4,129	47,167[1]	37,000	Lithuania
...	...	...	...	...	...	...	...	...	...	...	...	...	...	Luxembourg[2]
...	...	...	...	...	...	450	1,000	...	...	...	...	1,000	1,000	Macau
283	259	2,354[1]	1,251	176[1]	204	44,581[1]	3,000	121[1]	180	1,276	1,837	25,653	22,000	Macedonia
10,254	11,000	737	790	1,431	850	13,062	19,000	477	535	273	282	10,000	15,000	Madagascar
832	750	151	110	236	250	11,500	15,000	38	35	460	461	15,000	20,000	Malawi
677	748	212	175	2,577	1,829	62,377	125,000	29	43	486	478	287,000	420,000	Malaysia
...	...	...	...	...	...	...	...	...	...	...	...	...	...	Maldives
4,971	6,819	6,072	6,400	56	66	22,000	25,000	123	159	245	245	12,000	12,000	Mali
21	18	13	16	101	80	1,000	1,000	24	47	3,850	5,446	7,000	8,000	Malta
...	...	...	...	...	...	...	...	...	...	...	...	...	...	Marshall Islands
37	25	46	34	39	35	347	...	2	2	756	764	1,000	2,000	Martinique
1,350	1,500	5,067	7,600	...	...	3,800	4,000	97	116	350	350	4,000	5,000	Mauritania
29	28	6	7	12	21	2,200	4,000	12	5	1,878	1,175	4,000	5,000	Mauritius
...	...	...	...	...	...	...	...	...	...	...	...	...	...	Mayotte
32,194	30,600	5,862	6,150	15,715	17,750	240,218	496,000	6,336	9,501	992	1,397	1,066,000	1,882,000	Mexico
...	...	...	...	...	32	...	...	...	...	...	...	...	...	Micronesia
962[1]	405	1,300[1]	866	1,468[1]	543	183,980[1]	13,000	998[1]	575	2,476[1]	2,003	22,709[1]	28,000	Moldova
...	...	...	...	...	...	...	...	...	...	...	...	...	...	Monaco
2,694	2,054	14,266	15,667	166	16	351	...	268	385	348	316	2,000	...	Mongolia
3,284	2,670	13,528	17,300	9	8	71,200	137,000	929	1,150	521	879	171,000	235,000	Morocco
1,373	1,320	120	125	167	175	21,833	28,000	63	60	170	170	11,000	14,000	Mozambique
9,280	11,551	275	403	2,681	4,139	23,989	48,000	422	510	392	392	35,000	86,000	Myanmar (Burma)
2,104	2,509	3,289	2,200	18	18	1,717	2,000	76	75	401	403	1,000	2,000	Namibia
...	...	...	...	2	3	5	...	...	...	...	...	...	...	Nauru
6,274	6,979	903	850	571	913	12,000	20,000	252	343	366	402	16,000	25,000	Nepal
4,920	4,050	1,663	1,400	13,620	12,822	92,050	107,000	1,944	10,500	6,040	7,143	644,000	658,000	Netherlands, The
1	1	6	7	3	2	125	...	—	—	1,278	1,267	...	1,000	Netherlands Antilles
122	123	3	1	37	40	317	...	4	4	600	600	1,000	2,000	New Caledonia
7,987	9,633	57,861	43,987	404	354	9,067	13,000	7,544	13,162	2,835	3,700	46,000	54,000	New Zealand
2,833	3,350	4	4	565	400	4,000	17,000	162	238	797	914	26,000	31,000	Nicaragua

Crops and livestock (continued)

crops

country	grains production ('000 metric tons) 1989–91 average	grains production 2001	grains yield (kg/hectare) 1989–91 average	grains yield 2001	roots and tubers[a] production ('000 metric tons) 1989–91 average	roots and tubers[a] production 2001	roots and tubers[a] yield (kg/hectare) 1989–91 average	roots and tubers[a] yield 2001	pulses[b] production ('000 metric tons) 1989–91 average	pulses[b] production 2001	pulses[b] yield (kg/hectare) 1989–91 average	pulses[b] yield 2001	fruits[c] production ('000 metric tons) 1989–91 average	fruits[c] production 2001	vegetables[d] production ('000 metric tons) 1989–91 average	vegetables[d] production 2001
Niger	2,120	3,161	342	401	180	139	9,025	19,200	312	308	127	80	44	48	290	614
Nigeria	18,100	22,891	1,165	1,193	35,155	66,578	10,370	9,687	1,363	2,200	719	423	6,644	8,900	4,272	7,783
Northern Mariana Islands	...	...	...	...	...	...	...	...	...	...	...	...	99	26	182	131
Norway	1,410	1,307	3,943	3,962	452	388	24,246	25,000	—	...	...	...	185	318	155	193
Oman	5	5	2,124	2,271	5	16	25,208	29,091	...	...	...	...	...	...	...	...
Pakistan	21,038	27,820	1,784	2,287	1,052	2,134	11,467	17,015	1,044	740	553	510	3,871	4,817	3,193	4,912
Palau	...	...	...	...	...	...	...	...	...	...	...	...	...	...	...	...
Panama	336	317	1,884	3,138	66	76	5,901	11,537	9	9	526	416	1,225	726	65	160
Papua New Guinea	4	11	2,330	4,145	1,253	1,285	7,270	7,252	2	3	500	531	1,076	1,223	357	393
Paraguay	818	1,249	1,838	2,165	3,479	3,924	15,109	14,635	55	76	959	914	523	484	268	313
Peru	1,983	3,854	2,473	3,089	2,293	4,308	8,066	10,712	107	179	896	1,039	1,922	3,363	918	1,981
Philippines	14,350	17,480	2,018	2,668	2,761	2,575	6,851	6,398	60	54	908	747	8,340	11,053	4,211	4,911
Poland	27,594	27,231	3,231	3,087	33,247	20,401	18,350	17,083	635	323	1,857	2,230	1,792	3,180	5,797	5,513
Portugal	1,683	1,347	2,019	2,599	1,403	1,274	11,596	14,457	51	22	590	595	2,176	1,840	2,063	2,309
Puerto Rico	1	1	1,156	1,870	28	10	6,499	4,156	2	1	569	1,395	255	202	47	25
Qatar	3	6	2,910	3,418	—	...	9,611	10,143	7	8	1,832	1,841	8	18	30	55
Réunion	12	17	5,559	6,724	15	10	11,006	13,416	1	1	1,429	759	44	56	45	72
Romania	18,286	16,550	3,084	2,681	3,159	3,800	10,517	13,571	149	62	889	1,016	2,295	2,302	3,215	3,945
Russia	92,890[1]	83,622	1,612[1]	2,146	36,603[1]	34,500	10,686[1]	10,345	2,883[1]	1,278	1,383[1]	1,495	2,989[1]	3,445	10,390[1]	12,534
Rwanda	289	297	1,161	1,000	1,641	2,920	4,553	5,957	216	307	726	742	3,020	1,633	131	261
St. Kitts and Nevis	...	...	...	...	1	1	3,611	2,861	...	...	1,000	1,000	1	1	...	1
St. Lucia	—	—	...	...	11	11	4,350	4,050	...	...	2,133	2,000	176	118	1	1
St. Vincent and the Grenadines	2	2	3,409	3,333	19	13	4,539	4,547	...	...	1,000	1,000	78	49	3	4
Samoa	...	...	...	...	31	21	6,527	3,884	...	...	...	...	45	50	1	1
San Marino	...	...	...	...	...	...	...	...	...	...	...	...	...	...	...	...
São Tomé and Príncipe	3	2	2,015	2,230	6	33	7,346	9,054	...	...	...	...	10	22	3	6
Saudi Arabia	4,214	2,214	4,177	3,686	59	394	19,121	25,088	...	...	337	324	832	1,192	1,987	1,821
Senegal	996	1,026	823	879	67	141	3,990	5,089	19	48	...	...	105	129	197	227
Serbia and Montenegro	7,613[1]	9,144	3,099	3,767	766[1]	690	6,919	6,610	100[1]	107	1,439[1]	1,259	1,391[1]	1,124	1,037	1,106
Seychelles	...	...	...	...	...	...	5,000	5,000	...	...	...	...	2	2	2	2
Sierra Leone	566	222	1,224	1,078	139	...	5,220	4,671	38	52	652	673	163	162	189	182
Singapore	...	...	...	...	—	...	13,933	10,000	50	26	780	618	1	—	8	5
Slovakia	3,449[3]	3,478	4,041[3]	4,105	566[3]	401	13,057[3]	17,001	161[3]	69	2,347[3]	2,880	277[3]	273	458[3]	524
Slovenia	486[1]	499	4,150[1]	4,815	147[1]	191	12,416[1]	20,893	6[1]	4	1,277[1]	1,435	255[1]	296	77[1]	106
Solomon Islands	...	5	...	4,000	107	145	17,595	16,956	2	4	1,175	1,296	15	17	6	7
Somalia	497	313	715	565	50	76	10,421	10,000	13	15	312	263	271	216	65	73
South Africa	12,734	9,603	2,053	2,080	1,336	1,607	16,611	23,775	146	115	1,178	1,079	3,744	4,759	2,021	2,053
Spain	19,306	18,187	2,489	2,827	5,334	3,002	19,439	25,965	238	303	755	663	13,503	14,835	11,026	11,952
Sri Lanka	2,370	2,904	2,924	3,279	547	349	8,845	8,429	...	...	...	...	743	1,018	579	629
Sudan, The	2,771	3,365	497	509	137	171	2,670	2,614	103	262	1,064	1,588	773	980	922	1,145
Suriname	229	165	3,770	3,836	3	4	11,900	12,227	...	...	690	727	75	76	26	21
Swaziland	127	86	1,401	1,528	9	8	1,665	1,930	5	3	569	443	141	97	13	11
Sweden	5,677	5,548	4,594	4,668	1,132	912	32,977	28,697	91	101	2,494	2,787	132	37	261	284
Switzerland	1,331	1,106	6,352	6,220	731	526	37,867	37,571	8	10	4,264	3,750	634	454	308	283
Syria	2,597	5,158	668	1,689	407	480	17,543	20,870	131	193	577	667	1,370	1,858	1,690	1,868
Taiwan	...	...	...	...	...	...	...	...	...	...	...	...	...	...	...	...
Tajikistan	261[1]	316	1,012[1]	858	149[1]	305	12,031[1]	13,252	6[1]	6	560[1]	1,482	249[1]	157	622[1]	535
Tanzania	4,138	4,131	1,389	1,525	8,167	6,363	8,824	5,264	437	433	501	565	2,093	2,022	1,184	1,166
Thailand	23,624	30,111	2,149	2,713	21,784	18,492	14,241	15,832	377	273	751	834	6,371	7,557	2,557	2,870
Togo	505	740	809	1,107	913	1,289	7,992	6,796	22	51	202	297	49	49	152	131
Tonga	...	...	...	...	54	23	12,255	11,821	3	4	1,460	2,566	13	10	20	24
Trinidad and Tobago	17	12	2,816	2,929	10	12	9,757	10,315	...	...	...	...	62	80	17	25
Tunisia	1,624	1,820	1,112	1,232	205	330	12,592	12,222	73	92	616	888	719	991	1,480	2,195
Turkey	28,283	25,571	2,065	1,949	4,321	5,351	22,388	25,343	1,946	1,389	885	971	9,117	10,660	17,963	21,999
Turkmenistan	954[1]	1,299	2,385[1]	1,578	32[1]	30	7,325[1]	5,000	5[1]	15	2,425[1]	3,000	170[1]	179	538[1]	538
Tuvalu	...	...	...	...	—	—	...	...	...	...	...	...	1	1	—	...
Uganda	1,597	2,309	1,483	1,641	5,360	8,288	6,335	8,008	493	671	774	733	8,384	10,558	420	556
Ukraine	37,078[1]	38,837	2,952[1]	2,729	19,129[1]	13,500	12,044[1]	8,459	2,840[1]	880	2,298[1]	2,211	2,597[1]	2,152	5,750[1]	6,210
United Arab Emirates	2	...	1,912	691	4	5	19,300	19,464	...	...	...	...	205	378	270	1,129
United Kingdom	22,644	18,983	6,168	6,299	6,333	6,641	35,916	40,028	745	812	3,401	3,496	515	318	3,580	2,913
United States	292,220	325,315	4,579	5,886	18,530	20,828	32,069	38,545	1,623	1,228	1,839	1,829	25,256	29,863	31,092	35,513
Uruguay	1,230	2,053	2,411	3,968	215	171	7,514	11,409	6	6	986	982	394	511	117	147
Uzbekistan	2,281[1]	3,502	1,678[1]	2,920	468[1]	800	9,942[1]	14,545	6[1]	12	712[1]	2,400	1,000[1]	1,525	3,867[1]	3,298
Vanuatu	1	1	515	538	49	63	10,139	10,500	...	...	...	...	18	20	8	10
Venezuela	2,037	2,281	2,484	3,035	682	1,100	8,676	12,987	57	35	585	754	2,579	3,019	514	1,258
Vietnam	20,008	34,043	3,056	4,140	4,758	3,976	7,432	7,827	187	247	639	716	3,175	4,086	3,625	4,905
Virgin Islands (U.S.)	...	...	...	...	...	...	...	...	...	...	...	...	...	...	...	...
West Bank	28	30	...	...	16	17	...	...	2	2	...	...	164	153	194	228
Western Sahara	2	3	758	800	...	8,288	...	...	...	...	...	...	...	...	...	...
Yemen	693	672	871	1,085	153	211	12,233	12,373	64	63	1,424	1,219	314	591	536	584
Zambia	1,467	1,069	1,569	1,459	704	1,014	6,517	5,972	15	16	629	516	105	101	274	270
Zimbabwe	2,391	2,027	1,488	1,213	127	208	4,792	4,856	50	50	694	760	170	200	153	147

livestock														country
cattle		sheep		hogs		chickens		milk[e]				eggs[f]		
stock ('000 head)		stock ('000 head)		stock ('000 head)		stock ('000 head)		production ('000 metric tons)		yield (kg/animal)		production (metric tons)		
1989–91 average	2001	1989–91 average	2001	1989–91 average	2001	1989–91 average	2001	1989–91 average	2001	1989–91 average	2001	1989–91 average	2001	
1,712	2,260	3,100	4,500	37	39	17,833	24,000	140	184	393	400	8,000	10,000	Niger
13,974	20,000	12,477	20,500	3,319	4,855	122,120	126,000	350	386	239	243	313,000	435,000	Nigeria
...	...	...	...	...	...	...	...	...	...	...	...	...	...	Northern Mariana Islands
959	967	2,202	2,400	696	391	4,000	3,000	15,560	1,669	5,854	5,580	51,000	49,000	Norway
144	314	238	335	...	...	2,000	3,000	18	38	420	420	6,000	7,000	Oman
17,677	22,857	25,703	24,200	...	...	78,000	155,000	3,525	8,192	842	1,182	211,000	340,000	Pakistan
...	...	...	...	...	...	...	...	...	...	...	...	...	...	Palau
1,401	1,533	...	...	228	278	8,000	14,000	129	171	1,162	1,219	11,000	13,000	Panama
99	89	4	6	997	1,600	3,000	4,000	—	—	102	100	3,000	4,000	Papua New Guinea
7,985	9,900	422	402	2,443	2,700	15,065	15,000	224	330	1,904	2,399	35,000	68,000	Paraguay
4,126	4,950	12,484	14,500	2,417	2,800	62,406	90,000	788	1,075	1,323	2,067	104,000	160,000	Peru
1,664	2,548	30	30	7,968	11,063	77,000	115,000	15	11	2,298	2,571	297,000	445,000	Philippines
9,875	5,501	3,934	337	20,056	16,992	58,196	48,000	1,500	12,030	3,260	4,362	410,000	428,000	Poland
1,355	1,399	5,531	5,900	2,531	2,350	19,667	35,000	3,450	1,860	3,734	5,239	85,000	108,000	Portugal
595	390	9	16	204	118	11,241	12,000	396	377	4,233	3,660	17,000	15,000	Puerto Rico
10	15	126	215	...	...	2,932	4,000	10	11	1,592	1,493	3,000	4,000	Qatar
20	30	2	2	88	77	6,916	12,000	7	21	627	1,050	4,000	6,000	Réunion
6,029	2,800	15,236	7,800	12,675	5,076	121,000	74,000	...	5,047	1,867	3,154	354,000	305,000	Romania
51,939[1]	27,107	46,998[1]	14,000	31,820[1]	15,700	584,867[1]	325,000	45,088[1]	31,980	2,273[1]	2,460	2,259,433[1]	1,945,000	Russia
592	815	392	260	125	180	1,292	1,000	85	85	579	739	2,000	2,000	Rwanda
4	4	14	7	2	3	56	...	...	...	...	...	...	...	St. Kitts and Nevis
12	12	15	12	12	15	223	...	1	1	1,396	1,389	...	1,000	St. Lucia
6	6	13	13	10	10	205	...	1	1	1,351	1,370	1,000	1,000	St. Vincent and the Grenadines
24	28	...	...	185	170	356	...	1	2	1,000	1,000	...	...	Samoa
...	...	...	...	...	...	...	...	...	...	...	...	...	...	San Marino
4	4	2	3	3	2	124	...	—	...	170	170	...	...	São Tomé and Príncipe
195	330	6,370	7,576	...	...	76,000	130,000	274	601	6,254	8,035	113,000	136,000	Saudi Arabia
2,515	3,230	3,311	4,818	193	280	19,667	45,000	98	116	360	360	15,000	33,000	Senegal
1,925[1]	1,355	2,701[1]	1,917	3,876[1]	4,372	21,920[1]	21,000	1,841[1]	1,825	1,799	2,100	81,783	76,000	Serbia and Montenegro
3	1	...	...	18	18	293	1,000	...	...	533	564	1,000	2,000	Seychelles
333	400	271	365	50	52	6,000	6,000	17	21	250	250	7,000	8,000	Sierra Leone
—	—	—	—	300	190	2,000	2,000	...	...	...	...	17,000	16,000	Singapore
1,098[3]	608	492[3]	348	2,224[3]	1,488	7,128[3]	14,000	1,220[3]	1,102	3,254[3]	4,650	95,645[3]	67,000	Slovakia
488[1]	477	261	96	574[1]	604	5,533[1]	7,000	569[1]	649	2,650[1]	3,043	19,712[1]	23,000	Slovenia
11	13	...	...	53	67	144	...	1	1	650	650	...	...	Solomon Islands
4,100	5,300	12,783	13,200	9	4	2,833	3,000	425	530	398	400	2,000	2,000	Somalia
13,433	13,722	32,060	28,800	1,532	1,540	73,000	119,000	2,426	2,667	2,637	2,667	213,000	318,000	South Africa
5,125	6,411	23,280	24,400	16,509	23,348	111,000	128,000	6,100	6,294	3,728	4,842	649,000	560,000	Spain
1,690	1,565	25	11	88	68	9,000	11,000	172	221	271	321	46,000	52,000	Sri Lanka
21,080	38,325	21,304	47,000	...	...	32,371	38,000	2,252	3,072	480	480	33,000	46,000	Sudan, The
91	136	9	8	29	23	8,000	3,000	17	14	1,832	1,929	3,000	3,000	Suriname
712	615	24	32	23	34	1,133	3,000	42	38	274	288	...	1,000	Swaziland
1,704	1,638	408	452	2,243	1,891	11,433	7,000	3,401	3,300	6,097	7,759	116,000	98,000	Sweden
1,845	1,593	392	460	1,793	1,556	5,912	7,000	3,892	3,910	4,954	5,469	38,000	34,000	Switzerland
786	867	14,571	12,362	1	1	14,405	21,000	782	1,032	2,314	2,484	75,000	115,000	Syria
...	...	...	...	...	...	80,119	...	...	...	...	...	...	...	Taiwan
1,238[1]	1,091	2,245[1]	1,363	73[1]	1	5,167[1]	1,000	486[1]	316	886[1]	551	9,957[1]	2,000	Tajikistan
13,047	17,700	3,551	4,250	320	355	20,567	30,000	516	685	169	207	41,000	58,000	Tanzania
5,860	4,640	161	43	4,766	8,300	109,000	190,000	137	520	1,886	2,419	430,000	530,000	Thailand
244	278	1,153	1,000	404	289	6,070	8,000	7	9	225	225	6,000	6,000	Togo
11	11	...	...	94	81	221	...	—	—	1,500	1,480	...	...	Tonga
52	32	14	12	53	41	10,000	10,000	11	10	1,593	1,552	9,000	9,000	Trinidad and Tobago
626	760	5,935	6,600	6	6	39,367	43,000	401	980	1,449	1,782	52,000	79,000	Tunisia
12,037	10,548	43,195	29,435	10	5	73,181	220,000	8,183	8,600	1,352	1,593	369,000	715,000	Turkey
962[1]	860	5,793[1]	6,000	203[1]	45	6,900[1]	5,000	633[1]	830	1,506[1]	1,431	15,533[1]	15,000	Turkmenistan
...	...	...	...	12	13	29	...	...	...	...	...	...	...	Tuvalu
4,817	5,900	783	1,100	1,029	1,550	18,667	26,000	421	511	350	350	15,000	20,000	Uganda
...	9,421	6,658[1]	955	16,437[1]	9,078	1,803,520[1]	108,000	18,363[1]	13,200	2,273[1]	2,662	678,385[1]	525,000	Ukraine
49	100	255	467	...	...	7,000	15,000	5	9	210	157	10,000	13,000	United Arab Emirates
11,980	10,343	43,493	36,697	7,519	5,845	124,076	168,000	14,976	14,717	5,206	6,538	616,000	629,000	United Kingdom
96,316	96,700	11,128	6,965	54,557	59,138	1,333,000	1,830,000	66,423	75,025	6,673	8,226	4,048,000	5,080,000	United States
9,046	11,667	25,576	13,032	217	380	8,000	13,000	980	1,422	1,562	1,755	26,000	37,000	Uruguay
5,273[1]	5,400	8,681[1]	8,100	524[1]	89	26,933[1]	14,000	3,619[1]	3,700	1,639[1]	1,565	100,383[1]	70,000	Uzbekistan
124	151	...	...	59	62	306	...	2	3	202	207	...	...	Vanuatu
13,311	14,500	558	820	2,986	5,400	60,000	115,000	1,564	1,400	1,322	1,333	119,000	180,000	Venezuela
3,151	4,063	...	...	12,224	20,200	75,000	150,000	36	60	800	800	97,000	168,000	Vietnam
8	8	3	3	3	3	30	...	2	2	2,725	2,703	...	...	Virgin Islands (U.S.)
11	12	341	352	...	...	...	...	19	27	2,749	3,524	7,000	15,000	West Bank
...	...	27	33	...	...	...	...	...	...	...	...	...	...	Western Sahara
1,154	1,401	3,682	4,804	...	...	16,385	30,000	152	180	600	601	18,000	31,000	Yemen
2,845	2,600	59	150	296	340	16,033	30,000	77	64	300	300	26,000	46,000	Zambia
5,867	5,753	544	535	296	278	12,000	16,000	440	310	417	310	16,000	21,000	Zimbabwe

[1]1992–94 average. [2]Belgium includes Luxembourg. [3]1993–95 average. [4]Indonesia includes East Timor.

Extractive industries

Extractive industries are generally defined as those exploiting in situ natural resources and include such activities as mining, forestry, fisheries, and agriculture; the definition is often confined, however, to nonrenewable resources only. For the purposes of this table, agriculture is excluded; it is covered in the preceding table.

Extractive industries are divided here into three parts: mining, forestry, and fisheries. These major headings are each divided into two main subheadings, one that treats production and one that treats foreign trade. The production sections are presented in terms of volume except for mining, and the trade sections are presented in terms of U.S. dollars. Volume of production data usually imply output of primary (unprocessed) raw materials only, but, because of the way national statistical information is reported, the data may occasionally include some processed and manufactured materials as well, since these are often indistinguishably associated with the extractive process (sulfur from petroleum extraction, cured or treated lumber, or "processed" fish). This is also the case in the trade sections, where individual national trade nomenclatures may not distinguish some processed and manufactured goods from unprocessed raw materials.

Mining. In the absence of a single international source publication or standard of practice for reporting volume or value of mineral production, single-country sources predominantly have been used to compile mining production figures, supplemented by U.S. Bureau of Mines data, by the United Nations' *National Accounts Statistics* (annual; 2 parts), and by industry sources, especially *Mining Journal's Mining Annual Review*. Each

country has its own methods of classifying mining data, which do not always accord with the principal mineral production categories adopted in this table—namely, "metals," "nonmetals," and "energy." The available data have therefore been adjusted to accord better with the definition of each group. Included in the "metal" category are all ferrous and nonferrous metallic ores, concentrates, and scrap; the "nonmetal" group includes all nonmetallic minerals (stone, clay, precious gems, etc.) except the mineral fuels; the last group, "energy," is composed predominantly of the natural hydrocarbon fuels, though it may also include manufactured gas.

The contribution (value) of each national mineral sector to its country's gross domestic product is given, as is the distribution by group of that contribution (to gross domestic product and to foreign trade), although statistics regarding the value of mineral production are less readily available in country sources than those regarding trade or volume of minerals produced. Figures for value added by mineral output, though not always available, were sought first, as they provide the most consistent standard to compare the importance of minerals both within a particular national economy and among national mineral sectors worldwide. Where value added to the gross domestic product was not available, gross value of production or sales was substituted and the exception footnoted. Figures for value of production are reported here in millions of U.S. dollars to permit comparisons to be made from country to country. Comparisons can also be made as to the relative importance of each mineral group within a given country.

Extractive industries

country	mining							trade (value)								
	% of GDP, 1998	mineral production (value added)					year	exports					imports			
		year	total ('000,000 U.S.$)	by kind (%)				total ('000,000 U.S.$)	by kind (%)			total ('000,000 U.S.$)	by kind (%)		
				metals[a]	non-metals[b]	energy[c]			metals[a]	non-metals[b]	energy[c]		metals[a]	non-metals[b]	energy[c]
Afghanistan	...	...	...	...	...	...	1997	0.1	—	100.0	—	...	...	...	...	...
Albania	...	1994[1]	81.4	46.1	0.8	53.1	1997	16.5	93.9	6.1	—	12.9	—	34.9	65.1
Algeria	23.0	1998	10,895.7	—	—	100.0	1996	8,931.6	—	0.2	99.8	22.4	—	—	100.0
American Samoa	...	1998	...	...	100.0	—	...	...	...	...	...	...	...	...	...
Andorra	...	...	...	...	...	...	...	...	...	...	...	...	...	...	...
Angola	60.9[2]	1997	3,935.1	—	7.7	92.3	1997	212.6	—	90.4	9.6	...	...	...	...
Antigua and Barbuda	1.5	1998	9.0[12]	—	100.0	—	...	...	...	...	...	...	...	...	...
Argentina	2.4[2]	1997	7,821.8[3]	...	100.0	...	1997	2,429.7[4]	—	—	100.0[4]	419.5	65.2	1.6	33.2
Armenia	...	1998	...	—	100.0	—	1997	106.9	—	100.0	—	187.2	50.5	49.5	—
Aruba	...	1998	...	—	100.0	—	1997	1.4	—	100.0	—	...	...	...	...
Australia	4.4	1998	15,105.6	...	...	...	1997	17,083.6	40.1	3.6	56.3	3,181.5	3.4	9.0	87.6
Austria	0.5	1995	819.3	2.5	53.5	44.0	1997	484.0[4]	38.5[4]	61.2[4]	0.3[4]	3,055.2	16.7	10.2	73.1
Azerbaijan	...	...	...	...	...	...	1994	...	...	...	...	224.1	—	—	100.0
Bahamas, The	...	1998	...	—	100.0	—	1997	1.2	100.0	—	—	...	...	...	...
Bahrain	13.6	1998	841.2	—	1.5	98.5	1996	2,471.1[6]	0.6[6]	—	99.3[6]	2,002.2	15.8	0.6	83.7
Bangladesh	1.0	1997–98	417.6	—	47.4	52.6	1996	...	...	...	...	80.0	—	77.5	22.5
Barbados	1.0	1998	4.6[3]	—	100.0[3]	—	1997	0.1	100.0	—	...	8.3	—	43.4	56.6
Belarus	...	1998	...	—	100.0	—	1997	175.2	—	92.5	7.5	39.6	—	100.0	—
Belgium	0.3[2]	1997	617.8	—	100.0	—	1997	13,490.0	8.2	88.6	3.3	21,328.3	12.4	54.9	32.7
Belize	0.5	1998	2.5	—	100.0	—	1997	...	...	...	...	3.4	—	14.7	85.3
Benin	0.7[5]	1995	14.4[8]	—	100.0[8]	—	...	...	...	...	...	...	...	...	...
Bermuda	...	...	...	...	...	...	1997	...	...	...	...	14.0	—	100.0	...
Bhutan	2.3[2]	1997	8.5	—	100.0	—	1994	2.9	—	82.8	17.2	1.7	—	29.4	70.6
Bolivia	11.1	1998	686.1	—	49.5	50.5	1997	377.7	72.9	1.1	26.0	17.7	85.9	14.1	—
Bosnia and Herzegovina	...	...	...	...	...	...	1997	2.9	—	—	100.0	...	...	...	...
Botswana	37.6	1997–98	1,950.6	11.4[9]	88.0[9]	0.7[9]	[10]	...	...	...	...	...	...	...	...
Brazil	0.8[2]	1997	6,760.5	...	...	...	1997	3,454.5	92.4	7.6	—	5,433.9	8.2	4.4	87.4
Brunei	36.7	1998	1,777.6	—	8.5	91.5	1997	1,970.2[6]	—	—	100.0[6]	9.3	—	100.0	—
Bulgaria	1.4	1998	167.4	...	...	...	1997	120.4	37.7	62.3	—	1,166.2	13.4	3.4	83.2
Burkina Faso	...	1998	...	—	100.0	—	...	...	...	...	...	...	...	...	...
Burundi	0.6[2]	1995	6.2	...	...	...	...	...	...	...	...	...	...	...	...
Cambodia	0.3	1998	8.8	—	100.0	—	...	...	...	...	...	...	...	...	...
Cameroon	5.5	1997–98	491.5	—	—	100.0	1996	628.8	—	—	100.0	187.6	16.4	4.0	79.6
Canada	3.7	1998	21,998.8	19.4	12.0	68.6	1997	22,630.2	16.3	3.7	79.9	10,037.9	24.5	6.4	69.1
Cape Verde	0.3[9]	1994	0.9	—	100.0	—	...	...	...	...	...	...	...	...	...
Central African Republic	3.8	1998	39.8[11]	—	100.0[11]	—	1997	104.1	—	100.0	—	0.8[4]	—	100.0[4]	—
Chad	...	...	...	...	...	...	1997	...	...	...	...	...	...	...	...
Chile	8.5	1998	3,555.7	—	100.0	—	1997	2,553.3	96.9	3.1	—	1,505.5	4.1	—	95.9
China	...	...	...	...	...	...	1997	5,786.1	2.5	24.5	73.0	10,446.5	32.9	5.6	61.5
Colombia	5.5[4]	1996	4,735.4	...	...	...	1997	3,363.5	0.1	4.2	95.7	86.1	20.0	80.0	—
Comoros	—	1998	...	—	100.0	—	...	...	...	...	...	...	...	...	...
Congo, Dem. Rep. of the	22.8[6]	1995	288.6	—	100.0	—	1995	302.7	—	84.5	15.5	3.4	—	100.0	—
Congo, Rep. of the	40.6[13]	1996[13]	978.8[13]	...	...	...	1995	939.5	—	0.3	99.7	5.2	—	48.1	51.9
Costa Rica	...	...	...	...	...	...	1997	5.1	100.0	—	—	123.1[4]	—	7.0[4]	93.0[4]
Côte d'Ivoire	0.2[13]	1998[13]	28.1[13]	...	...	...	1997	132.0	—	100.0	—	489.9[4]	—	3.2[4]	96.8[4]
Croatia	0.4	1998	96.9	...	...	...	1997	135.0	23.1	14.1	62.8	772.7	—	7.3	92.7
Cuba	...	...	...	...	...	...	1997	...	...	...	...	13.3	—	100.0	—
Cyprus	0.3[14]	1998[14]	25.1	—	100.0	—	1997[14]	20.6	46.6	53.4	—	167.9	—	12.9	87.1
Czech Republic	...	...	...	...	...	...	1997	651.0	23.9	11.0	65.1	2,175.5	13.0	4.1	82.9
Denmark	1.4[2]	1997	2,023.8	—	100.0	—	1997	1,193.7	15.2	6.9	77.8	1,004.3	7.7	18.6	73.7
Djibouti	—	1998	...	—	100.0	—	...	...	...	...	...	...	...	...	...
Dominica	0.9	1998	2.0	—	100.0	—	1996	0.9	—	100.0	—	1.1	—	—	100.0
Dominican Republic	2.0	1998	309.3	—	100.0	—	1994	2.7	—	100.0	—	...	...	...	...
East Timor	...	...	...	...	...	...	...	...	...	...	...	...	...	...	...
Ecuador	7.8	1997	1,560.0	—	6.8[15]	93.2[15]	1997	1,404.8	—	—	100.0	95.0	—	9.4	90.6

Since the data for value of mineral production are obtained mostly from country sources, there is some variation (from a standard calendar year) in the time periods to which the data refer. In addition, the time period for which production data are available does not always correspond with the year for which mineral trade data are available.

The Standard International Trade Classification (SITC), Revision 3, was used to determine the commodity groupings for foreign trade statistics. The actual trade data for these groups is taken largely from the United Nations' *International Trade Statistics Yearbook* (2 vol.) and national sources.

Forestry. Data for the production and trade sections of forestry are based on the Food and Agriculture Organization (FAO) of the United Nations' *Yearbook of Forest Products*. Production of roundwood (all wood obtained in removals from forests) is the principal indicator of the volume of each country's forestry sector; this total is broken down further (as percentages of the roundwood total) into its principal components: fuelwood and charcoal, and industrial roundwood. The latter group was further divided to show its principal component, sawlogs and veneer; lesser categories of industrial roundwood could not be shown for reasons of space. These included pitprops (used in mining, a principal consumer of wood) and pulpwood (used in papermaking and plastics). Value of trade in forest products is given for both imports and exports, although exports alone tend to be the significant indicator for producing countries, while imports of wood are rarely a significant fraction of the trade of most importing countries.

Fisheries. Data for nominal (live weight) catches of fish, crustaceans, mollusks, etc., in all fishing areas (marine areas and inland waters) are taken from the FAO *Yearbook of Fishery Statistics* (*Catches and Landings*). Total catch figures are given in metric tons; the catches in inland waters and marine areas are given as percentages of the total catch, as are the main kinds of catch—fish, crustaceans, and mollusks. The total catch figures exclude marine mammals, such as whales and seals; and such aquatic animal products as corals, sponges, and pearls; but include frogs, turtles, and jellyfish. The subtotals by kind of catch, however, exclude the last group, which do not belong taxonomically to the fish, crustaceans, or mollusks.

Figures for trade in fishery products (including processed products and preparations like oils, meals, and animal feeding stuffs) are taken from the FAO's *Yearbook of Fishery Statistics* (*Commodities*). Value figures for trade in fish products are given for both imports and exports.

The following notes further define the column headings:
a. Includes ferrous and nonferrous metallic ores, concentrates, and scraps, such as iron ore, bauxite and alumina, copper, zinc, gold (except unwrought or semimanufactured), lead, or uranium.
b. Includes natural fertilizers; stone, sand, and aggregate; and pearls, precious and semiprecious stones, worked and unwrought.
c. Includes hydrocarbon solids, liquids, and gases.
1 cubic metre = 35.3147 cubic feet
1 metric ton = 1.1023 short tons

forestry						fisheries, 1999								country
production of roundwood, 2000				trade (value, '000 U.S.$), 1999		catch (nominal)						trade (value, '000 U.S.$)		
total ('000 cubic metres)	fuelwood, charcoal (%)	industrial roundwood (%)		exports	imports	total ('000 metric tons)	by source (%)		by kind of catch (%)			exports	imports	
		total	sawlogs, veneer				marine	inland	fish	crustaceans	mollusks			
8,283	78.8	21.2	10.3	...	1,090	1.2	—	100.0	100.0	—	—	...	...	Afghanistan
409	84.5	15.5	15.5	7,063	17,158	2.7	70.3	29.7	90.8	0.7	8.5	4,804	3,965	Albania
2,795	83.9	16.1	2.4	...	375,546	105.7	100.0	—	96.3	3.6	0.1	2,374	13,268	Algeria
...	...	...	...	...	302[2]	0.5	100.0	—	99.6	0.2	0.2	...	...	American Samoa
...	...	...	...	...	6,383	—	—	100.0	100.0	—	—	...	...	Andorra
6,676	83.3	16.7	1.0	1,635	5,124	177.5	96.6	3.4	98.3	1.4	0.3	10,043	14,523	Angola
...	...	...	...	...	4,604	3.2	100.0	—	69.3	29.2	1.4	644	2,373	Antigua and Barbuda
5,741	19.2	80.8	—	224,651	755,695	1,024.8	98.8	1.2	63.1	2.9	34.1	807,042	88,368	Argentina
36[5]	100.0[5]	—	—	...	386	0.4	—	100.0	100.0	—	—	494	3,136	Armenia
...	...	...	...	6	7,321	0.2	100.0	—	100.0	—	—	...	17,753	Aruba
22,938	11.8	88.2	43.5	709,553	1,523,192	216.3	98.6	1.4	61.5	25.8	12.7	899,040	485,072	Australia
13,276	21.5	78.5	60.5	4,085,669	2,318,823	0.4	—	100.0	100.0	—	—	10,689	204,997	Austria
...	...	...	...	206	28,116	4.7	—	100.0	100.0	—	—	3,850	846	Azerbaijan
17	—	100.0	100.0	...	30,414	10.5	100.0	—	16.9	78.5	4.5	69,591	4,400	Bahamas, The
—	—	—	—	...	25,821	10.3	100.0	—	65.5	34.1	0.4	6,925	3,203	Bahrain
33,629	98.1	1.9	0.5	14,405	92,529	924.1	37.0	63.0	96.6	3.4	—	297,585	2,050	Bangladesh
5	—	100.0	100.0	...	35,503	0.3	100.0	—	100.0	—	—	951	11,044	Barbados
6,136	15.1	84.9	51.6	73,918	63,254	0.5	—	100.0	88.9	—	11.1	14,028	54,905	Belarus
4,400	12.5	87.5	58.0	3,734,032[7]	4,136,516[7]	29.9	98.2	1.8	92.9	5.0	2.1	447,598[7]	1,063,195[7]	Belgium
188	67.2	32.8	32.8	3,763	4,003	39.9	100.0	—	64.3	5.4	30.3	21,163	1,724	Belize
6,140	94.6	5.4	0.6	931	12,324	38.5	22.2	77.8	80.1	19.9	—	1,928	3,457	Benin
...	...	...	...	...	...	0.5	100.0	—	91.1	8.9	—	...	7,569	Bermuda
1,751	97.4	2.6	1.0	156	2,159	0.3	—	100.0	100.0	—	—	...	...	Bhutan
1,906	72.7	27.3	26.3	25,409	40,384	6.1	—	100.0	100.0	—	—	4	2,938	Bolivia
40	...	100.0	100.0	72,219	23,986	2.5	—	100.0	100.0	—	—	...	9,781	Bosnia and Herzegovina
1,702	93.8	6.2	...	...	15,410	2.0	—	100.0	100.0	—	—	54	5,218	Botswana
197,897	57.6	42.4	23.6	2,579,776	811,923	655.0	73.3	26.7	90.6	8.7	0.6	138,232	289,808	Brazil
296	26.7	73.3	69.6	...	8,426	3.2	99.2	0.8	96.7	2.2	1.1	184	8,881	Brunei
4,766	44.2	55.8	34.1	75,289	77,741	10.6	76.6	23.4	64.0	—	36.0	5,774	13,307	Bulgaria
11,095	95.4	4.6	—	...	14,780	7.6	—	100.0	100.0	—	—	5	1,674	Burkina Faso
1,799	83.9	16.1	12.3	...	1,700	9.2	—	100.0	100.0	—	—	334	8	Burundi
8,157	87.3	12.7	5.0	35,010	8,910	269.1	14.2	85.8	98.0	1.3	0.7	30,525	2,796	Cambodia
15,279	82.0	18.0	11.6	386,415	18,650	95.0	63.2	36.8	99.6	0.4	—	6,152	19,783	Cameroon
185,659	2.6	97.4	78.9	25,469,746	3,777,382	1,021.9	96.0	4.0	62.5	26.2	11.4	2,617,759	1,338,973	Canada
...	...	...	...	2,519	3,760	10.4	100.0	—	99.6	0.4	—	1,852	1,013	Cape Verde
3,548	75.7	24.3	15.6	46,659	...	15.0	—	100.0	100.0	—	—	61	448	Central African Republic
1,969	61.4	38.6	0.7	116	1,650	84.0	—	100.0	100.0	—	—	...	28	Chad
27,972	38.6	61.4	42.1	1,530,190	185,022	5,050.5	100.0	—	97.1	0.8	2.1	1,696,819	54,569	Chile
291,330[12]	65.6[12]	34.4[12]	19.1[12]	6,778,898[12]	25,536,650[12]	17,240.0	98.3	1.7	69.9	17.6	12.5	2,959,530	1,127,412	China
17,845	95.4	4.6	4.5	78,486	316,615	117.9	75.6	24.4	94.8	5.0	0.2	183,668	71,028	Colombia
9	—	100.0	100.0	...	185	12.2	100.0	—	100.0	—	—	1	774	Comoros
50,754	92.7	7.3	0.5	20,754	3,968	208.4	1.9	98.1	99.8	0.2	—	431	41,905	Congo, Dem. Rep. of the
3,243	80.1	19.9	8.5	75,946	1,769	43.7	41.7	58.3	86.0	5.3	8.7	1,720	18,631	Congo, Rep. of the
5,397	69.0	31.0	25.9	20,837	240,616	25.7	90.4	9.6	96.1	3.6	0.3	148,321	25,359	Costa Rica
13,396	76.9	23.1	16.3	225,923	45,038	76.0	82.9	17.1	98.7	1.2	0.1	132,249	162,354	Côte d'Ivoire
3,486	31.4	68.6	54.9	229,147	290,892	19.3	97.9	2.1	93.0	1.5	5.5	34,845	34,825	Croatia
1,593	74.5	25.5	8.0	60	24,509	67.3	93.1	6.9	61.4	22.7	15.9	93,296	22,484	Cuba
25	26.4	73.6	579.7	2,127	37,192	5.3	98.7	1.3	93.8	2.8	3.4	4,343	31,891	Cyprus
14,441	6.5	93.5	55.5	868,057	667,290	4.2	—	100.0	100.0	—	—	25,922	73,795	Czech Republic
3,086	32.4	67.6	42.8	398,653	1,329,135	1,405.0	100.0	—	92.4	0.8	6.9	2,884,334	1,771,500	Denmark
—	—	—	—	...	4,475	0.4	100.0	—	100.0	—	—	130	1,253	Djibouti
...	...	...	...	...	8,358	1.2	100.0	—	100.0	—	—	...	1,595	Dominica
562	98.9	1.1	0.6	578	211,782	8.5	91.6	8.4	74.2	10.4	15.4	700	53,102	Dominican Republic
...	...	...	...	...	...	0.5	100.0	—	98.4	1.4	0.2	...	...	East Timor
11,340	47.8	0.1	45.6	72,103	224,328	497.9	99.9	0.1	99.6	0.4	—	954,471	5,060	Ecuador

Extractive industries (continued)

country	% of GDP, 1998	mineral production (value added) — year	total ('000,000 U.S.$)	by kind (%) metals[a]	non-metals[b]	energy[c]	trade (value) — year	exports total ('000,000 U.S.$)	metals[a]	non-metals[b]	energy[c]	imports total ('000,000 U.S.$)	metals[a]	non-metals[b]	energy[c]
Egypt	9.8[9]	1994	5,151.3	—	1.0	99.0	1997	704.6	—	5.2	94.8	381.9	40.7	19.2	40.1
El Salvador	0.4	1998	47.6	100.0	—	—	1997	...	...	...	...	151.9	—	5.4	94.6
Equatorial Guinea	61.3	1998	279.6	—	—	100.0	...	...	...	...	...	...	...	...	...
Eritrea	0.1	1998	0.5	100.0	—	—	1997	76.5	79.0	—	21.0	113.1	27.9	20.2	52.0
Estonia	1.0	1998	54.2	—	100.0	—	...	...	...	...	...	...	...	...	...
Ethiopia	0.5	1997–98	33.3	100.0	—	—	1995	...	...	...	...	68.4	—	—	100.0
Faroe Islands	0.2[4]	1996	1.7	...	...	...	1994	0.8	100.0	—	—	5.8	—	41.4	58.6
Fiji	3.4[4]	1996	42.5	100.0	—	—	...	...	...	...	...	...	...	...	...
Finland	0.2	1998	307.4	100.0	—	—	1997	295.9	64.2	33.1	2.8	3,383.4	28.5	8.5	63.1
France	0.8[6]	1995	11,521.0	4.8	14.3	81.0	1997	2,335.7	46.6	32.5	20.9	20,162.7	9.2	5.2	85.5
French Guiana	...	1998	...	100.0	—	—	...	...	...	...	...	...	...	...	...
French Polynesia	...	...	...	...	...	...	1997	191.4	—	100.0	—	...	...	...	...
Gabon	41.8[4]	1996	2,382.8	4.0	—	96.0	1996	2,621.1	2.4	—	97.6	6.7	—	50.7	49.3
Gambia, The	—	1998	...	—	100.0	—	1995	...	...	...	...	1.4	—	—	100.0
Gaza Strip	...	...	...	...	...	...	...	...	...	...	...	...	...	...	...
Georgia	...	...	...	...	...	...	1997	...	...	...	...	...	...	...	...
Germany	...	...	...	...	...	...	1997	5,631.4	43.6	21.0	35.3	30,568.8	16.3	5.6	78.1
Ghana	5.2	1998	388.6	100.0	—	—	1997	225.2	—	100.0	—	56.5	100.0	—	—
Greece	0.6[2]	1997	707.9	...	...	...	1997	310.3	40.9	35.9	23.2	1,393.2	6.9	7.2	85.9
Greenland	...	...	...	...	...	...	1997	...	...	...	...	1.6	—	100.0	—
Grenada	1.4	1998	1.3	—	100.0	—	1996	...	...	...	...	2.4	—	25.0	75.0
Guadeloupe	...	1998	...	—	100.0	—	...	...	...	...	...	...	...	...	...
Guam	...	1998	...	—	100.0	—	...	...	...	...	...	...	...	...	...
Guatemala	0.6	1998	30.0	...	...	...	1997	102.9	—	6.2	93.8	172.1	—	—	100.0
Guernsey	...	...	...	...	...	...	...	...	...	...	...	...	...	...	...
Guinea	15.7	1998	645.4[17]	100.0[17]	—	—	1997	396.7	80.3	19.7	—	...	...	...	...
Guinea-Bissau	...	1998	...	100.0	—	—	...	...	...	...	...	...	...	...	...
Guyana	13.6	1998	98.0	100.0	—	—	1997	94.3	100.0	—	—	...	...	...	...
Haiti	0.2	1998	1.8	—	100.0	—	...	...	...	...	...	10.1	—	—	100.0
Honduras	1.8	1998	82.3	100.0	—	—	1997	30.6	100.0	—	—	...	...	...	...
Hong Kong	0.02	1998	39.1	—	100.0	—	1997	2,264.8	27.2	72.8	—	4,639.9	12.9	75.8	11.2
Hungary	0.4[2]	1997	181.5	15.6	26.5	57.9	1997	136.5	99.6	—	0.4	1,747.1	1.9	3.5	94.6
Iceland	...	1998	...	—	100.0	—	1997	19.7	34.0	66.0	—	50.7	68.6	21.5	9.9
India	1.0	1996–97	3,268.9	...	...	...	1997	5,168.2	13.3	86.2	0.5	10,499.3[4]	7.8[4]	31.2[4]	61.0[4]
Indonesia	12.9	1998	12,704.4	34.7	—	65.3	1997	13,660.2	12.7	0.9	86.4	2,138.5	16.9	14.5	68.6
Iran	7.2	1998–99	13,441.8	9.1	—	90.9	1995	18,525.9	1.0	0.4	98.6	1,271.4	17.5	7.5	75.0
Iraq	...	...	...	...	...	...	1997	538.5	75.1	16.5	8.4	825.7	14.4	12.9	72.7
Ireland	...	1998	...	—	100.0	—	1997	6,948.8	0.5	99.5	—	7,117.3	0.2	73.3	26.5
Isle of Man	...	...	...	...	...	...	...	...	...	...	...	...	...	...	...
Israel	...	...	...	...	...	...	1997	...	...	...	...	...	...	...	...
Italy	...	...	...	...	...	...	1997	851.4	34.6	57.2	8.2	16,573.7	15.0	9.3	75.7
Jamaica	4.5	1998	310.3	97.2	2.8	...	1997	682.4	100.0	—	—	105.8	—	—	100.0
Japan	0.2[4]	1996	9,863.9	...	...	...	1997	1,315.4	44.0	56.0	—	67,595.7	12.8	5.8	81.4
Jersey	...	...	...	...	...	...	...	...	...	...	...	...	...	...	...
Jordan	3.3	1998	239.3	—	100.0	—	1997	353.6	5.0	95.0	—	416.7[6]	0.6[6]	8.6[6]	90.6[6]
Kazakhstan	...	...	...	...	...	...	1996	837.9	18.9	12.8	68.4	170.9	29.9	25.8	44.3
Kenya	0.2[6]	1995	14.1	100.0	—	—	1997	40.4	—	100.0	—	227.3[4]	—	2.6[4]	97.4[4]
Kiribati	...	...	...	...	...	...	1995	...	...	...	...	0.1	—	100.0	—
Korea, North	...	...	...	...	...	...	1997	90.6	30.8	36.9	32.3	52.7[6]	—	36.1[6]	63.9[6]
Korea, South	0.4	1998	1,141.7	...	...	...	1997	238.6	13.9	53.9	32.2	23,311.9[4]	12.8[4]	3.0[4]	84.2[4]
Kuwait	39.5[6]	1995	10,513.4	—	—	100.0	1997	14,130.4[4]	0.2[4]	—	99.8[4]	60.7	—	100.0	—
Kyrgyzstan	...	...	...	...	...	...	1996	15.8	75.9	—	24.1	118.2	2.5	4.8	92.7
Laos	0.4	1998	5.8	100.0	—	—	...	...	...	...	...	...	...	...	...
Latvia	0.5	1998	116.4	—	100.0	—	1997	32.3	85.1	—	14.9	148.9	13.7	8.1	78.2
Lebanon	...	...	...	...	...	...	1997	130.5	31.0	69.0	—	132.8	—	100.0	—
Lesotho	0.01[4]	1996	0.1	—	100.0	—	[10]	...	...	...	...	...	...	...	...
Liberia	2.4	1998	8.6	—	100.0	—	1997	15.7	100.0	—	—	14.8	—	100.0	—
Libya	25.8[4]	1996	8,441.7	—	7.1	92.9	1997	9,451.2[6]	—	—	100.0[6]	51.2	100.0	—	—
Liechtenstein	...	...	...	...	...	...	...	...	...	...	...	...	...	...	...
Lithuania	0.5	1998	49.3	...	33.9[2]	66.1[2]	1997	130.7	48.7	—	51.3	850.6	2.4	7.0	90.6
Luxembourg	0.2	1998	24.8	—	100.0	—	[7]	...	...	...	...	17.3	—	20.8	79.2
Macau	...	...	...	...	...	...	1997	...	...	...	...	41.8	6.7	39.5	53.8
Macedonia	...	...	...	...	...	...	1995	29.5	68.1	31.9	—	79.5	—	—	100.0
Madagascar	0.3[9]	1994	5.2	100.0	—	—	1997	26.6	40.6	59.4	—	5.1	—	62.7	37.3
Malawi	1.0[9]	1994	12.8	...	...	...	1995	...	...	...	...	...	...	...	...
Malaysia	7.9	1998	3,675.2[3]	...	...	...	1996	5,509.7	2.4	2.3	95.3	1,175.0	43.1	32.2	24.7
Maldives	1.6	1998	2.2	—	100.0	—	...	...	...	...	...	...	...	...	...
Mali	5.5	1998	81.7	100.0	—	—	1997	7.0	—	100.0	—	...	...	...	...
Malta	...	1998	...	—	100.0	—	1996	3.5[6]	97.9[6]	2.1[6]	—	10.2	—	100.0	—
Marshall Islands	0.3[6]	1995	0.3	—	100.0	—	...	...	...	...	...	...	...	...	...
Martinique	...	1998	...	—	100.0	—	1995	4.1	19.4	38.3	42.3	102.5	—	—	100.0
Mauritania	9.6[2]	1997	105.9	100.0	—	—	1997	301.6	100.0	—	—	...	...	...	...
Mauritius	0.1	1998	5.6	—	100.0	—	1996	56.2	—	73.8	26.2	56.2	—	73.8	26.2
Mayotte	...	...	...	...	...	...	...	...	...	...	...	...	...	...	...
Mexico	1.2	1998	5,128.4	...	...	...	1997	11,181.6	4.8	2.3	93.0	1,715.3	39.7	25.2	35.1
Micronesia	...	...	...	...	...	...	...	...	...	...	...	...	...	...	...
Moldova	...	1998	...	—	100.0	—	1997	18.7[6]	100.0[6]	—	—	147.5	—	—	100.0
Monaco	...	...	...	...	...	...	...	...	...	...	...	...	...	...	...
Mongolia	...	...	...	...	...	...	1996	254.1	90.9	9.1	—	...	...	...	...
Morocco	2.2[2]	1997	746.5	...	...	...	1997	751.1	23.6	76.4	—	1,449.6	—	11.3	88.7
Mozambique	...	...	...	...	...	...	1996	8.4	72.6	27.4	—	3.3	—	100.0	—
Myanmar (Burma)	0.4	1998–99	1,107.3	100.0	—	—	1997	39.0	—	100.0	—	...	...	...	...
Namibia	11.7[2]	1997	382.8	100.0	—	—	[10]	...	...	...	...	...	...	...	...
Nauru	...	1998	...	—	100.0	—	1997	151.6	—	100.0	—	...	...	...	...
Nepal	0.5	1998–99	26.8	100.0	—	—	1995	...	...	...	...	9.1	51.6	—	48.4

forestry						fisheries, 1999								country
production of roundwood, 2000				trade (value, '000 U.S.$), 1999		catch (nominal)						trade (value, '000 U.S.$)		
total ('000 cubic metres)	fuelwood, charcoal (%)	industrial roundwood (%)		exports	imports	total ('000 metric tons)	by source (%)		by kind of catch (%)			exports	imports	
		total	sawlogs, veneer				marine	inland	fish	crustaceans	mollusks			
2,883	95.4	4.6	—	11,855	794,951	380.5	40.8	59.2	94.5	4.1	1.4	1,442	153,061	Egypt
5,170	87.4	12.6	12.6	14,360	124,786	15.2	83.9	16.1	24.8	71.1	4.1	33,596	6,640	El Salvador
811	55.1	44.9	44.9	89,885	...	7.0	84.3	15.7	90.8	7.2	2.0	2,565	2,508	Equatorial Guinea
2,285	99.9	0.1	0.1	...	6,833	7.0	100.0	—	98.7	1.1	0.2	973	54	Eritrea
8,910	18.4	81.6	32.0	391,529	112,763	111.8	97.2	2.8	88.9	11.1	—	77,582	30,951	Estonia
89,925	97.3	2.7	—	...	8,894	15.9	—	100.0	100.0			...	42	Ethiopia
...	...	...	...	221	4,162	358.0	100.0	—	94.1	4.2	1.7	436,000	15,372	Faroe Islands
483	7.7	92.3	40.6	18,189	8,189	36.7	84.7	15.3	56.2	3.4	40.3	22,266	17,294	Fiji
54,263	7.6	92.4	47.9	10,925,450	887,491	160.6	77.1	22.9	99.9	0.1	—	21,493	118,244	Finland
50,170	22.0	78.0	52.8	5,683,978	7,492,308	578.1	99.2	0.8	86.4	3.5	10.1	1,107,169	3,280,940	France
120	49.8	50.2	42.6	2,481	2,424	7.7	100.0	—	45.5	54.5	—	40,495[2]	5,136[2]	French Guiana
...	...	...	...	...	22,201	12.4	99.6	0.4	99.5	0.4	0.1	2,263	6,891	French Polynesia
5,397	48.6	51.4	51.4	380,793	4,799	52.9	84.9	15.1	94.2	5.4	0.4	13,148	6,876	Gabon
618	81.8	18.2	17.2	...	1,416	30.0	91.7	8.3	97.9	1.8	0.3	4,643	848	Gambia, The
...	...	...	...	...	...	3.6	100.0	—	88.1	6.3	5.7	...	...	Gaza Strip
...	...	...	...	11,952	5,749	1.5	93.3	6.7	100.0	—	—	208	2,471	Georgia
37,634	6.8	93.2	62.2	9,923,976	10,776,915	238.9	90.4	9.6	92.0	8.0	—	966,300	2,288,523	Germany
21,907	94.4	5.6	5.2	187,175	24,016	492.8	84.9	15.1	99.1	0.9	—	95,813	20,321	Ghana
2,171	63.3	36.7	31.5	77,993	737,282	136.7	84.5	15.5	78.8	2.5	18.7	278,208	308,553	Greece
—	—	—	—	77	7,179	160.3	100.0	—	48.8	51.2	—	261,255	1,412	Greenland
...	...	...	...	—	5,167	1.6	100.0	—	95.2	4.4	0.4	3,530	2,534	Grenada
15	98.0	2.0	2.0	...	30,639	9.2	100.0	—	92.9	1.6	5.5	266[2]	30,393[2]	Guadeloupe
...	...	...	...	...	...	0.2	100.0	—	98.7	0.4	0.9	...	...	Guam
13,300	96.2	3.8	3.8	17,449	137,727	11.0	36.7	63.3	71.8	28.0	0.2	28,148	6,794	Guatemala
...	...	...	...	...	...	16	16	16	16	16	16	...	...	Guernsey
8,651	92.5	7.5	1.6	6,024	4,542	87.1	95.4	4.6	98.1	0.5	1.5	22,131	14,490	Guinea
592	71.3	28.7	6.8	610	...	5.0	96.0	4.0	81.3	2.4	16.3	6,318	487	Guinea-Bissau
467	2.4	97.6	93.1	36,047	3,239	53.8	98.9	1.1	77.7	22.3	—	34,461	475	Guyana
6,501	96.3	3.7	3.4	...	13,221	5.0	90.0	10.0	86.0	5.0	9.0	9,264	7,990	Haiti
7,413	88.5	11.5	11.5	43,309	59,836	7.2	98.6	1.4	53.7	21.8	24.4	97,207	14,805	Honduras
21[5]	100.0[5]	—	—	2,508,240[5]	3,101,116[5]	127.8	100.0	—	90.4	3.8	5.9	383,398	1,593,661	Hong Kong
5,902	44.0	56.0	23.4	353,145	618,345	7.5	—	100.0	97.6	—	2.4	6,948	39,552	Hungary
—	—	—	—	648	65,695	1,736.3	100.0	—	96.7	2.6	0.7	1,379,379	80,693	Iceland
302,794	92.1	7.9	6.1	54,971	789,321	3,316.8	79.2	20.8	89.3	7.9	2.8	1,019,579	20,188	India
190,601	83.5	16.5	13.0	4,757,769	947,593	4,149.4	92.9	7.1	90.9	6.6	2.6	1,527,092	86,555	Indonesia
1,151	16.5	83.5	26.9	...	201,165	387.2	63.0	37.0	97.3	1.2	1.5	23,945	58,002	Iran
177	66.7	33.3	14.1	...	4,341	24.6	53.2	46.8	100.0	—	—	...	1,277	Iraq
2,673	2.7	97.3	59.4	237,008	730,167	285.9	98.9	1.1	90.0	7.4	2.6	343,826	115,853	Ireland
...	...	...	...	...	...	2.6	100.0	—	3.6	9.0	87.3	...	...	Isle of Man
113	11.5	88.5	31.9	34,467	695,578	5.9	63.5	36.5	94.8	3.2	2.0	8,496	129,891	Israel
9,329	60.9	39.1	22.1	2,581,755	7,096,128	294.2	98.2	1.8	59.0	6.0	35.1	356,976	2,728,568	Italy
706	60.0	40.0	18.7	...	71,424	8.5	94.7	5.3	79.1	4.8	16.1	13,905	32,487	Jamaica
19,031	1.4	98.6	70.4	1,729,858	12,348,306	5,176.5	98.6	1.4	77.0	3.7	19.3	719,839	14,748,712	Japan
...	...	...	...	...	...	3.6[16]	100.0[16]	—[16]	25.7[16]	67.3[16]	7.0[16]	...	...	Jersey
11	63.6	36.4	—	5,420	104,204	0.5	31.4	68.6	100.0	—	—	1,231	21,020	Jordan
315[5]	100.0	—	—	598	48,398	25.8	—	100.0	100.0	—	—	12,257	11,903	Kazakhstan
29,908	93.4	6.6	1.5	2,064	38,124	205.3	3.2	96.8	99.5	0.4	0.2	32,415	5,339	Kenya
...	...	...	...	...	769[5]	48.2	100.0	—	97.0	—	3.0	5,611	299	Kiribati
7,000	78.6	21.4	14.3	15,192	8,781	210.0	90.5	9.5	95.2	—	4.8	71,535	2,579	Korea, North
1,722	1.6	98.4	36.1	1,515,287	2,967,578	2,119.7	99.7	0.3	64.0	4.4	31.5	1,393,428	1,140,022	Korea, South
...	...	...	...	13	97,708	6.3	100.0	—	88.5	11.5	—	4,721	22,111	Kuwait
42[5]	74.5[5]	25.5[5]	21.9[5]	225	9,892	—	100.0	100.0	100.0	—	—	...	2,287	Kyrgyzstan
4,869	82.2	17.8	15.1	26,657	1,704	30.0	—	100.0	100.0	—	—	99	1,157	Laos
14,488	11.6	88.4	58.7	600,131	47,946	125.4	99.5	0.5	97.5	2.5	—	51,849	36,097	Latvia
412	98.3	1.7	1.7	4,885	166,234	3.6	99.4	0.6	94.4	3.5	2.1	...	19,863	Lebanon
1,594	100.0	—	—	...	...	0.03	—	100.0	100.0	—	—	18	18	Lesotho
3,037	88.9	11.1	5.2	24,492	1,635	15.5	74.1	25.9	97.6	0.2	2.2	64	1,412	Liberia
652	82.2	17.8	9.7	...	33,260	32.5	100.0	—	100.0	—	—	32,654	12,561	Libya
13[5]	30.8[5]	69.2[5]	69.2[5]	...	...	—	...	...	...	...	...	...	...	Liechtenstein
5,346	22.0	77.6	52.4	171,231	113,279	33.6	94.9	5.1	87.6	12.4	—	33,560	52,499	Lithuania
259	6.9	93.1	43.6	[7]	[7]	—	...	...	...	...	...	[7]	[7]	Luxembourg
...	...	...	...	1,841	14,022	1.5	100.0	...	68.0	29.3	2.7	2,852	13,236	Macau
1,047	83.6	16.4	15.7	9,093	150,166	0.1	—	100.0	100.0	—	—	129	9,994	Macedonia
10,359	98.9	1.1	0.8	23,784	5,061	131.6	77.2	22.8	89.5	0.9	9.5	101,061	5,661	Madagascar
9,964	94.8	5.2	1.3	688	5,265	45.4	—	100.0	100.0	—	—	302	236	Malawi
29,461	26.2	73.8	68.6	3,114,963	1,000,476	1,251.8	99.7	0.3	78.3	8.5	13.2	299,437	258,747	Malaysia
...	...	...	...	14	4,220	133.5	100.0	—	99.6	—	0.4	38,907	...	Maldives
6,597	93.7	6.3	0.1	1,648	8,731	98.5	—	100.0	100.0	—	—	378	1,211	Mali
...	...	...	...	—	62,831	1.0	100.0	—	95.7	2.3	1.9	6,751	19,442	Malta
...	...	...	...	...	1,923	0.4	100.0	—	100.0	—	—	1,482	120	Marshall Islands
12	83.3	16.7	16.7	110	22,864	5.0	100.0	—	98.0	2.0	—	168[2]	38,658[2]	Martinique
16	62.5	37.5	6.3	...	6,000	47.8	89.5	10.5	64.7	—	35.2	99,348	524	Mauritania
25	48.0	52.0	28.0	3,741	67,773	12.0	100.0	—	97.2	0.3	2.5	38,558	32,642	Mauritius
...	...	...	...	...	...	1.5	100.0	—	100.0	—	—	3[2]	161[2]	Mayotte
24,122	67.1	32.9	27.0	281,218	2,106,097	1,202.2	92.4	7.6	80.6	7.7	11.7	649,787	125,723	Mexico
...	...	...	...	...	2,110	11.9	100.0	—	99.6	0.2	0.2	459	3,280	Micronesia
58	50.6	49.4	7.7	3,303	23,350	0.5	—	100.0	100.0	—	—	1,381	2,763	Moldova
...	...	...	...	...	...	0.004	100.0	—	100.0	—	—	...	...	Monaco
631	29.5	70.5	70.5	6,289	2,944	0.5	—	100.0	100.0	—	—	232	33	Mongolia
1,123	49.2	50.8	15.7	74,985	336,920	745.4	99.7	0.3	83.2	0.1	16.7	750,764	10,509	Morocco
18,043	92.7	7.3	0.7	14,072	10,075	35.6	69.8	30.2	100.0	—	—	76,861	10,341	Mozambique
22,574	85.2	14.8	10.4	239,712	18,874	851.6	84.8	15.2	98.7	1.3	0.1	158,560	559	Myanmar (Burma)
19	19	19	19	...	36,449	299.2	99.5	0.5	91.3	8.4	0.3	344,017	...	Namibia
...	...	...	...	23[5]	205[5]	0.3	100.0	—	100.0	—	—	...	...	Nauru
21,962	97.2	2.8	2.8	1,199	2,572	12.8	—	100.0	100.0	—	—	269	261	Nepal

Extractive industries (continued)

country	% of GDP, 1998	mineral production (value added)					trade (value)								
		year	total ('000,000 U.S.$)	by kind (%) metals[a]	non-metals[b]	energy[c]	year	exports total ('000,000 U.S.$)	by kind (%) metals[a]	non-metals[b]	energy[c]	imports total ('000,000 U.S.$)	by kind (%) metals[a]	non-metals[b]	energy[c]
Netherlands, The	2.7[6]	1995[3]	9,620.1[3]	...	...	...	1997	6,275.9	19.2	8.5	72.3	12,803.2	12.5	5.9	81.6
Netherlands Antilles	...	1998	...	—	100.0	—	1995	901.5	—	0.1	99.9	900.5	—	—	100.0
New Caledonia	10.7[2]	1997	352.1	100.0	—	—	1997	208.9	100.0	—	—	12.9	—	—	100.0
New Zealand	...	1996	...	—100.0—			1996	110.9	31.3	0.4	68.3	854.0	21.1	13.5	65.5
Nicaragua	1.6	1998	34.0	—100.0—			1997	4.0	100.0	—	—	130.0	—	4.6	95.4
Niger	3.5[9]	1994	62.5	—100.0—		—						19.9	1.5	98.5	...
Nigeria	26.0	1998	33,716.8	—	0.5	99.5	1995	11,131.5	...	...	100.0				
Northern Mariana Islands	...			...	...	...									
Norway	10.9	1998	16,068.2	—1.8		98.2	1997	24,255.2	0.4	1.0	98.6	1,820.3	73.2	11.3	15.5
Oman	40.6[2]	1997	6,361.2	—	0.7	99.3	1996	5,768.3	—	0.1	99.9	70.7	78.8	21.2	—
Pakistan	0.5	1997–98	301.4	...	...	...	1997	57.3	—	1.4	98.6	338.9	50.5	7.5	42.0
Palau	0.1	1998	0.1	—	100.0	—			...	...	...	324.5	...	...	100.0
Panama	0.2	1998	10.5	—100.0—			1996	6.7	100.0	—	—				
Papua New Guinea	26.0	1998	975.2	—64.0—		36.0	1995	1,123.1	48.0	—	52.0	124.9	...	66.9	33.1
Paraguay	0.3	1998	29.2	—	100.0		1996								
Peru	10.9	1998	2,378.8	—67.9[6, 20]—		32.1[6]	1997	1,150.6	79.1	0.1	20.8	564.2	0.4	—	99.6
Philippines	0.7	1998	489.1	57.7[6]	41.3[6]	1.0[6]	1997	567.7	55.4	25.5	19.1	4,078.1	14.2	4.1	81.7
Poland	2.9	1998	4,613.0	...	...	...	1997	1,400.6[4]	7.0[4]	11.6[4]	81.4[4]	3,751.2	11.7	6.5	81.8
Portugal	0.5[6]	1995	529.3	40.2	59.6	0.2	1997	391.8	57.0	35.6	7.5	2,369.2	0.7	7.7	91.6
Puerto Rico	...	...	...	...	...	...	...	...	...	...	...	...	...	...	...
Qatar	38.1[2]	1997	3,502.7[3]	...	...	...	1995	3,000.3	—	0.1	99.9	51.3[9]	75.3[9]	24.7[9]	—
Réunion	...	1998	...	—	100.0	—	1995	0.9	100.0	—	—	15.0	—	—	100.0
Romania	3.3[9]	1994	990.9	—	16.1	83.9	1997	75.6	62.6	37.4	—	1,723.1[9]	9.7[9]	3.7[9]	86.6[9]
Russia	...	...	...	...	...	...	1997	32,522.7	5.6	1.0	93.4	560.0[6]	60.2[6]	16.9[6]	23.0[6]
Rwanda	0.06	1998	1.2	...	...	...	...	...	...	...	...	...	...	...	...
St. Kitts and Nevis	0.3[6]	1995	0.6	—	100.0	—	1997	...	...	...	...	2.1	—	33.3	66.7
St. Lucia	0.5	1998	2.6	—	100.0	—	1996	...	...	...	...	5.1	—	49.0	51.0
St. Vincent	0.3	1998	0.9	—	100.0	—	1997	1.6	—	18.8	81.3	1.6[6]	—	18.8[6]	81.3[6]
Samoa	...	...	...	...	...	...	...	...	...	...	...	...	...	...	...
San Marino	...	...	...	...	...	...	...	...	...	...	...	...	...	...	...
São Tomé and Príncipe	...	1998	—	—	100.0	—	...	...	...	...	...	...	...	...	...
Saudi Arabia	37.2[2]	1997	54,352.5	—1.1		98.9	1997	50,116.9[2]	0.1[2]	...	99.9[2]	136.7	88.6	11.4	...
Senegal	0.2	1998	6.3	—	100.0	—	1995	55.8	7.3	92.7	—	102.6	—	13.5	86.5
Serbia and Montenegro	9.5[9]	1994	981.7	12.0	3.1	84.9	1997	16.8	32.1	—	67.9	708.7	23.6	5.9	70.6
Seychelles	...	1998	...	—	100.0	—	1996	...	...	...	...	0.5	—	100.0	—
Sierra Leone	16.8[22]	1994–95	117.7	—100.0—			1995	16.7	25.4	74.6	—	0.6	—	100.0	—
Singapore	0.02	1998	14.3	—	100.0	—	1997	787.1	31.0	41.7	27.3	8,895.9	0.7	9.0	90.3
Slovakia	0.9	1998	178.8	...	...	...	1997	68.5	28.0	72.0	—	1,106.3	8.9	4.1	87.0
Slovenia	1.0[2]	1997	182.6	...	...	...	1997	28.6	100.0	—	—	386.4	23.4	17.1	59.4
Solomon Islands	...	1998	...	—100.0[23]—		—	1996	...	...	...	...	2.0	—	—	100.0
Somalia	...	...	...	...	...	...	...	...	...	...	...	...	...	...	...
South Africa	6.5	1998	8,003.2	...	...	...	1997[10]	7,936.4	23.4	51.1	25.4	3,452.8	9.7	14.3	76.0
Spain	...	...	...	...	...	...	1997	771.2	39.7	55.0	5.3	12,200.5[4]	16.5[4]	4.2[4]	79.3[4]
Sri Lanka	1.9	1998	269.4[24]	—100.0[24]—			1995	216.5	—	100.0	...	271.1	—	40.0	60.0
Sudan, The	0.3	1998	27.4	...	...	...	1995	...	...	...	...	34.1	—	—	100.0
Suriname	10.9[4]	1996	58.9[25]	...	...	...	1997	594.7	100.0	—	—	15.9[6]	—	31.4[6]	68.6[6]
Swaziland	0.7	1998	8.9	...	...	...	[10]								
Sweden	0.3[6]	1995	634.3	59.2[9]	40.8[9]	—	1997	1,127.6	83.8	11.2	5.0	4,369.9	13.4	6.2	80.4
Switzerland	...	1998	...	—	100.0	—	1997	1,931.1	15.0	85.0	—	4,056.5	3.0	69.0	28.0
Syria	6.6[9]	1994	2,594.1[8]	—100.0[8]—			1995	2,675.5	—	1.4	98.6	21.6	—	—	100.0
Taiwan	0.3[6]	1995	791.6	—	79.6	20.4	1995	843.7	...	...	...	8,035.8	—35.8—		64.2
Tajikistan	...	...	...	...	...	...	1997	1.0	—	100.0	—	228.0[4]	—	100.0[4]	—
Tanzania	1.3	1998	111.9	...	...	...	...	...	...	...	...	...	...	...	...
Thailand	1.8[2]	1997	2,756.6	...	...	...	1997	1,334.0	9.3	74.9	15.7	5,929.7	4.7	14.2	81.1
Togo	5.8	1998	88.3	—	100.0	—	1997	145.3	—	100.0	—	...	...	...	...
Tonga	0.3[6]	1995	0.4	—	100.0	—	1995	0.1	—	100.0	—	1.3	—	46.2	53.6
Trinidad and Tobago	12.2	1998	708.6	—	—	100.0	1996	492.4	—	—	100.0	476.9	12.7	2.1	85.1
Tunisia	5.6	1998	1,456.4	—17.1—		82.9	1997	438.9	2.7	11.6	85.7	367.1	—	32.4	67.6
Turkey	1.1	1998	2,160.5	...	...	...	1997	325.8	61.7	38.3	—	5,709.8	21.0	3.3	75.7
Turkmenistan	9.7[2]	1997	204.0	...	...	...	1997	489.9	—	0.2	99.8	...	...	...	...
Tuvalu	0.9[6]	1995	0.1	—	100.0	—	...	...	...	...	...	...	...	...	...
Uganda	0.3[2,6]	1995–96	15.8	—100.0—			1996	...	...	...	...	11.2	—	100.0	—
Ukraine	...	...	...	...	...	...	1997	1,421.6	60.4	19.7	19.8	6,790.7	3.4	3.1	93.5
United Arab Emirates	33.4[9]	1994[3]	12,269.1[3]	...	...	...	1996	23,700.1	0.5	0.5	99.0	233.3	17.1	82.9	—
United Kingdom	1.7	1998	21,115.8	—8.5—		91.5	1997	18,681.6	5.5	32.6	61.8	16,302.2	16.2	38.7	45.1
United States	1.5[2]	1997	120,500.0	4.8	9.5	85.7	1997	13,394.6	35.4	33.2	31.4	80,065.7	5.6	12.8	81.6
Uruguay	0.2	1997	47.6	—	100.0	—	1997	...	...	...	...	229.7	—	6.4	93.6
Uzbekistan	...	...	...	...	...	...	1997	114.5	—	—	100.0	13.9	100.0	—	—
Vanuatu	...	1998	...	—	100.0	—	1994	...	...	...	...	0.5	—	—	100.0
Venezuela	12.1	1998	10,676.5	—6.4—		93.6	1997	12,510.3	1.8	—	98.2	132.3	41.5	58.5	—
Vietnam	6.2	1998	1,091.3	—9.4—		90.6	1997	103.2	1.8	—	98.8	32.1	—	100.0	—
Virgin Islands (U.S.)	...	1998	...	—	100.0	—	...	...	...	...	...	...	...	...	...
West Bank	...	...	...	...	...	...	...	...	...	...	...	...	...	...	...
Western Sahara	...	...	...	...	...	...	...	...	...	...	...	...	...	...	...
Yemen	9.8[9]	1994	1,788.2[8]	—	—100.0[8]—		1995	1,424.0	—	—	100.0	208.4	—	—	100.0
Zambia	6.1	1998	203.0	...	...	...	1995	12.9	—	100.0	—	1.7	100.0	—	—
Zimbabwe	6.9[9]	1994	336.1	...	...	...	1997	95.9	4.9	94.3	0.8	35.3[4]	17.8[4]	37.1[4]	45.0[4]

[1]Gross value of production (output). [2]1997. [3]Mostly crude petroleum and natural gas. [4]1996. [5]1998. [6]1995. [7]Belgium includes Luxembourg. [8]Mostly crude petroleum. [9]1994. [10]South Africa includes Botswana, Lesotho, Namibia, and Swaziland. [11]Mostly diamonds, some gold. [12]China includes Taiwan. [13]Petroleum sector only. [14]Republic of Cyprus only. [15]1993. [16]Jersey includes

forestry						fisheries, 1999								country
production of roundwood, 2000				trade (value, '000 U.S.$), 1999		catch (nominal)						trade (value '000 U.S.$)		
total ('000 cubic metres)	fuelwood, charcoal (%)	industrial roundwood (%)		exports	imports	total ('000 metric tons)	by source (%)		by kind of catch (%)			exports	imports	
		total	sawlogs, veneer				marine	inland	fish	crustaceans	mollusks			
1,039	15.4	84.6	55.1	2,706,468	5,705,731	514.6	99.6	0.4	87.2	2.8	9.9	1,744,665	1,304,585	Netherlands, The
...	...	...	...	1,535	19,459	0.9	100.0	—	99.4	—	0.6	1,198	6,380	Netherlands Antilles
5	—	100.0	58.3	...	11,595	3.2	100.0	—	96.1	2.8	1.1	18,766	5,677	New Caledonia
17,953	...	100.0	40.4	1,303,550	310,844	594.1	99.8	0.2	93.4	0.7	5.9	712,256	52,445	New Zealand
4,306	94.7	5.3	5.3	11,725	16,267	20.6	94.6	5.4	46.7	52.3	1.0	78,596	7,843	Nicaragua
6,666	93.8	6.2	—	...	6,334	11.0	—	100.0	100.0	—	—	154	458	Niger
100,637	90.6	9.4	7.1	33,457	172,331	455.6	69.4	30.6	92.0	7.2	0.8	19,662	209,959	Nigeria
...	...	...	...	...	51[5]	0.2	100.0	—	99.5	0.5	—	...	...	Northern Mariana Islands
8,173	8.1	91.9	50.1	1,831,746	1,009,845	2,620.1	100.0	—	97.5	2.5	—	3,764,790	612,469	Norway
...	...	...	...	...	17,179	108.8	100.0	—	92.6	0.5	6.9	38,243	5,077	Oman
33,075	92.7	7.3	5.4	...	137,040	654.5	72.5	27.5	93.6	4.9	1.6	141,476	816	Pakistan
...	...	...	...	...	1,123	1.8	100.0	—	98.0	2.0	—	290	87	Palau
1,052	96.7	3.3	3.3	5,440	67,462	120.5	100.0	—	90.8	7.7	1.5	194,898	15,125	Panama
8,597	64.4	35.6	35.6	168,807	12,439	53.7	74.9	25.1	96.9	3.1	—	25,173	7,819	Papua New Guinea
8,097	52.1	47.9	42.2	88,064	31,132	25.0	—	100.0	100.0	—	—	36	1,592	Paraguay
9,157	80.0	20.0	17.7	71,644	166,328	8,429.3	99.5	0.5	98.4	0.2	1.3	788,411	16,833	Peru
43,399	91.8	8.2	1.1	52,996	606,710	1,870.5	92.3	7.7	88.1	4.2	7.7	372,274	121,492	Philippines
25,652	6.0	94.0	44.1	862,220	1,251,300	235.1	94.1	5.9	89.6	8.3	2.1	282,354	260,653	Poland
9,878	6.1	84.8	32.7	1,185,978	913,640	207.7	100.0	—	90.3	2.3	7.4	278,586	1,017,066	Portugal
...	...	...	...	...	...	2.1	100.0	—	59.2	7.7	33.1	[21]	[21]	Puerto Rico
...	...	...	...	...	15,654	4.2	100.0	—	98.8	1.2	—	28	2,053	Qatar
36	85.9	14.1	11.6	342	69,029	5.8	100.0	—	95.5	4.5	—	19,662	33,053	Réunion
13,148	23.1	76.9	46.7	355,924	172,019	7.8	32.0	68.0	100.0	—	—	7,109	31,911	Romania
158,100	33.1	66.9	30.3	3,190,431	358,552	4,141.2	92.6	7.4	95.9	2.1	2.0	1,247,518	199,065	Russia
7,836	95.7	4.3	1.1	...	2,407	6.4	—	100.0	100.0	—	—	...	61	Rwanda
...	...	...	...	33	1,797	0.4	100.0	—	81.5	5.7	12.8	...	729	St. Kitts and Nevis
...	...	...	...	—	11,692	1.7	100.0	—	96.8	1.7	1.5	6,172	5,186	St. Lucia
...	...	...	...	8	18,545	15.6	100.0	—	100.0	—	—	927	1,537	St. Vincent
131	53.4	46.6	44.3	1,357	2,542	9.8	100.0	—	99.5	0.3	0.2	11,700	5,984	Samoa
...	...	...	...	...	...	—	100.0	—	100.0	—	—	...	...	San Marino
9	—	100.0	100.0	504[5]	196[5]	3.8	100.0	—	99.0	—	1.0	3,836	137	São Tomé and Príncipe
...	...	...	...	19,256	778,185	46.9	100.0	—	87.9	10.4	1.7	10,134	99,412	Saudi Arabia
5,037	84.2	15.8	0.8	...	45,293	418.1	90.4	9.6	87.8	1.5	10.7	301,498	3,784	Senegal
1,140	4.4	95.6	95.6	44,990	166,400	1.3	33.9	66.1	96.6	0.8	2.6	225	43,088	Serbia and Montenegro
...	...	...	...	99	1,416	37.8	100.0	—	99.7	—	0.2	12,318	12,904	Seychelles
3,419	96.4	3.6	0.1	1,264	2,053	59.4	75.6	24.4	94.9	3.9	1.2	15,654	3,267	Sierra Leone
120[5]	—	—	—	502,202	889,039	5.1	100.0	—	75.4	14.3	10.3	390,062	475,224	Singapore
5,783	5.9	94.1	42.2	431,828	237,213	1.4	—	100.0	100.0	—	—	1,895	32,269	Slovakia
2,253	23.6	76.4	49.7	399,531	296,900	2.0	88.8	11.2	98.6	—	1.4	6,597	29,280	Slovenia
872	15.8	84.2	84.2	51,070	...	82.3	100.0	—	99.9	—	0.1	64,170	75	Solomon Islands
8,329	98.7	1.3	0.3	132[5]	257[5]	20.3	98.8	1.2	95.6	2.0	2.5	4,058	170	Somalia
30,616[19]	39.2[19]	60.8[19]	19.6[19]	827,673	487,114	588.0	99.8	0.2	98.2	0.5	1.3	260,056[18]	55,691[18]	South Africa
14,810	11.1	88.9	38.4	1,626,053	3,813,488	1,167.2	99.3	0.7	86.8	3.1	10.1	1,604,237	3,286,831	Spain
10,344	93.9	6.1	0.6	2,862	81,534	271.6	90.1	9.9	98.7	1.1	0.2	74,120	59,775	Sri Lanka
9,682	77.6	22.4	1.3	1,040	16,928	49.5	11.1	88.9	99.7	—	0.3	88	280	Sudan, The
93	1.1	98.9	96.8	3,249	1,353	13.0	98.5	1.5	98.0	2.0	—	11,640	3,600	Suriname
890	62.9	37.1	29.2	62,000	—	0.1	—	100.0	100.0	—	—	2,242	9,738	Swaziland
61,800	9.5	90.5	49.7	9,720,885	1,615,641	351.3	99.6	0.4	98.9	1.1	—	477,992	715,463	Sweden
10,428	20.1	79.9	73.9	1,937,022	2,393,070	1.8	—	100.0	100.0	—	—	3,031	375,700	Switzerland
50	31.5	68.5	31.7	1,040	141,790	7.9	32.7	67.3	99.1	0.9	—	183	49,546	Syria
...	...	...	...	80	4,131	1,099.7	99.9	0.1	70.2	2.6	27.2	1,763,572	556,873	Taiwan
...	...	...	...	...	...	...	...	100.0	100.0	—	—	54	143	Tajikistan
39,846	94.2	5.8	0.8	5,939	22,531	310.0	16.1	83.9	99.1	—	0.9	60,202	1,975	Tanzania
36,631	92.2	7.9	0.1	758,925	1,006,210	3,004.9	92.5	7.5	86.7	4.3	9.0	4,109,860	840,679	Thailand
1,232	74.5	25.5	5.4	974	4,355	22.9	78.2	21.8	100.0	—	—	1,498	12,222	Togo
2	—	100.0	100.0	...	2,065	3.7	100.0	—	94.3	5.5	0.2	2,625	872	Tonga
44	22.7	77.3	77.3	2,032	65,952	15.0	100.0	—	95.0	5.0	—	12,315	8,009	Trinidad and Tobago
2,842	92.5	7.5	0.7	14,709	151,980	92.1	99.1	0.9	81.6	7.8	10.6	82,118	13,276	Tunisia
17,767	41.3	58.7	29.1	82,545	969,948	575.1	91.3	8.7	97.1	0.4	2.5	98,196	59,207	Turkey
...	...	...	...	501	3,880	8.8	—	100.0	100.0	—	—	316	99	Turkmenistan
...	...	...	...	—	323[5]	0.4	100.0	—	100.0	—	—	326	...	Tuvalu
16,998	81.3	18.7	6.2	...	17,781	226.1	—	100.0	100.0	—	—	24,221	78	Uganda
10,008	17.6	82.4	62.0	132,755	235,646	407.9	98.9	1.1	98.1	1.4	0.6	75,079	96,776	Ukraine
...	...	...	...	7,290	934,514	117.6	100.0	—	99.9	0.1	—	29,436	28,872	United Arab Emirates
7,451	3.1	96.9	57.1	2,192,065	8,983,465	837.8	99.8	0.2	85.3	7.5	7.2	1,427,853	2,276,998	United Kingdom
500,434	14.4	85.6	49.6	14,783,367	23,721,067	4,749.6	99.2	0.8	79.0	8.3	12.7	2,945,014[21]	9,407,307[21]	United States
6,163	70.3	29.7	22.3	77,918	97,102	103.0	97.6	2.4	79.7	3.3	17.0	98,981	13,418	Uruguay
...	...	...	...	240	37,231	2.9	—	100.0	100.0	—	—	44	2,688	Uzbekistan
63	38.0	62.0	62.0	3,074	...	94.6	100.0	—	99.1	0.3	0.6	738	681	Vanuatu
2,713	33.6	66.4	59.7	65,999	297,987	411.9	91.4	8.6	86.2	2.2	11.6	134,120	40,409	Venezuela
36,730	87.6	12.4	6.6	47,277	132,913	1,200.0	93.8	6.3	70.8	22.3	6.9	940,473	13,801	Vietnam
...	...	...	...	...	...	0.8	100.0	—	100.0	—	—	...	...	Virgin Islands (U.S.)
...	...	...	...	...	...	...	...	...	...	...	...	...	...	West Bank
...	...	...	...	...	...	...	...	...	...	...	...	...	...	Western Sahara
—	—	—	—	...	44,915	123.3	100.0	—	96.2	0.4	3.4	19,789	4,636	Yemen
8,053	89.6	10.4	4.0	...	8,809	67.3	—	100.0	100.0	—	—	205	1,404	Zambia
9,253	87.7	12.3	10.1	31,415	33,293	12.4	—	100.0	100.0	—	—	1,462	9,925	Zimbabwe

Guernsey. [17]Mostly bauxite and diamonds. [18]South Africa includes Lesotho. [19]South Africa includes Namibia. [20]Includes coal mining. [21]United States includes Puerto Rico. [22]1994–95.
[23]Mostly gold. [24]Mostly precious and semiprecious stones. [25]Mostly bauxite. [26]1995–96.

Manufacturing industries

This table provides a summary of manufacturing activity by industrial sector for the countries of the world, providing figures for total manufacturing value added, as well as the percentage contribution of 29 major branches of manufacturing activity to the gross domestic product. U.S. dollar figures for total value added by manufacturing are given but should be used with caution because of uncertainties with respect to national accounting methods; purchasing power parities; preferential price structures and exchange rates; labour costs; and costs for material inputs influenced by "most favoured" international trade agreements, barter, and the like.

Manufacturing activity is classified here according to a modification of the International Standard Industrial Classification (ISIC), revision 2, published by the United Nations. A summary of the 2-, 3-, and 4-digit ISIC codes (groups) defining these 29 sectors follows, providing definitional detail beyond that possible in the column headings. Recently available revision 3 data have also been modified to fit into this 29-sector breakdown.

The collection and publication of national manufacturing data is usually carried out by one of three methods: a full census of manufacturing (usually done every 5 to 10 years for a given country), a periodic survey of manufacturing (usually taken at annual or other regular intervals between censuses), and the onetime sample survey (often limited in geographic, sectoral, or size-of-enterprise coverage). The full census is, naturally, the most complete, but,

since up to 10 years may elapse between such censuses, it has sometimes been necessary to substitute a survey of more recent date but less complete coverage. In addition to national sources, data published by the United Nations Industrial Development Organization (UNIDO), especially its *International Yearbook of Industrial Statistics* and Geographical Reference Information Guide online; occasional publications of the International Monetary Fund (IMF); and other sources have been used.

ISIC code(s)	Products manufactured
31	Food, beverages, and tobacco
311 + 312	food including prepared animal feeds
313	alcoholic and nonalcoholic beverages
314	tobacco manufactures
32	Textiles, wearing apparel, and leather goods
321	spinning of textile fibres, weaving and finishing of textiles, knitted articles, carpets, rope, etc.
322	wearing apparel (including leather clothing; excluding knitted articles and footwear)
323 + 324	leather products (including footwear; excluding wearing apparel), leather substitutes, and fur products

Manufacturing industries

country	year	total manufacturing value added ('000,000 U.S.$)	(31) food (311 + 312)	bever-ages (313)	tobacco manufac-tures (314)	(32) textiles (exc. wearing apparel) (321)	wearing apparel (322)	leather and fur products (323 + 324)	(33) wood products (exc. furniture) (331)	wood furniture (332)	(34) paper, paper products (341)	printing and pub-lishing (342)	(35) industrial chemi-cals (351)	paints, soaps, etc. (352 exc. 3522)	drugs and medicines (3522)
Afghanistan	1988–89[1]	435	18.3	1.9	—	8.0	0.4	16.7	— 0.5 —		0.9	4.9	4.8	0.2	2.7
Albania	1998[2, 3, 4]	257	14.3	7.5	3.0	— 9.6 —		11.3	— 7.8 —		— 5.9 —		2.8[5]	[5]	[5]
Algeria	1997[3, 4, 7]	1,838	25.2	4.0	6.2	— 3.5 —		0.8	2.8	1.2	1.6	1.2	4.0	5.7	2.4
American Samoa	1998[8]	345	98.4	—	—		1.3		— 1.0 —		— 11.0 —		— 8.3 —		—
Andorra	1999[9]	41	— 10.4 —			7.6	— 2.4 —		— 1.0 —		— 11.0 —		— 8.3 —		—
Angola	1989	319	20.0	— 12.2 —		— 11.6 —			— 3.7 —		— 0.3 —		9.1[5]	[5]	[5]
Antigua and Barbuda	2000	13													
Argentina	1996[3, 7]	33,015	16.5	6.5	6.2	3.6	1.4	2.1	0.7	0.7[11]	2.6	4.1	4.3	— 10.6 —	
Armenia	2001[12]	358	— 55.0 —		4.4	0.7	1.2	0.2	0.7	...	0.2	2.3	— 4.4 —		
Aruba	1994	89[12]											...	...	...
Australia	2000–01	59,557	18.5	0.9	0.6	2.3	1.2	0.5	3.5	2.7[11]	3.2	9.5	3.1	2.4	2.3
Austria	1998[13, 14]	38,375	7.8	1.8	...	2.7	1.1	0.6	4.5	3.5[11]	3.9	...	2.0	1.2	2.4
Azerbaijan	2001[12]	1,325	— 34.0 —		4.2	1.8	0.6	0.2	0.2	...	0.1	0.7	— 9.4 —		
Bahamas, The	1992[14]	95	7.4	38.9		0.3	3.6		—	3.5	...	10.0	22.0		...
Bahrain	1992	761	5.0	1.1			6.5	0.1	0.1	8.4	0.4	4.4	5.6	—	
Bangladesh	1991–92[3, 7]	1,899	12.7	0.6	12.2	23.5	10.2	3.9	0.7	0.1	2.9	1.2	5.6	4.5	5.8
Barbados	1995	289	18.0	16.9	2.4	0.7	2.1		—	1.4	1.0	8.3	5.9	— 4.1 —	
Belarus	1994[2, 14, 15]	3,006	16.2	...	...	7.0	2.1	2.6	— 5.4[16]		— 16 —		16.3[5]	[5]	[5]
Belgium	1995	53,712	15.4	2.0	0.7	4.3	2.3	0.1	0.6	3.6	2.2	4.6	11.5	— 3.8 —	
Belize	1992[3]	59	45.9	7.5	3.9	— 3.8 —			5.5	2.7	1.1	1.5	— 14.1 —		
Benin	1990	59	20.6	13.1	—	3.2	5.5	6.9	3.6	5.2	—	2.5	— 9.5 —		
Bermuda	1995	170	...	...	...	...	...	...	...	...	...	...			
Bhutan	1989[3]	21	6.0	10.1	—	— 5.6 —			18.1	2.7	0.4	1.0	21.5	— 1.7 —	
Bolivia	1998[3, 19]	1,086	20.4	13.0	0.5	2.8	1.0	1.1	1.5	0.8[11]	1.7	1.9	0.5	2.6	2.0
Bosnia and Herzegovina	1991	4,021	9.1	2.6	1.7	5.9	4.5	3.3	6.3	4.2	3.9	1.4	5.5	— 4.1 —	
Botswana	1995	212	32.5	12.7	—	8.0	5.2	2.8	2.4	1.4	2.8	2.8	1.4	— 1.4 —	
Brazil	1996[13]	153,540	14.4	5.3	1.1	3.5	2.4	2.4	1.2	1.4[11]	4.0	4.7	— 12.5 —		
Brunei	1998[20]	151	...	...	...	...	...	...	...	...	...	...			
Bulgaria	1998[2]	7,669	14.8	5.8	4.8	3.5	3.5	1.3	1.4	1.1[11]	2.0	2.0	— 10.3 —		
Burkina Faso	1995	162	47.2	15.5	1.2	13.7	1.2	4.4	—	1.2	—	1.2	0.6	—	
Burundi	1995	117	54.7	21.4	5.1	9.4	—		0.9	—	—	0.9	— 1.7 —		
Cambodia	1995[3, 7]	71	— 14.2 —		5.9	0.7	— 21.7 —		— 10.4[21] —		21	0.5	— 0.3 —		
Cameroon	1997–98[3]	708	14.8	17.2	3.1	8.8	—	0.4	18.1	—	3.4	1.2	— 5.8 —		
Canada	1999[22]	112,037	10.0	2.5	0.8	2.0	2.2	0.2	4.7	2.6[11]	5.1	5.1	— 8.0 —		
Cape Verde	1997[2]	78	26.7	20.4	1.9	—	4.9	6.1	5.5	5.7	...	3.0	0.6	7.7	1.7
Central African Republic	1995	36	27.0	13.5	21.6	—	—	—	13.5	2.7	...	5.4	2.7	— 5.4 —	
Chad	2000	152	...	...	...	...	...	...	...	...	...	...	...	...	...
Chile	1997[3, 23]	18,472	21.9	7.0	3.6	2.1	2.1	1.3	3.6	0.8	6.1	3.3	5.2	5.2	2.0
China	1998[24]	182,196	6.7	3.6	5.9	6.7	— 5.0 —		0.8	0.5	2.1	1.2	— 11.4 —		
Colombia	1997[3, 7]	16,696	19.2	10.7	0.5	5.9	3.3	1.3	0.7	0.5	3.4	3.9	4.7	6.6	4.5
Comoros	2000	8.4	...	...	...	...	...	...	...	...	...	...	...	— 0.1 —	
Congo, Dem. Rep. of the	1990	808	86.7	5.4	1.9	0.6	0.2	0.6	0.1	0.2	—	0.1	0.9	— 0.1 —	
Congo, Rep. of the	1995	86	26.7	24.4	7.0	2.3	1.2	2.3	3.5	2.3	1.2	1.2	3.5	— 4.7 —	
Costa Rica	1997[3, 14]	1,412	27.7	15.5	2.8	1.7	3.8	0.6	1.5	0.9	4.2	3.8	6.8	4.4	1.7
Côte d'Ivoire	1997[14, 25]	857	31.3	5.2	5.5	7.6	1.7	0.8	11.2	0.1	2.7	2.3	6.1	6.0	—
Croatia	1999	3,363	— 18.7 —		1.5	2.1	5.0	1.5	3.2	26	1.8	7.3	— 10.8 —		
Cuba	1995	4,077[27]	15.7	5.4	39.9	3.6	1.9	1.2	1.0	0.8	0.2	1.2	1.9	— 7.8 —	
Cyprus	1999	971	19.5	8.6	8.8	2.0	6.0	1.9	6.3	5.2[11]	2.0	5.1	0.6	2.6	2.3
Czech Republic	1998[14]	12,920	9.0	2.9	1.4	3.8	1.7	0.9	2.8	2.0[11]	1.9	3.4	4.2	1.2	1.1
Denmark	1998	25,318	15.2	1.7	1.1	1.8	1.2	0.2	2.7	4.3[11]	2.5	8.6	2.4	2.2	4.1
Djibouti	1992[8]	13	— 5.0 —			— 3.0 —			—	—	— 0.3 —		— 1.0 —		
Dominica	2000[13]	20													
Dominican Republic	1990	1,298	31.9	13.8	5.2	3.5	1.2	3.0	0.2	1.5	2.9	1.7	1.6	— 3.4 —	
East Timor	1996	12	...	...	...	...	...	...	...	...	...	...	...	...	...
Ecuador	1998[3, 7]	4,680	13.7	8.2	0.1	2.2	0.4	0.5	0.9	0.5[11]	1.5	1.1	0.4	2.2	0.3
Egypt	1997–98[13]	6,768	17.1	0.8	0.6	8.7	4.2	0.4	—	0.5[11]	0.9	2.1	5.9	7.2	5.0
El Salvador	1998[3, 19, 29]	1,438	21.3	7.8	—	8.4	17.3	2.5	—	1.0	3.9	3.2	0.7	6.4	8.9
Equatorial Guinea	1990[2]	1.9	27.6	4.1	—		2.6		—	49.3	—	1.2	— 13.8 —		
Eritrea	1998[3, 7]	58	17.2	34.1	6.1	4.8	1.2	6.3	—	3.2[11]	0.3	1.6	0.4	6.1	—
Estonia	1998[2]	2,675	24.1	4.6		7.4	4.1	1.4	10.7	6.7[11]	2.0	5.3	1.7	4.1	0.3

ISIC code(s)	Products manufactured
33	Wood and wood products
331	sawlogs, wood products (excluding furniture), cane products, and cork products
332	wood furniture
34	Paper and paper products, printing and publishing
341	wood pulp, paper, and paper products
342	printing, publishing, and bookbinding
35	Chemicals and chemical, petroleum, coal, rubber, and plastic products
351	basic industrial chemicals (including fertilizers, pesticides, and synthetic fibres)
352 minus 3522	chemical products not elsewhere specified (including paints, varnishes, and soaps and other toiletries)
3522	drugs and medicines
353 + 354	refined petroleum and derivatives of petroleum and coal
355	rubber products
356	plastic products (excluding synthetic fibres)
36	Glass, ceramic, and nonmetallic mineral products
361 + 362	pottery, china, glass, and glass products
369	bricks, tiles, cement, cement products, plaster products, etc.
37	Basic metals
371	iron and steel
372	nonferrous basic metals and processed nickel and cobalt
38	Fabricated metal products, machinery and equipment
381	fabricated metal products (including cutlery, hand tools, fixtures, and structural metal products)
382 minus 3825	nonelectrical machinery and apparatus not elsewhere specified
3825	office, computing, and accounting machinery
383 minus 3832	electrical machinery and apparatus not elsewhere specified
3832	radio, television, and communications equipment (including electronic parts)
384 minus 3843	transport equipment not elsewhere specified
3843	motor vehicles (excluding motorcycles)
385	professional and scientific equipment; photographic and optical goods; watches and clocks
39	Other manufactured goods
390	jewelry, musical instruments, sporting goods, artists' equipment, toys, etc.

			(36)		(37)		(38)								(39)	
refined petroleum and products	rubber products	plastic products	pottery, china, and glass	bricks, tiles, cement, etc.	iron and steel	non-ferrous metals	fabricated metal products	nonelec-trical mach-inery	office equip., com-puters	electrical equip.	radio, tele-vision	transport equip. exc. motor vehicles	motor vehicles	profes-sional equip.	jewelry, musical instru-ments	country
(353 + 354)	(355)	(356)	(361 + 362)	(369)	(371)	(372)	(381)	(382 exc. 3825)	(3825)	(383 exc. 3832)	(3832)	(384 exc. 3843)	(3843)	(385)	(390)	
15.9	—	2.1		1.1	0.4	11.2[6]							0.1	—	37.1	Afghanistan
	[5]	[5]	8.0				[6]	1.7	2.3	4.3				...	0.4	Albania
...	0.1	1.1	0.5	21.4	6.4	1.3	0.5	1.7		4.3		0.1	2.3	1.2	0.3	Algeria
—	5.0		0.5		2.5[6]			14.6				19.6		7.2	9.8	American Samoa
																Andorra
20.0	[5]	[5]	11.3		1.9			5.0				4.7		[10]	0.3[10]	Angola
...															...	Antigua and Barbuda
11.6	1.0	2.5	4.2		4.1	0.6	2.9	3.9	0.1	1.9	1.2	0.5	5.6	0.3	0.4	Argentina
—	0.3		4.1		11.3		1.0	3.2	—	1.3	0.3	0.1		1.0	8.4	Armenia
...	...	...	...		...		...			...					...	Aruba
1.7	0.8	3.3	1.0	3.4	3.6	6.4	8.0	4.5	0.4	2.7	2.1	2.2	6.8	1.5	0.9	Australia
...	0.7	3.3	1.7	4.3	6.1		8.6	10.4	0.1	4.4	6.3	0.9	5.1	2.0	1.7	Austria
38.1	0.4		2.5		0.8		0.7	2.5	0.1	0.5	0.1	2.7	—	0.2	0.3	Azerbaijan
...	...	...	...	7.0	2.6	—	—	0.4		3.4	—	3.4	—	...	...	Bahamas, The
13.7	0.8			4.5	4.4	33.4	0.3	0.4		3.4	—	3.4	—		4.1	Bahrain
0.4	0.5	0.4	1.0	1.7	3.6	0.1	1.2	0.4		1.2	0.5	0.8	3.7	—	0.6	Bangladesh
—	6.6	14.9	0.7	2.8	—		6.9	3.8		2.4		1.0		—	0.3	Barbados
7.6	[5]	[5]	5.5		3.0			26.8							...	Belarus
1.0	0.6	5.4	2.5	2.1	4.7	1.8	7.1	7.1		7.8		7.0		0.5	1.3	Belgium
—	0.3[17]		[17]	6.2			2.0			0.1		4.2			1.1	Belize
—	—	—	0.5	24.6	—	—	4.8	—	—	—	—	—	—	—	0.9	Benin
...	...	...			...	...	...							...	...	Bermuda
...	0.7	2.2	29.0		...	...	...	1.0[18]						...	[18]	Bhutan
36.7	0.1	1.8	1.0	6.8	0.2	0.2	1.2	0.1		0.4			0.2		1.5	Bolivia
2.3	0.3	1.3	0.5	3.2	5.5	3.4	10.8	5.0		3.3		8.6		2.6	0.7	Bosnia and Herzegovina
—	0.5	0.5			—		2.4	0.9		0.9		1.4		—	19.8	Botswana
4.6	1.4	2.8	3.5		5.7		4.1	7.1	0.6	2.8	3.7	0.9	8.0	0.9	1.0	Brazil
...	...	...	...		...		...							...	...	Brunei
10.9	0.9	1.7	4.9		12.5		2.9	8.0	0.6	2.7	0.5	2.4	0.5	0.6	0.4	Bulgaria
—	1.2	0.6	—		1.2	—	0.6			0.6		1.2			8.1	Burkina Faso
—	—	0.9	—	1.7	—	—	2.6	—	—	—	—	—	—	—	0.9	Burundi
...	17.4		24.6		3.8		0.5	—	—	—	—	—	—	—	0.1	Cambodia
4.0	7.2	0.9	—	2.8	—	6.5	1.1	1.8		1.3		—	—	—	1.6	Cameroon
0.8	1.9	3.0	2.8		4.7		7.3	4.6		9.8		19.0		[10]	3.0[10]	Canada
...	0.3	...	0.6	1.5	0.1		5.6	0.1	...	—	...	4.1		3.5	—	Cape Verde
—	—	—	—		—	—	2.7	...	...	—	...	2.7		—	2.7	Central African Republic
...	...	...			...		...								...	Chad
3.4	0.9	2.4	0.9	3.6	2.3	12.3	3.9	2.0		1.1	0.2	0.8	1.6	0.2	0.2	Chile
3.5	1.4	2.4	1.5	4.5	6.5	2.2	3.3	7.8		13.3		7.2		1.1	1.4	China
5.8	1.1	4.1	2.4	5.7	2.0	0.4	3.4	1.9		2.0	0.4	0.7	3.4	0.7	0.8	Colombia
—	—	—			—										—	Comoros
0.1	—	—		0.2	...	...	0.4	0.3		0.2		0.5		—	1.5	Congo, Dem. Rep. of the
—	2.3	—		1.2	—		7.0	2.3		3.5		3.5		—	—	Congo, Rep. of the
2.9	1.8	4.4	1.3	2.9	...	0.1	2.5	1.8	...	1.0	4.6	1.0	0.1	...	0.2	Costa Rica
9.2	0.1	...	...	2.1	...		5.2	0.1		1.1		1.4	0.3	...	0.1	Côte d'Ivoire
11.2	2.5		6.0		2.1		6.7	3.8	0.7	4.0	1.9	5.0	0.6	0.8	2.8[26]	Croatia
...	2.4	2.1	0.5	1.9	0.7	0.9	1.7	1.7		0.9		3.5		0.3	3.0	Cuba
1.3	0.2	3.3	0.4	8.5	1.1		6.7	2.6	—	1.5	—	0.3	0.7	0.4	2.1	Cyprus[28]
...	1.5	2.9	8.3		7.9		9.6	11.3	0.1	5.8	1.6	1.3	8.2	2.2	1.6	Czech Republic
0.3	4.4		1.0	3.2	2.2		8.8	15.3	1.2	3.7	2.6	2.6	1.4	3.7	1.6	Denmark
—			0.1		0.1		13.0								77.5	Djibouti
...	...	...			...		...								...	Dominica
16.2	0.8	1.6	0.7	3.5	1.8	0.2	3.7	0.5		0.8		0.1		0.2	0.2	Dominican Republic
...	...	...			...		...								...	East Timor
56.2	0.3	2.4	0.5	2.9	0.8	0.3	1.4	0.6		0.5	—	0.1	1.7	—	0.2	Ecuador
13.7	0.7	1.2	1.7	8.7	4.4	1.3	2.1	3.9	0.4	3.1	0.8	1.0	2.9	0.4	0.2	Egypt
1.2	0.3	4.0	0.1	5.3	1.2	—	2.2	0.7		0.8	0.5	1.2	...	...	1.1	El Salvador
...	...	...	...	0.8	...	...	0.6	...		...		...		...	...	Equatorial Guinea
...	...	0.6	0.1	13.4	0.3	—	3.1	0.1	...	0.1	—	0.6	0.4	—	—	Eritrea
0.3	0.2	2.1	1.6	3.8	0.1	0.1	6.7	2.5	1.0	1.6	1.3	1.9	1.6	0.4	0.9	Estonia

Manufacturing industries (continued)

country	year	total manufacturing value added ('000,000 U.S.$)	(31) food (311 + 312)	(31) beverages (313)	(31) tobacco manufactures (314)	(32) textiles (exc. wearing apparel) (321)	(32) wearing apparel (322)	(32) leather and fur products (323 + 324)	(33) wood products (exc. furniture) (331)	(33) wood furniture (332)	(34) paper, paper products (341)	(34) printing and publishing (342)	(35) industrial chemicals (351)	(35) paints, soaps, etc. (352 exc. 3522)	(35) drugs and medicines (3522)
Ethiopia	1997–98[3,30]	449	28.2	20.6	5.7	6.9	0.6	5.4	0.8	2.0[11]	1.5	3.0	0.6	3.1	3.4
Faroe Islands	1999[8,31]	117	80.7	...	...	...	0.1	...	...	...	...	...	...	3.1	...
Fiji	1994	160	42.6	6.1	—	—13.8—		1.3	9.7	1.9	3.8	5.1	...	—5.3—	
Finland	2000	28,355	4.8	0.9	0.1	0.9	0.6	0.3	4.4	2.4[11,34]	17.8	5.2	...	—5.3—	
France	1998[13,35]	166,238[36]	...	...	...	2.8	1.8	0.9	1.1	1.7[11]	3.1	5.7	5.7	5.7	4.4
French Guiana	1996[14,37]	101	—8.5—			—38—			...	...	...	3.3[38]	...	...	...
French Polynesia	1993[14]	214	—27.2—						...	...	...	...	...	...	...
Gabon	1995	243	9.1	7.0	6.2	0.8	1.7	—	18.1	2.5	0.8	1.2	4.1	—1.7—	
Gambia, The	1995[3,19]	9.2	—65.0—			—8.3—			—6.2[39]—		—	4.2	8.8[5]	5	5
Gaza Strip[40]	...	...	...	...	...	...	...	...	...	...	...	...	...	...	...
Georgia	2001[2]	292	—47.8—		3.8	0.2	0.5	0.7	0.9	0.5[11,34]	0.4	3.0	—5.6—		
Germany	2000[35]	552,121	—8.1—		2.2	1.2	0.7	0.2	1.2	[41]	2.4	4.6	—11.4—		
Ghana	1993[3,35]	610	8.4	9.1	18.1	4.6	—0.5—		15.2	0.8	1.8	1.3	0.9	—8.9—	
Greece	1996[7,13]	10,948	18.3	6.6	2.0	6.6	5.0	1.4	1.5	1.5[11]	3.1	4.2	3.0	—8.9—	
Greenland	2000[14,43]	0.5	...	...	...	...	...	...	...	...	...	...	...	...	...
Grenada	1996[44,45]	21	31.5	51.2	2.0	—	—	—	...	...	6.5	...	—	8.8	...
Guadeloupe	1995[14]	290	—28.8—			...	[46]		...	[46]	...	24.4	...	[46]	
Guam	1997[1,14]	165	—14.8—												
Guatemala	1995	1,468	28.7	6.2	3.1	5.7	2.5	1.2	0.8	0.5	1.5	4.5	3.5	—16.4—	
Guernsey	2000[8,14]	68	...	[47]	...	[47]			...	7.2[47]	...	21.1	...	...	...
Guinea	1998	158	...	...	...	...	...	...	...	...	...	...	...	...	...
Guinea-Bissau	2001[48]	20	...	...	...	...	...	...	...	...	...	...	...	...	...
Guyana	2001[14,48]	58	46.4[49]						...	...	...	...	—	...	—6.3—
Haiti	1999[14]	197	—48.6—		3.8	—20.9—			...	...	...	...	...	...	...
Honduras	1996[13,19]	575	28.8	10.4	2.9	2.5	18.8	1.0	4.8	1.5	2.9	2.2	0.4	3.7	1.0
Hong Kong	1999[14]	8,477	7.9	[46]	[46]	11.1	11.0	0.1	0.1	0.1	1.3	16.3	—3.3—		
Hungary	1999	8,878	15.1	3.2	0.6	2.3	4.7	1.1	1.5	1.3	1.4	4.0	—7.0—		
Iceland	1996	998	43.6	2.1	—	2.4	1.6	1.2	0.2	3.6	1.1	10.4	1.2	2.0	—
India	1997–98[13,50]	34,090	9.1	1.3	1.7	9.6	1.8	0.8	0.2	0.1	1.4	1.4	9.2	4.1	4.9
Indonesia	1998[13,14,35]	14,799	12.1	0.4	8.8	10.5	3.4	3.7	6.8	2.8[11]	3.5	2.7	10.0	2.2	1.3
Iran	1996–97[7]	16,068	10.2	1.7	1.0	8.6	0.5	1.0	0.6	0.4[11]	1.7	0.9	11.8	3.5	1.6
Iraq	1995	567	9.9	3.4	1.2	3.5	1.2	3.5	—	0.2	3.5	1.4	9.2	—1.1—	
Ireland	1999	45,302	—15.1—		0.5	0.5	0.5	0.1	—0.6—		0.8	15.3	—35.5—		
Isle of Man	1998–99[13,14]	135	—19.9—			...	...	...	...	...	...	...	...	...	...
Israel	1998[19]	15,537	10.3	—1.7—		3.8	1.7	0.4	0.7	1.7[11]	2.3	4.8	—12.5—		
Italy	1998	161,544	7.2	1.4	0.4	6.3	4.0	2.8	1.1	2.5	2.6	3.3	3.6	—6.7—	
Jamaica	2001[13]	566	22.5	14.3	6.8	—2.5—		0.6	—2.7—		—2.9—		8.5[5]	5	5
Japan	1998	888,152	8.3	2.1	0.7	2.2	1.0	0.4	1.3	0.9[11]	2.6	6.1	3.6	2.9	3.2
Jersey	1996	46	...	...	...	...	...	...	...	...	...	...	...	...	...
Jordan	1998	1,262	10.2	5.7	13.3	2.2	2.0	0.9	1.0	2.6	2.7	2.8	6.9	2.7	5.1
Kazakhstan	1998[2,14]	5,660	12.9[14]	4.2	3.2	1.1[14]	0.4	0.2	0.4	0.2[11]	—[14]	2.2[14]	2.0	0.3[14]	0.2
Kenya	1998[4,13]	1,029	36.0	11.2	1.9	4.6	2.0	1.4	1.8	0.9	4.7	2.5	2.4	—6.4—	
Kiribati	1998	0.76	...	...	—	—	—	—	...	...	—	—	—	...	—
Korea, North	...	...	...	...	...	...	...	...	...	...	...	...	...	...	...
Korea, South	1999	168,813	—7.8—		1.1	5.5	1.9	1.0	0.6	[41]	2.3	2.5	—9.5—		
Kuwait	1997[7]	4,310	3.7	1.1	0.1	0.5	2.7	0.1	0.3	1.0	0.6	0.5	2.4	0.5	—
Kyrgyzstan	1998[2]	494	15.3	2.7	6.1	10.9	0.6	0.4	0.3	0.2[11]	—	0.7	—4.0—		0.1
Laos	1990[2]	66	4.5	7.4	16.3	—	5.1	0.3	40.1	5.0	—	1.2	—4.0—		
Latvia	1998[13,14]	1,125	23.3	12.2	—	5.9	4.6	0.5	16.1	2.2[11]	1.1	5.8	0.2	1.0	1.4
Lebanon	1994	1,679	—25.2—		1.9	3.3	9.6	3.0	—3.4—		2.4	2.4	2.4	—	
Lesotho	1995	134	43.3	28.4	...	10.4	3.0	2.2	...	0.7	...	1.5	—6.7—		
Liberia	1999	21	...	...	...	...	...	...	...	...	...	...	...	...	...
Libya	1995	857	4.3	2.2	9.4	3.7	3.3	8.5	0.3	0.2	0.3	1.0	7.0	—5.2—	
Liechtenstein	2000[8,14,53]	1,269	—6.1—			—1.7—			...	...	...	...	—10.0—		
Lithuania	1999[2]	4,552	—27.6—		[46]	6.6	10.9	1.2	5.7	[41]	1.4	3.8	—6.5—		
Luxembourg	1999	2,332	—11.0—			—10.0—			1.8	[41]	—7.5—		—6.4—		
Macau	2001	395	2.9	0.8	1.2	16.4	65.9	2.3	—	[41]	0.2	3.0	—2.3—		
Macedonia	1996	603	19.7	4.8	7.5	5.9	8.0	3.9	0.2	2.1	0.9	4.6	5.5	—5.1—	
Madagascar	1995	127	15.0	11.8	0.8	35.4	3.1	2.4	0.8	0.8	3.9	1.6	—	—6.3—	
Malawi	1998	105[13]	17.6	24.4	1.7	5.7	1.4	0.7	—2.0—		—6.5—		7.6[55]	—8.0—	
Malaysia	1997[13]	28,143	6.4	0.8	1.2	3.1	1.6	0.1	5.1	1.4	1.4	2.7	6.6	1.7	0.3
Maldives	2000	63[48]	...	...	...	...	...	...	...	...	...	...	...	...	...
Mali	1990	96	18.4	1.2	13.1	36.5	10.3	0.1	0.1	—	0.4	0.8	0.8	—0.7—	
Malta	1998	739	9.3	7.5	1.2	0.5	8.5	2.0	0.4	4.7[11]	1.4	7.0	1.4	1.6	1.9
Marshall Islands	1997	2.2	...	...	...	...	...	...	...	...	...	...	...	...	...
Martinique	1997	322	—39.8—			—0.4—			...	...	—3.9—		...	—14.5—	
Mauritania	1997	13	...	...	...	...	...	...	...	...	...	...	...	...	...
Mauritius	1998[7,57]	785	15.3	—6.8—		7.9	42.2	0.8	0.4	1.0[11]	1.5	3.3[57]	—4.6—		
Mayotte	1992	...	...	...	...	...	...	...	...	...	...	...	...	...	...
Mexico	1999[3,27]	41,861	8.4	8.9	3.8	1.9	0.5	0.3	0.1	0.2	2.3	0.5	8.8	—8.7—	
Micronesia	1996	2.6[6]	...	...	...	...	...	...	...	...	...	...	...	...	...
Moldova	1998[2,3,59]	752	39.8	25.8	5.8	1.6	1.4	2.0	0.5	1.1	1.5	1.6	—	0.4	0.9
Monaco	1992	689[1]	...	...	...	...	...	...	...	...	...	...	...	...	...
Mongolia	1998[3]	44	28.3	10.6	—	34.2	7.4	0.7	2.1	0.1[11]	—	2.6	—	0.2	2.9
Morocco	1998	5,484	16.9	4.7	12.2	8.3	8.8	1.3	1.5	0.3	2.6	1.2	9.8	3.4	2.0
Mozambique	2000[2]	490	15.7	22.4	1.9	4.4	2.6	...	4.5	0.1	—5.9—		—3.8—		
Myanmar (Burma)	1998	2,409[4]	4.0	19.9[4]	28.5	22.9	...	0.4	4.3	...	1.1[14]	...	...	5.4	6.9
Namibia	2001[14]	306	—70.8—		...	...	...	...	...	...	...	...	...	...	...
Nauru	1989	—	—	—	—	...	...	...	...	...	...	...	...	...	...
Nepal	1996–97[3,7,14]	381	13.6	9.1	12.0	25.9	6.3	1.3	1.4	0.9[11]	1.7	1.3	—	3.4	2.4
Netherlands, The	1999[3]	48,443	15.0	3.9	5.3	1.8	0.3	0.2	1.0	0.8	3.4	8.6	7.9	—5.5—	
Netherlands Antilles	1997	151	...	...	...	...	...	...	...	...	...	...	...	...	...
New Caledonia	1997[14]	375	—16.5—			...	...	...	...	...	...	...	...	...	...
New Zealand	1995	9,878	25.1	3.0	0.6	2.9	2.3	1.1	4.6	1.8	7.7	7.8	3.6	—3.1—	
Nicaragua	2000[14]	331	40.5	25.3	2.2	1.2	0.1	1.2	2.5	0.5	1.0	1.8	—3.9—		

refined petroleum and products (353 + 354)	rubber products (355)	plastic products (356)	(36) pottery, china, and glass (361 + 362)	(36) bricks, tiles, cement, etc. (369)	(37) iron and steel (371)	(37) non-ferrous metals (372)	(38) fabricated metal products (381)	nonelectrical machinery (382 exc. 3825)	office equip., computers (3825)	electrical equip. (383 exc. 3832)	radio, television (3832)	transport equip. exc. motor vehicles (384 exc. 3843)	motor vehicles (3843)	professional equip. (385)	(39) jewelry, musical instruments (390)	country
—	2.1	2.0	0.8	8.3	2.6	—	1.2	0.1	—	—	—	—	1.1	—	—	Ethiopia
…	…	…	…	…	…	…	…	…	…	…	…	14.3	…	…	4.9[32]	Faroe Islands
—	0.5	2.0	—	3.0[33]	[33]	—	3.2	1.2	…	…	…	0.4	1.0	…	1.2	Fiji
1.6	0.6	2.6	0.9	2.1	—4.5—		5.9	10.3	—	3.1	20.4	1.8	1.1	2.3	[34]	Finland
2.6	2.2	3.8	1.9	2.7	3.2	1.3	8.5	8.2	2.5	4.9	6.0	5.0	11.0	2.5	1.0	France
…	…	…	…	…	…	…	…	…	…	…	…	…	…	…	…	French Guiana
…	…	…	…	…	…	…	—35.4—								…	French Polynesia
10.3	—	—	0.8	5.8	2.1	2.1	8.7	—0.8—		—5.4—		—7.0—		0.4	3.3	Gabon
—	[5]	[5]	—	—	—1.8—		4.8	—0.8—						—	[39]	Gambia, The
…	…	…	…	…	…	…	…	…	…	…	…	…	…	…	…	Gaza Strip[40]
0.9	—1.9—		—8.7—		—12.5—		0.9	0.8	—	1.5	0.1	8.8	0.5	0.1	[34]	Georgia
5.1	—4.3—		—3.5—		—4.0—		6.7	13.0	1.1	7.0	2.9	2.0	13.1	3.0	2.3[41]	Germany
8.1	0.6	2.6	—4.4—		0.7	8.2	3.4	—0.3—		—1.5—		—0.6[42]—		—	[42]	Ghana
4.3	0.5	3.2	—7.3—		2.3	3.3	3.8	3.6	0.1	2.1	1.7	4.3	0.6	0.4	0.5	Greece
…	…	…	…	…	…	…	…	…	…	…	…	…	…	…	…	Greenland
—	…	…	—	—	…	…	—	—	…	…	—	—	—	—	…	Grenada
…	—	—	…	…	…	…	…	…	…	—46—		…	…	…	0.6	Guadeloupe
…	…	…	—10.3—		…	…	2.6	…	…	…	…	…	…	…	0.4	Guam
1.1	2.5	4.0	2.5	4.8	2.7	0.1	2.5	—0.8—		—3.4—		—0.3—		0.2	0.4	Guatemala
…	…	…	…	…	…	…	—9.3—		…	…	21.8	5.6	…	…	…	Guernsey
…	…	…	…	…	…	…	…	…	…	…	…	…	…	…	…	Guinea
…	…	…	…	…	…	…	…	…	…	…	…	…	…	…	…	Guinea-Bissau
—	…	—	—1.1—		…	…	2.0	…	…	…	…	…	…	…	…	Guyana
…	…	…	…	…	…	…	…	…	…	…	…	…	…	…	…	Haiti
0.2	1.1	3.3	0.1	7.5	0.5	0.2	3.6	0.7	—	0.9	0.1	—	0.2	0.1	0.7	Honduras
[46]	[46]	2.0	—4.2—		—1.0—		3.1	7.4	3.6	0.4	13.3	—4.6—		2.5	3.6	Hong Kong
15.0	0.3	3.5	1.7	2.2	1.3	1.2	3.8	—4.6—		—11.6—		—10.2—		2.1	0.4	Hungary
—	—	3.0	0.4	3.7	2.4	4.4	9.9	—	…	…	…	2.4	—	…	4.5	Iceland
2.2	2.2	1.7	0.7	3.7	13.1	2.6	2.4	6.3	0.7	5.1	2.3	3.3	6.2	0.6	1.3	India
1.7	2.0	1.9	…	…	2.5	1.5	2.6	1.3	—	1.4	4.8	6.9	1.4	0.4	1.3	Indonesia
1.9	1.8	1.3	1.4	8.4	15.3	3.1	5.1	6.2	0.1	2.6	1.2	0.8	6.5	0.6	0.2	Iran
25.2	0.5	1.4	0.7	18.2	4.1	—	4.8	—2.3—		—4.4—		—0.4—		…	0.6	Iraq
[51]	—1.2—		—1.7—		—0.4—		1.4	1.8	10.1	2.0	6.7	0.6	0.4	3.4	1.4[51]	Ireland
…	…	…	…	…	…	…	…	…	…	…	…	…	…	…	…	Isle of Man
—	…	—5.1—	—3.6—		—1.8—		10.6	—4.3—		2.4	14.4	—5.4—		11.2	1.3	Israel
2.1	1.7	3.0	1.6	4.3	3.5	1.2	7.4	—13.8—		—7.4—		—8.5—		2.6	1.1	Italy
14.1	[5]	[5]	—7.7—		[52]		—16.9[52]—								0.6	Jamaica
0.8	1.2	3.6	1.0	2.8	3.5	1.1	7.3	11.1	4.8	4.6	8.0	1.4	9.6	2.1	1.7	Japan
…	…	…	…	…	…	…	…	…	…	…	…	…	…	…	…	Jersey
6.5	0.2	3.0	1.1	13.5	2.2	0.7	9.1	—1.9—		—1.8—		…	1.2	0.1	0.6	Jordan
7.0[14]	0.3	0.3	0.1	2.6	9.3	20.7	1.6	1.9[14]	0.1	0.5	0.5	0.1[14]	0.1[14]	0.2	0.2[14]	Kazakhstan
0.8	3.1	3.8	0.5	3.8	…	…	6.8	—0.6—		…	…	—2.5—		0.1	2.2	Kenya
—	…	…	—	—	…	…	—	—	…	…	…	…	…	…	…	Kiribati
…	…	…	…	…	…	…	…	…	…	…	…	…	…	…	…	Korea, North
3.9	—4.2—		—3.9—		—6.6—		4.0	7.1	2.8	3.7	16.2	4.1	8.7	1.0	1.6[41]	Korea, South
75.2	0.1	1.3	0.3	3.4	0.3	—	2.8	1.3	—	1.0	—	0.4	0.1	—	0.5	Kuwait
0.6	—		1.2	9.3	—	40.8	0.4	3.2	0.2	4.3	0.1	—	0.8	1.4	0.4	Kyrgyzstan
—	—0.5—		0.1	3.8	—	—	10.8	—0.5—		—0.2—		—	—	…	0.1	Laos
0.1	0.1	1.0	1.2	2.1	—	0.1	4.0	3.7	0.1	2.3	0.8	3.2	0.5[14]	0.7	0.6	Latvia
1.6	—	3.2	—12.0—		—4.9—		8.9	—2.2—		—2.1—		—1.0—		…	10.5	Lebanon
…	…	…	…	0.7	…	…	3.0	…	…	…	…	…	…	…	…	Lesotho
…	…	…	…	…	…	…	…	…	…	…	…	…	…	…	…	Liberia
27.2	0.1	0.8	0.2	21.7	—	—	0.5	—	—	—	—	—	—	—	4.0	Libya
			—11.4—		0.6	1.5	17.6	—40.6—				—10.5—		…	[54]	Liechtenstein
13.1	—3.0—		—3.5—		—0.6—		2.0	2.4	0.2	2.3	3.0	2.0	0.1	1.1	3.0[41]	Lithuania
—12.1—			—8.6—		—17.3—		12.1	—7.6—		—4.0—		—0.5—		…	0.9[41]	Luxembourg
—	—	0.2	—1.3—		—	—	0.6	0.3	-0.1	—0.2—		—0.9—		…	1.5[41]	Macau
0.4	0.1	1.2	0.8	0.6	6.2	—	5.4	—1.1—		—9.5—		—4.7—		0.3	1.7	Macedonia
7.9	0.8	0.8	—	2.4	—	—	3.1	…	…	—2.4—		—0.8—		…	—	Madagascar
—	0.6	3.2	—	7.5	—	—	8.6	—4.5[56]—		[55]		[56]		…	—	Malawi
3.4	4.2	3.5	1.6	3.9	2.3	1.0	4.1	3.4	2.6	3.5	26.5	1.4	4.4	1.0	0.7	Malaysia
…	…	…	…	…	…	…	…	…	…	…	…	…	…	…	…	Maldives
0.7	0.3	0.4	—	1.3	—	—	6.2	—0.5—		—1.7—		—6.5—		…	…	Mali
—	3.9	2.1	0.6	2.0	—0.1—		3.4	2.0	0.2	6.0	20.1	2.8	0.2	4.2	5.1	Malta
…	…	…	…	…	…	…	…	…	…	…	…	…	…	…	…	Marshall Islands
…	…	…	…	…	…	…	…	…	…	…	…	…	…	…	…	Martinique
			—12.2—		…	…	…	—29.2—				…	…	…	…	Mauritania
			—5.3—		—1.5—		2.3	—0.6—		—1.4—		—0.4—		1.1	3.6	Mauritius
…	…	…	…	…	…	…	…	…	…	…	…	…	…	…	…	Mayotte
0.6[27,58]	1.3	1.5	2.7	3.7	7.6	3.1	4.1	—3.9—		—6.1—		—20.5—		0.4	0.3	Mexico
…	…	…	…	…	…	…	…	…	…	…	…	…	…	…	…	Micronesia
—	—	0.5	3.8	3.9	0.1	0.1	1.1	5.2	0.2	0.4	0.4	0.1	0.6	0.9	0.3	Moldova
…	…	…	…	…	…	…	…	…	…	…	…	…	…	…	…	Monaco
—	—	—	—	4.4	0.3	—	0.2	0.2	—	0.1	—	0.2	—	1.6	3.6	Mongolia
…	0.9	1.9	1.4	9.3	1.0	0.3	4.3	0.7	0.2	2.2	0.8	0.5	3.0	0.2	0.1	Morocco
0.4	1.1	1.8	—10.8—		0.1	0.1	23.9	—0.1—		—0.4—		—0.1—		…	0.1	Mozambique
—	1.7	1.0	…	…	1.3	…	0.1	…	…	0.6	…	…	0.9	…	0.9	Myanmar (Burma)
…	…	…	…	…	…	…	…	…	…	…	…	…	…	…	…	Namibia
…	…	…	…	…	…	…	…	…	…	…	…	…	…	…	…	Nauru
0.2	1.3	1.7	0.1	7.2	1.6	0.1	4.8	0.1	—	2.2	0.3	—	—	…	0.5	Nepal
1.8	0.6	3.2	1.6	2.3	—3.7—		6.2	—9.6—		—10.9—		—5.1—		0.9	0.3	Netherlands, The
…	…	…	…	…	…	47.9	…	…	…	…	…	…	…	…	…	Netherlands Antilles
…	…	…	…	…	…	…	…	…	…	—14.4—		…	…	…	…	New Caledonia
1.5	0.7	3.6	1.3	2.1	1.8	2.3	7.7	—4.8—		—4.4—		—4.4—		0.4	1.3	New Zealand
4.4	—0.1—		—10.9—		…	…	0.7	—0.3—		…	…	—0.2—		…	3.3	Nicaragua

Manufacturing industries (continued)

country	year	total manufacturing value added ('000,000 U.S.$)	(31) food (311+312)	beverages (313)	tobacco manufactures (314)	(32) textiles exc. wearing apparel (321)	wearing apparel (322)	leather and fur products (323+324)	(33) wood products exc. furniture (331)	wood furniture (332)	(34) paper, paper products (341)	printing and publishing (342)	(35) industrial chemicals (351)	paints, soaps, etc. (352 exc. 3522)	drugs and medicines (3522)
Niger	1998[3]	15	19.8			9.1			0.5		37.0		18.0		
Nigeria	1995	7,884	17.6	15.3	1.9	10.4	0.1	3.1	0.5	0.9	3.8	3.4	0.3	11.7	
Northern Mariana Islands	1997[1,14]	762	0.7			46	91.8	—	46	46	46	0.7	0.3		
Norway	1998[14]	17,647	12.4	3.9[14]		1.2	0.4	0.1	3.8	2.6[11]	4.3	9.9	4.9	1.2	1.6
Oman	1998	689	16.8	2.3	—	1.0	6.1	0.3	3.1	4.5[11]	1.4	3.1	1.0	4.3	0.8
Pakistan	1995–96[3,19]	6,307	15.2	1.6	6.2	23.5	1.4	1.3	0.2	—	1.6	2.0	8.5	3.0	4.8
Palau	2000	1.7	...	...	...	...	...[60]	...	...	...	...	...	...	...	...
Panama	1999	732	56.1			0.9	1.9	0.5	1.3	[41]	3.1	3.1	4.3		
Papua New Guinea	2000	318	...	...	...	...	...	...	...	...	...	...	...	...	...
Paraguay	2001	905	42.9	12.6	0.5	4.9	0.1	6.5	10.9	0.8		7.4	1.2	1.1	
Peru	1998	4,568	18.7	6.7		8.3	4.4	0.9	7.2		1.1	4.9	3.2	5.1	0.9
Philippines	2000	16,878	42.6	4.4	2.1	1.6	5.5		0.8	1.6	0.8	1.0	7.1		
Poland	1999	28,003	12.4	12.2	3.1	2.6	3.1	0.8	2.0	3.0	2.0	1.3	2.9	3.5	
Portugal	1997[3]	21,410	7.7	2.6	4.9	7.3	6.8	4.2	3.9	2.5[11]	3.2	4.9	2.2	1.6	2.0
Puerto Rico	1997[14]	36,427	4.0	5.7	...	0.2	1.9	0.6	...	0.1[11]	0.4	1.2	2.5	2.3	54.0
Qatar	1998	718	4.0	0.3	—	0.4	9.0	0.2	0.6	2.6	0.1	3.4	37.9	0.5	—
Réunion	1994	371	34.5	12.3		0.5			3.8		5.0[61]	6.3	3.7		
Romania	1997[62]	9,085	22.5	11.0	1.7	3.3	6.2	2.1	3.6	3.2[11]	1.0	1.7	2.3	1.5	1.2
Russia	1998	35,840[14]	16.4	4.2	1.5	1.3	1.0	0.4	1.9	0.9	2.4	1.1	5.6	2.3	1.5
Rwanda	1998	259	79.3			6.8	...	...	1.8		0.7		1.3		
St. Kitts and Nevis	2000[13]	30	9.3[64]	...	...	...	...	...	...	...	...	...	...	...	...
St. Lucia	1997	31	12.8	34.3	1.9	4.4	7.1	—	—	4.4	8.9	7.4	0.7	2.8	—
St. Vincent	2000[13]	15	...	...	...	...	...	...	...	...	...	...	...	...	...
Samoa	1998[15]	28	17.0	42.0	11.0	...	...	...	7.0	...	...	...	...	7.0	...
San Marino	...	...	...	...	...	...	...	...	...	...	...	...	...	...	...
São Tomé and Príncipe	2000[48]	2.5	...	...	...	...	...	...	...	...	...	...	...	...	...
Saudi Arabia	1998	12,542	7.9	2.8	—	1.0	0.1	0.2	0.3	0.8	2.5	1.3	26.7	4.0	
Senegal	1997[3]	341	36.6	4.1	3.1	5.2	—	—	0.2	0.1	1.9	2.5	19.8	4.3	2.1
Serbia and Montenegro	1999	3,591	28.6		2.4	4.6	3.5	2.3	2.2	6.1[34]	3.4	5.1	8.6		
Seychelles	1989	26[66]	79.6			0.6			2.1		6.0		4.1		
Sierra Leone	1993[3]	92	37.0	21.6	10.5	—	1.0	0.1	0.3	1.2	0.2	2.2	20.2		
Singapore	1998[7,13]	23,162	2.7	0.8	—	0.2	0.6	0.1	0.2	0.5[11]	1.0	4.2	1.9	4.1	6.5
Slovakia	1998[35]	3,047	9.5	2.9	...	2.5[4]	3.6	1.6	1.6	1.6[11]	5.9	2.6	3.3	1.2	2.2
Slovenia	1998[3]	4,927	11.8			8.7		1.6	3.7	5.0[34]	8.4		11.2		
Solomon Islands	2000	9.0	...	...	...	...	...	...	...	...	...	...	...	...	...
Somalia	1990	36	21.6	6.3	37.5	10.5	0.8	2.0	—	7.3	-0.6	0.3	0.4	5.1	
South Africa	1999[13]	22,833	9.7	4.7	0.4	2.9	2.9	1.1	1.8	1.3	4.6	2.9	4.4	5.1	
Spain	1998	108,953	9.5	4.1	4.8	2.6	2.2	1.5	2.1	2.6[11]	2.5	5.0	3.3	2.7	2.4
Sri Lanka	2001	2,009	30.2			39.7			0.9		1.7		10.7		
Sudan, The	1990	1,179	40.0	3.0	16.7	11.9	0.4	5.4	0.2	0.2	2.1	6.4	0.7	2.2	
Suriname	1992[2,13,44]	700	33.4	22.3	12.3	...	1.5	1.6	8.7	1.4	0.7	1.6	...	8.3	
Swaziland	1995[7,13,14]	335	27.5	42.0	...	0.4	3.0	...	1.2	0.8	17.9	1.1	—	0.2	...
Sweden	1999[3]	60,552	5.7	1.0	0.3	0.7	0.1	0.1	4.4	2.3[34,69]	9.8	5.8	3.0	5.7	
Switzerland	1999	49,667	9.6			1.7	0.5	0.2	3.5	[41]	2.6	6.8	18.0		
Syria	1995	3,805	12.0	5.8	3.8	20.2	1.2	2.1	2.2	0.2	0.4	0.8	0.2	0.9	
Taiwan	2001	70,798	5.8		1.2	5.3	1.5	0.4	0.2	1.0	2.0	0.9	7.3	2.6	
Tajikistan	1998[2]	679	35.8[4]	1.1[14]	0.1	18.3[4]	0.6	0.1[14]	—	—	...	0.1[14]	2.1[4]	...	...
Tanzania	1995	119	10.7	5.8	10.7	17.4	0.8	1.7	1.7	0.8	3.3	3.3	14.9	2.5	
Thailand	1996[3,7]	39,380	11.4	7.0	3.1	4.7	2.4	1.6	1.5	1.4[11]	3.2	3.0[4]	2.8	2.5	0.6
Togo	1998	138	50.9			6.0			5.8		5.6		4.4		
Tonga	1997[2,3]	15	51.3		—	0.8	1.6	1.1	1.6	4.3[34]	—	6.0	20.5		
Trinidad and Tobago	1995	862	12.0	9.1	3.3	0.2	0.9	0.2	0.4	1.0	2.8	2.5	36.5	1.4	0.1
Tunisia	1998[3]	4,977	10.2	3.3	6.4	7.7	15.9	4.5	5.4		2.1		4.6	2.8	1.0
Turkey	1998	36,678	9.3	1.8	1.5	11.4	5.1	0.7	0.6	0.8	1.3	1.7	3.8	6.2	
Turkmenistan	1992[2,14,15]	801	13.3	...	...	18.9	1.2	0.4	0.3[16]		[16]		3.2[5]	[5]	[5]
Tuvalu	1998	0.55	...	...	...	...	...	...	...	...	...	...	...	...	...
Uganda	1997[4]	346	27.9[4]	15.2[4]	3.5	5.6[4]		0.4	3.6[4]	3.4	1.2	5.3[4]	[4]	6.7[4]	0.9
Ukraine	1998[2,13,14]	23,163	19.4	3.5	1.4	0.8	0.9	0.4	1.0	0.6	1.0	0.8	4.8	1.1	1.1
United Arab Emirates	1998[7]	5,498	7.5			11.9			1.6		3.9		50.0		
United Kingdom	1998[13,14]	243,567	9.7[4]	2.3	0.9	2.6	1.8	0.5	1.5	2.6[11]	2.7	9.6	3.5	3.4	3.0
United States	1999	1,962,644	9.1	1.5	1.9	1.9	1.6	0.2	1.9	2.0[11]	3.8	3.2	3.9	4.0	3.8
Uruguay	1997[19]	3,069	21.4	10.2	5.9	6.7	2.8	2.8	0.2	0.6	2.0	3.7	1.4	6.5	
Uzbekistan	1992[2,14,15]	2,147	12.6	...	...	21.4	3.1	1.9	1.3[16]		[16]		5.4[5]	[5]	[5]
Vanuatu	1995[14]	16	35.9			3.2			23.5		6.9		4.7[74]		
Venezuela	1996[3,19]	15,621	11.3	4.0	12.7	1.8	1.9	0.9	0.4	0.5	1.7	1.5	7.8	3.4	1.3
Vietnam	1998[3,19,75]	2,532	13.2	10.2	6.8	8.3	6.2	7.3	1.1	0.8[11]	2.1	2.8	3.0	3.0	1.3
Virgin Islands (U.S.)	1997[1,14]	146	22.0				46	46	1.1	46		14.5	46		
West Bank[40]	1998	479	12.8	0.9	0.3	1.4	19.5	3.0	1.1	7.6	1.5	1.2	0.1	4.4	
Western Sahara	...	...	...	...	...	...	...	...	...	...	...	...	...	...	...
Yemen	2000	426	32.3		14.5	1.3	2.6	0.6	3.2	2.3[11]	0.5	3.6	1.9		
Zambia	1995	450	19.2	17.1	6.7	9.8	1.1	0.7	3.3	1.1	0.9	2.2	4.9	10.5	
Zimbabwe	1998[13]	1,088	13.6	15.7	4.7	9.1	3.0	2.5	2.9	2.0	2.1	2.8	3.7[76]	5.1	

[1]Gross output in value of sales. [2]Gross output of production. [3]In producer's prices. [4]Sum of available data. [5]351 includes 352, 355, and 356. [6]37 includes 381. [7]Establishments employing 10 or more persons. [8]Value of manufactured exports. [9]Value of manufactured exports (excluding duty-free reexports). [10]390 includes 385. [11]Includes metal furniture. [12]Estimated figure includes agriculture. [13]In factor values. [14]Complete ISIC detail is not available. [15]Includes extraction of petroleum, natural gas, metals, and nonmetals. [16]633 includes 34. [17]355 and 356 include 361 + 362. [18]338 includes 39. [19]Establishments employing five or more persons. [20]Includes mining and quarrying in other than petroleum and natural gas sectors. [21]133 includes 341. [22]In factor values at 1992 prices. [23]Establishments employing 50 or more persons. [24]All state-owned industrial enterprises and privately owned industrial enterprises with annual sales of more than U.S.$604,000. [25]Excludes traditional sector. [26]390 includes 332. [27]Excludes petroleum refining. [28]Republic of Cyprus only. [29]Excludes establishments processing coffee or cotton. [30]Establishments employing 10 or more persons and using power-driven machines. [31]Excludes frozen and chilled fish and crustaceans. [32]Remainder. [33]369 includes 371. [34]332 includes 390. [35]Establishments employing 20 or more persons. [36]Excludes unavailable data for food, beverages, and tobacco. [37]Establishments employing 6 or more persons. [38]342 includes 32. [39]933 includes 39. [40]West Bank includes Gaza

Manufacturing, by branch of industry — percentage of total value added in manufacturing (continued)

refined petroleum and products (353+354)	rubber products (355)	plastic products (356)	pottery, china, and glass (361+362)	bricks, tiles, cement, etc. (369)	iron and steel (371)	non-ferrous metals (372)	fabricated metal products (381)	nonelectrical machinery (382 exc. 3825)	office equip., computers (3825)	electrical equip. (383 exc. 3832)	radio, television (3832)	transport equip. exc. motor vehicles (384 exc. 3843)	motor vehicles (3843)	professional equip. (385)	jewelry, musical instruments (390)	country
			(36)		(37)		(38)								(39)	
—	1.9	2.8	0.4	5.8	1.0	1.9	3.7	1.1		2.0		9.8				Niger
[46]	[46]	[46]	2.8		—	—						0.2			0.5	Nigeria
															[46]	Northern Mariana Islands
1.1	0.2	1.8	0.6[14]	2.7[14]	2.3	5.2	6.1	8.2	0.3	3.8	1.7	11.6	1.4	2.1[14]	0.7	Norway
16.8	—	2.7	2.5	17.2	0.1	4.0	6.6	1.9	0.1	2.6	—	0.1	0.1		0.5	Oman
3.1	0.9	0.4	0.5	7.2	4.2	—	0.7	1.6	—	5.0	2.7	0.8	2.7	0.2	0.8	Pakistan
…	…	…	…	…	…	…	…	…	…	…	…	…	…	…	…	Palau
9.5	4.9		6.8		1.8		2.2	—		0.4		1.5	0.1	0.2	1.4[41]	Panama
…	…	…	…	…	…	…	…	…	…	…	…	…	…	…	…	Papua New Guinea
2.1		2.8	0.1	4.7	0.1	0.1	0.4	0.1				0.4			0.2	Paraguay
0.9	2.4		7.6		3.1	17.8	2.4	0.7		1.5		0.6			1.6	Peru
8.9	0.7		2.7		1.6		1.7	1.3		11.6		1.1			3.0	Philippines
6.5	1.8	2.6	1.8	2.7	3.8	0.6	6.7	6.8		6.8		9.5		1.0	0.6	Poland
10.5	0.6	1.7	2.7	5.6	1.1	0.5	5.7	4.4		3.0	2.5	1.4	4.8	0.6	1.1	Portugal
2.3	—	1.0	1.6		0.2		1.1	7.3		2.6	5.4	—	0.3	4.2	0.4	Puerto Rico
4.4	…	0.8	13.5		17.6	—	3.8	…	…	0.3		0.3	—	…	0.3	Qatar
—		[61]	…	16.8			12.2	5.0							—	Réunion
2.7	1.1	0.9	5.2		6.6		4.2	5.9	0.5	2.8	1.7	2.0	3.7	0.7	0.7	Romania
6.1	1.1	0.5	1.0	5.1	8.3	11.4	1.8	8.0	0.5	2.8	[46]	2.1[63]	7.1	1.0	1.9	Russia
…	…	…	8.0		1.9[6]			…	…	…	…	…	…	…	0.2	Rwanda
…	…	…	…	…	…	…	…	…	…	…	…	…	…	…	…	St. Kitts and Nevis
—	0.4	3.8	—	—	…	…	5.6	…	—	3.3	0.9	—	…	—	1.3	St. Lucia
…	…	…	…	10.0	…	…	1.0	…	…	…	…	…	…	…	5.0	St. Vincent
…	…	…	…	…	…	…	…	…	…	…	…	…	…	…	…	Samoa
																San Marino
															…	São Tomé and Príncipe
14.4	0.1	3.6	1.7	12.0	4.9	0.1	9.0	2.3		2.4		1.0		0.2	0.7	Saudi Arabia
3.7	—	1.9	—	6.9	2.7		4.1	0.4		0.8		1.8	0.4		—	Senegal
-0.1	4.7		7.3				4.5	3.8	1.5	3.2	1.3	0.6	2.3	1.4	[34]	Serbia and Montenegro
			5.2				2.4								—	Seychelles
			3.5				2.1								0.1	Sierra Leone
4.9	0.3	2.2	0.4	1.4	0.4	0.1	5.7	6.7	24.2	2.4	17.8	6.6	0.8	2.9	0.4	Singapore
5.9	2.4	2.2	2.0	5.2	7.6	2.7	5.4	9.2	0.3	4.4[4]	1.9	2.5[4]	6.3	2.3	0.6	Slovakia
0.3	5.8		4.6		13.6[6]		[6]	9.8[67]		11.3		4.2		[67]	[34]	Slovenia
—	—	—	—	—	—	—	[6]	…	…	…	…	…	…	…	—	Solomon Islands
1.6	—	0.5	—	3.0	—	—	1.1					0.9		—	1.7	Somalia
5.9	1.2	2.4	1.4	3.3	9.7	5.4	6.1	5.4		5.9		9.2		0.7	1.6	South Africa
8.7[14]	1.5	2.8	1.5	5.3	2.8	1.1	7.9	6.0	0.8	3.4	1.3	1.8	8.1	0.9	0.9	Spain
			8.9		0.7		4.9			2.3[68]					[68]	Sri Lanka
1.3	0.8	1.2	0.1	0.5	0.1	0.7	2.6	0.1		1.2		2.1			0.1	Sudan, The
…	0.7	0.6	5.3				2.2					0.9		0.2	0.5	Suriname
…	…	0.2	0.1	0.5	…	…	2.8	…	…	…	…	…	0.2	…	—	Swaziland
0.9	0.8	1.6	0.5	1.3	4.1	1.3	6.7	10.1	0.5	2.4	15.2	1.8	9.9	3.9	[34]	Sweden
3.2			2.3		2.2		10.5	14.5	5.8		3.1	1.4	0.5	10.7	3.0[41]	Switzerland
17.1	0.3	0.6	4.7	7.1	—	0.6	14.0	2.4		2.4		0.5			0.3	Syria
8.4	1.5	4.8	2.5		5.8		7.7	5.6		25.7		6.4		1.0	2.4	Taiwan
…	…	…	0.2[4]	1.1[4]	…	39.7	0.1[4]	0.3[4]		0.2[4]			0.2[4]		—	Tajikistan
4.1	0.8	1.7	—	5.8	1.7	2.5	4.1	0.8		1.7		3.3			—	Tanzania
3.3	3.6	2.7	1.3	5.2	1.5	0.3	3.5	3.9[4]	2.8	4.0		0.7[4]	14.0	1.2[4]	2.0	Thailand
			10.4		—	…	14.8	2.1[68]							[68]	Togo
—	—	0.5	8.3		—	—	2.8	0.3	—	1.4			—		[34]	Tonga
10.5	0.2	0.5	1.2	3.6	8.2	—	1.4	0.3	—	1.4	0.3	0.1	0.1	[10]	1.9[10]	Trinidad and Tobago
14.5	0.9	1.4[70]	2.9	3.5	1.4	3.1[71]	[71]	0.4		3.9	[72]	2.1		[72]	1.9[72]	Tunisia
15.5	2.0	1.8	2.6	4.7	5.7	1.0	3.2	4.5		5.1		8.6		0.5	0.5	Turkey
55.7	[5]	[5]	4.0		0.1		0.8								…	Turkmenistan
															…	Tuvalu
—	0.4[4]	1.1	4.9[4]	4.9[4]	…	10.9	…	…	…	3.7[4]	…	…	…	…	…	Uganda
5.4	2.0	0.5	1.0	4.4	25.6	1.9	5.1	6.6	0.1	2.2[4]		2.4	1.6	0.6[4]	0.1[4]	Ukraine
			7.0		6.6					9.9					1.6	United Arab Emirates
1.5	1.1	4.2	1.2	2.0	2.0	1.2	8.4	8.9	2.2	3.6	4.1	1.0[4,73]	6.3	3.2	1.3	United Kingdom
2.1	1.0	3.7	2.9		3.4		7.3	7.1	2.4	3.1	7.7	5.2	8.5	5.2	1.6	United States
18.8	0.9	2.9	0.9	2.9	1.9	0.2	2.8	0.7		1.2		1.5		0.6	0.5	Uruguay
12.4	[5]	[5]	5.4		12.2	[6]	13.2								…	Uzbekistan
			[74]		21.0[6]			…	…	…	…	…	…	…	…	Vanuatu
15.8	2.2	1.6	2.3	2.9	7.0	6.1	2.7	1.7		1.7	0.1	0.3	5.9	0.3	0.3	Venezuela
0.3	1.1	2.5	1.0	9.2	2.7	0.3	2.3	2.4	0.7	2.6	3.5	2.3	1.8	0.4	0.9	Vietnam
			15.0		—	—	2.3	[46]		—	1.9	3.4	0.3	19.8	1.9	Virgin Islands (U.S.)
—	0.1	4.7	0.5	25.4	0.1	—	11.7	1.1		1.9		0.3		0.2	0.2	West Bank[40]
															…	Western Sahara
8.2	…	3.3	…	18.8	…	…	6.0	0.4		0.3		0.2			…	Yemen
4.2	1.8	1.3	-0.2	3.3	1.3	—	5.3	1.1		3.3		0.7		—	0.2	Zambia
[76]	2.7	1.6	0.4	5.8	7.9	0.7	5.9	1.1		3.4		2.8		0.1	0.5	Zimbabwe

Strip. [41]390 includes 332. [42]384 includes 390. [43]Represents export value of clothing articles made from fur. [44]Selected industries only. [45]Total manufacturing value added (2000): U.S.$26,000,000. [46]Data withheld for reasons of confidentiality. [47]332 includes 313 and 321. [48]Includes public utilities. [49]Sugar and rice manufacturing only. [50]Establishments with electric power and employing 10 or more workers and all establishments employing 20 or more workers. [51]390 includes 353 + 354. [52]38 includes 37. [53]Excludes exports destined for Switzerland. [54]Complete data not available for professional equipment. [55]351 includes 383. [56]382 includes 384. [57]Excludes government printing. [58]Derivatives of petroleum and coal only. [59]Excludes Transdniester area and city of Tighina (Bendery). [60]Garment manufacturing accounts for most of manufacturing value added. [61]341 includes 356. [62]State enterprises only; state enterprises account for about 80% of all industrial output. [63]Excludes shipbuilding and aircraft (data withheld for reasons of confidentiality). [64]Refined sugar only. [65]Sector percentages are estimated figures. [66]Figure for 1999 is U.S.$88,000,000. [67]382 includes 385. [68]382 through 385 includes 390. [69]Includes recycling. [70]Includes synthetic fibres. [71]372 includes 381. [72]390 includes 3832 and 385. [73]Excludes railway equipment and aircraft. [74]35 includes 36. [75]17 provinces only covering about 80% of total industrial output. [76]351 includes 353 + 354.

Energy

This table provides data about the commercial energy supplies (reserves, production, consumption, and trade) of the various countries of the world, together with data about oil pipeline networks and traffic. Many of the data and concepts used in this table are adapted from the United Nations' *Energy Statistics Yearbook.*

Electricity. Total installed electrical power capacity comprises the sum of the rated power capacities of all main and auxiliary generators in a country. "Total installed capacity" (kW) is multiplied by 8,760 hours per year to yield "Total production capacity" (kW-hr).

Production of electricity comprises the total gross production of electricity by publicly or privately owned enterprises and also that generated by industrial establishments for their own use, but it usually excludes consumption by the utility itself. Measured in millions of kilowatt-hours (kW-hr), annual production of electricity ranges generally between 50% and 60% of total production capacity. The data are further analyzed by type of generation: fossil fuels, hydroelectric power, and nuclear fuel.

The great majority of the world's electrical and other energy needs are met by the burning of fossil hydrocarbon solids, liquids, and gases, either for thermal generation of electricity or in internal combustion engines. Many renewable and nontraditional sources of energy are being developed worldwide (wood, biogenic gases and liquids, tidal, wave, and wind power, geothermal and photothermal [solar] energy, and so on), but collectively these sources are still negligible in the world's total energy consumption. For this reason only hydroelectric and nuclear generation are considered here separately with fossil fuels.

Trade in electrical energy refers to the transfer of generated electrical output via an international grid. Total electricity consumption (residential and nonresidential) is equal to total electricity requirements less transformation and distribution losses.

Coal. The term coal, as used in the table, comprises all grades of anthracite, bituminous, subbituminous, and lignite that have acquired or may in the future, by reason of new technology or changed market prices, acquire an economic value. These types of coal may be differentiated according to heat content (density) and content of impurities. Most coal reserve data are based on proven recoverable reserves only, of all grades of coal. Exceptions are footnoted, with proven in-place reserves reported only when recoverable reserves are unknown. Production figures include deposits removed from both surface and underground workings as well as quantities used by the producers themselves or issued to the miners. Wastes recovered from mines or nearby preparation plants are excluded from production figures.

Natural gas. This term refers to any combustible gas (usually chiefly methane) of natural origin from underground sources. The data for production cover, to the extent possible, gas obtained from gas fields,

Energy

country	electricity installed capacity, 2002 ('000 kW)	production, 2002 capacity ('000,000 kW-hr)	production, 2002 amount ('000,000 kW-hr)	power source, 2002 fossil fuel (%)	power source, 2002 hydro power (%)	power source, 2002 nuclear fuel (%)	trade, 2002 exports ('000,000 kW-hr)	trade, 2002 imports ('000,000 kW-hr)	consumption amount, 2002 ('000,000 kW-hr)	consumption per capita, 2002 (kW-hr)	consumption residential, 1998 (%)	consumption non-residential, 1998 (%)	coal reserves, 2003 ('000,000 metric tons)	coal production, 2002 ('000 metric tons)	coal consumption, 2002 ('000 metric tons)
Afghanistan	661	5,790	475	33.7	66.3	—	—	92	567	28	...	...	71	1	1
Albania	1,892	16,574	3,686	4.7	95.3	—	58	2,163	5,791	1,844	...	...	850	87	100
Algeria	6,830	59,830	27,647	99.8	0.2	—	259	231	27,625	881	28.4	71.6	43	—	894
American Samoa	58	508	135	100.0	—	—	—	—	135	2,250	...	...	...	...	...
Andorra	...	...	...	...	...	...	...	...	...	...	...	...	...	...	...
Angola	460	4,030	1,786	36.0	64.0	—	—	—	1,786	135	...	...	...	...	...
Antigua and Barbuda	27	237	105	100.0	—	—	—	—	105	1,438	...	...	...	...	...
Argentina	27,864	244,089	84,492	50.5	42.5	7.0[1]	2,856	8,775	90,411	2,383	47.3	52.7	454	97	708
Armenia	3,329	29,162	5,519	28.6	30.0	41.4	660	306	5,165	1,554	...	...	...	...	...
Aruba	150	1,314	810	100.0	—	—	—	—	810	8,617	...	...	...	...	...
Australia	44,236	387,507	222,182	92.6	7.4	—	14,675	15,375	222,182	11,299	...	...	84,095	341,841	132,185
Austria	18,337	160,632	62,480	32.4	67.5	—[1]	925	2,375	63,179	7,845	...	...	21	1,412	5,477
Azerbaijan	5,390	47,216	19,543	89.7	10.3	—	—	—	20,993	2,579	...	...	...	...	...
Bahamas, The	401	3,513	1,886	100.0	—	—	—	—	1,886	6,084	...	...	...	...	...
Bahrain	1,366	11,966	7,278	100.0	—	—	—	—	7,278	10,830	...	...	...	...	...
Bangladesh	3,490	30,572	17,091	93.9	6.1	—	—	—	17,091	119	37.7	62.3	...	...	700
Barbados	166	1,454	859	100.0	—	—	—	—	859	3,193	78.4	21.6	...	...	...
Belarus	7,848	68,748	26,455	99.9	0.1	—	3,513	10,068	33,010	3,326	...	...	...	...	334
Belgium	15,721	137,716	82,614	40.8	1.8	57.4	9,070	16,658	90,202	8,749	...	...	...	173	9,246
Belize	43	377	162	38.3	61.7	—	—	27	189	713	71	29	...	...	...
Benin	56	491	92	97.8	2.2	—	—	533	625	92	64.1	35.9	...	...	...
Bermuda	146	1,279	630	100.0	—	—	—	—	630	7,778	...	...	...	...	...
Bhutan	362	3,171	1,898	—	100.0	—	1,420	16	494	236	...	...	...	52	62
Bolivia	1,274	11,160	4,188	47.4	52.6	—	—	9	4,197	485	49.0	51.0	1.0	...	...
Bosnia and Herzegovina	2,731	23,924	10,785	51.2	48.8	—	2,133	1,019	9,671	2,527	...	...	...	8,961	8,535
Botswana	2	2	2	2	2	2	2	2	2	2	26.3	73.7	43	2	2
Brazil	82,458	722,332	344,644	13.3	82.7	4.0	7	36,580	381,217	2,183	26.7	73.3	10,834	5,144	17,787
Brunei	509	4,459	3,036	100.0	—	—	—	—	3,036	8,903	53.7	46.3	...	...	...
Bulgaria	12,696	111,217	42,679	46.3	6.3	47.4	8,335	2,040	36,384	4,624	53.1	46.9	2,343	26,053	28,609
Burkina Faso	78	683	400	71.3	28.7	—	—	—	400	32	...	...	...	...	...
Burundi	44	385	129	1.6	98.4	—	—	36	164	25	73.8	26.2	...	...	...
Cambodia	35	307	129	72.9	27.1	—	—	—	129	10	...	...	...	...	...
Cameroon	905	7,927	3,249	2.0	98.0	—	—	—	3,249	207	...	...	...	1	1
Canada	113,116	990,896	601,523	28.9	58.4	12.7	36,117	16,088	581,494	18,541	...	...	7,047	66,493	61,715
Cape Verde	7	61	45	100.0	—	—	—	—	45	99	...	...	...	...	...
Central African Republic	43	377	108	23.1	76.9	—	—	—	108	28	69.3	30.7	2.9	...	...
Chad	29	254	98	100.0	—	—	—	—	98	12	...	...	...	...	...
Chile	11,146	97,639	45,483	49.0	51.0	—	—	—	45,483	2,918	30	70	1,265	433	3,629
China	239,170	2,095,129	1,928,912	83.8	14.9	1.3	9,704	2,300	1,921,508	1,484	25.3	74.7	123,000	1,397,849	1,313,899
Colombia	13,788	120,783	45,242	26.9	73.1	—	618	8	44,632	1,019	70.9	29.1	7,082	43,850	3,950
Comoros	6	53	19	89.5	10.5	—	—	—	19	25	...	...	...	...	...
Congo, Dem. Rep. of the	3,210	28,120	5,922	0.4	99.6	—	1,258	6	4,670	91	...	...	94	37	134
Congo, Rep. of the	121	1,060	399	0.8	99.2	—	—	364	763	210	...	...	...	...	...
Costa Rica	1,897	16,177	7,473	1.6	98.4	—	477	59	7,055	1,765	71.1	28.9	...	...	...
Côte d'Ivoire	1,203	10,538	4,788	63.9	36.1	—	1,565	—	3,223	197	26.1	73.9	...	...	...
Croatia	3,931	34,436	12,286	55.8	44.2	—	406	3,927	15,807	3,558	68	32	42	—	965
Cuba	3,959	34,681	15,699	99.3	0.7	—	—	—	15,699	1,395	52.8	47.2	...	...	26
Cyprus	1,005	8,804	3,785	100.0	—	—	—	—	3,785	5,323	82.4	17.6	...	...	54
Czech Republic	15,332	134,308	76,348	71.7	3.8	24.5	20,889	9,502	64,961	6,368	...	...	5,948	63,356	57,113
Denmark	13,295	116,464	39,245	87.5	0.1	12.4[4]	11,010	8,939	37,174	6,925	...	...	...	—	6,885
Djibouti	88	771	205	100.0	—	—	—	—	205	296	...	...	...	...	...
Dominica	14	123	85	65.9	34.1	—	—	—	85	1,197	...	...	...	...	...
Dominican Republic	5,112	44,781	11,510	92.4	7.6	—	—	—	11,510	1,326	72.3	27.7	...	...	233
East Timor	...	...	...	...	...	...	...	...	...	...	...	...	...	...	...
Ecuador	3,233	28,321	11,884	29.7	70.3	—	—	58	11,942	943	56.8	43.2	25	...	...

petroleum fields, or coal mines that is actually collected and marketed. (Much natural gas in Middle Eastern and North African oil fields is flared [burned] because it is often not economical to capture and market it.) Manufactured gas is generally a by-product of industrial operations such as refineries, gasworks, coke ovens, and blast furnaces. It is usually burned at the point of production and rarely enters the marketplace.

Crude petroleum. Crude petroleum is the liquid product obtained from oil wells; the term also includes shale oil, tar sand extract, and field or lease condensate. Production and consumption and consumption per capita data in the table refer, so far as possible, to the same year so that the relationship between national production and consumption patterns can be clearly seen; data are given in barrels.

Proven reserves are that oil remaining underground in known fields whose existence has been "proved" by the evaluation of nearby producing wells or by seismic tests in sedimentary strata known to contain crude petroleum, and that is judged recoverable within the limits of present technology and economic conditions (prices). The published proven reserve figures do not necessarily reflect the true reserves of a country, because government authorities or corporations often have political or economic motives for withholding or altering such data.

The estimated exhaustion rate of petroleum reserves is an extrapolated ratio of published proven reserves to the current rate of withdrawal/

production. Present world published proven reserves will last about 40 to 45 years at the present rate of withdrawal, but there are large country-to-country variations above or below the average.

Data on petroleum pipelines are provided because of the great importance to both domestic and international energy markets of this means of bringing these energy sources from their production or transportation points to refineries, intermediate consumption and distribution points, and final consumers. Their traffic may represent a very significant fraction of the total movement of goods within a country. Available data for petroleum pipelines traffic are often incomplete and their basis varies internationally, some countries reporting only international shipments, others reporting domestic shipments of 50 kilometres or more, and so on.

For data in the hydrocarbons portions of the table (coal, natural gas, and petroleum), extensive use has been made of a variety of international sources, such as those of the United Nations, the International Energy Agency (of the Organisation for Economic Co-operation and Development), and the World Energy Council (in its *World Energy Resources* [triennial]); of the U.S. Department of Energy (especially its *International Energy Annual*); and of various industry surveys, such as those published by the *International Petroleum Encyclopedia* and *World Oil*.

natural gas					crude petroleum								country
published proven reserves, 2005 ('000,000,-000 cu m)	production		consumption		reserves		produc-tion, 2002 ('000,000 barrels)	consump-tion, 2002 ('000,000 barrels)	consump-tion per capita (barrels)	refining capacity, 2005 ('000 barrels per day)	pipelines (latest)		
	natural gas, 2002 ('000,000 cu m)	manufac-tured gas, 2002 ('000,000 cu m)	natural gas, 2002 ('000,000 cu m)	natural gas per capita (cu m)	published proven, 2005 ('000,000 barrels)	years to exhaust proven reserves, 2002					length (km)	traffic ('000,000 metric ton-km)	
100	109	...	109	5.4	...	...	—	—	—	—	...	...	Afghanistan
2.8	14	9.7	14	4.4	165	204	2.6	2.6	0.8	26	207	8	Albania
4,531	81,227	11,857	22,942	732	11,800	34	362	163	5.2	450	6,496	...	Algeria
...	...	...	...	...	...	...	...	...	...	...	...	—	American Samoa
...	...	...	...	...	...	...	...	...	...	...	—	—	Andorra
46	604	93	604	13.2	5,412	27	326	15	1.2	39	887	—	Angola
...	...	...	...	...	...	...	...	...	...	...	—	—	Antigua and Barbuda
663	51,449	4,524	45,237	1,192	2,821	10	278	185	4.9	625	3,688	...	Argentina
...	...	...	1,022	308	...	...	—	...	...	...	—	—	Armenia
...	...	...	...	...	...	...	—	2.4	25.7	230	—	—	Aruba
2,549	36,849	6,498	25,753	1,310	3,500	10	227	244	12.4	755	4,773	...	Australia
15	2,052	1,167	8,496	1,055	62	13	7.2	63	7.9	209	663	8,165	Austria
850	4,900	213	5,100	1,064	7,000	63	113	64	5.8	399	1,518	1,900	Azerbaijan
...	...	...	...	...	...	...	...	...	...	...	—	—	Bahamas, The
92	9,622	511	9,622	14,100	125	2	11	91	135	249	53	...	Bahrain
300	11,472	19	11,472	79.8	56	82	2.2	11	0.1	33	—	—	Bangladesh
0.1	29	...	29	109	3.0	12	0.6	1.8	...	—	—	—	Barbados
2.8	254	736	18,448	1,768	198	15	13	116	11.3	493	2,443	...	Belarus
—	—	3,691	19,558	1,897	...	...	—	261	23.8	803	158	...	Belgium
—	...	...	...	...	...	...	—	—	—	—	—	—	Belize
1.2	...	...	...	0.6	8.0	24	0.3	—	—	—	—	—	Benin
...	...	...	...	...	...	...	—	—	—	—	—	—	Bermuda
...	...	...	...	...	...	...	—	—	—	—	—	—	Bhutan
680	6,724	593	2,704	313	441	38	12	9	1.1	47	2,457	...	Bolivia
...	...	...	302	78.9	...	...	—	—	—	—	174	—	Bosnia and Herzegovina
...	...	2	...	...	...	...	...	2	...	...	...	...	Botswana
240	8,205	12,020	13,435	73.7	8,500	18	536	597	3.4	1,920	5,212	1,446	Brazil
391	12,000	14	1,273	3,735	1,350	19	75	1.6	4.7	9	439	...	Brunei
5.9	21	661	3,184	405	15	54	0.4	31	4.9	115	495	295	Bulgaria
...	...	...	...	...	...	...	...	...	...	...	...	...	Burkina Faso
...	...	...	...	...	...	...	—	—	—	—	—	—	Burundi
...	...	...	...	...	...	...	—	—	—	—	—	—	Cambodia
110	...	21	...	...	400	9	52	11	0.6	42	—	—	Cameroon
1,673	180,500	35,224	87,400	2,393	178,800[3]	9	1,146	840	18.3	2,017	23,564	99,908	Canada
...	...	...	...	...	...	...	—	—	—	—	—	—	Cape Verde
...	...	...	...	...	...	...	—	—	—	—	—	—	Central African Republic
...	...	...	...	...	...	...	—	—	—	—	—	—	Chad
98	2,248	1,100	7,329	470	150	94	1.6	73	4.7	227	1,003	—	Chile
1,510	40,278	38,617	37,985	29.3	18,250	20	1,298	1,670	1.3	4,650	14,478	60,132	China
128	8,805	1,607	8,805	201	1,842	9	206	105	2.4	286	6,134	...	Colombia
...	...	...	...	...	...	...	—	—	—	—	—	—	Comoros
1.0	...	2.3	...	...	187	23	9.6	0.8	0	0	—	—	Congo, Dem. Rep. of the
91	127	3.5	127	34.9	1,506	18	82	6.3	1.7	21	646	...	Congo, Rep. of the
...	...	...	...	...	...	...	—	0.1	0.9	24	—	...	Costa Rica
30	1,542	110	1,512	94.3	100	51	6	22	1.3	65	—	—	Côte d'Ivoire
34	2,190	704	2,826	636	75	9	7.4	35	8.0	250	583	951	Croatia
71	585	189	585	52.0	750	32	26	33	2.9	301	—	—	Cuba
—	—	61	...	...	...	...	—	8.6	11.2	27	—	—	Cyprus
4.0	162	2,342	10,932	1,072	15	45	1.8	42	4.1	198	547	2,078	Czech Republic
74	9,064	521	5,517	1,028	1,277	9	140	60	11	176	455	1,385	Denmark
...	...	...	...	...	...	...	—	—	—	—	—	—	Djibouti
...	...	...	...	...	...	...	—	...	...	...	—	—	Dominica
—	...	44	...	...	...	...	—	14	1.7	48	104	...	Dominican Republic
...	...	...	...	...	...	...	—	—	—	—	...	—	East Timor
97	141	178	141	11.2	4,630	32	191	58	4.5	176	1,386	...	Ecuador

Energy   (continued)

country	electricity												coal		
	installed capacity, 2002 ('000 kW)	production, 2002 capacity ('000,000 kW-hr)	production, 2002 amount ('000,000 kW-hr)	power source, 2002 fossil fuel (%)	power source, 2002 hydro-power (%)	power source, 2002 nuclear fuel (%)	trade, 2002 exports ('000,000 kW-hr)	trade, 2002 imports ('000,000 kW-hr)	consumption amount, 2002 ('000,000 kW-hr)	consumption per capita, 2002 (kW-hr)	consumption resi-dential, 1998 (%)	consumption non-resi-dential, 1998 (%)	reserves, 2003 ('000,000 metric tons)	pro-duction, 2002 ('000 metric tons)	con-sump-tion, 2002 ('000 metric tons)
Egypt	16,961	148,578	85,954	82.1	17.9	—	417	228	85,765	1,287	74.4	25.6	22	48	1,354
El Salvador	1,051	9,207	3,952	46.1	28.8	25.1[4]	51	435	4,336	665	67.4	32.6	...	...	...
Equatorial Guinea	18	158	26	88.5	11.5	—	—	—	26	54	...	...	...	...	...
Eritrea	172	1,507	264	100.0	—	—	—	—	264	66	...	...	...	...	...
Estonia	2,545	22,294	8,527	99.9	0.1	—	1,102	412	7,837	5,767	55.4	44.6	...	12,400	13,088
Ethiopia	544	4,765	2,050	0.9	98.7	—[5]	—	—	2,050	32	35.65	64.45	...	...	...
Faroe Islands	93	815	195	54.9	44.1	—[6]	—	—	195	4,149	...	...	...	...	...
Fiji	200	1,752	520	18.5	81.5	—	—	—	520	625	22	78	...	...	15
Finland	16,569	145,144	74,899	55.8	14.4	29.7[1]	1,539	13,464	86,824	16,694	...	...	...	...	6,617
France	116,315[7]	1,018,919[7]	560,212[7]	10.1[7]	11.8[7]	78.1[1, 7]	79,900[7]	3,000[7]	483,312[7]	8,123[7]	...	...	17	2,067[7]	19,074[7]
French Guiana	140	1,226	477	100.0	—	—	—	—	477	2,725	55.42	44.62	...	...	...
French Polynesia	110	964	507	82.1	17.9	—	—	—	507	2,104	...	...	...	...	...
Gabon	415	3,635	1,513	43.5	56.5	—	—	—	1,513	1,226	41.9	58.1	...	...	...
Gambia, The	29	254	140	100.0	—	—	—	—	140	96	...	...	...	...	...
Gaza Strip	...	...	...	...	...	...	...	...	...	...	...	...	...	...	...
Georgia	4,456	39,035	7,357	8.0	92.0	—	—	452	7,809	1,786	...	...	...	7	27
Germany	125,665	1,100,825	566,540	61.5	5.2	33.3	38,272	49,370	576,538	6,989	...	...	7,219	210,987	246,131
Ghana	1,254	10,985	8,201	11.3	88.7	—	833	1,146	8,514	416	7.2	92.8	...	...	4
Greece	11,320	99,163	54,760	91.3	7.5	—[8]	1,706	4,602	57,656	5,247	...	...	4,178	70,468	69,682
Greenland	106	929	266	100.0	—	—	—	—	266	4,750	...	...	196	...	...
Grenada	27	237	153	100.0	—	—	—	—	153	1,913	72.9	27.1	...	...	...
Guadeloupe	420	3,679	1,160	100.0	—	—	—	—	1,160	2,654	...	...	...	...	...
Guam	400	3,504	1,745	100.0	—	—	—	—	1,745	10,839	...	...	...	...	...
Guatemala	1,513	13,254	8,301	74.6	25.4	—	440	55	7,916	660	67.3	32.7	...	...	...
Guernsey	...	...	...	...	...	...	...	...	...	...	...	...	...	...	...
Guinea	197	1,726	798	45.3	54.7	—	—	—	798	95	...	...	...	...	...
Guinea-Bissau	21	184	60	100.0	—	—	—	—	60	41	...	...	...	...	...
Guyana	309	2,707	924	99.5	0.5	—	—	—	924	1,195	...	...	...	...	...
Haiti	260	2,278	632	52.4	47.6	—	—	—	632	73	44.1	55.9	...	...	...
Honduras	912	7,989	4,247	42.2	57.8	—	—	415	4,662	696	69.5	30.5	...	...	141
Hong Kong	11,800	103,368	34,312	100.0	—	—	2,175	10,191	42,328	6,237	...	...	...	...	8,718
Hungary	8,524	74,670	36,156	60.9	0.5	38.6	8,349	12,605	40,412	3,972	65.5	34.5	3,596	13,027	14,054
Iceland	1,509	13,219	8,423	11.6	82.8	—	—	—	8,423	29,247	...	...	...	...	98
India	126,240	1,105,862	596,543	86.0	10.7	2.8[10]	175	1,520	597,888	569	53.5	46.5	99,034	364,904	386,506
Indonesia	25,284	221,488	97,765	83.3	14.1	—[11]	—	—	97,765	463	46.9	...	5,322	103,060	27,981
Iran	35,400	310,104	136,000	96.3	3.7	—	—	—	136,000	2,075	...	...	449	1,400	1,825
Iraq	9,500	83,220	37,021	98.3	1.7	—	—	—	37,021	1,542	...	...	...	...	...
Ireland	5,439	47,646	25,194	93.2	5.2	—[12]	62	565	25,697	6,560	...	...	15	—	2,770
Isle of Man	...	...	...	...	...	...	...	...	337	4,610	...	...	...	...	...
Israel	10,037	87,924	45,393	100.0	—	—	1,387	—	44,006	6,698	61.6	38.4	...	458	12,925
Italy	85,776[13]	751,398[13]	285,276[13]	78.9[13]	19.0[13]	—[14]	922[13]	51,519[13]	335,873[13]	5,840[13]	...	...	36[13]	163[13]	20,008[13]
Jamaica	1,348	11,808	6,934	97.8	2.2	—	—	—	6,934	2,640	36.2	63.8	...	...	88
Japan	260,885	2,285,353	1,097,167	64.4	8.4	26.9[15]	—	—	1,097,167	8,612	...	...	385	3,320	160,796
Jersey	...	...	...	...	...	...	...	...	557	6,265	...	...	...	...	...
Jordan	1,788	15,663	8,127	99.3	0.7	—	1	322	8,448	1,585	66.1	33.9	...	...	...
Kazakhstan	18,890	165,476	58,331	84.7	15.3	—	2,000	3,550	59,881	4,030	...	...	33,508	80,906	59,424
Kenya	1,148	10,056	4,678	25.0	66.7	—[16]	—	222	4,900	155	38.8	61.2	...	...	99
Kiribati	3	26	13	100.0	—	—	—	—	13	149	...	...	...	...	...
Korea, North	9,500	83,220	34,342	33.5	66.5	—	—	—	34,342	1,524	...	...	642	50,700	52,375
Korea, South	59,614	522,219	336,237	63.0	1.6	35.4	—	—	336,237	7,058	41.8	58.2	86	3,318	75,952
Kuwait	9,392	82,274	37,422	100.0	—	—	—	—	37,422	16,544	93.3	6.7	...	...	...
Kyrgyzstan	3,697	32,386	11,922	9.5	90.5	—	1,062	385	11,245	2,252	25.4	...	870	459	1,239
Laos	284	2,488	1,290	3.3	96.7	—	747	190	733	133	...	...	...	290	290
Latvia	2,117	18,545	3,975	37.8	62.2	—	490	2,838	6,323	2,703	59.5	40.5	...	...	102
Lebanon	2,297	20,122	9,660	87.2	12.8	—	—	532	10,192	2,834	...	...	...	...	200
Lesotho	2	2	2	2	2	2	2	2	2	2	...	...	...	2	2
Liberia	334	2,926	540	62.6	37.4	—	—	—	540	164	...	...	...	...	...
Libya	4,710	41,260	21,740	100.0	—	—	—	—	21,740	3,915	...	...	...	...	4
Liechtenstein	17	17	17	17	17	17	17	17	17	17	...	...	...	...	17
Lithuania	6,568	57,536	17,721	15.8	4.5	79.7	11,018	4,532	11,235	3,239	...	...	...	...	211
Luxembourg	1,244	10,897	1,245	24.1	72.7	—[18]	2,939	6,377	4,683	10,547	...	...	...	...	127
Macau	397	3,478	1,710	100.0	—	—	—	194	1,904	4,387	87.2	12.8	...	...	...
Macedonia	1,494	13,087	6,090	87.6	12.4	—	—	791	6,881	3,363	...	...	...	7,584	7,287
Madagascar	228	1,997	840	35.1	64.9	—	—	—	840	42	31.7	68.3	...	...	10
Malawi	196	1,717	893	2.6	97.4	—	2	—	891	80	67.4	32.6	1.9	...	18
Malaysia	15,671	137,278	77,501	93.1	6.9	—	—	—	77,501	3,234	48.4	51.6	4.0	318	5,251
Maldives	44	385	126	100.0	—	—	—	—	126	448	...	...	...	...	...
Mali	114	999	417	42.9	57.1	—	—	—	417	33	99	1	...	...	...
Malta	515	4,511	1,951	100.0	—	—	—	—	1,951	4,939	...	...	...	...	326
Marshall Islands	...	...	...	...	...	...	...	...	...	...	...	...	...	...	...
Martinique	396	3,469	1,180	100.0	—	—	—	—	1,180	3,033	...	...	...	...	...
Mauritania	115	1,007	165	79.4	20.6	—	—	—	165	58	...	...	...	...	6
Mauritius	660	5,782	1,974	96.0	4.0	—	—	—	1,974	1,631	64.7	35.3	...	...	315
Mayotte	...	...	...	...	...	...	...	...	77	491	...	...	...	...	...
Mexico	47,299	414,339	235,158	82.9	10.5	4.0[11]	344	546	235,360	2,280	...	...	1,297	10,984	14,134
Micronesia	...	...	...	...	...	...	...	...	...	...	...	...	...	...	...
Moldova	1,022	8,953	3,233	96.3	3.7	—	—	2,602	5,835	1,314	...	...	...	...	152
Monaco	7	7	7	7	7	7	7	7	7	7	...	...	...	7	7
Mongolia	901	7,893	3,112	100.0	—	—	16	187	3,263	1,318	...	...	...	5,668	5,668
Morocco	4,697	41,146	15,050	94.3	5.7	—	—	1,692	16,607	560	54.5	45.5	...	16	5,227
Mozambique	2,369	20,752	12,713	7.6	92.4	—	10,692	5,425	7,446	378	...	...	227	44	8
Myanmar (Burma)	1,581	13,850	6,614	66.3	33.7	—	—	—	6,614	135	75.5	24.5	2.0	115	115
Namibia	2	2	2	2	2	2	2	2	2	2	...	...	...	2	2
Nauru	10	88	30	100.0	—	—	—	—	30	2,308	...	...	...	...	...
Nepal	458	4,012	1,433	12.1	87.9	—	147	246	1,532	62	59.5	40.5	1.0	16	496

natural gas					crude petroleum									country
published proven reserves, 2005 ('000,000,000 cu m)	production		consumption		reserves		production, 2002 ('000,000 barrels)	consumption, 2002 ('000,000 barrels)	consumption per capita (barrels)	refining capacity, 2005 ('000 barrels per day)	pipelines (latest)		
	natural gas, 2002 ('000,000 cu m)	manufactured gas, 2002 ('000,000 cu m)	natural gas, 2002 ('000,000 cu m)	natural gas per capita (cu m)	published proven, 2005 ('000,000 barrels)	years to exhaust proven reserves, 2002					length (km)	traffic ('000,000 metric ton-km)	
1,657	26,034	2,542	26,034	391	3,700	14	250	234	3.5	726	5,032	...	Egypt
—	...	33	...	—	...	...	—	6.9	1.1	22	—	—	El Salvador
37	...	...	...	...	18	13	85	—	—	15	—	—	Equatorial Guinea
...	...	...	...	...	...	...	—	—	—	15	—	—	Eritrea
...	...	119	710	523	—	—	—	—	—	—	—	—	Estonia
25	...	3.5	4.7	...	0.4	...	—	5.5	0.1	—	—	—	Ethiopia
—	...	...	...	...	...	...	—	—	—	—	—	—	Faroe Islands
...	...	...	...	...	...	...	—	—	—	—	—	—	Fiji
...	—	1,394	4,392	855	...	...	—	82	15.8	252	—	—	Finland
14	2,832[7]	8,284[7]	13,736[7]	782[7]	148	16	8.5	597[7]	10[7]	1,951	3,024	24,429	France
...	...	...	...	...	...	...	—	—	—	—	—	—	French Guiana
...	...	...	...	...	...	...	—	—	—	—	—	—	French Polynesia
34	820	47	820	189	2,499	24	97	6.0	4.8	17	1,385	...	Gabon
...	...	...	...	...	...	...	—	...	...	—	—	—	Gambia, The
...	...	...	...	...	...	...	...	...	...	...	—	—	Gaza Strip
8.5	59	—	1,002	156	35	68	0.8	1.4	0.04	106	1,027	...	Georgia
306	24,486	17,526	95,519	1,403	442	17	30	784	9.4	2,323	3,540	37,250	Germany
24	...	69	...	—	17	10	0.7	13	0.6	45	—	—	Ghana
1.0	51	1,370	2,147	195	6.0	6	1.2	135	12.1	401	94	...	Greece
...	...	...	...	...	...	...	—	—	—	—	—	—	Greenland
...	...	...	...	...	...	...	—	—	—	—	—	—	Grenada
...	...	...	...	...	...	...	—	—	—	—	—	—	Guadeloupe
...	...	...	...	—	...	...	—	—	—	—	—	—	Guam
3.1	11	7	11	0.9	526	69	8.4	4.3	0.4	16	480	...	Guatemala
...	...	...	...	...	...	...	—	—	—	...	—	—	Guernsey
...	...	...	...	...	...	...	—	—	—	—	—	—	Guinea
...	...	...	...	...	...	...	—	—	—	—	—	—	Guinea-Bissau
...	...	...	...	...	...	...	—	—	—	—	—	—	Guyana
...	...	...	...	...	...	...	—	—	—	—	—	—	Haiti
...	...	...	...	...	...	...	—	—	—	—	—	—	Honduras
—	—	683	2,295	338	...	...	—	—	—	—	—	—	Hong Kong
34	3,020	979	13,858	1,362	102	21	7.0	40	4.0	161	848	2,470	Hungary
20	...	...	...	—	...	...	—	...	...	...	—	—	Iceland
853	26,293	8,684	26,293	25.0	5,371	22	250	874	0.8	2,255	5,613	...	India
2,557	86,400	3,378	55,300	111	4,700	13	452	432	1.7	993	7,472	...	Indonesia
26,618	69,928	4,426	74,757	1,131	125,800	78	1,374	502	7.7	1,474	8,256	22,882	Iran
3,115	2,900	2,725	5,141	214	115,000	129	891	193	8.0	598	5,418	...	Iraq
20	792	161	4,386	1,098	—	—	—	23	6.0	71	—	—	Ireland
...	...	...	...	...	...	...	—	...	...	...	—	—	Isle of Man
39	5.9	567	5.9	0.9	4.0	—	—	72	10.8	220	1,509	...	Israel
227	12,517	7,345	70,483[13]	1,226[13]	622	16	30	593[13]	10.3[13]	2,321	1,136	13,981	Italy
—	...	0.2	—	—	...	...	—	8.0	3.1	36	10	—	Jamaica
40	2,744	36,853	75,252	591	59	31	2.1	1,460	11.5	4,707	170	...	Japan
...	...	...	...	...	...	...	...	...	...	...	—	—	Jersey
6.2	223	257	223	41.9	1.0	...	—	28	5.3	90	743	...	Jordan
1,841	14,110	2,153	11,280	759	9,000	29	311	38	2.5	345	10,158	26,581	Kazakhstan
—	...	93	...	—	...	...	—	11	0.3	86	483	...	Kenya
...	...	...	...	...	...	...	—	—	—	—	—	—	Kiribati
...	...	...	...	...	...	...	—	19	0.8	71	154	...	Korea, North
—	—	19,620	23,931	502	...	...	—	788	16.5	2,544	452	...	Korea, South
1,572	9,983	3,673	9,983	4,413	99,000	142	680	320	142	889	540	...	Kuwait
5.7	30	...	886	177	40	66	0.6	0.8	0.2	10	13	—	Kyrgyzstan
...	...	...	...	...	...	...	—	—	...	—	136	—	Laos
...	...	...	1,540	658	40	...	—	—	—	—	409	6,450	Latvia
—	...	...	...	...	...	...	—	—	—	38	209	...	Lebanon
—	...	2	...	...	...	...	...	2	—	—	—	—	Lesotho
...	...	...	...	...	...	...	—	—	—	15	—	—	Liberia
1,314	5,850	1,691	5,044	920	36,000	70	504	143	26	380	7,252	...	Libya
...	...	17	...	...	...	...	...	17	17	—	—	—	Liechtenstein
—	...	784	2,617	754	12	147	3.2	47	13.7	263	331	2,960	Lithuania
...	...	—	1,229	2,767	...	...	—	—	—	—	—	...	Luxembourg
...	...	...	...	...	...	...	—	—	—	—	—	—	Macau
...	...	11	97	43.4	...	...	—	3.9	—	50	—	—	Macedonia
2.8	...	7	...	...	...	...	—	3.4	0.2	15	—	—	Madagascar
...	...	...	...	...	...	...	—	—	—	—	—	—	Malawi
2,124	48,284	2,849	28,017	1,169	3,000	11	275	181	7.5	545	1,841	...	Malaysia
...	...	...	...	...	...	...	—	—	—	—	—	—	Maldives
...	...	...	...	...	...	...	—	—	—	—	—	—	Mali
...	...	...	...	...	...	...	—	—	—	—	—	—	Malta
...	...	...	...	...	...	...	—	—	—	—	—	—	Marshall Islands
—	...	30	...	...	...	...	—	6.5	16.8	17	—	—	Martinique
...	...	48	...	...	...	...	—	7.2	2.5	—	—	—	Mauritania
...	...	...	...	...	...	...	—	—	—	—	—	—	Mauritius
...	...	...	...	...	...	...	...	...	...	...	—	—	Mayotte
424	34,050	9,730	40,473	392	14,600	14	1,156	498	4.8	1,684	28,200	...	Mexico
...	...	...	...	...	...	...	...	...	...	...	—	—	Micronesia
...	...	...	2,460	554	...	...	—	—	—	—	—	—	Moldova
...	...	7	7	...	...	...	—	7	7	—	—	—	Monaco
...	...	...	...	...	...	...	—	—	—	—	—	—	Mongolia
1.2	51	278	51	1.7	2.0	12	0.9	54	1.9	155	285	...	Morocco
127	2.4	...	2.4	0.1	...	...	—	—	—	—	—	—	Mozambique
346	6,483	18	1,199	24.8	50	14	3.5	7.3	0.1	57	558	...	Myanmar (Burma)
62	...	2	...	...	...	...	—	2	2	—	—	—	Namibia
...	...	...	...	...	...	...	—	—	—	—	—	—	Nauru
...	...	...	...	—	...	...	—	—	—	—	—	—	Nepal

Energy (continued)

country	electricity installed capacity, 2002 ('000 kW)	production, 2002 capacity ('000,000 kW-hr)	production, 2002 amount ('000,000 kW-hr)	power source, 2002 fossil fuel (%)	power source, 2002 hydro-power (%)	power source, 2002 nuclear fuel (%)	trade, 2002 exports ('000,000 kW-hr)	trade, 2002 imports ('000,000 kW-hr)	consumption amount, 2002 ('000,000 kW-hr)	consumption per capita, 2002 (kW-hr)	consumption residential, 1998 (%)	consumption non-residential, 1998 (%)	coal reserves, 2003 ('000,000 metric tons)	coal production, 2002 ('000 metric tons)	coal consumption, 2002 ('000 metric tons)
Netherlands, The	20,992	183,890	95,981	95.0	0.1	4.1[19]	4,488	20,870	112,363	6,958	...	...	533	...	13,466
Netherlands Antilles	210	1,840	1,000	100.0	—	—	—	—	1,000	4,566	...	...	...	...	...
New Caledonia	331	2,900	1,729	78.4	21.6	—	—	—	1,729	7,968	...	...	1.9	...	115
New Zealand	8,433	73,873	40,296	31.8	60.7	7.5[4]	—	—	40,296	10,301	...	...	611	4,459	2,445
Nicaragua	641	5,615	2,554	61.5	15.0	23.5[4]	7	15	2,562	496	70.7	29.3	...	...	...
Niger	105	920	243	100.0	—	—	—	215	458	40	56	44	75	178	178
Nigeria	5,881	51,518	18,125	61.8	38.2	—	—	—	18,125	149	...	...	203	62	62
Northern Mariana Islands	...	...	...	...	...	...	...	...	...	...	...	...	...	...	...
Norway	28,045	245,674	130,604	0.6	99.4	—	15,046	5,355	120,893	26,640	...	...	5.8	2,132	818
Oman	2,850	24,966	14,160	100.0	—	—	—	—	14,160	5,219	...	...	...	...	...
Pakistan	17,457	152,923	69,297	71.1	26.0	2.9	—	—	69,297	469	72.3	27.7	3,267	3,175	4,125
Palau	62	543	166	84.9	15.1	—	—	—	166	8,300	...	...	...	...	...
Panama	1,349	11,817	5,076	35.4	64.6	—	49	35	5,062	1,654	79.5	20.5	...	...	60
Papua New Guinea	472	4,135	1,390	33.6	66.4	—	—	—	1,390	249	27.9	72.1	...	...	...
Paraguay	7,416	64,964	48,251	0.1	99.9	—	41,770	—	6,481	1,129	79	21	...	...	...
Peru	5,913	51,798	24,266	16.2	83.8	—	—	—	24,266	907	67.74	32.34	1,135	22	910
Philippines	12,654	110,849	48,467	64.4	14.5	21.1[4]	—	—	48,467	610	65.34	34.74	253	1,665	8,627
Poland	30,598	268,038	144,126	97.2	2.8	—	11,537	4,469	137,058	3,549	41.84	58.24	14,998	161,915	140,426
Portugal	11,242	98,480	46,096	81.1	17.9	—[6]	3,430	5,329	47,995	4,647	...	...	39	—	5,668
Puerto Rico	4,901	42,933	22,100	99.2	0.8	—	—	—	22,100	5,727	...	...	...	...	176
Qatar	2,257	19,771	10,511	100.0	—	—	—	—	10,511	17,489	74.9	25.1	...	...	...
Réunion	439	3,846	1,613	64.4	35.6	—	—	—	1,613	2,156	...	...	...	...	...
Romania	21,904	191,879	54,935	60.8	29.2	10.0	3,290	436	52,081	2,385	27.1	72.9	530	30,414	34,254
Russia	212,768	1,863,848	891,285	65.7	18.4	15.9	18,097	5,154	878,342	6,062	36.1	63.9	168,202	240,980	224,100
Rwanda	43	377	172	2.3	97.7	—	4	20	188	23	...	...	...	...	...
St. Kitts and Nevis	20	175	110	100.0	—	—	—	—	110	2,619	...	...	...	...	...
St. Lucia	70	613	270	100.0	—	—	—	—	270	1,698	...	...	...	...	...
St. Vincent and the Grenadines	23	201	108	73.1	26.9	—	—	—	108	1,000	...	...	...	...	...
Samoa	24	210	105	66.7	33.3	—	—	—	105	597	...	...	...	...	...
San Marino	13	13	13	13	13	13	13	13	13	13	...	...	...	13	...
São Tomé and Príncipe	6	53	18	44.4	55.6	—	—	—	18	115	...	...	...	...	...
Saudi Arabia	24,100	211,116	145,631	100.0	—	—	—	—	145,631	6,620	...	...	...	...	...
Senegal	239	2,094	1,495	100.0	—	—	—	—	1,495	141	16.7	83.3	...	...	...
Serbia and Montenegro	11,779	103,184	33,163	68.5	31.5	—	1,054	5,713	37,822	3,460	24.3	75.7	17,773	35,896	36,177
Seychelles	93	815	219	100.0	—	—	—	—	219	2,704	24.3	75.7	...	...	...
Sierra Leone	130	1,139	257	100.0	—	—	—	—	257	54	...	...	...	...	...
Singapore	8,848	77,508	35,404	100.0	—	—	—	—	35,404	7,961	...	...	...	...	...
Slovakia	8,693	76,151	32,427	27.7	18.9	53.4	10,867	6,710	28,270	5,256	...	...	190	3,404	8,772
Slovenia	2,543	22,277	14,689	39.2	23.2	37.6	4,928	3,794	13,555	6,791	...	...	294	4,686	5,577
Solomon Islands	12	105	32	100.0	—	—	—	—	32	69	...	...	...	...	...
Somalia	80	701	282	100.0	—	—	—	—	282	33	...	...	...	...	...
South Africa	39,611[2]	346,992[2]	231,833[2]	92.0[2]	2.8[2]	5.2[2]	7,023[2]	12,114[2]	236,924[2]	4,715[2]	28.5	71.5	52,225	228,190	161,977
Spain	60,406	529,157	246,048	59.6	11.3	25.6[20]	7,175	12,504	251,377	6,154	...	...	568	22,034	46,241
Sri Lanka	2,768	24,248	6,951	61.2	38.8	—	—	—	6,951	366	62.7	37.3	...	...	1
Sudan, The	757	6,631	2,897	55.6	44.4	—	—	—	2,897	89	...	...	...	...	...
Suriname	389	3,408	1,921	17.6	82.4	—	—	—	1,921	4,447	...	...	...	...	...
Swaziland	2	2	2	2	2	2	2	2	2	2	...	...	223	2	2
Sweden	33,649	294,765	146,057	7.7	45.6	46.3[5]	14,754	20,110	151,413	16,995	...	...	1.0	—	3,021
Switzerland	17,969[17]	157,408[17]	66,649[17]	3.7[17]	55.4[17]	40.9[17]	32,308[17]	22,800[17]	62,143[17]	8,483[17]	...	...	...	...	168[17]
Syria	6,450	56,502	26,896	87.0	13.0	—	—	—	26,896	1,570	...	...	...	...	...
Taiwan	...	...	165,901	71.0	5.2	23.8	—	—	165,901	7,360	35.2	64.8	1.0	...	...
Tajikistan	4,443	38,921	15,241	2.3	97.7	—	4,019	5,240	16,462	2,559	...	...	...	131	131
Tanzania	543	4,757	2,994	8.6	91.4	—	...	...	2,994	83	...	...	214	83	83
Thailand	29,507	258,481	115,513	93.5	6.5	—	273	2,821	118,061	1,860	58.3	41.7	1,451	19,603	25,065
Togo	38	333	122	97.5	2.5	—	—	455	577	120	...	...	...	...	...
Tonga	8	70	36	100.0	—	—	—	—	36	340	...	...	...	...	...
Trinidad and Tobago	1,417	12,413	5,643	100.0	—	—	—	—	5,643	4,422	35.3	64.7	...	...	...
Tunisia	2,435	21,331	11,846	99.2	0.8	—	59	—	11,787	1,205	54.1	45.9	...	...	1
Turkey	31,853	279,032	129,400	73.8	26.2	—[1]	435	3,588	132,553	1,904	...	...	4,484	53,298	65,207
Turkmenistan	3,930	34,427	11,200	100.0	—	—	1,010	—	10,190	2,126	...	...	...	...	...
Tuvalu	...	...	...	...	...	...	...	...	...	...	...	...	...	...	...
Uganda	269	2,356	1,675	0.4	99.6	—	165	—	1,510	61	...	...	...	...	...
Ukraine	52,815	462,659	173,734	49.5	5.6	44.9	8,576	5,461	170,619	3,525	...	...	36,587	59,483	62,315
United Arab Emirates	5,880	51,509	41,750	100.0	—	—	—	—	41,750	14,215	...	...	...	...	...
United Kingdom	77,024	674,730	382,740	74.8	1.9	23.3	708	9,182	391,154	6,614	...	...	236	29,989	58,490
United States	917,876	8,040,594	3,858,452	72.3	7.1	20.2[5]	14,538	36,438	3,880,352	13,456	21.4	78.6	263,097	992,717	971,673
Uruguay	2,172	19,027	9,604	0.7	99.3	—	1,909	559	8,254	2,456	76	34	...	...	1
Uzbekistan	11,709	102,571	49,600	87.2	12.8	—	5,031	6,358	50,927	2,008	...	...	4,285	2,467	2,407
Vanuatu	12	105	43	100.0	—	—	—	—	43	208	...	...	...	...	...
Venezuela	20,577	180,255	87,406	32.9	67.1	—	—	—	87,406	3,484	23.8	76.2	513	7,369	25
Vietnam	5,029	44,054	31,215	38.4	59.5	2.1[4]	—	—	31,215	392	...	...	161	12,995	8,710
Virgin Islands (U.S.)	323	2,829	1,100	100.0	—	—	—	—	1,100	10,000	...	...	...	...	290
West Bank	...	...	...	...	...	...	...	...	...	...	...	...	...	...	...
Western Sahara	58	508	88	100.0	—	—	—	—	88	292	...	...	...	...	...
Yemen	810	7,096	3,094	100.0	—	—	—	—	3,094	159	...	...	...	...	...
Zambia	2,260	19,798	9,109	0.5	99.5	—	2,657	—	6,452	603	33	67	11	210	136
Zimbabwe	2,011	17,616	8,598	55.5	44.5	—	—	3,995	12,593	981	42.6	57.4	537	3,690	3,727

[1]In addition, geothermal equals 0.1%. [2]South Africa includes Botswana, Lesotho, Namibia, and Swaziland. [3]Includes 173,936,000,000 of Canadian oil sands. [4]Geothermal. [5]In addition, geothermal equals 0.4%. [6]In addition, geothermal equals 1.0%. [7]France includes Monaco. [8]In addition, geothermal equals 1.2%. [9]In addition, geothermal equals 5.6%. [10]In addition, geothermal equals 0.5%. [11]In addition, geothermal equals 2.6%. [12]In addition, geothermal equals 1.6%. [13]Italy includes San Marino. [14]In addition, geothermal equals 2.1%. [15]In addition, geothermal equals 0.3%.

natural gas					crude petroleum								country
published proven reserves, 2005 ('000,000,000 cu m)	production — natural gas, 2002 ('000,000 cu m)	production — manufactured gas, 2002 ('000,000 cu m)	consumption — natural gas, 2002 ('000,000 cu m)	consumption — natural gas per capita (cu m)	reserves — published proven, 2005 ('000,000 barrels)	reserves — years to exhaust proven reserves, 2002	production, 2002 ('000,000 barrels)	consumption, 2002 ('000,000 barrels)	consumption per capita (barrels)	refining capacity, 2005 ('000 barrels per day)	pipelines (latest) — length (km)	pipelines (latest) — traffic ('000,000 metric ton-km)	
1,756	79,776	13,932	52,682	3,262	106	7	15	331	20.5	1,228	590	5,503	Netherlands, The
—	...	127	...	...	...	...	—	107	492	320	—	—	Netherlands Antilles
...	...	...	...	...	...	...	—	...	...	—	—	—	New Caledonia
37	5,531	467	5,531	1,414	55	7	11	39	10.0	104	160	...	New Zealand
—	...	28	...	—	...	...	—	6.0	1.2	20	54	...	Nicaragua
...	...	...	...	...	...	...	...	...	...	—	—	—	Niger
4,502	14,347	388	6,426	52.5	25,000	43	716	79	0.6	439	3,638	...	Nigeria
—	...	...	...	—	...	...	—	...	...	—	—	—	Northern Mariana Islands
2,118	68,315	6,166	7,091	1,563	10,447	9	1,182	95	21.1	310	2,213	3,485	Norway
829	17,188	141	8,013	2,954	5,506	18	328	31	11.3	85	3,212	...	Oman
760	22,996	411	22,996	156	289	13	22	65	0.4	269	1,821	...	Pakistan
—	...	...	...	—	—	...	—	...	...	...	—	—	Palau
—	...	94	63	20.5	...	...	—	9.4	3.1	60	130	...	Panama
345	85	...	85	15.1	240	8	29	0.5	0.1	33	—	—	Papua New Guinea
—	...	...	...	—	...	...	—	0.7	0.1	8	—	—	Paraguay
247	907	1,087	907	33.9	285	9	37	59	2.2	193	1,157	...	Peru
107	370	863	370	4.7	152	22	2.0	100	1.3	333	135	...	Philippines
165	5,293	4,517	14,998	388	96	22	5.4	133	3.4	350	1,772	18,448	Poland
—	...	398	3,254	315	...	...	—	86	8.3	304	80	—	Portugal
...	...	99	...	...	...	...	—	19	4.9	110	—	—	Puerto Rico
25,768	29,300	2,992	11,629	19,350	15,207	65	230	24	40	200	702	...	Qatar
...	...	...	...	...	...	...	—	...	...	—	—	—	Réunion
101	12,001	2,125	15,538	712	956	17	44	91	4.2	517	2,427	2,257	Romania
47,573	484,470	28,007	329,003	2,271	60,000	22	2,705	1,391	9.6	5,433	75,539	1,980,000	Russia
57	0.3	...	0.3	...	...	...	—	...	...	—	—	—	Rwanda
...	...	...	...	...	...	...	—	—	—	—	—	—	St. Kitts and Nevis
...	...	...	...	...	...	...	—	—	—	—	—	—	St. Lucia
...	...	...	...	...	...	...	—	—	—	—	—	—	St. Vincent and the Grenadines
...	...	...	...	...	...	...	—	—	—	—	—	—	Samoa
...	...	...	[13]	...	...	...	...	[13]	[13]	—	—	—	San Marino
...	...	...	...	...	...	...	—	...	...	—	—	—	São Tomé and Príncipe
6,544	55,401	25,958	55,401	2,518	261,900	96	2,719	620	28	1,745	5,068	...	Saudi Arabia
—	0.9	19	0.9	...	...	...	—	6.8	0.6	27	—	—	Senegal
48	844	93	2,703	247	78	29	5.6	19	1.8	158	393	...	Serbia and Montenegro
...	...	...	...	...	...	...	—	...	...	—	—	—	Seychelles
—	...	...	...	—	...	...	—	1.9	0.4	10	—	—	Sierra Leone
—	—	1,083	4,411	992	...	...	—	298	67	1,337	—	—	Singapore
15	173	1,395	6,995	1,300	9.0	23	0.3	41	7.7	115	449	...	Slovakia
3.4	5.8	...	977	490	7.0	...	—	16	1.3	48	11	128	Slovenia
...	...	...	...	—	...	...	—	—	—	—	—	—	Solomon Islands
5.6	...	...	...	...	...	...	—	...	...	15	...	...	Somalia
2.8	2,371	4,227	2,371	47.2	16	1	58	209	4.2	490	847	...	South Africa
2.7	537	4,715	21,560	528	158	6	2.4	424	10.4	1,272	730	6,872	Spain
—	...	75	...	—	...	...	—	16	1.3	48	62	...	Sri Lanka
85	...	285	...	...	563	6	88	23	0.7	122	2,365	...	Sudan, The
—	...	...	...	...	111	42	3.8	3.3	7.7	7	—	—	Suriname
...	...	...	...	...	...	...	...	2	...	...	—	—	Swaziland
—	...	1,046	930	104	...	...	—	137	15.4	434	—	—	Sweden
—	—	478[17]	3,036[17]	414[17]	...	...	—	35[17]	4.8[17]	132	94	234	Switzerland
241	5,766	523	5,766	337	2,500	14	209	88	5.2	240	2,183	...	Syria
76	850	...	850	...	4.0	4	0.4	0.4	...	1,220	3,400	—	Taiwan
5.7	29	...	749	116	12	125	0.1	0.1	...	...	866	...	Tajikistan
2.3	...	...	...	...	...	...	—	—	...	15	...	...	Tanzania
378	19,223	4,452	26,488	417	583	21	25	267	4.2	703	67	...	Thailand
—	...	...	...	...	...	...	—	...	...	—	—	—	Togo
...	...	...	...	...	...	...	...	...	...	—	—	—	Tonga
733	18,043	1,037	18,043	14,140	990	15	48	55	43.4	165	478	...	Trinidad and Tobago
76	2,061	121	3,002	307	308	10	30	14	1.4	34	1,203	...	Tunisia
8.5	389	2,997	18,408	264	296	16	17	186	2.7	714	3,562	2,994	Turkey
2,011	51,850	453	14,421	3,008	546	8	69	48	10	237	1,395	694	Turkmenistan
...	...	...	...	...	...	...	...	—	—	—	—	—	Tuvalu
...	...	...	...	...	...	...	...	...	...	—	—	—	Uganda
1,121	18,679	4,918	73,317	1,515	395	75	19	154	3.2	880	4,540	38,402	Ukraine
6,006	44,071	10,155	36,958	12,584	97,800	134	729	166	57	514	2,936	...	United Arab Emirates
629	120,061	12,870	110,102	1,862	4,665	6	802	582	9.8	1,825	6,420	11,666	United Kingdom
5,353	559,907	117,226	673,226	2,334	21,374	13	2,078	5,600	19.4	17,125	244,620[21]	949,800[21]	United States
—	—	102	—	6.9	...	...	—	9.4	2.8	50	—	—	Uruguay
1,875	56,157	288	51,662	2,037	594	22	28	28	1.1	222	869	200	Uzbekistan
...	...	...	...	...	...	...	—	...	...	—	—	—	Vanuatu
4,191	23,113	90	23,113	921	77,800	79	965	301	12.0	1,282	7,360	...	Venezuela
193	2,064	309	2,064	25.9	600	19	126	—	—	—	3	...	Vietnam
...	...	...	...	...	...	...	—	—	1,353	495	—	—	Virgin Islands (U.S.)
...	...	...	...	...	...	...	—	—	—	—	—	—	West Bank
...	...	...	...	...	...	...	—	...	...	—	—	—	Western Sahara
479	...	91	...	...	4,000	21	194	33	1.7	130	1,174	—	Yemen
—	...	15	...	—	...	...	—	0.3	0.3	24	771	...	Zambia
...	...	111	...	—	...	...	—	...	...	—	—	—	Zimbabwe

[16]In addition, geothermal equals 8.3%. [17]Switzerland includes Liechtenstein. [18]In addition, geothermal equals 3.2%. [19]In addition, geothermal equals 0.8%. [20]In addition, geothermal equals 3.5%. [21]Mostly petroleum products.

Transportation

This table presents data on the transportation infrastructure of the various countries and dependencies of the world and on their commercial passenger and cargo traffic. Most states have roads and airports, with services corresponding to the prevailing level of economic development. A number of states, however, lack railroads or inland waterways because of either geographic constraints or lack of development capital and technical expertise. Pipelines, one of the oldest means of bulk transport if aqueducts are considered, are today among the most narrowly developed transportation modes worldwide for shipment of bulk materials. Because the principal contemporary application of pipeline technology is to facilitate the shipment of hydrocarbon liquids and gases, coverage of pipelines will be found in the "Energy" table. It is, however, also true that pipelines now find increasing application for slurries of coal or other raw materials.

While the United Nations' *Statistical Yearbook, Monthly Bulletin of Statistics,* and *Annual Bulletin of Transport Statistics* provide much data on infrastructure and traffic and have established basic definitions and classifications for transportation statistics, the number of countries covered is limited. Several commercial publications maintain substantial databases and publishing programs for their particular areas of interest: highway and vehicle statistics are provided by the International Road Federation's annual *World Road Statistics;* the International Union of Railway's *International Railway Statistics* and Jane's *World Railways* provide similar data for railways; Lloyd's *Register of Shipping Statistical Tables* summarizes the world's merchant marine; the *Official Airline Guide,* the International Civil Aviation Organization's *Digest of Statistics: Commercial Air Carriers,* and the International Air Transport Association's *World Air Transport Statistics* have also been used to supplement and update data collected by the UN. Because several of these agencies are commercially or insurance-oriented, their data tend to be more complete, accurate, and timely than those of intergovernmental organizations, which depend on periodic responses to questionnaires or publication of results in official sources. All of these international sources have been extensively supplemented by national statistical sources to provide additional data. Such diversity of sources, however, imposes limitations on the comparability of the statistics from country to country because the basis and completeness of data collection and the frequency and timeliness of analysis and publication may vary greatly. Data shown in italic are from 1994 or earlier.

The categories adopted in the table also have special problems of comparability. Total road length is subject to wide international variation of interpretation, as "roads" can mean anything from mere tracks to highly developed highways. Each country also has individual classifications that differ according to climate, availability of road-building materials, traffic patterns, administrative responsibility, and so on. "Paved roads," by contrast, is a much more tightly definable category, but the proportion of paved to total roads may be distorted by the less comparable total road statistics. Automobile and truck and bus fleet statistics, which are usually

Transportation

country	roads and motor vehicles (latest)								railroads (latest)					
	roads			motor vehicles			cargo		track length		traffic			
	length		paved (percent)	automobiles	trucks and buses	persons per vehicle	short ton-mi ('000,000)	metric ton-km ('000,000)	mi	km	passengers		cargo	
	mi	km									passenger-mi ('000,000)	passenger-km ('000,000)	short ton-mi ('000,000)	metric ton-km ('000,000)
Afghanistan	13,000	21,000	13	31,000	25,000	401	1,993	2,910	16	25	...	...	...	...
Albania	11,000	18,000	30	90,766	34,378	25	550	803	416	670	72	116	0.01	0.02
Algeria	63,643	102,424	69	725,000	780,000	19	9,589	14,000	2,451[2]	3,945[2]	1,135	1,826	1,465	2,139
American Samoa	217	350	43	4,672	199	11	...	...	—	—	—	—	—	—
Andorra	167	269	74	35,358	4,238	1.6			—	—	—	—	—	—
Angola	45,128	72,626	25	207,000	25,000	41	...	...	1,834[2]	2,952[2]	203	326	1,178	1,720
Antigua and Barbuda	155	250	...	13,588	1,342	4.3			—	—	—	—	—	—
Argentina	135,630	218,276	29	4,901,608	1,379,044	5.7	...	...	21,100[2]	33,958[2]	5,656	9,102	6,234	9,102
Armenia	5,238	8,431	100	1,300	4,460	655	146	213	516	830	29	46	201	324
Aruba	236	380	100	38,834	990	2.4	...	...	—	—	—	—	—	—
Australia	502,356	808,465	40	9,719,900	2,214,900	1.6	786,643	1,148,480	22,233[2,7]	35,780[2,7]	7,152	11,510	87,262	127,400
Austria	124,000	200,000	100	4,009,604	328,591	1.9	10,773	15,670	3,506	5,643	4,957[7]	7,971[7]	10,617[7]	15,500[7]
Azerbaijan	28,502	45,870	94	281,100	104,300	21	484	706	1,317	2,120	342	550	3,160	4,613
Bahamas, The	1,522	2,450	57	89,263	17,228	2.6	...	...	—	—	—	—	—	—
Bahrain	1,966	3,164	77	149,636	32,213	3.4	...	...	—	—	—	—	—	—
Bangladesh	126,773	204,022	12	54,784	69,394	991	...	...	1,699[2]	2,734[2]	3,094	4,980	567	828
Barbados	1,025	1,650	96	43,711	10,583	4.9	...	...	—	—	—	—	—	—
Belarus	33,186	53,407	99	1,132,843	8,867	8.9	6,323	9,232	3,410	5,488	10,485	16,874	20,911	30,529
Belgium	89,353	143,800	97	4,491,734	453,122	2.1	25,586	37,355	2,100[2]	3,380[2]	4,570	7,354	5,063	7,392
Belize	1,398	2,250	18	9,695	11,698	11	...	...	—	—	—	—	—	—
Benin	4,217	6,787	20	37,772	8,058	123	...	...	359	578	75.7	121.8	193.5	311.4
Bermuda	140	225	100	21,220	4,007	2.4	...	...	—	—	—	—	—	—
Bhutan	2,041	3,285	61	2,590	1,367	348	...	...	—	—	—	—	—	—
Bolivia	30,696	49,400	6	223,829	138,536	21	1,133	1,654	2,187[2]	3,519[2]	84.9	136.7	359.0	524.2
Bosnia and Herzegovina	13,574	21,846	52	96,182	10,919	30	2,708	3,954	641	1,031	19.3	31.1	63.6	92.8
Botswana	11,388	18,327	25	30,517	59,710	17	...	...	603	971	60	96	545	795
Brazil	1,030,652	1,658,677	9	21,313,351	3,743,836	6.5	178,359	260,400	18,458[2]	29,706[2]	8,676	12,667	96,741	141,239
Brunei	1,064	1,712	75	91,047	15,918	2.9	...	...	12[13]	19[13]	—	—	—	—
Bulgaria	23,190	37,320	92	1,730,506	251,382	4.2	4,300	6,278	4,020	6,470	2,341	3,767	3,071	4,484
Burkina Faso	7,519	12,100	16	38,220	17,980	190	...	...	386[2]	622[2]	126	202	31	45
Burundi	8,997	14,480	7	19,200	18,240	145	...	...	—	—	—	—	—	—
Cambodia	22,226	35,769	8	52,919	13,574	171	822	1,200	409	649	37	60	25	36
Cameroon	30,074	48,400	8	98,000	64,350	88	175	255	625[2]	1,006[2]	197	317	556	812
Canada	560,415	901,903	35	13,887,270	3,694,125	1.7	94,584	138,090	40,639	65,403	906	1,458	205,146	299,508
Cape Verde	680	1,095	78	3,280	820	94	...	...	—	—	—	—	—	—
Central African Republic	14,900	24,000	2	9,500	7,000	195	41	60	—	—	—	—	—	—
Chad	20,800	33,400	1	10,560	14,550	293	580	850	—	—	—	—	—	—
Chile	49,590	79,800	14	1,323,800	687,500	7.5	...	...	5,410[2]	8,707[2]	377	606	1,984	2,896
China	794,405	1,278,474	93	6,548,300	6,278,900	96	375,580	548,338	35,781	57,584	229,657	369,598	843,302	1,236,200
Colombia	71,808	115,564	12	762,000	672,000	27	21	31	2,007[2]	3,230[2]	9.6	15.5	504.3	736.2
Comoros	559	900	76	9,100	4,950	36	...	...	—	—	—	—	—	—
Congo, Dem. Rep. of the	95,708	154,027	2	787,000	60,000	55	...	...	3,193	5,138	18[14]	29[14]	121[14]	176[14]
Congo, Rep. of the	7,950	12,800	10	37,240	15,520	49	46	67	556	894	150	242	92	135
Costa Rica	22,119	35,597	17	294,083	163,428	7.6	2,103	3,070	590[2]	950[2]	3.7	5.9	45.8	66.8
Côte d'Ivoire	31,300	50,400	10	293,000	163,000	32	...	...	397[2]	639[2]	80[17]	129[17]	40[17]	58[17]
Croatia	17,475	28,123	82	1,124,825	117,794	3.4	1,774	2,590	1,694	2,726	619	996	1,321	1,928
Cuba	37,815	60,858	49	172,574	185,495	31	2,482	3,623	2,987	4,807	1,219	1,962	763	1,075
Cyprus	6,620	10,654	58	234,976	108,452	2.4	...	...	—	—	—	—	—	—
Czech Republic	78,234	125,905	44	3,695,792	426,684	2.5	23,227	33,911	6,469	9,444	4,323	6,957	11,447	16,713
Denmark	44,389	71,663	100	1,854,060	335,690	2.4	14,639	21,372	1,704[2]	2,743[2]	3,304	5,318	1,387	2,025
Djibouti	1,796	2,890	13	9,200	4,950	38	...	...	66	106	361	762	144	232
Dominica	485	780	50	6,581	2,825	7.8	...	...	—	—	—	—	—	—
Dominican Republic	7,829	12,600	49	224,000	151,550	21	...	...	1,083[2]	1,743[2]	...	...	...	...
East Timor	...	...	...	...	...	...			...	...	...	...	...	...
Ecuador	26,841	43,197	19	464,902	52,630	23	2,712	3,959	600[2]	966[2]	28	45	686	1,002

based upon registration, are relatively accurate, though some countries round off figures, and unregistered vehicles may cause substantial undercount. There is also inconsistent classification of vehicle types; in some countries a vehicle may serve variously as an automobile, a truck, or a bus, or even as all three on certain occasions. Relatively few countries collect and maintain commercial road traffic statistics.

Data on national railway systems are generally given for railway track length rather than the length of routes, which may be multitracked. Siding tracks usually are not included, but some countries fail to distinguish them. The United States data include only class 1 railways, which account for about 94 percent of total track length. Passenger traffic is usually calculated from tickets sold to fare-paying passengers. Such statistics are subject to distortion if there are large numbers of nonpaying passengers, such as military personnel, or if season tickets are sold and not all the allowed journeys are utilized. Railway cargo traffic is calculated by weight hauled multiplied by the length of the journey. Changes in freight load during the journey should be accounted for but sometimes are not, leading to discrepancies.

Merchant fleet and tonnage statistics collected by Lloyd's registry service for vessels over 100 gross tons are quite accurate. Cargo statistics, however, reflect the port and customs requirements of each country and the reporting rules of each country's merchant marine authority (although these, increasingly, reflect the recommendations of the International

Maritime Organization); often, however, they are only estimates based on customs declarations and the count of vessels entered and cleared. Even when these elements are reported consistently, further uncertainties may be introduced because of ballast, bunkers, ships' stores, or transshipped goods included in the data.

Airport data are based on scheduled flights reported in the commercial *Official Airline Guide* and are both reliable and current. The comparability of civil air traffic statistics suffers from differing characteristics of the air transportation systems of different countries; data for an entire country may be two to three years behind those for a single airport.

Outside of Europe, where standardization of data on inland waterways is necessitated by the volume of international traffic, comparability of national data declines markedly. Calculations as to both the length of a country's waterway system (or route length of river, lake, and coastal traffic) and the makeup of its stock of commercially significant vessels (those for which data will be collected) are largely determined by the nature and use of the country's hydrographic net—its seasonality, relief profile, depth, access to potential markets—and inevitably differ widely from country to country. Data for coastal or island states may refer to scheduled coastwise or interisland traffic.

merchant marine (latest)				air						canals and inland waterways (latest)				country
fleet (vessels over 100 gross tons)	total dead-weight tonnage ('000)	international cargo (latest)		airports with scheduled flights (latest)	traffic (latest)					length		cargo		
		loaded metric tons ('000)	off-loaded metric tons ('000)		passengers		cargo			mi	km	short ton-mi ('000,000)	metric ton-km ('000,000)	
					passenger-mi ('000,000)	passenger-km ('000,000)	short ton-mi ('000,000)	metric ton-km ('000,000)						
—	—	—	—	3	171.5[1]	276.0[1]	26[1]	38[1]		750	1,200	...	...	Afghanistan
24	81.0	120	2,040	1	2.2	3.5	0.22	0.32		46	74	24	35	Albania
149	1,093.4	63,110	15,700	28	1,803[3]	2,901[3]	12.5[3]	18.3[3]		...	...	...	...	Algeria
3	0.1	380	581	3	...	...	...	...		...	...	...	...	American Samoa
—	—	—	—	—	—	—	—	—		—	—	—	—	Andorra
123	73.9	23,288	1,261	17	385[4]	620[4]	60[4]	97[4]		805	1,295	...	...	Angola
292	997.4	28	113	2	157	252	0.1	0.2		...	...	...	...	Antigua and Barbuda
423	1,173.1	69,372	19,536	39	7,292[5]	11,735[5]	895[5]	1,307[5]		6,804	10,950	19,326	28,215	Argentina
...	...	...	...	1	356	572	5.9	9.5		...	...	...	...	Armenia
6	6	...	...	1	318	511	...	...		...	...	...	...	Aruba
695	3,857.3	35,664	43,360	400	46,647	75,071	1,156	1,688		5,200	8,368	31,891	46,560	Australia
26	208.5	1,479	5,766	6	7,742	12,460	247	361		218	351	7,938	11,590	Austria
69	...	...	...	3	1,025	1,650	125	183		...	...	3,112	5,008	Azerbaijan
1,061	33,081.7	5,920	5,705	22	87	140	0.32	0.455		...	...	...	...	Bahamas, The
87	192.5	13,285	3,512	1	1,762[8]	2,836[8]	81.3[8]	118.7[8]		...	...	...	...	Bahrain
301	566.8	948	10,404	8	2,154	3,466	95	139		5,000	8,046	...	...	Bangladesh
37	84.0	206	538	1	93[9]	149[9]	0.8[10]	1.1[10]		...	...	...	...	Barbados
...	18,373.0	...	...	1	864	1,390	7	10		1,092	1,757	71	103	Belarus
232	218.5	360,984	367,680	2	12,042	19,379	389	568		957	1,540	3,993	5,830	Belgium
32	45.7	255	277	9	...	...	...	...		513	825	...	...	Belize
12	0.2	339	1,738	1	160.5[11]	258.3[11]	8.4[11]	13.5[11]		...	...	...	...	Benin
94	5,206.5	130	470	1	29	46	...	...		...	...	...	...	Bermuda
—	—	—	—	1	29	46	—	—		—	—	—	—	Bhutan
1	15.8	...	...	14	1,223	1,968	28.7	41.9		6,214	10,000	90	132	Bolivia
...	...	...	...	1	25.1	40.4	0.29	0.43		...	...	...	...	Bosnia and Herzegovina
—	—	—	—	7	35.3[12]	56.8[12]	0.1[12]	0.2[12]		...	...	...	...	Botswana
635	9,348.3	239,932	146,452	139	21,765	35,028	891	1,031		31,069	50,000	56,030	81,803	Brazil
51	349.7	42	1,308	1	1,742	2,803	75.0	109.5		130	209	...	...	Brunei
107	391	5,290	20,080	3	1,259	2,026	18.9	30.4		292	470	487	711	Bulgaria
—	—	—	—	2	134.9	217.2	23.4	34.2		...	...	...	...	Burkina Faso
1	0.4	35	188	1	1.2	2.0	...	...		...	...	...	...	Burundi
3	3.8	11	95	8	26.1	42.0	0.3	0.4		2,300	3,700	51	75	Cambodia
47	39.8	2,385	2,497	5	348	560	57	91		1,299	2,090	...	...	Cameroon
1,185	2,896.8	187,716	94,536	269	42,379	68,202	1,224	1,787		1,860	3,000	...	...	Canada
42	30.9	144	299	9	106	171	13.2	19.2		...	...	...	...	Cape Verde
—	—	53	126	1	139.6[12]	224.7[12]	11.2[12]	16.4[12]		500	800	185	270	Central African Republic
—	—	—	—	1	145	233	25	37		1,240	2,000	...	...	Chad
392	854.9	29,532	18,144	23	6,618	10,651	1,443	2,107		450	725	5,629	8,218	Chile
2,390	20,658.0	1,146,084	101,688	113	49,725	80,024	2,291	3,345		68,537	110,300	1,329,187	1,940,580	China
101	403.0	49,332	15,288	43	3,723	5,991	573	836		11,272	18,140	1.7	2.5	Colombia
6	3.6	12	107	2	1.9	3.0	...	...		...	...	...	...	Comoros
27	30.7	2,395	1,453	22	173[15]	279[15]	29[15]	42[15]		9,300	15,000	678	990	Congo, Dem. Rep. of the
22	10.8	708	533	10	160[11]	258[11]	9.6	14		696	1,120	...	...	Congo, Rep. of the
24	8.4	3,017	3,972	14	2,167[16]	3,487[16]	61.9[16]	90.4[16]		454	730	...	...	Costa Rica
51	98.6	4,173	7,228	5	191[18]	307[18]	30[18]	44[18]		609	980	...	...	Côte d'Ivoire
203	140.9	4,416	7,680	4	474	763	2.0	3.0		580	933	43	63	Croatia
393	924.6	8,092	15,440	14	2,202	3,543	38.5	56.2		149	240	108	158	Cuba
1,416	36,198.1	1,344	4,308	2	1,685	2,711	26	38		...	...	...	...	Cyprus
18[19]	514.1[19]	759	409	2	2,705	4,354	21	30		413	664	627	915	Czech Republic
456	7,589.1	21,060	38,292	13	3,340[20]	5,376[20]	117[20]	171[20]		259	417	1,100	1,600	Denmark
10	4.1	414	958	1	42	67	4	6		...	...	...	...	Djibouti
7	3.2	103	181	2	...	...	...	...		...	...	...	...	Dominica
28	10.4	1,668	4,182	7	9.8	15.8	7.9	11.6		...	...	...	...	Dominican Republic
...	...	...	...		...	...	...	...		...	...	...	...	East Timor
154	504.1	11,783	1,958	14	574	924	79	116		932	1,500	...	...	Ecuador

Transportation (continued)

country	roads and motor vehicles (latest) roads length mi	km	paved (per-cent)	motor vehicles auto-mobiles	trucks and buses	persons per vehicle	cargo short ton-mi ('000,000)	metric ton-km ('000,000)	railroads (latest) track length mi	km	traffic passengers passen-ger-mi ('000,000)	passen-ger-km ('000,000)	cargo short ton-mi ('000,000)	metric ton-km ('000,000)
Egypt	39,800[21]	64,000[21]	78[21]	1,154,753	510,766	37	21,600	31,500	2,989	4,810	35,211	56,667	2,820	4,117
El Salvador	6,232	10,029	20	177,488	184,859	16	...	...	349[2]	562[2]	4.4	7.1	12	17
Equatorial Guinea	1,740	2,800	13	6,500	4,000	37	...	...	—	—	—	—	—	—
Eritrea	2,491	4,010	22	5,940	...	...	...	...	43	70	...	...	...	...
Estonia	10,209	16,430	51	451,000	86,900	2.7	2,691	3,929	636	1,024	149	238	4,808	7,020
Ethiopia	12,117	19,500	15	52,012	39,936	642	...	...	486[22]	782[22]	98	157	73	106
Faroe Islands	285	458	...	14,608	3,455	2.5	...	...	—	—	—	—	—	—
Fiji	3,200	5,100	20	49,712	33,928	9.4	...	...	370[13]	595[13]	—	—	—	—
Finland	48,340	77,900	65	2,069,055	300,048	2.2	19,884	29,030	3,626[2]	5,836[2]	2,122	3,415	6,680	9,753
France	547,200	893,500	100	27,480,000	5,610,000	1.8	114,382	166,995	19,486[2]	31,821[2]	40,100	64,500	37,000	54,000
French Guiana	706	1,137	40	29,100	10,600	3.2	...	...	—	—	—	—	—	—
French Polynesia	549	884	44	37,000	15,300	4.0	...	...	—	—	—	—	—	—
Gabon	4,760	7,670	8	24,750	16,490	28	...	...	506	814	53	85	345	503
Gambia, The	1,678	2,700	35	8,640	9,000	68	...	...	—	—	—	—	—	—
Gaza Strip	...	...	...	37,061	8,105	23	...	...	—	—	—	—	—	—
Georgia	12,862	20,700	93	427,000	41,510	11	288	420	961	1,546	219	349	2,150	3,139
Germany	143,372	230,735	99	42,323,672	2,550,222	1.8	176,337	257,447	54,188	87,207	41,321	66,500	48,875	71,356
Ghana	24,000	38,700	40	90,000	45,000	133	873	1,275	592[2]	953[2]	731.4	1,177	93.9	137.1
Greece	72,700	117,000	92	2,675,676	1,013,677	2.9	12,000	17,000	1,555[2]	2,503[2]	1,108	1,783	226	330
Greenland	93	150	60	2,242	1,474	15	...	...	—	—	—	—	—	—
Grenada	646	1,040	61	4,739	3,068	12	...	...	—	—	—	—	—	—
Guadeloupe	2,122	3,415	80	101,600	37,500	2.9	...	...	—	—	—	—	—	—
Guam	550	885	76	79,800	34,700	1.3	...	...	—	—	—	—	—	—
Guatemala	8,140	13,100	28	102,000	97,000	51	...	...	549[2]	884[2]	10.3	16.6	58.6	85.6
Guernsey	...	...	...	37,598	7,338	1.4	...	...	—	—	—	—	—	—
Guinea	18,952	30,500	16	14,100	21,000	219	...	...	411[2]	662[2]	25.8	41.5	5.0	7.3
Guinea-Bissau	2,734	4,400	10	7,120	5,640	91	...	...	—	—	—	—	—	—
Guyana	4,952	7,970	7	24,000	9,000	22	...	...	116[13]	187[13]	...	...	...	...
Haiti	2,585	4,160	24	32,000	21,000	121	...	...	—	—	—	—	...	...
Honduras	9,073	14,602	18	81,439	170,006	22	...	...	614	988	4.8	7.7	20.7	30.2
Hong Kong	1,183	1,904	100	332,000	133,000	14	...	...	21[2]	34[2]	2,231	3,591	68	99
Hungary	116,944	188,203	43	2,255,526	321,634	4.0	10,950	15,987	4,827[2]	7,768[2]	5,912	9,514	5,297	7,733
Iceland	7,691	12,378	25	151,409	19,428	1.6	318	464	—	—	—	—	—	—
India	2,062,727	3,319,644	46	4,189,000	2,234,000	148	656	958	39,028[2]	62,809[2]	261,254	420,449	209,259	305,513
Indonesia	212,177	341,467	56	2,734,769	2,189,876	41	17,000	25,000	4,013[2]	6,458[2]	11,548	18,585	3,449	5,035
Iran	102,976	165,724	50	1,793,000	692,000	24	46,750	68,250	3,915[2]	6,300[2]	3,792	6,103	9,863	14,400
Iraq	29,453	47,400	86	772,986	323,906	18	...	...	1,263[2]	2,032[2]	973	1,566	1,129	1,649
Ireland	57,477	92,500	94	1,269,245	188,814	2.6	4,041	5,900	1,209[2]	1,945[2]	870	1,400	342	500
Isle of Man	500	805	58	40,168	4,925	1.6	...	...	32[2]	52[2]	...	...	...	...
Israel	9,609	15,464	100	1,316,765	319,581	3.7	2,993	4,370	379[2]	610[2]	329	529	773	1,128
Italy	191,468	308,139	100	31,370,000	5,127,000	1.6	131,154	191,482	12,133	19,527	25,720	41,392	15,333	22,386
Jamaica	11,800	19,000	71	160,948	55,596	12	...	...	129[2]	208[2]	12.1	19.5	1.7	2.5
Japan	718,500	1,156,000	73	51,222,000	18,425,000	1.8	205,942	300,670	16,937	27,258	241,674	388,938	15,699	22,920
Jersey	346	557	100	58,491	9,922	1.3	...	...	—	—	—	—	—	—
Jordan	4,432	7,133	100	213,874	79,153	15	19,133	27,934	421[2]	677[2]	3.7	6.0	915	1,336
Kazakhstan	78,166	125,796	83	973,323	361,920	11	3,176	4,637	8,388[2]	13,500[2]	5,505	8,859	64,987	94,879
Kenya	39,060	63,800	14	278,000	81,200	78	134	196	1,885[2]	3,034[2]	239	385	813	1,309
Kiribati	416	670	5	222	115	260	...	...	—	—	—	—	—	—
Korea, North	14,526	23,377	8	248,000	...	...	...	...	5,302	8,533	2,100	3,400	6,200	9,100
Korea, South	55,162	88,775	76	8,084,000	3,938,000	3.9	51,031	74,504	4,165	6,703	18,686	30,072	8,704	12,708
Kuwait	2,765	4,450	81	747,042	140,480	2.3	...	...	—	—	—	—	—	—
Kyrgyzstan	11,445	18,500	91	146,000	...	...	695	1,015	264	424	58	93	323	472
Laos	13,870	22,321	14	16,320	4,200	242	16	23	—	—	—	—	—	—
Latvia	34,761	55,942	38	431,816	95,329	4.7	2,814	4,108	1,499	2,413	611	984	8,363	12,210
Lebanon	3,946	6,350	95	1,299,398	85,242	2.5	...	...	138	222	5.3	8.6	29	42
Lesotho	3,079	4,955	18	12,610	25,000	53	...	...	1.6	2.6	...	...	...	...
Liberia	6,600	10,600	6	9,400	25,000	59	...	...	304[2]	490[2]	...	...	534	860
Libya	50,704	81,600	57	809,514	357,528	4.0	...	...	—	—	—	—	—	—
Liechtenstein	201	323	...	21,150	2,684	1.4	...	...	12	19	...	...	...	...
Lithuania	44,350	71,375	91	980,910	105,022	3.4	3,843	5,611	1,241[2]	1,997[2]	463	745	5,376	7,849
Luxembourg	3,209	5,166	100	263,683	20,228	1.5	2,437	3,558	170[2]	274[2]	193	310	410	660
Macau	31	50	100	45,184	6,578	8.2	...	...	—	—	—	—	—	—
Macedonia	7,154	11,513	63	288,678	24,745	6.4	612	894	575	925	93	150	279	408
Madagascar	30,967	49,837	17	62,000	16,460	140	220	321	680[2]	1,095[2]	22	35	44	71
Malawi	10,222	16,451	19	27,000	29,700	171	—	—	495[2]	797[2]	16	26	34	49
Malaysia	41,282	66,437	76	3,517,484	644,792	5.1	...	...	1,384[2]	2,227[2]	828[31]	1,332[31]	625[31]	912[31]
Maldives	...	...	...	1,716	586	114	...	...	—	—	—	—	—	—
Mali	9,383	15,100	12	26,190	18,240	213	...	...	398[2]	641[2]	577.6	929.6	371	542.8
Malta	1,219	1,961	94	185,247	49,520	1.6	...	...	—	—	—	—	—	—
Marshall Islands	...	...	...	1,374	262	29	...	...	—	—	—	—	—	—
Martinique	1,299	2,091	75	108,300	32,200	2.6	...	...	—	—	—	—	—	—
Mauritania	4,760	7,660	11	18,810	10,450	82	...	...	437[2]	704[2]	...	...	1,603	2,340
Mauritius	1,184	1,905	93	46,300	12,100	20	...	...	—	—	—	—	—	—
Mayotte	145	233	77	— 6,553 —		20	...	...	—	—	—	—	—	—
Mexico	199,824	321,586	37	8,607,000	4,426,000	7.1	122,663	179,085	16,543[2]	26,623[2]	286	460	32,106	46,874
Micronesia	140	226	17	...	...	...	...	...	—	—	—	—	—	—
Moldova	7,643	12,300	87	166,757	67,638	18	697	1,018	819	1,318	213	343	816	1,191
Monaco	31	50	100	21,120	2,770	1.3	...	...	1	2	...	...	...	...
Mongolia	31,000	50,000	3	39,921	31,061	33	84.4	123.2	1,128	1,815	634	1,020	2,392	3,492
Morocco	35,921	57,810	52	1,018,146	278,075	21	1,429	2,086	1,099[2]	1,768[2]	1,104	1,776	3,258	4,757
Mozambique	18,890	30,400	19	4,900	7,520	1,431	75	110	1,940	3,123	317	510	781	1,140
Myanmar (Burma)	17,523	28,200	12	27,000	42,000	587	71	103.7	2,458[2]	3,955[2]	2,453	3,948	674	984
Namibia	40,526	65,220	8	74,875	66,500	12	...	...	1,480	2,382	21.6	34.7	738	1,077
Nauru	19	30	79	— 1,448 —		6.3	...	...	3[13]	5[13]	...	...	4.7	6.8
Nepal	4,785	7,700	42	47,541	29,371	306	984	1,437	37[2]	59[2]	...	...	...	...

merchant marine (latest) fleet (vessels over 100 gross tons)	total dead-weight tonnage ('000)	international cargo: loaded metric tons ('000)	off-loaded metric tons ('000)	air: airports with scheduled flights (latest)	traffic passengers passenger-mi ('000,000)	passenger-km ('000,000)	cargo short ton-mi ('000,000)	metric ton-km ('000,000)	canals length mi	km	cargo short ton-mi ('000,000)	metric ton-km ('000,000)	country
444	1,685.2	15,012	22,044	11	5,638	9,074	185	270	2,175	3,500	452	660	Egypt
15	...	221	1,023	1	1,355	2,181	10.9	16.0	...	...	...	...	El Salvador
3	6.7	110	64	1	4	7	0.7	1.0	...	...	...	...	Equatorial Guinea
...	...	...	...	2	...	...	...	...	...	...	...	...	Eritrea
234	680.4	30,024	5,784	1	103.6	166.7	0.6	0.9	199	320	1.4	2.1	Estonia
27	84.3	234	1,242	31	1,190	1,915	225	328	...	...	...	...	Ethiopia
191	59.8	223	443	1	...	...	...	...	...	...	...	...	Faroe Islands
64	60.4	568	625	13	742	1,195	51.6	75.4	126	203	...	...	Fiji
263	989.3	39,312	38,052	27	8,026	12,916	216	316	3,880	6,245	127,945	186,797	Finland
729	4,981.0	64,704	189,504	61	55,344[23]	89,067[23]	3,271[23]	4,775[23]	3,562	5,732	5,436	7,936	France
7	0.7	73	447	8	...	...	...	...	286	460	...	...	French Guiana
41	16.5	15	666	17	...	...	...	...	...	...	...	...	French Polynesia
29	30.2	12,828	212	17	452	728	68	100	994	1,600	...	...	Gabon
11	2.0	185	240	1	31	50	3	5	250	400	...	...	Gambia, The
—	...	...	...	1	...	...	...	...	—	—	...	...	Gaza Strip
54	1,108	...	...	1	78.9	127.1	0.5	0.8	...	...	3,740	5,460	Georgia
1,375	6,832.3	74,568	138,864	35	55,219	88,867	4,520	6,599	4,188	6,740	44,019	64,267	Germany
155	131.0	2,424	2,904	1	407	655	20	30	803	1,293	75	110	Ghana
1,872	45,276.6	16,464	45,024	36	5,160	8,305	71	103	50	80	585	854	Greece
82	17.2	298	288	18	104	167	0.23	0.34	...	...	...	...	Greenland
3	0.5	21	193	2	...	...	...	...	...	...	...	...	Grenada
20	4.4	349	2,285	7	...	...	...	...	...	...	...	...	Guadeloupe
5	0.1	195	1,524	1	...	...	...	...	...	...	...	...	Guam
8	0.4	2,096	3,822	2	311	500	48	70	162	260	...	...	Guatemala
—	—	...	...	2	...	...	...	...	...	...	...	...	Guernsey
23	1.7	16,760	734	1	32	52	3	5	805	1,295	...	...	Guinea
19	1.8	46	283	2	6.2	10.0	0.7	1.0	...	...	...	...	Guinea-Bissau
82	13.5	1,730	673	1	154	248	2.3	3.3	3,660	5,900	...	...	Guyana
4	0.4	170	704	2	...	...	...	...	60	100	...	...	Haiti
966	1,437.3	1,316	1,002	8	212[24]	341[24]	23[24]	33[24]	289	465	...	...	Honduras
387	11,688.6	36,13[25]	80,820[25]	1	...	...	...	...	...	...	...	...	Hong Kong
15	93.2	...	...	1	2,183	3,513	38	56	853	1,373	1,069	1,561	Hungary
394	114.9	1,162	1,733	24	2,273	3,658	50.9	74.4	...	...	58	84	Iceland
888	10,365.9	61,880	102,630	66	11,456	18,436	329	481	10,054	16,180	202,000	295,000	India
2,014	3,130.2	310,246	208,871	81	7,698	12,389	234	341	13,409	21,579	17,000	25,000	Indonesia
403	8,345.3	32,148	37,404	19	3,871	6,229	49	72	562	904	...	...	Iran
131	1,578.8	97,830	8,638	...	976	1,570	37.4	54.6	631	1,015	...	...	Iraq
189	208.6	6,367	17,637	9	4,018	6,466	88.8	129.6	435	700	...	...	Ireland
101	2,836.5	6	203	1	526.1	846.8	0.1	0.2	...	...	...	...	Isle of Man
58	723.4	12,876	20,916	7	8,777[26]	14,125[26]	882[26]	1,288[26]	...	...	...	...	Israel
1,966	7,149.5	48,252	234,120	34	18,312[27]	29,471[27]	835[27]	1,219[27]	918	1,477	85,681	125,092	Italy
12	16.2	8,802	5,285	4	1,038[28]	1,670[28]	20.2[28]	29.5[28]	...	...	...	...	Jamaica
6,140	16,198	124,548	754,464	73	97,745	157,305	4,920	7,183	1,100	1,770	155,468	226,980	Japan
...	...	...	...	1	...	...	...	...	...	...	...	...	Jersey
5	113.6	7,308	5,328	2	2,526	4,065	150.1	219.2	...	...	19,202	28,035	Jordan
...	...	...	...	20	1,509	2,429	162	237	2,425	3,903	97	141	Kazakhstan
29	11.6	1,596	3,228	11	1,062[29]	1,709[29]	126[29]	203[29]	...	...	...	...	Kenya
7	2.7	15	26	9	4.4	7.0	0.6	1.0	3	5	...	...	Kiribati
100	951.2	635	5,520	1	178	286	19	30	1,400	2,253	...	...	Korea, North
2,138	11,724.9	255,888	448,416	14	29,647	47,712	4,987	7,281	1,000	1,609	22,920	33,462	Korea, South
209	3,188.5	51,400	4,522	1	3,813	6,137	151	243	...	...	...	...	Kuwait
...	...	...	...	2	2,739	4,408	44.7	65.2	290	466	41	6.0	Kyrgyzstan
1	1.5	—	—	11	30	48	3	5	2,850	4,587	68	100	Laos
261	1,436.9	45,144	3,888	1	185	298	6	9	66	106	19,241	28,091	Latvia
163	438.2	152	1,150	1	1,315	2,116	218	319	...	...	...	...	Lebanon
—	—	—	—	1	3.9	6.2	0.4	0.6	—	—	—	—	Lesotho
1,672	97,374.0	21,653	1,608	1	4.3	7.0	0.7	1.0	...	...	...	...	Liberia
150	1,223.6	62,491	7,808	12	264[30]	425[30]	23[30]	34[30]	...	...	...	...	Libya
—	—	—	—	—	...	...	...	...	...	...	...	...	Liechtenstein
52	373.9	12,864	2,796	3	190.5	306.6	1.8	2.6	229	369	8.9	13	Lithuania
54	2,603.6	—	—	1	79.5	232	606.9	886.1	23	37	205	300	Luxembourg
6	0.1	755	3,935	—	...	...	...	...	...	...	...	...	Macau
...	...	...	...	2	553.5	890.7	239.2	349.2	...	...	...	...	Macedonia
85	82.1	540	984	44	519	836	20.2	29.5	...	...	1.2	1.8	Madagascar
1	0.3	...	...	5	68	110	10	14	89	144	1,683	2,457	Malawi
552	2,916.3	39,756	54,852	39	20,945	33,708	976	1,425	4,534	7,296	...	...	Malaysia
44	79.0	27	78	5	44	71	...	...	...	...	...	...	Maldives
—	—	—	—	9	150	242	26	38	1,128	1,815	18	27	Mali
889	17,073.2	309	1,781	1	1,173	1,888	7.7	11.2	...	...	...	...	Malta
35	4,182.4	29	123	25	17	28	0.003	0.005	...	...	...	...	Marshall Islands
6	1.1	960	1,584	1	...	...	...	...	...	...	...	...	Martinique
126	23.9	10,400	724	9	160.5	258.3	9.2	13.5	...	...	...	...	Mauritania
35	152.2	966	2,753	1	2,398	3,859	561.2	819.4	...	...	...	...	Mauritius
1	1.1	158	31	1	...	...	...	...	...	...	...	...	Mayotte
635	1,495.3	134,400	67,500	83	14,864	23,922	1,779	2,597	1,800	2,900	14,806	21,616	Mexico
19	9.2	...	...	4	...	...	...	...	...	...	...	...	Micronesia
1	...	...	...	1	0.1	0.2	0.7	1.0	263	424	172	251	Moldova
...	...	...	...	—	...	...	...	...	...	...	...	...	Monaco
1	...	...	...	1	326	525	33	48	247	397	0.1	0.2	Mongolia
492	586.2	24,228	27,972	11	2,789	4,489	260	380	...	...	...	...	Morocco
107	31.6	2,800	3,400	7	239	384	6	9	2,330	3,750	57	83	Mozambique
144	1,354.0	1,788	3,456	19	272	438	2.2	3.2	7,954	12,800	240	351	Myanmar (Burma)
30	5.9	1,132	644	11	470	756	16	23	...	...	...	...	Namibia
2	5.8	1,650	59	1	151[32]	243[32]	15[32]	24[32]	...	...	...	...	Nauru
—	—	—	—	24	532	856	64	93	...	...	...	...	Nepal

Transportation (continued)

country	roads and motor vehicles (latest)								railroads (latest)						
	roads			motor vehicles			cargo		track length		traffic				
	length		paved (per-cent)	auto-mobiles	trucks and buses	persons per vehicle	short ton-mi ('000,000)	metric ton-km ('000,000)	mi	km	passengers		cargo		
	mi	km									passen-ger-mi ('000,000)	passen-ger-km ('000,000)	short ton-mi ('000,000)	metric ton-km ('000,000)	
Netherlands, The	77,379	124,530	91	6,343,000	826,000	2.2	98,445	143,727	1,745	2,808	8,904	14,330	2,412	3,521	
Netherlands Antilles	367	590	51	75,105	17,753	2.2	...	...	—	—	—	—	—	—	
New Caledonia	3,582	5,764	52	56,700	21,200	2.6	...	...	—	—	—	—	—	—	
New Zealand	57,213	92,075	62	1,831,118	351,494	1.7	...	...	2,431²	3,912²	285	458	2,712	3,960	
Nicaragua	11,200	18,000	10	73,000	61,650	33	...	...	—	—	—	—	—	—	
Niger	6,276	10,100	8	38,220	15,200	169	1,044	1,524	—	—	—	—	—	—	
Nigeria	38,897	62,598	19	773,000	68,300	131	...	...	2,178	3,505	100	161	74	108	
Northern Mariana Islands	225	360	100	12,113	6,479	3.0	...	...	—	—	—	—	—	—	
Norway	56,470	90,880	74	1,813,642	447,583	2.0	10,086	14,726	2,489²	4,006²	1,609	2,589	1,467	2,142	
Oman	20,518	33,020	24	229,029	110,717	6.9	...	...	—	—	—	—	—	—	
Pakistan	149,679	240,885	55	1,167,635	251,407	95	66,304	96,802	5,452²	8,774²	11,908	19,164	2,753	4,020	
Palau	40	64	59	4,271		3.8	...	...	—	—	—	—	—	—	
Panama	7,022	11,301	33	203,760	74,637	9.4	...	...	220²	354²	242	389	1,096	1,600	
Papua New Guinea	12,263	19,736	6	13,000	32,000	93	...	...	—	—	—	—	—	—	
Paraguay	18,330	29,500	10	71,000	50,000	41	...	...	274²	441²	1.9	3.0	3.8	5.5	
Peru	45,836	73,766	12	557,042	359,374	26	...	...	1,238²	1,992²	132	212	0.8	1.1	
Philippines	124,243	199,950	39	745,144	263,037	73	...	...	557²	897²	7.5	12	452	660	
Poland	234,286	377,048	66	9,283,000	1,762,000	3.5	47,632	69,542	14,280	22,981	16,279	26,198	37,994	55,471	
Portugal	42,708	68,732	88	3,200,000	1,097,000	2.4	16,984	24,796	2,025²	3,259²	2,860	4,602	1,603	2,340	
Puerto Rico	8,948	14,400	100	878,000	190,000	3.5	...	...	—	—	—	—	—	—	
Qatar	764	1,230	90	126,000	64,000	2.9	...	...	—	—	—	—	—	—	
Réunion	1,711	2,754	79	190,300	44,300	3.0	...	...	—	—	—	—	—	—	
Romania	95,175	153,170	51	2,408,000	409,550	8.0	14,898	21,750	7,062	11,365	7,658	12,324	10,909	15,927	
Russia	354,628	570,719	79	19,717,800	5,021,000	5.9	14,384	21,000	93,800	151,000	88,048	144,700	825	1,205	
Rwanda	9,528	14,900	9	13,000	17,100	188	140	200	—	—	—	—	—	—	
St. Kitts and Nevis	199	320	43	5,200	2,300	5.3	...	...	22	36	—	—	—	—	
St. Lucia	750	1,210	5	14,783	1,020	9.5	...	...	—	—	—	—	—	—	
St. Vincent and the Grenadines	646	1,040	31	6,089	3,670	11	...	...	—	—	—	—	—	—	
Samoa	491	790	42	1,068	1,169	74	...	...	—	—	—	—	—	—	
San Marino	157	252	...	25,571	2,636	0.9	...	...	—	—	—	—	—	—	
São Tomé and Príncipe	199	320	68	4,040	1,540	24	...	...	—	—	—	—	—	—	
Saudi Arabia	101,000	162,000	43	1,744,000	1,192,000	6.6	57,859	84,473	864²	1,390²	138	222	586	856	
Senegal	9,134	14,700	29	85,488	36,962	72	375	547	761	1,225	128	206	476	695	
Serbia and Montenegro	31,377	50,497	60	1,400,000	132,000	6.9	852	1,244	2,528	4,069	1,003	1,614	1,760	2,570	
Seychelles	263	424	87	7,120	1,980	8.5	...	...	—	—	—	—	—	—	
Sierra Leone	7,270	11,700	11	17,640	10,890	163	36	53	52	84	...	...	...	...	
Singapore	1,875	3,017	97	413,545	147,325	5.8	...	...	73	117	31	31	31	31	
Slovakia	10,953	17,627	...	1,135,914	100,254	4.4	5,804	8,474	2,282	3,673	1,844	2,968	6,753	9,859	
Slovenia	7,771	12,507	81	829,674	67,111	2.2	1,986	2,900	746	1,201	388	625	1,907	2,784	
Solomon Islands	845	1,360	3	2,052	2,574	75	...	...	—	—	—	—	—	—	
Somalia	13,732	22,100	12	1,020	6,440	866	...	...	—	—	—	—	—	—	
South Africa	205,838	331,265	41	3,966,252	2,069,536	7.2	1,053	1,538	12,626²	20,319²	1,103	1,775	71,142	103,866	
Spain	215,335	346,548	99	16,847,000	3,659,000	2.0	85,801	125,268	8,595²	13,832²	11,525	18,547	7,959	11,620	
Sri Lanka	61,640	99,200	40	107,000	150,160	71	21	30	899²	1,447²	2,028	3,264	90	132	
Sudan, The	7,394	11,900	36	285,000	53,000	93	...	...	2,855²	4,595²	100	161	1,346	1,965	
Suriname	2,815	4,530	26	46,408	19,255	6.4	...	...	187	301	—	—	—	—	
Swaziland	2,367	3,810	29	31,882	32,772	17	...	...	187	301	752	1,210	1,993	2,910	
Sweden	130,500	210,000	74	3,890,159	352,897	2.1	22,798	33,285	6,811	10,961	4,746	7,638	13,074	19,088	
Switzerland	44,248	71,211	96	3,467,275	313,646	1.9	9,932	14,500	3,129	5,035	8,764	14,104	5,951	8,688	
Syria	25,756	41,451	23	138,900	282,664	37	1,075	1,570	1,507²	2,425²	113	182	934	1,364	
Taiwan	12,660	20,375	89	4,716,000	833,000	4.0	12,651	18,470	2,410	3,879	7,833	12,606	808	1,179	
Tajikistan	8,500	13,700	83	680	8,190	667	34	50	295	474	77	124	1,449	2,115	
Tanzania	54,805	88,200	4	23,760	115,700	229	...	...	2,218	3,569	2,324	3,740	927	1,354	
Thailand	40,141	64,600	98	1,661,000	2,855,000	14	...	...	2,873²	4,623²	6,636	10,680	1,940	2,832	
Togo	4,673	7,520	32	79,200	34,240	39	...	...	245²	395²	10.3	16.5	34	49	
Tonga	423	680	27	1,140	780	51	...	...	—	—	—	—	—	—	
Trinidad and Tobago	5,170	8,320	51	122,000	24,000	8.7	...	...	—	—	—	—	—	—	
Tunisia	14,354	23,100	79	269,000	312,000	16	678	990	1,348²	2,169²	743	1,196	1,620	2,365	
Turkey	238,380	383,636	25	4,283,080	1,488,016	11	104,255	152,210	5,388	8,671	3,804	6,122	6,871	10,032	
Turkmenistan	8,500	13,700	83	220,000	58,200	16	335	489	1,317	2,120	1,307	2,104	4,643	6,779	
Tuvalu	5	8	—	—	—	—	...	...	—	—	—	—	—	—	
Uganda	16,653	26,800	8	35,361	48,430	249	...	...	771²	1,241²	17	27	162	236	
Ukraine	107,111	172,378	95	4,885,691	...	...	12,534	18,300	14,021	22,564	29,577	47,600	107,081	156,336	
United Arab Emirates	2,356	3,791	100	201,000	56,950	9.6	...	...	—	—	—	—	—	—	
United Kingdom	231,096	371,914	100	23,393,000	2,368,000	2.3	117,504	171,553	23,518⁴⁵	37,849⁴⁵	23,800	38,300	12,603	18,400	
United States	3,906,292	6,286,396	91	131,839,000	79,778,000	1.3	1,051,045	1,534,500	137,900	222,000	14,000	22,500	1,421,000	2,075,000	
Uruguay	5,395	8,683	30	516,889	50,264	5.6	500	730	1,288²	2,073²	87.4	140.6	123	180	
Uzbekistan	52,444	84,400	87	865,300	14,500	25	1,248	1,822	2,271	3,655	1,553	2,500	11,580	16,907	
Vanuatu	665	1,070	24	4,000	2,600	27	...	...	—	—	—	—	—	—	
Venezuela	59,443	95,664	36	1,505,000	542,000	11	...	...	390²	627²	93.1	149.9	37.3	54.5	
Vietnam	58,000	93,300	25	200,000		358	1,462	2,134	1,952²	3,142²	1,694	2,727	958	1,398	
Virgin Islands (U.S.)	532	856	100	51,000	13,300	1.7	...	...	—	—	—	—	—	—	
West Bank	...	...	...	88,056	24,324	18	...	...	...	...	...	...	...	...	
Western Sahara	3,900	6,200	23	6,284	424	20	...	...	—	—	—	—	—	—	
Yemen	40,218	64,725	8	240,567	291,149	29	...	...	—	—	—	—	—	—	
Zambia	24,170	38,898	18	157,000	81,000	37	...	...	787	1,266	166	267	316	462	
Zimbabwe	11,395	18,338	47	323,000	32,000	31	...	...	1,714²	2,759²	253.6	408.2	3.2	4.6	

¹Ariana Afghan Airlines only.   ²Route length.   ³Air Algérie International flights only.   ⁴TAAG airline only.   ⁵Aerolineas Argentinas only.   ⁶Included in Netherlands Antilles.   ⁷Government railways only.   ⁸Portion of Gulf Air traffic.   ⁹Caribbean Airways only.   ¹⁰Caribbean Air Cargo only.   ¹¹Air Afrique only.   ¹²Air Botswana only.   ¹³For industrial purposes only.   ¹⁴Zaire National Railways only.   ¹⁵Air Zaire only.   ¹⁶LASCA only.   ¹⁷Traffic between Ouagadougou, Burkina Faso, and Abidjan, Côte d'Ivoire.   ¹⁸Air Ivoire only.   ¹⁹Data refer to former Czechoslovakia.   ²⁰Including SAS international and domestic traffic.   ²¹National roads only.   ²²Includes 62 mi (100 km) of the Chemin de Fer Djibouti-Ethiopien (CDE) in Djibouti.   ²³Air France and UTA only.   ²⁴TAN and SAHSA airlines only.   ²⁵Includes

fleet (vessels over 100 gross tons)	total dead-weight tonnage ('000)	international cargo (latest) loaded metric tons ('000)	international cargo (latest) off-loaded metric tons ('000)	airports with scheduled flights (latest)	passengers passenger-mi ('000,000)	passengers passenger-km ('000,000)	cargo short ton-mi ('000,000)	cargo metric ton-km ('000,000)	length mi	length km	cargo short ton-mi ('000,000)	cargo metric ton-km ('000,000)	country
399	2,874	91,920	305,232	6	36,109	58,112	2,679	3,911	3,135	5,046	27,887	40,714	Netherlands, The
154[33]	1,053.6[33]	215	517	6	234[34]	377[34]	1.2[34]	1.8[34]	...	...	...	...	Netherlands Antilles
17	18.1	1,040	930	11	145[35]	233[35]	3.4[35]	4.9[35]	...	...	...	...	New Caledonia
139	279.8	20,640	13,308	36	12,352	19,879	584	852	1,000	1,609	1,503	2,195	New Zealand
25	1.3	320	1,629	10	49	79	6	9	1,379	2,220	...	...	Nicaragua
—	—	—	—	6	160.5	258.3	9.3	13.5	186	300	14	20	Niger
271	733.3	86,993	11,346	12	70	112	1.3	2.1	5,328	8,575	...	...	Nigeria
2	0.9	33	205	2	...	...	...	...	...	...	...	...	Northern Mariana Islands
1,597	20,834	151,116	25,788	50	6,444[20]	10,371[20]	821[20]	1,199[20]	980	1,577	7,640	11,154	Norway
26	11.7	43,525	5,303	6	601[8]	968[8]	11[8]	18[8]	...	...	...	...	Oman
73	513.8	6,408	31,008	35	6,503	10,466	226	330	...	...	...	...	Pakistan
4	...	...	64	1	...	...	...	...	...	...	...	...	Palau
5,217	79,255.6	117,924	76,800	10	853	1,373	14.9	21.8	497	800	...	...	Panama
87	40.9	2,463	1,784	42	457	735	59	86	6,798	10,940	...	...	Papua New Guinea
38	38.5	...	...	5	134	215	13	19	1,900	3,100	...	...	Paraguay
623	615.6	10,197	5,077	27	1,637	2,634	172	251	5,300	8,600	...	...	Peru
1,499	13,807.1	16,980	52,596	21	6,395[36]	10,292[36]	165[36]	241[36]	2,000	3,219	...	...	Philippines
644	4,314.3	33,360	15,864	8	2,878	4,632	55	80	2,369	3,812	753	1,100	Poland
332	1,129.3	7,572	37,740	16	6,278	10,104	159	232	510	820	...	...	Portugal
13	...	...	...	7	...	...	...	...	...	...	...	...	Puerto Rico
64	744	18,145	2,588	1	1,776[8]	2,858[8]	72[8]	105[8]	...	...	...	...	Qatar
7	33.5	454	2,302	2	...	...	...	...	...	...	...	...	Réunion
439	4,845.5	11,676	18,972	12	1,446	2,327	33.8	49.4	1,002	1,613	2,947	4,302	Romania
4,543	16,592.3	7,092	744	75	33,181	53,400	1,575	2,300	55,357	89,089	44,962	65,643	Russia
				2	1.2	2.0	...	...	...	...	...	...	Rwanda
1	0.6	24	36	2	...	...	...	...	...	...	...	...	St. Kitts and Nevis
7	2.1	138	547	2	...	...	...	...	...	...	...	...	St. Lucia
946	1,253	72	128	5	...	...	...	...	...	...	...	...	St. Vincent and the Grenadines
7	6.5	48	144	3	165	265	18	26	...	...	...	...	Samoa
—	—	—	—	—	—	—	—	—	—	—	—	—	San Marino
4	2.3	16	45	2	6	9	0.7	1.0	...	...	...	...	São Tomé and Príncipe
279	1,278	214,070	46,437	28	11,774	18,949	1,815	2,650	...	...	...	...	Saudi Arabia
183	27.5	1,396	2,894	7	139.6[30]	224.7[30]	11.2[30]	16.4[30]	557	897	...	...	Senegal
462[37]	5,173.1[37]	360	972	5	551	887	4,112	6,003	365	587	905	1,322	Serbia and Montenegro
9	3.3	47	543	2	389	626	48	70	...	...	...	...	Seychelles
62	18.4	2,310	589	1	68[38]	110[38]	1.4[38]	2.0[38]	500	800	447	652	Sierra Leone
946	14,929.2	326,040	188,234	1	40,096	64,529	3,755	5,482	...	...	...	...	Singapore
...	...	...	...	2	143.8	231.4	0.5	0.7	107	172	1,046	1,527	Slovakia
13	346.5	2,460	5,952	3	517	832	2.8	4.2	...	...	21,900	31,973	Slovenia
33	5.0	278	349	21	29[39]	47[39]	0.9	1.3	...	...	...	...	Solomon Islands
28	18.5	324	1,007	1	81	131	3.0	5.0	...	...	...	...	Somalia
219	282.5	114,331	22,203	24	12,005[40]	19,320[40]	464[40]	677[40]	...	...	...	...	South Africa
2,190	5,077.3	55,752	169,848	25	37,715	60,696	4,388	6,407	649	1,045	21,836[41]	31,880[41]	Spain
66	472.6	9,288	16,632	1	3,204	5,156	459	670	267	430	0.7	1	Sri Lanka
16	62.2	1,543	4,300	3	330[42]	531[42]	14[42]	20[42]	3,300	5,310	...	...	Sudan, The
24	15.7	1,595	1,265	1	549[43]	883[43]	66[43]	106[43]	746	1,200	...	...	Suriname
—	—	—	—	1	30.7	49.4	0.09	0.1	—	—	—	—	Swaziland
430	2,881	61,320	75,528	48	6,997[20]	11,261[20]	196[20]	286[20]	1,275	2,052	5,708	8,334	Sweden
24	602.8	...	...	5	19,739	31,767	1,216	1,776	13	21	34	49	Switzerland
94	210.4	2,136	5,112	5	884	1,422	14	21	541	870	...	...	Syria
649	9,241.3	182,127	301,275	13	24,369	39,218	2,828	4,129	...	...	274	400	Taiwan
...	...	...	...	1	1,386	2,231	140	205	...	...	...	...	Tajikistan
43	48.5	1,249	2,721	11	114	184	2.0	2.9	...	...	...	...	Tanzania
351	1,194.5	42,495	74,579	25	23,826	38,345	1,145	1,671	2,300	3,701	...	...	Thailand
8	20.6	391	1,274	2	139.6	224.7	11.2	16.4	31	50	...	...	Togo
15	13.7	15	104	6	7	11	0.7	1.0	...	...	...	...	Tonga
53	17.5	9,622	10,961	2	1,783	2,869	38	55	...	...	...	...	Trinidad and Tobago
77	443.3	6,792	13,152	5	1,674	2,694	13	21	...	...	...	...	Tunisia
880	7,114.3	24,756	78,168	26	10,248[44]	16,492[44]	260[44]	380[44]	750	1,200	189	276	Turkey
...	...	...	...	1	970	1,562	98	143	240	387	5.5	8.0	Turkmenistan
6	16.0	...	...	1	...	...	...	...	...	...	...	...	Tuvalu
2	8.6	...	...	1	32.4	52.1	3	5	...	...	...	...	Uganda
...	...	77,004	7,116	12	1,225	1,972	18	27	2,734	4,400	3,973	5,800	Ukraine
276	1,491.7	88,153	9,595	6	12,150[8]	19,553[8]	978[8]	1,428[8]	...	...	...	...	United Arab Emirates
1,631	4,355	177,228	178,572	57	99,628	160,336	3,373	4,925	716	1,153	36,302	53,000	United Kingdom
509	18,585	392,076[46]	713,880[46]	834	619,500	997,000	18,116	26,449	25,778	41,485	356,188	520,026	United States
93	172.5	710[47]	1,450[47]	1	398	640	42	62	1,000	1,600	...	...	Uruguay
...	...	...	...	9	2,150	3,460	220	321	684	1,100	...	...	Uzbekistan
280	3,259.6	80	55	29	110.8	178.3	1.3	1.9	...	...	...	...	Vanuatu
271	1,355.4	101,435	17,932	20	3,600	5,800	438	639	4,400	7,100	8.9	13	Venezuela
230	872.8	303	1,510	12	2,380	3,831	67	98	11,000	17,702	1,339	1,955	Vietnam
1	...	105.5	648.3	2	...	...	...	...	...	...	...	...	Virgin Islands (U.S.)
—	—	—	—	—	—	—	—	—	—	—	—	—	West Bank
—	—	40	15	1	...	...	...	...	...	...	...	...	Western Sahara
40	13.7	1,936	7,829	12	978	1,574	22	32	...	...	...	...	Yemen
—	—	—	—	4	192	308	6.8	9.9	1,398	2,250	...	...	Zambia
—	—	—	—	7	544	875	24	35	...	...	...	...	Zimbabwe

transshipments. [26]El Al only. [27]Alitalia only. [28]Air Jamaica only. [29]Kenya Airways only. [30]International traffic only. [31]Peninsular Malaysia and Singapore. [32]Air Nauru only. [33]Includes Aruba. [34]Antillean Airlines only. [35]Air Caledonie only. [36]Philippine Air Lines only. [37]Data refer to pre-1991 Yugoslavia. [38]Sierra Leone Airlines international traffic only. [39]Solair only. [40]SAA only. [41]Coastal shipping only. [42]Sudan Airways only. [43]Suriname Airways only. [44]Turkish Airlines only. [45]British Railways only; excludes Northern Ireland. [46]Includes Puerto Rico. [47]Port of Montevideo only.

Communications

Virtually all the states of the world have a variety of communications media and services available to their citizens: book, periodical, and newspaper publishing (although only daily papers are included in this table); postal services; and telecommunications systems, that is, radio and television broadcasting, telephones (fixed and mobile), personal computers (PCs), and access to the Internet. Unfortunately, the availability of information about these services often runs behind the capabilities of the services themselves. Certain countries publish no official information; others publish data analyzed according to a variety of fiscal, calendar, religious, or other years; still others, while they possess such data almost simultaneously with the end of the business or calendar year, may not see them published except in company or parastatal reports of limited distribution. Even when such data are published in national statistical summaries, it may be only after a delay of up to several years.

The data also differ in their completeness and reliability. Figures for book production, for example, generally include all works published in separate bindings except advertising works, timetables, telephone directories, price lists, catalogs of businesses or exhibitions, musical scores, maps, atlases, and the like. The figures include government publications, school texts, theses, offprints, series works, and illustrated works, even those consisting principally of illustrations. Figures refer to works actually published during the year of survey, usually by a registered publisher, and deposited for copyright. A book is defined as a work of 49 or more pages; a work published simultaneously in more than one country is counted as having been published in each. A periodical is a publication issued at regular or stated intervals and, in Unesco's usage, directed to the general public. Newspaper statistics are especially difficult to collect and compare. Newspapers continually are founded, cease publication, merge, or change frequency of publication. Data on circulation are often incomplete, slow to be aggregated at the national level, or regarded as proprietary. In some countries no daily newspaper exists.

Post office statistics are compiled mainly from the Universal Postal Union's annual summary *Statistique des services postaux*. Postal services, unlike the other media discussed earlier, tend most often to be operated by

Communications

country	publishing (latest) books number of titles	books number of copies ('000)	periodicals number of titles	periodicals number of copies ('000)	daily newspapers number	total circulation ('000)	circulation per 1,000 adult persons	postal services post offices, 2004 number	persons per office	pieces of mail handled ('000,000)	pieces handled per person	telecommunications radio, 2000 receivers (all types; '000)	receivers per 1,000 persons
Afghanistan	2,795	3,741	...	...	12	113	5	410	69,693	2.4	0.03	2,950	114
Albania	381	5,710	143	3,477	21	76	29	563	5,527	7.6	1.8	756	243
Algeria	670	...	48	803	24	796	24	3,287	9,844	234	11	7,380	244
American Samoa	...	...	...	...	2	5.0	93	...	...	...	...	57	929
Andorra	57	...	...	...	2	17	227	...	...	...	...	16	227
Angola	22	419	...	...	5	128	11	55	281,637	0.7	0.05	750	54
Antigua and Barbuda	2	...	...	...	2	6.0	91	13	6,194	6.0	32	36	542
Argentina	9,850	39,663	...	...	182	2,200	75	5,689	6,745	393	9	24,300	681
Armenia	396[2]	20,212[2]	44	541	12	22	9	907	3,298	3.6	0.6	700	225
Aruba	...	...	...	...	13	73	852	4	17,100	12	94	50	557
Australia	10,835	...	...	...	49	2,934	182	3,844	5,188	5,727	261	36,700	1,908
Austria	25,358	...	2,792	...	16	2,720	394	1,999	4,088	2,054	252	6,050	753
Azerbaijan	542	2,643	49	801	24	132	23	1,311	6,373	7	1.2	177	22
Bahamas, The	...	...	...	...	4	39	130	62	5,141	26	46	215	739
Bahrain	40[2]	...	26	73	6	88	130	13	55,063	48	54	49	76
Bangladesh	...	...	...	...	37	6,880	53	9,995	13,928	290	2.1	6,360	49
Barbados	...	...	...	...	2	53	199	18	14,938	45	156	237	888
Belarus	3,809	59,073	155	3,765	10	1,101	127	3,784	2,593	876	51	2,990	299
Belgium	13,913	...	13,706	...	29	1,706	198	1,369	7,597	3,713[5]	346[5]	8,130	793
Belize	70	—	...	...	10	23.5	0.5	134[3]	1,720[3]	4.0[3]	12[3]	133	591
Benin	84[2]	42[2]	...	...	8	15	2.0	178	45,939	12	1.0	2,820	439
Bermuda	...	...	...	...	1	19	292	14[6]	4,500[6]	15[6]	240[6]	82	1,296
Bhutan	...	...	...	...	1	...	...	110	19,235	1.4	1.9	37	19
Bolivia	...	...	...	...	19	130	24	78	84,300	9.9[5]	0.75[5]	5,510	676
Bosnia and Herzegovina	...	...	...	...	7	106	26	245	15,957	29	13	900	243
Botswana	158[2]	...	14	177	2	76	49	181	9,773	39	22	254	155
Brazil	21,574[7]	104,397[7]	...	...	532	6,522	47	12,367	14,871	8,318	44	74,400	433
Brunei	45[2]	56[2]	15	132	2	25	94	32	11,428	10	26	93[3]	302[3]
Bulgaria	4,840	20,317	772	1,740	62	667	104	3,008	2,587	131	17	4,350	543
Burkina Faso	12[2]	14[2]	37	24	5	12	1.0	73	175,640	3.5	0.5	428	35
Burundi	...	...	...	...	1	11	2.0	32	227,557	16[1]	1.3[1]	1,260	220
Cambodia	...	...	...	...	6	36	3.0	79	174,660	3.7	0.2	1,480	119
Cameroon	...	...	...	...	3	35	2.0	377[3]	37,000[3]	6.1[3,8]	0.43[3,8]	2,410	163
Canada	19,900	...	1,400	37,108	100	5,350	199	18,607[9]	1,570[9]	10,715[10,11]	370[10,11]	32,200	1,047
Cape Verde	...	...	...	...	4	...	...	54[5]	7,780[5]	1.6[5]	2.1[5]	71[3]	179[3]
Central African Republic	...	...	...	...	6	7.0	2.0	24	166,082	...	...	280	80
Chad	...	...	...	...	1	2.0	0.2	42	224,951	10	0.6	1,990	236
Chile	2,469	4,095	417	3,450	59	816	68	710[5]	20,870[5]	343[5]	235[5]	5,230	354
China	130,613	7,240[12]	7,999	250,400	1,035	85,470	86	66,393	19,700	25,163	19	428,000	339
Colombia	1,481	11,314	...	...	24	1,093	25	1,996	22,500	97	2.0	21,600	544
Comoros	...	...	...	...	1	...	...	37[5]	17,800[5]	0.4[5]	0.3[5]	90[3]	170[3]
Congo, Dem. Rep. of the	64[2]	535[2]	...	...	8	146	3.0	497[5]	98,870[5]	...	...	18,700	386
Congo, Rep. of the	...	...	3	34	6	28	8.0	114[6]	22,720[6]	1.8[6]	0.5[6]	424	123
Costa Rica	963	...	...	...	7	275	96	149	28,544	26	6.2	3,200	816
Côte d'Ivoire	...	...	...	...	20	115	7	197	90,720	40	2.1	2,170	137
Croatia	1,718	...	352	6,357	12	508	102	1,158	3,920	367	65	1,510	340
Cuba	932	4,610	14	285	16	600	66	1,855[5]	5,990[5]	12[5]	1.1[5]	3,950	353
Cyprus	930	1,776	39	338	8	46	76	1,111	743	71	69	310[3]	406[3]
Czech Republic	10,244	...	1,168	81,387	81	1,861	213	3,419	2,992	3,364	303	8,230	803
Denmark	12,352	...	157	6,930	34	1,825	414	996	5,436	1,389	257	7,200	1,349
Djibouti	...	...	7	6.0	—	—	—	11	70,828	0.9	0.4	38	87
Dominica	...	...	...	...	—	—	—	64[9]	1,090[9]	2.9[6]	30[6]	46[3]	647[3]
Dominican Republic	...	...	...	...	11	230	27	278	31,539	6.6	0.6	1,510	181
East Timor	...	...	...	...	2	3	3	5	177,367	0.1	0.1	18[3]	21[3]
Ecuador	12[2]	19[2]	199	...	36	1,220	137	315[5]	38,600[5]	13[5]	0.45[5]	5,190	418
Egypt	2,215	92,353	258	2,373	17	2,000	31	5,615	12,937	312	3.2	21,900	339
El Salvador	...	...	45	774	5	250	59	317	21,333	9	0.8	2,970	478
Equatorial Guinea	...	...	...	...	...	...	...	20	24,612	...	...	180[3]	428[3]
Eritrea	106	420	...	...	—	—	—	66	64,114	2.8	0.4	1,650	444
Estonia	2,628	6,662	517	2,323	11	257	228	545	2,450	110	54	1,500	1,096

a single national service, to cover a country completely, and to record traffic data according to broadly similar schemes (although the details of *classes* of mail handled may differ). Some countries do not enumerate domestic traffic or may record only international traffic requiring handling charges. Data on mail traffic includes the number of copies of newspapers, and excludes advertising material and ordinary money orders.

Data for some kinds of telecommunications apparatus are relatively easy to collect; telephones, for example, must be installed, and service recorded so that it may be charged. But in most countries the other types of apparatus mentioned above may be purchased by anyone and used whenever desired. As a result, data on distribution and use of these types of apparatus may be collected in a variety of ways—on the basis of numbers of subscribers, licenses issued, periodic sample surveys, trade data, census or housing surveys, or private consumer surveys. Data on broadcast media refer to receivers; data on telephones to "main lines," or the lines connecting a subscriber's apparatus (fixed or mobile) to the public, switched net. The information provided for the number of PCs is estimated only.

"Users" refers to the number of people with access to computers connected to the Internet.

The *Statistical Yearbook* of Unesco contains extensive data on book, periodical, and newspaper publishing, and on radio and television broadcasting that have been collected from standardized questionnaires. The quality and recency of its data, however, depend on the completion and timely return of each questionnaire by national authorities. The commercially published annual *World Radio TV Handbook* (Andrew G. Sennitt, editor) is a valuable source of information on broadcast media and has complete and timely coverage. It depends on data received from broadcasters, but, because some do not respond, local correspondents and monitors are used in many countries, and some unconfirmed or unofficial data are included as estimates. The statistics on telecommunications apparatus and computers are derived mainly from the UN-affiliated International Telecommunication Union's *World Telecommunication Development Report* (annual).

... Not available.

— None, nil, or not applicable.

television, 2000		telephones, 2004		cellular phones, 2004		personal computers, 2004		Internet users, 2004		country
receivers (all types; '000)	receivers per 1,000 persons	main lines		cellular subscriptions ('000)	subscriptions per 1,000 persons	units ('000)	units per 1,000 persons	number ('000)	users per 1,000 persons	
		('000)	per 1,000 persons							
362	14	29[1]	1.3[1]	...	...	...	...	1.0	0.03	Afghanistan
383	123	255	83	1,100	358	36[1]	12[1]	75	23	Albania
3,330	110	2,200	69	4,683	145	290	9.0	845	26	Algeria
13	211	15[1]	252[1]	2.2[1]	38[1]	...	...	...	...	American Samoa
30	458	45	623	32	445	...	...	25	371	Andorra
193	19	96	6.7	940	67	27[1]	1.9[1]	172	12	Angola
33	501	38	494	54	701	...	...	20	260	Antigua and Barbuda
10,500	293	8,700	224	13,512	348	3,000[1]	82[1]	5,120	512	Argentina
759	244	583	190	203	67	200	66	150	49	Armenia
20[3]	204[3]	37	397	53	500	...	...	24	257	Aruba
14,200	738	10,872	546	16,449	826	13,720	689	13,000	653	Australia
4,310	536	3,763	463	7,990	984	3,420	421	3,900	480	Austria
2,080	259	984	116	1,783	211	149	18	408	48	Azerbaijan
75	247	140	441	186	587	...	...	93	293	Bahamas, The
256	402	192	259	650	879	121	164	153	207	Bahrain
909	7.0	827	5.5	4,238	29	1,650	11	300	2.0	Bangladesh
78[4]	290[4]	134	497	171	631	34	126	150	554	Barbados
3,420	342	3,071	311	1,118	113	109	11	1,600	162	Belarus
5,550	541	4,757	460	9,132	883	3,627	351	4,200	406	Belgium
42[4]	179[4]	34	129	98	375	35	127	35	134	Belize
289	45	73	11	236	34	30	4.3	100	14	Benin
66[5]	1,031[5]	56	872	30	476	34	535	35	543	Bermuda
13[4]	20[4]	30	13	18	7.7	11	4.7	20	8.6	Bhutan
970	119	625	70	1,801	201	190	23	350	39	Bolivia
411	111	938	245	1,050	274	...	...	225	54	Bosnia and Herzegovina
41	25	137	76	564	314	80	45	60	33	Botswana
58,900	343	42,382	235	65,605	363	19,350	107	22,000	122	Brazil
216	668	90	256	137	401	31	85	56	153	Brunei
3,600	449	2,770	354	4,730	604	461	59	461	281	Bulgaria
147	12	81	6.1	398	30	29	2.1	53	3.9	Burkina Faso
171	30	24	3.4	64	9.0	34	4.8	25	3.5	Burundi
100	8.0	36	2.6	498	35	38	2.6	41	2.8	Cambodia
503	34	93	5.9	1,537	94	160	9.8	167	10	Cameroon
21,700	716	20,068	633	14,984	472	22,390	705	20,000	630	Canada
2.0	4.6	73	156	66	139	48	10	25	53	Cape Verde
21	6.0	10	2.6	60	15	11	2.8	9.0	2.3	Central African Republic
8.4	1.0	12	1.3	65	8.0	15	1.7	60	6.8	Chad
3,580	242	3,318	215	9,567	621	2,138	139	4,300	279	Chile
370,000	293	312,443	238	334,824	255	52,990	40	94,000	72	China
11,200	282	8,768	195	10,401	232	2,996	67	3,586	80	Colombia
1.0[6]	1.8[3]	13	17	2	2.5	5.0	6.3	8.0	10	Comoros
150[13]	3.0[13]	10	0.2	1,000	19	...	...	50	0.9	Congo, Dem. Rep. of the
45	13	7	2	442	116	17	4.5	45	12	Congo, Rep. of the
907	231	1,343	316	923	217	1,014	239	1,000	235	Costa Rica
950	60	238	14	1,532	91	262	16	300	18	Côte d'Ivoire
1,300	293	1,700	389	2,553	584	842	191	1,303	295	Croatia
2,800	250	768	68	76	6.7	300	27	150	13	Cuba
120	180	418	518	641	794	249	309	298	370	Cyprus
5,200	508	3,450	337	10,771	1,053	2,450	240	4,800	469	Czech Republic
4,310	807	3,475	647	5,166	961	3,543	659	3,762	700	Denmark
31	71	11	16	33	34	21	31	9.0	13	Djibouti
16	220	21	295	42	589	9.0	127	18.5	261	Dominica
810	97	936	107	2,534	288	...	...	800	91	Dominican Republic
...	...	...	...	...	...	...	...	1.0	...	East Timor
2,710	218	1,612	122	4,544	344	734	55	625	47	Ecuador
12,200	189	9,464	135	7,643	109	2,300	33	3,900	56	Egypt
1,250	201	888	134	1,833	277	297	45	587	89	El Salvador
4.0[3]	9.0[3]	9.6	18	56	110	7.0	14	5.0	9.9	Equatorial Guinea
97	26	39	9.1	20	4.7	15	3.5	50	12	Eritrea
809	591	444	340	1,256	960	1,242	950	670	512	Estonia

Communications (continued)

country	publishing (latest)							postal services				telecommunications	
	books		periodicals		daily newspapers			post offices, 2004				radio, 2000	
	number of titles	number of copies ('000)	number of titles	number of copies ('000)	number	total circulation ('000)	circulation per 1,000 adult persons	number	persons per office	pieces of mail handled ('000,000)	pieces handled per person	receivers (all types; '000)	receivers per 1,000 persons
Ethiopia	240	674	...	...	5	92	1.4	650	116,307	29	0.3	11,800	189
Faroe Islands	...	...	...	...	1	6.0	136	33	1,416	11	271	102	2,222
Fiji	401	2,256	...	...	3	33	37	169	4,975	30	31	500[3]	636[3]
Finland	13,104	...	5,711	...	53	2,255	522	1,311	3,993	1,859	506	8,400	1,623
France	34,766	1,041	2,672	120,018	85	7,934	160	16,947	3,556	19,658	326	55,900	950
French Guiana	...	...	...	...	1	2.0	7.0	...	...	...	...	104[3]	650[3]
French Polynesia	...	...	...	...	2	24	108	975	2,370[5]	28[5]	102[5]	128[3]	574[3]
Gabon	...	...	...	...	1	22	16	60	22,706	6.6	3.7	630	501
Gambia, The	14[14]	10[14]	10	885	2	2.6	1.7	19	77,772	7.8	2.0	520	396
Gaza Strip[15]	...	...	...	...	...	...	...	...	...	...	...	...	...
Georgia	581[2]	834[2]	...	...	9	26	7	998	4,527	3,241	716	2,790	556
Germany	71,515	...	9,010	395,036	371	22,095	313	13,019	6,348	23,869	289	77,900	948
Ghana	28	648	121	774	7	160	8	721	30,048	125[16]	2.5[16]	13,900	710
Greece	4,225	...	...	...	32	618	68	2,200	5,045	734	54	5,220	478
Greenland	103	...	...	...	—	—	—	75	757	7.9	85	273[3]	482[3]
Grenada	...	...	4	89	—	—	—	53	1,929	8.9	51	57[3]	615[3]
Guadeloupe	...	...	...	...	1	35	81	...	...	...	...	113[3]	258[3]
Guam	...	...	...	...	1	26	180	...	...	...	...	221[3]	1,400[3]
Guatemala	...	...	...	...	6	417	31	436	28,199	34	2.1	902	79
Guernsey	...	...	...	...	...	...	...	12	5,000	56	642	...	...
Guinea	...	...	3	5.0	2	...	...	40	94,800	7.9[5]	0.4[5]	422	52
Guinea-Bissau	...	...	...	...	—	—	—	20	76,986	3[11,16]	0.3[6,16]	56	44
Guyana	42[2]	508[2]	...	...	3	42	50	71	10,567	15	13	420[3]	498[3]
Haiti	...	...	...	...	3	26	3.0	55	152,853	1.7	0.3	395	55
Honduras	22	80	...	...	6	223	34	435[6]	13,700[6]	35[6]	3.0[6]	2,620	412
Hong Kong	...	...	598	...	30	319	54	131	53,152	1,254[5]	175[5]	4,560	684
Hungary	9,193	53,194	1,203	14,927	32	1,820	216	2,824	3,585	2,202	135	7,050	690
Iceland	1,527	...	938	384	3	91	292	94	3,106	68	355	260	950
India	11,903	...	...	...	410	33,930	46	153,021[5]	6,240[5]	16,394[5]	16[5]	123,000	121
Indonesia	4,018[14]	8,103[14]	115	4,173	218	4,866	28	19,632	11,210	1,076	4.5	33,200	157
Iran	15,073	87,861	318	6,166	32	1,780	28	6,511	10,567	267	4.0	17,900	281
Iraq	...	...	...	...	11	...	...	278	100,924	695	2.1[5]	5,030	222
Ireland	...	...	...	...	7	742	234	1,604	2,543	749	184	2,660	695
Isle of Man	...	...	...	...	...	...	...	31	2,475	49	651	...	...
Israel	2,310[19]	9,368[19]	...	...	34	2,722	406	661	9,986	764	116	3,210	526
Italy	35,236	278,821	9,951	80,469	94	7,737	154	13,855	4,189	6,661	115	50,000	878
Jamaica	...	...	...	...	3	161	62	603	4,377	71	26	2,030	784
Japan	56,221[2]	400,013[2]	2,926	...	107	70,364	544	24,678	5,184	28,016	219	121,000	956
Jersey	...	...	...	...	...	...	...	21	4,190	62[3]	468[3]	...	...
Jordan	511	2,673[2]	31	43	4	383	77	392	12,941	24	4.8	1,850	372
Kazakhstan	1,226	21,014	...	...	4	500	30	3,733	3,975	153	10.1	6,270	422
Kenya	300[2]	452	...	...	5	315	10	865	38,691	136	4.1	6,760	223
Kiribati	...	...	...	...	—	—	—	25[3]	3,200[3]	1.9[3]	1.2[3]	33	386
Korea, North	...	...	...	...	3	4,500	208	...	...	...	...	3,330	154
Korea, South	30,487[2]	142,804[2]	...	...	136	18,500	393	3,692	12,905	4,952	103	48,600	1,033
Kuwait	196[20]	6,107[20]	...	...	7	390	173	59	44,177	32	12	1,400	624
Kyrgyzstan	351	1,980	...	...	3	73	15	922	5,644	28	5.6	542	111
Laos	88[2]	995[2]	...	...	4	22	4.0	234	24,751	1.1	0.2	781	145
Latvia	1,965	7,734	213	1,660	22	356	182	968	2,395	116	50	1,650	695
Lebanon	...	...	...	...	15	215	77	200	17,701	13	3.4	2,460	687
Lesotho	...	...	...	...	6	14	8.0	153	11,751	2.6	1.1	95	53
Liberia	...	...	...	...	3	33	12	34[13]	8,260[13]	...	...	863	274
Libya	26	2,645	...	...	5	79	15	360	15,945	50	8.8	1,430	273
Liechtenstein	...	...	...	...	2	19	606	12	2,850	34	977	21[3]	658[3]
Lithuania	3,645	14,915	269	...	19	101	29	955	3,606	175	51	1,750	500
Luxembourg	681	...	508	...	6	115	303	105	4,211	220	485	170	389
Macau	67	99	16	...	10	197	448	18	25,401	27	58	215	500
Macedonia	892	2,496	74	347	13	150	92	320	6,345	28	14	415	205
Madagascar	119	296	55	108	9	78	5.0	617	29,356	265	1.5[5]	3,350	216
Malawi	117[2,21]	9,174[2,21]	...	...	2	22	1.8	325	38,795	44[5]	3.4[5]	5,430	499
Malaysia	5,843	29,040	25	996	35	2,753	172	1,202	20,711	1,238	49	9,760	420
Maldives	...	...	...	...	3	5.0	18	216	1,487	1.4	4.8	343	129[3]
Mali	14[2]	28[2]	...	...	4	11	1.0	124[5]	86,200[5]	3.4[5]	0.2[5]	597	56
Malta	404	...	359	...	4	48	130	51	7,839	57	143	255[3]	669[3]
Marshall Islands	...	...	...	...	—	—	—	...	...	...	...	...	...
Martinique	...	...	...	...	1	30	78	...	...	...	...	82[3]	213[3]
Mauritania	...	...	...	...	3	1.0	0.5	26	114,629	0.3	0.1	371	149
Mauritius	80	163	62	...	2	60	65	125	9,865	74	60	450	379
Mayotte	...	...	...	...	...	...	...	...	...	...	...	50[13]	427[13]
Mexico	...	...	158	13,097	299	9,580	98	8,002	13,209	698	6.6	32,300	330
Micronesia	...	...	...	...	—	—	—	...	...	...	...	70[13]	667[13]
Moldova	921	2,779	76	196	6	75	21	1,146	3,681	99	24	3,250	758
Monaco	41	722	3	38	—	—	—	...	...	...	...	22	671
Mongolia	285[2]	959[2]	45	6,361	6	50	25	385	6,790	20	8.1	368	154
Morocco	918	1,836	...	...	20	355	10	1,653	18,766	284	9.5	6,920	243
Mozambique	...	3,490	...	...	6	16	1.0	299	64,963	8.9	0.5	778	44
Myanmar (Burma)	3,660	4,038	...	...	8	501	10	1,331	37,569	88[6]	1.9[6]	2,760	66
Namibia	106	...	...	...	5	35	19	118	17,028	79	39	258	141
Nauru	...	...	...	...	—	—	—	1	10,100	...	...	7.0[3]	609[3]
Nepal	...	...	...	...	29	250	11	4,156[5]	5,260[5]	74	2.8	883	39
Netherlands, The	34,067	...	367	19,283	36	4,712	351	3,188	5,090	5,303[22]	326[22]	15,600	980
Netherlands Antilles	...	...	...	...	3	70	334	15	12,058	24	132	217[3]	1,031[3]
New Caledonia	...	...	...	...	1	24	127	54	4,308	14	61	107[3]	527[3]
New Zealand	...	...	126	3,991	23	738	233	1,021	3,907	...	...	3,850	997
Nicaragua	...	...	...	...	6	95	18	183[5]	26,300[5]	8.3[5]	1.2[5]	1,370	270

| television, 2000 | | telephones, 2004 | | cellular phones, 2004 | | personal computers, 2004 | | Internet users, 2004 | | country |
receivers (all types; '000)	receivers per 1,000 persons	main lines ('000)	per 1,000 persons	cellular subscriptions ('000)	subscriptions per 1,000 persons	units ('000)	units per 1,000 persons	number ('000)	users per 1,000 persons	
376	6.0	435	6.3	178	2.5	225	3.1	113	1.6	Ethiopia
47	1,022	23[1]	482[1]	31[1]	644[1]	...	...	25	524	Faroe Islands
92	113	102	124	133	160	44	52	61	72	Fiji
3,580	692	2,368	454	4,988	956	2,515	482	3,286	630	Finland
37,000	628	33,870	577	44,552	737	29,410	487	25,000	414	France
30[3]	172[3]	51[1]	268[1]	138[1]	781[1]	...	...	3.2	143	French Guiana
45	189	54	214	90[1]	367[1]	78	315	61	246	French Polynesia
410	326	38	29	489	362	50	37	40	30	Gabon
3.9	3.0	38	29	175	120	23	16	49	34	Gambia, The
...	...	...	...	...	...	...	...	...	...	Gaza Strip[15]
2,380	474	683	135	841	166	192	38	176	35	Georgia
48,200	586	54,550	661	71,316	864	46,300	561	41,263	500	Germany
2,300	118	313	15	1,695	79	112	5.2	368	17	Ghana
5,330	488	5,158	470	11,044	1,006	986	90	1,955	178	Greece
22[3]	393[3]	26[17]	468[17]	17[17]	298[17]	...	...	10	180	Greenland
33[4]	355[4]	33	318	43	420	16	155	8.0	78	Grenada
118[4]	262[4]	210[17]	457[17]	324[1]	697[1]	100	217	20	43	Guadeloupe
106[4]	646[4]	80[18]	508[18]	33[1]	207[1]	...	...	50	319	Guam
697	61	1,132	89	3,168	250	231	18	597	60	Guatemala
...	...	55[17]	877[17]	32[1]	500[1]	...	...	30	596	Guernsey
357	44	26[1]	3.4[1]	112	14	44	55	46	58	Guinea
...	...	11	8.2	1.3	1	...	...	26	20	Guinea-Bissau
60[4]	70[4]	103	134	144	188	27	35	145	189	Guyana
36	5.0	140	17	400	47	...	...	500	59	Haiti
610	96	371	53	707	101	110	16	222	32	Honduras
3,290	493	3,780	531	8,149	1,145	4,187	589	3,480	489	Hong Kong
4,460	437	3,577	364	8,727	888	1,476	150	2,700	270	Hungary
143	509	191	650	291	994	138	471	226	770	Iceland
79,300	78	43,960	41	47,300	44	13,030	12	35,000	32	India
31,500	149	9,990	45	30,000	135	3,022	14	14,508	65	Indonesia
10,400	163	14,571	220	4,300	62	7,347	105	550	7.9	Iran
1,880	83	675[1]	25[1]	...	...	...	...	...	...	Iraq
1,530	399	2,019	505	3,780	945	2,011	503	1,080	270	Ireland
...	...	...	...	...	...	...	...	...	...	Isle of Man
2,040	335	3,000	437	7,188	1,047	5,037	734	3,200	466	Israel
28,100	494	25,957	453	62,750	1,094	18,150	317	28,870	503	Italy
502	194	500	187	2,200	822	166	62	1,067	399	Jamaica
92,000	725	58,788	460	91,474	716	69,200	542	75,000	587	Japan
...	...	74[17]	849[17]	61[17]	706[17]	...	...	8.0[18]	91[18]	Jersey
417	84	617	123	1,595	284	300	53	600	107	Jordan
3,580	241	2,500	162	2,759	179	...	...	400	36	Kazakhstan
758	25	299	9.2	2,546	79	441	14	1,500	46	Kenya
3	36	4.5[1]	51[1]	0.5[1]	6.0[1]	2.0[1]	23[1]	2.0[1]	23[1]	Kiribati
1,170	54	1,100[4]	50[4]	...	...	...	...	...	...	Korea, North
17,100	364	26,058	542	36,586	761	26,201	545	31,580	658	Korea, South
1,090	486	497	191	2,000	771	450	173	600	231	Kuwait
239	49	396	79	300	58	87	17	262	50	Kyrgyzstan
53	10	75	13	204	35	22	3.8	21	3.6	Laos
1,870	789	631	270	1,537	672	501	219	810	354	Latvia
1,200	335	630	178	888	250	400	113	600	169	Lebanon
29	16	37	21	159	88	...	...	43	24	Lesotho
79	25	6.8[17]	2.0[17]	...	...	...	...	1.0[1]	0.4[1]	Liberia
717	137	750	136	127	23	130	23	205	36	Libya
12[3]	375[3]	20[1]	583[1]	11[1]	333[1]	...	...	20[1]	585[1]	Liechtenstein
1,480	422	820	238	3,422	993	533	155	968	281	Lithuania
170	391	360	798	539	1,194	296	645	271	590	Luxembourg
123	286	174	372	432	926	130	278	150	321	Macau
571	282	525	258	776	372	140	68	769	77	Macedonia
372	24	60	3.6	334	19	91	5.1	90	5.0	Madagascar
33	3.0	93	7.5	222	18	20	1.6	46	3.7	Malawi
3,900	168	4,446	179	14,612	587	4,900	197	9,878	397	Malaysia
11	40	32	96	113	345	36	109	19	58	Maldives
130[5]	12[5]	75	3.8	400	36	42	3.8	50	4.5	Mali
217	556	208	521	290	725	126	318	301	660	Malta
...	...	4.5	83	0.6	11	5.0	88	2.0	35	Marshall Islands
66[3]	168[3]	172[18]	447[18]	320[1]	790[1]	52[1]	130[1]	40[1]	103[1]	Martinique
239	96	38	14	522	175	42	14	14	4.7	Mauritania
318	268	354	287	510	414	344	279	180	146	Mauritius
3.5[13]	30[13]	10[17]	70[17]	22[1]	15[1]	...	...	...	...	Mayotte
27,700	283	18,073	172	38,451	366	11,210	107	14,037	134	Mexico
2.2	20	10[1]	87[1]	1.8[1]	15[1]	...	...	10[1]	93[1]	Micronesia
1,270	297	863	203	787	185	112	26	406	95	Moldova
25[3]	758[3]	34[1]	1,040[1]	12[5]	364[5]	...	...	16[1]	494[1]	Monaco
155	65	138	56	319	130	312	119	200	76	Mongolia
4,720	166	1,309	44	9,337	312	620	21	3,500	117	Morocco
88	5.0	78	4.2	708	37	112	5.9	138	7.4	Mozambique
292	7.0	425	8.0	92	1.7	325	6.0	64	12	Myanmar (Burma)
69	38	128	64	286	142	220	109	75	37	Namibia
0.5[3]	0.1[3]	1.9[1]	160[1]	1.5[1]	130[1]	...	...	0.3[1]	26[1]	Nauru
159	7.0	400	16	179	7.0	118	4.6	175	6.8	Nepal
8,570	538	7,861	484	14,821	913	11,110	685	10,000	616	Netherlands, The
69[3]	321[3]	81.0	372	16[5]	74[5]	...	...	2.0	9.3	Netherlands Antilles
104	492	53	230	116	502	...	...	70	302	New Caledonia
2,010	522	1,801	461	3,027	775	1,924	493	3,200	819	New Zealand
350	69	215	38	739	132	200	36	125	22	Nicaragua

Communications (continued)

country	publishing (latest) books number of titles	books number of copies ('000)	periodicals number of titles	periodicals number of copies ('000)	daily newspapers number	daily newspapers total circulation ('000)	daily newspapers circulation per 1,000 adult persons	postal services post offices, 2004 number	persons per office	pieces of mail handled ('000,000)	pieces handled per person	telecommunications radio, 2000 receivers (all types; '000)	receivers per 1,000 persons
Niger	5[2]	11[2]	...	...	1	3.5	0.3	52	259,952	1.9	0.2	1,270	121
Nigeria	1,314	18,800	...	...	25	2,770	24	5,342	24,094	391[1]	2.0[1]	23,000	200
Northern Mariana Islands	...	...	...	...	...	...	...	...	...	...	...	11[13]	190[13]
Norway	6,900[19]	...	8,017	...	78	2,405	651	1,504	3,057	2,570	560	4,110	915
Oman	7[2]	21[2]	15	...	6	108	37	644	3,935	32	7.6	1,490	621
Pakistan	124	714	...	...	204	6,246	64	12,107	12,785	604	4.0	14,700	105
Palau	...	...	...	...	...	...	...	...	...	...	...	12[3]	663[3]
Panama	...	...	...	...	7	188	66	125	25,403	17	5.5	884	300
Papua New Guinea	122	...	...	...	2	51	9	108[23]	39,800[23]	39[23]	10[23]	446	86
Paraguay	152	...	...	...	4	227	43	264	22,792	4.6[5]	0.5[5]	961	182
Peru	612	1,836	...	...	73	4,250	154	1,947	14,156	21	0.7	7,080	273
Philippines	1,507[2]	14,718[2]	1,570	9,468	42	4,711	63	2,441	33,436	357	4.3	12,400	161
Poland	14,104	80,306	5,260	75,358	48	4,333	135	10,923	3,530	1,890	50	20,200	523
Portugal	7,868[7]	26,942[7]	984	10,208	16	680	77	3,026	3,451	1,950	186	3,080	304
Puerto Rico	...	...	...	...	5	624	173	...	...	...	...	2,830	742
Qatar	209[14]	2,205[14]	11	47	5	95	113	37	20,998	23	31	250[3]	432[3]
Réunion	69	...	...	...	3	55	83	...	...	...	...	173[3]	252[3]
Romania	7,199	38,374	987	...	51	1,148	61	6,821	3,195	402	19	7,310	334
Russia	36,237	421,387	2,751	387,832	485	15,300	105	40,140	3,585	4,634	34	61,100	418
Rwanda	...	...	15	101	1	0.5	0.1	19	467,493	2.5	0.3	587	76
St. Kitts and Nevis	...	...	10	44	1	...	...	7	6,027	3.1	66	28[3]	701[3]
St. Lucia	...	...	...	...	1	...	...	46	3,467	5.2	33	111[3]	746[3]
St. Vincent and the Grenadines	...	...	...	...	2	1.0	9.0	41[3]	2,680[3]	...	...	77[3]	690[3]
Samoa	...	...	...	...	2	...	...	38[1]	4,470[1]	0.9[1]	3.0[1]	178[3]	1,035[3]
San Marino	...	...	15	9	2	2.0	72	10[13]	3,000[13]	...	...	16[3]	610[3]
São Tomé and Príncipe	...	...	...	...	1	...	...	9	16,996	0.35	0.65	38[3]	272[3]
Saudi Arabia	3,900[2]	14,493[2, 21]	471	...	12	1,093	42	1,421[5]	14,200[5]	1,246[5]	455[5]	7,180	326
Senegal	...	...	...	...	18	47	5.0	137	83,109	12	1.1	1,320	141
Serbia and Montenegro	5,367	16,669	395	...	29	1,130	107	1,653	6,358	209	21	3,130	297
Seychelles	...	...	...	...	1	3.0	46	5	15,982	3.6	44	42[3]	560[3]
Sierra Leone	...	...	...	...	8	18	4.0	54[6]	83,500[6]	1.1[6]	0.1[6]	1,140	259
Singapore	...	...	...	...	11	1,542	415	138	30,961	834	197	2,700	672
Slovakia	3,800	6,139	424	8,725	12	480	107	1,598	3,380	517	96	5,200	965
Slovenia	3,441	6,267	784	...	7	360	208	557	3,532	849	425	792	405
Solomon Islands	...	...	...	...	1	5	16	127[5]	3,150[5]	4.3[6]	11[6]	57[3]	141[3]
Somalia	...	...	...	...	8	7.2	1.0	...	...	...	...	435	60
South Africa	5,418	31,349	11	2,149	18	1,406	46	2,449[5]	17,200[5]	2,700	56	16,800	338
Spain	46,330	192,019	...	...	136	4,240	123	3,291	12,958	5,871	135	13,500	333
Sri Lanka	4,115	19,650	...	...	13	493	33	4,680	4,395	411	20	3,870	208
Sudan, The	...	...	...	...	10	80	2	209	169,966	2.7	0.1	16,300	464
Suriname	47[2]	21[2]	...	...	3	50	116	42	10,630	...	...	300[3]	728[3]
Swaziland	...	...	...	...	2	27	26	51	20,280	14	14	169	162
Sweden	13,496	...	373	19,242	95	4,312	578	1,720[13]	5,140[13]	4,570[13]	503[13]	8,270	932
Switzerland	15,371	...	60	4,561	93	2,486	398	2,585	2,801	5,674	761	7,200	1,002
Syria	598	310[13]	30	192	4	326	20	604	30,765	16	0.9	4,500	276
Taiwan	...	...	...	...	30	4,000	188	9,976	2,270	5,973	264	8,620[13]	402[13]
Tajikistan	132[2]	997[2]	11	130	—	—	—	593	10,844	24	3.6	870	141
Tanzania	172[2]	364[2]	...	...	19	102	5.0	418	90,017	38	1.1	9,130	281
Thailand	8,142	...	1,522	...	34	11,753	187	4,478	14,224	1,491	24	14,700	235
Togo	...	...	...	...	1	20	4.0	55	108,880	5.0	0.9	1,330	265
Tonga	...	...	...	...	—	—	—	1.8[10]	55,600[10]	4.0[10]	40[10]	61[3]	400[3]
Trinidad and Tobago	26	30	...	...	4	137	125	245[5]	5,220[5]	30[6]	16[6]	672	532
Tunisia	720	6,000[21]	170	1,748	10	180	24	1,257	7,952	149	15	1,510	158
Turkey	6,546	...	3,554	...	81	4,948	96	4,381	16,485	925	13	38,600	573
Turkmenistan	450[2]	5,493[2]	...	...	2	45	14	190	25,084	91	19	1,190	256
Tuvalu	...	...	...	...	—	—	—	...	...	...	...	4.0[3]	384[3]
Uganda	288	2,229[19]	26	158	5	89	5.0	329	84,561	25	0.9	2,920	127
Ukraine	6,225	68,876	717	2,521	38	4,970	101	15,554	3,021	1,230	26	43,800	889
United Arab Emirates	293[21]	5,117[21]	80	922	6	423	168	356	12,035	164	38	1,030	318
United Kingdom	107,263	...	...	...	109	17,485	352	14,609	4,071	21,865	361	84,000	1,432
United States	68,175	...	11,593	...	1,457	54,626	233	37,159	7,950	206,649	703	598,000	2,118
Uruguay	934	1,970	...	...	4	973	293	1,409	1,245	18	5.4	2,000	603
Uzbekistan	1,003	30,914	81	684	5	74	3.0	2,961	8,851	77	3.0	11,300	456
Vanuatu	...	...	...	...	1	3	22	...	...	...	...	62	350
Venezuela	3,468[2]	7,420[2]	...	...	92	5,000	206	355	74,034	58	2.2	7,140	294
Vietnam	5,581	83,000	338	2,710	10	1,530	20	3,061	27,152	545	6.7	8,520	109
Virgin Islands (U.S.)	...	...	...	...	1	17	156	10	2,175	1.8	17	107	1,119
West Bank[15]	...	...	...	...	3	35	15	...	...	...	...	...	...
Western Sahara	...	...	...	...	1	...	...	...	...	...	...	56	211
Yemen	...	...	...	...	3	270	15	251	80,993	6.5	0.3	1,170	65
Zambia	...	...	...	...	3	55	9	195[5]	45,000[5]	20	1.8	1,510	145
Zimbabwe	232	...	28	680	3	122	10	1,162	11,133	137[5]	9.4[5]	4,110	362

television, 2000		telephones, 2004		cellular phones, 2004		personal computers, 2004		Internet users, 2004		country
receivers (all types; '000)	receivers per 1,000 persons	main lines ('000)	per 1,000 persons	cellular subscriptions ('000)	subscriptions per 1,000 persons	units ('000)	units per 1,000 persons	number ('000)	users per 1,000 persons	
388	37	24	1.9	148	12	9.0	0.7	24	1.9	Niger
7,840	68	1,028	8.1	9,147	72	867	6.8	1,770	14	Nigeria
...	...	271[8]	383[18]	3.0[18]	43[18]	...	...	10	0.1	Northern Mariana Islands
3,000	669	2,228	486	4,163	909	2,630	578	3,937	394	Norway
1,350	563	240	82	805	274	118	40	245	83	Oman
18,300	131	4,880	31	5,020	32	600[17]	4.2[17]	2,000	13	Pakistan
...	...	...	...	...	...	...	...	20[4]	1.2[4]	Palau
572	194	376	119	856	270	130	41	300	95	Panama
88	17	62	11	15	2.7	367	63	170	29	Papua New Guinea
1,200	218	281	47	1,768	294	356	59	150	25	Paraguay
3,840	148	2,050	74	4,093	149	2,689	98	3,220	117	Peru
11,100	144	3,438	42	32,936	399	3,684	45	4,400	53	Philippines
15,500	400	12,293	319	23,096	599	7,362	191	9,000	233	Poland
6,380	630	4,238	404	10,300	1,023	1,402	139	2,951	293	Portugal
1,260	330	1,330[17]	346[17]	1,211[17]	316[17]	...	...	1,000	257	Puerto Rico
503	869	191	308	490	792	133	215	165	267	Qatar
127[3]	184[3]	300[17]	410[17]	490[1]	66[1]	32[17]	45[17]	150[17]	202[17]	Réunion
8,340	381	4,389	197	10,215	459	2,450	110	4,500	201	Romania
61,500	421	36,993	253	74,420	516	19,010	132	16,000	111	Russia
10[3]	1.7[3]	23[1]	2.8[1]	150	18	...	...	38[1]	4.5[1]	Rwanda
12	260	24[1]	500[1]	10	217	11	239	40	870	St. Kitts and Nevis
32[3]	208[3]	52	315	93	620	26	173	55	367	St. Lucia
26	234	19	220	57	470	16	132	8.0	66	St. Vincent and the Grenadines
11	61	13	73	10[1]	58[1]	1[1]	6.7[1]	6.0	33	Samoa
9.0[3]	346[3]	21[1]	763[1]	17[1]	621[1]	...	...	14[1]	531[1]	San Marino
34	228	7	46	4.8	32	...	...	20	122	São Tomé and Príncipe
5,810	264	3,695	148	9,176	368	8,476	340	1,586	64	Saudi Arabia
376	40	229	21	1,028	99	242	23	482	47	Senegal
2,980	282	2,685	255	4,730	450	389	37	1,200	114	Serbia and Montenegro
16	203	21	262	49	608	15	185	20	247	Seychelles
57	13[17]	24[1]	4.8[1]	113	23	...	...	10	1.9	Sierra Leone
1,220	304	1,864	432	3,861	895	3,939	913	2,422	561	Singapore
2,190	407	1,250	231	4,275	791	1,595	295	2,276	421	Slovakia
720	368	872	407	1,739	871	704	355	950	480	Slovenia
9.6	23	6.2	13	1.5	3.7	20	41	3.0	6.1	Solomon Islands
102	14	100[1]	10[1]	35[1]	3.0[1]	6.2[1]	0.8[1]	89[1]	12[1]	Somalia
6,310	127	4,821	104	19,500	431	3,740	83	3,566	79	South Africa
24,000	591	17,752	432	38,623	939	10,957	266	13,000	316	Spain
2,060	111	991	51	2,211	115	530	28	280	15	Sri Lanka
9,580	273	1,029	30	1,049	30	606	18	1,140	33	Sudan, The
109	253	81	185	213	485	19	42	30	68	Suriname
124	119	46	44	113	104	36	33	36	33	Swaziland
5,090	574	6,873	766	9,302	1,032	6,861	761	6,800	755	Sweden
3,940	548	5,250	733	6,275	876	6,105	852	4,700	656	Switzerland
1,090	67	2,660	146	2,345	129	600	33	800	44	Syria
9,220[4]	417[4]	13,530	594	22,760	1,000	11,924	524	12,210	536	Taiwan
2,010	326	245	38	48	7.3	...	...	5.0	0.8	Tajikistan
650	20	149	4.2	1,640	44	278	7.4	333	8.8	Tanzania
17,700	284	6,724	106	28,000	441	3,716	59	6,970	110	Thailand
161	32	61	12	220	44	171	34	221	44	Togo
2.0[3]	20[3]	11[1]	113[1]	3.4[1]	34[1]	5.0	48	3.0	29	Tonga
429	340	321	246	648	496	137	105	160	122	Trinidad and Tobago
1,890	198	1,204	121	3,736	376	472	48	835	84	Tunisia
30,300	449	19,125	265	34,708	480	3,703	51	10,220	141	Turkey
911	196	376	77	9.2	1.9	...	...	36	7.3	Turkmenistan
0.1[13]	9.1[13]	0.7[1]	65[1]	...	...	...	...	...	...	Tuvalu
620	27	71	2.7	1,165	43	121	4.5	200	7.5	Uganda
22,500	456	12,142	252	13,735	285	1,327	28	3,750	78	Ukraine
948	292	1,188	273	3,683	847	450	120	1,385	319	United Arab Emirates
38,800[4]	652[4]	33,700	567	61,100	1,028	35,890	604	37,600	633	United Kingdom
241,000	854	177,947	599	181,105	610	220,000	741	185,000	623	United States
1,760	531	1,000	309	600	185	430	133	680	210	Uruguay
6,830	276	1,717	67	544	205	...	...	880	33	Uzbekistan
2.3	12	6.8	31	10.5	48	3	14	7.5	35	Vanuatu
4,490	185	3,347	128	8,421	322	2,145	82	2,313	88	Venezuela
14,500	185	10,125	123	4,960	60	1,044	13	5,870	71	Vietnam
65	594	69[17]	635[17]	41[17]	375[17]	...	...	30[1]	373[1]	Virgin Islands (U.S.)
...	...	357	97	974	26	169	46	160	43	West Bank[15]
6.0[13]	24[13]	...	...	...	...	...	...	...	...	Western Sahara
5,100	283	798	39	1,072	52	300	15	180	8.7	Yemen
1,400	134	88	7.9	300	28	113	10	231	21	Zambia
2,074[4]	183[4]	317	25	398	31	1,000	77	820	63	Zimbabwe

[1]2002. [2]First editions only. [3]1997. [4]1999. [5]1998. [6]1995. [7]Including reprints. [8]Foreign dispatched and foreign received only. [9]1994. [10]1993. [11]Domestic only. [12]Millions of copies. [13]1996. [14]School textbooks and government publications only. [15]West Bank includes Gaza Strip. [16]Foreign received only. [17]2001. [18]2000. [19]Excludes government publications and textbooks. [20]Government publications only. [21]School textbooks only. [22]Domestic and foreign received only. [23]1991.

Trade: external

The following table presents comparative data on the international, or foreign, trade of the countries of the world. The table analyzes data for both imports and exports in two ways: (1) into several major commodity groups defined in accordance with the United Nations system called the *Standard International Trade Classification* (SITC) and (2) by direction of trade for each country with major world trading blocs and partners. These commodity groupings are defined by the SITC code numbers beneath the column headings. The single-digit numbers represent broad SITC categories (in the SITC, called "sections"); the double-digit numbers represent subcategories ("divisions") of the single-digit categories (27 is a subcategory of 2); the three-digit number is a subcategory ("group") of the double-digit (667 is a subcategory of 66). Where a plus or minus sign is used before one of these SITC numbers, the SITC category or subcategory is being added to or subtracted from the aggregate implied by the total of the preceding sections. The SITC commodity aggregations used here are listed in the table at the end of this headnote. The full SITC commodity breakdown is presented in the United Nations publication *Standard International Trade Classification*.

The SITC was developed by the United Nations through its Statistical Commission as an outgrowth of the need for a standard system of aggregating commodities of external trade to provide international comparability of foreign trade statistics. The United Nations Statistical Commission has defined external merchandise trade as "all goods whose movement into or out of the customs area of a country compiling the statistics adds to or subtracts from the material resources of the country." Goods passing through a country for transport only are excluded, but goods entering for reexport, or deposited (as in a bonded warehouse, or free trade area) for reimport, are included. Statistics in this table refer only to goods and exclude purely financial transactions that are covered in the "Finance" and "National product and accounts" tables. Gold for fabrication (*e.g.*, as jewelry) is included; monetary and reserve gold are excluded.

For purposes of comparability of data, total value of imports and exports is given in this table in U.S. dollars. Conversions from currencies other than U.S. dollars are determined according to the average market rates for the year for which data are supplied; these are mainly as calculated by the International Monetary Fund (IMF) or other official sources. The commodity categories are given in terms of percentages of the total value of the country's import or export trade (with the exclusions noted above). Value is based on transaction value: for imports, the value at which the goods were purchased by the importer plus the cost of transportation and insurance to the frontier of the importing country (c.i.f. [cost, insurance, and freight] valuation); for exports, the value at which the goods were

Trade: external

country	year	imports total value ('000,000 U.S.$)	food and agricultural raw materials (0 + 1 + 2 − 27 − 28 + 4)	mineral ores and concentrates (27 + 28 + 667)	fuels and other energy (3)	manufactured goods totala (5 + 6 − 667 + 7 + 8 + 9)	of which chemicals and related products (5)	of which machinery and transport equipment (7)	of which othera (6 − 667 + 8 + 9)	from European Union (EU)b	from United States	from Japan	from China	from all otherc
Afghanistan	2001	576.5[1]	—— 19.9[2, 3] ——		2.7[2]	77.4[2, 4]	—	15.2[2]	62.2[2, 4]	8.2[1]	1.1[1]	8.6[1]	3.3[1]	78.8[1]
Albania	2002	1,503.7	21.1	0.6	9.0	69.2	7.0	21.4	40.9	74.0	1.7	0.6	2.5	21.2
Algeria	2000	9,152.1	30.8	0.2	1.4	67.6	11.6	34.5	21.6	58.7	11.4	3.0	2.3	24.6
American Samoa	2000[5]	505.9	—— 64.0[3, 6] ——		7.0[6]	29.0[4, 6]	...	6.0[6]	23.0[4, 6]	—	24.8	0.7	0.3	74.1
Andorra	2002	1,198.1	19.8	0.6	4.5	75.2	10.1	25.8	39.2	87.9	1.3	4.2	1.5	5.2
Angola	2001	3,179.2	—— 33.6[3, 7] ——		0.3[7]	66.1[4, 7]	9.1[7]	30.1[7]	26.9[4, 7]	42.5[1]	9.6[1]	1.1[1]	1.6[1]	45.3[1]
Antigua and Barbuda	1999	356.0	24.6	0.5	10.5	64.5	6.8	32.3	25.4	10.0	49.4	10.2	0.3	30.1
Argentina	2002	8,989.5	7.0	3.3	4.7	84.9	31.4	31.3	22.2	23.4	20.1	3.5	3.7	49.4
Armenia	2003	1,211.8	18.5	23.3	14.0	44.3	7.7	14.3	22.3	31.5	8.2	0.6	0.9	58.8
Aruba	1999	786.5[9]	21.7	4.1	—	74.2	10.4	36.9	26.9	14.6	66.1	1.4	0.2	17.7
Australia	2002	69,260.4	5.9	0.6	7.3	86.2	11.6	45.8	28.7	23.0	18.2	12.1	9.9	36.8
Austria	2002	68,227.9	9.1	0.7	6.4	83.8	11.0	39.7	33.2	77.0	5.0	2.3	1.9	13.8
Azerbaijan	2003	2,626.4	12.7	1.6	11.3	74.4	5.6	38.7	30.1	33.0	5.0	3.9	3.5	54.6
Bahamas, The	2001	1,927.3	19.6	0.3	15.2	64.9	7.6	26.9	30.4	2.1	83.3	1.2	—	13.4
Bahrain	2001	4,262.7	12.8	6.7	37.2	43.3	5.0	18.9	19.4	17.7	5.1	5.3	3.2	68.7
Bangladesh	2001	8,096.6	22.9	0.8	5.3	71.1	10.7	22.6	37.7	9.4	3.6	7.3	11.0	68.7
Barbados	2002	996.5	21.5	0.7	6.3	71.6	12.3	27.2	32.1	17.5	44.1	4.5	2.7	31.2
Belarus	2003	11,504.9	13.7	1.8	26.4	58.1	10.5	22.4	25.2	21.8	1.3	0.3	0.6	75.9[11]
Belgium	2001	178,698.4	10.3	7.7	8.6	73.3	17.8	31.7	23.8	71.6	7.0	2.9	2.2	16.3
Belize	2000	446.9	14.6	0.3	17.0	68.2	10.3	28.7	29.1	11.3	50.1	2.5	0.7	35.3
Benin	2001	601.9	25.4	0.9	17.3	56.4	11.1	16.3	29.0	44.7	4.3	3.1	8.0	40.0
Bermuda	1995	680.2	21.4	2.1	6.0	70.4	7.8	25.3	37.3	11.1	71.2	4.0	0.1	13.4
Bhutan	1999	182.1	19.2	0.6	10.4	69.9	6.1	41.7	22.0	1.3	0.3	3.3	0.9	94.2[14]
Bolivia	2002	1,769.3	14.3	0.2	5.0	80.4	15.7	29.4	35.4	8.5	15.6	5.5	4.8	65.5
Bosnia and Herzegovina	2003	3,311.9	21.2	1.6	7.7	69.5	11.3	25.3	32.9	57.6	1.5	0.9	1.8	38.2
Botswana	2001	1,810.8	14.7	2.4	6.7	76.1	7.2	32.0	37.0	11.5	1.8	0.3	0.4	86.1[17]
Brazil	2002	49,734.9	8.3	1.1	15.2	75.4	20.3	39.3	15.8	28.2	21.9	4.9	3.4	41.5
Brunei	1998	1,566.0	16.9	1.8	0.4	81.0	6.1	33.3	41.6	15.2	15.0	6.4	1.5	61.9
Bulgaria	2001	7,278.1	6.7	4.0	5.0	84.3	10.1	27.5	46.6	54.7	2.6	1.1	1.2	40.4
Burkina Faso	2001	788.4	15.6	0.4	25.1	58.9	9.2	33.3	16.3	37.3	3.6	11.8	3.3	44.0
Burundi	2001	138.9	15.6	1.5	12.5	70.3	18.3	23.4	28.6	35.9	3.1	4.4	4.1	52.4
Cambodia	1998	1,080.3	17.2[18, 19]	...	11.7[18]	...	6.5[18, 19]	17.0[18, 19]	...	8.3	3.6	6.6	8.9	72.7
Cameroon	2001	1,852.2	16.6	3.1	18.4	62.0	11.0	26.1	24.8	47.9	7.9	4.5	2.7	36.9
Canada	2002	222,240.9	7.3	1.4	4.9	86.4	9.7	49.3	27.4	11.4	62.6	4.4	4.6	17.0
Cape Verde	2001	247.5	36.2	0.2	5.6	58.0	6.4	27.9	23.7	74.2	3.2	—	7.4	15.2
Central African Republic	1996	179.9	25.9	0.4	8.1	65.6	7.9	37.4	20.3	48.7	1.7	8.7	0.3	40.6
Chad	1995	215.2	24.9	0.4	17.9	56.8	7.4	23.9	25.4	51.3	6.5	2.4	2.9	37.0
Chile	2002	15,383.4	9.1	0.5	16.4	73.9	13.4	35.6	25.0	19.7	16.6	3.5	7.2	53.1
China	2002	295,170.0	7.4	3.1	6.5	82.9	13.2	46.4	23.3	13.3	9.2	18.1	—	59.3
Colombia	2002	12,689.9	14.4	0.4	1.5	83.6	22.4	36.8	24.5	11.2	52.1	4.3	1.8	30.7
Comoros	2000	71.9	22.3	0.1	4.1	73.5	2.3	10.1	61.2	23.5	0.1	0.5	0.6	75.4
Congo, Dem. Rep. of the	2002	906.0	—— 20.0[22] ——		13.8[22]	66.2[22]	4.4[22]	45.5[22]	16.3[22]	41.8[1]	3.4[1]	1.5[1]	2.3[1]	51.0[1]
Congo, Rep. of the	2002	1,113.0	21.7[23]	0.4[23]	19.6[23]	58.3[23]	13.9[23]	20.2[23]	24.2[23]	49.5[1]	5.2[1]	0.7[1]	3.9[1]	40.7[1]
Costa Rica	2002	6,894.2	8.7	0.4	6.7	84.2	14.3	41.9	27.9	11.2	52.1	4.3	1.8	30.7
Côte d'Ivoire	2000	2,482.2	18.2	0.7	33.7	47.3	14.3	16.4	16.5	42.2	3.6	2.9	2.7	48.6
Croatia	2003	14,153.3	10.0	0.5	11.0	78.6	11.0	37.2	30.4	72.0	2.6	1.7	2.8	20.8
Cuba	2001	4,838.7	18.7	0.3	20.2	60.8	10.1	25.7	25.1	32.7	0.1	1.7	12.6	52.9
Cyprus[24]	2002	4,086.2	13.8	0.3	10.9	75.0	9.6	29.6	35.8	54.1	5.0	6.8	4.0	30.2
Czech Republic	2001	36,476.6	6.6	0.9	9.1	83.4	10.9	42.2	30.3	73.4	4.0	1.9	5.9	14.9
Denmark	2002	49,312.6	14.3	0.4	4.4	80.9	10.6	37.6	32.6	75.3	3.9	1.3	2.8	16.6
Djibouti	1999	52.5	37.7[21]	—[21]	8.1[21]	54.3[21]	6.8[21]	19.2[21]	28.3[21]	49.2[1]	2.0	3.3	2.4	43.0[1]
Dominica	2002	115.7	25.9	0.3	9.5	64.3	12.9	22.0	29.5	14.1	36.6	4.1	0.7	44.5
Dominican Republic	2001	5,496.7	14.1	0.1	22.5	63.2	11.1	29.6	22.6	10.8	44.8	3.9	1.0	39.4
East Timor	2001	237.0[1]	...	...	...	...	...	...	...	...	...	...	...	...
Ecuador	2003	6,534.4	10.7	0.3	10.2	78.7	16.9	37.1	24.8	12.8	21.4	4.2	4.6	56.9

sold by the exporter, including the cost of transportation and insurance to bring the goods onto the transporting vehicle at the frontier of the exporting country (f.o.b. [free-on-board] valuation).

The information presented here is obtained by processing detail from the United Nations' *International Trade Statistics Yearbook*, regional and national publications, and the Internet. In some cases where the original data were only available for an alternative trade classification, an approximation has been made of the SITC commodity groupings. For some countries, where the amounts involved are very small, estimates have been made for selected categories.

The notes that follow further define the column headings.
a. Also includes any unallocated commodities.
b. EU of 25 countries (Austria, Belgium, Cyprus (Republic of Cyprus), Czech Republic, Denmark, Estonia, Finland, France, Germany, Greece, Hungary, Ireland, Italy, Latvia, Lithuania, Luxembourg, Malta, The Netherlands, Poland, Portugal, Slovakia, Slovenia, Spain, Sweden, and the United Kingdom).
c. May include value of trade shown as not available (…) in any of the four preceding columns. May include any unspecified areas or countries.
… Not available.
— None, less than 0.05%, or not applicable.

Detail may not add to 100.0 or indicated subtotals because of rounding.

SITC category codes

0	Food and live animals
1	Beverages and tobacco
2	Crude materials, inedible, except fuels
27	Crude fertilizers, excluding chemical fertilizers, and crude minerals (excluding coal, petroleum, and precious stones)
28	Metalliferous ores and metal scrap
3	Mineral fuels, lubricants, and related materials (includes coal, petroleum, natural gas, electric current, etc.)
4	Animal and vegetable oils, fats and waxes
5	Chemicals and related products not elsewhere specified
6	Manufactured goods classified chiefly by material
667	Pearls, precious and semiprecious stones, unworked or worked
7	Machinery and transport equipment
8	Miscellaneous manufactured articles
9	Commodities and transactions not classified elsewhere in SITC

exports total value ('000,000 U.S.$)	food and agricultural raw materials (0 + 1 + 2 − 27 − 28 + 4)	mineral ores and concentrates (27 + 28 + 667)	fuels and other energy (3)	manufactured goods total[a] (5 + 6 − 667 + 7 + 8 + 9)	of which chemicals and related products (5)	of which machinery and transport equipment (7)	of which other[a] (6 − 667 + 8 + 9)	to European Union (EU)[b]	to United States	to Japan	to China	to all other[c]	country
89.3[1]	——25.0[1,2,3]——		…	75.0[1,2,4]	…	…	…	25.4[1]	0.7[1]	0.2[1]	0.2[1]	73.5[1]	Afghanistan
313.3	10.4	2.4	0.8	86.5	0.5	3.0	83.0	92.5	1.7	—	—	5.7	Albania
22,031.3	0.2	0.2	98.1	1.5	0.7	0.2	0.6	63.2	15.5	0.1	—	21.1	Algeria
346.3	100.0[1]	—	—	…	…	…	…	…	99.6	…	…	0.4	American Samoa
63.2	4.8	2.0	—	93.2	7.3	40.6	45.3	95.0	0.9	0.2	—	3.9	Andorra
6,379.8	0.3[8]	3.2[8]	96.5[8]	—[8]	—[8]	—[8]	—[8]	25.7[1]	46.7[1]	0.3[1]	10.3[1]	17.0[1]	Angola
15.0	8.4	2.3	0.6	88.7	11.5	39.6	37.6	30.4	21.1	0.2	—	48.3	Antigua and Barbuda
25,709.3	47.2	2.4	17.0	33.4	7.8	10.3	15.3	20.5	11.5	1.6	4.2	62.1	Argentina
667.9	12.6	47.6	2.0	37.9	0.4	3.5	33.9	38.7	8.2	—	0.7	52.4	Armenia
29.4[9]	35.2	16.4	…	48.3	2.4	19.0	26.9	12.4	45.9	—	—	41.7	Aruba
66,365.5	26.0	12.3	20.3	41.4	4.2	11.6	25.6	10.1	8.3	15.2	5.5	60.9	Australia
67,681.7	8.5	0.6	2.4	88.5	9.6	42.8	36.1	73.6	5.1	1.2	1.1	18.9	Austria
2,591.7	6.3	1.3	86.0	6.3	2.0	1.4	3.0	67.4	2.5	0.8	0.7	28.7	Azerbaijan
375.9	34.0	5.7	18.3	42.0	26.0	12.0	4.0	17.8	77.5	0.2	—	4.4	Bahamas, The
5,544.7	0.7	4.6	65.8	28.9	2.4	0.7	25.8	2.4	8.1	1.1	0.6	87.7[10]	Bahrain
5,681.8	8.2	—	0.2	91.7	1.3	0.9	89.5	45.2	39.0	1.8	0.2	13.9	Bangladesh
215.5	34.9	0.2	12.2	52.6	14.5	12.5	25.6	17.5	16.5	0.1	0.2	65.8	Barbados
9,964.3	12.2	0.7	22.0	65.2	11.9	22.8	30.6	35.8	1.0	—	1.6	61.5[12]	Belarus
190,308.8	10.6	6.8	4.0	78.6	21.0	31.2	26.4	77.7	5.6	1.0	0.8	14.9	Belgium
200.2	83.0	—	2.0	14.9	0.3	1.3	13.2	34.6	54.7	1.8	—	8.9	Belize
181.8[13]	88.4	0.1	—	11.5	0.8	1.0	9.7	18.2	0.1	0.1	0.2	81.4	Benin
62.9	1.5	—	—	98.5	—	—	98.5	6.3	49.7	—	—	44.1	Bermuda
116.0	15.0	3.1	41.9[15]	39.9	11.5	0.3	28.2	0.1	0.5	0.1	—	99.3[16]	Bhutan
1,371.6	34.0	14.8	25.0	26.3	0.9	3.0	22.5	7.1	14.1	0.4	0.6	77.8	Bolivia
1,027.5	18.4	3.0	6.1	72.4	2.3	17.5	52.7	53.1	0.9	—	—	46.0	Bosnia and Herzegovina
2,532.9	3.6	89.3	0.1	7.0	1.3	2.9	2.8	86.7	0.2	—	—	13.1	Botswana
60,361.8	31.8	6.3	4.9	57.0	6.0	24.4	26.6	25.5	25.7	3.5	4.2	41.1	Brazil
2,306.8	0.1	0.1	88.6	11.3	0.1	4.8	6.4	2.0	9.1	53.1	—	35.7	Brunei
5,113.9	12.0	2.3	9.0	76.7	9.1	11.0	56.7	58.2	5.6	0.3	0.2	35.8	Bulgaria
188.2	77.0	—	2.9	20.1	1.3	6.0	12.8	36.1	0.6	2.2	—	61.1	Burkina Faso
42.2	75.5	8.8	—	15.8	—	—	15.7	48.8	0.1	—	—	51.1	Burundi
796.1	88.9[18,20]	…	…	…	…	…	…	16.5	36.8	1.0	5.3	40.5	Cambodia
1,749.4	38.1	—	51.9	10.0	0.6	0.3	9.1	69.7	2.1	0.1	5.9	22.2	Cameroon
252,418.4	12.9	1.7	12.6	72.8	6.1	38.1	28.7	4.5	87.2	2.1	1.0	5.2	Canada
9.8[20]	3.5	—	—	96.5	0.3	2.2	94.0	80.6	17.7	—	—	1.7	Cape Verde
115.1	25.4	60.1	0.2	14.3	—	7.5	6.8	95.1	—	—	—	4.8	Central African Republic
251.6	88.2[21]	—[21]	—[21]	11.9[21]	6.5[21]	3.1[21]	2.3[21]	77.4[1]	2.4[1]	2.4[1]	1.0[1]	16.7[1]	Chad
17,423.1	37.7	13.3	1.2	47.8	6.2	2.5	39.1	24.4	20.0	11.1	7.0	37.5	Chile
325,595.9	5.8	0.7	2.6	91.0	4.7	39.0	47.3	16.1	21.5	14.9	—	47.5	China
11,897.5	24.5	1.1	35.9	38.4	11.2	5.6	21.7	13.8	44.8	1.6	0.2	39.5	Colombia
6.9	88.8	—	—	11.2	5.9	2.1	3.2	59.0	16.5	—	—	24.5	Comoros
1,415.0	13.1[21]	58.5[3,21]	11.1[21]	17.3[4,21]	0.2[21]	1.2[21]	15.9[4,21]	75.6[1]	10.7[1]	2.0[1]	0.8[1]	10.9[1]	Congo, Dem. Rep. of the
2,272.0	9.3[23]	0.3[23]	87.6[23]	2.7[23]	—[23]	0.4[23]	2.3[23]	21.1	8.4	3.3	9.3	57.9	Congo, Rep. of the
4,950.4	34.7	0.2	1.0	64.1	7.2	28.5	28.4	17.7	50.7	0.6	0.7	30.3	Costa Rica
3,627.9	63.6	0.2	20.3	15.9	4.2	1.0	10.7	45.8	8.3	0.2	0.1	45.6	Côte d'Ivoire
6,164.2	16.4	1.2	9.6	72.7	9.6	29.2	33.9	67.8	2.7	1.2	0.1	28.3	Croatia
1,660.6	59.4	29.1	1.5	10.1	3.2	1.1	5.8	41.1	—	1.7	4.3	52.9	Cuba
837.3	30.5	2.0	8.1	59.4	11.8	27.3	20.3	52.8	2.3	0.2	0.1	44.6	Cyprus[24]
33,384.2	5.8	0.7	3.0	90.4	6.4	47.4	36.6	85.4	3.0	0.4	0.5	10.8	Czech Republic
55,685.5	22.3	0.5	6.2	71.0	12.2	29.4	29.4	64.1	5.9	2.6	0.9	26.5	Denmark
151.1[1]	26.6[21,25]	0.1[21,25]	0.2[21,25]	73.1[21,25]	0.2[21,25]	7.9[21,25]	65.0[21,25]	24.8[1]	0.1[1]	—[1]	—[1]	75.1[1,26]	Djibouti
41.9	39.1	3.5	—	57.4	51.4	4.7	1.4	29.3	9.2	—	—	61.6	Dominica
814.3	42.4	1.4	15.8	40.4	6.6	1.4	32.4	18.8	40.2	1.2	—	39.7	Dominican Republic
8.0	…	…	…	…	…	…	…	…	…	…	…	…	East Timor
6,038.5	46.3	—	43.2	10.5	1.9	3.1	5.4	17.5	40.6	1.4	0.2	40.2	Ecuador

Trade: external (continued)

country	year	imports total value ('000,000 U.S.$)	Standard International Trade Classification (SITC) categories (%)							direction of trade (%)				
			food and agricultural raw materials (0 + 1 + 2 − 27 − 28 + 4)	mineral ores and concentrates (27 + 28 + 667)	fuels and other energy (3)	manufactured goods				from European Union (EU)[b]	from United States	from Japan	from China	from all other[c]
						total[a] (5 + 6 − 667 + 7 + 8 + 9)	of which chemicals and related products (5)	of which machinery and transport equipment (7)	of which other[a] (6 − 667 + 8 + 9)					
Egypt	2002	10,386.9	18.1	2.7	4.8	74.4	14.8	24.1	35.5	31.7	8.4	3.2	5.2	51.4
El Salvador	2002	3,907.3	20.2	0.3	12.9	66.6	15.9	23.3	27.4	7.9	33.6	3.5	2.8	52.2
Equatorial Guinea	2002	410.0	13.5[27]	3.4[27]	7.7[27]	75.4[27]	3.9[27]	58.2[27]	13.3[27]	55.2[1]	29.2[1]	0.4[1]	0.8[1]	14.4[1]
Eritrea	1998	526.8	——— 21.8[3] ———		1.5	76.7[4]	5.7	38.3	32.7[4]	32.3[29]	4.2	4.0	0.6	58.9
Estonia	2002	5,863.3	14.4	0.9	7.2	77.5	9.9	38.1	29.5	63.1	2.8	3.8	4.6	25.6
Ethiopia	2002	1,593.8	12.2	0.7	12.4	74.7	13.0	32.3	29.4	30.9	7.9	7.1	9.1	45.0
Faroe Islands	1999	477.5	22.7	0.4	8.1	68.8	7.0	36.6	25.2	55.3	1.3	2.4	1.3	39.8
Fiji	2003	1,068.6	18.6	0.3	12.2	68.9	8.1	27.9	32.9	2.2	9.2	5.4	3.1	80.2
Finland	2002	33,440.0	8.8	3.4	11.5	76.3	11.7	39.8	24.8	59.4	6.6	4.4	3.5	26.2
France[30]	2003	362,398.4	10.5	0.9	9.6	79.0	13.6	36.9	28.6	62.7	6.5	3.2	4.1	23.4
French Guiana	1995	783.3	18.8	0.1	5.3	75.8	8.0	42.2	25.6	77.0	3.3	1.4	0.6	17.6
French Polynesia	2003	1,306.4	18.7	0.1	6.3	74.8	7.5	43.3	24.0	55.3	8.9	3.1	3.7	29.0
Gabon	2000	956.1	19.0	0.3	4.1	76.6	8.6	47.9	20.1	59.7	11.1	—	0.7	28.5
Gambia, The	2000	189.4	35.2	0.2	11.9	52.7	5.6	21.9	25.2	53.1	4.0	2.7	7.5	32.7
Gaza Strip[31]	1994	339.3	…	…	…	…	…	…	…	…	…	…	…	100.0[32]
Georgia	2001	678.7	19.7	0.5	22.8	57.0	11.1	25.6	20.3	30.8	4.1	0.4	0.6	64.1
Germany	2003	601,761.1	8.9	1.1	8.6	81.3	10.5	37.2	33.6	60.0	7.0	3.6	4.7	24.8
Ghana	2000	2,933.2	15.1	2.4	21.4	61.0	9.8	30.4	20.8	43.3	7.5	1.8	3.2	44.3
Greece	2001	28,184.0	13.4	0.7	15.2	70.8	12.3	31.6	26.9	56.5	3.5	3.0	3.0	34.0
Greenland	2001	303.3	19.3	0.5	16.7	63.5	4.2	24.9	34.4	63.0	0.1	0.1	—	36.8
Grenada	2002	198.8	24.0	0.3	10.0	65.7	8.0	25.0	32.8	13.3	43.6	3.2	1.1	38.7
Guadeloupe	1995	1,901.3	22.6	0.3	5.8	71.3	9.5	32.0	29.8	78.1	3.3	2.2	0.8	15.6
Guam	2001	575.2	16.9[34]	0.1[34]	46.9[34]	36.2[34]	2.3[34]	19.1[34]	14.8[34]	1.3[1]	0.2[1]	22.6	—	75.9[1]
Guatemala	2002	6,074.5	14.6	0.4	12.7	72.3	17.0	30.1	25.2	11.0	36.2	5.6	3.3	43.9
Guernsey[35]	1998	…	…	…	…	…	…	…	…	…	…	…	…	…
Guinea	2001	600.8	24.6	0.2	18.6	56.6	11.5	24.9	20.1	49.2	7.1	3.9	5.4	34.5
Guinea-Bissau	2002	112.0	44.1[23]	0.1[23]	16.2[23]	39.7[23]	4.9[23]	22.9[23]	11.8[23]	37.8[1]	2.4[1]	1.2	3.8[1]	54.9[1]
Guyana	2002	564.5	16.2	0.2	22.2	61.4	12.0	24.1	25.3	13.5	34.7	4.0	3.4	44.5
Haiti	2002	1,181.0	——— 40.2[3, 36] ———		10.6[36]	49.3[4, 36]	7.3[36]	15.8[36]	26.1[4, 36]	9.9[1]	54.2[1]	0.2	2.2[1]	33.5[1]
Honduras	2002	3,105.3	16.8	0.2	12.9	70.1	17.2	28.3	24.6	6.3	39.0	5.4	0.6	48.7
Hong Kong	2003	233,193.9	4.6	2.6	2.0	90.8	5.8	48.2	36.8	8.5	5.5	11.8	43.3	30.9
Hungary	2002	37,611.6	4.5	0.3	7.4	87.8	9.1	51.6	27.1	63.7	3.7	4.2	5.5	22.9
Iceland	2003	2,792.9	12.2	3.9	7.8	76.1	10.4	35.3	30.4	63.8	7.5	3.8	3.6	21.4
India	2002	61,118.1	8.3	12.3	32.0	47.4	9.2	18.9	19.3	20.8	7.3	3.0	4.5	64.4
Indonesia	2002	31,288.8	16.8	1.7	21.0	60.5	16.9	27.5	16.2	12.6	8.5	14.1	7.8	57.1
Iran	2002	20,335.7	11.7	0.9	2.7	84.8	11.3	47.9	25.6	41.7	0.3	3.5	4.7	49.8
Iraq	2002	5,529.0	——— 31.5[3, 27] ———		0.4[27]	68.1[4, 27]	8.8[27]	30.3[27]	28.9[4, 27]	34.1[1]	0.6[1]	6.0	8.4[1]	50.9[1]
Ireland	2002	52,203.6	8.1	0.6	3.2	88.1	12.6	50.6	24.8	59.7	15.3	3.6	2.7	18.7
Isle of Man[35]	…	…	…	…	…	…	…	…	…	…	…	…	…	…
Israel	2002	33,105.9	7.0	22.1	9.4	61.4	9.8	31.5	20.2	41.7	18.5	2.4	2.4	35.0
Italy[38]	2002	242,744.0	12.4	1.5	9.0	77.1	12.9	33.3	30.8	59.8	4.8	2.1	3.2	30.1
Jamaica	2002	3,543.1	16.7	0.2	17.7	65.4	10.2	29.4	25.8	11.7	43.1	6.1	1.7	37.4
Japan	2003	383,452.0	15.2	3.1	21.2	60.5	7.7	27.6	25.3	13.1	15.6	—	19.7	51.6
Jersey	1980	537.1	23.9	0.4	9.3	66.5	6.5	24.8	35.2	84.9[39]	…	…	…	15.1
Jordan	2003	5,653.2	19.3	0.6	16.5	63.6	11.1	23.0	29.5	26.5	6.4	3.5	8.0	55.5
Kazakhstan	2001	6,355.9	8.9	1.8	12.6	76.7	11.4	38.2	27.1	26.6	5.4	2.2	2.8	63.0
Kenya	2002	3,074.6	14.4	0.2	16.7	68.6	16.2	31.8	20.7	33.4	6.9	6.2	2.4	51.1
Kiribati	1999	41.0	39.5	0.2	10.4	49.9	4.5	22.8	22.6	0.5	4.5	14.9	4.4	75.8
Korea, North	2002	2,179.0[1]	…	…	…	…	…	…	…	14.6[1]	1.3[1]	6.6	23.6[1]	54.0[1]
Korea, South	2002	149,572.3	8.9	2.9	21.3	66.9	9.3	34.9	22.7	11.5	15.3	19.7	11.6	41.8
Kuwait	1999	7,616.7	17.8	1.0	0.6	80.6	8.7	39.7	32.2	31.3	12.3	12.8	3.2	40.4
Kyrgyzstan	2002	579.4	15.2	2.1	26.2	56.5	13.8	21.2	21.6	14.9	8.2	1.1	10.2	65.6
Laos	2000	610.9	——— 36.8[3, 23] ———		6.1[23]	57.1[4, 23]	…	29.3[23]	27.8[4, 23]	7.1[1]	—	4.5	4.7	83.7
Latvia	2003	5,244.0	14.4	1.2	9.4	75.0	12.4	31.0	31.7	75.4	1.7	0.2	1.3	21.4
Lebanon	2001	7,290.3	18.7	1.6	17.7	62.0	9.9	23.6	28.5	43.7	7.1	3.2	5.6	40.4
Lesotho	2001	598.2	28.0	0.6	6.0	65.4	9.7	12.1	43.6	0.3	0.3	0.2	0.5	98.8[41]
Liberia	2002	4,614.0	——— 36.5[3, 43] ———		24.2[43]	39.2[4, 43]	7.1[43]	18.6[43]	13.6[4, 43]	32.1[1]	0.7[1]	17.9	0.7[1]	48.6[1]
Libya	1998	5,691.8	28.4	0.4	0.3	71.0	7.4	33.3	30.4	58.6	1.4	4.2	1.4	34.4
Liechtenstein	2002	872.9	3.9[1]	0.5[1, 3]	1.2[1]	94.4[1]	5.0[1]	46.0[1]	43.3[1, 4]	87.2[1]	3.3	0.8	0.6	8.2[1]
Lithuania	2001	6,352.8	12.1	0.9	20.3	66.7	12.2	28.2	26.3	63.6	1.9	0.1	0.7	33.6
Luxembourg	2001	10,942.5	10.9	4.3	5.6	79.2	9.8	39.2	30.2	87.8	6.1	1.1	0.4	4.6
Macau	2002	2,530.8	14.5	0.1	7.2	78.1	3.5	19.5	55.1	12.0	4.1	6.7	41.7	35.4
Macedonia	2003	2,299.9	15.7	0.8	14.0	69.5	11.1	18.8	39.6	53.1	2.5	0.8	2.1	41.5
Madagascar	1999	505.3	14.3	0.1	24.2	61.4	11.5	26.9	23.1	32.4	3.0	5.1	6.7	52.9
Malawi	2001	561.6	13.3	0.3	16.8	69.6	13.3	29.1	27.2	15.0	3.6	3.4	2.7	75.3
Malaysia	2002	79,359.4	6.5	0.9	4.8	87.9	7.1	61.5	19.2	11.7	16.9	18.0	7.8	45.5
Maldives	2003	470.8	23.2	1.8	11.8	63.3	5.4	27.2	30.6	11.2	1.3	2.2	0.6	84.7
Mali	1997	680.8	20.0	0.1	20.9	59.0	17.4	21.5	20.1	36.0	3.5	3.0	3.5	53.9
Malta	2001	2,726.8	11.6	0.3	8.3	79.8	7.3	49.4	23.1	64.4	11.6	2.1	2.0	19.9
Marshall Islands	2000	68.2	——— 19.4[3] ———		43.5	37.1[4]	—	16.9	20.2[4]	—	61.4	5.1	1.3	32.2
Martinique	1995	1,969.8	20.4	0.2	7.5	71.9	10.3	32.4	29.2	77.0	2.9	2.2	0.6	17.4
Mauritania	1996	426.7	26.9	0.1	29.3	43.8	3.0	24.8	15.9	64.6	0.3	0.8	5.6	28.7
Mauritius	2003	2,360.0	19.4	2.2	10.9	67.5	8.7	22.4	36.4	28.8	2.6	3.5	8.4	56.7
Mayotte	1997	141.1	——— 28.8[1, 3] ———		5.0	71.2[1, 4]	7.7	30.8	32.7[1, 4]	66.0[44]	…	…	…	34.0
Mexico	2002	168,650.5	7.5	0.7	2.6	89.2	9.8	51.1	28.2	10.0	63.4	5.5	3.7	17.4
Micronesia	1998	49.4	——— 37.3[3] ———		8.9	53.8[4]	3.6	20.0	30.2[4]	…	45.7	14.0	—	40.4
Moldova	2003	1,398.6	17.7	0.4	20.5	61.4	11.9	19.7	29.8	36.0	2.5	0.8	1.5	59.2
Monaco[30]	…	…	…	…	…	…	…	…	…	…	…	…	…	…
Mongolia	2001	630.1	18.6	0.3	22.1	59.0	5.5	29.3	24.3	12.7	2.3	8.8	19.0	57.2
Morocco	2002	11,878.2	17.3	1.3	15.5	65.9	9.8	25.6	30.5	57.5	4.3	1.7	2.9	33.6
Mozambique	2001	1,063.4	14.6	0.8	15.9	68.6	6.4	21.9	40.3	17.3	1.8	0.6	2.0	78.2
Myanmar (Burma)	1999	2,587.4	——— 8.7[3, 6] ———		4.46	86.9[4, 6]	8.6[6]	27.0[6]	51.3[4, 6]	3.1	3.5	11.1	9.6	72.6
Namibia	2001	1,552.9	13.7	2.0	10.3	73.9	10.7	34.4	28.8	6.1	0.9	0.1	1.1	91.8[45]
Nauru	2001	27.4	87.8[8]	…[8]	…[8]	12.2[8]	…[8]	2.8[8]	9.3[8]	9.1[1]	16.9	0.6	1.6	71.8[1]
Nepal	2000	1,557.9	15.4	1.3	15.2	68.2	10.7	17.2	40.3	7.4	1.5	2.6	7.5	80.9

exports								direction of trade (%)					country
total value ('000,000 U.S.$)	Standard International Trade Classification (SITC) categories (%)							to European Union (EU)[b]	to United States	to Japan	to China	to all other[c]	
	food and agricultural raw materials (0 + 1 + 2 − 27 − 28 + 4)	mineral ores and concentrates (27 + 28 + 667)	fuels and other energy (3)	manufactured goods									
				total[a] (5 + 6 − 667 + 7 + 8 + 9)	of which chemicals and related products (5)	of which machinery and transport equipment (7)	of which other[a] (6 − 667 + 8 + 9)						
4,009.3	2.9	2.4	39.2	55.5	7.6	1.7	46.2	28.8	8.7	1.3	4.9	56.2	Egypt
1,233.8	33.5	0.5	5.2	60.8	14.7	4.6	41.5	6.3	20.3	0.5	0.6	72.3	El Salvador
1,863.0	48.6[27]	—[27]	—[27]	51.4[27]	0.1[27]	39.8[27,28]	11.5[27]	34.7[1]	27.0[1]	2.5	16.6[1]	19.1[1]	Equatorial Guinea
27.9	——75.1[3]——		...	24.9[4]	2.1	2.4	20.4[4]	10.0[29]	2.0	13.2	—	74.8	Eritrea
4,336.3	20.5	1.6	5.3	72.7	5.6	27.6	39.5	72.1	2.2	0.6	0.5	24.6	Estonia
415.0	83.6	1.3	—	15.0	0.1	0.1	14.9	37.2	4.0	9.0	1.8	48.0	Ethiopia
477.9	94.7	—	—	5.3	0.1	3.8	1.4	83.8	4.6	1.2	0.1	10.2	Faroe Islands
494.4	51.7	0.2	—	48.1	1.4	0.6	46.2	22.2	24.5	4.5	0.8	47.9	Fiji
44,517.7	8.2	0.4	3.3	88.0	7.0	43.6	37.4	58.8	8.7	2.0	2.5	28.0	Finland
357,881.2	12.9	0.7	2.6	83.8	16.9	42.8	24.1	66.3	6.9	1.7	1.4	23.7	France[30]
158.2	33.6	0.1	0.2	66.1	1.4	33.0	31.7	77.5	1.0	—	—	21.5	French Guiana
125.2	16.7	64.8	—	18.5	1.6	12.5	4.5	16.2	14.6	30.3	0.7	38.3	French Polynesia
2,600.2	12.7	1.7	83.3	2.3	0.1	0.4	1.9	7.5	62.6	—	6.7	23.2	Gabon
16.2	82.0	—	0.1	17.9	9.6	4.7	3.5	32.4	1.8	0.2	0.1	65.5	Gambia, The
49.4	...	...	...	...	...	...	...	...	...	...	...	100.0[33]	Gaza Strip[31]
320.0	27.6	25.1	8.6	38.7	6.1	18.1	14.5	19.8	3.0	0.3	0.3	76.6	Georgia
748,531.3	5.1	0.6	1.5	92.8	12.9	50.3	29.6	62.7	9.2	1.8	2.7	23.6	Germany
1,670.9	37.2	2.8	4.9	55.1	0.6	1.2	53.3	47.3	5.9	1.4	1.7	43.8	Ghana
10,302.9	27.0	1.8	11.1	60.0	9.0	11.5	39.6	51.5	5.5	0.6	0.4	41.9	Greece
277.0	88.7	—	—	11.3	—	3.1	8.2	85.9	5.8	3.5	0.1	4.8	Greenland
38.3	65.3	—	0.1	34.7	8.0	14.2	12.5	35.7	29.3	0.6	—	34.4	Grenada
162.0	52.3	0.6	—	47.0	1.1	36.5	9.4	77.0	3.4	—	—	19.6	Guadeloupe
55.6	——69.5[3,21]——		0.7[21]	29.7[4,21]	0.7[21]	3.8[21]	25.2[4,21]	0.7[1]	1.3[1]	89.3	—	8.7[1]	Guam
2,277.5	57.4	0.3	6.9	35.4	14.7	3.5	17.2	5.5	30.3	1.3	—	62.9	Guatemala
93.0[1]	...	...	...	...	...	...	...	...	...	...	...	...	Guernsey[35]
574.9	2.1	53.9	0.8	43.2	17.2	2.1	24.0	64.1	16.9	—	—	19.1	Guinea
117.0	88.2[23]	0.1[23]	4.6[23]	7.2[23]	—[23]	6.6[23]	0.6[23]	5.9[1]	—[1]	—	—[1]	94.1[1]	Guinea-Bissau
446.5	52.2	11.3	—	36.6	1.0	2.3	33.2	25.2	25.5	0.2	0.4	48.7	Guyana
286.0	15.1	0.7	—	84.2	5.6	3.1	75.5	4.3[1]	83.9[1]	0.1	—[1]	11.7[1]	Haiti
1,248.3	53.5	4.4	—	42.0	4.8	2.4	34.9	14.6	54.8	1.4	0.1	29.1	Honduras
228,654.3	2.1	1.6	0.2	96.1	4.7	46.1	45.3	14.1	18.2	5.3	41.7	20.6	Hong Kong
34,336.6	8.2	0.4	1.5	89.9	6.2	58.6	25.1	81.8	3.5	0.6	0.5	13.7	Hungary
2,352.2	65.1	0.5	0.2	34.1	3.6	4.0	26.6	73.8	9.5	3.2	0.7	12.8	Iceland
52,471.4	13.4	17.6	5.1	63.8	11.2	8.4	44.2	22.5	20.7	3.5	3.7	49.5	India
57,158.7	15.8	3.6	24.3	56.3	5.2	17.1	34.0	14.3	13.2	21.1	5.1	46.3	Indonesia
28,355.8	4.1	0.3	86.5	9.1	2.0	0.7	6.4	36.2[37]	—[37]	16.5[37]	3.7[37]	43.6[37]	Iran
8,257.0	0.8[27]	0.3[1,27]	96.8[27]	2.1[1,27]	1.2[27]	0.2[27]	0.7[1,27]	29.1[1]	41.8[1]	1.2	1.1[1]	26.9[1]	Iraq
88,483.2	7.7	0.5	0.4	91.5	41.9	35.1	14.5	64.7	17.6	2.8	0.6	14.3	Ireland
...	...	...	...	...	...	...	...	...	...	...	...	...	Isle of Man[35]
29,511.4	5.4	35.8	0.4	58.5	13.7	28.7	16.1	26.3	40.2	2.2	1.4	29.8	Israel
251,003.2	7.4	0.3	1.8	90.5	10.4	37.5	42.6	58.2	9.7	1.7	1.5	28.9	Italy[38]
1,104.1	22.8	64.7	2.6	9.9	5.4	1.0	3.5	30.5	28.3	2.6	4.0	34.6	Jamaica
471,995.9	1.0	0.5	0.3	98.2	8.3	66.8	23.1	16.0	24.9	—	12.2	46.9	Japan
209.2	27.6	4.3[40]	—	68.0	1.2	31.1	35.7	67.3[39]	...	...	...	32.7	Jersey
3,081.6	14.4	11.8	0.2	73.5	19.9	10.7	42.9	3.4	21.5	0.5	1.2	73.5	Jordan
8,619.6	6.6	6.4	55.2	31.7	2.7	2.3	26.7	26.4	1.8	0.2	7.6	64.0	Kazakhstan
1,400.4	42.7	2.2	30.7	24.4	2.8	5.4	16.3	29.2	1.4	0.6	0.3	68.5	Kenya
9.1	92.6	0.1	—	7.3	—	—	7.3	10.3	13.4	1.5	—	74.8	Kiribati
1,028.0[1]	...	...	...	...	...	...	...	9.2[1]	—[1]	20.3	23.9[1]	46.5[1]	Korea, North
160,854.8	2.4	0.1	4.1	93.4	8.4	61.5	23.5	14.7	7.9	9.4	14.8	53.3	Korea, South
12,140.1	0.5	0.3	90.6	8.6	5.8	1.3	1.5	12.0[1]	11.6[1]	22.9[1]	1.1[1]	52.3[1]	Kuwait
460.3	26.4	2.9	12.6	58.1	1.6	10.6	45.8	5.4	6.3	—	8.7	79.6	Kyrgyzstan
186.1	——35.4[3,23]——		7.0[23]	57.5[4,23]	...	5.1[23]	52.4[4,23]	48.2[1]	4.7	6.3	3.6	37.2	Laos
2,893.7	35.9	1.1	1.4	61.6	6.1	9.1	46.4	79.3	2.9	0.9	0.6	16.4	Latvia
889.3	23.7	4.6	0.2	71.5	11.2	13.9	46.3	22.9	6.8	0.6	0.3	69.4	Lebanon
279.6	17.3	0.1	—	82.7	0.5	10.9	71.3	7.9	33.4	—	—	58.8[42]	Lesotho
1,044.0	——99.3[3,43]——		—[43]	0.7[4,43]	—[43]	—[43]	0.7[4,43]	81.7[1]	4.1[1]	—	4.8[1]	9.3[1]	Liberia
6,131.4	0.7	—	92.6	6.7	4.2	0.1	2.3	82.4	—	—	—	17.5	Libya
1,805.2	6.4[1]	0.4[1,3]	0.1[1]	93.1[1,4]	10.2[1]	59.4[1]	23.5[1,4]	63.0[1]	1.6	0.4	0.8	34.2[1]	Liechtenstein
4,583.0	16.6	1.5	23.1	58.7	7.5	19.9	31.4	70.9	3.8	0.4	—	24.9	Lithuania
8,387.0	7.1	0.5	0.1	92.3	6.0	29.7	56.6	85.6	3.5	0.6	0.6	9.7	Luxembourg
2,356.8	2.2	—	1.2	96.6	1.0	4.2	91.4	23.3	48.4	0.6	15.6	12.2	Macau
1,363.2	18.0	1.7	5.4	74.9	5.1	5.9	63.8	56.8	5.3	0.4	1.1	36.3	Macedonia
232.8	42.5	10.3	2.4	44.8	2.9	0.8	41.0	57.5	5.4	1.4	1.4	34.3	Madagascar
449.4	87.5	0.3	0.1	12.1	0.6	2.8	8.8	31.6	14.4	4.8	0.4	48.9	Malawi
93,281.3	9.8	0.1	8.7	81.4	4.7	59.8	16.9	12.8	20.2	11.2	5.6	50.2	Malaysia
113.0	67.7	0.3	—	32.0	—	—	32.0	15.6	32.3	10.3	—	41.7	Maldives
302.4	92.3	0.1	0.6	7.0	0.1	0.7	6.1	2.5	—	—	—	97.5	Mali
1,958.8	4.0	0.2	5.5	90.4	2.3	63.2	24.9	42.7	19.8	3.0	0.1	34.4	Malta
8.1	——98.7[3,36]——		—[36]	1.3[4,36]	—[36]	—[36]	1.3[4,36]	—[1]	71.0[1]	—[1]	—[1]	29.0[1]	Marshall Islands
241.9	62.3	1.0	17.8	18.9	2.1	13.0	3.8	78.0	2.6	—	—	19.3	Martinique
517.4	51.7	41.5	4.6	2.1	—	0.9	1.1	51.5	1.1	20.6	0.1	26.7	Mauritania
1,838.7	26.1	2.5	—	71.4	1.8	4.3	65.3	66.1	17.5	0.9	0.4	15.1	Mauritius
3.5	21.3[6,20]	—[6,20]	—[6,20]	78.7[6,20]	78.7[6,20]	—[6,20]	—[6,20]	80.0[44]	...	...	...	20.0	Mayotte
160,669.9	5.6	0.4	8.9	85.1	3.5	59.0	22.6	3.3	89.1	0.3	0.3	7.1	Mexico
3.3	——93.2[3]——		—	6.8[4]	...	...	6.8[4]	...	...	94.6	...	5.4	Micronesia
790.3	63.3	2.7	0.6	33.5	1.2	5.2	27.0	26.7	4.3	—	—	69.0	Moldova
...	...	...	...	...	...	...	...	...	...	...	...	...	Monaco[30]
448.5	24.9	39.1	0.9	35.1	0.7	1.0	33.4	9.1	21.3	3.5	51.6	14.4	Mongolia
7,850.3	23.0	6.7	3.7	66.6	11.2	12.6	42.8	73.8	3.1	3.6	0.3	19.2	Morocco
703.1	27.0	0.4	9.5	63.1	0.3	2.5	60.3	9.4	1.0	4.2	0.2	85.3	Mozambique
1,129.7	——77.2[3,6]——		0.5[6]	22.2[4,6]	—[6]	1.1[6]	21.1[4,6]	5.9	7.9	5.1	11.9	69.1	Myanmar (Burma)
1,404.5	37.1	40.4	0.7	21.8	0.5	3.9	17.5	55.5	3.0	0.7	0.5	40.4	Namibia
8.9	—[8]	100.0[8]	—[8]	—[8]	—[8]	—[8]	—[8]	1.3[1]	—[1]	6.9[1]	...[1]	91.7[1]	Nauru
708.8	10.4	0.2	—	89.4	8.5	0.5	80.4	22.7	27.1	1.4	—	48.8	Nepal

Trade: external   (continued)

country	year	imports											
		total value ('000,000 U.S.$)	Standard International Trade Classification (SITC) categories (%)							direction of trade (%)				
			food and agricultural raw materials (0 + 1 + 2 − 27 − 28 + 4)	mineral ores and concentrates (27 + 28 + 667)	fuels and other energy (3)	manufactured goods				from European Union (EU)[b]	from United States	from Japan	from China	from all other[c]
						total[a] (5 + 6 − 667 + 7 + 8 + 9)	of which chemicals and related products (5)	of which machinery and transport equipment (7)	of which other[a] (6 − 667 + 8 + 9)					
Netherlands, The	2002	163,367.4	13.6	1.1	11.8	73.4	12.7	36.1	24.7	56.5	9.9	3.4	4.9	25.3
Netherlands Antilles	1998	2,061.9	9.8	0.4	58.5	31.4	4.3	10.3	16.7	13.0	18.8	1.4	0.1	66.7
New Caledonia	2003	1,594.3	12.9	0.3	10.5	76.3	7.7	44.2	24.4	59.9	3.5	2.6	2.7	31.2
New Zealand	2002	15,044.1	9.5	1.7	9.3	79.4	12.1	39.8	27.5	19.5	13.6	12.0	8.0	46.9
Nicaragua	2002	1,802.2	16.2	0.1	13.1	70.6	15.9	26.2	28.6	7.2	27.6	5.1	2.1	57.9
Niger	2001	324.5	45.5	1.7	12.5	40.3	9.1	15.0	16.2	29.2	5.8	4.8	6.4	53.8
Nigeria	2000	5,805.4	20.8	0.6	1.7	76.8	20.2	33.6	22.9	48.4	11.4	4.9	4.3	31.0
Northern Mariana Islands	1997	836.2	— 11.8[3] —		8.2	80.0[4]	2.5	6.0	71.6[1, 4]	—	7.6	14.1	...	78.3
Norway	2002	34,889.4	9.5	4.2	3.5	82.8	9.5	40.5	32.9	70.4	6.2	3.1	5.3	15.1
Oman	2001	5,798.0	22.9	1.7	2.8	72.6	6.4	39.6	26.7	21.5	6.8	15.4	1.7	54.7
Pakistan	2003	13,013.4	16.2	1.4	23.6	58.8	18.2	24.6	16.1	16.9	6.0	6.6	7.3	63.2
Palau	2000	123.9	— 20.3[3] —		12.7	67.0[4]	6.3	27.8	32.9[4]	—	33.0	15.5	0.7	50.7
Panama	2003	3,124.1	15.0	0.2	11.7	73.0	14.1	29.4	29.6	7.4	35.0	6.2	1.5	49.8
Papua New Guinea	2000	1,035.1	19.0	0.6	22.1	58.3	7.1	29.5	21.6	2.4	6.6	11.3	2.0	77.8
Paraguay	2002	1,672.1	13.3	0.7	16.7	69.3	17.7	27.8	23.8	8.7	4.0	0.9	0.8	85.6
Peru	2003	8,469.7	14.3	0.4	17.4	67.9	16.5	28.4	23.0	13.2	18.6	4.4	7.7	56.2
Philippines	2002	35,426.5	8.6	1.1	9.3	81.0	7.5	60.3	13.2	7.9	20.6	20.4	3.5	47.6
Poland	2002	55,085.5	7.9	1.0	9.1	81.9	14.8	37.6	29.5	68.5	3.2	1.9	3.7	22.7
Portugal	2002	39,982.6	14.8	0.6	9.7	75.0	10.9	34.2	29.8	79.7	2.1	1.7	0.8	15.7
Puerto Rico	2003[48]	33,749.7	8.9	0.1	8.0	83.0	46.4	19.1	17.5	29.1	51.5	3.9	1.0	14.5
Qatar	2002	4,052.0	12.7	1.5	0.7	85.1	7.2	46.9	31.0	35.1	13.0	10.5	3.2	38.1
Réunion	1995	2,711.1	21.5	0.2	4.7	73.6	10.7	29.8	33.1	80.1	0.6	2.1	0.9	16.3
Romania	2003	24,003.1	8.3	1.6	10.9	79.2	10.3	29.6	39.4	67.3	2.3	1.2	2.8	26.4
Russia	2003	52,410.1	22.5	2.9	2.4	72.2	13.7	34.6	24.0	50.3	5.7	3.6	6.3	34.2
Rwanda	2002	251.2	19.9	1.5	16.2	62.4	13.6	25.2	23.6	27.8	2.4	2.5	2.0	65.3
St. Kitts and Nevis	2001	189.2	19.4	0.8	7.5	72.3	8.1	27.5	36.8	12.6	50.5	2.5	0.2	34.2
St. Lucia	2002	314.8	25.9	0.7	9.9	63.6	8.4	22.9	32.3	16.9	42.7	3.4	2.4	34.6
St. Vincent and the Grenadines	2003	201.1	24.4	0.3	9.8	65.5	8.8	24.8	31.9	12.8	41.2	3.3	0.9	41.9
Samoa	1999	115.9	— 35.0[3, 6] —		11.8[6]	53.2[4, 6]	—[1, 6]	16.9[1, 6]	36.3[4, 6]	3.2	11.9	14.4	1.2	69.3
San Marino[38]	1999	1,707.0	...	...	...	...	...	...	...	...	...	...	...	...
São Tomé and Príncipe	2003	42.2	39.5	0.2	10.5	49.8	5.5	24.0	20.3	78.2	—	6.3	0.1	15.3
Saudi Arabia	2002	32,333.2	17.0	0.4	0.2	82.3	9.6	43.6	29.0	32.7	16.3	11.1	5.3	34.6
Senegal	2001	1,730.2	28.7	1.2	16.8	53.3	11.2	22.8	19.3	52.1	4.2	2.7	2.4	38.6
Serbia and Montenegro	2000	3,710.6	12.9	2.3	20.1	64.7	15.0	22.1	27.7	49.4	2.0	1.3	2.1	45.1
Seychelles	2002	245.7	25.8	0.2	16.5	57.5	5.6	28.2	23.7	50.8	1.6	0.7	0.4	46.5
Sierra Leone	2002	481.0	— 47.9[3, 23] —		17.4[23]	34.8[4, 23]	7.6[23]	14.7[23]	12.5[4, 23]	63.8[1]	5.8[1]	0.2[1]	3.3[1]	26.9[1]
Singapore	2003	127,381.3	3.7	0.5	13.5	82.2	6.7	58.9	16.6	13.2	14.1	12.0	8.7	52.1
Slovakia	2003	22,171.2	6.2	1.7	12.0	80.1	9.8	41.1	29.2	73.7	1.9	1.9	2.5	20.0
Slovenia	2003	13,849.6	9.0	1.8	7.7	81.5	13.3	34.4	33.7	75.4	2.4	1.5	2.4	18.4
Solomon Islands	1997	182.6	— 18.0[3] —		8.6	73.4[4]	4.9	37.7	30.8[4]	3.1	2.1	14.9	—	79.9
Somalia	2002	354.0	30.3[49]	0.2[49]	4.6[49]	64.9[49]	5.1[49]	37.1[49]	22.7[49]	9.0[1]	1.9[1]	0.1	0.6[1]	88.4[1]
South Africa	2003	33,589.7	6.4	3.5	11.9	78.2	11.0	39.4	27.8	43.4	9.9	7.0	6.4	33.2
Spain	2002	165,919.5	12.0	1.6	10.8	75.5	12.6	38.0	25.0	66.0	4.1	2.4	3.3	24.1
Sri Lanka	2002	6,038.7	15.3	3.9	13.8	67.0	8.8	18.4	39.9	15.1	3.6	5.9	4.3	71.1
Sudan, The	2002	2,492.8	19.6	0.4	4.8	75.2	10.5	37.9	26.8	15.9	0.9	5.4	10.2	67.6
Suriname	2000	526.4	18.5	0.6	6.7	74.2	10.6	36.3	27.3	29.0	26.6	7.8	2.1	34.5
Swaziland	2002	890.7	20.5	0.5	12.7	66.3	11.7	22.6	32.0	2.0	0.2	0.9	1.4	95.5[50]
Sweden	2003	81,817.3	9.6	1.2	9.4	79.8	10.6	39.5	29.7	72.9	3.9	2.2	2.3	18.7
Switzerland[51]	2003	83,382.5	7.5	1.9	4.3	86.3	21.9	30.1	34.2	81.5	5.5	2.1	2.1	8.8
Syria	2002	4,277.5	20.1	0.5	3.0	76.4	13.2	24.1	39.1	29.9	6.9	3.7	5.9	53.5
Taiwan	2002	112,758.0	6.5	1.5	10.3	81.6	12.0	47.5	22.1	10.9	16.1	24.2	7.1	41.7
Tajikistan	2000	644.0	— 11.2[3] —		37.5	51.3[4]	36.4	9.6	5.4[4]	6.4	0.2	—	—	93.4
Tanzania	2003	2,192.9	15.0	0.2	18.5	66.2	12.4	31.9	21.9	19.9	3.2	7.7	5.3	63.9
Thailand	2001	62,057.5	7.8	2.2	12.0	78.0	10.7	45.3	22.0	12.6	11.6	22.4	6.0	47.5
Togo	2002	405.3	23.3	1.3	15.0	60.3	10.5	19.7	30.1	43.7	4.6	1.9	2.9	46.9
Tonga	2000	69.4	35.7	0.6[1]	16.3	47.4[1]	6.1	14.0	27.4[1]	0.4	10.4	5.3	1.7	82.1
Trinidad and Tobago	2001	3,932.1	9.6	0.4	23.4	66.6	7.5	40.2	18.9	18.1	34.4	3.5	1.7	42.3
Tunisia	2002	9,522.5	13.1	1.1	9.3	76.5	9.6	29.5	37.4	71.1	3.2	1.7	1.5	22.6
Turkey	2003	68,734.0	7.6	3.3	16.6	72.5	15.0	31.1	26.5	48.4	5.0	2.8	3.8	40.1
Turkmenistan	2000	1,785.5	12.1	0.4	1.2	86.3	8.9	43.8	33.5	13.0	3.5	8.1	0.9	74.5
Tuvalu	1999	8.1	35.2	0.6	9.2	55.1	4.8	24.7	25.6	1.8	0.3	6.1	1.9	89.9
Uganda	2002	1,073.7	16.6	0.9	16.3	66.2	12.1	26.5	27.6	18.4	3.3	8.1	4.1	66.0
Ukraine	2002	16,975.9	7.7	2.3[3]	39.2	50.8[4]	10.6	20.8	19.5[4]	32.2	2.7	1.1	1.5	62.4
United Arab Emirates	1999	25,911.3	— 33.6[3] —		0.9	65.4[4]	6.6	28.5	30.4[4]	36.2[1]	9.9	9.5	6.2	38.2[1]
United Kingdom[35]	2003	399,478.2	10.4	2.5	4.6	82.5	11.2	43.6	27.8	54.5	9.9	3.4	5.1	27.2
United States[54]	2003	1,305,091.5	5.9	1.5	12.5	80.1	8.0	40.9	31.2	19.9	—	9.3	12.5	58.3
Uruguay	2002	1,964.3	18.8	0.6	15.0	65.6	21.7	20.1	23.8	17.9	8.4	1.4	3.8	68.5
Uzbekistan	1998	3,288.7	19.3[1, 23]	1.3[1, 23]	1.4[23]	78.0[1, 23]	9.0[1, 23]	44.9[23]	24.1[1, 23]	21.9[1]	7.5	0.3	1.5	68.8[1]
Vanuatu	2000	86.7	— 24.0[3] —		15.1	60.9[4]	6.5	28.8	25.6[4]	6.3[1]	1.4	5.1	1.2	86.1
Venezuela	2002	11,673.3	14.0	0.5	2.6	82.9	16.0	43.1	23.7	20.4	32.9	3.7	1.9	41.0
Vietnam	1999	11,742.1	8.8	1.1	9.5	80.6	17.2	29.2	34.2	9.7	2.8	13.8	5.7	68.0
Virgin Islands (U.S.)	2003	5,570.4	...	...	80.3	...	...	...	...	...	10.9	...	...	...
West Bank[31]	1994	102.5[56]	...	...	...	...	...	...	...	...	...	...	...	...
Western Sahara	...	...	...	...	...	...	...	...	...	...	...	...	...	...
Yemen	2000	2,323.7	37.2	0.2	12.0	50.7	9.7	20.8	20.2	18.6	4.4	3.2	3.5	70.3
Zambia	2002	1,252.7	15.6	1.2	7.0	76.2	15.3	31.1	29.8	19.4	1.5	3.2	2.8	73.1
Zimbabwe	2002	2,466.7	13.0	1.3	8.3	77.5	18.7	34.3	24.4	17.0	3.5	2.9	1.9	74.7

[1]Estimate. [2]Year ending March 1996. [3]Excluding precious stones, etc. (667). [4]Including precious stones, etc. (667). [5]Year ending September 30. [6]1996. [7]1991. [8]1994. [9]Excluding mineral fuels; overall totals on a balance of payments basis, f.o.b.: imports U.S.$2,005,200,000, exports U.S.$1,413,500,000. [10]Includes 67.2% for areas unspecified (mainly petroleum and products). [11]Includes 65.7% from Russia. [12]Includes 49.2% to Russia. [13]Excluding reexports, estimated at 51.0% of total exports. [14]Includes 74.7% from India. [15]Mainly electricity. [16]Includes 94.4% to India. [17]Includes 77.5% from South Africa. [18]1993. [19]Main items only. [20]Domestic exports only. [21]1992. [22]1987. [23]1995. [24]Republic of Cyprus. [25]Excludes trade with Ethiopia via rail. [26]Includes 46.1% to Somalia. [27]1990. [28]Includes 38.7% for ships and boats. [29]Main countries only. [30]Figures for France include Monaco. [31]Total external trade for West Bank and Gaza Strip in 2000: imports U.S.$2,382,800,000, exports U.S.$400,900,000. [32]Includes 82.4% from Israel. [33]Includes 69.2% to Israel and 25.1% to Jordan. [34]1983. [35]Figures for United Kingdom include Guernsey, Isle of Man,

total value ('000,000 U.S.$)	food and agricultural raw materials (0+1+2-27-28+4)	mineral ores and concentrates (27+28+667)	fuels and other energy (3)	manufactured goods total[a] (5+6-667+7+8+9)	of which chemicals and related products (5)	of which machinery and transport equipment (7)	of which other[a] (6-667+8+9)	to European Union (EU)[b]	to United States	to Japan	to China	to all other[c]	country
175,385.2	21.3	0.9	7.0	70.8	17.7	32.2	20.9	74.9	5.4	1.1	0.7	17.8	Netherlands, The
1,169.2	4.5	0.5	84.8	10.2	0.8	2.4	7.0	14.6	17.4	0.1	—	68.0	Netherlands Antilles
739.6	4.0	24.7	1.2	70.1	0.2	2.7	67.3	35.8	1.4	21.4	1.3	40.1	New Caledonia
14,382.4	59.5	0.5	1.8	38.3	6.7	9.8	21.8	15.2	15.3	11.5	4.6	53.3	New Zealand
634.8	72.2	0.4	2.0	25.3	2.7	4.4	18.3	10.0	29.1	0.6	—	60.3	Nicaragua
154.0	40.7	56.5	—	2.8	0.2	1.2	1.4	40.4	0.3	16.5	—	42.8	Niger
27,055.2	0.1	—	99.6	0.2	—	0.1	0.1	23.0	42.6	0.4	0.5	33.5	Nigeria
263.0	—	—	—	100.0	—	—	100.0	—	100.0	—	—	—	Northern Mariana Islands
59,574.7	7.3	0.6	60.6	31.4	3.1	11.7	16.6	76.1	8.8	1.8	1.6	11.7	Norway
11,036.6	6.2	0.3	80.5	13.1	0.9	7.7	4.5	2.4	1.3	20.1	11.2	65.0	Oman
11,910.1	12.3	0.2	2.3	85.2	2.4	1.3	81.5	28.8	23.1	1.2	2.2	44.8	Pakistan
11.5	69.1[46]	—[46]	—[46]	30.9[46]	—[46]	—[46]	30.9[46]	—[46]	8.0[46]	58.8[46]	—[46]	33.2[46]	Palau
798.7	84.5	3.0	0.7	11.8	2.9	0.1	8.9	23.9	52.0	0.8	1.5	21.7	Panama
2,407.4	17.7	51.3	28.8	2.3	—	2.0	0.3	4.6	1.6	3.3	0.5	89.9[47]	Papua New Guinea
950.6	84.2	0.5	0.3	15.0	3.1	0.5	11.4	9.1	5.0	3.9	12.6	69.3	Paraguay
8,891.2	22.7	13.9	7.5	56.0	2.6	0.9	52.4	25.7	26.9	4.4	7.6	35.4	Peru
35,208.1	5.7	0.7	1.2	92.4	1.1	76.1	15.2	18.5	24.7	15.0	3.9	38.0	Philippines
40,253.9	8.9	1.0	5.1	85.0	6.3	37.8	40.9	80.7	2.7	0.2	0.5	15.9	Poland
26,485.0	9.9	1.0	1.9	87.2	5.7	35.9	45.5	81.6	5.6	0.3	0.3	12.1	Portugal
55,175.3	6.6	0.1	0.7	92.6	72.4	12.9	7.3	8.1	86.5	0.5	0.1	4.8	Puerto Rico
8,230.9	0.2	0.1	87.1	12.6	6.1	1.8	4.7	2.7	3.4	28.9	1.4	63.6	Qatar
208.7	78.6	0.6	0.2	20.6	1.7	12.7	6.2	80.7	0.6	6.1	—	12.6	Réunion
17,618.1	6.3	2.5	6.5	84.7	4.8	21.5	58.4	73.8	3.5	0.1	1.6	21.0	Romania
125,960.3	5.6	1.2	56.3	37.0	4.6	7.3	25.0	37.1[1]	2.4	1.8	6.2	52.4[1]	Russia
46.0	61.8	35.5	—	2.7	0.4	0.1	2.2	22.7	3.1	—	—	74.1	Rwanda
30.9	25.1	—	0.1	74.8	0.2	65.4	9.3	23.8	71.2	0.2	—	4.8	St. Kitts and Nevis
62.0	52.7	0.2	7.4	39.7	1.4	19.6	18.6	40.0	20.3	0.7	—	39.0	St. Lucia
38.1	73.5		0.1	26.4	0.5	13.6	12.3	30.2	13.2	—	—	56.5	St. Vincent and the Grenadines
18.1	—89.2[3,6]—		...	10.8[4,6]	...	...	10.8[4,6]	11.6	69.6	—	—	18.8	Samoa
1,679.0	...	...	...	...	...	...	...	...	...	...	...	...	San Marino[38]
6.6	95.0	—	—	5.0	—	4.3	0.7	93.9	2.9	0.2	—	3.0	São Tomé and Príncipe
61,932.3	1.0	0.2	86.0	12.8	8.2	1.6	2.9	12.9	20.9	14.8	—	51.4	Saudi Arabia
785.1	48.6	4.3	17.8	29.3	17.8	4.5	7.0	42.3	0.3	—	1.0	56.4	Senegal
1,711.1	22.7	1.2	0.3	75.8	8.5	12.6	54.7	48.1	0.2	—	0.7	51.0	Serbia and Montenegro
38.0	51.7	0.1	40.0	8.3	0.1	5.5	2.7	44.9	—	2.4	0.1	52.5	Seychelles
95.0	13.3[23]	77.0[23]	—[23]	9.7[23]	—[23]	—[23]	9.7[23]	82.5[1]	3.8[1]	0.8	0.1[1]	12.7[1]	Sierra Leone
143,561.4	2.3	0.4	8.5	88.9	11.8	61.1	16.0	14.2	14.3	6.7	7.0	57.8	Singapore
21,546.8	4.7	0.8	5.2	89.4	5.2	47.4	36.8	84.6	5.3	0.4	0.6	9.1	Slovakia
12,766.6	4.7	0.5	1.4	93.4	13.6	36.6	43.3	66.9	3.6	0.1	0.2	29.1	Slovenia
154.9	—96.5[3]—		—	3.5[4]	—	—	3.5[4]	24.7	0.1	39.7	—	35.5	Solomon Islands
97.0	95.4[21]	2.3[21]	—[21]	2.3[21]	—[21]	2.3[21]	—[21]	2.6[1]	0.3[1]	—	1.5[1]	95.6[1]	Somalia
30,897.2	13.4	10.6	9.8	66.2	7.6	20.7	37.9	35.9	12.2	9.9	2.8	39.1	South Africa
125,872.2	16.3	0.9	2.6	80.2	11.0	40.3	29.0	73.7	4.3	0.8	0.6	20.6	Spain
4,723.0	22.4	6.6	0.3	70.6	0.7	5.0	64.9	29.9	37.3	3.0	0.3	29.5	Sri Lanka
1,616.6	22.8	0.3	69.2	7.7	0.2	1.6	5.9	7.5	—	1.5	58.2	32.8	Sudan, The
514.0	15.1	62.1	6.7	16.1	0.9	2.6	12.6	31.1	20.1	4.1	0.3	44.4	Suriname
974.3	22.5	0.2	0.7	76.6	47.8	3.6	25.2	2.6	8.0	—	0.4	88.9	Swaziland
99,690.4	7.9	1.0	3.0	88.2	11.5	42.1	34.6	58.5	11.5	1.9	2.1	26.0	Sweden
87,156.1	3.1	1.2	0.3	95.5	34.3	26.9	34.3	62.3	11.3	4.0	2.1	20.3	Switzerland[51]
6,230.1	16.5	0.8	72.2	10.5	0.4	0.4	9.8	60.4	1.9	0.2	—	37.5	Syria
130,457.0	2.7	0.1	1.6	95.6	7.6	56.6	31.4	13.6	20.5	9.2	7.6	49.1	Taiwan
692.3	—16.6[3]—		13.3	70.1[4]	1.4	7.8	60.9[4]	35.2	0.1	—	—	64.7	Tajikistan
1,221.7	45.3	9.4	1.3	44.1	1.2	1.6	41.3	53.1	0.9	7.3	0.3	38.3	Tanzania
65,113.2	18.5	1.4	2.8	77.3	5.8	42.0	29.5	16.7	20.3	15.3	4.4	43.3	Thailand
250.6	39.5	16.7	0.5	43.3	1.3	2.4	39.6	11.0	0.4	—	1.0	87.6	Togo
8.9	95.3	—	—	4.7	2.6	—	2.1	2.5[1]	25.8	43.8	—	27.9	Tonga
5,113.4	5.2	0.1	51.9	42.8	16.2	16.0	10.6	8.8	42.3	3.0	—	45.8	Trinidad and Tobago
6,874.2	7.5	1.2	9.4	81.9	9.8	16.5	55.5	79.0	0.8	0.1	0.2	19.9	Tunisia
46,877.5	11.1	1.2	2.0	85.7	4.0	26.6	55.1	54.1	8.0	0.3	1.1	36.6	Turkey
2,505.5	10.2	0.4	81.0	8.4	0.4	0.6	7.4	18.9	0.5	—	0.3	80.3	Turkmenistan
1.4	92.2[52]	—[52]	—[52]	7.8[52]	—[52]	—[52]	7.8[52]	82.6	—	—	—	17.4	Tuvalu
467.4	72.9	1.6	5.7	19.9	1.5	2.4	15.9	34.0	2.0	2.9	0.2	61.0	Uganda
17,927.4	14.9	6.0[3]	9.2	69.9[4]	7.7	13.9	48.3[4]	33.0	2.8	0.5	3.7	60.0	Ukraine
22,344.0	—7.3[3]—		64.2	28.5[4]	2.0	8.8	17.7[4]	6.4[1,53]	2.5[53]	29.5[53]	0.6[53]	60.9[1,53]	United Arab Emirates
320,057.0	6.3	3.3	8.0	82.3	16.4	44.4	21.6	55.8	15.0	1.9	1.0	26.3	United Kingdom[35]
723,608.5	10.5	1.8	1.9	85.7	13.0	48.6	24.1	21.3	—	7.2	3.9	67.5	United States[54]
1,861.0	61.3	0.4	0.8	37.6	5.9	4.4	27.4	24.1	7.6	0.8	5.6	62.0	Uruguay
3,528.0	63.3[1,23]	4.1[1,23]	11.8[23]	20.8[1,23]	2.8[1,23]	2.7[23]	15.3[1,23]	29.2[1]	1.8	1.1[1]	1.0	67.0[1]	Uzbekistan
23.2	—86.6[3]—			13.4[4]	—	1.7	11.6[4]	18.8[1]	2.2	12.1	0.9	66.1	Vanuatu
23,293.3	1.9	0.9	81.4	15.8	3.7	2.3	9.9	8.2	56.3	0.3	0.4	34.8	Venezuela
11,541.4	30.1	0.6	20.5	48.8	1.2	8.4	39.1	22.9	4.4	15.5	6.5	50.8	Vietnam
5,560.8	...	...	86.3[55]	...	...	...	...	...	93.2	...	...	...	Virgin Islands (U.S.)
22.6[57]	...	...	...	...	...	...	...	...	...	...	...	...	West Bank[31]
...	...	...	...	...	...	...	...	...	...	...	...	...	Western Sahara
4,079.3	2.5	0.1	96.5	0.9	0.3	0.3	0.3	1.2	6.1	2.1	19.0	71.6	Yemen
929.5	12.1	4.8	2.1	81.0	1.0	4.9	75.2	47.8	0.6	0.8	0.3	50.5	Zambia
2,327.4	35.6	10.7	1.1	52.7	4.1	4.8	43.8	23.6	4.5	5.3	0.6	66.1	Zimbabwe

and Jersey (data for Jersey is also shown separately). [36]1997. [37]1999. [38]Figures for Italy include San Marino and Vatican City State. [39]United Kingdom only. [40]Including coins. [41]Includes 96.5% from South Africa. [42]Includes 53.0% to South Africa. [43]1997. Percentage based on total excluding trade in ships: imports U.S.$209,600,000; exports U.S.$99,300,000. [44]France only. [45]Includes 86.0% from South Africa. [46]1984. [47]Includes 75.8% for areas not specified. [48]Year ending June 30. [49]1986. [50]Includes 86.2% from South Africa. [51]Figures for Switzerland include Liechtenstein, also shown separately. [52]1989. [53]1998. [54]Figures for United States include Puerto Rico and Virgin Islands (U.S.), also shown separately. [55]Exports of refined petroleum to United States only. [56]Excluding imports from Israel (90.9% in 1987). [57]Excluding exports to Israel (70.3% in 1987).

Household budgets and consumption

This table provides international data on household income, on the consumption expenditure of households for goods and services, and on the principal object of such expenditure (in most countries), food consumption (by kind). For purposes of this compilation, income comprises pretax monetary payments and payment in kind. The first part of the table provides data on distribution of income by households and by sources of income; the second part analyzes the largest portion of income use—consumption expenditure. Such expenditure is defined as the purchase of goods and services to satisfy current wants and needs. This definition excludes income expended on taxes, debts, savings and investments, and insurance policies. The third and last part of the table focuses on food, which usually, and often by a wide margin, represents the largest share of consumer spending worldwide. The data provided include daily available calories per capita and consumption of major food groups.

For both sources of income and consumption expenditure, the primary basis of analysis for most countries is the household, an economic unit that can be as small as a single person or as large as an extended family. For some of the countries that do not compile information by household, the table provides data on personal income and personal expenditure—i.e., the income and expenditure of all the individuals constituting a society's households. When no expenditure data at all is available, the table reports the weights of each major class of goods and services making up a given country's consumer (or retail) price index (CPI). The weighting of the components of the CPI usually reflects household spending patterns within the country or its principal urban or rural areas.

The data on distribution of income show, collectively for an entire country, the proportion of total income earned (occasionally, expended) by households constituting the lowest quintile and highest decile (poorest 20% and wealthiest 10%) within the country. These figures show the degree to which either group represents a disproportionate share of poverty or wealth.

The data on sources of income illuminate patterns of economic structure in the gaining of an income. They indicate, for example, that in poor, agrarian countries income often derives largely from self-employment (usually farming) or that in industrial countries, with well-developed systems of salaried employment and social welfare, income derives mainly from wages and salaries and secondarily from transfer payments (see note a). Because household sizes and numbers of income earners vary so greatly internationally, and because the frequency and methodology of household and CPI surveys do not permit single-year comparisons for more than a few countries at once, no summary of total *household* income or expenditure was possible. Instead, U.S. dollar figures are supplied for *per capita* private final consumption expenditure (for a single, recent year) that are more comparable internationally and refer to the same date. The figures on distribution of consumption expenditure by end use reveal patterns of personal and family use of disposable income and indicate, inter alia, that in developing countries, food may absorb 50% or more of disposable income, while in the larger household budgets of the developed countries, by contrast, food purchases may account for only 20–30% of spending. Each category of expenditure betrays similar complexities of local habit, necessity, and aspiration.

The reader should exercise caution when using these data to make inter-country comparisons. Most of the information comes from single-country surveys, which often differ markedly in their coverage of economically or demographically stratified groups, in sample design, or in the methods

Household budgets and consumption

| country | income (latest) | | | | | | consumption expenditure | | | | | | |
| | percent received by | | by source (percent) | | | | per capita private final U.S.$ (1995) | by kind or end use (percent of household or personal budget; latest) | | | | | |
	lowest 20% of households	highest 10% of households	wages, salaries	self-em- ployment	transfer payments[a]	other[b]		food[c]	housing[d]	clothing[e]	health care	energy, water	educa- tion
Afghanistan	...	...	20.7	28.0	8.2	43.1	...	33.9	3.0	...	1.1	0.7	...
Albania	...	...	53.0	4.0	11.5	31.5	680	...	...	...	...	[2]	[3]
Algeria	7.0[1]	26.8[1]	43.1	38.3	18.6	1.8	810	52.3	6.7[2]	8.6	2.8		
American Samoa	...	...	...	...	...	...	1,880[4]	32.9	20.4[5]	5.2	...	...	...
Andorra	...	...	...	...	...	...	...	...	...	...	...	...	...
Angola	...	...	...	...	...	...	370	74.1[6]	10.2[2, 6]	5.5[6]	1.8[6]	[2, 6]	2.7[6]
Antigua and Barbuda	...	...	...	...	...	...	4,050	42.9	23.3	7.5	...	5.5	...
Argentina	4.4	35.2	53.9	31.5	1.5	12.7	6,620	40.1	9.3	8.0	7.9	9.0	2.6
Armenia	...	...	24.5	13.6[7]	5.5	56.4	360	69.6	...	17.4	...	...	...
Aruba	...	...	...	...	...	...	11,190	26.9	9.9	8.4	2.9	8.5	1.9
Australia	5.9	25.4	72.7	7.5	13.0	6.8	12,040	18.7	18.5	5.6	7.1	2.2	1.6
Austria	10.4	19.3	55.7	[8]	24.4	19.9[8]	16,020	28.1	14.5	8.5	5.8	4.0	0.4
Azerbaijan	...	...	70.2	10.8[7]	19.0	—	460	42.2	—	13.6	4.8	—	—
Bahamas, The	3.6	32.1	...	...	...	...	3,950[9]	13.8	32.8	5.9	4.4	...	5.3
Bahrain	...	...	...	...	...	...	2,240	32.4	21.2	5.9	2.3	2.2	2.3
Bangladesh	8.7[1]	28.6[1]	18.7	48.3	7.5	25.5	170[10]	63.3	8.8	5.9	1.1	8.4	1.2
Barbados	7.0	44.0[11]	...	...	...	...	4,860	45.8	16.8	5.1	3.8	5.2	[3]
Belarus	11.4[1]	20.0[1]	47.1	7.3[9]	45.6	—	610	29.0	2.7	...	...	...	...
Belgium	9.5[12]	20.2[12]	49.6	10.9	20.7	18.8	16,550	18.3	11.4	7.0	10.5	6.2	[3]
Belize	...	...	84.1	—— 15.9 ——			1,780	34.0	9.0	8.8	1.6	9.1	2.3
Benin	8.0	39.0	26.3	—— 73.7 ——			240	37.0	10.0	14.0	5.0	2.0	4.0
Bermuda	7.2	24.7	65.3	9.0	3.3	22.4	12,690[13]	14.6	27.7	4.9	7.6	3.3	3.8
Bhutan	...	...	...	...	...	...	170	72.3	...	21.2	...	3.7	...
Bolivia	5.6[12]	31.7[12]	...	...	...	...	690	46.6	7.8	5.1	2.1	4.7	0.3
Bosnia and Herzegovina	...	...	53.2	12.0	18.2	16.6	1,890[14]	44.7	1.6	8.3	3.4	7.8	[3]
Botswana	3.7	42.9	73.3	15.4	10.8	0.4	1,030	39.5[15]	11.8	5.6	2.3	2.5	4.9
Brazil	2.5[12]	47.6[12]	62.4	14.7	10.9	12.0	4,420	25.3	21.3[2]	12.9	9.1	[2]	...
Brunei	...	...	...	...	...	...		45.1	2.6	6.1	...	2.4	[3]
Bulgaria	8.5[1]	22.5[1]	34.7	23.6[7]	14.8	—	1,470	47.0	4.1	7.4	3.2	4.3	[3]
Burkina Faso	5.5[1]	39.5[1]	...	...	...	...	220	38.7[6]	5.1[6]	4.4[6]	5.2[6]	13.7[6]	[3]
Burundi	7.9[1]	26.6[1]	...	...	...	...	190	59.6[6]	4.4[6]	11.1[6]	...	5.8[6]	...
Cambodia	6.9[1]	33.8[1]	...	...	...	...	280	...	...	...	...	[2]	[3]
Cameroon	...	...	41.4	52.6	3.0	3.0	570	49.1	18.0[2]	7.6	8.6	[2]	...
Canada	7.5[12]	23.8[12]	57.0	13.7	20.7	8.6	11,460	13.4	24.5[2]	5.3	4.7	[2]	3.1
Cape Verde	...	...	...	...	...	...	920	60.0	8.5	2.5	0.5	4.9	[17]
Central African Republic	2.0[1]	47.7[1]	...	...	...	...	350	70.5[6]	0.6[6]	9.5[6]	1.0[6]	6.5[6]	...
Chad	8.0	30.0	...	...	...	...	170	45.3[6]	...	3.5[6]	11.9[6]	5.8[6]	...
Chile	3.5[12]	46.1[12]	—— 75.1 ——		12.0	12.9	2,940	27.9	15.2	22.5	...	...	...
China	5.9[12]	30.4[12]	21.6	72.2	—— 6.2 ——		260	49.9[15, 18]	6.8[18]	13.7[18]	2.9[18]	...	2.3[18]
Colombia	3.0[12]	46.1[12]	45.1	35.4	14.2	5.3	1,540	45.0	7.8	4.5	6.4	2.2	1.7
Comoros	...	...	25.6	64.5	8.7	1.2	350	67.3	2.3	11.6	3.2	3.8	[3]
Congo, Dem. Rep. of the	...	...	...	...	...	...	190	61.7	11.5[2]	9.7	2.6	[2]	[3]
Congo, Rep. of the	7.0	43.5	...	...	...	...	870	37.0	6.0	6.0	6.0	3.0	8.0
Costa Rica	4.0[12]	34.7[12]	61.0	22.6	9.6	6.8	1,600	39.1	12.1[2]	9.4	3.7	[2]	...
Côte d'Ivoire	7.1[1]	28.8[1]	44.9	49.9	—— 5.2 ——		480	48.0	7.8	10.0	0.7	8.5	...
Croatia	9.3[1]	21.6[1]	40.2	40.8	12.1	6.9	3,790	37.8	2.9	8.6	4.3	7.6	[3]
Cuba	...	...	57.3	—— 42.7 ——			1,510[9]	26.7	...	...	...	2.5	...
Cyprus	...	...	76.3	5.9	14.4	3.4	8,300	22.7	5.5	10.0	3.1	1.3	1.4
Czech Republic	10.3[12]	22.4[12]	—— 66.7 ——		27.6	5.7	2,620	26.7	5.5[2]	7.3	[19]	...	...
Denmark	9.6[12]	20.5[12]	63.3	14.6	25.9	-3.8	17,730	17.9	22.9	5.2	2.2	6.1	1.9
Djibouti	...	...	51.6	36.0	10.5	1.9	590	50.3	6.4	1.7	2.4	13.1	...
Dominica	...	...	...	...	...	...	2,110	43.1	16.1	6.5	...	5.4	...
Dominican Republic	4.3[12]	37.8[12]	41.7	31.8	1.5	25.0	1,150	46.0	10.0	3.0	5.0	5.0	3.0
East Timor	...	...	...	...	...	...	...	...	...	...	...	...	...
Ecuador	5.4[1]	33.8[1]	17.4	76.9	3.6	2.1	1,040	36.1	9.0	10.1	4.2	3.3	[17]

employed for collection, classification, and tabulation of data. Further, the reference period of the data varies greatly; while a significant portion of the data is from 1980 or later, information for some countries dates from the 1970s. This older information is typeset in italic. Finally, intercountry comparisons of annual personal consumption expenditure may be misleading because of the distortions of price and purchasing power present when converting a national currency unit into U.S. dollars.

The table's food consumption data include total daily available calories per capita (food supply), which amounts to domestic production and imports minus exports, animal feed, and nonfood uses, and a percentage breakdown of the major food groups that make up food supply.

The data for daily available calories per capita provide a measure of the nutritional adequacy of each nation's food supply. The following list, based on estimates from the United Nations Food and Agriculture Organization (FAO), indicates the regional variation in recommended daily minimum nutritional requirements, which are defined by factors such as climatic ambience, physical activity, and average body weight: Africa (2,320 calories), formerly Centrally Planned Asia (2,300 calories), Far East (2,240 calories), Latin America (2,360 calories), Near East (2,440 calories).

The breakdown of diet by food groups describes the character of a nation's food supply. A typical breakdown for a low-income country might show a diet with heavy intake of vegetable foods, such as cereals, potatoes, or cassava. In the high-income countries, a relatively larger portion of total calories derives from animal products (meat, eggs, and milk). The reader should note that these data refer to total national *supply* and often do not reflect the differences that may exist within a single country.

In compiling this table, Britannica editors rely on both numerous national

reports and principal secondary sources such as the World Bank's *World Development Report* (annual), the International Labour Organisation's *Sources and Methods: Labour Statistics vol. 1 Consumer Price Indices* (3rd ed.), the UN's *Yearbook of National Accounts Statistics* (annual) and *National Accounts Statistics: Compendium of Income Distribution Statistics,* and the FAO's *Food Balance Sheets.*

The following terms further define the column headings:
a. Includes pensions, family allowances, unemployment payments, remittances from abroad, and social security and related benefits.
b. Includes interest and dividends, rents and royalties, and all other income not reported under the three preceding categories.
c. Includes alcoholic and nonalcoholic beverages and meals away from home when identifiable. Excludes tobacco except as noted.
d. Rent, maintenance of dwellings, and taxes only; excludes energy and water (heat, light, power, and water) and household durables (furniture, appliances, utensils, and household operations), shown separately.
e. Includes footwear.
f. Furniture, appliances, and utensils; usually includes expenditure on household operation.
g. Includes expenditure on cultural activities other than education.
h. May include data not shown separately in preceding categories, including meals away from home (*see* note c).
i. Represents pure fats and oils only.
j. Consists mainly of peas, beans, and lentils; spices; stimulants; alcoholic beverages (when combined with "other"); sugars and honey; and nuts and oilseeds.

transportation, communications	household durable goods[f]	recreation[g]	personal effects, other[h]	daily available calories per capita	cereals	potatoes, cassava	meat, poultry	fish	eggs, milk	fruits, vegetables	fats, oils[i]	other[j]	country
...	...	...	61.3	1,716	83.4	1.1	4.1	—	2.4	2.6	3.8	2.6	Afghanistan
12.0	4.5	4.6[3]	8.5	2,976	51.1	1.8	5.1	0.1	16.9	6.0	9.0	10.0	Albania
17.8	5	1.1	22.6	3,020	60.3	2.2	2.7	0.3	6.1	5.1	13.8	9.5	Algeria
...	...	...	...	...	...	...	...	...	...	...	...	...	American Samoa
...	...	...	...	3,348	22.6	4.7	13.4	2.4	9.3	6.7	21.6	19.4	Andorra
3.9[6]	...	...	1.8[6]	...	...	...	...	...	...	...	...	...	Angola
10.0	...	...	10.8	2,450	25.8	1.0	15.8	1.7	11.3	7.9	16.4	20.2	Antigua and Barbuda
11.6	...	7.5	5.9	3,144	29.5	5.2	16.5	0.5	10.3	4.5	15.4	18.0	Argentina
...	6.6	...	28.7	2,356	52.3	6.7	5.3	0.1	7.0	6.5	11.7	10.4	Armenia
15.5	9.1	3.1	11.9	2,659	28.2	2.3	18.9	1.4	10.8	5.0	13.6	19.7	Aruba
15.1	7.0	7.5	16.7	3,190	22.7	3.2	15.5	0.8	11.8	5.3	17.0	23.5	Australia
16.3	7.8	7.1	7.5	3,531	20.7	3.1	13.8	0.6	11.4	5.5	21.5	23.4	Austria
5.1	6.5	0.7	27.1	2,191	66.6	2.7	4.6	0.1	9.7	5.1	2.8	8.4	Azerbaijan
14.8	8.9	4.9	9.2	2,546	30.1	1.4	18.8	1.1	5.9	8.6	9.3	24.9	Bahamas, The
8.5	9.8	6.4	9.0	...	...	...	...	...	...	...	...	...	Bahrain
0.9	...	...	10.4	2,050	81.6	1.3	0.8	0.9	1.5	1.1	5.6	7.2	Bangladesh
10.5	8.1	4.8[3]	—	2,978	31.6	3.9	12.6	2.3	6.6	3.4	12.8	26.8	Barbados
...	...	...	68.3	3,136	36.2	9.9	10.5	0.1	10.2	2.6	12.0	18.7	Belarus
13.4	10.6	6.8[3]	15.8	3,606	20.4	5.2	8.6	1.1	10.8	6.5	25.7	21.7	Belgium
13.7	8.0	...	9.4	2,922	34.0	1.4	6.3	0.4	7.5	9.6	10.2	30.7	Belize
14.0	5.0	...	9.0	2,571	37.5	36.9	2.2	0.7	0.8	2.6	5.3	14.0	Benin
7.3	16.6	10.8	3.4	2,921	22.8	2.6	15.7	2.7	7.8	12.4	15.2	20.8	Bermuda
...	0.7	...	2.1	...	...	...	...	...	...	...	...	...	Bhutan
17.7	9.7	2.7	3.3	2,214	40.7	6.6	11.2	0.1	3.7	8.6	11.4	17.7	Bolivia
6.0	4.1	3.5[3]	2.3	2,801	64.6	5.6	4.3	0.1	3.7	4.5	3.7	13.4	Bosnia and Herzegovina
13.1	13.8	3.1	3.4	2,159	46.9	1.8	6.3	0.5	8.9	2.5	11.6	21.6	Botswana
15.0	...	...	16.4	2,926	30.9	4.3	10.8	0.4	8.3	4.5	12.6	28.2	Brazil
17.2	8.3	8.9[3]	9.4	2,851	48.0	1.2	13.0	1.3	6.4	5.0	6.3	18.9	Brunei
6.6	4.0	3.0[3]	21.5	2,740	37.6	2.1	10.7	0.3	12.1	5.4	15.6	16.3	Bulgaria
18.6[6]	3.0[6]	2.3[3, 6]	9.0[6]	2,149	73.2	0.7	2.6	0.1	1.9	0.9	5.2	15.5	Burkina Faso
...	6.0[6]	...	13.1[6, 16]	1,578	16.7	30.0	1.3	0.4	0.8	10.3	1.5	39.0	Burundi
...	...	...	...	2,078	77.9	1.3	6.2	0.8	0.5	2.9	4.7	5.7	Cambodia
13.0	...	2.4	1.3	2,209	41.7	16.3	3.4	0.8	1.4	13.7	9.1	13.6	Cameroon
14.3	8.8	8.0	17.9	3,167	24.9	2.9	11.4	1.1	8.8	6.6	20.5	23.8	Canada
8.8	6.9	17	7.9[17]	3,099	40.3	2.5	5.8	1.5	4.9	3.1	17.6	24.2	Cape Verde
4.1[6]	0.8[6]	1.3[6]	5.7[6]	2,056	18.9	35.9	6.4	0.3	1.5	6.2	13.7	17.1	Central African Republic
...	...	...	33.5[6]	2,171	53.8	9.4	2.3	0.5	2.2	1.5	7.1	23.2	Chad
6.4	...	...	28.0	2,844	38.7	3.4	12.5	1.2	6.7	4.8	12.4	20.3	Chile
4.7[18]	5.3[18]	2.4[18]	12.0[18]	2,972	54.7	5.6	13.2	13.2	2.6	5.3	7.3	10.1	China
18.5	5.7	...	8.2	2,559	32.5	7.2	7.2	0.4	8.7	7.9	11.9	24.2	Colombia
2.2	3.0	2.5[3]	4.1	1,858	42.7	15.6	1.8	2.4	1.1	8.0	10.3	18.1	Comoros
5.9	4.8	3.8[3]	—	1,701	19.2	56.3	1.9	0.6	0.1	6.5	6.3	9.1	Congo, Dem. Rep. of the
15.0	4.0	...	15.0	2,241	25.4	37.9	3.1	2.2	1.5	6.2	11.7	11.9	Congo, Rep. of the
11.6	10.9	4.4[3]	8.8	2,781	32.9	1.9	5.3	0.5	9.5	5.0	14.1	30.9	Costa Rica
12.2	3.4	...	9.4	2,695	42.5	24.7	1.9	0.7	0.9	8.7	11.2	9.4	Côte d'Ivoire
9.3	4.5	4.1[3]	1.5	2,479	31.2	8.4	4.2	0.3	10.6	7.5	11.9	25.8	Croatia
5.4	...	...	65.4	2,473	37.3	5.3	5.3	0.8	4.9	5.1	9.6	31.7	Cuba
15.6	10.5	6.3	23.6	3,474	25.6	2.4	14.7	1.0	12.7	8.0	12.7	22.9	Cyprus
3.1	4.5	0.8[19]	52.7	3,292	27.6	4.4	10.1	0.7	9.6	4.3	17.9	25.4	Czech Republic
15.5	6.1	8.3	13.9	3,443	25.4	3.8	11.7	1.4	9.9	4.9	17.6	25.3	Denmark
...	1.5	...	24.6	2,074	51.3	0.2	4.6	0.2	4.8	1.6	17.9	19.4	Djibouti
11.6	6.0	...	11.3	2,996	23.9	9.1	10.6	1.6	8.7	12.5	6.9	26.7	Dominica
4.0	8.0	...	13.0	2,277	28.3	2.8	7.6	0.7	5.2	10.1	19.1	26.4	Dominican Republic
...	...	...	...	...	...	...	...	...	...	...	...	...	East Timor
12.8	5.5	17	19.0[17]	2,724	34.5	2.7	5.8	0.6	6.6	4.4	20.6	24.8	Ecuador

Household budgets and consumption   (continued)

country	income (latest)						consumption expenditure						
	percent received by		by source (percent)				per capita private final, U.S.$ (1995)	by kind or end use (percent of household or personal budget; latest)					
	lowest 20% of households	highest 10% of households	wages, salaries	self-employment	transfer payments[a]	other[b]		food[c]	housing[d]	clothing[e]	health care	energy, water	education
Egypt	9.8[1]	25.0[1]	...	...	...	...	740	50.2	10.5[2]	10.9	2.7	[2]	[3]
El Salvador	3.4[12]	40.5[12]	...	...	...	...	1,520	37.0[18]	12.1[18]	6.7[18]	4.2[18]	3.6[18]	3.7[18]
Equatorial Guinea	...	...	57.0[6]	42.0[6]	—	1.0[6]	310	62.0[6]	...	10.0[6]	6.0[6]	...	...
Eritrea	...	...	...	...	...	...	170	...	...	...	...	...	...
Estonia	6.2[12]	26.2[12]	53.0	5.7	12.8	28.5	1,390	41.0	9.6	8.4	[19]	6.5	3.1
Ethiopia	7.1[1]	33.7[1]	0.2	79.5	—	20.3	87	49.0	7.0	6.0	3.0	7.0	4.0
Faroe Islands	...	...	88.3	11.7	—	—	1,430[10]	40.9	11.0	8.0	...	18.9	...
Fiji	3.7	37.8	81.5	9.1	—	9.4		34.7	15.6[2]	9.3	2.4	[2]	[3]
Finland	10.0[12]	21.6[12]	70.3	7.4	9.7	12.6	13,260	22.5	16.9	5.0	4.8	4.6	[3]
France	7.2[12]	25.1[12]	51.1	14.1	27.5	7.3	15,810	17.4	16.2	6.1	9.8	3.8	0.7
French Guiana	...	...	74.6		—25.4—			30.0[15]	16.1[2]	6.7	4.4	[2]	[3]
French Polynesia	...	...	61.9	18.5	16.6	3.0	4,310[20]	39.6	9.7	6.3	1.0	8.1	1.0
Gabon	3.3	54.4	...	...	...	...	4,060	...	...	...	...	...	...
Gambia, The	...	...	...	...	...	...	330	58.0[21]	5.1[21]	17.5[21]	...	5.4[21]	...
Gaza Strip	...	...	...	...	...	...	910[22]	...	...	...	...	...	...
Georgia	...	...	34.5	21.6[7]	21.7	22.0	430	38.3	...	14.8	...	0.3	...
Germany	8.2[12]	23.7[12]	57.9	[8]	21.3	20.8[8]	16,850	19.0	16.9	7.9	3.5	4.1	[3]
Ghana	8.4[1]	26.1[1]	41.6[23]	47.1[23]	—	11.3[23]	290	57.4	11.5[2]	14.3	1.3	[2]	[3]
Greece	7.5[12]	25.3[12]	34.0	22.8	17.0	26.2	8,140	29.9	14.1	6.5	3.1	3.3	0.5
Greenland	...	...	...	...	...	...	11,110	30.1	10.0	7.7	0.3	5.4	...
Grenada	...	...	...	...	...	...	1,650	40.7[15]	11.9	5.2	[24]	3.9	[3]
Guadeloupe	...	...	78.9	13.7	7.4	—	4,080[27]	31.6[15]	11.3[2]	9.3	4.6	[2]	[3]
Guam	...	...	...	...	...	...		24.1	28.6	10.6	4.8	...	...
Guatemala	2.1[12]	46.6[12]	...	...	...	...	1,180	64.4	16.0[2]	3.1	0.6	[2]	0.3
Guernsey	...	...	...	...	...	...		23.7	12.1	7.5	...	8.2	...
Guinea	6.4[1]	32.0[1]	...	...	...	...	510	61.5	7.3[2]	7.9	11.1	[2]	...
Guinea-Bissau	2.1[1]	42.4[1]	...	...	...	...	230	...	...	...	...	...	...
Guyana	4.0	40.0[11]	73.0	...	6.3	20.7	...	42.5[15]	21.4	8.6	...	5.2	[3]
Haiti	...	...	...	...	...	...	320	51.1[15]	4.3	8.7	2.2	...	[3]
Honduras	3.4[12]	42.1[12]	58.3	[8]	1.8	39.9[8]	450	44.4	22.4[2]	9.1	7.0	[2]	[3]
Hong Kong	...	...					13,880	15.1	15.7[2]	21.3	5.0	[2]	0.5
Hungary	8.8[12]	24.8[12]	—55.0—		19.2	5.8	4,270	38.1	5.7	7.4	1.5	6.1	0.7
Iceland	4.7	27.3	73.1	2.7	10.2	14.0	15,850	31.3	16.0	7.5	2.3	2.9	1.3
India	8.1[1]	33.5[1]	42.2	39.7	—18.1—		210	52.2	6.1[25]	10.0	2.4	4.7[25]	1.8
Indonesia	8.0[12]	30.3[12]	42.1	41.5	2.5	13.9	640	47.5[18]	20.1[2, 18]	5.5[18]	...	[2]	...
Iran	3.8	41.7	37.4[18]	30.5[18]	—32.1[18]—		1,040	42.6[15]	24.9[2]	11.8	3.9	[2]	[3]
Iraq	...	...	23.9	33.9	23.0	18.6	1,710[13]	50.2	19.9[2]	10.6	1.6	[2]	[3]
Ireland	6.7[12]	27.4[12]	58.6	13.3	19.9	8.2	9,650	30.5	7.1	7.4	3.2	6.1	2.4
Isle of Man	6.4	26.6	64.1	6.6	16.9	12.4		31.0	7.9	7.0	...	11.0	...
Israel	6.9[12]	26.9[12]	63.4[18, 26]	14.6[18, 26]	18.9[18, 26]	3.1[18, 26]	9,930	23.8	19.8	5.3	6.2	2.4	2.9
Italy	8.7[12]	21.8[12]	41.7	25.9	20.3	12.1	11,860	19.5	10.0	9.8	6.7	3.8	0.7
Jamaica	7.0[1]	28.9[1]	63.6	13.9	14.0	8.5	1,770	35.7	5.7	4.6	2.8	4.9	0.2
Japan	10.6[12]	21.7[12]	59.3	11.1	19.5	10.1	24,670	22.6	6.7	6.0	2.7	5.6	5.3
Jersey	...	...	...	...	...	...		28.3	14.9	8.3	...	6.5	...
Jordan	7.6[1]	29.8[1]	51.4	11.1	13.7	23.8	1,020	40.6	15.8	6.7	2.2	5.0	3.5
Kazakhstan	6.7[1]	26.3[1]	67.7	5.8[7]	16.9	9.6	1,290	29.6	2.6	...	...	...	...
Kenya	5.0	34.9	...	...	...	...	220	46.5	10.0	7.7	2.2	2.6	1.0
Kiribati	...	...	69.7	21.4	6.0	2.9	370[4]	50.0[15]	7.5[2, 5]	8.0	...	[2]	...
Korea, North	...	...	...	...	...	...		46.5[27]	0.6[27]	29.9[27]	...	3.3[27]	...
Korea, South	7.5[1]	24.3[1]	53.8	25.1	13.1	8.0	5,390	29.7	4.1	7.7	5.0	4.0	14.2
Kuwait	...	...	53.8	20.8	—25.4—		...	28.1[15]	15.5	8.1	0.7	9.6	[3]
Kyrgyzstan	6.3[12]	31.7[12]	67.3		—32.7—		670	33.5	2.2	...	...	...	...
Laos	9.6[1]	26.4[1]	...	...	...	...	140[9]	...	...	...	...	...	...
Latvia	7.6[12]	25.9[12]	67.0	5.4[7]	17.4	10.2	2,400	51.6	...	...	...	...	...
Lebanon	5.0	45.0	27.9		3.0	69.1	3,010	42.8[6]	16.8[6]	8.6[6]	7.2[6]	4.5[6]	3.9[6]
Lesotho	2.8[1]	43.4[1]	22.4	27.8	44.7	5.1	530	48.0[15]	10.1	16.4	...	...	...
Liberia	5.0	73.0[11]	...	...	...	...	330[9]	34.4[6]	14.9[6]	13.8[6]	...	5.0[6]	...
Libya	...	...	...	...	...	...	2,330[9]	37.2[15]	32.2[2]	6.9	3.3	[2]	[3]
Liechtenstein	...	...	...	...	...	...		21.3[15]	18.0	6.6	7.7	4.4	[3]
Lithuania	7.8[1]	25.6[1]	66.4	9.7	18.7	5.2	1,910	50.3	...	...	...	...	...
Luxembourg	10.0	34.0[11]	67.1	4.8	28.1		15,140[28]	12.8	13.7	5.9	7.3	6.1	[3]
Macau	...	...	65.0	18.1	7.0	9.9	5,480	39.2[15]	17.5	6.8	4.0	5.2	[3]
Macedonia	...	...	57.7	17.2	16.2	9.0	1,010	40.6	1.9	7.8	3.0	7.8	[3]
Madagascar	5.1[1]	36.7[1]	58.8[6, 29]	14.1[6, 29]	—	27.1[6, 29]	220	59.0	6.0	6.0	2.0	6.0	4.0
Malawi	10.4	40.1	83.3	6.0	—	11.7	109	30.0	4.0	9.0	4.0	5.0	10.0
Malaysia	4.5[12]	37.9[12]	...	...	...	...	2,090	28.7	10.2[2]	4.3	2.5	[2]	0.6
Maldives	...	...	...	...	...	...	270[9]	57.4	1.6	8.0	2.5	...	[3]
Mali	4.6[1]	40.4[1]	...	...	...	...	200	57.0	2.0	6.0	2.0	6.0	4.0
Malta	...	...	63.8	19.3	—	16.9	5,380	31.2	3.5	7.6	3.5	2.0	0.4
Marshall Islands	...	...	...	...	...	...		57.7	15.6[2, 5]	12.0	...	[2]	...
Martinique	...	...	80.0	...	—	20.0	4,840[6]	32.1[15]	10.6[2]	8.0	5.2	[2]	[3]
Mauritania	6.2[1]	29.9[1]	...	...	...	...	470	73.1	2.5	8.1	0.9	7.7	0.4
Mauritius	4.0	46.7	51.7	29.0	11.2	8.1	2,290	41.9	8.8	8.4	3.0	6.4	2.9
Mayotte	...	...	...	...	...	...		42.2	...	31.5	...	6.8	...
Mexico	3.6[12]	42.8[12]	61.5	29.1	7.8	1.6	2,110	36.6[15]	13.3[2]	8.4	3.4	[2]	[3]
Micronesia	...	...	51.8	23.0	2.1	23.1		73.5	...	...	...	...	...
Moldova	6.9[12]	25.8[12]	41.2	10.4	15.3	33.1	220	...	...	...	...	...	...
Monaco	...	...	...	...	...	...		...	...	...	...	...	...
Mongolia	7.3[1]	24.5[1]	72.1	9.5[7]	9.7	8.7	230	39.1	5.9[2]	23.4	0.5	[2]	2.9
Morocco	6.5[1]	30.9[1]	...	...	...	...	900	38.0	7.0	11.0	5.0	2.0	8.0
Mozambique	6.5[1]	31.7[1]	51.6		—48.4—		57	74.6	11.7	3.7	0.8	...	[3]
Myanmar (Burma)	8.0	40.0[11]	...	...	...	...	750[28]	49.1[6]	10.4[6]	15.3[6]	2.4[6]	4.0[6]	5.9[6]
Namibia	...	...	67.1	27.5	5.4	...	1,050	...	...	...	...	...	...
Nauru	...	...	...	...	...	...		...	...	...	...	...	...
Nepal	7.6[1]	29.8[1]	25.1	63.4	—11.5—		170	61.2	17.3	11.7	3.7	...	[3]

transportation, communications	household durable goods[f]	recreation[g]	personal effects, other[h]	daily available calories per capita	cereals	potatoes, cassava	meat, poultry	fish	eggs, milk	fruits, vegetables	fats, oils[i]	other[j]	country
4.7	5.0	3.3[3]	12.7	3,282	65.4	1.6	2.9	0.6	2.1	6.9	6.1	14.3	Egypt
10.2[18]	5.7[18]	4.3[18]	12.5[18]	2,522	53.4	1.5	2.6	0.2	6.3	3.5	7.7	24.9	El Salvador
...	...	...	22.0[6]	...	...	...	...	...	...	...	...	...	Equatorial Guinea
...	...	...	...	1,744	73.4	4.4	0.6	0.0	1.9	0.1	0.7	18.8	Eritrea
9.2	2.3	5.0[19]	15.0	3,058	38.5	5.3	8.9	1.6	12.7	4.3	13.3	15.4	Estonia
8.0	2.0	...	14.0	1,805	66.3	13.1	3.2	0.0	1.9	0.6	2.8	12.1	Ethiopia
...	6.6	...	14.6	...	...	...	...	...	...	...	...	...	Faroe Islands
13.8	9.3	4.3[3]	10.6	2,852	42.3	6.9	8.5	1.4	3.0	1.8	18.7	17.3	Fiji
14.8	6.3	9.5[3]	15.6	3,180	33.6	4.2	16.3	2.0	15.7	3.9	12.9	18.6	Finland
16.1	7.7	6.9	15.3	3,541	24.3	3.4	16.5	1.2	12.0	4.7	19.7	18.3	France
17.5	7.9	6.2[3]	11.2	2,818	32.4	7.9	13.2	2.1	7.5	7.0	10.5	19.3	French Guiana
16.4	4.4	4.0	9.5	2,924	33.6	4.0	13.3	4.4	6.1	3.0	13.6	22.1	French Polynesia
...	...	...	...	2,560	29.5	17.9	7.3	3.1	2.4	16.4	7.9	15.5	Gabon
...	...	...	14.0[21]	2,559	54.0	0.7	1.3	1.9	1.4	0.9	17.7	22.1	Gambia, The
...	...	...	...	...	...	...	...	...	...	...	...	...	Gaza Strip
...	5.9	...	40.7	2,252	60.5	4.8	4.9	0.2	7.6	4.8	3.0	14.2	Georgia
17.8	9.4	10.6[3]	10.8	3,402	22.5	4.1	11.7	0.8	10.3	5.7	21.6	23.3	Germany
3.3	*3.8*	*3.9[8]*	*4.5*	2,684	26.2	48.2	1.2	1.8	0.2	9.6	4.6	8.3	Ghana
17.5	6.9	5.2	13.0	3,630	29.1	3.5	8.9	1.2	11.8	8.6	20.0	16.8	Greece
8.0	9.2	15.5	13.8	...	...	...	...	...	...	...	...	...	Greenland
9.1	13.7	4.6[3]	10.9[24]	2,681	25.3	2.5	9.1	1.5	9.5	9.2	13.1	29.8	Grenada
20.5	9.3	4.7[3]	8.7	2,732	37.8	2.6	10.8	2.6	8.5	8.4	13.1	16.1	Guadeloupe
18.0	...	*5.1*	*8.8*	...	...	...	...	...	...	...	...	...	Guam
7.0	5.0	0.9	2.7	2,159	55.3	0.4	3.6	0.1	5.1	3.1	7.0	25.4	Guatemala
15.7	8.3	...	24.7	3,257	22.8	6.1	14.4	1.0	11.6	5.0	19.1	20.0	Guernsey
5.1	*2.9*	*4.1*	*0.1*	2,315	42.9	15.6	0.9	1.2	1.0	13.0	14.7	10.8	Guinea
...	...	...	...	2,411	61.2	7.4	4.6	0.2	1.4	4.2	13.0	8.1	Guinea-Bissau
4.8	2.9	6.4[3]	8.2	2,476	47.3	3.8	4.8	4.2	5.4	2.8	4.1	27.6	Guyana
7.6	9.2	5.3[3]	11.6	1,876	46.7	8.8	3.3	0.3	2.0	7.4	8.8	22.8	Haiti
3.0	8.3	2.4[3]	3.1	2,343	46.7	0.3	3.6	0.3	8.6	6.7	11.9	21.9	Honduras
8.4	17.5	8.1	8.4	3,200	27.1	1.6	20.0	3.3	5.2	4.0	19.7	19.2	Hong Kong
15.2	8.8	5.9	10.6	3,408	25.4	3.6	10.1	0.2	8.4	5.4	22.7	24.1	Hungary
14.5	7.6	9.6	7.0	3,222	20.7	3.2	14.3	3.6	14.6	4.0	13.4	26.2	Iceland
10.6	3.1	1.8	5.7	2,466	62.7	1.6	0.9	0.4	4.5	3.2	8.5	18.3	India
...	2.9[18]	...	24.0	2,850	64.6	5.8	2.2	1.3	0.6	2.3	7.8	15.4	Indonesia
5.0	6.4	1.7[3]	3.7	2,822	51.2	3.2	4.3	0.3	3.8	11.2	10.8	15.1	Iran
6.5	6.7	0.8[3]	3.7	2,419	59.4	1.2	1.4	0.1	1.9	8.0	19.5	8.6	Iraq
14.0	7.2	8.9	13.1	3,622	26.8	6.0	13.1	0.8	11.3	4.0	16.5	21.4	Ireland
14.9	5.7	...	22.5	3,257	22.8	6.1	14.4	1.0	11.6	5.0	19.1	20.0	Isle of Man
12.9	10.8	4.3	11.6	3,466	33.5	2.5	8.2	0.9	7.6	8.6	18.3	20.3	Israel
13.2	9.5	8.4	18.4	3,608	31.8	1.9	11.1	1.1	8.9	7.2	22.0	15.9	Italy
12.4	5.5	2.1	26.1	2,711	30.5	9.3	8.5	0.8	5.3	7.2	13.1	25.3	Jamaica
11.0	3.7	9.5	26.9	2,874	40.7	2.5	5.8	6.3	6.5	4.3	12.0	21.8	Japan
13.9	*7.1*	...	*21.0*	3,257	22.8	6.1	14.4	1.0	11.6	5.0	19.1	20.0	Jersey
11.2	6.1	4.0	4.9	2,791	52.7	1.1	5.1	0.2	5.4	3.9	15.3	16.3	Jordan
...	...	...	67.8	2,517	54.4	4.1	9.1	0.2	12.0	2.1	7.4	10.8	Kazakhstan
8.4	9.4	3.1	9.1	1,968	52.4	8.6	3.7	0.5	7.2	3.2	9.3	15.3	Kenya
8.0	5	...	26.5	2,977	34.7	8.3	4.6	4.6	1.6	4.6	7.2	34.4	Kiribati
...	3.8[27]	...	15.9	1,899	64.5	1.1	3.1	1.3	1.0	7.6	5.8	15.5	Korea, North
11.3	5.0	—— 19.0 ——		3,069	49.7	1.1	9.6	3.0	2.2	7.1	9.7	17.7	Korea, South
13.7	11.2	5.2[3]	7.9	3,059	36.8	1.9	11.2	0.5	9.8	8.4	10.2	21.2	Kuwait
...	...	...	64.3	2,535	58.3	6.7	8.7	—	13.0	2.1	3.6	7.6	Kyrgyzstan
...	...	...	...	2,175	77.7	3.8	4.4	0.7	0.5	2.2	2.3	8.5	Laos
...	...	...	54.8	2,994	32.7	8.4	6.0	0.9	12.9	3.8	15.3	20.0	Latvia
5.4[6]	*2.6[6]*	*1.9[6]*	*6.3[6]*	3,285	34.6	3.9	4.9	0.4	5.2	15.9	13.9	21.2	Lebanon
4.7	11.9	...	8.8	2,210	75.5	4.3	3.4	—	1.1	1.4	3.1	11.2	Lesotho
...	6.1[6]	...	25.8[6]	1,979	41.5	20.4	2.0	0.4	0.5	5.5	19.8	10.0	Liberia
9.4	*4.6*	*8.5[3]*	*2.5*	3,267	46.3	2.0	4.8	0.3	5.7	7.3	17.0	16.7	Libya
13.3	5.8	16.3[3]	6.6	3,222	22.1	2.3	14.8	0.8	12.5	6.1	18.7	22.7	Liechtenstein
...	...	...	49.7	3,104	45.5	7.8	8.9	0.9	6.9	5.3	10.1	14.6	Lithuania
19.1	10.8	4.2[3]	20.1	3,606	20.4	5.2	8.6	1.1	10.8	6.5	25.7	21.7	Luxembourg
8.2	3.0	8.8[3]	7.3	2,471	36.3	0.7	15.7	2.3	4.7	3.7	20.7	15.8	Macau
6.5	4.2	3.3[3]	1.8	2,938	39.7	3.3	7.0	0.3	5.2	6.9	15.7	21.8	Macedonia
4.0	1.0	...	12.0	2,001	53.0	21.1	5.5	0.7	3.1	3.8	4.4	8.3	Madagascar
10.0	3.0	...	25.0	2,226	59.0	15.8	1.3	0.4	0.5	4.2	4.0	14.7	Malawi
20.9	7.7	11.0	14.1	2,901	41.6	2.1	9.2	3.1	5.2	3.4	12.5	22.8	Malaysia
2.6	17.0	5.9[3]	5.0	2,451	43.5	3.2	1.4	13.1	4.3	5.6	5.2	23.7	Maldives
10.0	1.0	...	12.0	2,118	69.9	0.5	4.2	0.8	4.6	1.2	7.4	11.3	Mali
16.4	9.9	7.1	18.4	3,382	30.8	4.0	8.8	1.6	11.3	7.9	11.5	24.0	Malta
...	5	...	14.7	...	...	...	...	...	...	...	...	...	Marshall Islands
20.7	9.4	5.4[3]	8.6	2,865	30.0	4.2	12.1	2.9	8.5	11.0	8.7	22.5	Martinique
2.0	1.2	4.0	0.1	2,640	54.8	0.4	4.0	0.9	10.8	1.2	9.9	18.1	Mauritania
10.0	6.4	—	12.2	2,944	44.7	1.3	4.8	1.2	6.3	3.0	16.6	22.2	Mauritius
5.1	8.8	...	5.6	...	...	...	...	...	...	...	...	...	Mayotte
10.0	11.8	5.5[3]	11.0	3,144	46.2	0.8	8.2	0.7	6.0	4.0	11.3	22.8	Mexico
...	...	...	26.5	...	...	...	...	...	...	...	...	...	Micronesia
...	...	...	...	2,763	48.4	4.2	4.0	0.1	8.9	6.6	8.2	19.7	Moldova
...	...	...	...	3,541	24.3	3.4	16.5	1.2	8.6	3.0	16.6	22.2	Monaco
3.5	8.0	0.4	16.2	2,010	47.0	2.2	27.2	—	10.4	1.2	4.7	7.2	Mongolia
8.0	5.0	...	16.0	3,165	59.7	2.0	2.8	0.5	2.0	5.4	10.4	17.3	Morocco
...	...	1.4[3]	7.9	1,911	41.2	37.3	1.4	0.2	0.6	1.4	8.9	9.1	Mozambique
3.8[6]	*0.5[6]*	*1.1[6]*	*7.5[6]*	2,832	76.3	0.5	2.0	1.0	0.9	2.6	7.0	9.6	Myanmar (Burma)
...	...	...	...	2,107	48.6	13.9	5.6	0.6	3.4	1.9	5.1	20.9	Namibia
...	...	...	...	...	...	...	...	...	...	...	...	...	Nauru
1.2	...	2.9[3]	2.0	2,170	76.8	3.4	2.0	0.1	3.8	2.5	4.4	7.0	Nepal

Household budgets and consumption (continued)

Columns are grouped as follows: **income (latest)** — *percent received by* (lowest 20% of households, highest 10% of households) and *by source (percent)* (wages/salaries, self-employment, transfer payments[a], other[b]); **consumption expenditure** — per capita private final, U.S.$ (1995), and *by kind or end use (percent of household or personal budget; latest)* (food[c], housing[d], clothing[e], health care, energy/water, education).

country	lowest 20% of households	highest 10% of households	wages, salaries	self-employment	transfer payments[a]	other[b]	per capita private final, U.S.$ (1995)	food[c]	housing[d]	clothing[e]	health care	energy, water	education
Netherlands, The	7.3[1]	25.1[1]	48.2	10.7	29.1	12.0	15,290	13.6	14.9	7.1	12.9	3.1	0.7
Netherlands Antilles	...	...	...	...	...	...	6,050[10]	24.4[30]	10.4[30]	8.7[30]	2.2[30]	8.3[30]	1.2[30]
New Caledonia	...	...	68.2	18.1	13.7	...	5,410[31]	25.9	23.3[2,5]	3.5	3.2	[2]	...
New Zealand	2.7[12]	29.8[12]	65.8	9.8	15.2	9.1	10,300	20.0	19.4	4.4	2.9	3.2	1.5
Nicaragua	4.2[1]	39.8[1]	...	...	...	...	360	...	...	...	...	...	...
Niger	2.6	35.4	...	...	...	...	210	50.5	19.1[5]	7.3	...	...	...
Nigeria	4.4[1]	40.8[1]	30.2[18]	46.3[18]	0.9[18]	22.6[18]	350[32]	48.0	3.0	5.0	3.0	1.0	4.0
Northern Mariana Islands	...	...	...	...	...	...	...	49.2[15]	19.5[2,5]	9.1	[19]	[2]	0.6
Norway	9.7[12]	21.8[12]	58.8	9.9	24.2	7.1	16,570	23.5	13.7	7.0	5.4	6.2	0.6
Oman	...	...	...	...	...	...	3,000	40.6	24.6	5.1	2.4	3.2	[3]
Pakistan	9.5[1]	27.6[1]	22.0	56.0	22.0		300	37.0	11.0	6.0	1.0	5.0	1.0
Palau	...	...	63.7	7.4	18.5	10.4	...	...	...	...	...	...	...
Panama	3.6[1]	35.7[1]	60.8[6]	12.8[6]	13.2[6]	13.2[6]	1,570	34.9	12.6[2]	5.1	3.5	[2]	[3]
Papua New Guinea	4.5[1]	40.5[1]	57.3	[8]	1.1	41.6[8]	1,140	40.9	12.5[5]	6.2	...	4.9	...
Paraguay	2.3	46.6	33.9	[8]	2.5	63.6[8]	1,590	48.7	16.4	9.7	3.4	—	1.5
Peru	4.4[12]	35.4[12]	31.2	65.1	3.7	...	1,820	44.1[15]	6.8[2]	10.1	2.7	[2]	[3]
Philippines	5.4[1]	36.6[1]	45.7	42.5	3.4	8.4	800	56.8	4.1[2]	3.9	...	[2]	[3]
Poland	7.7[1]	26.3[12]	34.0	4.3	20.7	41.0	1,940	41.2	2.8	10.9	8.1	1.0	...
Portugal	7.3[12]	28.4[12]	46.4	[8]	21.8	31.8[8]	6,860	34.8	2.0	10.3	4.5	3.0	1.4
Puerto Rico	3.2	34.7	56.3	6.4	29.5	7.8	5,640[10]	20.6	11.8[2]	7.4	11.6	[2]	3.1
Qatar	...	...	80.8	5.6	...	13.6	3,600[4]	24.5	35.1[5]	9.1	1.0	1.9	4.3
Réunion	...	...	68.9	[8]	16.0	15.1[8]	4,820[31]	22.4	11.8	7.9	2.2	2.2	[3]
Romania	8.9[12]	22.7[12]	62.6	37.4			1,570	51.1	16.4[2,5]	15.7	1.2	[2]	[3]
Russia	4.4[1]	38.7[1]	68.5	6.4	15.7	12.1	1,180	34.8	2.7	22.3	...	[2]	[3]
Rwanda	9.7[1]	24.2[1]	10.4[33]	47.7[33]	13.9[33]	28.0[33]	130	32.1[33]	13.1[33]	9.4[33]	1.3[33]	...	[33]
St. Kitts and Nevis	...	...	...	...	...	...	2,480[28]	55.6[15]	7.6	7.5	...	6.6	...
St. Lucia	...	...	...	...	...	...	...	49.6[15]	13.5	6.5	2.3	4.5	[3]
St. Vincent and the Grenadines	...	...	...	...	...	...	1,700	59.8	6.3	7.7	...	6.2	...
Samoa	...	...	49.4	22.8	...	27.8	710[1]	58.8	5.1[5]	4.2	...	5.0	...
San Marino	...	...	...	...	...	...	...	22.1	20.9[2]	8.0	2.6	[2]	[3]
São Tomé and Príncipe	...	...	...	...	...	...	270	...	...	...	...	...	...
Saudi Arabia	...	...	...	...	...	...	2,980	52.2[18,34]	17.2[18,34]	6.6[18,34]	2.1[18,34]	1.8[18,34]	1.1[18,34]
Senegal	6.4[1]	33.5[1]	51.6[6]	48.4[6]			380	49.0	7.0	11.0	2.0	4.0	6.0
Serbia and Montenegro	...	...	41.7	15.8	12.7	29.8	2,480[35]	51.6	1.4	7.4	5.2	8.4	[3]
Seychelles	4.1	35.6	77.2	3.8	3.2	15.8	3,410[32]	53.9	13.6	4.2	0.4	9.1	...
Sierra Leone	1.1[1]	43.6[1]	27.9	61.6	10.5		190	63.8	5.8[2]	7.3	4.5	[2]	[3]
Singapore	5.1	33.5	81.2	16.8	2.0		11,710	18.7	10.2[2]	7.1	4.6	[2]	1.4
Slovakia	11.9[12]	18.2[12]	76.7	[8]	8.7	14.4[8]	1,580	26.8	7.6[2]	8.9	...	[2]	...
Slovenia	8.4[12]	20.7[12]	52.4	13.0	23.4	11.2	5,460	30.8	18.3	8.5	5.0	7.3	[3]
Solomon Islands	...	...	74.1	25.9			820[4]	46.8	21.9[2,5]	5.7	[19]	[2]	...
Somalia	...	...	...	...	...	...	...	62.3[6,15]	15.3[6]	5.6[6]	...	4.3[6]	...
South Africa	2.9[1]	45.9[1]	73.6	[8]	4.9	21.5[8]	1,970	29.3	12.6[2]	7.5	4.5	[2]	1.4
Spain	7.5[12]	25.2[12]	48.5	27.5	19.5	4.5	8,840	21.6[15]	12.6[2]	8.6	4.7	[2]	[3]
Sri Lanka	8.0[1]	28.0[1]	48.5	[8]	9.7	41.8[8]	520	48.0	1.9	10.1	1.8	3.3	0.8
Sudan, The	4.0	34.6	...	...	...	...	1,050[35]	63.6	11.5	5.3	4.1	3.8	[3]
Suriname	...	...	74.6	...	3.2	22.2	5,960[10]	39.9[6]	4.4[6]	11.0[6]	3.6[6]	6.9[6]	2.6[6]
Swaziland	2.8	54.5	44.4	22.2	12.2	21.2	500	33.5[15]	13.4[2]	6.0	1.8	[2]	[3]
Sweden	9.6[12]	20.1[12]	58.9	9.7	25.8	5.6	13,680	21.3	19.9	8.6	3.2	4.9	0.1
Switzerland	6.9[12]	25.2[12]	63.6	[8]	16.5	19.9[8]	26,060	27.0[15]	13.1	4.4	9.9	7.7	[3]
Syria	...	...	40.7	...	25.1	34.2	2,210	58.8[15]	16.0[2]	7.5	...	[2]	[3]
Taiwan	7.1	25.5	64.5	19.7	4.5	11.3	12,230	26.8	22.5	5.6	7.8	3.0	5.6
Tajikistan	...	...	64.3	5.6[7]	30.1	—	340	65.3	...	...	...	...	...
Tanzania	6.8[1]	30.1[1]	28.1	34.2	3.5	34.2	150	66.7	8.3	9.9	1.3	7.6	...
Thailand	6.4[1]	32.4[1]	36.4	45.0	0.9	17.7	1,540	29.0	11.6	8.0	1.7	...	0.5
Togo	8.0	30.5	...	...	...	...	210	42.5[6]	13.4[2,6]	11.5[6]	5.0[6]	[2,6]	[3,6]
Tonga	...	...	...	...	...	...	...	49.3	10.5	5.6	0.3	2.7	...
Trinidad and Tobago	2.6	33.6	...	...	...	...	2,050	25.5[15]	21.6	10.4	[19]	...	1.5
Tunisia	5.9[1]	30.7[1]	...	...	...	...	1,260	39.0	10.7	6.0	3.0	5.1	1.8
Turkey	5.8[1]	32.3[1]	24.1	51.4	10.8	13.7	1,940	38.5	22.8[2]	9.0	2.6	[2]	1.4
Turkmenistan	6.1[1]	31.7[1]	56.6	26.0[7]	14.4	3.0	570[10]	...	...	...	...	...	...
Tuvalu	...	...	17.9	76.1	...	6.0	...	45.5	11.5[5]	7.5	...	...	...
Uganda	6.6[1]	31.2[1]	...	...	...	...	260	57.1[6,15]	5.5[6]	...	...	7.3[6]	...
Ukraine	8.6[1]	26.4[1]	66.4	9.3	13.4	10.9	490	41.3	1.7	...	...	...	[3]
United Arab Emirates	...	...	...	...	...	...	7,940	24.1	23.7	9.1	1.1	1.2	3.9
United Kingdom	6.6[12]	27.3[12]	66.2	9.8	13.9	11.0	12,020	17.1	21.7	6.0	...	4.6	...
United States	5.2[12]	30.5[12]	64.4	9.0	19.3	7.3	18,840	15.4	14.9	6.9	17.0	3.5	2.2
Uruguay	5.4[12]	32.7[12]	53.5	17.0	29.5		4,140	39.9	17.6[2]	7.0	9.3	[2]	1.3
Uzbekistan	7.4[12]	25.2[12]	59.8	18.5	21.7	...	950	30.5[15]	29.0[2,5]	4.7	[19]	[2]	0.8
Vanuatu	...	...	59.0	33.7	7.3		680	...	...	...	...	...	...
Venezuela	3.7[12]	37.0[12]	...	...	...	...	2,490	30.4	11.5	10.6	2.9	3.0	0.8
Vietnam	8.0[1]	29.9[1]	17.2	64.6	17.6	0.5	280	62.4	2.5	5.0	...	...	2.9
Virgin Islands (U.S.)	...	...	65.7	2.6	13.0	12.7	...	25.3[36]	24.9[36]	5.4[36]	...	6.5[36]	...
West Bank	...	...	...	...	...	...	1,380[22]	...	...	...	...	...	...
Western Sahara	...	...	...	...	...	...	...	...	...	...	...	...	...
Yemen	6.1[1]	30.8[1]	...	...	...	...	310	61.0[37]	13.2[37]	...	1.1[37]	6.1[37]	...
Zambia	4.2[1]	39.2[1]	79.9	17.8	1.3	1.0	220	36.0	7.0	10.0	8.0	4.0	14.0
Zimbabwe	4.0[1]	46.9[1]	92.0	1.0	...	7.0	580	30.1[15]	6.5	10.3	7.1	8.9	6.0

[1]Data refer to consumption shares by fractiles of persons. [2]Housing includes energy, water. [3]Recreation includes education. [4]1988. [5]Housing includes household durable goods. [6]Capital city only. [7]Agricultural self-employment only. [8]Other includes self-employment. [9]1989. [10]1993. [11]Highest 20%. [12]Data refer to income shares by fractiles of persons. [13]1985. [14]1990. [15]Includes tobacco. [16]Includes wage taxes. [17]Personal effects, other includes education and recreation. [18]Urban areas only. [19]Recreation includes health care. [20]1984. [21]Low-income population in Banjul

transportation, communications	household durable goods[f]	recreation[g]	personal effects, other[h]	food consumption, 1998 daily available calories per capita	percent of total calories derived from: cereals	potatoes, cassava	meat, poultry	fish	eggs, milk	fruits, vegetables	fats, oils[i]	other[j]	country
13.3	7.1	9.7	17.6	3,282	17.1	4.5	15.0	1.0	15.0	6.1	16.1	25.1	Netherlands, The
19.5[30]	10.0[30]	4.2[30]	10.1[30]	2,659	28.2	2.3	18.9	1.4	10.8	5.0	13.6	19.7	Netherlands Antilles
16.1	5	6.7	21.3	2,812	30.9	6.1	13.1	1.5	8.6	3.9	16.0	19.9	New Caledonia
17.1	10.9	—— 20.6 ——		3,315	22.1	4.1	15.1	1.3	11.1	7.4	16.8	22.3	New Zealand
...	...	...	...	2,208	50.4	1.3	2.4	0.1	4.3	2.7	10.9	27.9	Nicaragua
...	5	...	23.1	1,966	70.5	3.2	2.6	0.1	2.2	1.7	4.4	15.2	Niger
3.0	6.0	...	27.0	2,882	45.8	18.6	2.4	0.4	1.0	4.4	14.1	13.3	Nigeria
8.3	5	13.9[19]	—	...	...	...	...	...	...	...	...	...	Northern Mariana Islands
12.8	6.9	8.8	15.1	3,425	27.4	4.3	10.7	3.5	12.2	4.9	17.7	19.2	Norway
8.9	7.1	4.1[3]	4.0	...	...	...	...	...	...	...	...	...	Oman
13.0	5.0	...	21.0	2,447	57.0	0.9	3.1	0.2	8.5	2.9	13.2	14.3	Pakistan
15.1	8.4	11.7[3]	8.7	...	...	...	...	...	...	...	...	...	Palau
13.0	5	...	22.5	2,476	37.0	2.7	7.5	1.1	7.4	5.7	16.1	22.5	Panama
4.5	6.2	2.3	7.3	2,168	31.2	25.4	7.7	1.3	0.6	17.6	6.2	9.9	Papua New Guinea
				2,577	27.8	13.9	11.5	0.4	7.3	4.3	16.2	18.7	Paraguay
7.3	7.5	7.6[3]	13.9	2,420	35.7	13.4	4.3	1.8	4.5	6.4	11.6	22.4	Peru
5.0	12.8	...	17.3	2,280	51.7	4.2	8.8	3.0	2.2	8.3	5.9	15.9	Philippines
8.9	8.3	15.0[3]	3.8	3,351	34.4	7.4	10.4	1.0	8.6	4.5	15.6	18.0	Poland
15.4	8.6	4.4	15.6	3,691	28.6	6.3	10.8	2.4	8.3	7.1	17.0	19.6	Portugal
11.8	11.2	7.9	14.7	...	...	...	...	...	...	...	...	...	Puerto Rico
13.0	5	—— 11.1 ——		...	...	...	...	...	...	...	...	...	Qatar
24.9	6.0	10.1[3]	12.5	3,308	41.4	1.7	11.9	1.5	5.2	5.0	9.8	23.5	Réunion
6.6	5	4.5[3]	4.5	3,263	49.5	4.5	7.4	0.1	11.3	4.5	10.5	12.2	Romania
...	9.4	...	30.8	2,835	41.3	8.0	9.0	1.6	10.3	3.4	9.6	20.6	Russia
1.7[33]	5.3[33]	0.4[33]	35.5[33]	2,035	22.4	23.1	1.1	—	1.4	25.9	5.5	—	Rwanda
4.3	9.4	...	9.0	2,766	24.9	2.6	13.6	1.9	8.6	4.6	11.6	32.1	St. Kitts and Nevis
6.3	5.8	3.2[3]	8.3	2,842	34.3	4.8	14.0	1.3	6.8	9.3	6.9	22.7	St. Lucia
3.7	6.6	...	9.7	2,554	35.2	4.3	10.4	1.1	6.1	5.2	9.6	28	St. Vincent and the Grenadines
9.0	5	...	17.9	...	...	...	...	...	...	...	...	...	Samoa
17.6	7.2	7.1[3]	14.5	3,608	31.8	1.9	11.1	1.1	8.9	7.2	22.0	15.9	San Marino
4.5[18, 34]	5.9[18, 34]	...	8.6[18, 34]	2,201	28.3	15.4	1.4	2.1	0.8	17.0	10.6	24.3	São Tomé and Príncipe
5.0	2.0	...	12.0	2,888	46.6	1.1	7.3	0.4	4.9	10.1	11.4	18.2	Saudi Arabia
5.7	1.6	2.4[3]	16.3	2,277	57.5	1.0	3.7	2.8	2.4	2.0	18.7	11.9	Senegal
6.4	6.6	1.4	4.4	2,963	29.4	2.3	16.3	0.2	11.4	6.8	17.8	15.8	Serbia and Montenegro
				2,462	37.3	1.2	5.6	5.1	6.5	5.8	11.5	27.1	Seychelles
4.4	3.9	3.8[3]	4.8	2,045	53.4	10.4	1.0	1.4	0.6	2.9	17.6	12.8	Sierra Leone
13.8	8.9	13.1	23.3	...	...	...	...	...	...	...	...	...	Singapore
...	3.9	...	26.2	2,953	27.3	4.3	10.5	0.3	8.9	4.7	20.8	23.2	Slovakia
12.7	3.3	6.1[3]	8.0	2,950	35.4	3.5	11.1	0.4	12.0	5.3	15.2	17.2	Slovenia
9.9	5	19	15.7	2,130	33.3	36.3	3.1	3.7	0.6	2.7	2.9	17.4	Solomon Islands
...	...	...	12.1[6]	1,531	33.4	1.5	8.7	0.2	28.4	2.8	7.4	17.5	Somalia
16.7	10.0	6.3	11.7	2,909	53.0	2.0	7.0	0.5	4.8	2.8	11.7	18.1	South Africa
15.3	7.1	7.0[3]	23.1	3,348	22.6	4.7	13.4	2.4	9.3	6.7	21.6	19.4	Spain
17.0	3.9	2.4	10.8	2,314	51.3	2.9	0.9	1.9	3.4	4.5	2.9	32.3	Sri Lanka
1.5	5.5	0.7[3]	4.0	2,444	56.5	0.6	5.1	0.1	13.3	2.9	9.5	11.9	Sudan, The
9.5[6]	12.3[6]	5.8[6]	4.0[6]	2,633	41.2	2.3	7.0	1.6	4.8	6.2	12.5	24.5	Suriname
8.8	12.8	3.3[3]	20.4	2,503	48.1	1.3	6.4	—	5.2	1.8	6.2	31.0	Swaziland
15.7	6.6	10.9	8.8	3,114	25.6	3.6	10.2	1.8	14.1	5.2	18.9	20.7	Sweden
12.9	5.1	9.8[3]	10.1	3,222	22.1	2.3	14.8	0.8	12.5	6.1	18.7	22.7	Switzerland
2.4	5.8	2.1[3]	7.4	3,378	53.9	1.2	3.8	0.1	6.6	5.6	12.9	15.9	Syria
10.7	2.2	1.1	4.7	...	...	...	...	...	...	...	...	...	Taiwan
...	...	...	34.7	2,176	67.9	0.1	2.8	—	3.4	4.3	12.2	9.2	Tajikistan
4.1	1.4	0.7	—	1,999	49.0	19.5	2.6	1.1	2.2	5.4	6.8	13.6	Tanzania
12.9	10.9	4.2	14.9	2,462	47.1	1.9	6.6	2.6	2.8	5.7	6.1	27.3	Thailand
9.5[6]	4.4[6]	5.1[3, 6]	8.6[6]	2,513	50.7	29.2	2.3	1.3	0.6	1.3	7.2	7.5	Togo
5.8	10.6	0.5	14.7	...	...	...	...	...	...	...	...	...	Tonga
15.2	14.3	17	6.2[17]	2,711	36.8	2.8	4.5	0.9	6.8	3.8	14.6	29.9	Trinidad and Tobago
9.0	11.2	7.1	7.1	3,297	52.9	1.8	3.0	0.5	4.6	6.2	15.8	15.3	Tunisia
8.8	9.0	5.6	2.3	3,554	48.4	3.7	2.5	0.4	6.9	7.9	15.1	15.1	Turkey
...	...	...	...	2,684	57.7	0.5	7.6	0.1	8.2	3.4	16.4	6.1	Turkmenistan
10.5	5	...	25.0	...	...	...	...	...	...	...	...	...	Tuvalu
5.9[6]	...	...	24.2[6]	2,216	20.4	23.4	3.2	0.8	1.9	25.8	2.2	22.3	Uganda
...	6.8	6.3[3]	43.9	2,878	44.5	8.8	5.8	0.7	10.3	3.4	10.8	15.7	Ukraine
14.1	11.6	4.7	6.5	3,372	33.8	1.6	11.5	1.4	9.5	14.3	10.3	17.7	United Arab Emirates
15.1	8.0	15.9	11.6	3,257	22.8	6.1	14.4	1.0	11.6	5.0	19.1	20.0	United Kingdom
13.9	1.5	5.8	18.9	3,757	23.6	2.9	11.9	0.8	11.7	5.2	17.9	26.1	United States
10.4	6.3	3.1	5.1	2,866	28.9	3.7	19.1	0.6	12.3	4.0	11.0	20.3	Uruguay
...	...	...	...	2,564	55.8	2.1	6.9	—	9.4	4.1	15.3	6.2	Uzbekistan
13.2	5	12.3[19]	10.3	2,737	21.4	30.7	9.2	1.6	1.5	6.4	8.9	20.3	Vanuatu
7.1	4.5	2.7	26.4	2,358	34.9	3.1	6.6	1.7	6.5	7.3	15.2	24.7	Venezuela
...	4.6	...	22.6	2,422	70.9	4.0	7.6	1.3	0.5	3.9	3.2	8.6	Vietnam
11.7[36]	4.3[36]	...	21.9[36]	...	...	...	...	...	...	...	...	...	Virgin Islands (U.S.)
...	...	...	...	...	...	...	...	...	...	...	...	...	West Bank
...	...	...	...	...	...	...	...	...	...	...	...	...	Western Sahara
1.9[37]	3.0[37]	...	13.7[37]	2,087	68.7	1.0	2.7	0.7	1.8	3.0	8.2	13.9	Yemen
5.0	1.0	...	15.0	1,950	64.9	14.5	2.7	0.8	1.3	1.5	3.4	10.9	Zambia
1.1	12.9	0.6	16.5	2,153	60.5	2.1	2.3	0.3	3.1	1.0	11.9	18.8	Zimbabwe

and Kombo St. Mary only. [22]1986. [23]Urban areas of Eastern region only. [24]Personal effects, other includes health care. [25]Housing includes water. [26]Wage earners only. [27]Workers and clerical workers only. [28]1992. [29]Malagasy households only. [30]Curaçao only. [31]1987. [32]1994. [33]Rural areas only. [34]Middle-income population only. [35]1991. [36]St. Thomas only. [37]Data refer to former Yemen Arab Republic.

Health services

The provision of health services in most countries is both a principal determinant of the quality of life and a large and growing sector of the national economy. This table summarizes the basic indicators of health personnel; hospitals, by kind and utilization; mortality rates that are most indicative of general health services; external controls on health (adequacy of food supply and availability of safe drinking water); and sources and amounts of expenditure on health care. Each datum refers more or less directly to the availability or use of a particular health service in a country, and, while each may be a representative measure at a national level, each may also conceal considerable differences in availability of the particular service to different segments of a population or regions of a country. In the United States, for example, the availability of physicians ranges from about one per 730 persons in the least well-served states to one per 260 in the best-served, with a rate of one per 150 in the national capital. In addition, even when trained personnel exist and facilities have been created, limited financial resources at the national or local level may leave facilities underserved; or lack of good transportation may prevent those most in need from reaching a clinic or hospital that could help them.

Definitions and limits of data have been made as consistent as possible in the compilation of this table. For example, despite wide variation worldwide in the nature of the qualifying or certifying process that permits an individual to represent himself as a physician, organizations such as the World Health Organization (WHO) try to maintain more specific international standards for training and qualification. International statistics presented here for "physicians" refer to persons qualified according to WHO standards and exclude traditional health practitioners, whatever the local custom with regard to the designation "doctor." Statistics for health personnel in this table uniformly include all those actually working in the health service field, whether in the actual provision of services or in teaching, administration, research, or other tasks. One group of practitioners for whom this type of guideline works less well is that of midwives, whose training and qualifications vary enormously from country to country but who must be included, as they represent, after nurses, perhaps the largest and most important category of health auxiliary worldwide.

Hospitals also differ considerably worldwide in terms of staffing and services. In this tabulation, the term hospital refers generally to a permanent facility offering inpatient services and/or nursing care and staffed by at least one physician. Establishments offering only outpatient or custodial care are excluded. These statistics are broken down into data for general hospitals (those providing care in more than one specialty), specialized facilities (with care in only one specialty), local medical centres, and rural health-care centres; the last two generally refer to institutions that provide a more limited range of medical or nursing care, often less than full-time. Hospital data are further analyzed into three categories of administrative classification: public, private nonprofit, and private for profit. Statistics on number of beds refer to beds that are maintained and staffed on a full-time basis for a succession of inpatients to whom care is provided.

Data on hospital utilization refer to institutions defined as above. Admission and discharge, the two principal points at which statistics are normally collected, are the basis for the data on the amount and distribution of care by kind of facility. The data on numbers of patients exclude babies born during a maternal confinement but include persons who die before being discharged. The bed-occupancy and average length-of-stay statistics depend on the concept of a "patient-day," which is the annual total of daily censuses of inpatients. The bed-occupancy rate is the ratio of total patient-days to potential days based on the number of beds; the average length-of-stay rate is the ratio of total patient-days to total admissions. Bed-occupancy rates may exceed 100% because stays of partial days are counted as full days.

Two measures that give health planners and policy makers an excellent indication of the level of ordinary health care are those for mortality of children under age five and for maternal mortality. The former reflects the

Health services

country	health personnel							hospitals									
										kinds (%)			ownership (%)				
	year	physicians	dentists	nurses	pharmacists	midwives	population per physician	year	number	general	specialized	medical centres/other	public	private nonprofit	private for profit	total number of hospital beds	hospital beds per 10,000 pop.
Afghanistan	2002	3,617	630[1]	8,891	767	...	5,675	2002	73	...	...	277	77.0	—23.0—		12,668	16
Albania	2002	4,110	1,360[1]	12,570[2]	...	...	753	2002	51	...	...	...	100.0	—	...	9,514	31
Algeria	2002	28,642	8,618	87,571	5,198	...	1,095	2002	513	...	...	...	...	...	...	34,544	12
American Samoa	2003	49	15	127	2[1]	11	1,253	2003	1	100.0	—	—	100.0	—	...	128	21
Andorra	2003	244	42	194	64	10[2]	296	2003	2	100.0	—	—	50.0	—50.0—		233	33
Angola	1997	736	...	10,942	...	492	12,985	1990	58	...	...	...	...	...	...	11,857	12
Antigua and Barbuda	1999	76	12[3]	233	13[3]	31[3]	867	2003	3	50.0	50.0	—	100.0	—	...	255	25
Argentina	2002	99,358	28,900[1]	16,000[1]	...	...	373	2001	1,235[7]	...	...	...	56.8[7]	—43.2[7]—		115,803	20
Armenia	2003	11,728	710[9]	18,379	121	1,541[9]	256	2003	137	...	...	...	100.0	—	...	14,208	44
Aruba	2004	126	22	277	20	6	740	2004	3	50.0	—	50.0	100.0	—	...	305	32
Australia	2004	54,800	9,400	159,600	13,756	11,649[10]	375	2001–02	1,283	...	...	...	58.1	—41.9—		79,311	40
Austria	2004	37,447	4,029[10]	17,767[10]	1,581	1,579[10]	216	2003	310	40.1	—59.9—		...	...	...	71,741	81
Azerbaijan	2004	30,000	2,116[10]	59,872[10]	2,143	11,800	278	2003	735	...	...	...	100.0	—	...	68,500	83
Bahamas, The	2001	458	21[11]	1,323[11]	52[1]	...	672	2002	5	60.0	20.0	20.0	60.0	—40.0—		1,540	34
Bahrain	2003	1,189	144[10]	2,861[10]	131	...	580	2003	12	58.3	42.7	—	75.0	16.7	8.3	1,912	28
Bangladesh	2001	32,498	938[7]	18,135	7,485[4]	15,794	4,306	2001	568	...	...	...	69.3[7]	—30.7[7]—		44,030	3
Barbados	2002	376	63[1]	988[1]	138[12]	377[12]	721	2002	9	66.7	33.3	...	77.8	—	22.2	501	19
Belarus	2003	44,800	4,492	123,192[10]	3,001[10]	6,160[10]	220	2003	279	55.4[1]	—44.6[1]—		100.0	—	...	112,007	114
Belgium	2002	46,268	7,360[11]	109,187[11]	14,772	6,602[11]	223	2001	363[11]	80.4[11]	19.6[11]	—	38.6[11]	61.4[11]	—	71,907	70
Belize	2003	251	32[2]	303[2]	30[11]	230[11]	1,620	1999	7	...	...	...	100.0	—	—	598	25
Benin	2001	923	16[14]	5,003	85[14]	432[14]	7,183	2001	...	...	...	...	...	...	...	923	1
Bermuda	2003	121	22[3]	522[3]	29[3]	...	525	2003	2	50.0	50.0	—	...	...	...	226	36
Bhutan	2002	122	9[4]	500	5[4]	326[14]	6,019	2002	29	...	...	...	...	...	...	1,023	14
Bolivia	2002	2,987	692[10]	9,068[10]	...	...	2,827	2003	230	10.7[14]	8.9[14]	80.3[14]	...	...	...	12,464	15
Bosnia and Herzegovina	2003	5,576	679[10]	16,708[10]	350[10]	1,159[10]	691	2003	...	...	...	...	...	...	...	11,981	31
Botswana	2003	510	38[1]	4,090[1]	142[1]	...	3,261	2003	30[15]	53.3[15]	3.3[15]	43.3[15]	...	...	...	3,816	22
Brazil	2001	357,888	165,599	89,710	66,727	...	485	2002	6,493	—100.0—		—	35.0	—65.0—		487,058	27
Brunei	2003	309	64	1,678	90[2]	404[2]	870	2003	10	90.0	—	10.0	90.0	—10.0—		905	26
Bulgaria	2003	28,243	6,482[10]	35,621[10]	1,020[10]	3,518[10]	277	2004	258	54.7	—45.3—		...	...	...	49,171	70
Burkina Faso	2001[16]	490	36	3,381	60	476	23,943	2001	78[5]	—14.1[5]—		85.9[5]	100.0	—	—	15,801	19
Burundi	2000	323	9[4]	1,783	62	...	21,737	1999	...	...	...	...	...	...	...	3,380	6
Cambodia	2004	2,122	241	8,085[2]	564[1]	3,040[2]	6,173	2004	188[11]	...	...	...	100.0	—	—	7,482	6
Cameroon	1996	1,031	56	5,112	...	70	13,510	1988	629	—27.0—		73.0	72.3	—27.7—		29,285	27
Canada	2002	59,294	17,287[2]	310,733[2]	24,518[1]	358[2]	529	2002–03	1,079[3]	81.8[3]	16.6[3]	1.6[3]	95.8[3]	—	4.2[3]	115,120	36
Cape Verde	2001	123	...	1,907	6[3]	...	3,604	2000	65[3]	8.0[3]	—	92.0[3]	100.0	—	—	689	16
Central African Republic	2001	189	16[14]	217	22[4]	179	20,291	2001	255	—21.1[17]—		78.9[17]	79.7[17]	—20.3[17]—		4,126	11
Chad	2001	205	2[10]	1,220	38	161	42,700	2001	...	...	...	...	...	...	...	4,105	5
Chile	2003	17,250	6,750	10,000	1,830[3]	5,369[3]	925	2002	847	...	...	...	90.1	—9.9—		42,163	25
China	2002	2,122,019[18, 19]	19	1,345,706	368,852[1]	44,517[1]	687	2002	69,105[3]	11.2[3]	13.4[3]	75.4[3]	100.0	—	—	3,004,000	23
Colombia	2002	58,761	33,951	52,281	...	...	729	2003	1,165	...	...	...	...	...	...	49,000	12
Comoros	2004	48	6[4]	180[7]	6[4]	74[7]	12,417	1995	...	...	...	...	...	...	...	1,450	29
Congo, Dem. Rep. of the	1996	3,224	514	20,652	59[4]	...	14,492	1986	400	...	...	...	52.5	—47.5—		...	21
Congo, Rep. of the	1995	632	35[4]	4,663	175[4]	160	4,083	1990	...	...	...	...	...	...	...	4,817	33
Costa Rica	2004	6,600	1,594[1]	9,425[1]	1,289[1]	...	644	2003	29[1]	...	...	...	87.9[1]	—	12.1[1]	6,000	14
Côte d'Ivoire	2001	1,113	219[4]	6,110	135[4]	2,196[3]	14,297	2001	...	...	...	...	...	...	...	5,981	4
Croatia	2003	10,820	3,021[10]	22,185[10]	2,235	1,491[10]	410	2003	70	54.0	46.0	—	...	...	...	24,927	56
Cuba	2002	67,417	9,841	83,880	...	...	167	2003	266	...	...	...	100.0	—	...	69,534	62
Cyprus[21]	2000	1,800	619	2,931	584	120[22]	390	2003	115	71.8[7]	22.1[7]	6.1[7]	10.0[22]	0.9[22]	89.1[22]	1,236	57
Czech Republic	2003	44,106	6,698[10]	97,077[10]	5,199[10]	4,895[10]	230	2003	357	68.9	31.1	—	69.0	—31.0—		66,492	65
Denmark	2002	19,600	4,834	51,990	2,638	1,312	365	2002	69[10]	43.0[10]	57.0[10]	—	43.1[10]	56.9[10]	—	22,600	41

probability of a newborn infant dying before age five. The latter refers to deaths attributable to delivery or complications of pregnancy, childbirth, the puerperium (the period immediately following birth), or abortion. A principal source for the former data was UNICEF Child Mortality and for the latter, the UNICEF Report: Maternal Mortality in 2000.

Levels of nutrition and access to safe drinking water are two of the most basic limitations imposed by the physical environment in which health-care activities take place. The nutritional data are based on reported levels of food supply (whether or not actually consumed), referred to the recommendations of the United Nations' Food and Agriculture Organization for the necessary daily intake (in calories) for a moderately active person of average size in a climate of a particular kind (fewer calories are needed in a hot climate) to remain in average *good* health. Excess intake in the many developed countries ranges to more than 40% above the minimum required to maintain health (the excess usually being construed to diminish, rather than raise, health). The range of deficiency is less dramatic numerically but far more critical to the countries in which deficiencies are chronic, because the deficiencies lead to overall poor health (raising health service needs and costs), to decreased productivity in nearly every area of national economic life, and to the loss of social and economic potential through early mortality. By "safe" water is meant only water that has no substantial quantities of chemical or biological pollutants—*i.e.*, quantities sufficient to cause "immediate" health problems. Data refer to the proportion of persons having "reasonable access" to an "adequate" supply of water within a "convenient" distance of the person's dwelling, as these concepts are interpreted locally.

The data on health care expenditure were excerpted from a joint effort by the WHO and the World Bank to create better analytical tools by which the interrelations among health policy, health care delivery systems, and human health might be examined against the more general frameworks of government operations, resource allocation, and development process.

Expenditures were tabulated for direct preventative and curative activities and for public health and public education programs having direct impact on health status—family planning, nutrition, and health education—but not more indirect programs like environmental, waste removal, or relief activities. Public, parastatal (semipublic, *e.g.*, social security institutions), international aid, and household expenditure reports and surveys were utilized to build up a comprehensive picture of national, regional, and world patterns of health care expenditures and investment that could not have been assembled from any single type of source. For reasons of space, public and parastatal are combined as the former. A principal source for expenditures was the World Bank Group Statistical Database, which includes national statistics, UN databases, and World Bank surveys.

Internet resources for further information:
- WHO Global Health Atlas http://globalatlas.who.int
- WHO Regional Office for Africa http://www.afro.who.int
- WHO Regional Office for Europe http://www.euro.who.int
- WHO Regional Office for the Eastern Mediterranean http://www.emro.who.int/index.asp
- Pan American Health Organization http://www.paho.org
- WHO Regional Office for South-East Asia http://www.whosea.org
- ECOWAS Social and Economic Indicators http://www.ecostat.org/en/Socio-Economic/Health.pdf
- UNICEF Maternal Mortality in 2000. Annex Tables A, F; WHO, 2004 http://www.reliefweb.int/library/documents/2003/who-saf-22oct.pdf
- UNICEF Report on Child Mortality http://www.childinfo.org/areas/childmortality/u5data.php
- Human Development Report 2004 http://www.undp.org
- World Bank Database http://devdata.worldbank.org/hnpstats

No comparable source exists for hospitals.

admissions or discharges				bed occu- pancy rate (%)	aver- age length of stay (days)	mortality		popu- lation with access to safe water 2002 (%)	food supply (% of FAO require- ment) 2002	total health expenditures, 2001					country
rate per 10,000 pop.	by kinds of hospital (%)					under age 5 per 1,000 live newborn 2003	maternal mortality per 100,000 live births 2000			as percent of GDP	per capita (U.S.$)	by source (percent)			
	general	special- ized	medical centres/ other									public	private	external grants/ loans	
...	...	...	...	...	...	257	1,900	13	117	5.2	8	52.6	47.4	11.2	Afghanistan
...	...	...	...	...	...	21	55	97	118	3.7	45	64.6	35.4	3.4	Albania
371[13]	...	...	...	49.3[4]	5[4]	41	140	87	126	4.1	70	75.0	25.0	0.1	Algeria
965[5]	100.0	—	—	38.4[5]	4[5]	...	...	...	...	...	...	...	...	...	American Samoa
...	...	...	...	...	...	7	...	100	...	5.7	1,261	71.0	29.0	—	Andorra
238[6]	...	...	...	44.5[6]	16[6]	260	1,700	50	89	4.4	37	63.1	36.9	14.2	Angola
872[6]	...	...	...	50.0[3, 6]	8[3, 6]	12	150[3]	91	100	5.6	456	60.9	39.1	2.9	Antigua and Barbuda
560[6, 7]	...	...	...	52.0[6, 8]	6[6]	20	82	97[9]	127	9.5	680	53.4	46.6	0.3	Argentina
...	...	...	...	44.7	10	33	55	92	89	7.8	46	41.2	58.8	3.7	Armenia
1,183	...	...	...	88.7	8	...	...	100	...	...	...	...	...	...	Aruba
...	...	...	...	78.2	5	6	8	100	115	9.2	1,776	67.9	32.1	—	Australia
2,790	...	...	...	74.6	8	5	4	100	140	8.0	1,806	69.3	30.7	—	Austria
...	...	...	...	...	...	91	94	77	101	1.6	83	66.9	33.1	7.7	Azerbaijan
837[3, 8]	...	...	...	85.4[3, 8]	11[3, 8]	14	60	97	114	5.7	1,084	57.0	43.0	0.3	Bahamas, The
...	...	...	...	...	...	15	28	100[9]	...	4.1	490	69.0	31.0	—	Bahrain
...	...	...	...	...	...	69	300	99	95	3.5	11	44.2	55.8	13.3	Bangladesh
810[12]	93.5[12]	6.5[12]	—	88.3[12]	32[12]	13	95	100	128	6.5	634	66.3	33.7	4.8	Barbados
...	...	...	...	...	...	17	35	100	117	5.5	82	86.7	13.3	—	Belarus
1,963[11]	96.0[11]	4.0[11]	—	84.4[11]	12[11]	5	10	100	140	8.9	1,983	71.7	28.3	—	Belgium
265[13]	...	...	...	...	...	39	140	91	127	5.2	167	45.1	54.9	6.1	Belize
...	...	...	...	...	...	154	850	68	111	4.4	18	46.9	53.1	21.5	Benin
1,313[3]	97.0[3]	3.0[3]	—	75.0[3]	8[3]	...	...	...	88	...	...	...	...	...	Bermuda
...	...	...	...	...	...	85	420	62	...	3.9	9	90.6	9.4	38.2	Bhutan
250[3]	...	...	...	48.0[3]	6[3]	66	420	85	94	5.3	61	66.3	33.7	12.2	Bolivia
612[6]	...	...	...	...	...	17	31	98	114	7.5	113	36.8	63.2	2.4	Bosnia and Herzegovina
...	...	...	...	...	...	112	100	95	93	6.6	151	66.2	33.8	0.4	Botswana
740[7]	...	...	...	...	7	35	260	89	128	7.6	227	41.6	58.4	0.5	Brazil
...	...	...	...	...	...	6	37	90[9]	127	3.1	429	79.4	20.6	...	Brunei
...	...	...	...	...	...	15	32	100	114	4.8	112	82.1	17.9	2.1	Bulgaria
...	...	...	...	...	...	207	1,000	51	102	3.0	9	60.1	39.9	25.6	Burkina Faso
...	...	...	...	...	...	190	1,000	79	71	3.6	3	59.0	41.0	43.7	Burundi
...	...	...	...	...	...	140	450	34	92	11.8	30	85.1	14.9	19.7	Cambodia
...	...	...	...	...	...	166	730	63	98	3.3	28	37.1	62.9	6.3	Cameroon
860	...	...	...	82.5	7	6	6	100	135	9.5	2,124	70.8	29.2	—	Canada
...	...	...	...	...	...	35	150	80	138	4.5	64	83.9	16.1	16.6	Cape Verde
...	...	...	...	...	...	180	1,100	75	88	4.5	10	51.2	48.8	32.4	Central African Republic
...	...	...	...	...	...	200	1,100	34	89	2.6	12	78.0	24.0	62.0	Chad
749[3, 6]	...	...	...	69.9[3, 6]	7[3, 6]	9	31	95	117	7.0	253	44.0	56.0	0.1	Chile
418[14]	—60.4[14]—		39.6[14]	66.9[14]	15[14]	37	56	77	125	5.5	52	37.2	62.8	0.2	China
614[20]	41.4[20]	16.7[20]	41.9[20]	57.2[20]	6[20]	21	130	92	111	5.5	159	65.7	34.3	0.2	Colombia
...	...	...	...	...	...	73	480	94	75	3.1	7	60.0	40.0	39.9	Comoros
...	...	...	...	...	...	205	990	46	72	3.5	4	44.4	55.6	18.0	Congo, Dem. Rep. of the
...	...	...	...	...	...	108	510	46	97	2.1	17	63.8	38.2	3.3	Congo, Rep. of the
958[5]	...	...	...	78.2[5]	6[5]	10	43	97	128	7.2	358	68.5	31.5	1.3	Costa Rica
...	...	...	...	...	...	192	690	84	114	6.2	41	16.0	84	3.2	Côte d'Ivoire
1,700	72.0	28.0	—	82.0	11	7	8	96[9]	110	9.0	366	81.8	18.2	0.1	Croatia
1,376[5]	...	...	...	...	...	8	33	91	136	7.2	186	86.2	13.8	0.2	Cuba
522[7]	...	...	...	81.0	6	5	47	100	131	8.1	764	47.7	52.3	2.3	Cyprus[21]
1,835	98.0	2.0	—	81.2	9	4	9	100	128	7.4	408	91.4	8.6	—	Czech Republic
1,857	87.0	13.0	—	90.0	9	4	5	100	128	8.4	2,565	82.4	17.8	—	Denmark

Health services (continued)

country	health personnel							hospitals								total number of hospital beds	hospital beds per 10,000 pop.
	year	physicians	dentists	nurses	pharmacists	midwives	population per physician	year	number	kinds (%) general	specialized	medical centres/ other	ownership (%) public	private non-profit	private for profit		
Djibouti	1999	86	10	424	12	...	5,429	1999	8[3]	—25.0[3]—		75.0[3]	100.0	...	...	1,159	27
Dominica	2003	38	10	361	27[15]	...	1,580	2003	53[11]	1.9[11]	—98.1[11]—		100.0	—	—	270	30
Dominican Republic	2000	16,530	7,000	15,352	3,330	...	500	2003[8]	723[12]	—7.9[12]—		92.1[12]	...	...	...	9,395	11
East Timor	2002	47	...	...	...	...	17,355	1999	...				...	...	...	560	8
Ecuador	2002	20,592	2,062[2]	19,549[2]	906[22]	1,037[2]	627	2003	474[14]	17.0[14]	8.0[14]	75.0	26.0[14]	11.3[14]	62.7[14]	19,975	15
Egypt	2005	157,000	18,438[2]	188,000	46,096[2]	...	448	2005	5,072	4.5[11]	—95.5[11]—		87.9[11]	—12.1[11]—		170,000	24
El Salvador	2002	8,171	3,573	11,777	1,990	1,940[5]	798	2003	78	...	...	...	61.5[22]	1.3[22]	37.2[22]	4,625	7
Equatorial Guinea	2004	101	4[3]	169[3]	...	9[3]	5,070	1990	...	...	...	...	...	...	...	792	29
Eritrea	2000	173	4[3]	574[3]	...	79[3]	21,457	2000	10[3]	...	...	...	...	...	...	3,126	8
Estonia	2002	4,275	1,078	9,976	813[2]	453[10]	316	2003	51	...	...	...	87.2[11]	—12.8[11]—		8,248	61
Ethiopia	2002	1,971	61	13,018	125	1,142	34,473	2003	86	...	...	...	...	...	...	13,389	2
Faroe Islands	2003	83	38	360	10[14]	19[14]	518	2003	3	33.3[14]	—	66.7[14]	100.0	—	—	290	60
Fiji	2003	373	56	1,648	59[1]	...	2,229	1999	25	...	...	...	...	...	...	2,097	26
Finland	2003	16,633	4,607	112,637	7,756[10]	3,980[10]	313	2003	380	...	...	...	75.7	—24.3—		37,656	72
France	2004	196,000	40,935[23]	397,506	60,366	14,725[10]	306	2001	4,171	—100.0—			25.3	—74.7—		485,769	79
French Guiana	2003	319	38[15]	568	47[15]	40[15]	570	2003	25	...	...	...	...	...	...	764	42
French Polynesia	2004	447	113	824	82[2]	81[2]	562	2003	7	...	...	...	...	...	...	971	39
Gabon	2003	270	32[20]	759[20]	71[20]	240[20]	5,000	2003	27[17]	...	...	...	...	...	...	4,460	33
Gambia, The	2001	97	1,348	155[7]	6[7]	102[7]	14,000	2000	13[15]	15.4[15]	—	84.6[15]	...	...	...	1,140	8
Gaza Strip[24]	2001	...	...	...	...	...	...	2001	6	...	...	...	83.3[14]	—16.7[14]—		...	11
Georgia	2003	20,936	1,100	21,900	364[23]	1,500[23]	250	2003	422[4]	...	...	...	100.0	...	...	18,200	40
Germany	2003	304,000	63,854[10]	783,000[10]	53,000[10]	9,506[10]	271	2003	2,240	90.9[5]	9.1[5]	—	49.2[22]	36.0[22]	14.8[22]	541,901	66
Ghana	2002	975	36[3]	13,102	1,433	4,094	21,086	2001	121[5]	...	...	...	60.3[5]	—39.75—		18,448	9
Greece	2001	46,325	12,394	33,252	12,304	2,264	221	2001	337	53.1	46.9	—	43.0	—57.0—		51,500	49
Greenland	2003	91	34[10]	515	10[5]	11[7]	624	2001	16	6.3	—	93.7[4]	100.0	—	—	406	72
Grenada	2003	127	14[3]	232[3]	47[3]	...	803	2000	3	100.0	—	—	100.0	—	—	330	32
Guadeloupe	2003	924	129[3]	1,640[3]	220[3]	140[3]	477	2003	29	...	...	...	44.8[3]	—55.2[3]—		2,428	55
Guam	1999	166	31	647	57	24	1,169	2000	1	...	...	...	...	...	...	225	13
Guatemala	2003	11,700	2,046[1]	44,986[1]	...	18,924[22]	1,053	2003	35[14]	...	...	...	...	...	...	6,118	5
Guernsey	1999	93	...	418	...	...	654	2003	3	100.0	—	—	100.0	—	—	112,007	...
Guinea	2001	996	38	3,506	199[2]	299[2]	8,571	2004	38	—100.0—		...	100.0	—	—	2,990	3
Guinea-Bissau	2003	250	11[14]	1,769[10]	12[17]	148[3]	5,546	2001	16[22]	...	...	...	62.5[22]	—37.5[22]—		1,448	11
Guyana	2003	366	30	1,738	40[3]	165[3]	2,055	2002	30[15]	...	...	...	83.3[15]	—16.7[15]—		3,274	44
Haiti	1999	1,910	94[11]	834[11]	...	...	4,000	2000	49	...	...	...	...	...	...	6,431	8
Honduras	2001	1,680	989[7]	6,152[7]	975[22]	...	3,865	2003	68	...	...	...	41.2	—58.8—		5,158	16
Hong Kong	2003	11,016	1,848	43,782	1,412	136	621	2003	53	...	...	...	77.4	—22.6—		35,526	52
Hungary	2004	38,877	4,618[1]	84,947[10]	5,125	2,165	260	2003	167	60.0	—40.0—		97.3	—2.7—		79,610	78
Iceland	2003	1,047	283[2]	2,474	243[10]	219[10]	360	2003	57	89.0[11]	11.0[11]	—	...	...	...	2,432	85
India	2001[25]	555,060	19,523[22]	776,400	5,822[26]	16,103	1,853	2003	17,900[10]	...	...	...	55.0[5]	—45.0[5]—		903,900	9
Indonesia	2001	21,467	5,450	97,293	...	...	9,871	1999	1,215	...	...	...	55.4	—44.6—		124,834	6
Iran	1998	60,079	12,378	159,271	5,955[26]	7,387[7]	953	2003	733	79.8	—20.2—		84.5	—15.5—		111,552	17
Iraq	2003	16,594	2,689	69,525[1]	3,358	...	1,587	2003	196	...	...	...	66.8	—33.2—		34,505	13
Ireland	2003	10,270	2,006	63,474[2]	3,165	15,228[11]	389	2003	60[8]	100.0	—	—	100.0	—	—	13,020	35
Isle of Man	2004	143	24	41	24[26]	...	540	2003	3	—100.0—			100.0	—	—	505	70
Israel	2002	24,392	7,446	39,315	4,355	1,108	258	2003	356	18.5[14]	81.5[14]	—	71.3	—28.7—		40,116	61
Italy	2002	353,692	34,014	256,860	63,008	...	162	2003	1,410[10]	92.0[10]	8.0[10]	—	56.1[10]	—43.9[10]—		237,216	41
Jamaica	2003	2,253	212	4,374	52[3]	273[3]	1,193	2003	24[3]	75.0[3]	25.0[3]	—	75.0	—25.0—		3,795	14
Japan	2002	262,687	92,874	1,097,326	212,720	24,501[2]	489	2002	9,413[7]	88.7[7]	11.3[7]	—	73.5[7]	—26.5[7]—		1,646,797	128
Jersey	2001	174	...	...	...	...	500	1995	6	16.7	83.3	—	100.0	—	—	651	77
Jordan	2001	10,623	2,850	14,251	4,975	893	448	2003	95	...	...	...	43.1	—56.9—		8,982	17
Kazakhstan	2003	54,600	4,331[10]	113,400	2,672[10]	8,094[10]	274	2003	1,005	...	...	...	100.0	...	...	111,900	77
Kenya	2003	4,813	772	30,212	1,881	...	6,653	2003	649	—35.1[14]—		64.9[14]	...	...	...	60,657	19
Kiribati	2004	20	3	238	4[11]	...	4,545	2004	1	...	...	...	...	...	...	140	67
Korea, North	2002	70,870	...	59,900	...	12,931[14]	313	2002	...	...	...	...	...	...	...	292,340	131
Korea, South	2003	95,881	20,446	192,480	50,623[2]	8,728[2]	500	2003	1,302	21.7	—78.3—		10.0	—90.0—		426,489	88
Kuwait	2002	3,780	673[10]	9,197[10]	722[2]	19[1]	625	2002	23	...	...	...	66.7[15]	...	33.3[15]	5,200	22
Kyrgyzstan	2001	13,379	1,077	33,698	109	3,140	366	2003	348[14]	89.1	—	10.9	100.0	—	—	26,600	53
Laos	2003	1,283	83	5,291	...	...	2,207	2003	25	0.7[4]	—99.3[4]—		100.0	—	—	6,255	27
Latvia	2002	7,900	1,245[10]	11,954[10]	292[15]	501[10]	295	2003	153	51.2[15]	4.1[15]	28.8[15]	97.5[11]	2.5[11]	—	18,200	78
Lebanon	2001	11,505	4,283	4,157	3,359	...	298	2002	144	...	...	...	10.5[14]	—89.5[14]—		9,999	28
Lesotho	1995	105	10	1,169	60[16]	914	18,524	1987	22	90.9	9.1	—	54.5	45.5	—	2,400	13[12]
Liberia	2001	23	2[15]	2,800	...	997	116,667	1988	92	—37.0—		63.0	...	...	...	...	...
Libya	1997	6,092	619[3]	17,136[3]	1,095[3]	...	781	2002	...	...	...	...	...	...	...	18,100	39
Liechtenstein	2000	46	18[7]	...	27	...	710	2000	1	...	...	...	...	...	...	108	35
Lithuania	2004	13,682	2,490[10]	27,787[10]	2,266[10]	1,350[10]	252	2004	189	...	...	...	100.0	...	...	29,990	87
Luxembourg	2003	1,225	316	3,197	371	95[10]	367	2003	17	52.9	47.1	—	50.0	—50.0—		3,045	68
Macau	2004	1,006	137	1,043	48[7]	...	454	2004	2	—100.0—			50.0	—50.0—		1,114	21
Macedonia	2001	4,459	1,125	10,553	309	1,456	454	2002	58[3]	27.4[15]	24.2[15]	48.4[15]	100.0	—	—	10,248	49
Madagascar	2001	1,428	76	3,038	8	1,472	10,859	2000	...	...	...	...	...	...	...	7,043	5
Malawi	2003	187	4	3,094	39	...	64,775	1998	395	12.2	0.8	87.0	59.2	—40.8—		14,200	13
Malaysia	2003	18,191	2,418	36,784	2,333[10]	7,711[2]	1,406	2003	337[7]	...	...	...	35.1[7]	—64.9[7]—		47,406	19
Maldives	2003	315	8	785	141	409	905	2003	14	20.0	—	80.0	100.0	—	—	643	23
Mali	2001	781	9	2,652	57[14]	284[2]	13,214	1998	...	...	...	...	...	...	...	2,412	2
Malta	2001	1,144	158	1,473	750	291[11]	344	2003	7	...	...	...	71.4[3]	—28.6[3]—		2,140	48
Marshall Islands	2002	34	4	152[2]	2[10]	6	1,575	2002	2	100.0	—	—	100.0	—	—	140	26
Martinique	2000	762	130[3]	1,700[3]	230[3]	150[3]	507	2000	8	...	...	...	100.0	—	—	2,674	69
Mauritania	1995	323	47	1,461	65	237	7,251	1990	16	...	...	...	...	...	...	3,827	7
Mauritius	2004	1,303	167	2,774[28]	286	28	1,043	2004	14	57.1	28.6	14.3	68.7	—31.3—		3,677	31
Mayotte	1997	57	...	...	...	...	2,304	1997	2	100.0	—	—	100.0	—	—	186	14
Mexico	2002	140,286	9,108	192,828	...	6,558	734	2002	4,506[7]	...	...	...	34.2[7]	—65.8[7]—		76,529	11
Micronesia	2000	64	14	410	7[22]	7	1,678	2000	4	100.0	—	—	100.0	—	—	260	31
Moldova	2001	12,800	1,326	26,765	2,621	1,075	334	2003	312	...	...	...	100.0	...	...	25,000	67
Monaco	2002	156	21	500[14]	67[14]	11[14]	207	2001	1	100.0	—	—	100.0	...	...	521	161
Mongolia	2003	6,637	459	7,734	788	612	376	2002	390	...	...	...	...	...	...	18,180	74
Morocco	2003	13,955	2,304[10]	26,277	6,467	87[4]	2,123	2002[8]	201[7]	48.8[7]	—	51.2[7]	100.0	...	...	26,153	8

rate per 10,000 pop.	by kinds of hospital (%) general	special-ized	medical centres/other	bed occu-pancy rate (%)	aver-age length of stay (days)	under age 5 per 1,000 live newborn 2003	maternal mortality per 100,000 live births 2000	popu-lation with access to safe water 2002 (%)	food supply (% of FAO require-ment) 2002	as percent of GDP	per capita (U.S.$)	public	private	external grants/loans	country
1,026[11]	...	...	...	94.6[11]	8[11]	138	730	80	96	7.0	51	58.8	41.2	30.0	Djibouti
470[12]	...	...	...	...	...	14	657	97	114	6.0	203	71.3	28.7	0.9	Dominica
...	...	...	...	...	...	35	150	93	104	6.1	155	36.1	63.9	1.8	Dominican Republic
...	...	...	...	...	...	124	660	52	130	9.8	51	59.5	40.5	9.8	East Timor
508[14]	...	...	...	53.1[14]	6[14]	27	130	86	120	4.5	80	50.3	49.7	1.0	Ecuador
317[11]	...	...	...	...	...	39	84	98	133	3.9	59	48.9	51.1	2.0	Egypt
...	...	...	...	54.9[8,12]	6[8,12]	36	150	82	113	8.0	169	46.7	53.3	0.9	El Salvador
...	...	...	...	...	...	146	880	44	72	2.0	65	60.4	39.6	10.6	Equatorial Guinea
...	...	...	...	...	...	95	650	57	65	5.7	9	65.1	34.9	52.3	Eritrea
1,934	76.7[15]	21.5[15]	1.8[15]	67.7	9	9	63	100	117	5.5	224	77.8	22.2	—	Estonia
278	...	...	...	86.4[15]	12[15]	169	850	22	80	3.5	5	40.5	59.5	34.3	Ethiopia
278	...	...	...	86.4[15]	12[15]	...	...	...	...	...	...	...	...	...	Faroe Islands
...	...	...	...	...	...	20	75	45	127	4.0	79	67.1	32.9	10.1	Fiji
2,592	...	...	...	72.0	10	5	6	100	114	7.0	1,628	75.6	24.4	—	Finland
2,480	...	...	...	...	...	5	17	100	145	9.6	2,103	76.0	24.0	—	France
1,714[22]	...	...	...	70.3[22]	8[22]	...	...	88[9]	127	...	...	...	...	...	French Guiana
...	...	...	...	...	...	...	...	100	126	...	...	...	...	...	French Polynesia
...	...	...	...	...	...	91	420	87	113	3.6	151	47.9	52.1	1.8	Gabon
752[14]	...	...	...	74.9[14]	3[14]	123	540	82	96	6.4	21	49.4	50.6	26.6	Gambia, The
...	...	...	...	...	...	24	100	...	...	...	...	...	...	...	Gaza Strip
...	...	...	...	...	...	45	32	76	92	3.6	22	37.8	62.2	6.1	Georgia
1,812[22]	...	...	...	82.8[22]	13[22]	5	8	100	131	10.8	2,418	74.9	25.1	—	Germany
...	...	...	...	...	...	95	540	79	116	4.7	15	59.6	40.4	23.2	Ghana
1,530	83.4	16.6	—	75.0	8	5	9	99[9]	149	9.4	1,044	56.0	44.0	—	Greece
2,188	29.2	—	70.8	70.1	6	...	...	...	...	...	...	...	...	...	Greenland
774[5]	100.0	—	—	59.1[5]	7[5]	23	...	95	121	5.3	262	71.9	28.1	—	Grenada
2,154[3]	...	...	...	84.0[3]	10[3]	...	...	95[9]	113	...	...	...	...	...	Guadeloupe
...	...	...	...	...	...	...	...	100	...	...	...	...	...	...	Guam
...	...	...	...	...	...	47	240	95	101	4.8	86	48.3	51.7	1.4	Guatemala
1,115[1]	100.0	—	—	...	...	...	...	...	...	7.2	2,780	...	...	...	Guernsey
...	...	...	...	...	...	160	740	51	104	3.5	20	54.1	45.9	20.5	Guinea
...	...	...	...	...	...	204	1,100	59	88	5.9	9	53.8	46.2	38.6	Guinea-Bissau
...	...	...	...	...	...	69	170	83	119	5.3	50	79.9	20.1	2.2	Guyana
...	...	...	...	...	...	118	680	71	92	5.0	31	53.4	46.6	42.0	Haiti
459[22]	...	...	...	...	...	41	110	90	104	6.1	60	53.1	46.9	7.5	Honduras
1,917	...	...	...	...	...	6	7	100	134	4.7	720	19.5[1]	80.5[1]	—	Hong Kong
2,768	...	...	...	79.0	8	8	16	99	132	6.8	375	75.0	25.0	—	Hungary
2,828[12]	94.0[12]	6.0[12]	—	86.5[12]	12[12]	4	6	100	122	9.2	2,478	82.9	17.1	—	Iceland
...	...	...	...	...	...	87	540	86	111	5.1	29	17.9	82.1	0.4	India
...	...	...	...	...	...	41	230	78	134	2.4	21	25.1	74.9	6.5	Indonesia
...	...	...	...	...	...	39	76	93	128	6.3	79	43.5	56.5	0.1	Iran
645[4]	...	...	...	42.4[4]	4[4]	125	250	81	91	3.2	12	31.8	68.2	0.1	Iraq
1,520	100.0	—	—	84.5	7	6	5	100[9]	145	6.5	1,839	76.0	24.0	5.0	Ireland
...	...	...	...	...	...	...	...	...	...	...	...	...	...	...	Isle of Man
1,912	...	...	...	94.0	11	6	17	100	143	8.7	1,754	69.2	30.8	0.1	Israel
1,820[10]	91.1[10]	8.9[10]	—	73.7[10]	8[10]	4	5	100	146	8.4	1,562	75.3	24.7	—	Italy
242[3,8]	81.7[3,8]	18.3[3,8]	—	53.7[3]	5[3]	20	87	93	120	6.8	178	42.1	57.9	3.0	Jamaica
...	...	...	...	...	...	4	10	100	118	8.0	2,558	77.9	22.1	—	Japan
1,718[4]	84.0[4]	16.0[4]	—	...	...	...	...	...	...	7.5	2,600	...	...	...	Jersey
512	...	...	...	73.5	5	28	41	91	109	9.5	163	47.0	53.0	4.4	Jordan
...	...	...	...	...	...	73	210	86	105	3.1	48	60.4	39.6	3.5	Kazakhstan
...	...	...	...	...	...	123	1,000	62	90	7.8	18	21.4	78.6	9.8	Kenya
...	...	...	...	...	...	66	...	64	125	8.6	40	98.8	1.2	4.4	Kiribati
...	...	...	...	...	...	55	67	100	92	2.5	...	73.4	26.6	3.0	Korea, North
629[14]	97.5[14]	2.5[14]	—	65.5[14]	13[14]	5	20	92	130	6.0	524	44.4	55.6	—	Korea, South
950[8,15]	72.2[8,15]	27.8[8,15]	—	64.9[8,15]	7[8,15]	7	5	100	124	3.9	539	78.8	21.2	—	Kuwait
1,775	95.5	—	4.5	75.6	15	68	110	76	117	4.0	13	48.7	51.3	13.0	Kyrgyzstan
...	...	...	...	...	...	91	650	43	104	3.1	10	55.5	44.5	21.1	Laos
2,210	78.4[15]	4.6[15]	17.0[15]	76.5	13	12	42	100	115	6.4	190	52.5	47.5	0.7	Latvia
...	...	...	...	...	...	31	150	100	129	12.2	583	28.1	71.9	0.2	Lebanon
221[6]	...	...	...	...	...	84	550	76	116	5.5	23	78.9	21.1	6.0	Lesotho
...	...	...	...	...	...	235	760	62	82	4.3	5	75.9	24.1	57.2	Liberia
...	...	...	...	...	...	16	97	72	139	2.9	158	56.0	44.0	—	Libya
...	...	...	...	...	...	11	...	100	...	...	...	...	...	...	Liechtenstein
2,200[23]	...	...	...	76.9[23]	11[23]	11	13	100	130	6.0	216	70.5	29.5	1.0	Lithuania
1,941[15]	94.6[15]	5.4[15]	—	94.3	12	5	28	100	137	6.0	2,614	89.9	10.1	—	Luxembourg
726	...	...	...	64.4[15]	16[15]	...	...	...	108	...	...	...	...	...	Macau
995[15]	67.2[15]	6.1[15]	26.7[15]	68.5[3]	14[3]	11	23	...	105	6.8	102	84.9	15.1	6.8	Macedonia
...	...	...	...	...	...	126	55	45	88	2.0	5	65.9	34.1	36.8	Madagascar
...	...	...	...	...	...	178	1,800	67	93	7.8	14	35.0	65.0	26.5	Malawi
717[8,20]	...	...	...	...	...	7	41	95	129	3.8	143	53.7	46.3	—	Malaysia
413[27]	...	...	...	25.0[27]	3[27]	72	110	84	115	6.7	99	83.5	16.5	1.9	Maldives
...	...	...	...	...	...	220	1,200	48	93	4.3	11	38.6	61.4	20.8	Mali
...	...	...	...	...	...	6	21	100	145	8.8	830	68.5	31.5	—	Malta
1,060	...	...	...	...	4	61	...	85	...	9.8	190	64.7	35.3	25.4	Marshall Islands
2,092[14]	...	...	...	73.7[14]	10[14]	...	...	94[15]	118	...	...	...	...	...	Martinique
...	...	...	...	...	...	183	480	56	120	3.6	10	72.4	27.6	23.2	Mauritania
1,512[8]	...	...	...	74.6[8,15]	5[8,15]	18	24	100	130	3.4	107	59.5	40.5	1.6	Mauritius
...	...	...	...	...	...	...	...	...	...	...	...	...	...	...	Mayotte
560[8]	...	...	...	75.1	6	28	83	91	135	6.1	367	44.3	55.7	0.5	Mexico
1,118	...	...	...	51.4[7]	...	23	...	94	...	7.8	...	72.0	28.0	16.2	Micronesia
...	...	...	...	...	...	32	36	92	110	5.7	22	49.7	50.3	7.5	Moldova
...	...	...	...	...	...	4	...	100	139	7.6	3,051	56.1	43.9	—	Monaco
205[11]	...	...	...	...	...	68	110	62	93	6.4	25	72.3	27.7	15.4	Mongolia
255[7]	...	...	...	63.8[22]	8[22]	39	220	80	126	5.1	53	39.3	60.7	1.4	Morocco

Health services (continued)

country	year	physicians	dentists	nurses	pharmacists	midwives	population per physician	year	number	general (%)	specialized (%)	medical centres/other (%)	public (%)	private non-profit (%)	private for profit (%)	total number of hospital beds	hospital beds per 10,000 pop.
Mozambique	2003	500	138[2]	3,664[2]	419[2]	1,414[2]	37,000	1997	238	4.2	—95.8—		100.0	—	—	12,630	1
Myanmar (Burma)	2000	14,356	984[1]	12,642	...	10,307[2]	3,114	2000	737	...	...	...	...	...	...	28,943	6
Namibia	2000	620	677	3,800	915	1,954[7]	7,545	1992	47	...	...	...	91.5	—8.5—		6,379	40
Nauru	2003	15	1	64	...	...	672	2004	...	...	...	...	...	...	...	60	60
Nepal	2003	1,259	45[14]	6,216	21	1,621[14]	19,837	2003	83	94.0	—6.0—		...	...	...	5,190	2
Netherlands, The	2003	52,602	7,623	213,128[10]	3,148[23]	1,825	307	2002	129	67.3	32.7	—	...	...	...	90,747	57
Netherlands Antilles	2001	333	60	1,198	47	9	652	2001	13	30.8	53.8	15.4	...	...	...	1,466	78
New Caledonia	2002	476	126	1,128	91[10]	64[10]	454	2002	9	12.5[4]	12.5[4]	75.0[4]	62.5[4]	—37.5[4]—		888	41
New Zealand	2002	12,505	1,582	34,660	3,808[10]	2,288[10]	306	2002	445	...	...	...	19.1	—80.9—		23,825	60
Nicaragua	2003	8,986	1,585	5,862	...	...	2,538	2003	56[15]	46.4[15]	7.1[15]	46.4[15]	...	...	...	5,031	10
Niger	2002	386	21	2,668	63	461	30,977	2001	...	...	...	...	...	...	...		5
Nigeria	2002	25,914	2,180[2]	119,400[10]	8,642[2]	62,386[22]	4,722	2002	13,964[5]	6.4[5]	0.6[5]	93.0[5]	86.2[5]	—13.8[5]—		54,872	5
Northern Mariana Islands	1999	31	3	123	4	14	2,249	2002	1	100.0	—	—	100.0	—	—	82	11
Norway	2003	12,232	5,627[10]	92,791[10]	1,781[10]	3,089[10]	370	2003	...	...	...	...	...	...	...	22,662	43
Oman	2003	3,478	395	8,001	662	65[3]	659	2002	57	—8.4—		91.6	26.3	—73.7—		5,168	20
Pakistan	2002	101,635	4,560	44,520	45,390	23,084	1,516	2003	5,496	—16.5—		83.5	...	...	...	98,264	7
Palau	2003	21	2	26[11]	1	1	967	2003	1	...	...	...	...	...	...	70	50
Panama	2003	4,286	903	3,048	756[11]	...	727	2003	63	...	...	...	...	...	...	7,553	24
Papua New Guinea	2000	275	90	2,841	...	...	19,269	1993	...	...	...	...	...	...	...	14,119	34
Paraguay	2001	6,400	1,947	1,089	433[14]	1,547[14]	1,977	2002	...	...	...	...	...	...	...	6,759	12
Peru	2004	32,619	2,809[1]	17,108[1]	4,789[3]	3,832[3]	658	2003	481	...	...	...	50.2[3]	—49.8[3]—		43,074	14
Philippines	2004	93,862	45,903	352,398	47,463	14,675	885	2003	1,723	96.5[3]	3.1[3]	0.5[3]	38.4	—61.6—		91,000	11
Poland	2004	87,617	10,737	181,291	25,217	21,129	446	2004	782	93.6	6.4	—	84.4	—15.6—		188,038	69
Portugal	2001	35,536	4,370[2]	37,477[2]	8,056[2]	827[11]	310	2002	215	43.0[14]	18.8[14]	38.2[14]	74.3[14]	14.7[14]	11.0[14]	38,802	36
Puerto Rico	2001	5,980	2,507	11,959[7]	829[26]	120[20]	642	2002	68[7]	79.4[7]	—20.6[7]—		35.3[7]	—64.7[7]—		12,669	32
Qatar	2002	1,518	145	3,139	279	...	399	2002	5	25.0	75.0	—	60.0	—40.0—		1,357	24
Réunion	2003	1,179	382	2,027	277	176[11]	449	2000	18	85.5	—14.5—		71.0	—29.0—		2,124	30
Romania	2004	42,538	4,919	109,668	1,275	6,497[10]	511	2004	427	...	...	...	98.8	—1.2—		162,558	66
Russia	2003	686,000	46,209	1,551,000	10,215	67,825[10]	208	2003	10,100	37.4[15]	17.2[15]	45.4[15]	98.6	—1.4—		1,653,000	105
Rwanda	2002	155	4	1,735	11	10	52,722	1990	198	...	...	...	100.0	—	—	12,152	17
St. Kitts and Nevis	2001	49	15	294	21[11]	...	936	2003	4	50.0	—50.0—		...	...	...	178	55
St. Lucia	2002	92	9[10]	331[10]	13[7]	...	1,609	2002	6	25.0[12]	25.0[12]	50.0	...	...	...	285	19
St. Vincent	2003	61	6[11]	267[11]	27[5]	...	1,429	2003	11	...	...	...	77.8[12]	—22.2[12]—		209	15
Samoa	2002	43	6	333	5	3	4,115	2004	16[10]	12.5[10]	—87.5[10]—		100.0	—	—	661	36
San Marino	2002	117	...	...	6	...	230	2002	1	...	...	...	...	...	...	134	52
São Tomé and Príncipe	1998	63	7	171	2[26]	40	2,126	...	...	...	...	...	...	...	...		22
Saudi Arabia	2001	31,983	3,672[10]	69,421	5,420	...	650	2002	324	...	...	...	74.1[3]	—25.9[3]—		46,622	22
Senegal	2001	1,008	93[3]	4,339	322[3]	628	10,511	2003	18	...	...	...	...	...	...	3,582	4
Serbia and Montenegro	2001	27,769	4,209[2]	62,022	1,929	...	300	2002	...	...	...	...	...	...	...	51,785	60
Seychelles	2003	107	16	422	8	...	774	2003	7[8]	14.6[8]	14.6[8]	70.8[8]	100.0	—	—	419	51
Sierra Leone	2001	282	4	786	...	218[3]	16,333	2003	44	—25.6[14]—		74.4[14]	...	...	...	3,364	14
Singapore	2004	6,492	1,227	18,964	1,288	365	653	2004	29	55.6	—44.4—		44.8	—55.2—		11,795	34
Slovakia	2002	20,466	2,378	39,428	1,044[26]	965[10]	263	2003	111[11]	72.1[11]	27.9[11]	—	100.0	—	—	41,768	73
Slovenia	2002	4,636	1,199	14,205	778	...	430	2003	28	57.7	42.3	—	...	...	...	12,130	50
Solomon Islands	2003	57	26[1]	338[11]	28[1]	23[1]	8,491	2003	11	100.0	—	—	75.0	25.0	—	881	19
Somalia	1997	265	13	1,327	70	540[11]	25,034	1997	...	...	...	...	...	...	...	2,786	4
South Africa	2001	29,788	4,648	172,338	10,742	...	1,453	2001	612	...	...	...	51.1[11]	—48.9[11]—		144,364	35
Spain	2003	190,665	20,005	185,000	56,501	6,314[3]	223	2001	738	58.2	15.5	26.3	43.1	—56.9—		160,815	36
Sri Lanka	2002	9,518	461	16,924	830[1]	7,725[1]	2,492	2002	576	71.4	—28.6—		100.0	...	...	59,144	22
Sudan, The	2000	4,973	218	26,730	311	...	9,395	2002	...	...	...	...	...	...	...	36,419	7
Suriname	2000	313	4	688	14[3]	40[3]	2,000	2003	...	...	...	...	...	...	...	1,449	15
Swaziland	2000	184	20	3,345	46	...	5,560	2000	24[3]	—41.7[3]—		58.3[3]	...	...	...	1,570	15
Sweden	2001	25,200	13,446[2]	86,512[2]	5,317[2]	5,979[2]	354	2001	...	...	...	...	...	...	...	29,122	33
Switzerland	2002	25,921	3,468[2]	59,833[2]	4,450[2]	2,033[2]	281	2002	...	...	...	...	...	...	...	44,316	60
Syria	2003	25,147	12,206[10]	32,938[10]	8,862[10]	4,909[2]	699	2003	393	75.1	—24.9—		16.6	—83.4—		26,202	15
Taiwan	2003	20,020	5,220	57,820	13,670	490	714	2003	610	...	...	...	15.2	—84.8—		133,398	59
Tajikistan	2002	13,393	1,051[10]	26,887[10]	680	3,932[10]	472	2003	449[11]	...	...	...	98.2[15]	—1.8[15]—		40,387	61
Tanzania	2002	822	218[14]	1,392	365	13,953[14]	42,085	1993	173[5]	...	...	...	...	...	...		10
Thailand	2002	17,529	3,553	85,392	6,288	9,713[14]	3,589	2001	1,224	—100.0—			74.2	—25.8—		121,779	22
Togo	2001	289	25	1,230	141	346	17,887	2001	...	...	...	...	...	...	...		19
Tonga	2003	32	23	342	17[10]	19[10]	3,057	2004	4	...	...	...	...	...	...	296	29
Trinidad and Tobago	2001	1,234	216	1,936[28]	506	28	1,315	2003	71	...	...	...	...	...	...	4,384	33
Tunisia	2003	8,169	1,534	29,976	2,170	...	1,207	2003	168	—13.5[7]—		86.5[7]	100.0	—	—	16,682	17
Turkey	2001	82,920	15,866	162,597	22,922	41,586	826	2003	1,184	75.3[15]	8.8[15]	15.9[15]	84.3[15]	—15.7[15]—		156,549	26
Turkmenistan	1997	14,022	1,010	21,436	1,566	3,664	333	1994	368	...	...	...	100.0	—	—	46,000	115
Tuvalu	2003	7	2	30	1	10	1,591	2002	9	11.1[1]	—88.9[1]—		100.0	—	—	30	56
Uganda	2002	1,175	75	1,350	125	850	21,056	1996	81[20]	...	...	...	...	...	...	22,788	5
Ukraine	2002	224,000	20,800	526,000	23,488[11]	26,066[10]	214	2003	3,100	...	...	...	100.0	—	—	465,000	88
United Arab Emirates	2001	6,059	954	12,045	1,086	...	485	2002	143	...	...	...	74.0	—26.0—		7,448	22
United Kingdom	2002	80,306	22,194	367,520	40,028[28]	28	826	2002	...	...	...	...	...	...	...	186,290	38
United States	2002	853,200	168,000[2]	2,202,000	196,000[2]	3,000[14]	338	2002	5,794	94.4	5.6	—	34.6	52.2	13.2	976,000	34
Uruguay	2002	12,905	4,097	2,974	1,248	578	62	2003	107	...	...	...	44.8	—55.2—		6,695	19
Uzbekistan	2002	81,100	5,283	263,900	673	20,684	311	2003	192[14]	...	...	...	100.0	—	—		55
Vanuatu	2004	29	3[14]	312	6[1]	33[14]	7,407	2003	90[14]	5.6[14]	—94.4[14]—		100.0	—	—	573	31
Venezuela	2004	48,000	13,680	46,305[7]	8,571[7]	...	722	2003	556[7]	...	...	...	37.0[7]	—63.0[7]—		40,675	29
Vietnam	2003	47,587	...	48,157	5,977[10]	14,662[10]	1,700	2002	12,500[15]	...	...	...	...	...	...	184,440	23
Virgin Islands (U.S.)	2002	161	...	...	...	...	675	2004	2	...	...	...	...	...	...	329	30
West Bank[24]	2001	2,771	297	4,388	330	56[22]	1,186	2001	17	...	...	...	52.9[22]	—47.1[22]—			11
Western Sahara	1994	100	...	...	...	24	2,504	...	...	...	...	...	...	...	...	...	...
Yemen	2001	4,078	222	8,342	1,237[1]	385[15]	4,357	2001	121	...	...	...	...	...	...	9,802	6
Zambia	1995	601	26[4]	9,853	24[4]	311[4]	14,496	1993	994	8.2[33]	0.3	83.5[33]	80.9[33]	19.1[33]	—	22,927	29
Zimbabwe	2002	736	15	6,951	12	3,078[14]	16,205	1996[6]	1,378[22]	0.9[14]	2.6[14]	96.4[14]	...	...	...	22,973	20

[1]1999. [2]2000. [3]1996. [4]1990. [5]1991. [6]General hospitals only. [7]1997. [8]Government hospitals only. [9]Urban only. [10]2001. [11]1998. [12]1992. [13]Belize hospital only. [14]1995. [15]1994. [16]Government personnel only. [17]1988. [18]Includes doctors of traditional Chinese medicine. [19]Physicians includes dentists. [20]1989. [21]Republic of Cyprus only. [22]1993. [23]2002. [24]West Bank

rate per 10,000 pop.	general	special-ized	medical centres/other	bed occu-pancy rate (%)	aver-age length of stay (days)	under age 5 per 1,000 live newborn 2003	maternal mortality per 100,000 live births 2000	popu-lation with access to safe water 2002 (%)	food supply (% of FAO require-ment) 2002	as percent of GDP	per capita (U.S.$)	public	private	external grants/loans	country
...	...	...	...	...	...	158	1,000	42	89	5.9	10	67.4	32.5	36.9	Mozambique
...	...	...	...	68.0	9	107	360	80	136	2.1	229	17.8	82.2	0.2	Myanmar (Burma)
...	...	...	...	...	...	65	300	80	100	7.0	114	67.8	32.2	3.8	Namibia
...	...	...	...	...	...	30	...	...	...	7.5	...	88.7	11.3	—	Nauru
...	...	...	...	...	...	82	740	84	112	5.2	11	29.7	70.3	9.4	Nepal
939	95.4	4.6	—	65.8	9	5	16	100	125	8.9	1,974	63.3	36.7	—	Netherlands, The
1,165[4, 6]	...	...	...	84.8[4, 6]	84[4, 6]	...	...	...	106	...	...	...	...	...	Netherlands Antilles
1,332[3, 8]	...	...	...	64.0[3, 8]	63[3, 8]	6	7	100	116	8.3	1,056	76.8	23.2	—	New Caledonia
769[15]	—76.2[15]—		23.8[15]	...	...	38	230	81	122	7.8	59	48.5	51.5	7.7	New Zealand
									102						Nicaragua
...	...	...	...	...	...	262	1,600	46	91	3.7	7	39.1	60.9	16.9	Niger
...	...	...	...	...	...	198	800	60	116	3.4	20	23.2	76.8	7.1	Nigeria
1,670	100.0	—	—	56.4	4	...	...	98	...	...	...	...	...	...	Northern Mariana Islands
1,714	92.1	7.9	—	79.0[6]	5[6]	4	16	100	130	8.0	3,352	85.5	14.5	—	Norway
1,052	...	...	...	55.0	4	12	87	79	...	3.0	232	80.7	19.3	—	Oman
...	...	...	...	...	...	103	500	90	105	3.9	12	24.4	75.6	1.9	Pakistan
1,718	...	...	...	65.0	6	28	...	84	...	9.2	424	92.0	8.0	11.8	Palau
1,239[11]	...	...	...	52.5[11]	8[11]	24	160	91	98	7.0	336	69.0	31.0	0.6	Panama
...	...	...	...	...	...	93	300	39	95	4.4	24	89.0	11.0	21.2	Papua New Guinea
...	...	...	...	59.6	...	29	170	83	111	8.0	102	38.3	61.7	2.0	Paraguay
538[3]	...	...	...	62.1[3]	5[3]	34	410	81	109	4.7	94	55.0	45.0	1.7	Peru
1,730[6]	...	...	—	75.9[6]	8[6]	36	200	85	105	3.3	30	45.2	54.8	3.5	Philippines
1,146[14]	86.3[14]	10.5[14]	3.2[14]	74.5[14]	10[14]	7	13	100[9]	129	6.1	292	71.9	28.1	—	Poland
1,101[15]	94.0[15]	4.3[15]	1.7[15]	70.3[7]	6[7]	5	5	100[9]	153	9.2	994	69.0	31.0	—	Portugal
						...	25	...	...	...	...	...	...	...	Puerto Rico
364[29]	...	...	...	72.5[29]	7[29]	15	7	100	...	3.1	862	73.5	26.5	—	Qatar
2,011	...	...	...	71.8	6	...	41	...	146	...	...	...	...	...	Réunion
...	...	...	...	...	...	20	49	57	130	6.5	109	79.2	20.8	1.0	Romania
2,640	...	...	...	87.4	12	21	67	96	116	5.4	128	68.2	31.8	3.1	Russia
...	...	...	...	...	...	203	1,400	73	90	5.5	11	55.5	44.5	24.7	Rwanda
1,037	...	...	...	68.4	8	22	130[11]	99	108	4.8	443	66.3	33.7	5.6	St. Kitts and Nevis
983	...	...	...	...	...	18	30[7]	98	123	4.5	227	64.5	35.4	0.6	St. Lucia
728[7]	...	...	...	68.2[7]	7[7]	27	43[1]	93	107	6.1	166	63.5	36.5	0.3	St. Vincent
700[10]	70.8[12]	—	29.2[12]	32.9[12]	5[12]	24	...	88	122	5.8	74	82.2	17.8	15.6	Samoa
...	...	...	...	51.5	6	5	...	100	...	6.8	2,315	78.0	23.0	—	San Marino
...	...	...	...	...	...	118	...	79	105	2.3	33	67.7	32.3	56.4	São Tomé and Príncipe
...	...	...	...	...	...	26	23	97[9]	118	4.8	360	74.6	25.4	—	Saudi Arabia
...	...	...	...	...	...	137	690	72	96	4.8	25	58.8	41.2	20.2	Senegal
1,434	...	...	...	74.0	12	14	11	93	105	8.2	90	79.2	20.8	1.4	Serbia and Montenegro
1,346[30]	...	...	...	58.0[30]	5[30]	15	...	87	105	6.0	388	68.2	31.8	11.9	Seychelles
...	...	...	...	...	...	284	2,000	57	84	4.3	7	61.0	39.0	25.1	Sierra Leone
956	...	...	...	74.0	5	3	15	100	...	3.9	816	33.5	66.5	—	Singapore
1,720	95.1	4.9	—	74.9	11	8	10	100	117	5.6	223	89.3	10.7	—	Slovakia
1,710	...	...	...	75.2	10	4	17	100	118	8.4	821	74.9	25.1	—	Slovenia
...	...	...	...	...	...	22	130	70	99	5.0	38	93.5	6.5	15.9	Solomon Islands
...	...	...	...	...	...	225	1,100	29	71	2.6	6	44.6	55.4	9.3	Somalia
...	...	...	...	...	...	66	230	87	121	8.6	224	41.4	58.6	0.4	South Africa
1,123	...	...	...	79.6	9	4	4	100	137	7.6	1,065	71.4	28.6	—	Spain
2,043	...	...	...	...	...	15	92	78	103	3.6	30	48.9	51.1	3.1	Sri Lanka
...	...	...	...	...	...	93	590	69	95	3.5	18	18.7	81.3	2.7	Sudan, The
766[11, 31]	...	...	...	68.8[11, 31]	10[11, 31]	39	110	92	117	9.4	147	60.2	39.8	12.2	Suriname
...	...	...	...	...	...	153	370	52	103	3.3	73	68.5	31.5	7.9	Swaziland
1,906[15]	...	...	...	82.2[15]	8[15]	3	2	100	118	8.7	2,169	85.2	14.8	—	Sweden
...	...	...	...	83.0	10	5	7	100	131	11.0	3,774	57.1	42.9	—	Switzerland
1,058	...	...	...	75.5[8, 22]	3[8, 22]	18	160	79	123	5.4	61	43.9	56.1	0.3	Syria
...	...	...	...	...	...	8	8	100[9]	...	4.2	323	53.0	47.0	—	Taiwan
1,492[15]	...	...	...	70.2[15]	15[15]	118	100	58	71	3.3	6	71.1	28.9	7.4	Tajikistan
...	...	...	...	...	...	165	1,500	73	85	4.4	14	46.7	53.3	29.5	Tanzania
...	...	...	...	...	...	26	44	85	111	3.7	66	57.1	42.9	0.1	Thailand
...	...	...	...	...	...	140	570	51	102	2.8	88	48.6	51.4	8.1	Togo
622[12]	...	...	...	56.2[12]	10[12]	19	...	97	...	5.5	88	61.6	38.4	20.7	Tonga
1,050[6]	...	...	...	70.7[6, 8]	6[7, 8]	20	160	91	113	4.0	244	43.3	56.7	3.8	Trinidad and Tobago
...	...	...	...	...	...	24	120	82	135	6.4	120	75.7	24.3	0.6	Tunisia
709[15]	...	...	...	...	...	39	70	93	133	5.0	137	71.0	29.0	—	Turkey
...	...	...	...	...	...	102	31	71	107	4.1	58	73.3	26.7	0.6	Turkmenistan
1,368[1]	40.9[1]	—	59.1[1]	51.5[6]	12.2[6]	51	...	93	...	5.4	380	53.4	46.6	29.4	Tuvalu
...	...	...	...	...	...	140	880	56	103	5.9	18	57.5	42.5	24.8	Uganda
...	...	...	...	...	...	20	35	98	119	4.3	34	67.8	32.2	0.7	Ukraine
...	...	...	...	...	...	8	54	100	133	3.5	824	75.8	24.2	—	United Arab Emirates
...	...	...	...	...	...	6	13	100	135	7.6	1,837	82.2	17.8	—	United Kingdom
1,200[32]	...	...	...	62.4[32]	4.9[32]	8	17	100	143	14.9	4,873	45.9	54.1	—	United States
482	...	...	...	78.8[7, 8]	9[7, 8]	14	27	98	106	10.9	597	46.3	53.7	0.5	Uruguay
165	...	...	...	...	...	69	24	89	88	3.8	25	74.5	25.5	1.7	Uzbekistan
567[14]	...	...	...	41.9[14]	6[14]	38	...	60	113	3.8	42	59.2	40.8	8.4	Vanuatu
601[7, 8]	...	...	...	69.7[7, 8]	6[7, 8]	21	96	83	95	6.0	261	62.1	37.9	0.1	Venezuela
...	...	...	...	...	...	23	130	73	119	5.1	21	28.5	71.5	2.5	Vietnam
...	...	...	...	...	...	...	...	...	...	...	...	...	...	...	Virgin Islands (U.S.)
711[14]	...	...	...	80.9[14]	4[14]	24	100	94	...	...	...	...	...	...	West Bank[24]
...	...	...	...	...	...	...	...	...	...	...	...	...	...	...	Western Sahara
...	...	...	...	...	...	113	570	69	84	4.5	23	34.1	65.9	3.7	Yemen
1,249[33]	—75.7[33]—		24.3[33]	68.5[33]	7[33]	182	729	51	83	5.7	20	53.1	46.9	48.7	Zambia
546[22]	...	...	...	69.8[22]	7[22]	126	1,100	83	81	6.2	55	45.3	54.7	7.8	Zimbabwe

includes Gaza Strip. [25]Registered personnel; all may not be present and working in the country. [26]Number of pharmacies. [27]Central Hospital only. [28]Nurses include midwives. [29]Hamad General Hospital only. [30]Victoria Hospital only. [31]Paramaribo Hospital (1,213 beds) only. [32]4,927 community hospitals only. [33]1987.

Social protection

This table summarizes three principal areas of social protective activity for the countries of the world: social security, crime and law enforcement, and military affairs. Because the administrative structure, financing, manning, and scope of institutions and programmed tasks in these fields vary so greatly from country to country, no well-accepted or well-documented body of statistical comparisons exists in international convention to permit objective assessment of any of these subjects, either from the perspective of a single country or internationally. The data provided within any single subject area do, however, represent the most consistent approach to problems of international comparison found in the published literature for that field.

The provision of social security programs to answer specific social needs, for example, is summarized simply in terms of the existence or nonexistence of a specific type of benefit program because of the great complexity of national programs in terms of eligibility, coverage, term, age limits, financing, payments, and so on. Activities connected with a particular type of benefit often take place at more than one governmental level, through more than one agency at the same level, or through a mixture of public and private institutions. The data shown here are summarized from the U.S. Social Security Administration's *Social Security Programs Throughout the World* (regional coverage; Africa 2003, Asia 2002, Europe 2002, The Americas 2003). A bullet symbol (●) indicates that a country has at least one program within the defined area (a circle [○] indicates data is for 2003); in some cases it may have several. A blank space indicates that no program existed providing the benefit shown; ellipses [...] indicate that no information was available as to whether a program existed.

Data given for social security expenditure as a percentage of total central governmental expenditure are taken from the International Monetary Fund's *Government Finance Statistics Yearbook*, which provides the most comparable analytic series on the consolidated accounts of central governments, governmentally administered social security funds, and independent national agencies, all usually separate accounting entities, through which these services may be provided in a given country.

Data on the finances of social security programs are taken in large part from the International Labour Office's *The Cost of Social Security* (triennial), supplemented by national data sources.

Figures for criminal offenses known to police, usually excluding civil offenses and minor traffic violations, are taken in part from Interpol's *International Crime Statistics* (annual) and a variety of national sources. Statistics are usually based on the number of offenses reported to police, not the number of offenders apprehended or tried in courts. Attempted offenses are counted as the offense that was attempted. A person identified as having committed multiple offenses is counted only under the most serious offense. Murder refers to all acts involving the voluntary taking of life, including infanticide, but excluding abortion, or involuntary acts such as those normally classified as manslaughter. Assault includes "serious," or aggravated, assault—that involving injury, endangering life, or perpetrated with the use of a dangerous instrument. Burglary involves theft from the premises of another; although Interpol statistics are reported as "breaking and entering," national data may not always distinguish cases of forcible entry. Automobile theft excludes brief use of a car without the owner's

Social protection

country	social security — programs available, 2002 or 2003					expenditures, (latest) (% of total central govt.)[f]	finances — year	receipts — total ('000,000 natl. cur.)	insured persons (%)	employers (%)	government (%)	other (%)	expenditures — total ('000,000 natl. cur.)	benefits (%)	administration (%)	other (%)
	old-age, invalidity, death[a]	sickness and maternity[b]	work injury[c]	unemployment[d]	family allowances[e]											
Afghanistan	●	●	●		●	20.1	...	...	...	...	...	...	...	...	...	...
Albania	●	●	●	●	●		1990	967.0	—	—	88.8	11.2	1,440.0	61.8	——— 0.5 ———	
Algeria	○	○	○	○	○		1990	27,700.0	—	—	...	...	28,748.0	61.8	30.6	7.6
American Samoa	○	...	...	...	...		1990	...	...	...	...	...	13.0	100.0	—	—
Andorra	●	●	●	...	...		1993	11,832.2	...	...	...	...	7,937.2	90.2	4.6	5.2
Angola	...	...	...	...	...		1983	13.0	29.2	48.7	—	22.1	4.2	66.1	33.9	—
Antigua and Barbuda	○	○	...	...	...		1989	1,015,837.0	28.8	45.0	16.6	9.6	989,009.0	95.0	5.0	—
Argentina	○	○	○	○	○	47.8										
Armenia	●	●	●	●	●		1998	197.1	...	...	...	...	179.0	...	...	...
Aruba	○	...	○	...	...	5										
Australia	●	●	●	●	●	35.5	1998–99	...	...	...	...	1.9	41,825	99.6	0.3	—
Austria	●	●	●	●	●	46.3	1989	425,417.0	30.1	45.9	21.1	2.9	412,134.0	96.5	2.3	1.2
Azerbaijan	●	●	●	●	●	33.1										
Bahamas, The	○	○	○			6.9	1989	95.9	22.9	38.5	2.1	36.5	43.5	71.1	27.2	1.7
Bahrain	●		●			7.5	1989	39.6	12.3	40.2	—	47.5	9.7	69.8	20.9	9.3
Bangladesh	●	●	●	●		...	1989	73.6	12.4	37.5	2.4	47.7	34.1	94.0	...	...
Barbados	○	○	○	○		...	1989	191.7	38.0	40.8	1.5	19.7	149.1	93.5	5.8	0.7
Belarus	●	●	●	●	●	44.0	1986	3,199.0	—	—	93.2	6.8	3,199.0	100.0	—	—
Belgium	●	●	●	●	●		1986	1,347,070.0	24.4	39.7	31.6	4.3	1,322,636.0	94.5	4.3	1.2
Belize	○	○	○			5.9[6]	1989	15.3	8.9	53.2	—	38.0	3.9	56.7	43.3	—
Benin	○	7	○		○	...	1989	3,551.9	16.8	81.4	—	1.8	4,500.9	69.3	28.1	2.6
Bermuda	○	○	○	...	...	...										
Bhutan	...	...	...	...	...	...	1990	...	...	...	...	...	26.0[8]	...	...	...
Bolivia	○	○	○	...	○	20.6	1989	346.6	29.3	47.7	11.2	11.8	340.2	84.9	14.3	0.8
Bosnia and Herzegovina	●	●	●	●	●	...										
Botswana	○[10]		○			1.1[11]	1996	...	...	...	...	...	65.0[8]	...	...	...
Brazil	○	○	○	○	○	47.3[12]	1989	71,847.0	24.4	51.0	20.0	4.6	68,957.0	61.9	18.6	19.5
Brunei	●	...	...	...	...		1984	...	...	...	...	...	39.5	...	...	...
Bulgaria	●	●	●	●	●	35.5	1989	6,016.8	—	71.4	28.1	0.5	6,000.1	96.6	3.3	0.1
Burkina Faso	○	○	○		○	0.1[13]	1989	8,816.5	15.6	62.9	—	21.5	4,975.3	69.5	30.4	0.1
Burundi	○		○		○	5.1	1989	1,991.5	31.6	47.6	—	20.8	1,563.9	74.8	16.8	8.4
Cambodia	...	...	○	...	○											
Cameroon	○	...	○	○	○	0.5	1989	41,331.8	13.1	64.8	—	22.1	41,332.0	70.6	28.8	0.6
Canada	○	○	○	○	○	46.4	1989	130,306.6	9.9	15.6	64.4	10.1	115,764.2	96.9	2.5	0.6
Cape Verde	○	○	○		○	...	1989	697.7	26.5	58.5	—	15.0	316.7	82.4	16.1	1.5
Central African Republic	○	○	○		○	...	1989	3,604.0	8.4	76.0	—	15.6	3,247.0	64.6	32.9	2.5
Chad	○	○	○		○	...	1989	1,172.8	12.6	77.6	—	9.8	634.5	43.0	51.4	5.6
Chile	○	○	○	○	○	36.2	1989	1,186,056.0	32.8	2.7	37.9	26.6	798,770.0	83.9	14.7	1.4
China	●	●	●	●		22.4	1989	57,446.2	—	99.4	—	0.6	54,654	98.4	0.6	1.0
Colombia	○	○	○		○	12.1	1989	294,438.0	24.8	56.0	0.2	19.0	257,455.0	85.5	11.5	3.0
Comoros	○	...	...	...	...		1983	40.7	100.0	—	—	—	54.3	17.4	62.3	20.3
Congo, Dem. Rep. of the	○	...	○	...	○	0.1	1986	1,238.3	28.6	60.2	—	11.2	1,044.2	27.9	72.1	—
Congo, Rep. of the	○	○	○		○	...	1983	15,272.8	12.1	80.2	—	7.7	7,256.7	66.6	21.3	12.1
Costa Rica	○	○	○		○	21.3	1989	36,407.3	33.2	44.4	1.2	21.2	31,049.8	89.0	4.1	6.9
Côte d'Ivoire	○	○	○		○	...	1989	27,288.4	19.3	75.4	—	5.3	20,593.5	100.0	—	—
Croatia	●	●	●	●	●	42.8										
Cuba	○	○	○		○		1989	2,284.8	—	37.4	62.6	—	2,284.8	96.7	...	3.3
Cyprus[16]	●	●	●	●	●	24.5	1989	217.5	24.7	40.3	17.3	17.7	117.7	98.4	1.6	—
Czech Republic	●	●	●	●	●	35.3	1989[18]	132,740.0	—	3.9	96.1	—	132,748.0	99.7	0.3	—
Denmark	●	●	●	●	●	40.9	1989	225,965.6	4.3	5.0	88.2	2.5	218,258.2	97.0	3.0	—
Djibouti	●[19]	...	...	...	●[19]	...	1979	1,352.2	...	...	...	...	1,115.7	...	...	...
Dominica	○	○	○				1986	12.3	22.6	50.9	—	26.5	4.4	68.0	32.0	—
Dominican Republic	○	○	○			8.1	1986	77.9	20.1	72.9	—	6.8	74.3	75.9	24.1	—
East Timor[21]	...	...	...	...	...											
Ecuador	○	○	○		○	1.9[2]	1988	71,286.0	37.0	50.0	—	13.0	52,032.4	86.0	14.0	—

permission, "joyriding," and implies intent to deprive the owner of the vehicle permanently. Criminal offense data for certain countries refer to cases disposed of in court, rather than to complaints. Police manpower figures refer, for the most part, to full-time, paid professional staff, excluding clerical support and volunteer staff. Personnel in military service who perform police functions are presumed to be employed in their principal activity, military service.

The figures for military manpower refer to full-time, active-duty military service and exclude reserve, militia, paramilitary, and similar organizations. Because of the difficulties attached to the analysis of data on military manpower and budgets (including problems such as data withheld on national security grounds, or the publication of budgetary data specifically intended to hide actual expenditure, or the complexity of long-term financing of purchases of military matériel [how much was actually spent as opposed to what was committed, offset by nonmilitary transfers, etc.]), extensive use is made of the principal international analytic tools: publications such as those of the International Institute for Strategic Studies (*The Military Balance*) and the U.S. Arms Control and Disarmament Agency (*World Military Expenditures and Arms Transfers*), both annuals.

The data on military expenditures are from the sources identified above, as well as from the IMF's *Government Finance Statistics Yearbook* and country statistical publications.

The following notes further define the column headings:

a. Programs providing cash payments for *each* of the three types of long-term benefit indicated to persons (1) exceeding a specified working age (usually 50–65, often 5 years earlier for women) who are qualified by a term of covered employment, (2) partially or fully incapacitated for their usual employment by injury or illness, and (3) qualified by their status as spouse, cohabitant, or dependent minor of a qualified person who dies.

b. Programs providing cash payments (jointly, or alternatively, medical services as well) to occupationally qualified persons for *both* of the short-term benefits indicated: (1) illness and (2) maternity.

c. Programs providing cash or medical services to employment-qualified persons who become temporarily or permanently incapacitated (fully or partially) by work-related injury or illness.

d. Programs providing term-limited cash compensation (usually 40–75% of average earnings) to persons qualified by previous employment (of six months minimum, typically) for periods of involuntary unemployment.

e. Programs providing cash payments to families or mothers to mitigate the cost of raising children and to encourage the formation of larger families.

f. Includes welfare.

g. A police officer is a full-time, paid professional, performing domestic security functions. Data include administrative staff but exclude clerical employees, volunteers, and members of paramilitary groups.

h. Includes all active-duty personnel, regular and conscript, performing national security functions. Excludes reserves, paramilitary forces, border patrols, and gendarmeries.

crime and law enforcement (latest)					population per police officer[g]	military protection									country
offenses reported to the police per 100,000 population						manpower, 2003[h]		expenditure, 1999				arms trade, 1999 ('000,000 U.S.$)			
total	personal		property			total ('000)	per 1,000 population	total '000,000	per capita	% of central government expenditure	% of GDP or GNP	imports	exports		
	murder	assault	burglary	automobile theft											
...	...	...	...	...	540[1]	70	2.4	408[2]	...	...	...	0	0		Afghanistan
168.8	26.2	5.8	10.7	14.1	550	22.0	6.9	72	21	4.5	1.3	30	0		Albania
178.0	0.7	67.6	13.7	1.7	840	127.5	4.0	1,830	60	12.6	4.0	550	0		Algeria
3,006	8.0	494.0	588.0	6.0	460	3	3	—	—	—	—	...	...		American Samoa
2,616	0	16.7	515.2	110.6	220	—	—	...	...	...	...	...	...		Andorra
143.5	8.7	15.3	30.5	3.7	14[4]	131.0	12.2	2,460	248	41.1	21.2	350	0		Angola
4,977	4.7	475.0	1,984.4	35.9	120	0.2	2.2	...	...	...	...	...	...		Antigua and Barbuda
631.0	6.0	68.2	43.0	117.1	1,270	71.4	1.9	4,300	118	9.1	1.6	90	0		Argentina
264.4	4.1	4.7	16.6	0.7	...	44.7	14.6	570	170	20.2	5.8	10	0		Armenia
5,461	1.2	180.0	451.3	202.5	...	3	3	—	—	—	—	...	...		Aruba
7,003	3.7	708.5	2,926.2	684.8	438	53.7	2.7	7,060	372	7.6	1.8	1,100	550		Australia
6,095	1.4	3.0	944.0	34.7	470	34.6	4.3	1,690	208	1.5	0.8	30	30		Austria
176	4.2	2.4	10.3	0.4	...	66.5	8.1	927	120	24.4	6.6	10	0		Azerbaijan
4,870	27.1	61.5	1,560.2	415.7	125	0.9	2.7	...	...	...	...	...	...		Bahamas, The
1,390	1.6	0.5	380.1	207.6	180	11.2	16.6	415	666	18.9	8.1	70	0		Bahrain
90	2.8	4.3	4.3	1.1	2,560	125.5	0.9	624	5.0	10.1	1.3	80	0		Bangladesh
3,813	8.6	161.9	1,080.8	105.5	280	0.6	2.2	12	44	1.4	0.5	0	0		Barbados
1,282.4	11.6	20.6	197.9	59.9	...	72.9	7.4	925	89	4.1	1.3	0	310		Belarus
8,478	5.3	535.8	2,031.3	376.5	640	40.8	3.9	3,600	352	3.1	1.4	350	30		Belgium
...	12.8	20.0	600.0	4.0	290	1.1	3.9	11	47	5.4	1.6	0	0		Belize
297	5.1	102.0	4.6	0.6	3,250	4.6	0.6	34	5.0	8.3	1.4	5	0		Benin
8,871	5.1	221.7	1,949.2	...	370	3	3	—	—	...	...	0	0		Bermuda
...	...	...	...	...	...	...	...	...	...	...	...	0	0		Bhutan
660	28.6	59.4	0.9	...	...	31.5	3.7	148	18	8.0	1.8	10	0		Bolivia
402	2.5	2.6	...	...	...	19.8[9]	5.3[9]	276	75	24.3	4.5	40	0		Bosnia and Herzegovina
8,281	12.7	431.9	1.9	73.1	750	9.0	5.4	222	142	9.8	4.7	40	0		Botswana
779.1	11.2	255.7	5.2	61.2	...	287.6	1.6	9,920	58	5.5[6]	1.9	180	20		Brazil
932.9	1.5	1.2	79.8	57.5	100	7.0	20.0	295	897	11.5	4.0	20	0		Brunei
1,170.7	7.3	1.9	402.9	94.5	...	51.0	6.6	1,240	158	8.7	3.0	10	200		Bulgaria
9	0.4	1.7	—	—	...	10.8	0.8	42	4	5.9	1.6	0	0		Burkina Faso
156	9.7	10.8	2.0	0.2	1,980	50.5	8.3	49	8	26.7	7.0	60	0		Burundi
...	...	...	...	...	1,170	125	9.5	332	28	26.0	4.0	5	0		Cambodia
78	0.4	1.2	1.2	5.1	8,640	23.1	1.5	148	10	10.6	1.8	5	0		Cameroon
8,121	4.0	140.3	1,044.4	529.4	110	52.3	1.7	8,320	269	5.9	1.4	1,000	550		Canada
...	...	...	...	...	2,740[1]	1.2	2.7	5	13	2.2	0.9	5	0		Cape Verde
135	1.6	22.8	2.7	...	990	2.6	0.7	29	8	15.4	2.8	0	0		Central African Republic
...	...	...	...	...	470	30.4	3.3	37	5	12.7	2.4	10	0		Chad
1,366	4.5	84.8	488.0	12.9	1,360[14]	77.3	5.0	1,990	133	12.3	3.0	100	10		Chile
128	0.2	5.2	45.2	6.9	420	2,250.0	1.7	88,900	71	22.2	2.3	675	320		China
790	56.3	61.8	57.9	75.3	960	200.0	4.8	2,670	68	15.9	3.2	60	0		Colombia
...	...	...	...	...	910	—[15]	15	...	...	...	...	...	...		Comoros
32	1.5	4.7	0.2	0.2	870	97.8	1.9	5,150	102	41.4[6]	14.4	110	0		Congo, Dem. Rep. of the
868	5.3	11.1	232.4	23.1	480	10.0	2.7	58	21	8.4	3.5	0	0		Congo, Rep. of the
67	2.5	73.1	19.5	11.9	4,640	—	—	69	19	2.0	0.5	0	0		Costa Rica
1,216	6.1	24.1	290.9	38.6	...	17.1	1.0	82	5	3.4	0.8	0	0		Côte d'Ivoire
689	1.9	17.7	203.3	3.0	650	20.8	4.7	2,090	491	14.2	6.4	10	10		Croatia
4,142	2.6	71.7	831.4	263.0	180	46.0	4.1	630	57	...	1.9	0	0		Cuba
9,300	4.1	20.8	1,899	638.1	640[18]	10.0[17]	10.9[17]	309	411	9.3	3.4	340	0		Cyprus[16]
252	4.2	124.2	45.0	0.5	600	57.1	5.6	3,000	292	6.3	2.3	220	80		Czech Republic
9,567	7.9	682.4	1,736	77.6	...	22.9	4.2	2,780	524	4.2	1.6	290	10		Denmark
...	15.8	28.4	154.0	14.0	300	9.9	21.6	23	51	12.7	4.3	0	0		Djibouti
...	...	...	...	...	580	20	20	...	...	...	...	...	...		Dominica
587	25.9	35.6	164.5	52.9	260	24.5	2.8	123	15	4.4	0.7	20	0		Dominican Republic
...	...	...	...	...	...	0.7[22]	0.8[22]	...	...	...	...	...	...		East Timor[21]
...	...	...	...	...	...	59.5	4.6	479	38	16.2	3.7	20	0		Ecuador

Social protection (continued)

country	old-age, invalidity, death[a]	sickness and maternity[b]	work injury[c]	unemployment[d]	family allowances[e]	expenditures, (latest) (% of total central govt.)[f]	year	receipts total ('000,000 natl. cur.)	insured persons (%)	employers (%)	government (%)	other (%)	expenditures total ('000,000 natl. cur.)	benefits (%)	administration (%)	other (%)
Egypt	○	○	○	○		0.5[6]	1989	2,443.5	22.8	41.0	2.0	34.2	1,685.6	93.4	6.6	—
El Salvador	○	○	○			5.9	1989	465.3	27.1	51.7	—	21.2	368.3	78.1	21.9	—
Equatorial Guinea	○	○	○		○	...	1989	141.0	7.1	92.9	...	...	134.0	49.3	50.7	—
Eritrea	...	...	...	...		...	...	...	...	...	...	...	...	...	...	...
Estonia	●	●	●	●	●	31.4	...	90.1	...	...	...	...	...	...	...	...
Ethiopia	○		○			1.6[10]	1989[23]	190.9	32.8	65.3	—	1.9	153.7	98.3	1.7	—
Faroe Islands	○[19]	...	...	...	○[19]	...	...	...	...	...	...	...	...	...	...	...
Fiji	●		●			4.1[11]	1989	153.5	20.9	33.8	0.8	44.5	75.47	95.3	4.7	—
Finland	●	●	●	●	●	36.4	1989	118,589.0	7.7	41.1	44.0	7.2	106,235	96.3	3.7	—
France	●	●	●	●	●	38.8[24]	1989	1,700,202.0	77.7	—	20.4	1.9	1,669,096.0	95.5	3.7	0.8
French Guiana	○	...	○	...	○	...	1991	1,071.5	...	...	...	...	997.1	...	...	...
French Polynesia	○	...	...	...	○	...	1990	19,268.0	...	...	...	...	17,832.0	...	...	...
Gabon	○	○	○		○	...	1989	3,415.0	—	44.3	29.3	26.4	2,737.0	55.2	44.8	—
Gambia, The	○		○			1.0[2]	1982	—	...	...	...	...	5.6	...	...	...
Gaza Strip	...	...	...	...	...											
Georgia	●	●	●	●	●	29.7	...	...	...	...	...	...	...	...	...	...
Germany	●	●	●	●	●	50.0[11]	1989[25]	522,172.0	36.9	34.3	26.1	2.7	507,604.0	97.1	2.8	0.1
Ghana	○		○			7.1	1989	17,920.8	21.1	52.9	—	26.0	4,147.7	13.3	64.0	22.7
Greece	●	●	●	●	●	17.9[12]	1989	1,314,421.0	24.9	38.4	30.8	5.9	1,349,693.0	92.5	7.5	—
Greenland	○[19]	...	...	...	○[19]	...	...	...	...	...	...	...	...	...	...	...
Grenada	○	○	○			8.6[26]	1989	24.1	20.1	60.3	3.2	16.3	13.5	93.1	6.9	—
Guadeloupe	○	...	...	...	○	...	1994	2,607.3	...	...	...	...	5,883.4	...	...	...
Guam	○	...	...	...	○	...	1989	...	...	...	...	...	7.3	...	...	...
Guatemala	○	○	○			...	1989	348.5	29.1	54.8	—	16.1	279.7	82.7	14.6	2.7
Guernsey	●	●	●	●	●	...	1999	103,560	—45.0—		40.7	14.3	85,468	94.8	5.2	...
Guinea	○	○	○	...	○	...	1989	3,387.0	0.4	90.3	—	9.3	1,108.1	54.9	45.1	—
Guinea-Bissau	...	...	...		●	8.8[24]	1986	138.0	22.8	63.4	10.3	3.8	61.9	59.6	40.4	—
Guyana	○	○	○			...	1994	1,070.8	...	...	...	...	1,373.7	...	...	...
Haiti	○	7	○			5.1[27]	1977	60.5	—26.6—		69.9	3.5	52.4	92.7	7.3	—
Honduras	○	○	○			...	1986	166.2	23.9	40.8	3.3	32.0	76.8	84.6	15.4	—
Hong Kong	●	●	●	●	●	...	1998–99	...	...	...	...	...	26,939	...	...	...
Hungary	●	●	●	●	●	32.2	1994	798,000.0	...	...	...	...	737,000.0	...	...	...
Iceland	●	●	●	●	●	21.8	1997	14,799	—	—	—	—	96,094	98.2	1.8	—
India	●	●	●	●		...	1989	43,913.8	23.8	27.7	5.3	43.2	13,775.8	90.0	8.2	1.8
Indonesia	●		●			8.6	1989	239,477.0	50.7	49.3	...	...	181,499.0	12.3	15.8	71.9
Iran	●	●	●		●	16.5	1986	346,460.0	83.2	0.1	8.2	8.5	167,879.0	43.4	6.3	50.0
Iraq	●	●	●	●		...	1977	107.8	9.9	55.6	21.9	12.6	71.0	94.0	2.4	3.6
Ireland	●	●	●	●	●	25.9	1989	4,627.5	16.3	24.8	57.7	1.2	4,612.9	95.2	4.7	0.1
Isle of Man	●	●	●	●	●	...	1985	...	...	...	...	...	14.4	...	...	...
Israel	●	●	●	●	●	28.0	1989	13,851.1	31.1	27.7	35.0	6.2	13,593.3	81.7	15.4	2.9
Italy	●	●	●	●	●	1.0	1989	278,383.0	16.5	51.4	30.0	2.1	100,251.0	89.3	2.0	8.7
Jamaica	○	○	○			1.0	1989	374.3	11.5	13.6	43.8	31.1	273.6	92.6	7.4	—
Japan	●	●	●	●	●	36.8[26]	1989	59,571,299.0	27.4	31.6	26.4	14.6	46,684,159.0	94.3	1.7	4.0
Jersey	●	●	●	●	●	9.5[24, 27]	1991	60.9	—63.8—		23.4	12.8	52.8	...	...	...
Jordan	●		●			16.7	1986	53.6	28.7	55.3	—	16.0	9.5	77.4	14.0	8.6
Kazakhstan	●	●	●		●	32.8	...	...	...	...	...	...	...	...	...	...
Kenya	○	○	○			2.7	1989	4,262.0	18.2	13.7	10.0	58.1	1,857.8	53.8	46.1	0.1
Kiribati	●					...	...	...	...	...	...	...	...	...	...	...
Korea, North	...	...	...	...		...	...	...	...	...	...	...	...	...	...	...
Korea, South	●		●	●		10.8[6]	1996	7,425,400.0	—	62.2	—	—	9,656,600.0	...	...	...
Kuwait	●		●		●	20.4	1989	445.8	7.1	13.2	54.3	25.4	206.5	97.0	3.0	—
Kyrgyzstan	●	●	●	●	●	9.5	...	...	...	...	...	...	...	...	...	...
Laos	●	●	●	...	...	...	...	...	...	...	...	...	...	...	...	...
Latvia	●	●	●	●	●	40.8	...	...	...	...	...	...	...	...	...	...
Lebanon	●	●	●		●	5.4	...	...	...	...	...	...	...	...	...	...
Lesotho	...	...	...	...	...	1.1[31]	1992	...	...	...	...	...	12.0[8]	...	...	...
Liberia	○	○	○			...	1983	2.9	—	69.0	13.8	17.2	2.6	54.4	45.6	—
Libya	○	○	○			...	1989	314.3	21.6	25.4	50.2	2.8	260.0	77.5	19.5	3.0
Liechtenstein	●	●	●	●	●	...	...	...	...	...	...	...	...	...	...	...
Lithuania	●	●	●	●	●	35.5	...	...	...	...	...	...	24,981.7	...	...	...
Luxembourg	●	●	●	●	●	52.3[26]	1989	72,471.8	24.2	34.6	34.4	6.8	65,214.4	97.2	2.4	0.4
Macau	○	...	...	...	○	...	1998	223.2	...	...	...	...	207.4	...	...	...
Macedonia	○	○	○	○	○	...	1996	24,482	...	...	...	...	...	...	...	...
Madagascar	○	○	○		○	1.5	1989	15,229.0	22.2	77.8	—	—	14,542.0	81.2	18.8	—
Malawi			○			...	1986	—	...	...	...	...	5.4	...	...	...
Malaysia	●		●			7.2	1989	7,958.7	20.7	40.2	—	39.1	2,826.5	97.0	3.0	—
Maldives	...	...	...	...		2.4	1990	...	...	...	...	...	7.1	...	...	...
Mali	○	○	○		○	...	1986	8,128.8	16.6	74.3	—	9.1	7,924.6	63.7	34.7	1.6
Malta	●	●	●	●	●	34.0	1989	82.2	26.1	31.6	42.3	—	110.7	92.5	7.5	—
Marshall Islands	●					...	...	...	...	...	...	...	...	...	...	...
Martinique	○	...	...	...	○	...	1998	3,913.1	...	...	...	...	8,429.6	...	...	...
Mauritania	○	○	●		○	...	1989	808.4	1.5	90.4	—	8.1	735.2	63.5	31.2	5.3
Mauritius	○		○		○	21.4	1989	1,733.5	2.9	47.9	31.7	17.5	1,072.7	95.2	3.0	1.8
Mayotte	...	...	...	...		...	...	...	...	...	...	...	...	...	...	...
Mexico	○	○	○	○	○	20.1	1989	16,011,795.0	20.9	54.8	12.9	11.4	14,562,293.0	79.9	15.5	4.6
Micronesia	●					...	...	...	...	...	...	...	...	...	...	...
Moldova	●	●	●	●	●	42.4	...	...	...	...	...	...	...	...	...	...
Monaco	●	●	●	35	●	...	...	...	...	...	...	...	...	...	...	...
Mongolia	○	○	○		○	23.8	1989	2,431.6	—	—	20.8	79.2	2,304.6	100.0	...	...
Morocco	○	○	○		○	9.3	1989	4,660.5	20.6	47.5	12.9	19.0	3,040.7	94.8	5.0	0.2
Mozambique	○	...	...	...	...	...	1986	228.2	—	86.2	13.7	0.1	145.0	100.0	—	—
Myanmar (Burma)		○	○			2.3	1986	44.3	19.9	59.6	18.5	2.0	35.9	51.5	15.6	32.9
Namibia	○	○	○		○	6.8[13, 27]	...	...	...	...	...	...	...	...	...	...
Nauru	○	○	○		○	...	...	...	...	...	...	...	...	...	...	...
Nepal	●		●			4.6	1985	—	...	...	...	...	59.3	...	...	...

| offenses reported to the police per 100,000 population | | | | | population per police officer[g] | manpower, 2003[h] | | expenditure, 1999 | | | | arms trade, 1999 ('000,000 U.S.$) | | country |
| total | personal | | property | | | total ('000) | per 1,000 population | total '000,000 | per capita | % of central government expenditure | % of GDP or GNP | imports | exports | |
	murder	assault	burglary	automobile theft										
3,693	1.6	0.7	...	3.1	580	450.0	6.6	2,390	36	9.3[6]	2.7	700	0	Egypt
879	36.9	71.1	...	82.0	1,000	15.5	2.4	110	18	8.8	0.9	10	0	El Salvador
...	...	...	...	...	190	1.3	2.6	19	40	16.5	3.2	0	0	Equatorial Guinea
161.9	2.7	10.3	5.8	...	...	202.2	48.8	208	52	51.1	7.4	170	20	Eritrea
3,565	13.8	28.3	1,659.2	169.8	...	5.5	4.0	173	120	4.5	1.5	10	0	Estonia
258.3	6.5	77.8	1.4	1.4	1,100[23]	162.5	2.4	533	9	29.1	8.8	270	0	Ethiopia
...	...	...	...	...	...	[3]	[3]	—	—	—	—	...	...	Faroe Islands
2,370	2.9	44.1	427.9	44.4	407	3.5	4.2	35	42	5.4	2.0	0	0	Fiji
14,350	0.7	34.9	1,739.7	33.2	640	27.0	5.2	1,770	344	4.5	1.4	400	50	Finland
6,097	3.4	162.7	632.4	511.0	630	259.1	4.3	38,900	658	5.9	2.7	800	2,900	France
8,936	27.2	178.7	1,367.3	150.6	...	[3]	[3]	—	—	—	—	...	...	French Guiana
1,799	0.9	98.9	232.7	...	...	[3]	[3]	—	—	—	—	...	...	French Polynesia
114	1.4	17.9	2.3	7.5	1,290	4.7	3.5	93	78	7.3	2.4	0	0	Gabon
89	0.4	10.6	5.6	...	3,310	0.8	0.6	5	4	5.4	1.3	0	0	Gambia, The
4,355	...	...	...	...	...	—	—	...	...	...	...	...	...	Gaza Strip
286	4.7	99.5	21.1	0.8	...	17.5	3.5	165	33	7.0	1.2	10	30	Georgia
7,682	3.5	139.6	1,377.4	114.3	...	284.5	3.4	32,600	395	4.7	1.6	1,300	1,900	Germany
...	2.2	418.9	1.5	...	620	7.0	0.3	62	3	3.1	0.8	0	0	Ghana
3,641	3.0	68.2	356.8	166.5	380	177.6	16.1	6,060	573	16.4	4.7	1,900	90	Greece
9,360	18.1	845.0	1,883.5	...	340	[3]	[3]	—	—	—	—	...	...	Greenland
8,543	7.8	98.9	582.2	...	230	[20]	[20]	...	...	...	...	...	...	Grenada
5,793	13.2	215.2	821.5	453.9	...	[3]	[3]	—	—	—	—	...	...	Guadeloupe
10,080	7.9	169.3	634.2	333.6	...	[3]	[3]	—	—	—	—	...	...	Guam
510	27.4	77.1	27.9	58.1	670	31.4	2.5	121	10	5.0	0.7	0	0	Guatemala
...	...	...	...	...	...	[3]	[3]	...	...	...	...	...	...	Guernsey
18.4	0.5	0.7	0.7	0.1	1,140	9.7	1.1	54	7	7.4	1.6	0	0	Guinea
129	0.5	8.7	4.0	0.2	...	9.3	6.8	6	4	6.1	2.7	0	0	Guinea-Bissau
1,277	19.1	246.0	365.8	32.2	190	1.6	2.0	5	7	2.0	0.8	0	0	Guyana
701	...	...	...	...	400	[28]	[28]	...	...	...	...	0	0	Haiti
392	154.0	44.4	4.3	25.8	1,040	12.0	1.8	34	6	2.6	0.7	10	0	Honduras
1,122	1.0	117.1	133.4	15.3	221	[3]	[3]	...	...	...	...	0	0	Hong Kong
5,011	4.1	76.6	804.4	41.3	237	33.4	3.3	1,880	185	3.9	1.7	80	10	Hungary
31,332	0.7	15.8	920.3	...	940	—	—	—	—	—	—	10	0	Iceland
594	4.6	...	15.6	...	820	1,325.0	1.2	11,300	11	14.6	2.5	700	10	India
120.9	1.0	4.4	1.8	1.7	1,119	302	1.4	1,450	7	5.3	1.1	450	100	Indonesia
77	0.5	47.7	...	...	...	540.0	8.2	6,880	106	11.2	2.9	150	10	Iran
197	7.1	34.7	...	...	140	[29]	[29]	1,250	57	...	5.5	5	0	Iraq
1,696	1.4	12.4	479.8	16.3	310	10.5	2.6	779	208	2.6	1.0	40	0	Ireland
2,867	0.7	12.3	921.4	60.6	...	[3]	[3]	—	—	—	—	...	...	Isle of Man
6,254	2.2	491.8	990.1	501.7	210	167.6	25.9	8,700	1,510	18.5	8.8	2,400	600	Israel
4,214	4.4	46.4	...	537.0	680	200.0	3.5	23,700	412	4.7	2.0	700	380	Italy
1,871	37.2	511.4	135.7	7.2	430	2.8	1.1	51	19	2.1	0.8	10	0	Jamaica
1,773	1.0	16.0	206.0	34.0	480	239.9	1.9	43,200	342	6.1	1.0	3,000	20	Japan
...	...	...	...	...	...	[3]	[3]	—	—	—	—	...	...	Jersey
1,256	6.3	14.0	31.0	52.2	630	100.5	18.6	725	150	27.5	9.2	70	0	Jordan
932	15.9	...	...	3.4	...	65.8	4.4	671	40	5.3	0.9	160	10	Kazakhstan
484	6.4	54.1	76.9	9.7	1,500	24.1	0.8	200	7	7.1	1.9	5	0	Kenya
261	5.1	11.6	38.6	...	330	—	—	...	...	...	...	...	...	Kiribati
...	...	...	...	...	460	1,082.0	48.2	4,260	199	...	18.8	30	140	Korea, North
3,494	2.1	64.6	7.0	...	506	686.0	13.9	11,600	246	11.0	2.9	2,200	20	Korea, South
1,346	1.5	36.4	75.9	56.7	80	15.5	6.4	2,690	1,410	20.8	7.7	725	0	Kuwait
987	10.4[30]	12.6	482.4	...	...	10.9	2.2	285	62	14.0	2.4	0	0	Kyrgyzstan
...	...	...	...	...	280	29.1	5.1	28	5	11.1	2.0	0	0	Laos
2,097	9.3	18.6	56.1	129.0	...	4.9	2.1	144	59	2.3	0.9	5	0	Latvia
3,063	5.5	209.7	78.0	30.0	530	72.1	19.3	653	185	11.0	4.0	10	0	Lebanon
2,357	50.4	156.9	250.4	30.8	1,130	2.0	1.1	29	14	6.5	2.6	0	0	Lesotho
...	...	...	...	...	1,570	[32]	[32]	6	2	8.3	1.2	0	0	Liberia
1,065	2.1	5.4	...	...	...	76.0	13.7	1,490[6]	342[6]	19.7[6]	6.1[6]	20	30	Libya
...	...	114.3	614.3	153.6	660	[33]	[33]	—	—	—	—	...	...	Liechtenstein
2,029	9.0	10.4	585.6	96.7	...	12.7	3.7	314	87	3.9	1.3	20	0	Lithuania
6,280	17.2	89.0	1,152.8	182.0	829	0.9	2.0	141	326	2.0	0.8	50	0	Luxembourg
1,698	5.4	34.0	250.5	26.6	...	[3]	[3]	...	...	...	...	...	...	Macau
1,102	5.4	26.9	...	44.7	...	12.9	6.3	228	112	10.4	2.5	20	0	Macedonia
112	0.6	12.0	0.7	0.1	2,900	13.5	0.8	45	3	7.4	1.2	0	0	Madagascar
850	3.1	82.2	13.1	...	1,670	5.3	0.5	10	1	2.2	0.6	0	0	Malawi
604	3.1	25.9	155.6	20.8	760	104.0	4.1	1,660	78	9.3	2.3	925	0	Malaysia
2,353	1.9	3.3	36.1	...	35,710	—	—	...	...	...	...	...	...	Maldives
10.0	0.7	1.5	0.8	0.3	160	7.4	0.6	58	6	8.7	2.3	0	0	Mali
1,841	3.0	35.2	1,079.2	243.9	230	2.1	5.3	28	73	1.8	0.8	0	0	Malta
2,273	...	...	...	...	400	[34]	[34]	—	—	—	—	...	...	Marshall Islands
6,305	5.8	184.9	641.2	192.8	...	[3]	[3]	—	—	—	—	...	...	Martinique
95.4	0.8	27.0	7.3	2.5	710	15.8	5.9	37	14	18.9	4.0	0	0	Mauritania
2,712	2.9	7.8	116.0	...	240	—	—	9	7	0.9	0.2	0	0	Mauritius
...	...	...	...	...	...	[3]	[3]	...	...	...	...	...	...	Mayotte
108	7.3	30.2	...	...	...	192.8	1.9	2,700	27	3.8	0.6	160	30	Mexico
...	...	...	...	...	...	[34]	[34]	—	—	—	—	...	...	Micronesia
957	9.9	11.1	50.4	15.6	...	6.9	1.6	43	10	1.6	0.5	0	20	Moldova
3,430	—	46.7	106.7	70.0	...	...	...	...	...	...	...	...	...	Monaco
1,010	30.0	74.7	486.0	2.1	120	8.6	3.4	18	5	5.9	2.1	0	0	Mongolia
366	1.4	6.7	...	...	840	196.3	6.6	1,450	49	13.5	4.3	130	0	Morocco
166	4.2	9.2	45.9	...	...	8.2	0.4	94	5	9.1	2.5	5	0	Mozambique
64.5	1.9	26.9	0.1	0.1	650	488.0	11.5	4,650	112	189.3	7.8	60	0	Myanmar (Burma)
2,006	26.3	533.6	602.0	65.8	...	9.0	4.7	91	53	7.2	2.9	130	0	Namibia
...	25.0	400.0	100.0	0.8	110	...	...	...	...	...	...	...	...	Nauru
9	2.8	1.1	0.8	...	1,000	63.0	2.6	44	2	5.7	0.8	0	0	Nepal

Social protection (continued)

country	old-age, invalidity, death[a]	sickness and maternity[b]	work injury[c]	unemployment[d]	family allowances[e]	expenditures, (latest) (% of total central govt.)[f]	year	receipts total ('000,000 natl. cur.)	insured persons (%)	employers (%)	government (%)	other (%)	expenditures total ('000,000 natl. cur.)	benefits (%)	administration (%)	other (%)
Netherlands, The	●	●	●	●	●	37.4[6]	1989	154,427.0	37.3	30.3	19.0	13.4	135,609.0	96.9	3.1	—
Netherlands Antilles	...	...	○	○	...	12.9[5,26]	1998	317.0	100.0	—	—	—	275.0	...	...	...
New Caledonia	...	...	...	...	○	...	1987	15,834.0	...	...	...	...	14,598.0	...	...	...
New Zealand	●	●	●	●	●	37.9	1989	14,266.0	1.0	4.7	92.5	1.8	14,372.3	95.6	2.8	1.6
Nicaragua	○	○	○		○	14.7[26]	1989	647,454.8	13.5	49.1	7.6	29.8	452,038.6	82.4	17.6	—
Niger	○	○	○		○	...	1989	5,634.9	9.4	90.6	—	—	3,804.2	62.5	—	37.5
Nigeria	○		○			...	1989	54.0	50.0	50.0	—	—	22.6	42.5	57.5	—
Northern Mariana Islands	○		○	...	...	...										
Norway	○	○	○	○	○	40.0[12]	1989	158,105.0	18.3	31.4	46.6	3.7	131,578.2	98.7	1.3	—
Oman	●		●			5.6	1995	...	...	...	...	...	...	...	...	...
Pakistan	●	●	●	●		...	1989	9,321.4	1.3	8.0	84.3	6.4	8,092.0	97.4	1.2	1.4
Palau																
Panama	○	○	○			20.9	1989	496.7	31.0	39.5	7.1	22.4	452.8	94.0	4.8	1.2
Papua New Guinea	●		●			2.0	1983	45.0	40.5	32.1	8.0	19.4	9.4	82.3	9.7	8.0
Paraguay	○	○	○			16.2[24]	1993	...	...	...	...	...	253,341	...	...	...
Peru	○	○	○			...	1989	1,363,280.6	30.2	65.1	4.7	—	1,435,134.1	78.5	21.5	—
Philippines	●	●	●	●		3.9	1989	19,213.6	22.2	32.3	—	45.5	7,878.3	87.3	12.3	—
Poland	●	●	●	●	●	51.5	1989	11,572,248.0	2.1	70.2	25.1	2.6	11,452,165.0	98.8	1.2	—
Portugal	●	●	●	●	●	27.3[2]	1989	833,442.5	31.3	50.1	13.4	5.2	756,410.8	94.6	4.2	1.2
Puerto Rico	○	○	○	○	○	...	1980	...	...	...	...	...	1,041.3	100.0	—	—
Qatar	...	...	...	...	...	...	1986	80.0	—	—	100.0	—	80.0	100.0	—	—
Réunion	...	...	...	...	...	...	1998	...	...	...	...	...	13,200.0	...	...	...
Romania	●	●	●	●	●	31.4	1989	90,561.2	—	48.9	51.1	—	90,561.2	100.0	—	—
Russia	●	●	●	●	●	33.7										
Rwanda	○		○			...	1989	2,350.0	23.9	39.8	—	36.3	965.8	60.8	39.2	—
St. Kitts and Nevis	○	○	○			9.4	1989	14.3	...	...	...	...	7.9	...	...	...
St. Lucia	○	○	○			...	1986	14.6	28.6	28.6	—	42.8	3.4	61.4	38.6	—
St. Vincent and the Grenadines	○	○	○			8.8	1989	—	...	...	...	...	—	...	...	...
Samoa			●			—										
San Marino	●	●	●			...	1983	51,673.0	12.0	48.7	36.1	3.2	46,179.0	95.7	3.7	0.6
São Tomé and Príncipe	○	○	○			...	1986	46.4	37.7	56.3	—	6.0	23.7	100.0	—	—
Saudi Arabia	●	●	●			...	1989	1,761.4	26.8	73.2	—	—	4,292.9	100.0	—	—
Senegal	○	○	○		○	2.3[13,27]	1989	17,202.0	—	47.6	51.4	1.0	15,371.0	84.6	11.1	4.3
Serbia and Montenegro	●	●	●	●	●	6.0[39]	1986[39]	2,777,651.0	63.3	32.2	3.4	1.1	2,732,679.0	90.3	1.9	7.8
Seychelles	○	○	○			13.8	1983	69.1	30.1	60.2	—	9.7	42.7	69.6	4.9	25.5
Sierra Leone	○		○			0.1[12]	1990	...	...	...	...	...	153.00	100.00	—	—
Singapore	●	●	●			12.4	1989	7,531.9	49.1	35.3	0.1	15.6	5,045.8	78.0	0.6	21.4
Slovakia	●	●	●	●	●	30.2	1998	74,205	...	...	...	...	87,916	...	...	...
Slovenia	●	●	●	●	●	43.5										
Solomon Islands	●	○	○			...	1989	20.9	27.8	41.1	—	31.1	17.4	89.7	10.3	—
Somalia			○			...										
South Africa	○	○	○	○	○	4.2[6]	1994	2,034	—	100.0	—	—	2,260.0	...	...	...
Spain	●	●	●	●	●	39.6	1989	8,320,972.0	15.9	53.9	27.9	2.3	8,038,090.0	94.3	2.6	3.1
Sri Lanka	○	[7]	○		○	12.3	1989	15,399.9	22.0	24.4	29.1	24.5	5,819.0	98.5	1.3	0.2
Sudan, The	○		○			...	1989	62.0	24.9	0.5	—	74.6	14.7	37.5	62.5	—
Suriname	○	...	...	...	○	...	1989	73.0	24.7	75.3	—	—	70.6	100.0	—	—
Swaziland	○		○			0.4	1986	10.7	31.4	31.4	—	37.2	3.9	45.8	54.2	—
Sweden	●	●	●	●	●	46.3	1989	446,909.7	2.8	37.9	50.8	8.5	439,997.3	93.7	3.3	3.0
Switzerland	●	●	●	●	●	48.5	1989	45,800.1	45.6	22.6	25.9	5.9	41,745.7	91.5	3.0	5.5
Syria	●	●	●			5.3[12]	1989	3,147.9	30.4	60.9	—	5.6	1,455.9	95.7	4.2	0.1
Taiwan	●	●	●	●		13.8[2]										
Tajikistan	○	○	○	○		20.3										
Tanzania	○	○	○			...	1989	3,275.8	25.9	25.9	—	48.2	2,780.7	5.8	14.1	80.1
Thailand	●	●	●	●	●	6.0	1989	654.0	—	60.2	—	39.8	260.0	88.2	11.8	—
Togo	○	○	○	○		...	1989	10,162.0	8.1	61.5	—	30.4	5,844.0	77.5	22.5	—
Tonga						0.8[13]										
Trinidad and Tobago	○	○	○	○	○	14.3[26]	1989	584.9	12.0	24.1	39.7	24.2	438.4	85.6	11.1	3.3
Tunisia	○	○	○	○	○	18.8	1989	325.3	36.9	63.1	—	—	358.3	...	...	...
Turkey	●	●	●	●		5.9	1989	12,075,809.0	28.5	32.9	22.8	15.8	10,241,427.0	97.2	2.2	0.6
Turkmenistan	●	●	●	●		...										
Tuvalu	○	...	...	...	...	...	1981	...	...	...	...	...	0.1	67.6	32.4	—
Uganda	○		○			...	1989	265.9	32.1	64.3	1.1	2.5	145.0	0.3	76.8	22.9
Ukraine	●	●	●	●	●	43.2	1989	20,350.0	—	—	—	—	20,350.0	100.0	—	—
United Arab Emirates	...	...	...	...	...	3.2	1989	182.2	17.3	6.2	0.5	76.0	182.2	100.0	...	...
United Kingdom	●	●	●	●	●	36.5	1989	92,157.0	18.1	24.9	52.9	4.1	88,294.0	93.8	3.3	2.9
United States	○	○	○	○	○	28.3	1989	804,909.0	25.5	33.9	28.8	11.8	627,653.0	95.5	3.3	1.2
Uruguay	○	[43]	○	○	○	56.5	1989	535,507.0	31.4	37.3	26.0	5.3	548,591.0	93.6	5.4	1.0
Uzbekistan	●	●	●	●		...										
Vanuatu			●			...										
Venezuela	○	○	○	○	[43]	10.0	1986	7,457.6	21.3	40.7	12.7	25.3	6,355.7	86.1	14.9	—
Vietnam	●	●	●			10.5										
Virgin Islands (U.S.)	○	...	...	○	○	...										
West Bank	...	...	...	...	...											
Western Sahara	...	...	...	...												
Yemen	●	●	...			...										
Zambia	○		○			1.3	1986	179.2	28.4	28.4	—	43.2	67.7	40.6	59.4	—
Zimbabwe	○		○			18.2[26]	1983	167.0	25.9	7.6	64.2	2.3	112.2	93.7	6.2	0.1

[1] Rural areas. [2] 1990. [3] Political dependency; defense is the responsibility of the administering country. [4] Includes civilian militia. [5] Netherlands Antilles includes Aruba. [6] 1997. [7] Maternity benefits only. [8] Includes welfare. [9] In 2003 about 12,000 troops of the NATO-commanded Stabilization Forces were stationed in Bosnia and Herzegovina to assure implementation of the Dayton Accords. [10] Old age benefits only. [11] 1996. [12] 1998. [13] 1991. [14] Local officers only. [15] Military defense is the responsibility of France. [16] Republic of Cyprus only. [17] National Guard only. [18] Data refer to former Czechoslovakia. [19] 1999. [20] Paramilitary unit of country participating in the U.S.-sponsored Regional Security System, a defense pact among eastern Caribbean countries. [21] Indonesia includes East Timor, except where noted. [22] UN forces of 3,497 troops, including 104 observers, are stationed in East Timor. [23] Ethiopia includes Eritrea. [24] 1993. [25] Former West Germany. [26] 1995. [27] Social

total	murder	assault	burglary	automobile theft	population per police officer[g]	manpower, 2003[h] total ('000)	per 1,000 population	expenditure total '000,000	per capita	% of central government expenditure	% of GDP or GNP	imports	exports	country
7,808	10.9	242.8	3,100.4	239.0	510	53.1	3.3	7,030	445	5.9	1.8	775	140	Netherlands, The
5,574[36]	...	396	3,455	...	330	3	3	—	—	—	—	...	...	Netherlands Antilles
...	...	...	...	...	...	3	3	—	—	—	—	...	...	New Caledonia
13,854	3.9	546.3	2,352.9	788.6	630	8.6	2.1	587	156	3.5	1.2	575	0	New Zealand
1,069	25.6	203.8	110.7	...	90[4]	14	2.6	24	5	2.9	1.2	0	0	Nicaragua
99	0.9	16.6	1.0	0.7	2,350[37]	5.3	0.5	24	2	6.4	1.2	0	0	Niger
312	...	...	...	...	1,140	78.5	0.6	1,560	13	8.1	1.6	0	0	Nigeria
245	3.8	92.6	73.7	20.8	...	3	3	—	—	—	—	...	...	Northern Mariana Islands
9,769	2.3	66.1	95.0	465.8	660	26.6	5.8	3,310	742	5.0	2.2	480	20	Norway
331	1.5	1.8	...	14.9	430	41.7	15.9	1,780	726	36.3	15.3	30	0	Oman
318	7.1	2.2	10.4	9.0	720	620.0	4.2	3,520	25	27.9	5.9	1,000	10	Pakistan
...	...	...	323.0	...	...	34	34	—	—	—	—	...	...	Palau
419	2.0	11.8	25.1	77.7	180	—	—	124	45	5.1	1.4	5	0	Panama
766	8.6	66.7	63	22.0	720	3.1	0.6	36	7	3.7	1.1	0	0	Papua New Guinea
418	11.5	54.2	21.4	30.5	310	18.6	3.3	84	15	3.9	1.1	10	0	Paraguay
218	3.2	24.1	7.8	3.6	730	100.0	3.7	1,200	45	12.3	2.4	30	0	Peru
...	13.1	14.9	...	3.3	1,160	106.0	1.3	1,110	14	7.3	1.4	110	0	Philippines
2,901	2.8	79.2	936.8	185.0	370	163.0	4.2	6,690	173	6.1	2.1	40	30	Poland
661	3.1	1.5	115.3	40.4	660	44.9	4.4	2,410	240	5.4	2.1	60	0	Portugal
2,339	16.2	101.8	412.4	1,521	380	3	3	—	—	—	—	...	...	Puerto Rico
1,079	2.1	7.1	34.1	11.5	...	12.4	19.8	1,060	1,470	22.9	10.0	120	0	Qatar
2,097	7.8	123.1	181.3	137.9	220	3	3	—	—	—	—	...	...	Réunion
2,206	7.1	5.8	367.8	30.4	...	97.2	4.5	2,190	97	4.7	1.6	200	40	Romania
20,514	21.3	32.6	669.1	25.6	...	960.6	6.6	35,000	239	22.4	5.6	470	3,100	Russia
...	45.1	114.3	...	0.3	4,650	51.0	6.1	87	12	22.7	4.5	30	0	Rwanda
3,808	12.0	434.0	1,790	...	300	20	20	...	...	...	...	...	...	St. Kitts and Nevis
4,386	17.0	1,193.0	778.0	...	430	20	20	...	...	...	...	...	...	St. Lucia
3,977	10.3	986.9	...	...	250	20	20	...	...	...	...	...	...	St. Vincent and the Grenadines
...	...	...	...	...	...	38	38	—	...	...	...	...	...	Samoa
...	4.1	...	...	...	...	—	...	...	...	...	...	...	...	San Marino
558	4.0	...	...	...	400	14.0	—	1	3	1.3	1.2	0	0	São Tomé and Príncipe
149	0.5	0.2	...	45.4	280	124.5	5.2	21,200	996	43.2	14.9	7,700	0	Saudi Arabia
123	0.5	8.8	2.1	8.2	730	13.6	1.3	81	8	8.2	1.7	0	0	Senegal
1,268	...	...	...	...	140[39]	74.2	7.0	1,200[6]	114[6]	55.0[2,39]	4.9[2,39]	10	0	Serbia and Montenegro
5,361	3.7	43.4	378.0	40.9	120	0.4	4.9	...	...	...	...	...	...	Seychelles
...	...	...	...	...	600	14.0	2.8	20	4	13.5	3.0	10	0	Sierra Leone
783	1.0	2.4	40.1	55.2	230	72.5	17.1	4,400	1,100	20.5	4.8	950	20	Singapore
1,740	2.4	204.6	504.3	142.4	...	22.0	4.1	1,010	187	4.4	1.8	20	10	Slovakia
3,138	3.6	20.7	427.3	25.6	...	6.6	3.3	436	227	3.4	1.4	10	0	Slovenia
...	...	...	...	...	620	...	...	...	...	...	...	0	0	Solomon Islands
144	1.5	8.0	31.2	...	540	40	40	18[2]	3[2]	...	0.9[2]	20	0	Somalia
7,140.8	121.9	595.6	896.6	262.7	870	55.8	1.2	1,960	45	5.0	1.5	50	30	South Africa
4,449	2.7	23.4	562.8	343.3	580	150.7	3.5	7,560	192	6.1	1.3	750	70	Spain
280	8.2	10.8	54.7	...	860	152.3[41]	8.0[41]	729	38	18.4	4.7	40	0	Sri Lanka
...	10.2	46.3	66.6	4.7	740	104.5	2.7	424	12	46.8	4.8	10	0	Sudan, The
17,819	7.6	1,824.4	...	...	...	1.8	4.1	14	33	5.4	1.8	10	0	Suriname
3,962	18.1	471.7	706.8	54.1	610	—	—	21	20	4.6	1.5	0	0	Swaziland
12,982	4.5	42.5	1,615.1	658.9	330	27.6	3.1	5,330	601	5.5	2.3	230	675	Sweden
7,030	2.7	73.3	1,065.9	1,065.5	640	3.3	0.4	3,400	469	5.1	1.2	1,100	50	Switzerland
42	1.0	—	15.6	2.7	1,970	319.0	18.1	4,450	280	25.1	7.0	210	0	Syria
799	8.2	...	...	124.9	720	290.0	12.8	15,200	690	23.8[6]	5.2	2,600	20	Taiwan
317	2.5	4.6	...	...	...	6.0	0.9	80	13	9.4	1.3	0	0	Tajikistan
1,714	7.7	1.7	96.6	0.9	1,330	27.0	0.8	122	4	10.1	1.4	5	0	Tanzania
351	7.7	25.4	9.9	3.3	530	314.2	4.9	2,040	34	6.1	1.7	330	0	Thailand
11	...	...	...	...	1,970	8.6	1.6	25	5	9.4	1.8	0	0	Togo
2,727	1.0	108.5	541.7	14.8	330	38	38	—	—	—	—	...	...	Tonga
1,170	9.7	31.0	452.7	80.6	280	2.7	2.1	92	78	5.5	1.4	0	0	Trinidad and Tobago
1,419	1.2	165.1	60.1	10.2	340	35.0	3.5	357	38	5.4	1.8	10	0	Tunisia
547	3.9	120.0	...	28.9	1,570	514.9	7.3	9,950	154	13.9	5.3	3,200	70	Turkey
...	...	...	...	...	...	29.0	6.0	542	122	16.0	3.4	10	0	Turkmenistan
...	...	...	...	—	290	...	...	...	...	...	...	...	...	Tuvalu
316	9.9	54.8	19.3	8.3	1,090	60.0	2.4	140	6	13.9	2.3	30	0	Uganda
1,115	10.0	14.7	224.3	7.6	...	295.5	6.2	5,110	103	8.2	3.0	10	550	Ukraine
2,604.7	3.0	10.1	5.1	23.0	140	50.5	13.2	2,180	935	39.6	4.1	950	0	United Arab Emirates
9,823[42]	2.8[42]	405.2[42]	1,832.7[42]	752.9[42]	350	212.7	3.6	36,500	615	6.9	2.5	2,600	5,200	United Kingdom
5,374	9.0	430.2	1,041.8	591.2	318	1,427.0	4.9	281,000	1,030	15.7	3.0	1,600	33,000	United States
3,002	7.7	162.5	52.3	130.1	170	24.0	7.1	275	83	4.1	1.3	10	0	Uruguay
328	3.2	3.0	33.2	2.3	...	55.0	2.1	933	38	5.3	1.7	0	10	Uzbekistan
...	...	...	...	...	450	—	—	...	...	...	...	...	...	Vanuatu
1,106	22.1	152.2	358.2	239.4	320	82.3	3.2	1,420	61	7.1	1.4	310	0	Venezuela
74	1.5	8.5	...	...	...	484.0	5.9	3,230[6]	44[6]	11.6[6]	2.5[6]	70	0	Vietnam
10,441	22.3	1,943.2	3,183.7	954	240	3	3	—	—	—	—	...	...	Virgin Islands (U.S.)
2,226	...	...	...	...	...	...	...	...	...	...	...	...	...	West Bank
...	...	...	...	...	...	3	3	—	—	—	—	...	...	Western Sahara
63[44]	5.3	3.2	1.2	3.6	1,940	66.7	3.3	374	22	18.0	6.1	30	0	Yemen
666	9.8	9.5	153.5	9.6	540	18.1	1.7	31	3	3.5	1.0	0	0	Zambia
5,619	9.0	198.4	435.9	13.4	750	29.0	2.5	263	23	12.1	5.0	10	0	Zimbabwe

Security only.   [28]Haitian army was disbanded in 1995, and a National Police Force of 5,300 was formed.   [29]As of June 2004 U.S. and allied coalition forces numbered 140,000 and 23,000, respectively.   [30]Includes attempted murders.   [31]1992.   [32]As of September 2004 UN peacekeeping troops numbered 14,700.   [33]Military defense is the responsibility of Switzerland.   [34]Military defense is the responsibility of the United States.   [35]Coverage provided through France's program.   [36]Curaçao only.   [37]Includes paramilitary forces.   [38]Military defense is the responsibility of New Zealand.   [39]Data refer to Yugoslavia as constituted prior to 1991.   [40]Following the 1991 revolution, no national armed forces have yet been formed.   [41]Includes 42,300 recalled reservists.   [42]England and Wales.   [43]Coverage is provided under other programs.   [44]Former Yemen Arab Republic.

Education

This table presents international data on education analyzed to provide maximum comparability among the different educational systems in use among the nations of the world. The principal data are, naturally, numbers of schools, teachers, and students, arranged by four principal levels of education—the first (primary); general second level (secondary); vocational second level; and third level (higher). Whenever possible, data referring to preprimary education programs have been excluded from this compilation. The ratio of students to teachers is calculated for each level. These data are supplemented at each level by a figure for enrollment ratio, an indicator of each country's achieved capability to educate the total number of children potentially educable in the age group usually represented by that level. At the first and second levels this is given as a net enrollment ratio and at the third level as a gross enrollment ratio. Two additional comparative measures are given at the third level: students per 100,000 population and proportion (percentage) of adults age 25 and over who have achieved some level of higher or postsecondary education. Data in this last group are confined as far as possible to those who have completed their educations and are no longer in school. No enrollment ratio is provided for vocational training at the second level because of the great variation worldwide in the academic level at which vocational training takes place, in the need of countries to encourage or direct students into vocational programs (to support national development), and, most particularly, in the age range of students who normally constitute a national vocational system (some will be as young as 14, having just completed a primary cycle; others will be much older).

At each level of education, differences in national statistical practice, in national educational structure, public-private institutional mix, training and deployment of teachers, and timing of cycles of enrollment or completion of particular grades or standards all contribute to the problems of comparability among national educational systems.

Reporting the number of schools in a country is not simply a matter of counting permanent red-brick buildings with classrooms in them. Often the resources of a less developed country are such that temporary or outdoor facilities are all that can be afforded, while in a developed but sparsely settled country students might have to travel 80 km (50 mi) a day to find a classroom with 20 students of the same age, leading to the institution of measures such as traveling teachers, radio or televisual instruction at home under the supervision of parents, or similar systems. According to UNESCO definitions, therefore, a "school" is defined only as "a body of students . . . organized to receive instruction."

Such difficulties also limit the comparability of statistics on numbers of teachers, with the further complications that many at any level must work part-time, or that the institutions in which they work may perform a mixture of functions that do not break down into the tidy categories required by a table of this sort. In certain countries teacher training is confined to higher education, in others as a vocational form of secondary training, and so on. For purposes of this table, teacher training at the secondary level has been treated as vocational education. At the higher level, teacher training is classified as one more specialization in higher education itself.

The number of students may conceal great variation in what each country defines as a particular educational "level." Many countries do, indeed, have a primary system composed of grades 1 through 6 (or 1 through 8) that passes students on to some kind of postprimary education. But the age of intake, the ability of parents to send their children or to permit them to finish that level, or the need to withdraw the children seasonally for agricul-

Education

country	year	first level (primary)					general second level (secondary)					vocational second level[a]	
		schools	teachers[b]	students[c]	student/ teacher ratio	net enroll- ment ratio[d]	schools	teachers[b]	students[c]	student/ teacher ratio	net enroll- ment ratio[d]	schools	teachers[b]
Afghanistan	2002	4,876	58,312	3,900,000	52.9	29	1,994	34,271	400,000	18.1	14	...	...
Albania	2000–01	1,811	28,293	523,253	18.5	95	409[1]	5,780	100,082	17.3	77	...	2,174[1]
Algeria	2002–03	15,426[1]	167,529	4,612,574	27.5	95	3,954[1]	155,356	3,192,247	20.5	67	...	14,896
American Samoa	2001	32	524[2]	11,343	...	...	10	245[2]	4,217	...	...	1	21[2]
Andorra	1999–2000	12	...	5,996	...	89	6[1]	...	2,655[1]	...	71	...	...
Angola	1997–98	...	31,062[3]	1,342,116	...	61	...	5,138[3]	267,399	...	...	...	566[3]
Antigua and Barbuda	2000–01	55	525	10,427	19.9	...	14	381	5,794	10.0	...	1[4]	16[4]
Argentina	1999–2000	22,283	307,874	4,609,077	15.0	96	21,492[5]	127,718[5]	3,281,512[5]	25.7[5]	81	5	5
Armenia	2003–04	1,439[7]	46,000[7]	498,500[7]	10.8[7]	94	7	7	7	7	83	81	3,380
Aruba	2002	36	478	9,595	20.1	99	15	568	8,160	14.4	75	11	34
Australia	2003	9,607[7]	229,576[7]	3,330,300[7]	14.5[7]	97	7	7	7	7	88	1,949	32,300
Austria	2002–03	4,458[8]	67,152[8]	649,198[8]	9.7[8]	90	734[9]	41,840[9]	326,891[9]	7.8[9]	89	925	...
Azerbaijan	2004–05	4,553[7]	173,819[7]	1,634,341[7]	9.4[7]	80	7	7	7	7	76	59	7,028
Bahamas, The	2002–03	113[1]	2,029	34,079	16.8	86	37	2,135	31,975	15.0	76	...	...
Bahrain	2000–01	241	9,970	150,054	15.1	90	...	...	40,946	...	87	...	...
Bangladesh	2002–03	63,658[11]	315,055	17,561,828	55.7	84	16,095[11]	312,348	10,897,971	34.9	45	138[11]	8,431
Barbados	2002	109	1,823	29,502	16.2	100	32	1,389	21,436	15.4	90	...	...
Belarus	2003–04	4,460[7]	138,744[7]	1,369,000[7]	9.9[7]	94	7	7	7	7	85	248	14,772
Belgium	2002–03	4,596	89,445[12]	755,447	...	100	1,911	112,487	795,790	7.1	97	...	...
Belize	2003–04	275	2,618	62,074	23.7	99	43	1,074	15,344	14.3	69	...	...
Benin	2001–02	4,682	21,766	1,152,798	53.0	58	145[13]	4,447[1]	188,035[1]	42.0[1]	20	14[13]	283[13]
Bermuda	2002	26[1]	478[1]	10,474	...	100	...	355[1]	3,726[1]	10.5[1]	86	...	...
Bhutan	2004	433[7]	4,376[7]	135,988[7]	31.1[7]	...	7	7	7	7	...	8[13]	95[13]
Bolivia	2002	...	72,433	1,718,000	23.7	95	...	15,823	443,470	28.0	71	...	...
Bosnia and Herzegovina	2002–03	955[1]	20,874	365,072	17.4	98	184[1]	10,798	169,497	15.7	81	...	...
Botswana	2003	770	13,153	328,825	25.0	81	275	9,597	205,093	21.4	54	6	...
Brazil	2002	172,508	1,581,044	35,150,362	22.2	97	21,304	468,310	8,710,584	16.6	75	...	...
Brunei	2003	207[12]	4,828[12]	58,837[12]	12.2[12]	91	33	2,913	37,793	13.0	68	8	538
Bulgaria	2002–03	2,720[7]	61,354[7]	825,668[7]	13.5[7]	90	7	7	7	7	88	513	21,103
Burkina Faso	1996	3,568	14,037	702,204	50.0	36	252	4,152	137,257	33.0	9	41	731
Burundi	1998	1,512	12,107	557,344	46.0	57	400	3,548	56,872	16.0	9	...	...
Cambodia	2002–03	5,915	48,433	2,747,411	56.7	93	594	22,830	543,885	23.8	24	...	2,315[1]
Cameroon	2002–03	9,459[1]	49,042	2,798,523	57.1	67	700[4]	27,595	669,129	24.2	11[4]	32[4]	11,221
Canada	1999–2000	15,596[7]	302,977[7]	5,397,000[7]	17.8[7]	100	7	7	7	7	98	...	10,990[18]
Cape Verde	2002–03	370[19]	3,145	87,841	27.9	99	...	1,967	47,666	24.2	58	...	124
Central African Republic	1998	930[19]	3,125	284,398	91.0	53	46[19]	845[19]	42,253[2]	...	...	...	...
Chad	2002–03	2,660[20]	16,471	1,119,242	67.9	63	153[4]	2,595[14]	187,659	...	10	18[20]	148[14]
Chile	2003–04	8,702[4]	50,261	1,713,538	34.1	85	...	35,208	1,170,288	33.2	81	...	11,900
China	2003	425,846	5,703,000	116,897,000	20.5	100	79,490	4,537,000	85,832,000	18.9	73	9,908	488,000
Colombia	2003	33,957	190,961	5,207,772	27.3	87	12,293	168,587	3,603,949	21.4	56	...	...
Comoros	2002–03	346[17]	2,908	106,972	36.8	55	...	3,379	38,203	11.3	...	...	20
Congo, Dem. Rep. of the	1998	17,585	154,618	4,022,411	26.0	54	6,007	89,461	1,234,528	13.8	17[4]	...	...
Congo, Rep. of the	1998	1,166	4,515	270,451	59.9	96	...	5,094	114,450	22.5	...	...	1,746[14]
Costa Rica	2002–03	3,768[17]	24,142	545,509	22.6	90	468[17]	13,170	235,156	17.9	53	...	2,240
Côte d'Ivoire	2001–02	7,699[14]	40,529[20]	1,662,285[20]	41.0[20]	61	428[17]	15,959[20]	539,134	...	21	...	1,424[4]
Croatia	2003–04	2,138	28,335	393,421	13.9	89	665	20,073	195,340	9.7	87	442[21]	13,000[21]
Cuba	2002–03	9,397	86,641	925,325	10.9	94	2,032	80,372	938,047	11.7	86	...	27,267[20]
Cyprus[22]	2001	367	3,756	63,367	16.9	96	123	4,724	59,526	12.6	93	11	597
Czech Republic	2003–04	3,870	65,615	956,324	14.6	87	344	12,175	142,167	11.7	91	1,344	31,874
Denmark	2003	2,690[8]	33,100[8, 20]	705,974[8]	...	100	152	12,000[9, 20]	68,313[9]	...	96	157	13,100[20]

tural work all make even a simple enrollment figure difficult to assess in isolation. All of these difficulties are compounded when a country has instruction in more than one language or when its educational establishment is so small that higher, sometimes even secondary, education cannot take place within the country. Enrollment figures in this table may, therefore, include students enrolled outside the country.

Student-teacher ratio, however, usually provides a good measure of the ratio of trained educators to the enrolled educable. In general, primary and secondary students have been counted on the basis of full-time enrollment; tertiary students and teachers have been counted on the basis of both full-time and part-time enrollment or employment. At the primary and secondary levels, net enrollment ratio is the ratio of the number of children within the usual age group for a particular level who are actually enrolled to the total number of children in that age group (× 100). This ratio is usually less than (occasionally, equal to) 100 and is the most accurate measure of the completeness of enrollment at that particular level. It is not always, however, the best indication of utilization of teaching staff and facilities. Utilization, provided here for higher education only, is best seen in a gross enrollment ratio, which compares total enrollment (of all ages) to the population within the normal age limits for that level. For a country with substantial adult literacy or general educational programs, the difference may be striking: typically, for a less developed country, even one with a good net enrollment ratio of 90 to 95, the gross enrollment ratio may be 20%, 25%, even 30% higher, indicating the heavy use made by the country of facilities and teachers at that level.

Literacy data provided here have been compiled as far as possible from data for the population age 15 and over for the best comparability inter-nationally. Standards as to what constitutes literacy may also differ markedly; sometimes completion of a certain number of years of school is taken to constitute literacy; elsewhere it may mean only the ability to read or write at a minimal level testable by a census taker; in other countries studies have been undertaken to distinguish among degrees of functional literacy. When a country reports an official 100% (or near) literacy rate, it should usually be viewed with caution, as separate studies of "functional" literacy for such a country may indicate 10%, 20%, or even higher rates of inability to read, or write, effectively. Substantial use has been made of UNESCO literacy estimates, both for some of the least developed countries (where the statistical base is poorest) and for some of the most fully developed, where literacy is no longer perceived as a problem, thus no longer in need of monitoring.

Finally, the data provided for public expenditure on education are complete in that they include all levels of public expenditure (national, state, local) but are incomplete for certain countries in that they do not include data for private expenditure; in some countries this fraction of the educational establishment may be of significant size. Occasionally data for external aid to education may be included in addition to domestic expenditure.

The following notes further define the column headings:
a. Usually includes teacher training at the second level.
b. Full-time and part-time.
c. Full-time; may include students registered in foreign schools.
d. Latest.

| students[c] | student/ teacher ratio | third level (higher) | | | | | | | literacy (2000–04) over age 15 | | | public expenditure on education (percent of GNP)[d] | country |
		institutions	teachers[b]	students[c]	student/ teacher ratio	gross enroll-ment ratio[d]	students per 100,000 popula-tion[d]	percent of population age 25 and over with post-secondary education[d]	total (%)	male (%)	female (%)		
...	...	1	462	13,000	28.1	2	60	3.0	29.0	43.0	14.0	2.0	Afghanistan
18,495[1]	8.5[1]	...	2,927	42,160	14.4	16	1,367	...	98.7	99.2	98.3	3.2	Albania
356,237	23.9	...	57,747	682,775	11.8	21	2,176	...	69.8	79.5	60.1	4.9[1]	Algeria
160[2]	7.6[2]	1	77	1,178	15.3	...	2,003	22.6	99.4	99.4	99.5	8.1	American Samoa
...	...	1	...	1,341	...	...	2,093	...	100.0	100.0	100.0	...	Andorra
22,401[2]	...	1	776	8,327	10.7	1	87	...	66.8	82.1	53.8	3.4	Angola
46[4]	2.9[4]	11	161[1]	461[1]	2.9[1]	...	73	11.6	86.6	...	...	4.0	Antigua and Barbuda
5	5	1,744	126,224	1,336,800	10.6	60	3,673	17.0[6]	97.2	97.2	97.2	4.3	Argentina
28,600	8.4	20	6,628	55,900	8.4	27	1,863	20.3	99.4	99.7	99.2	3.1	Armenia
178	5.2	2	21	203	9.7	30	214	16.2	97.3	97.3	97.3	4.1	Aruba
1,717,800	53.8	46	84,435	929,752	11.0	74	4,671	31.0[6]	100.0	100.0	100.0	5.0	Australia
243,440	...	86	19,002	268,005	14.1	49	3,315	14.0	100.0	100.0	100.0	5.8	Austria
55,794	7.9	42	13,630	127,248	9.3	17	1,532	14.2	98.8	99.5	98.2	3.4	Azerbaijan
...	...	1[10]	160[1,10]	3,463[1,10]	21.6[1,10]	18	1,198	15.2[6]	95.5	94.7	96.4	4.0	Bahamas, The
3,522	...	2	696	14,187	20.4	33	2,225	12.5[6]	87.7	92.5	83.0	4.4[1]	Bahrain
126,355	15.0	13[11]	61,321	877,335	14.3	6	667	3.7	41.1	50.3	31.4	2.3	Bangladesh
...	...	4	339	11,226	33.1	38	4,143	11.2	99.7	99.7	99.7	7.9	Barbados
138,593	9.4	58	21,684	337,000	15.5	62	3,413	12.5	99.6	99.8	99.4	2.1	Belarus
...	...	226	26,454	298,387	11.3	61	2,888	33.0	100.0	100.0	100.0	6.2	Belgium
...	...	12[1]	228[1]	2,853	...	...	1,240	10.2	76.9	76.7	77.1	5.7	Belize
4,873[13]	17.2[13]	16[13]	962[14]	14,085[14]	14.6[14]	4	253	1.3	33.6	46.4	22.6	3.3	Benin
...	...	1	...	544	...	62	...	26.8[6]	98.0	98.0	98.0	3.7[1]	Bermuda
1,822[3]	12.2[3]	14	321	3,381	10.5	...	448	...	42.2	56.2	28.1	5.9	Bhutan
...	...	...	13,929	298,668	21.4	39	3,537	16.7[15]	86.5	92.9	80.4	6.5	Bolivia
...	...	56[1]	2,838	34,477	12.1	...	901	...	85.5	96.5	76.6	...	Bosnia and Herzegovina
2,899[16]	...	1	697[17]	12,286[16]	...	5	731	1.4	78.9	76.1	81.5	8.6[1]	Botswana
483,670	...	1,180	197,712	2,694,245	13.5	21	1,530	6.8	88.4	88.3	88.6	4.4	Brazil
3,024	5.6	2	392	3,805	9.7	13	1,090	12.9	92.7	95.2	90.2	3.0	Brunei
217,313	10.3	42	18,710	215,712	11.5	39	2,741	15.0	98.6	99.1	98.2	3.6	Bulgaria
9,539	13.0	9	632	9,531	15.1	1	84	...	26.6	36.8	16.6	3.6[14]	Burkina Faso
...	...	8	379	5,037	13.3	2	92	0.6	58.9	66.8	51.9	4.0	Burundi
9,983[1]	4.3[1]	...	1,001[1]	8,901[1]	8.9[1]	3	75	1.0	73.6	84.7	64.1	1.9	Cambodia
150,829	13.4	...	3,166	81,318	25.7	6	510	...	67.9	77.0	59.8	4.1	Cameroon
298,071[18]	27.1[18]	274	61,633	1,220,651	19.8	60	3,977	17.1	100.0	100.0	100.0	6.9	Canada
1,856	15.0	...	290	2,215	7.6	...	492	...	75.7	85.4	68.0	8.1	Cape Verde
...	...	1	154[16]	6,474[16]	42.0[16]	2	160	2.0	48.6	64.8	33.5	2.3[19]	Central African Republic
3,668	...	8	288[20]	5,901[17]	...	1	71	...	25.5	40.6	12.7	2.0	Chad
386,832	32.5	...	...	567,114	...	42	3,555	11.5	95.9	96.1	95.7	4.3	Chile
10,306,000	21.1	1,592	725,000	11,086,000	15.3	16	860	3.7	90.9	95.1	86.5	2.3	China
...	...	266[20]	75,568[20]	673,353[20]	8.9[20]	24	1,768	10.4	94.2	93.7	94.6	5.4	Colombia
69	3.5	...	125	1,707	13.7	2	298	0.2	56.2	63.5	49.1	3.9	Comoros
...	...	...	3,788	60,341	15.9	2	124	1.3	82.8	88.9	77.1	1.0	Congo, Dem. Rep. of the
23,606[14]	13.5[14]	...	1,341[4]	16,602[4]	12.4[4]	4	582	3.0	80.7	87.5	74.4	4.4	Congo, Rep. of the
53,809	24.0	52	3,874	77,283	19.9	19	1,910	12.7	95.8	95.7	95.9	5.2	Costa Rica
11,037[4]	7.8[4]	...	1,657[4]	87,565	...	7	396	0.9	48.1	60.1	38.2	4.8	Côte d'Ivoire
150,792[21]	11.6[21]	89[16]	7,622[16]	100,297[16]	13.2[16]	39	2,257	11.9	98.1	99.3	97.1	4.6	Croatia
244,253[20]	9.0[20]	64	24,199	235,997	9.8	34	2,110	5.9	99.8	99.8	99.8	8.7	Cuba
4,497	7.5	32	1,077	11,934	11.1	23	1,702	22.3	96.8	98.6	95.1	6.4	Cyprus[22]
399,524	12.5	193[23]	17,458	264,123	15.1	36	2,589	9.5	100.0	100.0	100.0	4.6	Czech Republic
172,225	...	162	9,600[20]	183,694	...	67	3,410	25.8	100.0	100.0	100.0	8.6	Denmark

Education   (continued)

country	year	first level (primary)					general second level (secondary)					vocational second level[a]	
		schools	teachers[b]	students[c]	student/ teacher ratio	net enrollment ratio[d]	schools	teachers[b]	students[c]	student/ teacher ratio	net enrollment ratio[d]	schools	teachers[b]
Djibouti	2000–01	73	1,127	37,938	33.7	36	26[5, 19]	628[4, 5]	16,121[5]	...	21	[5]	[5]
Dominica	2002–03	63[21]	550	10,460	19.0	81	15[21]	441	7,455	16.9	72	...	19
Dominican Republic	2002–03	4,001[4]	35,867	1,374,624	38.3	96	...	24,723[5]	658,164[5]	26.0[5]	36	[5]	[5]
East Timor	2003	...	4,080	183,600	45.0	...	...	1,103	38,180	34.6	20	...	...
Ecuador	2002–03	17,367[14]	83,736	1,987,465	23.7	99	...	73,284[5]	972,777[5]	13.3[5]	50	...	[5]
Egypt[24]	2002–03	24,198	533,831	11,433,939	21.4	91	1,942	91,458	1,249,706	13.7	81	1,959	151,792
El Salvador	2000	5,090	26,209	1,212,622	46.3	90	...	9,255[20]	147,867	...	49	...	...
Equatorial Guinea	1998	483	1,322	74,940	56.7	84	...	763	18,602	24.6	26	...	122[13]
Eritrea	2001–02	695	6,706	330,278	49.3	46	196	2,671	151,065	56.6	22	12	174
Estonia	2002–03	592	15,762[11]	200,500	...	95	284	10,361	106,000	10.2	88	79	1,779[11]
Ethiopia	1999–2000	11,490	115,777	6,462,503	55.8	51	410	13,154	571,719	43.5	18	62	1,309
Faroe Islands	2001–02	38	...	5,579	...	...	23	...	2,019	...	...	11	...
Fiji	2003	712	5,127	142,531	27.8	100	157	3,935	68,178	17.3	76	64	1,023[16]
Finland	2003	3,808	43,783[16]	597,414	...	98	440	7,480[16]	121,816	...	94	340	19,698[16]
France	2000–01	39,131[14]	211,192	3,839,770	18.2	99	11,052[14]	483,493	5,399,433	11.2	94	...	...
French Guiana	2001–02	92	1,871[12]	22,851	...	...	36	1,919	21,439	11.2	...	...	210[14]
French Polynesia	2000–01	173	2,811[14]	26,249	...	100	82	2,035[21]	24,743	...	64	...	316[2]
Gabon	2002–03	1,175	7,764	279,816	36.0	78	88	2,504	97,604	39.0	...	11[4]	412[4]
Gambia, The	2002–03	331[21]	4,708	178,288	37.9	79	85[21]	2,349	59,793	25.5	33	...	...
Gaza Strip[26]	2002–03	...	...	...	...	...	...	...	...	...	...	...	...
Georgia[27]	2003–04	3,148[7]	69,700[7]	654,600[7]	9.4[7]	77	[7]	[7]	[7]	[7]	74	85	2,146[14]
Germany	2002–03	17,829[21]	235,179	3,303,737	14.0	83	19,668[21]	515,596	6,716,720	13.1	88	9,754[21]	79,792
Ghana	2003–04	13,115[21]	71,330	2,678,912	37.6	59	8,906[21]	51,875	1,257,998	24.2	36[21]	99	453
Greece	2002–03	6,018	52,788	647,642	12.3	94	3,162	53,366	576,613	10.8	86	602	16,658
Greenland	2001–02	87[7]	1,191[7]	11,368[7]	9.5[7]	...	[7]	[7]	[7]	[7]	...	...	...
Grenada	2002–03	58[14]	888	16,598	18.7	84	19[4]	740	14,860	20.1	96	...	...
Guadeloupe	2001–02	348[17]	2,984	38,092[13]	...	...	88[5]	3,955[5]	51,366[3, 5]	...	...	[5]	[5]
Guam	2000–01	24	1,063	17,001	16.0	...	11	1,010	18,217	18.0	...	2	370[3]
Guatemala	2002–03	17,905[17]	68,901	2,075,694	30.1	87	3,118[5, 17]	44,435[5]	434,830[5]	9.8[5]	30	[5]	[5]
Guernsey[27]	2004	10	600[7]	9,000[7]	15.0[7]	...	6	[7]	[7]	[7]	...	...	...
Guinea	2002–03	5,765	23,859	1,073,458	45.0	66	557	8,360	301,491	36.1	21	41	1,268[20]
Guinea-Bissau	2000–01	...	3,518	155,033	44.1	45	...	1,783	25,648	14.4	9	...	...
Guyana	2002–03	428[28]	4,202	111,854	26.6	99	109[28]	3,321	69,426	20.9	78	7[28]	512[28]
Haiti	2002–03	360	30,205[4]	1,110,398[4]	36.8[4]	26	144	...	195,418[4]	...	22[4]	18	...
Honduras	2001	9,746	32,568	1,109,242	34.0	87	1,000	15,647	195,072	12.5	21[17]	...	...
Hong Kong	2002–03	803	23,988	468,800	19.5	98	542	25,742	471,100	18.3	74	1	1,008
Hungary	2003–04	3,747	89,784	913,000	10.2	91	1,622	38,479	531,400	13.8	94	622	9,716
Iceland	2002	193	4,437	44,695	10.1	100	36	2,258	21,379	9.5	86	...	...
India	2001–02	664,041	1,928,075	113,883,060	59.0	88	311,061	2,486,715	64,882,221	26.1	...	...	...
Indonesia	2001–02	148,516	1,164,808	25,850,849	22.2	92	28,627	700,976	10,490,634	15.0	54	4,522	139,359
Iran	2002–03	68,627	297,711	7,028,924	23.6	86	49,008	352,518	8,694,127	24.7	72	69	970
Iraq	2003–04	11,066	206,953	4,280,602	20.7	91	2,968	74,681	1,454,775	19.5	37	259	7,677
Ireland	2000–01	3,286	22,850	439,560	19.2	96	419	12,476	197,376	15.8	83	247	5,788
Isle of Man	2001	32	...	6,611	...	...	5	...	5,374	...	...	...	...
Israel	2002–03	2,178	60,600	758,798	12.5	19	1,768	75,938	451,027	5.9	89	180	...
Italy	2002–03	18,854[29]	256,650	2,778,877	10.8	100	7,906[29]	410,577	3,829,583	9.3	91	6,637[29]	307,279[29]
Jamaica	2002–03	788[2]	10,968	325,302	29.7	95	135[11]	11,315[5]	229,701[5]	20.3[5]	75	...	[5]
Japan	2003	23,633	414,000	7,227,000	17.5	100	16,584	511,000	7,558,000	14.8	100	62[1]	99,862[16]
Jersey	2002	21	...	7,380	...	...	10	...	5,715	...	...	...	...
Jordan	2002–03	2,708	55,900	1,222,400	21.9	92	912	15,200	179,800	11.8	80	214	3,026
Kazakhstan[27]	2002–03	8,254	60,509	1,120,000	18.5	92	...	170,190	1,976,400	11.6	87	357	5,893
Kenya	2002–03	15,906[4]	166,758	5,590,143	33.5	67	2,878[4]	57,181	1,362,131	23.8	25	62[4]	...
Kiribati	2002–03	88[30]	660	14,823	22.5	...	19[30]	324[30]	10,334[30]	31.9[30]	...	2[30]	39[30]
Korea, North	2000	4,886	59,000[31]	1,609,865	...	...	4,772	111,000[31]	2,181,524	...	...	...	...
Korea, South	2003	5,463	154,075	4,175,626	27.1	100	4,881	215,546	3,621,170	16.8	88	169	12,714
Kuwait[32]	2000–01	349[8]	17,385[8]	193,582[8]	11.1[8]	83	117[9]	9,234[9]	76,221[9]	8.3[9]	77	40	1,107
Kyrgyzstan	1999–2000	1,985	19,200	466,200	24.3	89	1,474[13]	36,600	633,900	17.3	...	53[13]	5,100
Laos	2002–03	7,896[14]	28,571	875,300	30.6	85	750[3]	13,421	348,309	30.0	35	...	350
Latvia	2004	1,026[7]	34,500[7]	301,000[7]	8.7[7]	86	[7]	[7]	[7]	[7]	88	103	3,666
Lebanon	2002–03	2,160[14]	26,428	449,311	17.0	91	...	34,613	350,211	10.1	...	275[14]	11,595
Lesotho	2002–03	1,249[14]	8,908	418,668	47.0	86	187[4]	3,384	81,130	24.0	23	9[13]	162
Liberia	1999–2000	...	10,047[21]	496,253	...	70	...	6,621[21]	84,643	...	18	...	...
Libya	2002–03	2,733[13]	122,020[20]	743,997	...	96[14]	...	17,668[20]	619,940	...	62[14]	480[20]	...
Liechtenstein	2003–04	14[21]	242	2,266	9.2	...	12[5]	198[5, 21]	4,113[5]	...	...	5	5
Lithuania	2002–03	2,172[7]	50,200[7]	594,300[7]	11.8[7]	91	[7]	[7]	[7]	[7]	94	82	4,700
Luxembourg	2002–03	...	2,966	32,004	10.8	90	...	3,279[5]	9,963	...	80	...	5
Macau	2003–04	82	1,615	39,378	24.4	87	47	1,666	41,830	25.1	74	2	125
Macedonia	2001–02	1,010	13,508	242,707	18.0	95	95	5,550[5]	92,068[5]	16.6[5]	53	5	5
Madagascar	2002–03	14,438[21]	55,309	2,856,480	51.6	79	...	19,471	436,211	22.4	...	...	1,092[21]
Malawi	2002–03	3,706[20]	45,780	2,846,589	62.2	100	...	11,360	517,690	45.6	29	...	475[20]
Malaysia	2003	7,498	174,189	2,996,780	17.2	93	1,682	113,032	1,951,225	17.3	70	86	7,126
Maldives	2000	230	2,221	68,242	30.7	92	298	2,212	52,327	23.7	51	...	...
Mali	2002–03	2,871[29]	22,557	1,294,672	57.3	45	307[2]	4,549[20]	311,717	...	5[21]	...	21,731[21]
Malta	1999–2000	126	1,501	34,261	22.8	96	75	2,561	27,354	10.7	87	23	526
Marshall Islands	2002–03	100	703	10,957	15.6	84	16	202	3,147	15.6	65	...	...
Martinique	2001–02	273	3,280	53,347	16.4	...	78	4,257	51,057	12.0	...	15[4]	896[4]
Mauritania	2002–03	2,676[21]	9,606	394,401	41.1	68	...	2,980	81,278	27.3	16	...	257
Mauritius	2002–03	291	5,256	132,432	25.2	97	175	5,553	99,687	18.0	74	114	433
Mayotte	2001–02	112	555[2]	28,591	...	...	14	246[2]	15,626	...	...	2[3]	17[3]
Mexico	2001–02	99,230	609,654	14,843,400	24.3	99	39,691	536,579	8,600,700	16.0	63	6,610[14]	65,712
Micronesia	1997–98	171	1,486	25,915	18.6	...	24	418	6,809	16.2	...	...	...
Moldova	2003–04	1,576[7]	42,600[7]	578,800[7]	13.6[7]	79	[7]	[7]	[7]	[7]	69	83	2,200
Monaco	2002–03	7	127[14]	1,899	...	...	4	192[14]	3,140	...	...	4[14]	89[14]
Mongolia	2001–02	700[7]	20,076[7]	510,300[7]	25.4[7]	79	[7]	[7]	[7]	[7]	77	32	985
Morocco	2002–03	6,565[28]	135,199	4,101,157	30.3	90	1,664[28]	87,887	1,679,077	19.1	37	69[28]	5,013

students[c]	student/teacher ratio	third level (higher) institutions	teachers[b]	students[c]	student/teacher ratio	gross enrollment ratio[d]	students per 100,000 population[d]	percent of population age 25 and over with post-secondary education[d]	literacy (2000–04) over age 15 total (%)	male (%)	female (%)	public expenditure on education (percent of GNP)[d]	country
5[5]	5	1[19]	13[19]	476	...	1	110	...	65.5	76.1	55.5	3.4	Djibouti
406	21.4	2[21]	34[2]	461[14]	14.2[2]	...	630	2.8	94.0	...	...	5.5	Dominica
5[5]	5	...	11,111	286,957	25.8	35	3,351	12.9	87.7	88.0	87.3	2.4	Dominican Republic
...	...	...	...	4,500[16]	...	12	552	1.4	58.6	65.0	52.0	...	East Timor
5[5]	5	21[14]	12,856[14]	115,554	...	20	894	15.5	91.0	92.3	89.7	1.1	Ecuador
2,214,152	14.6	293	...	1,239,441	...	29	1,842	4.6	55.6	67.2	43.6	4.8	Egypt[24]
...	...	...	7,501	114,675	15.3	17	1,827	6.4	79.7	82.4	77.1	2.9	El Salvador
2,105[13]	17.3[13]	...	58[13]	578[13]	10.0[13]	3	164	...	84.2	92.1	76.4	2.2	Equatorial Guinea
1,992	11.4	1[21]	198[21]	3,096[21]	15.6[21]	2	89	1.7	58.6	69.9	47.6	3.3	Eritrea
28,095	...	47	3,052	63,625	20.8	66	4,683	14.1	99.8	99.8	99.8	6.0	Estonia
12,551	9.6	6	1,779	40,894	23.0	2	64	1.4	41.5	49.2	33.8	4.6	Ethiopia
2,195[14]	...	1	19[14]	173[14]	9.1[14]	...	397	...	99.0	99.0	99.0	...	Faroe Islands
9,706	...	1	365[11]	15,393[11,25]	11.3[11]	12	1,856[25]	6.7	93.7	95.5	91.9	5.9	Fiji
304,688	...	20[11]	7,728[16]	169,846	...	88	3,258	28.0	100.0	100.0	100.0	6.4	Finland
...	...	1,062[4]	134,107	2,119,149	15.8	56	3,594	11.4	98.8	98.9	98.7	5.6	France
2,404[14]	11.4[14]	1	194	637	3.3	...	375	6.7	83.0	83.6	82.3	...	French Guiana
3,730[2]	11.8[2]	1	54	1,600	29.6	1	681	...	95.0	94.9	95.0	9.8[20]	French Polynesia
7,587	...	2[4,23]	585[23]	7,473[23]	12.6[23]	7	606	...	71.0	80.0	62.0	4.6	Gabon
428	...	4[21]	155[13]	1,169[21]	...	2	98	...	40.1	47.4	33.1	3.0	Gambia, The
...	...	...	...	...	...	...	...	...	...	...	...	...	Gaza Strip[26]
20,355	...	26	7,390	123,900	16.8	38	2,702	...	99.5	99.7	99.4	4.3	Georgia[27]
1,729,839	21.7	296[21]	284,116	2,334,569	8.2	51	2,829	23.0	100.0	100.0	100.0	4.6	Germany
18,672	41.2	15[21]	1,432[14]	25,372[14]	17.7[14]	3	147	...	54.1	62.9	45.7	4.2	Ghana
147,612	8.9	18	20,932[18]	272,037[18]	13.0[18]	74	2,480	9.0	91.0	94.0	88.3	4.0	Greece
...	...	1	14	100	7.1	...	177	...	100.0	100.0	100.0	...	Greenland
...	...	1	111	1,106	10.0	...	1,090	1.5	85.0	...	...	5.7	Grenada
5[5]	5	1	168	4,144	24.7	9	958	5.2	90.1	89.7	90.5	...	Guadeloupe
4,369[21]	...	1	192[3]	3,532[21]	...	...	2,343	39.9	99.0	99.0	99.0	8.5[21]	Guam
5[5]	5	...	13,105[17]	111,739	...	8	954	4.0	69.1	75.4	63.3	1.7[4]	Guatemala
...	...	1	...	...	...	...	...	...	100.0	100.0	100.0	...	Guernsey[27]
7,172	...	7	860	16,361	19.0	1	76	...	41.1	55.1	27.0	2.0	Guinea
...	...	...	...	...	...	...	...	0.1	36.8	53.0	21.4	2.3	Guinea-Bissau
6,266[28]	12.2[28]	1	371[28]	4,848	...	6	645	6.7	98.6	99.0	98.2	4.5	Guyana
...	...	2	899[4,23]	12,348[4,23]	13.7[4,23]	1.0	169	0.7	51.9	53.8	50.0	1.1	Haiti
...	...	10	3,704	64,142	17.3	15	982	3.1	80.0	79.8	80.2	3.6[17]	Honduras
59,400	58.9	9	5,620	86,900	14.9	31	1,280	13.4	93.5	96.5	90.2	4.3	Hong Kong
134,800	13.9	68	23,798	390,458	16.4	51	3,854	10.1	99.3	99.4	99.3	5.8	Hungary
...	...	11	2,620	13,884	5.3	63	4,820	19.9	100.0	100.0	100.0	7.8	Iceland
...	...	42,057	758,706	10,453,229	13.8	12	1,042	7.3	61.0	73.4	47.8	4.1	India
2,027,464	5	1,634[28]	194,828[28]	3,126,307[28]	16.0[28]	16	1,514	2.2	87.9	92.5	83.4	1.3	Indonesia
9,729	10.0	72[4]	84,579	1,673,757	19.8	21	2,476	...	77.0	83.5	70.4	4.9	Iran
128,981	16.8	65	14,700	288,670[11]	...	14	1,198	4.1	58.0	70.7	45.0	...	Iraq
96,842	16.7	29	6,925	119,131	17.2	52	3,134	21.0	100.0	100.0	100.0	5.3	Ireland
...	...	1	...	1,128[17]	...	...	1,512	...	...	...	...	...	Isle of Man
138,361	...	7	10,171	219,763	21.6	57	3,458	11.2	96.9	98.3	95.6	7.8	Israel
2,565,029[29]	8.3[29]	74[18]	54,856[18]	1,913,352	...	57	3,355	3.8	98.5	98.9	98.1	4.8	Italy
5[5]	5	1	2,006	45,770	22.8	18	1,717	4.2	87.6	83.8	91.4	5.3	Jamaica
1,047,720[16]	10.5[16]	1,227	170,000	3,054,000	18.0	51	2,395	34.4	100.0	100.0	100.0	3.5	Japan
...	...	1	...	582[30]	...	...	667	...	100.0	100.0	100.0	...	Jersey
43,861	14.5	22	6,036	153,965	25.5	35	3,076	9.4	89.9	95.1	84.7	5.0	Jordan
250,900	42.6	180	37,600	658,100	17.3	45	4,365	10.0	99.5	99.7	99.2	3.2	Kazakhstan[27]
27,687	...	14[23]	4,392[3,23]	98,607[23]	...	3	322	...	73.6	77.7	70.2	7.1	Kenya
1,501[30]	38.5[30]	—	—	—	...	...	...	...	90.0	...	...	6.3[14]	Kiribati
...	...	519[14]	27,000[31]	390,000[31]	14.4[31]	...	...	...	95.0	...	...	...	Korea, North
949,515	74.7	742[21]	163,606	3,223,431	19.7	85	6,736	21.1	97.8	99.2	96.4	4.2	Korea, South
2,997	2.7	1	918	17,747	19.0	21	...	16.4	82.9	84.7	81.0	5.0	Kuwait[32]
52,200	10.2	44	8,400	159,200	19.0	42	3,282	...	98.7	99.3	98.1	3.2	Kyrgyzstan
5,053	14.4	9[3]	1,794	28,117	15.7	5	508	0.4	68.7	77.0	60.9	2.8	Laos
45,000	12.3	56	5,360	131,000	24.4	73	5,670	13.9	99.7	99.8	99.7	5.8	Latvia
46,271	4.0	20[14]	11,196	144,050	12.9	44	4,152	0.6	87.4	93.1	82.2	2.7	Lebanon
1,128	7.0	1	545	6,108	11.2	3	298	...	81.4	73.7	90.3	8.4	Lesotho
45,067	...	...	633[21]	44,107	...	2	1,483	...	55.9	72.3	39.3	5.7	Liberia
178,052	...	13	...	375,028	...	58	6,795	2.7	81.7	91.8	70.7	7.1	Libya
5[5]	5	2	309	2,858[33]	7.5	...	8,269	11.6	100.0	100.0	100.0	...	Liechtenstein
44,400	9.4	15	14,200	168,200	11.8	72	4,849	12.6	99.6	99.6	99.6	6.0	Lithuania
22,093	...	5	...	8,644[34]	...	12	1,937	10.8	100.0	100.0	100.0	4.0	Luxembourg
2,349	18.8	7	1,164	13,680	11.8	81	2,460	5.9	91.3	95.3	87.8	3.0	Macau
5[5]	5	30	1,519	45,624	30.0	28	2,263	8.7[6]	96.1	98.2	94.1	3.5	Macedonia
8,138[21]	7.5[21]	6[21]	1,857	32,593	17.6	2	190	1.5[6]	70.6	76.4	65.2	2.9	Madagascar
2,228[20]	4.7[20]	6[20]	453	4,565	10.1	1	39	0.7	64.1	74.9	54.0	6.1	Malawi
38,387	5.4	48[14]	34,955	632,309	18.1	29	2,524	6.8	88.7	92.0	85.4	8.7	Malaysia
...	...	—	—	—	—	...	...	...	96.3	96.2	96.4	6.4[21]	Maldives
39,754	...	7[21]	1,312[29]	28,332	...	3	268	...	19.0	26.7	11.9	3.0	Mali
3,447	6.6	1	754	6,362	8.4	30	1,631	6.2[6]	87.9	86.4	89.2	4.6	Malta
...	...	1	...	3,131	...	...	5,841	2.6	91.2	92.4	90.0	9.1	Marshall Islands
7,661[20]	...	1	99[13]	11,755[20]	...	...	3,077	5.5[6]	97.6	97.2	98.0	...	Martinique
3,129	12.2	4	353	9,198	26.1	4	351	1.3	51.2	59.5	43.4	3.7	Mauritania
7,326	16.9	3	461[21]	16,764	...	15	1,384	1.9	84.3	88.2	80.5	4.7	Mauritius
1,733	...	—	—	—	—	...	...	...	91.9	...	...	...	Mayotte
1,448,550	22.0	4,183	216,804	2,147,100	9.9	22	2,115	11.0[6]	90.3	92.0	88.7	5.4	Mexico
...	...	1	71	1,884	26.5	...	1,744	...	92.4	92.9	91.9	6.2	Micronesia
22,800	10.4	100	7,700	122,700	15.9	30	2,900	11.3	96.2	97.5	95.0	4.5	Moldova
532[14]	6.0[14]	1	53	650	12.3	...	2,018	...	...	...	...	...	Monaco
15,000	15.2	178	5,400	92,300	17.1	37	3,806	7.6[6]	98.0	98.5	97.5	8.6	Mongolia
143,692	28.9	68[21]	10,064	276,018	27.4	11	951	...	50.7	63.3	38.3	6.6	Morocco

Education (continued)

country	year	first level (primary)					general second level (secondary)					vocational second level[a]	
		schools	teachers[b]	students[c]	student/teacher ratio	net enroll-ment ratio[d]	schools	teachers[b]	students[c]	student/teacher ratio	net enroll-ment ratio[d]	schools	teachers[b]
Mozambique	2001–02	8,165	38,762	2,555,975	65.9	55	75[14]	13,916	381,619	27.4	12	25[14]	862
Myanmar (Burma)	2002–03	35,877[21]	149,001	4,889,325	32.8	84	2,091[21]	73,062	2,382,608	32.6	35	103[4]	2,462[4]
Namibia	2002–03	1,362[17]	14,330	404,783	28.2	78	114[13]	5,869	138,099	23.5	44	17[13]	56[2]
Nauru	2002	5	64	1,566	24.5	81	4	40	609	15.2	...	1	6[30]
Nepal	2001–02	24,943	96,659	3,853,618	39.9	71	11,453	57,165	1,690,198	30.0	...	...	1,025
Netherlands, The	2002–03	7,039	...	1,290,625	...	99	692	72,296	925,726	12.8	89	137	35,853
Netherlands Antilles	2002–03	83[29]	1,145	22,687	19.8	88	23[29]	639	9,180	14.4	68	10[29]	542
New Caledonia	2001	289	1,837	36,996	20.1	98	64	2,371	29,036	12.2	72	14[20]	...
New Zealand	2003	2,177	23,358	456,782	19.6	100	333	15,596	257,586	16.5	93	24	4,714
Nicaragua	2002–03	7,224[14]	26,226	923,391	35.2	86	451[13]	10,401	364,012	35.0	39	...	899
Niger	2001–02	5,975	18,441	760,987	41.3	38	193	2,259	81,731	36.2	6	49	1,375
Nigeria	2002	49,343	537,741	29,575,790	55.0	67	10,000	187,126	7,485,072	40.0	29	...	...
Northern Mariana Islands	2001–02	37[7]	728[7]	13,323[7]	18.3[7]	...	7	7	7	7	...	...	...
Norway	2002–03	3,248	42,177	432,618	10.3	100	696[5, 29]	44,230[5]	385,009[5]	8.7[5]	96	5	5
Oman	2002–03	294[29]	14,911	314,064	21.1	72	177[28]	16,941	279,302	16.5	69	15[29]	1,072[30]
Pakistan	2000–01	165,700[12]	373,900[12]	20,999,000[12]	56.2[12]	59	31,600	320,100	6,576,000	20.5	...	580	7,062
Palau	2001–02	23	235	3,033	12.9	96	6	132	1,168	8.8	...	...	...
Panama	2002–03	2,866[14]	17,296	419,904	24.3	100	417[14]	15,613	147,878	9.5	63	...	5,664
Papua New Guinea	1999	2,790[4]	16,297	594,444	36.5	74	135[3]	3,046	74,042	24.3	24	117[3]	878[2]
Paraguay	2002–03	7,456[17]	35,709	962,661	27.0	89	1,844[17]	43,835	474,538	10.8	51	...	...
Peru	2002	33,734	177,257	4,219,800	23.8	100	9,168	139,349	2,302,099	16.5	69	2,425[4]	12,293[4]
Philippines	2002–03	41,267	337,082	12,962,745	38.5	94	7,893	119,235	6,032,440	50.6	59	...	...
Poland	2002–03	14,765	273,562	2,983,070	10.9	98	6,776	230,611	2,714,203	11.8	92	7,129	84,551
Portugal	2002–03	11,910	69,109	767,862	11.1	100	664	74,185	660,419	8.9	85	218	13,117
Puerto Rico	1998–99	2,101[7]	39,328[4, 7]	350,714	...	...	7	7	258,841	...	...	...	...
Qatar[27]	2002–03	174[20]	5,684	66,473	11.7	95	123[4]	4,990	51,331	10.3	82	3[20]	121
Réunion	2002–03	357	...	76,954	...	...	119	6,343[21]	100,020	...	...	...	1,120[20]
Romania	2002–03	12,456	154,197	2,198,312	14.3	89	1,388	60,988	740,404	12.1	81	113	7,559
Russia	2001–02	66,833[7]	1,350,200[7]	19,363,173[7]	14.3[7]	90	7	7	7	7	...	3,872	...
Rwanda	2002–03	1,710[2]	27,319	1,636,563	59.9	87	...	7,056	189,153	26.8	8[2]	...	...
St. Kitts and Nevis[27]	2001–02	24	301	5,608	18.6	100	7	389	4,445	11.4	95	...	...
St. Lucia	2000–01	82	1,052	28,618	27.2	99	18	678	12,865	19.0	76	1	27
St. Vincent and the Grenadines	2002–03	60	1,061	18,629	17.6	90	21	384	7,909	20.6	58	4	53
Samoa	2002–03	155[4]	1,121	30,164	26.9	98	...	1,074	22,941	21.4	62	...	...
San Marino	2002–03	14	242	1,343	5.5	...	7[5]	227[5]	2,162[5]	8.7[5]	...	5	5
São Tomé and Príncipe	2001–02	71[21]	881	28,780	32.7	97	11[21]	415[14]	7,327	...	29	...	11
Saudi Arabia	2002–03	12,815	198,181	2,342,214	11.8	54	10,270	165,152	1,927,009	11.7	53	95	6,128
Senegal	2002–03	5,670	26,325	1,287,093	48.9	58	579	7,601	306,026	40.3	16[14]	12[28]	384[28]
Serbia and Montenegro	2000–01	4,087	48,868	787,423	16.1	96	518	26,740	355,424	13.3	81	...	...
Seychelles	2003	26	675	9,477	14.0	100	12	552	7,551	13.7	100	11	193
Sierra Leone	2000–01	2,704	14,932	554,308	37.1	...	495	5,264	134,113	25.5	...	44[35]	709[35]
Singapore	2003	201[11]	12,025	299,939	24.9	93	180[11]	10,830	206,426	19.1	44	10[11]	1,956
Slovakia	2002	2,396	39,745[29]	602,360	...	86	220	6,259[29]	93,283	...	88	605	17,887
Slovenia	2002–03	811	6,884	87,085	12.7	93	143	8,482	103,538	12.2	93	...	5,986
Solomon Islands	2002	520[13]	2,514[13]	55,093	...	...	23[13]	618[13]	46,082	...	...	1[13]	...
Somalia	1990	1,125	8,208	377,000	20.9	10	82	2,109	44,000	20.3	3	21	498
South Africa	2000	17,213	183,639	6,266,223	34.1	89	10,547[38]	177,084[38]	5,588,866[38]	31.6[38]	66	187[13]	10,807[13]
Spain	2001–02	8,547	170,891	2,475,027	14.5	100	4,319[5]	264,484[5]	3,116,895[5]	11.8[5]	96	5	5
Sri Lanka	2000–01	10,977[7]	199,948[7]	4,337,161[7]	21.7[7]	...	7	7	7	7	...	36[21]	574
Sudan, The	1999–2000	11,923	117,151	3,137,494	26.8	54	1,694	21,114	401,424	19.0	...	...	761[14]
Suriname	2002–03	308[29]	3,324	64,659	19.5	97	141[29]	1,334	23,034	17.3	64	1	1,380
Swaziland	2001–02	541	6,594	212,064	32.2	75	182	3,647	61,335	16.8	32	5	228[13]
Sweden	2003–04	5,041[7]	110,157[7]	1,211,017[7]	11.0[7]	100	7	7	7	7	100	...	...
Switzerland	2001–02	...	39,363	536,423	13.6	99	...	36,767	375,424	10.2	87	...	11,239
Syria	2000	11,482	121,880	2,774,922	22.8	98	2,911	63,889	955,290	15.0	42	587	15,103
Taiwan	2003–04	2,638	102,793	1,912,791	18.4	...	1,192[5]	99,938[5]	1,745,073[5]	17.7[5]	...	5	5
Tajikistan	2001–02	660	100,200[7]	1,520,000[7]	15.2[7]	94	2,661	7	7	7	83	56	7
Tanzania[41]	2002–03	11,339[21]	112,860	5,981,338	53.0	82	4,911[13]	20,277	322,400	15.9	5	40[13]	1,062[20]
Thailand	2003–04	31,080	295,484	6,112,887	20.7	85	2,318[35]	194,298	4,385,297	22.6	...	679[35]	21,500
Togo	2002–03	4,701[21]	27,504	975,063	35.5	91	314[35]	9,001	334,864	37.2	27	...	653[14]
Tonga	1999	117	745	16,206	21.8	100	39	961	13,987	14.6	72	5	67
Trinidad and Tobago	2002–03	478[14]	7,623	141,036	18.5	91	101[14]	5,555	105,330	19.0	65	...	145
Tunisia	2001–02	4,518	60,566	1,325,707	21.9	97	1,356	57,821	1,074,391	18.6	...	...	237[20]
Turkey	2000	36,072	345,015	10,480,700	30.4	86	2,747	73,418	1,487,400	20.3	51	3,544	71,665
Turkmenistan	1995	1,900[7]	72,900[7]	940,600[7]	12.9[7]	...	7	7	7	7	79	78	...
Tuvalu	2001–02	12[21]	56	1,427	25.5	...	2[13]	36	912	25.3	...	1	10[3]
Uganda	2001	12,280	127,038	6,900,916	54.3	...	2,400	30,425	539,786	17.7	17	...	2,094[21]
Ukraine	2003–04	22,100[7]	551,000[7]	6,044,000[7]	11.0[7]	84	7	7	7	7	85	953	11,438[43]
United Arab Emirates	2001–02	...	18,704	285,473	15.3	83	...	17,563	224,740	12.8	71	9[14]	269
United Kingdom	2002–03	29,905[18]	262,390	4,488,162	17.1	100	...	326,095	4,404,569	13.5	95	...	157,751
United States	2002–03	118,531[7, 18]	1,667,417	24,848,518	14.9	92	7	1,599,303	23,854,458	14.9	88	...	...
Uruguay	2002	2,402	16,699	362,902	21.7	90	405	26,779	269,205	10.1	73	124	8,160
Uzbekistan	2001	9,788[7]	454,400[7]	6,076,400[7]	13.4[7]	...	7	7	7	7	...	440[20]	7,900
Vanuatu	2001–02	374[4]	1,241[7]	36,482	29.4	94	27[2]	7	8,743	...	28	2	80
Venezuela	2002–03	18,827[18]	186,658[1]	3,449,984	...	91	3,022[18]	61,781[1]	1,809,368	...	59	...	...
Vietnam	2002–03	13,092[13]	358,606	8,841,006	24.7	94	6,298[13]	351,900	8,955,994	25.4	65	451[13]	9,327
Virgin Islands (U.S.)	2000	289[7]	1,511[7]	25,620[7]	17.0[7]	...	7	7	7	7	...	—	—
West Bank[26]	2002–03	2,006[7]	35,287[7]	984,108[7]	27.9[7]	96	7	7	7	7	...	...	...
Western Sahara[27]	1995	40	925	32,257	34.9	...	13	1,267	10,541	8.3	...	...	...
Yemen[27]	2002–03	11,013[13]	113,812[18]	2,950,403	...	72	1,224[5]	14,083[18]	1,364,129	...	34	125[4]	1,406
Zambia	2002–03	4,221[21]	36,151	1,731,579	47.9	68	...	...	345,442	...	23	...	150
Zimbabwe	2003–04	4,706[21]	61,251	2,361,588	38.6	80	1,530[21]	33,964	758,229	22.3	34	25[2]	1,479[2]

[1]1997–98. [2]1992. [3]1990. [4]1995. [5]General second level includes vocational. [6]Age 15 and over. [7]Primary includes secondary. [8]Primary includes lower secondary. [9]Upper secondary only. [10]College of the Bahamas only. [11]2000. [12]Includes preprimary education. [13]1994. [14]1996–97. [15]Age 19 and over. [16]2002. [17]1999. [18]2001–02. [19]1991. [20]1996. [21]1998. [22]Republic of Cyprus only. [23]Universities only. [24]Data exclude 1,090,022 primary and 278,134 secondary students in the Al-Azhar education system. [25]Includes distance learning and 5,232 foreign students.

students[c]	student/ teacher ratio	third level (higher) institutions	teachers[b]	students[c]	student/ teacher ratio	gross enroll-ment ratio[d]	students per 100,000 popula-tion[d]	percent of population age 25 and over with post-secondary education[d]	literacy (2000–04) over age 15 total (%)	male (%)	female (%)	public expenditure on education (percent of GNP)[d]	country
20,880	24.2	3	954[14]	9,303[28]	...	1	54	0.2[6]	46.5	62.3	31.4	2.5	Mozambique
25,374[4]	10.3[4]	51[21]	17,089[21]	385,300[21]	22.5[21]	12	950	2.0	89.7	93.7	86.2	1.3	Myanmar (Burma)
1,503[13]	...	7[13]	931	13,536	14.5	8	686	4.0	85.0	86.8	83.5	7.1	Namibia
383[30]	6.3[30]	...	...	...	...	...	...	...	99.0	...	...	...	Nauru
20,546	20.0	2	4,925[19]	119,670	...	5	479	0.6	48.6	62.7	34.9	3.4	Nepal
489,444	13.7	12[23]	44,092	526,780	11.9	58	3,262	6.9[6]	100.0	100.0	100.0	5.3	Netherlands, The
6,088	...	1	340	2,286	6.7	14	1,295	11.4	96.7	96.7	96.7	...	Netherlands Antilles
5,916[20]	...	4[20]	55[11]	2,069[11]	37.6[11]	5	981	10.5[6]	96.2	96.8	95.5	11.6	New Caledonia
106,570	22.6	8[11]	13,360	184,000	13.8	74	4,600	39.1	100.0	100.0	100.0	7.1	New Zealand
18,939	21.1	108[30]	6,547	100,363	15.3	18	1,949	4.0	76.7	76.8	76.6	3.2	Nicaragua
18,400	13.4	2[21]	355[21]	5,569[21]	15.7[21]	2	56	0.2	14.4	19.6	9.4	2.4	Niger
...	...	158	35,115	947,538	27.0	8	770	...	66.8	74.4	59.4	0.7	Nigeria
...	...	129	504[29]	2,383[29]	4.7[29]	...	3,315	31.1	96.3	96.9	95.6	...	Northern Mariana Islands
5	5	71	17,903	212,335	11.9	81	4,679	18.7	100.0	100.0	100.0	7.6	Norway
16,472[30]	15.4[30]	1[23]	631	19,864	31.5	8	867	3.6[6]	74.4	82.0	65.4	4.8	Oman
75,000	10.6	1,187	41,673	1,087,999	25.6	3	777	2.5	48.6	61.7	35.2	1.8	Pakistan
...	...	1	25	598	23.9	...	3,054	10.0	97.6	98.3	96.6	10.7	Palau
103,350	18.2	14[14]	8,444	117,601	13.9	43	3,932	15.9	91.9	92.5	91.2	4.6	Panama
9,941[4]	12.9[2]	2[3]	815	13,761	16.9	2	264	...	57.3	63.4	50.9	2.4	Papua New Guinea
44,516	...	11[17]	1,135[17]	146,982	...	27	2,661	5.3[6]	91.6	93.1	90.2	4.4	Paraguay
270,576[4]	22.0[4]	2,161[11]	57,874[11]	1,495,957[11]	25.8[11]	32	5,764	20.4[6]	87.7	93.5	82.1	3.1	Peru
...	...	1,603[18]	109,979	2,427,211	22.1	30	3,046	8.0	92.6	92.5	92.7	2.9	Philippines
1,180,964	14.0	427	93,365	1,983,000	21.2	60	5,187	9.9	99.8	99.8	99.8	5.7	Poland
105,753	8.1	316	36,187	400,000	11.1	56	3,849	7.7	92.2	94.8	90.0	5.9	Portugal
...	...	44	...	171,625	...	...	4,539	28.7	94.1	93.9	94.4	7.8	Puerto Rico
557	4.6	1	650	7,826	12.0	22	1,146	13.3	89.2	...	...	3.6	Qatar[27]
13,547[20]	12.1[20]	1	286[21]	8,663[21]	30.3[21]	...	1,242	5.1[6]	88.4	86.3	90.2	...	Réunion
332,070	43.9	125	29,619	596,297	20.0	35	2,731	7.1	97.3	98.4	96.3	3.6	Romania
1,648,700	...	1,008	547,400	5,426,300	9.9	69	3,716	16.0[6]	99.4	99.8	99.2	3.8	Russia
...	...	...	1,348	20,393	15.1	3	250	...	64.0	70.5	58.8	2.8	Rwanda
...	...	1	51[35]	394[35]	7.7[35]	...	949	8.9	90.9	90.0	90.0	3.7	St. Kitts and Nevis[27]
808[35]	23.7[35]	1	127	1,403	11.0	...	899	2.7[6]	90.1	89.5	90.6	8.2	St. Lucia
1,715	32.3	...	...	...	...	...	...	2.6[36]	96.0	...	...	10.5	St. Vincent and the Grenadines
...	...	12[21]	28[21]	328[21]	11.7[21]	...	191	10.3[6]	98.7	98.9	98.4	4.8	Samoa
5	5	1	27	950	35.6	...	3,338	7.0[37]	98.7	98.9	98.4	...	San Marino
40	3.6	1	27	183	6.8	1	128	1.9	73.0	85.0	62.0	3.8[14]	São Tomé and Príncipe
68,434	11.2	92	23,350	525,344	22.5	25	2,455	...	79.4	87.1	69.3	8.2	Saudi Arabia
3,897	...	2[23,29]	963[23,29]	22,157[23,29]	23.0[23,29]	4	226	...	39.3	51.1	29.2	3.7	Senegal
...	...	51	1,612	50,901	31.6	36	507	9.3[6]	96.4	98.9	94.1	3.3	Serbia and Montenegro
1,652	8.6	...	...	...	...	...	...	4.6	91.9	91.4	92.3	5.7	Seychelles
21,454	...	1	1,198	8,795	7.3	2	194	1.5	29.6	39.8	20.5	3.8	Sierra Leone
23,708	12.1	8[11]	7,318[11]	111,538[11]	15.2[11]	39	2,776	17.8[6]	92.5	96.6	88.6	3.6	Singapore
217,849	12.2	20	13,166	152,182	11.6	34	2,829	9.5	99.7	99.7	99.6	4.4	Slovakia
86,638	14.5	49	3,109	87,205	28.0	68	4,369	10.4	99.7	99.7	99.6	6.1	Slovenia
9,560	...	...	...	...	...	...	...	2.6	54.1	62.4	44.9	3.4	Solomon Islands
10,400	9.7	1	549[19]	4,640[19]	8.5[19]	1	70	...	24.0	36.0	14.0	0.4	Somalia
140,531[13]	13.0[13]	21[23]	27,099[13]	617,897[13]	22.8[13]	15	1,664	8.5[6]	82.4	84.1	80.9	5.4	South Africa
5	5	...	98,587	1,508,116	15.3	62	3,703	13.5[39]	97.7	98.6	96.8	4.5	Spain
11,270	19.6	12	2,999	48,899	16.3	5	246	1.1	90.4	92.2	88.6	3.4	Sri Lanka
26,421[14]	34.7[14]	19	1,417[14]	52,260[14]	36.9[14]	7	272	0.8	59.0	69.2	49.9	1.4	Sudan, The
17,966	13.0	4	550	5,186[29]	...	12	1,126	...	92.2	93.6	90.7	3.5	Suriname
2,958[13]	13.0[13]	1	326	5,193	15.9	5	508	3.3	80.3	81.3	79.4	6.8	Swaziland
...	...	71	37,692	385,323	10.2	83	4,301	26.0[40]	100.0	100.0	100.0	7.7	Sweden
174,893	15.6	...	28,019	170,086	6.1	49	2,343	11.5	100.0	100.0	100.0	5.5	Switzerland
134,473	8.9	4	5,664	155,137	27.4	16	980	...	82.9	91.0	74.2	3.1	Syria
5	5	158	47,472	1,202,091	25.3	...	5,328	13.1[6]	94.6	97.6	91.4	5.2	Taiwan
29,600	...	35	6,100	118,400	19.4	16	1,875	11.7	99.5	99.7	99.3	2.9	Tajikistan
12,571[20]	11.8[20]	...	2,249	31,049	13.8	1	90	2.0	69.4	77.5	62.2	3.4[20]	Tanzania[41]
624,547	28.4	102[14]	65,548	2,251,453	34.3	38	3,558	5.1	92.6	94.9	90.5	4.7	Thailand
9,076[14]	13.8[14]	1	443[14]	11,639[14]	26.3[14]	4	317	1.3	53.0	68.5	38.3	2.7	Togo
755	11.3	1[2]	19[2]	225[2]	11.8[2]	4	234	2.8	98.9	98.8	99.0	5.0	Tonga
2,550	17.6	3[14]	969	12,316	12.7	9	965	3.4	98.5	99.0	97.9	4.6	Trinidad and Tobago
3,839[20]	16.2[20]	128	11,412	226,102	19.8	27	2,337	7.9[42]	74.3	83.4	65.3	6.7	Tunisia
875,200	12.2	1,273	67,880	1,607,400	23.7	28	2,384	10.8	88.3	95.7	81.1	3.7	Turkey
26,000	...	15	...	29,435[20]	...	22	689	...	98.8	99.3	98.3	3.9	Turkmenistan
58[19]	...	—	—	—	—	...	...	2.9[6]	95.0	...	...	...	Tuvalu
38,500[21]	18.4[21]	...	4,908	71,544	14.6	3	298	1.8	68.9	78.8	59.2	2.6	Uganda
326,213[43]	28.5[43]	1,007	177,644	2,269,800	12.8	62	4,761	...	99.6	99.7	99.2	5.5	Ukraine
1,667	6.2	4[14]	2,948	56,401	19.1	35	1,617	8.6[42]	77.3	75.6	80.7	2.4	United Arab Emirates
5,202,508	33.0	148	101,040	2,287,830	22.6	64	3,857	...	100.0	100.0	100.0	5.2	United Kingdom
...	...	4,197[30]	1,167,305	16,611,711	14.2	83	5,764	45.2	95.5	95.7	95.3	5.6	United States
65,567	8.0	6	10,524	98,798	9.4	37	3,063	17.2	97.7	97.3	98.1	2.6	Uruguay
214,500	27.2	61	18,400	183,600	10.0	16	732	...	99.3	99.6	98.9	7.9	Uzbekistan
892	11.2	1	27	675	25.0	4	351	5.2[6]	74.0	...	...	10.7	Vanuatu
56,746	...	144[18]	36,232[1]	983,217	...	40	3,879	10.0	93.0	93.3	92.7	5.2	Venezuela
309,807	33.2	104[13]	38,608	797,066	20.6	10	997	2.6	90.3	93.9	86.9	3.0[21]	Vietnam
—	—	1	266[14]	3,107	...	...	2,860	31.3	...	...	...	7.5[4]	Virgin Islands (U.S.)
...	...	36	2,286	83,408	36.5	...	2,443	...	...	...	...	...	West Bank[26]
1,222	...	—	...	...	...	...	...	...	...	...	...	...	Western Sahara[27]
15,074[18]	...	7[18]	3,429	184,072	53.7	11	953	2.7[42]	49.0	69.5	28.5	10.3	Yemen[27]
6,000	40.0	2[20]	640[20]	22,701[21]	...	2	242	1.5	67.9	76.1	59.7	2.1	Zambia
27,431[2]	18.5[2]	28[2]	3,581[4]	55,689	...	4	475	3.4	90.0	93.8	86.3	4.9	Zimbabwe

[26]Data include Gaza Strip and West Bank.   [27]Public schools only.   [28]1999–2000.   [29]2000–01.   [30]2001.   [31]1988.   [32]Government schools only; private education: 112 schools, 7,324 teachers, 128,204 students.   [33]Includes 511 students abroad.   [34]Includes 5,688 students abroad.   [35]1993.   [36]Employed only.   [37]Age 14 and over.   [38]Includes combined and intermediate schools.   [39]Age 16 and over.   [40]Ages 16–74.   [41]Mainland Tanzania only.   [42]Age 10 and over.   [43]2002–03.

BIBLIOGRAPHY AND SOURCES

The following list indicates the principal documentary sources used in the compilation of *Britannica World Data*. It is by no means a complete list, either for international or for national sources, but is indicative more of the range of materials to which reference has been made in preparing this compilation.

While *Britannica World Data* has long been based primarily on print sources, many rare in North American library collections, the burgeoning resources of the Internet can be accessed from any appropriately equipped personal computer (PC). At this writing, more than 100 national statistical offices had Internet sites and there were also sites for central banks, national information offices, individual ministries, and the like.

Because of the relative ease of access to these sites for PC users, uniform resource locators (URLs) for mainly official sites have been added to both country statements (at the end, in boldface) and individual Comparative National Statistics tables (at the end of the headnote) when a source providing comparable international data existed. Many sites exist that are narrower in coverage or less official and that may also serve the reader (on-line newspapers; full texts of national constitutions; business and bank sites) but space permitted the listing of only the top national and intergovernmental sites. Sites that are wholly or predominantly in a language other than English are so identified.

International Statistical Sources

Christian Research. *World Churches Handbook* (1997).
Comité Monétaire de la Zone Franc. *La Zone Franc: Rapport* (annual).
Eastern Caribbean Central Bank. *Report and Statement of Accounts* (annual).
Europa Publications Ltd. *Africa South of the Sahara* (annual); *The Europa Year Book* (2 vol.); *The Far East and Australasia* (annual); *The Middle East and North Africa* (annual).
Food and Agriculture Organization. *Food Balance Sheets; Production Yearbook; Trade Yearbook; Yearbook of Fishery Statistics* (2 vol.); *Yearbook of Forest Products.*
Global Airline Management. *Air Transport World* (monthly).
Her Majesty's Stationery Office. *The Commonwealth Yearbook.*
Instituts d'Émission d'Outre-Mer et des Départements d'Outre-Mer (France). *Bulletin trimestriel* (quarterly); *Rapport annuel.*
Inter-American Development Bank. *Economic and Social Progress in Latin America* (annual).
Inter-Parliamentary Union. *Chronicle of Parliamentary Elections and Developments* (annual); *World Directory of Parliaments* (annual).
International Air Transport Association. *World Air Transport Statistics* (annual).
International Civil Aviation Organization. *Civil Aviation Statistics of the World* (annual); *Digest of Statistics.*
International Institute for Strategic Studies. *The Military Balance* (annual).
International Monetary Fund. *Annual Report on Exchange Arrangements and Exchange Restrictions; Direction of Trade Statistics Yearbook; Government Finance Statistics Yearbook; International Financial Statistics* (monthly, with yearbook).
International Road Federation. *World Road Statistics* (annual).
International Telecommunication Union. *Yearbook of Statistics: Telecommunication Services* (annual).
Jane's Publishing Co., Ltd. *Jane's World Railways* (annual).
Keesing's Worldwide LLC. *Keesing's Record of World Events* (monthly except August).

Macmillan Press Ltd. *The Statesman's Year-Book.*
Middle East Economic Digest Ltd. *Middle East Economic Digest* (weekly).
Oxford University Press. *World Christian Encyclopedia* (David B. Barrett, ed. [2001, 2 vol.]).
PennWell Publishing Co. *International Petroleum Encyclopedia* (annual).
René Moreux et Cie. *Marchés tropicaux & Méditerranéens* (weekly).
United Nations (UN). *Demographic Yearbook; Industrial Commodities Statistics Yearbook; Energy Statistics Yearbook; International Trade Statistics Yearbook* (2 vol.); *Monthly Bulletin of Statistics; National Accounts Statistics* (2 parts; annual); *Population and Vital Statistics Report* (quarterly); *Statistical Yearbook; World Population Prospects 20** (biennial).
UN: Economic Commission for Latin America. *Economic Survey of Latin America and the Caribbean* (2 vol.; annual); *Statistical Yearbook for Latin America and the Caribbean.*
UN: Economic and Social Commission for Asia and the Pacific. *Asia-Pacific in Figures* (annual); *Statistical Yearbook for Asia and the Pacific.*
UN: Economic and Social Commission for Western Asia. *Demographic and Related Socio-Economic Data Sheets* (irreg.); *National Accounts Studies of the ESCWA Region* (irreg.); *The Population Situation in the ESCWA Region* (irreg.); *Statistical Abstract of the Region of the Economic and Social Commission for Western Asia* (annual).
United Nations Industrial Development Organization. *International Yearbook of Industrial Statistics.*
United States: Central Intelligence Agency, *The World Factbook* (annual); Dept. of Commerce, *World Population Profile* (biennial); Dept. of Health and Human Services, *Social Security Programs Throughout the World* (semiannual, 4 vol.); Dept. of Interior, *Minerals Yearbook* (3 vol. in 6 parts); Dept. of State, *World Military Expenditure and Arms Transfers* (annual).
World Association of Newspapers. *World Press Trends* (annual).
The World Bank Group. *World Bank Atlas* (annual); *Global Development Finance* (2 vol.; annual); *World Development Report* (annual).
World Tourism Organization. *Compendium of Tourism Statistics* (annual).

Internet Resources

Asian Development Bank: *Key indicators* (Asia and Pacific) http://www.adb.org/Documents/Books/Key_Indicators/2005/default.asp
Caribbean Development Bank (Caribbean) http://www.caribank.org
Thomas Brinkhoff: City Population (World) http://www.citypopulation.de
GeoHive (World) http://geohive.com
International Labour Organization: LABORSTA database (World) http://laborsta.ilo.org
Pan American Health Organization http://www.paho.org
Secretariat of the Pacific Community: Pacific Regional Information System (PRISM [Pacific]) http://www.spc.org.nc/prism/country/country.html
Stockholm International Peace Research Institute (SIPRI): SIPRI Military Database (World) http://www.sipri.org
United Nations Children Fund (UNICEF [World]) http://www.unicef.org
United Nations Development Programme (UNDP): *Human Development Report* (World) http://hdr.undp.org
United Nations Educational, Scientific, and Cultural Organization (UNESCO): Institute for Statistics database (World) http://www.uis.unesco.org
U.S. Census Bureau: International Data Base (World) http://www.census.gov/ipc/www/idbprint.html
The World Bank Group: World Bank Database (World) http://devdata.worldbank.org
The World Gazetteer (World) http://world-gazetteer.com/home.htm
World Health Organization (WHO) http://www.who.int/en
WHO Regional Office for Africa http://www.afro.who.int
WHO Regional Office for Europe http://www.euro.who.int
WHO Regional Office for the Eastern Mediterranean http://www.emro.who.int/index.asp

WHO Regional Office for South-East Asia http://www.whosea.org
WHO Regional Office for the Western Pacific http://www.wpro.who.int
WHO Global Health Atlas (World) http://globalatlas.who.int

National Statistical Sources

Afghanistan. *Afghanistan Statistical Yearbook* (annual).
Albania. *Population and Housing Census 2001; Statistical Yearbook of Albania.*
Algeria. *Annuaire statistique; Recensement général de la population et de l'habitat, 1998; Algeria: Recent Economic Developments* (IMF Country Staff Report [2001]).
American Samoa. *American Samoa Statistical Digest* (annual); *Report on the State of the Island* (U.S. Department of the Interior [annual]); *2000 Census of Population and Housing* (U.S.).
Andorra. *Anuari Estadístic* (annual); *Andorra Economic Report.*
Angola. *Angola—Selected Issues and Statistical Appendix* (IMF Staff Country Report [2005]); *Perfil estatístico de Angola* (irreg.).
Antigua. *Antigua and Barbuda—Statistical Appendix* (IMF Staff Country Report [2004]); *Statistical Yearbook; 2001 Population and Housing Census.*
Argentina. *Anuario estadístico de la República Argentina; Censo nacional de población, hogares y vivienda 2001.*
Armenia. *Statisticheskii Yezhegodnik Armenii* (Statistical Yearbook of Armenia); *Socio-Economic Situation of the Republic of Armenia* (annual).
Aruba. *Statistical Yearbook; Central Bank of Aruba Bulletin* (quarterly); *Fourth Population and Housing Census October 14, 2000.*
Australia. *Monthly Summary of Statistics, Australia; Social Indicators* (annual); *Year Book Australia; 2001 Census of Population and Housing.*
Austria. *Grosszählung 2001* (General Census 2001). *Sozialstatistische Daten* (irreg.); *Statistisches Jahrbuch für die Republik Österreich* (annual).
Azerbaijan. *Azerbaijan in Figures* (annual); *Statistical Yearbook of Azerbaijan.*
Bahamas, The. *Census of Population and Housing 2000; Statistical Abstract* (annual); *Quarterly Statistical Digest* (quarterly).
Bahrain. *Statistical Abstract* (annual); *The Population, Housing, Buildings and Establishments Census 2001; Bahrain in Figures* (annual).
Bangladesh. *Bangladesh Population Census, 2001; Statistical Yearbook of Bangladesh; Bangladesh Bank Annual Report* (annual).
Barbados. *Barbados Economic Report* (annual); *Monthly Digest of Statistics; Annual Statistical Digest* (annual).
Belarus. *Narodnoye Khozyaystvo Respubliki Belarus: Statisticheskiy Yezhegodnik* (National Economy of the Republic of Belarus: Statistical Yearbook).
Belgium. *Annuaire statistique de la Belgique; Recensement de la population et des logements au 1er oct. 2001; Statistical Bulletin* (quarterly).
Belize. *Belize Economic Survey* (annual); *Central Bank of Belize Annual Report and Accounts; 2000 Population Census: Major Findings.*
Benin. *Annuaire statistique; Recensement général de la population et de l'habitation* (2002).
Bermuda. *Bermuda Digest of Statistics* (annual); *Bermuda Facts and Figures* (annual); *The 2000 Census of Population and Housing.*
Bhutan. *Statistical Yearbook of Bhutan.*
Bolivia. *Anuario estadístico; Censo de población y vivienda 2001; Compendio estadístico* (annual); *Estadísticas socio-económicas* (annual).
Bosnia and Herzegovina. *Central Bank of Bosnia and Herzegovina Bulletin* (quarterly).
Botswana. *Statistical Bulletin* (quarterly); *2001 Population and Housing Census; Botswana—Selected Issues and Statistical Appendix* (IMF Staff Country Report [2004]).
Brazil. *Anuário Estatístico do Brasil; Censo Demográfico 2000.*
Brunei. *Brunei Statistical Yearbook; Brunei Darussalam Population and Housing Census 2001; Brunei Economic Bulletin* (quarterly).
Bulgaria. *Prebroyavaneto na naselenieto kŭm 01.03.2001 godina* (Census of Population of March 1, 2001); *Statisticheskii godishnik na Republika Bŭlgariya* (Statistical Yearbook of the Republic of Bulgaria).

Burkina Faso. *Burkina Faso: Statistical Annex* (IMF Staff Country Report [2004]); *Recensement général de la population du 10 au 20 decembre 1996.*

Burundi. *Annuaire statistique; Recensement général de la population, 1990; Burundi: Selected Issues and Statistical Appendix* (IMF Staff Country Report [2004]).

Cambodia. *1998 Population Census of Cambodia; Cambodia: Statistical Appendix* (IMF Staff Country Report [2004]).

Cameroon. *Cameroon—Statistical Appendix* (IMF Staff Country Report [2005]); *Recensement général de la population et de l'habitat 1987.*

Canada. *Canada Year Book* (biennial); *Census Canada 2001: Population.*

Cape Verde. *Cape Verde—Statistical Appendix* (IMF Staff Country Report [2003]); *O Recenseamento Geral da População e Habitação 2000.*

Central African Republic. *Annuaire statistique; Central African Republic: Selected Issues and Statistical Appendix* (IMF Staff Country Report [2004]); *Recensement général de la population 1988.*

Chad. *Annuaire statistique; Recensement general de la population et de l'habitat 1993; Chad: Statistical Appendix* (IMF Staff Country Report [2004]).

Chile. *Chile XVII censo nacional de población y VI de vivienda, 24 de abril 2002; Compendio estadístico* (annual).

China, People's Republic of. *China Statistical Yearbook; 2000 Population Census of the People's Republic of China.*

Colombia. *Colombia estadística* (annual); *Censo 93 informacion de vivienda; Colombia: Statistical Appendix* (IMF Staff Country Report [2001]).

Comoros. *Banque Centrale des Comoroes Rapport Annuel* (Central Bank of Comoros Annual Report); *Recensement général de la population et de l'habitat 15 septembre 2003.*

Congo, Dem. Rep. of the (Zaire). *Dem. Rep. of the Congo: Selected Issues and Statistical Appendix* (IMF Staff Country Report [2003]).

Congo, Rep. of the. *Annuaire statistique; Recensement général de la population et de l'habitat de 1984; Republic of Congo: Selected Issues and Statistical Appendix* (IMF Staff Country Report [2004]).

Costa Rica. *Anuario estadístico; Costa Rica at a Glance* (annual); *IX censo nacional de población y V de viviendas, 2000.*

Côte d'Ivoire. *Côte d'Ivoire—Statistical Appendix* (IMF Staff Country Report [2004]); *Recensement général de la population et de l'habitat 1998.*

Croatia. *Census of Population, Households and Dwellings 31st March 2001; Statistical Yearbook.*

Cuba. *Anuario estadístico; Censo de población y viviendas, 1981.*

Cyprus. *Census of Industrial Production* (annual); *Census of Population 2001; Economic Report* (annual); *Statistical Abstract* (annual).

Czech Republic. *Statistická ročenka České Republiky* (Statistical Yearbook of the Czech Republic).

Denmark. *Folke-og boligtaellingen, 2001* (Population and Housing Census); *Statistisk årbog* (Statistical Yearbook).

Djibouti. *Annuaire statistique de Djibouti; Djibouti: Banque Centrale de Djibouti Rapport Annuel* (annual).

Dominica. *Dominica—Statistical Appendix* (IMF Staff Country Report [2002]); *Population and Housing Census 1991; Statistical Digest* (irreg.).

Dominican Republic. *VIII censo nacional de población y vivienda, 2002.*

East Timor. *Economic Bulletin* (quarterly); *Democratic Republic of Timor-Leste: Statistical Appendix* (IMF Staff Country Report [2004]).

Ecuador. *Serie estadística* (quinquennial); *VI censo de población y V de vivienda 2001.*

Egypt. *Census Population, Housing, and Establishment, 1996; Statistical Yearbook.*

El Salvador. *Annual Economic Indicators; Censos nacionales: V censo de población y IV de vivienda* (1992); *El Salvador en cifras* (annual).

Equatorial Guinea. *Censos nacionales, I de población y I de vivienda—4 al 17 de julio de 1994; Equatorial Guinea: Statistical Appendix* (IMF Staff Country Report [2005]).

Eritrea. *Eritrea—Selected Issues and Statistical Appendix* (IMF Staff Country Report [2003]).

Estonia. *2000 Population and Housing Census; Eesti Statistika Aastaraamat* (Estonia Statistical Yearbook).

Ethiopia. *1994 Population and Housing Census of Ethiopia; Ethiopia Statistical Abstract* (annual); *Ethiopia—Statistical Appendix* (IMF Staff Country Report [2002]).

Faroe Islands. *Rigsombudsmanden på Færøerne: Beretning* (annual); *Statistical Bulletin* (annual); *Faroe Islands in Figures* (annual).

Fiji. *Key Statistics* (quarterly); *Current Economic Statistics* (quarterly); *1996 Census of the Population and Housing.*

Finland. *Economic Survey* (annual); *Population Census 1990; Statistical Yearbook of Finland; Finland in Figures* (annual).

France. *Annuaire statistique de la France; Données sociales* (triennial); *Recensement général de la population de 1999; Tableaux de l'Economie Française* (annual).

French Guiana. *Recensement général de la population de 1999; Tableaux economiques regionaux: Guyane* (biennial).

French Polynesia. *Résultats du recensement général de la population de la Polynésie Française, du 6 Septembre 1996; Tableaux de l'economie polynesienne* (irreg.); *Te avei'a: Bulletin d'information statistique* (monthly).

Gabon. *Recensement général de la population et de l'habitat 1993; Situation économique, financière et sociale de la République Gabonaise* (annual).

Gambia, The. *The Gambia—Selected Issues and Statistical Appendix* (IMF Staff Country Report [2004]).

Gaza Strip. *Judaea, Samaria, and Gaza Area Statistics Quarterly; Palestinian Statistical Abstract.*

Georgia. *Narodnoye Khozyaystvo Gruzinskoy SSR* (National Economy of the Georgian S.S.R. [annual]).

Germany. *Statistisches Jahrbuch für die Bundesrepublik Deutschland.*

Ghana. *Ghana—Selected Issues* (IMF Staff Country Report [2005]); *Population Census of Ghana, 2000; Quarterly Digest of Statistics.*

Greece. *Recensement de la population et des habitations, 2001; Statistical Yearbook of Greece.*

Greenland. *Grønland* (annual); *Grønlands befolkning* (Greenland Population [annual]).

Grenada. *Abstract of Statistics* (annual); *Grenada—Statistical Appendix* (IMF Staff Country Report [2003]). *2001 Population and Housing Census.*

Guadeloupe. *Recensement général de la population de 1999: Guadeloupe; Tableaux economiques regionaux: Guadeloupe* (biennial).

Guam. *Guam Annual Economic Review; 2000 Census of Population and Housing (U.S.).*

Guatemala. *Anuario estadística; Instituto nacional de estadística censos nationales XI de población y VI de habitación 2002.*

Guernsey. *Guernsey Census 2001; Statistical Digest* (annual); *Economic and Statistics Review* (annual).

Guinea. *Guinea—Statistical Appendix* (IMF Staff Country Report [2004]).

Guinea-Bissau. *Guinea-Bissau—Statistical Appendix* (IMF Staff Country Report [2002]); *Recenseamento Geral da População e da Habitação, 1991.*

Guyana. *Bank of Guyana: Annual Report and Statement of Accounts; Guyana: Statistical Annex* (IMF Staff Country Report [2001]).

Haiti. *Banque de la République d'Haiti: Rapport Annuel; Résultats préliminaires du 4ème recensement général de population et d'habitat* (August 2003).

Honduras. *Anuario estadístico; Censo nacional de población y vivienda, 2001; Honduras en cifras.*

Hong Kong. *Annual Digest of Statistics; Hong Kong* (annual); *Hong Kong 2001 Population Census; Hong Kong Social and Economic Trends* (biennial).

Hungary. *Statisztikai évkönyv* (Statistical Yearbook); *2001, Evi népszámlálás* (Census of Population 2001).

Iceland. *Landshagir* (Statistical Yearbook of Iceland); *Iceland in Figures* (annual).

India. *Census of India, 2001; Economic Survey* (annual); *Statistical Abstract* (annual).

Indonesia. *Indonesia: An Official Handbook* (irreg.); *Hasil Sensus penduduk Indonesia, 2000* (Census of Population); *Statistical Yearbook of Indonesia.*

Iran. *National Census of Population and Housing, October 1996; Iran Statistical Yearbook.*

Iraq. *Census of Population Oct. 1997; Central Bank of Iraq Annual Bulletin 2003; Statistical Bulletin 2003* (special issue).

Ireland. *Census of Population of Ireland, 2002; National Income and Expenditure* (annual); *Statistical Yearbook of Ireland* (annual).

Isle of Man. *Census Report 2001; Isle of Man Digest of Economic and Social Statistics* (annual).

Israel. *1995 Census of Population and Housing; Statistical Abstract* (annual).

Italy. *Statistica agrarie; Statistiche demografiche* (4 parts); *Statistiche dell'istruzione; Annuario statistico Italiano; 14º Censimento generale della popolazione e delle Abitazioni 21 Ottobre 2001.*

Jamaica. *Economic and Social Survey* (annual); *Statistical Abstract* (annual); *Statistical Yearbook of Jamaica; Population Census 2001.*

Japan. *Japan Statistical Yearbook; Statistical Indicators on Social Life* (annual); *1995 Population Census of Japan.*

Jersey. *Report of the Census for 2001; Statistical Review* (annual); *Jersey in Figures* (annual).

Jordan. *Population and Housing Census 1994; Central Bank of Jordan Report* (annual); *Statistical Yearbook; Jordan in Figures* (annual).

Kazakhstan. *Statistichesky Yezhegodnik* (Statistical Yearbook); *1999 Population Census.*

Kenya. *Economic Survey* (annual); *Population Census 1999; Statistical Abstract* (annual); *Kenya—Selected Issues and Statistical Appendix* (IMF Staff Country Report [2003]).

Kiribati. *Annual Abstract of Statistics; Kiribati Population Census 2000.*

Korea, North. *North Korea: A Country Study* (1994); *The Population of North Korea* (1990).

Korea, South. *Korea Statistical Yearbook; Social Indicators in Korea* (annual); *2000 Population and Housing Census.*

Kuwait. *Annual Statistical Abstract; General Census of Population and Housing and Buildings 1995; Kuwait: Statistical Appendix* (IMF Staff Country Report [2004]).

Kyrgyzstan. *Statistichesky Yezhegodnik Kyrgyzstana* (Statistical Yearbook of Kyrgyzstan).

Laos. *Lao People's Democratic Republic: Selected Issues and Statistical Appendix* (IMF Staff Country Report [2002]).

Latvia. *Statistical Yearbook of Latvia; Latvijas Republikas 2000 Iedzivotāju Skaits* (2000 Census of Population of the Republic of Latvia).

Lebanon. *Banque du Liban Annual Report.*

Lesotho. *Lesotho: Selected Issues and Statistical Appendix* (IMF Staff Country Report [2004]); *Statistical Yearbook; 2002 Population Census.*

Liberia. *Economic Survey* (annual); *Liberia: Selected Issues and Statistical Appendix* (IMF Staff Country Report [2003]).

Libya. *Libya Population Census, 1995.*

Liechtenstein. *Statistisches Jahrbuch; Volkszählung, 1990* (Census of Population); *Liechtenstein in Figures* (annual).

Lithuania. *Gyventojų ir Bustų Surašymu Skypūs 2001* (Population and Housing Census 2001); *Lietuvos Statistikos Metraštis* (Lithuanian Statistical Yearbook).

Luxembourg. *Annuaire statistique; Bulletin du STATEC* (monthly); *Recensement général de la population du 15 février 2001.*

Macau. *Anuário Estatístico; XIV Recenseamento Geral da População, 2001.*

Macedonia. *Former Yugoslav Republic of Macedonia: Selected Issues and Statistical Appendix* (IMF Staff Country Report [2003]); *Statistical Yearbook of the Republic of Macedonia.*

Madagascar. *Madagascar: Selected Issues and Statistical Appendix* (IMF Staff Country Report [2003]); *Recensement général de la population et de l'habitat, aout 1993; Situation économique.*

Malawi. *1998 Population and Housing Census; Malawi Statistical Yearbook; Malawi Yearbook; Malawi: Selected Issues and Statistical Appendix* (IMF Staff Country Report [2002]).

Malaysia. *Population and Housing Census of Malaysia 2000; Yearbook of Statistics; Malaysia: Statistical Appendix* (IMF Staff Country Report [2004]).

Maldives. *Population and Housing Census of Maldives 2000; Statistical Year Book of Maldives.*

Mali. *Annuaire statistique du Mali; Recensement general de la population et de l'habitat (du 1er au 9 mars 1998); Mali: Selected Issues and Statistical Annex* (IMF Staff Country Report [2004]).

Malta. *Annual Abstract of Statistics; Quarterly Digest of Statistics.*

Marshall Islands. *Marshall Islands Statistical Abstract* (annual); *Report on the State of the Islands* (U.S. Department of the Interior [annual]); *Population and Housing Census 1999.*

Martinique. *Recensement de la population de 1999. Martinique; Tableaux economiques regionaux: Martinique* (biennial).

Mauritania. *Recensement général de la population et de l'habitat 2000. Annuaire Statistique; Mauritania—Statistical Appendix* (IMF Staff Country Report [2003]).

Mauritius. *Annual Digest of Statistics; 2000 Housing and Population Census of Mauritius; Mauritius in Figures* (annual).

Mayotte. *Bulletin Trimestriel* (quarterly) and *Rapport Annuel* (Institut d'Emission, France); *Recensement de la population de Mayotte: juillet 2002.*

Mexico. *Anuario estadístico; XII Censo general de población y vivienda, 2000; Anuario estadístico de los Estados Unidos Mexicanos.*

Micronesia. *Micronesia—Recent Economic Developments* (IMF Staff Country Report [1998]); *FSM Statistical Yearbook* (annual).

Moldova. *Republic of Moldova: Statistical Appendix* (IMF Country Report [2004]); *Republica Moldova in Cifre* (annual).

Monaco. *Recensement general de la population 2000; Monaco en chiffres* (annual).

Mongolia. *Mongolian Statistical Yearbook* (annual); *Mongolia: Selected Issues and Statistical Appendix* (IMF Staff Country Report [2002]); *2000 Population and Housing Census of Mongolia.*

Morocco. *Annuaire statistique du Maroc; Recensement général de la population et de l'habitat de 1994; Morocco in Figures* (annual).

Mozambique. *Anuário Estatístico; Republic of Mozambique—Statistical Appendix* (IMF Staff Country Report [2004]); *II Recenseamento Geral da População e habitação, 1997.*

Myanmar (Burma). *Report to the Pyithu Hluttaw on the Financial, Social, and Economic Conditions for 20*** (annual); *Statistical Abstract* (irreg.); *1983 Population Census.*

Namibia. *2001 Population and Housing Census; Statistical/Economic Review* (annual).

Nauru. *Population Profile* (irreg.).

Nepal. *Economic Survey* (annual); *Statistical Yearbook of Nepal; National Population Census 2001; Nepal: Statistical Appendix* (IMF Staff Country Report [2003]).

Netherlands, The. *Statistical Yearbook of the Netherlands.*

Netherlands Antilles. *Fourth Population and Housing Census Netherlands Antilles 2001; Statistical Yearbook of the Netherlands Antilles.*

New Caledonia. *Images de la population de la Nouvelle-Calédonie principaux resultats du recensement 1996; Tableaux bilan economique* (annual); *New Caledonia Facts and Figures* (annual).

New Zealand. *2001 New Zealand Census of Population and Dwellings; New Zealand Official Yearbook.*

Nicaragua. *Censos Nacionales 1995; Compendio Estadístico* (annual).

Niger. *Annuaire statistique; Niger—Statistical Annex* (IMF Staff Country Report [2004]); *2ème Recensement général de la population 2001.*

Nigeria. *Annual Abstract of Statistics; Nigeria: Selected Issues and Statistical Appendix* (IMF Staff Country Report [2004]).

Northern Mariana Islands. *CNMI Population Profile; Report on the State of the Islands* (U.S. Department of the Interior [annual]); *2000 Census of Population and Housing (U.S.).*

Norway. *Folke-og boligtelling 2001* (Population and Housing Census); *Industristatistikk* (annual); *Statistisk årbok* (Statistical Yearbook).

Oman. *General Census of Population, Housing, and Establishments* (2003); *Statistical Yearbook; Bank of Oman Annual Report.*

Pakistan. *Economic Survey* (annual); *Pakistan Statistical Yearbook; Population Census of Pakistan, 1998.*

Palau. *Statistical Yearbook; Census 2000; Republic of Palau: Selected Issues and Statistical Appendix* (IMF Staff Country Report [2004]).

Panama. *Indicadores económicos y sociales* (annual); *X censo nacional de poblacion y vivienda realizados el 14 de mayo del 2000; Panama en cifras.*

Papua New Guinea. *Papua New Guinea: Selected Issues and Statistical Appendix* (IMF Staff Country Report [2004]); *Summary of Statistics* (annual); *2000 National Population Census.*

Paraguay. *Anuario estadístico del Paraguay; Censo nacional de población y viviendas, 2002; Paraguay: Statistical Appendix* (IMF Staff Country Report [2003]).

Peru. *Censos nacionales; IX de población: IV de vivienda, 11 de julio de 1993; Compendio estadístico* (3 vol.; annual); *Informe estadístico* (annual); *Peru: Selected Issues* (IMF Staff Country Report [2004]).

Philippines. *Philippine Statistical Yearbook; 2000 Census of Population and Housing.*

Poland. *Narodowy spis powszechny 2002* (National Population and Housing Census); *Rocznik statystyczny* (Statistical Yearbook).

Portugal. *Anuário Estatístico; XIV Recenseamento Geral da População: IV Recenseamento Geral da Habitação, 2001.*

Puerto Rico. *Estadísticas socioeconomicas* (annual); *Informe económico al gobernador* (Economic Report to the Governor [annual]); *2000 Census of Population and Housing (U.S.).*

Qatar. *Annual Statistical Abstract; Economic Survey of Qatar* (annual); *Qatar Year Book; Qatar Central Bank Annual Report; Population and Housing Census 1997.*

Réunion. *Recensement général de la population de 1999; Tableau Economique de la Réunion* (biennial).

Romania. *Anuarul statistic al României* (Statistical Yearbook); *Census of Population and Housing March 27, 2002.*

Russia. *Demograficheskiy Yezhegodnik Rossii* (Demographic Yearbook of Russia); *Rossiysky Statistichesky Yezhegodnik* (Russian Statistical Yearbook); *2002 All-Russian Population Census.*

Rwanda. *Bulletin de Statistique: Supplement Annuel; Recensement general de la population et de l'habitat 1991; Rwanda: Selected Issues and Statistical Appendix* (IMF Staff Country Report [2004]).

St. Kitts and Nevis. *Annual Digest of Statistics; St. Christopher and Nevis: Recent Economic Developments* (IMF Staff Country Report [2000]).

St. Lucia. *Annual Statistical Digest; St. Lucia: Statistical Appendix* (IMF Staff Country Report [2003]); *2001 Population and Housing Census.*

St. Vincent and the Grenadines. *Digest of Statistics* (annual); *Population and Housing Census 2001; St. Vincent and the Grenadines: Statistical Appendix* (IMF Staff Country Report [2003]).

Samoa (Western Samoa). *Annual Statistical Abstract; Census of Population and Housing, 2001; Samoa: Selected Issues and Statistical Appendix* (IMF Staff Country Report [2003]).

San Marino. *Bollettino di Statistica* (quarterly); *Annuario Statistico Demografico* (irreg.); *Republic of San Marino: Selected Issues and Statistical Appendix* (IMF Staff Country Report [2004]).

São Tomé and Príncipe. *1º Recenseamento Geral da População e da Habitação 2001; Sao Tome: Statistical Appendix* (IMF Staff Country Report [2004]).

Saudi Arabia. *Saudi Arabian Monetary Agency: Annual Report; Saudi Arabia Population and Housing Census 1992.*

Senegal. *Recensement de la population et de l'habitat 2001; Situation économique du Senegal* (annual); *Senegal: Statistical Appendix* (IMF Staff Country Report [2003]).

Serbia and Montenegro. *Census of Population, Households, and Housing 2002* (Serbia and Vojvodina only); *Statistički godišnjak Jugoslavije* (Statistical Yearbook of Yugoslavia).

Seychelles. *Statistical Abstract* (annual); *Seychelles in Figures* (annual); *National Population and Housing Census 2002.*

Sierra Leone. *Sierra Leone—Recent Economic Developments* (IMF Staff Country Report [1997]).

Singapore. *Census of Population, 2000; Singapore Yearbook; Yearbook of Statistics Singapore; Singapore: Selected Issues* (IMF Staff Country Report [2004]).

Slovakia. *Sčítanie Obyvateľov, Domov a Btov 2001* (Population and Housing Census 2001); *Statistical Yearbook of the Slovak Republic; Slovak Republic: Selected Issues and Statistical Appendix* (IMF Staff Country Report [2003]).

Slovenia. *Slovenija Popis 2002* (Slovenia Population Census 2002); *Statistični Letopis Republike Slovenija* (Statistical Yearbook of the Republic of Slovenia); *Republic of Slovenia: Selected Issues and Statistical Appendix* (IMF Staff Country Report [2004]).

Solomon Islands. *Solomon Islands 1999 Population Census; Solomon Islands: Selected Issues and Statistical Appendix* (IMF Staff Country Report [2004]).

Somalia. *Socio-Economic Survey 2002* (The World Bank Report No. 1, Somalia Watching Brief, 2003).

South Africa. *The People of South Africa Population Census, 2001; South Africa: Official Yearbook of the Republic of South Africa.*

Spain. *Anuario estadístico; Censo de población de 2001.*

Sri Lanka. *Census of Population and Housing, 2001; Sri Lanka Statistical Abstract* (irreg.); *Statistical Pocketbook of the Democratic Socialist Republic of Sri Lanka* (annual); *Sri Lanka: Selected Issues and Statistical Appendix* (IMF Staff Country Report [2004]).

Sudan, The. *Fourth Population Census, 1993; Sudan in Figures* (annual); *Sudan: Statistical Appendix* (IMF Staff Country Report [2000]).

Suriname. *General Population Census 1980; Statistisch Jaarboek van Suriname; Suriname—Selected Issues and Statistical Appendix* (IMF Staff Country Report [2003]).

Swaziland. *Annual Statistical Bulletin; Report on the 1997 Swaziland Population Census; Swaziland—Selected Issues and Statistical Appendix* (IMF Staff Country Report [2003]).

Sweden. *Folk-och bostadsräkningen, 1990* (Population and Housing Census); *Statistisk årsbok för Sverige* (Statistical Abstract of Sweden).

Switzerland. *Recensement fédéral de la population, 2000; Statistisches Jahrbuch* (Statistical Yearbook).

Syria. *General Census of Housing and Inhabitants, 1994; Statistical Abstract* (annual).

Taiwan. *Statistical Abstract* (annual); *Statistical Yearbook of the Republic of China; 1990 Census of Population and Housing.*

Tajikistan. *General Population Census of the Republic of Tajikistan 2000; Republic of Tajikistan: Statistical Appendix* (IMF Staff Country Report [2003]).

Tanzania. *Tanzania—Statistical Annex* (IMF Staff Country Report [2004]); *Tanzania in Figures* (annual); *Tanzania Statistical Abstract* (irreg.); *2002 Population Census.*

Thailand. *Statistical Handbook of Thailand* (annual); *Statistical Yearbook; Population and Housing Census 2000; Thailand: Statistical Appendix* (IMF Staff Country Report [2003]).

Togo. *Annuaire statistique du Togo; Recensement général de la population et de l'habitat 1993; Togo—Selected Issues* (IMF Staff Country Report [1999]).

Tonga. *Population Census, 1996; Tonga: Selected Issues and Statistical Appendix* (IMF Staff Country Report [2003]).

Trinidad and Tobago. *Central Bank of Trinidad and Tobago: Annual Economic Survey; 1990 Population and Housing Census; Trinidad and Tobago: Selected Issues and Statistical Appendix* (IMF Staff Country Report [2003]).

Tunisia. *Annuaire statistique de la Tunisie; Recensement général de la population et des logements, 1994; Tunisia: Selected Issues* (IMF Staff Country Report [2002]).

Turkey. *2000 Genel Nüfus Sayımı* (2000 Census of Population); *Türkiye İstatistik Yilliği* (Statistical Yearbook of Turkey).

Turkmenistan. *1995 Population and Housing Census of the Republic of Turkmenistan; Turkmenistan v tsifrakh* (Turkmenistan in figures [annual]).

Tuvalu. *Tuvalu Country Profile 2003.*

Uganda. *2002 National Population and Housing Census; Uganda: Statistical Appendix* (IMF Staff Country Report [2003]).

Ukraine. *Perepis Naselennya 2001* (Population Census 2001); *Statistichniy Shchorichnik Ukraini* (Statistical Yearbook of Ukraine).

United Arab Emirates. *Statistical Yearbook* (Abu Dhabi); *United Arab Emirates: Statistical Appendix* (IMF Staff Country Report [2004]); *Central Bank of UAE Report* (annual).

United Kingdom. *Annual Abstract of Statistics; Britain: An Official Handbook* (annual); *Census 2001; General Household Survey* series (annual).

United States. *Agricultural Statistics* (annual); *Current Population Reports; Digest of Education Statistics* (annual); *Minerals Yearbook* (3 vol. in 6 parts); *Statistical Abstract* (annual); *U.S. Exports: SIC-Based Products* (annual); *U.S. Imports: SIC-Based Products* (annual); *Vital and Health Statistics* (series 1–20); *2000 Census of Population and Housing.*

Uruguay. *Anuario estadístico; VII Censo general de poblacion III de hogares y V de viviendas, 22 de mayo de 1996; Uruguay—Recent Economic Developments* (IMF Country Report [2001]).

Uzbekistan. *Commonwealth of Independent States Statistical Yearbook; Republic of Uzbekistan; Uzbekistan—Recent Economic Developments* (IMF Staff Country Report [2000]).

Vanuatu. *National Population Census 1999; Vanuatu Statistical Yearbook; Vanuatu—Selected Issues and Statistical Appendix* (IMF Staff Country Report [2002]).

Venezuela. *Anuario estadístico; Censo general de la población y vivienda 2001; Encuesta de hogares por muestreo* (annual); *Encuesta industrial* (annual).

Vietnam. *Nien Giam Thong Ke* (Statistical Yearbook); *Tong Dieu Tra Dan So Viet Nam—1999* (Vietnam Population Census—1999).

Virgin Islands of the United States. *2000 Census of Population and Housing* (U.S.).

West Bank. *Population, Housing and Establishment Census—1997; Palestinian Statistical Abstract.*

Western Sahara. *Recensement general de la population et de l'habitat* (1994 [Morocco]).

Yemen. *Population of Yemen: 1994 Census; Republic of Yemen: Selected Issues* (IMF Country Staff Report [2001]).

Zambia. *Zambia: Selected Issues and Statistical Appendix* (IMF Staff Country Report [2004]); *2000 Census of Population, Housing, Agriculture.*

Zimbabwe. *Population Census 2002; Statistical Yearbook* (irreg.); *Zimbabwe: Statistical Appendix* (IMF Staff Country Report [2004]).

Index

This index covers both *Britannica Book of the Year* (cumulative for 10 years) and *Britannica World Data*. Biographies and obituaries are cumulative for 5 years.

Entries of major article topics in the *Book of the Year* are cumulative for 10 years; an accompanying year in **dark type** gives the year the reference appears, and the accompanying page number in light type shows the page on which the article appears. For example, "military affairs **06:**247; **05:**248; **04:**248; **03:**277; **02:**278; **01:**276; **00:**267; **99:**278; **98:**276; **97:**269" indicates that military affairs appeared every year from **1997** through **2006**. Other references that appear with a page number but without a year are references from the current yearbook.

Indented entries under a topic refer by page number to some other places in the yearbook text where the topic is discussed. Names of people covered in biographies and obituaries are usually followed by the abbreviation "(biog.)" or "(obit.)" with the year in **dark type** and a page number in light type, e.g., Parks, Rosa, *or* Rosa Louise McCauley (obit.) **06:**128. In the rare case where a person has both a biography and an obituary, both words appear under the main entry and are alphabetized accordingly, e.g.:

Newton, Helmut
  biography **02:**92
  obituary **05:**126
  photography 160

References to illustrations are by page number and are preceded by the abbreviation *il*.

The index uses word-by-word alphabetization (treating a word as one or more characters separated by a space from the next word). Please note that "St." is treated as "Saint." "Mc" is alphabetized as "Mc" rather than "Mac."

A

AACM: *see* Association for the Advancement of Creative Musicians
Aaliyah (obit.) **02:**104
AAP (Am. org.): *see* American Publishers, Association of
Abacha, Sani
  Nigeria 440
  Switzerland 466
Abbas, Abu, *or* Muhammad Abbas (obit.) **05:**98
Abbas, Mahmoud
  biography **04:**71
  Egypt 392
  Israel 413
  Jordan 418
Abbey Theatre (Irish thea. co.)
  Ireland 413
  theatre 261
Abbott, John: *see* Hunter, Evan
Abbou, Mohamed 470, *il.* 471
ABC (Am. corp.)
  football 311
  television 240
Abdella, Ali Said
  Eritrea 394
Abdul Aziz ibn Fahd
  King Fahd funeral *il.* 455
Abdul Kalam, A. P. J.
  biography **03:**67
  India 407
Abdullah, King, *or* Crown Prince Abdullah, *or* 'Abdullah ibn 'Abd al-'Aziz al Sa'ud
  biographies **06:**67; **03:**67
  Saudi Arabia 454
Abdullah II
  Jordan 418
  religion 278
Abe, Kazushige 238
Abe, Shinzo 417
Abelson, Philip Hauge (obit.) **05:**98
Abidjan (C.I.) 385
Abkhazia (rep., Georgia) 398
ABN Amro (Du. bank) 415
abnormal spindle-like microcephaly associated, *or* ASPM
  anthropology 148
Abobora, Lucia: *see* Santos, Lucia de Jesus dos

abortion
  United States 484
Aboulela, Leila
  Arabic literature 237
  Muslim writers 237
Abraham Lincoln Presidential Library (Springfield, Ill., U.S.)
  libraries *il.* 212
Abramoff, Jack 480
Abramovich, Roman 308
Abramovitz, Max (obit.) **05:**98
Abreu, Caio Fernando 234
ABT (Am. ballet co.): *see* American Ballet Theatre
Abū 'Alī Muṣṭafā (obit.) **02:**104
Abu-Assad, Hany 265, *il.* 264
Abu Dahdah, *or* Imad Eddin Barakat Yarkas 208
Abu Dhabi (U.A.E.) 475
Abu Ghraib prison (Iraq)
  court-martial prosecutions 288
  military affairs 248
Abu-Jaber, Diana 237
Abū Niḍāl (obit.) **03:**98
Abu Sayyaf (terrorist group) 446
Abubakar, Atiku 440
Abuja (Nig.) 440
AC Milan (It. football team) 308, *il.*
Academy Award
  Film Awards *table* 266
Accra (Ghana) 401
Aceh (prov., Indon.)
  Indonesia 409
  military affairs 248
acetylene (chem. compound) 268
Acholi (people)
  United Nations 351
acidity (chem.)
  wildlife conservation 193
ACT New Zealand (pol. party, N.Z.)
  New Zealand 438
ADA (1990, U.S.): *see* Americans with Disabilities Act
Adair, Red, *or* Paul Neal Adair (obit.) **05:**98
Adamkus, Valdas 427
Adams, Don, *or* Donald James Yarmy (obit.) **06:**98
Adams, Douglas (obit.) **02:**104
Adams, Eddie, *or* Edward Thomas Adams (obit.) **05:**98
Adams, Gerry 413
Adams, Michael 302

Adams, Robert 159
Adams, Victoria: *see* Beckham, Victoria
Addis Ababa (Eth.) 394
Adélie penguin 357
Adelphia Communications Corporation (Am. corp.) 209
Adere, Berhane *il.* 394
Adichie, Chimamanda Ngozi 227
Adidas (Ger. co.) 401
Adler, Larry (obit.) **02:**104
Adler, Mortimer J. (obit.) **02:**105
Admiral's Cup
  sailing 319
Adobe Systems (Am. co.)
  computers and information systems 164
adolescence
  childhood obesity 203
Advanced Micro Devices, *or* AMD (Am. co.)
  computer companies 163
advertising **99:**157; **98:**152; **97:**154
  computer security and crime 161
  magazines 245
  newspapers 243
  prescription drugs 204
  television 241
Aerosmith (biog.) **02:**73
aerospace industry **99:**158; **98:**153; **97:**155
Afghanistan **06:**359; **05:**359; **04:**358; **03:**390; **02:**384; **01:**387; **00:**378; **99:**399; **98:**389; **97:**388
  drug trafficking 208
  international law 206
  international relations
    Canada 377
    India 408
    New Zealand 438
    Pakistan 442
    Spain 462
    United Nations 350
  military affairs 248
  religion 277
  U.S. military bases and Taliban control *map* **02:**384
  see also WORLD DATA
"Afleet Alex" (racehorse) 305, *il.*
Afolabi, S. A.
  literature 227
Africa
  association football 309
  democracy (spotlight) **97:**416
  diamond trade controversy (sidebar) **01:**390, *map*
  economic affairs 173
  education 189
  food aid 144
  France's African policy (spotlight) **98:**466, *map* 467
  HIV and AIDS 201
  human rights 289
  international migration 292
  literature 227
  military affairs 248
  motion pictures 267
  peacekeeping operations 351
  popular music 252
  social protection 287
  struggle against AIDS (special report) **00:**450, *map*
  United Kingdom 478
  visit by Clinton (spotlight) **99:**441
"Africa Remix: Contemporary Art of a Continent" (art exhibition)
  "Cloth of Gold" *il.* 158
African American
  heart medication 218
African American History and Culture, National Museum of (museum) 214
African art
  "Cloth of Gold" *il.* 158
  museums 214
African Development Bank
  Ethiopia 395

African Financial Community franc (currency): *see* Communauté Financiére Africaine franc
African National Congress, *or* ANC (pol. party, S.Af.) 460
African Union, *or* AU
  international migration 292
  military affairs 248
  multinational and regional organizations 354
  Sudanese genocide 288
  Togo 469
African Union Mission in The Sudan, *or* AMIS II
  military affairs 248
  multinational and regional organizations 354
aftershock (geol.) 168
Afwerki, Isaias 393
Agar, John (obit.) **03:**98
Agassi, Andre 324
age discrimination (law)
  court cases 207
Ager, Shana: *see* Alexander, Shana
Agilent Technologies (Am. co.)
  computers and information systems 164
Agnelli, Giovanni (obit.) **04:**100
Agnelli, Umberto (obit.) **05:**98
Agrelo, Marilyn 267
agricultural subsidy
  European Union 353
agriculture **06:**144; **05:**144; **04:**146; **03:**146; **02:**152; **01:**146; **00:**128; **99:**124; **98:**123; **97:**123
  ancient grains (sidebar) **06:**145
  aquaculture (special report) **99:**132
  Bosnia and Herzegovina 371
  China 379
  commodities 180
  Cuba 387
  European Union 353
  genetically modified foods (special report) **01:**150
  Kenya 420
  livestock and disease (special report) **02:**154
  Morocco 435
  see also livestock
Agriculture, U.S. Department of, *or* USDA
  food-guide pyramid 204, *il.*
Ahanda, Joseph 375
Ahern, Bertie, *or* Bartholemew Ahern 412
AHL: *see* American Hockey League
Ahmadinejad, Mahmoud
  biography **06:**67
  Iran 409, *il.* 410
  Israel 414
Ahmadiyya (Islamic group) 367
Ahmed, Iajuddin 367
Ahn Hyun Soo 317
Ahonen, Janne 320
Ahtisaari, Martti
  Finland 395, *il.* 396
  Indonesia 409
Ai Confini tra Sardegna e Jazz Festival (It.) 252
AIA: *see* American Institute of Architects
AIDS (disease): *see* HIV/AIDS
Aiken, Joan Delano (obit.) **05:**98
Air National Guard (mil. org., U.S.): *see* National Guard
Airbus (Eur. consortium)
  business 185
airline industry
  business 185
  stock markets 177
airport
  Civil Engineering Projects *table* 153
Ajodhia, Jules Rattankoemar 464
Akayev, Askar 423, *il.*
Akesson, Birgit (obit.) **02:**105

---

ecology
  ecological restoration (special
    report) **99:**218
  ecotourism (special report)
    99:180
Economic and Financial Crimes
  Commission, *or* EFCC (pol.
  org., Nig.) 440
Economic Co-operation and
  Development, Organisation for,
  or OECD (internat. org.)
    Andorra 361
    economic affairs 171
    higher education 188
    Sweden 465
  economic growth **06:**171; **05:**172;
    04:173; **03:**185; **02:**188; **01:**186;
    00:170; **99:**191; **98:**185; **97:**188
    International Monetary Fund
      (special report) **99:**198, *map*
      199
    troubled world economy
      (spotlight) **99:**450
ecosystem
  environment 190
  "Ecstasy: In and About Altered
    States" (art exhibition) 157, *il.*
Ecuador **06:**391; **05:**391; **04:**391;
  03:425; **02:**417; **01:**423; **00:**416;
  99:431; **98:**421; **97:**414
    Colombia 383
    see also WORLD DATA
Ederle, Gertrude (obit.) **04:**111
Edinburgh (Scot., U.K.)
  architecture 152
Edinburgh Festival (festival,
  Edinburgh, Scot., U.K.)
    theatre 261
Editis (Fr. co.) 246
Edmonton Eskimos (Can. football
  team) 311
education **06:**187; **05:**188; **04:**187;
  03:204; **02:**206; **01:**204; **00:**191;
  99:209; **98:**201; **97:**203
    charter schools (sidebar) **04:**188
    cheating (special report) **03:**206
    home schooling (sidebar) **00:**193
    "No Child Left Behind" (sidebar)
      06:188
    Ph.D. job market (sidebar)
      98:201
    Slovakia 458
    Spain 462, *il.* 452
    Tanzania 468
    testing (special report) **02:**208
    United Kingdom 476
    United States 484
education, higher: *see* higher
  education
"Education of Arnold Hitler, The"
  (Estrin) 225
Edwards, Sir George Robert (obit.)
  04:111
Edwards, John, *or* John Reid
  Edwards (biog.) **05:**73
Edwards, Ralph Livingstone (obit.)
  06:110
EFCC (pol. org., Nig.): *see*
  Economic and Financial
  Crimes Commission
Egal, Muhammad Ibrahim (obit.)
  03:108
Egan, Msgr. John Joseph (obit.)
  02:117
Egypt **06:**392; **05:**392; **04:**392;
  03:426; **02:**418; **01:**423; **00:**416;
  99:432; **98:**421; **97:**414
    Arabic literature 236
    archaeology 148
    higher education 189
    Israel 414
    Syria 466
    terrorism 208
    see also WORLD DATA
Egyptian art
  museums 214
Ehrling, Evert Sixten (obit.)
  06:110

Eight, Group of, *or* G-8
  Benin 370
  Burkina Faso 374
  Ethiopia 395
  food aid 144
  Ghana 401
  human rights 289
  Mali 430
  multinational and regional
    organizations 354
  Nigeria 440
  popular music 253
  Sierra Leone 457
  United Kingdom 478
Einstein, Albert
  "Celebrating the Centennial of
    Einstein's 'Miraculous Year' "
    (special report) **06:**270, *ils.* 271
  classical music 250
  dance 256
Eisenman, Peter
  architecture 152
  Germany *il.* 401
Eisner, Will, *or* William Erwin
  Eisner (obit.) **06:**110
El Niño
  Oceania (spotlight) **99:**481
El Niño/Southern Oscillation, *or*
  ENSO (weather) 170
El Salvador **06:**393; **05:**393;
  04:393; **03:**427; **02:**419; **01:**425;
  00:417; **99:**432; **98:**422; **97:**415
    see also WORLD DATA
Elam, Jack (obit.) **04:**112
ElBaradei, Mohamed
  Iran 410
  Nobel Prize 62, *il.*
Elbaz, Alber 197
Elbegdorj, Tsahiagiyn 434
elderly: *see* old age
election
  Afghanistan 350, 359
  Albania 360
  Algeria 361
  Andorra 361
  Angola 362
  Argentina 362
  Austria 365
  Azerbaijan 365
  Belarus 368
  Belgium 369
  Bosnia and Herzegovina 371
  Botswana 372
  British election (sidebar) **02:**509
  Bulgaria 373
  Burkina Faso 374
  Burundi 374
  Canada 375
  Central African Republic 377
  Channel Islands 355
  Chile 378
  Colombia 383
  Congo, Democratic Republic of
    384, *il.*
  Côte d'Ivoire 385
  Czech Republic 388
  Denmark 389
  Djibouti 390
  Dominica 390
  Egypt 392
  Estonia 394
  Ethiopia 394
  French presidential race
    (sidebar) **03:**431
  Gambia, The 398
  Georgia 399
  Germany 179, 399, *il.* 400
  Guinea 404
  Guinea-Bissau 404, *il.*
  Haiti 405, *il.* 406
  Honduras 406
  Hungary 406
  Iran 410, *il.*
  Iraq 350, 411, 479, *ils.* 479, 11
  Israel 414
  Italy 414
  Jamaica 415
  Japan 416

Kazakhstan 419
Kuwait 422
Kyrgyzstan 423, *il.*
Latvia 424
Lebanon 425
Lesotho 425
Liberia 425, *il.* 426
Liechtenstein 427
Macedonia 428
Maldives 430
Mauritius 432
Mexico 432
Micronesia 433
Moldova 434
Mongolia 434
Mozambique 435
Nepal 437
New Zealand 438
Nicaragua 439
Niger 439
Northern Ireland 478
Norway 441
Pakistan 442
Papua New Guinea 444
Peru 445, *il.*
Philippines 445, *il.* 446
Poland 446
Portugal 447, *il.*
Russia 450
Singapore 458
Slovakia 458
Somaliland, Republic of 460
Spain 462
Sri Lanka 463
Suriname 464
Taiwan 467
Tajikistan 468
Tanzania 468
Thailand 469
Togo 469, *il.*
Trinidad and Tobago 470
Turkey 472
United Kingdom 475
  British election of 2005
    (sidebar) **06:**477
United States 482
  U.S. election of 2004
    (special report) **05:**484
  U.S. election reform debate
    (sidebar) **02:**517
  U.S. midterm elections
    (sidebar) **03:**517
  U.S. presidential race
    (special reports) **01:**514, *map*
    515; **97:**492, *map* 494
Uruguay 485
Venezuela 486
Zimbabwe 491
electric power **99:**164; **98:**159;
  97:161
  China 380
  Cuba 387
  Nicaragua 439
  North Korea 421
  Uganda 473
electricity grid
  U.S. electricity grid (sidebar)
    05:185
electromagnetic radiation
  Einstein 270
electron
  physics 272
electron transfer 269
electronic eavesdropping
  United States 481
electronic game: *see* computer
  game
electronic trading, *or* e-trading
  computers and information
    systems 164
  special report **00:**180
elementary education, *or* primary
  education **06:**187; **05:**188;
  04:187; **03:**204; **02:**206;
  01:204; **00:**191; **99:**209;
  98:201; **97:**203
Elitlopp (horse race) 307
Elizabeth (obit.) **03:**108

Elizabeth II (q. of U.K.)
  Antigua and Barbuda 362
  Australia 363
  Bahamas, The 366
  Barbados 367
  Belize 369
  biography **03:**71
  Canada 375
  Channel Islands 355
  Grenada 403
  Jamaica 415
  New Zealand 438
  Papua New Guinea 444
  Saint Kitts and Nevis 452
  Saint Lucia 453
  Saint Vincent and the
    Grenadines 453
  Solomon Islands 459
  Tuvalu 472
  United Kingdom 475
Ellroy, James (biog.) **02:**81
"Elsu" (racehorse) 307
"Emancipation of Mimi, The"
  (album) 254
Emanuel, Kerry 170
embargo
  Côte d'Ivoire 385
embezzlement
  Cameroon 375
  Hungary 406
  São Tomé and Príncipe 454
emergency management
  multinational and regional
    organizations 354
  "Preparing for Emergencies"
    (special report) **06:**182
  U.S. state governments 483
emerging market (econ.)
  stock markets 178
Emerson, Gloria (obit.) **05:**110
"Emily" (hurricane)
  Grenada 403
eminent domain
  court decisions 206
  United States 482
emissions trading
  Kyoto Protocol 194
Emmy Awards
  television 240, *il.*
employment
  Ph.D. job market (sidebar)
    98:201
  see also unemployment
"En Attendant Godot" (play): *see*
  Waiting for Godot"
EnCana (Can. co.) 391
"End of Time" (phot. exhibit)
  159
Endesa (Sp. co.) 181
"Endlich Stille" (Ott) 228
Enebish, Lhamsurengiyn (obit.)
  02:117
enemy combatant: *see* prisoner of
  war
energy conversion **99:**164; **98:**159;
  97:162
  business 180
  economic affairs 171
  environment 192
  Finland 395
  stock markets 175
  United States 480
Enewetak (atoll, Marshall Isls.)
  nuclear testing in the Pacific
    Islands, 1946–1996 *graph*
    99:247
"Enfant, L' " (motion picture) 264
  Belgium 369
England (constituent unit, U.K.)
  archaeology 149
  crime 208
  squash championship 321
  United Kingdom 477
England, Bank of (bank, U.K.)
  174
English Channel (chan., Eur.)
  Battle of Trafalgar anniversary *il.*
  31

J

---

junk-rated bond
stock markets 178
Jurado, Katy (obit.) **03:**117
Justice, Department of (U.S. govt.)
law enforcement 209
Justice, Donald Rodney (obit.)
05:116
Justice and Democracy, Military
Council for (Mauritanian org.)
431
Justicialist Party, *or* Peronist party,
or PJ (pol. party, Arg.) 362

K

Kabbah, Ahmad Tejan 457
Kabila, Joseph
biography **02:**86
Congo, Democratic Republic of
the 384
Kabila, Laurent (obit.) **02:**126
Kabuki
Kabuki in the U.S. (special
report) **06:**258
"Kabuki Lady Macbeth" (play)
Kabuki in the U.S. 258, *ils.* 258,
259
Kabul (Afg.) 359
Kabylia (reg., Alg.) 360
Kaczynski, Lech 446
Kadyrbekov, Ishenbay 423
Kael, Pauline (obit.) **02:**126
Kagame, Paul 452
Kahn, Louis 152
Kahn, Oliver (biog.) **03:**78
Kaiser Family Foundation (Am.
org.)
childhood obesity survey 203
Kaká, *or* Ricardo Izecson Santos
Leite 308
Kaliningrad (obl., Russ.) 427
Kalla, Jusuf 409
Kalu, Orji Uzor 440
Kalvitis, Aigars 424
"Kamataki" (motion picture) 264
Kamen, Dean (biog.) **03:**78
Kamen, Martin David (obit.)
03:118
Kampala (Ugan.) 473
Kamprad, Ingvar (biog.) **04:**83
kamut (plant) 145
Kan'an, Ghazi 467
Kanehara, Hitomi (biog.) **05:**79
Kanik, Ludovit 459
Kansas (state, U.S.)
same-sex marriage ban 484
Kansas City Chiefs (Am. football
team) 310
Kansfield, Norman J. 278
Kant, Krishan (obit.) **03:**118
Kaplan, Metin 399
Kapp, Andy 304
Kapranova, Olga *il.* 314
Karaca, Cem (obit.) **05:**117
Karadžić, Radovan 371
Karamanlis, Kostas, *or*
Konstantinos Karamanlis
biography **05:**80
Greece 402
Karami, Omar 424
Karat, Prakash 407
karate (martial art)
World Games 321
Karimov, Islam
Uzbekistan 485
Karlovic, Ivo
Davis Cup *il.* 52
Karlton, Lawrence 279
karsenia koreana: *see* Korean
crevice salamander
Karsh, Yousuf (obit.) **03:**118
Karume, Amani Abeid 468
Karzai, Hamid
Afghanistan 359
biography **02:**86
India 408
Kase, Toshikazu (obit.) **05:**117

Kashmir (state, India): *see* Jammu
and Kashmir
Kasner, Angela Dorothea: *see*
Merkel, Angela
Kasparov, Garry 302
Katayama, Satsuk *ils.* 416
Kathmandu (Nepal) 437
Kato, Shizue Hirota (obit.) **02:**126
"Katrina" (hurricane)
architecture 153
business 180
computer security and crime
161
Cuba 387
economic affairs 171
education 188
El Salvador 393
emergency management 182, *ils.*
183
fashions 199
football 310
jazz benefit concert 251, *il.* 252
libraries 213
magazines 245
mashups 163
meteorology and climate 169,
map 170, *il.* 169
military affairs 247, *il.*
museums 213
newspapers 244
stock markets 176
Thoroughbred racing 305
United States 480, 482, *il.* 483
Katz, Sir Bernard (obit.) **04:**120
Katz, Janina 229
Kauffman, Ross 267
Kaufman, Seymour: *see* Coleman,
Cy
"Kaun banega crorepati"
(television program) 241
Kawakami, Genichi (obit.)
03:118
Kawakuba, Rei *il.* 199
Kaye, M. M., *or* Mary Margaret
Kaye (obit.) **05:**117
Kazakhstan **06:**419; **05:**421;
04:423; **03:**454; **02:**451;
01:435; **00:**449; **99:**458;
98:450; **97:**439
bird flu 490
China 381
social protection 287
see also WORLD DATA
Kazan, Elia (obit.) **04:**120
Kazantzidis, Stelios (obit.) **02:**126
Kazuko Nakamura: *see* Nakamura,
Kiharu
KDH (pol. party, Slovakia): *see*
Christian Democratic
Movement
KDU-CSL (pol. party, Czech Rep.):
see Christian Democrats
Kebede, Liya 197
Keel, Howard, *or* Harold Clifford
Leek (obit.) **05:**117
Keeling, Charles David (obit.)
06:120
Keene, Carolyn: *see* Benson,
Mildred Augustine Wirt
Keeshan, Bob, *or* Robert James
Keeshan (obit.) **05:**117
Keflavík (Ice.) 407
Keidanren
Japan 416
Keita, Salif 253
Keïta, Seydou (obit.) **02:**126
Keke, Harold 459
Kelley, John Adelbert (obit.)
05:117
Kelly, Andrea 304
Kelly, Denis 257
Kelly, Margaret (obit.) **05:**117
Kelly, Michael (obit.) **04:**121
Kelly, Molly, *or* Molly Craig (obit.)
05:117
Kelly, Thomas Joseph (obit.)
03:118
Kelman, Charles (obit.) **05:**117

Kelo v. City of New London (law
case)
court decisions 206
U.S. state governments 482
Kemakeza, Sir Allan 459
Kempson, Rachel (obit.) **04:**121
Kempton Park (racecourse, Eng.,
U.K.) 306
Kennan, George Frost (obit.)
06:120
Kennedy, Anthony M. 207
Kennedy, Charles 477
Kennedy, Graham Cyril (obit.)
06:120
Kennedy, Rosemary (obit.) **06:**120
Kennedy Center for the
Performing Arts (thea., Wash.,
D.C., U.S.)
dance 254
Kenner, William Hugh (obit.)
04:121
Kent, Julie 254
Kente, Gibson, *or* "Bra Gib" (obit.)
05:118
Kentucky (state, U.S.) 207, 279
Kentucky Derby (horse race)
Sporting Record *tables* 334
Thoroughbred racing 305
Kenya **06:**420; **05:**422; **04:**424;
03:455; **02:**452; **01:**454;
00:452; **99:**459; **98:**450;
97:440
anthropology 147
death penalty 209
Morocco 435
Tanzania 468
track and field sports 325
see also WORLD DATA
Kenzaburō Ōe Prize
Japanese literature 238
Kepes, Gyorgy (obit.) **02:**127
Kérékou, Mathieu 369
Kerimov, Kerim (obit.) **04:**121
Kerr, Clark (obit.) **04:**121
Kerr, Jean Collins (obit.) **04:**121
Kerr-McGee (Am. co.) 366
Kerry, John, *or* John Forbes Kerry
biography **05:**80
U.S. election of 2004 (special
report) **05:**484
Kertész, André
photography 158, *il.* 159
Kesey, Ken (obit.) **02:**127
Kessel, Barney (obit.) **05:**118
Ketcham, Henry King (obit.)
02:127
Keys, Alicia, *or* Alicia Augello
Cook (biog.) **06:**83
Keys, Ancel (obit.) **05:**118
KHA-nyou: *see* Laotian rock rat
Khachiyan, Leonid Henry (obit.)
06:120
Khalifah, Hamad ibn Isa al- 366
Khalifah, Khalifah ibn Sulman al-
Bahrain 366
Khalifeh, Sahar (au.) 236
Khalilzad, Zalmay 359
Khalkhali, Sadeq (obit.) **04:**121
Khamenei, Ayatollah Sayyed Ali
409
Khamtay Siphandone 423
Khan, Vilayat Hussain (obit.)
05:118
Kharibian, Leo (obit.) **02:**127
Khartoum (Sud.) 463
Khatami, Mohammad 409
Khin Nyunt 436
Khodorkovsky, Mikhail
crime 209
Russia 449
Khoo Teck Puat (obit.) **05:**118
Kiam, Victor Kermit, II (obit.)
02:127
Kibaki, Mwai
biography **04:**84
Kenya 420
Kibria, S. A. M. S. 367
Kidjo, Angélique (biog.) **03:**79

kidnapping
Algeria 361
Brazil 372
Haiti 405
high seas piracy 211
Iraq 411
Paraguay 444
Venezuela 487
Kiev (Ukraine) 474
Kifaya Movement (pol. movement,
Egy.) 392
Kigali (Rw.) 452
Kiir Mayardit, Salva 464
Kikuyu (people)
Kenya 420
Kikwete, Jakaya 468
Kilburn, Tom (obit.) **02:**127
Kilby, Jack St. Clair (obit.) **06:**120
Kiley, Dan, *or* Daniel Urban Kiley
(obit.) **05:**118
Kilgore, Wyatt Merle (obit.) **06:**120
"Kilid" (Yārī) 236
Killingsworth, Edward Abel (obit.)
05:118
Kim Ga Young 299
Kim Jong Il
North Korea 421
Kimball, Ward (obit.) **03:**118
Kindleberger, Charles Poor, II
(obit.) **04:**121
King, Alan, *or* Irwin Alan Kniberg
(obit.) **05:**118
King, Earl (obit.) **04:**121
King, Michael (obit.) **05:**118
"King Kong" (motion picture) 262,
il. 263
King of Wartnaby, John Leonard
King, Baron (obit.) **06:**120
"Kingdom of Heaven" (motion
picture) 263
Kingston (Jam.) 415
Kingstown (St. Vincent and the
Grenadines) 453
"Kinky Boots" (motion picture)
264
Kinshasa (Con.K.) 384
Kipnis, Igor (obit.) **03:**119
Kirchhof, Paul 400
Kirchner, Néstor
Argentina 362
biography **04:**84
Latin American leaders 489, *il.*
488
Kiribati **06:**421; **05:**423; **04:**425;
03:456; **02:**453; **01:**455; **00:**453;
99:462; **98:**451; **97:**440
see also WORLD DATA
"Kirillow" (Maier) 227
Kirkpatrick, Clayton (obit.) **05:**118
Kishon, Ephraim, *or* Ferenc
Hoffmann (obit.) **06:**121
"Kiss Kiss Bang Bang" (motion
picture) 263
Kitagawa, Susumu 268
Kitano, Takeshi (biog.) **04:**84
Kittel, Frederick August: *see*
Wilson, August
KKE (pol. party, Gr.): *see*
Communist Party of Greece
Klaus, Josef (obit.) **02:**128
Klaus, Vaclav 388, *il.* 389
Klausner, Amos: *see* OZ, Amos
Klee, Paul 151, *il.* 152
Kleiber, Carlos (obit.) **05:**118
Klestil, Thomas (obit.) **05:**118
Klinger, Georgette (obit.) **05:**119
Klitschko, Vitali 301
Klochkova, Yana (biog.) **05:**80
Klossowski, Balthazar: *see* Balthus
Klüft, Carolina 326
KMT (pol. party, Tai.): *see*
Nationalist Party
Knapp, Jimmy (obit.) **02:**128
Knef, Hildegard Frieda Albertine
(obit.) **03:**119
Kniberg, Irwin Alan: *see* King,
Alan
Knight Ridder (Am. co.) 244

Qatar 448
Syria 466
Uganda 473
media and publishing
  books 246
  newspapers 244
  television 239
military affairs 249
religion 277
social protection 286
sports
  boxing 301
  cricket 303
  cycling 305
  rowing 318
  rugby football 312
  Thoroughbred racing 306
stock markets 179
see also WORLD DATA
United Methodist Church, *or* UMC
  278
United National Congress, *or* UNC
  (pol. party, Tr. and Tob.) 470
United Nations, *or* UN (internat.
  org.) **06:**350; **05:**350; **04:**346;
  03:380; **02:**374; **01:**376; **00:**368;
  99:386; **98:**376; **97:**376
China 382
Einstein centennial 270
environment 190
health and disease 200
human rights 288
international law 205
Japan 418
Latvia 424
Lebanon 424
Liberia 426
military affairs 247
Myanmar 436
Namibia 437
Nepal 437
Niger 439
Pakistan 442
Palau 443
Qatar 448
Rwanda 452
Security Council (special report)
  04:348
Sierra Leone 457
South Africa 461
Syria 466
United States 482
United Nations Children's Fund
  (internat. org.): *see* UNICEF
United Nations Convention
  Against Corruption (internat.
  org.)
  international law 206
United Nations Development
  Programme (internat.
  program)
  Roma 291
United Nations Educational,
  Scientific and Cultural
  Organization: *see* UNESCO
United Nations Environment
  Programme
  infectious diseases 351
United Nations High
  Commissioner for Refugees
  international migration 289
  United Nations 351
  Uzbekistan 486
United Nations Human
  Development Report
  Namibia 437
United Nations Mission in Eritrea
  and Ethiopia, *or* UNMEE
  Ethiopia 395
United Progressive Alliance, *or*
  UPA (pol. org., India) 407
United Progressive Party, *or* UPP
  (pol. party, Ant. and Barbuda)
  362
United Self-Defense Forces of
  Colombia, *or* AUC (paramil.
  org., Colom.) 382
  military affairs 248

United States **06:**479; **05:**480;
  04:482; **03:**513; **02:**511; **01:**511;
  00:509; **99:**513; **98:**495; **97:**490
agriculture and food production
  144
Arctic Regions 357
arts and entertainment
  dance 254
  literature 224
  motion pictures 262, *table* 266
  popular music 253
  theatre 261
    Kabuki (special report)
      06:258
Bush administration policies
  (special report) **04:**412
business 180
census of 2000 (special report)
  02:514, *maps* 515
Clinton's Africa trip (spotlight)
  99:441
Clinton's impeachment and trial
  (sidebar) **00:**513
computers and information
  systems 160, 164
  text messaging 165
death penalty 209
  executions (special report)
    03:230, *map* 231
economic affairs 171
  emergency management
    (special report) **06:**182
education 187
election reform (sidebar) **02:**517
environment 192
  carbon dioxide emissions *map*
    195
  Kyoto Protocol 194
gun control (special report)
  01:228
health and disease 200
  bird flu 490
  childhood obesity (sidebar)
    06:203
human rights 288
international law 206
international migration 289
international relations
  Afghanistan 350, 359
  Australia 364
  Azerbaijan 366
  Bahrain 367
  Cambodia 375
  Canada 377
  Cape Verde 377
  China 381
  Djibouti 390
  East Timor 391
  Fiji 396
  France 398
  Germany 401
  Guatemala 403
  Honduras 406
  Iceland 407
  India 408
  Iraq 411
  Israel 414
  Italy 414
  Japan 418
  Kenya 420
  Libya 426
  Lithuania 427
  Malta 431
  Marshall Islands 431
  Mauritius 432
  Mexico 433
  Micronesia 433
  multinational and regional
    organizations 354
  Myanmar 436
  Nepal 437
  Nicaragua 439
  Nigeria 440
  Oman 441
  Pakistan 443
  Palau 443
  Paraguay 444
  piracy 211

Qatar 448
Rwanda 452
São Tomé and Príncipe *il.* 454
Saudia Arabia 455
Slovakia 459
South Africa 461
South Korea 421
Spain 462
Syria 466
Turkey 472
Turkmenistan 472
Uganda 473
United Kingdom 478
United Nations 352
Uzbekistan 486
Venezuela 487
Vietnam 490
Yemen 491
media and publishing
  books 245
  magazines 245
  newspapers 244
  television 239
  midterm elections (sidebar)
    03:517
military affairs 247
military bases in Afghanistan
  map **02:**384
Office of the Independent
  Counsel (sidebar) **99:**515
presidential election (special
  reports) **05:**484; **01:**514, *map*
  515; **97:**492
September 11 terrorist attacks
  (special report) **02:**6, *map* 11
social protection 284
space exploration 275, *table*
sports
  associaton football 309
  automobile racing 294
  badminton 295
  baseball 295
  basketball 298
  bowling 300
  boxing 301
  equestrian 305
  fencing 307
  football 309
  golf 313
  gymnastics 314
  ice hockey 316
  rowing 318
  swimming 321
  tennis 323
  track and field sports 325
  volleyball 327, *il.* 326
  wrestling 327
stock markets 176
see also WORLD DATA
United States Air Force, The 249
  church and state 279
United States Coast Guard
  São Tomé and Príncipe *il.* 454
United States Congress: *see*
  Congress of the United States
United States Marine Corps, The
  Japan 418
United States Navy, The 249
  Japan 418
United Workers' Party, *or* UWP
  (pol. party, St. Lucia) 453
Unity, the Rule of Law,
  Development, Investment, and
  Employment, National
  Agreement for
  Mexico 433
universal jurisdiction
  international law 205
Universidad Católica (football
  team) 309
University Boat Race 319, *il.* 318
UNMEE (UN intervention): *see*
  United Nations Mission in
  Eritrea and Ethiopia
Unnewehr, Margaret: *see* Schott,
  Marge
Unseld, Siegfried (obit.) **03:**137
"Until I Find You" (Irving) 224

"Untitled" (sculp.) 155
UPA (pol. org., India): *see* United
  Progressive Alliance
UPP (pol. party, Ant. and
  Barbuda): *see* United
  Progressive Party
Uppman, Theodor (obit.) **06:**137
"Upside Down Mushroom Room"
  (art) 157, *il.*
uranium enrichment
  Iran 350, 410, 482
Urbani, Carlo (obit.) **04:**140
URhGe
  superconductivity 272
Uribe Vélez, Álvaro
  biography **03:**95
  Colombia 382, *il.* 383
Urich, Robert (obit.) **03:**137
Urquhart, Jane 226, *il.*
Urrea, Luis Alberto 224
Urrutia, Osmani 296
Uruguay **06:**485; **05:**488; **04:**488;
  03:519; **02:**519; **01:**519;
  00:517; **99:**519; **98:**502;
  97:500
Cuba 387
economic affairs 174
Latin American leaders 489
see also WORLD DATA
Urusemal, Joseph J. 433
US Airways (Am. co.) 185
U.S. Open (golf)
  golf 313, *il.* 312
  Sporting Record *tables* 338
U.S. Open (tennis) 324
  Sporting Record *tables* 345
USA PATRIOT Act (U.S. law)
  human rights 288
  libraries 212
  United States 481
USC (univ., Los Angeles, Calif.,
  U.S.): *see* Southern California,
  University of
USDA: *see* Agriculture, U.S.
  Department of
used book
  book publishing 246
Usher, *or* Usher Raymond IV
  biography **06:**95
  popular music 253
Uslar Pietri, Arturo (obit.) **02:**146
Ustinov, Sir Peter Alexander, *or*
  Peter Alexander Ustinov (obit.)
  05:138
Utaemon VI, Nakamura: *see*
  Nakamura Utaemon VI
Utah (state, U.S.) 484
Utah, University of (univ., Salt
  Lake City, Utah, U.S.)
  mascot name *il.* 189
Ute (people)
  athletic team names *il.* 189
Uttar Pradesh (state, India)
  Japanese encephalitis 202
UUP (pol. party, N.Ire., U.K.): *see*
  Ulster Unionist Party
UWP (pol. party, St. Lucia): *see*
  United Workers' Party
Uzaemon XVII, Ichimura: *see*
  Ichimura Uzaemon XVII
Uzbekistan **06:**485; **05:**488; **04:**488;
  03:519; **02:**519; **01:**519;
  00:517; **99:**519; **98:**503;
  97:500
China 380, 381
death penalty 209
military affairs 249
Persian literature 236
see also WORLD DATA

V

vaccine
  bird flu research 490
  health and disease 200
Vaduz (Liech.) 426
Vaiaku (Tuv.) 472

Index of Special Features in *Britannica Book of the Year,* 1997–2006